FOREIGN AFFAIRS BIBLIOGRAPHY
1962—1972

COUNCIL ON FOREIGN RELATIONS BOOKS

Founded in 1921, the Council on Foreign Relations, Inc. is a nonprofit and nonpartisan organization of individuals devoted to the promotion of a better and wider understanding of international affairs through the free interchange of ideas. The membership of the Council, which numbers about 1,600, is made up of men and women throughout the United States elected by the Board of Directors on the basis of an estimate of their special interest, experience and involvement in international affairs and their standing in their own communities. The Council does not take any position on questions of foreign policy, and no person is authorized to speak for the Council on such matters. The Council has no affiliation with and receives no funding from any part of the United States government.

The Council conducts a meetings program to provide its members an opportunity to talk with invited guests who have special experience, expertise or involvement in international affairs, and conducts a studies program of research directed to political, economic and strategic problems related to United States foreign policy. Since 1922 the Council has published the quarterly journal, *Foreign Affairs*. From time to time the Council also publishes books and monographs which in the judgment of the Committee on Studies of the Council's Board of Directors are responsible treatments of significant international topics worthy of presentation to the public. The individual authors of articles in *Foreign Affairs* and of Council books and monographs are solely responsible for all statements of fact and expressions of opinion contained in them.

The members of the Board of Directors of the Council as of September 1, 1975, are: Robert O. Anderson, W. Michael Blumenthal, Zbigniew Brzezinski, Douglas Dillon, Hedley Donovan, Elizabeth Drew, George S. Franklin, Edward K. Hamilton, Gabriel Hauge (Treasurer), Nicholas deB. Katzenbach, Bayless Manning (ex officio), Harry C. McPherson, Jr., Alfred C. Neal, James A. Perkins, Peter G. Peterson, Lucian W. Pye, David Rockefeller (Chairman), Robert V. Roosa, Marshall D. Shulman, Cyrus R. Vance (Vice Chairman), Paul A. Volcker, Martha R. Wallace, Paul C. Warnke, Franklin Hall Williams and Carroll L. Wilson.

FOREIGN AFFAIRS BIBLIOGRAPHY

A SELECTED AND ANNOTATED LIST OF BOOKS ON INTERNATIONAL RELATIONS
1962—1972

JANIS A. KRESLINS

Published for the Council on Foreign Relations by
R. R. Bowker Company
A Xerox Education Company
New York & London, 1976

Published by R. R. Bowker Co. (A Xerox Education Company)
1180 Avenue of the Americas, New York, N.Y. 10036
Copyright © 1976 by Council on Foreign Relations, Inc.
All rights reserved
Printed and bound in the United States of America.

Library of Congress Cataloging in Publication Data

Kreslins, Janis A
   Foreign affairs bibliography 1962–1972

   Includes indexes.
   1. International relations—Bibliography. I. Council on Foreign Relations. II. Title.
Z6461.K73   [JX1305]   016.327   75-29085
ISBN 0-8352-0784-6

CONTENTS

PREFACE   xix

FIRST PART
GENERAL INTERNATIONAL RELATIONS

I. GENERAL WORKS

    Reference Works 1
    Methodology and Theory 4
    General Treatments 7

II. POLITICAL FACTORS

    General 12
    Nationalism and Nationality 17
    Comparative Government 18
    Political Processes 20
    Political Philosophies and Ideologies
        General 21
        Democracy 23
        Liberalism; Conservatism 24
        Socialism 24
        Communism 26
        New Left; Anarchism; Student Politics 31
        Totalitarianism; Fascism 32
    The Problem of Authority; Violence and Revolution ... 34
    Colonial Problems; Decolonization 36
    Problems of New Nations 36

III. SOCIAL, CULTURAL AND RELIGIOUS FACTORS

    Society and Social Psychology 39
    Labor and Labor Movements 41
    Culture; Education; Public Opinion;
        Communications Processes 42
    Religious Problems 44

IV. GEOGRAPHIC, ETHNIC AND POPULATION FACTORS

    General Geography and Environment 45
    Ethnic Problems; The Jews 46
    Population Problems 47

V. ECONOMIC FACTORS

    General Economic Conditions and Tendencies 49
    Economic Theory 53
    Government and Economics; Planning 54

CONTENTS

International Trade	55
International Finance	59
Foreign Investment and Overseas Business; Multinational Corporations	65
Transport	67
Food and Agriculture	68
Raw Materials; Oil; Energy	70
Economic Growth and Development	71
Underdeveloped Economies	78
Economic Aid and Technical Assistance	81

VI. INTERNATIONAL LAW

General	83
Diplomacy and Diplomatic Practice	87
Law of War; Aggression	89
Maritime, Air, Space and Environmental Law	90
Treaties and Treaty Making	92
Human Rights	92
International Court of Justice	93
Miscellaneous	94

VII. INTERNATIONAL ORGANIZATION AND GOVERNMENT

General	96
United Nations	
General	99
Specialized Agencies and Activities	105
Peace-Keeping Forces and Operations	106

VIII. WAR AND PEACE

War

General	108
Theoretical Studies; Strategy	112
Naval Warfare	114
Aerial and Space Warfare and Technology	114
Nuclear Weapons; Missiles	115
Chemical and Biological Warfare	118
Guerrilla Warfare; Armed Insurrection	118
Propaganda; Psychological and Political Warfare	120
Intelligence	121
Peace; Disarmament; Arms Control	122

SECOND PART

THE WORLD SINCE 1914

I. GENERAL 129

CONTENTS

II. FIRST WORLD WAR
- Diplomatic History 131
- The Conduct of the War 136

III. INTER-WAR PERIOD 140

IV. SECOND WORLD WAR
- Immediate Origins and Outbreak 144
- General Accounts 146
- Diplomatic Aspects 148
- The Conduct of the War
  - Personal Narratives, Biographies and Reportage 154
  - Military Operations
    - General 156
    - Western Europe 159
    - Eastern Europe 161
    - Mediterranean; Greece; Crete; Italy 163
    - North and East Africa; Near and Middle East 165
    - The Pacific 165
    - Southeastern Asia; China; Burma 167
  - Aerial Operations 167
  - Naval Operations 168
  - Special Operations; Propaganda; Espionage; Intelligence 169
- Economic, Technical and Non-Military Aspects 172
- Resistance and Underground Movements 176

V. THE POSTWAR WORLD
- General 178
- East-West Relations
  - The Cold War; Peaceful Coexistence 180
  - Trade and Economic Problems 185
- The Third World; Nonalignment 186
- Western Defense; North Atlantic Treaty; Atlantic Community 188

THIRD PART

THE WORLD BY REGIONS

I. THE WESTERN HEMISPHERE
- General
  - Inter-American Relations
    - General 193
    - Regional Organizations 197
  - Latin America
    - General 200

CONTENTS

      Political and Constitutional Problems 203
      Economic and Social Problems 208
North America
  The United States
      General 213
      Recent History 214
      Biographies, Memoirs and Addresses
          Biographies 218
          Memoirs 223
          Addresses and Papers 227
      Foreign Policy
          General 229
          Relations with Western Europe 240
          Relations with Eastern Europe and the
            Soviet Union 241
          Relations with the Middle East and the
            Arab World 242
          Relations with Asia 243
          Relations with International Organizations ... 248
          Organization and Procedure 249
          Trade, Tariffs and Finance 251
          Aid and Assistance 254
      Military and Defense Policy 257
      Government and Constitutional Problems 264
      Questions of Subversion, Loyalty and Civil Liberties... 267
      Politics and Political Issues 268
      Economic Problems 274
      Social Questions 276
      Culture; Education; Press; Radio 278
      Science and Society 280
  Canada
      General 281
      Foreign Relations 282
      Military Policy 285
      Government and Politics 285
      Economic Problems 288
  Mexico
      General 289
      Foreign Relations 290
      Government, Constitution and Politics 290
      Economic and Social Problems 292
  Central America
      General 295
      British Honduras 297
      Costa Rica 297
      Guatemala 297
      Honduras 298
      Nicaragua 298
      Panama 299
      El Salvador 300

CONTENTS

West Indies and the Caribbean
    General 300
    Cuba
        General 302
        The Castro Regime 303
    Dominican Republic 307
    Haiti 309
    Jamaica 310
    Puerto Rico 311
    Other Islands 312

South America
    Argentina
        General 313
        Foreign Relations 314
        Government and Politics 314
        Perón and Peronismo 317
        Economic and Social Problems 317
    Bolivia
        General 319
        Foreign Relations 320
        Government and Politics 320
        Economic and Social Problems 322
    Brazil
        General 323
        Foreign Relations 324
        Government and Politics 325
        Economic and Social Problems 327
    Chile
        General 329
        Foreign Relations 332
    Colombia 333
    Ecuador 335
    The Guianas 336
    Paraguay 337
    Peru 338
    Uruguay 340
    Venezuela 341

II. EUROPE

General Surveys 344
Western Europe
    General Surveys and Political Problems 345
    Economic and Social Problems 347
    Integration
        General 349
        European Communities; European Economic
            Community; European Coal and Steel Community;
            European Atomic Energy Community; European
            Free Trade Association 353

CONTENTS

Eastern Europe and the Soviet Bloc
    General Surveys and Political Problems 358
    Economic Problems 362
    Council for Mutual Economic Assistance; Warsaw Treaty Organization 365

The European Nations
    Great Britain
        General 366
        Imperial and Commonwealth Relations; Colonial Policy 367
        Biographies, Memoirs and Addresses 369
        Foreign Policy 375
        Military Policy 378
        Government and Constitutional Problems 379
        Political Problems
            General 381
            Regional Issues 383
        Economic and Financial Problems 385
        Social and Cultural Problems 387
    Ireland 388
    The Netherlands 389
    Belgium 391
    Switzerland 393
    Liechtenstein 395
    France
        General 395
        Recent History 396
        Biographies, Memoirs and Addresses 400
        Foreign Policy 404
        Military Policy 407
        Politics and Government 408
        Economic Problems 415
        Social Problems 416
    The Mediterranean 417
    Malta 418
    Cyprus 418
    Italy
        General 419
        Biographies, Memoirs and Collected Writings 420
        Recent History 422
        Foreign Policy
            General 424
            Territorial Issues 425
        Political and Constitutional Problems 426
        Economic and Social Problems 429
        Regional Problems 431
    Vatican City 432
    Spain
        General 433
        The Republic and the Civil War 434
        The Franco Regime 437

CONTENTS

Foreign Relations	437
Economic and Social Problems	438
Regional Problems	439
Portugal	439
Scandinavia	
General	441
Denmark	442
Norway	444
Sweden	447
Finland	
General	449
Foreign Relations	452
Military Issues	454
Iceland	454
Baltic States	
General	455
Estonia	456
Latvia	458
Lithuania	461
Germany	
General	463
Recent History	465
The 1918 Revolution and the Weimar Republic	
General	468
Foreign Relations	473
The Nazi Era	
General	475
The Nazi Movement	478
Biographies, Memoirs and Collected Writings	480
Foreign Relations	482
Concentration Camps; Antisemitism; War Crimes	484
The Opposition	485
Post-World War II Era	
General	487
Germany under Occupation	488
The Soviet Zone and the German Democratic Republic	489
Berlin	493
Federal Republic of Germany	
General	495
Biographies, Memoirs and Collected Writings	496
Foreign Relations	498
Military Policy	502
Politics and Government	503
Economic and Financial Problems	506
Austria	
General	507
Post-World War II Developments	509
Hungary	
Recent History to 1945	511
Communism and the Communist Regime	513

CONTENTS

The 1956 Revolution	514
Foreign Relations	515

Czechoslovakia

Recent History to 1945	516
Communism and the Communist Regime	519
The 1968 Events	520
Nationalities and Regional Issues	522

Poland

General	523
Biographies, Memoirs and Collected Writings	524
Recent History	
To 1945	525
Since 1945	526
Foreign Relations	527
Economic Problems	529
Territorial, Frontier and Minority Problems	530

Union of Soviet Socialist Republics

General	531
Correspondents' Reports and Personal Accounts	532
Memoirs and Biographies	533
Recent History	
General	538
Revolution; Civil War; The Lenin Era	541
The Stalin Era	544
The Post-Stalin Years	545
Communist Party of the Soviet Union	546
Bolshevism and Soviet Marxism	547
Foreign Policy	
General	550
Relations with Western Europe	554
Relations with China	555
Relations with Other Countries	558
Foreign Economic Policy	560
Military Policy	561
Space Problems	563
Government; Constitution; Law	564
Secret Police; Political Trials; Espionage	566
Forced Labor; Prison Camps	567
Political Opposition; Defection	568
Economic Questions	
General	569
Agricultural Problems	574
Industry and Industrial Management	575
Manpower; Labor; Wages	576
Social Questions	576
Culture, Education and Religion	578
Regional, National and Minority Problems	
General	580
The Jews	581

CONTENTS

European Republics	
Ukrainian S.S.R.	582
Other Republics	584
Asian Republics	585
Rumania	588
Jugoslavia	
General	591
The Tito Regime	594
Bulgaria	596
Albania	600
Greece	
General	602
Biographies and Memoirs	604
World War II and the Civil War Period	605
Foreign Relations	606

III. ASIA AND THE PACIFIC AREA

General Surveys	607
Middle East	
General Surveys and Political Problems	611
Oil	615
The Arab World	616
Turkey	
General Surveys and Political Problems	622
Foreign Relations	625
Economic Problems	626
Syria	626
Lebanon	628
Israel	
General	629
Biographies, Memoirs and Collected Writings	630
Foreign Relations	
General	631
Arab-Israeli Conflict	
General	633
The 1956 Suez Crisis	637
Military Confrontations	638
Defense Policies	639
Politics and Government	640
Economic Problems	641
Social Problems	642
Jordan	643
Iraq	
General	644
The Kurdish Question	645
Saudi Arabia; United Arab Emirates (the former Trucial States); Kuwait; Southern Yemen; Yemen; Oman; Arabian Peninsula; Persian Gulf	646
Iran	649

CONTENTS

Central Asia and the Subcontinent of India
    General 652
    Afghanistan 653
    Tibet 654
    Nepal 655
    Sikkim; Bhutan 656
    India (Subcontinent and the Republic of India)
        General 656
        Recent History; Independence and Partition 657
        Biographies, Memoirs and Collected Writings 660
        Governmental, Constitutional and Political Problems .. 662
        Foreign Policy
            General 666
            Indian-Pakistani Relations; Kashmir Dispute . 668
            Indian-Chinese Relations 670
        Economic Problems 671
        Social Problems 674
    Pakistan
        General Surveys and Political Problems 675
        Foreign Relations 678
        Economic Problems 678
    Bangladesh 679
    Sri Lanka (Ceylon); Mauritius; Indian Ocean 680
Far East
    General 682
    China
        General 683
        Recent History 684
        Chinese Communism; The Communist Regime
            General 687
            The Cultural Revolution 695
        Biographies, Memoirs and Collected Writings 698
        Tourists' and Correspondents' Reports 700
        Foreign Relations 702
        Military Questions 705
        Economic and Social Problems 707
        Educational and Cultural Problems................... 710
        Overseas Chinese.................................... 711
        Sinkiang; National Minority Areas 711
        Taiwan (Formosa) 712
    Mongolian People's Republic 713
    Japan
        General 714
        Recent History
            General 715
            Since 1945 716
        Biographies and Memoirs 717
        Foreign and Defense Policies 718
        Politics and Government 721
        Economic Problems 723
        Social Problems 725

CONTENTS

Korea
- General 726
- The Korean War 728
- The *Pueblo* Affair 729
- Republic of Korea (South Korea) 730
- Democratic People's Republic of Korea (North Korea). 731

Southeastern Asia; East Indies
- General 733

Indochina
- General Surveys and the End of the French Rule 736
- Vietnam
  - General 738
  - The Vietnam War
    - General 739
    - U.S. Involvement 741
    - Military Aspects 745
  - Republic of Vietnam (South Vietnam) 746
  - Democratic Republic of Vietnam (North Vietnam) 747
- Laos 749
- Khmer Republic (Cambodia) 750

Thailand 751
Burma 753
Hong Kong 754
Singapore 755
Malaysia 756
Indonesia
- General 759
- Recent History 760
- Economic and Social Problems 762

Philippines 763

Australia and New Zealand
- General 766
- Australia
  - General 766
  - Foreign and Defense Policies 767
  - Politics and Government 769
  - Economic and Social Problems 770
- New Zealand 771

The Pacific Ocean
- General 772
- U.S. Territories 773
- Papua New Guinea 774
- Fiji; French Polynesia; New Caledonia; Western Samoa; Nauru 775

IV. AFRICA

General
- General Surveys 776
- Political Problems 779

CONTENTS

International Relations
- General 784
- Economic 787
- Economic and Social Problems 789

North Africa
- General 793
- Morocco 794
- Algeria 796
- Tunisia 799
- Libya 800
- Arab Republic of Egypt
  - General Surveys 801
  - Politics and Government 802
  - Foreign Relations 804
  - Economic and Social Conditions 804
- Sudan 806

West Africa
- General 807
- Guinea; Portuguese Guinea; Mali; Mauritania 809
- Ivory Coast; Togo; Dahomey; Upper Volta 810
- Senegal 811
- Sierra Leone; Gambia 812
- Liberia 813
- Ghana 814
- Nigeria
  - Politics and Government 816
  - The Civil War 818
  - Economic and Social Conditions 819
- Chad; Niger 821

Central Africa
- General 821
- Zaïre (Congo-Kinshasa) 822
- Congo-Brazzaville 824
- Cameroon 825
- Gabon; Central African Republic 825

East Africa
- General 826
- Ethiopia 827
- Somali Republic; The French Territory of the Afars and the Issas 829
- Kenya 829
- Uganda 831
- Rwanda; Burundi 832
- United Republic of Tanzania (Tanganyika; Zanzibar) 832

Southern Africa
- General 835
- Republic of South Africa
  - General 836
  - Apartheid 838
- Lesotho; Botswana; Swaziland 841
- South West Africa 841

Federation of Rhodesia and Nyasaland 842
Rhodesia... 843
Zambia 845
Malawi (Nyasaland) 846
Angola; Mozambique.................................... 846
Malagasy Republic (Madagascar) 847

V. POLAR REGIONS 848

Index to Authors 851

Index to Title Entries.................................. 918

PREFACE

In the Book of Ecclesiastes it is written: "Of making many books there is no end" (12:12). It was not an easy task to compile a bibliography that would continue the tradition of the earlier volumes of this series and provide an overview of the books and monographs published all over the world from 1962 to 1972. These publications deal with political, economic, and social developments and, particularly, with international relations in its many aspects since the beginning of World War I. The constant reorganization of the international state-system, especially since the end of World War II, and the ever-increasing output of books have affected the compilation of this volume in many ways. To note but one example: the recently established nations increasingly demanded and received recognition from observers everywhere and they themselves published more and more books in various languages on their history, achievements and goals.

The decade 1962-1972 also witnessed the start of the transformation of the international order established after World War II—a system that was characterized by the uncontested preeminence of the United States in all aspects of international politics and economics. For the bibliographer of contemporary history the changing world scene and the groping for new answers to international and national issues was reflected not only by a vast outpouring of books on various aspects of U.S. politics and foreign relations and such events as the Vietnam War, but also by new attempts and methods to reevaluate most international and national developments since World War II, or for that matter, since World War I. Though the world in the 1980s (a main concern in the present activities of the Council on Foreign Relations) will bear little resemblance to the world of the 1960s, it is hoped that the information provided by *Foreign Affairs Bibliography 1962-1972* will help guide us in coming events and to a better understanding of our past.

This is the fifth *Foreign Affairs Bibliography* prepared under the auspices of the Council on Foreign Relations. The first volume, for the years 1919-1932, was prepared by William L. Langer and the late Hamilton Fish Armstrong; the second, 1932-1942, by the late Robert Gale Woolbert; the third, 1942-1952, and the fourth, 1952-1962, by the late Henry L. Roberts. The present volume should be used in conjunction with the four previous volumes of this series and also with the special volume *The Foreign Affairs 50-Year Bibliography: New Evaluations of Significant Books on International Relations 1920-1970*, edited by the late Byron Dexter, that marked the fiftieth year of publication in October 1972 of the quarterly review *Foreign Affairs*. The student of contemporary history should always bear in mind that the *Foreign Affairs Bibliography* is compiled on a selective basis and includes only material published in book form, and that for any in-depth study of specific topics the user should also consult special subject bibliographies and reference works.

Foreign Affairs Bibliography 1962-1972 retains the outline and structure of its four predecessors. It is divided into three major sections: General International Relations, The World Since 1914, and The World by Regions, emphasizing respectively, analytical, chronological, and regional or national treatments. While these divisions, of course, cannot prevent overlapping classifications, the table of contents, the cross-references at the head of each section, and the index will guide the reader to the relevant material.

The volume considers books published in the years from 1962 (except for the 1962 titles appearing in the preceding volume) through 1972. Works published in 1973 and later have been included only if they are translations of works that appeared earlier, volumes whose publication completes a set, revised editions, or American editions of books first published elsewhere.

This bibliography is concerned only with the historical period since the outbreak of World War I. While its emphasis is upon international developments and foreign affairs, it includes the principal works on the politics, economy and social developments of nations throughout the world. The majority of the titles are in English and Western languages. However, as in the preceding volumes, an attempt was also made to list the significant books in other languages. Because more books dealing with contemporary history are being published in minor European and non-Western languages than ever before, the present bibliography contains more such titles than any of its predecessors.

For transliteration of titles printed in non-Western alphabets the Library of Congress transliteration systems, sometimes in modified versions, have been used. For capitalization of foreign language titles, contrary to the custom of the preceding volumes, the rules of the respective languages generally have been observed.

In general, this volume has followed its predecessors in not attempting to list the vast output of governmental publications, pamphlet material and textbooks. However, exceptions have been made for particularly significant books and series and for publications from countries where the distinction between the public and private domain is vague.

As was stated in the foreword to the first volume of *Foreign Affairs Bibliography*, the annotations are in the main descriptive and analytical, and are meant to indicate the nature of the book and the competence of the author.

Of the approximately 11,000 titles included in the present volume, a little less than half were listed in the Recent Books section of the *Foreign Affairs* quarterly. These titles, which form the basis of the volume, were selected and annotated primarily by the late Henry L. Roberts (who was solely responsible for the Recent Books section of *Foreign Affairs* from 1950 to 1967), by John G. Stoessinger (who coordinated and guided the section between 1967 and early 1972) and by the following contributors: Lewis C. Austin, William P. Bundy, John C. Campbell, Robert D. Crassweller, Pamela Day, William Diebold, Jr., Joseph A. Ellis, Robert Gilpin, Howard Linton, Richard H. Nolte, Andrew J. Pierre, Edward Schumacher, Gaddis Smith, Fritz Stern, Robert W. Valkenier, Jennifer Seymour Whitaker and Frank Wolf.

In order to get a representative selection of books for this volume, many scholars and the resources of countless institutions and libraries were consulted. Among the institutions and libraries that have provided aid and cooperation, I have to mention the Columbia University Libraries and, particularly, its reference department for a never-failing courtesy and willingness to provide assistance. Equally helpful over a period of many years has been the staff of the Italian Cultural Institute in New York. Other institutions and libraries which have been of great assistance are: Académie Royale des Sciences, des Lettres et des Beaux-arts de Belgique, Office Internationale de Librairie, Brussels; Bulgarian Academy of Sciences, Institute of History, Sophia; Department of International Affairs, Wellington; Forschungsinstitut der Deutschen Gesellschaft für Auswärtige Politik, Bonn; German Information Center, New York; Hunter College Library, New York; Institut Royal des Relations Internationales, Brussels; Det Kongelige Bibliotek, Copenhagen; Landsbókasafn Íslands, Reykjavik; The Library of the Australian Information Service, New York; The Library of Congress, Washington, D.C.; The Library of the Consulate General of Canada, New York; Nederlandsch Genootschap voor Internationale Zaken, The Hague; The New York Public Library; Det Norske Nobelinstituut, Oslo; The Romanian Library, New York; Stato Maggiore della Marina, Ufficio Storico Marina Militare, Rome; Utrikespolitiska Institutet, Stockholm; and the Zionist Archives and Library, New York.

The following scholars have provided advice, comments and contributions: Olavi Arens, Armstrong State College; George Atiyeh, Near Eastern Section, The Library of Congress; Paul H. Borsuk, Wellesley College; Lenard J. Cohen, Simon Fraser University; Emmanuel Coppieters, Institut Royal des Relations Internationales, Brussels; Olafur F. Hjartar, Landsbókasafn Íslands; Reuben B. Johnson, III, Center for Policy Research, New York; Kemal H. Karpat, University of Wisconsin; John I. Kolehmainen, Heidelberg College; Sylvia Landress, Zionist Archives and Library, New York; Juan Linz, Yale University; Vojtech Mastny, University of Illinois; Alfred Natali, Brooklyn College; Brit Roeck Odeen, Utrikespolitiska Institutet, Stockholm; Nissan Oren, The Hebrew University of Jerusalem; Juhani Paasivirta, University of Turku; Peter Prifti, Massachusetts Institute of Technology; Daisy Robers, Nederlandsch Genootschap voor Internationale Zaken, The Hague; Rouhollah K. Ramazani, University of Virginia; Paul A. Shapiro, Columbia University; Elsa Skarprud, Det Norske Nobelinstituut, Oslo; Richard Sorich, Columbia University; Adolf Sprudzs, University of Chicago Law School Library; Rudolf Tökés, University of Connecticut; V. Stanley Vardys, University of Oklahoma; Knud Vohn, Det Kongelige Bibliotek, Copenhagen; Piotr S. Wandycz, Yale University; Douglas L. Wheeler, University of New Hampshire; Stephen G. Xydis, Hunter College; and Frank T. Yorichika, East Asian Library, Columbia University.

I am particularly grateful to Jean Gunther, who was my mentor and close collaborator for many years in my bibliographic ventures at the Council on Foreign Relations. Jean Gunther carried the major burden in preparing the material for the two preceding volumes of the *Foreign Affairs Bibliography* and for the Recent Books section in *Foreign Affairs* from 1947 to 1972. In addition, Dzintra Bungs devoted more than a year to this undertaking. In the final phase, the dedication and perseverance of Randi Crawford considerably lightened my bibliographical and editorial chores. Finally, I have to thank the members of the staff of the Council on Foreign Relations for their assistance: Donald Wasson, Janet Rigney, Virginia Etheridge and Sally Parsons of the Library; William P. Bundy, John Temple Swing, Doris E. Forest, Grace Darling Griffin, Elizabeth H. Bryant, Helena Stalson, Vivian Kardaras and Robert W. Valkenier.

—Janis A. Kreslins

New York City, July 1975

FIRST PART:

GENERAL INTERNATIONAL RELATIONS

I. GENERAL WORKS

REFERENCE WORKS

See also (Political Factors) General, p. 12; General Geography and Environment, p. 45; General Economic Conditions and Tendencies, p. 49; Underdeveloped Economies, p. 78; International Law, p. 83; International Organization and Government, p. 96; War and Peace, p. 108; The World Since 1914, p. 129.

The Annual Register of World Events. New York: St. Martin's Press.
 The volume for 1972 of this venerable reference work, edited by Sir Ivison Macadam, is the 214th consecutive issue.

Current Biography. New York: H. W. Wilson.
 Well-researched biographical articles on persons prominent in the news. Monthly and annual issues; cumulative indexes. Published since 1940.

Dexter, Byron, *ed.*; assisted by Bryant, Elizabeth H. and Murray, Janice L. **The Foreign Affairs 50-Year Bibliography: New Evaluations of Significant Books on International Relations, 1920-1970.** New York: Bowker (for the Council on Foreign Relations), 1972, 936 p.
 This major undertaking provides the reader with a selection and appraisal of the most consequential and lasting works on foreign affairs that have appeared in the last half-century. Some 400 scholars have written new reviews and considerations of the 2,130 books chosen.

Documents on International Affairs, 1928-1963. New York: Oxford University Press (for the Royal Institute of International Affairs), 1929-73, 31 v.
 A very useful annual series of documents covering the period from 1928 through 1963 and supplementing and illustrating the corresponding volumes in the "Survey of International Affairs." For index covering the volumes 1928 to 1938, see the note under the "Survey of International Affairs."

The Europa Year Book. London: Europa Publications.
 This annual survey in two volumes, published since 1959, is a most useful reference work for the political, economic, social and cultural affairs of the contemporary world. Volume I of the 1972 edition contains information about international organizations and individual European countries; Volume II covers the states and territories of Africa, the Americas, Asia and Australasia.

Facts on File. New York: Facts on File.
 A digest of world news, published weekly since 1941, with semimonthly, quarterly and annual indexes.

The Far East and Australasia, 1969–. London: Europa Publications, 1969–.
 A solid reference work on "the states and territories of the area extending eastwards from Afghanistan and fanning out in the north through the Soviet Union to the Bering Strait, and in the south through Southern Asia to Australia, New Zealand and the Pacific territories." Through 1973 five volumes have been published.

Gilbert, Martin. **Recent History Atlas: 1870 to the Present Day.** New York: Macmillan, 1969, 121 p.
 A thorough reference prepared by a historian at Oxford University.

Gould, Julius and Kolb, William Lester, *eds.* **A Dictionary of the Social Sciences.** New York: Free Press of Glencoe, 1964, 761 p.
 A reference volume defining approximately one thousand basic concepts used in the

social sciences. It has been compiled by two groups of social scientists, one in the United Kingdom and the other in the United States, and was published under the auspices of UNESCO.

Harmon, Robert Bartlett. **Political Science: A Bibliographical Guide to the Literature.** New York: Scarecrow Press, 1965, 388 p.
A reference tool for students.

The Indian Year Book of International Affairs. Madras: University of Madras, Indian Study Group of International Affairs.
Collections of articles on international law and international relations published annually from 1952 to 1959, irregularly since 1960. Edited since 1962 by T. S. Rama Rao. Volume XV-XVI, covering the years 1966-67, was published in 1970.

International Encyclopedia of the Social Sciences. New York: Macmillan, 1968, 17 v.
A massive reference work, containing a wealth of information on contemporary political thought and developments. Edited by David L. Sills.

The International Who's Who. London: Europa Publications.
Biographical information about distinguished people in every country. Published annually since 1935.

Die internationale Politik: Jahrbücher des Forschungsinstituts der deutschen Gesellschaft für Auswärtige Politik. Bonn: Deutsche Gesellschaft für Auswärtige Politik, 1958–.
Yearbooks of the Deutsche Gesellschaft für Auswärtige Politik, published irregularly since 1958. Each yearbook consists of a volume of articles dealing with international affairs and with developments in the various countries of the world and of two supplementary volumes of documents and chronologies. Eight issues of the main volume have appeared through 1973 covering the years from 1955 to 1967. The supplementary volumes published through 1973 cover the years from 1961 to 1971.

Keesing's Contemporary Archives. London: Keesing's Publications.
A very thorough and detailed weekly digest of world events, published since 1931, with cumulative subject and name indexes.

Kernig, Claus Dieter, *ed.* **Marxism, Communism and Western Society: A Comparative Encyclopedia.** New York: McGraw-Hill, 1972-74, 8 v.
A massive encyclopedia that compares Soviet and Western concepts of history, politics, psychology and other social sciences. The German original appeared as "Sowjetsystem und demokratische Gesellschaft: eine vergleichende Enzyklopädie" (Freiburg: Herder, 1966-72, 6 v.).

Langer, William L., *comp.* and *ed.* **An Encyclopedia of World History.** Boston: Houghton, 5th rev. and enl. ed., 1972, 1,569 p.
The revised fifth edition of an indispensable work of reference, first published in 1940.

Mason, John Brown. **Research Resources: Annotated Guide to the Social Sciences. Volume I: International Relations & Recent History; Indexes, Abstracts & Periodicals.** Santa Barbara: American Bibliographical Center–Clio Press, 1968, 243 p.
This bibliography, in the words of the editors, "is designed for use of upper and lower division students, graduate students, and professors."

Mezhdunarodnyi ezhegodnik: politika i ekonomika, 1958–. Moscow: Izd-vo Politicheskoi Literatury, 1958–.
An annual comprising articles on international politics and summaries of major events in socialist, capitalist and developing states. Compiled by the Institute of World Economy and International Relations, this series is a useful reference for tracing the evolution of Moscow's view of world politics. Title varies.

Political Handbook and Atlas of the World, 1963–. New York: Harper and Row; Simon and Shuster (for the Council on Foreign Relations), 1963–.
This standard annual reference work, published formerly as "Political Handbook of the World," provides detailed information on all of the world's countries and dependent territories, plus basic data on the leading intergovernmental organizations. Edited from 1963 to 1968 by Walter H. Mallory. The volume for 1969 was not published. The 1970 issue and the supplementary annual volumes "The World This Year" for 1971-73 were edited by Richard P. Stebbins and Alba Amoia.

Prescott, John Robert Victor. **The Geography of Frontiers and Boundaries.** Chicago: Aldine Publishing Co., 1965, 190 p.

GENERAL WORKS

A convenient reference for geographers and political scientists, by an Australian scholar.

Roberts, Henry Lithgow and Others. **Foreign Affairs Bibliography.** New York: Bowker (for the Council on Foreign Relations), 1964, 752 p.

An extensive annotated bibliography of books published during the decade 1952–62 in international affairs, contemporary history and related fields. Based mainly on notes appearing in *Foreign Affairs*, this volume also contains several thousand additional titles.

The Statesman's Year Book: Statistical and Historical Annual of the States of the World. New York: St. Martin's Press.

A most useful annual reference volume containing historical, political, economical and statistical information on international organizations and the states of the world. Edited by Sigfrid Heinrich Steinberg from 1946 to 1969, since then by John Paxton.

Survey of International Affairs, 1920/23–. New York: Oxford University Press (for the Royal Institute of International Affairs), 1925–.

A well-known and valuable review of international affairs. Forty-four volumes covering the developments from 1920 to 1962 have been published through 1972. The volume for 1963 will be the concluding one of this impressive series. There is a "Consolidated Index to the Survey of International Affairs, 1920–1938, and Documents on International Affairs, 1928–1938," compiled by E. M. R. Ditmas.

Toscano, Mario. **The History of Treaties and International Politics. I: An Introduction to the History of Treaties and International Politics; The Documentary and Memoir Sources.** Baltimore: Johns Hopkins Press, 1966, 685 p.

A translation of Professor Toscano's important introduction to diplomatic documents and sources. The Italian original, first published in 1958, appeared in an enlarged edition as "Storia dei trattati e politica internazionale. I: Parte generale; introduzione allo studio della 'Storia dei trattati e politica internazionale' –le fonti documentarie e memorialistiche" (Turin: Giappichelli, 2d rev. and enl. ed., 1963, 850 p.).

Who's Who. New York: St. Martin's Press.

An annual British biographical dictionary containing information not only about persons prominent in Great Britain, but also in other countries. The 1972–73 volume was the 124th consecutive issue.

Who's Who in America. Chicago: Marquis.

A standard reference work. Published biennially since 1899.

Who's Who in the World, 1971–1972–. Chicago: Marquis, 1970–.

A new biographical dictionary, listing "those individuals who are of current reference interest and inquiry throughout the world."

Winchell, Constance M. **Guide to Reference Books.** Chicago: American Library Association, 8th ed., 1967, 741 p.

A very well-organized and indispensable vade mecum to reference books in all fields of knowledge. For students of contemporary history and international politics particularly useful are the sections dealing with history and area studies, economics, political science, law, geography, bibliography, and library resources. Three supplementary volumes, covering the years from 1965 to 1970 and compiled by Eugene P. Sheehy, were published from 1968 to 1972.

World Index of Social Science Institutions. Paris: UNESCO, 1970–.

A card index of social science research, advanced training and documentation institutions, based on information available in the UNESCO Social Science Documentation Centre.

The World of Learning. London: Europa Publications.

A massive, well-prepared and well-indexed listing of international and national learned societies, research institutes, libraries, archives, museums and universities. The volume for 1973–74, published in two parts, is the 24th consecutive edition.

The Year Book of World Affairs. New York: Praeger (for the London Institute of World Affairs).

An annual volume of articles on political, legal, economic and cultural problems. This series, edited by George W. Keeton and Georg Schwarzenberger, has been published since 1947.

GENERAL INTERNATIONAL RELATIONS

Yearbook of International Organizations. Brussels: Union of International Associations.
An indispensable reference work, published since 1948 and covering intergovernmental and nongovernmental organizations. The 14th edition (1972–73) was published in 1972.

Zawodny, Janusz Kazimierz. **Guide to the Study of International Relations.** San Francisco: Chandler, 1966, 151 p.
A reference volume designed to aid the student and researcher in finding materials dealing with contemporary international relations.

METHODOLOGY AND THEORY

See also General Treatments, p. 7; Political Factors, p. 12; Economic Factors, p. 49; International Law, p. 83; International Organization and Government, p. 96; War and Peace, p. 108.

Aron, Raymond. **Peace and War: A Theory of International Relations.** Garden City: Doubleday, 1966, 820 p.
A translation of a major study of the theory, sociology and history of international relations by an eminent French political scientist. The work appeared originally as "Paix et guerre entre les nations" (Paris: Calman-Lévy, 1962, 794 p.).

Burton, John Wear. **Conflict and Communication.** New York: Free Press, 1969, 246 p.
An analysis of conflict resolution. In his case materials the British scholar explores various patterns of interaction that nations in conflict might usefully apply in their efforts to reduce tensions between them.

Burton, John Wear. **International Relations: A General Theory.** New York: Cambridge University Press, 1965, 288 p.
In this significant work, the author offers a critique of orthodox power theory and its application, and turns to new models involving decision-making, communications, nonalignment and a system of state relations not dependent upon power.

Burton, John Wear. **Systems, States, Diplomacy and Rules.** New York: Cambridge University Press, 1968, 251 p.
A brave attempt to relate systems theory to contemporary international relations. Only partially successful but refreshingly free of jargon.

Burton, John Wear. **World Society.** New York: Cambridge University Press, 1972, 180 p.
An agreeable introduction to recent approaches to the study of world affairs.

Butterfield, Herbert and Wight, Martin, eds. **Diplomatic Investigations: Essays in the Theory of International Politics.** Cambridge: Harvard University Press, 1966, 227 p.
A stimulating if inconclusive collection of essays by a distinguished group of scholars wrestling with the problem why there is no adequate, or even real, theory of international politics.

Crawford, Elisabeth T. and Biderman, Albert D., eds. **Social Scientists and International Affairs.** New York: Wiley, 1969, 333 p.
A somewhat labored effort by 23 scholars to develop a "sociology of social science."

Deutsch, Karl W. **The Analysis of International Relations.** Englewood Cliffs: Prentice-Hall, 1968, 214 p.
A sophisticated introduction to international relations. The author makes discriminating use of quantitative data, communications, conflict and game theory.

Duchacek, Ivo D. **Comparative Federalism: The Territorial Dimension of Politics.** New York: Holt, Rinehart and Winston, 1970, 370 p.
A study of the multifaceted relationship between geography and power in the modern world.

Flechtheim, Ossip Kurt. **Eine Welt oder keine? Beiträge zur Politik, Politologie und Philosophie.** Frankfurt/Main: Europäische Verlagsanstalt, 1964, 266 p.
A collection of articles on contemporary political and philosophical problems by the father of "futurology." Professor Flechtheim is known for his advocacy of a more systematic approach to the exploration and planning of the future.

GENERAL WORKS

Forward, Nigel. **The Field of Nations.** Boston: Little, Brown, 1971, 207 p.
A British scholar surveys the leading game-theory and mathematical approaches to international politics, using the Cuban missile crisis as a model. The book cuts through a great deal of jargon with considerable insight and a welcome sense of humor.

Giffin, Sidney F. **The Crisis Game: Simulating International Conflict.** Garden City: Doubleday, 1965, 191 p.
A helpful introduction to an evaluation of the techniques and utility of political and military gaming, by a former U.S. Air Force general.

Goldmann, Kjell. **International Norms and War between States: Three Studies in International Politics.** Stockholm: Läromedelsförlagen, 1971, 368 p.
An attempt to quantify political decision-making in the international system by a Swedish scholar. Sponsored by the Center for International Affairs, Harvard University, and the Swedish Institute of International Affairs.

Guetzkow, Harold and Others. **Simulation in Social and Administrative Science.** Englewood Cliffs: Prentice-Hall, 1972, 768 p.
An extensive survey and appraisal of the state of the art of simulation.

Harrison, Horace Virgil, ed. **The Role of Theory in International Relations.** Princeton: Van Nostrand, 1964, 118 p.
Papers by Quincy Wright, Kenneth W. Thompson, William T. R. Fox and Hans J. Morgenthau, originally presented at a symposium given at the University of Maryland in the spring of 1961.

Hermann, Charles F., ed. **International Crises: Insights from Behavioral Research.** New York: Free Press, 1972, 334 p.
A well-orchestrated symposium on international crises, and a landmark study in the multidisciplinary and behavioral approaches to the subject. Heavy on methodology and statistics, and frequently jargon-ridden, this study illustrates both the strengths and limitations of the behavioral approach to international relations.

Hoffmann, Stanley, ed. **Conditions of World Order.** Boston: Houghton, 1968, 397 p.
An uneven symposium with contributions by 21 scholars. The most significant essays are those by Raymond Aron, Stanley Hoffmann and Henry A. Kissinger.

Holsti, K. J. **International Politics: A Framework for Analysis.** Englewood Cliffs: Prentice-Hall, 1967, 505 p.
The organization of this competent and useful textbook is based on two questions: "Why do states conduct their relations in specified ways, and how do they conduct their relations?"

Holsti, Ole R. **Crisis Escalation War.** Montreal: McGill-Queen's University Press, 1972, 290 p.
Using as case studies the crisis of 1914, which led to war, and the Cuban missile crisis of 1962, which did not, the author seeks to cast some light on decision-making in moments of mounting tension.

Hugo, Grant. **Appearance and Reality in International Relations.** New York: Columbia University Press, 1971, 207 p.
A somewhat discursive though intelligent treatment of the role of misunderstanding among nations, with illustrations taken from different periods of history.

Iklé, Fred Charles. **How Nations Negotiate.** New York: Harper and Row (for the Center for International Affairs, Harvard University), 1964, 274 p.
An analytical study of "the process and effects of negotiation between governments." Although the author is interested in the theory of negotiation, the book is grounded in a useful exploration of practical experience.

Jervis, Robert. **The Logic of Images in International Relations.** Princeton: Princeton University Press, 1970, 281 p.
This study explores the many intricate patterns in which nations manipulate other nations' political and strategic expectations, thus deriving advantages in the formulation of their own strategies and policies. Written under the auspices of the Center for International Affairs, Harvard University.

Kaplan, Morton A., *ed*. **New Approaches to International Relations.** New York: St. Martin's Press, 1968, 518 p.
Fourteen essays strung together in a highly uneven symposium, with a strong mathematical bent.

Kelman, Herbert C., *ed*. **International Behavior: A Social-Psychological Analysis.** New York: Holt, Rinehart and Winston (for the Society for the Psychological Study of Social Issues), 1965, 626 p.
A loose-jointed discussion, by a number of contributors, of the social-psychological approach to the study of international relations.

Klineberg, Otto. **The Human Dimension in International Relations.** New York: Holt, Rinehart and Winston, 1964, 173 p.
An eminent psychologist, convinced that war is not inevitable, appeals for an intelligent new approach to the conduct of international relations.

Knorr, Klaus Eugen and Rosenau, James N., *eds*. **Contending Approaches to International Politics.** Princeton: Princeton University Press (for the Princeton Center of International Studies), 1969, 297 p.
Essays emphasizing the compatibility of tradition and science in the study of international politics.

Konstantinov, Fedor Vasil'evich and Others, *eds*. **Sotsiologicheskie problemy mezhdunarodnykh otnoshenii.** Moscow: Izd-vo "Nauka," 1970, 326 p.
A collection of theoretical essays by leading Soviet scholars on critical problems in international relations, including peaceful coexistence of competing systems, the origins of militarism, the role of nationalism in the non-capitalist path of development, and disarmament.

Lieber, Robert J. **Theory and World Politics.** Cambridge (Mass.): Winthrop Publishers, 1972, 166 p.
A discussion of the possibility of a "scientific" theory of international relations, including such likely contenders as game theory, integration theory, cybernetics and systems theory.

Morgan, Roger, *ed*. **The Study of International Relations: Essays in Honour of Kenneth Younger.** New York: Oxford University Press (for the Royal Institute of International Affairs), 1972, 309 p.
A *Festschrift* in honor of the former director of Chatham House by authors closely associated with its work. Each has assessed the literature of his particular specialty, indicated subjects for future exploration and placed the research activities of Chatham House in context. Of interest to specialists and generalists alike.

Platig, Emil Raymond. **International Relations Research: Problems of Evaluation and Advancement.** Santa Barbara: Clio Press (for Carnegie Endowment for International Peace), 1967, 211 p.
A most useful and comprehensive analytical overview of the state of international relations as a discipline.

Rosecrance, Richard Newton. **Action and Reaction in World Politics.** Boston: Little, Brown, 1963, 314 p.
An effort to provide an analysis of international relations based on the data and perspectives of the historical experience of the last two centuries. In contrast to a number of writers, the author places considerable weight on the importance of domestic changes affecting the pattern of foreign affairs.

Rosenau, James N., *ed*. **International Politics and Foreign Policy: A Reader in Research and Theory.** New York: Free Press, rev. ed., 1969, 740 p.
The primary goal of this completely revised edition of an important reader (the first edition was published in 1961) is "to heighten the interdependence of theory and research" in the study of international politics and foreign policy. Fifty-two of the 57 selections are new.

Rosenau, James N. **The Scientific Study of Foreign Policy.** New York: Free Press, 1971, 472 p.
This is a brave and ambitious effort by an intelligent scholar who labors mightily to show that foreign policy is more science than art. The case is not proven in this book.

GENERAL WORKS

Rothstein, Robert L. **Planning, Prediction, and Policymaking in Foreign Affairs: Theory and Practice.** Boston: Little, Brown, 1972, 215 p.
An earnest brief for true long-range planning, lifted out of the State Department but using the combined services of practitioners and theoreticians.

Russett, Bruce Martin. **International Regions and the International System: A Study in Political Ecology.** Chicago: Rand McNally, 1967, 252 p.
An effort to apply quantitative and mathematical models to regional groupings.

Russett, Bruce Martin, ed. **Peace, War and Numbers.** Beverly Hills: Sage Publications, 1972, 352 p.
Papers originally presented at the September 1970 annual meeting of the American Political Science Association in Los Angeles. The authors, making use of the tools of modern social science, deal with current international problems in a highly theoretical manner.

Said, Abdul A., ed. **Theory of International Relations: The Crisis of Relevance.** Englewood Cliffs: Prentice-Hall, 1968, 191 p.
This anthology is a useful companion piece to Stanley Hoffmann's more thorough collection "Contemporary Theory in International Relations" (Englewood Cliffs: Prentice-Hall, 1960, 293 p.).

Singer, J. David. **Quantitative International Politics: Insights and Evidence.** New York: Free Press, 1968, 394 p.
Ten attempts to measure international relationships.

Singer, Marshall R. **Weak States in a World of Powers: The Dynamics of International Relationships.** New York: Free Press, 1972, 431 p.
A well-argued thesis that strong powers can be more effective in influencing and assisting weak powers by using "attractive" instruments of power (economic aid and cultural ties especially) than coercive ones.

Spiegel, Steven L. **Dominance and Diversity: The International Hierarchy.** Boston: Little, Brown, 1972, 309 p.
A careful, occasionally original analytic treatment of the nature of power today. Balanced but slightly jargon-laden, as in the conclusion that the future "will be determined by a dialectic between the distribution of power in the international hierarchy and the behavioral implications of particular strategies pursued by specific states."

Tanter, Raymond and Ullman, Richard H., eds. **Theory and Policy in International Relations.** Princeton: Princeton University Press (for the Center of International Studies, Princeton University), 1972, 250 p.
A collection of essays written with the intention "to bridge the gap between the community of policy-makers and the community of theorists."

Young, Oran R. **The Intermediaries: Third Parties in International Crises.** Princeton: Princeton University Press (for the Center of International Studies, Princeton University), 1967, 427 p.
A highly sophisticated though over-theoretical effort to explore the possibilities of third-party intervention in different types of international crises. Borrows heavily from the insights of Thomas Schelling.

GENERAL TREATMENTS

See also Methodology and Theory, p. 4; (Political Factors) General, p. 12; Economic Factors, p. 49; (The World Since 1914) General, p. 129.

Beaton, Leonard. **The Reform of Power: A Proposal for an International Security System.** New York: Viking, 1972, 242 p.
Beaton's premature death deprived us of a knowing and deep thinker on problems of international security. Fortunately, he left this statement of a philosophy and strategy for building a structure of world order, one which accepts the existence of national nuclear forces but which also suggests long-term arms-control measures.

GENERAL INTERNATIONAL RELATIONS

Beilenson, Laurence W., assisted by Dain, Bernard M. **The Treaty Trap.** Washington: Public Affairs Press, 1969, 344 p.
A well-researched indictment of uncritical reliance upon treaties in matters of vital national interest. The author maintains that most states are habitual treaty-breakers if the national interest so dictates.

Bell, Coral. **The Conventions of Crisis.** New York: Oxford University Press (for the Royal Institute of International Affairs), 1971, 131 p.
An illuminating study of the recently developing techniques of "managing" diplomatic crises.

Bennett, John Coleman. **Foreign Policy in Christian Perspective.** New York: Scribner, 1966, 160 p.
A thoughtful, somewhat Niebuhrian exploration of major world problems. The author argues the relevance of Christian ethics to foreign policy and urges Christians to take part in guiding the decisions of policy-makers.

Black, Cyril E. and Others. **Neutralization and World Politics.** Princeton: Princeton University Press, 1968, 195 p.
A first-rate analysis of the experience with neutralization arrangements.

Black, Joseph E. and Thompson, Kenneth W., *eds.* **Foreign Policies in a World of Change.** New York: Harper and Row, 1963, 756 p.
This volume comprises substantial statements on the foreign policies of 24 nations, all (except for Nigeria and Communist China) prepared for the book by scholars or statesmen of the countries covered. Includes pieces on the U.S.S.R. and Jugoslavia.

Bonante, Luigi. **La politica della dissuasione.** Turin: Giappichelli, 1971, 429 p.
An extended analysis and critique of the theory and practice of deterrence in international affairs.

Brown, Constantine. **The Coming of the Whirlwind.** Chicago: Regnery, 1964, 381 p.
A half-century of memoirs by a long-time correspondent and journalist, dealing in considerable measure with foreign affairs.

Brown, Lester R. **World without Borders.** New York: Random House, 1972, 395 p.
No major concern of contemporary society is omitted in this capacious book: environment, population, social justice, poverty, hunger, raw materials, the multinational corporation and more. The problems, admirably described and elegantly interrelated, impose solutions which we "must" find. However, the author fails to come to grips with the fact that it is the nation-states that will have to do the work.

Brucan, Silviu. **The Dissolution of Power: A Sociology of International Relations and Politics.** New York: Knopf, 1971, 388 p.
A Rumanian scholar concludes that "the UN must be given the authority to plan, to make decisions, and to enforce them—or it will disappear altogether."

Cot, Jean-Pierre. **La conciliation internationale.** Paris: Pedone, 1968, 389 p.
A careful historical survey, from a primarily legal point of view, of the practices of mediation and conciliation among states.

Czempiel, Ernst-Otto, *ed.* **Die anachronistische Souveränität: zum Verhältnis von Innen- und Aussenpolitik.** Cologne: Westdeutscher Verlag, 1969, 304 p.
In this collection of studies, originally prepared for conferences of the Deutsche Vereinigung für Politische Wissenschaft in 1966–69, an attempt is made to analyze how the international political situation and the internal political and economic conditions determine the formulation of foreign policy of the modern state.

Fisher, Roger Drummer, *ed.* **International Conflict and Behavioral Science: The Craigville Papers.** New York: Basic Books, 1964, 290 p.
A wide-ranging set of papers by a number of psychologists, sociologists, political scientists and economists and dealing with such themes as the nature of international conflict, handling conflicts, international community, decision-making and public influence.

Fisher, Roger Drummer. **International Conflict for Beginners.** New York: Harper and Row, 1969, 231 p.
A refreshingly simple yet politically sophisticated book.

GENERAL WORKS

Fliess, Peter J. **International Relations in the Bipolar World.** New York: Random House, 1968, 221 p.
A survey of contemporary world politics in a bipolar frame of reference.

Franck, Thomas M. **The Structure of Impartiality.** New York: Macmillan (for the Center for International Studies, New York University), 1968, 344 p.
A plea for judicial arbitration of the world's great political problems. A heroic effort, but one which will not convince those adherents of the Realpolitik school whom the author tries—not very successfully—to demolish.

Franck, Thomas M. and Weisband, Edward. **Word Politics: Verbal Strategy among the Superpowers.** New York: Oxford University Press, 1971, 176 p.
A fine analysis of the role of rhetoric in world politics. The authors argue that words may be as important as actions in the foreign policy calculations of states. Good case studies provide excellent empirical illustrations.

Frankel, Joseph. **The Making of Foreign Policy: An Analysis of Decision-Making.** New York: Oxford University Press, 1963, 231 p.
This addition to the studies of "decision-making" lies somewhere between traditional approaches and the efforts to provide a theoretical scheme. In the author's words, "It is an attempt to interpret international politics in terms of decision-making but in a non-technical manner and with a minimum of special terminology."

Franz, Günther, *ed.* **Teilung und Wiedervereinigung: eine weltgeschichtliche Übersicht.** Göttingen: Musterschmidt, 1963, 299 p.
A collection of essays, chiefly by German historians, on examples of national partition and reunification, such as nineteenth-century Poland and Italy or contemporary Korea and Vietnam.

Grewe, Wilhelm G. **Spiel der Kräfte in der Weltpolitik.** Düsseldorf: Econ-Verlag, 1970, 668 p.
A thorough survey of modern international politics by a leading German scholar-diplomat.

Gross, Feliks. **World Politics and Tension Areas.** New York: New York University Press, 1966, 377 p.
A work dealing with and classifying antagonisms arising between ethnic groups and those between ideological groups. It consists largely of a wide range of case studies from the tribal to the international.

Hall, Gus. **Imperialism Today: An Evaluation of Major Issues and Events of Our Time.** New York: International Publishers, 1972, 384 p.
Contemporary international relations as seen by the General Secretary of the Communist Party of the United States.

Hamon, Léo, *ed.* **L'Élaboration de la politique étrangère.** Paris: Presses Universitaires, 1969, 338 p.
Proceedings of a conference organized by the Centre d'Études des Relations Politiques at the University of Dijon on the role of public opinion, military considerations and political factors in the making of foreign policy. Among the participants there were Professor Duroselle, General Gallois and General Beaufre.

Hekhuis, Dale J. and Others, *eds.* **International Stability: Military, Economic and Political Dimensions.** New York: Wiley, 1964, 296 p.
The authors of these thoughtful studies argue that the emergence of new nation states, population growth and armaments race will not contribute to international stability.

Hinsley, Francis Harry. **Power and the Pursuit of Peace: Theory and Practice in the History of Relations Between States.** New York: Cambridge University Press, 1963, 416 p.
An impressive study by a professor at Cambridge University. After a historical critique of peace proposals since the seventeenth century, Mr. Hinsley examines the structure of the modern states' system and the progress of international relations in our century. In all these areas he offers many fresh and perceptive observations, including a most interesting discussion of the origins of the Second World War.

Horowitz, Irving Louis. **Three Worlds of Development: The Theory and Practice of International Stratification.** New York: Oxford University Press, 2d ed., 1972, 556 p.
: A sociologist examines the characteristics and interaction of "three worlds of development" —the United States and its Western allies, the U.S.S.R. and its Eastern bloc allies and the Third World of Latin America, Asia and Africa.

Iyer, Raghavan, ed. **The Glass Curtain Between Asia and Europe.** New York: Oxford University Press, 1965, 356 p.
: A symposium on the historical encounters and attitudes of the peoples of the East and the West, from the Greeks to the present.

Joyce, James Avery. **End of an Illusion.** Indianapolis: Bobbs-Merrill, 1969, 274 p.
: "The alliance system has had its day," the author argues, not very convincingly.

Klein, Robert A. **The Idea of Equality in International Politics: The Tension between the Concept of Great-Power Primacy and the Concept of Sovereign Equality.** Geneva: Université de Genève, Institut de Hautes Études Internationales, 1966, 264 p.
: The author concludes his investigation by stating that in the contemporary world "in terms of the two Great Powers, with their intercontinental ballistic missiles, . . . the nation-states of the rest of the world have largely become obsolete as sovereign independent entities."

Koebner, Richard and Schmidt, Helmut Dan. **Imperialism: The Story and Significance of a Political Word, 1840-1960.** New York: Cambridge University Press, 1964, 432 p.
: Working from the late Professor Koebner's notes and excerpts on the theme, Mr. Schmidt has followed his mentor's "semantic approach" in tracing the meaning of imperialism since the mid-nineteenth century.

Kulski, Władysław Wszebór. **International Politics in a Revolutionary Age.** New York: Lippincott, 2d rev. ed., 1968, 742 p.
: An updated version of a general guide first published in 1964.

Levy, Marion Joseph, Jr. **Modernization and the Structure of Societies: A Setting for International Affairs.** Princeton: Princeton University Press, 1966, 2 v.
: A study in somewhat opaque and abstract prose of the relevance of the backgrounds of various societies, modernized and not, to the arena of international affairs.

Luykx, Theo. **Geschiedenis van de internationale betrekkingen.** Brussels: Elsevier-Sequoia, 1971, 608 p.
: A substantial history of international relations since the Congress of Vienna. There is a very useful chronology.

MacIver, Robert Morrison. **Power Transformed: The Age-Slow Deliverance of the Folk and Now the Potential Deliverance of the Nations from the Rule of Force.** New York: Macmillan, 1964, 244 p.
: The author contends that in the gradual alteration of the forms of power, knowledge has taken the place of force as power's truest expression, and, with the use of the world's technical resources, knowledge may provide the resolution of the pressing problems of society.

Malik, Charles. **Man in the Struggle for Peace.** New York: Harper and Row, 1963, 242 p.
: In a mixture of philosophical reflection and political reminiscence the former Foreign Minister of Lebanon and former President of the U.N. General Assembly discusses some of the major themes of our time: the problem of peace, the role of the United Nations, the cold war and the challenge of communism.

Mark, Max. **Beyond Sovereignty.** Washington: Public Affairs Press, 1965, 178 p.
: A book arguing the thesis that while we are living in the "post-nation-state" era, the movement away from the nation state will not be smooth or even; some type of dialectical process is needed to achieve accommodation between nationalism and transnationalism.

Marshall, Charles Burton. **The Exercise of Sovereignty.** Baltimore: Johns Hopkins Press, 1965, 282 p.
: A collection of essays and papers on various aspects of foreign policy and international crisis.

Mathisen, Trygve. **The Functions of Small States in the Strategies of the Great Powers.** Oslo: Universitetsforlaget, 1971, 287 p.

The briefly sketched examples are mainly instances of overbearing conduct on the part of the United States and the U.S.S.R. toward smaller neighbors.

Northedge, F. S. and Grieve, M. J. **A Hundred Years of International Relations.** New York: Praeger, 1972, 397 p.
A general view, giving greater emphasis to the evolving structure of international relations than to the details of diplomatic history.

Northedge, F. S. and Donelan, M. D. **International Disputes: The Political Aspects.** New York: St. Martin's Press (for the David Davies Memorial Institute of International Studies), 1971, 349 p.
Based on case studies of fifty important international disputes since the Second World War, this book undertakes to examine their origins, whether within or between states, their development and their eventual solution.

Padelford, Norman Judson and Lincoln, George A. **The Dynamics of International Politics.** New York: Macmillan, 2d ed., 1967, 617 p.
A revised edition of a well-balanced examination of the major factors that affect international relations.

Pearson, Lester Bowles. **Peace in the Family of Man.** New York: Oxford University Press, 1969, 104 p.
The 1968 Reith lectures on international politics by the former Canadian Prime Minister; good common sense but no original ideas.

Penrose, Ernest Francis. **The Revolution in International Relations: A Study in the Changing Nature and Balance of Power.** New York: Humanities Press, 1966, 290 p.
A well-written survey by a British scholar.

Porter, Brian Ernest, *ed.* **The Aberystwyth Papers: International Politics, 1919-1969.** New York: Oxford University Press, 1972, 390 p.
Well-edited and generally high-quality essays by leading scholars. The volume was published in honor of the fiftieth anniversary of the founding at the University College of Wales of the world's first Chair of International Politics.

Renouvin, Pierre and Duroselle, Jean-Baptiste. **Introduction to the History of International Relations.** New York: Praeger, 1967, 432 p.
A leading French historian here undertakes, in collaboration with the Director of the Centre d'Études des Relations Internationales in Paris, a systematic study of the basic forces underlying international affairs and the role of the statesman in dealing with them. The French edition appeared as "Introduction à l'histoire des relations internationales" (Paris: Colin, 1964, 520 p.).

Rosenau, James N. and Others, *eds.* **The Analysis of International Politics.** New York: Free Press, 1972, 397 p.
A *Festschrift* honoring Harold and Margaret Sprout.

Rosenau, James N. *ed.* **Linkage Politics: Essays on the Convergence of National and International Systems.** New York: Free Press (for the Princeton Center of International Studies), 1969, 352 p.
Twelve imaginative essays exploring the boundaries between national and international systems.

Rothstein, Robert L. **Alliances and Small Powers.** New York: Columbia University Press, 1968, 331 p.
Drawing his materials from the classical as well as the contemporary period, the author advances a number of fertile theoretical propositions about the role of small powers in the international system.

Russett, Bruce Martin. **Trends in World Politics.** New York: Macmillan, 1965, 156 p.
A concise account of changes in the international political system, particularly since 1945, together with an introduction to some of the newer empirical techniques for the study of international relations. For the future he sees a trend away from the bipolarity of recent decades.

Schou, August and Brundtland, Arne Olav, *eds.* **Small States in International Relations.** New York: Wiley, 1971, 250 p.
A substantial collection of papers prepared for an international symposium under the auspices of the Norwegian Nobel Institute.

Scott, Andrew McKaye. **The Functioning of the International Political System.** New York: Macmillan, 1967, 244 p.

The author, a professor at the University of North Carolina, attempts to apply systems analysis to international politics.

Skolnikoff, Eugene B. **The International Imperatives of Technology.** Berkeley: University of California, Institute of International Studies, 1972, 194 p.

An analysis of the probable impact of technological advances on international political systems and their doubtfully adequate institutions.

Spiegel, Steven L. and Waltz, Kenneth Neal, *eds.* **Conflict in World Politics.** Cambridge (Mass.): Winthrop Publishers, 1971, 474 p.

An imaginatively compiled group of 22 articles analyzing types of conflict characteristic of the contemporary world.

Syed, Anwar Hussain. **Walter Lippmann's Philosophy of International Politics.** Philadelphia: University of Pennsylvania Press, 1964, 358 p.

The author concludes his ambitious study by stating that "Lippmann's theory of international politics is predominantly British."

Vital, David. **The Inequality of States: A Study of the Small Power in International Relations.** New York: Oxford University Press, 1967, 198 p.

Though the author belabors the obvious, i.e., that "the smaller the human and material resources of a state the greater are the difficulties it must surmount if it is to maintain any valid political options," this is a stimulating study of a neglected subject.

Vital, David. **The Survival of Small States: Studies in Small Power/Great Power Conflict.** New York: Oxford University Press, 1971, 136 p.

A realistic appraisal of the options for maneuver open to small states. The author's view of the world takes their interests and aims very much into account.

Ward, Barbara (Lady Jackson). **Spaceship Earth.** New York: Columbia University Press, 1966, 152 p.

A discussion by a noted English economist of whether modern science and technology force us toward a more coördinated world community. The sixth of the George B. Pegram Lectures at the Brookhaven National Laboratory.

Yost, Charles Woodruff. **The Insecurity of Nations: International Relations in the Twentieth Century.** New York: Praeger (for the Council on Foreign Relations), 1968, 276 p.

This is a far-ranging essay on the state of the postwar world. In speculating on the causes of national insecurity, the author draws heavily on the insights of the Austrian naturalist Konrad Lorenz. He then proceeds to an analysis of the three great upheavals of our time: the cold war in Europe, the victory of Chinese Communism and its impact on Asia, and the rise of independent Africa.

Young, Oran R. **The Politics of Force: Bargaining During International Crises.** Princeton: Princeton University Press (for the Center of International Studies), 1969, 438 p.

An excellent analysis of bargaining under international crisis conditions, making fine use of case materials.

II. POLITICAL FACTORS

GENERAL

See also General Works, p. 1; Political Philosophies and Ideologies, p. 21; Society and Social Psychology, p. 39; Economic Factors, p. 49; International Organization and Government, p. 96; The World Since 1914, p. 129.

Adler, Mortimer J. **The Common Sense of Politics.** New York: Holt, Rinehart and Winston, 1971, 265 p.

This excursion into political philosophy includes a naive plea for world government and some very ambitious suggestions for improving mankind's political institutions.

Ake, Claude Eleme. **A Theory of Political Integration.** Homewood (Ill.): Dorsey Press, 1967, 164 p.
A highly abstract, heavily behavioral, and very generalized excursion into empirical political theory.

Akzin, Benjamin. **State and Nation.** London: Hutchinson, 1964, 214 p.
A concise but able study of the relations between state and nation, by a professor of political science and constitutional law at the Hebrew University of Jerusalem.

Allardt, Erik and Rokkan, Stein, *eds.* **Mass Politics: Studies in Political Sociology.** New York: Free Press, 1970, 400 p.
A dozen essays in political sociology by a group of scholars assembled from eight different countries. The standard of the contributions is, on the whole, very high.

Banks, Arthur S. and Textor, Robert B. **A Cross-Polity Survey.** Cambridge: M.I.T. Press, 1963, 1,416 p.
Although this book in its appearance resembles a quasi-arithmetical "Finnegans Wake"—it is a 7090 computer "printout"—it comprises a great deal of data on comparative politics.

Beck, Carl and McKechnie, J. Thomas. **Political Elites: A Select Computerized Bibliography.** Cambridge: M.I.T. Press, 1968, 661 p.
This bibliography, which covers the whole world, was constructed "by systematically searching lists of books in print, other bibliographies, and approximately 100 social science journals published in English from 1945 to mid-1967."

Beloff, Max. **The Intellectual in Politics and Other Essays.** New York: Library Press, 1971, 346 p.
A series of fairly disconnected pieces dealing with a number of political problems. Only the opening chapter deals with the role of the intellectual in politics. The other chapters are reprints of lectures and essays, most of them published before.

Bergstraesser, Arnold. **Weltpolitik als Wissenschaft: geschichtliches Bewusstsein und politische Entscheidung.** Cologne: Westdeutscher Verlag, 1965, 268 p.
Essays on various issues of contemporary world politics, by a leading German political scientist who died in 1964. This volume includes a bibliography of Professor Bergstraesser's writings.

Berle, Adolf Augustus, Jr. **Power.** New York: Harcourt, Brace and World, 1969, 603 p.
A brave attempt to construct a general theory of power through "five laws" which are seen by the author as universally valid in human society.

Binder, Leonard and Others. **Crises and Sequences in Political Development.** Princeton: Princeton University Press, 1971, 326 p.
This volume in the series "Studies in Political Development" centers on five crises—labeled as identity, legitimacy, participation, penetration and distribution—which appear to have arisen historically in the process of political development and state building, and which may fall into significant sequential patterns.

Bracher, Karl Dietrich and Others, *eds.* **Die moderne Demokratie und ihr Recht. Modern Constitutionalism and Democracy. Festschrift für Gerhard Leibholz zum 65. Geburtstag.** Tübingen: Mohr, 1966, 2 v.
A wealth of contributions on political theory and international law by authors from all over the world.

Crozier, Brian. **The Masters of Power.** Boston: Little, Brown, 1969, 416 p.
The author presents several case studies in the uses of "internal" and "international" power.

Curry, R. L., Jr. and Wade, L. L. **A Theory of Political Exchange: Economic Reasoning in Political Analysis.** Englewood Cliffs: Prentice-Hall, 1968, 130 p.
A pioneering study of political systems from the perspective of economic theory.

Duverger, Maurice. **The Idea of Politics.** Indianapolis: Bobbs-Merrill, 1966, 238 p.
An impressive analysis of the forms of political conflict and hopes for the establishment of a society without conflict. The French original was published as "Introduction à la politique" (Paris: Gallimard, 1964, 382 p.).

Enzensberger, Hans Magnus. **Politik und Verbrechen.** Frankfurt/Main: Suhrkamp Verlag, 1964, 393 p.

GENERAL INTERNATIONAL RELATIONS

Essays on the theme of the relationship of crime to politics, drawing on such divergent cases as the Trujillo dictatorship, Chicago gangsters, the case of Wilma Montesi and the prerevolutionary Russian terrorists.

Farrell, Robert Barry, ed. **Approaches to Comparative and International Politics.** Evanston: Northwestern University Press, 1966, 368 p.

A collection of papers dealing with a wide variety of topics—theories of foreign policy, the politics of developing nations, types of political societies and areas providing "research challenges."

Faure, Edgar. **The Heart of the Battle ... For a New Social Contract.** New York: McGraw-Hill, 1972, 255 p.

Whether or not the former French Premier has drawn up an adequate new social contract, the reader will admire his skill in grappling with Marxism and the post-Marxian critiques of technological and consumer society, his prescriptions for "dis-alienating" man, and his suggestions for combatting the entropy of political democracy.

Feibleman, James K. **The Reach of Politics.** New York: Horizon Press, 1969, 335 p.

An impressive but occasionally too imaginative potpourri of political and social philosophy converging on the role of the state in human society.

Finlay, David James and Others. **Enemies in Politics.** Chicago: Rand McNally, 1967, 257 p.

A group of three case studies making some fine efforts at conceptualization. Ole R. Holsti's essay on John Foster Dulles and Russia is a valuable contribution to empirical theory.

Friedrich, Carl Joachim. **Man and His Government: An Empirical Theory of Politics.** New York: McGraw-Hill, 1963, 737 p.

Based on a lifetime's study of politics and political theory, this is an ambitious effort to draw some general conclusions from "the political experience of mankind."

Friedrich, Carl Joachim. **The Pathology of Politics: Violence, Betrayal, Corruption, Secrecy, and Propaganda.** New York: Harper and Row, 1972, 287 p.

Reflections on the diseases of the body politic by a distinguished political theorist.

Friedrich, Carl Joachim. **Trends of Federalism in Theory and Practice.** New York: Praeger, 1968, 193 p.

Essays on selected themes and countries pertaining to the debate on the nature of federalism.

Golembiewski, Robert T. and Others. **A Methodological Primer for Political Scientists.** Chicago: Rand McNally, 1968, 484 p.

The authors attempt to chart a course through the labyrinth of recent methodological work in political science. They exhibit a strong preference for the behavioral persuasion and dismiss the more traditional theorists somewhat cavalierly.

Greenstein, Fred I. **Personality and Politics.** Chicago: Markham, 1969, 200 p.

A somewhat turgid and inconclusive study of the impact of personality on politics. The author deals with his subject in highly theoretical terms.

Grosser, Alfred. **Au nom de quoi? Fondements d'une morale politique.** Paris: Éditions du Seuil, 1969, 332 p.

Mature reflections on moral issues in politics by a leading French student of contemporary Germany.

Howard, Nigel. **Paradoxes of Rationality: Theory of Metagames and Political Behavior.** Cambridge: M.I.T. Press, 1971, 248 p.

A quite technical work, presupposing familiarity with game theory, but indicating some interesting approaches to problem-solving in the "real world."

Katz, Milton. **The Things That Are Caesar's.** New York: Knopf, 1966, 227 p.

This study takes off from the author's topic sentences: "It takes qualities of one kind to face an electorate and win elective office in the United States today. It takes qualities of another kind to govern." In discussing this disparity, Mr. Katz ranges widely from Sulla and Caesar to the American Founding Fathers.

Knutson, Jeanne N. **The Human Basis of the Polity: A Psychological Study of Political Men.** Chicago: Aldine-Atherton, 1972, 360 p.

Proceeding from an analysis of Abraham Maslow's motivation theory, the author moves to a general consideration of the efforts to provide the "psychic dimensions of political man." Valuable as a critical review of the literature and as an original contribution.

Krieger, Leonard and Stern, Fritz Richard, eds. **The Responsibility of Power: Historical Essays in Honor of Hajo Holborn.** Garden City: Doubleday, 1968, 464 p.
Twenty-four historical essays on the manifold aspects of political power, drawn largely from the European experience.

Lane, Robert E. **Political Thinking and Consciousness.** Chicago: Markham, 1969, 348 p.
A study exploring the wellsprings of the political ideas of college students. The book is a valuable contribution to the bridge-building process between politics and social psychology.

Lasswell, Harold Dwight. **The Future of Political Science.** New York: Atherton Press, 1963, 256 p.
Imaginative suggestions by a well-known scholar.

Lipset, Seymour Martin, ed. **Politics and the Social Sciences.** New York: Oxford University Press, 1969, 328 p.
Ten essays—all on a high intellectual plane—seeking to relate economics, history, anthropology, psychology, psychiatry, sociology and statistics to the study of politics.

Lucas, John Randolph. **The Principles of Politics.** New York: Oxford University Press, 1967, 380 p.
A systematic survey of basic political concepts by an Oxford don who regards Anglo-Saxon institutions as the best and acknowledges his indebtedness to Edmund Burke.

Miliband, Ralph. **The State in Capitalist Society.** New York: Basic Books, 1969, 292 p.
A Marxist study of the nature of advanced capitalist societies by a senior lecturer in political science at the London School of Economics.

Mills, Charles Wright. **Power, Politics, and People: Collected Essays.** New York: Oxford University Press, 1963, 657 p.
Posthumously published collection of representative works by a well-known sociologist, left-wing intellectual and political activist. Edited by Irving Louis Horowitz.

Modelski, George Alexander. **Principles of World Politics.** New York: Free Press, 1972, 370 p.
An unorthodox interpretation which attempts to get away from concepts like nation-state and sovereignty to the ingredients of a more complex and pluralistic world order reflecting new conditions.

Nettl, John Peter. **Political Mobilization: A Sociological Analysis of Methods and Concepts.** New York: Basic Books, 1967, 442 p.
A massive effort, written in neo-Parsonian idiom, reaching fairly commonplace conclusions.

Organski, A. F. K. **The Stages of Political Development.** New York: Knopf, 1965, 229 p.
In this work, the intent of which is "to provide a new theoretical framework for the study of comparative politics," the author focuses on the themes of "primitive unification," industrialization, national welfare and abundance.

Organski, A. F. K. **World Politics.** New York: Knopf, 1968, 509 p.
A general survey of international politics, including a series of predictions on the shape of things to come. A revised edition of a work first published in 1958.

Osgood, Robert Endicott and Tucker, Robert W. **Force, Order, and Justice.** Baltimore: Johns Hopkins Press, 1967, 374 p.
The authors, in an ambitious effort to assess the role of force in world politics before and after the advent of the nuclear age, display great learning in history, philosophy and law. The book is not a compendium, however, but a challenging and frequently profound exploration in political thought.

Parsons, Talcott. **Politics and Social Structure.** New York: Free Press, 1969, 557 p.
A political scientist, William C. Mitchell, has selected 17 previously published essays by the eminent sociologist that are relevant to political thought and practical politics.

Politicheskie partii zarubezhnykh stran: spravochnik. Moscow: Izd-vo Politicheskoi Literatury, 1967, 349 p.

A Soviet handbook containing more than 500 entries describing the political parties of countries outside the U.S.S.R.

Pye, Lucian Wilmot and Verba, Sidney, *eds.* **Political Culture and Political Development.** Princeton: Princeton University Press, 1965, 574 p.
This volume in a series on political development is made up of essays by a number of specialists dealing with the relationship between the "political culture" of a nation and its political development. Ten nations are selected for consideration.

Rajan, M. S., *ed.* **Studies in Politics: National and International.** Delhi: Vikas Publications, 1970, 512 p.
A *Festschrift* honoring Dr. A. Appadori, a leading Indian student of international relations.

Robbins, Lionel Charles Robbins, Baron. **Politics and Economics: Papers in Political Economy.** New York: St. Martin's Press, 1963, 230 p.
In this collection of papers the distinguished British political economist writes on a variety of fundamental problems—liberty, equality, art, order, international integration and the relation between economics and politics—as well as on some financial issues.

Rosinski, Herbert. **Power and Human Destiny.** New York: Praeger, 1965, 206 p.
This posthumously edited study is a valuable and wide-ranging analysis of the problem and meaning of power in man's history.

Russett, Bruce Martin and Others. **World Handbook of Political and Social Indicators.** New Haven: Yale University Press, 1964, 373 p.
The first major publication of the Political Data Program at Yale University, including 75 data series embracing 141 independent nations and dependent territories.

Sawer, Geoffrey. **Modern Federalism.** London: C. A. Watts, 1969, 204 p.
The author, an Australian professor of law, states that "the main purpose of the work is to put forward some ideas about the dynamics of federalism" and "to give a compendious account of existing federal forms and their historical origins." He succeeds well.

Sellars, Roy Wood. **Social Patterns and Political Horizons.** Nashville: Aurora Publishers, 1970, 408 p.
A learned though rather diffuse survey of the main political systems and their philosophical bases in Western history.

Sharma, Brij Mohan and Choudhry, L. P. **Federal Polity.** London: Asia Publishing House, rev. ed., 1967, 384 p.
A completely revised and updated edition of a study of the development of the federal concept in which the authors deal sceptically with the idea of a world state. The first edition of this study appeared in 1931. There is an introduction by the well-known German scholar K. D. Bracher.

Silone, Ignazio. **Emergency Exit.** New York: Harper and Row, 1968, 207 p.
Essays on political and moral problems of our times. Of particular interest are the chapters describing the author's exit from the Communist Party. The Italian original was published as "Uscita di sicurezza" (Florence: Vallecchi, 1965, 9th ed., 241 p.).

Silvert, Kalman H. **Man's Power: A Biased Guide to Political Thought and Action.** New York: Viking, 1970, 163 p.
A highly subjective and challenging effort to explore the relations between constraint and freedom in man's political universe.

Spanier, John Winston. **World Politics in an Age of Revolution.** New York: Praeger, 1967, 434 p.
In this lucid and well-organized introduction to world politics, the author, a professor at the University of Florida, focuses on the three major forces in the postwar world that have profoundly altered international politics: the revolution in military technology, the permanent revolution of communism, and the national and social revolution throughout the underdeveloped areas.

Spiro, Herbert John. **World Politics: The Global System.** Homewood (Ill.): Dorsey Press, 1966, 345 p.
In this monograph a professor at the University of Pennsylvania argues "that the conditions which once brought about [the] difference between the study of the internal politics of states and the study of relations among states have evaporated."

Stoessinger, John G. **The Might of Nations: World Politics in Our Time.** New York: Random House, 3rd ed., 1969, 455 p.
  A treatment of world politics in terms of three conceptual principles: the struggle for power and order; the East-West and colonial-anticolonial struggles; and the gaps between perception and reality and their impact on world politics.

Thoenes, Piet. **The Élite in the Welfare State.** New York: Free Press, 1966, 236 p.
  An eminent Dutch sociologist considers the question of whether the welfare state and democracy can coëxist. The Dutch original was published as "De elite in de verzorgingsstaat: sociologische proeve van een terugkeer naar domineesland" (Leiden: Stenfert Kroese, 1962, 268 p.).

Thompson, Kenneth Winfred. **The Moral Issue in Statecraft: Twentieth-Century Approaches and Problems.** Baton Rouge: Louisiana State University Press, 1966, 127 p.
  An exploration of the relevance of moral standards to national politics and international diplomacy, by a former vice president of the Rockefeller Foundation. Based on the author's Rockwell Lectures, delivered at Rice University.

Thorbecke, Willem Johan Rudolf. **A New Dimension in Political Thinking.** Dobbs Ferry (N.Y.): Oceana Publications, 1965, 226 p.
  In this important and challenging volume a former Dutch diplomat applies Father P. Teilhard de Chardin's theories of evolution to the study of present-day political thought and world affairs.

Waelder, Robert. **Progress and Revolution: A Study of the Issues of Our Age.** New York: International Universities Press, 1967, 372 p.
  A somewhat diffuse though learned and frequently brilliant survey of major international political forces by a leading psychoanalyst.

Westin, Alan F. **Privacy and Freedom.** New York: Atheneum, 1967, 487 p.
  A penetrating analysis of major unresolved conflicts between the right to individual privacy and modern technological devices to invade it. The author makes thoughtful suggestions on how to restore the balance.

NATIONALISM AND NATIONALITY

See also (General Works) Methodology and Theory, p. 4; General Treatments, p. 7; Political Philosophies and Ideologies, p. 21; Problems of New Nations, p. 36; (International Organization and Government) General, p. 96; and the sections for specific countries and regions.

Deutsch, Karl W. **Nationalism and Its Alternatives.** New York: Knopf, 1969, 200 p.
  In this essay on nationalism a leading authority on the subject combines traditional and modern behavioral research techniques.

Doob, Leonard William. **Patriotism and Nationalism: Their Psychological Foundations.** New Haven: Yale University Press, 1964, 297 p.
  The author undertakes to view "patriotism and nationalism as they function inside patriots and nationalists." The study is based in part upon data gathered in South Tyrol.

Gordon, David C. **Self-Determination and History in the Third World.** Princeton: Princeton University Press, 1971, 219 p.
  In this scholarly study, the author shows how a number of new nations have used history for the purpose of strengthening national cohesion and how, in attempting to free themselves from colonial myths, national leaders often found it necessary to fashion counter-myths.

Hinsley, Francis Harry. **Sovereignty.** London: Watts, 1966, 255 p.
  A concise, tightly reasoned and original exploration of the concept of sovereignty, and its relation to society and the state.

Kohn, Hans. **Living in a World Revolution: My Encounters with History.** New York: Trident Press, 1964, 211 p.
  An admirable autobiography in which the late Professor Kohn, born in Prague but a

long-time resident in the United States, traces the historical and intellectual influences which brought about his interest in the problems of nationalism.

Schuster, Derek V. **Bad Blood among Brothers: An inside View behind Today's Separatist Movements.** New York: Vantage Press, 1972, 253 p.
A brief look at cultural conflicts in Cyprus, Northern Ireland, Canada, Belgium and Switzerland.

Shafer, Boyd C. **Faces of Nationalism: New Realities and Old Myths.** New York: Harcourt Brace Jovanovich, 1972, 535 p.
Long a student of nationalism, the author, for many years editor of *The American Historical Review*, here traces the evolution of that protean and myth-ridden phenomenon from the late Middle Ages to the present.

Silvert, K. H. *ed.* **Expectant Peoples: Nationalism and Development.** New York: Random House, 1963, 489 p.
The pregnant theme of this excellent volume of studies by the American Universities Field Staff is the role and quality of nationalism in the developing countries. While the topic is developed thematically, all the essays deal with individual countries in the Middle East, Latin America, Asia and Africa.

Smith, Anthony D. **Theories of Nationalism.** New York: Harper and Row, 1971, 344 p.
A sociologist probes into the theoretical literature on nationalism, finds much of it ill-informed, establishes his own typology of nationalist movements and comes up with a theory of his own.

Snyder, Louis L. **The New Nationalism.** Ithaca: Cornell University Press, 1968, 387 p.
An ambitious effort to assess the phenomenon of nationalism since 1945 on a global scale. Much depth despite the broad coverage.

COMPARATIVE GOVERNMENT

See also (General Works) Methodology and Theory, p. 4; (Political Factors) General, p. 12; Economic Growth and Development, p. 71; and the sections for specific countries and regions.

Aron, Raymond. **Democracy and Totalitarianism.** New York: Praeger, 1969, 262 p.
The French Fourth Republic and the Soviet system serve as models in this fertile and imaginative study in comparisons. Originally published as "Démocratie et totalitarisme" (Paris: Gallimard, 1965, 378 p.).

Bayne, Edward A. **Four Ways of Politics: State and Nation in Italy, Somalia, Israel, Iran.** New York: American Universities Field Staff, 1965, 320 p.
Although the author grants the disparateness of the four countries discussed, he would argue that there are relevant comparabilities, especially in the continuing tension between tradition and modernization.

Brogan, Sir Denis William and Verney, Douglas V. **Political Patterns in Today's World.** New York: Harcourt, 1963, 274 p.
A study of the political systems in Great Britain, France, Sweden and the United States, and a comparison of the Western liberal democracy with the communist political system in the Soviet Union.

Brzezinski, Zbigniew Kazimierz and Huntington, Samuel Phillips. **Political Power: USA/USSR.** New York: Viking, 1964, 461 p.
In this work two leading students of Soviet and American politics have joined forces to make an ambitious comparative study of the two countries' political systems, with an eye to similarities and differences, strengths and weaknesses, and the prospects of increasing convergence. Their expectations are undramatic: both systems have been, for their respective purposes, quite successful, each is likely to evolve, but it seems unlikely that they will become increasingly similar, in role or purpose.

Edinger, Lewis Joachim, *ed.* **Political Leadership in Industrialized Societies: Studies in Comparative Analysis.** New York: Wiley, 1967, 376 p.
Twelve contributors present case studies. Of particular interest is Stanley Hoffmann's essay on "heroic leadership" in modern France.

Epstein, Leon David. **Political Parties in Western Democracies.** New York: Praeger, 1967, 374 p.
A well-known American political scientist presents a comprehensive, scholarly survey of all aspects of contemporary parties, focusing particularly on Britain and America. Informative and quite readable.

Field, George Lowell. **Comparative Political Development: The Precedent of the West.** Ithaca: Cornell University Press, 1967, 247 p.
A brave but somewhat labored effort to forge new conceptual tools for comparative political analysis.

Fraenkel, Ernst. **Deutschland und die westlichen Demokratien.** Stuttgart: Kohlhammer, 1964, 205 p.
A collection of stimulating essays comparing German political institutions to those of older Western democracies.

Frank, Elke, ed. **Lawmakers in a Changing World.** Englewood Cliffs: Prentice-Hall, 1966, 186 p.
Eight essays examining the nature of the legislative bodies of the European Communities, the United Nations, Great Britain, France, West Germany, the United States and the U.S.S.R.

Friedrich, Carl Joachim. **The Impact of American Constitutionalism Abroad.** Boston: Boston University Press, 1968, 112 p.
The author argues that the main American ideas that have had a significant impact abroad have been presidentialism, federalism and the judicial review of human rights.

Kaltefleiter, Werner. **Die Funktionen des Staatsoberhauptes in der parlamentarischen Demokratie.** Opladen: Westdeutscher Verlag, 1970, 306 p.
A comparative study of the functions of the head of state in West European parliamentarian democracies.

Kerstiens, Thom. **The New Elite in Asia and Africa: A Comparative Study of Indonesia and Ghana.** New York: Praeger, 1966, 282 p.
An interesting effort to analyze comparatively the origins of new élites in Indonesia and Ghana during the colonial period, their contribution to the growth of nationalism, and their role after independence.

Lipset, Seymour Martin and Rokkan, Stein, eds. **Party Systems and Voter Alignments: Cross-National Perspectives.** New York: Free Press, 1967, 554 p.
A comparative analysis of voting patterns and social bases of party support in the English-speaking democracies, continental Europe, northern Europe and the emerging nations. The editors have attempted to place the eleven contributions into a common conceptual framework. An ambitious and useful work.

Merritt, Richard L. and Rokkan, Stein, eds. **Comparing Nations: The Use of Quantitative Data in Cross-National Research.** New Haven: Yale University Press, 1966, 584 p.
An extensive and in places quite technical symposium dealing with the use of quantitative indicators of political and social change in "cross-national" research.

Parliaments. London: Cassell (for the Inter-Parliamentary Union), 2d rev. and enl. ed., 1966, 346 p.
In this comparative study of representative institutions in 55 countries there is much useful information on the structure and organization of parliaments, the legislative function, powers in financial matters and control of the executive. The French original appeared as "Parlements" (Paris: Presses Universitaires, 2d rev. and enl. ed., 1966, 378 p.).

Peaslee, Amos Jenkins. **Constitutions of Nations.** The Hague: Nijhoff, 3rd rev. ed., 1965–70, 4 v. in 7 pts.
This new and updated edition of an indispensable reference work was prepared by Dorothy Peaslee Xydis.

Renesse, Ernst Albrecht von and Others. **Unvollendete Demokratien.** Opladen: Westdeutscher Verlag (for the Institut für öffentliches Recht und Politik der Universität Münster), 1965, 429 p.
An extensive survey of forms of organization and power structures in the non-communist countries of South and Southeast Asia, the Middle East and North Africa, and West Africa.

Singh, Nagendra. **The Defence Mechanism of the Modern State.** New York: Asia Publishing House (for the Indian Council of World Affairs), 1964, 479 p.

A comparative, but quite technical study of the Chiefs of Staff Committee as the "link between the political and the military wheels of the State" in the major military powers.

Smith, Bruce L. R. and Hague, D. C., eds. **The Dilemma of Accountability in Modern Government.** New York: St. Martin's Press, 1971, 391 p.

A very able collection of papers on the differences in the British and American experience with accountability.

Verkade, Willem. **Democratic Parties in the Low Countries and Germany: Origins and Historical Developments.** Leyden: Universitaire Pers, 1965, 331 p.

According to the author, this study is "a sociological analysis of the internal structure of the Liberal, the Socialist, the Catholic and the Christian type of parties" in Germany, Belgium and the Netherlands.

Waltz, Kenneth Neal. **Foreign Policy and Democratic Politics: The American and British Experience.** Boston: Little, Brown, 1967, 331 p.

On the basis of a thoughtful comparative analysis, the author concludes that "in matters of foreign policy (and of domestic policy as well) the American Presidential system is superior to British Parliamentary government." A startling thesis persuasively argued.

Wheare, K. C. **Legislatures.** New York: Oxford University Press, 1963, 247 p.

A broadly conceived comparative study of governments in which legislatures are now and have for some time been an important part of the governmental structure.

POLITICAL PROCESSES

See also (General Works) Methodology and Theory, p. 4; General Treatments, p. 7; (Political Factors) General, p. 12; Society and Social Psychology, p. 39; (The United States) Politics and Political Issues, p. 268.

Arora, Satish K. and Lasswell, Harold Dwight. **Political Communication.** New York: Holt, Rinehart and Winston, 1969, 312 p.

A study of the public utterances of top Indian and U.S. figures placed in an analytical framework designed to reveal differences or agreements on key issues. Main sources were *The New York Times* and *The Times of India*.

Becker, Theodore L., ed. **Political Trials.** Indianapolis: Bobbs-Merrill, 1971, 255 p.

A selection of 11 political trials in different political and national settings. Fascinating and valuable material, but an analytical conclusion to the book would have been most welcome.

Dahl, Robert Alan, ed. **Political Oppositions in Western Democracies.** New Haven: Yale University Press, 1966, 458 p.

An extensive collection of essays dealing with the apparently self-evident but frequently denied or circumscribed right of oppositions to appeal for votes against the party in power. Treatment is chiefly by country.

Dahl, Robert Alan. **Polyarchy: Participation and Opposition.** New Haven: Yale University Press, 1971, 257 p.

A tightly woven exploration of the conditions under which cultures that do not tolerate political opposition may be transformed into societies that do.

Ehrlich, Stanislaw. **Die Macht der Minderheit: die Einflussgruppen in der politischen Struktur des Kapitalismus.** Vienna: Europa Verlag, 1966, 331 p.

A study of the role of pressure groups in capitalistic-democratic societies, by a professor at Warsaw University. The Polish original was published as "Grupy nacisku w strukturze politycznej kapitalizmu" (Warsaw: Państwowe Wydawnictwo Naukowe, 1962, 382 p.).

Gellhorn, Walter. **Ombudsmen and Others: Citizens' Protectors in Nine Countries.** Cambridge: Harvard University Press, 1966, 448 p.

A study of efforts to lessen conflicts between citizens and administrators in nine countries: Denmark, Finland, New Zealand, Norway, Sweden, Jugoslavia, Poland, the Soviet Union and Japan.

Glick, Edward Bernard. **Peaceful Conflict: The Non-Military Use of the Military.** Harrisburg: Stackpole, 1967, 223 p.
A case for the involvement of the military in constructive civic action programs, especially in developing countries.

Kautsky, John H. **The Political Consequences of Modernization.** New York: Wiley, 1972, 267 p.
An extended essay that seeks to serve as an introduction to the subject and to provide a theory of political change.

La Palombara, Joseph G. and Weiner, Myron, *eds.* **Political Parties and Political Development.** Princeton: Princeton University Press, 1966, 487 p.
An international conference resulted in these papers on political parties, their role, development and effectiveness in various societies throughout the world.

Lipson, Leslie. **The Democratic Civilization.** New York: Oxford University Press, 1964, 614 p.
An ambitious study in comparative government, by a professor of political science at the University of California, Berkeley, concerned centrally with the democratic forms of government and a possible theory of the political process.

Pye, Lucian Wilmot, *ed.* **Communications and Political Development.** Princeton: Princeton University Press, 1963, 381 p.
This is a symposium of theoretically oriented papers dealing with the relationship of social communication in its various forms to political articulation and development.

Ritter, Gerhard A. and Ziebura, Gilbert, *eds.* **Faktoren der politischen Entscheidung.** Berlin: De Gruyter, 1963, 451 p.
A distinguished *Festschrift* for Ernst Fraenkel on both the theory and practice of political decision-making. Contributors include Hans Kelsen, Karl Dietrich Bracher, Richard Löwenthal and Gerhard A. Ritter.

Rowat, Donald Cameron, *ed.* **The Ombudsman: Citizen's Defender.** Toronto: University of Toronto Press, 1965, 348 p.
A symposium on existing, related and proposed systems making use of the Swedish Ombudsman—"an officer appointed by the legislature to receive and investigate complaints from citizens against unjust administrative action."

Scott, James C. **Comparative Political Corruption.** Englewood Cliffs: Prentice-Hall, 1972, 166 p.
Seeing corruption as a prevalent, perhaps necessary, lubricant for a society, the author compares such diverse cases as Stuart England, Thailand and urban America.

Tompkins, E. Berkeley, *ed.* **Peaceful Change in Modern Society.** Stanford: Hoover Institution Press, 1971, 158 p.
Essays commemorating the fiftieth anniversary of the Hoover Institution. Contributors include Anthony Eden, Sidney Hook and Bertrand de Jouvenel.

Wriggins, W. Howard. **The Ruler's Imperative: Strategies for Political Survival in Asia and Africa.** New York: Columbia University Press, 1969, 275 p.
The author has identified and researched eight different strategies employed by modern African and Asian leaders to obtain and keep political power.

POLITICAL PHILOSOPHIES AND IDEOLOGIES

General

See also (Political Factors) General, p. 12; Problems of New Nations, p. 36; Labor and Labor Movements, p. 41; Economic Theory, p. 53; The Postwar World, p. 178.

Apter, David Ernest, *ed.* **Ideology and Discontent.** New York: Free Press, 1964, 342 p.
An interdisciplinary symposium on the role of ideology both in newly emerging countries and in advanced industrial states; includes a chapter on the radical right in the United States.

Benson, Leonard Glenn. **National Purpose: Ideology and Ambivalence in America.** Washington: Public Affairs Press, 1963, 229 p.
A discussion of the function of ideologies in the contemporary world and particularly in the United States.

Cardonnel, Jean and Others. **L'Homme chrétien et l'homme marxiste.** Paris: Éditions de la Palatine, 1964, 268 p.
An effort to provide a "dialogue amical et difficile" between Christians and Marxists, on such themes as materialism and transcendence, morality and practice, and the Calvinist heritage.

Connolly, William E. **Political Science and Ideology.** New York: Atherton, 1967, 179 p.
A fine essay on empirical theory, casting some complex concepts into readily understandable terms, yet without oversimplification.

Djilas, Milovan. **The Unperfect Society: Beyond the New Class.** New York: Harcourt, Brace and World, 1969, 267 p.
Intended originally as a sequel to his "The New Class," the present work has a quite different intellectual framework, reflecting the author's departure from Marxism. The most interesting portions of the book are the most personal—Djilas' internal and external struggles over the last decade or so, years largely spent in prison.

Driberg, Thomas Edward Neil. **The Mystery of Moral Re-armament.** New York: Knopf, 1965, 317 p.
An extremely critical appraisal, by a British Labour M.P. and journalist, of the late Frank Buchman and his movement.

Heer, Friedrich. **Europa—Mutter der Revolutionen.** Stuttgart: Kohlhammer, 1964, 1,028 p.
An ambitious, though controversial, interpretation of the ideological movements of the nineteenth and twentieth centuries, by a very prolific Austrian historian.

Ionescu, Ghiţa and Gellner, Ernest, *eds.* **Populism: Its Meaning and National Characteristics.** New York: Macmillan, 1969, 263 p.
A fascinating collection of essays on the elusive concept of populism, based on papers presented at a conference at the London School of Economics in May 1967. The editors argue that populism during the nineteenth and twentieth centuries "has been more fundamental to the shaping of the political mind than is generally acknowledged."

Lange, Peer H. **Stalinismus versus "Sozialfaschismus" und "Nationalfaschismus."** Göppingen: Kümmerle, 1969, 367 p.
An analysis of ideology and practice during the left-swing of the late 1920s and early 1930s.

Meynaud, Jean. **Technocracy.** New York: Free Press, 1969, 315 p.
An impassioned plea to rescue politics from the technocrats and "electronic fascism" and to give it back to the politicians who are responsible to the people. The author, a French scholar, generalizes his findings to all modern democracies in the West, but much of the evidence is marshalled from the experience of his homeland. The French original appeared as "La Technocracie: mythe ou réalité?" (Paris: Payot, 1964, 297 p.).

Mitin, M. B., *ed.* **Sovremennye burzhuaznye teorii o sliianii kapitalizma i sotsializma: kriticheskii analiz.** Moscow: Nauka, 1970, 243 p.
This book contains the report of a conference sponsored by the Academy of Science of the U.S.S.R. on the theory of U.S.-Soviet convergence. The main targets for criticism are Raymond Aron, John Kenneth Galbraith, Adolf A. Berle and Zbigniew Brzezinski.

Muller, Herbert Joseph. **Freedom in the Modern World.** New York: Harper and Row, 1966, 559 p.
This work completes the author's trilogy dealing with the history of freedom since ancient times. It covers the nineteenth and twentieth centuries—from the French Revolution to the problem of freedom in the non-Western world.

Seton-Watson, Hugh. **Nationalism and Communism: Essays 1946-1963.** New York: Praeger, 1964, 253 p.
A collection of Professor Seton-Watson's essays and articles on the themes of nationalism, Eastern Europe, communism and international affairs.

Wagar, W. Warren. **Building the City of Man.** New York: Grossman, 1971, 180 p.
"Our goal," says the author, "must be, quite simply, a new organic world civilization," and he prescribes the wholesale revolutionary measures needed to create it. An enthusiastically total critique of the existing state of affairs.

Wilhelm, Donald, Jr. **The West Can Win: A Study in Science and World Power.** New York: Praeger, 1966, 208 p.
While the title is somewhat sensational, Mr. Wilhelm's purpose is a serious one: to develop, on the basis of science and scientific thought, a new political outlook and creed commensurate with the times and able to meet the appeals of Marxism.

Democracy

See also (Political Factors) General, p. 12; Comparative Government, p. 18; Political Processes, p. 20; (Political Philosophies and Ideologies) General, p. 21.

Almond, Gabriel Abraham and Verba, Sidney. **The Civic Culture: Political Attitudes and Democracy in Five Nations.** Princeton: Princeton University Press, 1963, 562 p.
This is "a study of the political culture of democracy and of the social structures and processes that sustain it," based on several thousand interviews in Germany, Italy, Mexico, Great Britain and the United States.

Butt, Ronald. **The Power of Parliament.** New York: Walker, 1969, 468 p.
This valuable study, written in a spirit of respect for Parliament and its traditions, seeks "to make it easier to judge the validity of allegations that Parliament has declined and the relevance of particular schemes of reform."

Ellul, Jacques. **The Political Illusion.** New York: Knopf, 1967, 258 p.
A fierce indictment of the modern democratic state, based largely on the experience with *dirigisme* in France. The French original appeared as "L'Illusion politique: essai" (Paris: Laffont, 1964, 265 p.).

Goerner, E. A., *ed.* **Democracy in Crisis.** Notre Dame: University of Notre Dame Press, 1971, 199 p.
Essays examining and interpreting recent "challenges to democracy" in Western Europe and the United States.

Julien, Claude. **Le Suicide des democraties.** Paris: Grasset, 1972, 316 p.
A wide-ranging inventory of the ills of Western industrial society, and particularly the United States, by a persistent critic of American power and civilization.

Lindblom, Charles Edward. **The Intelligence of Democracy: Decision Making through Mutual Adjustment.** New York: Free Press, 1965, 352 p.
The author, a professor at Yale University, argues that political systems should rely on dispersion of power for establishing rational and efficient governments.

Lippincott, Benjamin Evans. **Democracy's Dilemma: The Totalitarian Party in a Free Society.** New York: Ronald Press, 1965, 293 p.
A study of the dilemma confronting democratic societies based on traditional liberalism in dealing with the erosive presence of totalitarian parties, especially the communist, in their midst.

Niebuhr, Reinhold and Sigmund, Paul E. **The Democratic Experience: Past and Prospects.** New York: Praeger, 1969, 192 p.
This book presents a succinct analysis of the relevance—or irrelevance—of Western democracy to the developing world.

Pickles, Dorothy Maud. **Democracy.** New York: Basic Books, 1971, 200 p.
A broad discussion of the meaning, historical forces and problems of democracy, by a leading British political scientist.

Reed, Edward, *ed.* **Challenges to Democracy: The next Ten Years.** New York: Praeger, 1963, 245 p.
Papers delivered in honor of the 10th anniversary of the Fund for the Republic at a convocation organized by the Center for the Study of Democratic Institutions. Introduction by Robert M. Hutchins.

Tinker, Hugh. **Ballot Box and Bayonet: People and Government in Emergent Asian Countries.** New York: Oxford University Press (for the Royal Institute of International Affairs), 1964, 126 p.

Mr. Tinker refutes the popular statement that democracy has failed in Asia and Africa. His own thesis is that the essential and universal elements of democracy have been retained, and that those elements peculiar to Western countries, necessarily and understandably unworkable in the non-European new states, have been replaced by new, indigenous concepts of democracy.

Wheeler, Harvey. **Democracy in a Revolutionary Era: The Political Order Today.** New York: Praeger, 1968, 224 p.
The author attempts to prove, not very successfully, that democracy is the certain outcome of the development process and that balance-of-power politics is obsolete in today's world.

Liberalism; Conservatism

See also the sections for specific countries and regions.

Burnham, James. **Suicide of the West: An Essay on the Meaning and Destiny of Liberalism.** New York: Day, 1964, 312 p.
Part of Mr. Burnham's continuing indictment, this work, as he says, "is a set of variations on a single and simple underlying thesis: that what Americans call 'liberalism' is the ideology of Western suicide."

The Conservative Papers. Garden City: Doubleday, 1964, 268 p.
A collection of essays on various themes relating to the cause of American conservatism, with an introduction by Melvin R. Laird.

Kendall, Willmoore. **The Conservative Affirmation.** Chicago: Regnery, 1963, 272 p.
An extensive discussion of both the premises and politics of conservatism.

MacCallum Scott, John Hutchinson. **Experiment in Internationalism: A Study in International Behavior.** New York: Hillary House, 1967, 223 p.
A sympathetic, though on the whole objective, account of the history of the Liberal International by one of its moving spirits.

Meyer, Frank S. **The Conservative Mainstream.** New Rochelle: Arlington House, 1969, 488 p.
A collection of articles from *National Review* advertised by the publisher as "the conservative *summa*."

Meyer, Frank S., ed. **What is Conservatism?** New York: Holt, Rinehart, and Winston, 1964, 242 p.
A useful symposium.

Minogue, Kenneth R. **The Liberal Mind.** New York: Random House, 1964, 204 p.
A critical essay analyzing the nature of liberalism and its internal conflicts.

Röpke, Wilhelm, Theodor. **Fronten der Freiheit: Wirtschaft—internationale Ordnung—Politik.** Stuttgart: Seewald, 1965, 278 p.
A selection of writings on contemporary economic and political trends, by a well-known German liberal economist.

Socialism

See also (Political Philosophies and Ideologies) General, p. 21; Communism, p. 26; Totalitarianism; Fascism, p. 32; Society and Social Psychology, p. 39; General Economic Conditions and Tendencies, p. 49; Economic Theory, p. 53; and the sections for specific countries and regions.

Braunthal, Julius. **History of the International.** New York: Praeger, 1967, 2 v.
The English translation of the first two volumes of a massive history of the Marxist Internationals. The German original appeared as "Geschichte der Internationale" (Hannover: Dietz, 1961-71, 3 v.).

Conquest, Robert. **Marxism To-day.** London: Ampersand, 1964, 88 p.
A critical presentation of "the essentials of Marx's thought and of the ways in which it is currently applied," by a British scholar.

Crossman, Richard Howard Stafford. **The Politics of Socialism.** New York: Atheneum, 1965, 252 p.

Essays and articles of the 1950s and 1960s by the late maverick member of the British Labour Party. The two prominent themes are the rethinking of socialism—a much needed enterprise—and thoughts on the cold war.

Donneur, André. **Histoire de l'union des partis socialistes pour l'action internationale (1920-1923).** Sudbury (Ont.): Librairie de l'Université Laurentienne, 1967, 434 p.
A well-documented monograph on the history of the International Union of Socialist Parties, also known as the Two-and-a-Half International or the Vienna International. It was established in February 1921 by representatives of 19 socialist groups and parties for the purpose of creating unity in the international socialist movement.

Drachkovitch, Milorad M., ed. **Marxism in the Modern World.** Stanford: Stanford University Press (for the Hoover Institution on War, Revolution, and Peace), 1965, 293 p.
Essays on variant forms of Marxism in the twentieth century. The able group of contributors includes Raymond Aron, Bertram D. Wolfe, Boris Souvarine, Merle Fainsod, Adam B. Ulam, Arthur A. Cohen, Theodore Draper and Richard Löwenthal.

Fromm, Erich, ed. **Socialist Humanism.** Garden City: Doubleday, 1965, 420 p.
This symposium, which attempts to assess the "humanist" strain of Marxist thought, contains contributions by prominent neo-Marxist philosophers from Poland, Jugoslavia and Czechoslovakia.

Garaudy, Roger. **L'Alternative.** Paris: Laffont, 1972, 251 p.
The alternative (to both the jungle laws of capitalism, however refined, and to neo-Stalinist bureaucratic centralism) that Garaudy sketches is "Socialist self-management," to be initiated by a general strike of workers, intellectuals and those in the tertiary sector, in order to institute the "great social, political and cultural mutation that will put at the service of man the gigantic productive forces" of society.

Halévy, Élie. **The Era of Tyrannies: Essays on Socialism and War.** New York: New York University Press, 1966, 324 p.
A welcome translation of pieces ranging over the period from 1902 to 1936, by the late eminent French historian. The French original was published in 1938 as "L'Ère des tyrannies: études sur le socialisme et la guerre."

Harrington, Michael. **Socialism.** New York: Saturday Review Press, 1972, 436 p.
A leading American socialist reviews the socialist tradition, defends Marx against detractors and Stalinists and urges the need and relevance of socialism for the future. An important and well-argued statement of belief.

Humbert-Droz, Jules. **L'Origine de l'Internationale communiste: de Zimmerwald à Moscou.** Neuchâtel: La Baconnière, 1968, 255 p.
A collection of documents and speeches illustrating socialist attitudes during World War I, by a former Swiss Communist and a Comintern functionary.

Laidler, Harry Wellington. **History of Socialism.** New York: Crowell, 1968, 970 p.
A survey of "socialist thinking through its various stages of development from utopianism to the present day," published originally as "Social-Economic Movements" (New York: Crowell, 1944, 826 p.). The author is a prominent American socialist.

Leser, Norbert. **Zwischen Reformismus und Bolschewismus: der Austromarxismus als Theorie und Praxis.** Vienna: Europa Verlag, 1968, 600 p.
A detailed study of the Austrian variety of Marxism, both in its theoretical and organizational aspects, particularly as exemplified by the thinking and political activities of Karl Renner, Otto Bauer and Max Adler.

Löbl, Eugen. **Conversations with the Bewildered.** Cambridge: Schenkman, 1972, 192 p.
Advice from the disillusioned Old Left to the inexperienced New Left. Löbl, once one of Czechoslovakia's leading Marxists, calls for a new socialist humanism.

Martinet, Gilles. **Marxism of Our Time or the Contradictions of Socialism.** New York: Monthly Review Press, 1964, 126 p.
A stimulating essay by the Marxist editor of *France Observateur* on the contradictions that have beset the Marxist movement and on the possibilities of a renovation.

Miliband, Ralph and Saville, John, eds. **The Socialist Register, 1964–.** New York: Monthly Review Press; Humanities Press, 1964–.
An annual volume of essays, mostly written from a radical Marxist point of view, on socialism and contemporary politics.

Mossé, Robert. **L'économie socialiste: perspectives de l'an 2000.** Paris: Librairie Générale de Droit, 1968, 328 p.
Papers by a leading French economist on the problems of creating a democratic, consumer-oriented socialism.

Radice, Giles. **Democratic Socialism: A Short Survey.** New York: Praeger, 1966, 164 p.
A useful introduction to the subject by a member of the British Labour Party.

Šik, Ota. **Der dritte Weg.** Hamburg: Hoffmann und Campe, 1972, 450 p.
A well-argued critique of Marxist theory, and some practice, makes up most of this book. The eminent Czech reformer, now in exile in Switzerland, also sketches the main features of "the third way," a democratic, participatory market socialism with Jeffersonian overtones.

Stojanović, Svetozar. **Izmedju ideala i stvarnosti.** Belgrade: "Prosveta," 1969, 223 p.
A controversial and lucid analysis of contemporary developments in socialism, by a Marxist philosopher at Belgrade University. The English translation appeared as "Between Ideals and Reality: A Critique of Socialism and its Future" (New York: Oxford University Press, 1973, 222 p.).

Stoyanovitch, Constantin. **Marxisme et droit.** Paris: Librairie Générale de Droit, 1964, 406 p.
A critical examination of the Marxist theory of law.

Tamedly, Elisabeth. **Socialism and International Economic Order.** Geneva: Université de Genève, Institut Universitaire de Hautes Études Internationales, 1968, 299 p.
The history of ideas, theory and present practice are subjected to an analysis that stresses the conflict between economic and state interest and the lack of a rational basis for resolving it.

Thomas, Norman Mattoon. **Socialism Re-examined.** New York: Norton, 1963, 280 p.
The leader of American socialism for more than 40 years offers new directions for all socialists, particularly in the struggle to maintain peace.

Wolfe, Bertram David. **Marxism: One Hundred Years in the Life of a Doctrine.** New York: Dial Press, 1965, 404 p.
An able and most interesting tracing of the ambiguities of the Marxist heritage as it evolved from certain contradictory aims and impulses in Marx and Engels themselves.

Zhukov, Evgenii Mikhailovich, *ed.* **Sovremennye teorii sotsializma "natsional'nogo tipa."** Moscow: Izd-vo "Mysl'," 1967, 286 p.
A collection of articles on varieties of socialism "of a national type," as pursued in Algeria, Egypt, Guinea, Burma and a number of other countries.

Communism

See also General Works, p. 1; (Political Factors) General, p. 12; Political Philosophies and Ideologies, p. 21; Society and Social Psychology, p. 39; Labor and Labor Movements, p. 41; Culture; Education; Public Opinion; Communications Processes, p. 42; General Economic Conditions and Tendencies, p. 49; (International Law) General, p. 83; (War) Guerrilla Warfare; Armed Insurrection, p. 118; Propaganda; Psychological and Political Warfare, p. 120; Peace; Disarmament; Arms Control, p. 122; Inter-War Period, p. 140; Second World War, p. 144; The Postwar World, p. 178; and the sections for specific countries and regions.

Black, Cyril Edwin and Thornton, Thomas P., eds. **Communism and Revolution: The Strategic Uses of Political Violence.** Princeton: Princeton University Press, 1964, 467 p.
A substantial symposium by a number of knowledgeable authors on the "Communist experience in influencing political change by violent methods." The treatment is both historical and regional.

Bocheński, Innocentius M. and Niemeyer, Gerhart, eds. **Handbook on Communism.** New York: Praeger, 1962, 686 p.
The English translation of a massive handbook dealing with various aspects of international Communism. The German original appeared as "Handbuch des Weltkommunismus" (Freiburg: Alber, 1958, 762 p.).

Buber-Neumann, Margarete. **Kriegsschauplätze der Weltrevolution: ein Bericht aus der Praxis der Komintern 1919–1943.** Stuttgart: Seewald, 1967, 522 p.

A historical survey of the Comintern, filled with personal reminiscences, by the wife of the prominent German Communist Heinz Neumann, who disappeared in Stalin's purges in 1937.

Cheverny, Julien. **Les deux stratégies du communisme.** Paris: Julliard, 1965, 349 p.
An essay on the different strategic and foreign policy concepts of the Russian and Chinese brands of communism in a world political situation characterized by a balance of power achieved between the United States and the Soviet Union and the rift between Moscow and Peking.

Colby, Roy. **Conquest With Words: How the Communist Lingo Promotes World Revolution.** Arlington (Va.): Crestwood Books, 1967, 186 p.
A former Foreign Service officer discusses the semantics of communist terminology.

Crozier, Brian. **Since Stalin.** New York: Coward-McCann, 1970, 247 p.
A general, knowledgeable survey of recent developments in the communist world, in various communist movements and in the New Left. In the author's view the cold war is neither over nor on its way out.

Dallin, Alexander and Others, *eds.* **Diversity in International Communism.** New York: Columbia University Press (for the Research Institute on Communist Affairs, Columbia University), 1963, 867 p.
An extensive documentary record of the issues that have troubled and divided the international communist movement since the autumn of 1961.

Dallin, Alexander and Breslauer, George W. **Political Terror in Communist Systems.** Stanford: Stanford University Press, 1970, 172 p.
A concise but thoughtful discussion of the functions of terror at various stages in the gaining, maintenance and consolidation of power.

De George, Richard T. **The New Marxism.** New York: Pegasus, 1968, 170 p.
A concise account of developments and divergencies in Marxist theory in Eastern Europe and the Soviet Union since 1956.

Degras, Jane (Tabrisky), *ed.* **The Communist International, 1919-1943: Documents. Volume III, 1929-1943.** New York: Oxford University Press (for the Royal Institute of International Affairs), 1965, 494 p.
This valuable selection of documents on the Comintern covers the years from the disastrous turn to the left through the period of the popular front to the formal dissolution of the organization in 1943.

Deutscher, Isaac. **Ironies of History: Essays on Contemporary Communism.** New York: Oxford University Press, 1966, 278 p.
A collection of Mr. Deutscher's stimulating, and often provacative and irritating, essays since 1955 on communist affairs, international relations and cultural developments in the U.S.S.R.

Drachkovitch, Milorad M. and Lazitch, Branko, *eds.* **The Comintern: Historical Highlights.** New York: Praeger (for the Hoover Institution on War, Revolution, and Peace), 1966, 430 p.
A collection of essays, recollections and documents concerning various turning points and crises of the Comintern.

Drachkovitch, Milorad M., *ed.* **The Revolutionary Internationals, 1864-1943.** Stanford: Stanford University Press (for the Hoover Institution on War, Revolution, and Peace), 1966, 256 p.
Essays on aspects of the history of the three internationals.

Fischer, Ernst. **Erinnerungen und Reflexionen.** Reinbek b. Hamburg: Rowohlt, 1969, 477 p.
Soul-searching memoirs of a former Austrian Communist and a leading Marxist thinker who for many years lived in the Soviet Union where he worked for the Comintern.

Flechtheim, Ossip Kurt. **Weltkommunismus im Wandel.** Cologne: Wissenschaft und Politik, 1965, 255 p.
Although the author is an able student of communism, the fact that these chapters were written over a wide span of years—since the late 1930s—leads to a somewhat uneven and at times anachronistic coverage.

Fleron, Frederic J., Jr., *ed.* **Communist Studies and the Social Sciences: Essays on Methodology and Empirical Theory.** Chicago: Rand McNally, 1969, 481 p.

This collection of essays centering on methodological, conceptual and theoretical issues in the social sciences as they bear on the study of communism is probably for the specialist, but it contains material of real interest, presented by some able authors.

Freymond, Jacques, *ed*. **Contributions à l'histoire du Comintern.** Geneva: Droz (for the Institut de Hautes Études Internationales), 1965, 267 p.

A collection of memoirs and documents, with contributions, among others, by Boris Nikolaevskii, Angelica Balabanoff, Boris Souvarine and M. N. Roy on the history of the Comintern and some of its "founding fathers."

Garaudy, Roger. **Le Grand tournant du socialisme.** Paris: Gallimard, 1970, 315 p.

A prominent and long-standing French communist intellectual wrestles earnestly with a number of contemporary crises within the communist movement. The book has subsequently been charged with right-wing deviationism.

Gross, Babette. **Willi Münzenberg: eine politische Biographie.** Stuttgart: Deutsche Verlags-Anstalt (for the Institut für Zeitgeschichte), 1967, 352 p.

A biography of a leading Comintern functionary who in the late 1930s broke with Stalin and in 1940 died under mysterious circumstances. The author was Münzenberg's companion for many years.

Gruber, Helmut, *comp*. **International Communism in the Era of Lenin: A Documentary History.** Ithaca: Cornell University Press, 1967, 512 p.

Documents and commentary by Helmut Gruber and others. Chiefly for the general reader.

Hazard, John N. **Communists and Their Law.** Chicago: University of Chicago Press, 1969, 560 p.

A longtime and leading student of Soviet law here undertakes a "search for the common core of the family of Marxian socialist legal systems." Broadly based on a comparison of theory and practice in Eastern Europe, Asia and Africa, the approach is essentially thematic: the rule, or role, of law in the various fields of application.

Hillmann, Günther. **Selbstkritik des Kommunismus.** Reinbek bei Hamburg: Rowohlt, 1967, 251 p.

A useful collection of documents, with connecting commentary, concerning oppositional currents in communism since 1917 — in Russia and various other countries and in the international movement.

Hulse, James W. **The Forming of the Communist International.** Stanford: Stanford University Press, 1964, 275 p.

A scholarly study of the nascent Communist International in the period between the First and Second Congresses in 1919-1920.

Humbert-Droz, Jules. **Mémoires.** Neuchâtel: La Baconnière, 1969-73, 4 v.

The memoirs by the former Swiss Protestant pastor who for ten years was secretary of the Communist International. Volume I, "Mon Évolution du tolstoïsme au communisme, 1891-1921" (1969, 443 p.), covers his early years, his conversion to communism and his entry into the Comintern; volume II, "De Lénine à Staline: dix ans au service de l'Internationale communiste, 1921-1931" (1971, 509 p.), deals with his activities in the Comintern; volume III, "Dix ans de lutte antifasciste, 1931-1941" (1972, 431 p.), describes his gradual disillusionment with Stalin, and volume IV, "Le Courronnement d'une vie de combat, 1941-1971" (1973, 452 p), was compiled by Humbert-Droz's widow and covers the last thirty years of his life.

International Meeting of Communist and Workers' Parties, Moscow 1969. Prague: Peace and Socialism Publishers, 1969, 679 p.

The complete proceedings of the 1969 Moscow meeting of leftist parties. Included is the text of the conference declaration on present-day imperialism.

Johnson, Chalmers A., *ed*. **Change in Communist Systems.** Stanford: Stanford University Press, 1970, 368 p.

Some 12 specialists tackle in their respective essays the problem of defining, identifying and measuring political and economic change in the world's 14 communist nations. Part of their effort is to work toward more appropriate theoretical models in dealing with communist régimes.

Kanet, Roger E., *ed*. **The Behavioral Revolution and Communist Studies.** New York: Free Press, 1971, 376 p.
A collection of articles suggesting applications of behavioral research to communist systems.

Kautsky, John H. **Communism and the Politics of Development: Persistent Myths and Changing Behavior.** New York: Wiley, 1968, 216 p.
A collection of the author's articles since the early 1950s dealing broadly with the theme of the title.

King, Edmund James, *ed*. **Communist Education.** Indianapolis: Bobbs-Merrill, 1963, 309 p.
A collection of articles by Western authorities on various phases of education as observed at first-hand in Russia and other communist countries.

Kirkpatrick, Jeane J., *ed*. **The Strategy of Deception: A Study in World-Wide Communist Tactics.** New York: Farrar, Straus, 1963, 444 p.
This volume of essays on the communist movement outside the U.S.S.R. deals with the general theory of revolutionary strategy and with the efforts and failures of the communists in the various regions of the world and in the U.N.

Kolarz, Walter, *ed*. **Books on Communism.** New York: Oxford University Press, 1964, 568 p.
A very useful annotated bibliography of some 2,500 English-language publications.

Kolarz, Walter. **Communism and Colonialism.** New York: St. Martin's Press, 1964, 147 p.
Posthumously published essays dealing, through a variety of specific instances and issues, with the dubious right of Soviet Communism to pose as "anti-colonial."

Kurzman, Dan. **Subversion of the Innocents: Patterns of Communist Penetration in Africa, the Middle East, and Asia.** New York: Random House, 1963, 570 p.
A combination of good journalism and assiduous pursuit of facts and figures, this panorama of many countries gives a broad and generally accurate picture of the scope of Soviet and Chinese efforts and of the local factors which facilitate or hinder their success.

Labedz, Leopold, *ed*. **International Communism after Khrushchev.** Cambridge: M.I.T. Press, 1965, 232 p.
Articles dealing both with the vicissitudes of international communism as a movement and with the state of the parties in various parts of the world.

Lazitch, Branko and Drachkovitch, Milorad M. **Lenin and the Comintern. Volume I.** Stanford: Hoover Institution Press, 1972, 683 p.
An important work bringing to light much new material, though of course the basic Soviet sources remain unavailable. This volume, to be followed by another covering the years to 1924, concludes with a detailed study of the attempted revolution in Germany in 1921 and Lenin's change of line.

Lengyel, Emil. **Nationalism—The Last Stage of Communism.** New York: Funk & Wagnalls, 1969, 369 p.
A readable, though in places somewhat cursory, survey of the metamorphoses of the communist movement, with emphasis on the period of polycentrism.

Löwenthal, Richard. **World Communism: The Disintegration of a Secular Faith.** New York: Oxford University Press, 1964, 296 p.
A leading Western student of communist affairs traces what he takes to be the irreversible disintegration of world communism over the years since 1955. Originally appeared as "Chruschtschow und der Weltkommunismus" (Stuttgart: Kohlhammer, 1963, 245 p.).

Lukács, Georg. **History and Class Consciousness: Studies in Marxist Dialectics.** Cambridge: M.I.T. Press, 1971, 356 p.
A welcome, if long overdue, translation of Lukács' classic and enormously influential study. Includes the author's important preface to the 1967 German edition: "Geschichte und Klassenbewusstsein: Studien über marxistische Dialektik" (Berlin: Luchterhand, 1967, 733 p.).

McKenzie, Kermit Eubank. **Comintern and World Revolution, 1928-1943: The Shaping of Doctrine.** New York: Columbia University Press, 1964, 368 p.
A close study of the question of world revolution in communist theory as reflected in the Comintern during the years 1928-1943.

Mayer, Peter. **Cohesion and Conflict in International Communism: A Study of Marxist-Leninist Concepts and their Applications.** The Hague: Nijhoff, 1968, 257 p.
The author seeks to determine the influence of Marxist-Leninist thought on Soviet policies relating to international communism. In doing that, he underrates the strategic, economic and political considerations of the Soviet state.

Merleau-Ponty, Maurice. **Humanism and Terror: An Essay on the Communist Problem.** Boston: Beacon Press, 1969, 189 p.
A French philosopher of the Left attacks the anti-communist implications of Koestler's "Darkness at Noon" and demands greater awareness of Western wickedness and of the humanistic basis of Soviet life, despite terror. The French original was published as "Humanisme et terreur: essai sur le problème communiste" (Paris: Gallimard, 1947, 206 p.).

Nettl, John Peter. **Rosa Luxemburg.** New York: Oxford University Press, 1966, 2 v.
An ambitious and valuable biography and interpretation of the life and political views of one of the most remarkable and intelligent figures in the Marxist movement.

Niemeyer, Gerhart. **Deceitful Peace: A New Look at the Soviet Threat.** New Rochelle: Arlington House, 1971, 201 p.
In this extended essay Professor Niemeyer argues the continuing danger of communism, and the basic irrationality of its central premises.

Parkinson, G. H. R., *ed.* **George Lukács: The Man, His Work and His Ideas.** New York: Random House, 1970, 254 p.
A welcome set of essays on various facets of the thought of a leading Marxist theoretician.

Pirker, Theo, *ed.* **Utopie und Mythos der Weltrevolution: zur Geschichte der Komintern 1920-1940.** Munich: Deutscher Taschenbuch Verlag, 1964, 303 p.
A selection of articles from the official publications of the Communist International in the years from 1920 to 1940.

Rühle, Jürgen. **Literature and Revolution.** New York: Praeger, 1969, 520 p.
An encyclopedic survey of the tortured relationship of important twentieth-century writers to communism. The author, a West German critic, devotes most of his attention to Russian and German authors. The German original, of which the English edition is a revised version, was published as "Literatur und Revolution: die Schriftsteller und der Kommunismus" (Cologne: Kiepenheuer und Witsch, 1960, 610 p.).

Schneider, Wolfgang, *ed.* **Kommunismus International 1950-1965: Probleme einer gespaltenen Welt.** Cologne: Verlag Wissenschaft und Politik, 1965, 255 p.
A collection of essays, by various authors, analyzing the developments and policies of communism both in the free world and in the communist-ruled countries from 1950 to 1965.

Sobolev, Aleksandr Ivanovich and Others. **Outline History of the Communist International.** Moscow: Progress Publishers, 1971, 563 p.
This is the Soviet version of the history of the Comintern. The original appeared as "Kommunisticheskii Internatsional: kratkii istoricheskii ocherk" (Moscow: Izd-vo Politicheskoi Literatury, 1969, 599 p.).

Stawar, Andrzej, *pseud.* (Edward Janus). **Libres essais marxistes.** Paris: Éditions du Seuil, 1963, 284 p.
A collection of articles on contemporary political issues, primarily on communism, by a well-known Polish Marxist, who did not return to Gomulka's Poland after a study trip to France. The Polish original was published as: "Pisma ostatnie" (Paris: Instytut Literacki, 1961, 274 p.).

Sworakowski, Witold S. **The Communist International and Its Front Organizations: A Research Guide and Checklist of Holdings in American and European Libraries.** Stanford: The Hoover Institution on War, Revolution, and Peace, 1965, 493 p.
A comprehensive bibliography of the publications by and on the Communist International and its front organizations.

Treadgold, Donald W., *ed.* **Soviet and Chinese Communism: Similarities and Differences.** Seattle: University of Washington Press, 1967, 452 p.
  A symposium based on a conference of Russian and Chinese specialists in 1965, dealing centrally with a comparison of Soviet and Chinese Communism in their history, changes, power structure, economic policies and international behavior.

Triska, Jan F., *ed.* **Communist Party-States: Comparative and International Studies.** Indianapolis: Bobbs-Merrill, 1969, 392 p.
  A collection of essays that emanate from the Stanford Studies of the Communist System.

Tucker, Robert C. **The Marxian Revolutionary Idea.** New York: Norton, 1969, 240 p.
  Interesting essays on Marxian theory, its role as ideology and its place in communist revolutions.

Ul'ianovskii, R. A. **Sotsializm i osvobodivshiesia strany.** Moscow: Glavnaia Redaktsiia Vostochnoi Literatury, 1972, 557 p.
  A politically authoritative writer interprets Leninist theory on socialism, national liberation and the noncapitalist development with specific attention to such questions as agrarian reform and economic independence in Asian countries.

Wolfe, Bertram David. **Strange Communists I Have Known.** New York: Stein and Day, 1965, 222 p.
  A portrait gallery of unconventional communists, including John Reed, Angelica Balabanoff, Rosa Luxemburg, Maxim Litvinov and Leon Trotsky.

World Communist Movement: Selective Chronology 1818-1957. Washington: G.P.O., 1961-65, 4 v.
  A useful chronology, prepared by the Legislative Reference Service at the Library of Congress. The four published volumes cover the years from 1818 to 1955.

Yearbook on International Communist Affairs, 1966–. Stanford: Hoover Institution on War, Revolution, and Peace, 1968–.
  This useful reference series is designed to be a "continuing publication in English on the international political activities of the various communist parties, or on the relations among communists themselves." The volume for 1966 was edited by Milorad M. Drachkovitch; for 1968, by Richard V. Allen. Since 1969 Richard F. Staar has been the editor.

Zagladin, Vladimir Viktorovich, *ed.* **Mezhdunarodnoe kommunisticheskoe dvizhenie: ocherk strategii i taktiki.** Moscow: Izd-vo Politicheskoi Literatury, 2d rev. ed., 1972, 503 p.
  A survey of the history and present state of the international communist movement, containing prescriptions for the struggle against "Left opportunists" within foreign communist parties.

New Left; Anarchism; Student Politics

See also (Political Factors) General, p. 12; Socialism, p. 24; Communism, p. 26; Totalitarianism; Fascism, p. 32; The Problem of Authority; Violence and Revolution, p. 34; Problems of New Nations, p. 36; Society and Social Psychology, p. 39; (Latin America) Political and Constitutional Problems, p. 203; (The United States) Foreign Policy, p. 229; Politics and Political Issues, p. 268; Social Questions, p. 276; (Chile) General, p. 329; (France) Politics and Government, p. 408; (Spain) The Republic and the Civil War, p. 434; (Federal Republic of Germany) Politics and Government, p. 503; (Union of Soviet Socialist Republics) Revolution; Civil War; The Lenin Era, p. 541; (China) Chinese Communism; The Communist Regime, p. 687; Republic of Korea, p. 730.

Apter, David Ernest and Joll, James, *eds.* **Anarchism Today.** Garden City: Doubleday, 1972, 274 p.
  Essays providing a world tour of present-day anarchist movements and moods.

Cohn-Bendit, Daniel and Cohn-Bendit, Gabriel. **Obsolete Communism: The Left-Wing Alternative.** New York: McGraw-Hill, 1969, 255 p.
  A revolutionary youth leader, known for his role in the student strikes in France in 1967-68, discusses with the help of his brother his revolutionary activities and ethos.

Cranston, Maurice, *ed.* **The New Left.** New York: Library Press, 1971, 208 p.
  Six essays on leading figures of the New Left in America, Europe and the Third World.

GENERAL INTERNATIONAL RELATIONS

Emmerson, Donald K., *ed.* **Students and Politics in Developing Nations.** New York: Praeger, 1968, 444 p.
The editor skillfully blends together eleven essays on student politics in eleven different countries.

Feuer, Lewis S. **The Conflict of Generations: The Character and Significance of Student Movements.** New York: Basic Books, 1969, 543 p.
In this fine survey of student movements in the West during the last two centuries, the author identifies a common thread of the parricide wish everywhere.

Gerassi, John, *ed.* **The Coming of the New International.** New York: World Publishing Co., 1971, 610 p.
A broadly representative anthology of revolutionary writings, selected from more than 20 countries.

Hope, Marjorie. **Youth Against the World.** Boston: Little, Brown, 1970, 409 p.
An eyewitness report of youth protest around the world, written with considerable empathy and verve.

Jacobs, Dan Norman, *ed.* **The New Communisms.** New York: Harper and Row, 1969, 326 p.
Essays by several authors on strains and mutations of communism throughout the world.

Joll, James. **The Anarchists.** Boston: Atlantic (Little Brown), 1965, 303 p.
An able, if not definitive general history of the anarchist movement in the nineteenth and first third of the twentieth centuries.

Kepplinger, Hans Mathias. **Rechte Leute von links: Gewaltkult und Innerlichkeit.** Olten: Walter-Verlag, 1970, 327 p.
A useful analysis of the affinity between the New Left and the old and largely discredited Right. Unlikely to become popular reading among either group.

King, Richard. **The Party of Eros: Radical Social Thought and the Realm of Freedom.** Chapel Hill: University of North Carolina Press, 1972, 227 p.
The core of this book is a critical analysis of the social thought of Paul Goodman, Herbert Marcuse and Norman O. Brown.

Lipset, Seymour Martin, *ed.* **Student Politics.** New York: Basic Books, 1967, 403 p.
Fifteen social scientists examine student political movements ranging from Berkeley to France, India and Latin America.

Pfaff, William. **Condemned to Freedom.** New York: Ramdom House, 1971, 210 p.
The New Left, the Right backlash and the New Populism, the author asserts, are all symptoms of the despair of liberalism. He argues forcefully that liberalism, to survive, must embrace radical change.

Read, Herbert. **Anarchy and Order: Essays in Politics.** Boston: Beacon Press, 1971, 235 p.
Herbert Read, who died in 1968, is best known for his writings on art. He was also a philosophical anarchist. This book, which first appeared in England in 1954, assembles his various essays on the theme of anarchism.

Woddis, Jack. **New Theories of Revolution: A Commentary on the views of Frantz Fanon, Regis Debray and Herbert Marcuse.** New York: International Publishers, 1972, 415 p.
A communist critique of three leading contemporary advocates of revolution who reject the organized working-class movement.

Totalitarianism; Fascism

See also Comparative Government, p. 18; (Political Philosophies and Ideologies) General, p. 21; Democracy, p. 23; Socialism, p. 24; Communism, p. 26; Problems of New Nations, p. 36; Society and Social Psychology, p. 39; Inter-War Period, p. 140; Second World War, p. 144; The Postwar World, p. 178; and the sections for specific countries and regions.

Boca, Angelo del and Giovana, Mario. **Fascism Today: A World Survey.** New York: Pantheon Books, 1969, 532 p.

POLITICAL FACTORS 33

A comparative study of right-wing ideologies and movements in the world over the last fifty years. Originally published as "I 'figli del sole.' Mezzo secolo di nazifascismo nel mondo" (Milan: Feltrinelli, 1965, 610 p.).

Buchheim, Hans. **Totalitarian Rule: Its Nature and Characteristics.** Middletown: Wesleyan University Press, 1968, 112 p.
A fine theoretical exploration, though heavily indebted to Hannah Arendt's "The Origins of Totalitarianism." Somewhat discursive but full of insight.

Carsten, Francis Ludwig. **The Rise of Fascism.** Berkeley: University of California Press, 1967, 256 p.
A short, responsible survey of how fascism came to power in Italy and Germany, with some valuable comparative data on fascist movements in other European countries.

Diggins, John P. **Mussolini and Fascism: The View from America.** Princeton: Princeton University Press, 1972, 524 p.
An important study of America's far from uniformly hostile attitude to Italian Fascism—a sobering work that enhances our understanding of the appeals of fascism and of the nature of American society, by a young scholar.

Eisenberg, Dennis. **The Re-Emergence of Fascism.** New York: A. S. Barnes, 1968, 348 p.
A revealing though somewhat exaggerated account of neo-Nazi, fascist and other extreme right-wing groups in the world today.

Fetscher, Iring, *ed.* **Rechtsradikalismus.** Frankfurt/Main: Europäische Verlagsanstalt, 1967, 252 p.
A collection of articles on the right-wing political movements in Germany, the United States and France, written to explain the unforseen gains of the National Democratic Party in Germany in the middle 1960s.

Galkin, Aleksandr Abramovich. **Sotsiologiia neofashizma.** Moscow: Izd-vo "Nauka," 1971, 197 p.
A brief examination of right-wing movements in Europe and the United States through the prism of current Soviet beliefs about the origins and significance of fascism in a capitalist system.

Gregor, A. James. **The Ideology of Fascism: The Rationale of Totalitarianism.** New York: Free Press, 1969, 493 p.
In this study the author provides a detailed account of the ideology of Mussolini's Fascism and points out the affinities that exist between fascism and various Marxist and contemporary radical left ideologies.

Hamilton, Alastair. **The Appeal of Fascism: A Study of Intellectuals and Fascism, 1919-1945.** New York: Macmillan, 1971, 312 p.
The political irresponsibility and anti-intellectualism of intellectuals is a fascinating subject, here treated by an English writer with moderate success. He examines intellectuals in Italy, Germany, England and France.

Huntington, Samuel P. and Moore, Clement H., *eds.* **Authoritarian Politics in Modern Society.** New York: Basic Books, 1970, 533 p.
Fifteen political scientists evaluate the different ways in which one-party political systems adapt or fail to adapt to socio-economic change. The case studies are well chosen and the quality of research and analysis is high.

Kedward, H. R. **Fascism in Western Europe, 1900-1945.** Glasgow: Blackie, 1969, 260 p.
A brief but useful discussion of the ideas of the extreme Right in the first half of the twentieth century. The author is a British scholar.

Ledeen, Michael Arthur. **Universal Fascism.** New York: Howard Fertig, 1972, 200 p.
A study of the futile efforts to construct a Fascist International on the basis of an ideology of corporatism and the cult of youth in the middle 1930s.

Nolte, Ernst. **Die Krise des liberalen Systems und die faschistischen Bewegungen.** Munich: Piper, 1968, 475 p.
After his much-acclaimed theoretical analysis of fascism, Nolte now turns to an examination of the historical conditions which favored its rise. He also gives brief summaries of every fascist movement in Europe.

Nolte, Ernst, *ed.* **Theorien über den Faschismus.** Cologne: Kiepenheuer, 1967, 513 p.
An anthology of writings on fascism, both by advocates and critics of the doctrine.

Nolte, Ernst. **Three Faces of Fascism: Action Française, Italian Fascism, National Socialism.** New York: Holt, Rinehart and Winston, 1966, 561 p.
An ambitious attempt to analyze and describe the theory and practice of fascism in France, Italy and Germany. Like Hannah Arendt's "Origins of Totalitarianism," Nolte's book has a tremendous sweep and is at once philosophical and historical. A thoughtful, important and uneven work. The German original appeared as "Der Faschismus in seiner Epoche" (Munich: Piper, 1963, 633 p.).

Pirker, Theo, *ed.* **Komintern und Faschismus: Dokumente zur Geschichte und Theorie des Faschismus.** Stuttgart: Deutsche Verlags-Anstalt (for the Institut für Zeitgeschichte), 1965, 203 p.
A selection of documents from the Comintern publications "Inprekorr" and "Rundschau" on Italian Fascism and National-Socialism. Introduction and commentaries are provided by the editor.

Sugar, Peter F., *ed.* **Native Fascism in the Successor States 1918-1945.** Santa Barbara: ABC-Clio, 1971, 166 p.
A symposium of papers by East European and Western scholars, dealing with Fascist and right-radical movements in Austria, Czechoslovakia, Hungary, Poland, Rumania and Jugoslavia, chiefly in the interwar years.

Woolf, Stuart Joseph, *ed.* **European Fascism.** New York: Random House, 1969, 387 p.
A series of essays on fascism in various countries, with a valuable, concluding essay on "Fascism in Contemporary Europe."

THE PROBLEMS OF AUTHORITY; VIOLENCE AND REVOLUTION

See also (General Works) Methodology and Theory, p. 4; General Treatments, p. 7; (Political Factors) General, p. 12; Political Philosophies and Ideologies, p. 21; Problems of New Nations, p. 36; (International Law) General, p. 83; (War) General, p. 108; Guerrilla Warfare; Armed Insurrection, p. 118; Inter-War Period, p. 140; Second World War, p. 144; The Postwar World, p. 178; and the sections for specific countries and regions.

Arendt, Hannah. **On Revolution.** New York: Viking, 1963, 343 p.
One of the most penetrating and original thinkers of our time here deals with the phenomenon of revolution—its meaning, and the vicissitudes of the revolutionary tradition. An important contribution.

Arendt, Hannah. **On Violence.** New York: Harcourt, Brace and World, 1970, 106 p.
The central argument of this brilliant essay is that "violence appears where power is in jeopardy," that "every decrease in power is an open invitation to violence."

Dunn, John. **Modern Revolutions.** New York: Cambridge University Press, 1972, 346 p.
A penetrating analysis, through historical case studies, of modern revolution and revolutionary ideology.

Eckstein, Harry Horace, *ed.* **Internal War: Problems and Approaches.** New York: Free Press of Glencoe, 1964, 339 p.
A symposium of essays, some of them very theoretically oriented, on the theme of violence, rebellion, revolution.

Friedrich, Carl Joachim, *ed.* **Revolution.** New York: Atherton Press, 1966, 246 p.
Eleven thoughtful essays on many varieties of revolution, considered in the light of both past developments and future prospects. Published as the eighth volume of the "NOMOS" Yearbook of the American Society for Political and Legal Philosophy.

Gurr, Ted Robert. **Why Men Rebel.** Princeton: Princeton University Press (for the Center of International Studies), 1970, 421 p.
An effort, behaviorally oriented, to construct theoretical models for the study of political violence.

Johnson, Chalmers A. **Revolutionary Change.** Boston: Little, Brown, 1966, 191 p.
A study by a professor at the University of California of "the interrelationships be-

tween value, economic necessity, acceptable personality configurations, social control, and historical actions" which determine revolutionary change.

Kelly, George A. and Brown, Clifford W., Jr., *eds*. **Struggles in the State: Sources and Patterns of World Revolution.** New York: Wiley, 1970, 511 p.
Two dozen essays on revolution by both activists and scholars, past and present. The editors' introductory notes to each essay provide a useful analytical framework.

Lasswell, Harold Dwight and Lerner, Daniel, *eds*. **World Revolutionary Elites: Studies in Coercive Ideological Movements.** Cambridge: M.I.T. Press, 1965, 478 p.
Studies of four classic political uprisings and of the élites who led them: the Communists in Russia, the Nazis in Germany, the Fascists in Italy and the Kuomintang and Communists in China.

Latey, Maurice. **Patterns of Tyranny.** New York: Atheneum, 1969, 331 p.
A well-written and closely argued examination of the problem of tyranny throughout the ages. The English edition was published as "Tyranny: A Study in the Abuse of Power" (London: Macmillan, 1969, 328 p.).

Leiden, Carl and Schmitt, Karl M., *eds*. **The Politics of Violence: Revolution in the Modern World.** Englewood Cliffs: Prentice-Hall, 1968, 244 p.
A valuable contribution to the growing literature on the causes and current development of revolution, including case studies of Mexico, Turkey, Egypt and Cuba.

Leites, Nathan and Wolf, Charles, Jr. **Rebellion and Authority.** Chicago: Markham Publishing Co., 1970, 174 p.
An original and analytical approach to the general problem of insurgency. The authors have attempted to do for the understanding of insurgent conflicts what Thomas Schelling and Herman Kahn have done for the field of strategic nuclear conflict.

L'Etang, Hugh. **The Pathology of Leadership.** New York: Hawthorn Books, 1970, 215 p.
A British physician argues, on the basis of several tantalizing vignettes, that doctors may have the obligation, in the public interest, to jettison the Hippocratic Oath and reveal the medical histories and prognoses of national leaders.

Lipset, Seymour Martin. **Revolution and Counterrevolution: Change and Persistence in Social Structures.** New York: Basic Books, 1968, 466 p.
A collection of twelve major essays in political sociology.

Marek, Franz. **Philosophie der Weltrevolution: Beitrag zu einer Anthologie der Revolutionstheorien.** Vienna: Europa Verlag, 1966, 140 p.
An anthological survey of the revolutionary theories of the modern world, by an Austrian Communist.

Meisel, James Hans. **Counterrevolution: How Revolutions Die.** New York: Atherton Press, 1966, 237 p.
A study of twelve episodes in history, ranging from Cicero to de Gaulle, dealing with the ways revolutions may die or be aborted.

Pennock, James Roland and Chapman, John W., *eds*. **Coercion.** Chicago: Aldine-Atherton, 1972, 328 p.
Papers dealing with the role and meaning of coercion in human affairs, including international relations.

Sanger, Richard H. **Insurgent Era: New Patterns of Political, Economic, and Social Revolution.** Washington: Potomac Books, 1967, 231 p.
A study of both communist and non-communist revolt in Asia, Africa and Latin America since World War II, by a former U.S. Foreign Service officer.

Walter, Eugene Victor. **Terror and Resistance: A Study of Political Violence.** New York: Oxford University Press, 1969, 385 p.
Using primitive African societies and particularly the Zulu kingdom, the author attempts to discover why men who hold authority choose to rule by violence and terror. While the cases are confined to traditional societies, the author seeks a general theory applicable to all political systems.

West, Dame Rebecca. **The New Meaning of Treason.** New York: Viking, 1964, 374 p.
This book by a brilliant writer is a revised and expanded version of a work first published in 1947. Centrally a report on some of the most famous treason cases since World War II—William Joyce, Alan Nunn May, Klaus Fuchs, Burgess and Maclean among others—it is also a most provocative and probing discussion of the implications of treason in an age of mass culture and technological explosion.

COLONIAL PROBLEMS; DECOLONIZATION

See also (Political Factors) General, p. 12; Nationalism and Nationality, p. 17; Communism, p. 26; Problems of New Nations, p. 36; Society and Social Psychology, p. 39; Economic Factors, p. 49; (International Law) Miscellaneous, p. 94; United Nations, p. 99; The Postwar World, p. 178; and the sections for specific countries and regions.

Albertini, Rudolf von. **Decolonization: The Administration and Future of the Colonies, 1919–1960.** Garden City: Doubleday, 1971, 680 p.
This treatment of the decolonization policies of the European imperial powers, especially those of Britain and France, is a first-rate piece of scholarship. The German original was published as "Dekolonisation: die Diskussion über Verwaltung und Zukunft der Kolonien 1919–1960" (Opladen: Westdeutscher Verlag, 1966, 607 p.).

Berque, Jacques; Charnay, Jean-Paul and Others. **De l'impérialisme à la décolonisation.** Paris: Editions de Minuit, 1965, 501 p.
A collection of essays on problems of colonialism and decolonization in Asia and Africa.

Berque, Jacques. **Dépossession du monde.** Paris: Éditions du Seuil, 1964, 214 p.
A dozen eloquent essays dealing with the problems of contemporary man by a distinguished French scholar and orientalist who hopes that his work will be "a first approach to a sociology of decolonization."

Imam, Zafar. **Colonialism in East-West Relations: A Study of Soviet Policy towards India and Anglo-Soviet Relations, 1917–1947.** New Delhi: Eastman Publications, 1969, 531 p.
A well-researched study, based on extensive use of Russian, British and Indian sources. The author is convinced that Soviet interest in colonial affairs did exercise a remarkable influence on the whole process of the break-up of the colonial system in general and of the British rule in India in particular.

Lichtheim, George. **Imperialism.** New York: Praeger, 1971, 183 p.
An excellent essay on a much-debated theme.

Merle, Marcel, *ed.* **Les Églises chrétiennes et la décolonisation.** Paris: Colin, 1967, 519 p.
A well-documented study of the attitudes of various Christian churches in Western Europe and America toward decolonisation in the contemporary world.

Nkrumah, Kwame. **Neo-colonialism: The Last Stage of Imperialism.** New York: International Publishers, 1966, 280 p.
Most of this volume consists of detailed descriptions of the financial and ownership structure of international big business in Africa, the aim of which is to expose the sinister dynamics of neo-colonialism and especially the dominant role of American capital and U.S. Government agencies. This statement of Nkrumahism combines fact and fancy into an ideology which is unlikely to enter its "last stage" for some time to come.

Symonds, Richard. **The British and Their Successors: A Study in the Development of the Government Services in the New States.** Evanston: Northwestern University Press, 1966, 286 p.
A discussion of how the British approached the problem of the development of government services in their former possessions in Asia and Africa, with reference to the French, Belgian, American and Dutch experience in their colonial empires.

PROBLEMS OF NEW NATIONS

See also (Political Factors) General, p. 12; Nationalism and Nationality, p. 17; Democracy, p. 23; New Left; Anarchism; Student Politics, p. 31; Culture; Education; Public Opinion; Communications Processes, p. 42; (International Law) Miscellaneous, p. 94; United Nations, p. 99; Inter-War Period, p. 140; The Postwar World, p. 178; and the sections for specific countries and regions.

Alderfer, Harold Freed. **Local Government in Developing Countries.** New York: McGraw-Hill, 1964, 251 p.

A concise, general description of the patterns of local government in Latin America, Africa, the Middle East, Asia and selected communist states.

Anderson, James Norman Dalrymple, *ed*. **Changing Law in Developing Countries.** New York: Praeger, 1963, 292 p.
A collection of lectures given at the School of Oriental and African Studies of the University of London detailing various aspects of legal problems and problems arising from legal change in the new states. Of particular interest to the African specialist are the essays by Professor Anderson on Islamic law and by Professor Allott on legal development and economic growth.

Apter, David Ernest. **The Politics of Modernization.** Chicago: University of Chicago Press, 1965, 481 p.
A somewhat theoretically oriented study of the problem of modernization, the methods for mobilizing a society, and the adequacy of traditional democratic practices in achieving the needed results.

Ashford, Douglas Elliott. **National Development and Local Reform: Political Participation in Morocco, Tunisia, and Pakistan.** Princeton: Princeton University Press, 1967, 439 p.
A solid comparative study which gets to the roots of some of the problems obstructing steady development in the new nations.

Bienen, Henry, *ed*. **The Military Intervenes.** New York: Russell Sage Foundation, 1968, 175 p.
Six social scientists examine the role of the military in the modernization process in selected developing countries.

Butwell, Richard A., *ed*. **Foreign Policy and the Developing Nation.** Lexington: University of Kentucky Press, 1969, 236 p.
A symposium on the politics of development and modernization in selected developing countries.

Crozier, Brian. **The Morning After: A Study of Independence.** New York: Oxford University Press, 1963, 299 p.
An informed journalist's pessimistic assessment of newly independent Asian and African states and their leaders who fought for and achieved independence only to find themselves in the midst of new problems and threats.

Deutsch, Karl Wolfgang and Foltz, William J., *eds*. **Nation-Building.** New York: Atherton Press, 1963, 167 p.
A series of brief essays on the creation of nations and the meaning of nationalism, resulting from a 1962 panel discussion of the American Political Science Association.

Duroselle, Jean-Baptiste and Meyriat, Jean, *eds*. **La Communauté internationale face aux jeunes états.** Paris: Colin, 1964, 417 p.
———. **Politiques nationales envers les jeunes états.** Paris: Colin, 1964, 347 p.
Two volumes of essays on problems of new states from symposia sponsored by the Centre d'Étude des Relations Internationales.

Geertz, Clifford, *ed*. **Old Societies and New States.** New York: Free Press of Glencoe, 1963, 310 p.
Eight studies on some of the social-political problems faced by less developed, former colonial Asian and African countries in their "quest for modernity."

Gutteridge, William Frank. **Military Institutions and Power in the New States.** New York: Praeger, 1965, 182 p.
An examination of the nature, role and influence of the armed forces in the newly independent states.

Huntington, Samuel P. **Political Order in Changing Societies.** New Haven: Yale University Press, 1968, 488 p.
In this brilliant though somewhat disjointed work, the author makes a major contribution to the literature on the politics of modernization.

Janowitz, Morris. **The Military in the Political Development of New Nations: An Essay in Comparative Analysis.** Chicago: University of Chicago Press, 1964, 134 p.
A sociologist's comparative study of the role of the military in the political life of the new nations of Asia and Africa analyzing the "political capacities of the military to rule and to modernize."

McCord, William. **The Springtime of Freedom: Evolution of Developing Societies.** New York: Oxford University Press, 1965, 330 p.
A discussion of the political and social problems in the new nations, in which the author takes issue with the view that "political tyranny and economic centralization" are the only paths. He hopes for a pluralistic program and the growth of freedom.

Mair, Lucy Philip. **New Nations.** Chicago: University of Chicago Press, 1963, 235 p.
Miss Mair, a social anthropologist, uses "the extension of social relationships" as her frame of reference and discusses "society" in the developing countries. Examples are drawn from the Near and Far East as well as from Africa.

Neufeld, Maurice F. **Poor Countries and Authoritarian Rule.** Ithaca: New York State School of Industrial and Labor Relations, Cornell University, 1965, 240 p.
A discussion, by a professor of industrial and labor relations at Cornell, of the relationship between poverty in emerging countries with strong nationalistic expectations and the turn to authoritarian rule and governmental coercion.

Oglesby, Carl and Shaull, Richard. **Containment and Change.** New York: Macmillan, 1967, 248 p.
Two intellectual leaders of the "New Left" address themselves to the challenge of understanding social revolution in the developing nations.

Pennock, James Roland, *ed.* **Self-Government in Modernizing Nations.** Englewood Cliffs: Prentice-Hall, 1964, 119 p.
Contributors to this volume are Lucian W. Pye, Francis X. Sutton, Thomas L. Hodgkin, Zbigniew Brzezinski and W. Howard Wriggins. There is an introduction by the editor.

Polk, William Roe, *ed.* **Developmental Revolution: North Africa, Middle East, South Asia.** Washington: Middle East Institute, 1963, 269 p.
Consisting of papers presented by a variety of authorities at the Middle East Institute's seventeenth annual conference in 1963, this volume surveys the social pressures for development and discusses methods, resources and ways of payment.

Riggs, Fred Warren. **Administration in Developing Countries: The Theory of Prismatic Society.** Boston: Houghton, 1964, 477 p.
A study of political development in transitional societies by an imaginative and prolific theorist.

Rustow, Dankwart A. **A World of Nations: Problems of Political Modernization.** Washington: Brookings Institution, 1967, 306 p.
A first-rate comparative analysis of modernization as a political phenomenon. The book is empirically solid and written in good clear English happily devoid of technical jargon.

Sigmund, Paul Eugene. **The Ideologies of the Developing Nations.** New York: Praeger, rev. ed., 1967, 428 p.
An anthology of ideological statements and pronouncements by political leaders in the fermenting areas of Asia, the Middle East, Africa and Latin America.

Sinai, Isaac Robert. **The Challenge of Modernisation: The West's Impact on the Non-Western World.** New York: Norton, 1964, 256 p.
Mr. Sinai, journalist and lecturer at the New School, argues that the non-Western world revolutions, communist or not, are directed against the values which make up Western societies. The West, he says, is fighting a war of survival to defend those values.

Sinai, Isaac Robert. **In Search of the Modern World.** New York: New American Library, 1967, 226 p.
Analyzing the responses to modernization in Russia, China, Japan, Mexico and Turkey, the author concludes that economic advance is not going to help in establishing a single and unitary form of world civilization.

Swerdlow, Irving, *ed.* **Development Administration: Concepts and Problems.** Syracuse: Syracuse University Press, 1963, 162 p.
A collection of succinct essays demonstrating the "need and usefulness of the concept of development administration as a particular type of public administration" in developing countries with their particular political, cultural and economic problems.

Von der Mehden, Fred R. **Politics of the Developing Nations.** Englewood Cliffs: Prentice-Hall, 1964, 140 p.
A carefully documented study of the political instability and disunity of many of the new nations, analyzed in terms of colonial heritage, the search for national identity, varying national politics and ideologies.

III. SOCIAL, CULTURAL AND RELIGIOUS FACTORS

SOCIETY AND SOCIAL PSYCHOLOGY

See also (General Works) Reference Works, p. 1; Methodology and Theory, p. 4; (Political Factors) General, p. 12; Nationalism and Nationality, p. 17; Colonial Problems; Decolonization, p. 36; Problems of New Nations, p. 36; Population Problems, p. 47; Economic Factors, p. 49; War and Peace, p. 108; (The World Since 1914) General, p. 129; Inter-War Period, p. 140; The Postwar World, p. 178.

Alford, Robert R. **Party and Society: The Anglo-American Democracies.** Chicago: Rand McNally, 1963, 396 p.
A study of how social factors determine party preferences in Great Britain, the United States, Canada and Australia.

Aron, Raymond. **Dix-huit leçons sur la société industrielle.** Paris: Gallimard, 1962, 375 p.
———. **La Lutte de classes: nouvelles leçons sur les sociétés industrielles.** Paris: Gallimard, 1964, 377 p.
———. **Démocratie et totalitarisme.** Paris: Gallimard, 1965, 378 p.
A lucid and penetrating inquiry into industrial and industrializing societies, with particular reference to class struggle, social mobility, ruling élites and political systems. This series is based on lectures the author delivered at the Sorbonne from 1955 to 1958.

Aron, Raymond. **The Industrial Society: Three Essays on Ideology and Development.** New York: Praeger, 1967, 183 p.
Perceptive and balanced comment on the rich and poor nations and what we do and don't know about development. The French original appeared as "Trois essais sur l'âge industriel" (Paris: Plon, 1965, 241 p.).

Aron, Raymond. **Progress and Disillusion: The Dialectics of Modern Society.** New York: Praeger, 1968, 230 p.
An impressive though unnecessarily prolix examination of the relationships between the individual and political and social institutions in modern technological societies.

Balandier, Georges. **Political Anthropology.** New York: Pantheon Books, 1971, 214 p.
The value of this original study lies in its emphasis on the political patterns of non-Western societies, formerly described as "primitive." In addition to suggesting some interesting methodological innovations, the author reveals that the power structures of the societies he scrutinizes are quite sophisticated. The French edition appeared as "Anthropologie politique" (Paris: Presses Universitaires, 2d rev. ed., 1969, 244 p.).

Berger, Peter L., ed. **Marxism and Sociology: Views from Eastern Europe.** New York: Appleton, 1969, 246 p.
A symposium of essays by ten East European sociologists centering on some of the theoretical issues between Marxist and non-Marxist sociology.

Cantril, Albert Hadley. **The Pattern of Human Concerns.** New Brunswick: Rutgers University Press, 1966, 427 p.
In this ambitious work, Professor Cantril "attempts to provide a systematic psychological study" of what the various nations and peoples are feeling, seeking and hoping for at this point in history. Case studies are drawn from a number of highly dissimilar countries.

Diebold, John. **Man and the Computer: Technology as an Agent of Social Change.** New York: Praeger, 1969, 157 p.
Papers on the impact of technology on education, business and international relations.

Etzioni, Amitai. **The Active Society: A Theory of Societal and Political Processes.** New York: Free Press, 1968, 698 p.
An important landmark in social science theory.

Hartz, Louis and Others. **The Founding of New Societies: Studies in the History of the United States, Latin America, South Africa, Canada, and Australia.** New York: Harcourt, Brace and World, 1964, 336 p.
The author and four contributors present a theory of the formation and cultural development of five societies which claim their birth from European emigration: the United States, Latin America, South Africa, Canada and Australia.

Haskins, Caryl Parker. **The Scientific Revolution and World Politics.** New York: Harper and Row (for the Council on Foreign Relations), 1964, 115 p.
In these lectures Dr. Haskins, a biologist and President of the Carnegie Institution of Washington, offers a panoramic review of the impact of science and technology upon contemporary human societies, including the new and "intermediate" nations, and upon the relations between societies.

Hoselitz, Berthold Frank and Moore, Wilbert Ellis, *eds*. **Industrialization and Society.** Paris: UNESCO-Mouton, 1963, 437 p.
A substantial UNESCO symposium of 15 papers dealing with entrepreneurship, innovation, consumption and investment, public administration, urbanization and education.

Hsu, Francis Lang Kwang. **Americans and Chinese: Purpose and Fulfillment in Great Civilizations.** Garden City: Natural History Press (for the American Museum of Natural History), 1970, 493 p.
The author—a leading Chinese anthropologist—engages in a multifaceted exploration of the strengths and weaknesses of the American "individual-centered" society by contrasting it with the "situation-centered" ethic of his native China. The result is an original—and disturbing—perspective on the American way of life by a friendly, sensitive and concerned observer. A revised edition of "Americans and Chinese: Two Ways of Life" (1953).

Mason, Philip. **Patterns of Dominance.** New York: Oxford University Press (for the Institute of Race Relations), 1970, 377 p.
A sophisticated analysis of various types of institutionalized inequality in different societies, both ancient and modern, by the Director of the Institute of Race Relations in London. Though somewhat marred, perhaps, by a pervasive pessimism, this is a wise and valuable work.

Moore, Barrington, Jr. **Social Origins of Dictatorship and Democracy: Lord and Peasant in the Making of the Modern World.** Boston: Beacon Press, 1966, 559 p.
In this important work a Harvard sociologist examines the roles played by landowners and peasants in the transformation from agrarian to industrial societies, and the role of these groups in the processes making for democracy or dictatorship.

Niemeyer, Gerhart. **Between Nothingness and Paradise.** Baton Rouge: Louisiana State University Press, 1971, 226 p.
In this extended essay Professor Niemeyer analyzes the tradition of "total critique of society" and consequent totalitarian activism, and then outlines the criteria and limits of nondestructive social critique.

Parkin, Frank. **Class Inequality and Political Order.** New York: Praeger, 1971, 205 p.
Essays by a British sociologist dealing with some questions of social stratification in both capitalist and socialist societies.

Psychiatry and Public Affairs. Chicago: Aldine Publishing Co., 1966, 465 p.
This substantial volume of reports and symposia, prepared under the auspices of the Group for the Advancement of Psychiatry, covers such fields in the area of public affairs as desegregation, international relations, forceful indoctrination and nuclear war. A mixed serving but with some stimulating contributions.

Riesman, David. **Abundance for What?** Garden City: Doubleday, 1964, 610 p.
This selection of Mr. Riesman's essays, written in the main during the last decade,

SOCIAL, CULTURAL AND RELIGIOUS FACTORS

covers a very wide variety of topics, but tends to cluster around two main themes—the cold war, and the problem of living in a society of economic abundance.

Snow, C. P. **Public Affairs.** New York: Scribner, 1971, 224 p.
An eloquent and multifaceted plea for bridging the gulf between science and the humanities. The author is particularly concerned about the relationship between the scientist and government.

Touraine, Alain. **The Post-Industrial Society.** New York: Random House, 1971, 244 p.
A French sociologist probes the ills of modern Western societies and concludes that the sociologist has a significant role to play in deepening our understanding of these new forces and in affecting our power to shape them. Originally published in France as "La Société post-industrielle" (Paris: Denoël, 1969, 319 p.).

Toynbee, Arnold Joseph. **Surviving the Future.** New York: Oxford University Press, 1971, 164 p.
Seven discursive essays on man and society which originated from a dialogue with Japanese intellectuals.

Tucker, Frank H. **The White Conscience.** New York: Ungar, 1968, 353 p.
Guided by Carl Jung's analysis of the white man's mind and conduct, the author perceptively examines the unattractive manifestations of Western civilization: imperialism, totalitarianism and racism.

Willener, Alfred. **The Action-Image of Society: On Cultural Politicization.** New York: Pantheon Books, 1971, 336 p.
A Swiss sociologist, deeply impressed by the 1968 student-worker revolt in France, argues that the young generation can be understood by the sociologist only if he broadens and updates his research tools.

LABOR AND LABOR MOVEMENTS

See also Political Philosophies and Ideologies, p. 21; (International Organization and Government) General, p. 96; (United Nations) Specialized Agencies and Activities, p. 105; and the sections for specific countries and regions.

Kassalow, Everett M., *ed.* **National Labor Movements in the Postwar World.** Evanston: Northwestern University Press, 1963, 256 p.
Unions in underdeveloped countries get a good bit of attention in this collection but there are also essays on Norway, Japan, Belgium and France, international labor organizations, ideological issues and communist tactics. The scope and approach of the essays vary greatly but there is much of interest.

Landelius, Torsten. **Workers, Employers and Governments: A Comparative Study of Delegations and Groups at the International Labour Conference, 1919-1964.** Stockholm: Norstedt, 1965, 553 p.
A useful monograph on the International Labor Conference, by a Swedish scholar.

Millen, Bruce Hiram. **The Political Role of Labor in Developing Countries.** Washington: Brookings Institution, 1963, 148 p.
A solid study by a former U.S. State Department official with experience as a labor attaché.

Roberts, Benjamin Charles. **Labour in the Tropical Territories of the Commonwealth.** Durham: Duke University Press, 1964, 426 p.
A specialist in the field of industrial relations traces the history of trade unions and their effect on the political evolution of the territories formerly in the British colonial empire. He also writes at length on the development of labor policy and administration, labor law and industrial relations. Treatment is by subject rather than by area.

Sturmthal, Adolf Fox, *ed.* **White-Collar Trade Unions.** Urbana: University of Illinois Press, 1966, 412 p.
A collection of essays covering such advanced industrial societies as Australia, Austria, France, Germany, United Kingdom, Japan, Sweden and the United States. The editor concludes with a comparative essay.

Sturmthal, Adolf Fox. **Workers Councils: A Study of Workplace Organization on Both Sides of the Iron Curtain.** Cambridge: Harvard University Press, 1964, 217 p.
A comparative study of workers councils in France, Germany, Poland and Jugoslavia.

CULTURE; EDUCATION; PUBLIC OPINION; COMMUNICATIONS PROCESSES

See also (General Works) Reference Works, p. 1; General Treatments, p. 7; Political Processes, p. 20; Communism, p. 26; Society and Social Psychology, p. 39; Economic Growth and Development, p. 71; Economic Aid and Technical Assistance, p. 81; Maritime, Air, Space and Environmental Law, p. 90; (United Nations) Specialized Agencies and Activities, p. 105; (War) Propaganda; Psychological and Political Warfare, p. 120; (Second World War) Special Operations; Propaganda; Espionage; Intelligence, p. 169; The Postwar World, p. 178; and the sections for specific countries and regions.

Adams, Walter, *ed.* **The Brain Drain.** New York: Macmillan, 1968, 273 p.
    A symposium analyzing the causes of the brain drain from developing countries through a number of case studies. French language edition: "L'Exode des cerveaux" (Lausanne: Centre de Recherches Européennes, 1968, 309 p.).

Ashby, Sir Eric with Anderson, Mary. **Universities: British, Indian, African: A Study in the Ecology of Higher Education.** Cambridge: Harvard University Press, 1966, 558 p.
    A comprehensive history and analysis of higher education in the English-speaking world with particular attention to the impact of British institutions and practices on the universities of the Commonwealth, especially in formerly British Africa.

Beglov, Spartak Ivanovich. **Monopolii slova.** Moscow: Izd-vo "Mysl'," 2d ed., 1972, 454 p.
    A prominent Soviet journalist and commentator on international affairs looks at the "word monopolies," his term for the Western publishing and broadcasting media, and assesses their role in serving the propaganda requirements of imperialist "ruling circles."

Coleman, James Smoot, *ed.* **Education and Political Development.** Princeton: Princeton University Press, 1965, 620 p.
    A number of able scholars have contributed essays to this inquiry into the relationship between the educational process and political development. A major part of the work is devoted to the emergent states, but there are also chapters on the Soviet Union, Japan and Communist China.

Dizard, Wilson P. **Television: A World View.** Syracuse: Syracuse University Press, 1966, 349 p.
    An effort, by an editor of the *Washington Post*, to measure the prospects and impact of international television.

Emerson, Thomas I. **The System of Freedom of Expression.** New York: Random House, 1971, 754 p.
    According to the author, Lines Professor of Law at the Yale School of Law, the main purpose of this substantial monograph "has been to formulate the legal foundations for an effective system of freedom of expression."

Fischer, Heinz Dietrich. **Die grossen Zeitungen: Porträts der Weltpresse.** Munich: Deutscher Taschenbuch-Verlag, 1966, 305 p.
    Data about thirteen leading newspapers of the world: *Berlingske Tidende, Neue Zürcher Zeitung, The Times, Die Presse, The New York Times, La Prensa, Corriere della Sera, Svenska Dagbladet, Pravda, Le Monde, Die Welt, Ren Min Ribao* and *Frankfurter Allgemeine Zeitung.*

Fraser, Stewart, *ed.* **Governmental Policy and International Education.** New York: Wiley, 1965, 373 p.
    A symposium dealing with problems and successes of various governments in promoting international education and educational exchange.

Geldard, Frank Arthur and Others, *eds.* **Communication Processes.** New York: Pergamon Press (for Division of Scientific Affairs, Science Committee, North Atlantic Treaty Organization), 1965, 299 p.
    A symposium considering a variety of communications problems and prospects: data presentation and transmission, language barriers, group communication, and the use of computers in communication.

Haberer, Joseph. **Politics and the Community of Science.** New York: Van Nostrand Reinhold, 1969, 337 p.

SOCIAL, CULTURAL AND RELIGIOUS FACTORS

A fine scholarly treatment of the relationship between scientist and government in different times and different political settings. Two case studies on German science and on J. Robert Oppenheimer are particularly well done. Unfortunately, there is almost no analysis of Soviet science.

Hoffman, Arthur S., ed. **International Communication and the New Diplomacy.** Bloomington: Indiana University Press, 1968, 206 p.
Thirteen scholars assess the impact of communications technology on modern diplomacy.

Hohenberg, John. **Foreign Correspondence: The Great Reporters and Their Times.** New York: Columbia University Press, 1964, 502 p.
An able and by its nature most interesting history of foreign reporting from the turn of the eighteenth century to the present.

Hohenberg, John. **Free Press/Free People: The Best Cause.** New York: Columbia University Press, 1971, 514 p.
This is a broad-brush survey of recent world history, from the vantage point of a sensitive journalist much concerned with the integrity and freedom of the press and the news media throughout the world.

Jeffries, Sir Charles Joseph. **Illiteracy: A World Problem.** New York: Praeger, 1967, 204 p.
A former Deputy Under-Secretary of State in the British Colonial Office discusses the problem of illiteracy in the modern world and describes some of the most successful literacy campaigns.

Kertesz, Stephen D., ed. **The Task of Universities in a Changing World.** Notre Dame: University of Notre Dame Press, 1971, 503 p.
Essays on university problems in North and South America, Europe, Asia and Africa originally presented at conferences held at the University of Notre Dame Center for Continuing Education in 1969 and 1970 and at the Rockefeller Foundation's Villa Servelloni, Bellagio, Italy, in 1969.

Lee, John, ed. **The Diplomatic Persuaders.** New York: Wiley, 1968, 205 p.
Informative glimpses into government-mass media relations in fifteen countries.

Magnelia, Paul Francis. **The International Union of Students.** Menlo Park (Cal.): Peninsula Lithograph Co. (for the Université de Genève, Institut Univesitaire de Hautes Études Internationales), 1967, 193 p.
A detailed study of the communist-dominated international student organization, especially of how it was affected by the conflicts that occurred within the Communist bloc.

Markham, James Walter. **Voices of the Red Giants: Communications in Russia and China.** Ames: Iowa State University Press, 1967, 513 p.
An investigation, by a professor of journalism at the University of Iowa, of communist mass-communication systems in the Soviet Union and China.

Merritt, Richard L., ed. **Communication in International Politics.** Urbana: University of Illinois Press, 1972, 461 p.
Papers relating to various aspects of the title: people-to-people exchanges, influencing domestic and foreign opinion, government-to-government communication.

Paulu, Burton. **Radio and Television Broadcasting on the European Continent.** Minneapolis: University of Minnesota Press, 1967, 290 p.
A useful survey.

Pool, Ithiel de Sola and Others. **The Prestige Press: A Comparative Study of Political Symbols.** Cambridge: M.I.T. Press, 1970, 359 p.
A content analysis of political symbols that appear in the leading newspapers of a number of major countries.

Ritchie-Calder, Peter Ritchie Ritchie-Calder, Baron. **How Long Have We Got?** Montreal: McGill-Queen's University Press, 1972, 88 p.
Three imaginative and elegant lectures on the global impact of science and technology delivered at McGill University. The answer to the question in the title is not apocalyptic: with the dangers now well recognized, how much time we have depends upon what we do with it.

Schramm, Wilbur Lang. **Mass Media and National Development: The Role of Information in the Developing Countries.** Stanford: Stanford University Press, 1964, 333 p.

A wide-ranging and over-optimistic survey, by the Director of the Institute for Communication Research at Stanford University.

Westin, Alan F., *ed.* **Information Technology in a Democracy.** Cambridge: Harvard University Press, 1971, 499 p.

The editor, long concerned with the government's relation to the citizen's privacy, has assembled almost 50 essays dealing with the effects of control technology and "data banks" on the democratic process. The selections are well chosen and represent a broad spectrum of opinion.

Zuckerman, Solly Zuckerman, Baron. **Scientists and War.** New York: Harper and Row, 1967, 177 p.

The Chief Scientific Adviser to the British Government from 1964 to 1971 here provides a series of essays dealing with the two major themes of the impact of science on military affairs and the role of science in society.

RELIGIOUS PROBLEMS

See also (Political Philosophies and Ideologies) General, p. 21; Colonial Problems; Decolonization, p. 36; Economic Growth and Development, p. 71; and the sections for specific countries and regions.

Cragg, Kenneth. **Counsels in Contemporary Islam.** Chicago: Aldine Publishing Co., 1965, 255 p.

Islam today is "between past and present, between apprehension and confidence, between the stuff of events and the dictates of the spirit." Dr. Cragg's thoughtful essays illuminate aspects of Islam's continuing effort to survive and absorb the pressures of the modern world.

Fyzee, Asaf Ali Asghar. **A Modern Approach to Islam.** New York: Asia Publishing House, 1964, 127 p.

Four essays on the theme that the creed of Islam today needs reinterpretation. An Indian Muslim, Professor Fyzee has had an impressive career as public servant and scholar.

Houtart, François and Rousseau, André. **The Church and Revolution.** Maryknoll (N.Y.): Orbis Books, 1971, 371 p.

A study in search of answers to the question, "Why is it that Christianity, a proclamation of man's total liberation, historically finds itself in opposition to the movements which attempt to give concrete expression to this liberation?"

Hutten, Kurt. **Christen hinter dem Eisernen Vorhang: die christliche Gemeinde in der kommunistischen Welt.** Stuttgart: Quell-Verlag, 1962–1963, 2 v.

A valuable, largely factual two-volume history of the position of the Christian churches under communism.

Lochman, Jan Milič. **Church in a Marxist Society: A Czechoslovak View.** New York: Harper and Row, 1970, 198 p.

Reflections by a leading Czech theologian on the experiences of the Christian church in a radically secular society where "God is not quite dead."

Nolde, O. Frederick. **The Churches and the Nations.** Philadelphia: Fortress Press, 1970, 184 p.

The fundamental theme of this collection of essays is the obligation of the church to share in the secular quest for the improvement of man's lot in the political world.

Proctor, Jesse Harris, *ed.* **Islam and International Relations.** New York: Praeger, 1965, 221 p.

An examination of Islam as a factor in world and inter-Arab politics in essays by well-qualified authorities: H.A.R. Gibb, Majid Khadduri, Dankwart Rustow, Fayez Sayegh, Bayard Dodge, P. J. Vatikiotis, Vernon McKay and T. Cuyler Young.

Rosenthal, Erwin Isak Jakob. **Islam in the Modern National State.** New York: Cambridge University Press, 1966, 416 p.

The confusion and crisis of contemporary Islam brought on by the secular infiltration of the West and all its works are described and analyzed in this major study by a senior British orientalist. Required reading for serious students of Islam and the contemporary Muslim world.

Sopher, David E. **Geography of Religion.** Englewood Cliffs: Prentice-Hall, 1967, 118 p.
This pioneering study is an indispensable reference for students of religion and human geography.

IV. GEOGRAPHIC, ETHNIC AND POPULATION FACTORS

GENERAL GEOGRAPHY AND ENVIRONMENT

See also (General Works) Reference Works, p. 1; Methodology and Theory, p. 4; Population Problems, p. 47; International Trade, p. 55; Maritime, Air, Space and Environmental Law, p. 90.

Broek, Jan O. M. and Webb, John W. **A Geography of Mankind.** New York: McGraw-Hill, 1968, 527 p.
A very well-researched and well-written treatise, with excellent maps, diagrams and bibliographies.

Caldwell, Lynton K. **In Defense of Earth.** Bloomington: Indiana University Press, 1972, 295 p.
A good bit of history and some philosophy are rather attractively deployed to introduce the author's fairly concrete proposals for new and more effective national and international arrangements to protect the biosphere.

Chase, Allan. **The Biological Imperatives: Health, Politics, and Human Survival.** New York: Holt, Rinehart and Winston, 1971, 399 p.
The author argues that environmental disease factors are now multiplying at rates that threaten the biological future of man. He makes a powerful case for reversing national priorities which now place military might above good health.

Cohen, Saul Bernard. **Geography and Politics in a World Divided.** New York: Random House, 1963, 347 p.
A geographer's study of a politically divided world, with special emphasis on three "power cores": the United States, Maritime Europe and the Soviet Union.

Falk, Richard A. **This Endangered Planet.** New York: Random House, 1971, 495 p.
The distinctive feature of this thoughtful book is the development of the concept of ecological politics: the need to enlarge the political frame of reference everywhere to include environmental issues.

Gullion, Edmund A., ed. **Uses of the Seas.** Englewood Cliffs: Prentice-Hall (for the American Assembly, Columbia University), 1968, 202 p.
Six essays exploring the strategic, political and economic implications of future ocean science.

Kasperson, Roger E. and Minghi, Julian V., eds. **The Structure of Political Geography.** Chicago: Aldine Publishing Co., 1969, 527 p.
The aim of the editors of this collection of readings and annotated bibliographies is "to involve political geography in the mainstream of current social science theory and research."

Kay, David A. and Skolnikoff, Eugene B., eds. **World Eco-Crisis: International Organizations in Response.** Madison: University of Wisconsin Press, 1972, 324 p.
Articles discussing the role of international organizations in dealing with ecological problems.

Kneese, Allen V. and Others, eds. **Managing the Environment: International Economic Cooperation for Pollution Control.** New York: Praeger (for the Atlantic Council of the United States and Battelle Memorial Institute), 1971, 356 p.
A sample of the literature that has to be read by those who want to get below the surface in understanding the international aspects of ecology.

Laffin, John. **New Geography, 1966-67–**. New York: Abelard-Schuman, 1967, 237 p.
A biennial series presenting the latest geographical information.

Man in the Living Environment. Madison: University of Wisconsin Press (for the Institute of Ecology), 1972, 288 p.
This set of recommendations concerning environmental quality and management is the result of a workshop on global ecological problems.

Mills, Clarence Alonzo. **World Power Amid Shifting Climates.** Boston: Christopher, 1963, 171 p.
A medical authority here analyzes the influence which changing climatic conditions may have on the future world power structure.

Taylor, Gordon Rattray. **The Doomsday Book: Can the World Survive?** New York: World Publishing Co., 1970, 335 p.
A wide-ranging, impassioned polemic against man's heedless abuse of his natural environment.

Ward, Barbara (Lady Jackson) and Dubos, René. **Only One Earth.** New York: Norton, 1972, 225 p.
Two leading scholars in their fields, with the assistance of many distinguished consultants, have prepared this succinct statement on "The Care and Maintenance of a Small Planet," reviewing the wide range of environmental and demographic problems the world faces.

Wenk, Edward, Jr. **The Politics of the Ocean.** Seattle: University of Washington Press, 1972, 590 p.
A detailed examination of the domestic and international politics of ocean policy, which is as much a work of political science as of oceanography. The author skillfully examines the experience of the past decade, and proposes initiatives for future U.S. oceanographic policy and its governmental formulation.

Westermann Lexikon der Geographie. Brunswick: Georg Westermann Verlag, 1968–72, 5 v.
A five-volume geographical encyclopedia, written by an international team of scholars. The articles in this impressive reference work are based on up-to-date information and are supplemented with maps, statistical tables and bibliographies. Edited by Wolf Tietze.

Wilson, Thomas W., Jr. **International Environmental Action: A Global Survey.** New York: Dunellen, 1971, 364 p.
A timely assessment of the global imperatives of the environmental crisis followed by a useful summary of the leading international agencies attempting to cope with it today.

Zelinsky, Wilbur and Others, *eds.* **Geography and a Crowding World.** New York: Oxford University Press, 1970, 601 p.
Papers presented at a symposium at the Pennsylvania State University in 1967 on population pressures upon physical and social resources in the developing lands.

ETHNIC PROBLEMS; THE JEWS

See also (General Works) General Treatments, p. 7; First World War, p. 131; Inter-War Period, p. 140; Second World War, p. 144; The Postwar World, p. 178; and the sections for specific countries and regions.

Banton, Michael P. **Race Relations.** London: Tavistock Publications, 1967, 434 p.
A detached survey, including a discussion of race issues in contemporary Great Britain.

The Black Man in Search of Power. London: Nelson, 1968, 182 p.
Seven correspondents of *The Times* survey racial conflict between dominant whites and increasingly politically conscious non-whites in Britain, the United States and southern and central Africa.

Franklin, John Hope, *ed.* **Color and Race.** Boston: Houghton, 1968, 391 p.
Papers presented at the 1965 Copenhagen Conference on Race and Color.

Friedmann, Georges. **The End of the Jewish People?** Garden City: Doubleday, 1967, 307 p.

GEOGRAPHIC, ETHNIC AND POPULATION FACTORS

The author, a French sociologist, argues that because of the establishment of the state of Israel and the lessening of anti-Semitism all over the world, the Jews are in the process of losing their historical identity. An important study. The French edition appeared as "Fin du peuple juif?" (Paris: Gallimard, 1965, 376 p.).

Ingram, Derek. **Commonwealth for a Colour-Blind World.** New York: Humanities Press, 1965, 224 p.
The author argues that the Commonwealth can work more effectively to reduce racial tensions than any other grouping of states in existence today.

Laqueur, Walter Ze'ev. **A History of Zionism.** New York: Holt, Rinehart and Winston, 1972, 640 p.
A full and dispassionate treatment of the movement of Jewish national revival from its diffuse origins in eighteenth-century Europe to the creation of the Israeli state in 1948. Especially interesting is the description of struggles within Zionism and of the reluctance of many Jews at various times to espouse the idea.

Lendvai, Paul. **Anti-Semitism without Jews: Communist Eastern Europe.** Garden City: Doubleday, 1971, 393 p.
A most interesting study of the situation of the remaining Jewish population in Poland, Czechoslovakia, Hungary and Rumania. The story is remarkably different in each case, and for reasons that might not have been expected a decade ago.

Levin, Nora. **The Holocaust: The Destruction of European Jewry, 1933-1945.** New York: Crowell, 1968, 768 p.
A well-written but somewhat sloppily researched account of the destruction of European Jewry under Nazi rule.

Litvinoff, Barnet. **A Peculiar People.** New York: Weybright and Talley, 1969, 308 p.
A valuable and highly informative account of Jewish communities in the modern world. The author predicts greater assimilation for American Jewry.

Litvinoff, Barnet. **To the House of Their Fathers: A History of Zionism.** New York: Praeger, 1965, 311 p.
A convinced Zionist reviews the development of modern Zionism from 1880 to 1950.

Morse, Arthur D. **While Six Million Died: A Chronicle of American Apathy.** New York: Random House, 1968, 420 p.
This is a deeply tragic book. Its thrust is that the White House and the U.S. State Department, though largely aware of the fate of the Jews under Hitler, failed to alleviate the horror by opening wide the doors of sanctuary.

Robinson, Jacob. **And the Crooked Shall be Made Straight: The Eichmann Trial, the Jewish Catastrophe, and Hannah Arendt's Narrative.** New York: Macmillan, 1965, 406 p.
A sharp, detailed, at times pedantic, critique of Hannah Arendt's book on the Eichmann trial ("Eichmann in Jerusalem"), which not infrequently misses the point of her report.

Segal, Ronald. **The Race War.** New York: Viking, 1967, 416 p.
A passionate, single-factor interpretation of recent world history as a conflict between whites and non-whites, with the moment of truth close at hand.

POPULATION PROBLEMS

See also Religious Problems, p. 44; General Geography and Environment, p. 45; Food and Agriculture, p. 68; Economic Growth and Development, p. 71; Underdeveloped Economies, p. 78; Maritime, Air, Space and Environmental Law, p. 90; (The World Since 1914) General, p. 129; and the sections for specific countries and regions.

Berelson, Bernard and Others, eds. **Family Planning and Population Programs: A Review of World Developments.** Chicago: University of Chicago Press, 1966, 848 p.
A massive survey dealing in turn with the achievements and problems of various national programs, their organization and administration, the implications of different contraceptive methods and, finally, the problems of research in this sensitive but vital topic. The proceedings of the International Conference on Family Planning Programs that was held in Geneva in 1965.

Borgstrom, Georg Arne. **The Hungry Planet: The Modern World at the Edge of Famine.** New York: Macmillan, 1965, 487 p.

A very grim estimate of the world's demographic and nutritional prospects: "Completely defiant of all facts, we still preach about an 'abundant world' when only a few strongly armored oases remain on the globe."

Bouscaren, Anthony Trawick. **International Migrations since 1945.** New York: Praeger, 1963, 176 p.

A brief review of postwar migrations, including refugee movements, throughout the world.

Bouthoul, Gaston. **La Surpopulation: l'inflation démographique.** Paris: Payot, 1964, 250 p.

A leading French sociologist discusses the political and international implications of the world's rapid population expansion and the indispensability of "planification démographique."

Chamberlaine, Neil W. **Beyond Malthus: Population and Power.** New York: Basic Books, 1971, 214 p.

The population explosion per se, the author argues, is not a very reliable indicator for the future. Rather, the specific impact of population growth on the political and economic power distributions within a given society provides much better clues for neo-Malthusian analysts.

Davis, Kingsley. **World Urbanization, 1950-1970.** Berkeley: University of California Press, 1969-72, 2 v.

An indispensable reference by a professor at the University of California. Volume I is entitled "Basic Data for Cities, Countries and Regions"; volume II, "Analysis of Trends, Relationships and Development."

Ehrlich, Paul and Ehrlich, Ann. **Population, Resources, Environment.** San Francisco: W. H. Freeman, 1970, 383 p.

A powerful work, exploring the impact of the population crisis on the environment. Even though the authors may somewhat exaggerate the Malthusian peril, their book is one of the most thoroughly researched and persuasively argued polemics currently available. Good bibliographies accompany each chapter.

Fraser, Dean. **The People Problem.** Bloomington: Indiana University Press, 1971, 248 p.

One of the most impressive of the numerous neo-Malthusian analyses currently available.

Greep, Roy Orval, *ed.* **Human Fertility and Population Problems.** Cambridge: Schenkman Publishing Co., 1963, 278 p.

The papers and remarks of authorities participating in a 1963 conference on problems relating to the "unprecedented multiplication of the human species." The conference was sponsored by the American Academy of Arts and Sciences.

Hauser, Philip Morris, *ed.* **The Population Dilemma.** Englewood Cliffs: Prentice-Hall (for the American Assembly), 1963, 188 p.

Background papers on critical phases of the "accelerating population growth," prepared by 11 authorities for the Twenty-third American Assembly in May 1963.

Heer, David M. **After Nuclear Attack: A Demographic Inquiry.** New York: Praeger, 1965, 405 p.

A study of the demographic consequences of two hypothetical nuclear attacks, one aimed at military and industrial targets, the other at military targets alone. Fatality rates ranged from 18 to 30 percent of the population—probably an underestimate.

The International Migration of High-Level Manpower. New York: Praeger (in coöperation with Education and World Affairs), 1970, 738 p.

This massive collection of essays is concerned primarily with the impact of international migration of highly trained people on the less developed countries. It has been prepared by the Committee on the International Migration of Talent.

McCormack, Arthur. **The Population Problem.** New York: Crowell, 1970, 264 p.

A Catholic priest who emphasizes positive measures for dealing with growth, welfare and hunger concludes that "in certain areas of the world a population-restriction policy is urgently needed."

Moran, William E., Jr., *ed.* **Population Growth—Threat to Peace?** New York: Kenedy (for the Catholic Association for International Peace), 1965, 192 p.

A Catholic-sponsored symposium on the world's population growth, its implications, and what can or should be done about it.

Mudd, Stuart and Others, *eds*. **The Population Crisis and the Use of World Resources.** The Hague: W. Junk, 1964, 562 p.
This large volume represents the combined efforts of the World Academy of Art and Science and a group of Stanford University students in bringing together important statements by many authorities.

Ohlin, Goran. **Population Control and Economic Development.** Paris: Development Centre of the Organisation for Economic Co-operation and Development, 1967, 138 p.
The author of this thorough survey argues that "population control seems to hold out enormous promise to governments willing to launch such an enterprise."

Petersen, William. **Population.** New York: Macmillan, 2d rev. ed., 1969, 735 p.
A considerably revised and updated edition of a general textbook, the first edition of which appeared in 1961.

Rapid Population Growth: Consequences and Policy Implications. Baltimore: Johns Hopkins Press (for the National Academy of Sciences), 1971, 696 p.
This impressive attempt "to define and describe the problems resulting from today's unprecedented rates of human population increase" consists of a collection of 17 essays by leading scholars, a summary and recommendations.

Schechtman, Joseph B. **The Refugee in the World: Displacement and Integration.** New York: A. S. Barnes, 1964, 424 p.
A comprehensive, disturbing study of the attempts made to solve the refugee problems which developed from 1945 to 1963 in Europe, Asia and Africa; Cuban refugees are treated in an appendix.

Singer, S. Fred, *ed*. **Is There an Optimum Level of Population?** New York: McGraw-Hill, 1971, 426 p.
A number of authors analyze different aspects of a key question in a clarifying and enlightening way.

Valentei, Dmitrii Ignat'evich, *ed*. **Marksistsko-leninskaia teoriia narodonaseleniia.** Moscow: Izd-vo "Mysl'," 1971, 460 p.
A Soviet discussion of the principles of demography.

Volkmann, Hans-Erich. **Die russische Emigration in Deutschland 1919-1929.** Würzburg: Holzner, 1966, 154 p.
A brief but useful account of the Russian emigrants in Germany in the years from 1919 to 1929, with emphasis on their political and cultural activities.

Wyman, David S. **Paper Walls: America and the Refugee Crisis 1938-1941.** Amherst: University of Massachusetts Press, 1968, 306 p.
A critical study of American refugee policy.

Yarwood, A. T. **Asian Migration to Australia: The Background to Exclusion, 1896-1923.** New York: Cambridge University Press, 1964, 210 p.
After presenting background material on the Immigration Restriction Act of 1901 and how it was administered, the author devotes chapters to Japanese, Chinese, Indian and Syrian immigrants, indicating domestic and foreign pressures influencing their differing treatment.

V. ECONOMIC FACTORS

GENERAL ECONOMIC CONDITIONS AND TENDENCIES

See also (General Works) General Treatments, p. 7; Society and Social Psychology, p. 39; Labor and Labor Movements, p. 41; International Trade, p. 55; Foreign Investment and Overseas Business; Multinational Corporations, p. 65; International Organization and Government, p. 96; War and Peace, p. 108; (The World Since 1914) General, p. 129; The Postwar World, p. 178.

Baade, Fritz. **Dynamische Weltwirtschaft.** Munich: List Verlag, 1969, 503 p.
A senior German economist, formerly the head of the Institut für Weltwirtschaft in Kiel, argues that the dynamic world economy is capable of supporting a great increase

in population with rising living standards. He devotes most of his space to food, energy, raw materials and transportation, but calls for the industrialization of the less developed countries as well.

Bailey, Richard. **Problems of the World Economy.** Baltimore: Penguin, 1968, 201 p.
A solid survey with an emphasis on technology.

Bain, Joe Staten. **International Differences in Industrial Structure.** New Haven: Yale University Press, 1966, 209 p.
Plants and companies in Canada, France, India, Italy, Japan, Sweden, the United Kingdom and the United States are compared as to size and degrees of concentration. Inadequacies and discrepancies in data limit the results and force the author to give a good bit of attention to method. A pioneering effort.

Balogh, Thomas. **The Economics of Poverty.** New York: Macmillan, 1967, 381 p.
Twenty papers dealing with poverty and wealth, mostly in an international setting, by a fellow of Balliol College at Oxford, who was an economic adviser to the Labour Cabinet from 1964 to 1967.

Balogh, Thomas. **Unequal Partners.** Oxford: Blackwell, 1963, 2 v.
A selection of writings, very often of polemic nature, on contemporary economic and trade problems. Volume I, "The Theoretical Framework," contains articles published from 1949 to 1960; volume II, "Historical Episodes," covers the period from 1931 to the Bretton Woods conference.

Bhagwati, Jagdish N., *ed.* **Economics and World Order: From the 1970's to the 1990's.** New York: Macmillan, 1972, 365 p.
Fifteen economists of different nations, ages and ideologies are not likely to converge in their views of the world economy for the rest of the century—but a number of them say interesting things.

Boulding, Kenneth E. and Mukerjee, Tapan, *eds.* **Economic Imperialism.** Ann Arbor: University of Michigan Press, 1972, 338 p.
Some classicists, some critics, some historians and some quantifiers provide a stimulating interchange on an old subject that has come alive again.

Brown, Ernest Henry Phelps with Browne, Margaret H. **A Century of Pay.** New York: St. Martin's Press, 1969, 476 p.
A major study of wages in relation to production in France, Germany, Sweden, Britain and the United States from 1860 to 1960.

Clark, Colin and Stuvel, Geer, *eds.* **Income Redistribution and the Statistical Foundations of Economic Policy.** New Haven: International Association for Research in Income and Wealth, 1964, 353 p.
The main subjects of these papers are national accounts in policy-making and domestic redistribution of income in various countries.

Harrison, Anthony John. **The Framework of Economic Activity.** New York: St. Martin's Press, 1967, 189 p.
Excellent summary history of international economic relations in the twentieth century and the changing role of governmental policy.

Heilbroner, Robert L. **Between Capitalism and Socialism.** New York: Random House, 1970, 294 p.
Stimulating pieces by an excellent writer who uses economics "to elucidate the problem of large-scale historical and social change."

Horowitz, David. **The Abolition of Poverty.** New York: Praeger, 1969, 178 p.
The former Governor of the Bank of Israel prescribes for a massive increase in production and consumption throughout the world.

Johnson, Harry Gordon. **The World Economy at the Crossroads.** New York: Oxford University Press, 1966, 106 p.
An excellent short survey by a leading Canadian economist of the basic problems of international economic policy facing the advanced countries: monetary organization, trade barriers and discrimination, and trade and financial relations with the less developed countries.

Katona, George and Others. **Aspirations and Affluence: Comparative Studies in the United States and Western Europe.** New York: McGraw-Hill, 1971, 239 p.
Does increasing affluence make Europeans more like Americans? Sometimes yes and

sometimes no and it depends in part on where you live, according to this interesting book which looks at the attitudes of consumers as well as their economic behavior.

Kindleberger, Charles P. and Shonfield, Andrew, *eds*. **North American and Western European Economic Policies.** New York: St. Martin's Press, 1971, 551 p.
Good papers and excellent discussion skillfully edited to bring out salient issues about the economic relations among the industrialized countries and the substantial differences between "European regionalists and American cosmopolitans."

Kirschen, Etienne Sadi and Others. **Economic Policy in Our Time.** Amsterdam: North-Holland Publishing Co., 1964, 3 v.
Nine economists from the Common Market, Britain, Norway and the United States make a comparative study of national economic policies from 1949 to 1961. Volume I is devoted to general theory; volumes 2 and 3 comprise country studies.

Lambert, Richard David and Hoselitz, Berthold Frank, *eds*. **The Role of Savings and Wealth in Southern Asia and the West.** New York: UNESCO, 1963, 432 p.
A series of national studies, and an over-all evaluation, on differing social and cultural patterns which help to explain relative poverty and wealth.

Lange, Oscar Richard. **Political Economy.** New York: Macmillan; Elmsford (N.Y.): Pergamon, 1963-72, 2 v.
A restatement of Marxist economics by an influential Polish economist. The Polish original appeared as "Ekonomia polityczna" (Warsaw: Państwowe Wydawnictwo Naukowe, 2d ed., 1961–68, 2 v.).

Lenz, Friedrich. **Weltwirtschaft im Umbruch.** Velbert: S. Kappe, 1964, 382 p.
A treatise that ties together international economics, politics and social analysis.

Liubimov, Nikolai Nikolaevich, *ed*. **Mezhdunarodnye ekonomicheskie otnosheniia.** Moscow: Izd-vo "Mezhdunarodnye Otnosheniia," 1969, 494 p.
An introductory text in international economics that examines relations within and between the socialist and capitalist communities and discusses the prospective role of Third World countries in world economy. A concluding chapter summarizes the economic activities of international organizations.

Myrdal, Gunnar. **The Challenge of World Poverty: A World Anti-Poverty Program in Outline.** New York: Pantheon Books, 1970, 518 p.
The author dissects and explores with relentless logic most of the traditional approaches to world poverty. He himself attacks the problem through sociological analyses and the tools of economic science.

Papanicolaou, Efstathios E. **Coopération internationale et développement économique.** Geneva: Droz, 1963, 357 p.
Pertinent observations on international economic coöperation by an author with many years of experience in OEEC and GATT.

Peccei, Aurelio. **The Chasm Ahead.** New York: Macmillan, 1969, 297 p.
An Italian industrialist and a champion of Atlantic coöperation critically examines the role of technology in the modern world.

Perkins, James Oliver Newton. **International Policy for the World Economy.** London: Allen and Unwin, 1969, 232 p.
An Australian scholar discusses contemporary developments of world economy, suggests policies for international arrangements and strongly criticizes Britain's joining the E.E.C.

Prochnow, Herbert Victor, *ed*. **World Economic Problems and Policies.** New York: Harper and Row, 1965, 382 p.
Mr. Prochnow, who was once in charge of foreign economic policy in the U.S. State Department, has assembled the views of practitioners and a few academic experts on some major economic issues.

Pryor, Frederic L. **Public Expenditures in Communist and Capitalist Nations.** Homewood (Ill.): Irwin, 1968, 543 p.
A major venture in comparative economics, inevitably heavily laden with analytical apparatus. It breaks down some stereotypes but produces only a few conclusions to replace them.

Ranis, Gustav, *ed*. **The Gap between Rich and Poor Nations.** New York: St. Martin's Press, 1972, 439 p.
Papers by a group of excellent economists.

Reynolds, Lloyd G. **The Three Worlds of Economics.** New Haven: Yale University Press, 1971, 344 p.

Professor Reynolds of Yale compares the economic structures of the rich countries, the poor countries and the socialist countries and then their economic policies and problems. He asks how much of "Western" economics—analytical tools and theories, both—can usefully be applied to the other parts of the world. A book that deals with fundamentals.

Robbins, Lionel Charles Robbins, Baron. **Autobiography of an Economist.** New York: St. Martin's Press, 1972, 301 p.

———. **Money, Trade and International Relations.** New York: St. Martin's Press, 1971, 282 p.

In a remarkable retrospect, one of England's leading economists reassesses his own major works. By regrouping earlier essays and providing a new commentary on them, the other volume gives us an up-to-date statement of the author's views.

Röpke, Wilhelm. **Economics of the Free Society.** Chicago: Regnery, 1963, 273 p.

The first American edition of a book published in Vienna in 1937 ("Die Lehre von der Wirtschaft") in which the well-known German economist sets down his basic views.

Roll, Sir Eric. **The World after Keynes: An Examination of the Economic Order.** New York: Praeger, 1968, 193 p.

Sir Eric, a former professor who spent several decades in government service and has been a director of the Bank of England since 1968, surveys the state of economic thought but puts his emphasis on the problems of present and future policy. The book will be chiefly valued for the author's analysis and judgment on international affairs.

Sampedro, José Luis. **Decisive Forces in World Economics.** New York: McGraw-Hill, 1967, 256 p.

Having surveyed in a provocative fashion the economic and social developments in the modern world, the Spanish author predicts the emergence of a new socialism "blending the rationality and techniques of Western civilization with the natural art of living which has been better preserved by other cultures."

Shonfield, Andrew. **Modern Capitalism: The Changing Balance of Public and Private Power.** New York: Oxford University Press (for the Royal Institute of International Affairs), 1965, 456 p.

"What was it that converted capitalism from the cataclysmic failure which it appeared to be in the 1930s into the great engine of prosperity of the postwar Western world?" In pursuit of that question, the Director of the Royal Institute of International Affairs has written a remarkable book examining in depth the postwar economic policies and practices of Britain, France, Germany and the United States (and several other countries more briefly).

Simai, Mihály. **A harmadik évezred felé.** Budapest: Kossuth Könyvkiadó, 1971, 375 p.

Basing his analysis on a study of the world economy since the end of the war, Professor Simai of the Karl Marx University in Budapest attempts to discern the patterns and trends that will dominate the rest of the century.

The Technology Gap: U.S. and Europe. New York: Praeger, 1970, 158 p.

The authors of this symposium agree that the most significant technology gap between the United States and Europe is not one of knowledge, but one of failure to utilize available knowledge to the full by the Europeans. Prepared by the Atlantic Institute.

Usher, Dan. **The Price Mechanism and the Meaning of National Income Statistics.** New York: Oxford University Press, 1969, 180 p.

The British author, who has advised governments of less developed countries, shows that the poor are not quite as poor as they seem and the rich not as rich, and explains why.

Varga, Evgenii Samuilovich. **Ocherki po problemam politekonomii kapitalizma.** Moscow: Izd-vo Politicheskoi Literatury, 1965, 382 p.

Professor Varga, at one time a controversial figure among Soviet academics and a target of Stalinist repression, probes the nature of economics and politics under modern capitalism.

Weiller, Jean. **L'Économie internationale depuis 1950: du Plan Marshall aux grandes négociations commerciales entre pays inégalement développés.** Paris: Presses Universitaires, 1965, 250 p.

A French scholar covers the broad subject of the politics of international economic coöperation with a wealth of references to the conflicting views that he and other economists have held over the years.

ECONOMIC THEORY

See also (Political Factors) General, p. 12; Political Philosophies and Ideologies, 21; Society and Social Psychology, p. 39; Foreign Investment and Overseas Business; Multinational Corporations, p. 65; Economic Growth and Development, p. 71; Underdeveloped Economies, p. 78.

Baldwin, Robert Edward and Others. **Trade, Growth, and the Balance of Payments: Essays in Honor of Gottfried Haberler.** Chicago: Rand McNally, 1965, 267 p.

One of the most esteemed American teachers of international economics is honored by theoretical and practical papers by some of his distinguished students and associates.

Barna, Tibor and Others, *eds*. **Structural Interdependence and Economic Development.** New York: St. Martin's Press, 1963, 365 p.

These papers presented at an international conference on input-output techniques deal both with theoretical models and with their application to regional and national planning. The conference was sponsored by the Secretariat of the United Nations and by the Harvard Economic Research Project.

Čobeljić, Nikola and Stojanović, Radmila. **The Theory of Investment Cycles in a Socialist Economy.** White Plains: International Arts and Sciences Press, 1969, 168 p.

Two Jugoslav economists survey a wide range of theoretical and empirical material from a number of countries in order to "contribute to the overall development of the economic theory of socialism."

Fleming, J. Marcus. **Essays in International Economics.** Cambridge: Harvard University Press, 1971, 358 p.

The Deputy Director of Research of the International Monetary Fund, who was formerly a British civil servant, has written many first-rate articles linking economic theory and practice. Those in this volume deal largely with import restrictions, liquidity and exchange rates.

Les Fondements philosophiques des systèmes économiques. Paris: Payot, 1967, 523 p.

A *Festschrift* comprising a number of papers (some unpublished) by the French economist, Jacques Rueff, and articles about him and his work by an impressive list of authors from many countries.

Friedman, Milton and Roosa, Robert V. **The Balance of Payments: Free Versus Fixed Exchange Rates.** Washington: American Enterprise Institute for Public Policy Research, 1967, 192 p.

The record of a classic debate.

Galbraith, John Kenneth. **The New Industrial State.** Boston: Houghton, 2d rev. ed., 1971, 423 p.

A provocative and witty study by a well-known American economist and public figure.

Hicks, Sir John Richard. **Capital and Growth.** New York: Oxford University Press, 1965, 339 p.

A theoretical book about a subject that, according to the author, "has no particular bearing on underdevelopment economics."

Hoselitz, Berthold Frank, *ed*. **Economics and the Idea of Mankind.** New York: Columbia University Press, 1965, 277 p.

Several essays that try to illuminate the problems of thinking about economic questions in global terms.

Hutt, William Harold. **Keynesianism—Retrospect and Prospect: A Critical Restatement of Basic Economic Principles.** Chicago: Regnery, 1963, 447 p.

A lengthy discourse by an anti-Keynesian economist.

54 GENERAL INTERNATIONAL RELATIONS

Lekachman, Robert. **The Age of Keynes.** New York: Random House, 1966, 324 p.
 An evaluation of John Maynard Keynes' life and work and a penetrating account of the influence of his economic ideas on the contemporary world, by a professor at the State University of New York at Stony Brook.

Leontief, Wassily W. **Essays in Economics: Theories and Theorizing.** New York: Oxford University Press, 1966, 252 p.
 Often quite theoretical, this book by the creator of input-output analysis has several pieces of broad interest, notably those on Marxian and Soviet economics.

Lowe, Adolph. **On Economic Knowledge: Toward a Science of Political Economics.** New York: Harper and Row, 1965, 329 p.
 This monograph, in the words of the author, a German-born economist who for many years taught at the New School for Social Research in New York, "is the fruit of forty years of reflection about the subject matter and the method of a science of Economics."

Mundell, Robert A. **International Economics.** New York: Macmillan, 1968, 332 p.
 An outstanding younger economist has collected and adapted his papers to make a substantial treatise that is largely theoretical.

Myrdal, Gunnar. **Challenge to Affluence.** New York: Pantheon Books, 1963, 172 p.
 In his usual forthright manner, the Swedish economist prescribes various dosages of several different medicines for a patient he has treated before.

Röpke, Wilhelm. **Against the Tide.** Chicago: Regnery, 1969, 251 p.
 Essays spread over 30 years that give a good sampling of the German economist's leadership in neo-liberal thought.

Russett, Bruce Martin, *ed.* **Economic Theories of International Politics.** Chicago: Markham Publishing Co., 1968, 542 p.
 A collection of some interesting, often unsatisfactory, attempts to apply economic theory to political problems.

Salin, Edgar. **Politische Ökonomie: Geschichte der wirtschaftspolitischen Ideen von Platon bis zur Gegenwart.** Tübingen: Mohr, 5th rev. and enl. ed., 1967, 205 p.
 In the fifth edition of a book that first appeared in 1923, the gifted Swiss economist and sociologist updates his analytical history of economic thought, understood in its broadest sense, in relation to society and politics.

Sherman, Howard. **Radical Political Economy.** New York: Basic Books, 1972, 431 p.
 Mr. Sherman, a professor of economics at the University of California, believes that his "independent and nondogmatic" Marxism is "indistinguishable from the mainstream of radical Left thought in the United States."

Theobald, Robert. **Free Men and Free Markets.** New York: Potter, 1963, 203 p.
 Mr. Theobald convincingly questions many conventional economic theories as he ponders the changes which abundance and the "scientific revolution will require in the socioeconomic system of Western countries."

Wiles, Peter John de la Fosse. **Communist International Economics.** New York: Praeger, 1969, 566 p.
 A wide-ranging, sometimes idiosyncratic treatise by a professor at the University of London.

GOVERNMENT AND ECONOMICS; PLANNING

See also (Political Factors) Problems of New Nations, p. 36; Labor and Labor Movements, p. 41; Economic Theory, p. 53; Foreign Investment and Overseas Business; Multinational Corporations, p. 65; Economic Growth and Development, p. 71; and the sections for specific countries and regions.

Hesse, Kurt. **Planungen in Entwicklungsländern.** Berlin: Duncker, 1965, 618 p.
 Detailed studies of planning in India, Iran, Spain, Turkey, Senegal and Israel.

Honey, John C. **Planning and the Private Sector: The Experience in Developing Countries.** New York: Dunellen, 1970, 108 p.
 A succinct collection that covers much ground.

Marchal, Jean and Ducros, Bernard, eds. **The Distribution of National Income.** New York: St. Martin's Press, 1968, 733 p.
Facts, theories, interrelations and policies—in 26 papers presented at a conference held by the International Economic Association.

Margolis, Julius and Guitton, H., eds. **Public Economics.** New York: St. Martin's Press, 1969, 574 p.
These proceedings of an International Economic Association conference include several interesting papers on state enterprises as well as East-West comparisons and discussions of planning.

Millikan, Max Franklin, ed. **National Economic Planning.** New York: National Bureau of Economic Research, 1967, 413 p.
Four country studies and five functional analyses make up a major addition to the literature of planning.

Olson, Mancur, Jr. **The Economics of the Wartime Shortage.** Durham: Duke University Press, 1963, 152 p.
"A History of British Food Supplies in the Napoleonic War and in World Wars I and II," with emphasis on comparisons in each situation and the differing ways in which the shortages were overcome.

Saint-Geours, Jean. **La Politique économique des principaux pays industriels de l'occident.** Paris: Sirey, 1969, 576 p.
A systematic treatise on economic policy-making with much comparative data.

Tinbergen, Jan. **Central Planning.** New Haven: Yale University Press, 1964, 150 p.
The former chief planner for the Netherlands, who has also advised many underdeveloped countries, has condensed great experience in this compact book. A description of how planning is done is followed by his own prescription for "optimal planning."

INTERNATIONAL TRADE

See also General Economic Conditions and Tendencies, p. 49; International Finance, p. 59; Raw Materials; Oil; Energy, p. 70; Economic Growth and Development, p. 71; Underdeveloped Economies, p. 78; Economic Aid and Technical Assistance, p. 81; (International Law) Miscellaneous, p. 94; (United Nations) Specialized Agencies and Activities, p. 105; (The Postwar World) Trade and Economic Problems, p. 185; (The United States) Trade, Tariffs and Finance, p. 251; European Communities; European Economic Community; European Coal and Steel Community; European Atomic Energy Community; European Free Trade Association, p. 353; Council for Mutual Economic Assistance; Warsaw Treaty Organization, p. 365; and the sections for specific countries and regions.

Alexandersson, Gunnar and Norström, Göran. **World Shipping: An Economic Geography of Ports and Seaborne Trade.** New York: Wiley, 1963, 507 p.
An absorbing and important survey of the world-wide movement of ships, cargo and freight, followed by regional studies of individual ports—their historical development and role in international trade.

Alting von Geusau, Frans A. M., ed. **Economic Relations after the Kennedy Round.** Leyden: Sijthoff, 1969, 224 p.
Papers prepared for an international conference reflecting many different points of view.

Aubrey, Henry G. **Atlantic Economic Cooperation: The Case of the OECD.** New York: Praeger (for the Council on Foreign Relations), 1967, 214 p.
This first full-length study of the OECD shows how the organization works and the ways in which it influences—or might influence—national policies on a number of quite different kinds of issues.

Balassa, Bela A. and Others. **Studies in Trade Liberalization: Problems and Prospects for the Industrial Countries.** Baltimore: Johns Hopkins Press, 1967, 346 p.
Most of these papers assess the effects of tariff reduction on specific industrial countries, but two authors deal separately with non-tariff barriers and fiscal and social charges. The studies were made in preparation of Balassa's "Trade Liberalization among Industrial Countries."

Balassa, Bela A. **Trade Liberalization among Industrial Countries: Objectives and Alternatives.** New York: McGraw-Hill (for the Council on Foreign Relations), 1967, 251 p.
This book includes an extensive statistical investigation of the consequences of liberalizing trade in manufactured goods among industrialized countries. On the basis of the results—and of more general political and economic considerations—Professor Balassa evaluates alternative trade policies for the United States.

Baldwin, Robert Edward. **Nontariff Distortions of International Trade.** Washington: Brookings Institution, 1970, 210 p.
An excellent book on nontariff barriers and related practices that interfere with international trade, such as subsidies and taxes. The author is a University of Wisconsin professor with governmental experience.

Bhagwati, Jagdish N. **Trade, Tariffs and Growth: Essays in International Economics.** Cambridge: M.I.T. Press, 1970, 371 p.
Collected papers by an M.I.T. professor who is one of the best experts in the field.

Brown, Alan A. and Neuberger, Egon, *eds.* **International Trade and Central Planning.** Berkeley: University of California Press, 1968, 455 p.
Some 25 economists, most of them specialists on Russia, China or Eastern Europe, have combined forces to make this book a major contribution to the understanding of the interplay of foreign trade, planning and centralized control in the communist economies.

Burenstam Linder, Staffan. **Trade and Trade Policy for Development.** New York: Praeger, 1967, 179 p.
Increasingly the feeling grows that the trade problems of underdeveloped countries are different from those of industrialized nations. Here a Swedish economist constructs a theory that takes account of some of the differences and leads to different policy conclusions from those implied by classical theory.

Corbet, Hugh, *ed.* **Trade Strategy and the Asian-Pacific Region.** Toronto: University of Toronto Press, 1971, 221 p.
A revision of three studies originally published separately by a British group interested in worldwide trade liberalization.

Corden, W. M. **The Theory of Protection.** New York: Oxford University Press, 1971, 263 p.
"Effective protection"—which takes account of tariffs and quotas on inputs as well as outputs—turns out to be as promising and as full of difficulties in theoretical analysis as in practical application.

Curzon, Gerard. **Multilateral Commercial Diplomacy: An Examination of the Impact of the General Agreement on Tariffs and Trade on National Commercial Policies and Techniques.** New York: Praeger, 1966, 367 p.
This well-done study fills a large gap in the literature and provides a thorough analysis of some of the activities since the late 1940s of an agency once thought of as temporary and transitional.

Cutajar, Michael Zammit and Franks, Alison. **The Less Developed Countries in World Trade: A Reference Handbook.** London: Overseas Development Institute, 1967, 209 p.
A valuable compendium of facts and condensed statements of issues.

Dam, Kenneth W. **The GATT: Law and International Economic Organization.** Chicago: University of Chicago Press, 1970, 480 p.
In the course of studying the roles of substantive and procedural rules of law and a kind of "pragmatism" that sets itself against "legalism," Professor Dam gives a very full account of the activity and problems of the General Agreement on Tariffs and Trade.

Faaland, Just. **Essays in the Theory of Trade Discrimination.** Bergen: Grieg (for Chr. Michelsens Institutt), 1964, 213 p.
Neglected points, new statements, some quantification and a conclusion in which "The Pilgrim's Progress" is introduced into economic literature as effectively as "Alice in Wonderland" was a generation ago.

Flory, Thiébaut. **Le G.A.T.T.: droit international et commerce mondial.** Paris: Librairie Générale de Droit, 1968, 306 p.

A thorough analysis that deals more with the practice and procedures of the General Agreement on Tariffs and Trade than with traditional legal questions.

Franck, Thomas M. and Weisband, Edward, eds. **A Free Trade Association.** New York: New York University Press, 1968, 239 p.
This group of studies is generally favorable to the idea of a Free Trade Association centering on the North Atlantic. Several papers inevitably overlap similar work done in Britain and Canada but the two main contributions (by the editors) are new in their emphasis on political aspects and the implications of the proposal for the American economy.

Gupta, Kulawant Rai. **A Study of General Agreement of Tariffs and Trade.** New Delhi: S. Chand, 1967, 239 p.
A full, careful and usually quite balanced account of what GATT has done, with special attention, naturally, to the interests of the less developed countries.

Harrod, Sir Henry Roy Forbes with Hague, Douglas C., eds. **International Trade Theory in a Developing World.** New York: St. Martin's Press, 1963, 570 p.
A valuable collection of papers by leading economists followed by a summary of their discussion at a conference by the International Economic Association in 1961.

Hesse, Helmut. **Strukturwandlungen im Welthandel, 1950–1960/61.** Tübingen: Mohr, 1967, 425 p.
A comprehensive effort to account for changes in the share of world exports provided by nine groups of countries over the decade of the 1950s. East-West trade is not included.

Hirsch, Seev. **Location of Industry and International Competitiveness.** New York: Oxford University Press, 1967, 133 p.
An interesting contribution, combining theory and cases, to the growing understanding of the relation between industrial technology, stages of production and the different advantages enjoyed by developed and less developed countries in world trade.

Jaeger, Franz. **GATT, EWG und EFTA.** Bern: Stämpfli, 1970, 399 p.
A careful attempt, going beyond purely formal legal reasoning, to demonstrate the compatibility of the European Community and EFTA with GATT on all but a few points.

Johnson, Harry G., ed. **New Trade Strategy for the World Economy.** Toronto: University of Toronto Press, 1969, 344 p.
Four studies (previously published as pamphlets) with a stimulating essay by one of the champions of the idea of a multilateral free trade association.

Kellenberger, Eduard. **Aussenhandel.** Bern: Stämpfli, 1966, 385 p.
A theory of foreign trade, favoring protectionistic tariff policies.

Kenen, Peter Bain and Lawrence, Roger, eds. **The Open Economy: Essays on International Trade and Finance.** New York: Columbia University Press, 1968, 391 p.
Interesting technical papers coming out of Columbia's International Economics Workshop.

Kock, Karin. **International Trade Policy and the GATT 1947–1967.** Stockholm: Almqvist, 1969, 334 p.
Valuable analysis focusing on half a dozen of the key problems encountered in the General Agreement on Tariffs and Trade. The author is a Swedish economist who has also been a civil servant, diplomat and cabinet member.

Kravis, Irving B. **Domestic Interests and International Obligations: Safeguards in International Trade Organizations.** Philadelphia: University of Pennsylvania Press, 1963, 448 p.
A major study of the safeguards provided by GATT, the OECD, the Coal and Steel Community and the European Common Market for the protection of domestic interests.

Ladreit de Lacharrière, Guy. **Commerce extérieur et sous-développement.** Paris: Presses Universitaires, 1964, 279 p.
A survey of the trading arrangements that are of special interest to the less developed countries.

LaFave, Wayne R. and Hay, Peter, eds. **International Trade, Investment, and Organization.** Urbana: University of Illinois Press, 1967, 506 p.
A wide range of issues considered largely from a legal standpoint.

Lary, Hal B. **Imports of Manufactures from Less Developed Countries.** New York: National Bureau of Economic Research, 1968, 286 p.

A very careful study of a major economic problem. Original statistical work focuses on the possibilities of developing exports of labor-intensive goods from the poor countries.

Liebich, Ferdinand K. **Die Kennedy Runde: eine Analyse des weltweiten genfer Zollsenkungsabkommens.** Freudenstadt: Eurobuch-Verlag Lutzeyer, 1968, 237 p.

Useful statistical analysis and concise commentary about the major trading countries and most products.

Lloyd, Peter J. **International Trade Problems of Small Nations.** Durham: Duke University Press, 1968, 140 p.

Original analysis and a review of literature enable this economist to demonstrate that size and various economic characteristics are not as uniformly related as is generally believed.

Maizels, Alfred with Others. **Exports and Economic Growth of Developing Countries.** New York: Cambridge University Press, 1969, 443 p.

A major study of past and projected exports of sterling area countries and their relation to growth. Commodity prospects, the supply positions of individual countries, and policy issues for both the industrialized and the less developed countries are examined.

Maizels, Alfred. **Industrial Growth and World Trade.** New York: Cambridge University Press, 1963, 563 p.

This massive and impressive study examines the relation between industrial production and international trade in manufactured goods since the beginning of the century. On the basis of his interesting findings Mr. Maizels suggests possibilities for the next few decades.

Mandel, Ernest. **Europe vs. America: Contradictions of Imperialism.** New York: Monthly Review Press, 1970, 160 p.

A sophisticated Belgian Marxist analyzes the relations between American and European business in ways that would be in large part acceptable to observers of other persuasions. His prescription for "the socialist alternative" and how it may be brought about is something else again.

Meier, Gerald Marvin. **International Trade and Development.** New York: Harper and Row, 1963, 208 p.

Proceeding largely through an extension and modification of trade theory, Professor Meier reaches conclusions that challenge the emphasis frequently put on import restrictions, and suggest that the main problem may be how to communicate the benefits from expanded international trade to more than the export sectors of the underdeveloped countries.

New Directions for World Trade: Proceedings of a Chatham House Conference, Bellagio, 16–24 September 1963. New York: Oxford University Press (for the Royal Institute of International Affairs), 1964, 241 p.

In advance of the U.N. Conference on Trade and Development a group of economists from a number of countries, under the chairmanship of Andrew Shonfield, explored the central issues of trade between industrialized and underdeveloped countries. This valuable volume includes their papers, conclusions and a summary of the discussion.

Ohlin, Bertil Gotthard. **Interregional and International Trade.** Cambridge: Harvard University Press, rev. ed., 1967, 324 p.

A slightly abridged edition of a classic study, with a substantial essay giving the author's present views.

Patterson, Gardner. **Discrimination in International Trade: The Policy Issues, 1945–1965.** Princeton: Princeton University Press, 1966, 414 p.

What governments have sought to accomplish by trade discrimination and, so far as one can tell, what the effects have been are the points of enquiry of this major book. Writing with access to GATT documents and a fine sense of balance, Professor Patterson has produced what will surely be the definitive work for a long time to come on a central problem of postwar international trade.

Preeg, Ernest H. **Traders and Diplomats.** Washington: Brookings Institution, 1970, 320 p.

ECONOMIC FACTORS

An excellent history and analysis of the Kennedy Round by a young U.S. Foreign Service officer who took part in it. Disclosing no great secrets, he gives the flavor as well as an authoritative account of the main events and a valuable statistical analysis of the results. The author was the first International Relations Fellow of the Council on Foreign Relations.

Richter, John Hans. **Agricultural Protection and Trade: Proposals for an International Policy.** New York: Praeger, 1964, 148 p.
A former official of the U.S. Department of Agriculture, with much European experience, surveys the problems of international trade in farm products against an assessment of past national policies and their future evolution.

Samuelson, Paul A., ed. **International Economic Relations.** New York: St. Martin's Press, 1969, 281 p.
Papers on a number of major issues and summaries of discussions by some leading economists. (Proceedings of the Third Congress of the International Economic Association.)

Travis, William Penfield. **The Theory of Trade and Protection.** Cambridge: Harvard University Press, 1964, 296 p.
An interesting effort to make the theory of international trade more realistic by bringing protection into it. This also permits an assessment of the significance of protection.

Uri, Pierre, ed. **Trade and Investment Policies for the Seventies: New Challenges for the Atlantic Area and Japan.** New York: Praeger (in coöperation with the Atlantic Institute), 1971, 286 p.
A familiar subject enhanced by some good papers and more than the usual quota of Japanese contributions.

Vajda, Imre and Simai, Mihály, eds. **Foreign Trade in a Planned Economy.** New York: Cambridge University Press, 1971, 221 p.
A basic subject treated flexibly and interestingly by a number of Hungarian economists, including the late Professor Vajda, an outstanding figure.

Vajda, Imre. **The Role of Foreign Trade in a Socialist Economy: New Essays in Persuasion.** Budapest: Corvina Press, 1965, 336 p.
Essays by a leading Hungarian economist.

Vanek, Jaroslav. **General Equilibrium of International Discrimination: The Case of Customs Unions.** Cambridge: Harvard University Press, 1965, 234 p.
Viner's "trade creation" and "trade diversion" remain central to the analysis of customs unions, but Vanek's elaborations and refinements carry the study to new ground.

Wionczek, Miguel S., ed. **Economic Cooperation in Latin America, Africa, and Asia.** Cambridge: M.I.T. Press, 1969, 566 p.
A valuable collection of documents on trade, finance, banking and development, including the texts of all major agreements.

INTERNATIONAL FINANCE

See also General Economic Conditions and Tendencies, p. 49; Economic Theory, p. 53; Economic Growth and Development, p. 71; (International Law) Miscellaneous, p. 94; (The Postwar World) Trade and Economic Problems, p. 185; and the sections for specific countries and regions.

Adler, John H. with Kuznets, Paul W., eds. **Capital Movements and Economic Development.** New York: St. Martin's Press, 1967, 497 p.
Excellent papers from many countries, originally presented at a conference held by the International Economic Association.

Aliber, Robert Z. **The Future of the Dollar as an International Currency.** New York: Praeger, 1966, 169 p.
Tightly-written discussion of international monetary arrangements and a range of possible alternatives. Mr. Aliber, an economist at the University of Chicago, poses a set of policy choices for the United States, all of them likely in his view to make the dollar more important as an international currency.

Aliber, Robert Z., *ed.* **The International Market for Foreign Exchange.** New York: Praeger (in coöperation with the Graduate School of Business, University of Chicago), 1969, 272 p.
Papers and a summary of conference discussions dealing with the exchange market in a number of major countries.

Aubrey, Henry G. **The Dollar in World Affairs: An Essay in International Financial Policy.** New York: Harper and Row (for the Council on Foreign Relations), 1964, 295 p.
In examining the central issues of United States foreign financial policy, Dr. Aubrey stresses their relation to foreign policy as a whole. Exploring the implications of the position of the dollar as a reserve currency, he sees it as a financial instrument that serves the common objectives of the Western world, and not just those of the United States.

Aufricht, Hans. **The International Monetary Fund: Legal Bases, Structure, Functions.** New York: Praeger (for the London Institute of World Affairs), 1964, 126 p.
A concise survey.

Baker, James C. **The International Finance Corporation: Origin, Operations, and Evaluation.** New York: Praeger, 1968, 271 p.
A full-length account of the work of the World Bank's affiliate that helps finance private business.

Bochud, François, *ed.* **Fundamentale Fragen künftiger Währungspolitik.** Basel: Kyklos-Verlag (for the List Gesellschaft), 1965, 230 p.
The gold price, flexible exchange rates and related matters as discussed by a group of experts in March 1965.

Bosman, Hans W. J. and Alting von Geusau, Frans A. M., *eds.* **The Future of the International Monetary System.** Lexington (Mass.): Heath Lexington Books, 1970, 180 p.
In addition to papers by leading authorities on familiar topics, this book contains a contribution by two Czech economists on possible future relations between the COMECON countries and the international monetary system.

Brahmananda, P. R. **The Gold-Money Rift: A Classical Theory of International Liquidity.** Bombay: Popular Prakashan, 1969, 351 p.
Combining theory and observation, an Indian economist ranges widely over the problems that beset the international monetary system.

Brandes, Henning. **Der Euro-Dollarmarkt.** Wiesbaden: Gabler, 1968, 383 p.
A detailed analysis of the rise and operation of the Eurodollar market (to mid 1967) with some discussion of its effect on banks, central banks and governmental policies.

Brittan, Samuel. **The Price of Economic Freedom: A Guide to Flexible Rates.** New York: St. Martin's Press, 1971, 103 p.
According to this British journalist, the balance of payments is a pseudo problem which has been handled in ways that make real problems harder to solve. Flexible exchange rates, he argues, will help bring matters into a proper focus.

Cameron, Rondo, *ed.* **Banking and Economic Development: Some Lessons of History.** New York: Oxford University Press, 1972, 267 p.
The experiences of seven countries in the nineteenth century analyzed in the hope of throwing light on present problems.

Carreau, Dominique. **Souveraineté et coopération monétaire internationale.** Paris: Éditions Cujas, 1970, 530 p.
A massive treatise aimed primarily at French jurists who have neglected the impact on their subject of international monetary coöperation.

Carreau, Dominique. **Le Système monétaire international.** Paris: Colin, 1972, 397 p.
An examination of the *aspects juridiques* of the international monetary system, including a critique of the United States.

Cassell, Francis. **Gold or Credit? The Economics and Politics of International Money.** New York: Praeger (for the Federal Trust for Education and Research, London), 1965, 216 p.
A former editor of *The Banker* traces the history of the post-World War II monetary system and argues against the return to the gold standard.

Cheng, Hang-sheng. **International Bond Issues of the Less-Developed Countries: Diagnosis and Prescription.** Ames: Iowa State University Press, 1969, 95 p.
Rejecting the usual explanations for the slight use of international bond issues by developing countries, the author, an economics professor, propounds a novel scheme for channeling capital into bonds under World Bank surveillance.

Cohen, Stephen D. **International Monetary Reform, 1964–69: The Political Dimension.** New York: Praeger, 1970, 201 p.
An economist with treasury and banking experience gives a sober account of negotiations about gold, the dollar and Special Drawing Rights, with emphasis on the fact that control over money is power.

Crick, Wilfred Frank, ed. **Commonwealth Banking Systems.** New York: Oxford University Press, 1965, 536 p.
This basic survey largely replaces the volume edited by Professor R. S. Sayers: "Banking in the British Commonwealth" (New York: Oxford University Press, 1953, 486 p.).

Crochat, Max. **Le Marché des eurodevises.** Paris: Éditions de l'Épargne, 1969, 252 p.
Useful history and survey of the emergence and use of Eurodollars and other Euromonies.

Delaume, Georges René. **Legal Aspects of International Lending and Economic Development Financing.** Dobbs Ferry (N.Y.): Oceana Publications (for the Parker School of Foreign and Comparative Law, Columbia University), 1967, 371 p.
A clear and comprehensive summary.

Einzig, Paul. **The Case against Floating Exchanges.** New York: St. Martin's Press, 1970, 211 p.
Remembering the competitive devaluations of the past, a veteran financial journalist vigorously attacks the idea of making exchange rates more flexible.

Einzig, Paul. **The Euro-Dollar System: Practice and Theory of International Interest Rates.** New York: St. Martin's Press, 2d ed., 1965, 182 p.
An indefatigable English writer on financial questions gives us an account of a major innovation in international finance.

Einzig, Paul. **Foreign Dollar Loans in Europe.** New York: St. Martin's Press, 1965, 159 p.
In his pursuit of the newest practices in world money markets, the British journalist has some interesting things to say about the practice of issuing loans in Europe denominated in dollars.

Einzig, Paul. **Foreign Exchange Crises: An Essay in Economic Pathology.** New York: St. Martin's Press, 1968, 205 p.
A clear and remarkably complete *catalogue raisonnée* of the elements of the problem.

Einzig, Paul. **Leads and Lags: The Main Cause of Devaluation.** New York: St. Martin's Press, 1968, 169 p.
In this study the author puts new emphasis on the familiar phenomenon of speeding up or slowing down payments when a currency seems weak.

Fellner, William; Machlup, Fritz; Triffin, Robert and Others. **Maintaining and Restoring Balance in International Payments.** Princeton: Princeton University Press, 1966, 259 p.
These comprehensive papers prepared for discussions with officials and central bankers working on international monetary adjustments are an example of a valuable interplay between academic and governmental work on a tough subject.

Ferris, Paul. **The Money Men of Europe.** New York: Macmillan, 1969, 278 p.
A popularly written behavioral study of the gnomes of Zurich and their cousins in other countries.

Fromm, Gary, ed. **Transport Investment and Economic Development.** Washington: Brookings Institution, 1965, 314 p.
A number of authors tackle different aspects of a difficult problem.

Gardner, Richard N. **Sterling-Dollar Diplomacy: The Origins and the Prospects of Our International Economic Order.** New York: McGraw-Hill, 1969, 423 p.
The original text of this standard work which first appeared in 1956, plus a long introduction reassessing some points and bringing others up to date.

Garelli, François. **Pour une monnaie européenne.** Paris: Éditions du Seuil, 1969, 155 p.

This tract argues that Europe's need for a common money can be met before countries are ready for full political and economic fusion. But the formula proposed calls for a high degree of coördination of national policies, and the implications of this course are not very fully examined.

Goldsmith, Raymond W. **Financial Structure and Development.** New Haven: Yale University Press, 1969, 561 p.

A weighty comparative study with material from many countries put together in unfamiliar patterns.

Gowda, Krishnadasa Gowda Venkatagiri. **International Currency Plans and Expansion of World Trade.** New York: Asia Publishing House, 1964, 216 p.

Lucid discussion of the Triffin Plan and its rivals.

Green, Timothy. **The World of Gold.** New York: Walker, 1968, 242 p.

Producing, buying, selling and smuggling gold can be a rather romantic business if facts and stories are allowed to outweigh the problems of the international monetary system.

Hahn, L. Albert. **Fünfzig Jahre zwischen Inflation und Deflation.** Tübingen: Mohr, 1963, 247 p.

A prominent anti-Keynesian banker and economist reminisces on international financial and economic trends since World War I.

Hahn, L. Albert. **Geld und Gold: Vorträge und Aufsätze 1962-1968.** Basel: Kyklos-Verlag, 1969, 285 p.

Papers on monetary issues of the 1960s.

Halm, George N., ed. **Approaches to Greater Flexibility of Exchange Rates: The Bürgenstock Papers.** Princeton: Princeton University Press, 1970, 436 p.

A wide range of views and the high level of expertise make this an important contribution to the discussion of flexible exchange rates. The papers were arranged by C. Fred Bergsten, George N. Halm, Fritz Machlup and Robert V. Roosa.

Harrod, Sir Henry Roy Forbes. **Reforming the World's Money.** New York: St. Martin's Press, 1965, 181 p.

An eminent British economist argues that the world's financial ills will be cured by reform of the International Monetary Fund and, failing that, by raising the price of gold.

Heilperin, Michael A. **Aspects of the Pathology of Money.** London: Michael Joseph (for the Graduate Institute of International Studies, Geneva), 1968, 296 p.

A selection from the author's academic and journalistic writings from the late 1930s to the mid 1960s, including several previously unpublished papers.

Hinshaw, Randall Weston, ed. **The Economics of International Adjustment.** Baltimore: Johns Hopkins Press, 1971, 184 p.

Excellent editing of tape-recorded discussions by a stellar group of economists make this report a valuable contribution to the mounting discussion of how to make the international monetary system work more smoothly and safely.

Hinshaw, Randall Weston, ed. **Inflation as a Global Problem.** Baltimore: Johns Hopkins University Press, 1972, 163 p.

A well-edited report of a discussion among major authorities.

Hinshaw, Randall Weston, ed. **Monetary Reform and the Price of Gold: Alternative Approaches.** Baltimore: Johns Hopkins Press, 1967, 180 p.

Debate among highly articulate protagonists.

Hirsch, Fred. **Money International.** Garden City: Doubleday, 1969, 420 p.

A former editor of *The Economist* surveys the world of international money and finance for the benefit of the layman. An introductory chapter by Richard Cooper brings the 1966 British edition up to date.

Horie, Shigeo. **The International Monetary Fund: Retrospect and Prospect.** New York: St. Martin's Press, 1964, 208 p.

An eminent Japanese banker discusses not only the past and present of the Fund but also the future of the international monetary system.

Jacobsson, Per. **International Monetary Problems, 1957-1963.** Washington: International Monetary Fund, 1964, 368 p.

This collection includes most of the major speeches made by the late Swedish economist while he was Managing Director of the International Monetary Fund.

Kindleberger, Charles P. **Power and Money.** New York: Basic Books, 1970, 246 p.
A good introductory treatment of "the economics of international politics and the politics of international economics" by a gifted expositor.

Lipfert, Helmut. **Internationale Finanzmärkte: Probleme und Entwicklungen eines Jahrzehnts.** Frankfurt/Main: Knapp, 1964, 534 p.
Collected papers by a man involved in foreign exchange as a practitioner as well as an economic analyst.

McDaniels, John F. and Others, *eds.* **International Financing and Investment.** Dobbs Ferry (N.Y.): Oceana Publications (for the World Community Association), 1964, 738 p.
Useful papers of varying approach, level and content, and a long bibliography.

Machlup, Fritz. **The Alignment of Foreign Exchange Rates.** New York: Praeger, 1972, 94 p.
An eloquent and pithy statement of why an alteration of exchange rates is usually the best way to deal with balance-of-payments troubles that do not seem otherwise likely to go away.

Machlup, Fritz. **International Payments, Debts, and Gold.** New York: Scribner, 1964, 472 p.
Professor Machlup's originality and ingenuity extend to the form of this collection as well as its content. The papers, dating from 1929 to 1963, are shuffled, spliced, commented on anew and meticulously annotated to show how they have been revised.

Machlup, Fritz. **Remaking the International Monetary System: The Rio Agreement and Beyond.** Baltimore: Johns Hopkins Press (with the Committee for Economic Development), 1968, 161 p.
By pursuing "linguistic pragmatism" the world's monetary statesmen have shown "how to get agreement by avoiding excessively clear language." Professor Machlup sets matters right by a very clear exposition, commentary and critique of a plan he approves because it is based on "a genuine breakthrough in monetary thinking."

Meyer, Richard Hemmig. **Bankers' Diplomacy: Monetary Stabilization in the Twenties.** New York: Columbia University Press, 1970, 170 p.
A survey of the behavior of major central bankers in the twenties.

Mikesell, Raymond Frech. **Public International Lending for Development.** New York: Random House, 1966, 244 p.
A solid study of past and present practices and unsolved problems.

Mossé, Robert. **Les Problèmes monétaires internationaux.** Paris: Payot, 1967, 318 p.
A French expert wants to move away from gold toward a true international clearing system.

Mundell, Robert A. and Swoboda, Alexander K., *eds.* **Monetary Problems of the International Economy.** Chicago: University of Chicago Press, 1969, 405 p.
Papers presented at a conference attended by leading economists from all over the world at the University of Chicago in September 1966.

Munier, Bertrand. **Le Cambisme et le jeu monétaire international.** Paris: Presses Universitaires, 1970, 383 p.
Uncertainty makes foreign exchange dealing a good subject to approach through game theory. In doing so this young French academic brings to bear a good deal of practical knowledge.

Musgrave, Richard A. **Fiscal Systems.** New Haven: Yale University Press, 1969, 397 p.
A thoroughgoing comparative study dealing with developed and less developed countries and also with problems of international coördination.

Perera, Phillips. **Development Finance: Institutions, Problems, and Prospects.** New York: Praeger, 1968, 440 p.
A wide-ranging study, interesting notably for its material on development banks and other efforts to mobilize capital in a number of countries.

Prochnow, Herbert V., *ed.* **The Eurodollar.** Chicago: Rand McNally (for the Graduate School of Banking at the University of Wisconsin), 1970, 418 p.

A wide-ranging collection of views by an international group of economists and bankers.

Rolfe, Sidney E. with Hawkins, Robert G. **Gold and World Power: The Dollar, the Pound, and the Plans for Reform.** New York: Harper and Row, 1966, 276 p.
Far less political than the title promises, this book provides a very clear discussion of the U.S. balance of payments, the British economy's place in the world, and the proposals for international monetary reform.

Roosa, Robert V. **The Dollar and World Liquidity.** New York: Random House, 1967, 367 p.
Papers by the former Under Secretary of the Treasury for Monetary Affairs tracing the development of U.S. policy toward international monetary reform during the crucial years of the early 1960s.

Roosa, Robert V. **Monetary Reform for the World Economy.** New York: Harper and Row (for the Council on Foreign Relations), 1965, 173 p.
These lectures lay out the conditions for a proper international monetary order, appraise the many schemes for reform that have been advanced and set forth the author's own proposals.

Rueff, Jacques. **The Age of Inflation.** Chicago: Regnery, 1964, 175 p.
Six papers by an eminent French economist centering on the importance of finance in human affairs and the virtues of the gold standard. The French original appeared as "L'Âge de l'inflation" (Paris: Payot, 3rd ed., 1963, 144 p.).

Rueff, Jacques. **Balance of Payments: Proposals for the Resolution of the Most Pressing World Economic Problems of Our Time.** New York: Macmillan, 1967, 215 p.
A number of papers, some prewar, are put together as an exposition of the author's theory of how monetary factors determine the balance of payments. The French original appeared as "Le Lancinant problème des balances de paiements" (Paris: Payot, 1965, 233 p.).

Rueff, Jacques and Others. **Inflation und Weltwährungsordnung.** Erlenbach-Zurich: Rentsch, 1963, 231 p.
Papers by authorities on international monetary matters followed by a record of a discussion between them and Professor Triffin.

Rueff, Jacques. **Le Péché monétaire de l'occident.** Paris: Plon, 1971, 285 p.
Though no one has doubted the consistency of the eminent French economist in demonstrating why the gold exchange standard is a transgression and the efforts at reform of the 1960s no better, it is useful to have this documented record. It is made up of past articles, retrospective commentary and some previously unpublished advice to the French governments.

Saint Marc, Michèle. **Zone franc et décolonisation.** Paris: Société d'Édition d'Enseignement Supérieur, 1964, 259 p.
A study of the role of the French franc in former French colonies.

Schmitz, Wolfgang, ed. **Convertibility, Multilateralism and Freedom: World Economic Policy in the Seventies; Essays in Honour of Reinhard Kamitz.** New York: Springer, 1972, 426 p.
Distinguished contributors, many of them European liberals, honor the Austrian central banker, Reinhard Kamitz.

Scitovsky, Tibor. **Money and the Balance of Payments.** Chicago: Rand McNally, 1969, 188 p.
In this study the author emphasizes the role of market forces and the difficulties they encounter internationally.

Shoup, Carl Sumner, ed. **Fiscal Harmonization in Common Markets.** New York: Columbia University Press, 1967, 2 v.
An effort to advise the EEC about harmonizing taxes led Professor Shoup and others to see how little theoretical or practical work had been done on a subject that increases in interest as trade barriers fall. To fill the void they produced this impressive study which concentrates on the European Community but also deals with EFTA, Latin America, East Africa and COMECON.

Triffin, Robert. **Our International Monetary System: Yesterday, Today, and Tomorrow.** New York: Random House, 1968, 206 p.

With his usual clarity one of the most articulate participants in "the marathon debate on international monetary reform" puts the issues in bright historical perspective.

Triffin, Robert. **The World Money Maze: National Currencies in International Payments.** New Haven: Yale University Press, 1966, 585 p.
Valuable and often controversial papers on problems of international finance.

Ward, Richard Joseph. **International Finance.** Englewood Cliffs: Prentice-Hall, 1965, 213 p.
A description of the international monetary mechanism, with particular emphasis on the international operations of commercial banks and the foreign exchange markets.

Wasserman, Max Judd and Ware, Ray M. **The Balance of Payments: History, Methodology, Theory.** New York: Simmons-Boardman, 1965, 481 p.
A comprehensive attempt to show the development of the concept of the balance of payments from its earliest beginning to the present.

Wells, Louis T., Jr., ed. **The Product Life Cycle and International Trade.** Boston: Harvard University, Graduate School of Business Administration, Division of Research, 1972, 259 p.
This collection brings together most of the basic works concerning one of the principal contributions to new thought made by the Harvard Business School.

White, John. **Regional Development Banks.** New York: Praeger (in association with the Overseas Development Institute), 1972, 204 p.
The author, an English economist, argues that the creation of regional banks should not be regarded as an effort to create little World Banks, but as "an act of political resistance against the developed countries' hegemony in the world."

Zawadzki, Krzysztof Konrad Feliks. **The Economics of Inflationary Processes.** New York: Praeger, 1966, 288 p.
A detailed analysis of the causes, mechanics and effects of inflationary processes of various types.

FOREIGN INVESTMENT AND OVERSEAS BUSINESS; MULTINATIONAL CORPORATIONS

See also Colonial Problems; Decolonization, p. 36; Economic Theory, p. 53; International Trade, p. 55; International Finance, p. 59; Raw Materials; Oil; Energy, p. 70; Underdeveloped Economies, p. 78; (International Law) Miscellaneous, p. 94; and the sections for specific countries and regions.

Béguin, Jean-Pierre. **Les Entreprises conjointes internationales dans les pays en voie de développement.** Geneva: Institut Universitaire de Hautes Études Internationales, 1972, 271 p.
A legal study of international joint ventures in the developing countries.

Behrman, Jack N. **National Interests and the Multinational Enterprise: Tensions Among the North Atlantic Countries.** Englewood Cliffs: Prentice-Hall, 1970, 194 p.
An original and somewhat disturbing analysis of the impact of multinational business enterprises on governments. The author concludes that, generally, the business enterprises determine economic patterns by pursuing their own interests while governments lag behind.

Behrman, Jack N. **Some Patterns in the Rise of the Multinational Enterprise.** Chapel Hill: University of North Carolina, Graduate School of Business Administration, 1969, 180 p.
A former U.S. Assistant Secretary of Commerce makes a very useful contribution to the discussion of international business.

Brooke, Michael Z. and Remmers, H. Lee. **The Strategy of Multinational Enterprise.** Harlow: Longman, 1970, 389 p.
Having interviewed executives of many multinational corporations, the authors attempt to derive an analytical model of the operations of such enterprises.

Dunning, John H., *ed*. **The Multinational Enterprise.** New York: Praeger, 1971, 368 p.
   A leading British academic authority on investment has brought together a good team for a study of an increasingly important topic.

Eells, Richard. **Global Corporations: The Emerging System of World Economic Power.** New York: Interbook, 1972, 242 p.
   A veteran student of corporations discusses broad political, social and even philosophical issues of global corporations.

Fayerweather, John. **International Business Management: A Conceptual Framework.** New York: McGraw-Hill, 1969, 220 p.
   This effort to find a broad and consistent basis for looking at problems of international business reflects the widely felt need for theory in the social sciences.

Friedmann, Wolfgang Gaston and Béguin, Jean-Pierre. **Joint International Business Ventures in Developing Countries.** New York: Columbia University Press, 1971, 448 p.
   Case studies covering the last decade, a follow-up volume to "Joint International Business Ventures," edited by W. G. Friedman and G. Kalmanoff and published in 1961.

Günter, Hans, *ed*. **Transnational Industrial Relations: The Impact of Multi-national Corporations and Economic Regionalism on Industrial Relations.** New York: St. Martin's Press, 1972, 479 p.
   Will the multinational corporation someday face the multinational labor union? The most interesting papers in this volume deal with aspects of that question.

Hellmann, Rainer. **The Challenge to U.S. Dominance of the International Corporation.** New York: Dunellen, 1971, 348 p.
   Many facts and figures about American investment in Europe, and some about European investment in America, make up the bulk of this book by a German economic journalist.

Johnstone, Allan W. **United States Direct Investment in France: An Investigation of the French Charges.** Cambridge: M.I.T. Press, 1965, 109 p.
   This book examines the complaint in some French quarters that U. S. investment is a threat to French economic sovereignty.

Kapoor, Ashook and Grub, Phillip D., *eds*. **The Multinational Enterprise in Transition.** Princeton: Darwin Press, 1972, 505 p.
   An excellent comprehensive collection.

Kindleberger, Charles P., *ed*. **The International Corporation: A Symposium.** Cambridge: M.I.T. Press, 1970, 415 p.
   First-rate essays that cover the major aspects of an increasingly popular subject.

Kronfol, Zouhair A. **Protection of Foreign Investment: A Study in International Law.** Leyden: Sijthoff, 1972, 176 p.
   Careful investigation of the many different legal devices for protecting investment leads to an emphasis on their limited effectiveness.

Lillich, Richard Bonnot. **The Protection of Foreign Investment: Six Procedural Studies.** Syracuse: Syracuse University Press, 1965, 222 p.
   A study of the protection of American private interests against acts of foreign governments and the pursuit of subsequent claims.

McCreary, Edward A. **The Americanization of Europe: The Impact of Americans and American Business on the Uncommon Market.** Garden City: Doubleday, 1964, 295 p.
   This informative study covers both the activities of American businessmen in Europe and the development there of practices and attitudes in production, consumption and distribution that have been thought of as especially American.

Martyn, Howe. **International Business: Principles and Problems.** New York: Free Press of Glencoe, 1964, 288 p.
   A survey covering a wide range of subjects.

Mikesell, Raymond F. and Others. **Foreign Investment in the Petroleum and Mineral Industries: Case Studies of Investor-Host Country Relations.** Baltimore: Johns Hopkins Press (for Resources for the Future), 1971, 459 p.
   A solid contribution to the literature of international investment. Case studies in-

volving five commodities and seven countries provide a basis for analytical and prescriptive conclusions.

Neufeld, Edward Peter. **A Global Corporation: A History of the International Development of Massey-Ferguson Limited.** Toronto: University of Toronto Press, 1969, 427 p.
This detailed history of the Canadian-based producer of farm equipment stresses the effect of international horizons on its development.

Rolfe, Sidney E. and Damm, Walter, eds. **The Multinational Corporation in the World Economy: Direct Investment in Perspective.** New York: Praeger (for the Atlantic Institute, the Committee for Atlantic Economic Cooperation and the Atlantic Council of the United States), 1970, 169 p.
Useful papers with special emphasis on foreign investment in the United States.

Schwarzenberger, Georg. **Foreign Investments and International Law.** New York: Praeger, 1969, 237 p.
A thorough review of postwar British practice serves as a basis for criticism of proposed international arrangements to safeguard investment.

Stephenson, Hugh. **The Coming Clash: The Impact of Multinational Corporations on National States.** New York: Saturday Review Press, 1972, 185 p.
A useful study by a British editor.

Tugendhat, Christopher. **The Multinationals.** New York: Random House, 1972, 242 p.
Lucidly, as befits a former financial journalist, the Conservative MP for the Cities of London and Westminster discusses the activities of the big international companies and makes moderate proposals for national and international measures that will strengthen the hands of governments in dealing with them.

Vernon, Raymond. **The Economic and Political Consequences of Multinational Enterprise.** Boston: Harvard University, Graduate School of Business Administration, Division of Research, 1972, 236 p.
Major articles by a leading member of Harvard's Graduate School of Business Administration.

Whitman, Marina Von Neumann. **Government Risk-Sharing in Foreign Investment.** Princeton: Princeton University Press, 1965, 358 p.
The most comprehensive account we have of the devices—other than tax incentives—by which the U.S. Government and several international agencies have sought to encourage private investment abroad. Professor Whitman's careful analysis shows how hard it is to get a clear assessment of the effects of these measures.

Wilkins, Mira and Hill, Frank Ernest. **American Business Abroad: Ford on Six Continents.** Detroit: Wayne State University Press, 1964, 541 p.
An absorbing history of the Ford Motor Company's multiple international projects, the growth and development of which reflect many of the world's economic and political problems.

TRANSPORT

See also General Economic Conditions and Tendencies, p. 49; International Finance, p. 59; Maritime, Air, Space and Environmental Law, p. 90; and the sections for specific countries and regions.

Colby, Charles Carlyle. **North Atlantic Arena.** Carbondale: Southern Illinois University Press, 1966, 253 p.
A wide-ranging historical and geographical study of water transport, including the development of inland waterways, from the Mediterranean to North America.

Lawrence, S. A. **International Sea Transport: The Years Ahead.** Lexington (Mass.): Lexington Books, 1972, 316 p.
A thorough description of things as they are with some projection of economic, technological and political possibilities.

O'Connor, William E. **Economic Regulation of the World's Airlines: A Political Analysis.** New York: Praeger, 1971, 189 p.
    An official of the Civil Aeronautics Board sifts many proposals to find the most efficient and economic method of regulating international airlines.

Owen, Wilfred. **Strategy for Mobility.** Washington: Brookings Institution, 1964, 249 p.
    A study of the special problems transportation poses in working out a strategy for investment for development.

FOOD AND AGRICULTURE

See also Population Problems, p. 47; General Economic Conditions and Tendencies, p. 49; Government and Economics; Planning, p. 54; International Trade, p. 55; Economic Growth and Development, p. 71; Underdeveloped Economies, p. 78; Maritime, Air, Space and Environmental Law, p. 90; (International Organization and Government) General, p. 96; (United Nations) Specialized Agencies and Activities, p. 105; (The United States) Aid and Assistance, p. 254; and the sections for specific countries and regions.

Badouin, Robert. **Agriculture et accession au développement.** Paris: Pedone, 1967, 228 p.
    A monograph on the important place of agriculture in development.

Bartz, Fritz. **Die grossen Fischereiräume der Welt.** Wiesbaden: F. Steiner, 1964–65, 2 v.
    A comprehensive and well-documented survey of the fisheries of the world. A standard reference.

Brown, Lester R. **Seeds of Change: The Green Revolution and Development in the 1970's.** New York: Praeger (for the Overseas Development Council), 1970, 205 p.
    Succinct and readable account of the contemporary revolution in agriculture, by a former official of the U.S. Department of Agriculture. Optimistic in tone, it stresses the problems resulting from increased productivity and makes proposals for dealing with some of them.

Clark, Colin and Haswell, Margaret Rosary. **The Economics of Subsistence Agriculture.** New York: St. Martin's Press, 1964, 218 p.
    Data on the conditions of life and production of a large part of the world's farmers.

Clark, Colin. **Starvation or Plenty?** New York: Taplinger, 1970, 180 p.
    A senior British agricultural economist restates his basically optimistic views about the ability of the world to feed its people.

Cochrane, Willard W. **The World Food Problem: A Guardedly Optimistic View.** New York: Cromwell, 1969, 331 p.
    Neither alarmist nor complacent, this agricultural economist and former government official argues that neither birth control nor miracle grains can solve the food problem. That can only be done as part of general development policy for which both rich and poor nations must share responsibility.

Coppock, John O. **Atlantic Agricultural Unity: Is It Possible?** New York: McGraw-Hill (for the Council on Foreign Relations in coöperation with the Food Research Institute, Stanford University), 1966, 238 p.
    The author charts a course away from price supports and the attendant trade barriers and emphasizes national action more than detailed international bargaining.

Dumont, René and Rosier, Bernard. **The Hungry Future.** New York: Praeger, 1969, 271 p.
    In this study two distinguished French agronomists urge that the eradication of hunger becomes the primary objective of the last third of the twentieth century and outline prescriptions for the elimination of the coming food crisis. The French original appeared as "Nous allons à la famine" (Paris: Éditions du Seuil, 1966, 281 p.).

Fisher, Bart S. **The International Coffee Agreement: A Study in Coffee Diplomacy.** New York: Praeger, 1972, 287 p.
    A clearly argued and well-informed analysis of that *rara avis*, a durable commodity agreement. The young author recommends that the agreement be extended through most of the 1970s and suggests some improvements.

Freeman, Orville L. **World Without Hunger.** New York: Praeger, 1968, 190 p.
In typically hard-hitting fashion, a former Secretary of Agriculture poses the world's food problems, reviews what is being done about them and proposes specific greater efforts. He puts the United States in the role of leader, teacher and to some degree financier of these efforts, not that of supplier.

Garst, Jonathan. **No Need for Hunger.** New York: Random House, 1964, 182 p.
The successful Iowa-born agricultural expert states that "hunger, misery, and the population explosion are all one problem and a problem to be solved first by the production of more food."

Hardin, Clifford M., ed. **Overcoming World Hunger.** Englewood Cliffs: Prentice-Hall (for the American Assembly, Columbia University), 1969, 177 p.
Leading authorities analyze the food and population problem, mostly in less developed countries.

Hayami, Yujiro and Ruttan, Vernon W. **Agricultural Development: An International Perspective.** Baltimore: Johns Hopkins Press, 1971, 367 p.
This inquiry into productivity in agriculture, based on American and Japanese experience, stresses the importance of economic incentives and the organization of governmental research.

Hopcraft, Arthur. **Born to Hunger.** Boston: Houghton, 1968, 258 p.
A journalist's account of hunger and efforts to deal with it in a number of countries. Written for the Freedom from Hunger Campaign, United Kingdom Committee.

Idyll, Clarence P. **The Sea Against Hunger.** New York: Cromwell, 1970, 221 p.
This excellent book by a distinguished oceanographer demonstrates that the sea alone cannot save the world from hunger. It can, however, if sensibly harvested, become a valuable ally in the battle.

Jackson, W. A. Douglas, ed. **Agrarian Policies and Problems in Communist and Non-Communist Countries.** Seattle: University of Washington Press, 1971, 488 p.
Papers originally delivered at a conference at the University of Washington in 1967.

McGovern, George Stanley. **War Against Want: America's Food for Peace Program.** New York: Walker, 1964, 148 p.
Senator McGovern, who was the first director of the Food for Peace Program, describes the international food situation and its frightening future implications.

Millikan, Max Franklin and Hapgood, David. **No Easy Harvest: The Dilemma of Agriculture in Underdeveloped Countries.** Boston: Little, Brown, 1967, 178 p.
A condensation of expert thought on the whole range of factors that make agricultural development difficult.

Nair, Kusum. **The Lonely Furrow: Farming in the United States, Japan and India.** Ann Arbor: University of Michigan Press, 1969, 314 p.
The author concludes that different farmers have different responses to the same national policies.

Paddock, William and Paddock, Paul. **Famine—1975! America's Decision: Who Will Survive?** Boston: Little, Brown, 1967, 276 p.
Convinced that a time of famines lies ahead and that the United States will be the only major source of free grain, the authors combine their agricultural and diplomatic experience to propose guidelines for American decisions as to who shall starve and who be fed, and add some thoughts as to how this plight may be turned into a "catalyst for American greatness."

Papi, Ugo and Nunn, Charles, eds. **Economic Problems of Agriculture in Industrial Societies.** New York: St. Martin's Press, 1969, 671 p.
These papers were originally presented at a conference of the International Economic Association.

Pirie, Norman W. **Food Resources: Conventional and Novel.** Baltimore: Penguin, 1969, 208 p.
The author argues for increased food production.

Rowe, John Wilkinson Foster. **The World's Coffee.** London: H.M.S.O., 1963, 200 p.
These studies of the coffee industries of Brazil, Colombia, Costa Rica, Kenya, Tanganyika and Uganda are the outcome of a survey initiated by the Colonial Research Committee appointed by the British Secretary of the State for the Colonies.

Schultz, Theodore William. **Economic Crises in World Agriculture.** Ann Arbor: University of Michigan Press, 1965, 114 p.

A senior agricultural economist argues that increasing production in underdeveloped countries is not a matter of using existing resources better but of providing new imputs with high returns.

Stakman, Elvin Charles and Others. **Campaigns Against Hunger.** Cambridge: Harvard University Press, 1967, 328 p.

A history of the Rockefeller Foundation's work on increasing food production begun in Mexico in the 1940's and now extended to other countries.

Tuma, Elias H. **Twenty-Six Centuries of Agrarian Reform.** Berkeley: University of California Press, 1965, 309 p.

A study of land-reform movements from the Greeks to the present. At the end the author suggests some elements for a general theory of agrarian reform. On the whole he is not very sanguine about the efficacy of reform attempts.

Warriner, Doreen. **Land Reform in Principle and Practice.** New York: Oxford University Press, 1969, 457 p.

A leading student of land reform deals with the basic problems of this complicated subject and analyzes the experience of a number of countries.

Weitz, Raanan. **From Peasant to Farmer: A Revolutionary Strategy for Development.** New York: Columbia University Press, 1971, 292 p.

An Israeli specialist stresses people, organization, community-building and coöperation as elements in making agriculture a key to development.

RAW MATERIALS; OIL; ENERGY

See also General Geography and Environment, p. 45; Population Problems, p. 47; General Economic Conditions and Tendencies, p. 49; Foreign Investment and Overseas Business; Multinational Corporations, p. 65; (International Law) Miscellaneous, p. 94; (War) Nuclear Weapons and Missiles, p. 115; and the sections for specific countries and regions.

Acosta Hermoso, Eduardo. **Análisis histórico de la O.P.E.P.** Mérida: Universidad de los Andes, Facultad de Economía, 1969, 129 p.

A history of the Organization of Petroleum Exporting Countries from its creation in 1960 to its third conference in Tehran.

Adelman, Morris Albert. **The World Petroleum Market.** Baltimore: Johns Hopkins University Press (for Resources for the Future), 1972, 438 p.

Professor Adelman of MIT, one of the leading academic experts on the oil industry, has long examined the intricacies of prices, costs, taxes and the structure of the market. His conclusions are not those of the American oil industry and at key points they challenge the widely held view that there is an energy crisis.

Clawson, Marion, *ed.* **Natural Resources and International Development.** Baltimore: Johns Hopkins Press (for Resources for the Future), 1964, 462 p.

A collection of ten essays resulting from the 1963 Resources for the Future Forum on natural resources and world-wide economic growth.

Darmstadter, Joel and Others. **Energy in the World Economy: A Statistical Review of Trends in Output, Trade, and Consumption Since 1925.** Baltimore: Johns Hopkins Press (for Resources for the Future), 1972, 876 p.

An impressive collection of statistics plus an interpretive essay by a senior research associate of Resources for the Future.

Friedensburg, Ferdinand. **Die Bergwirtschaft der Erde: Bodenschätze, Bergbau und Mineralienversorgung der einzelnen Länder.** Stuttgart: Enke, 6th rev. ed., 1965, 566 p.

A completely revised edition of a useful reference work on the world's mining and mineral resources.

Guyol, N. B. **The World Electric Power Industry.** Berkeley: University of California Press, 1969, 366 p.

Statistics and description for a large number of countries.

Lutfi, Ashraf. **OPEC Oil.** Beirut: Middle East Research and Publishing Center, 1968, 120 p.
   A former Secretary General of the Organization of Petroleum Exporting Countries speaks bluntly on many of the problems of the oil producing countries.

Manners, Gerald. **The Changing World Market for Iron Ore, 1950-1980.** Baltimore: Johns Hopkins Press (for Resources for the Future), 1971, 384 p.
   Growth, technological change and politics are all taken into account in this valuable addition to Resources for the Future's series of commodity studies.

Mikdashi, Zuhayr and Others, *eds.* **Continuity and Change in the World Oil Industry.** Beirut: Middle East Research and Publishing Center, 1970, 233 p.
   Papers from a seminar at American University, Beirut.

Odell, Peter R. **An Economic Geography of Oil.** New York: Praeger, 1964, 219 p.
   A study of the world's oil supply, demand, refining, transport and distribution.

Odell, Peter R. **Oil and World Power: A Geographical Interpretation.** New York: Taplinger, 1971, 188 p.
   An informative survey.

Penrose, Edith T. **The Large International Firm in Developing Countries: The International Petroleum Industry.** London: Allen and Unwin, 1968, 311 p.
   A clearly stated and well-argued study of the post-World War II changes in the petroleum industry.

Rachkov, Boris Vasil'evich. **Neft' i mirovaia politika.** Moscow: Izd-vo "Mezhdunarodnye Otnosheniia," 1972, 272 p.
   A discussion of oil and world politics from a Soviet perspective.

Rouhani, Fuad. **A History of O.P.E.C.** New York: Praeger, 1971, 281 p.
   A study of the establishment, structure and functions of the Organization of Petroleum Exporting Countries—up to the successful negotiations with the major oil companies in 1971.

Tanzer, Michael. **The Political Economy of International Oil and the Underdeveloped Countries.** Boston: Beacon Press, 1969, 435 p.
   The author, a Harvard trained economist, examines the major forces determining the international oil trade, especially as they affect the underdeveloped countries: international corporations, Western governments, the Soviet Union, oil-exporting countries and international organizations.

Tomashpol'skii, Leonid Markovich. **Neft' i gaz v mirovom energeticheskom balanse (1900-2000 gg.).** Moscow: Izd-vo "Nedra," 1968, 263 p.
   A Soviet author examines problems of energy supply that may confront socialist, capitalist and developing states in the next decades.

Tumiati, Peter. **Il petrolio e gli arabi.** Milan: Longanesi, 1971, 190 p.
   A study which uncovers the obvious: the world is growing increasingly dependent on Arab oil.

Willrich, Mason. **Global Politics of Nuclear Energy.** New York: Praeger, 1971, 204 p.
   An inquiry into the implications for the world community of the advances in nuclear energy and technology for non-military purposes in the 1970s.

ECONOMIC GROWTH AND DEVELOPMENT

See also (General Works) General Treatments, p. 7; Communism, p. 26; Problems of New Nations, p. 36; Society and Social Psychology, p. 39; Population Problems, p. 47; Economic Theory, p. 53; International Trade, p. 55; International Finance, p. 59; Food and Agriculture, p. 68; Underdeveloped Economies, p. 78; Economic Aid and Technical Assistance, p. 81; United Nations, p. 99; (The Postwar World) General, p. 178; (The United States) Aid and Assistance, p. 254; and the sections for specific countries and regions.

Adelman, Irma and Morris, Cynthia Taft. **Society, Politics and Economic Development.** Baltimore: Johns Hopkins Press, 1967, 307 p.
   This careful quantitative work produces not novelty but support for some widely-held views on the relation between economic and political development.

Adler, John H., *ed.* **International Development, 1968: Accomplishments and Apprehensions.** Dobbs Ferry (N.Y.): Oceana Publications, 1969, 351 p.
Rich material on a wide range of subjects by many first-rate people. (The Proceedings of the Society for International Development's Tenth Anniversary World Conference.)

Alexander-Frutschi, Marian Crites, *ed.* **Human Resources and Economic Growth.** Menlo Park (Calif.): Stanford Research Institute, 1963, 398 p.
An extensive, annotated bibliography of the increasing body of literature dealing with education and training in support of economic and social development.

Alpert, Paul. **Economic Development: Objectives and Methods.** New York: Free Press of Glencoe, 1963, 308 p.
An introduction, with theoretical background, to the problems facing underdeveloped countries.

Bairoch, Paul. **Diagnostic de l'évolution économique du tiers-monde 1900–1966.** Paris: Gauthier-Villars, 1967, 228 p.
This rather daring effort to treat the less developed countries as a whole produces some interesting statistics and suggestive ideas.

Bangs, Robert B. **Financing Economic Development: Fiscal Policy for Emerging Countries.** Chicago: University of Chicago Press, 1968, 212 p.
A U.S. government economist with experience in less developed countries discusses tax and spending policies to promote growth under different conditions.

Basch, Antonín. **Financing Economic Development.** New York: Macmillan, 1964, 334 p.

──. **A Pragmatic Approach to Economic Development.** New York: Vantage Press, 1970, 247 p.
A long-time official of the World Bank analyzes the accomplishments and problems connected with economic development.

Bauer, Pèter Tamàs. **Dissent on Development.** Cambridge: Harvard University Press, 1972, 550 p.
A collection of essays by a champion of liberalism and the market who has long been a sharp critic of planning, foreign aid and other major development orthodoxies.

Berrill, Kenneth, *ed.* **Economic Development, with Special Reference to East Asia.** New York: St. Martin's Press, 1964, 434 p.
Papers submitted at the International Economic Association meeting held at Gamagori, Japan, together with summaries of discussions by economists specializing in growth and development in East Asia. Emphasis is on Japan and India.

Birmingham, Walter Barr and Ford, Alec George, *eds.* **Planning and Growth in Rich and Poor Countries.** New York: Praeger, 1966, 267 p.
Studies of Britain, India, Ghana, Sierra Leone and New Zealand lead to the conclusion that "economic growth is far too important . . . to be left to" decentralized decisions and markets.

Boserup, Ester. **Woman's Role in Economic Development.** New York: St. Martin's Press, 1970, 283 p.
The first large comparative study of what economic development does to women and how they affect it. The author is an experienced Danish economist.

Bryce, Murray D. **Policies and Methods for Industrial Development.** New York: McGraw-Hill, 1965, 309 p.
A very practical book by an experienced Canadian on how to discover the best possibilities for industrial development.

Chenery, Hollis B. and Others, *eds.* **Studies in Development Planning.** Cambridge: Harvard University Press (for the Center for International Affairs), 1971, 422 p.
This collection of articles reflects the important work done by the Project for Quantitative Research in Economic Development at Harvard.

Currie, Lauchlin Bernard. **Accelerating Development: The Necessity and the Means.** New York: McGraw-Hill, 1966, 255 p.
Mr. Currie, a former leading New Deal economist, has quite clear ideas about how to overcome the under-utilization of resources that is the nub of underdevelopment. He rejects, often pithily, some of the orthodoxies of development economics.

Currie, Lauchlin Bernard. **Obstacles to Development.** East Lansing: Michigan State University Press, 1968, 139 p.
Papers on social and political factors that interfere with economic development.

Denison, Edward Fulton with Poullier, Jean-Pierre. **Why Growth Rates Differ: Postwar Experience in Nine Western Countries.** Washington: Brookings Institution, 1967, 494 p.
Mr. Denison looks separately at a number of sources of growth in eight European countries. That most of them grew faster than the United States between 1950 and 1962 was not the result of superior policies, he concludes, but of different circumstances and opportunities.

Economic Development Issues: Greece, Israel, Taiwan, and Thailand. New York: Praeger, (for the Committee for Economic Development), 1968, 215 p.
Thoughtful, critical case studies helpful in understanding the role of aid and investment in growth.

Enke, Stephen. **Economics for Development.** Englewood Cliffs: Prentice-Hall, 1963, 616 p.
Intended as a text, this book stresses the role of private initiative.

Falkowski, Mieczyslow. **Les Problèmes de la croissance du tiers monde vus par les économistes des pays socialistes.** Paris: Payot, 1968, 221 p.
A survey by a Polish economist of what the economists in the Soviet bloc countries think about economic development in the Third World.

Forrester, Jay W. **World Dynamics.** Cambridge: Wright-Allen Press, 1971, 142 p.
The predecessor of the Meadows study "The Limits to Growth"; more detailed in some respects, but less refined in others.

Furtado, Celso. **Development and Underdevelopment.** Berkeley: University of California Press, 1964, 181 p.
Drawing on classical, Keynesian and Marxian economics and his own experience of the underdeveloped world, a leading Brazilian economist sets out his views on some major problems of growth. The book first appeared in Brazil as "Desenvolvimento e subdesenvolvimento" (Rio de Janeiro: Editóra Fundo de Cultura, 1961, 288 p.).

Furtado, Celso. **Théorie du développement économique.** Paris: Presses Universitaires, 1970, 264 p.
The views of a leading Brazilian economist on major controversies about economic development. The original appeared as "Teoria e política do desenvolvimento econômico" (São Paulo: Companhia Editóra Nacional, 1967, 262 p.).

Ginzberg, Eli. **Manpower for Development.** New York: Praeger, 1971, 331 p.
A rich volume discussing significant aspects of development.

Goulet, Denis. **The Cruel Choice: A New Concept in the Theory of Development.** New York: Atheneum, 1971, 362 p.
A discussion of the ethics of development.

Guernier, Maurice. **La Dernière chance du tiers monde.** Paris: Laffont, 1968, 339 p.
Eloquent plea by a former French official for a global development strategy emphasizing common markets, education, self-help and unpolitical multilateral aid.

Haan, Roelf L. **Special Drawing Rights and Development.** Leyden: Stenfert Kroese, 1971, 184 p.
A discussion of many arguments leads to the conclusion that all future SDRs should be assigned initially to international agencies financing development.

Hagen, Everett Einar, *ed.* **Planning Economic Development.** Homewood (Ill.): Irwin, 1963, 380 p.
Case studies of various types of economic planning as practiced in Burma, Pakistan, India, Japan, Mexico, Jugoslavia, Iran, Nigeria, and Great Britain.

Hallowell, John Hamilton, *ed.* **Development: For What?** Durham: Duke University Press (for the Lilly Endowment Research Program in Christianity and Politics), 1964, 241 p.
Papers on political, economic and religious implications of development.

Harbison, Frederick Harris and Myers, Charles Andrew. **Education, Manpower, and Economic Growth: Strategies of Human Resource Development.** New York: McGraw-Hill, 1964, 229 p.

———. **Manpower and Education.** New York: McGraw-Hill, 1965, 343 p.
Major studies attempting to define the manpower needs of countries in different stages of development and the requisite priorities for education and training.

Heilbroner, Robert Louis. **The Great Ascent: The Struggle for Economic Development in our Time.** New York: Harper and Row, 1963, 189 p.
The author tackles some of the formidable objective and subjective programs involved in the effort of underdeveloped nations to achieve self-sustaining economic development.

Hicks, Ursula Kathleen (Webb). **Development Finance: Planning and Control.** New York: Oxford University Press, 1965, 187 p.
A straightforward and systematic discussion of development finance based on the author's experience in advising governments of developing countries.

Higgins, Benjamin. **Economic Development: Principles, Problems, and Policies.** New York: Norton, rev. ed., 1968, 918 p.
A considerably revised edition of one of the most comprehensive books in the field. (First published in 1959.)

Hirschman, Albert O. **Development Projects Observed.** Washington: Brookings Institution, 1967, 197 p.
A major contribution, based on first-hand experience, by an authority on the subject.

Hodder, Bramwell William. **Economic Development in the Tropics.** London: Methuen, 1968, 258 p.
At the end, the author remarks that "to write about 'tropical' as quite distinct from any other kind of development is impossible." Rejecting the idea that one can generalize about the tropics, he sees no greater obstacles to development there than elsewhere.

Hunt, Chester Leigh. **Social Aspects of Economic Development.** New York: McGraw-Hill, 1966, 255 p.
A study of the social factors that are influencing the rate of economic growth in developing countries. The author is a professor at Western Michigan University.

Hunter, Guy. **Modernizing Peasant Societies: A Comparative Study in Asia and Africa.** New York: Oxford University Press (for the Institute of Race Relations), 1969, 324 p.
An interesting study of pitfalls to be avoided when developing countries at different stages of development and with different cultural backgrounds attempt to borrow ideas, institutions and technology from developed countries.

Jacoby, Erich H. with Jacoby, Charlotte F. **Man and Land: The Essential Revolution.** New York: Knopf, 1971, 400 p.
A refreshingly pragmatic study of land reform in developing countries, concluding with a set of sensible recommendations.

Johnson, Edgar Augustus Jerome. **The Organization of Space in Developing Countries.** Cambridge: Harvard University Press, 1970, 452 p.
A many-sided analysis of a complex of issues that have quite a bit to do with the quality of life in poor countries.

Jones, Graham. **The Role of Science and Technology in Developing Countries.** New York: Oxford University Press (for the International Council of Scientific Unions), 1971, 174 p.
A fine and objective assessment of the ways in which modern science and technology can help to promote social and economic growth in poor but developing countries. The author's broad conclusion is that aid and trade may be more helpful than research.

Kindleberger, Charles P. **Economic Growth in France and Britain, 1851-1950.** Cambridge: Harvard University Press, 1964, 378 p.
A well-known economist refutes most of the explanations that have been advanced for the differences in economic growth between Britain and France.

Kindleberger, Charles P. **Europe's Postwar Growth: The Role of Labor Supply.** Cambridge: Harvard University Press, 1967, 270 p.
With his customary perception and vigor, the author presses the case for attributing much of the rapid growth in postwar Europe to a plentiful supply of labor. He discusses the implications of the end of "supergrowth" and tells about the migration of labor within Europe.

King, John A., Jr. **Economic Development Projects and Their Appraisal: Cases and Principles from the Experience of the World Bank.** Baltimore: Johns Hopkins Press (for the Economic Development Institute, International Bank for Reconstruction and Development), 1967, 530 p.
Thirty cases chosen to show how the World Bank analyzes its economic development projects.

Kuznets, Simon Smith. **Economic Growth of Nations: Total Output and Production Structure.** Cambridge: Belknap Press of Harvard University Press, 1971, 363 p.
The Nobel Prize winner presents some of the major results of a massive inquiry into the increase in production in the industrial nations since the nineteenth century.

Kuznets, Simon Smith. **Modern Economic Growth: Rate, Structure, and Spread.** New Haven: Yale University Press, 1966, 529 p.
A basic examination of what is known about growth in non-communist developed countries, with briefer consideration of the position of less developed countries.

Kuznets, Simon Smith. **Postwar Economic Growth.** Cambridge: Harvard University Press, 1964, 148 p.
These lectures by a leading authority are the results of a vast amount of work.

Lewis, Sir William Arthur. **Development Planning: The Essentials of Economic Policy.** New York: Harper and Row, 1966, 278 p.
A remarkable *tour de force* explaining with great clarity the steps in making a national economic plan.

Lewis, Sir William Arthur, ed. **Tropical Development 1880-1913.** Evanston: Northwestern University Press, 1971, 346 p.
A leading authority on development, and some of his students, demonstrate how the growth of demand for tropical products in the late nineteenth century brought significant growth to a number of countries in Asia, Africa and Latin America.

Lundberg, Erik. **Instability and Economic Growth.** New Haven: Yale University Press, 1968, 433 p.
A well-known Swedish economist buttresses a general treatment of economic instability in the inter-war and postwar periods and its relation to growth with chapters on Britain, Sweden, the Netherlands, Japan and relations between Canada and the United States.

MacBean, Alasdair I. **Export Instability and Economic Development.** Cambridge: Harvard University Press, 1967, 367 p.
For a long time it has been generally accepted that countries producing primary products are more vulnerable to short-term market fluctuations than industrial countries and that this fact jeopardizes their chances of development. MacBean's extensive statistical analysis shows the error of these views. An important book.

Madan, Balkrishna. **Aspects of Economic Development and Policy.** Bombay: Allied Publishers, 1964, 363 p.
Essays by an economist instrumental in the formulation of India's monetary and economic issues.

Maddison, Angus. **Economic Growth in Japan and the USSR.** New York: Norton, 1969, 174 p.
Good historical sketches, condensed data and reasonable explanations by a well-known scholar.

Maddison, Angus. **Economic Growth in the West: Comparative Experience in Europe and North America.** New York: Twentieth Century Fund, 1964, 246 p.
In seeking explanations for growth, and particularly for differences in national growth rates, Mr. Maddison sets forth analyses and arguments with a clarity that helps define the issues whether one agrees with his conclusions or not.

Maddison, Angus. **Economic Progress and Policy in Developing Countries.** New York: Norton, 1971, 313 p.
In this study the author argues that not only the economic conditions in the poor countries have improved, but that also a better understanding of their problems has been gained.

Markham, Jesse W. and Papanek, Gustav F., *eds.* **Industrial Organization and Economic Development: In Honor of E. S. Mason.** Boston: Houghton, 1970, 422 p.
Since Edward S. Mason of Harvard taught so many excellent economists, it is not

surprising that this book should be a great deal more interesting than the usual *Festschrift*. About half the pieces deal with international issues.

Meadows, Donella H. and Others. **The Limits to Growth.** New York: Universe Books, 1972, 205 p.
A pessimistic survey of "the present growth trends in world population, industrialization, pollution, food production, and resource depletion." Prepared as a report for the Club of Rome's Project on the Predicament of Mankind.

Meier, Richard L. **Developmental Planning.** New York: McGraw-Hill, 1965, 420 p.
Education, administration and social factors rather than economics are at the center of this analysis.

Montgomery, John Dickey and Siffin, William J., *eds.* **Approaches to Development: Politics, Administration, and Change.** New York: McGraw-Hill, 1966, 299 p.
An examination of public administration as an instrument for achieving political and economic goals in developing countries, based on seminars at Indiana University.

Oser, Jacob. **Promoting Economic Development: With Illustrations from Kenya.** Evanston: Northwestern University Press, 1967, 242 p.
Professor Oser combines an interesting discussion of the theoretical issues of economic growth with a critical account of development policies in Kenya.

Papanek, Gustav F., *ed.* **Development Policy—Theory and Practice.** Cambridge: Harvard University Press, 1968, 367 p.
Ten papers evaluating development experience in Argentina, Colombia, Liberia and Pakistan, prepared under the auspices of the Center for International Affairs, Harvard University.

Phillips, Hiram S. **Guide for Development: Institution-Building and Reform.** New York: Praeger, 1969, 282 p.
An experienced aid official provides "a practical guide" for those trying to create institutions that will bring about development and reform. Several case studies.

Powelson, John P. **Institutions of Economic Growth: A Theory of Conflict Management in Developing Countries.** Princeton: Princeton University Press, 1972, 281 p.
An ingenious effort to construct a theory of institutions for economic growth that takes account of conflicting interests, administrative capacity, quasi-rational behavior and the need for consensus.

Ranis, Gustav, *ed.* **Government and Economic Development.** New Haven: Yale University Press, 1971, 567 p.
The experience of many countries is used to throw light on a key controversy: the proper role of government in development.

Rao, Vijendra Kasturi Ranga Varadaraja. **Essays in Economic Development.** New York: Asia Publishing House, 1964, 333 p.
A dozen major papers by a leading Indian economist. Theory largely takes second place to application and the discussion of policy.

Riggs, Fred Warren, *ed.* **Frontiers of Development Administration.** Durham: Duke University Press, 1971, 623 p.
A number of scholarly essays on development policy and bureaucracy in various political settings.

Robinson, Edward Austin Gossage, *ed.* **Problems in Economic Development: Proceedings of a Conference Held by the International Economic Association.** New York: St. Martin's Press, 1965, 625 p.
An impressive array of economists from all over the world contribute papers on many major issues of economic development, as well as on some very special subjects.

Robinson, Ronald, *ed.* **Developing the Third World: The Experience of the Nineteen-Sixties.** New York: Cambridge University Press, 1971, 289 p.
Since the editor thought that "there is little hope of success if economists can talk only to economists and administrators will talk only with God," he invited a group of practitioners and scholars to review their experience with development problems in the Third World.

Rosenstein-Rodan, P. N., *ed.* **Capital Formation and Economic Development.** Cambridge: M.I.T. Press, 1964, 164 p.
Technical papers based on Indian experience.

Rostow, Walt Whitman, *ed.* **The Economics of Take-off into Sustained Growth.** New York: St. Martin's Press, 1963, 481 p.

Walt Rostow's idea of a "take-off" in economic development has rapidly passed into common use, but the specialists have been skeptical. In this important volume, papers by leading authorities are followed by a long summary of ten days' discussion. In his own paper and in answering the critics, Rostow restates his views with some refinements and elaboration.

Rubin, Seymour J. **The Conscience of the Rich Nations: The Development Assistance Committee and the Common Aid Effort.** New York: Harper and Row (for the Council on Foreign Relations), 1966, 164 p.

This volume is directed to the problem of the widening gap between rich and poor nations and of ways to meet it. The author was from 1962 to 1964 U.S. Representative on the Development Assistance Committee, the central agency discussed.

Sachs, Ignacy, *ed.* **Studies in Developing Countries.** Warsaw: Polish Scientific Publishers, 1964–67, 3 v.

Polish-sponsored symposia, with contributions primarily by economists from underdeveloped countries. The volumes are entitled: vol. 1, "Planning and Economic Development" (1964, 259 p.); vol. 2, "Agriculture, Land Reforms and Economic Development" (1964, 284 p.); and vol. 3, "Obstacles to Growth: Demographic, Economic, and Social" (1967, 199 p.).

Sametz, Arnold W., *ed.* **Financial Development and Economic Growth: The Economic Consequences of Underdeveloped Capital Markets.** New York: New York University Press, 1972, 257 p.

Essays comparing the experience of rich and poor, market and Socialist countries that seem to show that growth is compatible with very different degrees of control over capital markets.

Schickele, Rainer. **Agrarian Revolution and Economic Progress.** New York: Praeger (in coöperation with the Agricultural Development Council), 1968, 410 p.

An American economist with great experience in less developed countries labels as "a primer" what is in fact a thoughtful and far more rounded and reflective book than most studies of agricultural development.

Scitovsky, Tibor. **Papers on Welfare and Growth.** Stanford: Stanford University Press, 1964, 274 p.

Collected papers by the Hungarian-born economist at Stanford University.

Shaffer, Harry G. and Prybyla, Jan S., *eds.* **From Underdevelopment to Affluence: Western, Soviet, and Chinese Views.** New York: Appleton, 1968, 441 p.

This collection of readings on development includes much Russian and Chinese material.

Singer, Hans Wolfgang. **International Development: Growth and Change.** New York: McGraw-Hill, 1964, 295 p.

A U.N. official examines major theoretical and practical problems of development and includes a number of papers on Africa and Northeast Brazil.

Skorov, G. E. **Razvivaiushchiesia strany: obrazovanie, zaniatost', ekonomicheskii rost.** Moscow: Izdatel'stvo "Nauka," 1971, 366 p.

A Soviet work on the place of education in economic development.

Solo, Robert A. and Rogers, Everett M. **Inducing Technological Change for Economic Growth and Development.** Lansing: Michigan State University Press, 1972, 238 p.

A solid collection of papers.

Southworth, Herman M. and Johnston, Bruce F., *eds.* **Agricultural Development and Economic Growth.** Ithaca: Cornell University Press, 1967, 608 p.

Thoroughgoing and authoritative analyses.

Spindler, Joachim von. **Das wirtschaftliche Wachstum der Entwicklungsländer.** Stuttgart: Kohlhammer, 1963, 304 p.

A survey of economic growth problems of the developing countries by a former German financial adviser to the government of Malaya.

Streeten, Paul. **The Frontiers of Development Studies.** New York: Halsted/Wiley, 1972, 498 p.

A collection of stimulating essays by an author who has long chided Western economists for their failure to take adequate account of differences in societies and cultures.

Theberge, James D., ed. **Economics of Trade and Development.** New York: Wiley, 1968, 545 p.
Well-selected readings.

Vanek, Jaroslav with Bilsborrow, Richard. **Estimating Foreign Resource Needs for Economic Development: Theory, Method, and a Case Study of Colombia.** New York: McGraw-Hill, 1967, 180 p.
The author's purpose is "to explore, both in theory and in practice, the interdependence between economic development and the requirements of foreign resources called for by that development."

Ward, Barbara (Lady Jackson). **The Lopsided World.** New York: Norton, 1968, 126 p.
These 1965 Christian A. Herter Lectures are essentially a sequel to the author's "The Rich Nations and the Poor Nations" (New York: Norton, 1962, 159 p.).

Ward, Barbara (Lady Jackson) and Others, eds. **The Widening Gap: Development in the 1970's.** New York: Columbia University Press, 1971, 372 p.
Out of a mountain of paper generated for a major conference, the editors have fashioned a readable book in which a number of authorities delineate the major issues and their conflicting views on what should be done.

Wilson, George W. and Others. **The Impact of Highway Investment on Development.** Washington: Brookings Institution, 1966, 226 p.
Focused largely on Bolivia, Guatemala and El Salvador, these thoughtful—and sobering—case studies examine the role which highway systems have played in the economy of an underdeveloped country.

Zebot, Cyril Anthony. **The Economics of Competitive Coexistence: Convergence through Growth.** New York: Praeger, 1964, 262 p.
To achieve satisfactory economic growth the underdeveloped countries must improve their human resources, the communist countries must give consumers and managers a greater share in decisions, and the West must check inflation by more understanding between labor and capital.

Zolōtas, Xenophōn Euthymiou. **Monetary Equilibrium and Economic Development: With Special Reference to the Experience of Greece, 1950-1963.** Princeton: Princeton University Press, 1965, 223 p.
A Greek economist combines a study of his country's postwar experience with a contribution to the more general problem of the interplay of stable money and economic growth.

UNDERDEVELOPED ECONOMIES

See also (Political Factors) General, p. 12; Problems of New Nations, p. 36; Society and Social Psychology, p. 39; Population Problems, p. 47; General Economic Conditions and Tendencies, p. 49; International Trade, p. 55; International Finance, p. 59; Foreign Investment and Overseas Business; Multinational Corporations, p. 65; Food and Agriculture, p. 68; Raw Materials; Oil; Energy, p. 70; Economic Growth and Development, p. 71; Economic Aid and Technical Assistance, p. 81; United Nations, p. 99; and the sections for specific countries and regions.

Abellan, Victoria, ed. **Las N.U. y el tercer mundo.** Barcelona: Ediciones Japizua (for the Departamento de Derecho Internacional de la Universidad de Barcelona), 1971, 661 p.
This University of Barcelona's comprehensive but rather prosaic volume on development problems is of interest primarily as a sampling of Spanish thought in the field.

Bachmann, Hans. **The External Relations of Less-Developed Countries.** New York: Praeger, 1968, 341 p.
A Swiss economist has been remarkably successful in making this "manual of economic policies" for people in less developed countries not just a training tool but a ready reference that tells not only what issues are important but how they need to be thought about.

Balassa, Bela A. **Trade Prospects for Developing Countries.** Homewood (Ill.): Irwin, 1964, 450 p.
A set of statistical projections of export possibilities of the less developed countries, with some comment on the results.

Bandera, Vladimir Nicholas. **Foreign Capital as an Instrument of National Economic Policy.** The Hague: Nijhoff, 1964, 155 p.
An effort to bring East European experience between the wars to bear on problems of underdeveloped countries.

Baranson, Jack. **Industrial Technologies for Developing Economies.** New York: Praeger, 1969, 168 p.
Interesting discussion by a World Bank official of the problems of determining the technologies best suited to different developing countries, the obstacles to their use and the ways of fostering improvement.

Beckford, George L. **Persistent Poverty.** New York: Oxford University Press, 1972, 303 p.
A Jamaican economist presents "a genuinely Third World perspective" on plantation economics and the resulting persistance of underdevelopment.

Behrendt, Richard Fritz Walter. **Soziale Strategie für Entwicklungsländer.** Frankfurt/Main: S. Fischer, 1965, 639 p.
The author, with many years' experience in Latin America, summarizes his views on the social processes of the developing countries and on ways to deal with them.

Bhagwati, Jagdish N. **The Economics of Underdeveloped Countries.** New York: McGraw-Hill, 1966, 254 p.
A well-presented introduction. Many charts and tables.

Bryant, John. **Health and the Developing World.** Ithaca: Cornell University Press, 1970, 345 p.
A physician's diagnosis of the "vast gap that exists between biomedical knowledge and our capability for bringing this knowledge within effective reach of the world's people." The author's prescriptions seem persuasive and realistic.

Dell, Sidney Samuel. **Trade Blocs and Common Markets.** New York: Knopf, 1963, 384 p.
An English economist argues for the formation of economic blocs among the underdeveloped countries.

Desai, A. R., *ed.* **Essays on Modernization of Underdeveloped Societies.** New York: Humanities Press, 1972, 2 v.
To celebrate its 50th anniversary, the Department of Sociology of the University of Bombay invited an extraordinary number of specialists to write on a wide variety of subjects.

Firth, Raymond William and Yamey, B. S., *eds.* **Capital, Saving and Credit in Peasant Societies: Studies from Asia, Oceania, the Caribbean and Middle America.** Chicago: Aldine Publishing Co., 1964, 400 p.
Solid studies trying to link anthropology and economics.

Frank, Charles R., Jr.; Bhagwati, Jagdish N.; Shaw, Robert d'A. and Malmgren, Harald B. **Assisting Developing Countries: Problems of Debts, Burden-Sharing, Jobs, and Trade.** New York: Praeger (in coöperation with the Overseas Development Council), 1972, 482 p.
Four first-rate studies previously published as pamphlets.

Fritsch, Bruno, *ed.* **Entwicklungsländer.** Cologne: Kiepenheuer, 1968, 460 p.
A collection of papers on development economics.

Gabriel, Peter Paul. **The International Transfer of Corporate Skills: Management Contracts in Less Developed Countries.** Boston: Harvard University, Division of Research, Graduate School of Business Administration, 1967, 230 p.
A favorable view of management contracts as an alternative to direct investment as a means for getting know-how and technology into less developed countries.

Ghaussy, Abdul Ghanie. **Das Genossenschaftswesen in den Entwicklungsländern.** Breisgau: Rombach, 1964, 341 p.
A German-educated Afghan surveys the place of coöperatives in underdeveloped countries.

Haller, Albert von. **Die Letzten wollen die Ersten sein: der Westen und die Revolution der farbigen Völker.** Düsseldorf: Econ-Verlag, 1963, 297 p.
A realistic appraisal of the aspirations of the people in developing countries and of the ways in which the West can most effectively provide help.

Hla Myint, U. **The Economics of the Developing Countries.** New York: Praeger, 1965, 192 p.

——. **Economic Theory and the Underdeveloped Countries.** New York: Oxford University Press, 1971, 353 p.

Substantial discussions of the basic issues faced by the developing countries, by a well-known Burmese economist.

Krivine, David, *ed.* **Fiscal and Monetary Problems in Developing States: Proceedings of the Third Rehovoth Conference.** New York: Praeger, 1967, 404 p.

Solid studies by authorities from all over the world.

Lebret, Louis Joseph. **The Last Revolution: The Destiny of Over- and Underdeveloped Nations.** New York: Sheed, 1965, 213 p.

A French Dominican who has influenced development planning in a number of countries denounces the Western world for unconcern, materialism and betrayal of its own values. Originally published in France as "Le Drame du siècle: misère, sous-développement, inconscience, espoir" (Paris: Éditions Ouvrières, 1960, 190 p.).

Lerner, Daniel and Schramm, Wilbur Lang, *eds.* **Communication and Change in the Developing Countries.** Honolulu: East-West Center Press, 1967, 333 p.

A useful though uneven symposium of eighteen essays growing out of a conference held at the East-West Center in 1964.

Meier, Gerald Marvin. **Leading Issues in Development Economics.** New York: Oxford University Press, 2d ed., 1970, 758 p.

This considerably revised and expanded edition of readings, with commentary by the author, "is more concerned with the strategic policy problems that experience has revealed to be especially pressing in many of the less-developed countries."

Mountjoy, Alan B. **Industrialization and Underdeveloped Countries.** Chicago: Aldine Publishing Co., 2d rev. ed., 1967, 200 p.

An economic geographer discusses the problems faced by developing nations on the road to industrialization.

Paddock, William and Paddock, Paul. **Hungry Nations.** Boston: Little, Brown, 1964, 344 p.

An agricultural expert and his brother, formerly in the U.S. Foreign Service, pool their experiences to say what is wrong about economic development and how to put it right: more stress on agriculture, more research to find what is best suited to each place, fewer dreams of industry and less emphasis on political prestige.

Perroy, Henri. **L'Europe devant le tiers monde.** Paris: Aubier-Montaigne, 1971, 320 p.

A discussion by a French scholar and publicist of West European relations with the underdeveloped countries, with gloomy prognostications for the latter's economic future.

ReQua, Eloise G. and Statham, Jane. **The Developing Nations: A Guide to Information Sources Concerning Their Economic, Political, Technical and Social Problems.** Detroit: Gale Research Co., 1965, 339 p.

A bibliography covering a wide range of materials in English dealing with underdeveloped areas, the processes of economic development and problems in foreign aid policy.

Robinson, Edward Austin Gossage, *ed.* **Backward Areas in Advanced Countries.** New York: St. Martin's Press, 1969, 474 p.

Papers that provide a useful comparison of experience in a number of capitalist and socialist countries.

Robinson, Richard D. **International Business Policy.** New York: Holt, Rinehart and Winston, 1964, 252 p.

A wide-ranging attempt to explain the difficult position in which foreign businesses often find themselves in underdeveloped countries.

Sachs, Ignacy. **Foreign Trade and Economic Development of Underdeveloped Countries.** New York: Asia Publishing House, 1966, 136 p.

The author of this study, in which the massive burden of backwardness facing the developing countries has been ignored, is a Polish economist. The original was published as "Handel zagraniczny a rozwój gospodarczy" (Warsaw: Państowe Wydawn. Ekonomiczne, 1963, 141 p.).

Staley, Eugene and Morse, Richard McGee. **Modern Small Industry for Developing Countries.** New York: McGraw-Hill, 1965, 435 p.
A thorough study, based on evaluating the experience of India and some other countries.

Wilber, Charles K. **The Soviet Model and Underdeveloped Countries.** Chapel Hill: University of North Carolina Press, 1969, 241 p.
The author constructs a model of economic development which he finds implicit in the Soviet experience and then checks its credentials as a guide for underdeveloped areas. Includes a pertinent look at Soviet Central Asia.

ECONOMIC AID AND TECHNICAL ASSISTANCE

See also Economic Growth and Development, p. 71; Underdeveloped Economies, p. 78; United Nations, p. 99; (The United States) Aid and Assistance, p. 254; and the sections for specific countries and regions.

Arnold, Harry John Philips. **Aid for Development: A Political and Economic Study.** Chester Springs (Pa.): Dufour Editions, 1966, 256 p.
An assessment of American and other aid programs, with emphasis on East-West comparisons. Carries through to 1965 the author's "Aid for Developing Countries" (1962).

Badeau, John Stothoff and Stevens, Georgiana G., *eds*. **Bread from Stones: Fifty Years of Technical Assistance.** Englewood Cliffs: Prentice-Hall, 1966, 133 p.
Twelve essays reflect the experience harvested by the Near East Foundation during its half-century of devotion to technical assistance and rural development overseas.

Bass, Lawrence Wade. **The Management of Technical Programs: With Special Reference to the Needs of Developing Countries.** New York: Praeger, 1965, 138 p.
A detailed and practical guide based on the overseas experience of the Arthur D. Little Company.

Bhagwati, Jagdish N. **Amount and Sharing of Aid.** Washington: Overseas Development Council, 1970, 197 p.
Rich in interesting compilations and original calculations showing who is giving and receiving what.

Boserup, Ester and Sachs, Ignacy, *eds*. **Foreign Aid to Newly Independent Countries. Aide extérieure aux pays récemment indépendants.** The Hague: Mouton, 1971, 184 p.
Boserup (a Dane) and Sachs (a Pole) have coördinated studies by a number of scholars from Eastern and Western Europe that throw light on the ability of poor countries to absorb aid.

Bräker, Hans. **Multilaterale Hilfeleistung für Entwicklungsländer.** Opladen: Westdeutscher Verlag, 1968, 192 p.
A comprehensive survey of the multilateral aid programs for the developing countries administered by the United Nations and other important international organizations.

Cerych, Ladislav. **Problems of Aid to Education in Developing Countries.** New York: Praeger (for the Atlantic Institute), 1965, 213 p.
An effort to analyze the body of experience with respect to educational aid to developing countries—its role at various levels, forms and means, and problems of creating appropriate organizational and institutional frameworks.

Dillon, Wilton. **Gifts and Nations: The Obligation to Give, Receive and Repay.** The Hague: Mouton, 1968, 113 p.
In this original case study drawn from Franco-American relations during the Marshall Plan period, the author suggests that donor nations must find ways to let recipients somehow reciprocate for gifts received or else face a "Gaullist" backlash triggered by wounded self-esteem.

Domergue, Maurice. **Technical Assistance: Theory, Practice, and Policies.** New York: Praeger, 1968, 196 p.
A practical guide by an OECD official.

Esman, Milton Jacob and Cheever, Daniel Sargent. **The Common Aid Effort: The Development Assistance Activities of the Organization for Economic Co-operation and Development.** Columbus: Ohio State University Press, 1967, 421 p.
An economist and a political scientist combine forces in a thorough analysis of the work of the Development Assistance Committee and related OECD and consortia activities.

Friedmann, Wolfgang Gaston; Kalmanoff, George and Meagher, Robert F. **International Financial Aid.** New York: Columbia University Press, 1966, 498 p.
The authors, who conducted a Columbia University Law School study of the giving and receiving of aid, give the gist of reports on the experience of individual countries along with a discussion of programs and an analysis of key policy issues.

Gray, Clive S. **Resource Flows to Less-Developed Countries: Financial Terms and Their Constraints.** New York: Praeger, 1969, 305 p.
How much a developing country gets out of aid depends on the forms in which resources are transferred (grants, hard and soft loans, etc.) and the conditions attached by the countries exporting the capital. This effort to provide quantitative measures is comprehensive, thoughtful and technical.

Hayter, Teresa. **Aid as Imperialism.** Baltimore: Penguin, 1971, 221 p.
The thesis implied in the title is not well argued but there are interesting points about the leverage exercised by the World Bank and other aid agencies in Latin America. The English author, originally helped in her inquiry by World Bank officials, later became a member of the International Marxist Group.

Johnson, Harry Gordon. **Economic Policies toward Less Developed Countries.** Washington: Brookings Institution, 1967, 279 p.
Impressive economic analysis combined with some political assessment leads the author to general and specific policy conclusions favoring commodity agreements that support prices and tariff preferences for manufactured goods.

Keenleyside, Hugh Llewellyn. **International Aid: A Summary, with Special Reference to the Programmes of the United Nations.** New York: James H. Heineman, 1966, 343 p.
The former Director General of Technical Assistance at the United Nations combines a comprehensive and clear summary of what aid is and how it has been given, with some straightforward advice about carrying out the unfinished business.

Legum, Colin, *ed.* **The First U.N. Development Decade and its Lessons for the 1970's.** New York: Praeger (in coöperation with the Vienna Institute for Development), 1970, 312 p.
An Austrian institute inspired by Nehru brought together an interesting group of people from developed and less developed countries of a wide political spectrum; papers plus summaries of discussions.

Little, Ian Malcolm David and Clifford, Juliet Mary. **International Aid: A Discussion of the Flow of Public Resources from Rich to Poor Countries.** Chicago: Aldine Publishing Co., 1966, 302 p.
Comprehensive, balanced and commonsensical, this useful book supports the view that sound economics is apt to be good politics. (The English edition of 1965 has two additional chapters about British aid.).

Mason, Edward Sagendorph. **Foreign Aid and Foreign Policy.** New York: Harper and Row (for the Council on Foreign Relations), 1964, 118 p.
A leading student of aid and development in his Elihu Root lectures at the Council on Foreign Relations gives balanced answers to questions about the relation of foreign aid to foreign policy.

Masson, Paul. **L'Aide bilatérale: assistance, commerce ou stratégie?** Paris: Presses Universitaires, 1967, 332 p.
General reflections built around useful summaries of the aid policies of more than a dozen countries (not including France).

Montgomery, John Dickey. **Foreign Aid in International Politics.** Englewood Cliffs: Prentice-Hall, 1967, 118 p.
A thoughtful essay devoted largely to American aid programs, though some space is given to European, communist and multilateral efforts. The author's conclusions about the future success of American aid programs are cautiously optimistic.

Müller, Kurt. **The Foreign Aid Programs of the Soviet Bloc and Communist China.** New York: Walker, 1967, 331 p.
A translation, with some additional material, of an important survey of the strategy and activities of the Soviet bloc countries in the underdeveloped nations of the world. It contains a very extensive selection of relevant treaties and agreements. The German original was published as "Über Kalkutta nach Paris? Strategie und Aktivität des Ostblocks in den Entwicklungsländern" (Hanover: Verlag für Literatur und Zeitgeschehen, 1964, 584 p.).

Pearson, Lester B. **The Crisis of Development.** New York: Praeger (for the Council on Foreign Relations), 1970, 117 p.
The former Chairman of the Commission on International Development, in this personal synopsis of the Commission's Report, argues for increased aid programs for the developing countries as a matter of enlightened self-interest for the world's wealthy nations.

Pincus, John A. **Economic Aid and International Cost Sharing.** Baltimore: Johns Hopkins Press, 1965, 221 p.
A first-rate study that asks interesting questions about the real cost of aid and the extent to which there are burdens to be shared in trade policy.

Pincus, John A. **Trade, Aid and Development: The Rich and Poor Nations.** New York: McGraw-Hill (for the Council on Foreign Relations), 1967, 400 p.
An imaginative study of the nature of the developed countries' political and economic interest in poor countries and an examination of what classic and contemporary economic theory teaches about trade and development.

Spencer, Daniel L. and Woroniak, Alexander, *eds.* **The Transfer of Technology to Developing Countries.** New York: Praeger, 1967, 209 p.
In this survey the emphasis is more on history, theory and method than on practical experience.

Tansky, Leo. **U.S. and U.S.S.R. Aid to Developing Countries: A Comparative Study of India, Turkey, and the U.A.R.** New York: Praeger, 1967, 192 p.
Interesting comparisons and useful data on Soviet aid occupy relatively small space compared to more general accounts of the three countries' development.

Walters, Robert S. **American and Soviet Aid: A Comparative Analysis.** Pittsburgh: University of Pittsburgh Press, 1970, 299 p.
Point-by-point comparisons of aid-giving practice lead to an emphasis on similarities rather than differences, with the United States having the advantage of wealth.

Weaver, James Hill. **The International Development Association: A New Approach to Foreign Aid.** New York: Praeger, 1965, 268 p.
A clearly written history of the World Bank's "soft loan" affiliate, with some account of its practices.

Weidner, Edward William. **Technical Assistance in Public Administration Overseas: The Case for Development Administration.** Chicago: Public Administration Service, 1964, 247 p.
A description of major American and U.N. programs of technical assistance in public administration and an examination of their disappointing impact, by an author with considerable experience in the field.

VI. INTERNATIONAL LAW

GENERAL

See also (General Works) General Treatments, p. 7; (Political Factors) General, p. 12; International Organization and Government, p. 96; Peace; Disarmament; Arms Control, p. 122; (The World Since 1914) General, p. 129.

Akehurst, Michael. **A Modern Introduction to International Law.** New York: Atherton Press, 1971, 367 p.

A useful survey by a Cambridge trained British scholar, trying "to bridge the gap between international law and international relations."

Annuaire français de droit international. Paris: Centre National de la Recherche Scientifique.
An annual volume of essays, chronology and bibliography dealing with international law, published since 1956.

Black, Cyril E. and Falk, Richard A., eds. **The Future of the International Legal Order.** Princeton: Princeton University Press, 1969–.
The following four of the projected five volumes have been published through 1972: "Vol. I: Trends and Patterns" (1969, 618 p.); "Vol. II: Wealth and Resources" (1970, 343 p.); "Vol. III: Conflict Management" (1971, 413 p.); "Vol IV: The Structure of the International Environment" (1972, 637 p.). Written under the auspices of the Center of International Studies, Princeton University.

Bowett, Derek William. **The Law of International Institutions.** New York: Praeger (for the London Institute of World Affairs), 1963, 347 p.
A textbook on the rapidly expanding branch of international law dealing with international organizations—global, regional and judicial.

Bozeman, Adda B. **The Future of Law in a Multicultural World.** Princeton: Princeton University Press, 1971, 229 p.
A challenging work which argues forcefully that a global legal system which is not authentically based on the multiplicity of cultures that comprise the world can never be recognized as binding or even persuasive.

Briggs, Herbert Whittaker. **The International Law Commission.** Ithaca: Cornell University Press, 1965, 380 p.
A scholarly exposition of the origins, the statute and the procedures and methods of the International Law Commission, the guiding function of which is "the promotion of the progressive development of international law and its codification."

The British Yearbook of International Law. New York: Oxford University Press (for the Royal Institute of International Affairs).
An annual volume of essays and book reviews published since 1920. The volumes since 1962 were edited by Sir Humphrey Waldock and R. Y. Jennings.

The Canadian Yearbook of International Law; Annuaire Canadien de Droit International, 1963–. Vancouver, B.C.: The University of British Columbia (for the Canadian Branch, International Law Association), 1963–.
A substantial collection of articles and book reviews, published annually and edited by C. B. Bourne. Volume IX, covering the year 1971, was published in 1972.

Chayes, Abram; Ehrlich, Thomas and Lowenfeld, Andreas F., comps. **The International Legal Process.** Boston: Little, Brown, 1968–69, 3 v.
According to the authors, "the aim of these materials is to provide a general introduction to the range and reach, the adequacies and failings, of the international legal system." The work will be of particular use to scholars concerned with international economic law.

Chou, Keng-sheng. **Hsien-tai Ying Mei kuo-chi fa ti ssŭ-hsiang tung-hsiang.** Peking: Shih-chieh Chih-shi Ch'u-pan-she, 1963, 71 p.
This booklet is one of the few known Chinese Communist analyses of trends in contemporary Anglo-American thought on international law. Covering sovereignty, international law and related problems, the author adopts a negative stand on the value of world law and world government.

Cohen, Jerome Alan, ed. **China's Practice of International Law: Some Case Studies.** Cambridge: Harvard University Press, 1972, 417 p.
Aspects of Chinese foreign policy involving international law—notably disputes with Russia, Japan and India, as well as cases dealing with foreign diplomats and foreign organizations. Cohen and his collaborators conclude that China's approach to the law, like that of other countries, is pragmatic, not principled.

Coplin, William D. **The Functions of International Law.** Chicago: Rand McNally, 1966, 294 p.
A study that undertakes both to be an introduction to international law and to provide a theoretical framework for its analysis. Contains a useful annex of important conventions and charters.

Dutoit, Bernard. **Coexistence et droit international à la lumière de la doctrine soviétique.** Paris: Pedone, 1966, 179 p.
A review of the changing Soviet concepts of international law.

Elias, Taslim Olawale. **Africa and the Development of International Law.** Dobbs Ferry (N.Y.): Oceana, 1972, 261 p.
A useful study by a professor at the University of Lagos.

En hommage à Paul Guggenheim: recueil d'études de droit international. Geneva: Institut Universitaire de Hautes Études Internationales, 1968, 901 p.
A massive *Festschrift* honoring the Swiss scholar, Paul Guggenheim, containing articles on international law and related topics.

Engel, Salo with Métall, Rudolf A., eds. **Law, State, and International Legal Order.** Knoxville: University of Tennessee Press, 1964, 365 p.
A *Fetschrift* of 28 essays honoring Hans Kelsen.

Erickson, Richard J. **International Law and the Revolutionary State: A Case Study of the Soviet Union and Customary International Law.** Dobbs Ferry (N.Y.): Oceana, 1972, 254 p.
Thorough research into Soviet writings and practice underlies this comprehensive study, the main theme of which is the Soviet Union's general acceptance, with due concern for its ideology and political aims, of much of customary international law.

Falk, Richard A. **Legal Order in a Violent World.** Princeton: Princeton University Press (for the Center of International Studies, Princeton University), 1968, 610 p.
An exploration of international violence from the perspective of international law.

Falk, Richard A. **The Status of Law in International Society.** Princeton: Princeton University Press (for the Center of International Studies, Princeton University), 1970, 678 p.
A collection of essays by a leading scholar.

Friedmann, Wolfgang Gaston. **The Changing Structure of International Law.** New York: Columbia University Press, 1964, 410 p.
An important, wide-ranging analysis of the many significant revisions injected into traditional international law as a result of rapid changes in international society and international groupings.

Gould, Wesley L. and Barkun, Michael. **International Law and the Social Sciences.** Princeton: Princeton University Press, 1970, 338 p.
An effort to examine the main problems of international law in terms of systems theory. While the methodology is somewhat unfamiliar, the substantive conclusions reached by the authors are not.

Gould, Wesley L. and Barkun, Michael. **Social Science Literature: A Bibliography for International Law.** Princeton: Princeton University Press (for the American Society of International Law), 1972, 641 p.
An annotated bibliography of books and articles published primarily in the period from 1955 to 1965. A companion volume to the authors' "International Law and the Social Sciences" (1970).

Grzybowski, Kazimierz. **Soviet Public International Law: Doctrines and Diplomatic Practice.** Leyden: Sijthoff, 1970, 544 p.
A massive study of the history and evolution of Soviet concepts of international law.

Head, Ivan L., ed. **This Fire-Proof House: Canadians Speak Out About Law and Order in the International Community.** Dobbs Ferry (N.Y.): Oceana Publications (for the World Law Foundation), 1967, 176 p.
A presentation of the views of Canadian lawyers and scholars on law and order in the international community.

Henkin, Louis. **How Nations Behave: Law and Foreign Policy.** New York: Praeger (for the Council on Foreign Relations), 1968, 324 p.
In these well-argued essays, the author demonstrates the importance and application of law in the day-to-day dealings among nations and weighs its successes and failures in helping to keep the peace in the face of divisive political pressures.

Higgins, Rosalyn. **The Development of International Law Through the Political Organs of the United Nations.** New York: Oxford University Press (for the Royal Institute of International Affairs), 1963, 402 p.
A pioneering study by an English international lawyer.

Jahrbuch für internationales Recht. Göttingen: Vandenhoeck.
A German yearbook of international law, containing articles, documents, book reviews and bibliographies; published since 1948.

Jenks, Clarence Wilfred. **Law in the World Community.** New York: McKay, 1968, 164 p.
A series of lectures on international law delivered by the author in twelve world capitals during 1965 and 1966.

Jessup, Philip C. **The Price of International Justice.** New York: Columbia University Press, 1971, 82 p.
The former U.S. Judge on the International Court of Justice has compressed much wisdom about the future of the rule of law into this slender volume.

Kunz, Josef Laurenz. **The Changing Law of Nations: Essays on International Law.** Columbus: Ohio State University Press, 1968, 970 p.
A collection of essays by a leading scholar who emphasizes the continuity of international law from its beginning to World War I and describes the subsequent transformations and crises.

Mansūr, 'Ali 'Ali. **al-Sharī'ah al-Islāmīyah wa al-qānūn al-dūwalī al-'ām.** Cairo: The Higher Council for Islamic Affairs, 1971, 410 p.
A comparative study of Islamic and public international law.

Maurach, Reinhart and Meissner, Boris, eds. **Völkerrecht in Ost und West.** Stuttgart: Kohlhammer, 1967, 248 p.
A collection of essays discussing the divergent conceptions of international law in the Western World and the Soviet Bloc, originally presented at a conference of the Deutsche Gesellschaft für Osteuropakunde in 1965.

Merillat, Herbert Christian Laing, ed. **Legal Advisers and Foreign Affairs.** Dobbs Ferry (N.Y.): Oceana Publications (for the American Society of International Law), 1964, 162 p.
The purpose of this conference report is "to help clarify the role of the legal adviser and to provide for an informal exchange of views and experience among some of those responsible for advising their governments on the legal aspects of international dealings."

O'Connell, Daniel Patrick. **International Law.** Dobbs Ferry (N.Y.): Oceana Publications, 1965, 2 v.
A massive and comprehensive survey of all aspects of international law.

Ramundo, Bernard A. **Peaceful Coexistence: International Law in the Building of Communism.** Baltimore: Johns Hopkins Press (in coöperation with Institute for Sino-Soviet Studies, George Washington University), 1967, 262 p.
An attempt to demonstrate that Soviet jurists are dedicated to the promotion of "peaceful coexistence" as the governing principle of contemporary international law.

Rhyne, Charles S. **International Law: The Substance, Processes, Procedures and Institutions for World Peace with Justice.** Washington: CLB Publishers, 1971, 656 p.
A very comprehensive treatment of the subject, including discussions of non-Western principles and experiences in international law.

Robinson, Jacob. **International Law and Organization: General Sources of Information.** Leyden: Sijthoff, 1967, 560 p.
A most useful bibliographical tool, containing an annotated list of general books on international law and information about bibliographies, periodicals, yearbooks and the publications of international legal associations and research institutes.

Scheinman, Lawrence and Wilkinson, David. **International Law and Political Crisis: An Analytic Casebook.** Boston: Little, Brown, 1968, 273 p.
Seven well-chosen case studies illustrating the complex relationships between power and law in world politics.

Schwarzenberger, Georg. **The Inductive Approach to International Law.** Dobbs Ferry (N.Y.): Oceana Publications (for the London Institute of World Affairs), 1965, 209 p.
A leading student of international law defines the inductive approach to the subject and defends it against objections that have been raised against this method.

Schwarzenberger, Georg. **International Law and Order.** New York: Praeger, 1971, 298 p.
A highly sophisticated and up-to-date treatment of the subject.

Schweizerisches Jahrbuch für internationales Recht. Zurich: Polygraphischer Verlag.
A Swiss yearbook of international law, published since 1944.

al-Shaybānī, Muhammad ibn al-Hassan. **The Islamic Law of Nations: Shaybānī's Siyar.** Baltimore: Johns Hopkins Press, 1966, 311 p.
The works of an eminent eighth-century Muslim jurist with a useful introduction by Majid Khadduri. Of interest to all who seek to understand contemporary Islamic conceptions of international law.

Sørensen, Max, *ed.* **Manual of Public International Law.** New York: St. Martin's Press, 1968, 930 p.
A textbook sponsored by the Carnegie Endowment for International Peace. It includes contributions by twelve authorities from all over the world.

Sovetskii ezhegodnik mezhdunarodnogo prava. Moscow: Izd-vo Akademii Nauk SSSR.
A Soviet yearbook of international law, published since 1958.

Thirlway, H.W.A. **International Customary Law and Codification.** Leyden: Sijthoff, 1972, 158 p.
A study of the continuing role of unwritten law created by custom.

Tung, William L. **International Law in an Organizing World.** New York: Crowell, 1968, 604 p.
A scholarly treatment of the subject.

Tunkin, Grigorii Ivanovich. **Droit international public: problèmes théoriques.** Paris: Pedone, 1965, 250 p.
A translation of a standard Soviet treatise on international law and diplomacy in the contemporary world. The Russian original was published as "Voprosy teorii mezhdunarodnogo prava" (Moscow: Gos. Izd-vo Iurid. Lit-ry, 1962, 329 p.).

Tunkin, Grigorii Ivanovich. **Teoriia mezhdunarodnogo prava.** Moscow: Mezhdunarodnye Otnosheniia, 2d rev. and enl. ed., 1970, 510 p.
An authoritative survey of Soviet conceptions of international law. An updated and revised German version appeared as "Völkerrechtstheorie" (Berlin: Berlin Verlag, 1972, 492 p.).

Visscher, Charles de. **Problèmes d'interprétation judiciaire en droit international public.** Paris: Pedone, 1963, 269 p.
An important contribution on the question of judicial interpretation in international law, by an eminent Belgian lawyer.

Visscher, Charles de. **Theory and Reality in Public International Law.** Princeton: Princeton University Press, rev. ed., 1968, 527 p.
A highly sophisticated analysis of the role of international law in world politics. A translation of the third French edition "Théories et réalités en droit international public" (Paris: Pedone, 3rd rev. ed., 1960, 534 p.).

Whiteman, Marjorie M., *ed.* **Digest of International Law.** Washington: Department of State, 1963–73, 15 v.
An indispensable reference, the purpose of which is to reflect the status of international law in our time.

DIPLOMACY AND DIPLOMATIC PRACTICE

See also Culture; Education; Public Opinion; Communications Processes, p. 42; International Organization and Government, p. 96; War and Peace, p. 108; (First World War) Diplomatic History, p. 131; Inter-War Period, p. 140; (Second World War) Diplomatic Aspects, p. 148; The Postwar World, p. 178; and the sections for specific countries and regions.

Braunias, Karl and Meraviglia, Peter, *eds.* **Modern Science and the Tasks of Diplomacy.** Graz: Verlag Styria, 1965, 238 p.
A trilingual—German, French and English—symposium on a variety of themes related to the title.

Busk, Sir Douglas Laird. **The Craft of Diplomacy.** New York: Praeger, 1967, 293 p.
A former British diplomat has written a witty but serious exposition of what it takes to have a good foreign service. Lessons are chiefly drawn from the British service but could apply to others as well.

Cottam, Richard Walter. **Competitive Interference and Twentieth Century Diplomacy.** Pittsburgh: University of Pittsburgh Press, 1967, 243 p.

"Competitive interference" is a mixture of counter-insurgency, and political, economic and psychological manipulation. The author discusses its increasing importance in modern diplomacy, primarily in theoretical terms though with special reference to the American experience in Iran.

Eubank, Keith. **The Summit Conferences, 1919-1960.** Norman: University of Oklahoma Press, 1966, 225 p.
The author sketches vignettes of seven diplomatic "summits" and concludes—not surprisingly—that "the formal summit conference could serve as the occasion for the signing of a final agreement, not the negotiation which should have been pursued by the professionals."

Fisher, Glen H. **Public Diplomacy and the Behavioral Sciences.** Bloomington: Indiana University Press, 1972, 180 p.
In this introductory effort to develop a "behavioral science for the diplomat," the author, himself a U.S. Foreign Service officer, examines the areas of perception, preconception and language and their bearing on the behavior of nations.

Fisher, Roger Drummer. **Basic Negotiating Strategy: International Conflict for Beginners.** London: Allen Lane, 1971, 194 p.
An introduction into the art of negotiation. The author draws his examples primarily from recent great power diplomacy.

Gamboa, Melquiades Jereos. **Elements of Diplomatic and Consular Practice: A Glossary.** Dobbs Ferry (N.Y.): Oceana Publications, 1967, 489 p.
A useful reference volume, compiled by a Philippine scholar and diplomat.

Gromyko, Andrei Andreevich and Others, *eds.* **Diplomaticheskii slovar'.** Moscow: Izd-vo Politicheskoi Literatury, 1971, 3 v.
A new edition of a Soviet diplomatic dictionary, providing compact reference to the events, personalities, treaties, and basic concpets, both historical and current, that are deemed important by the makers of Soviet foreign policy.

Hardy, Michael. **Modern Diplomatic Law.** Dobbs Ferry (N.Y.): Oceana Publications, 1968, 150 p.
This monograph contains much useful technical information.

Harmon, Robert B. **The Art and Practice of Diplomacy.** Metuchen (N.J.): Scarecrow Press, 1971, 355 p.
A well-annotated bibliography of some 900 selected works.

Johnson, Edgar Augustus Jerome, *ed.* **The Dimensions of Diplomacy.** Baltimore: Johns Hopkins Press, 1964, 135 p.
Six lectures on various facets of diplomacy, power and foreign policy by McGeorge Bundy, Henry A. Kissinger, W. W. Rostow, James R. Killian, Jr., Adolf A. Berle and Livingston Merchant.

Kaufmann, Johan. **Conference Diplomacy.** Dobbs Ferry (N.Y.): Oceana Publications, 1968, 222 p.
Part manual and part analysis, this is an unusual and often witty book reflecting the author's experiences as a Dutch diplomat.

Krekeler, Heinz Ludwig. **Die Diplomatie.** Munich: Olzog, 1965, 254 p.
A compact survey of the history of diplomacy and its contemporary practice by a veteran German diplomat who for many years represented his country in Washington.

Lall, Arthur Samuel. **Modern International Negotiation: Principles and Practice.** New York: Columbia University Press, 1966, 404 p.
A substantial inquiry into the increasingly complex patterns and modes of international negotiation in recent years. For a number of years the author was India's Ambassador to the U.N.

Lee, Luke T. **Vienna Convention on Consular Relations.** Leyden: Sijthoff, 1966, 315 p.
In the words of the author, this study "is a description and analysis of the salient features of the Convention [1963] against the backgrounds of the Vienna Conference, state practice, juridical doctrines, and draft codes."

Moussa, Farag. **Diplomatie contemporaine: guide bibliographique.** Geneva: Centre Européen de la Dotation Carnegie pour la Paix Internationale, 1964, 199 p.
A brief but systematic introduction, followed by a useful annotated bibliography, to problems of contemporary diplomacy, by an Arab scholar and diplomat.

Nascimento e Silva, G. E. do. **Diplomacy in International Law.** Leyden: Sijthoff, 1972, 217 p.
A useful reference work on the law of diplomatic practice and institutions.

Schütz, Walter J., ed. **Aus der Schule der Diplomatie: Beiträge zu Aussenpolitik, Recht, Kultur, Menschenführung.** Düsseldorf: Econ-Verlag, 1965, 712 p.
A *Festschrift*, containing articles on diplomatic practice and international relations, published in honor of Peter H. Pfeiffer, a German diplomat who after World War II played a leading role in the establishment of the West German diplomatic service.

Sen, Biswanath. **A Diplomat's Handbook of International Law and Practice.** The Hague: Nijhoff, 1965, 522 p.
Intended by its author, an Indian lawyer, to serve as a reference volume for foreign service officers in their day-to-day work.

Vagts, Alfred. **The Military Attaché.** Princeton: Princeton University Press, 1967, 408 p.
Both a historical outline of the development of the service attaché and a discussion of his function and field of activities.

Waters, Maurice. **The Ad Hoc Diplomat: A Study in Municipal and International Law.** The Hague: Nijhoff, 1963, 233 p.
An examination of the politics and procedures concerning the creation of special agents in international affairs. The personalities and careers of two men in particular, Colonel House and Harry Hopkins, are studied in depth.

Wilson, Clifton E. **Diplomatic Privileges and Immunities.** Tucson: University of Arizona Press, 1967, 300 p.
A detailed and useful compendium.

Wood, John R. and Serres, Jean. **Diplomatic Ceremonial and Protocol.** New York: Columbia University Press, 1970, 378 p.
A diplomat's Emily Post-type guide to international good manners.

LAW OF WAR; AGGRESSION

See also War and Peace, p. 108; First World War, p. 131; Inter-War Period, p. 140; Second World War, p. 144; The Postwar World, p. 178; Arab-Israeli Conflict, p. 633; The Korean War, p. 728; The Vietnam War, p. 739.

Bailey, Sydney D. **Prohibitions and Restraints in War.** New York: Oxford University Press (for the Royal Institute of International Affairs), 1972, 194 p.
A historical and legal examination of the concept of restraints and human rights in times of armed conflict.

Brownlie, Ian. **International Law and the Use of Force by States.** New York: Oxford University Press, 1963, 532 p.
A scholarly monograph in development of the author's starting observation that "the law is, very nearly, all that we possess by way of a common language for a community of states the co-existence of which would otherwise depend too much on the uncertainties arising from political competition."

Falk, Richard A., ed. **The International Law of Civil War.** Baltimore: Johns Hopkins Press (for the American Society of International Law), 1971, 452 p.
Six case studies, exploring the complex relationship between international law and civil war and ranging from the American Civil War to Vietnam.

Gerlach, Axel. **Die Intervention: Versuch einer Definition.** Frankfurt/Main: Metzner, 1967, 257 p.
A study of intervention in international law.

Lazareff, Serge. **Status of Military Forces Under Current International Law.** Leyden: Sijthoff, 1971, 458 p.
An extended analysis on recent developments in international law relating to the status of military forces stationed in another country.

Luard, David Evan Trant. **The International Regulation of Civil Wars.** New York: New York University Press, 1972, 240 p.
Essays examining a number of recent civil wars (in Spain, Greece, Lebanon, Laos,

Congo, Yemen and Cyprus), their impact on international relations and the problem of regulating them through law or institutions.

Meier, Walter. **Die Bestimmungen über das Kriegsverbrechens- und Besetzungsstrafrecht in den Genfer Abkommen zum Schutze der Kriegsopfer von 1949.** Winterthur: Keller, 1964, 239 p.
A discussion of the sections dealing with war crimes and occupation in the 1949 Geneva Convention for the Protection of War Victims.

Poulantzas, Nicholas M. **The Right of Hot Pursuit in International Law.** Leyden: Sijthoff, 1969, 451 p.
The definitive monograph on the subject.

Schwarzkopf, Dietrich. **Atomherrschaft.** Stuttgart: Seewald, 1969, 279 p.
An ambitious effort, by a West German journalist, to adjust international legal concepts, diplomacy and strategy to the nuclear age.

MARITIME, AIR, SPACE AND ENVIRONMENTAL LAW

See also International Organization and Government, p. 96; Aerial and Space Warfare and Technology, p. 114; (The Postwar World) General, p. 178; (Canada) Foreign Relations, p. 282; (Bolivia) Foreign Relations, p. 320; (Chile) Foreign Relations, p. 332; (Union of Soviet Socialist Republics) Government; Constitution; Law, p. 564; Polar Regions, p. 848.

Alexander, Lewis M., ed. **The Law of the Sea.** Columbus: Ohio State University Press, 1967, 321 p.
A very useful though somewhat uneven symposium on offshore boundaries, fisheries, the sea-bed, continental shelf and other problems of sea law.

Alexandrowicz, Charles Henry. **The Law of Global Communications.** New York: Columbia University Press, 1971, 195 p.
A definitive monograph on the international legal provisions governing postal communications, radio transmissions, civil aviation, satellite communications and maritime transport.

Andrassy, Juraj. **International Law and the Resources of the Sea.** New York: Columbia University Press, 1970, 191 p.
A first-rate scholarly monograph.

Baxter, Richard Reeve. **The Law of International Waterways.** Cambridge: Harvard University Press, 1964, 371 p.
A well-documented study of existing laws pertaining to international waterways—straits, canals and rivers—the various organizations which administer them, the obstacles to international administration. Special attention is given to the rules guiding the use of the Suez, Panama and Kiel canals.

Borgese, Elisabeth Mann, ed. **Pacem in Maribus.** New York: Dodd, Mead, 1972, 382 p.
A useful collection of papers on maritime law. The text culminates in a draft statute, prepared by Mrs. Borgese, for an ocean regime.

Brown, Edward Duncan. **The Legal Regime of Hydrospace.** London: Stevens (for the London Institute of World Affairs), 1971, 236 p.
An analysis of some of the important current problems relating to the international law of the sea, the seabed and its subsoil, the delimitation of the continental shelf, deep-sea mining, and oil and nuclear pollution.

Buergenthal, Thomas. **Law-Making in the International Civil Aviation Organization.** Syracuse: Syracuse University Press, 1969, 247 p.
A solid and scholarly monograph, mostly of a technical nature. Lacking is a discussion of the problem of airplane hijacking.

Burke, William Thomas. **Towards a Better Use of the Ocean: Contemporary Legal Problems in Ocean Development.** New York: Humanities Press, 1969, 231 p.
Proceedings of a symposium held in Stockholm in June 1968. A publication of the Stockholm International Peace Research Institute.

Butler, William E. **The Soviet Union and the Law of the Sea.** Baltimore: Johns Hopkins Press, 1971, 245 p.
An analysis of Soviet doctrines and practices relating to territorial waters, inland seas, the continental shelf and the high seas.

Friedmann, Wolfgang Gaston. **The Future of the Oceans.** New York: Braziller, 1971, 132 p.
A passionate plea, based on deep knowledge of the subject, for an international regime for the oceans. The author deplores the trend toward partition of large portions of the seabed among competing nation-states.

Gál, Gyula. **Space Law.** Dobbs Ferry (N.Y.): Oceana Publications, 1969, 320 p.
A comprehensive monograph.

Gureev, Sergei Aleksandrovich. **Kollizionnye problemy morskogo prava.** Moscow: Izd-vo "Mezhdunarodnye Otnosheniia," 1972, 221 p.
A Soviet monograph on variations between socialist and capitalist maritime laws, designed to be of service to the masters of Soviet vessels as well as to international affairs specialists.

Kehrberger, H. Peter. **Legal and Political Implications of Space Research; Space Law and its Background: Political, Military, Economical Aspects and Techno-Scientific Problems of Astronautics.** Hamburg: Verlag Weltarchiv, 1965, 365 p.
An informative survey and a bibliography of Eastern and Western sources.

Lee, Luke T. and Larson, Arthur, *eds*. **Population and Law.** Durham (N.C.): Rule of Law Press, 1971, 452 p.
A survey, organized on a geographical basis, of current law relating to population. Prepared under the auspices of the Rule of Law Research Center of Duke University on a grant by the Population Council.

McDougal, Myres Smith and Others. **Law and Public Order in Space.** New Haven: Yale University Press, 1963, 1,147 p.
A massive and systematic attempt to produce a "framework of inquiry for study of the law and public order of space in their larger context." Includes a chapter on potential interaction with advanced forms of non-earth life.

Matte, Nicolas Mateesco. **Aerospace Law.** Toronto: Carswell, 1969, 501 p.
An exhaustive compendium.

Matte, Nicolas Mateesco. **Deux frontières invisibles: de la mer territoriale à l'air "territorial."** Paris: Pedone, 1965, 296 p.
A study of the law of the territorial sea and of the territorial air. The author strongly opposes the exclusive sovereignty of states over the air space above their territory.

Mensbrugghe, Yves van der. **Les Garanties de la liberté de navigation dans le canal de Suez.** Paris: Librairie Générale de Droit, 1964, 430 p.
A technical study of the guarantees of freedom to navigate in the Suez Canal.

Morenoff, Jerome. **World Peace through Space Law.** Charlottesville (Va.): Michie Co., 1967, 329 p.
The author makes a survey of space law and argues for a "United Nations Reconnaissance Agency."

Oda, Shigeru. **International Control of Sea Sources.** Dobbs Ferry (N.Y.): Oceana Publications, 1963, 215 p.
The author capably expresses his concern for recent trends in international law on matters relating to the vast resources under the sea.

Plender, Richard. **International Migration Law.** Leyden: Sijthoff, 1972, 339 p.
An exposition of an increasingly important subject. The references take in over 100 countries, and the introductory chapters on nationality law in general, and on the historical background of restrictions on migration, are particularly useful.

Schwartz, Mortimer D., *ed*. **Proceedings of the Conference on Space Science and Space Law.** South Hackensack (N.J.): Rothman, 1964, 176 p.
Papers presented at the conference of June 18–20, 1963, at the University of Oklahoma where legal and scientific experts met to discuss ways "to close the gap between science and law."

White, Irvin L. **Decision-Making for Space: Law and Politics in Air, Sea, and Outer Space.** West Lafayette: Purdue University Press, 1970, 277 p.
This monograph sets forth the main legal and political problems in outer space and the main legal rules covering international air and sea. It also attempts to explain why national decision-makers either accept or reject these rules.

TREATIES AND TREATY MAKING

See also (General Works) Reference Works, p. 1; General Treatments, p. 7; International Organization and Government, p. 96; (First World War) Diplomatic History, p. 131; Inter-War Period, p. 140; (Second World War) Diplomatic Aspects, p. 148; The Postwar World, p. 178.

Bot, Bernard R. **Nonrecognition and Treaty Relations.** Dobbs Ferry (N.Y.): Oceana Publications, 1968, 286 p.
A useful monograph with a heavy legal emphasis.

Chiu, Hung-ta. **The Capacity of International Organizations to Conclude Treaties, and the Special Legal Aspects of the Treaties so Concluded.** The Hague: Nijhoff, 1966, 225 p.
A comprehensive study of treaties concluded by international organizations, by a Harvard trained professor at the National Taiwan University.

McDougal, Myres S.; Lasswell, Harold Dwight and Miller, James C. **The Interpretation of Agreements and World Public Order.** New Haven: Yale University Press, 1967, 410 p.
The authors of this impressive study, which is written in highly esoteric language, subordinate the interpretation of a treaty to the attainment of certain objectives.

Renoux, Yvette with Yates, Janine, *comps.* **Glossary of International Treaties in French, English, Spanish, Italian, Dutch, German and Russian.** New York: Elsevier Publishing Co., 1970, 198 p.
A handy reference manual of the most important words and phrases found in recent international treaties.

Rönnefarth, Helmuth K. G. and Euler, Heinrich. **Konferenzen und Verträge. Teil II. Band 4 B: Neueste Zeit 1959-1963.** Würzburg: Ploetz, 1963, 735 p.
A well-documented reference volume on the international conferences and agreements in the period from 1959 to 1963.

Schweisfurth, Theodor. **Der internationale Vertrag in der modernen sowjetischen Völkerrechtstheorie.** Cologne: Verlag Wissenschaft und Politik, 1968, 349 p.
An extended and quite detailed analysis of the place of treaties in Soviet theory of international law.

Treaties and Alliances of the World: An International Survey Covering Treaties in Force and Communities of State. New York: Scribner, 1974, 235 p.
A reference volume "designed to present the state of affairs with regard to groupings of States and their principal treaties with each other in force at Jan. 1, 1973." A revised edition of a work published originally in 1968.

Voïcu, Ioan. **De l'interprétation authentique des traités internationaux.** Geneva: Université de Genève, Institut Universitaire de Hautes Études Internationales, 1967, 245 p.
A thesis on the interpretation of international treaties, by a Rumanian scholar.

HUMAN RIGHTS

See also Political Philosophies and Ideologies, p. 21; Ethnic Problems; The Jews, p. 46; United Nations, p. 99; and the sections for specific countries and regions.

Brownlie, Ian, *ed.* **Basic Documents on Human Rights.** New York: Oxford University Press, 1971, 531 p.
A convenient handbook of sources on human rights, with brief annotations by the editor.

Eide, Asbjörn and Schou, August, *eds*. **International Protection of Human Rights.** New York: Wiley, 1968, 300 p.
Fourteen essays on human rights prepared under the auspices of the Norwegian Nobel Institute.

Fawcett, J. E. S. **The Application of the European Convention on Human Rights.** New York: Oxford University Press, 1969, 368 p.
In the words of the author, "This is an analytical survey, Article by Article and clause by clause, of the application in practice of the European Convention on Human Rights by its appointed organs from 1954 until the end of 1967."

Haas, Ernst B. **Human Rights and International Action: The Case of Freedom of Association.** Stanford: Stanford University Press, 1970, 184 p.
An excellent analysis of the problems involved in the development of common international criteria for the observance and implementation of fundamental human rights.

Kutner, Luis, *ed*. **The Human Right to Individual Freedom: A Symposium on World Habeas Corpus.** Coral Gables: University of Miami Press, 1970, 249 p.
Pleadings by leading jurists and legal scholars for the establishment of a world court of habeas corpus.

La Chapelle, Philippe de. **La Déclaration universelle des droits de l'homme et le catholicisme.** Paris: Librairie Générale de Droit, 1967, 490 p.
An analysis of the Universal Declaration of Human Rights, from a Catholic point of view.

Luard, David Evan Trant, *ed*. **The International Protection of Human Rights.** New York: Praeger, 1967, 384 p.
A comprehensive and well-organized symposium.

Robertson, Arthur Henry. **Human Rights in the World.** New York: Humanities Press, 1972, 280 p.
An exploration and analysis of the principal covenants, conventions and declarations relating to the international protection of human rights.

The United Nations and Human Rights. Dobbs Ferry (N.Y.): Oceana Publications, 1968, 239 p.
A forward-looking report of the Commission to Study the Organization of Peace.

Van Dyke, Vernon. **Human Rights, the United States, and World Community.** New York: Oxford University Press, 1970, 292 p.
This informative monograph addresses itself to three basic questions: first, what are human rights? second, what is the nature of international obligation? and third, what is being done in the area of implementation?

Vasak, Karel. **La Convention européenne des droits de l'homme.** Paris: Librairie Générale de Droit, 1964, 325 p.
A history and analysis of the European Convention for Human Rights.

Weil, Gordon Lee. **The European Convention on Human Rights: Background, Development and Prospects.** Dobbs Ferry (N.Y.): Oceana Publications, 1963, 260 p.
An informative and well-researched study.

INTERNATIONAL COURT OF JUSTICE

See also (Western Europe) Integration, p. 349.

Douma, J., *comp*. **Bibliography on the International Court, Including the Permanent Court, 1918-1964.** Leyden: Sijthoff, 1966, 387 p.
An extensive bibliography, containing more than 3,500 titles of documents, books and review articles published all over the world.

Günther, Manfred. **Der Sondervoten sowjetischer Richter am internationalen Gerichtshof: zugleich ein Beitrag zur Stellung der Sowjetunion zum Völkerrecht.** Cologne: Verlag Wissenschaft und Politik, 1966, 156 p.
A monograph on the votes of Soviet members of the International Court of Justice.

Katz, Milton. **The Relevance of International Adjudication.** Cambridge: Harvard University Press, 1968, 165 p.
  A valuable monograph, including an analysis of the South West African cases before the International Court of Justice.

Kitchel, Denison. **Too Grave a Risk: The Connally Amendment Issue.** New York: Morrow, 1963, 128 p.
  An essay in defense of the Connally Amendment with respect to the jurisdiction of the World Court.

Rosenne, Shabtai. **The Law and Practice of the International Court.** Leyden: Sijthoff, 1965, 2 v.
  An indispensable reference and source book by an Israeli diplomat and lawyer.

Verzijl, Jan Hendrik Willem. **The Jurisprudence of the World Court: A Case by Case Commentary.** Leyden: Sijthoff, 1965–66, 2 v.
  Analyses of the judgements, orders and advisory opinions of both the Permanent Court of International Justice and the World Court, by a prominent Dutch professor of international law.

Visscher, Charles de. **Aspects récents du droit procédural de la Cour internationale de justice.** Paris: Pedone, 1966, 220 p.
  Observations on the character of international disputes and a discussion of the effect of international judicial decisions. The study covers the jurisprudence of both the World Court and its predecessor, the Permanent Court of International Justice. The author, a Belgian international law expert, is a former judge of both these courts.

Yearbook. The Hague: International Court of Justice.
  A comprehensive annual reference volume on the organization and activities of the International Court of Justice. Includes information about the publications of the Court. The twenty-seventh volume, for the years 1972-73, was published in 1973.

MISCELLANEOUS

Blittersdorf, Winrich Freiherr von. **Das internationale Plebiszit: praktische Fragen und Technik der Verwirklichung des Selbstbestimmungsrechts.** Hamburg: Forschungsstelle für Völkerrecht und Ausländisches Öffentliches Recht, Universität Hamburg, 1965, 285 p.
  A general study of the problems of self-determination, and the various means and difficulties of achieving a free plebiscite.

Blum, Yehuda Z. **Historic Titles in International Law.** The Hague: Nijhoff, 1965, 360 p.
  An attempt to show that the question of historic titles deserves to be considered as a whole and not exclusively in a maritime context.

Bridel, Renée. **Neutralité: une voie pour le tiers monde?** Lausanne: Éditions L'Age d'Homme, 1968, 288 p.
  A French scholar examines the problem of neutrality in the contemporary world, especially as it concerns the new nations.

Chapal, Philippe. **L'Arbitrabilité des différends internationaux.** Paris: Pedone, 1967, 294 p.
  A monograph on international arbitration. The author pleads for an increased role for supranational bodies in settling international disputes.

D'Amato, Anthony. **The Concept of Custom in International Law.** Ithaca: Cornell University Press, 1971, 286 p.
  An imaginative study of an elusive subject.

Dawson, Frank Griffith and Head, Ivan L. **International Law, National Tribunals and the Rights of Aliens.** Syracuse: Syracuse University Press, 1971, 334 p.
  Lawyers, laymen and corporations who venture abroad or who become involved in litigation abroad will find this study most valuable.

Falk, Richard A. **The Role of Domestic Courts in the International Legal Order.** Syracuse: Syracuse University Press, 1964, 184 p.
  This well-documented study on the proper role of domestic courts in the evolution of

international order is the third volume in the Procedural Aspects of International Law Series sponsored by Syracuse University's College of Law's International Legal Studies Program.

Frowein, Jochen Abraham. **Das De Facto-Regime im Völkerrecht: eine Untersuchung zur Rechtsstellung "Nichtanerkannter Staaten" und ähnlicher Gebilde.** Cologne: Heymanns, 1968, 243 p.
A detailed discussion of the problem of recognition in international law.

Grieves, Forest L. **Supranationalism and International Adjudication.** Urbana: University of Illinois Press, 1969, 266 p.
A valuable monograph analyzing the political premises, constitutional bases and judicial practices of five international tribunals. The author concludes that only the Court of the European Communities is truly supranational.

Higgins, Rosalyn. **Conflict of Interests: International Law in a Divided World.** Chester Springs (Pa.): Dufour Editions, 1965, 170 p.
A pithy study addressed to the questions: "Do agreed rules of law really govern relations between states which have few interests in common? And . . . do they really apply . . . where there is a conflict of interests?"

Jenks, Clarence Wilfred. **The Prospects of International Adjudication.** Dobbs Ferry (N.Y.): Oceana Publications, 1964, 805 p.
A massive exploration of the prospects for further advances in international adjudication, especially with respect to increasing the effectiveness of the International Court as an instrument for the rule of law.

Jennings, Robert Yewdall. **The Acquisition of Territory in International Law.** Dobbs Ferry (N.Y.): Oceana Publications, 1963, 130 p.
A series of lectures drawing "attention to certain difficulties and problems of general principle which require consideration" in the matter of territorial acquisition.

Koziebrodski, Leopold Bolesta. **Le Droit d'asile.** Leyden: Sijthoff, 1962, 374 p.
A comprehensive discussion of the right of asylum.

Luard, David Evan Trant, *ed*. **The International Regulation of Frontier Disputes.** New York: Praeger, 1970, 247 p.
Seven specialists compare the approaches to frontier disputes of the League of Nations, the United Nations and regional organizations and then examine the relative merits of mediation, arbitration and judicial settlement.

Meissner, Boris, *ed*. **Das Selbstbestimmungsrecht der Völker in Osteuropa und China.** Cologne: Verlag Wissenschaft und Politik, 1968, 236 p.
Essays on the right of self-determination in the Soviet Union, Eastern Europe and Communist China.

Metzger, Stanley D. **International Law, Trade and Finance: Realities and Prospects.** Dobbs Ferry (N.Y.): Oceana Publications, 1963, 184 p.
A well-documented study of the steps by which "international tranquility" has been achieved through international agreements in the expanding field of commercial and economic transactions.

Nehrt, Lee Charles. **International Marketing of Nuclear Power Plants.** Bloomington: Indiana University Press, 1966, 405 p.
A discussion of domestic and international atomic energy laws and treaties, with emphasis on the way they affect the foreign marketing of nuclear power plants.

Ni, Chêng-yü. **Kuo-chi fa chung ti ssŭ-fa kuan-hsia wên-t'i.** Peking: Shih-chieh Chih-shih Ch'u-pan-she, 1964, 136 p.
This short study of jurisdiction in international law is one of the rare known Chinese Communist studies on international legal questions.

O'Brien, William Vincent, *ed*. **The New Nations in International Law and Diplomacy.** New York: Praeger (for the Institute of World Polity, Georgetown University), 1965, 323 p.
This collection, published as Volume III of "The Yearbook of World Polity," contains the following essays: "Independence and Problems of State Succession," by D. P. O'Connell; "Military Servitudes and the New Nations," by Albert J. Esgain; "United States Recognition Policy Toward the New Nations," by William V. O'Brien and Ulf H. Goebel; and "The New States and the United Nations," by J. E. S. Fawcett.

Rubin, Seymour J., *ed*. **Foreign Development Lending—Legal Aspects.** Dobbs Ferry (N.Y.): Oceana Publications, 1972, 352 p.
This volume of papers and discussions, sponsored by the American Society of International Law, covers both international agencies and national practices.

White, Gillian Mary. **The Use of Experts by International Tribunals.** Syracuse: Syracuse University Press, 1965, 259 p.
A study of the use of experts, their competence, role privileges and immunities.

Zivier, Ernst Renatus. **Die Nichtanerkennung im modernen Völkerrecht: Probleme staatlicher Willensäusserung.** Berlin: Berlin Verlag, 1967, 311 p.
A very useful study of the legal and political practices of non-recognition, with emphasis on Germany.

VII. INTERNATIONAL ORGANIZATION AND GOVERNMENT

GENERAL

See also General Works, p. 1; (Political Factors) General, p. 12; General Geography and Environment, p. 45; Economic Factors, p. 49; International Law, p. 83; United Nations, p. 99; (The World Since 1914) General, p. 129; Inter-War Period, p. 140; Second World War, p. 144; The Postwar World, p. 178; and the sections for specific countries and regions.

Barros, James. **Betrayal from Within.** New Haven: Yale University Press, 1969, 289 p.
A case study of Joseph Avenol, the second Secretary-General of the League of Nations (1933–1940), who is pictured as having helped to undermine the organization by collaborating with the Axis powers behind the scenes. Unfortunately, the author generalizes from this and speaks out strongly against a politically active Secretary-Generalship. (Written under the auspices of the Center of International Studies, Princeton University.)

Bloch, Roger and Lefèvre, Jacqueline. **La Fonction publique internationale et européenne.** Paris: Librairie Générale de Droit, 1963, 219 p.
A legal study of the regulations governing personnel serving in the rapidly proliferating international organizations.

Codding, George Arthur. **The Universal Postal Union: Coordinator of the International Mails.** New York: New York University Press, 1964, 296 p.
A useful study.

Cox, Robert W., *ed*. **The Politics of International Organizations.** New York: Praeger, 1970, 319 p.
A high-level symposium focusing on social and economic agencies and their advances toward multilateral integration.

Douglas, William O. **Towards a Global Federalism.** New York: New York University Press, 1968, 177 p.
A passionate plea for a world rule of law, by an Associate Justice of the U.S. Supreme Court.

Doxey, Margaret P. **Economic Sanctions and International Enforcement.** New York: Oxford University Press (for the Royal Institute of International Affairs), 1971, 162 p.
A solid study of an old subject, covering the League, the United Nations and the efforts of single nations and groups of them. Not surprisingly, the Canadian professor's emphasis is on the limited usefulness of sanctions. Good bibliography.

Etzioni, Amitai. **Political Unification: A Comparative Study of Leaders and Forces.** New York: Holt, Rinehart and Winston, 1965, 346 p.
A study, both theoretical and empirical, of regional associations as an approach to political unification. Case studies include the United Arab Republic, the Federation of the West Indies, the Nordic Council and the European Economic Community.

Etzioni, Minerva M. **The Majority of One: Towards a Theory of Regional Compatibility.** Beverly Hills: Sage Publications, 1970, 238 p.
Basing her conceptualizations primarily on the relationship between the Organization of American States and the United Nations, the author has produced an original work about the compatibility of regional and global pathways to world order.

Fleiner, Thomas. **Die Kleinstaaten in den Staatenverbindungen des zwanzigsten Jahrhunderts.** Zurich: Polygraphischer Verlag, 1966, 384 p.
A monograph on the role of small states in twentieth-century international organizations.

Franck, Thomas M., *ed.* **Why Federations Fail: An Inquiry into the Requisites for Successful Federalism.** New York: New York University Press, 1968, 213 p.
A systematic analysis, through four case studies, of the reasons for the disintegration of federations.

Gardner, Richard Newton and Millikan, Max F., *eds.* **The Global Partnership.** New York: Praeger, 1968, 498 p.
A symposium dealing with problems of international agencies and economic development.

Haas, Ernst Bernard. **Beyond the Nation-State: Functionalism and International Organization.** Stanford: Stanford University Press, 1964, 595 p.
An extended inquiry into the prospects and measures for furthering the growth of "mutual deference and institutional mingling" between nations, with special emphasis on the International Labor Organization.

Haas, Michael. **International Organization: An International Bibliography.** Stanford: Hoover Institution Press, 1971, 944 p.
A massive reference volume, containing nearly 8,000 titles and ranging from early periods of international history to the present.

Hamzeh, Fuad Said. **International Conciliation.** The Hague: Drukkerij Pasmans, 1963, 177 p.
A study of international conciliation as "a powerful procedure that can bring harmony and understanding between disputants," with particular emphasis on the work of the U.N. Conciliation Commission for Palestine.

Harris, Errol Eustace. **Annihilation and Utopia: The Principles of International Politics.** New York: Humanities Press, 1966, 331 p.
An effort, as the title suggests, to put forward some new principles of international politics under the threat of nuclear holocaust. The author points to world government as the only way out.

Hay, Peter. **Federalism and Supranational Organizations: Patterns for new Legal Structures.** Urbana: University of Illinois Press, 1966, 335 p.
Essays on the role of supranational organizations, especially the European communities, in international law and in the legal structure of their constituents.

Hevesy, Paul de. **The Unification of the World: Proposals of a Diplomatist.** New York: Pergamon Press, 1966, 356 p.
A former Hungarian diplomat argues that international coöperation combined with improved food production and free agricultural trade will solve most of the problems of the modern world.

Hovey, J. Allan, Jr. **The Superparliaments: Interparliamentary Consultation and Atlantic Cooperation.** New York: Praeger, 1966, 202 p.
A study of the development of "international regional assemblies of members of national legislatures convened regularly to investigate and debate international problems."

Jacob, Philip E. and Atherton, Alexine L. **The Dynamics of International Organization: The Making of World Order.** Homewood (Ill.): Dorsey Press, 1965, 723 p.
A pragmatic study of the nature and scope of the tasks and of the performance of international organizations in coping with them.

Keohane, Robert O. and Nye, Joseph S., Jr., *eds.* **Transnational Relations and World Politics.** Cambridge: Harvard University Press, 1972, 428 p.
Essays directed toward the evidently important if somewhat uncertain area of transnational relations, organizations and coalitions. Written under the auspices of the Center for International Affairs, Harvard University.

Lador-Lederer, J. Josef. **International Non-Governmental Organizations and Economic Entities.** Leyden: Sijthoff, 1963, 403 p.
A study of the activities of non-state organizations and their impact on international relations and law.

Langrod, Jerzy Stefan. **The International Civil Service: Its Origins, Its Nature, Its Evolution.** Dobbs Ferry (N.Y.): Oceana Publications, 1963, 358 p.
A thorough survey of the administrative and political aspects of international secretariats and the personalities involved. The French original appeared as "La Fonction publique internationale: sa genèse, son essence, son évolution" (Leyden: Sijthoff, 1963, 387 p.).

Luard, David Evan Trant, ed. **The Evolution of International Organizations.** New York: Praeger, 1966, 342 p.
An uneven symposium by the editor and ten collaborators, including a fine essay on the Security Council by Inis L. Claude, Jr.

Luard, David Evan Trant. **Nationality and Wealth: A Study in World Government.** New York: Oxford University Press, 1964, 370 p.
The author argues for an increased role of international organizations and for a global redistribution of income and wealth.

Meerhaeghe, Marcel Alfons Gilbert van. **International Economic Institutions.** New York: Wiley, 1967, 404 p.
Essentially a handbook that summarizes organizations and agreements and provides a compendium of concepts and theories. The Dutch original was published as "Internationale economische betrekkingen en instellingen" (Leyden: H. E. Stenfert Kroese, 1964, 327 p.).

Morozov, Grigorii Iosifovich. **Mezhdunarodnye organizatsii: nekotorye voprosy teorii.** Moscow: Izd-vo "Mysl'," 1969, 231 p.
A Soviet study of the origins, status and influence of international organizations in contemporary world politics.

Pham-Thi-Tu. **La Coopération intellectuelle sous la Société des Nations.** Geneva: Droz, 1963, 268 p.
A history of the brief life of the Committee for Intellectual Cooperation under the League of Nations.

Plano, Jack Charles and Riggs, Robert E. **Forging World Order: The Politics of International Organization.** New York: Macmillan, 1967, 600 p.
A general survey of contemporary international organizations.

Plischke, Elmer, ed. **Systems of Integrating the International Community.** Princeton: Van Nostrand, 1964, 198 p.
Papers presented at a University of Maryland symposium in December 1962 on practical and theoretical aspects of international confederation.

Rovine, Arthur W. **The First Fifty Years.** Leyden: Sijthoff, 1970, 498 p.
A thorough, conscientiously researched, though somewhat ponderous work on the Secretaries-General of the League of Nations and the United Nations.

Siotis, Jean. **Essai sur le secretariat international.** Geneva: Droz, 1963, 272 p.
A historical and analytical survey of administrative and executive international secretariats, from the Congress of Vienna to the United Nations.

Stošić, Borko D. **Les Organisations non gouvernementales et les Nations Unies.** Geneva: Droz, 1964, 367 p.
A thesis covering private international organizations and their connection with the agencies of the United Nations.

Szawlowski, Richard. **Les Finances et le droit financier d'une organisation internationale inter-gouvernementale.** Paris: Cujas, 1971, 221 p.
Using the World Health Organization as his main focus, the author looks more closely than others have done at the income, outgo and budgeting of international organizations.

Virally, M. and Others. **Les Missions permanentes auprès des organisations internationales.** Brussels: Bruylant (for the Dotation Carnegie pour la Paix Internationale), 1971—.
This survey of the history, organization and functions of the missions at the inter-

national organizations is the definitive work on the subject. Two volumes published through 1973.

Woodhouse, Christopher Montague. **The New Concert of Nations.** Chester Springs (Pa.): Dufour, 1964, 103 p.
A brief but forceful book by a Conservative M.P. and former Director-General of the Royal Institute of International Affairs calling for effective international action to replace the current disequilibrium among nations.

Yalem, Ronald Joseph. **Regionalism and World Order.** Washington: Public Affairs Press, 1965, 160 p.
A study both of the theoretical premises of regionalism and of regional organizations and their operation under the League of Nations and the United Nations.

UNITED NATIONS

General

See also General Works, p. 1; Political Factors, p. 12; International Law, p. 83; (International Organization and Government) General, p. 96; Peace; Disarmament; Arms Control, p. 122; (Second World War) Diplomatic Aspects, p. 148; The Postwar World, p. 178; and the sections for specific countries and regions.

L'Adaptation de L'O.N.U. au monde d'aujourd'hui. Paris: Pedone, 1965, 230 p.
Proceedings of an international conference on the role of the United Nations in the contemporary world, held in Nice from May 27 to 29, 1965.

Alker, Hayward Rose, Jr. and Russett, Bruce Martin. **World Politics in the General Assembly.** New Haven: Yale University Press, 1965, 326 p.
A serious effort to use some quite sophisticated quantitative techniques in describing and analyzing the political process in the General Assembly.

Annual Review of United Nations Affairs. Dobbs Ferry (N.Y.): Oceana Publications.
An annual series, started in 1950. The volumes covering the period from 1962 to 1972 were edited by Richard N. Swift, Barbara A. Kulzer and Florence Remz.

Aulén, Gustaf. **Dag Hammarskjold's White Book.** Philadelphia: Fortress Press, 1969, 154 p.
A profound interpretation of "Markings," the very personal book of the late Secretary-General of the United Nations, by a leading theologian of Sweden.

Bailey, Sydney D. **Voting in the Security Council.** Bloomington: Indiana University Press, 1970, 275 p.
A meticulous vote-by-vote analysis of Security Council Resolutions from 1946 through 1967. The author regards the veto as an integral part of the Security Council and suggests that even if it were abolished from the Charter, a Big Power veto would still exist in the Realpolitik of international life.

Baker, William Gedney. **The United States and Africa in the United Nations.** Geneva: Université de Genève, 1968, 241 p.
This political science doctoral thesis by an American at the University of Geneva concentrates on the period 1960–63, with particular attention to the Fifteenth General Assembly in 1960–61.

Barros, James, ed. **The United Nations: Past, Present, and Future.** New York: Free Press, 1972, 279 p.
Six experts assess the contemporary role and accomplishments of the six chief organs of the United Nations. The major accomplishment: that the U.N. has survived.

Becker, Benjamin M. **Is the United Nations Dead?** Philadelphia: Whitmore Publishing Co., 1969, 163 p.
A well-reasoned plea for strengthening the United Nations, aimed at the general reader.

Bingham, June Rossbach. **U Thant: The Search for Peace.** New York: Knopf, 1966, 300 p.
An interim biography of the Secretary-General of the U.N. by the wife of a former U.S. Ambassador to the organization.

Bolintineanu, A. and Malița, Mircea. **Carta ONU—document al erei noastre.** Bucharest: Editura Politica, 1970, 360 p.

Two leading Rumanian scholars discuss the achievements and disappointments of the United Nations, with special emphasis on the contributions made by Rumania.

Boyd, Andrew. **Fifteen Men on a Powder Keg.** New York: Stein and Day, 1971, 383 p.

A lively and highly informative study of the U.N. Security Council.

Carey, John. **UN Protection of Civil and Political Rights.** Syracuse: Syracuse University Press, 1970, 205 p.

The author traces the efforts made by the United Nations on many fronts to protect individuals from their own governments. The conclusions are both realistic and constructive.

Castañeda, Jorge. **Legal Effects of United Nations Resolutions.** New York: Columbia University Press, 1970, 243 p.

A careful legal analysis of six types of U.N. General Assembly resolutions which, in the author's opinion, "produce true juridical effects against which members have no legal recourse."

Cordier, Andrew W. and Maxwell, Kenneth L., eds. **Paths to World Order.** New York: Columbia University Press, 1967, 161 p.

This volume comprises the Dag Hammarskjöld Memorial Lectures, presented in 1965, and deals both with the late Secretary-General's life and work and with some of the major issues he was concerned with or involved in.

Cordier, Andrew W. and Foote, Wilder, eds. **Public Papers of the Secretaries-General of the United Nations.** New York: Columbia University Press, 1969.

A well-prepared collection including "all texts believed by the editors to be essential or most likely to be useful in study and research about the United Nations." The following volumes have been published through 1973: "Volume I: Trygve Lie, 1946–1953" (1969, 535 p.); "Volume II: Dag Hammarskjöld, 1953–1956" (1972, 716 p.); "Volume III: Dag Hammarskjöld, 1956–1957" (1973, 729 p.).

Cosgrove, Carol Ann and Twitchett, Kenneth J., eds. **The New International Actors: The United Nations and the European Economic Community.** New York: St. Martin's Press, 1970, 272 p.

This book brings together some excellent articles on the United Nations and the European Economic Community. The authors fail, however, in their efforts to build a common analytical framework for the two institutions.

Coyle, David Cushman. **The United Nations and How It Works.** New York: Columbia University Press, rev. ed., 1969, 256 p.

A revised edition of a useful introductory survey of which the first edition appeared in 1961.

De Guinsbourg, Victor. **The Eternal Machiavelli in the United Nations World.** Scarsdale (N.Y.): The Author, 1969, 899 p.

A collection of salient U.N. documents and proverbs assembled by a former member of the U.N. Military Staff Committee.

Donovan, Frank Robert. **Mr. Roosevelt's Four Freedoms: The Story behind the United Nations Charter.** New York: Dodd, 1966, 245 p.

A discussion of how Roosevelt's political ideas and ideals influenced the formation of the United Nations.

Eichelberger, Clark Mell. **New Dimensions for the United Nations: The Problems of the Next Decade.** Dobbs Ferry (N.Y.): Oceana Publications, 1966, 225 p.

The seventeenth report of the Commission to Study the Organization of Peace, supplemented with a collection of essays by various authors.

Eichelberger, Clark Mell. **UN: The First Twenty-five Years.** New York: Harper and Row, rev. ed. 1970, 178 p.

A revision and updating of one of the best popular books on the United Nations for the general reader.

El-Ayouty, Yassin. **The United Nations and Decolonization.** The Hague: Nijhoff, 1971, 286 p.

This scholarly study reveals the catalytic role of the Afro-Asian states in the decolonization process.

Everyman's United Nations: A Complete Handbook of the Activities and Evolution of the United Nations during its First Twenty Years, 1945-1965. New York: United Nations, 8th ed., 1968, 634 p.

A useful reference volume, supplemented by "Everyman's United Nations: A Summary of the Activities of the United Nations During the Five-Year Period 1966-1970" (New York: United Nations, 1971, 248 p.).

Farajallah, Samaan Boutros. **Le Groupe afro-asiatique dans le cadre des Nations Unies.** Geneva: Droz, 1963, 511 p.

An analysis of the formation and structure of the Afro-Asian group in the United Nations, based on documentary sources and taking into account national political events which affect the attitudes and actions of the group.

Gavshon, Arthur L. **The Last Days of Dag Hammarskjold.** London: Barrie, 1963, 259 p.

An examination of the circumstances surrounding the death in an air crash of the former Secretary-General of the United Nations.

Goodrich, Leland M.; Hambro, Edvard and Simons, Anne Patricia. **Charter of the United Nations: Commentary and Documents.** New York: Columbia University Press, 3rd rev. ed., 1969, 732 p.

This classic interpretation of the U.N. Charter traces in a definitive manner the constitutional evolution of the United Nations.

Gordenker, Leon, *ed.* **The United Nations in International Politics.** Princeton: Princeton University Press, 1971, 241 p.

Six first-rate essays by leading scholars of the United Nations, exploring the present and future role of the world organization in the international political system.

Gordenker, Leon. **The UN Secretary-General and the Maintenance of Peace.** New York: Columbia University Press, 1967, 380 p.

A thoughtful study of three Secretaries-General and how they viewed their political functions.

Halderman, John W. **The United Nations and the Rule of Law: Charter Development through the Handling of International Disputes and Situations.** Dobbs Ferry (N.Y.): Oceana Publications, 1967, 248 p.

This substantial monograph is a product of the United Nations Studies Program of the Rule of Law Research Center at Duke University.

Hammarskjöld, Dag. **Markings.** New York: Knopf, 1964, 221 p.

These posthumously published jottings and entries by the late Secretary-General of the United Nations contain virtually nothing about his public activities, but a great deal about his inner state of mind—"a sort of *white book* concerning my negotiations with myself—and with God." They are of considerable importance to one's picture of the whole man, and yet the bafflement and perplexity of most reviewers suggest the difficulty of interpreting them.

Hammarskjöld, Dag. **Servant of Peace: A Selection of the Speeches and Statements of Dag Hammarskjöld, Secretary-General of the United Nations, 1953-1961.** New York: Harper and Row, 1962, 388 p.

A selection of the speeches and statements of the late Secretary-General, edited and introduced by Wilder Foote.

Han, Henry H. **International Legislation by the United Nations.** New York: Exposition Press, 1971, 221 p.

An examination of the U.N. machinery for international legislative functions, with recommendations for improvement, by a Korean-born professor at Central Michigan University.

Kahng, Tae Jin. **Law, Politics, and the Security Council.** The Hague: Nijhoff, 1964, 252 p.

An attempt by a Korean scholar to clarify the practice of the Security Council in the handling of legal questions that includes, among others, examinations of the Suez, the Congo and the Cuban crises. Introduced by Professor Leland M. Goodrich.

Kay, David A. **The New Nations in the United Nations, 1960-1967.** New York: Columbia University Press, 1970, 254 p.

The main preoccupations of the United Nations, in the author's view, are no longer peacekeeping and the composition of East-West disputes, but economic development and decolonization. These shifts in emphasis are largely the result of the new nations' exercise of political influence in the world organization. A careful and scholarly study.

Kay, David A., ed. **The United Nations Political System.** New York: Wiley, 1967, 419 p.
Twenty-four judiciously selected essays.

Kelen, Imre. **Hammarskjöld.** New York: Putnam, 1966, 316 p.
A journalistic account by a former director and producer of television at the U.N.

Lee, Marc J. **The United Nations and World Realities.** New York: Pergamon Press, 1965, 255 p.
An examination of the efforts of the United Nations to solve various political, social and cultural problems during the first twenty years of its existence, by a lecturer in international politics at Southampton University. For the general reader.

The Maxwell School Series on the Administration of Foreign Policy through the United Nations. Syracuse: Syracuse University, Maxwell School of Citizenship and Public Affairs, 1966–69.
In this series of country studies the following volumes have appeared: "The Administration of United Kingdom Foreign Policy Through the United Nations," by Rosalyn Higgins (1966, 63 p.); "The Administration of United States Foreign Policy Through the United Nations," by Donald Gordon Bishop (1967, 112 p.); and "The Administration of Indian Foreign Policy Through the United Nations," by Charles P. Schleicher and J. S. Bains (1969, 130 p.).

Miller, Linda B. **World Order and Local Disorder.** Princeton: Princeton University Press (for the Center of International Studies, Princeton University), 1967, 235 p.
A good factual account of the role the United Nations has played or failed to play in internal conflicts. Somewhat lacking in analytical depth.

Morozov, Grigorii Iosifovich and Others, eds. **OON: itogi, tendentsii, perspektivy. (K 25-letiiu OON).** Moscow: Izd-vo "Mezhdunarodnye Otnosheniia," 1970, 544 p.
An assessment of the United Nations at its twenty-fifth anniversary, by a team of Soviet and Eastern European observers. A bibliography of Soviet works on the United Nations is included.

National Studies on International Organization. New York: Manhattan Publishing Co. (for the Carnegie Endowment for International Peace).
The two concluding volumes of the 24-volume series of studies, dealing with the relations of a group of states with the United Nations and other international organizations, were published as: "The United States and the United Nations: The Search for International Peace and Security," by Lawrence D. Weiler and Anne Patricia Simons (1967, 589 p.); and "The Federal Republic of Germany and the United Nations," by Heinz Dröge, Fritz Münch and Ellinor von Puttkamer, for the Deutsche Gesellschaft für Auswärtige Politik (1967, 206 p.).

Pfahlberg, Bernhard. **Zur Politik afro-asiatischer Staaten in den Vereinten Nationen, 1945–1960.** Baden-Baden: Nomos Verlagsgesellschaft, 1966, 283 p.
A well-documented study of the foreign policies of the Afro-Asian states as demonstrated by their participation in the work of the United Nations from 1945–60.

Prokof'ev, B. P. **OON—25 let.** Moscow: Izdatel'stvo "Mezhdunarodnye Otnosheniia," 1970, 80 p.
A Soviet account of the United Nations' first 25 years. The author is optimistic about the organization's future.

Prosser, Michael H., ed. **Sow the Wind, Reap the Whirlwind.** New York: Morrow, 1970, 2 v.
One-hundred fifty speeches by heads of state who have addressed the United Nations during its first 25 years.

Ross, Alf. **The United Nations: Peace and Progress.** Totowa (N.J.): The Bedminster Press, 1966, 443 p.
A Danish professor argues that American-Russian rapprochement is the only sure foundation for world peace and a successful United Nations.

Schlüter, Hilmar Werner. **Diplomatie der Versöhnung: die Vereinten Nationen und die Wahrung des Weltfriedens.** Stuttgart: Seewald, 1966, 440 p.
A systematic description of the efforts of the United Nations to maintain and secure peace in the world.

Sen, Sudhir. **United Nations in Economic Development—Need for a New Strategy.**
Dobbs Ferry (N.Y.): Oceana Publications, 1969, 351 p.
A practical and constructive study by a former official of the U.N. Technical Assistance Board.

Sharma, D. N. **Afro-Asian Group in the U.N.** Allahabad: Chaitanya Publishing House, 1969, 411 p.
The author's survey of the major questions of concern to the Afro-Asian group at the United Nations reflects most of the ingredients of the anti-colonial position. He also tends to regard the group as much more monolithic than it actually is.

Sharp, Walter R. **The United Nations Economic and Social Council.** New York: Columbia University Press, 1969, 322 p.
A straightforward description and analysis of ECOSOC, the first such book to appear in the literature on the United Nations.

Siegler, Heinrich, Freiherr von. **Die Vereinten Nationen: eine Bilanz nach zwanzig Jahren.** Bonn: Siegler, Verlag für Zeitarchive, 1966, 195 p.
A survey of the origins, operations and accomplishments of the United Nations.

Smouts, Marie-Claude. **Le Secrétaire général des Nations Unies.** Paris: Colin, 1971, 298 p.
A dissertation on the role played by the Secretaries-General of the United Nations in resolving international conflicts.

Stevenson, Adlai Ewing. **Looking Outward: Years of Crisis at the United Nations.** New York: Harper and Row, 1963, 295 p.
A selection of Governor Stevenson's eloquent speeches in the years that he was U.S. Ambassador to the United Nations. While he deals chiefly with international themes, there is also a section on American problems and a selection of playful miscellany.

Stoessinger, John George and Others. **Financing the United Nations System.** Washington: Brookings Institution, 1964, 348 p.
Professor Stoessinger, in collaboration with ten experts, examines closely the many ramifications of the financial plight of the United Nations operations and possible ways to solve the situation, which he holds is above all a "political crisis over the proper role the United Nations is to play in the national policies of its member states."

Stoessinger, John George with McKelvey, Robert C. **The United Nations and the Superpowers.** New York: Random House, 2d rev. ed., 1970, 210 p.
Case studies illustrating various patterns of U.S.-Soviet political interaction at the United Nations.

Sud, Usha. **United Nations and the Non-Self-Governing Territories.** Jullundur: University Publications, 1965, 219 p.
In the words of the author, an American-trained Indian scholar, "the purpose of this book is to introduce the reader to the provisions of Chapter XI of the United Nations Charter which deals with non-self governing territories, and its subsequent elaboration."

Tavares de Sá, Hernane. **The Play within the Play: The Inside Story of the UN.** New York: Knopf, 1966, 309 p.
An urbane, witty, and often quite critical account of the activities of the United Nations, by its former Under-Secretary for Public Information (1960–65), who is also a well-known Brazilian journalist and publisher.

Tetlow, Edwin. **The United Nations: The First 25 Years.** London: Peter Owen, 1970, 208 p.
A curious mixture of wisdom, humor and popular gossip, instructive and entertaining for the general reader.

Tobiassen, Leif Kr. **The Reluctant Door: The Right of Access to the United Nations.** Washington: Public Affairs Press, 1969, 413 p.
A detailed examination of the access rights to the United Nations "in terms of the provisions included in the UN Charter and in the 1947 UN Headquarters Agreement, and in terms of the situation in the United States."

Townley, Ralph. **The United Nations: A View from Within.** New York: Scribner, 1969, 353 p.
A competent survey of the United Nations for the general reader.

Tung, William L. **International Organization under the United Nations System.** New York: Crowell, 1969, 415 p.

A scholarly treatment of the subject, with a strong legal and structural emphasis.

Twichett, Kenneth J., ed. **The Evolving United Nations: A Prospect for Peace?** New York: St. Martin's Press (for the David Davies Memorial Institute of International Studies), 1971, 239 p.

Essays by nine hands appraising the role of the United Nations.

Urquhart, Brian. **Hammarskjold.** New York: Knopf, 1972, 630 p.

A superior account of Hammarskjöld's eight years as Secretary-General of the United Nations. The author, a long time U.N. official, was close enough to his subject to give great warmth and humanity to the story, not so close as to distort. Unpublished material from the Hammarskjöld private papers is used throughout to enrich interpretation and break new historical ground.

Van Dusen, Henry P. **Dag Hammarskjöld: The Statesman and His Faith.** New York: Harper and Row, 1967, 240 p.

The former president of New York's Union Theological Seminary traces the interrelation between Dag Hammarskjöld's public career and his private meditations, "Markings," published after the Secretary-General's death in 1961.

Van Langenhove, Fernand. **Le Rôle proéminent du secrétaire général dans l'opération des Nations Unies au Congo.** Brussels: Institut Royal des Relations Internationales, 1964, 260 p.

The growth in the role of the Secretary-General of the United Nations through the involvement of the U.N. in the Congo is lucidly and authoritatively treated by the former Permanent Representative of Belgium to the United Nations.

Van Panhuys, H. F.; Brinkhorst, L. J. and Maas, H. H., eds. **International Organisation and Integration: A Collection of the Texts of Documents Relating to the United Nations, its Related Agencies and Regional Organisations; with Annotations.** Leyden: Sijthoff (for the Cornelis van Vollenhoven Foundation, Leyden, and the Europe Institute, Leyden), 1968, 1,141 p.

The fourth edition of a valuable reference volume which first appeared in 1950 under the title "United Nations Textbook."

Wadsworth, James Jeremiah. **The Glass House: The United Nations in Action.** New York: Praeger, 1966, 224 p.

A personal account of the U.N., based on the author's quite extensive experiences from 1953 to 1961, including those of Chief of U.S. Mission and Permanent U.S. Representative.

Wainhouse, David Walter. **Remnants of Empire: The United Nations and the End of Colonialism.** New York: Harper and Row (for the Council on Foreign Relations), 1964, 153 p.

A close look at what remains of the process of decolonization, with particular attention to the role of the United Nations and the policy issues for the United States. The author was closely associated with the background of these issues as a U.S. State Department official.

Waters, Maurice, ed. **The United Nations: International Organization and Administration.** New York: Macmillan, 1967, 583 p.

A collection of readings by various authors illustrating the activities of the United Nations.

Yearbook of the United Nations, 1946-47—. New York: Office of Public Information, United Nations, 1947—.

An indispensable reference for the many-sided activities of the United Nations and the related inter-governmental organizations. Published annually. The volume for 1971 appeared in 1974.

Zacher, Marc W. **Dag Hammarskjold's United Nations.** New York: Columbia University Press, 1970, 295 p.

A scholarly and measured defense of the Hammarskjöld administration.

Specialized Agencies and Activities

See also Economic Factors, p. 49; International Court of Justice, p. 93; (International Organization and Government) General, p. 96; (United Nations) General, p. 99; Aerial and Space Warfare and Technology, p. 114; and the sections for specific countries and regions.

Ahluwalia, Kuljit. **The Legal Status, Privileges and Immunities of the Specialized Agencies of the United Nations and Certain Other International Organizations.** The Hague: Nijhoff, 1964, 230 p.
A competent study.

Alcock, Antony. **History of the International Labor Organization.** New York: Octagon Books, 1971, 384 p.
A first-rate scholarly monograph, though the author does not pay sufficient attention to the ILO's financial problems, particularly in its relationship to the United States.

Alexander, Yonah. **International Technical Assistance Experts: A Case Study of the U.N. Experience.** New York: Praeger, 1966, 223 p.
A study of the U.N. technical assistance programs and their administration.

Friedeberg, Alfred Salomon. **The United Nations Conference on Trade Development of 1964.** Rotterdam: Rotterdam University Press, 1968, 241 p.
A survey of the first UNCTAD conference.

Gosovic, Branislav. **UNCTAD: Conflict and Compromise.** Leyden: Sijthoff, 1972, 349 p.
An exceptionally thorough analysis of the work of UNCTAD up to 1970, by a Jugoslav author, stressing substantive issues, the development of the organization and the resolution of conflicts among the members.

Hagras, Kamal M. **United Nations Conference on Trade and Development: A Case Study in U.N. Diplomacy.** New York: Praeger, 1965, 171 p.
This study by an official of the United Arab Republic is primarily a straightforward account of the conference proceedings and results.

Johnston, George Alexander. **The International Labour Organisation: Its Work for Social and Economic Progress.** London: Europa Publications, 1970, 363 p.
An excellent monograph on the history, structure and activities of the ILO, by a British scholar.

Jones, Joseph Marion. **The United Nations at Work: Developing Land, Forests, Oceans, and People.** New York: Pergamon Press, 1965, 238 p.
An account of the problems confronting the F.A.O. and other U.N. agencies in their efforts to help the developing countries to speed social and economic progress, by a professor at the Fletcher School of Law and Diplomacy, Tufts University.

Kirdar, Üner. **The Structure of United Nations Economic-Aid to Underdeveloped Countries.** The Hague: Nijhoff, 1966, 361 p.
After a comprehensive and largely descriptive account of the organization of aid, a Turkish official makes a series of proposals for improvement.

Koh, Byung Chul. **The United Nations Administrative Tribunal.** Baton Rouge: Louisiana State University Press, 1966, 176 p.
The author argues that the Tribunal makes a modest contribution to the rule of law at the international level.

Landy, Ernest Alfred. **The Effectiveness of International Supervision: Thirty Years of I.L.O. Experience.** Dobbs Ferry (N.Y.): Oceana Publications (for the Université de Genève, Institut Universitaire de Hautes Études Internationales), 1966, 268 p.
A systematic attempt to measure the effectiveness of international supervisory arrangements of the International Labour Organization.

Maheu, René. **La Civilisation de l'universel.** Paris: Laffont, 1966, 282 p.
A collection of writings by the former Director-General of UNESCO.

Mangone, Gerard Joseph, *ed.* **UN Administration of Economic and Social Programs.** New York: Columbia University Press, 1966, 291 p.
Six specialists write chapters on the organization, coördination and field administration of U.N. social and economic programs.

Morozov, Grigorii Iosifovich and Others, *eds*. **Spetsializirovannye uchrezhdeniia OON v sovremennom mire.** Moscow: Izd-vo "Nauka," 1967, 402 p.
A Soviet survey of the specialized agencies of the United Nations.

Morse, David Abner. **The Origin and Evolution of the I.L.O. and its Role in the World Community.** Ithaca: New York State School of Industrial and Labor Relations, Cornell University, 1969, 125 p.
A useful study.

Račić, Obrad. **Odnos izmedju Ujedinjenih Nacija specijalizovanih ustanova.** Belgrade: Institut za medjunarodnu politiku, 1966, 303 p.
A Jugoslav study of the relationship between the United Nations and various international specialized agencies.

Sathyamurthy, T. V. **The Politics of International Cooperation: Contrasting Conceptions of U.N.E.S.C.O.** Geneva: Droz, 1964, 313 p.
A thoughtful and well-conceived examination of UNESCO, and a review of the attitudes of the United States, the United Kingdom, the U.S.S.R., France, Brazil and India toward that organization. There is a useful bibliography.

Sewell, James Patrick. **Functionalism and World Politics: A Study Based on United Nations Programs Financing Economic Development.** Princeton: Princeton University Press, 1966, 359 p.
The core of this book is a good history of development activities in the U.N., the World Bank and its affiliates.

Shkunaev, Vladimir Glebovich. **Mezhdunarodnaia organizatsiia truda vchera i segodnia.** Moscow: Mezhdunarodnaia Otonosheniia, 1968, 247 p.
A former member of the Soviet delegation to the ILO has written an historical survey of ILO with emphasis on the Soviet role.

Shuster, George Nauman. **UNESCO: Assessment and Promise.** New York: Harper and Row (for the Council on Foreign Relations), 1963, 130 p.
An American educator associated with UNESCO from its beginnings gives his considered views on the purposes and achievements of that organization and its role in world affairs. The book pays special attention to implications for U.S. foreign policy.

Tickner, Frederick James. **Technical Cooperation.** New York: Praeger (in coöperation with the United Nations, Special Projects Office), 1966, 206 p.
A professor at the State University of New York, who was associated with the U.N. technical aid program for ten years, writes about the transfer of technical knowledge and skills to developing nations.

Peace-Keeping Forces and Operations

See also Law of War; Aggression, p. 89; (International Organization and Government) General, p. 96; War and Peace, p. 108; Cyprus, p. 418; Arab-Israeli Conflict, p. 633; The Korean War, p. 728; Zaïre, p. 822.

Attia, Gamal el Din. **Les Forces armées des Nations Unies en Corée et au Moyen-Orient.** Geneva: Droz, 1963, 467 p.
An analysis of the legal aspects of the U.N. intervention in Korea and the Middle East.

Ballaloud, Jacques. **L'ONU et les opérations de maintien de la paix.** Paris: Pedone, 1971, 239 p.
A rather general discussion of the development of the U.N. peace-keeping functions.

Bloomfield, Lincoln P. with Others. **The Power to Keep Peace.** Berkeley: World Without War Council, 1971, 249 p.
The principal author's optimism about prospects for a U.N. police force is balanced by more melancholy assessments by three other scholars. An interesting essay by a psychiatrist concludes the symposium. An updated version of a work which appeared originally as "International Military Forces" (Boston: Little, Brown, 1964, 296 p.).

Bowett, Derek William and Others. **United Nations Forces: A Legal Study of United Nations Practice.** New York: Praeger (for the David Davies Memorial Institute), 1964, 579 p.
A comprehensive discussion, both historical and prescriptive, of the use of U.N. forces in maintaining the peace. The author, an international lawyer, spent two years in the U.N. Secretariat.

Boyd, James M. **United Nations Peace-Keeping Operations: A Military and Political Appraisal.** New York: Praeger, 1971, 261 p.
A U.S. Air Force officer analyzes the United Nations peace-keeping operations, as Leland M. Goodrich states in the foreword, "against the background of his own extensive and varied military experience."

Burns, Arthur Lee and Heathcote, Nina. **Peace-Keeping by U.N. Forces: From Suez to the Congo.** New York: Praeger (for the Center of International Studies, Princeton University), 1963, 256 p.
A good study of the uses to which the U.N. has put military forces at its disposal in recent years: in Suez, Lebanon, Jordan and the Congo. A concluding chapter considers the limitations and possibilities of such forces.

Cox, Arthur M. **Prospects for Peacekeeping.** Washington: Brookings Institution, 1967, 178 p.
A useful, if somewhat superficial, interpretive essay on United Nations peace-keeping operations with emphasis on their significance in the context of American foreign policy.

Fabian, Larry L. **Soldiers Without Enemies: Preparing the United Nations for Peacekeeping.** Washington: Brookings Institution, 1971, 315 p.
An informative survey of U.N. peace-keeping operations. The author emphasizes political and military preparedness for peace-keeping and concludes his analysis with some practical suggestions for the future.

Harbottle, Michael. **The Blue Berets.** Harrisburg: Stackpole, 1972, 157 p.
A brief guide to the more significant U.N. peace-keeping efforts since 1946.

Harbottle, Michael. **The Impartial Soldier.** New York: Oxford University Press (for the Royal Institute of International Affairs), 1970, 210 p.
The author, Chief of Staff of the U.N. Force in Cyprus from 1966 to 1968, describes his experiences as an idealist without illusions.

Higgins, Rosalyn. **United Nations Peacekeeping 1946–1967: Documents and Commentary.** New York: Oxford University Press (for the Royal Institute of International Affairs).
An invaluable reference work, planned in three volumes. Through 1973 the following volumes have appeared: vol. I, "The Middle East" (1969, 674 p.) and vol. II, "Asia" (1970, 486 p.).

Horn, Carl C. von. **Soldiering for Peace.** New York: McKay, 1967, 402 p.
Memoirs of the Swedish general who had been the military commander of U.N. forces in Palestine, Congo and Yemen. A useful source for the study of international peace-keeping operations.

Hymoff, Edward. **Stig von Bayer: International Troubleshooter for Peace.** New York: James H. Heineman, 1965, 368 p.
A study of the U.N. peace-keeping forces in the Congo and Cyprus, centered around the career and adventures of a young Swedish officer.

James, Alan. **The Politics of Peace-Keeping.** New York: Praeger (for the Institute for Strategic Studies), 1969, 452 p.
In this study the author combines thorough factual information with intelligent analysis and suggests that great-power consensus will continue to provide the best context for U.N. peace-keeping operations.

Karaosmanoğlu, Ali L. **Les Actions militaires coercitives et non coercitives des Nations Unies.** Geneva: Droz, 1970, 320 p.
A solid examination of the legal aspects of the U.N. peace-keeping operations involving military forces.

Larus, Joel, ed. **From Collective Security to Preventive Diplomacy: Readings in International Organization and the Maintenance of Peace.** New York: Wiley, 1965, 556 p.
Readings illustrating the peace-keeping operations at the League of Nations and the United Nations.

Legault, Albert. **Peace-Keeping Operations: Bibliography.** Paris: International Information Center on Peace-Keeping Operations, 1967, 203 p.
A useful reference.

Rosner, Gabriella. **The United Nations Emergency Force.** New York: Columbia University Press, 1963, 294 p.

A comprehensive record of UNEF (United Nations Emergency Force), created in November 1956 to cope with the Suez crisis, and a strong recommendation for a permanent international force.

Taylor, Alastair and Others. **Peacekeeping: International Challenge and Canadian Response.** Toronto: Canadian Institute of International Affairs, 1968, 211 p.
A valuable account of the Canadian contribution to U.N. peace-keeping operations.

Williams, Walter L. **Intergovernmental Military Forces and World Public Order.** Dobbs Ferry (N.Y.): Oceana Publications, 1971, 703 p.
The author analyzes contemporary intergovernmental military forces and pleads for their strengthening.

VIII. WAR AND PEACE

WAR

General

See also General Works, p. 1; Law of War; Aggression, p. 89; (The World Since 1914) General, p. 129; First World War, p. 131; Second World War, p. 144; The Postwar World, p. 178; and the sections for specific countries and regions.

The Arms Trade with the Third World. New York: Humanities Press (for the Stockholm International Peace Research Institute), 1971, 910 p.
A massive compilation of information on the arms trade from industrialized to underdeveloped countries since 1945.

Art, Robert J. and Waltz, Kenneth Neal, *eds.* **The Use of Force: International Politics and Foreign Policy.** Boston: Little, Brown, 1971, 547 p.
A widely representative symposium on the uses of military power in world politics today.

Buchan, Alastair Francis. **War in Modern Society: An Introduction.** New York: Harper and Row, 1968, 207 p.
A thoughtful introductory essay by a British scholar. (First published in England in 1966.)

Calder, Nigel, *ed.* **Unless Peace Comes.** New York: Viking, 1968, 243 p.
A grim forecast about the weapons of the 1980s. Samples include "robots on the march," "psychic poisons" and "infectious clouds."

Clarke, Robin. **The Science of War and Peace.** New York: McGraw-Hill, 1972, 335 p.
After a review, largely familiar but still chilling, of the disasters that threaten to overtake humanity, the author turns to the various intellectual efforts that are being made to find a way to avert catastrophe.

Coste, René. **Mars ou Jésus? La Conscience chrétienne juge la guerre.** Lyons: Chronique Sociale de France, 1963, 208 p.
A theologian attempts to deal with the problem of war from the Christian point of view and more specifically through the ideas of Pope Pius XII.

Craig, Gordon Alexander. **War, Politics, and Diplomacy.** New York: Praeger, 1966, 297 p.
A collection of essays on war, civil-military relations and diplomacy by a leading American historian.

Dupuy, Trevor Nevitt and Others. **The Almanac of World Military Power.** Dunn Loring (Va.): T. N. Dupuy Associates (in association with Stackpole Books), 1971, 338 p.
A useful geopolitical assessment of the power capabilities of the world's nations.

Erickson, John and Others, *eds.* **The Military-Technical Revolution: Its Impact on Strategy and Foreign Policy.** New York: Praeger (for the Institute for the Study of the U.S.S.R.), 1966, 284 p.

A symposium based on a 1964 conference. Almost half the contributions deal specifically with the Soviet Union.

Feld, Bernard Taub and Others, *eds.* **Impact of New Technologies on the Arms Race.** Cambridge: M.I.T. Press, 1971, 379 p.
Papers and discussion from the 10th Pugwash Symposium held in June 1970.

Frank, Jerome D. **Sanity and Survival: Psychological Aspects of War and Peace.** New York: Random House, 1968, 330 p.
A welcome effort to build a bridge between psychiatry and international politics.

Frank, Lewis A. **The Arms Trade in International Relations.** New York: Praeger, 1969, 266 p.
The author concludes his well-documented study by saying that the only really effective control over the arms trade "will reside with the principal supplier countries who maintain sufficient power and military strength to encourage the pursuit of more nonmilitary goals by those seeking additional weapons."

Fried, Morton and Others, *eds.* **War: The Anthropology of Armed Conflict and Aggression.** New York: The Natural History Press (for the American Museum of Natural History), 1968, 262 p.
A collection of papers originally delivered in 1967 at a symposium of the American Anthropological Association.

Getlein, Frank. **Playing Soldier: A Diatribe.** New York: Holt, Rinehart and Winston, 1971, 168 p.
The universal appeal of war, the author asserts, is in its game quality: "War is hell, said Sherman, who was in a good position to know, but there is a long tradition in life and letters that chooses hell over heaven because it's a livelier place. The games are better down there."

Harkabi, Yehoshafat. **Nuclear War and Nuclear Peace.** New York: Daniel Davey, 1966, 303 p.
An introduction to the study of modern strategy within the framework of international relations, by an Israeli general.

Herzog, Arthur. **The War-Peace Establishment.** New York: Harper and Row, 1965, 271 p.
A journalist's effort to identify, describe and appraise the various schools of thought engaged in the "arms debate."

Higham, Robin David Stewart, *ed.* **Civil Wars in the Twentieth Century.** Lexington: University Press of Kentucky, 1972, 260 p.
A collection of essays covering the civil wars in Russia, China, Vietnam, Spain, Ireland and Nigeria.

Horsburgh, H. J. N. **Non-Violence and Aggression: A Study of Gandhi's Moral Equivalent of War.** New York: Oxford University Press, 1968, 207 p.
A discussion of the ethical and religious presuppositions of Satyagraha (reform through friendly passive resistance), of Gandhi's application of that concept, and the practicability of its substitution for armed force.

Howard, Michael Eliot. **Studies in War and Peace.** New York: Viking, 1971, 262 p.
A collection of thoughtful essays by a British military historian with a pronounced philosophical bent.

Iklé, Fred Charles. **Every War Must End.** New York: Columbia University Press, 1971, 160 p.
A valuable analysis of the tormented process through which wars in the twentieth century have been brought to a close. The author concludes, on the basis of the evidence, that "wars must be ended before they start."

Kahn, Herman. **On Escalation: Metaphors and Scenarios.** New York: Praeger, 1965, 308 p.
The author of "On Thermonuclear War" here turns to an analysis in his characteristic fashion—through metaphors and scenarios—of the problem of escalation, the product of "competition in risk-taking."

Kimminich, Otto. **Rüstung und politische Spannung: Studien zum Problem der internationalen Sicherheit.** Gütersloh: Bertelsmann, 1964, 296 p.

A historical and theoretical discussion of the interrelationship between armament and international tensions, by a German scholar.

Knorr, Klaus Eugen. **On the Uses of Military Power in the Nuclear Age.** Princeton: Princeton University Press (for the Princeton Center of International Studies), 1966, 185 p.
An essay examining "trends discernible in the nature of military conflict, in political attitudes toward war as a method for settling disputes, and hence trends affecting the place of military power in international relations."

Leckie, Robert. **Warfare.** New York: Harper and Row, 1970, 206 p.
This little book about war contains a great deal of knowledge and wisdom. The author rejects the myth of "a world without war" but maintains that, since wars have become less useful to policy-makers because of their greater destructiveness, there might be fewer of them in the future.

Luttwak, Edward. **A Dictionary of Modern War.** New York: Harper and Row, 1971, 224 p.
A lavishly illustrated guide covering hardware and organization as well as concepts of modern war.

McClintock, Robert. **The Meaning of Limited War.** Boston: Houghton, 1967, 239 p.
A fine series of eight case studies of limited war in the nuclear age, with a concluding prescription on how to keep wars of the future limited as well.

McCormick, Donald. **Peddler of Death: The Life and Times of Sir Basil Zaharoff.** New York: Holt, Rinehart and Winston, 1965, 255 p.
An effort to trace the still murky career of the arms merchant who sold weapons from the Boer War to World War I.

McNeil, Elton Burbank, *ed.* **The Nature of Human Conflict.** Englewood Cliffs: Prentice-Hall, 1965, 315 p.
An inter-disciplinary effort to get at the roots of human conflict, especially in war and international relations.

Martin, Thomas Lyle, Jr. and Latham, Donald C. **Strategy for Survival.** Tucson: University of Arizona Press, 1963, 389 p.
A handbook on civil defense and thermonuclear war, with a principal intention of demonstrating the need and feasibility of civil defense measures.

The Military Balance, 1960–. London: The Institute for Strategic Studies, 1960–.
As stated by the compilers of this most useful reference, this annual publication is a "quantitative assessment of the military power and defence expenditure of countries throughout the world."

Montgomery of Alamein, Bernard Law Montgomery, 1st Viscount. **A History of Warfare.** Cleveland: World Publishing Co., 1968, 584 p.
In this beautifully illustrated book, the old British soldier provides a stimulating survey of the major wars and battles throughout history.

Moulton, James Louis. **Defence in a Changing World.** London: Eyre, 1964, 191 p.
A former British officer explains the purpose of defense, treating with clarity the questions of deterrence and disarmament and offering suggestions for the organization of armed forces.

Mydans, Carl and Mydans, Shelley. **The Violent Peace.** New York: Atheneum, 1968, 478 p.
A broad survey, in sharply etched vignettes and numerous superb photographs, of 25 scattered wars around the globe since 1945.

Nerlich, Uwe, *ed.* **Beiträge der Sozialwissenschaft.** Gütersloh: Bertelsmann, 1966, 2 v.
A collection of 51 essays on peace and war by leading American and European scholars. Vol. 1 is entitled "Krieg und Frieden im industriellen Zeitalter," vol. 2, "Krieg und Frieden in der modernen Staatenwelt."

O'Brien, William V. **War and/or Survival.** Garden City: Doubleday, 1966, 289 p.
An intelligent and well-conceptualized probing into the dilemmas of war, morality and law, by a Catholic scholar.

Owen, David. **The Politics of Defence.** New York: Taplinger, 1972, 249 p.
The author, a former Minister for the Royal Navy, finds the present machinery for

defense decision-making to be disturbingly defective, especially in its potential for dangerous escalation.

Palit, Dharitri Kumar. **War in the Deterrent Age.** South Brunswick (N.J.): A. S. Barnes, 1968, 224 p.
The author, a general in the Indian Army, writes that it has been his purpose "to suggest that the establishment of a balance of deterrents in nuclear strategy does not necessarily create a historical condition in which other forms of war become outlawed."

Pruitt, Dean G. and Snyder, Richard C., eds. **Theory and Research on the Causes of War.** Englewood Cliffs: Prentice-Hall, 1969, 314 p.
An uneven collection of essays with a pronounced behavioral bent.

Ramsey, Paul. **The Just War: Force and Political Responsibility.** New York: Scribner, 1968, 554 p.
A Protestant theologian wrestles with the problems of force, justice and peace and concludes that no easy generalizations are possible.

Reid, Robert William. **Tongues of Conscience: Weapons Research and the Scientists' Dilemma.** New York: Walker, 1969, 351 p.
This book consists of a number of essays about great men of science who have been involved in weapons research. Of the dozen sketches drawn by the author, the best are of Alfred Nobel, Albert Einstein and J. Robert Oppenheimer.

Roberts, Adam, ed. **Civilian Resistance as a National Defense: Non-Violent Action Against Aggression.** Harrisburg: Stackpole, 1968, 320 p.
Twelve experts on non-violent resistance contribute case studies from recent history. The English edition appeared as "The Strategy of Civilian Defence" (London: Faber, 1967, 320 p.).

Rosenau, James N., ed. **International Aspects of Civil Strife.** Princeton: Princeton University Press, 1964, 322 p.
A symposium that endeavors to define the "sociological, systematic, legal, political, strategic and moral links between internal wars and international processes."

Schelling, Thomas C. **Arms and Influence.** New Haven: Yale University Press (for the Center for International Affairs, Harvard University), 1966, 293 p.
A leading student of strategic theory here studies the principles that underlie the "diplomacy of violence"—"the bargaining power that comes from the physical harm a nation can do to another nation."

Sergeev, P. I., ed. **Vooruzhenye sily kapitalisticheskikh gosudarstv.** Moscow: Voennoe Izd-vo, 1971, 488 p.
A systematic survey of the military forces and strategic doctrines of the major Western states, intended to serve as a handbook for Soviet officers.

Singer, J. David and Small, Melvin. **The Wages of War, 1816–1965: A Statistical Handbook.** New York: Wiley, 1972, 419 p.
A statistical survey of wars, much of it computer-generated. Behavioralist-oriented scholars will find this useful.

SIPRI Yearbook of World Armaments and Disarmament, 1968/69–. New York: Humanities Press (for the Stockholm International Peace Research Institute), 1969–.
An informative annual publication, prepared by an international group of scholars, the purpose of which is "to provide a synoptic view of world armaments and military expenditure, and of the progress made, if any, in limiting or reducing them." Particularly valuable are the many statistical tables.

Speier, Hans. **Force and Folly.** Cambridge: M.I.T. Press, 1969, 342 p.
Occasional essays on war, international affairs and intellectual history, by a member of the Research Council of the RAND Corporation.

Strategic Survey, 1966–. London: The Institute for Strategic Studies, 1967–.
A very useful annual publication reviewing "developments, during the preceding calendar year, in strategic policy, doctrine and weapons in the most significant powers and areas."

Strokov, Aleksandr Aleksandrovich, ed. **Istoriia voennogo iskusstva.** Moscow: Voennoe Izd-vo, 1966, 654 p.
A Soviet history of warfare, with heavy emphasis on the "Great Patriotic War" of

1941-45. A concluding chapter summarizes contemporary military doctrines of the major capitalist powers.

Ten Eyck, John C. **The Law of Diminishing War Power: From Troy to Vietnam.** New York: Pageant Press International, 1970, 273 p.
In a number of case studies drawn from different historical periods and geographic locales, the author demonstrates that too many military successes may lead to the kind of overconfidence that ultimately invites military disaster.

Timasheff, Nicholas Sergeyevitch. **War and Revolution.** New York: Sheed and Ward, 1965, 339 p.
A Russian-born scholar, before his retirement Professor of Sociology at Fordham University, attempts to describe the social phenomena involved in the human processes related to war, revolution and peace.

Tompkins, John S. **The Weapons of World War III: The Long Road Back From the Bomb.** Garden City: Doubleday, 1966, 340 p.
In this discussion of the relation between weapons and tactics, the author looks into the weapons that could permit tactical choices short of nuclear war.

Van Doorn, Jacques, *ed.* **Armed Forces and Society: Sociological Essays.** The Hague: Mouton, 1968, 386 p.
A wide-ranging and substantial collection of essays.

Wolf, Eric R. **Peasant Wars of the Twentieth Century.** New York: Harper and Row, 1969, 328 p.
An anthropologist compares with great skill six recent peasant revolutions—in Mexico, Russia, China, Vietnam, Algeria and Cuba.

Theoretical Studies; Strategy

See also Law of War; Aggression, p. 89; War, p. 108; First World War, p. 131; Second World War, p. 144; The Cold War; Peaceful Coexistence, p. 180; (The United States) Military and Defense Policy, p. 257; (Great Britain) Military Policy, p. 378; (Union of Soviet Socialist Republics) Military Policy, p. 561; (China) Military Questions, p. 705; The Korean War, p. 728; The Vietnam War, p. 739.

Barringer, Richard E. and Ramers, Robert K. **War: Patterns of Conflict.** Cambridge: M.I.T. Press, 1972, 2 v.
An ambitious, very technical effort to demonstrate that conflict is a systematic phenomenon and hence subject to reliable and automated techniques capable of manipulating the multitude of variables involved. The accompanying technical manual provides the requisite computer programs.

Beaufre, André. **An Introduction to Strategy.** New York: Praeger, 1965, 138 p.
———. **Deterrence and Strategy.** New York: Praeger, 1966, 173 p.
———. **Strategy of Action.** New York: Praeger, 1967, 136 p.
A trilogy on strategic thought by a leading French military writer. The original editions appeared as: "Introduction à la stratégie" (Paris: Colin, 1963, 127 p.); "Dissuasion et stratégie" (Paris: Colin, 1964, 207 p.); and "Stratégie de l'action" (Paris: Colin, 1966, 144 p.).

Bokarev, Viktor Andreevich. **Kibernetika i voennoe delo: filosofiskii ocherk.** Moscow: Voennoe Izd-vo, 1969, 287 p.
An introductory inquiry into the military applications of cybernetics, including a discussion of weapons development, simulation, modelling, and problems of command.

Brown, Neville. **Strategic Mobility.** New York: Praeger (for the Institute for Strategic Studies), 1964, 254 p.
A British student of military affairs discusses the possibilities and limits of mobile forces and operations.

Coats, Wendell J. **Armed Force as Power.** New York: Exposition Press, 1967, 432 p.
A broadly conceived essay on the theory of war.

Däniker, Gustav. **Strategie des Kleinstaats: politisch-militärische Möglichkeiten schweizerischer Selbstbehauptung im Atomzeitalter.** Frauenfeld: Huber, 1966, 230 p.
A stimulating discussion, by a Swiss military analyst, of the strategic opportunities available to a small power in the nuclear age.

Dahm, Helmut. **Abschreckung oder Volkskrieg.** Olten: Walter-Verlag, 1968, 414 p.
An extensively documented presentation of Soviet and Communist Chinese strategic and military doctrine.

Duncker, Joachim Zachris. **Eine neue Aera der Kriegführung? Finnische Gedanken zum modernen Kriegsbild.** Darmstadt: Wehr und Wissen Verlagsgesellschaft, 1963, 205 p.
A Finnish officer's view of contemporary warfare and strategy.

Eccles, Henry Effingham. **Military Concepts and Philosophy.** New Brunswick: Rutgers University Press, 1965, 339 p.
Admiral Eccles undertakes to establish the framework for a comprehensive theory of conflict under conditions of modern technology—an effort to relate classic concepts to current reality.

Galula, David. **Counterinsurgency Warfare: Theory and Practice.** New York: Praeger, 1964, 143 p.
An effort "to define the laws of counterrevolutionary warfare, to deduce from them its principles, and to outline the corresponding strategy and tactics."

Hoffmann, Stanley. **The State of War: Essays on the Theory and Practice of International Politics.** New York: Praeger, 1965, 276 p.
A collection of significant essays by a Harvard professor.

Howard, Michael Eliot, *ed.* **The Theory and Practice of War.** New York: Praeger, 1966, 376 p.
A symposium of essays on a wide variety of military themes, historical and strategic, appropriately presented as a *Festschrift* to Captain B. H. Liddell Hart.

Kingston-McCloughry, Edgar James. **The Spectrum of Strategy: A Study of Policy and Strategy in Modern War.** London: Cape, 1964, 223 p.
In this survey of modern strategy the author, a British Air Vice-Marshal, is very much concerned with contemporary problems that affect NATO and East-West relations.

Legault, Albert. **Le Concept de la dissuasion: ses exigences stratégiques et ses incidences sur la politique.** Ambilly-Annemassee: Presses de Savoie, 1964, 177 p.
An elaborate study on deterrence, with extensive documentation and a bibliography.

McGuire, Martin C. **Secrecy and the Arms Race.** Cambridge: Harvard University Press, 1965, 249 p.
An effort to present a theory of the arms race, with particular reference to the role played in it by information and secrecy. A quite technical study using a number of tools of economic analysis.

Problems of Modern Strategy. New York: Praeger (for the Institute for Strategic Studies), 1970, 219 p.
These papers prepared by nine leading theorists of modern strategy for the 1968 Conference of the Institute for Strategic Studies are distinguished by their broadly conceived nontechnical approach. Foreword by Alastair Buchan.

Rapoport, Anatol. **Strategy and Conscience.** New York: Harper and Row, 1964, 323 p.
A critique of contemporary strategic thinking and its premises.

Rosecrance, Richard Newton, *ed.* **The Future of the International Strategic System.** San Francisco: Chandler (for the Institute of International Studies, University of California, Berkeley), 1972, 219 p.
Essays exploring the implications of a multipolar strategic world.

Ruge, Friedrich. **Politik und Strategie: strategisches Denken und politisches Handeln.** Frankfurt/Main: Bernard und Graefe (for the Arbeitskreis für Wehrforschung), 1967, 319 p.
In this survey of contemporary strategic doctrines, Admiral Ruge, a veteran of the German Navy, devotes a great deal of attention to questions of subversion and political warfare.

Sun-tzŭ. **The Art of War.** New York: Oxford University Press, 1963, 197 p.
A new translation, with an extensive introduction by Samuel B. Griffith II, of a classic Chinese study on the fundamentals of warfare written in the sixth century B.C.

Šveics, Vilnis. **Small Nation Survival: Political Defense in Unequal Conflicts.** New York: Exposition Press, 1970, 271 p.
The author suggests, on the basis of a number of case studies of unequal conflicts, that

small nations may use their political strength as a decisive strategic element in their military struggle against a great-power aggressor.

Wilson, Andrew. **The Bomb and the Computer: Wargaming from Ancient Chinese Mapboard to Atomic Computer.** New York: Delacorte Press, 1969, 218 p.
An intelligent survey of the uses and abuses of war games in strategic analysis. Easily understandable by the layman.

Wylie, Joseph Caldwell. **Military Strategy: A General Theory of Power Control.** New Brunswick: Rutgers University Press, 1967, 111 p.
In this essay a prominent American naval officer questions the validity of old concepts and pleads for the reintroduction of intellectual order into modern military strategy.

Naval Warfare

See also (First World War) The Conduct of the War, p. 136; (Second World War) Naval Operations, p. 168; and the sections for specific countries.

Cable, James. **Gunboat Diplomacy: Political Applications of Limited Naval Force.** New York: Praeger (for the Institute for Strategic Studies), 1971, 251 p.
An attempt to develop a doctrine of limited use of naval force. Well endowed with illustrative case materials, the analysis is particularly enlightening on the enigma of Soviet naval power.

Gretton, Sir Peter. **Maritime Strategy: A Study of Defense Problems.** New York: Praeger, 1965, 210 p.
A British naval officer seeks "to discover whether the expression 'Maritime Strategy' has any modern relevance," and if so, whether its principles still apply as far as the defense problems of Britain are concerned.

Hezlet, Sir Arthur Richard. **The Submarine and Sea Power.** New York: Stein and Day, 1967, 278 p.
A most thorough analysis of the role of the submarine in the last two world wars. The author sees the nuclear submarine as the supreme arbiter in any future struggle for control of the sea.

Jane's Fighting Ships. New York: Franklin Watts.
The standard reference of the world's navies. The 75th annual volume, edited by John E. Moore, was published in 1974.

Kuenne, Robert Eugene. **The Attack Submarine: A Study in Strategy.** New Haven: Yale University Press, 1965, 215 p.
A technical approach to the problem of deploying attack submarines.

Martin, Laurence W. **The Sea in Modern Strategy.** New York: Praeger, 1967, 190 p.
An impressive study of seapower in the nuclear age by a British scholar, particularly good on blockades and seaborne nuclear forces.

Sanguinetti, Tony. **Atome et batailles sur mer.** Paris: Hachette, 1965, 285 p.
A French naval officer discusses the implications of nuclear power on sea warfare. The concluding chapter deals with the conversion of the French Navy.

Whitehouse, Arthur George Joseph. **Amphibious Operations.** Garden City: Doubleday, 1963, 346 p.
An historical survey of sea-borne landings and movements, from the Romans to General MacArthur.

Aerial and Space Warfare and Technology

See also (First World War) The Conduct of the War, p. 136; (Second World War) Aerial Operations, p. 167; and the sections for specific countries.

Emme, Eugene Morlock, *ed.* **The History of Rocket Technology.** Detroit: Wayne State University Press (in coöperation with the Society for the History of Technology), 1964, 320 p.
A useful and not unduly technical series of knowledgeable articles on the development of rocketry, U.S. rocket programs and manned flight.

WAR AND PEACE

Evans, F. T. and Howard, H. D. **Outlook on Space.** New York: Hillary House, 1965, 179 p.
A non-technical introduction to the growing relationship between space research and international organizations.

Frutkin, Arnold Wolfe. **International Cooperation in Space.** Englewood Cliffs: Prentice-Hall, 1965, 186 p.
An introduction, by a NASA official, including a chapter on coöperation with the Soviet Union.

Goldsen, Joseph M., ed. **Outer Space in World Politics.** New York: Praeger, 1963, 180 p.
A collection of essays by knowledgeable writers.

Hezlet, Sir Arthur Richard. **Aircraft and Sea Power.** New York: Stein and Day, 1970, 370 p.
An illuminating analysis of the past and future role of aircraft at sea, by a leading British expert.

Kash, Don E. **The Politics of Space Cooperation.** Lafayette (Ind.): Purdue University Studies, 1967, 137 p.
A good survey, despite minor inaccuracies, of NASA's record and of U.S. space projects with the Soviet Union and the United Nations.

Klass, Philip J. **Secret Sentries in Space.** New York: Random House, 1971, 236 p.
The thesis of this informative book is that reconnaissance and surveillance satellites have been and can continue to be a powerful force for peace.

Levy, Lillian, ed. **Space: Its Impact on Man and Society.** New York: Norton, 1965, 228 p.
A symposium discussing a variety of questions—legal, economic, political, military and moral—relating to space exploration.

Ossenbeck, Frederick J. and Kroeck, Patricia C., eds. **Open Space and Peace.** Stanford: Hoover Institution, 1964, 227 p.
A symposium on the political, technical and military aspects of satellite observation from open space.

Quester, George H. **Deterrence before Hiroshima: The Airpower Background of Modern Strategy.** New York: Wiley, 1966, 196 p.
The author, a Research Associate of the Harvard Center for International Affairs, attempts to prove that atomic weapons have not changed "air strategy enough to preclude any interesting or valuable analogies with the past."

Taubenfeld, Howard Jack, ed. **Space and Society.** Dobbs Ferry (N.Y.): Oceana Publications, 1964, 172 p.
Papers prepared for the Seminar on Problems of Outer Space under the sponsorship of the Carnegie Endowment for International Peace.

Von Braun, Wernher. **Space Frontier.** New York: Holt, Rinehart and Winston, 1967, 216 p.
The Director of NASA's George C. Marshall Space Flight Center from 1960–70, formerly of V-2 fame at Peenemünde, has written a primer on space flight for the layman.

Nuclear Weapons; Missiles

See also Population Problems, p. 47; Law of War; Aggression, p. 89; War and Peace, p. 108; Second World War, p. 144; The Postwar World, p. 178; (The United States) Foreign Policy, p. 229; Military and Defense Policy, p. 257; (Canada) Military Policy, p. 285; (Great Britain) Military Policy, p. 378; (France) Foreign Policy, p. 404; Military Policy, p. 407; (Union of Soviet Socialist Republics) Foreign Policy, p. 550; Military Policy, p. 561; (China) Military Questions, p. 705; (Australia) Foreign and Defense Policies, p. 767.

Aron, Raymond. **The Great Debate: Theories of Nuclear Strategy.** Garden City: Doubleday, 1965, 265 p.
In this book—based on lectures for a French audience—M. Aron reviews, with his customary lucidity, the recent developments of strategic theory, the European reaction to the McNamara doctrine, the pros and cons of an independent French deterrent and the

future of the Atlantic Alliance. The French original appeared as "Le Grand débat: initiation à la stratégie atomique" (Paris: Calmann-Lévy, 1963, 274 p.).

Bader, William B. **The United States and the Spread of Nuclear Weapons.** New York: Pegasus (for the Center of International Studies, Princeton University), 1968, 176 p.
The author argues for a more pragmatic American attitude toward non-proliferation.

Barnaby, Charles Frank and Boserup, A., eds. **Implications of Anti-ballistic Missile Systems.** New York: Humanities Press, 1969, 246 p.
This symposium by an international group of scholars and scientists makes a valuable contribution to the ABM debate. A Pugwash monograph.

Barnaby, Charles Frank, ed. **Preventing the Spread of Nuclear Weapons.** New York: Humanities Press, 1969, 374 p.
A symposium by leading scientists. The contributions are mostly technical in nature. A Pugwash monograph.

Boskey, Bennett and Willrich, Mason, eds. **Nuclear Proliferation: Prospects for Control.** New York: Dunellen Co. (for the American Society of International Law), 1970, 191 p.
A symposium focusing on the control aspects of the Treaty on the Non-Proliferation of Nuclear Weapons.

Brodie, Bernard. **Escalation and the Nuclear Option.** Princeton: Princeton University Press, 1966, 151 p.
A knowledgeable writer on contemporary strategic issues presents his views on the problem of escalation and the use of tactical nuclear weapons, which he feels should be retained as one of the American options.

Brown, Neville. **Nuclear War: The Impending Strategic Deadlock.** New York: Praeger, 1965, 238 p.
A British writer on military affairs assesses the strategic balance between East and West and looks forward to a reasonably stable stalemate.

Buchan, Alastair Francis, ed. **A World of Nuclear Powers?** Englewood Cliffs: Prentice-Hall (for the American Assembly, Columbia University), 1966, 176 p.
A useful symposium dealing with most of the central issues of nuclear proliferation.

Curtis, Richard and Hogan, Elizabeth. **Perils of the Peaceful Atom: The Myth of Safe Nuclear Power Plants.** Garden City: Doubleday, 1969, 274 p.
A passionate plea against nuclear power.

Delcoigne, Georges and Rubinstein, Georges. **Non-prolifération des armes nucléaires et systèmes de contrôle.** Brussels: Éditions de l'Institut de Sociologie, 1970, 214 p.
A concise and clear survey and reference dealing with the problem of the non-proliferation of nuclear weapons.

Gallois, Pierre M. **Paradoxes de la paix.** Paris: Presses du Temps Présent, 1967, 369 p.
A challenging analysis, by a leading advocate of an independent French nuclear deterrent, of the impact of atomic power on military alliances.

Goldschmidt, Bertrand. **Les Rivalités atomiques, 1939–1966.** Paris: Fayard, 1967, 340 p.
A French scientist surveys the role of nuclear weapons and energy in international politics in the period from 1939 to 1966.

Green, Philip. **Deadly Logic: The Theory of Nuclear Deterrence.** Columbus: Ohio State University Press, 1966, 361 p.
A critique of the theory and theorists of nuclear deterrence, with Herman Kahn as the central target.

Groueff, Stéphane. **Manhattan Project.** Boston: Little, Brown, 1967, 372 p.
The author, a French journalist, recounts the dramatic story of the building of the first atomic bomb.

Harkabi, Yehoshafat. **Nuclear War and Nuclear Peace.** Jerusalem: Israel Program for Scientific Translations, 1966, 303 p.
An attempt by an Israeli scientist to systematize and explain various concepts of nuclear strategy. The original of this study was written in Hebrew.

Hasson, Joseph Albert. **The Economics of Nuclear Power.** London: Longmans, 1965, 160 p.
Essays directed toward a methodology for evaluating nuclear power, its costs, its role in economic welfare and the question of choice among alternative fuels.

Heilbrunn, Otto. **Conventional Warfare in the Nuclear Age.** New York: Praeger, 1965, 164 p.
A thoughtful and penetrating discussion of the problems of conventional warfare under the shadow of nuclear power.

Kramish, Arnold. **The Peaceful Atom in Foreign Policy.** New York: Harper and Row (for the Council on Foreign Relations), 1963, 276 p.
A physicist with wide experience in government examines American and Soviet policies, the International Atomic Energy Agency, EURATOM, and the military and political implications of the peaceful uses of atomic energy.

Lamont, Lansing. **Day of Trinity.** New York: Atheneum, 1965, 333 p.
Although the story has been told before, this is a remarkably gripping, dramatic and informative reconstruction of the events leading to the first atomic explosion in New Mexico in July 1945.

Larus, Joel. **Nuclear Weapons Safety and the Common Defense.** Columbus: Ohio State University Press, 1967, 171 p.
A discerning analysis of the problems and prospects of reducing the possibility of nuclear weapons accidents.

Lifton, Robert Jay. **Death in Life: Survivors of Hiroshima.** New York: Random House, 1968, 594 p.
The author treats a terrible subject with brilliance, compassion and restraint. Hiroshima, in his view, was an "end of the world" experience for its survivors. For us, the survivors in a larger sense, it signifies the "last chance" to learn.

Lilienthal, David Eli. **Change, Hope, and the Bomb.** Princeton: Princeton University Press, 1963, 168 p.
Mr. Lilienthal, first chairman of the Atomic Energy Commission, expresses his belief that there is hope in a world threatened by the atom bomb.

Morris, Christopher. **The Day They Lost the H-Bomb.** New York: Coward-McCann, 1966, 192 p.
A journalist's account of the loss and recovery of the missing H-bomb off the Spanish coast in early 1966.

Moss, Norman. **Men Who Play God.** New York: Harper and Row, 1969, 352 p.
A fast-paced though well-researched book about the birth of the H-Bomb and the statesmen and scientists who have thought most about its implications.

Mullenbach, Philip. **Civilian Nuclear Power.** New York: Twentieth Century Fund, 1963, 406 p.
A serious study of the multitude of economic issues and questions of policy formation that have been involved in the reactor power development.

O'Brien, William V. **Nuclear War, Deterrence and Morality.** Westminster (Md.): Newman, 1967, 120 p.
A Roman Catholic view of various aspects of the nuclear dilemma.

Rosecrance, Richard Newton, *ed.* **The Dispersion of Nuclear Weapons: Strategy and Politics.** New York: Columbia University Press, 1964, 343 p.
A number of essays on the problems resulting from the spread of nuclear weapons to an increasing number of states.

Ryan, William L. and Summerlin, Sam. **The China Cloud: America's Tragic Blunder and China's Rise to Nuclear Power.** Boston: Little, Brown, 1968, 309 p.
The story of how some 80 American-trained Chinese scientists, who were forced to leave the United States in the late 1940s and the early 1950s, helped to make China a nuclear power.

Wentz, Walter B. **Nuclear Proliferation.** Washington: Public Affairs Press, 1968, 216 p.
The author argues that the policy of advocating the non-proliferation of atomic weapons is "both unrealistic and contrary to American interests."

York, Herbert. **Race to Oblivion: A Participant's View of the Arms Race.** New York: Simon and Schuster, 1970, 256 p.
A former Director of Defense Research and Engineering in the U.S. Department of Defense reminisces on his experience in developing advanced weaponry and criticizes the growth of nuclear weapons arsenals all over the world.

Chemical and Biological Warfare

See also (The United States) Military and Defense Policy, p. 257; The Vietnam War, p. 739.

Brown, Frederic J. **Chemical Warfare: A Study in Restraints.** Princeton: Princeton University Press, 1968, 355 p.
The definitive study of the policy of international restraint in the use of poison gas after World War I.

Clarke, Robin. **The Silent Weapons.** New York: McKay, 1968, 270 p.
A British scientist appeals to the world's scientific community to deny its coöperation in the development of chemical and biological warfare arsenals.

Cookson, John and Nottingham, Judith. **A Survey of Chemical and Biological Warfare.** New York: Monthly Review Press, 1971, 420 p.
Two British scholars have undertaken a painstaking study of the manufacture, availability and use of CBW, particularly in the United States, Canada and Europe.

McCarthy, Richard D. **The Ultimate Folly: War by Pestilence, Asphyxiation, and Defoliation.** New York: Knopf, 1969, 176 p.
A passionate and forcefully argued plea against the stockpiling and possible use of chemical and biological weapons.

Rose, Steven with Pavett, David, *eds*. **CBW: Chemical and Biological Warfare.** Boston: Beacon Press, 1969, 209 p.
A symposium dealing with the legal and ethical dimensions of CBW and its use in Vietnam and Yemen.

Rothschild, Jacquard Hirshorn. **Tomorrow's Weapons, Chemical and Biological.** New York: McGraw-Hill, 1964, 271 p.
The former Commanding General of the U.S. Army Chemical Corps Research and Development Command discusses the potentialities of biological and chemical weapons and the moral and political aspects of their employment.

Thomas, Ann Van Wynen and Thomas, A. J., Jr. **Legal Limits on the Use of Chemical and Biological Weapons.** Dallas: Southern Methodist University Press, 1970, 332 p.
This carefully researched monograph provides a valuable legal guide for all those who wish to curtail the manufacture and prevent the use of chemical and biological weapons.

Guerrilla Warfare; Armed Insurrection

See also Second World War, p. 144; (Inter-American Relations) General, p. 193; (Latin America) Political and Constitutional Problems, p. 203; Nicaragua, p. 298; (Cuba) Castro Regime, p. 303; (Bolivia) Government and Politics, p. 320; Uruguay, p. 340; (Great Britain) Regional Issues, p. 383; Ireland, p. 388; (France) Recent History, p. 396; Biographies, Memoirs and Addresses, p. 400; (Greece) World War II and the Civil War Period, p. 605; Arab-Israeli Conflict, p. 633; (China) Military Questions, p. 705; (Southeastern Asia; East Indies) General, p. 733; (Indochina) General Surveys and the End of the French Rule, p. 736; The Vietnam War, p. 739; Malaysia, p. 756; Philippines, p. 763; (Africa) Political Problems, p. 779; Algeria, p. 796; Nigeria, p. 816; Zaïre, p. 822; Kenya, p. 829.

Beaufre, André. **La Guerre révolutionnaire: les formes nouvelles de la guerre.** Paris: Fayard, 1972, 305 p.
General Beaufre examines the theory of revolutionary war, giving particular importance to psychological factors, and then demonstrates how it has been applied, from the Middle Ages to the present.

Beilenson, Laurence W. **Power through Subversion.** Washington: Public Affairs Press, 1972, 299 p.
Lenin is seen as the master theorist and practitioner of subversion in this highly conceptualized historical study. The author calls for a doctrine of "foreign aid for freedom" and concludes that the United States should exert its own power through subversion.

Bell, John Bowyer. **The Myth of the Guerrilla.** New York: Knopf, 1971, 285 p.
A debunking study contrasting the myth and the reality of the guerrilla fighter. Sponsored by Harvard's Center for International Affairs.

Campbell, Arthur. **Guerillas: A History and Analysis.** New York: Day, 1968, 344 p.
A series of vignettes about guerrilla warfare since the Boer War.

Cross, James Eliot. **Conflict in the Shadows: The Nature and Politics of Guerrilla War.** Garden City: Doubleday, 1963, 180 p.
A resumé of the history of guerrilla warfare and a plea for greater appreciation of the political and military significance of this form of warfare.

Ebert, Theodor. **Gewaltfreier Aufstand: Alternative zum Bürgerkrieg.** Freiburg: Rombach, 1968, 408 p.
This "Intelligent Man's Guide to Non-Violent Insurrection" is lucidly written and based on Indian and American experience.

Gann, Lewis Henry. **Guerrillas in History.** Stanford: Hoover Institution Press, 1971, 99 p.
A brief but incisive and quite comprehensive survey of guerrilla warfare in history, by a British scholar.

Grivas, George. **General Grivas on Guerrilla Warfare.** New York: Praeger, 1965, 109 p.
Drawing on his experience as leader of the Cyprus liberation campaign, General Grivas discusses guerrilla warfare as an unorthodox but increasingly important form of combat. An English edition appeared under the title "Guerrilla Warfare and EOKA's Struggle" (London: Longmans, 1964, 109 p.).

Hahlweg, Werner. **Guerilla Krieg ohne Fronten.** Stuttgart: Kohlhammer, 1968, 297 p.
A concise factual overview of guerrilla warfare from ancient times to the war in Vietnam.

Heilbrunn, Otto. **Warfare in the Enemy's Rear.** New York: Praeger, 1964, 231 p.
A highly skilled evaluation of guerrilla warfare in World War II combined with a search for a doctrine to guide the future use of forces in the rear.

Hyde, Douglas A. **The Roots of Guerrilla Warfare.** London: Bodley Head, 1968, 159 p.
Observations on guerrilla warfare in Asia and Latin America, based on first-hand experience.

Kitson, Frank. **Low Intensity Operations: Subversion, Insurgency, Peace-Keeping.** Harrisburg: Stackpole, 1971, 208 p.
Drawing on his experiences in Kenya, Malaya, Cyprus and Northern Ireland, Brigadier Kitson seeks to outline "the steps which should be taken now in order to make the army ready to deal with subversion, insurrection, and peacekeeping operations during the second half of the 1970's."

Klonis, N. I., *pseud.* **Guerrilla Warfare: Analysis and Projections.** New York: Speller, 1972, 401 p.
The first half of the book is historical, from the Napoleonic Wars to Vietnam; the second has detailed "how to do it" operational guidelines.

Luttwak, Edward. **Coup d'État: A Practical Handbook.** New York: Knopf, 1969, 209 p.
A recipe book on how to overthrow governments. Cold-blooded and impressive.

McCuen, John J. **The Art of Counter-Revolutionary War.** Harrisburg: Stackpole, 1967, 349 p.
Drawing his examples from Greece, Algeria, Indochina and Malaya, the author has written a solid text on counter-revolutionary strategy. There is a foreword by Sir Robert Thompson.

Mallin, Jay, *ed.* **Strategy for Conquest.** Coral Gables: University of Miami Press, 1970, 381 p.
Well-annotated selections from the works of seven leading communist ideologues on guerrilla warfare.

Mallin, Jay, *ed.* **Terror and Urban Guerrillas: A Study of Tactics and Documents.** Coral Gables: University of Miami Press, 1972, 176 p.
An anthology of writings by leading contemporary practitioners of urban guerrilla warfare.

Marighela, Carlos. **For the Liberation of Brazil.** Baltimore: Penguin, 1971, 191 p.
A collection of guidelines for urban guerrilla warfare and other revolutionary activities. The author, a Brazilian revolutionary, was killed in 1967.

Martínez Codó, Enrique. **Guerrillas tras la Cortina de Hierro.** Buenos Aires: Instituto Informativo—Editorial Ucranio, 1966, 419 p.

A study of guerrilla warfare during and after World War II in the territories of the Soviet Union. Special attention is devoted to the Soviet "forced migration" programs that eliminated popular support to the anti-communist guerrillas.

Moss, Robert. **The War for the Cities.** New York: Coward, McCann and Geoghegan, 1972, 288 p.

In this useful book on urban guerrilla warfare the author anticipates that this may come to be the most prevalent form of political violence in the coming decade.

Neuberg, A. **Armed Insurrection.** New York: St. Martin's Press, 1971, 285 p.

This revolutionary manual for communists was first published by Comintern agents in 1928. Of particular interest is the description of the planning and execution of the communist uprising in Tallinn, Estonia, in 1924, and the chapter on peasant insurrections by Ho Chi Minh.

Paget, Julian. **Counter-Insurgency Operations: Techniques of Guerrilla Warfare.** New York: Walker, 1967, 189 p.

A well-done British view of the subject, based on the experiences with insurgency in Malaya, Kenya and Cyprus.

Pomeroy, William J., *ed.* **Guerrilla Warfare and Marxism.** New York: International Publishers, 1968, 336 p.

Selections from the writings of several strategists of revolutionary warfare.

Pustay, John S. **Counterinsurgency Warfare.** New York: Free Press, 1965, 236 p.

A study centering on the means by which a regime can defend itself against communist-initiated insurgency warfare.

Robinson, Donald, *ed.* **The Dirty Wars.** New York: Delacorte Press, 1968, 356 p.

A useful collection of essays on guerrilla wars around the globe since World War II.

Scott, Andrew M. and Others. **Insurgency.** Chapel Hill: University of North Carolina Press, 1970, 139 p.

This analysis of insurgent warfare is heavily indebted to systems theory. The authors pride themselves on their conceptual rigor, yet their substantive conclusions are not particularly original.

Thayer, Charles Wheeler. **Guerrilla.** New York: Harper and Row, 1963, 195 p.

Mr. Thayer, who has had military, diplomatic and O.S.S. experience—and commands a lively style—discusses the conditions under which guerrilla warfare may thrive, its potentialities and limitations and the prerequisites for counter-guerrilla measures.

Thompson, Sir Robert Grainger Ker. **Revolutionary War in World Strategy 1945-1969.** New York: Taplinger, 1970, 171 p.

The head of the British Advisory Mission to Vietnam from 1961 to 1965 surveys guerrilla warfare since World War II and concludes by defending American policies in Vietnam.

Tinker, Jerry M. and Others, *eds.* **Strategies of Revolutionary Warfare.** New Delhi: S. Chand, 1969, 382 p.

Essays by American scholars on the tactics and strategy of revolutionary warfare. In the words of the editors, the essential theme of the volume is "that revolutions do not just 'happen,' but are the result of the carefully planned use of the political and military techniques of insurgency."

Trinquier, Roger. **Guerre, subversion, révolution.** Paris: Laffont, 1968, 285 p.

A treatise on revolutionary warfare by a French officer who had served in Indochina and Algeria.

Propaganda; Psychological and Political Warfare

See also Political Factors, p. 12; (Second World War) Special Operations; Propaganda; Espionage; Intelligence, p. 169; (The Postwar World) The Cold War; Peaceful Coexistence, p. 180; and the sections for specific countries and regions.

Blackstock, Paul W. **Agents of Deceit: Frauds, Forgeries and Political Intrigue among Nations.** Chicago: Quadrangle Books, 1966, 315 p.

WAR AND PEACE

A discussion of frauds and fake documents in the underworld of international affairs; many of the items relate to Russia and communism.

Brown, James Alexander Campbell. **Techniques of Persuasion: From Propaganda to Brainwashing.** Baltimore: Penguin, 1963, 325 p.
A survey of methods and results, historical and contemporary.

Choukas, Michael. **Propaganda Comes of Age.** Washington: Public Affairs Press, 1965, 299 p.
An extensive discussion of propaganda and propaganda techniques, particularly interesting for its rich—and repellent—collection of examples and illustrations.

Clews, John C. **Communist Propaganda Techniques.** New York: Praeger, 1964, 326 p.
A general survey together with a case history charging that the United States was using bacterial weapons in the Korean War.

Davison, Walter Phillips. **International Political Communication.** New York: Praeger (for the Council on Foreign Relations), 1965, 404 p.
This study analyzes both deliberate and inadvertent uses of information to influence political attitudes in foreign countries.

Ellul, Jacques. **Propaganda: The Formation of Men's Attitudes.** New York: Knopf, 1965, 320 p.
A scholarly and challenging study of the characteristics of contemporary propaganda. The French original was published as "Propagandes" (Paris: Colin, 1962, 335 p.).

Havighurst, Clark C., *ed.* **International Control of Propaganda.** Dobbs Ferry (N.Y.): Oceana Publications, 1968, 196 p.
Most of the papers in this symposium were presented at a conference organized by the International Law Society at the Duke University Law School in February 1966.

Michie, Allan Andrew. **Voices through the Iron Curtain: The Radio Free Europe Story.** New York: Dodd, 1963, 304 p.
A report by the former deputy director of Radio Free Europe on the success of this "unique venture in psychological warfare." The chapters on Poland and Hungary are most revealing of the effectiveness of the agency.

Murty, B. S. **Propaganda and World Public Order: The Legal Regulation of the Ideological Instrument of Coercion.** New Haven: Yale University Press, 1968, 310 p.
An excellent and exhaustive study exploring the manifold problems of regulating propaganda. The author draws for his conclusions on political science, sociology, psychology, communications research and law.

Whitton, John Boardman and Larson, Arthur. **Propaganda: Towards Disarmament in the War of Words.** Dobbs Ferry (N.Y.): Oceana Publications (for the World Rule of Law Center, Duke University), 1964, 305 p.
An analysis of "the rules, principles and remedies available to control propaganda of a kind that threatens the peace." Principal dangers are seen in warmongering, subversion and defamation.

Intelligence

See also (Political Factors) General, p. 12; (Second World War) Special Operations; Propaganda; Espionage; Intelligence, p. 169; and the sections for specific countries.

Blackstock, Paul W. **The Secret Road to World War Two: Soviet Versus Western Intelligence, 1921-1939.** Chicago: Quadrangle Books, 1969, 384 p.
An informative book on the struggle between Soviet and Western espionage services during the inter-war period.

Blackstock, Paul W. **The Strategy of Subversion: Manipulating the Politics of Other Nations.** Chicago: Quadrangle Books, 1964, 351 p.
A general discussion of "covert political operations" as practiced by various powers. The author thinks that their value has been greatly overestimated.

Dulles, Allen Welsh. **The Craft of Intelligence.** New York: Harper and Row, 1963, 277 p.
Drawing in part from his own extensive experience in diplomacy and intelligence, the former head of the Central Intelligence Agency has written his informed, sensible and quite unsensational observations on the gathering, organizing and evaluating of open and secret information.

Dulles, Allen Welsh, ed. **Great True Spy Stories.** New York: Harper and Row, 1968, 393 p.
Thirty-nine true "whodunits," some of which are stranger than fiction.

Elliott-Bateman, Michael, ed. **The Fourth Dimension of Warfare. Volume I: Intelligence, Subversion, Resistance.** New York: Praeger, 1970, 181 p.
Essays on intelligence operations in various political settings.

Gunzenhäuser, Max. **Geschichte des geheimen Nachrichtendienstes.** Frankfurt/Main: Bernard und Graefe (for the Bibliothek für Zeitgeschichte), 1968, 434 p.
An exhaustive and critical bibliography of the literature on secret service work and espionage. There are subject, geographic and author indexes.

Ind, Allison. **A Short History of Espionage.** New York: McKay, 1963, 337 p.
Colonel Ind, an American intelligence officer in the Far East in World War II, has written a good book on espionage from the Trojan Horse through 1961.

Kahn, David. **The Codebreakers: The Story of Secret Writing.** New York: Macmillan, 1967, 1,164 p.
A history of "secret communication from ancient times to the threshold of outer space."

Orlov, Alexander. **Handbook of Intelligence and Guerrilla Warfare.** Ann Arbor: University of Michigan Press, 1963, 187 p.
This work was written by a former Soviet intelligence agent and guerrilla fighter who later defected to the West. It compares the Western and Soviet intelligence operations and explains in detail the methods taught to and used by Soviet spies.

Page, Bruce and Others. **The Philby Conspiracy.** Garden City: Doubleday, 1968, 300 p.
The well-told tale, at once humorous and terrifying, of one of the great feats of duplicity in modern espionage.

Ronblöm, Hans Krister. **The Spy without a Country.** New York: Coward-McCann, 1965, 222 p.
The story of the Swedish Air Attaché, Colonel Stig Wennerström, a quite successful double agent until his arrest in 1963.

Strong, Sir Kenneth. **Men of Intelligence.** New York: St. Martin's Press, 1972, 183 p.
A study of the roles of some chiefs of intelligence, in Germany, Britain, France and the United States, since World War I.

Wilensky, Harold L. **Organizational Intelligence: Knowledge and Policy in Government and Industry.** New York: Basic Books, 1967, 226 p.
A sociological analysis of the process of intelligence gathering and use both in government and industry.

Wise, David and Ross, Thomas B. **The Espionage Establishment.** New York: Random House, 1967, 308 p.
A chatty survey of spying in the Soviet Union, Great Britain, the United States and Communist China.

PEACE; DISARMAMENT; ARMS CONTROL

See also General Works, p. 1; United Nations, p. 99; War and Peace, p. 108; Inter-War Period, p. 140; The Postwar World, p. 178; and the sections for specific countries and regions.

Aboltin, V. Ia., ed. **Politika gosudarstv i razoruzhenie.** Moscow: Izd-vo "Nauka," 1966-67, 3 v.
A survey of problems and prospects of disarmament, centering on the Third World, the Soviet-American relationship, and Western Europe.

Aboltin, V. Ia. and Others. **Sovremennye problemy razoruzheniia.** Moscow: Izd-vo "Mysl'," 1970, 397 p.
A collective of Soviet authors discusses current problems of disarmament, including accidental war and its prevention, Warsaw Pact–NATO relations, and "imperialist concepts" of the arms race.

Aronowitz, Dennis S. **Legal Aspects of Arms Control Verification in the United States.**
Dobbs Ferry (N.Y.): Oceana Publications, 1965, 222 p.
A study conducted under contract with the U.S. Arms Control and Disarmament Agency.

Barker, Charles Albro, ed. **Problems of World Disarmament: A Series of Lectures Delivered at the Johns Hopkins University.** Boston: Houghton, 1963, 170 p.
A series of lectures on types of contemporary warfare and aspects of arms control and disarmament.

Barnet, Richard Joseph and Falk, Richard A., eds. **Security in Disarmament.** Princeton: Princeton University Press (for the Princeton Center of International Studies), 1965, 441 p.
A symposium on three general themes: inspection, the protection of states in the course of disarmament and the question of security in circumstances of total disarmament.

Benoit, Emile and Boulding, Kenneth Ewart, eds. **Disarmament and the Economy.** New York: Harper and Row, 1963, 310 p.
These significant studies are based on the premise that: "The political problems of disarmament are the most difficult and the most important, and the economic problems will rise in importance only as the political problems are solved. It is essential, however, to know we *can* solve the economic problems concerned."

Benoit, Emile, ed. **Disarmament and World Economic Interdependence.** New York: Columbia University Press, 1967, 260 p.
Papers prepared for the Conference on Economic Aspects of World Disarmament and Interdependence which took place during August and September, 1965, in Oslo, under the sponsorship of the Program of Research on International Economics of Disarmament and Arms Control and the International Peace Research Institute.

Biddle, W. F. **Weapons Technology and Arms Control.** New York: Praeger, 1972, 355 p.
A detailed analysis of the scientific and technological aspects of the control of strategic and tactical nuclear weapons. Particular attention is given to warheads and their delivery systems, but not to the politics or history of arms control.

Bosc, Robert. **Sociologie de la paix.** Paris: Spes, 1965, 252 p.
A Catholic analysis of the state and dynamics of contemporary international society, and of actions to maintain or restore peace.

Cordier, Andrew Wellington and Foote, Wilder, eds. **The Quest for Peace.** New York: Columbia University Press, 1965, 390 p.
This volume comprises 24 Dag Hammarskjöld Memorial Lectures on a wide variety of themes relating to the search for and maintenance of international peace. Among the contributors are U Thant, Adlai Stevenson, Dean Rusk, Lester B. Pearson and Muhammad Zafrulla Khan.

Crosser, Paul K. **War is Obsolete: The Dialectics of Military Technology and its Consequences.** Amsterdam: Grüner, 1972, 244 p.
The author of this tract argues that "massive disarmament will have to replace massive rearmament before the Twentieth Century comes to a close."

Dean, Arthur Hobson. **Test Ban and Disarmament: The Path of Negotiation.** New York: Harper and Row (for the Council on Foreign Relations), 1966, 153 p.
Ambassador Dean gives his views on the negotiating process and on the major political and other problems related to the nuclear test ban, limited arms control and general disarmament.

Documents on Disarmament. Washington: United States Arms Control and Disarmament Agency.
A most useful annual collection of documents on arms control and disarmament developments, published since 1960.

Dougherty, James E. and Lehman, John F., Jr., eds. **Arms Control for the Late Sixties.** Princeton: Van Nostrand, 1967, 265 p.
Papers originally presented at the Third International Arms Control Symposium, held in Philadelphia in 1966.

Dougherty, James E. and Lehman, John F., Jr., eds. **The Prospects for Arms Control.** New York: Macfadden, 1965, 270 p.

Essays based on papers presented at the Philadelphia Collegiate Disarmament Conference in 1964.

Driver, Christopher P. **The Disarmers: A Study in Protest.** London: Hodder, 1964, 255 p.
An account and appraisal of the Campaign for Nuclear Disarmament in Britain in the years since 1957.

The Economic Effects of Disarmament. Toronto: University of Toronto Press (for the Economist Intelligence Unit), 1963, 224 p.
The first part of this study assesses the effect of defense expenditure on the British economy as a whole and on specific industries. The second part estimates the consequences of alternative policies of re-deploying resources in the event of disarmament.

Edwards, David V. **Arms Control in International Politics.** New York: Holt, Rinehart and Winston, 1969, 200 p.
A serious and realistic study of the present limitations and the future possibilities of arms control.

Epstein, William. **Disarmament: Twenty-five Years of Effort.** Toronto: Canadian Institute of International Affairs, 1971, 97 p.
A succinct and useful survey of recent progress in arms control, with emphasis on the constructive role of the United Nations.

Fischer, Georges. **The Non-Proliferation of Nuclear Weapons.** New York: St. Martin's Press, 1972, 270 p.
A thorough study of the efforts to control the spread of nuclear weapons since the signing of the partial test ban in August 1963; an updated translation of "La Non-prolifération des armes nucléaires" (Paris: Librairie Générale de Droit, 1969, 242 p.).

Forndran, Erhard. **Probleme der internationalen Abrüstung.** Frankfurt/Main: Metzner (for the Deutsche Gesellschaft für Auswärtige Politik), 1970, 450 p.
A detailed study of nuclear arms control negotiations between 1962 and 1968, by a German scholar.

Forndran, Erhard. **Rüstungskontrolle: Friedenssicherung zwischen Abschreckung und Abrüstung.** Düsseldorf: Bertelsmann Universitätsverlag, 1970, 272 p.
A wise assessment of American deterrence and arms-control policies during the Eisenhower and Kennedy administrations.

García Robles, Alfonso. **El Tratado de Tlatelolco.** Mexico City: El Colegio de México, 1967, 339 p.
Speeches and documents, compiled by one of Mexico's leading proponents of nuclear disarmament, tracing the successful effort to bar nuclear weapons from Latin America.

Gardner, Richard Newton, *ed.* **Blueprint for Peace.** New York: McGraw-Hill, 1966, 404 p.
A volume drawn from the reports and proposals presented at the White House Conference on International Coöperation, November 29–December 1, 1965.

Genovés, Santiago. **Is Peace Inevitable? Aggression, Evolution, and Human Destiny.** New York: Walker, 1970, 194 p.
The author argues that man is not aggressive by nature. Aggression is learned, and war is a social disease. The book is at sharp variance with the thesis advanced by Konrad Lorenz in his "On Aggression."

Gotlieb, Allan. **Disarmament and International Law: A Study of the Role of Law in the Disarmament Process.** Toronto: Canadian Institute of International Affairs, 1965, 232 p.
An official of the Canadian Department of External Affairs and a participant in the Eighteen Nation Disarmament Committee from 1962 to 1964 combines theory and practice in assessing basic questions concerning and prospects for general and complete disarmament.

Halperin, Morton H. and Perkins, Dwight H. **Communist China and Arms Control.** New York: Praeger (for the East Asian Research Center and the Center for International Affairs, Harvard University), 1965, 191 p.
A coöperative effort with the U.S. Arms Control and Disarmament Agency to identify and clarify factors affecting the formulation of Communist China's policies toward arms control and disarmament issues.

Höglund, Bengt and Ulrich, Jörgen Willian, eds. **Conflict Control and Conflict Resulution.** Copenhagen: Munksgaard, 1972, 240 p.
A symposium—both a stocktaking and a critique—on peace research.

Holcombe, Arthur Norman. **A Strategy of Peace in a Changing World.** Cambridge: Harvard University Press, 1967, 332 p.
A collection of essays by a Harvard professor on the requirements of an organized world peace. Of particular interest is the article analyzing voting patterns in the U.N. General Assembly.

Iwan, Joachim H. **Die Abrüstung: die Bemühungen um Friedenssicherung durch Rüstungsbeschränkung und -kontrolle.** Munich: Beck, 1965, 270 p.
A study of the attempts to institute international armaments control in the time span from the Baruch Plan in 1942 to the Moscow Nonproliferation Treaty of 1962.

Jacobson, Harold Karan and Stein, Eric. **Diplomats, Scientists, and Politicians: The United States and the Nuclear Test Ban Negotiations.** Ann Arbor: University of Michigan Press, 1966, 538 p.
An extensive and thorough account of the background and events that led up to the 1963 treaty.

Khaitsman, Viktor Moiseevich. **SSSR i problema razoruzheniia, 1945-1959: istoriia mezhdunarodnykh peregovorov.** Moscow: Izd-vo "Nauka," 1970, 478 p.
A history of East-West disarmament negotiations from 1945 to 1959, forcefully presenting the Soviet perspective.

Klein, Jean. **L'Entreprise du désarmement depuis 1945.** Paris: Éditions Cujas, 1964, 325 p.
A compact history of international concern for disarmament from 1945 to 1964.

Kolkowicz, Roman and Others. **The Soviet Union and Arms Control: A Superpower Dilemma.** Baltimore: Johns Hopkins Press, 1970, 212 p.
An effort by several authors to elucidate the elements in the Soviet approach to strategic arms limitations: Soviet-American strategic relations, nuclear proliferation, the China factor and Soviet policy toward Europe.

Leachman, Robert B. and Althoff, Philip, eds. **Preventing Nuclear Theft: Guidelines for Industry and Government.** New York: Praeger, 1972, 377 p.
The topics of these essays range from the political aspects of the safeguard system in the nonproliferation treaty to measuring nuclear fuel cycles, and include discussion of the projected dangers of nuclear material after their theft.

Lieberman, Joseph I. **The Scorpion and the Tarantula: The Struggle to Control Atomic Weapons, 1945-1949.** Boston: Houghton, 1970, 460 p.
In this case study of the failure to control atomic weapons in the immediate postwar period, the author maintains that the responsibility for this tragedy falls equally upon the United States and the Soviet Union.

Luard, David Evan Trant, ed. **First Steps to Disarmament: A New Approach to the Problems of Arms Reductions.** New York: Basic Books, 1965, 277 p.
Assuming that the realization of complete disarmament is unattainable, the authors in this collection of essays offer suggestions of a restricted and specific nature.

Mallan, Lloyd. **Peace is a Three-Edged Sword.** Englewood Cliffs: Prentice-Hall, 1964, 253 p.
A popular, and optimistic, account of U.S. deterrent capabilities.

Mark, David Everett. **Die Einstellung der Kernwaffenversuche: Probleme und Ergebnisse der bisherigen Verhandlungen.** Frankfurt/Main: Metzner (for the Forschungsinstitut der Deutschen Gesellschaft für Auswärtige Politik), 1965, 436 p.
The background of the test-ban treaty, by a member of the U.S. Foreign Service who participated in the negotiations. A collection of important documents is appended.

Millis, Walter and Real, James. **The Abolition of War.** New York: Macmillan, 1963, 217 p.
The authors state in their opening sentence: "It is the contention of this book that the world has reached a point, no doubt for the first time in history, at which it is possible to think and talk seriously about the abolition of organized war."

Millis, Walter. **An End to Arms.** New York: Atheneum (for the Center for the Study of Democratic Institutions), 1965, 301 p.

The author of numerous books on the subject of war and peace makes a general inquiry "into possible demilitarization of the international politics system, rather than merely into its disarmament."

Mitrany, David. **A Working Peace System.** Chicago: Quadrangle Books, 1966, 221 p.

Essays by a long-standing advocate of the "functional" approach to international organization and peace.

Moch, Jules Salvador. **Destin de la paix.** Paris: Mercure de France, 1969, 301 p.

A French representative at the U.N. Disarmament Commission in the 1950s reviews his experience in search of negotiated disarmament.

Nye, Joseph Samuel, Jr. **Peace in Parts: Integration and Conflict in Regional Organization.** Boston: Little, Brown, 1971, 210 p.

An effort to assess the past and future role of international regional organizations in promoting world peace. Written under the auspices of Harvard's Center for International Affairs.

Pearson, Lester Bowles. **The Four Faces of Peace, and the International Outlook.** New York: Dodd, 1964, 267 p.

A compilation of speeches on peace and international affairs by the former Canadian Prime Minister.

Rehm, Georg Wilhelm. **Rüstungskontrolle im Weltraum.** Bonn: Siegler (for the Deutsche Gesellschaft für Auswärtige Politik), 1965, 129 p.

A substantially documented analysis of post-World War II efforts at arms control.

Roberts, Chalmers M. **The Nuclear Years: The Arms Race and Arms Control, 1945-70.** New York: Praeger, 1970, 159 p.

This factual survey of 25 years of U.S.-Soviet nuclear relations is especially useful for the general reader.

Rotblat, Joseph. **Scientists in the Quest for Peace.** Cambridge: M.I.T. Press, 1972, 399 p.

A useful documentary history of the 21 Pugwash conferences held since 1957.

Shore, William I. **Fact-Finding in the Maintenance of International Peace.** Dobbs Ferry (N.Y.): Oceana Publications, 1970, 183 p.

A useful historical review of the development of impartial fact-finding machinery.

Siegler, Heinrich, Freiherr von, *ed.* **Dokumentation zur Abrüstung und Sicherheit.** Bonn: Siegler, 1960–.

A massive collection of documents dealing with problems of international security and disarmament. The first three volumes cover the period from 1943 to 1965. Beginning with volume 4, the collection appears annually.

Stone, Jeremy J. **Containing the Arms Race.** Cambridge: M.I.T. Press, 1966, 252 p.

The author concentrates here on two relatively specific but much debated issues: the freeze of strategic delivery systems, and a U.S.-Soviet agreement not to deploy missile defense systems. This study was prepared under the auspices of the Center for International Affairs at Harvard University.

Stone, Jeremy J. **Strategic Persuasion: Arms Limitations through Dialogue.** New York: Columbia University Press, 1967, 176 p.

An essay discussing the communications, both official and unofficial, between the Americans and the Russians on matters of strategy and arms control. A companion volume to the author's "Containing the Arms Race."

Strachey, Evelyn John St. Loe. **On the Prevention of War.** New York: St. Martin's Press, 1963, 334 p.

In this thoughtful essay the late British socialist author and politician discusses the stability of the international power balance, the prospects for disarmament in light of the intentions of the great powers, and the possibilities for safely coming through our perilous times.

Thant, U. **Toward World Peace.** New York: Yoseloff, 1964, 404 p.

A selection of U Thant's speeches and public statements both as the Permanent Representative of Burma to the United Nations and as Secretary-General of that organization.

Volle, Hermann and Duisberg, Claus-Jürgen. **Probleme der internationalen Abrüstung.** Frankfurt/Main: Metzner, 1964, 2 v.
An extended analysis, with selected but voluminous documents, on efforts at disarmament and security in the U.N. from 1945 to 1961.

Wainhouse, David Walter and Others. **Arms Control Agreements.** Baltimore: Johns Hopkins Press, 1968, 179 p.
The authors of this valuable study focus on the problems of inspection and verification of arms-control agreements. They conclude with a recommendation for a single international verification organization.

Wainhouse, David Walter and Others. **International Peace Observation: A History and Forecast.** Baltimore: Johns Hopkins Press (in coöperation with the Washington Center of Foreign Policy Research), 1966, 663 p.
A solid study of the past experience and the possible future role of "peace observation." A large part of the book comprises case studies since the 1920s.

Wright, Sir Michael. **Disarm and Verify.** New York: Praeger, 1964, 255 p.
A retired British Foreign Service officer discusses the central obstacles that have confronted the disarmament negotiations and the possible means of overcoming them.

Young, Elizabeth. **A Farewell to Arms Control?** Baltimore: Penguin, 1972, 255 p.
In this history of the nuclear policies of the five atomic powers the British author emphasizes the role of intellectual fashions, especially in the United States, and concludes that the arms race is not about to end.

SECOND PART:

THE WORLD SINCE 1914

I. GENERAL

See also General Works, p. 1; (Political Factors) General, p. 12.

Armstrong, Hamilton Fish and Others, *eds.* **Fifty Years of Foreign Affairs.** New York: Praeger (for the Council on Foreign Relations), 1972, 501 p.
A selection of 31 distinguished articles from the pages of the quarterly *Foreign Affairs* over the half-century 1922–1972. Each is preceded by a brief note placing it in the context of its time.

Barraclough, Geoffrey. **An Introduction to Contemporary History.** New York: Basic Books, 1965, 272 p.
A leading British historian sketches some of the central themes of twentieth-century history.

Black, Cyril Edwin. **The Dynamics of Modernization: A Study in Comparative History.** New York: Harper and Row, 1966, 207 p.
In this extended essay a Princeton historian develops his theme that the problem of modernization provides the best key to an understanding of the crises and turbulences of recent history. A publication of the Center of International Studies, Princeton University.

Bliven, Bruce. **The World Changers.** New York: Day, 1965, 418 p.
A former editor of *The New Republic* reviews the 1930s and 1940s in the form of biographical sketches of Roosevelt, Churchill, Hitler, Stalin, Mussolini, Gandhi, Chiang Kai-shek and Hirohito.

Boulding, Kenneth Ewart. **The Meaning of the Twentieth Century: The Great Transition.** New York: Harper and Row, 1964, 199 p.
A gallant if not particularly satisfying effort to identify the major "traps" confronting mankind—war, demographic suffocation, the exhaustion of energy resources, and ideological delusions—and to suggest ways of avoiding them.

Broszat, Martin and Heiber, Helmut, *eds.* **Weltgeschichte des 20. Jahrhunderts.** Munich: Deutscher Taschenbuch Verlag, 1966–70, 14 v.
This massive history of the twentieth century comprises the following volumes: vol. 1, "Der Erste Weltkrieg" (1968, 370 p.), by Hans Herzfeld; vol. 2, "Revolutionen und Friedensschlüsse 1917–1920" (1967, 300 p.), by Gerhard Schulz; vol. 3, "Die Republik von Weimar" (1966, 282 p.), by Helmut Heiber; vol. 4, "Die faschistischen Bewegungen" (1966, 333 p.), by Ernst Nolte; vol. 5, "Europa zwischen den Kriegen" (1969, 400 p.), by Hermann Graml; vol. 6, "Der Ferne Osten in der Weltpolitik des industriellen Zeitalters" (1970, 527 p.), by Gottfried Karl Kindermann; vol. 7, "Die Vereinigten Staaten von Amerika" (1966, 295 p.), by Erich Angermann; vol. 8, "Sowjetrussland" (1967, 290 p.), by Karl Heinz Ruffmann; vol. 9, "Der Staat Hitlers" (1969, 472 p.), by Martin Broszat; vol. 10, "Der Zweite Weltkrieg" (1967, 525 p.), by Lothar Gruchmann; vol. 11, "Das geteilte Deutschland" (1966, 287 p.), by Thilo Vogelsang; vol. 12, "Konflikte der Weltpolitik nach 1945" (1970, 306 p.), by John Adalbert Lukacs; vol. 13, "Auflösung der Kolonialreiche" (1966, 307 p.), by Franz Ansprenger; vol. 14, "Europa zwischen Aufbruch und Restauration" (1968, 342 p.), by Wolfgang Wagner.

Clark, Ronald W. **Einstein: The Life and Times.** New York: World Publishing Co., 1971, 718 p.
A comprehensive and well-written biography. The author emphasizes Einstein's youth in the context of the rise of modern Germany, his middle years in the pursuit of the relativity theory and the dilemma of nuclear weapons, and his last years devoted to the cause of Zionism.

Duché, Jean. **L'Histoire du monde. Tome IV: Le Grand tournant. Deuxième partie (de 1914 à nos jours).** Paris: Flammarion, 1966, 634 p.

The concluding volume of a general survey of world history, covering the period from 1914 to 1965.

Keep, John Leslie Howard and Brisby, Liliana, *eds.* **Contemporary History in the Soviet Mirror.** New York: Praeger, 1964, 331 p.

A symposium of papers by a number of leading British and American scholars dealing with recent trends in Soviet historiography on a variety of recent and contemporary topics, including diplomacy and international affairs.

Knapp, Wilfrid. **A History of War and Peace, 1939-1965.** New York: Oxford University Press (for the Royal Institute of International Affairs), 1967, 639 p.

A comprehensive narrative of world politics since 1939 by a British scholar who covers familiar ground in a straightforward manner.

Launay, Jacques de. **Histoire contemporaine de la diplomatie secrète, 1914-1945.** Lausanne: Éditions Rencontre, 1965, 517 p.

A popular survey, occasionally providing interesting documentation, of secret diplomacy in the period from 1914 to 1945.

McNeill, William Hardy. **The Rise of the West: A History of the Human Community.** Chicago: University of Chicago Press, 1963, 829 p.

Neither a textbook nor an exercise in metahistory, Professor McNeill's remarkably unified review of world history represents the effort of an intelligent and trained historian to encompass in a single narrative the development and diffusion of Western culture, techniques and social organization.

Mowat, Charles Loch, *ed.* **The Shifting Balance of World Forces, 1898-1945.** London: Cambridge University Press, 2d ed., 1968, 844 p.

A new version of the last volume of Lord Acton's "Cambridge Modern History," now entitled "New Cambridge Modern History." Though some of the contributions are very good, the new volume is not as distinguished as its predecessor.

Mowat, Robert Case. **Ruin and Resurgence: 1939-1965.** New York: Harper and Row, 1968, 406 p.

A straightforward history of the Second World War and of the subsequent renaissance of Europe.

Nitschke, August. **Der Feind: Erlebnis, Theorie und Begegnung; Formen politischen Handelns im 20. Jahrhundert.** Stuttgart: Kohlhammer, 1964, 268 p.

Interesting reflections on the attitudes of some of the most influential men of the twentieth century (Charles de Gaulle, Adolf Hitler, Benito Mussolini, Sigmund Freud, etc.) toward their enemies, by a German medievalist.

Possony, Stefan Thomas. **Zur Bewältigung der Kriegsschuldfrage: Völkerrecht und Strategie bei der Auslösung zweier Weltkriege.** Opladen: Westdeutscher Verlag, 1968, 350 p.

A discussion of the various theories concerning the origin of both world wars. The author is convinced that the Russians were implicated in the Sarajevo murder and rejects the attempts by Dedijer and other writers to prove the contrary.

Renouvin, Pierre. **War and Aftermath: 1914-1929.** New York: Harper and Row, 1968, 369 p.

———. **World War II and its Origins: International Relations, 1929-1945.** New York: Harper and Row, 1969, 402 p.

A concise and balanced review of international politics during both world wars and the inter-war period, by an eminent French diplomatic historian. The French original appeared as "Les Crises du XXe siècle" (Paris: Hachette, 1957-58, 2 v.).

Rougemont, Denis de. **Journal d'une époque (1926-1946).** Paris: Gallimard, 1968, 599 p.

The record of a writer's thoughts and experiences, first in Europe and then, during World War II, in the Americas. Uneven in depth, but thoroughly absorbing and interesting.

Schroeder, Felix von, *ed.* **Weltgeschichte der Gegenwart.** Berne: Francke, 1962-63, 2 v.

This is a massive collaborative handbook of contemporary world history. The first volume is organized by country and region. The second comprises studies on various leading themes and issues.

Stillman, Edmund O. and Pfaff, William. **The Politics of Hysteria: The Sources of Twentieth-Century Conflict.** New York: Harper and Row, 1964, 273 p.
A critical appraisal of the West, its limitless creative and destructive energy, its internecine conflicts and its devastating impact on the rest of the world. The prognosis is not very hopeful.

Toscano, Mario. **Pagine di storia diplomatica contemporanea.** Milan: Giuffrè, 1963, 2 v.
A collection of articles in two volumes, "Origini e vicende della Prima Guerra Mondiale" and "Origini e vicende della Seconda Guerra Mondiale," on the causes and conduct of the two world wars, by a leading European diplomatic historian.

Toynbee, Arnold Joseph. **Change and Habit: The Challenge of our Time.** New York: Oxford University Press, 1966, 240 p.
In these lectures Mr. Toynbee reasons within his own universe of discourse, developed in his classic "A Study of History," and stresses the need for conscious change if we are to survive.

Watt, Donald Cameron; Spencer, Frank and Brown, Neville. **A History of the World in the Twentieth Century.** New York: Morrow, 1968, 864 p.
This solid survey by three British scholars "concerns itself mainly with the political and power relationships between the recognized component political units of the twentieth century world."

Wheeler-Bennett, Sir John Wheeler. **A Wreath to Clio: Studies in British, American and German Affairs.** New York: St. Martin's Press, 1967, 224 p.
Thoughts and vignettes on British politics, German leaders and the American Civil War, by a veteran historian, writing with his customary perspicacity.

Zhukov, Evgenii Mikhailovich, *ed.* **Osnovnye etapy razvitiia mirovogo revoliutsionnogo protsessa posle Oktiabria.** Moscow: Izd-vo "Mysl'," 1968, 616 p.
A Soviet scholar attempts to schematize the process of the world-wide anti-capitalist and anti-colonial revolution, begun in 1917 with the Russian October Revolution.

II. FIRST WORLD WAR DIPLOMATIC HISTORY

See also (The World Since 1914) General, p. 129; Inter-War Period, p. 140; and the sections for specific countries and regions.

Baumgart, Winfried. **Deutsche Ostpolitik 1918: von Brest-Litowsk bis zum Ende des Ersten Weltkrieges.** Munich: Oldenbourg, 1966, 462 p.
A major contribution to the diplomatic and political history of World War I dealing with German policies in Russia in 1918. The author analyzes with great clarity the many-layered German plans in Russia and shows how the German Foreign Office, in spite of opposition from the Army High Command and certain diplomatic representatives in Russia, gave support to the Bolsheviks in order to keep Russia weak and to prevent the pro-Allied forces from toppling Lenin's régime.

Baumgart, Winfried, *ed.* **Von Brest-Litovsk zur deutschen Novemberrevolution.** Göttingen: Vandenhoeck und Ruprecht, 1971, 750 p.
This well-edited and significant book comprises three diaries written in Russia—of a journalist, Alfons Paquet; a general, Wilhelm Groener; and an admiral, Albert Hopman—for the period from March to November 1918. A valuable source for this rather murky period of the Russian Revolution and German-Soviet relations.

Biase, Corrado de. **L'Italia dalla neutralità all'intervento nella Prima Guerra Mondiale.** Modena: S.T.E.M. Mucchi, 1965-66, 2 v.
A critical and well-documented study of the interaction between Italy's foreign policy and domestic political developments during the nine months preceding Italy's entry into the First World War in May 1915.

Bihl, Wolfdieter. **Österreich-Ungarn und die Friedensschlüsse von Brest-Litovsk.** Vienna: Böhlau, 1970, 192 p.
A study of the Austro-Hungarian role and interests in the Brest-Litovsk negotiations.

Borowsky, Peter. **Deutsche Ukrainepolitik 1918.** Lübeck: Matthiesen Verlag, 1970, 316 p.

A monograph on German policy in the Ukraine in the months of the Rada and Skoropadsky régimes, with appropriate emphasis on economic and agricultural affairs.

Cohen, Warren I. **The American Revisionists: The Lessons of Intervention in World War I.** Chicago: University of Chicago Press, 1967, 252 p.

An exposition of the thought of five Americans—H. E. Barnes, C. A. Beard, C. H. Grattan, W. Millis and C. C. Tansill—who considered U.S. intervention in World War I a mistake.

Czernin von und zu Chudenitz, Ferdinand, Graf. **Versailles, 1919: The Forces, Events and Personalities that Shaped the Treaty.** New York: Putnam, 1964, 437 p.

The aim of this study is "to show by documentary evidence how the five main, and most controversial, clauses of the Treaty of Versailles came to be written the way they were."

Dallin, Alexander and Others. **Russian Diplomacy and Eastern Europe, 1914-1917.** New York: King's Crown Press (Columbia University), 1963, 305 p.

A collection of six essays on various facets of Russian policy in Central and Eastern Europe between the outbreak of the First World War and the coming of the Revolution.

Dedijer, Vladimir. **The Road to Sarajevo.** New York: Simon and Schuster, 1966, 550 p.

This work, by the author of a biography of Tito and a member of the wartime Jugoslav partisan movement, is of special interest both because of the particular background and vantage point from which Mr. Dedijer writes and because of the book's intensive inquiry into the mood and mentality of the Bosnian revolutionary youths responsible for the assassination of Franz Ferdinand.

Edwards, Marvin L. **Stresemann and the Greater Germany, 1914-1918.** New York: Bookman Associates, 1963, 245 p.

A carefully documented study of Stresemann's annexationist activities during the First World War.

Fedyshyn, Oleh S. **Germany's Drive to the East and the Ukrainian Revolution, 1917-1918.** New Brunswick: Rutgers University Press, 1971, 401 p.

An extensive, well-researched inquiry into German *Ostpolitik* before and during the occupation of the Ukraine.

Fischer, Fritz. **Germany's Aims in the First World War.** New York: Norton, 1967, 652 p.

The author, on the basis of a mass of new—and to Germany damaging—archival evidence, suggests that German expansionism, closely related to the industrial interests of the country, was a continuous policy throughout the first half of the twentieth century. This important work that stimulated new researches in Germany and elsewhere must be regarded as fundamental to an understanding of German and European history in our time. The German original appeared as "Griff nach der Weltmacht: die Kriegszielpolitik des kaiserlichen Deutschland, 1914-1918" (Düsseldorf: Droste, 3d rev. ed., 1964, 902 p.).

Fischer, Fritz. **Krieg der Illusionen: die deutsche Politik von 1911 bis 1914.** Düsseldorf: Droste, 1969, 805 p.

An analysis of the aggressive German prewar policies. A major work on the still explosive issue of the origins of the First World War.

Fischer, Fritz. **Weltmacht oder Niedergang: Deutschland im Ersten Weltkrieg.** Frankfurt/Main: Europäische Verlagsanstalt, 1965, 109 p.

The author answers his critics and repeats his thesis about Germany's purposeful expansionist policies. The English translation appeared as "World Power or Decline: The Controversy over Germany's Aims in the First World War" (New York: Norton, 1974, 131 p.).

Fowler, Wilton Bonham. **British-American Relations, 1917-1918: The Role of Sir William Wiseman.** Princeton: Princeton University Press, 1969, 334 p.

Sir William Wiseman, who was head of British intelligence operations in the United States and enjoyed Colonel House's patronage, played an important role in British-American wartime diplomacy because, "having decided that House was the best approach to Wilson, the British government routed its most urgent petitions to him through Wiseman." This volume, based primarily on unpublished sources, appeared as a supplementary volume to "The Papers of Woodrow Wilson."

Futrell, Michael. **Northern Underground.** New York: Praeger, 1963, 240 p.
An important study of the channels and devices used in Scandinavia and Finland by Russian revolutionaries to smuggle correspondence, arms, and propaganda into Russia. The story centers on the First World War and such figures as Shlyapnikov, Kesküla and Fürstenberg (Hanecki).

Geiss, Imanuel, *ed.* **Julikrise und Kriegsausbruch 1914: eine Dokumentensammlung.** Hanover: Verlag für Literatur und Zeitgeschehen, 1963-64, 2 v.
A collection of German documents, with explanatory remarks, dealing with the diplomatic and political developments pertaining to the outbreak of World War I. A one volume English edition, with a new introductory chapter, was published as "July 1914; The Outbreak of the First World War: Selected Documents" (New York: Scribner, 1967, 400 p.).

Goldberg, George. **The Peace to End Peace.** New York: Harcourt, Brace and World, 1969, 221 p.
A cursory and rather chatty account of the Paris Peace Conference of 1919, with emphasis on the three main protagonists, Woodrow Wilson, Georges Clemenceau and David Lloyd George.

Hankey, Maurice Pascal Alers Hankey, 1st Baron. **The Supreme Control at the Paris Peace Conference 1919.** London: Allen and Unwin, 1963, 206 p.
A valuable commentary on the organization and functioning of the Paris Peace Conference from the vantage point of the head of the secretaryship of the British Empire Delegation.

Hantsch, Hugo. **Leopold Graf Berchtold: Grandseigneur und Staatsmann.** Graz: Verlag Styria, 1963, 2 v.
A well-researched and well-written biography of Count Berchtold, Minister of Foreign Affairs of Austria-Hungary at the outbreak of World War I.

Haselmayr, Friedrich. **Der Weg in die Katastrophe.** Munich: Bruckmann, 1963-64, 2 v.
A diplomatic history of Germany before and during World War I, the sixth and concluding volume (in two parts) of "Diplomatische Geschichte des Zweiten Reichs von 1871-1918."

Hazlehurst, Cameron. **Politicians at War: July 1914 to May 1915; A Prologue to the Triumph of Lloyd George.** New York: Knopf, 1971, 346 p.
On the basis of carefully assembled new sources, a young English historian presents an intimate picture of how the British cabinet entered the war in August 1914 and waged it.

Headlam-Morley, Sir James Wycliffe. **A Memoir of the Paris Peace Conference 1919.** London: Methuen, 1972, 230 p.
Letters and diary entries, written by a member of the British delegation to the Paris Peace Conference of 1919, of particular interest because Headlam-Morley was a dominant figure in the New States Committee. The volume has been edited by Agnes Headlam-Morley, Russel Bryant and Anna Maria Cienciala.

Höglinger, Felix. **Ministerpräsident Graf Clam-Martinic.** Graz: Böhlau, 1964, 236 p.
A scholarly biography of Count Clam-Martinic (1863-1932), an important politician at the end of the Dual Monarchy, Prime Minister from December 1916 to June 1917 and Military Governor of Montenegro from 1917 to 1919.

Janssen, Karl-Heinz. **Macht und Verblendung.** Göttingen: Musterschmidt, 1963, 342 p.
A study of the role and influence of Bavaria, Saxony and other *Bundesstaaten* on German war aims in 1914-1918.

Kann, Robert A. **Die Sixtusaffäre und die geheimen Friedensverhandlungen Österreich-Ungarns im Ersten Weltkrieg.** Munich: Oldenbourg, 1966, 94 p.
A very informative study, based on recently discovered documents, on the secret negotiations in which Austria-Hungary was engaged during World War I.

Kantorowicz, Hermann. **Gutachten zur Kriegsschuldfrage 1914.** Frankfurt/Main: Europäische Verlagsanstalt, 1967, 447 p.
A most interesting study dealing with the war-guilt problem in 1914. The author, a German professor of law who left his native country in 1933, prepared this survey for a commission of the Reichstag in 1927. The chief culprit in the author's view is the Austro-Hungarian Count Berchtold. The manuscript has been edited by Imanuel Geiss.

Koch, H. W., ed. **The Origins of the First World War: Great Power Rivalry and German War Aims.** New York: Taplinger, 1972, 374 p.
An intellectually stimulating symposium devoted to Fritz Fischer's now classic revisionist analysis of Germany's war aims and responsibility for the First World War which has profoundly altered contemporary German diplomatic history.

Krug von Nidda, Roland. **Der Weg nach Sarajewo: Franz Ferdinand.** Vienna: Amalthea Verlag, 1964, 319 p.
A biography of Archduke Franz Ferdinand, whose assassination provided the spark for the outbreak of World War I.

Louis, William Roger. **Great Britain and Germany's Lost Colonies, 1914–1919.** New York: Oxford University Press, 1967, 167 p.
A fine analysis, based on much new evidence, of Britain's colonial aims during the First World War. According to the author, Great Britain never wavered in its desire for the German colonies.

Lowe, Peter. **Great Britain and Japan, 1911-1915: A Study of British Far Eastern Policy.** London: Macmillan, 1969, 343 p.
The author concludes in his study that British policy in the Far East from 1911 to 1915 was basically defensive and sought to preserve stability in the region.

Mantoux, Paul Joseph. **Paris Peace Conference 1919.** Geneva: Droz, 1964, 227 p.
This is a translation of the first part (March 24–April 18) of Paul Mantoux' important "Notes" on the sessions of the Council of Four. The French edition was published as "Les Délibérations du Conseil des quatre, 24 mars–28 juin 1919" (Paris: Editions du Centre National de la Recherche Scientifique, 1955, 2 v.).

Mayer, Arno J. **Politics and Diplomacy of Peacemaking: Containment and Counterrevolution at Versailles, 1918–1919.** New York: Knopf, 1967, 918 p.
A carefully researched reassessment of the Versailles peace negotiations. By highlighting domestic pressures and conflicts, the author has prepared a most valuable case study demonstrating the primacy of domestic politics in international relations.

Monticone, Alberto. **La Germania e la neutralità italiana: 1914–1915.** Bologna: Il Mulino, 1971, 644 p.
A well-documented monograph on Germany's effort to mediate Austro-Italian differences prior to Italy's entry in the First World War.

O'Grady, Joseph P., ed. **The Immigrants' Influence on Wilson's Peace Policies.** Lexington: University of Kentucky Press, 1967, 329 p.
Eleven essays on the attempts of various American ethnic groups, mostly of East European origin, to influence President Wilson's foreign policies during World War I. The editor of this volume claims that the Poles and the Jews were more successful than the others.

Renouvin, Pierre. **L'Armistice de Rethondes: 11 novembre 1918.** Paris: Gallimard, 1968, 486 p.
A solid history, by a renowned French scholar, of the Armistice that was signed by the French and the Germans on November 11, 1918.

Riezler, Kurt. **Tagebücher, Aufsätze, Dokumente.** Göttingen: Vandenhoeck und Ruprecht, 1972, 766 p.
Diaries, articles and documents written by a close collaborator of Chancellor Bethmann-Hollweg during World War I. After the Bolshevik Revolution, Riezler, a counselor at the German Embassy in Moscow and, after the murder of Count Mirbach, the chargé d'affaires, played a prominent role in the formulation of the German policies toward Russia. The volume has been edited by Karl Dietrich Erdmann.

Rössler, Hellmuth, ed. **Ideologie und Machtpolitik 1919: Plan und Werk der Pariser Friedenskonferenzen 1919.** Göttingen: Musterschmidt (for the Ranke-Gesellschaft), 1966, 273 p.
Papers and discussions on the 1919 Paris Peace Conference from an international symposium, held under the auspices of the Ranke-Gesellschaft, which took place in October 1964 in Schwäbisch Hall.

Ropp, Friedrich von der. **Zwischen Gestern und Morgen: Erfahrungen und Erkenntnisse.** Stuttgart: Steinkopf, 2d ed., 1963, 261 p.

Memoirs by a Baltic German citizen of Tsarist Russia who at the beginning of World War I on behalf of the German government travelled to England to explore the possibilitites of a separate peace, and who later, in order to weaken the Russian war effort, helped to support the organizations of various non-Russian nationalities that asked for the right of self-determination.

Rothwell, Victor Howard. **British War Aims and Peace Diplomacy 1914-1918.** New York: Oxford University Press, 1971, 315 p.
This well-documented study, according to the author, "is a history of British official thinking on war aims in the First World War and of the British part in the attempts which were made to end the war by negotiation." The emphasis is on British policies toward Austria-Hungary, Turkey and Bulgaria.

Scherer, André and Grunewald, Jacques, eds. **L'Allemagne et les problèmes de la paix pendant la Première guerre mondiale. Tome 2: De la Guerre sous-marine à outrance à la revolution soviétique (1er février 1917 - 7 novembre 1917).** Paris: Presses Universitaires, 1966, 579 p.
A selection of documents from the archives of the German Foreign Ministry dealing with German peace moves in the period from February to November 1917. Volume I was published in 1962 and volume III is in preparation.

Schlarp, Karl-Heinz. **Ursachen und Enstehung des Ersten Weltkrieges im Lichte der sowjetischen Geschichtsschreibung.** Frankfurt/Main: Metzner (for the Institut für Auswärtige Politik, Hamburg), 1971, 289 p.
A useful survey of Soviet scholarship dealing with the causes and outbreak of World War I.

Seymour, Charles. **Letters from the Paris Peace Conference.** New Haven: Yale University Press, 1965, 289 p.
Valuable for the historian of the Peace Conference of 1919, this volume comprises letters which the late Charles Seymour, a member of the Inquiry, wrote to his family during his stay in Paris. The book has been edited by Harold B. Whiteman, Jr.

Shepherd, Gordon. **The Last Hapsburg.** New York: Weybright and Talley, 1968, 358 p.
A well-documented and vivid story of the personal and political tragedy of Charles I, the last Hapsburg Emperor, who succeeded Emperor Franz Josef in November 1916. Particular attention is devoted to Charles' secret wartime diplomacy and his two attempts to restore the monarchy in 1921.

Silberstein, Gerard E. **The Troubled Alliance: German-Austrian Relations, 1914 to 1917.** Lexington: University Press of Kentucky, 1970, 366 p.
A well-documented and systematic examination of the German and Austrian efforts during World War I to secure the allegiance of Turkey and the Balkan states.

Smith, Gaddis. **Britain's Clandestine Submarines, 1914-1915.** New Haven: Yale University Press, 1964, 155 p.
An interesting study of the secret submarine contract concluded by Charles Schwab of the Bethlehem Steel Corporation and Admiral Fisher during the early months of World War I.

Steglich, Wolfgang. **Die Friedenspolitik der Mittelmächte, 1917/1918.** Wiesbaden: Franz Steiner, 1964, 593 p.
A solid monograph on the diplomacy of Germany and Austria-Hungary during 1917 and 1918.

Thompson, John M. **Russia, Bolshevism, and the Versailles Peace.** Princeton: Princeton University Press, 1967, 429 p.
A first-rate account of the Russian question at the Paris Peace Conference of 1919.

Trask, David F. **General Tasker Howard Bliss and the "Sessions of the World," 1919.** Philadelphia: American Philosophical Society, 1966, 80 p.
An important study of General Bliss's activities at the Paris Peace Conference.

Trumpener, Ulrich. **Germany and the Ottoman Empire, 1914-1918.** Princeton: Princeton University Press, 1968, 433 p.
A valuable contribution to the study of imperialism in the First World War. New evidence suggests that German efforts in Turkey were often haphazard and less successful than hitherto assumed.

Vietsch, Eberhard von. **Bethmann Hollweg: Staatsmann zwischen Macht und Ethos.** Boppard am Rhein: Boldt, 1969, 348 p.

A monograph on Bethmann-Hollweg, Chancellor of the German Reich from 1909 to 1917. Of particular interest are the discussions of Bethmann-Hollweg's policies at the outbreak of, and during World War I. The author claims that the Chancellor was never convinced of a German victory in World War I and defends him against accusations that he was pursuing annexationist aims.

Vietsch, Eberhard von, *ed.* **Gegen die Unvernunft: der Briefwechsel zwischen Paul Graf Wolff Metternich und Wilhelm Solf 1915-1918, mit zwei Briefen Albert Ballins.** Bremen: Schünemann, 1964, 145 p.

A collection of letters, containing information about Germany's foreign policy during World War I, exchanged between Count Metternich, a former German ambassador in London, and Wilhelm Solf, Secretary of State of the German Foreign Office in 1918. The editor of this volume is also the author of a biography of Wilhelm Solf: "Wilhelm Solf: Botschafter zwischen den Zeiten" (Tübingen: Wunderlich, 1961, 402 p.).

Weber, Frank G. **Eagles on the Crescent: Germany, Austria, and the Diplomacy of the Turkish Alliance, 1914-1918.** Ithaca: Cornell University Press, 1970, 284 p.

A valuable addition to the diplomatic history of World War I, based primarily on unpublished records of the German and Austrian foreign ministries.

Williamson, Samuel R., Jr. **The Politics of Grand Strategy: Britain and France Prepare for War, 1904-1914.** Cambridge: Harvard University Press, 1969, 409 p.

This scholarly work on Anglo-French military and naval conversations before World War I illustrates the primacy of domestic politics and bureaucracy in the determination of alliance policy, even in times of great stress and danger.

Zechlin, Egmont. **Die deutsche Politik und die Juden im Ersten Weltkrieg.** Göttingen: Vandenhoeck, 1969, 592 p.

A well-documented survey of the role of the Jews in Germany and German occupied territories during World War I, and a description of the German efforts to use the Jewish problem all over the world as a means for enhancing their chances for victory.

Zeman, Zbyněk Anthony Bohuslav. **The Gentlemen Negotiators.** New York: Macmillan, 1971, 402 p.

The author offers fascinating insights into the diplomatic negotiations taking place in nine world capitals during World War I. A fine scholarly contribution.

Zeman, Zbyněk Anthony Bohuslav and Scharlau, W. B. **The Merchant of Revolution: The Life of Alexander Israel Helphand (Parvus) 1867-1924.** New York: Oxford University Press, 1965, 306 p.

An important and well-documented study of the fantastic career of Helphand-Parvus, a Russian-German socialist thinker, revolutionary and businessman, who during World War I advised German governmental agencies on how to weaken the Russian Empire internally and who transmitted German subsidies to Lenin's Bolshevik organizations. The original German version appeared as "Freibeuter der Revolution: Parvus-Helphand" (Cologne: Verlag Wissenschaft und Politik, 1964, 381 p.).

Živojnović, Dragan R. **America, Italy and the Birth of Yugoslavia (1917-1919).** Boulder (Colo.): East European Quarterly, 1972, 338 p.

A detailed monograph on the Adriatic question, concentrating on Wilson's policy and the dispute with Italy at the Peace Conference.

THE CONDUCT OF THE WAR

See also (The World Since 1914) General, p. 129; (The United States) Biographies, Memoirs and Addresses, p. 218; Military and Defense Policy, p. 257; (Great Britain) Biographies, Memoirs and Addresses, p. 369; (France) Biographies, Memoirs and Addresses, p. 400; The Baltic States, p. 455; (Poland) Recent History to 1945, p. 525.

Agar, Augustus Willington Shelton. **Baltic Episode: A Classic of Secret Service in Russian Waters.** London: Hodder, 1963, 255 p.

An exciting tale of the deft maneuvers of the British Navy against the Russians during the confused Baltic events of 1919.

FIRST WORLD WAR

Asprey, Robert Brown. **At Belleau Wood.** New York: Putnam, 1965, 375 p.
An account of the American Marine Corps offensive at Belleau Wood in June 1918.

Barker, Arthur J. **The Bastard War: The Mesopotamian Campaign of 1914-1918.** New York: Dial Press, 1967, 449 p.
An authoritative study of the battles waged over the Mesopotamian oil fields between Turkey and Great Britain during World War I. The British edition is entitled "The Neglected War: Mesopotamia, 1914-1918" (London: Faber, 1967, 534 p.).

Barnett, Correlli. **The Swordbearers: Supreme Command in the First World War.** New York: Morrow, 1964, 392 p.
A study of four supreme commanders—Moltke, Pétain and Ludendorff on the Western Front and Jellicoe at the Battle of Jutland.

Beaver, Daniel R. **Newton D. Baker and the American War Effort, 1917-1919.** Lincoln: University of Nebraska Press, 1966, 273 p.
While this excellent book centers on the person and activities of Wilson's Secretary of War, it also has much to say about other leading actors in 1917-1918, such as Generals Pershing and Bliss.

Bennett, Geoffrey Martin. **The Battle of Jutland.** London: Batsford, 1964, 208 p.
Another interpretation of the controversial World War I sea battle, evaluated in the light of new evidence.

Bennett, Geoffrey Martin. **Cowan's War: The Story of British Operations in the Baltic, 1918-1920.** London: Collins, 1964, 254 p.
An account of British naval operations, directed by Admiral Cowan, in the midst of confusing political events in the Eastern Baltic Area.

Coffman, Edward M. **The War to End All Wars.** New York: Oxford University Press, 1968, 412 p.
A first-rate study of the military experience of the United States in the First World War.

DeWeerd, Harvey Arthur. **President Wilson Fights His War.** New York: Macmillan, 1968, 457 p.
A fine military history of the background and impact of the American war effort in Europe during World War I. President Wilson and General Pershing emerge as the author's heroes.

Faldella, Emilio. **La grande guerra.** Milan: Longanesi, 1965, 2 v.
A dispassionate narrative of Italy's military campaigns in the First World War, by a veteran of that conflict. The first volume, "Le battaglie dell'Isonzo, 1915-17," details the eleven unsuccessful Italian offensives along the Isonzo River; the second, "Da Caporetto al Piave, 1917-18," traces the causes of the Caporetto disaster and the stabilization of the Italian army along the Piave River.

Falls, Cyril Bentham. **Armageddon: 1918.** Philadelphia: Lippincott, 1964, 200 p.
A tribute to the "shock action" of British and Arab troops under Allenby and the last great cavalry charge in the Palestine offensive of September 1918 in which the Turks were rapidly defeated. This monograph was published as a volume in "The Great Battles of History" series and is the work of the official historian of the Palestine campaign.

Feldman, Gerald D. **Army, Industry and Labor in Germany, 1914-1918.** Princeton: Princeton University Press, 1966, 572 p.
A pioneering study of the struggles and changing fortunes of major interest groups and their impact on wartime and revolutionary Germany, by an American historian.

Fredette, Raymond H. **The Sky on Fire: The First Battle of Britain 1917-1918 and the Birth of the Royal Air Force.** New York: Holt, Rinehart and Winston, 1966, 289 p.
An account of the little-known story of the German air raids—mostly by Gothas or Giants—during the last two years of the First World War.

Führ, Christoph. **Das K.u.K. Armeeoberkommando und die Innenpolitik in Österreich, 1914-1917.** Graz: Böhlau, 1968, 190 p.
A well-documented study of the relations between the Government and the Army High Command in the Dual Monarchy in the first three years of the war.

Gardner, Brian. **The Big Push.** New York: Morrow, 3rd ed., 1963, 176 p.
A critical analysis of the planning and strategy of the British command in the Battle

of the Somme (July 1–November 18, 1916) in which the British lost 20,000 soldiers on the first day of the "big push."

Gardner, Brian. **On to Kilimanjaro: The Bizarre Story of the First World War in East Africa.** Philadelphia: Macrae Smith, 1963, 284 p.
An account of the German campaign in East Africa, under the imaginative leadership of General von Lettow-Vorbeck, to keep the British from reaching the Western Front. The English edition appeared as "German East: The Story of the First World War in East Africa" (London: Cassell, 1963, 213 p.).

Gatti, Angelo. **Caporetto: dal diario di guerra inedito, maggio-dicembre 1917.** Bologna: Il Mulino, 4th ed., 1964, 477 p.
This important diary, with an introduction by Alberto Monticone, chronicles Italy's war-weariness and military ineptness in the months preceding and following the Caporetto disaster in October 1917.

Gibbs, Sir Philip Hamilton. **The War Dispatches.** London: Anthony Gibbs and Phillips, 1964, 409 p.
A famous war correspondent reflects on the hazards of his profession during World War I.

Goodspeed, Donald James. **Ludendorff: Genius of World War I.** Boston: Houghton, 1966, 335 p.
A Canadian officer and military historian appraises the outstanding German general of the First World War. While regarding him as a brilliant tactician and "one of the very greatest military organizers of all time," the author feels he was "completely unequipped ... to cope with political problems"—a disaster for Germany and the world. The British edition is entitled "Ludendorff: Soldier, Dictator, Revolutionary" (London: Hart-Davis, 1966, 272 p.).

Guinn, Paul Spencer. **British Strategy and Politics, 1914 to 1918.** New York: Oxford University Press, 1965, 359 p.
A study of the political background of Britain's strategic planning in the Great War, written with verve and objectivity, and based on new sources.

Higgins, Trumbull. **Winston Churchill and the Dardanelles: A Dialogue in Ends and Means.** New York: Macmillan, 1963, 308 p.
An account of the political background of the Gallipoli disaster.

Hoyt, Edwin Palmer. **Kreuzerkrieg.** Cleveland: World Publishing Co., 1968, 340 p.
The story, well told, of the German East Asia Cruiser Squadron in World War I. The hero clearly is Admiral Maximilian Graf von Spee.

James, Robert Rhodes. **Gallipoli.** New York: Macmillan, 1965, 384 p.
Although there have been many histories of the Gallipoli campaign, this is certainly one of the best and makes use of a number of private unpublished papers of the principal participants. Excellent maps and illustrations.

Kielmansegg, Peter, Graf von. **Deutschland und der Erste Weltkrieg.** Frankfurt/Main: Athenaion, 1968, 747 p.
A scholarly and comprehensive account of Germany's role in World War I, based on a judicious scrutiny of the mass of new material published since the end of World War II.

Klein, Fritz and Others, *eds*. **Deutschland im Ersten Weltkrieg.** Berlin: Akademie-Verlag (for the Institut für Geschichte in der Deutschen Akademie der Wissenschaften), 2d rev. ed., 1970, 3 v.
A massive study of Germany's role in World War I, with enormous attention given to the activities of the German Communists during that period.

Koeltz, Louis. **La Guerre de 1914-1918: les opérations militaires.** Paris: Sirey, 1966, 653 p.
A military history of World War I, by a French general. A volume in the series "L'Histoire du XXe siècle."

Laffargue, André Charles Victor. **Foch et la bataille de 1918.** Paris: Arthaud, 1967, 399 p.
A battle-by-battle account of the fighting on the Western Front in 1918, with Marshal Foch as the hero.

Marder, Arthur Jacob. **From the Dreadnought to Scapa Flow: The Royal Navy in the Fisher Era, 1904-1919.** New York: Oxford University Press, 1961-70, 5 v.

The author, a professor at the University of California, Irvine, has "chronicled the story of the Royal Navy in 1914–18, as well as the crucially important pre-war decade and the immediate aftermath of the war." A major and well-documented study.

Mosley, Leonard Oswald. **Duel for Kilimanjaro: An Account of the African Campaign, 1914-1918.** London: Weidenfeld, 1963, 244 p.
The efforts of the Germans and their capable General von Lettow-Vorbeck are well recounted here in this tale of the German-British campaigns in German East Africa during World War I.

Murray, Joseph. **Gallipoli as I Saw It.** London: Kimber, 1965, 192 p.
A participant of the Gallipoli campaign reminisces on what he experienced during this tragedy.

Nobécourt, René Gustave. **L'Année du 11 novembre 1918.** Paris: Laffont, 1968, 439 p.
In this account of the last months of World War I in France Marshal Foch is depicted as the outstanding military leader.

Norman, Aaron. **The Great Air War.** New York: Macmillan, 1968, 558 p.
The romantic and personal stories of the great air aces of World War I. Fast-paced and well-researched.

Pedroncini, Guy. **Les Mutineries de 1917.** Paris: Presses Universitaires, 1967, 328 p.
A detailed survey of the mutinies in the French Army in 1917 (in which approximately 30–40,000 soldiers participated) and of the measures Marshal Pétain took to reëstablish order.

Plaschka, Richard Georg. **Cattaro, Prag: Revolte und Revolution; Kriegsmarine und Heer Österreich-Ungarns im Feuer der Aufstandsbewegungen vom 1. Februar und 28. Oktober 1918.** Graz: Böhlau, 1963, 313 p.
Monographs on two events relating to the collapse of the Hapsburg Monarchy: the sailors' revolt at Cattaro in February 1918 and the Prague uprising of October 1918.

Roesler, Konrad. **Die Finanzpolitik des Deutschen Reiches im Ersten Weltkrieg.** Berlin: Duncker, 1967, 237 p.
A monograph on the financial policies of Germany during World War I.

Rössler, Hellmuth, *ed.* **Weltwende 1917: Monarchie, Weltrevolution, Demokratie.** Göttingen: Musterschmidt (for the Ranke-Gesellschaft), 1965, 214 p.
Essays on the cataclysmic events of the last year of the First World War.

Schettini, Mario. **La Prima Guerra Mondiale: storia, letteratura.** Florence: Sansoni, 1965, 713 p.
A history of the First World War on the Austro-Italian front, told through the diaries, letters and memoirs of the combatants on both sides of the trenches.

Stallings, Laurence. **The Doughboys.** New York: Harper and Row, 1963, 404 p.
A well-told tale of the two million men of the American Expeditionary Forces who fought in Europe from 1917–1918 under General Pershing.

Taylor, Alan John Percivale. **Illustrated History of the First World War.** New York: Putnam, 1964, 224 p.
A generously illustrated account of each year of battle in World War I. The English edition was entitled "The First World War: An Illustrated History" (London: Hamilton, 1963, 224 p.).

Taylor, Alan John Percivale. **Politics in Wartime and Other Essays.** New York: Atheneum, 1965, 207 p.
A collection of essays by a lively British historian, a producer, as he says, of "dry biscuits" rather than "rich plum puddings." The larger part of the book is devoted to the First World War and its immediate antecedents.

Terraine, John. **Ordeal of Victory.** Philadelphia: Lippincott, 1963, 508 p.
A massive and detailed study of Field Marshal Douglas Haig's role in the First World War. The author does much to clear Haig of the very considerable abuse to which he has been subjected: Lloyd George, on the other hand, appears in a most unattractive light.

Terraine, John. **The Western Front: 1914-1918.** Philadelphia: Lippincott, 1965, 230 p.
A collection of the author's able essays dealing with various aspects of the "grotesquely static nature" of the war on the Western Front.

Vigezzi, Brunello. **L'Italia di fronte alla Prima Guerra Mondiale.** Milan: Ricciardi, 1966–.
A comprehensive study of the Italian experience during the First World War. The first volume, "L'Italia neutrale," which incorporates a wide variety of sources, describes the political events which caused Italy to abandon the Triple Alliance, adhere to neutrality and finally to intervene in the war on the side of the Triple Entente.

Watt, Richard M. **Dare Call It Treason.** New York: Simon and Schuster, 1963, 344 p.
An interesting investigation of the 1917 mutinies in the French Army, their immediate cause, their earlier roots in the structure of the French military and political system, and the reconstruction of order and morale by Pétain and Clemenceau.

Weber, Hellmuth. **Ludendorff und die Monopole: deutsche Kriegspolitik 1916-1918.** Berlin: Akademie-Verlag, 1966, 174 p.
An East German study of political developments in Germany from 1916 to 1918.

Woodward, Sir Ernest Llewellyn. **Great Britain and the War of 1914-1918.** New York: Barnes and Noble, 1967, 610 p.
A comprehensive account of Great Britain's efforts in World War I, by a distinguished British historian.

III. INTER-WAR PERIOD

See also Socialism, p. 24; Communism, p. 26; Totalitarianism; Fascism, p. 32; (International Organization and Government) General, p. 96; (War) Propaganda; Psychological and Political Warfare, p. 120; (The United States) Foreign Policy, p. 229; (Europe) General Surveys, p. 344; (Great Britain) Biographies, Memoirs and Addresses, p. 369; Foreign Policy, p. 375; Military Policy, p. 378; Belgium, p. 391; Switzerland, p. 393; (France) Recent History, p. 396; Biographies, Memoirs and Addresses, p. 400; Military Policy, p. 407; (Italy) Biographies, Memoirs and Collected Writings, p. 420; Foreign Policy, p. 424; (Spain) The Republic and the Civil War, p. 434; Norway, p. 444; The Baltic States, p. 455; (Germany) Recent History, p. 465; The 1918 Revolution and the Weimar Republic, p. 468; The Nazi Era, p. 475; (Austria) General, p. 507; (Hungary) Foreign Relations, p. 515; (Czechoslovakia) Recent History to 1945, p. 516; (Poland) Recent History to 1945, p. 525; Foreign Relations, p. 527; (Union of Soviet Socialist Republics) Memoirs and Biographies, p. 533; Foreign Policy, p. 550; Rumania, p. 588; Jugoslavia, p. 591; Bulgaria, p. 596; (Greece) General, p. 602; Foreign Relations, p. 606; (China) Recent History, p. 684; (Japan) Recent History, p. 715.

Aigner, Dietrich. **Das Ringen um England.** Munich: Bechtle, 1969, 444 p.
A discussion of German-British relations from 1933 to 1939. The author thinks that Hitler suffered his first important foreign policy defeat when the makers of British public opinion wrecked German attempts to establish good relations with Great Britain.

L'altra Europa 1922-45: momenti e problemi. Turin: Giappichelli, 1967, 294 p.
Six well-known Italian historians consider the theme of Europe's opposition to fascism during the inter-war period.

Armstrong, Hamilton Fish. **Peace and Counterpeace: From Wilson to Hitler.** New York: Harper and Row, 1971, 585 p.
The memoirs of the man who for half a century was the editor of *Foreign Affairs*. They provide important information on many personalities who helped to shape twentieth-century history and tell the story of the journal and some of its illustrious contributors—Poincaré, Masaryk, Venizelos, Stresemann, Bukharin, Radek, Paderewski, Austin Chamberlain, Sforza, Beneš and many more.

Barros, James. **The Corfu Incident of 1923: Mussolini and the League of Nations.** Princeton: Princeton University Press, 1965, 339 p.
A monograph centering on the League of Nations' role in the handling, or mishandling, of the Corfu Incident.

Barros, James. **The League of Nations and the Great Powers: The Greek-Bulgarian Incident, 1925.** New York: Oxford University Press, 1970, 143 p.
A good monograph on the successful handling of a very touchy border incident.

Baumont, Maurice. **Les Origines de la Deuxième guerre mondiale.** Paris: Payot, 1969, 363 p.
A study of the origins of World War II by a veteran French specialist on inter-war history. It is intended for a less scholarly public than his "La Faillite de la paix" of which the 5th revised edition appeared in 1967.

Carsten, Francis Ludwig. **Revolution in Central Europe, 1918-1919.** Berkeley: University of California Press, 1972, 360 p.
A comparative study of the revolutionary possibilities in the immediate aftermath of the First World War, with particular emphasis on the role of workers' and soldiers' councils. A judicious appraisal, based on much new archival material.

Casella, Alessandro. **Le Conflit sino-japonais de 1937 et la Société des Nations.** Paris: Librairie Générale de Droit et de Jurisprudence, 1968, 151 p.
A survey of how the League of Nations reacted to the Sino-Japanese conflict of 1937. Useful bibliography.

Colvin, Ian Goodhope. **None So Blind: A British Diplomatic View of the Origins of World War II.** New York: Harcourt, Brace and World, 1965, 360 p.
The central figure, and Cassandra-like hero, of this review of the origins of World War II is Lord Vansittart, Permanent Under-Secretary for Foreign Affairs from 1930 to 1938.

Compton, James V. **The Swastika and the Eagle: Hitler, the United States, and the Origins of World War II.** Boston: Houghton, 1967, 297 p.
A scholarly elaboration on Hitler's attitude and policies toward the United States in the years before Pearl Harbor.

Dexter, Byron. **The Years of Opportunity: The League of Nations, 1920-1926.** New York: Viking, 1967, 264 p.
The author, formerly Managing Editor of *Foreign Affairs*, argues that Locarno was the 1925 watershed between a successful League based on "a core of organized power" and a League that became the instrument of Hitler.

Eubank, Keith. **Munich.** Norman: University of Oklahoma Press, 1963, 322 p.
A serious and scholarly though not a path-breaking view of the Munich Agreement and of some of the mythology associated with it.

Fry, Michael G. **Illusions of Security: North Atlantic Diplomacy 1918-22.** Toronto: University of Toronto Press, 1972, 221 p.
An investigation of the efforts to establish close coöperation between the British Empire and the United States in the aftermath of World War I.

Funke, Manfred. **Sanktionen und Kanonen: Hitler, Mussolini und der internationale Abessinienkonflikt 1934-36.** Düsseldorf: Droste, 1970, 220 p.
A major and well-documented study of the Italian-German relations during the Abyssinian war. The author shows that Hitler did not support Mussolini during the Italian campaign in Africa but, on the contrary, supplied armaments to Abyssinia. He also argues that the Rome-Berlin Axis was not a result of German-Italian coöperation at that time.

Gannon, Franklin Reid. **The British Press and Germany, 1936-1939.** New York: Oxford University Press, 1971, 314 p.
A close examination of Britain's national press shows that the attitudes toward Nazi Germany were more complex and less divided than had once been assumed.

Gilbert, Martin and Gott, Richard. **The Appeasers.** Boston: Houghton, 1963, 444 p.
Although the two authors were born in the late 1930s and have no personal recriminations, this cool and able account of Britain's appeasers—"decayed serving men"—in the face of Hitler's mounting threat is altogether devastating.

Gilbert, Martin. **The Roots of Appeasement.** New York: New American Library, 1967, 254 p.
In this study of the origins and development of appeasement, both as a policy and as a state of mind, the author makes a sharp distinction between the earlier attitudes based on hope and the later ones that were based on weakness and led to Munich.

Hauser, Oswald. **England und das Dritte Reich.** Stuttgart: Seewald, 1972, 317 p.
This first of a two-volume study of Britain's policy of appeasement, covering the years 1933-1936, provides fuller insight (from Cabinet and Foreign Office minutes) into a policy that was as much "realistic" choice as "optimistic" drift.

Jacobson, Jon. **Locarno Diplomacy: Germany and the West, 1925-1929.** Princeton: Princeton University Press, 1972, 420 p.
The promise and the realities of the great détente in Europe in the 1920s are examined closely and intelligently, with much attention paid to new primary sources.

Jaenicke, Wolfgang Albert. **Das Ringen um die Macht im Fernen Osten.** Würzburg: Holzner, 1963, 194 p.

An account of the background of the Chinese-Japanese conflict of 1937.

Jarausch, Konrad Hugo. **The Four Power Pact 1933.** Madison: State Historical Society of Wisconsin (for the Department of History, University of Wisconsin), 1965, 265 p.

A study of Europe's response to Hitler's seizure of power and of the diplomatic failures of 1933 that "were the first in a chain of disasters leading to the outbreak of World War II."

Koginos, Manny T. **The *Panay* Incident: Prelude to War.** Lafayette: Purdue University Studies, 1967, 154 p.

The author maintains that the sinking of the American gunboat *Panay* in 1937 was provoked by Japanese military extremists, not the Japanese government as a whole. An interesting, closely-reasoned interpretation of an episode on the road to Pearl Harbor.

Král, Václav, *ed.* **Das Abkommen von München 1938.** Prague: Academia, 1968, 369 p.

A collection of documents, mainly from the archives of the Prague Foreign Office, published in order to discredit the policies of the Czechoslovak government and of the Western powers during the 1938 crisis. Despite its bias, the volume includes many sources indispensable for the elucidation of Czechoslovakia's much-misunderstood part in the Munich story.

Kutakov, Leonid Nikolaevich. **Japanese Foreign Policy on the Eve of the Pacific War: A Soviet View.** Tallahassee (Fla.): Diplomatic Press, 1972, 241 p.

A Soviet scholar and diplomat argues, not always convincingly, that the Pacific War was facilitated by the unavailing U.S. and British attempts to arrange a peaceful settlement with Japan, and that the Western powers only joined the Soviet Union when vital Anglo-American interests were threatened. The manuscript for this study was edited and translated by George Alexander Lensen.

Lafore, Laurence Davis. **The End of Glory.** Philadelphia: Lippincott, 1970, 280 p.

A very well-written and lively effort to reëxamine the origins of the Second World War. While he offers no surprises, the author has succeeded in painting a compelling portrait of Western Europe on the edge of the abyss during the 1920s and 1930s.

Liubimov, Nikolai Nikolaevich and Erlikh, Aleksandr Nikolaevich. **Genuezskaia konferentsiia.** Moscow: Izd-vo Instituta Mezhdunarodnykh Otnoshenii, 1963, 156 p.

Memoirs of the Genoa Conference of 1922 by two diplomats who served as junior members of the Soviet delegation.

Lundgreen, Peter. **Die englische Appeasement-Politik bis zum Münchener Abkommen: Voraussetzungen, Konzeption, Durchführung.** Berlin: Colloquium Verlag, 1969, 153 p.

Refraining from criticism, the author attempts to analyze the defense, economic and foreign policy factors that contributed toward the formulation of Chamberlain's appeasement policies against Hitler.

Middlemas, Keith. **The Strategy of Appeasement: The British Government and Germany, 1937-39.** Chicago: Quadrangle Books, 1972, 510 p.

Solidly based on newly opened British archives, this probing study of how the Chamberlain government formulated and conducted its foreign policy is first-rate, both as history and as political science.

Montigny, Jean. **Le Complot contre la paix, 1935-1939.** Paris: Éditions de la Table Ronde, 1966, 352 p.

An anti-British and anti-American account of the international politics preceding the outbreak of World War II, by a Frenchman who was a Radical-Socialist Deputy in the National Assembly from 1924 to 1942 and who in 1939 opposed his country's entrance into the war.

Nasarski, Peter, *ed.* **Deutsche Jugendbewegung in Europa.** Cologne: Verlag Wissenschaft und Politik, 1967, 415 p.

A collection of essays on youth organizations in Austria and of the German minorities in Poland, the Baltic States, Czechoslovakia, Italy and France between both world wars. The authors do not pay enough attention to the very successful efforts of the National Socialists to gain influence in these organizations.

Nelson, Harold Ira. **Land and Power: British and Allied Policy on Germany's Frontiers, 1916-19.** Toronto: University of Toronto Press, 1963, 402 p.
In focusing on a key issue Professor Nelson also illuminates many hitherto neglected aspects of British planning for a European order after World War I. An important and lucid book based on extensive research.

Newman, William J. **The Balance of Power in the Interwar Years, 1919-1939.** New York: Random House, 1968, 239 p.
A study of the Locarno Pact and its collapse in the 1930s, by a professor at Boston University.

Noguères, Henri. **Munich: "Peace for Our Time."** New York: McGraw-Hill, 1965, 423 p.
A retelling of the Munich story, emphasizing the fleeting popularity of "the peacemakers" in the Western countries.

Offner, Arnold A. **American Appeasement: United States Foreign Policy and Germany, 1933-1938.** Cambridge: Belknap Press of Harvard University Press, 1969, 328 p.
This study of American policy toward Germany in the 1930s systematically sets forth the crimes of omission committed by the American leadership which, in the author's view, further weakened Britain and France and further whetted Hitler's appetite for aggression.

Perry, Hamilton Darby. **The Panay Incident: Prelude to Pearl Harbor.** New York: Macmillan, 1969, 295 p.
The publisher of *American Heritage* tells the story well, largely from the American point of view. The book complements the study by Manny T. Koginos, who is more thorough on the Japanese side.

Peters, Ihor Andrianovych. **SSSR, Chekhoslovakia, i evropeiskaia politika nakanune Miunkhena.** Kiev: Izd-vo "Naukova Dumka," 1971, 190 p.
A vigorous defense of the Soviet concepts of Czechoslovakia's role in European politics between 1934 and 1938.

Robbins, Keith. **Munich 1938.** London: Cassell, 1968, 398 p.
According to the author, an Oxford-trained English historian, the purpose of this informative and readable study is "to look at the development of the Munich crisis without the hindering concept of 'appeasement', and certainly without 'the appeasers'."

Rössler, Hellmuth, *ed.* **Die Folgen von Versailles 1919-1924.** Göttingen: Musterschmidt, 1969, 195 p.
Papers and discussions by leading European historians on the consequences of the Treaty of Versailles, from a conference sponsored by the Ranke-Gesellschaft.

Rössler, Hellmuth, *ed.* **Locarno und die Weltpolitik 1924-1932.** Göttingen: Musterschmidt, 1969, 213 p.
Papers and discussions on world politics in the period after Locarno from a conference sponsored by the Ranke-Gesellschaft. Among the participants there were not only leading French and German historians, but also personalities who took part in the formulation of the foreign policies of their countries in the 1920s.

Roskill, Stephen Wentworth. **Naval Policy Between the Wars. I: The Period of Anglo-American Antagonism, 1919-1929.** New York: Walker, 1969, 638 p.
A first-rate account of British naval policy after World War I, with emphasis on the Anglo-American competition for mastery of the seas after the Washington Conference of 1921-22.

Schmidt, Royal Jae. **Versailles and the Ruhr: Seedbed of World War II.** The Hague: Nijhoff, 1968, 310 p.
The author of this monograph locates the origins of World War II in the Franco-Belgian occupation of the Ruhr in 1923. Conscientiously researched but not particularly original.

Secchia, Pietro, *ed.* **Enciclopedia dell'antifascismo e della Resistenza.** Milan: La Pietra, 1968–.
An encyclopedia attempting to cover all aspects of political and military history since the First World War, with special emphasis on Italy and Europe. The late editor was an important member of the Italian Communist Party. Two volumes have been published through 1972.

Sontag, Raymond J. **A Broken World, 1919-1939.** New York: Harper and Row, 1971, 415 p.
A remarkable synthesis of the inter-war period by a well-known historian; appearing in the distinguished series "The Rise of Modern Europe."

Spengler, Erhard. **Zur Frage des völkerrechtlich gültigen Zustandekommens der deutsch-tschechoslowakischen Grenzneuregelung von 1938.** Berlin: Duncker & Humblot, 1967, 171 p.
A legal study of the Czech-German border revision agreement of 1938.

Thompson, Laurence Victor. **The Greatest Treason: The Untold Story of Munich.** New York: Morrow, 1968, 298 p.
A British journalist's account of the liquidation of the Czechoslovak state in 1938, based on extensive interviews and published sources. The author shows understanding for Chamberlain, considers, of course, Hitler the villain and is rather critical of Beneš and his policies.

Thorne, Christopher. **The Limits of Foreign Policy: The West, the League and the Far Eastern Crisis of 1931-1933.** London: Hamilton, 1972, 442 p.
An important study in which the author utilizes the full range of Western-language sources as well as a formidable array of private papers to put events into their contemporary setting. While none of his conclusions are strikingly new, the work illuminates not only one crisis but a generation of British and American policy in Asia.

Vogt, Martin, *ed.* **Die Entstehung des Youngplans: dargestellt vom Reichsarchiv 1931-1933.** Boppard: Boldt, 1970, 396 p.
A substantial history of the Young Plan, prepared by the Reichsarchiv in the 1930s but never before published.

Wendt, Bernd Jürgen. **Economic Appeasement: Handel und Finanz in der britischen Deutschland-Politik 1933-1939.** Düsseldorf: Bertelsmann Universitätsverlag, 1971, 695 p.
A detailed and well-documented study of how trade and financial considerations influenced British policies toward Germany from 1933 to 1939.

Wendt, Bernd Jürgen. **München 1938: England zwischen Hitler und Preussen.** Frankfurt/Main: Europäische Verlagsanstalt, 1965, 150 p.
In this study the author shows how in 1938 leaders of the conservative anti-Nazi opposition sought British help for overthrowing Hitler and why they failed. A volume in the series "Hamburger Studien zur neueren Geschichte," edited by Fritz Fischer.

Wilson, Hugh Robert, Jr. **Disarmament and the Cold War in the Thirties.** New York: Vantage Press, 1963, 87 p.
A brief, informative survey of disarmament negotiations and international developments in the 1930s, based on the papers of Hugh R. Wilson, Sr., a senior American diplomat who was Minister to Switzerland from 1927 to 1937 and Ambassador to Germany from 1938 to 1939.

IV. SECOND WORLD WAR

IMMEDIATE ORIGINS AND OUTBREAK

See also (General Works) General Treatments, p. 7; Inter-War Period, p. 140; (The United States) Biographies, Memoirs and Addresses, p. 218; Foreign Policy, p. 229; (Great Britain) Biographies, Memoirs and Addresses, p. 369; Foreign Policy, p. 375; Belgium, p. 391; Switzerland, p. 393; (France) Recent History, p. 396; Biographies, Memoirs and Addresses, p. 400; (Italy) Recent History, p. 422; Baltic States, p. 455; (Germany) The Nazi Era, p. 475; (Hungary) Recent History to 1945, p. 511; (Czechoslovakia) Recent History to 1945, p. 516; (Poland) Recent History to 1945, p. 525; (Union of Soviet Socialist Republics) Memoirs and Biographies, p. 533; Foreign Policy, p. 550; Jugoslavia, p. 591; Greece, p. 602; (Japan) Recent History, p. 715.

Baker, Leonard. **Roosevelt and Pearl Harbor.** New York: Macmillan, 1970, 356 p.
A spirited defense of FDR's gradual rejection of isolationism and preparations for war during 1941.

Ball, Adrian. **The Last Day of the Old World.** Garden City: Doubleday, 1963, 278 p.
A reconstruction of the events of September 3, 1939.

Cienciala, Anna M. **Poland and the Western Powers, 1938-1939: A Study in the Interdependence of Eastern and Western Europe.** Toronto: University of Toronto Press, 1968, 310 p.
A penetrating analysis of the crisis confronting Polish diplomacy just before the Second World War.

Farago, Ladislas. **The Broken Seal: The Story of "Operation Magic" and the Pearl Harbor Disaster.** New York: Random House, 1967, 439 p.
A fascinating and, on the whole, well-documented story of the competition between American and Japanese code breakers between 1923 and December 7, 1941. The author served as chief of research and planning in the office of U.S. Naval Intelligence during World War II.

Glasebock, Willy. **War Deutschland am 2. Weltkrieg allein schuld? Von Versailles bis Danzig.** Niederpleis b. Siegburg: Ring-Verlag Helmut Cramer, 1964, 581 p.
German innocence and Anglo-Polish responsibility for the Second World War constitute the principal conclusions of this study which owes much to David L. Hoggan.

Glaser, Kurt. **Der Zweite Weltkrieg und die Kriegsschuldfrage. (Die Hoggan-Kontroverse).** Würzburg: Marienburg-Verlag, 1965, 167 p.
A discussion, itself bound to raise controversy, of the dispute over the "war guilt" question, centering on David L. Hoggan's book that was originally published in 1961: "Der erzwungene Krieg: die Ursachen und Urheber des 2. Weltkriegs" (Tübingen: Verlag der deutschen Hochschullehrer-Zeitung, 6th ed., 1964, 925 p.).

Hayashi, Fusao, *pseud.* **Dai Tōa Sensō kōtei ron.** Tokyo: Pancho Shobō, 1964–65, 2 v.
A Japanese study of the causes of the Pacific War.

Hoehling, Adolph A. **The Week Before Pearl Harbor.** New York: Norton, 1963, 238 p.
A well-researched examination of the activities of the principal characters involved in events in the week preceding the attack on Pearl Harbor; another attempt to determine why the United States was caught off guard when so much evidence existed that an attack was imminent.

Ike, Nobutaka, ed. **Japan's Decision for War: Records of the 1941 Policy Conferences.** Stanford: Stanford University Press, 1967, 306 p.
Translation of the detailed notes taken at 57 crucial liaison conferences attended by representatives of the Japanese Cabinet and Army and Navy Chiefs and Vice-Chiefs of Staff, and at five Imperial conferences at which high-level decisions were ratified in the presence of the Emperor. Very important for the study of American-Japanese relations.

Kennan, George Frost. **From Prague After Munich: Diplomatic Papers, 1938-1940.** Princeton: Princeton University Press, 1968, 266 p.
These papers written by Mr. Kennan, the distinguished American diplomat and writer, during a period of diplomatic service in Czechoslovakia in the years following Munich are a significant historical source.

Libal, Michael. **Japans Weg in den Krieg: die Aussenpolitik der Kabinette Konoye 1940/1941.** Düsseldorf: Droste, 1971, 261 p.
In this study of the Japanese foreign policies during the last two years before the attack on Pearl Harbor the author argues that the decision to attack the United States was made by the cabinets of Prince Konoye before September 1941.

McSherry, James E. **Stalin, Hitler, and Europe.** New York: World Publishing Co., 1968–70, 2 v.
A history of Nazi-Soviet relations by a former U.S. State Department official. The author thinks that "Stalin's encouragement may have been a decisive factor" for Hitler's decision to start World War II.

Mosley, Leonard. **On Borrowed Time: How World War II Began.** New York: Random House, 1969, 509 p.
This book covers familiar terrain in a competent and readable manner. The "weakness, stupidity, ignorance and maladroitness" of the French and British leaders made World War II inevitable, in the author's view.

Parkinson, Roger. **Peace for Our Time: Munich to Dunkirk—The Inside Story.** New York: McKay, 1972, 411 p.
    A familiar, if still gripping, story of futility, put together with the help of some new evidence.

Petrov, Vladimir. **"June 22, 1941": Soviet Historians and the German Invasion.** Columbia: University of South Carolina Press, 1968, 322 p.
    A translation, with commentary, of A. M. Nekrich's book "1941 22 iiunia" (Moscow: "Nauka," 1965, 171 p.) on the background of the German invasion of Russia, and of some of the critical reviews and attacks which ensued. Interesting for the controversies surrounding de-Stalinization.

Ribbentrop, Annelies von. **Deutsch-englische Geheimverbindungen.** Tübingen: Verlag der Deutschen Hochschullehrer-Zeitung (for the Insitut für Deutsche Nachkriegsgeschichte), 1967, 644 p.
    The widow of Hitler's Minister for Foreign Affairs discusses the German-British negotiations, both official and unofficial, shortly before the outbreak of World War II and concludes that the British bear a major part of the responsibility for starting the war.

Rozanov, German Leont'evich. **Plan "Barbarossa": zamysly i final.** Moscow: Izd-vo "Mezhdunarodnye Otnosheniia," 1970, 136 p.
    A compact presentation of the Soviet version of the inception, execution, and ultimate failure of the German invasion of the U.S.S.R. in June 1941, with emphasis on diplomatic activity and military planning leading up to the actual assault.

Saitō, Takashi. **Dainiji sekai taisen zen shi kenkyū.** Tokyo: Tōkyō Daigaku Shuppankai, 1965, 328 p.
    A Japanese study of the outbreak of World War II in the Pacific.

Schäfer, Emil Philipp. **13 Tage Weltgeschichte: wie es zum Zweiten Weltkrieg kam.** Düsseldorf: Econ-Verlag, 1964, 376 p.
    A detailed study of the events from August 22 to September 3, 1939, that led to the outbreak of World War II.

Soviet Peace Efforts on the Eve of World War II (September 1938–August 1939): Documents and Records. Moscow: Novosti Press Agency Publishing House (for the Ministry for Foreign Affairs of the U.S.S.R.), 1973, 2 v.
    An official collection of documents endeavoring to vindicate the record of Soviet foreign policy between Munich and the Molotov-Ribbentrop Pact. Edited by V. M. Falin, A. A. Gromyko and others. The Russian original appeared as "SSSR v bor'be za mir nakanune Vtoroi mirovoi voiny (sentiabr' 1938 g.–avgust 1939 g.): dokumenty i materialy" (Moscow: Izd-vo Politicheskoi Literatury, 1971, 736 p.).

Thorne, Christopher. **The Approach of War, 1938-1939.** New York: St. Martin's Press, 1967, 232 p.
    A brief account of the diplomatic activities of the last two years before the outbreak of World War II, including a guide to important writings on the subject. A volume in the series "The Making of the Twentieth Century."

Walendy, Udo. **Wahrheit für Deutschland: die Schuldfrage des Zweiten Weltkrieges.** Vlotho/Weser: Verlag für Volkstum und Zeitgeschichtsforschung, 1964, 399 p.
    A study seeking to exculpate Hitler and implicate Roosevelt for bringing about World War II. An appalling example of specious scholarship in the service of threadbare revisionism.

GENERAL ACCOUNTS

See also (The World Since 1914) General, p. 129; Inter-War Period, p. 140; (Second World War) Military Operations, p. 156; and the sections for specific countries and regions.

Adams, Henry H. **Years of Deadly Peril.** New York: McKay, 1969, 559 p.
    A survey of the events from the Nazi invasion of Poland to Pearl Harbor. The author covers familiar ground in a familiar manner, but his research is sound and his style is brisk and readable.

Bauer, Eddy and Others. **Histoire controversée de la Deuxième guerre mondiale, 1939-1945.** Monaco: J.-C. Polus, 1966-67, 7 v.
A lavishly produced and richly illustrated journalistic history of World War II.

Brooks, Lester. **Behind Japan's Surrender: The Secret Struggle That Ended an Empire.** New York: McGraw-Hill, 1968, 428 p.
A study of internal political developments in Japan between the bombing of Hiroshima and surrender.

Buchanan, Albert Russell. **The United States and World War II.** New York: Harper and Row, 1964, 2 v.
A useful and concise account of the role of the United States in the Second World War, based on a wide use of the official and other military histories.

Calvocoressi, Peter and Wint, Guy. **Total War: The Study of World War II.** New York: Pantheon, 1972, 959 p.
The authors present the broad themes and many of the detailed incidents of the war in Europe and Asia with flair and authority.

Cartier, Raymond. **La Seconde guerre mondiale.** Paris: Larousse—"Paris Match," 1965-66, 2 v.
A richly illustrated history of World War II by a well-known French writer.

Dahms, Hellmuth Günther. **Geschichte des Zweiten Weltkriegs.** Tübingen: Wunderlich, rev. and enl. ed., 1965, 917 p.
A completely revised and expanded history of World War II.

Dupuy, Richard Ernest. **World War II: A Compact History.** New York: Hawthorn, 1969, 334 p.
A succinct survey.

Hillgruber, Andreas and Hümmelchen, Gerhard. **Chronik des Zweiten Weltkrieges.** Frankfurt/Main: Bernard und Graefe, 1966, 196 p.
A chronicle of the military and diplomatic events of World War II. A useful reference.

Hillgruber, Andreas, *ed.* **Probleme des Zweiten Weltkrieges.** Cologne: Kiepenheuer, 1967, 455 p.
A representative selection of studies, mostly reprints from standard works and scholarly magazines, on various problems of World War II. Very useful bibliography.

Jacobsen, Hans-Adolf. **Zur Konzeption einer Geschichte des Zweiten Weltkrieges 1939-1945.** Frankfurt/Main: Bernard und Graefe, 1964, 176 p.
A most useful attempt to survey the literature dealing with the military and diplomatic history of World War II, including chapters on the official military histories, the series of foreign policy documents and the holdings of archives in Germany and the United States.

Michel, Henri. **La Seconde guerre mondiale.** Paris: Presses Universitaires, 1968-69, 2 v.
A standard history of World War II.

Salis, Jean Rodolphe von. **Weltchronik 1939-1945.** Zurich: Orell Füssli Verlag, 1966, 556 p.
A selection of the weekly reports on international developments that were delivered during World War II over radio Beromünster by the Swiss historian Salis and were initiated by the Bundespräsident Marcel Pilet-Golaz.

SSSR v Velikoi otechestvennoi voine 1941-1945 gg.: kratkaia khronika. Moscow: Voennoe Izd-vo, 2d enl. ed., 1970, 856 p.
A day-by-day chronicle of the Soviet Union's military operations and major policy decisions during the Second World War, offering a wealth of detail.

Werth, Alexander. **Russia at War, 1941-1945.** New York: Dutton, 1964, 1,100 p.
A very full and ambitious reconstruction, based both on the author's experiences as a war correspondent in the U.S.S.R. and his very considerable use of subsequently published Soviet materials. The interpretations of a number of Stalin's diplomatic and military policies should definitely be questioned.

Wright, Gordon. **The Ordeal of Total War, 1939-1945.** New York: Harper and Row, 1968, 315 p.
An analysis of all facets of European society at war.

DIPLOMATIC ASPECTS

See also (General Works) General Treatments, p. 7; Inter-War Period, p. 140; (The United States) Biographies, Memoirs and Addresses, p. 218; Foreign Policy, p. 229; (Europe) General Surveys, p. 344; (Great Britain) Biographies, Memoirs and Addresses, p. 369; Foreign Policy, p. 375; The Netherlands, p. 389; Belgium, p. 391; Switzerland, p. 393; (France) Recent History, p. 396; Biographies, Memoirs and Addresses, p. 400; Foreign Policy, p. 404; (Italy) Biographies, Memoirs and Collected Writings, p. 420; Recent History, p. 422; Foreign Policy, p. 424; Denmark, p. 442; Norway, p. 444; Sweden, p. 447; Finland, p. 449; Baltic States, p. 455; (Germany) The Nazi Era, p. 475; Hungary, p. 511; Czechoslavakia, p. 516; Poland, p. 523; (Union of Soviet Socialist Republics) Memoirs and Biographies, p. 533; Recent History, p. 538; Foreign Policy, p. 550; Rumania, p. 588; Jugoslavia, p. 591; Bulgaria, p. 596; Greece, p. 602; India, p. 656; China, p. 638; Japan, p. 714.

Actes et documents du Saint Siège relatifs à la Seconde guerre mondiale. Vatican City: Libreria Editrice Vaticana (for the Secrétairerie d'État de sa Sainteté), 1965—.
A collection of documents and correspondence dealing with the diplomacy of Vatican shortly before and during World War II. The following volumes have been published through 1974: vol. 1, "Le Saint Siège et la guerre en Europe, mars 1939–août 1940" (1965, 552 p.); vol. 2, "Lettre de Pie XII aux évêques allemands 1939–1944" (1966, 452 p.); vol. 3, "Le Saint Siège et la situation religieuse en Pologne et dans les Pays Baltes, 1939–1945" (1967, 2 pts.); vol. 4, "Le Saint Siège et la guerre en Europe, juin 1940–juin 1941" (1967, 622 p.); vol. 5, "Le Saint Siège et la guerre mondiale, juillet 1941–octobre 1942" (1969, 794 p.); vol. 6, "Le Saint Siège et les victimes de la guerre, mars 1939–décembre 1940" (1972, 557 p.); vol. 7, "Le Saint Siège et la guerre mondiale, novembre 1942–décembre 1943" (1973, 765 p.).; and vol. 8, "Le Saint Siège et les victimes de la guerre, janvier 1941–décembre 1942" (1974, 806 p.). The volumes have been edited by Pierre Blet, Robert A. Graham, Angelo Martini and Burkhart Schneider.

Alperovitz, Gar. **Atomic Diplomacy: Hiroshima and Potsdam: The Use of the Atomic Bomb and the American Confrontation with Soviet Power.** New York: Simon and Schuster, 1965, 317 p.
As the author observes, the ultimate point of his study "is that the atomic bomb played a role in the formulation of policy, particularly in connection with Truman's only meeting with Stalin, the Potsdam Conference."

Anglin, Douglas George. **The St. Pierre and Miquelon *Affaire* of 1941.** Toronto: University of Toronto Press, 1966, 219 p.
A monograph on the diplomatic repercussions of the Free French seizure of St. Pierre and Miquelon in December 1941.

Avantaggiato Puppo, Franca. **Gli armistizi francesi del 1940.** Milan: Giuffrè, 1963, 336 p.
A scholarly study of the peace treaties signed by France with Italy and Germany in 1940.

Beitzell, Robert. **The Uneasy Alliance: America, Britain, and Russia, 1941–1943.** New York: Knopf, 1972, 404 p.
A competent retelling based on published sources only. Sound judgments, no surprises, strongest on setting the military background. Does not supersede Herbert Feis' "Churchill–Roosevelt–Stalin" (1957) or William H. McNeill's "America, Britain, and Russia" (1953).

Berezhkov, Valentin Mikhailovich. **In diplomatischer Mission bei Hitler in Berlin 1940–1941.** Frankfurt/Main: Stimme-Verlag, 1967, 112 p.
The First Secretary at the Soviet Embassy in Berlin in 1940–1941 reminisces about the Nazi-Soviet diplomatic relations during that period. The Russian original was published in 1965 in the periodical *Novyi Mir*.

Béthouart, Marie Émile. **Cinq années d'espérance: mémoires de guerre 1939–1945.** Paris: Plon, 1968, 359 p.
Memoirs by a French general covering many World War II battlefields and conferences. Of particular interest are the descriptions of the French-American negotiations in Washington.

Birse, Arthur Herbert. **Memoirs of an Interpreter.** New York: Coward-McCann, 1967, 254 p.

SECOND WORLD WAR

Mr. Birse, who was one of Churchill's Russian interpreters during World War II, recounts his impressions of the conferences at Yalta, Potsdam and Tehran and of the statesmen who attended them.

Böhme, Hermann. **Der deutsch-französische Waffenstillstand im Zweiten Weltkrieg. Erster Teil: Entstehung und Grundlagen des Waffenstillstandes von 1940.** Stuttgart: Deutsche Verlags-Anstalt (for the Institut für Zeitgeschichte), 1966, 464 p.

A fascinating and detailed account of the Franco-German armistice negotiations of June 1940 and of the immediate post-armistice period, with particular emphasis on the impact of the English attack on the French fleet at Mers-el-Kébir in July 1940. By a former German officer, a participant of these negotiations, who has carefully studied non-German sources as well.

Boyle, John Hunter. **China and Japan at War, 1937-1945: The Politics of Collaboration.** Stanford: Stanford University Press, 1972, 430 p.

A substantial and well-documented monograph on a neglected subject: the Chinese collaboration with the Japanese, particularly as exemplified by China's Pétain, Wang Ching-wei.

Bunker, Gerald E. **The Peace Conspiracy: Wang Ching-wei and the China War, 1937-1941.** Cambridge: Harvard University Press, 1972, 327 p.

A well-researched study of the futile attempts of Wang Ching-wei, who was a disciple of Sun Yat-sen and one of the most influential statesmen of Nationalist China, to save China by collaborating with the Japanese.

Burdick, Charles Burton. **Germany's Military Strategy and Spain in World War II.** Syracuse: Syracuse University Press, 1968, 228 p.

A thoroughly researched study of the various levels of German efforts to gain military control of Spain during World War II, by a professor at San Jose State College.

Cadogan, Sir Alexander George Montagu. **The Diaries of Sir Alexander Cadogan, O.M., 1938-1945.** New York: Putnam, 1972, 881 p.

As Permanent Undersecretary of the Foreign Office during the last war, Cadogan was ideally placed for first-hand observation of men and events. The diaries, here reproduced in abbreviated form and edited by David Dilks, suggest that his rather conventional prejudices and personal likes and dislikes narrowed his outlook.

Chadwin, Mark Lincoln. **The Hawks of World War II.** Chapel Hill: University of North Carolina Press, 1968, 310 p.

A scholarly monograph on the interventionist movement in the United States prior to Pearl Harbor. The book focuses on the Century Group and the Fight for Freedom Committee.

Chautemps, Camille. **Cahiers secrets de l'armistice 1939-1940.** Paris: Plon, 1963, 330 p.

M. Chautemps, four times the Radical Premier of France, revives the debate on the political, diplomatic and military errors committed in the period leading to the 1940 Armistice.

Clemens, Diane Shaver. **Yalta: A Study in Soviet-American Relations.** New York: Oxford University Press, 1970, 356 p.

A well-researched and substantial study.

Conte, Arthur. **Yalta ou le partage du monde (11 février 1945).** Paris: Laffont, 1964, 376 p.

In this study of the Yalta Conference the author argues that the agreements reached there by Stalin, Roosevelt and Churchill had ominous consequences for postwar Europe, permitted Stalin to pursue his imperialistic goals and assured the eventual victory of the Communists in China.

Deuerlein, Ernst. **Deklamation oder Ersatzfrieden? Die Konferenz von Potsdam 1945.** Stuttgart: Kohlhammer, 1970, 203 p.

A well-documented study of the Potsdam Conference of 1945. There is a very useful evaluation of the sources pertaining to the subject.

Divine, Robert A. **Roosevelt and World War II.** Baltimore: Johns Hopkins Press, 1969, 107 p.

A reappraisal of Roosevelt's policy regarding World War II.

Douglas-Hamilton, James. **Motive for a Mission: The Story behind Hess's Flight to Britain.** New York: St. Martin's Press, 1971, 290 p.

The circumstances of Hess's flight are scrupulously set forth, with the help of new material. A fine study, dramatic and illuminating, by the son of one of the English principals in this extraordinary story.

Falconi, Carlo. **The Silence of Pius XII.** Boston: Little, Brown, 1970, 430 p.
After having conducted original research in Jugoslavia and Poland, the author concludes that the Vatican was well aware of the Nazi atrocities in these two countries.

Fehrenbach, Theodore Reed. **F.D.R.'s Undeclared War, 1939 to 1941.** New York: McKay, 1967, 344 p.
The author attempts to "reveal" FDR's plans to lead the American people into the Second World War.

Feis, Herbert. **The Atomic Bomb and the End of World War II.** Princeton: Princeton University Press, 1966, 213 p.
Using new information, the author rewrites much of his "Japan Subdued," published in 1961.

Fischer, Alexander, *ed.* **Teheran, Jalta, Potsdam: die sowjetischen Protokolle von den Kriegskonferenzen der "Grossen Drei."** Cologne: Verlag Wissenschaft und Politik, 1968, 414 p.
A translation of the Soviet protocols of the conferences at Tehran, Yalta and Potsdam. The editor compares the Soviet versions with the American and British conference records and provides useful critical notes.

Gambino, Antonio. **Le conseguenze della Seconda Guerra Mondiale: l'Europa da Yalta a Praga.** Bari: Laterza, 1972, 324 p.
An Italian journalist maintains that the decisions taken at the Yalta Conference were unplanned, but that they effectively divided Europe into a Soviet sphere, primarily political and military, and an American sphere, primarily cultural and economic.

Gardner, Brian. **The Year That Changed the World: 1945.** New York: Coward-McCann, 1964, 356 p.
A popular account of the international events of the year 1945, which brought an end to war and the beginning of an uneasy peace.

Goodhart, Philip Carter. **Fifty Ships That Saved the World: The Foundation of the Anglo-American Alliance.** Garden City: Doubleday, 1965, 267 p.
A concise but absorbing account of the transfer of 50 American destroyers to Great Britain in 1940, an action which, in the author's view, was one of the "principal foundation stones of the Anglo-American alliance."

Hacker, Jens. **Sowjetunion und DDR zum Potsdamer Abkommen.** Cologne: Verlag Wissenschaft und Politik, 1968, 175 p.
A collection of documents, with commentaries by the author, illustrating the Soviet and East German interpretations of the Potsdam Treaty.

Hansen, Reimer. **Das Ende des Dritten Reiches: die deutsche Kapitulation 1945.** Stuttgart: Klett, 1966, 247 p.
In this well-documented monograph on the final months of Nazi Germany the author discusses the Allied demand for unconditional surrender, Hitler's reaction to it, unofficial German attempts to find better terms for ending the war, Admiral Dönitz's 23-day-rule and the actual surrender.

Henry-Haye, G. **La Grande eclipse franco-americaine.** Paris: Plon, 1972, 393 p.
Vichy France's ambassador to Washington in 1940–1942 presents his apologia and an account of how the United States, and especially FDR, willfully misunderstood the French situation in those years.

Hentsch, Guy. **Staline négociateur: une diplomatie de guerre.** Neuchâtel: Éditions de la Baconnière, 1967, 382 p.
A monograph on Stalin as a wartime diplomatic negotiator, with particular reference to his performance at the Tehran, Yalta and Potsdam conferences.

Higgins, Trumbull. **Hitler and Russia: The Third Reich in a Two-Front War, 1937–1943.** New York: Macmillan, 1966, 310 p.
An account of how Hitler managed to get himself into a two-front war.

Hillgruber, Andreas, *ed.* **Staatsmänner und Diplomaten bei Hitler.** Frankfurt/Main: Bernard und Graefe, 1967–70, 2 v.

The German protocols of Hitler's conversations with foreign statesmen from the outbreak of the European war to 1944. An indispensable source.

Israelian, Viktor Levonovich. **The Anti-Hitler Coalition: Diplomatic Co-operation between the USSR, USA, and Britain during the Second World War 1941-1945.** Moscow: Progress Publishers, 1971, 422 p.
A Soviet diplomatic historian chronicles the wartime alliance of the "Big Three," accusing the Western Allies of duplicity and inefficiency. The original appeared in Russian as "Antigitlerovskaia koalitsiia" (Moscow: Izd-vo "Mezhdunarodnye Otnosheniia," 1964, 607 p.).

Israelian, Viktor Levonovich and Kutakov, Leonid Nikolaevich. **Diplomacy of Agression: Berlin-Rome-Tokyo Axis; Its Rise and Fall.** Moscow: Progress Publishers, 1970, 438 p.
A diplomatic history of the Axis powers from 1939 to 1945, tracing their mutual relations through military success and failure. A concluding chapter treats Japan's attempts to achieve a "compromise peace" after the fall of Nazi Germany. The Russian original appeared as "Diplomatiia agressorov: germano-italo-iaponskii fashistskii blok; istoriia ego vosniknoveniia i krakha" (Moscow: Izd-vo "Nauka," 1967, 436 p.).

Klafkowski, Alfons. **The Potsdam Agreement.** Warsaw: Polish Scientific Publishers, 1963, 340 p.
A legal study of the Potsdam agreement, by a prominent Polish Communist scholar. The Polish original appeared as "Umowa Poczdamska z dnia 2. VIII. 1945 r." (Warsaw: Instytut Wydawniczy Pax, 1960, 629 p.).

Kolko, Gabriel. **The Politics of War.** New York: Random House, 1969, 685 p.
A substantial and carefully researched analysis of American policy, 1943-1945, particularly good on the interplay between domestic and international forces in the shaping of foreign policy. The author suggests that the American leaders, in their efforts to build a *Pax Americana*, refused to see the limits of American power in the postwar world.

Kuznets, Iurii L'vovich. **Ot Perl-Kharbora do Potsdama: ocherk vneshnei politiki SShA.** Moscow: Izd-vo "Mezhdunarodnye Otnosheniia," 1970, 351 p.
A Soviet assessment of U.S. foreign policy during the Second World War. The author suggests that only the rise of the American military-industrial complex destroyed the spirit of coöperation introduced by Franklin D. Roosevelt into American-Soviet relations.

Lebra, Joyce C. **Jungle Alliance: Japan and the Indian National Army.** Singapore: Donald Moore for Asia Pacific Press, 1971, 255 p.
The best treatment in English so far of the curious joint diplomatic and military enterprises of the Japanese Empire and the Indian colony during the Pacific War.

Lee, Raymond E. **The London Journal of General Raymond E. Lee, 1940-1941.** Boston: Little, Brown, 1971, 489 p.
Voluminous journals of the American military attaché in London during the 18 months from Dunkirk to Pearl Harbor, edited by James Leutze. A portrait of an interventionist and an important source for the history of the time.

Lensen, George Alexander. **The Strange Neutrality: Soviet-Japanese Relations during the Second World War, 1941-1945.** Tallahassee (Fla.): Diplomatic Press, 1972, 332 p.
A revealing diplomatic history based on both Soviet and Japanese sources.

Mallaby, Sir Howard George Charles. **From My Level: Unwritten Minutes.** London: Hutchinson, 1965, 222 p.
The author's level as wartime secretary to the British Joint Chiefs of Staff and other posts was high enough to see Churchill, Attlee and the top military leaders at close quarters, and his intelligence and perception make his recollections of these leaders agreeable and important reading.

Marienfeld, Wolfgang. **Konferenzen über Deutschland.** Hanover: Verlag für Literatur und Zeitgeschehen, 1963, 385 p.
An extensive account of Allied plans and conferences with respect to Germany from 1941 to 1949.

Martin, Bernd. **Deutschland und Japan im Zweiten Weltkrieg.** Göttingen: Musterschmidt, 1969, 326 p.
An exhaustive analysis of Japanese-German alliance policy during World War II. The

author dissects the many conflicts that characterized the alliance, even during its greatest wartime successes.

Meskill, Johanna Margarete Menzel. **Hitler and Japan: The Hollow Alliance.** New York: Atherton, 1966, 245 p.

The author concludes her study of German-Japanese collaboration during World War II by saying: "The German-Japanese alliance was a failure, not only because each power failed separately to attain the goals it had set itself, but because as allies the powers failed to take advantage of their association."

Miles, Milton E. **A Different Kind of War.** Garden City: Doubleday, 1967, 629 p.

A searing indictment of U.S. China policy during World War II, by the commander of the U.S. Navy's guerrilla forces in China. Prepared by Hawthorne Daniel from the original manuscript.

Neumann, William Louis. **After Victory: Churchill, Roosevelt, Stalin and the Making of the Peace.** New York: Harper and Row, 1967, 212 p.

Covers the same ground as Herbert Feis' "Churchill—Roosevelt—Stalin" (1957) but not with the same thoroughness.

O'Connor, Raymond G. **Diplomacy for Victory: FDR and Unconditional Surrender.** New York: Norton, 1971, 143 p.

In contrast to many historians, Mr. O'Connor regards Roosevelt's "unconditional surrender" policy in a positive light, as providing flexibility and permitting the Allies to maintain their tenuous relationship until victory.

Okumura, Fusao. **Nichi-Bei kōshō to Taiheiyō sensō.** Tokyo: Maino Shoten, 1970, 651 p.

A study of Japanese-American diplomacy and World War II in the Pacific.

Orlow, Dietrich. **The Nazis in the Balkans: A Case Study of Totalitarian Politics.** Pittsburgh: University of Pittsburgh Press, 1968, 235 p.

A study of the role of a subordinate Nazi agency, the *Südosteuropa-Gesellschaft*, in formulating plans and policies for the Balkans.

Plehwe, Friedrich-Karl von. **The End of an Alliance: Rome's Defection from the Axis in 1943.** New York: Oxford University Press, 1971, 161 p.

A member of the German military mission in Rome reconstructs the aftermath of Mussolini's ouster in July 1943, emphasizing particularly Hitler's brutal reaction to Italian developments. A useful commentary on a hitherto obscure aspect of World War II. The German original was published as "Schicksalsstunden in Rom: Ende eines Bündnisses" (Berlin: Propyläen Verlag, 1967, 316 p.).

Ressing, Gerd. **Versagte der Westen in Jalta und Potsdam? Ein dokumentierter Wegweiser durch die alliierten Kriegskonferenzen.** Frankfurt/Main: Akademische Verlagsgesellschaft Athenaion, 1970, 173 p.

The German author attempts to demolish the legend that Western leaders capitulated to the Soviets at the conferences of Yalta and Potsdam.

Russett, Bruce Martin. **No Clear and Present Danger: A Skeptical View of the United States Entry into World War II.** New York: Harper and Row, 1972, 111 p.

A bold dissent from the sacrosanct assumption that participation in the war against Hitler was a strategic necessity for the United States. Russett's arguments against interventionism go beyond those of Robert W. Tucker in his "A New Isolationism" (1972).

Sanakoev, Shalva Parsadanovich and Tsybulevskii, B. L., *eds.* **Tegeran, Ialta, Potsdam: sbornik dokumentov.** Moscow: Izd-vo "Mezhdunarodnye Otnosheniia," 2d ed., 1970, 416 p.

The minutes of the proceedings of the three major wartime conferences at Tehran, Yalta and Potsdam, as taken from Soviet archives, with an introductory essay defending the Soviet interpretation of the agreements reached among the Allies.

Smith, Gaddis. **American Diplomacy during the Second World War, 1941-1945.** New York: Wiley, 1965, 194 p.

A brief review, with considerable stress on the illusions entertained by U.S. leaders.

Snell, John L. **Illusion and Necessity: The Diplomacy of Global War, 1939-1945.** Boston: Houghton, 1963, 229 p.

A composite, fact-crammed record of the diplomacy of all World War II belligerents.

Tanaka, Masaaki. **Nihon muzai ron.** Tokyo: Shin Jinbutsu Ōraisha, 1972, 260 p.
The author analyzes the theory that Japan is without guilt for starting the war in the Pacific.

Theoharis, Athan G. **The Yalta Myths.** Columbia: University of Missouri Press, 1970, 263 p.
An interesting attempt to analyze the techniques used by both Democrats and Republicans in their efforts to manipulate the Yalta Conference for their respective political campaign purposes.

Tillmann, Heinz. **Deutschlands Araberpolitik im Zweiten Weltkrieg.** Berlin: Deutscher Verlag der Wissenschaften, 1965, 473 p.
An East German historian's heavily documented study of Germany's expansionist policy in the Near East during World War II. Drawing mainly on German Foreign Office archives and I.G. Farben records, the author lists also as sources 31 "Classics of Marxism-Leninism."

Toscano, Mario. **Dal 25 luglio all'8 settembre: nuove rivelazioni sugli armistizi fra l'Italia e le Nazioni Unite.** Florence: Le Monnier, 1966, 232 p.
A description of Badoglio's vain attempts in 1943 to join the Allies and to help them to expell the Germans from Italy after the coup d'état which overthrew Mussolini. The author argues that the Allies were not interested in Badoglio's proposals because they wanted to draw into Italy as many German divisions as possible in order to weaken the defense of the Channel coast.

Toscano, Mario. **Designs in Diplomacy: Pages from European Diplomatic History in the Twentieth Century.** Baltimore: Johns Hopkins Press, 1971, 433 p.
Most of these previously published essays deal with Italy's diplomatic relations during World War II. The quality of research and analysis reveals the hand of a fine historian.

Viorst, Milton. **Hostile Allies: FDR and Charles de Gaulle.** New York: Macmillan, 1965, 280 p.
A spirited study of the conflict between the two leaders from 1940 to 1945, with little sympathy for FDR's "courtship of the dishonorable" (Vichy) and with admiration for the difficult but determined de Gaulle.

Walendy, Udo, ed. **Europa in Flammen, 1939–1945.** Vlotho/Weser: Verlag für Volkstum und Zeitgeschichtsforschung, 1966–67, 2 v.

———. **Wahrheit für Deutschland: die Schuldfrage des Zweiten Weltkrieges.** Vlotho/Weser: Verlag für Volkstum und Zeitgeschichtsforschung, 1965, 2d rev. ed., 496 p.
These compilations are of interest only because they constitute one of the most extensive attempts to prove that Nazi Germany was not guilty of the outbreak of World War II and for the many crimes committed during that period.

White, Dorothy Shipley. **Seeds of Discord: De Gaulle, Free France and the Allies.** Syracuse: Syracuse University Press, 1964, 471 p.
A thorough reconstruction of the first disputes between de Gaulle and England and America from June 1940 to the Allied landing in North Africa in 1942.

Wilson, Theodore A. **The First Summit: Roosevelt and Churchill at Placentia Bay 1941.** Boston: Houghton, 1969, 344 p.
A workmanlike monograph on the August 1941 meeting between Churchill and Roosevelt. Good portraits of the two leaders as the bond between them deepened.

Wojcik, Andrzej. **The War Settlement in Eastern Europe.** New York: Czas Publishing Co., 1964, 124 p.
An analysis of the evolution of American and British public opinion concerning the Polish frontier question in the years from 1939 to 1944.

Woodward, Sir Ernest Llewellyn. **British Foreign Policy in the Second World War.** London: H.M.S.O., 1970– .
An authoritative history, based mainly on British materials and written between 1942 and 1950 for official use. Of the planned five volumes three have been published through 1972. A one-volume abridgement appeared in 1962.

THE CONDUCT OF THE WAR

Personal Narratives, Biographies and Reportage

See also other sections for the Second World War and the sections for specific countries.

Bialer, Seweryn, *ed.* **Stalin and His Generals.** New York: Pegasus, 1969, 644 p.
  A selection of military memoir material from the writings of leading Soviet officers. Well-introduced and well-edited, the book adds considerably to our knowledge of Stalin's leadership in the war.

Biriuzov, Sergei Semenovich. **Surovyi gody.** Moscow: Izd-vo "Nauka," 1966, 558 p.
  The memoirs of World War II campaigns in the Ukraine and Balkans by a Soviet commander who was serving as Chief of Staff at the time of his death in a plane crash in 1964.

Chennault, Anna. **Chennault and the Flying Tigers.** New York: Paul S. Eriksson, 1963, 298 p.
  A biography of the "Flying Tiger of them all, Chennault of China," by his wife who used her own recollections checked, where necessary, against official papers, diaries and other private papers.

Chuikov, Vasilii Ivanovich. **Nachalo puti.** Volgograd: Nizhne-Volzhskoe Izd-vo, 3rd rev. ed., 1967, 380 p.
  The Soviet hero of Stalingrad describes his impressions of the battle that marked the "beginning of the path" toward Berlin. An earlier edition has been translated into English as "The Battle for Stalingrad" (New York: Holt, Rinehart and Winston, 1964, 364 p.). The Soviet marshal has described the subsequent military events of World War II in a series of articles, "Konets Tret'ego Reikha" (*Oktiabr'*, 1965), of which the American edition appeared as "The Fall of Berlin" (New York: Holt, Rinehart and Winston, 1968, 261 p.) and the English edition as "The Fall of the Third Reich" (London: Panther, 1969, 252 p.).

De Guingand, Sir Francis Wilfred. **Generals at War.** London: Hodder, 1964, 256 p.
  Wartime reminiscences and an attempt to reassess the war record of Lord Wavell, by the former Chief of Staff of the British 8th Army and the 21st Army Group.

Eisenhower, Dwight David. **The Papers of Dwight David Eisenhower: The War Years.** Baltimore: Johns Hopkins Press, 1970, 5 v.
  A well-edited collection of documents, containing a wealth of information about Eisenhower as a military commander and grand strategist during World War II.

Frankenberg und Proschlitz, Egbert von. **Meine Entscheidung.** Berlin: Deutscher Militärverlag, 1963, 372 p.
  A polemical memoir by a German officer who, while in a Soviet prison camp, joined the anti-Nazi League of German Officers.

Görlitz, Walter. **Paulus and Stalingrad.** New York: Citadel, 1964, 301 p.
  A documentary biography of Field Marshal Paulus up to his capture after the battle of Stalingrad. The German edition appeared as "Paulus: 'Ich stehe hier auf Belfehl!'" (Frankfurt/Main: Bernard und Graefe, 1960, 272 p.).

Grechko, Andrei Antonovich. **Battle for the Caucasus.** Moscow: Progress Publishers, 1971, 366 p.
  An abridged version of the memoirs of a Soviet military leader dealing with the Soviet campaign of 1942–43 to hold and reverse the German advances in the Caucasus. The author became Soviet Minister of Defense in 1967. The original appeared as "Bitva za Kavkaz" (Moscow: Voennoe Izd-vo, 2d ed., 1969, 494 p.).

Halder, Franz. **Kriegstagebuch: Tägliche Aufzeichnungen des Chefs des Generalstabes des Heeres 1939-1942.** Stuttgart: Kohlhammer, 1962-64, 3 v.
  The important war diary of the Chief of the German General Staff from 1939 to 1942.

Konev, Ivan Stepanovich. **Sorok piatyi.** Moscow: Voennoe Izd-vo, 2d rev. and enl. ed., 1970, 286 p.
  Memoirs of the Soviet conquest of Berlin and Prague in 1945 by a senior commander

who later served as Chief of Staff of the Warsaw Pact armed forces. The English translation of an earlier edition was published as "Year of Victory" (Moscow: Progress Publishers, 1969, 248 p.).

Kopański, Stanisław. **Wspomnienia wojenne, 1939-1946.** London: Veritas, 1962, 394 p.
Valuable memoirs by a high-ranking Polish officer who was Chief of Staff of the Polish armed forces from August 1943 until the end of the war.

Lasch, Otto. **Zuckerbrot und Peitsche: ein Bericht aus russischer Kriegsgefangenschaft – 20 Jahre danach.** Pfaffenhofen: Ilmgau Verlag, 1965, 202 p.
A German general who in April 1945, disobeying the orders of Hitler, surrendered Königsberg to the Russians, describes the fate of high-ranking German officers in Russian captivity.

Lewin, Ronald. **Rommel as Military Commander.** Princeton: Van Nostrand, 1968, 262 p.
The author assesses Rommel as one of the great commanders of all time and as a man who preserved his honor to the end.

Mellnik, Stephen Michael. **Philippine Diary, 1939-1945.** New York: Van Nostrand Reinhold, 1969, 316 p.
An absorbing account of how this officer escaped from internment after the fall of Corregidor, directed guerrilla forces and returned to recapture this stronghold.

Nelson, James, *ed.* **General Eisenhower on the Military Churchill: A Conversation with Alistair Cooke.** New York: Norton, 1970, 94 p.
A sensitively illustrated personal memoir elicited by Alistair Cooke from General Eisenhower about his wartime comrade-in-arms, Winston Churchill.

Panter-Downes, Mollie. **London War Notes: 1939-1945.** New York: Farrar, Straus and Giroux, 1971, 378 p.
Week after week, the London correspondent of *The New Yorker* wrote about London life and morale during the war. This collection of her pieces constitutes a readable, informative record. Edited by William Shawn.

Pawle, Gerald. **The War and Colonel Warden.** New York: Knopf, 1963, 422 p.
An intimate account of Churchill (Colonel Warden was his favorite pseudonym) in the war based on recollections of Commander C. R. Thompson, his personal assistant from 1940 to 1945.

Rokossovskii, Konstantin Konstantinovich. **A Soldier's Duty.** Moscow: Progress Publishers, 1970, 340 p.
The war memoirs of a popular Soviet commander during the Polish campaigns of World War II. The author later served as Poland's Minister of Defense. The original appeared in Russian as "Soldatskii dolg" (Moscow: Voennoe Izd-vo, 1968, 380 p.).

Shtemenko, Sergei Matveevich. **General'nyi shtab v gody voiny.** Moscow: Voennoe Izd-vo, 1968, 415 p.
A significant memoir by the former chief of operations of the Soviet General Staff during World War II.

Tedder, Arthur William Tedder, Baron. **With Prejudice: The War Memoirs.** Boston: Little, Brown, 1967, 692 p.
Detailed and frank memoirs, covering the years from 1932 to 1945, by a distinguished Royal Air Force officer who at the end of World War II was the Deputy Supreme Commander of the Allied Forces.

Thompson, Laurence Victor. **1940.** New York: Morrow, 1966, 256 p.
An absorbing account by a British journalist of the critical year 1940 in Great Britain.

Warlimont, Walter. **Inside Hitler's Headquarters, 1939-45.** New York: Praeger, 1964, 658 p.
The author was a deputy to General Jodl in Hitler's headquarters from September 1939 to September 1944. His personal recollections, supplemented by other evidence, provide an important account of Hitler's relations to his generals.

Warner, Oliver. **Admiral of the Fleet: Cunningham of Hyndhope; The Battle for the Mediterranean.** Athens: Ohio University Press, 1967, 301 p.
A pleasant memoir of an outstanding British naval commander during World War II, known particularly for his exploits in the Mediterranean.

Military Operations

General

See also other sections for the Second World War and the sections for specific countries.

Adams, Henry Hitch. **1942: The Year That Doomed the Axis.** New York: McKay, 1967, 522 p.
A teacher at the U.S. Naval Academy reviews the military events of the year at the beginning of which the Axis was winning on every front and at the end of which the tables were turned.

Ambrose, Stephen E. **The Supreme Commander: The War Years of General Dwight D. Eisenhower.** Garden City: Doubleday, 1970, 732 p.
This is very much the official history of General Eisenhower from 1941 to 1945. The author has researched his subject with meticulous care and considerable erudition, but his judgments are uncritical to the point of adulation.

Australia in the War of 1939-1945. Canberra: Australian War Memorial.
The official history of Australian participation in the Second World War, planned in five series: 1) Army; 2) Navy; 3) Air; 4) Civil; and 5) Medical. For volumes published before 1963, see "Foreign Affairs Bibliography, 1952-1962." In the Army series, the last two of the seven planned volumes were published since 1963: vol. 3, "Tobruk and El Alamein," by Barton Maughan (1966, 854 p.) and vol. 7, "The Final Campaigns," by Gavin M. Long (1963, 667 p.). In the Navy series, the last of the planned two volumes appeared in 1968: vol. 2, "Royal Australian Navy, 1942-1945," by G. Hermon Gill (753 p.). In the Air series, the last of the planned four volumes was published in 1963: vol. 4, "Air Power over Europe, 1944-1945," by John Herington (539 p.). In the Civil series, the next to the last of the planned five volumes appeared in 1970: vol. 2, "The Government and the People, 1942-1945," by Paul Hasluck (771 p.). The volumes in the Medical series are not listed in this bibliography.

Baldwin, Hanson Weightman. **Battles Lost and Won.** New York: Harper and Row, 1966, 532 p.
An appraisal and evaluation, by the former military editor of *The New York Times*, of eleven crucial battles—land, sea and air—of the Second World War.

Barclay, Cyril Nelson. **On Their Shoulders: British Generalship in the Lean Years, 1939-1942.** London: Faber, 1964, 184 p.
A defense of the leading British generals in the years of Britain's defeats "who—short of men, weapons and allies—held our enemies at bay and made possible the victories of their successors."

Collier, Basil. **The Second World War: A Military History.** New York: Morrow, 1967, 640 p.
A very handy summary of events from Munich to Hiroshima by a British scholar, containing useful maps and appendixes.

Davis, Kenneth Sydney. **Experience of War: The U.S. in World War II.** Garden City: Doubleday, 1965, 704 p.
An informative and well-rounded compendium of the total U.S. war effort.

Greenfield, Kent Roberts. **American Strategy in World War II: A Reconsideration.** Baltimore: Johns Hopkins Press, 1963, 145 p.
In this brief volume the former Chief Historian of the U.S. Department of the Army presents some of his well-informed reflections and views on World War II strategy.

Hillgruber, Andreas. **Hitlers Strategie: Politik und Kriegführung 1940-1941.** Frankfurt/Main: Bernard und Graefe, 1965, 715 p.
A massive, heavily documented volume on Hitler's strategy and policies in the critical year between the fall of France and the attack on the U.S.S.R. A major contribution.

History of the Second World War: United Kingdom Military Series. London: H.M.S.O.
An important official history of the military aspects of Britain's war efforts, edited by Sir James Ramsay Montagu Butler and planned "to provide a broad survey of events from an inter-service point of view rather than separate accounts of the parts played by each of the three services." For volumes published before 1963, see "Foreign Af-

fairs Bibliography, 1952–1962." In the subseries "Grand Strategy," planned in six volumes, the following volumes have been published since 1963: "Vol. III: June 1941–August 1942," by J. M. A. Gwyer and J. R. M. Butler (1964, 2 pts.); "Vol. IV: August 1942–August 1943," by Michael Eliot Howard (1972, 804 p.). In the subseries "Campaigns" the following volumes have been published since 1963: "The Mediterranean and Middle East," by Ian Stanley Ord Playfair and others (vol. IV, 1966, 556 p.); "The War against Japan," by Stanley Woodburn Kirby and others (vol. IV, 1965, 568 p. and vol. V, 1969, 650 p., completing the set); "Victory in the West," by Lionel Frederick Ellis and others (vol. II, 1969, 476 p., completing the set). In the subseries "Civil Affairs and Military Government," the following volume has been published since 1963: "Civil Affairs and Military Government: Central Organisation and Planning," by F. S. V. Donnison (1966, 400 p.).

Hoyle, Martha Byrd. **A World in Flames.** New York: Atheneum, 1970, 356 p.
A comprehensive military history of World War II. An excellent reference work for the general reader.

Istoriia Velikoi otechestvennoi voiny Sovetskogo Soiuza, 1941–1945. Moscow: Voennoe Izd-vo, 1960–65, 6 v.
This is the official Soviet history of military operations during the "Great Patriotic War." Edited by P. N. Pospelov and others.

Jacobsen, Hans-Adolf and Rohwer, Jürgen, *eds.* **Decisive Battles of World War II: The German View.** New York: Putnam, 1965, 509 p.
A revised English edition of an earlier German symposium on the battles in Europe from Dunkirk to the Battle of the Bulge, written by leading German experts.

Klietmann, Kurt-Gerhard. **Die Waffen-SS: eine Dokumentation.** Osnabrück: Verlag "Der Freiwillige," 1965, 519 p.
A manual providing information on the organization, structure and numerical strength of the *Waffen-SS* units during World War II.

Leyen, Ferdinand, Prinz von der. **Rückblick zum Mauerwald: vier Kriegsjahre im OKH.** Munich: Biederstein, 1965, 183 p.
Critical reflections on Nazi military leadership by a reserve officer who spent four years at the Headquarters of the German Army during World War II.

Liddell Hart, Sir Basil Henry. **History of the Second World War.** New York: Putnam, 1971, 768 p.
A splendid history by one of the most influential military writers of our time who died shortly after the completion of this volume.

MacDonald, Charles Brown. **The Mighty Endeavor: American Armed Forces in the European Theater in World War II.** New York: Oxford University Press, 1969, 564 p.
A comprehensive history of the American military contribution in World War II.

Majdalany, Fred. **The Fall of Fortress Europe.** Garden City: Doubleday, 1968, 442 p.
A fast-paced, well-written history of the gradual collapse of the *Wehrmacht*.

Matt, Alphons. **Zwischen allen Fronten: der Zweite Weltkrieg aus der Sicht des Büros Ha.** Frauenfeld: Huber, 1969, 329 p.
Revealing extracts from the archives of "Büro Ha," the Swiss Information Agency during World War II, about major military developments on both the Eastern and Western fronts.

Müller-Hillebrand, Burkhart. **Der Zweifrontenkrieg: das Heer vom Beginn des Feldzuges gegen die Sowjetunion bis zum Kriegsende.** Frankfurt/Main: Mittler, 1969, 325 p.
A detailed account of the organization of the *Wehrmacht* during World War II. Volume III of "Das Heer 1933–1945."

Official History of New Zealand in the Second World War, 1939–45. Wellington: Department of International Affairs, War History Branch.
The following volumes of the history of New Zealand in the Second World War have appeared since 1962: "The New Zealand People at War: War Economy," by John Victor T. Baker (1965, 660 p.); "Italy. Volume II: From Casino to Trieste," by Robin L. Kay (1967, 639 p.); and "Alam Halfa and Alamein," by Ronald Walker (1967, 507 p.). As part of this history, but not listed in this bibliography, there were also published a number of unit histories. Furthermore, a collection of documents on New Zealand during the War was completed: "Documents Relating to New Zealand's Participation in the Second World War, 1939–45" (1949–63, 3 v.).

Official History of the Indian Armed Forces in the Second World War, 1939-45. Calcutta: Orient Longmans (for the Combined Inter-Services Historical Section, India and Pakistan).

An official history of the part played by pre-partition India and its armed forces in the Second World War, edited by Bisheshwar Prasad. For volumes of this history published before 1963, see "Foreign Affairs Bibliography, 1952-1962." In the series "Campaigns in the Western Theatre" the last of the four volumes was published in 1963: "East African Campaign, 1940-41," edited by Bisheshwar Prasad (180 p.). In the series "General War Administration and Organisation" the following volumes were published since 1962: "Indian War Economy," by Nirmal Chandra Sinha and P. N. Khera (1962, 551 p.) and "Defence of India: Policy and Plans," by Bisheshwar Prasad (1963, 278 p.).

Schoenfeld, Maxwell Philip. **The War Ministry of Sir Winston Churchill.** Ames: Iowa State University Press, 1972, 283 p.

A useful survey by a professor at the University of Wisconsin.

Schramm, Percy Ernst and Others, *eds.* **Kriegstagebuch des Oberkommandos der Wehrmacht, 1940-1945.** Frankfurt/Main: Bernard und Graefe, 1961-65, 4 v. in 7 parts.

The records and logs of the High Command of the *Wehrmacht* during World War II, together with valuable introductions and commentaries by the editor and his associates, Hans-Adolf Jacobsen, Andreas Hillgruber and Walther Hubatsch.

Sekistov, Vasilii Anatol'evich, *ed.* **Bol'shaia lozh' o voine.** Moscow: Voennoe Izd-vo, 1971, 368 p.

A vituperative defense of Soviet historiography of the Second World War against the "attacks" of the military historians in the United States, Great Britain, France and West Germany.

Stein, George H. **The Waffen SS: Hitler's Elite Guard at War, 1939-1945.** Ithaca: Cornell University Press, 1966, 330 p.

A scholarly and conscientious effort to trace the history of the *Waffen-SS*, the military branch of Hitler's élite guard, in its complex and confusing relations with the *Wehrmacht* in the course of the war.

Thompson, Reginald William. **Churchill and the Montgomery Myth.** New York: M. Evans, 1968, 276 p.

A scathing criticism of Field Marshal Montgomery's strategies in the period between August 1942 and December 1943. The English edition appeared as "The Montgomery Legend" (London: Allen and Unwin, 1967, 276 p.).

Trevor-Roper, Hugh Redwald, *ed.* **Blitzkrieg to Defeat: Hitler's War Directives, 1939-1945.** New York: Holt, Rinehart and Winston, 1965, 231 p.

The text of Hitler's secret directives to his army commanders. An important source for Hitler's conduct of the war, rendered more valuable by Trevor-Roper's excellent introduction and elucidating commentaries. The original German edition, containing more documentation, was edited by Walter Hubatsch and appeared as "Hitlers Weisungen für die Kriegsführung, 1939-1945" (Frankfurt/Main: Bernard und Graefe, 1962, 330 p.).

United States Army in World War II. Washington: Department of the Army, Office of the Chief of Military History.

A monumental multi-volume official history, edited successively by Kent Roberts Greenfield, Stetson Conn and Maurice Matloff. The work consists of the following subseries: The War Department, The Army Air Forces (edited by Wesley F. Craven and James L. Cate and published by the University of Chicago Press), The Army Ground Forces, The Army Service Forces, The Western Hemisphere, The War in the Pacific, The European Theater of Operations, The Mediterranean Theater of Operations, The Middle East Theater, China-Burma-India Theater, The Technical Services, Special Studies, Pictorial Record. Volumes which had appeared from 1963 to 1972 are arranged according to their subseries and are noted in the appropriate sections of this bibliography. A master index and reader's guide is in preparation. For volumes published before 1963, see other volumes of the "Foreign Affairs Bibliography."

United States Army in World War II: The War Department. Washington: Department of the Army, Office of the Chief of Military History.

The concluding volume in the subseries "The War Department" appeared in 1969: "Global Logistics and Strategy: 1943-1945," by Robert W. Coakley and Richard M. Leighton (889 p.).

United States Army in World War II: The Western Hemisphere. Washington: Department of the Army, Office of the Chief of Military History.
Only one volume in the subseries "The Western Hemisphere" appeared in the period between 1963 and 1972: "Guarding the United States and its Outposts," by Stetson Conn, Rose C. Engelman and Byron Fairchild (1964, 592 p.).

Die Wehrmacht in Kampf. Neckargemünd: Vowinckel, 1954-74, 50 v.
A comprehensive series of monographs on important battles and problems of the Second World War, edited by Hermann Teske. The authors of most of the volumes are German officers who actively participated in the events they describe.

Young, Peter, ed. **Decisive Battles of the Second World War.** London: Arthur Barker, 1967, 439 p.
A collection of descriptions of the important World War II battles by leading military commanders. Of particular interest are the Japanese accounts, not available in other Western publications.

Young, Peter. **World War 1939-45.** New York: Crowell, 1966, 447 p.
A concise but well-done history of the war in all its theaters.

Western Europe

See also other sections for the Second World War and the sections for specific countries.

Adleman, Robert H. and Walton, George. **The Champagne Campaign.** Boston: Little, Brown, 1969, 298 p.
A lively account of the American parachute drop into southern France in late 1944.

Ambrose, Stephen E. **Eisenhower and Berlin, 1945: The Decision to Halt at the Elbe.** New York: Norton, 1967, 119 p.
A spirited defense of Eisenhower's decision not to try for Berlin, against the advice of Patton and Montgomery.

Ash, Bernard. **Norway, 1940.** London: Cassell, 1964, 340 p.
A very detailed study of the disastrous campaign of 1940 in Norway; the reading is difficult, but there is much valuable information not previously available.

Azeau, Henri. **La Guerre franco-italienne, juin 1940.** Paris: Presses de la Cité, 1967, 389 p.
A study of a little-known episode of World War II, the French-Italian military encounter in June 1940.

Beaufre, André. **1940: The Fall of France.** New York: Knopf, 1968, 215 p.
Recollections and reflections on the catastrophe of 1940 and its background, by a leading French writer on military strategy. Originally published as "Le Drame de 1940" (Paris: Plon, 1965, 273 p.).

Blumenson, Martin. **The Duel for France, 1944.** Boston: Houghton, 1963, 423 p.
A balanced popular account of the battle for France in the summer of 1944. The author is a military historian who wrote "Breakout and Pursuit" (1961), the official U.S. Army history dealing with the liberation of France.

Eisenhower, John S. D. **The Bitter Woods.** New York: Putnam, 1969, 506 p.
In this account of Hitler's 1944 Ardennes offensive, well-told from the Allied point of view, the author concludes that the German attack in the West permitted the Russians to advance farther into Germany, with far-reaching results for the postwar division of Europe.

Elstob, Peter. **Hitler's Last Offensive.** New York: Macmillan, 1971, 413 p.
A British tank commander during the Battle of the Bulge has rendered a fascinating account of that epic encounter in the Ardennes. The author demonstrates that the battle was lost for Hitler after the first three days and that the ironic end result was that the Russians, rather than the Americans, captured Berlin.

Essame, Hubert. **The Battle for Germany.** New York: Scribner, 1969, 228 p.
A British general reviews the fighting in Germany from 1944 until the end of the war. He praises Montgomery for his strategic concepts and criticizes Eisenhower for ignoring Soviet aims in Europe.

Giles, Janice Holt. **The Damned Engineers.** Boston: Houghton, 1970, 409 p.
The heroes of this fast-paced account of the Battle of the Bulge are the American combat engineers. Well-researched and well-written.

Haupt, Werner. **Berlin 1945: Hitlers letzte Schlacht.** Rastatt: Pabel, 1963, 240 p.
An account of Hitler's last stand in Berlin in 1945.

Horne, Alistair. **To Lose a Battle: France 1940.** Boston: Little, Brown, 1969, 647 p.
A splendid chronicle of the German defeat of France in 1940. The sharp contrast between the deadly efficiency of the German generals and the obsolescence of the French military emerges with devastating clarity.

Jung, Hermann. **Die Ardennen-Offensive 1944/45: ein Beispiel für die Kriegführung Hitlers.** Göttingen: Musterschmidt, 1971, 406 p.
A well-documented study of the last important German offensive against the Western Allies during World War II. The author concludes that the desperate undertaking in the Ardennes in December 1944, a brain-child of Hitler, bereft the Germans of all military reserves and enabled Stalin to advance rapidly toward Berlin.

Kimche, Jon. **The Unfought Battle.** New York: Stein and Day, 1968, 168 p.
The author argues, not very convincingly, that Britain and France could have overrun the German lines in September 1939 and finished the war right then and there, but failed to do so because of faulty intelligence systems.

McKee, Alexander. **Caen: Anvil of Victory.** London: Souvenir, 1964, 368 p.
A vivid description of the savage battle for Caen in the summer of 1944, the outcome of which opened the way for the liberation of France.

Minott, Rodney Glisan. **The Fortress that Never Was: The Myth of Hitler's Bavarian Stronghold.** New York: Holt, Rinehart and Winston, 1964, 208 p.
A harsh and not altogether peruasive indictment of American military intelligence which at the end of the war took seriously the possibility of a German "redoubt" in Bavaria. The author claims that this was a gratuitous miscalculation which weakened our postwar political position in Central Europe.

Mordal, Jacques, *pseud.* (Hervé Cras). **La Bataille de France, 1944-1945.** Paris: Arthaud, 1964, 456 p.
A history of military operations in France from D-Day to liberation, based on familiar sources.

Moulton, James Louis. **The Norwegian Campaign of 1940: A Study of Warfare in Three Dimensions.** London: Eyre, 1966, 328 p.
A study of a campaign first involving sea, land and air at once.

Nobécourt, Jacques. **Hitler's Last Gamble: The Battle of the Bulge.** New York: Schocken Books, 1967, 302 p.
This detailed and well-written account of the last German offensive of World War II originally appeared as "Le Dernier coup de dés de Hitler: la bataille des Ardennes" (Paris: Laffont, 1962, 438 p.).

Rauchensteiner, Manfried. **Krieg in Österreich 1945.** Vienna: Oesterreichischer Bundesverlag (for the Heeresgeschichtliches Museum in Wien), 1970, 388 p.
A thorough and well-documented survey of the military operations in Austria in the final period of World War II.

Robichon, Jacques. **The Second D-Day.** New York: Walker, 1969, 314 p.
An account of the Allied reconquest of southern France in 1944. Originally published as "Le Débarquement de Provence: 15 août 1944" (Paris: Laffont, 1962, 372 p.).

Ryan, Cornelius. **The Last Battle.** New York: Simon and Schuster, 1966, 571 p.
An absorbing account of the assault and capture of Berlin in 1945; much more than purely military history is included.

Taylor, Telford. **The Breaking Wave: The Second World War in the Summer of 1940.** New York: Simon and Schuster, 1967, 378 p.
An absorbing study of the German-British conflict in the critical summer of 1940, with particular emphasis on the German side of the story of the Battle of Britain "which was planned . . . but never executed."

United States Army in World War II: The European Theater of Operations. Washington: Department of the Army, Office of the Chief of Military History.
The following volumes in the subseries "The European Theater of Operations" of the official history "United States Army in World War II" appeared in the period from 1963 to 1973: "The Siegfried Line Campaign," by Charles B. MacDonald (1963, 670 p.); "The Ardennes: Battle of the Bulge," by H. M. Cole (1965, 720 p.); and "The Last Offensive," by Charles B. MacDonald (1973, 532 p.).

William, John. **The Ides of May: The Defeat of France, May–June 1940.** New York: Knopf, 1968, 385 p.
A dramatic recital of the sudden collapse of French political and military leadership in the spring of 1940.

Eastern Europe

See also other sections for the Second World War and the sections for specific countries.

Aaken, Wolf van. **Hexenkessel Ostfront: von Smolensk nach Breslau.** Rastatt/Baden: Pabel, 1964, 223 p.
A rather impressionistic account of critical episodes in the German-Soviet war.

Bagramian, Ivan Khristoforovich. **Tak nachinalas' voina.** Moscow: Voennoe Izd-vo, 1971, 512 p.
A Soviet marshal gives his account and explanation of the early reverses suffered by the defenders of the Ukraine at the time of the 1941 German attack and details the efforts to retain the city of Kiev.

Carell, Paul, *pseud.* (Paul Karl Schmidt). **Hitler Moves East: 1941–1943.** Boston: Little, Brown, 1965, 640 p.
An extensive but somewhat episodic and anecdotal account of the Nazi campaign in Russia to 1943 by a prolific German author. A translation of "Unternehmen Barbarossa" (Frankfurt/Main: Ullstein, 1963, 559 p.).

Carell, Paul, *pseud.* (Paul Karl Schmidt). **Scorched Earth.** Boston: Little, Brown, 1970, 556 p.
This volume covers the Russo-German war from the battle of Kursk in 1943, which the author describes as the beginning of the German defeat, to the Russian advance into East Prussia in 1944. A thorough and conscientious study. Originally published as "Verbrannte Erde: Schlacht zwischen Wolga und Weichsel" (Berlin: Ullstein, 1966, 511 p.).

Clark, Alan. **Barbarossa: The Russian-German Conflict, 1941–45.** New York: Morrow, 1965, 522 p.
A quite readable and informed account, by a British military historian, of the German attack on Russia and its eventual defeat.

Eremenko, Andrei Ivanovich. **Stalingrad: notes du commandant en chef.** Paris: Plon, 1964, 513 p.
An account of the Battle of Stalingrad (August 1942–February 1943), told by Marshal Eremenko, commander of the Soviet operations. The Russian edition appeared as "Stalingrad" (Moscow: Voennoe Izd-vo, 1961, 502 p.).

Fabry, Philipp Walter. **Balkan-Wirren 1940–41: diplomatische und militärische Vorbereitung des deutschen Donauüberganges.** Darmstadt: Wehr und Wissen Verlagsgesellschaft, 1966, 195 p.
A thorough and well-documented study of the diplomatic and military preparations preceding the German attack on Greece in the spring of 1941.

Grechko, Andrei Antonovich, *ed.* **Osvoboditel'naia missiia sovetskikh vooruzhennykh sil vo Vtoroi Mirovoi Voine.** Moscow: Izd-vo Politischeskoi Literatury, 1971, 518 p.
A collection of studies dealing with the Soviet conquest of Eastern Europe during World War II.

Haupt, Werner. **Baltikum 1941: die Geschichte eines ungelösten Problems.** Neckargemünd: Vowinckel, 1963, 200 p.
A survey of Nazi military operations in the Baltic States in 1941.

Hnilicka, Karl. **Das Ende auf dem Balkan 1944/45.** Göttingen: Musterschmidt, 1970, 404 p.

A study, based primarily on German sources, of the retreat of the German military forces from Jugoslavia in 1944-45.

Kissel, Hans. **Die Katastrophe in Rumänien 1944.** Darmstadt: Wehr und Wissen Verlagsgesellschaft, 1964, 287 p.
A description of the military aspects of the decision of King Michael of Rumania to fight the Germans in 1944.

Klink, Ernst. **Das Gesetz des Handelns: die Operation "Zitadelle" 1943.** Stuttgart: Deutsche Verlags-Anstalt, 1966, 356 p.
A well-documented study of the German attempts to regain initiative in the military operations on the Eastern Front in the summer of 1943.

Malinovskii, Rodion Iakovlevich, *ed.* **Budapesht, Vena, Praga: istoriko-memuarnyi trud.** Moscow: Izd-vo "Nauka," 1965, 381 p.
A narrative of the Soviet advance through Central Europe in 1944-45, with emphasis on the liberation of Budapest, Vienna and Prague.

Meier-Welcker, Hans, *ed.* **Abwehrkämpfe am Nordflügel der Ostfront, 1944-1945.** Stuttgart: Deutsche Verlags-Anstalt, 1963, 459 p.
Three technical studies, based almost exclusively on German sources, on military developments in the northern section of the Eastern front from 1944 to 1945. Karl Köhler has written the chapter on the role of the German air force, Helmuth Forwick deals with the retreat of the German armies to Latvia, and Rudolf Kabath and Friedrich Forstmeier describe the battle for East Prussia.

Otechestvenata voina na Bulgariia, 1944-1945. Sofia: Durzhavno voenno izdatelstvo (for the Ministerstvoto na narodnata otbrana), 1961-1966, 3 v.
A detailed official military history of Bulgaria's war against the Germans under the Soviet command during 1944-1945.

Pavlov, Dmitrii Vasil'evich. **Leningrad 1941: The Blockade.** Chicago: University of Chicago Press, 1965, 186 p.
An account of the three-year siege of Leningrad by the Soviet chief of food supplies for the city during the blockade. A useful contribution to this epic story. The Russian original appeared as "Leningrad v blokade, 1941 god" (Moscow: Voennoe Izd-vo, 2d enl. ed., 1961, 198 p.).

Rawski, Tadeusz and Others. **Wojna wyzwoleńcza narodu polskiego w latach 1939-1945: węzłowe problemy.** Warsaw: Ministerstwa Obrony Narodowey, 1963-1966, 2 v.
A history of the Polish struggle against the Nazis during World War II, written by a group of scholars at the Military Historical Institute in Warsaw.

Reinhardt, Klaus. **Die Wende vor Moskau: das Scheitern der Strategie Hitlers im Winter 1941/42.** Stuttgart: Deutsche Verlags-Anstalt (for the Militärgeschichtliches Forschungsamt), 1972, 355 p.
The author of this very well-documented study argues that the battle for Moscow in the winter of 1941/42 decided the outcome of World War II and that the Germans failed to capture the Russian capital because of faulty strategic conceptions and inadequate supplies.

Saint-Loup, Stanislas de, *pseud.* (Marc Augier). **Les Volontaires.** Paris: Presses de la Cité, 1963, 506 p.
An account of the *Légion des volontaires français contre le bolchevisme* in the German attack on the Soviet Union.

Salisbury, Harrison Evans. **The 900 Days: The Siege of Leningrad.** New York: Harper and Row, 1969, 635 p.
An extensive and fascinating account of the classic siege, based on a wide range of Soviet sources.

Seaton, Albert. **The Russo-German War 1941-45.** New York: Praeger, 1971, 628 p.
A thorough history. The author's conclusions are not startling: Hitler was solely responsible for the outbreak of the war and for the disaster at Stalingrad.

Seth, Ronald. **Operation Barbarossa: The Battle for Moscow.** London: Blond, 1964, 191 p.
An able brief account of the background and operations of the German attack on Russia in 1941.

Terzić, Velimir and Others, *eds.* **Oslobodilački rat naroda Jugoslavije, 1941–1945.**
Belgrade: Vojnoistorijski institut, 2d rev. and enl. ed., 1963–65, 2 v.
This is the official Jugoslav history of World War II in Jugoslavia.

Turney, Alfred W. **Disaster at Moscow: Von Bock's Campaigns 1941–1942.** Albuquerque: University of New Mexico Press, 1970, 228 p.
Based in part upon General von Bock's war diary, this is a close study of his campaigns against Moscow, the reasons for their failure, and his qualities as a commander.

Valori, Francesco. **Gli italiani in Russia: la campagna dello C.S.I.R. e dell' A.R.M.I.R.** Milan: Bietti, 1967, 426 p.
A dispassionate and well-documented account of the campaigns of Italian military units on the Eastern Front during the Second World War.

Wagener, Carl. **Moskau 1941: der Angriff auf die russische Hauptstadt.** Bad Nauheim: Podzun, 1965, 3rd ed., 214 p.
An account of the battle for Moscow in the winter of 1941/42, based on German sources.

Zakharov, Matvei Vasil'evich, *ed.* **Osvobozhdenie iugo-vostochnoi i tsentral'noi Evropy voiskami 2-go i 3-go ukrainskikh frontov, 1944–1945.** Moscow: Izd-vo "Nauka," 1970, 676 p.
A history of the Soviet campaigns in the Balkans, Austria and Czechoslovakia in 1944–1945. The editor of the volume, Marshal Zakharov, was Chief of Staff of the Second Ukrainian Front at that time.

Zhilin, Pavel Andreevich, *ed.* **Velikaia otechestvennaia voina: kratkii nauchno-populiarnyi ocherk.** Moscow: Izd-vo Politicheskoi Literatury, 1970, 638 p.
An illustrated history of the Soviet Union's "Great Patriotic War," marking the twenty-fifth anniversary of the victory over Nazi Germany.

Zhukov, Georgii Konstantinovich. **Marshal Zhukov's Greatest Battles.** New York: Harper and Row, 1969, 304 p.
A translation of Marshal Zhukov's important articles on the battles of Moscow, Stalingrad, Kursk and Berlin, with helpful commentary by Harrison E. Salisbury.

Ziemke, Earl F. **Stalingrad to Berlin: The German Defeat in the East.** Washington: Office of the Chief of Military History, United States Army, 1968, 549 p.
The author states in the preface that his purpose is "to describe the manner in which the Soviet Union emerged as the predominant military power in Europe." The volume was published in the "Army Historical Series."

Mediterranean; Greece; Crete; Italy

See also other sections for the Second World War and the sections for specific countries.

Adleman, Robert H. and Walton, George. **Rome Fell Today.** Boston: Little, Brown, 1968, 336 p.
An excellent and eminently readable account of "the first time in history that Rome was taken from the south."

Baudino, Carlo. **Una guerra assurda: la campagna di Grecia.** Milan: Istituto Editoriale Cisalpino, 1965, 286 p.
A vigorous analysis of Italy's military fiasco in Greece in October 1940.

Böhmler, Rudolf. **Monte Cassino.** London: Cassell, 1964, 314 p.
An account of the Cassino-Anzio campaigns, written by a German officer in the Parachute Division. The original was published as "Monte Casino" (Frankfurt/Main: E. S. Mittler, 2d ed., 1963, 253 p.).

Cervi, Mario. **Storia della guerra Grecia.** Milan: Sugar Editore, 1965, 515 p.
A frankly and dispassionately told story of Mussolini's ill-conceived and miserable campaign against Greece in 1940.

Ceva, Bianca, *ed.* **Cinque anni di storia italiana 1940–1945: da lettere e diari di caduti.** Milan: Edizioni di Comunità, 1964, 350 p.
A collection of excerpts from letters and diaries of Italians who fought and died on both the Fascist and anti-Fascist sides during World War II.

Connell, Charles. **Monte Cassino: The Historic Battle.** London: Elek, 1963, 206 p.
  This account records in detail the assault and the bravery of the Second Polish Corps at Monte Cassino.

O Ellinikos Stratos kata ton B' Pagkosmion Polemon. Athens, 1967, 256 p.
  A factual account of the Greek Army during World War II, prepared by its General Staff.

Higgins, Trumbull. **Soft Underbelly: The Anglo-American Controversy over the Italian Campaign 1939-1945.** New York: Macmillan, 1968, 275 p.
  A balanced explanation of the reasons for the British determination to divert the Allies from an invasion of France to a land offensive in the Mediterranean during World War II.

Howard, Michael Eliot. **The Mediterranean Strategy in the Second World War.** New York: Praeger, 1968, 82 p.
  A dispassionate assessment of the Allied failure to adopt British plans to invade Europe through its "soft underbelly," the Balkans.

Jackson, William Godfrey Fothergill. **The Battle for Italy.** New York: Harper and Row, 1967, 372 p.
  A very substantial history of the Italian campaign in World War II.

Jackson, William Godfrey Fothergill. **The Battle for Rome.** New York: Scribner, 1969, 224 p.
  A study of the military activities that culminated in the capture of Rome on June 4, 1944, by a British general who writes from first-hand experience. Of particular interest because of the author's critique of the American General Mark Clark.

Kurowski, Franz. **Der Kampf um Kreta.** Herford: Maximilian-Verlag, 1965, 244 p.
  A blow-by-blow account of the German conquest of Crete in May 1941.

Lombardi, Gabrio. **L'8 settembre fuori d'Italia.** Milan: Mursia, 1967, 463 p.
  This balanced narrative of Italy's surrender in World War II examines in detail the dilemma of the Italian army units still fighting on foreign soil, primarily in Russia, at the time of the armistice.

Mahas, D. **O Ellinoïtalikos polemos 1940-1941.** Athens, 1967, 2 v.
  A history of the Greek-Italian war in 1940–41, by the Chief of Staff of the Second Greek Army Corps during these operations.

Papakonstantinou, Theophylaktos. **I machi tis Ellados 1940-1941.** Athens: Galaxias, 1966, 438 p.
  Well-researched and well-written account of the Greek fight against the Axis in 1940–1941.

Schröder, Josef. **Italiens Kriegsaustritt 1943: die deutschen Gegenmassnahmen im italienischen Raum; Fall "Allarich" und "Achse."** Göttingen: Musterschmidt (for the Arbeitskreis für Wehrforschung, Stuttgart), 1969, 412 p.
  A very thorough and well-documented study of the gradual disintegration of the German-Italian axis during World War II which came to an end with the capitulation of Italy on August 9, 1943. The author claims that the Italian withdrawal from the war did not affect considerably the German fighting against the Allies.

Shepperd, Gilbert Alan. **The Italian Campaign, 1943-45: A Political and Military Reassessment.** New York: Praeger, 1968, 450 p.
  A British Army officer renders a detailed and dispassionate account of the campaign from the Sicilian landings to final victory.

Stewart, Ian McDougall Guthrie. **The Struggle for Crete: 20 May-1 June 1941; A Story of Lost Opportunity.** London: Oxford University Press, 1966, 518 p.
  A well-written account of the conquest of Crete by German air-borne troops. The author states that in Crete the British and Germans "learnt much that was to influence them for the rest of the war."

Strel'nikov, Vasilii S. and Cherepanov, Nikolai M. **Voina bez riska: deistviia anglo-amerikanskikh voisk v Italii v 1943-45 godakh.** Moscow: Voennoe Izdatel'stvo Ministerstva Oborony SSSR, 1965, 278 p.
  This Soviet study of the Allied war effort in Italy challenges the Anglo-American view that the peninsular operation was a calculated risk. The authors assert that the Allied

landing in Italy was but a marginal risk which served only to prolong the war and to secure the establishment of an orthodox bourgeois regime in Italy.

United States Army in World War II: The Mediterranean Theater of Operations. Washington: Department of the Army, Office of the Chief of Military History.
The following volumes in the subseries "The Mediterranean Theater of Operations" of the official history "United States Army in World War II" appeared from 1963 to 1972: "Sicily and the Surrender of Italy," by Howard McGaw Smyth and Albert N. Garland (1965, 609 p.) and "Salerno to Cassino," by Martin Blumenson (1969, 491 p.).

North and East Africa; Near and Middle East

See also other sections for the Second World War and the sections for specific countries.

Barker, A. J. **Eritrea 1941.** London: Faber, 1966, 248 p.
A comprehensive and well-written account of the British conquest of Eritrea in 1941.

Blumenson, Martin. **Kasserine Pass.** Boston: Houghton, 1967, 341 p.
An account of the significance of the critical battle of Kasserine Pass in Tunisia in 1943—a shock treatment for the American forces.

Caccia Dominioni di Sillavengo, Paolo, Conte. **Alamein, 1933–1962: An Italian Story.** London: Allen and Unwin, 1966, 289 p.
A popular narrative of the Battle of Alamein (October 1942), written by an Italian veteran of the African campaign and a career officer since World War I. The Italian edition appeared as "Alamein (1932–1962)" (Milan: Longanesi, 8th rev. and enl. ed., 1964, 604 p.).

Carver, Michael. **Tobruk.** Chester Springs (Pa.): Dufour, 1964, 271 p.
An account of the battles at Tobruk in 1941–42, written by a distinguished British military historian and general.

Kinghorn, Alan. **The Dynamic War.** New York: Exposition Press, 1967, 121 p.
A succinct survey of the British-German campaigns in North Africa in World War II.

Koenig, Marie Pierre Joseph François. **Bir-Hakeim, 10 Juin 1942.** Paris: Laffont, 1971, 427 p.
A posthumously published account of the battle of Bir-Hakeim by a well-known French general.

Majdalany, Fred. **The Battle of El Alamein: Fortress in the Sand.** Philadelphia: Lippincott, 1965, 168 p.
A concise account, published in "The Great Battles of History" series.

Mast, Charles Emmanuel. **Histoire d'une rébellion: Alger, 8 novembre 1942.** Paris: Plon, 1969, 525 p.
A description of the Anglo-American invasion of Morocco and Algeria on November 8, 1942, and of its political repercussions, by the general who was in charge of the French forces coöperating with the Allies.

Tuker, Sir Francis Ivan Simms. **Approach to Battle.** London: Cassell, 1963, 410 p.
A critical analysis of the British Eighth Army campaigns in North Africa and the Western Desert from 1941 to the capture of Tunis.

The Pacific

See also other sections for the Second World War and the sections for specific countries.

Bateson, Charles. **The War with Japan.** London: Barrie and Rockliff, the Cresset Press, 1968, 417 p.
A lucid history of the Pacific War. The Australian author criticizes the intransigent decision of Roosevelt and Churchill that only unconditional surrender of Japan was acceptable and emphasizes the contribution to victory of America's allies: India, Australia, Britain, New Zealand and China.

Brownlow, Donald Grey. **The Accused: The Ordeal of Rear Admiral Husband Edward Kimmel, U.S.N.** New York: Vantage Press, 1968, 190 p.

A defense of Admiral Kimmel, Commander-in-Chief of the Pacific Fleet at the time of the Pearl Harbor debacle.

Coffey, Thomas M. **Imperial Tragedy: Japan in World War II; The First Days and the Last.** New York: World Publishing Co., 1970, 531 p.
A useful and informative survey by a journalist with first-hand experience in Japan.

Craig, William. **The Fall of Japan.** New York: Dial Press, 1967, 368 p.
A popular history of events in Tokyo and in Washington signaling the end of the war in the Pacific. Mr. Craig's many sources include interviews with Japanese and Americans, official documents and diaries.

Dai Tōa sensō senshi sōsho. Tokyo: Asagumo Shimbunsha, 1966– .
A massive Japanese history of World War II in East Asia. Through 1974, 77 volumes have been published.

Davis, Burke. **Get Yamamoto.** New York: Random House, 1969, 231 p.
A fast-paced story of the successful mission to shoot down the planner of Pearl Harbor.

Garfield, Brian Wynne. **The Thousand-Mile War: World War II in Alaska and the Aleutians.** Garden City: Doubleday, 1969, 351 p.
This is the first history of the Aleutian campaign, fought against Japan for 15 months in 1942–43, off the coast of Alaska. An impressive book about an almost forgotten struggle.

Griffith, Samuel B., II. **The Battle for Guadalcanal.** Philadelphia: Lippincott, 1963, 282 p.
A colorful but objective recounting of the many months of military action at Guadalcanal, told by a retired U.S. Marine general who participated in the campaign.

Hattori, Takushirō. **Dai Tōa Sensō zenshi.** Tokyo: Hara Shobō, 1965, 1,086 p.
A comprehensive history of World War II in East Asia with emphasis on military affairs.

Kaneko, Toshio. **Karafuto 1945 nen natsu.** Tokyo: Kōdansha, 1972, 409 p.
A Japanese study of the end of World War II in Sakhalin.

Leckie, Robert. **Challenge for the Pacific: Guadalcanal—The Turning Point of the War.** Garden City: Doubleday, 1965, 372 p.
A military historian, using Japanese and Western-language sources, gives convincing evidence that the hundred-day Guadalcanal battle marked the beginning of the end for the Imperial Japanese forces.

Lockwood, Douglas. **Australia's Pearl Harbour: Darwin, 1942.** Melbourne: Cassell, 1966, 232 p.
An account of the Japanese air raids on Darwin on February 19, 1942, the aim of which was to eliminate any possibility of Allied interference with the Japanese occupation of the Netherlands East Indies.

Lord, Walter. **Incredible Victory.** New York: Harper and Row, 1967, 331 p.
A well-researched narrative of the "closest squeak and the greatest victory"—the Battle of Midway.

Marx, Joseph Laurance. **Nagasaki: The Necessary Bomb?** New York: Macmillan, 1971, 239 p.
An inside view of the Japanese government just before V-J Day. The author maintains that the Nagasaki bomb gave the military in Japan a chance to save face and an excuse to accept Hirohito's wish to surrender.

Newcomb, Richard Fairchild. **Iwo Jima.** New York: Holt, Rinehart and Winston, 1965, 338 p.
An account of the fierce and bloody battle for Iwo Jima in February 1945.

Oya, Sōichi, *ed*. **Japan's Longest Day.** London: Souvenir, 1968, 279 p.
An attempt to reconstruct the events in the 24 hours preceding Emperor Hirohito's broadcast of World War II surrender decision on August 15, 1945. Based on interviews with the surviving participants. The Japanese original was published as "Nihon no ichiban nagai hi" (Tokyo: Bungei Shunju, 1965, 225 p.).

Satō, Kanryō. **Dai tōa Sensō kaikoroku.** Tokyo: Tokuma Shoten, 1966, 426 p.
A study of the causes and events of World War II in the Pacific, by a former Japanese War Ministry official who also examines the Tokyo War Crimes Trial and the problem of Japan's war guilt.

SECOND WORLD WAR

Swinson, Arthur. **Four Samurai.** London: Hutchinson, 1968, 266 p.
Profiles of Generals Homma, Yamashita, Mutaguchi and Honda—four high-ranking Japanese officers during World War II.

Tomioka, Sadatoshi. **Kaisen to shusen.** Tokyo: Mainichi Shimbunsha, 1968, 246 p.
Memoirs of the war in the Pacific by a Japanese admiral.

United States Army in World War II: The War in the Pacific. Washington: Department of the Army, Office of the Chief of Military History.
The concluding volume in the subseries "The War in the Pacific" of the official history "United States Army in World War II" appeared in 1963: "Triumph in the Philippines," by Robert Ross Smith (756 p.).

Southeastern Asia; China; Burma

See also other sections for the Second World War and the sections for specific countries.

Barber, Noël. **A Sinister Twilight: The Fall of Singapore, 1942.** Boston: Houghton, 1968, 364 p.
This is the definitive account of the conquest of Singapore by the Japanese in 1942, "the greatest debacle in the history of British arms."

Collier, Basil. **The War in the Far East 1941-1945: A Military History.** New York: Morrow, 1969, 530 p.
An impressive military history, by a former official historian to the British Cabinet Office.

Dorn, Frank. **Walkout: With Stilwell in Burma.** New York: Crowell, 1971, 258 p.
A personal account of the Burma Campaign by General Stilwell's senior aid-de-camp.

Kirby, Stanley Woodburn. **Singapore: The Chain of Disaster.** New York: Macmillan, 1971, 270 p.
An authoritative account of the loss of Singapore to the Japanese during World War II. The author, a British general with first-hand experience in Malaya, blames the British governments of the inter-war years for making decisions which inevitably led to "the greatest national humiliation suffered by Britain since Yorktown."

Leasor, James. **Singapore: The Battle that Changed the World.** Garden City: Doubleday, 1968, 325 p.
A study of the Japanese capture of Singapore in February 1942 by an author who argues that the famous British fortress could have been defended successfully.

Liang, Chin-tung. **General Stilwell in China 1942-1944: The Full Story.** New York: St. John's University Press, 1972, 321 p.
Having had access to Generalissimo Chiang Kai-shek's archives, the author, a former official of the Republic of China, has written a critical account of General Stilwell's role in China during World War II.

Peers, William R. and Brelis, Dean. **Behind the Burma Road: The Story of America's Most Successful Guerrilla Force.** Boston: Atlantic (Little, Brown), 1963, 246 p.
A full account of the complex 1943-1945 guerrilla operations in Burma.

Zakharov, Matvei Vasil'evich and Others. **Final: istoriko-memuarnyi ocherk o razgrome Imperialisticheskoi Iaponii v 1945 godu.** Moscow: Izd-vo "Nauka," 2d rev. and enl. ed., 1969, 415 p.
A history of Soviet operations against Japan in Manchuria during August 1945.

Aerial Operations

See also (War) Aerial and Space Warfare and Technology, p. 114; (Second World War) Military Operations, p. 156.

Bekker, Cajus, *pseud.* (Hans Dieter Berenbrok). **The Luftwaffe War Diaries.** Garden City: Doubleday, 1968, 399 p.
A comprehensive but rather popular account of the German Air Force during World War II. The original was published as "Angriffshöhe 4000: ein Kriegstagebuch der deutschen Luftwaffe" (Hamburg: G. Stalling, 1964, 484 p.).

Giovannitti, Len and Freed, Fred. **The Decision to Drop the Bomb.** New York: Coward-McCann, 1965, 348 p.
A study dealing with the complex of considerations that led to the decision to use the atomic bomb against Japan.

Irving, David John Cawdell. **The Destruction of Dresden.** New York: Holt, Rinehart and Winston, 1964, 255 p.
A reconstruction of the bombing of Dresden on February 13 and 14, 1945, during which time British and U.S. bombers killed 135,000 people. The author (along with many others) does not believe that the raids were justified or contributed to the military effort of the Allies.

Lukas, Richard C. **Eagles East.** Tallahassee: Florida State University Press, 1970, 256 p.
An extensive account of American air force relations with the Soviet Union between 1941 and 1945, years of intermittent coöperation, frustration and obstruction.

Mosley, Leonard. **Backs to the Wall.** New York: Random House, 1971, 430 p.
A deeply moving portrait of London under German aerial siege. The essence of the city is captured by the following comment by a Londoner: "We have not starved. We have not been herded into gas ovens. We have seen our beloved London stand up and take it."

Tantum, William H., IV and Hoffschmidt, E. J., eds. **The Rise and Fall of the German Air Force (1933 to 1945).** Old Greenwich (Conn.): WE, Inc., 1969, 422 p.
This operational history of the German Air Force during World War II is based on German documents and statistics and was written at the command of the Air Council of Great Britain. (Reprint of an earlier edition that was prepared for official use.)

Verrier, Anthony. **The Bomber Offensive.** New York: Macmillan, 1969, 373 p.
This may well be the definitive account of the Anglo-American air offensive against Germany in World War II.

Naval Operations

See also (War) Naval Warfare, p. 114; (Second World War) Diplomatic Aspects, p. 148; Military Operations, p. 156.

Alman, Karl. **Angriff, ran, versenken! Die U-Boot-Schlacht im Atlantik.** Rastatt: Pabel-Verlag, 1965, 326 p.
A review of the achievements of the German submarine fleet during World War II, with an introduction by Admiral Dönitz.

Ansel, Walter. **Hitler and the Middle Sea.** Durham: Duke University Press, 1972, 514 p.
In this companion volume to his "Hitler Confronts England" (1960), Admiral Ansel discusses Hitler's strategy and activities in the Mediterranean, centering on the invasion of Crete.

Creswell, John. **Sea Warfare 1939-1945.** Berkeley: University of California Press, rev. and enl. ed., 1967, 343 p.
A succinct, strictly factual overview of World War II at sea.

Gallagher, Thomas. **The X-Craft Raid.** New York: Harcourt Brace Jovanovich, 1971, 170 p.
The story—well told—of the British midget submarines which put the impregnable German battleship *Tirpitz* out of action in World War II.

Gemzell, Carl-Axel. **Raeder, Hitler und Skandinavien: der Kampf für einen maritimen Operationsplan.** Lund: Gleerup, 1965, 390 p.
An able study of German naval strategy, centering on Admiral Raeder, with particular reference to the plans and reasons for the invasion of Norway and Denmark.

Hoyt, Edwin Palmer. **How They Won the War in the Pacific.** New York: Weybright and Talley, 1970, 554 p.
The undisputed hero of this well-written history of the American naval forces in the Pacific during World War II is Admiral Chester W. Nimitz.

Iachino, Angelo. **Tramonto di una grande marina.** Milan: Mondadori, 1966, 318 p.
A partisan account of the exploits and demise of the Italian fleet during World War II.

Lockwood, Charles Andrews and Adamson, Hans Christian. **Battles of the Philippine Sea.** New York: Crowell, 1967, 229 p.
A good account of the great sea battles of mid-1944.

La Marina Italiana nella Seconda Guerra Mondiale. Rome: Ufficio Storico della Marina Militare.
A multi-volume official record of the Italian Navy in the Second World War, published irregularly since 1950. Of the planned 21 volumes all have been published through 1973, with the exception of vol. 20 and vol. 21, pts. 2 and 3.

Morison, Samuel Eliot. **The Two-Ocean War: A Short History of the U.S. Navy in the Second World War.** Boston: Atlantic (Little, Brown), 1963, 611 p.
The author of the magistral 15-volume "History of United States Naval Operations in World War II" (1947–62) here offers a hefty, one-volume survey of the major campaigns and battles.

Piterskii, Nikolai Alekseevich and Others, *eds*. **Boevoi put' sovetskogo voenno-morskogo flota.** Moscow: Voen. Izd-vo, 2d enl. ed., 1967, 588 p.
A survey of the Soviet Navy during World War II. The German translation, with commentaries by Jürgen Rohwer, appeared as "Die Sowjet-Flotte im Zweiten Weltkrieg" (Oldenburg: G. Stalling for the Arbeitskreis für Wehrforschung, 1966, 581 p.).

Raiola, Giulio. **Quelli di Betasom.** Rome: Volpe, 1966, 223 p.
A study of Italian submarine activity in the North Atlantic during World War II.

Rohwer, Jürgen and Hümmelchen, Gerhard. **Chronik des Seekriegs: 1939–1945.** Oldenburg: Stalling (for the Arbeitskreis für Wehrforschung and the Bibliothek für Zeitgeschichte), 1968, 655 p.
A detailed chronicle of naval warfare during World War II.

Salewski, Michael. **Die deutsche Seekriegsleitung 1935–1945. Band I: 1935–1941.** Frankfurt/Main: Bernard und Graefe, 1970, 595 p.
The first volume of a well-documented study of the German Naval Staff covering the period from 1935 to 1941.

Smith, William Ward. **Midway: Turning Point of the Pacific.** New York: Crowell, 1966, 174 p.
The story of the battle of Midway in June 1942, by one of the four participating U.S. flag officers.

Thomas, David Arthur. **The Battle of the Java Sea.** New York: Stein and Day, 1969, 259 p.
An account of the naval operations in the Java Sea from the outbreak of war in the Pacific on December 7, 1941 until March 1, 1942 and the resulting destruction of the Allied fleet assembled to oppose the Japanese Navy.

Von der Porten, Edward P. **The German Navy in World War II.** New York: Crowell, 1969, 274 p.
A readable general survey, based on many interviews with former German naval officers and published sources. The author, an American schoolteacher, has a high regard for German naval strategy.

Winton, John, *pseud.* **The Forgotten Fleet.** New York: Coward-McCann, 1970, 433 p.
An effort to fill a "blind spot" in the history of World War II: the role of the Royal Navy in the Pacific. The British at first were regarded as "the poor relations" of the United States, but their contribution gradually won the Americans' respect and admiration.

Special Operations; Propaganda; Espionage; Intelligence

See also (War) Guerrilla Warfare; Armed Insurrection, p. 118; Intelligence, p. 121 (The United States) Culture; Education; Press; Radio, p. 278.

Accoce, Pierre and Quet, Pierre. **A Man Called "Lucy": 1935–1945.** New York: Coward-McCann, 1967, 250 p.
The story of the German master spy, Rudolf Roessler, in Switzerland, who during World War II supplied the Russians and the Swiss with information that he received from the highest German military circles. A widely discussed book in which some

facts are mixed with a good deal of fiction. The French original appeared as "La Guerre a été gagnée en Suisse: l'affaire Roessler" (Paris: Perrin, 1966, 317 p.).

Bazna, Elyesa with Nogly, Hans. **I Was Cicero.** New York: Harper and Row, 1962, 212 p.
An engaging story of espionage and rascality by the man who lifted documents from the British Ambassador in Turkey and sold them to the Nazis. The general lines of the story are familiar from "Operation Cicero," by L. C. Moyzisch (1951). The German edition appeared as "Ich war Cicero: die Bekenntnisse des grössten Spions des Zweiten Weltkrieges" (Munich: Kindler, 1962, 295 p.).

Boelcke, Willi A., *ed*. **The Secret Conferences of Dr. Goebbels: The Nazi Propaganda War 1939-43.** New York: Dutton, 1970, 364 p.
Documentation on the organization and activities of Dr. Goebbels' Ministry for Propaganda from 1939 to 1943, including a selection of the minutes of the ministerial meetings for that period. The English edition is an abridged translation of "Wollt Ihr den totalen Krieg? Die geheimen Goebbels-Konferenzen, 1939–1943" (Stuttgart: Deutsche Verlags-Anstalt, 1967, 362 p.), with supplementary material translated from the complete edition of the minutes of Goebbels' conferences from 1939 to 1941, "Kriegspropaganda 1939–1941: Geheime Ministerkonferenzen im Reichspropagandaministerium" (Stuttgart: Deutsche Verlags-Anstalt, 1966, 794 p.). Both these volumes were also edited by Willi A. Boelcke.

Budkevich, Sergei Leonidovich. **"Delo Zorge": sledstvie i sudebnyi protzess.** Moscow: Izd-vo "Nauka," 1969, 231 p.
An interpretive study, based on documents, of the trial and execution of Soviet master spy Richard Sorge in Japan during World War II.

Cookridge, Edward Henry, *pseud*. (Edward Spiro). **Set Europe Ablaze.** New York: Crowell, 1967, 410 p.
An account of the successes and failures of Britain's "Special Operations Executive," the espionage ring that operated in Nazi-occupied Europe during World War II. The English edition appeared under the title "Inside S.O.E.: The story of Special Operations in Western Europe, 1940–45" (London: Barker, 1966, 640 p.).

Deakin, Frederick William and Storry, George Richard. **The Case of Richard Sorge.** New York: Harper and Row, 1966, 373 p.
An able and scholarly account of Richard Sorge's extraordinary espionage activities in the Far East on behalf of the Soviet Union.

Deakin, Frederick William. **The Embattled Mountain.** New York: Oxford University Press, 1971, 284 p.
The author of this valuable personal account (reinforced by much subsequent research and discussion) was a member of the first British mission to Tito's headquarters in 1943.

Dulles, Allen Welsh. **The Secret Surrender.** New York: Harper and Row, 1966, 268 p.
An absorbing account, by the guiding participant, of the secret negotiations, via the O.S.S., for the surrender of the German forces in Italy. Of interest, too, in casting light on one of the early occasions for Soviet-Western friction as the war approached its end.

Foot, Michael Richard Daniel. **SOE in France.** London: H.M.S.O., 1966, 550 p.
A detailed and masterly history of the clandestine British secret service unit for organizing subversion and resistance in France during World War II. A volume in the "History of the Second World War" series that appears under British government auspices.

Ford, Corey. **Donovan of OSS.** Boston: Little, Brown, 1970, 366 p.
A biography of the founder of the U.S. Office of Strategic Services.

Fujiwara, Iwaichi. **Hiroku Daihon'ei no misshi.** Tokyo: Dancho Shobō, 1972, 252 p.
A memoir dealing with the Japanese secret service and its work with underground movements in Southeast Asia in World War II. First published under the title " F Kikan."

Ganier-Raymond, Philippe. **The Tangled Web.** New York: Pantheon Books, 1968, 203 p.
The story of how the Germans captured a radio operator of the Dutch Section of the British Special Operations Executive and forced him to send false messages and receive valuable information. The French original was published as "Le Réseau étranglé" (Paris: Fayard, 1967, 270 p.).

SECOND WORLD WAR

Garder, Michel. **La Guerre secrète des services spéciaux français, 1935–1945.** Paris: Plon, 1967, 522 p.
The story of the dramatic exploits of the French secret service, continued clandestinely under the German occupation. The author is a former member who unfortunately gives few indications of his sources.

Garliński, Jozef. **Poland, S.O.E., and the Allies.** London: Allen and Urwin, 1969, 248 p.
An informative study of the Polish underground during World War II, with particular attention to the activities of the British Special Operations Executive. The Polish original was published as "Politycy i żołnierze" (London: Polska Fundacja Kulturalna, 1968, 320 p.).

Irving, David John Cawdell. **Accident: The Death of General Sikorski.** London: Kimber, 1967, 231 p.
The author of this inconclusive study suspects that British intelligence services were instrumental in causing the aircraft crash at Gibraltar in July 1943 in which General Sikorski, a Polish exile leader, was killed.

Höhne, Heinz. **Codeword: Direktor; The Story of the Red Orchestra.** New York: Coward, McCann and Geoghegan, 1971, 310 p.
A German journalist argues that the mysterious *Rote Kapelle* in Nazi Germany during World War II was not a democratic resistance organization but a group working for the Soviet espionage service. The German original was published as "Kennwort: Direktor; die Geschichte der Roten Kapelle" (Frankfurt/Main: S. Fischer Verlag, 1970, 335 p.).

Kirkpatrick, Lyman B., Jr. **Captains without Eyes.** New York: Macmillan, 1969, 303 p.
The author presents five cases of intelligence failures in World War II. His analyses of Hitler's invasion of Russia and of the Japanese attack on Pearl Harbor are impressive, though somewhat padded. The treatment of Dieppe, Arnheim and the Battle of the Bulge is a bit thin.

Kurz, Hans Rudolf. **Nachrichtenzentrum Schweiz.** Frauenfeld: Huber, 1972, 131 p.
A thorough, though brief, account of the activities of the Swiss and various foreign intelligence services in Switzerland during World War II. Written with the coöperation of the Swiss Bundesrat.

Lomax, Sir John Garnett. **The Diplomatic Smuggler.** London: Arthur Barker, 1965, 288 p.
Reminiscences by a British Foreign Service officer who during World War II was a commercial counsellor in the British Embassy in Berne. The volume deals primarily with the author's efforts to smuggle certain high-precision Swiss instruments through the German blockade.

McLachlan, Donald. **Room 39: A Study in Naval Intelligence.** New York: Atheneum, 1968, 438 p.
A thorough study of British Naval Intelligence during World War II, by an English writer and journalist who served on the personal staff of the Director of Naval Intelligence from 1940 to 1945.

Mader, Julius and Others. **Doktor Sorge funkt aus Tokyo.** Berlin: Deutscher Militärverlag, 4th rev. and enl. ed., 1970, 474 p.
An East German version of the achievements of the communist master spy Richard Sorge, executed by the Japanese on November 7, 1944. The volume includes a selection of Sorge's writings.

Masterman, J. C. **The Double-Cross System—In the War of 1939 to 1945.** New Haven: Yale University Press, 1972, 203 p.
This report, kept secret for over 25 years, advances the bold claim that British Intelligence managed to control the entire apparatus of Nazi espionage in Britain and, moreover, convinced Hitler that the D-Day landings would take place at Calais rather than in Normandy.

Meo, Lucy D. **Japan's Radio War on Australia, 1941–1945.** Melbourne: Melbourne University Press, 1968, 300 p.
A careful survey of the ineffective Japanese wartime propaganda, based on the transcripts of the Japanese broadcasts to Australia that were made in the Listening Post of the Commonwealth Department of Information.

Perrault, Gilles. **The Red Orchestra.** New York: Simon and Schuster, 1969, 512 p.
  An account of a famous Soviet spy ring in Nazi Germany, and especially of its Jewish leader, Leopold Trepper. The original French edition appeared as "L'Orchestre rouge" (Paris: Fayard, 1967, 577 p.).

Radó, Sándor. **Dóra jelenti . . .** Budapest: Kossuth Könyvkiadó, 1971, 398 p.
  Wartime memoirs of the head of a Soviet spy ring working in Switzerland. Some parts of the narrative appear authentic while others are impossible to verify.

Scheurig, Bodo. **"Free Germany": The National Committee and the League of German Officers.** Middletown (Conn.): Wesleyan University Press, 1969, 311 p.
  A well-documented history of the Free Germany movement in the Soviet Union during World War II. The German original appeared as "Freies Deutschland: das Nationalkomitee und der Bund Deutscher Offiziere in der Sowjetunion 1939–1945" (Munich: Nymphenburger Verlagshandlung, 1960, 268 p.).

Schnabel, Reimund, *ed*. **Missbrauchte Mikrofone: deutsche Rundfunkpropaganda im Zweiten Weltkrieg.** Vienna: Europa Verlag, 1967, 506 p.
  A collection of documents on Nazi foreign language broadcasting during World War II.

Steenberg, Sven. **Vlasov.** New York: Knopf, 1970, 230 p.
  The story of General Andrei Vlasov, a Soviet war hero who defected and attempted to organize a movement for the overthrow of the Stalinist régime. The author was a Wehrmacht officer and interpreter in German-occupied Russia. The German original appeared as "Wlassow: Verräter oder Patriot?" (Cologne: Verlag Wissenschaft und Politik, 1968, 255 p.).

Strik-Strikfeldt, Wilfred. **Against Stalin and Hitler: Memoir of the Russian Liberation Movement, 1941–1945.** New York: John Day, 1973, 270 p.
  The story of the Vlasov army told by a German officer attached to it. The German original appeared as: "Gegen Stalin und Hitler: General Wlassow und die russische Freiheitsbewegung" (Mainz: Von Hase und Koehler, 1970, 287 p.).

Strong, Sir Kenneth. **Intelligence at the Top: The Recollections of an Intelligence Officer.** Garden City: Doubleday, 1969, 366 p.
  The bulk of the book is concerned with World War II, when the author, a British major general, served with General Eisenhower as his Chief of Intelligence.

Sweet-Escott, Bickham. **Baker Street Irregular.** London: Methuen, 1965, 278 p.
  An attempt to describe the Special Operations Executive, formed during World War II to help resistance movements in enemy-occupied territories, by one of its organizers.

ECONOMIC, TECHNICAL AND NON-MILITARY ASPECTS

See also other sections for the Second World War and the sections for specific countries.

Anders, Leslie. **The Ledo Road: General Joseph W. Stilwell's Highway to China.** Norman: University of Oklahoma Press, 1965, 255 p.
  A former historian in the Office of the Chief of Engineers describes the building of the 500-mile supply line to China by the U.S. Army Engineers.

Argenti, Philip Pandely. **The Occupation of Chios by the Germans and Their Administration of the Island: Described in Contemporary Documents.** New York: Cambridge University Press, 1967, 375 p.
  A collection of documents, with a brief introductory survey.

Benda, Harry Jindrich and Others, *eds*. **Japanese Military Administration in Indonesia: Selected Documents.** Detroit: Cellar Book Shop (for Yale University, Southeast Asia Studies), 1965, 279 p.
  Translations, mainly from the Japanese but a few from Dutch and Indonesian, of 83 primary documents dating from 1941 to 1944, showing how Indonesia was ruled under occupation. The editors caution that the Japanese destroyed many of their own records, and that the whole story will have to await the ferreting out of materials from other sources.

Bernhardt, Friedrich. **Die "Kollaboration" asiatischer Völker mit der japanischen Besatzungsmacht im Zweiten Weltkrieg als Glied im Dekolonisationsprozess.** Hamburg: Institut für Asienkunde, 1971, 103 p.
This is one of the few studies which views the "collaboration" of Asians with the Japanese in World War II as a part of the process of decolonialization. The study concentrates mainly on Burma, Indonesia and India, with some attention to Malaya and the Philippines.

Bosch, William J. **Judgment on Nuremberg.** Chapel Hill: University of North Carolina Press, 1970, 272 p.
The author of this well-researched monograph examines the attitudes of American policy-makers, legislators, lawyers, military people, historians and men of God toward the Nuremberg Trials. He considers the trial "a test of men's basic concepts of law, politics, and morality."

Brougher, William Edward. **South to Bataan: North to Mukden.** Athens: University of Georgia Press, 1971, 207 p.
A terse but revealing diary by a high-ranking American prisoner of war, Brigadier General W. E. Brougher, all of it written while in Japanese prison camps from 1942 to 1945. Edited by Dorris Clayton James.

Calder, Angus. **The People's War: Britain—1939–1945.** New York: Pantheon Books, 1969, 656 p.
A history of the domestic aspects of the war, with more than a touch of social criticism.

Fireside, Harvey. **Icon and Swastika.** Cambridge: Harvard University Press, 1971, 242 p.
An illuminating study of a relatively untouched field—the experiences of the Russian Orthodox Church, and its various factions, under German occupation in the Second World War.

Gascar, Pierre. **Histoire de la captivité des français en allemagne (1939–1945).** Paris: Gallimard, 1967, 317 p.
A sensitive and intelligent reconstruction of the collective fate of a million and a half French prisoners in Germany.

Girdner, Audrie and Loftis, Anne. **The Great Betrayal.** New York: Macmillan, 1969, 562 p.
A well-researched study of the relocation of Japanese-Americans during World War II.

Haight, John McVickar, Jr. **American Aid to France, 1938–1940.** New York: Atheneum, 1970, 278 p.
A study by a professor at Lehigh University of an important chapter of World War II that started with the French purchase of 100 American fighter planes in the spring of 1938 and that came to an end with the Battle of France in May and June 1940.

Hartcup, Guy. **The Challenge of War.** New York: Taplinger, 1970, 295 p.
A survey of Britain's successful mobilization of its scientific talent during World War II.

Hartendorp, A. V. H. **The Japanese Occupation of the Philippines.** Manila: Bookmark, 1967, 2 v.
A Philippine editor's history, written in secret during his three-year imprisonment, of the Santo Tomas Internment Camp and of Japanese rule of the country as told to him by people entering the camp. A portion of this work was published in 1964: "The Santo Tomas Story" (New York: McGraw-Hill, 446 p.).

History of the Second World War: United Kingdom Civil Series. London: H.M.S.O.
An official history of the civil aspects of Britain's war efforts, edited by Sir William Keith Hancock. The concluding volumes of this series are: "Oil: A Study in Wartime Policy and Administration," by D. J. Payton-Smith (1971, 520 p.) and "Design and Development of Weapons: Studies in Government and Industrial Organisation," by M. M. Postan and others (1964, 579 p.). For volumes published before 1963, consult other volumes of "Foreign Affairs Bibliography."

Irving, David John Cawdell. **The German Atomic Bomb: The History of Nuclear Research in Nazi Germany.** New York: Simon and Schuster, 1968, 329 p.
An account of the German attempt to manufacture an atomic bomb in World War II, based on interviews with leading German scientists and unpublished documents in Germany and the United States.

Janssen, Gregor. **Das Ministerium Speer: Deutschlands Rüstung im Krieg.** Berlin: Ullstein, 1968, 446 p.

A well-documented history of German armaments efforts during World War II, with emphasis on the career of Hitler's Armaments Minister, Albert Speer.

Jones, Robert Huhn. **The Roads to Russia.** Norman: University of Oklahoma Press, 1969, 326 p.

A scholarly account of U.S. lend-lease to Russia during World War II.

Kannapin, Hans-Eckhardt. **Wirtschaft unter Zwang.** Cologne: Deutsche Industrieverlagsgesellschaft, 1966, 334 p.

This is primarily a study of the role of foreign laborers and concentration camp inmates in the German economy during World War II.

Kimball, Warren F. **The Most Unsordid Act: Lend-Lease, 1939-1941.** Baltimore: Johns Hopkins Press, 1969, 281 p.

The author of this well-researched monograph maintains that the Lend-Lease Act "was the most significant of all the steps toward war taken before December 7, 1941." The case is argued most persuasively.

Kravchenko, Grigorii Sergeevich. **Ekonomika SSSR v gody Velikoi otechestvennoi voiny (1941-1945 gg.).** Moscow: Izd-vo "Ekonomika," 2d rev. and enl. ed., 1970, 389 p.

A general economic history of the Soviet Union during World War II.

Kwiet, Konrad. **Reichskommissariat Niederlande.** Stuttgart: Deutsche Verlags-Anstalt, 1968, 172 p.

This scholarly study of early and abortive Nazi efforts at governing conquered Holland with some measure of popular support is a valuable contribution to the literature on occupied Europe.

Maginnis, John J. **Military Government Journal: Normandy to Berlin.** Amherst: University of Massachusetts Press, 1971, 351 p.

A day-by-day account of U.S. military government operations from the invasion of Normandy to the occupation of Berlin. General Maginnis' journal was edited by Robert A. Hart.

Milward, Alan Steele. **The German Economy at War.** New York: Oxford University Press, 1965, 214 p.

Drawn largely from documents of the Speer Ministry, this study supports previous analyses of the less-than-total mobilization of the German war economy and shows how resistance to adequate concentration of power in any part of the government helped produce that result.

Miyamoto, Kazuo. **Hawaii: End of the Rainbow.** Rutland: Tuttle, 1964, 509 p.

A factual, dispassionate story of life in American concentration camps, written by a Hawaiian physician of Japanese ancestry interned in Pearl Harbor and later removed to mainland relocation centers for three years.

Mühlen, Patrik von zur. **Zwischen Hakenkreuz und Sowjetstern: der Nationalismus der sowjetischen Orientvölker im Zweiten Weltkrieg.** Düsseldorf: Droste Verlag, 1971, 256 p.

A survey of German policies toward the Caucasian and Turkic people of the Soviet Union during World War II.

Myer, Dillon S. **Uprooted Americans.** Tucson: University of Arizona Press, 1971, 360 p.

The former Director of the War Relocation Authority for Japanese-Americans during World War II reflects on his experiences. The result is a compassionate account of what America did to 110,000 of her citizens.

Petrov, Vladimir. **Money and Conquest: Allied Occupation Currencies in World War II.** Baltimore: Johns Hopkins Press (in coöperation with the Institute for Sino-Soviet Studies, George Washington University), 1967 282 p.

A critical view of the planning and execution of Allied financial policies.

Pfahlmann, Hans. **Fremdarbeiter und Kriegsgefangene in der deutschen Kriegswirtschaft: 1939-1945.** Darmstadt: Wehr und Wissen Verlagsgesellschaft, 1968, 238 p.

A survey of the significant contribution of prisoners of war and foreign workers to the German economy during World War II.

Polenberg, Richard, *ed.* **America at War: The Home Front, 1941-1945.** Englewood Cliffs: Prentice-Hall, 1968, 175 p.

Nostalgic vignettes from the American home front during World War II.

Rhode, Horst. **Das deutsche Wehrmachttransportwesen im Zweiten Weltkrieg.** Stuttgart: Deutsche Verlags-Anstalt (for the Militärgeschichtliches Forschungsamt), 1971, 439 p.
A well-documented study of German military transportation during World War II.

Ross, David R. B. **Preparing for Ulysses: Politics and Veterans during World War II.** New York: Columbia University Press, 1969, 315 p.
An excellent monograph on the successful American experience in reintegrating the veterans of World War II into society.

Steinert, Marlis G. **Hitlers Krieg und die Deutschen.** Düsseldorf: Econ-Verlag (for the Institut Universitaire de Hautes Études Internationales), 1970, 646 p.
In this study of German public opinion during World War II the author shows that the workers were more loyal in obeying the regulations of Hitler's state than the peasantry and the bourgeoisie.

Thomsen, Erich. **Deutsche Besatzungspolitik in Dänemark 1940-1945.** Düsseldorf: Bertelsmann Universitätsverlag, 1971, 277 p.
A solid survey of German policies in Denmark during World War II. The author also shows in great detail how the Danes managed to preserve their sovereignty without becoming too subservient to the German wishes.

Trunk, Isiah. **Judenrat: The Jewish Councils in Eastern Europe under Nazi Occupation.** New York: Macmillan, 1972, 664 p.
A painstaking inquiry into the role of the councils through which the Nazis applied their solutions to "the Jewish problem." Facing forthrightly the moral and other questions this subject has raised, the author concludes that Jewish participation or nonparticipation in the deportations had no substantial influence on the final outcome of the holocaust.

Umbreit, Hans. **Der Militärbefehlshaber in Frankreich 1940-1944.** Boppard: Boldt, 1968, 360 p.
A well-documented monograph on the German military government in France during World War II.

United States Army in World War II: Special Studies. Washington: Department of the Army, Office of the Chief of Military History.
The following volumes in the subseries "Special Studies" of the official history "United States Army in World War II" appeared in the period from 1963 to 1972: "Buying Aircraft: Matériel Procurement for the Army Air Forces," by Irving Brinton Holley, Jr. (1964, 625 p.); "Civil Affairs: Soldiers Become Governors," by Harry L. Coles and Albert K. Weinberg (1964, 930 p.) and "The Employment of Negro Troops," by Ulysses Lee (1966, 740 p.).

United States Army in World War II: The Technical Services. Washington: Department of the Army, Office of the Chief of Military History.
The following volumes in the subseries "The Technical Services" of the official history "United States Army in World War II" appeared in the period from 1963 to 1972: "The Chemical Warfare Service: Chemicals in Combat," by Brooks E. Kleber and Dale Birdsell (1965, 673 p.); "The Corps of Engineers: The War Against Japan," by Karl C. Dod (1966, 759 p.); "The Medical Department: Medical Service in the Mediterranean and Minor Theaters," by Charles M. Willtse (1966, 664 p.); "The Ordnance Department: On Beachhead and Battlefront," by Lida Mayo (1968, 523 p.); "The Quartermaster Corps: Operations in the War Against Germany," by William F. Ross and Charles F. Romanus (1965, 798 p.) and "The Signal Corps: The Outcome (July 1943 through 1945)," by George Raynor Thompson and Dixie R. Harris (1966, 693 p.).

Vegesack, Siegfried von. **Als Dolmetscher im Osten: ein Erlebnisbericht aus den Jahren 1942-43.** Hanover-Döhren: Verlag Harro von Hirschheydt, 1965, 265 p.
A description of the criminal policies of the German administration in the occupied territories of Russia and the Baltic States during World War II.

Velden, Doetje van. **De japanse interneringskampen voor burgers gedurende de Tweede Wereldoorlog.** Groningen: Wolters, 1963, 628 p.
A careful and detailed study of the governing of internment camps in all Japanese-occupied areas in 1942-45, the treatment accorded the prisoners and their physical and mental conditions and the varying degrees of adherence by the Japanese to international conventions.

Wilmington, Martin W. **The Middle East Supply Centre.** Albany: State University of New York Press, 1971, 248 p.

The only complete treatment of this Allied-operated economic structure which proved indispensable to victory in the Second World War. The author regrets the failure to transform it to peacetime usage. Edited by Laurence Evans.

RESISTANCE AND UNDERGROUND MOVEMENTS

See also other sections for the Second World War and the sections for specific countries.

Armstrong, John Alexander, *ed.* **Soviet Partisans in World War II.** Madison: University of Wisconsin Press, 1964, 792 p.

This very substantial volume is the outcome of a group of postwar studies devoted to an analysis of the Soviet partisan movement. In addition to Mr. Armstrong, the contributors are Kurt DeWitt, Earl Ziemke, Alexander Dallin, Ralph Mavrogordato, Wilhelm Moll and Gerhard L. Weinberg.

Bartoszewski, Władyslaw and Lewin, Zofia, *eds.* **Righteous among Nations: How Poles Helped the Jews, 1939-1945.** London: Earlscourt Publications, 1969, 834 p.

A compilation of documents describing the assistance given by Poles to Jews during the Nazi occupation. The original Polish edition appeared as "Ten jest ojczyzny mojej: Polacy z pomocą Żydom, 1939-45" (Cracow: Znak, 1966, 633 p.).

Bartoszewski, Władyslaw. **Warsaw Death Ring, 1939-1944.** Warsaw: Interpress Publishers, 1968, 450 p.

A detailed account of the staggering tragedies and horrors that befell the inhabitants of Warsaw from the time of the occupation of the capital by the Germans in October 1939 up to, but not including, the uprising of 1944. A translation of "Warszawski pierścień śmierci, 1939-1944" (Warsaw: Zachodnia Agencja Prasowa, 1967, 404 p.).

Battaglia, Roberto. **Risorgimento e resistenza.** Rome: Riuniti, 1964, 395 p.

A collection of essays on the Resistance Movement in Italy from 1943 to 1945. The author, who died in 1963, was a prominent historian, anti-Fascist and a partisan leader. Edited by Ernesto Ragionieri.

Bennett, Jeremy. **British Broadcasting and the Danish Resistance Movement, 1940-1945: A Study of the Wartime Broadcasts of the B.B.C. Danish Service.** New York: Cambridge University Press, 1966, 266 p.

A pioneering study of British broadcasting to Europe during World War II.

Bocca, Giorgio. **Storia dell'Italia partigiana: settembre 1943-maggio 1945.** Bari: Laterza, 2d ed., 1966, 675 p.

A comprehensive, well-documented and artfully written history of Italian resistance to German occupation and Mussolini's Social Republic.

Bravo, Anna. **La repubblica partigiana dell'alto Monferrato.** Turin: Giapichelli, 1964, 269 p.

A study of the anti-Fascist resistance movement in the Alto Monferrato in 1944. This work demonstrates the extensive support given the partisans by the conservative and apolitical peasants of the region.

Denis, Henri. **Le Comité parisien de la libération.** Paris: Presses Universitaires, 1963, 259 p.

A careful, scholarly history of the Liberation Committee of Paris, formed in September 1943 to coördinate resistance activities, and its subsequent divisions and decline.

European Resistance Movements, 1939-45. Oxford: Pergamon Press, 1964, 663 p.

This second volume on European wartime resistance contains the documented papers presented at the Second International Conference on the History of the Resistance Movements held in Milan in 1961. The reports are in French and English.

Flender, Harold. **Rescue in Denmark.** New York: Simon and Schuster, 1963, 281 p.

The amazing story of the spontaneous efforts of the Christian population of Denmark to hide the 8,000 Jews there when the Nazis came to arrest and deport them in 1943.

Hesse, Erich. **Der sowjetrussische Partisanenkrieg 1941 bis 1944.** Göttingen: Musterschmidt, 1969, 292 p.
A dissertation on the origins and development of Soviet partisan warfare, as reflected in the German military and political documents.

Jewish Resistance during the Holocaust. Jerusalem: Yad Vashem, 1971, 562 p.
Papers delivered at a conference in Jerusalem in 1968.

Katz, Robert. **Death in Rome.** New York: Macmillan, 1966, 334 p.
An account of the Ardeatine Caves massacre in March 1944.

Kédros, André. **La Résistance grecque, 1940-1944.** Paris: Laffont, 1966, 543 p.
A detailed and well-researched study of the Greek resistance movement during World War II, by a Greek historian who witnessed the events described.

Lampe, David. **The Last Ditch.** New York: Putnam, 1968, 250 p.
A study of the Nazi guidelines for the invasion and occupation of Great Britain and of the British countermeasures for such an eventuality.

Mayer, Daniel. **Les Socialistes dans la Résistance.** Paris: Presses Universitaires, 1968, 247 p.
A short account of the Socialist role in the French Resistance, by one of the major leaders. Illuminating documents, some never before published, are appended.

Michel, Henri. **Jean Moulin, l'unificateur.** Paris: Hachette, 1964, 222 p.
An account of the activities and death of Jean Moulin, one of the most important resistance leaders in German-occupied France during World War II and the organizer of the National Council of the Resistance.

Michel, Henri. **The Shadow War: European Resistance 1939-1945.** New York: Harper and Row, 1972, 416 p.
A comprehensive, analytical survey of this pan-European phenomenon, by the doyen of French historians of the Resistance and the Second World War. The French original appeared as "La Guerre de l'ombre" (Paris: Grasset, 1970, 420 p.).

L'occupazione in Europa. Rome: Riuniti, 1964, 617 p.
A collection of papers dealing with the Nazi occupation of Europe, presented at the Third International Conference on the History of the Resistance Movements held in Karlovy Vary on September 2-4, 1964.

Perrone Capano, Renato. **La resistenza in Roma.** Naples: Macchiaroli, 1963, 2 v.
A chronicle of the German occupation of Rome from September 1943 to June 1944 and of the Italian resistance movement.

Quazza, Guido. **La resistenza italiana.** Turin: Giappichelli (for the Istituto di Storia of the Università di Torino), 1966, 267 p.
A brief survey of the Italian resistance movement during World War II. There is a useful chronology and an appendix of documents.

La resistenza e gli alleati in Toscana. I C.L.N. della Toscana nei rapporti col governo dell' Italia liberata. Florence: Istituto storico della resistenza in Toscana, 1964, 305 p.
A collection of papers presented at the Historical Institute of the Resistance in Tuscany dealing with the relations between the partisan movement in Tuscany on the one hand and the Italian Royal Government in the South and the Allies on the other.

Tys-Krokhmaliuk, Yuriy. **UPA Warfare in Ukraine.** New York: Society of Veterans of Ukrainian Insurgent Army, 1972, 449 p.
An attempt to describe the armed resistance of the Ukrainian Insurgent Army against the Nazi and Soviet regimes in the years from 1942 to 1952.

Venohr, Wolfgang. **Aufstand für die Tschechoslowakei.** Hamburg: Wegner, 1969, 372 p.
An extensive account of the relatively little-known armed anti-German uprising in Slovakia in the autumn of 1944.

V. THE POSTWAR WORLD

GENERAL

See also General Works, p. 1; Political Factors, p. 12; Economic Factors, p. 49; International Organization and Government, p. 96; War and Peace, p. 108; East-West Relations, p. 180; Western Europe, p. 345; Eastern Europe and the Soviet Bloc, p. 358.

Beaufre, André. **L'Enjeu du désordre: de la contagion révolutionnaire à la guerre atomique.** Paris: Grasset, 1969, 189 p.
A leading French military writer attempts to diagnose the ills of the Western nations and speculates about the coming crises in the Soviet Union, the United States and Western Europe.

Bloomfield, Lincoln Palmer and Leiss, Amelia C. **Controlling Small Wars: A Strategy for the 1970's.** New York: Knopf, 1969, 421 p.
From a number of well-researched case studies the authors draw inferences for the future that exhibit an unusual combination of conceptual imagination and practical sense.

Böttcher, Winfried and Others, *eds.* **Das grosse Dreieck.** Stuttgart: Deutsche Verlags-Anstalt, 1971, 208 p.
Essays on the Washington-Moscow-Peking triangle, an appropriate *Festschrift* for Klaus Mehnert.

Borch, Herbert von. **Friede trotz Krieg: Spannungsfelder der Weltpolitik seit 1950.** Munich: Piper, 1966, 375 p.
Reflections on the great issues of world politics in the period from 1950 to 1965, by a German journalist and editor of *Aussenpolitik* who for many years reported from Washington.

Borisov, Iurii Vasil'evich; Gromyko, Anatolii Andreevich and Israelian, Viktor Levonovich, *eds.* **Diplomatiia sovremennogo imperializma: liudi, problemy, metody.** Moscow: Izd-vo "Mezhdunarodnye Otnosheniia," 1969, 415 p.
A survey of the foreign policy goals and diplomatic methods of "contemporary imperialism," i.e., the United States, Great Britain, France, West Germany and Japan.

Burgess, Warren Randolph and Huntley, James Robert. **Europe and America—The Next Ten Years.** New York: Walker, 1970, 232 p.
This projection of relations within the Atlantic Community during the coming decade places great emphasis on economic instruments of coöperation and better education in international affairs for the young.

Calvocoressi, Peter. **International Politics since 1945.** New York: Praeger, 1968, 480 p.
A competent factual summary by a British scholar.

Deutscher, Isaac. **Russia, China, and the West: A Contemporary Chronicle, 1953–1966.** New York: Oxford University Press, 1970, 360 p.
A selection of the late Isaac Deutscher's articles and essays on current affairs from 1953 to 1966. Edited by Fred Halliday.

Dönhoff, Marion, Gräfin. **Welt in Bewegung: Berichte aus vier Erdteilen.** Düsseldorf: Diederichs Verlag, 1965, 364 p.
Perceptive observations on contemporary international developments, by a leading German journalist; published originally in *Die Zeit* from 1951 to 1965.

Dolci, Danilo. **A New World in the Making.** New York: Monthly Review Press, 1965, 327 p.
The author of several widely discussed books on Sicilian poverty here reflects on travels in the early 1960s to Russia, Jugoslavia, Senegal and Ghana.

Douglas, William O. **International Dissent: Six Steps toward World Peace.** New York: Random House, 1971, 155 p.
The author urges the abolition of military pacts, a stronger World Court, more multilateral aid, the end of colonialism, recognition of Communist China and an international regime for the oceans.

Geiger, Theodore. **The Conflicted Relationship: The West and the Transformation of Asia, Africa and Latin America.** New York: McGraw-Hill (for the Council on Foreign Relations), 1967, 303 p.
  A study, designed for the general reader interested in public affairs, dealing with American and Western economic and political relations with Asia, Africa and Latin America.

Grossner, Claus and Others, *eds.* **Das 198. Jahrzehnt.** Hamburg: Wegner, 1969, 590 p.
  Twenty-six writers from Europe and America present their reasoned and often provocative prognoses of particular aspects of the 1970s. A *Festschrift* for Countess Dönhoff, a prominent German journalist and writer.

Hagemann, Max. **Der provisorische Frieden.** Erlenbach-Zurich: Rentsch, 1964, 744 p.
  A massive analysis by a Swiss scholar of the problems of international order and organization confronting the world since 1945.

Hilsman, Roger and Good, Robert Crocker, *eds.* **Foreign Policy in the Sixties.** Baltimore: Johns Hopkins Press, 1965, 299 p.
  These essays in honor of Arnold Wolfers are directed toward three main themes: the contemporary international arena, the instrumentalities of foreign policy and the moral issues in statecraft.

Hofer, Walther. **Perspektiven der Weltpolitik.** Zurich: Fretz und Wasmuth Verlag, 1964, 152 p.
  A stimulating collection of essays on some of the most important issues in post-World War II international relations, by a well-known Swiss historian.

Holbraad, Carsten, *ed.* **Super Powers and World Order.** Canberra: Australian National University Press, 1971, 161 p.
  A symposium of papers dealing with various aspects of recent great-power relations.

Horowitz, David. **Empire and Revolution: A Radical Interpretation of Contemporary History.** New York: Random House, 1969, 274 p.
  A highly polemical and unoriginal broadside against imperialism, both Western and Soviet, with a pronounced Trotskyist bias. The British edition appeared as "Imperialism and Revolution" (London: Allen Lane, 1969, 274 p.).

Howe, Quincy. **Ashes of Victory: World War II and its Aftermath.** New York: Simon and Schuster, 1972, 542 p.
  A sweeping, richly written narrative for the general reader. In evaluating the U.S. policies, the author states that "far from having betrayed Franklin Roosevelt, all his successors in the White House had remained stubbornly true to his legacy."

Hudson, Geoffrey Francis. **The Hard and Bitter Peace.** New York: Praeger, 1967, 319 p.
  An overview of world politics since 1945 by a British scholar.

Kahn, Herman and Bruce-Briggs, B. **Things to Come: Thinking about the Seventies and Eighties.** New York: Macmillan, 1972, 262 p.
  In this contribution to futurology, Mr. Kahn has programmed his tripod for the 1970s and 1980s. An engaging, irritating and thought-provoking book.

Kahn, Herman and Wiener, Anthony J. **The Year 2000.** New York: Macmillan, 1967, 431 p.
  The authors, both mainstays of the Hudson Institute, have undertaken to create "a framework for speculation on the next thirty-three years," under the auspices of the Commission on the Year 2000. The book contains more technical brilliance than political wisdom.

Kertesz, Stephen Denis. **The Quest for Peace through Diplomacy.** Englewood Cliffs: Prentice-Hall, 1967, 182 p.
  A fairly straightforward descriptive account with emphasis on modern multilateral diplomacy in the United Nations and in Western Europe.

Kreisky, Bruno. **Die Herausforderung: Politik an der Schwelle des Atomzeitalters.** Düsseldorf: Econ-Verlag, 1963, 188 p.
  A discussion of contemporary international relations by the Austrian Foreign Minister from 1959 to 1966 and Chancellor of his country since 1970.

Laloy, Jean. **Entre guerres et paix, 1945-1965.** Paris: Plon, 1966, 380 p.
: A perceptive analysis of the main trends in international politics in the period between 1945 and 1965, by a prominent French diplomatist and student of Soviet affairs. An important book.

Laqueur, Walter Ze'ev. **Out of the Ruins of Europe.** Freeport (N.Y.): The Library Press, 1971, 520 p.
: A collection of nostalgic essays and reviews which reflect the life and intellectual interests of a well-known writer, born in Germany, and now at home in Israel, England and America.

Madariaga, Salvador de. **Weltpolitisches Kaleidoskop: Reden und Aufsätze.** Zürich: Fretz und Wasmuth Verlag, 1965, 223 p.
: Articles and addresses dealing with problems of the cold war and contemporary politics, by the eminent Spanish liberal.

Rostow, Walt Whitman. **Politics and the Stages of Growth.** New York: Cambridge University Press, 1971, 410 p.
: The author suggests that the 1970s ought to be the decade of political development in the sense that the 1960s was the decade of economic development. His data, based on the experiences of eight countries, lead him to guardedly optimistic conclusions.

Schmeltz, Guy Willy. **La Politique mondiale contemporaine.** Paris: La Colombe, 1963, 613 p.
: An attempt to interpret the major currents in the contemporary world: the trends toward unity, toward division and toward a "third world."

Swearingen, Rodger, *ed.* **Soviet and Chinese Communist Power in the World Today.** New York: Basic Books, 1966, 127 p.
: A series of lectures on the changes in the communist world and their implications for U.S. policy, by Max Frankel, Philip E. Mosely, George E. Taylor, Marshall Shulman and the editor.

Wheeler-Bennett, Sir John Wheeler and Nicholls, Anthony. **The Semblance of Peace: The Political Settlement after the Second World War.** New York: St. Martin's Press, 1972, 878 p.
: A well-documented and stylishly written study of the "origins and significance of the uneasy and interrupted peace" since 1945. The authors see the genesis of the cold war in events before rather than after 1945.

Willrich, Mason. **Global Politics of Nuclear Energy.** New York: Praeger, 1971, 204 p.
: An inquiry into the implications for the world community of the advances in nuclear energy and technology for nonmilitary purposes in the 1970s.

Zhurkin, V. V. and Primakov, E. M., *eds.* **Mezhdunarodnye konflikty.** Moscow: Mezhdunarodnye Otnosheniia, 1972, 238 p.
: A Soviet study of the international crises of the past decade in Cuba, Indochina, the Middle East and South Asia.

EAST-WEST RELATIONS

The Cold War; Peaceful Coexistence

See also General Works, p. 1; Political Factors, p. 12; International Law, p. 83; International Organization and Government, p. 96; War and Peace, p. 108; (The Postwar World) General, p. 178; Western Defense; North Atlantic Treaty; Atlantic Community, p. 188; (The United States) Biographies, Memoirs and Addresses, p. 218; Foreign Policy, p. 229; Military and Defense Policy, p. 257; Western Europe, p. 345; Eastern Europe and the Soviet Bloc, p. 358; Great Britain, p. 366; France, p. 395; Germany, p. 463; (Union of Soviet Socialist Republics) Foreign Policy, p. 550.

Abel, Elie. **The Missile Crisis.** Philadelphia: Lippincott, 1966, 220 p.
: A journalist's well-informed and absorbing account of the October 1962 Cuban missile crisis—two weeks on the brink of the ultimate holocaust.

Allison, Graham T. **Essence of Decision: Explaining the Cuban Missile Crisis.** Boston: Little, Brown, 1971, 338 p.
: A thorough and sophisticated monograph on the Cuban missile crisis.

Arbatov, Georgi A. **The War of Ideas in Contemporary International Relations: The Imperialist Doctrine, Methods and Organisation of Foreign Political Propaganda.** Moscow: Progress Publishers, 1973, 317 p.
A leading Soviet scholar discusses the role of ideology in international relations. Despite continuing ideological barriers, the author is hopeful about prospects for Soviet-American rapprochement. The Russian original was published as "Ideologicheskaia bor'ba v sovremennykh mezhdunarodnykh otnosheniiakh" (Moscow: Izd-vo Politicheskoi Literatury, 1970, 351 p.).

Bar-Zohar, Michel. **The Hunt for German Scientists.** New York: Hawthorn Books, 1967, 207 p.
In this story of the search for German atom and rocket scientists and technicians in the aftermath of World War II, the author shows that the Russians were the chief beneficiaries. The French original appeared as "La Chasse aux savants allemands (1944–1960)" (Paris: Fayard, 1965, 285 p.).

Barnet, Richard J. and Raskin, Marcus G. **After 20 Years: Alternatives to the Cold War in Europe.** New York: Random House, 1965, 243 p.
The two authors, formerly in government service, argue that the effort to "build an Atlantic Community" and to "win the arms race" is both obsolete and dangerous. The core of the book is, as the subtitle indicates, a search for alternatives.

Bell, Coral. **Negotiation from Strength: A Study in the Politics of Power.** New York: Knopf, 1963, 248 p.
A quite critical study of Western policy vis-à-vis the Soviet Union since 1950, centering on the goal of "negotiation from strength"—a goal the author feels to have been both ambiguous and probably impossible of realization.

Bergeron, Gérard. **La Guerre froide inachevée.** Montreal: Les Presses de l'Université de Montréal, 1971, 315 p.
A retrospective survey of 27 years of "classical cold war" and a prognosis of the international scene in 1985, when, according to the French-Canadian author, the nineteenth-century principles of balance of power again will prevail.

Bērziņš, Alfreds. **The Two Faces of Co-existence.** New York: Speller, 1967, 335 p.
A former minister of Latvia argues "that the communist leaders in Moscow are still at the centre of the world communist conspiracy, in spite of the ideological differences or power struggles that can be discerned between Russia and China."

Birnbaum, Karl E. **Peace in Europe: East-West Relations 1966–1968 and the Prospects for a European Settlement.** New York: Oxford University Press (in coöperation with the Royal Institute of International Affairs), 1970, 159 p.
A thoughtful essay on the premises and perceptions of leading statesmen in East and West in the years of new efforts at détente by a Swedish scholar, familiar with America and Europe. Written under the auspices of the Harvard Center for International Affairs.

Bottome, Edgar M. **The Balance of Terror: A Guide to the Arms Race.** Boston: Beacon Press, 1971, 215 p.
A succinct history of nuclear diplomacy since the end of World War II.

Brandt, Willy. **The Ordeal of Coexistence.** Cambridge: Harvard University Press, 1963, 112 p.
In these lectures, delivered at Harvard in October 1962, the German statesman deals with the problem and meanings of "coexistence" and their implications for Berlin, Germany and the West.

Bredow, Wilfred von. **Vom Antagonismus zur Konvergenz?** Frankfurt/Main: Metzner, 1972, 218 p.
After examining various aspects of the convergence theories, the author of this substantial study proposes the term "antagonistic co-operation" for designating East-West relations in the 1970s.

Bromke, Adam and Uren, Philip E., eds. **The Communist States and the West.** New York: Praeger, 1967, 242 p.
A collection of twelve essays, predominantly by Canadian scholars, on relations between the Communist bloc and the Western powers.

Donnelly, Desmond. **Struggle for the World: The Cold War, 1917-1965.** New York: St. Martin's Press, 1965, 511 p.
   The history of the cold way by a British journalist and a former Labour M.P. who in 1971 joined the Conservative Party.

Dulles, Eleanor Lansing and Crane, Robert Dickson, *eds.* **Détente: Cold War Strategies in Transition.** New York: Praeger (for the Center for Strategic Studies, Georgetown University), 1965, 307 p.
   A symposium dealing with the prospects for an international détente and some of the strategic implications for both the Communist and Western powers.

Egorov, Valerii Nikolaevich. **Mirnoe sosushchestvovanie i revoliutsionnyi protsess.** Moscow: Izd-vo "Mezhdunarodnye Otnosheniia," 1971, 224 p.
   The author examines the concept of peaceful coexistence, contrasting "mistaken" Western views with a proper Leninist understanding.

Etzioni, Amitai. **Winning Without War.** Garden City: Doubleday, 1964, 271 p.
   A thoughtful essay on the East-West conflict, critical of the "duopolist" strategies of both the "protracted conflict" and the conflict-resolution schools. The author seeks a third course aiming at non-armed rather than armed conflict and competition.

Feis, Herbert. **From Trust to Terror: The Onset of the Cold War, 1945-1950.** New York: Norton, 1970, 428 p.
   The customary thoroughness of the author's research and the even-handedness of his analysis make this book one of the finest treatments of the start of the cold war.

Fontaine, André. **History of the Cold War.** New York: Pantheon Books, 1968-69, 2 v.
   The foreign editor and diplomatic correspondent of *Le Monde* reviews the history of the cold war, the origins of which he pushes back to the Russian October Revolution. The wane of Europe is seen as the main cause of the cold war; the rise of Europe between the superpowers is the author's hope. The French original appeared as "Histoire de la guerre froide" (Paris: Fayard, 1966-67, 2 v.).

Fulbright, James William. **Prospects for the West.** Cambridge: Harvard University Press, 1963, 132 p.
   In these William L. Clayton Lectures the former Chairman of the U.S. Senate Committee on Foreign Relations discusses Soviet-Western relations, the United States and its allies and the domestic tasks confronting the United States.

Gamson, William A. and Modigliani, Andre. **Untangling the Cold War: A Strategy for Testing Rival Theories.** Boston: Little, Brown, 1971, 222 p.
   An attempt to develop new methods for the study of the cold war.

Gardner, Lloyd C.; Schlesinger, Arthur Meier, Jr. and Morgenthau, Hans J. **The Origins of the Cold War.** Waltham (Mass.): Ginn-Blaisdell, 1970, 122 p.
   These three essays and the rejoinders to them strike a felicitous balance between revisionism and traditionalism.

Greig, Ian. **The Assault on the West.** Petersham (Surrey): The Foreign Affairs Publishing Co., 1968, 357 p.
   In this volume, introduced by Sir Alec Douglas-Home, the author attempts to inform the reader about the many-sided Communist campaigns against the West.

Halle, Louis Joseph. **The Cold War as History.** New York: Harper and Row, 1967, 434 p.
   The central thesis of this fair and admirable effort at historical interpretation: "Since the end of the eighteenth century four great wars have been fought to maintain or restore the European balance of power. The fourth was the Cold War, which began almost immediately after World War II."

Herz, Martin Florian. **Beginnings of the Cold War.** Bloomington: Indiana University Press, 1966, 214 p.
   A brief summary of the events and disputes, chiefly in early 1945, that set the stage for the cold war.

Jalée, Pierre. **Imperialism in the Seventies.** New York: Third Press, 1972, 226 p.
   A study by a French Marxist author.

Kennan, George Frost. **On Dealing with the Communist World.** New York: Harper and Row (for the Council on Foreign Relations), 1964, 57 p.

In these lectures, entitled "The Rationale of Coexistence," "East-West Trade" and "Polycentrism and Western Policy," Mr. Kennan wrestles with the continuing problem of dealing with the Communist world and with the need, as he sees it, to surmount a number of traditional clichés and stereotypes which inhibit our ability to perceive, and act upon, the factor of change.

Kennedy, Robert Francis. **Thirteen Days: A Memoir of the Cuban Missile Crisis.** New York: Norton, 1969, 224 p.

The late U.S. Senator adds some new insights to the political and military record of the Cuban missile confrontation.

Kirsch, Botho. **Sturm über Eurasien.** Stuttgart: Seewald, 1970, 286 p.

The ex-foreign editor of *Der Spiegel* argues that Bonn's policy of accommodation with Moscow is tragically mistaken. The conflict between China and Russia is irreconcilable and détente in the West only opens the way for Russian aggression in the East.

Korbel, Josef. **Detente in Europe: Real or Imaginary?** Princeton: Princeton University Press, 1972, 302 p.

"The policy of détente is both a hope and a danger," according to this assessment which stresses American disengagement from Europe as a major factor in the present trend.

Krockow, Christian, Graf von. **Soziologie des Friedens: Drei Abhandlungen zur Problematik des Ost-West-Konflikts.** Gütersloh: Bertelsmann, 1962, 221 p.

An attempt to describe and analyze, with the help of the theories of Thomas Hobbes, Ralf Dahrendorf, Talcott Parsons and others, the contemporary "sociological aspects" of the East-West conflict.

LaFeber, Walter. **America, Russia, and the Cold War: 1945–1966.** New York: Wiley, 2d ed., 1972, 339 p.

An able essay emphasizing the impact of domestic politics on foreign policy.

LaFeber, Walter, *ed.* **The Origins of the Cold War, 1941–1947.** New York: Wiley, 1971, 172 p.

A balanced selection of documents and articles.

Larson, David Lloyd, *ed.* **The "Cuban Crisis" of 1962.** Boston: Houghton, 1963, 333 p.

A compilation, without commentary but with a chronology, of public statements and documents relating to the Soviet-U.S. confrontation over Cuba.

Lasby, Clarence G. **Project Paperclip: German Scientists and the Cold War.** New York: Atheneum, 1971, 338 p.

A broad view of American efforts to capture leading German scientists and bring hundreds of them to this country. Sensibly set against the background of the emergent cold war and based on interviews and government documents, by an American historian.

Lerche, Charles Olsen. **The Cold War . . . and After.** Englewood Cliffs: Prentice-Hall, 1965, 150 p.

An essay on the roots and nature of the cold war.

Luard, David Evan Trant, *ed.* **The Cold War.** New York: Praeger, 1964, 347 p.

A symposium of British essays surveying the history of the cold war and its possible future course. The treatment is chiefly by geographic regions.

McWhinney, Edward, *ed.* **Law, Foreign Policy, and the East-West** *Détente.* Toronto: University of Toronto Press, 1964, 123 p.

A collection of essays, stemming from the Conference on Law and World Affairs at the University of Toronto in January 1964, on "the response of the West in general, and of Canada in particular" to shifts in the cold war.

Mayrzedt, Hans and Romé, Helmut, *eds.* **Koexistenz zwischen Ost und West: Konflikt, Kooperation, Konvergenz.** Vienna: Europa Verlag, 1967, 346 p.

Papers on problems of coexistence, East-West trade and economic trends in Eastern Europe, delivered at a conference held at Graz in 1965 that was sponsored by the Institut für Europäische Studien.

Miksche, Ferdinand Otto. **Kapitulation ohne Krieg: die Jahre 1970–1980.** Stuttgart: Seewald, 1965, 258 p.

A projection of the possibilities of big power constellations in the 1970s and a plea for the strengthening of Western Europe. The author is an Austrian-born French military expert.

Miksche, Ferdinand Otto. **Rüstungswettlauf: Ursachen und Auswirkungen.** Stuttgart: Seewald, 1972, 452 p.
A survey of contemporary armaments race, a criticism of the military planning of the Western World and a plea for a stronger and more united Western Europe.

Naimy, Mikhail. **Ab'ad min Muskū wa min Washintun.** Beirut: Dār Sādir, 1966, 205 p.
The reflections of a leading Lebanese writer on his experiences in Russia and the United States. He sees their conflict as passing.

Nalin, Iu. and Nikolaev, A. **Sovetskii Soiuz i evropeiskaia bezopasnost'.** Moscow: Izd-vo "Mezhdunarodnye Otnosheniia," 1971, 104 p.
An advertisement for the Soviet conception of a European security system, holding out the prospect of large-scale economic relations between East and West.

Pachter, Henry Maximilian. **Collision Course: The Cuban Missile Crisis and Coexistence.** New York: Praeger, 1963, 261 p.
A short study of the Cuban missile crisis and its implications for the nuclear age, strengthened by documents pertaining to "the momentous events that shook the world in the last two weeks of October, 1962."

Petrov, Fedor Pavlovich. **Mezhdunarodnoe nauchno-tekhnicheskoe sotrudnichestvo: sostoianie, tseli, i perspektivy.** Moscow: Izd-vo "Mezhdunarodnye Otnosheniia," 1971, 357 p.
A summary of the Soviet conception of the nature and possibilities of technical and scientific coöperation among nations, including the capitalist states of Western Europe and North America.

Planck, Charles R. **Sicherheit in Europa: die Vorschläge für Rüstungsbeschränkung und Abrüstung 1955–1965.** Munich: R. Oldenbourg (for the Deutsche Gesellschaft für Auswärtige Politik), 1968, 224 p.
An American scholar analyzes the proposals for the renunciation of force and arms control in Europe in the decade from 1955 to 1965.

Popov, Viktor Ivanovich., *ed.* **Sovetskaia vneshnaia politika i evropeiskaia bezopasnost'.** Moscow: Izd-vo "Mezhdunarodnye Otnosheniia," 1972, 253 p.
A discussion of the Soviet proposals for a European security system.

Power, Thomas Sarsfield with Arnhym, Albert A. **Design for Survival.** New York: Coward-McCann, 1965, 255 p.
The retired Commander in Chief of the U.S. Strategic Air Command urges the need for the maintenance of overwhelming military superiority in face of the continuing Communist militancy.

Quester, George H. **Nuclear Diplomacy: The First Twenty-Five Years.** New York: Dunellen (for the Center for International Affairs, Harvard University), 1971, 327 p.
An analytical study of the Soviet-American nuclear relationship since the end of World War II.

Rock, Vincent P. **A Strategy of Interdependence.** New York: Scribner, 1964, 399 p.
An ambitious and serious effort to devise a strategy, and an international setting for it, that may help control international conflict and more particularly the U.S.-Soviet confrontation. The author's basic premise is of international society as a rapidly developing community.

Rotblat, Joseph. **Pugwash—The First Ten Years: History of the Conferences of Science and World Affairs.** New York: Humanities Press, 1968, 244 p.
A systematic survey of the evolution, organization and activities of the Pugwash conferences at which leading scientists from both East and West discuss disarmament and other important contemporary political and social problems.

Rubinstein, Alvin Zachary and Ginsburgs, George, *eds.* **Soviet and American Policies in the United Nations: A Twenty-Five-Year Perspective.** New York: New York University Press, 1971, 211 p.
A thoughtful assessment of superpower relations at the United Nations during the recent past.

Sakharov, Andrei Dmitrievich. **Progress, Coexistence, and Intellectual Freedom.** New York: Norton, 1968, 158 p.
: An eloquent plea for superpower collaboration as the key to a better world, by an outstanding Soviet scientist. Capably annotated by Harrison E. Salisbury. The Russian original appeared as "Razmyshlenia o progresse, mirnom sosyshchestvovanii i intellektual'noi svobode" (Frankfurt: Possev, 1968, 61 p.).

Seabury, Paul. **The Rise and Decline of the Cold War.** New York: Basic Books, 1967, 171 p.
: The author locates the beginnings of the cold war—which he regards as a specific historical phenomenon—in 1946 or 1947. The book complements the one by Louis J. Halle. While factually not as thorough, it is conceptually somewhat more daring. Prepared under the auspices of the Center for International Affairs, Harvard University.

Stanley, Timothy W. and Whitt, Darnell M. **Detente Diplomacy: United States and European Security in the 1970's.** New York: Dunellen (for the Atlantic Council of the United States), 1970, 170 p.
: An historical analysis of the main problems confronting the architects of East-West détente in Europe.

Steinicke, Dietrich with Harbeck, Wolfdieter. **Quellenindex zur Cubakrise.** Frankfurt/Main: Metzner (for the Forschungsstelle für Völkerrecht und ausländisches öffentliches Recht der Universität Hamburg), 1969, 400 p.
: A guide to the published official documents dealing with the 1962 Cuban missile crisis.

Stoessinger, John George. **Nations in Darkness: China, Russia, and America.** New York: Random House, 1971, 197 p.
: The author presents ten original case studies in Chinese-American and Russo-American relations which demonstrate how misperceptions of "the other side" have led to disaster in the recent past. A set of guidelines to statesmen who wish to avoid such pitfalls concludes the book.

Wesson, Robert Gale. **The American Problem: The Cold War in Perspective.** New York: Abelard-Schuman, 1963, 288 p.
: The author argues that the American influence in the world is in a state of decline.

Whitton, John Boardman, ed. **Propaganda and the Cold War: A Princeton University Symposium.** Washington: Public Affairs Press, 1963, 119 p.
: These papers dealing chiefly with American propaganda efforts, achievements and shortcomings in the setting of the cold war present quite diverse views.

Willrich, Mason. **Non-Proliferation Treaty: Framework for Nuclear Arms Control.** Charlottesville: Michie Co., 1969, 341 p.
: In the words of the author, Professor of Law at the University of Virginia, "The purpose of this book is to analyze the Non-Proliferation Treaty, to ascertain its meaning and explore its potentialities in terms of the specific problems which will be encountered if it is implemented."

Wolfers, Arnold, ed. **Changing East-West Relations and the Unity of the West.** Baltimore: Johns Hopkins Press, 1964, 242 p.
: The existence and nature of détente, the Sino-Soviet dispute and future prospects are discussed in eight papers presented to the European-American Colloquium at the Washington Center of Foreign Policy Research in May 1964.

Trade and Economic Problems

See also Economic Factors, p. 49; (The Postwar World) General, p. 178; Western Defense; North Atlantic Treaty; Atlantic Community, p. 188; (Latin America) Economic and Social Problems, p. 208; (The United States) Trade, Tariffs and Finance, p. 251; Aid and Assistance, p. 254; (Western Europe) Economic and Social Problems, p. 347; Council for Mutual Economic Assistance; Warsaw Treaty Organization, p. 365; (Union of Soviet Socialist Republics) Foreign Economic Policy, p. 560.

Adler-Karlsson, Gunnar. **Western Economic Warfare 1947–1967: A Case Study in Foreign Economic Policy.** Stockholm: Almqvist, 1968, 319 p.
: A study of the American led effort to restrict exports to the communist countries. Critical in tone, it is careful in its use of evidence.

Berg, Michael von. **Die strategische Bedeutung des Ost-West-Handels im Rahmen der weltpolitischen Auseinandersetzung.** Leyden: Sijthoff, 1966, 205 p.

A summary of communist ideas about foreign trade and some useful statistics.

Domdey, Karl Heinz and Others. **Gegenwartsprobleme der internationalen Handelsbeziehungen.** Berlin: Verlag Die Wirtschaft, 1964, 300 p.

An East German collection of essays on East-West trade and on international trade and monetary organizations.

Dopfer, Kurt. **Ost-West-Konvergenz.** Zurich: Polygraphischer Verlag, 1970, 571 p.

The author of this wide-ranging survey examines the problem of the convergence of the economic systems of East and West.

Lange-Prollius, Horst. **Ostwesthandel für die 70er Jahre.** Bad Harzburg: Verlag für Wissenschaft, Wirtschaft und Technik, 1971, 467 p.

A *vade mecum* for East-West trade by an experienced businessman.

Pisar, Samuel. **Coexistence and Commerce: Guidelines for Transactions Between East and West.** New York: McGraw-Hill, 1970, 558 p.

A comprehensive treatise on doing business with Russia and Eastern Europe. The author, an American lawyer based in Europe, concludes by proposing a "code of fair practices" for the future. About half the book is on legal matters.

Sawyer, Carole A. **Communist Trade with Developing Countries: 1955-65.** New York: Praeger, 1966, 126 p.

A useful study that gives all the statistics but goes beyond them to interpret what has not happened in a segment of trade where appraisals are more likely to be politically distorted than rationally balanced.

Standke, Klaus-Heinrich. **Der Handel mit dem Osten: die Wirtschaftsbeziehungen mit den Staatshandelsländern.** Baden-Baden: Nomos, 2d rev. ed., 1972, 327 p.

A thorough, detailed survey of East-West trade.

Uren, Philip E., *ed.* **East-West Trade.** Toronto: Canadian Institute of International Affairs, 1966, 181 p.

A symposium in which Canadians (and a few Americans) discuss economic, strategic and legal aspects of trade with the Communist countries and examine the prospects for its expansion.

Wasowski, Stanislaw, *ed.* **East-West Trade and the Technology Gap: A Political and Economic Appraisal.** New York: Praeger (in coöperation with the Institute for Defense Analyses), 1970, 214 p.

Interesting papers with detailed material on the state of technology in Eastern Europe and its bearing on trade, economic reforms and coöperation among the Eastern countries and between them and the West.

Wilczynski, Jozef. **The Economics and Politics of East-West Trade.** New York: Praeger, 1969, 416 p.

A comprehensive but uneven survey by an Australian scholar.

THE THIRD WORLD; NONALIGNMENT

See also General Works, p. 1; Political Factors, p. 12; Economic Factors, p. 49; (Internal Law) Miscellaneous, p. 83; International Organization and Government, p. 96; (The United States) Foreign Policy, p. 229; (Union of Soviet Socialist Republics) Foreign Policy, p. 550; Rumania, p. 588; (Jugoslavia) The Tito Regime, p. 594; (Middle East) The Arab World, p. 616; (India) Foreign Policy, 666; (China) Foreign Relations, p. 702; (Africa) International Relations, p. 784.

Aćimović, Ljubivoje, *ed.* **Nonalignment in the World of Today.** Belgrade: Institute of International Politics and Economics, 1969, 274 p.

A multifaceted view of nonalignment, by a group of leading scholars, predominantly from small and middle powers.

Burton, John Wear, *ed.* **Nonalignment.** New York: James H. Heineman, 1967, 142 p.

This volume contains eight short essays on the political and economic aspects of nonalignment in Africa and Asia.

Crabb, Cecil Van Meter, Jr. **The Elephants and the Grass: A Study of Nonalignment.** New York: Praeger, 1965, 237 p.
Arguing that most Western views of nonalignment or neutralism are prejudiced or cliché-ridden, the author makes a sympathetic study of the neutralist credo. The title is explained by the African proverb: When two elephants fight, it is the grass that suffers.

Gafurov, B. G. and Others, *eds.* **Natsional'no-osvoboditel'noe dvizhenie v Azii i Afrike.** Moscow: Glavnaia Redaktsiia Vostochnoi Literatury, 1967–68, 3 v.
A Soviet history of colonialism and national liberation movements in Asia and Africa.

Grubbe, Peter, *pseud.* (Klaus Volkmann). **Herrscher von Morgen? Macht und Ohnmacht der blockfreien Welt.** Düsseldorf: Econ-Verlag, 1964, 411 p.
A German correspondent's report on and appraisal of the peoples and nations of the Third World.

Jansen, G. H. **Nonalignment and the Afro-Asian States.** New York: Praeger, 1966, 432 p.
An Indian journalist tells of the steps by which a number of newly independent countries of Asia and Africa came to adopt the practice of nonalignment vis-à-vis the "imperial" powers.

Labin, Suzanne. **Le Tiers Monde entre l'est et l'ouest: vivre en dollars, voter en roubles.** Paris: Éditions de la Table Ronde, 1964, 235 p.
The author argues that the communists are gaining adherents in the underdeveloped countries not because they give more economic aid, but because they concentrate on propaganda and the support for pro-communist groups and individuals.

Lacouture, Jean. **The Demigods: Charismatic Leadership in the Third World.** New York: Knopf, 1970, 300 p.
This is a successful effort to apply the Weberian charisma analysis to four Third World leaders: Nasser, Nkrumah, Sihanouk and Bourguiba. The author is also indebted to the "psychohistorical" approach of Erik Erikson. Translation of "Quatre hommes et leurs peuples" (Paris: Éditions du Seuil, 1969, 282 p.).

Lavrishchev, A. A. and Others, *eds.* **Razvivaiushchiesia strany v mirovoi politike.** Moscow: Izd-vo "Nauka," 1970, 260 p.
A Soviet study of the role of the developing countries in world politics.

London, Kurt, *ed.* **New Nations in a Divided World: The International Relations of the Afro-Asian States.** New York: Praeger (for the Institute for Sino-Soviet Studies, George Washington University), 1964, 336 p.
Papers presented at an international conference in Athens in September 1962 on various political problems of the Afro-Asian states and their relations with the Communist bloc.

Mates, Leo. **Nonalignment: Theory and Current Policy.** Dobbs Ferry (N.Y.): Oceana, 1972, 543 p.
In the wake of great-power détente and increasing divergence among the nonaligned countries, the former Jugoslav Ambassador to the United States seeks to restore the faith, and, one might add, Jugoslav leadership, of the nonaligned world.

Miller, John Donald Bruce. **The Politics of the Third World.** New York: Oxford University Press (for the Royal Institute of International Affairs), 1967, 126 p.
A balanced though somewhat cursory survey, by an Australian scholar, of the disparate policies of the Afro-Asian countries. Whatever unity of purpose one perceives in these nations, the author contends, exists not in their politics but in their common quest for economic development.

Miller, Norman and Aya, Roderick, *eds.* **National Liberation: Revolution in the Third World.** New York: Free Press, 1971, 307 p.
Eight essays on revolutionary movements in different Third World countries. The quality of the contributions is uniformly high.

Mirskii, G. I. **Armiia i politika v stranakh Azii i Afriki.** Moscow: Izd-vo "Nauka," 1970, 348 p.
A study on the role of the military in the developing countries by a leading Soviet expert on the Middle East.

Modrzhinskaia, Elena Dmitrievna. **Raspad kolonial'noi sistemy i ideologiia imperializma.** Moscow: Izd-vo "Nauka," 1965, 341 p.
    A Soviet study of how "imperialist" countries are trying to reëstablish their influence in the countries of the Third World.

Queuille, Pierre. **Histoire de l'afro-asiatisme jusqu'à Bandoung: la naissance du tiers-monde.** Paris: Payot, 1965, 326 p.
    A study by a French diplomat of the political trend toward an Afro-Asian bloc in the decades leading up to Bandung. A part of the book is devoted to the Afro-Asian group in the U.N.

Rossi, Mario. **The Third World: The Unaligned Countries and the World Revolution.** New York: Funk & Wagnalls, 1963, 209 p.
    A study, based largely on interviews, of the attitude of the leaders of the unaligned countries to the international situation, the cold war and the U.N.

Schröder, Dieter. **Die Konferenzen der "Dritten Welt": Solidarität und Kommunikation zwischen nachkolonialen Staaten.** Hamburg: Forschungsstelle für Völkerrecht und Ausländisches Öffentliches Recht der Universität Hamburg, 1968, 343 p.
    An informative survey of the anti-colonial and solidarity movements in the Third World, especially since World War II.

Shchetinin, Valentin Dmitrievich, *ed.* **Ekonomicheskoe planirovanie i diplomatiia: rol' mezhdunarodnykh otnoshenii, vneshnei politiki i diplomatii v planirovanii razvitiia molodykh natsional'nykh gosudarstv.** Moscow: Izd-vo "Mezhdunarodnye Otnosheniia," 1970, 279 p.
    A group of Soviet analysts assesses the degree to which the foreign policy aims of developing countries are conditioned by requirements of obtaining capital investment and trade stability.

Smets, Paul F. **De Bandoeng à Moshi: contribution à l'étude des conférences afro-asiatiques (1955–1963).** Brussels: Université Libre de Bruxelles, Institut de Sociologie, 1964, 154 p.
    A detailed and well-documented evaluation of the achievements of the conferences of Bandung, Cairo, Conakry, Belgrade and Moshi.

Thornton, Thomas Perry, *ed.* **The Third World in Soviet Perspective.** Princeton: Princeton University Press, 1964, 355 p.
    A sample of Soviet writings on the problems of the developing areas in Asia, Africa and Latin America.

Worsley, Peter. **The Third World.** Chicago: University of Chicago Press, 1965, 317 p.
    Sympathizing with the grievances, ideas and aspirations of the people of the underdeveloped part of the world, and believing in the need for social revolution, the author, a British sociologist, discusses the new international role of the Third World.

WESTERN DEFENSE; NORTH ATLANTIC TREATY; ATLANTIC COMMUNITY

See also Internation Organization and Government, p. 96; War and Peace, p. 108; (The United States) Biographies, Memoirs and Addresses, p. 218; Foreign Policy, p. 229; Military and Defense Policy, p. 257; (Canada) Foreign Relations, p. 282; Military Policy, p. 285; Western Europe, p. 345; (Great Britain) Biographies, Memoirs and Addresses, p. 369; Foreign Policy, p. 375; Military Policy, p. 378; (France) Biographies, Memoirs and Addresses, p. 400; Foreign Policy, p. 404; Military Policy, p. 407; (Italy) Foreign Policy, p. 424; (Germany) Post-World War II Era, p. 487; Berlin, p. 493; Federal Republic of Germany, p. 495; (Greece) Foreign Relations, p. 606; (Turkey) Foreign Relations, p. 625; (Australia and New Zealand) General, p. 766.

Alting von Geusau, Frans A. M., *ed.* **NATO and Security in the Seventies.** Lexington (Mass.): Heath, 1971, 158 p.
    Papers dealing with NATO's ability to meet certain regional and crisis situations in the next decade.

Amme, Carl H., Jr. **NATO without France: A Strategic Appraisal.** Stanford: Hoover Institution on War, Revolution, and Peace, 1967, 195 p.

Leaning heavily on the "graduated deterrence" thesis developed by Henry Kissinger in "Nuclear Weapons and Foreign Policy" in 1957, the author argues that NATO should be prepared to use tactical nuclear weapons to prevent major conventional wars.

Das atlantische Dilemma: Aggressivität und Krise der NATO, 1949–1969. Berlin: Staatsverlag der DDR (for the Deutsches Institut für Zeitgeschichte), 1969, 469 p.
An East German interpretation of NATO.

Beaufre, André. **NATO and Europe.** New York: Knopf, 1966, 170 p.
Suggestions on how to solve the NATO crisis and to improve American-European relations, by a noted French military strategist. Originally published as "L'O.T.A.N. et l'Europe" (Paris: Calmann-Lévy, 1966, 239 p.).

Beer, Francis A. **Integration and Disintegration in NATO.** Columbus: Ohio State University Press, 1969, 330 p.
A solid and thorough study concentrating on organizational and administrative problems faced by the alliance.

Bell, Coral. **The Debatable Alliance.** New York: Oxford University Press (for the Royal Institute of International Affairs), 1964, 130 p.
An Australian scholar examines with much perception the tribulations of Anglo-American relations "as an element in the central power-balance."

Broekmeijer, M. W. J. M. **Developing Countries and N.A.T.O.** Dobbs Ferry (N.Y.): Oceana Publications, 1963, 208 p.
A Dutch air force officer studies the strategic, economic and political importance of the developing nations to the Atlantic Community and NATO defense. The relationship is recognized as important but no very startling conclusions emerge.

Buchan, Alastair Francis and Windsor, Philip. **Arms and Stability in Europe.** New York: Praeger (for the Institute for Strategic Studies, London), 1963, 236 p.
A discussion of the present confrontation, and future prospects for lessening tensions, between NATO and the Warsaw Pact countries.

Burrows, Sir Bernard and Irwin, Christopher. **The Security of Western Europe: Towards a Common Defence Policy.** London: Charles Knight, 1972, 189 p.
An eloquent and informed study by a former British ambassador to NATO and the Deputy Director of the U.K. Federal Trust. The authors believe in the need for greater defense coördination because of the East-West negotiations on security and the evolution of the Common Market, and call for the eventual establishment of a European Defense Agency.

Catlin, George Edward Gordon. **The Stronger Community.** New York: Hawthorn Books, 1967, 217 p.
A plea for a stronger Atlantic Community and a forceful attack on both the personality and the policies of General de Gaulle. The English edition was entitled "The Grandeur of England and the Atlantic Community" (Oxford: Pergamon, 1966, 217 p.).

Cerny, Karl H. and Briefs, Henry W., *eds.* **NATO in Quest of Cohesion.** New York: Praeger (for the Hoover Institution on War, Revolution, and Peace), 1965, 476 p.
The record of a conference on many aspects of NATO's future, comprising excerpts from actual discussions and specially prepared papers on various topics by 23 qualified authors.

Cleveland, Harlan. **NATO: The Transatlantic Bargain.** New York: Harper and Row, 1970, 204 p.
An intelligent and pragmatic political analysis of alliance management between the United States and its European allies.

Cooper, Richard N. **The Economics of Interdependence: Economic Policy in the Atlantic Community.** New York: McGraw-Hill (for the Council on Foreign Relations), 1968, 302 p.
A stimulating and original study by a former U.S. Deputy Assistant Secretary of State, now a professor at Yale University.

Cottrell, Alvin J. and Dougherty, James E. **The Politics of the Atlantic Alliance.** New York: Praeger, 1964, 264 p.
A concise but useful political guide. The British edition was entitled "The Atlantic Alliance: A Short Political Guide" (London: Pall Mall, 1964, 264 p.).

Cromwell, William C., ed. **Political Problems of Atlantic Partnership: National Perspectives.** Bruges: College of Europe, 1969, 458 p.

A look at the Atlantic Community from the American, British and German points of view.

Deutsch, Karl Wolfgang. **Arms Control and the Atlantic Alliance: Europe Faces Coming Policy Decisions.** New York: Wiley, 1967, 167 p.

The author has employed quantitative research methods and élite interviews in Germany and France to arrive at his findings.

Freund, Ludwig. **Politische Waffen: Grundkonzeptionen der westlichen Verteidigungsstrategie.** Frankfurt/Main: Bernard und Graefe, 1966, 280 p.

Reflections on the political and military strategies that have been developed by the United States and its allies for confronting the Soviet threat to the Western world. The author is particularly critical of the views of those whom he calls the "neo-isolationists": George Kennan, Walter Lippmann, Hans Morgenthau, Jr. and J. William Fulbright.

Furniss, Edgar Stephenson, Jr., ed. **The Western Alliance: Its Status and Prospects.** Columbus: Ohio State University Press, 1965, 182 p.

A collection of papers prepared for colloquia at Ohio State University and dealing with a number of problems relative to NATO—its military features, the role of certain members and its prospects.

Herter, Christian Archibald. **Toward an Atlantic Community.** New York: Harper and Row (for the Council on Foreign Relations), 1963, 107 p.

The late U.S. Secretary of State pleads the cause of Atlantic solidarity through the greater unity of Western Europe and a partnership between Europe and the United States.

Houssiaux, Jacques, ed. **Les Politiques économiques dans la zone atlantique.** Paris: Sirey, 1970, 303 p.

Articles on international economic relations and organizations in the Western World presented at a conference of the International Economic Association in September 1969.

Hunter, Robert Edwards. **Security in Europe.** Bloomington: Indiana University Press, 2d ed., 1972, 281 p.

A revised edition of a study, first published in 1969, in which the author "undertakes to explore some of the major questions raised by the development of security for the European Continent in the years following the Second World War."

Ipsen, Knut. **Rechtsgrundlagen und Institutionalisierung der atlantisch-westeuropäischen Verteidigung.** Hamburg: Hansischer Gildenverlag (for the Institut für internationales Recht an der Universität Kiel), 1967, 223 p.

A legal study of the supranational organs of Western defense.

Jackson, Henry Martin, ed. **The Atlantic Alliance.** New York: Praeger, 1967, 309 p.

Testimony on NATO before the Jackson Subcommittee of the U.S. Senate by Richard E. Neustadt, Dean Acheson, Christian A. Herter, Lauris Norstad, Thomas C. Schelling, Malcolm W. Hoag, John J. McCloy, Dean Rusk and Robert S. McNamara.

Jordan, Robert S. **The NATO International Staff/Secretariat 1952-1957: A Study in International Administration.** New York: Oxford University Press, 1967, 307 p.

A substantial study of Lord Ismay's impact on the NATO Staff/Secretariat.

Kissinger, Henry Alfred. **The Troubled Partnership: A Re-appraisal of the Atlantic Alliance.** New York: McGraw-Hill (for the Council on Foreign Relations), 1965, 266 p.

In this volume in "The Atlantic Policy Studies," sponsored by the Council on Foreign Relations, a leading student of U.S. foreign and military policy and subsequently the Secretary of State in the Nixon and Ford administrations re-examines the Atlantic Alliance, its structural problems, the major political and strategic issues and the prospects for the future.

McCloy, John Jay. **The Atlantic Alliance: Its Origin and Its Future.** New York: Columbia University Press (for Carnegie-Mellon University), 1969, 83 p.

A reasoned case for the continuing existence and development of NATO as the best guarantor of peaceful U.S.-Soviet relations.

Middleton, Drew. **The Atlantic Community: A Study in Unity and Disunity.** New York: McKay, 1965, 303 p.
A *New York Times* correspondent's informed but rather pessimistic account of the problems confronting the Atlantic Community.

Munk, Frank. **Atlantic Dilemma: Partnership or Community?** Dobbs Ferry (N.Y.): Oceana Publications, 1964, 177 p.
An analysis of the various schemes for increasing political integration in the Atlantic Community. The author, a professor of political science, was a Research Fellow at the Atlantic Institute in Paris, which sponsored this study, from 1961 to 1962.

Neustadt, Richard E. **Alliance Politics.** New York: Columbia University Press, 1970, 167 p.
A most illuminating book on crisis politics in NATO. The author deals with Anglo-American relations during the Suez crisis and with the Skybolt affair.

Newhouse, John and Others. **U.S. Troops in Europe: Issues, Costs, and Choices.** Washington: Brookings Institution, 1971, 177 p.
The authors of this balanced work conclude that there is a continuing need for a substantial number of U.S. forces in Europe and recommend a number of steps to share the cost more evenly.

Pfaltzgraff, Robert L., Jr. **The Atlantic Community: A Complex Imbalance.** New York: Van Nostrand Reinhold, 1969, 216 p.
A succinct history of NATO, with emphasis on the U.S.-European relationship. The author is heavily indebted to Henry Kissinger's "The Troubled Partnership."

Planck, Charles R. **Sicherheit in Europa: Die Vorschläge für Rüstungsbeschränkung und Abrüstung, 1955–1965.** Munich: Oldenbourg (for the Deutsche Gesellschaft für Auswärtige Politik), 1968, 224 p.
In this study an American scholar attempts to review systematically and critically the proposals dealing with European security and disarmament in the decade from 1955 to 1965.

Richardson, James L. **Germany and the Atlantic Alliance: The Interaction of Strategy and Politics.** Cambridge: Harvard University Press (for the Center for International Affairs, Harvard University), 1966, 403 p.
A study of the interrelationships of "the orientation of Germany and the political and strategic implications of nuclear weapons," by a British scholar.

Ruge, Friedrich, **Politik, Militär, Bündnis.** Stuttgart: Deutsche Verlags-Anstalt, 1963, 157 p.
Admiral Ruge analyzes specific historical examples of the relationship between the military and the political and discusses the contemporary concern over the role of the military in the NATO organization.

Schneider, Fernand Marie Thiébaut. **Stratégie pour l'occident: l'U.R.S.S. dans l'OTAN? Essai politique et militaire.** Paris: Charles-Lavauzelle, 1965, 214 p.
Reflections on NATO and Western defense concepts, by a French military expert who is a keen advocate of the Atlantic Community.

Stanley, Timothy W. **NATO in Transition: The Future of the Atlantic Alliance.** New York: Praeger (for the Council on Foreign Relations), 1965, 417 p.
The author, a former high civilian official of the U.S. Defense Department, argues that NATO should be transformed from an alliance cemented by fear to a partnership for building a stable world based on hope.

Stehlin, Paul. **Retour à zéro: l'Europe et sa défense dans le compte à rebours.** Paris: Laffont, 1968, 387 p.
Reflections on European defense, East-West relations and French foreign policy, by a French officer who before World War II was a military attaché in Berlin and who from 1960 to 1963 was Chief of Staff of the French Air Force.

Sternberg Montaldi, Annamaria. **Le Rôle de l'opinion publique dans la Communauté Atlantique.** Leyden: Sijthoff, 1963, 291 p.
A faculty member of the University of Florence has made a study of mass opinion in 13 NATO countries to determine what people think of NATO and its purposes and to ascertain what media shape their opinions.

Strauch, Rudolf. **Die atlantische Wirtschaftszusammenarbeit.** Zurich: Polygraphischer Verlag, 1970, 331 p.
A useful if rather elaborately organized account of private efforts and public accomplishments in Atlantic economic coöperation.

Strausz-Hupé, Robert and Others. **Building the Atlantic World.** New York: Harper and Row, 1963, 400 p.
An inquiry into the history of the North Atlantic Alliance and a plea for "the Atlantic Community, the Closer Union," as a successor to NATO.

Szent-Miklósy, István. **The Atlantic Union Movement: Its Significance in World Politics.** New York: Fountainhead Publishers, 1965, 264 p.
A description of the historical development, cultural foundations, economic and political objectives of the Atlantic Union movement, by a Hungarian émigré scholar.

Von Riekhoff, Harald. **NATO: Issues and Prospects.** Toronto: Canadian Institute of International Affairs, 1967, 170 p.
An intelligent analysis by a Canadian scholar of NATO's possible contributions toward East-West détente in Europe.

Westeuropäische Verteidigungskooperation. Munich: Oldenbourg (for the Deutsche Gesellschaft für Auswärtige Politik), 1972, 256 p.
A detailed examination, from a West German perspective, of the opportunities and pitfalls of European defense coöperation—in both nuclear weapons and conventional armaments.

Wilcox, Francis Orlando and Haviland, Henry Field, Jr., *eds.* **The Atlantic Community: Progress and Prospects.** New York: Praeger, 1963, 294 p.
A symposium by a number of distinguished and competent European and American contributors.

THIRD PART:

THE WORLD BY REGIONS

I. THE WESTERN HEMISPHERE

GENERAL

INTER-AMERICAN RELATIONS

General

See also the sections for specific countries and regions.

Aguilar Monteverde, Alonso. **Pan-Americanism from Monroe to the Present.** New York: Monthly Review Press, 1968, 192 p.
A revised English version of an anti-United States account of American policies toward Latin America. The original was published as "El panamericanismo de la doctrina Monroe a la doctrina Johnson" (Mexico City: Cuadernos Americanos, 1965, 186 p.).

Arévalo, Juan José. **Anti-Kommunism in Latin America: An X-ray of the Process Leading to a New Colonialism.** New York: Lyle Stuart, 1964, 224 p.
An attack on American foreign policies and the traditional Latin American power elites, by the former President of Guatemala. The original was published as "Antikomunismo en América Latina: radiografía del proceso hacia una nueva colonización" (Havana: Ediciones la Tertulia, 3rd ed., 1960, 206 p.).

Astiz, Carlos Alberto with McCarthy, Mary F., *eds.* **Latin American International Politics.** Notre Dame: University of Notre Dame Press, 1969, 343 p.
Sixteen authors describe various aspects of the foreign policies of Mexico, Brazil and Argentina.

Barber, Willard Foster and Ronning, C. Neale. **Internal Security and Military Power: Counterinsurgency and Civic Action in Latin America.** Columbus: Ohio State University Press, 1966, 338 p.
In this study of United States policies toward Latin America the authors examine the contradiction resulting from economic programs designed to promote social reform and military assistance deemed necessary for internal security.

Barclay, Glen St. John. **Struggle for a Continent: The Diplomatic History of South America, 1917-1945.** New York: New York University Press, 1972, 213 p.
An introductory survey by an Australian scholar.

Barnes, William Sprague and Others. **Tax Policy on United States Investment in Latin America.** Princeton: Tax Institute of America, 1963, 275 p.
A symposium of papers by an able group of specialists.

Belaúnde, Víctor Andrés. **20 años de Naciones Unidas.** Madrid: Ediciones Cultura Hispánica, 1966, 398 p.
A Peruvian diplomat analyzes the development of the United Nations and the crises it has faced in the first 20 years. He also discusses Latin American relations with the United Nations.

Bethel, Paul D. **The Losers.** New Rochelle: Arlington House, 1969, 615 p.
A strong indictment of U.S. foreign policy toward Cuba and Latin America. The author, who was press officer at the U.S. Embassy in Havana when relations with Cuba were broken, is convinced that the final target of the communists is the conquest of the United States itself.

Burr, Robert N. **Our Troubled Hemisphere: Perspectives on United States–Latin American Relations.** Washington: Brookings Institution, 1967, 256 p.
In this historical study the author concludes that solutions for improvement lie in a stronger O.A.S., a strengthened Alliance for Progress and a better understanding by the United States of its hemispheric neighbors.

Callcott, Wilfrid Hardy. **The Western Hemisphere: Its Influence on United States Policies to the End of World War II.** Austin: University of Texas Press, 1968, 506 p.
In the words of the author, a professor at the University of South Carolina, this study is "an effort to sketch the frequently erratic steps that led in the direction of a hemisphere policy for the United States as it attempted to meet the changing conditions that developed by the middle of the twentieth century."

Ciria, Alberto. **Cambio y estancamiento en América Latina.** Buenos Aires: Editorial Jorge Alvarez, 1967, 164 p.
An analysis of the forces causing and obstructing change in Latin America, with a discussion of what role the United States can play in Latin American development.

Cosío Villegas, Daniel. **American Extremes.** Austin: University of Texas Press, 1964, 227 p.
Essays by an influential Mexican intellectual examining some of Latin America's internal and external problems. In the author's view, while the United States has increased its political and economic hegemony in the Western hemisphere, it has also "become the most persuasive exponent of the worst faults of Western civilization and the weakest exponent of its best achievements."

Cúneo, Dardo. **La batalla de América Latina.** Buenos Aires: Ediciones Siglo Veinte, 1964, 239 p.
Observations on U.S.-Latin American relations, by a former Argentine diplomat and political commentator.

Eisenhower, Milton Stover. **The Wine Is Bitter: The United States and Latin America.** Garden City: Doubleday, 1963, 342 p.
A report of Dr. Eisenhower's extensive activities and observations in Latin America during his brother's administration.

Franco, Pablo. **La influencia de los Estados Unidos en América Latina.** Montevideo: Ediciones Tauro, 1967, 130 p.
A critique of United States cultural, political and economic influence in Latin America.

García Robles, Alfonso. **The Denuclearization of Latin America.** New York: Carnegie Endowment for International Peace, 1967, 167 p.
A discussion of a 1963 proposal for the creation of a nuclear free zone in Latin America. Spanish original: "La desnuclearización de la América Latina" (Mexico City: Colegio de México, 2d rev. ed., 1966, 154 p.).

Glinkin, Anatolii Nikolaevich and Others, *eds.* **Strany Latinskoi Ameriki v sovremennykh mezhdunarodnykh otnosheniakh.** Moscow: Izd-vo "Nauka," 1967, 510 p.
A comprehensive Soviet assessment of international relations in Latin America.

Goldhamer, Herbert, **The Foreign Powers in Latin America.** Princeton: Princeton University Press (for the RAND Corporation), 1972, 321 p.
A detailed and scholarly volume.

Green, David. **The Containment of Latin America.** Chicago: Quadrangle Books, 1971, 370 p.
The theme: the Good Neighbor policy failed because FDR and Truman used it to strengthen U.S. control over Latin American economies, thereby intensifying nationalism and instability.

Grunwald, Joseph and Others. **Latin American Economic Integration and U.S. Policy.** Washington: Brookings Institution, 1972, 216 p.
A useful survey.

Herrera Lane, Felipe. **Nacionalismo, regionalismo, internacionalismo: América Latina en el contexto internacional.** Buenos Aires: Banco Interamericano de Desarrollo, Instituto para la Integración de América Latina, 1970, 449 p.
A collection of speeches and articles on Latin America's role in the world economic system, by the President of the Inter-American Development Bank from 1960 to 1970.

Hirsch-Weber, Wolfgang. **Lateinamerika: Abhängigkeit und Selbstbestimmung.** Opalden: Leske (for the Deutsche Gesellschaft für Auswärtige Politik), 1972, 170 p.
A well-researched survey of the international relations of the Latin American countries, with emphasis on the role of the United States on the subcontinent.

Kane, William Everett. **Civil Strife in Latin America: A Legal History of U.S. Involvement.** Baltimore: Johns Hopkins University Press, 1972, 240 p.
The author of this excellent work sees U.S. interventions in Latin America resulting primarily from strategic rather than economic concerns.

Lieuwen, Edwin. **U.S. Policy in Latin America: A Short History.** New York: Praeger, 1965, 149 p.
This brief and factual historical account of U.S. hemispheric policies stresses the "ever-increasing United States concern over Latin America."

Lodge, George Cabot. **Engines of Change: United States Interests and Revolution in Latin America.** New York: Knopf, 1970, 411 p.
An eloquent plea for the alignment of the United States with the forces of nontotalitarian revolutionary change in politics, religion and society, with proposals for new administrative techniques and structures.

MacEoin, Gary. **Revolution Next Door: Latin America in the 1970s.** New York: Holt, Rinehart and Winston, 1971, 243 p.
Critical reflections on American involvement in Latin America by an Irish-born American journalist.

Manger, William, ed. **The Two Americas: Dialogue on Progress and Problems.** New York: Kenedy, 1965, 144 p.
Lectures delivered at Georgetown University during 1963 and 1964, in which six distinguished statesmen and Latin American specialists discuss contemporary inter-American problems.

Morrison, DeLesseps Story. **Latin American Mission: An Adventure in Hemisphere Diplomacy.** New York: Simon and Schuster, 1965, 288 p.
These first-hand accounts and personal reflections, compiled by the late deLesseps Morrison while U.S. Ambassador to the O.A.S. (1961–63), center around the Cuban problem and the Punta del Este Conference.

Munro, Dana Gardner. **Intervention and Dollar Diplomacy in the Caribbean, 1900–1921.** Princeton: Princeton University Press, 1964, 553 p.
A scholarly examination of U.S. foreign policy toward Central America which contends that concern for North American security, and not business interests, guided U.S. actions during the early twentieth century.

Petras, James and LaPorte, Robert, Jr. **Cultivating Revolution: The United States and Agrarian Reform in Latin America.** New York: Random House, 1971, 469 p.
Analysis of agricultural reform in Chile, Peru and Cuba, with the conclusion that only the revolutionary approach to tenure problems will prove adequate.

Queuille, Pierre. **L'Amérique Latine; la doctrine Monroe et le panaméricanisme: le conditionnement historique du Tiers-Monde latino-américain.** Paris: Payot, 1969, 288 p.
A detailed study of the impact of the Monroe Doctrine on Latin American politics and a survey of the development of Pan-American organizations.

Ramírez Necochea, Hernán. **Los Estados Unidos y América Latina, 1930–1965.** Santiago: Editora Austral, 1965, 298 p.
A Marxist interpretation of U.S.-Latin American relations between 1930–1965.

Romualdi, Serafino. **Presidents and Peons: Recollections of a Labor Ambassador in Latin America.** New York: Funk and Wagnalls, 1967, 524 p.
The author, the representative of the American Federation of Labor in Latin America from 1946 to 1965, states that "the main purpose of this book is to highlight the activities and achievements of the United States labor movement in combating the attempts of Communists and other totalitarian forces to gain control of organized labor in Latin America since 1946."

Ronning, C. Neale. **Law and Politics in Inter-American Diplomacy.** New York: Wiley, 1963, 167 p.
A study of contemporary interpretations of inter-American law caused by changing political, social and economic conditions in the Western Hemisphere.

Sanz de Santamaría, Carlos. **Revolución silenciosa.** Mexico City: Fondo de Cultura Económica, 1971, 265 p.
   The author, one-time President of the Inter-American Committee of the Alliance for Progress, discusses Latin America's problems and inter-American relations and argues that coöperation between the United States and Latin America is mutually beneficial.

Shapiro, Samuel, *ed*. **Cultural Factors in Inter-American Relations.** Notre Dame: University of Notre Dame Press, 1968, 368 p.
   Papers presented at the fifth annual meeting of the Catholic Inter-American Coöperation Program.

Tarasov, Konstantin Sergeevich. **SShA i Latinskaia Amerika: voenno-politicheskie i voenno-ekonomicheskie otnosheniia.** Moscow: Izd-vo Politicheskoi Literatury, 1972, 359 p.
   A Soviet criticism of U.S. economic and military policies in Latin America.

Trask, David F. and Others, *comps*. and *eds*. **A Bibliography of United States-Latin American Relations Since 1810.** Lincoln: University of Nebraska Press, 1968, 441 p.
   A valuable annotated bibliography organized chronologically, topically and along national lines.

Trías, Vivian. **Imperialismo y geopolítica en América Latina.** Buenos Aires: Editorial Jorge Alvarez, 1969, 310 p.
   A leftist analysis of the changing nature of United States imperialism in Latin America and of the role of Brazil as a U.S. ally. An appendix deals with the consequences of these developments for Uruguay.

Tulchin, Joseph S. **The Aftermath of War: World War I and U.S. Policy Toward Latin America.** New York: New York University Press, 1971, 287 p.
   The author examines how the securing of petroleum and cables and the providing of bank loans affected U.S. policies toward Latin America during World War I and its immediate aftermath.

Vernon, Raymond, *ed*. **How Latin America Views the U.S. Investor.** New York: Praeger (in coöperation with the Harvard University Graduate School of Business Administration), 1966, 117 p.
   Four papers drawn from the 1965 Leatherbee Lectures at Harvard University examine the impact of foreign investment upon Latin America; the stress is upon the investor's obligations rather than his rights.

Wagner, Robert Harrison. **United States Policy Toward Latin America: A Study in Domestic and International Politics.** Stanford: Stanford University Press, 1970, 246 p.
   The economic policies of the United States toward Latin America between World War II and the coming of the Alliance for Progress are traced in craftsmanlike detail, with particular reference to the effect of American domestic considerations.

Wood, Bryce. **The United States and Latin American Wars, 1932-1942.** New York: Columbia University Press, 1966, 519 p.
   A well-documented, informative and scholarly diplomatic study of the Chaco War, the Leticia dispute and the Marañón conflict. In noting the failure of the United States to prevent violence, given its "narrow view of the range of its obligations," the author relates the general inability to resolve these disputes to the formation of the Organization of American States.

Wright, Theodore Paul. **American Support of Free Elections Abroad.** Washington: Public Affairs Press, 1964, 184 p.
   A survey, through case studies in eight Latin American nations, of American efforts to promote democracy in other countries.

Wythe, George. **The United States and Inter-American Relations.** Gainesville: University of Florida Press, 1964, 251 p.
   This is a sober and analytical study of hemispheric relations and the complex problems posed when one of the partners is so overwhelmingly dominant.

Regional Organizations

See also International Organization and Government, p. 96; and the sections for specific countries and regions.

Agudelo Villa, Hernando. **La Revolución del desarrollo: origen y evolución de la Alianza Para el Progreso.** Mexico City: Editorial Roble, 1966, 453 p.
An analysis of the Alliance for Progress written by one of the nine "wise men" of the Inter-American Committee of the Alliance. The concept of the Alliance is praised, but its actual functioning is criticized.

Alba, Víctor. **Alliance Without Allies: The Mythology of Progress in Latin America.** New York: Praeger, 1965, 244 p.
A translation of "Parásitos, mitos y sordomudos"(Mexico City: Centro de Estudios y Documentacion Sociales, 1964, 287 p.) , this book is a polemical condemnation of the Alliance for Progress. While the author accepts the objectives of the Alliance, he believes these goals have been denied by the actions of the oligarchic élite in Latin America and by U.S. policies which fail to reach the masses.

Ball, Mary Margaret. **The OAS in Transition.** Durham: Duke University Press, 1969, 721 p.
A scholarly treatment—massive, diligent, well-documented—of all aspects of the Organization of American States, past and present.

Canelas O., Amado. **Radiografía de la Alianza para el Atraso.** La Paz: Librería "Altiplano," 1963, 311 p.
A leftist analysis of the Alliance for Progress.

Connell-Smith, Gordon. **The Inter-American System.** New York: Oxford University Press (for the Royal Institute of International Affairs), 1966, 376 p.
The author of this cogent study contends that the United States fostered Pan Americanism primarily to gain Latin American support for its own policy of limiting extra-continental influence in the Western Hemisphere.

Dell, Sidney Samuel. **The Inter-American Development Bank: A Study in Development Financing.** New York: Praeger, 1972, 255 p.
The English author, a long-time U.N. official, concentrates on appraising the performance of the oldest of the regional banks and makes a good case for his view that more innovation and flexibility are needed if the I.D.B. is to keep abreast of current problems.

Dell, Sidney Samuel. **A Latin American Common Market?** New York: Oxford University Press (for the Royal Institute of International Affairs), 1966, 336 p.
In this analysis of the problems facing efforts at regional integration, the author notes that only far-reaching reforms in land tenure, tax structure and distribution of income can insure the success of Latin America's common markets.

Fernández-Shaw, Félix Guillermo. **La Organización de los Estados Americanos (O.E.A.): una nueva visión de América.** Madrid: Ediciones Cultura Hispánica, 2d ed., 1963, 989 p.
An updated edition of a comprehensive work on the history and functioning of the Organization of American States. Contains many documents.

Fuentes Irurozqui, Manuel. **La integración económica de América Latina.** Madrid: Ediciones Cultura Hispánica, 1967, 280 p.
A Spanish economist calls for the inclusion of Spain and Portugal in Latin America's plans for economic integration.

Gardner, Mary A. **The Inter American Press Association: Its Fight for Freedom of the Press, 1926–1960.** Austin: University of Texas Press, 1967, 217 p.
A useful study of a neglected field of inter-American relations, by a professor at Michigan State University.

Garrié Faget, Rodolfo. **Organismos militares interamericanos.** Buenos Aires: Ediciones Depalma, 1968, 102 p.
A description of the various inter-American military organizations.

Gordon, Lincoln. **A New Deal for Latin America.** Cambridge: Harvard University Press, 1963, 146 p.

These lectures, delivered before Brazilian audiences by the President of Johns Hopkins University, the U.S. Ambassador to Brazil from 1961 to 1966, deal with the Alliance for Progress, its purposes, methods and prospects.

Gregg, Robert W., ed. **International Organization in the Western Hemisphere.** Syracuse: Syracuse University Press, 1968, 262 p.
Thoughtful essays critically examining the inter-American system as well as the dominant role played by the United States in hemispheric relations.

Hanson, Simon Gabriel. **Dollar Diplomacy Modern Style: Chapters in the Failure of the Alliance for Progress.** Washington: Inter-American Affairs Press, 1970, 189 p.
Harsh criticism of the Alliance for Progress. The primary indictments concern intervention, confusion of public and private interest and the use of taxpayers' money to bail out investors.

Hanson, Simon Gabriel. **Five Years of the Alliance for Progress.** Washington: Inter-American Affairs Press, 1967, 210 p.
An observer of hemispheric economic development examines in detail the impact which the Alliance for Progress has had upon Latin America. His thoughtful, highly critical assessment is that the program has been used "to reward rather than to penalize resistance to change."

Herrera Lane, Felipe and Others. **Integration in Lateinamerika.** Zurich: Orell Füssli, 1965, 193 p.
An examination of the state of Latin America's common markets by Felipe Herrera, Mateo Magariños de Mello, Abrahán Bennatón and Christoph Eckenstein, along with supplementary documents concerning the organizations of the Latin American Free Trade Association and the Central American Common Market. The contributions are based on papers delivered at a conference in Switzerland in 1964.

Hilton, Ronald, ed. **The Movement Toward Latin American Unity.** New York: Praeger (in coöperation with the California Institute of International Studies), 1969, 561 p.
A collection of articles on almost every aspect of Latin American integration.

Inman, Samuel Guy. **Inter-American Conferences 1826–1954: History and Problems.** Washington: University Press of Washington, D.C., 1965, 282 p.
Published posthumously, this optimistic history of the inter-American system is highlighted by the personal experiences of a man long identified with and sympathetic to Latin America, its people and its problems.

Jiménez Lazcano, Mauro. **Integración económica é imperialismo.** Mexico City: Editorial Nuestro Tiempo, 1968, 163 p.
A study of Latin American economic integration which argues that integration will lead to increased foreign control rather than economic development.

Jose, James R. **An Inter-American Peace Force Within the Framework of the Organization of American States.** Metuchen (N.J.): Scarecrow Press, 1970, 334 p.
The concept of the often-mooted Peace Force is examined from every angle. The author concludes that it is not likely to be conjured into early existence.

Kaplán, Marcos. **Problemas del desarrollo y de la integración en América Latina.** Caracas: Monte Avila Editores, 1968, 255 p.
Essays on development problems and the prospects for economic integration in Latin America.

Kruse-Rodenacker, Albrecht. **Die Interamerikanische Entwicklungsbank.** Hamburg: Übersee-Verlag (for the Institut für Iberoamerika-Kunde, Hamburg), 1968, 116 p.
A brief guide to the history and activities of the Inter-American Development Bank.

Kutzner, Gerhard. **Die Organisation der Amerikanischen Staaten (OAS).** Hamburg: Hansischer Gildenverlag, 1970, 399 p.
A history of inter-American coöperation and a detailed survey of the structure and activities of the Organization of American States.

Levinson, Jerome and Onís, Juan de. **The Alliance That Lost Its Way: A Critical Report on the Alliance for Progress.** Chicago: Quadrangle Books, 1970, 381 p.
The authors conclude that the Alliance attempted too much and that development efforts, properly divorced from security considerations, should concentrate on assistance to countries able and willing to pursue economic and social reforms by democratic means.

Manger, William, ed. **The Alliance for Progress: A Critical Appraisal.** Washington: Public Affairs Press, 1963, 131 p.
  Papers from a conference on Latin America at Georgetown University in June 1961.

Maritano, Nino and Obaid, Antonio H. **An Alliance for Progress: The Challenge and the Problem.** Minneapolis: T. S. Denison and Co., 1963, 205 p.
  This study on the Alliance for Progress—its origins, development and problems—concludes that U.S. willingness to help Latin Americans "far exceeds their efforts and willingness to help themselves."

Maritano, Nino. **A Latin American Economic Community.** Notre Dame: University of Notre Dame Press, 1970, 265 p.
  An informative and competent account covering the history, status and contributions of the various hemispheric integration movements, regional and subregional. Useful tables and basic documents are included.

Maschke, Arturo. **La creación del Banco Interamericano de Desarrollo.** Mexico City: Centro de Estudios Monetarios Latinoamericanos, 1966, 290 p.
  A history of the establishment of the Inter-American Development Bank, by a former Chilean Minister of Finance.

May, Herbert K. **Problems and Prospects of the Alliance for Progress: A Critical Examination.** New York: Praeger, 1968, 252 p.
  A review of the establishment and accomplishments of the Alliance for Progress, by a former Deputy Assistant Secretary of State for Inter-American Affairs.

Mayobre, José Antonio and Others. **Hacia la integración acelerada de América Latina: proposiciones a los presidentes latinoamericanos.** Mexico City: Fondo de Cultura Económica, 1965, 195 p.
  Four prominent Latin American economists—José Antonio Mayobre, Felipe Herrera, Carlos Sanz de Santamaría and Raúl Prebisch—survey the state of Latin America's common markets.

Perloff, Harvey S. **Alliance for Progress: A Social Invention in the Making.** Baltimore: Johns Hopkins Press (for Resources for the Future), 1969, 253 p.
  A favorable appraisal of the Alliance for Progress.

Rogers, William D. **The Twilight Struggle: The Alliance for Progress and the Politics of Development in Latin America.** New York: Random House, 1967, 301 p.
  A sober assessment of the Alliance for Progress—its history, accomplishments and prospects.

Schreiber, Anna P. **The Inter-American Commission on Human Rights.** Leyden: Sijthoff, 1970, 187 p.
  A detailed and thorough study of the creation, structure and operational patterns of the Inter-American Commission on Human Rights.

Slater, Jerome. **The OAS and United States Foreign Policy.** Columbus: Ohio State University Press, 1967, 315 p.
  In the author's view, U.S. policy toward the O.A.S. has vacillated among three objectives: internal collective security in the hemisphere, anti-communism and anti-dictatorship. This cogently reasoned study suggests that the United States has been most effective when pursuing the first objective but has tended to split the alliance when pursuing the second and third.

Stoetzer, O. Carlos. **The Organization of American States: An Introduction.** New York: Praeger, 1965, 213 p.
  A study of the history, structure and accomplishments of the Organization of American States. The German original appeared as "Panamerika: Idee und Wirklichkeit" (Hamburg: Übersee Verlag, 1964, 176 p.).

Thomas, Ann Van Wynnen and Thomas, A. J., Jr. **The Organization of American States.** Dallas: Southern Methodist University Press, 1963, 530 p.
  A thoughtful and well-documented study on the origins and growth of the Pan American system; this work examines in detail the organizational structure and functions of the O.A.S.

Veneroni, Horacio Luis. **Fuerza militar interamericana.** Buenos Aires, 1966, 184 p.
  A criticism of the proposal to establish an inter-American peace-keeping force.

Wionczek, Miguel S., *ed*. **Latin American Economic Integration: Experiences and Prospects.** New York: Praeger, 1966, 310 p.
Originally published as "Integración de la América Latina: experiencias y perspectivas" (Mexico City: Fondo de Cultura Económica, 1964, 381 p.), this revised and updated collection of essays examines both the achievements and the difficulties of Latin America's two regional economic organizations, the Latin American Free Trade Association and the Central American Common Market.

LATIN AMERICA

General

See also (The World Since 1914) General, p. 129; Inter-American Relations, p. 193; (Central America) General, p. 295; (West Indies and the Caribbean) General, p. 300.

Adams, Mildred, *ed*. **Latin America: Evolution or Explosion?** New York: Dodd (for the Council on World Tensions), 1963, 277 p.
A collection of papers by a distinguished group of participants in a conference at the University of Bahia, sponsored by the Council on World Tensions during the summer of 1962.

Alba, Víctor. **The Latin Americans.** New York: Praeger, 1969, 392 p.
An overview, both in time and in space, of Latin American life in all of its facets.

Alba, Víctor. **Nationalists without Nations.** New York: Praeger, 1968, 248 p.
A plea for political and economic integration of Latin America and for abolishing the oligarchies which, in the author's opinion, are the chief obstacle to economic, social and political progress in the southern half of the Western Hemisphere.

Alexander, Robert Jackson. **Today's Latin America.** New York: Praeger, 2d rev. ed., 1968, 261 p.
An updated edition of a survey of contemporary Latin America.

Andreski, Stanislav. **Parasitism and Subversion: The Case of Latin America.** New York: Pantheon Books, 1967, 303 p.
An imaginative and wide-ranging analysis—pessimistic in its conclusions—by a Polish-born British sociologist. Of particular value because the author relates the phenomena of Latin American society to similar phenomena in other countries.

Bailey, Norman A., *ed*. **Latin America: Politics, Economics, and Hemispheric Security.** New York: Praeger (for the Center for Strategic Studies), 1965, 289 p.
Papers originally presented at a conference at Georgetown University in July 1964.

Betancourt, Rómulo. **Hacia América Latina democrática é integrada.** Madrid: Taurus Ediciones, 3rd ed., 1969, 265 p.
The ex-President of Venezuela sets forth his thoughts on Latin American political issues and economic unity.

Briano, Justo P. **Geopolítica y geoestrategia americana.** Buenos Aires: Editorial Pleamar, 1966, 338 p.
A discussion of Latin America's relations with other parts of the world and of future power relations in Latin America from a geopolitical perspective.

Calvert, Peter. **Latin America: Internal Conflict and International Peace.** New York: St. Martin's Press, 1969, 231 p.
A very large subject compressed within a narrow space.

Chaunu, Pierre. **L'Amérique et les Amériques.** Paris: Colin, 1964, 470 p.
A broad historical survey of the Western Hemisphere; interesting for its noticeable anti-Yankee approach and its European assessment of New World history.

Cline, Howard Francis, *comp*. and *ed*. **Latin American History: Essays on its Study and Teaching, 1898-1965.** Austin: University of Texas Press (for the Conference on Latin American History), 1967, 2 v.
An analysis of the changing North American attitudes toward Latin American history. Supplemental historiographical material makes this work indispensable for the specialist in Latin American studies.

Cunill Grau, Pedro. **L'Amérique andine.** Paris: Presses Universitaires, 1966, 308 p.
A geographically oriented study of Andean Latin America.

D'Antonio, William V. and Pike, Frederick B., *eds*. **Religion, Revolution, and Reform: New Forces for Change in Latin America.** New York: Praeger, 1964, 276 p.
The general theme of these thoughtful essays reflects the belief that only "if the Church in Latin America commits itself clearly, unequivocally, and immediately to the attainment of social pluralism, then religion has some chance of being a factor in social change."

Davis, Harold Eugene. **Latin American Thought: A Historical Introduction.** Baton Rouge: Louisiana State University Press, 1972, 269 p.
This highly competent work, reaching back to pre-Colombian antecedents, is a welcome addition to Latin American intellectual history.

Der deutsche Faschismus in Lateinamerika: 1933–1943. Berlin: Humboldt-Universität, 1966, 203 p.
An East German collection of articles on Nazi activities in Latin America in the years from 1933 to 1943.

Douglas, William O. **Holocaust or Hemispheric Co-op: Cross Currents in Latin America.** New York: Random House, 1971, 216 p.
A plea, animated by idealism and good will, for basic reordering of Latin American life. The author is a Justice of the U.S. Supreme Court.

Gunther, John. **Inside South America.** New York: Harper and Row, 1967, 610 p.
In these perceptive and comprehensive observations, based largely on numerous interviews and direct experience, Mr. Gunther presents a valuable assessment of contemporary South America.

Handbook of Latin American Studies. Gainesville: University of Florida Press.
An indispensable guide to all branches of Latin American studies. Prepared for the Hispanic Foundation in the Library of Congress, and published annually since 1935, it lists books and articles under topical and regional headings with brief critical summaries. The volumes published since 1963 have been edited by Earl J. Pariseau, Henry E. Adams and Donald E. J. Stewart. The "Author Index to Handbook of Latin American Studies, Nos. 1-28: 1936–1966," compiled by Francisco José and Maria Elena Cardona, was published in 1968 (421 p.).

Hector, Cary. **Der Staatsstreich als Mittel der politischen Entwicklung in Südamerika.** Berlin: Colloquium Verlag, 1964, 227 p.
A study of economic, social and political conditions in Latin America, and an analysis of the role of the *coup d'état* in political developments in Argentina and Bolivia from 1930 to 1955.

Herrera Lane, Felipe. **Nacionalismo latinoamericano.** Santiago: Editorial Universitaria, 1967, 224 p.
The former president of the Inter-American Development Bank discusses the broad national and international problems which must be overcome before Latin America can achieve its much-needed economic integration.

Johnson, Cecil Earle. **Communist China and Latin America, 1959–1967.** New York: Columbia University Press, 1970, 324 p.
A scholarly study.

Kaplán, Marcos. **Formación del estado nacional en América Latina.** Santiago: Editorial Universitaria, 1969, 320 p.
An analysis of the formation of nation-states in Argentina, Brazil, Mexico, and Chile.

Lambert, Jacques. **Latin America: Social Structures and Political Institutions.** Berkeley: University of California Press, 1967, 413 p.
A survey of contemporary Latin America. The French original was published as "Amérique Latine: structures sociales et institutions politiques" (Paris: Presses Universitaires, 1963, 448 p.).

Maurer, Gerhard. **Blickpunkt Südamerika: die Revolution der steigenden Erwartungen.** Cologne: Kiepenheuer, 1967, 149 p.
A brief but thorough survey of the complicated political, economic and social problems of Latin America. The author describes clearly the goals, tactics and achievements of both the Moscow and Peking brands of communism, advocates agrarian

reforms and writes favorably about the entrepreneurship of the often denounced oligarchies.

Nehemkis, Peter. **Latin America: Myth and Reality.** New York: Knopf, 1964, 286 p.
A perceptive and thoughtful examination of contemporary Latin America. The author, an institutional lawyer long experienced in Latin American affairs, provides reasoned insights along with practical suggestions for bettering a deteriorating hemispheric situation.

Okinshevich, Leo, *comp.* and Carlton, Robert G., *ed.* **Latin America in Soviet Writings: A Bibliography.** Baltimore: Johns Hopkins Press (for the Library of Congress), 1966, 2 v.
Prepared by the Hispanic Foundation in coöperation with the Slavic and Central European Division of the Library of Congress, this fundamental bibliography of writings concerning Latin America in the Russian language also contains Soviet translations of studies by Latin American authors. Volume I covers the period 1917–1958; Volume II, 1959–1964.

Oswald, Joseph Gregory, *comp.* and Carlton, Robert G., *ed.* **Soviet Image of Contemporary Latin America: A Documentary History, 1960-1968.** Austin: University of Texas Press (for the Conference on Latin American History), 1971, 365 p.
A compilation and translation of Soviet writings on Latin America.

Plaza, Galo. **Latin America: Today and Tomorrow.** Washington: Acropolis Books, 1971, 229 p.
A distinguished statesman speaks out for democratic processes and for a liberal, evolutionary approach to political, social and economic problems.

Ramos, Jorge Abelardo. **Historia de la nación latinoamericana.** Buenos Aires: A. Peña Lillo Editor, 1968, 601 p.
A Marxist history of Latin America, with emphasis on the various movements for Latin American unification.

Ribeiro, Darcy. **The Americas and Civilization.** New York: Dutton, 1971, 510 p.
A Brazilian anthropologist surveys the hemisphere in space and time. The treatment is passionately leftist, with a tendency to mythology and factual error. Translation of "As Américas e a civilização; processo de formação e causas do desenvolvimento desigual dos povos americanas" (Rio de Janeiro: Civilizaçao Brasileira, 1970, 660 p.).

Rudel, Christian. **L'Amérique Latine entre hier et demain.** Paris: Éditions du Centurion, 1965, 191 p.
Scattered journalistic reflections on the revolutionary nature of contemporary Latin America, with an optimistic assessment of the role being played by the Christian Democratic movement.

Sable, Martin Howard. **A Guide to Latin American Studies.** Los Angeles: Latin American Center, University of California, 1967, 2 v.
The author states in the preface that "the Guide is meant to facilitate research at the undergraduate and graduate levels in any discipline/or professional field related to Latin America." It contains approximately 5000 annotations of books, pamphlets, periodical articles and government documents published in various languages.

Schneider, Ronald M. and Kingsbury, Robert C. **An Atlas of Latin American Affairs.** New York: Praeger, 1965, 136 p.
A useful reference.

Schurz, William Lytle. **Latin America: A Descriptive Survey.** New York: Dutton, rev. ed., 1963, 373 p.
An extensively revised edition of a work first published in 1941, this broad descriptive survey was completed shortly before the death of Dr. Schurz in 1962. The work represents the results of a lifetime of study and travel in Latin America by a respected and noted scholar.

Shapiro, Samuel. **Invisible Latin America.** Boston: Beacon Press, 1963, 180 p.
In this concise but useful study, an American professor analyzes the traditional obstacles to Latin American progress in five representative countries—Guatemala, Peru, Venezuela, Cuba and Mexico. The Alliance for Progress is examined as it has affected Bolivia.

Symposium on Latin America. Wellesley: Wellesley College, 1963, 223 p.
Papers on contemporary Latin America.

TePaske, John Jay and Fisher, Sidney Nettleton, *eds*. **Explosive Forces in Latin America.** Columbus: Ohio State University Press, 1964, 196 p.
This collection of papers, from a conference held at Ohio State University in 1962, deals with institutional and social forces responsible for change in Latin America.

Toulat, Jean. **Espérance en Amérique du Sud.** Paris: Perrin, 1965, 330 p.
Optimistic reflections by a French priest concerning the future of South America.

Toynbee, Arnold J. **Between Maule and Amazon.** New York: Oxford University Press, 1967, 154 p.
Pleasant vignettes, gleaned from past travel experiences in Latin America, by a renowned historian.

Véliz, Claudio, *ed*. **Latin America and the Caribbean: A Handbook.** New York: Praeger, 1968, 840 p.
These essays, by some eighty specialists, are encyclopedic in extent. A basic reference work, supplemented by statistical and bibliographical materials.

Véliz, Claudio, *ed*. **Obstacles to Change in Latin America.** New York: Oxford University Press (for the Royal Institute of International Affairs and St. Antony's College, Oxford University), 1965, 263 p.
Drawn from the London Conference on Obstacles to Change in Latin America, 1965, these essays, by prominent Latin American academicians from different disciplines, emphasize the need for fundamental institutional change in Latin America and the necessity for Latin America to find indigenous solutions for her problems.

Wagley, Charles. **The Latin American Tradition.** New York: Columbia University Press, 1968, 242 p.
Reflective essays on cultural patterns within Latin America. The emphasis is on continuity rather than change in traditional attitudes and values.

Wendt, Herbert. **The Red, White, and Black Continent: Latin America—Land of Reformers and Rebels.** Garden City: Doubleday, 1966, 526 p.
A perceptive journalistic study of Latin America. The original was published in German as "Der schwarz-weiss-rote Kontinent: Lateinamerika—Reformer und Rebellen" (Oldenburg: Stalling, 1964, 518 p.).

Political and Constitutional Problems

See also Political Factors, p. 12; (War) Guerrilla Warfare; Armed Insurrection, p. 118; (Union of Soviet Socialist Republics) Relations with Other Countries. p. 558; (China) Foreign Relations, p. 702; and the sections for specific countries and regions.

Agor, Weston H., *ed*. **Latin American Legislatures: Their Role and Influence.** New York: Praeger, 1971, 523 p.
A pioneering study of the character, role and functions of national legislatures in Chile, Costa Rica, Uruguay, Argentina, Brazil, Guatemala, Peru, Colombia and Venezuela.

Alba, Víctor. **Politics and the Labor Movement in Latin America.** Stanford: Stanford University Press, 1968, 404 p.
This useful and comprehensive survey with an extensive bibliography is an updated translation of "Historia del movimiento obrero en América Latina" (Mexico City: Libreros Mexicanos Unidos, 1964, 598 p.).

Alexander, Robert Jackson. **Latin-American Politics and Government.** New York: Harper and Row, 1965, 184 p.
Part of "Harper's Comparative Government Series," this brief primer surveys the political background of contemporary Latin America.

Bambirra, Vania and Others. **Diez años de insurrección en América Latina.** Santiago: Ediciones Prensa Latinoamérica, 1971, 2 v.
A series of articles by leftist authors analyzing the causes of the failure of guerrilla movements during the 1960s in Guatemala, Venezuela, Peru, Uruguay, Brazil and Colombia.

Bernard, Jean-Pierre and Others. **Tableau des partis politiques en Amérique du Sud.** Paris: Colin, 1969, 429 p.
A systematic description of the political parties in South America, including a wealth of statistical information.

Bourne, Richard. **Political Leaders of Latin America.** New York: Knopf, 1970, 310 p.
An examination of the lives and careers of Guevara, Stroessner, Frei, Kubitschek, Eva Perón and Carlos Lacerda.

Burnett, Ben G.; Johnson, Kenneth F. and Others. **Political Forces in Latin America: Dimensions of the Quest for Stability.** Belmont (Calif.): Wadsworth, 2d ed., 1970, 699 p.
Interdisciplinary studies focusing on the problem of "political instabillity" in Latin America.

Busey, James Lynn. **Latin America: Political Institutions and Processes.** New York: Random House, 1964, 184 p.
This general survey treats in detail the political structure and experience of Mexico, Costa Rica, Brazil, Argentina and Uruguay.

Clark, Gerald. **The Coming Explosion in Latin America.** New York: McKay, 1963, 436 p.
The editor of *The Montreal Star* reports on a 50,000-mile trip through Latin America. The author argues the need for radical reform.

Debray, Régis. **Revolution in the Revolution? Armed Struggle and Political Struggle in Latin America.** New York: Monthly Review Press, 1967, 126 p.
A tract, of which the Cuban-sponsored Spanish edition has been widely distributed in Latin America. The author, a French Marxist-Leninist well-known for his visit to Che Guevara and his subsequent arrest and trial, argues that the revolution in Latin America will be accomplished only with the help of guerrilla warfare. The French original appeared as "Révolution dans la révolution? Lutte armée et lutte politique en Amérique Latine" (Paris: Maspéro, 1967, 144 p.).

Debray, Régis. **Strategy for Revolution.** New York: Monthly Review Press, 1970, 255 p.
Essays on Latin American politics. The French original appeared as "Essais sur l'Amérique Latine" (Paris: Maspéro, 1967, 219 p.).

Donovan, John. **Red Machete: Communist Infiltration in the Americas.** Indianapolis: Bobbs-Merrill, 1963, 310 p.
A surface study of communist infiltration in Latin America, based primarily on travel experiences and "first-hand" contacts.

Dubois, Jules. **Operation America: The Communist Conspiracy in Latin America.** New York: Walker, 1963, 361 p.
A survey of communism in Latin American countries by a Latin American journalist.

Fagen, Richard R. and Cornelius, Wayne A., Jr. *eds.* **Political Power in Latin America: Seven Confrontations.** Englewood Cliffs: Prentice-Hall, 1970, 419 p.
Seven recent power confrontations—in Chile, Venezuela, Argentina, Brazil, Mexico, Cuba and the Dominican Republic—are illuminated by extensive excerpts from variegated accounts and studies, many by observers and scholars in Latin America.

Ferguson, J. Halcro. **The Revolutions of Latin America.** London: Thames and Hudson, 1963, 189 p.
A former member of the British Foreign Service surveys unevenly political developments in Latin America from their colonial origins to the present.

Frank, Andre Gunder. **Latin America: Underdevelopment or Revolution.** New York: Monthly Review Press, 1970, 409 p.
Polemical essays by an author who argues that there is a need for revolution in Latin America.

Gerassi, John. **The Great Fear: The Reconquest of Latin America by Latin Americans.** New York: Macmillan, 1963, 457 p.
A provocative study of the political climate in Latin America which concludes that the region's social change can be effected only by the "extreme left" or by the "extreme nationalists" and not by Latin America's "democratic forces."

Goldenberg, Boris. **Kommunismus in Lateinamerika.** Stuttgart: Kohlhammer (for the Friedrich-Ebert-Stiftung and the Bundesinstitut für Ostwissenschaftliche und Internationale Studien), 1971, 639 p.

A substantial and well-documented history of communism in Latin America from 1918 to 1968. The author, a West German journalist and scholar, discusses the organizational role of the Comintern, describes the relations among the various communist parties, and surveys the most important Latin American communist parties and their splinter groups.

Gott, Richard. **Guerrilla Movements in Latin America.** Garden City: Doubleday, 1971, 626 p.

A long and uncritical panegyric extolling violent revolution.

Hauberg, Clifford A. **Latin American Revolutions.** Minneapolis: Denison, 1968, 303 p.

Descriptions of revolutionary movements in Mexico, Central America and the Caribbean. The sources are secondary, and the treatment conventional and cursory.

Horowitz, Irving Louis and Others, *eds.* **Latin American Radicalism: A Documentary Report on Left and Nationalist Movements.** New York: Random House, 1969, 653 p.

In this compilation of representative writings, the unifying theme is the inevitability of revolution in Latin America. The diversity of opinion, ranging from Christian Democratic to Maoist views, emphasizes the pluralistic nature of the Left.

Houtart, François and Pin, Émile. **The Church and the Latin American Revolution.** New York: Sheed and Ward, 1965, 264 p.

In this study two priests discuss the role of the Catholic Church in the contemporary social revolution of Latin America and note that, while centers of resistance remain, progressive forces within the Church are succeeding in identifying it with the developing revolution in Latin America. The original appeared as "L'Église à l'heure de l'Amérique Latine" (Tournai: Casterman, 1965, 265 p.).

Humphreys, Robert Arthur. **Tradition and Revolt in Latin America and other Essays.** New York: Columbia University Press, 1969, 264 p.

Graceful essays, largely historical in content and reaching back to the eighteenth century. The author is an eminent British authority on Latin America.

Jackson, D. Bruce. **Castro, the Kremlin, and Communism in Latin America.** Baltimore: Johns Hopkins Press (for the Washington Center of Foreign Policy Research, School of Advanced International Studies), 1969, 163 p.

The political interactions of the Russian, Cuban and Latin American governments are set forth in an authoritative, concise and clear manner.

Johnson, John J. **The Military and Society in Latin America.** Stanford: Stanford University Press, 1964, 308 p.

In this thoughtful examination the author argues that the role of the military, increasingly influenced by the urban middle-class, will continue to be important in unstable Latin American societies.

Jorrín, Miguel and Martz, John D. **Latin-American Political Thought and Ideology.** Chapel Hill: University of North Carolina Press, 1970, 453 p.

A useful examination into the theoretical and philosophical basis of political thought in Latin America, through analysis of the writings and themes of the region's foremost thinkers.

Lamberg, Robert F. **Die castritische Guerilla in Lateinamerika: Theorie und Praxis eines revolutionären Modells.** Hanover: Verlag für Literatur un Zeitgeschehen, 1971, 173 p.

A thorough study of Castroite guerrilla warfare in Latin America. The author concludes by saying that the Castroites, having mostly middle-class and upper middle-class backgrounds, have failed almost everywhere to establish a close relationship with the masses.

Landsberger, Henry A., *ed.* **Latin American Peasant Movements.** Ithaca: Cornell University Press, 1969, 476 p.

Ten essays, generally thorough and well-documented, in which competent contributors describe peasant movements in Venezuela, Mexico, Bolivia, Chile, Peru, Guatemala and Brazil.

Liebman, Arthur and Others. **Latin American University Students: A Six Nation Study.** Cambridge: Harvard University Press (for the Center for International Affairs), 1972, 296 p.

A comparative study of student movements and attitudes in six countries selected for their diverse political and university systems: Colombia, Panama, Paraguay, Puerto Rico, Uruguay and Mexico.

Lieuwen, Edwin. **Generals vs. Presidents: Neomilitarism in Latin America.** New York: Praeger, 1964, 160 p.

Continuing his studies on the role of the armed forces in contemporary Latin America, Professor Lieuwen in this volume deals with the resurgence of the military in politics and its ominous implications for both Latin America and the United States.

Lipset, Seymour Martin and Solari, Aldo E., eds. **Elites in Latin America.** New York: Oxford University Press, 1967, 531 p.

Fifteen perceptive essays by respected North American and Latin American social scientists examining the varied nature of élite groups in Latin America and their role in decision-making processes. Emphasis is also given to the role education has played in affecting these élites.

Maier, Joseph Ben and Weatherhead, Richard W., eds. **Politics of Change in Latin America.** New York: Praeger, 1964, 258 p.

A well-balanced collection of essays by prominent Latin American specialists, including Gilberto Freyre, Charles Wagley, Germán Arciniegas, Richard M. Morse, Victor L. Urquidi and Stanley R. Ross.

Mander, John. **The Unrevolutionary Society: The Power of Latin American Conservatism in a Changing World.** New York: Knopf, 1969, 331 p.

An imaginative inquiry into the entire Latin American scene, with particular emphasis upon nine of the more important nations, by an author who takes all life and all literature as his domain. His conclusions stress the continuity and enduring tenacity of the culture pattern.

Masur, Gerhard. **Nationalism in Latin America: Diversity and Unity.** New York: Macmillan, 1966, 278 p.

In this informative study of contemporary nationalistic trends in Latin America, the author views the principal issue as one of finding a "satisfactory basis for harmonious coexistence throughout the hemisphere."

Mercier Vega, Luis. **Guerrillas in Latin America: The Technique of the Counter-State.** New York: Praeger, 1969, 246 p.

An analysis of guerrilla movements, their potentialities and their variations, in Venezuela, Argentina, Bolivia, Guatemala, Paraguay, Brazil, Colombia and Peru. The French original appeared as "Technique du contre-état" (Paris: Belfond, 1968, 255 p.).

Mercier Vega, Luis. **Roads to Power in Latin America.** New York: Praeger, 1969, 208 p.

An excellent book that provides an analysis of the Latin American state and its functioning as a society in its own right. The French original was published as "Mécanismes du pouvoir en Amérique Latine" (Paris: Éditions Universitaires, 1967, 231 p.).

Mutchler, David E. **The Church as a Political Factor in Latin America.** New York: Praeger, 1971, 460 p.

The Church, seeking survival, has tended in the author's opinion to serve the interests of U.S. and European policies, thereby weakening reformist and populist movements.

Needler, Martin C. **Latin American Politics in Perspective.** New York: Van Nostrand, rev. ed., 1967, 191 p.

A survey of politics and administration in Latin America, by a professor at the University of New Mexico.

Needler, Martin C. **Political Development in Latin America: Instability, Violence and Evolutionary Change.** New York: Random House, 1968, 210 p.

A useful survey, written under the auspices of the Center for International Affairs, Harvard University.

Needler, Martin C., ed. **Political Systems of Latin America.** New York: Van Nostrand-Reinhold, 2d ed., 1970, 621 p.

A comprehensive introduction to Latin American politics and government.

Petras, James and Zeitlin, Maurice, eds. **Latin America: Reform or Revolution?** Greenwich (Conn.): Fawcett, 1968, 511 p.
Penetrating studies from the Left; the mood is pessimistic, the ideological theme that of necessary conflict.

Petras, James. **Politics and Social Structure in Latin America.** New York: Monthly Review Press, 1970, 382 p.
Essays directed to sociology, politics and U.S.-Latin American relations. The author takes his firm stance on the Left, and tends to overestimate economic motivations and causations.

Pike, Frederick Braun, ed. **The Conflict Between Church and State in Latin America.** New York: Knopf, 1964, 239 p.
This collection of studies traces the political, social and economic relationships between church and state in Latin America from the colonial beginnings to the present.

Poppino, Rollie E. **International Communism in Latin America: A History of the Movement 1917–1963.** New York: Free Press of Glencoe, 1964, 247 p.
A scholarly study.

Samuel, Albert. **Castrisme, communisme, démocratie chrétienne en Amérique Latine.** Lyons: Chronique Sociale de France, 1965, 209 p.
In this evaluation of Latin America's contemporary problems, the author focuses upon the impact of Castroism and the developing Christian Democratic movement.

Schmitt, Karl Michael and Burks, David D. **Evolution or Chaos: Dynamics of Latin American Government and Politics.** New York: Praeger, 1963, 308 p.
In this comprehensive survey of political, social and economic institutions in Latin America, two discerning American professors relate political developments to hemispheric revolutionary pressures.

Sigmund, Paul E., ed. **Models of Political Change in Latin America.** New York: Praeger, 1970, 338 p.
Excerpts from source materials, linked by short commentaries, illuminating political developments in nine Latin American nations.

Szulc, Tad. **The Winds of Revolution: Latin America Today—and Tomorrow.** New York: Praeger, 1963, 308 p.
In this thoughtful examination Mr. Szulc, formerly Latin American correspondent for *The New York Times*, contends that the United States, in its inability to understand Latin America's social revolution, has failed to provide a positive ideological alternative to Castro and communism in the hemisphere.

Turner, Frederick C. **Catholicism and Political Development in Latin America.** Chapel Hill: University of North Carolina Press, 1971, 272 p.
A competent and scholarly description of attitudes toward social change held by progressive Roman Catholic leaders and their movements. Much use is made of pastoral messages and other ecclesiastical source materials.

Véliz, Claudio, ed. **The Politics of Conformity in Latin America.** New York: Oxford University Press (for the Royal Institute of International Affairs), 1967, 291 p.
These well-written essays examine power élites, from military officers to spokesmen for emerging political sectors. In general, the studies conclude that stability characterizes the Latin American value system and that integration into existing structures rather than violent revolutionary change is the goal of diverse social groups.

Whitaker, Arthur Preston and Jordan, David C. **Nationalism in Contemporary Latin America.** New York: Free Press, 1966, 229 p.
Written by two respected scholars, this thoughtful work is of particular value in its examination of the varying impact nationalism has had upon specific Latin American countries.

Williams, Edward J. **Latin American Christian Democratic Parties.** Knoxville: University of Tennessee Press, 1967, 305 p.
A pioneering and well-documented study of the Christian Democratic parties in Latin America. The author, a professor at the University of Arizona, is convinced that the ideological bent of the Christian Democratic movement "is remarkably appropriate" to the continent.

Zea, Leopoldo. **The Latin-American Mind.** Norman: University of Oklahoma Press, 1963, 308 p.

A competent and much-needed translation of "Dos etapas del pensamiento en Hispanoamérica" (1949), an incisive and analytical examination of those intellectual considerations which have shaped political history in Latin America.

Economic and Social Problems

See also Problems of New Nations, p. 36; Society and Social Psychology, p. 39; Economic Factors, p. 49; Inter-American Relations, p. 193; and the sections for specific countries and regions.

Aguilar Monteverde, Alonso. **Problemas estructurales del subdesarrollo.** Mexico City: Universidad Nacional Autónoma de México, Instituto de Investigaciones Económicas, 1971, 327 p.

The author discusses a number of general topics—the Alliance for Progress, the demographic explosion, the relevance of Marxism for developing countries—and also analyzes in some detail Mexico's development problems. He argues that structural changes are needed in Latin America and in Mexico.

Alba, Víctor. **Los Subamericanos.** Mexico City: Costa-Amic, 1964, 324 p.

A prolific writer sketchily examines the present state of Latin America and concludes that both "classic" capitalism and "inhuman" communism have failed to provide the means for Latin America's development and that another route must be found to resolve Latin America's social and economic problems.

Alemann, Roberto T. and Others. **Economic Development Issues: Latin America.** New York: Praeger, 1967, 341 p.

These studies, prepared for the Committee for Economic Development, survey the economies of Mexico, Peru, Colombia, Chile, Argentina and Brazil.

Alexander, Robert Jackson. **Organized Labor in Latin America.** New York: Free Press, 1965, 274 p.

In this sympathetic view of the role of labor in Latin America's changing social, economic and political order, the author focuses attention on the processes of collective bargaining.

Anderson, Charles W. **Politics and Economic Change in Latin America: The Governing of Restless Nations.** Princeton: Van Nostrand, 1967, 388 p.

A study of the "potential, performance, and role of government as an instrument of economic change in Latin America." The author believes that "pragmatic" and "prudent" reforms, under state aegis, give the best promise for Latin America's economic and social development.

Aspectos financieros de las economías latinoamericanas. Mexico City: Centro de Estudios Monetarios Latinoamericanos, 1956—.

A series, issued irregularly, examining Latin America's economy.

Baerresen, Donald Walter and Others. **Latin American Trade Patterns.** Washington: Brookings Institution, 1965, 329 p.

This study, primarily a compilation of statistical materials pertaining to Latin American trade, examines the problems of economic integration of the region.

Beaulac, Willard Leon. **A Diplomat Looks at Aid to Latin America.** Carbondale: Southern Illinois University Press, 1970, 148 p.

The author of this urbane volume pleads for the continuing need for aid, administered with understanding and sophistication.

Bell, Harry H. **Tariff Profiles in Latin America: Implications for Pricing Structures and Economic Integration.** New York: Praeger, 1971, 168 p.

An interesting contribution to the growing discussion of the impact of tariffs and other import restrictions on development. The author is a former U.S. Foreign Service officer.

Blasier, Stewart Cole, *ed.* **Constructive Change in Latin America.** Pittsburgh: University of Pittsburgh Press, 1968, 243 p.

A collection of essays on social change, based on University of Pittsburgh Latin American seminars. Of particular interest are the studies on economics by John P. Powelson and on the Latin American intellectual by Germán Arciniegas.

Brown, Robert T. **Transport and the Economic Integration of South America.** Washington: Brookings Institution, 1966, 288 p.
In this examination of the relationship between various modes of transportation and Latin America's economic integration, the author notes that the failure to eliminate artificial political and economic barriers between countries has contributed largely to the inefficient use of existing transport facilities.

Campos, Roberto de Oliveira. **Reflections on Latin American Development.** Austin: University of Texas Press (for the Institute of Latin American Studies), 1967, 168 p.
Informative essays by Brazil's Minister of Planning during the régime of Castello Branco.

Carnoy, Martin. **Industrialization in a Latin American Common Market.** Washington: Brookings Institution, 1972, 267 p.
Research institutions in ten Latin American countries and the United States have combined efforts to devise a method of showing where industries can be most economically located (and how to estimate the cost of locating them elsewhere). The method is then tried out on six industries.

Chonchol, Jacques. **El desarrollo de América Latina y la reforma agraria.** Santiago: Editorial del Pacífico, 1964, 112 p.
The author, who later became Minister of Agriculture in Chile, argues that agrarian reforms are necessary for economic development in Latin America.

Cole, John P. **Latin America: An Economic and Social Geography.** Washington: Butterworths, 1965, 468 p.
A factual textbook buttressed with numerous maps, charts, drawings, statistics and a selected bibliography.

Delgado, Oscar, *ed*. **Reformas agrárias en la América Latina.** Mexico City: Fondo de Cultura Económica, 1965, 756 p.
A comprehensive study of agrarian conditions and agrarian reform programs in Latin America.

Development Problems in Latin America: An Analysis by the United Nations Economic Commission for Latin America. Austin: University of Texas Press (for the Institute of Latin American Studies), 1970, 318 p.
These studies summarize the first two decades of E.C.L.A.'s activities and achievements.

Edel, Matthew. **Food Supply and Inflation in Latin America.** New York: Praeger, 1969, 214 p.
The "structuralist" thesis of agricultural lag as a cause of inflation is analyzed in light of the larger countries. Technical, with an abundance of statistics.

Farley, Rawle. **The Economics of Latin America: Development Problems in Perspective.** New York: Harper and Row, 1972, 400 p.
In this comprehensive study the author scrutinizes both the achievements of the past and the ambiguities of the future.

Form, William Humbert and Blum, Albert Alexander, *eds*. **Industrial Relations and Social Change in Latin America.** Gainesville: University of Florida Press, 1965, 177 p.
Drawn essentially from lectures given at Michigan State University (1962–63), these essays examine the implications which radical social change holds for the pattern of industrial relations in Latin America.

Frank, Andre Gunder. **Capitalism and Underdevelopment in Latin America: Historical Studies of Chile and Brazil.** New York: Monthly Review Press, rev. ed., 1969, 344 p.
Four essays, framed in Marxian terms, examining the "Indian Problem" in Latin America and various aspects of economic development in Chile and Brazil. The author contends that only by the destruction of the capitalist system would it be possible to solve the economic issues of Latin America.

Furtado, Celso. **Subdesenvolvimento e estagnação na América Latina.** Rio de Janeiro: Editôra Civilização Brasileira, 1966, 127 p.
Observations on the problems of economic development by a well-known Brazilian economist and former Minister of Planning under Goulart.

García, Antonio. **Reforma agraria y economía empresarial en América Latina.** Santiago: Editorial Universitaria, 1967, 305 p.
Statistics and pertinent bibliography back up this solid interpretive study of traditional and modern systems of land tenure in Latin America.

Geyer, Georgie Anne. **The New Latins: Fateful Change in South and Central America.** Garden City: Doubleday, 1970, 340 p.
The author describes social and psychological change in Latin America, in a vividly written first-hand account.

Glade, William P., Jr. **The Latin American Economies: A Study of their Institutional Evolution.** New York: American Book, 1969, 665 p.
This study of Latin American economic development emphasizes the role of the state and covers the period since the colonial times.

Goldenberg, Boris. **Gewerkschaften in Lateinamerika.** Hanover: Verlag für Literatur und Zeitgeschehen (for the Forschungsinstitut der Friedrich-Ebert-Stiftung), 1964, 197 p.
A country-by-country discussion of labor unions in Latin America since the First World War.

Gordon, Wendell Chaffee. **The Political Economy of Latin America.** New York: Columbia University Press, 1965, 401 p.
In this survey of Latin American economic problems, the author argues that "the tendency of the privileged and their cohorts to resist fanatically any minor abatement of their privileges is a heavy hand stifling the progress of Latin America."

Gozard, Gilles. **Demain, l'Amérque Latine.** Paris: Presses Universitaires, 1964, 249 p.
A survey in which the author views, with subdued optimism, Latin America's contemporary state and potential economic developments, particularly those of interest to Europe and France.

Griffin, Keith. **Underdevelopment in Spanish America.** Cambridge: M.I.T. Press, 1970, 288 p.
Believing that underdevelopment is implicit in present national and international structures, the author outlines various proposals for fundamental changes in existing systems.

Grunwald, Joseph and Musgrove, Philip. **Natural Resources in Latin American Development.** Baltimore: Johns Hopkins Press (for Resources for the Future), 1970, 494 p.
A useful survey, including detailed statistical information—by country and commodity.

Hirschman, Albert O. **A Bias for Hope.** New Haven: Yale University Press, 1971, 374 p.
The distinguished Harvard authority on Latin American development has gathered here a harvest of his shorter writings, published over a period of almost two decades. A new "Introduction: Political Economics and Possibilism" serves as a focus and unifying element.

Hirschman, Albert O. **Journeys Toward Progress: Studies of Economic Policy-Making in Latin America.** Twentieth Century Fund, 1963, 308 p.
In this study Professor Hirschman analyzes the policy-making process in Latin America as it relates to economic reform and development; based on the experience of Brazil, Colombia and Chile.

Horowitz, Irving Louis, *ed.* **Masses in Latin America.** New York: Oxford University Press, 1970, 608 p.
Sixteen studies of the social, political and economic characteristics and functions of the Latin American masses. The stress is predominantly sociological, and the tone academic.

Johnson, John J., *ed.* **Continuity and Change in Latin America.** Stanford: Stanford University Press, 1964, 282 p.
These papers, presented in January 1963 at a conference sponsored by the Joint Committee on Latin American Studies, examine changes in the status and behavior of various social groups in contemporary Latin America.

Joslin, David. **A Century of Banking in Latin America.** New York: Oxford University Press, 1963, 307 p.
This study, commemorating the centennial of the Bank of London & South America Ltd., traces the development and activities of this institution in the region.

Kahl, Joseph Alan. **The Measurement of Modernism: A Study of Values in Brazil and Mexico.** Austin: University of Texas Press (for the Institute of Latin American Studies), 1968, 210 p.

An empirical study of the impact which industrialization has had upon the worker.

Lateinamerika und Europa: Probleme und Möglichkeiten der Zusammenarbeit. Olten: Vereinigung Christlicher Unternehmer der Schweiz, 1963, 215 p.

A symposium chiefly devoted to the problems and prospects of economic coöperation between Europe and Latin America.

Lauterbach, Albert T. **Enterprise in Latin America: Business Attitudes in a Developing Economy.** Ithaca: Cornell University Press, 1966, 207 p.

An analysis of business attitudes in Latin America, drawn from interviews and personal conversations with businessmen.

Léon, Pierre. **Économies et sociétés de l'Amérique Latine.** Paris: Société d'Édition d'Enseignement Supérieur, 1969, 480 p.

A century and a half of complex social, political and economic development is summarized by a French academic. An able and thoughtful volume.

Mander, John. **Static Society: The Paradox of Latin America.** London: Gollancz, 1969, 348 p.

The author argues that, in spite of many revolutionary developments, Latin America has a profoundly static society.

Menjívar, Rafael. **Reforma agraria: Guatemala, Bolivia, Cuba.** San Salvador: Editorial Universitaria de El Salvador, 1969, 475 p.

The theme of this book is the necessity and inevitability of agrarian reform in Latin America. The author, a Marxist, sees the destruction of the landlord class as the first objective of an agrarian reform and takes Cuba as an example of a successful reform, in contrast to the cases of Bolivia and Guatemala.

Mörner, Magnus, *ed.* **Race and Class in Latin America.** New York: Columbia University Press, 1970, 309 p.

Thirteen papers of professional quality assess race relations, slavery and social classes in selected countries and time periods.

Nisbet, Charles T., *ed.* **Latin America: Problems in Economic Development.** New York: Free Press, 1969, 357 p.

The problems considered are population, agriculture, inflation, exports, industrialization and growth. The essays are competent and sometimes directed to technically cognizant readers.

Onufriev, Iu. G. and Others, *eds.* **Agrarnyi vopros i problemy osvoboditel'nogo dvizheniia v stranakh Latinskoi Ameriki.** Moscow: Izd-vo "Nauka," 1968, 194 p.

A group of Soviet specialists on Latin America deal with the relationship of land tenure to revolutionary change and assess the role of the labor movement and leftist political parties in various Latin American countries.

Pazos y Roque, Felipe. **Medidas para detener la inflación crónica en América Latina.** Mexico City: Centro de Estudios Monetarios Latinoamericanos, 1969, 222 p.

A discussion of the problem of inflation in Latin America.

Piedra, Alberto Martinez, *ed.* **Socio-Economic Change in Latin America.** Washington: Catholic University of America Press, 1970, 271 p.

Most of the essays in this collection were originally presented in 1968 and 1969 at a series of seminars sponsored by the Latin American Institute of the Catholic University of America in Washington, D.C.

Poblete Tronsoso, Moisés. **La explosión demográfica en América Latina.** Buenos Aires: Editorial Schapire, 1967, 204 p.

An examination of demographic trends in Latin America and of attempts to deal with the population explosion.

Powelson, John P. **Latin America: Today's Economic and Social Revolution.** New York: McGraw-Hill, 1964, 303 p.

A North American professor with long experience in Latin American universities knowledgeably analyzes the problems of Latin American economic development and attempts to reconcile divergencies in economic thought between Latin America and the United States.

Prebisch, Raúl. **Change and Development—Latin America's Great Task.** New York: Praeger, 1971, 293 p.

A detailed study prepared by the author, a leading economist and Director-General of the Latin American Institute for Economic and Social Planning, for the Inter-American Development Bank.

Problemas de pagos en América Latina. Mexico City: Centro de Estudios Monetarios Latinoamericanos, 1964, 298 p.

These papers, delivered at a meeting held by the Bancos Centrales del Continente Americano in Rio de Janeiro in October 1963, explore the question of bank payments and examine the means by which international financial coördination can be achieved.

Ramos, Joseph R. **Labor and Development in Latin America.** New York: Columbia University Press, 1970, 281 p.

A very technical analysis of labor force characteristics and employment tendencies, presented with precision and clarity.

Ruiz García, Enrique. **América Latina: anatomía de una revolución.** Madrid: Ediciones Guadarrama, 1966, 539 p.

A general discussion of the economic and social forces producing the revolutionary events in Latin America.

Santos, Theotonio dos. **La crisis norteamericana y América Latina.** Santiago: Editorial Prensa Latinoamericana, 1971, 159 p.

A well-known economist presents a theoretical analysis of economic crises in underdeveloped countries and examines the multiple consequences of the economic developments in the United States on Latin America.

Santos, Theotonio dos. **Dependencia económica y cambio revolucionario en América Latina.** Caracas: Editorial Neuva Izquierda, 1970, 152 p.

Essays on models of economic development, the economic dependency of Latin America, and possible alternative paths of development.

Smith, Thomas Lynn. **Studies of Latin American Societies.** Garden City: Doubleday, 1970, 412 p.

Analyses of social form and function in Latin America, with emphasis upon Colombia and Brazil.

Sosa-Rodriguez, Raul. **Les problèmes structurels des relations économiques internationales de l'Amérique Latine.** Geneva: Droz, 1963, 252 p.

A statistical study of Latin America's twentieth-century pattern of foreign trade and commerce which concludes that rapid industrialization—despite economic imbalance, declining values of traditional exports, currency and financing difficulties—remains the goal for Latin American nations.

Stein, Stanley J. and Stein, Barbara H. **The Colonial Heritage of Latin America: Essays on Economic Dependence in Perspective.** New York: Oxford University Press, 1970, 222 p.

The theme of this study is the influence of colonial rule and of neo-colonialist forces since 1700. The authors favor structural change—radical revision in economic and social policy—over evolutionary development.

Stycos, J. Mayone and Arias, Jorge, eds. **Population Dilemma in Latin America.** Washington: Potomac Books, 1966, 249 p.

Presented at the Pan American Assembly on Population held in Cali, Colombia, during the summer of 1965 and sponsored by the American Assembly of Columbia University, the Universidad del Valle and the Association of Colombian Medical Schools, this collection of papers examines various aspects of the demographic crisis in Latin America.

Tamagna, Frank M. **La banca central en América Latina.** Mexico City: Centro de Estudios Monetarios Latinoamericanos, 1963, 597 p.

A comparison of central banking systems and procedures in Latin America.

Urquidi, Victor L. **The Challenge of Development in Latin America.** New York: Praeger, 1964, 209 p.

In this study a prominent Latin American economist examines the state of Latin American economy and concludes that the Alliance for Progress "is the only road open to Latin America that guarantees us democracy, liberty, and personal dignity."

The Spanish original was published as "Viabilidad económica de América Latina" (Mexico City: Fondo de Cultura Económica, 1962, 205 p.).

Vekemans, Roger and Others. **L'Amérique Latine en devenir.** Paris: Fayard, 1963, 223 p.
A discussion of contemporary Latin America, with emphasis on religious and economic problems.

Withers, William. **The Economic Crisis in Latin America.** New York: Free Press of Glencoe, 1964, 307 p.
The author argues that the defeat of communism in the hemisphere depends upon intelligent U.S. leadership and upon the ability of Latin America's middle class to follow the Mexican policy of "combining Latin American nationalism with capitalism and socialism in a workable combination emphasizing capitalism."

Yudelman, Montague with Howard, Fredric. **Agricultural Development and Economic Integration in Latin America.** London: Allen and Unwin, 1970, 336 p.
A useful introductory survey.

NORTH AMERICA

THE UNITED STATES

General

See also The World Since 1914, p. 129.

Blum, John Morton. **The Promise of America: An Historical Inquiry.** Boston: Houghton, 1966, 206 p.
An American historian undertakes "to define American aspirations and to measure American achievements in terms of men who exemplified the best and the less-than-best in the national past."

Brogan, Sir Denis William. **American Aspects.** New York: Harper and Row, 1964, 195 p.
A selection of essays on American life and culture by a well-known British scholar.

Gardner, John William. **The Recovery of Confidence.** New York: Norton, 1970, 189 p.
An essay ranging over most of the problem areas that bedevil contemporary American society.

Goodman, Paul. **New Reformation: Notes of a Neolithic Conservative.** New York: Random House, 1970, 208 p.
The theme of this book is that there is in America today a crisis of belief comparable to that of the times just before the Reformation. The author does not engage much in the prescription of remedies.

Hacker, Andrew. **The End of the American Era.** New York: Atheneum, 1970, 239 p.
In this neo-Spenglerian essay, the author predicts middle age and inevitable decline for the United States.

Kennedy, Edward Moore. **Decisions for a Decade: Policies and Programs for the 1970s.** Garden City: Doubleday, 1968, 222 p.
A survey, by a U.S. Senator, of the problems that, in his view, will confront America in the 1970s.

Lipset, Seymour Martin. **The First New Nation.** New York: Basic Books, 1963, 366 p.
In this historical and comparative analysis of the American nation, a prominent sociologist deals both with the question of America as an "exceptional" society and with the problem of achieving stability in the midst of change.

Lyons, Gene Martin, *ed.* **America: Purpose and Power.** Chicago: Quadrangle Books, 1965, 384 p.
A selection of essays, sponsored by the Public Affairs Center at Dartmouth College, dealing with the general theme of changing forces in American society.

May, Ernest R., *ed.* **The American Image Series.** New York: Braziller, 1963, 4 v.
This series, under the general editorship of Ernest R. May and comprising four volumes, was designed as an introduction for the general, and especially the foreign, reader. The titles are: "The American Society," edited by Kenneth S. Lynn (245 p.); "The American Foreign Policy," edited by Ernest R. May (248 p.); "The American Political Process," edited by Leonard W. Levy and John P. Roche (246 p.); and "The American Economy," edited by Jesse W. Markham (274 p.).

Morgenthau, Hans Joachim, *ed.* **The Crossroad Papers: A Look into the American Future.** New York: Norton, 1965, 279 p.
Initiated by the Americans for Democratic Action, this collection of essays seeks to come to grips with some of the major issues that will confront the United States in the areas of economics, international relations, race, education and government.

Morison, Samuel Eliot. **The Oxford History of the American People.** New York: Oxford University Press, 1965, 1,150 p.
An excellent one-volume interpretation of the American past and present by an outstanding historian.

Peirce, Neal R. **The Megastates of America: People, Politics, and Power in the Ten Great States.** New York: Norton, 1972, 745 p.
The author pays tribute to John Gunther's "Inside U.S.A." and provides detailed portraits of New York, Massachusetts, New Jersey, Pennsylvania, Ohio, Illinois, Michigan, Florida, Texas and California.

Priestland, Gerald. **America: The Changing Nation.** New York: Barnes and Noble, 1969, 341 p.
The Washington correspondent of the BBC paints a broad-brush, generally not unattractive, picture of American responses to domestic and international crises.

Salisbury, Harrison E. **The Many Americas Shall Be One.** New York: Norton, 1971, 204 p.
A far-ranging survey by the well-known and influential former editor and correspondent of *The New York Times*.

Segal, Ronald. **The Americans: A Conflict of Creed and Reality.** New York: Viking, 1969, 340 p.
A polemic against modern America, capped by a defense of the American dream. The author, a South African living in Britain, writes with the invective of the betrayed lover. Originally published as "America's Receding Future" (London: Weidenfeld and Nicolson, 1968, 323 p.).

Snowman, Daniel. **America since 1920.** New York: Harper and Row, 1969, 192 p.
A perceptive essay by a British scholar. Originally published as "USA: The Twenties to Vietnam" (London: Batsford, 1968, 192 p.).

Tyrmand, Leopold. **Notebooks of a Dilettante.** New York: Macmillan, 1970, 240 p.
Random observations about America by a Polish immigrant determined to "defend America against itself."

Recent History

See also General Works, p. 1; Political Factors, p. 12; The World Since 1914, p. 129; (The United States) Biographies, Memoirs and Addresses, p. 218; Foreign Policy, p. 229; Politics and Political Issues, p. 268; The Vietnam War, p. 739.

Baker, Leonard. **The Johnson Eclipse: A President's Vice Presidency.** New York: Macmillan, 1966, 280 p.
An account of Lyndon Johnson's rather shadowy and overshadowed role as Vice President in the Kennedy Administration.

Bell, Jack. **The Johnson Treatment.** New York: Harper and Row, 1965, 305 p.
An interim report, by a Washington correspondent, on the style of the Johnson Administration.

Brandt, Willy. **Begegnungen mit Kennedy.** Munich: Kindler, 1964, 242 p.
A tribute to President Kennedy by the former West German Chancellor.

Chester, Lewis; Hodgson, Godfrey and Page, Bruce. **An American Melodrama: The Presidential Campaign of 1968.** New York: Viking Press, 1969, 814 p.
A lively, informative and intelligently written instant history by a team of journalists from the London *Sunday Times.*

Cummings, Milton Curtis, Jr., *ed.* **The National Election of 1964.** Washington: Brookings Institution, 1966, 295 p.
A collection of studies on various aspects of the 1964 election.

Daniels, Jonathan. **The Time between the Wars: Armistice to Pearl Harbor.** Garden City: Doubleday, 1966, 372 p.
An American newspaper editor, and son of Wilson's Secretary of the Navy, reviews America between the two wars.

Donahoe, Bernard F. **Private Plans and Public Dangers: The Story of FDR's Third Nomination.** Notre Dame: University of Notre Dame Press, 1965, 256 p.
In this well-documented study the author argues that FDR would have run in 1940 without the encouragement he received from the international developments in order to block a conservative upsurgence.

Evans, Rowland and Novak, Robert D. **Nixon in the White House: The Frustration of Power.** New York: Random House, 1971, 431 p.
A disturbing portrait of a man "flawed by an instinct" seeking tactical short-range advantages without proper attention to long-range strategic considerations. The authors charge that Nixon's vision was often blurred by self-pity and fear of the press.

Faber, Harold, *ed.* **The Road to the White House.** New York: McGraw-Hill, 1965, 305 p.
A substantial account of the 1964 election campaign, "a team effort of members of the staff of *The New York Times.*"

Feis, Herbert. **1933: Characters in Crisis.** Boston: Little, Brown, 1966, 366 p.
As Economic Adviser of the State Department, Mr. Feis was carried over from the Hoover to the Roosevelt Administration. Close enough to the problems to understand them thoroughly and high enough to know what the great folk said and did about them, he gives us a most valuable account of the tempestuous events of 1933.

Freeland, Richard M. **The Truman Doctrine and the Origins of McCarthyism.** New York: Knopf, 1972, 419 p.
The author advances the thesis that Truman used anti-communism as a political tactic to rally support for his policies in Western Europe and thus, unwittingly, prepared the ground for the excesses of McCarthyism.

Goldman, Eric Fredrick. **The Tragedy of Lyndon Johnson.** New York: Knopf, 1969, 531 p.
The author sees President Johnson as a tragic figure not because of what he *did* but because of what he *was.*

Gromyko, Anatolii Andreevich. **1036 dnei Prezidenta Kennedi.** Moscow: Izd-vo Politicheskoi Literatury, 1968, 279 p.
A political biography of John F. Kennedy and a foreign policy analysis of his administration, with an interesting narrative of the Cuban missile crisis from a Soviet perspective. The author is a prominent international affairs specialist and also the son of the Foreign Minister of the U.S.S.R. The English translation appeared as "Through Russian Eyes: President Kennedy's 1036 Days" (Washington: International Library, 1973, 227 p.).

Halberstam, David. **The Best and Brightest.** New York: Random House, 1972, 688 p.
In this volume Halberstam interweaves a narrative of the Kennedy and Johnson years with biographies of the decision-makers: Robert McNamara, Walt Rostow, Dean Rusk, McGeorge and William Bundy and scores of less prominent men.

Heren, Louis. **No Hail, No Farewell.** New York: Harper and Row, 1970, 275 p.
This sympathetic appraisal of the Johnson Administration by a leading British journalist retells the hard facts of the Johnson years in easy prose.

Herzog, Arthur. **McCarthy for President.** New York: Viking, 1969, 309 p.
A key figure in the McCarthy candidacy of 1968 has written an intimate account of the campaign from New Hampshire to California.

Kirkendall, Richard Stewart, *ed.* **The Truman Period as a Research Field.** Columbia: University of Missouri Press, 1967, 284 p.
   This volume, the outgrowth of a conference of historians, political scientists and archivists held in the Truman Library in 1966, is a reference source for scholars of the Truman Presidency.

Koch, Thilo. **Tagebuch aus Washington.** Hamburg: Wegner, 1963–64, 3 v.
   A German journalist's diary of the Washington scene from January 20, 1961 to December 10, 1963.

Krock, Arthur. **In the Nation: 1932-1966.** New York: McGraw-Hill, 1966, 455 p.
   Essays and columns on American politics and foreign policy by a distinguished journalist who for many years was the head of the Washington bureau of *The New York Times*.

Lane, Mark. **Rush to Judgment.** New York: Holt, Rinehart and Winston, 1966, 478 p.
   The much disputed critique of the Warren Commission inquiry into the assassination of President Kennedy.

Larson, Arthur. **Eisenhower: The President Nobody Knew.** New York: Scribner, 1968, 210 p.
   A competent defense of the Eisenhower Presidency.

Leuchtenburg, William Edward. **Franklin D. Roosevelt and the New Deal, 1932-1940.** New York: Harper and Row, 1963, 393 p.
   In this volume of "The New American Nation Series," Professor Leuchtenburg has succeeded in presenting a brief, lively and very well-informed survey of the New Deal era.

Levin, Murray Burton. **Kennedy Campaigning.** Boston: Beacon Press, 1966, 313 p.
   A study of the Kennedy system of campaigning and its use by Edward Kennedy in the 1962 Senatorial campaign.

Livermore, Seward W. **Politics is Adjourned: Woodrow Wilson and the War Congress, 1916-1918.** Middletown (Conn.): Wesleyan University Press, 1966, 324 p.
   A study of the causes underlying the Republican victory in the Congressional election of 1918—a fateful event that undermined Woodrow Wilson's position as war leader.

Lurie, Leonard. **The King Makers.** New York: Coward, McCann and Geoghegan, 1971, 271 p.
   A hard-hitting account of the 1952 Republican Convention with particular emphasis on Nixon's relentless pursuit of the vice-presidential nomination. The author's main target for criticism, however, is the convention system itself.

McCarthy, Eugene J. **The Year of the People.** Garden City: Doubleday, 1969, 323 p.
   A pleasant and low-keyed report of the 1968 Presidential campaign by the Senator from Minnesota who sought the Democratic Party nomination.

Manchester, William Raymond. **The Death of a President: November 20–November 25, 1963.** New York: Harper and Row, 1967, 710 p.
   A staggering mass of data on the assassination of President Kennedy.

Moley, Raymond with Rosen, Elliot A. **The First New Deal.** New York: Harcourt, Brace and World, 1966, 577 p.
   A useful contribution on the first years of the FDR Administration by the chief Brains-Truster of that time.

Moscow, Warren. **Roosevelt and Willkie.** Englewood Cliffs: Prentice-Hall, 1968, 210 p.
   In this story of the 1940 contest, the author concludes that Willkie's campaign to win the nomination was superbly skillful but that his election campaign was inept.

Mowrer, Edgar Ansel. **Triumph and Turmoil: A Personal History of Our Time.** New York: Weybright and Talley, 1968, 454 p.
   A reporter's survey of contemporary history, marked by a strong anti-Kennedy bias.

Newman, Albert H. **The Assassination of John F. Kennedy: The Reasons Why.** New York: Clarkson N. Potter, 1970, 622 p.
   This thorough and searching inquiry confirms most of the basic conclusions of the Warren Commission.

The Official Warren Commission Report on the Assassination of President John F. Kennedy. Garden City: Doubleday, 1964, 888 p.
   This edition of the report includes a brief analysis and commentary by Louis Nizer.

The body of the text is a full reproduction of the official U.S. Government edition. The hearings before the President's Commission on the Assassination of President Kennedy were published as "Investigation of the Assassination of President John F. Kennedy" (Washington: G.P.O., 1964, 26 v.).

O'Neill, William L. **Coming Apart: An Informal History of America in the 1960's.** Chicago: Quadrangle Books, 1971, 442 p.
The main thesis of this chronicle is that the nation went on a kind of "binge" during the 1960s in which both Left and Right participated.

Osborne, John. **The Nixon Watch.** New York: Liveright, 1970, 201 p.
———. **The Second Year of the Nixon Watch.** New York: Liveright, 1971, 207 p.
———. **The Third Year of the Nixon Watch.** New York: Liveright, 1972, 216 p.
———. **The Fourth Year of the Nixon Watch.** New York: Liveright, 1973, 218 p.
Annual compilations of the author's essays in *The New Republic*, a readable diary of Nixon's presidency.

Phillips, Cabell B. H. **The New York Times Chronicle of American Life: From the Crash to the Blitz, 1929-1939.** New York: Macmillan, 1969, 596 p.
A dramatic popular history.

Phillips, Cabell B. H. **The Truman Presidency.** New York: Macmillan, 1966, 463 p.
A well-told narrative of Harry Truman's remarkable and hardly-to-be-expected success in the Presidency, in sharp contrast to the disasters that befell two other immediate postwar presidents, Andrew Johnson and Warren Harding.

Reston, James Barrett. **Sketches in the Sand.** New York: Knopf, 1967, 479 p.
A fine and sensitively balanced selection of Reston's writings, largely drawn from his column in *The New York Times*.

Ross, Irwin. **The Loneliest Campaign: The Truman Victory of 1948.** New York: New American Library, 1968, 304 p.
An arresting account of the stunning upset-victory of Harry Truman in the 1948 Presidential election.

Salinger, Pierre Emil George. **With Kennedy.** Garden City: Doubleday, 1966, 391 p.
Memoirs of the Kennedy Administration, by the late President's press secretary.

Schlesinger, Arthur Meier, Jr. **A Thousand Days: John F. Kennedy in the White House.** Boston: Houghton, 1965, 1,087 p.
This account of the Kennedy Administration by the late President's Special Assistant is both absorbing reading and a very important source for American domestic and foreign policies in those years.

Seligman, Lester G. and Cornwell, Elmer E., Jr., eds. **New Deal Mosaic: Roosevelt Confers with His National Emergency Council, 1933-1936.** Eugene: University of Oregon Books, 1965, 578 p.
The text, with introduction and notes, of the Proceedings of the National Emergency Council. A valuable verbatim source for the history of the New Deal years.

Sidey, Hugh. **A Very Personal Presidency.** New York: Atheneum, 1968, 305 p.
An attempt to fathom the complex personality of Lyndon B. Johnson in the Presidency.

Sorensen, Theodore Chaikin. **The Kennedy Legacy.** New York: Macmillan, 1969, 414 p.
An affectionate profile of the two assassinated Kennedy brothers and a somewhat labored effort to project their influence into the future. The author also claims that John Kennedy would not have Americanized the Vietnamese war.

Stone, Isidor Feinstein. **In a Time of Torment.** New York: Random House, 1967, 463 p.
A collection of writings by the well-known editor covering issues and personalities of the 1960s.

Tugwell, Rexford Guy. **The Brains Trust.** New York: Viking, 1968, 538 p.
This valuable personal narrative throws much light on Roosevelt's campaign for the Presidency in 1932.

Tugwell, Rexford Guy. **FDR: Architect of an Era.** New York: Macmillan, 1967, 270 p.
A member of the original Roosevelt "Brains Trust" surveys the achievements of FDR.

Tugwell, Rexford Guy. **In Search of Roosevelt.** Cambridge: Harvard University Press, 1972, 313 p.

Warm, nostalgic personal essays, mostly written in the 1950s and now conveniently assembled, by a member of the original "Brains Trust." The theme is Roosevelt's lack of scruples about means and deep conviction about ends.

Voorhis, Jerry. **The Strange Case of Richard Milhous Nixon.** New York: Paul S. Eriksson, 1972, 341 p.
The author, defeated by Richard Nixon in the 1946 congressional election and active since then in promoting coöperative community action, views his subject's career with profound alarm.

Warren, Frank A., III. **Liberals and Communism: The "Red Decade" Revisited.** Bloomington: Indiana University Press, 1966, 276 p.
Having analyzed the extent of communist influence on liberal thinking in the U.S. in the thirties, the author concludes that it was great but by no means pervasive. The author's sympathies lie with the anti-communist liberals.

Warren, Sidney. **The Battle for the Presidency.** Philadelphia: Lippincott, 1968, 426 p.
An accurate and most readable account of ten presidential campaigns from Jefferson to Goldwater.

White, Theodore Harold. **The Making of the President 1964.** New York: Atheneum, 1965, 431 p.
While the present book is a chronological sequel to Mr. White's report on the 1960 Presidential campaign, its flavor is quite different, partly because of the difference in the campaigns, partly because the author views 1964 less as a contest than as a part of the turbulent procession of American history.

White, Theodore Harold. **The Making of the President 1968.** New York: Atheneum, 1969, 459 p.
The author argues that Nixon's "strategy of blandness" defeated Humphrey's "gypsy carnival." The book is better and more revealing on Robert Kennedy and Eugene McCarthy than on the two main contenders. On the whole, this is the most personal and the least objective of Mr. White's post-mortems published through 1972.

Williams, William Appleman. **Some Presidents: Wilson to Nixon.** New York: The New York Review, 1972, 122 p.
Six sprightly essay-reviews by a veteran revisionist historian, including a particularly perceptive and sympathetic piece on Herbert Hoover.

Witcover, Jules. **85 Days: The Last Campaign of Robert Kennedy.** New York: Putnam, 1969, 347 p.
A personal and often moving account. The eyewitness account of the assassination is detailed and harrowing.

Wolfskill, George and Hudson, John A. **All but the People: Franklin D. Roosevelt and His Critics, 1933-39.** New York: Macmillan, 1969, 386 p.
The entire spectrum of criticism of FDR's policies from 1933 to 1939. The savagery of the attacks is equally fierce from both Left and Right extremists.

Biographies, Memoirs and Addresses

Biographies

See also First World War, p. 131; Second World War, p. 144; (The United States) Recent History, p. 214.

Anson, Robert Sam. **McGovern: A Biography.** New York: Holt, Rinehart and Winston, 1972, 303 p.
A biography of Senator McGovern, the unsuccessful Democratic presidential candidate in 1972.

Ayer, Fred, Jr. **Before the Colors Fade.** Boston: Houghton, 1964, 266 p.
An affectionate but quite candid portrait of the late General George S. Patton, by his nephew.

Bellush, Bernard. **He Walked Alone.** The Hague: Mouton, 1968, 246 p.
An authoritative biography of the statesman and diplomat John Gilbert Winant, with a moving foreword by Allan Nevins.

Blum, John Morton. **From the Morgenthau Diaries.** Boston: Houghton, 1959–67, 3 v.
A political biography of Roosevelt's Secretary of the Treasury, Henry Morgenthau, Jr., based on his extensive diaries. The titles of the individual volumes are: vol. 1, "Years of Crisis, 1928–1938" (1959, 583 p.); vol. 2, "Years of Urgency, 1938–1941" (1965, 443 p.) and vol. 3, "Years of War, 1941–1945" (1967, 526 p.). A one volume revision and condensation was published as "Roosevelt and Morgenthau" (Boston: Houghton, 1970, 686 p.).

Burns, James MacGregor. **Roosevelt: The Soldier of Freedom.** New York: Harcourt, Brace and World, 1970, 722 p.
This splendid biography does justice to the enormous complexity of FDR's character. In the author's view, Roosevelt's vacillation between a bold global vision and a narrow pursuit of *Realpolitik* contributed to the coming of the cold war.

Cannon, Lou. **Ronnie and Jesse: A Political Odyssey.** Garden City: Doubleday, 1969, 340 p.
Political portraits of Jesse Unruh and Ronald Reagan.

Cochran, Bert. **Adlai Stevenson: Patrician among the Politicians.** New York: Funk & Wagnalls, 1969 424 p.
A well-researched political biography. The author concludes with the controversial thought that "Stevenson's tragedy would have been more brutal had he attained the pinnacle of power."

Coffin, Tristram. **Senator Fulbright: Portrait of a Public Philosopher.** New York: Dutton, 1966, 378 p.
In this adoring biography Fulbright is described as "a modern Prometheus" who "defies the gods and myths of modern society to save man from the horror of atomic doom."

Dallek, Robert. **Democrat and Diplomat: The Life of William E. Dodd.** New York: Oxford University Press, 1968, 415 p.
The biography of a Wilsonian liberal who was President Roosevelt's Ambassador to Germany from 1933 to 1938.

Davis, Kenneth Sydney. **FDR: The Beckoning of Destiny, 1882–1928; A History.** New York: Putnam, 1972, 936 p.
A gushing, breathless "life and times" for the general reader.

Davis, Kenneth Sydney. **The Politics of Honor: A Biography of Adlai E. Stevenson.** New York: Putnam, 1967, 543 p.
An updated version of the author's "A Prophet in His Own Country," published in 1957.

Davis, Nuel Pharr. **Lawrence and Oppenheimer.** New York: Simon and Schuster, 1968, 384 p.
This book offers some extraordinary insights into the minds and careers of two men who helped to usher in the atomic age. Particularly revealing on Oppenheimer.

De Toledano, Ralph. **One Man Alone: Richard Nixon.** New York: Funk & Wagnalls, 1969, 386 p.
A worshipful biography.

De Toledano, Ralph. **R.F.K.: The Man Who Would be President.** New York: Putnam, 1967, 381 p.
A superficial biography of the late Senator Robert F. Kennedy.

Dulles, Eleanor Lansing. **John Foster Dulles: The Last Year.** New York: Harcourt, Brace and World, 1963, 244 p.
Although devoted chiefly to Mr. Dulles' activities in 1958, the year before his death, this modest but illuminating and affectionate memoir by his sister, herself a member of the State Department at the time, also provides a number of insights into the late Secretary's background and earlier career.

Evans, Rowland and Novak, Robert D. **Lyndon B. Johnson: The Exercise of Power.** New York: New American Library, 1966, 597 p.
A comprehensive political biography by two well-known American columnists, written while President Johnson was still in office.

Farago, Ladislas. **Patton: Ordeal and Triumph.** New York: Obolensky, 1964, 885 p.
An ambitious, lively, though somewhat overwritten and occasionally inaccurate biography of the late General Patton.

Fleischman, Harry. **Norman Thomas: A Biography.** New York: Norton, 1964, 320 p.
An admiring and uncritical biography faithfully reporting the many and untiring undertakings of the eminent Socialist.

Freud, Sigmund and Bullitt, William C. **Thomas Woodrow Wilson, Twenty-eighth President of the United States: A Psychological Study.** Boston: Houghton, 1967, 307 p.
The central theme of this sketchy book is Wilson's need both to emulate and destroy his "incomparable father."

Furgurson, Ernest B. **Westmoreland: The Inevitable General.** Boston: Little, Brown, 1968, 347 p.
An adoring biography of a prominent American officer who was commander of the U.S. Military Assistance Command in Vietnam from 1964 to 1968.

Gregory, Ross. **Walter Hines Page: Ambassador to the Court of St. James's.** Lexington: University Press of Kentucky, 1970, 236 p.
A carefully researched biography of the American Ambassador to Britain during World War I. Page is portrayed as an ardent Anglophile whose futile efforts to persuade President Wilson to intervene in the war doomed his embassy to frustration.

Guhin, Michael A. **John Foster Dulles: A Statesman and His Times.** New York: Columbia University Press, 1972, 404 p.
The author depicts Dulles as closer to "a thoroughly pragmatic craftsman whose approach to international politics was unimpaired by ideological or moral precepts" than the rigid ideologue imagined by some contemporaries and historians. The prose is heavy; the portrait convincing.

Heinrichs, Waldo Huntley, Jr. **American Ambassador: Joseph C. Grew and the Development of the U.S. Diplomatic Tradition.** Boston: Little, Brown, 1966, 460 p.
A solid account of the forty-year career of Joseph C. Grew in the American diplomatic service. The author contends that Grew played an important role in the establishment of American diplomacy on a professional career basis.

Hess, Stephen. **America's Political Dynasties: From Adams to Kennedy.** Garden City: Doubleday, 1966, 736 p.
In the author's words, this is an effort "to bring together for the first time the panorama of American political dynasties from colonial days to the present; to investigate their roles in shaping the nation; and to recount the lives of some two hundred often engaging, usually ambitious, sometimes brilliant, occasionally unscrupulous individuals."

Israel, Fred L. **Nevada's Key Pittman.** Lincoln: University of Nebraska Press, 1963, 210 p.
A critical portrayal of a "political realist" who was head of the Senate Committee on Foreign Relations from 1933 to 1940.

James, Dorris Clayton. **The Years of MacArthur. Volume I: 1880–1941.** Boston: Houghton, 1970, 740 p.
This first volume of a projected two-volume biography is one of the leading works to have appeared thus far on the controversial general. The research is thorough, and judgments are balanced and without prejudice.

Johnpoll, Bernard K. **Pacifist's Progress: Norman Thomas and the Decline of American Socialism.** Chicago: Quadrangle Books, 1970, 336 p.
In this study the author asserts that "Thomas's failure as a politician was a reflection of his success as a human being."

Johnson, Haynes Bonner and Gwertzman, Bernard M. **Fulbright: The Dissenter.** Garden City: Doubleday, 1968, 321 p.
A well-researched, well-written though somewhat worshipful biography of the former Senator from Arkansas.

Katcher, Leo. **Earl Warren: A Political Biography.** New York: McGraw-Hill, 1967, 502 p.
This biography is better on Warren the politician than on Warren the Supreme Court Justice.

Kearney, James R. **Anna Eleanor Roosevelt: The Evolution of a Reformer.** Boston: Houghton, 1968, 332 p.
An objective study.

Keeley, Joseph Charles. **The China Lobby Man: The Story of Alfred Kohlberg.** New Rochelle: Arlington House, 1969, 421 p.
An apotheosis of Alfred Kohlberg, a moving spirit behind the "China Lobby," with vicious attacks on former Foreign Service officers and China scholars.

Kendrick, Alexander. **Prime Time: The Life of Edward R. Murrow.** Boston: Little, Brown, 1969, 548 p.
A somewhat overlong chronicle of the great broadcaster's career. The highlights are well told: "This is London," the confrontation with Joe McCarthy, Korea, and the USIA.

Landau, David. **Kissinger: The Uses of Power.** Boston: Houghton Mifflin, 1972, 270 p.
Landau, who began this study while still a Harvard undergraduate, is informative about Kissinger's pre-White House career, appreciative of his skill but critical of intellectual qualities which allegedly inhibited an early settlement of the Vietnam War.

Lash, Joseph P. **Eleanor and Franklin.** New York: Norton, 1971, 765 p.
——. **Eleanor: The Years Alone.** New York: Norton, 1972, 368 p.
A massive, well-documented and admiring biography of Eleanor Roosevelt, the wife of President Franklin D. Roosevelt.

Lasky, Victor. **J.F.K.: The Man and the Myth.** New York: Macmillan, 1963, 653 p.
An extensively researched attack on the late President Kennedy.

Link, Arthur Stanley. **The Higher Realism of Woodrow Wilson and Other Essays.** Nashville: Vanderbilt University Press, 1971, 425 p.
Essays on Wilson, by the leading authority on the twenty-eighth President of the United States.

Link, Arthur Stanley. **Wilson.** Princeton: Princeton University Press.
Since 1963 the following volumes have been published of this authoritative biography of Woodrow Wilson: "Confusions and Crises, 1915–1916" (1964, 386 p.) and "Campaigns for Progressivism and Peace, 1916–1917" (1965, 464 p.). For earlier volumes, consult "Foreign Affairs Bibliography, 1952–1962."

Long, Gavin Merrick. **MacArthur as Military Commander.** Princeton: Van Nostrand and Reinhold, 1969, 243 p.
An objective and straightforward narrative of the general's career.

Lunt, Richard D. **The High Ministry of Government: The Political Career of Frank Murphy.** Detroit: Wayne State University Press, 1965, 263 p.
A study of the political career of a man who served as mayor of Detroit, Governor-General of the Philippines, Governor of Michigan, U.S. Attorney General and eventually Justice of the U.S. Supreme Court.

Lyons, Eugene. **Herbert Hoover.** Garden City: Doubleday, 1964, 444 p.
A largely rewritten and expanded biography first published in 1948.

McCoy, Donald Richard. **Calvin Coolidge: The Quiet President.** New York: Macmillan, 1967, 472 p.
This may well be the definitive biography of the "quiet President." The author's scholarship is impeccable, the style smooth, the central conclusion not surprising: "Coolidge's failure was the failure of a President who does not look ahead and does not fight to head off the problems of the future."

Mazlish, Bruce. **In Search of Nixon: A Psychohistorical Inquiry.** New York: Basic Books, 1972, 187 p.
A bold attempt to use psychoanalysis and the imperfectly defined technique of "psychohistory" to understand President Nixon's behavior.

Mazo, Earl and Hess, Stephen. **Nixon: A Political Portrait.** New York: Harper and Row, 1968, 334 p.
A revision of Mazo's "Richard Nixon: A Political and Personal Portrait" (New York: Harper, 1959, 309 p.). A useful study, but certainly not the definitive biography.

Michelmore, Peter. **The Swift Years: The Robert Oppenheimer Story.** New York: Dodd, 1969, 273 p.
An Australian journalist has produced a very personal, sympathetic and highly readable biography of the controversial physicist.

Miller, William J. **Henry Cabot Lodge.** New York: James H. Heineman, 1967, 449 p.
An adoring biography of a distinguished statesman and diplomat.

Morrison, Joseph L. **Josephus Daniels: The Small-D Democrat.** Chapel Hill: University of North Carolina Press, 1966, 316 p.
A biography of Josephus Daniels (1862–1948), a North Carolina newspaperman who was Secretary of the Navy during both of Wilson's administrations and served as ambassador to Mexico during the first nine years of FDR's administration.

Muller, Herbert Joseph. **Adlai Stevenson: A Study in Values.** New York: Harper and Row, 1967, 338 p.
A fine, though frankly admiring, political biography.

Nevins, Allan. **Herbert H. Lehman and His Era.** New York: Scribner, 1963, 456 p.
A detailed description of the many public service contributions of Herbert Lehman, a leading Democrat and a former governor of the State of New York.

Newfield, Jack. **Robert Kennedy: A Memoir.** New York: Dutton, 1969, 318 p.
This biography is an affectionate tribute to the man "who might have united the black and white poor into a new majority for change."

Patterson, James T. **Mr. Republican: A Biography of Robert A. Taft.** Boston: Houghton Mifflin, 1972, 749 p.
A work of superior scholarship and sound judgment about a Senator whose intelligence and industry were unrivaled, but whose impact was limited by the incongruity between his ideas and the times. The book was authorized by the Taft family but neither the research nor the resulting text was controlled by them in any way.

Pogue, Forrest C. **George C. Marshall.** New York: Viking, 1963–.
The definitive biography of the late general, based upon Marshall's papers and a number of interviews. Through 1973 the following volumes have appeared: "Education of a General, 1880–1939" (1963, 421 p.); "Ordeal and Hope, 1939–1942" (1966, 491 p.) and "Organizer of Victory, 1943–1945" (1973, 683 p.).

Rogow, Arnold A. **James Forrestal: A Study of Personality, Politics, and Policy.** New York: Macmillan, 1963, 397 p.
The author attempts to probe the late Secretary of Defense Forrestal's personality to get at the background to his tragic suicide in 1949 and to find the relationship between his temper and character and his role in national policy.

Schapsmeier, Edward L. and Schapsmeier, Frederick H. **Prophet in Politics: Henry A. Wallace and the War Years, 1940–1965.** Ames: Iowa State University Press, 1971, 268 p.
A worshipful account of Henry Wallace's political career during the Second World War and cold war years.

Shannon, William Vincent. **The Heir Apparent: Robert Kennedy and the Struggle for Power.** New York: Macmillan, 1967, 309 p.
A sympathetic political biography of the late Robert F. Kennedy, by a member of the editorial board of *The New York Times*.

Sherrill, Robert and Ernst, Harry W. **The Drugstore Liberal.** New York: Grossman, 1968, 200 p.
A biography of Senator Humphrey, Vice President of the United States from 1965 to 1969.

Smith, Gene. **When the Cheering Stopped: The Last Years of Woodrow Wilson.** New York: Morrow, 1964, 307 p.
An overly dramatic account of those years in President Wilson's life which have already been more accurately recorded.

Sorensen, Theodore Chaikin. **Kennedy.** New York: Harper and Row, 1965, 783 p.
A highly informative portrait of John F. Kennedy as politician, candidate and President, by a close associate of the late President.

Steinberg, Alfred. **Sam Johnson's Boy: A Close-up of the President from Texas.** New York: Macmillan, 1968, 871 p.
In this stinging biography the author reaches the conclusion that "Sam Johnson's boy could not become more than the President from Texas" and "failed to emerge as a President of the United States."

Sternsher, Bernard. **Rexford Tugwell and the New Deal.** New Brunswick: Rutgers University Press, 1964, 535 p.
A comprehensive study of Tugwell's activities as a leading figure in the New Deal; an effort to "set the record straight."

Stevenson, Adlai Ewing. **The Papers of Adlai E. Stevenson.** Boston: Little, Brown, 1972–.
A documentary biography of Governor Stevenson, planned in eight volumes and edited by Walter Johnson. Through 1973, the following volumes have appeared: "Beginnings of Education, 1900–1941" (1972, 568 p.); "Washington to Springfield, 1941–1948" (1973, 620 p.) and "Governor of Illinois, 1949–1953" (1973, 621 p.).

Tompkins, C. David. **Senator Arthur H. Vandenberg: The Evolution of a Modern Republican, 1884–1945.** Lansing: Michigan State University Press, 1970, 312 p.
A solid political biography providing perspective and information not available in "The Private Papers of Senator Vandenberg" (1952).

Walton, Richard J. **The Remnants of Power: The Tragic Last Years of Adlai Stevenson.** New York: Coward-McCann, 1968, 255 p.
Stevenson's years at the United Nations, in the author's view, were marked by a profound inner conflict between the public and the private man over some of the main policy directions of the Johnson administration.

Weaver, John Downing. **Warren: The Man, the Court, the Era.** Boston: Little, Brown, 1967, 406 p.
This biography of the former Chief Justice includes a first-rate assessment of the Warren Commission Report on the assassination of President Kennedy.

Whitman, Alden Rogers and Others. **Portrait—Adlai E. Stevenson: Politician, Diplomat, Friend.** New York: Harper and Row, 1965, 289 p.
A sketch of Stevenson's role as a politician, diplomat and personal friend, drawn in large measure from coverage provided by *The New York Times.*

Wills, Garry. **Nixon Agonistes: The Crisis of the Self-made Man.** Boston: Houghton, 1970, 617 p.
A biography of Richard M. Nixon and a profound analysis of the political forces in America that made him President.

Witcover, Jules. **The Resurrection of Richard Nixon.** New York: Putnam, 1970, 479 p.
A straightforward account of the political peregrinations of Richard Nixon.

Witcover, Jules. **White Knight: The Rise of Spiro Agnew.** New York: Random House, 1972, 465 p.
A study of the controversial Vice President, based primarily on interviews with 120 of his friends, enemies and associates. More than half the book deals with the years before 1969. The author is a veteran Washington journalist.

Memoirs

See also (The World Since 1914) General, p. 129; Inter-War Period, p. 140; Second World War, p. 144.

Acheson, Dean Gooderham. **Morning and Noon.** Boston: Houghton, 1965, 288 p.
These ably written memoirs of the youth and early career of the former Secretary of State are pleasantly revealing of the man, but stop at 1941 when Mr. Acheson became Assistant Secretary of State for Economic Affairs.

Acheson, Dean Gooderham. **Present at the Creation: My Years at the State Department.** New York: Norton, 1969, 798 p.
A rich and detailed memoir about the author's years in the State Department, with affectionate emphasis on the Truman years. The forceful personality of the former Secretary of State emerges most clearly from these pages.

Bowles, Chester. **Promises to Keep: My Years in Public Life, 1941–1969.** New York: Harper and Row, 1971, 657 p.
This memoir by a distinguished public servant and diplomat is an important source for the study of American politics and foreign relations.

Braden, Spruille. **Diplomats and Demagogues.** New Rochelle (N.Y.): Arlington House, 1971, 496 p.
Memoirs by a former U.S. diplomat with many years of service in various Latin American countries who from 1946–47 was also the Assistant Secretary of State for American Republic Affairs.

Briggs, Ellis Ormsbee. **Farewell to Foggy Bottom.** New York: McKay, 1964, 306 p.
Unusually lively, humorous and often caustic diplomatic memoirs by a former U.S. Foreign Service officer and ambassador whose stations included much of Latin America, Czechoslovakia and Korea.

Bush, Vannevar. **Pieces of the Action.** New York: Morrow, 1970, 366 p.
A salty autobiography, written with humor and optimism, by a leading scientist, administrator and chairman of the National Defense Research Commission during World War II.

Childs, James Rives. **Foreign Service Farewell: My Years in the Near East.** Charlottesville: University Press of Virginia (for Randolph-Macon College), 1969, 192 p.
Reminiscences of his many years of service in the Middle East by a veteran American diplomat.

Christian, George. **The President Steps Down: A Personal Memoir of the Transfer of Power.** New York: Macmillan, 1970, 282 p.
LBJ's last hundred days, recounted by his former press secretary.

Conant, James Bryant. **My Several Lives: Memoirs of a Social Inventor.** New York: Harper and Row, 1970, 701 p.
The author explores at a leisurely pace his three careers as scientist, educator and statesman.

Cutler, Robert. **No Time for Rest.** Boston: Atlantic (Little, Brown), 1966, 421 p.
The political memoirs of a Bostonian become national public servant, who served with Stimson, Marshall, Forrestal and ultimately as Special Assistant to President Eisenhower.

Douglas, Paul H. **In the Fullness of Time.** New York: Harcourt Brace Jovanovich, 1972, 642 p.
Senator Douglas reviews his life—personal, academic, military and above all political—in frank and fascinating detail and provides an invaluable source for a history of the Senate and its major legislative achievements in the years 1949–66.

Du Bois, William Edward Burghart. **The Autobiography of W. E. B. Du Bois.** New York: International Publishers, 1968, 448 p.
This autobiography was written at the age of ninety by a black American writer and leader who helped found the National Association for the Advancement of Colored People. In his later years Mr. Du Bois joined the Communist Party and became a citizen of Ghana.

Einstein, Lewis. **A Diplomat Looks Back.** New Haven: Yale University Press, 1968, 269 p.
The evocative and perceptive memoirs of a distinguished American diplomat, spanning half a century. Edited by Lawrence E. Gelfand.

Eisenhower, Dwight David. **At Ease: Stories I Tell to Friends.** Garden City: Doubleday, 1967, 400 p.
The late President Eisenhower reminisces in an easygoing manner about his childhood, his military career and the years after World War II before he became a Republican Presidential candidate.

Eisenhower, Dwight David. **The White House Years.** Garden City: Doubleday, 1963–65, 2 v.
The first volume of the detailed and informative memoirs of the late President Eisenhower is entitled "Mandate for Change, 1953–1956" (1963, 650 p.), the second, "Waging Peace, 1956–1961" (1965, 741 p.).

Frankel, Charles. **High on Foggy Bottom: An Outsider's Inside View of the Government.** New York: Harper and Row, 1969, 240 p.
A philosophy professor's log of his experiences as Assistant Secretary of State for Educational and Cultural Affairs in the Johnson administration.

Galbraith, John Kenneth. **Ambassador's Journal: A Personal Account of the Kennedy Years.** Boston: Houghton, 1969, 656 p.
An interesting if wry memoir by the prominent American economist who was the U.S. Ambassador to India during the Kennedy administration.

Hoover, Calvin Bryce. **Memoirs of Capitalism, Communism, and Nazism.** Durham: Duke University Press, 1965, 302 p.
A prominent economist and intelligence officer appraises capitalism, communism and Nazism and provides useful information on his many important assignments during and after World War II.

Hughes, Emmet John. **The Ordeal of Power: A Political Memoir of the Eisenhower Years.** New York: Atheneum, 1963, 372 p.
Mr. Hughes, who for a time was a speech writer and adviser to President Eisenhower, here offers his memoirs of the latter's administration. The late John Foster Dulles is the central villain of the piece.

Johnson, Claudia A. (Taylor). **A White House Diary.** New York: Holt, Rinehart and Winston, 1970, 806 p.
This diary by President Johnson's wife reveals the character of a devoted, loving and powerful woman, and provides an intimate perspective of the Johnson household during the Presidency.

Johnson, Edgar Augustus Jerome. **American Imperialism in the Image of Peer Gynt.** Minneapolis: University of Minnesota Press, 1971, 352 p.
A memoir by a liberal scholar-bureaucrat with a literary flair and considerable political experience.

Johnson, Lyndon Baines. **The Vantage Point: Perspectives of the Presidency, 1963-1969.** New York: Holt, Rinehart and Winston, 1971, 636 p.
A volume of political memoirs by the late President. Only three chapters deal with the war in Vietnam.

Kennan, George Frost. **Memoirs.** Boston: Atlantic (Little, Brown), 1967-72, 2 v.
Well-written reminscences, covering the years from 1925 to 1963, by a distinguished U.S. diplomat who is also known for his writings on U.S. foreign policy and contemporary history.

Krock, Arthur. **Memoirs: Sixty Years on the Firing Line.** New York: Funk & Wagnalls, 1968, 508 p.
The testament and testimony of one of the great American journalists of the twentieth century. Arthur Krock, who spent almost 40 years with *The New York Times*—for many years as the head of its Washington Bureau—provides in his recollections fascinating characterizations of many leading Americans and laments the drift toward mass democracy.

LeMay, Curtis Emerson with Kantor, MacKinlay. **Mission with LeMay: My Story.** Garden City: Doubleday, 1965, 581 p.
This autobiography is more revealing of the personality and life of the former Air Force Chief of Staff than of the military history he experienced before, during and after World War II.

Lilienthal, David Eli. **The Journals of David E. Lilienthal.** New York: Harper and Row, 1964-71, 5 v.
The first volume of Mr. Lilienthal's well-written and remarkably frank private journals, "The TVA Years, 1939-1945," covers the latter part of his directorship of the Tennessee Valley Authority; the second volume, "The Atomic Energy Years, 1945-1950," his experiences as first chairman of the Atomic Energy Commission; the third volume, "Venturesome Years, 1950-1955," the beginnings of the author's career in private business; the fourth volume, "The Road to Change, 1955-1959," his experiences in establishing the Development and Resources Corporation and travels to various underdeveloped countries; the fifth volume, "The Harvest Years, 1959-1963," deals with the Development and Resources Corporation and offers glimpses into the author's relationship with John F. Kennedy.

Lindbergh, Charles August. **The Wartime Journals of Charles A. Lindbergh.** New York: Harcourt Brace Jovanovich, 1970, 1,038 p.

These journals by the famous aviator and public figure are an important source for the history of our times.

Long, Breckinridge. **The War Diary of Breckinridge Long: Selections from the Years 1939-1944.** Lincoln: University of Nebraska Press, 1966, 410 p.
Selections from the diary of an American diplomat and policy-maker who was President Roosevelt's Assistant Secretary of State from 1940 to 1944. Edited by Fred L. Israel.

MacArthur, Douglas. **Reminiscences.** New York: McGraw-Hill, 1964, 438 p.
These personal memoirs, written shortly before his death, reveal much about the personality of the late general, one of America's greatest military leaders, and provide a good deal of material for the historian, though as a source the book must be used with caution and checked against other military records.

McCarthy, Abigail. **Private Faces, Public Places.** Garden City: Doubleday, 1972, 448 p.
A moving autobiography by a thoughtful woman, the ex-wife of former Senator Eugene McCarthy.

Matthews, Herbert L. **A World in Revolution: A Newspaperman's Memoir.** New York: Scribner, 1972, 462 p.
The author's observations on a number of countries in revolutionary ferment are not particularly revealing, but his analyses of the changing editorial policies of *The New York Times*, for which he worked for 45 years, are penetrating and instructive.

Meyers, Joan Simpson, *ed.* **John Fitzgerald Kennedy: As We Remember Him.** New York: Atheneum, 1965, 241 p.
A memorial volume. The pictures of the late President are accompanied by a text based largely on interviews and memoranda prepared for the purpose by friends and members of the President's family.

Murphy, Robert Daniel. **Diplomat among Warriors.** Garden City: Doubleday, 1964, 470 p.
Important and substantial memoirs by a veteran Foreign Service officer whose diplomatic and trouble-shooting assignments brought him close to an extraordinary number of central issues of the wartime and post-World War II years.

O'Donnell, Kenneth P. and Powers, David F. **"Johnny, We Hardly Knew Ye": Memories of John Fitzgerald Kennedy.** Boston: Little, Brown, 1972, 434 p.
O'Donnell and Powers—both Irish, both from Massachusetts—were John F. Kennedy's intimate political aides and personal friends from 1946 until his death. Their recollections are poignant, rollicking, uncritical and revealing.

Perkins, Dexter. **Yield of the Years: An Autobiography.** Boston: Little, Brown, 1969, 245 p.
Fifty years of history—in education, politics and foreign policy—as seen through the eyes of a leading American historian.

Riegle, Donald with Armbrister, Trevor. **O Congress.** Garden City: Doubleday, 1972, 297 p.
The lively diary from April 1971 to March 1972 of a young, unorthodox Republican Congressman: his disenchantment with the Nixon administration, his alliance with the McCloskey campaign, crises in his personal life.

Strausz-Hupé, Robert. **In My Time.** New York: Norton, 1965, 284 p.
This autobiography of the Austrian-born director of the Foreign Policy Research Institute at the University of Pennsylvania, who in 1969 became the U.S. Ambassador to Morocco, contains a wealth of observations on twentieth-century political developments.

Sulzberger, Cyrus Leo. **A Long Row of Candles: Memoirs and Diaries, 1934-1954.** New York: Macmillan, 1969, 1,061 p.
———. **The Last of the Giants.** New York: Macmillan, 1970, 1,063 p.
Commentaries on international relations and accounts of interviews with leading statesmen all over the world, by the well-known columnist of *The New York Times*.

Swing, Raymond. **"Good Evening!"** New York: Harcourt, Brace and World, 1964, 311 p.
Memoirs and reflections on his profession by a foreign correspondent who achieved greatest prominence as a radio news commentator.

Taylor, Edmond Lapierre. **Awakening from History.** Boston: Gambit, 1969, 522 p.
An American foreign correspondent of many years' standing has written an autobiography which, in his words, bears witness to "some of the transformations that have taken place in the mind of my generation since it came of age forty-odd years ago."

Taylor, Maxwell D. **Swords and Plowshares.** New York: Norton, 1972, 434 p.
General Taylor in this autobiographical and didactic essay discusses the uses and misuses of power.

Vandegrift, Alexander Archer with Asprey, Robert Brown. **Once a Marine: The Memoirs of General A. A. Vandegrift.** New York: Norton, 1964, 338 p.
Memoirs, mainly of the Second World War, by the former Commandant of the U.S. Marine Corps.

Addresses and Papers

See also Inter-War Period, p. 140; Second World War, p. 144; (The United States) Foreign Policy, p. 229.

Acheson, Dean Gooderham. **Fragments of My Fleece.** New York: Norton, 1971, 222 p.
A collection of stories, articles and personal glimpses by the former Secretary of State.

Blumenson, Martin. **The Patton Papers, 1885–1940.** Boston: Houghton, 1972, 996 p.
The largest portion of this volume, consisting mostly of diaries and family letters, traces General Patton's participation in the First World War.

Bullitt, Orville H., *ed.* **For the President—Personal and Secret: Correspondence between Franklin D. Roosevelt and William C. Bullitt.** Boston: Houghton Mifflin, 1972, 655 p.
Lengthy, colorful, imaginative and, at times, outrageous letters from Ambassador Bullitt with a few brief replies by President Roosevelt. The bulk of the material deals with Bullitt's years in Moscow and Paris. Good reading and valuable for historians.

Burns, James MacGregor, *ed.* **To Heal and to Build: The Programs of President Lyndon B. Johnson.** New York: McGraw-Hill, 1968, 506 p.
This volume brings together the main programs and speeches of President Johnson.

Chambers, Whittaker. **Odyssey of a Friend: Whittaker Chambers' Letters to William F. Buckley, Jr. 1954–1961.** New York: Putnam, 1970, 303 p.
These letters, edited by the recipient, reveal the brilliant and tortured mind of Whittaker Chambers even more clearly than his "Witness" (1952). They contain many important footnotes to the recent history of the United States.

Cooke, Alistair. **Talk about America.** New York: Knopf, 1968, 310 p.
Forty-one broadcasts, all given on the BBC.

Cousins, Norman. **Present Tense: An American Editor's Odyssey.** New York: McGraw-Hill, 1967, 679 p.
The editorial page from the *Saturday Review* from Pearl Harbor to Vietnam. The author's major thesis: the world has become one, but has not become whole.

Coyne, John R., Jr. **The Impudent Snobs.** New Rochelle (N.Y.): Arlington House, 1972, 524 p.
A compilation of the former Vice President Agnew's speeches preceded by an admiring analysis and elaboration of his attack on the press and television. The author, a conservative journalist, once served on the Vice President's staff.

Daniels, Josephus. **The Cabinet Diaries of Josephus Daniels, 1913–1921.** Lincoln: University of Nebraska Press, 1963, 648 p.
A source for the Wilson era by the Secretary of the Navy in both administrations. Edited by Edmund David Cronon.

Dobney, Frederick J., *ed.* **Selected Papers of Will Clayton.** Baltimore: Johns Hopkins Press, 1971, 298 p.
Carefully chosen excerpts from speeches and sparse but revealing unpublished papers of an architect of foreign policy in the Truman years. Clayton's efforts to create an environment favorable to American capitalism are displayed.

Fosdick, Raymond B. **Letters on the League of Nations: From the Files of Raymond B. Fosdick.** Princeton: Princeton University Press, 1966, 171 p.
Letters from and to Raymond B. Fosdick, chiefly in 1919 and 1920, relating to the establishment of the League of Nations and the question of American participation.

Freedman, Max. **Roosevelt and Frankfurter: Their Correspondence, 1928-1945.** Boston: Atlantic (Little, Brown), 1968, 772 p.
This is a poignant and moving book, in essence the story of a friendship, but illuminated with flashes of insight into the personalities and politics of the President and the Justice.

Fulbright, James William. **Fulbright of Arkansas.** Washington: Robert B. Luce, 1963, 279 p.
A good selection of Senator Fulbright's important public speeches on foreign and domestic policy. Edited by Karl Ernest Meyer.

Goldberg, Arthur J. **The Defenses of Freedom.** New York: Harper and Row, 1966, 342 p.
A collection of the public papers of the former Supreme Court Justice who was U.S. Permanent Representative at the United Nations from 1965 to 1968.

Hobbs, Joseph Patrick. **Dear General: Eisenhower's Wartime Letters to Marshall.** Baltimore: Johns Hopkins Press, 1971, 255 p.
These letters reveal General Eisenhower's growth as man and military commander. Marshall's singular role as his mentor emerges with great clarity.

Kennedy, Robert Francis. **To Seek a Newer World.** Garden City: Doubleday, 1967, 233 p.
A judicious selection from the late Senator's papers and speeches since January 1965.

Lindsay, John Vliet. **Journey into Politics: Some Informal Observations.** New York: Dodd, 1967, 152 p.
A collection of essays written during Lindsay's seven years as a member of Congress. A brief concluding chapter offers reflections on his experience as Mayor of New York City.

Lippmann, Walter. **Conversations with Walter Lippmann.** Boston: Atlantic (Little, Brown), 1965, 242 p.
A collection of the well-known columnist's periodic C.B.S. television interviews since August 1960.

Lippmann, Walter. **Early Writings.** New York: Liveright, 1970, 356 p.
Writings from the author's mid-twenties. Mr. Schlesinger's sensitive annotations are most helpful.

Lippmann, Walter. **The Essential Lippmann: A Political Philosophy for Liberal Democracy.** New York: Random House, 1963, 552 p.
A substantial selection of Walter Lippmann's writings on various political themes. Edited by Clinton Lawrence Rossiter and James Lare.

Luce, Henry Robinson. **The Ideas of Henry Luce.** New York: Atheneum, 1969, 405 p.
The writings of the founder and long-time editor of *Time*, selected from a span of almost half a century by John K. Jessup, the former chief editorial writer of *Life*.

MacArthur, Douglas. **A Soldier Speaks: Public Papers and Speeches of General of the Army Douglas MacArthur.** New York: Praeger, 1965, 367 p.
A selection of the late general's public papers and speeches, arranged chronologically over his long career from 1908 to 1964. Edited by Vorin E. Whan, Jr.

Murrow, Edward Roscoe. **In Search of Light.** New York: Knopf, 1967, 364 p.
The great broadcast journalist's reports from 1938 to 1961.

Peabody, James Bishop, *ed.* **The Holmes-Einstein Letters.** New York: St. Martin's Press, 1964, 377 p.
The correspondence of Justice Oliver Wendell Holmes and the much younger American diplomat Lewis Einstein, carried on from 1903 to 1935, resulted in a brilliant running discourse on multiple personal, national and international topics.

Public Papers of the Presidents of the United States. Washington: G.P.O.
A compilation of most of the public messages and statements of the Presidents of the United States. The series was begun in 1957 in response to a recommendation of the

THE WESTERN HEMISPHERE

National Historical Publications Commission. The volumes published through 1972 cover the years of President Truman from 1945 to 1953, of President Eisenhower from 1953 to 1961, of President Kennedy from 1961 to 1963, of President Johnson from 1963 to 1969, and of President Nixon from 1969 to 1971.

Roosevelt, Anna Eleanor. **Tomorrow is Now.** New York: Harper and Row, 1963, 139 p.
Just before her death Mrs. Roosevelt completed the draft of this brief but eloquent plea to look back into history for the lessons to be found there, to realize that we must face the unknown "as our ancestors faced the unknown, with imagination and integrity, with courage and a high heart."

Rusk, Dean. **The Winds of Freedom.** Boston: Beacon Press, 1963, 363 p.
A selection of the speeches and statements of the former Secretary of State from January 1961 to August 1962.

Smith, Margaret Chase. **Declaration of Conscience.** Garden City: Doubleday, 1972, 512 p.
A collection of speeches, a few letters and memoranda and brief comments by the former Senator. Edited by William C. Lewis, Jr.

Foreign Policy
General

See also General Works, p. 1; Political Factors, p. 12; International Law, p. 83; International Organization and Government, p. 96; War and Peace, p. 108; The World Since 1914, p. 129; Inter-American Relations, p. 193; (The United States) General, p. 213; Recent History, p. 214; Biographies, Memoirs and Addresses, p. 218; Military and Defense Policy, p. 257; Politics and Political Issues, p. 268; Culture; Education; Press; Radio, p. 278; and the sections for specific countries and regions.

Adler, Selig. **The Uncertain Giant: 1921-1941.** New York: Macmillan, 1966, 340 p.
This work, "intended primarily for the nonspecialist," provides a concise review of U.S. foreign policy between the two world wars.

American Foreign Policy: Current Documents, 1956-67. Washington: G.P.O. (for the Department of State), 1959-69, 12 v.
An official collection of documents on the "scope, goals, and implementation of the foreign policy of the United States," continuing the series which began with "A Decade of American Foreign Policy: Basic Documents, 1941-1949" (Washington: G.P.O., 1950, 1,381 p.) and "American Foreign Policy, 1950-1955: Basic Documents" (Washington: G.P.O., 1957, 2 v.).

Amerika no taigai seisaku. Tokyo: Kajima Kenkyūjo Shuppankai, 1971, 474 p.
A substantial collection of essays on contemporary U.S. foreign policy prepared by the Area Studies Group of Keio University.

Appleton, Sheldon. **United States Foreign Policy.** Boston: Little, Brown, 1968, 624 p.
An introductory book with imaginative use of case studies. The author states that "the outbreaks of violence in our own cities and in foreign lands have common causes."

Ball, George W. **The Discipline of Power: Essentials of a Modern World Structure.** Boston: Atlantic (Little, Brown), 1968, 363 p.
In this sane and balanced book a distinguished American diplomat and statesman suggests that America has tended to use her power not arrogantly, but exuberantly. In his quest for a new world power balance, Mr. Ball's central concern is the need for progress toward European unity.

Barnet, Richard J. **Intervention and Revolution: The United States in the Third World.** Cleveland: World Publishing Co., 1968, 302 p.
An indictment of "the militarist analysis of the world environment" and a plea that the United States intervene less in the revolutions of other nations.

Bartlett, Ruhl Jacob. **Policy and Power: Two Centuries of American Foreign Relations.** New York: Hill and Wang, 1963, 303 p.
A brief but useful survey of the history of U.S. foreign relations.

Bowie, Robert Richardson. **Shaping the Future: Foreign Policy in an Age of Transition.** New York: Columbia University Press, 1964, 118 p.

In these lectures a Harvard professor concisely summarizes the principal requisites for a foreign policy, for success in achieving an Atlantic order and for organizing and managing foreign policy.

Braeman, John; Bremner, Robert H. and Brody, David, *eds.* **Twentieth-Century American Foreign Policy.** Columbus: Ohio State University Press, 1971, 567 p.
Eleven essays on various aspects of American foreign policy. The volume is the third in the series "Modern America," dealing with the problems of change and continuity in twentieth-century U.S. history.

Brandon, Donald Wayne. **American Foreign Policy: Beyond Utopianism and Realism.** New York: Appleton, 1966, 295 p.
A critique of U.S. foreign policy and attitudes in the present century, stressing the realist and utopian approaches, and advocating the tradition of "prudential judgment."

Brown, Seyom. **The Faces of Power: Constancy and Change in United States Foreign Policy from Truman to Johnson.** New York: Columbia University Press, 1968, 397 p.
In this valuable book, the author, a RAND Corporation analyst, examines the uses of power in the foreign policy decision-making processes of Presidents Truman, Eisenhower, Kennedy and Johnson.

Brzezinski, Zbigniew Kazimierz. **Between Two Ages: America's Role in the Technetronic Era.** New York: Viking, 1970, 334 p.
The author projects the impact of technology and electronics upon society in the United States, the Soviet Union and other "post-industrial" states. A most original study of global society in transition.

Buckley, Thomas H. **The United States and the Washington Conference, 1921-1922.** Knoxville: University of Tennessee Press, 1970, 222 p.
The author of this meticulously researched monograph takes the reader step by step through the arduous negotiations of the Washington Conference of 1921-1922. The assessment of the arms limitation agreements that emerged from the conference is balanced and realistic.

Canham, Erwin D. **The Ethics of United States Foreign Relations.** Columbia: University of Missouri Press, 1966, 93 p.
Lectures by the editor of *The Christian Science Monitor.*

Cantril, Albert Hadley. **The Human Dimension: Experiences in Policy Research.** New Brunswick: Rutgers University Press, 1967, 202 p.
The author argues for the inclusion of "all necessary psychological factors" in the formulation of foreign policy in order to avoid disasters like the Bay of Pigs.

Chomsky, Noam. **American Power and the New Mandarins.** New York: Pantheon Books, 1969, 404 p.
The author, a well-known linguist who passionately opposed the war in Vietnam, attacks the American intellectual establishment for misguiding the makers of U.S. foreign policy.

Cleveland, Harlan. **The Obligations of Power: American Diplomacy in the Search for Peace.** New York: Harper and Row, 1966, 168 p.
The former U.S. Ambassador to NATO offers an informal and perhaps overly sanguine essay on the goals and requirements of American foreign policy.

Cooper, John Milton, Jr. **The Vanity of Power: American Isolationism and the First World War, 1914-1917.** Westport (Conn.): Greenwood, 1969, 271 p.
The author of this fine scholarly book argues that the isolationist position that formed during the First World War and lasted until the Second belonged to a particular moment in American history and is not likely to be resurrected in contemporary America.

Czempiel, Ernst Otto. **Das amerikanische Sicherheitssystem 1945-1949: Studie zur Aussenpolitik der bürgerlichen Gesellschaft.** Berlin: De Gruyter, 1966, 442 p.
A carefully researched survey of the U.S. role in world affairs from World War II to the birth of NATO.

Davydov, Iu. P. and Rudnev, V. S., *eds.* **SShA: regional'nye problemy vneshnei politiki.** Moscow: Izd-vo "Nauka," 1971, 215 p.
A Soviet critique of the United States foreign policy as it enters the 1970s. Published for the Institute of the United States of America.

Dmitriev, Boris Dmitrievich. **SShA: politiki, generaly, diplomaty; chetvert' veka politiki "s pozitsii sily."** Moscow: Izd-vo "Mezhdunarodnye Otnosheniia," 1971, 350 p.
A chronological and analytical Soviet study of the evolution of U.S. foreign policy since 1945. Persistence in the unattainable goal of confronting the Soviet Union "from a position of strength" is said to assure the failure of American strategy, regardless of tactical shifts.

Documents on American Foreign Relations. New York: Harper and Row; Simon and Schuster (for the Council on Foreign Relations).
A most useful annual selection of documents, begun in 1939. The volumes published from 1963 through 1972, covering the years from 1962 to 1969, were prepared by Richard P. Stebbins and Elaine P. Adam, with the exception of the 1964 annual which was edited by Jules Davids and Elaine P. Adam.

Donelan, Michael Denis. **The Ideas of American Foreign Policy.** London: Chapman, 1963, 272 p.
A British review of the leading ideas and viewpoints affecting U.S. foreign policy between 1945 and 1962.

Duroselle, Jean-Baptiste. **From Wilson to Roosevelt: Foreign Policy of the United States, 1913-1945.** Cambridge: Harvard University Press, 1963, 499 p.
A translation of an important study of U.S. foreign policy in the period encompassing the two world wars, written by a leading French student. The original appeared as "De Wilson à Roosevelt: politique extérieure des États-Unis, 1913-1945" (Paris: Colin, 1960, 494 p.).

Edwards, Jerome E. **The Foreign Policy of Col. McCormick's Tribune, 1929-1941.** Reno: University of Nevada Press, 1971, 232 p.
An informative study of the foreign policies of one of the leading isolationist newspapers in the United States during the administrations of Herbert Hoover and Franklin Roosevelt.

Ellis, Lewis Ethan. **Republican Foreign Policy, 1921-1933.** New Brunswick: Rutgers University Press, 1968, 404 p.
A sympathetic and balanced appraisal of the "back to normalcy" period in American foreign policy.

Ferrell, Robert Hugh, ed. **The American Secretaries of State and Their Diplomacy.** New York: Cooper Square Publishers, 1963—.
A continuation of the series that was edited by Samuel Flagg Bemis and published in ten volumes under the same title by Knopf from 1927 to 1929. The new sequence comprises the following volumes: vol. XI, "Frank B. Kellogg, Henry L. Stimson," by Robert Hugh Ferrell (1963, 360 p.); vol. XII-XIII, "Cordell Hull, 1933-44," by Julius William Pratt (1964, 2 v.); vol. XIV, "E. R. Stettinius, Jr.," by Richard L. Walker and "James F. Byrnes," by George Curry (1965, 423 p.); vol. XV, "George C. Marshall," by Robert Hugh Ferrell (1966, 326 p.); vol. XVI, "Dean Acheson," by Gaddis Smith (1972, 473 p.); vol. XVII, "John Foster Dulles," by Louis L. Gerson (1968, 372 p.); and vol. XVIII, "Christian A. Herter," by G. Bernard Noble (1970, 333 p.).

Finletter, Thomas Knight. **Interim Report: On the U.S. Search for a Substitute for Isolation.** New York: Norton, 1968, 185 p.
An experienced public servant reviews the main lines of contemporary U.S. foreign policy.

Fisher, Sydney Nettleton, ed. **New Horizons for the United States in World Affairs.** Columbus: Ohio State University Press, 1966, 162 p.
Papers by Robert R. Bowie, Arthur Larson, John S. Badeau and others presented at the fourth annual conference of the Graduate Institute for World Affairs of Ohio State University, November 12-14, 1964.

FitzSimons, Louise. **The Kennedy Doctrine.** New York: Random House, 1972, 275 p.
A largely unsuccessful attempt to demonstrate that "President Kennedy's policies were as dominated by cold-war thinking as were those of his predecessors."

Foreign Relations of the United States. Washington: G.P.O. (for the Department of State).
An important collection of official papers relating to the foreign relations of the United States, comprising a series of volumes compiled on an annual basis plus special volumes

on particular topics. Volumes published in the period from 1963 through 1973 cover the years from 1941 to 1948. The special volumes published during this decade are: "The Conferences at Washington, 1941–1942, and Casablanca, 1943" (1968, 895 p.); "The Conferences at Washington and Quebec, 1943" (1970, 1,382 p.); and "The Conference at Quebec, 1944" (1972, 527 p.).

Frankel, Charles. **The Neglected Aspect of Foreign Affairs.** Washington: Brookings Institution, 1966, 156 p.
Professor Frankel, a philosopher and a former Assistant Secretary of State for Educational and Cultural Affairs, argues that our educational and cultural policy abroad has been badly neglected or poorly defined. He concludes with some recommended principles and practices.

Fulbright, James William. **The Arrogance of Power.** New York: Random House, 1967, 264 p.
This book is the outgrowth of the three Christian A. Herter Lectures the former Senator delivered at the Johns Hopkins School of Advanced International Studies in 1966. It is a passionate indictment of interventionist America, especially in Asia and Latin America.

Fulbright, James William. **The Crippled Giant: American Foreign Policy and its Domestic Consequences.** New York: Random House, 1972, 292 p.
The author reflects in a familiar, dour fashion on postwar U.S. history and concludes that "we are going to have to recover our mistrust of power—in the Presidency and wherever else it is found."

Fulbright, James William. **Old Myths and New Realities.** New York: Random House, 1964, 147 p.
A critique of American foreign policies in the early 1960s, by the Chairman of the Senate Foreign Relations Committee during that period.

Gallagher, Hugh Gregory. **Advise and Obstruct.** New York: Delacorte Press, 1969, 338 p.
Seven case studies of the Senate's role in foreign policy from the Jay Treaty in 1795 to Tonkin Gulf crisis in 1964.

Gelfand, Lawrence E. **The Inquiry: American Preparations for Peace, 1917–1919.** New Haven: Yale University Press, 1963, 387 p.
The first solid study of the American group entrusted with the task of preparing a peace program following the U.S. entry into the First World War.

George, Alexander L. and Others. **The Limits of Coercive Diplomacy: Laos, Cuba, Vietnam.** Boston: Little, Brown, 1971, 268 p.
A critical assessment, emerging from a research program at Stanford University, of recent U.S. attempts to exercise coercive diplomacy.

Geyelin, Philip L. **Lyndon B. Johnson and the World.** New York: Praeger, 1966, 309 p.
A critical appraisal of President Johnson's handling of foreign affairs, by a correspondent of *The Wall Street Journal*.

Glad, Betty. **Charles Evans Hughes and the Illusions of Innocence: A Study in American Diplomacy.** Urbana: University of Illinois Press, 1966, 365 p.
A study of the thought and policies of Charles Evans Hughes as they bore on U.S. diplomacy up through his resignation as Secretary of State in 1925.

Goldwin, Robert A., ed. **Beyond the Cold War.** Chicago: Rand McNally, 1965, 235 p.
Essays on American foreign and military policy in a changing world.

Goodfriend, Arthur. **The Twisted Image.** New York: St. Martin's Press, 1963, 264 p.
As the title vaguely suggests, this book deals with what President Johnson has called "America's failure to put across to millions of people overseas its desires and real objectives." It is based chiefly on the author's experiences as Public Affairs Officer with USIA in India.

Gregg, Robert W. and Kegley, Charles W., Jr., eds. **After Vietnam: The Future of American Foreign Policy.** Garden City: Doubleday, 1971, 343 p.
A collection of papers originally delivered in 1970 at the Maxwell Graduate School of Citizenship and Public Affairs, Syracuse University, supplemented with other essays previously published by leading students of international politics.

Grenville, John Ashley Soames and Young, George Berkeley. **Politics, Strategy, and American Diplomacy: Studies in Foreign Policy, 1873-1917.** New Haven: Yale University Press, 1966, 352 p.
Having examined eleven episodes in U.S. diplomacy, the authors conclude that "the harmonization of strategy and foreign policy was more often a matter of chance than of design."

Hancock, M. Donald and Rustow, Dankwart A., eds. **American Foreign Policy in International Perspective.** Englewood Cliffs: Prentice-Hall, 1971, 375 p.
A symposium by leading scholars in the field.

Hartmann, Frederick H. **The New Age of American Foreign Policy.** New York: Macmillan, 1970, 399 p.
The author of this survey of contemporary U.S. foreign policy issues intends to provide "a frame of reference and a set of criteria for assessing and choosing among the grand alternative foreign policy choices open to the United States." The study is based on lectures delivered at the Naval War College.

Heller, Deane and Heller, David. **Paths of Diplomacy: America's Secretaries of State.** Philadelphia: Lippincott, 1967, 192 p.
Thumbnail sketches from the careers of twenty Secretaries of State from Thomas Jefferson to Dean Rusk.

Hero, Alfred Olivier, Jr. and Starr, Emil. **The Reuther-Meany Foreign Policy Dispute: Union Leaders and Members View World Affairs.** Dobbs Ferry (N.Y.): Oceana Publications, 1970, 228 p.
An empirical study of the foreign policy postures of the AFL and the CIO before and after their merger.

Hero, Alfred Olivier, Jr. **The Southerner and World Affairs.** Baton Rouge: Louisiana State University Press, 1965, 676 p.
An interesting study "of the behavior of Southerners and their Congressmen toward world affairs since the mid-1930's."

Hilsman, Roger. **To Move a Nation: The Politics of Foreign Policy in the Administration of John F. Kennedy.** Garden City: Doubleday, 1967, 602 p.
The author, who was head of Intelligence in the State Department and then Assistant Secretary of State for the Far East in the Kennedy Administration, writes about specific crises such as Laos, Cuba One and Two, the Congo and Vietnam. The role of the CIA looms large in the story.

Horowitz, David, ed. **Containment and Revolution: Western Policy Towards Social Revolution, 1917 to Vietnam.** Boston: Beacon Press, 1967, 252 p.
Leaders of the New Left attempt to prove in this polemic that the United States has followed an imperialist path during the last half century.

Horowitz, David. **The Free World Colossus: A Critique of American Foreign Policy in the Cold War.** New York: Hill and Wang, 1965, 451 p.
Blaming the United States for launching the cold war, and using one-sided documentation, the author argues that American policy since 1945 has been aimed not at containing the expansion of communism but at containing social revolution within foreign countries.

Iakovlev, Aleksandr Nikolaevich. **Pax Americana: imperskaia ideologiia.** Moscow: Izdatel'stvo "Molodaia Gvardiia," 1969, 367 p.
A Soviet critique of America's conception of herself as "world policeman." Henry Kissinger, Walt Rostow and Dean Acheson are singled out for particular attention.

Janis, Irving L. **Victims of Groupthink: A Psychological Study of Foreign-Policy Decisions and Fiascoes.** Boston: Houghton Mifflin, 1972, 277 p.
A noted social psychologist, after careful study of six major episodes since 1941, concludes that fiascoes often result when decision-makers are more concerned with retaining the approval of groups than with the substance of the problem.

Jonas, Manfred. **Isolationism in America, 1935-1941.** Ithaca: Cornell University Press, 1966, 315 p.
The bulk of this book consists of a first-rate analysis of the isolationism of the 1930s as a political phenomenon.

Julien, Claude. **America's Empire.** New York: Pantheon Books, 1971, 442 p.
The foreign editor of *Le Monde* argues the paradoxical thesis that America's idealism and liberalism inherently led to her quest for empire. The author's emphasis is analytical rather than polemical. Though he covers much ground that is familiar, he does it in a balanced and interesting manner. The French original was published as "L'Empire américain" (Paris: Grasset, 1968, 419 p.).

Kiernan, Bernard P. **The United States, Communism, and the Emergent World.** Bloomington: Indiana University Press, 1972, 248 p.
The United States should, says the author, hold an "open door to revolution" and deliberately relinquish some of its power in the emergent world.

Kissinger, Henry Alfred. **American Foreign Policy.** New York: Norton, 1969, 143 p.
These three essays by the Harvard professor who became Secretary of State in Nixon's administration are largely drawn from previously published articles and books.

Kolko, Gabriel. **The Roots of American Foreign Policy: An Analysis of Power and Purpose.** Boston: Beacon Press, 1969, 166 p.
In this sophisticated and polemical book "the predominance of the economic ruling class" is seen as the key to politics at home and policy abroad.

Kolko, Joyce and Kolko, Gabriel. **The Limits of Power: The World and United States Foreign Policy 1945-1954.** New York: Harper and Row, 1972, 820 p.
Two leading revisionist historians diagnose the postwar decade as the crucial period during which "America's basic problems—and failures—emerged."

Krippendorff, Ekkehart. **Die amerikanische Strategie: Entscheidungsprozess und Instrumentarium der amerikanischen Aussenpolitik.** Frankfurt/Main: Suhrkamp, 1970, 495 p.
This is a deeply pessimistic analysis of American foreign policy during the 1960s. The author concludes that the United States is willing to pay the price of considerable political repression and would risk atomic war in order to preserve the capitalist system.

Kuehl, Warren F. **Seeking World Order: The United States and International Organization to 1920.** Nashville: Vanderbilt University Press, 1969, 385 p.
A history of the American peace movement from 1815 to 1920. The author is particularly good in his analysis of the diversity of the movement and in his appraisal of President Wilson.

Lane, Thomas A. **America on Trial: The War for Vietnam.** New Rochelle (N.Y.): Arlington House, 1971, 227 p.
A very critical review of recent American foreign policies in general and of those toward Vietnam in particular. The author, a retired general who during World War II served on the staff of General Douglas MacArthur, is convinced that the leaders of the communist countries have never abandoned their aims to destroy the Free World.

Lerche, Charles Olsen. **The Uncertain South: Its Changing Patterns of Politics in Foreign Policy.** Chicago: Quadrangle Books, 1964, 324 p.
On the basis of roll-call votes of Southern Congressmen from 1953 to 1962, Professor Lerche challenges the "myth" of Southern internationalism and describes the drift of the South's politicians and constituents toward "unilateralism" in world affairs.

Levin, Norman Gordon, Jr. **Woodrow Wilson and World Politics: America's Response to War and Revolution.** New York: Oxford University Press, 1968, 340 p.
The author argues that Wilson's foreign policy was marked by a major effort to avoid the dangers to America from both the European nationalism of the Right and Lenin's revolutionary radicalism of the Left.

Lippmann, Walter. **The Cold War: A Study in U.S. Foreign Policy.** New York: Harper and Row, 1972, 81 p.
A republication of Lippmann's rigorous and prophetic critique in 1947 of George Kennan's famous "X" article (also included). A primary source for the intellectual history of post-1945 American foreign policy. Introduction by Ronald Steel.

Liska, George. **Imperial America.** Baltimore: Johns Hopkins Press, 1967, 115 p.
This book powerfully argues a challenging and original thesis: America today is an imperial, though nonimperialistic power, analogous to ancient Rome.

Loewenheim, Francis L., *ed.* **The Historian and the Diplomat.** New York: Harper and Row, 1967, 213 p.
Essays relating to the role of history and historians in American foreign policy.

Lowenstein, Linda, *comp.* **Government Resources Available for Foreign Affairs Research.** Washington: Department of State, Bureau of Intelligence and Research, Office of External Research, 1965, 56 p.
A very useful directory of government facilities and a bibliography of government resources available for research on foreign affairs.

McCarthy, Eugene J. **The Limits of Power: America's Role in the World.** New York: Holt, Rinehart and Winston, 1967, 246 p.
The former Senator from Minnesota argues for a more restrained foreign policy in Asia and urges larger roles for the Senate and for international agencies as vehicles of U.S. foreign policy.

Maddox, Robert James. **William E. Borah and American Foreign Policy.** Baton Rouge: Louisiana State University Press, 1970, 272 p.
A respectable monograph on the controversial Senator's career. It treats Borah's opposition to the League, his stand on neutrality and analyzes the Idahoan's campaign to recognize the Soviet government.

Martin, James Joseph. **American Liberalism and World Politics, 1931-1941.** New York: Devin-Adair, 1965, 2 v.
A massive indictment of the attitudes of American liberals toward foreign policy and of their intellectual hegemony since 1917.

Masters, Roger D. **The Nation is Burdened: American Foreign Policy in a Changing World.** New York: Knopf, 1967, 319 p.
An eloquent appeal to base U.S. foreign policy on the defense of the national interest in a world that is still governed by the principle of the balance of power.

Mel'nikov, Iurii Mikhailovich. **Vneshnepoliticheskie doktriny SShA: proiskhozhdenie i sushnost' programmy "Novykh Rubezhei" prezidenta D. Kenedi.** Moscow: Izd-vo "Nauka," 1970, 494 p.
A lengthy discussion of U.S. foreign policy in the last years of the Eisenhower administration and during the Kennedy years. The author argues that the trend toward peaceful coexistence with the Soviet bloc became more pronounced with the policies of the "New Frontier," especially after the Cuban missile crisis.

Morgenthau, Hans Joachim. **A New Foreign Policy for the United States.** New York: Praeger (for the Council on Foreign Relations), 1969, 252 p.
A bold reëxamination of five basic issues confronting American foreign policy: the Atlantic Alliance, communism, the uncommitted nations, nuclear power and the problem of national priorities.

Morgenthau, Hans Joachim. **Truth and Power.** New York: Praeger, 1970, 449 p.
Forceful essays on the main controversies besetting American foreign policy and politics during the 1960s.

Morris, Bernard S. **International Communism and American Policy.** New York: Atherton Press, 1966, 179 p.
An essay on the schism in the international communist movement and its implications for U.S. policy. The author has had long experience in the Department of State.

Nixon, Edgar Burkhardt, *ed.* **Franklin D. Roosevelt and Foreign Affairs.** Cambridge: Belknap Press of Harvard University Press, 1969, 3 v.
These volumes cover the four years of FDR's first term. The documents collected here shed considerable light on America's reactions to the rise of Hitler and Mussolini, the Italo-Ethiopian war, war debts and the birth of the Good Neighbor Policy toward Latin America.

Osgood, Robert Endicott. **Alliances and American Foreign Policy.** Baltimore: Johns Hopkins Press, 1968, 171 p.
A thoughtful essay on the changing nature of alliances since the advent of the atomic age and a thought-provoking look into their possible future.

Osgood, Robert Endicott and Others. **America and the World: From the Truman Doctrine to Vietnam.** Baltimore: Johns Hopkins Press (in collaboration with the Washing-

ton Center of Foreign Policy Research, School of Advanced International Studies, Johns Hopkins University), 1970, 434 p.
Substantial essays on American foreign policy by professors associated with The Johns Hopkins University.

Parenti, Michael. **The Anti-Communist Impulse.** New York: Random House, 1970, 333 p.
The author argues that mindless anti-communism has been the propellent for many tragic misadventures in recent American foreign policy.

Parmet, Herbert S. **Eisenhower and the American Crusades.** New York: Macmillan, 1972, 660 p.
A full and well-researched study of the Eisenhower presidency. The author argues that Eisenhower, not John Foster Dulles, was in command of foreign policy and that his apparent lack of sophistication was a cultivated political asset.

Payne, James L. **The American Threat.** Chicago: Markham, 1970, 241 p.
A sophisticated exploration, with a pronounced theoretical bent, of "our nation's most powerful foreign policy instrument: the threat of war." The author strikes a felicitous balance in his use of illustrative case materials.

Perkins, Dexter. **The Diplomacy of a New Age: Major Issues in U.S. Policy Since 1945.** Bloomington: Indiana University Press, 1967, 190 p.
These essays were originally presented at Indiana University in 1966.

Pfeffer, Richard M., ed. **No More Vietnams? The War and the Future of American Foreign Policy.** New York: Harper and Row (for the Adlai Stevenson Institute of International Affairs), 1968, 299 p.
Twenty-six scholars explore the lessons of Vietnam. The spectrum of views is fairly wide, with a pronounced tendency toward the critical.

Pratt, Julius William. **Challenge and Rejection: The United States and World Leadership, 1900-1921.** New York: Macmillan, 1967, 248 p.
This volume in the "American Diplomatic History Series" covers the period from the death of President McKinley to the inauguration of President Harding.

Pusey, Merlo J. **The U.S.A. Astride the Globe.** Boston: Houghton, 1971, 247 p.
The author tries "to assess some of the consequences of our excessive preoccupation with military force in the name of peace and freedom."

Quigg, Philip W. **America the Dutiful.** New York: Simon and Schuster, 1971, 223 p.
A positive assessment of American foreign policy since 1945.

Radosh, Ronald. **American Labor and United States Foreign Policy.** New York: Random House, 1970, 463 p.
The author argues that the American labor movement from Samuel Gompers onward has always supported official American foreign policy in order to secure for the worker a part of "the great American pie."

Reuss, Henry S. **The Critical Decade.** New York: McGraw-Hill, 1964, 227 p.
A forthright and well-informed statement on the central issues of U.S. foreign and domestic economic policy, the organization of free world coöperation and the reform of Congress, by the Democratic Representative from Wisconsin.

Riencourt, Amaury de. **The American Empire.** New York: Dial Press, 1968, 366 p.
The author attempts to prove that America is destined to rule half of the earth. The other half will probably be ruled by the Soviet Union. The scholarship is sketchy.

Rivera, Joseph Hosmer de. **The Psychological Dimension of Foreign Policy.** Columbus: Merrill, 1968, 441 p.
A welcome, and in places even pioneering, contribution.

Rosenau, James N. **National Leadership and Foreign Policy.** Princeton: Princeton University Press, 1963, 409 p.
A case study of the mobilization of public support, based on a questionnaire sent to the 1,067 national leaders (647 responded) who were convened by the White House in 1958 for a discussion of the requirements of U.S. foreign economic policy.

Rostow, Eugene Victor. **Law, Power, and the Pursuit of Peace.** Lincoln: University of Nebraska Press, 1968, 133 p.
A spirited defense of Presidents Truman (in Korea, Berlin, Greece, Turkey and Iran),

Kennedy (in Cuba) and Johnson (in the Middle East and in Vietnam), by the former Under Secretary of State for Political Affairs.

Rostow, Eugene Victor. **Peace in the Balance: The Future of American Foreign Policy.** New York: Simon and Schuster, 1972, 352 p.
The author's ideal American diplomatist was Dean Acheson. Here he adopts his mentor's tone and manner to attack critics and argue that the only foundation of peace is a balance of power maintained by American military force.

Rostow, Walt Whitman. **The Diffusion of Power: An Essay in Recent History.** New York: Macmillan, 1972, 739 p.
This huge book is part personal memoir, part a continuation of "The United States in the World Arena" (1960), and above all an argument and apologia for an interventionist foreign policy. The author is a former Chairman of the Policy Planning Council in the State Department.

Rostow, Walt Whitman. **View from the Seventh Floor.** New York: Harper and Row, 1964, 178 p.
In this brief book the author undertakes to explain U.S. foreign policy, its objectives and measures, since 1960.

Rovere, Richard Halworth. **Waist Deep in the Big Muddy: Personal Reflections on 1968.** Boston: Atlantic (Little, Brown), 1968, 116 p.
A critique of American foreign policy, focusing primarily on the war in Vietnam.

Rustow, Dankwart A., *ed*. **America's Role in World Affairs Series.** Englewood Cliffs: Prentice-Hall, 1967–.
Of this series on U.S. foreign policies since World War II the following volumes have been published through 1972: "Africa and United States Policy," by Rupert Emerson (1967, 117 p.); "Cold War and Coexistence: Russia, China, and the United States," by William E. Griffith (1971, 115 p.); "The Web of Interdependence: The United States and International Organization," by Ernst B. Haas (1970, 115 p.); "Foreign Aid in International Politics," by John Dickey Montgomery (1967, 118 p.); "Asia and United States Policy," by Wayne Ayres Wilcox (1967, 116 p.); and "American Foreign Policy in International Perspective," ed. by M. Donald Hancock and Dankwart A. Rustow (1971, 375 p.).

Schlesinger, Arthur Meier, Jr. **The Bitter Heritage: Vietnam and American Democracy, 1941-1966.** Boston: Houghton, 1967, 126 p.
This brief and critical book is drawn from articles by Mr. Schlesinger reflecting his concern with developments in American foreign policy and their impact domestically.

Seabury, Paul. **Power, Freedom, and Diplomacy.** New York: Random House, 1963, 424 p.
In this thoughtful study the author's purpose is to "define and analyze the sources of American conduct in world affairs and the manner in which American interests, conduct, and purposes fit into the broader patterns of world politics."

Seabury, Paul and Wildavsky, Aaron B., *eds*. **U.S. Foreign Policy: Perspectives and Proposals for the 1970s.** New York: McGraw-Hill, 1969, 215 p.
Ten distinguished political scientists reflect on the American foreign policy in the world's pivotal areas.

Shepherd, George W., Jr., *ed*. **Racial Influences on American Foreign Policy.** New York: Basic Books, 1971, 238 p.
Nine essays exploring the impact of the racial factor in various lands on American foreign policy.

Sommer, Walter. **Die Weltmacht USA im Urteil der französischen Publizistik, 1924-1939.** Tübingen: Mohr, 1967, 248 p.
A well-documented study of how the French press evaluated the United States as a world power in the years from 1924 to 1939.

Steel, Ronald. **Imperialists and Other Heroes: A Chronicle of the American Empire.** New York: Random House, 1971, 447 p.
American foreign policy from Truman through Nixon, the author asserts, has been a policy of empire. "John F. Kennedy," he writes, "was firmly committed to the imperial foreign policy evolved by Acheson and Dulles in the late forties and early fifties."

Steel, Ronald. **Pax Americana.** New York: Viking, 1967, 371 p.
: This is a highly polemical, but cogently argued indictment of U.S. foreign policies, similar in conclusions to Senator Fulbright's "The Arrogance of Power."

Stillman, Edmund O. and Pfaff, William. **Power and Impotence: The Failure of America's Foreign Policy.** New York: Random House, 1966, 244 p.
: A wholesale onslaught on U.S. foreign policy.

Stromberg, Roland Nelson. **Collective Security and American Foreign Policy: From the League of Nations to NATO.** New York: Praeger, 1963, 301 p.
: A history of U.S. attitudes toward collective security from the creating of the League of Nations through the Suez and Congo crises.

Sulzberger, Cyrus Leo. **Unfinished Revolution: America and the Third World.** New York: Atheneum, 1965, 304 p.
: A widely travelled and experienced foreign affairs columnist of *The New York Times* looks at what he calls "the Revolution of Self-Determination" and the so-called Third World it has created.

Swomley, John M., Jr. **The American Empire: The Political Ethics of Twentieth-Century Conquest.** New York: Macmillan, 1970, 250 p.
: A revisionist history of American foreign policy since 1939. The author maintains that "it has been in the interest of military and financial circles to make war and to garrison other lands, quite as much for the expansion of American control as for the destruction of Fascism and the containment of Communism."

Taylor, Arnold H. **American Diplomacy and the Narcotics Traffic, 1900–1939.** Durham: Duke University Press, 1969, 370 p.
: A detailed discussion of "the nature and extent of the activities of the United States in promoting consideration and solution of the [narcotics traffic] problem."

Taylor, Maxwell Davenport. **Responsibility and Response.** New York: Harper and Row, 1967, 84 p.
: These lectures by the former Chairman of the Joint Chiefs of Staff and author of "The Uncertain Trumpet" put forward a doctrine of national policy based on the situation in a "multipolar power relationship."

Terchek, Ronald J. **The Making of the Test Ban Treaty.** The Hague: Nijhoff, 1970, 211 p.
: An analysis of the roles played in the United States by the various political participants in the ratification of the treaty.

Trivers, Howard. **Three Crises in American Foreign Affairs and a Continuing Revolution.** Carbondale: Southern Illinois University Press, 1972, 220 p.
: Reflections on the Berlin Wall issue, the Cuban missile crisis and the Vietnam War, by a former Foreign Service officer.

Tucker, Robert W. **Nation or Empire? The Debate Over American Foreign Policy.** Baltimore: Johns Hopkins Press (for the Washington Center of Foreign Policy Research), 1968, 160 p.
: In this cogently reasoned essay, the author concludes that an imperial American foreign policy would lead to further Vietnams.

Tucker, Robert W. **A New Isolationism: Threat or Promise?** New York: Universe Books, 1972, 127 p.
: A brief, provocative attack on the shibboleth that isolationism and security are mutually exclusive. The author contends that the strategic conditions that required the abandonment of isolationism in 1939 no longer exist.

Tucker, Robert W. **The Radical Left and American Foreign Policy.** Baltimore: Johns Hopkins Press (for the Washington Center of Foreign Policy Research, School of Advanced International Studies, Johns Hopkins University), 1971, 156 p.
: The author concludes that radical-left criticism, as distinguished from conventional liberal criticism, assumes that foreign policy flows inexorably from the structure of society; only by radical change in society can foreign policy be changed. The comments are sometimes trenchant, although the number of critics discussed is very small.

Tugwell, Rexford G. **Off Course: From Truman to Nixon.** New York: Praeger, 1971, 326 p.
: In this survey the author concludes that Richard Nixon was confronted with the challenge of returning to Roosevelt's policy of coexistence with the communist nations.

The United States in World Affairs. New York: Harper and Row; Simon and Schuster (for the Council on Foreign Relations).
: A valuable annual survey of the foreign policy of the United States and international developments, begun in 1931. Richard P. Stebbins wrote all the volumes published in the decade between 1963 and 1972, with the exception of the volume for 1964, prepared by Jules Davids, and of that for 1970, prepared by William P. Lineberry. Volumes for 1968 and 1969 were not published through 1972.

Venkataramani, M. S. **Undercurrents in American Foreign Relations.** New York: Asia Publishing House, 1965, 218 p.
: Four episodes as viewed by an Indian scholar: the Roosevelt administration and the Indian famine, the U.S. and India's food crisis in 1946, the Suez crisis, and the U-2 incident.

Vukadinović, Radovan. **Sila i interesi vanjska politika SAD.** Zagreb: Centar za Kulturnu Djelatnost Omladine, 1972, 398 p.
: An informed and comprehensive Jugoslav study of American foreign policy.

Walton, Richard J. **Cold War and Counterrevolution: The Foreign Policy of John F. Kennedy.** New York: Viking, 1972, 250 p.
: A rebuttal to the rather worshipful accounts of the Kennedy administration by Arthur M. Schlesinger, Jr. and Theodore Sorensen (both 1965).

Warburg, James Paul. **The United States in the Postwar World: What We Have Done, What We Have Left Undone, and What We Can and Must Do.** New York: Atheneum, 1966, 327 p.
: A study of American foreign policies in the post-World War II period. The author's basic argument is that American foreign policy has been dictated by an excessive and unjustified fear of communism.

Warren, Sidney. **The President as World Leader.** Philadelphia: Lippincott, 1964, 480 p.
: A highly readable analysis of the new responsibilities faced by the American presidents since Theodore Roosevelt. The evaluation of Franklin Delano Roosevelt's approach to foreign policy during his terms in office is of particular interest.

Weintal, Edward and Bartlett, Charles. **Facing the Brink: An Intimate Study of Crisis Diplomacy.** New York: Scribner, 1967, 248 p.
: Two journalists discuss five international crises since World War II and the handling of them by the responsible persons in Washington.

Whitworth, William. **Naive Questions about War and Peace.** New York: Norton, 1970, 126 p.
: The author elicits Eugene V. Rostow's views on American foreign policy around the globe.

Wittner, Lawrence S. **Rebels against War.** New York: Columbia University Press, 1969, 339 p.
: A scholarly assessment of the American peace movement from Pearl Harbor to 1960. The author concludes that "the peace movement proved considerably more sophisticated than is commonly thought."

Wolf, Charles, Jr. **United States Policy and the Third World: Problems and Analysis.** Boston: Little, Brown, 1967, 204 p.
: This book is an outgrowth of several RAND research studies and memoranda in which the author purports to test the "value" of the Third World to the United States, largely through the technique of "systems analysis."

Yost, Charles W. **The Conduct and Misconduct of Foreign Affairs.** New York: Random House, 1972, 234 p.
: The author, a Foreign Service officer for nearly 40 years, expresses a deep unease over a foreign policy which is dependent on domestic opinion.

Relations with Western Europe

See also The World Since 1914, p. 129; (The United States) Biographies, Memoirs and Addresses, p. 218; Military and Defense Policy, p. 257; Western Europe, p. 345; and the sections for specific countries.

Beloff, Max. **The United States and the Unity of Europe.** Washington: Brookings Institution, 1963, 124 p.
In this concise but perceptive essay Mr. Beloff discusses the "conscious, if intermittent" effort of the United States since 1945 to persuade the European countries of the advantage of integration.

Brzezinski, Zbigniew Kazimierz. **Alternative to Partition: For a Broader Conception of America's Role in Europe.** New York: McGraw-Hill (for the Council on Foreign Relations), 1965, 208 p.
In this study Professor Brzezinski advocates a policy of "peaceful engagement" involving measures that at once may help to end the partition of Europe and also to relieve certain mounting problems that American policy has been facing in Western Europe.

Bykov, Oleg Nikolaevich and Others. **Zapadnaia Evropa i SShA: ocherk politicheskikh vzaimootnoshenii.** Moscow: Izd-vo "Mysl," 1968, 447 p.
A group of Soviet international affairs specialists examines the crisis of American "Atlantic policy" during the years 1956–1966, proceeding on the premise that divergent aims held by Great Britain, France and West Germany will continue to undermine American efforts to forge a united Europe.

Calleo, David P. **The Atlantic Fantasy: The U.S., NATO, and Europe.** Baltimore: Johns Hopkins Press (for the Washington Center of Foreign Policy Research, School of Advanced International Studies), 1970, 182 p.
A revisionist critique of American attitudes and policies toward Europe.

Cleveland, Harold Van B. **The Atlantic Idea and Its European Rivals.** New York: McGraw-Hill (for the Council on Foreign Relations), 1966, 186 p.
A concise but comprehensive analysis of the salient problems of American relations with Europe.

Fox, William Thornton Rickert and Fox, Annette Baker. **NATO and the Range of American Choice.** New York: Columbia University Press, 1967, 352 p.
In this substantial study the emphasis is upon the policy process rather than upon the policies themselves.

Hoffmann, Stanley. **Gulliver's Troubles, or the Setting of American Foreign Policy.** New York: McGraw-Hill (for the Council on Foreign Relations), 1968, 556 p.
The purpose of this brilliant analysis, in the words of the author, is "to determine what the United States, with its enormous power, can attempt and expect to achieve in the Atlantic area."

Kleiman, Robert. **Atlantic Crisis: American Diplomacy Confronts a Resurgent Europe.** New York: Norton, 1964, 158 p.
An American journalist's informed and generally judicious account of the political aftermath of Britain's exclusion from the Common Market. General de Gaulle is the central figure of the piece. Prepared originally as a background paper for the Atlantic Study of the Council on Foreign Relations.

Kottman, Richard Norman. **Reciprocity and the North Atlantic Triangle, 1932–1938.** Ithaca: Cornell University Press, 1968, 294 p.
Materials from U.S. archives and private papers about the interplay of trade policy and foreign policy in American-British-Canadian relations in the 1930s.

Lerche, Charles Olsen. **Last Chance in Europe: Bases for a New American Policy.** Chicago: Quadrangle Books, 1967, 221 p.
The late author argues that the United States must be prepared to change its policies fundamentally to accept the new concept of partnership with Europe.

Nunnerly, David. **President Kennedy and Britain.** New York: St. Martin's Press, 1972, 242 p.
A historical essay on Britain's "special relationship" with the United States in the Kennedy years. Based chiefly on systematic interviews with many of the principals involved.

Radkau, Joachim. **Die deutsche Emigration in den USA.** Düsseldorf: Bertelsmann Universitätsverlag, 1971, 378 p.
A detailed study of the influence the refugees from Nazi Germany exercized on the formulation of U.S. policies toward Europe in the years from 1933 to 1945.

Steel, Ronald. **The End of Alliance: America and the Future of Europe.** New York: Viking, 1964, 148 p.
A former American Foreign Service officer argues that NATO has outlived its usefulness and that American policy must not be wedded to past postures and premises.

Relations with Eastern Europe and the Soviet Union

See also Political Philosophies and Ideologies, p. 21; International Organization and Government, p. 96; War and Peace, p. 108; The World Since 1914, p. 129; (The United States) Biographies, Memoirs and Addresses, p. 218; Military and Defense Policy, p. 257; Eastern Europe and the Soviet Bloc, p. 358; and the sections for specific countries.

Arbatov, G. A. and Others. **"Doktrina Niksona."** Moscow: Izd-vo "Nauka," 1972, 232 p.
The origins and consequences of the Nixon Doctrine in U.S. foreign policy are assessed in a collective work by the most prominent Soviet specialists in American affairs; published shortly after President Nixon's visit to Moscow in 1972.

Bennett, Edward Moore. **Recognition of Russia: An American Foreign Policy Dilemma.** Waltham (Mass.): Blaisdell Publishing Co., 1970, 226 p.
A concise review and analysis.

Bishop, Donald Gordon. **The Roosevelt-Litvinov Agreements: The American View.** Syracuse: Syracuse University Press, 1965, 297 p.
A study of the problems and differences arising in conjunction with the implementation of the agreements reached at the time of the American recognition of the Soviet Union in 1933.

Bohlen, Charles Eustis. **The Transformation of American Foreign Policy.** New York: Norton, 1969, 130 p.
Five lectures on U.S.-Soviet relations, delivered at Columbia University in 1969 by the former ambassador to Moscow.

Bose, Tarun Chandra. **American Soviet Relations, 1921–1933.** Calcutta: Mukhopadhyay, 1967, 228 p.
A scholar at Jadavpur University, Calcutta, undertakes a topical analysis of American-Soviet relations during the years of non-recognition. Considerable stress on economic factors.

Byrnes, Robert F., *ed.* **The United States and Eastern Europe.** Englewood Cliffs: Prentice-Hall (for the American Assembly, Columbia University), 1967, 176 p.
Chapters by a number of specialists, prepared as background papers for a meeting of the American Assembly, dealing with such themes as political change, economic modernization, cultural change and international and intra-bloc relations.

Campbell, John Coert. **American Policy toward Communist Eastern Europe: The Choices Ahead.** Minneapolis: University of Minnesota Press, 1965, 136 p.
Essentially a background paper, analyzing the situation in Communist Eastern Europe and the alternative policies that may be open to the United States.

Druks, Herbert. **Harry S. Truman and the Russians, 1945–1953.** New York: Speller, 1967, 291 p.
A scholarly survey of President Truman's major confrontations with Stalin.

Farnsworth, Beatrice. **William C. Bullitt and the Soviet Union.** Bloomington: Indiana University Press, 1967, 244 p.
A concise, informative monograph on the late diplomat's attitudes toward and relations with revolutionary Russia, from his ill-starred mission of 1919 through his bitter disillusionment as ambassador in the 1930s. Based on considerable use of unpublished documents.

Filene, Peter G. **Americans and the Soviet Experiment, 1917–1933.** Cambridge: Harvard University Press, 1967, 389 p.
An informative history of the evolution of attitudes in various groups of American society toward the Soviet Union during the years of non-recognition and of marked changes in both the Russian and American scenes.

Gaddis, John Lewis. **The United States and the Origins of the Cold War, 1941–1947.** New York: Columbia University Press, 1972, 396 p.

The author, avoiding the single-cause explanations of some economic determinists, stresses domestic political pressures on American leaders and the influence of lessons "learned" from the Second World War as factors that contributed to the genesis of the cold war.

Gardner, Lloyd C. **Architects of Illusion: Men and Ideas in American Foreign Policy, 1941–1949.** Chicago: Quadrangle Books, 1970, 365 p.

A revisionist history of the origins of the cold war. The author finds more fault with the United States than with the Soviet Union.

Harriman, William Averell. **America and Russia in a Changing World: A Half Century of Personal Observation.** Garden City: Doubleday, 1971, 218 p.

In this volume the distinguished American statesman and diplomat proclaims his impatience with outworn ideological slogans and his determination to base policies on objective realities.

Jados, Stanley S. **Documents on Russian-American Relations: Washington to Eisenhower.** Washington: Catholic University of America Press, 1965, 416 p.

An uneven and highly selective collection of various official documents pertaining to American-Russian relations primarily in the period since World War I.

Paterson, Thomas G., ed. **Cold War Critics: Alternatives to American Foreign Policy in the Truman Years.** Chicago: Quadrangle Books, 1971, 313 p.

A selection of revisionist historians writing on various aspects of the early cold war period. All are highly critical of American policy toward the Soviet Union and eager for reconciliation between the superpowers.

Rapoport, Anatol. **The Big Two: Soviet-American Perceptions of Foreign Policy.** New York: Pegasus, 1971, 249 p.

An intelligent, though rather discursive, assessment of Soviet-American relations, with a heavy emphasis on game-theory methodology.

Ulam, Adam B. **The Rivals: America and Russia since World War II.** New York: Viking, 1971, 405 p.

The author of important studies of Bolshevism and Soviet foreign policy here traces the recent history of Soviet-U.S. relations. He finds few heroes on either side, but many foibles and misconceptions.

Relations with the Middle East and the Arab World

See also International Organization and Government, p. 96; The World Since 1914, p. 129; (The United States) Biographies, Memoirs and Addresses, p. 218; Middle East, p. 611; and the sections for specific countries.

Badeau, John Stothoff. **The American Approach to the Arab World.** New York: Harper and Row (for the Council on Foreign Relations), 1968, 209 p.

Mature reflections based on the author's long and deep acquaintance with the Arab world as scholar, administrator and U.S. ambassador. Without prescribing detailed policies, he sets forth the elements of an approach attuned both to basic American interests and to the nature of Arab society and politics in a time of constant and often unpredictable change.

DeNovo, John August. **American Interests and Policies in the Middle East, 1900–1939.** Minneapolis: University of Minnesota Press, 1963, 447 p.

A substantial description and assessment of American relations with the Middle East up to the Second World War.

Evans, Laurence. **United States Policy and the Partition of Turkey, 1914–1924.** Baltimore: Johns Hopkins Press, 1965, 437 p.

A thoroughgoing study of U.S. Middle East policy, its genesis, motivation, implementation and effect during the postwar settlement of the "Eastern question."

Howard, Harry Nicholas. **The King-Crane Commission: An American Inquiry in the Middle East.** Beirut: Khayats, 1963, 369 p.

A carefully researched, fully documented study of President Wilson's attempt, in support of his self-determination principle during the World War I peace settlement, to ascertain the wishes of the populations in post-Ottoman Syria, Palestine and Mesopotamia.

Polk, William Roe. **The United States and the Arab World.** Cambridge: Harvard University Press, rev. ed., 1969, 377 p.
In this revised edition of his 1965 book, the author, a well-known scholar and a former member of the State Department's Policy Planning Council, presents three new chapters describing and analyzing the main events of the 1960s.

Stevens, Georgiana G., *ed.* **The United States and the Middle East.** Englewood Cliffs: Prentice-Hall, 1964, 182.
An authoritative discussion prepared for the Twenty-fourth American Assembly (October 1963).

Relations with Asia

See also The World Since 1914, p. 129; (The United States) Biographies, Memoirs and Addresses, p. 218; The Korean War, p. 728; The Vietnam War, p. 739; and the sections for specific countries and regions.

The Amerasia Papers: A Clue to the Catastrophe of China. Washington: G.P.O. (for the Subcommittee to Investigate the Administration of the Internal Security Act and Other Internal Security Laws of the Committee on the Judiciary, U.S. Senate), 1970, 2 v.
A massive collection of documents on the Far Eastern policy of the U.S. government during World War II, including the official dispatches of John Stewart Service and papers seized by the Federal Bureau of Investigation from the office of *Amerasia*.

Barnett, Arthur Doak. **A New U.S. Policy Toward China.** Washington: Brookings Institution, 1971, 132 p.
Prescriptions for U.S. diplomacy toward China by a leading American China expert.

Barnett, Arthur Doak and Reischauer, Edwin Oldfather, *eds.* **The United States and China: The Next Decade.** New York: Praeger, 1970, 250 p.
This volume is the outgrowth of a conference on United States-China relations held in March 1969 in New York. While the editors have done a fine job in organizing the material for publication, the contributions remain uneven.

Beal, John Robinson. **Marshall in China.** Garden City: Doubleday, 1970, 385 p.
The author maintains that twice during 1946 Marshall almost succeeded in bringing off a coalition between the Chinese Nationalists and the Communists. Chiang Kai-shek passed up the first opportunity and the Communists rejected the second. The author seems to attribute more direct political influence to Marshall than the General actually may have exercised in China at the time.

Blum, Robert. **The United States and China in World Affairs.** New York: McGraw-Hill (for the Council on Foreign Relations), 1966, 287 p.
A serious effort to analyze Sino-American relations and find new approaches and initiatives in U.S. policy toward China. After the author's death, the study was completed and edited by Arthur Doak Barnett.

Borg, Dorothy. **The United States and the Far Eastern Crisis of 1933-1938: From the Manchurian Incident through the Initial Stage of the Undeclared Sino-Japanese War.** Cambridge: Harvard University Press, 1964, 674 p.
A scholarly work describing in detail the aims of the United States during a critical period in its foreign relations.

Bose, Nemai Sadhan. **American Attitude and Policy to the Nationalist Movement in China (1911-1921).** Calcutta: Orient Longmans, 1970, 282 p.
A Jadavpur University professor labels as hypocritical the support and sympathy for Chinese republicanism which were professed by Taft and Wilson. He claims that their prime concerns were American stability, prosperity in trade and investment, and unimpaired missionary activities.

Buhite, Russell D. **Nelson T. Johnson and American Policy Toward China, 1925-1941.** East Lansing: Michigan State University Press, 1969, 163 p.

A study of the career of a former chief of the State Department's Far Eastern Division and Minister to China.

Campbell, Alex. **Unbind Your Sons: The Captivity of America in Asia.** New York: Liveright, 1970, 366 p.
A general indictment of American policies in the Middle East and in Asia, by the managing editor of *The New Republic*.

Caridi, Ronald J. **The Korean War and American Politics: The Republican Party as a Case Study.** Philadelphia: University of Pennsylvania Press, 1969, 319 p.
A fine case study illustrating the primacy of partisan politics in the shaping of foreign policy.

Chang Hsin-hai. **America and China: A New Approach to Asia.** New York: Simon and Schuster, 1966, 288 p.
Dr. Chang, once a high-ranking Nationalist China diplomat, calls on the United States to surrender Formosa to Peking, speed Communist China's admission to the United Nations, give up the Vietnam struggle, and abandon Japan.

China, Vietnam, and the United States. Washington: Public Affairs Press, 1966, 218 p.
The statements of participants in the February-March 1966 Congressional hearings on U.S. policies in Asia, especially in Southeast Asia.

Ch'ing, Ju-chi. **Mei-kuo ch'in Hua shih.** Peking: Jen-min ch'u-pan She, 1962, 2 v.
A detailed historical record of U.S. "imperialist" actions against China from 1784 to the 20th century.

Chou, Chih-ming, ed. **T'ai-p'ing-yang hsüeh-hui yü Fei-cheng-ch'ing chi-t'uan.** Taipei: Hua Lung Wen-hua Shih-yeh Co., Ltd., 1968–1969, 3 v.
A Nationalist Chinese attack on the Institute of Pacific Relations and the "clique" of Harvard's John King Fairbank for selling out China to the communists.

Cohen, Warren I. **America's Response to China: An Interpretative History of Sino-American Relations.** New York: Wiley, 1971, 242 p.
An attempt "to explain American policy toward China in a broad international setting."

Davis, Forrest and Hunter, Robert A. **The Red China Lobby.** New York: Fleet, 1963, 287 p.
Through an examination of Sino-American relations during the last century, the authors argue against the admission of Communist China to the United Nations. Admiral Radford, in a foreword, concurs.

Dulles, Foster Rhea. **American Policy Toward Communist China, 1949–1969.** New York: Crowell, 1972, 273 p.
A solid, factual introduction. The author, who died in 1970, was a prolific historical writer and a cousin of Secretary of State Dulles.

Fairbank, John King. **China: The People's Middle Kingdom and the U.S.A.** Cambridge: Harvard University Press (Belknap Press), 1967, 145 p.
Eleven historical essays, updated and reëdited since their original publication in various journals (mostly in 1966). Many of them give fuller treatments to topics discussed by the Harvard sinologist in his testimony before the Senate Committee on Foreign Relations.

Fairbank, John King. **The United States and China.** Cambridge: Harvard University Press, 3rd rev. ed., 1971, 500 p.
This book, completely revised since its last edition in 1958, still remains the most balanced and informative work on American relations with China.

Fifield, Russell Hunt. **Southeast Asia in United States Policy.** New York: Praeger (for the Council on Foreign Relations), 1963, 488 p.
A penetrating examination of Southeast Asia with suggestions for developing and implementing a rationale for American policy in that area. Professor Fifield, long a specialist in Asian studies and former government official, predicts marked changes in the American outlook on Asia and success in American aims.

Fleming, Denna Frank. **America's Role in Asia.** New York: Funk & Wagnalls, 1969, 209 p.
Essays by a persistent opponent of the American involvement in Vietnam.

Friedman, Edward and Selden, Mark, eds. **America's Asia: Dissenting Essays on Asian-American Relations.** New York: Pantheon Books, 1971, 458 p.
Twelve younger scholars accuse their teachers of witting or unwitting complicity in an aggressive U.S. foreign policy in Asia.

Gordon, Bernard K. **Toward Disengagement in Asia: A Strategy for American Foreign Policy.** Englewood Cliffs: Prentice-Hall, 1969, 186 p.
A persuasive argument that Asian effort and Asian manpower must gradually become the primary means of providing Asian security.

Greene, Felix. **A Curtain of Ignorance: How the American Public Has Been Misinformed about China.** Garden City: Doubleday, 1964, 340 p.
A study by a former head of BBC's New York office.

Greene, Fred. **U.S. Policy and the Security of Asia.** New York: McGraw-Hill (for the Council on Foreign Relations), 1968, 429 p.
After treating the role of security in foreign relations in general, Mr. Greene shows how and to what extent America's traditional involvement in Asia has developed, identifies threats to its interests there and discusses effects of possible changes in commitments and alignments.

Gupta, D. C. **United States Attitude Towards China.** Delhi: S. Chand, 1969, 445 p.
This study covers the period from the Yalta Agreement in February 1945 to the outbreak of the Korean War in June 1950.

Gurtov, Melvin. **Southeast Asia Tomorrow: Problems and Prospects for US Policy.** Baltimore: Johns Hopkins Press, 1970, 114 p.
An assessment of the prospective security environment in Southeast Asia over the next decade, with suggestions for policy changes based on a more closely defined decision on the scope and nature of American interests.

Henderson, William, ed. **Southeast Asia: Problems of United States Policy.** Cambridge: M.I.T. Press, 1964, 273 p.
Eleven chapters, by 13 highly regarded specialists, stemming from an Asia House conference in May 1963 on U.S. political, strategic, economic and socio-cultural policies toward Southeast Asia. The editor concludes with a review of past policy and suggested factors for consideration by American policy-makers in the future.

Hess, Gary R. **America Encounters India, 1941-1947.** Baltimore: Johns Hopkins Press, 1971, 211 p.
A monograph on the American popular and official attitudes toward political developments in India during World War II and its immediate aftermath. The author argues that for the Americans at that time their association with Great Britain was more important than the development of good relations with the Indian nationalists.

Hohenberg, John. **Between Two Worlds: Policy, Press, and Public Opinion in Asian-American Relations.** New York: Praeger (for the Council on Foreign Relations), 1967, 507 p.
The author, drawing on his experience of 25 years as a newspaperman and from a journey through seven Asian countries, explores the impact of foreign correspondence on foreign policy in American-Asian relations.

Hope, A. Guy. **America and Swaraj.** Washington: Public Affairs Press, 1968, 136 p.
A study of the formation of American attitudes toward the evolvement of Indian independence, emphasizing the part played by Ambassador William Phillips in carrying out President Roosevelt's policy.

Israel, Jerry. **Progressivism and the Open Door: America and China, 1905-1921.** Pittsburgh: University of Pittsburgh Press, 1971, 222 p.
A workmanlike monograph which rejects the traditional notion that the American Open Door policy was unique and different from the general Western political and industrial penetration of China.

Kalb, Marvin and Abel, Elie. **Roots of Involvement: The U.S. in Asia, 1784-1971.** New York: Norton, 1971, 336 p.
The authors assert that the Indochina war is only a link in a chain of "America's swashbuckling adventures in Asia." Truman, Eisenhower, Kennedy, Johnson and Nixon are all taken to task for blundering ever deeper into the quicksands of Asian wars.

Kubek, Anthony. **How the Far East Was Lost: American Policy and the Creation of Communist China.** Chicago: Regnery, 1963, 480 p.
An extremely critical, "revisionist" review of U.S. policy in China in the 1940s. The late General George C. Marshall is seen as "perhaps the key figure in the China debacle."

Lansdale, Edward Geary. **In the Midst of Wars: An American's Mission to Southeast Asia.** New York: Harper and Row, 1972, 386 p.
Memoirs of an American practitioner of counterinsurgency and covert operations in the Philippines and Vietnam. The author does not mention his important role in shaping policy toward Vietnam in the 1960s and limits his account to the 1950s.

Liu, Kwang-Ching. **Americans and Chinese: A Historical Essay and a Bibliography.** Cambridge: Harvard University Press, 1963, 211 p.
A Harvard historian surveys the impact of Americans in China and Chinese in America in 40 pages, and appends a 152-page bibliography which forms a useful guide for the study of modern China and Sino-American relations.

MacFarquhar, Roderick, *ed.* **Sino-American Relations, 1949-71.** New York: Praeger (for the Royal Institute of International Affairs), 1972, 267 p.
This volume contains a useful compendium of documents on the postwar course of Sino-American relations as well as essays by Morton Halperin, A.M. Halpern and Donald W. Klein which attempt to assess the consequences of this course.

May, Ernest R. and Thomson, James C. Jr., *eds.* **American-East Asian Relations: A Survey.** Cambridge: Harvard University Press, 1972, 425 p.
Historiographical essays, organized chronologically and with predominant emphasis on relations with China.

Middleton, Drew. **America's Stake in Asia.** Philadelphia: Lippincott, 1968, 240 p.
A cogently reasoned argument in favor of a continuing American presence in Asia.

Moorsteen, Richard H. and Abramowitz, Morton. **Remaking China Policy: U.S.-China Relations and Governmental Decisionmaking.** Cambridge: Harvard University Press, 1971, 136 p.
A realistic and tersely argued plan of action for a new Asian—not just China—policy.

Neumann, William Louis. **America Encounters Japan: From Perry to MacArthur.** Baltimore: Johns Hopkins Press, 1963, 353 p.
A controversial study of the effects of American attitudes toward Japan (many of them deep-rooted and misconceived) on the development of American foreign policy.

O'Connor, Richard. **Pacific Destiny: An Informal History of the U.S. in the Far East: 1776-1968.** Boston: Little, Brown, 1969, 505 p.
The story of the evolution of the United States as a Pacific rather than an Atlantic power.

Palmer, Norman Dunbar. **South Asia and United States Policy.** Boston: Houghton, 1966, 332 p.
This study deals primarily with the internal dynamics and the external policies of India and Pakistan and the implications of the situation of South Asia for U.S. foreign policy.

Passin, Herbert, *ed.* **The United States and Japan.** Englewood Cliffs: Prentice-Hall, 1966, 174 p.
An important discussion of Japanese-American social, political and economic relations as they have developed since the end of World War II.

Rankin, Karl Lott. **China Assignment.** Seattle: University of Washington Press, 1964, 343 p.
Mr. Rankin was U.S. Consul General in Canton and Hong Kong at the time of the Chinese Communist takeover of the Mainland, and subsequently Minister and Ambassador to the Nationalist Government. His is a sincerely conceived history of U.S. relations with China during the decade 1949-1959. Recognizing the shortcomings of the Chiang régime, he considers American support of it essential.

Rappaport, Armin. **Henry L. Stimson and Japan, 1931-33.** Chicago: University of Chicago Press, 1963, 238 p.
A history professor at Berkeley, using government documents and private papers, traces the development of Stimson's reactions—from calmness to outraged moral indignation—to the historic Mukden Incident and Japan's occupation of Manchuria.

Ravenal, Earl C., ed. **Peace with China? U.S. Decisions for Asia.** New York: Liveright, 1971, 242 p.
Eighteen scholars and government officials discuss the future of U.S. China policy. The level of discourse is almost uniformly high.

Reischauer, Edwin Oldfather. **Beyond Vietnam: The United States and Asia.** New York: Knopf, 1967, 242 p.
A plea for a less haphazardly conceived foreign policy in Asia by the former U.S. Ambassador to Japan.

Sanders, Sol. **A Sense of Asia.** New York: Scribner, 1969, 339 p.
A Bangkok-based journalist deplores American foreign policy but believes that national security demands U.S. involvement in Asian problems.

Schweitzer, Carl-Christoph. **Amerikas chinesisches Dilemma.** Opladen: Westdeutscher Verlag. 1969, 341 p.
The author of this extensive study examines the American-Chinese relations in the period between the proclamation of the Peoples' Republic of China in October 1949 and the outbreak of the Korean War in June 1950. He pays particular attention to the influence exercised by internal political developments on the official attitude of the United States toward China. There is also a comparison of the British and American China policies of that time.

Sergeichuk, S. **SShA i Kitai.** Moscow: Izd-vo "Mezhdunarodnye Otnosheniia," 2d enl. and rev. ed., 1973, 236 p.
A detailed treatment of American policy toward China since 1949, as seen through decidedly unsympathetic Soviet eyes. The transformation of Washington-Peking relations under the Nixon Administration is deemed a cynical maneuver that answers the needs and ambitions of both parties.

Service, John S. **The Amerasia Papers: Some Problems in the History of US-China Relations.** Berkeley: Center for Chinese Studies, University of California, 1971, 220 p.
The publication in 1970 by the Internal Security Subcommittee of "The Amerasia Papers: A Clue to the Catastrophe of China" reopened the controversy over who "lost China." In this monograph Mr. Service, who was discharged from the Foreign Service in 1951 for his views on China, offers his version of the U.S.-China relations in the aftermath of World War II.

Shewmaker, Kenneth E. **Americans and Chinese Communists, 1927-1945.** Ithaca: Cornell University Press, 1971, 387 p.
A professor at Dartmouth evaluates the mostly favorable reporting on Chinese Communists by such American travelers as Agnes Smedley, Evans F. Carlson, Anna Louise Strong, Edgar and Helen Snow and others.

Smith, David S., ed. **The Next Asia: Problems for U.S. Policy.** New York: Columbia University, 1969, 316 p.
Political, economic, military and cultural problems facing the United States and major Asian nations as seen by ten participants of the 1967–68 seminar held by the International Fellows Program of Columbia University. Mostly on or involving China.

Steele, Archibald Trojan. **The American People and China.** New York: McGraw-Hill (for the Council on Foreign Relations), 1966, 325 p.
An examination of American public attitudes toward China and U. S. China policy, based upon interviews with persons in leadership positions and opinion surveys.

Tsou, Tang. **America's Failure in China, 1941-50.** Chicago: University of Chicago Press, 1963, 614 p.
A well-documented review and critique of American policy toward China during the 1940s. Of special value are the author's insights into Chinese domestic politics.

Tuchman, Barbara Wertheim. **Stilwell and the American Experience in China, 1911–45.** New York: Macmillan, 1971, 621 p.
The theme of this poignant historical assessment is that "China was a problem for which there was no American solution."

Vorontsov, Vladilen Borisovich. **"Kumiry" bez prikras: D. Makartur i dal'nevostochnaia politika SShA.** Moscow: Izd-vo "Mezhdunarodnye Otnosheniia," 1968, 216 p.
A critical assessment of the views and role of General Douglas MacArthur during the U.S. post-World War II engagement in the Far East.

Vorontsov, Vladilen Borisovich. **Tikhookeanskaia politika SShA 1941-1950.** Moscow: Izd-vo "Nauka," 1967, 317 p.

A conventional Soviet attack on American policies in the Pacific during and after World War II, with special attention to Korea, Japan and Indochina. Although almost entirely dependent on Western sources, a bibliography of works in Russian is included.

Young, Kenneth Todd. **Negotiating with the Chinese Communists: The United States Experience, 1953-1967.** New York: McGraw-Hill (for the Council on Foreign Relations), 1968, 461 p.

An account and appraisal of the 130 or more secret Ambassadorial Talks, held first in Geneva, then in Warsaw, at which American and Chinese representatives discussed their governments' positions on important, timely issues.

Relations with International Organizations

See also International Organization and Government, p. 96; The Postwar World, p. 178; Inter-American Relations, p. 193; (The United States) Biographies, Memoirs and Addresses, p. 218; and other subsections under (The United States) Foreign Policy.

Bloomfield, Lincoln Palmer. **The United Nations and U.S. Foreign Policy: A New Look at the National Interest.** Boston: Little, Brown, rev. ed., 1967, 268 p.

A completely revised and updated edition of a study, originally published in 1960, of the U.S. participation in the United Nations. Mr. Bloomfield, the author of numerous books and articles on international affairs, served in the State Department from 1946 to 1957.

Divine, Robert A. **Second Chance: The Triumph of Internationalism in America During World War II.** New York: Atheneum, 1967, 371 p.

A description of the successful struggle waged by individuals and groups in the United States during World War II to prepare the ground for American participation in a new world organization. The struggle, the author shows, was not between internationalism and isolationism, but over the form that internationalism would take.

Finkelstein, Lawrence S., ed. **The United States and International Organization: The Changing Setting.** Cambridge: M.I.T. Press, 1969, 216 p.

A collection of essays.

Gardner, Richard Newton. **In Pursuit of World Order: U.S. Foreign Policy and International Organizations.** New York: Praeger, 2d rev. ed., 1966, 278 p.

An informed appraisal, by the Deputy Assistant Secretary of State for International Organization Affairs from 1961 to 1965, of the positive contribution of international organizations in conjunction with American objectives and purposes.

Gross, Franz Bruno, ed. **The United States and the United Nations.** Norman: University of Oklahoma Press, 1964, 356 p.

Essays prepared under the auspices of the Foreign Policy Research Institute of the University of Pennsylvania and dealing from a wide range of perspectives with the impact of the U.N. on American policy.

Haas, Ernst B. **Tangle of Hopes: American Commitments and World Order.** Englewood Cliffs: Prentice-Hall, 1969, 306 p.

A systematic analysis of American involvements in international organizations with some thoughtful policy recommendations.

Riggs, Robert E. **US/UN: Foreign Policy and International Organization.** New York: Appleton-Century-Crofts, 1971, 347 p.

A solid study of the pursuit of American policy objectives through the United Nations.

Russell, Ruth B. **The United Nations and United States Security Policy.** Washington: Brookings Institution, 1968, 510 p.

A carefully researched study advancing the thesis that American security interests would be better served by using the United Nations as a means to create an East-West détente rather than to advance cold war objectives.

Stone, Ralph A. **The Irreconcilables: The Fight Against the League of Nations.** Lexington: University Press of Kentucky, 1970, 208 p.

This well-written monograph analyzes the role of the 16 Senators who, during the fight between Wilson and the Senate over the League of Nations, were known as the "irreconcilables."

Weiler, Lawrence Duffield and Simons, Anne Patricia. **The United States and the United Nations.** New York: Manhattan Publishing Co. (for Carnegie Endowment for International Peace), 1967, 589 p.
A comprehensive study of U.S. peace and security policies in the United Nations during the organization's first ten years.

Organization and Procedure

See also (General Works) Methodology and Theory, p. 4; and other subsections under (The United States) Foreign Policy.

Bailey, Thomas Andrew. **The Art of Diplomacy: The American Experience.** New York: Appleton, 1968, 303 p.
A charming and witty collection of maxims culled from the American diplomatic experience.

Barnett, Vincent M., Jr., *ed.* **The Representation of the United States Abroad.** New York: Praeger (for the American Assembly, Columbia University), rev. ed., 1965, 251 p.
Papers dealing with various aspects of U.S. representation—diplomatic, economic, military and cultural. Based on background papers first published in 1956.

Beaulac, Willard Leon. **Career Diplomat: A Career in the Foreign Service of the United States.** New York: Macmillan, 1964, 199 p.
A guide for those contemplating a career in diplomatic service, by a long-time Foreign Service officer and ambassador.

Beichman, Arnold. **The "Other" State Department.** New York: Basic Books, 1968, 221 p.
A crisply written account of the structure, activities and main personalities of the U.S. Mission to the United Nations.

Berding, Andrew Henry Thomas. **Dulles on Diplomacy.** Princeton: Van Nostrand, 1965, 184 p.
The former Assistant Secretary of State for Public Affairs made extensive shorthand notes of conversations with the late Secretary Dulles. These notes are the basis for this informal but informative presentation of Dulles' views on his tasks as a diplomat.

Blancké, W. Wendell. **The Foreign Service of the United States.** New York: Praeger, 1969, 286 p.
An instructive and entertaining study by a retired Foreign Service officer.

Briggs, Ellis Ormsbee. **Anatomy of Diplomacy: The Origin and Execution of American Foreign Policy.** New York: McKay, 1968, 248 p.
A chatty account of the execution of American foreign policy, by a former ambassador.

Burke, Lee H. **Ambassador at Large: Diplomat Extraordinary.** The Hague: Nijhoff, 1972, 176 p.
A study of a new diplomatic office that was officially institutionalized in the United States in 1949.

Campbell, John Franklin. **The Foreign Affairs Fudge Factory.** New York: Basic Books, 1971, 292 p.
A trenchant critique of the bureaucratic dimension of American foreign policy by the late editor of *Foreign Policy*.

Chittick, William O. **State Department, Press and Pressure Groups: A Role Analysis.** New York: Wiley-Interscience, 1970, 373 p.
An analysis of the roles of different actors in and close to the State Department as they affect the policy-making process.

Clark, Keith C. and Legere, Laurence J., *eds.* **The President and the Management of National Security: A Report.** New York: Praeger (for the Institute of Defense Analyses), 1969, 274 p.

An informative study on the "nuts and bolts" of the policy-planning and coördination process in national security matters. After an exhaustive scrutiny of the available machinery, the authors conclude that "the force of personality of the President and his principal advisers" is more important than any formal organization procedures.

Destler, Irving McArthur. **Presidents, Bureaucrats, and Foreign Policy.** Princeton: Princeton University Press, 1972, 329 p.
This study contains both a critical history of the numerous and ineffective proposals since 1945 to reform the conduct of U.S. foreign policy and a sophisticated proposal for enhancing the role of a Secretary of State responsive to presidential needs.

Dulles, Eleanor Lansing. **American Foreign Policy in the Making.** New York: Harper and Row, 1968, 370 p.
A workmanlike survey of the foreign policy-making process, including some useful case studies.

Gerberding, William P. **United States Foreign Policy: Perspectives and Analysis.** New York: McGraw-Hill, 1966, 383 p.
In this textbook the author deals with policy formulation processes in the U.S. and discusses some of the major foreign policy problems of the contemporary world.

Harr, John Ensor. **The Professional Diplomat.** Princeton: Princeton University Press, 1969, 404 p.
An excellent in-depth analysis of the Foreign Service officer corps of the U.S. Foreign Service. The author concludes with some managerial recommendations.

Henkin, Louis. **Foreign Affairs and the Constitution.** Mineola (N.Y.): Foundation Press, 1972, 553 p.
The author's defense of executive power from the constitutional standpoint, including its use in Vietnam, will be challenged by some, but his reasonable tone and careful citations should make the work standard for some time to come.

Hill, Norman Llewellyn. **Mr. Secretary of State.** New York: Random House, 1963, 185 p.
A critical commentary on the changing role of the Secretary of State.

Hilsman, Roger. **The Politics of Policy Making in Defense and Foreign Affairs.** New York: Harper and Row, 1971, 198 p.
This book sheds light on the limitations on presidential policy-making through the bureaucracy and the Congress. It echoes, in many of its conclusions, the insights of Richard Neustadt in "Presidential Power."

Jackson, Henry Martin, ed. **The Secretary of State and the Ambassador.** New York: Praeger, 1964, 203 p.
——. **The National Security Council.** New York: Praeger, 1965, 311 p.
These two volumes of knowledgeable papers and analyses were prepared under the auspices of subcommittees of the Senate Committee on Government Operations, chaired by Senator Jackson.

Johnson, Richard A. **The Administration of United States Foreign Policy.** Austin: University of Texas Press, 1971, 415 p.
The author, a former State Department career administrator and diplomatist, reviews his country's foreign policy and argues that the future security of the United States depends in part on abandoning the "luxury of conducting its overseas affairs as a projection of domestic bureaucratic rivalries."

Landecker, Manfred. **The President and Public Opinion: Leadership in Foreign Affairs.** Washington: Public Affairs Press, 1968, 133 p.
In this study the author attempts to determine how Presidents Roosevelt and Truman assessed and aroused public opinion in the formulation of their respective foreign policies.

Leacacos, John P. **Fires in the In-Basket: The ABC's of the State Department.** Cleveland: World Publishing Co., 1968, 552 p.
A balanced study of the State Department.

Lisagor, Peter and Higgins, Marguerite. **Overtime in Heaven: Adventures in the Foreign Service.** Garden City: Doubleday, 1964, 275 p.
A colorful record of the hazards and sacrifices entailed in the life of the Foreign Service officer while serving his country.

McCamy, James Lucian. **Conduct of the New Diplomacy.** New York: Harper and Row, 1964, 303 p.
An analysis of problems faced by the Executive Branch in administering U.S. foreign policy.

Rosenau, James Nathan, *ed.* **Domestic Sources of Foreign Policy.** New York: Free Press (for the Princeton Center of International Studies), 1967, 340 p.
A group of ten scholars and the editor attempt to demonstrate the primacy of domestic politics in the foreign policy decision-making process. Useful though uneven.

Sapin, Burton M. **The Making of United States Foreign Policy.** Washington: Brookings Institution, 1966, 415 p.
A sophisticated assessment of the foreign policy machinery of the United States.

Shvedkov, Iu. A., and Others. **SShA: vneshnopoliticheskii mekhanizm; organizatsiia, funktsii, upravlenie.** Moscow: Izd-vo "Nauka," 1972, 367 p.
A survey of United States foreign policy, particularly of its organizational framework and functions, as seen by a group of Soviet analysts associated with the Institute of the United States of America.

Simpson, Smith. **Anatomy of the State Department.** Boston: Houghton, 1967, 285 p.
A fierce critique of the Department of State.

Stennis, John C. and Fulbright, James William. **The Role of Congress in Foreign Policy.** Washington: American Enterprise Institute for Public Policy Research, 1971, 139 p.
Two prominent legislators debate the nature of the balance between Congress and the President in foreign policy. Stennis, on the whole, approves the present system, but Fulbright diagnoses executive usurpation.

Villard, Henry Serrano. **Affairs at State.** New York: Crowell, 1965, 254 p.
A career Foreign Service officer of long standing, Ambassador Villard here discusses the professional diplomatic service of the United States, defends it against many charges, gives his views of the reasons for the periodic slumps in morale, and offers a number of reforms.

Wilcox, Francis O. **Congress, the Executive, and Foreign Policy.** New York: Harper and Row (for the Council on Foreign Relations), 1971, 179 p.
This brief book offers a constructive treatment of the foreign policy implications of the separation of powers.

Trade, Tariffs and Finance

See also International Trade, p. 55; International Finance, p. 59; Foreign Investment and Overseas Business; Multinational Corporations, p. 65; Inter-American Relations, p. 193; (The United States) Economic Problems, p. 274; other subsections under (The United States) Foreign Policy; and the sections for specific countries and regions.

Aharoni, Yair. **The Foreign Investment Decision Process.** Boston: Harvard University, Division of Research, Graduate School of Business Administration, 1966, 362 p.
An Israeli scholar comments on the process by which American firms decide to go abroad.

Bradley, Gene E., *ed.* **Building the American-European Market: Planning for the 1970's.** Homewood (Ill.): Dow Jones-Irwin (for the Atlantic Council of the United States), 1967, 272 p.
A rather optimistic review of the major transatlantic economic issues.

Cahill, Harry A. **The China Trade and U.S. Tariffs.** New York: Praeger, 1973, 161 p.
A survey of U.S.-China trade and a plea to grant the most-favored nation status to China, by an American Foreign Service officer.

Clabaugh, Samuel F. and Feulner, Edwin J., Jr. **Trading with the Communists.** Washington Center for Strategic Studies, 1968, 254 p.
This review of developments in trading with the communists since 1964 includes also congressional viewpoints, a summary of legislation affecting U.S. trade with communist nations and a useful bibliography.

Cohen, Benjamin J., *ed.* **American Foreign Economic Policy.** New York: Harper and Row, 1968, 442 p.

According to the editor, the purpose of this collection of essays "is to give some insights into the major issues confronting the policymakers of the world's richest and most powerful nation in the third decade of the postwar era."

Cohen, Jerome B., ed. **Pacific Partnership: United States-Japan Trade.** Lexington (Mass.): Lexington Books (for the Japan Society), 1972, 270 p.
Professor Cohen has assembled leading authorities who thoroughly cover the leading issues of today and the future.

Curtis, Thomas B. and Vastine, John Robert, Jr. **The Kennedy Round and the Future of American Trade.** New York: Praeger, 1971, 239 p.
When he was in Congress, Mr. Curtis of Missouri was one of the hardest-working supporters of liberal trade policies and Mr. Vastine was his assistant. This book, based on reports made to the House, is especially valuable for its material on specific industries and commodities.

Danielian, N. R., ed. **The United States Balance of Payments: An Appraisal of U.S. Economic Strategy.** Washington: International Economic Policy Association, 1966, 200 p.
The authors recommend tackling the balance of payments problem by reducing military expenditures abroad, tying aid more effectively than before, abandoning most-favored-nation treatment and making balance of payments considerations the main guide of trade policy.

Diebold, William, Jr. **The United States and the Industrial World: American Foreign Economic Policy in the 1970s.** New York: Praeger (for the Council on Foreign Relations), 1972, 463 p.
An examination of the nature and possibilities of U.S. economic policies, by a Senior Research Fellow at the Council on Foreign Relations.

Douglas, Paul Howard. **America in the Market Place: Trade, Tariffs and the Balance of Payments.** New York: Holt, Rinehart and Winston, 1966, 381 p.
A clear exposition of the history and economics of American involvement in international trade, aid and finance, by a former Senator who is also a distinguished economist.

Evans, John W. **The Kennedy Round in American Trade Policy: The Twilight of the GATT?** Cambridge: Harvard University Press (for the Center for International Affairs), 1971, 383 p.
A major addition to the literature of American foreign trade policy by a man who has had many years of experience as an official and negotiator. Although the focus is on the Kennedy Round, the book provides an informed analysis of the main features of American policy throughout the postwar period (and, indeed, since 1934).

Fatemi, Nasrollah Saifpour; Saint Phalle, Thibaut de and Keeffe, Grace M. **The Dollar Crisis: The United States Balance of Payments and Dollar Stability.** New York: Fairleigh Dickinson University Press, 1964, 317 p.
Pessimistic about the future course of the U.S. balance of payments, the authors recommend a series of fairly drastic measures affecting investment, aid and military spending abroad.

Gardner, Lloyd C. **Economic Aspects of New Deal Diplomacy.** Madison: University of Wisconsin Press, 1964, 409 p.
An extensively documented, though not very substantial, survey.

Garretson, Robert C. **The Abundant Peace.** Cleveland: World Publishing Co., 1965, 255 p.
An executive of the Carling Brewing Company compares the trends of economic growth in the U.S.S.R. and the U.S.A. from 1929 to 1964 and pleads for better relations between the two countries.

Harvey, Mose L. **East-West Trade and United States Policy.** New York: National Association of Manufacturers, 1966, 175 p.
In this major study a former member of the Policy Planning Council of the State Department, writing for the National Association of Manufacturers, stresses the political aspects of trading with communist countries.

Hawkins, Robert G. and Walter, Ingo, eds. **The United States and International Markets.** Lexington (Mass.): Lexington Books, 1972, 417 p.
Essays, sponsored by the Center for International Studies of New York University, on

major problems in international commercial policy facing the United States in the coming decade.

Hellmann, Rainer. **Amerika auf dem Europamarkt: US-Direktinvestitionen im Gemeinsamen Markt.** Baden-Baden: Nomos, 1966, 237 p.
A balanced study of American direct investment and the controversies it has given rise to.

Hinshaw, Randall Weston. **The European Community and American Trade: A Study in Atlantic Economics and Policy.** New York: Praeger (for the Council on Foreign Relations), 1964, 188 p.
This concisely written study covers American trade relations with the European Economic Community and European Free Trade Association and explores major alternatives for the future of American trade policy.

Hogan, John D. **The U.S. Balance of Payments and Capital Flows.** New York: Praeger, 1967, 199 p.
A standard treatment.

Hudson, Michael. **Super Imperialism: The Economic Strategy of American Empire.** New York: Holt, Rinehart and Winston, 1972, 304 p.
A very critical survey of American foreign economic policies from the First World War debts to the inconvertibility of the dollar.

Kelly, William Boland, Jr., *ed*. **Studies in United States Commercial Policy.** Chapel Hill: University of North Carolina Press, 1963, 262 p.
Harry Hawkins and John Leddy, who for many years had key roles in shaping trade policy in the State Department, contribute the three central papers, on the successive Trade Agreements Acts, the escape clause and peril points, and agricultural problems. The editor writes on the period between 1922 and 1934 and Don Humphrey on the Common Market and British Commonwealth problems.

Kindleberger, Charles P. **American Business Abroad: Six Lectures on Direct Investment.** New Haven: Yale University Press, 1969, 225 p.
Wide-ranging lectures by a leading economist.

Krause, Lawrence B. **European Economic Integration and the United States.** Washington: Brookings Institution, 1968, 265 p.
A major study with emphasis on measuring the effects of the formation of the Common Market and EFTA on American foreign trade.

Lary, Hal Buckner. **Problems of the United States as World Trader and Banker.** New York: National Bureau of Economic Research, 1963, 175 p.
The author of one of the basic studies of the U.S. balance of payments during the inter-war period traces postwar developments, assesses the strength and weaknesses of the American position and puts the appraisals of the more recent troubles in a balanced perspective.

Lawrence, Samuel A. **United States Merchant Shipping Policies and Politics.** Washington: Brookings Institution, 1966, 405 p.
A thoroughgoing analysis of a generally neglected subject.

Lipsey, Robert E. **Price and Quantity Trends in the Foreign Trade of the United States.** Princeton: Princeton University Press, 1963, 487 p.
A valuable study sponsored by the National Bureau of Economic Research.

Malmgren, Harald B. **International Economic Peacekeeping in Phase II.** New York: Quadrangle Books (for the Atlantic Council of the United States), 1972, 267 p.
Between leaving the Johnson administration and his 1972 appointment as Deputy Special Representative for Trade Negotiations, Mr. Malmgren became a prolific and vigorous commentator on American foreign economic policy. This book is a clear, well-argued and well-informed analysis of the best ways of negotiating trade issues in the years to come.

Malmgren, Harald B., *ed*. **Pacific Basin Development: The American Interests.** Lexington (Mass.): Lexington Books (for the Overseas Development Council), 1972, 148 p.
Focusing on Japan, Mr. Malmgren's team of scholars examine American economic interests in the Pacific region.

Markham, Jesse William and Others. **The Common Market: Friend or Competitor?** New York: New York University Press, 1964, 123 p.

The false antithesis of the title is not pursued in the three lectures which emphasize competition within the European Economic Community, American investment and U.S. exports.

Metzger, Stanley D. **Trade Agreements and the Kennedy Round.** Fairfax (Va.): Coiner Publications, 1964, 119 p./104 p.
A valuable legal exposition of the Trade Expansion Act of 1962, with sensible political and psychological commentary, followed by relevant documents.

Plotnick, Alan R. **Petroleum: Canadian Markets and United States Foreign Trade Policy.** Seattle: University of Washington Press, 1965, 172 p.
A close examination of domestic and foreign markets for Canadian oil, now and in the future, and some exposition of Canadian and U.S. national policies.

Polk, Judd and Others. **U.S. Production Abroad and the Balance of Payments: A Survey of Corporate Investment Experience.** New York: National Industrial Conference Board, 1966, 200 p.
An analysis of the relationship of private investment to the domestic economy.

Robinson, Stuart W., Jr. **Multinational Banking.** Leyden: Sijthoff, 1972, 316 p.
An American lawyer examines American banking in France, Britain and Switzerland and shows how national laws have shaped international functions.

Salant, Walter S. and Others. **The United States Balance of Payments in 1968.** Washington: Brookings Institution, 1963, 298 p.
A wide-ranging analysis by six leading economists of the U.S. financial and trade programs in the post-World War II era, with projections for 1968.

Shaffer, Edward H. **The Oil Import Program of the United States: An Evaluation.** New York: Praeger, 1968, 257 p.
A helpful guide to the intricacies of the oil import quotas.

Strackbein, Oscar Robert. **American Enterprise and Foreign Trade.** Washington: Public Affairs Press, 1965, 193 p.
A well-informed protectionist spokesmen argues against trade-barrier reduction largely on grounds of the effect on employment and the demand necessary for growth.

Terpstra, Vern. **American Marketing in the Common Market.** New York: Praeger, 1967, 168 p.
A study of how American firms have coped with their European opportunities.

Vernon, Raymond. **Sovereignty at Bay: The Multinational Spread of U.S. Enterprises.** New York: Basic Books, 1971, 326 p.
Focusing mainly on American-controlled multinational enterprises, Professor Vernon deals comprehensively with their character, their impact on the world economy and national political and economic reactions to them.

Weintraub, Sidney. **Trade Preferences for Less-Developed Countries: An Analysis of United States Policy.** New York: Praeger, 1967, 231 p.
A solid study, reflecting the author's experience in the State Department.

Wilkins, Mira. **The Emergence of Multinational Enterprise: American Business Abroad from the Colonial Era to 1914.** Cambridge: Harvard University Press, 1970, 310 p.
A major work that does much to explain as well as describe the growth of direct foreign investment by Americans up to 1914.

Wilson, Joan Hoff. **American Business and Foreign Policy, 1920-1933.** Lexington: University Press of Kentucky, 1971, 339 p.
A well-documented history which demonstrates the complexity of business views and influences.

Aid and Assistance

See also Economic Aid and Technical Assistance, p. 81; United Nations, p. 99; other subsections under (The United States) Foreign Policy and the sections for specific countries.

Achterberg, Erich. **General Marshall macht Epoche: Konferenzen, Gestalten, Hintergründe.** Frankfurt/Main: Ullstein, 1964, 295 p.
A review and appraisal of the Marshall Plan.

Arkes, Hadley. **Bureaucracy, the Marshall Plan, and the National Interest.** Princeton: Princeton University Press, 1972, 395 p.

An ingenious use of the organization of the Economic Coöperation Administration as an indicator of how the Marshall Plan was to express the national interest.

Ashabranner, Brent. **A Moment in History.** Garden City: Doubleday, 1971, 392 p.

A constructively critical account of the first ten years of the Peace Corps. One poignant observation: "It is impossible to imagine the Peace Corps being born in today's America, but fortunately it already exists."

Asher, Robert E. **Development Assistance in the Seventies: Alternatives for the United States.** Washington: Brookings Institution, 1970, 248 p.

This well-informed study deals with all the central issues of U.S. aid policies, weighs the evidence of experience and shows the implications of alternative choices.

Baldwin, David Allen. **Economic Development and American Foreign Policy, 1943–62.** Chicago: University of Chicago Press, 1966, 291 p.

A useful discussion of the place of soft loans in American foreign policy.

Black, Lloyd D. **The Strategy of Foreign Aid.** Princeton: Van Nostrand, 1968, 176 p.

A survey of the history, use and results of foreign aid, with the emphasis on development.

Brynes, Asher. **We Give to Conquer.** New York: Norton, 1966, 219 p.

The author argues that "All unilateral foreign aid to poorer nations . . . seeks to create, maintain, and defend spheres of influence and thus under the guise of philanthropy it carries on the old statecraft in a new way."

Carey, Robert G. **The Peace Corps.** New York: Praeger, 1970, 274 p.

A good straightforward description and analysis of the Corps' record.

Clark, Paul G. **American Aid for Development.** New York: Praeger (for the Council on Foreign Relations), 1972, 231 p.

Contrary to widespread impressions, many poor countries made marked economic progress in the 1960s. They and others could make good use of increased foreign aid to grow further in the 1970s. These conclusions by the head of the Center of Development Economics at Williams College (and a former AID official) lead to concrete recommendations for the reshaping of American aid policies.

Coffin, Frank Morey. **Witness for Aid.** Boston: Houghton, 1964, 273 p.

A former Congressman, who represented the United States on the Development Assistance Committee of the OECD, writes vigorously in support of an aid program that emphasizes long-run development, professionalism in administration, and realistic expectations of what can be accomplished.

Curti, Merle Eugene. **American Philanthropy Abroad.** New Brunswick: Rutgers University Press, 1963, 651 p.

A substantial history by a leading American historian of nongovernmental programs for relief and technical aid abroad from the days of the Greek revolution and the Irish famine to the present.

Elliott, William Yandell, ed. **Education and Training in the Developing Countries: The Role of U.S. Foreign Aid.** New York: Praeger, 1966, 399 p.

A symposium of distinguished contributions.

Feis, Herbert. **Foreign Aid and Foreign Policy.** New York: St. Martin's Press, 1964, 246 p.

A balanced, reflective commentary on the political and economic aspects of foreign aid, by an author with long experience of foreign economic policy.

Fuchs, Lawrence H. **"Those Peculiar Americans": The Peace Corps and American National Character.** New York: Meredith Press, 1967, 232 p.

A case study gleaned from the author's personal experience as Peace Corps Director in the Philippines.

Hapgood, David and Bennett, Meridan. **Agents of Change: A Close Look at the Peace Corps.** Boston: Little, Brown, 1968, 244 p.

The authors interviewed several hundred Peace Corps volunteers in seventeen programs all over the world. The result is a useful and informative book largely reflecting the views of the volunteers themselves.

Hapgood, David, *ed*. **The Role of Popular Participation in Development.** Cambridge: M.I.T. Press, 1969, 222 p.
Experts and practitioners attempt to determine how to increase the role of local people in the programs of AID.

Hayes, Samuel P., *ed*. **The Beginning of American Aid to Southeast Asia.** Lexington (Mass.): Heath Lexington, 1971, 336 p.
This volume contains the reports of the Griffin Mission (1950) and retrospective comment by French, Vietnamese and Burmese officials. The author/editor was deputy chief of the mission.

Hinkel, Günter. **Die Auslandshilfe der USA.** Berlin: Deutscher Verlag der Wissenschaften, 1972, 238 p.
An East German analysis of American foreign aid programs as instruments of imperialism in the Kennedy and Johnson administrations.

Hoopes, Roy, *ed*. **The Peace Corps Experience.** New York: Clarkson N. Potter, 1968, 309 p.
A book written from the volunteers' point of view.

Hoover, Herbert Clark. **An American Epic. Volume IV: The Guns Cease Killing and the Saving of Life from Famine Begins, 1939–1963.** Chicago: Regnery, 1964, 322 p.
In this fourth volume of his series on American efforts to combat famine caused by war, the late President writes of the program started in 1939 to aid the small democracies and carries the story on through postwar international efforts to provide relief from starvation.

Hunter, Robert E. and Rielly, John E., *eds*. **Development Today: A New Look at U.S. Relations with the Poor Countries.** New York: Praeger (in coöperation with the Overseas Development Council), 1972, 286 p.
A well-conceived collection of papers, most of them prepared for a seminar of the Overseas Development Council.

Kaplan, Jacob Julius. **The Challenge of Foreign Aid: Policies, Problems, and Possibilities.** New York: Praeger, 1967, 405 p.
A solid study, drawing on a wide range of the national experience and emphasizing economics.

Kretzschmar, Winfried W. **Auslandshilfe als Mittel der Aussenwirtschafts- und Aussenpolitik.** Munich: Oldenbourg, 1964, 256 p.
Addressed primarily to a German audience, this very competent analysis of American aid treats the period of the British loan, the Marshall Plan and aid to China before 1949.

McGuire, Edna. **The Peace Corps: Kindlers of the Spark.** New York: Macmillan, 1966, 224 p.
The story of a three-month "pilgrimage made to see the Peace Corps in action"— in Ecuador, Sierra Leone, Tunisia, India and Malaysia. As the subtitle indicates, the observations are very positive.

Mikesell, Raymond Frech. **The Economics of Foreign Aid.** Chicago: Aldine Publishing Co., 1968, 300 p.
A thorough study with fairly concrete recommendations for the best use of aid at different stages of development.

Moomaw, I. W. **The Challenge of Hunger: A Program for More Effective Foreign Aid.** New York: Praeger, 1966, 222 p.
Like many people with a long experience of privately-run aid programs, Dr. Moomaw, an agricultural specialist, believes that the way out of U.S. foreign aid troubles is to separate military from economic aid, stick to the original principles of Point IV, emphasize direct contact with people, and give well-selected men in the field greater freedom from Washington's dictates.

Nelson, Joan M. **Aid, Influence, and Foreign Policy.** New York: Macmillan, 1968, 149 p.
This book deals very concretely with the limits and possibilities of using aid to influence political and development policies. The author was formerly in the Agency for International Development. Prepared under the auspices of the Center for International Affairs, Harvard University.

O'Leary, Michael Kent. **The Politics of American Foreign Aid.** New York: Atherton Press, 1967, 172 p.
An instructive inquiry "into the mood of the public concerning foreign aid."

Poats, Ruther M. **Technology for Developing Nations: New Directions for U.S. Technical Assistance.** Washington: Brookings Institution, 1972, 255 p.
The author, an experienced aid administrator, sees a "renaissance in technical assistance" and suggests how it ought to be organized to make more use of U.S. non-governmental talents.

Rubin, Jacob A. **Your Hundred Billion Dollars: The Complete Story of American Foreign Aid.** Philadelphia: Chilton, 1964, 299 p.
A popular treatment stressing humanitarian and educational elements.

Texter, Robert B., ed. **Cultural Frontiers of the Peace Corps.** Cambridge: M.I.T. Press, 1966, 363 p.
A book by a number of authors dealing with the overseas activities and problems of the Peace Corps, with particular attention to the qualities and characteristics of 13 selected host countries.

Thompson, Kenneth W. **Foreign Assistance: A View from the Private Sector.** Notre Dame: University of Notre Dame Press, 1972, 160 p.
Drawing principally on the work of the Rockefeller Foundation in international health and agriculture programs, the author points to useful lessons which privately financed foreign aid can offer to government operations.

Thorp, Willard L. **The Reality of Foreign Aid.** New York: Praeger (for the Council on Foreign Relations), 1971, 370 p.
The former chairman of the Development Assistance Committee (and onetime Assistant Secretary of State for Economic Affairs) draws on his extensive governmental and academic experience for a comprehensive analysis of the process of economic development and the ways rich countries can help poor ones.

Toma, Peter A. **The Politics of Food for Peace: Executive-Legislative Interaction.** Tucson: University of Arizona Press, 1967, 195 p.
A detailed analysis by a professor at the University of Arizona of the politics involved in providing food aid for foreign nations.

Tully, Andrew and Britten, Milton. **Where Did Your Money Go? The Foreign Aid Story.** New York: Simon and Schuster, 1964, 223 p.
Less sensational than it sounds, this journalistic effort at "constructive muckraking" draws together material that goes well beyond aid into other foreign policy difficulties.

Verein, Andrei Vladimirovich. **"Apostoly Mira" na trekh kontinentakh: neokolonialistskaia sushchnost' amerikanskogo "Korpusa Mira."** Moscow: Izd-vo "Mezhdunarodnye Otnosheniia," 1971, 239 p.
A vituperative Soviet attack on the Peace Corps, which in the author's opinion is a tool of U.S. imperialism.

Military and Defense Policy

See also General Works, p. 1; Law of War; Aggression, p. 89; United Nations, p. 99; War and Peace, p. 108; First World War, p. 131; Second World War, p. 144; The Postwar World, p. 178; (The United States) Recent History, p. 214; Biographies, Memoirs and Addresses, p. 218; Foreign Policy, p. 229; Politics and Political Issues, p. 268; The Korean War, p. 728; The Pueblo Affair, p. 729; The Vietnam War, p. 739; and the sections for specific countries and regions.

Abshire, David M. and Allen, Richard V., eds. **National Security: Political, Military, and Economic Strategies in the Decade Ahead.** New York: Praeger (for the Hoover Institution on War, Revolution and Peace), 1963, 1,039 p.
A huge symposium on a wide range of issues relating to U.S. national security. The papers are based on a conference at the Center for Strategic Studies of Georgetown University in January 1963.

Ackley, Charles Walton. **The Modern Military in American Society.** Philadelphia: Westminster Press, 1972, 400 p.
A study emphasizing the fact that the U.S. military establishment is in a period of trial and transition in the wake of Vietnam, rising defense budgets and the adoption of the all-volunteer armed forces concept.

Adams, Benson D. **Ballistic Missile Defense.** New York: American Elsevier, 1971, 274 p.
  This competent and technically highly informative monograph focuses on the Nike-Zeus, Nike-X, Sentinel and Safeguard missile systems.

Armacost, Michael H. **The Politics of Weapons Innovation.** New York: Columbia University Press, 1969, 304 p.
  This case study of the Thor-Jupiter controversy illuminates the complex interaction between the political process and weapons policies in the United States. More broadly, the book offers some valuable insights into the relationship of politics to technology.

Art, Robert J. **The TFX Decision: McNamara and the Military.** Boston: Little, Brown, 1968, 202 p.
  A case study of civil-military relations in the American government. Prepared under the auspices of the Center for International Affairs at Harvard University.

Baldwin, Hanson W. **Strategy for Tomorrow.** New York: Harper and Row, 1970, 377 p.
  The author argues forcefully for U.S. military superiority. In its general approach, the book warns against what the author sees as the futile hope for a brave new warless world.

Baldwin, William Lee. **The Structure of the Defense Market, 1955–1964.** Durham: Duke University Press, 1967, 249 p.
  An analysis, from an economist's point of view, of the structure of the defense market during a decade of cold war.

Barnet, Richard Joseph. **The Economy of Death.** New York: Atheneum, 1970, 201 p.
  A powerful polemic against the "military-industrial complex" and a "dangerously irrational" defense policy, by a former member of the Department of State.

Barnet, Richard Joseph. **Roots of War.** New York: Atheneum, 1972, 350 p.
  The author of this revisionist synthesis argues that American business interests influence but do not dictate foreign policy. He is more persuasive than rigid economic determinists like Joyce and Gabriel Kolko.

Bletz Donald F. **The Role of the Military Professional in U.S. Foreign Policy.** New York: Praeger, 1972, 320 p.
  A professional soldier for thirty years advocates "the thorough integration of political and military considerations at the national level."

Bobrow, Davis B., ed. **Weapons System Decisions: Political and Psychological Perspectives on Continental Defense.** New York: Praeger, 1969, 282 p.
  A volume of studies, based on a research project sponsored by the Oak Ridge National Laboratories in 1965, urging "the use of behavioral science expertise to improve the bases for decision between national security postures."

Braisted, William Reynolds. **The United States Navy in the Pacific, 1910–1922.** Austin: University of Texas Press, 1971, 741 p.
  The author of this substantial survey states that it has been his "principal concern to show how American naval men sought to provide security for American interests against a possible Japanese attack by developing the Navy's capacity ultimately to win and to retain control of the western Pacific."

Caraley, Demetrios. **The Politics of Military Unification: A Study of Conflict and the Policy Process.** New York: Columbia University Press, 1966, 345 p.
  A close study of the intense struggle that took place in the United States between 1943 and 1947 over the issue of the unification of the military services.

Chayes, Abram and Wiesner, Jerome B., eds. **ABM: An Evaluation of the Decision to Deploy an Anti-Ballistic Missile System.** New York: Harper and Row, 1969, 282 p.
  A group of scholars, scientists and statesmen attack the decision to deploy the ABM system on grounds of strategic soundness, economic and technical feasibility, as well as political and diplomatic wisdom.

Cochran, Bert. **The War System.** New York: Macmillan, 1965, 274 p.
  A sharp critique of the "militarization" of American life: "The first duty of the political analyst is to expose the hollowness and the sham of the diplomacy and military system that is supposed to save us from war."

Coffey, J. I. **Strategic Power and National Security.** Pittsburgh: University of Pittsburgh Press, 1971, 214 p.

The author argues that current and projected levels of U.S. nuclear capability far exceed rational requirements and therefore are detrimental to national security.

Davis, Vincent. **The Admirals Lobby.** Chapel Hill: University of North Carolina Press, 1967, 329 p.
A valuable study of the Navy's officer corps as a political pressure group.

Davis, Vincent. **Postwar Defense Policy and the U.S. Navy, 1943-1946.** Chapel Hill: University of North Carolina Press, 1966, 371 p.
A study of the Navy's efforts, from midway in the Second World War, to plan and prepare for its postwar role.

Deitchman, Seymour J. **Limited War and American Defense Policy: Building and Using Military Power in a World at War.** Cambridge: M.I.T. Press, 2d rev. ed., 1969, 302 p.
An extensive study of "problems of military function and systems, and the application of the systems to tactics and strategy" within the framework of limited warfare.

Donovan, James A. **Militarism, U.S.A.** New York: Scribner, 1970, 288 p.
A former marine asserts that "America has become a militaristic and agressive nation," and warns against the temptation to assume the role of world policeman.

Donovan, James A. **The United States Marine Corps.** New York: Praeger, 1967, 246 p.
A frankly admiring history of the Corps, its famous battles, doctrines and traditions.

Dupuy, Richard Ernest and Baumer, William H. **The Little Wars of the United States.** New York: Hawthorn Books, 1968, 226 p.
Seven vignettes ranging from the war with France in 1798 to the intervention in Russia in 1918.

Duscha, Julius. **Arms, Money, and Politics.** New York: Ives Washburn, 1965, 210 p.
The author, a reporter for *The Washington Post*, discusses the politics and economics of defense spending and proposes solutions for some of the problems raised by this vast and complex area of national effort.

Englebardt, Stanley L. **Strategic Defenses.** New York: Crowell, 1966, 168 p.
A brief survey of the U.S. strategic defense systems, emphasizing the communications networks.

Felix, Christopher, *pseud.* **A Short Course in the Secret War.** New York: Dutton, 1963, 314 p.
A former U.S. intelligence agent has written an account of the principles underlying American intelligence operations and an exciting tale of personal involvement in espionage in Soviet-controlled Hungary in 1946 and 1947. The British edition was entitled "The Spy and his Masters: A Short Course in the Secret War" (London: Secker and Warburg, 1963, 287 p.).

Fulbright, James William. **The Pentagon Propaganda Machine.** New York: Liveright, 1970, 166 p.
This book comprises a series of speeches given by the author on the Senate floor in December 1969. In essence, it is an exposé of the Defense Department's high-powered public relations activities.

Gerhardt, James M. **The Draft and Public Policy: Issues in Military Manpower Procurement, 1945-1970.** Columbus: Ohio State University Press, 1971, 425 p.
A scholarly monograph on the history of the draft since World War II.

Ginsburgh, Robert N. **U.S. Military Strategy in the Sixties.** New York: Norton, 1965, 160 p.
Modestly described as a "primer," this is a concise and lucid discussion of U.S. strategic policies and problems.

Goulding, Phil G. **Confirm or Deny: Informing the People on National Security.** New York: Harper and Row, 1970, 369 p.
An account of news management under the Johnson administration. The missing H-Bomb, the bombing of Hanoi, McNamara's fight for deëscalation, the capture of the *Pueblo*, and Clark Clifford's role in reversing Vietnam policy—are all discussed with considerable originality and a commendable sense of balance.

Halperin, Morton H. **Defense Strategies for the Seventies.** Boston: Little Brown (for the Center for International Affairs, Harvard University), 1971, 149 p.
A revision of the author's lucid "Contemporary Military Strategy" (1967) incorporat-

ing material on the Nixon administration. The book is primarily an analytical review of the permutations of strategic doctrines since 1945 rather than speculation about the future.

Halperin, Morton H. **Limited War in the Nuclear Age.** New York: Wiley, 1963, 191 p.
Based upon an examination of contemporary limited wars, this study offers some recommendations for an American "local-defense" strategy.

Hersh, Seymour M. **Chemical and Biological Warfare: America's Hidden Arsenal.** Indianapolis: Bobbs-Merril, 1968, 354 p.
A well-documented inventory.

Hitch, Charles Johnston. **Decision-Making for Defense.** Berkeley: University of California Press, 1965, 83 p.
Concise but important lectures by a former Assistant Secretary of Defense.

Holst, Johan Jørgen and Schneider, William, Jr., eds. **Why ABM? Policy Issues in the Missile Defense Controversy.** New York: Pergamon Press, 1969, 321 p.
A collection of papers prepared under the aegis of the Hudson Institute. The nine contributors, including Donald G. Brennan, Herman Kahn and Albert Wohlstetter, are all in favor of some kind of missile defense.

Hovey, Harold A. **United States Military Assistance: A Study of Policies and Practices.** New York: Praeger, 1965, 306 p.
Written by a former Pentagon aid official, this book is a comprehensive history of military assistance programs. It concludes that military aid should be more sharply separated from economic aid.

Howe, Jonathan Trumbull. **Multicrises.** Cambridge: M.I.T. Press, 1971, 412 p.
A naval man argues for a stronger Navy. He maintains that Soviet naval expansion and British naval contraction have made the United States vulnerable, especially when simultaneous crises erupt.

Infield, Glenn B. **Unarmed and Unafraid.** New York: Macmillan, 1970, 308 p.
An informative book on aerial reconnaissance, shedding new light on the technical aspects of the U-2 episode, the Cuban missile crisis and the Vietnam War.

Jordan, Amos A., Jr., ed. **Issues of National Security in the 1970's: Essays Presented to Colonel George A. Lincoln on His Sixtieth Birthday.** New York: Praeger, 1967, 336 p.
A collection of fifteen essays in honor of the late soldier and professor at West Point.

Just, Ward. **Military Men.** New York: Knopf, 1970, 256 p.
In a series of sharply etched profiles of army men from generals down to privates, the author has assembled a vivid portrait of the U.S. Army.

Kaufmann, William Weed. **The McNamara Strategy.** New York: Harper and Row, 1964, 339 p.
This is chiefly a presentation, much of it in McNamara's own words, of the changes brought about in the Defense Department by the former Secretary of Defense.

King, Edward L. **The Death of the Army: A Pre-Mortem.** New York: Saturday Review Press, 1972, 246 p.
A veteran's scathing "pre-mortem" of the U.S. Army. Of interest to anyone concerned with the impact of the Vietnam War upon the American military establishment.

Kintner, William Roscoe. **Peace and the Strategy Conflict.** New York: Praeger, 1967, 264 p.
A plea that the United States maintain its strategic superiority vis-à-vis the Soviet Union. The book contains a number of recommendations, including the deployment of a ballistic missile defense system against both China and the Soviet Union.

Kirkpatrick, Lyman B., Jr. **The Real CIA.** New York: Macmillan, 1968, 312 p.
This study by a former high CIA official blends scholarship and personal experience.

Knoll, Erwin and McFadden, Judith Nies. **American Militarism 1970.** New York: Viking, 1969, 150 p.
A report on the Conference on the American Defense Establishment held in Washington in the spring of 1969. In his epilogue, Senator Fulbright stresses the need to reassert control over the military.

Kolodziej, Edward A. **The Uncommon Defense and Congress, 1945–1963.** Columbus: Ohio State University Press, 1966, 630 p.

A lengthy inquiry into "Congress' use of . . . power . . . to influence military force levels, weapons systems, and strategic policy."

Kuenne, Robert Eugene. **The Polaris Missile Strike: A General Economic Systems Analysis.** Columbus: Ohio State University Press, 1967, 434 p.
A study, quite technical in parts, of the Polaris deterrence system.

Kyre, Martin and Kyre, Joan. **Military Occupation and National Security.** Washington: Public Affairs Press, 1968, 198 p.
A study of U.S. military government policies from the Mexican War through Vietnam. The author emphasizes the relationship between national politics at home and occupation policies abroad.

Lapp, Ralph Eugene. **Arms beyond Doubt: The Tyranny of Weapons Technology.** New York: Cowles Book Co., 1970, 210 p.
The author, a distinguished nuclear physicist, argues persuasively that Congress tends to vote for new weapons largely out of fear and ignorance. He also suggests that once a new weapon enters the development phase, it develops a momentum of its own which is difficult if not impossible to reverse.

Lapp, Ralph Eugene. **The Weapons Culture.** New York: Norton, 1968, 230 p.
The author suggests that the United States has become "arms-maker and arms merchant to the world."

Leckie, Robert. **The Wars of America.** New York: Harper and Row, 1968, 1,052 p.
This book traces American military involvements from colonial times to Vietnam. The factual exposition is generally accurate, the analysis frequently controversial.

LeMay, Curtis E. with Smith, Dale O. **America is in Danger.** New York: Funk & Wagnalls, 1968, 346 p.
The former Air Force Chief of Staff attacks the defense policies of the Kennedy and Johnson administrations and advocates the reëstablishment of American military superiority in the world.

Levine, Robert Arthur. **The Arms Debate.** Cambridge: Harvard University Press, 1963, 347 p.
The author undertakes to sort out and analyze the intellectual content of the leading schools of thought on the arms debate.

Licklider, Roy E. **The Private Nuclear Strategists.** Columbus: Ohio State University Press, 1972, 213 p.
A study of the makeup of that significant group of individuals, not employed by the government, who have been professionally concerned with nuclear strategy and disarmament.

Lowe, George E. **The Age of Deterrence.** Boston: Little, Brown, 1964, 324 p.
The author, a former Foreign Service officer, discusses the U.S. debate on strategy and defense theory since 1952. His reduction of the various positions to the dual classification of Utopian and Traditionalist is hardly helpful in dealing with a subject of such intricacy.

McBride, James Hubert. **The Test Ban Treaty: Military, Technological, and Political Implications.** Chicago: Regnery, 1967, 197 p.
This book, largely an echo of Dr. Edward Teller's arguments before the Senate Foreign Relations Committee in 1963, concludes that "the Nuclear Test Ban Treaty was a serious mistake and a threat to the future security of the nation."

MacCloskey, Monro. **The United States Air Force.** New York: Praeger, 1967, 244 p.
A succinct history of American air power.

McNamara, Robert S. **The Essence of Security: Reflections in Office.** New York: Harper and Row, 1968, 176 p.
The former Defense Secretary discusses U.S. security and related topics.

Melman, Seymour. **Pentagon Capitalism: The Political Economy of War.** New York: McGraw-Hill, 1970, 290 p.
A passionate indictment of what the author describes as the expansion of the Pentagon into all aspects of American life.

Morison, Samuel Eliot; Merk, Frederick and Freidel, Frank. **Dissent in Three American Wars.** Cambridge: Harvard University Press, 1970, 104 p.

Three Harvard scholars take the measure of popular American dissent during the War of 1812, the Mexican War and the Spanish-American War. Frank Freidel suggests some interesting analogies between the Philippine insurrection and the Vietnam War.

Nelkin, Dorothy. **The University and Military Research: Moral Politics at M.I.T.** Ithaca: Cornell University Press, 1972, 195 p.
A case study, centering on the 1969–70 controversy at M.I.T. over military-related research on campus.

Possony, Stefan T. and Pournelle, J. E. **The Strategy of Technology: Winning the Decisive War.** New York: Dunellen, 1971, 189 p.
A hard-headed assessment in which the authors assert that the United States must make full use of its weapons technology if a third world war is to be averted.

Posvar, Wesley W. and Others. **American Defense Policy.** Baltimore: Johns Hopkins Press, 1965, 471 p.
A very useful collection of articles, by many specialists, on various aspects of U.S. defense policy and strategy.

Powers, Francis Gary with Gentry, Curt. **Operation Overflight.** New York: Holt, Rinehart and Winston, 1970, 375 p.
The story of the U-2 spy pilot's flight over the Soviet Union, capture and return home.

Powers, Patrick W. **A Guide To National Defense.** New York: Praeger, 1964, 326 p.
A guide for the citizen to the U.S. defense program, its direction, employment, support and possible roles.

Ransom, Harry Howe. **The Intelligence Establishment.** Cambridge: Harvard University Press, rev. ed., 1970, 309 p.
A revision of the author's excellent earlier study, "Central Intelligence and National Security" (1958).

Raymond, Jack. **Power at the Pentagon.** New York: Harper and Row, 1964, 363 p.
An experienced correspondent for *The New York Times* discusses the Pentagon and its inhabitants.

Ries, John Charles. **The Management of Defense: Organization and Control of the U.S. Armed Services.** Baltimore: Johns Hopkins Press, 1964, 228 p.
A wide-ranging review, with emphasis on problems created by centralization.

Rodberg, Leonard S. and Shearer, Derek, *eds.* **The Pentagon Watchers: Students Report on the National Security State.** Garden City: Doubleday, 1970, 416 p.
An uneven symposium of ten highly polemical essays, all very critical of the defense establishment.

Roherty, James Michael. **Decisions of Robert S. McNamara: A Study of the Role of the Secretary of Defense.** Coral Gables: University of Miami Press, 1970, 223 p.
In this effort to construct a general theory of civil-military relations the most valuable parts are two first-rate case studies, one on the decision not to build a manned bomber and the other on the decision to build a nuclear carrier.

Roscoe, Theodore. **On the Seas and in the Skies.** New York: Hawthorn Books, 1970, 690 p.
A history of U.S. naval aviation.

Russett, Bruce Martin. **What Price Vigilance?** New Haven: Yale University Press, 1970, 261 p.
A behaviorally oriented analysis, largely based on roll-call data, of Congressional voting patterns on issues of national defense.

Scherer, Frederic M. **The Weapons Acquisition Process: Economic Incentives.** Boston: Harvard University, Graduate School of Business Administration, Division of Research, 1964, 447 p.
A solid and rather technical study of the problem of providing economic incentives for the maintenance of the development and production of advanced weapons systems in the United States.

Schwarz, Urs. **American Strategy: A New Perspective.** Garden City: Doubleday, 1966, 178 p.
A lucid and objective survey of American strategic thought, with emphasis on the atomic era, by the former foreign editor of the *Neue Zürcher Zeitung*. German edition: "Strategie gestern, heute, morgen" (Düsseldorf: Econ-Verlag, 1965, 291 p.).

Smith, Dale Orville. **The Eagle's Talons: A Military View of Civil Control of the Military.** Washington: Spartan Books, 1966, 368 p.

A retired Air Force general questions the growing civil control of the U.S. Armed Forces. The study has been prefaced by Barry Goldwater.

Smith, Mark E., III and Johns, Claude J., Jr., *eds*. **American Defense Policy.** Baltimore: Johns Hopkins Press, 2d ed., 1968, 551 p.

A systematic study of U.S. defense and security policy.

Smith, Perry McCoy. **The Air Force Plans for Peace, 1943–1945.** Baltimore: Johns Hopkins Press, 1970, 132 p.

The author concludes that "since the planners could not accurately anticipate American postwar foreign policy and since they were reluctant to confer with State Department officials to gain insights into the possible policy problems of the postwar world, they decided to design a force which would be so large that it could handle every conceivable contingency."

Smith, R. Harris. **OSS: The Secret History of America's First Central Intelligence Agency.** Berkeley: University of California Press, 1972, 458 p.

A mine of detail—names, dates, operations large and small—but devoid of interpretation or reflection. The author corresponded with and interviewed nearly 200 former members of the Office of Strategic Services.

Stambuk, George. **American Military Forces Abroad.** Columbus: Ohio State University Press, 1963, 252 p.

A effort to study the impact on the Western state system and on the "sovereign territorial state" of American military forces in peacetime in foreign territory.

Stein, Harold, *ed*. **American Civil-Military Decisions: A Book of Case Studies.** University: University of Alabama Press (in coöperation with the Inter-University Case Program), 1963, 705 p.

This massive volume comprises 11 case studies involving American civil-military decisions ranging from the Far Eastern crisis of 1931–32 to the decisions to rearm West Germany and establish bases in Spain. The purpose of the study is to illustrate the processes by which such decisions, containing both military and civil issues, are arrived at.

Swomley, John M., Jr. **The Military Establishment.** Boston: Beacon Press, 1964, 266 p.

A sounding of the alarm against the danger of military predominance in American life by an author who describes himself frankly as "a participant in the struggle to prevent the adoption of peacetime conscription and other steps toward military control."

Thayer, Frederick C., Jr. **Air Transport Policy and National Security.** Chapel Hill: University of North Carolina Press, 1965, 352 p.

A discussion of the multiple relationships between military airlift policy and commercial air transport policy. The author tends to be quite critical of past U.S. policies in these matters.

Thayer, George. **The War Business: The International Trade in Armaments.** New York: Simon and Schuster, 1969, 417 p.

The author maintains that U.S. arms policy is "overblown, overstaffed, misguided and almost out of control" and argues for a "flexible, reasonable and minimal" arms policy.

Trewhitt, Henry L. **McNamara.** New York: Harper and Row, 1971, 307 p.

The former Defense Secretary is given high marks for rationality in his nuclear policy vis-à-vis the Soviet Union and China.

Tuleja, Thaddeus Vincent. **Statesmen and Admirals: Quest for a Far Eastern Naval Policy.** New York: Norton, 1963, 256 p.

A balanced analysis of the frustrations involved in trying to formulate a strong U.S. naval policy in the Pacific in the 1930s.

Twining, Nathan Farragut. **Neither Liberty nor Safety: A Hard Look at U.S. Military Policy and Strategy.** New York: Holt, Rinehart and Winston, 1966, 320 p.

The former Chairman of the Joint Chiefs of Staff criticizes the U.S. defense policies.

Ushakov, Georgii. **Tainy Lengli.** Moscow: Izd-vo Politicheskoi Literatury, 1971, 256 p.

A Soviet exposé of the "sinister" activities of the Central Intelligence Agency.

Voss, Earl H. **Nuclear Ambush: The Test-Ban Trap.** Chicago: Regnery, 1963, 612 p.
An extensive account, analysis and critique of the movement for nuclear test ban and the negotiations relating to it, written before the signing of the Test Ban Treaty.

Walt, Lewis W. **America Faces Defeat.** Woodbridge (Conn.): Apollo Books, 1972, 209 p.
General Walt, USMC (Ret.), believes the United States is militarily "overpowered by the Soviets." He urges vast increases in the Navy, Marines, and air lift capacity for the Army.

Weigley, Russell Frank. **History of the United States Army.** New York: Macmillan, 1967, 688 p.
A thoroughgoing study of the Army from colonial days to the present, though somewhat thin on counterinsurgency warfare. The author's main thesis: the partnership between the professional and the citizen soldier that is the distinctive feature of the United States Army must remain unimpaired despite the perplexities of the war in Vietnam.

Wheeler, Gerald E. **Prelude to Pearl Harbor: The United States Navy and the Far East, 1921-1931.** Columbia: University of Missouri Press, 1963, 212 p.
A well-documented account of the U.S. Navy's difficult efforts to maintain strength in the Pacific in the era between the Washington Naval Conference and Japan's invasion of Manchuria.

Wilson, Thomas Williams, Jr. **The Great Weapons Heresy.** Boston: Houghton, 1970, 275 p.
This book focuses on J. Robert Oppenheimer's "heretical" belief that national security may not necessarily lie in the attainment of military superiority over presumed enemies.

Wolfers, Arnold and Others. **The United States in a Disarmed World.** Baltimore: Johns Hopkins Press, 1966, 236 p.
These essays dealing with problems of disarmament were prepared at the Washington Center of Foreign Policy Research.

Yarmolinsky, Adam. **The Military Establishment: Its Impacts on American Society.** New York: Harper and Row, 1971, 434 p.
This is a broadly conceived, measured and calm assessment of the multifaceted role of the military in the United States.

Government and Constitutional Problems

See also General Works, p. 1; Political Factors, p. 12; (The United States) Recent History, p. 214; Biographies, Memoirs and Addresses, p. 218; Foreign Policy, p. 229; Questions of Subversion, Loyalty and Civil Liberties, p. 267; Politics and Political Issues, p. 268.

Abels, Jules. **The Degeneration of Our Presidential Election.** New York: Macmillan, 1968, 322 p.
An urgent plea for shorter, calmer and less cliché-ridden presidential campaigns.

Baker, Leonard. **Back to Back.** New York: Macmillan, 1967, 311 p.
A thoroughly researched account of the "court-packing" battle between FDR and the Supreme Court. The author, incidentally, suggests that Lyndon Johnson won his seat in Congress in 1937 primarily by supporting Roosevelt's campaign to enlarge the Court.

Barker, Carol M. and Fox, Matthew H. **Classified Files: The Yellowing Pages.** New York: Twentieth Century Fund, 1972, 115 p.
A very useful description, analysis and critique of the government's procedures in withholding and granting access to its records.

Bayh, Birch Evans. **One Heartbeat Away: Presidential Disability and Succession.** Indianapolis: Bobbs-Merrill, 1968, 372 p.
The Indiana Senator recounts in lively prose his crucial role in the passage of the Twenty-Fifth Amendment in Feburary 1967.

Binkley, Wilfred Ellsworth. **The Man in the White House: His Powers and Duties.** New York: Harper and Row, rev. ed., 1964, 274 p.
A revised edition of a useful general appraisal of the institution of the Presidency.

Bolling, Richard. **House Out of Order.** New York: Dutton, 1965, 253 p.
  The Democratic Representative from Missouri, who has served in the House since 1948, casts a critical eye on that body and its operations. Quoting Gambetta, he finds it a "broken mirror in which the Nation cannot recognize its own image."

Bundy, McGeorge. **The Strength of Government.** Cambridge: Harvard University Press, 1968, 113 p.
  These 1968 Godkin Lectures are a reasoned plea for strength in government at the national, state and local levels. The author urges maximum political participation in order to ensure that such strength serves the cause of freedom.

Burns, James MacGregor. **Presidential Government: The Crucible of Leadership.** Boston: Houghton, 1965, 366 p.
  A study of the Presidency by the author of several major works on American politics and political figures. One of his aims is to "help fashion a theory of the American Presidency."

Cary, William Lucius. **Politics and the Regulatory Agencies.** New York: McGraw-Hill, 1967, 149 p.
  The former Chairman of the Securities Exchange Commission deals, partly on the basis of his own experience, with the interplay of politics and the federal regulatory agencies.

Charles, Searle Franklin. **Minister of Relief: Harry Hopkins and the Depression.** Syracuse: Syracuse University Press, 1963, 286 p.
  A review of the administrative aspects of Hopkins's work as federal relief administrator during 1933-1938.

Clapp, Charles L. **The Congressman: His Work as He Sees It.** Washington: Brookings Institution, 1963, 452 p.
  An important and revealing study on the role of the members of the House of Representatives, the result of a conference at the Brookings Institution where Congressmen discussed with candor their problems and responsibilities.

Clark, Joseph S. **Congress: The Sapless Branch.** New York: Harper and Row, 1964, 268 p.
  The former liberal Democratic Senator from Pennsylvania has written a well-informed volume on the workings of both houses of Congress.

Cronin, Thomas E. and Greenberg, Sanford D., *eds.* **The Presidential Advisory System.** New York: Harper and Row, 1969, 375 p.
  An authoritative collection of essays, many by former presidential advisers, all previously published.

Cox, Archibald. **The Warren Court: Constitutional Decision as an Instrument of Reform.** Cambridge: Harvard University Press, 1968, 144 p.
  The author, who was Solicitor General of the United States from 1961 to 1965 and director of the Office of the Watergate Special Prosecution Force in 1973, acclaims the Warren Court's record on civil rights, criminal procedure and political democracy.

Cummings, Milton C., Jr. **Congressmen and the Electorate: Elections for the U.S. House and the President, 1920-1964.** New York: Free Press, 1966, 233 p.
  A study of elections to the U.S. House of Representatives and their relationship to votes for the Presidency.

Dahl, Robert Alan. **Pluralist Democracy in the United States: Conflict and Consent.** Chicago: Rand McNally, 1967, 471 p.
  A solid introduction to the American political system.

Dietze, Gottfried. **America's Political Dilemma: From Limited to Unlimited Democracy.** Baltimore: Johns Hopkins Press, 1968, 298 p.
  The author of this essay argues that American democracy has strayed from the original ideas of the Founding Fathers.

Fenno, Richard Francis, Jr. **The Power of the Purse.** Boston: Little, Brown, 1966, 704 p.
  A solid study of appropriations politics in Congress.

Flash, Edward Serrill, Jr. **Economic Advice and Presidential Leadership: The Council of Economic Advisers.** New York: Columbia University Press, 1965, 382 p.
  More interesting as history than as an analysis of the Council's influence or its place in the government machine, this useful study covers the period from 1946 to 1962.

Heren, Louis. **The New American Commonwealth.** New York: Harper and Row, 1968, 366 p.
    This is a balanced essay on the American political system by the former Washington correspondent of the London *Times*.

Horn, Stephen. **Unused Power.** Washington: Brookings Institution, 1970, 285 p.
    An excellent monograph arguing for an enhanced role for the Senate Committee on Appropriations.

Karl, Barry Dean. **Executive Reorganization and Reform in the New Deal: The Genesis of Administrative Management, 1900-1939.** Cambridge: Harvard University Press, 1963, 292 p.
    A history of the reform of the executive branch, with special attention given to the rise of social scientists in the Roosevelt administration.

Koenig, Louis William. **The Chief Executive.** New York: Harcourt, Brace and World, 1964, 435 p.
    An extensive study of the U.S. Presidency, its powers, responsibilities and the roadblocks it encounters. The author definitely favors a strong Presidency.

McInnis, Mary, ed. **We Propose: A Modern Congress.** New York: McGraw-Hill, 1966, 338 p.
    Twenty-one articles by members and former members of Congress on the work, procedures and problems of the Congress.

MacNeil, Neil. **Forge of Democracy: The House of Representatives.** New York: McKay, 1963, 496 p.
    A good description of the organization, operations and climate of the House, by a veteran journalist with inside knowledge of the Congress.

Mann, Dean E. with Doig, Jameson W. **The Assistant Secretaries: Problems and Processes of Appointment.** Washington: Brookings Institution, 1965, 310 p.
    A systematic study of recruitment processes and the type of men who, appointed by the President, fill the offices of the departmental under secretaries, assistant secretaries and their counterparts in the independent agencies.

Morrow, William Lockhart. **Congressional Committees.** New York: Scribner, 1969, 261 p.
    A descriptive and analytical study of the Congressional Committees, in the author's opinion "the most significant voices of authority speaking for an essential independent branch of government."

Murphy, Paul L. **The Constitution in Crisis Times, 1918-1969.** New York: Harper and Row, 1972, 570 p.
    A history of constitutional evolution in the United States during the past half-century.

Navasky, Victor S. **Kennedy Justice.** New York: Atheneum, 1971, 482 p.
    A substantial study of Robert Kennedy as Attorney General. The reader also learns much about the way decisions were made near the top of the Kennedy administration.

Nelson, William H., ed. **Theory and Practice in American Politics.** Chicago: University of Chicago Press (for William Marsh Rice University), 1964, 149 p.
    Originally presented as lectures in a series given at Rice University in 1962, these essays examine the relationship between constitutional theory and American political tradition.

Peirce, Neal R. **The People's President.** New York: Simon and Schuster, 1968, 400 p.
    This is a well-researched study on the role of the Electoral College in American history. The author strongly favors a Constitutional amendment that would provide a direct vote for President by the American people.

Perloff, Harvey S., ed. **The Future of the United States Government: Toward the Year 2000.** New York: Braziller, 1971, 388 p.
    Essays prepared by members of the Commission on the Year 2000 of the Academy of Arts and Sciences.

Pomper, Gerald. **Nominating the President: The Politics of Convention Choice, With a New Postscript on 1964.** New York: Norton, 2d ed., 1966, 304 p.
    An extensive analysis of the practice of selecting the national candidates and suggestions for possible changes in nominating methods, by a professor at Rutgers University. An updated edition of a work originally published in 1963.

Pusey, Merlo John. **The Way We Go to War.** Boston: Houghton, 1969, 202 p.
A Pulitzer-Prize-winning editor of *The Washington Post* urges a rethinking of the constitutional principles dealing with the power to declare war.

Reedy, George E. **The Twilight of the Presidency.** New York: World Publishing Co., 1970, 205 p.
A concerned and skeptical look at the Presidency, which the author describes as "the American Monarchy."

Riddle, Donald H. **The Truman Committee.** New Brunswick: Rutgers University Press, 1964, 207 p.
A study of the Senate Special Committee to Investigate the National Defense Program, better known as the Truman Committee, from 1941 to 1948.

Schlesinger, Arthur Meier, Jr. and De Grazia, Alfred. **Congress and the Presidency: Their Role in Modern Times.** Washington: American Enterprise Institute for Public Policy Research, 1967, 192 p.
The book is the result of a debate between the two scholars, with Schlesinger generally favoring a strong executive and De Grazia arguing that the Presidency today has too much power.

Seidman, Harold. **Politics, Position, and Power: The Dynamics of Federal Organization.** New York: Oxford University Press, 1970, 311 p.
An excellent description of "the Federal scene as observed for almost a quarter of a century through a particular window in the Bureau of the Budget."

Sorensen, Theodore Chaikin. **Decision-Making in the White House: The Olive Branch or the Arrows.** New York: Columbia University Press, 1963, 94 p.
In these lectures the Special Counsel to President Kennedy puts forward his thoughtful observations on the factors and conditions that shape presidential decisions.

Truman, David Bicknell, *ed.* **The Congress and America's Future.** Englewood Cliffs: Prentice-Hall, 1965, 185 p.
Eight critical essays on the functions and procedures of Congress, designed as background reading for the American Assembly meetings dealing with the subject of congressional reform.

White, William Smith. **Home Place: The Story of the U.S. House of Representatives.** Boston: Houghton, 1965, 175 p.
The author of "Citadel" (1957), a study of the U.S. Senate, has turned to the House of Representatives, its tone, the types who sit in it, its strengths and weaknesses.

Questions of Subversion, Loyalty and Civil Liberties

See also Human Rights, p. 92; (Second World War) Economic, Technical and Non-Military Aspects, p. 172; (The United States) Recent History, p. 214; Biographies, Memoirs and Addresses, p. 218; Social Questions, p. 276.

Abraham, Henry Julian. **Freedom and the Court: Civil Rights and Liberties in the United States.** New York: Oxford University Press, 1967, 335 p.
A useful and balanced survey of the Supreme Court's impact on civil rights and liberties.

Bosworth, Allan R. **America's Concentration Camps.** New York: Norton, 1967, 283 p.
The depressing story, well told, of the relocation centers for over 100,000 Americans of Japanese ancestry during World War II.

Cook, Fred J. **The Nightmare Decade.** New York: Random House, 1971, 626 p.
A story of the 1950s and the omnipresent figure of Joseph McCarthy, as seen through the eyes of a first-rate reporter.

Goodman, Walter. **The Committee.** New York: Farrar, Straus and Giroux, 1968, 564 p.
A negative verdict on the record of the House Committee on Un-American Activities.

Griffith, Robert. **The Politics of Fear: Joseph R. McCarthy and the Senate.** Lexington: University Press of Kentucky, 1971, 362 p.
An excellent scholarly study in which the author concludes that McCarthy's power "was the consequence of Republican partisanship and, after 1950, of Democratic acquiescence."

Humphrey, Hubert Horatio. **Beyond Civil Rights: A New Day of Equality.** New York: Random House, 1968, 193 p.
A passionate plea for real equality for all American citizens.

Konvitz, Milton Ridvas. **Expanding Liberties: Freedom's Gains in Postwar America.** New York: Viking, 1966, 429 p.
A study of the new freedoms that have emerged since the end of World War II. The discussion centers on First Amendment rights, civil rights and the international protection of human rights.

Latham, Earl. **The Communist Controversy in Washington.** Cambridge: Harvard University Press, 1966, 446 p.
This book, one of the studies on communism in America originally sponsored by the Fund for the Republic, deals with the bitter controversy over communism in and out of government that raged from the latter years of the New Deal to the flowering of McCarthy.

Levin, Murray Burton. **Political Hysteria in America: The Democratic Capacity for Repression.** New York: Basic Books, 1971, 312 p.
This fine case study of the "Red Scare" of 1919-20 is used by the author as a searchlight for the illumination of the darker recesses of the American political mind.

Major, John. **The Oppenheimer Hearing.** New York: Stein and Day, 1971, 336 p.
A Cambridge-trained historian reëxamines the Oppenheimer case and its background and comes to the conclusion that it may be "that the interests of the state could not be reconciled with the freedom of an individual."

Potter, Charles Edward. **Days of Shame.** New York: Coward-McCann, 1965, 304 p.
The former Senator from Michigan gives an account, from his perspective as a member of the Senate Government Operations Committee, of the dramatic Army-McCarthy hearings in 1954.

Preston, William, Jr. **Aliens and Dissenters: Federal Suppression of Radicals, 1903-1933.** Cambridge: Harvard University Press (for the Center for the Study of the History of Liberty in America, Harvard University), 1963, 352 p.
A well-researched study.

Roche, John Pearson. **The Quest for the Dream: The Development of Civil Rights and Human Relations in Modern America.** New York: Macmillan, 1963, 308 p.
Mr. Roche, formerly chairman of the Americans for Democratic Action, upturns traditional views on civil liberties in this century; where others see evidence of decline, he notes significant progress.

Stern, Philip M. with Green, Harold P. **The Oppenheimer Case: Security on Trial.** New York: Harper and Row, 1969, 591 p.
The author of this persuasively argued and detailed narrative delivers a strong indictment of the American loyalty-security system.

Theoharis, Athan George. **Seeds of Repression: Harry S. Truman and the Origins of McCarthyism.** Chicago: Quadrangle Books, 1971, 238 p.
The author argues that the Truman administration was more cause than victim of McCarthyism.

Politics and Political Issues

See also Political Factors, p. 12; Society and Social Psychology, p. 39; (The United States) General, p. 213; Recent History, p. 214; Biographies, Memoirs and Addresses, p. 218; Foreign Policy, p. 229; Military and Defense Policy, p. 257; Government and Constitutional Problems, p. 264; Science and Society, p. 280; The Vietnam War, p. 739.

Alsop, Stewart Johonnot Oliver. **The Center: People and Power in Political Washington.** New York: Harper and Row, 1968, 365 p.
A chatty "inside" book of Washington politics by a well-known journalist.

Ambrose, Stephen E. **Institutions in Modern America: Innovation in Structure and Process.** Baltimore: Johns Hopkins Press, 1967, 145 p.

Four essays dealing with the labor movement, the pattern of modern politics, the large industrial corporation and the rise of military power.

Anderson, John Bayard, *ed.* **Congress and Conscience.** Philadelphia: Lippincott, 1970, 192 p.
Six Congressmen explore the relationship between politics and ethics in a number of different fields.

Anderson, Patrick. **The Presidents' Men.** Garden City: Doubleday, 1968, 420 p.
An informative book about presidential assistants from Harry Hopkins to Jack Valenti.

Arendt, Hannah. **Crises of the Republic.** New York: Harcourt Brace Jovanovich, 1972, 240 p.
A collection of recent essays, all focused on the United States, by an eminent political philosopher; includes her famous reflections "On Lying in Politics" and "On Violence."

Aya, Roderick and Miller, Norman, *eds.* **The New American Revolution.** New York: Free Press, 1971, 342 p.
This symposium on revolutionary movements in the United States focuses largely on black militants and the young intelligentsia.

Baus, Herbert M. and Ross, William B. **Politics Battle Plan.** New York: Macmillan, 1968, 399 p.
An account of campaign management at the top political level.

Bernstein, Barton J., *ed.* **Politics and Policies of the Truman Administration.** Chicago: Quadrangle Books, 1970, 330 p.
Eight carefully researched and well-documented essays on different aspects of the Truman Administration.

Buckley, William Frank, Jr., *comp.* **Did You Ever See a Dream Walking? American Conservative Thought in the Twentieth Century.** Indianapolis: Bobbs-Merrill, 1970, 554 p.
A useful anthology.

Buckley, William Frank, Jr. **The Governor Listeth: A Book of Inspired Political Revelations.** New York: Putnam, 1970, 447 p.
——. **The Jeweler's Eye.** New York: Putnam, 1969, 342 p.
——. **Rumbles Left and Right: A Book about Troublesome People and Ideas.** New York: Putnam, 1963, 251 p.
Essays on contemporary American politics by the editor of the *National Review*.

Burns, James MacGregor. **The Deadlock of Democracy: Four-Party Politics in America.** Englewood Cliffs: Prentice-Hall, 1963, 388 p.
In this stimulating study of American politics, Professor Burns develops the idea that the largely independent congressional and presidential wings of both the Republican and Democratic Parties can be considered as separate political parties.

Burns, James MacGregor. **Uncommon Sense.** New York: Harper and Row, 1972, 196 p.
A critique of American pragmatism in domestic and foreign affairs and a cry for new leadership based on carefully examined principles, by a noted biographer of FDR.

Cater, Douglass. **Power in Washington: A Critical Look at Today's Struggle to Govern in the Nation's Capital.** New York: Random House, 1964, 275 p.
The correspondent on national affairs for *The Reporter* describes the "subgovernments" of power which exist within the office of the President, the Congress, the Pentagon, political parties, the press and the Washington lobbies.

Dawidowicz, Lucy S. and Goldstein, Leon J. **Politics in a Pluralist Democracy: Studies of Voting in the 1960 Election.** New York: Institute of Human Relations Press, 1963, 100 p.
This brief, competent survey of the 1960 election analyzes voting results in five major cities, the influence of Kennedy's religion on specific rural groups, and the Jewish vote.

Donovan, John C. **The Policy Makers.** New York: Pegasus, 1970, 255 p.
A balanced primer on the policy-making process in the United States.

Douglas, William Orville. **Points of Rebellion.** New York: Random House, 1970, 97 p.
A sympathetic view of dissent by a great dissenter. The Justice inveighs against the

Vietnam War, segregation, pollution and poverty, and exhorts the Establishment to respond forcefully or else risk revolution.

Dutton, Frederick G. **Changing Sources of Power: American Politics in the 1970s.** New York: McGraw-Hill, 1971, 263 p.

A warning that the real danger to the American polity is neither revolution nor depression, but aimlessness, stalemate and drift—in the author's words, "public impotence."

Eldredge, Hanford Wentworth. **The Second American Revolution.** New York: Morrow, 1964, 403 p.

Fearing collapse and defeat by default for democratic Western society, the author, a Dartmouth professor, criticizes what he calls the eighteenth-century models of traditional democracy and pleads for a fundamental revamping of American political institutions and the conscious development of superlative leadership.

Free, Lloyd Arthur and Cantril, Albert Hadley. **The Political Beliefs of Americans: A Study of Public Opinion.** New Brunswick: Rutgers University Press, 1967, 239 p.

One melancholy conclusion of this study is that "a surprising number of Americans are abysmally ignorant of the specifics of international affairs, even at the most elementary level."

Gerson, Louis L. **The Hyphenate in Recent American Politics and Diplomacy.** Lawrence: University of Kansas Press, 1964, 325 p.

An attempt "to appraise the nature and scope of ethnic-group activity—particularly as it affects and is affected by the American political parties—and its impact on the formation and execution of foreign policy."

Gilder, George F. and Chapman, Bruce K. **The Party That Lost Its Head.** New York: Knopf, 1966, 331 p.

Republicans discuss ills and schisms of the G.O.P. and make a number of proposals for reform.

Goldwater, Barry. **The Conscience of a Majority.** Englewood Cliffs: Prentice-Hall, 1970, 248 p.

Informative observations on American political and social issues by the Senator from Arizona and the 1964 presidential candidate.

Gordon, Kermit, *ed.* **Agenda for the Nation.** Washington: Brookings Institution, 1968, 620 p.

Essays of high quality on major domestic and foreign policy issues.

Harrington, Michael. **Toward a Democratic Left: A Radical Program for a New Majority.** New York: Macmillan, 1968, 314 p.

The author urges a new "first party" that must go "beyond Franklin Roosevelt in political strategy as well as in social and economic program."

Harris, Richard. **Justice: The Crisis of Law, Order and Freedom in America.** New York: Dutton, 1970, 268 p.

A polemic against President Nixon's and Attorney General Mitchell's treatment of the "law and order" issue.

Hart, Jeffrey. **The American Dissent: A Decade of Modern Conservatism.** Garden City: Doubleday, 1966, 262 p.

A sympathetic discussion of recent American conservative and right-wing thought, with particular attention to the writers and writings appearing in the *National Review*.

Hickel, Walter J. **Who Owns America?** Englewood Cliffs: Prentice-Hall, 1971, 328 p.

The Secretary of Interior of the early Nixon administration, who was also the Governor of Alaska from 1966 to 1969, describes his battles on behalf of youth, conservation and open communications.

Janson, Donald and Eismann, Bernard. **The Far Right.** New York: McGraw-Hill, 1963, 259 p.

A report on ultraconservative currents and personalities on the American scene.

Javits, Jacob Koppel. **Order of Battle: A Republican's Call to Reason.** New York: Atheneum, 1964, 328 p.

An appraisal of the principles of the Republican Party by the Senator from New York.

Jones, J. Harry, Jr. **The Minutemen.** Garden City: Doubleday, 1968, 426 p.
Some frightening insights into the leading personalities and objectives of the American Far Right.

Kaplan, Morton A. **Dissent and the State in Peace and War: An Essay on the Grounds of Public Morality.** New York: Dunellen, 1970, 172 p.
An exploration of major political dilemmas facing the United States at home and abroad.

Kennan, George Frost and Others. **Democracy and the Student Left.** Boston: Atlantic (Little, Brown), 1968, 239 p.
Thirty-nine letters by students and teachers written in response to Mr. Kennan's "Rebels Without a Program," published in *The New York Times Magazine* on January 21, 1968. The book concludes with a reply by Mr. Kennan.

Kessel, John Howard. **The Goldwater Coalition: Republican Strategies in 1964.** Indianapolis: Bobbs-Merrill, 1968, 371 p.
A post-mortem on the formation of the political coalition that won Senator Goldwater the Presidential nomination in 1964.

Kirk, Russell and McClellan, James. **The Political Principles of Robert A. Taft.** New York: Fleet Press Corp., 1963, 213 p.
This volume, sponsored by The Robert A. Taft Institute of Government, attempts to describe the late Republican Senator's political convictions, influence and his endeavors to present a conservative foreign policy.

Kraft, Joseph. **Profiles in Power: A Washington Insight.** New York: New American Library, 1966, 192 p.
A series of perceptive essays by a well-known journalist.

Laird, Melvin R., *ed*. **Republican Papers.** New York: Praeger, 1968, 500 p.
The Republican credo on most of the crucial questions of domestic and foreign policy is set forth here in 29 "discussion papers."

Lipset, Seymour Martin and Raab, Earl. **The Politics of Unreason.** New York: Harper and Row, 1970, 547 p.
A comprehensive historical study of right-wing extremism in America. The authors examine the sociopolitical bases of this phenomenon from 1790 to the John Birch Society and conclude that "the American population is still highly vulnerable to political extremism; the American political system is less so, but scarcely fail-safe."

Lowi, Theodore J. **The Politics of Disorder.** New York: Basic Books, 1971, 193 p.
In a well-written polemic, the author argues that major changes in the American system have often come about by going outside traditional institutions. What the Americans need, the author claims, is not law and order, but law and disorder.

Lubell, Samuel. **The Hidden Crisis in American Politics.** New York: Norton, 1970, 306 p.
The well-known expert on American public opinion advocates a "consciously thought-through effort to reunite the nation."

McPherson, Harry. **A Political Education.** Boston: Atlantic (Little, Brown), 1972, 467 p.
Well-written and informative observations on American politics by an author who came to Washington in 1956 as a staff assistant to Senator Lyndon Johnson and after service in the Defense and State Departments was special counsel to LBJ, 1965–69.

Mayer, George Hillman. **The Republican Party, 1854–1964.** New York: Oxford University Press, 1964, 563 p.
A scholarly, event-crammed narrative of the fortunes of the Republican Party, dealing very heavily with elections and legislative controversies.

Moley, Raymond, Jr. **The American Legion Story.** New York: Duell, 1966, 443 p.
A very favorable account of the American Legion.

Monsen, R. Joseph, Jr. and Cannon, Mark W. **The Makers of Public Policy: American Power Groups and Their Ideologies.** New York: McGraw-Hill, 1965, 355 p.
This study is directed to public policy at the national level, and considers the various formal and informal power groups—business, labor, agriculture, Blacks, public school teachers, intellectuals, and the civil and military bureaucracies.

Neuhaus, Richard. **In Defense of People: Ecology and the Seduction of Radicalism.** New York: Macmillan, 1971, 315 p.
An attack on the ecology movement as "a seductive diversion from the political tasks of our time," by a Lutheran pastor.

Newman, William J. **Liberalism and the Retreat from Politics.** New York: Braziller, 1964, 190 p.
An essay on some of the problems and quandaries of contemporary American liberalism, with particular attention to such figures as David Riesman, C. Wright Mills, Paul Goodman and Hannah Arendt.

Nichols, Roy Franklin. **The Invention of the American Political Parties.** New York: Macmillan, 1967, 416 p.
This is a thorough study of the birth of the American two-party system. The author shows its European antecedents and then leads us with a sure hand through the numerous improvisations that marked the evolution of the system from its beginnings in mid-nineteenth century Virginia to its consolidation a century later.

Overstreet, Harry Allan and Overstreet, Bonaro (Wilkinson). **The Strange Tactics of Extremism.** New York: Norton, 1964, 315 p.
The authors of popular but useful studies on contemporary communism here turn their attention to the American radical right, including a lengthy section on the John Birch Society.

Paolucci, Henry. **War, Peace, and the Presidency.** New York: McGraw-Hill, 1968, 241 p.
The political credo of a conservative on the major domestic and foreign policy issues confronting the United States.

Petrov, Petr Sergeevich. **Vozniknovenie Kommunisticheskoi partii SShA i ee bor'ba za legalizatsiiu.** Moscow: Izd-vo "Mysl'," 1971, 279 p.
A Soviet inquiry into the origins and early history of the Communist Party of the United States.

Phillips, Kevin P. **The Emerging Republican Majority.** New Rochelle (N.Y.): Arlington House, 1969, 482 p.
The author, who manages to marshall impressive evidence in support of his thesis from voting pattern projections, predicts an overall national trend in favor of the Republican Party during the 1970s.

Polsby, Nelson W. and Wildavsky, Aaron B. **Presidential Elections: Strategies of American Electoral Politics.** New York: Scribner, 3d ed., 1971, 332 p.
A stimulating effort to "make plain the context within which the battle for Presidential office is waged."

Ransom, Harry Howe. **Can American Democracy Survive Cold War?** Garden City: Doubleday, 1963, 270 p.
This book arises from the author's expressed concern "that in periods of obsessive fear or true national emergency, radical changes will occur in our institutions—in the name of national security—that will severely damage the democratic framework." He argues that these dangers can be averted by "organizational foresight."

Record, Wilson. **Race and Radicalism: The NAACP and the Communist Party in Conflict.** Ithaca: Cornell University Press, 1964, 237 p.
A history of the efforts of the Communist Party to influence, penetrate or wreck the N.A.A.C.P. and other civil rights organizations. A volume in the series "Communism in American Life."

Reifenberg, Jan. **Notiert in Washington 1955-1963; von Eisenhower zu Kennedy.** Stuttgart: Steingrüben Verlag, 1963, 342 p.
Observations on the American political scene, by the former Washington correspondent of the *Frankfurter Allgemeine Zeitung*.

Revel, Jean-François. **Without Marx or Jesus: The New American Revolution has Begun.** Garden City: Doubleday, 1971, 269 p.
The author, a French journalist, maintains that thorough-going reform is possible only in the United States. An arresting, though often glibly optimistic polemic. French edition, "Ni Marx ni Jésus" (Paris: Laffont, 1970, 263 p.).

Rogin, Michael Paul. **The Intellectuals and McCarthy: The Radical Specter.** Cambridge: M.I.T. Press, 1967, 366 p.

This is a fine book with a misleading title. The author hardly deals at all with McCarthy's impact on the intellectual community, but is primarily concerned with the socio-political roots of his electoral successes.

Rubenstein, Richard E. **Rebels in Eden: Mass Political Violence in the United States.** Boston: Little, Brown, 1970, 201 p.

The author argues that political violence in the United States is a tradition and that minority groups have almost always resorted to violence before gaining a measure of power in the political process.

Scammon, Richard M. and Wattenberg, Ben J. **The Real Majority.** New York: Coward-McCann, 1970, 347 p.

Any candidate for political office who courts the Right or the Left will be defeated, in the authors' view. The secret of political success lies in listening to, and then leading, the center.

Schlesinger, Arthur Meier, Jr. **The Crisis of Confidence: Ideas, Power and Violence in America.** Boston: Houghton, 1969, 313 p.

These essays by the well-known historian and public figure deal with violence in America, the role of the intellectual, college unrest, the cold war, Vietnam and the prospects for American politics.

Schlesinger, Arthur Meier, Jr. **The Politics of Hope.** Boston: Houghton, 1963, 298 p.

A selection of Mr. Schlesinger's essays on American history, politics and personalities, written in the decade before he went to Washington to be President Kennedy's Special Assistant.

Schlesinger, Joseph Abraham. **Ambition and Politics: Political Careers in the United States.** Chicago: Rand McNally, 1966, 226 p.

A highly technical, behaviorally oriented analysis of the careers of major party candidates for governor and senator in 48 states.

Scott, Hugh Doggett. **Come to the Party.** Englewood Cliffs: Prentice-Hall, 1968, 269 p.

The former National Chairman of the Republican Party argues for a broadly based G.O.P. The right wing is treated with an acid pen.

Seale, Bobby. **Seize the Time.** New York: Random House, 1970, 429 p.

The story of the Black Panther Party, by one of its leading members.

Sherwin, Mark. **The Extremists.** New York: St. Martin's Press, 1963, 242 p.

The late news editor of the *New York Post* surveys the American political Right and especially the more extreme and frantic manifestations.

Starobin, Joseph R. **American Communism in Crisis, 1943-1957.** Cambridge: Harvard University Press, 1972, 331 p.

An informed analysis of the internal factionalism, stultifying concepts and rigidities of the Communist Party of the United States of America. The author, a political scientist, is a former foreign editor of the *Daily Worker*.

Storing, Herbert J., ed. **What Country Have I?** New York: St. Martin's Press, 1970, 235 p.

A selection of political writings by Black Americans.

Sundquist, James L. **Politics and Policy: The Eisenhower, Kennedy, and Johnson Years.** Washington: Brookings Institution, 1968, 560 p.

The author of this solid study maintains that the legislative successes of the Johnson administration on matters of domestic policy were attributable primarily to the political activists within the Congress.

Thayer, George. **The Farther Shores of Politics: The American Political Fringe Today.** New York: Simon and Schuster, 1967, 610 p.

An examination of minor political groups in the United States.

White, William S. **The Responsibles.** New York: Harper and Row, 1972, 275 p.

The author emphasizes the positive sides of five American leaders—Truman, Taft, Eisenhower, Kennedy and Johnson—to make the point that the American political system is still capable of producing greatness.

Wicker, Tom. **JFK and LBJ: The Influence of Personality Upon Politics.** New York: Morrow, 1968, 297 p.

The author sheds new light on the two Presidents by studying what he considers their greatest failures: Kennedy's disappointing relationship with Congress and Johnson's inability to forge political consensus on his Vietnam policy.

Withers, William. **Freedom Through Power.** New York: Day, 1965, 245 p.
An effort by an economist to define and analyze the nature of "power" in the United States and its bearing upon democracy and the freedom of the individual.

Wriston, Henry Merritt. **Policy Perspectives.** Providence: Brown University Press, 1964, 178 p.
The former president of Brown University and of the Council on Foreign Relations has selected from his writings nine perceptive pieces on public policy, education and foreign affairs.

Economic Problems

See also Economic Factors, p. 49; United Nations, p. 99; (Second World War) Economic, Technical and Non-Military Aspects, p. 172; (East-West Relations) Trade and Economic Problems, p. 185; Inter-American Relations, p. 193; (The United States) General, p. 213; Recent History, p. 214; Biographies, Memoirs and Addresses, p. 218; Foreign Policy, p. 229; Military and Defense Policy, p. 257; Government and Constitutional Problems, p. 264; Politics and Political Issues, p. 268; (Western Europe) Integration, p. 349; (Great Britain) Economic and Financial Problems, p. 385.

Ahearn, Daniel S. **Federal Reserve Policy Reappraised, 1951-1959.** New York: Columbia University Press, 1963, 376 p.
A broad survey centering on the Federal Reserve's use of monetary instruments and controls over financial variables.

Baker, Leonard. **The Guaranteed Society.** New York: Macmillan, 1968, 276 p.
A scathing polemic against government "giveaway" programs.

Bauer, Raymond Augustine and Others. **American Business and Public Policy.** New York: Atherton Press, 1963, 499 p.
An examination, based on extensive interviews and polls, of the politics of the foreign trade issue from 1952 to 1962.

Berle, Adolph Augustus, Jr. **The American Economic Republic.** New York: Harcourt, Brace and World, 1963, 247 p.
An effort to sketch "the theory and practice of the American economic system as it actually functions," by a well-known lawyer with many years of government experience.

Brundage, Percival Flack. **The Bureau of the Budget.** New York: Praeger, 1970, 327 p.
A scholarly study by a former director of the Budget Bureau.

Clarke, Stephen V. O. **Central Bank Cooperation, 1924-31.** New York: Federal Reserve Bank of New York, 1967, 234 p.
A history based on the records of the Federal Reserve Bank of New York and private papers.

Edwards, Edgar Owen, ed. **The Nation's Economic Objectives.** Chicago: University of Chicago Press (for William Marsh Rice University), 1964, 167 p.
The following leading economists have written contributions to this volume: Edward S. Mason, Simon Kuznets, Lester V. Chandler, Arthur F. Burns, Fritz Machlup, Kenneth E. Boulding, Seymour E. Harris and Jacob Viner.

Eldridge, Hope Tisdale and Thomas, Dorothy Swaine. **Population Redistribution and Economic Growth: United States, 1870-1950. III: Demographic Analyses and Interrelations.** Philadelphia: American Philosophical Society, 1964, 368 p.
The concluding volume of a major study of which the first two parts were prepared by Simon S. Kuznets and other scholars.

Friedman, Milton and Schwartz, Anna Jacobson. **A Monetary History of the United States, 1867-1960.** Princeton: Princeton University Press (for the National Bureau of Economic Research), 1963, 860 p.
A massive, authoritative work in which the authors "provide a prologue and background for a statistical analysis of the secular and cyclical behavior of money in the United States."

Harris, Seymour Edwin. **Economics of the Kennedy Years, and a Look Ahead.** New York: Harper and Row, 1964, 273 p.
A favorable review of President Kennedy's economic policies. There is also a discussion of the economic education of the late President.

Heilbroner, Robert Louis. **The Limits of American Capitalism.** New York: Harper and Row, 1966, 148 p.
A provocative essay suggesting that American capitalism may not be able to broaden its ideology enough to assert control over the application of science to society's problems.

Heller, Walter Wolfgang. **New Dimensions of Political Economy.** Cambridge: Harvard University Press, 1966, 203 p.
At the core of these expanded Godkin Lectures is a clear exposition of what is new about the "new economics" and wherein it differs from the oversimplified Keynesianism most people believe it to be.

Heller, Walter Wolfgang, *ed.* **Perspectives on Economic Growth.** New York: Random House, 1968, 237 p.
Nine essays by economists who for the most part had some hand in the Kennedy adminstration's focus on growth.

Janeway, Eliot. **The Economics of Crisis: War, Politics, and the Dollar.** New York: Weybright and Talley, 1968, 317 p.
An interesting, sometimes controversial, history that stresses the place of war in expanding the American economy.

Kreinin, Mordechai Elihau. **Alternative Commercial Policies—Their Effect on the American Economy.** East Lansing: Michigan State University, Graduate School of Business Administration, 1967, 154 p.
A careful effort to measure the effects on the United States of the creation of an Atlantic Free Trade Area and comparisons with some alternative courses.

Landsberg, Hans H. and Others. **Resources in America's Future: Patterns of Requirements and Availabilities, 1960-2000.** Baltimore: Johns Hopkins Press, 1963, 1,017 p.
The core of this massive study is a set of projections of the demand and supply of natural resources—products and services as well as land, water and minerals—to the year 2000 for the United States.

Matusow, Allen Joseph. **Farm Policies and Politics in the Truman Years.** Cambridge: Harvard University Press, 1967, 267 p.
An authoritative work.

Melman, Seymour. **Our Depleted Society.** New York: Holt, Rinehart and Winston, 1965, 366 p.
The author describes his book as "an economic audit of the price that America has paid for twenty years of cold war."

Men'shikov, Stanislav Mikhailovich, *ed.* **Ekonomicheskaia politika pravitel'stva Kennedi, 1961-1963.** Moscow: Izd-vo "Mysl'," 1964, 412 p.
A study of the economic policies of the Kennedy administration, by a collective of economists at the Institute of World Economy and International Relations of the Soviet Academy of Sciences.

Men'shikov, Stanislav Mikhailovich, *ed.* **Noveishie tendentsii v organizatsii upravleniia krupnymi firmami v SShA.** Moscow: Izd-vo "Nauka," 1966, 321 p.
A survey of new trends in the organization and management of large industrial enterprises in the United States, prepared at the Institute of World Economy and International Relations of the Soviet Academy of Sciences.

Men'shikov, Stanislav Mikhailovich and Mnogolet, N. I., *eds.* **SShA: ekonomicheskie rychagi v upravlenii firmami.** Moscow: Izd-vo "Nauka," 1971, 352 p.
A serious Soviet assessment of the significance of recent developments in industrial management in the United States, with special emphasis on the growth of major corporations and conglomerates and on the role of the Federal government in regulating the economy.

Nash, Gerald D. **United States Oil Policy, 1890-1964: Business and Government in Twentieth Century America.** Pittsburgh: University of Pittsburgh Press, 1968, 286 p.

A useful history that concentrates on the quest for "coöperation," inside the industry and between it and the government, and the emergence of the government as arbiter of the industry.

Nevins, Allan and Hill, Frank Ernest. **Ford: Decline and Rebirth, 1933-1962.** New York: Scribner, 1963, 508 p.
The final volume of a history of the Ford empire.

Nossiter, Bernard D. **The Mythmakers: An Essay on Power and Wealth.** Boston: Houghton, 1964, 244 p.
An assessment of the economic policies of President Kennedy and his predecessors. The author, national economics reporter for *The Washington Post* from 1955 to 1964, is convinced that much of contemporary economic theory is irrelevant for solving real problems.

Proxmire, William. **Report from Wasteland: America's Military-Industrial Complex.** New York: Praeger, 1970, 248 p.
Senator Proxmire, Chairman of the Subcommittee on Priorities and Economy in Government of the Joint Economic Committee, concludes his somber report with some practical proposals for bringing a runaway budget under control.

Romasco, Albert U. **The Poverty of Abundance.** New York: Oxford University Press, 1965, 282 p.
A reappraisal of the consequences and impact of the Great Depression during the years of the Hoover Administration and of the efforts made to recover from it.

Schultze, Charles L. with Hamilton, Edward K. and Schick, Allen. **Setting National Priorities: The 1971 Budget.** Washington: Brookings Institution, 1970, 192 p.
An interesting demonstration of how the apparently pedestrian task of making the budget in fact involves major policy choices, not only about who gets what in the economy but about the defense posture of the United States quite a few years in the future. Mr. Schultze was Director of the Bureau of the Budget, 1965–68.

Silk, Leonard. **Nixonomics: How the Dismal Science of Free Enterprise Became the Black Art of Controls.** New York: Praeger, 1972, 212 p.
A brisk, witty, slightly disorganized account of how policy changed, by a *New York Times* man who understands economic ideas as well as political forces.

Tanzer, Michael. **The Sick Society: An Economic Examination.** New York: Holt, Rinehart and Winston, 1971, 260 p.
The author argues that American society is dominated by profit-seeking corporations owned by a "tiny upper-income elite."

Woytinsky, Emma (Shadkhan). **Profile of the U.S. Economy: A Survey of Growth and Change.** New York: Praeger, 1967, 601 p.
A comprehensive presentation of figures with text tracing changes in the American economy over fifty years and often much longer.

Social Questions

See also Society and Social Psychology, p. 39; Labor and Labor Movements, p. 41; Ethnic Problems; The Jews, p. 46; (Second World War) Economic, Technical and Non-Military Aspects, p. 172; (The United States) General, p. 213; Biographies, Memoirs and Addresses, p. 218; Questions of Subversion, Loyalty and Civil Liberties, p. 267; Politics and Political Issues, p. 268; Economic Problems, p. 274.

Bell, Daniel and Kristol, Irving, *eds.* **Confrontation: The Student Rebellion and the Universities.** New York: Basic Books, 1969, 191 p.
A symposium on student unrest by nine contributors.

Bennett, Lerone, Jr. **Confrontation: Black and White.** Chicago: Johnson Publishing Co., 1965, 312 p.
In discussing the racial issue in the United States, a senior editor of *Ebony* stresses "the idea of forcing men to confront the gap between word and deed, promise and performance."

Bennett, Marion Tinsley. **American Immigration Policies: A History.** Washington: Public Affairs Press, 1963, 362 p.

A documented history, focusing chiefly on debates over restrictions on immigration since 1941.

Carmichael, Stokely and Hamilton, Charles V. **Black Power: The Politics of Liberation in America.** New York: Random House, 1967, 198 p.
A powerful statement of the authors' revolutionary position. A searing indictment of "White Power" and a fierce call to the Black community to "become their own men and women . . . by whatever means necessary."

The Changing Values on Campus. New York: Washington Square Press, 1972, 246 p.
The results of an intensive survey of the shifting attitudes of American college students over the years 1968 to 1971, prepared for the JDR 3rd Fund by Daniel Yankelovich, Inc. Among the conclusions: decreasing pessimism, polarization and acceptance of violence.

Day, Lincoln Hubert and Day, Alice Taylor. **Too Many Americans.** Boston: Houghton, 1964, 298 p.
The authors worry about the population trends in the United States and urge the early attainment of stability.

Domhoff, G. William. **The Higher Circles: The Governing Class in America.** New York: Random House, 1970, 367 p.
This book is a theoretical amplification and updating of the thesis advanced by C. Wright Mills in his "The Power Elite."

Fermi, Laura. **Illustrious Immigrants: The Intellectual Migration from Europe, 1930-41.** Chicago: University of Chicago Press, 1968, 440 p.
This is the story of Hitler's rejects who replenished America's intellectual arsenal in virtually every field of human endeavor during the 1930s.

Flynn, George Q. **American Catholics and the Roosevelt Presidency, 1932-1936.** Lexington: University Press of Kentucky, 1968, 272 p.
In the words of the author, "This study attempts to discuss Catholic reaction to the major events of the period and the reasons for their particular response."

Fuchs, Lawrence H. **John F. Kennedy and American Catholicism.** New York: Meredith Press, 1967, 271 p.
The author explores the interaction among three factors—the American national character, the Roman Catholic Church and John F. Kennedy.

Gross, Bertram Myron, ed. **A Great Society?** New York: Basic Books, 1968, 362 p.
Thirteen scholars in as many original essays address themselves to the problems of America's future.

Lewis, Norman. **The Honored Society.** New York: Putnam, 1964, 318 p.
A breezy yet informative account of the history and contemporary role of the Mafia, by a contributor to *The New Yorker*.

Reich, Charles A. **The Greening of America: How the Youth Revolution is Trying to Make America Livable.** New York: Random House, 1970, 399 p.
The author asserts that the youth revolution is the only constructive alternative to the "wasteland of the corporate state."

Rose, Arnold M., ed. **Assuring Freedom to the Free: A Century of Emancipation in the USA.** Detroit: Wayne State University Press, 1964, 306 p.
A collection of lectures in celebration of the centenary of the Emancipation Proclamation and dealing with a variety of topics relating to the vicissitudes of the Blacks in America.

Short, James F., Jr. and Wolfgang, Marvin E., eds. **Collective Violence.** Chicago: Aldine, Atherton, 1972, 387 p.
A wide-ranging collection of papers dealing with the phenomenon of collective violence in the United States.

Wattenberg, Ben J. with Scammon, Richard M. **This U.S.A.** Garden City: Doubleday, 1965, 520 p.
A lively account of some of the findings about American life to be drawn from the 1960 census. Mr. Wattenberg, a journalist, was assisted in this endeavor by Mr. Scammon, the Director of the Bureau of the Census, 1961-65.

Williams, Roger Neville. **The New Exiles.** New York: Liveright, 1971, 401 p.
   A report on self-exiled American war resisters in Canada, all of whom, the author asserts, have the inalienable right to return.

Culture; Education; Press; Radio

See also Culture; Education; Public Opinion; Communications Processes, p. 42; (The United States) Biographies, Memoirs and Addresses, p. 218; Foreign Policy, p. 229.

Aronson, James. **Deadline for the Media: Today's Challenges to Press, TV and Radio.** Indianapolis: Bobbs-Merrill, 1972, 327 p.
   An attack, written with old-time indignation, on encroachments by government and other interests against freedom of the press.

Braisted, Paul J., ed. **Cultural Affairs and Foreign Relations.** Washington: Columbia Books, rev. ed. 1968, 211 p.
   A group of essays, prepared for the American Assembly, dealing with various facets of international cultural relations, education and science, and suggesting principles for use in the development of national policies. The first edition of this volume, edited by Robert Blum, appeared in 1963.

Capps, Finis Herbert. **From Isolationism to Involvement: The Swedish Immigrant Press in America, 1914-1945.** Chicago: Swedish Pioneer Historical Society, 1967, 238 p.
   A thorough analysis of the attitudes of the Swedish-Americans toward the foreign policy of the United States from 1914 to 1945, by a specialist on Scandinavia in the Department of State.

Ch'ien, Ts'un-hsün and Winger, Howard W., eds. **Area Studies and the Library.** Chicago: The University of Chicago Press, 1966, 184 p.
   Papers, delivered at a conference organized by the Graduate Library School of the University of Chicago, discussing the area study programs at American universities and the problems of building up collections of research materials in the many languages of Asia, the Near East, Africa, Latin America, the Soviet Union and Eastern Europe.

Cohen, Bernard Cecil. **The Press and Foreign Policy.** Princeton: Princeton University Press, 1963, 288 p.
   A study based on interviews with foreign affairs reporters and responsible government officials to evaluate the impact of the press on American foreign policy.

Coombs, Philip H. **The Fourth Dimension of Foreign Policy: Educational and Cultural Affairs.** New York: Harper and Row (for the Council on Foreign Relations), 1964, 158 p.
   A former Assistant Secretary of State assesses past efforts of U.S. foreign policy and advocates a considerable expansion of America's cultural contacts with other nations.

Cornwell, Elmer Eckert, Jr. **Presidential Leadership of Public Opinion.** Bloomington: Indiana University Press, 1965, 370 p.
   An able and interesting study of the means and techniques used by Presidents since Theodore Roosevelt to guide and influence public opinion from the "bully pulpit" of the White House.

Dickson, Paul. **Think Tanks.** New York: Atheneum, 1971, 369 p.
   A critical survey of the activities and importance of the élite group of American research and development institutions known as think tanks.

Elder, Robert Ellsworth. **The Information Machine.** Syracuse: Syracuse University Press, 1968, 356 p.
   A scholarly study of the U.S. Information Agency and its role in American foreign policy.

Fox, William Thornton Rickert. **The American Study of International Relations.** Columbia: University of South Carolina, Institute of International Studies, 1968, 116 p.
   Six splendid essays by a well-known Columbia University professor.

Henderson, John W. **The United States Information Agency.** New York: Praeger, 1969, 324 p.
   A factual, straightforward and, on the whole, favorable assessment of the USIA.

Johnson, Walter and Colligan, Francis J. **The Fulbright Program: A History.** Chicago: University of Chicago Press, 1965, 380 p.
A history of the program, properly associated with the name of Senator Fulbright, that initiated, under Public Law 584 of the Seventy-Sixth Congress (1946), vastly expanded American activities in the fields of international educational and scholarly exchange.

Lyons, Gene Martin and Morton, Louis. **Schools for Strategy: Education and Research in National Security Affairs.** New York: Praeger, 1965, 356 p.
A valuable review of the intellectual role of American universities and research groups in contributing to national security activities in recent years.

McGaffin, William and Knoll, Erwin. **Anything but the Truth: The Credibility Gap—How the News is Managed in Washington.** New York: Putnam, 1968, 250 p.
A somewhat sensationalist account of news management in Washington during the Eisenhower, Kennedy and Johnson administrations.

Mickelson, Sig. **The Electric Mirror: Politics in an Age of Television.** New York: Dodd, Mead, 1972, 304 p.
An examination of the immense influence television exercises on American political mechanisms and processes.

Minor, Dale. **The Information War.** New York: Hawthorn Books, 1970, 212 p.
In this study the author blames both the government and the news media for news censorship, distortion and manipulation.

Nielsen, Waldemar A. **The Big Foundations.** New York: Columbia University Press (for the Twentieth Century Fund), 1972, 475 p.
An informative and much-needed analysis of the 33 largest American foundations: Ford, Rockefeller, Duke, *et al.* The author finds many of the giants unresponsive to social needs, afflicted by archaic attitudes and incompetently staffed.

Patrick, Charles William. **The American Press and the European Army Plan: A Study of the Reaction of the American Press with Respect to the European Defense Community, 1950-1954.** Ambilly: Les Presses de Savoie (for the Université de Genève, Institut Universitaire de Hautes Études Internationales), 1965, 183 p.
An extensive and well-documented analysis.

The Professional School and World Affairs. Albuquerque: University of New Mexico Press, 1968, 408 p.
A useful symposium based on the premise that exposure to international affairs should extend to professional schools, especially those in business, public administration, law, agriculture, engineering, medicine and education.

Reston, James Barrett. **The Artillery of the Press: Its Influence on American Foreign Policy.** New York: Harper and Row (for the Council on Foreign Relations), 1967, 116 p.
With apt examples from his own experience, the noted journalist shows how contemporary conditions have heightened the conflict between the people's right to know and the government's need for secrecy in the conduct of foreign affairs. One conclusion: the power of the President to influence opinion is more to be feared than that of the press.

Rivers, William L. **The Opinionmakers.** Boston: Beacon Press, 1965, 207 p.
A report on the Washington press corps, including such influential figures as James Reston, Walter Lippmann and David Brinkley.

Rubin, Ronald I. **The Objectives of the U.S. Information Agency: Controversies and Analysis.** New York: Praeger, 1968, 251 p.
The author explores the role of the USIA in the American political system.

Schiller, Herbert I. **Mass Communications and American Empire.** New York: Augustus Kelley, 1969, 170 p.
A critical examination of the economic and political functions of mass communications in the United States.

Selltiz, Claire and Others. **Attitudes and Social Relations of Foreign Students in the United States.** Minneapolis: University of Minnesota Press, 1963, 434 p.
This final volume of a series of monographs sponsored by the Committee on Cross-Cultural Education of the Social Science Research Council deals broadly with the

problems involved in the adjustment of foreign students to university life in the United States and to the American scene.

Smith, Bruce L. R. **The RAND Corporation.** Cambridge: Harvard University Press, 1966, 332 p.
An illuminating case study of an important postwar phenomenon: the emergence of the nonprofit research or advisory corporation, chiefly in conjunction with military and strategic affairs.

Sorensen, Thomas C. **The Word War: The Story of American Propaganda.** New York: Harper and Row, 1968, 337 p.
This book tells the story of American propaganda abroad since World War I. In the author's view, propaganda, in the best sense of the term, is a continuing necessity.

Thomson, Charles Alexander and Laves, Walter H. C. **Cultural Relations and U.S. Foreign Policy.** Bloomington: Indiana University Press, 1963, 227 p.
A study of the evolution of the U.S. Government's programs, started in 1938, "to stimulate, encourage, and channel cultural activities in line with foreign policy."

The University Looks Abroad. New York: Walker, 1965, 300 p.
The result of a study conducted by Education and World Affairs on the international activities and interests of six American universities—Cornell, Indiana, Michigan State, Stanford, Tulane and Wisconsin.

Wilson, Howard Eugene and Wilson, Florence H. **American Higher Education and World Affairs.** Washington: American Council on Education, 1963, 158 p.
This is the concluding volume in a series sponsored by the Carnegie Endowment for International Peace on higher education and world affairs.

Science and Society

See also Society and Social Psychology, p. 39; Culture; Education; Public Opinion; Communications Processes, p. 42; (The United States) Biographies, Memoirs and Addresses, p. 218; Military and Defense Policy, p. 257; Questions of Subversion, Loyalty and Civil Liberties, p. 267.

Brooks, Harvey. **The Government of Science.** Cambridge: M.I.T. Press, 1968, 343 p.
Ten papers exploring the multiple relationships between science and government.

Cox, Donald William. **America's New Policy Makers: The Scientists' Rise to Power.** Philadelphia: Chilton, 1964, 298 p.
A popularly written tract on the U.S. Government's involvement in scientific affairs since 1790, largely concentrating on the importance and role of the space scientist working with and for the government.

Etzioni, Amitai. **The Moon-Doggle: Domestic and International Implications of the Space Race.** Garden City: Doubleday, 1964, 198 p.
Professor Etzioni argues that the space race is "not a propellent but a drag" and has "proved to be a monumental misdecision."

Galloway, Jonathan F. **The Politics and Technology of Satellite Communications.** Lexington (Mass.): Lexington Books, 1972, 247 p.
A scholarly analysis of the decision-making process in U.S. national and international communication satellites policy, which criticizes the lack of central direction and goals in U.S. policy and characterizes the decision-making process as "legislative rather than hierarchical-executive."

Gilpin, Robert George and Wright, Christopher, *eds*. **Scientists and National Policy-Making.** New York: Columbia University Press, 1964, 307 p.
A symposium on the activities of natural scientists in a growing number of areas of national policy.

Gould, Jay Martin. **The Technical Elite.** New York: Kelley, 1966, 178 p.
A study of the élite status being achieved by American scientists and engineers and some of the implications for our society.

Grodzins, Morton Melvin and Rabinowitch, Eugene, *eds*. **The Atomic Age: Scientists in National and World Affairs.** New York: Basic Books, 1963, 616 p.
A collection of significant articles from the *Bulletin of the Atomic Scientists* since 1945.

Hewlett, Richard G. and Duncan, Francis. **Atomic Shield, 1947/1952: A History of the United States Atomic Energy Commission.** University Park: Pennsylvania State University, 1969, 718 p.
   The second volume of this impressive work carries the story from 1947, when the Commission assumed responsibility for the nation's atomic energy program, to 1952, when the first thermonuclear device was detonated. The first volume, "The New World, 1939–1946," was published in 1962.

Horowitz, Irving Louis, *comp*. **The Rise and Fall of Project Camelot: Studies in the Relationship between Social Science and Practical Politics.** Cambridge: M.I.T. Press, 1967, 385 p.
   An analysis of the short-lived Project Camelot—financed by the U.S. Department of the Army in 1964—aimed at assessing attitudes toward social change in Latin America.

Horowitz, Irving Louis, *ed*. **The Use and Abuse of Social Science.** New Brunswick: Transaction Books, 1971, 350 p.
   Critical essays on the involvement of social scientists in national policy-making.

Logsdon, John M. **The Decision to Go to the Moon: Project Apollo and the National Interest.** Cambridge: M.I.T. Press, 1970, 187 p.
   A well-researched study, discussing the impact of Project Apollo on the American political system.

Schaffter, Dorothy. **The National Science Foundation.** New York: Praeger, 1969, 278 p.
   This detailed and comprehensive study is particularly instructive on the educational activities of the N.S.F.

Skolnikoff, Eugene Bertram. **Science, Technology, and American Foreign Policy.** Cambridge: M.I.T. Press, 1967, 330 p.
   The author, who served for five years on the White House staff to assist the President's Science Advisory Committee, presents his reflections and conclusions on the significance of "the role of science in foreign affairs."

Smith, Alice Kimball. **A Peril and a Hope: The Scientists' Movement in America, 1945–47.** Chicago: University of Chicago Press, 1965, 591 p.
   A study of the beginning of the dramatic change in the relation of the scientist and the scientific community to public affairs.

Van Dyke, Vernon. **Pride and Power: The Rationale of the Space Program.** Urbana: University of Illinois Press, 1964, 285 p.
   A political scientist looks into our space program to ascertain the political motives involved in its initiation, support, organization and implementation.

Wiesner, Jerome Bert. **Where Science and Politics Meet.** New York: McGraw-Hill, 1965, 302 p.
   Papers on science, education, society and disarmament, written for the most part while the author was Special Assistant for Science and Technology to Presidents Kennedy and Johnson.

CANADA

General

See also (Canada) Government and Politics, p. 285.

Canadian Annual Review. Toronto: University of Toronto Press.
   A useful handbook on Canadian politics, foreign relations, economic, social and cultural developments, published annually since 1961 and edited by John Saywell. Since 1972, beginning with volume covering the year 1971, the handbook is entitled "Canadian Annual Review of Politics and Public Affairs."

Clark, Gerald. **Canada: The Uneasy Neighbor.** New York: McKay, 1965, 433 p.
   A leading Canadian correspondent here discusses two central areas of tension and anxiety—English Canada vis-à-vis French Canada and Canada as a whole vis-à-vis the United States.

Creighton, Donald. **Canada's First Century, 1867-1967.** New York: St. Martin's Press, 1970, 372 p.
: A well-known Canadian historian concludes his review of the last hundred years of Canadian history with very pessimistic thoughts about his country's future.

Fraser, Blair. **The Search for Identity: Canada, 1945-1967.** Garden City: Doubleday, 1967, 325 p.
: A fast-paced journalistic account of Canada's recent history through the eyes of the late Ottawa correspondent of *Maclean's*.

Hawkins, Freda. **Canada and Immigration: Public Policy and Public Concern.** Quebec: McGill-Queen's University Press (for the Institute of Public Administration of Canada), 1972, 444 p.
: This thorough analysis of immigration into Canada since 1945 is skillfully set in an international context.

Leach, Richard H., *ed.* **Contemporary Canada.** Durham: Duke University Press (for the Duke University Commonwealth-Studies Center), 1967, 328 p.
: Papers on contemporary Canadian economic, social and political problems originally presented in 1966 at a seminar sponsored by the Committee on Commonwealth Studies of Duke University.

McNaught, Kenneth. **The Pelican History of Canada.** Baltimore: Penguin Books, 1969, 336 p.
: A useful general survey by a professor at the University of Toronto.

Morton, William Lewis. **The Kingdom of Canada: A General History from Earliest Times.** Toronto: McClelland & Stewart, 1963, 556 p.
: A well-balanced history emphasizing the characteristics which have molded Canada into a distinctly individual nation.

Report of the Royal Commission on Bilingualism and Biculturalism. Ottawa: Queen's Printer, 1967-70, 5 v. in 6 pts.
: A major investigation of almost every aspect of contemporary Canadian society.

Schwartz, Mildred A. **Public Opinion and Canadian Identity.** Berkeley: University of California Press, 1967, 263 p.
: Using the results of public-opinion polls, the author tries to answer the question of how the Canadians define their national identity.

Urquhart, Morris C. with Buckley, K. A. H., *eds.* **Historical Statistics of Canada.** New York: Cambridge University Press, 1965, 672 p.
: A wide range of statistical information on Canada covering the period from 1867 to 1960. The volume has been sponsored by the Canadian Political Science Association and the Social Science Research Council of Canada.

Wilson, Edmund. **O Canada: An American's Notes on Canadian Culture.** New York: Farrar, Straus and Giroux, 1965, 245 p.
: The eminent literary critic's excursions into Canadian literature include discussions of Canadian politics and the French separatist struggle.

Foreign Relations

See also (International Law) General, p. 83; (United Nations) Peace-Keeping Forces and Operations, p. 106; (Canada) General, p. 281; Military Policy, p. 285; (Great Britain) Imperial and Commonwealth Relations; Colonial Policy, p. 367; The 1956 Suez Crisis, p. 637; Polar Regions, p. 848.

Balawyder, Aloysius. **Canadian-Soviet Relations between the World Wars.** Toronto: University of Toronto Press, 1972, 248 p.
: The author of this well-researched study demonstrates that Canada lacked a coherent policy toward the Soviet Union, except for measures calculated to avoid discord at home.

Bédard, Charles. **Le Régime juridique des Grands Lacs de l'Amérique du Nord et du Saint-Laurent.** Quebec: Presses de l'Université Laval, 1966, 178 p.
: A legal study of the Canadian and U.S. agreements concerning the Great Lakes and the St. Lawrence Seaway, by a French-Canadian lawyer and diplomat.

Canada in World Affairs. Toronto: Oxford University Press (for the Canadian Institute of International Affairs).
Detailed surveys of Canada's participation in world affairs. The following volumes have been published since 1963: vol. X, "1957–1959," by Trevor Lloyd (1968, 253 p.); vol. XI, "1959–1961," by Richard A. Preston (1965, 300 p.); and vol. XII, "1961–1963," by Peyton V. Lyon (1968, 555 p.).

Clarkson, Stephen, *ed.* **An Independent Foreign Policy for Canada?** Toronto: McClelland, 1968, 290 p.
Twenty-six Canadian scholars explore the possibilities of a greater degree of autonomy for their country's foreign policy.

Craig, Gerald M. **The United States and Canada.** Cambridge: Harvard University Press, 1968, 376 p.
The author argues that success in strengthening American-Canadian ties will depend on an appreciation of differences as well as similarities between the two nations.

Crispo, John H. G. **International Unionism: A Study in Canadian-American Relations.** Toronto: McGraw-Hill Company of Canada, 1967, 327 p.
A careful and pioneering study of the American-controlled Canadian labor unions.

Deener, David Russell, *ed.* **Canada-United States Treaty Relations.** Durham: Duke University Press (for Duke University Commonwealth-Studies Center), 1963, 250 p.
A symposium on a wide variety of historical and topical themes bearing on the treaty relations between the United States and Canada.

Dickey, John Sloan, *ed.* **The United States and Canada.** Englewood Cliffs: Prentice-Hall, 1964, 184 p.
An appraisal by seven contributors, prepared under the auspices of the American Assembly, of various aspects of Canadian-U.S. relations.

Dobell, Peter C. **Canada's Search for New Roles: Foreign Policy in the Trudeau Era.** New York: Oxford University Press (for the Royal Institute of International Affairs), 1972, 161 p.
A vigorous discussion of Canada's abandonment of her role as a uniquely moral "middle power."

Documents on Canadian External Relations. Ottawa: Department of External Affairs, 1967–.
A massive collection of documents "intended to illustrate the formulation and implementation of Canadian policy in the field of external relations." Six volumes, covering the period from 1909 to 1939, have been published through 1973.

Eayrs, James George. **In Defence of Canada.** Toronto: University of Toronto Press, 1964–.
A monumental and readable history of Canada's external and defense policies, by the leading scholar in this field. Through 1972 the following volumes have been published: vol. I: "From the Great War to the Great Depression" (1964, 382 p.); vol. II: "Appeasement and Rearmament" (1965, 261 p.); and vol. III: "Peacemaking and Deterrence" (1972, 448 p.).

Farrell, Robert Barry. **The Making of Canadian Foreign Policy.** Scarborough: Prentice-Hall of Canada, 1969, 181 p.
The principal concern of this study "is the Department of External Affairs and the Foreign Service Officers who run that Department."

Gordon, J. King, *ed.* **Canada's Role as a Middle Power: Papers Given at the Third Annual Banff Conference on World Development, August 1965.** Toronto: Canadian Institute of International Affairs, 1966, 212 p.
Papers on Canadian foreign policies by Lester B. Pearson and other prominent Canadians.

Gordon, Walter Lockhart. **A Choice for Canada: Independence or Colonial Status.** Toronto: McClelland, 1966, 125 p.
As he showed when he was Finance Minister, Mr. Gordon is much concerned about Canada's economic dependence on the United States and the extent to which American firms own substantial slices of Canadian mining and industry.

Julien, Claude. **Canada: Europe's Last Chance.** New York: St. Martin's, 1968, 178 p.
An editor of *Le Monde* pleads for greater European interest in Canadian independence. The French original appeared as "Le Canada: dernière chance de l'Europe" (Paris: Grasset, 1965, 204 p.).

Le Gris, Claude. **L'Entrée du Canada sur la scène internationale (1919-1927).** Paris: Presses Universitaires, 1966, 93 p.
A succinct account of Canada's foreign policy between the Treaty of Versailles and the Statute of Westminster.

Lyon, Peyton Vaughan. **The Policy Question: A Critical Appraisal of Canada's Role in World Affairs.** Toronto: McClelland, 1963, 128 p.
The Canadian author asks for "a more accurate appraisal of our diplomatic assets and opportunities."

Martin, Paul Joseph James. **Canada and the Quest for Peace.** New York: Columbia University Press, 1967, 93 p.
Three lectures by the former Canadian Minister of External Affairs on Canada's role in world affairs.

Merchant, Livingston Tallmadge, *ed*. **Neighbors Taken for Granted.** New York: Praeger (for the School of Advanced International Studies, Johns Hopkins University), 1966, 166 p.
A collection of essays by Canadian and American experts, among them Dean Acheson, General Charles Faulkes and James B. Reston, examining the myths and realities—economic, political and psychological—that threaten the American-Canadian friendship.

Page, Donald M., *comp*. **A Bibliography of Works on Canadian Foreign Relations, 1945-1970.** Toronto: Canadian Institute of International Affairs, 1973, 441 p.
A valuable reference.

Piper, Don Courtney. **The International Law of the Great Lakes: A Study of Canadian-United States Co-operation.** Durham: Duke University Press (for the Duke University Commonwealth-Studies Center), 1967, 165 p.
In the words of the author, this study is "an attempt to extract from the conventional rules and customary principles of international law that govern Canadian-American relations those rules, principles, and practices that are applicable specifically to the Great Lakes."

Preston, Richard A., *ed*. **The Influence of the United States on Canadian Development: Eleven Case Studies.** Durham: Duke University Press, 1972, 269 p.
An uneven but often original potpourri—including studies of the U.S. impact on aspects of Canadian scholarship, labor, literature, language, politics and the economy.

Reford, Robert William. **Canada and Three Crises.** Toronto: Canadian Institute of International Affairs, 1968, 246 p.
An examination of Canadian foreign policies during three world crises: the confrontation over the off-shore islands of China, Suez in 1956, and the Cuban missile crisis.

Spicer, Keith. **A Samaritan State? External Aid in Canada's Foreign Policy.** Toronto: University of Toronto Press, 1966, 272 p.
A review and appraisal of Canada's performance in providing foreign aid. The author finds the record relatively good.

Thomson, Dale C. and Swanson, Roger F. **Canadian Foreign Policy: Options and Perspectives.** Toronto: McGraw-Hill Ryerson, 1971, 170 p.
A most useful review of Canadian foreign policies, written as a commentary to a series of foreign policy papers published by the Government of Canada in June 1970.

Thordarson, Bruce. **Trudeau and Foreign Policy: A Study in Decision-Making.** Toronto: Oxford University Press, 1972, 231 p.
In his discussion of Trudeau's foreign policies the author employs approaches drawn explicitly from recent work in political science.

Tupper, Stanley R. and Bailey, Douglas L. **Canada and the United States—The Second Hundred Years.** New York: Hawthorn Books, 1967, 189 p.
The authors urge the citizens of both countries to educate themselves about each other.

Military Policy

See also (United Nations) Peace-Keeping Forces and Operations, p. 106; (Canada) General, p. 281; Foreign Relations, p. 282; The Korean War, p. 728.

Eggleston, Wilfrid. **Canada's Nuclear Story.** Toronto: Clarke, Irwin, 1965, 368 p.
This history of Canadian nuclear research includes a survey of Anglo-American coöperation in nuclear research and development during World War II when Canada was the main Allied source of uranium.

Gray, Colin S. **Canadian Defence Priorities: A Question of Relevance.** Toronto: Clarke, Irwin, 1972, 293 p.
An imaginative, nonpolemical discussion based on the assumption that for "a country like Canada, defence policy really equals equipment." The author suggests that the Canadian military will have "an increasing number of essentially civilian duties to perform."

McLin, Jon B. **Canada's Changing Defense Policy, 1957-1963: The Problems of a Middle Power in Alliance.** Baltimore: Johns Hopkins Press (in coöperation with the Washington Center of Foreign Policy Research, School of Advanced International Studies, Johns Hopkins University), 1967, 251 p.
A well-documented study, with special attention to the role of the United States in the formation of Canadian defense policies.

Preston, Richard A. **Canada and "Imperial Defense": A Study of the Origins of the British Commonwealth's Defense Organization, 1867-1919.** Durham: Duke University Press (for the Duke University Commonwealth-Studies Center), 1967, 576 p.
An attempt to reinterpret the history of the defense system of the British Commonwealth, with emphasis on military developments in Canada.

Stacey, Charles Perry. **Arms, Men and Governments: The War Policies of Canada, 1939-1945.** Ottawa: Minister of National Defence, 1970, 681 p.
An official and very well-documented history of the military policies of Canada during World War II. The author, former Director of the Historical Section of the General Staff of the Canadian Army, surveys also Canada's relations with its allies so far as they affected the conduct of the war.

Warnock, John W. **Partner to Behemoth: The Military Policy of a Satellite Canada.** Toronto: New Press, 1970, 340 p.
A former U.S. Foreign Service officer who has become a Canadian citizen combines a useful factual narrative of Canadian defense policy with some strong nationalist and socialist sentiments and a dash of revisionist history.

Government and Politics

See also Nationalism and Nationality, p. 17; Society and Social Psychology, p. 39; (Canada) General, p. 281.

Aitchison, James Hermiston. **The Political Process in Canada.** Toronto: University of Toronto Press, 1963, 193 p.
A symposium of essays, in honor of R. MacGregor Dawson, dealing with a variety of historical, political and regional topics.

Beal, John Robinson. **Pearson of Canada.** New York: Duell, 1964, 210 p.
A popularly written biography of an outstanding statesman up to the time he became Prime Minister in 1963.

Bergeron, Gérard. **Le Canada français après deux siècles de patience.** Paris: Éditions du Seuil, 1967, 283 p.
A professor at the University of Laval in Quebec reviews the history of French Canada and writes about the political aspirations of the French Canadians.

Bernard, Michel. **Le Québec change de visage.** Paris: Plon, 1964, 217 p.
A French author's report on Quebec and the French Canadians: history, culture, frustrations and the question of "separatism."

Burns, Ronald M., *ed*. **One Country or Two?** Montreal: McGill-Queen's University Press, 1971, 287 p.
A dozen high-quality essays by English-speaking Canadians examining the consequences for the rest of Canada of the separation of Quebec. None of the authors favors "two countries," but all agree on the necessity of planning for what is a strong possibility although not an immediate probability.

Carr, David William. **Recovering Canada's Nationhood.** Ottawa: Canada Publishing Company, 1971, 222 p.
An impassioned plea for Canadians to begin effective resistance to American influence. The author denounces the idea that Canadian economic autonomy is impossible.

Carrigan, D. Owen, *comp*. **Canadian Party Platforms: 1867-1968.** Urbana: University of Illinois Press, 1968, 363 p.
A most useful reference volume, including also the election results for the period covered.

Chadwick, Gerald William St. John. **Newfoundland: Island into Province.** New York: Cambridge University Press, 1967, 268 p.
A comprehensive and well-documented history, with emphasis on constitutional developments. The author served the British Government in Newfoundland and was involved in the establishment of the union of Newfoundland with Canada.

Corbett, Edward M. **Quebec Confronts Canada.** Baltimore: Johns Hopkins Press, 1968, 336 p.
In this fine and scholarly book, the author concludes that the future of the Canadian federation will depend on the English majority's readiness to meet the demands of the French minority.

Crépeau, Paul André and Macpherson, C. B., *eds*. **The Future of Canadian Federalism. L'Avenir du fédéralisme canadien.** Toronto: University of Toronto Press, 1965, 188 p.
Papers presented at meetings of the Association of Canadian Law Teachers and the Canadian Political Science Association in 1964 on the cultural, political and economic relations between the French and English Canadians.

Gotlieb, Allan, *ed*. **Human Rights, Federalism and Minorities. Les Droits de l'homme, le fédéralisme et les minorités.** Toronto: Canadian Institute of International Affairs, 1970, 268 p.
A collection of essays by prominent Canadians on the protection of human rights in Canada.

Heeney, Arnold. **The Things that are Caesar's: The Memoirs of a Canadian Public Servant.** Toronto: University of Toronto Press, 1972, 218 p.
During much of the middle third of this century the late author served as Secretary to the Canadian Cabinet, a post consciously modeled on Lord Hankey's role in London. His memoirs are orderly and discreet as befits a classic public servant.

Hogan, George. **The Conservative in Canada.** Toronto: McClelland, 1963, 130 p.
A brief history of Canadian conservatism and an analysis of the attitudes and principles of members of the Progressive Conservative Party.

Horowitz, Gad. **Canadian Labour in Politics.** Toronto: University of Toronto Press, 1968, 273 p.
In the words of the Canadian author, "this is a historical study of the relationship between the labour movement and the socialist party in Canada."

Hutchison, Bruce. **Mr. Prime Minister: 1867-1964.** New York: Harcourt, Brace and World, 1965, 394 p.
A lively history, by a leading Canadian journalist, of the origins and development of the Prime Ministry in Canada.

Kunz, F. A. **The Modern Senate of Canada, 1925-1963: A Reappraisal.** Toronto: University of Toronto Press, 1965, 395 p.
The author states that it is his purpose "to place the discussion of the structure and functioning of the modern Senate in a broad theoretical setting."

Kwavnick, David. **Organized Labour and Pressure Politics: The Canadian Labour Congress 1956-1968.** Montreal: McGill-Queen's University Press, 1972, 287 p.
A critical study of the Canadian Labour Congress as an organization more concerned with the appearance of status than with attempting to exercise real power.

Mallory, James Russell. **The Structure of Canadian Government.** New York: St. Martin's Press, 1971, 418 p.
A detailed and systematic survey of "the machinery of government in Canada." The author, a Canadian scholar, concludes his study with a plea for the strengthening of the "forces of unity."

Massey, Vincent. **What's Past is Prologue: The Memoirs of the Right Honourable Vincent Massey.** New York: St. Martin's Press, 1964, 540 p.
This is an important contribution by the distinguished Canadian public servant who for many years served his country and the Commonwealth. His last official assignment was as Governor-General of Canada, from which he retired in 1959.

Neatby, H. Blair. **William Lyon Mackenzie King: A Political Biography. Vol. II. 1924–1932: The Lonely Heights.** Toronto: University of Toronto Press, 1963, 452 p.
The second volume of a scholarly and well-researched biography of the late Canadian Prime Minister. The author of the first volume, published in 1958, was Robert MacGregor Dawson.

Newman, Peter Charles. **A Nation Divided: Canada and the Coming of Pierre Trudeau.** New York: Knopf, 1969, 469 p.
An account of the Liberal regime of Lester Pearson, by a well-known Canadian newspaper editor and correspondent. Originally published as "The Distemper of Our Times: Canadian Politics in Transition, 1963–1968" (Toronto: McClelland, 1968, 558 p.).

Newman, Peter Charles. **Renegade in Power: The Diefenbaker Years.** Indianapolis: Bobbs-Merrill, 1964, 414 p.
A critical examination of the years in power—1957 to 1963—of Canada's buoyant, controversial Prime Minister, John Diefenbaker. Mr. Newman successfully depicts the many contradictions in the character of the Progressive Conservative leader.

Pearson, Lester Bowles. **Mike: The Memoirs of the Right Honourable Lester B. Pearson. Volume I: 1897–1948.** New York: Quadrangle Books, 1972, 301 p.
A straightforward account of a rising career with the Canadian foreign service— especially good on wartime London and Washington. The account stops with 1947, but two more posthumous volumes are planned, covering Pearson's years as Secretary of State for External Affairs and as Prime Minister.

Pearson, Lester Bowles. **Words and Occasions.** Cambridge: Harvard University Press, 1970, 296 p.
The writings and public speeches of the former Prime Minister of Canada over the past half century, intelligently annotated by himself.

Pickersgill, John Whitney and Forster D. F. **The Mackenzie King Record.** Toronto: University of Toronto Press, 1960–70, 4 v.
The record of the activities of Canada's Prime Minister Mackenzie King from 1939 to 1948, based on his diaries.

Quinn, Herbert Furlong. **The Union Nationale: A Study in Quebec Nationalism.** Toronto: University of Toronto Press, 1963, 249 p.
A political history of Quebec from the First World War to the 1960 elections, with particular attention to the rise of the Union Nationale.

Rodney, William. **Soldiers of the International: A History of the Communist Party of Canada, 1919–1929.** Toronto: University of Toronto Press, 1968, 204 p.
A solid and well-documented study of the first decade of the Canadian Communist Party.

Sevigny, Pierre. **This Game of Politics.** Toronto: McClelland and Stewart, 1965, 324 p.
The story of the political career of John Diefenbaker who as the leader of the Progressive Conservative Party was Canadian Prime Minister from 1957 to 1963. The author is a French-Canadian member of Diefenbaker's party.

Simeon, Richard. **Federal-Provincial Diplomacy: The Making of Recent Policy in Canada.** Toronto: University of Toronto Press, 1972, 324 p.
An original approach, with data taken from the 1960s, to an essential aspect of Canadian government and the general nature of federalism.

Smiley, Donald V. **The Canadian Political Nationality.** Toronto: Methuen, 1967, 142 p.
A concise and balanced history of the Canadian federation by a Canadian scholar.

Stewart, Walter. **Trudeau in Power.** New York: Outerbridge and Dienstfrey, 1972, 240 p.
A critique of the Canadian Prime Minister's performance since election in 1968. The author argues that Trudeau is an autocrat who has evaded or mismanaged the nation's most serious problems. Published in Canada as "Shrug: Trudeau in Power" (Toronto: New Press, 1971).

Sullivan, Martin. **Mandate '68.** Garden City: Doubleday, 1968, 439 p.
An admiring account of Pierre Elliott Trudeau's rise to power in Canadian politics.

Thomson, Dale C. **Louis St. Laurent: Canadian.** New York: St. Martin's Press, 1968, 564 p.
A biography of a distinguished Canadian statesman who had served his country as Minister of Justice, Secretary of State for External Affairs and Prime Minister (November 15, 1948–June 21, 1957). The author, a professor at the University of Montreal, was St. Laurent's secretary from 1953 to 1958.

Trudeau, Pierre Elliott. **Federalism and the French Canadians.** New York: St. Martin's Press, 1968, 212 p.
In these essays the Canadian Prime Minister sets forth his views on Canadian federalism.

Economic Problems

See also General Economic Conditions and Tendencies, p. 49; Economic Growth and Development, p. 71; (The United States) Trade, Tariffs and Finance, p. 251; (Canada) General, p. 281.

Armstrong, Muriel. **The Canadian Economy and its Problems.** Scarborough: Prentice-Hall of Canada, 1970, 257 p.
An introductory survey.

Bonin, Bernard. **L'Investissement étranger à long terme au Canada.** Montreal: Presses de l'École des Hautes Études Commerciales de Montréal, 1967, 462 p.
A history and analysis of foreign capital investment in Canada.

Camu, Pierre and Others. **Economic Geography of Canada.** New York: St. Martin's Press, 1964, 393 p.
This reference book contains a wealth of information and data on Canada's natural and historical setting, on economic geography in general, and on the 68 individual regions into which the authors have divided the country.

Caves, Richard E. and Reuber, Grant L. with Others. **Capital Transfers and Economic Policy: Canada, 1951-1962.** Cambridge: Harvard University Press, 1971, 432 p.
This study is important for an understanding of the Canadian economy, with implications for broader questions of international economics as well.

Currie, Archibald William. **Canadian Transportation Economics.** Toronto: University of Toronto Press, 1967, 719 p.
A comprehensive and detailed study.

Gray, Earle. **The Great Canadian Oil Patch.** Toronto: Maclean-Hunter, 1970, 355 p.
Popular history of the Canadian oil industry by the editor of a trade journal.

Johnson, Harry Gordon. **The Canadian Quandary: Economic Problems and Policies.** Toronto: McGraw-Hill, 1963, 352 p.
A collection of essays and speeches on Canada's domestic and international economic problems, many attacking economic nationalism as harmful to competition and to growth.

Kilbourn, William. **Pipeline.** Toronto: Clarke, Irwin, 1970, 222 p.
A lively history of the controversy about building a gas pipeline across Canada.

Levitt, Kari. **Silent Surrender: The Multinational Corporation in Canada.** New York: St. Martin's Press, 1970, 185 p.
The author, a professor of economics at McGill, argues that "political mobilization around a new nationalism is the only way" to regain Canadian control of Canada.

Safarian, A. E. **Foreign Ownership of Canadian Industry.** Toronto: McGraw-Hill, 1967, 346 p.
This book by a leading Canadian economist throws more light on the behavior of foreign-owned companies in Canada than most of the writing and talking that has preceded it.

Thompson, Robert Wendell. **International Trade and Domestic Prosperity: Canada 1926-38.** Toronto: University of Toronto Press, 1970, 139 p.
A careful, fairly technical study of the mechanism and policy implications of Canada's dependence on the outside world's economy.

Tremblay, Rodrigue. **Indépendance et Marché Commun: Québec—É.-U.** Montreal: Éditions du Jour, 1970, 127 p.
A well-qualified economist demonstrates the cost to Quebec of Canadian tariffs and argues that the province would be better off in a customs union with the United States—whether the rest of Canada joined or not.

Wilson, George Wilton and Others. **Canada: An Appraisal of its Needs and Resources.** New York: Twentieth Century Fund, 1965, 453 p.
A valuable and statistic-crammed study, prepared by a team of Canadian economists.

Wonnacott, Gordon Paul. **The Canadian Dollar, 1948-1962.** Toronto: University of Toronto Press, 1965, 339 p.
An earlier book on Canada's experience with flexible exchange rates ("The Canadian Dollar, 1948-1958") is reproduced here with an additional hundred pages on what happened after the country returned to a fixed rate in 1958, plus a discussion of the key issues of the future.

Wonnacott, Ronald J. and Wonnacott, Gordon Paul. **Free Trade between the United States and Canada: The Potential Economic Effects.** Cambridge: Harvard University Press, 1967, 430 p.
A careful analysis by two Canadian scholars.

Woods, Harry Douglas and Ostry, Sylvia. **Labour Policy and Labour Economics in Canada.** New York: St. Martin's Press, 1963, 534 p.
In this collaborative work by two Canadian economists, Professor Woods deals with labor policy and the general question of public interest in industrial relations, and Professor Ostry treats labor supply, employment and wages. A revised edition of the first part of this volume was prepared by H. D. Woods and was published as "Labour Policy in Canada" (New York: St. Martin's Press, 1973, 377 p.). A revised edition of the second part was prepared by H. D. Woods, Sylvia Ostry and Mahmood A. Zaidi and appeared as "Labour Economics in Canada" (New York: St. Martin's Press, 1972, 354 p.).

MEXICO

General

See also (War) General, p. 108; Latin America, p. 200.

Alba, Víctor. **The Mexicans: The Making of a Nation.** New York: Praeger, 1967, 268 p.
A useful primer for understanding the Mexican nation and its people.

Cumberland, Charles Curtis. **Mexico: The Struggle for Modernity.** New York: Oxford University Press, 1968, 394 p.
A survey of Mexican history.

Lincoln, John, *pseud.* (Maurice Cardif). **One Man's Mexico: A Record of Travels and Encounters.** New York: Harcourt, Brace and World, 1968, 238 p.
Vignettes of Mexico by a professional writer and traveler.

Nicholson, Irene. **The X in Mexico: Growth within Tradition.** Garden City: Doubleday, 1966, 295 p.
A potpourri of Mexico, past and present, written by a long-time resident.

Silva Herzog, Jesús. **El pensamiento económico, social y político de México, 1810-1964.** Mexico City: Instituto Mexicano de Investigaciones Económicas, 1967, 748 p.
An analysis of the economic, social and political thought of prominent Mexicans of the nineteenth and twentieth centuries.

Wilgus, Alva Curtis, *ed.* **Mexico Today.** Gainesville: University of Florida Press, 1964, 232 p.
Papers on economic, political, social and cultural trends of contemporary Mexico prepared for the annual conference on the Caribbean at the University of Florida (1963). A volume in the series "The Caribbean."

Foreign Relations

See also Inter-American Relations, p. 193.

Calvert, Peter. **The Mexican Revolution, 1910-1914: The Diplomacy of Anglo-American Conflict.** New York: Cambridge University Press, 1968, 330 p.
This study of the divergent interests and policies of Great Britain and the United States in Mexico during the Revolution pays more attention to individuals than to ideologies and political trends.

Corominas, Enrique V. **México, Cuba, y la O.E.A.** Buenos Aires: Ediciones Política, Economía y Finanzas, 1965, 236 p.
An important analysis and defense of Mexico's foreign policies toward Cuba and other Latin American countries by a former Mexican delegate to the Organization of American States.

Cosío Villegas, Daniel. **Cuestiones internacionales de México: una bibliografía.** Mexico City: Secretaría de Relaciones Exteriores, 1966, 588 p.
An extensive and useful bibliography, without annotations, of books and articles dealing with Latin American and Mexican international relations.

Gómez Robledo, Antonio. **México y el arbitraje internacional.** Mexico City: Editorial Porrúa, 1965, 412 p.
A thorough study of three international arbitration issues in which Mexico was involved: the Piadoso Fund of California, the Chamizal and the Passion Island cases.

Hundley, Norris, Jr. **Dividing the Waters: A Century of Controversy between the United States and Mexico.** Berkeley: University of California Press, 1966, 266 p.
A thoughtful and detailed study on the Colorado, Rio Grande and Tijuana rivers in U.S.-Mexican Relations.

James, Daniel. **Mexico and the Americans.** New York: Praeger, 1963, 472 p.
A perceptive American journalist surveys the history of U.S.-Mexican relations, with particular emphasis upon Mexico's evolutionary development since the Revolution of 1910 and the impact this has had upon twentieth-century social revolutions.

Liss, Sheldon B. **A Century of Disagreement: The Chamizal Conflict 1864-1964.** Washington: University Press of Washington, D.C. (for the Latin American Institute), 1965, 167 p.
A concise and studious appraisal of the thorny Chamizal dispute between the United States and Mexico, its origins and final settlement during the Kennedy administration, supplemented by statistical materials and two inadequate maps.

Meyer, Lorenzo. **México y Estados Unidos en el conflicto petrolero, 1917-1942.** Mexico City: El Colegio de México, 1968, 273 p.
A detailed history of the Mexican-United States controversy over Mexican oil.

Ulloa Ortiz, Berta. **La Revolución intervenida: relaciones diplomáticas entre México y Estados Unidos, 1910-1914.** Mexico City: El Colegio de México, 1971, 394 p.
A scholarly history of United States intervention in the Mexican Revolution between 1910 and 1914.

Ulloa Ortiz, Berta. **Revolución Mexicana, 1910-1920.** Mexico City: Secretaría de Relaciones Exteriores, 1963, 538 p.
A guide to 259 volumes of the "Mexican Revolution" section of the Archives of the Secretary of Foreign Relations.

Zorrilla, Luis G. **Historia de las relaciones entre México y los Estados Unidos de América, 1800-1958.** Mexico City: Editorial Porrúa, 1965-66, 2 v.
An excellent scholarly study of Mexican-U.S. relations between 1800 and 1958.

Government, Constitution and Politics

See also The Problem of Authority; Violence and Revolution, p. 34; Latin America, p. 200.

Atkin, Ronald. **Revolution! Mexico 1910-20.** New York: Day, 1970, 354 p.
A colorful account of the dramatic revolutionary decade in Mexico, with well-selected pictures.

Blanco Moheno, Roberto. **El cardenismo.** Mexico City: Libro Mex Editores, 1963, 365 p.
A leftist analysis of the Cárdenas period.

Díaz Ordaz, Gustavo. **Ideas políticas del presidente Gustavo Díaz Ordaz.** México: Editorial Ruta, 1966, 365 p.
A collection of statements by President Díaz Ordaz on a variety of political, economic and social themes. Edited by Robert Amorós.

Documentos históricos de la Revolución Mexicana. Mexico City: Fondo de Cultura Económica; Editorial Jus (for the Comision de Ivestigaciones Históricas de la Revolución Mexicana), 1960– .
A multi-volume collection of documents pertaining to the Mexican Revolution. The first five volumes were edited by Isidro Fabela; the subsequent, by Josefina E. Fabela.

Ezcurdia, Mario. **Análisis teórico del Partido Revolucionario Institucional.** Mexico City: B. Costa-Amič Editor, 1968, 181 p.
A study of the Institutional Revolutionary Party (P.R.I.) of Mexico, stressing its uniqueness.

González Casanova, Pablo. **Democracy in Mexico.** New York: Oxford University Press, 2d ed., 1970, 245 p.
A leading Mexican scholar examines social and political life in his country since 1910, with particular reference to power mechanisms and the prospects for a wider democracy. The original edition appeared as "La democracia en México" (Mexico City: Ediciones ERA, 1965, 261 p.).

González Navarro, Moisés. **La Confederación Nacional Campesina: un grupo de presión en la reforma agraria Mexicana.** Mexico City: B. Costa-Amič Editor, 1968, 333 p.
A thorough study of the Confederacion Nacional Campesina emphasizing its development and relations with other political pressure groups and the P.R.I.

Horn, Hans Rudolf. **México: Revolution und Verfassung.** Hamburg: Übersee-Verlag, 1969, 164 p.
A study of the 1917 Mexican Constitution and a survey of 50 years of Mexican political, economic and social developments.

Horta, Arnaldo Pedroso d'. **México: uma revolução insolúvel.** Rio de Janeiro: Editôra Saga, 1965, 276 p.
An evaluation of the Mexican Revolution and its political and social consequences, by a Brazilian scholar.

Lieuwen, Edwin. **Mexican Militarism: The Political Rise and Fall of the Revolutionary Army, 1910-1940.** Albuquerque: University of New Mexico Press, 1968, 194 p.
Professor Lieuwen, author of the pioneering work "Arms and Politics in Latin America" (1960), describes civil-military relations in Mexico from the years before World War I when the Mexican Army of the Revolution seized power to the election of 1940 when civilians regained control of the government.

Lombardo Toledano, Vicente. **¿Moscú o Pekín? La vía mexicana hacia el socialismo.** Mexico City: Partido Popular Socialista, 1963, 187 p.
A discussion of the future course which Mexican socialism should follow by the leader of the Partido Popular Socialista.

Lozoya, Jorge Alberto. **El ejército mexicano, 1911-1965.** Mexico City: El Colegio de México, 1970, 128 p.
A brief account of the role of the military in Mexican politics between 1911 and 1965.

Meyer, Michael C. **Huerta: A Political Portrait.** Lincoln: University of Nebraska Press, 1972, 272 p.
A scholarly biography of Victoriano Huerta (1854-1916), an important Mexican general who was also his country's President at a very critical time.

México: realidad política de sus partidos. Mexico City: Instituto Mexicano de Estudios Politícos, 1970, 318 p.
A historical and institutional analysis of Mexican political parties, including an examination of their positions on major issues.

Millon, Robert Paul. **Mexican Marxist: Vicente Lombardo Toledano.** Chapel Hill: University of North Carolina Press, 1966, 222 p.

Based on his numerous writings and personal interviews, this is a clearly stated exposition of Vicente Lombardo Toledano's thought. The author's frankly sympathetic bias prevents a critical analysis of the socialist leader's important role in Mexico's contemporary development.

Millon, Robert Paul. **Zapata: The Ideology of a Peasant Revolutionary.** New York: International Publishers, 1969, 159 p.
An account of the program, tactics and thought of the peasant revolutionary Zapata.

Moreno, Daniel. **Los partidos políticos del México contemporáneo, 1926-1970.** Mexico City: B. Costa-Amič Editor, 1970, 289 p.
A study of the establishment and evolution of political parties in Mexico between 1926 and 1970, of presidential campaigns between 1934 and 1970, and of leftist groups in Mexican politics.

Moya Palencia, Mario. **La reforma electoral.** Mexico City: Ediciones Plataforma, 1964, 206 p.
An analysis of the Mexican electoral reform of 1962 and its effects on the political system.

Padgett, Leon Vincent. **The Mexican Political System.** Boston: Houghton, 1966, 244 p.
An introductory survey.

Portes Gil, Emilio. **Autobiografía de la Revolución Mexicana: un tratado de interpretación histórica.** Mexico City: Instituto Mexicano de Cultura, 1964, 865 p.
A history of the Revolution as interpreted by an important revolutionary and former President of Mexico.

Los presidentes de México ante la nación: informes, manifiestos y documentos de 1821 a 1966. Mexico City: Presidente, 1966, 5 v.
Extensive collection of Presidential decrees, statements and documents from 1821 to 1966.

Schmitt, Karl Michael. **Communism in Mexico: A Study in Political Frustration.** Austin: University of Texas Press, 1965, 290 p.
In this factual account of the failings of communism in Mexico, the author concludes that the communist movement has been unable to offer "substantial and meaningful opposition to the government party and the basic power structure of Mexico."

Turner, Frederick C. **The Dynamic of Mexican Nationalism.** Chapel Hill: University of North Carolina Press, 1968, 350 p.
An analysis and description of Mexican nationalism. The author argues that the 1910 Revolution and the subsequent civil war were the catalysts that helped to develop its contemporary form.

Valadés, José C. **El presidente de México en 1970.** Mexico City: Editores Mexicanos Unidos, 1969, 184 p.
An analysis of contemporary Mexican presidential selection system.

Vasconcelos, José. **A Mexican Ulysses: An Autobiography.** Bloomington: Indiana University Press, 1963, 288 p.
A well-done abridgement and translation by W. Rex Crawford of the autobiography of José Vasconcelos (1881-1959), an illustrious Mexican patriot. The original version, "Ulises criollo" (4 v.), has appeared in many editions.

Wilkie, James Wallace and Michaels, Albert L., eds. **Revolution in Mexico: Years of Upheaval, 1910-1940.** New York: Knopf, 1969, 300 p.
Forty-eight short selections, covering Mexican life in its full heterogeneity, by participants, scholars and other commentators.

Womack, John, Jr. **Zapata and the Mexican Revolution.** New York: Knopf, 1969, 435 p.
A penetrating, scholarly and warmly written study of Zapata—the man and the times. Supplemented with documents and bibliography.

Economic and Social Problems

See also Problems of New Nations, p. 36; Economic Growth and Development, p. 71; (Latin America) Economic and Social Problems, p. 208.

Ashby, Joe C. **Organized Labor and the Mexican Revolution under Lázaro Cárdenas.** Chapel Hill: University of North Carolina Press, 1967, 350 p.

A study of Cárdenas' policies toward organized labor in the 1930s, a period when "the Mexican labor movement attained its highest form of organization, prestige, and influence in national economic policy."

Bazant, Jan. **Historia de la deuda exterior de México, 1823-1946.** Mexico City: El Colegio de México, 1968, 277 p.
A history of Mexico's foreign debt.

Bennett, Robert Lee. **The Financial Sector and Economic Development: The Mexican Case.** Baltimore: Johns Hopkins Press, 1965, 210 p.
A statistical examination of Mexico's financial institutions and their role in the country's period of industrial growth following World War II.

Bermúdez, Antonio J. **The Mexican National Petroleum Industry: A Case Study in Nationalization.** Stanford: Stanford University, Institute of Hispanic American and Luso-Brazilian Studies, 1963, 269 p.
Supported by charts and statistics, this detailed study traces the development of Petróleos Mexicanos during the period (1946-1958) when the author headed Mexico's nationalized oil industry.

Brothers, Dwight S. and Solís M., Leopoldo. **Mexican Financial Development.** Austin: University of Texas Press, 1966, 236 p.
A detailed study of Mexico's financial system, chiefly in the years since 1940.

Carmona, Fernando. **El drama de América Latina: el caso de México.** Mexico City: Cuadernos Americanos, 1964, 277 p.
An analysis of Mexican economic development. The author argues that Mexico must break free of dependence on foreign economic ties in order to develop a dynamic economy.

Carmona, Fernando and Others. **El milagro mexicano.** Mexico City: Editorial Nuestro Tiempo, 1970, 363 p.
These essays dealing with economic, social and political conditions in Mexico attempt to show that the "Mexican Miracle" is a myth and that the real miracle is that the Mexican people tolerate their backwardness.

Cole, William Earle. **Steel and Economic Growth in Mexico.** Austin: University of Texas Press (for the Institute of Latin American Studies), 1967, 173 p.
A detailed study of the Mexican steel industry and the role which the government has played in its development. Statistical and bibliographical materials supplement a scholarly analysis of the industry's impact on the economy.

Eckstein, Salomón. **El ejido colectivo en México.** Mexico City: Fondo de Cultura Económica, 1966, 511 p.
A study of the economic efficiency of the *ejido* system and of some of its social effects. Translation of a Harvard doctoral dissertation.

Freithaler, William O. **Mexico's Foreign Trade and Economic Development.** New York: Praeger, 1968, 160 p.
A factual, statistical study. The author concludes optimistically that, despite external trade difficulties, Mexico will continue a sustained economic growth.

Glade, William P., Jr. and Anderson, Charles W. **The Political Economy of Mexico: Two Studies.** Madison: University of Wisconsin Press, 1963, 242 p.
In this volume Mr. Glade discusses the relation of the Mexican Revolution to economic development, while Mr. Anderson deals more narrowly with the development of public credit institutions.

Guillén Romo, Arturo. **Planificación económica a la mexicana.** Mexico City: Editorial Nuestro Tiempo, 1971, 143 p.
A critical discussion of economic planning in Mexico.

Hansen, Roger D. **The Politics of Mexican Development.** Baltimore: Johns Hopkins Press, 1971, 267 p.
The author criticizes the Mexican Revolution for its failure to diminish the gap between rich and poor, and assigns the principal blame to nineteenth-century, self-seeking entrepreneurial attitudes of the traditional Mexican élite.

Ibarra, David and Others. **El perfil de México en 1980.** Mexico City: Siglo Veintiuno Editores, 1970, 2 v.
A useful study of economic trends in Mexico.

La Cascia, Joseph S. **Capital Formation and Economic Development in Mexico.** New York: Praeger, 1969, 190 p.

A technical investigation, with extensive statistical analysis, of changing patterns of Mexican capital formation during 1959–1966.

Link, Max. **Die Ursachen des industriellen Aufstiegs Mexikos.** Zurich: Orell Füssli, 1970, 229 p.

An economic history of Mexico, with emphasis on the growth of the industries. Many statistical tables.

López Rosado, Diego G. **Problemas económicos de México.** Mexico City: Universidad Nacional Autónoma de México, 1963, 340 p.

A useful reference on Mexican economic problems.

Meister, Albert. **Le Système mexicain: les avatars d'une participation populaire au développement.** Paris: Éditions Anthropos, 1971, 190 p.

A sociological study of modern Mexico.

Meléndez, Hugo Tulio. **Estudio comparativo de la reforma agraria de México y Yugoslavia.** Mexico City: Ediciones Oasis, 1965, 123 p.

A comparative analysis of agrarian reforms in Mexico and Yugoslavia.

Oldman, Oliver Sanford and Others. **Financing Urban Development in Mexico City: A Case Study of Property Tax, Land Use, Housing, and Urban Planning.** Cambridge: Harvard University Press, 1967, 356 p.

A detailed and careful examination of the impact which fiscal and legal policies have had upon the growth of Mexico's capital.

Padilla Aragón, Enrique. **México: desarrollo con pobreza.** Mexico City: Siglo Veintiuno Editores, 1969, 179 p.

An analysis of Mexico's uneven economic growth over the past 30 years, with policy recommendations on how to solve major problems.

Peña, Moisés T. de la. **El pueblo y su tierra: mito y realidad de la reforma agraria en México.** Mexico City: Cuadernos Americanos, 1964, 895 p.

A noted Mexican economist examines in detail the problem of land and its distribution in Mexico. A valuable study.

Pérez López, Enrique and Others. **Mexico's Recent Economic Growth: The Mexican View.** Austin: University of Texas Press (for the Institute of Latin American Studies), 1967, 217 p.

Six prominent Mexican economists examine varied aspects of the Mexican economy.

Poleman, Thomas Theobald. **The Papaloapan Project: Agricultural Development in the Mexican Tropics.** Stanford: Stanford University Press, 1964, 167 p.

A factual study of Mexico's attempt to develop a humid, tropical region. A publication of Stanford's Food Research Institute.

Quirarte, Martín. **El problema religioso en México.** Mexico City: Instituto Nacional de Antropología e Historia, 1967, 408 p.

A scholarly study of the history of the Catholic Church in Mexico.

Reynolds, Clark W. **The Mexican Economy: Twentieth-Century Structure and Growth.** New Haven: Yale University Press, 1970, 468 p.

An intensive and able economic study, with unusual attention to social aspects. One important conclusion is that "although no major economic obstacles stand in the way of sustained growth, political pitfalls abound."

Ross, John B. **The Economic System of Mexico.** Stanford: California Institute of International Studies, 1971, 131 p.

The author reviews the growth of the Mexican economy since Cárdenas and describes the purposes and functions of the government in the development process.

Seoane Corrales, Edgardo. **El ejemplo mexicano.** Lima: Moncloa Editores, 1967, 244 p.

A former ambassador to Mexico and Vice President of Peru finds the Mexican model of development suitable for the rest of Latin America.

Shafer, Robert Jones. **Mexico: Mutual Adjustment Planning.** Syracuse: Syracuse University Press, 1966, 214 p.

A detailed, scholarly study of the role played by the Mexican Government in shaping the country's economic structure.

Silva Herzog, Jesús. **Historia de la expropiación de las empresas petroleras.** Mexico City: Instituto Mexicano de Investigaciones Económicas, 3rd ed., 1964, 205 p.
A comprehensive study of the Mexican oil expropriation and the context in which it took place.

Silva Herzog, Jesús. **Inquietud sin tregua: ensayos y artículos escogidos, 1937-1965.** Mexico City: Cuadernos Americanos, 1965, 367 p.
A selection of essays and articles on Mexican economic and political affairs, by a distinguished Mexican intellectual who is critical of a rightward trend in governmental policy.

Singer, Morris. **Growth, Equality, and the Mexican Experience.** Austin: University of Texas Press (for the Institute of Latin American Studies), 1970, 341 p.
An attempt to discern the relationship between economic growth and equality in the Mexican experience from 1939 to 1961.

Solís M., Leopoldo. **La realidad económica mexicana: retrovisión y perspectivas.** Mexico City: Siglo Veintiuno Editores, 1970, 356 p.
An analysis of the Mexican economy, including a discussion of future prospects.

Strassmann, Wolfgang Paul. **Technological Change and Economic Development: The Manufacturing Experience of Mexico and Puerto Rico.** Ithaca: Cornell University Press, 1968, 353 p.
An inquiry into the diffusion, innovation and absorption of technology with some suggestions for improving these very imperfect processes.

Vernon, Raymond. **The Dilemma of Mexico's Development: The Roles of the Private and Public Sectors.** Cambridge: Harvard University Press, 1963, 226 p.
In this careful analysis of contemporary Mexican economic development the author concludes that the bureaucratic Mexican government, because of its unwillingness to offend existing interests, is incapable of modifying an increasingly outdated agricultural policy.

Vernon, Raymond, *ed.* **Public Policy and Private Enterprise in Mexico.** Cambridge: Harvard University Press, 1964, 324 p.
A supplement to Professor Vernon's "The Dilemma of Mexico's Development" (1963), this collection of essays examines more closely the nature of the relationship between the public and private sectors of the Mexican economy.

Wilkie, James Wallace. **The Mexican Revolution: Federal Expenditure and Social Change since 1910.** Berkeley: University of California Press, 2d rev. ed., 1970, 337 p.
Drawn from a careful examination of projected and actual budgetary expenditures, this study attempts to measure revolutionary myths against social realities.

Wionczek, Miguel S. **El nacionalismo mexicano y la inversión extranjera.** Mexico City: Siglo Veintiuno Editores, 1967, 314 p.
"Mexicanization," the gradual absorption of foreign-owned industries by the government, is studied in historical perspective in the sugar, electric and extractive industries.

Wright, Harry K. **Foreign Enterprise in Mexico.** Chapel Hill: University of North Carolina Press, 1971, 425 p.
A broad inquiry into legal, institutional and social factors that constitute the environment for investment in Mexico.

CENTRAL AMERICA

General

See also Underdeveloped Economies, p. 78; Latin America, p. 200.

Castillo, Carlos M. **Growth and Integration in Central America.** New York: Praeger, 1966, 188 p.
A carefully phrased monograph by a leading Costa Rican economist and statesman observing that there is "not as yet any real interdependence among the Central American economies and their behavior is only starting to adjust to the newly acquired dimensions."

Cochrane, James David. **The Politics of Regional Integration: The Central American Case.** New Orleans: Tulane University, 1969, 225 p.
A balanced account of the status and significance of the Central American Common Market.

Fernández-Shaw, Félix Guillermo. **La integración de Centroamérica.** Madrid: Ediciones Cultura Hispánica, 1965, 1,086 p.
An exhaustive compilation of documents pertaining to the history of the economic and political integration of Central America, each prefaced by background information.

Helfritz, Hans. **Zentralamerika: die Länderbrücke im Karibischen Raum.** Berlin: Safari-Verlag, 1963, 439 p.
Brief surveys of Costa Rica, Nicaragua, Honduras, El Salvador, Guatemala, British Honduras and Cuba.

Kennedy, Paul P. **The Middle Beat.** New York: Teachers College Press, 1971, 235 p.
A *New York Times* correspondent recalls the drama of events in Mexico, Guatemala and El Salvador from 1954 to 1965. Edited by Stanley R. Ross.

McCamant, John F. **Development Assistance in Central America.** New York: Praeger, 1968, 351 p.
A study of the impact which aid projects have had upon economic and political development in Central America.

McClelland, Donald H. **The Central American Common Market.** New York: Praeger, 1972, 243 p.
A detailed discussion of the experience in economic integration in Central America.

Orantes, Isaac Cohen. **Regional Integration in Central America.** Lexington (Mass.): Lexington Books, 1972, 126 p.
An informative overview and synthesis.

Parker, Franklin Dallas. **The Central American Republics.** New York: Oxford University Press (for the Royal Institute of International Affairs), 1964, 348 p.
A general historical survey of Central America stressing contemporary developments in each of the five republics. The author is optimistic about future economic and political integration.

Ramsett, David E. **Regional Industrial Development in Central America.** New York: Praeger, 1969, 133 p.
A useful discussion of industrialization within the Central American Common Market countries.

Rodríguez, Mario. **Central America.** Englewood Cliffs: Prentice-Hall, 1965, 178 p.
In this survey of Central American history the author optimistically assesses those political and economic factors binding the nations together, while warning that U.S. policies, in emphasizing military solutions, can only undermine "the moderate democratic elements, and force them into the neutralist camp."

Torres-Rivas, Edelberto. **Procesos y estructuras de una sociedad dependiente (centroamericana).** Santiago: Ediciones Prensa Latinoamericana, 1969, 210 p.
A leftist view of the history of Central America, with emphasis on the economic structure of the area, economic change, and the effects of these factors on politics and social life.

Villagrán Kramer, Francisco. **Integración económica centroamericana: aspectos sociales y políticos.** Guatemala: Universidad de San Carlos de Guatemala, 1967, 374 p.
An analysis of the structure of the Central American Common Market.

Wynia, Gary W. **Politics and Planners: Economic Development Policy in Central America.** Madison: University of Wisconsin Press, 1972, 227 p.
A study of the role of the *técnicos* in relation to the Central American Common Market and regional development in the Isthmus area.

Zeledón, Marco Tulio. **La ODECA: sus antecedentes históricos y su aporte al derecho internacional americano.** San José: Colegio de Abogados de Costa Rica, 1966, 192 p.
A history of proposals and attempts to form Central American regional institutions between 1824 and the mid-1960s. The author is a former Secretary General of the Organization of Central American States.

British Honduras

See also Inter-American Relations, p. 193; Latin America, p. 200; (Central America) General, p. 295.

Gall, Francis. **Belice, tierra nuestra.** Guatemala: Centro Editiorial José de Pineda Ibarra, 1962, 197 p.
   A documented presentation of the Guatemalan view of the British Honduras problem in Central American relations.
Gregg, Algar Robert. **British Honduras.** London: H.M.S.O., 1968, 158 p.
   A brief but solid survey of the historical, political, economic and social development of British Honduras.
Minkel, Clarence W. and Alderman, Ralph H. **A Bibliography of British Honduras, 1900-1970.** East Lansing: Latin American Studies Center, Michigan State University, 1970, 93 p.
   An unannotated, but most useful bioliography.

Costa Rica

See also Food and Agriculture, p. 68; Inter-American Relations, p. 193; Latin America, p. 200; (Central America) General, p. 295.

Arias Sánchez, Oscar. **Grupos de presión en Costa Rica.** San José (Costa Rica): Editorial Costa Rica, 1971, 130 p.
   Although primarily a theoretical discussion of the nature and function of interest groups in modern society, this study presents some empirical material on Costa Rican interest groups.
Bell, John Patrick. **Crisis in Costa Rica: The 1948 Revolution.** Austin: University of Texas Press (for the Institute of Latin American Studies), 1971, 192 p.
   The most thorough account yet available concerning the origins and role of the National Liberation Movement in Costa Rica and the rise of José Figueres to political preëminence.
Blutstein, Howard I. and Others. **Area Handbook for Costa Rica.** Washington: G.P.O., 1970, 323 p.
   A useful compendium of information on Costa Rica, including an extensive bibliography. Prepared by the Foreign Area Studies of the American University.

Guatemala

See also Economic Growth and Development, p. 71; Inter-American Relations, p. 193; Latin America, p. 200; (Central America) General, p. 295.

Adams, Richard Newbold. **Crucifixion by Power: Essays on Guatemalan National Social Structure, 1944-1966.** Austin: University of Texas Press, 1970, 553 p.
   A distinguished social anthropologist analyzes Guatemalan peasant life and development using the power structure on the national level as a framework.
Dombrowski, John and Others. **Area Handbook for Guatemala.** Washington: G.P.O., 1970, 361 p.
   A useful compendium of information on Guatemala, with an extensive bibliography. Prepared by the Foreign Area Studies at the American University.
Galeano, Eduardo. **Guatemala: clave de Latinoamérica.** Montevideo: Ediciones de la Banda Oriental, 1967, 166 p.
   A polemic denouncing political repression and imperialist influence in Guatemala.
Maestre Alfonso, Juan. **Guatemala: subdesarrollo y violencia.** Madrid: I.E.P.A.L., 1969, 250 p.
   A general introduction to Guatemala. The influence of the United States and of foreign business interests is seen as a primary cause of Guatemala's underdevelopment and political instability.
Melville, Thomas and Melville, Marjorie. **Guatemala: The Politics of Land Ownership.** New York: The Free Press, 1971, 320 p.

In this study of contemporary Guatemala two former Catholic missionaries with first-hand experience in Guatemala express their concern about the country's social, economic and political inequities.

Paredes Moreira, José Luis. **Reforma agraria: una experiencia en Guatemala.** Guatemala: Universidad de San Carlos de Guatemala, 1963, 195 p.

An analysis and defense of the Guatemalan agrarian reform program of the Arbenz government and a criticism of subsequent agrarian policy.

Rodman, Selden. **The Guatemala Traveler: A Concise History and Guide.** New York: Meredith Press, 1967, 127 p.

An introduction to the Guatemalan past and present, designed for both student and traveler, and marked with perceptive comments on Guatemalan political developments.

Ydígoras Fuentes, Miguel with Rosenthal, Mario. **My War with Communism.** Englewood Cliffs: Prentice-Hall, 1963, 238 p.

A former president of Guatemala describes his years in office and the unceasing internal pressures from Castro's Cuba.

Honduras

See also Inter-American Relations, p. 193; Latin America, p. 200; (Central America) General, p. 295.

Blutstein, Howard I. and Others. **Area Handbook for Honduras.** Washington: G.P.O., 1971, 225 p.

A useful compendium of information on Honduras, including an extensive bibliography. Prepared by the Foreign Area Studies of the American University.

Hidalgo, Carlos F. **De estructura económica y Banca Central: la experiencia de Honduras.** Madrid: Gráficas Ibarra, 1963, 133 p.

A well-documented study of the economic structure of Honduras and of the policies of the Central Bank since 1950. The author calls for more vigorous development efforts and for measures to diversify the economy.

Mariñas Otero, Luis. **Las constituciones de Honduras.** Madrid: Ediciones Cultura Hispánica, 1962, 466 p.

An indispensable reference volume containing the texts of the constitutions and fundamental charters adopted by Honduras. Of particular importance are the preliminary remarks that contain valuable information about the political and historical developments of the country.

Mariñas Otero, Luis. **Honduras.** Madrid: Ediciones Cultura Hispánica, 1963, 399 p.

A survey of Honduras from pre-Colombian times to the 1960s.

Paredes, Lucas. **Liberalismo y nacionalismo: transfugismo político.** Tegucigalpa: Imprenta Honduras, 1963, 399 p.

A political history of Honduras between the 1930s and 1960s.

Zaldívar Guzmán, Raul. **Liberalismo en Honduras.** Tegucigalpa: Asociación Liberal de Profesionales, 1964, 104 p.

A collection of articles originally published in *El Pueblo*, the official organ of the Liberal Party, dealing with the history, programs and principles of the Liberal Party.

Nicaragua

See also Inter-American Relations, p. 193; Latin America, p. 200; (Central America) General, p. 295.

Chamorro Cardenal, Pedro Joaquín. **Diario de un preso.** Managua: Editorial Nuevos Horizontes, 1963, 232 p.

A critic of the Somozas presents his views on politics and the corruption of the ruling regime, taken from notes he wrote while in prison.

Cuadra Pasos, Carlos. **Historia de medio siglo.** Managua: Editorial Unión, 1964, 2d ed., 173 p.

A study of Nicaraguan politics and foreign relations between 1900 and the 1930s, by a conservative ex-Foreign Minister.

Kamman, William. **A Search for Stability: United States Diplomacy Toward Nicaragua, 1925-1933.** Notre Dame: University of Notre Dame Press, 1968, 263 p.
A detailed, ponderous study, including a useful, critical bibliography.

Macaulay, Neill. **The Sandino Affair.** Chicago: Quadrangle Books, 1967, 319 p.
A detailed study of Augusto C. Sandino's military activities against the U.S. Marines from 1927 until his death in 1933. The author sees Sandinismo as one of the nationalistic precursors "of modern revolutionary guerrilla warfare" and condemns the role of the United States in Nicaragua during that period.

Murillo Valladares, Gilberto. **Transición.** Managua: Editora Nacional de Publicaciones, 1963, 214 p.
A defense of the Somoza governments in the period from 1950 to 1963.

Ryan, John Morris and Others. **Area Handbook for Nicaragua.** Washington: G.P.O., 1970, 393 p.
A useful compendium of information on Nicaragua, with bibliographies. Prepared by Johnson Research Associates for the American University.

Panama

See also Inter-American Relations, p. 193; Latin America, p. 200; (Central America) General, p. 295.

Alba C., Manuel María. **Cronología de los gobernantes de Panamá, 1510-1967.** Panama City: Imprenta Nacional, 1967, 399 p.
A reference work providing basic information on the men who have governed Panama since 1510.

Castillero R., Ernesto J. **El Canal de Panamá.** Panama City: Editora Humanidad, 1964, 204 p.
An introductory history of the Panama Canal, covering the period from Colonial times to 1964.

Guizado, José Ramón. **El extraño asesinato del Presidente Remón.** Barcelona: Editorial Linomonograph, 1964, 295 p.
A detailed study of the assassination of President Remón. The author was the first Vice President of Panama under Remón.

Fernández-Shaw, Félix Guillermo. **Panamá y sus relaciones centroamericanas.** Madrid: Ediciones Cultura Hispánica, 1964, 329 p.
An analysis of Panama's attitudes toward Central American integration movements since World War II. The author, a Spanish diplomat, sees Panama becoming more favorable to integration.

Klette, Immanuel J. **From Atlantic to Pacific: A New Interocean Canal.** New York: Harper and Row (for the Council on Foreign Relations), 1967, 143 p.
A careful exploration of the major alternatives faced by the United States in planning the construction of a new sea-level waterway.

Liss, Sheldon B. **The Canal: Aspects of United States-Panamanian Relations.** Notre Dame: University of Notre Dame Press, 1967, 310 p.
A useful survey, including excerpts from treaties between the United States and Panama, the United States and Colombia, and Colombia and Panama.

Mellander, Gustavo Adolfo. **The United States in Panamanian Politics: The Intriguing Formative Years.** Danville (Ill.): Interstate Printers and Publishers, 1971, 215 p.
This account of the U.S. presence in Panamanian affairs from 1903-08 serves as useful background for contemporary Canal negotiations.

Niemeier, Jean Gilbreath. **The Panama Story.** Portland (Ore.): Metropolitan Press, 1968, 303 p.
This informative history, drawn primarily from the files of the *Star and Herald* of Panama City and its Spanish sister-paper, *La Estrella de Panamá*, covers the period from 1849 to the present.

Panamá y los Estados Unidos de América ante el problema del Canal. Panama City: Imprenta Nacional (for the Panamá Universidad, Facultad de Derecho y Ciencias Políticas), 1966, 523 p.

A collection of documents and articles stating the Panamanian case in the Canal dispute.

Pippin, Larry LaRae. **The Remón Era: An Analysis of a Decade of Events in Panama, 1947-1957.** Stanford: Institute of Hispanic American and Luso-Brazilian Studies, 1964, 200 p.
A detailed study of contemporary Panamanian political history.

Weil, Thomas E. and Others. **Area Handbook for Panama.** Washington: G.P.O., rev. ed., 1972, 415 p.
A useful compendium of information on Panama, with an extensive bibliography. Prepared by the Foreign Area Studies at the American University.

El Salvador

See also Economic Growth and Development, p. 71; Inter-American Relations, p. 193; Latin America, p. 200; (Central America) General, p. 295.

Blutstein, Howard I. and Others. **Area Handbook for El Salvador.** Washington: G.P.O., 1971, 259 p.
A useful compendium of information on El Salvador, including an extensive bibliography. Prepared by the Foreign Area Studies of the American University.

Browning, David. **El Salvador: Landscape and History.** Oxford: Clarendon Press, 1971, 329 p.
A well-researched monograph on land use in El Salvador from pre-Columbian era to the present. An indispensable reference for the student of contemporary history of El Salvador.

Raynolds, David R. **Rapid Development in Small Economies: The Example of El Salvador.** New York: Praeger, 1967, 124 p.
El Salvador's experience stimulates a former U.S. embassy official to think about the advantages of small economies.

Spaeth, Carl B.; Manning, Bayless and Rowles, James P. **The El Salvador-Honduras Conflict of 1969 and the International Legal Process.** Stanford: Stanford School of Law, 1971, 329 p.
A precise inquiry "into the nature of the specific successes achieved and the specific failures suffered by the OAS at various stages in the dispute—both before and after the invasion."

WEST INDIES AND THE CARIBBEAN

General

See also Underdeveloped Economies, p. 78; (International Organization and Government) General, p. 96; Inter-American Relations, p. 193; Latin America, p. 200.

Bell, Wendell, ed. **The Democratic Revolution in the West Indies: Studies in Nationalism, Leadership, and the Belief in Progress.** Cambridge: Schenkman Publishing Co., 1967, 232 p.
These essays examine the nature of the West Indian élites and the impact nationalism had upon the region during the more optimistic early 1960s.

Bosch, Juan. **De Cristóbal Colón a Fidel Castro: el Caribe, frontera imperial.** Madrid: Ediciones Alfaguara, 1970, 740 p.
A general history of the Caribbean from the discovery to the present.

Comitas, Lambros. **Caribbeana 1900-1965: A Topical Bibliography.** Seattle: University of Washington Press (for the Research Institute for the Study of Man), 1968, 909 p.
This important bibliography on the non-Hispanic territories of the Caribbean is arranged by subject and contains over 7000 references to books, monographs, reports, articles and miscellaneous publications. There are author and geographical indexes.

Corkran, Herbert, Jr. **Patterns of International Cooperation in the Caribbean, 1942–1969.** Dallas: Southern Methodist University Press, 1970, 285 p.
 The author describes regional integration strategies and alignments against the background of earlier Caribbean organizations.

Crassweller, Robert D. **The Caribbean Community.** New York: Praeger (for the Council on Foreign Relations), 1972, 470 p.
 The author of this study urges the development of a "Caribbean Community" characterized by greatly increased regional coördination and joint action over a wide range of economic and social activities.

De Kadt, Emanuel J., *ed.* **Patterns of Foreign Influence in the Caribbean.** New York: Oxford University Press (for the Royal Institute of International Affairs), 1972, 188 p.
 Interesting essays on geopolitical relationships and the U.S. role in the Caribbean accompany studies of Jamaica, Cuba, Guatemala and the Dutch and French Caribbean.

Henry, Zin. **Labour Relations and Industrial Conflict in Commonwealth Caribbean Countries.** Port-of-Spain (Trinidad): Columbus Publishers, 1972, 283 p.
 The subject of this study is important, among other reasons, because of the intimate connection between the labor-union movement and the political process in the Commonwealth Caribbean.

Knowles, Yereth Kahn. **Beyond the Caribbean States: A History of Regional Cooperation in the Commonwealth Caribbean.** San German (Puerto Rico): Caribbean Institute and Study Center for Latin America, 1972, 275 p.
 The author of this history of the "efforts to bring unity of some kind to the British Caribbean area" argues that "neo-colonialism" limits the region's potential for true integration.

Mitchell, Sir Harold Paton, 1st Bart. **Contemporary Politics and Economics in the Caribbean.** Athens: Ohio University Press, 1968, 520 p.
 Each Caribbean country and territory is competently considered in its political and economic aspects. Region-wide analyses are also provided in particular fields. A useful volume.

Mitchell, Sir Harold Paton, 1st Bart. **Europe in the Caribbean.** Geneva: Institut Universitaire de Hautes Études Internationales, 1963, 211 p.
 A doctoral thesis which surveys the colonial policies of Britain, France and the Netherlands in the Caribbean, with particular emphasis upon contemporary developments.

Mordecai, Sir John. **Federation of the West Indies.** Evanston: Northwestern University Press, 1968, 484 p.
 One of the leading proponents of the West Indian federalist movement examines its failure.

Perkins, Dexter. **The United States and the Caribbean.** Cambridge: Harvard University Press, rev. ed., 1967, 197 p.
 A revised and updated version of an earlier study (1947) by a well-informed and respected scholar.

Rickards, Colin. **Caribbean Power.** London: Dobson, 1963, 247 p.
 A London correspondent in the Caribbean gives interesting, lively, but abbreviated sketches of 23 leaders.

Segal, Aaron. **Politics and Population in the Caribbean.** Río Piedras: University of Puerto Rico, Institute of Caribbean Studies, 1969, 158 p.

———. **Politics of Caribbean Economic Integration.** Río Piedras: University of Puerto Rico, Institute of Caribbean Studies, 1968, 156 p.
 Useful studies of contemporary Caribbean political, social and economic problems.

Sherlock, Philip Manderson. **West Indies.** New York: Walker, 1966, 215 p.
 A readable introductory survey of the history and contemporary political, social, cultural and economic problems of the West Indies, by a noted Jamaican scholar and academician.

Szulc, Tad, *ed.* **The United States and the Caribbean.** Englewood Cliffs: Prentice Hall, 1971, 212 p.
 These papers by Caribbean specialists were prepared for the thirty-eighth American Assembly in October–November 1970.

Theberge, James D., ed. **Soviet Seapower in the Caribbean: Political and Strategic Implications.** New York: Praeger (in coöperation with the Center for Strategic and International Studies, Georgetown University), 1972, 175 p.
A useful volume, of particular interest to students of developments in U.S.-Soviet relations in the Caribbean.

Wilgus, Alva Curtis, ed. **The Caribbean.** Gainsville: University of Florida Press, 1951-67, 17 v.
Papers presented at the annual Caribbean conferences at the University of Florida, covering a wide range of subjects.

Williams, Eric Eustace. **From Columbus to Castro: The History of the Caribbean, 1492-1969.** New York: Harper and Row, 1971, 576 p.
A substantial history by the Prime Minister of Trinidad and Tobago.

Cuba

General

See also The Problem of Authority; Violence and Revolution, p. 34; Latin America, p. 200; (The United States) Foreign Policy, p. 229; (Mexico) Foreign Relations, p. 290; (West Indies and the Caribbean) General, p. 300.

Aguilar, Luis E. **Cuba 1933: Prologue to Revolution.** Ithaca: Cornell University Press, 1972, 256 p.
An analysis of the 1933 Cuban Revolution by a Cuban-born and Cuban-trained scholar now living in the United States. The author argues that the 1933 events "formed the essential prologue" for Castro's take-over and he pays particular attention to the activities of Sumner Welles, the American ambassador in Havana at that time.

Alvarez Díaz, José R. and Others. **Cuba: geopolítica y pensamiento económico.** Miami: Colegio de Economistas de Cuba en el Exilio, 1964, 576 p.
An attempt to relate the history of the development of the Cuban economy and Cuban economic thought to the island's geopolitical setting. The authors argue that Castro's relationship with the Soviet bloc is contrary to Cuba's economic and political interests.

Alvarez Díaz, José R., ed. **A Study on Cuba.** Coral Gables: University of Miami Press, 1965, 774 p.
An abridged English translation of a statistical survey of the development of the Cuban economy, past and present. The book first appeared as "Un estudio sobre Cuba; colonia, república, experimento socialista: estructura económica, desarrollo institucional, socialismo y regresión" (Coral Gables: University of Miami Press, for the Grupo Cubano de Investigaciones Económicas de University of Miami, 1963, 1,703 p.).

Batista y Zaldivar, Fulgencio. **The Growth and Decline of the Cuban Republic.** New York: Devin-Adair, 1964, 300 p.
The former chief of state of Cuba reflects on his regime and on the reasons for his deposal. The Spanish original was published as "Piedras y leyes" (Mexico City: Ediciones Botas, 1961, 495 p.).

Blutstein, Howard I. and Others. **Area Handbook for Cuba.** Washington: G.P.O., 1971, 505 p.
A useful compendium of information on Cuba, including an extensive bibliography. Prepared by the Foreign Area Studies at the American University.

García Montes, Jorge and Alonso Avila, Antonio. **Historia del Partido Comunista de Cuba.** Miami: Rema Press, 1970, 559 p.
A history of the Communist Party of Cuba and its precursors from 1860 to 1961. The authors are anti-Castro Cuban exiles.

Guerra y Sánchez, Ramiro. **Sugar and Society in the Caribbean: An Economic History of Cuban Agriculture.** New Haven: Yale University Press, 1964, 218 p.
With a useful background provided by Sidney W. Mintz, this translation of a classic study on the Cuban economy by a noted Cuban historian remains as valuable today as when first published in 1927 as "Azúcar y población en las Antillas."

Langley, Lester D. **The Cuban Policy of the United States: A Brief History.** New York: Wiley, 1968, 203 p.
A solid, factual survey.

Le Riverend, Julio. **Historia económica de Cuba.** Havana: Editorial Nacional de Cuba, 2d ed., 1965, 280 p.
A Marxist interpretation of Cuban economic history from colonial times to the Castro Revolution.

Plank, John Nathan, ed. **Cuba and the United States: Long-Range Perspectives.** Washington: Brookings Institution, 1967, 265 p.
Substantial studies examining various aspects of Cuban-U.S. relations. Of particular interest are the essay by Henry Wriston dealing with the historical framework and Bayless Manning's overall summarization of the Cuban problem.

Riera Hernández, Mario. **Historial obrero cubano, 1574–1965.** Miami: Rema Press, 1965, 303 p.
A history of the Cuban labor movement, mainly of the twentieth century pre-Castro period.

Santovenia, Emeterio S. and Shelton, Raúl M. **Cuba y su historia.** Miami: Rema Press, 1965, 3 v.
A comprehensive history of Cuba from pre-discovery to Fidel Castro.

Thomas, Hugh. **Cuba: The Pursuit of Freedom.** New York: Harper and Row, 1971, 1,696 p.
A majestic study of Cuban history since 1762, with somewhat lesser stress upon the period since 1960.

The Castro Regime

See also Population Problems, p. 47; United Nations, p. 99; The Postwar World, p. 178; Inter-American Relations, p. 193; Latin America, p. 200; (The United States) Foreign Policy, p. 229; (Canada) Foreign Relations, p. 282; Guatemala, p. 297; (West Indies and the Caribbean) General, p. 300; (Bolivia) Government and Politics, p. 320; (Chile) Foreign Relations, p. 332; (Union of Soviet Socialist Republics) Foreign Policy, p. 550.

Aranda, Sergio. **La revolución agraria en Cuba.** Mexico City: Siglo Veintiuno Editores, 1968, 240 p.
A sympathetic account of agrarian reform in Cuba, including a discussion of the social effects of the program.

Arredondo, Alberto. **Reforma agraria: la experiencia cubana.** Río Piedras (Puerto Rico): Editorial San Juan, 1969, 318 p.
A polemical study that concludes that Cuba's agrarian reform has been a failure. The reason for its lack of success is its dogmatic adherence to Marxist-Leninist precepts.

Bonsal, Philip W. **Cuba, Castro, and the United States.** Pittsburgh: University of Pittsburgh Press, 1971, 318 p.
A former U.S. Ambassador to Cuba has written an eloquent first-hand account of Castroite Cuba and its relations with its northern neighbor.

Boorstein, Edward. **The Economic Transformation of Cuba.** New York: Monthly Review Press, 1968, 303 p.
A defense of Cuba's socialist experiment, based on the author's experiences in Cuba from 1960 to 1963.

Castro, Fidel. **Revolutionary Struggle: Volume I (1947–1958) of the Selected Works of Fidel Castro.** Cambridge: M.I.T. Press, 1972, 471 p.
A useful and substantial collection of Castro's numerous communications, from ten-line personal letters to "History Will Absolve Me," preceded by more than 100 pages of historical and biographical material. Edited by Rolando E. Bonachea and Nelson P. Valdés.

Clytus, John and Rieker, Jane. **Black Man in Red Cuba.** Coral Gables: University of Miami Press, 1970, 158 p.
A cry of disillusionment from an American Black who sought justice in Castro's Cuba.

Dewart, Leslie. **Christianity and Revolution: The Lesson of Cuba.** New York: Herder & Herder, 1963, 320 p.
A philosophical enquiry into the Cuban Revolution and its relations with the Catholic Church.

Draper, Theodore. **Castroism: Theory and Practice.** New York: Praeger, 1965, 263 p.
As with the author's earlier volume on the Cuban Revolution, this concise analytical study on the nature of Castro's Cuba and its peculiar relationship to the communist movement is essential reading for the serious student of Latin American affairs.

Dumont, René. **Cuba: socialisme et développement.** Paris: Éditions du Seuil, 1964, 189 p.
A sympathetic assessment of the Cuban Revolution and its failings in the agricultural sector.

Fagen, Richard R. and Others. **Cubans in Exile: Disaffection and the Revolution.** Stanford: Stanford University Press, 1968, 161 p.
A statistical survey, based on questionnaires, of the attitudes of Cuban exiles in the United States concerning the Castro Revolution. A final chapter considers the meaning and consequences of the exodus.

Fagen, Richard R. **The Transformation of Political Culture in Cuba.** Stanford: Stanford University Press, 1969, 271 p.
A scholarly study, basically sympathetic, of what the author deems "the most profound social transformation ever seen in the Americas."

Franco, Victor. **The Morning After: A French Journalist's Impressions of Cuba Under Castro.** New York: Praeger, 1963, 248 p.
A French correspondent writes of his personal experiences in Cuba during 1961 and bitterly relates how enthusiasm for the Castro régime became complete disillusionment. The French original appeared as "La Révolution sensuelle" (Paris: Grasset, 1962, 334 p.).

Furtak, Robert K. **Kuba und der Weltkommunismus.** Opladen: Westdeutscher Verlag, 1967, 194 p.
A solid study of the Cuban Revolution. The author argues that Havana has become the fourth center of world communism, next to Moscow, Peking and Belgrade, and describes the growing reliance of Latin American communists on Cuban leadership.

Gambini, Hugo. **El Ché Guevara.** Buenos Aires: Editorial Paidós, 1968, 513 p.
A biography of Ché Guevara beginning with his youth in Argentina and ending with his attempt to form a guerrilla movement in Bolivia.

Goldenberg, Boris. **The Cuban Revolution and Latin America.** New York: Praeger, 1965, 376 p.
A knowledgeable study of Latin America's social and political problems, and the background and evolution of Castro's Revolution, by a Russian-born, German-educated author who spent the years 1941–1960 in Cuba. The German original appeared as "Lateinamerika und die Kubanische Revolution" (Cologne: Kiepenheuer, 1963, 519 p.).

Guevara, Ernesto. **Che: Selected Works of Ernesto Guevara.** Cambridge: M.I.T. Press, 1969, 456 p.
A collection of the writings, speeches, interviews and letters of Ché Guevara. The Bolivian diary is not included. Edited by Rolando E. Bonachea and Nelson P. Valdés.

Halperin, Maurice. **The Rise and Decline of Fidel Castro: An Essay in Contemporary History.** Berkeley: University of California Press, 1972, 380 p.
The author, six years a resident of Cuba, describes the rise of Castro and adumbrates the decline of the Revolution. The period covered is 1959–1964; a companion volume will follow. The analysis is good and so is the extensive selection of speeches and documents.

James, Daniel. **Ché Guevara: A Biography.** New York: Stein and Day, 1969, 380 p.
A full-length study of the myth-enshrouded *guerrillero* whom the author sees as "more the apostle of violence than the maker of revolution, more the agent of destruction than the builder of a continent."

Johnson, Haynes Bonner and Others. **The Bay of Pigs: The Leaders' Story of Brigade 2506.** New York: Norton, 1964, 368 p.

This detailed account of the abortive invasion of Cuba is based primarily on interviews with the leaders Manuel Artime, José Peréz San Román, Erneido Oliva, and Enrique Ruiz-Williams, and the survivors of the highly idealistic but inadequately prepared Brigade 2506.

Karol, K. S., *pseud.* (Karol Kewes). **Guerrillas in Power: The Course of the Cuban Revolution.** New York: Hill and Wang, 1970, 624 p.
A notable contribution to the history of the Revolution, blending love of its lost possibilities with rancorous dislike and distrust of the Soviet Union; written with a pro-Maoist bias. The French original appeared as "Les Guérilleros au pouvoir; l'itinéraire politique de la révolution cubaine" (Paris: Laffont, 1970, 606 p.).

Krakau, Knud. **Die Kubanische Revolution und die Monroe Doktrin: eine Herausforderung der Aussenpolitik der Vereinigten Staaten.** Frankfurt/Main: Metzner, 1968, 220 p.
A well-documented study of the application by the United States of the Monroe Doctrine to Castro's Cuba.

Lataste Hoffer, Alban. **Cuba: ¿Hacia una nueva economía política del socialismo?** Santiago: Editorial Universitaria, 1968, 177 p.
A sympathetic study of Cuba's attempt to construct a socialist economy, with emphasis on Cuba's deviation from European models.

Lazo, Mario. **Dagger in the Heart: American Policy Failures in Cuba.** New York: Funk & Wagnalls, 1968, 426 p.
A former Havana lawyer, born, raised and educated in the United States, assesses the "totalitarian" nature of Castro's Cuba. He believes that the liberal establishment in the United States was the basic factor which "delivered Cuba to Communism."

Lockwood, Lee. **Castro's Cuba, Cuba's Fidel.** New York: Macmillan, 1967, 288 p.
An American journalist's report and pictorial study of contemporary Cuba, drawn largely from a trip made during 1965. The book depicts the human side of the Cuban Revolution, and includes lengthy and informative interviews with Fidel Castro.

López-Fresquet, Rufo. **My 14 Months with Castro.** Cleveland: World Publishing Co., 1966, 223 p.
Cuba's Minister of the Treasury from January 8, 1959 to March 17, 1960, who subsequently left the country, has written a useful account of his experience. Commissioned by the Hoover Institution on War, Revolution, and Peace at Stanford University.

Macaulay, Neill. **A Rebel in Cuba: An American's Memoir.** Chicago: Quadrangle Books, 1970, 199 p.
An American who fought in Castro's rebel army describes his experiences and offers his interpretations of the Cuban Revolution.

Mallin, Jay. **Fortress Cuba: Russia's American Base.** Chicago: Regnery, 1965, 192 p.
Journalistic reflections on the communist takeover in Cuba and the subversive Soviet operations in the Western Hemisphere. The author asks the United States to return to the policies of Teddy Roosevelt.

Matthews, Herbert Lionel. **Fidel Castro.** New York: Simon and Schuster, 1969, 382 p.
An admiring biography by the veteran *New York Times* correspondent whose dispatches from the Sierra Maestra in 1957 brought Fidel Castro to general public notice.

Meneses, Enrique. **Fidel Castro.** New York: Taplinger, 1968, 238 p.
An assessment of Castroism by a journalist for *Paris Match* who was in the Sierra Maestra from December 1957 through March 1958. The original appeared as "Fidel Castro: siete años de poder" (Madrid: Aguado, 1966, 270 p.).

Mesa-Lago, Carmelo. **The Labor Sector and Socialist Distribution in Cuba.** New York: Praeger (for the Hoover Institution on War, Revolution, and Peace), 1968, 250 p.
In this well-documented study of the economic conditions in Castro's Cuba the author concludes that "the uprooting of private property and individual material interest and the substitution of collective property and social-moral interest . . . precipitated immediate drops in production, productivity, and quality."

Mesa-Lago, Carmelo. **Revolutionary Change in Cuba.** Pittsburgh: University of Pittsburgh Press, 1971, 544 p.
Essays on political, social and economic aspects in contemporary Cuba.

Monahan, James and Gilmore, Kenneth O. **The Great Deception: The Inside Story of How the Kremlim Took Over Cuba.** New York: Farrar, Straus, 1963, 213 p.
Two editors of the *Reader's Digest* reconstruct, chiefly on the basis of interviews with exiled Cubans, the dismal course of the Cuban Revolution since the beginning of 1959.

Nelson, Lowry. **Cuba: The Measure of a Revolution.** Minneapolis: University of Minnesota Press, 1972, 242 p.
A well-known sociologist, returning to the subject of his classic study of rural Cuba, examines Castro's Revolution. His assessment: "deprivation, disillusionment, and increasing suppression."

O'Connor, James R. **The Origins of Socialism in Cuba.** Ithaca: Cornell University Press, 1970, 338 p.
A laudatory explanation of Cuban developments since 1959, rooted in the premise that only through socialism could ancient ills be overcome.

Petit, Antoine G. **Castro, Debray contre le marxisme-léninisme: lettres à un ami vénézuélien.** Paris: Laffont, 1968, 206 p.
A Haitian exile, with personal experiences in both Cuba and China, denies the validity of viewing the Cuban Revolution in Maoist terms. He also rejects Castroism as a possible model for contemporary Latin America.

Phillips, R. Hart. **The Cuban Dilemma.** New York: Obolensky, 1963, 357 p.
This first-hand account of the Castro régime traces its consolidation of power and the domination of the revolution by communism. A provocative book, published after Mrs. Phillips had left Cuba and had become head of *The New York Times* bureau in Miami.

Roa, Raúl. **Retorno a la alborada.** Santa Clara (Cuba): Editora del Consejo Nacional de Universidades, 2d ed., 1964, 2 v.
A selection of the speeches and writings of Castro's Foreign Minister, including much data on foreign affairs.

Rojo, Ricardo. **My Friend Ché.** New York: Dial Press, 1968, 220 p.
An intimate story of the life and thought of Ché Guevara, by an Argentinian lawyer and long-time friend of the revolutionary. Translation of "Mi amigo el Ché" (Buenos Aires: Alvarez, 1968, 266 p.).

Ruiz, Ramón Eduardo. **Cuba: The Making of a Revolution.** Amherst: University of Massachusetts Press, 1968, 190 p.
A thoughtful examination of the social, economic and political factors responsible for the Cuban Revolution.

Sauvage, Léo. **Autopsie du castrisme.** Paris: Flammarion, 1962, 348 p.
As New York correspondent for *Le Figaro* Léo Sauvage made several visits to Cuba between January 1959 and March 1962. His book, carefully documented and convincingly argued, disputes several popular notions about relations between Castro, communism and the United States.

Seers, Dudley, *ed.* **Cuba: The Economic and Social Revolution.** Chapel Hill: University of North Carolina Press, 1964, 432 p.
This useful economic and social assessment, based on trips made to Cuba during the summer of 1962 by Dudley Seers, Andrés Bianchi, Richard Jolly and Max Nolff, and amplified by numerous statistics and charts, deals with agricultural, educational and industrial developments since the Revolution.

Semidei, Manuela. **Les États-Unis et la révolution cubaine, 1959-1964.** Paris: Colin, 1968, 207 p.
The author contends that the United States was unable to accept an "independent" Cuba and that its determination to retain "colonial" controls forced Castro to seek new alliances.

Smith, Earl E. T. **The Fourth Floor: An Account of the Castro Communist Revolution.** New York: Random House, 1963, 242 p.
A subjective but interesting first-hand account of the Castro Revolution during its formative years, 1957-59, by the United States Ambassador to Cuba at the time.

Suárez, Andrés. **Cuba: Castroism and Communism, 1959-1966.** Cambridge: M.I.T. Press, 1967, 266 p.

A thoughtful assessment of the Cuban Revolution, by a former member of the Castro government. Based upon a close study of the Cuban press and personal experiences, the author views a charismatic Castro's reluctance to delegate authority and institutionalize the Revolution as a reflection of his personal love of power.

Suchlicki, Jaime, ed. **Cuba, Castro, and Revolution.** Coral Gables: University of Miami Press, 1972, 250 p.
The scholarship in these seven essays devoted to political, social and economic structures in Cuba is solid and well-grounded. Three of them focus on the Soviet presence in the Revolution.

Suchlicki, Jaime. **University Students and Revolution in Cuba, 1920–1968.** Coral Gables: University of Miami Press, 1969, 177 p.
A balanced account, free of fanaticism and dogma, of the student movement in the context of Cuban life.

Sutherland, Elizabeth. **The Youngest Revolution: A Personal Report on Cuba.** New York: Dial Press, 1969, 277 p.
This account of Cuba under Castro is impressionistic, reportorial, subjective and sympathetic to the Revolution.

Tetlow, Edwin. **Eye on Cuba.** New York: Harcourt, Brace and World, 1966, 291 p.
A British journalist assesses the human costs of the Cuban Revolution.

Torres Ramírez, Blanca. **Las relaciones cubano-soviéticas (1959–1968).** Mexico City: Colegio de México, Centro de Estudios Internacionales, 1971, 142 p.
An analysis of relations between the Soviet Union and Castro's Cuba. The study focuses on the apparent contradiction between Cuba's economic and military dependence and its political and ideological independence.

Urrutia Lleó, Manuel. **Fidel Castro & Company, Inc.: Communist Tyranny in Cuba.** New York: Praeger, 1964, 217 p.
A bitter personal account of the Cuban Revolution betrayed, written by the man who was Castro's first president during the early months of 1959.

Valdés, Nelson P. and Lieuwen, Edwin. **The Cuban Revolution: A Research-Study Guide (1959–1969).** Albuquerque: University of New Mexico Press, 1971, 230 p.
According to the authors, "the purpose of this guide is to provide a useful bibliographical tool for all those interested in developing their interest, pursuing research, or teaching courses on the Cuban revolution."

Yglesias, José. **In the Fist of the Revolution: Life in a Cuban Country Town.** New York: Pantheon Books, 1968, 307 p.
An account of life in Cuba based on the author's experiences in the town of Mayarí in 1967.

Zeitlin, Maurice and Scheer, Robert. **Cuba: Tragedy in Our Hemisphere.** New York: Grove Press, 1963, 316 p.
The authors of this study argue that the majority of the Cuban people support and have benefited from the Revolution and that continued "misunderstanding" of the Revolution by the United States will have profound international consequences.

Zeitlin, Maurice. **Revolutionary Politics and the Cuban Working Class.** Princeton: Princeton University Press, 1967, 306 p.
Drawing on random samplings taken during the summer of 1962, the author concludes that socialization of industry and overall revolutionary ideology has had a profound and positive influence upon the Cuban working class.

Dominican Republic

See also *Inter-American Relations, p. 193; Latin America, p. 200; (The United States) Foreign Policy, p. 229; (West Indies and the Caribbean) General, p. 300; Haiti, p. 309.*

Atkins, G. Pope and Wilson, Larman C. **The United States and the Trujillo Regime.** New Brunswick: Rutgers University Press, 1972, 245 p.
A sound study of U.S.-Dominican relations during the era of Trujillo, with appropriate reference to pre-Trujillo developments.

Bosch, Juan. **Pentagonism: A Substitute for Imperialism.** New York: Grove Press, 1968, 141 p.
    A harsh criticism of U.S. policy in the Dominican Republic by ex-President Bosch. The original was published as "El Pentagonismo: sustituto del imperialismo" (Mexico City: Siglo Veintiuno Editores, 1968, 147 p.).

Bosch, Juan. **The Unfinished Experiment: Democracy in the Dominican Republic.** New York: Praeger, 1965, 239 p.
    A terse and cogent story of the post-Trujillo period, from May 1961 to May 1964. The Spanish original was published as "Crisis de la democracia de América en la República Dominicana" (Mexico City: Centro de Estudios y Documentación Sociales, 3rd ed., 1965, 226 p.).

Campillo Pérez, Julio G. **El grillo y el ruiseñor: elecciones presidenciales dominicanas.** Santo Domingo: Editora del Caribe, 1966, 366 p.
    A study of the electoral process in the Dominican Republic from 1848 to 1962, including extensive electoral statistics.

Chang-Rodríguez, Eugenio, ed. **The Lingering Crisis: A Case Study of the Dominican Republic.** New York: Las Americas Publishing Co., 1969, 178 p.
    Essays provoked by the 1965 civil war, some marked by an evident attempt at impartiality, some by visible devotion to the Bosch cause and philosophy.

Crassweller, Robert D. **Trujillo: The Life and Times of a Caribbean Dictator.** New York: Macmillan, 1966, 468 p.
    A vividly written, terse account of the Trujillo era. The author, while noting certain positive governmental actions, observes that "against these must be balanced the gravest of crimes and abuses, which outweigh the achievements."

Draper, Theodore. **The Dominican Revolt: A Case Study in American Policy.** New York: Commentary, 1968, 208 p.
    A perceptive analysis of the nature of the U.S. intervention during the Dominican crisis, based largely on articles published in *Commentary*.

Franco, Franklin J. **República Dominicana: clases, crisis y comandos.** Havana: Casa de las Américas, 1966, 274 p.
    A Marxist study of political, economic and social change in the Dominican Republic between 1930 and 1965.

Franco, Pericles A. **Mi protesta contra el golpe militar.** Santo Domingo: Editora del Caribe, 1964, 130 p.
    A collection of essays from *Listín Diario* criticizing the military coup of 1963.

Grabendorf, Wolf. **Bibliographie zu Politik und Gesellschaft der Dominikanischen Republik.** Munich: Weltforum Verlag (for the Arnold-Bergstraesser-Institut), 1973, 103 p.
    A very thorough bibliography of political, social, economic and foreign policy developments in the Dominican Republic since the fall of Trujillo. Most entries deal with the U.S. intervention in 1965.

Kurzman, Dan. **Santo Domingo: Revolt of the Damned.** New York: Putnam, 1965, 310 p.
    A sober, analytical assessment of the Dominican crisis, by a correspondent of *The Washington Post*.

Lowenthal, Abraham F. **The Dominican Intervention.** Cambridge: Harvard University Press, 1972, 246 p.
    A judicious and well-documented study of the U.S. intervention in 1965.

Martin, John Bartlow. **Overtaken by Events: The Dominican Crisis from the Fall of Trujillo to the Civil War.** Garden City: Doubleday, 1966, 821 p.
    A detailed study of the events from the assassination of Trujillo to American intervention, by a former ambassador to the Dominican Republic who later became President Johnson's personal envoy charged with resolving the political crisis.

Niedergang, Marcel. **La Révolution de Saint-Domingue.** Paris: Plon, 1966, 230 p.
    A correspondent for *Le Monde* surveys the Dominican Revolution, condemns the intervention by the United States, and concludes that these tragic events are but a further indication of the revolutionary nature of contemporary Latin America.

Pattee, Richard. **La República Dominicana.** Madrid: Ediciones Cultura Hispánica, 1967, 361 p.
A history of the Dominican Republic from discovery to 1961.

Roberts, T. D. and Others. **Area Handbook for Dominican Republic.** Washington: G.P.O., 1967, 446 p.
A useful compendium of information on the Dominican Republic, with bibliographies. Prepared by the Foreign Area Studies at the American University.

Rodman, Selden. **Quisqueya: A History of the Dominican Republic.** Seattle: University of Washington Press, 1964, 202 p.
An introductory history of the Dominican Republic.

Slater, Jerome. **Intervention and Negotiation: The United States and the Dominican Revolution.** New York: Harper and Row, 1970, 254 p.
A study of the controversial American intervention in the Dominican Republic in 1965. The approach is judicious, the tone temperate and the research soundly based.

Szulc, Tad. **Dominican Diary.** New York: Delacorte Press, 1965, 306 p.
A perceptive first-hand account of the Dominican tragedy in 1965 by a correspondent for *The New York Times*. The author contends that the U.S. inability to comprehend the nature of the struggle, caused in large measure by fear of another Cuba, resulted in actions which only strengthened extremist groups of both Left and Right.

Thomas, Aaron Joshua, Jr. and Thomas, Ann Van Wynnen. **The Dominican Republic Crisis 1965: Background Paper and Proceedings of the Ninth Hammarskjöld Forum.** Dobbs-Ferry (N.Y.): Oceana Publications (for the Association of the Bar of the City of New York), 1967, 164 p.
This background paper and the resulting panel discussion examine international legal implications of the Dominican crisis. Of particular interest is the dialogue between two Columbia University law professors—Adolf A. Berle, who defends U.S. intervention, and Wolfgang Friedmann, who denies its justification.

Wiarda, Howard J. **Dictatorship and Development: The Methods of Control in Trujillo's Dominican Republic.** Gainesville: University of Florida Press, 1968, 224 p.
A carefully researched and useful study, containing interpretations that on occasion run counter to generally held views.

Wiarda, Howard J. **The Dominican Republic: Nation in Transition.** New York: Praeger, 1969, 249 p.
A brief survey of the Dominican Republic.

Haiti

See also Inter-American Relations, p. 193; Latin America, p. 200; (West Indies and the Caribbean) General, p. 300.

Castor, Suzy. **La ocupación norteamericana de Haití y sus consecuencias, 1915-1934.** Mexico City: Siglo Veintiuno Editores, 1971, 230 p.
A leftist criticism of the United States' occupation of Haiti from 1915 to 1934. The author charges that the United States helped to prevent social change.

Diederich, Bernard and Burt, Al. **Papa Doc: The Truth about Haiti Today.** New York: McGraw-Hill, 1969, 393 p.
The rather lurid story of mid-century Haiti and Duvalier's first ten years of dictatorship. The treatment is journalistic and somewhat brash, but vivid and informed.

Duvalier, François. **Éléments d'une doctrine.** Port-au-Prince: Presses Nationales d'Haïti, 3rd ed., 1968, 921 p.

——. **La Marche à la présidence.** Port-au-Prince: Presses Nationales d'Haïti, 3rd ed., 1968, 619 p.

——. **Mémoires d'un leader du Tiers Monde: mes négociations avec le Saint-Siège; ou, une tranche d'histoire.** Paris: Hachette, 1969, 383 p.
Writings by the man who ruled Haiti from 1957 to 1971.

Leyburn, James Graham. **The Haitian People.** New Haven: Yale University Press, rev. ed., 1966, 342 p.

A new edition of a classic treatise, published originally in 1941. There is a new introduction by Sidney W. Mintz describing recent developments in Haiti and an updated bibliography.

Logan, Rayford Whittingham. **Haiti and the Dominican Republic.** New York: Oxford University Press (for the Royal Institute of International Affairs), 1968, 220 p.
A comparative political history of the two disparate countries which share the island of Hispaniola.

Moore, O. Ernest. **Haiti: Its Stagnant Society and Shackled Economy.** New York: Exposition Press, 1972, 281 p.
Authoritative but less massively detailed than the Rotberg study, this volume is a useful introduction to the many-sided Haitian dilemma.

Pierre-Charles, Gérard. **L'Économie haïtienne et sa voie de développement.** Paris: G.-P. Maisonneuve et Larose, 1967, 271 p.
A broad study of the Haitian economy and of the history of its growth. The author attributes the shortcomings of Haitian economy to American policies and the nature of the capitalist world economy.

Rotberg, Robert I. with Clague, Christopher K. **Haiti: The Politics of Squalor.** Boston: Houghton, 1971, 456 p.
An exhaustive study, researched extensively and in depth, covering almost all internal aspects of Haitian life and development.

Schaedel, Richard P., ed. **Research and Resources of Haiti.** New York: Research Institute for the Study of Man, 1969, 624 p.
Papers, some in English and some in French, providing detailed analyses of Haitian politics, demography, language and literacy, nutrition and health.

Schmidt, Hans. **The United States Occupation of Haiti, 1915–1934.** New Brunswick: Rutgers University Press, 1971, 303 p.
A well-researched account of the long Marine occupation, based on archival sources hitherto largely ignored.

Jamaica

See also Inter-American Relations, p. 193; Latin America, p. 200; (West Indies and the Caribbean) General, p. 300.

Bell, Wendell. **Jamaican Leaders: Political Attitudes in a New Nation.** Berkeley: University of California Press, 1964, 229 p.
A sociological study of Jamaican nationalism, based on interviews and questionnaires. The author expresses cautious optimism that Jamaican leaders will avoid the cynicism toward political democracy so damaging to new nations.

Black, Clinton Vane de Brosse. **The Story of Jamaica: From Prehistory to the Present.** London: Collins, rev. ed., 1965, 255 p.
An introductory survey.

Carley, Mary Manning. **Jamaica: The Old and the New.** New York: Praeger, 1963, 212 p.
A brief, sympathetic survey, with bibliography.

Hamilton, B. L. St. John. **Problems of Administration in an Emergent Nation: A Case Study of Jamaica.** New York: Praeger, 1965, 218 p.
A study examining the governmental and administrative problems of a recently independent nation.

Harrod, Jeffrey. **Trade Union Foreign Policy.** Garden City: Doubleday, 1972, 485 p.
An extensive analysis of the influence of British and American trade unions on the Jamaican labor movement. One unexpected finding: contrary to precedent in their home countries, unions and corporations tend to coöperate in foreign environments.

Nettleford, Rex M. **Identity, Race and Protest in Jamaica.** New York: Morrow, 1972, 256 p.
Essays on Jamaican social and political problems by an author whose attainments extend to fields as diverse as trade unions and the dance.

Palmer, Ransford W. **The Jamaican Economy.** New York: Praeger, 1968, 185 p.
Numerous tables accompany this technical analysis of industry, agriculture, the public sector, foreign trade and financing.

Widdicombe, Stacey H., Jr. **The Performance of Industrial Development Corporations: The Case of Jamaica.** New York: Praeger, 1972, 418 p.
An intensive inquiry into the successful Jamaican experience with institutions promoting industrial development.

Puerto Rico

See also Inter-American Relations, p. 193; Latin America, p. 200; The United States, p. 213; (West Indies and the Caribbean) General, p. 300.

Aitken, Thomas, Jr. **Poet in the Fortress: The Story of Luis Muñoz Marín.** New York: New American Library, 1964, 241 p.
A biographical eulogy of Luis Muñoz Marín, for many years the Governor of Puerto Rico and a leading figure of the Popular Democratic Party.

Anderson, Robert William. **Party Politics in Puerto Rico.** Stanford: Stanford University Press, 1965, 269 p.
A worthwhile examination of political parties in Puerto Rico—from 1940 through 1964.

Friedlander, Stanley L. **Labor Migration and Economic Growth: A Case Study of Puerto Rico.** Cambridge: M.I.T. Press, 1965, 181 p.
A theoretical analysis, buttressed with statistics, on the effects of emigration upon Puerto Rico's development. The author concludes that emigration has been beneficial to the island's people and its economy.

García Angulo, Efraín. **Puerto Rico, estado federado o república autónoma.** New York: Las Americas Publishing Co., 1964, 247 p.
A discussion of the various options—statehood, sovereignty, or association—open to Puerto Rico. The author criticizes the present legal arrangement and supports statehood.

García Passalacqua, Juan M. **La crisis política en Puerto Rico, 1962-1966.** San Juan: Ediciones Edil, 1970, 184 p.
An account of politics in Puerto Rico between 1962-1966, by a member of the P.P.D. (Partido Popular Democrático).

Goodsell, Charles True. **Administration of a Revolution.** Cambridge: Harvard University Press, 1965, 254 p.
Professor Goodsell argues that Governor Tugwell's efforts in restructuring an essentially colonial political bureaucracy into an effective administrative apparatus provided the basis for Puerto Rico's rapid socio-economic development under the leadership of Muñoz Marín.

Lewis, Gordon K. **Puerto Rico: Freedom and Power in the Caribbean.** New York: Monthly Review Press, 1963, 626 p.
A British author concludes that Puerto Rico's peculiar political arrangement with the United States has had a retarding effect upon the island's long-term economic progress and upon the cultural integrity of the Puerto Rican people.

Liebman, Arthur. **The Politics of Puerto Rican University Students.** Austin: University of Texas Press (for the Institute of Latin American Studies), 1970, 205 p.
The author demonstrates that students at the University of Puerto Rico, unlike their activist Latin American peers, are moderate and career-oriented, reflecting a pragmatic and basically conservative society.

López Tamés, Román. **El estado libre asociado de Puerto Rico.** Oviedo (Spain): Publicaciones del Instituto de Estudios Jurídicos, 1965, 284 p.
A study of the legal status of Puerto Rico as a Commonwealth and as an independent nation.

Maldonado-Denis, Manuel. **Puerto Rico: mito y realidad.** Barcelona: Ediciones Peninsula, 1969, 269 p.

A Puerto Rican nationalist and advocate of independence denounces U.S. imperialism in Puerto Rico.

Maldonado-Denis, Manuel. **Puerto Rico: A Socio-Historic Interpretation.** New York: Random House, 1972, 336 p.
This study is basically an attack on what the author, a professor at the University of Puerto Rico, calls the North American domination of his native island. The Spanish original was published as "Puerto Rico: una interpretación histórico-social" (Mexico City: Siglo Veintiuno Editores, 1969, 255 p.).

Ramos de Santiago, Carmen. **El gobierno de Puerto Rico.** San Juan: Editorial Universitaria, Universidad de Puerto Rico, 2d rev. ed., 1970, 813 p.
A valuable reference book on Puerto Rican government and politics, including information on government structures, parties and elections.

Sánchez Tarniella, Andrés. **Nuevo enfoque sobre el desarrollo político de Puerto Rico.** Madrid: Afrodisio Aguado, 2d rev. ed., 1971, 189 p.
An interpretation of the political development of Puerto Rico from 1868 to 1970. The author finds the political forces in contemporary Puerto Rico to be conservative.

Wagenheim, Kal. **Puerto Rico: A Profile.** New York: Praeger, 1970, 286 p.
A short but competent treatment of all phases of Puerto Rican life.

Wells, Henry. **The Modernization of Puerto Rico: A Political Study of Changing Values and Institutions.** Cambridge: Harvard University Press, 1969, 440 p.
A solid and well-written study of the vast changes, particularly in politics and culture, that modernization and the American presence have brought to Puerto Rico.

Other Islands

See also Inter-American Relations, p. 193; Latin America, p. 200; (West Indies and the Caribbean) General, p. 300.

Brisk, William J. **The Dilemma of a Ministate: Anguilla.** Columbia: University of South Carolina, Institute of International Studies, 1969, 93 p.
A study of the Anguilla issue in international politics in the 1960s.

Farrugia, Laurent. **Le Fait national guadeloupéen.** Ivry-sur-Seine: The Author, 1968, 203 p.
A survey of the history and contemporary politics of Guadeloupe, by an author with a pro-independence viewpoint.

Lewis, Gordon K. **The Growth of the Modern West Indies.** New York: Monthly Review Press, 1968, 506 p.
A critical and pessimistic survey of the English-speaking Antilles during the last 50 years.

Lewis, Gordon K. **The Virgin Islands.** Evanston: Northwestern University Press, 1972, 382 p.
A worthwhile study by a Caribbean scholar.

O'Loughlin, Carleen. **Economic and Political Change in the Leeward and Windward Islands.** New Haven: Yale University Press, 1968, 260 p.
An expert and clearly written analysis of an area long neglected by American scholars.

Oxaal, Ivar. **Black Intellectuals Come to Power: The Rise of Creole Nationalism in Trinidad and Tobago.** Cambridge: Schenkman Publishing Co., 1968, 194 p.
A first-hand observer describes the development of society and culture in Trinidad and Tobago up to 1962.

Robinson, A. N. R. **The Mechanics of Independence: Patterns of Political and Economic Transformation in Trinidad and Tobago.** Cambridge: M.I.T. Press, 1971, 200 p.
The author of this study, who has served as Minister of External Affairs and Minister of Finance in the government of Trinidad and Tobago, surveys briefly his country's political history and pleads for political union of the whole Caribbean region.

Ryan, Selwyn D. **Race and Nationalism in Trinidad and Tobago.** Toronto: University of Toronto Press, 1972, 509 p.
A thorough account of political life in Trinidad and Tobago from the end of the First World War to the present.

Singham, A. W. **The Hero and the Crowd in a Colonial Polity.** New Haven: Yale University Press, 1968, 389 p.
A detailed study of the British colony of Grenada, by a professor at the University of the West Indies.

Williams, Eric Eustace. **Inward Hunger: The Education of a Prime Minister.** Chicago: University of Chicago Press, 1971, 352 p.
The political autobiography of the Prime Minister of Trinidad and Tobago.

SOUTH AMERICA

ARGENTINA

General

See also (Latin America) General, p. 200.

Alexander, Robert Jackson. **An Introduction to Argentina.** New York: Praeger, 1969, 197 p.
A discussion of all aspects of the Argentine nation and people, past and present.

Caldas Villar, Jorge. **Nueva historia argentina.** Buenos Aires: Juan C. Granda y Jorge R. Corvalán Editores, 1966, 4 v.
A balanced account of Argentine history from pre-Columbian times to 1965.

Ferns, Henry Stanley. **Argentina.** New York: Praeger, 1969, 284 p.
A British scholar presents Argentina in its variety and complexity, from colonial times to Onganía.

Grondona, Mariano Carlos. **La Argentina en el tiempo y en el mundo.** Buenos Aires: Editorial Primera Plana, 1967, 254 p.
An analysis of Argentina's internal politics, changing social and economic problems and foreign policies.

Historia argentina contemporánea, 1862–1930. Buenos Aires: El Ateneo (for the Academia Nacional de la Historia), 1963–67, 4 v. in 7 pts.
A detailed political, cultural, economic and geographical history of Argentina from 1862 to 1930.

Munson, Frederick P. and Others. **Area Handbook for Argentina.** Washington: G.P.O., 1969, 446 p.
A useful compendium of information on Argentina, with an extensive bibliography. Prepared by the Foreign Area Studies at the American University.

Ramos, Jorge Abelardo. **Revolución y contrarrevolución en la Argentina.** Buenos Aires: Editorial del Mar Dulce, 4th rev. ed., 1970– .
A massive history of Argentina from a Marxist viewpoint. Three of the five planned volumes that have been published through 1972 have appeared in many revised editions and cover the period from 1810 to 1922.

Scobie, James R. **Argentina: A City and a Nation.** New York: Oxford University Press, 2d rev. ed., 1971, 323 p.
This historical survey examines Argentina's transition from an agricultural to an industrial economy. Emphasizing the country's formative years—the nineteenth century—the author is particularly concerned with the transformation of the pampas and the rapid growth of Buenos Aires. There is a very useful selective guide to the literature on Argentina.

Tella, Torcuato S. di and Others. **Argentina: sociedad de masas.** Buenos Aires: Editorial Universitaria de Buenos Aires, 3rd ed., 1966, 284 p.
Essays on Argentine history and contemporary politics by some of Argentina's most distinguished social scientists.

Whitaker, Arthur Preston. **Argentina.** Englewood Cliffs: Prentice-Hall, 1964, 184 p.
An introductory historical survey.

Foreign Relations

See also Inter-American Relations, p. 193; (Argentina) General, p. 313; (Chile) Foreign Relations, p. 332; Paraguay, p. 337; (Germany) The Nazi Era, p. 475; Polar Regions, p. 848.

Caillet-Bois, Ricardo R. **Cuestiones internacionales, 1852-1966.** Buenos Aires: Editorial Universitaria de Buenos Aires, 1970, 115 p.
A short summary of Argentine border disputes over the last century.

Conil Paz, Alberto and Ferrari, Gustavo. **Argentina's Foreign Policy, 1930-1962.** Notre Dame: University of Notre Dame Press, 1966, 240 p.
A well-researched study of Argentine foreign policy during a turbulent period of Argentine history. The Spanish original appeared as "Política exterior argentina, 1930-1962" (Buenos Aires: Editorial Huemul, 1964, 277 p.).

Cúneo, Dardo. **Las nuevas fronteras.** Buenos Aires: Ediciones Transición, 1963, 230 p.
A discussion of Argentine politics and foreign policy, by a writer and political activist who has served as a delegate to the O.A.S.

Fitte, Ernesto J. **La disputa con Gran Bretaña por la islas del Atlántico Sur.** Buenos Aires: Emecé Editores, 1968, 261 p.
An analysis of the dispute between Britain and Argentina over the Malvinas Islands (Falkland Islands).

García Lupo, Rogelio. **História de unas malas relaciones.** Buenos Aires: Jorge Alvarez Editor, 1964, 112 p.
A history of United States-Argentine relations by a critic of American influence in Argentina.

Peterson, Harold Ferdinand. **Argentina and the United States, 1810-1960.** Albany: State University of New York, 1964, 627 p.
A wide-ranging and scholarly survey.

Rizzo Romano, Alfredo. **La cuestión de límites con Chile en la zona del Beagle.** Buenos Aires: Editorial Pleamar, 1968, 234 p.
A well-documented study of Argentine-Chilean border disputes in the Beagle Channel area.

Government and Politics

See also (Latin America) Political and Constitutional Problems, p. 203; (Argentina) General, p. 313; Perón and Peronismo, p. 317.

Agulla, Juan Carlos. **Federalismo y centralismo.** Buenos Aires: Ediciones Líbera, 1967, 164 p.
Addresses on the meaning of federalism in Argentina, delivered at a symposium.

Alende, Oscar Eduardo. **Punto de partida.** Buenos Aires: Editorial Santiago Rueda, 1965, 417 p.
A long-time leader of the Radical Party discusses Argentina's political crisis of the early 1960s.

Alende, Oscar Eduardo. **Los que mueven las palancas.** Buenos Aires: A. Peña Lillo, 1971, 192 p.
A survey of recent political history in Argentina. The author is sharply critical of "liberals" who follow a policy of free trade and open up the country to foreign investors and political influence.

Bustos Fierro, Raúl. **Desde Perón hasta Onganía.** Buenos Aires: Ediciones Octubre, 1969, 492 p.
A Peronist account of the political history of Argentina between 1955 and 1966.

Canton, Darío. **El parlamento argentino en épocas de cambio: 1890, 1916 y 1946.** Buenos Aires: Editorial del Instituto, 1966, 208 p.
A study of changes in the composition of the Argentine Congress and of the characteristics of its members at three critical periods in Argentine history.

Canton, Darío. **La política de los militares argentinos, 1900-1971.** Buenos Aires: Siglo Veintiuno, 1971, 161 p.

An analysis of the political role of the Argentine military between 1900 and 1971. The author argues that the military has become the arbiter of social change and has acted to preserve its own preëminence at the expense of the rest of the society.

Carri, Roberto. **Sindicatos y poder en la Argentina.** Buenos Aires: Editorial Sudestada, 1967, 187 p.
A useful account of the role of unions in Argentine politics between 1955 and 1967.

Ceresole, Norberto. **Ejército y política nacionalista.** Buenos Aires: Editorial Sudestada, 1968, 363 p.
An analysis of the role of the armed forces in Argentine politics between 1955–1966. The author calls on the armed forces to break their dependency on the United States, to pursue a nationalist policy and to ally with the working class.

Ciria, Alberto. **Partidos y poder en la Argentina moderna, 1930–1946.** Buenos Aires: Editorial Jorge Alvarez, 2d rev. ed., 1968, 379 p.
An interpretation of Argentine politics between 1930 and 1946, discussing the roles of political parties, the military, business interests, the Church, and labor organizations. A final chapter analyzes recent political developments.

Díaz Araujo, Enrique. **La conspiración del '43; el GOU: una experiencia militarista en La Argentina.** Buenos Aires: La Bastilla, 1971, 341 p.
A detailed examination of the circumstances and intrigues which led to the military coup of 1943 in Argentina and to the subsequent emergence of Perón as a national leader.

Evers, Tilman Tönnies. **Militärregierung in Argentinien: das politische System der "Argentinischen Revolution."** Frankfurt/Main: Metzner, 1972, 288 p.
A critical and well-documented examination of the political and economic developments in Argentina since 1966. The author claims that Argentinean politicians are applying outdated techniques in attempting to solve their country's problems.

Fayt, Carlos S. **El político armado.** Buenos Aires: Ediciones Pannedille, 1971, 248 p.
An excellent account of Argentine political history of the 1960s, including discussions of the causes of the 1966 coup, the role of the armed forces in politics, and the problems of the Onganía government.

Florit, Carlos A. **Las fuerzas armadas y la guerra psicológica.** Buenos Aires: Ediciones Arayú, 1963, 155 p.
A criticism of the army's role in Argentine politics.

Frondizi, Arturo. **Estrategia y táctica del movimiento nacional.** Buenos Aires: Editorial Desarrollo, 1964, 179 p.
Former President Frondizi argues that a strong, united nationalist movement can be constructed in Argentina on the foundations established by the governments of Yrigoyen and Perón.

Goldwert, Marvin. **Democracy, Militarism, and Nationalism in Argentina, 1930–1966.** Austin: University of Texas Press (for the Institute of Latin American Studies), 1972, 253 p.
The military, and its relationship to the totality of political and social life, are examined in an attempt to explain the course of Argentine history since the fall of Yrigoyen.

Marianetti, Benito. **Argentina: realidad y perspectivas.** Buenos Aires: Editorial Platina, 1964, 554 p.
The memoirs of a socialist and former member of the Central Committee of the Communist Party.

Melo, Carlos R. **Los partidos políticos argentinos.** Córdoba (Argentina): Universidad Nacional de Córdoba, 4th rev. ed. 1970, 313 p.
An excellent enlarged and updated study of Argentine political parties. Originally published in 1943.

Navarro Gerassi, Marysa. **Los nacionalistas.** Buenos Aires: Editorial Jorge Alvarez, 1969, 251 p.
An important study of rightist nationalist movements in Argentina since 1930.

Orona, Juan V. **La logia militar que enfrentó a Hipólito Yrigoyen.** Buenos Aires, 1965, 193 p.

——. **La revolución del 6 de septiembre.** Buenos Aires, 1966, 244 p.
——. **La logia militar que derrocó a Castillo.** Buenos Aires, 1966, 140 p.
——. **La dictadura de Perón.** Buenos Aires, 1970, 374 p.
——. **La revolución del 16 de septiembre.** Buenos Aires, 1971, 317 p.
 A series of studies of military involvement in Argentine politics from the 1920s to 1955. The author, a retired army colonel, is anti-Peronist and applauds the military for having overthrown Perón, but criticizes the military for failing to produce economic and political stability.

Orsolini, Mario Horacio. **Ejército argentino y crecimiento nacional.** Buenos Aires: Ediciones Arayú, 1965, 281 p.
 An analysis of the role of the Argentine armed forces in politics and in the economic development of the country.

Parera, Ricardo Gregorio. **Democrácia Cristiana en la Argentina: los hechos y la ideas.** Buenos Aires: Editorial Nahuel, 1967, 375 p.
 A basic source for the history, policies and principles of the Argentine Christian Democratic Party.

Peña, Milcíades. **Masas, caudillos, y elites: la dependencia argentina de Yrigoyen a Perón.** Buenos Aires: Ediciones Fichas, 1971, 133 p.
 An interpretation of Argentine politics between 1916 and 1955. The author argues that Perón's government was not revolutionary and that Argentina remained under the control of large landowners, industrialists and foreign capitalists throughout the period.

Potash, Robert A. **The Army and Politics in Argentina, 1928-1945: Yrigoyen to Perón.** Stanford: Stanford University Press, 1969, 314 p.
 A detailed and scholarly analysis of the political role of the Argentine military.

Prieto, Ramón. **El pacto: 8 años de política argentina.** Buenos Aires: Editorial "En Marcha," 1963, 236 p.
 A left-wing nationalist analyzes Argentina's politics during the eight years following the overthrow of Perón.

Puiggrós, Rodolfo. **Historia crítica de los partidos políticos argentinos.** Buenos Aires: Editorial Jorge Alvarez, new ed., 1965–.
 An updated and greatly expanded history of Argentine political parties and Argentine society up through the Peronist period. Five of the six planned volumes have been published through 1972.

Quintero, Carlos Alberto. **História reciente: la crisis política argentina de 1955-1966.** Buenos Aires: Librería Huemul, 1970, 286 p.
 A chronological study of Argentine political history between 1955 and 1966.

Ramos, Jorge Abelardo. **La lucha por un partido revolucionario.** Buenos Aires: Ediciones Pampa y Cielo, 1964, 143 p.
 A Trotskyite account of the efforts to form a revolutionary party in Argentina after 1945.

La **"Revolución Argentina": análisis y prospectiva.** Buenos Aires: Ediciones Depalma (for the Instituto de Ciencias Políticas of the Universidad del Salvador), 1966, 210 p.
 A collection of essays examining the Argentine Revolution of 1966 from legal, political and sociological points of view.

Romero, Luis Alberto and Others. **El radicalismo.** Buenos Aires: Carlos Pérez Editor, 1969, 318 p.
 A series of essays on the development of the Radical Party between 1910 and 1966, by sympathetic authors.

Selser, Gregorio. **Argentina a precio de costo: el gobierno de Frondizi.** Buenos Aires: Ediciones Iguazú, 1965, 302 p.
 An analysis of the Frondizi government which argues that Frondizi betrayed the country and the hopes of his own supporters.

Tella, Torcuato S. di and Halperín Donghi, Tulio. **Los fragmentos del poder: de la oligarquía a la poliarquía argentina.** Buenos Aires: Editorial Jorge Alvarez, 1969, 535 p.
 A volume of articles by sixteen prominent scholars on social, economic and political change in Argentina.

Vazeilles, José. **Los socialistas.** Buenos Aires: Editorial Jorge Alvarez, 1968, 320 p.
An account of the development of the Socialist Party in Argentina by a union organizer and party member.

Perón and Peronismo

See also (Argentina) Government and Politics, p. 314.

Borroni, Otelo and Vacca, Roberto. **La vida de Eva Perón.** Buenos Aires: Editorial Galerna, 1971, 348 p.
A well-documented study of Eva Perón's role in Argentine life between 1946 and 1952.

Cárdenas, Gonzalo and Others. **El peronismo.** Buenos Aires: Carlos Pérez Editor, 1969, 338 p.
Essays and documents on Peronism.

Ciria, Alberto. **Perón y el justicialismo.** Mexico City: Siglo Veintiuno, 1971, 193 p.
An excellent study of the Peronist ideology, *justicialismo*, which helps to clarify its basic principles.

Cook, John William. **Peronismo y revolución.** Buenos Aires: Ediciones Papiro-Galerna, 1971, 236 p.
A Peronist theoretician analyzes the Revolution of 1966 and its significance for the labor movement.

Fayt, Carlos S. **Naturaleza del peronismo.** Buenos Aires: Viracocha Editores, 1967, 414 p.
An important analysis of the social causes and nature of the Peronist movement.

Firpo, M. Eduardo. **Perón y los peronistas.** Buenos Aires: Talleres Gráficos Alberde, 1965, 255 p.
A Peronist discusses Peronism and its development since 1955.

Gazzera, Miguel and Ceresole, Norberto. **Peronismo: autocrítica y perspectivas.** Buenos Aires: Editorial Descartes, 1970, 316 p.
Essays by Peronists on the history and future prospects of their movement.

Guardo, Ricardo C. **Horas difíciles.** Buenos Aires: A. Peña Lillo, 1963, 370 p.
A former president of the Chamber of Deputies (1946–1952) defends Peronism and recounts the experiences of the "difficult hours" between 1955 and 1962.

Kirkpatrick, Jeane J. **Leader and Vanguard in Mass Society: A Study of Peronist Argentina.** Cambridge: M.I.T. Press, 1971, 262 p.
A well-researched study.

Luna, Félix. **El 45: crónica de un año decisivo.** Buenos Aires: Editorial Jorge Alvarez, 1969, 637 p.
A detailed account of the political events of 1945, the year that Perón made his successful bid for power.

Lux Wurm, Pedro Carlos. **Le Péronisme.** Paris: Librairie Générale de Droit, 1965, 273 p.
An account of the Peronist movement—its origins, content and structure.

Perón, Juan Domingo. **Conducción política.** Buenos Aires: Editorial Freeland, new ed., 1971, 368 p.
A republication of a work originally published in 1952 in which Perón explains his political beliefs.

Rodríguez de Martínez Paiva, Celina E. and Pizzuto de Rivero, María Rosa. **La verdad: vida y obra de Eva Perón.** Buenos Aires: Editorial Austral, 1967, 248 p.
A eulogistic appraisal of Eva Perón's role as a social activist and fighter for women's rights.

Economic and Social Problems

See also Economic Growth and Development, p. 71; (Latin America) Economic and Social Problems, p. 208; (Argentina) General, p. 313.

Abellá Blasco, Mario. **Historia del sindicalismo: los obreros, la economía, la política.** Buenos Aires: A. Peña Lillo, 1967, 204 p.

A general discussion of the development of trade unions in Argentina and in the world.

Antonio, Jorge. **Argentina en venta: la desintegración del estado liberal.** Buenos Aires: Editorial Jorge Alvarez, 1968, 203 p.
A Peronist critique of liberal economic policies which "sell" Argentina to foreign interests.

Bagú, Sergio. **Evolución histórica de la estratificación social en la Argentina.** Caracas: Instituto de Investigaciones Económicas y Sociales, 1969, 145 p.
An analysis of changes in the social structure of Argentina between 1880-1930.

Broner, Julio and Larriqueta, Daniel E. **La revolución industrial argentina.** Buenos Aires: Editorial Sudamericana, 1969, 195 p.
A discussion of economic development in Argentina. The author argues that the goal of increasing economic wealth should be secondary to the goal of achieving economic autarky.

Cuccorese, Horacio Juan. **Historia de los ferrocarriles en la Argentina.** Buenos Aires: Editorial Macchi, 1969, 159 p.
A history of Argentine railroads from the 1850s to their nationalization in 1947.

Cúneo, Dardo. **Comportamiento y crisis de la clase empresaria.** Buenos Aires: Editorial Pleamar, 1967, 319 p.
A well-researched study of Argentine industrial, commercial and agricultural interest groups. The author concludes that Argentine "entrepreneurs" have failed as directors of the country's economic development.

Díaz Alejandro, Carlos F. **Essays on the Economic History of the Argentine Republic.** New Haven: Yale University Press, 1970, 549 p.
A detailed and expert treatment of economic developments in Argentina since 1860.

Ferrer, Aldo. **The Argentine Economy.** Berkeley: University of California Press, 1967, 239 p.
An Argentinian economist examines the country's stagnation from a historical perspective, which shows, in his belief, that contemporary economic difficulties reflect inadequate solutions to problems of an agricultural society in transition to an industrial one.

Fienup, Darrell Fischer and Others. **The Agricultural Development of Argentina: A Policy and Development Perspective.** New York: Praeger, 1969, 437 p.
A thorough study, including recommendations for future agricultural policies.

Frigerio, Rogelio. **Estatuto del subdesarrollo: las corrientes del pensamiento económico argentino.** Buenos Aires: Jorge Alvarez, 1967, 128 p.
An analysis and critique of various schools of economic thought in contemporary Argentina. Frigerio is a former advisor to Arturo Frondizi and a "developmentist" economist.

Frondizi, Arturo. **Petróleo y nación.** Buenos Aires: Ediciones Transición, 1963, 180 p.
A collection of former President Frondizi's public statements on economic development and, especially, on the controversial issue of the petroleum contracts with foreign companies.

Frondizi, Arturo. **Política económica nacional.** Buenos Aires: Ediciones Arayú, 1963, 316 p.
A selection of speeches on economic affairs made by Frondizi during his presidency (1958-1962).

García Lupo, Rogelio. **Contra la ocupación extranjera.** Buenos Aires: Editorial Centro, 1971, 3rd ed., 189 p.
A collection of articles by a leftist nationalist purporting to show that the Argentine government of General Onganía was controlled by foreign economic interests.

García Martínez, Carlos. **La inflación argentina.** Buenos Aires: Consejo Empresario de Cooperación, 1965, 400 p.
An analysis of the causes and consequences of inflation in Argentina.

García Zamor, Jean Claude. **Public Administration and Social Changes in Argentina, 1943-1955.** Rio de Janeiro: Editora Mory, 1968, 190 p.
A political and social history of Argentina during the Perón régime.

Germani, Gino. **Política y sociedad en una epoca de transición: de la sociedad tradicional a la sociedad de masas.** Buenos Aires: Editorial Paidos, 2d ed., 1965, 266 p.
A collection of articles on social change in Argentina.

Imaz, José Luis de. **Los que mandan (Those Who Rule).** Albany: State University of New York Press, 1970, 279 p.
An important study of the Argentine political, military, economic, social, religious and labor élites from 1936 to 1964. The author concludes that Argentina lacks a cohesive ruling élite and that a generation of leaders has failed. Spanish original: "Los que mandan" (Buenos Aires: Editorial Universitaria de Buenos Aires, 1964, 250 p.).

Marotta, Sebastián. **El movimiento sindical argentino: su génesis y desarrollo.** Buenos Aires: Ediciones "Lacio," 1960–70, 3 v.
A prominent labor leader's history of the Argentine labor movement. The author died after completing volume 3, which ended with 1935, but his followers have promised to finish his work.

Olarra Jiménez, Rafael. **Evolución monetaria argentina.** Buenos Aires: Editorial Universitaria de Buenos Aires, 1968, 187 p.
An important study of the monetary and banking systems in Argentina.

Rotondaro, Rubén. **Realidad y cambio en el sindicalismo.** Buenos Aires: Editorial Pleamar, 1971, 426 p.
An excellent study of the development of Argentine labor unions.

Sánchez Jáuregui, Francisco J. **El desaliento argentino.** Buenos Aires: Editorial Jorge Alvarez, 1968, 180 p.
An analysis of Argentina's economic problems by a businessman and Radical Party (U.C.R.P.) activist. He argues that Argentina can overcome its problems if the government will provide incentives and formulate a consistent economic policy.

Smith, Peter H. **Politics and Beef in Argentina: Patterns of Conflict and Change.** New York: Columbia University Press, 1969, 292 p.
An analysis of the developments and crises within the Argentine beef industry, a mainstay of the national economy, in the years from 1900 to 1946.

Tella, Guido di and Zymelman, Manuel. **Las etapas del desarrollo económico argentino.** Buenos Aires: Editorial Universitaria de Buenos Aires, 1967, 540 p.
An important historical study, employing a Rostowian "stages of development" framework, of the growth of the Argentine economy.

Tella, Torcuato S. di. **El sistema político argentino y la clase obrera.** Buenos Aires: Editorial Universitaria de Buenos Aires, 1964, 127 p.
A sociological analysis of the Argentine working class and its political history.

BOLIVIA

General

See also Latin America, p. 200.

Barton, Robert. **A Short History of the Republic of Bolivia.** La Paz: Los Amigos del Libro, 2d ed., 1968, 343 p.
An introductory study, containing an appendix listing diplomatic agents of the United States who served in Bolivia from 1948 to 1968.

Fellman Velarde, José. **Historia de Bolivia.** La Paz: Editorial "Los Amigos del Libro," 1968–70, 3 v.
A Marxist interpretation of Bolivian history from pre-history to 1956.

Fifer, J. Valerie. **Bolivia: Land, Location, and Politics since 1825.** New York: Cambridge University Press, 1972, 301 p.
A British scholar examines the geographical factors that have determined recent Bolivian politics and foreign relations.

Malloy, James M. and Thorn, Richard S., eds. **Beyond the Revolution: Bolivia since 1952.** Pittsburgh: University of Pittsburgh Press, 1971, 402 p.

This collection of studies on Bolivian political, economic and social developments since 1952 is an outgrowth of a seminar sponsored by the Center for International Studies and the Center for Latin American Studies at the University of Pittsburgh.

Foreign Relations

See also Inter-American Relations, p. 193; (Latin America) General, p. 200; (Chile) Foreign Relations, p. 332.

Araníbar, Eufronio. **La historia de nuestro mar.** Cochabamba: Editorial Canelas, 1966, 194 p.
A history of how and why Bolivia lost its outlet to the sea.

Escobari Cusicanqui, Jorge. **El derecho al mar.** La Paz: Librería Juventud, 1964, 281 p.
A detailed presentation of the Bolivian right to access to the sea, with a discussion of the history of the problem.

Espinosa Moraga, Oscar. **Bolivia y el mar, 1810–1964.** Santiago: Editorial Nascimiento, 1964, 551 p.
A well-researched account of Bolivia's diplomatic and political efforts to gain a Pacific seaport, written by an unsympathetic Chilean.

Fernández, Carlos José. **La guerra del Chaco.** Buenos Aires, 1955–67, 4 v.
A comprehensive military history of the Chaco War from the Paraguayan point of view.

Garner, William R. **The Chaco Dispute: A Study of Prestige Diplomacy.** Washington: Public Affairs Press, 1966, 151 p.
A description of the origins and course of the Chaco War between Paraguay and Bolivia in the 1930s, with emphasis on the negotiations between the United States and Argentina concerning this wasteful conflict.

Iturralde Chinel, Luis de. **La desviación del Río Lauca por Chile.** La Paz, 1963, 374 p.
A well-documented study of the Bolivian position in the dispute with Chile over the use of the waters of the Río Lauca.

Lang, Gerhard. **Boliviens Streben nach freiem Zugang zum Meer.** Hamburg: Hamburger Gesellschaft für Völkerrecht und Auswärtige Politik, 1966, 94 p.
A most useful survey of Bolivia's never-ending aspirations for free access to the sea.

Querejazu Calvo, Roberto. **Masamaclay: historia política, diplomática y militar de la guerra del Chaco.** La Paz, 1965, 484 p.
A detailed political, diplomatic and military history of the Chaco War.

Rout, Leslie B., Jr. **Politics of the Chaco Peace Conference 1935–1939.** Austin: University of Texas Press (for the Institute of Latin American Studies), 1970, 268 p.
A well-documented study of the efforts to terminate the war between Paraguay and Bolivia, particularly at the Chaco Peace Conference which, according to the author, "remains one of the few contemporary conferences that has provided a lasting settlement to an international crisis."

Vittone, Luis. **La guerra del Chaco: aspectos y episodios sobresalientes.** Asunción: Imprenta Militar, 1964, 197 p.
A study of the Chaco War.

Government and Politics

See also Latin America, p. 200; Cuba, p. 302.

Bonifaz, Miguel. **Bolivia, frustración y destino.** Sucre: Imprenta Universitaria, 1965, 301 p.
A political history of Bolivia, especially useful for information on the numerous parties of the Left between 1936 and 1965.

González, Luis J. and Sánchez Salazar, Gustavo A. **The Great Rebel: Che Guevara in Bolivia.** New York: Grove Press, 1969, 254 p.
Two Bolivian journalists present a sympathetic account of the 1967 insurgency in which the career of Guevara, the Argentine-born Latin American revolutionary leader, came to its end.

Guevara, Ernesto. **The Complete Bolivian Diaries of Ché Guevara and Other Captured Documents.** New York: Stein and Day, 1968, 330 p.
  This translation also includes a preface by the editor and the diaries of three of Guevara's advisers. Edited by Daniel James.

Guevara, Ernesto. **El diario del Ché en Bolivia: noviembre 7, 1966 a octubre 7, 1967.** Havana: Instituto del Libro, 1968, 346 p.
  The official Cuban version of Ché Guevara's Bolivian diary.

Gutiérrez, Mario R. **Predestinación histórica de Bolivia: libertad y dictadura.** La Paz: Talleres Gráficos Bolivianos, 1966, 346 p.
  A leader of the conservative Falange Socialista Boliviana party interprets political events between 1952 and 1966.

Harris, Richard. **Death of a Revolutionary: Che Guevara's Last Mission.** New York: Norton, 1970, 219 p.
  A sympathetic account of the controversial revolutionary and his attempt to start a revolution in Bolivia.

Klein, Herbert Sanford. **Parties and Political Change in Bolivia, 1880-1952.** New York: Cambridge University Press, 1970, 451 p.
  The author traces in full detail the antecedent forces of the 1952 Revolution. The comments on the seminal function of the Chaco War are particularly interesting.

Landívar Flores, Hernán. **Infierno en Bolivia.** La Paz: Editorial Difusión, 1964, 412 p.
  A survey of contemporary Bolivian political history which is highly critical of past Presidents Paz Estenssoro and Siles Zuazo.

Llosa M., José Antonio. **René Barrientos Ortuño: paladín de la bolivianidad.** La Paz: Empresa Editora "Novedades," 1966, 298 p.
  The author of this study of contemporary political history argues that René Barrientos Ortuño, of the Movimiento Nacionalista Revolucionario, exemplifies the revolution.

Lora, Guillermo. **La revolución boliviana: análisis crítico.** La Paz: Editorial Difusión, 1964, 408 p.
  A leftist critique of the Movimiento Nacionalista Revolucionario and its attempts to govern. The author is a Trotskyite politician and labor historian.

Malloy, James M. **Bolivia: The Uncompleted Revolution.** Pittsburgh: University of Pittsburgh Press, 1970, 396 p.
  The author believes that Bolivia has been continuously in a revolutionary situation since 1936. Political and economic events are traced to 1964, with emphasis upon the "will, capacities and orientation of the active contestants."

Marof, Tristán, *pseud*. (Gustavo Adolfo Navarro). **Victor Paz Estenssoro: vida y trasfondo de la política boliviana.** La Paz: Librería y Editorial Juventud, 1965, 208 p.
  A socialist critique of the Movimiento Nacionalista Revolucionario government and of its leader Paz Estenssoro.

Pando Monje, Mario. **Los movimientistas en el poder; la revolución boliviana: sus grandezas y frustraciones.** La Paz: Editorial El Siglo, 1969, 270 p.
  A defense of the Movimiento Nacionalista Revolucionario governments (1952-1964) by a member of this party.

Peñaloza, Luis. **Historia del Movimiento Nacionalista Revolucionario, 1941-1952.** La Paz: Editorial Librería Juventud, 1963, 293 p.
  A history of the M.N.R. between 1941 and 1952, when the party seized power.

Quebracho, *pseud*. (Liborio Justo). **Bolivia: la revolución derrotada.** Buenos Aires: Juarez Editor, 2d ed., 1971, 321 p.
  An account of how the "first proletariat revolution in Latin America," the Bolivian Revolution of 1952, failed by ceding power to the Movimiento Nacionalista Revolucionario. The author is critical of the ideology and strategy of the Bolivian Trotskyite Revolutionary Workers Party (P.O.R.).

Rolón Anaya, Mario. **Política y partidos en Bolivia.** La Paz: Librería Editorial Juventud, 1966, 587 p.
  A political history of Bolivia from the 1940s to the 1960s.

Sandoval Rodríguez, Isaac. **Nacionalismo en Bolivia.** La Paz: Cooperativa de Artes Gráficas E. Burillo Ltda., 1970, 277 p.
  A short political history of Bolivia from the establishment of independence to 1969.

Economic and Social Problems

See also Economic Growth and Development, p. 71; (Latin America) Economic and Social Problems, p. 208.

Abadie-Aicardi, Raúl Federico. **Economía y sociedad de Bolivia en el siglo XX: el antiguo régimen.** Montevideo: Ediciones del Rio de la Plata, 1966, 123 p.

An account of Bolivian society and the Bolivian economy before the 1952 Revolution.

Almaraz Paz, Sergio. **El poder y la caída: el estaño en la historia de Bolivia.** La Paz: Los Amigos del Libro, 1967, 260 p.

A history of Bolivian tin mining from its origin to nationalization in 1952.

Bedregal, Guillermo. **Bolivia: imperialismo y revolución; estructura y tipología de un pais neocolonial.** La Paz: Los Amigos del Libro, 1970, 284 p.

A social and economic survey of contemporary Bolivia. The author views Bolivia as a dependent country subjected to neocolonialist foreign domination.

Bedregal, Guillermo. **Monopolio contra países pobres: la crisis mundial del estaño.** Mexico City: Siglo Veintiuno Editores, 1967, 269 p.

A leftist analysis of the world tin market and how it works against the interests of Colombia. The author is a former manager of COMIBOL, the Bolivian state mining corporation.

Canelas O., Amado. **Mito y realidad de la industrialización Boliviana.** Cochabamba: Los Amigos del Libro, 1966, 478 p.

———. **Mito y realidad de la reforma agraria.** La Paz: Los Amigos del Libro, 1966, 305 p.

———. **Nacionalización de las minas de Bolivia: historia de una frustración.** La Paz: Librería Altiplano, 1963, 285 p.

A Bolivian leftist analyzes industrialization, agrarian reform and nationalization of mining in Bolivia.

Eder, George Jackson. **Inflation and Development in Latin America: A Case History of Inflation and Stabilization in Bolivia.** Ann Arbor: University of Michigan, Program in International Business, Graduate School of Business Administration, 1968, 822 p.

An extremely detailed and authoritative analysis of the Bolivian monetary stabilization program of 1956–57 and related political and economic matters.

Heath, Dwight B. and Others. **Land Reform and Social Revolution in Bolivia.** New York: Praeger, 1969, 464 p.

A detailed description of agricultural and social systems in Bolivia, together with proposals for change.

Lora, Guillermo. **Historia del movimiento obrero boliviano.** La Paz: Los Amigos del Libro, 1967–.

A history of the Bolivian labor movement, planned in four volumes. Three volumes, covering the period from 1848 to 1933, have been published through 1972.

Mariaca Bilboa, Enrique. **Mito y realidad del petróleo boliviano.** La Paz: Los Amigos del Libro, 1966, 538 p.

A history of the Bolivian state oil corporation, with a discussion of foreign oil interests in Bolivia.

Puhle, Hans-Jürgen. **Tradition und Reformpolitik in Bolivien.** Hanover: Verlag für Literatur und Zeitgeschehen, 1970, 89 p.

A very well-documented survey of economic development policies in contemporary Bolivia.

Urquidi Morales, Arturo. **El feudalismo en America y la reforma agraria boliviana.** Cochabamba: Los Amigos del Libro, 1966, 411 p.

A sociologist and former rector of the University of Cochabamba gives a historical view of the "feudalistic" base from which land reform emerged in post-revolutionary Bolivia. One of the authors of the agrarian reform law of 1953, the writer broadly surveys its subsequent impact upon the Bolivian nation.

Villarroel Claure, Ramiro. **Mito y realidad del desarrollo en Bolivia.** Cochabamba: Los Amigos del Libro, 1969, 299 p.

A Marxist interpretation of Bolivian problems of development in the 1950s and 1960s.

Wilkie, James W. **The Bolivian Revolution and U.S. Aid since 1952: Financial Background and Context of Political Decisions.** Los Angeles: University of California, Latin American Center, 1969, 114 p.

An examination of "the nature of and patterns in Bolivian Central Government expenditure," with emphasis on budgetary matters. There are many charts and statistical tables.

Zondag, Cornelius Henry. **The Bolivian Economy, 1952-65: The Revolution and its Aftermath.** New York: Praeger, 1966, 262 p.

A former official of the Agency for International Development in Bolivia examines the social, economic and political impact of the Bolivian Revolution. The overall tone is guardedly optimistic.

BRAZIL

General

See also (Latin America) General, p. 200.

Baklanoff, Eric Nicolas, ed. **New Perspectives of Brazil.** Nashville: Vanderbilt University Press, 1966, 328 p.

Ten Brazilian scholars, representing varied disciplines, survey the country's socio-economic, political, demographic and cultural problems.

Baklanoff, Eric Nicolas, ed. **The Shaping of Modern Brazil.** Baton Rouge: Louisiana State University Press (for the Latin American Studies Institute), 1969, 164 p.

Essays covering the country's history, politics, economics, geography and educational system.

Bello, José Maria. **A History of Modern Brazil, 1889-1964.** Stanford: Stanford University Press, 1966, 362 p.

A useful history, particularly informative for the period before 1930. The concluding chapter, covering the years from 1954 to 1964, was written by Rollie E. Poppino. The original edition appeared as "História da república, 1889-1954, síntese de sessenta e cinco anos de vida brasileira" (São Paulo: Companhia Editora Nacional, 4th ed., 1959, 405 p.).

Burns, E. Bradford. **A History of Brazil.** New York: Columbia University Press, 1971, 449 p.

A scholarly history that brings the Brazilian narrative up to 1970.

Cruz Costa, Joao. **A History of Ideas in Brazil: The Development of Philosophy in Brazil and the Evolution of National History.** Berkeley: University of California Press, 1964, 427 p.

A substantial study of Brazil's intellectual history, with emphasis on European influences. First published as "Contribuçao à história das idéias no Brasil: o desenvolvimento da filosofia no Brasil e a evoluçao histórica nacional" (Rio de Janeiro: Olympio, 1956, 484 p.).

Dos Passos, John Roderigo. **Brazil on the Move.** Garden City: Doubleday, 1963, 205 p.

In these personal reflections based on travels in Brazil the distinguished American author expresses guarded optimism, sympathy and understanding.

Faust, Jean-Jacques. **Le Brésil: une Amérique pour demain.** Paris: Éditions du Seuil, 1966, 252 p.

A thoughtful assessment of contemporary Brazil by a French journalist.

Graham, Richard, ed. **A Century of Brazilian History since 1865: Issues and Problems.** New York: Knopf, 1969, 233 p.

Essays on Brazilian politics and culture during the last hundred years.

Pereira, Luiz Carlos Bresser. **Desenvolvimento e crise no Brasil.** São Paulo: Editôra Brasiliense, 2d rev. ed., 1970, 214 p.

An analysis of Brazil's economic, social, and political development since 1930.

Poppino, Rollie E. **Brazil: The Land and People.** New York: Oxford University Press, 1968, 370 p.
: A concise survey of Brazilian history and institutions, supplemented by a bibliographical guide.

Prado Júnior, Caio. **A revolucão brasileira.** São Paulo: Editôra Brasiliense, 1966, 332 p.
: An interpretation of recent Brazilian history. The author, a Marxist, argues that Brazil is not being transformed from a feudal to a capitalist society but has always been part of the world-wide capitalist system.

Rodrigues, José Honório. **The Brazilians: Their Character and Aspirations.** Austin: University of Texas Press, 1968, 186 p.
: A perceptive analysis by a respected historian. A translation of "Aspirações nacionais: interpretação histórico-política" (São Paulo: Editôra Fulgor, 1963, 162 p.).

Roett, Riordan, *ed.* **Brazil in the Sixties.** Nashville: Vanderbilt University Press, 1972, 434 p.
: A collection of essays which, in the words of the editor, "tries to illuminate some of the complexities of change in Brazil and, simultaneously, to indicate the future course of modernization."

Rondière, Pierre. **Délirant Brésil?** Paris: Hachette, 1964, 336 p.
: Vividly sketched images of Brazil's past and present, based on a traveler's experiences from Rio to the Amazon.

Rosenbaum, H. Jon and Tyler, William G., *eds.* **Contemporary Brazil: Issues in Economic and Political Development.** New York: Praeger, 1972, 438 p.
: A collection of articles on a wide range of problems that have confronted contemporary Brazil.

Saunders, John, *ed.* **Modern Brazil: New Patterns and Development.** Gainesville: University of Florida Press, 1971, 350 p.
: Studies on Brazil's progress on the road to great-power status.

Smith, Thomas Lynn. **Brazil: People and Institutions.** Baton Rouge: Louisiana State University Press, 4th rev. ed., 1972, 778 p.
: An updated edition of a standard survey, including new chapters on Brazil's development during the 1960s.

Wagley, Charles. **An Introduction to Brazil.** New York: Columbia University Press, 2d rev. ed., 1971, 341 p.
: A sympathetic and knowledgeable survey of the land and people of Brazil by a respected North American anthropologist who has had long contact with this nation.

Weil, Thomas E. and Others. **Area Handbook for Brazil.** Washington: G.P.O., 1971, 645 p.
: A useful compendium of information on Brazil, with an extensive bibliography. Prepared by the Foreign Area Studies at the American University.

Foreign Relations

See also Inter-American Relations, p. 193; (Brazil) General, p. 323; Government and Politics, p. 325; Paraguay, p. 337; Portugal, p. 439.

Alencastre, Amilcar. **O Brasil, a Africa e o futuro.** Rio de Janeiro: Laemmert, 1969, 230 p.
: In this discussion of Brazil's policies towards Africa, the author argues that Brazil's interests could be impaired by too close an identification with Portuguese colonialism.

Morel, Edmar. **O golpe começou em Washington.** Rio de Janeiro: Editôra Civilização Brasileira, 1965, 276 p.
: A journalist attempts to prove that the military coup of 1964 began in Washington.

Penna, José Osvaldo de Meira. **Política externa: segurança & desenvolvimento.** Rio de Janeiro: Agir Editôra, 1967, 216 p.
: A Brazilian diplomat offers his ideas on the future foreign policies of his country and pleads for the establishment of closer ties with Portugal and its African communities.

Rodrigues, José Honório. **Brazil and Africa.** Berkeley: University of California Press, 1965, 382 p.
A history of Brazil's relations with Africa, emphasizing contemporary issues. The Brazilian original: "Brasil e África: outro horizonte" (Rio de Janeiro: Editôra Civilização Brasileira, 2d rev. and enl. ed., 1964, 2 v.).

Rodrigues, José Honório. **Interêsse nacional e política externa.** Rio de Janeiro: Editôra Civilização Brasileira, 1966, 232 p.
A respected Brazilian historian examines the economic and political forces which have shaped the foreign policies of contemporary Brazil and condemns the Castello Branco military coup of April 1964.

Segundo Silioni, Rolando. **La diplomacia luso-brasileña en la cuenca del Plata.** Buenos Aires: Círculo Militar, 1964, 250 p.
A study of Brazilian diplomacy in the River Plate region since colonial times.

Government and Politics

See also Guerrilla Warfare; Armed Insurrection, p. 118; (Latin America) Political and Constitutional Problems, p. 203; (Brazil) General, p. 323.

Antoine, Charles. **Church and Power in Brazil.** Maryknoll (N.Y.): Orbis Books, 1973, 275 p.
A highly critical account by a French priest of the Catholic Church in Brazil from 1964 to the beginning of the third military presidency in 1969. The French original was published as "L'Eglise et le pouvoir au Brésil: naissance du militarisme" (Paris: Desclée de Brouwer, 1971, 269 p.).

Bastos, J. Justino Alves. **Encontro com o tempo.** Porto Alegre: Editôra Globo, 1965, 393 p.
These memoirs by a former Brazilian officer describe the internal structure of the Brazilian Army and contain useful information about the political views of the military.

Burns, E. Bradford. **Nationalism in Brazil: A Historical Survey.** New York: Praeger, 1968, 158 p.
A study of Brazilian nationalism—from its origins through twentieth-century developments—with a critical bibliographical essay.

Café Filho, João. **Do sindicato ao catete: memórias políticas e confissões humanas.** Rio de Janeiro: J. Olympio, 1966, 2 v.
Memoirs of Vargas' Vice-President who was the President of Brazil for a short period after Vargas' suicide.

Carneiro, Glauco. **História das revoluções brasileiras.** Rio de Janeiro: Edições O Cruzeiro, 1965, 2 v.
A survey of the Brazilian revolutionary movements and revolts since 1889 that includes a discussion of the 1964 coup.

Carneiro, Levi. **Uma experiência de parlamentarismo.** São Paulo: Martins, 1965, 312 p.
An experienced politician analyzes Brazil's experiment with a parliamentary system of government in the period from 1960 to 1962.

Carone, Edgard. **A Premeira República, 1889-1930: texto e contexto.** São Paulo: Difusão Européia do Livro, 1969, 303 p.
A useful collection of essays and documents on Brazil's major political and economic problems during the First Republic.

Carone, Edgard. **Revoluções do Brasil contemporâneo, 1922-1938.** São Paulo: Editôra São Paulo, 1965, 174 p.
A study of anti-régime movements in Brazil between 1922 and 1938.

Dines, Alberto and Callado, Antonio. **Os idos de março e a queda em abril.** Rio de Janeiro: José Alvaro Editôr, 1964, 403 p.
Interpretations of the meaning of the Brazilian Revolution of 1964.

Dubnic, Vladimir Reisky de. **Political Trends in Brazil.** Washington: Public Affairs Press, 1968, 184 p.

A knowledgeable account of contemporary Brazilian politics, centering upon the Quadros, Goulart and Castello Branco regimes.

Dulles, John W. F. **Unrest in Brazil: Political-Military Crises 1955–1964.** Austin: University of Texas Press, 1970, 449 p.
A well-written and elaborate description of Brazilian political factions and struggles, from the suicide of Vargas to the coming of the military government.

Dulles, John W. F. **Vargas of Brazil.** Austin: University of Texas Press, 1967, 395 p.
A biography of Getúlio Vargas, the dictatorial and revolutionary statesman and politician who centralized Brazil and dominated its politics from 1930 until 1954.

Faust, Jean-Jacques. **A revolução devora seus presidentes.** Rio de Janeiro: Editôra Saga, 1965, 162 p.
A French journalist's account of the events preceeding, accompanying and following the 1964 coup.

Fiechter, Georges-André. **Le Régime modernisateur du Brésil, 1964–1972.** Leyden: Sijthoff, 1972, 296 p.
A description of the modernization process in Brazil carried on by the military regime in the period from 1964 to 1972.

Freyre, Gilberto. **Order and Progress: Brazil from Monarchy to Republic.** New York: Knopf, 1970, 422 p.
A leading Brazilian social historian, emphasizing the persistence of traditional social forms and practices, delineates his country's gradual modernization. A condensed translation of "Ordem e progresso" (Rio de Janeiro: J. Olympio, 1959, 2 v.).

Graham, Lawrence S. **Civil Service Reform in Brazil: Principles Versus Practice.** Austin: University of Texas Press (for the Institute of Latin American Studies), 1968, 233 p.
The author notes the failure of Brazilian efforts, especially in the years from 1945 to 1964, to incorporate into their administrative practices North American patterns of "economy and efficiency."

Henriques, Affonso. **Ascensão e queda de Getúlio Vargas.** Rio de Janeiro: Distribuidora Record, 1966, 3 v.
A history of the political career of Getúlio Vargas by an unsympathetic author.

Horowitz, Irving Louis. **Revolution in Brazil: Politics and Society in a Developing Nation.** New York: Dutton, 1964, 430 p.
A collection of writings and articles by Brazilian political and intellectual leaders on Brazil's political, social and economic problems, supplemented by Professor Horowitz's assessment of the problems and prospects of contemporary Brazil.

Ianni, Octávio. **Crisis in Brazil.** New York: Columbia University Press, 1970, 244 p.
The author, analyzing the political and economic causes and consequences of the 1964 coup, views the subsequent administrations as fascist systems characterized by foreign dependency, and predicts that they may terminate in a socialist society. Translation of "O colapso do populismo no Brasil" (Rio de Janeiro: Editôra Civilização Brasileira, 1968, 236 p.).

Ianni, Octávio and Others. **Política e revolução social no Brasil.** Rio de Janeiro: Editôra Civilização Brasileira, 1965, 198 p.
Essays on economic development, social structure and the nationalist Left in Brazil.

Jurema, Abelardo. **Sexta-Feira, 13: os últimos dias do govêrno João Goulart.** Rio de Janeiro: Edicões O Cruzeiro, 1964, 241 p.
An account of the last year of Goulart's government by a member of his cabinet.

Lacerda, Carlos. **Palavras e ação.** Rio de Janeiro: Distribuidora Record, 1965, 202 p.
A collection of essays both by and about Lacerda, one of Brazil's best known politicians.

Lavenère-Wanderley, Nelson Freire. **História da Fôrça Aérea Brasileira.** Rio de Janeiro: Ministério da Aeronáutica, 1967, 450 p.
A basic study of the origins, organization and history of the Brazilian Air Force.

Levine, Robert M. **The Vargas Regime: The Critical Years, 1934–1938.** New York: Columbia University Press, 1970, 270 p.
A well-documented investigation of the politics and ideology of the first Vargas government and its policies.

Mário, Victor, *pseud.* **Cinco años que abalaram o Brasil.** Rio de Janeiro: Editôra Civilização Brasileira, 1965, 631 p.
   A chronological account of political events in Brazil between 1960 and 1964.

Nasser, David. **A revolução que se perdeu a si mesma: diário de um repórter.** Rio de Janeiro: Edicões O Cruzeiro, 1965, 424 p.
   A popular account of Brazilian political history in the early 1960s.

Pedreira, Fernando. **Março 31: civis e militares no processo da crise brasileira.** Rio de Janeiro: José Alvaro, 1964, 207 p.
   A discussion of Brazilian politics since 1930 and the causes of the coup of 1964, including an analysis of factionalism in the military.

Ramos, Alberto Guerreiro. **Mito e verdade da revolução brasileira.** Rio de Janeiro: Zahar Editôres, 1963, 218 p.
   A discussion of the meaning of revolution in Brazil by a sociologist and Labor Party (P.T.B.) congressman.

Schneider, Ronald M. **The Political System of Brazil.** New York: Columbia University Press, 1971, 431 p.
   A scholarly investigation into the evolution of authoritarian military regimes in Brazil since 1964.

Silva, Hélio. **O ciclo de Vargas.** Rio de Janeiro: Editôra Civilização Brasileira, 1964—.
   In this massive and comprehensive survey of the era of Vargas 12 volumes have been published through 1972.

Simão, Azis. **Sindicato e estado: suas relações na formação do proletariado de São Paulo.** São Paulo: Dominus Editôra, 1966, 245 p.
   A study of relations between labor and the Brazilian government primarily in São Paulo before 1940.

Skidmore, Thomas E. **Politics in Brazil, 1930–1964: An Experiment in Democracy.** New York: Oxford University Press, 1967, 446 p.
   Attempting to investigate the causes of the fall of President João Goulart in 1964, the author, a professor of history at the University of Wisconsin, has written a detailed interpretation of what he regards "as the most important factors determining the trend of Brazilian politics since the Revolution of 1930." Comprehensive bibliography.

Sodre, Nelson Werneck. **História militar do Brasil.** Rio de Janeiro: Editôra Civilização Brasileira, 1965, 439 p.
   A Marxist account of the history of the Brazilian Army and state militias from colonial days to the 1960s.

Stepan, Alfred. **The Military in Politics: Changing Patterns in Brazil.** Princeton: Princeton University Press, 1971, 313 p.
   This scholarly study suggests that "the mode of military involvement in Latin American politics may well shift increasingly from that of system-maintenance to that of system-transformation." A RAND Corporation Research Study.

Economic and Social Problems

See also Food and Agriculture, p. 68; Economic Growth and Development, p. 71; (Latin America) Economic and Social Problems, p. 208; (Brazil) General, p. 323; Government and Politics, p. 325.

Baer, Werner. **The Development of the Brazilian Steel Industry.** Nashville: Vanderbilt University Press, 1969, 202 p.
   A well-documented review of the growth of the Brazilian steel industry, the largest in Latin America.

Campos, Roberto de Oliveira. **Economia, planejamento e nacionalismo.** Rio de Janeiro: APEC Editôra, 1963, 324 p.

———. **Ensaios contra maré.** Rio de Janeiro: APEC Editôra, 1969, 410 p.
   Essays analyzing Brazilian economic and political problems, written by a former Planning Minister and architect of the Castello Branco economic program.

Cardoso, Fernando Henrique. **Empresário industrial e desenvolvimento econômico no Brasil.** São Paulo: Difusão Européia do Livro, 1964, 196 p.
   A study of the Brazilian industrial élite.

Daland, Robert T. **Brazilian Planning: Development Politics and Administration**. Chapel Hill: University of North Carolina Press, 1967, 231 p.

An attempt to examine the role of planning in a developing society such as Brazil's. The author's premise reflects his belief that "the relation between planning and consequent development patterns is yet to be established."

Ellis, Howard Sylvester, ed. **The Economy of Brazil**. Berkeley: University of California Press, 1969, 408 p.

Contributions by Brazilian and American economists on Brazil's post-World War II economic development.

Fernandes, Florestan. **Sociedade de classes e subdesenvolvimento**. Rio de Janeiro: Zahar Editôres, 1968, 256 p.

Essays on contemporary Brazilian social problems by a well-known Brazilian sociologist.

Ferreira, Pinto. **Capitais estrangeiros e dívida externa do Brasil**. São Paulo: Editôra Brasiliense, 1965, 230 p.

A study of foreign investment in Brazil since the period of the Empire.

Freitas, José-Itamar de, ed. **Brasil año 2000: o futuro sem fantasia**. Rio de Janeiro: Editôra Monterrey Limitada, 1969, 327 p.

A speculative description of social and economic conditions in Brazil in the year 2000 based on projections of the country's growth trends.

Havighurst, Robert James and Moreira, J. Roberto. **Society and Education in Brazil**. Pittsburgh: University of Pittsburgh Press, 1965, 263 p.

A statistically oriented study of contemporary Brazilian institutions and social forces.

Hopper, Janice H., ed. **Indians of Brazil in the Twentieth Century**. Washington: Institute for Cross-Cultural Research, 1967, 256 p.

A compilation of data and statistics dealing with the Brazilian Indians.

Ianni, Octávio. **Estado e planejamento econômico no Brasil, 1930-1970**. Rio de Janeiro: Editôra Civilização Brasileira, 1971, 316 p.

An analysis of the changing role of the state in the Brazilian economy between 1930 and 1970.

Ianni, Octávio. **Industrialização e desenvolvimento social no Brasil**. Rio de Janeiro: Editôra Civilização Brasileira, 1963, 269 p.

An analysis of the impact of industrialization on social structure in Brazil.

Jaguaribe, Hélio. **Economic and Political Development: A Theoretical Approach and a Brazilian Case Study**. Cambridge: Harvard University Press, 1968, 202 p.

In this study a Brazilian political scientist concludes that Brazil's economic and political development can be furthered only through state intervention or a more pronounced assertion of national consciousness. A revised translation of a work published in Brazil as "Desenvolvimento econômico e desenvolvimento politíco" (Rio de Janeiro: Editôra Fundo de Cultura, 1962, 224 p.).

Keith, Henry H. and Edwards, S. F., eds. **Conflict and Continuity in Brazilian Society**. Columbia: University of South Carolina Press, 1969, 312 p.

Historical essays, each rounded out with a separate commentary by another author, tracing themes in the Brazilian past that illuminate the present. The principal rubrics include the economy, the church and the polity.

Leff, Nathaniel H. **The Brazilian Capital Goods Industry, 1929-1964**. Cambridge: Harvard University Press, 1968, 186 p.

A technical examination of a sector of Brazil's industrialization process.

Leff, Nathaniel H. **Economic Policy-Making and Development in Brazil, 1947-1964**. New York: Wiley, 1968, 201 p.

A perceptive study which notes that "the Brazilian government has had a substantial degree of autonomy from interest groups or socioeconomic class pressures in the making of economic policy."

Leite, Antônio Dias. **Caminhos do desenvolvimento**. Rio de Janeiro: Zahar Editôres, 1966, 227 p.

A critical analysis of the Castello Branco government's economic development program.

McMillan, Claude, Jr. and Gonzalez, Richard F. **International Enterprise in a Developing Economy: A Study of U.S. Business in Brazil**. East Lansing: Michigan State University, Bureau of Business and Economic Research, 1964, 247 p.

Based essentially on questionnaires and interviews of U.S. executives in Brazil, this study examines the nature, organization and beneficial impact of North American corporate enterprise upon the Brazilian economy.

Mangabeira, Francisco. **Imperialismo, petróleo, Petrobrás.** Rio de Janeiro: Zahar Editôres, 1964, 210 p.
A Brazilian nationalist and former president of Petrobrás offers his views on the importance and operation of the oil industry.

Martins, Luciano. **Industrialização, burguesia nacional e desenvolvimento: introdução à crise brasileira.** Rio de Janeiro: Editôra Saga, 1968, 167 p.
A study of the upper economic strata in Brazil and the attitudes of their members toward development.

Raposo, Ben-Hur. **Reforma agrária para Brasil.** Rio de Janeiro: Editôra Fondo de Cultura, 1965, 165 p.
A useful collection of data on agrarian reform policies and laws in Brazil.

Robock, Stefan Hyman. **Brazil's Developing Northeast: A Study of Regional Planning and Foreign Aid.** Washington: Brookings Institution, 1963, 213 p.
In this study the author traces governmental reforms during the Kubitschek administration which led to the establishment of a regional developmental agency, SUDENE (Superintendencia do Disenvolvimento do Nordeste), in 1959.

Rodrigues, José Albertino. **Sindicato e desenvolvimento no Brasil.** São Paulo: Difusão Européia do Livro, 1968, 215 p.
An analysis of the role of labor unions in the Brazilian development process, with a history of labor legislation and organization.

Rodrigues, Leôncio Martins. **Conflito industrial e sindicalismo no Brasil.** São Paulo: Difusão Européia do Livro, 1966, 222 p.
A history of the development of trade unionism in Brazil.

Schmitter, Philippe C. **Interest Conflict and Political Change in Brazil.** Stanford: Stanford University Press, 1971, 499 p.
This is an elaborate and somewhat technically oriented investigation of the functions and significance of interest groups and their relation to economic and social development.

Schuh, G. Edward with Alves, Eliseu Roberto. **The Agricultural Development of Brazil.** New York: Praeger, 1970, 456 p.
A thorough and detailed analysis.

Simonsen, Mário Henrique. **Inflação: gradualismo x tratamento de choque.** Rio de Janeiro: APEC Editôra, 1970, 215 p.
A theoretical and empirical examination of inflation by a leading Brazilian economist.

Sodre, Nelson Werneck. **História da burguesia brasileira.** Rio de Janeiro: Editôra Civilização Brasileira, 1964, 418 p.
An important work on the history of the Brazilian bourgeoisie and its role in politics.

Willoquet, Gaston. **L'Économie brésilienne.** Paris: Nouvelles Éditions Latines, 1965, 156 p.
A brief, optimistic primer on the nature and state of the Brazilian economy.

Wirth, John D. **The Politics of Brazilian Development, 1930-1954.** Stanford: Stanford University Press, 1970, 278 p.
A study of economic policy-making during the Vargas era, with particular reference to steel, petroleum and foreign trade.

CHILE
General

See also Latin America, p. 200.

Alessandri Palma, Arturo. **Recuerdos de gobierno.** Santiago: Editorial Nascimiento, 1967, 3 v.
Memoirs and documents of Alessandri's two presidential terms.

Angell, Alan. **Politics and the Labour Movement in Chile.** New York: Oxford University Press (for the Royal Institute of International Affairs), 1972, 289 p.

An account of the contributions of Chile's deeply politicized labor unions to the "revolution in liberty." The author concludes that the unions have gone beyond the function of conflict regulation and have provided direct support for political "revolutionary activity," however defined.

Bonilla, Frank and Glazer, Myron. **Student Politics in Chile.** New York: Basic Books, 1970, 367 p.
A study of the development of student organizations since 1918 and a survey of student activity in the presidential campaign of 1964.

Burnett, Ben G. **Political Groups in Chile.** Austin: University of Texas Press (for the Institute of Latin American Studies), 1970, 319 p.
This craftsmanlike analysis of the sources of radical sentiment and political change during the 1960s includes much comment on parties and interest groups.

Cademártori, José. **La economía chilena.** Santiago: Editorial Universitaria, 1968, 293 p.
A Marxist survey of the Chilean economy.

Chile: A Critical Survey. Santiago: Institute of General Studies, 1972, 324 p.
Allende's regime in Chile is convincingly depicted in these detailed and careful studies, whose combined scope covers the entire national life. The 16 authors are respected scholars and others prominent in public affairs.

Debray, Régis. **The Chilean Revolution: Conversations with Allende.** New York: Pantheon Books, 1972, 201 p.
A well-known French leftist interviews President Allende on his regime and policies in Chile. The French original appeared as "Entretien avec Allende sur la situation au Chili" (Paris: Maspéro, 1971, 128 p.).

Echaiz, René León. **Evolución histórica de los partidos políticos chilenos.** Santiago: Editorial Francisco de Aguirre, 1971, 187 p.
An account of the evolution of the Chilean political party system.

Foxley, Alejandro and Others. **Chile: búsqueda de un nuevo socialismo.** Santiago: Ediciones Nueva Universidad, 1971, 266 p.
Essays by 12 authors, including both supporters and opponents of the Allende government, on how to establish a socialist economy in Chile.

Gil, Federico Guillermo. **The Political System of Chile.** Boston: Houghton, 1966, 323 p.
A comprehensive survey and description of the social, economic and historical influences shaping the political system in Chile.

Grayson, George W., Jr. **El Partido Demócrata Cristiano Chileno.** Buenos Aires: Editorial Francisco de Aguirre, 1968, 517 p.
A eulogistic account, originally written as a thesis at Johns Hopkins University, of the Christian Democratic Party—its origins and development. The author views the movement as offering a positive alternative to Castroism's threat in the hemisphere.

Gross, Leonard. **The Last, Best Hope: Eduardo Frei and Chilean Democracy.** New York: Random House, 1967, 240 p.
A journalistic survey of Eduardo Frei's regime.

Halperin, Ernst. **Nationalism and Communism in Chile.** Cambridge: M.I.T. Press, 1965, 267 p.
The focal point of this analytical assessment of the forces shaping the political structure of Chile is the presidential election of 1964. In the author's view, the Christian Democratic victory reflected the ebbing influence of extreme nationalism and communism in the hemisphere.

Horne, Alistair. **Small Earthquake in Chile: Allende's South America.** New York: Viking, 1972, 349 p.
A balanced and colorful account by a keen and well-informed observer.

Joliat, Jérôme. **Inflation et développement économique: la cas du Chili.** Lausanne: Payot (for the Université de Genève, Institut Universitaire de Hautes Études Internationales), 1966, 296 p.
A study of economic development in Chile.

Joxe, Alain. **Las fuerzas armadas en el sistema político chileno.** Santiago: Editorial Universitaria, 1970, 176 p.
An analysis of the role of the armed forces in Chilean politics originally written in French.

Kaufman, Robert R. **The Politics of Land Reform in Chile, 1950-1970.** Cambridge: Harvard University Press, 1972, 321 p.
In this study, the author traces with scholarly competence the impact of land-reform proposals upon Chilean politics during the two decades prior to Allende's election.

Mamalakis, Markos and Reynolds, Clark Winton. **Essays on the Chilean Economy.** Homewood (Ill.): Irwin, 1965, 409 p.
This volume, sponsored by the Economic Growth Center of the Department of Economics at Yale University, contains the following essays: "Public Policy and Sectorial Development: A Case Study of Chile 1940-1958," by Markos Mamalakis, and "Development Problems of an Export Economy: The Case of Chile and Copper," by Clark Winton Reynolds.

Nunn, Frederick M. **Chilean Politics 1920-1931: The Honorable Mission of the Armed Forces.** Albuquerque: University of New Mexico, 1970, 219 p.
A study of Colonel Carlos Ibáñez del Campo who dominated Chilean politics in the 1920s. The author states that "military deliberation of political matters became necessary in the 1920s because civilian leaders proved unable (in some cases unwilling) to carry on the affairs of state."

Petras, James and Merino, Hugo Zemelman. **Peasants in Revolt: A Chilean Case Study, 1965-1971.** Austin: University of Texas Press (for the Institute of Latin American Studies), 1972, 154 p.
A sociological analysis.

Petras, James. **Politics and Social Forces in Chilean Development.** Berkeley: University of California Press, 1969, 377 p.
A careful study, emphasizing the role of "statism" in the Chilean economy.

Pinto, Aníbal. **Chile: una economía difícil.** México: Fondo de Cultura Económica, 1964, 184 p.
An examination of Chile's economic problems. Pinto argues that Chile must follow new policies which involve development of internal markets.

Pinto, Aníbal and Others. **Chile hoy.** Santiago: Siglo Veintiuno Editores, 1970, 407 p.
Leftist analyses of Chile's social, political and economic problems.

Puga Vega, Mariano. **El cobre chileno.** Santiago: Editorial Andrés Bello, 1965, 144 p.
An analysis of Chile's agreements with U.S. copper companies.

Puga Vega, Mariano. **El petróleo chileno.** Santiago: Editorial Andrés Bello, 1964, 144 p.
A study of the development of the oil industry in Chile and of the state oil company, E.N.A.P.

Ramírez Necochea, Hernán. **Origen y formación del Partido Comunista de Chile.** Santiago: Editora Austral, 1965, 319 p.
A history of Chile's Communist Party written by a professor who is also a party member.

Rogers, Jorge. **Dos caminos para la reforma agraria en Chile, 1945-1965.** Santiago: Editorial Orbe, 1966, 342 p.
A conservative attack on the Frei government's agrarian reform program.

Sierra, Enrique. **Tres ensayos de estabilización en Chile: las políticas aplicadas en el decenio 1956-1966.** Santiago: Editorial Universitaria, 1970, 213 p.
An evaluation of three anti-inflation policies applied in Chile during the decade 1956-1966.

Silvert, Kalman Hirsch. **Chile: Yesterday and Today.** New York: Holt, Rinehart and Winston, 1965, 218 p.
An informative introduction to problems of Chile's national development.

Thiesenhusen, William C. **Chile's Experiments in Agrarian Reform.** Madison: University of Wisconsin Press (for *Land Economics*), 1966, 230 p.
In the words of the author: "The study is based on the assumption that, if Chile wants development, it is doubtful whether she can afford to maintain agricultural workers in their present state of poverty and economic non-participation."

Urzúa Valenzuela, Germán. **Los partidos políticos chilenos.** Santiago: Editorial Jurídica de Chile, 1968, 222 p.
A useful study of the history and evolution of Chilean political parties.

Vitale, Luis. **Esencia y apariencia de la democracia cristiana.** Santiago: Arancibia Hnos., 1964, 161 p.
A Marxist criticism of the Christian Democratic Party of Chile. The author traces the history of Christian Democracy in the world and its development in Chile.

Zorina, Irina Nikolaevna. **Revoliutsiia ili reforma v Latinskoi Amerike: kritika reformizma chiliiskoi khristianskoi demokratii.** Moscow: Izd-vo "Nauka," 1971, 263 p.
A Soviet critique of the Christian Democrats in Chile and their failure to come to grips with the real problems of the country. The book concludes with a brief description of the 1970 electoral victory of Salvador Allende.

Foreign Relations

See also Inter-American Relations, p. 193; (Argentina) Foreign Relations, p. 314; (Bolivia) Foreign Relations, p. 320.

Barros, Mario. **Historia diplomática de Chile, 1541-1938.** Barcelona: Ediciones Ariel, 1970, 781 p.
An extensive examination of the diplomatic history of Chile from colonial days to the Popular Front (1938).

La cuestión del Río Lauca. Santiago: Ministerio de Relaciones Exteriores, 1963, 327 p.
A well-documented presentation of the Chilean position on the Río Lauca dispute with Bolivia.

Encina, Francisco A. **Las relaciones entre Chile y Bolivia, 1841-1963.** Santiago: Editorial Nascimiento, 1963, 287 p.
A history of relations between Chile and Bolivia from 1841 to the Río Lauca incident.

Eyzaguirre, Jaime. **Breve historia de las fronteras de Chile.** Santiago: Editorial Universitaria, 1967, 107 p.
A study of Chilean boundaries.

Lagos Carmona, Guillermo. **Las fronteras de Chile.** Santiago: Editora Zig-Zag, 1966, 256 p.
A well-documented account of Chile's border disputes, particularly those involving Argentina.

Marín Madrid, Alberto. **Los problemas fronterizos en pocas líneas.** Santiago: Editorial Orbe, 1966, 155 p.
A scholarly discussion of three Chilean border disputes with Argentina: Palena, Laguna del Desierto and the Beagle Channel.

Pike, Fredrick B. **Chile and the United States, 1880-1962.** Notre Dame: University of Notre Dame Press, 1963, 466 p.
A study of Chilean relations with the United States since the last decades of the nineteenth century. The author devotes considerable attention to domestic issues that found reflection in the foreign field.

Ramírez Necochea, Hernán. **Historia del imperialismo en Chile.** Santiago: Editora Austral, 2d ed., 1970, 352 p.
A Marxist study of English, German, and American influences on Chilean development and politics.

Teitelboim Volsky, Sergio. **Chile y la soberanía en el mar.** Santiago: Editorial Andrés Bello, 1966, 219 p.
A review of the evolution of the Chilean conceptions of international law regarding territorial waters, the continental shelf and fishing rights.

Wolpin, Miles D. **Cuban Foreign Policy and Chilean Politics.** Lexington (Mass.): Heath Lexington Books, 1972, 414 p.
In this study of recent Chilean political developments the author argues that "great power infusions are of major importance to internal political conflicts and outcomes."

COLOMBIA

See also Food and Agriculture, p. 68; Economic Growth and Development, p. 71; Inter-American Relations, p. 193; Latin America, p. 200.

Agudelo Villa, Hernando. **Cuatro etapas de la inflación en Colombia.** Bogotá: Ediciones Tercer Mundo, 1967, 316 p.
The Minister of Finance during the presidency of Alberto Lleras Camargo examines post-World War II inflationary trends in Colombia.

Andrade S., Francisco. **Demarcación de las fronteras de Colombia.** Bogotá: Ediciones Lerner, 1965, 627 p.
A history of Colombia's border disputes and their settlements.

Bird, Richard Miller. **Taxation and Development: Lessons from Colombian Experience.** Cambridge: Harvard University Press, 1970, 277 p.
A thorough analysis of Colombian taxation policies and reforms, and their relationship to economic growth. Written under the auspices of the Center for International Affairs, Harvard University.

Consuegra, José. **Apuntes de economía política.** Bogotá: Ediciones Pensamiento Económico y Social, 1963, 382 p.
A useful discussion of Colombian economic problems, mainly after 1950.

Dix, Robert Heller. **Colombia: The Political Dimensions of Change.** New Haven: Yale University Press, 1967, 452 p.
A solid study of the process of modernization—industrialization and urbanization—in Colombia.

Duff, Ernest A. **Agrarian Reform in Colombia.** New York: Praeger, 1968, 240 p.
An examination of the problems delaying real agrarian reform; the strength of the study is in its statistics.

Echavarría Olózoga, Felipe. **Una economía en crisis.** Roma, 1963, 213 p.
A Colombian journalist's analysis of economic and political problems in Colombia.

Fals Borda, Orlando. **Subversion and Social Change in Colombia.** New York: Columbia University Press, 1969, 238 p.
An attempt by a Colombian sociologist to delineate the constructive contributions of subversion to the life of his country, today and in the past. The treatment is scholarly, the viewpoint left of center. Translation of "La subversión en Colombia: visión del cambio social en la historia" (Bogotá: Departmento de Sociologiá, Facultad de Ciencias Humanas, Universidad Nacional, 1967, 293 p.).

Galbraith, W. O. **Colombia: A General Survey.** New York: Oxford University Press (for the Royal Institute of International Affairs), 2d ed., 1966, 177 p.
This revised edition of an earlier work (1953) contains updated material on political and economic developments. A useful introduction to contemporary Colombia.

Guillén Martínez, Fernando. **Raíz y futuro de la revolución.** Bogotá: Ediciones Tercer Mundo, 1963, 234 p.
An analysis of the processes of social and political change in contemporary Colombia.

Guzmán Campos, Germán. **La violencia en Colombia: parte descriptiva.** Cali: Ediciones Progreso, 1968, 509 p.
An expanded version of Guzmán Campos' contribution to a multi-authored study "La violencia" which was first published in 1962 and is recognized as a major work on Colombian history from 1948 to 1958.

Habegger, Norberto. **Camilo Torres, el cura guerrillero.** Buenos Aires: A. Peña Lillo Editor, 1967, 312 p.
A eulogistic appraisal of the role and philosophy of Camilo Torres, the late guerrilla priest.

Havens, Arthur Eugene and Flinn, William L., *eds.* **Internal Colonialism and Structural Change in Colombia.** New York: Praeger, 1970, 250 p.
Abundant data are marshalled in support of a plea for structural changes in Colombian society. For the technically prepared reader.

Holt, Pat M. **Colombia Today—and Tomorrow.** New York: Praeger, 1964, 209 p.
A brief survey of contemporary Colombia, touching upon, among other things, the politics of the National Front, the Peace Corps, coffee, and the "conservative" Church. The author leaves unanswered the question "whether the bursting, shifting population of Colombia, now awakening after centuries of slumber," can evolve peacefully.

Il'ina, Nina Georgievna. **Politicheskaia bor'ba v Kolumbii, 1946-1957.** Moscow: Izd-vo "Nauka," 1968, 243 p.
A Soviet interpretation of internal conflict and political dictatorship in Colombia during the 1946-1957 period of "la violencia," with special reference to problems of the Left.

Lleras Restrepo, Carlos. **Hacia la restauración democrática y el cambio social: nuevo testimonio sobre la política colombiana.** Bogotá: Editorial Agra, 1963, 2 v.
A collection of speeches and articles, written between 1955 and 1963, by a leader of the Liberal Party who subsequently became President of Colombia (1966-1970).

López Michelson, Alfonso. **Colombia en la hora cero: proceso y enjuiciamiento del Frente Nacional.** Bogotá: Ediciones Tercer Mundo, 1963, 2 v.
A collection of papers and speeches by the leader of the leftist Movimiento Revolucionario Liberal.

Mohr, Hermann J. **Economia colombiana: una estructura en crisis.** Bogotá: Ediciones Tercer Mundo, 1972, 315 p.
A German economist, who since 1966 has been associated with the Centro de Investigacion y Accion Social in Bogotá, analyzes the present economic conditions in Colombia and offers some thoughts on the prospects of economic development in that country.

Nelson, Richard R. and Others. **Structural Change in a Developing Economy: Colombia's Problems and Prospects.** Princeton: Princeton University Press, 1971, 322 p.
A discussion of the links between development and various social and economic phenomena in Colombia, based on a RAND Corporation study.

Ospina Vásquez, Luis. **Plan agrícola.** Medellín (Colombia): Editorial Granamérica, 1963, 183 p.
A thorough examination of a proposed agricultural reform program for Colombia.

Parra Sandoval, Rodrigo, *ed.* **Dependencia externa y desarrollo político en Colombia.** Bogotá: Imprenta Nacional, 1970, 222 p.
A series of articles on Colombian politics and intellectual life. The authors argue that both are shaped by Colombia's position of "dependence", or lack of national autonomy.

Payne, James L. **Patterns of Conflict in Colombia.** New Haven: Yale University Press, 1968, 358 p.
An examination of the attitudes which motivate politicians in Colombia. American norms provide the criteria for the author's assessments.

Pinto, Luiz de Aguiar Costa. **Voto y cambio social: el caso colombiano en el contexto latinoamericano.** Bogotá: Ediciones Tercer Mundo, 1971, 92 p.
An analysis of the political system of Colombia during the National Front period and of the election of April 1970 which marked its end.

Ruiz Novoa, Alberto. **El gran desafío.** Bogotá: Ediciones Tercer Mundo, 1965, 146 p.
A former Colombian general who became impatient with the rate of social change offers his view on needed reforms in Colombia.

Sanz de Santamaría, Carlos. **Una época difícil.** Bogotá: Ediciones Tercer Mundo, 1965, 380 p.
A survey of political and economic events in Colombia from 1962 to 1963 when the author was the Minister of the Treasury.

Sepúlveda Niño, Saturnino. **Las elites colombianas en crisis: de partidos policlasistas a partidos monoclasistas.** Bogotá, 1970, 196 p.
A leftist exposé of the Colombian "power élite" and an analysis of the 1970 election.

Smith, Thomas Lynn. **Colombia: Social Structure and the Process of Development.** Gainesville: University of Florida Press, 1967, 389 p.
This scholarly study by a respected sociologist examines Colombian systems of land tenure and their social ramifications.

Torres Restrepo, Camilo. **Christianismo y revolución.** Mexico City: Ediciones Era, 1970, 611 p.

———. **Revolutionary Priest: The Complete Writings and Messages of Camilo Torres.** New York: Random House, 1971, 460 p.
Speeches and writings by a well-known priest who was a revolutionary leader in Colombia.

Urrutia, Miguel. **The Development of the Colombian Labor Movement.** New Haven: Yale University Press, 1969, 297 p.
A serious examination of the growth of the Colombian labor movement since 1850.

Villaveces, Jorge. **La derrota: 25 años de historia.** Bogotá: Editorial Jorvi, 1963, 177 p.
A critical analysis of Colombian politics between 1938 and 1963, by a follower of Gaitán.

Weil, Thomas E. and Others. **Area Handbook for Colombia.** Washington: G.P.O., 1970, 595 p.
A useful compendium of information on Colombia with an extensive bibliography. Prepared by the Foreign Area Studies at the American University.

Wurfel, Seymour W. **Foreign Enterprise in Colombia: Laws and Policies.** Chapel Hill: University of North Carolina Press, 1965, 563 p.
A detailed study.

ECUADOR

See also Inter-American Relations, p. 193; Latin America, p. 200; (The United States) Aid and Assistance, p. 254.

Bialek, Robert W. **Catholic Politics: A History Based on Ecuador.** New York: Vantage, 1963, 144 p.
A history of the relations between the Catholic Church and state in Ecuador.

Erickson, Edwin E. and Others. **Area Handbook for Ecuador.** Washington: G.P.O., 1967, 561 p.
A useful compendium of information on Ecuador, with bibliographies. Prepared by the Foreign Area Studies at the American University.

Galarza Arízaga, Rafael. **Esquema político del Ecuador.** Guayaquil: Editorial Alberada, 1963, 198 p.
A general introduction to politics in Ecuador, including chapters on the political parties and political groups.

Gibson, Charles R. **Foreign Trade in the Economic Development of Small Nations: The Case of Ecuador.** New York: Praeger, 1971, 327 p.
The author concludes his examination of Ecuadorian foreign trade in the post-World War II period by saying that "the evidence indicates rather conclusively . . . that Ecuador has not developed through international trade."

Hurtado, Oswaldo. **Dos mundos superpuestos: ensayo de diagnóstico de la realidad ecuatoriana.** Quito: Instituto Ecuatoriano de Planificación para el Desarrollo Social, 1969, 258 p.
A good introduction to the economic, social and political problems in Ecuador.

Pérez Concha, Jorge. **Ensayo histórico-crítico de las relaciones diplomáticas del Ecuador con los estados limítrofes.** Quito: Editorial Casa de la Cultura Ecuatoriana, 1958–64, 2 v.
A well-researched study of Ecuador's territorial claims and border disputes with neighboring countries since 1810.

Salgado, Germánico. **Ecuador y la integración económica de América Latina.** Buenos Aires: Instituto para la Integración de América Latina, Banco Interamericano de Desarrollo, 1970, 330 p.
A careful investigation of the structure and development possibilities of the Ecuadorian economy, including a discussion of the significance for Ecuador of the Latin American Free Trade Association and the Andean Pact.

Silva, Rafael Euclides. **Derecho territorial ecuatoriano.** Guayaquil: Universidad de Guayaquil, 1962, 526 p.
A detailed study of Ecuador's case in the Peruvian-Ecuadorian boundary dispute.

Watkins, Ralph James. **Expanding Ecuador's Exports: A Commodity-By-Commodity Study with Projections to 1973.** New York: Praeger, 1967, 430 p.
This study, undertaken by Surveys and Research Corporation for the Government of Ecuador, contains a wealth of information on the country's economy and foreign trade.

Weil, Thomas E. and Others. **Area Handbook for Ecuador.** Washington: G.P.O., rev. ed., 1973, 403 p.
A useful compendium of information on Ecuador, with an extensive bibliography. Prepared by the Foreign Area Studies at the American University.

Zook, David Hartzler. **Zärumilla-Marañón: The Ecuador-Peru Dispute.** New York: Bookman Associates, 1964, 331 p.
A well-documented monograph.

THE GUIANAS

See also Latin America, p. 200; West Indies and the Caribbean, p. 300.

Andic, Fuat M. and Andic, Suphan. **Government Finance and Planned Development: Fiscal Surveys of Surinam and the Netherlands Antilles.** Río Piedras: University of Puerto Rico, Institute of Caribbean Studies, 1968, 395 p.
A detailed examination of the relationship between public and private economic sectors in the Dutch South American possessions.

Burnham, Forbes. **A Destiny to Mould: Selected Speeches by the Prime Minister of Guyana.** New York: Africana Publishing Corp., 1970, 275 p.
A collection of speeches by a leading political figure of Guyana covering the period from 1955 to 1969. Compiled and annotated by C. A. Nascimento and R. A. Burrowes.

David, Wilfred L. **The Economic Development of Guyana, 1953–1964.** New York: Oxford University Press, 1969, 399 p.
The author concludes his informative and well-documented study by saying that "the heavy investment in Guyana has not proved to be a sufficient condition for, or a decisive determinant of, rapid growth in income and employment."

Despres, Leo Arthur. **Cultural Pluralism and Nationalist Politics in British Guiana.** Chicago: Rand McNally, 1967, 310 p.
A scholarly study of the impact which ethnic and cultural factors have had upon the political system of Guyana.

Hansen, Han and Wagt, Gabri de. **Wat doen we in Suriname?** Hilversum: Brand, 1967, 176 p.
An introduction to contemporary Surinam, with emphasis on the benefits that Dutch rule has brought to this country.

Irving, Brian, ed. **Guyana: A Composite Monograph.** Hato Rey (Puerto Rico): Inter-American University Press, 1972, 87 p.
Short chapters covering politics, economics and social aspects.

Jagan, Cheddi. **The West on Trial: My Fight for Guyana's Freedom.** London: Michael Joseph, 1966, 471 p.
In these personal reflections Guyana's first Premier and the leader of the pro-communist People's Progressive Party blames big business, Britain and the United States for his inability to stay in power.

Mitchell, William B. and Others. **Area Handbook for Guyana.** Washington: G.P.O., 1969, 378 p.
A useful compendium of information on Guyana, with a bibliography. Prepared by the Foreign Area Studies at the American University.

Newman, Peter Kenneth. **British Guiana: Problems of Cohesion in an Immigrant Society.** New York: Oxford University Press (for the Institute of Race Relations), 1964, 104 p.
In this primer dealing with the political, economic, social and demographic background of British Guiana, the author concludes that the real danger is not a "takeover" by any single clique but "simply the prospect of breakdown of any effective government at all."

Reno, Philip. **The Ordeal of British Guiana.** New York: Monthly Review Press, 1964, 132 p.
This eulogy of the Jagan regime in British Guiana depicts the Guyanese people as "determined to move ahead to the new day . . . in spite of British obstruction and United States intervention."

Simms, Peter. **Trouble in Guyana: An Account of People, Personalities and Politics as They Were in British Guiana.** London: Allen and Unwin, 1966, 198 p.
A thoughtful examination of political developments leading to Guyana's independence. The author ascribes the declining fortunes of the People's Progressive Party to Dr. Cheddi Jagan's inability to form a national political movement.

PARAGUAY

See also Inter-American Relations, p. 193; Latin America, p. 200; (Bolivia) Foreign Relations, p. 320.

Bejarano, Ramón César. **El Paraguay en busca del mar.** Asunción: Casa Editorial Toledo, 1965, 109 p.
A short history of Paraguay's claim of right to access to the sea and of her relations with Brazil and Argentina concerning that claim.

Cardozo, Efraím. **Breve história del Paraguay.** Buenos Aires: Editorial Universitaria de Buenos Aires, 1965, 169 p.
An introductory survey of the history of Paraguay.

Cardozo, Efraím. **Los derechos del Paraguay sobre los Saltos del Guairá.** Asunción: Biblioteca Guaireña "Cirilo Cáceres Zorrilla," 1965, 279 p.
A presentation of the Paraguayan case in the dispute with Brazil over possession of the Saltos del Guairá.

Ceuppens, Henry D. **Paraguay año 2000.** Asunción: Artes Gráficas Zamphirópolos, 1971, 285 p.
A compendium of data on Paraguayan politics, society, economics, foreign relations and foreign investment, with projections for the year 2000. The author strongly supports the Stroessner regime.

Lewis, Paul H. **The Politics of Exile: Paraguay's Febrerista Party.** Chapel Hill: University of North Carolina Press, 1968, 209 p.
Based upon interviews with Paraguayan exiles in Argentina, this is an able analysis of contemporary Paraguayan politics. While internal struggles and long years in exile have weakened the Febrerista movement, the author concludes that, given the "modernist attitudes" of its members, the party "will probably continue to play an important role in the nation's politics, either in legality or in exile."

Pendle, George. **Paraguay: A Riverside Nation.** New York: Oxford University Press (for the Royal Institute of International Affairs), 3rd ed., 1967, 96 p.
An updated revision (earlier edition published in 1956) of a primer on Paraguayan history.

Pincus, Joseph. **The Economy of Paraguay.** New York: Praeger, 1968, 517 p.
A description and evaluation of economic developments and policies in Paraguay. The author concludes that "moderate optimism in Paraguay's economic future would be well justified."

Weil, Thomas E. and Others. **Area Handbook for Paraguay.** Washington: G.P.O., 1972, 316 p.
A useful compendium of information on Paraguay, with an extensive bibliography. Prepared by the Foreign Area Studies at the American University.

PERU

See also Inter-American Relations, p. 193; Latin America, p. 200; Ecuador, p. 335.

Astiz, Carlos Alberto. **Pressure Groups and Power Elites in Peruvian Politics.** Ithaca: Cornell University Press, 1969, 316 p.
The author concludes that revolutionary change in Peru, from above or below, is unlikely.

Belaúnde Terry, Fernando. **Peru's own Conquest.** Lima: American Studies Press, 1965, 219 p.
In these provocative and revealing personal reflections, the former president of Peru writes of his country—its problems and his plans.

Bourricaud, François. **Power and Society in Contemporary Peru.** New York: Praeger, 1970, 356 p.
In this thorough social and political analysis, the author discerns the politicization of the Peruvian masses and the differentiation and socialization of the oligarchy. The 1968 Revolution is not covered. A translation of "Pouvoir et société dans le Pérou contemporain" (Paris: Colin, 1967, 317 p.).

Carey, James Charles. **Peru and the United States, 1900-1962.** Notre Dame: University of Notre Dame Press, 1964, 243 p.
A study of the economic development of Peru and the role therein of the United States. The author believes that "private economic interests have been more of a liability than an asset in the relations between Washington and Lima."

Ceresole, Norberto. **Peru o el nacimiento del sistema latinoamericano.** Buenos Aires: Editorial Galerna, 1971, 397 p.
An analysis of the 1968 Peruvian Revolution which praises the military's nationalistic policies and sees the military's role there as a model for other Latin American countries, especially Argentina.

Dew, Edward. **Politics in the Altiplano: The Dynamics of Change in Rural Peru.** Austin: University of Texas Press (for the Institute of Latin American Studies), 1969, 216 p.
A meticulous account of social, economic and political change among the Indians and Mestizos of southeastern Peru during 1956–66.

Las empresas estatales en el Perú. Lima: Centro de Documentación Económico-Social, 1965, 219 p.
Published by an agency dedicated to the defense of free enterprise, this book examines various state enterprises (*i.e.* steel, oil, electric power, banks, housing, tourism, etc.) and concludes that these "state enterprises dedicated to industrial or commercial operations have retarded rather than aided the development of Peru."

Frías, Ismael. **La revolución peruana y la vía socialista.** Lima: Editorial Horizonte, 1970, 277 p.
A collection of articles on the 1968 Revolution and the possibility of establishing socialism in Peru, by a prominent leftist intellectual.

Hilliker, Grant. **The Politics of Reform in Peru.** Baltimore: Johns Hopkins Press, 1971, 201 p.
This study, centering around the Peruvian Aprista Party, throws light on the relative lack of efficiency of broadly based reformist parties in creating change in Latin America.

Kilty, Daniel R. **Planning for Development in Peru.** New York: Praeger, 1967, 196 p.
A study of public agencies involved in Peruvian developmental planning.

Malpica Silva Santisteban, Carlos. **El mito de la ayuda exterior.** Lima: Francisco Moncloa Editores, 1967, 239 p.
A study of the various types of foreign aid—loans, direct investment, grants, services—which Peru receives and of their effects on the Peruvian economy. Malpica argues that capital outflows exceed inflows, that Peru exports technicians, and that, in general, "foreign aid" is a misnomer.

Marett, Sir Robert Hugh Kirk. **Peru.** New York: Praeger, 1969, 288 p.
The former British ambassador to Peru writes interestingly and well of the heritage, history, politics, sociology and economy of a complex country.

Martin Saunders, César. **Dichos y hechos de la política peruana.** Lima, 1963, 188 p.
A political history of Peru in the turbulent years from 1962 to 1963, based on numerous interviews with important political leaders.

Owens, Ronald Jerome. **Peru.** New York: Oxford University Press (for the Royal Institute of International Affairs), 1963, 195 p.
This concise survey in the series of Chatham House books on Latin America deals with the land, people, history, politics and economics of Peru.

Payne, James L. **Labor and Politics in Peru: The System of Political Bargaining.** New Haven: Yale University Press, 1965, 292 p.
An informative study of the Peruvian labor movement and its position in the nation's political life.

Peterson, Harries-Clichy and Unger, Tomás. **Petróleo: hora cero.** Lima: Distribuidora Inca, 1964, 368 p.
This factual and statistical study of the Peruvian oil industry, written by a Peruvian and a North American, concludes that political factors have outweighed economic considerations and have hindered the development of the oil industry in Peru.

Pike, Fredrick Braun. **The Modern History of Peru.** New York: Praeger, 1967, 386 p.
A readable, concise history of Peru since independence—the stress is upon political considerations.

Ramírez Novoa, Ezequiel. **Recuperación de la brea y pariñas: soberanía nacional y desarrollo económico.** Lima: Ediciones 28 de Julio, 1964, 181 p.
A study of how Standard Oil obtained and kept title to Peruvian oil reserves. The author calls for nationalization of foreign oil companies in Peru.

Robinson, David A. **Peru in Four Dimensions.** Lima: American Studies Press, 1964, 424 p.
A guide to contemporary Peru.

Roel Pineda, Virgilio. **La planificación económica en el Perú.** Lima: Editorial Gráfica Labor, 1968, 195 p.
A history of attempts to establish economic planning as part of the policy-making process in Peru between 1961–1966 and critical analyses of three development plans.

Seoane Corrales, Edgardo. **Surcos de paz.** Lima: Talleres de Industrial Gráfica, 1963, 355 p.
An analysis of the distribution of wealth and of agricultural problems in Peru, by a former vice president of that country.

Sharp, Daniel A., *ed.* **U.S. Foreign Policy and Peru.** Austin: University of Texas Press (for the Institute of Latin American Studies), 1972, 485 p.
A competent collection of studies covering the main aspects of the interplay between post-revolutionary Peruvian developments and U.S. policy.

Spaey, Philippe. **L'Élite politique péruvienne.** Paris: Éditions Universitaires, 1972, 242 p.
A critical account of the role of the political élite in contemporary Peru.

Stephens, Richard H. **Wealth and Power in Peru.** Metuchen (N.J.): Scarecrow Press, 1971, 219 p.
The characteristics, significance and increasing power of the Peruvian landed class are described with a fine understanding of cultural and psychological intangibles. Unfortunately, there is no reference to the impact of the 1968 Revolution upon this élite.

Tullis, F. LaMond. **Lord and Peasant in Peru: A Paradigm of Political and Social Change.** Cambridge: Harvard University Press, 1970, 295 p.
The author examines the possibilities of reform from below, through peasant and village initiative, as a means of effecting change in the Peruvian land-tenure system. Sponsored by Harvard's Center for International Affairs.

Villanueva, Víctor. **Hugo Blanco y la rebelión campesina.** Lima: Librería-Editorial Juan Mejía Baca, 1967, 197 p.
An account of the peasant revolt in the Peruvian Andes in the 1960s which was led by Hugo Blanco.

Wagner de Reyna, Alberto. **Historia diplomática del Perú, 1900–1945.** Lima: Ediciones Peruanas, 1964, 2 v.
A diplomatic history of Peru from 1900 to 1945 by an eminent Peruvian historian and

diplomat, with useful annexes containing bibliographies, indexes of treaties and chronologies.

Weil, Thomas E. and Others. **Area Handbook for Peru.** Washington: G.P.O., rev. ed., 1972, 429 p.
A useful compendium of information on Peru, with an extensive bibliography. Prepared for the Foreign Area Studies at the American University.

URUGUAY

See also Inter-American Relations, p. 193; Latin America, p. 200.

Alisky, Marvin. **Uruguay: A Contemporary Survey.** New York: Praeger, 1969, 174 p.
A summary of all aspects of Uruguayan life, including its geographical basis, economy, politics, culture and foreign relations.

Arapey, *pseud.* (Abraham Guillén). **Uruguay: país en crisis.** Montevideo: Nativa Libros, 1966, 244 p.
A leftist view of Uruguay's economic problems.

Arismendi, Rodney. **La revolución uruguaya en la hora del Frente Amplio.** Montevideo: Ediciones Pueblos Unidos, 1971, 94 p.
The views of the Secretary General of the Uruguayan Communist Party in support of the creation of a united leftist coalition as a means of taking power.

Batlle Berres, Luis. **Pensamientos y acción: discursos y artículos.** Montevideo: Editorial Alfa, 1965–66, 2 v.
A selection of speeches and articles written by a former Uruguayan president (1947–1950).

Benvenuto, Luis Carlos and Others. **Uruguay hoy.** Buenos Aires: Siglo Veintiuno, 1971, 455 p.
A collection of essays on contemporary political, social and economic problems in Uruguay from a leftist perspective.

Brannon, Russell H. **The Agricultural Development of Uruguay: Problems of Government Policy.** New York: Praeger, 1968, 366 p.
In this factual study responsibility for Uruguay's economic problems is attributed to governmental policies which traditionally have favored urban rather than rural sectors.

Buzzetti, José L. **Historia económica y financiera del Uruguay.** Montevideo, 1969, 335 p.
An economic history of Uruguay from 1726 to the present.

Campiglia, Néstor. **Los grupos de presión y el proceso político: la experiencia uruguaya.** Montevideo: Arca, 1969, 230 p.
A general study of the role of pressure groups in Uruguayan society and of their effects on political life. Pressure groups are seen as an important factor in maintaining political stability.

Campiglia, Néstor. **El Uruguay movilizado.** Montevideo: Editorial Giron, 1971, 175 p.
An analysis of the breakdown of Uruguay's political system during the 1960s. The author argues that increased political participation undermined the previously stable system of bargaining and compromise.

Durán, José Luis. **Por un Uruguay mejor.** Montevideo: Imprenta Letras, 1966, 268 p.
An analysis of the causes of Uruguay's underdevelopment. The author argues that agrarian reform is a necessity if Uruguay is to develop.

Faraone, Roque. **El Uruguay en que vivimos, 1900–1968.** Montevideo: Arca, 2d ed., 1968, 141 p.
A general analysis of the antecedents of the Uruguayan crisis of the 1960s.

Fernández Cabrelli, Alfonso. **De Batlle a Pacheco Areco: etapas de la lucha entre oligarquía y pueblo.** Montevideo: Imprenta Norte, 1969, 273 p.
A political history of Uruguay from the beginning of the century to 1968. The author calls on the people to resist the resurgent oligarchy as Batlle did in his day.

Kerbusch, Ernst-Joseph. **Das uruguayische Regierungssystem: der zweite Colegiado, 1952–1967.** Cologne: Heymanns Verlag (for the Forschungsinstitut für Politische Wissenschaft und Europäische Fragen der Universität Köln), 1971, 212 p.

A thorough and well-documented study of the organization and functions of the government of Uruguay. The author concludes his study by stating that the present system of government is highly inadequate for the contemporary needs of Uruguay.

Louis, Julio A. **Batlle y Ordóñez, apogeo y muerte de la democracia burguesa.** Montevideo: Nativa Libros, 1969, 206 p.
A Marxist analysis of Uruguay's development which argues that Batlle's model of bourgeois democracy failed to solve major problems and no longer satisfies Uruguayan needs.

Mercader, Antonio and Vera, Jorge de. **Tupamaros: estrategia y acción.** Montevideo: Editorial Alfa, 1969, 174 p.
An examination of the goals, strategy and development of the Tupamaro urban guerrilla movement.

Nuñez, Carlos. **Los Tupamaros: vanguardia armada en el Uruguay.** Montevideo: Provincias Unidas, 3rd ed., 1969, 148 p.
An analysis of the origins, the actions, the methods, and the significance of the Tupamaro urban guerrilla movement.

Oddone, Juan Antonio. **La formación del Uruguay moderno: la immigración y el desarrollo económico-social.** Buenos Aires: Editorial Universitaria de Buenos Aires, 1966, 106 p.
A brief account of Uruguay's economic and social development, with emphasis on immigration and its consequences.

El proceso económico del Uruguay: contribución al estudio de su evolución y perspectivas. Montevideo: Fundación de Cultura Universitaria (for the Universidad de la República, Instituto de Economía), 1969, 423 p.
An excellent, comprehensive study of the development and problems of the Uruguayan economy.

Ramírez, Gabriel. **Las fuerzas armadas uruguayas en la crisis continental.** Montevideo: Tierra Nueva, 1971, 341 p.
An analysis of the Uruguayan military and its role in internal politics. The author argues that the military's political interventions and conservativism coincide with the interests of the United States and are encouraged and supported by the U.S. military and government.

Segundo, Juan Luis and Others. **Uruguay 67: una interpretación.** Montevideo: Editorial Alfa, 1967, 125 p.
Three essays on Uruguay's physical and human resources which offer some tentative hypotheses about contemporary problems and prospects for future development.

Solari, Aldo E. **El desarrollo social del Uruguay en la postguerra.** Montevideo: Editorial Alfa, 1967, 225 p.
A study of social change in Uruguay since World War II.

Trias, Vivian. **Economía y política en el Uruguay contemporáneo.** Montevideo: Ediciones de la Banda Oriental, 1968, 178 p.
A Marxist history of Uruguayan political development in the years from 1965 to 1968.

Weil, Thomas E. and Others. **Area Handbook on Uruguay.** Washington: G.P.O., 1971, 439 p.
A useful compendium of information on Uruguay, with an extensive bibliography. Prepared by the Foreign Area Studies at the American University.

VENEZUELA

See also Raw Materials; Oil; Energy, p. 70; Inter-American Relations, p. 193; Latin America, p. 200.

Acedo Mendoza, Carlos. **Venezuela: ruta y destino.** Barcelona: Ediciones Ariel, 1966, 2 v.
An analysis of Venezuela's development problems by a prominent Social Christian intellectual.

Alexander, Robert Jackson. **The Venezuelan Democratic Revolution: A Profile of the Regime of Rómulo Betancourt.** New Brunswick: Rutgers University Press, 1964, 345 p.

A prolific writer on contemporary Latin American developments examines the "democratic left" in Venezuela and notes that agrarian reform has been the most fundamental economic and social change brought about by Betancourt's democratic revolution.

Barrios, Gonzalo. **Los días y la política.** Caracas: Editorial Arte, 1963, 463 p.
An analysis of the post-Pérez Jiménez period by one of the founders of Acción Democrática.

Betancourt, Rómulo. **La revolución democrática en Venezuela: documentos del gobierno presidido por Rómulo Betancourt, 1959-1964.** Caracas: Imprenta Nacional, 1968, 4 v.
Four volumes of Betancourt's speeches and other public statements made while he was the president of Venezuela (1959-1964).

Brito Figueroa, Federico. **Historia económica y social de Venezuela: una estructura para su estudio.** Caracas: Dirección de Cultura, Universidad Central de Venezuela, 1966, 2 v.
A Marxist social and economic history of Venezuela from colonial times to the present.

Burggraaff, Winfield J. **The Venezuelan Armed Forces in Politics, 1935-1959.** Columbia: University of Missouri Press, 1972, 241 p.
A description of the evolutionary changes in the relationships between the military and the rest of society in Venezuela.

Carrillo Batalla, Tomás Enrique. **Crisis y administración fiscal.** Caracas: Universidad Central de Venezuela, Instituto de Investigaciones de la Facultad de Economía, 1964, 870 p.
An ex-Minister of Finance analyzes Venezuela's economic and administrative problems.

Diagnóstico de la economía venezolana. Caracus: Universidad Central de Venezuela (for the Colegio de Economistas de Venezuela), 1964, 176 p.
Compiled by a study group from an association of Venezuelan university economists, this statistical analysis of the Venezuelan economy covers the years 1955 through 1961.

Giménez Landínez, Victor Manuel. **La reforma agraria integral.** Caracas: Ministerio de Agricultura y Cría, 1963-64, 2 v.
A collection of public statements on agricultural policy and problems by a Venezuelan Minister of Agriculture (1959-1963).

Heaton, Louis E. **The Agricultural Development of Venezuela.** New York: Praeger, 1969, 320 p.
A study, sponsored by the Ford Foundation, examining the changes in Venezuela's agricultural output and productivity.

Levy, Fred D., Jr. **Economic Planning in Venezuela.** New York: Praeger, 1968, 204 p.
In this study based upon interviews the author concludes that the Venezuelans should pay more attention to political considerations in formulating their economic policies.

López Contreras, Eleazar. **Gobierno y administración, 1936-1941.** Caracas: Editorial Arte, 1966, 158 p.
Memoirs by an ex-President (1936-1941).

Luzardo, Rodolfo. **Notas histórico-económicas, 1928-1963.** Caracas: Editorial Sucre, 1963, 262 p.
A detailed political history of Venezuela between 1928 and 1963.

Márquez, Pompeyo. **Imperialismo, dependencia, latifundismo.** Caracas: Ediciones La Muralla, 1968, 258 p.
A member of the Communist Party of Venezuela analyzes three contemporary economic problems: imperialism, economic dependence and land tenure.

Marrero, Levi. **Venezuela y sus recursos.** Caracas: Cultural Venezolana, 1964, 699 p.
A comprehensive collection of data on the geography and resources of Venezuela.

Martinez, Anibal R. **Our Gift, Our Oil.** Vienna: O.P.E.C., 1966, 199 p.
A study of Venezulean petroleum policies.

Martz, John D. **Acción Democrática: Evolution of a Modern Political Party in Venezuela.** Princeton: Princeton University Press, 1966, 443 p.

This factual and objective study traces the origins and rise to power of Venezuela's National Revolutionary Party. The author concludes that Acción Democrática "is no longer Venezuela's only modern party, however, and the battle to remain the country's leading party is therefore more difficult than before."

Mayobre, José Antonio. **Las inversiones extranjeras en Venezuela: estudio.** Caracas: Monte Ávila Editores, 1970, 103 p.
A Venezuelan central banker who was formerly Minister of Finance analyzes foreign investment in Venezuela, balances the advantages and disadvantages and sets forth a program of moderate policies for his country.

Maza Zavala, Domingo F. **Venezuela: una economía dependiente.** Caracas: Universidad Central de Venezuela, 1964, 378 p.
A leftist analysis of the structure of the Venezuelan economy.

Mieres, Francisco. **El petroleo y la problemática estructural venezolana.** Caracas: Universidad Central de Venezuela, Instituto de Investigaciones, 1969, 403 p.
A scholarly study of the economic development of Venezuela, with particular emphasis on Venezuela's petroleum policies.

Mijares, Augusto. **La evolución política de Venezuela, 1810–1960.** Buenos Aires: Editorial Universitaria de Buenos Aires, 1967, 199 p.
A study of the political development of Venezuela between 1810 and 1960.

Parra Aranguren, Gonzalo. **La nacionalidad venezolana originaria.** Caracas: Universidad Central de Venezuela, 1964, 2 v.
A detailed analysis of Venezuelan concepts of nationality.

Pérez Alfonzo, Juan Pablo. **El pentágono petrolero.** Caracas: Ediciones Revista Política, 1967, 214 p.
A former Minister of Mines discusses petroleum policies and argues for decreased dependence on petroleum exports.

Pérez Alfonzo, Juan Pablo. **Petróleo y dependencia.** Caracas: Síntesis Dos Mil, 1971, 247 p.
An analysis of Venezuela's petroleum policy and of its effects on the country's development. The author, a member of the Acción Democrática party and former Minister of Mines and Hydrocarbons, argues against granting concessions to foreign companies and for a cautious, long-range petroleum policy which will provide a solid basis for the economic development of Venezuela.

The Politics of Change in Venezuela. Cambridge: M.I.T. Press, 1967–71, 3 v.
This study is a result of a coöperative project initiated in 1963 between M.I.T. and Venezuela's Central University. Vol. 1, "A Strategy for Research on Social Policy" (1967), was written by Frank Bonilla and José A. Silva Michelena; vol. 2, "The Failure of Elites" (1970), by Frank Bonilla; and vol. 3, "The Illusion of Democracy in Dependent Nations" (1971), by José A. Silva Michelena.

Quijada, Ramón. **Reforma agraria en Venezuela.** Caracas: Editorial Arte, 1963, 254 p.
A collection of statements on agrarian reform by a well-known member of Acción Democrática.

Rangel, Domingo A. **Los andinos en el poder: balance de una hegemonía, 1899–1945.** Caracas: Talleres Gráficos Universitarios, 1964, 329 p.
A history of the abuse of power in twentieth-century Venezuela.

Rangel, Domingo A. **Capital y desarrollo.** Caracas: Universidad Central de Venezuela, Instituto de Investigaciones Económicas y Sociales, 1969–71, 3 v.
A Marxist study of economic development in Venezuela.

Rangel, Domingo A. **El proceso del capitalismo contemporáneo en Venezuela.** Caracas: Dirección de Cultura, Universidad Central de Venezuela, 1968, 284 p.
A history of the development of capitalism in Venezuela.

Rangel, Domingo A. **La revolución de las fantasías.** Caracas: Ediciones Ofidi, 1966, 260 p.
A disillusioned interpretation of the failure of the Acción Democrática Party and of the revolution which overthrew Jiménez in 1958.

Sáder Pérez, Rubén. **Petróleo nacional y opinión pública.** Caracas: Ediciones Ofidi, 1966, 222 p.

A study of the Venezuelan State Oil Company and of Venezuela's role in the Organization of Petroleum Exporting Countries.

Weil, Thomas E. and Others. **Area Handbook for Venezuela.** Washington: G.P.O., 1971, 525 p.
A useful compendium of information on Venezuela, with an extensive bibliography. Prepared by the Foreign Area Studies at the American University.

Wilgus, Alva Curtis, ed. **Venezuelan Development: A Case History.** Gainesville: University of Florida Press, 1963, 301 p.
A collection of papers resulting from the annual Caribbean Conference held in December 1962 at the University of Florida. A volume in the series "The Caribbean."

II. EUROPE

GENERAL SURVEYS

See also General Works, p. 1; Culture; Education; Public Opinion; Communications Processes, p. 42; Population Problems, p. 47; (The World Since 1914) General, p. 129; First World War, p. 131; Inter-War Period, p. 140; Second World War, p. 144; The Postwar World, p. 178; (The United States) Relations with Western Europe, p. 240.

Burks, Richard Voyles, ed. **The Future of Communism in Europe.** Detroit: Wayne State University Press, 1968, 283 p.
Lectures on various features of East and West European communism by Kevin Devlin, Michael Petrovich, Gregory Grossman, Arnold Horelick and the editor.

Gilbert, Martin. **The European Powers 1900–45.** New York: The New American Library, 1965, 308 p.
A survey of European politics.

Griffith, William E., ed. **Communism in Europe: Continuity, Change, and the Sino-Soviet Dispute.** 1964–66, 2 v.
Substantial studies on developments in Jugoslavia, Poland, Hungary, Italy, East Germany, Czechoslovakia, Norway, Sweden and Finland.

Lichtheim, George. **Europe in the Twentieth Century.** New York: Praeger, 1972, 409 p.
A wide-ranging survey by a neo-Marxist writer. The author's emphasis on "the transformation of inherited life styles under the impact of social and technological change" is not so persuasive as his summarization of the political and economic developments and his rendering of intellectual movements and the cultural climate.

Lüthy, Herbert. **Nach dem Untergang des Abendlandes.** Cologne: Kiepenheuer, 1964, 453 p.
Perceptive essays on recent European history by a well-known Swiss historian.

Lukacs, John Adalbert. **Decline and Rise of Europe.** Garden City: Doubleday, 1965, 295 p.
A very personal, cultivated and suggestive essay about Europe's recent past and the growth of a European consciousness, by a Hungarian-born American historian.

Mutton, Alice Florence Adelaide. **Central Europe: A Regional and Human Geography.** New York: Praeger, 2d rev. ed., 1968, 488 p.
A useful introduction by a veteran geographer to some aspects of the Alpine, Czechoslovak, Germanic and Benelux countries.

Olson, Kenneth Eugene. **The History Makers: The Press of Europe from Its Beginnings through 1965.** Baton Rouge: Louisiana State University Press, 1966, 471 p.
A wide-ranging, historical survey of the press in 24 European countries, from Norway to Bulgaria.

Parker, Robert Alexander Clarke. **Europe 1919–45.** New York: Delacorte Press, 1969, 396 p.
A useful survey. The author rejects A. J. P. Taylor's thesis that Hitler's foreign policies were no more unscrupulous than those of any other major power.

Pounds, Norman John Greville. **An Atlas of European Affairs.** New York: Praeger, 1964, 135 p.
A useful guide to postwar Europe.

Rogger, Hans and Weber, Eugen Joseph, *eds.* **The European Right: A Historical Profile.** Berkeley: University of California Press, 1965, 589 p.
An analysis by American and European scholars of the diverse manifestations of right-wing movements in 11 East and West European countries, chiefly in this century.

Rougemont, Denis de. **The Idea of Europe.** New York: Macmillan, 1966, 434 p.
A French-Swiss journalist and political scientist presents a sensitive historical review "of how men from the time of Homer to the present day have come to think of Europe as a cultural entity."

Rougemont, Denis de. **The Meaning of Europe.** New York: Stein and Day, 1965, 126 p.
Brilliant reflections on the unique history of Europe, which the author defines as "the creator of the world." Originally published as "Les Chances de l'Europe" (Neuchâtel: La Baconnière, 1962, 90 p.).

Schieder, Theodor, *ed.* **Europa im Zeitalter der Nationalstaaten und europäische Weltpolitik bis zum Ersten Weltkrieg.** Stuttgart: Union Verlag, 1968, 655 p.
A survey of European history covering the last third of the nineteenth century and the period of the twentieth century that came to an end with the conclusion of World War I. Extensive bibliographies. Published as Volume 6 of the "Handbuch der europäischen Geschichte."

Silvestri, Stefano. **La sicurezza europea: modelli di situazioni internazionali in Europa negli anni '70.** Bologna: Il Mulino, 1969, 181 p.
An analysis of the possible ways in which global strategies may shift vis-à-vis Europe in the 1970s.

Strauss, Franz Josef. **Challenge and Response: A Programme for Europe.** New York: Atheneum, 1970, 175 p.
Germany's relentlessly controversial politician argues for a European policy, based on hostility to Russia and suspicion of its likely partner, America. A translation of "Herausforderung und Antwort: ein Programm für Europa" (Stuttgart: Seewald, 1968, 231 p.).

Taylor, Alan John Percivale. **From Sarajevo to Potsdam.** New York: Harcourt, Brace and World, 1966, 216 p.
A popular, lively and richly illustrated historical survey by a well-known English historian.

Visine, François. **A.B.C. de L'Europe.** Paris: Librairie Générale de Droit, 1967–72, 5 v. in 8 pts.
A compendium of information on contemporary European political, legal, economic, scientific and military institutions and problems.

Voyenne, Bernard. **Histoire de l'idée européenne.** Paris: Payot, 1964, 249 p.
A revised edition of an earlier survey of the idea of Europe from the Greeks to de Gaulle.

Wiskemann, Elizabeth. **The Europe I Saw.** New York: St. Martin's Press, 1968, 255 p.
Intimate glimpses of Europe before World War II, by a British journalist and historian who, from the early 1930s on, understood and struggled against the fascist threat.

Wiskemann, Elizabeth. **Europe of the Dictators, 1919–1945.** New York: Harper and Row, 1966, 287 p.
A book for the general reader by an author well-equipped to handle the intricacies of Central and Eastern European history.

WESTERN EUROPE

General Surveys and Political Problems

See also Political Philosophies and Ideologies, p. 21; (The World Since 1914) General, p. 129; First World War, p. 131; Inter-War Period, p. 140; Second World War, p. 144; The Postwar World, p. 178.

Alexander, Lewis M. **Offshore Geography of Northwestern Europe: The Political and Economic Problems of Delimitation and Control.** Chicago: Rand McNally (for the Association of American Geographers), 1963, 162 p.

A valuable regional study emphasizing political control over the offshore areas in the maritime basin created by the North Sea and the adjoining bodies of water off the coasts of Northwestern Europe.

Bahne, Siegfried, ed. **Origines et débuts des partis communistes des pays latins (1919-1923** Dordrecht: Reidel, 1969, 655 p.
An important collection of documents from the archives of Jules Humbert-Droz dealing with the organization of the communist parties in France, Italy, Spain, Portugal and Belgium.

Brunner, Erich Edwin. **Die Problematik der verfassungsrechtlichen Behandlung extremistischer Parteien in den westeuropäischen Verfassungsstaaten.** Zurich: Schulthess, 1965, 324 p.
A comparative study of the handling of extremist parties in selected Western European constitutional states—the German Federal Republic, Austria, France and Switzerland.

Buchan, Alastair F., ed. **Europe's Futures, Europe's Choices: Models of Western Europe in the 1970s.** New York: Columbia University Press (for the Institute of Strategic Studies, London), 1969, 167 p.
A sober and suggestive appraisal, not of what European powers ought to do but of what they can do—and with what likely harm and benefit to themselves and others.

Calleo, David Patrick. **Europe's Future: The Grand Alternatives.** New York: Horizon Press, 1965, 192 p.
A fresh look at the options before Europe, by an American scholar.

Calmann, John, ed. **Western Europe: A Handbook.** New York: Praeger, 1967, 697 p.
Uneven articles on individual countries and common trends, supplemented by useful statistics.

Crouzet, Maurice. **The European Renaissance since 1945.** New York: Harcourt Brace Jovanovich, 1970, 216 p.
A French historian and veteran administrator of French education has written a spirited synthesis, with equal emphasis on politics and culture.

Freymond, Jacques. **Western Europe since the War: A Short Political History.** New York: Praeger, 1964, 236 p.
Not a history of Europe, but a series of intelligent essays focused on the development of "Atlantic Europe."

Graubard, Stephen Richards, ed. **A New Europe?** Boston: Houghton, 1964, 691 p.
This symposium of 26 essays, written by leading figures from academic and public life on both sides of the Atlantic, deals with some of the central aspects of Europe's cultural, social and political transformation. A valuable introduction to the study of contemporary Europe.

Heath, Edward Richard George. **Old World, New Horizons: Britain, Europe, and the Atlantic Alliance.** Cambridge: Harvard University Press, 1970, 89 p.
The 1967 Godkin Lectures by the Prime Minister of Great Britain from 1970 to 1974.

Henig, Stanley and Pinder, John, eds. **European Political Parties: A Handbook.** New York: Praeger, 1970, 565 p.
A comparative study of parties in 10 countries and in the European assemblies, by well-known, mostly British, scholars.

Kitzinger, Uwe W. **Britain, Europe and Beyond.** Leyden: Sijthoff, 1964, 222 p.
A series of informative and urbane essays and broadcasts on various aspects of European politics, by a leading British political scientist.

Laqueur, Walter Ze'ev. **The Rebirth of Europe.** New York: Holt, Rinehart and Winston, 1970, 434 p.
An intelligent and comprehensive survey of Europe since the end of World War II. The author, at home in Europe and America, covers economic and cultural as well as political developments.

Lerner, Daniel and Gorden, Morton. **Euratlantica: Changing Perspectives of the European Elites.** Cambridge: M.I.T. Press, 1969, 447 p.
Two American social scientists, using interviews and survey data, seek to establish the changing attitudes of British, French and German élites in the decade 1955-1965.

Lichtheim, George. **The New Europe: Today—and Tomorrow.** New York: Praeger, 1963, 232 p.
: A quick review of the historical background, the political origins and contemporary problems of Europe.

Mayne, Richard. **The Recovery of Europe: From Devastation to Unity.** New York: Harper and Row, 1970, 375 p.
: A very well-informed monograph on post-World War II European history by an Englishman who was present at the birth of both the Coal and Steel Community and the Common Market and was closely associated with Jean Monnet.

Sampson, Anthony. **Anatomy of Europe: A Guide to the Workings, Institutions and Character of Contemporary Western Europe.** New York: Harper and Row, 1969, 462 p.
: A penetrating look at the new Europe, at its architects, its characteristic institutions and its ways of life—and at its student critics who would lead it into different paths. Intelligent and readable, and highly informative, by a veteran observer of the British anatomy. The British edition was published as "The New Europeans" (London: Hodder and Stoughton, 1968, 462 p.).

Sérant, Paul. **Les Vaincus de la libération.** Paris: Laffont, 1964, 422 p.
: An account of the purges of the collaborators with Germans in Western Europe after the end of World War II. The author's sympathies are with the collaborators.

Warnecke, Steven Joshua, *ed.* **The European Community in the 1970's.** New York: Praeger, 1972, 228 p.
: A wide-ranging and thoughtful series of essays on various aspects of European-American relations. Contributors include Ralf Dahrendorf, William Diebold, Uwe Kitzinger, Harald Malmgren, Andrew Pierre and the editor.

Weil, Gordon Lee. **The Benelux Nations: The Politics of Small-Country Democracies.** New York: Holt, Rinehart and Winston, 1970, 260 p.
: A compact survey of contemporary Belgium, Netherlands and Luxembourg.

Economic and Social Problems

See also Economic Factors, p. 49; Western Defense; North Atlantic Treaty; Atlantic Community, p. 188; (Latin America) Economic and Social Problems, p. 208; (The United States) Trade, Tariffs and Finance, p. 251; (Western Europe) Integration, p. 349; (Middle East) Oil, p. 615; (Africa) Economic and Social Problems, p. 789.

Armand, Louis and Drancourt, Michel. **The European Challenge.** New York: Atheneum, 1970, 256 p.
: A suggestive sketch of what a united Europe could do to respond to the cultural and economic challenges of contemporary technology. Translation of "Le Pari européen" (Paris: Fayard, 1968, 315 p.).

Böhning, W. R. **The Migration of Workers in the United Kingdom and the European Community.** New York: Oxford University Press (for the Institute of Race Relations), 1972, 167 p.
: An excellent analysis of what appears to be a lasting feature of Western Europe's economy—foreign workers.

Catalano, Franco. **Europa e Stati Uniti negli anni della guerra fredda: economia e politica, 1944-1956.** Milan: ILI, 1972, 446 p.
: A noted Italian scholar traces American economic domination of Western Europe, beginning with the monetary agreement of Bretton Woods.

Denton, Geoffrey and Others. **Economic Planning and Policies in Britain, France and Germany.** London: Allen and Unwin (for P.E.P.), 1968, 424 p.
: A useful comparative study, with a discussion of problems of planning in the European Economic Community.

Eight European Central Banks. New York: Praeger (for the Bank for International Settlements), 1963, 336 p.

A study of the organization and activities of banks on the Board of the Bank for International Settlements—the central banks of England, Sweden, Switzerland and the Common Market countries. The volume comprises individual authoritative studies clearly explaining international monetary coöperation.

Gordon, Richard L. **The Evolution of Energy Policy in Western Europe.** New York: Praeger, 1970, 330 p.
A valuable contribution to an important topic that casts much light on many aspects of "the reluctant retreat from coal."

Kindleberger, Charles P. **Europe and the Dollar.** Cambridge: M.I.T. Press, 1966, 297 p.
Papers by a well-known economist at the Massachusetts Institute of Technology.

Kleps, Karlheinz. **Langfristige Wirtschaftspolitik in Westeuropa: die neuen wirtschaftspolitischen Konzeptionen und ihre Problematik.** Freiburg: Rombach, 1966, 524 p.
A thorough and quite critical survey of national and international long-term economic planning in Western Europe, by a German economist.

MacLennan, Malcolm and Others. **Economic Planning and Policies in Britain, France and Germany.** New York: Praeger, 1969, 424 p.
An interesting comparison that looks more at practice than theory and draws some sensible conclusions.

Oxford Regional Economic Atlas: Western Europe. New York: Oxford University Press, 1971, 96 p.
A useful volume.

Postan, Michael Moïssey. **An Economic History of Western Europe, 1945-1964.** London: Methuen, 1967, 382 p.
A leading British economic historian examines alternative explanations of growth and other economic developments, emphasizes the differences in national performance, stresses management and explores the social aspects of economic changes.

Reed, Laurance Douglas. **Europe in a Shrinking World: A Technological Perspective.** London: Oldbourne, 1967, 208 p.
A rapid survey of the technological gap which, according to the British author, only European union can fill.

Rees, Graham L. **Britain and the Postwar European Payments Systems.** Cardiff: University of Wales Press, 1963, 291 p.
This study deals primarily with the European Payments Union and its liquidation in 1958 when, in the author's words, "the importance of purely European payments arrangements finally came to an end with the declaration of non-resident covertibility by the major O.E.E.C. countries."

Servan-Schreiber, Jean-Jacques. **The American Challenge.** New York: Atheneum, 1968, 291 p.
To avoid becoming an economic satellite of the United States, Europe must emulate, not exclude, American business. To do so requires more integration, the right governmental policies, and a degree of mobility that the author thinks is more likely to be provided by men of the Left than of the Right. The French original appeared as "Le Défi américain" (Paris: Denoël, 1967, 343 p.).

Tracy, Michael. **Agriculture in Western Europe.** New York: Praeger, 1964, 415 p.
A comprehensive history of farm production and policies since 1880, including prescriptions for the future.

Ulman, Lloyd and Flanagan, Robert J. **Wage Restraint: A Study of Incomes Policies in Western Europe.** Berkeley: University of California Press, 1971, 257 p.
A clearly written analysis commissioned by the U.S. Council of Economic Advisers.

Vellas, Pierre. **L'Europe face à la révolution technologique américaine.** Paris: Dunod, 1969, 192 p.
In this study a French economist departs from the common prescription that Europe must unite to overcome the technological lead of the United States. He also analyzes the strengths and weaknesses of Euratom, OECD, the Concorde project, work on space and communications and other efforts of international coöperation.

Integration

General

See also International Organization and Government, p. 96; Western Defense; North Atlantic Treaty; Atlantic Community, p. 188; (The United States) Relations with Western Europe, p. 240; (Western Europe) General Surveys and Political Problems, p. 345; European Communities; European Economic Community; European Coal and Steel Community; European Atomic Energy Community; European Free Trade Association, p. 353; Eastern Europe and the Soviet Bloc, p. 358; and the sections for specific countries.

Albonetti, Achille. **Preistoria degli Stati Uniti d'Europa.** Milan: Giuffrè, 2d enl. ed., 1964, 416 p.
A leading Italian "Eurocrat" writes the political history of the movement for European unity from 1945 to 1963.

Albrecht-Carrié, René. **One Europe: The Historical Background of European Unity.** Garden City: Doubleday, 1965, 346 p.
A judicious and informative survey of Europe's common traditions and divergent national histories, with particular emphasis on the last 150 years. Professor Albrecht-Carrié, a well-known historian, is a partisan of European unity, but points to the many difficulties on the path to it.

Alting von Geusau, Frans A. M. **Beyond the European Community: A Case of Political Unification.** Leyden: Sijthoff, 1969, 247 p.
Emphasizing the negative, a Dutch political scientist stresses the limits of European integration, the failure of economic coöperation and the unsuitability of Europe as a unit for dealing with some major political issues.

Beck, Robert Holmes and Others. **The Changing Structure of Europe.** Minneapolis: University of Minnesota Press, 1970, 286 p.
Five American scholars look at Western European integration and major trends in politics, economics and education.

Beugel, Ernst Hans van der. **From Marshall Aid to Atlantic Partnership: European Integration as a Concern of American Foreign Policy.** New York: Elsevier, 1966, 480 p.
A balanced study, by a former Minister of State for Foreign Affairs of the Netherlands, of American-European relations since 1945.

Bloes, Robert. **Le "Plan Fouchet" et le problème de l'Europe politique.** Bruges: College of Europe, 1970, 542 p.
A detailed discussion of the problem of European political unification, with emphasis on the development of the Fouchet Plan, a proposal originally advanced by France in 1961 that asked for an increased role for the European Community in foreign policy and defense matters.

Bromberger, Merry and Bromberger, Serge. **Jean Monnet and the United States of Europe.** New York: Coward-McCann, 1969, 349 p.
An account of the activities and achievements of Jean Monnet, one of Europe's great planners, set against the background of postwar politics, by two well-known French journalists. Translation of "Les Coulisses de l'Europe" (Paris: Presses de la Cité, 1968, 419 p.).

Brugmans, Hendrik. **Vingt ans d'Europe: témoignages, 1946-1966.** Bruges: De Tempel, 1966, 362 p.
Essays and speeches, primarily on the subject of European integration, by a leading member of the European Movement and the Rector of the College of Europe from 1950 to 1972.

Buerstedde, Sigismund. **Der Ministerrat im konstitutionellen System der Europäischen Gemeinschaften.** Bruges: De Tempel, 1964, 251 p.
A history and a description of the tasks of the various councils of ministers of the European Communities.

Cartou, Louis. **Organisations européennes.** Paris: Dalloz, 1965, 478 p.
A convenient introduction to the various European organizations.

Colebrook, Mulford Jay. **Franco-British Relations and European Integration 1945-50.** Geneva: Blanc-Wittwer (for the Institut Universitaire de Hautes Études Internationales), 1971, 308 p.
A rather pedestrian thesis on the immediate postwar years, when neither power was interested in building a new Europe.

Cook, Don. **Floodtide in Europe.** New York: Putnam, 1965, 384 p.
A book "about the men and the affairs that have shaped the present state of Europe since Jean Monnet tapped that first blast furnace at Esch-sur-Alzette in 1953."

Coudenhove-Kalergi, Richard Nicolaus, Graf von. **Weltmacht Europa.** Stuttgart: Seewald, 1971, 195 p.
A plea for European unity by a leading and tireless proponent of that cause.

Crawford, Oliver. **Done This Day: The European Idea in Action.** New York: Taplinger, 1970, 399 p.
Both an historical account of the work of the Council of Europe and a plea for a federated Europe, by a well-informed Englishman.

Dehousse, Jean-Maurice, *comp.* **La Fusion des communautés européennes au lendemain des accords de Luxembourg.** The Hague: Nijhoff (for the Institut d'Études Juridiques Européennes, Liège), 1967, 284 p.
Proceedings of a conference held in Liège in April 1966 dealing with various aspects of European integration and the future of European democracy.

De la Mahotière, Stuart. **Towards One Europe.** Baltimore: Penguin, 1970, 331 p.
An Englishman, with much experience in European affairs, analyzes the political and economic context of the European Economic Community.

Deutsch, Karl Wolfgang and Others. **France, Germany and the Western Alliance: A Study of Elite Attitudes on European Integration and World Politics.** New York: Scribner, 1967, 324 p.
A report on the findings of a group of social scientists on the attitudes of French and West German "élites" about such major issues as European integration and arms control.

Dutoit, Bernard. **L'Union Soviétique face à l'intégration européenne.** Lausanne: Université, École des H.E.C., Centre de Recherches Européennes, 1964, 237 p.
A study of the Soviet analysis of and response to the various moves toward European integration.

Friedrich, Carl Joachim. **Europe: An Emergent Nation?** New York: Harper and Row, 1969, 269 p.
A German-American political scientist examines the informal bases of an emergent European community and notes far more progress than a narrowly political perspective would reveal. A sober and suggestive work.

Furler, Hans. **Im neuen Europa: Erlebnisse und Erfahrungen im Europäischen Parlament.** Frankfurt/Main: Societäts-Verlag, 1963, 271 p.
A former president of the European Coal and Steel Community and the European Parliament reminisces about his efforts on behalf of European integration. The volume includes a collection of Mr. Furler's speeches.

La Fusion des communautés européennes. The Hague: Nijhoff, 1965, 295 p.
A symposium on the legal aspects of the fusion of the European communities, held in April 1965 under the auspices of the Institut d'Études Juridiques Européennes of the University of Liège.

Ganshof van der Meersch, W. J. **Organisations européennes. I: Les Institutions.** Brussels: Bruylant, 1966, 580 p.
A thorough description of the history, structure and functions of the more important West and East European international organizations, by a professor at the Institute of European Studies the University of Brussels.

Gladwyn, Hubert Miles Gladwyn Jebb, 1st Baron. **Europe after De Gaulle.** New York: Taplinger, 1969, 169 p.
An author, who firmly believes that Europe with Britain will supplant the narrower Gaullist vision, dissects de Gaulle's foreign policy.

Gladwyn, Hubert Miles Gladwyn Jebb, 1st Baron. **The European Idea.** New York: Praeger, 1966, 159 p.
A political tract dedicated to the hope that the European idea can yet be translated into political reality. The former British ambassador to Paris recognizes the many obstacles and argues that Britain must help build a supranational Europe in partnership with America.

Hogan, Willard Newton. **Representative Government and European Integration.** Lincoln: University of Nebraska Press, 1967, 246 p.
Theoretical and practical considerations on how democratic, representative control can be added to transnational political authority, with contemporary Western Europe as the main focus.

Imbert, Armand. **L'Union de l'Europe occidentale.** Paris: Librairie Générale de Droit, 1968, 238 p.
A scholarly analysis of the political vicissitudes of the first of the European organizations, the Western European Union.

Kuby, Heinz. **Provokation Europa: die Bedingungen seines politischen Überlebens.** Cologne: Kiepenheuer, 1965, 391 p.
A strong plea for a politically integrated Europe that can accomodate a reunified Germany.

Layton, Christopher. **European Advanced Technology: A Programme for Integration.** New York: Humanities Press, 1969, 293 p.
A British author provides facts and analyses about European experience and makes proposals based on the record of success and failure.

Lindberg, Leon N. **The Political Dynamics of European Economic Integration.** Stanford: Stanford University Press, 1963, 367 p.
The main purpose of the author is to contribute to the formation of a theory of international integration.

Lipgens, Walter, *ed.* **Europa-Föderationspläne der Widerstandsbewegungen 1940-1945.** Munich: Oldenbourg (for the Deutsche Gesellschaft für Auswärtige Politik), 1968, 547 p.
A German scholar, working on the origins of European union, presents a carefully selected collection of the plans and hopes for a united Europe drawn up by the leading resistance movements in Hitler's Europe.

Liska, George. **Europe Ascendant: The International Politics of Unification.** Baltimore: Johns Hopkins Press, 1964, 182 p.
Drawing rather heavily on historical analogy, Professor Liska tries to establish some general conclusions about the conditions of European unification and its possible forms. The result is an interesting and suggestive book that gives higher marks to de Gaulle than most American treatments of the subject.

Malvestiti, Piero. **Costruire l'Europa.** Milan: Giuffrè, 1963, 475 p.
Writings and speeches on political and economic integration of Europe by an Italian statesman who from 1958 to 1959 was Vice-President of the Commission of the European Economic Community and from 1959 to 1963 President of the High Authority of the European Coal and Steel Community.

Mayrzedt, Hans and Binswanger, Hans Christoph, *eds.* **Die Neutralen in der europäischen Integration.** Vienna: Wilhelm Braumüller (for the Österreichische Gesellschaft für Aussenpolitik und Internationale Beziehungen), 1970, 496 p.
A detailed examination, by Austrian, Swiss and Swedish experts, of the attitudes of European neutral countries toward European integration.

Morgan, Roger. **West European Politics since 1945: The Shaping of the European Community.** London: Batsford, 1972, 243 p.
In this survey the author focuses on the internal politics of the six original members of the European Community.

Nême, Jacques and Nême, Colette. **Économie européenne.** Paris: Presses Universitaires, 1970, 560 p.
A description and history of supranational European economic organizations, the Common Market, EFTA and COMECON.

Paklons, L. L. **Bibliographie européenne - European Bibliography.** Bruges: De Tempel, 1964, 217 p.
   An unannotated, but useful listing of publications on European integration held by the College of Europe library.

Palmer, Michael; Lambert, John and Others. **A Handbook of European Organizations.** New York: Praeger, 1968, 519 p.
   A useful survey of the origins, evolution and functioning of the chief European organizations. The English edition appeared as "European Unity: A Survey of the European Organisations" (London: Allen and Unwin, for Political and Economic Planning, 1968, 519 p.).

Pinto, Roger. **Les Organisations européennes.** Paris: Payot, 1963, 443 p.
   A study chiefly of the legal aspects of the several European organizations by a professor of law at the Sorbonne. Particularly valuable is his detailed analysis of the Council of Europe and its role in the protection of human rights.

Robertson, Arthur Henry. **European Institutions: Cooperation, Integration, Unification.** New York: Praeger, 2d ed., 1966, 427 p.
   An updated edition of a concise description of the structure and functions of the leading European organizations. The first edition appeared in 1959.

Sartorelli, Fausto. **L'Europa è viva.** Rome: Centro Italiano di Studi e Documentazione, 1970, 328 p.
   A study of the evolution of European unity.

Sattler, Andreas. **Das Prinzip der funktionellen Integration und die Einigung Europas.** Göttingen: Schwartz, 1967, 234 p.
   In this difficult but valuable study the author is primarily concerned about the effect of the integration of Europe on the political life of the West European states.

Scheingold, Stuart A. **The Rule of Law in European Integration: The Path of the Schuman Plan.** New Haven: Yale University Press, 1965, 331 p.
   A significant study of the political and economic aspects of the work of the Court of Justice of the European Communities after the establishment of a common market for coal and steel.

Schmid, Karl. **Europa zwischen Ideologie und Verwirklichung: psychologische Aspekte der Integration.** Zurich: Artemis Verlag, 1966, 192 p.
   A well-known Swiss professor of German literature at the Technische Hochschule in Zurich writes with erudition about the various concepts of European unification and the psychological problems relevant to the realization of this goal.

Schuman, Robert. **Pour l'Europe.** Paris: Les Éditions Nagel, 2d ed., 1964, 205 p.
   A plea for French-German understanding and European integration, by the late French Premier and Foreign Minister and originator of the plan for the European Coal and Steel Community.

Sidjanski, Dusan. **Dimensions européennes de la science politique: questions méthodologiques et programme de recherches.** Paris: Librairie Générale de Droit, 1963, 187 p.
   A political scientist suggests an elaborate program for the study of European integration.

Siegler, Heinrich, Freiherr von, *ed.* **Europäische politische Einigung 1949-1968: Dokumentation von Vorschlägen und Stellungnahmen.** Bonn: Siegler, Verlag für Zeitarchive, 1968, 435 p.
   A collection of documents on European integration and coöperation covering the years from 1949 to 1968.

Spinelli, Altiero. **The Eurocrats: Conflict and Crisis in the European Community.** Baltimore: Johns Hopkins Press, 1966, 229 p.
   A description of the centers of united European action, how they are connected, and how they have fared. The Italian author has long been active in the European federalist movement.

Uri, Pierre. **Partnership for Progress: A Program for Transatlantic Action.** New York: Harper and Row (for the Atlantic Institute), 1963, 126 p.
   In this study Mr. Uri succinctly sets forth specific proposals for strengthening the economic unity of members of the Atlantic Community.

Willis, Frank Roy. **France, Germany, and the New Europe, 1945–1963.** Stanford: Stanford University Press, rev. ed., 1968, 431 p.
A lucid history of the partial unification of Europe as achieved through the rapprochement of two former enemies, by an American historian.

European Communities; European Economic Community; European Coal and Steel Community; European Atomic Energy Community; European Free Trade Association

See also Comparative Government, p. 18; General Economic Conditions and Tendencies, p. 49; International Trade, p. 55; International Finance, p. 59; International Organization and Government, p. 96; (War) Nuclear Weapons; Missiles, p. 115; (The United States) Foreign Policy, p. 229; (Western Europe) General Surveys and Political Problems, p. 345; Economic and Social Problems, p. 347; and the sections for specific countries and regions.

Ananiadès, Léonide C. **L'Association aux communautés européennes.** Paris: Librairie Générale de Droit, 1967, 352 p.
A thorough examination, largely juridical, of the different kinds of associations existing or envisaged in the treaties of the European communities.

Balekjian, Wahé Hagop. **Legal Aspects of Foreign Investment in the European Economic Community.** Dobbs Ferry (N.Y.): Oceana Publications, 1968, 356 p.
A detailed summary by country of laws on exchange control, taxation, the treatment of foreign-owned firms and related matters.

Barzanti, Sergio. **The Underdeveloped Areas within the Common Market.** Princeton: Princeton University Press, 1965, 437 p.
This study deals primarily with southern Italy and some areas of France.

Bell, Coral, *ed*. **Europe without Britain.** Melbourne: Cheshire (for the Australian Institute of International Affairs), 1963, 120 p.
Essays dealing chiefly with the diplomatic and political aspects of the breakdown of the negotiations for Britain's entry into the Common Market in the early 1960s.

Blake, Harlan Morse, *ed*. **Business Regulation in the Common Market Nations.** New York: McGraw-Hill, 1969, 4 v.
This valuable series was sponsored by a special committee of the Association of the Bar of the City of New York. Volume 1, "Belgium, The Netherlands, Luxembourg," edited by Ruth B. Ginsburg and others (1969, 576 p.); vol. 2, "France, Italy," edited by Barbara B. Blake and Joseph M. Perillo (1969, 601 p.); vol. 3, "West Germany," edited by Kim Ebb and others (1969, 437 p.); and vol. 4, "Common Market and American Antitrust: Overlap and Conflict," edited by James A. Rahl (1970, 476 p.).

Bodenheimer, Susanne J. **Political Union: A Microcosm of European Politics, 1960–1966.** Leyden: Sijthoff, 1967, 229 p.
A study of the difficulties of establishing political union among the members of the European Economic Community.

Bourrinet, Jacques. **Le Problème agricole dans l'intégration européenne.** Paris: Cujas, 1964, 337 p.
A discussion of West European agricultural policies up to the end of 1963.

Butterwick, Michael and Rolfe, Edmund Neville. **Food, Farming, and the Common Market.** New York: Oxford University Press, 1968, 259 p.
Essentially a reference work comparing agriculture in Britain and the Common Market as to policy, production and trade.

Campbell, Alan. **Restrictive Trading Agreements in the Common Market.** South Hackensack (N.J.): Rothman, 1964, 228 p.
Texts and commentaries of the Rome Treaty and action taken under it.

Campbell of Eskan, Baron and Others. **Britain, the EEC and the Third World.** New York: Praeger (in association with the Overseas Development Institute), 1972, 95 p.
Very good for data and arguments about the effect on poor countries of Britain's entry into the European Community.

Camps, Miriam. **Britain and the European Community, 1955-1963.** Princeton: Princeton University Press, 1964, 547 p.
A first-rate study by an American authority who has been a close observer of both the development of the European Community and the evolution of British policy toward it.

Camps, Miriam. **European Unification in the Sixties: From the Veto to the Crisis.** New York: McGraw-Hill (for the Council on Foreign Relations), 1966, 273 p.
A discussion of the implications for European integration of de Gaulle's veto on British entry and of the Community's 1965 crisis.

Camps, Miriam. **What Kind of Europe? The Community Since de Gaulle's Veto.** New York: Oxford University Press (for the Royal Institute of International Affairs), 1965, 140 p.
After reviewing the two years following de Gaulle's veto of British entry into the Common Market, the author expresses the conviction that "the 'federalizing' process of the Community" is going to continue, "albeit more slowly than many would wish."

Casadio, Gian Paolo. **Una politica agricola per l'Europa: i problemi del finanziamento.** Bologna: Il Mulino (for Istituto Affari Internazionali, Rome), 1967, 267 p.
A detailed study of the intricate arrangements for financing the European Community's common agricultural policy.

Clark, William Hartley. **The Politics of the Common Market.** Englewood Cliffs: Prentice-Hall, 1967, 180 p.
A combination of introductory survey and perceptive comment.

Coffey, Peter and Presley, John R. **European Monetary Integration.** New York: St. Martin's Press, 1972, 131 p.
Concise history and quick, crisp arguments for moving ahead faster.

Constant, S. C. and Others. **L'Europe du charbon et de l'acier.** Paris: Presses Universitaires, 1968, 199 p.
A broad economic and geographical survey of the six countries of the European Community.

Coombes, David L. **Politics and Bureaucracy in the European Community.** London: Allen and Unwin, 1970, 343 p.
A serious and well-written analysis.

Corbet, Hugh and Robertson, David, *eds.* **Europe's Free Trade Area Experiment.** Elmsford (N.Y.): Pergamon Press, 1970, 258 p.
Papers on EFTA experience and prospects by close observers.

Davidson, Ian. **Britain and the Making of Europe.** New York: St. Martin's Press, 1972, 150 p.
The European editor of the *Financial Times* gives a lucid account of the functions of the European Community, with some sober thoughts on how Britain's entry could affect the Community's open-ended future.

Drouin, Pierre. **L'Europe du Marché Commun.** Paris: Julliard, 1963, 350 p.
A survey of the Common Market by a well-informed French journalist.

Ellis, Harry Bearse. **The Common Market.** Cleveland: World Publishing Co., 1965, 204 p.
A readable, comprehensive and optimistic survey.

Ernst, Heiner. **Die grüne Front: Probleme der Agrarpolitik der EWG.** Vienna: Europa-Verlag, 1965, 212 p.
A study of the agricultural policies of the European Common Market.

The European Free Trade Association and the Crisis of European Integration: An Aspect of the Atlantic Crisis? London: Michael Joseph (for the Graduate Institute of International Studies, Geneva), 1968, 323 p.
Exploring possible steps in European integration, the authors advocate a broad, rather loose grouping comprising EFTA and the European Community, with politics played down and bridges being built to the East. The study also surveys the position of each EFTA country.

Feld, Werner Joachim. **The European Common Market and the World.** Englewood Cliffs: Prentice-Hall, 1967, 184 p.
A solid survey by a close student of the subject.

Feld, Werner Joachim. **Transnational Business Collaboration Among Common Market Countries.** New York: Praeger, 1970, 139 p.
   This study is not the definitive treatment of an important topic.

Fischer, Fritz. **Die institutionalisierte Vertretung der Verbände in der Europäischen Wirtschaftsgemeinschaft.** Hamburg: Hansischer Gildenverlag (for the Institut für Internationales Recht, Universität Kiel), 1965, 207 p.
   Useful description of relations between groups representing private economic interests and the organs of the European Economic Community.

Freisberg, Ernst. **Die grüne Hürde Europas: deutsche Agrarpolitik und EWG.** Cologne: Westdeutscher Verlag, 1965, 214 p.
   A German socialist and agricultural expert discusses the difficulties the European Common Market has encountered, especially as relating to Germany, in formulating its agrarian policies.

Green, Andrew Wilson. **Political Integration by Jurisprudence.** Leyden: Sijthoff, 1969, 847 p.
   A massive study of the impact of the Court of Justice of the European Communities on European political integration, by an American scholar.

Hallstein, Walter. **Europe in the Making.** New York: Norton, 1973, 343 p.
   A former president of the European Economic Community surveys the history, problems and achievements of that organization. The German original appeared as "Der unvollendete Bundesstaat: europäische Erfahrungen und Erkenntnisse" (Düsseldorf: Econ-Verlag, 1969, 283 p.).

Holt, Stephen. **The Common Market: The Conflict of Theory and Practice.** London: Hamish Hamilton, 1967, 207 p.
   Among the strong points of this book are its detailed treatment of some of the decision-making procedures inside the Community, the make-up of its staff, functional representation and the federal and non-federal elements in its organization.

Houben, Petrus Henricus Johannes Maria. **Les Conseils de ministres des communautés européennes.** Leyden: Sijthoff, 1964, 259 p.
   An examination of the juridical structure and functioning of the Councils of Ministers of the three European Communities—Coal and Steel, Atomic Energy and Common Market. By a member of the Dutch Foreign Office.

Houdbine, Anne-Marie and Vergès, Jean-Raymond. **Le Parlement européen dans la construction de l'Europe des six.** Paris: Presses Universitaires, 1966, 184 p.
   Two short, scholarly studies on how democratic and how effective the European Parliament is.

Jegouzo, Y. **L'Élaboration de la politique de développement dans l'Europe communautaire.** Paris: Librairie Générale de Droit, 1970, 521 p.
   An exhaustive examination of who does what in European development planning and administration.

Jensen, Finn B. and Walter, Ingo. **The Common Market: Economic Integration in Europe.** Philadelphia: Lippincott, 1965, 278 p.
   A comprehensive introduction.

Junckerstorff, Henry Alfred Kurt with Mihanovich, Clement S., *eds.* **International Manual on the European Economic Community.** St. Louis: St. Louis University Press, 1963, 521 p.
   A practical guide, compiled by European and American authors, on the objectives and initial success of the Common Market.

Kaiser, Karl. **EWG und Freihandelszone.** Leyden: Sijthoff, 1963, 270 p.
   A solid study of the European Economic Community and the free-trade-area negotiations.

Kirschen, Étienne-Sadi with Others. **Financial Integration in Western Europe.** New York: Columbia University Press, 1969, 144 p.
   Useful as a succinct, documented account of the harmonization of economic policies in the Common Market countries, the development of European capital markets, and the work of common financial organizations such as the European Investment Bank.

Kohnstamm, Max. **The European Community and its Role in the World.** Columbia: University of Missouri Press, 1964, 82 p.
A Dutchman, who has devoted years to European integration at the side of Jean Monnet, reviews succinctly the problem of European unification.

Kovar, Robert. **Le Pouvoir réglementaire de la Communauté européenne du charbon et de l'acier.** Paris: Librairie Générale de Droit, 1964, 348 p.
A legal study of the European Coal and Steel Community.

Lambrinidis, John S. **The Structure, Function, and Law of a Free Trade Area: The European Free Trade Association.** New York: Praeger (for the London Institute of World Affairs), 1965, 303 p.
A Greek barrister with British experience provides a detailed exegesis of the EFTA treaty and the practices under it.

Lang, John Temple. **The Common Market and Common Law: Legal Aspects of Foreign Investment and Economic Integration in the European Community, with Ireland as a Prototype.** Chicago: University of Chicago Press, 1966, 573 p.
A broad study of legal and economic issues involved in British and Irish membership in the European Common Market.

Lindberg, Leon N. and Scheingold, Stuart A. **Europe's Would-Be Polity: Patterns of Change in the European Community.** Englewood Cliffs: Prentice-Hall, 1970, 314 p.
Two veteran students of the European Community have digested a mass of fragmentary evidence in an effort to analyze how it works and how it may change. For the political scientist rather than the general reader.

Manzanarès, Henri. **Le Parlement européen.** Paris: Berger-Levrault, 1964, 321 p.
A comprehensive scholarly study of the organization and functions of the European Parliament.

Melchior de Molènes, Charles. **L'Europe de Strasbourg.** Paris: Éditions Roudil, 1971, 774 p.
A study of the history, structure and activities of the Council of Europe.

Meynaud, Jean and Sidjanski, Dusan. **L'Europe des affaires: rôle et structure des groupes.** Paris: Payot, 1967, 247 p.
A study of large industrial groups and organizations in the European Community. The authors conclude that economic integration will not lead to political unity.

Meynaud, Jean and Sidjanski, Dusan. **Les Groupes de pression dans la Communauté européenne, 1958-1968.** Brussels: Éditions de l'Institut de Sociologie, 1971, 733 p.
A comprehensive study of the influence of organized labor, professional societies, the press, financial institutions and industrial enterprises and organizations on the activities of the European Economic Community in the period from 1958 to 1968.

Neunreither, Karlheinz. **Das Europa der Sechs ohne Aussenpolitik.** Cologne: Westdeutscher Verlag, 1964, 191 p.
A comprehensive and knowledgeable review of the political and economic relations between the European Economic Community and the rest of the world.

Newhouse, John. **Collision in Brussels: The Common Market Crisis of 30 June 1965.** New York: Norton, 1967, 195 p.
A detailed account, with much inside information, of the background and working out of a crisis that changed life in the Common Market.

Oudenhove, Guy van. **The Political Parties in the European Parliament: The First Ten Years, September 1952-September 1962.** Leyden: Sijthoff, 1965, 268 p.
A pioneering study by a Belgian political scientist of the European Parliament and of the emergence of supranational parties in that body.

Parker, Geoffrey. **An Economic Geography of the Common Market.** New York: Praeger, 1969, 178 p.
A comprehensive study by a British author.

Pflimlin, Pierre and Legrand-Lane, Raymond. **L'Europe communautaire.** Paris: Plon, 1966, 398 p.
A prominent French statesman and advocate of European unity surveys, with the

help of a colleague, the post-World War II developments that led to the establishment of the Common Market.

Polach, Jaroslav George. **EURATOM: Its Background, Issues and Economic Implications.** Dobbs Ferry (N.Y.): Oceana Publications, 1964, 232 p.
A detailed study of the European Atomic Energy Community.

Ramazani, Rouhollah Karegar. **The Middle East and the European Common Market.** Charlottesville: University Press of Virginia, 1964, 152 p.
An informative study by an Iranian-born professor at the University of Virginia.

Rangnekar, D. K. **India, Britain and European Common Market.** New Delhi: R. and K. Publishing House (for the National Institute of Public Affairs, New Delhi), 1963, 236 p.
An Indian economist reflects on the exclusiveness of the Common Market and makes important proposals concerning economic coöperation among underdeveloped nations.

Raux, Jean. **Les Relations extérieures de la Communauté économique européenne.** Paris: Cujas, 1966, 557 p.
A detailed survey of the external relations of the European Economic Community.

Sarmet, Marcel. **L'Épargne dans le Marché commun: comparaison avec la Grande-Bretagne et les États-Unis.** Paris: Éditions Cujas, 1963, 506 p.
A statistical and theoretical study of the economies of the Common Market, Great Britain and the United States.

Schneider, Herbert. **Grossbritanniens Weg nach Europa.** Freiburg: Rombach, 1968, 253 p.
A study of the British attitude toward European economic integration in the years from 1955 to 1961.

Stohler, Jacques. **Die Integration des Verkehrs: europäische Erfahrungen und Probleme.** Basel: Kyklos-Verlag; Tübingen: Mohr, 1963, 180 p.
A thoroughgoing review of the integration of transportation in the Common Market.

Walsh, A. E. and Paxton, John. **The Structure and Development of the Common Market.** London: Hutchinson, 1968, 232 p.
A comprehensive British survey.

Walter, Ingo. **The European Common Market: Growth and Patterns of Trade and Production.** New York: Praeger, 1967, 212 p.
Statistical analysis of the impact of the Common Market on trade among its members.

Wasserman, Max Judd and Others. **The Common Market and American Business.** New York: Simmons-Boardman, 1964, 300 p.
Clear-cut presentation of basic data and broad analysis to help the businessman trade or invest in Western Europe.

Weil, Gordon Lee. **A Foreign Policy for Europe? The External Relations of the European Community.** Bruges: College of Europe, 1970, 324 p.
An analysis of the uneven, and on the whole disappointing, beginnings of a common foreign policy for the European Community. An informative study by a close American observer.

Weil, Gordon Lee, ed. **A Handbook on the European Economic Community.** New York: Praeger (in coöperation with the European Community Information Service), 1965, 479 p.
The Information Service's former Director of Research and Studies has arranged complete documents and excerpts to give a full and fairly detailed picture of the growth and operations of the European Economic Community. There is a bibliography of the published official documents of the Community.

Willemsen, Adriaan. **Wettbewerbstheorie—Wettbewerbspolitik.** Bern: Stämpfli, 1971, 313 p.
A comparison of theory, policy and law on competition in the European Community and EFTA that emphasizes the different purposes of the two bodies.

Zeller, Adrien with Giraudy, Jean-Louis. **L'Imbroglio agricole du Marché commun.** Paris: Calmann-Lévy, 1970, 316 p.
A very critical analysis of the European Community's common agricultural policy.

EASTERN EUROPE AND THE SOVIET BLOC

General Surveys and Political Problems

See also General Works, p. 1; Political Factors, p. 12; International Law, p. 83; International Organization and Government, p. 96; The World Since 1914, p. 129; and the sections for specific countries.

Adams, Arthur Eugene and Others. **An Atlas of Russian and East European History.** New York: Praeger, 1967, 204 p.
A useful reference covering more than 1500 years of Russian and East European history.

Bender, Peter. **6 x Sicherheit.** Cologne: Kiepenheuer (for the Institute for Strategic Studies, London), 1971, 250 p.
A study of the individual efforts of the six East European states of the Warsaw Pact to achieve security against various real or perceived threats in the postwar years.

Blumenfeld, Yorick. **Seesaw: Cultural Life in Eastern Europe.** New York: Harcourt, Brace and World, 1968, 276 p.
A journalist's report on the highly interesting cultural ferment in Eastern Europe in the 1960s—in the arts, cinema, theater and politics—and on the efforts to stifle or contain it.

Bromke, Adam and Rakowska-Harmstone, Teresa, *eds.* **The Communist States in Disarray, 1965-1971.** Minneapolis: University of Minnesota Press, 1972, 363 p.
Essays on tensions and conflicts within the Communist world in the second half of the 1960s.

Brown, James F. **The New Eastern Europe: The Khrushchev Era and After.** New York: Praeger, 1966, 306 p.
A survey of developments in Eastern Europe during and since the Khrushchev era.

Brzezinski, Zbigniew Kazimierz. **The Soviet Bloc: Unity and Conflict.** Cambridge: Harvard University Press, rev. and enl. ed., 1967, 599 p.
A considerably revised and enlarged edition of an important study, first published in 1960.

Collier, David S. and Glaser, Kurt, *eds.* **Berlin and the Future of Eastern Europe.** Chicago: Regnery (in coöperation with Foundation for Foreign Affairs), 1963, 251 p.
A collection of conference papers dealing with a variety of issues: European unity, Berlin, the East-West conflict, Eastern Europe and German-Slav relations.

Collier, David S. and Glaser, Kurt, *eds.* **Elements of Change in Eastern Europe: Prospects for Freedom.** Chicago: Regnery (in coöperation with Foundation for Foreign Affairs), 1968, 251 p.
Papers presented at an international congress in Wiesbaden in September 1966.

Collier, David S. and Glaser, Kurt, *eds.* **Western Integration and the Future of Eastern Europe.** Chicago: Regnery (in coöperation with Foundation for Foreign Affairs), 1964, 207 p.
Papers presented at an international conference held in Wiesbaden in September 1963.

Collier, David S. and Glaser, Kurt, *eds.* **Western Policy and Eastern Europe.** Chicago: Regnery (in coöperation with Foundation for Foreign Affairs), 1966, 245 p.
Papers from a German-American conference held in March 1965.

Czerwinski, E. J. and Piekalkiewicz, Jaroslaw A., *eds.* **The Soviet Invasion of Czechoslovakia: Its Effects on Eastern Europe.** New York: Praeger, 1972, 210 p.
Essays dealing with various aspects of the impact of the 1968 invasion on the other states of Eastern Europe.

Farrell, Robert Barry, *ed.* **Political Leadership in Eastern Europe and the Soviet Union.** Chicago: Aldine Publishing Co., 1970, 359 p.
A collection of papers dealing with the theoretical bases of Soviet and East European leadership, types of leaders and their relation to society.

Fejtö, François. **A History of the People's Democracies: Eastern Europe Since Stalin.** New York: Praeger, 1971, 374 p.
A translation of a substantial study, "Histoire des démocraties populaires; II: Après

Staline, 1953–1968" (Paris: Éditions du Seuil, 1969, 533 p.), in which a leading student of Eastern Europe picks up the thread of the first volume of this study (published in 1952) and carries it through to the Soviet occupation of Czechoslovakia.

Fischer-Galati, Stephen Alexander, *ed*. **Eastern Europe in the Sixties.** New York: Praeger, 1963, 239 p.
A cross-country survey, by nine authors, of contemporary Eastern Europe.

Frenzke, Dietrich and Uschakow, Alexander, *eds*. **Macht und Recht im kommunistischen Herrschaftssystem.** Cologne: Verlag Wissenschaft und Politik, 1965, 334 p.
A collection of essays on Soviet and East European law and politics, published in honor of Boris Meissner, a leading German scholar of East European law and history.

Geyer, Dietrich, *ed*. **Wissenschaft in kommunistischen Ländern.** Tübingen: Wunderlich, 1967, 309 p.
Essays by German scholars on philosophical, scientific, political and literary thought in the communist countries of Europe.

Hoffman, George W., *ed*. **Eastern Europe.** New York: Praeger, 1971, 502 p.
Essays, with comments, on various aspects of geography and geographical scholarship in East Central and Southeastern Europe.

Horecky, Paul Louis, *ed*. **Southeastern Europe: A Guide to Basic Publications.** Chicago: University of Chicago Press, 1969, 755 p.

———. **East Central Europe: A Guide to Basic Publications.** Chicago: University of Chicago Press, 1969, 956 p.
Most useful reference volumes "containing a highly selective and judiciously evaluated inventory of the most important publications" relating to Eastern Europe. These surveys were initiated by the Subcommittee on East Central and Southeast European Studies of the American Council of Learned Societies and the Social Science Research Council.

Iatrides, John O. **Balkan Triangle: Birth and Decline of an Alliance Across Ideological Boundaries.** The Hague: Mouton, 1968, 211 p.
A monograph centering on the pact of coöperation and the military alliance concluded in 1953 and 1954 among Jugoslavia, Greece and Turkey.

Ionescu, Ghita. **The Break-Up of the Soviet Empire in Eastern Europe.** Baltimore: Penguin, 1965, 168 p.
A balanced survey of the dramatic and far-reaching changes within the Soviet bloc since the end of World War II, by a former Rumanian diplomat now teaching in England.

Ionescu, Ghita. **The Politics of the European Communist States.** New York: Praeger, 1967, 303 p.
An analysis of the relation between state and society in the communist states of Eastern Europe, excluding the Soviet Union. The treatment is topical and deals centrally with the question of state power and the checks upon it through dissent or countervailing influences.

Jackson, George D. **Comintern and Peasant in East Europe, 1919–1930.** New York: Columbia University Press, 1966, 339 p.
A scholarly account of the efforts of the Comintern and of the various peasant parties to master or gain the support of the important peasant movement in Eastern Europe in the first decade after World War I.

Jamgotch, Nish, Jr. **Soviet-East European Dialogue: International Relations of a New Type?** Stanford: Hoover Institution on War, Revolution, and Peace, 1968, 165 p.
An essay centering on the theme that "Soviet interaction with East European states bears an inherent theoretical content and built-in proposition which underpins the Soviet political system itself."

Kase, Francis Joseph. **People's Democracy: A Contribution to the Study of the Communist Theory of State and Revolution.** Leyden: Sijthoff, 1968, 223 p.
A critical analysis of the theory of "people's democracy" and its application in the various stages of the Communist takeover in Eastern Europe after World War II. The last portion of the book looks at the area outside Europe.

Lendvai, Paul. **Eagles in Cobwebs: Nationalism and Communism in the Balkans.** Garden City: Doubleday, 1969, 396 p.

An interesting discussion, by a Hungarian-born journalist, of the recent and diverse trends in Jugoslavia, Rumania, Albania and Bulgaria.

Lewis, Flora. **Red Pawn: The Story of Noel Field.** Garden City: Doubleday, 1965, 283 p.
An able and most interesting effort to unravel the mysteries and political ramifications of the disappearances, arrests and reappearances in Communist Eastern Europe of Noel Field, his wife and brother.

Liess, Otto Rudolf. **Südosteuropa: Befund und Deutung.** Vienna: Wollzeilen Verlag, 1968, 399 p.
A general survey of contemporary Southeast Europe, by topic and by country, from Czechoslovakia to Turkey.

London, Kurt, ed. **Eastern Europe in Transition.** Baltimore: Johns Hopkins Press, 1966, 364 p.
A group of papers, covering various facets of change in Eastern Europe, based on the Fifth International Conference on World Politics held in the Netherlands in September 1965.

Lukaszewski, Jerzy, ed. **The People's Democracies after Prague: Soviet Hegemony, Nationalism, Regional Integration?** Bruges: De Tempel, 1970, 330 p.
Papers originally presented at a symposium, sponsored by the Collège d'Europe in Bruges, relating to trends and prospects in Eastern Europe, especially in light of the events of 1968.

McNeal, Robert Hatch, ed. **International Relations among Communists.** Englewood Cliffs: Prentice-Hall, 1967, 181 p.
A collection of documents concerning relations between communist states since the end of the Second World War.

Meier, Viktor E. **Neuer Nationalismus in Südosteuropa.** Opladen: Leske (for the Forschungsinstitut der Deutschen Gesellschaft für Auswärtige Politik), 1968, 154 p.
A concise study of nationalism in contemporary Southeast European politics.

Národní fronta a komunisté: Československo, Jugoslávie, Polsko, 1938-1945. Prague: Naše vojsko, 1968, 716 p.
Papers and comments from a conference of Czechoslovak, Polish and Jugoslav historians, held in Belgrade in October 1966, to discuss the origins of the National Front concept and its relationship to the communist seizure of power in Czechoslovakia, Jugoslavia and Poland. The National Fronts are seen as products of domestic political conditions, rather than of Moscow's guidance. A few of the contributions, however, hint cautiously that for the Soviet Union the National Front was part of a long-term strategy. Records from the national party archives, but not from the Comintern and Soviet files, had been accessible to many of the participants.

Opat, Jaroslav ed. **Střední a jihovýchodní Evropa ve válce a v revoluci, 1939-1945: Československo, Polsko, Jugoslávie, Albánie, Rumunsko, Bulharsko, Maďarsko.** Prague: Academia, 1969, 561 p.
An important collection of essays by Czechoslovakia's "liberal" Marxist historians. Intent to legitimize the communists' rise to power after World War II, the authors stress the allegedly decisive role of communist-dominated resistance movements rather than the importance of the conquest of East Central Europe by the Red Army. Despite the ensuing distortions, the essays present an impressive amount of annotated factual data.

Paikert, G. C. **The Danube Swabians: German Populations in Hungary, Rumania and Yugoslavia and Hitler's Impact on Their Patterns.** The Hague: Nijhoff, 1967, 324 p.
A thorough study of the German minorities in Hungary, Rumania and Jugoslavia from the eighteenth century to the end of World War II. The author, a Hungarian scholar, pays particular attention to the Nazi successes in penetrating their political and cultural organizations and describes the tragic fate that overtook them at the end of the war when most of them were expelled from their homelands and a considerable number was massacred.

Pounds, Norman John Greville. **Eastern Europe.** Chicago: Aldine Publishing Co., 1969, 912 p.
This volume in the series of "Geographies for Advanced Study" is an authoritative survey both of the region as a whole and of the constituent countries—East Germany, Poland, Czechoslovakia, Hungary, Rumania, Jugoslavia, Bulgaria and Albania.

Raupach, Hans. **Wirtschaft und Politik in Osteuropa.** Berlin: Duncker, 1968, 204 p.
A collection of Hans Raupach's essays on East European and Soviet economic and political problems published in celebration of the author's 65th birthday. Edited by Werner Gumpel and Dietmar Keese.

Roberts, Henry L. **Eastern Europe: Politics, Revolution, and Diplomacy.** New York: Knopf, 1970, 324 p.
A selection of the late author's essays written since 1951 and dealing with the historiography, politics and diplomacy of Eastern Europe and the Soviet Union.

Ross, Thomas. **Osteuropa kehrt zurück.** Vienna: Molden, 1965, 359 p.
A German journalist reports on the winds of change in the communist states of Eastern Europe.

Roucek, Joseph Slabey and Lottich, Kenneth V. **Behind the Iron Curtain.** Caldwell (Idaho): Caxton Printers, 1964, 631 p.
Most of the chapters in this volume deal with education and cultural indoctrination in the communist countries.

Schöpflin, George, *ed.* **The Soviet Union and Eastern Europe.** New York: Praeger, 1970, 614 p.
A substantial handbook, with chapters by numerous specialists.

Shaffer, Harry G., *ed.* **The Communist World.** New York: Appleton, 1967, 558 p.
A survey of the U.S.S.R. and other communist countries, comprising both Marxist and non-Marxist views.

Shub, Anatole. **An Empire Loses Hope: The Return of Stalin's Ghost.** New York: Norton, 1970, 474 p.
An extensive, well-informed and largely personal report on developments in Eastern Europe and the Soviet Union in the 1960s. The author, an able American journalist, was in the area for most of the period.

Singleton, Frederick Bernard. **Background to Eastern Europe.** New York: Pergamon Press, 1965, 226 p.
A short introduction to the historical, political, geographic and economic problems of contemporary Eastern Europe, by an English scholar.

Skilling, Harold Gordon. **Communism, National and International: Eastern Europe after Stalin.** Toronto: University of Toronto Press (in association with the Canadian Institute of International Affairs), 1964, 168 p.
An informed appraisal of developments in Eastern Europe by a scholar who has traveled widely in the area.

Skilling, Harold Gordon. **The Governments of Communist East Europe.** New York: Crowell, 1966, 256 p.
A concise but useful study, handled topically rather than by country.

Staar, Richard Felix, *ed.* **Aspects of Modern Communism.** Columbia: University of South Carolina Press, 1968, 416 p.
Papers and discussions relating to political, economic and military developments in the Soviet Union, Eastern Europe and communist Asia.

Staar, Richard Felix. **The Communist Regimes in Eastern Europe.** Stanford: Hoover Institution on War, Revolution and Peace, 2d rev. ed., 1971, 304 p.
An introductory survey.

Ströhm, Carl Gustaf. **Zwischen Mao und Chruschtschow: Wandlungen des Kommunismus in Südosteuropa.** Stuttgart: Kohlhammer, 1964, 303 p.
A penetrating analysis of political developments in post-War War II Southeastern Europe, with special emphasis on Jugoslavia and its variety of communism.

Sugar, Peter F. and Lederer, Ivo J. *eds.* **Nationalism in Eastern Europe.** Seattle: University of Washington Press, 1969, 465 p.
This volume comprises essays by very competent specialists on the emergence of nationalism in a rich variety of modes in Albania, Bulgaria, Czechoslovakia, Greece, Hungary, Jugoslavia, Poland and Rumania.

Toma, Peter A., *ed.* **The Changing Face of Communism in Eastern Europe.** Tucson: University of Arizona Press, 1970, 413 p.
The papers in this collection were originally presented at a summer institute at the University of Arizona in 1969.

Triska, Jan F., *ed.* **Constitutions of the Communist Party-States.** Stanford: Hoover Institution on War, Revolution, and Peace, 1968, 541 p.
A convenient collection and translation of the texts, past and present, of the constitutions of states ruled by communist parties.

Urban, George R., *ed.* **Scaling the Wall: Talking to Eastern Europe.** Detroit: Wayne State University Press, 1964, 303 p.
A selection of broadcasts from Radio Free Europe. The English edition appeared under the title "Talking to Eastern Europe" (London: Eyre, 1964, 303 p.).

Volkmann, Hans-Erich, *ed.* **Die Krise des Parlamentarismus in Ostmitteleuropa zwischen den beiden Weltkriegen.** Marburg/Lahn: Herder-Institut, 1967, 184 p.
A study of the crisis that befell the parliamentary system in Poland, Czechoslovakia and the Baltic States in the inter-war years.

Vukadinović, Radovan. **Odnosi medju evropskim socijalističkim državama SEV i Varšavski ugovor.** Zagreb: Školska knjiga, 1970, 328 p.
A comprehensive and very carefully researched Jugoslav study concerned with political and economic relations among the European communist states. There is an appendix of the most important COMECON and Warsaw Pact documents and a bibliography.

Zsolnay, Vilmos von. **Die Wissenschaft in Osteuropa.** Mainz: v. Hase and Koehler, 1967, 230 p.
A survey of the role of organization of the sciences in the U.S.S.R., Poland, Hungary, Czechoslovakia and Rumania.

Economic Problems

See also Economic Factors, p. 49; Second World War, p. 144; The Postwar World, p. 178; (The United States) Foreign Policy, p. 229; (Eastern Europe and the Soviet Bloc) General Surveys and Political Problems, p. 358; Council for Mutual Economic Assistance; Warsaw Treaty Organization, p. 365; and the sections for specific countries.

Adams, Arthur E. and Adams, Jan S. **Men Versus Systems.** New York: Free Press, 1971, 327 p.
A comparative study of the agricultural systems of the Soviet Union, Poland and Czechoslovakia, based in part on the authors' personal observations and interviews in 1967.

Ebel, Robert E. **Communist Trade in Oil and Gas.** New York: Praeger, 1970, 447 p.
An effort to project the future export capability of the Soviet bloc.

Fox, Ursula. **Das Bankwesen der europäischen Volksdemokratien.** Wiesbaden: Gabler, 1967, 209 p.
This useful study of the structure and activity of banking in Eastern Europe includes an examination of international coöperation in these matters.

Gamarnikow, Michael. **Economic Reforms in Eastern Europe.** Detroit: Wayne State University Press, 1968, 204 p.
A report on economic reforms and the conflict between "dogmatic sclerosis and pragmatic drive."

Grossman, Gregory, *ed.* **Money and Plan: Financial Aspects of East European Economic Reforms.** Berkeley: University of California Press, 1969, 188 p.
Studies of high quality about the place of money and credit in the East European economies.

Harbron, John D. **Communist Ships and Shipping.** New York: Praeger, 1963, 262 p.
A discussion of post-World War II shipbuilding and shipping in Russia, Poland, East Germany, Bulgaria, China and the smaller communist block countries.

Höhmann, Hans-Hermann and Others. **Die Wirtschaftsordnungen Osteuropas im Wandel: Ergebnisse und Probleme der Wirtschaftsreformen.** Freiburg: Rombach, 1972, 2 v.
A substantial collection of country studies and general papers, written by scholars in West Germany and Great Britain, on the economic reforms in Eastern Europe.

Hoffman, George W. **Regional Development Strategy in Southeast Europe: A Comparative Analysis of Albania, Bulgaria, Greece, Romania and Yugoslavia.** New York: Praeger, 1972, 322 p.

This ambitious book brings together a wealth of data and makes some interesting comparisons. Though it is essentially a summary of economic planning and reforms, the geographer's approach and the author's firsthand acquaintance with the area add other dimensions.

Karcz, Jerzy F., ed. **Soviet and East European Agriculture.** Berkeley: University of California Press, 1967, 445 p.

A volume of contributions originally presented at a conference on Soviet agriculture in 1965. While primary emphasis is on the U.S.S.R., there are chapters on Jugoslavia, Poland and Czechoslovakia.

Kaser, Michael Charles, ed. **Economic Development for Eastern Europe.** New York: St. Martin's Press, 1968, 329 p.

These proceedings of a 1964 conference held in Bulgaria by the International Economic Association deal with a variety of theoretical and practical issues.

Köhler, Heinz. **Economic Integration in the Soviet Bloc: With an East German Case Study.** New York: Praeger, 1966, 402 p.

Using developments in East Germany for illustrative purposes, the author describes how the economic integration within the Communist bloc was advanced by the Soviet demand for reparations and the establishment of the Council for Mutual Economic Assistance.

Kretschmar, Robert S., Jr. and Foor, Robin. **The Potential for Joint Ventures in Eastern Europe.** New York: Praeger, 1972, 153 p.

A useful compilation of facts, figures and terminology.

Marer, Paul and Eubanks, Gary J. **Soviet and East European Foreign Trade, 1946-1969: Statistical Compendium and Guide.** Bloomington: Indiana University Press, 1972, 408 p.

A major source of otherwise unobtainable trade data about Eastern Europe.

May, Jacques M. **The Ecology of Malnutrition in Five Countries of Eastern and Central Europe.** New York: Hafner, 1963, 292 p.

A study of food resources and nutritional levels in East Germany, Poland, Jugoslavia, Albania and Greece.

Meier, Jens and Howlowitsch, Johann, eds. **Die Aussenwirtschaft Südosteuropas: Entwicklung—Probleme—Perspektiven.** Cologne: Verlag Wissenschaft und Politik, 1970, 180 p.

Brief essays on the foreign trade of Hungary, Rumania, Bulgaria, Albania, Jugoslavia, Greece and Turkey. Useful statistical tables.

Miller, Margaret and Others. **Communist Economy under Change.** London: Deutsch (for the Institute of Economic Affairs), 1963, 272 p.

Four thoughtful "studies in the theory and practice of markets and competition in Russia, Poland and Yugoslavia."

Pryor, Frederic L. **The Communist Foreign Trade System.** Cambridge: M.I.T. Press, 1963, 296 p.

A satisfactory study of both the national and international aspects of the Communist block trade system.

Raupach, Hans and Others, eds. **Jahrbuch der Wirtschaft Osteuropas; Yearbook of East-European Economics, 1970-.** Munich: Olzog (for the Osteuropa-Institut, München), 1970-.

An annual collection of articles on East European economics.

Reimann, Günter. **Der rote Profit: Preise, Märkte, Kredite im Osten.** Frankfurt/Main: Knapp, 1968, 236 p.

Essays on the economy, finance and foreign trade of Soviet bloc countries. The author, who has traveled widely in Eastern Europe, thinks that unless the profit motive is introduced in communist countries, there is not much hope for the construction of healthy economies.

Selucky, Radoslav. **Economic Reforms in Eastern Europe.** New York: Praeger, 1972, 179 p.

An émigré from Czechoslovakia in 1968 stresses the inevitable connection of economic reform and political relations and the choice between "Sovietizing East European economies" and "Europeanizing the Soviet economy."

Spulber, Nicolas. **Socialist Management and Planning.** Bloomington: Indiana University Press, 1971, 235 p.
  An authority on Soviet and East European economies here examines "the key directions of change in planning, management, and performance control in 'Soviet-type' socialist economies."

Stojković, Momir M. **Medjunarodnopravni položaj Dunava s osvrtom na ekonomski i politički značaj.** Belgrade, 1970, 146 p.
  A survey of the general economic and political importance of the Danube as an international waterway. The study focuses particularly on the activities and problems of the Danube Commission.

Surányi-Unger, Theo. **Studien zum Wirtschaftswachstum Südosteuropas.** Stuttgart: Fischer, 1964, 216 p.
  On economic growth in Communist Hungary, Rumania, Bulgaria and Albania.

Thalheim, Karl Christian. **Beiträge zur Wirtschaftspolitik und Wirtschaftsordnung.** Berlin: Duncker, 1965, 440 p.
  The range of subjects covered by the author over 35 years is wide, but the postwar papers concentrate on the economies of the Soviet Union and Eastern Europe.

Thalheim, Karl Christian, *ed.* **Wachstumsprobleme in den osteuropäischen Volkswirtschaften.** Berlin: Duncker (for the Gesellschaft für Wirtschafts- und Sozialwissenschaften), 1968–70, 2 v.
  Studies on problems of economic growth in Eastern Europe. The first volume deals with the Soviet Union, the second with the German Democratic Republic, Czechoslovakia, Hungary, Jugoslavia, Rumania and Bulgaria. There is also an extensive bibliography.

Thalheim, Karl Christian and Höhmann, Hans-Hermann, *eds.* **Wirtschaftsreformen in Osteuropa.** Cologne: Verlag Wissenschaft und Politik, 1968, 309 p.
  Nine substantial country studies and two more general papers on the economic reforms in Communist countries.

Vásárhelyi, Miklós. **Die Entwicklung des sowjetischen Aussenhandels mit den europäischen Ostblockstaaten seit der Gründung des COMECON (1949–1963).** Aarau: Keller, 1967, 221 p.
  Detailed review of trade among the Communist countries of Europe, stressing Soviet domination of their coöperative measures. Statistics by product and country to 1963.

Weber, Eckhard. **Stadien der Aussenhandelsverflechtung Ostmittel- und Südosteuropas.** Stuttgart: G. Fischer, 1971, 308 p.
  A significant study of the evolution of foreign trade patterns in East Central and Southeastern Europe in the years of Soviet hegemony.

Wellisz, Stanisław Henryk. **The Economies of the Soviet Bloc.** New York: McGraw-Hill, 1964, 245 p.
  An introduction to the operation of Soviet-type economies with particular reference to decision-making and resource allocation. The Polish experience receives most attention.

Wilczynski, J. **Socialist Economic Development and Reforms.** New York: Praeger, 1972, 350 p.
  A systematic analysis of recent economic reforms in the eight socialist countries of Eastern Europe.

Wrangel, Georg von. **Wird der Ostblock kapitalistisch? Die kommunistischen Wirtschaftsreformen und ihre Bedeutung.** Munich: Moderne Verlag, 1966, 263 p.
  A survey of economic reforms in the Soviet bloc countries. The author concludes that the communists have not changed their basic economic ideas.

Zauberman, Alfred. **Industrial Progress in Poland, Czechoslovakia, and East Germany, 1937–1962.** New York: Oxford University Press (for the Royal Institute of International Affairs), 1964, 338 p.
  The energy, metal and chemical industries receive special attention in this detailed study which also devotes chapters to the labor force, foreign trade and the effect of planning and other governmental measures.

Council for Mutual Economic Assistance; Warsaw Treaty Organization

See also Economic Factors, p. 49; War and Peace, p. 108; The Postwar World, p. 178; Western Europe, p. 345; (Eastern Europe and the Soviet Bloc) General Surveys and Political Problems, p. 358; Economic Problems, p. 362; and the sections for specific countries.

Ágoston, István. **Le Marché commun communiste: principes et pratique du COMECON.** Geneva: Droz, 1964, 353 p.
A substantial dissertation on COMECON. Useful bibliography.

Barkovskii, Anatolii Nikolaevich and Others. **Problemy koordinatsii narodno-khoziaistvennykh planov stran SEV.** Moscow: Izd-vo "Mezdunarodnye Otnosheniia," 1968, 325 p.
An examination of the practical as well as the theoretical problems of coördinating the central planning processes of states belonging to the Council for Mutual Economic Assistance.

Caillot, Jean. **Le C.A.E.M.** Paris: Librairie Générale de Droit, 1971, 413 p.
A juridical examination of the structure and extent of integration of COMECON.

Grzybowski, Kazimierz. **The Socialist Commonwealth of Nations: Organizations and Institutions.** New Haven: Yale University Press, 1964, 300 p.
The author discusses the "legal unity" of the "socialist commonwealth," and of such organs as the Council for Mutual Economic Assistance and the Warsaw Treaty Organization. Prepared under the auspices of the American Society of International Law.

Hacker, Jens and Uschakow, Alexander. **Die Integration Osteuropas 1961 bis 1965.** Cologne: Verlag Wissenschaft und Politik, 1966, 323 p.
Two studies on East European military and economic integration in the period from 1961 to 1965, supplemented with documents and bibliographies. Jens Hacker has described the Warsaw Pact and Alexander Uschakow the COMECON.

Kaser, Michael Charles. **COMECON: Integration Problems of the Planned Economies.** New York: Oxford University Press (for the Royal Institute of International Affairs), 2d ed., 1967, 279 p.
A standard study of the Council for Mutual Economic Assistance, by an Oxford don who spent a number of years on the staff of the U.N. Economic Commission for Europe.

Meissner, Boris, ed. **Der Warschauer Pakt: Dokumentensammlung.** Cologne: Verlag Wissenschaft und Politik (for the Seminar für Politik, Gesellschaft und Recht Osteuropas der Universität Kiel), 1962, 203 p.
A study of the history, organization and goals of the Warsaw Pact. There is a documentary supplement and a chronology.

Menzhinskii, V. I., ed. **Mezhdunarodnye organizatsii sotsialisticheskikh stran: pravovye voprosy organizatsii i deiatel'nost'.** Moscow: Izd-vo "Mezhdunarodnye Otnosheniia," 1971, 221 p.
A survey of international organizations that serve the socialist countries of Eastern Europe.

Pommer, Hans Jörg. **Politik und Wirtschaft im Sowjetblock dargestellt am Beispeil des Rates für gegenseitige Wirtschaftshilfe (COMECON).** Mainz: v. Hase & Koehler, 1966, 219 p.
An introduction to the history and organization of COMECON.

Remington, Robin Alison. **The Warsaw Pact: Case Studies in Communist Conflict Resolution.** Cambridge: M.I.T. Press, 1971, 268 p.
An interesting analysis of the manner in which the Soviet Union uses the Pact to contain intra-bloc conflict. In the concluding chapter, the author suggests that "great power crisis management in the Dominican Republic in 1965 and in Czechoslovakia in 1968 had a depressing sameness."

Ribi, Rolf C. **Das COMECON.** Zurich: Polygraphischer Verlag, 1970, 462 p.
A detailed analysis of the Council for Mutual Economic Assistance by a Swiss economist.

Schaefer, Henry Wilcox. **COMECON and the Politics of Integration.** New York: Praeger, 1972, 200 p.
  The principal value of this book by an analyst for Radio Free Europe is the use it makes of public statements by officials and commentators in COMECON countries for the period from the invasion of Czechoslovakia to the adoption of the "complex program" of integration in 1971.

Teich, Gerhard. **Der Rat für Gegenseitige Wirtschaftshilfe 1949-1963.** Kiel: Institut für Weltwirtschaft, Bibliothek, 1966, 445 p.
  A very useful bibliography, arranged chronologically, of publications dealing with the Council for Mutual Economic Assistance.

Uschakow, Alexander. **Der Ostmarkt im COMECON.** Baden-Baden: Nomos Verlagsgesellschaft, 1972, 486 p.
  A valuable collection of documents about the Council for Mutual Economic Assistance and some related matters.

THE EUROPEAN NATIONS

GREAT BRITAIN

General

See also The World Since 1914, p. 129; (Europe) General Surveys, p. 344; Western Europe, p. 345.

Calleo, David Patrick. **Britain's Future.** New York: Horizon Press, 1969, 252 p.
  A brief but brilliant inquiry by an American political scientist who fully understands the importance and nature of British cultural traditions.

Crick, Bernard Rowland, *ed.* **Essays on Reform, 1967: A Centenary Tribute.** New York: Oxford University Press, 1967, 222 p.
  A collection of informative essays dedicated to the belief that Britain needs to embark on new reforms if it is "to continue to be a worthy place in which a good life can be led."

Gilbert, Bentley Brinkerhoff. **Britain since 1918.** New York: Harper and Row, 1968, 206 p.
  A critical history of Britain's domestic and foreign policies. A feat of compression.

Gowing, Margaret Mary. **Britain and Atomic Energy, 1939-1945.** New York: St. Martin's Press, 1964, 464 p.
  The official history of Britain's efforts in the nuclear field.

Hartley, Anthony. **A State of England.** New York: Harcourt, Brace and World, 1963, 255 p.
  A clever and restrained analysis of what is wrong with postwar Britain, especially with its intellectuals, by one of them.

Medlicott, William Norton. **Contemporary England, 1914-1964.** New York: McKay, 1967, 614 p.
  A sound survey of the contemporary history of England. Mr. Medlicott is more cautious in his judgment than Mr. Taylor in his "English History, 1914-1945."

Seaman, Lewis Charles Bernard. **Post-Victorian Britain, 1902-1951.** London: Methuen, 1966, 531 p.
  A general survey of British history in the first half of the twentieth century.

Taylor, Alan John Percivale. **English History, 1914-1945.** New York: Oxford University Press, 1965, 708 p.
  A highly readable history, by one of Britain's ablest and most controversial historians.

Imperial and Commonwealth Relations; Colonial Policy

See also Political Factors, p. 12; Ethnic Problems; The Jews, p. 46; (Great Britain) Biographies, Memoirs and Addresses, p. 369; Foreign Policy, p. 375; Military Policy, p. 378; and the sections for specific countries and regions.

Arnold, Guy. **Economic Co-operation in the Commonwealth.** New York: Pergamon Press, 1967, 184 p.
The author argues that economic links "are not sufficient reason for the Commonwealth's existence" and that its long-term justification must rest on the contribution it can make to race relations.

Ball, M. Margaret. **The "Open" Commonwealth.** Durham: Duke University Press (for the Duke University Commonwealth-Studies Center), 1971, 286 p.
According to the author, a professor at Duke University, this monograph "represents an introduction to the study of the Commonwealth of Nations as an international organization."

Barnett, Correlli. **The Collapse of British Power.** New York: Morrow, 1972, 643 p.
A controversial analysis of Britain's fall from Empire, concentrating on the inter-war period. Barnett seeks an explanation in Britain's "national character" and faults British public schools for educating an élite with strong pacifist and romantic beliefs.

Beloff, Max. **Imperial Sunset. Volume I: Britain's Liberal Empire, 1897-1921.** New York: Knopf, 1970, 387 p.
An important and well-wrought contribution to literature on decolonization. This study, by a well-known British scholar, helps to explain the relative ease with which Britain took the end of Empire.

Burns, Sir Alan Cuthbert. **Parliament as an Export.** London: Allen and Unwin, 1966, 271 p.
A symposium dealing with the question of whether the United Kindom Westminster model has been followed by other countries in the Commonwealth.

Cross, Colin. **The Fall of the British Empire, 1918-1968.** New York: Coward-McCann, 1969, 359 p.
The last half-century of Empire, depicted with a fine eye for the telling detail of social history, by a British journalist.

Eayrs, James George, *ed*. **The Commonwealth and Suez: A Documentary Survey.** New York: Oxford University Press, 1964, 483 p.
Successive phases of the 1956-57 Suez crisis as viewed by eight Commonwealth countries. Selected statements and speeches are supplemented by a well-written commentary.

Fischer, Georges. **Le Parti travailliste et la décolonisation de l'Inde.** Paris: Maspero, 1966, 341 p.
A study dealing with how ideology and politics of the British Labor Party influenced the decolonization of India.

Goldsworthy, David. **Colonial Issues in British Politics, 1945-1961: From 'Colonial Development' to 'Wind of Change.'** New York: Oxford University Press, 1971, 425 p.
A careful and revealing account of how domestic pressures influenced Britain's policy of liquidating the remaining Empire.

Gowda, Krishnadasa Gowda Venkatagiri. **Commonwealth Common Market: A Proposal.** Mysore: Rao and Raghavan, 1964, 189 p.
"Written under the spell of the collapse" of the negotiations for British entry into the European Common Market, this book proposes a Commonwealth alternative.

Griffiths, Sir Percival Joseph. **Empire into Commonwealth.** London: Benn, 1969, 391 p.
Sir Percival Griffiths, who had a distinguished career in the Indian Civil Service, evaluates with pride the achievements of imperial Britain.

Hall, H. Duncan. **Commonwealth: A History of the British Commonwealth of Nations.** New York: Van Nostrand Reinhold, 1971, 1,015 p.
This massive work surveys the Commonwealth from the beginning of the century to the 1950s. Centering on the development of the association rather than upon the

individual members, it makes extensive use of the minutes of the Prime Ministers' meetings.

Hamilton, William Baskerville and Others, eds. **A Decade of the Commonwealth, 1955–1964.** Durham: Duke University Press (for the Duke University Commonwealth-Studies Center), 1966, 567 p.

A symposium on the challenges and changes confronting the Commonwealth since 1955, in the creation of new states, in intra-Commonwealth relations and in the international field.

Kirkman, William Patrick. **Unscrambling an Empire: A Critique of British Colonial Policy, 1956–1966.** London: Chatto, 1966, 214 p.

A well-informed and polemical study by an ex-correspondent of *The Times* who is critical of the British policies favoring unstable federations.

Lee, John Michael. **Colonial Development and Good Government.** New York: Oxford University Press, 1968, 311 p.

A well-documented study of British colonial experience, emphasizing the achievements of the Colonial Service.

Livingston, William Samuel, ed. **Federalism in the Commonwealth.** New York: Oxford University Press (for the Hansard Society), 1963, 237 p.

Critical bibliographical essays by 11 scholars on different aspects of federalism in Commonwealth countries.

McIntyre, William David. **Colonies into Commonwealth.** New York: Walker, 1967, 391 p.

A professor at the University of Canterbury, New Zealand, surveys the liquidation of the British Colonial Empire and the emergence of the new grouping of states that form the Commonwealth today.

Mansergh, Philip Nicholas Seton. **The Commonwealth Experience.** New York: Praeger, 1969, 471 p.

The gradual transition from Empire to Commonwealth, described and analyzed in this comprehensive survey of Britain's progress in turning some colonial dependents into equal partners. Informative and readable, by a well-known British historian.

Mansergh, Philip Nicholas Seton, ed. **Documents and Speeches on Comonwealth Affairs, 1952–1962.** New York: Oxford University Press (for the Royal Institute of International Affairs), 1963, 775 p.

The third volume of a series devoted to the history of Commonwealth relations since 1931. A valuable and comprehensive collection which encompasses Commonwealth repercussions on Britain's application for entry into the Common Market.

Miller, John Donald Bruce. **Britain and the Old Dominions.** Baltimore: Johns Hopkins Press, 1967, 286 p.

A study, by an Australian scholar, of Britain's recent relations with Canada, Australia, New Zealand and South Africa.

Perham, Dame Margery Freda. **Colonial Sequence, 1930 to 1949.** New York: Barnes and Noble, 1968, 351 p.

This volume, subtitled "A Chronological Commentary upon British Colonial Policy especially in Africa," contains some important articles and letters written and published mainly in *The Times* during the 1930s and 1940s. They provide a fascinating retrospect into the British colonial period through the eyes of a knowledgeable student.

Streeten, Paul and Corbet, Hugh, eds. **Commonwealth Policy in a Global Context.** London: Frank Cass, 1971, 232 p.

Explorations of the extent to which the Commonwealth continues to provide a useful framework for coöperation.

Wilson, Robert R. **International Law and Contemporary Commonwealth Issues.** Durham: Duke University Press (for the Duke University Commonwealth-Studies Center), 1971, 245 p.

This volume by a former chairman of the Committee on Commonwealth Studies at Duke University examines how the problems of state succession, communalism, secession, migration and defense in the British Commonwealth test the relevance of international law.

Biographies, Memoirs and Addresses

See also First World War, p. 131; Inter-War Period, p. 140; Second World War, p. 144.

Avon, Anthony Eden, 1st Earl of. **The Reckoning: The Memoirs of Anthony Eden, Earl of Avon.** Boston: Houghton, 1965, 716 p.
This volume of the former Prime Minister's memoirs covers the climactic period of his career—from his resignation as Foreign Secretary under Neville Chamberlain to the end of the Second World War. While not stylistically on the level of the Churchill memoirs for the same period, they are an indispensable source for the war and the diplomacy of those years, with many items of interest about leading personalities and powers.

Barman, Thomas. **Diplomatic Correspondent.** New York: Macmillan, 1969, 273 p.
The somewhat meandering, though often amusing and informative memoirs of a former diplomatic correspondent for the BBC covering his many assignments all over the world in the period from 1929 to the early 1960s.

Beaverbrook, William Maxwell Aitken, 1st Baron. **The Decline and Fall of Lloyd George.** New York: Duell, 1963, 320 p.
This is an absorbing account of the political clashes and maneuvers that led to Lloyd George's extraordinary fall from power in the course of the years 1921–1922. Lord Beaverbrook is in a position to write intimately of these events, and he has appended a fascinating selection of documents, letters, diary entries from the key figures of the time.

Berlin, Sir Isaiah. **Mr. Churchill in 1940.** Boston: Houghton, 1964, 38 p.
In this evocative essay, Sir Isaiah Berlin does justice to his subject.

Birkenhead, Frederick Winston Furneaux Smith, 2d Earl of. **Halifax: The Life of Lord Halifax.** Boston: Houghton, 1966, 626 p.
A full and friendly biography of a cautious and religious man who "had held three of the highest offices of the State"—leaving a major mark on none.

Bonham-Carter, Victor. **The Strategy of Victory 1914–1918; The Life and Times of the Master Strategist of World War I: Field-Marshal Sir William Robertson.** New York: Holt, Rinehart and Winston, 1964, 417 p.
A detailed biographical review of the life of the distinguished Field-Marshal Sir William Robertson, Chief of the Imperial General Staff in World War I; more revealing of the events than of the master strategist himself. The British edition was entitled "Soldier True: The Life and Times of Field-Marshal Sir William Robertson" (London: Muller, 1964, 417 p.).

Bonham-Carter, Lady Violet (Asquith). **Winston Churchill: An Intimate Portrait.** New York: Harcourt, Brace and World, 1965, 413 p.
Moving and perspicacious recollections by the daughter of Prime Minister Asquith. This volume ends with Churchill's involuntary exile from the government in 1916.

Brodrick, Alan Houghton. **Near to Greatness: A Life of the Sixth Earl Winterton.** London: Hutchinson, 1965, 272 p.
A biography of a British statesman who in the 1920s twice served as the Under-Secretary for India.

Bullock, Alan Louis Charles. **The Life and Times of Ernest Bevin. Volume Two: Minister of Labour, 1940–1945.** London: Heinemann, 1967, 407 p.
The second volume of a well-researched and sympathetic biography of an important Labour leader and statesman who died in 1951.

Butler of Saffron Walden, Richard Austen Butler, Baron. **The Art of the Possible: The Memoirs of Lord Butler.** London: Hamish Hamilton, 1971, 274 p.
Recollections of a leading Conservative that tell us little about his many experiences and important involvements.

Caradon, Hugh Mackintosh Foot, Baron. **A Start in Freedom.** New York: Harper and Row, 1964, 256 p.
This autobiography is an eloquent tribute to the final decades of the British colonial period, to British efforts to leave something of value to people about to receive independence, and to Britain's continuing concern for the well-being of new nations. The author's own career with the British Colonial Service started in 1929 in Palestine;

his final post was as Governor of Cyprus. From 1964 to 1970 the author was the Permanent Representative of the United Kingdom at the United Nations.

Chandos, Oliver Lyttelton, 1st Viscount. **The Memoirs of Lord Chandos: An Unexpected View from the Summit.** New York: New American Library, 1963, 430 p.
The very agreeable and intermittently important recollections of the former Oliver Lyttelton, who held various posts in Churchill's cabinets.

Churchill, Randolph Spencer and Gilbert, Martin. **Winston S. Churchill.** Boston: Houghton, 1966– .
A magisterial biography of the great Englishman, of which three volumes have appeared through 1972. The first two volumes, "Youth, 1874–1900" (1966, 614 p.) and "Young Statesman, 1901–1914" (1967, 763 p.), were written by Winston's son Randolph, after whose death Martin Gilbert took over. Volume III is entitled "The Challenge of War, 1914–1916" (1971, 988 p.). The authors of these three volumes have also prepared a companion collection of letters and documents (1967–73, 3 v. in 7 pts.).

Citrine, Walter McLennan, 1st Baron. **Two Careers.** London: Hutchinson, 1967, 384 p.
The memoirs of a British trade-union leader, known particularly for his efforts during World War II to establish good relations between Britain and the Soviet Union.

Clark, Ronald William. **Tizard.** Cambridge: M.I.T. Press, 1965, 458 p.
A sympathetic and well-documented biography of Sir Henry Tizard that includes a discussion of his role in the perfection of radar as an operating defense system during the Battle of Britain and of his feud with Churchill's personal scientific adviser Lord Cherwell (Lindemann).

Cole, John Alfred. **Lord Haw-Haw and William Joyce: The Full Story.** New York: Farrar, Straus and Giroux, 1965, 316 p.
The life of William Joyce, the British traitor and fascist, who was executed after World War II for his broadcasting from Germany. The volume contains vivid descriptions of pre-World War II Britain and its fascist movement.

Connell, John, *pseud.* (John Henry Robertson). **Wavell: Scholar and Soldier.** New York: Harcourt, Brace and World, 1965, 573 p.
An impressive and admiring biography of an outstanding soldier, based in part on Wavell's papers. The book ends in June 1941, when Churchill sent Wavell from Egypt to India.

Cross, Colin. **Philip Snowden.** London: Barrie and Rockliff, 1966, 356 p.
A scholarly biography of a prominent British socialist and statesman.

Devlin, Bernadette. **The Price of My Soul.** New York: Knopf, 1969, 224 p.
This autobiographical volume by the Member of Parliament from Mid Ulster from 1969 to 1974 is an evocative picture of the conditions of Northern Ireland and of a temperament that rebelled against them.

Dickie, John. **The Uncommon Commoner: A Study of Sir Alec Douglas-Home.** New York: Praeger, 1964, 224 p.
An account of Sir Alec's career before his appointment as Prime Minister in 1963.

Dixon, Piers. **Double Diploma; the Life of Sir Pierson Dixon: Don and Diplomat.** London: Hutchinson, 1968, 321 p.
A biography of a senior British diplomat whose career began before Munich and ended in 1964; written by his son and based largely on Sir Pierson Dixon's own elegant recollections of men and events.

Douglas, Sholto, Baron Douglas of Kirtleside, with Wright, Robert. **Combat and Command: The Story of an Airman in Two World Wars.** New York: Simon and Schuster, 1966, 806 p.
Memoirs by a prominent British soldier who ended his military career as military governor and commander in chief of the British Zone in Germany. The English edition was published as "Years of Combat" (London: Collins, 1963, 384 p.) and "Years of Command" (London: Collins, 1966, 382 p.).

Evans, Sir Geoffrey Charles. **Slim as Military Commander.** Princeton: Van Nostrand, 1969, 239 p.
An excellent though somewhat worshipful biography of the British Field-Marshal, written by his Divisional Commander in Burma.

Foot, Paul. **The Rise of Enoch Powell: An Examination of Enoch Powell's Attitude to Immigration and Race.** Baltimore: Penguin, 1969, 142 p.
A polemic against England's controversial Conservative politician.

Gardner, Brian. **Allenby of Arabia: Lawrence's General.** New York: Coward-McCann, 1966, 314 p.
"What an idol the man was to us," wrote Lawrence of his commander General Allenby, the victor in Palestine in 1918. To Lawrence, Allenby remarked, "In fifty years your name will be a household word; to find out about Allenby they will have to go to the War Museum." Not so if this able biography of an outstanding officer has the attention it deserves.

Gardner, Brian. **Churchill in Power: As Seen by His Contemporaries.** Boston: Houghton, 1970, 349 p.
A respectful effort at debunking the Churchill legend, emphasizing that after 1940 Churchill was no longer the acknowledged embodiment of a united people.

George-Brown, George Alfred George-Brown, Baron. **In My Way: The Political Memoirs of Lord George-Brown.** New York: St. Martin's Press, 1972, 299 p.
The spirited memoirs of Britain's famously volatile former Foreign Secretary. Candid and often uncomplimentary vignettes of Britain's politics and politicians.

Gladwyn, Hubert Miles Gladwyn Jebb, 1st Baron. **The Memoirs of Lord Gladwyn.** New York: Weybright and Talley, 1972, 422 p.
A rich diplomatic life recounted in an elegant patrician style. Of particular interest are the descriptions of the author's contributions to the creation of the United Nations and NATO.

Gollin, Alfred M. **Proconsul in Politics: A Study of Lord Milner in Opposition and in Power.** New York: Macmillan, 1964, 627 p.
An important and thorough study. Lord Milner's role in the First World War and his response to the Russian Revolutions of 1917 are of particular interest.

Harvey, Oliver. **The Diplomatic Diaries of Oliver Harvey, 1937–1940.** New York: St. Martin's Press, 1972, 448 p.
Harvey was Principal Private Secretary to the British Foreign Secretary and, at the end of the period here covered, Minister in Paris. His diary, edited by John Harvey, is a highly readable and interesting source, not likely to give much comfort to latter-day apologists for appeasement.

Heuston, R. F. V. **Lives of the Lord Chancellors, 1885–1940.** New York: Oxford University Press, 1964, 632 p.
These felicitous biographical essays of the 12 lord chancellors, based largely on private papers, illuminate some important aspects of British politics.

Higham, Robin David Stewart. **The Military Intellectuals in Britain, 1918–1939.** New Brunswick: Rutgers University Press, 1966, 267 p.
A study of the ideas and work of such men as Sir Herbert Richmond, J. F. C. Fuller and B. H. Liddell Hart.

Hyde, Harford Montgomery. **Lord Reading: The Life of Rufus Isaacs, First Marquess of Reading.** New York: Farrar, Straus and Giroux, 1968, 454 p.
A biography of Lord Reading (1860–1935), a prominent British statesman who was the first Jew to become successively Attorney-General, Lord Chief Justice, Ambassador to the United States, Viceroy of India and Foreign Secretary.

Jackson, W. G. F. **Alexander of Tunis as Military Commander.** New York: Dodd, Mead, 1972, 344 p.
A well-written and admiring biography of Field-Marshal Harold Alexander by a general who once served under him. Considerable attention, including maps, is given to Alexander's battlefield tactics and to his personal qualities of leadership.

James, Robert Rhodes. **Churchill: A Study in Failure, 1900–1939.** London: Weidenfeld and Nicolson, 1970, 372 p.
An outstanding study of the career of Churchill in the years from 1900 to 1939, written without anticipating the Churchill of World War II fame.

Jenkins, Roy. **Asquith: Portrait of a Man and an Era.** New York: Chilmark Press, 1965, 572 p.
A brilliantly persuasive biography of the last great Liberal leader of England, with much new information on his premiership and its end in the First World War.

Jenkins, Roy. **Essays and Speeches.** New York: Chilmark Press, 1968, 288 p.
> A fine collection on many themes from aviation and crime to politics and politicians, by a prominent member of the Labour Party.

Jones, Thomas. **Whitehall Diary.** New York: Oxford University Press, 1969-71, 3 v.
> Intimate glimpses of the workings of the British government, especially valuable for the First World War and the immediate postwar period, by a member of the Cabinet Secretariat, who on his appointment in 1916 resolved "to act as a fluid person moving about among people who mattered." Volume I covers the period 1916-1925; volume II, 1926-1930; volume III deals with Anglo-Irish relations and covers the period 1918-1925. Edited by Keith Middlemas.

Kilmuir, David Patrick Maxwell Fyfe, 1st Earl of. **Political Adventure: The Memoirs of the Earl of Kilmuir.** London: Weidenfeld, 1964, 356 p.
> The candid reminiscences of a staunchly loyal Tory Party member who was Lord Chancellor under Churchill, Eden and Macmillan.

Lee, Jennie. **This Great Journey: A Volume of Autobiography, 1904-45.** London: MacGibbon, 1963, 230 p.
> Miss Lee writes of her own career in public service, and that of her husband, Aneurin Bevan.

Liddell Hart, Sir Basil Henry. **The Liddell Hart Memoirs.** New York: Putnam, 1966, 2 v.
> Readable and illuminating memoirs by one of the most influential, though at times disregarded, strategic thinkers and military historians of our time.

McCormick, Donald. **The Mask of Merlin: A Critical Biography of David Lloyd George.** New York: Holt, Rinehart and Winston, 1964, 343 p.
> A quite harsh, frequently entertaining, but hardly definitive appraisal.

McFadyean, Sir Andrew. **Recollected in Tranquillity.** London: Pall Mall Press, 1964, 287 p.
> The benign memoirs of a versatile British Liberal who negotiated German reparations in the early 1920s and helped German refugees.

Macmillan, Harold. **[Memoirs.]** New York: Harper and Row, 1966— .
> The lucidly written and very informative political memoirs of the former Prime Minister. Through 1972 the following volumes have been published: vol. I, "Winds of Change, 1914-1939" (1966, 584 p.); vol. II, "The Blast of War, 1939-1945" (1968, 623 p.); vol. III, "Tides of Fortune, 1945-1955" (1969, 729 p.); vol. IV, "Riding the Storm, 1956-1959" (1971, 786 p.); and vol. V, "Pointing the Way, 1959-1961" (1972, 504 p.).

Middlemas, Keith and Barnes, John. **Baldwin: A Biography.** New York: Macmillan, 1970, 1,149 p.
> A massive and well-documented biography of a man who was Prime Minister of Great Britain three times in the period from 1922 to 1937.

Moran, Charles McMoran Wilson, Baron. **Churchill: Struggle for Survival, 1940-1965; Taken from the Diaries of Lord Moran.** Boston: Houghton, 1966, 877 p.
> In May 1940 Lord Moran became Winston Churchill's personal physician. These diary entries, covering the subsequent two decades, have been the object of some criticism as being by their nature in doubtful taste. Still, they do provide significant information about a central historical figure of our century.

Mosley, Sir Oswald Ernald, 6th Bart. **My Life.** New Rochelle (N.Y.): Arlington House, 1972, 521 p.
> The revealing memoirs of an exceptionally intelligent British politician who compromised his career by becoming the leader of the British fascists in the 1930s. A commentary on half a century of history and on men Mosley knew, including Roosevelt, Mussolini and Hitler.

Nicolson, Sir Harold George. **Diaries and Letters.** New York: Atheneum, 1966-68, 3 v.
> An entertaining and historically revealing commentary on British life and politics, by a well-known writer and public figure, covering the years from 1930 to 1962. Edited by the author's son, Nigel Nicolson.

Pound, Reginald. **Evans of the Broke: A Biography of Admiral Lord Mountevans, K.C.B., D.S.O., L.L.D.** New York: Oxford University Press, 1963, 323 p.
> A biography of an unusual British admiral, known for his exploits in the Antarctic and for his many years of service in various posts of responsibility.

Powell, John Enoch. **Freedom and Reality.** New Rochelle (N.Y.): Arlington House, 1970, 264 p.
A collection of speeches, addresses and articles by the influential former Conservative Member of the Parliament. Edited by John Wood.

Powell, John Enoch. **A Nation Not Afraid: The Thinking of Enoch Powell.** London: Batsford, 1965, 156 p.
A collection of speeches and articles, edited by John Wood, in which the controversial British Conservative argues "that in a free society achievement and satisfaction come in response to the freely expressed wishes of people, as a spontaneous process, not as a result of political activity and administrative decisions at the centre."

Reed, Bruce and Williams, Geoffrey. **Denis Healey and the Policies of Power.** London: Sidgwick and Jackson, 1971, 286 p.
The career of a prominent Labour Secretary of State for Defense is examined in the context of his principal policy decisions.

Rock, William R. **Neville Chamberlain.** New York: Twayne, 1969, 242 p.
The author thinks that Neville Chamberlain's contributions to English life and politics were noteworthy and that his appeasement policies do not exemplify "the full story of his existence."

Rogers, William Thomas, ed. **Hugh Gaitskell, 1906-1963.** London: Thames, 1964, 167 p.
A collection of essays by friends and associates honoring the late leader of the British Labour Party.

Roskill, Stephen W. **Hankey: Man of Secrets.** New York: St. Martin's Press, 1972–.
The authorized biography of Lord Hankey, based largely on diaries and personal papers, by a distinguished naval historian. An extraordinary man, Hankey was at the center of Britain's foreign policy machinery from 1908 to 1942 under six Prime Ministers. Of special interest to students of the First World War. Two volumes have been published through 1973.

Sampson, Anthony. **Macmillan: A Study in Ambiguity.** New York: Simon and Schuster, 1967, 256 p.
A study of the career of the British statesman and Prime Minister (1957-1963) by the author of well-known works on contemporary England.

Scott, Charles Prestwich. **The Political Diaries of C. P. Scott, 1911-1928.** Ithaca: Cornell University Press, 1970, 509 p.
Portions of the hitherto unpublished diary and correspondence of the *Manchester Guardian's* famous editor. Friend and critic of Lloyd George, Scott was close to the British government, and his accounts reveal the reactions of a liberal mind to leading men and events. An important source, especially on the style of British policy. Edited by Trevor Wilson.

Smith, Dudley. **Harold Wilson: A Critical Biography.** London: Hale, 1964, 224 p.
A biography of the Labour leader and Prime Minister, written by "a politician in the opposite camp." Useful, but not the definitive study.

Smith, Leslie. **Harold Wilson: The Authentic Portrait.** New York: Scribner, 1965, 231 p.
A biography of the leader of Britain's Labour Party and his country's Prime Minister from 1964 to 1970, and again from 1974.

Sparrow, Gerald. **"R.A.B.": Study of a Statesman; The Career of Baron Butler of Saffron Walden, C. H.** London: Odhams, 1965, 253 p.
An attempt to assess the career of Richard Austen Butler, for many years a leading member of the Conservative Party.

Spears, Sir Edward Louis, 1st Bart. **Two Men Who Saved France: Pétain and De Gaulle.** New York: Stein and Day, 1966, 222 p.
A British general reminisces on his role as a senior liaison officer between the British and French armies during both World Wars.

Stevenson, Frances. **Lloyd George: A Diary.** New York: Harper and Row, 1972, 338 p.
A remarkable work, absorbing and illuminating. Frances Stevenson was both mistress and confidential secretary to Lloyd George—and apparently a model in both roles. An invaluable source on Lloyd George and world events from the First to the Second World War. Edited by A. J. P. Taylor.

Swinton, Philip Cunliffe-Lister, 1st Earl of, with Margach, James D. **Sixty Years of Power: Some Memories of the Men Who Wielded It.** New York: James H. Heineman, 1967, 265 p.
Intimate studies of the Prime Ministers of Great Britain since the beginning of this century, by a statesman with many years of government experience.

Taylor, Alan John Percivale. **Beaverbrook.** New York: Simon and Schuster, 1972, 712 p.
An adulatory biography of Lord Beaverbrook, the Canadian-born British newspaper magnate, politician, financier and philanthropist, efficient cabinet minister in two world wars, confidant of the powerful, bon vivant and raconteur.

Taylor, Alan John Percivale and Others. **Churchill Revised: A Critical Assessment.** New York: Dial Press, 1969, 274 p.
The inevitable effort at revision, pressed with vigor and considerable insight. Five essays of uneven quality, including a suggestive interpretation of the man behind the legend by Anthony Storr, a British psychiatrist.

Thompson, Reginald William. **Montgomery, the Field Marshal.** New York: Scribner, 1970, 344 p.
A fair critique of Lord Montgomery's generalship, especially in the battles in Northwest Europe in 1944-45. The author is a former British intelligence officer and an experienced war correspondent.

Toynbee, Arnold Joseph. **Experiences.** New York: Oxford University Press, 1969, 417 p.
Thoughts and maxims on a vast variety of subjects by the well-known British historian.

Trevelyan, Humphrey Trevelyan, Baron. **Living with the Communists: China 1953-5, Soviet Union 1962-5.** Boston: Gambit, 1972, 320 p.
An astute and sensitive memoir, crisply presented by a leading British diplomatist, of political conditions in China during the mid-1950s and in the Soviet Union during the mid-1960s.

Wheeler-Bennett, Sir John Wheeler, *ed.* **Action This Day: Working with Churchill.** New York: St. Martin's Press, 1969, 272 p.
Six wartime associates recall their chief, remembering his courage, his zest and his untidiness as an administrator.

Whitwell, John. **British Agent.** London: Kimber, 1966, 224 p.
A British intelligence agent reminisces on his activities in Prague and Riga before World War II.

Williams, Marcia. **Inside Number 10.** New York: Coward, McCann and Geoghegan, 1972, 384 p.
A gossipy volume of reminiscences by the Personal and Political Secretary to Prime Minister Wilson covering the period from October 1964 to June 1970.

Wilson, Harold. **A Personal Record: The Labour Government, 1964-1970.** Boston: Atlantic (Little, Brown), 1971, 836 p.
Recollections of trying years, with no small thought given to personal reputation. Little drama or reflections, many details.

Wilson, Harold. **Purpose in Politics.** Boston: Houghton, 1964, 270 p.
——. **Purpose and Power.** Boston: Houghton, 1966, 194 p.
Selected speeches and articles by the leader of Britain's Labour Party since 1963 and repeatedly his country's Prime Minister.

Young, Kenneth. **Churchill and Beaverbrook: A Study in Friendship and Politics.** New York: James H. Heineman, 1967, 349 p.
A moving and absorbing study of the vicissitudes of friendship that for 55 years linked two giants of English life. Based principally on hitherto unpublished letters in the Beaverbrook archives.

Foreign Policy

See also General Works, p. 1; International Organization and Government, p. 96; War and Peace, p. 108; First World War, p. 131; Inter-War Period, p. 140; Second World War, p. 144; The Postwar World, p. 178; Western Europe, p. 345; (Great Britain) Imperial and Commonwealth Relations; Colonial Policy, p. 367; Biographies, Memoirs and Addresses, p. 369; Military Policy, p. 378; and the sections for specific countries and regions.

Austin, Dennis. **Britain and South Africa.** New York: Oxford University Press (for the Royal Institute of International Affairs), 1966, 191 p.
A British political scientist evaluates proposed alternatives for British policy toward South Africa on the basis of a dispassionate and highly competent appraisal of the precise nature of Britain's economic, political and strategic interests in southern Africa.

Barclay, Glen St. John. **Commonwealth or Europe.** St. Lucia (Australia): University of Queensland Press (for the Australian Institute of International Affairs), 1970, 210 p.
An Australian with a practical and academic background presents an acerbic picture of Britain's relations with Europe.

Barker, Elisabeth. **Britain in a Divided Europe, 1945-1970.** London: Weidenfeld, 1971, 316 p.
A straightforward study of British foreign policies after World War II. The author argues that Britain was expected to play a role for which it no longer had the resources.

Beloff, Max. **The Future of British Foreign Policy.** New York: Taplinger, 1969, 154 p.
A leading scholar urges a European course for Britain, convinced that there has been a "sudden tearing down of the veils between Britain's true position and the way in which her people have perceived it."

Busch, Briton Cooper. **Britain, India, and the Arabs, 1914-1921.** Berkeley: University of California Press, 1971, 522 p.
A first-rate monograph on the role of India in the formation of the foreign policies of Great Britain toward the Arab Near East during World War I and its immediate aftermath.

Carter, William Horsfall. **Speaking European: The Anglo-Continental Cleavage.** New York: Humanities Press, 1966, 223 p.
As the author says, this is "an analysis and assessment of the Channel Gap . . . the gulf between English and Continental thought-processes." He advises the English to speak European and pay more heed to de Gaulle.

Clifford, Nicholas Rowland. **Retreat from China: British Policy in the Far East, 1937-1941.** Seattle: University of Washington Press, 1967, 222 p.
A competent and well-documented study.

Collier, Basil. **The Lion and the Eagle: British and Anglo-American Strategy, 1900-1950.** New York: Putnam, 1972, 499 p.
A British military historian surveys the international developments that marked the decline of the British Empire and the ascendancy of the United States as a world power.

Colvin, Ian Goodhope. **The Chamberlain Cabinet.** New York: Taplinger, 1971, 286 p.
On the basis of newly opened Cabinet papers, Colvin adds important details to the familiar picture of the appeasement years.

Documents on British Foreign Policy, 1919-1939. London: H.M.S.O.
An indispensable collection of documents for the study of British foreign policy and of many aspects of international affairs during the inter-war period. Originally published simultaneously in three series, and later in four, starting, respectively, with 1919, 1925, 1929 and 1938. In the decade from 1963 through 1973 the following volumes, edited by Rohan Butler, J. P. T. Bury, M. E. Lambert, W. N. Medlicott and Douglas Dakin, were published: First Series: vols. XIII-XVIII, covering the period from 1920 to 1923 (1963-72); Series IA: vols. I-V, covering the period from 1925 to 1928 (1966-73); Second Series: vols. IX-XIII, covering the period from 1931 to 1936 (1965-73); the Third Series was completed in 1961. For volumes published before 1963, consult earlier volumes of the "Foreign Affairs Bibliography."

Gelber, Lionel Morris. **The Alliance of Necessity: Britain's Crisis, the New Europe and American Interests.** New York: Stein and Day, 1966, 192 p.
The Canadian author fears that membership in the Common Market would mean the Europeanization of Britain and the stilling of its independent voice in the world. He would prefer Britain where it has always been, partly in and partly out of Europe.

George, Margaret. **The Warped Vision: British Foreign Policy, 1933-1939.** Pittsburgh: University of Pittsburgh Press, 1965, 238 p.
An effort to probe the motivations that impelled the British appeasers to appease.

Gordon, Michael R. **Conflict and Consensus in Labour's Foreign Policy, 1914-1965.** Stanford: Stanford University Press, 1969, 333 p.
An informative study, cogently argued and well written, by an American political scientist. Of interest to anyone concerned with the ambivalent role of ideals in the discussion of foreign policy.

Hugo, Grant. **Britain in Tomorrow's World: Principles of Foreign Policy.** New York: Columbia University Press, 1969, 256 p.
An inquiry into the theoretical assumptions that help forge British foreign policy.

Index to the Correspondence of the Foreign Office, 1920–. Nedeln (Liechtenstein): Kraus-Thomson (by arrangement with Her Majesty's Stationery Office), 1969–.
An indispensable guide to the dispatches and correspondence of the Foreign Office of Great Britain, a reprint of the volumes issued for restricted use within the Foreign Office. The publication of this index reflects the new policy of the British government reducing from 50 to 30 years the period during which its official papers and correspondence are closed to public inspection. The index for the period from 1920 to 1938 was published in 77 volumes in 1969; subsequent volumes are published on an annual basis, as documents are declassified under the 30-year rule.

Kaiser, Karl and Morgan, Roger, *eds.* **Britain and West Germany: Changing Societies and the Future of Foreign Policy.** New York: Oxford University Press (for the Royal Institute of International Affairs), 1971, 294 p.
An Anglo-German team examines the changing determinants of foreign policies in the two countries. A superb book. The German edition was published as "Strukturwandlungen der Aussenpolitik in Grossbritannien und der Bundesrepublik" (Munich: Oldenbourg, for the Deutsche Gesellschaft für Auswärtige Politik, 1970, 264 p.).

Lieber, Robert J. **British Politics and European Unity: Parties, Elites, and Pressure Groups.** Berkeley: University of California Press, 1970, 317 p.
An American political scientist investigates the influence of British parties and pressure groups on government policies concerning Europe.

Louis, William Roger. **British Strategy in the Far East, 1919-1939.** New York: Oxford University Press, 1971, 284 p.
Written for the Yale Far Eastern History Seminar, this lucid analysis argues that racism in the United States and Great Britain was the most important single factor in the dropping of the Anglo-Japanese Alliance and the subsequent failures to achieve conciliation and to satisfy the Japanese need for a feeling of equality.

McDermott, Geoffrey Lyseter. **The Eden Legacy and the Decline of British Diplomacy.** London: Frewin, 1969, 240 p.
A former British Foreign Service officer argues that British diplomacy has been inadequate to the international problems confronting the contemporary world.

Mander, John. **Great Britain or Little England?** Boston: Houghton, 1964, 206 p.
Starting with England's at first hostile response to President Kennedy's conduct of the second Cuban crisis, the author critically examines his countrymen's views on foreign policy.

Manderson-Jones, R. B. **The Special Relationship: Anglo-American Relations and Western European Unity, 1947-56.** New York: Crane, Russak, 1972, 168 p.
This valuable work examines the conflicting American and British attitudes with respect to Britain's role in Western Europe and the nature of the "special relationship."

Marett, Sir Robert Hugh Kirk. **Through the Back Door: An Inside View of Britain's Overseas Information Services.** New York: Pergamon Press, 1968, 224 p.
Pleasantly instructive memoirs of more than thirty years in Britain's information services.

Middleton, Drew. **The Supreme Choice: Britain and Europe.** New York: Knopf, 1963, 292 p.
The author, for many years chief of the London bureau of *The New York Times*, discusses the thorny problem of Britain's relation to the developing European Community. It is a mature and serious work that touches on many of the major problems of international relations.

Miller, Kenneth E. **Socialism and Foreign Policy: Theory and Practice in Britain to 1931.** The Hague: Nijhoff, 1967, 301 p.
An examination of the British Labour Party's "early efforts to apply socialist theories to foreign policy actions."

Monroe, Elizabeth. **Britain's Moment in the Middle East, 1914-1956.** Baltimore: Johns Hopkins Press, 1963, 254 p.
The author combines originality, personal experience and first-class scholarship in her study of Britain's period of supremacy in the Middle East.

Naylor, John F. **Labour's International Policy.** Boston: Houghton, 1969, 380 p.
A competent study of the Labour Party's muddled and insular thinking on foreign affairs in the 1930s, by an American scholar. There is a valuable bibliographic essay.

Nicholas, Herbert George. **Britain and the U.S.A.** Baltimore: Johns Hopkins Press, 1963, 191 p.
This volume treats Britain's dealings with the United States since the beginning of World War II. The coverage is selective and topical, but handled with grace and perception.

Nish, Ian. H. **Alliance in Decline: A Study in Anglo-Japanese Relations, 1908-23.** New York: Humanities Press, 1972, 424 p.
A well-documented history of an alliance whose disappearance was considered an important event in American diplomatic history. The author is a Senior Lecturer at the London School of Economics and Political Science.

Northedge, Frederick Samuel. **The Troubled Giant: Britain Among the Great Powers, 1916-1939.** New York: Praeger (for the London School of Economics and Political Science), 1966, 657 p.
A substantial though compressed account of Britain's foreign policy from the middle of the First World War to the outbreak of the Second—a period seen as one of relative decline not merely of resources but in ability to adjust ideas to new circumstances.

Pfaltzgraff, Robert L., Jr. **Britain Faces Europe.** Philadelphia: University of Pennsylvania Press, 1969, 228 p.
A study of British foreign policy toward Europe in the years between 1957 and 1967, a period characterized by "the substitution of regional European interests for the global perspective which once guided British foreign policy."

Pickles, William. **Britain and Europe—How Much Has Changed?** Oxford: Blackwell, 1967, 119 p.
"Not enough," would appear to be the answer of this British political scientist who opposes his country's entry into the Common Market.

Platt, Desmond Christopher St. Martin. **The Cinderella Service: British Consuls since 1825.** Hamden (Conn.): Archon Books, 1971, 272 p.
A pioneering, but certainly not definitive study of the British Consular Service. The author, whose point of view is described by the title of this survey, is particularly critical of the 1943 Foreign Service reforms.

Porter, Brian Ernest. **Britain and the Rise of Communist China: A Study of British Attitudes, 1945-1954.** New York: Oxford University Press, 1967, 195 p.
This volume, in the words of the author, "is a study of British attitudes, as reflected in Government policy, parliamentary debate, and public opinion, towards the emergence of Communist China as a great power and the issues, wars, and problems which accompanied that momentous event."

Richards, Peter G. **Parliament and Foreign Affairs.** Toronto: University of Toronto Press, 1967, 191 p.
With this survey of how the British Parliament considers foreign affairs, the author intends to provide "a bridge between the study of political institutions and the study of international politics."

Russett, Bruce Martin. **Community and Contention: Britain and America in the Twentieth Century.** Cambridge: M.I.T. Press, 1963, 252 p.
A rather theoretically oriented analysis of the factors determining the relations between Britain and the United States in the present century.

Steiner, Zara Shakow. **The Foreign Office and Foreign Policy, 1898-1914.** New York: Cambridge University Press, 1970, 262 p.
A monograph on the civil servants in the Foreign Office: their collective origins, their views and roles, their impact.

Thompson, Neville. **The Anti-Appeasers: Conservative Opposition to Appeasement in the 1930s.** New York: Oxford University Press, 1971, 256 p.
The widely held view that a few Conservatives were consistent anti-appeasers is scrutinized and adjudged to have been "rather like a mirage."

Ullman, Richard H. **Anglo-Soviet Relations, 1917-1921.** Princeton: Princeton University Press, 1961-72, 3 v.
The author of this major and very well-documented study has sought, in his own words, "to place emphasis upon the making of policy within the government in London and the relationship to that process of the perceptions and actions of British public servants, military and civilian, in the field."

Vital, David. **The Making of British Foreign Policy.** New York: Praeger, 1968, 119 p.
A lucid introduction by an Israeli official and specialist in international affairs.

Watt, Donald Cameron. **Britain Looks to Germany.** London: Wolff, 1965, 164 p.
A valuable work of synthesis assessing the development of British policy toward Germany since the Second World War.

Watt, Donald Cameron. **Personalities and Policies.** Notre Dame: University of Notre Dame Press, 1965, 275 p.
A series of perceptive essays on various aspects of British foreign policy. Important for the light they shed on particular problems—such as the influence of the Commonwealth on Munich—and highly suggestive for the student of foreign policy of any period. The author is an English historian and political scientist.

Younger, Kenneth Gilmour. **Changing Perspectives in British Foreign Policy.** New York: Oxford University Press (for the Royal Institute of International Affairs), 1964, 139 p.
An admirable, realistic appraisal of Britain's need for new directions in foreign policy after de Gaulle's veto of her long-delayed entry into Europe, by a former director of Chatham House.

Military Policy

See also War and Peace, p. 108; First World War, p. 131; Inter-War Period, p. 140; Second World War, p. 144; The Postwar World, p. 178; Western Europe, p. 345; (Great Britain) Imperial and Commonwealth Relations; Colonial Policy, p. 367; Biographies, Memoirs and Addresses, p. 369; Foreign Policy, p. 375; and the sections for specific countries and regions.

De Kadt, Emanuel Jehuda. **British Defence Policy and Nuclear War.** London: Frank Cass, 1964, 148 p.
A careful analysis of Britain's problems in the face of the threat of nuclear war. The author concludes that there is no justification for nuclear independence.

Dennis, Peter. **Decision by Default: Peacetime Conscription and British Defence, 1919-39.** Durham: Duke University Press, 1972, 243 p.
A lively scholarly study of inter-war British military policy using the perspective of conscription as a political issue. There are some interesting parallels between the revulsion against conscription following Britain's vast losses of men in 1914-1918 and the motivation for a U.S. all-volunteer army after Vietnam.

Higham, Robert David Stewart. **Armed Forces in Peacetime; Britain, 1918-1940: A Case Study.** Hamden (Conn.): Archon Books, 1963, 332 p.
A critical examination of Britain's inter-war defense policy, marked, in the author's judgment, by a "reckless economizing upon defence in the names of disarmament by example and of orthodox finance."

Howard, Michael E. **The Continental Commitment.** London: Temple Smith, 1972, 176 p.
Six essays on British defense policy between 1900 and the start of World War II. Howard demonstrates convincingly that Britain's well-known difficulties in maintaining its postwar world role had their roots in the tension between the requirements of imperial defense, the security of the British Isles and the maintenance of the prewar balance of power in Europe.

Luvaas, Jay. **The Education of an Army.** Chicago: University of Chicago Press, 1964, 454 p.
A well-written historical survey by an American scholar of the evolution of military thinking in Great Britain from Waterloo to World War II.

Pierre, Andrew J. **Nuclear Politics.** New York: Oxford University Press, 1972, 378 p.
A detailed examination of the British experience with respect to the development of an independent nuclear capability.

Rosecrance, Richard Newton. **Defense of the Realm: British Strategy in the Nuclear Epoch.** New York: Columbia University Press, 1968, 308 p.
A review of Britain's military planning and its political background, principally in the first post-World War II decade.

Snyder, William Paul. **The Politics of British Defense Policy, 1945-1962.** Columbus: Ohio State University Press, 1965, 284 p.
A clear and useful survey of the evolution of British defense planning in a period of shrinking power, by a West Point graduate.

Verrier, Anthony. **An Army for the Sixties: A Study in National Policy, Contract and Obligation.** London: Secker and Warburg, 1966, 288 p.
A contribution to the ongoing debate about the role to be played by the British Army in the contemporary world, with some proposed reforms and an appraisal of the commitments it should attempt to undertake.

Government and Constitutional Problems

See also Comparative Government, p. 18; (Great Britain) Biographies, Memoirs and Addresses, p. 369; Political Problems, p. 381.

Berkeley, Humphry. **The Power of the Prime Minister.** London: Allen and Unwin, 1968, 128 p.
The author, a former Conservative Member of Parliament who joined the Labour Party in 1970, argues "that the basic defect in the British system of Government is the supra-presidential power of the Prime Minister."

Birch, Anthony Harold. **The British System of Government.** New York: Praeger, 1967, 284 p.
An introductory survey.

Birch, Anthony Harold. **Representative and Responsible Government: An Essay on the British Constitution.** Toronto: University of Toronto Press, 1964, 252 p.
In his thoughtful and important book, Professor Birch examines the different theories and expectations concerning representative government and measures them against prevailing practices.

Bridges, Edward Ettingdene Bridges, Baron. **The Treasury.** New York: Oxford University Press, 1964, 248 p.
This study was written by a former Permanent Secretary to the Treasury.

Bulmer-Thomas, Ivor. **The Growth of the British Party System.** New York: Humanities Press, 1966, 2 v.
An industrious attempt to trace the long history of the British party system from 1640 to the present. The second volume deals with the years since 1924.

Butt, Ronald. **The Power of Parliament.** London: Constable, 1967, 468 p.
A study of the British Parliament by a constitutional historian, written in a spirit of respect for this ancient institution.

Charlot, Monica. **La Démocratie à l'anglaise: les campagnes électorales en Grande-Bretagne depuis 1931.** Paris: Colin, 1972, 442 p.
A technical survey of British election campaigns since 1931.

Crick, Bernard Rowland. **The Reform of Parliament.** Garden City: Doubleday, 1965, 297 p.
   A successful interpretation of the British parliamentary system and an advocacy that it should be reformed, by a professor at the University of London.

Crossman, Richard H. S. **The Myths of Cabinet Government.** Cambridge: Harvard University Press, 1972, 126 p.
   In these revised Godkin Lectures a prominent member of the Labour Party attempts a new interpretation of British politics, arguing that power rests with the Prime Minister and not with the cabinet.

Daalder, Hans. **Cabinet Reform in Britain, 1914-1963.** Stanford: Stanford University Press, 1963, 381 p.
   A Dutch political scientist carefully analyzes the changes, actual and proposed, in Britain's cabinet, particularly in light of war and defense needs.

Guttsman, Wilhelm L. **The British Political Elite.** New York: Basic Books, 1964, 398 p.
   A well-written sociological survey of the recruitment of the British political élite since the Reform Act of 1832.

Heussler, Robert. **Yesterday's Rulers: The Making of the British Colonial Service.** Syracuse: Syracuse University Press, 1963, 260 p.
   A fine contribution to an important and fascinating subject.

Inglis, Brian. **Abdication.** New York: Macmillan, 1966, 433 p.
   An ably written and absorbing account of the background and circumstances of Edward VIII's abdication in 1936.

Laundy, Philip. **The Office of Speaker.** New York: Oxford University Press, 1965, 488 p.
   A history of the office of the Speaker in the British Parliament, with a concluding section on the speakership in the Commonwealth and other parliaments.

Lees, John D. and Kimber, Richard, eds. **Political Parties in Modern Britain: An Organizational and Functional Guide.** London: Routledge, 1972, 288 p.
   A useful reference.

Leonard, R. L. **Elections in Britain.** Princeton: Van Nostrand, 1968, 192 p.
   A systematic though introductory survey of contemporary British elections.

Mackintosh, John Pitcairn. **The British Cabinet.** London: Stevens, 2d rev. ed., 1968, 651 p.
   A revised and updated edition of a thorough study of the evolution of the British Cabinet, first published in 1962. The author is a British scholar and a Labour MP.

Nicholson, Max. **The System: The Misgovernment of Modern Britain.** New York: McGraw-Hill, 1969, 455 p.
   A radical indictment of how traditional forms and principles have hobbled British life in the last decades.

Pritt, Denis Nowell. **The Labour Government, 1945-51.** New York: International Publishers, 1963, 467 p.
   A study of the Labour Party's campaigns, policies, parliamentary sessions from 1945 to its defeat in the General Election of 1951, by a former MP known for his activities on behalf of various causes of the Left.

Pulzer, Peter G. J. **Political Representation and Elections: Parties and Voting in Great Britain.** New York: Praeger, 1968, 165 p.
   A lucid introduction to the different aspects of the British electoral process.

Ranney, Austin. **Pathways to Parliament.** Madison: University of Wisconsin Press, 1965, 298 p.
   An American political scientist analyzes how English parties select their candidates and whom they select.

Richards, Peter Godfrey. **Patronage in British Government.** Toronto: University of Toronto Press, 1963, 284 p.
   A critical and interesting assessment of the continuing importance of governmental patronage in Britain.

Sampson, Anthony. **Anatomy of Britain Today.** New York: Harper and Row, rev. ed., 1965, 720 p.
   A completely revised and updated edition of a guide to Britain's ruling Establishment.

Stacey, Frank A. **The Government of Modern Britain.** New York: Oxford University Press, 1968, 419 p.
An introductory survey with useful bibliographies, by a British scholar.

Thornton, Archibald Paton. **The Habit of Authority: Paternalism in British History.** Toronto: University of Toronto Press, 1966, 402 p.
A well-known student of British imperialism analyzes the history of successful paternalism in Great Britain from the Norman Conquest to the present.

Wilding, Norman and Laundy, Philip. **An Encyclopaedia of Parliament.** New York: St. Martin's Press, 4th rev. ed., 1971, 931 p.
A completely revised and greatly enlarged edition of a very useful reference volume on the British Parliament and its proliferations in the Commonwealth.

Wiseman, Herbert Victor. **Parliament and the Executive.** New York: Humanities Press, 1966, 271 p.
An analysis of the problem of executive-legislative relations in Great Britain, supplemented by an anthology of extracts from the writings and speeches of leading historians and statesmen.

Political Problems
General

See also Political Factors, p. 12; (Great Britain) Biographies, Memoirs and Addresses, p. 369; Foreign Policy, p. 375; Government and Constitutional Problems, p. 379.

Blake, Robert. **The Conservative Party from Peel to Churchill.** New York: St. Martin's Press, 1971, 305 p.
A portrait of a party, by a fine historian, author of the well-known "Disraeli."

Boyd, Francis. **British Politics in Transition, 1945–63.** New York: Praeger, 1964, 253 p.
Mr. Boyd, a leading British correspondent, analyzes Britain's political machinery and the key issues which successive governments faced since 1945. He maintains that the system has functioned well, despite defects.

Brand, Carl Fremont. **The British Labour Party: A Short History.** Stanford: Stanford University Press, 1964, 340 p.
A useful summary of the Labour Party after 1914, written by a scholar in the field and designed for the general reader.

Butler, David Edgeworth and King, Anthony. **The British General Election of 1964.** New York: St. Martin's Press, 1965, 401 p.
The authoritative analysis of Britain's 1964 election.

Butler, David Edgeworth and Pinto-Duschinsky, Michael. **The British General Election of 1970.** New York: St. Martin's Press, 1971, 493 p.
In the greatest upset since World War II, the Tories won an "unpopularity contest" and this study explains the reasons for the reversal. A fine, literate study of an election and of British politics in general.

Butler, David Edgeworth and Freeman, Jennie. **British Political Facts, 1900–1960.** New York: St. Martin's Press, 1963, 245 p.
A most useful compilation of facts and figures on British political life.

Butler, David Edgeworth and Stokes, Donald E. **Political Change in Britain: Forces Shaping Electoral Choice.** New York: St. Martin's Press, 1969, 516 p.
Two well-known political scientists present an inquiry into the political behavior of the British electorate. A joint Anglo-American effort.

Chester, Lewis and Others. **The Zinoviev Letter.** Philadelphia: Lippincott, 1968, 218 p.
Not the last word on the supposedly anti-communist forgery of 1924 which had wide ramifications in Britain's domestic politics.

Cline, Catherine Ann. **Recruits to Labour: The British Labour Party, 1914–1931.** Syracuse: Syracuse University Press, 1963, 198 p.
A brief study of the Liberals and few Conservatives who joined the British Labour Party after the First World War, and of their impact on Labour policies.

Cowie, Harry. **Why Liberal?** Baltimore: Penguin, 1964, 155 p.
A guide to the policies and attitudes of the Liberal Party, prepared with the 1964 general election in mind, by a member of its research department.

Cowling, Maurice. **The Impact of Labour 1920-1924: The Beginning of Modern British Politics.** New York: Cambridge University Press, 1971, 570 p.
A detailed study of British politics during a crucial period of postwar regrouping. A British historian adduces new evidence and offers an important new perspective.

Deakin, Nicholas, *ed.* **Colour and the British Electorate, 1964.** New York: Praeger (for the Institute of Race Relations, London), 1965, 172 p.
The electoral campaigns in six constituencies with a relatively large colored population are sensibly analyzed by different authors, determined to see what the impact of colored immigration is on British politics.

Einzig, Paul. **Decline and Fall? Britain's Crisis in the Sixties.** New York: St. Martin's Press, 1969, 244 p.
In this angry diagnosis of the British situation in the 1960s, the writer blames the Labour Party for placing party interests above national interests.

Epstein, Leon David. **British Politics in the Suez Crisis.** Urbana: University of Illinois Press, 1964, 220 p.
A thorough examination of the British domestic response to the Suez Crisis of 1956, placed in the context of the British system and of lingering imperialist sentiments. Professor Epstein is struck by a "rigidly partisan political world" that determined parliamentary response.

Francis-Williams, Edward Francis Williams, Baron. **A Pattern of Rulers.** London: Longmans, 1965, 272 p.
In examining the careers of Stanley Baldwin, Ramsay MacDonald, Neville Chamberlain, Montagu Norman and Lord Halifax, a former editor of the *Daily Herald* has provided an introduction to British politics in the 1930s.

Gilmour, Ian Hedworth John Little. **The Body Politic.** London: Hutchinson, 1969, 496 p.
A detailed examination of the contemporary British political system by a Conservative Member of Parliament.

Grimond, Joseph. **The Liberal Challenge.** London: Hollis, 1963, 317 p.
The leader of the Liberal Party in Great Britain from 1956 to 1967 outlines a program for his party.

Hall, Peter Geoffrey, *ed.* **Labour's New Frontiers.** New York: London House and Maxwell, 1964, 180 p.
Ten essays, by men close to the Labour Party, who try to define Britain's problems and Labour's possible answers, and who seek collectively to remedy what one contributor calls the "constrictedness of imagination and aspiration" prevalent in contemporary British society.

Hoffman, J. D. **The Conservative Party in Opposition, 1945-51.** London: MacGibbon, 1964, 288 p.
A Canadian political scientist examines the ways in which Britain's Conservative Party responded to its great defeat of 1945 and how through the reorganization of party and platform and the pursuit of parliamentary opposition it prepared its return to power.

Howard, Anthony and West, Richard. **The Road to Number 10.** New York: Macmillan, 1965, 317 p.
Though marked by occasional unfairness, it is a readable account of the British election campaign of 1964, from start to finish. The British edition was published as "The Making of the Prime Minister" (London: Cape, 1965, 239 p.).

James, Robert Rhodes. **Ambitions and Realities: British Politics 1964-70.** New York: Harper and Row, 1972, 311 p.
The author tends to view history through personalities—a perfectly valid approach, as it includes broader political, economic and social considerations as well. There are excellent sketches of Wilson, Heath and Powell.

Macfarlane, L. J. **The British Communist Party: Its Origin and Development until 1929.** London: MacGibbon and Kee, 1966, 338 p.
The author states that he has approached his subject "from the point of view of an

informed British socialist of the nineteen twenties, accepting the broad principles of Marxism, sympathetic to the aims of the Communist Party, but awake of its shortcomings."

Maude, Angus. **The Common Problem.** London: Constable, 1969, 307 p.
A Conservative MP offers a perceptive critique of existing society and of its dominant interpreters, the social scientists. In presenting the first major restatement of modern conservatism in Britain in many years, he also proposes specific, radical reforms.

Nordlinger, Eric A. **The Working-Class Tories: Authority, Deference and Stable Democracy.** Berkeley: University of California Press, 1967, 276 p.
Analyzing the results of national surveys, conducted by the National Opinion Polls, Ltd., in 1963, the author tries to answer the question why one third of the English working class is voting for the Conservative Party.

Parkin, Frank. **Middle Class Radicalism: The Social Bases of the British Campaign for Nuclear Disarmament.** New York: Praeger, 1968, 207 p.
An investigation based on survey techniques.

Parkinson, Cyril Northcote. **Left Luggage: A Caustic History of British Socialism from Marx to Wilson.** Boston: Houghton, 1967, 236 p.
A critical and eccentric discussion of British socialism, with Beatrice and Sidney Webb as the author's main targets.

Skidelsky, Robert Jacob Alexander. **Politicians and the Slump: The Labour Government of 1929-1931.** London: Macmillan, 1967, 431 p.
In this well-documented study of the British Labour Government from 1929 to 1931 the Oxford-trained author concentrates his attention on the Government's handling of the unemployment problem. In the author's opinion the Labour Government failed because it could not "bring together socialism on the one hand with economic reality and parliamentary democracy on the other."

Stewart, Michael. **The British Approach to Politics.** London: Allen and Unwin, 6th rev. ed., 1967, 309 p.
A revised edition of an introductory, if informative, survey of British politics, originally published in 1938. The author is a former British Foreign Secretary.

Thayer, George. **The British Political Fringe: A Profile.** London: Anthony Blond, 1965, 256 p.
A compendium of information about a multitude of "movements" on the fringe of British politics, by an American student of the British political system.

Watkins, K. W. **Britain Divided: The Effect of the Spanish Civil War on British Political Opinion.** New York: Nelson, 1963, 270 p.
In this scholarly study the author argues and demonstrates in detail that the Spanish Civil War had the most damaging and divisive effects on British political life.

Wilson, Trevor. **The Downfall of the Liberal Party, 1914-1935.** Ithaca: Cornell University Press, 1966, 415 p.
An account of the fate that befell the historic Liberal Party.

Wootton, John Graham George. **The Politics of Influence.** Cambridge: Harvard University Press, 1963, 301 p.
A political scientist studies the impact of British ex-servicemen's organizations on British politics and culture.

Wootton, John Graham George. **Workers, Unions and the State.** New York: Schocken Books, 1967, 173 p.
A wide-ranging and thoughtful study of the relations among workers, unions and the government in Great Britain.

Regional Issues

See also Nationalism and Nationality, p. 17; (War) Guerrilla Warfare; Armed Insurrection, p. 118; (Great Britain) Biographies, Memoirs and Addresses, p. 369; Ireland, p. 388.

Fergusson of Kilkerran, Sir James. **The Curragh Incident.** London: Faber, 1964, 236 p.
A recounting of the critical events involving the Asquith cabinet and the British officer corps in their handling of the issue of Home Rule for Ulster in the months preceding the outbreak of World War I.

Gray, Tony. **The Orange Order.** London: The Bodley Head, 1972, 292 p.
An objective account of the root cause of Ulster's intransigence, indicating how—and, to some degree, why—the Orangeman's pertinacious dogmatism has remained basically unchanged throughout three centuries.

Hanham, Harold John. **Scottish Nationalism.** Cambridge: Harvard University Press, 1969, 250 p.
A sympathetic study of Scottish nationalism, its history and present cultural and political basis.

Hastings, Max. **Barricades in Belfast: The Fight for Civil Rights in Northern Ireland.** New York: Taplinger, 1970, 211 p.
A young British journalist gives a good example of instant history, drawing on his own reporting from Ulster in 1969.

Kellas, James G. **Modern Scotland: The Nation since 1870.** New York: Praeger, 1968, 284 p.
A study of Scottish society, emphasizing the continued separate identity of the Scottish nation.

Lawrence, Reginald James. **The Government of Northern Ireland: Public Finance and Public Services, 1921-1964.** New York: Oxford University Press, 1966, 198 p.
An inquiry into the system known as "parliamentary devolution," a process that has given Northern Ireland a unique status in the Commonwealth.

MacCormick, Neil, *ed.* **The Scottish Debate: Essays on Scottish Nationalism.** New York: Oxford University Press, 1970, 160 p.
According to the editor, the aim of this collection is "to contribute to a clearer understanding of the nature of the Scottish national movement in historical and comparative terms."

Morgan, Kenneth O. **Wales in British Politics, 1868-1922.** Cardiff: University of Wales Press, 1963, 353 p.
An excellent and much needed reference work on the leading Welsh figures and the issues important to Wales in British politics.

Northern Ireland: A Report on the Conflict. New York: Random House, 1972, 316 p.
A much-expanded version of a special report for the London *Sunday Times*. An informative mixture of instant history and hard-hitting reporting, with no effort to minimize the horrors and the dangers or to exculpate the British.

O'Neill, Terence Marne. **Ulster at the Crossroads.** New York: Humanities Press, 1969, 201 p.
The often eloquent speeches of Ulster's former Prime Minister who resigned in 1969, thwarted by opposition within his own party. In an introduction, John Cole concludes that "O'Neill's drive towards liberalism was hindered more by the pusillanimousness of the middle classes" than by the extremists of either camp.

Rose, Richard. **Governing without Consensus: An Irish Perspective.** Boston: Beacon Press, 1971, 567 p.
An original case study of the dynamics of political authority in Northern Ireland, containing much of value in a wider context.

The Ulster Debate. London: The Bodley Head (in association with the Institute for the Study of Conflict), 1972, 160 p.
A study discussing various facets of the situation in Northern Ireland—political alternatives, military aspects and economic implications (including Ireland's membership in the EEC).

Wolfe, J. N., *ed.* **Government and Nationalism in Scotland.** Edinburgh: Edinburgh University Press, 1969, 205 p.
Papers on Scottish nationalism originally delivered at the Fifth Edinburgh Seminar in the Social Sciences in 1968.

Economic and Financial Problems

See also Economic Factors, p. 49; Inter-War Period, p. 140; (Second World War) Economic, Technical and Non-Military Aspects, p. 172; East-West Relations, p. 180; (Great Britain) Biographies, Memoirs and Addresses, p. 369; Foreign Policy, p. 375; Political Problems, p. 381.

Aldcroft, Derek H. **The Inter-War Economy: Britain, 1919-1939.** New York: Columbia University Press, 1971, 441 p.
A useful and very informative survey.

Armitage, Susan. **The Politics of Decontrol of Industry: Britain and the United States.** London: Weidenfeld (for the London School of Economics and Political Science), 1969, 213 p.
Interesting comparisons of experience at the end of the First World War based partly on new material.

Barry, E. Eldon. **Nationalisation in British Politics: The Historical Background.** Stanford: Stanford University Press, 1965, 397 p.
An important and thorough study of British plans for nationalization, from the dreams of land nationalization in the nineteenth century to the postwar realization of some socialist schemes and the decline of interest and hope in nationalization.

Beckerman, Wilfred and Others. **The British Economy in 1975.** New York: Cambridge University Press, 1965, 631 p.
An ambitious attempt to forecast the state of British economy in the mid-1970s, by a group at the National Institute for Economic and Social Research.

Brandon, Henry. **In the Red: The Struggle for Sterling, 1964-1966.** Boston: Houghton, 1967, 114 p.
An interesting, slightly gossipy account of how the Labour government dealt with the sterling crisis with the help of the United States and continental Europe.

Brittan, Samuel. **Steering the Economy: The British Experiment.** New York: Library Press, 3rd ed., 1971, 504 p.
A close look at the British Treasury's activities since the early 1950s, with a good bit of emphasis on errors and limitations. A new version of a work first published in 1964.

Caves, Richard Earl and Others. **Britain's Economic Prospects.** Washington: Brookings Institution, 1968, 510 p.
A major work on the British economy by a group of American economists. Their prescriptions for policy emphasize growth through increased efficiency rather than the stimulation of investment or demand.

Cohen, Benjamin J. **The Future of Sterling as an International Currency.** New York: St. Martin's Press, 1971, 260 p.
A first-rate analysis of the costs and benefits to Britain of the pound's various roles as an international currency. Professor Cohen wrote the book while he was an International Affairs Fellow of the Council on Foreign Relations.

Conan, Arthur Robert. **The Problem of Sterling.** New York: St. Martin's Press, 1966, 122 p.
A devastating critique of Great Britain's financial policies since World War II.

Corbet, Hugh, *ed.* **Trade Strategy and the Asian-Pacific Region.** Toronto: University of Toronto Press, 1971, 221 p.
Essays, sponsored by the Atlantic Trade Study Group of London, arguing that Britain's future lies in the open environment of a free-trade treaty linking the United States, Japan and the Commonwealth.

Croome, David R. and Johnson, Harry G., *eds.* **Money in Britain, 1959-1969.** New York: Oxford University Press, 1970, 304 p.
The tenth anniversary of the Radcliffe Report provided the occasion for a sophisticated set of discussions of British monetary policy.

Donaldson, Peter. **Guide to the British Economy.** Baltimore: Penguin, 1965, 255 p.
An introduction to contemporary issues of British economy.

Dow, J. C. R. **The Management of the British Economy, 1945-60.** New York: Cambridge University Press, 1964, 443 p.
A major critical study of governmental policies and measures.

Grant, Alexander Thomas Kingdom. **The Machinery of Finance and the Management of Sterling.** New York: St. Martin's Press, 1967, 189 p.
An analysis by a Cambridge economist with more than twenty-five years experience in the British government.

Harrod, Sir Henry Roy Forbes. **The British Economy.** New York: McGraw-Hill, 1963, 240 p.
A critical evaluation of official British economic policy since World War II, with comparisons of American and British problems.

Harrod, Sir Henry Roy Forbes. **Towards a New Economic Policy.** New York: Kelley, 1967, 70 p.
The eminent Oxford economist prefers import controls and export incentives to deflation if international monetary reform does not provide enough liquidity to permit Britain to make full use of its resources without running into balance of payments difficulties.

Huet, Philippe. **Politique économique de la Grande-Bretagne depuis 1945.** Paris: Colin, 1969, 582 p.
A scholarly survey of Britain's political economy, intended as a factual contribution to the debate on England's entry into Europe.

Kelf-Cohen, Reuben. **Twenty Years of Nationalisation: The British Experience.** New York: St. Martin's Press, 1969, 339 p.
An undogmatic review of the premises of nationalization and the actual results achieved in British industry. By a former civil servant with considerable experience in this tangled field.

Lamfalussy, Alexandre. **The United Kingdom and the Six.** Homewood (Ill.): Irwin, 1963, 147 p.
This is an important book into which a Belgian economist has distilled a great deal of his own and others' work on comparisons of growth rates in Britain and the Common Market. His conclusions point toward the importance of export expansion as a prime mover in growth.

Leruez, Jacques. **Planification et politique en Grande-Bretagne, 1945-1971.** Paris: Colin, 1972, 314 p.
A critical study of the theoretical and practical aspects of economic planning in Great Britain since the end of World War II.

Livingstone, J. M. **Britain and the World Economy.** Baltimore: Penguin, 1966, 233 p.
A short survey of the part played by Great Britain in the world economy since the end of World War II.

McMahon, Christopher William. **Sterling in the Sixties.** New York: Oxford University Press (for the Royal Institute of International Affairs), 1964, 118 p.
An intelligent discussion of the problems of achieving a long-run improvement in the British balance of payments.

McMillan, James and Harris, Bernard. **The American Take-Over of Britain.** New York: Hart, 1968, 252 p.
A plea by two British journalists that Britain ward off American commercial domination.

Pelling, Henry Mathison. **A History of British Trade Unionism.** New York: St. Martin's Press, 1963, 287 p.
An informative history by a Fellow of St. John's College at Cambridge University.

Revell, Jack and Others. **The Wealth of the Nation: The National Balance Sheet of the United Kingdom, 1957-1961.** New York: Cambridge University Press, 1967, 484 p.
This useful study focuses on assets and liabilities instead of income and production.

Scott, Maurice FitzGerald. **A Study of United Kingdom Imports.** New York: Cambridge University Press, 1963, 269 p.
Economic history is combined with econometrics in this detailed examination of the behavior of British imports.

Shanks, Michael, ed. **The Lessons of Public Enterprise.** London: Cape, 1963, 314 p.
A Fabian Society study of the important aspects of British experience with nationalization of industries. The various contributors dissect the failures and suggest revisions for the future.

Strange, Susan. **Sterling and British Policy: A Political Study of an International Currency in Decline.** New York: Oxford University Press (for the Royal Insitute of International Affairs), 1971, 363 p.

A stimulating analysis of what has been wrong with the pound (and the British economy) since the war. Prescriptions for a more optimistic future include a floating exchange rate, consolidation of debt and a more nationalistic use of financial controls.

Wells, Sidney John. **British Export Performance: A Comparative Study.** New York: Cambridge University Press, 1964, 235 p.

An excellent analysis of the decline in the competitive strength of British exports in the 1950s.

Wells, Sidney John. **Trade Policies for Britain: A Study in Alternatives.** New York: Oxford University Press (for the Royal Institute of International Affairs), 1966, 137 p.

The conclusions of this study underline the importance of Europe to Britain. Originally prepared as a contribution to the trade project of the Council on Foreign Relations' Atlantic Policy Studies.

Worswick, George David Norman and Ady, P. H., *eds.* **The British Economy in the Nineteen-Fifties.** New York: Oxford University Press, 1963, 564 p.

This volume of essays, an excellent sequel to a preceding volume on 1945–50, presents a rather dreary picture of British economy and economic policy in the 1950s.

Social and Cultural Problems

See also Culture; Education; Public Opinion; Communications Processes, p. 42; Ethnic Problems; The Jews, p. 46; (Second World War) Economic, Technical and Non-Military Aspects, p. 172; (Great Britain) Political Problems, p. 381.

Cockburn, Patricia Arbuthnot. **The Years of the Week.** London: Macdonald, 1968, 287 p.

The fascinating story of a London news-sheet which in the 1930s dug up and occasionally invented news to promote radical anti-fascism. Told with verve and insight by the editor's wife.

Desai, Rashmi H. **Indian Immigrants in Britain.** New York: Oxford University Press (for the Institute of Race Relations), 1963, 154 p.

An Indian anthropologist examines the life of his compatriot-immigrants in Britain.

Hopkins, Harry. **The New Look: A Social History of the Forties and Fifties in Britain.** Boston: Houghton, 1964, 512 p.

A perceptive and entertaining inquiry into England's social revolution since the war.

Huxley, Elspeth Josceline (Grant). **Back Street New Worlds.** New York: Morrow, 1965, 190 p.

A review of the status and welfare of the various minorities from all over the world who have settled in Great Britain.

Levin, Bernard. **Run It Down the Flagpole: Britain in the Sixties.** New York: Atheneum, 1971, 450 p.

Instant social history by a well-known British journalist.

Marwick, Arthur. **Britain in the Century of Total War: War, Peace and Social Change, 1900-1967.** Boston: Atlantic (Little, Brown), 1968, 511 p.

A spirited and controversial account, by a Scottish historian, of the changes that two wars wrought in British society.

Peach, Ceri. **West Indian Migration to Britain: A Social Geography.** New York: Oxford University Press (for the Institute of Race Relations), 1968, 122 p.

A thorough and suggestive study of the causes and social consequences of West Indian migration, which was due not so much to native conditions but to "the expansion of the British economy [which] has created gaps at the lower end of the occupational and residential ladder to which West Indian and other coloured immigrants have been drawn in as a replacement population."

Rose, Eliot Joseph Benn with Deakin, Nicholas and Others. **Colour and Citizenship: A Report on British Race Relations.** New York: Oxford University Press (for the Institute of Race Relations), 1969, 815 p.

IRELAND

See also (War) General, p. 108; (Western Europe) Integration, p. 349; (Great Britain) Biographies, Memoirs and Addresses, p. 369; Foreign Policy, p. 375; Regional Issues, p. 383.

Ayearst, Morley. **The Republic of Ireland: Its Government and Politics.** New York: New York University Press, 1970, 241 p.
An introductory treatise, with some attention to Irish history and society.

Bell, John Bowyer. **The Secret Army: The IRA 1916-1970.** New York: Day, 1971, 404 p.
The story of a revolutionary movement, based largely on extensive interviews with its members. The reader is left with the impression of the futility of so much suffering.

Boyce, D. G. **Englishmen and Irish Troubles: British Public Opinion and the Making of Irish Policy 1918-22.** Cambridge: MIT Press, 1972, 253 p.
A successful attempt to investigate the victory of Sinn Féin "from a British rather than an Irish angle."

Bromage, Mary (Cogan). **Churchill and Ireland.** Notre Dame: University of Notre Dame Press, 1964, 222 p.
A well-researched study tracing the course of Winston Churchill's official policies toward Ireland, from his advocacy of Home Rule through his handling of the delicate situation causing new strains during World War II.

Caulfield, Malachy Francis. **The Easter Rebellion.** New York: Holt, Rinehart and Winston, 1963, 375 p.
A vivid and sympathetic reconstruction of the uprising in Dublin by an Irish-born journalist in England.

Chubb, Basil. **The Government and Politics of Ireland.** Stanford: Stanford University Press, 1970, 364 p.
A valuable study of the Irish political system, by a political scientist in Dublin.

Coogan, Timothy Patrick. **The I.R.A.** New York: Praeger, 1970, 373 p.
A leading Irish journalist presents a history of the Irish Republican underground. Though asserting that "the I.R.A. tradition is one of physical action and separatism," Coogan also discusses the ideological divisions and nascent Marxism influencing the movement.

Coogan, Timothy Patrick. **Ireland since the Rising.** New York: Praeger, 1966, 355 p.
A serious, searching, cheerful account of Ireland in the half-century since the Easter Rising. The author believes "her long hard climb to economic prosperity is nearing success" and with it, modernizing social change.

Duff, Charles. **Six Days to Shake an Empire.** Cranbury (N.J.): A. S. Barnes, 1967, 210 p.
An account of the Easter Rising in Dublin in 1916 and of its influence on the British dependencies in Africa and Asia.

FitzGerald, Garret. **Towards a New Ireland.** London: Charles Knight, 1972, 190 p.
A noted Irish economist and Minister of Foreign Affairs since 1973 reviews the causes and effects of political division on both North and South, and urges all factions to work for the creation of a "new" Ireland—a nonsectarian, pluralist, participatory society, united politically without sacrifice of its religious tradition or denial of its mixed inheritance.

Gray, Tony. **The Irish Answer: An Anatomy of Modern Ireland.** Boston: Little, Brown, 1966, 429 p.
Following a brief historical introduction, the author presents an interesting and informative account of contemporary Ireland—its economy, the disputed matter of public opinion and censorship, and the domestic affairs of the nation.

Greaves, C. Desmond. **The Irish Crisis.** New York: International Publishers, 1972, 222 p.
For the author of this study "English monopoly capitalism" is the villain responsible for unrest in contemporary Ireland.

EUROPE

Harkness, D. W. **The Restless Dominion: The Irish Free State and the British Commonwealth of Nations, 1921-31.** London: Macmillan, 1969, 312 p.
The author of this scholarly study argues that Irish diplomacy was the main factor in securing the sovereign equality of the Dominions.

Kee, Robert. **The Green Flag: The Turbulent History of the Irish National Movement.** New York: Delacorte Press, 1972, 877 p.
Irish nationalism from Wolfe Tone to Partition, told at length by a British journalist. In its largely successful attempt to separate myth from reality, the book performs a service to the cause of Irish historiography.

Langrod, Jerzy Stefan and Clifford-Vaughan, M. **L'Irlande.** Paris: Librairie Générale de Droit, 1968, 303 p.
A survey of Ireland's past and present, based on wide reading; strong on social developments.

Leon, Donald E. **Advisory Bodies in Irish Government.** Dublin: Institute of Public Administration, 1963, 180 p.
A study of the organization and operation of the increasingly important groups—"adjuncts of the administration"—responsible for advising the government of Ireland.

Longford, Francis Aungier Pakenham, 7th Earl of and O'Neill, Thomas P. **Eamon de Valera.** Boston: Houghton, 1971, 499 p.
An authorized and authoritative biography of Ireland's master statesman, affording a sweeping portrait of Irish politics as well.

Mansergh, Philip Nicholas Seton. **The Irish Question, 1840-1921.** Toronto: University of Toronto Press, rev. ed., 1965, 316 p.
An intelligent and informative interpretation of the Irish question, by a Cambridge scholar who has often and expertly dealt with specific aspects of Irish history. A revised edition of "Ireland in the Age of Reform and Revolution," published in 1940.

Nowlan, Kevin Barry and Williams, T. Desmond, *eds.* **Ireland in the War Years and After, 1939-51.** Notre Dame: University of Notre Dame Press, 1970, 216 p.
A series of essays, mostly by Irish scholars on the political and cultural changes before and after Ireland's withdrawal from the Commonwealth.

O'Brien, Conor Cruise. **States of Ireland.** New York: Pantheon, 1972, 336 p.
A cogent, impartial and highly personalized appraisal of the state of the Catholic and Protestant "states" of Ireland, by the former international civil servant and a member of the Daíl. Dr. O'Brien has hope, not for unity, but for rational and palatable diversity.

Williams, Desmond, *ed.* **The Irish Struggle, 1916-1926.** London: Routledge, 1966, 193 p.
A collection of 15 essays, reflecting many viewpoints and dealing "with the period between the Easter Rising of 1916 and the first years of the new Irish Free State governments."

Younger, Calton. **A State of Disunion: Arthur Griffith, Michael Collins, James Craig, Eamon de Valera.** London: Muller, 1972, 349 p.
A treatment of early Irish statehood through studies of four of its major figures.

THE NETHERLANDS

See also Comparative Government, p. 18; Colonial Problems; Decolonization, p. 36; Economic Growth and Development, p. 71; Second World War, p. 144; The Postwar World, p. 178; West Indies and the Caribbean, p. 300; The Guianas, p. 336; Western Europe, p. 345; Indonesia, p. 759.

Abert, James Goodear. **Economic Policy and Planning in the Netherlands, 1950-1965.** New Haven: Yale University Press, 1969, 282 p.
A solid account of one of the most interesting European efforts at planning in a country heavily dependent on the international economy.

Beyen, Johan Willem. **Het spel en de knikkers: een kroniek van vijftig jaren.** Rotterdam: Donker, 1968, 304 p.
The memoirs of a Dutch banker, diplomat and a former Minister of Foreign Affairs.

Bloema, K. P. **Moderne politieke strategieën: een kritiek op het defensie- en het buitenlandse beleid.** The Hague: Nijgh & Ditmar, 1968, 163 p.
In this critique of Dutch defense and foreign policies the author pleads for a United Europe, comprising both the Eastern and Western parts.

Geismann, Georg. **Politische Struktur und Regierungssystem in den Niederlanden.** Frankfurt/Main: Athenaeum, 1964, 337 p.
An informative study, by a German political scientist, of the structure of contemporary Dutch politics, with a brief sketch of the historical and social background.

Hartog, F. **Nederland en de Euromarkt.** Leyden: Kroese, 1971, 176 p.
A study of the role of the Netherlands in the formation and the development of the European Economic Community.

Hollander, A. N. J. den and Others, eds. **Drift en koers: een halve eeuw sociale verandering in Nederland.** Assen: van Gorcum/Prakke, 2d ed., 1962, 331 p.
A collection of essays, published on the 25th anniversary of the Dutch Sociological Association, describing the changes which took place in Dutch society during the last 50 years.

Jong, L. de. **Het Koninkrijk der Nederlanden in de Tweede Wereldoorlog 1939-1945.** The Hague: Nijhoff (for the Rijksinstituut voor Oorlogsdocumentatie), 1969–.
The official history of the Kingdom of the Netherlands in the Second World War. Four volumes have been published through 1972.

Jonkman, Jan Anne. **Het oude Nederlands-Indië.** Assen: Van Gorcum, 1971, 327 p.
Memoirs of a former Dutch Minister for Overseas Territories, dealing with the Indonesian question after the Second World War.

Keuning, Hendrick Jakob. **Het Nederlandse volk in zijn woongebied: hoofdlijnen van een economische en sociale geografie van Nederland.** The Hague: Leopold, 3rd ed., 1970, 487 p.
A socio-geographic review of the Netherlands.

Lijphart, Arend. **The Politics of Accommodation: Pluralism and Democracy in the Netherlands.** Berkeley: University of California Press, 1968, 222 p.
A political scientist explains the reasonably successful workings of Dutch democracy.

Luns, Joseph Marie Antoine Hubert. **Ik herinner mij . . . .** Leyden: Sijthoff, 1971, 269 p.
Reminiscences by a leading Dutch diplomat who was his country's Minister of Foreign Affairs from 1952 to 1971.

Maass, Walter B. **The Netherlands at War, 1940-1945.** New York: Abelard-Schuman, 1970, 264 p.
An informative survey by an Austrian-born member of the Dutch resistance movement during World War II.

Nederlandse buitenlandse politiek: aspecten en achtergronden. The Hague: Nederlandsch Genootschap voor Internationale Zaken, 1970, 99 p.
Essays on Dutch foreign policy, based on discussions held by the Netherlands Institute of International Affairs.

Presser, Jacob. **The Destruction of the Dutch Jews.** New York: Dutton, 1969, 556 p.
A scholarly study by a Dutch historian who as a Jew suffered through the years of Nazi occupation.

Rijkens, P. **Handel en wandel: nagelaten geschriften 1888-1965.** Rotterdam: Donker, 1965, 185 p.
Writings on recent economic and political history of the Netherlands by a Dutch industrialist and public figure.

Schermerhorn, Willem. **Het dagboek van Schermerhorn.** Groningen: Wolters-Noordhoff, 1970, 2 v.
The diaries and reports of Schermerhorn, chairman of the Commission for the Dutch East Indies from September 1946 to October 1947.

Schokking, J. J., ed. **Nederland, Europa en de wereld: ons buitenlands beleid in discussie.** Meppel: Boom en Zoon, 1970, 232 p.
A collection of essays on Dutch foreign policy since 1945.

Stikker, Dirk Uipko. **Men of Responsibility: A Memoir.** New York: Harper and Row, 1966, 418 p.
Wartime and postwar memoirs by the Dutch statesman and former Secretary-General of NATO.

Warmbrunn, Werner. **The Dutch under German Occupation, 1940–1945.** Stanford: Stanford University Press, 1963, 338 p.
A scholarly and judicious inquiry into all aspects of Dutch life, with particular emphasis on collaboration and resistance.

BELGIUM

See also Nationalism and Nationality, p. 17; Comparative Government, p. 18; Colonial Problems; Decolonization, p. 36; Labor and Labor Movements, p. 41; Inter-War Period, p. 140; Second World War, p. 144; The Postwar World, p. 178; Western Europe, p. 345; (Central Africa) General, p. 821; Zaïre, p. 822; Rwanda; Burundi, p. 832.

Arango, Ergasto Ramón. **Leopold III and the Belgian Royal Question.** Baltimore: Johns Hopkins Press, 1963, 234 p.
A broad, balanced and informative inquiry into the controversies surrounding the conduct of King Leopold of Belgium during and after the Second World War.

Baudhuin, Fernand. **Histoire économique de la Belgique 1957–1968.** Brussels: Emile Bruylant, 1970, 514 p.
A survey of economic developments in Belgium from 1957 to 1968.

Capelle, Robert. **Dix-huit ans auprès du Roi Léopold.** Paris: Fayard, 1970, 418 p.
A strong defense of the policies of King Leopold, particularly of his neutralist stance in 1940, by his former private secretary.

Les Conséquences d'ordre interne de la participation de la Belgique aux organisations internationales. Brussels: Institut Royal des Relations Internationales, 1964, 366 p.
A pioneering study of the effects of Belgium's participation in international organizations on its domestic institutions.

Dayez, Étienne-Charles. **La Belgique est-elle morte?** Paris: Fayard, 1969, 173 p.
A survey of the Flemish-Walloon controversy, based on the author's interviews with thirteen well-known Belgian politicians.

Du Roy, Albert. **La Guerre des belges.** Paris: Éditions du Seuil, 1968, 238 p.
A detailed study of the Flemish-Walloon conflict.

Evalenko, René. **Régime économique de la Belgique.** Brussels: Vander, 1968, 554 p.
A detailed discussion of the structure and trends of the contemporary Belgian economy.

Gérard-Libois, Jules and Gotovitch, José. **L'An 40, la Belgique occupée.** Brussels: Centre de Recherches et d'Information Socio-Politiques, 1971, 517 p.
A study of Belgium during the German occupation in World War II.

Huggett, Frank Edward. **Modern Belgium.** New York: Praeger, 1969, 296 p.
An informative survey of contemporary Belgium, divided by linguistic and nationalistic barriers, by a British author.

Kieft, David Owen. **Belgium's Return to Neutrality.** New York: Oxford University Press, 1972, 201 p.
A valuable monograph on Belgian foreign policy in the 1930s; the author's persuasive thesis is that the decision to go neutral was largely determined by domestic crises.

Luykx, Theo. **Politieke geschiedenis van belgië van 1789 tot heden.** Brussels: Elsevier, 1964, 559 p.
A political history of Belgium since the French Revolution.

Lyon, Margot. **Belgium.** New York: Walker, 1971, 204 p.
A highly readable account of the problems of Belgium, past and present, by a seasoned British journalist.

Mallinson, Vernon. **Belgium.** New York: Praeger, 1970, 240 p.
An introduction to Belgium's history and contemporary predicaments, by a British scholar who has known the country for decades.

Martin, Marie-Madeleine. **Baudouin Ier et la Belgique.** Paris: Flammarion, 1964, 248 p.
A pleasant little book that tries to describe Baudouin I and the history of Belgium.

Meynaud, Jean and Others, eds. **La Décision politique en Belgique: le pouvoir et les groupes.** Paris: Colin (for the Centre de Recherche et d'Information Socio-politiques), 1965, 403 p.
A summary of the bases of Belgian politics and an analysis of the politics of major decisions since 1945.

L'Opinion publique belge: le Parlement, l'Europe, les finances publiques, la politique culturelle. Brussels: Éditions de l'Institut de Sociologie de l'Université de Bruxelles, 1971, 354 p.
A collection of papers on Belgian public opinion originally presented at a conference organized by the Institut de Sociologie of the University of Brussels.

Les Relations militaires franco-belges de mars 1936 au 10 mai 1940. Paris: Éditions du Centre National de la Recherche Scientifique, 1968, 198 p.
A survey, supplemented with documents, by a group of Belgian and French historians, of the negotiations concerning the defense of their countries from 1936 to 1940.

Spaak, Paul-Henri Charles. **Combats inachevés.** Paris: Fayard, 1969, 2 v.
Memoirs of the Belgian statesman who for nearly thirty years directed Belgian foreign policy and had considerable influence on the whole Atlantic world. A major historical source for the world since 1940. An abridged English version was published as "The Continuing Battle: Memoirs of a European, 1936-1966" (Boston: Little, Brown, 1972, 512 p.).

Van den Bulcke, D. **De buitenlandse ondernemingen in de Belgische industrie.** Ghent: SERUG - Seminarie voor Toegepaste Economie bij de Rijksuniversiteit de Gent, 1971, 339 p.
A survey of foreign-owned Belgian industrial enterprises.

Van Langenhove, Fernand. **La Belgique et ses garants: l'été 1940; contribution à l'histoire de la politique extérieure de la Belgique pendant la Seconde guerre mondiale.** Brussels: Palais des Académies, 1972, 228 p.
A substantial study of Belgian foreign policy in the tragic summer of 1940.

Van Langenhove, Fernand. **La Sécurité de la Belgique: contribution à l'histoire de la période 1940-1950.** Brussels: Éditions de l'Université de Bruxelles, 1971, 263 p.
Belgium's move from neutrality and war to a new policy of close alliance in Europe and within NATO is here depicted by the former secretary-general of the Belgian Foreign Office. An informative and useful work.

Van Wauwe, Ludo. **Fédéralisme: utopie ou possibilité?** Paris: Librairie Générale de Droit, 1971, 223 p.
A plea for a federal solution to the strife between the Flemings and the Walloons.

Visscher, Charles de and Van Langenhove, Fernand, eds. **Documents diplomatiques belges 1920-1940: la politique de sécurité extérieure.** Brussels: Académie Royale des Sciences, des Lettres et des Beaux-Arts de Belgique, Commission Royale d'Histoire, 1964-66, 5 v.
A massive collection of documents dealing with Belgian foreign policy in the period from 1920-1940.

Wigny, Pierre Louis. **La Troisième révision de la constitution.** Brussels: Émile Bruylant, 1972, 449 p.
A study of the Belgian Constitution.

SWITZERLAND

See also Nationalism and Nationality, p. 17; International Organization and Government, p. 96; (Second World War) Special Operations; Propaganda; Espionage; Intelligence, p. 169; Western Europe, p. 345; Nepal, p. 655.

Bonjour, Edgar. **Geschichte der schweizerischen Neutralität: vier Jahrhunderte eidgenössischer Aussenpolitik.** Basel: Helbing und Lichtenhahn, 1946-74, 7 v.
   A very well-prepared review of the foreign policy of Switzerland from the seventeenth century to the end of World War II. The author, a professor at the University of Basel, was commissioned by the Swiss Federal Council to undertake this monumental task. Most of the volumes have appeared in revised editions.

Bringolf, Walther. **Mein Leben: Weg und Umweg eines schweizer Sozialdemokraten.** Bern: Scherz, 1965, 509 p.
   The autobiography of a Swiss Social Democrat ranging from the years of the First World War up to the 1960s. Particularly interesting because Switzerland served as a place of refuge for so many revolutionaries and exiles during that time.

Chaudet, Paul. **La Suisse et notre temps: du souvenir à la réflexion.** Paris: Laffont, 1970, 254 p.
   An analysis of the Swiss political experience as a possible model for a new Europe, by a former President of the Swiss Confederation.

Chopard, Théo, *ed.* **Switzerland Present and Future: A Small Country Reexamines Itself.** Berne: New Helvetic Society, 1963, 216 p.
   Distinguished citizens of Switzerland interpret various facets of their country's life and wonder what the Swiss response to the new Europe should be. A thoughtful symposium.

Dargeant, Robert. **Les Suisses.** Paris: Gallimard, 1966, 191 p.
   Sprightly reflections on the Swiss character, helpful for understanding Swiss behavior on the international scene.

Ehni, Reinhart. **Die Schweiz und die Vereinten Nationen von 1944-1947.** Tübingen: Mohr, 1967, 147 p.
   A solid study of the foreign policies of Switzerland in the years from 1944 to 1947, a period when Switzerland redefined its concepts of neutrality and decided not to join the United Nations.

Glaus, Beat. **Die Nationale Front: eine schweizer faschistische Bewegung, 1930-1940.** Zurich: Benziger, 1969, 504 p.
   A study of Swiss fascism in the 1930s.

Gruber, Christian. **Die politischen Parteien der Schweiz im Zweiten Weltkrieg.** Zurich: Europa Verlag, 1966, 267 p.
   A well-documented history of the political parties of Switzerland during the Second World War.

Gruner, Erich. **Die Parteien in der Schweiz.** Bern: Francke, 1969, 277 p.
   A valuable survey of Swiss political parties.

Haas, Leonhard. **Carl Vital Moor, 1852-1932: ein Leben für Marx und Lenin.** Zurich: Benziger, 1970, 372 p.
   A carefully researched biography of a tempestuous Swiss socialist who was a helper of Lenin and an occasional agent of the Germans in their dealings with the Bolsheviks.

Henecka, Hans Peter. **Die jurassischen Separatisten.** Meisenheim am Glan: Anton Hain, 1972, 320 p.
   A solid study of the French speaking separatists of the Jura region in Switzerland.

Hubert-de Perrot, Francine. **La Suisse et la coopération avec les pays en voie de développement.** Geneva: Imprimerie Centrale, 1964, 246 p.
   An introductory survey of Swiss aid to developing countries.

Iklé, Max. **Switzerland: An International Banking and Finance Center.** Stroudsburg (Pa.): Dawden, Hutchinson & Ross, 1972, 156 p.

A study of the origins and functioning of the Swiss banking system by a leading Swiss financier. The German original was published as "Die Schweiz als internationaler Bank- und Finanzplatz" (Zürich: Orell Füssli, 1971, 187 p.).

Kurz, Hans Rudolf. **Bewaffnete Neutralität.** Frauenfeld: Huber, 1967, 150 p.
A good exposition of the military implications of Swiss neutrality.

Kurz, Hans Rudolf. **General Henri Guisan.** Zurich: Musterschmidt, 1965, 97 p.
A brief biography of the Commander-in-Chief of the Swiss Army during World War II.

Liniger-Goumaz, Max. **La Suisse, sa neutralité et l'Europe.** Geneva: Éditions du Temps, 1964, 102 p.
A Swiss educator wrote this defense of continued Swiss neutrality and independence while teaching at the National Pedagogical Institute in Léopoldville.

McRae, Kenneth Douglas. **Switzerland: Example of Cultural Coexistence.** Toronto: Canadian Institute of International Affairs, 1964, 74 p.
A brief, useful survey of Switzerland's way of accommodating several languages in one state, by a Canadian political scientist.

Masnata, François. **Le Parti Socialiste et la tradition démocratique en Suisse.** Paris: Colin, 1963, 332 p.
A well-documented study of the Socialist Party of Switzerland.

Meier, Heinz K. **Friendship under Stress: U.S.-Swiss Relations 1900–1950.** Bern: Lang, 1970, 423 p.
A detailed, scholarly account of the surprisingly complicated relations between the two countries, by a Swiss-American historian.

Meyer, Alice. **Anpassung oder Widerstand: die Schweiz zur Zeit des deutschen Nationalsozialismus.** Frauenfeld: Huber, 1965, 227 p.
A well-documented and absorbing study of Swiss reactions to Hitler's Germany, and of the struggle between the advocates of accommodation and resistance.

Rahm, Werner. **Le Marché suisse du fer et la construction de l'Europe.** Lausanne: Centre de Recherches Européennes, 1964, 294 p.
History of the Swiss iron industry and analysis of its contemporary problems, mostly in relation to the European Coal and Steel Community.

Rings, Werner. **Advokaten des Feindes: das Abenteuer der politischen Neutralität.** Düsseldorf: Econ-Verlag, 1966, 207 p.
Interviews with prominent Swiss, German and Allied diplomats, Red Cross officials and public figures dealing with the Swiss efforts during World War II on behalf of prisoners-of-war, concentration camp inmates and various internees all over the world.

Roethlisberger, Eric. **La Suisse dans l'AELE 1960–1966: 7 ans d'intégration économique dans un cadre européen restreint.** Neuchâtel: La Baconnière, 1969, 310 p.

———. **Mot d'ordre intégration? La Suisse et l'AELE 1967–1969: préparation à un grand marché intégré en Europe.** Neuchâtel: La Baconnière, 1970, 201 p.
The first study is a well-informed examination of the effects of Switzerland's adaptation to the European Free Trade Association in the years from 1960 to 1966. The second, a continuation of the first, covers the period from 1967 to 1969 and discusses possible future relations of Switzerland with the Common Market.

Rohr, Jean. **La Suisse contemporaine: société et vie politique.** Paris: Colin, 1972, 349 p.
A wide-ranging survey of the changing structure of Swiss society and its complex political life, counterpointing the myth with the current malaise.

Rougemont, Denis de. **La Suisse: ou, l'histoire d'un peuple heureux.** Paris: Hachette, 1965, 305 p.
A survey of Swiss culture and a fervent argument that that happily diverse country should become a model for a federated Europe.

Schmid-Ammann, Paul. **Die Wahrheit über den Generalstreik von 1918: seine Ursachen, sein Verlauf, seine Folgen.** Zurich: Morgarten Verlag, 1968, 440 p.
A solid study of the Swiss General Strike in 1918, containing a wealth of information on Swiss politics, foreign relations and the international communist movement.

Schumann, Klaus. **Das Regierungssystem der Schweiz.** Cologne: Heymanns, 1971, 369 p.
A thorough examination of the structure, operation and politics of the Swiss federal system.

Sell, Manfred. **Die neutralen Alpen.** Stuttgart: Seewald, 1965, 241 p.
    A short account of the virtues of Swiss neutrality and a plea for an extension of neutrality throughout the Alpine area.
Senn, Alfred Erich. **The Russian Revolution in Switzerland, 1914–1917.** Madison: University of Wisconsin Press, 1971, 250 p.
    An able study of the activities of the revolutionary emigration from Tsarist Russia in Switzerland during the vitally important years 1914–1917.
Sorell, Walter. **The Swiss: A Cultural Panorama of Switzerland.** Indianapolis: Bobbs-Merrill, 1972, 303 p.
    An engaging "cultural Baedeker" that demonstrates that civic stability is the precondition for fostering high culture.
Steiner, Jürg. **Gewaltlose Politik und kulturelle Vielfalt: Hypothesen, entwickelt am Beispiel der Schweiz.** Bern: Haupt, 1970, 365 p.
    A solid study of the political structure of Switzerland. A revised and enlarged English translation appeared as "Amicable Agreement versus Majority Rule: Conflict Resolution in Switzerland" (Chapel Hill: University of North Carolina Press, 1974, 312 p.).
Steiner, Jürg, *ed.* **Das politische System der Schweiz.** Munich: Piper, 1971, 240 p.
    A substantial collection of essays on the political system of Switzerland, written with the intent to contribute new ideas to the development of the theory of comparative politics and international relations.
Tschopp, Peter. **Inflation et politique monétaire: le cas de la Suisse.** Geneva: Éditions Générales, 1967, 226 p.
    A study of how Switzerland coped with domestic and international inflationary pressures in the 1950s and 1960s.
Veyrassat, Paul. **La Suisse et la création de l'AELE: une page d'intégration européenne.** Neuchâtel: La Baconnière, 1969, 238 p.
    A systematic and thorough study of the choices Switzerland faced when it considered joining the European Free Trade Association.
Vogel, René M. W. **Politique commerciale Suisse.** Montreux: Ed. Léman, 1966, 498 p.
    A massive study of Swiss foreign trade since the beginning of the nineteenth century. The bulk of the study deals with contemporary developments.
Wüst, René-Henri. **Alerte en pays neutre: la Suisse en 1940.** Lausanne: Payot, 1966, 159 p.
    An attempt to describe Swiss military and foreign policy in the eleven weeks following the German attack on the Western Allies in May 1940.

LIECHTENSTEIN

Havrincourt, Hubert d'. **Liechtenstein.** Lausanne: Éditions Rencontre, 1964, 192 p.
    An introductory survey.
Raton, Pierre. **Liechtenstein: History and Institutions of the Principality.** Vaduz: Liechtenstein-Verlag, 1970, 150 p.
    A useful study. The original appeared as "Le Liechtenstein: histoire et institutions" (Geneva: Droz, 2d ed., 1967, 179 p.).

FRANCE

General

See also (Europe) General Surveys, p. 344; Western Europe, p. 345; (France) Politics and Government, p. 408.

L'Année politique, économique, sociale et diplomatique en France. Paris: Presses Universitaires.
    A useful annual chronological review of political, economic, diplomatic and social developments in France. Published since 1946.

Ardagh, John. **The New French Revolution.** New York: Harper and Row, 1969, 501 p.
A study of contemporary French society and of its leap to modernity. The well-informed British author covers all facets of French life, neglecting only politics and de Gaulle as having been studied to excess.

Brinton, Clarence Crane. **The Americans and the French.** Cambridge: Harvard University Press, 1968, 305 p.
A pleasant introduction to France and Franco-American relations by a knowledgeable Harvard historian. A volume in "The American Foreign Policy Library."

Cairns, John Campbell. **France.** Englewood Cliffs: Prentice-Hall, 1966, 180 p.
A brief but sensitive introduction to contemporary France.

Cobb, Richard Charles. **A Second Identity: Essays on France and French History.** New York: Oxford University Press, 1969, 316 p.
Spirited and learned essays on French history, by a British scholar with an exceptional knowledge of France and French life.

Cobban, Alfred. **A History of Modern France, 1715-1962.** New York: Braziller, rev. and enl. ed., 1965, 3 v.
An excellent history, by a veteran student of France.

Faure, Edgar. **Prévoir le présent.** Paris: Gallimard, 1966, 255 p.
A prominent French statesman, at the time of the publication of this volume de Gaulle's Minister of Agriculture, holds forth on world politics and French economic and political problems.

Hoffmann, Stanley and Others. **In Search of France.** Cambridge: Harvard University Press, 1963, 443 p.
A solid symposium on contemporary France prepared under the auspices of the Center for International Affairs at Harvard University.

Nourissier, François. **The French.** New York: Knopf, 1968, 309 p.
A witty, well-written and quite informative survey of contemporary France and the French. The original appeared as "Les Français" (Lausanne: Éditions de Rencontre, 1968, 191 p.).

Pflimlin, Pierre and Uhrich, René. **L'Alsace: destin et volonté.** Paris: Calmann-Lévy, 1963, 262 p.
A brief, useful survey of Alsatian life, past and present.

Revel, Jean-François. **The French.** New York: Braziller, 1966, 117 p.
As one reviewer has said, the author "describes France and the French as one might imagine Lucifer discoursing on faith." Though an angry book, and full of overstatements, it was widely discussed when published in France. French edition: "En France: la fin de l'opposition" (Paris: Julliard, 1965, 201 p.).

Recent History

See also Political Factors, p. 12; The World Since 1914, p. 129; Western Europe, p. 345; (France) General, p. 395; Biographies, Memoirs and Addresses, p. 400; Foreign Policy, p. 404; Military Policy, p. 407; Politics and Government, p. 408; The 1956 Suez Crisis, p. 637; Indochina, p. 736; Algeria, p. 796.

Aron, Robert. **Histoire de l'épuration. I: De l'indulgence aux massacres, novembre 1942–septembre 1944.** Paris: Fayard, 1967, 661 p.
A volume by a veteran chronicler of Vichy and the liberation of France on one of the most controversial episodes in recent French politics: the purges of collaborators in North Africa and in France.

Aron, Robert. **Nouveaux grands dossiers de l'histoire contemporaine.** Paris: Librairie Académique Perrin, 1963, 312 p.
Ten studies, principally on France and de Gaulle since 1940.

Astier de la Vigerie, Emmanuel d'. **De la chute à la libération de Paris, 25 août 1944: trente journées qui ont fait la France.** Paris: Gallimard, 1965, 397 p.
A devoted Gaullist and a leader of the French Resistance outlines the history of France under Nazi occupation.

Barsalou, Joseph. **La Mal-aimée: histoire de la IVe République.** Paris: Plon, 1964, 333 p.
A political history of the Fourth Republic, focused largely on the men who ran it, and

on the communists and Gaullists who sought to wreck it. The author, a leading journalist, acknowledges its many achievements, especially in the domestic sphere.

Bechtel, Guy. **Laval, vingt ans après.** Paris: Laffont, 1963, 373 p.
A French journalist, who was only 14 at the time of Laval's execution, undertakes a reappraisal of the latter's career.

Benoit-Guyod, Georges. **L'Invasion de Paris (1940-1944).** Paris: Éditions du Scorpion, 1962, 319 p.
The day-by-day observations and reactions of a Parisian who stayed in the capital throughout the war and German occupation.

Berl, Emmanuel. **La Fin de la IIIe République: 10 juillet 1940.** Paris: Gallimard, 1968, 366 p.
A study of the political aftermath of France's military defeat—or the road to Vichy.

Bonnefous, Edouard. **Histoire de la Troisième République.** Paris: Presses Universitaires, 1956-67, 7 v.
The concluding volumes of this parliamentary history of the Third Republic are entitled: vol. 6, "Vers la guerre: du Front Populaire à la conférence de Munich (1936-1938)" (1965, 451 p.) and vol. 7, "La Course vers l'abîme: la fin de la IIIe République (1938-1940)" (1967, 464 p.). For titles of earlier volumes, consult "Foreign Affairs Bibliography, 1952-1962."

Boyer de Latour, Pierre. **Le Drame français.** Paris: Au Fil d'Ariane, 1963, 269 p.
A bitter critique of the policies and government of de Gaulle by a former official of the Fourth Republic.

Burman, Ben Lucien. **The Generals Wear Cork Hats: An Amazing Adventure That Made World History.** New York: Taplinger, 1963, 257 p.
Breezy impressions of de Gaulle and his Free French in wartime Africa.

Buron, Robert. **Les Dernières années de la IVe République.** Paris: Plon, 1968, 249 p.
The last five years of the Fourth Republic, as reflected in excerpts from the diary of a leading parliamentarian and sometime minister.

Chapman, Guy. **Why France Fell: The Defeat of the French Army in 1940.** New York: Holt, Rinehart and Winston, 1969, 403 p.
A close analysis of France's military defeat, ". . .the result of twenty years' blindness to the facts of 1914-18." Written by a veteran of the First World War and a student of French affairs.

Christian, William A., Jr. **Divided Island: Faction and Unity on Saint Pierre.** Cambridge: Harvard University Press, 1969, 212 p.
The author of this searching analysis of the Pétainist-Gaullist division on the French island of Saint Pierre maintains that the divisions that plagued the island were those of France herself in microcosm.

Collins, Larry and Lapierre, Dominique. **Is Paris Burning?** New York: Simon and Schuster, 1965, 376 p.
An American and a French journalist tell the dramatic story of the narrow margin by which Paris avoided being destroyed by Hitler at the time of the Nazi withdrawal in August 1944.

Confer, Vincent. **France and Algeria: The Problem of Civil and Political Reform, 1870-1920.** Syracuse: Syracuse University Press, 1966, 148 p.
A study of the middle years of French power in Algeria, a period in which the opportunity to facilitate a harmonious political evolution of Moslem Algeria and metropolitan France was lost.

Cotta, Michèle. **La Collaboration, 1940-1944.** Paris: Colin, 1964, 333 p.
A study of the politicians and journalists who were "collaborationists" and the diverse reasons for their favoring alignment with the Axis powers.

Duquesne, Jacques. **Les Catholiques français sous l'occupation.** Paris: Grasset, 1966, 477 p.
A balanced study of the conflicting forces operating within the Catholic Church of France after June 1940.

Elgey, Georgette. **Histoire de la IVe République.** Paris: Fayard, 1965, 2 v.
Having interviewed many leading politicians of the Fourth Republic, the author pro-

vides a skillful and detailed account of French politics after World War II. Volume I of her study is entitled "La République des illusions, 1945–1951" (1965, 555 p.), and volume II, "La République des contradictions, 1951–1954" (1965, 654 p.).

Fabre-Luce, Alfred. **Vingt-cinq années de liberté.** Paris: Julliard, 1962–64, 3 v.
Lengthy memoirs, covering the period from 1936 through 1961 and containing vivid observations on French politics and politicians, by a remorseless critic of General de Gaulle. The volumes are entitled: "Le Grand jeu, 1936–1939," "L'Épreuve, 1939–1946" and "La Récompense, 1946–1961."

Faillant de Villemarest, Pierre. **L'Espionnage soviétique en France, 1944–1969.** Paris: Nouvelles Éditions Latines, 1969, 316 p.
An alarmist account of Soviet subversion in France in the years from 1944 to 1969, by a French journalist.

Goguel–Nyegaard, François, ed. **Le Référendum du 8 avril 1962.** Paris: Colin, 1963, 221 p.
A comprehensive and valuable study of all aspects of de Gaulle's referendum on Algerian independence, by a well-known French political scientist.

Gounelle, Claude. **Le Dossier Laval.** Paris: Plon, 1969, 764 p.
A dossier of documents on the question of Laval's collaboration with the Germans, by an author who is convinced that Marshal Pétain's successor as head of the Vichy government did not get a chance to present his case before the court that condemned him to death.

Hänsch, Klaus. **Frankreich zwischen Ost und West.** Berlin: Walter de Gruyter, 1972, 287 p.
A study of French politics and foreign policies in the years from 1946 to 1948, a period of increased tensions in East-West relations.

Hess, John L. **The Case for De Gaulle: An American Viewpoint.** New York: Morrow, 1968, 154 p.
A well-argued defense of de Gaulle's domestic and foreign policies, by a former Paris correspondent of *The New York Times*.

Jäckel, Eberhard. **Frankreich in Hitlers Europa: die deutsche Frankreich-Politik im 2. Weltkrieg.** Stuttgart: Deutsche Verlags-Anstalt (for the Institut für Zeitgeschichte), 1966, 396 p.
A serious and well-documented study of France in Hitler's Europe, based primarily on German sources.

Jamet, Claude, ed. **Le Rendez-vous manqué de 1944.** Paris: Éditions France-Empire, 1964, 317 p.
A survey, based on many interviews, of French political attitudes during World War II.

Jeanneney, Jules Émile. **Journal politique: septembre 1939–juillet 1942.** Paris: Armand Colin, 1972, 514 p.
A leading French politician and a veteran member of the Parliament reviews the events in France from 1940 to 1942.

Jeantet, Gabriel. **Pétain contre Hitler.** Paris: Éditions de la Table Ronde, 1966, 337 p.
A confidant of Pétain describes the Marshal's secret diplomacy after the Allied landing in North Africa in 1942.

Julliard, Jacques. **La IVe République (1947–1958).** Paris: Calmann-Lévy, 1968, 370 p.
A series of essays on the Fourth Republic by a French scholar of the Christian Left.

Kaspi, André. **La Mission de Jean Monnet à Alger, mars–octobre 1943.** Paris: Éditions Richelieu, 1971, 240 p.
A monograph on Jean Monnet's significant role in Algiers in 1943, making use of his personal papers.

Launay, Jacques de. **Le Dossier de Vichy.** Paris: Julliard, 1967, 317 p.
A collection of texts illustrating various aspects of the Vichy government, especially its links with both previous and subsequent republics.

Laurent, Jacques. **Année 40: Londres, de Gaulle, Vichy.** Paris: Éditions de la Table Ronde, 1965, 414 p.
A right-wing author, hostile to de Gaulle, reviews the events of 1940.

Macridis, Roy C. and Brown, Bernard E. **Supplement to the De Gaulle Republic: Quest for Unity.** Homewood (Ill.): Dorsey Press, 1963, 141 p.
New chapters to the volume the authors published in 1960.

Menard, Orville D. **The Army and the Fifth Republic.** Lincoln: University of Nebraska Press, 1968, 265 p.
A description of the role of the army in restoring de Gaulle to power in 1958 and in attempting to topple him in April 1961.

Michel, Henri. **Vichy année 40.** Paris: Laffont, 1966, 451 p.
A survey of the first six months of the Vichy government, a period witnessing the beginning of the "Révolution Nationale," the cutting of all ties with Great Britain and the collaboration with the Nazi regime.

Mohler, Armin. **Die Fünfte Republik: Was steht hinter de Gaulle?** Munich: Piper, 1963, 331 p.
A perceptive German journalist tries to grasp the social and historical background of the Fifth Republic and the person of de Gaulle.

Mollet, Guy. **13 mai 1958-13 mai 1962.** Paris: Plon, 1962, 244 p.
The first four years of the Fifth Republic as seen by a leading French statesman and a member of de Gaulle's government.

Morland; Barangé and Martinez. **Histoire de l'Organisation de l'armée secrète.** Paris: Julliard, 1964, 605 p.
A record of the O.A.S., "a private enterprise of unlimited irresponsibility" in the authors' final judgment, which wrought a nightmare of senseless bloodshed and destruction in Algeria and brought France itself to the edge of disaster.

Noguères, Henri and Others. **Histoire de la résistance en France de 1940 à 1945.** Paris: Laffont, 1967–.
A history of the resistance movement in France during World War II. Three volumes have been published through 1972, covering the period from June 1940 to September 1943.

Novick, Peter. **The Resistance Versus Vichy: The Purge of Collaborators in Liberated France.** New York: Columbia University Press, 1968, 245 p.
A well-researched and balanced study.

Ophuls, Marcel. **The Sorrow and the Pity.** New York: Outerbridge and Lazard, 1972, 194 p.
This script of Marcel Ophuls' documentary film on the fall of France and the German occupation demonstrates the intensity and persistence of the divisions in the French body politic. There is an introduction by Stanley Hoffmann.

Paillat, Claude. **Vingt ans qui déchirèrent la France. Tome I: Le Guêpier.** Paris: Laffont, 1969, 628 p.
A French journalist, quoting extensively from documents and letters written by French officials, comments on the dissolution of the French empire after World War II.

Paxton, Robert Owen. **Parades and Politics at Vichy: The French Officer Corps under Marshal Pétain.** Princeton: Princeton University Press, 1966, 472 p.
A well-documented and well-written history of the French Army during the Vichy regime. The author has been "concerned less with 'battles and leaders' than with the tone of an important social group and its part in public life."

Paxton, Robert Owen. **Vichy France: Old Guard and New Order, 1940-1944.** New York: Knopf, 1972, 399 p.
This volume, particularly well-written and well-documented, is scathing in its presentation of evidence, especially German, which has recently become available. Pétain took advantage of a foreign army to carry out domestic reforms, but any benefits he thought he could gain from collaboration turned out to be illusory.

Pomaret, Charles. **Le Dernier témoin: fin d'une guerre, fin d'une république, juin et juillet 1940.** Paris: Presses de la Cité, 1968, 313 p.
The author was a minister in the last two French governments before the capitulation, and he also served in Marshal Pétain's first cabinet. In this volume Mr. Pomaret briefly reminisces on his experience in a very tragic period in recent French history.

Raïssac, Guy. **Un Combat sans merci: l'affaire Pétain–de Gaulle.** Paris: Michel, 1966, 527 p.
A study of the relations between Pétain and de Gaulle. The author has had access to the archives of the Vichy government.

Rémy, *pseud.* (Gilbert Renault-Roulier). **La Ligne de démarcation.** Paris: Perrin, 1964 –.
A massive survey of the events concerning the border that was established on June 22, 1940 between Vichy and German-occupied France. Twenty-one volumes have been published through 1972.

Roy, Jules. **The Trial of Marshal Pétain.** New York: Harper and Row, 1968, 263 p.
The day-by-day reconstruction of Pétain's controversial trial, by a well-known writer who, once a follower of the Marshal, is now critical of him and his judges. Translation of "Le Grand naufrage" (Paris: Julliard, 1966, 316 p.).

Saint-Paulien, J., *pseud.* (Maurice-Ivan Sicard). **Histoire de la collaboration.** Paris: Éditions de l'Esprit Nouveau, 1964, 610 p.
A massive history of French collaboration with the Germans during World War II, written by a collaborator.

Shirer, William Lawrence. **The Collapse of the Third Republic: An Inquiry into the Fall of France in 1940.** New York: Simon and Schuster, 1969, 1,082 p.
A detailed but highly readable account of the French political scene in the years before the debacle of 1940. The veteran journalist turned historian sticks quite closely to the colorful political surface.

Soustelle, Jacques. **A New Road for France.** New York: Speller, 1965, 278 p.
A bitter indictment of the Gaullist road, by a former close associate of the General in the Resistance. Soustelle broke with de Gaulle over Algeria and still thinks the Algerian settlement "the greatest crime in the history of France." Embittered in exile, he is nevertheless an intelligent spokesman of the irreconcilable opposition to de Gaulle and decolonization. The French original appeared as "Sur une route nouvelle" (Paris: Éditions du Fuseau, 1964, 315 p.).

Soustelle, Jacques. **Vingt-huit ans de Gaullisme.** Paris: Éditions de la Table Ronde, 1968, 473 p.
A very personal and extremely hostile evaluation of de Gaulle and his policies.

Viard, René. **La Fin de l'empire colonial français.** Paris: G.-P. Maisonneuve et Larose, 1963, 160 p.
A good summary, by one close to the men and to the events, of the dissolution of the French colonial empire in the years following the Brazzaville conference of 1944.

Warner, Geoffrey. **Pierre Laval and the Eclipse of France.** New York: Macmillan, 1969, 461 p.
An absorbing and judicious account of the life and times of a controversial figure.

Williams, Philip Maynard. **Crisis and Compromise.** Hamden (Conn.): Shoe String Press, 1964, 546 p.
An analysis of the political machinery of the Fourth Republic, by an English scholar who knows France exceptionally well. This book encompasses entirely revised parts of his earlier "Politics in Post-War France" (1954) and 11 new chapters.

Biographies, Memoirs and Addresses

See also First World War, p. 131; Inter-War Period, p. 140; Second World War, p. 144; Indochina, p. 736; Algeria, p. 796.

Aron, Robert. **An Explanation of De Gaulle.** New York: Harper and Row, 1966, 210 p.
An essay, based partly on four interviews with the great "unknown." The French original appeared as "Charles de Gaulle" (Paris: Perrin, 1964, 262 p.).

Beaufre, André. **Mémoires: 1920–1940–1945.** Paris: Presses de la Cité, 1969, 514 p.
Eloquent and informative recollections of a French general who before and during the Second World War played a major role in military and political affairs.

Beaufre, André. **La Revanche de 1945.** Paris: Plon, 1965, 313 p.
General Beaufre's memoirs and reflections on the period 1940–1945 in France and the French resistance abroad.

Bidault, Georges. **Resistance: The Political Autobiography of Georges Bidault.** New York: Praeger, 1967, 348 p.
 The spiteful memoirs of a chief figure of the Fourth Republic, who was a resistance leader with de Gaulle during World War II and because of the General's Algerian policy opposed him later. The French original was published as "D'une résistance à l'autre" (Paris: Presses du Siècle, 1965, 382 p.).

Blum, Léon. **Oeuvres.** Paris: Michel, 1954– .
 The collected writings of Léon Blum, French Socialist, statesman and man of letters. Seven volumes have been published through 1972.

Bonnet, Georges Étienne. **De Munich à la guerre: défense de la paix.** Paris: Plon, rev. ed., 1967, 585 p.
 Appointed Foreign Minister in April 1938, Bonnet helped shape France's hapless policies that led to Munich and the war. A revised and enlarged edition of recollections published in 1948 as "Défense de la paix" (Geneva: Éditions du Cheval Ailé, 1946–48, 2 v.).

Bonnet, Georges Étienne. **Vingt ans de vie politique, 1918-1938: de Clemenceau à Daladier.** Paris: Fayard, 1969, 286 p.
——. **Dans la tourmente (1938-1948).** Paris: Fayard, 1970, 319 p.
 Memoirs by a French diplomat and statesman who was Foreign Minister of his country at a very critical time (1938–1939).

Boris, Georges. **Servir la République.** Paris: Julliard, 1963, 493 p.
 A collection of texts and personal accounts by a French economist who was a participant in French governments for 40 years.

Bromberger, Merry. **Le destin secret de Georges Pompidou.** Paris: Fayard, 1965, 349 p.
 A biography of Georges Pompidou, de Gaulle's Prime Minister and successor who died in 1974.

Challe, Maurice. **Notre révolte.** Paris: Presses de la Cité, 1968, 444 p.
 Written in prison, these notes of General Challe include reflections on the Suez affair, the war in Algeria, his role in the revolt of 1961 and a variety of other subjects. They provide an inside view of the French Army in Algeria and above all of the General himself.

Chambe, René. **Le Maréchal Juin, "Duc du Garigliano."** Paris: Presses de la Cité, 1968, 438 p.
 A biography of Marshal Juin, a leading French officer during World War II. General Chambe, the author of this volume, is a friend of the Marshal and a well-known military historian.

Chauvel, Jean. **Commentaire.** Paris: Fayard, 1971–72, 2 v.
 Memoirs by a veteran French diplomatist, who had served as his country's representative in Berne, Vienna, London and at the United Nations, covering the years from 1938 to 1952.

Cole, Hubert. **Laval: A Biography.** New York: Putnam, 1963, 314 p.
 Less general than the title would suggest, this is chiefly an account, and a good one, of Pierre Laval's disastrous but not frivolous career during the Vichy years, 1940–1944.

Colton, Joel. **Léon Blum: Humanist in Politics.** New York: Knopf, 1966, 512 p.
 A substantial, sympathetic though not uncritical political biography, by a professor of history at Duke University.

Crawley, Aidan. **De Gaulle.** Indianapolis: Bobbs-Merrill, 1969, 510 p.
 A well-researched biography of General de Gaulle, presenting, as the author, a former Member of Parliament, says, "an English point of view."

Duclos, Jacques. **Mémoires.** Paris: Fayard, 1968– .
 Memoirs by a veteran leader of the French Communist Party. Six volumes have been published through 1972.

Ély, Paul. **Mémoires.** Paris: Plon, 1964–69, 2 v.
 Volume 1 of General Ély's memoirs is entitled "L'Indochine dans la tourmente" (360 p.) and deals with the author's experience in Indochina; vol. 2, "Suez . . . le 13 mai" (504 p.), covers his service as Chief of Staff from 1956 to 1960; most of it is about Algeria, but a detailed account of the Suez affair as seen from his position is included.

Flanner, Janet. **Paris Journal, 1944-1965.** New York: Atheneum, 1965, 615 p.
 A selective and intelligent portrait of postwar France, drawn by *The New Yorker*'s Genêt, who began her Paris reporting in 1925. Her letters range from the wretched gloriousness of the Liberation to the prosperous uncertainties of the mid-1960s.

Fouchet, Christian. **Mémoires d'hier et de demain: au service du Général de Gaulle.** Paris: Plon, 1971, 297 p.
 Fouchet, a dedicated Gaullist and "old companion" from the dark days of June 1940 and an efficient envoy and minister, reverently and discreetly recollects several "historical turning points" in the career of his hero, saving for a second volume his part in certain Gaullist reforms for "mustering the French people."

Gaulle, Charles André Joseph Maria de. **De Gaulle: Implacable Ally.** New York: Harper and Row, 1966, 248 p.
 A collection of excerpts from de Gaulle's writings and speeches, including snippets from his "Memoirs," intended to illustrate his views on a host of subjects. Edited by Roy C. Macridis.

Gaulle, Charles André Joseph Maria de. **Discours et messages.** Paris: Plon, 1970, 5 v.
 A collection of General de Gaulle's formal speeches, from the day in June 1940 when he first spoke " in the name of France" to his resignation 29 years later. A testament of greatness.

Gaulle, Charles André Joseph Maria de. **Memoirs of Hope: Renewal and Endeavor.** New York: Simon and Schuster, 1972, 392 p.
 Memoirs covering the years of de Gaulle's second effort to raise France to his level of sublime expectation. An indispensable source and an evocation of style and spirit. The first volume of the French original appeared as "Mémoires d'espoir: le renouveau 1958-1962" (Paris: Plon, 1970, 314 p.), and the first two chapters of the projected second volume as "Mémoires d'espoir: l'effort 1962" (Paris: Plon, 1971, 223 p.).

Griffiths, Richard. **Pétain: A Biography of Marshal Philippe Pétain of Vichy.** Garden City: Doubleday, 1972, 379 p.
 A balanced, scholarly study of the Marshal, the "incarnation" of France in victory in World War I, in defeat in 1940, and of Vichy's collaboration with the Nazis. Especially illuminating on the continuity in the ideas and ethos of the traditional Right.

Lacouture, Jean. **De Gaulle.** New York: New American Library, 1966, 215 p.
 A series of essays by a prominent French journalist, for many years with *Le Monde*, tracing the complex course of de Gaulle's life and thought. The French original was published as "De Gaulle" (Paris: Éditions du Seuil, 1965, 188 p.).

La Gorce, Paul Marie de. **De Gaulle entre deux mondes: une vie et une époque.** Paris: Fayard, 1964, 766 p.
 An attempt to describe General de Gaulle's personality, philosophy and statesmanship on the background of World War II and subsequent French history.

Langlade, Paul de. **En Suivant Leclerc.** Paris: Au Fil d'Ariane, 1964, 428 p.
 An account of Leclerc's great military career from North Africa to the liberation of France, by a fellow-general.

Lapie, Pierre Olivier. **Herriot.** Paris: Fayard, 1967, 342 p.
 A biography of Éduard Herriot (1872-1957), a prominent French statesman, repeatedly premier of France and the leader of the Radical Socialist Party.

Lecoeur, Auguste. **Le Partisan.** Paris: Flammarion, 1963, 314 p.
 The frankly told story of the author's life as a Communist Party member. Lecoeur fought in the International Brigade in Spain, took an active part in the resistance in France's northern mining region and became an important party official before his expulsion from the party in the mid-1950s over an organizational issue.

Malraux, André. **Anti-Memoirs.** New York: Holt, Rinehart and Winston, 1968, 420 p.
 In this first of four projected volumes, the eminent French writer and statesman uses the episodes of his rich life as illustrations or signposts of the human condition. The French original appeared as "Antimémoires" (Paris: Gallimard, 1967, 604 p.).

Malraux, André. **Felled Oaks: Conversation with De Gaulle.** New York: Holt, Rinehart and Winston, 1972, 128 p.
 The record of Malraux's last extended conversation with de Gaulle, as well as the epitome of a close association of two self-consciously great men. A moving work of po-

etry and truth and an important source on what de Gaulle thought on topics ranging from the basis of his rule—"I had a contract with France"—to his views on politics and literature, on history and hippies, on the future and himself. The French original was published as "Les Chênes qu'on abat" (Paris: Gallimard, 1971, 235 p.).

Mannoni, Eugène. **Moi, Général de Gaulle.** Paris: Éditions du Seuil, 1964, 154 p.
A rather breezy yet intelligent and revealing analysis of the inscrutable de Gaulle and particularly of his rhetoric, by a veteran French journalist.

Mauriac, Claude. **Un Autre de Gaulle: journal 1944-1954.** Paris: Hachette, 1971, 408 p.
Appointed to de Gaulle's secretariat in 1944, the young Mauriac had ample chance to observe him and converse with him. Mauriac's journal makes clear that he took full advantage of his opportunities.

Mauriac, François. **De Gaulle.** Garden City: Doubleday, 1966, 229 p.
A famous French writer records and analyzes his admiration for de Gaulle, and compares his portrait with de Gaulle's own sense of himself, as revealed in the latter's spoken and written word. The French original was published as "De Gaulle" (Paris: Grasset, 1964, 345 p.).

Mauriac, François. **Mémoires politiques.** Paris: Grasset, 1967, 476 p.
A collection of articles, originally published between 1933 and 1953. These controversial essays furnish an elegant commentary on the great political themes of those years.

Mengin, Robert. **No Laurels for de Gaulle.** New York: Farrar, Straus and Giroux, 1966, 402 p.
A strong anti-Gaullist appraisal based on the diary of a French journalist during the years 1939-43.

Mitterrand, François. **Ma Part de vérité: de la rupture à l'unité.** Paris: Fayard, 1969, 206 p.
A mixture of autobiography and political apologia by a leader of the French Left and a candidate in the 1965 presidential elections.

Moch, Jules Salvador. **Rencontres avec Darlan et Eisenhower.** Paris: Plon, 1968, 345 p.
Reminiscences on Admiral Darlan and General Eisenhower by a prominent French statesman.

Moch, Jules Salvador. **Rencontres avec De Gaulle.** Paris: Plon, 1971, 406 p.
A veteran French Socialist recalls his many interviews with de Gaulle, whom he supported during the war and criticized during the Fifth Republic. Few political revelations, but memorable examples of de Gaulle's sublime egotism.

Moch, Jules Salvador. **Rencontres avec Léon Blum.** Paris: Plon, 1970, 363 p.
Evocations of the author's 24 years of collaboration and friendship with Léon Blum.

Molchanov, Nikolai Nikolaevich. **General de Goll'.** Moscow: Izd-vo "Mezhdunarodnye Otnosheniia," 1972, 496 p.
A Soviet study of the career of General de Gaulle.

Monnerville, Gaston. **Clemenceau.** Paris: Fayard, 1968, 766 p.
An admiring biography of the French statesman who was Premier of his country from 1906 to 1909, and again from 1917 to 1920. The author, a well-known French public figure, was President of the Senate from 1958 to 1968.

Nantet, Jacques. **Pierre Mendès-France.** Paris: Éditions du Centurion, 1967, 272 p.
A biography of the lawyer, economist and politician who was the Premier of France from June 1954 to February 1955. Based on ten long conversations with him.

Rochefort, Robert. **Robert Schuman.** Paris: Éditions du Cerf, 1968, 383 p.
A biography of the Lorraine-born French statesman who as Premier, Minister of Foreign Affairs and Minister of Finance played a prominent role in French politics after World War II and was a leading proponent of European unity.

Ryan, Stephen. **Pétain the Soldier.** South Brunswick (N.J.): A. S. Barnes and Co., 1969, 315 p.
A study of the military career and doctrines of Henri Philippe Pétain, Marshal of France. Commenting briefly on Pétain's role during World War II, the author writes that "by providing a scapegoat in his person, he could help his people rationalize their breakdown and restore their pride."

Salan, Raoul. **Mémoires: fin d'un empire.** Paris: Presses de la Cité, 1970–.
Memoirs by a leading French soldier whose career ended in jail after his participation in the Algerian uprising of 1961. Through 1972 three of the four planned volumes have appeared dealing with Salan's long missions in Indochina and Algeria.

Salem, Daniel. **Pierre Mendès France et le nouveau socialisme.** Paris: Presses Universitaires, 1969, 158 p.
A collection of Mendès-France's statements, illustrating his gradual elaboration of a new brand of democratic socialism.

Schoenbrun, David. **The Three Lives of Charles De Gaulle.** New York: Atheneum, 1966, 373 p.
An anecdotal biography, by a veteran reporter who admires his subject.

Thyraud de Vosjoli, P. L. **Lamia.** Boston: Little, Brown, 1970, 344 p.
The highly readable and controversial memoirs of a former French underground agent who rose in de Gaulle's intelligence service only to denounce it eventually as being Soviet-infiltrated.

Tournoux, Jean-Raymond. **Jamais dit.** Paris: Plon, 1971, 490 p.
A collection of facts, hitherto unpublished documents, anecdotes and observations on Charles de Gaulle.

Tournoux, Jean-Raymond. **Sons of France: Pétain and De Gaulle.** New York: Viking Press, 1966, 245 p.
A lively and well-documented study of the relationship between Pétain and de Gaulle. A somewhat abridged translation of "Pétain et de Gaulle" (Paris: Plon, 1964, 556 p.).

Tournoux, Jean-Raymond. **La Tragédie du Général.** Paris: Plon, 1967, 704 p.
De Gaulle's incisive, often ironic, comments, woven together to make an intellectual biography of sorts.

Werth, Alexander. **De Gaulle: A Political Biography.** New York: Simon and Schuster, 1966, 416 p.
A workmanlike and generally favorable biography of de Gaulle, whom the author sees as essentially a perennial rebel.

Wolf, Dieter. **Die Doriot-Bewegung: ein Beitrag zur Geschichte des französischen Faschismus.** Stuttgart: Deutsche Verlags-Anstalt (for the Institut für Zeitgeschichte), 1967, 408 p.
A comprehensive and well-documented biography of Doriot, France's leading fascist and wartime collaborator, who began his career as a communist functionary in 1920.

Wormser, Georges. **Georges Mandel, l'homme politique.** Paris: Plon, 1967, 316 p.
A biography of a French statesman, principal private secretary of Clemenceau and a member of various French cabinets at the outbreak of World War II. Mandel was assassinated in 1944 during the German occupation.

Ziebura, Gilbert. **Léon Blum: Theorie und Praxis einer sozialistischen Politik. Band I: 1872 bis 1934.** Berlin: De Gruyter, 1963, 526 p.
In this first of a projected two-volume biography, a German political scientist rightly emphasizes the constant tension between Blum's socialist aspirations and the political realities of the Third Republic. A careful and reflective narrative with valuable insights into all aspects of recent French history.

Foreign Policy

See also General Works, p. 1; International Organization and Government, p. 96; War and Peace, p. 108; First World War, p. 131; Inter-War Period, p. 140; Second World War, p. 144; The Postwar World, p. 178; (France) Recent History, p. 396; Biographies, Memoirs and Addresses, p. 400; Military Policy, p. 407; Politics and Government, p. 408; Economic Problems, p. 415; and the sections for specific countries and regions.

Bjøl, Erling. **A France devant l'Europe: la politique européenne de la IVe République.** Copenhagen: Munksgaard, 1966, 456 p.
A study by a Danish scholar of French policy in respect to questions of European coöperation, chiefly between 1950 and 1957.

Bonnefous, Edouard. **Les Milliards qui s'envolent: l'aide française aux pays sous-développés.** Paris: Fayard, 1963, 293 p.

An appeal, nationalist in tone, against French aid to underdeveloped countries.

Carmoy, Guy de. **The Foreign Policies of France, 1944-1968.** Chicago: University of Chicago Press, 1970, 510 p.

A useful survey of the pro-European policies of a feeble Fourth Republic contrasted with the Gaullist drive to independence, by a French scholar and former official. The French original was published as "Les Politiques étrangères de la France, 1944-1966" (Paris: Éditions de la Table Ronde, 1967, 520 p.).

Chernikov, Gennadii Pavlovich and Chernikova, Diana Aleksandrovna. **Storoniki i protivniki franko-sovetskogo sotrudnichestva.** Moscow: Izd-vo "Mezhdunarodnye Otnosheniia," 1971, 256 p.

A Soviet assessment of the domestic political trends in France and a plea for improved relations between France and the U.S.S.R.

Cocatre-Zilgien, André. **Diplomatie française et problèmes internationaux contemporains.** Paris: Éditions Cujas, 1970, 264 p.

A collection of lively essays on various aspects of French foreign affairs and world politics, by a French academic.

Couve de Murville, Maurice. **Une Politique étrangère, 1958-1969.** Paris: Plon, 1971, 499 p.

The reflections of de Gaulle's Foreign Minister, whose tenure at the Quai d'Orsay was the longest since the French Revolution. Offers interesting perspectives on the traditional French outlook on diplomacy and on de Gaulle's ideas and practices.

Dantsig, Boris Moiseevich and Others, *eds.* **Politika Frantsii v Azii i Afrike, 1945-1964 gg.** Moscow: Izd-vo "Nauka," 1965, 406 p.

A comprehensive Soviet survey of French colonial policies between 1945 and 1964.

DePorte, Anton William. **De Gaulle's Foreign Policy, 1944-1946.** Cambridge: Harvard University Press, 1968, 327 p.

A balanced study of de Gaulle's first ventures in foreign policy, placing them in the tradition of such predecessors as Barthou and Poincaré. The author is a U.S. State Department official.

Documents diplomatiques français, 1932-1939. Paris: Imprimerie Nationale (for the Ministère des Affaires Étrangères, Commission de Publication des Documents Relatifs aux Origines de la Guerre 1939-1945), 1964–.

Documents on French foreign policy in the years from 1932 to 1939, published by the French Ministry of Foreign Affairs. In the "Ire Série (1932-1935)," six volumes have been published through 1972 covering the period from July 9, 1932 to July 26, 1934. In the "2e Série (1936-1939)," eight volumes have been published through 1973 covering the period from January 1, 1936 to March 20, 1938.

Fagerberg, Elliott Pennell. **The "Anciens Combattants" and French Foreign Policy.** Geneva: Université de Genève, Institut Universitaire de Hautes Études Internationales, 1966, 353 p.

An investigation of the influence of the French veterans' organizations on the formulation of French foreign policy.

Fisher, Sydney Nettleton, *ed.* **France and the European Community.** Columbus: Ohio State University Press, 1965, 176 p.

Culture, law, security, agriculture, economics, integration and relations with the Soviet bloc are some of the subjects explored in this symposium that took place in the fall of 1963.

Ghébali, Victor-Yves. **La France en guerre et les organisations internationales, 1939-1945.** The Hague: Mouton, 1969, 273 p.

A scholarly study of Vichy's and de Gaulle's wartime relations with the League of Nations in neutral Switzerland. Not surprisingly, Vichy broke with the League and the Free French sought to coöperate with it.

Grosser, Alfred. **French Foreign Policy under de Gaulle.** Boston: Little, Brown, 1967, 175 p.

An updated translation of a realistic and informative appraisal of French foreign policy since 1958. The author, a well-known political scientist and student of French politics, emphasizes the continuity of policies from the Fourth to the Fifth Republic and hints that even after de Gaulle a radical change may not take place. The French original was published as "La Politique extérieure de la Ve République" (Paris: Éditions du Seuil, 1965, 189 p.).

Hayter, Teresa. **French Aid.** London: Overseas Development Institute, 1966, 229 p.
A comprehensive and well-researched study of France's aid programs.

Kohl, Wilfrid L. **French Nuclear Diplomacy.** Princeton: Princeton University Press, 1971, 412 p.
A scholarly study of the different stages and purposes of the French nuclear program and of its impact on French relations with other powers.

Kulski, Władysław Wszebór. **De Gaulle and the World: The Foreign Policy of the Fifth French Republic.** Syracuse: Syracuse University Press, 1966, 428 p.
An extensive appraisal, which strives hard to discriminate between the negative and positive features of de Gaulle's foreign policy in light of their bearing upon French national interests.

La Gorce, Paul-Marie de. **La France contre les empires.** Paris: Grasset, 1969, 365 p.
An examination of French foreign policies in the post-World War II years. The author argues that they were more than just the expression of General de Gaulle's ideas and personality.

Lipschits, Isaac. **La Politique de la France au Levant, 1939-1941.** Paris: Pedone, 1963, 240 p.
A study of Britain, the Free French and Vichy in Syria and Lebanon.

Massip, Roger. **De Gaulle et l'Europe.** Paris: Flammarion, 1963, 204 p.
A lucid appraisal of de Gaulle which concentrates on the period since his return to power in 1958. The author traces de Gaulle's sustained policy of seeking to put France and West Germany in control of a loose confederation of sovereign European states.

Mourin, Maxime. **Les Relations franco-soviétiques (1917-1967).** Paris: Payot, 1967, 371 p.
A concise survey of Franco-Russian relations since the eve of the 1917 Revolution.

Newhouse, John. **De Gaulle and the Anglo-Saxons.** New York: Viking, 1970, 371 p.
An intelligent and readable analysis of tripartite policies in the Gaullist era from 1958 to 1969, years which saw a historic drifting apart, due principally to de Gaulle's aim "to liberate France from the Anglo-Saxons."

Osswald, Klaus-Dieter and Others. **Frankreichs Entwicklungshilfe: Politik auf lange Sicht?** Cologne: Westdeutscher Verlag (for the Arnold-Bergstraesser-Institut), 1967, 321 p.
A comprehensive survey of the history and achievements of the French aid programs for the developing nations.

Pickles, Dorothy Maud. **The Uneasy Entente: French Foreign Policy and Franco-British Misunderstandings.** New York: Oxford University Press (for the Royal Institute of International Affairs), 1966, 180 p.
An expert on French government and politics tries to answer the question of where Great Britain fits into General de Gaulle's Grand Design.

Reynaud, Paul. **The Foreign Policy of Charles de Gaulle.** New York: Odyssey Press, 1964, 160 p.
An important and eloquent indictment of de Gaulle's foreign policy, by an erstwhile supporter and former Prime Minister. The French original appeared as "La Politique étrangère du gaullisme" (Paris: Julliard, 1964, 269 p.).

Saint Robert, Philippe de. **Le Jeu de la France en Méditerranée.** Paris: Julliard, 1970, 302 p.
A collection of reports and essays strongly defending General de Gaulle's policies toward the Arabs and Israel, with the specter of American world hegemony hovering overhead.

Serfaty, Simon. **France, de Gaulle and Europe: The Policy of the Fourth and Fifth Republics toward the Continent.** Baltimore: Johns Hopkins Press, 1968, 176 p.
A survey of French foreign policy. The author differentiates between France in a period of decline before 1958 and in a period of ascendancy after de Gaulle's return to power.

Tint, Herbert. **French Foreign Policy since the Second World War.** New York: St. Martin's Press, 1972, 273 p.
A brief account, by a British political scientist, of how France has tried to expand her influence abroad.

Volkov, Nikolai Vasil'evich. **Frantsiia i sotsialisticheskie strany Evropy: ekonomicheskie i nauchno-tekhnicheskie sviazy.** Moscow: Izd-vo "Mezhdunarodnye Otnosheniia," 1971, 280 p.
A serious examination of the problems of and prospects for French trade and technical coöperation with Eastern Europe.

Zimmermann, Ludwig. **Frankreichs Ruhrpolitik: von Versailles bis zum Dawesplan.** Göttingen: Musterschmidt, 1971, 299 p.
A study of French policies toward Germany in the immediate post-World War I years, written during World War II when the author had the opportunity to work in French archives which have not been open to scholars after the conclusion of the war.

Military Policy

See also War and Peace, p. 108; First World War, p. 131; Inter-War Period, p. 140; Second World War, p. 144; The Postwar World, p. 178; Western Europe, p. 345; (France) Recent History, p. 396; Biographies, Memoirs and Addresses, p. 400; Foreign Policy, p. 404; Politics and Government, p. 408; The 1956 Suez Crisis, p. 637; Indochina, p. 736; Algeria, p. 796; and the sections for specific countries and regions.

Ailleret, Charles. **L'Aventure atomique française.** Paris: Grasset, 1968, 400 p.
A survey of French efforts to develop a nuclear force, by a prominent French general who was killed in an air accident in 1968.

Bankwitz, Philip Charles Farwell. **Maxime Weygand and Civil-Military Relations in Modern France.** Cambridge: Harvard University Press, 1967, 445 p.
A study of the turbulent relations between the French civilian and military authorities in the inter-war period and of the career and thinking of General Weygand, Commander-in-Chief of the French Army during the tragic days of June 1940 and the chief advocate for signing the armistice with the Germans.

Chantebout, Bernard. **L'Organisation générale de la défense nationale en France depuis la fin de la Seconde guerre mondiale.** Paris: Librairie Générale de Droit, 1967, 500 p.
A painstaking study of the postwar French defense establishment in all its aspects.

Dulac, André. **Nos Guerres perdues: Levant 1941, Indochine 1951-1953, Algérie 1958-1960.** Paris: Fayard, 1969, 209 p.
First-hand experiences of defeat, by a general who entered St. Cyr in 1925. Over half the book is devoted to the Algerian struggle in which Dulac played an important role.

Furniss, Edgar Stephenson, Jr. **De Gaulle and the French Army: A Crisis in Civil-Military Relations.** New York: Twentieth Century Fund, 1964, 331 p.
A thoughtful and spirited account of de Gaulle's struggle with the Army over Algeria, by a veteran student of French affairs.

Gaulle, Charles André Joseph Marie de. **Trois études: précédées du mémorandum du 26 janvier 1940.** Paris: Plon, 1971, 253 p.
Three essays on military themes, written with the General's usual breadth and incisiveness, and an analysis of France's precarious position in January 1940.

Girardet, Raoul and Others. **La Crise militaire française, 1945-1962: aspects sociologiques et idéologiques.** Paris: Colin, 1964, 235 p.
An exemplary study of the recruitment, way of life, and intellectual and political outlook of the French Army in its period of great social and moral crisis from the end of the Second World War to the end of the Algerian war.

Hughes, Judith M. **To the Maginot Line: The Politics of French Military Preparation in the 1920's.** Cambridge: Harvard University Press, 1971, 300 p.
A perceptive and well-documented study of the causes and consequences of French military planning in the inter-war years, by a young American historian.

Kelly, George Armstrong. **Lost Soldiers: The French Army and Empire in Crisis, 1947-1962.** Cambridge: M.I.T. Press, 1965, 404 p.
An informative and well-written study of the travail of the French Army from the war in Indochina to the Algerian conflict.

Lacoste Lareymondie, Marc de. **Mirages et réalités: l'arme nucléaire française.** Paris: Éditions de la Serpe, 1964, 215 p.
A judicious and informative critique of French nuclear policy, by a St. Cyr graduate who for many years was involved in atomic studies and policies.

La Gorce, Paul-Marie de. **The French Army: A Military-Political History.** New York: Braziller, 1963, 568 p.
A balanced and comprehensive history of the French Army from the Dreyfus Affair to the defeat in Algeria, with a welcome focus on the political milieu of the times. The French original appeared as "La République et son armée" (Paris: Fayard, 1963, 708 p.).

Mendl, Wolf. **Deterrence and Persuasion: French Nuclear Armament in the Context of National Policy, 1945-1969.** New York: Praeger, 1970, 256 p.
An analysis of why France developed a nuclear force. The author concludes that "a military justification has followed rather than preceded" the existence of nuclear weapons.

Moch, Jules Salvador. **Non à la force de frappe.** Paris: Laffont, 1963, 272 p.
In this volume a prominent French socialist advocates nuclear disarmament and loyalty to existing international security arrangements.

Paret, Peter. **French Revolutionary Warfare from Indochina to Algeria.** New York: Praeger (for the Center of International Studies, Princeton University), 1964, 163 p.
A brief study of French strategic thought on how to fight the type of subversive war experienced in Indochina and Algeria.

Scheinman, Lawrence. **Atomic Energy Policy in France under the Fourth Republic.** Princeton: Princeton University Press, 1965, 259 p.
The origins of French atomic policy depicted against the background of domestic politics, by a political scientist.

Politics and Government

See also Political Factors, p. 12; (France) Recent History, p. 396; Biographies, Memoirs and Addresses, p. 400; Foreign Policy, p. 404; Military Policy, p. 407; Economic Problems, p. 415.

Alexandre, Philippe. **The Duel: De Gaulle and Pompidou.** Boston: Houghton, 1972, 360 p.
A description of the complicated relations between de Gaulle and his successor.

Ambler, John Steward. **The French Army in Politics, 1945-1962.** Columbus: Ohio State University Press, 1966, 427 p.
An able study of the problem of civilian control over the French military establishment during those critical and hectic years when the army ceased to be "a docile servant of the state."

Andrieu, René. **Les Communistes et la révolution.** Paris: Julliard, 1968, 315 p.
Reflections on the role of the Communist Party in the politics of France by the editor of *L'Humanité*. Mr. Andrieu provides an explanation of why the communists were reluctant to support the revolutionaries during the events of May 1968.

Aron, Raymond. **La Révolution introuvable: réflexions sur les événements de mai.** Paris: Fayard, 1968, 187 p.
Aron was one of the few intellectuals in France who openly proclaimed his hostility to what he called the "revolutionary carnival" of the students in May 1968. Appalled by his colleagues' facile admiration for the young, and worried by what they welcomed, Aron entered the fray with controversial articles, reprinted here.

Avril, Pierre. **Le Régime politique de la Ve République.** Paris: Librairie Générale de Droit, 1964, 398 p.
A clear and critical analysis of the elusive form of government which de Gaulle has given France.

Barale, Jean. **La Constitution de la IVe République à l'épreuve de la guerre.** Paris: Librairie Générale de Droit, 1963, 526 p.
A substantial study of the influence of the cold war and colonial wars in undermining the political institutions of the Fourth Republic.

Barjonet, André. **Le Parti Communiste Français.** Paris: John Didier, 1970, 236 p.
An intelligent, Marxist analysis of the premises and policies of today's French Communist Party, by a former member who left the party because of its anti-revolutionary stance in the putative revolution of 1968.

Berger, Suzanne. **Peasants against Politics: Rural Organization in Brittany, 1911-1967.** Cambridge: Harvard University Press, 1972, 298 p.
This monograph offers new perspectives on the politics of France and the various theories of modernization. Written under the auspices of the Center for International Affairs, Harvard University.

Bloch, Roger. **Histoire du Parti Radical-Socialiste.** Paris: Librairie Générale de Droit, 1968, 190 p.
A brief survey of the Radical-Socialist Party of France, the predominant party of the Third Republic.

Bloch-Morhange, Jacques. **Le Gaullisme.** Paris: Plon, 1963, 238 p.
This study discovers that Gaullism is but the invention and appeal of a remarkable man.

Bortoli, Gilbert. **Sociologie du référendum dans la France moderne.** Paris: Librairie Générale de Droit, 1965, 412 p.
A sociological analysis of seven referenda in post-World War II France, only one of which took place during General de Gaulle's political absence.

Brower, Daniel Roberts. **The New Jacobins: The French Communist Party and the Popular Front.** Ithaca: Cornell University Press, 1968, 265 p.
A useful study of communist tactics which prescribed support of non-radical governments.

Caute, David. **Communism and the French Intellectuals, 1914-1960.** New York: Macmillan, 1964, 412 p.
A detailed and judicious study of the relations of French intellectuals to communism. The author, an English historian, sets the story in the broadest context and even tries to assess what happened to the work of individual intellectuals because of their adherence to communism.

Charlot, Jean. **The Gaullist Phenomenon.** New York: Praeger, 1971, 205 p.
A study of the transformation of French politics from the characteristic ideological, multiparty government by assembly toward the establishment of a majority parliamentary system. The French original appeared as "Le Phénomène gaulliste" (Paris: Fayard, 1970, 206 p.).

Charlot, Jean. **L'Union pour la Nouvelle République: étude du pouvoir au sein d'un parti politique.** Paris: Colin, 1967, 361 p.
A detailed and well-documented history of the Union for the New Republic (U.N.R.), the party that was established by Jacques Soustelle on October 1, 1958 in order to unify the Gaullist forces.

Charnay, Jean-Paul. **Les Scrutins politiques en France de 1815 à 1962: contestations et invalidations.** Paris: Colin, 1965, 281 p.
A technical study of the French elections.

Charnay, Jean-Paul. **Société militaire et suffrage politique en France, depuis 1789.** Paris: Service d'Édition et de Vente des Publications de l'Éducation Nationale, 1964, 319 p.
A scholarly study of the impact of changing forms of suffrage on military-civilian relations in France since the Revolution.

Charnay, Jean-Paul. **Le Suffrage politique en France.** Paris: Mouton, 1965, 832 p.
A study of the history of French elections, with particular attention to the incidence of contested and invalid results.

Dansette, Adrien. **Mai 1968.** Paris: Plon, 1971, 473 p.
   A well-known historian gives us a reliable historical account and analysis of the events of May 1968.

Debré, Michel. **Au Service de la nation: essai d'un programme politique.** Paris: Stock, 1963, 279 p.
   A close collaborator of General de Gaulle and a former Prime Minister writes about the future role of France.

L'Élection présidentielle des 5 et 19 décembre 1965. Paris: Colin (for the Centre d'Étude de la Vie Politique Française), 1970, 548 p.
   Comprehensive documentation on, and detailed analysis of, the presidential election in France in December 1965.

Fabre-Luce, Alfred. **The Trial of Charles de Gaulle.** New York: Praeger, 1963, 270 p.
   This book takes the form of an imaginary trial, with "testimony" from public statements of Mollet, Soustelle and others, charging de Gaulle with giving away Algeria and assorted breaches of the constitution. All copies of the original "Haute Cour" (Paris: Julliard, 1962, 288 p.) were seized by the French authorities and the author was prosecuted and fined for defamation of the head of state.

Fauvet, Jacques with Duhamel, Alain. **Histoire du Parti Communiste Français.** Paris: Fayard, 1964–65, 2 v.
   The editor of *Le Monde*, in collaboration with Alain Duhamel, has written the first comprehensive history of the French Communist Party, concentrating chiefly on its role in French politics.

Fejtö, François. **The French Communist Party and the Crisis of International Communism.** Cambridge: M.I.T. Press, 1967, 225 p.
   A brief survey of the French Communist Party from Stalin's death to Khrushchev's fall. The author emphasizes the relations between the French and the Italian Communist parties.

Ferniot, Jean. **Mort d'une révolution: la gauche de mai.** Paris: Denoël, 1968, 237 p.
   In this study de Gaulle's victory in May–June 1968 is seen as a consequence of the disarray of the French Left, for which "nothing is possible without the Communists, [and] nothing is possible with them."

Fields, Adolph Belden. **Student Politics in France: A Study of the Union Nationale des Étudiants de France.** New York: Basic Books, 1970, 198 p.
   An American political scientist studies the national organization of French students. Completed before the May 1968 upheavals, the book nevertheless sheds some light on subsequent events.

Fontaine, André. **La Guerre civile froide.** Paris: Fayard, 1969, 193 p.
   Reflections on the May 1968 events in France, by the editor-in-chief of *Le Monde*.

Fossaert, Robert. **Le Contrat socialiste.** Paris: Éditions du Seuil, 1969, 285 p.
   An analysis of the disarray of the French Left in the 1960s and bold speculation on how it should define its future role and program.

Fougeyrollas, Pierre. **La Conscience politique dans la France contemporaine.** Paris: Denoël, 1963, 337 p.
   A social scientist combines a methodological inquiry with a brief report on political consciousness in the various French parties.

Fougeyrollas, Pierre. **Pour une France fédérale: vers l'unité européenne par la révolution régionale.** Paris: Denoël, 1968, 211 p.
   The author argues that there is too much centralism in France and pleads for a federal system with more political, economic and cultural rights for the regions of France.

Goguel-Nyegaard, François and Grosser, Alfred. **La Politique en France.** Paris: Colin, 1964, 298 p.
   An excellent survey of French political life, by two leading political scientists.

Goguel-Nyegaard, François, *ed.* **Le Référendum d'octobre et les élections de novembre 1962.** Paris: Colin, 1965, 437 p.
   A team of political scientists presents impressive studies of various aspects of the referendum confirming de Gaulle's wish for the direct election of the President and of the subsequent parliamentary election which brought defeat to the "old parties."

Graham, Bruce Desmond. **The French Socialists and Tripartisme, 1944-1947.** Toronto: University of Toronto Press, 1965, 299 p.
A penetrating analysis of French socialism and its short-lived hope after World War II to govern together with communists and liberal Catholics.

Greene, Nathanael. **Crisis and Decline: The French Socialist Party in the Popular Front Era.** Ithaca: Cornell University Press, 1969, 361 p.
A thorough story, ably recounted by an American historian.

Guérin, Daniel. **Front Populaire: révolution manquée.** Paris: Julliard, 1963, 325 p.
Controversial reflections on French left-wing politics in the 1930s, by a militant socialist whose occasional hero was Trotsky.

Halbecq, Michel. **L'État, son autorité, son pouvoir (1880-1962).** Paris: Librairie Générale de Droit, 1965, 651 p.
In this lengthy study the author elaborates the idea of authority in relation to a general theory of the state, emphasizing the developments in France in the course of 80 years.

Hartley, Anthony. **Gaullism: The Rise and Fall of a Political Movement.** New York: Outerbridge and Dienstfrey, 1971, 373 p.
A thorough study of a fascinating subject, by an experienced British journalist and editor.

Humbert-Droz, Jules. **"L'Œil de Moscou" à Paris, 1922-1924.** Paris: Julliard, 1964, 265 p.
A collection of documents from the archives of Jules Humbert-Droz, a Swiss national who was a member of the secretariat of the Communist International and its delegate to the French party from 1921 to 1925. Especially important for the study of the French Communist Party in the early 1920s.

Johnson, Richard. **The French Communist Party Versus the Students: Revolutionary Politics in May-June 1968.** New Haven: Yale University Press, 1972, 215 p.
A detailed analysis of the conflicts between "proletarian apparatchiks" and left-wing students filled with anarchist ideas and yearnings.

Kessler, Marie-Christine. **Le Conseil d'État.** Paris: Colin, 1968, 390 p.
A political sociologist examines the reputation and effectiveness of the prestigious Conseil d'État. Based on interviews carried out in 1963 and 1964.

Kriegel, Annie. **Aux Origines du communisme français, 1914-1920; contribution à l'histoire du mouvement ouvrier français.** Paris: Mouton, 1964, 2 v.
A substantial history of the early years of the French Communist Party by a former communist.

Kriegel, Annie. **Le Congrès de Tours (décembre 1920), naissance du Parti Communiste Français.** Paris: Julliard, 1964, 258 p.
An abbreviated version, with a useful introduction, of the official record of the Tours congress of December 1920, when a majority of the French Socialist Party decided to break away from the parent party and establish a French Communist Party.

Kriegel, Annie. **The French Communists: Profile of a People.** Chicago: University of Chicago Press, 1972, 408 p.
A splendid work on the character and history of the party, by a well-known scholar who fuses analytical insights with her personal experiences in the party. Originally published in France as "Les Communistes français: essai d'ethnographie politique" (Paris: Éditions du Seuil, 1968, 320 p.).

Larmour, Peter J. **The French Radical Party in the 1930's.** Stanford: Stanford University Press, 1964, 327 p.
A scholarly study of the leading French party of the 1930s, with particular attention to its parliamentary manoeuvring. It illuminates the author's dubious contention that "the Third Republic was not overthrown by the German invasion; it went under because of peacetime crisis."

Lefranc, Georges. **Histoire du Front Populaire (1934-1938).** Paris: Payot, 1965, 501 p.
A somewhat personal history of the Popular Front in France, from its origins to early demise, by a socialist teacher who participated in some of the events of the time and who remembers the period "as a great adventure."

Lefranc, Georges. **Le Mouvement socialiste sous la Troisième République (1875-1940).** Paris: Payot, 1963, 444 p.

The author of this study provides interesting data on French socialism at the time of the Third Republic.

Leites, Nathan. **The Rules of the Game in Paris.** Chicago: University of Chicago Press, 1970, 355 p.
An American political scientist attempts to evoke the subtleties and nuances of French political life by assembling characteristic utterances from French life and literature.

Lichtheim, George. **Marxism in Modern France.** New York: Columbia University Press, 1966, 212 p.
A critical analysis of the adaptations of Marxist theory to French conditions and of the resulting changes in both, by a well-known writer on Marxism and other contemporary issues.

MacRae, Duncan, Jr. **Parliament, Parties, and Society in France, 1946–1958.** New York: St. Martin's Press, 1967, 375 p.
An analysis, much of it statistical, of the travails of the Fourth Republic by a political scientist at the University of North Carolina.

Manin, Phillippe. **Le R.P.F. (Rassemblement du Peuple Français) et les problèmes européens.** Paris: Presses Universitaires, 1966, 140 p.
A study of the attitudes of the Rassemblement du Peuple Français toward European problems, primarily in the years from 1948 to 1953 when the Atlantic Union, OEEC, NATO and the Council of Europe were established.

Mendès-France, Pierre. **A Modern French Republic.** New York: Hill and Wang, 1963, 205 p.
A reaffirmation of the author's beliefs in democratic ideals, with proposals for a real democracy in which citizens would play an effective role and coöperate fully with the government to plan for the good of all. The French original appeared as "La République moderne: propositions" (Paris: Gallimard, 1962, 251 p.).

Micaud, Charles Antoine. **Communism and the French Left.** New York: Praeger, 1963, 308 p.
The author analyzes French communism in the context of the peculiar weaknesses of French society and politics. Mr. Micaud, who wrote an earlier study "The French Right and Nazi Germany," is a close and knowledgeable observer of French politics.

Mitterrand, François. **Le Coup d'état permanent.** Paris: Plon, 1964, 279 p.
Witty and polemical observations on French politics by a leading French statesman.

Moneta, Jakob. **Die Kolonialpolitik der französischen KP.** Hanover: Verlag für Literatur und Zeitgeschehen, 1968, 302 p.
An impressive collection of documents on the attitude of the French Communist Party toward colonialism.

Montalais, Jacques de. **Qu'est-ce que le gaullisme?** Paris: Éditions Mame, 1969, 216 p.
A fervent Gaullist and a well-known journalist attempts to define his party's philosophy.

Mossuz, Janine. **André Malraux et le gaullisme.** Paris: Colin, 1970, 312 p.
A doctoral thesis on Malraux's relations with de Gaulle, concerned particularly with the question of whether Malraux had betrayed his prewar ideals in embracing the General's politics.

Nobécourt, Jacques and Planchais, Jean. **Une Histoire politique de l'armée.** Paris: Éditions du Seuil, 1967, 2 v.
A history of the political role of the French Army from 1919 to 1967, by two correspondents of *Le Monde*. Vol. 1, "De Pétain à Pétain, 1919–1942," was written by Jacques Nobécourt and vol. 2, "De de Gaulle à de Gaulle, 1940–1967," by Jean Planchais.

Noonan, Lowell G. **France: The Politics of Continuity in Change.** New York: Holt, Rinehart and Winston, 1970, 528 p.
A comprehensive introduction to contemporary French politics by an American political scientist.

Philip, André. **La Gauche: mythes et réalités.** Paris: Aubier, 1964, 228 p.
A collection of essays on contemporary political, social and economic issues, by one of the leading figures of the Fourth Republic.

Pickles, Dorothy Maud. **The Government and Politics of France. Volume I: Institutions and Parties.** London: Methuen, 1972, 433 p.
Now that the Fifth Republic has survived the passing of de Gaulle, this solid study by a noted scholar reassesses with insight the viability and continuity of France's institutions, parties and interest groups; a second volume will examine political, economic, social and foreign policies.

Pierce, Roy. **Contemporary French Political Thought.** New York: Oxford University Press, 1966, 276 p.
An exceptionally able critical exposition of the political thought of Emmanuel Mounier, Simone Weil, Albert Camus, Jean-Paul Sartre, Bertrand de Jouvenel and Raymond Aron.

Pierce, Roy. **French Politics and Political Institutions.** New York: Harper and Row, 1968, 275 p.
A brief survey of French political life.

Posner, Charles, ed. **Reflections on the Revolution in France: 1968.** Baltimore: Penguin, 1970, 317 p.
A group of authors survey and analyze the May 1968 events. The central assumption is that France will never be the same again.

Rémond, René. **La Droite en France: de la Première Restauration à la Ve République.** Paris: Aubier, 2d rev. and enl. ed., 1963, 414 p.
An informed discussion of French right-wing political activities.

Ridley, F. F. **Revolutionary Syndicalism in France: The Direct Action of its Time.** New York: Cambridge University Press, 1971, 279 p.
A fine study of an important subject. A British scholar sets syndicalism in the broadest cultural and political context and emphasizes the present-day echoes of the earlier mood and movement.

Rioux, Lucien and Backmann, René. **L'Explosion de mai: 11 mai 1968—histoire complète des "événements."** Paris: Laffont, 1969, 614 p.
A vivid depiction of the May 1968 events by two French journalists from *Le Nouvel Observateur*.

Ritsch, Frederick F. **The French Left and the European Idea, 1947-1949.** New York: Pageant, 1967, 277 p.
A rather pedestrian account of the split between the French Socialist and Communist Parties over the issue of European alignments at the beginning of the cold war.

Scholl-Latour, Peter. **Im Sog des Generals: von Abidjan nach Moskau.** Stuttgart: Deutsche Verlags-Anstalt, 1966, 363 p.
Informative reporting on de Gaulle and French politics and foreign policies from July 1965 to July 1966, by the former head of the bureau of West German television in Paris.

Schwartzenberg, Roger-Gérard. **La Campagne présidentielle de 1965.** Paris: Presses Universitaires, 1967, 182 p.
An analysis of the 1965 French presidential campaign.

Seale, Patrick and McConville, Maureen. **Red Flag/Black Flag: French Revolution, 1968.** New York: Putnam, 1968, 252 p.
An account of the turbulent May 1968 events in France by two correspondents of *The Observer* who think that the lessons of those days "must be carefully pondered because they carry a hint of what politics in the West may be like in the 1970s."

Servan-Schreiber, Jean-Jacques and Albert, Michel. **The Radical Alternative.** New York: Norton, 1971, 204 p.
A catalog of French social ills and prescriptions for what is to be done. The French original appeared as "Ciel et terre: manifeste radical" (Paris: Denoël, 1970, 298 p.).

Servan-Schreiber, Jean-Jacques. **The Spirit of May.** New York: McGraw-Hill, 1969, 116 p.
A passionate defense of the May 1968 student uprising. The author cites his "The American Challenge" to prove that he had diagnosed the deep dissatisfactions before the eruption. Translated from "Le Réveil de la France: mai-juin 1968" (Paris: Denoël, 1968, 127 p.).

Simmons, Harvey G. **French Socialists in Search of a Role, 1956–1967.** Ithaca: Cornell University Press, 1970, 313 p.
A rather spirited analysis of the decline of French socialism in the years since the socialist Mollet helped to launch the Suez campaign. A scholarly work, by a professor of political science in Canada.

Singer, Daniel. **Prelude to Revolution: France in May 1968.** New York: Hill and Wang, 1970, 434 p.
A rhapsodic and absorbing account of May 1968, by a European journalist who believes the outburst of those days prefigured a real revolution.

Taÿ, Hugues. **Le Régime présidentiel et la France: étude d'histoire des idées juridiques et politiques.** Paris: Librairie Générale de Droit, 1967, 334 p.
An historical analysis of the various proponents of a presidential regime, particularly after 1940. A useful background to the present and future controversy concerning this fundamental question in French politics.

Touraine, Alain. **The May Movement: Revolt and Reform.** New York: Random House, 1971, 373 p.
A well-known French sociologist offers at once a description of the May 1968 events and an analysis of their long-term significance. The French original was published as "Le Mouvement de mai ou le communisme utopique" (Paris: Éditions du Seuil, 1968, 298 p.).

Vaudiaux, Jacques. **Le Progressisme en France sous la 4e République: les hommes—l'organisation—les électeurs.** Paris: Cujas, 1968, 261 p.
A scholarly study of a small group of left-wing deputies who, while insisting on their independence, usually sided with the Communists.

Viansson-Ponté, Pierre. **Bilan de la Ve République: les politiques.** Paris: Calmann-Lévy, 1967, 276 p.
Nine years of Gaullist rule thoughtfully and knowledgeably assessed by a leading writer of *Le Monde*. A chronology of the Fifth Republic further enhances the value of this important book.

Viansson-Ponté, Pierre. **The King and His Court.** Boston: Houghton, 1965, 250 p.
An entertaining yet instructive guide to de Gaulle's style as ruler and to his entourage. The French original appeared as "Les Gaullistes, rituel et annuaire" (Paris: Éditions du Seuil, 1963, 189 p.).

Waterman, Harvey. **Political Change in Contemporary France: The Politics of an Industrial Democracy.** Columbus (Ohio): Merrill, 1969, 256 p.
Analyzing the politics of contemporary France, the author discerns "a tendency away from extreme political beliefs, attitudes and opinions."

Williams, Philip Maynard. **The French Parliament: Politics in the Fifth Republic.** New York: Praeger, 1968, 136 p.
The Gaullist parliament, analyzed and compared to French antecedents and English experience.

Williams, Philip Maynard with Others. **French Politicians and Elections, 1951–1961.** New York: Cambridge University Press, 1970, 312 p.
Twenty-five essays by an English academic who catches the spirit and the substance of French politics with rare and delightful lucidity.

Williams, Philip Maynard and Harrison, Martin. **Politics and Society in de Gaulle's Republic.** Garden City: Doubleday, 1972, 393 p.
An incisive analysis of a decade of French politics, by two English experts on France.

Williams, Philip Maynard. **Wars, Plots and Scandals in Post-War France.** New York: Cambridge University Press, 1970, 232 p.
A guide through the maze of French plots and conspiracies, most of which were connected with unpopular wars.

Wilson, Frank L. **The French Democratic Left 1963–1969: Toward a Modern Party System.** Stanford: Stanford University Press, 1971, 258 p.
Despite successive efforts at reform, the non-communist Left in France remained for a long time splintered and powerless. An American political scientist seeks to analyze

the reasons for the failure and offers some general comments on the problems of transforming parties.

Wohl, Robert. **French Communism in the Making, 1914-1924.** Stanford: Stanford University Press, 1966, 530 p.
A welcome study, detailed and well-documented, of the background, origins and early history of the French Communist Party.

Zürn, Peter. **Die republikanische Monarchie.** Munich: Beck, 1965, 347 p.
A comprehensive study of the history and structure of the constitution of the Fifth Republic, by a student of Armin Mohler.

Economic Problems

See also Economic Factors, p. 49; Western Europe, p. 344; (France) Recent History, p. 396; Biographies, Memoirs and Addresses, p. 400; Foreign Policy, p. 404.

Amselek, Paul. **Le Budget de l'état sous la Ve République.** Paris: Librairie Générale de Droit, 1967, 657 p.
A detailed study of the financial policies of the Fifth Republic.

Bleton, Pierre. **Le Capitalisme français.** Paris: Éditions Ouvrières, 1966, 261 p.
An introductory survey of the financial and commercial policies of large French enterprises and a discussion of the role of the state in the French economy.

Bonnaud, Jacques. **Le Ve Plan: une stratégie de l'expansion.** Paris: Éditions de l'Épargne, 1967, 313 p.
A description and evaluation of the fifth French economic plan.

Closon, Francis-Louis and Filippi, Jean, eds. **L'Économie et les finances: le ministre et le ministère, l'administration centrale, les services.** Paris: Presses Universitaires, 1968, 515 p.
A description of the work of the French Ministry of Economy and Finance.

Cohen, Stephen S. **Modern Capitalist Planning: The French Model.** Cambridge: Harvard University Press, 1970, 310 p.
This stimulating study stresses the way French economic planning is shaped by "the power structure of the modern capitalist political economy."

Ducouloux, Claude. **Les Sociétés d'économie mixte en France et en Italie.** Paris: Librairie Générale de Droit, 1963, 283 p.
A study of the economies of France and Italy comparing the respective governments' legal controls over private enterprise.

Fourastié, Jean and Courthéoux, Jean-Paul. **La Planification économique en France.** Paris: Presses Universitaires, 1963, 208 p.
A compact study on the origins, the execution and the results of economic planning in France.

Gilpin, Robert George. **France in the Age of the Scientific State.** Princeton: Princeton University Press, 1968, 474 p.
A wide-ranging inquiry into French efforts to organize scientific resources in order to resist American domination.

Hackett, John and Hackett, Anne-Marie. **Economic Planning in France.** Cambridge: Harvard University Press, 1963, 418 p.
A thoroughgoing study of how French planning is carried on, with first-hand information and interesting reflections on the character of the process.

Hansen, Niles Maurice. **French Regional Planning.** Bloomington: Indiana University Press, 1968, 319 p.
A solid study of France's far-reaching efforts at regional planning, written primarily for economists, but of general political interest.

Lattre, André de. **Politique économique de la France depuis 1945.** Paris: Sirey, 1966, 521 p.
A survey of France's economic policies, financial problems and foreign trade since 1945, by a leading French banker and economist.

Lipiansky, Edmond and Rettenbach, Bernard. **Ordre et démocratie.** Paris: Presses Universitaires, 1967, 176 p.
A description of the ideas of L'Ordre Nouveau and Club Jean-Moulin, two influential groups that asked for profound reforms of the French political and economic systems.

Lutz, Vera C. **Central Planning for the Market Economy: An Analysis of the French Theory and Experience.** London: Longmans (in association with the Institute of Economic Affairs), 1969, 194 p.
According to this analysis, French "indicative planning" never lived up to its reputation and has been replaced by a kind of "soft" and semi-secret interventionism in which the state gives favors to private enterprises in return for promised performance.

McArthur, John H. and Scott, Bruce R. **Industrial Planning in France.** Boston: Harvard University, Graduate School of Business Administration, Division of Research, 1969, 592 p.
Two professors at the Harvard Business School challenge some of the received wisdom about the French economy.

Mittelstädt, Axel. **Frankreichs Währungspolitik von Poincaré zu Rueff.** Frankfurt/Main: Knapp, 1967, 257 p.
A study of internal and external monetary policies of France from 1918 to 1958.

Peikert, Helmut. **Frankreichs Wirtschaft Heute: Struktur und Tendenzen.** Mainz: Krausskopf-Verlag, 2d rev. ed., 1963, 272 p.
An informed account of the structure and growth of the contemporary French economy.

Sauvy, Alfred. **Histoire économique de la France entre les deux guerres.** Paris: Fayard, 1965–67, 2 v.
A well-documented economic history of France in the inter-war period.

Scargill, David Ian. **Economic Geography of France.** New York: St. Martin's Press, 1968, 148 p.
A good survey with maps and pictures.

Sheahan, John. **Promotion and Control of Industry in Postwar France.** Cambridge: Harvard University Press, 1963, 301 p.
A close analysis of the remarkable French economic performance in the decade 1950–1960 and the bearing on this of the new promotion and control techniques that have been applied by the government and privately.

Stoleru, Lionel. **L'Impératif industriel.** Paris: Éditions du Seuil, 1969, 294 p.
This merciless but understanding analysis of French industrial policy provides a foundation for solid proposals on how to do better in the future.

Szokolóczy-Syllaba, János. **Les Organisations professionnelles françaises et le Marché Commun.** Paris: Colin (for the Fondation Nationale des Sciences Politiques), 1965, 372 p.
French industrialists were generally opposed to the Common Market or at least worried about it, but they adapted to the change rather well and developed more favorable views. The author documents this process with valuable studies of the cotton, woolen, automobile and electrical industries, describing their economic problems and pressure-group activities.

Social Problems

See also Labor and Labor Movements, p. 41; (France) Recent History, p. 396; Politics and Government, p. 408.

Batailler, Francine and Others. **Analyses de presse.** Paris: Presses Universitaires, 1963. 236 p.
Four sociological essays on contemporary French journals, including a particularly interesting one on "The Ideology of the *Canard Enchaîné.*"

Crozier, Michel. **La Société bloquée.** Paris: Éditions du Seuil, 1970, 251 p.
Essays on French society and sociology, by a leading French sociologist, reflecting his scholarly pursuits and his "frustrations as a citizen."

Domenach, Jean-Marie and Montvalon, Robert de, *comps.* **The Catholic Avant-Garde: French Catholicism Since World War II.** New York: Holt, Rinehart and Winston, 1967, 245 p.
A valuable collection of writings showing how French Catholic writers are seeking new paths in thought and action.

Drancourt, Michel. **Les Clés du pouvoir.** Paris: Fayard, 1964, 238 p.
A brief essay on contemporary French society, with particular emphasis on the role of the business élite, and a plea for an integrated European economy that would be strong enough to offer a third form of industrial civilization, qualitatively different from American and Soviet examples.

Hughes, Henry Stuart. **The Obstructed Path: French Social Thought in the Years of Desperation 1930–1960.** New York: Harper and Row, 1968, 304 p.
An impressive survey by a scholar with an intimate knowledge of modern France.

Rémond, René, *ed.* **Forces religieuses et attitudes politiques dans la France contemporaine.** Paris: Colin, 1965, 397 p.
A collection of papers, by scholars from different countries and disciplines, on the relationship of religious movements to political attitudes, chiefly in France since 1945. The book grew out of an international colloquium in Strasbourg in 1963.

Sérant, Paul. **La France des minorités.** Paris: Laffont, 1965, 411 p.
A survey of the cultural and political situation and expectations of the very sizable groups in France speaking other languages than French.

Talbott, John E. **The Politics of Educational Reform in France, 1918–1940.** Princeton: Princeton University Press, 1969, 283 p.
A young American historian analyzes the efforts to democratize French education, especially secondary education, in the inter-war years. A versatile study, lucidly written, and of absorbing interest.

THE MEDITERRANEAN

See also (Second World War) Military Operations, p. 156; and the sections for specific countries and regions.

Höpker, Wolfgang. **Wie rot ist das Mittelmeer? Europas gefährdete Südflanke.** Stuttgart: Seewald, 1968, 164 p.
A study of the Soviet attempts to establish their presence in the Mediterranean, particularly in the 1960s.

Potre, Rock. **Mediterraneo forza 8?** Florence: Licosa-Sansoni, 1971, 367 p.
This study advances the idea that the Mediterranean, and especially the Suez, will constitute the major focus of Soviet diplomatic activity in the 1970s.

Salomon, Michel. **Méditerranée rouge: un nouvel empire soviétique?** Paris: Laffont, 1970, 399 p.
A study of the Soviet presence in the Mediterranean and the Near East, by a well-informed French writer.

Stewart, John David. **Gibraltar: The Keystone.** Boston: Houghton, 1967, 335 p.
The author, an Irish engineer and writer, has written an informal history and a memoir of his stay on the Rock from 1952 until 1961.

Silvestri, Stefano, *ed.* **Mediterraneo: economia, politica, strategia.** Bologna: Il Mulino, 1969, 310 p.
This volume, sponsored by the Institute for International Affairs in Rome, examines the economy, politics and military position of the Mediterranean vis-à-vis the rest of the world.

MALTA

Blouet, Brian. **A Short History of Malta.** New York: Praeger, 1967, 253 p.
An introductory study of Malta's geography and history of its position in the contemporary world.

Dobie, Edith. **Malta's Road to Independence.** Norman: University of Oklahoma Press, 1967, 286 p.
A brief history of Maltese politics and British responses, particularly since the Second World War.

CYPRUS

See also Nationalism and Nationality, p. 17; (United Nations) Peace-Keeping Forces and Operations, p. 106; (War) Guerrilla Warfare; Armed Insurrection, p. 118; (Greece) General, p. 602; (Middle East) General Surveys and Political Problems, p. 611.

Adams, Thomas W. **AKEL: The Communist Party of Cyprus.** Stanford: Hoover Institution Press, 1971, 284 p.
The most complete and enlightening book on the subject.

Émelianidès, Achille. **Histoire de Chypre.** Paris: Presses Universitaires, 1963, 126 p.
A short, competent history of Cyprus by a noted Cypriote lawyer.

Foley, Charles. **Legacy and Strife: Cyprus from Rebellion to Civil War.** Baltimore: Penguin, rev. ed., 1964, 187 p.
A British journalist's well-informed account of events in Cyprus up to mid-1964. The original edition was entitled "Island in Revolt" (London: Longmans, 1962, 248 p.).

Georghiades, Antonios. **Die Zypernfrage.** Bonn: Bouvier, 1963, 156 p.
A useful study dealing with the history of Cyprus since 1878 and the efforts to resolve the Cyprus problem in the decade preceding 1959.

Grivas, George. **The Memoirs of General Grivas.** New York: Praeger, 1965, 226 p.
The character of the General, brave, self-righteous, opinionated, cunning, and murderously ruthless in his pursuit of *enosis*, becomes chillingly clear in this one-sided account of the EOKA campaign to force the British out of Cyprus. Edited by Charles Foley.

Ierodiakonou, Leontios. **The Cyprus Question.** Stockholm: Almqvist, 1971, 311 p.
A generally reliable account, detailed up to 1959 and sketchy thereafter. The author is critical of British policy in the 1950s for denying self-determination to the people of Cyprus.

Kyriakides, Stanley. **Cyprus: Constitutionalism and Crisis Government.** Philadelphia: University of Pennsylvania Press, 1968, 212 p.
Essentially an analysis of the Constitution of 1960, with good coverage of background material and some suggestions for the future. The international aspects are less deeply explored.

Leonidov, S. M. **Kipr v bor'be za nezavisimost'.** Moscow: Institut Mezhdunarodnykh Otnoshenii, 1963, 138 p.
A Soviet account of the international aspects of the Cypriote struggle for independence.

Maier, Franz Georg. **Cypern: Insel am Kreuzweg der Geschichte.** Stuttgart: Kohlhammer, 1964, 189 p.
A German scholar's compressed history of Cyprus from the earliest times up to independence in 1960.

Purcell, Hugh Dominic. **Cyprus.** New York: Praeger, 1968, 416 p.
A historical survey of Cyprus since Neolithic times, with emphasis on contemporary developments.

Salih, Halil Ibrahim. **Cyprus: An Analysis of Cypriot Political Discord.** Brooklyn: Gaus, 1968, 184 p.
The author surveys the recent history of Cyprus and argues that the Greek and Turkish

Cypriots, having completely different political, religious and cultural backgrounds, cannot coexist under a single political system.

Stegenga, James A. **The United Nations Force in Cyprus.** Columbus: Ohio State University Press, 1968, 227 p.
A case study of the U.N. peace-keeping force in Cyprus that was established in 1964.

Stephens, Robert Henry. **Cyprus; A Place of Arms: Power Politics and Ethnic Conflict in the Eastern Mediterranean.** New York: Praeger, 1966, 232 p.
An able presentation of the Cyprus problem in the setting of the island's variegated and troubled history.

Ténékidès, Georges. **Chypre: histoire récente et perspectives d'avenir.** Paris: Éditions Nagel, 1964, 292 p.
A study of the Cyprus problem and of its solution from a Greek point of view.

Vanezis, P. N. **Makarios: Faith and Power.** New York: Abelard-Schuman, 1972, 196 p.
A brief sketch of Cypriote history and a favorable portrayal of Archbishop Makarios.

Xydis, Stephen George. **Cyprus: Conflict and Conciliation, 1954-1958.** Columbus: Ohio State University Press, 1967, 704 p.
Meticulous in attention to detail, this massive monograph is devoted to Greece's diplomatic strategy in putting its case on Cyprus to the United Nations. Based on published documents and on the papers of Averoff-Tossizza, the former Greek Foreign Minister.

ITALY

General

See also (Europe) General Surveys, p. 344; Western Europe, p. 345.

Barzini, Luigi Giorgio. **The Italians.** New York: Atheneum, 1964, 352 p.
A highly entertaining, but ultimately quite serious and even somber appraisal of Italians by a distinguished journalist and a former Liberal deputy in the Italian Parliament.

Clough, Shepard Bancroft and Saladino, Salvatore. **A History of Modern Italy: Documents, Readings, and Commentary.** New York: Columbia University Press, 1968, 657 p.
This broad survey of modern Italy covers diplomatic, political, social, economic and cultural developments.

Grindrod, Muriel. **Italy.** New York: Praeger, 1968, 260 p.
A compact and readable survey of modern Italy, with particular attention to developments after 1945.

Hearder, Harry and Waley, Daniel Philip, *eds.* **A Short History of Italy: From Classical Times to the Present Day.** New York: Cambridge University Press, 1963, 263 p.
A cursory account, originally prepared for the Naval Intelligence Division of the British Admiralty.

Hughes, Henry Stuart. **The United States and Italy.** Cambridge: Harvard University Press, rev. ed., 1965, 297 p.
A revised and updated version of a solid and well-written study originally published in 1953. A volume in "The American Foreign Policy Library."

Hughes, Serge. **The Fall and Rise of Modern Italy.** New York: Macmillan, 1967, 322 p.
An uneven effort to illuminate Italian politics since 1890 against the background of Italian culture. The author argues that "modern Italian history consists basically of two periods" and that the second period began with the left-center collaboration of the early 1960s.

Ragionieri, Ernesto, *comp.* **Italia giudicata 1861-1945, ovvero la storia degli italiani scritta dagli altri.** Bari: Laterza, 1969, 873 p.
A history of Italy from unification to the end of the Second World War as seen through the eyes of foreigners.

Romano, Salvatore. **L'Italia del novocento.** Rome: Biblioteca di Storia Patria, rev. ed., 1966–67, 2 v.
A searching examination of the crisis of the Italian liberal state. The first volume, "L'età giolittiana, 1900–14," reveals the constitutional weaknesses which were apparent before the First World War; the second volume, "Dalla Prima guerra mondiale alla costituzione republicana," describes the failure of the post-World War I parliamentary governments, the rise and fall of fascism, and the birth of the Italian Republic.

Salvadori, Massimo. **Italy.** Englewood Cliffs: Prentice-Hall, 1965, 184 p.
A short sketch of contemporary Italy and its historical background.

Biographies, Memoirs and Collected Writings

Berio, Alberto. **Dalle Ande all'Himalaya: ricordi di un diplomatico.** Naples: Edizioni Scientifiche Italiane, 1961, 189 p.
These memoirs of Italy's former ambassador to Chile, India, Ethiopia and Jugoslavia shed some light on Mussolini's secret diplomacy.

Calamandrei, Piero. **Scritti e discorsi politici.** Florence: La Nuova Italia, 1966, 2 v. in 3 pts.
These volumes, edited by Norberto Bobbio, contain a large part of the speeches and writings of Piero Calamandrei (1889–1956), a Florentine jurist, vigorous anti-fascist, an organizer of the partisan movement during World War II in Tuscany, and a deputy in the postwar Republican legislature. They reveal the twin themes of his life: peace through federalism and socialism through parliamentary democracy.

Cammett, John M. **Antonio Gramsci and the Origins of Italian Communism.** Stanford: Stanford University Press, 1967, 306 p.
An excellent study of the life of one of the more remarkable and original communist thinkers.

Carrillo, Elisa Anna. **Alcide De Gasperi: The Long Apprenticeship.** Notre Dame: University of Notre Dame Press, 1965, 185 p.
A narrow, but well-documented study of De Gasperi's political career, from his membership in the Austro-Hungarian Reichsrat to his selection as Italian Premier in 1945.

Catti de Gasperi, Maria Romana. **De Gasperi, uomo solo.** Milan: Mondadori, 1964, 418 p.
The daughter of the late Italian Prime Minister has written a warm and intimate biography, with much original material from private papers, underscoring those courses of conduct which exemplified De Gasperi, as a statesman, "alone."

Collier, Richard. **Duce! A Biography of Benito Mussolini.** New York: Viking, 1971, 447 p.
A racy book, stronger on Mussolini's sexual exploits than on the nature of his rule or the character of Italian fascism.

De Felice, Renzo and Mariano, Emilio, *eds.* **Carteggio D'Annunzio-Mussolini (1919–1938).** Milan: Mondadori, 1971, 511 p.
The correspondence between the Italian poet and adventurer Gabriele D'Annunzio and his admirer and political ally Benito Mussolini. Each editor has contributed an introduction.

De Felice, Renzo. **Mussolini.** Turin: Einaudi, 1965–.
A major biography of Mussolini. Volume I, "Mussolini il rivoluzionario, 1883–1920" (1965, 773 p.), covers Mussolini's early career, when he was a revolutionary of the Left, and his break to the Right in the period of the First World War; vol. II, "Mussolini il Fascista" (1966–69, 2 pts.), deals with Mussolini's conquest of power and the organization of the Fascist state until 1929; two more volumes are in preparation.

Einaudi, Luigi. **Opere.** Turin: Einaudi, 1956–.
The collected writings of the President of the Italian Republic from 1948 to 1955, published since 1956. Thirteen volumes have appeared through 1973.

Fiori, Giuseppe. **Antonio Gramsci: Life of a Revolutionary.** New York: Dutton, 1971, 304 p.
A sympathetic and moving biography of Antonio Gramsci, one of the founders of the

Italian Communist Party and a leading Marxist theorist. The Italian original appeared as "Vita di Antonio Gramsci" (Bari: Laterza, 1966, 362 p.).

Firpo, Luigi, ed. **Bibliografia degli scritti di Luigi Einaudi (dal 1893 al 1970).** Turin: Pubblicazione Promossa dalla Banca d'Italia, 1971, 909 p.
An exhaustive register of the writings of Luigi Einaudi, renowned economist and first President of the Italian Republic, published between 1893 and 1970.

Fornari, Harry. **Mussolini's Gadfly: Roberto Farinacci.** Nashville: Vanderbilt University Press, 1971, 237 p.
A study of one of the most pro-German and antisemitic Italian fascist leaders, known as being more fascist than the Duce himself.

Frankel, Paul H. **Mattei: Oil and Power Politics.** New York: Praeger, 1966, 190 p.
An account of the remarkable career of Enrico Mattei and his influence in the world of international oil interests.

Kirkpatrick, Sir Ivone Augustine. **Mussolini: A Study in Power.** New York: Hawthorn Books, 1964, 726 p.
The late distinguished British diplomat has written a gripping account of the Duce, whose "driving force . . . was ambition and lust for power for power's sake." The author draws on his personal experience and postwar publications, and he interprets the evidence in a detached, sometimes compassionate, manner.

Leone, Giovanni. **Testimonianze.** Milan: Mondadori, 1963, 421 p.
A collection of speeches, on a variety of themes, by the former Italian Prime Minister.

MacGregor-Hastie, Roy. **The Day of the Lion: The Life and Death of Fascist Italy, 1922-1945.** New York: Coward-McCann, 1964, 395 p.
MacGregor-Hastie, a British journalist at home in Italy, has written a breezy but not altogether satisfactory biography of Mussolini. He emphasizes Mussolini's efforts to be a peacemaker in the 1930s and that "Fascism did not lead inevitably to war." He merely summarizes the years after 1940.

Mussolini, Benito. **Opera omnia.** Florence: La Fenice, 1951-63, 36 v.
The collected writings of Benito Mussolini, edited by Edoardo and Duilio Susmel.

Quaroni, Pietro. **Diplomatic Bags: An Ambassador's Memoirs.** New York: D. White, 1966, 158 p.
Illuminating and informative, though rather scattered reminiscences by a veteran Italian diplomat, consisting of selections that were originally published in "Ricordi di un ambasciatore" (Milan: Garzanti, 1954, 186 p.) and "Valigia diplomatica" (Milan: Garzanti, 1956, 302 p.).

Salvadori, Massimo. **Gaetano Salvemini.** Turin: Einaudi, 1963, 264 p.
A biography of the prominent Italian intellectual and historian.

Salvemini, Gaetano. **Opere.** Milan: Feltrinelli, 1962– .
The collected works of Gaetano Salvemini (1873-1957), an indefatigable critic of the Fascist regime in Italy, who lived for many years in the United States and was a professor of Italian civilization at Harvard. The following sections of his collected works deal with contemporary history and foreign affairs: series II, "Scritti di storia moderna e contemporanea"; series III, "Scritti di politica estera"; and series VI, "Scritti sul fascismo."

Saragat, Giuseppe. **Quaranta anni di lotta per la democrazia: scritti e discorsi, 1925-1965.** Milan: Mursia, 1965, 674 p.
A collection of the political writings and speeches of Giuseppe Saragat, a former President of the Italian Republic. Edited by Luigi Preti and Italo De Feo.

Sonnino, Sidney. **Diario, 1914-1916.** Bari: Laterza, 1972– .
The first volume of the complete works of Sidney Sonnino (1847-1922), a conservative statesman and Italy's Foreign Minister during the First World War. Sonnino's diary, edited by Benjamin Brown, recounts the tortuous path of Italian diplomacy before and during Italy's participation in World War I.

Sturzo, Luigi. **Opera omnia.** Bologna: Zanichelli.
The collected works of Luigi Sturzo (1871-1959), a well-known Italian political theorist, anti-fascist leader and the founder of the Italian Popular Party, the predecessor of the present Christian Democratic Party. Sturzo's writings have been published

since 1954 and they are divided in three series: of the first, "Opere," vols. 1-7, 9-10 and 12 have been published through 1973; of the second "Saggi, discorsi, articoli," vols. 1, 3-6 and 9-13; and of the third, "Scritti vari," only vol. 3.

Togliatti, Palmiro. **Opere.** Rome: Riuniti, 1967– .
The collected writings of Palmiro Togliatti (1893-1964), one of the founders of the Italian Communist Party and its leader after World War II. Through 1972 two volumes have been published covering the period up to 1940; four additional volumes are expected.

Turati, Filippo. **Lettere dall'esilio.** Milan: Pan Editrice, 1968, 246 p.
A collection of letters by Filippo Turati, leader of the moderate wing of the Italian Socialist Party, written during his exile in France in the late 1920's. Edited by Bianca Pittoni.

Recent History

See also Political Factors, p. 12; The World Since 1914, p. 129; Western Europe, p. 344; (Italy) General, p. 419; Biographies, Memoirs and Collected Writings, p. 420; Foreign Policy, p. 424; Political and Constitutional Problems, p. 426; Ethiopia, p. 827.

Araldi, Vinicio. **La crisi italiana del '43.** Milan: Silva, 1964, 251 p.
This study focuses on the political and military crisis of July 1943 which brought about the fall of Mussolini. An appendix provides useful biographical data on the principal figures.

Aroma, Nino d'. **Un popolo alla prova: dieci anni di guerra, 1935-1945.** Palermo: Editore Cusimano, 1968, 4 v.
A comprehensive and sympathetic history of a ten-year ordeal for the Italian people engaged almost continuously in war: in Ethiopia, Spain, Albania, Greece, France, North Africa, Russia, and finally in Italy itself.

Bandini, Franco. **Tecnica della sconfitta: storia dei quaranta giorni che precedettero e seguirono l'entrata dell'Italia in guerra.** Milan: Sugar, 2d ed., 1964, 914 p.
An examination of the political and military decisions made by Italy prior to and immediately following its entry into World War II.

Collotti, Enzo. **L'amministrazione tedesca dell'Italia occupata, 1943-45: studio e documenti.** Milan: Lerici, 1963, 607 p.
A study of Nazi rule in Italy following the Italian surrender, by a leftist historian.

Dalla Tana, Luciano. **Mussolini massimalista.** Parma: Guanda, 1963, 173 p.
A study of Mussolini's revolutionary and intransigent early socialism.

De Biase, Carlo. **L'aquila d'oro: storia dello Stato maggiore italiano (1861-1945).** Milan: Edizioni del Borghese, 1970, 473 p.
A balanced and well-documented history of the Italian General Staff from unification to the end of the Second World War. The author suggests that the caste character of the officer corps resulted in continuous deficiencies in the command structure.

Gallo, Max. **L'Italie de Mussolini: vingt ans d'ère fasciste.** Paris: Perrin, 1964, 555 p.
A young French historian retells the political history of Italian fascism.

Il governo dei C.L.N.: atti del convegno dei comitati di liberazione nazionale. Turin: Giappichelli, 1966, 255 p.
The first part of this book contains papers by Guido Quazza, Leo Valiani and Edoardo Volterra read at the 1965 Congress of the Committees of National Liberation (CLN); the authors demonstrate that the Italian partisan movement was not only anti-German, but anti-fascist as well. The second part is comprised of further proceedings of that meeting.

Lussu, Emilio. **Sul Partito d'Azione e gli altri: note critiche.** Milan: Mursia, 1968, 263 p.
A critical and well-documented account of the role of the Party of Action in the Italian resistance movement during World War II.

Mack Smith, Denis. **Italy: A Modern History.** Ann Arbor: University of Michigan Press, rev. ed., 1969, 542 p.

This volume, originally published in 1959 as part of "The University of Michigan History of the Modern World," provides the reader with a major reassessment of the coming of fascism in Italy. Far from regarding fascism as an aberration in the great march forward of Italian liberal democracy, the author sees it arising out of structural weaknesses rooted in the constitutional and social edifice of the state.

Melograni, Piero. **Storia politica della grande guerra, 1915-1918.** Bari: Laterza, 2d ed., 1969, 579 p.
A study analyzing the relationships between Italy's political, social and military institutions during the First World War.

Palermo, Ivan. **Storia di un armistizio: gli avvenimenti dell'8 settembre 1943 ricostruiti sulla base di una fondamentale documentazione finora inedita.** Milan: Mondadori, 1967, 618 p.
In addition to a sound treatment of the controversial armistice of Cassibile, the author reproduces the depositions and interrogations of the Committee of Inquiry which was established to examine the failure of the Royal Italian Army to defend the capital against German occupation. The author assigns much of the blame to the King and to Badoglio, both of whom were unable to issue consistent directives to their subordinates.

Pansa, Giampaolo. **L'esercito di Salò: la storia segreta dell'ultima battaglia di Mussolini.** Milan: Mondadori, 1970, 250 p.
A military history of the Italian Social Republic established at Salo by Mussolini in 1943.

Répaci, Antonino. **La marcia su Roma: mito e realtà.** Rome: Canesi, 1963, 2 v.
An exhaustive documentary study of Mussolini's march on Rome.

Rosengarten, Frank. **The Italian Anti-Fascist Press (1919-1945): From the Legal Opposition Press to the Underground Newspapers of World War II.** Cleveland: Press of Case Western Reserve University, 1968, 263 p.
This study of the anti-fascist press reveals the deep and wide-ranging revulsion of many segments of Italian society to Mussolini's regime.

Santarelli, Enzo. **Storia del movimento e del regime fascista.** Rome: Editori Riuniti, 1967, 2 v.
An attempt to reconstruct the formation and evolution of the Fascist movement in Italy.

Tompkins, Peter. **Italy Betrayed.** New York: Simon and Schuster, 1966, 352 p.
A former O.S.S. agent here criticizes, in a vigorous and personal narrative, the failure, quite unnecessary in his eyes, of the Allies to take full advantage of Mussolini's fall. The policy of working with Victor Emmanuel and Badoglio comes in for particular criticism.

Valiani, Leo. **Il partito socialista italiano nel periodo della neutralità, 1914-1915.** Milan: Feltrinelli, 1963, 135 p.
This work, based primarily on unpublished sources, identifies the positions taken by the leading members of the Italian Socialist Party on the question of Italy's intervention in World War I.

Vivarelli, Roberto. **Il dopoguerra in Italia e l'avvento del fascismo (1918-1922).** Naples: Istituto Italiano per gli Studi Storici, 1967—.
An impressive, thorough and synthetic study of the critical post-World War I period in Italy. The first of the planned three volumes, "Dalla fine della guerra all'impresa di Fiume," contains masterful portraits of D'Annunzio, Nitti, Giolitti, Orlando and Mussolini.

Woolf, S. J., ed. **The Rebirth of Italy, 1943-50.** New York: Humanities Press, 1972, 264 p.
An excellent collection of essays on the transition from fascism to a capitalist, parliamentary democracy—more rewarding than most symposia because of the expertness of the contributors and the briefness of the period treated.

Zangrandi, Ruggero. **Il lungo viaggio attraverso il fascismo: contributo alla storia di una generazione.** Milan: Feltrinelli, 3rd ed., 1963, 610 p.
An attempt to reconstruct the long voyage of a generation of Italians reaching adulthood during the Fascist period from 1922 to 1943.

Foreign Policy

General

See also General Works, p. 1; International Organization and Government, p. 96; War and Peace, p. 108; First World War, p. 131; Inter-War Period, p. 140; Second World War, p. 144; The Postwar World, p. 178; (Italy) Biographies, Memoirs and Collected Writings, p. 420; Recent History, p. 422; Territorial Issues, p. 425; Political and Constitutional Problems, p. 426; Vatican City, p. 432; Ethiopia, p. 827; Somali Republic, p. 829; and the sections for specific countries and regions.

Bonanni, Massimo, *ed.* **La politica estera della Repubblica Italiana.** Milan: Edizioni di Comunità, 1967, 3 v.
A voluminous collection of essays on Italian foreign policy and foreign service in the post-World War II period, based on papers submitted to a conference that took place in Rome in 1967 and was sponsored by the Istituto Affari Internazionali.

Carocci, Giampiero. **La politica estera dell'Italia fascista (1925-1928).** Bari: Laterza, 1969, 391 p.
A detailed survey of Mussolini's foreign policy from the Treaty of Locarno to the second half of 1928 when Italian relations with Ethiopia and Jugoslavia were temporarily stabilized. The author pays particular attention to the interaction between domestic and foreign policy.

Cassels, Alan. **Mussolini's Early Diplomacy.** Princeton: Princeton University Press, 1970, 425 p.
A scholarly and original study of the first four years of the Duce's foreign policy. They were not as restrained as had once been assumed.

D'Amoja, Fulvio. **Declino e prima crisi dell'Europa di Versailles: studio sulla diplomazia italiana ed europea (1931-1933).** Milan: Giuffrè, 1967, 510 p.
A very well-documented diplomatic history of Italy from 1931 to 1933. The author, who describes in great detail Italy's maneuvering between Great Britain and France on the one side and Germany on the other, is very critical of Mussolini's foreign policies.

D'Amoja, Fulvio. **La politica estera dell'impero: storia della politica estera fascista dalla conquista dell'Etiopia all'Anschluss.** Padua: CEDAM, 1967, 194 p.
A survey of Italian diplomacy from the conquest of Ethiopia to the Anschluss. It tells of the increasing collaboration between Hitler and Mussolini and the Italian acquiescence in the German annexation of Austria.

De Biase, Carlo. **L'impero di "Faccetta Nera."** Milan: Edizione del Borghese, 1966, 213 p.
A well-documented account of how Italy won, administered, and then left undefended her empire in East Africa.

Di Capua, Giovanni. **Come l'Italia aderì al Patto atlantico.** Rome: La Base, 1969, 253 p.
A revealing and well-documented account of the domestic pressures which caused the Italian government to join the NATO. The author regards Italy's membership in this alliance as an aberration and maintains that traditionally Italian foreign policy has been based on the principle of non-alignment.

I documenti diplomatici italiani. Rome: Libreria dello Stato (for the Ministero degli Affari Esteri, Commissione per la Pubblicazione dei Documenti Diplomatici).
A well-prepared and important collection of documents dealing with Italian foreign relations. It is published in nine series, of which the last five cover the period since the beginning of World War I. In the years from 1963 through 1973 the following volumes have appeared: in the "Quarta serie: 1908-1914," edited by Augusto Torre, vol. XII "28 giugno-2 agosto 1914" (1964, 581 p.); in the "Quinta serie: 1914-1918," edited by Augusto Torre and Ettore Anchieri, vol. IV "25 maggio-23 ottobre 1915" (1973, 668 p.); in the "Settima serie: 1922-1935," edited by Ruggero Moscati and Giampiero Carocci, vol. V "7 febbraio-31 dicembre 1927" (1967, 704 p.); vol. VI "1 gennaio-23 settembre 1928" (1967, 660 p.); vol. VII "24 settembre 1928-12 settembre 1929" (1970, 691 p.); vol. VIII "13 settembre-14 aprile 1930" (1972, 678 p.); and in the "Nona serie: 1939-1943," edited by Mario Toscano, vol. V "11 giugno-28 ottobre 1940" (1965, 833 p.). For previously published volumes consult earlier editions of "Foreign Affairs Bibliography."

Ferrara, Mario. **La politica estera dell'Italia libera (1945-1971).** Milan: Pan, 1972, 286 p.
One of the few narrative histories of Italian foreign policy since the end of the Second World War.

Graziano, Luigi. **La politica estera italiana nel dopoguerra.** Padua: Marsilio, 1968, 189 p.
A revisionist examination of Italy's postwar foreign policy. The author asserts that equating goodness with the West and evil with the East has long been an outmoded fairy tale designed for popular consumption; Italy's true interest, he continues, would best be served by seeking an accomodation with Russia and Third World countries.

L'Italia in Africa. Rome: Istituto Poligrafico dello Stato (for the Comitato per le documentazione dell'opera dell'Italia in Africa), 1955–.
A documentary history of Italy's role in Africa, planned in many volumes.

Jacomini di San Savino, Francesco. **La politica dell'Italia in Albania nelle testimonianze del luogotenente del Re Francesco Jacomini di San Savino.** Bologna: Cappelli, 1965, 380 p.
Memoirs describing Mussolini's takeover of Albania. The author was the Italian Ambassador and later the Viceroy in Albania.

Kirova, Kira Emmanuilovna. **Russkaia revoliutsiia i Italiia, mart-oktiabr' 1917.** Moscow: Izd-vo "Nauka," 1968, 323 p.
A monograph on Russo-Italian relations in 1917, by a Soviet scholar.

Kogan, Norman. **The Politics of Italian Foreign Policy.** New York: Praeger, 1963, 178 p.
A useful study of decision-making.

Laurens, Franklin D. **France and the Italo-Ethiopian Crisis, 1935–36.** The Hague: Mouton, 1967, 432 p.
This exhaustive monograph describes the relations between Mussolini and Pierre Laval, the French Foreign Minister, during the Italo-Ethiopian crisis. The author seems to suggest that had not Britain and France abandoned the Hoare-Laval scheme for carving up Ethiopia, Mussolini might have been more willing to maintain the Stresa Front against Nazi Germany.

Miège, J.-L. **L'Impérialisme colonial italien de 1870 à nos jours.** Paris: Société d'Édition d'Enseignement Supérieur, 1968, 419 p.
A survey of Italian colonial policies since 1870, including a useful bibliography and a supplement of documents and maps.

Minerbi, Sergio. **L'Italie et la Palestine, 1914–1920.** Paris: Presses Universitaires de France, 1970, 297 p.
A study dealing with Italy's ambitions in the Near East during and after World War I and the frustration of her diplomatic efforts by Great Britain and France.

Pastorelli, Pietro. **L'Albania nella politica estera italiana (1914–1920).** Naples: Jovene, 1970, 418 p.
In this study Italy emerges as the protector of Albanian independence from Serbian and Greek encroachments during and after the First World War.

Rumi, Giorgio. **Alle origini della politica estera fascista (1918–1923).** Bari: Laterza, 1968, 327 p.
A study tracing the origins of the aggressive nationalistic component of Mussolini's foreign policy.

Toscano, Mario. **The Origins of the Pact of Steel.** Baltimore: Johns Hopkins Press, 1968, 417 p.
A definitive, though slightly apologetic, account of the background to the Hitler-Mussolini alliance. The Italian original was published as "Le origini diplomatiche del Patto d'Acciaio" (Florence: Sansoni, 2d ed., 1956, 414 p.).

Willis, F. Roy. **Italy Chooses Europe.** New York: Oxford University Press, 1971, 373 p.
An analysis of Italy's important role in promoting European institutions, set against the background of her own economic and political conditions.

Zamboni, Giovanni. **Mussolinis Expansionspolitik auf dem Balkan.** Hamburg: Helmut Buske Verlag, 1970, 514 p.
A useful study of Italy's policy toward Albania in the 1920s.

Territorial Issues

Barros, James. **The Corfu Incident of 1923: Mussolini and the League of Nations.** Princeton: Princeton University Press, 1965, 339 p.
A scholarly monograph on Mussolini's first belligerent venture in international affairs: the occupation of Corfu.

Burger, Norbert. **Südtirol—wohin? Ein politisches Problem unserer Zeit, und seine Lösung.** Leoni am Starnberger See: Druffel, 1966, 212 p.
An active leader of the South Tyrol freedom fighters, or terrorists, presents his version of the case for internationally guaranteed autonomy for the German-Austrian South Tyrol.

Duroselle, Jean-Baptiste. **Le Conflit de Trieste: 1943-1954.** Brussels: Éditions de l'Institut de Sociologie de l'Université Libre de Bruxelles, 1966, 648 p.
A comprehensive, fair-minded and well-documented account of the Trieste dispute by a leading French scholar. The study was sponsored by the Carnegie Foundation.

Fenet, Alain. **La Question du Tyrol du Sud: un problème de droit international.** Paris: Librairie Générale de Droit, 1968, 369 p.
An historical and juridical inquiry into the fate of South Tyrol, called Alto Adige by the Italians who annexed it in 1919. The author acknowledges grounds for Austrian grievances.

Huter, Franz, *ed.* **Südtirol: eine Frage des europäischen Gewissens.** Munich: Oldenbourg, 1965, 616 p.
A massive collection of essays on the history, geography, economics and culture of South Tyrol. The emphasis is on the history of the area under Italian rule.

Novak, Bogdan Cyril. **Trieste, 1941-1954: The Ethnic, Political, and Ideological Struggle.** Chicago: University of Chicago Press, 1970, 526 p.
The fate of a city and its hinterland, depicted with scholarly detachment by a native of the area who has become an American professor of history.

Ritschel, Karl Heinz. **Diplomatie um Südtirol: politische Hintergründe eines europäischen Versagens.** Stuttgart: Seewald, 1966, 796 p.
A massive survey of the South Tyrol problem, with particular attention to Austrian-Italian negotiations since World War II. The author is a champion of the cause of the German-speaking South Tyrolese.

Rusinow, Dennison I. **Italy's Austrian Heritage, 1919-1946.** New York: Oxford University Press, 1969, 423 p.
A thorough work on Italy's territorial gains at Austria's—and her own—expense. The thesis is that the annexations of Alto Adige and Venezia Giulia encouraged Italian "irrational nationalist passion" and proved "a source of political weakness at home and abroad."

Toscano, Mario. **Storia diplomatica della questione dell'Alto Adige.** Bari: Laterza, 1967, 745 p.
A diplomatic history of the problem of South Tyrol in the period between World War I and 1965, by a leading Italian scholar.

Political and Constitutional Problems

See also Political Factors, p. 12; (Italy) Biographies, Memoirs and Collected Writings, p. 420; Recent History, p. 422; Foreign Policy, p. 424; Economic and Social Problems, p. 429.

Aquarone, Alberto. **L'organizzazione dello stato totalitario.** Turin: Einaudi, 1965, 620 p.
This scholarly study explains the organization of the Fascist state, its relationship to the Fascist party and to then existing social and political institutions.

Bartolotta, Francesco. **Parlamenti e governi d'Italia dal 1948 al 1970.** Rome: Vito Bianco, 1971, 2 v.
An important compendium of documents, statistics and tables listing Italy's operative political statutes, legislative enactments, and ministerial coalitions from 1948 to 1970.

Bassani, M. and Others. **I partiti politici: legge e statuti.** Milan: Istituto Editoriale Cisalpino, 1966, 454 p.
An analytical study of the internal dynamics of Italian political parties and their functioning within constitutional and statutory norms.

Berstein, Serge and Milza, Pierre. **L'Italie fasciste.** Paris: Armand Colin, 1970, 416 p.
A valiant attempt to reconcile the conflicting interpretations of Italian fascism. The authors suggest that there is both continuity and discontinuity in the Fascist movement and in the regime itself.

Berti, Giuseppe, *ed.* **I primi dieci anni di vita del P.C.I.: documenti inediti dell'archivio Angelo Tasca.** Milan: Feltrinelli, 1967, 524 p.
A documentary history of the first decade of the life of the Italian Communist Party, told through the unedited papers of Angelo Tasca (1892–1960), the right-wing leader of the party until his expulsion in 1929.

Blackmer, Donald L. M. **Unity in Diversity: Italian Communism and the Communist World.** Cambridge: M.I.T. Press, 1968, 434 p.
A thorough, thoughtful study of the evolution of Italian communism in the post-Stalin era, when national and international verities of the past no longer could guide the party's course. The author concludes that "the PCI has in practice become a revisionist party."

Catalano, Franco. **Storia dei partiti politici italiani.** Turin: ERI, 1965, 378 p.
A brief but solid survey of the evolution of Italy's political parties.

Ciani, Ansaldo. **Il partito liberale italiano: da Croce a Malagodi.** Naples: Edizioni scientifiche italiane, 1968, 271 p.
This work describes the destruction of the Italian Liberal Party during the Fascist period, its reconstruction after World War II, and its present role in parliamentary life.

Facchi, Paolo and Galli, Giorgio. **La sinistra democristiana.** Milan: Feltrinelli, 1962, 470 p.
A straightforward account of the ideological and political maneuvers of the left wing of Italy's Christian Democratic Party from 1943 to 1960.

Fried, Robert C. **The Italian Prefects: A Study in Administrative Politics.** New Haven: Yale University Press, 1963, 343 p.
A narrow survey of Italy's administrative development from unification in 1861 to the present.

Galli, Giorgio and Prandi, Alfonso. **Patterns of Political Participation in Italy.** New Haven: Yale University Press, 1970, 364 p.
A team of Italian political scientists presents much useful data on the structure of Italian politics. The authors stress the stability of postwar politics; their research was completed in 1965.

Godechot, Thierry. **Le Parti démocrate-chrétien italien.** Paris: Librairie Générale de Droit, 1964, 303 p.
An important, scholarly study of the Christian Democratic Party, Italy's leading party.

König, Helmut. **Lenin und der italienische Sozialismus 1915–1921: ein Beitrag zur Gründungsgeschichte der kommunistischen Internationale.** Tübingen: Arbeitsgemeinschaft für Osteuropaforschung, 1967, 240 p.
A well-documented study of how Lenin influenced the organization and growth of the Italian Socialist Party. The author pays particular attention to the role of the Comintern in causing the split within the Italian Socialist Party in 1921 and in the subsequent establishment of the Italian Communist Party.

Kogan, Norman. **A Political History of Postwar Italy.** New York: Praeger, 1966, 252 p.
A brief survey, cautiously optimistic, by a professor of political science at the University of Connecticut.

La Palombara, Joseph G. **Interest Groups in Italian Politics.** Princeton: Princeton University Press, 1964, 452 p.
A political scientist examines the impact of Italian interest groups on politics, with particular emphasis on the Confederation of Italian Industry and on Catholic Action.

Leoni, Francesco. **Storia dei partiti politici italiani.** Naples: Guida, 1971, 415 p.
A balanced account of the origins and development of political parties in Italy.

Lopukhov, Boris Removich. **Fashizm i rabochie dvizhenie v Italii, 1919–29.** Moscow: Izd-vo "Nauka," 1968, 415 p.
This study of Italian fascism by a Soviet scholar explains the rise of a mass right wing movement in a Marxist-Leninist framework. The author argues that the primary social base of Mussolini's movement was composed of the petty bourgeoisie, the economic losers in the development of industrial capitalism.

Mammarella, Giuseppe. **Italy After Fascism: A Political History, 1943–1963.** Notre Dame: University of Notre Dame Press, rev. and enl. ed., 1966, 377 p.
This broad chronological survey of Italian history during the last years of World War II and the postwar period is a useful introduction to contemporary Italian politics.

Manacorda, Gastone. **Il socialismo nella storia d'Italia: storia documentaria dal Risorgimento alla Repubblica.** Bari: Laterza, 1966, 873 p.
A prominent Italian historian provides a documentary history of the origins and vicissitudes of the socialist movement in Italy, from unification to the establishment of the Republic.

Melito, Archimede. **Da Giolitti a De Gasperi: avvenimenti e considerazioni, 1903-1953.** Rome: Libreria Editrice Romana, 1964, 195 p.
A brief history of Italian parliamentary vicissitudes in the first half of the twentieth century.

Melograni, Piero. **Gli industriali e Mussolini: rapporti tra Confindustria e fascismo dal 1919 al 1929.** Milan: Longanesi, 1972, 325 p.
A penetrating examination of the relationship between the Fascist movement and the Confederation of Italian Industry. The author demonstrates with careful documentation that the industrialists threw their support behind Mussolini only after his consolidation of power.

Nenni, Pietro. **Il socialismo nella democrazia: realtà del presente.** Florence: Vallecchi, 1966, 387 p.
A collection of articles and speeches by the leader of the Italian Socialist Party, Pietro Nenni. This volume, edited by Giuseppe Tamburrano, demonstrates the evolutionary nature of Italian socialism and the willingness of the party to collaborate with other political parties in the task of genuine social and economic reform.

Paulson, Belden H. and Ricci, Athos. **The Searchers: Conflict and Communism in an Italian Town.** Chicago: Quadrangle Books, 1966, 360 p.
A book arising from the question of why the little hill town of Castelfuoco, near Rome, votes more than 70 percent Communist.

Santarelli, Enzo. **La revisione del marxismo in Italia: studi di critica storica.** Milan: Feltrinelli, 1964, 346 p.
An essay on the development of Marxist thought in Italy.

Sarti, Roland. **Fascism and the Industrial Leadership in Italy, 1919-1940.** Berkeley: University of California Press, 1971, 154 p.
A brief account of the complex relationship between worried industrialists and ambitious fascists, by an American historian born in Italy. He concludes that "by the Second World War, the industrialists were more entrenched in the economic and social system than they were when fascism came to power."

Scoppola, Pietro, *ed.* **Chiesa e stato nella storia d'Italia: storia documentaria dall'unità alla Repubblica.** Bari: Laterza, 1967, 861 p.
A collection of documents, supplemented by narrative history, on Church-State relations focusing upon areas of tension and conflict. The author believes that only a strong Fascist state felt secure enough to grant the Church sufficient freedom and autonomy in the Lateran Treaty of 1929.

Scoppola, Pietro. **Coscienza religiosa e democrazia nell'Italia contemporanea.** Bologna: Il Mulino, 1966, 429 p.
In this collection of essays, a noted Catholic scholar examines the relationship between religious consciousness and political democracy in contemporary Italy.

Secchia, Pietro. **L'azione svolta dal partito communista in Italia durante il fascismo (1927-1932): ricordi, documenti inediti e testimonianze.** Milan: Feltrinelli, 1970, 557 p.
A documentary history of the Italian Communist Party during the critical years from 1927 to 1932 when most of its members were in prison, in exile, or in the underground.

Seton-Watson, Christopher. **Italy from Liberalism to Fascism, 1870-1925.** New York: Barnes and Noble, 1967, 772 p.
A political history of splendid thoroughness and perception, written with critical command of all sources and infused with the author's intimate knowledge of contemporary Italy. The English scholar is more generous in his assessment of the achievements of the liberal half-century than has been customary in recent literature.

Settembrini, Domenico. **La Chiesa nella politica italiana (1944-1963).** Pisa: Nistri-Lischi, 1964, 422 p.

An attempt to survey the role of the Catholic Church in Italian politics in the period from 1944 to 1963.

Spartaro, Giuseppe. **I democratici cristiani dalla dittatura alla repubblica.** Milan: Mondadori, 1968, 435 p.
A comprehensive examination of the origins and development of the Christian Democratic Party in Italy.

Spriano, Paolo. **L'occupazione delle fabbriche: settembre 1920.** Turin: Einaudi, 1968, 230 p.
A scholarly account of the Italian labor movement in the critical post-World War I period culminating in the occupation of the factories in northern Italy in 1920.

Spriano, Paolo. **Storia del Partito Comunista Italiano.** Turin: Einaudi, 1967– .
A well-documented history of the Italian Communist Party since 1917 by a member of the party. Four volumes published through 1973.

Spriano, Paolo. **Storia di Torino operaia e socialista: da De Amicis a Gramsci.** Turin: Einaudi, 1972, 509 p.
A communist history of the labor movement in the key industrial city of Turin during the first quarter of the twentieth century.

Susmel, Dulio. **Nenni e Mussolini, mezzo secolo di fronte.** Milan: Rizzoli, 1969, 356 p.
An analysis of the political struggle between Mussolini and Pietro Nenni, the leader of the Socialist Party, two Italian political leaders who in their early years had similar ideological views.

Tedeschi, Mario. **La guerra dei generali.** Milan: Edizioni del Borghese, 1968, 212 p.
An attempt to unravel the inner workings of the Italian intelligence agency. The author notes that intelligence gathering is more frequently directed against domestic political opponents than foreign governments.

Economic and Social Problems

See also General Economic Conditions and Tendencies, p. 71; (Western Europe) Integration, p. 349; (France) Economic Problems, p. 415.

Catalano, Francesco. **Aspetti dell'Italia sotto il fascismo e la resistenza.** Milan: La Goliardica, 1967, 296 p.
A balanced monograph of Italian society on the eve of and during the Second World War.

Catalano, Franco. **L'economia italiana di guerra: la politica economico-finanziaria del fascismo dalla guerra d'Etiopia alla caduta del regime, 1935-1943.** Milan: Istituto Nazionale per la Storia del Movimento di Liberazione, 1969, 143 p.
A noted Italian economic historian examines how the Italian economy was geared toward the Fascist war effort from 1935 to the fall of the régime.

Catalano, Franco. **Potere economico e fascismo: la crisi del dopoguerra, 1919-1921.** Milan: Lerici, 1964, 340 p.
A critical study of the post-World War I economic crisis in Italy and its relationship to the rise of the Fascist movement.

Clough, Shepard Bancroft. **The Economic History of Modern Italy.** New York: Columbia University Press, 1964, 458 p.
An important and comprehensive survey of Italy's economic development since unification. Professor Clough, an economic historian, is particularly concerned with the problems of Italy's economic growth.

Colombo, Emilio. **Linee di una politica industriale (1959-1962).** Bologna: Cappelli, 1963, 746 p.
A selection of speeches and writings covering the four-year period when the author was Minister of Industry and Trade.

Corbino, Epicarmo. **L'economia italiana dal 1860 al 1960.** Bologna: Zanichelli, 1962, 389 p.
A magisterial survey of Italian economic development from the founding of the unitary state in 1860-61 up to 1960.

Forte, Francesco. **La congiuntura in Italia, 1961–1965.** Turin: Einaudi, 1966, 505 p.
A description of Italy's boom-bust economic cycle from the 1950s to the mid-1960s.

Gaetani d'Aragona, Gabriele. **Politica dello sviluppo agricolo.** Milan: Giuffrè, 1964, 158 p.
An examination of the historical reasons for Italy's rural backwardness, especially in the South.

Hildebrand, George Herbert. **Growth and Structure in the Economy of Modern Italy.** Cambridge: Harvard University Press, 1965, 475 p.
Out of their dismal postwar situation, the Italians produced a remarkable recovery and expansion. With a mastery of his material that reflects the years this book was in the making, Professor Hildebrand explains and analyzes how it was done—and what remains undone. An important contribution to the history of postwar Europe.

Horowitz, Daniel L. **The Italian Labor Movement.** Cambridge: Harvard University Press, 1963, 356 p.
A valuable study of the history of Italian trade unionism in relation to the social, political, and economic environment. A central concern of the author is the reason for communist domination of the movement in much of the postwar period.

La Malfa, Ugo. **La politica economica in Italia, 1946–1962.** Milan: Edizioni di Comunità, 1963, 542 p.
Writings and speeches on the development of the Italian economy since World War II.

La Palombara, Joseph G. **Italy: The Politics of Planning.** Syracuse: Syracuse University Press, 1966, 184 p.
A political scientist at Yale looks into the political features and implications of economic planning in postwar Italy.

Lenti, Libero. **Inventario dell'economia italiana.** Milan: Garzanti, 1966, 279 p.
Thirty-nine short essays by a liberal professor and journalist on many phases of the Italian economy.

Morandi, Rodolfo. **Storia della grande industria in Italia.** Turin: Einaudi, 1966, 249 p.
This balanced study of Italy's industrial development was originally published in 1959 as the second volume of the author's "Opere."

Poggi, Gianfranco. **Catholic Action in Italy: The Sociology of a Sponsored Organization.** Stanford: Stanford University Press, 1967, 280 p.
A study of the lay organization, Azione Cattolica Italiana, its relationship to the Catholic Church and to the society as a whole, dealing chiefly with the period 1944–58.

Posner, M. V. and Woolf, S. J. **Italian Public Enterprise.** Cambridge: Harvard University Press, 1967, 160 p.
A brief survey and evaluation of Italian economic development, especially in the public sector, from 1945 to 1963.

Rochat, Giorgio. **L'esercito italiano da Vittorio Veneto a Mussolini (1919–1925).** Bari: Laterza, 1967, 609 p.
This exhaustive study documents the relationship between the Italian military and civil society from the end of the First World War to Mussolini's consolidation of power.

Romeo, Rosario. **Breve storia della grande industria in Italia.** Rome: Edindustria, 1967, 272 p.
A brief but solid history of the development of heavy industry in Italy by a noted economic historian.

Saraceno, Pasquale. **Ricostruzione e pianificazione (1943–1948).** Bari: Laterza, 1969, 494 p.
An important collection of essays, edited by Piero Barucci, dealing with the economic reconstruction of Italy during and immediately following the Second World War.

Stern, Robert Mitchell. **Foreign Trade and Economic Growth in Italy.** New York: Praeger (in coöperation with University of Michigan Graduate Research Seminar in International Economics), 1967, 216 p.
This study measures the importance of exports in stimulating Italian economic growth.

Tremelloni, Roberto. **L'Italia in una economia aperta.** Milan: Garzanti, 1963, 431 p.
Papers on Italy's economic problems by a well-known socialist economist who has frequently held ministerial and other governmental posts.

Votaw, Dow. **The Six-Legged Dog: Mattei and ENI—A Study in Power.** Berkeley: University of California Press, 1964, 172 p.
This is a good start toward understanding the blend of politics, finance and entrepreneurship exhibited by Italy's government-owned energy corporation and its first president, the late Enrico Mattei.

Regional Problems

Apih, Elio. **Italia: fascismo e antifascismo nella Venezia Giulia (1918-1943).** Bari: Laterza, 1966, 480 p.
A study of the Italianization of, and of the imposition of fascism upon, Fiume, Istria and Trieste after 1918.

Colapietra, Raffaele. **Napoli tra dopoguerra e fascismo.** Milan: Feltrinelli, 1962, 323 p.
This study, based primarily on the regional press, describes how the Fascist Party supplanted the politically bankrupt Liberal Party in the South in the years from 1919 to 1923.

Corbino, Epicarmo. **Cinquant'anni di vita economica italiana, 1915-1965.** Naples: Edizioni Scientifiche Italiane, 1966, 2 v.
A collection of articles written by Professor Corbino of the University of Naples providing useful information on merchant shipping, banking policy and economic development in the South.

Dolci, Danilo. **Waste: An Eye-Witness Report on Some Aspects of Waste in Western Sicily.** New York: Monthly Review Press, 1964, 352 p.
A compassionate, yet critical inquiry into the appalling poverty and wasted lives of Sicily, by a well-known reformer.

Labini, Sylos, *ed.* **Problemi dell'economia siciliana.** Milan: Feltrinelli, 1966, 1,482 p.
This exhaustive documentary study, commissioned by the Feltrinelli Institute, examines the difficulties of industrializing Sicily, an economically backward region.

Martellaro, Joseph Alexander. **Economic Development in Southern Italy, 1950-1960.** Washington: Catholic University of America Press, 1965, 123 p.
An assessment of what has been done in the Mezzogiorno.

Pantaleone, Michele. **The Mafia and Politics.** New York: Coward-McCann, 1966, 255 p.
A Sicilian journalist, long an enemy of the Mafia, writes a most illuminating and significant history of the Sicilian underworld and its social and economic background. The Italian original was published as "Mafia e politica, 1943-1962" (Turin: Einaudi, 1962, 286 p.).

Saville, Lloyd Blackstone. **Regional Economic Development in Italy.** Durham: Duke University Press, 1967, 191 p.
Detailed proposals for an approach applicable to a number of regions, including developed ones, not just the much-written-about South.

Schachter, Gustav. **The Italian South: Economic Development in Mediterranean Europe.** New York: Random House, 1965, 244 p.
A study of the economic conditions of southern Italy and a short presentation of the economic problems of other Mediterranean regions.

Tarrow, Sidney. **Peasant Communism in Southern Italy.** New Haven: Yale University Press, 1967, 389 p.
This scholarly study examines the growth of the Italian Communist Party among the backward peasants of southern Italy. The author points out that Communist gains resulted from long-standing social and economic grievances of the rural masses and from the efforts of Communist leaders, especially Antonio Gramsci, who recognized the necessity of a worker-peasant alliance.

Vito, Francesco and Others, *eds.* **Problemi economici e finanziari delle regioni.** Milan: Società Editrice Vita e Pensiero, 1966, 147.
——. **Lo sviluppo economico regionale.** Milan: Società Editrice Vita e Pensiero, 1967, 199 p.
Collections of essays on regional economic progress and problems in Italy. Published in the series "I problemi economici d'oggi," the purpose of which is to confront

laissez-faire economic theory with the raw data of regional underdevelopment; therefore, state planning emerges as a secondary theme.

VATICAN CITY

See also (Second World War) Diplomatic Aspects, p. 148; (Germany) Recent History, p. 465.

Bull, George. **Vatican Politics at the Second Vatican Council, 1962-5.** New York: Oxford University Press (for the Royal Institute of International Affairs), 1966, 157 p.
A concise but informative account.

Cardinale, Igino. **Le Saint-Siège et la diplomatie.** Paris: Desclée, 1962, 342 p.
The Vatican Chief of Protocol under the late Pope John XXIII surveys the nature and practice of papal diplomacy.

Castiglione, Luigi. **Pio XII e il nazismo.** Turin: Borla, 1965, 331 p.
This volume, based on diplomatic dispatches, demonstrates the deteriorating relationship between Hitler and the Vatican prior to the outbreak of World War II. The author, a partisan of Pius XII, defends the diplomatic posture taken by the Papacy toward Nazi Germany.

Cavallari, Alberto. **The Changing Vatican.** Garden City: Doubleday, 1967, 215 p.
A study of the Vatican coming to grips with the realities of twentieth century life. The original appeared as "Il Vaticano che cambia" (Milan: Mondadori, 2d ed., 1967, 220 p.).

Falconi, Carlo. **The Popes in the Twentieth Century.** Boston: Little, Brown, 1968, 400 p.
This book contains short biographical sketches of five Popes: Pius X, Benedict XV, Pius XI, Pius XII and John XXIII. The Italian original appeared as "I Papi de ventesimo secolo" (Milan: Feltrinelli, 1967, 398 p.).

Falconi, Carlo. **The Silence of Pius XII.** Boston: Little, Brown, 1970, 430 p.
The author maintains that Pius XII was well aware of Nazi atrocities, but felt that to speak out would have been both useless and counter-productive. He believes, however, that Pacelli's diplomatic background caused him to place excessive faith in the efficacy of diplomatic channels. The Italian original appeared as "Il silenzio di Pio XII" (Milan: Sugar, 1965, 566 p.).

Friedländer, Saul. **Pius XII and the Third Reich: A Documentation.** New York: Knopf, 1966, 238 p.
An important contribution to the controversy about Pope Pius XII's views and policies toward the Third Reich. The author presents new documents, chiefly drawn from the Nazi Foreign Office records and indicating that the Germans at least believed the Pope had understanding and even sympathy for their cause. The author is aware of the limitations of his evidence. The French original was published as "Pie XII et le IIIe Reich: documents" (Paris: Éditions du Seuil, 1964, 235 p.).

Gollin, James. **Worldly Goods.** New York: Random House, 1971, 531 p.
A painstakingly researched account of the Vatican's financial policy. While the Church has been a superb money manager—increasing the value of its portfolio even during the Depression—its officials in general have placed Christian charity first.

Guerry, Émile Maurice. **The Popes and World Government.** Baltimore: Helicon, 1964, 254 p.
In this book which traces the concern of the Papacy for a world organization to assure world peace, the author draws mainly on the pronouncements of Pope Pius XII who for 20 years repeatedly expressed the need for individuals to assume international responsibility, recognize mankind's interdependence and work for a world government. The original appeared as "L'Église et la communauté des peuples" (Paris: Bonne Presse, 1958, 347 p.).

Margiotta Broglio, Francesco. **L'Italia e la Santa Sede dalla Grande Guerra alla conciliazione.** Bari: Laterza, 1966, 567 p.
A preliminary investigation of the origins of the Lateran Treaties of 1929 which brought to an end the long-standing feud between Church and state in Italy.

Mourin, Maxime. **Le Vatican et l'U.R.S.S.** Paris: Payot, 1965, 298 p.
  A history of Soviet relations with the Vatican. The author tends to defend the Russian policies, and argues that the Soviets have merely taken over the long-established Russian tradition of suspicion of Papal designs.

Nichols, Peter. **The Politics of the Vatican.** New York: Praeger, 1968, 373 p.
  A non-Catholic British journalist offers a sympathetic view of the contemporary Church, torn from some of her historic moorings by the need to engage more closely with present-day society—in Pope Paul's words, "to get to grips with it, almost to run after it."

Nobécourt, Jacques. **"Le Vicaire" et l'histoire.** Paris: Éditions du Seuil, 1964, 381 p.
  An editor of *Le Monde* summarizes the international debate occasioned by Hochhuth's play "Deputy" and gives his own trenchant interpretation of Pope Pius XII's views and policies toward the Nazis.

Rynne, Xavier, *pseud*. **Letters from Vatican City: Vatican Council II (First Session); Background and Debates.** New York: Farrar, Straus, 1963, 289 p.
  "An essay in theological journalism" recounting and interpreting the events of the eight week session of the Ecumenical Council called by Pope John XXIII in the closing months of 1962.

Winter, Eduard. **Rom und Moskau: ein halbes Jahrtausend Weltgeschichte in ökumenischer Sicht.** Wien: Europa Verlag, 1972, 490 p.
  Although much of this book by a well-known East German historian deals with the period before 1917, the latter part of it is of interest to the student of the relations between the Kremlin and the Vatican.

SPAIN

General

See also (Europe) General Surveys, p. 344; Western Europe, p. 345.

Carr, Raymond. **Spain 1808–1939.** New York: Oxford University Press, 1966, 766 p.
  A splendid history of Spain from the turn of the nineteenth century up to the Civil War of the 1930s.

Clissold, Stephen. **Spain.** New York: Walker, 1969, 211 p.
  Spain, its past and present, in seven pleasant, compressed chapters.

Comín Colomer, Eduardo. **Historia del Partido Comunista de España.** Madrid: Editora Nacional, 1965–67, 3 v.
  A massive history of the Spanish Communist Party from April 1920 to July 1936.

Crow, John Armstrong. **Spain: The Root and the Flower.** New York: Harper and Row, 1963, 412 p.
  A good general history of Spanish civilization, of which the last third is devoted to Spain in the twentieth century.

Hermet, Guy. **Les Communistes en Espagne.** Paris: Colin, 1971, 215 p.
  A useful study of the Spanish Communist Party during its period of illegality and exile.

Hills, George. **Spain.** New York: Praeger, 1970, 480 p.
  A useful survey of twentieth-century Spain, set against the background of earlier history.

Jackson, Gabriel. **Historian's Quest.** New York: Knopf, 1969, 234 p.
  This complementary volume to the author's earlier, widely praised study of the Spanish Republic, offers an autobiographical perspective on modern Spain and on the contemporary practice of history.

Michener, James Albert. **Iberia: Spanish Travels and Reflections.** New York: Random House, 1968, 818 p.
  The many faces of Spain, affectionately depicted and handsomely illustrated.

Pabón y Suárez de Urbina, Jesús. **Cambó.** Barcelona: Alpha, 1952–69, 2 v. in 3 pts.
  This biography of Francisco Cambó, the leader of the Catalan bourgeoisie, is one of the best political histories of modern Spain.

Payne, Stanley G. **Politics and the Military in Modern Spain.** Stanford: Stanford University Press, 1967, 574 p.
A welcome scholarly study of the role played by the military as a political influence in Spain from the beginning of the nineteenth century to the present.

Petrie, Sir Charles. **King Alfonso (XIII) and His Age.** London: Chapman and Hall, 1963, 247 p.
A biography of Alfonso XIII, King of Spain in 1931 when the monarchy was overthrown. The British author, who had discussed with Don Alfonso "the more momentous events of his reign," concludes that "very few monarchs would have done better, and the vast majority would have done a great deal worse."

Pike, Fredrick B. **Hispanismo, 1898-1936: Spanish Conservatives and Liberals and Their Relations with Spanish America.** Notre Dame: University of Notre Dame Press, 1971, 486 p.
The author of this extensive survey, which is based on published materials, is convinced that by studying Spanish politics one gains a much better understanding of the history of the Spanish-speaking areas of the New World.

Reventlow, Rolf. **Spanien in diesem Jahrhundert: Bürgerkrieg, Vorgeschichte und Auswirkungen.** Vienna: Europa Verlag, 1968, 504 p.
A German Social Democrat, who participated in the Spanish Civil War on the Republican side, combines his reminiscences with an interpretation of modern Spanish history.

Schulte, Henry F. **The Spanish Press, 1470-1966: Print, Power, and Politics.** Urbana: University of Illinois Press, 1968, 280 p.
A study of the Spanish press, with emphasis on censorship during the Franco regime, by an American foreign correspondent and professor of journalism.

Smith, Rhea Marsh. **Spain: A Modern History.** Ann Arbor: University of Michigan Press, 1965, 508 p.
A compact history of Spain from the Visigoths to Franco.

Welles, Benjamin. **Spain: The Gentle Anarchy.** New York: Praeger, 1965, 386 p.
A pleasant introduction to contemporary Spain, by a *New York Times* correspondent who liked his six-year stint there.

The Republic and the Civil War

See also (War) General, p. 108; Inter-War Period, p. 140; (Great Britain) Political Problems, p. 381; (Spain) The Franco Regime, p. 437.

Azaña, Manuel. **Obras completas.** Mexico City: Oasis, 1966–.
The works of Manuel Azaña, Prime Minister and second President of the Republic, with a scholarly introduction by Juan Marichal. Four volumes have been published.

Bolin, Luis A. **Spain: The Vital Years.** Philadelphia: Lippincott, 1967, 396 p.
A study of the Civil War by an Anglo-Spanish aristocrat who served as Franco's Press Officer from 1936 to 1938.

Brome, Vincent. **The International Brigades: Spain 1936-1939.** New York: Morrow, 1966, 317 p.
This account, though useful, is not the definitive study of the subject.

Carr, Raymond, ed. **The Republic and the Civil War in Spain.** New York: St. Martin's Press, 1971, 275 p.
A superb collection of nine essays containing fresh insights and based on sound scholarship.

Chapaprieta Torregrosa, Joaquín. **La paz fue posible: memorias de un político.** Barcelona: Ariel, 1971, 436 p.
Memoirs by the liberal bourgeois Minister of Finance and Prime Minister during the period of the Second Republic.

Cierva y de Hoces, Ricardo de la, ed. **Bibliografía general sobre la Guerra de España (1936-1939) y sus antecedentes históricos: fuentes para la historia contemporánea de España.** Barcelona: Ariel, 1968, 729 p.

──────. **Los documentos de la primavera trágica: análisis documental de los antecedentes inmediatos del 18 de julio de 1936.** Madrid: Ministerio de Información y Turismo, 1967, 747 p.

Two basic reference volumes for the period leading to the Civil War and the war itself.

Cierva y de Hoces, Ricardo de la. **Historia de la Guerra Civil española. Vol. I: 1898–1936.** Madrid: San Martín, 1969, 826 p.

The most complete and documented history of the Second Republic.

Delperrie de Bayac, Jacques. **Les Brigades internationales.** Paris: Fayard, 1968, 466 p.

A partisan history of the international brigades that fought for the Republicans in the Spanish Civil War.

Eby, Cecil de Grotte. **Between the Bullet and the Lie: American Volunteers in the Spanish Civil War.** New York: Holt, Rinehart and Winston, 1969, 342 p.

A thorough study of the organization, battle record and the tragic fate of the American volunteers—most but not all of whom were communists—who fought for the Republican side.

Eby, Cecil de Grotte. **The Siege of the Alcázar.** New York: Random House, 1966, 242 p.

A depiction of the Republican attack on the Nationalist-held military academy in Toledo in the summer of 1936.

Fraser, Ronald. **In Hiding: The Life of Manuel Cortes.** New York: Pantheon, 1972, 238 p.

These skillfully rendered interviews with the Cortes family chronicle how the events of the 1930s, and their consequences, were lived by working-class Spaniards in rural Andalusia.

García Durán, Juan. **Bibliografía de la Guerra civil española, 1936–1939.** Montevideo: El Siglo Ilustrado, 1964, 559 p.

A bibliography on the Spanish Civil War.

Gaya Delrue, Marcelo. **Combattre pour Madrid: mémoires d'un officier franquiste.** Paris: Éditions de la Pensée Moderne, 1964, 253 p.

Memoirs of the Civil War, by one of Franco's officers.

Gil-Robles y Quiñones, José María. **No fue posible la paz.** Barcelona: Ariel, 1968, 851 p.

The memoirs of the leader of the C.E.D.A., the dominant Catholic party of the Right, during the period of the Second Republic.

Harper, Glenn T. **German Economic Policy in Spain During the Spanish Civil War, 1936–1939.** The Hague: Mouton, 1967, 150 p.

A monograph on the economic aspects of German intervention. The author concludes that "Debts of gratitude and debts of reichsmarks were not sufficient to make Spain an economic satellite of the German Reich."

Ibarruri, Dolores. **They Shall Not Pass: The Autobiography of La Pasionaria.** New York: International Publishers, 1966, 351 p.

Primarily an interpretation of the Spanish Civil War by a leading Spanish communist who for many years has been living in Moscow. The Spanish original was published as "El único camino" (Havana: Impr. Nacional de Cuba, 1962, 462 p.).

Jackson, Gabriel. **The Spanish Republic and the Civil War, 1931–1939.** Princeton: Princeton University Press, 1965, 578 p.

An important, thoughtful reassessment of Spanish politics before and during the Civil War, by an American historian who supplemented earlier published accounts with recent interviews. Strongly Republican in his sympathies, he is historical in his method and judgments.

Johnston, Verle B. **Legions of Babel: The International Brigades in the Spanish Civil War.** University Park: Pennsylvania State University Press (for the Hoover Institution on War, Revolution, and Peace), 1968, 228 p.

A brief, scholarly account of a great adventure characterized by an extraordinary mélange of men and motives.

Landis, Arthur H. **The Abraham Lincoln Brigade.** New York: Citadel Press, 1967, 677 p.

A partisan history of the American volunteers who fought on the Republican side during the Spanish Civil War, by a veteran of the Canadian Battalion of the International Brigade.

Lerma, José Larios Fernandez de Villavicencio, Duque de. **Combat over Spain.** New York: Macmillan, 1966, 308 p.
The Civil War memoirs of a bomber and fighter pilot in Franco's air force, based largely on the author's diaries and letters of the time.

Lorenzo, César M. **Les Anarchistes espagnols et le pouvoir (1868-1969).** Paris: Éditions du Seuil, 1969, 429 p.
Chiefly an examination of the activities of the Spanish anarchists in the period from May 1937 to the end of the Civil War. An important secondary source.

Mancisidor, José Maria. **Frente a frente.** Madrid: The Author, 1963, 364 p.
A chapter from the history of the Spanish Civil War: the trial and execution of the young Falangist José-Antonio Primo de Rivera.

Nellessen, Bernd. **Die verbotene Revolution: Aufstieg und Niedergang der Falange.** Hamburg: Leibniz-Verlag, 1963, 216 p.
A thoughtful study of the Falange Movement before the outbreak of the Spanish Civil War. The author argues that Franco distorted and largely destroyed the original aims and ideals of the Falange.

Payne, Stanley George. **The Spanish Revolution.** New York: Norton, 1970, 398 p.
A veteran student of modern Spain presents a survey of Spanish leftist revolutionary movements.

Robinson, Richard A. H. **The Origins of Franco's Spain: The Right, The Republic and Revolution, 1931-1936.** Pittsburgh: University of Pittsburgh Press, 1971, 475 p.
A serious inquiry into the causes of the Spanish Civil War, scrutinizing especially the diverse parties of the Right. A revisionist work which argues that much of the responsibility for the failure of the Republic lay with the Left Republicans themselves.

Saborit, Andrés. **Julián Besteiro.** Buenos Aires: Losada, 1967, 325 p.
This biography of the centrist P.S.O.E. leader Julián Besteiro contains information on the Spanish Socialist Party during the Republican period.

Sánchez, José M. **Reform and Reaction: The Politico-Religious Background of the Spanish Civil War.** Chapel Hill: University of North Carolina Press, 1964, 241 p.
In the author's opinion, the Spanish Civil War was the "focal point for all the brewing discontents of two centuries of Spanish history."

Sedwick, Frank. **The Tragedy of Manuel Azaña and the Fate of the Spanish Republic.** Columbus: Ohio State University Press, 1964, 295 p.
A sympathetic biography of Azaña, whom Madariaga describes in the foreword as "The biggest mind and the noblest heart among the leaders of the Republic."

Southworth, Herbert Rutledge. **Le Mythe de la croisade de Franco.** Paris: Ruedo Ibérico, 1964, 327 p.
A valuable review of literature on the Spanish Civil War and a vigorous refutation of various attempts to depict Franco's struggle as something other than a fascist onslaught. A shorter version of this book appeared in Spanish: "El mito de la cruzada de Franco: crítica bibliográfica" (Paris: Ruedo Ibérico, 1963, 314 p.).

Stansky, Peter David Lyman and Abrahams, William Miller. **Journey to the Frontier: Two Roads to the Spanish Civil War.** Boston: Atlantic (Little, Brown), 1966, 430 p.
The dual biography of two young Englishmen—Julian Bell and John Cornford—who died in the Spanish Civil War.

Watters, William E. **An International Affair: Non-Intervention in the Spanish Civil War, 1936-1939.** New York: Exposition Press, 1971, 423 p.
A rather narrow study of the events surrounding the International Non-Intervention Agreement of the Spanish Civil War, by a long-time soldier turned historian.

Weintraub, Stanley. **The Last Great Cause: The Intellectuals and the Spanish Civil War.** New York: Weybright and Talley, 1968, 340 p.
A pro-Loyalist evocation of the "Legend of Spain" and of the writers and artists who created it.

The Franco Regime

See also Inter-War Period, p. 140; Second World War, p. 144; (Spain) The Republic and the Civil War, p. 434.

Crozier, Brian. **Franco.** Boston: Little, Brown, 1968, 589 p.
 A well-written, somewhat superficial account of Franco's career, by an English journalist whose feelings for Franco while writing the book "changed from antipathy to grudging admiration."

Díez Alegría, Manuel. **Ejército y sociedad.** Madrid: Alianza Editorial, 1972, 207 p.
 A collection of essays by the Chief of Staff of the Army; it deserves notice as an example of the changing mentality in the armed forces.

Fernández-Carvajal, Rodrigo. **La constitución española.** Madrid: Editora Nacional, 1969, 182 p.
 A scholarly study of the constitution of Franco's Spain.

Fraga Iribarne, Manuel and Others, *eds.* **La España de los años 70. I: La sociedad.** Madrid: Moneda y Crédito, 1972, 1,018 p.
 A collection of papers on contemporary Spanish society.

Gallo, Max. **Histoire de l'Espagne franquiste.** Paris: Laffont, 1969, 491 p.
 A popular history of Franco's Spain, by a French author who is not an admirer of the Caudillo.

García Venero, Maximiano. **La Falange en la guerra de España: la unificación y Hedilla.** Paris: Ruedo Ibérico, 1967, 502 p.
 An account of the events in 1937 leading to the incorporation of the Falange into an official party under the leadership of Franco.

Hills, George. **Franco: The Man and His Nation.** New York: Macmillan, 1968, 464 p.
 A biography of the generalissimo based on research and extensive interviews with Franco and his close associates. Much useful emphasis on Franco's career before 1936.

Iglesias Selgas, Carlos. **Los sindicatos en España: origen, estructura y evolución.** Madrid: Ediciones del Movimiento, 1965, 479 p.

——. **La via española a la democracia.** Madrid: Ediciones del Movimiento, 1968, 327 p.
 Studies dealing with the institutions of the Franco regime.

Ledesma Ramos, Ramiro. **Fascismo en España? Discurso a las juventudes de España.** Barcelona: Ariel, 1968, 334 p.
 These writings of a leading syndicalist contain useful information on fascism in Spain.

Paniker, Salvador. **Conversaciones en Cataluña.** Barcelona: Kairos, 1966, 275 p.

——. **Conversaciones en Madrid.** Barcelona: Kairos, 2d ed., 1969, 367 p.
 Interviews with leaders of the opposition, cabinet members, intellectuals and artists.

Trythall, J. W. D. **El Caudillo: A Political Biography of Franco.** New York: McGraw-Hill, 1970, 304 p.
 A self-consciously dispassionate biography of Franco, concentrating on his role since the Civil War.

Vilar, Sergio. **Protagonistas de la España democrática: la oposición a la dictadura, 1939–1969.** Barcelona: Ediciones Sociales, 1968, 745 p.
 A survey of the different tendencies within the opposition from a leftist perspective.

Foreign Relations

See also Inter-War Period, p. 140; Second World War, p. 144; The Postwar World, p. 178; Norway, p. 444.

Armangué Rius, Gil. **Gibraltar y los españoles.** Madrid: Aguilar, 1964, 733 p.
 A short history of Gibraltar and a voluminous collection of quotations selected with the purpose of demonstrating the necessity of the return of the Rock to Spain.

Rico, Gumersindo. **La población de Gibraltar.** Madrid: Editora Nacional, 1967, 282 p.
 An anti-British tract discussing the present status of Gibraltar, with emphasis on population problems.

Rio Cisneros, Agustín del. **Viraje politico español durante la II guerra mundial 1942-1945: replica al cerco internacional 1945-1946.** Madrid: Ediciones del Movimiento, 1965, 609 p.
A collection of articles and speeches on the foreign policy of Spain during World War II, by a writer who hails the achievements of Franco.

Szulc, Tad. **The Bombs of Palomares.** New York: Viking, 1967, 274 p.
A former *New York Times* correspondent reconstructs the chilling story of the U.S. loss in Spain of two planes and four hydrogen bombs in January 1966.

Traina, Richard P. **American Diplomacy and the Spanish Civil War.** Bloomington: Indiana University Press, 1968, 301 p.
This monograph displays considerable analytical depth and balance. The author reveals the bewildering complexities of the dilemma which the United States faced in Spain, but is reluctant to judge or to condemn.

Economic and Social Problems

See also Government and Economics; Planning, p. 54; (Inter-American Relations) Regional Organizations, p. 197; Western Europe, p. 345.

Anderson, Charles W. **The Political Economy of Modern Spain: Policy-Making in an Authoritarian System.** Madison: University of Wisconsin Press, 1970, 282 p.
A painstaking study of the political factors in Spain's economic progress from 1957 to 1967.

Chilcote, Ronald H. **Spain's Iron and Steel Industry.** Austin: University of Texas, Bureau of Business Research, 1968, 174 p.
A detailed view, with attention to the implications of Spanish experience for the place of steel production in developing nations.

Duocastella, Rogelio and Others. **Análisis sociológico del catolicismo español.** Barcelona: Nova Terra and Instituto de Sociología y Pastoral Aplicadas, 1967, 165 p.
A descriptive study of the Spanish catholicism, with a detailed bibliography.

The Economic Development of Spain. Baltimore: Johns Hopkins Press, 1963, 416 p.
A report of a mission organized by the International Bank for Reconstruction and Development to advise the government of Spain on economic development plans.

Estruch, Juan. **Los protestantes españoles.** Barcelona: Nova Terra, 1968, 217 p.
A sociological study of contemporary Spanish protestantism.

García-Echevarría, Santiago. **Wirtschaftsentwicklung Spaniens unter dem Einfluss der europäischen Integration.** Opladen: Westdeutscher Verlag, 1964, 186 p.
A study of Spain's economic growth and of the problems and prospects of its trade with the Common Market and EFTA.

Hergel, Horst Hans. **Industrialisierungspolitik in Spanien seit Ende des Bürgerkrieges.** Cologne: Westdeutscher Verlag, 1963, 352 p.
An extensive study of Spanish economic policy, especially with respect to economic growth, since the Civil War.

Informe sociológico sobre la situación social de España. Madrid: Euramérica, 1966, 361 p.

Informe sociólogico sobre la situación social de España 1970. Madrid: Euramérica, 1970, 1,634 p.
These reports of the FOESSA Foundation, directed by Professor Amando de Miguel, are the basic source for the study of the social structure of Spain in all its aspects. They are based on public statistics, national sample surveys and secondary literature.

Irizarry, Carmen. **The Thirty Thousand: Modern Spain and Protestantism.** New York: Harcourt, Brace and World, 1966, 399 p.
A journalist's informed exploration of contemporary Spain's relation to its protestants.

Malefakis, Edward E. **Agrarian Reform and Peasant Revolution in Spain: Origins of the Civil War.** New Haven: Yale University Press, 1970, 469 p.
The author's analysis of the political consequences of antiquated land tenure is basic to an understanding of Spain in the 1930s.

Sociología española de los años setenta. Madrid: Confederación Española de Cajas de Ahorros, 1971, 842 p.
A bibliography of writings by Spanish sociologists and a collection of essays on Spanish social structure.

Tuñón de Lara, Manuel. **Medio siglo de cultura española (1885-1936).** Madrid: Tecnos, 1970, 293 p.
A sociologically oriented review of Spanish nineteenth- and twentieth-century intellectual history.

Tuñón de Lara, Manuel. **El movimiento obrero en la historia de España.** Madrid: Taurus, 1972, 963 p.
A valuable study of the Spanish labor movement up to the Republican period.

Velarde Fuertes, Juan. **Sobre la decadencia económica de España.** Madrid: Editorial Tecnos, 1967, 654 p.
A voluminous collection of essays on economic problems in contemporary Spain.

Regional Problems

Azaola, José Miguel de. **Vasconia y su destino. I: La regionalización de España.** Madrid: Revista de Occidente, 1972, 551 p.
A study of the economic relations between the Basque country and Spain.

García Venero, Maximiano. **Historia del nacionalismo catalán.** Madrid: Editora Nacional, 2d ed., 1967, 2 v.
A general history of Catalan nationalism.

García Venero, Maximiano. **Historia del nacionalismo vasco.** Madrid: Editora Nacional, 1968, 664 p.
A general history of Basque nationalism.

Hurtado, Amadeu. **Quaranta anys d'advocat: historia del meu temps.** Barcelona: Ariel, 1969, 2 v.
The memoirs of a Catalan politician covering the period of the 1930s.

Lisón Tolosana, Carmelo. **Antropología cultural de Galicia.** Madrid: Siglo Veintiuno de España, 1971, 408 p.
This study of Galicia by an anthropologist provides the background for better understanding the anti-centralist sentiment in that region.

Miguel, Amando de and Salcedo, Juan. **Dinámica del desarrollo industrial de las regiones españoles.** Madrid: Tecnos, 1972, 337 p.
A study of regional differences in socio-economic development, with interesting comparisons with Italy.

Molas, Isidre. **Lliga Catalana: un estudi d'estasiologia.** Barcelona: Edicions 62, 1972, 2 v.
A historical, political and sociological study of the Catalan bourgeois regionalist party that played a preëminent role in the period of the Monarchy and the Republic.

PORTUGAL

See also The Postwar World, p. 178; (Inter-American Relations) Regional Organizations, p. 197; (Western Europe) General Surveys and Political Problems, p. 345; (India) Foreign Policy, p. 666; (Africa) International Relations, p. 784; (West Africa) General, p. 807; Guinea; Portuguese Guinea; Mali; Mauritania, p. 809; Sierra Leone; Gambia, p. 812; (Central Africa) General, p. 821; Angola; Mozambique, p. 846.

Caetano, Marcello. **Ensaios pouco políticos.** Lisbon: Verbo, 2d ed., 1971, 217 p.
A selection of speeches made between 1930 and 1967 by the successor of Salazar. More liberal and cosmopolitan than his predecessor, Caetano favors consulting public opinion to a greater degree than did Salazar, but emphasizes an authoritarian executive power.

Caetano, Marcello. **História breve das constituições portuguesas.** Lisbon: Verbo, 3rd rev. ed., 1971, 141 p.
A succinct history of Portugal's constitutional development since 1822, including a discussion of the 1971 revisions of the 1933 Salazar constitution.

Costa, José Maria da. **Historia breve do movimento operário português.** Lisbon: Verbo, 1964, 143 p.
  A former labor leader discusses working class movements in Portugal with emphasis on the years from 1900 to 1926.

Delgado, Humberto. **The Memoirs of General Delgado.** London: Cassell, 1964, 234 p.
  Rambling thoughts and recollections of one of Salazar's leading opponents who was murdered in 1965.

Dez anos de política externa (1936-1947). Libson: Ministério dos Negócios Estrangeiros, 1961-65, 5 v.
  An official collection of documents on Portugal's diplomatic policies in the period from 1936 to 1947.

Godinho, Vitorino de Magalhães. **O socialismo e o futuro da peninsula.** Lisbon: Livros Horizonte, 2d ed., 1969, 122 p.
  A distinguished Portuguese historian writes about the past, the present and the future of Portugal. The author is very critical of Salazar's economic policies.

Kay, Hugh. **Salazar and Modern Portugal.** New York: Hawthorn, 1970, 478 p.
  A sober, full-length study of Portugal's late controversial leader, by a British journalist.

Leal, Francisco Pinto da Cunha. **As minhas memórias.** Lisbon: The Author, 1966-68, 3 v.
  Verbose but fascinating reminiscences of a former Premier of the first Portuguese Republic (1910-26) who in the post-1930 era became an adversary of Salazar. The most revealing memoirs published by a former Republican Premier.

Livermore, Harold Victor. **A New History of Portugal.** New York: Cambridge University Press, 2d ed., 1966, 365 p.
  A considerably revised version of Professor Livermore's well-known history, but without a great deal on the twentieth century.

Lupi, Luís C. **Memórias: diário de um inconformista (1910-1938).** Lisbon: The Author, 1971– .
  Memoirs of a noted journalist who made his name as a successful propagandist for the New State under Salazar. Two volumes have been published through 1972.

Mar, Naum Iosifovich. **Liudi kak skaly.** Moscow: Izd-vo Politicheskoi Literatury, 1967, 317 p.
  A Soviet study of contemporary Portuguese politics, with emphasis on the activities of the Portuguese Communist Party.

Marques, Antonio Henrique de Oliveira. **História de Portugal.** Lisbon: 1972-73, 2 v.
  A formidable though controversial general history of Portugal from ancient times to 1969, the year following Premier Caetano's appointment to succeed Salazar. An abbreviated English edition was published as "History of Portugal" (New York: Columbia University Press, 1972-73, 2 v.).

Marques, Antonio Henrique de Oliveira. **A primeira república portuguesa (para uma visão estrutural).** Lisbon: Livros Horizonte, 1971, 204 p.
  A revisionist essay on the history of the first Republic. The author emphasizes social and economic history and opposes traditional conservative interpretations.

Moreira, Adriano. **Portugals Überseepolitik.** Baden-Baden: Lutzeyer, 1963, 168 p.
  A series of essays by a Portuguese ethnologist and former Minister for Overseas Territories on Portugal's relations with its overseas possessions.

Moura, Francisco Pereira da. **Por onde a economia portuguesa?** Lisbon: Publicações Dom Quixote, 3rd rev. ed., 1970, 213 p.
  A discussion by an eminent Portuguese economist of Portugal's post-1945 economy.

Nogueira, Franco. **As crises e os homens.** Lisbon: Ática, 1971, 545 p.
  A lengthy investigation of the Portuguese tradition in international affairs, by a former Foreign Minister.

Nogueira, Franco. **The Third World.** London: Johnson, 1967, 154 p.
  A defense of the policies of Portugal toward her overseas territories. Translation of "Terceiro mundo" (Lisbon: Ática, 1961, 212 p.).

Nogueira, Franco. **The United Nations and Portugal: A Study of Anti-Colonialism.** London: Sidgwick and Jackson, 1963, 188 p.

A defense of Portugal's attitude toward U.N.'s concern with her African territories. Translation of "As Nações Unidas e Portugal" (Lisbon: Ática, 2d rev. ed., 1962, 234 p.).

Pereira, Pedro Teotónio. **Memórias.** Lisbon: Verbo, 1972, 345 p.
The first volume of the memoirs of a leading diplomat and minister who died in November 1972. Pereira was Portugal's "man in Madrid" during the important years from 1937 to 1945 and was later ambassador in Brazil, the United States and the United Kingdom. In the 1930s he was a cabinet minister close to Salazar and instrumental in establishing the corporative system.

Ploncard d'Assac, Jacques. **Salazar.** Paris: Éditions de la Table Ronde, 1967, 350 p.
An admiring account of the politics and philosophy of the authoritarian statesman who was Prime Minister of Portugal from 1932 to 1968.

Rao, R. P. **Portuguese Rule in Goa, 1510-1961.** New York: Asia Publishing House, 1963, 242 p.
The Goan scene in its "natural all-India setting" from Portuguese occupation to the controversial use of force by India to bring Goa officially into the Union.

Revisão constituicional 1971: textos e documentos. Lisbon: Secretaria de Estado da Informação e Turismo, 1971, 411 p.
Official record of the 1971 revisions of the 1933 Salazar constitution, including the original text of that document and the debates and discussions of the 1971 changes in such organs as the National Assembly and the Corporative Chamber. There is also a list of deputies who composed the National Assembly in 1971.

Rudel, Christian. **Le Portugal et Salazar.** Paris: Éditions Ouvrières, 1968, 158 p.
The principal aspects of Portuguese society and politics briefly examined.

Sayers, Raymond S., *ed.* **Portugal and Brazil in Transition.** Minneapolis: University of Minnesota Press, 1968, 367 p.
A potpourri—the result of papers and discussions drawn from the 1966 Colloquium of Luso-Brazilian Studies. Focus is on present and future trends, the framework being "the world the Portuguese created."

Serrão, Joel. **Do sebastianismo ao socialismo em Portugal.** Lisbon: Livros Horizonte, 2d ed., 1969, 113 p.
A classic study of four ideologies or ideas which have strongly influenced politics in Portugal since the late 16th century: sebastianism (a kind of popular, atavistic messianism), liberalism, republicanism and socialism.

Serrão, Joel. **Emigração portuguesa.** Lisbon: Livros Horizonte, 1969, 167 p.
An eminent social historian discusses a major problem of contemporary Portugal: emigration to Europe and the Americas. Useful and reliable tables of statistics.

Soares, Mário. **Le Portugal bailloné: un témoignage.** Paris: Calmann-Levy, 1972, 314 p.
The leading Socialist wrote from exile in Paris an extensive and detailed history of the opposition's activities since 1945.

SCANDINAVIA

General

See also (International Organization and Government) General, p. 96; (First World War) Diplomatic History, p. 131; (Europe) General Surveys, p. 344; Western Europe, p. 345.

Anderson, Stanley V. **The Nordic Council: A Study of Scandinavian Regionalism.** Seattle: University of Washington Press, 1967, 194 p.
A political scientist analyzes the evolution of this major regional body, composed of deputies from the five Scandinavian parliaments. It epitomizes the coöperation of the Nordic countries and their discovery of a middle way between anarchy and integration: "Among themselves, they will neither fight nor unite."

Andrén, Nils Bertel Einar. **Government and Politics in the Nordic Countries: Denmark, Finland, Iceland, Norway, Sweden.** Stockholm: Almqvist & Wiksell, 1964, 241 p.
A solid introduction.

Connery, Donald S. **The Scandinavians.** New York: Simon and Schuster, 1966, 590 p.
A readable and informative survey of contemporary Denmark, Norway, Sweden, Finland and Iceland. An informal work based largely on personal observations.

Fusilier, Raymond. **Les Pays nordiques: Danemark, Finlande, Norvège, Suède, Islande.** Paris: Librairie Générale de Droit, 1965, 295 p.
A French scholar offers a brief, useful survey of the political institutions of the five Nordic countries.

Legrand, André. **L'Ombudsman scandinave.** Paris: Librairie Générale de Droit, 1970, 549 p.
A detailed examination of the highly developed grievance-handling mechanisms in the administrative and political institutions of the Scandinavian countries.

Scandinavian Political Studies, 1966—. New York: Columbia University Press, 1966—.
A yearbook published by the Political Science Associations in Denmark, Finland, Norway and Sweden, including articles on Scandinavian political problems, recent political developments, and a very useful bibliography.

Sømme, Axel Christian Zellitz, *ed.* **A Geography of Norden: Denmark, Finland, Iceland, Norway, Sweden.** New York: Wiley, 1962, 363 p.
A solid introduction to the physical and economic geography of the Scandinavian countries.

Sparring, Åke, *ed.* **Kommunisten im Norden.** Cologne: Verlag Wissenschaft und Politik, 1967, 167 p.
Four valuable studies of Communist parties in postwar Scandinavia.

Wuorinen, John Henry. **Scandinavia.** Englewood Cliffs: Prentice-Hall, 1965, 146 p.
A comprehensive introduction, by a well-known scholar in the field.

Zorgbibe, Charles. **Les États-unis scandinaves.** Paris: Pedone, 1968, 141 p.
A discussion of the idea of the Scandinavian Union in general and of the Nordic Council in particular.

Denmark

See also Political Processes, p. 20; (Second World War) Naval Operations, p. 168; Economic, Technical and Non-Military Aspects, p. 172; Resistance and Underground Movements, p. 176; Western Europe, p. 345; (Scandinavia) General, p. 441; Polar Regions, p. 848.

Borre, Ole and Stehouwer, Jan. **Partistyrke og social struktur.** Aarhus: Akademisk Boghandel, 1968, 183 p.
A study of party strength and social structure in Denmark based on data from the 1960 general election.

Dansk sikkerhedspolitik 1948-1966. Copenhagen: Udenrigsministeriet, 1968, 2 v.
A discussion of the Danish security problems in the years from 1948 to 1966, supplemented with a volume of pertinent documents. Published by the Danish Ministry of Foreign Affairs.

Dau, Mary. **Danmark og Sovjetunionen 1944-49.** Copenhagen: Munksgaard (for the Dansk Udenrigspolitisk Institut), 1969, 291 p.
A survey of Danish relations with the Soviet Union during and immediately following World War II.

Fink, Troels Marstrand Trier. **Deutschland als Problem Dänemarks: die geschichtlichen Voraussetzungen der dänischen Aussenpolitik.** Flensburg: Wolff, 1968, 125 p.
A survey of Germany's role in Danish foreign policy.

Frederiksen, Bjarne W. **Danmarks Sydslesvigpolitik efter det tyske sammenbrud i 1945.** Copenhagen: Munksgaard, 1971, 210 p.
A study of Danish border policies after the German capitulation in 1945.

Hæstrup, Jørgen. **. . . til Landets Bedste: hovedtræk af departementschefsstyrets virke 1943-45.** Copenhagen: Gyldendal, 1966-71, 2 v.
A study of Danish central administration during the last part of the German occupation.

Jørgensen, Harald. **Genforeningens statspolitiske baggrund: tilblivelsen af Versaillestraktatens slesvigske bestemmelser.** Copenhagen: D.B.K., 1970, 414 p.
  A study of the origins and background of the provisions in the Versailles Treaty relating to Slesvig and the reunification of the northern part of Slesvig with Denmark.

Jones, W. Glyn. **Denmark.** New York: Praeger, 1970, 256 p.
  A rapid glance at the history and present politics of Denmark.

Kaarsted, Tage. **Påskekrisen 1920.** Aarhus: Universitetsforlaget, 1968, 427 p.
  A monograph on a major crisis in Danish parliamentary government in 1920.

Kaarsted, Tage. **Regeringskrisen 1957: en studie i regeringsdannelsens proces.** Aarhus: Institut for Presseforskning og Samtidshistorie, 1964, 196 p.
  A study of cabinet formation in Denmark in 1957.

Karup Pedersen, Ole. **Udenrigsminister P. Munchs opfattelse af Danmarks stilling i international politik.** Copenhagen: Gad, 1970, 650 p.
  A comprehensive discussion of Danish foreign policy and of the views of the Danish Foreign Minister P Munch in the years from 1929 to 1940.

Løkkegaard, Finn. **Det danske gesandtskab i Washington 1940-1942: Henrik Kaufmann som uafhængig dansk gesandt i USA 1940-1942 og hans politik vedrørende Grønland og de oplagte danske skibe i Amerika.** Copenhagen: Gyldendal, 1968, 644 p.
  A historical study of the policies carried out by Henrik Kaufmann, Danish envoy to the United States during the first years of World War II, relating to the position of Greenland and the Danish merchant vessels in American ports.

Miller, Kenneth E. **Government and Politics in Denmark.** Boston: Houghton, 1968, 308 p.
  A well-written and informative introduction to the contemporary politics of Denmark.

Munch, Peter. **Erindringer.** Copenhagen: Nyt Nordisk Forlag, 1959-67, 8 v.
  The memoirs of a leading Danish statesman through the period of two world wars.

Nissen, Henrik and Poulsen, Henning. **På dansk friheds grund: Dansk Ungdomssamvirke og De ældres Råd 1940-1945.** Copenhagen: Gyldendal, 1963, 328 p.
  A historical study of the efforts of Danish youth organizations to promote support for Danish government during the German occupation.

Poulsen, Henning. **Besættelsesmagten og de danske nazister: det politiske forhold mellem tyske myndigheder og nazistiske kreds i Danmark 1940-1943.** Copenhagen: Gyldendal, 1970, 499 p.
  A monograph on the relations between the German occupation authorities in Denmark and Danish supporters of the Nazi movement.

Rasmussen, Erik. **Velfærdsstaten på vej, 1913-1939.** Copenhagen: Politikens Forlag, 1971, 512 p.
  A general treatment of Danish history during the period from 1913 to 1939. Published as volume 13 of "Danmarks historie," edited by John Danstrup and Hal Koch.

Sjøqvist, Viggo. **Danmarks udenrigspolitik 1933-1940.** Copenhagen: Gyldendal, 1966, 417 p.
  A historical study of Danish foreign policy during the years from 1933 to 1940.

Sørensen, Max. **Statsforfatningsret.** Copenhagen: Juristforbundets Forlag, 1969, 431 p.
  A major treatise on the Danish constitution.

Svensson, Bjørn. **Derfor gik det sådan 9. april.** Copenhagen: Branner & Koch, 1965, 249 p.
  A careful analysis of the events leading to the German occupation of Denmark on April 9, 1940.

Thomsen, Niels. **Dagbladskonkurrencen 1870-1970: politik, journalistik og økonomi i dansk dagspresses strukturudvikling.** Copenhagen: Gad, 1972, 2 v.
  An analysis of the Danish press during the last hundred years.

Thygesen, Niels. **The Sources and the Impact of Monetary Changes: An Empirical Study of Danish Experiences 1951-1968.** Copenhagen: Gad, 1971, 332 p.
  A technical study of Danish financial policies.

Trommer, Aage. **Jernbanesabotagen i Danmark under den anden verdenskrig: en krigshistorisk undersøgelse.** Odense: Odense Universitetsforlag, 1971, 323 p.
  A study of sabotage against the Danish railway system during the Second World War.

Wendt, Frantz. **Besættelse og atomtid, 1939-1970.** Copenhagen: Politikens Forlag, 1972, 547 p.
A general treatment of Danish history during the period from 1939 to 1970. Published as volume 14 of "Danmarks historie," edited by John Danstrup and Hal Koch.

Westergård Andersen, Harald. **Dansk politik—igår og idag, 1920-1966.** Copenhagen: Fremad, 1966, 258 p.
A historical survey of Danish politics since 1920.

Yahil, Leni. **Test of a Democracy: The Rescue of Danish Jewry in World War II.** Jerusalem: The Magus Press, 1966, 316 p.
A survey of the Danish attitudes and policies towards the Jews during the German occupation.

Norway

See also Political Processes, p. 20; Labor and Labor Movements, p. 41; (Second World War) Western Europe, p. 159; Naval Operations, p. 168; (Europe) General Surveys, p. 344; Western Europe, p. 345; (Scandinavia) General, p. 441; Polar Regions, p. 848.

Åmlid, Johanne. **Ut av kurs: en førstehånds beretning fra Arbeiderpartiets lukkede landsmøte i 1949 der avgjørelsen om norsk medlemskap i NATO i realiteten ble tatt.** Oslo: Pax, 1966, 126 p.
A first-hand report from the Labor Party's closed meeting in 1949, the result of which was Norway's participation in NATO. The author was against it.

Andenæs, Johannes and Others. **Norway and the Second World War.** Oslo: Tanum, 1966, 167 p.
A scholarly inquiry into the history of Norway during World War II, with emphasis on the story of collaboration with the enemy.

Andreassen, Tormod. **Forsvarets virkinger på norsk økonomi.** Oslo: Statistisk sentralbyrå, 1972, 141 p.
A study of the impact of defense expenditures on the Norwegian economy.

Benum, Edgeir. **Maktsentra og opposisjon: Spaniasaken i Norge 1946 og 1947.** Oslo: Universitetsforlaget, 1969, 151 p.
A study of Norway's diplomatic relations with Spain in the years from 1946 to 1947.

Berggrav, Eivind Josef. **Front—fangenskap—flukt, 1942-1945.** Oslo: Land og kirke, 1966, 162 p.
Memoirs covering the period of World War II by a prominent Norwegian clergyman.

Bjerke, Juul. **Langtidslinjer i norsk økonomi 1865-1960. Trends in Norwegian Economy, 1865-1960.** Oslo: Statistisk sentralbyrå, 1966, 152 p.
A useful survey of Norwegian economic development.

Børde, Ketil. **Norge i FN 1945-1970.** Oslo: Aschehoug, 1970, 168 p.
A summary of Norwegian opinions on international problems as expressed in the United Nations.

Bratland, Per. **Hvem har makt i Norge?** Oslo: Aschehoug, 1965, 131 p.
A study of decision-making in Norway.

Brundtland, Arne Olav. **Sikkerhetspolitisk omprøving? En analyse av norske sikkerhetsproblemer og utviklingen i Europa.** Oslo: NUPI, 1968, 254 p.
A scholarly analysis of Norwegian security problems.

Burgess, Philip M. **Elite Images and Foreign Policy Outcomes: A Study of Norway.** Columbus: Ohio State University Press, 1968, 179 p.
A study of Norway's shift from traditional neutrality to membership in NATO, with special emphasis on the changing élite conceptions of the country's strategic interests.

Dahl, Hans Fredrik. **Norge mellom krigene: det norske samfunn i krise og konflikt 1918-1940.** Oslo: Pax, 1971, 124 p.
A social and political analysis of Norway between the two world wars.

Eckstein, Harry Horace. **Division and Cohesion in Democracy: A Study of Norway.** Princeton: Princeton University Press, 1966, 293 p.
An examination, by a Princeton political scientist, designed as a case study in the area of comparative politics.

Eriksen, Knut Einar. **DNA og NATO: en redegjørelse for debatten og vedtakene i det Norske arbeiderparti 1948-49.** Oslo: Gyldendal, 1972, 328 p.
A survey of the debates and decisions in the Labor Party that lead to Norway's membership in NATO.

Eriksen, Knut Einar and Lundestad, Geir, *comps.* **Norsk utenrikspolitikk.** Oslo: Universitetsforlaget, 1972, 236 p.
Documents concerning Norway's role in Nordic and European coöperation.

Fostervoll, Kåre. **Norges sosialdemokratiske arbeidarparti, 1921-1927.** Oslo: Samlaget, 1969, 147 p.
The story of the Norwegian Social Democratic Labor Party, founded in 1921 in protest against the revolutionary leadership of the Labor Party.

Frydenlund, Knut. **Norsk utenrikspolitikk i etterkrigstidens internasjonale samarbeid.** Oslo: NUPI, 1966, 147 p.
A short study of Norwegian postwar foreign policy, written by a Norwegian Minister of Foreign Affairs.

Furre, Berge. **Norsk historie, 1905-1940.** Oslo: Samlaget, 1971, 342 p.
A survey of Norwegian history from 1905 to 1940.

Gabrielsen, Bjørn Vidar. **Menn og politikk: Senterpartiet 1920-1970.** Oslo: Aschehoug, 1970, 221 p.
The story of the old Peasants Party which in 1959 changed its name to Center Party.

Garbo, Gunnar. **I brennpunktet: innlegg om utenrikspolitikk.** Oslo: Epoke, 1969, 121 p.
The opinions of a prominent member of the Liberal Party on foreign policy.

Gerhardsen, Einar. **Erindringer.** Oslo: Tiden, 1970—.
Memoirs by a Norwegian statesman who was his country's Prime Minister from 1945 to 1951 and from 1955 to 1965. Through 1972 three of the planned four volumes have been published.

Hambro, Carl Joachim. **Dagboksblade og aktstykker til regjeringsdannelsen i 1945.** Oslo: Gyldendal, 1964, 119 p.
Diaries and documents on the establishment of the first post-World War II government, by a former president of the *Storting*.

Hayes, Paul M. **Quisling: The Career and Political Ideas of Vidkun Quisling, 1887-1945.** Bloomington: Indiana University Press, 1972, 368 p.
A scholarly and judicious biography of a complicated traitor, based on some new evidence.

Heradstveit, Per Øyvind, *ed.* **Partiene og utenrikspolitikken.** Oslo: Aschehoug, 1965, 90 p.
A collection of articles by prominent members of different political parties in Norway on their concepts of foreign policy.

Hewins, Ralph. **Quisling: Prophet without Honour.** New York: Day, 1966, 384 p.
A British journalist's effort to rehabilitate in some measure a man whose name became an international epithet.

Holst, Johan Jørgen. **Norsk sikkerhetspolitikk i strategisk perspektiv.** Oslo: NUPI, 1967, 2 v.
A scholarly analysis, with documentation, of Norway's security problems.

Ingebrigtsen, Arnulf. **De som styrer Norge.** Oslo: Cappelen, 1968, 259 p.
An attempt to discover the real decision-makers in Norway.

Koritzinsky, Theo. **Velgere, partier og utenrikspolitikk: analyse av norske holdninger 1945-1970.** Oslo: Pax, 1970, 182 p.
A survey of Norwegian conceptions of foreign policy.

Larssen, Olav. **Sti gjennom ulendt terreng: læretid, partistrid, ny vekst.** Oslo: Aschehoug, 1969, 214 p.

——. **Mennesker ved skillevei.** Oslo: Aschehoug, 1971, 186 p.
Memoirs by a prominent member of the Labor Party who was the editor of the party's newspaper from 1949 to 1963.

Lie, Trygve. **Oslo—Moskva—London.** Oslo: Tiden, 1968, 183 p.
A volume of memoirs by the Norwegian Foreign Minister during World War II who subsequently became the Secretary-General of the United Nations.

Lindboe, Asbjørn. **Fra de urolige tredveårene: dagboksnedtegnelser og kommentarer.** Oslo: Tanum, 1965, 262 p.
Diaries and commentaries of the Minister of Justice from 1931 to 1935, the time of the dispute over the sovereignty of East Greenland.

Løchen, Einar. **Norway in European and Atlantic Co-operation.** Oslo: Universitetsforlaget, 1964, 88 p.
A study of Norway's membership in international organizations.

Loock, Hans-Dietrich. **Quisling, Rosenberg und Terboven.** Stuttgart: Deutsche Verlags-Anstalt, 1970, 587 p.
An analysis of the abortive attempt to establish a national socialist regime in Norway. Using much new material, a German historian portrays the lives of Quisling and of his German partners against the background of political and military conditions. A controversial study of absorbing interest.

Lyng, John. **Brytningsår: erindringer.** Oslo: Cappelen, 1972–.
Memoirs by a Conservative statesman who had served as his country's Prime Minister for a few weeks in 1963 and as Foreign Minister from 1965 to 1970. Through 1973 two volumes have been published.

Milward, Alan Steele. **The Fascist Economy in Norway.** New York: Oxford University Press, 1972, 317 p.
Using new archival material, a leading scholar inquires into the character and impact of German economic policy in Norway from 1940 to 1945, with interesting observations on what the Norwegian example shows about the nature of fascism.

Nordahl, Konrad. **Med LO for friheten.** Oslo: Tiden, 1969, 245 p.
Memoirs by a prominent member of the Labor Party, for many years chairman of the Norwegian Trade Union.

Norges økonomi etter krigen. Oslo: Aschehoug (for the Statistisk sentralbyrå), 1965, 437 p.
A very informative survey of economic developments in post-World War II Norway. There is an English summary.

Ørvik, Nils. **Alternativer for sikkerhet.** Oslo: Mortensen, 1970, 264 p.
A discussion of the Norwegian security alternatives: NATO, Nordic defense coöperation and European defense coöperation in EEC.

Ørvik, Nils, ed. **Fears and Expectations: Norwegian Attitudes toward European Integration.** Oslo: Universitetsforlaget, 1972, 370 p.
Norway's decision not to join the European Economic Community can be better understood after reading this book. The authors have analyzed the Norwegian debate on this question, giving particular attention to the attitudes of élites toward loss of sovereignty and political integration.

Paulsen, Helge, ed. **Norge og den 2. verdenskrig: mellom nøytrale og allierte.** Oslo: Universitetsforlaget, 1968, 299 p.
A study of Norway's relations with the Allies and the neutrals during World War II.

Popperwell, Ronald G. **Norway.** New York: Praeger, 1972, 335 p.
A general survey of Norwegian history, published in "Nations of the Modern World" series. Only about one-fifth of the text covers the post-World War II years.

Skodvin, Magne. **Norden eller NATO? Utenriksdepartementet og allianse-spørsmålet 1947–1949.** Oslo: Universitetsforlaget, 1971, 354 p.
Should Norway prefer Nordic coöperation or NATO? A scholarly interpretation of documents from the Foreign Office of Norway.

Valen, Henry and Katz, Daniel. **Political Parties in Norway: A Community Study.** Oslo: Universitetsforlaget; London: Tavistock Publications, 1964, 383 p.
A Norwegian and an American political scientist join in a broadly gauged study of the structure and functioning of Norwegian parties, based largely on research of the Stavanger region in the general election of 1957.

Wyller, Thomas Christian. **Frigjøringspolitikk: regjeringsskiftet sommeren 1945.** Oslo: Universitetsforlaget, 1963, 219 p.
A history of the political events in Norway from May 8 to June 23, 1945, and of the establishment of the new Norwegian government.

Sweden

See also Comparative Government, p. 18; Political Processes, p. 20; Labor and Labor Movements, p. 41; General Economic Conditions and Tendencies, p. 49: (Europe) General Surveys, p. 344; Western Europe, p. 345; (Scandinavia) General, p. 441; (Finland) Foreign Relations, p. 452.

Andreen, Per G. **De mörka åren: perspektiv på svensk utrikespolitik våren 1940-nyåret 1942.** Stockholm: Norstedt & Söner, 1971, 200 p.
 A detailed account of important events in Swedish foreign policy from 1940 to 1942, the period of coalition government. Based on diaries and memoirs, notably those of Gösta Bagge, leader of the Conservative Party.

Andrén, Nils Bertel Einar. **Power-Balance and Non-Alignment: A Perspective on Swedish Foreign Policy.** Stockholm: Almqvist & Wiksell, 1967, 212 p.
 A study, supplemented with documents, of Swedish foreign policy since World War II.

Andrén, Nils Bertel Einar. **Svensk statskunskap.** Stockholm: Utbildningsförlaget, 5th rev. ed., 1972, 397 p.
 A thorough introduction to Swedish constitution and political institutions, by a prominent Swedish scholar of political science.

Andrén, Nils Bertel Einar and Landqvist, Åke. **Svensk utrikespolitik efter 1945.** Stockholm: Almqvist & Wiksell, 1965, 294 p.
 A scholarly study, including documents, of Swedish foreign policy since 1945.

Arpi, Gunnar. **Sveriges nutida näringsliv.** Stockholm: P. A. Norstedt & Söner, 7th rev. ed., 1971, 207 p.
 A classic description of Sweden's contemporary trade and economy, with emphasis on Sweden's international economic profile and Sweden's part in world production.

Assarson, Vilhelm. **I skuggan av Stalin.** Stockholm: Bonniers, 1963, 237 p.
 Reminiscences of the Swedish envoy in Moscow from 1940 to 1943.

Back, Pär-Erik. **Det svenska partiväsendet.** Stockholm: Almqvist & Wiksell, 3rd rev. ed., 1972, 171 p.
 A survey of the Swedish party system, written by a professor of political science.

Bergström, Villy. **Den ekonomiska politiken i Sverige och dess verkningar.** Stockholm: Almqvist & Wiksell, 1969, 151 p.
 A study of Swedish monetary and fiscal policies, published under the auspices of the Industrial Research Association. The main part deals with the inter-war and postwar periods.

Björkman, Leif. **Sverige inför Operation Barbarossa: svensk neutralitetspolitik 1940–41.** Stockholm: Almänna förlaget, 1971, 519 p.
 A study of the 1940–41 foreign policy debate in the Swedish government, parliament, political parties and the Military Council. Part I of the research project: "Sweden during the Second World War."

Board, Joseph B., Jr. **The Government and Politics of Sweden.** Boston: Houghton, 1970, 270 p.
 A well-documented introduction to Swedish politics.

Boheman, Erik. **På vakt.** Stockholm: Norstedt & Söner, 1963–64, 2 v.
 Reminiscences of a Swedish politician and diplomat, formerly Swedish envoy to Ankara, Sofia, Athens, Warsaw and Bucharest. The first part, "Från attaché till sändebud," ends in 1937, while the second, "Kabinettssekreterare under andra världskriget," covers the Second World War period when the author served as Undersecretary of State for Foreign Affairs.

Documents on Swedish Foreign Policy. Stockholm: Royal Ministry for Foreign Affairs, 1950– .
 Annual volumes of important official documents, speeches and statements and other matters of importance. The Swedish edition appears as "Utrikesfrågor: offentliga dokument m.m. rörande svenska utrikespolitiska frågor."

Elmer, Åke. **Från Fattigsverige till välfärdsstaten: sociala förhållanden och socialpolitik i Sverige under nittonhundratalet.** Stockholm: Aldus/Bonniers, 1969, 4th rev. ed., 144 p.
 As the title suggests, "From Poverty to Welfare State" deals with social conditions and

social welfare policy in Sweden during the twentieth century. The author, an associate professor in social policy, describes the development of social welfare in Sweden and analyzes contemporary social legislation.

Elvander, Nils. **Intresseorganisationerna i dagens Sverige.** Lund: Gleerup, 2d rev. ed., 1972, 346 p.
A methodical survey, based mainly on primary research, of the Swedish organizations that play an important role in Swedish state and society.

Elvander, Nils. **Svensk skattepolitik 1945-1970: en studie i partiers och organisationers funktioner.** Stockholm: Rabén & Sjögren, 1972, 405 p.
A detailed analysis of Swedish fiscal policy during the postwar period.

Erlander, Tage. **Tage Erlander 1901-1939.** Stockholm: Tiden, 1972, 320 p.
Political memoirs of one of Sweden's most prominent Social Democrats who was his country's Prime Minister from 1946 to 1969.

Ferlet, Tyra. **Miracle de la Suède: un pays pauvre devient riche.** Paris: Arthaud, 1969, 325 p.
A popular study of life in contemporary Sweden, covering various aspects from industry to nudity.

Fleisher, Frederic. **The New Sweden: The Challenge of a Disciplined Democracy.** New York: McKay, 1967, 365 p.
The lessons of contemporary Sweden in sixteen informative chapters, ranging from politics to the new morality, by an American student and long-term resident.

Grenholm, Gunvor, ed. **Den svenska historien.** Stockholm: Bonniers, 1966-68, 10 v.
An illustrated description of all phases of Swedish history and national life by a number of well-known specialists. The tenth volume, "Vår egen tid från 1920 till 1960-talet" (1968, 381 p.), covers the period from 1920 to the 1960's.

Hadenius, Stig; Molin, Björn and Wieslander, Hans. **Sverige efter 1900: en modern politisk historia.** Stockholm: Aldus/Bonniers, 4th ed., 1971, 326 p.
An analysis of the domestic political developments in Sweden during the twentieth century. The study concentrates on the political parties and the governments.

Hägglöf, Gunnar. **Möte med Europa: Paris-London-Moskva-Genève-Berlin, 1926-1940.**
Stockholm: Norstedt & Söner, 1971, 231 p.
———. **Samtida vittne, 1940-1945.** Stockholm: Norstedt & Söner, 1972, 247 p.
Memoirs of a leading Swedish diplomat who held sensitive posts in Europe during the 1930s and the Second World War. The first volume appeared in English as "Diplomat" (London: Bodley Head, 1972, 221 p.).

Höjer, Karl J. **Den svenska socialpolitiken: en översikt.** Stockholm: Norstedt & Söner, 9th rev. ed., 1969, 199 p.
A survey of the origin and development of Swedish social welfare policy. The author served for several years as head of the National Welfare Board. This revised edition has been prepared by Karl-Erik Herngård.

Lewin, Leif and Others. **The Swedish Electorate, 1887-1968.** Stockholm: Almqvist & Wiksell, 1972, 293 p.
An empirical study of the political behaviour of Sweden's electorate.

Lindbeck, Assar. **Samhällsekonomisk politik.** Stockholm: Rabén & Sjögren, 1971, 315 p.
An analysis and criticism of Sweden's economic policy and contemporary economic situation.

Lindbeck, Assar. **Svensk ekonomisk politik: problem och teorier under efterkrigstiden.** Stockholm: Aldus/Bonniers, 2d ed., 1969, 233 p.
The author, a prominent economist, discusses economic policies and problems in Sweden during the postwar period.

Lundberg, Erik and Others. **Svensk finanspolitik i teori och praktik.** Stockholm: Aldus/Bonniers, 1971, 457 p.
The aim of this substantial study, prepared under the auspices of the Business Research Institute of the Stockholm School of Economics, is to analyze Swedish finances during the postwar period.

Norgren, Marie and Norgren, Christian. **Svensk industri: struktur och omvandling.** Stockholm: Rabén & Sjögren, 1970, 187 p.
A description of contemporary Swedish industry.

Nyman, Olle. **Ny författning: frågeställningar i reformdiskussion.** Stockholm: Aldus/Bonniers, 1969, 240 p.
A summary of and comments on the Swedish debate concerning a new constitution and the role of monarchy, with emphasis on the period since 1954 when a state committee for the investigation of the constitution was established.

Oakley, Stewart. **A Short History of Sweden.** New York: Praeger, 1966, 292 p.
An introduction for the general reader.

Ohlin, Bertil Gotthard. **Memoarer: ung man blir politiker.** Stockholm: Bonniers, 1972, 356 p.
In the first volume of his memoirs, the author, a prominent economist, describes his political career up to 1945. In 1944 Ohlin became leader of the Liberal Party as well as Secretary of Commerce in the coalition government.

Ruin, Olof. **Mellan samlingsregering och tvåpartisystem: den svenska regeringsfrågan 1945-1960.** Stockholm: Bonniers, 1968, 398 p.
An account of Swedish party politics during the period from 1945 to 1960.

Schnitzer, Martin. **The Economy of Sweden.** New York: Praeger, 1970, 252 p.
A study, based on a first-hand knowledge of the country, of how Sweden has combined many of the institutions of capitalism and socialism into a highly developed economic and political system.

Södersten, Bo, *ed*. **Svensk ekonomi.** Stockholm: Rabén & Sjögren, 1970, 368 p.
Essays by a number of Swedish economists on the structure and development of Swedish economy.

Tomasson, Richard F. **Sweden: Prototype of Modern Society.** New York: Random House, 1970, 302 p.
An American sociologist presents a useful survey of Sweden.

Uhlin, Åke. **Februarikrisen 1942: svensk säkerhetspolitik och militär planering 1941-1942.** Stockholm: Allmänna förlaget, 1972, 264 p.
This volume in the research project "Sweden during the Second World War" analyzes Swedish security policies and military preparations.

Undén, Östen. **Tankar om utrikespolitik.** Stockholm: Rabén & Sjögren, 1963, 148 p.
Selected speeches by a former Foreign Minister on Sweden's international relations after the Second World War.

Wahlbäck, Krister. **Finlandsfrågan i svensk politik 1937-40.** Stockholm: Norstedt, 1964, 464 p.
A detailed doctoral dissertation of the Finnish issue in Swedish politics, 1937-40.

Westerlind, Erik and Beckman, Rune. **Sveriges ekonomi: struktur och utvecklingstendenser.** Stockholm: Prisma, 6th rev. ed., 1968, 128 p.
A study of the main features of Swedish economic structure and development.

Whiteside, Thomas. **An Agent in Place: The Wennerström Affair.** New York: Viking, 1966, 150 p.
The story of the career of Colonel Stig Wennerström, the one-time Swedish air attaché in Washington, who after his arrest in 1963 confessed that he had transmitted highly important NATO and Swedish military secrets to the Russians.

Finland

General

See also Political Processes, p. 20; (Europe) General Surveys, p. 344; Western Europe, p. 345; (Scandinavia) General, p. 441; (Union of Soviet Socialist Republics) Memoirs and Biographies, p. 533.

Ahtokari, Reijo. **Punainen Valpo.** Helsinki: Otava, 1969, 220 p.
An account of the role of the Finnish secret police in domestic politics during the postwar years from 1944 to 1948.

Blomstedt, Yrjö. **K. J. Ståhlberg: valtiomieselämäkerta.** Helsinki: Otava, 1969, 549 p.
    A solid biography of K. J. Ståhlberg, Finland's first President.

Borg, Olavi. **Suomen puolueideologiat: periaateohjelmien sisältöanalyyttinen vertailu sekä katsaus niiden historialliseen taustaan ja syntyprosessiin.** Porvoo: Söderström, 1964, 317 p.
    A useful guide to Finnish political parties and their programs.

Dey, Reinhold. **Finnland heute: ein Land bewältigt seine Gegenwart.** Düsseldorf: Econ-Verlag, 1965, 296 p.
    A general survey of postwar Finland by a German journalist who knows the country well.

Hakalehto, Ilkka. **Suomen Kommunistinen Puolue ja sen vaikutus poliittiseen ja ammatilliseen työväenliikkeeseen 1918-1928.** Porvoo: Söderström, 1966, 324 p.
    A serious attempt to analyze communism in Finland in the years from 1918 to 1928. The author has based his research on material found in the archives of the Finnish State Police.

Hall, Wendy. **The Finns and Their Country.** New York: Eriksson, 1968, 224 p.
    An informal but well-informed general survey of the Finns and Finland.

Heikkilä, Toivo. **Paasikivi peräsimessä.** Helsinki: Otava, 1965, 365 p.
    Memoirs of Ambassador Toivo Heikkilä, secretary to J. K. Paasikivi and Mauno Pekkala, two Prime Ministers of Finland.

Hodgson, John Helms. **Communism in Finland: A History and Interpretation.** Princeton: Princeton University Press, 1967, 261 p.
    A comprehensive history of the Finnish Communist Party.

Hulkko, Jouko and Others, eds. **Finland 1917-1967: An Assessment of Independence.** Helsinki: Kirjayhtymä, 1967, 171 p.
    A collection of essays by leading Finnish scholars and diplomats on Finnish politics and foreign policy.

Hyvämäki, Lauri. **Sinistä ja mustaa: tutkielmia Suomen oikeisto radikalismista.** Helsinki: Otava, 1971, 282 p.
    An account by a historian of the right-wing political currents in Finland during the 1920s and 1930s.

Jägerskiöld, Stig. **Den unge Mannerheim.** Helsinki: Schildt, 1964, 349 p.
———. **Gustaf Mannerheim 1906-1917.** Helsinki: Schildt, 1965, 357 p.
———. **Gustaf Mannerheim 1918.** Helsinki: Schildt, 1967, 410 p.
———. **Riksföreståndaren Gustaf Mannerheim 1919.** Helsinki: Schildt, 1969, 334 p.
———. **Mannerheim mellan världskrigen.** Helsinki: Schildt, 1972, 325 p.
    A massive and well-documented biography of Marshal Mannerheim.

Junnila, Tuure. **Freiheit im Vorfeld: Finnlands Kampf um Sicherheit und Neutralität.** Vienna: Europa Verlag, 1967, 129 p.
    A Finnish conservative politician surveys the development of Finland since 1944. The original edition appeared as "Suomen taistelu turvallisuudestaan ja puolueettomuudestaan" (Porvoo: Söderström, 1964, 153 p.).

Jutikkala, Eino Kaarlo Ilmari and Others. **Kaksi vuosikymmentä Suomen sisäpolitiikkaa 1919-1939.** Porvoo: Söderström, 1964, 228 p.
    Essays on domestic politics during the inter-war years.

Kallas, Hillar and Nickels, Sylvie, eds. **Finland: Creation and Construction.** New York: Praeger, 1968, 366 p.
    A general survey of the country, its people and culture by a number of specialists.

Kholodkovskii, V. M. **Revoliutsiia 1918 v Finliandii i germanskaia interventsiia.** Moscow: "Nauka," 1967, 387 p.
    A monograph on the Finnish Civil War in 1918 and on the role of Germany in it. The author, who has had access to Soviet archives but has not acquainted himself with material to be found in Finnish and German archives, concludes that the time has arrived in Finland for a peaceful transition to socialism.

Kivimäki, Toivo Mikael. **Suomalaisen poliitikon muistelmat.** Porvoo: Söderström, 1965, 316 p.

The engrossing and valuable memoirs of Professor Kivimäki, who served Finland in a number of high posts: Prime Minister, Minister of interior and of justice, and ambassador to Germany during the war years.

Kuusinen, Aino. **Der Gott stürzt seine Engel.** Vienna: Molden, 1972, 352 p.
Important memoirs by a former Finnish Communist. Her husband Otto Kuusinen was a Comintern functionary in the interwar period and head of the Soviet-sponsored Finnish government at the beginning of World War II.

Linkomies, Edwin. **Vaikea aika: Suomen pääministerinä sotavuosina 1943-44.** Helsinki: Otava, 1970, 445 p.
The memoirs of Finland's wartime premier Edwin Linkomies, written in prison but withheld from publication until 1970.

Mead, William Richard. **Finland.** New York: Praeger, 1968, 256 p.
A concise, knowledgeable survey, in part historical, of the land and its people.

Nousiainen, Jaakko. **The Finnish Political System.** Cambridge: Harvard University Press, 1971, 454 p.
A very solid work, originally written as an introduction for Finnish students to their system of government and politics. The author is a professor of political science at the University of Turku. The Finnish original appeared as "Suomen poliittinen järjestelmä" (Porvoo: Söderström, 3rd rev. ed., 1967, 501 p.).

Pesonen, Pertti. **An Election in Finland.** New Haven: Yale University Press, 1968, 416 p.
An intensive and skillful study of party activities and voting behavior in the Finnish electoral process.

Puntila, Lauri Aadolf. **Suomen poliittinen historia 1809-1966.** Helsinki: Otava, 5th rev. ed., 1971, 260 p.
An excellent survey of Finnish political developments, written by one of the country's leading political historians. The French edition, translated from an earlier Finnish edition, appeared as "Histoire politique de la Finlande de 1809 à 1955" (Neuchâtel: Éditions de la Baconnière, 1966, 286 p.).

Rintala, Marvin. **Four Finns: Political Profiles.** Berkeley: University of California Press, 1969, 120 p.
A study of the political careers of Gustaf Mannerheim, Väinö Tanner, K. J. Ståhlberg and J. K. Paasikivi. Particular attention is devoted to their successes, or failures, in reaching an accommodation with the Soviet Union.

Screen, J.E.O. **Mannerheim: The Years of Preparation.** London: C. Hurst, 1970, 158 p.
The author argues that Mannerheim's service in Tsarist Russia influenced his outlook and policies in independent Finland.

Simonen, Seppo. **Paluu Karjalaan: palautetun alueen historiaa, 1941-1944.** Helsinki: Otava, 1965, 337 p.
A detailed study of the Karelian refugees' return to their homes for three years of valiant reconstruction work, followed by a second flight, 1941-44.

Toivonen, Anna Leena. **Etelä-Pohjanmaan valtamerentakainen siirtolaisuus, 1867-1930.** Helsinki: Suomen Historiallinen Seura, 1963, 294 p.
An analysis of the forces and circumstances behind Finnish emigration to the United States and Canada.

Upton, Anthony Frederick. **Finland in Crisis, 1940-1941: A Study in Small-Power Politics.** Ithaca: Cornell University Press, 1965, 318 p.
An able original study of Finnish affairs during the interlude between the end of the Winter War of 1939-40 and the renewal of hostilities in June 1941.

Wagner, Ulrich. **Finnlands Kommunisten.** Stuttgart: Kohlhammer, 1971, 198 p.
A welcome study of the recent history of the Finnish Communist Party and the effort to recreate, in the second half of the 1960s, a popular front.

Warner, Oliver. **Marshal Mannerheim and the Finns.** Helsinki: Otava, 1967, 232 p.
An admiring biography by a British author of the Finnish soldier and statesman who led his country's forces in the fight for independence during both world wars and who was also president of Finland from 1944 to 1946.

Wuorinen, John Henry. **A History of Finland.** New York: Columbia University Press, (for the American-Scandinavian Foundation), 1965, 548 p.
A broad-gauge history of Finland and its people by a leading American student of the country. About three-fifths of the volume deals with Finnish history since independence.

Foreign Relations

See also Sweden, p. 447; (Baltic States) General, p. 455; Estonia, p. 456; (Union of Soviet Socialist Republics) Foreign Policy, p. 550.

Apunen, Osmo. **Kansallinen realismi ja puolueettomuus Suomen ulkopoliittisina valintoina: tutkimus Suomen ulkopoliittisen toimintaohjelman rakenteesta ja funktioista I Paasikiven linja.** Tampere: Tampereen Yliopisto, 1972, 268 p.
A study of Finnish foreign policy in the immediate aftermath of World War II.

Apunen, Osmo. **Suomi keisarillisen Saksan politiikassa 1914-1915.** Helsinki: Tammi, 1968, 307 p.
A monograph on the German policies toward Finland at the beginning of World War I.

Aspelmeier, Karl Friedrich Dieter. **Deutschland und Finnland während der beiden Weltkriege.** Hamburg-Volksdorf: Von der Ropp (for the Finnlandinstitut in Köln), 1967, 178 p.
A survey of German-Finnish relations during both world wars.

Barros, James. **The Åland Islands Question: Its Settlement by the League of Nations.** New Haven: Yale University Press, 1968, 362 p.
A comprehensive study of the Finnish-Swedish conflict over the Åland Islands in the immediate aftermath of World War I.

Blinnikka, Aulis. **Valvontakomission aika.** Helsinki: Söderström, 1969, 194 p.
A journalist's account of the activities of the Allied Control Commission in Finland from 1944 to 1947.

Gripenberg, Georg A. **Finland and the Great Powers: Memoirs of a Diplomat.** Lincoln: University of Nebraska Press, 1965, 380 p.
The diplomatic memoirs of Finland's envoy to London, the Vatican and Stockholm during the Second World War. The Swedish original was entitled "Diplomatisk vardag" (Helsinki: Söderström, 1964, 239 p.).

Halsti, Wolfgang Hallsten. **Me, Venäjä ja muut.** Helsinki: Otava, 1969, 313 p.
The first full-length inquiry into the meaning of the Finnish-Soviet Friendship and Mutual Assistance Treaty, by a knowledgeable military writer.

Jakobson, Max. **Finnish Neutrality: A Study of Finnish Foreign Policy since the Second World War.** New York: Praeger, 1969, 116 p.
Informative essays on Finnish foreign policy since the Second World War. The author was Finland's Ambassador to the United Nations from 1965 to 1972.

Jalanti, Heikki. **La Finlande dans l'étau germano-soviétique, 1940-1941.** Neuchâtel: Éditions de la Baconnière, 1966, 380 p.
A well-documented account of Finland's relations with Germany and the Soviet Union in the uneasy period between March 1940, the end of the Winter War, and June 1941, when the Germans invaded the Soviet Union.

Käkönen, Uljas Antero. **Moskovassa ja Arkangelissa talvella 1941.** Helsinki: Otava, 1969, 142 p.

———. **Sotilasasiamiehenä Moskovassa 1939.** Helsinki: Otava, 1966, 222 p.
Reminiscences of a Finnish military attaché in Moscow at the beginning of World War II.

Kalela, Jorma. **Grannar på skilda vägar: det finländsk-svenska samarbetet i den finländska och svenska utrikespolitiken 1921-1923.** Helsinki: The Finnish Historical Society, 1971, 313 p.
A study of Finnish-Swedish relations from 1921 to 1923.

Korhonen, Keijo. **Suomi neuvostodiplomatiassa: Tartosta talvisotaan 1920-1939.** Lahti: Tammi, 1966-71, 2 v.
A wide-ranging study of Finnish-Soviet relations in the inter-war period.

Krosby, Hans Peter. **Finland, Germany, and the Soviet Union, 1940-1941: The Petsamo Dispute.** Madison: University of Wisconsin Press, 1968, 276 p.
A careful and thorough investigation of the Petsamo nickel deposits as a crucial issue in the tense relations between Finland, the Soviet Union and Germany in the period between the Winter War and the renewal of hostilities in 1941.

Krosby, Hans Peter. **Suomen valinta 1941.** Helsinki: Kirjayhtymä, 1967, 410 p.
A well-documented study dealing with the Finnish-German relations in 1940-41.

Nevakivi, Jukka. **Apu jota ei pyydetty: liittoutuneet ja Suomen talvisota, 1939-1940.** Helsinki: Tammi, 1972, 305 p.
The author of this solid study argues that the Western Allies offered military aid to Finland in early 1940 in order to establish their presence in Scandinavia prior to the Germans, and that Finland's refusal of this offer prevented the spread of World War II to Sweden.

Ørvik, Nils. **Sicherheit auf finnisch: Finnland und die Sowjetunion.** Stuttgart: Seewald, 1972, 210 p.
A probing study of the interaction of Finland's neutrality and its Treaty of Friendship and Coöperation with the Soviet Union, which details the effects on Finland's security and defense, economic relations and domestic politics as well as the implications for Scandinavia and other European countries.

Paasikivi, Juho Kusti. **Am Rande der Supermacht: Behauptung durch Diplomatie.** Hamburg: Holsten, 1972, 442 p.
The German edition of the important memoirs of the late Prime Minister and President of Finland, dealing primarily with Finnish-Russian relations, was edited by Gösta von Uexküll. The Finnish original appeared as "Toimintani Moskovassa ja Suomessa 1939-41" (Helsinki: Söderström, 1958, 2 v.).

Paasivirta, Juhani. **L'Administration des affaires étrangères et la politique extérieure de la Finlande depuis le début de l'indépendance nationale en 1917 jusqu'à la guerre russo-finlandaise de 1939-40.** Turku: Turun Yliopisto, 1966, 207 p.
A study of the organization and performance of the Finnish foreign service in the period from 1917 to 1940.

Paasivirta, Juhani. **The Victors in World War I and Finland: Finland's Relations with the British, French and United States Governments in 1918-1919.** Helsinki: Finnish Historical Society, 1965, 198 p.
A solid study originally published as "Ensimmäisen maailmansodan voittajat ja Suomi: Englannin, Yhdysvaltain ja Ranskan sekä Suomen suhteita vv. 1918-1919" (Porvoo: Söderström, 1961, 270 p.).

Polvinen, Tuomo. **Finland i stormaktspolitiken 1941-1944: bakgrunden till fortsättningskriget.** Helsinki: Schildt, 1969, 281 p.
An investigation of the Finnish problem in Great Power politics during World War II. The Finnish original appeared as "Suomi suurvaltojen politiikassa, 1941-1944; jatkosodan tausta" (Helsinki: Söderström, 1964, 330 p.).

Polvinen, Tuomo. **Suomi suurvaltojen politiikassa, 1941-1944.** Helsinki: Söderström, 1964, 330 p.
A valuable monograph on Finland's foreign relations during the Continuation War, 1941-44.

Polvinen, Tuomo. **Venäjän vallankumous ja Suomi 1917-1920.** Helsinki: Söderström, 1967-71, 2 v.
A study of Finnish-Russian relations from 1917 to 1920.

Väyrynen, Raimo. **Conflicts in Finnish-Soviet Relations: Three Comparative Case Studies.** Tampere: University of Tampere, 1972, 270 p.
An investigation of the conflict factors in Finnish-Soviet relations in 1948-49, 1958-59 and 1961-62.

Wuorimaa, Aarne. **Lähettiläänä Hitlerin Saksassa.** Helsinki: Otava, 1967, 208 p.
An account of a Finnish diplomat's seven-year service in Hitler's Germany.

Military Issues

See also (Second World War) Military Operations, p. 156.

Chew, Allen F. **The White Death.** East Lansing: Michigan State University Press, 1971, 313 p.
A historian reviews the Soviet-Finnish Winter War and finds the reality to have been nearly as heroic and remarkable as described in the myths that sprang up about it.

Clark, Douglas. **Three Days to Catastrophe.** London: Hammond, 1966, 228 p.
An account of how Britain and France very nearly got involved in the Finnish-Russian war of 1939-40.

Halsti, Wolfgang Hallsten. **Lapin sodassa.** Helsinki: Otava, 1972, 300 p.
A distinguished Finnish military historian presents an excellent account of the military events in Lapland during World War II.

Käkönen, Uljas Antero. **Miehityksen varalta-päämajan tiedustelua 1943-1945.** Helsinki: Otava, 1971, 250 p.
A valuable description of Finnish military operations during 1943-1945.

Mäkelä, Jukka L. **Im Rücken des Feindes: der finnische Nachrichtendienst im Krieg.** Frauenfeld: Huber, 1967, 206 p.
A brief survey of the activities of the Finnish intelligence services during World War II. The Finnish original was published as "Osku: tiedustelua ja kaukopartiointia välirauhan ja jatkosodan Ajalta" (Porvoo: Söderström, 1966, 205 p.).

Pakaslahti, Aaro. **Talvisodan poliittinen näytelmä.** Helsinki: Söderström, 1970, 340 p.
The posthumously published Winter War memoirs of the chief of the political division of Finland's Foreign Ministry.

Peltier, Marius Adolphe. **La Finlande dans la tourmente.** Paris: Éditions France-Empire, 1966, 301 p.
An account of the Winter War and its continuation in 1941-44. The author has served as French naval attaché in both Helsinki and Moscow.

Perko, Touko. **Aseveljien kuva.** Porvoo: Söderström, 1971, 257 p.
A study of the relations between Finnish and German armed forces during the war of 1941-44. There is a German summary.

Seppälä, Helge. **Taistelu Leningradista ja Suomi.** Helsinki: Söderström, 1969, 280 p.
A monograph on how Finland's political and military policies have been influenced by the adjacent Neva region. Utilizing to advantage recently published Soviet studies, the book, written by a high-ranking officer, sheds much new light, especially on Finland's role in the siege of Leningrad.

Tervasmäki, Vilho. **Eduskuntaryhmät ja maanpuolustus valtiopäivillä, 1917-1939.** Helsinki: Söderström, 1964, 356 p.
A study of how two Finnish parties, the Social Democratic and the Agrarian, changed the stands on national defense appropriations before World War II.

Tuompo, Wiljo Einar. **Päiväkirjani päämajasta 1941-1944.** Helsinki: Söderström, 1968, 305 p.
A high-ranking staff officer's diary, viewing military and political developments from within Mannerheim's headquarters during the Continuation War and throwing new light on the Finnish commander-in-chief.

Iceland

See also Western Defense; North Atlantic Treaty; Atlantic Community, p. 188; (Scandinavia) General, p. 441; Polar Regions, p. 848.

Benediktsson, Bjarni. **Land og lýdveldi.** Reykjavík: Almenna bókafélagid, 1965, 2 v.
Essays on Icelandic history, politics and foreign affairs.

Björnsson, Ólafur. **Thjódarbúskapur Íslendinga.** Reykjavík: Hladbúd, 2d ed., 1964, 423 p.
An economic survey of Iceland.

Griffiths, John Charles. **Modern Iceland.** New York: Praeger, 1969, 226 p.
An introduction to contemporary Iceland by an English writer.

Gröndal, Benedikt. **Iceland: From Neutrality to NATO Membership.** Oslo: Universitetsforlaget, 1971, 106 p.
  The author discusses Iceland's development from the policy of "eternal neutrality" adopted in 1918 to membership in the North Atlantic Treaty Organization in 1949. He maintains that Iceland is essential to the security of her fellow members of the North Atlantic Alliance.

Hansen, Haye Walter. **Island, von der Wikingerzeit bis zur Gegenwart.** Frankfurt/Main: Cate, 1965, 244 p.
  A brief but informative history and survey of Iceland.

Hansson, Ólafur. **Facts about Iceland.** Reykjavík: Bókaútgáfa Menningarsjóds, 13th ed., 1967, 72 p.
  An introduction to Iceland.

Jónsson, Agnar K. **Stjórnarrád Íslands 1904-1964.** Reykjavík: Sögufélagid, 1969, 1,046 p.
  A history of the Cabinet of Iceland from 1904 to 1964.

Magnúss, Gunnar M. **Árin, sem aldrei gleymast.** Reykjavík: Skuggsjá, 1964-65, 2 v.
  A history of Iceland during two world wars.

Stefánsson, Bernhard. **Endurminningar ritadar af honum sjálfum.** Akureyri: Kvöldvökuútgáfan, 1961-64, 2 v.
  The autobiography of a leading figure of the Progressive Party, member of Parliament for more than thirty years.

Stefánsson, Stefan Jóhann. **Minningar Stefáns Jóhanns Stefánssonar.** Reykjavík: Setberg, 1966-67, 2 v.
  The autobiography of a leader of the Labor Party who was also a member of the Parliament, a diplomat, and Prime Minister of Iceland from 1947 to 1949.

Thórarinsson, Thórarinn. **Sókn og sigrar: saga Framsóknarflokksins; fyrra bindi.** Reykjavík: Framsóknarflokkurinn, 1966, 272 p.
  The first volume of the history of the Progressive Party which was founded in 1916.

BALTIC STATES

General

See also (War) Guerrila Warfare; Armed Insurrection, p. 118; (First World War) The Conduct of the War, p. 136; Inter-War Period, p. 140; (Second World War) Diplomatic Aspects, p. 148; Military Operations, p. 156; Economic, Technical and Non-Military Aspects, p. 172; Eastern Europe and the Soviet Bloc, p. 358; Union of Soviet Socialist Republics, p. 531.

Acta Baltica: Liber Annalis Instituti Baltici, 1960/61—. Königstein im Taunus: Institutum Balticum, 1962—.
  An annual collection of articles on the recent history of the Baltic States and the current political, economic, legal and cultural problems of the Soviet Baltic republics.

Blanckenhagen, Herbert von. **Am Rande der Weltgeschichte: Erinnerungen aus Alt-Livland, 1913-1923.** Göttingen: Vandenhoeck, 1966, 363 p.
  Reminiscences on the complicated military, political and social developments in Latvia and Estonia during World War I and its aftermath. The author, a Baltic German, fought against the establishment of the independent Baltic republics and in January 1918 negotiated secretly with members of Count Mirbach's mission in Petrograd.

Grimm, Claus. **Vor den Toren Europas, 1918-1920: Geschichte der Baltischen Landeswehr.** Hamburg: Velmede, 1963, 320 p.
  A partisan history of the role of the Baltic German military units which fought against the Bolsheviks and the armies of Latvia and Estonia in the aftermath of World War I.

Hehn, Jürgen von and Others, *eds*. **Von den Baltischen Provinzen zu den Baltischen Staaten.** Marburg/Lahn: Herder-Institut (for the Baltische Historische Kommission), 1971, 341 p.
  A solid and well-documented collection of articles dealing with the political activities of Estonians, Latvians and Baltic Germans and with the policies of Great Powers in 1917-18 that led to the establishment of the independent states of Latvia and Estonia.

Loeber, Dietrich A., *ed*. **Diktierte Option: die Umsiedlung der Deutsch-Balten aus Estland und Lettland, 1939-1941.** Neumünster: Karl Wachholtz Verlag, 1972, 787 p.
A massive compilation of documents dealing with the transfer of Baltic German minorities from Latvia and Estonia to Germany and German-controlled territories in the years from 1939 to 1941. According to the editor, the resettlement was a consequence of the Nazi-Soviet agreements of 1939.

Mann, Bernhard. **Die Baltischen Länder in der deutschen Kriegszielpublizistik, 1914-1918.** Tübingen: Mohr, 1965, 161 p.
An excellent monograph describing how various German political factions and leading publicists during World War I developed their views on the future political and social order of the Baltic States.

Poska, Jüri G., *ed*. **Pro Baltica: mélanges dédiés à Kaarel R. Pusta; in memoriam.** Stockholm: Publication du Comité des Amis de K. R. Pusta, 1965, 244 p.
This *Festschrift*, honoring the Estonian diplomat Kaarel Pusta, contains articles on the foreign policy of Estonia and the Baltic States.

Rauch, Georg von. **Geschichte der Baltischen Staaten.** Stuttgart: Kohlhammer, 1970, 224 p.
A solid history of the Baltic States from the establishment of their independence in the end-phase of World War I to their occupation by the Soviets in May 1940. The author is a professor of East European history at the University of Kiel. The English translation appeared as "The Baltic States; the Years of Independence: Estonia, Latvia, Lithuania, 1917-1940" (Berkeley: University of California Press, 1974, 265 p.).

Rei, August. **The Drama of the Baltic Peoples.** Stockholm: Kirjastus Vaba Eesti, 1970, 384 p.
A survey of the history of the Baltic States in the twentieth century, emphasizing the events preceding their incorporation into the Soviet Union. The author was a prominent Estonian Social Democrat, who at various times served as the Speaker of the Estonian Constituent Assembly, Head of State, and ambassador to Moscow. There is a concluding chapter, describing developments in Estonia since 1940, by Evald Uustalu.

Sprudzs, Adolf and Rusis, Armins, *eds*. **Res Baltica.** Leyden: Sijthoff, 1968, 303 p.
Essays in English on Baltic affairs, in memory of Alfred Bilmanis, the late Latvian statesman and diplomat.

Tarulis, Albert N. **American-Baltic Relations 1918-1922: The Struggle over Recognition.** Washington: Catholic University of America Press, 1965, 386 p.
A well-documented account of the attitude of the Wilson and Harding administrations toward the Baltic States, and a detailed description of the efforts of various Baltic organizations and diplomats to obtain from Washington *de jure* recognition of the new republics.

Volkmann, Hans-Erich. **Die deutsche Baltikumpolitik zwischen Brest-Litovsk und Compiègne.** Cologne: Böhlau, 1970, 283 p.
A detailed and well-documented study of German policies toward Latvia and Estonia in the period between the signing of the treaties of Brest-Litovsk and Compiègne. The author disagrees with the well-known thesis of Fritz Fischer that German policy toward the Baltic region was completely annexationist.

Estonia

See also Eastern Europe and the Soviet Bloc, p. 358; (The Baltic States) General, p. 455; Latvia, p. 458; Union of Soviet Socialist Republics, p. 531.

Arumäe, Heino. **Za kulisami "Baltiiskogo Soiuza": iz istorii vneshnei politiki burzhuaznoi Estonii v 1920-1925 gg.** Tallinn: Kirjastus Eesti Raamat, 1966, 278 p.
A Soviet account of the Estonian foreign policy between 1920 and 1925, and of the attempts to form a Baltic Union including not only Estonia, Latvia and Lithuania, but also Finland and Poland.

Eesti nõukogude entsüklopeedia. Tallinn: Kirjastus Valgus, 1968-.
A Soviet Estonian encyclopedia containing a wealth of information on Estonian his-

tory and politics. Of the planned eight volumes, six have been published through 1974.

Estonian Official Guide: Eesti Vabariigi administratsiooni retrospektne informatsioon. Baltimore: Baltimore Estonian Society, 1972, 144 p.
This useful reference work is a partial reprint of an official directory published by the Estonian government in 1938. It contains a description of the entire structure of the Estonian governmental and administrative system in 1938, with the names of all important officials. There is also a list of important non-governmental organizations.

Küng, Andres. **Estland—en studie i imperialism.** Stockholm: Aldus/Bonniers, 1971, 243 p.
This book is based upon two visits which the author as an editor of the Swedish state radio made to Soviet Estonia in 1970. Besides conversations with the Estonian man in the street, Küng was able to interview a number of Soviet Estonian officials. The author contends that present-day Estonia is the victim of Soviet imperialism.

Laaman, Eduard. **Eesti iseseisvuse sünd.** Stockholm: Kirjastus Vaba Eesti, 2d ed., 1964, 752 p.
A classic study of the creation of an independent Estonian state in the years from 1917 to 1920.

Laretei, Heinrich. **Saatuse mängukanniks: mällu jäänud märkmeid.** Lund: Eesti Kirjanike Kooperatiiv, 1970, 264 p.
Memoirs of an Estonian diplomat and statesman. Mr. Laretei was the Estonian ambassador in the Soviet Union from 1926 to 1928, in Lithuania from 1928 to 1930, and in Sweden from 1936 until the incorporation of Estonia into the Soviet Union. As he also served as the head of the Political Department of the Estonian Ministry for Foreign Affairs from 1930 to 1933, and was the Deputy Foreign Minister from 1933 to 1936, he is able to speak authoritatively on Estonian foreign policy during these years.

Larin, Peter Artem'evich. **Estonskii narod v Velikoi otechestvennoi voine, 1941-1945.** Tallinn: Akademiia Nauk Estonskoi SSR, 1964, 351 p.
The story of Estonian military units which were formed in the Red Army and which fought in Estonia against the Germans during World War II. The emphasis is on the formation of the 8th Estonian Rifle Corps in 1942 and the creation of a cadre of Communist Party members in its ranks.

Lebbin, H.-A. **Sotsiaaldemokratismi pankrot Eestis.** Tallinn: Kirjastus Eesti Raamat, 1970, 449 p.
A thoroughly documented Soviet study of the Estonian Social Democratic Worker's Party during the inter-war period.

Lundborg, Einar Paul Albert Muni. **Soomusautoga Eesti vabadussõjas: minu rindeelamusi 1919-1920.** Lund: Eesti Kirjanike Kooperatiiv, 1968, 279 p.
Reminiscences from the Estonian War of Independence in 1919-1920, by a Danish volunteer officer.

Maamägi, V. and Others, eds. **Eesti NSV ajalugu, III.** Tallinn: Kirjastus Eesti Raamat, 1971, 754 p.
A Soviet interpretation of the period of Estonian independence and the developments in Estonia during World War II. Published as the concluding volume of a general history of Estonia.

Maasing, Richard and Others, eds. **Eesti saatusaastad, 1945-60.** Stockholm: Kirjastus EMP, 1963-72, 6 v.
This is the continuation of the ten-volume work on Estonia during the Second World War published in Sweden from 1954 to 1962 ("Eesti Riik ja rahvas teises maailmasõjas"). The main subjects covered are the Estonian emigré activities in the early postwar period in Western Europe and conditions in Soviet Estonia after 1945. The articles on Soviet Estonia are extremely critical of Soviet policies.

Mägi, Artur. **Das Staatsleben Estlands während seiner Selbständigkeit; I: Das Regierungssytem.** Uppsala: Almqvist & Wiksells, 1967, 327 p.
The best study of the Estonian political system during the period of Estonian independence.

Nodel, Emanuel. **Estonia: Nation on the Anvil.** New York: Bookman Associates, 1963, 207 p.
A general history of Estonia during the last 100 years.

Panksejev, A. and Pesti, M., eds. **Ülevaade Eestimaa Kommunistliku Partei ajaloost; II: 1920-1940.** Tallinn: Eesti Riiklik Kirjastus, 1963, 406 p.
An official history of the Estonian Communist Party during the period of Estonian independence.

Piip, Ants. **Tormine aasta: ülevaade Eesti välispoliitika esiajast 1917-1918. aastal dokumentides ja mälestusis.** Örebro (Sweden): Kirjastus Vaba Eesti, 2d ed., 1966, 400 p.
An important memoir, supplemented with documents, dealing with the efforts of Estonian statesmen and diplomats in 1917-1918 to secure recognition for an independent Estonia.

Pusta, Kaarel R. **Saadiku päevik, I.** New York: Kirjastus Kultuur, 1964, 312 p.
Memoirs of an Estonian diplomat who was a member of the Estonian delegation at the Versailles Peace Conference and a long-time ambassador to France.

Siilivask, Karl. **Veebruarist oktoobrini.** Tallinn: Kirjastus Eesti Raamat, 1972, 498 p.
A well-documented Soviet study dealing with events in Estonia from February to October 1917. While stress is laid on the activities of Estonian Bolsheviks, some attention is paid to the activities of non-Bolshevik Estonian political groups.

Tomingas, William. **Mälestused.** Toronto: Oma Press, 1970, 342 p.
These memoirs by an Estonian officer and government official deal with the period from 1917 to 1920. Tomingas served as a secretary at the Tartu peace negotiations between the Estonian delegation headed by J. Poska and the Soviet delegation led by A. Joffe. The conference resulted in a peace treaty between Russia and Estonia that was signed on February 2, 1920, and according to which the Soviet Union unconditionally recognized the Estonian independent state.

Uustalu, Evald. **Eesti Vabariik, 1918-1940.** Lund: Eesti Kirjanike Kooperatiiv, 1968, 268 p.
The best history of the Estonian republic in the inter-war period covering internal and external politics, economics, and social and cultural life.

Warma, Aleksander. **Diplomaadi krooonika: ülestähendusi ja dokumente aastatest 1938-44.** Lund: Eesti Kirjanike Kooperatiiv, 1971, 275 p.
An important volume of memoirs by an Estonian diplomat covering the period from 1938 to 1944. Major attention is paid to the negotiations leading to the Soviet-Estonian Treaty of Mutual Assistance in September 1939 and to the World War II years Warma spent in Finland. The book includes the protocols of the various Soviet-Estonian negotiations in Moscow in September and October 1939.

Latvia

See also (Second World War) Military Operations, p. 156; Eastern Europe and the Soviet Bloc, p. 358; (Great Britain) Biographies, Memoirs and Addresses, p. 369; (The Baltic States) General, p. 455; Union of Soviet Socialist Republics, p. 531.

Aizsilnieks, Arnolds. **Latvijas saimniecības vēsture, 1914-1915.** Stockholm: Daugava, 1968, 983 p.
The first scholarly economic history of Latvia during World War I, the period of independence, Soviet rule from 1940 to 1941, and the German occupation from 1941 to 1945.

Andersons, Edgars. **Latvijas vēsture, 1914-1920.** Stockholm: Daugava, 1967, 754 p.
A detailed survey, with a comprehensive bibliography, of the complicated military, political and diplomatic events in Latvia during World War I and its immediate aftermath. The author is a professor of history at the San Jose State College in California.

Bastjānis, Valdemārs. **[Memoirs.]** Stockholm: Memento and Dr. Emīls Ogriņš, 1964-70, 3 v.
The author of these memoirs is a prominent Latvian Social Democrat and a former Finance Minister of Latvia who died in 1975 in the United States. "Dzīves straumē" (1970, 302 p.) deals with the author's youth, the 1905 Revolution, World War I and the Russian revolutions. "Demokratiskā Latvija" (1966, 323 p.) describes the establishment of the independence of Latvia and the parliamentarian period when the au-

thor was a member of the parliament and Minister of Finance from 1926 to 1928. "Gala sākums" (1964, 175 p.) is a very critical account of the authoritarian regime of Kārlis Ulmanis (1934-1940) and of the establishment of the Soviet rule. An important source for the recent history of Latvia.

Bērziņš, Alfreds. **The Unpunished Crime.** New York: Speller,.1963, 314 p.
Memoirs of a member of the last government of the Latvian independent state, includint descriptions of the Soviet takeover in 1940 and of the author's imprisonment by the Germans during World War II. The Latvian edition appeared as "Labie gadi: pirms un pēc 15. maija" (New York: Grāmatu Draugs, 1963, 414 p.). The author's post-World War II political activities are described in "Tāls ir ceļs atpakaļ uz dzimteni" (New York: Grāmatu Draugs, 1971, 327 p.).

Bērziņš, V. **Latviešu strēlnieki cīņā par Padomju Latviju 1919. gadā.** Riga: Zinātne, 1969, 263 p.
A Soviet monograph on the military developments in Latvia from the collapse of the German front in late 1918 to the conclusion of peace between independent Latvia and the Soviet Union in 1920. The author, though suffering from a communist self-righteousness, shows a thorough control of the primary and secondary sources on the subject.

Bobe, M. and Others, *eds*. **The Jews in Latvia.** Tel Aviv: Association of Latvian and Estonian Jews in Israel, 1971, 383 p.
A volume of essays providing a wealth of material on the political, social, cultural and religious life of the Latvian Jewry. Of particular value is the article by Professor Max M. Laserson: "The Jews and the Latvian Parliament, 1918-1934." There is also a bibliography and a short chapter on the Jews in Estonia.

Bukšs, Miķelis. **Francis Kemps: ceineitōjs par tautas tīseibom.** Munich: Latgaļu izdevnīceiba (for the Latgaļu Pētnīceibas Instituts), 1969, 380 p.
A monograph on Francis Kemps (1876-1952), a writer and statesman from the eastern and Catholic part of Latvia, Latgale. Useful information on the frequently neglected history of Latgale, particularly during 1917 and the time of Latvia's independence.

Cielēns, Fēlikss. **Laikmetu maiņā. III: Latvija Eiropas traģēdijā.** Lidingö (Sweden): Memento, 1964, 444 p.
The concluding volume of memoirs by Fēlikss Cielēns (1888-1962), a leading Latvian Social Democrat and a former Foreign Minister of Latvia, deals with the regime of Kārlis Ulmanis (1934-1939), when Cielēns lived in France, and with developments in Latvia during World War II.

Drīzulis, A., *ed*. **Sociālistiskās revolūcijas uzvara Latvijā 1940. gadā (20. VI.-5. VIII): dokumenti un materiāli.** Riga: Latvijas PSR Zinātņu Akadēmija, Vēstures Institūts, 1964, 543 p.
A Soviet version of how the communists in 1940 established their rule in Latvia.

Kiewisz, Leon. **Sprawy łotewskie w bałtyckiej polityce Niemiez w latach 1914-1919.** Poznan: Instytut Zachodni, 1970, 254 p.
A Polish study of German policies in Latvia during World War I. There is a bibliography.

King, Gundar Julian. **Economic Policies in Occupied Latvia: A Manpower Management Study.** Tacoma: Pacific Lutheran University Press, 1965, 304 p.
A study of economic problems in Soviet Latvia since the end of World War II.

Klīve, Ādolfs. **Brīvā Latvija.** New York: Grāmatu Draugs, 1969, 493 p.
Memoirs dealing with the establishment of the independent Baltic states. The author, a prominent Latvian statesman who died in New York in 1974, describes in particular the activities of those political forces which decided early in the First World War that the Western Allies would be the victors and, consequently, worked against the various German, Russian and Bolshevik schemes in the Baltic region.

Krastiņš, Jānis, *ed*. **Latviešu strēlnieku vēsture (1915-1920).** Riga: Izdevniecība Zinātne, 1970, 697 p.
A detailed history of the Latvian Rifles from their formation in 1915 to their last battles in the Russian Civil War in 1920. The emphasis is on the activities of those Latvian Rifle units which after the October Revolution, and the occupation of Latvia by the Germans, fought on Lenin's side. This volume contains a wealth of information

on the important role the Latvian Rifles exercised on behalf of the Soviet government in the Russian Civil War.

Krastiņš, Jānis, *ed*. **Latyshskie Strelki v bor'be za sovetskuiu vlast' v 1917–1920 godakh: vospominaniia i dokumenty.** Riga: Latvijas PSR Zinātņu Akadēmija, Vēstures Institūts, 1962, 526 p.
A collection of documents and articles on the participation of the Latvian Rifles in the Russian Revolution and the Civil War. The Latvian original appeared as "Latviešu strēlnieki cīņā par padomju varu, 1917.–1920. gadā: atmiņas un dokumenti" (Riga: Latvijas PSR Zinātņu Akadēmijas Izdevniecība, 1960, 565 p.).

Krieviņš, Edgars. **Viņas dienas.** Kew (Victoria, Australia): Austrālijas Latvietis, 1966, 332 p.
Memoirs by the Latvian Minister in Berlin in the 1930s. A useful source for the diplomatic history of that period, especially concerning the Nazi-Soviet agreement of 1939 and its Baltic repercussions.

Kripens, Arvids. **Kalpaka bataljons un Baloža brigāde.** Sidney (Australia): The Author, 1963, 212 p.
A survey of the events in the first half of 1919 in Courland, Latvia, where Latvian, German and Bolshevik troops, observed by the representatives of the Western Allies, were battling with each other in the political and military chaos created by the Russian and German revolutions.

Kroeger, Erhard. **Der Auszug aus der alten Heimat: die Umsiedlung der Baltendeutschen.** Tübingen: Verlag der Deutschen Hochschullehrer-Zeitung, 1967, 198 p.
Reminiscences by the unrepenting leader of the German Nazi movement in Latvia who after the conclusion of the Nazi-Soviet Pact in 1939 was instrumental in arranging with Himmler the resettlement of the Baltic Germans to formerly Polish territories.

Lasmanis, Aleksandrs. **Cerības un vilšanās.** Stockholm: Daugava, 1963, 272 p.
Memoirs of a Latvian officer, of particular interest for the description of events in German-held Courland during the last months of World War II.

Latvijas PSR mazā enciklopēdija. Riga: Zinātne (for the Latvijas PSR Zinātņu Akadēmija), 1967–72, 4 v.
An encyclopedia containing a wealth of information, that has been selected with the help of a Marxist-Leninist yardstick, on Latvian history, politics, economic and social conditions, and cultural affairs. Particularly useful are the biographical entries for Latvian communists.

Lejiņš, Jānis. **Mana dzimtene: atmiņu un pārdomu atspulgā.** Västerås (Sweden): Ziemeļblāzma, 1971, 333 p.
Memoirs, based on a carefully kept diary, by an active member of a leading Latvian political party, the Farmers' Union, and former member of the Latvian Parliament. A valuable, though not always reliable, source for the history of Latvia in the 1920s and 1930s.

Lejiņš, P., *ed*. **Julijs Feldmans.** Lincoln (Nebraska): Vaidava, 1963, 200 p.
A collection of articles commemorating Mr. Julijs Feldmans, the late Latvian Minister in Washington, and containing interesting information on the U.S. attitude toward the representatives of the Baltic States in Washington after World War II.

Millers, Visvaris. **Sozdanie sovetskoi gosudarstvennosti v Latvii.** Riga: Zinātne, 1967, 528 p.
An account of the unsuccessful attempts by the Bolsheviks to assume power in Latvia after 1917 and of the events leading to the more effective "revolution of 1940."

Rutkis, J., *ed*. **Latvia: Country and People.** Stockholm: Latvian National Foundation, 1967, 681 p.
An informative reference volume on Latvia and its people, with particular emphasis on Latvian life during the period of national independence. The treatment is topical.

Sīpols, Vilnis. **Dzimtenes nodevība: buržuāziskās Latvijas ārpolitika no 1933. līdz 1940. gadam.** Riga: Latvijas Valsts Izdevniecība, 1963, 259 p.
A communist history of the foreign policy of Latvia from 1933 to 1940.

Sīpols, Vilnis. **Tainaia diplomatiia: burzhuaznaia Latviia v antisovetskikh planakh imperialisticheskikh derzhav 1919–1940 gg.** Riga: Liesma, 1968, 347 p.
A Soviet study of the foreign policy of independent Latvia.

Šilde, Ādolfs. **Bez tiesībām un brīvības: Latvijas sovjetizācija 1944-1965.** Copenhagen: Imanta, 1965, 436 p.
  An account of the Sovietization of Latvia from 1944 to 1965, containing detailed information on the Communist Party of Latvia, economic and population problems, educational reforms and anti-Soviet resistance.

Šilde, Ādolfs. **Die Sowjetisierung Lettlands.** Bonn: Bundesinstitut für Ostwissenschaftliche und Internationale Studien, 1967, 162 p.
  A survey of how the Soviet regime was established in Latvia.

Spekke, Arnolds. **Atmiņu brīži.** Stockholm: Zelta Ābele, 1967, 601 p.
  Memoirs by a Latvian historian and diplomat who from 1954 to 1970 was the Latvian *chargé d'affaires* in Washington. There is valuable information on U.S. policies toward the Baltic States since their incorporation into the Soviet Union.

Stachko, Petr Ivanovich, ed. **Za sovetskuiu vlast' v Latvii, 1918-1920: sbornik statei.** Riga: Latviiskoe Gos. Izd-vo (for the Institut Istorii Partii pri TsK KP Latvii), 1964, 732 p.
  A collection of articles on the Bolshevik attempts to establish their rule in Latvia in the period from 1918 to 1920.

Šteimanis, Josifs. **Latvijas Komunistiskās Partijas taktika cīņā par padomju varas atjaunošanu, 1920-1940.** Riga: Latvijas KP CK Partijas Vēstures Institūts, 1965, 264 p.
  An account of the communist planning and strategy for the establishment of Soviet rule in Latvia between both world wars.

Unāms, Žanis. **Dzīvā Latvija.** Lincoln (Nebraska): Pilskalns, 1964, 335 p.
  A discussion of the problem of the Baltic States in contemporary international relations, and articles on leading political figures and developments in Latvia before World War II.

Lithuania

See also Eastern Europe and the Soviet Bloc, p. 358; (Baltic States) General, p. 455; (Poland) Foreign Relations, p. 527; Union of Soviet Socialist Republics, p. 531.

Audėnas, Juozas. **Paskutinis posėdis.** New York: Romuva, 1966, 277 p.
  Memoirs of the final years of independent Lithuania by its last Minister of Agriculture.

Budrys, Jonas. **Kontržvalgyba Lietuvoje.** New York: Darbininkas, 1967, 224 p.
  Memoirs about politics in Lithuania in the early 1920s, particularly valuable for the description of the annexation of the Klaipeda (Memel) region by Lithuania. The author, a former chief of the Lithuanian Army intelligence, commanded troops that seized Klaipeda and was Lithuania's Consul General in New York.

Bulavas, Juozas. **Vokiškųjų fašistų okupacinis Lietuvos valdymas (1941-1944m.).** Vilnius: Lietuvos TSR Mokslų Akademija, Ekonomikos Institutas, 1969, 294 p.
  A Soviet study of German occupied Lithuania, 1941-44.

Burokevičius, Mykolas. **Lietuvos KP ideologinis darbas su inteligentija 1940-65 m.** Vilnius: Mintis, 1972, 195 p.
  A short, but informative and important Soviet study of the efforts of the Communist Party in the years from 1940 to 1965 to influence the Lithuanian intelligentsia to work for the Soviet system.

Gaigalaitė, Aldona. **Klerikalizmas Lietuvoje 1917-1940.** Vilnius: Mintis, 1970, 312 p.
  A well-documented Soviet monograph on the Catholic Church and the Christian democratic parties in independent Lithuania.

Gerutis, Albertas, ed. **Lithuania: 700 Years.** New York: Manyland Books, 1969, 474 p.
  Despite the title, the bulk of the book is devoted to the last fifty years of Lithuanian history.

Hellmann, Manfred. **Grundzüge der Geschichte Litauens und des litauischen Volkes.** Darmstadt: Wissenschaftliche Buchgesellschaft, 1966, 179 p.
  A succinct but very useful survey of the history of Lithuania by a well-known German medievalist.

Kučas, Antanas, ed. **Amerikos Lietuvių istorija.** Boston: Lietuvių enciklopedijos leidykla, 1971, 639 p.
  A history of Lithuanian emigration into the United States.

Lietuvių enciklopedija. Boston: Lietuvių enciklopedijos leidykla, 1953-1969, 36 v.
An encyclopedia containing a wealth of information on Lithuanian history, economy, culture and social conditions. An abridged English version appears as "Encyclopedia Lituanica" (Boston: Juozas Kapočius, 1970— .). Three volumes have been published through 1974.

Linde, Gerd. **Die deutsche Politik in Litauen im Ersten Weltkrieg.** Wiesbaden: Harrassowitz, 1965, 265 p.
A well-documented monograph on German policies toward Lithuania during World War I.

Liulevičius, Vincentas, ed. **Lietuvių švietimas Vokietijoje.** Chicago: Kultūrai Remti Draugija, 1969, 639 p.
A survey of the network of educational institutions for Lithuanian refugees in Germany from 1945 to 1950.

Mažoji lietuviškoji tarybinė enciklopedija. Vilnius: Mintis, 1966-71, 3 v.
A Soviet Lithuanian encyclopedia. Limited in scope, it concentrates on the period of Soviet rule since 1940 and is very useful for its account of Communist Party activities.

Merkelis, Aleksandras. **Antanas Smetona: jo visuomeninė, kultūrinė ir politinė veikla.** New York: Amerikos Lietuvių Tautinė Sąjunga, 1964, 740 p.
A well-documented biography of the last President of independent Lithuania, written by his secretary. It contains a wealth of information on Lithuania's politics and includes texts of the President's speeches and letters.

Meskauskas, Kazys and Others, eds. **Litva za polveka novoi epokhi.** Vilnius: Mintis, 1967, 448 p.
An illustrated survey of Lithuania's industrial and agricultural development since the introduction of Soviet rule.

Musteikis, Kazys. **Prisiminimų fragmentai.** London: Nida, 1970, 126 p.
Short, concise and very informative memoirs by the last Minister of Defense of independent Lithuania. It covers mainly the crucial period of 1938-40.

Raštikis, Stasys. **Ivykiai ir žmones: iš mano užrašų.** Chicago: Akademines Skautijos Leidykla, 1972, 616 p.
The third volume of memoirs by the former Commander-in-Chief of the Lithuanian Army. The author not only explains the organization and administration of the Lithuanian armed forces, but also discusses the Army's influence in Lithuanian politics.

Sabaliūnas, Leonas. **Lithuania in Crisis: Nationalism to Communism, 1939-1940.** Bloomington: Indiana University Press, 1972, 293 p.
A critical analysis of Lithuanian domestic and foreign affairs in the inter-war period, the social and economic conditions in the last years of independence, and the crises leading to the loss of sovereignty.

Šarmaitis, Romas, ed. **Lietuvos komunistų partijos istorijos apybraiža.** Vilnius: Mintis, 1971, 525 p.
This is the first of the three planned volumes of the history of the Lithuanian Communist Party. It covers the period from 1887 to 1920.

Savasis, J. **The War Against God in Lithuania.** New York: Manyland Books, 1966, 134 p.
A survey of Soviet policies toward the Roman Catholic Church in Lithuania.

Senn, Alfred Erich. **The Great Powers, Lithuania and the Vilna Question 1920-1928.** Leyden: Brill, 1966, 239 p.
A thorough study of the Polish-Lithuanian dispute over Vilnius and of the efforts of the League of Nations to settle it. Particular attention is paid to the influence this conflict exercised on Lithuanian politics.

Šimutis, Leonardas. **Amerikos Lietuvių Taryba: 30 metų Lietuvos laisves kovoje.** Chicago: Amerikos Lietuvių Taryba, 1971, 499 p.
A study of the political activities of the American Lithuanian Council.

Skipitis, Rapolas. **Nepriklausomą Lietuvą statant.** Chicago: Terra, 1967-71, 2 v.
Memoirs by a former Minister of the Lithuanian government dealing with the democratic period in Lithuania's politics (1918-26).

Šliogeris, Vaclovas. **Antanas Smetona: žmogus ir valstybininkas.** Sodus: Juozas J. Bachunas, 1966, 181 p.
Informative memoirs about the last President of independent Lithuania, Antanas Smetona. The author was the President's military aide.

Sūduvis, N. E., *pseud*. **Vienų vieni: dvidešimt penkerių metų rezistencijoje.** New York: Į Laisvę Fondas Lietuviškai Kultūrai Ugdyti, 1964, 424 p.
A history of Lithuanian resistance against the Soviets and the Nazis since 1940, by a Lithuanian resistance leader.

Tarvydas, Stanislovas S. and Basalykas, Alfonsas B. **Litva.** Moscow: Mysl', 1967, 285 p.
A general Soviet survey of Lithuania. Though the chapters dealing with politics and history often contain incorrect information, the volume provides a good survey of Lithuanian natural resources, postwar economic development, population trends and the arts.

Vaitkevičius, Bronius. **Socialistinė revoliucija Lietuvoje 1918-1919 metais.** Vilnius: Mintis, 1967, 693 p.
A Marxist-Leninist interpretation of Communist efforts to establish Soviet rule in Lithuania in 1918-19, written by a Soviet Lithuanian historian and party functionary.

Vaitkus, Mykolas. **Nepriklausomybės saulėj, 1918-1940.** London: Nida Press, 1968, 2 v.
A Lithuanian poet and priest reminisces about the culture and the political developments of independent Lithuania.

Vardys, V. Stanley, *ed*. **Lithuania under the Soviets: Portrait of a Nation, 1940-65.** New York: Praeger, 1965, 299 p.
A well-documented survey of Lithuania's development from 1918 through World War II.

The Violations of Human Rights in Soviet Occupied Lithuania. Delran (N.J.): Lithuanian American Community, 1972—.
An annual documentation on religious and national dissent and struggle for civil rights in Soviet Lithuania. Through 1974 three volumes have been published covering the developments from 1971 to 1973.

Žiugžda, Juozas, *ed*. **Lietuvos TSR istorija. III Tomas: Nuo 1917 iki 1940 metų.** Vilnius: Mintis, 1965, 405 p.
A Soviet interpretation of the history of the independent Lithuanian state. Published as the third volume of a general history of Lithuania prepared under the auspices of the Academy of Sciences of the Lithuanian S.S.R.

Žiugžda, Juozas, *ed*. **Vilniaus miesto istorija nuo spalio Revoliucijos iki dabartinių dienų.** Vilnius: Mintis, 1972, 331 p.
A Soviet study of Vilnius since 1917. Prepared by the Institute of History of the Academy of Sciences of the Lithuanian S.S.R., it contains a wealth of information about Vilnius as an international issue during the inter-war period.

GERMANY

General

See also The World Since 1914, p. 129; Europe (General Surveys), p. 344; Western Europe, p. 345.

Abelein, Manfred. **Die Kulturpolitik des Deutschen Reiches und der Bundesrepublik Deutschland.** Cologne: Westdeutscher Verlag, 1968, 312 p.
A study of the role of government in formulating policies on educational, scientific and cultural development in the Weimar Republic, Nazi Germany and the Bundesrepublik. Of particular interest are the sections on cultural relations with foreign countries.

Batty, Peter. **The House of Krupp.** New York: Stein and Day, 1967, 333 p.
The story of the gigantic firm that has played a key role in Europe's military and political history, with emphasis on developments during World War II and its aftermath.

Bracher, Karl Dietrich. **Deutschland zwischen Demokratie und Diktatur.** Berne: Scherz, 1964, 415 p.

A collection of excellent essays on various aspects of German politics of the twentieth century by a leading student of the period. Particular attention is paid to the causes of the collapse of Weimar Republic and the rise of National Socialism.

Dahrendorf, Ralf. **Society and Democracy in Germany.** Garden City: Doubleday, 1967, 482 p.

A significant, if at times difficult and perplexing work, by a leading German sociologist on the social structure and attitudes in Germany and their impact on the development of political democracy since 1871. The German original was published as "Gesellschaft und Demokratie in Deutschland" (Munich: Piper, 1965, 516 p.).

Demeter, Karl. **The German Officer-Corps in Society and State, 1650–1945.** New York: Praeger, 1965, 414 p.

An English translation of a much-revised study, first published in 1930, which examines in commendable breadth the sociological and political aspects of the German officer corps. With a valuable introduction by Michael Howard.

Freund, Ludwig. **Deutschland im Brennpunkt: die amerikanische Politikwissenschaft und die deutsche Frage.** Stuttgart: Seewald, 1968, 195 p.

An account of what the author considers the unsatisfactory and even unfair record of American political scientists writing on Germany.

Hempel, Gustav. **Die deutsche Montanindustrie: ihre Entwicklung und Gestaltung.** Essen: Vulkan-Verlag Classen, 2d ed., 1969, 231 p.

History of the German coal and steel industries that is stronger on pre-1945 than on more recent developments.

Höhn, Reinhard. **Die Armee als Erziehungsschule der Nation: das Ende einer Idee.** Bad Harzburg: Verlag für Wissenschaft, Wirtschaft und Technik, 1963, 590 p.

In this thoroughly documented study the author describes how the Prussian idea of the army as a "school for the nation" influenced the development of the German armed forces. The volume covers the period from the beginning of the nineteenth century to World War I.

Hoffmann, Walther Gustav and Others. **Das Wachstum der deutschen Wirtschaft seit der Mitte des 19. Jahrhunderts.** Berlin: Springer-Verlag, 1965, 842 p.

An encyclopaedic survey of economic development in Germany since the middle of the nineteenth century.

Jacob, Herbert. **German Administration since Bismarck: Central Authority versus Local Autonomy.** New Haven: Yale University Press, 1963, 224 p.

A scholarly analysis of German administration from 1871 through the first ten years of the Federal Republic.

Loewenberg, Gerhard. **Parliament in the German Political System.** Ithaca: Cornell University Press, 1966, 463 p.

A substantial and scholarly study of the "continuities and discontinuities" of the German parliamentary tradition together with an interesting analysis of the Bundestag in the current German political system.

Mann, Golo. **The History of Germany Since 1789.** New York: Praeger, 1968, 547 p.

A solid history. An updated translation of "Deutsche Geschichte des neunzehnten und zwanzigsten Jahrhunderts" (Frankfurt/Main: S. Fischer, 1958, 989 p.).

Mauersberg, Hans. **Deutsche Industrien im Zeitgeschehen eines Jahrhunderts.** Stuttgart: G. Fischer, 1966, 584 p.

A survey of the industrialization of Germany through 1960. The author deals at great length with developments during both world wars and with the problems caused by Germany's defeat.

Pois, Robert A. **Friedrich Meinecke and German Politics in the Twentieth Century.** Berkeley: University of California Press, 1972, 164 p.

This volume traces the evolution of Meinecke's *Weltanschauung* from a great faith in the balance between *Macht* and *Kultur*, to recognition that an ideal balance is not possible, to efforts to divorce these concepts entirely. The author tries to show why Meinecke and his class, representatives of the educated liberal bourgeoisie, ultimately failed on all counts.

Ringer, Fritz K. **The Decline of the German Mandarins: The German Academic Community, 1890-1933.** Cambridge: Harvard University Press, 1969, 528 p.
A valuable scholarly study of the German professoriate in the decades before Hitler. Depicting an educational system in crisis and decline, the book has more than purely historical interest.

Ritter, Gerhard. **The Sword and the Scepter: The Problem of Militarism in Germany.** Coral Gables: University of Miami Press, 1969-73, 4 v.
A major study on German statecraft and militarism by an outstanding conservative historian. The last two volumes are a reinterpretation of German politics from the outbreak of the First World War to the November Revolution in 1918. The German original appeared as "Staatskunst und Kriegshandwerk: das Problem des 'Militarismus' in Deutschland" (Munich: Oldenbourg, 1964-68, 4 v.).

Schwarz, Max. **MDR: Bibliographisches Handbuch der Reichstage.** Hanover: Verlag für Literatur und Zeitgeschehen, 1965, 832 p.
A Who's Who of the members of the German Reichstag from 1848 to 1933, including statistical information on national elections. A useful reference.

Stern, Fritz R. **The Failure of Illiberalism: Essays on the Political Culture of Modern Germany.** New York: Knopf, 1972, 233 p.
A collection of essays dealing with the style and substance of German politics from Bismarck to Adenauer, by an historian writing for the general reader as well as for the specialist.

Stolper, Gustav and Others. **The German Economy: 1870 to the Present.** New York: Harcourt, Brace & World, 1967, 353 p.
A considerably expanded and updated edition of a standard history of German economy by a noted German economist and politician who died in 1947. The original English version was published as "German Economy, 1870-1940: Issues and Trends" (New York: Reynal & Hitchcock, 1940, 295 p.). The present revised English version is a translation of the German version: "Deutsche Wirtschaft seit 1870" (Tübingen: Mohr, 2d rev. ed., 1966, 384 p.).

Stucken, Rudolf. **Deutsche Geld- und Kreditpolitik, 1914 bis 1963.** Tübingen: Mohr, 3rd ed., 1964, 341 p.
A revised edition of a standard reference on German economic and financial policies.

Thomas, Georg Richard. **Geschichte der deutschen Wehr- und Rüstungswirtschaft (1918-1943/45).** Boppard: Boldt, 1966, 552 p.
General Thomas, an opponent of Hitler but a strong believer in German military strength, played a leading role in organizing the German armaments industries in the 1930s and during the first years of World War II. His account of German armaments industries since 1918, written in 1943 and 1944, has been introduced, edited and provided with copious notes by Wolfgang Birkenfeld.

Recent History

See also General Works, p. 1; Political Factors, p. 12; Population Problems, p. 47; The World Since 1914, p. 129; (Europe) General Surveys, p. 344; Western Europe, p. 345; (Finland) Foreign Relations, p. 452; Baltic States, p. 455; other subsections under Germany; (Union of Soviet Socialist Republics) Recent History, p. 538; United Republic of Tanzania, p. 832.

Akten zur deutschen auswärtigen Politik, 1918-1945.
A collection of documents from the archives of the German Foreign Ministry, originally sponsored by the governments of the United States, Great Britain and France, and published in English as "Documents on German Foreign Policy." When the captured German Foreign Ministry archives were returned to Germany, it was decided to continue to publish the documents, with the participation of the government of the Federal Republic of Germany, in the original German versions. Through 1973 the following volumes have appeared: in "Serie B: 1925-1933," five volumes of the German edition, covering the period from December 1925 to June 1927 (Göttingen: Vandenhoeck und Ruprecht, 1966–); in "Serie C: 1933-1937," three volumes of the German edition, covering the period from January 1933 to March 1935 (Göttingen: Vandenhoeck und Ruprecht, 1971–), and five volumes of the English edition, cover-

ing the period from January 1933 to October 1936 (Washington: G.P.O., 1957–); in "Serie D: 1937-1941," all volumes of both the German and English editions have been published (Baden-Baden: Imprimerie Nationale; Göttingen: Vandenhoeck und Rupprecht, 1950-70, 13 v.; Washington: G.P.O., 1949-64, 13 v.); and in "Serie E: 1941-1945," two volumes of the German edition, covering the period from December 1941 to June 1942 (Göttingen: Vandenhoeck und Rupprecht, 1969–).

Balfour, Michael L. G. **The Kaiser and His Times.** Boston: Houghton, 1964, 524 p.
A well-written, thoroughly researched biography of William II, particularly important because it clarifies the role of the complex German monarch in the area of foreign relations.

Borries, Kurt. **Deutschland im Kreis der europäischen Mächte: eine historisch-politische Analyse.** Stuttgart: Tauchnitz, 1963, 307 p.
Essays on German foreign policy in the nineteenth and twentieth centuries. The author thinks that it is the purpose of the Russians to get the Germans on their side after they become disillusioned with the West, particularly the United States.

Cecil, Lamar. **Albert Ballin: Business and Politics in Imperial Germany, 1888-1918.** Princeton: Princeton University Press, 1967, 388 p.
A welcome study of the relationship between the Imperial German government and big business as reflected in the activities of the shipping magnate, Albert Ballin. A good portion of the book deals with World War I.

Deuerlein, Ernst, *ed.* **Der Reichstag: Aufsätze, Protokolle und Darstellungen zur Geschichte der parlamentarischen Vertretung des deutschen Volkes, 1871-1933.** Frankfurt/Main: Athenäum, 1963, 307 p.
A study of the Reichstag as an institution and of the people prominent there from Bismarck through the burning of the parliament building in 1933.

Deutsche Geschichte seit dem Ersten Weltkrieg. Stuttgart: Deutsche Verlags-Anstalt (for the Institut für Zeitgeschichte), 1971-73, 3 v.
In the first two volumes, six colleagues at the Institute for Contemporary History present separate book-length studies of the Weimar Republic, inter-war European international relations, Hitler's Third Reich, the Second World War, Germany divided, and the development of the German economy since 1918—accounts which are balanced, coördinated and well-written. The third volume is a most useful survey of archives, libraries and research organizations specializing in contemporary German history.

Dokumentation zur Deutschlandfrage. Bonn: Siegler, 1961– .
A comprehensive and chronologically arranged collection of documents, compiled by Heinrich von Siegler, on the German problem in international relations since the signing of the Atlantic Charter in 1941. Volume V, published in 1970, covers the developments through October 1969. The first two volumes have appeared in an enlarged and revised edition.

Dokumente zur Deutschlandpolitik. Frankfurt/Main: Metzner (for the Bundesministerium für Gesamtdeutsche Fragen and, since 1971, for the Bundesministerium für Innerdeutsche Beziehungen), 1961– .
A massive collection of treaties, documents, letters, articles, speeches and interviews dealing with the German problem in international affairs since 1941. Planned in five series, only Reihe III, edited by Ernst Deuerlein, Hansjürgen Schierbaum and Gisela Biewer and covering the period from May 5, 1955 to November 9, 1958, has been completed through 1972 (4 v. in 9 pts., 1961-69). Five volumes of Reihe IV, edited by Ernst Deuerlein, Hannelore Nathan, Werner John and Günther Holzweissig and covering the period from November 10, 1958 to December 31, 1960, were published through 1973 (5 v. in 8 pts., 1971-73).

Ernst, Fritz. **The Germans and Their Modern History.** New York: Columbia University Press, 1966, 164 p.
In a series of widely acclaimed lectures, delivered in 1961 and 1962 at the University of Heidelberg, a professor of medieval and modern history attempts to reinterpret recent German history. German original: "Die Deutschen und ihre jüngste Geschichte: Beobachtungen und Bemerkungen zum deutschen Schicksal der letzten fünfzig Jahre" (Stuttgart: Kohlhammer, 1963, 162 p.).

Grobba, Fritz. **Männer und Mächte im Orient.** Göttingen: Musterschmidt, 1967, 339 p.
Diplomatic reminiscences covering the years from 1923 to 1947 when the author was German *chargé d'affaires* in Kabul and ambassador in Jidda and Baghdad. The volume includes a survey of the German negotiations with the Grand Mufti of Jerusalem during World War II.

Jacobsen, Hans-Adolf, *ed.* **Misstrauische Nachbarn: Deutsche Ostpolitik 1919/1970.** Düsseldorf: Droste, 1970, 504 p.
A selection of documents illustrating German relations with Eastern Europe in the period from 1919 to 1970. The emphasis is on German-Russian relations and on developments since World War II.

Kaltefleiter, Werner. **Wirtschaft und Politik in Deutschland: Konjunktur als Bestimmungsfaktor des Parteiensystems.** Opladen: Westdeutscher Verlag, 2d rev. ed., 1968, 190 p.
A discussion of the influence of economic developments on the political life of the Weimar Republic and the Bundesrepublik.

Kent, George O., *comp. and ed.* **A Catalog of Files and Microfilms of the German Foreign Ministry Archives, 1920-1945.** Stanford: The Hoover Institution, 1962-73, 4 v.
An indispensable reference listing all the files from the political archives of the German Foreign Ministry and the German missions and consulates for the years from 1920 to 1945 that were seized by the American and British armies at the end of World War II. It is a joint undertaking of the U.S. Department of State and the Hoover Institution on War, Revolution, and Peace.

Kochan, Lionel. **The Struggle for Germany, 1914-1945.** Chicago: Aldine Publishing Co., 1963, 150 p.
A brief but illuminating essay on the tug of war between Russia and the Western powers for the allegiance of Germany since the beginning of World War I.

Lesser, Jonas. **Germany: The Symbol and the Deed.** New York: Yoseloff, 1965, 601 p.
An Austrian-born writer appraises recent German history and concludes that the Germans have not learned much from their Nazi past.

Markert, Werner, *ed.* **Deutsch-russische Beziehungen von Bismarck bis zur Gegenwart.** Stuttgart: Kohlhammer, 1964, 236 p.
A collection of articles and conversations on Russo-German relations, chiefly since 1914, by leading experts of West Germany.

Mehnert, Klaus. **Der deutsche Standort.** Stuttgart: Deutsche Verlags-Anstalt, 1967, 415 p.
A survey of twentieth-century German history and a compendium of shrewd observations on contemporary German society.

Nehring, Walther K. **Die Geschichte der deutschen Panzerwaffe 1916 bis 1945.** Berlin: Propyläen Verlag, 1969, 328 p.
A German general, a leading strategist of tank warfare during World War II, reminisces on his military career and the development of German armored vehicles.

Osterroth, Franz and Schuster, Dieter. **Chronik der deutschen Sozialdemokratie.** Hanover: Dietz, 1963, 671 p.
A factual handbook on the German socialist movement since 1848, with emphasis on developments in the twentieth century.

Pross, Harry. **Jugend, Eros, Politik: die Geschichte der deutschen Jugendverbände.** Berne: Scherz, 1964, 520 p.
A study of the German youth movements of the twentieth century.

Schmokel, Wolfe William. **Dream of Empire: German Colonialism, 1919-1945.** New Haven: Yale University Press, 1964, 204 p.
The pervasive appeal of colonialism and Germany's diplomatic efforts to regain an overseas empire, both under Weimar and Hitler, are clearly depicted in this important scholarly monograph.

Veröffentlichungen der Kommission für Zeitgeschichte bei der Katholischen Akademie in Bayern. Mainz: Matthias-Grünewald-Verlag, 1965– .
A multi-volume collection of documents and studies on the situation of the Catholic Church in the Weimar Republic and in Nazi Germany and on the official relations between the Vatican and Hitler's government. Volume 15 of the "Reihe A: Quellen"

was published in 1973. Volume 13 of the "Reihe B: Forschungen" was published in 1972. The latter series includes also publications on pre-World War I and post-World War II topics concerning the German catholics.

Vogt, Hannah. **The Burden of Guilt: A Short History of Germany, 1914–1945.** New York: Oxford University Press, 1964, 318 p.
A candid survey, originally designed for German students. The German original appeared as "Schuld oder Verhängnis?" (Frankfurt a.M.: Diesterweg, 1961, 251 p.).

Weber, Hermann, ed. **Der deutsche Kommunismus.** Cologne: Kiepenheuer, 1963, 679 p.
A comprehensive collection of documents on the German communist movement and its splinter groups covering the years from 1919 to 1963, including annexes on the party congresses and leadership.

Weber, Hermann, ed. **Völker hört die Signale: der deutsche Kommunismus, 1916–1966.** Munich: Deutscher Taschenbuch Verlag, 1967, 411 p.
A useful collection of documents on German communism in the years from 1916 to 1966, with commentaries by the editor.

The 1918 Revolution and the Weimar Republic

General

See also First World War, p. 131; Inter-War Period, p. 140; (Finland) General, p. 449; (Germany) General, p. 463; Recent History, p. 465; The Nazi Era, p. 475.

Akten der Reichskanzlei: Weimarer Republik. Boppard am Rhein: Boldt (for the Historische Kommission bei der Bayerischen Akademie der Wissenschaften and the Bundesarchiv), 1968– .
A rich selection of documents from the archives of the German *Reichskanzlei* on the manifold activities of the German cabinets during the Weimar Republic. This important series is edited by Karl Dietrich Erdmann and Wolfgang Mommsen. Through 1973 the following volumes have appeared: "Das Kabinett Scheidemann: 13. Februar bis 20. Juni 1919," ed. by Hagen Schulze (1971, 554 p.); "Das Kabinett Müller I: 27. März bis 21. Juni 1920," ed. by Martin Vogt (1971, 375 p.); "Das Kabinett Cuno: 22 November 1922 bis 12. August 1923," ed. by Karl-Heinz Harbeck (1968, 799 p.); "Das Kabinett Müller II: 28. Juni 1928 bis 27. März 1930," ed. by Martin Vogt (1970, 2 v.); "Das Kabinett Fehrenbach: 25. Juni 1920 bis 4. Mai 1921," ed. by Peter Wulf (1972, 720 p.); "Die Kabinette Marx I und II: 30. November 1923 bis 3. Juni 1924; 3. Juni 1924 bis 15. Januar 1925," ed. by Günter Abramowski (1973, 2 v.). and "Die Kabinette Wirth I und II: 10. Mai 1921–26. Okt. 1921, 26. Okt. 1921–22. Nov. 1922," ed. by Hans Booms and Others (1973, 2 v.).

Angress, Werner T. **Stillborn Revolution: The Communist Bid for Power in Germany, 1921–1923.** Princeton: Princeton University Press, 1963, 513 p.
A thorough study of the German Communist Party in its revolutionary phase, when it prepared and tried to execute a revolution which Stalin prematurely hailed as "the most important world event in our time."

Badia, Gilbert. **Le Spartakisme: les dernières années de Rosa Luxemburg et de Karl Liebknecht, 1914–1919.** Paris: L'Arche, 1967, 438 p.

———, ed. **Les Spartakistes, 1918: l'Allemagne en révolution.** Paris: Julliard, 1966, 297 p.
Surveys of, and documentation on, the Spartacist movement in Germany in 1918 and 1919.

Brüning, Heinrich. **Memoiren 1918–1934.** Stuttgart: Deutsche Verlags-Anstalt, 1970, 721 p.
The revealing and in some ways self-incriminatory memoirs of Weimar's last constitutional chancellor provide a major historical source on the demise of the Weimar Republic. Brüning's policies can be said to have deepened the crisis which led to his own failure and thus to Hitler's triumph.

Brüning, Heinrich. **Reden und Aufsätze eines deutschen Staatsmanns.** Münster: Verlag Regensberg, 1968, 358 p.
  A selection of speeches by Heinrich Brüning, Reichskanzler of the Weimar Republic from March 30, 1930 to May 30, 1932. Edited by Wilhelm Vernekohl and Rudolf Morsey.

Carl Melchior: ein Buch des Gedenkens und der Freundschaft. Tübingen: Mohr, 1967, 140 p.
  A collection of essays commemorating Dr. Carl Melchior, a German banker and statesman, who played a prominent role in the diplomacy of the Weimar Republic. Useful information on the negotiations concerning the 1919 Peace Conference and the Dawes and Young plans.

Carsten, Francis Ludwig. **The Reichswehr and Politics, 1918-1933.** New York: Oxford University Press, 1966, 427 p.
  A well-documented history of the Reichswehr during the Weimar Republic, including a description of its secret activities in the Soviet Union. The author, a professor at the University of London, tries to answer the question why the Reichswehr failed to safeguard Germany from the National Socialist dictatorship. The German original: "Reichswehr und Politik, 1918-1933" (Cologne: Kiepenheuer, 1964, 484 p.).

Comfort, Richard A. **Revolutionary Hamburg: Labor Politics in the Early Weimar Republic.** Stanford: Stanford University Press, 1966, 226 p.
  A solid study describing the issues involved in the development of organized labor in Hamburg from late 1918 to the beginning of 1924.

Dederke, Karlheinz. **Reich und Republik: Deutschland 1917-1933.** Stuttgart: Klett Verlag, 1969, 316 p.
  Though planned as a text, this is a useful history of Germany from 1917 to 1933. Sponsored by the Deutsches Institut für Zeitgeschichte.

Dorpalen, Andreas. **Hindenburg and the Weimar Republic.** Princeton: Princeton University Press, 1964, 506 p.
  A scholarly biography of Hindenburg's unhappy career as German president. The author draws on some new material and his narrative illuminates some aspects of Weimar's decline.

Erdmann, Karl Dietrich. **Adenauer in der Rheinlandpolitik nach dem Ersten Weltkrieg.** Stuttgart: Klett, 1966, 386 p.
  A well-documented study of the role of Adenauer in the politics of Rhineland in the aftermath of World War I.

Erger, Johannes. **Der Kapp-Lüttwitz-Putsch: ein Beitrag zur deutschen Innenpolitik 1919/20.** Düsseldorf: Droste, 1967, 365 p.
  A thorough, well-balanced and well-documented monograph on the right-wing military insurrection of March 1920, its antecedents and its meaning for the development of parliamentary democracy in Germany.

Eschenburg, Theodor. **Die improvisierte Demokratie.** Munich: Piper, 1963, 305 p.
  A collection of stimulating essays—mostly biographical—on the Weimar Republic, by one of Germany's leading political scientists.

Fürstenberg, Hans. **Erinnerungen: mein Weg als Bankier und Carl Fürstenbergs Altersjahre.** Wiesbaden: Rheinische Verlags-Anstalt, 1965, 303 p.
  Memoirs of a banker, covering the period of the Weimar Republic.

Gay, Peter. **Weimar Culture: The Outsider as Insider.** New York: Harper and Row, 1968, 205 p.
  A spirited essay on a colorful cultural epoch, by a professor at Yale University.

Grossmann, Kurt Richard. **Ossietzky: ein deutscher Patriot.** Munich: Kindler, 1963, 580 p.
  A biography of Carl von Ossietzky, the well-known pacifist and editor of *Weltbühne* who in 1933 won the Nobel Peace Prize. Useful for the student of the Weimar Republic.

Guske, Claus. **Das politische Denken des Generals von Seeckt.** Lübeck: Matthiesen Verlag, 1971, 283 p.
  A detailed discussion of the political views of General von Seeckt, the highly capable

officer who was in charge of the Reichswehr in the early years of the Weimar Republic and who tried in a very subtle fashion to restore Germany's influence in European politics.

Haffner, Sebastian. **Failure of a Revolution: Germany 1918-19.** New York: Library Press, 1972, 205 p.
In this lively popular account of the political developments in Germany in 1918/19, the author argues that "a victorious German Revolution might have saved Germany" from subsequent disasters. The German original was published as "Die verratene Revolution: Deutschland 1918/19" (Munich: Scherz, 1969, 224 p.).

Hermens, Ferdinand Aloys and Schieder, Theodor, eds. **Staat, Wirtschaft und Politik in der Weimarer Republik: Festschrift für Heinrich Brüning.** Berlin: Duncker, 1967, 507 p.
A collection of historical essays and personal memoirs concerning Brüning's government and Weimar politics—in honor of the eightieth birthday of the unsuccessful statesman.

Hertzman, Lewis. **DNVP: Right-Wing Opposition in the Weimar Republic, 1918-1924.** Lincoln: University of Nebraska Press, 1963, 263 p.
A scholarly study, based on some new sources, of Germany's largest right-wing party and of its unfortunate role in the early life of the Weimar Republic.

Heuss, Theodor. **Erinnerungen 1905-1933.** Tübingen: Wunderlich, 1963, 459 p.
These valuable memoirs of the former President of the Federal Republic of Germany encompass the German political scene through the 1920s and the fatal collapse of the political party system.

Hoepke, Klaus-Peter. **Die deutsche Rechte und der italienische Faschismus.** Düsseldorf: Droste, 1968, 348 p.
One of the few serious discussions of the relations between the German Right and Italian Fascism during the Weimar Republic.

Hofer, Walther and Others, eds. **Der Reichstagsbrand.** Berlin: Arani, 1972, 293 p.
The Reichstag fire of February 27, 1933 remains a controversial subject among German historians; this collection of documents and commentary concludes that the Nazis were the arsonists.

Hubatsch, Walther. **Hindenburg und der Staat.** Göttingen: Musterschmidt, 1966, 397 p.
The purpose of this important collection of documents from Hindenburg's archives and of the editor's introductory essay is to explain Hindenburg's conception of the German state and of his responsibilities as its President.

Hunt, Richard Norman. **German Social Democracy, 1918-1933.** New Haven: Yale University Press, 1964, 292 p.
This careful account of the internal machinery of the largest democratic party in Weimar Germany explains the weaknesses which beset the party and thus burdened the first German Republic.

Ilsemann, Sigurd von. **Der Kaiser in Holland.** Munich: Biederstein, 1967-68, 2 v.
The diary of Sigurd von Ilsemann, *aide-de-camp* of Kaiser Wilhelm II while he lived in Holland from 1918 to 1941. A revealing record of the Kaiser's activities and views.

Kalbe, Ernstgert. **Freiheit für Dimitroff: der internationale Kampf gegen die provokatorische Reichstagsbrandstiftung und den Leipziger Prozess.** Berlin: Rütten und Loening, 1963, 359 p.
An East German account, using communist-oriented sources, of the Reichstag fire and the ensuing trial of Dimitroff.

Kessler, Harry. **In the Twenties: The Diaries of Harry Kessler.** New York: Holt, Rinehart and Winston, 1971, 535 p.
His diaries, at last translated into English, have long been hailed as a brilliant source for the inter-war period, particularly in Germany. Kessler was a shrewd observer of men and events, with an unfailing flair for being at the center of all that was important. The German edition appeared as "Tagebücher, 1918-1937" (Frankfurt/Main: Insel-Verlag, 2d rev. ed., 1961, 799 p.).

Knütter, Hans-Helmuth. **Die Juden und die deutsche Linke in der Weimarer Republik, 1918-1933.** Düsseldorf: Droste, 1971, 259 p.

A serious and well-documented study of the role of the Jews in the leftist politics in the Weimar Republic.

Lebovics, Herman. **Social Conservatism and the Middle Classes in Germany, 1914-1933.** Princeton: Princeton University Press, 1969, 248 p.
A monograph, of both historic and contemporary interest, on how the plight of Germany's middle classes inspired murky theories of a new social order that would be neither capitalistic nor socialist.

Luther, Hans. **Vor dem Abgrund, 1930-1933: Reichsbankpräsident in Krisenzeiten.** Berlin: Propylän Verlag, 1964, 316 p.
Sober and unintentionally revealing recollections of the three years' economic crisis before Hitler's accession to power, by the then president of the Reichsbank.

Meier-Welcker, Hans. **Seeckt.** Frankfurt/Main: Bernard und Graefe, 1967, 744 p.
A well-documented biography of one of Germany's foremost political generals, famous for his reticence and success. By a professional soldier turned military historian.

Mitchell, Allan. **Revolution in Bavaria, 1918-1919: The Eisner Regime and the Soviet Republic.** Princeton: Princeton University Press, 1965, 374 p.
An admirable and absorbing account of one of the most fascinating revolutionary upheavals in post-1918 Europe. The author contributes sound judgments on many hitherto obscure aspects of German history.

Morsey, Rudolf. **Die Deutsche Zentrumspartei, 1917-1923.** Düsseldorf: Droste, 1966, 651 p.
A scholarly monograph on the Catholic Center Party from 1917 to the fall of Stresemann's government in 1923.

Mosse, Werner E. and Paucker, Arnold, *eds.* **Deutsches Judentum in Krieg und Revolution, 1916-1923.** Tübingen: Mohr (for the Leo Baeck Institut), 1971, 704 p.
——. **Entscheidungsjahr 1932: zur Judenfrage in der Endphase der Weimarer Republik.** Tübingen: Mohr (for the Leo Baeck Institut), 2d rev. ed., 1966, 615 p.
Two collections of essays, treating a great variety of topics, on German Jewry during World War I and the Weimar Republic.

Netzband, Karl-Bernhard and Widmaier, Hans Peter. **Währungs- und Finanzpolitik der Ära Luther, 1923-1925.** Basel: Kyklos-Verlag, 1964, 286 p.
A technical study of the, in the author's opinion, very successful financial policies of the German Finance Minister, and subsequently Reichskanzler, Hans Luther, in the years from 1923 to 1925.

Neubauer, Helmut, *ed.* **Deutschland und die Russische Revolution.** Stuttgart: Kohlhammer, 1968, 112 p.
Essays on the reverberations in Germany of the Bolshevik October Revolution, originally presented at a conference of the Deutsche Gesellschaft für Osteuropakunde.

Niekisch, Ernst. **Die Legende von der Weimarer Republik.** Cologne: Verlag Wissenschaft und Politik, 1968, 238 p.
A criticism of German Social Democracy for its failure to defend the Weimar Republic and an indictment of the German bourgeoisie for its sheepishness in facing the menace of Hitler. The author, who died in 1967, was a Prussian left-wing socialist.

Paetel, Karl Otto. **Versuchung oder Chance? Zur Geschichte des deutschen Nationalbolschewismus.** Göttingen: Musterschmidt, 1965, 343 p.
A study of the German political groups in the years of the Weimar Republic that combined both radical right and radical left tendencies and were known as National Bolsheviks.

Papen, Franz von. **Vom Scheitern einer Demokratie, 1930-1933.** Mainz: Von Hase und Koehler, 1968, 408 p.
A greatly extended version of the second section of the author's "Der Wahrheit eine Gasse" (Munich: List, 1952, 677 p.). Though of questionable value as a historical survey, it throws light on the self-righteous thinking of the prominent conservative statesman who, though not an admirer of Hitler, helped the Nazis to assume power.

Pünder, Hermann. **Von Preussen nach Europa: Lebenserinnerungen.** Stuttgart: Deutsche Verlags-Anstalt, 1968, 571 p.

Memoirs by a prominent German public servant, Secretary of State under chancellors Marx, Müller and Brüning during the years of the Weimar Republic, and a leading statesman in the post-1945 period in the Federal Republic.

Rathenau, Walther. **Tagebuch 1907–1922.** Düsseldorf: Droste, 1967, 319 p.
These diaries of Walther Rathenau, covering the years from 1907 to 1922 and edited by Hartmut Pogge von Strandmann, contain useful information on German politics and diplomacy. There is an introduction by Professor Fritz Fischer.

Rohe, Karl. **Das Reichsbanner Schwarz Rot Gold.** Düsseldorf: Droste, 1966, 494 p.
A thorough history of the paramilitary organization Das Reichsbanner Schwarz Rot Gold organized in 1924 by the Social Democrats for the defense of the Weimar Republic.

Ryder, A. J. **The German Revolution of 1918: A Study of German Socialism in War and Revolt.** New York: Cambridge University Press, 1967, 303 p.
An informative and scholarly study. Half of this book deals with German socialism before 1918.

Saldern, Adelheid von. **Hermann Dietrich: ein Staatsmann der Weimarer Republik.** Boppard/Rhein: Boldt, 1966, 226 p.
A study of the career and achievements of a prominent member of the German Democratic Party who was minister in the Müller and Brüning cabinets during the Weimar Republic.

Schmädke, Jürgen. **Militärische Kommandogewalt und parlamentarische Demokratie: zum Problem der Verantwortlichkeit des Reichswehrministers in der Weimarer Republik.** Lübeck: Matthiesen Verlag, 1966, 216 p.
A well-documented study of the failure of the Weimar Republic to subordinate its armed forces to civilian and parliamentary control.

Schulz, Gerhard. **Zwischen Demokratie und Diktatur: Verfassungspolitik und Reichsreform in der Weimarer Republik. Band I: Die Periode der Konsolidierung und der Revision des Bismarckschen Reichsaufbaus, 1919–1930.** Berlin: De Gruyter, 1963, 678 p.
The first volume of a valuable and thorough analysis of the political ramifications of constitution-making and constitution-reforming in the first 11 years of Weimar, with foremost emphasis on the question of federalism.

Schulze, Hagen. **Freikorps und Republik, 1918–1920.** Boppard: Boldt, 1969, 363 p.
A meticulously documented monograph on the military forces, known as the Free Corps, organized in Germany after the November Revolution with the approval of the Socialist government and the Western Allies for suppressing uprisings of the radical left and for defending the eastern borders after the disintegration of the German Army.

Schwarz, Jürgen. **Studenten in der Weimarer Republik.** Berlin: Duncker, 1971, 488 p.
A study of the organizations, social background, political activities and views of the university students in the Weimar Republic during the turbulent years from 1918 to 1923.

Stürmer, Michael. **Koalition und Opposition in der Weimarer Republik, 1924–1928.** Düsseldorf: Droste, 1967, 319 p.
A well-documented study of the political processes in the Weimar Republic in the years from 1924 to 1928, a period of relative stability and calm.

Stumpf, Richard. **War, Mutiny and Revolution in the German Navy: The World War I Diary of Seaman Richard Stumpf.** New Brunswick: Rutgers University Press, 1967, 442 p.
The wartime diary of an unusually observant German seaman who describes his transformation from an "outspoken Wilhelminian nationalist into an antimilitarist and republican."

Thimme, Annelise. **Flucht in den Mythos: die Deutschnationale Volkspartei und die Niederlage von 1918.** Göttingen: Vandenhoeck, 1969, 195 p.
A study of the attitudes of the conservative and nationalistic upper-class dominated *Deutschnationale Volkspartei* during the Weimar Republic. In the author's opinion, this party contributed to Hitler's coming to power not because it approved of his goals, but because it was against all social change and uncompromisingly opposed all liberal and socialistic parties.

Tjaden, Karl Hermann. **Struktur und Funktion der "KPD-Opposition" (KPO): eine Organisationssoziologische Untersuchung zur "Rechts"-Opposition im deutschen Kommunismus zur Zeit der Weimarer Republik.** Meisenheim am Glan: Hain, 1964, 350 p.

A detailed and richly documented study of the "Rightist Opposition" group within the German Communist Party during the period of the Weimar Republic.

Tobias, Fritz. **The Reichstag Fire.** New York: Putnam, 1964, 348 p.

A thorough reconstruction of the events connected with the Reichstag fire. The author argues that van der Lubbe could have done the deed without accomplices—contrary to the assertions of Nazis and anti-Nazis at the time and of historians since then.

Treviranus, Gottfried Reinhold. **Das Ende von Weimar: Heinrich Brüning und seine Zeit.** Düsseldorf: Econ-Verlag, 1968, 431 p.

Informative reminiscences from the era of the Weimar Republic, by a close friend of Chancellor Brüning and a member of his cabinet.

Turner, Henry Ashby, Jr. **Stresemann and the Politics of the Weimar Republic.** Princeton: Princeton University Press, 1963, 287 p.

A thorough, if narrowly conceived, study of Stresemann's gradual, reluctant conversion to republicanism and of his decisive role in German domestic politics, 1918-1929. The unpublished Stresemann *Nachlass* served as the principal source.

Vogelsang, Thilo. **Kurt von Schleicher: ein General als Politiker.** Göttingen: Musterschmidt, 1965, 112 p.

A brief biography of the last Chancellor of the Weimar Republic, murdered by the Nazis on June 30, 1934.

Ziemer, Gerhard. **Inflation und Deflation zerstören die Demokratie.** Stuttgart: Seewald, 1971, 256 p.

In this collection of essays on the financial crises of the Weimar Republic the author argues that well-meaning politicians who were ignorant of the principles determining economic and financial affairs were the real grave diggers of the Weimar Republic.

Foreign Relations

See also First World War, p. 131; Inter-War Period, p. 140; (Germany) General, p. 463; Recent History, p. 465; The 1918 Revolution and the Weimar Republic, General, p. 468; The Nazi Era, p. 475; and the sections for specific countries.

Berg, Peter. **Deutschland und Amerika: über das deutsche Amerikabild der zwanziger Jahre.** Lübeck: Matthiesen, 1963, 163 p.

A straightforward study of German attitudes toward the United States in the years between the armistice and the depression.

Cahén, Fritz Max. **Der Weg nach Versailles: Erinnerungen 1912-1919.** Boppard am Rhein: Boldt, 1963, 383 p.

A memoir by a journalist who was an aide to German Foreign Minister Rantzau at Versailles.

Deutsch-sowjetische Beziehungen von den Verhandlungen in Brest-Litowsk bis zum Abschluss des Rapallovertrages: Dokumentensammlung. Berlin: Staatsverlag der Deutschen Demokratischen Republik (for the Ministerium für Auswärtige Angelegenheiten der UdSSR and the Ministerium für Auswärtige Angelegenheiten der DDR), 1967-71, 2 v.

A collection of documents tracing German-Soviet relations from the end of hostilities in 1917-1918 to the signing of the Rapallo Agreement in 1922, compiled under the joint auspices of the Soviet and East German foreign ministries. The Russian version appeared as "Sovetsko-germanskie otnosheniia ot peregovorov v Brest-Litovske do podpisaniia Rapall'skogo dogovora: sbornik dokumentov" (Moscow: Izd-vo Politicheskoi Literatury, 1968-71, 2 v.).

Dyck, Harvey Leonard. **Weimar Germany and Soviet Russia, 1926-1933: A Study in Diplomatic Instability.** New York: Columbia University Press, 1966, 279 p.

A monograph on the vicissitudes of German-Soviet relations between the treaty of

Berlin and the coming of Hitler. An appropriate sequel to Gerald Freund's "Unholy Alliance."

Favez, Jean-Claude. **Le Reich devant l'occupation franco-belge de la Ruhr en 1923.** Geneva: Droz, 1969, 409 p.
A well-planned and clearly written monograph on the political, economic and diplomatic problems of Germany before the French and Belgian occupation of the Ruhr in 1923.

Gottwald, Robert. **Die deutsch-amerikanischen Beziehungen in der Ära Stresemann.** Berlin: Colloquium Verlag, 1965, 167 p.
A revealing study of German-American relations and of the many influences which shaped them. The author, a German historian, used new German and American archival sources.

Kellermann, Volkmar. **Schwarzer Adler — weisser Adler.** Cologne: Markus Verlag, 1970, 196 p.
A very critical review of policies and attitudes in the Weimar Republic toward the Polish state.

Kimmich, Christoph M. **The Free City: Danzig and German Foreign Policy, 1919-1934.** New Haven: Yale University Press, 1968, 196 p.
According to the author, the purpose of this study is the examination of "the history of the Weimar Republic's attempt to revise the borders."

Link, Werner. **Die amerikanische Stabilisierungspolitik in Deutschland, 1921-32.** Düsseldorf: Droste, 1970, 704 p.
A very comprehensive and well-documented study of U.S. involvement in German economic problems during the Weimar Republic.

Linke, Horst Günther. **Deutsch-sowjetische Beziehungen bis Rapallo.** Cologne: Verlag Wissenschaft und Politik, 1970, 295 p.
A solid and well-documented survey of German-Rusian relations during the first four years of the Weimar Republic, by a young German historian.

Maxelon, Michael-Olaf. **Stresemann und Frankreich, 1914-1929.** Düsseldorf: Droste, 1972, 309 p.
A study of Stresemann's views on France and of his policies toward that country, when he was Germany's Foreign Minister.

Rosenbaum, Kurt. **Community of Fate: German-Soviet Diplomatic Relations, 1922-1928.** Syracuse: Syracuse University Press, 1965, 325 p.
This study provides some new documentary evidence from the German archives.

Salewski, Michael. **Entwaffnung und Militärkontrolle in Deutschland, 1919-1927.** Munich: Oldenbourg (for the Deutsche Gesellschaft für Auswärtige Politik), 1966, 421 p.
A thorough study of the system of controls that was designed to keep Germany disarmed after World War I.

Schwabe, Klaus. **Deutsche Revolution und Wilson-Frieden.** Düsseldorf: Droste, 1971, 711 p.
A massive study by a German historian of the changing relations between the United States and defeated Germany, seen in the context of ideological, political and economic factors.

Spenz, Jürgen. **Die diplomatische Vorgeschichte des Beitritts Deutschlands zum Völkerbund, 1924-1926.** Göttingen: Musterschmidt, 1966, 216 p.
A thorough study of the diplomatic developments preceding and concerning the admission of the Weimar Republic to the League of Nations in September 1926.

Teske, Hermann, *ed.* **General Ernst Köstring: der militärische Mittler zwischen dem deutschen Reich und der Sowjetunion, 1921-1941.** Frankfurt/Main: Mittler, 1966, 334 p.
These memoirs, letters and official reports of General Köstring, for many years the German military attaché in Moscow, contain valuable information on Soviet military developments and German-Soviet relations in the inter-war period.

Von Riekhoff, Harald. **German-Polish Relations, 1918-1933.** Baltimore: Johns Hopkins Press, 1971, 421 p.

A sober assessment of the diplomatic relations between the two countries, based on German and Polish sources, and set against the background of general European politics.

Walsdorff, Martin. **Westorientierung und Ostpolitik: Stresemanns Russland-Politik in der Locarno-Ära.** Bremen: Schünemann, 1971, 325 p.
A revisionist reconsideration of Stresemann's foreign policy as solely that of the "Good European."

Wandel, Eckhard. **Die Bedeutung der Vereinigten Staaten von Amerika für das deutsche Reparationsproblem, 1924–1929.** Tübingen: Mohr, 1971, 332 p.
The author argues that the reparations agreements made Germany financially dependent on the United States and that, consequently, the United States exercised considerable influence on the politics and foreign policies of the Weimar Republic.

Weidenfeld, Werner. **Die Englandpolitik Gustav Stresemanns: theoretische und praktische Aspekte der Aussenpolitik.** Mainz: Von Hase und Koehler, 1972, 382 p.
A well-documented and solid study of Stresemann's policies toward England.

Zsigmond, László. **Zur deutschen Frage, 1918–1923: die wirtschaftlichen und internationalen Faktoren der Wiederbelebung des deutschen Imperialismus und Militarismus.** Budapest: Akadémiai Kiadó, 1964, 345 p.
A study of the German problem in international relations from 1918 to 1923. The author, a Hungarian communist historian, contends that the First World War did not destroy German monopolistic capitalism and imperialism, and that the Western powers, being concerned about the rise of communism, helped Germany to regain a prominent role in European politics.

The Nazi Era

General

See also Political Philosophies and Ideologies, p. 21; Inter-War Period, p. 140; Second World War, p. 144; (Europe) General Surveys, p. 344; Western Europe, p. 345; and other subsections under Germany.

Absolon, Rudolf. **Die Wehrmacht im Dritten Reich.** Boppard: Boldt, 1969– .
A historical survey, planned in six volumes and prepared at the Archives of the Federal Republic, dealing with the organization of the armed forces in Hitler's Germany. The first two published volumes cover the period through August 2, 1934.

Adolph, Walter. **Hirtenamt und Hitler-Diktatur.** Berlin: Morus-Verlag, 1965, 183 p.
A study of the Catholic Church under the Nazi régime, with emphasis on the divergent views of Cardinal Bertram, Archbishop of Breslau, who thought that a modus vivendi was possible with the Nazis, and of Count Preysing, Bishop of Berlin, who did not have any illusions about the nature of Hitler's state.

Birkenfeld, Wolfgang. **Der synthetische Treibstoff, 1933–1945: ein Beitrag zur nationalsozialistischen Wirtschafts- und Rüstungspolitik.** Göttingen: Musterschmidt, 1964, 279 p.
This well-documented study traces the history of German synthetic fuel production through the whole Nazi period. The author suggests that the Allies were mistaken not to give this industry a higher priority as a bombing target.

Boberach, Heinz, ed. **Meldungen aus dem Reich: Auswahl aus den geheimen Lageberichten des Sicherheitsdienstes der SS, 1939–1944.** Neuwied: Luchterhand Verlag, 1965, 551 p.
A selection of the highly confidential German public opinion surveys that from 1939 to 1944 were compiled twice a week by Himmler's security police (SD).

Bracher, Karl Dietrich. **The German Dictatorship: The Origins, Structure, and Effects of National Socialism.** New York: Praeger, 1970, 553 p.
A thorough, incisive and scholarly synthesis of all aspects of the Nazi phenomenon, by Germany's leading expert on the subject. This study, likely to become a standard work, offers a further commentary on the precariousness of modern democracy and the ways by which it can be perverted. The German original appeared as "Die

deutsche Diktatur: Entstehung, Struktur, Folgen des Nationalsozialismus" (Cologne: Kiepenheuer, 1969, 580 p.).

Buchheim, Hans and Others. **Anatomie des SS-Staates.** Olten: Walter, 1965, 2 v.
A detailed description of the guiding principles, organization and activities of the SS establishment, prepared by a group of scholars from the Institut für Zeitgeschichte and the Deutsche Gesellschaft für Auswärtige Politik for use at German war crimes trials. Vol. I is entitled "Die SS—das Herrschaftsinstrument, Befehl und Gehorsam," (390 p.); Vol. II, "Konzentrationslager, Kommissarbefehl, Judenverfolgung" (458 p.). The English version appeared as "Anatomy of the SS State" (New York: Walker, 1968, 614 p.).

Carroll, Berenice A. **Design for Total War: Arms and Economics in the Third Reich.** The Hague: Mouton, 1968, 311 p.
This monograph on economic mobilization for war in Nazi Germany is primarily a study of the paradoxical career and plans of General Georg Thomas, the former head of the German Armed Forces' Economic and Armaments Office, who was a dedicated advocate of total economic mobilization and at the same time an opponent of Adolf Hitler. General Thomas was arrested in November 1944 for alleged complicity in the attempt upon Hitler's life on July 20, 1944.

Conway, John S. **The Nazi Persecution of the Churches, 1933-45.** New York: Basic Books, 1968, 474 p.
A study of collaboration and resistance of organized Christianity in the Third Reich by an English historian.

Die deutsche Justiz und der Nationalsozialismus. Stuttgart: Deutsche Verlags-Anstalt (for the Institut für Zeitgeschichte), 1968—.
A massive survey of law and justice under the Nazi regime. Two volumes have been published through 1972.

Göhring, Martin. **Alles oder Nichts: zwölf Jahre totalitären Herrschaft in Deutschland. Band I: 1933-1939.** Tübingen: Mohr, 1966, 354 p.
The first volume of a history of Nazi Germany by a leading German historian who pays particular attention to the influence exercised by internal German political developments on the formulation of Hitler's foreign policy. The author died before completing the second volume.

Heinz, Grete and Peterson, Agnes F., *comps.* **NSDAP Hauptarchiv: Guide to the Hoover Institution Microfilm Collection.** Stanford: Hoover Institution on War, Revolution, and Peace, 1964, 175 p.
An indispensable guide to German documents from various archives of the National Socialist Party available on microfilm at the Hoover Institution.

Homze, Edward L. **Foreign Labor in Nazi Germany.** Princeton: Princeton University Press, 1967, 350 p.
A study based largely on captured German records and reports, and dealing with the organization and administration of the Nazi foreign labor program and its relationship to the war economy.

Huber, Heinz and Müller, Artur, *eds.* **Das Dritte Reich: seine Geschichte in Texten, Bildern und Dokumenten.** Munich: Desch, 1964, 2 v.
A gripping and comprehensive record of the Third Reich, made up of objective commentary and illuminating pictures, originally prepared for a highly successful German TV series.

Lewy, Guenter. **The Catholic Church and Nazi Germany.** New York: McGraw-Hill, 1964, 416 p.
A major contribution to a bitter and important controversy. The author, a political scientist, had access to some hitherto unused sources. He more often indicts than explains Catholic accommodation to Hitler's regime.

Mau, Hermann and Krausnick, Helmut. **German History 1933-45: An Assessment by German Historians.** New York: Ungar, 1963, 157 p.
A brief attempt to evaluate the history of Hitler's Germany. Hermann Mau was a brilliant young historian who died before completing the German text. The German edition was entitled "Deutsche Geschichte der jüngsten Vergangenheit, 1933-45" (Tübingen: Wunderlich, 1956, 206 p.).

Mommsen, Hans. **Beamtentum im Dritten Reich.** Stuttgart: Deutsche Verlags-Anstalt (for the Institut für Zeitgeschichte), 1966, 246 p.
An incisive analysis of the relations between the Nazi regime and German bureaucracy, followed by a hundred pages of carefully selected documents. An important contribution to the history of the Third Reich.

Müller, Hans, *ed.* **Katholische Kirche und Nationalsozialismus.** Munich: Nymphenburger Verlagshandlung, 1963, 432 p.
A collection of articles and documents illustrating the relations between the Catholic Church and the National Socialists in the period from 1930 to 1935.

Müller, Klaus-Jürgen. **Das Heer und Hitler: Armee und nationalsozialistisches Regime, 1933-1940.** Stuttgart: Deutsche Verlags-Anstalt, 1969, 711 p.
A well-documented study of the relationship between the National Socialist regime and the Army from 1933 to the beginning of the campaign in the West in May 1940. Mr. Müller thinks that the leading German officers supported Hitler not because they were Nazis, but because they disapproved of the Weimar Republic, wanted to strengthen the German state and were not able to understand the revolutionary character of the Nazi movement.

O'Neill, Robert John. **The German Army and the Nazi Party, 1933-1939.** New York: James H. Heineman, 1967, 286 p.
An able and interesting study of the way in which Hitler, once in power, managed to achieve ascendancy over the leaders of the German Army.

Peterson, Edward Norman. **The Limits of Hitler's Power.** Princeton: Princeton University Press, 1969, 472 p.
Inspired by an unusual curiosity about human behavior and based on new sources, this scholarly work analyzes the far from efficient system of government which Hitler headed and which was often hobbled by local obstructionism and in-fighting.

Phillips, Walter Alfred Peter. **The Tragedy of Nazi Germany.** New York: Praeger, 1969, 241 p.
An essay on the deeper causes of Nazi evil, written out of fear that the West could produce another similar monstrosity. Controversial, moralistic and troubling.

Robertson, Esmonde Manning. **Hitler's Pre-War Policy and Military Plans, 1933-1939.** New York: Citadel Press, 1967, 207 p.
A closely reasoned study of Hitler's policies, critical of earlier notions that he followed some sort of master plan. "Hitler seldom looked more than one move ahead" is the theme of this important and illuminating book. First published in London in 1963.

Roh, Franz. **"Entartete" Kunst: Kunstbarbarei im Dritten Reich.** Hanover: Fackelträger-Verlag, 1962, 330 p.
A long-standing supporter of avant-garde art in modern Germany discusses the Nazi reaction against modern art.

Schoenbaum, David. **Hitler's Social Revolution: Class and Status in Nazi Germany, 1933-1939.** Garden City: Doubleday, 1966, 336 p.
An analytical treatment of the impact of National Socialism on the various sections of German society—labor, business, agriculture, women and the state itself.

Schorn, Hubert. **Die Gesetzgebung des Nationalsozialismus als Mittel der Machtpolitik.** Frankfurt/Main: Klostermann, 1963, 175 p.
A short but useful book by a retired judge on the legal methods used by the Nazi regime to secure its power.

Schweitzer, Arthur. **Big Business in the Third Reich.** Bloomington: Indiana University Press, 1964, 739 p.
A far-ranging analysis of big business and the Nazi state by an economist who tries to emulate Weber's sociological analysis of economic conditions. The author holds that from 1933 to 1939 Germany was governed by a "coalition of Nazis, generals, and big business," which left big business stronger and richer than before and its enemies, including the anti-capitalistic wing of the Nazis, defeated.

Steinert, Marlis G. **23 Days: The Final Collapse of Nazi Germany.** New York: Walker, 1969, 326 p.
In this study of the final days of the Third Reich particular attention is paid to the careers of the leading figures in German government and armed forces after Hitler's

suicide: Admiral Dönitz, Count Schwerin von Krosigk, Albert Speer, General Jodl and Field Marshal Keitel. In the author's opinion Admiral Dönitz saved Germany from total destruction and provided countless Germans with the opportunity to escape Soviet captivity. The German original was published as "Die 23 Tage der Regierung Dönitz" (Düsseldorf: Econ-Verlag, 1967, 426 p.).

Wheaton, Eliot Barculo. **Prelude to Calamity: The Nazi Revolution 1933-35: With a Background Survey of the Weimar Era.** Garden City: Doubleday, 1968, 523 p.
Summarizing the results of recent scholarship, the author presents a survey of the Nazi takeover of the Weimar Republic.

Wulf, Josef, *ed.* **Kunst und Kultur im Dritten Reich.** Gütersloh: Sigbert Mohn, 1963-64, 5 v.
Documentation on the arts, literature, theater, film, press and radio in Nazi Germany. The titles of the individual volumes are: vol. 1, "Die Bildenden Künste im Dritten Reich" (1963, 413 p.); vol. 2, "Musik im Dritten Reich" (1963, 446 p.); vol. 3, "Literatur und Dichtung im Dritten Reich" (1963, 471 p.); vol. 4, "Theater und Film im Dritten Reich" (1964, 437 p.); and vol. 5, "Presse und Funk im Dritten Reich" (1964, 390 p.).

The Nazi Movement

See also Totalitarianism; Fascism, p. 32; The Problem of Authority; Violence and Revolution, p. 34; Inter-War Period, p. 140; Second World War, p. 144; (Latin America) General, p. 200; (The United States) Biographies, Memoirs and Addresses, p. 218; Switzerland, p. 393; (Italy) Recent History, p. 422; other subsections under Germany.

Bennecke, Heinrich. **Hitler und die S.A.** Munich: Olzog, 1962, 264 p.
A study of the origins and functions of the S.A. in Hitler's Germany by a former member of the organization.

Bollmus, Reinhard. **Das Amt Rosenberg und seine Gegner: Studien zum Machtkampf im nationalsozialistischen Herrschaftssystem.** Stuttgart: Deutsche Verlags-Anstalt, 1970, 359 p.
A study of Alfred Rosenberg's organization for National Socialist ideology and a description of its importance within the Nazi hierarchy.

Bonnin, Georges. **Le Putsch de Hitler à Munich en 1923.** Les Sables-d'Olonne (France): The Author, 1966, 232 p.
For this collection of documents on Hitler's unsuccessful coup of November 1923 the author has made use of some hitherto little-known sources.

Boveri, Margret. **Wir lügen alle: eine Hauptstadtzeitung unter Hitler.** Olten: Walter, 1965, 744 p.
The story of how a leading liberal newspaper of Germany, the *Berliner Tageblatt*, tried to compromise with Goebbels after the Nazis came to power. The author, on the staff of this paper at that time, calls it "an attempt at the impossible."

Bramsted, Ernest Kohn. **Goebbels and National Socialist Propaganda, 1925-1945.** East Lansing: Michigan State University Press, 1965, 488 p.
A detailed study of the subject and a contribution to the general study of the functions of twentieth-century propaganda.

Burden, Hamilton Twombly. **The Nuremberg Party Rallies, 1923-39.** New York: Praeger, 1967, 206 p.
A well-documented study of the awesome Nazi Party rallies at Nuremberg where Hitler, using modern methods of organization and propaganda, displayed his talent for seducing the German masses.

Delarue, Jacques. **The Gestapo: A History of Horror.** New York: Morrow, 1964, 384 p.
A partial reconstruction of Gestapo's network of terror, with some new information on its activities in France. The French author, himself a victim of the German occupation, has written a book for the general reader, not the specialist. The original appeared in France as "Histoire de la Gestapo" (Paris: Fayard, 1962, 472 p.).

Eschenburg, Theodor and Others. **The Path to Dictatorship, 1918-1933.** Garden City: Doubleday, 1966, 217 p.

Essays by leading German students of the Nazi era on what lay behind Hitler's takeover. The German original was published as "Der Weg in die Diktatur, 1918 bis 1933" (Munich: Piper, 1962, 244 p.).

Gordon, Harold J., Jr. **Hitler and the Beer Hall Putsch.** Princeton: Princeton University Press, 1972, 666 p.

An exemplary investigation of the primary sources that provides an enlightening case study of the roots of power, the weaknesses of the Weimar Republic and Bavaria's position vis-à-vis National Socialism.

Grieswelle, Detlev. **Propaganda der Friedlosigkeit: eine Studie zu Hitlers Rhetorik, 1920-1933.** Stuttgart: Ferdinand Enke Verlag, 1972, 233 p.

A substantial study of Hitler's rhetoric and propaganda techniques during the Weimar Republic.

Hale, Oron James. **The Captive Press in the Third Reich.** Princeton: Princeton University Press, 1964, 353 p.

The Nazis first muzzled the once flourishing German press and then usurped the ownership as well. A dreary tale of power, cupidity and unprincipled subservience, told authoritatively and on the basis of extensive research by a well-known historian.

Heberle, Rudolf. **Landbevölkerung und Nationalsozialismus: eine soziologische Untersuchung der politischen Willensbildung in Schleswig-Holstein 1918 bis 1932.** Stuttgart: Deutsche Verlags-Anstalt (for the Institut für Zeitgeschichte), 1963, 171 p.

In this thorough sociological study the author attempts to explain why Schleswig-Holstein, in 1914 a stronghold of liberalism and in 1919/20 favoring the parties of the Left, became a bastion of National Socialism before 1933. A shortened English version appeared as "From Democracy to Nazism" (Baton Rouge: Louisiana State University Press, 1945, 130 p.).

Höhne, Heinz. **The Order of the Death's Head: The Story of Hitler's S.S.** New York: Coward-McCann, 1970, 690 p.

In contrast to the writers who claim that the SS was a monolithic and demonically well-organized body, the author demonstrates that it was a bizarre and irrationally governed organization and that its diverse membership comprised not only Nazi fanatics and criminals but also idealists, romantics, careerists and wartime conscripts. An expanded version of a series published in the weekly *Der Spiegel*. The German original was published as "Der Orden unter dem Totenkopf: die Geschichte der SS" (Gütersloh: Sigbert Mohn Verlag, 1967, 600 p.).

Holborn, Hajo, *ed.* **Republic to Reich: The Making of the Nazi Revolution.** New York: Pantheon Books, 1972, 491 p.

These essays, by leading German scholars, provide important new insights into the rise of Nazism. They were expertly selected and introduced by the late Hajo Holborn who had a profound impact on the study of this theme, here and abroad.

Horn, Wolfgang. **Führerideologie und Parteiorganisation in der NSDAP (1919-1933).** Düsseldorf: Droste, 1972, 451 p.

An attempt to describe how and why Hitler established his authority over the heterogeneous Nazi party before 1933.

Jochmann, Werner. **Nationalsozialismus und Revolution: Ursprung und Geschichte der NSDAP in Hamburg, 1922-1933; Dokumente.** Frankfurt/Main: Europäische Verlagsanstalt (for the Forschungsstelle für die Geschichte des Nationalsozialismus in Hamburg), 1963, 444 p.

Documents on the early years of the Nazi movement in north and northwest Germany where, more than in other parts of the country, the movement emphasized its socialistic and revolutionary impulses.

Kele, Max H. **Nazis and Workers: National Socialist Appeals to German Labor, 1919-1933.** Chapel Hill: University of North Carolina Press, 1972, 243 p.

A scholarly study of Nazi efforts to woo workers—and their success which the author argues has been considerably underestimated.

Klose, Werner. **Generationen im Gleichschritt: ein Dokumentarbericht.** Oldenburg: Stalling, 1964, 296 p.

An informative but not very scholarly survey of the history and organization of the Hitler youth movement.

Kühnl, Reinhard. **Die nationalsozialistische Linke, 1925–1930.** Meisenheim am Glan: Hain, 1966, 378 p.
   A thorough study of the development of the political ideas and activities of the leftist and anti-capitalistic North German wing of the NSDP. The leftist wing was active from 1925 to 1930, when Hitler succeeded in forcing its leader Otto Strasser to leave the Party.

Lutzhöft, Hans-Jürgen. **Der nordische Gedanke in Deutschland, 1920–1940.** Stuttgart: Klett, 1971, 439 p.
   A solid study of the development of the various German doctrines proclaiming the superiority of the Nordic race, including a description of the influence of such doctrines on the domestic and foreign policies of Nazi Germany.

Maser, Werner. **Die Frühgeschichte der NSDAP: Hitlers Weg bis 1924.** Frankfurt: Athenäum, 1965, 524 p.
   In this study of Hitler's youth and the early years of the Nazi Party the author claims that most of Hitler's biographers have relied too much on the Führer's own writings.

Mosse, George Lachmann. **The Crisis of German Ideology: Intellectual Origins of the Third Reich.** New York: Grosset and Dunlap, 1964, 373 p.
   An effort to trace the ideas in nineteenth- and early twentieth-century German thought that underlay the Nazi ideology.

Mosse, George Lachmann, ed. **Nazi Culture: Intellectual, Cultural and Social Life in the Third Reich.** New York: Grosset and Dunlap, 1966, 386 p.
   This collection of documents and readings on Nazi cultural and social life includes, among others, excerpts from the writings of Adolf Hitler, Alfred Rosenberg, Joseph Goebbels and Cardinal Faulhaber.

Orlow, Dietrich. **The History of the Nazi Party.** Pittsburgh: University of Pittsburgh Press, 1969–73, 2 v.
   In the words of the author, a professor of history at Syracuse University, this study attempts "to interrelate the more visible, propagandistic activities of the NSDAP with the less conspicuous organizational and structural developments."

Zeman, Zbynek Anthony Bohuslav. **Nazi Propaganda.** New York: Oxford University Press (in association with the Wiener Library), 1964, 226 p.
   A brief but suggestive study of the techniques and successes of Nazi propaganda in Germany and abroad.

Biographies, Memoirs and Collected Writings

See also Second World War, p. 144; other subsections under Germany.

Ackermann, Josef. **Heinrich Himmler als Ideologe.** Göttingen: Musterschmidt, 1970, 317 p.
   A study of the development of the horrifying ideological concepts of Heinrich Himmler, one of the most powerful and ruthless men in Nazi Germany. The author has had access to Himmler's personal papers.

Aronson, Shlomo. **Reinhard Heydrich und die Frühgeschichte von Gestapo und SD.** Stuttgart: Deutsche Verlags-Anstalt, 1971, 339 p.
   A study of the early years of Gestapo and the notorious SD leader Reinhard Heydrich.

Bezymenskii, Lev Aleksandrovich. **The Death of Adolf Hitler: Unknown Documents from Soviet Archives.** New York: Harcourt, Brace and World, 1968, 114 p.
   The official Soviet evidence, based on the autopsy and interviews, that Hitler killed himself by poisoning.

Bräutigam, Otto. **So hat es sich zugetragen. . . .** Würzburg: Holzner, 1968, 723 p.
   Memoirs of a German diplomat, a leading participant in the planning and execution of Nazi policies in Eastern Europe during World War II. A useful source.

Calic, Édouard. **Secret Conversations with Hitler: The Two Newly-Discovered 1931 Interviews.** New York: Day, 1971, 191 p.
   Hitler's calculated rantings against Jews, Marxists, foreign powers, and especially against the "rotten bourgeoisie" as delivered to a bourgeois editor. An important source for Hitler's views and tactics before gaining power. The German original was published as "Ohne Maske: Hitler—Breiting Geheimgespräche 1931" (Frankfurt/Main: Societäts-Verlag, 1968, 233 p.).

Cecil, Robert. **The Myth of the Master Race: Alfred Rosenberg and Nazi Ideology.** New York: Dodd, Mead, 1972, 266 p.

The first serious attempt to describe the life and ideology of Alfred Rosenberg, by a British scholar.

Dönitz, Karl. **Mein wechselvolles Leben.** Göttingen: Musterschmidt, 1968, 227 p.

The autobiography of Admiral Dönitz, commander of the Submarine Force of the German Navy from 1935 to 1943, subsequently the Commander-in-Chief of the German Navy and, for a few days, after Hitler's death, head of the German state. This volume contains very little on the Nazi years which the Admiral has described in his "Zehn Jahre und zwanzig Tage" (Bonn: Athenaeum, 1958, 512 p.).

Dollmann, Eugen. **Dolmetscher der Diktatoren.** Bayreuth: Hestia-Verlag, 1963, 253 p.

These memoirs by an official interpreter of Nazi Germany contain some information on the negotiations that led to the capitulation of the German troops in Italy during the end-phase of World War II.

Domarus, Max, *ed.* **Hitler: Reden und Proklamationen, 1932-1945; kommentiert von einem deutschen Zeitgenossen.** München: Süddeutscher Verlag, 2d ed., 1965, 2 v. in 4 pts.

Speeches and proclamations of Adolf Hitler from 1932 to 1945, with annotations and commentary by the editor.

Fest, Joachim C. **The Face of the Third Reich: Portraits of the Nazi Leadership.** New York: Pantheon Books, 1970, 402 p.

A series of biographical essays about Nazi leaders who together made up "the face of the Third Reich." The German original was published as "Das Gesicht des Dritten Reiches: Profile einer totalitären Herrschaft" (Munich: Piper, 1963, 513 p.).

Gisevius, Hans Bernd. **Adolf Hitler: Versuch einer Deutung.** Munich: Rütten und Loening, 1963, 565 p.

A substantial, though somewhat episodic and uneven biography of Adolf Hitler.

Hammerstein-Equord, Kunrat, Freiherr von. **Spähtrupp.** Stuttgart: Goverts, 1963, 311 p.

Six memoir episodes by a German officer originally drafted in the 1940s, and ranging from Hitler's takeover in 1933 to the abortive coup of July 20, 1944.

Hanfstaengl, Ernst. **Zwischen weissem und braunem Haus.** Munich: Piper, 1970, 402 p.

These memoirs provide useful information on the early years of the Nazi party and Hitler's regime. The author, a Harvard graduate and an early supporter of Adolf Hitler, left Germany in 1937 and spent part of the war years in the United States.

Heiber, Helmut. **Goebbels.** New York: Hawthorn, 1972, 387 p.

This biography by the editor of Goebbels' early diaries is most revealing about the propaganda techniques Goebbels perfected—and succumbed to—in excoriating the "bourgeois" pettiness and philistinism he himself so completely manifested. The German original was published as "Joseph Goebbels" (Berlin: Colloquium Verlag, 1962, 433 p.).

Heiber, Helmut, *ed.* **Reichsführer!** Stuttgart: Deutsche Verlags-Anstalt, 1968, 318 p.

A collection of letters written by and to Himmler which clearly demonstrate the evil banality of the Nazi leader's philosophy.

Hitler, Adolf. **Tischgespräche im Führerhauptquartier, 1941-1942.** Stuttgart: Seewald, new ed., 1963, 546 p.

A new and complete edition of Hitler's mealtime monologues at his headquarters in 1941 and 1942, including a widely discussed portrait of Hitler by Percy Ernst Schramm, who is also the editor of the new edition.

Keitel, Wilhelm. **The Memoirs of Field-Marshal Keitel.** New York: Stein and Day, 1966, 288 p.

Memoirs of the chief of the Wehrmacht who was executed as a war criminal in 1946, edited by Walter Görlitz. The German original was published as "Generalfeldmarschall Keitel: Verbrecher oder Offizier?" (Göttingen: Musterschmidt, 1961, 447 p.).

Lange, Karl. **Hitlers unbeachtete Maximen.** Stuttgart: Kohlhammer, 1968, 211 p.

The author of this provocative study argues that most of the disasters caused by Hitler and his regime were caused by the unwillingness of his followers and opponents to read carefully his "Mein Kampf."

McGovern, James. **Martin Bormann.** New York: Morrow, 1968, 237 p.
The author, a former CIA official in charge of the quest for Bormann, argues convincingly that the ruthless Nazi leader, who had hoped to become the successor to Hitler, took poison and that the Russians disposed of his body.

Manvell, Roger and Fraenkel, Heinrich. **Himmler.** New York: Putnam, 1965, 283 p.
The story of the evil man who was the leader of the SS and one of Hitler's chief lieutenants.

Maser, Werner. **Adolf Hitler: Legende, Mythos, Wirklichkeit.** Munich: Bechtle, 1971, 529 p.
A widely read and discussed study of Hitler's career, based on a wealth of newly discovered, but not always very well-digested documentation.

Maser, Werner. **Hitlers Mein Kampf.** Munich: Bechtle, 1966, 344 p.
Commentaries on the sources, style and contents of Hitler's "Mein Kampf."

Röhrs, Hans-Dietrich. **Hitlers Krankheit: Tatsachen und Legenden; medizinische und psychische Grundlagen seines Zusammenbruchs.** Neckargemünd: Vowinckel, 1966, 203 p.
The author, a German doctor, analyzes Hitler's medical history and comes to the conclusion that certain aberrations of his personality were the result of an indiscriminate use of drugs.

Schirach, Baldur von. **Ich glaubte an Hitler.** Hamburg: Mosaik Verlag, 1967, 367 p.
These meager memoirs are of interest only because they were written by an important Nazi official, the leader of Hitler's youth organization.

Senger und Etterlin, Fridolin von. **Neither Fear Nor Hope: The Wartime Career of General Frido von Senger und Etterlin, Defender of Cassino.** New York: Dutton, 1964, 368 p.
Important and well-written memoirs by a German general who fought on many battlefields of the Second World War. The German original was published as "Krieg in Europa" (Cologne: Kiepenheuer, 1960, 459 p.).

Smith, Bradley F. **Adolf Hitler: His Family, Childhood and Youth.** Stanford: Hoover Institution on War, Revolution, and Peace, 1967, 180 p.
The variegated experiences and impressions of the young "loner" in Austria, painstakingly depicted by an American historian.

Smith, Bradley F. **Heinrich Himmler: A Nazi in the Making, 1900-1926.** Stanford: Hoover Institution Press, 1971, 211 p.
An interesting and thoughtful attempt to analyze the psychological and social factors shaping Himmler's early career in Nazism, based on the quantities of biographical material assembled by the meticulous Himmler himself.

Speer, Albert. **Inside the Third Reich: Memoirs.** New York: Macmillan, 1970, 596 p.
Probably the most revealing memoirs of the Hitler regime, by its chief architect turned technocrat and organizer of armaments. As Hitler's confidant, he was close to important men and events, and he had a shrewd, surprisingly non-ideological perspective on the Third Reich. Translation of: "Erinnerungen" (Berlin: Propyläen-Verlag, 1969, 610 p.).

Foreign Relations

See also General Works, p. 1; Inter-War Period, p. 140; Second World War, p. 144; other subsections under Germany and the sections for specific countries and regions.

Ben-Elissar, Eliahu. **Le Facteur juif dans la politique étrangère du IIIe Reich (1933-1939).** Paris: Julliard, 1969, 521 p.
Based on German archival sources, this thesis by an Israeli scholar analyzes the impact of the Nazi treatment of Jews on German relations to other countries, including America. For many years, the Nazis were quite concerned about foreign responses.

Ebel, Arnold. **Die diplomatischen Beziehungen des Dritten Reiches zu Argentinien unter besonderer Berücksichtigung der Handelspolitik (1933-1939).** Geneva: Université de Genève, Institut Universitaire de Hautes Études Internationales, 1970, 472 p.

A detailed and well-documented history of the relations between Nazi Germany and Argentina.

Friedländer, Saul. **Prelude to Downfall: Hitler and the United States, 1939-1941.** New York: Knopf, 1967, 328 p.

An important study of German policy toward the United States, based in part on hitherto unavailable sources, especially German naval documents. Originally published as "Hitler et les États-Unis (1939-1941)" (Geneva: Droz, 1963, 298 p.).

Frye, Alton. **Nazi Germany and the American Hemisphere, 1933-1941.** New Haven: Yale University Press, 1967, 229 p.

A well-documented study of Nazi subversive efforts in the Western Hemisphere, epitomized by the campaign to defeat Roosevelt in 1940: "One of the most massive interferences in American domestic affairs in history." Also a thoughtful assessment of Hitler's likely—malevolent—intentions had he won the war in Europe.

Granzow, Brigitte. **A Mirror of Nazism: British Opinion and the Emergence of Hitler, 1929-1933.** London: Gollancz, 1964, 248 p.

An intelligent selection of articles by British correspondents for *The Times, The Observer, Manchester Guardian, Daily Telegraph* and *Economist,* used by the author to analyze the meaning for the British of Hitler's rise to power.

Hildebrand, Klaus. **Deutsche Aussenpolitik, 1933-1945: Kalkül oder Dogma?** Stuttgart: Kohlhammer, 1971, 186 p.

An attempt to interpret the basic premises and development of Nazi foreign policy, emphasizing its close relationship to the aims originally formulated in the 1920s.

Hildebrand, Klaus. **Vom Reich zum Weltreich: Hitler, NSDAP und koloniale Frage, 1919-1945.** Munich: W. Fink, 1969, 955 p.

In a massive work, based on vast, hitherto unused archival material, a German historian analyzes admirably the place of colonial aspirations in Hitler's shifting policies.

Hirszowicz, Łukasz. **The Third Reich and the Arab East.** Toronto: University of Toronto Press, 1966, 403 p.

A thoroughgoing examination of Nazi policy in the Middle East by a Polish scholar. The Polish edition appeared as "III Rzesza i Arabski Wschód" (Warsaw: Książka i Wiedza, 1963, 565 p.).

Jacobsen, Hans-Adolf. **Nationalsozialistische Aussenpolitik, 1933-1938.** Frankfurt/Main: Metzner, 1968, 944 p.

A most thorough and authoritative analysis of Hitler's foreign policy before 1938. Jacobsen stresses the continuity of revolutionary aims in Nazi policy from the early 1920s to the increasingly open aggressiveness, as manifested by the *Anschluss.*

Kuhn, Axel. **Hitlers aussenpolitisches Programm: Entstehung und Entwicklung, 1919-1939.** Stuttgart: Klett, 1970, 286 p.

A book in two parts: a short survey of Hitler's views on foreign policy before 1933 and an account of his policies toward England thereafter.

Schröder, Hans-Jürgen. **Deutschland und die Vereinigten Staaten, 1933-1939.** Wiesbaden: F. Steiner, 1970, 338 p.

A monograph on the relations between Nazi Germany and the United States, with emphasis on the economic aspects. Based on a thorough study of archival materials.

Schubert, Günter. **Anfänge nationalsozialistischer Aussenpolitik.** Cologne: Wissenschaft und Politik, 1963, 251 p.

A study of the early attempts of the Nazis to formulate their foreign policies.

Smith, Arthur Lee., Jr. **The Deutschtum of Nazi Germany and the United States.** The Hague: Nijhoff, 1965, 172 p.

A history of the attempts of the German Foreign Institute (Deutsches Ausland-Institut) to promote Nazi aims among Americans of German descent before and during World War II.

Weinberg, Gerhard L. **The Foreign Policy of Hitler's Germany: Diplomatic Revolution in Europe, 1933-36.** Chicago: University of Chicago Press, 1971, 397 p.

An intelligent analysis of Hitler's early triumphs, on the basis of new archival sources and of an admirable mastery of existing literature. A major contribution by an American historian.

Concentration Camps; Antisemitism; War Crimes

See also Ethnic Problems; The Jews, p. 46; Second World War, p. 144; other subsections under Germany and the sections for specific countries.

Arendt, Hannah. **Eichmann in Jerusalem: A Report on the Banality of Evil.** New York: Viking, rev. and enl. ed., 1964, 312 p.

While one may question some of Miss Arendt's historical observations and some of her quite striking conclusions on Eichmann's role in the Nazi extermination of Jews, this is an important, original and valuable study that should be read carefully and thoughtfully.

Billig, Joseph. **L'Hitlérisme et le système concentrationnaire.** Paris: Presses Universitaires, 1967, 321 p.

A history of the Nazi concentration camp system, based on secondary sources, by a scholar associated with the Centre de Documentation Juive Contemporaine.

Davidson, Eugene. **The Trial of the Germans.** New York: Macmillan, 1966, 636 p.

An ambitious account of the trial of the 22 major defendants at Nuremberg following World War II.

Hausner, Gideon. **Justice in Jerusalem.** New York: Harper and Row, 1966, 528 p.

The Attorney General of Israel from 1960 to 1963, with righteous anger and in overwhelming detail, re-prosecutes the case against Eichmann and the evil he represented.

Henkys, Reinhard and Others. **Die nationalsozialistischen Gewaltverbrechen: Geschichte und Gericht.** Stuttgart: Kreuz, 1964, 392 p.

A brief account of Nazi crimes and post-1945 prosecution of those responsible, by Protestant authors.

Hilberg, Raul, *ed.* **Documents of Destruction: Germany and Jewry, 1933-1945.** Chicago: Quadrangle Books, 1971, 242 p.

Representative documents from all over Europe, illustrating horror, degradation and death.

Langbein, Hermann, *comp.* **Der Auschwitzprozess.** Frankfurt/Main: Europäische Verlagsanstalt, 1965, 1,027 p.

A massive compilation of facts and documents on Auschwitz, Hitler's biggest death camp. The author of the volume is a former inmate who played a leading role in the preparation of the Frankfurt trial.

Naumann, Bernd. **Auschwitz: A Report on the Proceedings against Robert Karl Ludwig Mulka and Others before the Court at Frankfurt.** New York: Praeger, 1966, 433 p.

A lengthy report of the trial, concluded in August 1965, of a group of Nazi officials responsible for the liquidation of countless Jews and other inmates during World War II at one of the most notorious Nazi concentration camps. Based on a series of articles written for the *Frankfurter Allgemeine Zeitung.* The German original appeared as "Auschwitz: Bericht über die Strafsache gegen Mulka und andere vor dem Schwurgericht Frankfurt" (Frankfurt/Main: Athenaeum, 1965, 552 p.).

Pearlman, Moshe. **The Capture and Trial of Adolf Eichmann.** New York: Simon and Schuster, 1963, 666 p.

A lengthy recounting of the capture and trial of Eichmann well-told by a former Israeli government adviser who draws heavily on court room proceedings to prove Eichmann's leading and willing role in the Nazi atrocities against European Jews during World War II.

Sharf, Andrew. **The British Press and Jews under Nazi Rule.** New York: Oxford University Press (for the Institute of Race Relations), 1964, 228 p.

An Israeli scholar presents a sober and informative survey of how the British press reported and interpreted Nazi persecution of the Jews.

Steiner, Jean-François. **Treblinka.** New York: Simon and Schuster, 1967, 415 p.

A monograph on the notorious Nazi concentration camp.

Wechsberg, Joseph, *ed.* **The Murderers among Us: The Simon Wiesenthal Memoirs.** New York: McGraw-Hill, 1967, 340 p.

The grim story of the Nazi victim who now ferrets out his people's former tormentors, composed, perhaps inevitably but regrettably, as a kind of thriller.

Wormser-Migot, Olga. **Le Système concentrationnaire nazi (1933-1945).** Paris: Presses Universitaires, 1968, 660 p.

A detailed survey of the history and organization of Nazi concentration camps. There is a useful bibliography and chronology.

The Opposition

See also Second World War, p. 144; other subsections under Germany.

Baumont, Maurice. **La Grande conjuration contre Hitler.** Paris: Del Duca, 1963, 261 p.
  The author, a prominent French historian, presents the events of July 1944 and sees them not only as a military plot but as evidence of a wide-ranging political movement.

Brandt, Willy. **In Exile: Essays, Reflections and Letters, 1933-1947.** Philadelphia: University of Pennsylvania Press, 1971, 264 p.
  A record of former Chancellor Brandt's thoughts and activities as a young socialist before, during and immediately after exile. Under the trying conditions of the 1930s and the war, he had already fused idealism with a strong political intelligence.

Deutsch, Harold Charles. **The Conspiracy against Hitler in the Twilight War.** Minneapolis: University of Minnesota Press, 1968, 394 p.
  A careful and most readable reconstruction, based on new evidence, of conspiratorial efforts against Hitler in the first ten months of the war.

Ehlers, Dieter. **Technik und Moral einer Verschwörung: 20 Juli 1944.** Frankfurt/Main: Athenäum Verlag, 1964, 250 p.
  A profound examination of the moral issues encountered by the participants of the conspiracy against Hitler that came to an end with the attempt to assassinate Hitler on July 20, 1944.

Finker, Kurt. **Stauffenberg und der 20. Juli 1944.** Berlin: Union-Verlag, 1967, 419 p.
  According to this East German study, Stauffenberg, who attempted to assassinate Hitler on July 20, 1944, was favorably disposed toward the Soviet Union.

Friedländer, Saul. **Kurt Gerstein: The Ambiguity of Good.** New York: Knopf, 1969, 228 p.
  A painstaking reconstruction and analysis of the life of an SS officer who at great personal risk sought to warn the West about Nazi extermination of the Jews, which he himself witnessed at close quarters. Translation of "Kurt Gerstein ou l'ambiguité du bien" (Paris: Casterman, 1967, 205 p.).

Graml, Hermann and Others. **The German Resistance to Hitler.** Berkeley: University of California Press, 1970, 281 p.
  Four incisive studies of different aspects of the German resistance.

Groscurth, Helmuth. **Tagebücher eines Abwehroffiziers, 1938-1940.** Stuttgart: Deutsche Verlags-Anstalt (for the Institut für Zeitgeschichte), 1970, 594 p.
  These diaries and documents, edited by Helmut Krausnick and Harold C. Deutsch, by an *Abwehr* officer are an important source for the history of the German military opposition to Hitler and also of the criminal German policies in the conquered regions of Eastern Europe and the Soviet Union.

Hoffmann, Peter. **Widerstand—Staatsstreich—Attentat: der Kampf der Opposition gegen Hitler.** Munich: Piper, 1969, 988 p.
  A painstaking reconstruction of all internal attempts at overthrowing the Hitler regime.

Kempner, Benedicta Maria. **Priester vor Hitlers Tribunalen.** Munich: Rütten und Loening, 1966, 496 p.
  A collection of biographies of German priests executed by the Nazi regime.

Kopp, Otto, *ed.* **Widerstand und Erneuerung: neue Berichte und Dokumente vom inneren Kampf gegen das Hitler Regime.** Stuttgart: Seewald, 1966, 308 p.
  A collection of reminiscences and essays on the relations between the German industrialists and the Nazi regime.

Kramarz, Joachim. **Stauffenberg: The Architect of the Famous July 20th Conspiracy to Assassinate Hitler.** New York: Macmillan, 1967, 255 p.
  A well-documented biography of Count von Stauffenberg, the Swabian aristocrat and

general staff officer who almost succeeded in killing Hitler on July 20, 1944. Of particular interest are the chapters discussing Stauffenberg's plans for a future Germany and his relations with various German resistance groups. German original: "Claus Graf Stauffenberg" (Frankfurt/Main: Bernard und Graefe, 1965, 245 p.).

Krebs, Albert. **Fritz-Dietlof Graf von der Schulenburg: zwischen Staatsraison und Hochverrat.** Hamburg: Leibniz-Verlag, 1964, 338 p.

An associate's recollections of Count Schulenburg who in 1932 joined the Nazi party, in the mid-1930s served and feared the Nazi state, and in 1944 was executed as one of the leaders of the July 20 conspiracy against Hitler.

Manvell, Roger and Fraenkel, Heinrich. **The Canaris Conspiracy: The Secret Resistance to Hitler in the German Army.** New York: McKay, 1969, 267 p.

The story of the military opposition to Hitler, of which Admiral Canaris, head of Hitler's military intelligence, was one of the leaders. Based on interviews with the survivors and published sources.

Manvell, Roger and Fraenkel, Heinrich. **The Men Who Tried to Kill Hitler.** New York: Coward-McCann, 1964, 272 p.

A readable and reliable account of the final conspiracy against Hitler. The English edition has the title "The July Plot" (London: Bodley Head, 1964, 272 p.).

Müller, Christian. **Oberst i.G. Stauffenberg.** Düsseldorf: Droste, 1971, 623 p.

The definitive biography by a young Swiss historian of the German officer who on July 20, 1944, attempted to kill Hitler.

Reck-Malleczewen, Friedrich Percyval. **Diary of a Man in Despair.** New York: Macmillan, 1970, 219 p.

The reflections of a German conservative who detested the Nazis and considered them the products of 1789, of industrial capitalism, and of mass civilization. The author was executed by the Nazis in 1945. The German original was published as "Tagebuch eines Verzweifelten" (Stuttgart: Goverts, 1966, 203 p.).

Röder, Werner. **Die deutschen sozialistischen Exilgruppen in Grossbritannien.** Hanover: Verlag für Literatur und Zeitgeschehen (for the Friedrich-Ebert-Stiftung), 1968, 322 p.

A comprehensive survey of the German socialist exile groups in Great Britain from 1933 to the end of the Nazi rule.

Roon, Ger van. **German Resistance to Hitler: Count Von Moltke and the Kreisau Circle.** New York: Van Nostrand Reinhold, 1971, 400 p.

A detailed and well-documented description of the activities, goals and membership of the anti-Nazi Kreisauer circle in Germany during World War II. The German original was published as "Neuordnung im Widerstand: der Kreisauer Kreis innerhalb der deutschen Widerstandsbewegung" (Munich: Oldenbourg, 1967, 652 p.).

Scheurig, Bodo. **Ewald von Kleist-Schmenzin: ein Konservativer gegen Hitler.** Oldenburg: Stalling, 1968, 296 p.

A study of the conservative Prussian aristocrat Ewald von Kleist-Schmenzin, an inveterate enemy of the Nazi regime, who was executed by Hitler's authorities on April 9, 1945. It includes a description of his efforts in 1938 to establish contact with leading British public figures, including Winston Churchill.

Schlabrendorff, Fabian von. **The Secret War against Hitler.** New York: Pitman, rev. and enl. ed., 1965, 438 p.

A completely revised and enlarged edition of Schlabrendorff's personal recollections of the hopes and sufferings of the German resistance movement, published originally in German as "Offiziere gegen Hitler" (Zurich: Europa Verlag, 1946, 203 p.) and in English as "They Almost Killed Hitler" (New York: Macmillan, 1947, 150 p.). A valuable and poignant source.

Schmitthenner, Walter and Buchheim, Hans, *eds.* **Der deutsche Widerstand gegen Hitler.** Cologne: Kiepenheuer, 1967, 287 p.

Four essays of high quality on the German resistance to Hitler, emphasizing its conservative outlook and showing that many of the resistance leaders were interested in maintaining Germany's right to European hegemony.

Schramm, Wilhelm, Ritter von, *ed.* **Beck und Goerdeler: Gemeinschaftsdokumente für den Frieden, 1941-1944.** Munich: G. Müller, 1965, 285 p.

A collection of documents containing plans for the future of post-World War II Germany, written by two leading members of the anti-Nazi resistance.

Sykes, Christopher. **Tormented Loyalty: The Story of a German Aristocrat Who Defied Hitler.** New York: Harper and Row, 1969, 477 p.
A biographical account of Adam von Trott, a cosmopolitan German patriot executed by Hitler for his links to the conspirators of July 20.

Zahn, Gordon Charles. **In Solitary Witness: The Life and Death of Franz Jägerstätter.** New York: Holt, Rinehart, and Winston, 1964, 277 p.
A profile of an Austrian Catholic, based on his letters, who refused to fight in Hitler's armed forces and who consequently was executed by the Nazis in 1943.

Zeller, Eberhard. **The Flame of Freedom: The German Struggle against Hitler.** Coral Gables: University of Miami Press, 1969, 471 p.
A somewhat abridged translation of a study originally published in German as "Geist der Freiheit: der zwanzigste Juli" (Munich: Gotthold Müller Verlag, 5th rev. ed., 1965, 560 p.).

Zipfel, Friedrich. **Kirchenkampf in Deutschland, 1933-1945.** Berlin: De Gruyter, 1965, 571 p.
This volume deals with anti-Nazi resistance of various church groups in Hitler's Germany.

Post-World War II Era
General

See also (International Law) Miscellaneous, p. 94; The Postwar World, p. 178; Western Europe, p. 345; other subsections under Germany.

Binder, Gerhart. **Deutschland seit 1945.** Stuttgart: Seewald, 1969, 608 p.
A survey of developments in both West and East Germany since 1945. Planned as a popular reference volume, it contains many documents, maps, charts, chronologies and a bibliography.

Collotti, Enzo. **Storia delle due Germanie, 1945-1968.** Turin: Einaudi, 1968, 1,122 p.
A systematic study of the domestic and foreign policies of East and West Germany since the Second World War, by a leftist historian.

Dulles, Eleanor Lansing. **One Germany or Two: The Struggle at the Heart of Europe.** Stanford: Hoover Institution Press, 1970, 315 p.
Drawing on personal and family experience, Mrs. Dulles has written an analysis of the German problem, focusing on reunification, in the light of the whole postwar experience.

Elon, Amos. **Journey through a Haunted Land: The New Germany.** New York: Holt, Rinehart and Winston, 1967, 259 p.
An Israeli journalist reports on Germany, both East and West, in the mid-1960s. He is particularly concerned about the attitudes of the Germans toward their Nazi past. The German original appeared as "In einem heimsuchten Land: Reise eines israelischen Journalisten in beide deutsche Staaten" (Munich: Kindler, 1966, 387 p.).

Grabert, Herbert. **Sieger und Besiegte: der deutsche Nationalismus nach 1945.** Tübingen: Verlag der Deutschen Hochschullehrer-Zeitung, 1966, 420 p.
A neo-Nazi interpretation of recent German history.

Grosser, Alfred. **Germany in Our Time: A Political History of the Postwar Years.** New York: Praeger, 1971, 378 p.
A veteran analyst of German affairs presents a comprehensive survey of all aspects of the two Germanies since the war.

Guttenberg, Karl Theodor, Freiherr zu. **Wenn der Westen will: Plädoyer für eine mutige Politik.** Stuttgart: Seewald, 1964, 238 p.
The late conservative German politician presents a serious argument for a tougher policy toward communism as a means of strengthening the West and reunifying Germany.

Hauck, Christian W. **Endlösung Deutschland.** Munich: Droemer Knaur, 1963, 304 p.
A plea for German reunification in the context of a new *Mitteleuropa*.

Hofer, Walther, *ed.* **Europa und die Einheit Deutschlands.** Cologne: Verlag Wissenschaft und Politik, 1970, 366 p.
A group of leading historians from Europe and the United States discuss the problem of German unity in connection with the 100th anniversary of the establishment of Bismarck's Reich.

Holbik, Karel and Myers, Henry Allen. **Postwar Trade in Divided Germany: The Internal and International Issues.** Baltimore: Johns Hopkins Press, 1964, 138 p.
A useful study with emphasis on political and institutional aspects.

Kogon, Eugen. **Die unvollendete Erneuerung: Deutschland im Kräftefeld 1945–1963.** Frankfurt/Main: Europäische Verlagsanstalt, 1964, 257 p.
These searching essays by an outstanding German writer illuminate most of the central problems of recent German history.

Krülle, Siegrid. **Die völkerrechtlichen Aspekte des Oder-Neisse-Problems.** Berlin: Duncker, 1970, 391 p.
This legal study of the Oder-Neisse problem includes proposals for the settlement of the controversy over the German territories that were incorporated into the Soviet Union and Poland after World War II.

Landauer, Carl. **Germany: Illusions and Dilemmas.** New York: Harcourt, Brace and World, 1969, 360 p.
A veteran German-American scholar takes stock of the current scene in Germany and pleads for greater realism in Western initiatives to the East.

Lehndorff, Hans, Graf von. **East Prussian Diary.** London: Wolff, 1963, 252 p.
A harrowing account of how the Soviets established their rule in East Prussia in the period from 1944 to 1947, by a doctor who came to the West in 1947. The German original, which has been published in many editions, appeared originally as "Ein Bericht aus Ost- und Westpreussen, 1945–1947" (Bonn: Bundesministerium für Vertriebene, 1960, 255 p.).

Mosler, Hermann and Doehring, Karl. **Die Beendigung des Kriegszustands mit Deutschland nach dem Zweiten Weltkrieg.** Cologne: Heymann, 1963, 486 p.
A comprehensive survey and evaluation of the treaties terminating the state of war with Germany, including a discussion of the legal problems arising from the existence of the two Germanies.

Radcliffe, Stanley. **Twenty-five Years On: The Two Germanies 1970.** London: Harrap, 1972, 254 p.
A handbook of useful information about the development of the two Germanies.

Schwarz, Hans-Peter. **Vom Reich zur Bundesrepublik: Deutschland im Widerstreit der aussenpolitischen Konzeptionen in den Jahren der Besatzungsherrschaft, 1945–1949.** Neuwied am Rhein: Luchterhand, 1966, 884 p.
A detailed and well-documented discussion of the German problem in world politics in the period from 1945 to 1949, by a professor at the University of Hamburg.

Wettig, Gerhard. **Entmilitarisierung und Wiederbewaffnung in Deutschland, 1943–1955.** Munich: Oldenbourg (for the Deutsche Gesellschaft für Auswärtige Politik), 1967, 683 p.
How the wartime allies disarmed Germany and how the cold-war antagonists for their own purposes rearmed the two Germanies. A sober study, set in the context of East-West relations.

Germany Under Occupation

See also The Postwar World, p. 178; (The United States) Biographies, Memoirs and Addresses, p. 218; Foreign Policy, p. 229; (Great Britain) Biographies, Memoirs and Addresses, p. 369; Foreign Policy, p. 375; (France) Biographies, Memoirs and Addresses, p. 400; Foreign Policy, p. 404; (Union of Soviet Socialist Republics) Foreign Policy, p. 550; other subsections under Germany.

Backer, John H. **Priming the German Economy: American Occupational Policies, 1945–1948.** Durham: Duke University Press, 1971, 212 p.
An active participant, a former American Foreign Service officer, describes the diffi-

culties and successes of the American Military Government in reconstructing the German economy.

Balabkins, Nicholas. **Germany under Direct Controls: Economic Aspects of Industrial Disarmament, 1945-1948.** New Brunswick: Rutgers University Press, 1964, 265 p.
A survey of economic policies and conditions in the British and American zones.

FitzGibbon, Constantine. **Denazification.** New York: Norton, 1969, 222 p.
A survey of the American, British, French and Russian denazification programs in Germany after the end of World War II. The author, a British scholar, concludes that the French were the most successful because they placed "far greater emphasis on the educational, as opposed to the punitive, aspects of denazification than did the other three Allied administrations."

Gaal, Miklòs. **Die neue oekonomische Politik in Russland und die deutsche Währungs- und Wirtschaftsreform: Würdigung und Vergleich.** Winterthur: Schellenberg, 1965, 221 p.
A comparative study of the N.E.P. in Russia and the German post-1945 currency and economic reforms.

Gimbel, John. **The American Occupation of Germany: Politics and the Military, 1945-1949.** Stanford: Stanford University Press, 1968, 335 p.
An American scholar judiciously examines the formation and substance of U.S. policies which embodied national interests as well as ideals.

Kuklick, Bruce. **American Policy and the Division of Germany: The Clash with Russia over Reparations.** Ithaca: Cornell University Press, 1972, 286 p.
A critical study of American policy on the major issue of reparations, set in the general context of revisionist literature. The author contends—as has become fashionable—that "a hostile and belligerent American attitude ... and an unrealistic attitude ... were responsible for the partition of Germany and perhaps for the rigid division of Europe."

Pünder, Tilman. **Das bizonale Interregnum: die Geschichte des vereinigten Wirtschaftsgebiets 1946-1949.** Spich b. Köln: Grote, 1966, 404 p.
A solid survey of the economic region that was formed in 1946 from the British and American zones of occupation in Germany.

Schuster, Rudolf. **Deutschlands staatliche Existenz im Widerstreit politischer und rechtlicher Gesichtspunkte 1945-1963.** Munich: Oldenbourg, 1963, 308 p.
A scholarly inquiry into the political and especially the legal aspects of the present division of Germany.

Shears, David J. A. **The Ugly Frontier.** New York: Knopf, 1970, 233 p.
A British journalist describes conditions along the 858-mile frontier separating East and West Germany.

Váli, Ferenc Albert. **The Quest for a United Germany.** Baltimore: Johns Hopkins Press, 1967, 318 p.
The Hungarian-born author, a professor at the University of Massachusetts, concludes his solid study of the German problem since the end of World War II with a plea not to abandon the quest for German unity.

The Soviet Zone and the German Democratic Republic

See also (Second World War) Diplomatic Aspects, p. 148; The Postwar World, p. 178; (Europe) General Surveys, p. 344; Eastern Europe and the Soviet Bloc, p. 358; (Germany) Post-World War II Era, p. 487; Berlin, p. 493; Federal Republic of Germany, p. 495; (Poland) Foreign Relations, p. 527; (Union of Soviet Socialist Republics) Foreign Policy, p. 550.

Apel, Hans. **Wehen und Wunder der Zonenwirtschaft.** Cologne: Verlag Wissenschaft und Politik, 1966, 286 p.
An American economist of German origin analyzes the East German economy up to 1963 and, looking ahead, expects it to improve substantially.

Badia, Gilbert and LeFranc, Pierre. **Un Pays méconnu: la République Démocratique Allemande.** Leipzig: Edition Leipzig, 1963, 314 p.
A compilation of facts and statistics on the German Democratic Republic.

Baring, Arnulf. **Uprising in East Germany: June 17, 1953.** Ithaca: Cornell University Press, 1972, 194 p.
    An analysis of the causes, goals and results of the uprising of June 17, 1953. The German original appeared as "Der 17. Juni 1953" (Cologne: Kiepenheuer, rev. ed., 1965, 184 p.).

Barm, Werner. **Totale Abgrenzung.** Stuttgart: Seewald, 1971, 253 p.
    A former East German official, now living in the Federal Republic, writes about politics and his personal experiences in the German Democratic Republic.

Childs, David. **East Germany.** New York: Praeger, 1969, 286 p.
    This informative work pays particular attention to East German reactions to the Czech crisis of 1968.

Dasbach, Anita Mallinckrodt. **Wer macht Aussenpolitik der DDR? Apparat, Methoden, Ziele.** Düsseldorf: Droste, 1972, 364 p.
    A valuable study of decision-making and decision-makers of East German foreign policy.

Dönhoff, Marion, Gräfin; Leonhardt, Rudolf Walter and Sommer, Theo. **Reise in ein fernes Land.** Hamburg: Nannen, 1964, 143 p.
    Three distinguished West German editors report on their travels and talks in East Germany, a country they find 30 years behind the times in everyday life, and with which, according to them, West Germany should establish closer, if informal, ties. An intelligent travelogue and a persuasive plea.

Doernberg, Stefan. **Kurze Geschichte der DDR.** Berlin: Dietz, 1964, 557 p.
    This history of the German Democratic Republic is not a very impressive example of East German historiography, though some parts of this account of East German development may provide useful clues.

Dokumente zur Aussenpolitik der Regierung der Deutschen Demokratischen Republik. Berlin: Staatsverlag der Deutschen Demokratischen Republik (for the Institut für Internationale Beziehungen and the Ministerium für Auswärtige Angelegenheiten).
    A collection of documents relating to the foreign policy of the German Democratic Republic and reflecting the views of the Communist regime, published annually since 1954. Volume 18, in two parts, covers the year 1970 and was published in 1973.

Dornberg, John. **The Other Germany.** Garden City: Doubleday, 1968, 370 p.
    An East European specialist of *Newsweek* gives a breezy account of East Germany's "transformation from the grim last bastion of Stalinism to a country burgeoning with confidence and nascent nationalism."

Feddersen, Dieter. **Die Rolle der Volksvertretungen in der Deutschen Demokratischen Republik.** Hamburg: Hansischer Gildenverlag (for the Institut für Internationales Recht, Universität Kiel), 1965, 235 p.
    A monograph on representation in the D.D.R.

Förtsch, Eckart with Mann, Rüdiger. **Die SED.** Stuttgart: Kohlhammer, 1969, 198 p.
    A well-documented study of the history, structure and functions of the Socialist Unity Party.

Forster, Thomas M. **The East German Army: A Pattern of a Communist Military Establishment.** New York: A. S. Barnes, 1968, 255 p.
    A study of the history and organization of the National People's Army, by a West German author. The German original was published as "NVA: Die Armee der Sowjetzone" (Cologne: Markus, 2d rev. ed., 1965, 287 p.).

Fricke, Karl Wilhelm. **Warten auf Gerechtigkeit.** Cologne: Verlag Wissenschaft und Politik, 1971, 256 p.
    A documentary history of communist purges and rehabilitations, with particular attention to the SED in East Germany.

Gleitze, Bruno. **Die Industrie der Sowjetzone unter dem gescheiterten Siebenjahrplan.** Berlin: Duncker, 1964, 375 p.
    A well-documented survey of industrial development in the German Democratic Republic from 1959 to 1965.

Gniffke, Erich Walter. **Jahre mit Ulbricht.** Cologne: Verlag Wissenschaft und Politik, 1966, 375 p.

Memoirs on the political developments in the Soviet-occupied part of Germany between May 1945 and October 1948, when the author, who had played a leading part in reëstablishing the SPD under the Russian aegis, defected to the West.

Görlich, Johann Wolfgang. **Geist und Macht in der DDR: die Integration der kommunistischen Ideologie.** Olten: Walter-Verlag, 1968, 218 p.
A study of the return of Marxism to East Germany—under the auspices of Soviet disciples—after 1945.

Hamel, Hannelore. **Das sowjetische Herrschaftsprinzip des demokratischen Zentralismus in der Wirtschaftsordnung Mitteldeutschlands.** Berlin: Duncker, 1966, 210 p.
An analysis of the application of the principle of "democratic centralism" in the economic organization of the German Democratic Republic.

Hangen, Welles. **The Muted Revolution: East Germany's Challenge to Russia and the West.** New York: Knopf, 1966, 231 p.
Vignettes of life in East Germany by an able N.B.C. correspondent who was killed in Cambodia in 1970.

Havemann, Robert. **Fragen, Antworten, Fragen.** Munich: Piper, 1970, 301 p.
A well-known East German scientist of communist persuasion describes his attempts to reform Marxism and his difficulties with the political establishment of the German Democratic Republic.

Hindrichs, Armin. **Die Bürgerkriegsarmee: die militanten Kampfgruppen des deutschen Kommunismus.** Berlin-Grunewald: Arani, 1962, 174 p.
A description of the traditions, organization and tasks of the military units of the S.E.D. that were established in 1953 to aid the army and police in emergency situations.

Hornstein, Erika von. **Staatsfeinde: sieben Prozesse in der "DDR."** Cologne: Kiepenheuer, 1963, 317 p.
An account of the experiences of seven persons, each charged with being an "enemy of the state of the D.D.R."

Kabel, Rudolf. **Die Militarisierung der Sowjetischen Besatzungszone Deutschlands.** Bonn: Bundesministerium für Gesamtdeutsche Fragen, 1966, 316 p.
A collection of documents on the development and organization of the army and the various para-military workers' and youth organizations in the German Democratic Republic.

Kopp, Fritz. **Kurs auf ganz Deutschland? Die Deutschlandpolitik der SED.** Stuttgart: Seewald, 1965, 345 p.
A study of official documents and declarations of the Socialist Unity Party and the German Democratic Republic on problems of nationalism and reunification, by a consultant of the Archives for All-German Questions in Bonn.

Lippmann, Heinz. **Honecker and the New Politics of Europe.** New York: Macmillan, 1972, 272 p.
An informative biography of Ulbricht's successor, by a writer who once worked with him in the Communist Youth Movement. The German original was published as "Honecker: Porträt eines Nachfolgers" (Cologne: Verlag Wissenschaft und Politik, 1971, 271 p.).

Ludz, Peter Christian. **Parteielite in Wandel: Funktionsaufbau, Sozialstruktur und Ideologie der SED-Führung.** Opladen: Westdeutscher Verlag, 1968, 438 p.
A formidable study of the changing composition of East German élites and of the attendant changes in ideology. The author, a well-informed West German political scientist, combines empirical data with efforts at new theoretical formulations about totalitarian rule and stresses the emergence of "consultative authoritarianism" as a new and more efficient form of government in Ulbricht's Germany. An abbreviated and revised English version appeared as "The Changing Party Elite in East Germany" (Cambridge: M.I.T. Press, 1972, 509 p.).

Ludz, Peter Christian, *ed*. **Studien und Materialien zur Soziologie der DDR.** Cologne: Westdeutscher Verlag, 1964, 540 p.
A comprehensive survey of many aspects of East German society and ideology, mostly by highly qualified West German academics. An important contribution.

Martin, Alexander, *ed.* **Sicherheit und friedliche Zusammenarbeit in Europa: Dokumente 1954-1967.** Berlin: Staatsverlag der Deutschen Demokratischen Republik (for the Deutsches Institut für Zeitgeschichte), 1968, 412 p.
A collection of documents illustrating the views of the government of the German Democratic Republic on European security in the period from 1954 to 1967.

Mitzscherling, Peter and Others. **DDR-Wirtschaft: eine Bestandsaufnahme.** Frankfurt/Main: Fischer Bücherei, 1971, 383 p.
A useful survey of the character and progress of the East German economy.

Norden, Albert; Matern, Hermann and Ebert, Friedrich. **Zwei deutsche Staaten: die nationale Politik der DDR.** Vienna: Europa Verlag, 1967, 253 p.
Three prominent East German communists present their views on German reunification.

Polikeit, Georg. **Die sogenannte DDR: Zahlen, Daten, Realitäten: eine Landeskunde über den anderen Teil Deutschlands.** Jugenheim: Weltkreisverlag, 1966, 328 p.
A brief handbook on the German Democratic Republic. Useful for factual information. The chapters on the legal system and foreign policy are based primarily on official East German sources.

Pritzel, Konstantin. **Die Wirtschaftsintegration Mitteldeutschlands.** Cologne: Verlag Wissenschaft und Politik, 1969, 263 p.
A detailed account of East Germany's part in COMECON with material on its economic policies and political developments.

Propp, Peter Dietrich. **Zur Transformation einer Zentralverwaltungswirtschaft sowjetischen Typs in eine Marktwirtschaft.** Berlin: Duncker (for Osteuropa-Institut an der Freien Universität Berlin), 1964, 300 p.
An effort to think through the problems of transforming East Germany into a market economy.

Richert, Ernst. **Macht ohne Mandat: der Staatsapparat in der sowjetischen Besatzungszone Deutschlands.** Cologne: Westdeutscher Verlag, 2d rev. and enl. ed., 1963, 305 p.
A completely revised edition of a study of the political system in the German Democratic Republic.

Richert, Ernst. **Das zweite Deutschland: ein Staat, der nicht sein darf.** Gütersloh: Mohn, 1964, 341 p.
An informative and thoughtful analysis of East Germany's development. The author, a newspaper editor in East Germany until 1948, has written extensively on this subject, and is not uncritical of West German prejudices against the Ulbricht regime which, he finds, has made important progress.

Schenk, Fritz. **Das rote Wirtschaftswunder.** Stuttgart: Seewald, 1969, 247 p.
An extensive account of the development and achievements of centralized planning in the German Democratic Republic.

Schöneburg, Karl-Heinz and Others. **Vom Werden unseres Staates: eine Chronik.** Berlin: Staatsverlag der Deutschen Demokratischen Republik, 1966-67, 2 v.
A chronology, supplemented with documents, of the German Democratic Republic in the years from 1945 to 1955.

Smith, Jean Edward. **Germany beyond the Wall: People, Politics . . . and Prosperity.** Boston: Little, Brown, 1969, 338 p.
A general appraisal of East Germany by a political scientist who toured the country thoroughly and studied its problems.

Sontheimer, Kurt and Bleek, Wilhelm. **Die DDR: Politik, Gesellschaft, Wirtschaft.** Hamburg: Hoffmann und Campe, 1972, 259 p.
An informed, concise overview of East Germany's government, politics, society and economic system.

Stern, Carola, *pseud.* **Ulbricht: A Political Biography.** New York: Praeger, 1965, 231 p.
An informative biography, designed for the general reader, from Ulbricht's beginnings as a young Marxist to his role as old Stalinist. The author, a West German journalist who had escaped from Ulbricht's rule, sees him neither as a demon nor a hero, but a "politically dangerous, spiritually crippled and therefore pitiable, petty-bourgeois." The German original appeared as "Ulbricht" (Cologne: Kiepenheuer, 1963, 356 p.).

Storbeck, Dietrich. **Soziale Strukturen in Mitteldeutschland: eine sozialstatistische Bevölkerungsanalyse im gesamtdeutschen Vergleich.** Berlin: Duncker & Humblot, 1964, 323 p.
A description and analysis of the changes within the social structure of East Germany in the period since World War II.

Thalheim, Karl Christian. **Die Wirtschaft der Sowjetzone in Krise und Umbau.** Berlin: Duncker, 1964, 190 p.
A short survey of recent changes in the organization of the East German economy, by a leading West German scholar.

Weber, Hermann. **Von der SBZ zur "DDR." Band I: 1945-1955.** Hanover: Verlag für Literatur und Zeitgeschehen, 1966, 174 p.
A brief survey of the political developments in the Soviet occupied zone of Germany that led to the establishment of the German Democratic Republic.

Weber, Hermann and Oldenburg, Fred. **25 Jahre SED: Chronik einer Partei.** Cologne: Verlag Wissenschaft und Politik, 1971, 204 p.
A useful chronology, covering the years from 1946 to 1971, of the Socialist Unity Party of East Germany.

Woitzik, Karl-Heinz. **Die Auslandsaktivität der sowjetischen Besatzungszone Deutschlands: Organisationen-Wege-Ziele.** Mainz: v. Hase & Koehler, 1967, 283 p.
A study of the structure, organization and activities of the official and semi-official agencies and institutions in charge of conducting the foreign policies of the German Democratic Republic.

Berlin

See also (Second World War) Diplomatic Aspects, p. 148; The Postwar World, p. 178; (The United States) Biographies, Memoirs and Addresses, p. 218; Foreign Policy, p. 229; (Eastern Europe and the Soviet Bloc) General Surveys and Political Problems, p. 358; (Germany) Post-World War II Era, p. 487; The Soviet Zone and the German Democratic Republic, p. 489; Federal Republic of Germany, p. 495.

Bark, Dennis L. **Die Berlin-Frage, 1949-1955: Verhandlungsgrundlagen und Eindämmungspolitik.** Berlin: Walter de Gruyter (for the Historische Kommission zu Berlin), 1972, 544 p.
A comprehensive and thoroughly documented discussion by an American scholar of the Berlin problem in international politics in the period from 1949 to 1955.

Catudal, Honoré M., Jr. **Steinstücken: A Study in Cold War Politics.** New York: Vantage Press, 1971, 165 p.
The fascinating story of the political tribulations of a tiny West German village near Berlin, completely enclosed by East German territory.

Dulles, Eleanor Lansing. **Berlin: The Wall Is Not Forever.** Chapel Hill: University of North Carolina Press, 1967, 245 p.
An account of postwar Berlin, enlivened by the personal recollections of the author who, during many years at the State Department, helped shape U.S. German policy.

Fijalkowski, Jürgen and Others. **Berlin-Hauptstadtanspruch und Westintegration.** Opladen: Westdeutscher Verlag, 1967, 353 p.
A detailed and well-documented survey of the establishment and development of the political parties and labor unions in West Berlin after 1945, and a discussion of the economic, social and political relations and ties between West Berlin and the Federal Republic of Germany.

Friedensburg, Ferdinand. **Es ging um Deutschlands Einheit: Rückschau eines Berliners auf die Jahre nach 1945.** Berlin: Haude und Spener, 1971, 359.
The author, who was the mayor of Berlin in the immediate post-World War II years, reminisces on his political activities after 1945 and on the Berlin problem in East-West diplomacy.

Galante, Pierre with Miller, Jack. **The Berlin Wall.** Garden City: Doubleday, 1965, 277 p.
A journalist's story of the Wall and the people who have suffered from its existence.

Keller, John Wendell. **Germany, the Wall and Berlin: Internal Politics during an International Crisis.** New York: Vantage Press, 1964, 437 p.

A brief survey of reactions of German newspapers and party leaders to political changes affecting Germany, with particular attention to the repercussions after the building of the Berlin Wall.

Kuby, Erich. **The Russians and Berlin: 1945.** New York: Hill and Wang, 1968, 372 p.
A searing account of life in Berlin in the spring and summer of 1945, by a German journalist. Translated from "Die Russen in Berlin 1945" (Munich: Scherz, 1965, 426 p.).

McDermott, Geoffrey Lyster. **Berlin: Success of a Mission?** New York: Harper and Row, 1963, 147 p.
The author was British Deputy Commandant in Berlin from July 1961 until his sudden dismissal from the Foreign Service a year later. This is his incisive and valuable account of his year in Berlin; it concludes with his plan to end the "Western allies' policy of waffle."

Mampel, Siegfried. **Der Sowjetsektor von Berlin: eine Analyse eines äusseren und inneren Status.** Frankfurt/Main: Metzner, 1963, 496 p.
A useful study of the administration of East Berlin.

Plischke, Elmer. **Government and Politics of Contemporary Berlin.** The Hague: Nijhoff, 1963, 119 p.
A brief description of governmental authorities and political parties in postwar Berlin.

Riklin, Alois. **Das Berlinproblem: historisch-politische und völkerrechtliche Darstellung des Viermächtestatus.** Cologne: Verlag Wissenschaft und Politik, 1964, 446 p.
The tangled political and juridical problems of postwar Berlin lucidly analyzed by a Swiss scholar.

Schick, Jack M. **The Berlin Crisis, 1958-1962.** Philadelphia: University of Pennsylvania Press, 1971, 266 p.
A well-documented though conventional study of the Soviet attempts to create a crisis over the issue of Berlin from 1958 to 1962.

Schiller, Karl. **Berliner Wirtschaft und deutsche Politik: Reden und Aufsätze, 1961-1964.** Stuttgart: Seewald, 1964, 204 p.
A collection of important essays and speeches on contemporary problems of West Berlin by a leading German economist and the economic adviser to the S.P.D.

Schwoebel, Jean. **Les Deux K, Berlin et la paix.** Paris: Julliard, 1963, 328 p.
The diplomatic correspondent of *Le Monde* competently traces the course and the meaning of exchanges between Kennedy and Khrushchev on the issue of Berlin in 1961, 1962 and 1963.

Smith, Jean Edward. **The Defense of Berlin.** Baltimore: Johns Hopkins Press, 1963, 431 p.
A lucid and critical review of American policy concerning Berlin, from its wartime beginnings to the aftermath of the wall. The author was formerly a U.S. officer, stationed in Berlin.

Springer, Axel. **Von Berlin aus gesehen.** Stuttgart: Seewald, 1971, 319 p.
A collection of outspoken speeches, letters and interviews by the controversial publisher.

Stanger, Roland J., ed. **West Berlin: The Legal Context.** Columbus: Ohio State University Press, 1966, 133 p.
Essays originally presented at Ohio State University at a regional meeting of the American Society of International Law.

Thomas, Siegfried. **Entscheidung in Berlin: zur Entstehungsgeschichte der SED in der deutschen Hauptstadt 1945/46.** Berlin: Akademie-Verlag, 1964, 261 p.
An East German history of the formation of the Socialist Unity Party (S.E.D.) in 1945 and 1946 which purports to rectify the "falsifications" on the subject published in the West, particularly those written by Wolfgang Leonhard and Carola Stern.

Waldman, Eric. **Die Sozialistische Einheitspartei Westberlins und die sowjetische Berlinpolitik.** Boppard am Rhein: Harald Boldt Verlag, 1972, 336 p.
A useful case study of the S.E.W., the small pro-Soviet communist party of West Berlin.

Windsor, Philip. **City on Leave: A History of Berlin, 1945–1962.** New York: Praeger, 1963, 275 p.
A brief but very useful account of the political and diplomatic aspects of the Berlin problem since the war.

Federal Republic of Germany

General

See also other subsections under Germany.

Arntz, Helmut, *ed.* **Regierung Adenauer, 1949–1963.** Wiesbaden: Steiner, 1963, 983 p.
A comprehensive documentary survey of the 14 years of recent German history during which Adenauer was at the helm of the Federal German Republic.

Balfour, Michael Leonard Graham. **West Germany.** New York: Praeger, 1968, 344 p.
The Bonn record set against the background of Germany's dominant historical traditions. Informative and well-written.

Barzel, Rainer. **Gesichtspunkte eines Deutschen.** Düsseldorf: Econ-Verlag, 1968, 291 p.
A leading member of the Christian Democratic Union discusses a range of problems from the prospects for Europe to the seriousness of student unrest.

Bracher, Karl Dietrich. **Das deutsche Dilemma.** Munich: Piper, 1971, 470 p.
A collection of essays on the character of the Federal Republic and on its political antecedents, by a foremost political scientist and a forthright defender of democracy.

Chamberlin, William Henry. **The German Phoenix.** New York: Duell, 1963, 309 p.
An optimistic survey of postwar Germany by a veteran writer and journalist.

Dönhoff, Marion, Gräfin. **Die Bundesrepublik in der Ära Adenauer: Kritik und Perspektiven.** Reinbek bei Hamburg: Rowohlt, 1963, 281 p.
A collection of articles by a well-known German publicist on internal and external problems of Adenauer's Germany. Originally published in the weekly *Die Zeit*.

Froese, Leonhard and Gerken, Eike, *eds.* **Was soll aus Deutschland werden?** Munich: Goldmann, 1968, 295 p.
Fourteen essays, mostly by prominent but "non-Establishment" figures, on the need for new departures in German policies.

Gross, Johannes. **Die Deutschen.** Frankfurt/Main: Scheffler, 1967, 300 p.
Sober observations, with a dash of irony, on contemporary German politics, culture and social customs.

Grosser, Alfred. **The Federal Republic of Germany.** New York: Praeger, 1964, 150 p.
An informative survey by a leading French authority on contemporary Germany. The French original appeared as "La République Fédérale d'Allemagne" (Paris: Presses Universitaires, 1963, 124 p.).

Guttenberg, Karl Theodor, Freiherr zu. **Im Interesse der Freiheit.** Stuttgart: Seewald; Bonn: AZ Studio, 1970, 311 p.
Essays on German politics and foreign policy by a prominent member of the Christian Social Union who died in 1972.

Hammerschmidt, Helmut, *ed.* **Zwanzig Jahre danach: eine Deutsche Bilanz, 1945–1965.** Munich: Desch, 1965, 535 p.
Thirty-eight essays by different authors on the state of German life in the mid-1960s.

Harcourt, Robert d'. **L'Allemagne d'Adenauer à Erhard.** Paris: Flammarion, 1964, 219 p.
Well-informed commentary on the West German scene from 1961 to the death of Kennedy. This veteran observer concludes that "the German path of tomorrow is still obscure."

Hiscocks, Charles Richard. **The Adenauer Era.** Philadelphia: Lippincott, 1966, 312 p.
A sober, factual, but not particularly penetrating analysis of the Adenauer era, by a former British diplomat turned scholar. The British edition appeared as "Germany Revived: An Appraisal of the Adenauer Era" (London: Gollancz, 1966, 271 p.).

Jaspers, Karl. **Hoffnung und Sorge: Schriften zur deutschen Politik, 1945–1965.** Munich: Piper, 1965, 370 p.

———. **Wohin treibt die Bundesrepublik? Tatsachen, Gefahren, Chancen.** Munich: Piper, 1966, 280 p.

———. **Antwort zur Kritik meiner Schrift "Wohin treibt die Bundesrepublik?"** Munich: Piper, 1967, 234 p.

A collection of postwar writings on German politics by the eminent philosopher.

Koch, Thilo. **Wohin des Wegs Deutschland? Ein Wiedersehen.** Munich: Kindler, 1965, 286 p.

Clever comments on contemporary Germany by a columnist who is well acquainted with the United States.

Leonhardt, Rudolf Walter. **This Germany: The Story Since the Third Reich.** Greenwich (Conn.): New York Graphic Society Publishers, 1964, 275 p.

A portrait of Germany and its people by a well-known German journalist. Originally appeared as "X-mal Deutschland" (Munich: Piper, 1961, 532 p.).

Merkl, Peter Hans. **Germany: Yesterday and Tomorrow.** New York: Oxford University Press, 1965, 366 p.

An essay on postwar Germany, by a German-born professor at the University of California, Santa Barbara.

Netzer, Hans-Joachim, ed. **Adenauer und die Folgen.** Munich: Beck, 1965, 259 p.

Seventeen essays on political, economic and foreign policy issues in Adenauer's Germany. Among the authors are Theodor Eschenburg, Carlo Schmid, Waldemar Besson, Eugen Kogon and Thomas Dehler.

Neven-du Mont, Jürgen. **After Hitler: A Report on Today's West Germans.** New York: Pantheon Books, 1970, 319 p.

A well-known German journalist records 42 interviews with a wide variety of citizens in Heidelberg. The flavor is authentic and his conclusion significant: "I found little of the civic spirit and social initiative that are common in the Anglo-Saxon world." Translation of "Zum Beispiel 42 Deutsche: Bericht aus einer deutschen Stadt" (Munich: Nymphenburger Verlagshandlung, 1968, 331 p.).

Stahl, Walter, ed. **The Politics of Postwar Germany.** New York: Praeger (for Atlantik-Bruecke), 1963, 480 p.

A substantial though somewhat uneven collection of writings by German and foreign commentators dealing with various features of postwar Germany and its temper.

Witte, Barthold C. **Was ist des deutschen Vaterland?** Mainz: v. Hase & Koehler Verlag, 1967, 270 p.

A pessimistic survey of recent German history and a plea for a reëxamination of West German policies on German unification.

Biographies, Memoirs and Collected Writings

Adenauer, Konrad. **Erinnerungen.** Stuttgart: Deutsche Verlags-Anstalt, 1965–68, 4 v.

Memoirs by Chancellor Adenauer, covering the years from 1945 to 1963. In these recollections, an important source for the history of Germany and the Atlantic Community, the dominant themes are the author's passion for Europe and his fear of Soviet communism and of American withdrawal. The first volume has appeared in English as "Memoirs, 1945–1953" (Chicago: Regnery, 1966, 477 p.).

Augstein, Rudolf. **Konrad Adenauer.** London: Secker and Warburg, 1964, 128 p.

A slanted chronological account of Adenauer's life and a hostile summary of his career as Chancellor, by the editor of *Der Spiegel* who charges Adenauer with indifference to German reunification and with pervasive political amorality.

Cookridge, E. H, *pseud.* (Edward Spiro). **Gehlen: Spy of the Century.** New York: Random House, 1972, 402 p.

A British journalist writes a good story about the mysterious general who performed great feats of espionage for several masters—successively.

Dalberg, Thomas. **Franz Josef Strauss.** Gütersloh: Bertelsmann-Sachbuchverlag, 1968, 256 p.

An admiring biography of Franz Josef Strauss, the influential Bavarian statesman and leader of the Christian Social Union, who since 1949 has been a member of the Bundestag and has held various posts of cabinet rank in the federal government.

Edinger, Lewis Joachim. **Kurt Schumacher: A Study in Personality and Political Behavior.** Stanford: Stanford University Press, 1965, 390 p.
A thoughtful account of the brave and fascinating life of the leader of the German Socialists after 1945.

Ehlert, Nikolaus. **Grosse grusinische Nr. 17: deutsche Botschaft in Moskau.** Frankfurt/Main: Scheffler, 1967, 358 p.
Reminiscences by a West German diplomat and translator in Moscow from 1956 to 1963.

Frederik, Hans. **Franz Josef Strauss: das Lebensbild eines Politikers.** Munich-Inning: Humboldt Verlag, 2d rev. and enl. ed, 1965, 293 p.
A journalistic account of the stormy career of West Germany's controversial politician.

Gehlen, Reinhard. **The Service: The Memoirs of General Reinhard Gehlen.** New York: World Publishing Co., 1972, 386 p.
The memoirs of the controversial former chief of the West German Federal Intelligence Service, written partly in response to the allegations made in Heinz Höhne's and Hermann Zolling's "The General Was a Spy." The German original appeared as "Der Dienst: Erinnerungen, 1942–1971" (Mainz: Von Hase und Koehler, 1971, 424 p.).

Heuss, Theodor. **Geist der Politik: ausgewählte Reden.** Frankfurt/Main: Fischer Bücherei, 1964, 173 p.
Twelve speeches on a variety of general subjects, by the late President of the Bonn Republic.

Höhne, Heinz and Zolling, Hermann. **The General Was a Spy: The Truth about General Gehlen and his Spy Ring.** New York: Coward, McCann and Geoghegan, 1972, 347 p.
A journalistic study by two editors of *Der Spiegel* of the German superspy who served Nazi Germany, the CIA and the Federal Republic. The German original was published as "Pullach Intern" (Hamburg: Hoffmann und Campe, 1971, 378 p.).

John, Otto. **Twice Through the Lines.** New York: Harper and Row, 1972, 340 p.
The memoirs of a controversial German intelligence agent and executive, known particularly for his abduction to East Germany in 1954. The German original appeared as "Zweimal kam ich heim" (Düsseldorf: Econ-Verlag, 1969, 376 p.).

Kopp, Otto. **Adenauer.** Stuttgart: Seewald, 1963, 183 p.
A sympathetic biography of Adenauer, by a Swiss author.

Kroll, Hans. **Lebenserinnerungen eines Botschafters.** Cologne: Kiepenheuer, 2d ed., 1967, 611 p.
The long memoirs of a professional German diplomat who during his tenure in Moscow, from 1958 to 1962, attracted attention—and aroused Western concern—by his zealous efforts to promote better Russo-German relations.

Kuby, Erich. **Franz Josef Strauss.** Munich: Desch, 1963, 380 p.
An unflattering portrait of the former West German Minister of Defense.

Loewenstein, Hubertus, Prince. **Towards the Further Shore.** London: Gollancz, 1968, 448 p.
A civilized autobiography by a German nobleman who early recognized the evil nature of Nazism and who has been commenting prolifically on international events ever since.

Maier, Reinhold. **Ein Grundstein wird gelegt: die Jahre 1945–1947.** Tübingen: Wunderlich, 1964, 415 p.

———. **Erinnerungen, 1948–1953.** Tübingen: Wunderlich, 1966, 547 p.
Important recollections of a leading German politician who in the first years of the postwar occupation collaborated with American authorities in the establishment of a new *Land*, Württemberg-Baden.

Prittie, Terence C. F. **Konrad Adenauer, 1876–1967.** Chicago: Cowles Book Co., 1972, 334 p.
A British journalist, with decades of experience in Germany, presents a straightforward portrait, based in part on interviews with Adenauer's contemporaries.

Ollenhauer, Erich. **Reden und Aufsätze.** Hanover: Dietz, 1964, 357 p.
A collection of speeches and writings of a prominent German Social Democrat who died in 1963. Edited by Fritz Sänder.

Poppinga, Anneliese. **Meine Erinnerungen an Konrad Adenauer.** Stuttgart: Deutsche Verlags-Anstalt, 1970, 353 p.
Adenauer's secretary recalls his life in retirement and his conversations about all aspects of his career and his thoughts. A pleasant, unpretentious addition to Adenauer's "Memoirs."

Vogel, Georg. **Diplomat unter Hitler und Adenauer.** Düsseldorf: Econ-Verlag, 1969, 319 p.
Pedestrian but occasionally quite informative memoirs of a German diplomat who had spent 11 years in the foreign service of Nazi Germany and 12 years in the foreign service of the Federal Republic.

Wighton, Charles. **Adenauer: A Critical Biography.** New York: Coward-McCann, 1964, 389 p.
The book deals chiefly with Adenauer's chancellorship, and the subtitle of the original English edition, "democratic dictator," epitomizes the author's main contention.

Foreign Relations

See also (General Works) Reference Works, p. 1; United Nations, p. 99; The Postwar World, p. 178; Western Europe, p. 345; other subsections under Germany and the sections for specific countries.

Ashkenasi, Abraham. **Reformpartei und Aussenpolitik: die Aussenpolitik der SPD Berlin-Bonn.** Opladen: Westdeutscher Verlag, 1968, 220 p.
A study of the conflicts within the Social Democratic Party concerning foreign policy.

Aussenpolitische Perspektiven des Westdeutschen Staates. Munich: Oldenbourg (for the Deutsche Gesellschaft für Auswärtige Politik), 1971–72, 3 v.
A substantial and very comprehensive study of the foreign policy of the German Federal Republic prepared by leading German scholars in the field. Vol. 1, "Das Ende des Provisoriums," and vol. 2, "Das Vordringen neuer Kräfte," were edited by Ulrich Scheuner, and vol. 3, "Der Zwang zur Partnerschaft," was edited by Richard Löwenthal.

Die auswärtige Politik der Bundesrepublik Deutschland. Köln: Verlag Wissenschaft und Politik (for the Auswärtiges Amt), 1972, 989 p.
A survey of the foreign policies of the German Federal Republic since 1949, supplemented with documents, chronologies, statistics and maps. A very useful reference.

Bandulet, Bruno. **Adenauer zwischen West und Ost.** Munich: Weltforum Verlag, 1970, 315 p.
A scholarly assessment of Adenauer's foreign policy toward the United States, the Soviet Union and France, stressing his flexibility and readiness to adapt to changing conditions in Europe during his chancellorship.

Baring, Arnulf. **Aussenpolitik in Adenauers Kanzlerdemokratie.** Munich: Oldenbourg, 1969, 492 p.
A penetrating analysis of the early years of Adenauer's foreign policy, by a political scientist with literary flair.

Bender, Peter. **Offensive Entspannung: Möglichkeit für Deutschland.** Cologne: Kiepenheuer, 1964, 172 p.
The author argues that only a stable East Germany could become more liberal—hence Bonn should contemplate possible means for increasing contacts with East Germany.

Besson, Waldemar. **Die Aussenpolitik der Bundesrepublik: Erfahrungen und Massstäbe.** Munich: Piper, 1970, 493 p.
A leading political scientist presents an account and analysis of German foreign policy from 1949 to 1969, emphasizing the maxims of political realism which evolved in that period.

Birnbaum, Immanuel. **Entzweite Nachbarn: deutsche Politik in Osteuropa.** Frankfurt/Main: Scheffler, 1968, 188 p.
A sceptical review of German policies toward Eastern Europe, by a veteran German journalist.

Brandt, Willy. **A Peace Policy for Europe.** New York: Holt, Rinehart and Winston, 1969, 225 p.
  Germany's former Foreign Minister and Chancellor argues his policy of détente, especially in relation to the East. Originally written for a German audience. Translation of "Friedenspolitik in Europa" (Frankfurt/Main: Fischer, 1968, 223 p.).

Brandt, Willy. **Der Wille zum Frieden: Perspektiven der Politik.** Hamburg: Hoffmann und Campe, 1971, 379 p.
  This is a selection of Brandt's speeches and articles of the last thirty years, compiled after he received the Nobel Prize in 1971. The consistent emphasis throughout Brandt's career has been on peace and unity—for the two Germanies, within Europe, with the Atlantic Alliance, and with Eastern Europe.

Brentano, Heinrich von. **Germany and Europe: Reflections on German Foreign Policy.** New York: Praeger, 1964, 223 p.
  Speeches and articles, by the former German Foreign Minister, from his early pronouncement on denazification in 1947 to his letter of resignation in 1961. Originally published in German as "Deutschland, Europa und die Welt: Reden zur deutschen Aussenpolitik" (Bonn: Siegler, 1962, 415 p.).

Damm, Ulrich. **Die Bundesrepublik Deutschland und die Entwicklungsländer.** Geneva: Université de Genève, Institut Universitaire de Hautes Études Internationales, 1965, 167 p.
  A study of the relations between the Federal Republic of Germany and the developing countries.

Dönhoff, Marion, Gräfin. **Deutsche Aussenpolitik von Adenauer bis Brandt.** Hamburg: Wegner, 1970, 297 p.
  Masterful commentaries on German politics and foreign relations covering a quarter of century since the end of World War II, by a leading German publicist.

End, Heinrich. **Erneuerung der Diplomatie: der auswärtige Dienst der Bundesrepublik Deutschland—Fossil oder Instrument?** Neuwied am Rhein: Luchterhand, 1969, 185 p.
  A description and critique of the Foreign Service of the Federal Republic of Germany, including remarks on the art of diplomacy in general.

Erdmenger, Klaus. **Das folgenschwere Missverständnis: Bonn und die sowjetische Deutschlandpolitik, 1949-1955.** Freiburg im Breisgau: Rombach, 1967, 177 p.
  A provocative analysis of West German response to Soviet initiatives, by a political scientist.

Feld, Werner Joachim. **Reunification and West German-Soviet Relations.** The Hague: Nijhoff, 1963, 204 p.
  A political scientist analyzes Bonn's policy toward reunification in the larger context of its relations with the Soviet Union. A useful introduction to the tangled topic and its vast literature.

Haas, Wilhelm. **Beitrag zur Geschichte der Entstehung des Auswärtigen Dienstes der Bundesrepublik Deutschland.** Bonn: Köllen, 1969, 531 p.
  A senior German career diplomat reminisces on his part in the organization of the Foreign Office and diplomatic service of the Federal Republic. The bulk of the book consists of extensive documentation.

Hanrieder, Wolfram F. **West German Foreign Policy, 1949-1963: International Pressure and Domestic Response.** Stanford: Stanford University Press, 1967, 275 p.
  A political scientist uses new forms of analysis to illuminate West Germany's postwar foreign policy.

Henkys, Reinhard, *ed.* **Deutschland und die östlichen Nachbarn: Beiträge zu einer evangelischen Denkschrift.** Stuttgart: Kreuz-Verlag, 1966, 240 p.
  A collection of essays on problems raised by the 1965 memorandum of the German Evangelical Church on the refugee problem and Germany's relations with its eastern neighbors.

Hoffmann, Johannes. **Das Ziel war Europa: der Weg der Saar 1945-1955.** Munich: Olzog, 1963, 456 p.
  A valuable survey of the Saar problem in the decade after World War II, by a leading political figure in the region.

Holbik, Karel and Myers, Henry Allen. **West German Foreign Aid, 1956–1966: Its Economic and Political Aspects.** Boston: Boston University Press, 1969, 158 p.
A concise account, particularly interesting on German thinking about aid and development.

Huyn, Hans, Graf, *ed.* **Ostpolitik im Kreuzfeuer.** Stuttgart: Seewald, 1971, 235 p.
Nine essays challenging the *Ostpolitik* of Brandt and Scheel in its various aspects; factual and for the most part soberly argued in presenting the reservations of the opposition Christian Democratic Union.

Huyn, Hans, Graf. **Die Sackgasse: Deutschlands Weg in die Isolierung.** Stuttgart: Seewald, 1966, 503 p.
A rambling discourse on the vicissitudes of post-World War II German foreign policy. The main target of the author, a former German diplomat, is the former Foreign Minister Gerhard Schröder.

Kaiser, Karl. **German Foreign Policy in Transition: Bonn between East and West.** New York: Oxford University Press, 1968, 153 p.
A compact essay by a German political scientist at home on both sides of the Atlantic, written before the Soviet invasion of Czechoslovakia.

Kiep, Walther Leisler. **Good-Bye Amerika—was dann?** Stuttgart: Seewald, 1972, 229 p.
A leader of the Christian Democratic Union reflects soberly on West Germany's future in an era when the old alliance and complementary economic relations with the United States have eroded. The English edition, with a foreword by George W. Ball, appeared as "A New Challenge to Western Europe: A View from Bonn." (New York: Mason and Lipscomb, 1974, 217 p.).

Knusel, Jack L. **West German Aid to Developing Nations.** New York: Praeger, 1968, 214 p.
A useful study with statistical analysis.

Majonica, Ernst. **Bonn-Peking: die Beziehungen der Bundesrepublik Deutschland zur Volksrepublik China.** Stuttgart: Kolhammer, 1971, 259 p.
A scholarly investigation of the diplomacy of West Germany toward the People's Republic in the years from 1949 to 1966. The author was a C.D.U. member in the Bundestag from 1950 to 1972.

Majonica, Ernst. **East-West Relations: A German View.** New York: Praeger, 1969, 240 p.
A thorough discussion of Germany's international role in the 1960s, by a leading foreign policy expert of the C.D.U./C.S.U. faction in the German Bundestag. The German original appeared as "Deutsche Aussenpolitik: Probleme und Entscheidungen" (Stuttgart: Kohlhammer, 2d rev. ed., 1966, 327 p.).

Meissner, Boris, *ed.* **Die deutsche Ostpolitik 1961–1970: Kontinuität und Wandel.** Cologne: Verlag Wissenschaft und Politik, 1970, 447 p.
A collection of documents illustrating the evolution of the controversial *Ostpolitik*.

Rasch, Harold. **Bonn und Moskau: von der Notwendigkeit deutsch-sowjetischer Freundschaft.** Stuttgart: Seewald, 1969, 192 p.
The author, an active member of the German-Soviet Society in West Germany, argues that West German-Soviet relations will be improved only after the recognition of the Oder-Neisse Line and the German Democratic Republic, and after the abrogation of the 1938 Munich Treaty.

Reuther, Helmut, *ed.* **Deutschlands Aussenpolitik seit 1955.** Stuttgart: Seewald, 1965, 447 p.
Essays on the foreign policies of the German Federal Republic. Most of the authors share the editor's view that for the men in charge of West German foreign relations there is very little room for play and that it is in the interest of the United States to maintain the division of Germany.

Schmidt, Helmut. **Strategie des Gleichgewichts: deutsche Friedenspolitik und die Weltmächte.** Stuttgart: Seewald, 1969, 327 p.
The former German Defense Minister who became Chancellor in 1974 presents a comprehensive and realistic appraisal of the foreign policy options open to the Federal Republic.

Schröder, Gerhard. **Wir brauchen eine heile Welt: Politik in und für Deutschland.** Düsseldorf: Econ-Verlag, 1963, 283 p.

Excerpts from articles and speeches of the former West German Foreign Minister, with informative comments by the editor, Dr. Alfred Rapp.

Schütz, Wilhelm Wolfgang. **Modelle der Deutschlandpolitik: Wege zu einer neuen Aussenpolitik.** Cologne: Kiepenheuer, 1966, 191 p.
A plea for a more sophisticated and independent German foreign policy.

Schütz, Wilhelm Wolfgang. **Rethinking German Policy: New Approaches to Reunification.** New York: Praeger, 1967, 154 p.
A leading West German advocate of the reunification of Germany argues that the Soviet and American preoccupation with Asia is prolonging the division of his country and asks for increased efforts and concrete longterm planning to further reunification. A revised edition and translation of "Reform der Deutschlandpolitik" (Cologne: Kiepenheuer, 1965, 240 p.).

Schulz, Eberhard. **An Ulbricht führt kein Weg mehr vorbei: provozierende Thesen zur deutschen Frage.** Hamburg: Hoffmann und Campe, 1967, 271 p.
A prominent member of the Deutsche Gesellschaft für Auswärtige Politik writes pessimistically about the chances for reunification of Germany. He also urges the West Germans to establish trade, cultural and social relations with the German Democratic Republic.

Schwarzkopf, Dietrich and Wrangel, Olaf von. **Chancen für Deutschland: Politik ohne Illusionen.** Hamburg: Hoffmann und Campe, 1965, 327 p.
An informative and thorough study of the principles, instruments and perspectives of the foreign policies of the Federal Republic. The two authors are journalists who for many years have reported on foreign relations from Bonn. Mr. Wrangel has also been a member of the C.D.U. faction in the Bundestag since 1965.

Seelbach, Jörg. **Die Aufnahme der diplomatischen Beziehungen zu Israel als Problem der deutschen Politik seit 1955.** Meisenheim/Glan: Hain, 1970, 299 p.
A systematic study of the issues concerning the recognition of Israel in German politics.

Sethe, Paul. **Öffnung nach Osten: weltpolitische Realitäten zwischen Bonn, Paris und Moskau.** Frankfurt/Main: Scheffler, 1966, 203 p.
A plea to coördinate West German foreign policies with those of France in order to achieve gradual reunification of Germany.

Siegler, Heinrich, Freiherr von, *ed.* **Wiedervereinigung und Sicherheit Deutschlands.** Bonn: Siegler, 1967–.
A comprehensive collection of documents on German reunification, foreign and defense policies. The first volume, published in 1967 and covering the period from 1944 to 1963, is the sixth enlarged edition of a volume that appeared originally in 1955. The second volume, covering the years from 1964 to 1967, was published in 1968. Other volumes are in preparation.

Stehle, Hansjakob. **Nachbarn im Osten: Herausforderung zu einer neuen Politik.** Frankfurt/Main: S. Fischer Verlag, 1971, 284 p.
A gifted journalist, who is an authority on Poland, writes on *Ostpolitik* and its effects on the evolution of Eastern Europe (not including the G.D.R.). The book is dedicated to Willy Brandt and the conclusions are optimistic.

Strauss, Franz Josef. **The Grand Design: A European Solution to German Reunification.** New York: Praeger, 1966, 105 p.
The former West German Defense Minister outlines his activist program: the building of a European Federation, armed by Anglo-French nuclear weapons, allied to the United States, and strong enough to bring about German reunification.

Studnitz, Hans-Georg von. **Bismarck in Bonn: Bemerkungen zur Aussenpolitik.** Stuttgart: Seewald, 1964, 319 p.
Disturbing variations on the theme, "the vanquished retain the right to deny the legitimacy of realities which were created by force." A plea for a more militant policy toward reunification and the return of the eastern provinces.

Whetten, Lawrence L. **Germany's Ostpolitik: Relations between the Federal Republic and the Warsaw Pact Countries.** New York: Oxford University Press (for the Royal Institute of International Affairs), 1971, 244 p.

A timely analysis of the immediate origins of Brandt's policies, set in the context of changing power relations between and within the great blocs. A sober perspective on Germany's likely power in the future is included.

White, John. **German Aid: A Survey of the Sources, Policy and Structure of German Aid.** London: Overseas Development Institute, 1965, 221 p.
Detailed description plus an appraisal that emphasizes the sharp focus on economic objectives and the consequent characteristics that distinguish German aid from that of other countries.

Windelen, Heinrich. **SOS für Europa.** Stuttgart: Seewald, 1972, 228 p.
A severe critique of the former Chancellor Brandt's *Ostpolitik,* by a C.D.U. spokesman and member of the Bundestag.

Ziebura, Gilbert. **Die deutsch-französischen Beziehungen seit 1945: Mythen und Realitäten.** Pfullingen: Neske, 1970, 200 p.
A critical, revisionist perspective on Franco-German reconciliation, its successes and shortcomings. The author, a German political scientist, argues that the relations between the two countries must go far beyond their present stage in order to become truly exemplary.

Military Policy

See also Western Defense; North Atlantic Treaty; Atlantic Community, p. 188; other subsections under Federal Republic of Germany.

Baudissin, Wolf, Graf von. **Soldat für den Frieden.** Munich: Piper, 1969, 335 p.
A collection of important speeches and essays by a German general who played a leading role in trying to define a new democratic ethos for the West German army. Edited by Peter V. Schubert.

Dormann, Manfred. **Demokratische Militärpolitik: die alliierte Militärstrategie als Thema deutscher Politik, 1949-1968.** Freiburg: Rombach, 1970, 296 p.
A German political scientist analyzes the political context of Bonn's defense policies. A useful background to current debates about new departures.

Haftendorn, Helga. **Militärhilfe und Rüstungsexporte der BRD.** Düsseldorf: Bertelsmann Universitätsverlag, 1971, 144 p.
Useful data on military aid and arms sales of the Federal Republic of Germany.

Jansen, Thomas. **Abrüstung und Deutschland-Frage.** Mainz: Von Hase und Koehler, 1968, 206 p.
A study of the problem of disarmament in the foreign policy of West Germany in the years from 1954 to 1956.

Kahn, Helmut Wolfgang. **Die Russen kommen nicht.** Munich: Rütten und Loening, 1969, 263 p.
A scathing critique of the defense policies of the Federal Republic in the 1960s.

Karst, Heinz. **Das Bild des Soldaten: Versuch eines Umrisses.** Boppard/Rhine: Boldt, 1964, 372 p.
An attempt to describe the ideas, traditions and tasks influential in forming the attitudes of the soldiers and officers of the West German army.

McGeehan, Robert. **The German Rearmament Question: American Diplomacy and European Defense after World War II.** Urbana: University of Illinois Press, 1971, 280 p.
A somewhat narrow, scholarly study of America's role in pushing for German rearmament, a decisive and controversial event in postwar developments.

Mahncke, Dieter. **Nukleare Mitwirkung: die Bundesrepublik Deutschland in der Atlantischen Allianz, 1954-1970.** New York/Berlin: De Gruyter, 1972, 274 p.
The best and most complete analysis of Germany's role in the nuclear debate of the Atlantic Alliance.

Moch, Jules Salvador. **Histoire du réarmement allemand depuis 1950.** Paris: Laffont, 1965, 411 p.
A study of German rearmament and an indictment of the policies of the United States toward Germany primarily in the period from 1950 to 1955, by a former French Defense Minister and a leading member of the Socialist Party.

Schubert, Klaus von. **Wiederbewaffnung und Westintegration.** Stuttgart: Deutsche Verlags-Anstalt, 1970, 216 p.
A broad, scholarly analysis of one of the turning points of the postwar world: the decision to rearm West Germany.

Waldman, Eric. **The Goose Step is Verboten: The German Army Today.** New York: Free Press, 1964, 294 p.
An American political scientist tries to assess how the present West German army fits into Bonn's democratic state. He relies heavily on questionnaires and interviews and is satisfied by what these reveal.

Politics and Government

See also Comparative Government, p. 18; Totalitarianism; Fascism, p. 32; (Western Europe) General Surveys and Political Problems, p. 345; other subsections under Federal Republic of Germany.

Allemann, Fritz René. **Zwischen Stabilität und Krise: Etappen der deutschen Politik, 1955-1963.** Munich: Piper, 1963, 309 p.
A collection of thoughtful, incisive essays on German politics from 1956 to 1962, written by the author of "Bonn ist nicht Weimar."

Beyme, Klaus von. **Die politische Elite in der Bundesrepublik Deutschland.** Munich: Piper, 1971, 240 p.
The sociology of the political élite in the Federal Republic. A useful survey, by a young German sociologist.

Bölling, Klaus. **Republic in Suspense: Politics, Parties, and Personalities in Postwar Germany.** New York: Praeger, 1964, 276 p.
A useful, informative and sometimes critical review of political forces in West Germany since the war, by a German journalist.

Bott, Hermann. **Die Volksfeind-Ideologie: zur Kritik rechtsradikaler Propaganda.** Stuttgart: Deutsche Verlags-Anstalt (for the Institut für Zeitgeschichte), 1969, 147 p.
A study of the radical right ideologies, and their leading exponents, in the Federal Republic of Germany.

Braunthal, Gerard. **The West German Legislative Process.** Ithaca: Cornell University Press, 1972, 290 p.
A detailed study of the formulation of public policy in the Federal Republic.

Bunn, Ronald F. **German Politics and the Spiegel Affair: A Case Study of the Bonn System.** Baton Rouge: Louisiana State University Press, 1968, 230 p.
The author, a professor of history at the University of Houston, writes about the questions that were posed to the West German public by the confrontation between West German federal agencies and *Der Spiegel* for publishing alleged state secrets in October 1962.

Chalmers, Douglas A. **The Social Democratic Party of Germany: From Workingclass Movement to Modern Political Party.** New Haven: Yale University Press, 1964, 258 p.
A political scientist provides a useful analysis of the post-1945 changes in the German Social Democratic Party and adds reflections of a theoretical nature about his discipline.

Childs, David. **From Schumacher to Brandt: The Story of German Socialism, 1945-1965.** New York: Pergamon Press, 1966, 194 p.
A quick survey of the internal history of the German Socialist Party since 1945.

Domes, Jürgen. **Mehrheitsfraktion und Bundesregierung.** Cologne: Westdeutscher Verlag, 1964, 187 p.
A study of the organization, structure and performance of the C.D.U./C.S.U. faction in the second and third Bundestag.

Dreher, Klaus. **Der Weg zum Kanzler: Adenauers Griff nach der Macht.** Düsseldorf: Econ Verlag, 1972, 364 p.
A West German journalist offers some new information on the political activities of Adenauer in the immediate post-World War II years.

Ellwein, Thomas. **Das Regierungssystem der Bundesrepublik Deutschland.** Cologne: Westdeutscher Verlag, 2d rev. ed., 1965, 718 p.

A well-documented critical discourse on the political system of the Federal Republic of Germany.

Erler, Fritz. **Democracy in Germany.** Cambridge: Harvard University Press, 1965, 139 p.
Fritz Erler, a leading German Social Democrat, delivered these lectures, in briefer form, at Harvard in 1964. "Demokratie in Deutschland" was published in Stuttgart by Seewald (1965, 194 p.).

Erler, Fritz. **Politik für Deutschland.** Stuttgart: Seewald, 1968, 647 p.
Speeches and writings by a prominent German Social Democrat, a foreign policy expert and for many years the leader of the S.P.D. faction of the Bundestag. Mr. Erler died in 1967.

Gerken, Richard. **Spione unter uns: Methoden und Praktiken der roten Geheimdienste nach amtlichen Quellen; die Abwehrarbeit in der Bundesrepublik Deutschland.** Donauwörth: Cassianeum, 1965, 350 p.
A description of the activities of the Soviet and Eastern bloc intelligence service agents in the Federal German Republic.

Gerstenmaier, Eugen. **Neuer Nationalismus? Von der Wandlung der Deutschen.** Stuttgart: Deutsche Verlags-Anstalt, 1965, 136 p.
Eleven speeches and essays on contemporary German nationalism, by a former Speaker of the West German Bundestag.

Glaser, Hermann and Stahl, Karl Heinz, *eds.* **Opposition in der Bundesrepublik: ein Tagungsbericht.** Freiburg: Rombach, 1968, 222 p.
A collection of papers from a conference attended by journalists, academics, politicians and representatives of the New Left on the theme of opposition in the Bundesrepublik.

Grebing, Helga. **Konservative gegen die Demokratie.** Frankfurt/Main: Europäische Verlagsanstalt, 1971, 466 p.
A detailed theoretical discussion of conservative political conceptions in the Federal Republic since 1945.

Gutscher, Jörg Michael. **Die Entwicklung der FDP von ihren Anfängen bis 1961.** Meisenheim am Glan: Hain, 1967, 340 p.
A thorough history of the liberal Free Democratic Party, primarily in the period from 1945 to 1961.

Hättich, Manfred and Others. **Politische Bewegungen in Deutschland: Entwicklungen, Aufbau, Ziele.** Bonn: Eichholz, 1964, 480 p.
A survey of the development, organization and programs of the West German political parties.

Junker, Ernst Ulrich. **Die Richtlinienkompetenz des Bundeskanzlers.** Tübingen: Mohr, 1965, 140 p.
A solid study of the historical development and the constitutional position of the office of Chancellor within German parliamentary democracy.

Kaden, Albrecht. **Einheit oder Freiheit: die Wiedergründung der SPD 1945/46.** Hanover: Dietz, 1964, 367 p.
A valuable study of the formation of the West German Social Democratic Party in the immediate aftermath of World War II, emphasizing Schumacher's successful efforts to defend the party against the threat of communist infiltration.

Kühnl, Reinhard and Others. **Die NPD: Struktur, Ideologie und Funktion einer neofaschistischen Partei.** Frankfurt/Main: Suhrkamp, rev. ed., 1969, 397 p.
A completely revised edition of a Marxist study of right-wing radicalism in general and of the National Democratic Party in particular in the German Federal Republic.

Luchsinger, Friedrich. **Bericht über Bonn: deutsche Politik 1955-1965.** Zurich: Fretz, 1966, 383 p.
Ten years of the Federal Republic, as reflected in the sober and well-informed dispatches of the Bonn correspondent of the *Neue Zürcher Zeitung.*

Merkl, Peter Hans. **The Origin of the West German Republic.** New York: Oxford University Press, 1963, 269 p.
A carefully researched history of the political origins of the Bonn Constitution.

Mohler, Armin. **Was die Deutschen fürchten: Angst vor der Politik, Angst vor der Geschichte, Angst vor der Macht.** Stuttgart: Seewald, 1965, 249 p.

In this study a Swiss writer, the author of an important book on conservative political groups in the Weimar Republic, writes about post-World War II German politics.

Nagle, John David. **The National Democratic Party: Right Radicalism in the Federal Republic of Germany.** Berkeley: University of California Press, 1970, 221 p.
An American political scientist examines the neo-Nazi party in the wider context of Bonn politics.

Narr, Wolf-Dieter. **C D U-S P D: Programm und Praxis seit 1945.** Stuttgart: Kohlhammer, 1966, 327 p.
A comparative survey of the development of the Christian Democratic Union and the Social Democratic Party in the Federal Republic in the twenty years following the collapse of Nazi Germany.

Pinney, Edward L. **Federalism, Bureaucracy, and Party Politics in Western Germany.** Chapel Hill: University of North Carolina Press, 1963, 268 p.
This study is centrally concerned with the play of party politics and the role of federalism and bureaucracy in the functioning of the second chamber in the German Federal Republic, the Bundesrat.

Pirker, Theo. **Die SPD nach Hitler.** Munich: Rütten, 1965, 360 p.
A short history of the Social Democratic Party since 1945, written by a former left-wing member who in 1961 resigned in disillusionment with what he considered the party's weakness and lack of direction.

Richert, Fritz. **Die nationale Welle: Masche, Mythos und Misere einer neuen Rebellion von rechts.** Stuttgart: Seewald, 1966, 206 p.
A discussion of the reasons for the reëmergence of a radical right wing movement in Germany in the mid-1960s.

Roberts, Geoffrey K. **West German Politics.** New York: Taplinger, 1972, 206 p.
A concise survey of the operation of the country's political system, its parties and interest groups.

Schäfer, Friedrich. **Der Bundestag.** Cologne: Westdeutscher Verlag, 1967, 377 p.
A survey of the organization and workings of the Bundestag and a discussion of various reform proposals, by a prominent S.P.D. member.

Schäfer, Gert and Nedelmann, Carl, *eds.* **Der CDU-Staat: Studien zur Verfassungswirklichkeit der Bundesrepublik.** Munich: Szczesny Verlag, 1967, 354 p.
A series of essays on the correlation between the constitutional conceptions of democracy and the political and social realities in the Federal Republic of Germany.

Schellenger, Harold Kent, Jr. **The SPD in the Bonn Republic: A Socialist Party Modernizes.** The Hague: Nijhoff, 1968, 247 p.
In this study of the S.P.D. from 1945 to 1967 the author stresses the declining role of ideology. Based on party documents and interviews with party members.

Schmidt, Giselher. **Hitlers und Maos Söhne: NPD und neue Linke.** Frankfurt/Main: Scheffler, 1969, 275 p.
An analysis of what right and left extremism in Germany have in common: rejection of liberal tolerance, the glorification of violence and of the heroic aspects of life.

Schoenbaum, David. **The Spiegel Affair.** Garden City: Doubleday, 1968, 239 p.
An American journalist and historian writes on the confrontation in 1962 between West Germany's leading magazine and the government of the Federal Republic.

Schröder, Albrecht. **La Réaction du public allemand devant des oeuvres littéraires de caractère politique pendant la période 1945-1950.** Geneva: Université de Genève, Institut Universitaire de Hautes Études Internationales, 1964, 245 p.
A brief, somewhat narrow doctoral thesis on political attitudes in postwar Germany, particularly concerning the Nazi past. Valuable documentation.

Seifert, Jürgen and Others, *eds.* **Die Spiegel-Affäre.** Olten: Walter, 1966, 2 v.
Commentary and documents dealing with the controversy caused by the accusations of West German government officials that the German weekly *Der Spiegel* in its June 13, 1962 issue had betrayed state secrets.

Smoydzin, Werner. **NPD: Geschichte und Umwelt einer Partei.** Pfaffenhofen/Ilm: Ilmgau-Verlag, 1967, 281 p.
A study of the rise, organization and goals of the right-wing National Democratic Party of the Federal Republic of Germany.

Stackelberg, Karl-Georg, Freiherr von. **Attentat auf Deutschlands Talisman: Ludwig Erhards Sturz.** Stuttgart: Kohlhammer, 1967, 258 p.
A study of the causes and consequences of Ludwig Erhard's resignation as Chancellor of the Federal Republic in 1966.

Sternberger, Adolf. **Die Grosse Wahlreform: Zeugnisse einer Bemühung.** Cologne: Westdeutscher Verlag, 1964, 251 p.
A critique of the parliamentary system in the German Federal Republic and proposals for its revision.

Tauber, Kurt P. **Beyond Eagle and Swastika: German Nationalism since 1945.** Middletown (Conn.): Wesleyan University Press, 1967, 2 v.
An encyclopedic survey of rightist nationalism in West Germany since 1945.

Tilford, R. B. and Preece, R. J. C. **Federal Germany: Political and Social Order.** Chester Springs (Pa.): Dufour Editions, 1969, 176 p.
An introductory survey of West German politics and social institutions.

Vogel, Bernhard and Haungs, Peter. **Wahlkampf und Wählertradition.** Cologne: Westdeutscher Verlag, 1965, 531 p.
A detailed survey of the 1961 elections for the Bundestag.

Wildenmann, Rudolf. **Macht und Konsens als Problem der Innen- und Aussenpolitik.** Cologne: Westdeutscher Verlag, 2d ed., 1967, 361 p.
A study of the political system of the Bundesrepublik, particularly as it affects the formulation and execution of West German foreign policy.

Zöller, Josef Othmar. **Rückblick auf die Gegenwart: die Entstehung der Kanzlerdemokratie.** Stuttgart: Seewald, 1964, 416 p.
An intelligent commentary on the historical and sociological background of the Bonn Republic, by a well-known publicist.

Economic and Financial Problems

See also Labor and Labor Movements, p. 41; General Economic Conditions and Tendencies, p. 49; (Western Europe) Economic and Social Problems, p. 347; Integration, p. 349; other subsections under Federal Republic of Germany.

Bilger, François. **La Pensée économique libérale dans l'Allemagne contemporaine.** Paris: Librairie Générale de Droit, 1964, 318 p.
A valuable survey of the quite unexpected rise of liberal economic thought in postwar Germany, originally presented as a thesis at the Sorbonne.

Blauhorn, Kurt. **Ausverkauf in Germany?** Munich: Moderne Verlags GmbH., 1966, 265 p.
An editor of *Der Spiegel* writes with concern about the growth of American investments in the Federal Republic.

Boarman, Patrick M. **Germany's Economic Dilemma: Inflation and the Balance of Payments.** New Haven: Yale University Press, 1964, 344 p.
The reasons for the surplus in the German balance of payments, its internal effects and proposals for changing the situation are carefully examined from a point of view sympathetic to the Erhard policies.

Braunthal, Gerard. **The Federation of German Industry in Politics.** Ithaca: Cornell University Press, 1965, 389 p.
This balanced and interesting examination of the relation of German business to the executive, the legislature, the civil service, the parties and public opinion is firmly based on both a close study of the Bundesverband der Deutschen Industrie's activities and a familiar grasp of the key issues in postwar Germany's economic and political history.

Ehrenberg, Herbert. **Die Erhard-Saga: Analyse einer Wirtschaftspolitik, die keine war.** Stuttgart: Seewald, 1965, 271 p.
A critical account of the economic policies of former Chancellor Erhard.

Erhard, Ludwig. **The Economics of Success.** Princeton: Van Nostrand, 1963, 412 p.
Speeches and articles of the years from 1945 to 1962 by Germany's Chancellor from 1963 to 1966.

François-Poncet, Jean. **La Politique économique de l'Allemagne occidentale.** Paris: Sirey, 1970, 404 p.
  A systematic and well-documented introduction to the economy of the German Federal Republic.

Fritzsche, Bruno. **Deutschland wird zahlen: Geschichte und Probleme deutscher Währungspolitik.** Zurich: Benziger, 1970, 248 p.
  A Swiss scholar reviews the financial policies of the Federal Republic since the end of World War II.

Grossmann, Kurt Richard. **Die Ehrenschuld: Kurzgeschichte der Wiedergutmachung.** Berlin: Ullstein, 1967, 212 p.
  A brief, illuminating account of Bonn's restitution policy toward Jews and Israel, written by a Jewish participant in some of the negotiations.

Gutmann, Gernot and Others. **Die Wirtschaftsverfassung der Bundesrepublik Deutschland: Entwicklung und ordnungspolitische Grundlagen.** Stuttgart: G. Fischer, 1964, 453 p.
  A structural, institutional and legal discussion of the economic order of the Federal Republic.

Neelsen, Karl. **Wirtschaftsgeschichte der BRD.** Berlin: VEB Deutscher Verlag der Wissenschaften, 1971, 318 p.
  An East German study of the economic history of the Federal Republic.

Pounds, Norman John Greville. **The Economic Pattern of Modern Germany.** Chicago: Rand McNally, 1964, 133 p.
  A British-trained scholar, now chairman of the Department of Geography at Indiana University, discusses the economic resurgence of Germany since 1945 against the background of German economic history during this century and the last.

Roskamp, Karl W. **Capital Formation in West Germany.** Detroit: Wayne State University Press, 1965, 287 p.
  Interesting analysis that stresses the important role of the government in creating savings.

Schiller, Karl. **Der Ökonom und die Gesellschaft.** Stuttgart: G. Fischer, 1964, 249 p.
  Collected papers by a former Federal Minister of Economics and Finance and a leading economist of the Social Democratic Party.

Wadbrook, William Pollard. **West German Balance-of-Payments Policy: The Prelude to European Monetary Integration.** New York: Praeger, 1972, 340 p.
  A detailed and systematic analysis of goals, tactics and machinery of West German international financial policies from 1961 to 1971.

Zischka, Anton. **War es ein Wunder? Zwei Jahrzehnte deutschen Wiederaufstiegs.** Hamburg: Mosaik Verlag, 1966, 607 p.
  Essays on the economic development of Germany since World War II. The author pays particular attention to the economic policies of the Allies toward Germany.

AUSTRIA

General

See also Political Philosophies and Ideologies, p. 21; Labor and Labor Movements, p. 41; First World War, p. 131; Inter-War Period, p. 140; Second World War, p. 144; (Italy) Territorial Issues, p. 425; Germany, p. 463; (Hungary) Recent History to 1945, p. 511.

Andics, Hellmut. **Der Fall Otto Habsburg.** Vienna: Molden, 1965, 220 p.
  A study of the political ideas and activities of Crown Prince Otto von Habsburg, son of the last Emperor of the Austro-Hungarian monarchy.

Andics, Hellmut. **50 Jahre unseres Lebens: Österreichs Schicksal seit 1918.** Vienna: Molden, 1968, 740 p.
  A richly illustrated survey of political, cultural and social developments in Austria since 1918.

Andics, Hellmut. **Der Staat, den keiner wollte: Österreich, 1918-38.** Vienna: Herder, 1963, 562 p.
A balanced account of Austrian history from the fall of the Hapsburgs to the Nazi invasion.

Brook-Shepherd, Gordon. **The Anschluss.** Philadelphia: Lippincott, 1963, 222 p.
An able account, by a British journalist, of the fateful German takeover of Austria in March 1938.

Die Erhebung der österreichischen Nationalsozialisten im Juli 1934. Vienna: Europa-Verlag, 1965, 300 p.
A report, prepared by the Historical Commission of the SS Reichsführer in 1938 and rediscovered in 1964 in Czechoslovakia, on the Nazi attempt to overthrow the Austrian government on July 25, 1934. New information on the subversive activities of the Nazis in Austria.

Gehl, Jürgen. **Austria, Germany, and the Anschluss, 1931-1938.** New York: Oxford University Press, 1963, 212 p.
A brief but thoroughly documented study of efforts to bring about Austro-German union, culminating in Hitler's takeover of Austria in March 1938.

Hannak, Jacques. **Karl Renner und seine Zeit: Versuch einer Biographie.** Vienna: Europa-Verlag, 1965, 718 p.
A comprehensive study of Karl Renner, a leading Austrian socialist who was the Chancellor of Austria from 1918 to 1920 and the Federal President from 1945 to 1950.

Hoor, Ernst. **Österreich 1918-1938: Staat ohne Nation, Republik ohne Republikaner.** Vienna: Österreichischer Bundesverlag, 1966, 162 p.
A history of Austria covering the years from 1918 to 1938. The author is convinced that the main reason for the collapse of the first Austrian Republic was its lack of national consciousness.

Jacobsen, Hans-Adolf, *ed.* **Hans Steinacher: Bundesleiter des VDA, 1933-1937.** Boppard: Boldt, 1970, 623 p.
Memoirs, richly supplemented with documents, of an Austrian public figure who was a leader of the Organization of Germans in Foreign Countries in the 1930s.

Kerekes, Lajos. **Anschluss 1938: Ausztria és a nemzetközi diplomácia, 1933-1938.** Budapest: Akadémiai Kiadó, 1963, 407 p.
An account of Austrian-German diplomatic relations in the 1930s and of the Nazi takeover of Austria in 1938.

Kleinwaechter, Friedrich F. G. **Von Schönbrunn bis St. Germain.** Graz: Verlag Styria, 1964, 336 p.
A well-documented study of the establishment of the Austrian Republic in 1918, by a liberal who at that time did not believe in the existence of the Austrian state.

Kreissler, Felix. **Von der Revolution zur Annexion: Österreich 1918 bis 1938.** Vienna: Europa-Verlag, 1970, 334 p.
In this survey of the history of Austria between both world wars the author castigates the leaders of the Christian Socialists and the Social Democrats for their skepticism concerning the independence of the first Austrian republic.

Leichter, Otto. **Zwischen zwei Diktaturen: Österreichs revolutionäre Sozialisten, 1934-1938.** Vienna: Europa-Verlag, 1968, 468 p.
An admiring study of the Austrian revolutionary socialists in the 1930s.

Maass, Walter B. **Assassination in Vienna.** New York: Scribner, 1972, 180 p.
A study of the Nazi conspiracy against the Austrian government which culminated in the assassination of Dollfuss.

May, Arthur James. **The Passing of the Hapsburg Monarchy, 1914-1918.** Philadelphia: University of Pennsylvania Press, 1966, 2 v.
A sequel to the author's "Hapsburg Monarchy, 1867-1914" (Cambridge: Harvard University Press, 1951, 532 p.), this monograph deals with the final years of the Danube monarchy. While writing this study, the author had access to original sources in the Haus-, Hof- und Staatsarchiv in Vienna and in the archives of the late Professor Robert W. Seton-Watson.

Preradovich, Nikolaus von. **Die Wilhelmstrasse und der Anschluss Österreichs, 1918–1933.** Bern: Lang, 1971, 327 p.
A study of the attitude of the Foreign Ministry of the Weimar Republic toward Austria.

Reimann, Viktor. **Innitzer: Kardinal zwischen Hitler und Rom.** Vienna: Molden, 1967, 380 p.
A monograph on the controversial policies of the Austrian Cardinal Innitzer after the *Anschluss*, especially of his support for the Nazi plebiscite on April 10, 1938 which attempted to legalize the incorporation of Austria into the German Reich.

Reimann, Viktor. **Zu gross für Österreich: Seipel und Bauer im Kampf um die erste Republik.** Vienna: Molden, 1968, 414 p.
A study of the political struggles of post-1919 Austria, as reflected in the lives of the two principal antagonists, Ignaz Seipel, a cleric, and Otto Bauer, a socialist.

Schuschnigg, Kurt von. **The Brutal Takeover.** New York: Atheneum, 1971, 382 p.
Part recollections, part history, by Austria's former Chancellor. A useful record not so much for new evidence as for an evocation of the crisis months before the *Anschluss* in 1938. The German original was published as "Im Kampf gegen Hitler" (Vienna: Molden, 1969, 472 p.).

Stadler, Karl R. **Austria.** New York: Praeger, 1971, 335 p.
A useful history of twentieth-century Austria, by an Austrian scholar who studied and taught in England.

Stadler, Karl R. **The Birth of the Austrian Republic, 1918–1921.** Leyden: Sijthoff, 1966, 207 p.
A monograph on the Austrian problem at the Paris Peace Conference and the manner in which the Austrian Republic came into being.

Stadler, Karl R. **Österreich 1938–1945: im Spiegel der NS-Akten.** Vienna: Herold, 1966, 427 p.
A study of political developments in Nazi-ruled Austria from 1938 to 1945, based on official German documents now in various American, German and Austrian archives.

Vasari, Emilio. **Dr. Otto Habsburg oder die Leidenschaft für Politik.** Vienna: Herold, 1972, 400 p.
An admiring biography of the son of the last Emperor of Austria-Hungary, now active as a writer and as an advocate of European unity.

Von Klemperer, Klemens. **Ignaz Seipel: Christian Statesman in a Time of Crisis.** Princeton: Princeton University Press, 1972, 468 p.
A political biography of the Austrian Christian Socialist leader who served his country as Chancellor and Foreign Minister in a very difficult time in the inter-war period.

Post-World War II Developments

See also The Postwar World, p. 178; Western Europe, p. 345.

Allard, Sven. **Russia and the Austrian State Treaty: A Case Study of Soviet Policy in Europe.** University Park: Pennsylvania State University Press, 1970, 248 p.
The very knowledgeable former Swedish Ambassador in Vienna discusses the circumstances of the 1955 treaty restoring Austria's sovereignty, and offers his reflections on the nature of Soviet foreign policy, especially in Eastern Europe after 1945. The Swedish original was published as "Ryskt utspel i Wien" (Stockholm: P. A. Norstedt, 1965, 303 p.).

Ausch, Karl. **Erlebte Wirtschaftsgeschichte: Österreichs Wirtschaft seit 1945.** Vienna: Europa-Verlag, 1963, 359 p.
A former business editor of Vienna's Socialist newspaper *Wiener Arbeiter-Zeitung* has collected 150 of his articles published between 1947–1961 which chronicle Austria's economic chaos after the war and the subsequent recovery.

Bader, William B. **Austria Between East and West, 1945–1955.** Stanford: Stanford University Press, 1966, 250 p.
An analysis of the period of the postwar occupation of Austria, with particular emphasis on the revival of political life and the eventual Soviet withdrawal.

Behrmann, Lilly-Ralou; Proché, Peter and Strasser, Wolfgang. **Bibliographie zur Aussenpolitik der Republik Österreich seit 1945.** Vienna: Wilhelm Braumüller (for the Österreichische Gesellschaft für Aussenpolitik und Internationale Beziehungen), 1974, 505 p.
A very thorough bibliography of Austrian foreign relations since the end of World War II, including articles, pamphlets and monographs published through 1971.

Béthouart, Marie Émile. **La Bataille pour l'Autriche.** Paris: Presses de la Cité, 1965, 318 p.
A description of Austria under Allied occupation after World War II, by a French general who was his country's High Commissioner in Austria from 1945 to 1950.

Butschek, Felix, ed. **EWG und die Folgen: die Auswirkungen eines Abkommens zwischen Österreich und der Europäischen Wirtschaftsgemeinschaft.** Vienna: Molden, 1966, 413 p.
A thorough analysis of the probable impact on the Austrian economy of membership in the Common Market.

Kobliakova, I. K. and Others. **SSSR v bor'be za nezavisimost' Avstrii.** Moscow: Izd-vo Politicheskoi Literatury, 1965, 198 p.
An account of Soviet-Austrian relations prior to and following the State Treaty of 1955.

März, Eduard. **Österreichs Wirtschaft zwischen Ost und West.** Vienna: Europa-Verlag, 1965, 293 p.
A collection of essays on the post-World War II Austrian economy, by an economist who advocates the doctrines of socialism.

Marcic, René and Others, *eds.* **Zur Reform der österreichischen Innenpolitik, 1955-1965.** Vienna: Europa-Verlag, 1966-68, 2 v.
A voluminous collection of articles and documents concerning Austrian politics in the period from 1955 to 1965 and illustrating the conviction of the editors that the Austrian constitution should be rewritten.

Nassmacher, Karl-Heinz. **Das österreichische Regierungssystem: grosse Koalition oder alternierende Regierung?** Opladen: Westdeutscher Verlag, 1968, 243 p.
An effort to place Austria's practice of coalition governments in a general framework of parliamentary politics.

Puaux, Gabriel. **Mort et transfiguration de l'Autriche, 1933-1955.** Paris: Plon, 1966, 205 p.
The French Ambassador to Austria from 1933 to 1938 writes about his tour of duty and comments on the reëstablishment of the Austrian state after the conclusion of World War II.

Schärf, Adolf. **Erinnerungen aus meinem Leben.** Vienna: Verlag der Wiener Volksbuchhandlung, 1963, 176 p.
Memoirs by the third president of postwar Austria.

Schlesinger, Thomas O. **Austrian Neutrality in Postwar Europe: The Domestic Roots of a Foreign Policy.** Vienna: Braumüller, 1972, 158 p.
The author concludes his informative survey by stating that "Western tendencies to give Austrian neutrality a tongue-in-cheek treatment undermine its credibility in Eastern Europe."

Schulmeister, Otto. **Die Zukunft Österreichs.** Vienna: Molden, 1967, 392 p.
A soul-searching examination of Austria's contemporary situation and future prospects by a prominent liberal Catholic journalist.

Siegler, Heinrich, Freiherr von. **Austria: Problems and Achievements, 1945-1963.** Bonn: Siegler, 1964, 167 p.
A short chronicle of Austria's development since 1945, largely on the basis of official documents.

Siegler, Heinrich, Freiherr von. **Österreichs Souveränität, Neutralität, Prosperität.** Bonn: Siegler, 1967, 287 p.
A useful survey of the major aspects of Austrian political and economic developments since 1945.

Steiner, Kurt. **Politics in Austria.** Boston: Little, Brown, 1972, 443 p.
An analytically sophisticated volume which focuses on the metamorphosis of Austria's Second Republic from a "consociational" or coalition-type government into a "de-politicized" democracy.

Strasser, Wolfgang. **Österreich und die Vereinten Nationen: eine Bestandaufnahme von 10 Jahren Mitgliedschaft.** Vienna: Braumüller (for the Österreichische Gesellschaft für Aussenpolitik und Internationale Beziehungen), 1967, 439 p.
A thorough study of Austrian policy in the United Nations in its first decade of membership beginning in 1955. Not surprisingly, particular attention is paid to Austrian efforts concerning South Tyrol.

Vodopivec, Alexander. **Die Balkanisierung Österreichs: Folgen einer grossen Koalition.** Vienna: Molden, 1966, 406 p.
A discussion of Austrian life and politics.

Weber, Wilhelm. **Die Verstaatlichung in Österreich.** Berlin: Duncker, 1964, 501 p.
A massive study of the Austrian economy in the post-World War II years, with special attention to the nationalization policies.

Wlatnig, Friedrich. **Krise der Integration: Europa und Österreich.** Vienna: Europa-Verlag, 1967, 184 p.
A brief survey of Austria's foreign trade in the middle 1960s.

Wlatnig, Friedrich. **Die Quadratur der Integration: das Beispiel Österreich.** Vienna: Europa-Verlag, 1966, 194 p.
A survey of the foreign trade of Austria in the early 1960s and a discussion of the various supra-national organizations promoting economic integration of Europe and affecting Austrian neutrality, by a correspondent of the *Neue Zürcher Zeitung* who is a firm supporter of EFTA.

HUNGARY

Recent History to 1945

See also Political Philosophies and Ideologies, p. 21; First World War, p. 131; Inter-War Period, p. 140; Second World War, p. 144; (Europe) General Surveys, p. 344; (Austria) General, p. 507; (Jugoslavia) General, p. 591.

Braham, Randolph L. **The Destruction of Hungarian Jewry.** New York: Pro Arte (for the World Federation of Hungarian Jews), 1963, 2 v.
A documentary indictment of the SS and bureaucratic officials who joined in a systematic effort to eliminate Hungarian Jews. These documents cover events preceding the German occupation of Hungary in 1944 and the period of occupation.

Dósa, Rudolfné. **A MOVE: egy jellegzetes magyar fasiszta szervezet, 1918–1944.** Budapest: Akadémiai Kiadó, 1972, 228 p.
A history of a most influential political secret society in Horthy's Hungary. Well-documented and indispensable for the study of interest group politics.

Gazsi, József and Pintér, István, *eds.* **Fegyverrel a fasizmus ellen.** Budapest: Zrínyi Katonai Kiadó, 1968, 312 p.
Essays on anti-Nazi resistance in Hungary during World War II.

Hollós, Ervin. **Rendőrség, csendőrség, VKF 2.** Budapest: Kossuth Könyvkiadó, 1971, 431 p.
A well-researched account on the activities of the political police, the rural gendarmery and the military counterintelligence branch of the Hungarian General Staff, supplemented by six case studies of anti-leftist campaigns during the Second World War.

Horthy, Miklós. **Confidential Papers.** Budapest: Corvina Press, 1965, 439 p.
Documents from the archives of Admiral Horthy on miscellaneous domestic and foreign policy matters. The Hungarian edition appeared as "Horthy Miklós titkos iratai" (Budapest: Kossuth Könyvkiadó, 2d ed., 1963, 533 p.). Both editions were prepared by Miklós Szinai and László Szűcs.

Kónya, István. **A Magyar Református Egyház felső vezetésének politikai ideológiája a Horthy-korszakban.** Budapest: Akadémiai Kiadó, 1967, 243 p.
A critical analysis of the public posture of the Hungarian Reformed Church between 1919 and 1944, with particular attention to the teachings and political ideology of its most prominent spokesman Bishop László Ravasz.

Kónya, Sándor. **Gömbös kisérlete totális fasiszta diktatura megteremtésére.** Budapest: Akadémiai Kiadó, 1968, 201 p.
An analysis of the rise and fall of Prime Minister Julius Gömbös' radical right wing faction (1933-1936) in Hungarian politics.

Lackó, Miklós. **Nyilasok, nemzetiszocialisták, 1935-1944.** Budapest: Kossuth Könyvkiadó, 1966, 347 p.
An able sociological and historical survey and analysis of the politics, ideologies and personalities of the National Socialist movement and the Arrow Cross Party on the eve of and during the Second World War.

Márkus, László. **A Károlyi Gyula-kormány bel-és külpolitikája.** Budapest: Akadémiai Kiadó, 1968, 320 p.
A very thorough analysis of the personalities and domestic and foreign policies of Prime Minister Count Julius Károlyi's cabinet (1931-1932).

Nagy, Magda H. **A Válasz: Tanulmány.** Budapest: Szépirodalmi Könyvkiadó, 1963, 379 p.
A communist study of populist activities in the 1930s.

Nagy-Talavera, Nicholas M. **The Green Shirts and the Others: A History of Fascism in Hungary and Rumania.** Stanford: Hoover Institution Press, 1970, 427 p.
An insufficiently documented comparative study of the fascist moods, movements and parties that flourished in Hungary and Rumania in the inter-war years.

Pintér, István. **Ki volt Horthy Miklós?** Budapest: Zrínyi Katonai Kiadó, 1968, 350 p.
An interesting, though rather partisan, biography of Admiral Nicholas Horthy, former Regent of Hungary (1920-1944).

Serfőző, Lajos. **A Magyarországi Szociáldemokrata Párt a parlamentben, 1922-1926.** Budapest: Akadémiai Kiadó, 1967, 337 p.
A well-documented and reasonably objective account of the Hungarian Social Democratic Party's activities in the National Assembly between 1922 and 1926.

Sipos, Péter. **Imrédy Béla és a Magyar Megújulás Pártja.** Budapest: Akadémiai Kiadó, 1970, 261 p.
An in-depth analysis of the policies of Prime Minister Béla Imrédy (1938) and of the history of his Party of National Rejuvenation.

Szabolcs, Ottó. **Köztisztviselők as ellenforradalmi rendszer társadalmi bázisában, 1920-1926.** Budapest: Akadémiai Kiadó, 1965, 210 p.
An important sociological study on the structure, economic position, career patterns, educational and religious background of the Hungarian civil service personnel during the formative years of the Horthy regime.

Szinai, Miklós and Szűcs, László, *eds.* **Bethlen István titkos iratai.** Budapest: Kossuth Könyvkiadó, 1972, 493 p.
Documents from the archives of Prime Minister (1921-1931) Count István Bethlen on various internal social, economic and political matters and new information on the notorious "Franc Forgery Scandal" of 1926.

Tilkovszky, Loránt. **Revizió és nemzetiségpolitika Magyarországon, 1938-1941.** Budapest: Akadémiai Kiadó, 1967, 349 p.
A lucidly argued critical evaluation of policies toward national minorities that came under Hungarian control in Slovakia, Ruthenia and northern Transylvania following the Vienna Awards of 1938-1939. An important study.

Vasari, Emilio. **Ein Königsdrama im Schatten Hitlers: die Versuche des Reichsverwesers Horthy zur Gründung einer Dynastie.** Vienna: Herold, 1968, 205 p.
The story of the attempts to restore monarchy in Hungary after World War I, and particularly of the conflict between the two pretenders to the throne, Admiral Horthy and Charles I. The author is a pro-Hapsburg Hungarian writer.

Communism and the Communist Regime

See also Communism, p. 26; Ethnic Problems; The Jews, p. 46; (Europe) General Surveys, p. 344; Eastern Europe and the Soviet Bloc, p. 358; other subsections under Hungary.

Alton, Thad Paul and Others. **Hungarian National Income and Product in 1955.** New York: Columbia University Press, 1963, 254 p.
This volume, part of a larger study on the structure and growth of the economies of East Central Europe, analyzes the size, composition, sources and uses of the Hungarian national income as of 1955.

Dokumentumok a magyar forradalmi munkásmozgalom történetéből. Budapest: Kossuth Könyvkiadó (for the Magyar Szocialista Munkáspárt Párttörténeti Intézet), 1964, 3 v.
Documents on the activities of the underground Communist Party of Hungary.

Erdei, Ferenc, ed. **Information Hungary.** New York: Pergamon Press, 1968, 1,144 p.
An ambitious, informative but politically tendentious work of reference on nearly all aspects of Hungarian life, culture and history, compiled by a committee appointed by the Hungarian Academy of Sciences.

Erényi, Tibor and Rákosi, Sándor, eds. **Legyőzhetetlen erő: a magyar kommunista mozgalom szervezeti fejlődésének 50 éve.** Budapest: Kossuth Könyvkiadó, 1968, 294 p.
A collection of eight studies on the history of the Hungarian Communist Party's organizational development between 1918 and 1968. A very useful research tool for the study of Hungarian Communist politics.

Hidas, Antal. **A városligettől a csendes óceánig.** Budapest: Szépirodalmi Könyvkiadó, 1968, 373 p.
Memoirs of Béla Kun's son-in law covering his years in the Soviet Union, including the story of his imprisonment and subsequent rehabilitation.

Ignotus, Paul. **Hungary.** New York: Praeger, 1972, 333 p.
An illuminating history of Hungary by a journalist now living in London. Interesting introspective reflections on the events of 1956 and their aftermath.

Janos, Andrew C. and Slottman, William B., eds. **Revolution in Perspective.** Berkeley: University of California Press, 1971, 185 p.
Six essays on various aspects of the 1919 Hungarian Soviet Republic.

Kende, Peter. **Logique de l'économie centralisée; un exemple: la Hongrie.** Paris: Société d'Édition d'Enseignement Supérieur, 1964, 516 p.
An examination of Hungarian postwar planning and economic development.

Kovrig, Bennett. **The Hungarian People's Republic.** Baltimore: Johns Hopkins Press, 1970, 206 p.
This volume is one in a series of monographs designed to deal with "integration and community building among the communist party states of Eastern Europe."

Kun, Béláné. **Kun Béla: emlékezések.** Budapest: Magvető, 1966, 419 p.
A biography of the leader of the Hungarian Communist regime of 1919 who was liquidated by Stalin in 1937. In spite of the book's length, the author, Béla Kun's widow, provides very little new information on the politics and personality of her husband.

Liess, Otto Rudolf and Peschaut, Theodor. **Ungarn zwischen Ost und West.** Hanover: Niedersächsische Landeszentrale für Politische Bildung, 1963, 167 p.
A brief survey of Hungary's vicissitudes since 1945, with some attention to cultural policy.

Liptai, Ervinné. **A Magyarországi Szocialista Munkáspárt, 1925-1928.** Budapest: Kossuth Könyvkiadó, 1971, 284 p.
An interesting history of the Hungarian Socialist Workers Party, the outlawed Hungarian Communist Party's shortlived front organization in the 1920s.

Marosán, György. **Az uton végig kell menni.** Budapest: Magvető Könyvkiadó, 1972, 475 p.
The second volume of memoirs by a pro-communist former leader of the Hungarian Social Democratic Party covering the years between 1945 and 1958. An important contemporary document.

Nógrádi, Sándor. **Történelmi lecke.** Budapest: Kossuth Könyvkiadó, 1970, 466 p.
An updated synthesis of the two-volume memoir by a prominent pro-Muscovite leader of the Communist Party of Hungary, published in the early 1960s. A most useful work for the study of Communist Party history.

Nyers, Rezső. **The Cooperative Movement in Hungary.** Budapest: Pannonia Press, 1963, 260 p.
In addition to a general treatment on Hungarian coöperatives, the author presents an apologia for the Soviet-type agricultural collective.

Ságvári, Ágnes. **Népfront és koalíció Magyarországon, 1936-1948.** Budapest: Kossuth Könyvkiadó, 1967, 308 p.
The author seeks to and succeeds in demonstrating the underlying ideological continuity of the Hungarian Communist Party's Popular Front strategy and tactics between the party's dissolution in 1936 and its ascendance to power in 1948.

Savarius, Vincent, *pseud*. (Béla Sándor Szász). **Freiwillige für den Galgen.** Cologne: Verlag Wissenschaft und Politik, 1963, 251 p.
A former government official, imprisoned from 1949 to 1954, describes the persecutions and show-trials in Rakosi's Hungary.

Sik, Endre. **Vihar a levelet...** Budapest: Zrínyi Katonai Kiadó, 1970, 519 p.
Memoirs by an Hungarian communist scholar and diplomat (Sik was a leading Soviet Africanist in the 1930s and Hungarian ambassador in Washington after 1948) of his years in the Soviet Union during the great purges and the war. Extremely informative and useful for the understanding of postwar personality conflicts among Hungarian communist leaders.

Széchényi, Georg, Graf. **Ungarn zwischen Rot und Rot: ein Bericht aus den Jahren 1944-1956.** Munich: Biederstein, 1963, 183 p.
A Hungarian aristocrat's account of his country's tribulations between the end of the war and the 1956 Revolution. Imre Nagy is the hero of the piece.

Tökés, Rudolf Leslie. **Béla Kun and the Hungarian Soviet Republic: The Origins and Role of the Communist Party of Hungary in the Revolutions of 1918-1919.** New York: Praeger (for the Hoover Institution on War, Revolution, and Peace), 1967, 292 p.
An able investigation of the origins of the Hungarian Communist Party, centering on the figure of Béla Kun and concluding with the short-lived Hungarian Soviet Republic.

Tóth, István. **A Nemzeti Parasztpárt története, 1944-1948.** Budapest: Kossuth Könyvkiadó, 1972, 325 p.
A history of the Hungarian Peasant Party during the democratic interlude of 1944–1948 by a reasonably objective communist historian.

Vass, Henrik, *ed*. **A kommunista párt szövetségi politikája, 1936-1962.** Budapest: Kossuth Könyvkiadó, 1966, 316 p.
Four well-documented studies on the Hungarian Communist Party's policies of "class alliance" from Béla Kun to János Kádár.

Zsoldos, László. **The Economic Integration of Hungary into the Soviet Bloc: Foreign Trade Experience.** Columbus: Ohio State University, Bureau of Business Research, 1963, 149 p.
A monograph on Hungarian foreign trade between 1950 and 1960, with an eye to the question of the country's economic integration in the Soviet economic bloc.

The 1956 Revolution

See also East-West Relations, p. 180; Eastern Europe and the Soviet Bloc, p. 358; other subsections under Hungary.

Aczél, Tamás, *ed*. **Ten Years After.** New York: Holt, Rinehart and Winston, 1967, 253 p.
A series of essays commemorating the tenth anniversary of the 1956 Hungarian Revolution.

Marton, Endre. **The Forbidden Sky.** Boston: Little, Brown, 1971, 306 p.
Recollections of a Hungarian-born reporter for the Associated Press of the Hungarian revolt.

Meray, Tibor. **That Day in Budapest: October 23, 1956.** New York: Funk & Wagnalls, 1969, 503 p.
A retrospective on the 1956 Hungarian Revolution by a participant who has in subsequent years gained additional information about the events of those tragic weeks. Translation of "Budapest (23 octobre 1956)" (Paris: Laffont, 1966, 351 p.).

Molnár, Miklós. **Victoire d'une défaite: Budapest 1956.** Paris: Fayard, 1968, 363 p.
Reflections on the Hungarian Revolution by a Hungarian journalist.

Radványi, János. **Hungary and the Superpowers: The 1956 Revolution and Realpolitik.** Stanford: Hoover Institution Press, 1972, 197 p.
The author, a former Hungarian diplomat who served as *chargé d'affaires* in Washington from 1962 to 1967, here provides some extremely interesting information on the Hungarian crisis of 1956 and international affairs in the late 1950s and early 1960s.

Szikszoy, Joseph Alexander. **The Legal Aspects of the Hungarian Question.** Ambilly (France): Les Presses de Savoie, 1963, 220 p.
A detailed analysis of the legality of the Kadar government at the time of the 1956 uprising. Subsequent Soviet assistance to this government and the barring of United Nations interference are examined.

Wagner, Francis S., *ed.* **The Hungarian Revolution in Perspective.** Washington: Freedom Fighters' Memorial Foundation, 1967, 350 p.
A collection of articles on the Hungarian Revolution by scholars and public figures. The volume contains a useful bibliography compiled by I. L. Halasz de Beky which is a supplement to his "A Bibliography of the Hungarian Revolution 1956" (Toronto: University of Toronto Press, 1963, 179 p.).

Foreign Relations

See also Inter-War Period, p. 140; Second World War, p. 144; The Postwar World, p. 178; Eastern Europe and the Soviet Bloc, p. 358; other subsections under Hungary and the sections for specific countries and regions.

Ádám, Magda. **Magyarország és a kisantant a harmincas években.** Budapest: Akadémiai Kiadó, 1968, 389 p.
An informative and balanced account of Hungary's conflicts with the Little Entente in the 1930s.

Boros, Ferenc. **Magyar-csehszlovák kapcsolatok 1918-1921 - ben.** Budapest: Akadémiai Kiadó, 1970, 330 p.
An examination of Czechoslovak-Hungarian relations in the aftermath of World War I, a period when they were at their worst.

Diplomáciai iratok Magyarország külpolitikájához, 1936-1945. Budapest: Akadémiai Kiadó, 1962 - .
A collection of diplomatic documents concerning Hungary's foreign policy from 1936 to 1945. Through 1972 four volumes of the planned six have been published: vol. I, "A Berlin-Róma tengely kialakulása és Ausztria annexiója, 1936-1938," ed. by Lajos Kerekes (1962, 832 p.); vol. II, "A müncheni egyezmény létrejötte és Magyarorszag külpolitikája, 1936-1938," ed. by Magda Ádám (1965, 1,029 p.); vol. III, "Magyarország külpolitikája, 1938-1939," ed. by Magda Ádám (1970, 809 p.) and vol. IV, "Magyarország külpolitikája a II. világháború kitörésének időszakában, 1939-1940," edited by Gyula Juhász (1962, 904 p.).

Fenyo, Mario D. **Hitler, Horthy, and Hungary: German-Hungarian Relations, 1941-1944.** New Haven: Yale University Press, 1972, 279 p.
Relying on German documents and many other sources, Fenyo throws new light on some of the lesser-known episodes of wartime relations, especially the German occupation of Hungary in March 1944 and the abortive coup of October 15, 1944.

Hoensch, Jörg Konrad. **Der ungarische Revisionismus und die Zerschlagung der Tschechoslowakei.** Tübingen: Mohr, 1967, 323 p.
A study of Hungarian post-Trianon revisionism, with particular reference to the dismemberment of Czechoslovakia after Munich.

Il'ichev, L. F. and Others, *eds.* **Sovetsko-vengerskie otnosheniia 1945-1948 gg.: dokumenty i materialy.** Moscow: Izd-vo Politicheskoi Literatury, 1969, 355 p.
A collection of documents on the relations between the U.S.S.R. and Hungary in

the aftermath of World War II, published under the joint auspices of the Soviet and Hungarian foreign ministries. There is an appendix containing documents on the 1967 Soviet-Hungarian Friendship Treaty.

Juhász, Gyula. **Magyarország külpolitikája, 1919-1945.** Budapest: Kossuth Könyvkiadó, 1969, 374 p.
A concise and well-balanced history of Hungarian foreign policy between the wars.

Kerekes, Lajos, ed. **Allianz Hitler-Horthy-Mussolini: Dokumente zur ungarischen Aussenpolitik, 1933-1944.** Budapest: Akadémiai Kiadó, 1966, 409 p.
A collection of documents on Hungarian foreign policy in the years from 1933 to 1944, prepared at the Institute of History of the Hungarian Academy of Sciences.

Kis, Aladár. **Magyarország külpolitikája a második világháború előestéjén.** Budapest: Kossuth Könyvkiadó, 1963, 253 p.
A case study on the foreign policies of Prime Minister Count Pál Teleki between November 1938 and September 1939.

Ránki, György and Others, eds. **A Wilhelmstrasse és Magyarország.** Budapest: Kossuth Könyvkiadó, 1968, 1,005 p.
Annotated documents from the German Foreign Ministry's archives on German-Hungarian relations between 1933 and 1944.

Ránki, György. **Emlékiratok és a valóság Magyarország második világháborús szerepéről.** Budapest: Kossuth Könyvkiadó, 1964, 302 p.
An able critique of Western and Hungarian exile memoir literature on Hungary's foreign policies during the Second World War.

CZECHOSLOVAKIA

Recent History to 1945

See also Political Philosophies and Ideologies, p. 21; First World War, p. 131; Inter-War Period, p. 140; Second World War, p. 144; Eastern Europe and the Soviet Bloc, p. 358; (Great Britain) Biographies, Memoirs and Addresses, p. 369; (Germany) The Nazi Era, p. 475; (Hungary) Foreign Relations, p. 515; (Poland) Foreign Relations, p. 527; other subsections under Czechoslovakia.

Amort, Čestmír, ed. **Heydrichiáda.** Prague: Naše vojsko, 1965, 320 p.
A selection of Nazi documents illustrating the "breaking and bending" of the Czech people under the administration of Acting Reich Protector Reinhard Heydrich in 1941-42, particularly of his efforts to win the support of the working classes. The introductory essay by the editor, a Party historian notorious for licentious use of evidence, is of scant value.

Bartošek, Karel. **Pražské povstání 1945.** Prague: Naše vojsko, 2d rev. ed., 1965, 297 p.
The standard account of the Prague uprising of 1945, by a dogmatic communist historian turned liberal. A thoroughly rewritten version of a viciously anti-Western earlier edition, this is a much more balanced study demonstrating the spontaneous character of the uprising which caught both the communist and the non-communist resistance unprepared, embarrassed the Russians and the Western Allies, and was nearly defeated in the last days of World War II. The English version appeared as "The Prague Uprising" (Prague: Artia, 1965, 294 p.).

Beneš, Edvard. **Mnichovské dny: paměti.** Prague: Svoboda, 1968, 555 p.
This is the first volume of the memoirs by Czechoslovakia's President who died in 1948. Written during World War II without access to archival documents, the book presents a subjective and apologetic interpretation of the 1938 Czechoslovak crisis. The second volume appeared in English as "Memoirs: From Munich to New War and New Victory" (Boston: Houghton, 1954, 346 p.).

Brandes, Detlef. **Die Tschechen unter deutschem Protektorat: Teil I: Besatzungspolitik, Kollaboration und Widerstand im Protektorat Böhmen und Mähren bis Heydrichs Tod (1939-1942).** Munich: Oldenbourg, 1969, 372 p.
A scholarly study of Czech resistance to and collaboration with the Nazis in the period from 1939 to 1945.

Brod, Toman and Čejka, Eduard. **Na západní frontě: historie československých vojenských jednotek na Západě v letech druhé světové války.** Prague: Naše vojsko-- Svaz protifašistických bojovníků, 1963, 458 p.
   The story of the Czechoslovak troops in the West in World War II, co-authored by Brod, one of the liberal Czech Marxist historians. Based upon unpublished records from Prague archives.

Davenport, Marcia (Gluck). **Too Strong for Fantasy.** New York: Scribner, 1967, 483 p.
   In her autobiography the American writer and novelist describes at great length her encounters and conversations with Jan Masaryk, Foreign Minister of Czechoslovakia, during the last years of his life.

Doležal, Jiří. **Jediná cesta.** Prague: Naše vojsko, 1966, 324 p.
   A rambling and uncritical, but often informative survey of resistance activities in occupied Czechoslovakia in 1939-45. Includes annotated data from party, military and local administrative archives which are inaccessible elsewhere.

Feierabend, Ladislav Karel. **[Memoirs.]** New York and Washington: Universum and the Author, 1961-68.
   Memoirs, written in the United States, by a leading moderate member of Czechoslovakia's conservative Agrarian Party who had been minister in the Czechoslovak cabinet after Munich, in the "Protectorate" cabinet until his 1940 escape to London, and in Beneš' government-in-exile until 1945. It is a critical and well-informed personal account of the politics of Czechoslovakia's dramatic 1938-48 decade, supplemented by original documents from the author's archives. The titles of the individual volumes are: "Ve vládách Druhé republiky" (203 p.); "Ve vládě Protektorátu" (171 p.); "Z vlády doma do vlády v exilu" (162 p.); "Ve vládě v exilu" (2 v.); "Beneš mezi Washingtonem a Moskvou" (182 p.); "Soumrak československé demokracie" (183 p.) and "Pod vládou Národní fronty" (240 p.).

Fiš, Teodor. **Mein Kommandeur, General Svoboda: vom Ural zum Hradschin.** Vienna: Europa-Verlag, 1969, 158 p.
   An account of Ludvik Svoboda's activities in the war years as leader of Czechoslovak troops in the Soviet Union.

Grňa, Josef. **Sedm roků na domácí frontě.** Brno: Blok, 1968, 324 p.
   Memoirs by one of the leaders of the principal resistance organization in occupied Czechoslovakia in 1944-45. Long suppressed, the publication of the book during the Dubček reform era was a landmark in the rehabilitation of non-communist resistance. The volume includes important information about the extensive British activities in support of the underground, the political limitations of the British involvement, and the relations between the underground and the Soviet partisans.

Hoyt, Edwin Palmer. **The Army without a Country.** New York: Macmillan, 1967, 243 p.
   A popular account of the anabasis of the Czech Legion in revolutionary Russia.

Klimeš, Miloš and Others, *eds.* **Cesta ke Květnu: vznik lidové demokracie v Československu.** Prague: Academia, 1965, 2 v.
   A tendentious, yet highly informative selection of documents, mostly from Czechoslovak Communist Party archives, on the communist policies and the political struggle during the final phase of World War II. Although intended to document an irresistible development toward the communist seizure of power, allegedly foreseen and striven for by the Party and its Soviet sponsors, the volume gives evidence of improvisation and of the open-endedness of Moscow's policies in 1944-1945.

Kocman, Alois and Others, *eds.* **Boj o směr vývoje československého státu.** Prague: Academia, 1965-69, 2 v.
   Two volumes of documents on the foreign and domestic policies of Czechoslovakia during the first three years of its independence. Thin on foreign affairs, the collection consists mainly of sources selected to demonstrate the impact of the Russian Revolution and the Prague government's alleged preoccupation with an anti-Bolshevik crusade.

Křen, Jan. **Do emigrace: buržoazní zahraniční odboj, 1938-1939.** Prague: Naše vojsko, 1963, 579 p.

——. **V emigraci: západní zahraniční odboj, 1939-1940.** Prague: Naše vojsko, 1969, 612 p.

Two volumes of a history of the Czechoslovak resistance movement in the West from Munich until the formation of Beneš' government-in-exile in July 1940. Written by a leading Czech Marxist historian and based on extensive archival materials, this is the most detailed investigation of the subject.

Kvaček, Robert. **Nad Evropou zataženo: Československo a Evropa, 1933-1937.** Prague: Svoboda, 1966, 451 p.

A study of Czechoslovakia's desperate predicament in the power politics of the 1930s, by an able Czech diplomatic historian. Though written within the official interpretive framework that requires sharp criticism of the West, this work provides details from the Prague archives that add valuable insights on the course of Beneš' policy.

Lvová, Míla. **Mnichov a Edvard Beneš.** Prague: Svoboda, 1968, 285 p.

The most informative of the communist accounts of Czechoslovakia's part in the Munich crisis. Based on research in Prague government archives, the book criticizes Beneš for surrendering to blackmail and presumes that the Soviets were willing to assist Czechoslovakia single-handedly at that time.

Machotka, Otakar, ed. **Pražské povstání 1945.** Washington: Rada svobodného Československa, 1965, 149 p.

Articles and recollections by leading non-communist participants in the May 1945 anti-German uprising in Prague. Intended as a rebuttal to the communist version of the events ("Pražské povstání 1945," by Karel Bartošek), the book glorifies the uprising as an act of patriotic resistance and minimizes the communist share in its accomplishments.

Mastny, Vojtech. **The Czechs under Nazi Rule.** New York: Columbia University Press, 1971, 274 p.

An able monograph on Czech efforts at resistance under German occupation from 1939 till 1942 and the repressions following the assassination of Heydrich.

Odboj a revoluce, 1938-1945: nástin dějin československého odboje. Prague: Naše vojsko, 1965, 435 p.

A preliminary outline, intended as preview of an ambitious multi-volume history of Czechoslovakia during World War II planned by Czechoslovak historians during the reform era of the 1960s but never published in its final form. The short version is an interpretive survey without source references, overemphasizing the extent of the resistance and defending the legitimacy of the communist rise to power with arguments characteristic of the ideology of Czechoslovak reform communism.

Otáhalová, Libuše and Červinková, Milada. **Dokumenty z historie československé politiky, 1939-1943.** Prague: Academia, 1966, 2 v.

The first volume of this collection of documents concerns the wartime policies of Beneš' government-in-exile, as reflected especially in the extensive diary entries of his perceptive *chef de cabinet*, Jaromír Smutný. The second volume consists of contemporary records relating to the activities of the Czech government in the Nazi-occupied Protectorate of Bohemia and Moravia. Despite a tendentious commentary, the documentation is reliable and very informative not only on the two governments' unenviable predicaments, but also on a great many other aspects of wartime diplomacy, Nazi occupation policies, collaboration and resistance.

Pichlík, Karel. **Zahraniční odboj 1914-1918 bez legend.** Prague: Svoboda, 1968, 504 p.

A well-researched study of the activities of the Czechoslovak leaders, particularly of Masaryk, in exile during World War I. Based on archival materials in Prague and published during the brief period of the Czechoslovak Spring.

Rudé právo, 1939-1945. Prague: Svoboda, 1971, 688 p.

An edition of the underground issues of the Czechoslovak Communist Party's main periodical from the period of World War II. Long-delayed because of the political upheavals of the late 1960s, the publication omits controversial material indicative of the extraordinary penetration of the Czech Communist underground by Gestapo agents.

Thunig-Nittner, Gerburg. **Die tschechoslowakische Legion in Russland.** Wiesbaden: Harrassowitz, 1970, 209 p.

A detailed study of the Czechoslovak Legion in Russia during the Civil War period and its significance for the origins of the Czech Republic. An important contribution.

Vetiška, Rudolf. **Skok do tmy**. Prague: Nakladatelství politické literatury, 1966, 380 p.
The controversial memoirs of the Czech emissary who headed a Comintern mission and parachuted into German occupied Czechoslovakia in March 1943. Although considerably less than candid, the author describes the failure of the mission because of treason by some of its members and the infiltration of the Communist underground by undercover agents.

Willars, Christian. **Die böhmische Zitadelle: ČSR—Schicksal einer Staatsidee**. Vienna: Molden, 1965, 518 p.
A monograph on the role of Czechoslovakia in modern European history. The author is pleading for a West European orientation of the "Bohemian citadel."

Communism and the Communist Regime

See also Socialism, p. 24; Communism, p. 26; Religious Problems, p. 44; Second World War, p. 144; The Postwar World, p. 178; (Europe) General Surveys, p. 344; Eastern Europe and the Soviet Bloc, p. 358; (Union of Soviet Socialist Republics) Foreign Policy, p. 550; other subsections under Czechoslovakia.

Bittman, Ladislav. **The Deception Game: Czechoslovak Intelligence in Soviet Political Warfare**. Syracuse: Syracuse University Research Corporation, 1972, 246 p.
A former leading communist intelligence officer in Czechoslovakia, now living in the United States, recounts his activities in the Soviet-dominated Czechoslovak Intelligence Service before 1968.

Feiwel, George R. **New Economic Patterns in Czechoslovakia: Impact of Growth, Planning, and the Market**. New York: Praeger, 1968, 589 p.
A detailed inquiry into Czechoslovak economic policy and planning. The body of research relates to the period preceding the end of 1967.

Knapp, Viktor and Mlynář, Zdeněk. **La Tchécoslovaquie**. Paris: Librairie Générale de Droit, 1965, 262 p.
Two Czech scholars, at the Charles University in Prague, write on the theory and practice of Czech government and administration.

Krejčí, Jaroslav. **Social Change and Stratification in Postwar Czechoslovakia**. New York: Columbia University Press, 1972, 207 p.
The author of this study relates facts and analysis of Czech economics and social life to the broader subject of contemporary socialism.

Kuhn, Heinrich. **Handbuch der Tschechoslowakei**. Munich: Lerche (for the Collegium Carolinum), 1966, 1,021 p.
A detailed reference volume on the government, Communist Party and various organizations in Czechoslovakia since 1945. There is a useful section containing statistical information on the country's territory and population.

Kuhn, Heinrich. **Der Kommunismus in der Tschechoslowakei. Band I: Organisationsstatuten und Satzungen**. Cologne: Verlag Wissenschaft und Politik, 1965, 303 p.
The texts, with a lengthy introduction, of the organizational statutes and resolutions of the Czechoslovak Communist Party since 1920.

Kusin, Vladimir V. **Political Grouping in the Czechoslovak Reform Movement**. New York: Columbia University Press, 1972, 224 p.
A revealing study of the pluralism in Czechoslovak society which emerged with the gradual disintegration of the old structures of the Party, the trade unions and other monopolistic organizations before August 1968.

Löbl, Eugen. **Sentenced and Tried: The Stalinist Purges in Czechoslovakia**. London: Elek, 1969, 272 p.
A professional economist and a government official, now living in the West, describes his arrest, trial and confinement in Communist Czechoslovakia.

London, Artur Gerard. **The Confession**. New York: Morrow, 1970, 442 p.
A searing account, by one of the leading defendants in the Slansky trial, of his experiences as a prisoner of the State Security Police of Czechoslovakia. Terrifying and tragic.

Šik, Ota. **Plan and Market under Socialism**. White Plains (N.Y.): International Arts and Sciences Press, 1968, 382 p.

An attack on administrative planning and management in Czechoslovakia, followed by closely argued proposals for the introduction of certain kinds of market relations in socialist economies. The author was Deputy Premier in the Czech government before the Soviet invasion in August 1968. Translation and revision of "K problematice socialistických zbožních vztahů" (Prague: Nakl. Československé akademie věd, 1964, 400 p.).

Sterling, Claire. **The Masaryk Case.** New York: Harper and Row, 1970, 366 p.
An extensive effort to get at the facts in the death of Jan Masaryk in March 1948. The author has followed many clues, spoken with many people and concludes that it was murder, not suicide.

Suda, Zdeněk. **The Czechoslovak Socialist Republic.** Baltimore: Johns Hopkins Press, 1969, 180 p.
A useful introduction.

Szulc, Tad. **Czechoslovakia since World War II.** New York: Viking, 1971, 503 p.
A substantial history by a former foreign correspondent for *The New York Times* with particular emphasis on the events of 1968, to many of which Szulc was an eyewitness.

Ulč, Otto. **The Judge in a Communist State: A View from Within.** Athens: Ohio University Press, 1972, 307 p.
A former judge of Communist Czechoslovakia, who left his native country in 1959 and is now on the faculty of the State University of New York at Binghamton, reminisces on his practice of law in post-Stalinist Czechoslovakia. A unique and valuable source.

Zinner, Paul Ernest. **Communist Strategy and Tactics in Czechoslovakia, 1918-48.** New York: Praeger, 1963, 264 p.
A leading student of the politics and government of Eastern Europe here analyzes the development of Communist strategy and tactics in the Czechoslovak setting from the origins of the Party through the critical war years, to the seizure of power in 1948. An important contribution to the subject.

The 1968 Events

See also Socialism, p. 24; Communism, p. 26; East-West Relations, p. 180; Eastern Europe and the Soviet Bloc, p. 358; (Germany) The Soviet Zone and the German Democratic Republic, p. 489; (Union of Soviet Socialist Republics) Foreign Policy, p. 550; Political Opposition; Defection, p. 568; Rumania, p. 588.

Daix, Pierre. **Journal de Prague: (décembre 1967 - septembre 1968).** Paris: Julliard, 1968, 282 p.
A French journalist's personal account of events in Prague from December 1967 to September 1968.

Ello, Paul, *comp.* **Dubcek's Blueprint for Freedom.** London: Kimber, 1969, 352 p.
Key documents, with a useful introduction and commentaries by Hugh Lunghi, of the Czechoslovak democratization process that came to an end on August 21, 1968.

Garaudy, Roger, *ed.* **La Liberté en sursis: Prague 1968.** Paris: Fayard, 1968, 156 p.
A collection of Czech statements and texts relating to developments in Prague in 1968.

Golan, Galia. **The Czechoslovak Reform Movement.** New York: Cambridge University Press, 1971, 349 p.
A scholarly study of the powerful reform movement that developed within the Czechoslovak Communist Party from 1962 to 1968.

Gueyt, Rémi. **La Mutation tchécoslovaque, analysée par un témoin (1968-1969).** Paris: Éditions Ouvrières, 1969, 424 p.
A first-hand French observer reports on the events in Czechoslovakia in 1968 and 1969.

Haefs, Hanswilhelm. **Die Ereignisse in der Tschechoslowakei vom 27.6.1967 bis 18.10. 1968: ein dokumentarischer Bericht.** Bonn: Siegler, 1969, 319 p.
A chronologically arranged collection of documents on the events in Czechoslovakia from June 27, 1967 to October 18, 1968. The volume also includes biographies of the Czech leaders who played a prominent role in the days of the Russian invasion.

Hamšík, Dušan. **Writers against Rulers.** New York: Random House, 1971, 208 p.
An account of the preparation for the notable 1967 Congress of the Czech Writers' Union.

Jancar, Barbara Wolfe. **Czechoslovakia and the Absolute Monopoly of Power.** New York: Praeger, 1971, 330 p.
This detailed study of political power in a communist state is primarily concerned with the crisis of 1968.

Journalist M., *pseud.* (Josef Maxa). **A Year is Eight Months.** Garden City: Doubleday, 1970, 201 p.
A Czech journalist, an idealistic communist, reports on the political and cultural developments in Czechoslovakia during the eight months preceding the Warsaw Pact forces' invasion in August 1968. There is an introduction by Tad Szulc.

Kusin, Vladimir V. **The Intellectual Origins of the Prague Spring.** New York: Cambridge University Press, 1971, 153 p.
A serious effort to describe the evolution of reformist ideas among Czech intellectuals in the decade 1956-67.

Liehm, Antonín J. **The Politics of Culture.** New York: Grove Press, 1972, 412 p.
A translation of interviews with leading Czech writers and intellectuals in 1967-68.

Littell, Robert, *ed.* **The Czech Black Book.** New York: Praeger, 1969, 303 p.
An important source, with many documents, for the study of the Soviet invasion of August 1968, prepared by the Institute of History of the Czechoslovak Academy of Sciences. The original was published as "Sedm pražských dnů: 21.-27. srpen 1968" in Prague in 1968.

Löbl, Eugen and Grünwald, Leopold. **Die intellektuelle Revolution: Hintergründe und Auswirkungen des "Prager Frühlings."** Düsseldorf: Econ Verlag, 1969, 307 p.
An in-depth analysis of the 1968 events by two leading participants.

Marcelle, Jacques. **Le Deuxième coup de Prague.** Brussels: Les Éditions Vie Ouvrière, 1968, 295 p.
An interesting account of the rapid changes in Czech life and politics in the months preceding the Soviet invasion of August 20, 1968.

Mňačko, Ladislav. **The Seventh Night.** New York: Dutton, 1969, 220 p.
Reflections on the 1968 Soviet invasion of Czechoslovakia and on the political and cultural developments in that country since World War II. The author is a prominent Slovak communist writer who left his country after the Soviet occupation.

Ostrý, Antonín, *pseud.* **Československý problem.** Cologne: Index, 1972, 358 p.
A major analysis of the Prague Spring and the Russian-Czech confrontation, written by an author still living in Czechoslovakia.

Pelikán, Jiří, *ed.* **The Secret Vysocany Congress.** London: Allen Lane, 1971, 304 p.
A translation of the proceedings and documents of the Extraordinary Fourteenth Congress of the Communist Party of Czechoslovakia on August 22, 1968.

Pelikán, Jiří, *ed.* **Das unterdrückte Dossier.** Vienna: Europa Verlag, 1970, 442 p.
A German translation of a report commissioned by the Control Committee of the Czech Communist Party in 1968, and dealing with various delicate political issues, including the question of rehabilitation, in the years after 1948.

Piekalkiewicz, Jaroslaw A. **Public Opinion Polling in Czechoslovakia, 1968-69.** New York: Praeger, 1972, 357 p.
A technical analysis of surveys conducted during the Dubček era.

Remington, Robin Alison, *ed.* **Winter in Prague.** Cambridge: M.I.T. Press, 1969, 473 p.
A substantial selection of documents relating to the crisis in Czech communism in 1968.

Salomon, Michel. **Prague Notebook: The Strangled Revolution.** Boston: Little, Brown, 1971, 361 p.
A French journalist's informal account of what he saw and heard in Prague in 1967-68, published originally as "Prague: la révolution étranglée, janvier - août 1968" (Paris: Laffont, 1968, 381 p.).

Schwartz, Harry. **Prague's 200 Days: The Struggle for Democracy in Czechoslovakia.** New York: Praeger, 1969, 274 p.

A specialist on communist affairs for *The New York Times* effectively recounts the aborted Czechoslovak effort at "self-liberation" during the months from January to August 1968.

Shawcross, William. **Dubcek.** New York: Simon and Schuster, 1971, 317 p.
An English journalist's reconstruction of the political career of Alexander Dubček.

Šik, Ota. **Czechoslovakia: The Bureaucratic Economy.** White Plains (N.Y.): International Arts and Sciences Press, 1972, 138 p.
An English translation of Šik's important critical lectures, first delivered in the summer of 1968.

Sviták, Ivan. **The Czechoslovak Experiment, 1968-1969.** New York: Columbia University Press, 1971, 243 p.
The author, a former fellow of the Institute of Philosophy in Prague and now in exile, deals with a wide range of social and political issues of his country before the Soviet invasion.

Tatu, Michel. **L'Hérésie impossible: chronique du drame tchécoslovaque.** Paris: Grasset, 1968, 289 p.
Perceptive observations on the events in Czechoslovakia in 1968 by the East European correspondent of *Le Monde*.

Tigrid, Pavel. **Le Printemps de Prague.** Paris: Éditions du Seuil, 1968, 278 p.
A valuable documentary history of the background to the Dubček era, up to the Soviet intervention of August 1968.

Tigrid, Pavel. **Why Dubcek Fell.** London: Macdonald, 1971, 229 p.
A documented narrative of the Dubček experiment, the motives for the Soviet 1968 intervention and the dreary succession of events between the invasion and Dubček's elimination from public life a year later.

Windsor, Philip and Roberts, Adam. **Czechoslovakia 1968: Reform, Repression and Resistance.** New York: Columbia University Press (for the Institute for Strategic Studies, London), 1969, 199 p.
A survey of developments in Soviet-Czech relations between January and August 1968 that culminated in the Soviet invasion. There is a supplement of the basic documents pertaining to these developments.

Zartman, I. William, *ed.* **Czechoslovakia: Intervention and Impact.** New York: New York University Press, 1970, 127 p.
Papers by Jan Triska, Vernon V. Aspaturian, William E. Griffith, Andrew J. Pierre, Andrew M. Scott and the editor, dealing with the impact of the 1968 Soviet intervention in Czechoslovakia on contemporary international relations.

Zeman, Zbyněk Anthony Bohuslav. **Prague Spring.** New York: Hill and Wang, 1969, 167 p.
A Prague-born British scholar gives a personal account of the reform movement in Czechoslovakia that burgeoned and was crushed in 1968.

Nationalities and Regional Issues

See also Ethnic Problems; The Jews, p. 46; Second World War, p. 144; Eastern Europe and the Soviet Bloc, p. 358; (Germany) The Nazi Era, p. 475; other subsections under Czechoslovakia.

Brügel, Johann Wolfgang. **Tschechen und Deutsche, 1918-1938.** Munich: Nymphenburger Verlagshandlung, 1967, 662 p.
An impartial, well-documented study of Czech-German relations within the Czechoslovak Republic, from its inception to Munich. Written by a German from Czechoslovakia living in London, it emphasizes Czech reasonableness and German willingness to live in the new state, until Hitler destroyed the basis of coexistence.

Černý, Bohumil. **Most k novému zivotu: německá emigrace v ČSR v letech 1933-1939.** Prague: Lidová demokracie, 1968, 188 p.
An able account by a Czech Marxist historian of the many-sided activities of the anti-Nazi German refugees in Czechoslovakia during the 1930s.

Dress, Hans. **Slowakei und faschistische Neuordnung Europas, 1939-1941.** Berlin: Akademie-Verlag, 1972, 199 p.
An East German study of Slovakia during the early years of World War II.

Ďurica, Milan Stanislao. **La Slovacchia e le sue relazioni politiche con la Germania 1938-1945. Vol. I: Dagli accordi di Monaco all'inizio della Seconda Guerra Mondiale (ottobre 1938–settembre 1939).** Padova: Marsilio, 1964, 274 p.
A history of Slovakia's relations with Nazi Germany covering the period from the Munich Agreement to the outbreak of World War II.

Hoensch, Jörg Konrad. **Die Slowakei und Hitlers Ostpolitik: Hlinkas Slowakische Volkspartei zwischen Autonomie und Separation 1938/1939.** Cologne: Böhlau, 1965, 390 p.
A study of the development of Hlinka's Slovak People's Party and of Hitler's policies toward Czechoslovakia.

Husák, Gustáv. **Svedectvo o Slovenskom národnom povstaní.** Bratislava: Epocha, 2d rev. ed., 1969, 632 p.
An account of the Slovak resistance movement during World War II, by a leading participant and the present Secretary-General of the Communist Party of Czechoslovakia. The German edition appeared as "Der slowakische Nationalaufstand" (Berlin: Dietz, 1972, 740 p.).

Král, Václav, ed. **Die Deutschen in der Tschechoslowakei, 1933–1947: Dokumentensammlung.** Prague: Academia, 1964, 663 p.
Documents, mainly of German origin, illustrating Nazi policies toward Czechoslovakia before and during World War II. They are selected with the intent to exaggerate the extent of Czech resistance and the culpability of the Sudeten Germans for Nazi policies. Although the selection by the editor, an ultra-conservative communist polemicist-historian, is very one-sided, the publication provides much useful information.

Luža, Radomír. **The Transfer of the Sudeten Germans: A Study of Czech-German Relations, 1933–1962.** New York: New York University Press, 1964, 365 p.
A member of the Czech resistance movement during the war discusses the historical background for the Czech expulsion of the Sudeten Germans in 1945.

Mikus, Joseph A. **Slovakia: A Political History, 1918–1950.** Milwaukee: Marquette University Press, 1963, 392 p.
A discussion of Slovakia's difficult efforts at independence. A translation, with additions, of a book which first appeared as "La Slovaquie dans le drame de l'Europe: histoire politique de 1918 à 1950" (Paris: Les Iles d'Or, 1955, 475 p.).

Nittner, Ernst, comp. **Dokumente zur sudetendeutschen Frage 1916 bis 1967.** Munich: Ackermann-Gemeinde, rev. and enl. ed., 1967, 583 p.
A collection of documents on the Germans in Czechoslovakia covering the years from 1916 to 1967.

Orcival, François d'. **Le Danube était noir: la cause de la Slovaquie indépendante.** Paris: Éditions de la Table Ronde, 1968, 309 p.
A plea for the independence of Slovakia and a defense of Monseigneur Joseph Tiso and his Slovak state, established after the partition of Czechoslovakia on March 14, 1939.

Prečan, Vilém, ed. **Slovenské národné povstanie: dokumenty.** Bratislava: Vydavatel'stvo politickej literatúry, 1965, 1,218 p.
Edited by an open-minded Marxist historian, the volume consists of a balanced, diverse and detailed selection of documents about the 1944 anti-German uprising in Slovakia, the intriguing political and military planning by Beneš' government-in-exile, the Czechoslovak Communists, the Soviet Union and the Western Allies in the final stage of World War II.

POLAND

General

See also Political Processes, p. 20; (Europe) General Surveys, p. 344; Eastern Europe and the Soviet Bloc, p. 358.

Beneš, Václav L. and Pounds, Norman John Greville. **Poland.** New York: Praeger, 1970, 416 p.
A convenient general survey of the country's history, economic development and resources.

Bromke, Adam. **Poland's Politics: Idealism vs. Realism.** Cambridge: Harvard University Press, 1967, 316 p.

The subtitle indicates the underlying theme of this scholarly work: that the conflict between political idealism and political realism "stands out as the single most pervasive phenomenon in modern Polish political life." Emphasis is on the post-1945 period.

Droga przez półwiecze: o Polsce lat 1918-1968. Warsaw: Państwowy Instytut Wydawniczy, 1969, 319 p.

A collection of essays by leading Polish historians delivered at a joint session of the Academy of Sciences and Warsaw University on the 50th anniversary of Poland's recovery of independence.

Hartmann, Karl. **Polen.** Zurich: Christiana-Verlag, 1966, 498 p.

An overall historical survey of Polish culture, including the post-1945 period.

Kowalczyk, Stanisław; Borkowski, Jan and Others. **Zarys historii polskiego ruchu ludowego.** Warsaw: Ludowa Spółdzielnia Wydawnicza, 1963-1970, 2 v.

This important outline history of the Polish peasant movement covers the period from the 1860s to 1939 and contains much useful material.

Rhode, Gotthold. **Geschichte Polens.** Darmstadt: Wissenschaftliche Buchgesellschaft, 2d rev. ed., 1966, 543 p.

A concise but valuable general history by a leading German historian.

Roos, Hans. **A History of Modern Poland: From the Foundation of the State in the First World War to the Present Day.** New York: Knopf, 1966, 303 p.

An excellent and well-balanced history of Poland since the founding of the republic in the First World War. The German original appeared as "Geschichte der polnischen Nation, 1916-1960: von der Staatsgründung im Ersten Weltkrieg bis zur Gegenwart" (Stuttgart: Kohlhammer, 1961, 263 p.).

Syrop, Konrad. **Poland: Between the Hammer and the Anvil.** London: Hale, 1968, 208 p.

A concise and readable survey of Polish history, of which the last quarter is devoted to events since 1945.

Woods, William Howard. **Poland: Eagle in the East.** New York: Hill and Wang, 1968, 272 p.

An informal portrayal of contemporary Poland.

Biographies, Memoirs and Collected Writings

See also Second World War, p. 144.

Bethell, Nicholas. **Gomułka: His Poland, His Communism.** New York: Holt, Rinehart and Winston, 1969, 296 p.

A substantial biography of the Polish Communist leader, by a British journalist.

Bielecki, Tadeusz. **W szkole Dmowskiego.** London: Polska Fundacja Kulturalna, 1968, 317 p.

A collection of essays on Roman Dmowski, the leader of the Polish National Democratic Movement, by a prominent politician of this orientation.

Blit, Lucjan. **The Eastern Pretender: Boleslaw Piasecki: His Life and Times.** London: Hutchinson, 1965, 223 p.

The biography of the former Polish fascist leader who after World War II became the head of the pro-communist Catholic PAX organization.

Korboński, Stefan. **Warsaw in Exile.** New York: Praeger, 1966, 325 p.

Personal reminiscences and sidelights on major events of recent history, by a prominent member of the Polish Peasant Party who was also a leading figure in the Assembly of Captive European Nations. The present volume, published originally as "W imieniu Polski walczącej" (London: B. Świderski, 1963, 756 p.), covers primarily the period since 1949 and is a continuation of the author's "Fighting Warsaw: The Story of the Polish Underground State, 1939-1945" (1956) and "Warsaw in Chains" (1959).

Kukiel, Marian. **Generał Sikorski.** London: Instytut Polski i Muzeum im. Gen. Sikorskiego, 1970, 280 p.

This first biography of General Sikorski, written by a close friend and associate, places its emphasis on the Second World War period. It provides important insights.

Micewski, Andrzej. **Roman Dmowski.** Warsaw: "Verum," 1971, 423 p.
A solid biography of Roman Dmowski, the leader of the National Democrats.

Raina, Peter K. **Gomulka.** Cologne: Verlag Wissenschaft und Politik, 1970, 191 p.
A political biography by an Indian historian who lived five years in Poland.

Rataj, Maciej. **Pamiętniki.** Warsaw: Ludowa Spółdzielnia Wydawnicza, 1965, 484 p.
These memoirs by an outstanding Populist leader cover the years from 1918 to 1927.

Retinger, Joseph Hieronim. **Joseph Retinger—Memoirs of an Eminence Grise.** Brighton: Sussex University Press, 1972, 265 p.
Autobiographical notes by an adventurous Pole, who during World War II was active in Polish politics and diplomacy in Great Britain, Russia and the United States, and was a supporter of General Sikorski. Edited by John Pomian.

Szembek, Jan. **Diariusz i teki Jana Szembeka.** London: Instytut Polski i Muzeum im. Gen. Sikorskiego, 1964-72, 4 v.
A massive diary of the Polish Under Secretary of State for Foreign Affairs in the 1930s, accompanied by additional documents. It replaces the short French version "Journal 1933-1939" (Paris: Plon, 1952, 504 p.) and is one of the richest sources for Polish inter-war diplomacy. Volumes 1-3 are edited by Tytus Komarnicki, and volume 4 by Jozef Zarański.

Witos, Wincenty. **Moje wspomnienia.** Paris: Instytut Literacki, 1964-65, 3 v.
Important memoirs of the chief figure in the Polish Peasant Party, written mostly in exile in Czechoslovakia.

Recent History

To 1945

See also Political Philosophies and Ideologies, p. 21; First World War, p. 131; Inter-War Period, p. 140; Second World War, p. 144; Eastern Europe and the Soviet Bloc, p. 358; (Germany) The 1918 Revolution and the Weimar Republic, p. 468; The Nazi Era, p. 475; other subsections under Poland.

Ajnenkiel, Andrzej. **Od "rządów ludowych" do przewrotu majowego: zarys dziejów politycznych Polski, 1918-1926.** Warsaw: Wiedza Powszechna, 1964, 339 p.
An able survey of Polish political history prior to Piłsudski's coup of 1926.

Batowski, Henryk. **Agonia pokoju i początek wojny.** Poznań: Wydawnictwo Poznańskie, 1969, 502 p.
A detailed story of the three weeks preceeding and following the outbreak of the Second World War, by a well-known diplomatic historian.

Ciechanowski, Jan M. **Powstanie warszawskie: zarys podłoża politycznego i dyplomatycznego.** London: Odnowa, 1971, 399 p.
A well-documented and thoughtful, although controversial, study of the origins of the Warsaw Uprising of 1944.

Holzer, Jerzy and Molenda, Jan. **Polska w pierwszej wojnie światowej.** Warsaw: Wiedza Powszechna, 1963, 380 p.
A very useful survey of Poland during the First World War.

Jabłoński, Henryk. **Narodziny Drugiej Rzeczypospolitej, 1918-1919.** Warsaw: Wiedza Powszechna, 1962, 311 p.
A stimulating analysis of the rebirth of Poland, by a leading Marxist historian and politician.

Johnpoll, Bernard K. **The Politics of Futility.** Ithaca: Cornell University Press, 1967, 298 p.
An investigation of the General Jewish Workers Bund of Poland during the inter-war period. The author is critical of the policies and political premises of the Bund as a party in evading the practical task of influencing the direction of the Polish state.

Leczyk, Marian. **Komitet Narodowy Polski a Ententa i Stany Zjednoczone, 1917-1919.** Warsaw: Państwowe Wydawnictwo Naukowe, 1966, 326 p.
A pioneering study of Dmowski's National Committee in the years from 1917 to 1919.

Madajczyk, Czesław. **Polityka III Rzeszy w okupowanej Polsce.** Warsaw: Państwowe Wydawnictwo Naukowe, 1970, 2 v.
   A voluminous study of German policy in occupied Poland during the Second World War. The author is the director of the Historical Institute of the Polish Academy of Sciences in Warsaw.

Micewski, Andrzej. **W cieniu marszałka Piłsudskiego.** Warsaw: Czytelnik, 1969, 427 p.
   A study on Polish inter-war politics, emphasizing the Piłsudski tradition, by a gifted historian-journalist.

Micewski, Andrzej. **Z geografii politycznej II Rzeczypospolitej.** Warsaw: "Znak," 1964, 406 p.
   A pioneering and stimulating study of Polish inter-war politics, with emphasis on the parties of the Right.

Moczulski, Leszek. **Wojna polska.** Poznań: Wydawnictwo Poznańskie, 1972, 222 p.
   Interestingly written and implicitly defying official interpretations, this work on the 1939 War by a well-known journalist was quickly withdrawn from circulation.

Montfort, Henri Archambault de. **Le Massacre de Katyn: crime russe ou crime allemand?** Paris: Éditions de la Table Ronde, 1966, 198 p.
   The author examines the documents dealing with the Katyn massacre of Polish officers and concludes that the Soviets were responsible for it.

Polonsky, Antony. **Politics in Independent Poland, 1921-1939.** New York: Oxford University Press, 1972, 572 p.
   A thorough study of political life in inter-war Poland, giving particular attention to the disintegration of Piłsudski's "guided democracy" in the years after the May 1926 coup.

Rothschild, Joseph. **Piłsudski's Coup D'Etat.** New York: Columbia University Press, 1966, 435 p.
   A scholarly, but quite dramatic account of the "causes, events, and consequences" of Józef Piłsudski's coup d'état of May 1926.

Stawecki, Piotr. **Następcy komendanta: wojsko a polityka wewnętrzna Drugiej Rzeczpospolitej w latach 1935-1939.** Warsaw: Ministerstwo Obrony Narodowej, 1969, 323 p.
   An inquiry into the role of the army in Polish politics in the 1930s. Not the last word on the subject.

Wiśniewski, Ernest, *ed.* **Wojna wyzwoleńcza narodu polskiego w latach 1939-1945.** Warsaw: Ministerstwo Obrony Narodowej, 1966, 881 p.
   An official history of Poland's struggle during the Second World War.

Zabiełło, Stanisław. **W kręgu historii.** Warsaw: Pax, 1970, 219 p.
   A collection of articles on themes relating mainly to the Second World War, by a prewar Polish diplomat turned amateur historian.

Żarnowski, Janusz. **Struktura społeczna inteligencji w Polsce w latach 1918-1939.** Warsaw: Państwowe Wydawnictwo Naukowe, 1964, 362 p.
   An important study of the inter-war Polish intelligentsia by a noted social historian.

Since 1945

See also Socialism, p. 24; Communism, p. 26; The Postwar World, p. 178; Eastern Europe and the Soviet Bloc, p. 358; other subsections under Poland.

Gelberg, Ludwik. **Die Entstehung der Volksrepublik Polen.** Frankfurt/Main: Athenäum, 1972, 175 p.
   A combined legal and political study dealing with the position of the government-in-exile, the institutions of the provisional regime in Lublin and Warsaw, and the establishment of the new frontiers.

Hiscocks, Charles Richard. **Poland: Bridge for the Abyss?** New York: Oxford University Press, 1963, 359 p.
   The author of this survey argues that Poland can serve as a bridge between the communist world and the West.

Jedlicki, Witold. **Klub Krzywego Koła.** Paris: Instytut Literacki, 1963, 168 p.
   A history of the "Crooked Circle Club," dissolved by the Polish authorities in 1962, by one of its members.

Jordan, Zbigniew A. **Philosophy and Ideology: The Development of Philosophy and Marxism-Leninism in Poland Since the Second World War.** Dordrecht: Reidel, 1963, 600 p.
A useful survey by a Polish scholar.

Laeuen, Harald. **Polen nach dem Sturz Gomulkas.** Stuttgart: Seewald, 1972, 260 p.
An informed and sympathetic account of the first year of Gierek's rule. Most of it deals with internal affairs but the final two chapters touch on Eastern Europe and on policy toward Germany.

Markiewicz, Stanisław. **Stato e chiesa in Polonia.** Padua: Marsilio Editori, 1967, 249 p.
Though biased, this study by a Polish Communist official contains useful information on the important role of the Catholic Church in present-day Poland. Translated from "Sprzeczności we współczesnym katolicyzmie" (Warsaw: Książka i Wiedza, 1964, 246 p.).

Mieroszewski, Juliusz. **Ewolucjonizm.** Paris: Instytut Literacki, 1964, 69 p.
A collection of articles by a leading and influential emigré political writer arguing for an evolutionist development of Polish communism.

Pirages, Dennis Clark. **Modernization and Political-Tension Management; A Socialist Society in Perspective: Case Study of Poland.** New York: Praeger, 1972, 260 p.
Using the latest in social science methods, the author attempts to fathom the Polish political and economic system and to throw light on the key question of the relationship of industrial modernization to political change and reform.

Raina, Peter K. **Die Krise der Intellektuellen: die Rebellion für die Freiheit in Polen.** Olten: Walter-Verlag, 1968, 128 p.
A brief account of the conflict between the Polish regime and the liberal intellectuals in 1966–67.

Rozmaryn, Stefan. **La Pologne.** Paris: Librairie Générale de Droit, 1963, 363 p.
A description of the political institutions of Communist Poland by a professor at the University of Warsaw.

Singer, Gusta. **Teacher Education in a Communist State: Poland 1956–1961.** New York: Bookman Associates, 1965, 282 p.
An analysis of the organization and curricula of teacher education institutions from 1956 to 1961, including a survey of the whole educational system in Communist Poland.

Stehle, Hansjakob. **The Independent Satellite: Society and Politics in Poland since 1945.** New York: Praeger, 1965, 361 p.
An able report on post-World War II Poland by a German journalist, including a perceptive account of contemporary German-Polish relations. The German version appeared as "Nachbar Polen" (Frankfurt/Main: Fischer, enl. ed., 1968, 434 p.).

Szczepański, Jan. **Rozważania o Rzeczypospolitej.** Warsaw: Państwowy Instytut Wydawniczy, 1971, 145 p.
A collection of articles and essays on contemporary Poland by a leading sociologist.

Foreign Relations

See also (General Works) Reference Works, p. 1; The World Since 1914, p. 129; other subsections under Poland and the sections for specific countries and regions.

Balcerak, Wiesław. **Polityka zagraniczna Polski w dobie Locarna.** Warsaw: Ossolineum, 1967, 244 p.
A solid study of Polish foreign policy of the Locarno period, with a good appraisal of Foreign Minister Skrzyński.

Bregman, Aleksander. **Jak świat światem? Stosunki polsko-niemieckie wczoraj, dziś i jutro.** London: Nakładem Polskiej Fundacji Kulturalnej, 1964, 274 p.
An important study of Polish-German relations after World War II and a plea for reconciliation, by a well-known Polish journalist and a former editor of the London *Dziennik Polski*.

Budurowycz, Bohdan B. **Polish-Soviet Relations, 1932–1939.** New York: Columbia University Press, 1963, 229 p.

A judicious and scholarly monograph on the course of Polish-Soviet relations from the conclusion of the 1932 Nonaggression Pact to the partition of Poland in 1939.

Ciałowicz, Jan. **Polsko-francuski sojusz wojskowy, 1921-1939.** Warsaw: Państwowe Wydawnictwo Naukowe, 1970, 423 p.
A pioneering study of the Franco-Polish military alliance in the inter-war period, by a former staff officer.

Documents on Polish-Soviet Relations, 1939-1945. Volume II: 1943-1945. London: Heinemann (for the General Sikorski Historical Institute), 1967, 866 p.
The second and final volume of a substantial collection of documents on relations between the Polish Government in London and the Soviet Government. Volume I was published in 1961.

Dokumenty i materiały do historii stosunków polsko-radzieckich. Warsaw: Książka i Wiedza (for the Polska Akademia Nauk, Pracownia Historii Stosunków Polsko-Radzieckich and Akademia Nauk ZSRR, Instytut Słowianoznawstwa), 1962-.
A massive collection of documents on Soviet-Polish relations in the period from March 1917 to 1945. Through 1973 eight volumes have appeared. There is also a Russian edition, but the Polish one prints all documents in their original language.

Dziewanowski, M. K. **Joseph Pilsudski: A European Federalist, 1918-1922.** Stanford: Hoover Institution, 1969, 379 p.
A study of Piłsudski's futile attempts to convince the Lithuanians and Byelorussians to federate with Poland.

Gostyńska, Weronika. **Stosunki polske-radzieckie 1918-1919.** Warsaw: Książka i Wiedza, 1972, 400 p.
A well-documented Marxist history of Polish-Soviet relations in the years from 1918 to 1920.

Horák, Stephan. **Poland's International Affairs, 1919-1960.** Bloomington: Indiana University, 1964, 248 p.
A useful annotated calendar of Polish international agreements.

Korbel, Josef. **Poland Between East and West: Soviet and German Diplomacy Toward Poland, 1919-1933.** Princeton: Princeton University Press, 1963, 321 p.
A scholarly study in diplomatic history dealing with the complex and shifting policies of Germany and the Soviet Union from the end of the First World War to the Polish-German Nonaggression Pact.

Kowalski, Włodzimierz T. **Walka dyplomatyczna o miejsce Polski w Europie 1939-1945.** Warsaw: Książka i Wiedza, 4th ed., 1972, 877 p.
A detailed study of Poland in the diplomacy of the Second World War. The author heads the Institute on Soviet-Polish Relations in Warsaw.

Kozeński, Jerzy. **Czechosłowacja w polskiej polityce zagranicznej w latach 1932-1938.** Poznań: Instytut Zachodni, 1964, 317 p.
A well-documented monograph on Polish policy toward Czechoslovakia in the 1930s.

Krasuski, Jerzy. **Stosunki polsko-niemieckie.** Poznań: Instytut Zachodni, 1962-64, 2 v.
A solid study of German-Polish relations before Hitler's advent to power.

Kukułka, Józef. **Francja a Polska po traktacie wersalskim 1919-1922.** Warsaw: Książka i Wiedza, 1970, 623 p.
An exhaustive, though somewhat pedestrian, study of Franco-Polish relations after the Treaty of Versailles.

Kuźmiński, Tadeusz. **Polska, Francja, Niemcy 1933-1935.** Warsaw: Państwowe Wydawnictwo Naukowe, 1963, 259 p.
A study on Polish diplomatic history in the years from 1933 to 1935, by a noted historian.

Lewandowski, Józef. **Federalizm: Litwa i Białoruś w polityce obozu belwederskiego.** Warsaw: Państwowe Wydawnictwo Naukowe, 1962, 271 p.
A stimulating although controversial analysis of the much discussed ideas of Piłsudski and his entourage concerning the plans for federation with Lithuania and Byelorussia in the years from 1918 to 1920.

Lipski, Józef. **Diplomat in Berlin, 1933-1939: Papers and Memoirs of Józef Lipski, Ambassador of Poland.** New York: Columbia University Press, 1968, 679 p.
Józef Lipski, who died in 1958, was Polish Ambassador to Germany from 1933 to

1939. The translation and publication of his papers for those years—reports, instructions from Warsaw, documents, lectures, etc.—provide an important source for Polish-German and international relations in the 1930s. Edited by Wacław Jędrzejewicz.

Łukasiewicz, Juliusz. **Diplomat in Paris, 1936-1939: Papers and Memoirs of Juliusz Łukasiewicz, Ambassador of Poland.** New York: Columbia University Press, 1970, 408 p.
Posthumously edited memoirs and papers of the former Polish Ambassador to France dealing with the occupation of the Rhineland, the Teschen dispute and the mounting crisis from March to September 1939. A valuable companion piece to the memoirs of Józef Lipski. Edited by Wacław Jędrzejewicz.

Pajewski, Janusz. **Wokół sprawy polskiej: Paryż-Lozanna-Londyn 1914-1918.** Poznań: Wydawnictwo Poznańskie, 1970, 254 p.
An excellently written and well-documented study of the Polish question in the Allied camp during the First World War, by a prominent historian.

Pułaski, Michał. **Stosunki dyplomatyczne polsko-czecho-słowacko-niemieckie od 1933 do wiosny 1938.** Poznań: Wydawnictwo Poznańskie, 1967, 222 p.
A solid study of Polish-Czechoslovak-German relations in the Hitler era.

Rachocki, Janusz, ed. **Volksrepublik Polen, Bundesrepublik Deutschland: Probleme der Normalisierung gegenseitiger Beziehungen.** Poznań: Instytut Zachodni, 1972, 287 p.
A collection of articles and documents illustrating the official Polish conceptions of contemporary German-Polish relations.

Stanisławska, Stefania. **Polska a Monachium.** Warsaw: Książka i Wiedza, 1967, 467 p.
A discussion of the controversial part played by Polish diplomacy in the Munich crisis of 1938.

Szklarska-Lohmannowa, Alina. **Polsko-czechosłowackie stosunki dyplomatyczne w latach 1918-1925.** Wrocław: Ossolineum, 1967, 180 p.
A balanced and judicious study of Polish-Czechoslovak relations in the post-Versailles period.

Vierheller, Viktoria. **Polen und die Deutschland-Frage, 1939-1949.** Cologne: Verlag Wissenschaft und Politik, 1970, 183 p.
A study of the position of the various Polish regimes between 1939 and 1949 with respect to the German question and Polish-German relations.

Wandycz, Piotr Stefan. **Soviet-Polish Relations, 1917-1921.** Cambridge: Harvard University Press, 1969, 403 p.
Following a concise review of the long and troubled course of Russian-Polish relations, Professor Wandycz of Yale University makes a detailed and scholarly study of diplomatic and military affairs in the crucial years when both the Polish Republic and the Soviet regime were struggling into existence.

Weit, Erwin. **At the Red Summit: Interpreter behind the Iron Curtain.** New York: Macmillan, 1973, 226 p.
Memoirs of a translator for the Polish regime from 1956 to 1969, dealing particularly with Polish-East German meetings and conversations. The German original was published as "Ostblock intern" (Hamburg: Hoffmann und Campe, 1970, 273 p.).

Wojciechowski, Marian. **Stosunki polsko-niemieckie 1933-1938.** Poznań: Instytut Zachodni, 1965, 571 p.
An important study of German-Polish relations in the Hitler period by a noted historian.

Economic Problems

See also Labor and Labor Movements, p. 41; Eastern Europe and the Soviet Bloc, p. 358.

Alton, Thad Paul and Others. **Polish National Income and Product in 1954, 1955, and 1956.** New York: Columbia University Press, 1965, 252 p.
This volume in a series of studies on the national income of countries in East Central Europe provides "a cross-section view of economic activity as it is summarized in the gross national product."

Feiwel, George R. **Poland's Industrialization Policy: A Current Analysis.** New York: Praeger, 1971, 747 p.

———. **Problems in Polish Economic Planning.** New York: Praeger, 1971, 454 p.
These two volumes constitute a massive and informative study of the Polish economy.

Korbonski, Andrzej. **Politics of Socialist Agriculture in Poland, 1945-1960.** New York: Columbia University Press, 1965, 330 p.
A scholarly inquiry into the interplay of politics and economics in Poland's postwar agriculture, with particular attention to the collapse of collectivization after October 1956.

Landau, Zbigniew and Tomaszewski, Jerzy. **Anonimowi władcy: z dziejów kapitału obcego w Polsce 1918-1939.** Warsaw: Wiedza Powszechna, 3rd ed., 1968, 220 p.
A preliminary inquiry into the controversial subject of foreign capital in Poland during the inter-war period, by two prominent economic historians.

Landau, Zbigniew and Tomaszewski, Jerzy. **Zarys historii gospodarczej Polski 1918-1939.** Warsaw: Książka i Wiedza, 1971, 321 p.
An outline of the economic history of inter-war Poland.

Territorial, Frontier and Minority Problems

See also Ethnic Problems; The Jews, p. 46; First World War, p. 131; Second World War, p. 144; Eastern Europe and the Soviet Bloc, p. 358; Lithuania, p. 461; Germany, p. 463; Czechoslovakia, p. 516; Union of Soviet Socialist Republics, p. 531.

Bahr, Ernst and König, Kurt. **Niederschlesien unter polnischer Verwaltung.** Frankfurt/Main: Metzner (for the Johann Gottfried Herder Forschungsrat), 1967, 442 p.
A detailed review of the political, economic, demographic and cultural changes brought about by the Polish rule in the formerly Prussian province of Lower Silesia.

Bluhm, Georg. **Die Oder-Neisse-Linie in der deutschen Aussenpolitik.** Freiburg: Rombach, 1963, 204 p.
A thorough discussion of the political and moral aspects of the Oder-Neisse line in the context of world politics. The author argues that the former German territories now constitute an indisputable, vital interest of the Polish nation which the Germans must come to recognize.

Bohmann, Alfred. **Menschen und Grenzen: Strukturwandel der deutschen Bevölkerung im polnischen Staats- und Verwaltungsbereich.** Cologne: Verlag Wissenschaft und Politik, 1969, 448 p.
An extensive demographic study of the changes in the structure of the German population in Poland since 1919.

Buchhofer, Ekkehard. **Die Bevölkerungsentwicklung in den polnisch verwalteten deutschen Ostgebieten von 1956-1965.** Kiel: Neue Universität, Geographisches Institut, 1967, 279 p.
A study of population developments from 1956 to 1965 in the former German territories east of the Oder-Neisse line.

Kruszewski, Z. Anthony. **The Oder-Neisse Boundary and Poland's Modernization.** New York: Praeger, 1972, 245 p.
A useful study of the complex and important role that the transfer of German territory, and the relocation of some 4.5 million Poles, played in the postwar modernization of Poland.

Labuda, Gerard. **Polska granica zachodnia: tysiąc lat dziejów politycznych.** Poznań: Wydawnictwo Poznańskie, 1971, 453 p.
A comprehensive history of the Polish western frontier by an outstanding historian.

Wrzesiński, Wojciech. **Ruch polski na Warmii, Mazurach i Powiślu w latach 1920-1939.** Poznań: Instytut Zachodni, 1963, 436 p.
A detailed and well-documented study of the attempt by the Polish minority in East Prussia to preserve and further Polish national consciousness in the period 1920-1939.

Zdziechowski, Georges. **Le Problème clef de la construction européenne: la Pologne sur l'Oder.** Paris: Pedone, 1965, 228 p.
A presentation of the Polish case in the Oder-Neisse question.

UNION OF SOVIET SOCIALIST REPUBLICS

General

See also General Works, p. 1; Political Factors, p. 12; The World Since 1914, p. 129; Eastern Europe and the Soviet Bloc, p. 358; (Union of Soviet Socialist Republics) Recent History, p. 538.

Anderson, Thornton. **Russian Political Thought: An Introduction.** Ithaca: Cornell University Press, 1967, 444 p.
   This history, beginning with Kievian Rus', emphasizes the "Greek-Mongol-Russian tradition as a distinct body of political thought." Emphasis is on the pre-Soviet periods.

Bol'shaia Sovetskaia Entsiklopediia. Moscow: Izd-vo "Sovetskaia Entsiklopediia," 3rd ed., 1970—.
   By the middle of 1973 eight volumes of the new edition of "The Great Soviet Encyclopedia" were published. This version is less polemical and more informative than the previous ones.

Cole, John P. **A Geography of the U.S.S.R.** Baltimore: Penguin, 1967, 326 p.
   A concise regional geography, stressing economic features.

Curtiss, John Shelton, *ed.* **Essays in Russian and Soviet History.** New York: Columbia University Press, 1963, 345 p.
   This symposium of 20 pieces on modern and contemporary Russian and Soviet history was organized as a *Festschrift* for a leading scholar in the field, Geroid Tanquary Robinson.

Gregory, James Stothert. **Russian Land, Soviet People.** New York: Pegasus, 1968, 947 p.
   An extensive general and regional geographic survey of the U.S.S.R.

Harris, Chauncy Dennison. **Cities of the Soviet Union.** Chicago: Rand McNally (for the Association of American Geographers), 1970, 484 p.
   A leading American student of Soviet geography offers a valuable study of the "economic functions, size relations, distributional patterns, and growth" of some 1,247 cities and towns of the U.S.S.R.

Horecky, Paul Louis, *ed.* **Russia and the Soviet Union.** Chicago: University of Chicago Press, 1965, 473 p.
   This valuable annotated bibliographic guide to Western-language publications is a companion volume to the editor's "Basic Russian Publications" (1962).

Kohler, Foy D. **Understanding the Russians: A Citizen's Primer.** New York: Harper and Row, 1970, 441 p.
   On the basis of his extended diplomatic career, including a number of years in Moscow—as Counselor of Embassy (1947–49) and Ambassador (1962–66)—Mr. Kohler surveys the history and nature of the Soviet system. He is definitely anti-revisionist in his view of the origins and the continuation of the cold war.

Maichel, Karol. **Guide to Russian Reference Books. Vol. II: History, Auxiliary Historical Sciences, Ethnography, and Geography.** Stanford: Stanford University, The Hoover Institution on War, Revolution, and Peace, 1964, 297 p.
   A useful reference.

Mellor, Roy E. H. **Geography of the U.S.S.R.** New York: St. Martin's Press, 1964, 402 p.
   An examination of problems affected by geography in the Soviet Union, by a British scholar.

Sedlmeyer, Karl. **Landeskunde der Sowjetunion.** Frankfurt/Main: Bernard und Graefe, 1968, 218 p.
   A useful introduction to the physical and economic geography of the Soviet Union.

Seton-Watson, Hugh. **The Russian Empire 1801–1917.** New York: Oxford University Press, 1967, 813 p.
   In this third volume of the "Oxford History of Modern Europe," Professor Seton-Watson has presented a massive and balanced general survey of Russian history from the accession of Alexander I to the end of the monarchy in the February Revolution.

Taaffe, Robert N. and Kingsbury, Robert C. **An Atlas of Soviet Affairs.** New York: Praeger, 1965, 143 p.
   A useful reference.

Utechin, Sergej V. **Russian Political Thought.** New York: Praeger, 1964, 320 p.
A concise introduction to Russian political thought from medieval times to the present.

Whiting, Kenneth R. **The Soviet Union Today.** New York: Praeger, rev. and enl. ed., 1966, 423 p.
A revised and expanded edition of a handbook "intended for the person seeking an introduction to things Soviet."

Correspondents' Reports and Personal Accounts

Barwich, Heinz and Barwich, Elfi. **Das rote Atom.** Bern: Scherz, 1967, 277 p.
A German scientist's personal account of his experiences in connection with Soviet atomic developments in the two postwar decades.

Behrens, Erwin. **Tagebuch aus Moskau.** Hamburg: Wegner, 1964, 227 p.
Reportage on Moscow and parts of the U.S.S.R. between October 1961 and January 1964.

Botting, Douglas. **One Chilly Siberian Morning.** New York: Macmillan, 1967, 192 p.
An engaging account of a British traveler's experience in northern Siberia.

De Mauny, Erik. **Russian Prospect: Notes of a Moscow Correspondent.** New York: Atheneum, 1970, 320 p.
Interesting reflections on the changing world of Russia in the 1960s by a BBC correspondent who was there before and after the fall of Khrushchev.

Dornberg, John. **The New Tsars: Russia under Stalin's Heirs.** Garden City: Doubleday, 1972, 470 p.
A rather somber account of the Soviet Union in the late 1960s, by the former chief of *Newsweek*'s Moscow bureau.

Kalb, Marvin. **The Volga: A Political Journey Through Russia.** New York: Macmillan, 1967, 191 p.
A C.B.S. correspondent's account of a voyage upstream from Volgograd to Moscow, with a good deal of political and historical discussion.

Levine, Isaac Don. **I Rediscover Russia.** New York: Duell, 1964, 216 p.
An account of a visit to the Soviet Union by an old Russia hand well known for his vigorous anti-Stalinist writings.

Meier, Viktor E. **Fassade und Wirklichkeit der Sowjetunion.** Zurich: Buchverlag der Neuen Zürcher Zeitung, 1965, 190 p.
Able reporting on the Soviet scene in 1964 by a correspondent for the *Neue Zürcher Zeitung*.

Mihajlov, Mihajlo. **Moscow Summer.** New York: Farrar, Straus and Giroux, 1965, 220 p.
The internationally debated report of a Jugoslav teacher on a visit to the Soviet Union in the summer of 1964.

Nerhood, Harry W., *comp*. **To Russia and Return.** Columbus: Ohio State University Press, 1969, 367 p.
An annotated bibliography of "reports of journeys to Russia that have been published in the English language," from earliest times to the present. Approximately half of the entries are accounts of travels to the Soviet Union.

Ronchey, Alberto. **Russia in the Thaw.** New York: Norton, 1964, 249 p.
An Italian journalist's perceptive account of the Soviet scene in 1959–1961. The Italian original appeared as "La Russia del disgelo" (Milan: Garzanti, 1963, 242 p.).

Scheffer, Paul. **Augenzeuge im Staate Lenins.** Munich: Piper, 1972, 449 p.
Reprinted dispatches from Russia in the 1920s by the correspondent of the *Berliner Tageblatt*. Scheffer's personal ties with leading Soviet personalities and with the German Embassy, described in Margret Boveri's introduction, gave him a unique semi-political role.

Schiller, Ulrich. **Zwischen Moskau und Jakutsk.** Hamburg: Wegner, 1970, 212 p.
A German correspondent's report on contradictory trends and impulses in Soviet life.

Shub, Anatole. **The New Russian Tragedy.** New York: Norton, 1969, 128 p.
A depressing reportage on the Soviet scene, by a well-trained observer who was the

Moscow correspondent for *The Washington Post* from 1967 to 1969, when he was expelled.

Specovius, Günther. **Die Russen sind anders: Mensch und Gesellschaft im Sowjetstaat.** Düsseldorf: Econ-Verlag, 1963, 639 p.
An extensive and quite lively survey of the Soviet Union by a German journalist.

Van der Post, Laurens. **A View of all the Russias.** New York: Morrow, 1964, 374 p.
A most valuable and informative portrait of the Soviet Union and its inhabitants.

Memoirs and Biographies

See also Socialism, p. 24; Communism, p. 26; Second World War, p. 144; Bulgaria, p. 596.

Abrikosov, Dmitrii Ivanovich. **Revelations of a Russian Diplomat: The Memoirs of Dmitrii I. Abrikossow.** Seattle: University of Washington Press, 1964, 329 p.
The author of these recollections had served for more than 20 years in the Russian diplomatic corps and ended his career in 1925 as *chargé d'affaires* in Tokyo when the Japanese government recognized the Soviet régime. Edited by George Alexander Lensen.

Allilueva, Svetlana. **Only One Year.** New York: Harper and Row, 1969, 444 p.
Recollections by Stalin's daughter covering the period from December 1966 to December 1967 during which she left Russia for India and made her decision to come to the United States. The book contains numerous flashbacks to events and personalities in the Stalin and Khrushchev years. The Russian original appeared as "Tol'ko odin god" (New York: Harper and Row, 1969, 381 p.).

Allilueva, Svetlana. **Twenty Letters to a Friend.** New York: Harper and Row, 1967, 246 p.
Although Stalin's daughter provides little political insight and her book is scarcely a literary masterpiece, it is, for all its disconcerting qualities, a significant and moving document. The Russian original appeared as "Dvadtsat' pisem k drugu" (London: Hutchinson, 1967, 222 p.).

Amal'rik, Andrei. **Involuntary Journey to Siberia.** New York: Harcourt Brace Jovanovich, 1970, 297 p.
The courageously nonconformist author of "Will the Soviet Union Survive Until 1984?" reports on his imprisonment, trial and exile to Siberia in the mid-1960s. Not surprisingly he was rearrested, tried and imprisoned. Translated from "Nezhelannoe puteshestvie v Sibir' " (New York: Harcourt Brace Jovanovich, 1970, 294 p.).

Balabanoff, Angelica. **Impressions of Lenin.** Ann Arbor: University of Michigan Press, 1964, 152 p.
Quite revealing personal memoirs of Lenin by a onetime secretary of the Comintern who early broke with the movement.

Berezhkov, Valentin Mikhailovich. **Gody diplomaticheskoi sluzhby.** Moscow: Izd-vo "Mezhdunarodnye Otnosheniia," 1972, 367 p.
The memoirs of the Soviet diplomat and journalist Valentin Berezhkov, including his accounts of service in the Soviet embassy in Berlin in 1941, at the Tehran Conference of 1943, and in the United Nations during its first days.

Berger, Joseph. **Nothing but the Truth.** New York: Day, 1971, 286 p.
Memoirs of a founding member of the Communist Party of Palestine and a veteran Comintern functionary who spent 22 years in Soviet concentration camps and exile.

Chaney, Otto Preston, Jr. **Zhukov.** Norman: University of Oklahoma Press, 1971, 512 p.
This substantial biography of Marshal Zhukov is considerably more extensive in coverage and scope than Zhukov's own rather flat memoirs.

Crankshaw, Edward. **Khrushchev: A Career.** New York: Viking, 1966, 311 p.
A biography of Nikita Khrushchev by a correspondent of the London *Observer*. A substantial study, but not the definitive biography.

Crowley, Edward L. and Others, *eds*. **Prominent Personalities in the USSR: A Biographic Dictionary.** Metuchen (N.J.): Scarecrow Press, 1968, 792 p.

A biographic reference work in a series compiled at the Institute for the Study of the U.S.S.R. in Munich, Germany.

Deutscher, Isaac. **Lenin's Childhood.** New York: Oxford University Press, 1970, 67 p.
A fragment, posthumously published, of what was intended to be a major biography of Lenin.

Deutscher, Isaac. **Stalin: A Political Biography.** New York: Oxford University Press, 2d ed., 1967, 661 p.
This second edition of a well-known biography first published in 1949 is virtually unchanged with the exception of an extensive postscript covering Stalin's last years.

Ehrenburg, Il'ia Grigor'evich. [**Memoirs.**] New York: Knopf; Cleveland: World Publishing Co., 1962-67, 4 v.
These memoirs of a leading Soviet writer and journalist, who died in 1967, cover a vast sweep of Soviet history. A significant though not always reliable document. The volumes of the American edition are entitled: "People and Life, 1891-1921" (1962, 453 p.); "Memoirs: 1921-1941" (1964, 543 p.); "The War: 1941-1945" (1965, 198 p.); and "Post-War Years, 1945-1954" (1967, 349 p.). The various Russian original versions were edited by the author for the English translation.

Fischer, Louis. **The Life of Lenin.** New York: Harper and Row, 1964, 703 p.
Mr. Fischer's study stresses Lenin's years in power after 1917 and is, in fact, almost a history of the early Soviet state. For Lenin's early career and the origins of Bolshevism the reader should still refer to the works of Haimson, Keep, Treadgold, Ulam, and Wolfe.

Fleming, Robert Peter. **The Fate of Admiral Kolchak.** New York: Harcourt, Brace and World, 1963, 253 p.
Colonel Fleming admirably unravels the confused and tragic story of Admiral Aleksandr Kolchak, who for less than one year (1919-20) was Supreme Ruler of Russia in the civil war against the new Bolshevik government.

Frankland, Mark. **Khrushchev.** New York: Stein and Day, 1967, 213 p.
This "essay in biography" by the former Moscow correspondent for the London *Observer* is particularly useful in its account of the last phases of Khrushchev's career.

Getzler, Israel. **Martov: A Political Biography of a Russian Social Democrat.** New York: Cambridge University Press, 1967, 246 p.
A detailed monograph on a leading Menshevik's ideas and activities in the Russian revolutionary movement and in international socialism.

Ginzburg, Evgeniia Semenovna. **Journey into the Whirlwind.** New York: Harcourt, Brace and World, 1967, 418 p.
A perceptive account, by a Russian woman, a party member and wife of an official in Kazan, of eighteen years of concentration camp life during and after the Great Purges. The Russian original appeared as "Krutoi marshrut" (Milan: Mondadori, 1967, 474 p.).

Gorbatov, Aleksandr Vasil'evich. **Years Off My Life: The Memoirs of General of the Soviet Army A. V. Gorbatov.** New York: Norton, 1965, 222 p.
These recollections deal with the author's arrest and conviction during the Stalinist purges, his prison ordeal and rehabilitation at the beginning of World War II. First published in the Moscow periodical *Novyi Mir* in the spring of 1964.

Haupt, Georges and Marie, Jean-Jacques, *eds.* **Les Bolchéviks par eux-mêmes.** Paris: Maspéro, 1969, 398 p.
An indispensable reference volume containing biographies and autobiographies of Soviet leaders of the period of Revolution, Civil War and the immediate post-World War I years, translated from the now extremely rare "Entsiklopedicheskii Slovar" published in the 1920s in Moscow. There are extensive notes by the editors.

Hayter, Sir William Goodenough. **The Kremlin and the Embassy.** New York: Macmillan, 1967, 160 p.
Informal and rather slight diplomatic memoirs by the British Ambassador to Moscow from 1953-57.

Hyde, H. Montgomery. **Stalin: The History of a Dictator.** New York: Farrar, Straus and Giroux, 1972, 679 p.
A lengthy biography reflecting much consultation of available sources but tending to be anecdotal rather than analytical in its study of the formidable subject.

Kerensky, Aleksandr Fedorovich. **Russia and History's Turning Point.** New York: Duell, 1965, 558 p.
  Readable and historically informative memoirs of the leading figure in Russia's Provisional Government following the fall of the Tsar.

Khatskevich, Aleksandr Fedorovich. **Soldat velikikh boev: zhizn' i deiatelnost' F. E. Dzerzhinskogo.** Minsk: Izd-vo "Nauka i Tekhnika," 3rd ed., 1970, 478 p.
  A biography of Feliks Dzerzhinskii, first head of the Soviet secret police, commemorated today as the "first Chekist" and the founder of a great tradition in defense of the Revolution.

Khrushchev, Nikita Sergeevich. **Krushchev Remembers.** Boston: Little, Brown, 1970, 639 p.
  These controversial memoirs by the Soviet leader, first published in the West, provide a fascinating exploration of the late Stalin years. However, there are many things the author does not say, much that is self-serving, and much that is contradictory to known facts.

Kondrat'ev, Nikolai Dmitrievich. **Marshal Bliukher.** Moscow: Voennoe Izd-vo, 1965, 292 p.
  A biography of Marshal V. K. Bliukher, early Soviet military commander and victim of Stalin's purge of the armed forces in 1938.

Leonhard, Wolfgang. **Nikita Sergejewitsch Chruschtschow.** Lucerne: Bucher, 1965, 191 p.
  A knowledgeable student of Kremlin politics writes of Khrushchev's rise and fall. Profusely and effectively illustrated.

Lerner, Warren. **Karl Radek: The Last Internationalist.** Stanford: Stanford University Press, 1970, 240 p.
  A solid political biography of one of the most intelligent of the Old Bolsheviks who perished in the great purges.

Lewin, Moshé. **Lenin's Last Struggle.** New York: Pantheon Books, 1968, 193 p.
  An able account of the last phase of Lenin's career, the agonizing year before his completely disabling stroke of March 1923. Translation of "Le Dernier combat de Lénine" (Paris: Éditions de Minuit, 1967, 173 p.).

Lockhart, Sir Robert Hamilton Bruce. **The Two Revolutions: An Eye-witness Study of Russia 1917.** Chester Springs (Pa.): Dufour Editions, 1967, 144 p.
  A brief assessment of the revolutionary changes in Russia in 1917. Sir Robert, author of "Memoirs of a British Agent," was British Consul-General in Moscow in 1917 and in 1918 headed a special mission to the Soviet Government.

Löwy, Adolf Georg. **Die Weltgeschichte ist das Weltgericht; Bucharin: Vision des Kommunismus.** Zurich: Europa Verlag, 1969, 419 p.
  An extensive study of the career of Bukharin, with particular emphasis on the development of his thought.

M. V. Frunze: vospominaniia druzei i soratnikov. Moscow: Voennoe Izd-vo, 1965, 328 p.

Mikhail Vasil'evich Frunze: vospominaniia rodnykh, blizkikh, soratnikov. Frunze: Izd-vo "Kyrgyzstan," 1969, 223 p.
  Two collections of the reminiscences of associates and friends of M. V. Frunze, revolutionary hero and a major early theorist of Soviet military doctrine.

McNeal, Robert Hatch. **Bride of the Revolution: Krupskaya and Lenin.** Ann Arbor: University of Michigan Press, 1972, 326 p.
  A serious biography of Lenin's wife and collaborator, Nadezhda Krupskaya.

Maiskii, Ivan Mikhailovich. **[Memoirs.]**
  The Soviet Ambassador to London from 1932 to 1943 details his efforts to forge an anti-German alliance between Britain, France and the U.S.S.R. before and during the first years of World War II in the following volumes: "Who Helped Hitler?" (London: Hutchinson, 1964, 216 p.), of which the Russian edition appeared as "Kto pomogal Gitleru?" (Moscow: Izd-vo Instituta Mezhdunarodnykh Otnoshenii, 1962, 197 p.); "Memoirs of a Soviet Ambassador: The War, 1939–43" (New York: Scribner, 1968, 408 p.), of which the Russian original was published as "Vospominaniia sovetskogo posla: voina 1939–43" (Moscow: Nauka, 1965, 405 p.). These volumes should be used together with the revised and expanded one volume Russian version "Vospominaniia sovetskogo diplomata 1925–1945 gg." (Moscow: Nauka, 1971, 711 p.).

Mandel'shtam, Nadezhda. **Hope Against Hope: A Memoir.** New York: Atheneum, 1970, 431 p.

A masterful memoir by the widow of the great Russian poet Osip Mandelstam dealing with the tragic life of her husband and the developments in the Soviet state, particularly during the Stalin reign. Indispensable for understanding the contemporary Soviet society and politics. The Russian original was published as "Vospominaniia" (New York: Izd-vo Im. Chekhova, 1970, 429 p.).

Marie, Jean-Jacques. **Staline.** Paris: Éditions du Seuil, 1967, 306 p.

In contrast to most of the earlier biographers of Stalin, the author of this volume has had the advantage of utilizing sources published after Stalin's death.

Menon, Kumara Padmanabha Sivasankara. **The Flying Troika.** New York: Oxford University Press, 1963, 330 p.

This book comprises extracts from the political memoirs kept by the Indian Ambassador to the Soviet Union in the years 1952-1961. A condensed version of this volume, including also material from the author's "Russian Panorama" (1962), was published as "The Lamp and the Lampstand" (London: Oxford University Press, 1968, 343 p.).

Meretskov, Kirill Afanas'evich. **Na sluzhbe narodu: stranitsy vospominanii.** Moscow: Izd-vo Politicheskoi Literatury, 1968, 464 p.

Memoirs of Marshal K. A. Meretskov, a Soviet officer who held important commands in the Baltic area and the Far East during World War II and was a high-ranking military adviser to the Loyalist side during the Spanish Civil War.

Mikoian, Anastas Ivanovich. **Dorogoi bor'by.** Moscow: Izd-vo Politicheskoi Literatury, 1971, 589 p.

This initial volume of the memoirs of Anastas Mikoian, a veteran Bolshevik, carries the reader through the October Revolution.

Miliukov, Pavel Nikolaevich. **Political Memoirs, 1905-1917.** Ann Arbor: University of Michigan Press, 1967, 508 p.

A translation of the memoirs of a Russian historian and a leader of the Constitutional Democratic Party, first published in 1955 as "Vospominaniia, 1859-1917" (New York: Izd-vo Im. Chekhova, 2 v.). Edited by Arthur P. Mendel.

Nekrasov, Viktor Platonovich. **Both Sides of the Ocean.** New York: Holt, Rinehart and Winston, 1964, 191 p.

An account of a Soviet writer's travels in Italy and the United States, originally published in the November 1962 issue of *Novyi Mir*, for which the author was taken to task by Mr. Khrushchev in his speech before writers, artists and ideologists on March 8, 1963.

Ordzhonikidze, Zinaida Bavrilovna. **Put' bol'shevika: stranitsy iz zhizni G. K. Ordzhonikidze.** Moscow: Izd-vo Politicheskoi Literatury, 1967, 400 p.

A study of the revolutionary career of G. K. Ordzhonikidze, early Bolshevik leader and hero of the Russian Civil War, written by his widow. This new edition includes previously unpublished chapters on Ordzhonikidze's activities on behalf of the Party in the Caucasus during the years 1921-1925.

Paustovskii, Konstantin Georgievich. **The Story of a Life.** New York: Pantheon, 1964, 661 p.

Vivid memoirs of imperial Russia, war and revolution by a leading and respected Soviet writer. The Russian original appeared as "Povest' o zhizni" (Moscow: Izd-vo Khudozh. Lit-ry, 1962, 2 v.).

Payne, Pierre Stephen Robert. **The Life and Death of Lenin.** New York: Simon and Schuster, 1964, 672 p.

The work, while quite readable, is somewhat less sure-footed than other contemporary biographies of Lenin and tends to rather sensational conclusions.

Payne, Pierre Stephen Robert. **The Rise and Fall of Stalin.** New York: Simon and Schuster, 1965, 767 p.

A massive but quite unsatisfactory biography by a very prolific writer.

Pineau, Christian. **Nikita Sergueevitch Khrouchtchev.** Paris: Perrin, 1965, 286 p.

A study of Khrushchev by a French writer, statesman and former foreign minister who writes with first-hand knowledge of Russia and his subject.

Pospelov, Petr Nikolaevich and Others. **Vladimir Il'ich Lenin: biografiia.** Moscow: Izd-vo Politicheskoi Literatury, 4th ed., 1970, 720 p.
An amply illustrated official Soviet biography of the chief architect of the Russian Revolution, issued in a new edition to coincide with the hundreth anniversary of Lenin's birth.

Possony, Stefan Thomas. **Lenin: The Compulsive Revolutionary.** Chicago: Regnery, 1964, 418 p.
The author of this monograph is particularly concerned with the underground aspects of Lenin's career and he emphasizes the role of German money in financing Lenin's plans.

Robien, Louis, Comte de. **The Diary of a Diplomat in Russia, 1917-1918.** New York: Praeger, 1970, 318 p.
This is a day-by-day report on the Russian Revolution in 1917-1918 by a young French official in the Petrograd Embassy. The original appeared as "Journal d'un diplomate en Russie (1917-1918)" (Paris: A. Michel, 1967, 347 p.).

Rosmer, Alfred. **Moscow under Lenin.** New York: Monthly Review Press, 1972, 253 p.
Pro-Leninist, anti-Stalinist recollections of Russia in the early 1920s, by an old French militant. The French original appeared as "Moscou sous Lénine: les origines du communisme" (Paris: Horay, 1953, 316 p.).

Schapiro, Leonard Bertram and Reddaway, Peter, *eds.* **Lenin: The Man, the Theorist, the Leader.** New York: Praeger (in association with the Hoover Institution on War, Revolution, and Peace), 1967, 317 p.
A superior set of papers, chiefly by British scholars, reappraising various facets of Lenin's abilities, policies and career.

Simmonds, George W., *ed.* **Soviet Leaders.** New York: Crowell, 1967, 405 p.
Biographical sketches of 42 leading figures in various areas of Soviet life: political, military, scientific and cultural.

Smirnov, V. **Lenin Suomen vaiheissa.** Helsinki: Otava, 1970, 220 p.
Lenin took refuge in Finland some 20 times during 1905 and 1917, and Smirnov's account brings together what information is accessible concerning these episodes.

Smith, Edward Ellis. **The Young Stalin: The Early Years of an Elusive Revolutionary.** New York: Farrar, Straus and Giroux, 1967, 470 p.
An ambitious effort to reconstruct Stalin's early life—from his birth in 1879 to the Bolshevik seizure of power in 1917. In the author's view Stalin in these prerevolutionary years also served as a police agent.

Smith, Homer. **Black Man in Red Russia.** Chicago: Johnson Publishing Co., 1964, 221 p.
An American Black gives a straightforward account of his 14 years in Soviet Russia.

Tschebotarioff, Gregory Porphyriewitch. **Russia, My Native Land.** New York: McGraw-Hill, 1964, 384 p.
Quite interesting memoirs of imperial Russia, the Revolution and Civil War, by a Cossack officer who subsequently became an American engineer.

Tsereteli, Iraklii Georgievich. **Vospominaniia o Fevral'skoi revoliutsii.** Paris: Mouton, 1963, 2 v.
Recollections, supplemented with many documents, by a Georgian and Russian Menshevik leader who played a prominent role in the political events in Russia between the February and October revolutions. A very important source.

Valentinov, Nikolay, *pseud.* (Nikolai Vladislavovich Vol'skii). **Encounters with Lenin.** New York: Oxford University Press, 1968, 273 p.
A welcome translation of the memoirs of the author's association and eventual break with Lenin in the years before 1914. The Russian original, first published in New York, appeared as "Vstrechi s Leninym" (New York: Izd-vo Im. Chekhova, 1953, 355 p.).

Vishniak, Mark Ven'iaminovich. **Gody emigratsii, 1919-1969: Parizh—N'iu-Iork (vospominaniia).** Stanford: Hoover Institution Press, 1970, 276 p.
Reminiscences and observations by a prominent Russian Jew, member of the Constituent Assembly in 1918, who has spent more than 50 years in emigration. An important source for the history of the Russian emigration.

Voroshilov, Klement Efremovich. **Rasskazy o zhizni (vospominaniia).** Moscow: Izd-vo Politicheskoi Literatury, 1968, 366 p.
    The first volume of the memoirs of the late Marshal Voroshilov.

Warth, Robert D. **Joseph Stalin.** New York: Twayne, 1969, 176 p.
    The author claims that in his biography of Stalin he has used primary materials unavailable to previous biographers. There is a useful bibliography.

Wittlin, Thaddeus. **Commissar: The Life and Death of Lavrenty Pavlovich Beria.** New York: Macmillan, 1972, 566 p.
    The story of Beria's four decades of intrigue and murder on behalf of Stalin and himself. Worth reading despite the author's failure to give the reader any help in determining what is fact and what is surmise.

Wolfe, Bertram David. **The Bridge and the Abyss: The Troubled Friendship of Maxim Gorky and V. I. Lenin.** New York: Praeger (for the Hoover Institution on War, Revolution, and Peace), 1967, 180 p.
    An illuminating account of the strained, ambivalent but protracted friendship between Lenin and Maxim Gorky.

Woytinsky, Emma Shadkhan. **Two Lives In One.** New York: Praeger, 1965, 324 p.
    The widow of W. S. Woytinsky writes of their life together in revolutionary Russia, in Europe and later in the New World. A fitting companion piece to Woytinsky's "Stormy Passage" (1961).

Zarnitskii, Stanislav Vasil'evich and Sergeev, Anatolii Nikolaevich. **Chicherin.** Moscow: Izd-vo "Molodaia Gvardiia," 1966, 253 p.
    A biography of G. V. Chicherin, Foreign Minister of the U.S.S.R. from 1918 to 1930, who conducted vital negotiations with the Western powers and fostered the professionalization of foreign affairs in the U.S.S.R.

Zhukov, Georgii Konstantinovich. **The Memoirs of Marshal Zhukov.** New York: Delacorte Press, 1971, 703 p.
    These memoirs by Marshal Zhukov, probably the most famous Russian military leader during World War II, end with the conclusion of hostilities in 1945. An important source, though suffering from political editing, for the military and political history of the Soviet Union. The Russian original appeared as "Vospominaniia i razmyshleniia" (Moscow: Izd. Agenstva Pechati "Novosti," 1969, 751 p.).

Zhukov, Iuri Aleksandrovich. **Liudi 30-kh godov.** Moscow: Izd-vo "Sovetskaia Rossiia," 1966, 572 p.

——. **Liudi 40-kh godov: zapiski voennogo korrespondenta.** Moscow: Izd-vo "Sovetskaia Rossiia," 1969, 672 p.
    Reflections on the 1930s and 1940s in Russia by a prominent Soviet commentator, concentrating on the accomplishments rather than the shortcomings of the Soviet system.

Recent History

General

See also General Works, p. 1; Political Factors, p. 12; The World Since 1914, p. 129; Eastern Europe and the Soviet Bloc, p. 358; other subsections under the Union of Soviet Socialist Republics.

Annuaire de l'U.R.S.S.: droit, économie, sociologie, politique, culture, 1965–. Paris: Éditions du Centre National de la Recherche Scientifique, 1965–.
    A wide-ranging annual collection of articles on legal, economic, social, political and cultural problems of the Soviet Union, prepared by the Centre de recherche sur l'U.R.S.S. et les pays de l'Est of the University of Strasbourg. It supersedes a two-volume publication entitled "L'U.R.S.S.: droit, économie, sociologie, politique, culture" (1962–64) that was prepared by the same research institute.

Berkhin, Il'ia Borisovich. **Geschichte der UdSSR, 1917–1970.** Berlin: Dietz, 1971, 914 p.
    A massive survey of Soviet history, originally published in Russian. A revised and updated Russian edition appeared as "Istoriia SSSR (1917–1971 gg.)" (Moscow: Izd-vo "Vysshaia Shkola," 2d rev. and enl. ed., 1972, 726 p.).

Carr, Edward Hallett. **The October Revolution: Before and After.** New York: Knopf, 1969, 178 p.
Somewhat controversial essays on the achievements of the Bolshevik Revolution by a leading student of Soviet Russia. The author is more concerned with the industrial achievements than with the lack of civil liberties and the oppressive features of the Soviet regime. The English edition was published as "1917: Before and After" (London: Macmillan, 1969, 178 p.).

Crowley, Edward L. and Others, *eds.* **Party and Government Officials of the Soviet Union, 1917-1967.** Metuchen (N.J.): Scarecrow Press, 1969, 214 p.
A most useful reference work, tracing the composition of the leading governmental and Party organs of the Soviet Union. Compiled by the Institute for the Study of the U.S.S.R., Munich.

Dallin, David J. **From Purge to Coexistence: Essays on Stalin's and Khrushchev's Russia.** Chicago: Regnery, 1964, 289 p.
A posthumously published collection of the late author's essays on a variety of Soviet themes. The book includes a bibliography of his writings.

Deutscher, Isaac. **The Unfinished Revolution: Russia 1917-1967.** New York: Oxford University Press, 1967, 115 p.
In these George Macaulay Trevelyan Lectures, Mr. Deutscher reviews from a Marxist perspective the achievements and failures of the Soviet Union since the Revolution.

Drachkovitch, Milorad M., *ed.* **Fifty Years of Communism in Russia.** University Park: Pennsylvania State University Press (for the Hoover Institution on War, Revolution, and Peace), 1968, 316 p.
Papers by a distinguished group of scholars, dealing with various aspects of Soviet life, thought and policy, over the half-century since 1917.

Grey, Ian. **The First Fifty Years: Soviet Russia 1917-67.** New York: Coward-McCann, 1967, 558 p.
A sympathetic survey of the course of Soviet history.

Hendel, Samuel and Braham, Randolph L., *eds.* **The U.S.S.R. after 50 Years: Promise and Reality.** New York: Knopf, 1967, 299 p.
A collection of essays.

Hudson, Geoffrey Francis. **Fifty Years of Communism: Theory and Practice, 1917-1967.** New York: Basic Books, 1968, 234 p.
A concise, knowledgeable essay on the development of the theory and practice of communism since 1917.

Laird, Roy D. **The Soviet Paradigm.** New York: Free Press, 1970, 272 p.
It is the author's thesis that "the Soviet political system stands out as a unique paradigm of a successful centralized monohierarchical polity."

Levi, Arrigo. **Il potere in Russia: da Stalin a Brezhnev.** Bologna: Il Mulino, 2d rev. ed., 1967, 740 p.
An extensive study of power—personal, political, economic—in the Soviet Union from the Stalin era to Brezhnev.

Lewin, Moshé. **Russian Peasants and Soviet Power: A Study of Collectivization.** Evanston: Northwestern University Press, 1968, 539 p.
The author, who has lived for some years in the Soviet Union, describes in this study the social structure of the peasant society before collectivization and the political and punitive measures taken by the Soviet authorities in the late 1920s. The French original appeared as "La Paysannerie et la pouvoir soviétique, 1928-1930" (The Hague: Mouton, 1966, 480 p.).

London, Kurt, *ed.* **The Soviet Union: A Half-Century of Communism.** Baltimore: Johns Hopkins Press (in coöperation with the Institute for Sino-Soviet Studies, George Washington University), 1968, 493 p.
A selection of papers reviewing Soviet politics and foreign relations, originally delivered in West Berlin in September 1967.

Lyons, Eugene. **Workers' Paradise Lost: Fifty Years of Soviet Communism: A Balance Sheet.** New York: Funk & Wagnalls, 1967, 387 p.
The title indicates the author's verdict, and he anticipates troubled days ahead.

Margulies, Sylvia R. **The Pilgrimage to Russia: The Soviet Union and the Treatment of Foreigners, 1924-1937.** Madison: University of Wisconsin Press, 1968, 290 p.
A study of the Soviet attitude toward foreign visitors who made the "pilgrimage" between 1924 and 1937.

Mosely, Philip Edward, *ed.* **The Soviet Union, 1922-1962: A Foreign Affairs Reader.** New York: Praeger (for the Council on Foreign Relations), 1963, 497 p.
A collection of 30 articles from *Foreign Affairs* dealing with the Soviet Union and Soviet-American relations. Edited and introduced by the late Professor Philip Mosely.

Nettl, John Peter. **The Soviet Achievement.** New York: Harcourt, Brace and World, 1968, 288 p.
An able and readable interpretation of Soviet history in the half-century since the Revolution. Designed for the interested general reader but containing many views and insights that will be of interest to the specialist.

Nicolaevsky, Boris I. **Power and the Soviet Elite: "The Letter of an Old Bolshevik" and Other Essays by Boris I. Nicolaevsky.** New York: Praeger (for the Hoover Institution on War, Revolution, and Peace), 1965, 275 p.
A valuable collection of Mr. Nicolaevsky's articles over the last 25 years on the struggle for power in the Kremlin, edited by Janet D. Zagoria.

Oberländer, Erwin and Others, *eds.* **Russia Enters the Twentieth Century, 1894-1917.** New York: Schocken Books, 1971, 352 p.
The principal intent of these essays by an able group of scholars is to counteract the tendency to view these years as a mere prelude to revolution.

Pethybridge, Roger William. **A History of Postwar Russia.** New York: New American Library, 1966, 263 p.
A brief survey by a British political scientist of developments in Russia between 1945 and the Twenty-second Party Congress in 1961.

Pietromarchi, Luca. **The Soviet World.** New York: A. S. Barnes, 1965, 462 p.
The Italian Ambassador in Moscow from 1958 to 1961 appraises the Soviet Union. The Italian original was published as "Il mondo sovietico" (Milan: Bompiani, 2d ed., 1963, 700 p.).

Salisbury, Harrison Evans., *ed.* **The Soviet Union: The Fifty Years.** New York: Harcourt, Brace and World, 1967, 484 p.
An extensive survey of the Soviet Union fifty years after the Revolution, by a group of *The New York Times* reporters sent to the U.S.S.R. in 1967.

Sorlin, Pierre. **The Soviet People and their Society.** New York: Praeger, 1969, 293 p.
A sympathetic account, by a French sociologist, of the trials and tribulations of the Soviet people in the years since 1917. Translation of "La Société soviétique, 1917–1967" (Paris: A. Colin, 2d rev. ed., 1967, 285 p.).

Treadgold, Donald Warren, *ed.* **The Development of the USSR: An Exchange of Views.** Seattle: University of Washington Press, 1964, 399 p.
A series of discussions on a wide range of Russian and Soviet topics, originally appearing in the *Slavic Review*.

Von Laue, Theodore Hermann. **Why Lenin? Why Stalin? A Reappraisal of the Russian Revolution, 1900-1930.** Philadelphia: Lippincott, 1964, 242 p.
An interesting, original and sometimes debatable explanation of the circumstances conducive to the appearance of such figures as Lenin and Stalin in the seats of power in Russia.

Werth, Alexander. **Russia: Hopes and Fears.** New York: Simon and Schuster, 1969, 352 p.
This posthumously published book by a prolific and generally pro-Soviet observer attempts to sum up Soviet progress in the years since World War II.

Westwood, J. N. **Russia: 1917-1964.** New York: Harper and Row, 1966, 208 p.
A brief survey of Soviet history.

Wolfe, Bertram David. **An Ideology in Power: Reflections on the Russian Revolution.** New York: Stein and Day, 1969, 406 p.
A substantial collection of Mr. Wolfe's essays on Marxism, revolution and the Soviet system. They have been written over a period of 25 years, but demonstrate a remarkable unity of perspective and insight.

Revolution; Civil War; the Lenin Era

See also Political Factors, p. 12; War and Peace, p. 108; First World War, p. 131; Inter-War Period, p. 140; (The United States) Foreign Policy, p. 229; Military and Defense Policy, p. 257; Switzerland, p. 393; (Italy) Foreign Policy, p. 424; Political and Constitutional Problems, p. 426; The Baltic States, p. 455; (Germany) The 1918 Revolution and the Weimar Republic, p. 468; (Czechoslovakia) Recent History to 1945, p. 516; (Poland) Foreign Relations, p. 527; Bulgaria, p. 596; (Japan) Foreign and Defense Policies, p. 718; other subsections under the Union of Soviet Socialist Republics.

Avrich, Paul Henry. **Kronstadt 1921.** Princeton: Princeton University Press, 1970, 271 p.
A scholarly examination and interpretation of the sailors' revolt against the Bolshevik government, a critical point in the history of the Revolution.

Avrich, Paul Henry. **The Russian Anarchists.** Princeton: Princeton University Press, 1967, 303 p.
An able work, centering chiefly on the often neglected Russian anarchist activities during the revolutions of 1905 and 1917.

Les Bolchéviks et la révolution d'octobre. Paris: Maspero, 1964, 361 p.
The French translation of the protocols of the Central Committee of the Bolshevik Party covering the period from August 1917 to February 1918. Edited by Giuseppe Boffa, an Italian Communist leader. The Russian original appeared as "Protokoly, avgust 1917–fevral' 1918" (Moscow: Institut Marksizma-Leninizma pri TSK KPSS, 1958, 307 p.).

Bradley, John. **Allied Intervention in Russia.** New York: Basic Books, 1968, 251 p.
A concise but serious history of the Allied intervention in Russian revolutionary developments from 1917 to 1920.

Brahm, Heinz. **Trotzkijs Kampf um die Nachfolge Lenins: die ideologische Auseinandersetzung 1923-1926.** Cologne: Verlag Wissenschaft und Politik, 1964, 231 p.
After a discussion of Trotsky's varied relations with Lenin in the years 1902–1921, the author turns to his battle with Stalin, Zinoviev and Kamenev for Lenin's succession.

Brinkley, George A. **The Volunteer Army and Allied Intervention in South Russia, 1917-1921: A Study in the Politics and Diplomacy of the Russian Civil War.** Notre Dame: University of Notre Dame Press, 1966, 446 p.
A learned study, by a professor at the University of Notre Dame, of General Denikin's Volunteer Army, the major anti-Bolshevik force in southern Russia during the Russian Civil War.

Daniels, Robert Vincent. **Red October: The Bolshevik Revolution of 1917.** New York: Scribner, 1967, 269 p.
In this important and absorbing study Mr. Daniels traces the confused course of events immediately preceding the Bolshevik seizure of power and finds that this momentous event was far from a well-planned coup.

Ellis, Charles Howard. **The British "Intervention" in Transcaspia, 1918-1919.** Berkeley: University of California Press, 1963, 175 p.
An interesting account, based in part on the author's own recollections, of the British operations in Transcaspia and the Caucasus in 1918 and 1919.

Fediukin, Sergei Alekseevich. **Sovetskaia vlast' i burzhuaznye spetsialisty.** Moscow: Izd-vo "Mysl'," 1965, 253 p.
An analysis of one of the most acute problems that faced the new Bolshevik regime: the necessity of employing non-communist "bourgeois" technicians and professionals in the attempt to reconstruct the economy.

Ferro, Marc. **The Russian Revolution of February 1917.** Englewood Cliffs: Prentice-Hall, 1972, 292 p.
An admirable history, broad in scope, well-written and using new material, of the first half of the revolutionary year—from the fall of the Tsar to the end of the brief "honeymoon" period in June. The French original contains bibliographic notes that were omitted from the English translation. It appeared as: "La Révolution de 1917: la chute du tsarisme et les origines d'octobre" (Paris: Aubier-Montaigne, 1967, 606 p.).

Flerov, Vasilii Sergeevich, *ed.* **Bor'ba za vlast' sovetov v Sibirii i na dal'nem vostoke.** Tomsk: Izd-vo Tomskogo Universiteta, 1968, 181 p.
A collection of historical essays on the events of 1917-1918 in Siberia and the Far East, drawn largely from the archives of local revolutionary organizations.

Golinkov, David L'vovich. **Krakh vrazheskogo podpol'ia: iz istorii bor'by s kontrrevoliutsiei v Sovetskoi Rossii v 1917-1924 gg.** Moscow: Izd-vo Politicheskoi Literatury, 1971, 368 p.
A detailed account of the successful struggle against all forms of anti-Bolshevik activity between 1917 and 1924. This glorification of the achievements of the Chekists serves to remind the Soviet reader that similar vigilance may be required today.

Katkov, George. **Russia 1917: The February Revolution.** New York: Harper and Row, 1967, 489 p.
A major study of the immediate causes and the course of the 1917 February Revolution in Russia. The author, a fellow at St. Antony's College, Oxford, demolishes countless current assumptions about the "democratic and bloodless" nature of the February Revolution, adds substantially to our knowledge of the German and German-supported Bolshevik influence on political developments in Russia and provides considerable detail on how the fabrication of rumors contributed to the downfall of the Tsarist regime. Of particular value is the annotated bibliography.

Kenez, Peter. **Civil War in South Russia, 1918.** Berkeley: University of California Press, 1971, 351 p.
This study concentrates on the creation of the Volunteer Army in the first year of the Civil War.

Laqueur, Walter Ze'ev. **The Fate of the Revolution: Interpretations of Soviet History.** New York: Macmillan, 1967, 216 p.
Reflections on the historiography of the Russian Revolution, Lenin and Stalin.

Lenin, Vladimir Il'ich. **[Collected Works.]**
The latest compilation of Lenin's complete works appeared as "Polnoe sobranie sochinenii" (Moscow: Izd-vo Politicheskoi Literatury, 5th ed., 1958-65, 55 v.). The previous edition, "Sochineniia," also has been completed (Moscow: Izd-vo Politicheskoi Literatury, 4th ed., 1941-64, 45 v.). The most recent English translation has appeared as "Collected Works" (Moscow: Foreign Languages Publishing House, 1960-70, 45 v.). An index to both the 4th and 5th editions of Lenin's works was edited by M. M. Vasser and others: "Spravochnyi tom k polnomu sobraniiu sochinenii V. I. Lenina" (Moscow: Izd-vo Politicheskoi Literatury, 1969-70, 2 v.).

Lenin, Vladimir Il'ich. **Lenin, unbekannte Briefe, 1912-1914.** Einsiedeln: Benziger Verlag, 1967, 156 p.
A scholarly edition, with German translation, of a number of hitherto unpublished letters by Lenin during the critical years 1912-1914. Of considerable importance for the history of the man and his movement. Edited and translated by Leonhard Haas.

Luckett, Richard. **The White Generals.** New York: Viking, 1971, 413 p.
An English historian's ambitious effort to cover the vast expanse of the Russian Civil War and the vicissitudes of the various "White" leaders.

Meijer, Jan Marinus, *ed.* **The Trotsky Papers, 1917-1922.** The Hague: Mouton, 1964-71, 2 v.
This excellently edited collection of documents in the possession of the International Institute of Social History in Amsterdam comprises centrally the correspondence of the Bolshevik leaders during the years of the Civil War. The material is presented in the original and in English translation.

Melgunov, Sergei Petrovich. **The Bolshevik Seizure of Power.** Santa Barbara (Calif.): ABC-Clio Press, 1972, 260 p.
The English translation of a significant historical work first published in Russian as "Kak Bol'sheviki zakhvatili vlast': oktiabr'skii perevorot 1917 goda" (Paris: Renaissance, 1953, 390 p.). The author, a liberal democrat, was an active participant in the revolutionary events of 1917-1920. Edited by Sergei G. Pushkarev.

Mints, I. I. and Others, *eds.* **Sverzhenie samoderzhaviia: sbornik statei.** Moscow: Izd-vo "Nauka," 1970, 328 p.

An anthology of Soviet writings on the February Revolution of 1917, adapted from the proceedings of a conference marking the fiftieth anniversary of the fall of the Russian monarchy.

Narkiewicz, Olga A. **The Making of the Soviet State Apparatus.** Manchester: Manchester University Press, 1970, 238 p.
A monograph reëxamining the social, economic and political conditions in town and countryside during the NEP period.

Pietsch, Walter. **Revolution und Staat: Institutionen als Träger der Macht in Sowjetrussland, 1917-1922.** Cologne: Verlag Wissenschaft und Politik, 1969, 172 p.
An interesting analysis of the formation of the Bolshevik regime and the Soviet state, emphasizing the role of institutions as the necessary means for gaining and establishing power.

Pipes, Richard, ed. **Revolutionary Russia.** Cambridge: Harvard University Press, 1968, 365 p.
Thirteen papers, with comments and discussion, relating to the Russian Revolution. The symposium is based on a conference of leading scholars held in Cambridge, Massachusetts, in April 1967.

Rabinowitch, Alexander. **Prelude to Revolution: The Petrograd Bolsheviks and the July 1917 Uprising.** Bloomington: Indiana University Press, 1968, 299 p.
An able and scholarly inquiry into the perplexing abortive Petrograd uprisings of June and July 1917.

Radkey, Oliver Henry. **The Sickle under the Hammer.** New York: Columbia University Press, 1963, 525 p.
In this work, the sequel to his "The Agrarian Foes of Bolshevism," Professor Radkey traces, with an enormous fund of scholarship, the fate of the Russian Socialist Revolutionaries between the Bolshevik seizure of power and the dissolution of the Constituent Assembly in January 1918.

Shukman, Harold. **Lenin and the Russian Revolution.** New York: Putnam, 1967, 224 p.
A brief, popular survey of the twentieth-century background to the Russian Revolution and the victory of Lenin.

Silverlight, John. **The Victors' Dilemma.** New York: Weybright and Talley, 1970, 392 p.
A solid study of Allied, especially British, intervention in the Russian Civil War. Makes extensive use of recently available documents in the British Public Record Office.

Singer, Ladislaus. **Raubt das Geraubte: Tagebuch der Weltrevolution 1917.** Stuttgart: Seewald, 1967, 296 p.
This survey of revolutionary developments in Russia from February to October 1917 includes documentation on how the Germans, hoping to speed up the disintegration of Russia, provided financial support to the Bolsheviks.

Suny, Ronald Grigor. **The Baku Commune, 1917-1918.** Princeton: Princeton University Press, 1972, 412 p.
An able monograph on the revolution in a provincial capital that was also an oil center and a focus of national antagonisms.

Tompkins, Stuart Ramsay. **The Triumph of Bolshevism: Revolution or Reaction?** Norman: University of Oklahoma Press, 1967, 331 p.
An interpretation of "Lenin's tortuous and devious road to victory," by a professor emeritus at the University of Oklahoma.

Ulam, Adam Bruno. **The Bolsheviks: The Intellectual and Political History of the Triumph of Communism in Russia.** New York: Macmillan, 1965, 598 p.
An exceptionally solid and perceptive account of the rise and triumph of the Bolsheviks in Russia. Lenin, appropriately, is the central figure of the piece.

Vladimirtsev, I. N. and Others, eds. **Sovetskoe sodruzhestvo narodov: ob'edinitel'noe dvizhenie i obrazovanie SSSR; sbornik dokumentov 1917-1922.** Moscow: Izd-vo Politicheskoi Literatury, 1972, 335 p.
A useful compilation of documents, some of which are said to be published for the first time, relating to the successful establishment of the Union of Soviet Socialist Republics as "the world's first multinational socialist state" during the years 1917-1922.

Wade, Rex A. **The Russian Search for Peace, February–October 1917.** Stanford: Stanford University Press, 1969, 196 p.
A study centering on the efforts of the moderate socialists to deal with the baffling problem of war and peace in the critical months between the two revolutions.

Zlatopol'skii, David L'vovich and Christiakov, Oleg Ivanovich. **Obrazovanie Soiuza SSR.** Moscow: Izd-vo "Iuridicheskaia Literatura," 1972, 319 p.
A compact history of events that led up to the foundation of the Union of Soviet Socialist Republics in 1922.

The Stalin Era

See also General Works, p. 1; Political Factors, p. 12; The World Since 1914, p. 129; (The United States) Relations with Eastern Europe and the Soviet Union, p. 241; Finland, p. 449; Baltic States, p. 455; Germany, p. 463; Hungary, p. 511; Czechoslovakia, p. 516; Poland, p. 523; Rumania, p. 588; Jugoslavia, p. 591; Bulgaria, p. 596; (India) Biographies, Memoirs and Collected Writings, p. 660; China, p. 683; Japan, p. 714; other subsections under the Union of Soviet Socialist Republics.

Arsić, Draginja. **Društveno-ekonomski koreni staljinizma.** Belgrade: Institut za medjunarodnu politiku i privredu, 1972, 284 p.
A Jugoslav view on the political, social and economic sources of "bureaucratization" in the Soviet Union during the Stalinist period.

Astier de la Vigerie, Emmanuel d'. **Sur Staline.** Paris: Plon, 1963, 220 p.
A brief but vivid history of the Stalin era, including numerous references to the great leader.

Carr, Edward Hallett. **Socialism in One Country, 1924–1926. Volume Three.** New York: Macmillan, 1964, 2 pts.
This volume, in two parts, is a continuation, at the same impressive level, of Mr. Carr's magistral, multi-volume "History of Soviet Russia." It deals with external affairs—both the foreign policy of the Soviet state and the activities of Comintern—during the critical years 1924–1926. Part I treats Soviet relations with the West; Part II, with the East.

McNeal, Robert Hatch, *comp.* **Stalin's Works: An Annotated Bibliography.** Stanford: The Hoover Institution on War, Revolution, and Peace, 1967, 197 p.
A useful reference.

Medvedev, Roi Aleksandrovich. **Let History Judge: The Origins and Consequences of Stalinism.** New York: Knopf, 1972, 566 p.
The first serious and sustained effort by a Soviet scholar to describe and analyze the crimes and excesses of Stalinism. Published first in the West with the authorization of the author. Well-edited, with useful explanatory material, by David Joravsky and Georges Haupt.

Randall, Francis Ballard. **Stalin's Russia: An Historical Reconsideration.** New York: Free Press, 1965, 328 p.
An essay in reconsideration of the Stalin era that starts with the challenging statement "Stalin was probably the most important man who ever lived." The author concludes that he was also "one of the two or three worst men who ever lived."

Stalin, Iosif V. **Sochinennia.** Stanford: The Hoover Institution on War, Revolution, and Peace, 1967, 3 v.
A collection of Stalin's writings not included in his collected works published in Moscow from 1946 to 1951. Edited by Robert H. McNeal.

Tucker, Robert Charles. **The Soviet Political Mind.** New York: Norton, rev. ed., 1972, 304 p.
A collection of Professor Tucker's perceptive and provocative essays on Stalin, Stalinism and changes in the post-Stalin era.

Werth, Alexander. **Russia: The Post-War Years.** New York: Taplinger, 1971, 446 p.
A journalist of long residence and good standing in Moscow gives an account of the years of the origins of the cold war, 1945–48. Much of the blame falls on the United States, but, unlike American revisionists, Werth also shows that Stalin's tough policies were no mere reaction to unexpected American hostility.

The Post-Stalin Years

See also Political Factors, p. 12; The Postwar World, p. 178; Eastern Europe and the Soviet Bloc, p. 358; Baltic States, p. 455; other subsections under the Union of Soviet Socialist Republics.

Achminow, German Fedor. **Breschnew und Kossygin: die neuen Männer im Kreml?** Diessen/Ammersee: v. Tucher, 1964, 155 p.
An effort to appraise the power struggle in the Kremlin in the immediate aftermath of Khrushchev's fall.

Boettcher, Erik and Others, *eds.* **Bilanz der Ära Chruschtschow.** Stuttgart: Kohlhammer, 1966, 391 p.
Papers, originally delivered at a conference of the Deutsche Gesellschaft für Osteuropakunde in 1964, assessing the changes in Soviet politics, foreign relations, cultural affairs and economy that took place during the reign of Khrushchev.

Braverman, Harry. **The Future of Russia.** New York: Macmillan, 1963, 175 p.
An effort to predict the evolution of the Soviet society, economy and state in coming decades. It is the author's expectation that the Russians may "reconstitute for the world the image of socialism which their own development shattered."

Brezhnev, Leonid Il'ich. **Following Lenin's Course: Speeches and Articles.** Moscow: Progress Publishers, 1972, 499 p.
Major speeches and writings by the General Secretary of the Communist Party of the Soviet Union covering the years 1967–1971. A more comprehensive edition of Brezhnev's writings since 1964, but only ranging through 1970, is available as "Leninskom kursom" (Moscow: Izd-vo Politicheskoi Literatury, 1970, 2 v.).

Brezhnev, Leonid Il'ich. **Molodym—Stroit' Kommunizm.** Moscow: Politizdat, 1970, 399 p.
A selection of addresses and reports by the First Secretary of the Central Committee of the Communist Party on Soviet topics that have special relevance to the role of the Komsomol and the problems and prospects of Soviet youth.

Brumberg, Abraham, *ed.* **In Quest of Justice.** New York: Praeger, 1970, 477 p.
Introduced by some brief but useful Western commentaries on contemporary dissent, protest and counterattack in the U.S.S.R., the volume comprises a rich selection of pertinent documents: trials, protests and petitions, material on national and religious dissent and the views of writers and their censors.

Conquest, Robert. **Russia after Khrushchev.** New York: Praeger, 1965, 267 p.
The author of "Power and Policy in the U.S.S.R." here pursues his analysis of Soviet politics, with particular emphasis on changes and continuities since Stalin, the characteristics of the new leadership and the persistent jockeying for position.

Dallin, Alexander and Larson, Thomas B., *eds.* **Soviet Politics since Khrushchev.** Englewood Cliffs: Prentice-Hall, 1968, 181 p.
A series of essays discussing major areas of Soviet policies and politics in the last half-decade. Three chapters deal with military and foreign affairs.

Dirscherl, Denis, *ed.* **The New Russia: Communism in Evolution.** Dayton: Pflaum Press, 1968, 203 p.
A collection of writings, some previously published, on recent changes in Soviet life and ideology.

Féron, Bernard. **L'U.R.S.S. sans idole: de Staline à Brejnev et Kossyguine.** Paris: Casterman, 1966, 229 p.
A French journalist reviews the Khrushchev era.

Hindus, Maurice Gerschon. **The Kremlin's Human Dilemma: Russia after Half a Century of Revolution.** Garden City: Doubleday, 1967, 395 p.
A quite revealing report, by an old Russia hand, based on journeys in 1962, 1963 and 1965. He surveys developments in town and country and also discusses the implications of Khrushchev's fall and prospects for the future.

Hyland, William and Shryock, Richard Wallace. **The Fall of Khrushchev.** New York: Funk & Wagnalls, 1968, 209 p.
An effort, only moderately successful, to trace the decline and fall of Nikita Sergeievich in the two years following the Cuban missile crisis.

Linden, Carl A. **Khrushchev and the Soviet Leadership, 1957–1964.** Baltimore: Johns Hopkins Press (in coöperation with the Institute for Sino-Soviet Studies, George Washington University), 1966, 270 p.

A valuable analysis of the nature of Khrushchev's leadership, his victory in 1957 and his abrupt fall in 1964.

Löwenthal, Richard and Vogel, Heinrich, eds. **Sowjetpolitik der 70er Jahre.** Stuttgart: Kohlhammer, 1972, 153 p.
Essays on Soviet foreign and domestic policies by well-known authors—the results of a conference held in October 1971.

Medvedev, Zhores Aleksandrovich. **The Medvedev Papers.** New York: St. Martin's Press, 1971, 470 p.
This book is a translation of two manuscripts by a leading Soviet biochemist; prepared originally for private circulation. An important example of *samizdat* criticism of the Soviet bureaucrats and censors on scientific inquiry.

Medvedev, Zhores Aleksandrovich and Medvedev, Roi Aleksandrovich. **A Question of Madness.** New York: Knopf, 1971, 223 p.
An account by a prominent Soviet biochemist, and his twin brother, of his being diagnosed as an "incipient schizophrenic" and railroaded into a mental institution, for evident political reasons.

Morozow, Michael. **Das sowjetische Establishment.** Stuttgart: Seewald, 1971, 198 p.
A study of the persons making up the leadership of the Soviet party and bureaucratic hierarchies.

Page, Martin and Burg, David. **Unpersoned: The Fall of Nikita Sergeyevitch Khrushchev.** London: Chapman and Hall, 1966, 174 p.
An attempt to describe Khrushchev's fall from power by a former *Daily Express* Moscow correspondent and a Russian-born student of Soviet affairs.

Strong, John W., ed. **The Soviet Union Under Brezhnev and Kosygin: The Transition Years.** New York: Van Nostrand Reinhold, 1971, 277 p.
Essays by a number of scholars dealing with various facets of Soviet life and politics in the post-Khrushchev years.

Tatu, Michel. **Power in the Kremlin: From Khrushchev to Kosygin.** New York: Viking, 1969, 570 p.
A translation of an important study, by a French correspondent for *Le Monde*, of the Soviet leadership in the 1960s. The French original was published as "Le Pouvoir en U.R.S.S.: du déclin de Khrouchtchev à la direction collective" (Paris: Grasset, 1967, 604 p.).

Ulam, Adam Bruno. **The New Face of Soviet Totalitarianism.** Cambridge: Harvard University Press, 1963, 233 p.
Essays, by a professor of government at Harvard, on contemporary Soviet politics.

Whitney, Thomas P., ed. **Khrushchev Speaks.** Ann Arbor: University of Michigan Press, 1963, 466 p.
An anthology, with commentary, of Khrushchev's speeches, articles, press conferences and comments between 1949 and the end of the Twenty-second Party Congress in 1961.

Communist Party of the Soviet Union

See also (General Works) Reference Works, p. 1; Socialism, p. 24; Communism, p. 26; Eastern Europe and the Soviet Bloc, p. 358; other subsections under the Union of Soviet Socialist Republics.

Avtorkhanov, Abdurakhman. **The Communist Party Apparatus.** Chicago: Regnery (in coöperation with the Foundation for Foreign Affairs), 1966, 422 p.
A study of the theoretical background, organization, functions and evolution of the Communist Party in the Soviet Union, including an analysis of the relations between Soviet foreign policy and the communist theory of world revolution. The author, a graduate of the Institute of Red Professors in Moscow, was a member of the Munich Institute for the Study of the U.S.S.R.

Gehlen, Michael P. **The Communist Party of the Soviet Union.** Bloomington: Indiana University Press, 1969, 161 p.
An exercise in functional analysis.

Hough, Jerry F. **The Soviet Prefects.** Cambridge: Harvard University Press, 1969, 416 p.
A close and scholarly examination of the role of local party organs in industrial decision-making. Of particular interest in the light it casts on the actual functioning and structure of the bureaucracy.

Kolkowicz, Roman. **The Soviet Military and the Communist Party.** Princeton: Princeton University Press, 1967, 429 p.
A very substantial study, analytical and historical, of the ambiguous and changing relationship between the Communist Party and the military establishment in the Soviet Union.

Lewytzkyj, Borys. **Die Kommunistische Partei der Sowjetunion.** Stuttgart: Klett, 1967, 312 p.
The author, a Ukrainian scholar, surveys the social structure of the Communist Party of the Soviet Union and concludes that its members form a self-perpetuating élite very much concerned with maintaining its privileged role within the Soviet system.

Materialy XXIII s'ezda KPSS. Moscow: Izd-vo Politicheskoi Literatury, 1966, 303 p.
Major documents, directives and addresses of the Twenty-third Congress of the Communist Party of the Soviet Union, held in March-April 1966.

Materialy XXIV s'ezda KPSS. Moscow: Izd-vo Politicheskoi Literatury, 1971, 319 p.
Major documents, directives and addresses of the Twenty-fourth Congress of the Communist Party of the Soviet Union, held in March-April 1971.

Ponomarev, Boris Nikolaevich and Others, *eds.* **Istoriia Kommunisticheskoi Partii Sovetskogo Soiuza.** Moscow: Izd-vo Politicheskoi Literatury, 4th ed., 1971, 735 p.
This is the latest version of the comprehensive official history of the Communist Party of the Soviet Union, representing a minor updating of the 1969 edition.

Rigby, Thomas Harold. **Communist Party Membership in the U.S.S.R., 1917-1967.** Princeton: Princeton University Press, 1968, 573 p.
A comprehensive and thorough history and analysis of "recruitment to the Soviet Communist Party and the composition of the party" by a leading authority on the subject.

Schapiro, Leonard Bertram. **The Communist Party of the Soviet Union.** New York: Random House, 1971, 2d rev. and enl. ed., 686 p.
A revised and updated edition of a standard history, first published in 1960.

Schapiro, Leonard Bertram, *ed.* **The U.S.S.R. and the Future.** New York: Praeger (for the Institute for the Study of the U.S.S.R., Munich), 1963, 324 p.
A substantial symposium of essays analyzing the 1961 program of the Communist Party of the Soviet Union. Appendices include texts of the 1919 and 1961 programs.

Solov'ev, A. A., *ed.* **KPSS: spravochnik.** Moscow: Izd-vo Politicheskoi Literatury, 3rd rev. and enl. ed., 1971, 415 p.
A compact guide to the major events in the history of the Communist Party of the Soviet Union. This latest edition encompasses the Twenty-fourth Congress of 1971.

Westen, Klaus. **Die Kommunistische Partei der Sowjetunion und der Sowjetstaat: eine verfassungsrechtliche Untersuchung.** Cologne: Verlag Wissenschaft und Politik, 1968, 349 p.
A historical and legal study of the relationship between the Communist Party of the Soviet Union and the Soviet State. An important contribution.

Bolshevism and Soviet Marxism

See also (General Works) Reference Works, p. 1; Political Philosophies and Ideologies, p. 21; other subsections under the Union of Soviet Socialist Republics.

Achminow, German Fedor. **Die Totengräber des Kommunismus.** Stuttgart: Steingrüben, 1964, 486 p.
A sociological inquiry into Soviet communism, which the author sees to have been a sort of "Ersatz-Frühkapitalismus" that cannot lead to communism's goals.

Blakeley, Thomas J. **Soviet Theory of Knowledge.** Dordrecht: Reidel, 1964, 203 p.
A survey and evaluation of contemporary Soviet theory of knowledge. Technical but by no means irrelevant to our general understanding of the Soviet outlook.

Bocheński, Innocentius M. **Soviet Russian Dialectical Materialism (Diamat)**. Dordrecht: Reidel, 1963, 185 p.
A concise critique of the philosophical premises of Marxism and Leninism. The German original was published as "Der sowjetrussische dialektische Materialismus (Diamat)" (Berne: Francke, 4th ed., 1962, 213 p.).

Chkhikvadze, Viktor Mikhailovich, *ed*. **Leninskoe uchenie o diktature proletariata**. Moscow: Izd-vo "Nauka," 1970, 255 p.
A group of authors discuss the concept of "the dictatorship of the proletariat," the doctrine that legitimizes class-based terror as necessary to the transition from capitalism to socialism.

Conquest, Robert, *ed*. **The Politics of Ideas in the U.S.S.R.** New York: Praeger, 1967, 175 p.
A factual and concise survey of the role of ideology in the Soviet state.

Dahm, Helmut. **Die Dialektik im Wandel der Sowjetphilosophie**. Cologne: Verlag Wissenschaft und Politik, 1963, 151 p.
A study of dialectical materialism in the Soviet Union since Stalin's death, by a Catholic scholar.

De George, Richard T. **Patterns of Soviet Thought: The Origins and Development of Dialectical and Historical Materialism**. Ann Arbor: University of Michigan Press, 1966, 293 p.
A comprehensive and competent survey of the background and development of dialectical and historical materialism, from Marxism to Stalinism.

Denno, Theodore Freed. **The Communist Millennium: The Soviet View**. The Hague: Nijhoff, 1964, 166 p.
This writer's purpose is "to present as complete a picture as possible of what that new organization of human life under communism is to be according to the views of Marx and Engels, Lenin, Trotsky, Bukharin, Stalin and the present Soviet Communist leadership."

Fedoseev, Petr Nikolaevich. **Marksizm v XX veke: Marks, Engel's, Lenin i sovremennost'**. Moscow: Izd-vo "Mysl," 1972, 582 p.
A broad survey of Marxism in the Soviet mold. The role of the party in linking revolutionary theory to practice is emphasized, with specific references to the Russian experience since 1917.

Fedoseev, Petr Nikolaevich and Others. **Nauchnyi kommunizm**. Moscow: Izd-vo Politicheskoi Literatury, 1972, 496 p.
An official text for the study of Marxism-Leninism in the U.S.S.R.

Flechtheim, Ossip Kurt. **Bolschewismus 1917–1967: von der Weltrevolution zum Sowjetimperium**. Frankfurt/Main: Europa Verlag, 1967, 255 p.
A general survey and interpretation of Soviet communism by an able historian.

Hollander, Gayle Durham. **Soviet Political Indoctrination: Developments in Mass Media and Propaganda Since Stalin**. New York: Praeger, 1972, 244 p.
An inquiry into the process the sociologists call "political socialization," and how it works from above through agit-prop and the mass media.

The Impact of the Russian Revolution, 1917–1967: The Influence of Bolshevism on the World Outside Russia. New York: Oxford University Press (for the Royal Institute of International Affairs), 1967, 357 p.
A collection of essays by Arnold J. Toynbee, Neil McInnes, Hugh Seton-Watson, Peter Wiles and Richard Löwenthal.

Jaworskyj, Michael, *ed*. **Soviet Political Thought**. Baltimore: Johns Hopkins Press, 1968, 621 p.
An extensive collection of materials translated from the Russian by the editor and organized chronologically, covering the period from 1917 to 1961.

Kaltakhchian, Suren Tigranovich. **Leninizm o sushchnosti natsii i puti obrazovaniia internatsional'noi obschnosti liudei**. Moscow: Izd-vo Moskovskogo Universiteta, 1969, 461 p.

The author discusses the concept of internationalism in utopian terms and argues that national differentiations are an invariable feature of capitalism.

Kool, Frits and Oberländer, Erwin, eds. **Arbeiterdemokratie oder Parteidiktatur.** Olten: Walter-Verlag, 1967, 535 p.
Documents on the opposition within the Bolshevik party in the years following the 1917 Revolution.

Laloy, Jean. **Le Socialisme de Lénine.** Paris: Desclée, De Brouwer, 1967, 319 p.
A prominent French diplomat and student of Soviet affairs summarizes Lenin's philosophical and political ideas and discusses the way they have changed the course of modern history.

Lieber, Hans Joachim and Ruffmann, Karl Heinz, eds. **Der Sowjetkommunismus: Dokumente.** Cologne: Kiepenheuer, 1963–64, 2 v.
An extensive collection of documents on Soviet communism.

Makarov, Aleksei Dmitrievich and Others, ed. **Marksistsko-leninskaia filosofiia: dialekticheskii materializm.** Moscow: Izd-vo "Mysl'," 1970, 366 p.
A survey of the philosophic tenets of contemporary Marxism-Leninism in the U.S.S.R.

Malafeev, Aleksei Nikolaievich and Others. **Politicheskaia ekonomika: uchebnik dlia shkol osnov marksizma-leninizma.** Moscow: Izd-vo Politicheskoi Literatury, 3rd ed., 1971, 367 p.
A standard Soviet textbook for the required study of Marxism-Leninism.

Parry, Albert. **The New Class Divided: Science and Technology Versus Communism.** New York: Macmillan, 1966, 364 p.
The author's theme is stated at the outset: "My purpose is to investigate the possibility that the [Soviet] scientific-technical personnel is essentially a group distinct, or potentially distinct, from the Party zealots." He foresees an increasingly important and oppositional role for this key group.

Ponomarev, Boris Nikolaevich and Others, eds. **Mezhdunarodnoe revoliutsionnoe dvizhenie rabochego klassa.** Moscow: Izd-vo Politicheskoi Literatury, 3rd rev. ed., 1966, 446 p.
A survey of the state of proletarian internationalism and the worldwide working class movement.

Richards, David John. **Soviet Chess.** New York: Oxford University Press, 1965, 201 p.
A most interesting effort both to analyze the ideological background of Soviet chess and its remarkable achievements, and to study Soviet chess as an "illustration of the workings of the Soviet mind."

Rumiantsev, Aleksei Matveevich, ed. **Nauchnyi kommunizm: slovar'.** Moscow: Izd-vo Politicheskoi Literatury, 1969, 368 p.
A compact dictionary of communism, defining key concepts of Soviet Marxism-Leninism.

Trapeznikov, Sergei Pavlovich. **Na krutykh povorotakh istorii (iz urokov bor'by s revizionizmom vnutri marksistsko-leninskogo dvizheniia).** Moscow: Izd-vo "Mysl'," 1971, 271 p.
A collection of essays by one of the foremost defenders of ideological orthodoxy in the U.S.S.R. that reflects unceasing vigilance against revisionism of both the Left and the Right within the international communist movement.

Vigor, Peter Hast. **A Guide to Marxism and its Effects on Soviet Development.** New York: Humanities Press, 1966, 253 p.
A presentation of the main tenets of Marxist-Leninist theory and an attempt to show some of the effects of this theory upon Soviet practice, by a British writer.

Wetter, Gustavo Andrea. **Soviet Ideology Today.** New York: Praeger, 1966, 334 p.
Father Wetter, author of a classic study of dialectial materialism, here turns to an analysis and critique of the philosophical doctrines of Soviet ideology. The original appeared as "Dialektischer und historischer Materialismus" (Frankfurt/Main: Fischer Bücherei, 1962, 339 p.).

Za chistotu marksizma-leninizma. Moscow: Izd-vo "Mysl'," 1964, 327 p.
An anthology of essays attacking "left-wing" and "petit-bourgeois" concepts of Maoism.

Foreign Policy
General

See also General Works, p. 1; Political Factors, p. 12; International Law, p. 83; International Organization and Government, p. 96; War and Peace, p. 108; The World Since 1914, p. 129; other subsections under the Union of Soviet Socialist Republics and the sections for specific countries and regions.

Airapetian, Mikhail Ervanovich and Sukhodeev, Vladimir Vasil'evich. **Novyi tip mezhdunarodnykh otnoshenii.** Moscow: Izd-vo "Mysl'," 1964, 278 p.
This study advances the argument that the Soviet approach to the conduct of international relations differs qualitatively from that of capitalist states, and that the emerging pattern is most visible in fraternal relations among members of the socialist community. Written during the Khrushchev period.

Arbatov, G. A. **Ideologicheskaia bor'ba v sovremennykh mezhdunarodnykh otnosheniiakh.** Moscow: Izd-vo Politicheskoi Literatury, 1970, 351 p.
The chief of the Soviet Union's Institute for the United States of America probes a key question in Moscow's assessment of contemporary international politics: how does the struggle between two competing systems continue after the threat of nuclear war has abated?

Aspaturian, Vernon V. and Others. **Process and Power in Soviet Foreign Policy.** Boston: Little, Brown, 1971, 939 p.
An impressive selection of essays by the author and other leading American experts on Soviet politics and foreign relations dealing "extensively with the linkages and interrelationships between domestic social demands and pressures, internal factional politics, and Soviet foreign policy." Most of the contributions have been published before but are not easily accessible in their original versions.

Barghoorn, Frederick Charles. **Soviet Foreign Propaganda.** Princeton: Princeton University Press, 1964, 329 p.
This study by Professor Barghoorn of Yale University deals in a conscientious and scholarly manner with the purposes, themes, techniques and organization of the formidable Soviet propaganda operations.

Bestuzhev-Lada, Igor' Vasil'evich and Others. **Vneshniaia politika Sovetskogo Soiuza: aktualnye problemy (1967–1970).** Moscow: Izd-vo "Mezhdunarodnye Otnosheniia," 1970, 262 p.
A general survey of the principles, programs and problems of Soviet foreign policy, produced at the Institute of International Relations of Moscow University.

Carroll, Eber Malcolm. **Soviet Communism and Western Opinion, 1919–1921.** Chapel Hill: University of North Carolina Press, 1965, 302 p.
A posthumously edited account of the divisions in Western policies and opinions regarding the nascent Soviet state. Edited by Frederic B. M. Hollyday.

Chubar'ian, Aleksandr Oganovich. **V. I. Lenin i formirovanie sovetskoi vneshnei politiki.** Moscow: Izd-vo "Nauka," 1972, 315 p.
A serious and well-organized study of the initial period in Soviet foreign policy. The author's focus is largely on the Brest-Litovsk and Rapallo treaties.

Crowley, Edward L., ed. **The Soviet Diplomatic Corps, 1917–1967.** Metuchen (N.J.): Scarecrow Press (for the Institute for the Study of the U.S.S.R., Munich), 1970, 240 p.
A useful reference on the organization and personnel of the U.S.S.R. Ministry of Foreign Affairs in the years from 1917 to 1967. This work also contains a chronology of the most noteworthy Soviet diplomatic acts and events.

Dokumenty Vneshnei Politiki SSSR. Moscow: Izd-vo Polit. Lit-ry (for the Ministerstvo Inostrannykh Del SSSR), 1957– .

A collection of documents from the archives of the Soviet Ministry of Foreign Affairs. Through 1973 18 volumes have been published, covering the period from November 7, 1917 to December 31, 1934.

Eudin, Xenia Joukoff and Slusser, Robert Melville. **Soviet Foreign Policy, 1928-1934: Documents and Materials.** University Park: Pennsylvania State University Press, 1966-67, 2 v.
A useful selection of documents, with narrative summary, covering a particularly critical turning point in Soviet foreign policy. A publication of the Hoover Institution on War, Revolution, and Peace.

Fischer, Louis. **The Road to Yalta: Soviet Foreign Relations, 1941-1945.** New York: Harper and Row, 1972, 238 p.
This book, planned as the second volume of a history of Soviet foreign relations from 1917 to the present, was uncompleted at the time of the author's death in January 1970. The narrative runs from the German assault on the Soviet Union to the eve of the Yalta conference.

Fischer, Louis. **Russia's Road from Peace to War: Soviet Foreign Relations, 1917-1941.** New York: Harper and Row, 1969, 499 p.
Mr. Fischer here returns to the scene of his earlier "The Soviets in World Affairs" (first published in 1930), and presents a wide-ranging, informed but essentially informal history of Soviet foreign relations up to the German attack in June 1941.

Gehlen, Michael P. **The Politics of Coexistence: Soviet Methods and Motives.** Bloomington: Indiana University Press, 1967, 334 p.
An examination of the Soviet theory of "peaceful coexistence" and its application in foreign policy.

Geyer, Dietrich, *ed.* **Sowjetunion: Aussenpolitik 1917-1955.** Cologne: Böhlau, 1972, 618 p.
A reference volume, written by leading West German scholars, surveying Soviet foreign policy in the period from 1917 to 1955. Published in the series "Osteuropa-Handbuch."

Hammond, Thomas Taylor, *comp.* and *ed.* **Soviet Foreign Relations and World Communism.** Princeton: Princeton University Press, 1965, 1,240 p.
This major reference work is an annotated bibliography of 7,000 books in some 30 languages, covering Soviet foreign relations by period and by region, international communism and a number of related topics.

Hanak, H. **Soviet Foreign Policy Since the Death of Stalin.** Boston: Routledge and Kegan Paul, 1972, 340 p.
A useful selection of documents, with introductions, to illustrate Soviet foreign policy since 1953.

Harvey, Mose L. and Others. **Science and Technology as an Instrument of Soviet Policy.** Coral Gables (Fla.): Center for Advanced International Studies, University of Miami, 1972, 219 p.
A summary and analysis based on Soviet public statements at a time when the transfer of technology is assuming a prominent place in Soviet-American relations.

Hayter, Sir William Goodenough. **Russia and the World: A Study in Soviet Foreign Policy.** New York: Taplinger, 1970, 133 p.
Reflections by the former British Ambassador in Moscow on the "conservative" as opposed to the "revolutionary" components in contemporary Soviet foreign policy.

Hyde, Douglas Arnold. **The Peaceful Assault: The Pattern of Subversion.** London: Bodley Head, 1963, 127 p.
The author, a former member of the Communist Party of Great Britain, analyzes various techniques of communist strategy and concludes that Soviet adherence to peaceful coexistence is misleading.

Ioffe, Aleksandr Evseevich. **Internatsional'nye, nauchnye i kulturnye sviazi Sovetskogo Soiuza 1928-1932.** Moscow: Izd-vo "Nauka," 1969, 200 p.
Though the First Five-Year Plan (1928-1932) represents a period of relative isolation in Soviet foreign policy, the author seeks to demonstrate continuance of the pursuit of outside contacts at that time.

Ioffe, Aleksandr Evseevich. **Vneshnaia politika Sovetskogo Soiuza, 1928-1932 gg.** Moscow: Izd-vo "Nauka," 1968, 487 p.
An extensive survey of Soviet foreign policy between 1928 and 1932. A lengthy bibliographic essay is included.

Jacobsen, C. G. **Soviet Strategy—Soviet Foreign Policy: Military Considerations Affecting Soviet Policy-Making.** Glasgow: MacLehose/The University Press, 1972, 236 p.
An expert inquiry, based on a Glasgow University Ph.D. thesis.

Lebedev, Viacheslav Vladimirovich. **Mezhdunarodnoe polozhenie Rossii nakanune Oktiabr'skoi Revoliutsii.** Moscow: Izd-vo "Nauka," 1967, 311 p.
A serious and well-documented analysis of the foreign policies of the Provisional Government and the Bolsheviks between February and October 1917.

Letopis' sovetskoi vneshnei politiki 1917-1967: daty i fakty. Moscow: Izd-vo Politicheskoi Literatury, 1968, 120 p.
A descriptive and selective chronology of Soviet foreign policy, covering the fifty years since the Revolution.

Librach, Jan. **The Rise of the Soviet Empire.** New York: Praeger, rev. ed., 1965, 399 p.
A useful outline, by a former Polish diplomat, of the history of Soviet foreign policy.

Markert, Werner and Geyer, Dietrich, eds. **Sowjetunion; Verträge und Abkommen: Verzeichnis der Quellen und Nachweise 1917-1962.** Cologne: Böhlau, 1967, 611 p.
A guide to the treaties and international agreements of the Soviet state concluded in the period from November 7, 1917 to December 31, 1962. The main part contains descriptions of the treaties, arranged chronologically, with bibliographical notes about the sources and commentaries. There is also a chronology and a listing of the treaties and agreements by country. This volume, in the series "Osteuropa-Handbuch," has been compiled by Jörg Konrad Hoensch and Helmut König.

Meissner, Boris. **Die Breshnew-Doktrin.** Cologne: Verlag Wissenschaft und Politik, 1969, 189 p.
Documents, with a useful introduction, relating to the background and enunciation of the so-called Brezhnev doctrine, including responses from other communist regimes. A shorter version of this volume appeared as "The Brezhnev Doctrine" (Kansas City: Park College, Governmental Research Bureau, 1970, 80 p.).

Meissner, Boris and Rhode, Gotthold, eds. **Grundfragen sowjetischer Aussenpolitik.** Stuttgart: Kohlhammer, 1970, 175 p.
Essays by a group of German scholars on "continuity and change" in Russian and Soviet policy toward such neighbors as Poland, Germany and China.

Mezhdunarodnye otnosheniia posle Vtoroi Mirovoi Voiny. Moscow: Izd-vo Politicheskoi Literatury, 1962-65, 3 v.
These three volumes on international relations after the Second World War, prepared by the Institute of World Economy and International Relations, cover, from the Soviet perspective, the years 1945 to 1965. A substantial work, with quite extensive documentation.

Mironov, Nikolai Vladimirovich. **Pravovoe regulirovanie vneshnikh snoshenii SSSR, 1917-1970 gg.** Moscow: Izd-vo "Mezhdunarodnye Otnosheniia," 1971, 294 p.
A study of legal problems associated with various processes of Soviet international relations.

Nikhamin, V. P. and Others, eds. **Sovremennye mezhdunarodnye otnosheniia i vneshniaia politika Sovetskogo Soiuza: uchebnoe posobie.** Moscow: Izd-vo "Mysl'," 1972, 335 p.
An official Communist Party text on international politics and Soviet foreign policy, written to incorporate the results of the Twenty-fourth Party Congress and to reflect the emergence of Party Secretary Brezhnev into foreign policy leadership.

Novikov, K. V. and Others, eds. **50 let bor'by SSSR za razoruzhenie: sbornik dokumentov.** Moscow: Izd-vo "Nauka," 1967, 690 p.
A collection of Soviet documents on problems of peace and disarmament, from the first "Decree of Peace" of the Bolsheviks in 1917 to Soviet proposals for nuclear disarmament and European security arrangements in 1967. A short bibliography of Soviet sources on disarmament is included.

Osakwe, Chris. **The Participation of the Soviet Union in Universal International Organizations.** Leyden: Sijthoff, 1972, 194 p.

The author examines in detail the Soviet role in three organizations (ILO, WHO and UNESCO), taking full account of the ideological and political premises of Soviet policy.

Oznobishin, Dmitrii Vladimirovich. **Ot Bresta do Iur'eva: iz istorii sovetskoi vlasti, 1917–1920 gg.** Moscow: Izd-vo "Nauka," 1966, 326 p.
A study of Soviet foreign policy from the Treaty of Brest-Litovsk to the recognition of Estonia in 1920.

Pächter, Heinz. **Weltmacht Russland: aussenpolitische Strategie in drei Jahrhunderten.** Oldenburg: Stalling-Verlag, 1968, 399 p.
A discussion of Tsarist and Soviet foreign policies. The author warns against making concessions to the Russians in the hope that they will reciprocate them, and expresses the conviction that the liberalization of the Soviet system of government will not change its foreign policies.

Phelps-Fetherston, Iain. **Soviet International Front Organizations: A Concise Handbook.** New York: Praeger, 1965, 178 p.
A useful reference volume on various international organizations that defend the policies of the Soviet Union.

Ponomarev, Boris Nikolaevich; Gromyko, Andrei Andreevich and Khvostov, Vladimir Mikhailovich, *eds.* **Istoriia vneshnei politika Sovetskogo Soiuza.** Moscow: Izd-vo "Nauka," 1966–71, 2 v.
An official history of Soviet foreign policy since 1917, characterized as a coherent movement toward peace and progress in spite of fascist aggression and imperialist nuclear blackmail. The first volume is available in English translation as "History of Soviet Foreign Policy, 1917–1945" (Moscow: Progress Publishers, 1969, 497 p.).

Popov, Viktor Ivanovich, *ed.* **Leninskaia diplomatiia mira i sotrudnichestva.** Moscow: Izd-vo "Nauka," 1965, 244 p.
An anthology of essays by Soviet diplomatic historians on the establishment of diplomatic relations between the U.S.S.R. and the Western powers and Japan during 1924–25.

Rubinstein, Alvin Zachary. **The Soviets in International Organizations.** Princeton: Princeton University Press, 1964, 380 p.
A well-documented study of post-Stalinist Soviet policies and actions in those agencies and commissions of the U.N. having chiefly to do with underdeveloped countries.

Schickling, Willi. **Die Chruschtschow-Orgel: das Spiel auf den Nerven der Menschheit.** Stuttgart: Seewald, 1963, 168 p.
The author studies several international crises in relation to Soviet propaganda policy and views Khrushchev as a shrewd combatant in a "war of nerves" with the West.

Shulman, Marshall Darrow. **Stalin's Foreign Policy Reappraised.** Cambridge: Harvard University Press, 1963, 320 p.
In this scholarly work Professor Shulman argues that a major evolution in Soviet foreign policy occurred in the last three years of Stalin's life and not, as is so often supposed, after his death.

Törnudd, Klaus. **Soviet Attitudes Towards Non-Military Regional Co-operation.** Helsinki: Societas Scientiarum Fennica, 2d rev. ed., 1963, 324 p.
This study by a Finnish scholar is based on research done in the United States and the Soviet Union.

Triska, Jan F. and Finley, David D. **Soviet Foreign Policy.** New York: Macmillan, 1968, 518 p.
The authors of this advanced textbook, for many years associated with the Stanford Institute of Political Studies, attempt to introduce new techniques of political analysis in their discussion of Soviet foreign policies.

Ulam, Adam Bruno. **Expansion and Coexistence: Soviet Foreign Policy, 1917–73.** New York: Praeger, 2d ed., 1974, 797 p.
A massive and impressive study by a Harvard University professor, first published in 1968.

Vneshniaia politika Sovetskogo Soiuza i mezhdunarodnye otnosheniia: sbornik dokumentov, 1961–. Moscow: Izd-vo "Mezhdunarodnye Otnosheniia", 1962–.

An annual compilation of significant documents on Soviet foreign policy, including texts of treaties and official declarations.

Vygodskii, Semen Iul'evich. **U istokov sovetskoi diplomatii.** Moscow: Izd-vo Politicheskoi Literatury, 1965, 350 p.
A history of the first years of Soviet involvement in world affairs, with special attention to the creation of a new diplomatic service and a restructured foreign ministry.

Warth, Robert Douglas. **Soviet Russia in World Politics.** New York: Twayne, 1963, 544 p.
An introduction to the history of Soviet foreign relations.

Weeks, Albert Loren. **The Other Side of Coexistence.** New York: Pitman, 1970, 304 p.
An analysis of Soviet foreign policy, especially in respect to relations with the United States. As the author looks forward into the 1970s he finds Russia facing some crossroads and paradoxes—a common plight of states, it appears.

Wesson, Robert G. **Das Grundproblem der sowjetischen Aussenpolitik.** Frankfurt/Main: Athenäum Verlag, 1970, 199 p.
A succinct survey of the main issues of Soviet foreign policy.

Wettig, Gerhard. **Europäische Sicherheit: das europäische Staatensystem in der sowjetischen Aussenpolitik, 1966–1972.** Düsseldorf: Bertelsmann Universitätsverlag, 1972, 213 p.
A thorough exposition of Soviet proposals, aims and tactics on the question of European security, with a consideration of alternatives for the West.

Zimmerman, William. **Soviet Perspectives on International Relations, 1956–1967.** Princeton: Princeton University Press, 1969, 336 p.
A study of changes in the outlook of the Soviet leadership with respect to the nature and management of international relations. The author is particularly concerned with the degree to which ideology continues to play a role in the post-Stalin era.

Relations with Western Europe

See also General Works, p. 1; Political Factors, p. 12; International Law, p. 83; International Organization and Government, p. 96; War and Peace, p. 108; The World Since 1914, p. 129; other subsections under the Union of Soviet Socialist Republics and the sections for specific countries and regions.

Anderle, Alfred, ed. **Rapallo und die friedliche Koexistenz.** Berlin: Akademie-Verlag, 1963, 295 p.
An East German study of Russo-German relations in the 1920s. Useful bibliography.

Embree, George Daniel, ed. **The Soviet Union and the German Question, September 1958–June 1961.** The Hague: Nijhoff, 1963, 330 p.
A collection of Soviet documents and statements tracing the course of Soviet policy toward Germany and Berlin.

Fabry, Philipp W. **Die Sowjetunion und das Dritte Reich: eine dokumentierte Geschichte der deutsch-sowjetischen Beziehungen von 1933 bis 1941.** Stuttgart: Seewald, 1971, 485 p.
This survey of German-Russian relations in the period from 1933 to 1941 provides many new details on the intricate, paradoxical, dishonest but very often quite close coöperation between the Nazi and Soviet leaders.

Galkin, Aleksandr Abramovich and Mel'nikov, Daniil Efimovich. **SSSR, zapadnye derzhavy, i germanskii vopros.** Moscow: Izd-vo "Nauka," 1966, 261 p.
A Soviet examination of the German question in the post-World War II period.

Grunwald, Constantin de. **Les Alliances franco-russes: neuf siècles de malentendus.** Paris: Plon, 1965, 405 p.
A history of Franco-Russian relations, spanning nine centuries and emphasizing the continuity in Russian and Soviet foreign policies.

Hartl, Hans and Marx, Werner. **Fünfzig Jahre sowjetische Deutschlandpolitik.** Boppard: Boldt, 1967, 648 p.
An extensive though politically loaded survey of Soviet policies toward Germany since 1917.

Krummacher, F. A. and Lange, Helmut. **Krieg und Frieden.** Munich: Bechtle, 1970, 564 p.
   A substantial review, though not a major scholarly study, of German-Soviet relations from "Brest-Litovsk to Operation Barbarossa."

Laqueur, Walter Ze'ev. **Russia and Germany: A Century of Conflict.** Boston: Little, Brown, 1965, 367 p.
   In the words of the author, the Breslau-born director of the London Institute for Contemporary History, this study deals "with the historical origins of Russophobia in Germany, and of anti-Germanism in Russia" and "with the confrontation of Nazism and Bolshevism that culminated in the Second World War."

Meyer, Gerd. **Die sowjetische Deutschland-Politik im Jahre 1952.** Tübingen: Arbeitsgemeinschaft für Osteuropaforschung, 1970, 181 p.
   A close examination and appraisal of the Soviet initiatives in 1952 regarding the reunification of Germany.

Niclauss, Karlheinz. **Die Sowjetunion und Hitlers Machtergreifung.** Bonn: Röhrscheid, 1966, 208 p.
   A monograph on German-Russian relations from 1929 to 1935.

Nikolaev, Pavel Alekseevich. **Politika Sovetskogo Soiuza v germanskom voprose 1945-1964.** Moscow: Izd-vo "Nauka," 1966, 397 p.
   A historical study of Soviet policy on the German question between 1945 and 1964, arguing that the constant goal of the U.S.S.R. had always been the establishment of a stable peace in Europe.

Popov, Viktor Ivanovich. **Diplomaticheskie otnosheniia mezhdu SSSR i Angliei (1929-1939 gg.).** Moscow: Izd-vo "Mezhdunarodnye Otnosheniia," 1965, 515 p.
   A Soviet interpretation of Anglo-Soviet relations in the years preceding the Second World War, based largely on published British documents.

Rosenko, Ivan Arkhipovich. **Sovetsko-germanskie otnosheniia (1921-1922 gg.).** Leningrad: Izd-vo Leningradskogo Universiteta, 1965, 157 p.
   A discussion of early Soviet-German relations that characterizes the Treaty of Rapallo as a great victory of the Leninist policy of peaceful coexistence with states of divergent social systems.

Vehviläinen, Olli. **Kansallissosialistinen Saksa ja Neuvostoliitto 1933-34, Hitlerin valtaantulosta Baltian pöytäkirjaa koskevien neuvottelujen raukeamiseen.** Helsinki: Söderström, 1966, 281 p.
   A Finnish study of the Baltic question in German-Soviet relations from 1933 to 1934.

Volkov, Fedor Dmitrievich. **SSSR—Angliia 1929-1945 gg.** Moscow: Izd-vo "Mezhdunarodnye Otnosheniia," 1964, 558 p.
   A survey of Anglo-Soviet relations before and during World War II, claiming to reveal the "aggressive character of English imperialism."

Weingartner, Thomas. **Stalin und der Aufstieg Hitlers.** Berlin: De Gruyter, 1970, 302 p.
   A valuable study of Soviet and Comintern policy toward Germany during the crucial years from 1929 to 1934.

Wolfe, Thomas W. **Soviet Power and Europe, 1945-1970.** Baltimore: Johns Hopkins Press, 1970, 534 p.
   A detailed and well-documented examination of Soviet policies toward Europe since World War II, with emphasis on military and strategic matters.

Relations with China

See also The Postwar World, p. 178; (Europe) General Surveys, p. 344; Bulgaria, p. 596; Albania, p. 600; China, p. 683; Vietnam, p. 738; other subsections under the Union of Soviet Socialist Republics.

Akimova, Vera Vladimirovna (Vishniakova). **Two Years in Revolutionary China, 1925-1927.** Cambridge: East Asian Research Center, Harvard University, 1971, 352 p.
   The memoirs of the secretary of the Soviet military advisory group in China from 1925 to 1927. The Russian original appeared as "Dva goda v vosstavshem Kitae, 1925-1927" (Moscow: "Nauka," 1965, 389 p.).

Baby, Jean. **La Grande controverse sino-soviétique: 1956–1966.** Paris: Grasset, 1966, 444 p.
   A skillful presentation of the Chinese side of the argument concerning the Sino-Soviet controversy in the decade from 1956 to 1966.

Borisov, Oleg Borisovich and Koloskov, Boris Trofimovich. **Sovetsko-kitaiskie otnoshenii, 1945–1970: kratkii ocherk.** Moscow: Izd-vo "Mysl'," 1971, 479 p.
   A lengthy and detailed analysis of Soviet relations with China since 1945 and a forceful critique of the ambitions of Maoism.

Borodin, Boris Aleksandrovich. **Pomoshch' SSSR kitaiskomu narodu v antiiaponskoi voine, 1937–1941.** Moscow: Izd-vo "Mysl'," 1965, 198 p.
   This historical study of the assistance given by the Soviet Union to Chiang Kai-shek in his fight against Japan after the formation of a "united front" in 1937 sheds light on a previously unexamined period in Sino-Soviet relations.

Bromke, Adam, *ed.* **The Communist States at the Crossroads: Between Moscow and Peking.** New York: Praeger, 1965, 270 p.
   A collection of papers dealing with the impact of the Sino-Soviet rift on the Communist world. Treatment is chiefly by individual country.

Chêng, Chu-yüan. **Economic Relations between Peking and Moscow, 1949–63.** New York: Praeger (for the Institute for Sino-Soviet Studies, George Washington University), 1964, 119 p.
   A well-documented study of Soviet economic pressure on Communist China.

Cherepanov, Aleksandr Ivanovich. **Severnyi pokhod Natsional'no-revoliutsionnoi armii Kitaia: Zapiski voennogo sovetnika.** Moscow: "Nauka," 1968, 303 p.
——. **Zapiski voennogo sovetnika v Kitae (1926–1927).** Moscow: "Nauka," 2d rev. and enl. ed., 1971, 311 p.
   Memoirs by a Soviet military advisor to Sun Yat-sen's government in the 1920s. The first volume has appeared in English as "Notes of a Military Advisor in China" (Taipei: Office of Military History, 1970, 381 p.).

Chin, Shen-pao. **1917–1927 nien chih Chung-Su kuan-hsi.** Taipei: Chia-hsin Shui-ni Kung-ssu, 1966, 187 p.
   A study of Sino-Soviet relations from 1917 to 1927, based on Chinese and Western sources.

Clemens, Walter C., Jr. **The Arms Race and Sino-Soviet Relations.** Stanford: Hoover Institution on War, Revolution, and Peace, 1968, 335 p.
   An examination of the possible relationship between the issue of nuclear arms control and the crisis in Sino-Soviet relations.

Clubb, O. Edmund. **China and Russia: The "Great Game."** New York: Columbia University Press, 1971, 578 p.
   A sweepingly panoramic view of the 800-year history of Sino-Soviet relations. The author suggests that while sources of conflict will continue to bedevil both giant neighbors, the odds, after Mao's passing, are in favor of China's coöperation with the United States.

Crankshaw, Edward. **The New Cold War: Moscow v. Pekin.** Baltimore: Penguin, 1963, 167 p.
   The *Observer*'s correspondent on Soviet affairs, formerly attached to the British Military Mission in Moscow, uses Soviet and Chinese press sources and Communist Party policy documents to trace the development of the Sino-Soviet rift.

Dapčević-Oreščanin, Sonja. **Sovjetsko-kineski spor i problemi razvoja socializma.** Belgrade: Institut za medjunarodnu politiku i privredu, 1963, 219 p.
   A well-documented Jugoslav analysis of the Sino-Soviet conflict.

Fejtö, François. **Chine—URSS: la fin d'une hégémonie.** Paris: Plon, 1964–66, 2 v.
   A Hungarian-born commentator on East European affairs describes the Sino-Soviet rift from 1950 to 1966, with extensive documentary annexes.

Floyd, David. **Mao against Khrushchev: A Short History of the Sino-Soviet Conflict.** New York: Praeger, 1964, 456 p.
   Mr. Floyd, a specialist on communist affairs for the London *Daily Telegraph*, skillfully traces the developing conflict between the Russian and Chinese communists from the death of Stalin to the open polemics of mid-1963. Of particular value are the chronology and selected documentation that comprise about half the book.

Garthoff, Raymond Leonard, *ed.* **Sino-Soviet Military Relations.** New York: Praeger, 1966, 285 p.
   A collection of studies on the politico-military features of Sino-Soviet relations from 1917 up to the present. The concluding chapter contemplates some of the factors that might be involved in an open armed conflict between the two states.

Gittings, John. **Survey of the Sino-Soviet Dispute: A Commentary and Extracts from the Recent Polemics, 1963-1967.** New York: Oxford University Press (for the Royal Institute of International Affairs), 1968, 410 p.
   A useful selection of some 138 Soviet and Chinese documents.

Griffith, William E. **The Sino-Soviet Rift.** Cambridge: M.I.T. Press, 1964, 508 p.
——. **Sino-Soviet Relations, 1964-1965: Analyzed and Documented.** Cambridge: M.I.T. Press, 1967, 504 p.
   A professor of political science at M.I.T. surveys in these two volumes Sino-Soviet relations from 1962 through 1965.

Halperin, Morton H., *ed.* **Sino-Soviet Relations and Arms Control.** Cambridge: M.I.T. Press, 1967, 342 p.
   A collection of papers designed to "elucidate the impact of the Sino-Soviet dispute on prospects for arms control and disarmament." Prepared under the auspices of the Center for International Affairs and the East Asian Research Center, Harvard University.

Iurkov, S. G. **Pekin: novaia politika?** Moscow: Izd-vo Politicheskoi Literatury, 1972, 270 p.
   A Soviet attempt to gain insight into Peking's domestic and foreign policies and to discredit Mao's China in the eyes of the Soviet public and the world at large.

Kartunova, Anastasiia Ivanovna. **V. K. Bliukher v Kitae, 1924-1927 gg.** Moscow: "Nauka," 1970, 185 p.
   Documents and commentaries concerning the activities of the Soviet Marshal Bliukher in China in the 1920s.

Klein, Sidney. **The Road Divides: Economic Aspects of the Sino-Soviet Dispute.** Hong Kong: International Studies Group, 1966, 178 p.
   This useful analysis by a professor at Rutgers University includes detailed statistics on trade, technical assistance and aid. The author is convinced that the Sino-Soviet estrangement will continue well into the 1970s.

Labedz, Leopold and Urban, G. R., *eds.* **The Sino-Soviet Conflict.** Chester Springs (Pennsylvania): Dufour, 1965, 192 p.
   Eleven round-table discussions commissioned by Radio Free Europe containing commentaries and analytical reflections on various manifestations of the Sino-Soviet rivalry.

Lévesque, Jacques. **Le Conflit sino-soviétique et l'Europe de l'Est.** Montreal: Presses de l'Université de Montréal, 1970, 387 p.
   A serious analysis of the impact of the Sino-Soviet conflict upon Soviet relations with the East European states, more particularly Poland and Rumania.

Mehnert, Klaus. **Peking and Moscow.** New York: Putnam, 1963, 522 p.
   An analysis of the cultural, historical and ideological differences between China and the U.S.S.R., together with clarification of their significance to the West. The German original appeared as "Peking und Moskau" (Stuttgart: Deutsche Verlags-Anstalt, 1962, 605 p.).

Méray, Tibor. **Politik ohne Gnade.** Zurich: Schweizer Verlagshaus, 1965, 476 p.
   A history of recent Soviet-Chinese relations, by a Hungarian writer who covered the Korean War from the communist side but left Hungary after the 1956 Revolution.

The Polemic on the General Line of the International Communist Movement. Peking: Foreign Languages Press, 1965, 585 p.
   An official Chinese collection of documents illustrating the dispute between the Chinese and Soviet Communist parties.

Pommerening, Horst. **Der chinesisch-sowjetische Grenzkonflikt: das Erbe der ungleichen Verträge.** Olten: Walter, 1968, 266 p.
   A history of Tsarist expansion in Central Asia, Siberia and the Far East, and a study of Russian-Chinese relations. The author, a German scholar who has lived in the Far East and had been associated with the Center for International Affairs at Harvard

University, has supplemented his well-researched monograph with maps and an extensive bibliography.

Quaroni, Pietro. **Russia e Cina.** Milan: Garzanti, 1967, 329 p.
An Italian diplomat examines the historical and ideological causes of the Sino-Soviet split.

Reuther, Helmut, *ed.* **Moskau—Peking.** Olten: Walter-Verlag, 1965, 152 p.
A collection of 18 papers presented at an international seminar. Emphasis is on the Moscow-Peking rift, its causes and effects. Short biographical sketches of the authors permit some judgment on their qualifications and on their point of view.

Salisbury, Harrison Evans. **War between Russia and China.** New York: Norton, 1969, 224 p.
The author, for many years a leading writer for *The New York Times*, analyzes the causes of the Sino-Soviet differences (which, he believes, may well lead to war) and suggests how the United States can influence—and will be influenced by—the struggle.

Saran, Vimla. **Sino-Soviet Schism: A Bibliography, 1956–1964.** New York: Asia Publishing House, 1971, 162 p.
This useful bibliography of both communist and non-communist literature that has appeared in English was issued under the auspices of the School of International Studies, Jawaharlal Nehru University.

Schatten, Fritz. **Der Konflikt Moskau-Peking.** Munich: Piper, 1963, 212 p.
A documentary analysis of the Moscow-Peking ideological schism during the period from April 1960 to August 1963, with a very useful introduction on the background to these events by the author, a writer for *Neue Zürcher Zeitung*.

Schwartz, Harry. **Tsars, Mandarins, and Commissars: A History of Chinese-Russian Relations.** Philadelphia: Lippincott, 1964, 252 p.
This survey by Mr. Schwartz, a Soviet specialist for *The New York Times*, is concerned with the background and causes for the Sino-Soviet schism.

Sladkovskii, M. I., *ed.* **Leninskaia politika SSSR v otnoshenii Kitaia.** Moscow: Izd-vo "Nauka," 1968, 257 p.
A collection of articles justifying Moscow's policies toward China since the 1920s.

Tasca, Carlo. **Origini e storia del dissidio cino-sovietico.** Rome: Edizioni Cinque Lune, 1965, 200 p.
According to this interpretive essay, the essence of the Sino-Soviet split lies in China's appetite for Russia's sparsely populated territory.

Zablocki, Clement J., *ed.* **Sino-Soviet Rivalry: Implications for U.S. Policy.** New York: Praeger (for the Center for Strategic Studies, Georgetown University), 1966, 242 p.
A collection of articles, based on a series of hearings on the Sino-Soviet conflict before the House Foreign Affairs Subcommittee on the Far East and Pacific.

Zagoria, Donald S. **The Sino-Soviet Conflict, 1956–1961.** New York: Atheneum, 1964, 484 p.
A standard work on Sino-Soviet relations by a leading scholar.

Relations with Other Countries

See also General Works, p. 1; Political Factors, p. 12; International Law, p. 83; International Organization and Government, p. 96; War and Peace, p. 108; The World Since 1914, p. 129; other subsections under the Union of Soviet Socialist Republics and the sections for specific countries and regions.

Clissold, Stephen, *ed.* **Soviet Relations with Latin America 1918–1968: A Documentary Survey.** New York: Oxford University Press (for the Royal Institute of International Affairs), 1970, 313 p.
A useful volume of Soviet, Comintern and Latin American documents, with explanatory notes and an extended introduction.

Cohn, Helen Desfosses. **Soviet Policy toward Black Africa: The Focus on National Integration.** New York: Praeger, 1972, 316 p.
Theory and practice during the 1960s, from Khrushchev's adventures in the Congo to the more cautious policies of Brezhnev.

Duncan, W. Raymond, *ed.* **Soviet Policy in Developing Countries.** Waltham (Mass.): Ginn-Blaisdell, 1970, 350 p.
Thirteen essays by various hands on Soviet strategies, policies and quandries in the Third World.

Genelin, Rafail Sholomovich. **Rossiia i SShA, 1914-1917 gg.: ocherki istorii russko-amerikanskikh otnoshenii.** Leningrad: Izd-vo "Nauka," 1969, 417 p.
An academic study of the economic and political relations between the United States and Russia during the years 1914-1917. The author pays particular attention to the interests of American corporations and financial institutions doing business in Russia.

Gvishiani, Liudmila Alekseevna. **Sovetskaia Rossiia i SShA (1917-1920).** Moscow: Izd-vo "Mezhdunarodnye Otnosheniia," 1970, 327 p.
A presentation of U.S.-Soviet relations in the period immediately following the Bolshevik Revolution, with a routine interpretation that does not match the rich sources cited. The author, a prominent Soviet expert on American affairs, is the daughter of Soviet Premier Aleksei Kosygin.

Hoetzsch, Otto. **Russland in Asien: Geschichte einer Expansion.** Stuttgart: Deutsche Verlags-Anstalt, 1966, 176 p.
A history of Russian expansion in Asia by a leading German student of East European history who died in 1946. Though the volume deals primarily with nineteenth-century developments, it contributes greatly to a better understanding of present-day relations between Russia and various Asiatic countries, especially China.

Kapur, Harish. **Soviet Russia and Asia 1917-1927: A Study of Soviet Policy towards Turkey, Iran, and Afghanistan.** Geneva: Université de Genève, 1965, 265 p.
A well-documented study which concludes that "the Bolsheviks saw in their policy in Asia an essential unity of the two basic objectives—the objective of safeguarding the security of the Soviet State and the objective of world revolution."

Kheifets, Aleksandr Naumovich. **Sovetskaia diplomatiia i narody Vostoka, 1921-1927.** Moscow: Izd-vo "Nauka," 1968, 327 p.
A diplomatic history of initial Soviet contacts with the nations of Asia, including a discussion of the events that lead up to the Sino-Soviet agreement of May 31, 1924.

Kheifets, Aleksandr Naumovich. **Sovetskaia Rossiia i sopredel'nye strany vostoka v gody Grazhdanskoi Voiny (1918-1920).** Moscow: Izd-vo "Nauka," 1964, 470 p.
The author suggests that from the very outset Soviet foreign policy emphasized peaceful coexistence, specifically with states bordering Russia in Asia.

Laqueur, Walter Ze'ev. **The Struggle for the Middle East: The Soviet Union in the Mediterranean, 1958-1968.** New York: Macmillan, 1969, 360 p.
This study by a perceptive student of both Soviet and Middle Eastern affairs is essentially a continuation of the author's "The Soviet Union and the Middle East," published in 1959. Written under the auspices of the Center for Strategic and International Studies, Georgetown University.

Legvold, Robert. **Soviet Policy in West Africa.** Cambridge: Harvard University Press, 1970, 372 p.
A study of Soviet interest in and policy toward Guinea, Ghana, the Ivory Coast, Mali, Nigeria and Senegal in the years from 1957 to 1968.

Lenin, Vladimir Il'ich. **Lenin on the United States: Selected Writings.** New York: International Publishers, 1970, 674 p.
These writings, compiled from Lenin's "Collected Works," are useful for understanding "the place the United States held in his thinking at various times."

Lensen, George Alexander. **Russian Diplomatic and Consular Officials in East Asia: A Handbook of the Representatives of Tsarist Russia and the Provisional Government in China, Japan and Korea from 1858 to 1924 and of Soviet Representatives in Japan from 1925 to 1968.** Tokyo: Sophia University (in coöperation with the Diplomatic Press, Tallahassee), 1968, 294 p.
A useful reference.

McLane, Charles Bancroft. **Soviet Strategies in Southeast Asia: An Exploration of Eastern Policy under Lenin and Stalin.** Princeton: Princeton University Press, 1966, 563 p.
A Dartmouth College professor, whose sources include unpublished documents and interviews, identifies and interprets the origins of Russia's shift in attention to the

emerging nations of the East. Short biographies of important personalities and chronologies are appended.

Morison, David L. **The U.S.S.R. and Africa.** New York: Oxford University Press (for the Institute of Race Relations and the Central Asian Research Centre), 1964, 124 p.
An analysis of Soviet aims in and attitudes toward Africa; an appendix quotes or paraphrases Soviet views on each African country.

Naik, J. A. **Soviet Policy towards India: From Stalin to Brezhnev.** Delhi: Vikas Publications, 1970, 201 p.
An Indian scholar's analysis of the course of Soviet policy toward his country, chiefly in the last three decades.

Nollau, Günther and Wiehe, Hans Jürgen. **Russia's South Flank.** New York: Praeger, 1963, 171 p.
A somewhat sketchy appraisal of the "Soviet threat to Iran, Turkey, and Afghanistan," based in part on the authors' travels to these areas.

Oswald, J. Gregory and Strover, Anthony J., eds. **The Soviet Union and Latin America.** New York: Praeger, 1970, 190 p.
Papers originally presented at an international symposium at the Institute for the Study of the U.S.S.R. in Munich, Germany, on May 20 and 21, 1968.

Segesvary, Victor. **Le Réalisme khrouchtchévien.** Neuchâtel: La Baconnière, 1968, 253 p.
An extensive study of Soviet policy vis-à-vis the Arab states of the Middle East and of the Soviet entry into that region of international conflict during the Khrushchev era.

Ulianovskii, Rastislav Aleksandrovich and Others, eds. **Komintern i Vostok: bor'ba za leninskuiu strategiiu i taktiku v natsional'no-osvoboditel'nom dvizhenii.** Moscow: Izd-vo "Nauka," 1969, 513 p.
A collection of essays on Comintern activities in Asia and the contemporary Soviet policies toward the Third World.

Vel'tov, Nikolai. **Uspekhi sotsializma v SSSR i ikh vliianie na SShA.** Moscow: Izd-vo "Mezhdunarodnye Otnosheniia," 1971, 216 p.
The author tries to describe how 50 years of Soviet power have influenced economic and political developments in the United States.

Foreign Economic Policy

See also International Trade, p. 55; International Finance, p. 59; Raw Materials; Oil; Energy, p. 70; Economic Aid and Technical Assistance, p. 81; East-West Relations, p. 180; Eastern Europe and the Soviet Bloc, p. 358; (Union of Soviet Socialist Republics) Foreign Policy, p. 550; and the sections for specific countries and regions.

Biskup, Reinhold. **Sowjetpolitik und Entwicklungsländer.** Freiburg im Breisgau: Rombach, 1970, 212 p.
An unfriendly view of Soviet ideology and strategy with respect to developing countries.

Carter, James Richard. **The Net Cost of Soviet Foreign Aid.** New York: Praeger, 1971, 134 p.
According to the author, the purpose of this well-documented study "is to examine some aspects of the reciprocal relationship that exists between the Soviet economic aid program and the volume of Soviet foreign trade" in the period from 1955 through 1968.

Freedman, Robert Owen. **Economic Warfare in the Communist Bloc: A Study of Soviet Economic Pressure against Yugoslavia, Albania, and Communist China.** New York: Praeger, 1970, 192 p.
The author states that "the major conclusion to be drawn from this study is that the Soviet leadership has gradually become more sophisticated in its use of economic pressure since 1948."

Giffen, James Henry. **The Legal and Practical Aspects of Trade with the Soviet Union.** New York: Praeger, rev. ed., 1971, 366 p.
An effort to "eliminate some of the misunderstanding which has too long shrouded U.S.-Soviet trade transactions by examining such transactions in detail."

Goldman, Marshall Irwin. **Soviet Foreign Aid.** New York: Praeger, 1967, 265 p.
Two chapters on the aid element in Soviet economic relations with other communist countries are followed by detailed examinations of Soviet aid to the U.A.R., India, Afghanistan and Indonesia and shorter accounts of Russian and Chinese activities in other less developed countries.

Jacobson, Harold Karan. **The USSR and the UN's Economic and Social Activities.** Notre Dame: University of Notre Dame Press, 1963, 309 p.
"This study," in the words of the author, "is an analysis of the Soviet Union's policies with respect to the economic and social activities of the United Nations, the reactions of other states to these policies, and the impact of the resulting interaction on the UN's institutions and functions."

Kumykin, P. N. and Others, *eds.* **50 let sovetskoi vneshnei torgovli.** Moscow: Izd-vo "Mezhdunarodnye Otnosheniia," 1967, 319 p.
An official history of Soviet foreign trade, with an introductory chapter by Minister of Foreign Trade N. S. Patolichev.

Pozdniakov, Vladimir Sergeevich. **Gosudarstvennaia monopoliia vneshnei torgovli v SSSR.** Moscow: Izd-vo "Mezhdunarodnye Otnosheniia," 1969, 199 p.
A concise description of the origins, structure and rationale of the Soviet foreign trade apparatus.

Shishkin, Valerii Aleksandrovich. **Sovetskoe gosudarstvo i strany zapada v 1917-1923 gg.: ocherki istorii stanovleniia ekonomicheskikh otnoshenii.** Leningrad: Izd-vo "Nauka," 1969, 440 p.
A serious treatise on the establishment of economic relations between Soviet Russia and the Western powers in the early 1920s.

Sladkovskii, M. I. **History of Economic Relations between Russia and China.** New York: Daniel Davey, 1967, 299 p.
A translation of a study originally published in Russian as "Ocherki ekonomicheskikh otnoshenii SSSR s Kitaem" (Moscow: Vneshtorgizdat, 1957, 454 p.). In spite of the fact that the monograph was written to prove the thesis "that the development of economic ties between the Soviet Union and China is the logical outcome of a centuries-old friendship," it is a work of considerable scholarship. The English edition was prepared in Jerusalem under the sponsorship of Israel Program for Scientific Translations.

Vneshniaia torgovlia SSSR: statisticheskii sbornik, 1918-1966. Moscow: Izd-vo "Mezhdunarodnye Otnosheniia" (for the Ministerstvo Vneshnei Torgovli, Plannovo-Ekonomicheskoe Upravlenie), 1967, 241 p.
A useful statistical guide to Soviet foreign trade, with breakdowns by period, trading partner and commodity. An appendix surveys Tsarist Russia's foreign trade in 1913.

Zenz, Gisela. **Sowjetische Entwicklungshilfe: Organisation und Vertragsrecht.** Cologne: Verlag Wissenschaft und Politik, 1970, 125 p.
A legal study of Soviet technical and economic assistance activities.

Military Policy

See also War and Peace, p. 108; Second World War, p. 144; The Postwar World, p. 178; (The United States) Military and Defense Policy, p. 257; Eastern Europe and the Soviet Bloc, p. 358; other subsections under the Union of Soviet Socialist Republics and the sections for specific countries.

Andolenko, Serge. **Histoire de l'armée russe.** Paris: Flammarion, 1967, 477 p.
A general survey of the Russian army since the time of Peter the Great. The last fifty pages deal with the Soviet period.

Bloomfield, Lincoln Palmer and Others. **Khrushchev and the Arms Race.** Cambridge: M.I.T. Press, 1966, 338 p.
This study from the Arms Control Project at M.I.T. comprises an analysis of the Soviet interests, motivations and outlook on questions of disarmament and arms control during the "Khrushchev decade."

Breyer, Siegfried. **Die Seerüstung der Sowjetunion.** Munich: Lehmann, 1964, 269 p.
A reference manual on the Soviet Navy.

Chernenko, K. U. and Savinkin, N. I., *eds.* **KPSS o vooruzhennykh silakh Sovetskogo Soiuza: dokumenty 1917-1968.** Moscow: Voennoe Izd-vo, 1969, 471 p.
A collection of official documents and decrees on the relations between the Communist Party and the Soviet military since 1917.

Dallin, Alexander and Others. **The Soviet Union and Disarmament.** New York: Praeger (for the School of International Affairs, Columbia University), 1964, 282 p.
A report based on working papers and discussions of a group of scholars and specialists and dealing with the attitudes and possible intentions of the U.S.S.R. in the question of disarmament and arms control.

Eller, Ernest McNeill. **The Soviet Sea Challenge.** Chicago: Cowles, 1971, 315 p.
The author describes the rapid growth of the Soviet sea power and argues that the United States should maintain and modernize its own forces to meet the Soviet challenge.

Fairhall, David. **Russian Sea Power.** Boston: Gambit, 1971, 286 p.
An able and broadly conceived study of Soviet maritime power and prospects— mercantile as well as naval—by the defense correspondent of *The Guardian*.

Garder, Michel. **A History of the Soviet Army.** New York: Praeger, 1966, 226 p.
A thorough study of the Soviet military system from the October Revolution to the fall of Khrushchev, by a Russian-born French military expert. A revised and updated version of "Histoire de l'armée soviétique" (Paris: Plon, 1959, 308 p.).

Garthoff, Raymond Leonard. **Soviet Military Policy: A Historical Analysis.** New York: Praeger, 1966, 276 p.
A leading student of Soviet military affairs here traces the continuities and discontinuities in Russian and Soviet military policy. The volume includes some comparative information on Communist China.

Gasteyger, Curt, *ed.* **Strategie und Abrüstungspolitik der Sowjetunion: ausgewählte sowjetische Studien und Reden.** Frankfurt/Main: Metzner (for the Deutsche Gesellschaft für Auswärtige Politik), 1964, 346 p.
A collection of Soviet speeches and writings on disarmament. The editor has provided a fine introduction and a helpful bibliography.

Herrick, Robert Waring. **Soviet Naval Strategy: Fifty Years of Theory and Practice.** Annapolis: United States Naval Institute, 1968, 197 p.
A detailed analysis of the evolution of Soviet naval strategy. The author's conclusions concerning the Soviet Navy's strategic role have been the occasion for some debate in U.S. Navy circles.

Höpker, Wolfgang. **Weltmacht zur See: die Sowjetunion auf allen Meeren.** Stuttgart: Seewald, 1971, 211 p.
A German journalist's alarmed view of the expansion and implications of Soviet sea power.

Horelick, Arnold Lawrence and Rush, Myron. **Strategic Power and Soviet Foreign Policy.** Chicago: University of Chicago Press, 1966, 225 p.
A knowledgeable analysis of the interrelation of Soviet strategic military power and foreign policy in the "years since the advent of nuclear weapons made strategic power seem too destructive to employ militarily and yet too dangerous to ignore in political calculations."

Jacobs, Walter Darnell. **Frunze: The Soviet Clausewitz, 1885-1925.** The Hague: Nijhoff, 1969, 235 p.
An analysis of Frunze's role in developing a military doctrine for the Red Army.

Joshua, Wynfred and Gilbert, Stephen P. **Arms for the Third World: Soviet Military Aid Diplomacy.** Baltimore: Johns Hopkins Press, 1969, 169 p.
A study of military aid as a component of contemporary Soviet foreign policy in the Middle East, Africa, Asia and Latin America.

Kintner, William Roscoe and Scott, Harriet Fast, *eds.* **The Nuclear Revolution in Soviet Military Affairs.** Norman: University of Oklahoma Press, 1968, 420 p.
Translations of articles by Soviet specialists reflecting the important developments in military strategy and concepts since Khrushchev.

Korablev, Iurii Ivanovich. **V. I. Lenin i sozdanie Krasnoi Armii.** Moscow: Izd-vo "Nauka," 1970, 462 p.

A detailed historical analysis of Lenin's decisions on military policy and the organization of the Red Army during the Russian Civil War.

Larson, Thomas B. **Disarmament and Soviet Policy, 1964–1968.** Englewood Cliffs: Prentice-Hall, 1969, 280 p.

This study of Soviet attitudes toward disarmament since Khrushchev is designed as a sequel to Alexander Dallin's "The Soviet Union and Disarmament" (1964).

Lewytzkyj, Borys. **Die Marschälle und die Politik: eine Untersuchung über den Stellenwert des Militärs innerhalb des sowjetischen Systems seit dem Sturz Chruschtschews.** Cologne: Markus-Verlag, 1971, 196 p.

In this study of the role of the military in Soviet political decisions the main argument is that they are less a pressure group than an integral part of the policy structure.

Lototskii, S. S. and Others. **The Soviet Army.** Moscow: Progress Publishers, 1971, 350 p.

A concise history of the Soviet Army crediting military successes predictably to the strengths of a socialist society. The original appeared as "Armiia sovetskaia" (Moscow: Izd-vo Politicheskoi Literatury, 1969, 445 p.).

Mackintosh, Malcolm. **Juggernaut: A History of the Soviet Armed Forces.** New York: Macmillan, 1967, 320 p.

A brief history, from the formation of the Red Army to the present, much of it dealing with campaigns in the Second World War.

O'Ballance, Edgar. **The Red Army.** New York: Praeger, 1964, 237 p.

A concise, though somewhat uneven history and appraisal of the Soviet armed forces, by a British officer and military author.

Ra'anan, Uri. **The USSR Arms the Third World.** Cambridge: M.I.T. Press, 1969, 256 p.

Two carefully researched case studies: the 1955 Soviet arms deal with Egypt, and the military relationship between the U.S.S.R. and Indonesia from 1956 to 1960.

Ritter, Gerhard. **Das Kommunemodell und die Begründung der Roten Armee im Jahre 1918.** Wiesbaden: Harrassowitz (for the Osteuropa-Institut an der Freien Universität Berlin), 1965, 262 p.

A discussion of the theoretical concepts of Marx, Engels and Lenin that influenced to a certain degree the formation of the Red Army in 1918.

Sokolovskii, Vasilii Danilovich, *ed*. **Military Strategy: Soviet Doctrine and Concepts.** New York: Praeger, 1963, 396 p.

———. **Soviet Military Strategy.** Englewood Cliffs: Prentice-Hall, 1963, 544 p.

Two translations of an authoritative work on contemporary Soviet military thought and doctrine, prepared by 15 Soviet specialists and theoreticians. The first has an introduction by Raymond L. Garthoff. The second, a RAND Corporation Research Study, has an analytical introduction, annotations and supplementary material by Herbert S. Dinerstein, Leon Gouré and Thomas W. Wolfe. The Russian original appeared as "Voennaia strategiia" (Moscow: Voennoe Izd-vo, 1962, 457 p.).

Wolfe, Thomas W. **Soviet Strategy at the Crossroads.** Cambridge: Harvard University Press, 1964, 342 p.

An able, informed and well-balanced discussion, by a staff member of the RAND Corporation, of developments and debates in Soviet military policy and strategy, chiefly since the 1962 Cuban crisis.

Woodward, David. **The Russians at Sea: A History of the Russian Navy.** New York: Praeger, 1966, 254 p.

A history of the Russian Navy since Peter the Great that concentrates on naval battles.

Zakharov, Matvei Vasil'evich and Others, *eds*. **50 let vooruzhennykh sil SSSR.** Moscow: Voennoe Izd-vo, 1968, 583 p.

A history of the Soviet armed forces, published on the fiftieth anniversary of their founding. Great achievements gain great attention here, but the decimation of the Soviet high command during the Stalinist purges merits exactly three sentences.

Space Problems

See also Aerial and Space Warfare and Technology, p. 114.

Daniloff, Nicholas. **The Kremlin and the Cosmos.** New York: Knopf, 1972, 258 p.

A journalist's account of the development of the Russian space program.

Sheldon, Charles S., II. **Review of the Soviet Space Program.** New York: McGraw-Hill, 1968, 152 p.
A useful reference book, including comparative data for the U.S. programs.

Stoiko, Michael. **Soviet Rocketry: Past, Present, and Future.** New York: Holt, Rinehart and Winston, 1970, 272 p.
A very thorough analysis of the Soviet space program, including valuable comparisons with the American experience.

Government; Constitution; Law

See also Comparative Government, p. 18; Political Processes, p. 20; Communism, p. 26; (International Law) General, p. 83; Maritime, Air, Space and Environmental Law, p. 90; International Court of Justice, p. 93; Eastern Europe and the Soviet Bloc, p. 358; other subsections under the Union of Soviet Socialist Republics.

Armstrong, John Alexander. **Ideology, Politics, and Government in the Soviet Union: An Introduction.** New York: Praeger, rev. ed., 1967, 173 p.
An extensively revised edition of a concise survey of the Soviet political system.

Azrael, Jeremy R. **Managerial Power and Soviet Politics.** Cambridge: Harvard University Press, 1966, 258 p.
A stimulating inquiry into the role of Soviet managers in the policy-making process and in becoming spokesmen for a "new class" within the society. A volume in Harvard's "Russian Research Center Studies."

Barghoorn, Frederick Charles. **Politics in the USSR: A Country Study.** Boston: Little, Brown, 1966, 418 p.
A study of the Soviet state in its relations with Soviet society, by a well-known professor at Yale University. Written for "The Little, Brown Series in Comparative Politics," the purpose of which is to meet the needs of teachers in their introductory course offerings.

Berman, Harold Joseph and Quigley, John B., Jr., *eds*. **Basic Laws on the Structure of the Soviet State.** Cambridge: Harvard University Press, 1969, 325 p.
A useful collection of laws and decrees relating to the legislative, administrative and judicial aspects of the Soviet state.

Berman, Harold Joseph and Maggs, Peter B. **Disarmament Inspection under Soviet Law.** Dobbs Ferry (N.Y.): Oceana Publications, 1967, 154 p.
An analysis of Soviet law with respect to its relevance, as a channel for, or an obstacle to, disarmament inspection.

Berman, Harold Joseph. **Soviet Criminal Law and Procedure: The RSFSR Codes.** Cambridge: Harvard University Press, 1966, 501 p.
A translation of the 1960 codes of criminal law and procedure in the largest of the Soviet Republics, as amended to 1965, with an extended introduction by a leading American student of Soviet law.

Brzezinski, Zbigniew Kazimierz, *ed*. **Dilemmas of Change in Soviet Politics.** New York: Columbia University Press, 1969, 163 p.
Essays and debate on the nature, reality and possible direction of political change in the Soviet Union, originally appearing in the journal *Problems of Communism*.

Butler, William E. **The Law of Soviet Territorial Waters: A Case Study of Maritime Legislation and Practice.** New York: Praeger, 1968, 192 p.
An analysis of the Soviet regime of territorial waters.

Chkhikvadze, Viktor Mikhailovich. **Gosudarstvo, demokratiia, zakonnost'.** Moscow: Izd-vo "Iuridicheskaia Literatura," 1967, 503 p.
A general treatise on concepts of legality and authority under the Soviet system, by a leading Soviet legal scholar.

Churchward, L. G. **Contemporary Soviet Government.** New York: American Elsevier Publishing Co., 1968, 366 p.
A textbook on the Soviet political system since the death of Stalin. The author, an Australian scholar, pays particular attention to political and legal theory.

Conquest, Robert, *ed.* **Justice and the Legal System in the U.S.S.R.** New York: Praeger, 1968, 152 p.
──. **The Soviet Police System.** New York: Praeger, 1968, 103 p.
──. **The Soviet Political System.** New York: Praeger, 1968, 144 p.
  Brief but useful surveys, prepared by a well-informed British scholar.
Fainsod, Merle. **How Russia Is Ruled.** Cambridge: Harvard University Press, rev. ed., 1963, 684 p.
  This revised edition of an excellent work on the Soviet government takes account of developments since the appearance of the first edition in 1953.
Feifer, George. **Justice in Moscow.** New York: Simon and Schuster, 1964, 353 p.
  An American student's interesting first-hand account of the operations of the court system in Moscow, based on his attendance of numerous trials and legal proceedings.
Gečys, Kazys. **Two Worlds.** New York: Fordham University, Institute of Contemporary Russian Studies, 1964, 414 p.
  A study of communist theory of government and a demonstration of how Soviet political institutions and social organizations actually perform, by a professor at Fordham University.
Grottian, Walter. **Das sowjetische Regierungssystem: die Grundlagen der Macht der kommunistischen Parteiführung.** Cologne: Westdeutscher Verlag, 2d rev. ed., 1965, 586 p.
  A survey, with extensive documentation, of the Soviet system of government. This is a completely revised edition of the 1956 original publication.
Juviler, Peter Henry and Morton, Henry Walter, *eds.* **Soviet Policy-Making: Studies of Communism in Transition.** New York: Praeger, 1967, 274 p.
  A symposium dealing with influences on the Soviet political process.
Kositsyn, Aleksandr Pavlovich. **Sotsialisticheskoe gosudarstvo: zakonomernosti, vozniknoveniia, i razvitiia.** Moscow: Izd-vo "Iuridicheskaia Literatura," 1970, 415 p.
  A study of the origins and role of the state apparatus under socialism, with an outline of the presumed evolution toward a "self-directed" communist society.
Kulichenko, M. I. and Others, *eds.* **Mnogonatsional'noe sovetskoe gosudarstvo.** Moscow: Izd-vo Politicheskoi Literatury, 1972, 430 p.
  A lengthy definition of the political and ethnic character of the U.S.S.R.
LaFave, Wayne R., *ed.* **Law in the Soviet Society.** Urbana: University of Illinois Press, 1965, 297 p.
  A symposium on various features of Soviet law.
Lapenna, Ivo. **State and Law: Soviet and Yugoslav Theory.** New Haven: Yale University Press, 1964, 135 p.
  A monograph on Jugoslav and Soviet interpretations of the state and law and the difficulty of reconciling Marxist theory with actual practice.
Maurach, Reinhart and Meissner, Boris, *eds.* **50 Jahre Sowjetrecht.** Stuttgart: Kohlhammer, 1969, 192 p.
  Essays on the evolution of various facets of Soviet public, civil and criminal laws.
Meissner, Boris. **Sowjetunion und Selbstbestimmungsrecht.** Cologne: Verlag Wissenschaft und Politik (for the Seminar für Politik, Gesellschaft und Recht Osteuropas der Universität Kiel), 1962, 463 p.
  A survey of the changing Soviet conceptions of self-determination, with a voluminous documentary appendix.
Meissner, Boris, *ed.* **Sowjetunion und Völkerrecht, 1917 bis 1962.** Cologne: Verlag Wissenschaft und Politik (for the Seminar für Politik, Gesellschaft und Recht Osteuropas der Universität Kiel), 1963, 622 p.
  A massive bibliography of Soviet writings on international law and diplomacy, with a most useful introduction by the editor. The section dealing with the works published from 1917 to 1957 is based on a Soviet bibliography compiled by Professor V. N. Durdenevskii. The period covering the years from 1958 to 1962 was compiled by Alexander Uschakow.
Meyer, Alfred George. **The Soviet Political System: An Interpretation.** New York: Random House, 1965, 494 p.

A serious effort "to present a general picture of the entire Soviet system and to acquaint the student with its most important components, including institutions, practices, processes, and the very vocabulary of Soviet government and politics."

Rush, Myron. **Political Succession in the USSR.** New York: Columbia University Press, 1965, 223 p.
An able effort "to present a theoretical analysis and historical account of the problem of succession in the USSR." While the author had not expected Khrushchev's ouster, he feels that his argument is not weakened by it.

Schapiro, Leonard Bertram. **The Government and Politics of the Soviet Union.** New York: Random House, 1965, 191 p.
A useful and concise introduction by a leading scholar in the field.

Skilling, H. Gordon and Griffiths, Franklyn, *eds*. **Interest Groups in Soviet Politics.** Princeton: Princeton University Press, 1971, 433 p.
Essays by 11 specialists on the role of such interest groups as the *apparatchiki*, the military, the managers, the writers and the jurists.

Wannow, Marianne. **Das Selbstbestimmungsrecht im sowjetischen Völkerrechtsdenken.** Göttingen: Institut für Völkerrecht der Universität Göttingen, 1965, 287 p.
A monograph on Soviet theories of self-determination.

Secret Police; Political Trials; Espionage

See also Communism, p. 26; (Second World War) Special Operations; Propaganda; Espionage; Intelligence, p. 169; Eastern Europe and the Soviet Bloc, p. 358; (France) Recent History, p. 396; Biographies, Memoirs and Addresses, p. 400; Sweden, p. 447; other subsections under the Union of Soviet Socialist Republics.

Andics, Hellmut. **Rule of Terror: Russia under Lenin and Stalin.** New York: Holt, Rinehart and Winston, 1969, 208 p.
An effort to trace the history of terror as an instrument of Soviet policy: ideological origins, the creation of techniques and their application domestically and abroad. The German original appeared as "Der grosse Terror" (Vienna: Molden, 1968, 416 p.).

Bernikow, Louise. **Abel.** New York: Trident Press, 1970, 347 p.
The author attempts to uncover the human being under the mask of the Soviet master spy. On one level, the book is a fascinating spy story; on another, a sophisticated, often quite moving inquiry into the problem of human identity.

Conquest, Robert. **The Great Terror.** Harmondsworth: Penguin, rev. ed., 1971, 830 p.
A major and comprehensive study of Stalin's purges in the 1930s, making use of memoirs and other Soviet material.

Donovan, James Britt. **Strangers on a Bridge: The Case of Colonel Abel.** New York: Atheneum, 1964, 432 p.
The point of view of the defense counsel adds interest to this true spy story. The volume describes some episodes that offer food for thought on the manner of negotiating with the Russians.

Hayward, Max, *ed*. **On Trial: The Soviet State Versus "Abram Tertz" and "Nikolai Arzhak."** New York: Harper and Row, rev. and enl. ed., 1967, 310 p.
A translation, with extensive introduction, of the trial, conviction and sentencing in February 1966 of the Soviet writers Andrei Sinyavsky ("Abram Tertz") and Yuli Daniel ("Nikolai Arzhak").

Katkov, George. **The Trial of Bukharin.** New York: Stein and Day, 1969, 255 p.
A well-known student of Russian history at Oxford University describes the trial of Nikolai Bukharin, a victim of Stalin and one of the leading Bolsheviks during the early years of the Soviet state.

Kolesnikova, Mariia Vasil'evna and Kolesnikov, Mikhail Sergeevich. **Rikhard Zorge.** Moscow: Izd-vo "Molodaia Gvardiia," 1971, 297 p.
A biography of the Soviet master spy Richard Sorge.

Kriegel, Annie. **Les Grands procès dans les systèmes communistes: la pédagogie infernale.** Paris: Gallimard, 1972, 189 p.

Illuminating essays on the phenomenon of purges and terror in the U.S.S.R. and Eastern Europe from the 1930s to the 1960s.

Lewytzkyj, Borys. **The Uses of Terror: The Soviet Secret Police 1917-1970.** New York: Coward, McCann and Geoghegan, 1972, 349 p.
This English translation of a serious history of the Soviet political police carries the story down to mid-1970. The German original was published as "Die rote Inquisition: die Geschichte der sowjetischen Sicherheitsdienste" (Frankfurt: Societäts-Verlag, 2d rev. ed., 1967, 395 p.).

Penkovskii, Oleg Vladimirovich. **The Penkovskiy Papers.** Garden City: Doubleday, 1965, 411 p.
A volume dealing with the remarkable activities of Colonel Oleg Penkovskii, a senior officer in Soviet military intelligence who spied for the West and was sentenced to death in Moscow in 1963.

Poretsky, Elisabeth K. **Our Own People: A Memoir of 'Ignace Reiss' and His Friends.** Ann Arbor: University of Michigan Press, 1970, 278 p.
An absorbing account of Soviet intelligence in the 1920s and 1930s, by the wife of Ignace Reiss, a Polish communist who departed from the NKVD in 1937 and from this life very shortly after.

Scharndorff, Werner. **Moskaus permanente Säuberung.** Munich: Olzog, 1964, 389 p.
A well-documented treatise on political succession in the Soviet Union. The author, an Austrian scholar, emphasizes that the system of the "permanent purge" was instituted by Lenin and not by his successors.

Seth, Ronald. **Unmasked! The Story of Soviet Espionage.** New York: Hawthorn Books, 1965, 306 p.
The author concludes his survey of Soviet espionage activities by saying that "the greatest danger from Soviet spying lies not in the operation of the professional agents, but in the hidden sympathizers who are in positions to pass secrets on." The British edition appeared as "Forty Years of Spying" (London: Cassell, 1965, 294 p.).

Smith, Edward Ellis with Lednicky, Rudolf. **"The Okhrana": The Russian Department of Police; A Bibliography.** Stanford: Hoover Institution on War, Revolution, and Peace, 1967, 280 p.
A bibliography on the Imperial Russian Secret Police, based on the collections in the library and archives of the Hoover Institution. Important for providing information on Okhrana's interest in the revolutionary organizations of Russia both before and during World War I.

Soviet Intelligence and Security Services, 1964-70: A Selected Bibliography of Soviet Publications, with Some Additional Titles from Other Sources. Washington: G.P.O., 1972, 289 p.
A comprehensive bibliography of books and articles, primarily in Russian and in the languages of the Soviet Baltic republics, prepared by the Congressional Research Service of the Library of Congress for the Senate Subcommittee to Investigate the Administration of the Internal Security Act and Other Internal Security Laws.

Tucker, Robert C. and Cohen, Stephen F., eds. **The Great Purge Trial.** New York: Grosset, 1965, 725 p.
The text of the Soviet translation of the 1938 purge trial of Bukharin and others, together with annotations, explanatory notes, and an introductory essay by Professor Tucker.

Forced Labor; Prison Camps

See also Baltic States, p. 455; other subsections under the Union of Soviet Socialist Republics.

Bunyan, James. **The Origin of Forced Labor in the Soviet State, 1917-1921.** Baltimore: Johns Hopkins Press (in coöperation with the Hoover Institution on War, Revolution, and Peace), 1967, 276 p.
A collection of documents, with introductions, depicting the development of Bolshevik policy toward labor in the first years of the Soviet regime.

Conquest, Robert. **The Nation Killers.** New York: Macmillan, 1971, 222 p.
The author of the well-known massive study of the Great Purges here assembles the

evidence on the deportation of the Crimean Tatars, the Chechens and other Soviet nationalities.

Marchenko, Anatolii Timofeevich. **My Testimony.** New York: Dutton, 1969, 415 p.
An account of conditions in Soviet prison camps in the post-Stalin years, by a former inmate. The Russian original appeared as "Moi pokazaniia" (Frankfurt/Main: Posev, 1969, 420 p.).

Štajner, Karlo. **7,000 dana u Sibiru.** Zagreb: Globus, 1971, 474 p.
A Jugoslav author describes his sojourn of twenty years in Soviet prisons and detention camps during the Stalinist period.

Swianiewicz, S. **Forced Labour and Economic Development: An Enquiry into the Experience of Soviet Industrialization.** New York: Oxford University Press (for the Royal Institute of International Affairs), 1965, 321 p.
A Polish economist who spent three years as a Russian prisoner combines an economic explanation of why the U.S.S.R. resorted to forced labor with a warning that developing countries may be pushed in the same direction by the effort to industrialize rapidly.

Thomsen, Alexander. **... Aber die Liebe war stärker: als Rote-Kreuz Arzt zehn Jahre in sowjetischer Gefangenschaft.** Darmstadt: Schneekluth, 1962, 364 p.
A description of Soviet concentration camps and prisons by a Danish doctor who spent ten years after World War II in Vorkuta, Stalino and Sverdlovsk. First published in Danish as "I menneskelighedens navn" (Copenhagen: E. Wangel, 1960, 462 p.).

Wigmans, Johan H. **Ten Years in Russia and Siberia.** London: Darton, Longmans and Todd, 1964, 234 p.
Through a confusing set of circumstances the author, a young Dutchman, who sought to join the Dutch armed forces in Britain during World War II, landed in Russian prison camps and stayed there for ten years. His tale is an account of prison life in Russia before Khrushchev's rise to power. The Dutch original was published as "Ik was een der miljoenen" (Tielt: Lannoo, 1954, 299 p.).

Political Opposition; Defection

See also (The Postwar World) The Cold War; Peaceful Coexistence, p. 180; Eastern Europe and the Soviet Bloc, p. 358; Baltic States, p. 455; other subsections under the Union of Soviet Socialist Republics.

Amal'rik, Andrei. **Will the Soviet Union Survive Until 1984?** New York: Harper and Row, 1970, 93 p.
A young Russian writer's bleakly apocalyptic view of the Soviet future. It was only published abroad, and Amalrik was subsequently incarcerated. A significant oppositional tract. The Russian original appeared as "Prosushchestvuet li Sovetskii Soiuz do 1984 goda?" (Amsterdam: Fond Im. Gertsena, 1969, 71 p.).

Gaucher, Roland. **Opposition in the U.S.S.R., 1917–1967.** New York: Funk & Wagnalls, 1969, 547 p.
An extended account of the numerous oppositional individuals and movements, through the course of Soviet history: Whites, Kronstadt rebels, Makhno, Trotsky, Vlasov, Ukrainian nationalists and many others. The French original appeared as "L'Opposition en U.R.S.S., 1917–1967" (Paris: A. Michel, 1967, 431 p.).

Gerstenmaier, Cornelia. **The Voices of the Silent.** New York: Hart, 1972, 587 p.
The history of intellectual dissent—liberal, Christian and Marxist—in the Soviet Union from Pasternak to Solzhenitsyn. The author, well informed and sympathetic, may overestimate the effects of this "democratic movement" on the regime's durability. First published in German as "Die Stimme der Stummen" (Stuttgart: Seewald, 2d enl. ed., 1971, 395 p.).

Gorbanevskaya, Natalia. **Red Square at Noon.** New York: Holt, Rinehart and Winston, 1972, 288 p.
An account, by one of the participants subsequently adjudged insane by the authorities, of the brief 1968 demonstration in Red Square protesting the Soviet invasion of Czechoslovakia.

Labedz, Leopold, ed. **Solzhenitsyn: A Documentary Record.** New York: Harper and Row, 1971, 229 p.
Documents on Solzhenitsyn's continuing battle for creative freedom, from his rehabilitation in 1956, through his mounting troubles in the 1960s, to the Nobel prize award in 1970.

Reddaway, Peter, ed. **Uncensored Russia: Protest and Dissent in the Soviet Union.** New York: American Heritage Press, 1972, 499 p.
A translation, with commentary, of the underground *Chronicle of Current Events* for the period April 1968–December 1969.

Rothberg, Abraham. **The Heirs of Stalin: Dissidence and the Soviet Regime, 1953-1970.** Ithaca: Cornell University Press, 1972, 450 p.
A valuable account of the Soviet leadership's responses to artistic, political and scientific dissidence since Stalin's death.

Economic Questions

General

See also Problems of New Nations, p. 36; Economic Factors, p. 49; (Second World War) Economic, Technical and Non-Military Aspects, p. 172; Eastern Europe and the Soviet Bloc, p. 358; (Germany) Post-World War II Era, p. 487; other subsections under the Union of Soviet Socialist Republics.

Ames, Edward. **Soviet Economic Processes.** Homewood (Ill.): Irwin, 1965, 257 p.
A theoretical work by a professor of economics at Purdue, but directed to providing "an explanation of the behavior of Soviet producing enterprises and of the nature of general economic equilibrium in the Soviet system."

Athay, Robert E. **The Economics of Soviet Merchant-Shipping Policy.** Chapel Hill: University of North Carolina Press, 1971, 150 p.
An examination of the economic role of the Soviet Union's rapidly expanding merchant-shipping activities.

Balinky, Alexander and Others. **Planning and the Market in the U.S.S.R.: The 1960's.** New Brunswick: Rutgers University Press, 1967, 132 p.
An inquiry by four specialists into the Soviet economic reforms of the first half of the 1960s.

Becker, Abraham Samuel. **Soviet National Income, 1958-1964.** Berkeley: University of California Press, 1969, 608 p.
A calculation of national accounts for each of the years of the Seven Year Plan, 1959–1965, aimed at ascertaining the pattern of change in Soviet national income and output. Based upon, and continuing, the procedures developed by Abram Bergson.

Bergson, Abram and Kuznets, Simon Smith, eds. **Economic Trends in the Soviet Union.** Cambridge: Harvard University Press, 1963, 392 p.
A substantial assessment, by a number of leading students of the Soviet economy. The material was originally prepared for a conference held in the spring of 1961.

Bergson, Abram. **The Economics of Soviet Planning.** New Haven: Yale University Press, 1964, 394 p.
In this volume a leading authority on the Soviet economy deals centrally with the actual operation of the system, how it is organized, how it handles questions of management and incentive in industry and agriculture and how efficiently it promotes the aims of the regime.

Bergson, Abram. **Planning and Productivity Under Soviet Socialism.** New York: Columbia University Press, 1968, 95 p.
A careful assessment of the productivity of the Russian economic system, with some international comparisons. A publication of Carnegie-Mellon University.

Bernard, Philippe J. **Destin de la planification soviétique.** Paris: Éditions Ouvrières, 1963, 326 p.

An extended appraisal of the Soviet planned economy, based in part on a two-month stay at the Institute of Economy in Moscow. The author, a French economist, has served in the Commissariat Général du Plan.

Bor, Mikhail Zakharovich. **Aims and Methods of Soviet Planning.** New York: International Publishers, 1967, 255 p.

An introductory survey by a Soviet economist. The Russian original appeared as "Ocherki po metodologii i metodike planirovaniia" (Moscow: Izd-vo "Ekonomika," 1964, 277 p.).

Borisov, Evgenii Filipovich and Others, eds. **Politekonomicheskii slovar'.** Moscow: Izd-vo Politicheskoi Literatury, 2d ed., 1972, 367 p.

An official dictionary of major terms and concepts employed in economic analysis in the U.S.S.R.

Campbell, Robert Wellington. **Accounting in Soviet Planning and Management.** Cambridge: Harvard University Press, 1963, 315 p.

An interesting and fruitful approach to an understanding of the Soviet economy by way of an analysis of Soviet cost accounting. It is the author's conclusion that Soviet accounting has important failings both in providing information and in exerting control.

Carr, Edward Hallett and Davies, R. W. **Foundations of a Planned Economy, 1926–1929.** New York: Macmillan, 1971, 1 v. in 2 pts.

In this first volume of the continuation of his vast "A History of Soviet Russia," Mr. Carr, now with R. W. Davies as collaborator, turns to economic developments in the crucial three years preceding the spring of 1929. The treatment is by topic; concurrent domestic politics will be dealt with in a subsequent volume.

Chambre, Henri. **Union Soviétique et développement économique.** Paris: Aubier-Montaigne, 1967, 430 p.

A French student of Marxism and the Soviet Union here deals with two problems: the economic development of the U.S.S.R. itself, and the relevance of Soviet concepts and methods to the needs of underdeveloped countries.

Degras, Jane (Tabrisky), ed. **Soviet Planning.** New York: Praeger, 1965, 225 p.

An appropriate and well-deserved *Festschrift* for Naum Jasny.

Drogichinskii, Nikolai Emel'ianovich and Starodubrovskii, B. G., eds. **Osnovy i praktika khoziaistvennoi reformy v SSSR.** Moscow: Izd-vo "Ekonomika," 1971, 520 p.

A general survey of the fundamental principles and practices of a planned economy in the present-day U.S.S.R.

Efimov, Anatolii Nikolaevich. **Ekonomika i planirovanie sovetskoi promyshlennosti.** Moscow: Izd-vo "Ekonomika", 1970, 334 p.

An important treatment of Soviet industrial planning, by the director of the Economic Research Institute of Gosplan.

Ellman, Michael. **Soviet Planning Today.** New York: Cambridge University Press, 1971, 219 p.

A technical analysis of recent Soviet efforts to develop a theory of an optimally functioning socialist economy.

Feiwel, George R. **The Soviet Quest for Economic Efficiency: Issues, Controversies, and Reforms.** New York: Praeger, 2d rev. and enl. ed., 1972, 790 p.

A considerably expanded and updated edition of a monograph on "the Soviet industrial planning system and its reform." The first edition appeared in 1967.

Felker, Jere L. **Soviet Economic Controversies: The Emerging Marketing Concept and Changes in Planning, 1960–1965.** Cambridge: M.I.T. Press, 1966, 172 p.

Good summary, drawing on many sources.

Goldman, Marshall Irwin. **The Soviet Economy: Myth and Reality.** Englewood Cliffs: Prentice-Hall, 1968, 176 p.

A volume dealing with various major questions concerning the performance of the Soviet economy.

Goldman, Marshall Irwin. **Soviet Marketing: Distribution in a Controlled Economy.** New York: Free Press of Glencoe, 1963, 229 p.

A valuable study, based in good part on first-hand observation, of Soviet marketing since World War II; comparisons with U.S. developments in the same period are especially informative.

Goldman, Marshall Irwin. **The Spoils of Progress.** Cambridge: M.I.T. Press, 1972, 372 p.
Appropriately dedicated to Lake Baikal, this is a serious study of environmental pollution in the Soviet Union. It is evident that state ownership of the means of production is not in itself a remedy.

Gosudarstvennyi piatiletnii plan razvitiia narodnogo khoziaistva SSSR na 1971-1975 gody. Moscow: Izd-vo Politicheskoi Literatury, 1972, 455 p.
The text of the Soviet Union's Ninth Five-Year Plan, adopted in 1971, and other documents and addresses pertaining to the subject.

Hahn, Gerhard. **Investitionslenkung im sowjetischen Wirtschaftssystem.** Stuttgart: G. Fischer, 1967, 243 p.
A technical inquiry into governmental planning in the Soviet economic process.

Hanson, Philip. **The Consumer in the Soviet Economy.** Evanston: Northwestern University Press, 1968, 249 p.
An essay, by a British economist, addressed to the question: "What has been the effect so far of the general pattern of Soviet economic development on Soviet citizens as consumers?"

Hunter, Holland. **Soviet Transport Experience: Its Lessons for Other Countries.** Washington: Brookings Institution, Transport Research Program, 1968, 194 p.
An able study of Soviet railway policy and its rather impressive achievements.

Hutchings, Raymond. **Soviet Economic Development.** New York: Barnes and Noble, 1971, 314 p.
A concise account of the origins, progress and characteristics of Soviet economic development. A useful introduction to the subject.

Ingram, David. **The Communist Economic Challenge.** New York: Praeger, 1965, 168 p.
This concise examination of Soviet growth and policies concludes that although we may not be economically buried in the Khrushchevian manner, we face problems that require the best possible use of our own resources.

Jasny, Naum. **Soviet Economists of the Twenties.** New York: Cambridge University Press, 1972, 217 p.
This posthumously edited and published study deals with such nonconformist economists as Groman, Bazarov, Ginzburg and Kondratiev.

K novym rubezham (razvitie narodnogo khoziaistva SSSR v deviatoi piatiletke). Moscow: Izd-vo "Ekonomika," 1971, 206 p.
A general survey of the problems and prospects of the Soviet Ninth Five-Year Plan (1971-1975), produced by the staff of the Gosplan.

Katz, Abraham. **The Politics of Economic Reform in the Soviet Union.** New York: Praeger, 1972, 230 p.
A brief survey of basic economic policies since 1917, followed by analysis of the reforms of 1965 and their outcome.

Khrushchev, Nikita Sergeevich. **Stroitel'stvo kommunizma v SSSR i razvitie sel'skogo khoziaistva.** Moscow: Izd-vo Politicheskoi Literatury, 1962-64, 8 v.
The collected works of the late Soviet leader on topics of industrial and agricultural development in the U.S.S.R.

Lagutkin, Vladimir Martynovich and Others, *eds.* **Proizvodstvennie ob'edineniia: problemy i perspektivy.** Moscow: Izd-vo "Mysl'," 1971, 316 p.
A survey of current efforts to employ sophisticated methods of economic planning and mathematical modelling to further the development of Soviet industrial enterprises.

Liberman, E. G. **Economic Methods and the Effectiveness of Production.** White Plains: International Arts and Sciences Press, 1972, 180 p.
The Soviet economist, frequently considered the intellectual father of his country's industrial reforms, here corrects misinterpretations (in both East and West) of his ideas about the use of "profit."

Markert, Werner, *ed.* **Sowjetunion: das Wirtschaftssystem.** Cologne: Böhlau (for the Arbeitsgemeinschaft für Osteuropaforschung), 1965, 587 p.

This volume in the valuable series "Osteuropa-Handbuch" deals with the various facets of the Soviet economic system, each chapter prepared by a specialist in his field.

Masnata, Albert. **Le Système socialiste-soviétique: essai d'une étude générale de son économie.** Neuchâtel: La Baconnière, 1965, 348 p.
A survey, sponsored by the Swiss National Fund for Scientific Research, of the development, organization, achievements and shortcomings of the economic system of the Soviet Union.

Menz, Gertraud. **Das sowjetische Bankensystem.** Berlin: Duncker (for the Osteuropa-Institut an der Freien Universität Berlin), 1963, 196 p.
A sketch of the history of the Soviet banking organization is followed by an inquiry into the function of banking and monetary policy in contemporary Soviet planning.

Moorsteen, Richard Harris and Powell, Raymond P. **The Soviet Capital Stock, 1928-1962.** Homewood (Ill.): Irwin, 1966, 671 p.
A solid and important statistical contribution in working out Soviet capital stock estimates and their bearing on the growth of the Soviet economy.

Notkin, Aleksandr Il'ich, ed. **Faktory ekonomicheskogo razvitiia SSSR.** Moscow: Izd-vo "Ekonomika," 1970, 256 p.
Eleven Soviet economists discuss some of the problems of economic growth in the U.S.S.R., including labor productivity, regional specialization and changing patterns of consumer demand.

Nove, Alec. **An Economic History of the U.S.S.R.** Baltimore: Penguin, 1969, 416 p.
A well-organized survey by a leading British student of Soviet economy.

Nove, Alec. **Economic Rationality and Soviet Politics: Or, Was Stalin Really Necessary?** New York: Praeger, 1964, 316 p.
A collection of perceptive and informative papers.

Nove, Alec. **The Soviet Economy.** New York: Praeger, 2d rev. ed., 1969, 373 p.
A considerably revised edition of an introduction to the Soviet economy. The first edition appeared in 1961.

Omarovskii, Aleksandr Grigor'evich and Others, eds. **Ekonomika sotsialisticheskoi promyshlennosti.** Moscow: Izd-vo Moskovskogo Gosudarstvennogo Universiteta, 1971, 424 p.
An introduction to Soviet economics and industrial organization, published under the auspices of the Economics Faculty of Moscow University.

Ottone, Piero. **La nuova Russia.** Milan: Longanesi, 1967, 182 p.
An Italian economist notes the gradual decentralization and the increase of individual initiative in the Soviet economy.

Petrakov, Nikolai Iakovlevich. **Khoziaistvennaia reforma: plan i ekonomicheskaia samostoiatel'nost'.** Moscow: Izd-vo "Mysl'," 1971, 134 p.
An outline of the theory and practice of recent economic reforms in management and marketing in the U.S.S.R., tracing new concepts of decentralization back to Lenin's New Economic Policy of the early 1920s.

Pryde, Philip R. **Conservation in the Soviet Union.** New York: Cambridge University Press, 1972, 301 p.
A geographer writes on the history, theory and practice of the Soviet Union in conserving its natural resources, weighing those factors which are general to all countries and those which are peculiar to the Soviet system of government.

Roberts, Paul Craig. **Alienation and the Soviet Economy.** Albuquerque: University of New Mexico Press, 1971, 121 p.
An effort "to explain the operation of the Soviet economy in terms of its organizational principles and Marxian aspirations."

Romensky, Serge. **L'U.R.S.S. à 50 ans: les révisionnistes conservateurs.** Paris: Éditions du Seuil, 1967, 233 p.
A French foreign correspondent reviews Soviet reforms in industry and agriculture in the years from 1964 to 1966. Emphasis is on the contradictions in party policy.

Rosenko, Margarita Nikolaevna. **Stroitel'stvo kommunizma v SSSR i zakonomernosti razvitiia sotsialisticheskikh natsii.** Leningrad: Izd-vo Leningradskogo Universiteta, 1968, 224 p.

A theoretical study of how economic development influences the multinational character of the Soviet Union.

Schwartz, Harry. **An Introduction to the Soviet Economy.** Columbus (Ohio): Merrill, 1968, 168 p.
According to the author, this study is a successor to his "Russia's Soviet Economy" (New York: Prentice-Hall, 1954, 2d ed., 682 p.) and a companion volume to "The Soviet Economy since Stalin."

Schwartz, Harry. **The Soviet Economy Since Stalin.** Philadelphia: Lippincott, 1965, 256 p.
An informed review of the accomplishments and failures of the Soviet economy in the period between Stalin's death and Khrushchev's fall.

Sharpe, Myron E., *ed.* **Planning, Profit and Incentives in the USSR.** White Plains (N.Y.): International Arts & Sciences Press, 1966, 2 v.
A collection of articles, speeches and laws originally published in various Soviet collections and journals and pertaining to new developments and reforms in Soviet economic planning. The titles of the two volumes are: vol. I, "The Liberman Discussion: A New Phase in Soviet Economic Thought" (314 p.), and vol. II, "The Reform of Soviet Economic Management" (337 p.).

Sherman, Howard J. **The Soviet Economy.** Boston: Little, Brown, 1969, 371 p.
In the words of the author, this study "is an attempt at a detailed coverage of all of the main aspects and approaches to the Soviet economy."

Spulber, Nicolas. **The Soviet Economy: Structure, Principles, Problems.** New York: Norton, rev. ed., 1969, 329 p.
A revised edition of a general introduction to the Soviet economy by a professor at Indiana University. The first edition appeared in 1962.

Spulber, Nicolas. **Soviet Strategy for Economic Growth.** Bloomington: Indiana University Press, 1964, 175 p.

———, *ed.* **Foundations of Soviet Strategy for Economic Growth.** Bloomington: Indiana University Press, 1964, 530 p.
In the first book Professor Spulber discusses the Soviet debate in the 1920s on the goals and means of economic planning and development. The companion volume presents a substantial selection of Soviet essays from that period by such men as Leontief, Preobrazhensky and Groman.

Sutton, Anthony C. **Western Technology and Soviet Economic Development.** Stanford: Hoover Institution on War, Revolution, and Peace, 1968-73, 3 v.
An extensive empirical presentation and analysis of the role of foreign concessions and technological transfers in the development of the Soviet economy from 1917 to 1965.

Tolkachev, Aleksandr Sergeevich. **Ekonomicheskie problemy material'no-tekhnicheskoi bazy kommunizma v SSSR.** Moscow: Izd-vo "Mysl'," 1971, 358 p.
An examination of contemporary Soviet economic problems.

Treml, Vladimir G., *ed.* **The Development of the Soviet Economy: Plan and Performance.** New York: Praeger (for the Institute for the Study of the U.S.S.R.), 1968, 298 p.
Essays, mostly rather critical, concerning the achievements and shortcomings of the Soviet economy in the various sectors.

Treml, Vladimir G. and Hardt, John P., *eds.* **Soviet Economic Statistics.** Durham: Duke University Press, 1972, 457 p.
Conference papers discussing the "availability, reliability, and credibility of Soviet economic statistics."

Tsapkin, Nikolai Varlaamovich, *ed.* **Planirovanie narodnogo khoziaistva SSSR: uchebnoe posobie.** Moscow: Izd-vo "Mysl'," 1972, 479 p.
A survey of economic planning and administration in the U.S.S.R., prepared as a textbook for use in training courses for Communist Party officials.

Wagener, Hans-Jürgen. **Wirtschaftswachstum in unterentwickelten Gebieten.** Berlin: Duncker and Humblot, 1972, 192 p.
A well-documented study of economic growth rates in the various republics of the Soviet Union.

Westwood, J. N. **Soviet Railways Today**. New York: Citadel Press, 1964, 192 p.
A survey stressing the technical and operational rather than economic features of Soviet railroads.

Zaleski, Eugène. **Planning for Economic Growth in the Soviet Union, 1918-1932**. Chapel Hill: University of North Carolina Press, 1971, 425 p.
An updated translation of an important study, originally published as volume 1 of "Planification de la croissance et fluctuations économiques en U.R.S.S." (Paris: Société d'Édition d'Enseignement Supérieur, 1962, 372 p.).

Zaleski, Eugène. **Planning Reforms in the Soviet Union, 1962-1966**. Chapel Hill: University of North Carolina Press, 1967, 203 p.
An analysis of recent reforms in Soviet economic planning and management.

Zverev, Arsenii Grigor'evich. **Natsional'nyi dokhod i finansy SSSR**. Moscow: Izd-vo Finansy, 2d rev. and enl. ed., 1970, 312 p.
An analysis of Soviet government expenditures by an author who served as Minister of Finance of the U.S.S.R. between 1938 and 1960.

Agricultural Problems

See also Eastern Europe and the Soviet Bloc, p. 358; other subsections under the Union of Soviet Socialist Republics.

Bronger, Dirk. **Der Kampf um die sowjetische Agrarpolitik, 1925-1929**. Cologne: Verlag Wissenschaft und Politik, 1967, 318 p.
A substantial study of the formulation and execution of Soviet agrarian policies in the years from 1925 to 1929, with special attention to the views of the various oppositional groups within the Communist Party.

Dumont, René. **Sovkhoz, kolkhoz: ou, le problématique communisme**. Paris: Éditions du Seuil, 1964, 380 p.
An agronomist's candid report on his 1962 tour of Russian farm lands; first-hand observations led him to believe that the agricultural goal set for 1980 probably will not be achieved unless vital changes are introduced.

Hahn, Werner G. **The Politics of Soviet Agriculture, 1960-1970**. Baltimore: Johns Hopkins University Press, 1972, 311 p.
This detailed study shows how the fortunes of Soviet political leaders were affected by agricultural issues and decisions.

Jasny, Naum. **Khrushchev's Crop Policy**. Glasgow: Outram (for the Institute of Soviet and East European Studies, University of Glasgow), 1965, 243 p.
A pioneer student of the Soviet economy and more particularly of Soviet agriculture discusses Khrushchev's policies with respect to food and feed crops.

Kerblay, Basile H. **Les marchés paysans en U.R.S.S.** Paris: Mouton, 1968, 517 p.
An extensive study of a significant but infrequently treated subject—the evolution and function of peasant markets (including the broader questions of flow and exchange of goods) in the Soviet economy.

Laird, Roy D., *ed.* **Soviet Agricultural and Peasant Affairs**. Lawrence: University of Kansas Press, 1963, 335 p.
A symposium, based on papers presented at a conference held in 1962 and dealing with various aspects of Russia's perennial agricultural problems—administration, incentives, output, agronomy and the politics of agriculture.

Laird, Roy D. and Crowley, Edward L., *eds.* **Soviet Agriculture: The Permanent Crisis**. New York: Praeger (for the Institute for the Study of the U.S.S.R. in coöperation with the University of Kansas), 1965, 209 p.
A collection of papers and commentaries on various aspects of Soviet agriculture.

Laird, Roy D. and Laird, Betty A. **Soviet Communism and Agrarian Revolution**. Baltimore: Penguin, 1970, 157 p.
A brief but critical survey of the inadequacies of communist agricultural policies.

Millar, James R., *ed.* **The Soviet Rural Community**. Urbana: University of Illinois Press, 1971, 420 p.

A substantial symposium of studies on Soviet agricultural policy, rural administration and trends in village life.

Miller, Robert F. **One Hundred Thousand Tractors.** Cambridge: Harvard University Press, 1970, 423 p.
An extensive monograph on the history of the machine-tractor stations (MTS) and their very important administrative and economic roles in Soviet agriculture until their liquidation under Khrushchev.

Ploss, Sidney I. **Conflict and Decision-Making in Soviet Russia: A Case Study of Agricultural Policy, 1953-1963.** Princeton: Princeton University Press, 1965, 312 p.
The author, formerly a professor at the George Washington University and at the University of Pennsylvania, aims with this well-written study to further our understanding of contemporary Soviet politics. He reconstructs from the official records disputes over agricultural policy in the post-Stalin era and argues that the most important reason for the challenge to Khrushchev's leadership was the controversy over investment policy.

Strauss, Erich. **Soviet Agriculture in Perspective.** New York: Praeger, 1969, 328 p.
A broad review of the history of Soviet agriculture, its ups and downs, with some concluding thoughts about present problems and future prospects.

Volin, Lazar. **A Century of Russian Agriculture: From Alexander II to Khrushchev.** Cambridge: Harvard University Press, 1970, 644 p.
A major study of Russian agriculture in both the imperial and Soviet periods, by a leading authority on the subject, who died in 1966.

Wädekin, Karl-Eugen. **The Private Sector in Soviet Agriculture.** Berkeley: University of California Press, 2d rev. ed., 1973, 407 p.
An enlarged and revised translation of a serious inquiry into the scope, significance and importance of the private sector in Soviet agriculture. The German original appeared as "Privatproduzenten in der sowjetischen Landwirtschaft" (Cologne: Verlag Wissenschaft und Politik, 1967, 271 p.).

Industry and Industrial Management

See also Eastern Europe and the Soviet Bloc, p. 358; other subsections under the Union of Soviet Socialist Republics.

Campbell, Robert Wellington. **The Economics of Soviet Oil and Gas.** Baltimore: Johns Hopkins Press (for Resources for the Future), 1968, 279 p.
This study emphasizes the decision-making process in Soviet oil and gas industries.

Chapelle, Jean with Ketchian, Sonia. **URSS: second producteur de pétrole du monde.** Paris: Éditions Technip, 1963, 314 p.
A French oil expert surveys the Soviet petroleum industry—production, refining, transportation and trade.

Mazanova, Margarita Borisovna, *ed.* **Problemy razvitiia vostochnikh raionov SSSR.** Moscow: Izd-vo "Nauka," 1971, 179 p.
A collection of articles dealing with industrial development in Siberia and Soviet Central Asia.

Richman, Barry M. **Soviet Management, with Significant American Comparisons.** Englewood Cliffs: Prentice-Hall, 1965, 279 p.
A monograph on the processes and problems of Soviet industrial management and the role and significance of management in the economic progress of the Soviet Union, by a professor at the University of California.

Shabad, Theodore. **Basic Industrial Resources of the U.S.S.R.** New York: Columbia University Press, 1969, 393 p.
A useful survey by type of resource and by region.

Shashin, Valentin Dmitrievich and Others, *eds.* **Neftedobyvaiushchaia promyshlennost' SSSR 1917-1967.** Moscow: Izd-vo "Nedra," 1968, 319 p.
A comprehensive history of the Soviet oil industry.

Verre, Éveline. **L'Entreprise industrielle en Union Soviétique: nouvelles méthodes de gestion.** Paris: Sirey, 1965, 266 p.
A detailed examination of Soviet industrial policies and achievements.

Manpower; Labor; Wages

See also Eastern Europe and the Soviet Bloc, p. 358; other subsections under the Union of Soviet Socialist Republics.

Brown, Emily Clark. **Soviet Trade Unions and Labor Relations.** Cambridge: Harvard University Press, 1966, 394 p.
An appraisal, by a professor emeritus at Vassar, of Soviet unions and industrial relations, with emphasis on the years since 1953.

Chapman, Janet Goodrich. **Real Wages in Soviet Russia since 1928.** Cambridge: Harvard University Press, 1963, 395 p.
An important though quite technical study which undertakes to present and analyze the statistical data on the real wages of the Soviet worker since the beginning of the Five Year Plans.

Conquest, Robert, *ed.* **Agricultural Workers in the U.S.S.R.** New York: Praeger, 1969, 139 p.
A concise account of the vicissitudes of the Russian peasant since 1917, but with emphasis on the post-Stalin years.

Conquest, Robert, *ed.* **Industrial Workers in the U.S.S.R.** New York: Praeger, 1967, 203 p.
A well-documented survey.

Dodge, Norton T. **Women in the Soviet Economy.** Baltimore: Johns Hopkins Press, 1966, 331 p.
A substantial inquiry, rich in statistical information, into the role of Soviet women in the various areas of economic, professional and scientific activity.

McAuley, Mary. **Labour Disputes in Soviet Russia, 1957-1965.** New York: Oxford University Press, 1969, 269 p.
An effort to surmount both Soviet mythology and Western stereotypes, and to get at the realities of labor disputes and the means for dealing with them.

Osipov, Gennadii Vasil'evich, *ed.* **Industry and Labour in the U.S.S.R.** London: Tavistock Publications, 1966, 297 p.
A selection of translations of a number of papers by Soviet specialists dealing with a variety of questions relating to labor and industry.

Stanley, Emilo J. **Regional Distribution of Soviet Industrial Manpower, 1940-60.** New York: Praeger, 1968, 208 p.
A monograph dealing with the graphic presentation of the geographic distribution of industrial manpower in the U.S.S.R.

Social Questions

See also Eastern Europe and the Soviet Bloc, p. 358; other subsections under the Union of Soviet Socialist Republics.

Andreev, Edvard Pavlovich and Others. **Modelirovanie sotsial'nykh protsessov.** Moscow: Izd-vo "Nauka," 1970, 228 p.
A highly technical but politically and ideologically significant collection of papers on the topic of "modelling of social processes," using quantitative methods where ideological assertion might once have sufficed.

Connor, Walter D. **Deviance in Soviet Society.** New York: Columbia University Press, 1972, 327 p.
A sociological study of juvenile delinquency, alcoholism and crime, and efforts at their prevention or control.

Field, Mark George. **Soviet Socialized Medicine: An Introduction.** New York: Free Press, 1967, 231 p.
An introductory study, intended for the layman, of the Soviet health service.

Fischer, George. **The Soviet System and Modern Society.** New York: Atherton Press, 1968, 199 p.

Using as his basic data the careers of some 300 top party executives, the author pushes his analysis in two directions: toward the detection of trends in Soviet society and toward a refinement of models for social structures.

Inkeles, Alex. **Social Change in Soviet Russia.** Cambridge: Harvard University Press, 1968, 475 p.
A collection of essays over the last two decades by a leading American student of Soviet society.

Kassof, Allen Howard, ed. **Prospects for Soviet Society.** New York: Praeger (for the Council on Foreign Relations), 1968, 586 p.
A comprehensive inquiry into many aspects of Soviet life, from politics, economics and the military to science, social attitudes, the family and the literary scene.

Kassof, Allen Howard. **The Soviet Youth Program: Regimentation and Rebellion.** Cambridge: Harvard University Press, 1965, 206 p.
An able analysis by a sociologist of the purposes, methods, consequences and prospects of the vast Soviet effort to mould and direct its youth. A volume in the series of the Harvard Russian Research Center.

Kim, M. P. and Others, eds. **Sovetskaia intelligentsiia: istoriia formirovaniia i rosta 1917–1965 gg.** Moscow: Izd-vo "Mysl'," 1968, 432 p.
The history of the emergence and growth of a "Soviet intelligentsia" since 1917.

Konstantinov, O. A., ed. **Geografiia naseleniia i naselennykh punktov SSSR.** Leningrad: Izd-vo "Nauka," 1967, 291 p.
A collection of scholarly papers on population problems in the U.S.S.R. English summaries of each contribution are included.

Kozlov, Viktor Ivanovich. **Dinamika chislennosti narodov: metodologiia issledovaniia i osnovnye faktory.** Moscow: Izd-vo "Nauka," 1969, 406 p.
A serious study of the relationship between demographic processes and ethnic factors, using various regions of the U.S.S.R. as examples.

Kurman, Mikhail Veniaminovich and Lebedinskii, Ivan Vasil'evich. **Naselenie bol'shogo sotsialisticheskogo goroda.** Moscow: Izd-vo "Statistika," 1968, 198 p.
A Soviet study of the social process of urbanization of large cities, with particular attention paid to the problems of the Ukrainian city of Kharkov.

Lane, David. **The End of Inequality? Stratification under State Socialism.** Baltimore: Penguin, 1971, 156 p.
A British scholar argues in this examination of Soviet society that "inequality is a characteristic of state-socialist society as it is of the capitalist."

Lane, David. **Politics and Society in the USSR.** New York: Random House, 1971, 616 p.
This substantial survey, while designed as a textbook, has the advantage of emphasizing some of the significant sociological features: class, status, pressure groups and family functions.

Madison, Bernice Q. **Social Welfare in the Soviet Union.** Stanford: Stanford University Press, 1968, 298 p.
A solid historical and functional study of social welfare programs and services.

Male, D. J. **Russian Peasant Organisation before Collectivisation: A Study of Commune and Gathering, 1925–1930.** New York: Cambridge University Press, 1971, 253 p.
A very useful study of the role of the Russian commune, as a landholding organ and a unit of local administration, in the last half decade before the onset of collectivization.

Matthews, Mervyn. **Class and Society in Soviet Russia.** New York: Walker, 1972, 366 p.
This professional study provides useful background for consideration of Soviet domestic and foreign policies.

Meissner, Boris, ed. **Social Change in the Soviet Union: Russia's Path toward an Industrial Society.** Notre Dame: University of Notre Dame Press, 1972, 247 p.
This collection of essays, originally presented at a conference in Germany in 1963 and subsequently considerably revised, provides a survey "of Soviet society, its evolution and change from its prerevolutionary origins to recent times." The German edition appeared as "Sowjetgesellschaft im Wandel: Russlands Weg zur Industriegesellschaft" (Stuttgart: Kohlhammer, 1966, 205 p.).

Osborn, Robert J. **Soviet Social Policies: Welfare, Equality, and Community.** Homewood (Ill.): Dorsey Press, 1970, 294 p.
An inquiry into the way the Soviet government influences the peoples' "choices" in such matters as expenditures, education, jobs and residence.

Pokshishevskii, Vadim Viacheslavovich. **Geografiia naseleniia SSSR: ekonomiko-geograficheskie ocherki.** Moscow: Izd-vo "Proveshchenie," 1971, 174 p.
A compact demographic survey of the Soviet Union.

Simirenko, Alex, ed. **Social Thought in the Soviet Union.** Chicago: Quadrangle Books, 1969, 439 p.
A collection of essays by twelve specialists on the state of the discipline in the various social sciences.

Vladimirov, Leonid. **The Russians.** New York: Praeger, 1968, 249 p.
A volume by a well-informed former Soviet journalist.

Wesson, Robert G. **Soviet Communes.** New Brunswick: Rutgers University Press, 1963, 275 p.
A monograph on the Soviet experience with and abandonment of communes in the 1920s.

Zaslavskaia, T. I., ed. **Migratsiia sel'skogo naseleniia.** Moscow: Izd-vo "Mysl'," 1970, 348 p.
An attempt to determine patterns in the migration of the Soviet Union's rural populace. Field research was conducted by the Siberian branch of the U.S.S.R. Academy of Sciences.

Culture, Education and Religion

See also Communism, p. 26; Culture; Education; Public Opinion; Communications Processes, p. 42; Religious Problems, p. 44; (Second World War) Economic, Technical and Non-Military Aspects, p. 172; (Eastern Europe and the Soviet Bloc) General Surveys and Political Problems, p. 358; other subsections under the Union of Soviet Socialist Republics.

Ahlberg, René. **Entwicklungsprobleme der empirischen Sozialforschung in der UdSSR (1917–1966).** Berlin: Osteuropa-Institut, 1968, 237 p.
An historical analysis of the vicissitudes of empirical social research in the U.S.S.R.

Andronov, Sergei Antipovich and Others, eds. **KPSS vo glave kul'turnoi revoliutsii v SSSR.** Moscow: Izd-vo Politicheskoi Literatury, 1972, 376 p.
This text argues that the U.S.S.R. has undergone a profound cultural, economic and political revolution, involving the fulfillment by the Communist Party of the Leninist vision of mass education and the propogation of a proletarian world-view in the arts and sciences.

Anweiler, Oskar. **Geschichte der Schule und Pädagogik in Russland.** Heidelberg: Quelle und Meyer, 1964, 482 p.
An excellent study, by the author of an outstanding work on the Soviets, on Russian education and pedagogy from the last years of Tsarism through the experiments and reversals of the 1920s.

Benton, William. **The Teachers and the Taught in the U.S.S.R.** New York: Atheneum, 1966, 174 p.
A personal discussion of education, science and indoctrination, based largely on Mr. Benton's visit to the Soviet Union in 1964.

Billington, James H. **The Icon and the Axe.** New York: Knopf, 1966, 786 p.
An excellent, provocative, well-written and sometimes controversial survey of the history of Russian culture.

Bourdeaux, Michael. **Patriarch and Prophets: Persecution of the Russian Orthodox Church Today.** New York: Praeger, 1970, 359 p.
A documentary history of Soviet church-state relations.

Burlatskii, Fedor Mikhailovich. **Lenin, gosudarstvo, politika.** Moscow: Izd-vo "Nauka," 1970, 522 p.
A Soviet sociologist argues for the establishment of the discipline of political science in the U.S.S.R.

De George, Richard T. **Soviet Ethics and Morality.** Ann Arbor: University of Michigan Press, 1969, 184 p.
An exposition and evaluation of Marxist-Leninist writings on ethical theory and the official stance on communist morality.

Fitzpatrick, Sheila. **The Commissariat of Enlightenment.** New York: Cambridge University Press, 1971, 380 p.
A scholarly account of the establishment of the Soviet commissariat for education in the years 1917–21. The central figure is Lunacharsky, "a large, untidy man with pince-nez and a benevolent expression."

Fletcher, William Catherwood and Strover, Anthony J., eds. **Religion and the Search for New Ideals in the USSR.** New York: Praeger, 1967, 135 p.
Papers delivered at a conference held at the Institute for the Study of the U.S.S.R. in Munich in April 1966.

Fletcher, William Catherwood. **A Study in Survival: The Church in Russia, 1927–1943.** New York: Macmillan, 1965, 168 p.
A monograph on the Russian Orthodox Church's struggle for survival in the Stalin era, with particular attention to the work of Metropolitan Sergii.

Graham, Loren R. **Science and Philosophy in the Soviet Union.** New York: Knopf, 1972, 584 p.
This impressive study investigates the complex interplay between some of the leading themes of twentieth-century science and the principles of Marxist philosophy. Mr. Graham, a professor at Columbia University, is far less concerned with such scandals as the Lysenko affair than with the serious intellectual endeavors of the best Soviet scientific minds.

Graham, Loren R. **The Soviet Academy of Sciences and the Communist Party, 1927–1932.** Princeton: Princeton University Press, 1967, 255 p.
A serious, scholarly study of the vicissitudes of the highly important Soviet Academy of Sciences during the crucial turning point of the First Five-Year Plan.

Gurevich, Semen Moiseevich, ed. **Problemy informatsii v pechati: ocherki teorii i praktiki.** Moscow: Izd-vo "Mysl'," 1971, 310 p.
A group of Soviet professional journalists and academics argue that the informational process has to serve the requirements of building socialism.

Hayward, Max and Fletcher, William Catherwood, eds. **Religion and the Soviet State: A Dilemma of Power.** New York: Praeger (for the Centre de Recherches et d'Étude des Institutions Religieuses), 1969, 200 p.
A collection of able essays dealing with various aspects of contemporary religious and intellectual life in the Soviet Union.

Heer, Nancy Whittier. **Politics and History in the Soviet Union.** Cambridge: M.I.T. Press, 1971, 319 p.
An interesting study of the peculiar role of historiography in the Soviet Union, with particular attention to the vicissitudes of party history in the decade following Khrushchev's 1956 denunciation of Stalin.

Johnson, Priscilla and Labedz, Leopold, eds. **Khrushchev and the Arts: The Politics of Soviet Culture, 1962–1964.** Cambridge: M.I.T. Press, 1965, 300 p.
A selection of Soviet documents, with an extensive introductory essay.

Joravsky, David. **The Lysenko Affair.** Cambridge: Harvard University Press, 1970, 459 p.
An exceptionally fine work, by a leading student of the history of Soviet science, which goes far beyond scandalmongering or muckraking to wrestle with the root causes of the disasters symbolized by Lysenkoism.

Korol, Alexander G. **Soviet Research and Development: Its Organization, Personnel, and Funds.** Cambridge: M.I.T. Press, 1965, 375 p.
A serious effort to ascertain the magnitude and distribution of the national resources devoted to scientific research and development in the Soviet Union. A valuable contribution. A study sponsored by the Office of Economic and Manpower Studies, National Science Foundation.

Kultura, nauka, iskusstvo SSSR: slovar'-spravochnik. Moscow: Izd-vo Politicheskoi Literatury, 1965, 318 p.

A handbook of the official institutions and ideological concepts of Soviet science, education, communications, literature, art, sports and physical culture.

Kuz'min, Mikhail Sergeevich. **Deiatel'nost' partii i sovetskogo gosudarstva po razvitiiu mezhdunarodnykh nauchnykh i kulturnykh sviazei SSSR (1917–1932 gg.).** Leningrad: Izd-vo Leningradskogo Universiteta, 1971, 149 p.
A survey of the early work of VOKS, the All-Union Society for Cultural Contacts, which facilitated cultural and technical exchanges between Russia and the capitalist countries.

Medvedev, Zhores Aleksandrovich. **The Rise and Fall of T. D. Lysenko.** New York: Columbia University Press, 1969, 284 p.
A translation of a Soviet scientist's account of the ravages wrought by Lysenkoism in Soviet biology and of the struggle to eliminate it. The manuscript has not been published in the U.S.S.R.

Mickiewicz, Ellen Propper. **Soviet Political Schools.** New Haven: Yale University Press, 1967, 190 p.
A study of Soviet schools for the instruction and indoctrination of adults.

Morton, Henry W. **Soviet Sport: Mirror of Soviet Society.** New York: Collier Books, 1963, 221 p.
A history of attitudes and patterns in the contemporary Soviet Union, as reflected by athletic competitions.

Romanovskii, Sergei Kalistratovich. **Mezhdunarodnye kulturnye i nauchnye sviazi SSSR.** Moscow: Izd-vo "Mezhdunarodnye Otnosheniia," 1966, 238 p.
A survey of Soviet cultural and technical exchange programs.

Rudman, Herbert C. **The School and State in the USSR.** New York: Macmillan, 1967, 286 p.
A study concentrating on the organization and management of the Soviet educational system.

Simirenko, Alex, *ed.* **Soviet Sociology: Historical Antecedents and Current Appraisals.** Chicago: Quadrangle Books, 1966, 384 p.
An anthology of writings by Western and Soviet scholars providing background material for an understanding of Soviet sociology in perspective of its historical antecedents.

Social Sciences in the USSR. Paris: Mouton, 1965, 297 p.
A survey of the historical, philosophical, economic and juridical sciences, prepared by the U.S.S.R. Academy of Sciences at UNESCO's request and designed for the Western reader.

Stroyen, William B. **Communist Russia and the Russian Orthodox Church, 1943–1962.** Washington: Catholic University of America Press, 1967, 161 p.
A gloomy account of the interaction between the Russian Orthodox Church and the Soviet regime. The author concludes by saying that "the future of the Orthodox Church depends upon its participation in the objectives of the government and upon the courage of the people to express their need for religion."

Zatko, James J. **Descent into Darkness.** Notre Dame: University of Notre Dame Press, 1965, 232 p.
A scholarly account of the tribulations of the Roman Catholic Church in Russia in the period from the February Revolution to 1923, with brief chapters on the relations of the Catholic Church with the Imperial Russian government and on developments from 1924 to 1931.

Regional, National and Minority Problems

General

See also (International Law) Miscellaneous, p. 94; Eastern Europe and the Soviet Bloc, p. 358; The Baltic States, p. 455; other subsections under the Union of Soviet Socialist Republics.

Allworth, Edward, *ed.* **Soviet Nationality Problems.** New York: Columbia University Press, 1971, 296 p.

This symposium of essays, growing out of a continuing seminar at Columbia University, emphasizes general problems raised by the question of nationality in the U.S.S.R.

Armstrong, Terence. **Russian Settlement in the North.** New York: Cambridge University Press, 1965, 223 p.
A thorough description of the Russian penetration of Northern Siberia, both under the Tsarist and the Soviet regimes.

Conolly, Violet. **Beyond the Urals.** New York: Oxford University Press, 1967, 420 p.
An extensive survey of Soviet economic resources, achievements and goals in Asiatic Russia.

Conquest, Robert, *ed.* **Soviet Nationalities Policy in Practice.** New York: Praeger, 1967, 160 p.
A factual and concise survey.

Dibb, Paul. **Siberia and the Pacific: A Study of Economic Development and Trade Prospects.** New York: Praeger, 1972, 288 p.
Useful background information for understanding the Soviet efforts to obtain Western and Japanese assistance for the exploitation of Siberian natural resources.

Fumoto, Masayoshi, *ed.* **Shiberia no shigen kaihatsu.** Tokyo: Ajia Keizai Kenkyūjo, 1972, 324 p.
———, *ed.* **Shiberia no chiiki kaihatsu.** Tokyo: Ajia Keizai Kenkyūjo, 1972, 395 p.
Substantial Japanese studies of Siberian regional development and natural resources.

Goldhagen, Erich, *ed.* **Ethnic Minorities in the Soviet Union.** New York: Praeger (for the Institute of East European Jewish Studies of the Philip W. Lown School of Near Eastern and Judaic Studies, Brandeis University), 1968, 351 p.
Essays by an able group, dealing both with general questions concerning the ethnic minorities in the U.S.S.R. and with particular ethnic groups.

Kim, Maksim Pavlovich and Others, *eds.* **SSSR—velikoe sodruzhestvo narodov-brat'ev.** Moscow: Izd-vo "Nauka," 1972, 338 p.
An anthology of essays celebrating the Leninist principles on the nationality question, selected to greet the fiftieth anniversary of the founding of the Union of Soviet Socialist Republics.

Makarova, Galina Petrovna. **Osushchestvlenie leninskoi natsional'noi politiki v pervye gody sovetskoi vlasti (1917–1920 gg.).** Moscow: Izd-vo "Nauka," 1969, 268 p.
A narrative of the first steps of Soviet nationalities policy during the period of "War Communism," featuring the victorious struggle against such enemies as the "bourgeois-nationalist parties" in the minority regions.

Rashidov, Sharaf Rashidovich. **Znamia druzhby.** Moscow: Izd-vo Politicheskoi Literatury, 1967, 230 p.
An Uzbek member of the Soviet leadership marks the fiftieth anniversary of the October Revolution with an exposition of Soviet nationalities policy, emphasizing the fraternal ties between minority groups and their Great Russian "older brothers."

Saiadov, Saiad Atosh Oglu. **Natsional'naia politika KPSS i druzhba narodov SSSR.** Baku: Izd-vo "Azerneshr," 1969, 167 p.
This treatise on the Soviet Union's Leninist nationalities policy reiterates the thesis that the Communist Party of the Soviet Union safeguards vital minority rights while fostering national unity on the basis of fraternal exchanges and economic coöperation.

St. George, George. **Siberia: The New Frontier.** New York: McKay, 1969, 374 p.
An informal account.

Tillett, Lowell. **The Great Friendship: Soviet Historians on the Non-Russian Nationalities.** Chapel Hill: University of North Carolina Press, 1969, 468 p.
A study of the vicissitudes of Soviet historiography with respect to Russian colonialism and the non-Russian nationalities.

The Jews

See also Ethnic Problems; The Jews, p. 46.

Baron, Salo Wittmayer. **The Russian Jew under Tsars and Soviets.** New York: Macmillan, 1964, 427 p.

A general history of Russian Jewry, from the earliest settlements to the present, by an outstanding student of Jewish history.

Cang, Joel. **The Silent Millions.** New York: Taplinger, 1970, 246 p.
A brief history of Soviet Jewry by a British journalist.

Eliav, Arie L. **Between Hammer and Sickle.** New York: New American Library, rev. ed., 1969, 237 p.
A report on the fate of Russia's Jews, by an Israeli writer and government official who was First Secretary to the Israeli Embassy in Moscow from 1958 to 1960.

Gitelman, Zvi Y. **Jewish Nationality and Soviet Politics.** Princeton: Princeton University Press, 1972, 573 p.
An excellent monograph on the place of the Jews in the Soviet society of the 1920s. The theme is the interplay of the Soviet Communist Party, the Jewish Communist leaders and the Jewish community in the combined process of modernization and Bolshevization of a minority not easily torn from its religious identity.

Kochan, Lionel, ed. **The Jews in Soviet Russia since 1917.** New York: Oxford University Press (for the Institute of Jewish Affairs, London), 2d ed., 1972, 377 p.
A substantial volume of essays dealing with various aspects of the situation of the Jews in the Soviet period of Russian history.

Rubin, Ronald I., ed. **The Unredeemed: Anti-Semitism in the Soviet Union.** Chicago: Quadrangle Books, 1968, 316 p.
A selection of essays dealing with the vicissitudes of Soviet Jewry, including the impact of international tensions.

Smolar, Boris. **Soviet Jewry Today and Tomorrow.** New York: Macmillan, 1971, 228 p.
A bleak picture by a Russian-born American journalist, editor of the Jewish Telegraphic Agency until his retirement in 1967.

The European Republics
Ukrainian S.S.R.

See also First World War, p. 131; Second World War, p. 144; Eastern Europe and the Soviet Bloc, p. 358; other subsections under the Union of Soviet Socialist Republics.

Adams, Arthur E. **Bolsheviks in the Ukraine.** New Haven: Yale University Press, 1963, 440 p.
A solid study of the Bolsheviks' second, and temporarily abortive, effort to gain control of the Ukraine in the months immediately following the end of the First World War—November 1918 to June 1919.

Bilinsky, Yaroslav. **The Second Soviet Republic: The Ukraine after World War II.** New Brunswick: Rutgers University Press, 1964, 539 p.
An excellent study of political, economic and cultural developments in the Ukraine since 1945. Extensive bibliography.

Browne, Michael, ed. **Ferment in the Ukraine.** New York: Praeger, 1971, 267 p.
Documents on political and intellectual protest in the Ukraine in the 1960s, and the counterattack through political trials and repression.

Chornovil, Viacheslav, comp. **The Chornovil Papers.** New York: McGraw-Hill, 1968, 246 p.
Quite revealing documents—memoranda, petitions and the like—by a Ukrainian journalist and other intellectuals who suffered incarceration in connection with the on-going tensions between Moscow and the Ukraine.

Dubyna, K. K., ed. **Istoriia Ukraïns'koi RSR.** Kiev: Nauk. Dumka, 1967, 2 v.
A general Soviet version of Ukrainian history.

Dziuba, Ivan. **Internationalism or Russification? A Study in the Soviet Nationalities Problem.** London: Weidenfeld, 1968, 240 p.
A Soviet Ukrainian literary critic voices his alarm at communist nationality policies in the Ukraine.

Hornykiewicz, Theophil, ed. **Ereignisse in der Ukraine 1914–1922: deren Bedeutung und historische Hintergründe.** Philadelphia: W. K. Lypynsky East European Research Institute, 1966-69, 4 v.

A massive collection of documents from the Austrian State Archives on the Ukrainian problem during World War I and its aftermath.

Kolasky, John. **Education in Soviet Ukraine.** Toronto: Peter Martin Associates, 1968, 238 p.
An indictment, on grounds of discrimination and Russification, of Soviet educational policy in the Ukraine, by a former Canadian Communist of Ukrainian background.

Kolasky, John. **Two Years in Soviet Ukraine.** Toronto: Peter Martin Associates, 1970, 264 p.
The story of the author's two disillusioning years as a student in the Soviet Ukraine.

Korolivskii, S. M., *ed.* **Grazhdanskaia voina na Ukraine, 1918–1920.** Kiev: Nauk. Dumka, 1967, 3 v. in 4 pts.
A collective effort to describe the Civil War period in the Ukraine from a communist perspective.

Korolivskii, S. M. and Others. **Pobeda sovetskoi vlasti na Ukraine.** Moscow: Izd-vo "Nauka," 1967, 579 p.
An official history of the Bolshevik seizure of power in the Ukraine.

Koropeckyj, I. S. **Location Problems in Soviet Industry before World War II: The Case of the Ukraine.** Chapel Hill: University of North Carolina Press, 1971, 219 p.
A monograph on the industrial growth of the Ukraine in the years of the First and Second Five-Year Plans.

Kubijovyč, Volodymyr, *ed.* **Ukraine: A Concise Encyclopedia.** Toronto: University of Toronto Press (for the Ukrainian National Association), 1963–71, 2 v.
A major reference including information on Ukrainian geography, economy, language, history, culture, literature and Ukrainians abroad.

Lewytzkyj, Borys. **Die Sowjetukraine 1944–1963.** Cologne: Kiepenheuer, 1964, 443 p.
A study of economic and political developments in the Ukraine from 1944 to 1963.

Mazlakh, Serhii and Shakhrai, Vasyl'. **On the Current Situation in the Ukraine.** Ann Arbor: University of Michigan Press, 1970, 220 p.
An eloquent statement on the question of self-determination and a study of Ukrainian nationalism of the 1917–1918 period. The authors, two old Bolsheviks, published the volume originally in Saratov in 1919. The present edition was prepared and annotated by Peter J. Potichyj.

Nahayewsky, Isidore. **History of the Modern Ukrainian State, 1917–1923.** Munich: Ukrainian Free University and Academy of Arts and Sciences, 1966, 317 p.
A monograph by an émigré historian.

Nesterenko, Oleksii Oleksilovych, *ed.* **Natsional'nyi dokhod Ukraïns'koï RSR v period rozhornutoho budivnytstva komunizmu.** Kiev: Vid-vo Akademiï Nauk Ukr. RSR, 1963, 333 p.
An important study of Ukrainian economy.

Pidhainy, Oleh Semenovych. **The Formation of the Ukrainian Republic.** New York, Toronto: New Review Books, 1966, 685 p.
A detailed history of the establishment of the Ukrainian state in the aftermath of the Bolshevik Revolution. The author pays particular attention to how the Ukrainian Republic was recognized by Great Britain, France, the Central Powers and the Bolsheviks, but does not treat adequately the subsequent relations between the new state and the German military authorities.

Russian Oppression in Ukraine: Reports and Documents. London: Ukrainian Publishers, 1963, 576 p.
A Ukrainian émigré publication.

Skaba, A. D., *ed.* **Ukraïns'ka RSR v period hromadians'koï viïny.** Kiev: Vyd-vo Polit. Lit-ry Ukraïny, 1967–70, 3 v.
A massive survey of political and military developments in the Ukraine during the Civil War.

Sosnovskyi, Mykhailo. **Ukraïna na mizhnarodnii areni, 1945–1965.** Toronto: Vyd-vo Doslidnoho Instytutu Studiium, 1966, 272 p.
A Canadian-Ukrainian scholar describes the Ukrainian problem in international rela-

tions from 1945 to 1965 and the activities of the Ukrainian organizations in the Western world on behalf of Ukrainian independence.

Suprunenko, Nikolai Ivanovich. **Ocherki istorii Grazhdanskoi Voiny i inostrannoi voennoi interventsii na Ukraine (1918-1920).** Moscow: Izd-vo "Nauka," 1966, 454 p.
A survey of the military events in Ukraine in the aftermath of World War I.

Symonenko, Rem Heorhiiovych. **Proval polityky mizhnarodnoho imperializmu na Ukraïni.** Kiev: Nauk. Dumka, 1965, 302 p.
A Soviet study of the military and political activities of the "imperialist" states in the Ukraine from 1919 to 1921.

Other Republics

See also Second World War, p. 144; Eastern Europe and the Soviet Bloc, p. 358; The Baltic States, p. 455; other subsections under the Union of Soviet Socialist Republics.

Balagurov, Ia. A. and Mashezerskov, V. I. **Kareliia v period grazhdanskoi voiny i inostrannoi interventsii, 1918-1920.** Petrozavodsk: Karel'skoe Knizhnoe Izd-vo, 1964, 647 p.
A Soviet survey of political and military developments in Karelia in the aftermath of World War I.

Basov, G. F. and Others, *eds.* **Organy gosudarstvennogo upravleniia Belorusskoi SSR.** Minsk: Nauka i Tekhnika, 1968, 327 p.
A study of the administrative apparatus of the Byelorussian S.S.R.

Cherepnin, Lev Vladimirovich and Trapeznikov, Sergei Pavlovich, *eds.* **Istoriia Moldavskoi S.S.R.** Kishinev: Kartia Moldoveniaske, 2d rev. ed., 1965-68, 2 v.
A history of Moldavia, prepared under the auspices of the Moldavian Academy of Sciences.

Khalikov, A. Kh. and Others. **Istoriia Tatarskoi ASSR.** Kazan: Tatknigoizdat, 1968, 719 p.
A history of the Tatar Autonomous Soviet Socialist Republic.

Konanau, Hauryla Mikhailavich, *comp.* **Nasha respublika: tsifry i fakty.** Minsk: Belarus', 1967, 196 p.
Basic facts on the Byelorussian S.S.R.

Krupenikov, Igor' Arkad'evich and Others. **Moldaviia.** Moscow: Mysl', 1970, 253 p.
A general survey of the Moldavian S.S.R.

Lazarev, Artem Markovich. **Vossoedinenie moldavskogo naroda v edinoe Sovetskoe gosudarstvo.** Kishinev: Kartia Moldoveniaske, 1965, 204 p.
A Soviet view of the "unification of the Moldavian people," brought about by the introduction of Soviet power in former Rumanian territories.

Lubachko, Ivan S. **Belorussia under Soviet Rule, 1917-1957.** Lexington: University Press of Kentucky, 1972, 219 p.
A survey of his nation's recent vicissitudes under Soviet, Polish and German rules, by a native Byelorussian now teaching in the United States.

Martinkevich, F. S., *ed.* **Ekonomika Sovetskoi Belorussii.** Minsk: Nauka i Tekhnika, 1967, 571 p.
An economic history of the Byelorussian S.S.R.

Martinkevich, F. S., *ed.* **Sotsial'no-ekonomicheskie preobrazovaniia v Belorusskoi SSR za gody sovetskoi vlasti.** Minsk: Nauka i Tekhnika, 1970, 528 p.
A survey of the economic transformation of Byelorussia under the Soviet rule.

Mints, Isaak Izrailevich and Others, *eds.* **Pobeda sovetskoi vlasti v Belorussii.** Minsk: Nauka i Tekhnika, 1967, 506 p.
A history of the establishment of Soviet rule in Byelorussia.

Surilov, A. V., and Stratulat, N. P. **O natsionalno-gosudarstvennom samopredelenii moldavskogo naroda.** Kishinev: Kartia Moldoveniaske, 1967, 147 p.
A brief survey of the establishment of the Moldavian S.S.R.

EUROPE

Asian Republics

See also Second World War, p. 144; Eastern Europe and the Soviet Bloc, p. 358; (Asia and the Pacific Area) General Surveys, p. 607; (Middle East) General Surveys and Political Problems, p. 611; (Central Asia and the Subcontinent of India) General, p. 652; (China) Sinkiang; National Minority Areas, p. 711; other subsections under the Union of Soviet Socialist Republics.

Abaeva, Dina Mikhailovna. **Razvitie obshchestvennogo uzstroistva Turkmenskoi SSR (1924-1964 gg.).** Ashkhabad: Ylym, 1968, 187 p.
A survey of the establishment of the Turkmen S.S.R.

Agzamkhodzhaev, Anvar. **Obrazovanie i razvitie Uzbekskoi SSR.** Tashkent: Izd-vo "Fan," 1971, 342 p.
A constitutional and political history of Uzbekistan.

Allworth, Edward, *ed*. **Central Asia: A Century of Russian Rule.** New York: Columbia University Press, 1967, 552 p.
A solid work on the land and peoples of Central Asia, especially the effects of Russian influence on its social, political, economic, religious and literary development since the fall of Tashkent in 1865.

Allworth, Edward. **Nationalities of the Soviet East: Publications and Writing Systems; A Bibliographical Directory and Transliteration Tables for Iranian- and Turkic-Language Publications, 1818-1945, Located in U.S. Libraries.** New York: Columbia University Press, 1971, 440 p.
A useful reference.

Aminov, A. M., *ed*. **Ekonomicheskaia istoriia Sovetskogo Uzbekistana (1917-1965 gg.).** Tashkent: Izd-vo "Fan," 1966, 370 p.
An economic history of the Uzbek S.S.R.

Aminova, R. Kh., *ed*. **Istoriia Uzbekskoi S.S.R.** Tashkent: Izd-vo "Fan," rev. ed., 1967-68, 4 v.
A Soviet history of the Uzbek S.S.R.

Amirkhanyan, Savarsh Megrabovich. **Iz istorii bor'by za sovetskuiu vlast' v Armenii.** Erevan: Izd-vo "Aiastan," 1967, 186 p.
The memoirs of the struggle for power in post-1917 Armenia by a high official in the Cheka. Though written many years later and published posthumously, they are a contribution to the history of the region as well as of the Soviet secret police.

Bacon, Elizabeth Emaline. **Central Asians under Russian Rule: A Study in Culture Change.** Ithaca: Cornell University Press, 1966, 273 p.
The author concludes that the Tajiks, Uzbeks, Kazakhs, Kirghiz, Turkomans and Karakalpaks have not lost their sense of ethnic identity and are not likely to become merged with the Russians.

Badalyan, Kh. H., *comp*. **Iz istorii inostrannoi interventsii v Armenii v 1918 godu.** Erevan: Izd-vo Erevanskogo Universiteta, 1970, 248 p.
A collection of materials on the activities of foreign powers in Armenia in 1918.

Baishev, S. B., *ed*. **Istoriia Kazakhskoi S.S.R.: epokha sotsializma.** Alma-Ata: Nauka, 3rd rev. ed., 1967, 751 p.
A history of Kazakhstan under the Soviet regime.

Baishev, S. B. and Chulanov, G. C., *eds*. **Razvitie narodnogo khoziaistva Kazakhstana za 50 let sovetskoi vlasti.** Alma-Ata: Nauka, 1967, 462 p.
An economic history of Soviet Kazakhstan.

Becker, Seymour. **Russia's Protectorates in Central Asia: Bukhara and Khiva, 1865-1924.** Cambridge: Harvard University Press, 1968, 416 p.
A scholarly study of the khanates of Bukhara and Khiva under imperial and early Soviet rule.

Bennigsen, Alexandre and Lemercier-Quelquejay, Chantal. **Islam in the Soviet Union.** New York: Praeger (in association with the Central Asian Research Centre, London), 1967, 272 p.
An historical survey, by two leading specialists, of the vicissitudes of the Muslim peoples of the Soviet Union.

Carrère d'Encausse, Hélène. **Réforme et révolution chez les Musulmans de l'Empire russe: Bukhara, 1867-1924.** Paris: Colin, 1966, 313 p.
  A history of the Muslim Emirate of Bukhara since its conquest by the Russians in the middle of the nineteenth century and of its successor state, which came to an end in 1924, the People's Republic of Bukhara. Particular attention is paid to the reformist movement known as Jadidism.

Cherseev, Dzhumasiat. **Kul'turnaia revoliutsiia v Turkmenistane.** Ashkhabad: Turkmenistan, 1970, 199 p.
  A study of communist cultural reforms in Turkmenistan in the years from 1925 to 1937.

Dzhamgerchinov, B. D. and Others, *eds*. **Istoriia Kirgizskoi SSR.** Frunze: "Kyrgyzstan," 1968, 2 v.
  A Soviet history of the Kirghiz S.S.R., prepared under the auspices of the Kirghiz Academy of Sciences.

Dzhaoshvili, Vakhtang Sh. **Naselenie Gruzii.** Tbilisi: Metsniereba, 1968, 398 p.
  A monograph on demographic problems in the Georgian S.S.R.

Gafurov, B. G. and Litvinskov, B. A., *eds*. **Istoriia tadzhikskogo naroda.** Moscow: Izd-vo Vostochnoi Literatury "Nauka," 1963-65, 3 v. in 5 pts.
  A comprehensive general survey of the history of the Tadzhiks.

Gidney, James B. **A Mandate for Armenia.** Kent (Ohio): Kent State University Press, 1967, 270 p.
  A study, based primarily on American sources, of the American involvement in the Armenian problem during and after World War I. The author is critical of the Allied policies toward Armenia.

Gugushvili, Paata Vissarionovich, *ed*. **Gruzinskaia SSR: kratkii istoriko-ekonomicheskii ocherk.** Tbilisi: Merani, 1971, 232 p.
  A historical survey of the economic development of the Georgian S.S.R.

Guliev, Dzhamil' Bakhadur ogly. **Bor'ba Kommunisticheskoi Partii za osushchestvlenie leninskoi natsional'noi politiki v Azerbaidzhane.** Baku: Azerbaidzhanskoe Gosudarstvennoe Izd-vo, 1970, 706 p.
  The author marks the fiftieth anniversary of Soviet power in Azerbaijan by providing a lengthy and heavily documented account of the local struggle against "reactionary elements" during the Civil War period.

Guseinov, I. A. and Others, *eds*. **Istoriia Azerbaidzhana.** Baku: Akademiia Nauk Azerbaidzhanskoi SSR, 1958-63, 3 v.
  A Soviet history of Azerbaijan.

Hayit, Baymirza. **Sowjetrussischer Kolonialismus und Imperialismus in Turkestan.** Oosterhout (Netherlands): Anthropological Publications, 1965, 117 p.
  Dr. Hayit, a Turkestani Muslim trained in Germany and author of several books and monographs on the history of Turkestan, enlarges on the theme that the U.S.S.R., anti-imperialist in Asia and Africa, none the less practices a rigorous imperialism of its own in Turkestan.

Hovannisian, Richard G. **Armenia on the Road to Independence, 1918.** Berkeley: University of California Press, 1967, 364 p.
  This detailed account of the Armenian question during the First World War and the events leading to the brief period of independence of the "Armenian Republic" is a significant contribution to the political and diplomatic history of the period.

Hovannisian, Richard G. **The Republic of Armenia. Volume I: The First Year, 1918-1919.** Berkeley: University of California Press, 1972, 547 p.
  The author's previous work, "Armenia on the Road to Independence, 1918," was the forerunner to this thoroughly researched description of the tribulations of the ill-fated independent state's first year.

Iarmukhamedov, Mukhtamid Shamukhamedovich. **Ekonomicheskaia geografiia Kazakhskoi S.S.R.** Alma-Ata: Mektep, 1964, 249 p.
  An economic geography of the Kazakh S.S.R.

Inoiatov, Khamid Sharapovich. **Pobeda sovetskoi vlasti v Uzbekistane.** Tashkent: Izd-vo "Uzbekistan," 1967, 247 p.

This narrative of the events of 1917–1918 in Uzbekistan, leading to the successful assumption of power in Central Asia by the Bolsheviks, is presented not only for historical interest but also with the intent of suggesting a parallel path of development for ex-colonial areas of the present day.

Karryev, Aga, *ed*. **Istoriia Sovetskogo Turkmenistana.** Ashkhabad: Ylym, 1970, 2 v.
A general Soviet history of the Turkmen S.S.R.

Kiikbaev, Nigmet. **Torzhestvo leninskoi natsional'noi politiki v Kazakhstane (1917–1967 gg.).** Alma-Alta: Izd-vo "Kazakhstan," 1968, 342 p.
A Soviet study of Kazakhstan as an example of the success of Leninist policies toward national minorities.

Kirakosyan, Jon Sahaki. **Zapadnaia Armeniia v gody Pervoi mirovoi voiny.** Erevan: Izd-vo Erevanskogo Universiteta, 1971, 475 p.
A Soviet study of the Armenian question during World War I.

Kuliev, N. M. **Istoriia Azerbaidzhana (1921–1961): bibliografiia.** Baku: Elm, 1970, 287 p.

——— and Others. **Velikii oktiabr' i Azerbaidzhan (1917–1967): bibliografiia.** Baku: Akademiia Nauk Azerbaidzhanskoi SSR, 1967, 172 p.
Useful bibliographies on the Soviet rule in Azerbaijan.

Makharadze, N. B. **Pobeda sotsialisticheskoi revoliutsii v Gruzii.** Tbilisi: Sabchota Sakartvelo, 1965, 449 p.
A study of the establishment of Soviet rule in Georgia.

Nove, Alec and Newth, J. A. **The Soviet Middle East: A Communist Model for Development.** New York: Praeger, 1967, 160 p.
An inquiry by two well-qualified scholars into economic and social development in the national republics of Central Asia and Transcaucasian Asia and the mixed blessings of Russian participation and control.

Nurmukhamedov, Suniiat Bekmashevich. **Ocherki istorii sotsialisticheskogo stroitel'stva v Kazakhstane, 1933–1944 gg.** Alma-Ata: Nauka, 1966, 279 p.
A study of economic developments in Kazakhstan from 1933 to 1944.

Pobeda sovetskoi vlasti v Srednei Azii i Kazakhstane. Tashkent: Izd-vo "Fan," 1967, 768 p.
This official narrative of the struggle for Soviet power in Central Asia and Kazakhstan against forces of the White armies and local nationalists was published as part of the fiftieth anniversary observances of the October Revolution.

Radzhabov, Zarif Sharipovich, *ed*. **Istoriia Tadzhikskoi S.S.R.** Dushanbe: Irfon, 1965, 450 p.
A Soviet history of the Tadzhik S.S.R.

Rakowska-Harmstone, Teresa. **Russia and Nationalism in Central Asia: The Case of Tadzhikistan.** Baltimore: Johns Hopkins Press (in coöperation with the Institute for Sino-Soviet Studies, George Washington University), 1970, 325 p.
An intensive study, focusing on Tadzhikistan in the decade 1946–56, of Soviet nationality policy and native response in Central Asia.

Rywkin, Michael. **Russia in Central Asia.** New York: Collier Books, 1963, 191 p.
A tightly knit history of Russia's penetration into Central Asia.

Samedov, Teimur Gazanfarovich. **Ekonomicheskoe i kul'turnoe razvitie Turkmenistana v gody zaversheniia stroitel'stva sotsializma v SSSR (1945–1958 gg.).** Ashkhabad: Turkmenskii Gosudarstvennyi Universitet Im. A. M. Gor'kogo, 1970, 185 p.
A study of economic and cultural developments in the Turkmen S.S.R. from 1945 to 1958.

Samedov, Vitalii Iunusovich. **Rasprostranen'ie marksizma-leninizma v Azerbaidzhane.** Baku: Azerbaidzhanskoe Gos. Izd-vo, 1962–66, 2 v.
A history of socialism and Marxism in Azerbaijan.

Togan, Ahmed Zeki Velidi. **Hâtıralar: Türkistan ve diğer Müslüman doğu Türklerinin milli varlık ve kültür mücadeleleri.** Istanbul: Hikmet Gazetecilik Ltd., 1969, 643 p.
Memoirs by the former President of the short-lived Bashkirian Republic, subsequently professor at the University of Istanbul until his death in 1972. Excellent information about the Turkic speaking nations of the U.S.S.R. and their struggle for liberation, chiefly in the period from 1900 to 1922.

Vaidyanath, R. **The Formation of the Soviet Central Asian Republics: A Study in Soviet Nationalities Policy, 1917-1936.** New Delhi: People's Publishing House, 1967, 297 p.
  An Indian scholar, who lived for an extended period in the Soviet Union, describes in this well-documented study the implementation of the Soviet nationalities policies in the Central Asian region that was formerly known as Turkestan.

Viatkin, M. P. and Others, *eds.* **Istoriia Kirgizii.** Frunze: Kirgizskoe Gos. Izd-vo, 1963, 2 v.
  A general history of the Kirghiz S.S.R., prepared under the auspices of the Kirghiz Academy of Sciences.

Wheeler, Geoffrey Edleston. **The Modern History of Soviet Central Asia.** New York: Praeger, 1964, 272 p.
  A useful introduction, by a leading British authority, to the five Central Asian republics of the Soviet Union.

Wheeler, Geoffrey Edleston. **The Peoples of Soviet Central Asia.** Chester Springs (Pa.): Dufour Editions, 1966, 126 p.
  A brief history of the Muslim peoples inhabiting the Soviet Socialist Republics of Kazakhstan, Uzbekistan, Kirghizia, Tadzhikistan and Turkmenistan since they came under Russian domination in the eighteenth and nineteenth centuries. The author was the Director of the Central Asian Research Centre in London from 1953 to 1968.

RUMANIA

See also Political Factors, p. 12; Ethnic Problems; The Jews, p. 46; Inter-War Period, p. 140; Second World War, p. 144; Eastern Europe and the Soviet Bloc, p. 358; (Hungary) Recent History to 1945, p. 511; (Union of Soviet Socialist Republics) Foreign Policy, p. 550.

Apostol, Georghe P. and Others. **Județele României Socialiste.** Bucharest: Editura Politică, 2d ed., 1972, 593 p.
  A very useful detailed economic survey of Rumania by administrative district, balancing recent statistical data with historical accounts of local developments.

Basic Principles of Romania's Foreign Policy: Communiqué on the Joint Meeting of the Central Committee of the Romanian Communist Party, the State Council, and the Romanian Government, August 21, 1968; Special Session of the Grand National Assembly of the Socialist Republic of Romania, August 22, 1968. Bucharest: Meridiane Publishing House, 1968, 99 p.
  The main speeches and resolutions prepared in immediate reaction to the Warsaw Pact invasion of Czechoslovakia. These documents represent the most outspoken expression of Rumania's independent course in international relations.

Braham, Randolph L. **Education in Romania: A Decade of Change.** Washington: G.P.O., 1972, 145 p.

———. **Education in the Rumanian People's Republic.** Washington: G.P.O., 1963, 229 p.
  Studies on the evolution of educational policies in Rumania.

Ceaușescu, Nicolae. **Romania on the Way of Completing Socialist Construction: Reports, Speeches, Articles.** Bucharest: Meridiane Publishing House, 1969—.
  Reports, speeches and articles by the President of the State Council and General Secretary of the Central Committee of the Rumanian Communist Party covering the period since July 1965. Through 1973 seven volumes have been published. The Rumanian edition appears as "România pe drumul desăvîrșirii construcției socialiste: rapoarte, cuvîntari, articole" (Bucharest: Editura Politică, 1969—). The title for both editions varies.

Cioranesco, George and Others. **Aspects des relations russo-roumaines: rétrospectives et orientations.** Paris: Minard, 1967, 276 p.
  Chapters by a number of authors on the history of Russo-Rumanian relations from the first contacts at the time of Peter the Great to the present.

Conferința națională a Partidului Comunist Român: Lucrări; București, 19-21 iulie 1972. Bucharest: Editura Politică (for the Partidul Comunist Român), 1972, 565 p.

The debates and major resolutions of a decisive conference of the Rumanian Communist Party which adopted economic guidelines and standards of party behavior for the coming decade.

Constantinescu-Iaşi, Petre and Others, eds. **Istoria României.** Bucharest: Editura Academiei Republicii Populare Române, 1960–72, 5 v.
The official Marxist historical synthesis of Rumania from the beginning of primitive habitation to the completion of national unity after World War I.

Dezvoltarea economică a României, 1944–1964. Bucharest: Editura Academiei Republicii Populare Române (for the Academia Republicii Populare Române, Institutul de Cercetări Economice), 1964, 787 p.
A comprehensive volume of essays on Rumanian economy. Should be consulted jointly with the following more specialized studies: "Dezvoltarea economiei româneşti, 1966–1970" (Bucharest: Editura Politică, 1971, 160 p.); "Industria României, 1944–1964," edited by Vasile Malinschi and Others (Bucharest: Editura Academiei RPR, 1964, 803 p.); "Industria României, 1966–1970," edited by Constantin Ionescu (Bucharest: Editura Politică, 1971, 272 p.); and "Agricultura României, 1944–1964," by Nicolae Giosan and Others (Bucharest: Editura Agro-Silvică, 1964, 389 p.).

Documente din Istoria Partidului Comunist şi a Mişcării Muncitoreşti Revoluţionare din România. Bucharest: Editura Politică (for the Institutul de Studii Istorice şi Social-Politice de pe lîngă C.C. al P.C.R.), 1966–.
An extensive collection of documents of the Rumanian Communist Party to replace the four volumes of a similar collection published from 1953 to 1957. The five volumes which have appeared through 1973 cover the period from 1893 to 1924.

Fischer-Galati, Stephen Alexander. **The New Rumania: From People's Democracy to Socialist Republic.** Cambridge: M.I.T. Press, 1967, 126 p.
A concise but very informative analysis of the evolution of communist Rumania, with particular and much-needed emphasis on the role of the late leader Gheorghiu-Dej, a little-known and underestimated figure.

Fischer-Galati, Stephen Alexander. **Twentieth Century Rumania.** New York: Columbia University Press, 1970, 248 p.
A thoughtful interpretation of the profound changes in Rumanian life and politics in this century, but with an eye to the significant elements of continuity that have survived and reëmerged in the communist era.

Floyd, David. **Rumania: Russia's Dissident Ally.** New York: Praeger, 1965, 144 p.
A writer for the London *Daily Telegraph* briefly reviews the steps by which the Rumanian Communist regime has, since 1962, gained a considerable measure of diplomatic and economic independence.

Georgescu, Titu and Others. **Partidul Comunist Român în viaţa social-politică a României, 1921–1944: culegere de studii.** Bucharest: Editura Militară (for the Institutul de Studii Istorice şi Social-Politice de pe lîngă C.C. al P.C.R.), 1971, 423 p.
A collection of articles which makes substantial concessions to the *sine qua non* of party adulation but which nevertheless presents considerable new material on inter-war party activities and policies, with moderate documentation from party archives.

Gusti, Dimitrie. **Opere.** Bucharest: Editura Academiei Republicii Socialiste România, 1968–71, 5 v.
A collection, with introduction and extensive notes, of the works of Dimitrie Gusti (1880–1955), Rumania's most eminent 20th century sociologist. It reflects the renaissance of interest in sound sociological research which has taken place since 1965. Edited by Ovidiu Bădina and Octavian Neamţu.

Holt, Dumitru and Others. **Administraţia de stat în Republica Socialistă România.** Bucharest: Editura Academiei Republicii Socialiste România, 1968, 360 p.
A valuable study of the Rumanian state administrative structure, including sections on cadres, governmental responsibilities, agencies and basic statutes.

Ionescu, Ghita. **Communism in Rumania, 1944–1962.** New York: Oxford University Press (for the Royal Institute of International Affairs), 1964, 378 p.
An able, scholarly and much needed study which provides a history both of the Rumanian Communist Party and of Rumania's vicissitudes under the Communist regime.

Ionescu, Ghita. **The Reluctant Ally: A Study of Communist Neo-colonialism.** London: Ampersand, 1965, 133 p.
A useful survey of the Rumanian-COMECON conflict in the early 1960s, by a Rumanian exile scholar teaching in England.

Jowitt, Kenneth. **Revolutionary Breakthroughs and National Development: The Case of Romania, 1945-1965.** Berkeley: University of California Press, 1971, 317 p.
The first work which attempts to apply modern political science methodology to the realities of Rumanian development under socialism. Sometimes puzzling, but very stimulating and thought-provoking.

Kopanskii, Iakov Mikhailovich and Levit, Iziaslav Elikovich. **Sovetsko-rumynskie otnosheniia, 1929-34 gg.** Moscow: Izd-vo "Nauka," 1971, 187 p.
A detailed diplomatic history of the events leading up to the establishment of normal relations between Rumania and the Soviet Union in 1934.

Malița, Mircea and Others, eds. **Reprezentanțele Diplomatice ale României.** Bucharest: Editura Politică, 1967-69, 2 v.
A survey of the activities of Rumanian diplomatic missions abroad from the unification of Moldavia and Wallachia in 1859 to the present. The first volume covers the period from 1859 to 1917, the second, from 1911 to 1939.

Matei, Horia C. and Others. **Chronological History of Romania.** Bucharest: Editura Enciclopedică Română, 1972, 524 p.
A useful reference. The chapters on contemporary history have been compiled by Ioan Chiper and Ion Alexandrescu.

Moisuc, Viorica. **Diplomația României și problema apărării suveranității și independenței naționale în perioada martie 1938-mai 1940.** Bucharest: Editura Academiei Republicii Socialiste România, 1971, 324 p.
An excellent and well-documented study of Rumanian diplomacy from Munich to the fall of France, after which Rumania moved rapidly to full alignment with Germany. The best study of this critical period yet available.

Moisuc, Viorica and Others. **Probleme de politică externă a României, 1919-1939: culegere de studii.** Bucharest: Editura Militară (for the Institutul de Studii Istorice și Social-Politice de pe lîngă C.C. al P.C.R.), 2d ed., 1971, 473 p.
Nine substantial articles, with extensive and detailed documentation, on Rumanian foreign policy in the inter-war period.

Montias, John Michael. **Economic Development in Communist Rumania.** Cambridge: M.I.T. Press, 1967, 327 p.
A leading student of the economics of Eastern Europe provides both a wealth of information and a general summing up.

Niri, A. **Istoricul unui tratat înrobitor: tratatul economic româno-german din martie 1939.** Bucharest: Editura Științifică, 1965, 309 p.
One of the first Rumanian attempts after 1945 to deal in a scholarly fashion with major inter-war events as they concerned Rumania.

Organizații de masă legale și ilegale create, conduse sau influențate de P.C.R., 1921-1944. Bucharest: Editura Politică (for the Institutul de Studii Istorice și Social-Politice de pe lîngă C.C. al P.C.R.), 1970, 579 p.
The first volume of a projected two-volume work which will trace the development of communist and communist-inspired movements in inter-war Rumania. This volume covers 18 organizations founded before the end of 1933, including Petru Groza's Ploughmen's Front (Frontul Plugarilor).

Pearton, Maurice. **Oil and The Roumanian State.** Oxford: Clarendon Press, 1971, 361 p.
A solid history of the Rumanian oil industry before, during and after World War II.

Popișteanu, Cristian. **România și Antanta Balcanică: momente și semnificații de istorie diplomatică.** Bucharest: Editura Politică, 2d ed., 1971, 357 p.
A useful study of Rumania's role in Balkan politics from Versailles to World War II.

Rădulescu, Ilie. **Funcția economică organizatorică a statului socialist.** Bucharest: Editura Academiei Republicii Socialiste România, 1967, 335 p.
Theoretical discussions of Rumanian economic policy since 1960.

Le Régime et les institutions de la Roumanie. Brussels: Université Libre de Bruxelles, Institut de Sociologie, 1966, 180 p.

Papers, mostly by Rumanian scholars, delivered in November 1964 in Brussels at a study conference on political and economic problems of the Rumanian People's Republic.

România în războiul antihitlerist, 23 august 1944–9 mai 1945. Bucharest: Editura Militară (for the Institutul de Studii Istorice şi Social-Politice de pe lîngă C.C. al P.C.R.), 1966, 813 p.
A military history of Rumania's participation in the final campaigns of World War II. The starting point is the coup against Antonescu on August 23, 1944.

Samuelli, Annie. **The Wall Between.** Washington: Robert B. Luce, 1967, 227 p.
An appalling personal account of political imprisonment in Rumania in the 1950s and early 1960s.

Statement on the Stand of the Romanian Workers' Party Concerning the Problems of the World Communist and Working-Class Movement, Endorsed by the Enlarged Plenum of the Central Committee of the Romanian Workers' Party Held in April 1964. Bucharest: Romanian News Agency (for the Partidul Muncitoresc Român), 1964, 54 p.
This famous "declaration of independence" states the principles which Rumania has attempted to espouse in international and interparty relations.

Stoicoiu, Virgiliu. **Legal Sources and Bibliography of Romania.** New York: Praeger, 1964, 237 p.
A bibliography of Rumanian legal sources from the seventeenth century to the mid-1960s, by the Rumanian law bibliographer at the U.S. Library of Congress.

Titulescu, Nicolae. **Discursuri.** Bucharest: Editura Ştiinţifică, 1967, 620 p.
A collection of speeches of Rumania's foremost inter-war diplomat.

Titulescu, Nicolae. **Documente Diplomatice.** Bucharest: Editura Politică, 1967, 893 p.
A carefully chosen selection of documents from Titulescu's career, edited by George Macovescu.

Vîntu, I. and Others. **Sfaturile populare, organe locale ale puterii de stat în Republica Populară România.** Bucharest: Editura Academiei Republicii Populare Române, 1964, 450 p.
A detailed study of the origins, organization, and functioning of local government organs in Rumania, published by the Institute for Legal Research of the Rumanian Academy.

JUGOSLAVIA

General

See also Political Factors, p. 12; Labor and Labor Movements, p. 41; Economic Growth and Development, p. 71; First World War, p. 131; Inter-War Period, p. 140; Second World War, p. 144; The Postwar World, p. 178; (Mexico) Economic and Social Problems, p. 292; (Europe) General Surveys, p. 344; Eastern Europe and the Soviet Bloc, p. 358; (Italy) Foreign Policy, p. 424; (Union of Soviet Socialist Republics) Foreign Policy, p. 550; Government; Constitution; Law, p. 564; (Jugoslavia) The Tito Regime, p. 594.

Auty, Phyllis. **Yugoslavia.** New York: Walker, 1965, 251 p.
A concise but informed and informative general history, with emphasis on the period since 1945.

Boban, Ljubo. **Sporazum Cvetković-Maček.** Belgrade: Institut društvenih nauka, 1965, 435 p.
A political analysis of the Serbo-Croat question during the years 1938 and 1939.

Božić, Ivan; Čirković, S.; Ekmečić, M. and Dedijer, V. **Istorija Jugoslavije.** Belgrade: "Prosveta," 1972, 606 p.
A history of the political, cultural, social and economic development of the Jugoslav peoples from the time they settled in the Balkan region up to the end of the Second World War. The book includes 59 maps.

Clissold, Stephen, *ed.* **A Short History of Yugoslavia: From Early Times to 1966.** New York: Cambridge University Press, 1966, 279 p.

The major part of this useful introductory survey, written by R. W. Seton-Watson, H. C. Darby and R. G. D. Laffan, was originally published in 1944 by the Naval Intelligence Division of the British Admiralty. Stephen Clissold and Phyllis Auty have contributed chapters on Jugoslav history during and after World War II. Excellent maps.

Čulinović, Ferdo. **Okupatorska podjela Jugoslavije.** Belgrade: Vojnoizdavački Zavod, 1970, 688 p.
A comprehensive and well-researched analysis of the Axis occupation of Jugoslavia during World War II.

Djordjevic, Jovan. **La Yougoslavie.** Paris: Librairie Générale de Droit, 1967, 482 p.
A systematic analysis of the political and constitutional systems of contemporary Jugoslavia.

Donlagić, Ahmet and Others. **Yugoslavia in the Second World War.** Belgrade: Međunarodna Štampa—Interpress, 1967, 245 p.
The official English version of a Jugoslav history of World War II developments in Jugoslavia.

Eterovich, Francis Hyacinth and Spalatin, Christopher, *eds.* **Croatia: Land, People, Culture.** Toronto: University of Toronto Press, 1964–70, 2 v.
This reference work covers geography, demography, archaeology, history, economic development, the arts and Croatian migration to the United States and Canada.

Gligorijević, Branislav. **Demokratska stranka i politički odnosi u Kraljevini Srba Hrvata i Slovenaca.** Belgrade: Institut za savremenu istoriju, 1970, 620 p.
The definitive study of the activities of the Democratic Party in the period from 1918 to 1929; there is an excellent bibliography.

Hory, Ladislaus and Broszat, Martin. **Der kroatische Ustascha-Staat 1941–1945.** Stuttgart: Deutsche Verlags-Anstalt (for the Institut für Zeitgeschichte), 1964, 183 p.
A substantial account, based largely on German records, of the Pavelić régime during the Second World War.

Jukić, Ilija. **Pogledi na prošlost, sadašnjost i budućnost hrvatskog naroda.** London: Hrvatska politička knjižnica, 1965, 268 p.
A polemical survey of Croat history, by a former Undersecretary of State in the Royal Jugoslav government.

Kulundžić, Zvonimir. **Atentat na Stjepana Radića.** Zagreb: "Stvarnost," 1967, 614 p.
A well-researched study of the events surrounding the assassination of the Croatian Peasant Party leader Stjepan Radić in 1928.

Lederer, Ivo John. **Yugoslavia at the Paris Peace Conference: A Study in Frontiermaking.** New Haven: Yale University Press, 1963, 351 p.
This scholarly and balanced study of Jugoslav territorial issues at the end of World War I and in the peacemaking is a welcome addition to the studies treating the experiences of the various nations at the Versailles settlement. Bordering seven states, Jugoslavia's frontiers presented a particularly knotty issue, but Professor Lederer, making good use of new Jugoslav archival sources, has done much to clarify the picture.

Mitrović, Andrej. **Jugoslavija na konferenciji mira 1919–1920.** Belgrade: Zavod za izdavanje udžbenika SRS, 1969, 276 p.
A study of the activities of various Jugoslav political groups at the Peace Conference in Paris after World War I, and a discussion of the geopolitical problems of the new Jugoslav state.

Morača, Pero. **Jugoslavija 1941.** Belgrade: Institut za savremenu istoriju, 1971, 784 p.
The official history of the role played by the Jugoslav Communist Party in the first year of the war against the Axis powers.

Mužić, Ivan. **Hrvatska politika i jugoslavenska ideja.** Split: Ivan Mužić, 1969, 319 p.
A historical survey of the development of the concept of Jugoslavism, in particular as it affected Croatian politics. There is a substantial bibliography.

Palmer, Stephen E., Jr. and King, Robert R. **Yugoslav Communism and the Macedonian Question.** Hamden (Conn.): Archon Books, 1971, 247 p.
An historical study of Jugoslav communist policy in and concerning Macedonia between the wars, during World War II and in the Tito era. The authors see the area as still a potential point of conflict.

Pavlowitch, Stevan K. **Yugoslavia.** New York: Praeger, 1971, 416 p.
A substantial survey, in the "Nations of the Modern World" series, by a Belgrade-born author teaching in England.

Pertot, Vladimir. **Ekonomika medjunarodne razmjene Jugoslavije.** Zagreb: "Informator," 1970-71, 2 v.
A comprehensive study, including a volume of documents, of Jugoslav foreign economic relations from the First World War to the late 1960s.

Prcela, John and Guldescu, Stanko, eds. **Operation Slaughterhouse: Eyewitness Accounts of Postwar Massacres in Yugoslavia.** Philadelphia: Dorrance, 1970, 557 p.
Documents on the execution and imprisonment of Croats by Tito's partisan troops after the end of World War II. The editors blame the British military authorities for refusal to protect the Croats, of whom a considerable number had collaborated with the Germans, from Tito's vengeance.

Ristić, Dragisa N. **Yugoslavia's Revolution of 1941.** University Park: Pennsylvania State University Press (for the Hoover Institution on War, Revolution, and Peace), 1966, 175 p.
A useful and revealing eyewitness account, but well-documented also, of the Simović coup d'état of March 27, 1941, an event which was to have fateful and worldwide repercussions.

Šepić, Dragovan. **Italija, saveznici i Jugoslovenko pitanje 1914-1918.** Zagreb: Školska Knjiga, 1970, 431 p.
A detailed study of the Jugoslav issues in foreign relations in the Adriatic area during World War I.

Stojadinović, Milan M. **Ni rat ni pakt: Jugoslavija izmedju dva rata.** Buenos Aires, 1963, 760 p.
Important memoirs of a Serbian politician who from 1935 to 1939 was the head of the Jugoslav government.

Stojkov, Todor. **Opozicija u vreme šestojanuarske diktature 1929-1935.** Belgrade: "Prosveta," 1969, 356 p.
A substantial historical analysis of political opposition during the period of royal dictatorship from 1929 to 1938.

Vinaver, Vuk. **Jugoslavia i Madjarska 1918-1933.** Belgrade: Institut za savremenu istoriju, 1971, 574 p.
A detailed study of Jugoslav-Hungarian foreign relations and their importance to European diplomatic developments from 1918 to 1933.

Vlahov, Dimitar. **Memoari na Dimitar Vlahov.** Skoplje: Nova Makedonija, 1970, 370 p.
This autobiography of a leading functionary of the Macedonian Federal Republic in Tito's Jugoslavia covers the period up to 1935. Important for the history of the pro-communist wing of the Internal Macedonian Revolutionary Organization, the Comintern stand on the Macedonian problem and the conflicts between the Sofia and Skoplje communists.

Wuescht, Johann. **Jugoslawien und das Dritte Reich.** Stuttgart: Seewald, 1969, 359 p.
A history, with documents, of Jugoslav-German relations from 1933 to 1945. The documents are important, the interpretation is bound to be controversial.

Zbornik dokumenata i podataka o narodnooslobodilačkom ratu jugoslovenskih naroda. Belgrade: Vojnoistorijiski institut, 1949–.
A multi-volume history of documents and materials on World War II military and political developments in Jugoslavia. Ten volumes have been published through 1974.

Živković, Dušan. **Postanak i razvitak narodne vlasti u Jugoslaviji, 1941-1942.** Belgrade: Institut za savremenu istoriju, 1969, 683 p.
A detailed analysis of the establishment and consolidation of partisan organizations on liberated territory during the first years of World War II.

The Tito Regime

See also Second World War, p. 144; The Postwar World, p. 178; Eastern Europe and the Soviet Bloc, p. 358; (Union of Soviet Socialist Republics) Foreign Policy, p. 550; (Jugoslavia) General, p. 591.

Adamović, Mihajlo, *ed.* **Ekonomski odnosi Jugoslavije sa zemljama u razvoju.** Ljubljana: Centar za proučevanje sodelvanja z dželami v razvoju, 1971, 312 p.
Papers on the nature and problems of Jugoslavia's economic relations with the developing nations.

Adizes, Ichak. **Industrial Democracy: Yugoslav Style.** New York: Free Press, 1971, 297 p.
A look at "industrial democracy" in Jugoslavia by means of case studies of the operation of two companies in 1967.

Auty, Phyllis. **Tito: A Biography.** New York: McGraw-Hill, 1970, 343 p.
The author, a leading British specialist on Jugoslavia, modestly calls this an "interim historical biography—between those written in the nineteen-fifties, especially those of V. Dedijer, Sir Fitzroy Maclean and K. Zilliacus—and the many that will come later." It is in fact a very substantial, scholarly contribution.

Avakumović, Ivan. **History of the Communist Party of Yugoslavia.** Aberdeen: Aberdeen University Press, 1964, 207 p.
This first volume of a scholarly history carries the story up to the beginning of 1941, by which time this singularly faction-ridden body had been purged and Bolshevized.

Bilandžić, Dušan. **Borba za samoupravni socijalizam u Jugoslaviji, 1945-1969.** Zagreb: Institut za historiju radničkog pokreta Hrvatske, 1969, 146 p.
A concise historical overview of political and socio-economic changes in Jugoslavia after World War II, with major emphasis on the introduction of the system of workers' self-management and the changing role of the Jugoslav Communist Party.

Bombelles, Joseph T. **Economic Development of Communist Yugoslavia, 1947-1964.** Stanford: Hoover Institution on War, Revolution, and Peace, 1968, 219 p.
Details of Jugoslavia's effort to work out its own methods in applying socialism in the 1950s and 1960s.

Broekmeyer, M. J., *ed.* **Yugoslav Workers' Selfmanagement.** Dordrecht: Reidel, 1970, 267 p.
The proceedings of a symposium held in Amsterdam in 1970 by Jugoslav and foreign scholars.

Campbell, John Coert. **Tito's Separate Road: America and Yugoslavia in World Politics.** New York: Harper and Row (for the Council on Foreign Relations), 1967, 180 p.
A balanced consideration of American policies toward Jugoslavia in the postwar years.

Dedijer, Vladimir. **The Battle Stalin Lost: Memoirs of Yugoslavia, 1948-1953.** New York: Viking, 1971, 341 p.
These are informal, personal but informative recollections of the years 1948-1953 when Stalin tried vainly to unseat the Tito regime. Dedijer was first disillusioned with the Soviet government in 1948 when he belatedly discovered the extent of Soviet attempts to exploit the Jugoslav economy. Translation of "Izgubljena bitka J. V. Staljina" (Sarajevo: Svjetlost, 1969, 435 p.).

Fisher, Jack C. **Yugoslavia—A Multinational State: Regional Difference and Administrative Response.** San Francisco: Chandler, 1966, 244 p.
A student of city and regional planning undertakes "to examine the effects of the uniform system of local administration which was superimposed over the country's heterogeneous cultural and economic matrix after World War II."

Hamilton, F. E. Ian. **Yugoslavia: Patterns of Economic Activity.** New York: Praeger, 1968, 384 p.
A solid study of the economic geography of Jugoslavia and of the development of policy with respect to economic planning and management since 1945.

Hondius, Frederik Willem. **The Yugoslav Community of Nations.** The Hague: Mouton, 1968, 375 p.
A legal-constitutional study of the development of Jugoslavia as a federal, "multinational" system.

Horvat, Branko. **An Essay on Yugoslav Society.** White Plains (N.Y.): International Arts and Sciences Press, 1969, 245 p.
  A series of papers by a noted Jugoslav Marxist economist. Translation of "Ogled o jugoslavenskom društvu" (Zagreb: "Mladost," 1969, 303 p.).

Johnson, A. Ross. **The Transformation of Communist Ideology: The Yugoslav Case, 1945-1953.** Cambridge: M.I.T. Press, 1972, 269 p.
  One of the many merits of this careful analysis of Jugoslav ideology, against the background of the relationship with the Soviet Union, is the attention given to the statements and undercurrents of the period from 1945-1948.

Macesich, George. **Yugoslavia: The Theory and Practice of Development Planning.** Charlottesville: University Press of Virginia, 1964, 227 p.
  A survey of the various facets of the contemporary Jugoslav economy, with particular attention paid to problems of economic development and planning. The work is based in part on several visits to the country.

Meister, Albert. **Où va l'autogestion yougoslave?** Paris: Anthropos, 1970, 386 p.
  An updated study of workers' participation in management in Jugoslavia.

Milenkovitch, Deborah D. **Plan and Market in Yugoslav Economic Thought.** New Haven: Yale University Press, 1971, 323 p.
  A detailed and able monograph on Jugoslav theories and views on the organization of a socialist society.

Pašic, Najdan. **Klase i politika: elementi marksističke političke nauke.** Belgrade: "Rad," 1968, 421 p.
  A thoughtful discussion of Jugoslav Marxist theory and the self-management system, by a prominent Jugoslav scholar and political activist.

Pejovich, Svetozar. **The Market-Planned Economy of Yugoslavia.** Minneapolis: University of Minnesota Press, 1966, 160 p.
  A study of the uniqueness of the Jugoslav economic system with its particular mixture of central planning and a free-market economy.

Petranović, Branko. **Politička i ekonomska osnova narodne vlasti u Jugoslaviji za vreme obnove.** Belgrade: Institut za savremenu istoriju, 1969, 464 p.
  An important study of Jugoslav political, economic and social development under the Communist regime immediately after World War II.

Petranović, Branko. **Političke i pravne prilike za vreme privremene vlade DFJ.** Belgrade: Institut društvenih nauka, 1964, 232 p.
  A description of the political and legal organization of Jugoslavia after World War II.

Popović, Nenad D. **Yugoslavia: The New Class in Crisis.** Syracuse: Syracuse University Press, 1968, 240 p.
  A former Jugoslav official, who defected in 1961, argues that the regime of Jugoslavia's new class "in its dialectical transformations, unavoidably develops those forces that will eventually bury both the new class and communism."

Pribičević, Branko. **Sukob komunističke partije Jugoslavia i kominforma.** Belgrade: "Komunist," 1972, 60 p.
  A short survey of the main issues in the conflict between Jugoslavia and the Soviet-bloc countries in the period from 1948 to 1955.

Rubinstein, Alvin Zachary. **Yugoslavia and the Nonaligned World.** Princeton: Princeton University Press, 1970, 353 p.
  A substantial study of the origins and development of Jugoslavia's foreign policy toward the new nations of Asia and Africa.

Shoup, Paul. **Communism and the Yugoslav National Question.** New York: Columbia University Press, 1968, 308 p.
  A careful and original study of national rivalries within Jugoslavia and of the efforts of Tito's regime to deal with them.

Sukijasović, Miodrad. **Yugoslav Foreign Investment Legislation at Work.** Dobbs Ferry (N.Y.): Oceana, 1970, 178 p.
  An analysis of the legal complexities and practical issues concerning the investment of foreign capital in the Jugoslav economy.

Tito, Josip Broz. [**Works.**]
> Of the official collection of the Jugoslav leader's writings published as "Sabrana dela" (Belgrade: Kultura, 1947–), 20 volumes have been published through 1972. Tito's speeches and articles appear as "Govori i članci" (Zagreb: Naprijed, 1959–); 21 volumes have appeared through 1972. The following selections of his writings and speeches have appeared in English: "Selected Speeches and Articles, 1941–1961" (Zagreb: Naprijed, 1963, 459 p.); "Selected Military Works" (Belgrade: Vojnoizdavački Zavod, 1966, 336 p.); and "The Essential Tito," edited by Henry M. Christman (New York: St. Martin's Press, 1970, 197 p.).

Tornquist, David. **Look East, Look West: The Socialist Adventure in Yugoslavia.** New York: Macmillan, 1966, 310 p.
> A personal but informative report on contemporary Jugoslavia, based on the author's experience in the country as a translator.

Vinterhalter, Vilko. **Tito: der Weg des Josip Broz.** Zurich: Europa Verlag, 1969, 363 p.
> A translation of a Slovenian historian's analysis of Tito's political evolution over his long career.

Vrtačič, L. **Einführung in den jugoslawischen Marxismus-Leninismus.** Dordrecht: Reidel (for the Osteuropa-Institut der Universität Fribourg/Schweiz), 1963, 208 p.
> An introduction to the study of philosophy in Jugoslavia after World War II, with a bibliographical survey of the philosophical literature, primarily Marxist, published from 1945 to 1959.

Vucinich, Wayne S., *ed.* **Contemporary Yugoslavia: Twenty Years of Socialist Experiment.** Berkeley: University of California Press, 1969, 441 p.
> A substantial and very knowledgeable collection of essays by an outstanding group on various facets of Jugoslav life since 1939.

Vukmanović-Tempo, Svetozar. **Mein Weg mit Tito.** Munich: Droemer/Knaur, 1972, 408 p.
> A one volume version of the memoirs of a leading Jugoslav communist. The original appeared as "Revolucija koja teče: memoari" (Belgrade: Kommunist, 1971, 2 v.).

Žarko D. and Others, *eds.* **Socijalistički i radnički pokret i Komunistička partija Jugoslaviji 1867–1969: bibliografija posebnih izdanja (1945–1969).** Belgrade: Institut za savremenu istoriju, 1972, 790 p.
> A comprehensive and well-organized annotated bibliography of Jugoslav publications concerning the international workers' movement and the Communist Party of Yugoslavia.

BULGARIA

See also Inter-War Period, p. 140; Second World War, p. 144; The Postwar World, p. 178; Eastern Europe and the Soviet Bloc, p. 358.

Atanasov, Shteriu. **Pokhod na Zapad: spomeni.** Sofia: Durzhavno voenno izdatelstvo, 1966, 205 p.
> After receiving his military and political training in the Soviet Union, Atanasov, a Bulgarian communist émigré, served as the political commissar of the First Bulgarian Army which fought against the Germans in 1944–45 on Jugoslav, Hungarian and Austrian territory under the command of Marshal Tolbukhin. The memoir is important for the description of the relations between the professional commanders and their communist aides.

Avramov, Petur. **Bulgarskata komunisticheska partiia i formirane na sotsialisticheskata inteligentsiia.** Sofia: Bulgarska komunisticheska partiia, 1966, 277 p.
> A study of the formation, development and composition of the new socialist intelligentsia in Bulgaria.

Berov, Liuben. **Polozhenieto na rabotnicheskata klasa v Bulgariia pri kapitalizma.** Sofia: Partizdat, 1968, 342 p.
> A Marxist history of the working class in Bulgaria under capitalism.

Biriuzov, S. S. **Sovetskii soldat na Balkanakh.** Moscow: Voennoe Izdatal'stvo Ministerstva Oborony SSSR, 1963, 335 p.
  Marshal Biriuzov led the Red Army into Bulgaria in September 1944 and became the actual head of the Allied Control Commission which ruled the country during the communist takeover. The author's experiences are of particular value for the study of the political developments in Bulgaria and the conflicts between Soviet and Western interests in the country.

Brown, J. F. **Bulgaria under Communist Rule.** New York: Praeger, 1970, 339 p.
  An analysis of the years of communist rule in Bulgaria from 1953 to 1968. A useful sequel to earlier studies on the nation and the party by Dellin and Rothschild.

Chary, Frederick B. **The Bulgarian Jews and the Final Solution, 1940-1944.** Pittsburgh: University of Pittsburgh Press, 1972, 246 p.
  The best scholarly treatment of what happened to the Bulgarian Jewish community in Hitler's Europe.

Confino, Baruch. **Aliya "B" mehupey Bulgariyah, 1938-1940, 1947-1948.** Jerusalem: Achiasaf Publishing House, 1965, 135 p.
  An account of the illegal Jewish emigration from Bulgaria to Palestine, by one of its organizers.

Dimitrov, Ilcho. **Burzhoaznata opozitsiia v Bulgariia, 1939-1944.** Sofia: Nauka i izkustvo, 1969, 251 p.
  A substantial monograph on the Bulgarian non-communist political factions and their leaders during World War II.

Dragoicheva, Tsola. **Po velia na dulga: spomeni i razmisli.** Sofia: Partizdat, 1972, 599 p.
  This is the first volume of an autobiography by Bulgaria's foremost communist woman revolutionary and a leading functionary.

Georgeoff, Peter John. **The Social Education of Bulgarian Youth.** Minneapolis: University of Minnesota Press, 1968, 329 p.
  An extensive description of the form, content and purpose of contemporary Bulgarian public education.

Georgiev, Velichko. **Burzhoaznite i drebno burzhoaznite partii v Bulgariia, 1934-1939.** Sofia: Nauka i izkustvo, 1971, 466 p.
  An important and well-documented monograph of the non-communist political groupings and factions in Bulgaria, covering the period of King Boris' dictatorship from the coup of 1934 to the outbreak of the Second World War.

Giovanna di Bulgaria. **Memorie.** Milano: Rizzoli, 1964, 226 p.
  Reminiscences by King Boris' widow.

Gornenski, Nikifor. **Klasite v Bulgaria i borbite im, 1934-1944.** Sofia: Nauka i izkustvo, 1967, 211 p.
  A standard Marxist analysis of the class struggle in Bulgaria during the decade preceding the communist takeover.

Grubcheva-Ogniana, Mitka. **V imeto na naroda: spomeni.** Sofia: Bulgarska komunisticheska partiia, 1964, 543 p.
  An autobiography by a Bulgarian communist woman partisan, a member of the communist execution squads during the Second World War.

Il'ichev, L. F. and Others, *eds.* **Sovetsko-bolgarskie otnosheniia 1944-1948 gg.: dokumenty i materialy.** Moscow: Izd-vo Politicheskoi Literatury, 1969, 508 p.
  A collection of documents on the emergence of the Soviet-backed postwar regime in Bulgaria and its formal relations with Moscow.

Isusov, Mito. **Rabotnicheskata klasa v Bulgariia, 1944-1947.** Sofia: Bulgarska akademiia na naukite, 1971, 289 p.
  A detailed monograph on the working class in Bulgaria during the first three years of the communist rule.

Izvestiia na instituta po istoriia na Bulgarskata Komunisticheska Partiia. Sofia: Bulgarska komunisticheska partiia, 1957– .
  Published by the Institute for the History of the Bulgarian Communist Party, this collection of articles, brief monographs, documents, archival materials and book re-

views is the most important official source for the history of Bulgarian communism. Through 1972, 28 volumes have been published.

Keshales, Haim. **Korot Yehudey Bulgariya.** Tel Aviv: Davar, 1969-72, 4 v.
A general history of the Jews in Bulgaria, including a discussion of the fate of the Jewish community during the Second World War and under the communist rule.

Khadzhinikolov, Veselin and Others. **Georgi Dimitrov: biografiia.** Sofia: Partizdat, 1972, 644 p.
A well-documented official political biography of the late Georgi Dimitrov, the former General Secretary of the Comintern and Bulgaria's Premier in the post-Second World War period. An important source for the history of Bulgarian communism and the Comintern in the 1930s and early 1940s.

Khristov, Khristo and Others, *eds.* **Sotsialisticheskata revolutsiia v Bulgariia: istoricheski studii.** Sofia: Bulgarska akademiia na naukite, 1965, 556 p.
A valuable collection of articles by leading Bulgarian historians and social scientists covering various aspects of the political, ideological and socio-economic transformations of Bulgaria under socialism from 1944 through the late 1950s.

Kolarov, Vasil. **Spomeni.** Sofia: Bulgarska komunisticheska partiia, 1968, 642 p.
The autobiography of the veteran Bulgarian communist leader and Comintern functionary, covering the early years of his life up to the mid-1920s.

Kosev, D. and Others, *eds.* **Istoria na Bulgariia.** Sofia: Nauka i izkustvo (for the Bulgarska Akademiia na Naukite), 2d rev. ed., 1962-64, 3 v.
A revised edition of a standard history of Bulgaria published by the Bulgarian Academy of Sciences.

Kostov, Traicho. **Traicho Kostov: izbrani statii, dokladi, rechi.** Sofia: Bulgarska komunisticheska partiia, 1964, 962 p.
A collection of writings and speeches of Traicho Kostov, the former General Secretary of the Bulgarian Communist Party, who was tried for treason and executed in 1949. Some of Kostov's most significant writings, such as his opening report before the Eighth Plenum of the Bulgarian Communist Party in March 1945, as well as his significant wartime correspondence with Tito and the Jugoslav Macedonians, have not been included in this collection.

Kukov, K. **Razgrom na burzhoaznata opozitsiia, 1944-1947.** Sofia: Bulgarska komunisticheska partiia, 1966, 230 p.
A standard communist account of the rise and destruction of the anti-communist opposition in Bulgaria after World War II.

Mizov, Nikolai. **Islamut v Bulgariia.** Sofia: Bulgarska komunisticheska partiia, 1965, 231 p.
A Marxist study of the role of Islam among Bulgaria's Turkish minority.

Natan, Zhak and Others, *eds.* **Ikonomika na Bulgariia.** Sofia: Nauka i izkustvo, 1969–.
A very comprehensive and ambitious Marxist economic history of Bulgaria, planned in six volumes. Through 1972 two volumes have appeared covering the period from antiquity to the 1950s.

Natan, Zhak. **Pametni vremena: spomeni.** Sofia: Bulgarska komunisticheska partiia, 1970, 303 p.
This memoir by Bulgaria's foremost Marxist historian and communist functionary covers the author's political career up to 1944. It is significant primarily for a description of the Bulgarian communist exiles in Soviet Russia during the 1920s, and the political struggles between Jewish communists and Zionists in inter-war Bulgaria.

Oliver, Khaim D. **We Were Saved: How the Jews in Bulgaria Were Kept from the Death Camps.** Sofia: Foreign Languages Press, 1967, 169 p.
A popular account of the fate of the Bulgarian Jews during the Second World War. The original appeared as "Nie, spasenite" (Sofia: Izdatelstvo za literatura na chuzhdi ezitsi, 1967, 184 p.).

Oren, Nissan. **Bulgarian Communism: The Road to Power, 1934-1944.** New York: Columbia University Press, 1972, 293 p.
This excellent monograph, which serves as a sequel to Joseph Rothschild's work on the earlier history of Bulgarian communism, follows the development of the Party in the

decade leading to the establishment of communist rule in the country at the end of the Second World War.

Penkov, Penko and Others, eds. **Vunshnata turgoviia na Narodna Republika Bulgariia.** Sofia: Nauka i izkustvo, 1970, 369 p.
An official discussion of Bulgaria's foreign trade problems in the period from 1944 to 1968.

Petrova, Dimitrina V. **Bulgarskiiat Zemedelski Naroden Suiuz i Narodniiat front, 1934–1939.** Sofia: Bulgarski zemedelski naroden suiuz, 1967, 187 p.
This monograph dealing with the relations between the Bulgarian Agrarian Union and the Bulgarian communists during the mid-1930s is important more for its factual data than for its interpretations.

Petrova, Dimitrina V. **Bulgarskiiat Zemedelski Naroden Suiuz v kraia na burzhoaznoto gospodstvo v Bulgariia.** Sofia: Bulgarski zemedelski naroden suiuz, 1970, 228 p.
A biased but useful history of the various agrarian parties in Bulgaria during the Second World War.

Piti, Buko. **Te, spasitelite.** Tel Aviv, 1969, 252 p.
An account of how the Bulgarian Jews escaped deportation during the Second World War.

Romano, A. and Others, eds. **Yahadut Bulgariyah.** Jerusalem: Encyclopedia of the Jewish Diaspora, 1967, 1,018 p.
A comprehensive study of the history of the Jewish community in Bulgaria from the earliest times, sponsored by the Union of Bulgarian Immigrants in Tel Aviv, Israel.

Roussinov, Spas. **Economic Development of Bulgaria after the Second World War.** Sofia: Sofia Press, 1969, 251 p.
A useful general survey.

Sharova, K. and Others. **Istoriia na Bulgarskata Komunisticheska Partiia.** Sofia: Bulgarska komunisticheska partiia, 2d ed., 1973, 708 p.
The latest edition of an official history of the Bulgarian Communist Party.

Shterev, Pantelei. **Obshti borbi na bulgarskiia i grutskiia narod sreshtu khitlerofashistkata okupatsiia.** Sofia: Bulgarska akademiia na naukite, 1966, 178 p.
A Bulgarian view of the Greek resistance in northern Greece during the Second World War and its relations with the Bulgarian communist resistance movement. Important for the study of the Bulgarian withdrawal from Thrace and Greek Macedonia in the fall of 1944.

Siegert, Heinz. **Bulgarien heute: rotes Land am Schwarzen Meer.** Düsseldorf: Econ-Verlag, 1964, 269 p.
A Viennese journalist's informative account of contemporary Bulgaria.

Sovetsko-Bolgarskie otnosheniia, 1944–1948: dokumenty i materialy. Moscow: Izdatel'stvo Politicheskoi Literatury (for the Ministerstvo inostrannykh del S.S.S.R. and the Ministerstvo inostrannykh del N.R.B.), 1969, 508 p.
An important selection of documents on Soviet-Bulgarian relations in the post-World War II period.

Stefanov, G. **Mezhdunarodni otnosheniia i vunshna politika na Bulgariia, 1870–1957.** Sofia: Nauka i izkustvo, 1965, 267 p.
A standard diplomatic history of Bulgaria, reflecting the official ideology of contemporary Bulgaria.

Trunski, Slavcho. **Neotdavna, 1942–1943–1944.** Sofia: Bulgarski pisatel, 1965, 728 p.
Wartime reminiscences by Bulgaria's most successful communist partisan leader.

Ustanoviavane i ukrepvane na narodnodemokratichnata vlast, septembri 1944–mai 1945: sbornik dokumenti. Sofia: Bulgarska akademiia na naukite, 1969, 763 p.
An important collection of documents on the politics of the communist takeover in Bulgaria covering the critical first nine months after the entry of the Red Army into the country.

Vinarov, Ivan. **Boitsi na tikhiia front: spomeni na razuznavacha.** Sofia: Bulgarska komunisticheska partiia, 1969, 648 p.
An interesting and readable memoir by a Bulgarian communist who for almost 20

years lived as a political exile in the Soviet Union and served as a Soviet intelligence agent in China and Central Europe.

Vranchev, Petur. **Spomeni.** Sofia: Durzhavno voenno izdatelstvo, 1968, 637 p.
A detailed and instructive memoir by a professional revolutionary who was promoted to the rank of general upon the entry of the Red Army in Bulgaria in 1944. Vranchev's story is of particular significance for a description of the communist relations with the Zveno group and the Military League from the late 1930s to the September coup of 1944.

Vunshna politika na Narodna Republika Bulgaria. Sofia: Nauka i izkustvo (for the Ministerstvo na vunshnite reboti), 1970– .
A standard collection of documents, agreements and treaties pertaining to Bulgaria's foreign relations in the post-World War II period. Through 1972 two volumes have been published covering the period from 1944 to 1969.

ALBANIA

See also Inter-War Period, p. 140; Second World War, p. 144; The Postwar World, p. 178; Eastern Europe and the Soviet Bloc, p. 358; (Italy) Foreign Policy, p. 424; (Union of Soviet Socialist Republics) Foreign Policy, p. 550; Foreign Economic Policy, p. 560; (China) Foreign Relations, p. 702.

Benanti, Franco. **La guerra più lunga: Albania 1943-1948.** Milan: Mursia, 1966, 327 p.
The author, a medic in the Italian army occupying Albania during the Second World War, narrates the dissolution of Italy's military forces in the Balkans after September 1943. In addition, since the author remained in Albania until the summer of 1948, he was able to observe at close range the formation of the Hoxha government.

Dodic, Lazar. **Historischer Rückblick auf die Stellung Albaniens im Weltkommunismus (1941-1968): mit Dokumentation.** Trittau: Scherbarth, 1970, 142 p.
A brief survey of Albanian political developments from 1941 to 1968, and an attempt to answer the question why Albania has established close ties with Communist China. There is a supplement of documents.

Dokumenta kryesore të Partisë së Punës të Shqipërisë. Tirana: Instituti i Historisë së Partisë Pranë K. Q. të PPSH.
A collection of documents, resolutions and other materials of the Albanian Communist Party. Since 1961 the following volumes have been published: vol. II (1961, 555 p.), covering the period from 1949 to 1956; vol. III (1970, 589 p.), covering the period from 1957 to 1961 and including the correspondence with the Communist Party of the Soviet Union at the inception of Soviet-Albanian differences; and vol. IV (1970, 618 p.), covering the developments from 1961 to 1965.

Ekonomia politike e socializmit. Tirana: Botim i Universitetit Shtetëror te Tiranës, 1972, 464 p.
An attempt to present "the categories and economic laws of socialism," as formulated by the classics of Marxism-Leninism, and in the light of Albania's experience in building socialism.

Gardiner, Leslie. **The Eagle Spreads His Claws.** Edinburgh: Blackwood, 1966, 286 p.
A history of the prolonged Corfu Channel dispute and of Albania's relations with the West from 1945 to 1965, by a former British naval officer.

Griffith, William E. **Albania and the Sino-Soviet Rift.** Cambridge: M.I.T. Press, 1963, 423 p.
A first-rate study with voluminous documents of the background and significance of the Albanian break with the Soviet Union and the alliance with Communist China, prepared under the auspices of the Center for International Studies at M.I.T.

Hako, Hulusi. **Akuzojmë fenë.** Tirana: Shtëpia Botonjëse "Naim Frashëri," 1968, 180 p.
A shrill, polemic attack on religion, which nonetheless gives much information on the political and ideological motives that led the Albanian leadership to abolish the religious establishment in 1967.

Hamm, Harry. **Albania–China's Beachhead in Europe.** New York: Praeger, 1963, 176 p.
A German journalist's informative report on Albania, based in part on a visit to the country in 1961. The German original appeared as "Rebellen gegen Moskau:

Albanien—Pekings Brückenkopf in Europa" (Cologne: Wissenschaft und Politik, 1962, 189 p.).

History of the Party of Labor of Albania. Tirana: Institute of Marxist-Leninist Studies, 1971, 691 p.
The official version of the history of the Albanian Communist Party from its beginnings in 1929 through the cultural revolution in the late 1960s. The Albanian original appeared as: "Historia e Partisë së Punës të Shqioërisë" (Tirana: Instituti i Studimeve Marksiste-Leniniste pranë KQ të PPSH, 1968, 544 p.).

Hoxha, Enver. **Speech Delivered at the Meeting of 81 Communist and Workers' Parties in Moscow on November 16, 1960.** Tirana: The "Naim Frashëri" Publishing House, 1969, 144 p.
A full text of the Albanian leader's vitriolic attack on Khrushchev and the Soviet leadership, accusing them of revisionism and anti-Marxism.

Hoxha, Enver. **Twenty Five Years of Struggles and Victories on the Road to Socialism.** Tirana: The "Naim Frashëri" Publishing House, 1969, 96 p.
An interesting review by Albania's leader of the course travelled and the gains achieved by the Albanian people under the leadership of the Communist Party since liberation in 1944.

Hoxha, Enver. **Vepra.** Tirana: Instituti i Studimeve Marksiste-Leniniste pranë KQ të PPSH, 1968—.
The collected works of Hoxha, Secretary of the Albanian Communist Party. By the end of 1972, eleven volumes had been published, covering the period up to August 1954.

Italiaander, Rolf, *ed.* **Albanien—Vorposten Chinas.** Munich: Delp, 1970, 282 p.
A collection of travel reports, documents and commentaries on Albania and its external relations.

Kadare, Ismail. **General of the Dead Army.** New York: Grossman, 1972, 255 p.
Widely regarded as an original work of prose, Kadare's book is also of interest to students of Albanian political problems because it develops the theme that the Albanian people will not endure subjugation. The Albanian original was published as "Gjenerali i ushtrisë së vdekur" (Tirana: Shtëpia Botonjëse "Naim Frashëri," new ed., 1967, 242 p.).

Keefe, Eugene K. and Others, *eds.* **Area Handbook for Albania.** Washington: G.O.P., 1971, 223 p.
Prepared by Foreign Area Studies of the American University, this volume is a compilation of data on the social, economic, political and military institutions of communist Albania.

Kessle, Gun and Myrdal, Jan. **Albansk utmaning.** Stockholm: PAN/Norstedt, 1970, 213 p.
The authors of this illustrated volume argue that socialist Albania, by virtue of its very existence and daring political and economic policies, presents a challenge to the "power politics" of the United States and the Soviet Union.

Kongresi i pestë i Partisë së Punës të Shqipërisë. Tirana: Shtëpia Botonjëse "Naim Frashëri," 1967, 404 p.
Proceedings of the Fifth Congress of the Albanian Communist Party, held in November 1966. Interesting especially for the impact on the congress of the Cultural Revolution then current in Communist China and Albania.

Mury, Gilbert. **Albanie, terre de l'homme nouveau.** Paris: F. Maspéro, 1970, 175 p.
An uncritical and idealistic account of life and developments in contemporary Albania, by a militant French sociologist.

Pano, Nicholas C. **The People's Republic of Albania.** Baltimore: Johns Hopkins Press, 1968, 185 p.
A useful survey of Albanian political developments during and after the Second World War, with the emphasis on the role and line of the Albanian Communist Party.

Pernack, Hans-Joachim. **Probleme der wirtschaftlichen Entwicklung Albaniens.** Munich: Südosteuropa-Gesellschaft, 1972, 196 p.
A survey of Albania's economic history.

Republika Popullore e Shqipërisë në jubileun e 30 vjetorit të themelimit të PPSH. Tirana: Drejtoria e Statistikes, 1971, 175 p.

A publication of the Directorate of Statistics on the occasion of the 30th anniversary of the Albanian Communist Party. Contains tables, illustrated charts and commentary intended to show the economic and cultural progress made under the people's rule.

Ruches, Pyrrhus J. **Albania's Captives.** Chicago: Argonaut, 1965, 213 p.
A hardly dispassionate plea for the return of "Northern Epirus" to Greece.

Skendi, Stavro. **The Albanian National Awakening, 1878-1912.** Princeton: Princeton University Press, 1967, 498 p.
Moving into unexplored territory, Professor Skendi traces the belated but real upsurge of Albanian national affirmation and desire for independence in the decades after the Congress of Berlin. An important contribution, indispensable for understanding contemporary developments.

Thomas, John I. **Education for Communism: School in the People's Republic of Albania.** Stanford: Hoover Institution Press, 1969, 131 p.
A study of education and the school system in Communist Albania, based largely on Albanian-language sources.

GREECE

General

See also Economic Growth and Development, p. 71; Inter-War Period, p. 140; Second World War, p. 144; The Postwar World, p. 178; Eastern Europe and the Soviet Bloc, p. 358; other subsections under Greece.

Bakojannis, Pavlos. **Militärherrschaft in Griechenland.** Stuttgart: Kohlhammer, 1972, 218 p.
A sensible but pretentious effort to get beyond the clichés about the Colonels' regime and to see their coup and subsequent rule in relation to preceding conditions.

Campbell, John Kennedy and Sherrard, Philip. **Modern Greece.** New York: Praeger, 1968, 426 p.
A concise but informative survey of Greek history since the beginning of the nineteenth century. Nearly half the volume is devoted to events since 1948.

Candilis, Wray O. **The Economy of Greece, 1944-66: Efforts for Stability and Development.** New York: Praeger, 1968, 238 p.
A somewhat technical analysis, with much statistical data.

Carey, Jane Perry (Clark) and Carey, Andrew Galbraith. **The Web of Modern Greek Politics.** New York: Columbia University Press, 1968, 240 p.
A useful history of modern Greek politics.

Cervi, Mario. **Dove va la Grecia? Dal colpo di stato al referendum.** Milan: Mursia, 1968, 323 p.
An Italian scholar traces the origins of the Colonels' regime in Greece to the lack of material progress, political instability and social injustice.

Chauvel, Jean-François. **La Grèce à l'ombre des épées.** Paris: Laffont, 1968, 280 p.
A French journalist's account of events in Greece from the coup of April 21, 1967, to the departure of the King in December.

Clogg, Richard and Yannopoulos, George, *eds.* **Greece under Military Rule.** New York: Basic Books, 1972, 272 p.
A collection of critical articles reviewing the Greek military regime's first five years in power.

Coutsoumaris, George and Others. **Analysis and Assessment of the Economic Effects of the U.S. PL 480 Program in Greece.** Athens: Center of Planning and Economic Research, 1965, 293 p.
A study originally commissioned by the U.S. Department of Agriculture.

Coutsoumaris, George. **The Morphology of Greek Industry: A Study in Industrial Development.** Athens: Center of Economic Research, 1963, 430 p.
A detailed empirical and statistical analysis of the structure and performance of Greek industry.

Ellis, Howard S. and Others. **Industrial Capital in Greek Developments.** Athens: Center of Economic Research, 1971, 335 p.
  A case study of economic development in Greece through an analysis of the role and deficiencies of the capital market.

Holden, David. **Greece without Columns.** Philadelphia: Lippincott, 1972, 336 p.
  The chief foreign correspondent of the London *Sunday Times* is not happy with the condition of democracy in contemporary Greece, but he blames the old political establishment and the lethargy of the Greek population as much as the regime of the Colonels.

Katris, John A. **Eyewitness in Greece: The Colonels Come to Power.** St. Louis: New Critics Press, 1971, 317 p.
  A Greek journalist and editor presents his view of the background to the Colonels' coup.

Kofos, Evangelos. **Nationalism and Communism in Macedonia.** Thessaloniki: Institute for Balkan Studies, 1964, 251 p.
  A history of Macedonia from the early nineteenth century to 1962, containing much information hitherto unavailable in English.

Kousoulas, Dimitrios George. **Revolution and Defeat.** New York: Oxford University Press, 1965, 306 p.
  An excellent, authoritative history of the fortunes and misfortunes of the Greek Communist Party. About half the volume is devoted to the years since 1941.

Legg, Keith R. **Politics in Modern Greece.** Stanford: Stanford University Press, 1969, 367 p.
  An analysis of the Greek political system as a rather distinct but not unique type in the contemporary world.

Marceau, Marc. **La Grèce des colonels.** Paris: Laffont, 1968, 273 p.
  An Athens correspondent for *Le Monde* reports on and analyzes the coup of April 21, 1967.

Markezinis, Spyros V. **Politiki istoria tis neoteras Ellados 1828-1964.** Athens: Papyros, 1966-70, 5 v.
  A massive political history of modern Greece. The author believes that the role of the Great Powers in Greek politics has been overestimated.

Meynaud, Jean and Others. **Les forces politiques en Grèce.** Lausanne: Études de Science Politique, 1965, 530 p.
  A detailed examination of contemporary Greek politics, with many charts and statistical tables.

Papandreou, Andreas George. **Democracy at Gunpoint: The Greek Front.** Garden City: Doubleday, 1970, 365 p.
  The author, a Harvard-trained Greek political figure, gives his intimate view of Greek politics in the 1960s. He is very hostile to U.S. policy; the CIA is a principal target.

Pentzopoulous, Dēmētrēs. **The Balkan Exchange of Minorities and Its Impact Upon Greece.** The Hague: Mouton, 1962, 293 p.
  A scholarly study of the exchange of Greek and Turkish minorities after World War I and of the problems of resettlement and adaptation.

Psaros, Dimitrios. **I anatheorissis tou Syntagmmatos: politiki analysis kai nomiki ermineia en syngrisei pros to proïschyon Syntagma 1864-1911-1952.** Athens: P. Kleissiounis, 1969, 542 p.
  A massive study of the Constitution of 1968, which, though never fully implemented and based on the principle of a "crowned republic," contains many provisions on civil rights and the position of the military as guardians of the Constitution.

Rallis, Konstantinos. **Psifos, eklogai kai synchrona eklogika systimata.** Athens, 1966, 455 p.
  An important monograph on the election systems in modern Greece.

Rousseas, Stephen Williams and Others. **The Death of a Democracy: Greece and the American Conscience.** New York: Grove Press, 1967, 268 p.
  A vehement indictment of the military coup of April 21, 1967, by a professor of economics at New York University, a strong partisan of Andreas Papandreou.

Skriver, Ansgar. **Soldaten gegen Demokraten: Militärdiktatur in Griechenland.** Cologne: Kiepenheuer, 1968, 197 p.
A German journalist's presentation of the events of the first year following the April 1967 coup in Athens.

Stockton, Bayard. **Phoenix with a Bayonet.** Ann Arbor (Mich.): Georgetown Publications, 1971, 306 p.
An American journalist's relatively favorable appraisal of the military group that took power in Greece in the coup of April 1967.

Tassoulis, Georgios, *ed.* **O Archiepiskopos Athinon Chryssanthos o apo Trapezoundos. I Ethniki kai Ekklisiastiki Drassis tou 1881-1949.** Athens, 1970-72, 2 v.
This monograph on the political and religious activities of Archbishop of Athens Chryssanthos of Trebizond provides valuable documentation and information about the project of an independent Trebizond after World War I, the Cyprus issue in 1931, and the Archbishop's attitude toward the Germans, who removed him from his position in 1941.

Triantis, Stephen G. **Common Market and Economic Development: The E.E.C. and Greece.** Athens: Center of Planning and Economic Research, 1965, 232 p.
A professor at the University of Toronto, working with a Greek research organization, stresses the disadvantages of an underdeveloped country in a single market area and concludes that association with the European Common Market will hurt the Greek economy.

Tsoucalas, Constantine. **The Greek Tragedy.** Baltimore: Penguin, 1969, 207 p.
A Greek lawyer provides a concise, informed historical background to the military coup of April 21, 1967. Of particular interest is the account of the emergence of a center-left group in the early 1960s.

Woodhouse, Christopher Montague. **A Short History of Modern Greece.** New York: Praeger, 1968, 318 p.
A concise, knowledgeable survey, the last third of which deals with Greece in the twentieth century.

Young, Kenneth. **The Greek Passion: A Study in People and Politics.** London: Dent, 1969, 542 p.
A controversial presentation of the Greek political climate over the ages. The author concludes that "the lamentable political history of the Greeks suggests that in a free society they are incapable of ruling themselves."

Zotos, Stephanos. **The Greeks: Dilemma between Past and Present.** New York: Funk & Wagnalls, 1969, 270 p.
A Greek newspaperman undertakes an informal portrait of his nation, its culture and habits.

Biographies and Memoirs

See also (Greece) World War II and the Civil War Period, p. 605.

Dafnis, Grigorios. **Sofoklis Eleftheriou Venizelos.** Athens: Ikaros, 1970, 662 p.
A well-documented biography of Sophocles Venizelos, the son of the great liberal Greek statesman, who between 1944 and 1952 served for several times as Prime Minister and Foreign Minister. Written by one of the outstanding Greek historians, it provides important insights into the Greek political process and contains useful information on U.S.-Greek relations.

Danglis, G. Panayotis. **Anamniseis, engrafa, allilografia.** Athens, 1965, 2 v.
The author of these reminiscences, documents and correspondence was one of the members of the triumvirate which established the provisional Greek government in Thessaloniki in 1916. Important for students interested in the role of the military in Greek politics.

Frederica, Queen of the Hellenes. **A Measure of Understanding.** New York: St. Martin's Press, 1972, 270 p.
A chatty book of memoirs dealing with Queen Frederica's life up to the death of her husband, King Paul, in 1964. It includes her correspondence with General Marshall in the late 1940s.

Grigoropoulos, Theodoros. **Apo tin koryfi tou lofou.** Athens, 1966, 581 p.
   The memoirs of a general who once represented Greece as a NATO member in Washington.
Pyromaglou, Komninos. **O G. Kartalis kai i epochi tou, 1934–1944.** Athens, 1965, 680 p.
   The first volume of a sympathetic biography of G. Kartalis, a well-to-do politician from central Greece who set up a republican party in the postwar period and died in 1957.
Streit, Georgios. **Imerologion-Archeion.** Athens, 1964–66, 2 v. in 3 pts.
   This diary by one of the confidential advisers of King Constantine I and the Greek Minister of Foreign Affairs in 1914 provides important information on Greek politics and foreign relations during World War I.
Tsirimokos, Ilias. **Alexandros Svolos.** Athens, 1963, 144 p.
   The socialist leader, who served briefly as Prime Minister in 1965 after the downfall of A. Papandreou, eulogizes Alexandros Svolos, an eminent professor of constitutional law at the University of Athens who served as President and Minister of Foreign Affairs of the short-lived P.E.E.A. (Political Committee of National Liberation) set up under communist and E.A.M. auspices in March 1944.
Venezis, Ilias. **Emmanouil Tsouderos.** Athens, 1966, 524 p.
   A sympathetic and well-documented biography of E. T. Tsouderos, Prime Minister of the Greek government-in-exile from 1941 to 1944, by a well-known novelist.

World War II and the Civil War Period

See also (War) Guerrilla Warfare; Armed Insurrection, p. 118; Inter-War Period, p. 140; Second World p. 144; The Postwar World, p. 178; Bulgaria, p. 596; other subsections under Greece.

Enepekidis, P. **Oi diogmoi ton evraion en Elladi 1941–1944.** Athens: Papazissis, 1969, 199 p.
   This study, based on documents from the Bundesarchiv in Coblentz and the Institut für Zeitgeschichte in Munich, describes the deportations and extermination of the Jews in Greece during World War II.
Eudes, Dominique. **Les Kapétanios: la guerre civile grecque (1943–1949).** Paris: Fayard, 1970, 493 p.
   In this informative account of the Greek Civil War the author glorifies the guerrillas and glosses over their excesses.
Grigoriadis, Ph. N. **Istoria tou emphyliou polemou 1945–1949: to deftero andartiko.** Athens, 1964–65, 2 v.
———. **To andartiko ELAS-EDES-EKKA.** Athens, 1963, 2 v.
   Two massive studies of the Greek resistance movement during World War II and the following Civil War, emphasizing the communist side of the picture.
Kanellopoulos, Panayotis. **Ta chronia tou Megalou Polemou 1939–1944.** Athens, 1964, 232 p.
   The last Prime Minister before the military coup of April 21, 1967 depicts in sweeping brush-strokes World War II from the Greek vantage point.
Karalis, Konstantinos. **Istoria ton dramatikon gegonoton tis Peloponnissou 1943–1949.** Athens, 1967, 2 v.
   A description of the emergence and activities of E.A.M. and other resistance movements in the Peloponnese.
Kosmas, Georgios. **Oi ellinikoi polemoi, Valkanikoi-Ellinoitalikos-Symmoritopolemos.** Athens: Ellinikon Fos, 1967, 478 p.
   In this study of the military activities in Greece during World War II and its aftermath particularly interesting is the account of the counter-guerrilla operations in the late 1940s. The author was Chief of Staff of the Greek Army in 1948.
Matthews, Kenneth. **Memories of a Mountain War: Greece, 1944–1949.** London: Longman, 1972, 284 p.
   A BBC correspondent places the Greek Civil War in a long and clear perspective.

O'Ballance, Edgar. **The Greek Civil War 1944-1949.** New York: Praeger, 1966, 237 p.
   The author of studies of the Soviet and Chinese armies here recounts the story of the Greek Civil War that erupted intermittently between 1944 and 1949.

Tsakalotos, Thrasyvoulos. **1944 Dekemvrios: I machi ton Athinon.** Athens, 1969, 66 p.
   In this slim volume, the author, head of a Greek military brigade, describes its role during the communist-led uprising in Athens in December 1944, a traumatic event for the course of post-World War II Greek politics.

Zotos, Stephanos. **Greece: The Struggle for Freedom.** New York: Crowell, 1967, 194 p.
   A Greek journalist, formerly Director of the Information Service of the Greek Embassy in Washington, reviews the tragic period between the Italian attack in October 1940 and the 1949 failure of the communists in the civil war.

Foreign Relations

See also Inter-War Period, p. 140; Second World War, p. 144; The Postwar World, p. 178; and the sections for specific countries and regions.

Barros, James. **The Corfu Incident of 1923: Mussolini and the League of Nations.** Princeton: Princeton University Press, 1965, 339 p.
   A monograph centering on the League of Nations' role in the handling or mishandling of the Corfu Incident.

Christidis, Christos. **Kypriako kai Ellinotourkika.** Athens, 1967, 528 p.
   A close observer of the various phases of the Cyprus question terms its handling by the Greek government a "course toward national bankruptcy" and emphasizes the need for good Greek-Turkish relations.

Couloumbis, Theodore A. **Greek Political Reaction to American and NATO Influences.** New Haven: Yale University Press, 1966, 250 p.
   A study emphasizing the reactions of Greek politicians and the press to Greek postwar foreign policies.

Kitsikes, Demetrios. **Propagande et pressions en politique internationale: la Grèce et ses revendications à la conférence de la paix (1919-1920).** Paris: Presses Universitaires, 1963, 538 p.
   The author contends that the use of propaganda by Greece during the Paris Peace Conference achieved a measure of success among the British, thus prompting Lloyd George to aid the Greeks against Turkey.

Korozis, Athanasios. **Ellinotourkikoi agones kai filiai 1914-1940.** Athens, 1967, 819 p.
   In this account of the Greek-Turkish relations from 1914 to 1940, the author, a military man, emphasizes the role of the Great Powers.

Kyrou, Alexis A. **Oneira kai pragmatikotis: Chronia diplomatikis zoïs 1923-1953.** Athens: Kleissiouni, 1972, 398 p.
   Reminiscences of a diplomat who served in several important diplomatic posts at various critical moments in modern Greek history. His death in 1970 did not permit him to cover the period since 1954 when he was a close adviser of Prime Minister Alexander Papagos.

Melas, Michail K. **Anamniseis enos diplomatou.** Athens, n. d., 258 p.
   A diplomat, the scion of one of the great families of Greece, gives an entertaining and witty account of his experiences in Albania, Great Britain, Turkey and Egypt.

Psomiades, Harry J. **The Eastern Question: The Last Phase; A Study in Greek-Turkish Diplomacy.** Thessaloniki: Institute for Balkan Studies, 1968, 145 p.
   A monograph on the role played by Greece after World War I in the struggle for the Ottoman succession, with emphasis on the 1923 Lausanne settlement.

Theodoulou, Christos. **Greece and the Entente: August 1, 1914 - September 25, 1916.** Thessaloniki: Institute for Balkan Studies, 1971, 379 p.
   The author concludes his very well-documented study of Greco-Entente relations during World War I by condemning modern Greece's traditional dependence on the Great Powers.

Walder, David. **The Chanak Affair.** New York: Macmillan, 1969, 379 p.
   An account by a British historian of the British involvement in the Greek-Turkish

confrontation in 1922 which brought Britain to the brink of war with Turkey, resulted in the destruction of the imperial ambitions of Greece, and marked the emergence of modern Turkey.

Xydis, Stephen George. **Greece and the Great Powers, 1944–1947: Prelude to the "Truman Doctrine."** Thessaloniki: Institute for Balkan Studies, 1963, 758 p.
In this massive and scholarly study Dr. Xydis analyzes the course of Greek relations with the Great Powers during the critical years from the country's liberation to the advent of the Truman Doctrine. Of particular value for its extensive use of Greek foreign policy materials.

III. ASIA AND THE PACIFIC AREA

GENERAL SURVEYS

See also General Works, p. 1; Political Factors, p. 12; Geographic, Ethnic and Population Factors, p. 45; Economic Factors, p. 49; International Organization and Government, p. 96; War and Peace, p. 108; First World War, p. 131; Inter-War Period, p. 140; Second World War, p. 144; The Postwar World, p. 178; and the sections for specific countries and regions.

Asian Development after Vietnam. Tokyo: Asahi Evening News Co., 1968, 184 p.
Proceedings and lectures of the Asian Development Symposium, held in Tokyo in 1968, the aim of which was "to search for guidelines toward a new pattern of social and economic development in Asia in anticipation of the cessation of hostilities in Vietnam."

Badgley, John. **Asian Development: Problems and Prognosis.** New York: Free Press, 1971, 210 p.
This gloomy analysis leads the author to two conclusions: U.S. involvement with Asia should increase, not decline; and effective development is more likely on the local than on the national scale.

Barnett, Arthur Doak, *ed.* **Communist Strategies in Asia: A Comparative Analysis of Governments and Parties.** New York: Praeger, 1963, 293 p.
Eight essays, all written by top Asian area specialists and edited by a Senior Fellow at the Brookings Institution.

Bellah, Robert Neelly, *ed.* **Religion and Progress in Modern Asia.** New York: Free Press, 1965, 246 p.
An evaluation, based on a 1963 international conference in Manila, of the cultural and religious aspects of modernization and how they help or hinder progress.

Benz, Ernst. **Buddhism or Communism: Which Holds the Future of Asia?** Garden City: Doubleday, 1965, 234 p.
A study of Buddhism from Ceylon to Japan and of its exploitation by Red China.

Bibliography of Asian Studies, 1969–. Ann Arbor (Mich.): Association for Asian Studies, 1971–.
A comprehensive annual reference volume, published formerly as a separate issue of *The Journal of Asian Studies*. The volume for 1969 was edited by Richard C. Howard; subsequent volumes were prepared by Thein Swe.

Braibanti, Ralph J. D., *ed.* **Asian Bureaucratic Systems Emergent from the British Imperial Tradition.** Durham: Duke University Press (for the Duke University Commonwealth-Studies Center), 1966, 733 p.
Following introductory essays on "Structure of the British Imperial Heritage" and "Recruitment and Training of British Civil Servants in India 1600–1860," there are chapters on the higher bureaucracy in India, Pakistan, Burma, Ceylon, Malaya and Nepal.

Brecher, Michael. **The New States of Asia: A Political Analysis.** New York: Oxford University Press, 1963, 226 p.
Six essays by a McGill University political scientist on Southern Asian countries which have achieved independence since World War II.

Chandrasekhar, Sripati, *ed.* **Asia's Population Problems: With a Discussion of Population and Immigration in Australia.** New York: Praeger, 1967, 311 p.
Essays by an Indian scholar.

Elliott-Bateman, Michael. **Defeat in the East: The Mark of Mao Tse-Tung on War.** New York: Oxford University Press, 1967, 270 p.
The author urges the West to discard traditional tactics and to adopt Mao's military philosophy which has been successfully applied by smaller forces in Southeast Asia.

Far Eastern Affairs: Number Three. Carbondale: Southern Illinois University Press, 1963, 144 p.

——: **Number Four.** New York: Oxford University Press, 1968, 117 p.
Collections of essays on contemporary Far Eastern affairs by scholars at St. Antony's College, Oxford. Edited by Geoffrey Francis Hudson.

Grant, Margaret, *ed.* **South Asia Pacific Crisis: National Development and the World Community.** New York: Dodd (for the Council on World Tensions), 1964, 314 p.
This book results from a University of Malaya Conference on Development and Coöperation in the South Asia Pacific Region, attended by specialists from six continents. South Asia in this study includes Japan, Australia and New Zealand.

Harcourt, François d'. **Asia: Awakening of a World.** New York: Harcourt, Brace and World, 1964, 295 p.
A French journalist's narrative of a journey in 1961 from Galilee to Japan.

Hildebrandt, Walter. **Siegt Asien in Asien? Traditionalismus, Nationalismus, Kommunismus: Strukturprobleme eines Kontinents.** Göttingen: Musterschmidt, 1966, 618 p.
After a wide-ranging and somewhat chaotic discussion of a multitude of problems facing modern Asia, the author, a German professor of sociology, comes to the conclusion that the growing nationalism of the Asian nations will decide the fate of that continent.

Hohenberg, John. **New Era in the Pacific: An Adventure in Public Diplomacy.** New York: Simon and Schuster, 1972, 539 p.
The author, a professor of journalism, weaves personal interviews with many Asian leaders into an historical tour of the Pacific and South Asian horizon since World War II. He concludes that the United States should willingly contribute to the coming era when Asians "become the masters of their own continent."

Italiaander, Rolf. **Die neuen Männer Asiens.** Düsseldorf: Econ-Verlag, 1964, 445 p.
Profiles of political and intellectual leaders from 17 Asian countries who have played a prominent part in the decolonization of Asia after World War II.

Kennedy, Joseph. **Asian Nationalism in the Twentieth Century.** New York: St. Martin's Press, 1968, 244 p.
A survey with writings by Asian leaders from the first half of this century.

Kirby, Edward Stuart. **Economic Development in East Asia.** New York: Praeger, 1967, 253 p.
An uneven survey of the economic development from 1945 to 1965 of fifteen Asian countries. Figures and statements are mostly from official sources; inferences, comments and evaluations are the author's own.

Koh, Sung Jae. **Stages of Industrial Development in Asia: A Comparative History of the Cotton Industry in Japan, India, China, and Korea.** Philadelphia: University of Pennsylvania Press, 1966, 461 p.
A specialist in comparative economic studies in Asian countries selects the cotton industry to prove his point that indiscriminate adoption of Western methods in economic growth, to the neglect of lessons learned from indigenous experiences, is not always wise.

Lamb, Alastair. **Asian Frontiers: Studies in a Continuing Problem.** New York: Praeger, 1968, 246 p.
A study of the patterns of evolution of boundary disputes along Asian borders.

Lent, John A., *ed.* **The Asian Newspapers' Reluctant Revolution.** Ames: Iowa State University Press, 1971, 373 p.
An introductory survey of the press in Asia by American and Asian scholars.

Levi, Werner. **The Challenge of World Politics in South and Southeast Asia.** Englewood Cliffs: Prentice-Hall, 1968, 184 p.
A study by a professor at the University of Hawaii.

Levkovskii, Aleksei Ivanovich, *ed.* **Ekonomicheskaia politika i gosudarstvennyi kapitalizm v stranakh vostoka.** Moscow: Izd-vo "Nauka," 1972, 403 p.
A Soviet anthology of articles on economic planning and state capitalism in Asia and the Middle East.

Löwenthal, Richard, *ed.* **Issues in the Future of Asia: Communist and Non-Communist Alternatives.** New York: Praeger, 1969, 177 p.
Five essays on questions of potentially vital importance to the political, economic and cultural life of Asia.

Maude, Angus. **South Asia: A Background Book.** Chester Springs (Pa.): Dufour Editions, 1966, 176 p.
A British journalist and a Conservative Member of Parliament surveys briefly South Asia's past and present and concludes by advocating the containment of China by complete neutralization of South Asia under a joint Western and Soviet guarantee.

Miller, John Donald Bruce, *ed.* **India, Japan, Australia: Partners in Asia?** Canberra: Australian National University Press, 1968, 214 p.
Fourteen political and economic specialists discuss how these three countries with distinct national interests and outlooks respond to major developments in world affairs.

Myrdal, Gunnar. **Asian Drama: An Inquiry into the Poverty of Nations.** New York: Twentieth Century Fund, 1968, 3 v.
A description of the economic conditions in South and Southeast Asia in their demographic, social and political setting, together with an account of the prospects for development and the main policy alternatives facing the governments.

Nakamura, Hajime. **Ways of Thinking of Eastern Peoples: India, China, Tibet, Japan.** Honolulu: East-West Center Press, rev. ed., 1964, 712 p.
Professor Nakamura of Tokyo University, with the help of Professor Philip P. Wiener, has completely revised his original Japanese study of thought-patterns in Asian countries.

Nunn, G. Raymond. **Asia: A Selected and Annotated Guide to Reference Works.** Cambridge: M.I.T. Press, 1971, 223 p.
A useful reference tool, listing primarily books and periodicals published in English and Japanese.

Okumura, Fusao. **Kokusai seiji to Ajia.** Tokyo: Maeno Shoten, 1971, 281 p.
A study of international politics in Asia, with emphasis on processes of modernization and development.

Onslow, Cranley, *ed.* **Asian Economic Development.** New York: Praeger, 1965, 242 p.
Case studies of postwar economic development in Burma, Ceylon, India, Malaya, Pakistan and Thailand by leading economists in each of those countries. The final chapter, a comparative analysis by the editor, urges greater initiative from the more developed countries and a change in their aid programs.

Rawson, Robert Rees. **The Monsoon Lands of Asia.** Chicago: Aldine Publishing Co., 1963, 256 p.
A geographic survey of the area from Pakistan to Japan, sustaining nearly half the world's population, by a British scholar.

Roberts, Harold Selig and Brissenden, Paul F., *eds.* **The Challenge of Industrial Relations in the Pacific-Asian Countries.** Honolulu: East-West Center Press, 1965, 259 p.
Papers from a 1962 conference sponsored by the Institute of Advanced Projects of the East-West Center in Honolulu. Discussion centered around problems arising from rapid industrialization, with emphasis on labor dispute settlements.

Robinson, Edward Austin Gossage and Kidron, Michael, *eds.* **Economic Development in South Asia.** New York: St. Martin's Press, 1971, 585 p.
A collection of papers presented at a conference of the International Economic Association at Kandy, Ceylon.

The Role of Science in the Development of Natural Resources with Particular Reference to Pakistan, Iran and Turkey. Oxford: Pergamon Press, 1964, 454 p.
Papers presented at a 1962 symposium.

Rose, Saul, ed. **Politics in Southern Asia.** New York: St. Martin's Press, 1963, 386 p.
Sixteen papers presented at a St. Antony's College symposium on the political evolution of each country in the region from Pakistan to the Philippines, by area specialists drawn from different disciplines.

Scalapino, Robert Anthony, ed. **The Communist Revolution in Asia: Tactics, Goals, and Achievements.** Englewood Cliffs: Prentice-Hall, 1965, 405 p.
Professor Scalapino starts off this volume with a succinct comparative analysis of left-wing movements in Asia. He is followed by other scholars who describe and analyze, country by country, the structure, leadership and operations of Communist Party organizations in the East, from China to India. Stress is on the interrelationship of the parties.

Schram, Stuart R. and Carrère d'Encausse, Hélène, eds. **Le Marxisme et l'Asie, 1853–1964.** Paris: Colin, 1965, 493 p.
A most handy reference work, in which the authors, researchers for the Fondation Nationale des Sciences Politiques, provide French versions of 80 texts dating from 1853 (Marx's *New York Daily Tribune* article on British domination in India) to July 13, 1964 (Peking's *Jen-min jih-pao* article on Khrushchev's "pseudo-communism"), all relevant to Marxist views on Asia.

Shamsul Huq, Muhammad. **Education and Development Strategy in South and South East Asia.** Honolulu: East-West Center Press, 1965, 286 p.
An examination of the national plans for education in Pakistan, India, Indonesia and the Philippines. Particular attention is paid to determining the economic value of education.

Shand, Richard Tregurtha, ed. **Agricultural Development in Asia.** Berkeley: University of California Press, 1969, 360 p.
Ten specialists discuss the main technical, economic and socio-political ingredients of an effective approach to the solution of the problem of poverty in post-World War II Asia.

Singh, Lalita Prasad. **The Politics of Economic Cooperation in Asia: A Study of Asian International Organizations.** Columbia: University of Missouri Press, 1966, 271 p.
A pioneer study of regional economic coöperation in Asia, with emphasis on the Economic Commission for Asia and the Far East.

Singh, Patwant. **The Struggle for Power in Asia.** London: Hutchinson, 1971, 208 p.
In this wide-ranging appraisal of possible developments in Asian international relations, the author warns of the dangers inherent in the struggle for power among China, Japan and the Soviet Union, and calls on India to accept the responsibilities of the great-power status.

Sinha, Krishna Kishore, ed. **Problems of Defence of South and East Asia.** Bombay: Manaktalas, 1969, 479 p.
A study of the regional defense arrangements among Asian nations. Emphasis is on India, with China's crucial role also in the forefront.

Spencer, Robert F., ed. **Religion and Change in Contemporary Asia.** Minneapolis: University of Minnesota Press, 1971, 172 p.
Case studies of the function of religion in promoting or hindering political and social change in modern China, Japan, Vietnam, India, Burma, Pakistan and Indonesia.

Studies on Asia 1960–1967. Lincoln: University of Nebraska Press, 1960–68, 8 v.
Annual collections of essays on Asian affairs. Volumes 1–7 were edited by Robert K. Sakai; volume 8, by Sidney Devere Brown.

Taiheiyō Sensō Shi. Tokyo: Aoki Shoten, 1971–73, 6 v.
A Japanese history of the wars in the Pacific during the twentieth century. The last volume deals with the Korean War and it also includes an index to all volumes.

Tinker, Hugh. **Re-orientations: Essays on Asia in Transition.** New York: Praeger, 1965, 175 p.
A survey of the transformation of Asian government and society and of the interaction between community and authority in times of internal and international tensions.

Tinker, Hugh. **South Asia: A Short History.** New York: Praeger, 1966, 287 p.
A professor at the University of London, who served during the last days of British rule in India in its army and civil service, describes the economic, religious, social and political events in South Asia over the past 50 years.

Varma, Shanti Prasad and Misra, Kashi Prasad, *eds.* **Foreign Policies in South Asia.** New Delhi: Orient Longmans (for South Asia Studies Centre, University of Rajasthan, Jaipur), 1969, 403 p.
A collection of papers stemming from a 1968 seminar on foreign policy at the University of Rajasthan.

Ward, Barbara E. (Lady Jackson), *ed.* **Women in the New Asia.** New York: UNESCO, 1963, 529 p.
This study had its origins at the UNESCO-sponsored conference held in Calcutta in 1958 and is an informative inquiry into "the impact of the new public status of women upon the private, domestic lives of both sexes in the various countries of South and South-East Asia."

Weidner, Edward W., *ed.* **Development Administration in Asia.** Durham: Duke University Press (in coöperation with the Comparative Administration Group of the American Society for Public Administration), 1970, 431 p.
A study of the distinctive roles, and modification of roles, of Asian administrators under conditions of rapid change and development.

Wightman, David. **Toward Economic Cooperation in Asia.** New Haven: Yale University Press (for the Carnegie Endowment for International Peace), 1963, 400 p.
A historical appraisal of the first 15 years of E.C.A.F.E. (Economic Commission for Asia and the Far East) which describes and analyzes the purposes, structure, functions and problems of the organization.

Wilcox, Wayne Ayres and Others. **Asia and the International System.** Cambridge: Winthrop Publishers, 1972, 383 p.
Thorough, careful and generally unimaginative analyses of the foreign policies of 19 Asian nations.

Wilson, Dick. **Asia Awakes: A Continent in Transition.** New York: Weybright and Talley, 1970, 460 p.
The author concludes his study by saying that despite some progress, "we have a long way to go before we acquire a minimally realistic assessment of Asia."

Wint, Guy, *ed.* **Asia: A Handbook.** New York: Praeger, 1966, 856 p.
More than 60 outstanding experts collaborate to provide a valuable reference work.

MIDDLE EAST

GENERAL SURVEYS AND POLITICAL PROBLEMS

See also General Works, p. 1; Political Factors, p. 12; Geographic, Ethnic and Population Factors, p. 45; Economic Factors, p. 49; International Organization and Government, p. 96; War and Peace, p. 108; First World War, p. 131; Inter-War Period, p. 140; Second World War, p. 144; The Postwar World, p. 178; and the sections for specific countries.

Adams, Michael, *ed.* **The Middle East: A Handbook.** New York: Praeger, 1971, 633 p.
A useful reference, a volume in the "Handbooks to the Modern World" series.

Binder, Leonard. **The Ideological Revolution in the Middle East.** New York: Wiley, 1964, 287 p.
A political scientist seeks an explanation of the process of ideological change through an examination of political developments in the modern Middle East.

Curtis, Michael, *ed.* **People and Politics in the Middle East.** New Brunswick (N.J.): Transaction Books, 1971, 325 p.
The proceedings of the 1970 conference of the American Academic Association for Peace in the Middle East.

Ducruet, Jean. **Les Capitaux européens au Proche-Orient.** Paris: Presses Universitaires, 1964, 468 p.
The history of European financing of the Ottoman Empire is followed by an examination of contemporary problems of investment in the successor states.

Farnie, D. A. **East and West of Suez: The Suez Canal in History, 1854-1956.** New York: Oxford University Press, 1969, 860 p.
A well-documented and extensive survey of the effect upon world trade and politics of the Suez Canal.

Fisher, Sydney Nettleton, *ed.* **The Military in the Middle East.** Columbus: Ohio State University Press, 1963, 138 p.
Eight essays dealing with the role of the military in Turkey, Iraq, Syria, Egypt, Israel and the area in general by well-known authorities.

Fitzsimons, Matthew Anthony. **Empire by Treaty.** Notre Dame: University of Notre Dame Press, 1964, 235 p.
A well-done history of British policy in the postwar Middle East, leading the author to conclude that the surprising thing was not the decline of British influence, but the fact that it could be maintained so long in the absence of real power.

Grabill, Joseph L. **Protestant Diplomacy and the Near East: Missionary Influence on American Policy, 1810-1927.** Minneapolis: University of Minnesota Press, 1971, 395 p.
Thorough research marks this detailed account of missionary "diplomacy," particularly its intense though fruitless lobbying for direct American governmental support of national minorities in the collapsing Ottoman Empire.

Haddad, George Meri. **Revolutions and Military Rule in the Middle East: The Northern Tier.** New York: Speller, 1965, 251 p.
A comparative study of revolutions and military coups in Turkey, Iran, Afghanistan and Pakistan. Professor Haddad finds, against the view that military élites have been the chief instrument of reform and change, that their vices outweigh their virtues.

Halpern, Manfred. **The Politics of Social Change in the Middle East and North Africa.** Princeton: Princeton University Press, 1963, 431 p.
A major attempt to apply the categories of political science to the thoroughgoing transformation of Middle Eastern and North African society now in process.

Henle, Hans. **Der neue Nahe Osten.** Frankfurt/Main: Suhrkamp, rev. ed., 1972, 526 p.
This review of Middle East politics since World War II stresses the trends of nationalism and socialism, the leading role of Nasser, and the futility of neocolonialism. Henle's original book was published in 1966; Curt Ullerich brings the story to 1971.

Hershlag, Zvi Yehuda. **Introduction to the Modern Economic History of the Middle East.** Leyden: Brill, 1964, 419 p.
An important study designed to provide a framework for further researches in economic history of the modern Middle East.

Hottinger, Arnold. **Fellachen und Funktionäre: Entwicklungswege im Nahen Osten.** Munich: Kösel, 1967, 211 p.
A seasoned journalist's essay on modernization and development in the Middle East.

Hurewitz, Jacob Coleman. **Middle East Politics: The Military Dimension.** New York: Praeger (for the Council on Foreign Relations), 1969, 553 p.
In this penetrating inquiry the author devotes special attention to the arms races, military aid programs and the interaction of great-power and local interest. The narrative covers each country separately, from Morocco to Afghanistan.

Hurewitz, Jacob Coleman, *ed.* **Soviet-American Rivalry in the Middle East.** New York: Praeger (for the Academy of Political Science, Columbia University), 1969, 250 p.
In this well-planned volume a dozen authors assess the state of the cold war in the Middle East and engage in some speculation on its future. The papers on arms competition and the military balance are particularly informative.

Imhoff, Christoph Hans, Freiherr von. **Duell im Mittelmeer: Moskau greift nach dem Nahen und dem Mittleren Osten.** Freiburg: Rombach, 1968, 434 p.
A generally successful attempt by a writer who knows the area to place developments in the Middle East in the framework of great-power relationships. Solid information is combined with informed speculation.

Karpat, Kemal H., ed. **Political and Social Thought in the Contemporary Middle East.** New York: Praeger, 1968, 397 p.

A welcome collection of essays and articles, primarily by Arab and Turkish scholars.

Kedourie, Elie. **The Chatham House Version and other Middle-Eastern Studies.** New York: Praeger, 1970, 488 p.

These essays by a well-known scholar include a criticism of the interpretations of the Middle East in publications of the Royal Institute of International Affairs, particularly those written by Arnold Toynbee, as superficial, eccentric and doctrinaire.

Kermani, Taghi T. **Economic Development in Action: Theories, Problems, and Procedures as Applied in the Middle East.** Cleveland: World Publishing Co., 1967, 236 p.

In this study the author discusses primarily the economic development of Iran, Iraq and Jordan.

Kimche, Jon. **The Second Arab Awakening.** New York: Holt, Rinehart and Winston, 1970, 288 p.

A study of the policies and diplomacy of the Great Powers in the Middle East, especially Great Britain, with the main focus on Palestine and Egypt.

Klieman, Aaron S. **Soviet Russia and the Middle East.** Baltimore: Johns Hopkins Press (for the Washington Center of Foreign Policy Research, Johns Hopkins University), 1970, 107 p.

A good short treatment of the subject.

Lenczowski, George. **Soviet Advances in the Middle East.** Washington: American Enterprise Institute for Public Policy Research, 1972, 176 p.

A veteran observer draws on data from many sources and wisely refrains from over-interpretation of the facts. The result is a most informative book.

Lewis, Bernard. **The Middle East and the West.** Bloomington: Indiana University Press, 1964, 160 p.

A brief study of Middle Eastern society and its reactions to Western influences, by a leading British orientalist and historian.

Longrigg, Stephen Hemsley. **The Middle East: A Social Geography.** Chicago: Aldine Publishing Co., 2d rev. ed., 1970, 291 p.

A well-written, well-informed and sympathetic account of the modern Middle East based on many years of firsthand experience in the area by a British observer and author.

al-Marayati, Abid A., comp. **Middle Eastern Constitutions and Electoral Laws.** New York: Praeger, 1968, 483 p.

Useful collection of English translations of constitutions and other major political documents from eleven Middle Eastern countries.

Merlin, Samuel, ed. **The Big Powers and the Present Crisis in the Middle East.** Rutherford (N.J.): Fairleigh Dickinson University Press, 1968, 201 p.

Record of a colloquium held in December 1967, with brief presentations by distinguished panelists (including Richard H. Nolte, Cecil Hourani and General E. L. M. Burns) and a general discussion reported verbatim.

The Middle East: Economic and Political Problems and Prospects. New York: American Elsevier, 1971– .

A distinguished series, planned in five volumes, prepared under the auspices of RAND and Resources for the Future. Through 1972 the following volumes have been published: "The Agricultural Potential of the Middle East," by Marion Clawson and others (1971, 312 p.); "Middle Eastern Oil and the Western World: Prospects and Problems," by Sam H. Schurr and Paul T. Homan with others (1971, 206 p.); "Economic Development and Population Growth in the Middle East," edited by Charles A. Cooper and Sidney S. Alexander (1972, 620 p.); and "Political Dynamics in the Middle East," edited by Paul Y. Hammond and Sidney S. Alexander (1972, 666 p.).

Middle East Record. Jerusalem: Israel Universities Press (for the Shiloah Center for Middle Eastern and African Studies, Tel Aviv University).

A valuable and indispensable reference series presenting information on Middle Eastern politics. Since 1962 three volumes have been published covering the developments through 1968.

Middle Eastern Affairs: Number Three. Carbondale: Southern Illinois University Press, 1963, 184 p.
——: **Number Four.** New York: Oxford University Press, 1965, 165 p.
Collections of essays on the contemporary Middle East by scholars at St. Antony's College, Oxford. Edited by Albert Habib Hourani.

Nader, Claire and Zahlan, A. B., eds. **Science and Technology in Developing Countries.** New York: Cambridge University Press, 1969, 588 p.
Application of advanced scientific and technological methods to the development problems of the Middle East is discussed by a group of specialists, primarily American and Arab. Proceedings of a conference held at the American University, Beirut, in 1967.

Nevakivi, Jukka. **Britain, France and the Arab Middle East, 1914-1920.** New York: Oxford University Press, 1969, 284 p.
This monograph on the bargaining and maneuvering leading up to the division of the former Ottoman provinces into British and French mandates supplements the earlier works of Kedourie, Zeine and others.

Nolte, Richard H., ed. **The Modern Middle East.** New York: Atherton Press (for the American Association for Middle East Studies), 1963, 218 p.
Essays dealing with the Middle East at large and the problems of modernization.

Peretz, Don. **The Middle East Today.** New York: Holt, Rinehart and Winston, 2d ed. 1971, 496 p.
An introductory survey, dealing with developments since World War I.

Pounds, Norman John Greville. **An Atlas of Middle Eastern Affairs.** New York: Praeger, 1963, 117 p.
Maps, graphs and brief commentaries depicting selected features of Middle Eastern history, geography, climate, population, resources and politics make this a useful quick reference for non-specialists.

Ramazani, Rouhollah Karegar. **The Northern Tier: Afghanistan, Iran, and Turkey.** Princeton: Van Nostrand, 1966, 142 p.
The author of this informative introductory survey states in the preface that "although there are numerous factors and forces that now tend to militate against the union of Afghanistan, Iran, and Turkey, there are also significant reasons to justify the hope for such a fusion before too long."

Rivlin, Benjamin and Szyliowicz, Joseph S., eds. **The Contemporary Middle East: Tradition and Innovation.** New York: Random House, 1965, 576 p.
A comprehensive volume of writings on the modern Middle East. The underlying theme is the transition from traditionalism to modernity.

Sachar, Howard Morley. **The Emergence of the Middle East, 1914-1924.** New York: Knopf, 1969, 518 p.
In a dramatic presentation of what was in itself high drama, the end of the Ottoman Empire and the emergence of the many conflicts born of its collapse, the author draws on recent research by many scholars and thus provides a new and welcome addition to the earlier standard works on the period.

Sachar, Howard Morley. **Europe Leaves the Middle East, 1936-1954.** New York: Knopf, 1972, 687 p.
This comprehensive history of "eighteen years of equivocal and hopelessly convoluted Western disengagement" is a solid work of scholarship, though bound to be controversial on some points of fact and interpretation. The author sees the chief Western legacy as one of "gall and venom."

Thornburg, Max Weston. **People and Policy in the Middle East.** New York: Norton, 1964, 249 p.
Based on the author's 20 years of experience in the Middle East as an engineer, adviser and administrator, this is a perceptive and readable "inquiry into the behavior of people in the process of change."

Trevelyan, Humphrey Trevelyan, Baron. **The Middle East in Revolution.** Boston: Gambit, 1970, 275 p.
A British diplomat describes three assignments—Cairo at the time of Suez, post-revolution Baghdad, and Aden—the waning stages of Britain's moment in the Middle East.

Tütsch, Hans Emanuel. **From Ankara to Marrakesh: Turks and Arabs in a Changing World.** London: Allen and Unwin (for the Congress for Cultural Freedom), 1964, 224 p.
Articles dealing with the Arab world, Turkey and Cyprus in 1959–63, first published in the *Neue Zürcher Zeitung*.

Tweedy, Owen. **Gathering Moss: A Memoir of Owen Tweedy.** London: Sidgwick and Jackson, 1967, 345 p.
This memoir of Owen Tweedy, who was secretary to Lord Allenby and later served as an information officer in Palestine and the Middle East, contains valuable information on the Allenby to Lloyd period in Egypt and on the Arab-Jewish struggle in Palestine before 1948.

Vatikiotis, P. J., ed. **Revolution in the Middle East and Other Case Studies.** Totowa (N.J.): Rowman and Littlefield, 1972, 231 p.
Thoughtful essays by well-known experts exploring a number of theoretical and practical questions on revolution in several Middle Eastern countries, with comparative discussions of revolutions in Eastern Europe, Latin America and China.

Vernier, Bernard. **Armée et politique au Moyen-Orient.** Paris: Payot, 1966, 252 p.
The army considered as an engine of modernization in nine Middle Eastern countries, by a member of the Paris Centre d'Études de Politique Étrangère.

OIL

See also Raw Materials; Oil; Energy, p. 70; (The United States) Trade, Tariffs and Finance, p. 251; (Middle East) General Surveys and Political Problems, p. 611; The Arab World, p. 616; Arab-Israeli Conflict, p. 633; (Iraq) General, p. 644.

Amin, Mahmūd. **al-Batrūl wa iqtiṣādiyāt mawārīdihi.** Cairo: Dār al-Ma'ārif, 1968, 264 p.
A study of the oil economics in the world in general and of their economic importance to the Arabs in particular.

Aramco Handbook: Oil and the Middle East. Dhahran: Arabian American Oil Company, rev. ed., 1968, 279 p.
A useful reference.

al-Barrāwī, Rāshid. **Harb al-batrūl fi al-'ālam.** Cairo: The Anglo-Egyptian Bookshop, 1968, 325 p.
A leading Egyptian economist surveys the oil problems all over the world and how they affect the Arabs.

Cattan, Henry. **The Evolution of Oil Concessions in the Middle East and North Africa.** Dobbs Ferry (N.Y.): Oceana Publications (for the Parker School of Foreign and Comparative Law), 1967, 173 p.
Useful summary by a long-time legal adviser to Aramco and Tapline.

Dhahab, Sāhib. **al-Batrūl al-'Arabī al-khām fī al-sūq al-'ālamīyah.** Cairo: al-Maṭba'ah al-'Alamīyah, 1969, 592 p.
A historical and analytical study of crude oil production in the Middle East and a discussion of the conflict of interests between international oil companies and the Arab governments.

Frank, Helmut Jack. **Crude Oil Prices in the Middle East: A Study in Oligopolistic Price Behavior.** New York: Praeger, 1966, 209 p.
Professor Frank discusses price developments reflecting the sweeping changes in the political and economic conditions in the Middle East and assesses oil company price policies and practices.

Ḥamdān, Jamāl. **Batrūl al-'Arab, dirāsah fī al-jughrafīyah al-basharīyah.** Cairo: Dār al-Ma'rifah, 1964, 306 p.
In this study of the oil problems in the Arab World the author concludes that oil will be the cement that will hold together Arab nationalism.

Hirst, David. **Oil and Public Opinion in the Middle East.** New York: Praeger, 1966, 127 p.
A study of the nature, extent and causes of Arab distrust of the Western oil industry.

Issawi, Charles and Yeganeh, Mohammed. **The Economics of Middle Eastern Oil.** New York: Praeger, 1963, 230 p.

This work by two professional economists deals directly and knowledgeably with the problems of the oil industry in the Middle East, chiefly in the Persian Gulf area.

Lubell, Harold. **Middle East Oil Crises and Western Europe's Energy Supplies.** Baltimore: Johns Hopkins Press, 1963, 233 p.

A detailed analysis of the role of oil in Western security. The author notes the dependence of the NATO countries on Middle Eastern oil exports and argues that the danger of an interrupted oil flow is great enough to justify stockpiling and a vigorous effort to develop alternative sources of energy.

Mikdashi, Zuhayr. **A Financial Analysis of Middle Eastern Oil Concessions, 1901–65.** New York: Praeger, 1966, 340 p.

A straightforward effort to "analyze and interpret the determinants of methods and rates of payments of major oil concessions . . . and the financial performance of the parties concerned."

Mughraby, Muhamad A. **Permanent Sovereignty over Oil Resources: A Study of Middle East Oil Concessions and Legal Change.** Beirut: Middle East Research and Publishing Center, 1966, 233 p.

The changing principles of ownership and sovereignty over natural resources, the development of joint-venture agreements in the oil industry, and the evolution and promise of collective bargaining techniques are usefully examined by a Lebanese legal scholar.

Philby, Harry St. John Bridger. **Arabian Oil Ventures.** Washington: Middle East Institute, 1964, 134 p.

A brief volume by the great chronicler of Arabia and the House of Saud, published posthumously, dealing with early attempts to exploit oil in both Western and Eastern Arabia.

Sarkis, Nicolas. **Le Pétrole et les économies arabes.** Paris: Librairie Générale de Droit, 1963, 279 p.

An analysis of the relationship between oil-producing countries and the oil companies and a discussion of the oil industry's impact on economies of the Middle East as a whole.

Sayegh, Kamal S. **Oil and Arab Regional Development.** New York: Praeger, 1968, 357 p.

A description of the workings of the international oil industry in the Arab world, and of ways in which Arab participation may be increased, with a proposed new approach or "model" leading to an Arab Oil Community and an Arab Common Market.

Stocking, George W. **Middle East Oil: A Study in Political and Economic Controversy.** Nashville: Vanderbilt University Press, 1970, 485 p.

A distinguished economist's impartial and readable account of past and present problems faced by the industry and by producing countries, presented against the background of political events.

THE ARAB WORLD

See also Religious Problems, p. 44; (International Law) General, p. 83; International Organization and Government, p. 96; Second World War, p. 144; The Postwar World, p. 178; (The United States) Relations with the Middle East and the Arab World, p. 242; (Great Britain) Foreign Policy, p. 375; (France) Foreign Policy, p. 404; (Germany) The Nazi Era, p. 475; (Union of Soviet Socialist Republics) Foreign Policy, p. 550; Middle East, p. 611; (China) Foreign Relations, p. 702; North Africa, p. 793.

Abd al-Hakim, Muḥammad Ṣubhi and Others. **al-Mawārid al-iqtiṣādīyah li al-waṭan al-'Arabī.** Cairo: Dār al-Qalam, 1966, 538 p.

A description and analysis of the economic resources of the Arab countries.

Abdel-Malek, Anouar, *ed.* **La Pensée politique arabe contemporaine.** Paris: Éditions du Seuil, 1970, 378 p.

A most useful collection of articles on contemporary Arab political thought, with an introduction by the editor.

Abdulrahman, A. J. **Guide to Arabic Reference Books.** Basrah (Iraq): Modern Press, 1970, 556 p.
An annotated bibliography of reference books in Arabic and Western languages on philosophy, psychology, religion, social sciences, applied sciences, fine art, literature and history.

Abu Jaber, Kamel S. **The Arab Ba'th Socialist Party: History, Ideology, and Organization.** Syracuse: Syracuse University Press, 1966, 218 p.
A well-researched study of the genesis, development and character of the Ba'th and its radical Arab socialism.

Adams, Michael. **Chaos or Rebirth: The Arab Outlook.** London: British Broadcasting Corporation, 1968, 170 p.
An informative survey of contemporary Arab politics and Arab-Israeli relations, resulting from a broadcasting project on the Third Program of the B.B.C.

Agwani, Mohammed Shafi. **Communism in the Arab East.** New York: Asia Publishing House (for the Indian School of International Studies), 1970, 259 p.
An Indian scholar's informative study, using many Arabic sources, which concentrates on the communist parties rather than on Soviet policy.

A'māl mu'tamar al-iqtiṣādiyīn al-'Arab al-thānī. Baghdad: Government Press, 1969, 709 p.
Proceedings of the 2d Arab Economists Conference held in Baghdad, March 8–13, 1969, on coöperation among Arabs, petroleum problems, and political and security dimensions of economic planning in various Arab countries.

'Ammash, Salih Mahdi. **al-Wiḥdah 'askarīyah, al-maḍmūn al-'askarī lil-wiḥdah al-'Arabīyah.** Beirut: al-Ṭali'ah, 1967, 164 p.
A former defense minister of Iraq and a high army officer discusses Arab military coöperation.

Anabtawi, M. F. **Arab Unity in Terms of Law.** The Hague: Nijhoff, 1963, 263 p.
A competent guide to developments which gave substance to Arab unity from the creation of the Arab League to Syria's break with the U.A.R. in 1961.

al-Arsūzī, Zakī. **al-Mu'allafāt al-kāmilah.** Damascus, 1972, 435 p.
The first volume of the complete works of one of the intellectual founders of the Ba'th movement.

al-'Aẓm, Ṣādiq Jalāl. **Naqd al-fikr al-dīnī.** Beirut: Dār al-Ṭalī'ah, 1969, 231 p.
Criticism of religious thinking in general and of Islam in particular. The author, a Muslim intellectual, blames Islam for most of the ills of the Arab world. The book caused a furor and generated lengthy discussions.

Azzam, Abdel Rahman. **The Eternal Message of Muhammad.** New York: Devin-Adair, 1964, 297 p.
An interpretation by an Arab statesman of the contemporary importance of the "Eternal Message."

Baer, Gabriel. **Population and Society in the Arab East.** New York: Praeger, 1964, 275 p.
A careful and thorough study of Arab society. The author shows that, great and rapid change notwithstanding, old traditions and social patterns continue and that amalgamation of a new Arab society has yet to be completed. The Hebrew original was entitled "Arve ha-Mizraḥ ha-Tikhon" (Tel-Aviv, 1960, 267 p.).

al-Bahi, Muḥammad. **al-Fikr al-Islāmī wa al-mujtama' al-mu'āṣir, mushkilāt al-ḥukm wa al-tawjīh.** Cairo: al-Dār al-Qawmīyah, 1966, 624 p.
A study of the conceptions of government wealth distribution in Islam. The author concludes that Islam is the only religion that fulfills the intellectual as well as the instinctive needs of man.

Bakhīt, Abd al-Ḥamīd. **al-Mujtama' al-'Arabī wa al-Islāmī.** Cairo: Dār al-Ma'ārif, 1965–66, 2 v.
Studies of contemporary Arab society, politics and foreign relations.

al-Barrāwī, Rāshid. **al-Iqtiṣād al-'Arabī mina al-khalij ilā al-muḥīṭ.** Cairo: Renaissance Bookshop, 1964, 397 p.
A survey of the economic situation in the Arab world. The author concludes that the new trends favor economic independence, economic growth through planning, and economic coöperation among the Arabs.

al-Barūdī, 'Alī. **Fī al-ishtirākīyah al-'Arabīyah.** Alexandria: Munsha'at al-Ma'ārif, 1967, 262 p.
A university professor explains Arab socialism and compares it with other socialist systems.

Bashir, al-Shāfi'ī Muhammad. **Nazarīyat al-ittihad bayna al-duwal wa tatbīqātuha bayana al-duwal al-'Arabīyah.** Alexandria: Munsh'at al-Ma'arif, 1963, 390 p.
A study of different types of federations and their possible application in the Arab countries. A special chapter is dedicated to the League of Arab States.

Be'eri, Eliezer. **Army Officers in Arab Politics and Society.** New York: Praeger, 1970, 514 p.
In this detailed treatment an Israeli scholar analyzes the origins, motives and achievements of the officer class in the Arab countries and finds military dictatorship neither an admirable nor an inevitable development of Arab society.

Berger, Morroe, ed. **The New Metropolis in the Arab World.** New Delhi: Allied Publishers, 1963, 254 p.
Essays in urban planning written by Arab authors for an international seminar held in Cairo in 1960.

Berque, Jacques. **The Arabs: Their History and Future.** New York: Praeger, 1964, 310 p.
A study of the Arab world, by a leading French orientalist and sociologist. The French original appeared as "Les Arabes d'hier à demain" (Paris: Éditions du Seuil, 1960, 284 p.).

Beyssade, Pierre. **La Ligue arabe.** Paris: Éditions Planète, 1968, 261 p.
Essentially a survey of inter-Arab politics since World War II, well informed and without illusions. The theme is the dream of unity versus the reality of disunity, both reflected in the League.

al-Bitār, Nadīm. **al-Fa'ālīyah al-thawrīyah fī al-nakbah.** Beirut: Dār àl-Ittihād, 1965, 163 p.
A philosophical discussion of the influence of Arab revolutionary thinking on Arab political developments caused by the Palestine problem.

al-Būtī, Muhammad Sa'īd Ramadān. **Dawābit al-maslahah fī al-sharī'ah àl-Islāmīyah.** Damascus: al-Maktabah al-Umawīyah, 1966–67, 466 p.
The author discusses the limits of *al-Maslaha*, the theory that what is beneficial to the community may be religiously sanctioned.

Carmichael, Joel. **The Shaping of the Arabs: A Study in Ethnic Identity.** New York: Macmillan, 1967, 407 p.
Sweeping through history from Muhammad to Nasser, a journalist and political analyst undertakes the impossible task of disentangling the strands of religion, language, cultural identity and political and social organization in the "shaping" of the Arabs over the centuries.

Clayton, Sir Gilbert Falkingham. **An Arabian Diary.** Berkeley: University of California Press, 1969, 379 p.
An account of two diplomatic missions undertaken during the 1920s by one of Britain's outstanding Near Eastern hands. The long introduction by Robert O. Collins is a useful survey of some aspects of British-Arab relations during World War I and after.

Cleveland, William L. **The Making of an Arab Nationalist.** Princeton: Princeton University Press, 1971, 211 p.
An excellent biography, describing the trends and forces that nurtured the thought of Sati' al-Husri, the most influential ideologist of Arab nationalism.

Cremeans, Charles Davis. **The Arabs and the World: Nasser's Arab Nationalist Policy.** New York: Praeger (for the Council on Foreign Relations), 1963, 338 p.
The author, an American with long teaching and governmental experience in Egypt, discusses Arab nationalism and foreign policy as it has emerged in recent decades. It is his well-considered view that there is "a foreign policy of Arab nationalism as consistent and as firmly based on doctrine and interests as Western foreign policies."

Diab, Muhammad Amine. **Inter-Arab Economic Cooperation, 1951–1960.** Beirut: Economic Research Institute, American University of Beirut, 1963, 319 p.
A concise survey of the voluminous trade agreements among the Arab states and a collection of statistics covering trade among Egypt, Iraq, Jordan, Lebanon, Saudi Arabia and Syria.

Flory, Maurice and Mantran, Robert. **Les Régimes politiques des pays arabes.** Paris: Presses Universitaires, 1968, 469 p.
A combined handbook and history, packed with information and bibliographical references, of the Arab world from Morocco to Muscat.

Gabrieli, Francesco. **The Arabs: A Compact History.** New York: Hawthorn Books, 1963, 215 p.
A panoramic view of the Arabs in history from pre-Islamic times up to the present by an Italian scholar. The Italian original appeared as "Gli arabi" (Florence: Sansoni, 1957, 235 p.).

Ghālī, Shukrī. **Amrīka wa al-ḥarb al-fikrīyyah.** Cairo: al-Mu'assasah al-Misrīyah al-'Ammah, 1967, 106 p.
An Egyptian writer exposes what he calls the American intellectual war against the Arab culture. He sees the American educational institutions, pro-Western periodicals and the movies as weapons used to destroy what is genuinely Arabic.

Hottinger, Arnold. **The Arabs: Their History, Culture and Place in the Modern World.** Berkeley: University of California Press, 1963, 344 p.
The result of a Swiss observer's long experience and scholarly devotion, this volume is a multi-faceted portrait of the Arab and his society.

Hujayr, Mubārak. **al-Mustaqbal al-iqtiṣādī wal al-mālī lil-dūwal al-'Arabīyah.** Cairo: The Anglo-Egyptian Bookshop, 1969, 281 p.
A study of the economic future of the Arab world. The author's forecast is based on the examination of present economic situation and developmental trends in the Arab countries.

al-Huṣarī, Abū Khaldūn Sāṭi'. **Mudhakkirātī fī al-'Iraq.** Beirut: Dār al-Ṭali'ah, 1967, 2 v.
Memoirs by the theoretician of secular Arab nationalism shedding new information on the events of the 1920s and 1930s.

al-Husary, Khaldun. **Three Reformers: A Study in Modern Arab Political Thought.** Beirut: Khayats, 1966, 176 p.
A lucid account of the ideas of the Egyptian Rifa'ah al-Tahtawi, the Tunisian Khayr al-Din and the Syrian al-Kawakibi, three reformers who advocated the assimilation of Western culture within the framework of Islam.

Husayn, Ahmad. **al-Ummah al-insānīyah.** Cairo: al-Matba'ah al-'Alamīyah, 1966, 474 p.
The author, once a leader of a fascist-like organization who later became a devout Muslim, calls for the removal of national barriers.

'Imārah, Muḥammad. **al-Ummah al-'Arabīyah wa qaḍīyat al-tawḥīd.** Cairo: al-Dār al-Miṣrīyah lil-Ta'līf, 1966, 224 p.
A study of the basic concepts of Arab nationalism: historical community, one language, one land and one social psychology.

Ismā'il, 'Adil. **al-Sīyāsah al-dūwalīyah fī al-sharq al-'Arabī, 1789–1958.** Beirut: Dār al-Nashr li-al-Sīyasah wa-al-Tarīkh, 1964, 320 p.
The fourth volume of a political history of the Arab East from 1866 to 1918 dealing with the events leading to the British occupation of Egypt, the proliferation of European interests, and Arab-Turkish relations.

al-Jamal, Shawqī. **al-Tadāmun al-Asyawī al-Afrīqī wa athāruhu fī al-qadayā al-'Arabīyah.** Cairo: al-Mu'assasah al-Misrīyah lil-Ta'līf, 1964, 354 p.
A survey of the proceedings and resolutions of the first three meetings of the Permanent Organization for Afro-Asian Peoples Solidarity, with emphasis on the effect of these meetings on Arab affairs.

Kerr, Malcolm H. **The Arab Cold War: Gamal'Abd Al-Nasir and His Rivals, 1958–1970.** New York: Oxford University Press (for the Royal Institute of International Affairs), 3rd rev. ed., 1971, 166 p.
A compact and authoritative interpretation of inter-Arab rivalries, by an American political scientist of long experience in the Arab world. This latest edition adds a chapter describing the lineup that emerged after the Six-Day War: in brief, Nasser and Hussein in coöperation against the fedayeen.

Khadduri, Majid. **Political Trends in the Arab World: The Role of Ideas and Ideals in Politics.** Baltimore: Johns Hopkins Press, 1970, 298 p.
A comprehensive treatment of political ideologies, including nationalism, constitutional democracy, Islamic reformism, Marxism and Arab socialism. The author de-

velops a thesis for a new social democracy which he considers suited to the Arab future.

al-Kharbutly, 'Ali Husnī. **al-Tārikh al-mūwaḥḥad lil ummah al-'Arabīyah.** Cairo: al-Hay'ah al-Miṣrīyah al-'Ammah, 1970, 321 p.
A historical survey of concepts of Arab unity, by an Egyptian professor.

Klieman, Aaron S. **Foundations of British Policy in the Arab World: The Cairo Conference of 1921.** Baltimore: Johns Hopkins Press, 1970, 322 p.
A careful account, based in part on published British documents, of a much ignored event in British-Arab affairs. The Cairo Conference sharpened and gave direction to a hesitant British policy in the area, but the result, in ignoring some of the basic Arab aspirations of the day, gave rise to many later problems.

Koury, Enver M. **The Patterns of Mass Movements in Arab Revolutionary-Progressive States.** The Hague: Mouton, 1970, 308 p.
A belabored attempt to explain the social and psychological determinants of Arab revolutionary behavior.

Koury, Enver M. **The Super-Powers and the Balance of Power in the Arab World.** Beirut: Catholic Press, 1970, 208 p.
A study of the relationship between the international system as represented by the U.S. and U.S.S.R. and the regional sub-system represented by the Arab world. The author affirms that the idea of balance of power is still valid despite the constant shifts in alliances.

Laroui, Abdallah. **L'Idéologie arabe contemporaine: essai critique.** Paris: Maspéro, 1967, 225 p.
The author of this analysis of contemporary Arab ideologies considers Marxism without its totalitarian frame as the most suitable ideology for the Arab world.

MacDonald, Robert W. **The League of Arab States: A Study in the Dynamics of Regional Organization.** Princeton: Princeton University Press, 1965, 407 p.
A careful examination of the founding, structure and operation of the Arab League up through 1964, with the conclusion that it has been successful in asserting Arab dignity and power in the world, and ought now to become a main channel for economic and social modernization.

Mansoor, Menahem. **Political and Diplomatic History of the Arab World, 1900–1967: A Chronological Study.** Washington: NCR/Microcard Editions, 1972, 7 v.
A massive reference, "developed pursuant to a contract between the United States Office of Education and the University of Wisconsin."

The Middle East and North Africa. London: Europa Publications.
A most useful reference work, formerly published under the title "The Middle East." The 20th edition of this publication, covering the years 1973–74 and dealing with Middle East and North African politics, economic life and cultural activities, was published in 1973.

Monteil, Vincent. **Le Monde musulman.** Paris: Horizons de France, 1963, 287 p.
A rewarding, comprehensive study, well-illustrated, of Muslims in the Arab world and in Turkey, Iran, Malay and North Africa.

Mousa, Sulaiman. **al-Ḥarakah al-'Arabīyah, sirat al-mirhalah al-'ūlā lil-nahḍah al-'Arabīyah al-ḥadithah.** Beirut: Dār al-Nahar, 1970, 680 p.
A history of the formative years of the Arab nationalist movement. Based on archival materials in England and the Arab world, the author gives an Arab point of view of the developments between 1908 and 1924.

Muhyī al-Dīn, Khalid. **Ḥarakat al-salām, al-fikrah, wa al-takwīn, wa al-manhaj.** Cairo: al-Hay'ah al-Miṣrīyah al-'Ammah, 1967, 132 p.
Essays by a leading Egyptian leftist on the peace movement and its relation with the liberation movements in the Arab world.

Murqus, Ilyas. **Tārīkh al-aḥzāb al-shūyū'īyah fī al-waṭan al-'Arabī.** Beirut: Dār al-Ṭab'ah, 1964, 312 p.
A history of the communist parties in the Arab countries, by a well-known Marxist.

Musrey, Alfred G. **An Arab Common Market: A Study in Inter-Arab Trade Relations, 1920–67.** New York: Praeger, 1969, 274 p.
An American economist's careful account of how political and economic differences

have prevented economic integration among the Arab states despite the number of agreements concluded toward that end. The essential element, a sufficient community of interests to apply vast oil revenues to regional development, has been lacking.

Nawfal, al-Sayyid Muḥammad A. **al-'Amal al-'Arabi al-mushtarak fī al-majāl al-dūwalī.** Cairo: Institute of Arab Studies and Research, 1968, 202 p.
The Deputy Secretary General of the League of Arab States discusses common Arab action in international affairs. His chapters on the League's agencies and institutions are most informative.

Niḍāl al-Ba'th fī sabīl al wiḥdah, al-hurrīyah, al-ishtirākīyah (Wathā' iq Hizb al-Ba'th al-'Arabī al-Ishtirākī). Beirut: Dār al-Ṭali'ah (for the Hizb al-Ba'th al-'Arabī al-Ishtirākī), 1963–72, 9 v.
A collection of documentary materials consisting of Syrian and Iraqi statements, resolutions and editorials on the struggle of the Ba'th to achieve unity, freedom and socialism.

Nutting, Anthony. **The Arabs: A Narrative History from Mohammed to the Present.** New York: Potter, 1964, 424 p.
A useful general history. The author resigned as British Minister of State for Foreign Affairs in protest against Eden's policy during the Suez crisis of 1956.

Qubain, Fahim Issa. **Education and Science in the Arab World.** Baltimore: Johns Hopkins Press, 1966, 539 p.
A pioneering effort to collect information on education and manpower in all the Arab countries except Tunisia, Algeria and Morocco.

Rahman, Fazlur. **Islam.** New York: Holt, Rinehart and Winston, 1967, 271 p.
A survey of the historical development of Islam, both doctrine and practice, by a Pakistani scholar. His final chapters argue for the internal reconstruction of society in the individual Muslim countries.

Rifā'ī, Muḥammad 'Ali. **al-Jāmi'ah al-'Arabīyah wa qaḍayā al-taḥrir.** Cairo, 2d rev. ed., 1972, 610 p.
A description and documentation of the participation of the League of Arab States in the decolonization process.

Rodinson, Maxime. **Marxisme et monde musulman.** Paris: Éditions du Seuil, 1972, 699 p.
A collection of Rodinson's past writings on many aspects of Marxism as related to the Muslim world, tied together by a preface and comments on each piece in its contemporary setting.

Ronart, Stephan and Ronart, Nandy. **Concise Encyclopaedia of Arabic Civilization: The Arab West.** New York: Praeger, 1966, 410 p.
A useful companion volume to the authors' earlier encyclopedia dealing with the Arab East.

Ṣaab, Hassan. **Naẓrah ilā al-ittiḥad al-'Arabi al-mashrū' al-waḥdawī al-Nāṣiri ba'd 'Abd al-Nāsir.** Tripoli: Maktabat al-Farjānī, 1971, 304 p.
A look at the projected union between Libya, Egypt and Syria after the death of Abdel Nasser.

Sayegh, Fayez Abdullah, ed. **The Dynamics of Neutralism in the Arab World: A Symposium.** San Francisco: Chandler (for the Council on International Perspectives), 1964, 275 p.
The editor and eight Arab scholars, diplomats and political figures contribute essays toward a definition and rationale of neutralism as a cold war phenomenon.

Sayf al-Dawlah, 'Ismat. **'Usus al-ishtirakīyah al-'Arabīyah.** Cairo: al-Hay'ah, 2d ed., 1971, 394 p.
An analytical essay on Arab socialism by an Egyptian professor. The author concludes that the future of the struggle for liberation and unity depends on the application of the three basic principles of the Arab socialist movement: freedom, unity and socialism.

Schechtman, Joseph B. **The Mufti and the Fuehrer: The Rise and Fall of Haj Amin El-Husseini.** New York: Yoseloff, 1965, 336 p.
Haj Amin, the Grand Mufti of Jerusalem, long regarded by Zionists and their sup-

porters as evil incarnate, is given an unjustified importance in this one-sided and incomplete biography.

Sharabi, Hisham Bashir. **Nationalism and Revolution in the Arab World.** Princeton: Van Nostrand, 1966, 176 p.
A concise and well-done handbook of contemporary politics in the Middle East and North Africa by the author of "Government and Politics of the Middle East in the Twentieth Century."

al-Ṭamāwī, Sulaymān Muḥammad. **al-Sulṭāt al-thalāth fī al-dasātīr al-'Arabīyah al-mu'āṣirah wa fī al-fikr al-sīyāsī al-Islāmī.** Cairo: Dār al-Fikr al-'Arabī, rev. ed., 1973, 600 p.
A comparative study of the legislative, executive and judiciary powers of the Arab countries.

Tibi, Bassam. **Nationalismus in der Dritten Welt am arabischen Beispiel.** Frankfurt/Main: Europäische Verlagsanstalt, 1971, 288 p.
A convenient summary of varying interpretations of nationalism in the Arab world, with emphasis on the writings and influence of Sati'al-Husri.

Tütsch, Hans Emanuel. **Facets of Arab Nationalism.** Detroit: Wayne State University Press, 1965, 157 p.
This well-informed study is based on a decade of travel and observation in North Africa and the Middle East for the *Neue Zürcher Zeitung*.

'Urwadkī, Yaḥya. **al-Sūq al-'Arabīyah al-mushtarakah.** Damascus: Ministry of Culture, 1970, 392 p.
A comprehensive study of the Arab Common Market established in 1965.

al-Wathā'iq al-'Arabīyah, 1963– . Beirut: American University of Beirut, Jafet Memorial Library, 1963– .
An annual collection of government policy declarations, communiques and decrees, speeches of leading figures, party manifestos and statements, conventions and constitutions. Three volumes (1963–65) have appeared both in Arabic and English. The English title of this collection is "Arab Political Documents."

Who's Who in the Arab World, 1971–1972. Beirut: Publitec Publications, 3rd rev. ed., 1971, 1,567 p.
A survey of 15 Arab countries and a biographical dictionary listing more than 3,000 leading personalities in the Arab world.

TURKEY

General Surveys and Political Problems

See also The Problem of Authority; Violence and Revolution, p. 34; First World War, p. 131; Second World War, p. 144; The Postwar World, p. 178; Eastern Europe and the Soviet Bloc, p. 358; (Middle East) General Surveys and Political Problems, p. 611; The Arab World, p. 616; (Japan) Politics and Government, p. 721.

Ağaoğlu, Samet. **Arkadaşım Menderes.** Istanbul: Rek-Turk, 1967, 204 p.
A biography of Adnan Menderes, Prime Minister of Turkey from 1950 to 1960, by a close associate and an important figure in the Democratic Party.

Ağaoğlu, Samet. **Aşına yüzler.** Istanbul: Ağaoğlu Yayınevi, 1965, 229 p.
Useful but partisan portraits of some leading contemporary Turkish politicians.

Atatürk, Kemâl. **Atatürk'ün Hatıra Defteri.** Ankara: Türk Tarih Kurumu, 1972, 223 p.
A note-book by Atatürk, including references to personalities and events associated with the early history of the Republic. Edited by Şükrü Tezer.

Avcıoğlu, Doğan. **Türkiye'nin düzeni, dün, bugün, yarın.** Ankara: Bilgi Yayınevi, 2d ed., 1971, 770 p.
This very popular study was published originally in 1968. It represents the socialistic-nationalistic thinking that ideologically nurtured the political events from 1965 to 1971. Using a great deal of economic and historical data, the author attempts to prove that Turkey has become subservient to the West.

Aydemir, Şevket Süreyya. **Tek adam: Mustafa Kemal'in hayatı.** Istanbul: Remzi Kitabevi, 1963–65, 3 v.

———. **İkinci adam: İsmet İnönü.** Istanbul: Remzi Kitabevi, 1966–68, 3 v.
———. **Menderes'in dramı.** Istanbul: Remzi Kitabevi, 1969, 559 p.
Aydemir, an important figure in the ideological history of the country, attempts in these volumes to provide a political history of the Turkish modernization through the study of key personalities guiding modern Turkey: Atatürk, İnönü and Menderes. The author uses often original documents and interprets Turkish politics from a nationalistic and semi-Marxist point of view. These studies have played a major role in educating the Turkish public to see their recent history in a new light. Indispensable for any study of modern Turkey.

Baban, Cihat. **Politika galerisi: büstler ve portreler.** Istanbul: Remzi Kitabevi, 1970, 459 p.
Excellent but subjective protraits of some leading Turkish politicians, by a journalist and former minister.

Bahrampour, Firouz. **Turkey: Political and Social Transformation.** Brooklyn: Gaus, 1967, 100 p.
A brief description of developments since Atatürk's revolution.

Basgil, Ali Fuad. **La Révolution militaire de 1960 en Turquie (ses origines).** Geneva: Perret-Gentil, 1963, 206 p.
A review of the military takeover in Turkey in 1960.

Bayar, Celâl. **Başvekilim Adnan Menderes.** Istanbul: Baha Matbaası, 1969, 176 p.
A useful discussion of Menderes, a prominent Turkish statesman and one of the founders of the Democratic Party who died in 1961. It reflects a growing Menderes cult which has reached some segments of the intelligentsia after striking deep roots among the villagers.

Bayar, Celâl. **Ben de yazdım.** Istanbul: Baha Matbaası, 1965–69, 7 v.
Reminiscences and an attempt to survey the Turkish War of Liberation by the third President of Turkey and a former leader of the Democratic Party.

Berkes, Niyazi. **The Development of Secularism in Turkey.** Montreal: McGill University Press, 1964, 537 p.
"The transformation of Turkey from a traditional to a secular state illustrates the complex relations between economic and technical changes and political and religious changes. For this reason it presents a valuable case history." This is the theme, and Professor Berkes' study of the process is impressive in scope and authority.

Bülent, Nuri Esen. **La Turquie.** Paris: Librairie Générale de Droit, 1970, 276 p.
An introduction to the politics and government of Turkey, by a professor at the University of Ankara.

Cem, İsmail. **Türkiye'de geri kalmışlığın tarihi.** Istanbul: Cem Yayınevi, 1970, 428 p.
A historical and ideological study of the causes of underdevelopment in Turkey. Though factually unreliable, it is useful for understanding the political thinking prevailing in Turkey during the 1960s.

Dewdney, J. C. **Turkey: An Introductory Geography.** New York: Praeger, 1971, 214 p.
This introduction to the physical, human and economic geography of Turkey is the first of its kind that has been published in English. The author is a British scholar.

Dodd, Clement Henry. **Politics and Government in Turkey.** Berkeley: University of California Press, 1969, 335 p.
A study of domestic political scene in the 1960s, competently and soberly viewed through the prism of constitutional law and practice, parties and elections, and public administration.

Eren, Nuri. **Turkey Today and Tomorrow: An Experiment in Westernization.** New York: Praeger, 1963, 276 p.
A Turkish diplomat examines the salient features of contemporary Turkey against a somewhat idealized image of Western democratic society, and finds much to criticize as well as approve.

Frey, Frederick Ward. **The Turkish Political Elite.** Cambridge: M.I.T. Press, 1965, 483 p.
This analysis of the social background of Turkish legislators from 1920 onwards is at the same time a valuable summary of political evolution in Turkey.

Goloğlu, Mahmut. **Milli Mücadele tarihi.** Ankara: Nüve-Başmur Matbaası, 1968–71, 5 v.
A solid study of the Turkish War of Liberation.

Harris, George S. **The Origins of Communism in Turkey.** Stanford: Hoover Institution on War, Revolution, and Peace, 1967, 215 p.
   This account of the early years of the communist movement, told for the first time in revealing detail, throws light on the broader questions of Turkey's politics and its relations with Russia.

İnönü, İsmet. **Hatıralarım.** Istanbul: Istanbul Matbaası, 1969, 263 p.
   Memoirs by the second President of Turkey and a leading statesman.

İsen, Can Kaya. **Geliyorum diyen ihtilâl, 22 subat 21-mayıs.** Istanbul: Tan Matbaası, 1964, 368 p.
   A detailed account of the abortive military coups in the early 1960s.

Kazamias, Andreas Michael. **Education and the Quest for Modernity in Turkey.** Chicago: University of Chicago Press, 1967, 304 p.
   The historical chapters of this book, using both Turkish and foreign works, describe the educational aspects of the reform movement in the Ottoman Empire and the Turkish Republic. The chapters on the contemporary scene are based in part on personal observation and field research.

Kinross, John Patrick Douglas Balfour, 3rd Baron. **Ataturk: A Biography of Mustafa Kemal, Father of Modern Turkey.** New York: Morrow, 1965, 615 p.
   This definitive and absorbing biography is the first to live up to the Churchillian dimensions of its subject.

Köprülü, Mehmet Fuat. **Demokrasi yolunda.** The Hague: Mouton, 1964, 928 p.
   A collection of newspaper articles on Turkish politics and international relations, published between 1945 and 1950, by a distinguished Turkish historian, statesman and one of the founders of the Democratic Party. This compendium appeared under the auspices of Columbia University's Department of Near and Middle East Languages and the Near and Middle East Institute and was edited by Tophyan T. Halasi-Kun.

Lewis, Bernard. **The Emergence of Modern Turkey.** New York: Oxford University Press (for the Royal Institute of International Affairs), 2d ed., 1968, 524 p.
   An extensively revised edition of an authoritative study of the emergence of modern Turkey.

Nayir, Yaşar Nabi, ed. **Atatürkçülük nedir?** Istanbul: Varlık Yayınevi, 1969, 217 p.
   A series of essays searching for a new definition of Atatürk's political philosophy.

Robinson, Richard Dunlop. **The First Turkish Republic: A Case Study in National Development.** Cambridge: Harvard University Press, 1963, 367 p.
   An interpretive history in which the author's long experience and intimate knowledge of modern Turkey are brought to bear on the theme that the evolution of Turkey from Atatürk until the military takeover in 1960 can be viewed as an instructive test case of accelerated development under Western-oriented leadership.

Selek, Sabahattin. **Anadolu ihtilâli.** Istanbul: Burçak Yayınevi, 1968, 736 p.
   An important and influential monograph on the social origins of the Turkish War of Liberation from 1919 to 1922. The author's populist conclusions differ from the élitist interpretations that prevailed until recently in Turkey.

Szyliowicz, Joseph S. **Political Change in Rural Turkey: Erdemli.** The Hague: Mouton, 1966, 218 p.
   A study tracing the development of political activity in a closely knit village group of southwestern Turkey from 1941 to 1957.

Tevetoğlu, Fethi. **Türkiye'de sosyalist ve komünist faâliyetler 1910-1960.** Ankara: Ayyıldız Matbaası, 1967, 720 p.
   A major book published by the rightist organization "Komünizmle Mücadele Derneği" (Association to Combat Communism). The author, in spite of his biases, has provided useful information on the communist and socialist movements in Turkey.

Toker, Metin. **İsmet Paşayla 10 yıl 1954-1964.** Ankara: Akis Yayınları, 1966-69, 4 v.
   İnönü's son-in-law reminisces about his father-in-law and provides information about political events in the period from 1954 to 1964 when İnönü was the head of the Republican People's Party and then Prime Minister after the revolution of 1960.

Toker, Metin. **Solda ve sağda vuruşanlar.** Ankara: Akis Yayınları, 1971, 171 p.
   A useful though superficial account of the rightist and leftist groups fighting each other and the parliamentary system in the late 1960s.

Tunçay, Mete. **Türkiye'de sol akımlar, 1908-1925.** Ankara: Sevinç Matbassı, 2d ed., 1967, 218 p.
　One of the best studies of the early leftist movements in Turkey.
Turan, Osman. **Türkiye'de mânevî buhran: din ve lâiklik.** Ankara: Hilâl Yayınları, 1964, 296 p.
──. **Türkiye'de siyâsî buhranın kaynakları.** Istanbul: Neşriyat Yurdu, 1969, 195 p.
　These studies by a conservative professor of history at the University of Ankara represent a rather rare effort to visualize the political conflicts and cultural crises in Turkey as the consequence of changes in the system of values and social anomy.
Ülken, Hilmi Ziya. **Türkiye'de çağdaş düşünce tarihi.** Istanbul: Ahmet Sait Matbaası, 1966, 2 v.
　A history of ideas in Turkey by a well-known educator familiar both with Western and Eastern cultures.
Weiker, Walter F. **The Turkish Revolution 1960-1961: Aspects of Military Politics.** Washington: Brookings Institution, 1963, 172 p.
　A study in detail of the political problems involved in the 1960-61 military takeover and the implications for U.S. policies.
Yalman, Ahmet Emin. **Yakın tarihte gördüklerim ve geçirdiklerim.** Istanbul: Yenilik Basımevi, 1970-71, 4 v.
　Memoirs by a well-known Turkish journalist who died in 1973. The author was particularly active from 1947 to 1950 in supporting the opposition Democratic Party.

Foreign Relations

See also Second World War, p. 144; The Postwar World, p. 178; and the sections for specific countries and regions

Erkin, Feridun Cemal. **Les Relations turco-soviétiques et la question des détroits.** Ankara: Başnur Matbaası, 1968, 540 p.
　A substantial study by a former Foreign Minister of Turkey of Turkish-Soviet relations, concentrating on the crisis of 1945-1946. The Turkish original was published as "Türk-Sovyet ilişkileri ve Boğazlar messelesi" (Ankara: Başnur Matbaası, 1968, 452 p.).
Harris, George S. **Troubled Alliance: Turkish-American Problems in Historical Perspective, 1945-1971.** Washington: American Enterprise Institute for Public Policy Research; Stanford: Hoover Institution on War, Revolution and Peace, 1972, 263 p.
　A running account of a whole gamut of difficulties—from the status of the U.S. military forces in Turkey to the opium trade—that have plagued Turkish-American ties. The author sees a waning, though not an end, of the association, and an eventual tilt on Turkey's part toward Europe.
Krecker, Lothar. **Deutschland und die Türkei im Zweiten Weltkrieg.** Frankfurt/Main: Klostermann, 1964, 293 p.
　A monograph on German-Turkish relations, based chiefly on German published and unpublished sources.
Kürkçüoğlu, Ömer E. **Türkiye'nin Arap Orta Doğusuna karşı politikası (1945-1970).** Ankara: Sevinç Matbaası, 1972, 210 p.
　The first detailed and reliable study of Turkish foreign policy toward the Arab nations after World War II.
Massigli, René Lucien Daniel. **La Turquie devant la guerre: mission à Ankara, 1939-1940.** Paris: Plon, 1964, 511 p.
　The detailed autobiographical record of a French diplomat's struggle in Ankara (1939-1940) against the intrigues of the Nazis and the bureaucratic hesitations of his own government.
Olaylarla Türk Dış Politikası 1919-1965. Ankara: Dışişleri Bakanlığı Matbaası, 1968, 428 p.
　A substantial collection of studies on Turkish foreign policy by leading Turkish scholars.
Sezer, Duygu. **Kamu oyu ve Dış politika.** Ankara: Sevinç Matbaası, 1972, 584 p.
　A study of Turkish public attitudes toward foreign policy.

Trask, Roger R. **The United States Response to Turkish Nationalism and Reform, 1914-1939.** Minneapolis: University of Minnesota Press, 1971, 280 p.
  A detailed treatment of many aspects of Turkish-American relations.

The Turkish Yearbook of International Relations, 1960–. Ankara: University of Ankara, Institute of International Relations, 1961–.
  An annual collection of articles, documents, chronologies, book reviews and bibliographies.

Váli, Ferenc A. **Bridge Across the Bosporus: The Foreign Policy of Turkey.** Baltimore: Johns Hopkins Press, 1971, 410 p.
  A well-informed and methodical survey of Turkey's postwar foreign policy.

Váli, Ferenc A. **The Turkish Straits and NATO.** Stanford: Hoover Institution Press, 1972, 348 p.
  The Montreux Convention, Soviet expansion in the Middle East, NATO strategy and Turkey's choices all receive sober though rather brief treatment. Documents, all previously published, make up the second half of the book.

Economic Problems

See also Problems of New Nations, p. 36; (Economic Factors) Government and Economics; Planning, p. 54; Economic Aid and Technical Assistance, p. 81; (Eastern Europe and the Soviet Bloc) Economic Problems, p. 362; (Asia and the Pacific Area) General Surveys, p. 607.

Cohn, Edwin J. **Turkish Economic, Social, and Political Change.** New York: Praeger, 1970, 196 p.
  The author argues that rapid economic development and progress toward a more open society can go hand in hand in Turkey.

Eldem, Vedat. **Osmanlı imparatorluğunun iktisadi şartları hakkında bir tetkik.** Ankara: Türkiye İş Bankası, 1970, 327 p.
  An original, though somewhat careless economic history of the Ottoman State during its last decades. Useful for understanding the economic policies of modern Turkey.

Hershlag, Zvi Yehuda. **Turkey: The Challenge of Growth.** Leyden: Brill, 2d ed., 1968, 406 p.
  A thoroughly revised edition of the author's "Turkey, an Economy in Transition" (1958).

Rivkin, Malcolm D. **Area Development for National Growth: The Turkish Precedent.** New York: Praeger, 1965, 228 p.
  The lessons drawn from Turkish efforts over 40 years to stimulate the development of its interior regions are of clear import to other similarly motivated nations.

SYRIA

See also (The United States) Relations with the Middle East and the Arab World, p. 242; (France) Foreign Policy, p. 404; Military Policy, p. 407; (Middle East) General Surveys and Political Problems, p. 611; The Arab World, p. 616; Arab-Israeli Conflict, p. 633.

'Alam al-Dīn, Wajīh. **Marāhil istiqlāl dawlatay Lubnān wa-Sūrīyā, 1922-1943.** Beirut: The Author, 1967, 308 p.
  A documentary history of the struggle of Lebanon and Syria to obtain their independence, covering the period from the beginning of the mandate in 1922 to the declaration of independence in 1943.

Davet, Michel-Christian. **La Double Affaire de Syrie.** Paris: Fayard, 1967, 360 p.
  A study of the takeover of Syria by British and Free French forces in 1941 and of the crisis involving the British, de Gaulle and the Syrian nationalists in 1945. The use of unpublished material and interviews with participants makes this a valuable book.

Hilan, Rizkallah. **Culture et développement en Syrie et dans les pays retardés.** Paris: Éditions Anthropos, 1969, 388 p.
A study of cultural and economic development of underdeveloped countries in general and of Syria in particular.

al-Ḥuṣarī, Abū Khaldūn Sāṭiʻ. **The Day of Maysalūn: A Page from the Modern History of the Arabs.** Washington: Middle East Institute, 1966, 187 p.
Reminiscences of the first independent Arab government in Syria 1919–1920 by a well-known Arab nationalist. There is an appendix of documents.

Le Corbeiller, Jacques. **La guerre de Syrie: juin-juillet 1941.** Paris: Éditions du Fuseau, 1967, 200 p.
An account of the complicated warfare in Syria in June and July 1941 which resulted in the termination of the authority of the French Vichy government by the Free French and British forces.

Mahr, Horst. **Die Baath-Partei.** Munich: Olzog, 1971, 181 p.
A competent summary, based on Western sources, of the history and organization of the Baʻth, mainly in Syria but with some mention of its activities in other Arab states.

Nyrop, Richard F. and Others. **Area Handbook for Syria.** Washington: G.P.O., 1971, 357 p.
A useful reference volume with a bibliography, prepared by the Foreign Area Studies at the American University.

Petran, Tabitha. **Syria.** New York: Praeger, 1972, 284 p.
Generally an informative historical and political survey, although the author does not muffle her antipathy to Western policies, to Israel and to certain Arab leaders.

Rabinovich, Itamar. **Syria under the Baʻth 1963-66: The Army-Party Symbiosis.** Jerusalem: Israel Universities Press/New York: Halsted Press, 1972, 276 p.
This well-documented account dispels much of the confusion about what happened to the country, the party and the military during the first factious years of Baʻth rule.

Saab, Édouard. **La Syrie ou la révolution dans la rancoeur.** Paris: Julliard, 1968, 309 p.
A review of two decades (1948–67) of politics and government in Syria by a prominent Beirut editor and correspondent of *Le Monde*.

Sanjian, Avedis Krikor. **The Armenian Communities in Syria under Ottoman Dominion.** Cambridge: Harvard University Press, 1965, 390 p.
A definitive history of the Orthodox Armenian communities in Syria, their internal organization and social institutions, and their evolution during four centuries of Ottoman rule.

Seale, Patrick. **The Struggle for Syria: A Study of Post-War Arab Politics 1945–1958.** New York: Oxford University Press (for the Royal Institute of International Affairs), 1965, 344 p.
The Observer's veteran Middle East correspondent's brilliant examination of Syria as the "head and heart" of the Arab national movement.

Tibawi, A. L. **A Modern History of Syria: Including Lebanon and Palestine.** New York: St. Martin's Press, 1970, 441 p.
A general history covering the nineteenth and twentieth centuries. The author's main interest is in the period of World War I and its aftermath when the Western powers broke up the unity of the Arab East.

Torrey, Gordon H. **Syrian Politics and the Military, 1945–1958.** Columbus: Ohio State University Press, 1964, 438 p.
A valuable and pioneering record of political developments in postwar Syria.

Zuwiyya-Yamak, Labib. **The Syrian Social Nationalist Party: An Ideological Analysis.** Cambridge: Harvard University Press (for the Center for Middle Eastern Studies, Harvard University), 1966, 177 p.
The author states that his "primary purpose is to examine the doctrine of Syrian nationalism as stated by Antun Sa'adih, discuss his political philosophy, and give a brief description of the organizational structure of the SSNP" which was "the first organized party in the Arab East to have a definite national doctrine and a well structured ideology."

LEBANON

See also (The United States) Relations with the Middle East and the Arab World, p. 242; (France) Foreign Policy, p. 404; Military Policy, p. 407; (Middle East) General Surveys and Political Problems, p. 611; The Arab World, p. 616; Syria, p. 626; Arab-Israeli Conflict, p. 633.

Abu-Izzedin, Halim S. **Siyāsat Lubnān al-khārijīyah.** Beirut: Dār al-'Ilm lil-Malāyyīn, 1966, 271 p.
An articulate explanation of the principles that guided Lebanon's foreign policy in the 1960s.

Agwani, Mohammed Shafi, ed. **The Lebanese Crisis, 1958: A Documentary Study.** New York: Asia Publishing House (for the Indian School of International Studies), 1965, 407 p.
An Indian scholar's reconstruction of a Lebanese crisis which became, with the landing of U. S. troops, a major cold-war confrontation.

Binder, Leonard, ed. **Politics in Lebanon.** New York: Wiley, 1966, 345 p.
This well-edited volume presents a comprehensive exploration and analysis of the politics of contemporary Lebanese democracy.

Chamoun, Camille. **Crise au Moyen-Orient.** Paris: Gallimard, 1963, 436 p.
The former President of Lebanon (1952–58) presents an outspoken inside history of postwar Lebanon culminating with the international crisis of 1958 and the landing of American troops. Nasser is his chief villain and U. S. policy his despair.

Chamoun, Camille. **Mudhakkirāti.** Beirut, 1969, 307 p.
The first volume of the memoirs by the Lebanese statesman deals with the struggle for independence during the years from 1943 to 1946.

Hachem, Nabil. **Libanon: sozio-ökonomische Grundlagen.** Opladen: Leske (for the Deutsches Orient-Institut), 1969, 374 p.
A solid survey of economic and social conditions in Lebanon.

al-Hasan, Hasan. **al-Anzimah al-sīyāsīyah wa-al-dusturīyah fī Lubnān wa sā'ir al-buldan al-'Arabīyah.** Beirut: al-Dār al-Lubnānīyah lil-Ṭibā'ah, 1967, 496 p.
A survey of the political and constitutional systems of Lebanon and other countries of the Arab world.

Hitti, Philip Khûri. **A Short History of Lebanon.** New York: St. Martin's Press, 1965, 248 p.
A lively condensation of the authoritative "Lebanon in History" (1957) by Princeton's grand old man of Arab letters.

Hudson, Michael Craig. **The Precarious Republic: Political Modernization in Lebanon.** New York: Random House (for the Center for International Affairs, Harvard University), 1968, 364 p.
Utilizing modern political science concepts, the author has written a substantial study of Lebanese social and political problems. Based on a thorough study of sources.

Lyautey, Pierre. **Liban moderne.** Paris: Julliard, 1964, 157 p.
An informative study of the modernization of Lebanon by a French scholar who knows the country well.

Meo, Leila M. T. **Lebanon: Improbable Nation; A Study in Political Development.** Bloomington: Indiana University Press, 1965, 246 p.
A lively history of modern Lebanon culminating in the crisis of 1958 and the landing of U.S. Marines. The author is a Palestinian by birth.

Rizk, Charles. **Le Régime politique libanais.** Paris: Librairie Générale de Droit, 1966, 170 p.
A capable description of the confessionally based, socially heterogeneous Lebanese political system, by a Lebanese scholar and television commentator.

Salibi, Kamal Suleiman. **The Modern History of Lebanon.** New York: Praeger, 1965, 227 p.
A well-written study by a leading Lebanese scholar.

Suleiman, Michael W. **Political Parties in Lebanon: The Challenge of a Fragmented Political Culture.** Ithaca: Cornell University Press, 1967, 326 p.

A scholarly, documented description and analysis of Lebanon's political parties, legal and illegal, that tells a great deal about the politics of other Arab states as well.

Ziadé, Pierre. **Histoire diplomatique de l'indépendance du Liban (avec un recueil de documents).** Beirut: al-Maṭābʻah al-Ahlīyah, 1969, 320 p.
An account of the diplomatic efforts that culminated in the French promise to give Lebanon its independence. Almost half of the book consists of pertinent documents.

ISRAEL

General

See also (Germany) The Nazi Era, p. 475; (Middle East) General Surveys and Political Problems, p. 611; Syria, p. 626.

Aron, Raymond. **De Gaulle, Israel and the Jews.** New York: Praeger, 1969, 160 p.
A collection of Aron's articles, written during the Six-Day War and here republished with some earlier pieces on Israel, and a long, poignant preface analyzing and criticizing de Gaulle's description of the "élitist" Jewish people. The French original appeared as "De Gaulle, Israël et les Juifs" (Paris: Plon, 1968, 186 p.).

Eban, Abba Solomon. **My Country: The Story of Modern Israel.** New York: Random House, 1972, 304 p.
A well-written and informative study, by a leading Israeli statesman, Foreign Minister of his country from 1966 to 1974.

Elston, D. R. **Israel: The Making of a Nation.** New York: Oxford University Press (for the Anglo-Israel Association), 1963, 159 p.
An introductory survey, brief but balanced, of modern Israel.

Emanuel, Muriel, ed. **Israel: A Survey and Bibliography.** New York: St. Martin's Press, 1971, 309 p.
This reference volume contains brief essays, with bibliographies, on Israeli history, government, economy, science, education and social conditions.

Fein, Leonard J. **Israel: Politics and People.** Boston: Little, Brown, 1968, 338 p.
An attempt, in general successful, to apply the methods of modern political science in describing Israel's political system and society: parties, coöperative institutions, the West-East gap, the generational gap and the nature of the "establishment."

Frei, Bruno. **Israel zwischen den Fronten: Utopie und Wirklichkeit.** Vienna: Europa Verlag, 1965, 200 p.
Reflections of a senior Austrian foreign correspondent, editor, author and publisher on some of the problems besetting modern Israel.

Gervasi, Frank. **The Case for Israel.** New York: Viking, 1967, 258 p.
Israel's story from the Balfour Declaration to the Six-Day War. The writing is lively, the argument strictly partisan.

Glubb, Sir John Bagot. **Peace in the Holy Land: An Historical Analysis of the Palestine Problem.** London: Hodder, 1971, 384 p.
General Glubb, who knows the Middle East very well and is best known for his service as commander of the Arab Legion, outlines 4,000 years of Palestine's history and proposes solutions for the conflict in that area.

Hillel, Marc. **Israël en danger de paix.** Paris: Fayard, 1969, 350 p.
A journalist's thoughtful book on the fundamental problems that confront Israel as a society and as a state.

Korn, Yitzhak. **Dor bema'avako: hatenuah hatziyonit bitekufat hamedinah.** Tel Aviv: Otpaz, 1970, 367 p.
A plea for the necessity of having close relations between the Diaspora and the State of Israel in order to preserve the national values and aspirations of the Jewish people.

Latour, Anny. **La Résurrection d'Israël.** Paris: Julliard, 1965, 387 p.
A history of the Zionist movement and the establishment of the State of Israel.

McIntyre, Ian C. **The Proud Doers: Israel after Twenty Years.** London: British Broadcasting Corporation, 1968, 192 p.

An informative and perceptive survey, by the BBC's special emissary to Israel after the Six-Day War.

Orni, Ephraim and Efrat, Elisha. **Geography of Israel.** Jerusalem: Israel Universities Press, 3rd rev. ed., 1971, 551 p.
This solid survey includes also information about the administered areas.

Petuchowski, Jakob Josef. **Zion Reconsidered.** New York: Twayne, 1967, 143 p.
This small book, in the author's words, "represents a testing of Zionist pronouncements by the touchstone of Israeli realities."

Prittie, Terence Cornelius Farmer. **Israel: Miracle in the Desert.** New York: Praeger, rev. ed., 1968, 260 p.
A journalist, author of several books on Germany, takes an overall look at Israel, generally supporting Israel's policies.

Sachar, Howard Morley. **From the Ends of the Earth: The Peoples of Israel.** Cleveland: World Publishing Co., 1964, 510 p.
A sequel to the author's "Aliyah: The Peoples of Israel" (1961), this volume is an evocation of modern Israel through the stories of representative citizens of diverse origin. It includes a detailed account of the "Lavon Affair," the abortive 1954 sabotage effort in Egypt and its political repercussions in Israel.

Sanders, Ronald. **Israel: The View from Masada.** New York: Harper and Row, 1966, 310 p.
The story of Jewish national rebirth.

Sontheimer, Kurt, *ed*. **Israel: Politik, Gesellschaft, Wirtschaft.** Munich: Piper, 1968, 364 p.
Essays on the political, social and economic problems of Israel prepared by a team of scholars at the Free University of Berlin.

Soustelle, Jacques. **The Long March of Israel.** New York: American Heritage Press, 1969, 254 p.
Always a man with a cause, Soustelle gives a sympathetic, almost lyrical account of the Zionist movement and the Jewish community in Palestine up to 1949. The French original was published as "La Longue marche d'Israël" (Paris: Fayard, 1968, 338 p.).

Sykes, Christopher. **Cross Roads to Israel.** London: Collins, 1965, 479 p.
A well-written story of Britain in Palestine and of the growth of the Zionist party into the state of Israel.

Talmon, J. L. **Israel among the Nations.** New York: Macmillan, 1971, 199 p.
A general survey of Jewish thought and political activities since the 19th century. While reviewing favorably the establishment of the Jewish state, the author criticizes some of the Israeli policies toward the Arabs after the Six-Day War.

Biographies, Memoirs and Collected Writings

See also (Germany) The Nazi Era, p. 475.

Bar-Zohar, Michel. **Ben-Gurion: The Armed Prophet.** Englewood Cliffs: Prentice-Hall, 1968, 296 p.
A labor of love, this biography "does not pretend to be objective" but is nevertheless informative and useful. The French version appeared as "Ben Gourion: le prophète armé" (Paris: Fayard, 1966, 412 p.).

Ben-Gurion, David. **Ben Gurion Looks Back: In Talks with Moshe Pearlman.** New York: Simon and Schuster, 1965, 260 p.
Reminiscences, philosophy and opinions, by the Israeli leader, compiled by Moshe Pearlman.

Ben-Gurion, David. **Igrot David Ben-Gurion, kines velivah he'arot Yehudah Erez.** Tel Aviv: Am Oved veUniversitat Tel Aviv, 1971, 458 p.
A collection of letters by the Israeli leader, covering his childhood in Plonsk, studies in Turkey, service in the Jewish Legion and activities in the United States.

Ben-Gurion, David. **Israel: A Personal History.** New York: Funk & Wagnalls, 1971, 862 p.
"Epic history" and a good deal of autobiography. The fuller original version appeared as "Medinat Yisrael hamehudeshet" (Tel Aviv: Am Oved, 1969, 2 v.).

Ben-Gurion, David. **Israel: Years of Challenge.** New York: Holt, Rinehart and Winston, 1963, 240 p.
This autobiographical account by the Israeli statesman reveals much but omits much and is imbued throughout both with the author's famous sense of mission and his implacable scorn for those with contrary views.

Ben-Gurion, David. **Letters to Paula.** Pittsburgh: University of Pittsburgh Press, 1972, 259 p.
Letters written in the period 1919-39 which provide some interesting insights into the future Prime Minister's struggles to establish a Jewish state.

Bentwich, Norman de Mattos and Bentwich, Helen. **Mandate Memories, 1918-1948.** New York: Schocken, 1965, 231 p.
A distinguished Anglo-Zionist reminisces with his wife on British administration in Palestine.

Furlonge, Sir Geoffrey. **Palestine Is My Country: The Story of Musa Alami.** New York: Praeger, 1969, 244 p.
The life of Musa Bey Alami has been so closely interwoven with the story of the Palestine Arabs that this sympathetic biography serves also as a history of the times.

Goldmann, Nahum. **The Autobiography of Nahum Goldmann: Sixty Years of Jewish Life.** New York: Holt, Rinehart and Winston, 1969, 358 p.
Why Goldmann has been both a leader in world Zionism and a controversial figure in Israel emerges clearly from this autobiography in which he gives, in addition to fascinating detail on his diplomatic activity in the cause of the Jewish state, his considered views on the complex relationship between Israel and the Diaspora.

Katz, Samuel. **Days of Fire.** Garden City: Doubleday, 1968, 317 p.
A memoir, with much fascinating detail, of a career devoted to the cause of Irgun Zvai Leumi in its fight against the Arabs, the British and the Jewish "establishment."

Lau-Lavie, Naphtali. **Moshe Dayan: A Biography.** London: Vallentine, 1968, 223 p.
An admiring biography of an Israeli military hero and a former Defense Minister.

Prittie, Terence Cornelius Farmer. **Eshkol: The Man and the Nation.** New York: Pitman, 1969, 368 p.
A hasty biography of a leading Israeli statesman.

St. John, Robert. **Eban.** Garden City: Doubleday, 1972, 542 p.
This lengthy but lively biography is at its best in its portrayal of the former Foreign Minister's diplomatic activities during the Six-Day War and its aftermath.

Syrkin, Marie. **Golda Meir: Woman with a Cause.** New York: Putnam, 1964, 320 p.
This authorized biography of the former Prime Minister of Israel is an admiring and interesting, albeit not overly critical, account of that formidable lady.

Weisgal, Meyer Wolfe and Carmichael, Joel, eds. **Chaim Weizmann: A Biography by Several Hands.** New York: Atheneum, 1963, 346 p.
Laudatory essays on the Zionist leader.

Weizmann, Chaim. **The Letters and Papers of Chaim Weizmann.** London: Oxford University Press, 1968– .
These writings by a foremost Jewish leader are an important source for the history of Zionism and Jews in the contemporary world. Through 1972 three volumes have been published, edited by Barnet Litvinoff, Leonard Stein, Meyer Weisgal, and Gedalia Yogev.

Foreign Relations

General

See also United Nations, p. 99; The Postwar World, p. 178; (The United States) Relations with the Middle East and the Arab World, p. 242; (France) Foreign Policy, p. 404; (Federal Republic of Germany) Foreign Relations, p. 498; Economic and Financial Problems, p. 506; (Middle East) General Surveys and Political Problems, p. 611; Nepal, p. 655; (Africa) International Relations, p. 784; other subsections under Israel.

Bar-Zohar, Michel. **Gesher al ahyam hatihon: yahase Yisrael-Tzarfat, 1947-1963.** Tel Aviv: Am Hasefer, 1964, 266 p.
A study of French-Israeli relations, particularly at the time of the Sinai Campaign in 1956.

Brecher, Michael. **The Foreign Policy System of Israel: Setting, Images, Process.** New Haven: Yale University Press, 1972, 693 p.

A disquisition on personalities, institutions and modes of thought, with an admixture of tables and computations on decision-making.

Dagan, Avigdor. **Moscow and Jerusalem.** New York: Abelard-Schuman, 1970, 255 p.

A pro-Israel analysis of Soviet-Israeli relations since 1948, by a veteran Israeli diplomat.

Deutschkron, Inge. **Bonn and Jerusalem: The Strange Coalition.** Philadelphia: Chilton, 1970, 357 p.

A fact-filled account of the difficult course of postwar relations between two countries separated by the chasm of genocide. By a German-born Israeli journalist.

Draper, Theodore. **Israel and World Politics: Roots of the Third Arab-Israeli War.** New York: Viking, 1968, 278 p.

An attempt to put together from published material the story of the events leading up to the Six-Day War of 1967 against the background of the earlier "rounds" of 1948 and 1956.

Feis, Herbert. **The Birth of Israel: The Tousled Diplomatic Bed.** New York: Norton, 1969, 90 p.

A historical essay on Anglo-American controversies concerning Israel in the 1946–48 period.

Friedländer, Saul. **Réflexions sur l'avenir d'Israël.** Paris: Éditions du Seuil, 1969, 190 p.

A pessimistic discussion of the foreign policy and political alternatives Israel faces in the future.

Jansen, G. H. **Zionism, Israel and Asian Nationalism.** Beirut: Institute for Palestine Studies, 1971, 347 p.

An indictment of Israel as a foreign intrusion in Asia by a one-time pro-Zionist Indian.

Jansen, Michael E. **The United States and the Palestinian People.** Beirut: Institute for Palestine Studies, 1970, 215 p.

A review of the Palestine question, strongly critical of U.S. policy as pro-Zionist and unfair to the Palestine Arabs.

Kimche, Jon. **The Unromantics: The Great Powers and the Balfour Declaration.** London: Weidenfeld, 1968, 87 p.

The story of the deployment of political and economic influence by the Zionists, especially in Germany and Great Britain, that led to the signing of the Balfour Declaration and the establishment of the State of Israel. The author is convinced that the German Zionists were very influential in shaping German policies in the war against Russia.

Kreinin, Mordechai Elihau. **Israel and Africa: A Study in Technical Cooperation.** New York: Praeger, 1964, 206 p.

Professor Kreinin's study, based on interviews in Africa and Israel, is a useful exploration of the subject.

Laufer, Leopold. **Israel and the Developing Countries: New Approaches to Cooperation.** New York: Twentieth Century Fund, 1967, 298 p.

A straightforward description of Israel's wide-ranging technical assistance operations.

Safran, Nadav. **The United States and Israel.** Cambridge: Harvard University Press, 1963, 341 p.

This volume in "The American Foreign Policy Library" deals quite extensively with domestic affairs in Israel as well as with its external relations.

Shinnar, Felix Eliezer. **Bericht eines Beauftragten: die deutsch-israelischen Beziehungen, 1951–1966.** Tübingen: Wunderlich, 1967, 209 p.

The former head of the Israeli mission to Germany describes Israeli-German relations from 1951 to 1966, with emphasis on the implementation of reparations under his leadership.

Tsur, Jacob. **Prélude à Suez: journal d'une ambassade, 1953–1956.** Paris: Presses de la Cité, 1968, 448 p.

This diary of Israel's Ambassador to France during the years preceding the Sinai-Suez crisis touches on both French and Israeli politics as well as international affairs.

Vogel, Rolf, *ed.* **The German Path to Israel: A Documentation.** Chester Springs (Pa.): Dufour, 1969, 325 p.

Documents and writings on West German-Israeli relations, emphasizing the role of Konrad Adenauer in bringing about the signing of the reparations agreement of 1952. The German original was published as "Deutschlands Weg nach Israel" (Stuttgart: Seewald, 1967, 350 p.).

Arab-Israeli Conflict
General

See also United Nations, p. 99; The Postwar World, p. 178; (The United States) Relations with the Middle East and the Arab World, p. 242; and the subsections under the Middle East, Israel and North Africa.

'Abd al-Mun'im, Muḥammad Fayṣal. **Naḥnu wa Isrā'īl fī ma'rakat al-maṣīr.** Cairo: Dār al-Sha'b, 1968, 444 p.
A discussion of the Arab struggle against Israel. The book is divided into two parts, one dealing with the goals of Zionism and imperialism, the other with the Arab sources of strength.

Abu-Lughod, Ibrahim, ed. **The Transformation of Palestine.** Evanston: Northwestern University Press, 1971, 522 p.
These essays on the origin and development of the Arab-Israeli conflict have been written from a pro-Arab point of view. There is an introduction by Professor Arnold Toynbee.

Abū Yaṣīr, Ṣāliḥ Mas'ūd. **Jihād sha'b Filasṭin khilāl niṣf qarn.** Beirut: Dār al-Fatḥ, 1968, 617 p.
The author, a former foreign minister of Lybia, surveys the history of the Palestinian question and the Arab struggle against the establishment of a Jewish state.

Aldouby, Zwy and Ballinger, Jerrold. **The Shattered Silence: The Eli Cohen Affair.** New York: Coward, McCann and Geoghegan, 1971, 453 p.
The story of an intelligence agent who provided Israel with important information on Syrian defense. Eli Cohen was captured and executed.

Arnoni, M. S. **Rights and Wrongs in the Arab-Israeli Conflict.** Passaic (N.J.): The Minority of One Press, 1968, 191 p.
A polemic full of condemnations (of the U.S. State Department, the Soviet Union, the Arab governments, the oil industry and some of the leaders of Israel), with suggestions for a Middle East settlement.

Assaf, Michael. **Hayehasim ben Arvim veYehudim b'Eretz-Yisrael (1860-1948).** Tel Aviv: Tarbut vehinuh, 1970, 453 p.
A history of Arab-Jewish relations in Palestine from 1860 to 1948.

Avineri, Shlomo, ed. **Israel and the Palestinians.** New York: St. Martin's Press, 1971, 168 p.
A collection of articles by Israelis (including Moshe Dayan and Arie Eliav) and Arab Palestinians, which tend to bear out the editor's view that moderate views concerning the Palestinian question are held both on the Israeli and the Arab side.

Avnery, Uri. **Israel Without Zionists: A Plea for Peace in the Middle East.** New York: Macmillan, 1968, 215 p.
An Israeli author speaks out against a Zionist Israel and pleads for a federation between Israel and a Palestinian Arab state.

Azcárate y Flórez, Pablo de. **Mission in Palestine, 1948-1952.** Washington: Middle East Institute, 1966, 211 p.
A valuable source for students of the Palestine problem and a case history of how an international body can and cannot act, by the Principal Secretary of the Palestine Conciliation Commission, 1949-1952.

Bar-Yaacov, Nissim. **The Israel-Syrian Armistice: Problems of Implementation, 1949-1966.** Jerusalem: Magnes Press, Hebrew University, 1967, 377 p.
While the conclusions of this work consistently support official Israeli positions, the individual chapters provide detailed factual treatment of all the main items of dispute: drainage of Lake Hula, the use of Jordan water, the demilitarized zones, infiltration and reprisal, etc. Valuable background for any consideration of the broader Arab-Israeli conflict.

Bar-Zohar, Michel. **Embassies in Crisis: Diplomats and Demagogues behind the Six-Day War.** Englewood Cliffs: Prentice-Hall, 1971, 279 p.
Politics and diplomacy of the period before and during the June war described by a talented Israeli journalist and biographer.

Barcata, Louis. **Arabien nach der Stunde Null.** Vienna: Molden, 1968, 383 p.
A veteran Austrian journalist's report on attitudes and conditions in thirteen Arab states since the Six-Day War.

Ben-Gurion, David. **My Talks with Arab Leaders.** Jerusalem: Keter Books, 1972, 342 p.
Ben-Gurion's recollections of his efforts to reach an understanding with Arab leaders from 1933, when he became a member of the Jewish Agency Executive, to 1963, when he retired from the premiership of Israel.

Berger, Earl. **The Covenant and the Sword: Arab-Israeli Relations, 1948-56.** Toronto: University of Toronto Press, 1965, 245 p.
A Canadian scholar-journalist's narrative of events from the armistice agreements of 1949 to the eve of Israel's invasion of Egypt in 1956.

Bovis, H. Eugene. **The Jerusalem Question, 1917-1968.** Stanford: Hoover Institution Press, 1971, 175 p.
The merit of this compact book is its straight, factual story of the problem from 1917 to 1968. The question of a settlement is discussed, but no specific solution is pressed.

Brook, David. **Preface to Peace: The United Nations and the Arab-Israel Armistice System.** Washington: Public Affairs Press, 1964, 151 p.
A sketch of the historical background and an explanation of the purposes and principles of the machinery which was established when Israel signed armistice agreements with four Arab states in 1949.

Buehrig, Edward H. **The UN and the Palestinian Refugees: A Study in Non-Territorial Administration.** Bloomington: Indiana University Press, 1971, 215 p.
Concentrating on the experience of the United Nations Relief and Works Agency for Palestine Refugees, the author touches rather lightly on such matters as the U.N. relations with the Israeli government after 1967 and the role of the camps in the activities of the fedayeen.

Burdett, Winston. **Encounter with the Middle East: An Intimate Report on What Lies Behind the Arab-Israeli Conflict.** New York: Atheneum, 1969, 384 p.
The author has done some careful research to supplement his own observations on the critical events of 1966 and 1967.

Cattan, Henry. **Palestine, the Arabs and Israel: The Search for Justice.** London: Longmans, 1969, 281 p.
A presentation of the case of the Palestinian Arabs.

Cohen, Aharon. **Israel and the Arab World.** New York: Funk and Wagnalls, 1970, 576 p.
A book notable for its comprehensive coverage and independent judgment. The viewpoint is generally that of Mapam, concerned over Israel's independence but seeking rapprochement with the Arabs and critical of Western and official Israeli policies.

Davis, John Herbert. **The Evasive Peace: A Study of the Zionist-Arab Problem.** London: Murray, 1968, 124 p.
The former Director of the United Nations Relief and Works Agency for Palestine Refugees in the Near East calls for justice for the Arab refugees and de-Zionization of Israel.

Dodd, Charles Harold and Sales, Mary E. **Israel and the Arab World.** New York: Barnes and Noble, 1970, 247 p.
A useful collection of documents, with commentaries, on the Israeli-Arab conflict.

Douglas-Home, Charles. **The Arabs and Israel: A Background Book.** Chester Springs (Pa.): Dufour Editions, 1969, 121 p.
This little book by a correspondent of *The Times* of London combines the bare bones of "background" with some personal views.

Fawdah, 'Izz al-Dīn. **al-Iḥtilāl al-Isrā'īlī wa al-muqāwamah al-Filasṭīnīyah fi ḍaw' al-qānūn al-dūwalī al-'Āmm.** Beirut: Research Centre, Palestine Liberation Organization, 1969, 176 p.
A legal essay on the Israeli occupation of Arab territories and the Palestinians right, according to international law, to defend themselves.

Feinberg, Nathan. **Eretz-Yisrael bitekufat hamandat umedinat Yisrael: beayot bamishpat habenleumi.** Jerusalem: Hotzoat sefarim al shem J. L. Magnes, Hauniversita Halvrit, 1963, 311 p.
A professor at the Hebrew University of Jerusalem discusses the problems of international law concerning Palestine and the State of Israel.

Fisher, Roger. **Dear Israelis, Dear Arabs: A Working Approach to Peace.** New York: Harper and Row, 1972, 166 p.
In an attempt to bypass the stalemate and polemics of the past, as well as utopian goals for the future, Professor Fisher writes a series of letters to Middle Eastern, U.S. and U.N. leaders proposing specific operational moves in which each party can help bring about solutions to pieces of the many-faceted larger problem.

Forsythe, David P. **United Nations Peacemaking: The Conciliation Commission for Palestine.** Baltimore: Johns Hopkins University Press (in coöperation with the Middle East Institute), 1972, 201 p.
A detailed history of the work of the C.C.P. in 1949, the conclusions of which are relevant to later attempts at peacemaking.

Hadawi, Sami. **Bitter Harvest: Palestine Between 1914-1967.** New York: New World Press, 1967, 355 p.
Half a century of the Palestine problem described by a Christian Palestinian Arab, whose feelings of outrage over the Zionist intrusion and bitterness at Western policy provide the theme.

Halderman, John W., ed. **The Middle East Crisis: Test of International Law.** Dobbs Ferry: Oceana Publications, 1969, 193 p.
A symposium which concentrates on the legal aspects of the Arab-Israeli dispute but does not neglect their political context. Contributors include Arab and Israeli scholar-diplomats and American experts in international law.

Harkabi, Yehoshafat. **Arab Attitudes to Israel.** New York: Hart, 1972, 527 p.
An Israeli general, who is a veteran Arabist, has gone through mountains of Arab writings to produce this monograph.

International Documents on Palestine, 1967-. Beirut: Institute for Palestine Studies, 1970-.
Documents on the policies and attitudes of various countries throughout the world, including the Arab states and Israel, on the Palestine question. Through 1972 three volumes have appeared.

Jacobs, Paul. **Between the Rock and the Hard Place.** New York: Random House, 1970, 155 p.
The account of an ill-fated attempt by the Center for Democratic Institutions to hold a conference of nongovernmental Arabs and Israelis; of interest mainly for the conversations the author had with individual Israelis and with Palestinian Arabs (including al-Fatah representatives).

Jargy, Simon. **Guerre et paix en Palestine ou l'histoire du conflit israélo-arabe (1917-1967).** Neuchâtel: Éditions de la Baconnière, 1968, 218 p.
A well-told story of the Arab-Israeli conflict from 1917 to 1967.

Kanovsky, Eliyahu. **The Economic Impact of the Six-Day War: Israel, the Occupied Territories, Egypt, Jordan.** New York: Praeger, 1970, 451 p.
In this detailed study, which takes account also of the pre-1967 period, the author takes issue with some views widely held after the June war, for example, that the Jordanian economy would be unable to survive without the West Bank.

Khadduri, Majdia D., ed. **The Arab-Israeli Impasse.** Washington: Robert B. Luce, 1969, 223 p.
A collection of previously presented essays and lectures representing what might be called the moderate position, taking full account of the Arab point of view and intended by the editor to counterbalance the torrent of pro-Israel publications since June 1967. Glubb Pasha, Arnold Toynbee, John S. Badeau and Harry N. Howard are among the authors.

Khouri, Fred John. **The Arab-Israeli Dilemma.** Syracuse: Syracuse University Press, 1968, 436 p.
The author concludes his thorough examination by saying that "the ideal, long-term

solution for the Arab-Israeli dilemma would be the establishment of a federal union of the Arab states and Israel."

al-Khūlī, Luṭfī. **Khamsah Yūnyū . . . al-ḥaqīqah . . . wa-al-mustaqbal.** Cairo: Dār al-Kātib al-'Arabī, 1968, 208 p.
An examination of the meaning of the June war to Egypt and the Arabs. The author concludes that the Arab-Israeli conflict is not caused by religious differences but is the result of power politics and imperialist designs.

Lall, Arthur Samuel. **The UN and the Middle East Crisis, 1967.** New York: Columbia University Press, 1968, 322 p.
A detailed account of the United Nations' activities in the Middle East from the withdrawal of U.N.E.F. in May 1967 to the establishment of the Jarring mission six months later.

Laqueur, Walter Ze'ev, ed. **The Israel-Arab Reader: A Documentary History of the Middle East Conflict.** New York: Citadel Press, 1969, 371 p.
A convenient collection of documents, plus significant articles and speeches previously published but often not easily available.

Laqueur, Walter Ze'ev. **The Road to Jerusalem: The Origins of the Arab-Israeli Conflict, 1967.** New York: Macmillan, 1968, 368 p.
A study of the origins and immediate antecedents of the war of June 1967. The account of the crisis is based largely on the contemporary press.

Laron, Ram. **Hama'atzamot vehamizrah hatihon.** Tel Aviv: Bronfman, 1970, 208 p.
A survey of international relations in the Middle East. The author claims that intervention by the Great Powers is the main cause of the Arab-Israeli conflict.

Lilienthal, Alfred M. **The Other Side of the Coin: An American Perspective of the Arab-Israeli Conflict.** New York: Devin-Adair, 1965, 420 p.
A substantial manifestation (earlier volumes: "What Price Israel?" 1953; "There Goes the Middle East," 1957) of the author's dogged struggle to warn America against Zionism, Israel and their undue influence on U.S. policy.

Mehdi, Mohammad Taki. **Peace in the Middle East.** New York: New World Press, 1967, 109 p.
A tract by the founder of the Action Committee on American-Arab Relations proposing the return of Arab refugees to their homes in Palestine and the voluntary emigration of Israeli Jews to countries of their origin or of their choice.

Merlin, Samuel. **The Search for Peace in the Middle East: The Story of President Bourguiba's Campaign for a Negotiated Peace Between Israel and the Arab States.** South Brunswick: Yoseloff, 1968, 490 p.
A blow-by-blow account of the few months in 1965 when the Tunisian leader urged the Arab world to take a new and realistic look at the Palestine problem, with additional comment on his political philosophy. The author is an Israeli citizen.

Palestine: International Documents on Human Rights, 1948-1972. Beirut: Institute for Palestine Studies, 1972, 424 p.
A collection of reports, studies and recommendations issued by international organizations dealing with violations of the human rights of the Palestinian people.

The Palestine Question. Beirut: The Institute for Palestine Studies, 1968, 203 p.
A legal essay based on the deliberations of a seminar held in Algiers, July 22-27, 1967.

Reisman, Michael. **The Art of the Possible: Diplomatic Alternatives in the Middle East.** Princeton: Princeton University Press, 1970, 161 p.
The author, a professor at the Yale Law School, suggests that the Big Powers "help create the conditions for minimum order in the region" and "resolve the major moral and human problem—the plight of the Palestine refugees." There is an appendix of documents on the problem of Palestine since 1920.

Rodinson, Maxime. **Israel and the Arabs.** New York: Pantheon, 1969, 239 p.
Written by a well-known French Marxist scholar of the Islamic world, this is a serious study of the Arab-Israeli conflict. Understanding of both sides, Rodinson is fair and balanced in his judgments but never fearful of stating his own conclusions. The French original was published as "Israël et le refus arabe: 75 ans d'histoire" (Paris: Éditions du Seuil, 1968, 249 p.).

Safran, Nadav. **From War to War: The Arab-Israeli Confrontation, 1948–1967.** New York: Pegasus, 1969, 464 p.
  A solid study of the Arab-Israeli conflict, inter-Arab disputes and great-power competition in the Near East.

Saliba, Samir N. **The Jordan River Dispute.** The Hague: Nijhoff, 1968, 164 p.
  A study of the conflict over the "distribution and place of use of the Jordan waters" among Syria, Lebanon, Jordan and Israel. The author concludes by saying that the settlement of this issue would be a simple matter after the cessation of the Arab-Israeli hostilities.

Schleifer, Abdullah. **The Fall of Jerusalem.** New York: Monthly Review Press, 1972, 247 p.
  Using Jerusalem as the principal illustration of the invasion and denial of Arab rights by Israel, a radical poet and journalist makes the case for the Palestinian guerrillas.

Sharabi, Hisham Bashir. **Palestine and Israel: The Lethal Dilemma.** New York: Pegasus, 1969, 224 p.
  This sharp and inevitably controversial book contains a strong critique of U.S. policy toward the Arab world since World War II, a sympathetic and penetrating examination of the roots of Arab attitudes, and the author's own conclusions on the main elements of the Arab-Israeli conflict, including the phenomenon of the Palestinian liberation movements.

Stock, Ernest. **Israel on the Road to Sinai, 1949–1956: With a Sequel on the Six-Day War, 1967.** Ithaca: Cornell University Press, 1967, 284 p.
  Careful attention to the press and parliamentary debates in Israel gives this competent account of Israel's foreign policy the added dimension of linkage to domestic politics.

al-Ṭarīqī, 'Abd Allah. **al-Batrūl al-'Abrabī, silāh fī al-ma'rakah.** Beirut: Palestine Liberation Organization Research Centre, 1967, 77 p.
  A study of the role which Arab oil can play in the Arab-Israeli conflict. The author was the Saudi Minister of Oil and Mineral Wealth and has been the major advocate of the use of oil for bargaining political advantages.

Verg, Erik. **Halbmond um den Davidstern: die arabische Welt und Israel.** Berlin: Ullstein, 1964, 228 p.
  A well-traveled journalist reports his impressions of Israel and the surrounding crescent of Arab states and his reflections on the quarrel that divides them.

Wagenlehner, Günther. **Eskalation im Nahen Osten.** Stuttgart: Seewald, 1968, 284 p.
  This study attempts to trace the interaction of interests and attitudes of the local contestants and outside powers in the Arab-Israeli conflict.

Wagner, Heinz. **Der arabisch-israelische Konflikt im Völkerrecht.** Berlin: Duncker, 1971, 475 p.
  A detailed legal examination of the Arab-Israeli conflict.

Warburg, James Paul. **Crosscurrents in the Middle East.** New York: Atheneum, 1968, 244 p.
  The author's primer shows understanding and moderation in its treatment of Arabs and Jews, reserving its harshest judgments for the policies of outside powers, particularly the United States.

Wilson, Evan M. **Jerusalem, Key to Peace.** Washington: Middle East Institute, 1970, 176 p.
  A tempered combination of personal reminiscence, capsule history and recommendations for a settlement in Jerusalem by a former U.S. diplomat who was Consul General there during the 1960s.

The 1956 Suez Crisis

See also United Nations, p. 99; The Postwar World, p. 178; (The United States) Relations with the Middle East and the Arab World, p. 242; (Canada) Foreign Relations, p. 282; (Great Britain) Foreign Policy, p. 375; Political Problems, p. 381; (France) Biographies, Memoirs and Addresses, p. 400; Foreign Policy, p. 404; and the subsections under the Middle East, Israel and North Africa.

Barker, Arthur J. **Suez: The Seven Day War.** New York: Praeger, 1965, 223 p.
  A British officer's review of operation "Musketeer," the abortive Anglo-French invasion of Suez in 1956.

Beaufre, André. **The Suez Expedition, 1956.** New York: Praeger, 1970, 161 p.
   The commander of the French invasion force tells his story of the "short-lived but brilliant military success" which ended in total political defeat. He is outspoken in pointing out the errors of political decision, command organization and timing which led to failure. The French original appeared as "L'Expédition de Suez" (Paris: Grasset, 1967, 253 p.).

Clark, D. M. J. **Suez Touchdown: A Soldier's Tale.** London: Davies, 1964, 183 p.
   The author records his experiences during the 1956 British landings at Port Said, and his indignation at not being able to "finish the job."

Dayan, Moshe. **Diary of the Sinai Campaign.** New York: Harper and Row, 1966, 236 p.
   A candid narrative of the eight-day conquest of Sinai in 1956, blunders and all, by the man who planned and directed it. The original appeared as "Yoman ma'arahat Sinai" (Tel Aviv: Am Hasefer, 1965, 224 p.).

Finer, Herman. **Dulles Over Suez: The Theory and Practice of His Diplomacy.** Chicago: Quadrangle Books, 1964, 538 p.
   An extended and harsh indictment of John Foster Dulles' role in the 1956 Suez crisis.

Haykal, Muhammad Hasanayn. **Khabāya al-Sūways.** Cairo: Dār al-'Aṣr al-Ḥadith, 1967, 158 p.
   The first part of this work by the editor of *al-Ahram* gives an Egyptian view of the Suez crisis, while the second part contains comments on Hugh Thomas' "Suez."

Love, Kennett. **Suez: The Twice-Fought War: A History.** New York: McGraw-Hill, 1969, 767 p.
   A massive study of the crisis of 1955–56, especially illuminating in connection with the author's interviews with Eisenhower, Eden, Nasser and others of the cast.

Moncrieff, Anthony, *ed*. **Suez: Ten Years After.** New York: Pantheon Books, 1967, 160 p.
   An analysis and assessment of the 1956 Suez crisis by means of a series of BBC broadcasts, using interviews with such principal figures as Nasser, Ben-Gurion and Pineau (but not Eden), and a review of the evidence by experts. Introduced by Peter Calvocoressi.

Nutting, Anthony. **No End of a Lesson: The Story of Suez.** New York: Potter, 1967, 205 p.
   The former Minister of State who resigned at the time of Suez tells his story of what happened within the British Government before and during the crisis. If any question remains about the fact of collusion with France and Israel, this book dispels it with full clarity of detail as to time and place.

Robertson, Terence. **Crisis: The Inside Story of the Suez Conspiracy.** New York: Atheneum, 1965, 349 p.
   A Canadian writer's study of the 1956 Suez crisis, with a useful stress on the Canadian role in helping to resolve it.

Thomas, Hugh. **Suez.** New York: Harper and Row, 1967, 261 p.
   An account of the British side of the Suez fiasco of 1956. Its virtues and weaknesses derive from the author's method and from the time of writing—ten years after the event (midway between "the snipers of contemporary politics and journalism" and "the artillery of history").

Military Confrontations

See also the subsections under the Middle East, Israel and North Africa.

'Abd al-Mun'im, Muhammad Fayṣal. **Asrār 1948.** Cairo: Maktabat al-Qāhirah al-Ḥadithah, 1968, 702 p.
   This extensive work gives an Arab point of view of what actually hapened before and during the 1948 war. The author is an Egyptian army officer who is also a historian.

Abu-Lughod, Ibrahim, *ed*. **The Arab-Israeli Confrontation of June 1967: An Arab Perspective.** Evanston: Northwestern University Press, 1970, 201 p.
   According to the editor, the objective of this volume of essays by Arab scholars living in the United States and Britain is to "provide a badly needed antidote to the one-sided and selective attention given in this country to the Middle East conflict."

ASIA AND THE PACIFIC AREA

Allon, Yigal. **Ma'arahot Palmah: megamot uma'as.** Tel Aviv: Hakibbutz Hameuchad, 1965, 319 p.
An account of the campaign of Palmach in the War of Independence, by the Commander-in-Chief of the Israeli Army at that time.

Byford-Jones, Wilfred. **The Lightning War.** Indianapolis: Bobbs-Merrill, 1968, 229 p.
A popular account of the Six-Day War in 1967, written in frank admiration of Israel's military achievement. The author, a retired officer, is a British journalist.

Chaliand, Gérard. **The Palestinian Resistance.** Baltimore: Penguin, 1972, 189 p.
A journalist's informative account of the Palestinian guerrilla organizations.

Churchill, Randolph Spencer and Churchill, Winston Spencer. **The Six Day War.** Boston: Houghton, 1967, 250 p.
A good preliminary account of the war by two well-known Englishmen.

Dīrī, Akram and al-Ayyūbī, Haytham. **Naḥwā istrātījīyah 'Arabīyah jadīdah.** Beirut: Dār al-Ṭali'ah, 1969, 294 p.
A criticism of Arab strategy in the confrontation with Israel. The authors draw a comprehensive plan according to which the totality of the political, economic and military resources of the Arabs should be used.

Harakat al-muqāwamah al-Filasṭīnīyah fī waqi'īhā al-rāhin. Beirut: Dār al Ṭali'ah (for al-Jabhah al-Sha'bīyah al-Dīmuqrāṭīyah li-Taḥrīr Filasṭīn), 1970, 167 p.
An analysis of the contradictions within the Palestine resistance movement as seen by the Marxist-oriented Popular Democratic Front for the Liberation of Palestine.

Hashavia, Arye. **A History of the Six-Day War.** Tel Aviv: Ledory, 1969, 414 p.
A member of the International Institute for Strategic Studies describes the events of the Six-Day War.

Kimche, David and Bawly, Dan. **The Sandstorm: The Arab-Israeli War of June 1967: Prelude and Aftermath.** New York: Stein and Day, 1968, 319 p.
An informative description of the war, its antecedents and aftermath. The author blames the al-Fatah, the Palestinian underground terrorist organization, for bringing about a military confrontation between the Arab states and Israel.

Kurzman, Dan. **Genesis 1948: The First Arab-Israeli War.** New York: World Publishing Co., 1970, 750 p.
An attempt to recreate the events surrounding the birth of Israel. It is popularized history, consisting mainly of vignettes and dramatic episodes, but it includes information gained in many interviews.

MacLeish, Roderick. **The Sun Stood Still.** New York: Atheneum, 1967, 174 p.
A reporter's vivid first-hand impressions from Cairo on the eve of the Six-Day War in 1967 and from Israel during the fighting.

O'Ballance, Edgar. **The Third Arab-Israeli War.** Hamden (Conn.): Archon Books, 1972, 288 p.
This careful account of Israel's victory profits from assistance given to the author by Israeli participants, but he had no comparable help from the other side in chronicling the Arab defeat.

Rouleau, Eric and Others. **Israel et les arabes: le 3e combat.** Paris: Éditions du Seuil, 1967, 187 p.
Instant history of the Six-Day War by well-informed French journalists.

Young, Peter. **The Israeli Campaign 1967.** London: Kimber, 1967, 192 p.
A useful account by a British soldier and military historian.

Defense Policies

See also other subsections under Israel.

Allon, Yigal. **The Making of Israel's Army.** New York: Universe Books, 1970, 273 p.
The development of Israel's armed forces and military doctrine in the context of that country's unique strategic needs, briefly described by an Israeli statesman and soldier.

Allon, Yigal. **Shield of David: The Story of Israel's Armed Forces.** New York: Random House, 1970, 272 p.
A leading Israeli soldier describes the development of Israel's military doctrines from

the time of the first Jewish settlements in Palestine to the Six-Day War. The original appeared as "Keshet lohamim" (Jerusalem: Weidenfeld veNikolson, 1972, 272 p.).

Dayan, David. **Bitahon le-lo shalom: sipurim shel 20 shanim loatot.** Tel Aviv: Massada, 1968, 231 p.

A correspondent of the Israeli Army Broadcast Service discusses the security problems of Israel.

Kagan, Binyamin. **The Secret Battle for Israel.** Cleveland: World Publishing Co., 1966, 299 p.

The story of the inception and growth of the Israeli Air Force, by an Israeli officer who during World War II fought with the Polish Army and subsequently was a member of the Haganah. The French original was published as "Combat secret pour Israël" (Paris: Hachette, 1963, 285 p.).

Khaṭṭāb, Maḥmūd Shīt. **al-'Askariyyah al-Isrā'īliyyah.** Beirut: Dār al-Ṭali'ah, 1968, 416 p.

A serious study of Israeli militarism and military strategy by a high-ranking Iraqi officer who participated in the 1948 Palestinian War and the 1958 Iraqi Revolution.

Peres, Shimon. **David's Sling.** New York: Random House, 1971, 322 p.

New light on Israel's negotiations for arms abroad and build-up of an arms industry at home by one who was an architect of both endeavors. The original was published as "Kela David" (Jerusalem: Weidenfeld veNikolson, 1970, 261 p.).

Peres, Shimon. **Hashalav haba.** Tel Aviv: Am Hasefer, 1965, 272 p.

A collection of essays on defense problems of Israel by a former Deputy Defense Minister and one of the leaders of Rafi.

Perlmutter, Amos. **Military and Politics in Israel: Nation-Building and Role Expansion.** New York: Praeger, 1969, 161 p.

A study of civil-military relations in Israel in all their complexity.

Politics and Government

See also Political Factors, p. 12; other subsections under Israel.

Arazi, Arieh. **Le Système électoral israélien.** Geneva: Droz, 1963, 209 p.

A description and analysis of the Israeli electoral system.

Arian, Alan, *ed.* **The Elections in Israel, 1969.** Jerusalem: Jerusalem Academic Press, 1972, 311 p.

A collection of articles on the 1969 elections.

Arian, Alan. **Ideological Change in Israel.** Cleveland: Press of Case Western Reserve University, 1968, 220 p.

A study of, in the author's opinion, very slow political and ideological transitions in Israel in the first half of the 1960s.

Badi, Joseph. **The Government of the State of Israel.** New York: Twayne, 1963, 307 p.

A straightforward account of Israel's political structure.

Birnbaum, Ervin. **The Politics of Compromise: State and Religion in Israel.** Rutherford: Fairleigh Dickinson University Press, 1970, 348 p.

A study of how the religious parties of Israel have managed "to extract substantial concessions from their main coalition partner, the Mapai." Useful charts on the distribution of portfolios in the Israeli cabinets and on the Knesset elections and membership.

Dinur, Ben-Zion, *ed.* **Sefer Toldot Hahagana.** Tel Aviv: Ma'arahot and Am Oved, 1954–72, 3 v.

A comprehensive history of the Hagana from 1882 to 1947.

Freudenheim, Yehoshu'a. **Government in Israel.** Dobbs Ferry (N.Y.): Oceana, 1967, 309 p.

A useful reference. The Hebrew original appeared as "Ha-Shilton bi-Medinat Yisrael" (Jerusalem, 1956, 351 p.).

Israel Government Yearbook. Jerusalem: Central Office of Information, Ministry of Education and Culture.

A valuable annual review of the activities of the Israeli government, published since 1950.

Israel Yearbook. Tel Aviv: Israel Yearbook Publications in coöperation with the Jewish Agency.
An annual, published since 1950, containing short articles by government officials and scholars on the economy, social conditions, science, arts and legal structure of Israel.

Landau, Jacob M. **The Arabs in Israel: A Political Study.** New York: Oxford University Press (for the Royal Institute of International Affairs), 1969, 300 p.
A competent study of a difficult subject, analyzing *inter alia* Arab leadership, intellectual trends, voting patterns and political activity. The author eschews definite conclusions, but his hope that "confrontation may well change into coöperation, and thence into integration" hardly seems justified by his evidence.

Medding, Peter Y. **Mapai in Israel: Political Organisation and Government in a New Society.** New York: Cambridge University Press, 1972, 326 p.
A detailed study of Israel's major political party, devoted largely to its structure and internal politics but with some attention to external problems that have had an impact on the party's leadership.

Niv, David. **Ma'arahot haIrgun hatzevai haleumi.** Tel Aviv: Mosad Klausner, 1965–.
A comprehensive work on the history of the Irgun from 1931 to 1944. Through 1972 three volumes have been published.

Waelès, Raoul. **Israël.** Paris: Librairie Générale de Droit, 1969, 310 p.
An introduction to the administration and organization of the State of Israel.

Zidon, Asher. **Knesset: The Parliament of Israel.** New York: Herzl Press, 1967, 342 p.
An inside view of the Knesset, by its Deputy Secretary for many years. The Hebrew original appeared as "Bet hanivharim: more netive Hakneset bahakika uvamimshal" (Jerusalem: Achiasaf, 1964, 480 p.).

Economic Problems

See also Economic Factors, p. 49; other subsections under Israel.

Akzin, Benjamin and Dror, Yehezkel. **Israel: High-Pressure Planning.** Syracuse: Syracuse University Press, 1966, 90 p.
Two political scientists review the development of economic planning in Israel.

Balabkins, Nicholas. **West German Reparations to Israel.** New Brunswick: Rutgers University Press, 1971, 384 p.
The documented story of the 1952 Luxembourg Treaty and its fulfillment, stressing the effects on the Israeli economy.

Frey, René Leo. **Strukturwandlungen der israelischen Volkswirtschaft, global und regional, 1948–1975.** Basel: Kyklos-Verlag, 1965, 142 p.
A study of economic trends in Israel, including forecasts for the future.

Hadawi, Sami. **Palestine: Loss of a Heritage.** San Antonio: Naylor, 1963, 148 p.
The former Official Land Valuer and Inspector of Tax Assessments of the (British) Government of Palestine 1937–48 presents the facts of land ownership up to 1948 and argues the injustices committed against Arab property-owners by Israel since then.

Halevi, Nadav and Klinov-Malul, Ruth. **The Economic Development of Israel.** New York: Praeger (in coöperation with the Bank of Israel), 1968, 321 p.
A detailed survey of Israel's rapid economic growth from 1948 to 1965, together with comments on policy covering public finance, foreign exchange and inflation.

Horowitz, David. **The Economics of Israel.** New York: Pergamon Press, 1967, 193 p.
A handbook of basic data with many useful tables, accompanied by comment on Israel's economic policies by the former Governor of the Bank of Israel.

Horowitz, David. **The Enigma of Economic Growth: A Case Study of Israel.** New York: Praeger, 1972, 157 p.
An eminent Israeli economist describes his country's development over the past two decades.

Israel Economic Development: Past Progress and Plan for the Future. Jerusalem: Prime Minister's Office, Economic Planning Authority, 1968, 551 p.
  A survey and analysis of the economic development of Israel from 1948 to 1967 and the plans for future economic development.

Kanovsky, Eliyahu. **The Economy of the Israeli Kibbutz.** Cambridge: Center for Middle Eastern Studies, 1966, 169 p.
  A look at a unique but not wholly successful institution.

Klatzmann, Joseph. **Les Enseignements de l'expérience israélienne.** Paris: Presses Universitaires, 1963, 297 p.
  An enthusiastic study of agricultural development in Israel.

Lifschitz, Yaakov. **Hahitpathut hakalkalit bashetahim hamuhzakim, 1967–1969.** Tel Aviv: Ma'arahot, 1970, 298 p.
  A noted economist presents an analysis of the economic development in the areas that have come under Israeli administration as a result of the Six-Day War.

Ofer, Gur. **The Service Industries in a Developing Economy: Israel as a Case Study.** New York: Praeger (in coöperation with the Bank of Israel), 1967, 167 p.
  A detailed study by an Israeli economist explaining, among other things, why services occupy so large a segment of the economy.

Pack, Howard. **Structural Change and Economic Policy in Israel.** New Haven: Yale University Press, 1971, 273 p.
  A professional economist's careful study of Israel's growth from independence to 1967, with some attention to the factors of governmental leadership and outside aid.

Weitz, Raanan and Rokach, Avshalom. **Agricultural Development: Planning and Implementation.** New York: Praeger, 1968, 404 p.
  A fundamental study of the economic and social aspects of the development of agriculture in Israel. The experience in the Lakhish area is described as the best concrete example of regional planning.

Social Problems

See also Ethnic Problems; The Jews, p. 46; (Union of Soviet Socialist Republics) The Jews, p. 581; other subsections under Israel.

Antonovsky, Aaron and Arian, Alan. **Hopes and Fears of Israelis: Consensus in a New Society.** Jerusalem: Jerusalem Academic Press, 1972, 222 p.
  A valuable sociological study of the Israeli society. The authors conclude that despite the heterogeneous population there is a high degree of social cohesion and stability.

Berler, Alexander. **New Towns in Israel.** Jerusalem: Israel Universities Press, 1970, 353 p.
  An outline of the geographical, social and economic development of the new urban settlements since 1948.

Darin-Drabkin, H. **The Other Society.** New York: Harcourt, Brace and World, 1963, 356 p.
  A quite comprehensive account of the Israeli kibbutzim: their structure, social role and economic efficiency.

Derogy, Jacques and Saab, Édouard. **Les deux exodes.** Paris: Denoël, 1968, 286 p.
  Two essays by a Jewish and an Arab author, one on the Jewish migration to Palestine in 1946–48, the other on the plight of the Palestine Arab refugees.

Eisenstadt, Schmuel Noah and Others, *eds*. **Integration and Development in Israel.** New York: Praeger, 1970, 703 p.
  A collection of sociological, socio-psychological and demographic studies on modern Israel.

Eisenstadt, Schmuel Noah. **Israeli Society.** New York: Basic Books, 1967, 451 p.
  A leading sociologist at the Hebrew University discusses problems of Israeli society. The Hebrew original was published as "Ha-Hevrah hayisre'elit: reka, hitpathut uveayot" (Jerusalem: Hotzoat sefarim al shem J. L. Magnes, Hauniversita Haivrit, 1967, 388 p.).

Elon, Amos. **The Israelis: Founders and Sons.** New York: Holt, Rinehart and Winston, 1971, 359 p.
A fascinating discussion of Israel's society.

Imhoff, Christoph Hans, Freiherr von. **Israel—die zweite Generation.** Stuttgart: Deutsche Verlags-Anstalt, 1964, 291 p.
A perceptive examination of Israel, its people and institutions, and its problems, internal and external.

Matras, Judah. **Social Change in Israel.** Chicago: Aldine Publishing Co., 1965, 211 p.
A study of the social structure and dynamics of a successful new nation in the midst of rapid growth and change, by an Israeli sociologist.

Merhav, Peretz. **Toldot tenuat hapoalim be-Eretz Yisrael: hahitpathut hara'ayonit-hamedinit, perakim uteudot (1905-1965).** Merhaviah: Sifriat Poalim, 1967, 415 p.
A history of the labor movement in Palestine and Israel from 1905 to 1965.

Segre, V. D. **Israel: A Society in Transition.** New York: Oxford University Press, 1971, 277 p.
A general survey of the establishment and development of the Jewish state up to 1957, including its foreign relations, with some interesting reflections on "the search for an identity."

Selzer, Michael. **The Aryanization of the Jewish State.** New York: Black Star, 1967, 126 p.
Despite the title, the author offers much food for thought, especially on the place of the Oriental Jews in Israel and in the Arab-Jewish relationship.

Sitton, Shlomo. **Israël: immigration et croissance, 1948-1958; suivi d'un bref aperçu de la période 1959-1961.** Paris: Cujas, 1963, 389 p.
An important study of immigration into Israel.

Stern, Boris. **The Kibbutz That Was.** Washington: Public Affairs Press, 1965, 158 p.
A useful study of the changes that have come about in the organization and activities of the kibbutz.

Viteles, Harry. **A History of the Co-operative Movement in Israel.** London: Vallentine, 1967-70, 7 v.
A survey of the various types of coöperative movements in Israel, including the kibbutz, from its origins to the present. Massive in its detail, it is an invaluable collection of source material.

Weingrod, Alex. **Israel: Group Relations in a New Society.** New York: Praeger (for the Institute of Race Relations, London), 1965, 82 p.
A brief but substantial study of Israel's multi-ethnic society.

Willner, Dorothy. **Nation-Building and Community in Israel.** Princeton: Princeton University Press, 1969, 478 p.
Primarily a specialized work on land settlement and social structure, this book also relates immigration and settlement to the ideology and politics of the Zionist movement and the Jewish community in Palestine both before and after independence.

JORDAN

See also (Middle East) General Surveys and Political Problems, p. 611; The Arab World, p. 616; Arab-Israeli Conflict, p. 633.

Abidi, Aqil Hyder Hasan. **Jordan: A Political Study, 1948-1957.** New York: Asia Publishing House (for the Indian School of International Studies), 1965, 251 p.
A solid study by an Indian scholar.

Aruri, Naseer H. **Jordan: A Study in Political Development (1921-1965).** The Hague: Nijhoff, 1972, 206 p.
A study of the various factors—internal and external—that limited domestic consensus and thus inhibited Jordan's attainment of nationhood.

Goichon, A. M. **Jordanie réelle.** Paris: Desclée, De Brouwer, 1967-72, 2 v.
A massive handbook containing material on nearly every aspect of government and society in Jordan.

Hussein, King of Jordan. **My "War" with Israel.** New York: Morrow, 1969, 170 p.
A frank exposition of the King's views, written in coöperation with Vick Vance and Pierre Lauer. The French original appeared as "Ma Guerre avec Israël" (Paris: A. Michel, 1968, 223 p.).

Jum'ah, Sa'd. **al-Mu'āmarah wa ma'rakat al-maṣīr.** Beirut: Dār al-Kātib al-'Arabī, 1968, 272 p.
The author, Prime Minister of Jordan during the June war with Israel, tells his side of the story. Complements King Hussein's "My 'War' with Israel."

Lyautey, Pierre. **La Jordanie nouvelle.** Paris: Julliard, 1966, 155 p.
A brief and readable survey of modern Jordan by a prolific author.

Reese, Howard C. and Others. **Area Handbook for Hashemite Kingdom of Jordan.** Washington: G.P.O., 1970, 370 p.
A useful reference, with bibliographies. Prepared by Systems Research Corporation under the auspices of Foreign Area Studies at the American University.

Sanger, Richard Harlakenden. **Where the Jordan Flows.** Washington: Middle East Institute, 1963, 397 p.
An introduction to modern Jordan and a guidebook to its past.

Snow, Peter. **Hussein: A Biography.** Washington: Robert B. Luce, 1972, 256 p.
A sympathetic account by a British journalist. It is at its best in treating the King's chronic difficulties with the Palestinians.

Vatikiotis, P. J. **Politics and the Military in Jordan: A Study of the Arab Legion 1921–1957.** New York: Praeger, 1967, 169 p.
A study of the Arab Legion's military structure and political role during its evolution from an élite corps to a national army. Mr. Vatikiotis, author of an earlier work on the Egyptian army, provides also a good account of the crisis of the 1950s involving the King, the Legion, the Arab nationalists and the forces pressing on Jordan from outside.

IRAQ

General

See also (Middle East) General Surveys and Political Problems, p. 611; The Arab World, p. 616; Arab-Israeli Conflict, p. 633.

Alnasrawi, Abbas Abdul-Karim. **Financing Economic Development in Iraq: The Role of Oil in a Middle Eastern Economy.** New York: Praeger, 1967, 188 p.
A monograph which seeks to explain Iraq's development policies and programs both before and after the change of regime in 1958.

Dann, Uriel. **Iraq under Qassem: A Political History, 1958–1963.** New York: Praeger, 1969, 405 p.
A detailed study by an Israeli scholar most of which is devoted to the stormy events of Kassem's first year and the struggles of Nasserists, Ba'thists and communists about him and against him.

Didden, Horst. **Irak—eine sozio-ökonomische Betrachtung.** Opladen: Leske (for the Deutsches Orient-Institut), 1969, 278 p.
A solid survey of the social and economic problems of contemporary Iraq.

Gallman, Waldemar J. **Iraq under General Nuri.** Baltimore: Johns Hopkins Press, 1964, 241 p.
A revealing memoir, rather flattering to the murdered Prime Minister, by the U.S. Ambassador to Iraq at the time of Kassem's revolt in 1958.

Gehrke, Ulrich and Kuhn, Gustav. **Die Grenzen des Irak.** Stuttgart: Kohlhammer, 1963, 2 v.
A history of Iraqi boundary disputes with Kuwait and Iran.

Ghālib, Ṣubayḥ'Ali. **Qiṣat thawrat 14 Tammūz wa-al-ḍubbāṭ al-aḥrār.** Beirut: Dār al-Ṭalī'ah, 1968, 110 p.
The author describes his role in the Iraqi revolution of July 14, 1958, and discusses his underground activities between 1952 and 1958.

Haseeb, K. **The National Income of Iraq, 1953-1961.** New York: Oxford University Press (for the Royal Institute of International Affairs), 1964, 184 p.
A technical study.

al-Hāshimi, Taha. **Mudhakkirāt Taha al-Hāshimi, 1914-1943.** Beirut: Dār al-Ṭali'ah, 1968, 504 p.
The memoirs of a former Chief of Staff and Prime Minister of Iraq, covering the period between 1919 and 1943.

al-Jamālī, Muḥammad Fāḍil. **al-'Irāq al-ḥadith: arā' wa muṭala'āt fī shū'unihi al-maṣīrīyah.** Beirut, 1969, 237 p.
A former Prime Minister and Minister of Foreign Affairs of Iraq discusses the politics and foreign policy of modern Iraq.

Jawdat, 'Ali. **Dhikrīyāt 'Ali Jawdat, 1908-1958.** Beirut: Dār al-Kitāb al-Jadīd, 1967, 336 p.
Memoirs covering the period from the declaration of the Ottoman constitution in 1908 to the Iraqi revolution in 1958. The author was a companion of King Faysal I and later held a number of ministerial positions including that of Foreign Minister.

Khadduri, Majid. **Republican 'Iraq: A Study in 'Iraqi Politics since the Revolution of 1958.** New York: Oxford University Press (for the Royal Institute of International Affairs), 1969, 318 p.
An attempt to unravel the complex web of plots, coups and revolts that began with the overthrow of the monarchy.

Kimball, Lorenzo Kent. **The Changing Pattern of Political Power in Iraq, 1958 to 1971.** New York: Robert Speller, 1972, 246 p.
A monograph on the politics of Iraq since the revolution of 1958, with some theoretical discussion thrown in.

Mukhlis, Jāsīm, *ed*. **Mudhakkirāt al-tabaqchalī.** Sidon: al-Maktabah al-'Aṣrīyah, 1969, 586 p.
Documents and memoirs of an Iraqi army officer and lawyer known for his participation in the court-martial of Nāẓim Kāmil al-Ṭabaqjali and his group in 1959.

al-Mumayyiz, Amīn. **al-Mamlakah al-'Arabīyah al-Sa'ūdīyah kamā 'araftuhā: mudhakkirāt diblūmāsīyah.** Beirut, 1963, 637 p.
This record, kept by the head of the Iraqi mission to Saudi Arabia from 1954 to 1956, is most important for its candid explanation of the unfortunate impact of the Baghdad Pact on relations between Saudi Arabia and Iraq.

Smith, Harvey H. and Others. **Area Handbook for Iraq.** Washington: G.P.O., 1971, 413 p.
A useful reference volume with a bibliography, prepared by the Foreign Area Studies at the American University.

al-Suwaydī, Tawfiq. **Mudhakkīrātī, niṣf qarn min tārikh al-'Iraq wa al-qaḍīyah al-'Arabīyah.** Beirut: Dār al-Kātib al-'Arabī, 1969, 647 p.
The memoirs of a well-known political leader and economic policy-maker in modern Iraq. In addition to representing Iraq in the League of Nations and the United Nations, the author has been Foreign Minister and Prime Minister of his country.

Vernier, Bernard. **L'Irak d'aujourd'hui.** Paris: Colin, 1963, 494 p.
A useful handbook on modern Iraq, principally devoted to the period 1958-62 under Kassem.

The Kurdish Question

Adamson, David. **The Kurdish War.** New York: Praeger, 1965, 215 p.
A lively and balanced account by a British journalist based on his travels in rebel Kurdistan in 1962.

Arfa, Hassan. **The Kurds.** New York: Oxford University Press, 1966, 178 p.
A brief but useful account by an Iranian statesman and soldier (Iranian Chief of Staff 1944–46) of a turbulent people from its vague pre-Islamic origins down to its contemporary struggle for autonomy.

Chériff Vanly, Ismet. **Le Kurdistan irakien entité nationale: étude de la révolution de 1961.** Neuchâtel: Éditions de la Baconnière, 1970, 419 p.

A representative of Barzani's movement defends the Kurdish national cause and provides a wealth of information on Kurdish-Iraqi relations and negotiations.

Eagleton, William, Jr. **The Kurdish Republic of 1946.** New York: Oxford University Press (for the Royal Institute of International Affairs), 1963, 142 p.
A monograph on the short-lived Republic of Mahabad, created in northwest Iran immediately after the war.

al-Ghamrāwī, Amīn Sāmī. **Qiṣṣat . . . al-akrād fī shamāl al-'Irāq.** Cairo: Dār al-Nahḍah al-'Arabīyah, 1967, 442 p.
A general survey of the Kurds in Iraq and of their conflict with the Iraqi government.

Ghassemlou, Abdul Rahman. **Kurdistan and the Kurds.** Prague: Czechoslovak Academy of Sciences, 1965, 304 p.
A thorough survey, reflecting the Marxist orientation of its publisher.

Haraldsson, Erlendur. **Land im Aufstand . . . Kurdistan.** Hamburg: Matari-Verlag, 1966, 226 p.
Observations on the Kurdish fight against the Iraqi government troops in the early 1960s and a survey of the Kurdish problem in the modern world, by an Icelandic journalist who sympathizes with the Kurdish nationalist movement.

Kinnane, Derk. **The Kurds and Kurdistan.** New York: Oxford University Press (for the Institute of Race Relations), 1964, 85 p.
A well-done introductory essay with a chapter on the war in Iraq bringing the story up to mid-June 1964.

Mauriès, René. **Le Kurdistan ou la mort.** Paris: Laffont, 1967, 240 p.
An eye-witness account of the warfare between the Kurds and the forces of the Iraqi government.

Rooy, Silvio van and Tamboer, Kees, *eds.* **ISK's Kurdish Bibliography.** Amsterdam: International Society Kurdistan, 1968, 2 v.
A useful reference.

Schmidt, Dana Adams. **Journey among Brave Men.** Boston: Atlantic (Little, Brown), 1964, 298 p.
The lively narrative of correspondent Schmidt's clandestine six weeks in 1962 among the insurgent Kurds of northeastern Iraq and the story of their struggle for self-determination.

SAUDI ARABIA; UNITED ARAB EMIRATES (THE FORMER TRUCIAL STATES); KUWAIT; SOUTHERN YEMEN; YEMEN; OMAN; ARABIAN PENINSULA; PERSIAN GULF

See also Raw Materials; Oil, Energy, p. 70; Economic Aid and Technical Assistance, p. 81; United Nations, p. 99; (War) Chemical and Biological Warfare, p. 118; (The United States) Relations with the Middle East and the Arab World, p. 242; (Middle East) General Surveys and Political Problems, p. 611; Oil, p. 615; The Arab World, p. 616; Arab-Israeli Conflict, p. 633; Iraq, p. 644; Iran, p. 649.

Albaharna, Husain M. **The Legal Status of the Arabian Gulf States.** Dobbs Ferry (N.Y.): Oceana Publications, 1969, 351 p.
An investigation of the many and complex problems of the small Arab states of the Persian Gulf in their relations to Britain, to the world community and to each other.

Area Handbook for Peripheral States of Arabian Peninsula. Washington: G.P.O., 1971, 201 p.
A useful reference, prepared for the American University by the Stanford Research Institute.

Assah, Ahmed. **Miracle of the Desert Kingdom.** London: Johnson, 1969, 330 p.
An uncritical but quite informative account of the views and achievements of the Saudi regime headed by King Faysal.

Deffarge, Claude and Troeller, Gordian. **Yemen 62–69: de la révolution sauvage à la trêve des guerriers.** Paris: Laffont, 1969, 304 p.
First-hand impressions of the civil war in the 1960s in Yemen by a well-known team of French journalists.

De Gaury, Gerald. **Faisal: King of Saudi Arabia.** New York: Praeger, 1967, 191 p.
This biography of the Arab ruler includes a bibliography on Saudi Arabia in the twentieth century.

The Economic Development of Kuwait. Baltimore: Johns Hopkins Press, 1965, 194 p.
A report of a mission organized by the International Bank for Reconstruction and Development.

El Mallakh, Ragaei. **Economic Development and Regional Cooperation: Kuwait.** Chicago: University of Chicago Press, 1968, 265 p.
A comprehensive examination of this oil-rich Arab nation's economy and rapid domestic development.

Ḥawātimah, Nāyif. **Azmat al-Thawrah fi al-janūb al-Yamanī: taḥlil wa naqd.** Beirut: Dār al-Ṭali'ah, 1968, 255 p.
The author, a Marxist leader of the Popular Democratic Front for the Liberation of Palestine, examines the National Liberation Movement in Southern Yemen and its influential middle class elements.

Hawley, Donald. **The Trucial States.** New York: Twayne, 1971, 379 p.
A useful though not a definitive reference volume.

Holden, David. **Farewell to Arabia.** New York: Walker, 1966, 268 p.
A vivid portrait of the peninsula by a correspondent of the London *Sunday Times*.

Hopwood, Derek, *ed.* **The Arabian Peninsula: Society and Politics.** Totowa (N.J.): Rowman and Littlefield, 1972, 320 p.
A collection of essays of generally high quality, some historical (R. M. Burrell's contribution on the Persian Gulf deserves special mention) and some contemporary.

Howarth, David Armine. **The Desert King: Ibn Saud and His Arabia.** New York: McGraw-Hill, 1964, 307 p.
This biography of "the great king" is at the same time a lively and authoritative history of the Saudi state he created.

Ingrams, William Harold. **The Yemen: Imams, Rulers, and Revolutions.** New York: Praeger, 1964, 164 p.
An account of Yemen history and politics by a British administrator and writer.

al-Jāsim, Muḥamad 'Ali Riḍa. **Muqaddimat fi iqtiṣādīyat al-mamlakah al-'Arabīyah al-Sa'ūdīyah.** Cairo: The League of Arab States, 1972, 246 p.
An introduction to Saudi Arabia's economy.

Johnston, Sir Charles Hepburn. **The View from Steamer Point.** New York: Praeger, 1964, 224 p.
The former Governor and High Commissioner of Aden describes the British plans for merging Aden with the Federation of South Arabia as a device for maintaining the British base against the forces of Arab nationalism.

Kelly, John Barrett. **Eastern Arabian Frontiers.** New York: Praeger, 1964, 319 p.
An able study of the Buraimi dispute—in detail, and in historical and political perspective.

King, Gillian. **Imperial Outpost—Aden.** New York: Oxford University Press (for the Royal Institute of International Affairs), 1964, 93 p.
A brief examination of the British position in Aden.

Landen, Robert Geran. **Oman since 1856: Disruptive Modernization in a Traditional Arab Society.** Princeton: Princeton University Press, 1967, 488 p.
A scholarly political and economic history of Muscat and Oman, primarily during the latter half of the nineteenth century, with a brief chapter on more recent developments. An extensive annotated bibliography is included.

Little, Tom. **South Arabia: Arena of Conflict.** New York: Praeger, 1968, 196 p.
A seasoned journalist's straightforward presentation of the main events in the recent history of South Arabia, concluding with the departure of the British and the establishment of the People's Republic of Southern Yemen in November 1967.

Macro, Eric. **Yemen and the Western World Since 1571.** New York: Praeger, 1968, 150 p.
  A chronicle of Yemen's episodic relations with the West over the centuries. The treatment of recent decades is casual, but good on the military problems of the Aden-Yemen frontier.

Mann, Clarence. **Abu Dhabi: Birth of an Oil Sheikhdom.** Beirut: Khayats, 1964, 152 p.
  An introductory history by a U.S. Army officer.

Nawfal, al-Sayyid Muḥammad A. **al-Khalīj al-'Arabī aw al-hudūd al-sharqīyah lil waṭan al-'Arabī.** Beirut: Dār al-Ṭali'ah, 1969, 528 p.
  A comprehensive study of the history and importance of the Arab Gulf.

Nish'at, Ṣādiq. **Tārīkh-i Sīyāsī-i Khalīj- Fārs.** Tehran: Shirkat-i Nasbi-ye Kānun-i Kitāb, 1965–66, 681 p.
  A history of the Persian Gulf from ancient times to the present, with maps and photographs.

O'Ballance, Edgar. **The War in the Yemen.** Hamden (Conn.): Archon Books, 1971, 218 p.
  A British author describes the military events in Yemen after the 1962 *coup d'état*. He does not spare criticism of all parties to the conflict—royalist, republican and Egyptian alike.

Paget, Julian. **Last Post: Aden 1964–1967.** London: Faber, 1969, 276 p.
  The military story of the last four years of Britain's empire in South Arabia, by a British officer.

Phillips, Wendell. **Oman: A History.** New York: Raynal, 1968, 246 p.
  A representative for the King of Oman and Dependencies presents a history of that country from earliest times through the crises that brought it to the world's attention during the 1950s.

Riḍā, 'Adil. **'Umān wa al-khalij, qaḍayā wa munaqashāt.** Cairo: Dār al-Kātib al-'Arabī, 1969, 245 p.
  The author looks at Oman and the Gulf States and discusses the international power politics in the area. His sympathies are on the side of the revolutionary forces.

Schmidt, Dana Adams. **Yemen: The Unknown War.** New York: Holt, Rinehart and Winston, 1968, 316 p.
  A veteran correspondent's detailed, first-hand account of Yemen's civil war. Sympathetic to the royalist side in the struggle, the author is critical of the United States for having recognized the republican regime, as well as of the United Nations for having failed to cope effectively with the problem.

Shibr, Sābā Jūrj. **The Kuwait Urbanization: Documentation, Analysis, Critique.** Kuwait: Kuwait Government Printing Press, 1964, 643 p.
  A very large "paperback" which records the development of modern Kuwait with the multifold assistance of maps, drawings, photographs, sketches, charts and 29 appendices. The author, trained at M.I.T. and Cornell, has been architectural and city-planning adviser to the Government of Kuwait.

al-Shu'aybī, Muḥammad 'Ali. **Jumhurīyat al-Yamen al-Dimūqrāṭīyah al-Sha'bīyah: dirāsat fī al-tanmīyah al-iqlimīyah wa-mashākiliha.** Cairo: Arab Renaissance Bookstore, 1971, 262 p.
  Studies in regional planning and economic development in the Peoples Republic of Southern Yemen.

Soulié, G. Jean-Louis and Champenois, Lucien. **Le Royaume d'Arabie saoudite face à l'islam révolutionnaire, 1953–1964.** Paris: Colin, 1966, 134 p.
  A brief discussion of "the fundamental problem" of Saudi Arabia: "Can it move resolutely forward while at the same time safeguarding its spiritual rear?"

Ṭaher, Abdulhady Hassen. **Istrātijiyat al-tanmīyah wa-al-batrūl fī al-mamlakah al-'Arabīyah al-Sa'ūdīyah.** Jeddah: The Sa'ūdi Publishing House, 1970, 243 p.
  An attempt to define the economic interests of Saudi Arabia.

Trevaskis, Sir Gerald Kennedy. **Shades of Amber: A South Arabian Episode.** London: Hutchinson, 1968, 256 p.
  An autobiographical account of the author's experiences over a 13-year period as a

British Colonial Service officer in South Arabia, with emphasis on the formation of the short-lived South Arabian Federation.

Walpole, Norman C. and Others. **Area Handbook for Saudi Arabia.** Washington: G.P.O., 1971, 373 p.
A useful reference volume with bibliographies, prepared by the Foreign Area Studies at the American University.

Wenner, Manfred W. **Modern Yemen: 1918-1966.** Baltimore: Johns Hopkins Press, 1967, 257 p.
A study of Yemen's politics, national and international, especially during the reigns of the Imams Yahya and Ahmad, based on both Western and Arabic sources.

Wepf, Reinhold. **Yemen: Land der Königin von Saba.** Berne: Kümmerly, 1966, 108 p.
Personal impressions and a historical survey of Yemen by a Swiss doctor who went there in 1964 with an International Red Cross mission to help the wounded of the war between the Royalists and the Republicans.

Winstone, H. V. F. and Freeth, Zahra. **Kuwait: Prospect and Reality.** New York: Crane, Russak, 1972, 232 p.
An introductory survey of Kuwait's social, economic and political development.

IRAN

See also Comparative Government, p. 18; Government and Economics; Planning, p. 54; Economic Growth and Development, p. 71; Diplomacy and Diplomatic Practice, p. 87; Second World War, p. 144; (Union of Soviet Socialist Republics) Relations with Other Countries, p. 558; (Asia and the Pacific Area) General Surveys, p. 607; (Middle East) General Surveys and Political Problems, p. 611; Oil, p. 615; The Arab World, p. 616; (Iraq) General, p. 644.

Agaev, Semen L'vovich. **Iran v period politicheskogo krizisa 1920-1925 gg. (Voprosy vneshnei politiki).** Moscow: Izd-vo "Nauka," 1970, 210 p.

———. **Iran: vneshniaia politika i problemy nezavisimosti 1925-1941 gg.** Moscow: Izd-vo "Nauka," 1971, 360 p.
Two volumes of historical interpretation of Iran's foreign policy from 1925 to 1941 by a Soviet scholar.

Āli-i Aḥmad, Jalāl. **Gharbzadigī.** Tehran, 1962-63, 116 p.
One of the most provocative criticisms of westernization in Iran.

Amuzegar, Jahangir. **Technical Assistance in Theory and Practice: The Case of Iran.** New York: Praeger, 1966, 275 p.
An Iranian Ambassador-at-Large and Chief of the Iranian Economic Mission in Washington explores and documents the uses and limitations of foreign technical assistance from the point of view of a developing country.

Arasteh, A. Reza with Arasteh, Josephine. **Man and Society in Iran.** Leyden: Brill, 1964, 193 p.
An informative effort to "define the place of man in Iran in relation to his society and cultural achievement" by methods of "historical, statistical, descriptive and speculative analysis."

Arfa, Hassan. **Under Five Shahs.** London: Murray, 1964, 457 p.
Lively personal memoirs spanning 70 years and the evolution of medieval Persia into modern Iran by a soldier-diplomat close to the center of events.

Armajani, Yahya. **Iran.** Englewood Cliffs: Prentice-Hall, 1972, 182 p.
An introduction to Iranian history, by a professor at Macalester College. There is a useful bibliography.

Avery, Peter. **Modern Iran.** New York: Praeger, 1965, 527 p.
A British scholar who has spent a number of years in Iran describes the transformation of Persia from a quarreled-over remnant of empire into the vital and rapidly modernizing Iran of today.

Āzarī, S. 'Alī. **Qīām-i Shaīkh Muḥammad-i Khīābānī dar Tabrīz.** Tehran: Chāpkhānih-ye Sā'ib, 1965/66, 515 p.
A discussion of the thoughts and life of Muḥammad-i Khīābānī, leader of the National

Democratic Movement of Iran at the end of World War I. The author of this monograph, one of the few reliable political biographies published in Iran, is a renowned scholar.

Bahār, Mehdī. **Mīrās-khawr-i Istiʻmār.** Tehran, 1965–66, 656 p.
A leftist criticism of the United States, with particular reference to its role in Iran. This book was much discussed in Iran during the late 1960s.

Baldwin, George Benedict. **Planning and Development in Iran.** Baltimore: Johns Hopkins Press, 1967, 212 p.
The author, who participated in the formulation of Iran's 1962–67 Development Plan, describes the difficulties of carrying out comprehensive planning amid "the unhappy condition of Iranian politics and administration."

Barzīn, Masʻod. **Sayrī dar matbuʻāt-i Irān.** Tehran: Chāpkhānih-ye Rāstī, 1965–66, 172 p.
A valuable analysis of the Iranian press, though limited in historical perspective.

Bayne, Edward A. **Persian Kingship in Transition.** New York: American Universities Field Staff, 1968, 288 p.
An analysis of twenty years of Muhammad Reza Shah Pahlavi's reign. The chapter "The Strains of Foreign Policy" throws a revealing light on Iran's international role as the Shah has conceived and pursued it.

Benedick, Richard Elliot. **Industrial Finance in Iran.** Boston: Harvard University, 1964, 274 p.
A first-rate study of the financial sector of a developing economy and at the same time an intimate portrait of modern Iran.

Bharier, Julian. **Economic Development in Iran 1900–1970.** New York: Oxford University Press, 1971, 314 p.
This comprehensive study, rich in statistics, foresees a somewhat slower rate of economic growth over the coming decade than the remarkable progress of the recent past.

Bill, James Alban. **The Politics of Iran: Groups, Classes and Modernization.** Columbus (Ohio): Merrill, 1972, 174 p.
A historical survey and case studies of contemporary Iranian politics by a professor at the University of Texas.

Cottam, Richard Walter. **Nationalism in Iran.** Pittsburgh: University of Pittsburgh Press, 1964, 332 p.
A study of nationalism as a twentieth-century phenomenon in Iran and of its effects on Iranian political behavior. Professor Cottam is a political scientist with experience in Iran as an American Foreign Service officer.

Fakhrāʼī, Ibrāhīm. **Sardār-i Jangal.** Tehran: Inteshārat-i Jāvīdān, 1965–66, 490 p.
A competent biographical and historical account of the life of the well-known Mīrzā Kuchik Khān, the leader of the Jangali movement.

Farahmand, Sohrab. **Der Wirtschaftsaufbau des Iran.** Basel: Kyklos-Verlag; Tübingen: Mohr, 1965, 179 p.
This compressed study is a well-grounded contribution to the literature of the economic development of Iran.

Iusopov, Iskander Azimovich. **Ustanovlenie i razvitie sovetsko-iranskikh otnoshenii (1917–1927 gg.).** Tashkent: Izd-vo "Fan" Uzbekskoi SSR, 1969, 227 p.
The establishment of Soviet-Iranian relations by treaty in 1921 is credited with propelling Iran away from the imperialist orbit and toward true independence. A bibliography of Western, Soviet and Persian materials is included.

Jacobs, Norman. **The Sociology of Development: Iran as an Asian Case Study.** New York: Praeger, 1966, 541 p.
Professor Jacobs asks himself why European countries and Japan have been successful in economic development while others have not despite significant economic and political assistance. In his case study of Iran he finds some useful answers.

Lambton, Ann Katherine Swynford. **The Persian Land Reform, 1962–1966.** Oxford: Clarendon Press, 1969, 386 p.
A solid investigation by a leading student of Iran at the University of London.

Marlowe, John, *pseud*. **Iran: A Short Political Guide.** New York: Praeger, 1963, 144 p.
A brisk and well-wrought history of contemporary Iran notable for its compression, scope and authority.

Masa'il-i ijtimā'ī-ye shahr-i Tihrān. Tehran: Chāpkhānih-ye Danishgāh, 1964–65, 553 p.
A study of social and economic problems of the capital city of Tehran, based on the reports of a group of research scholars at the Institute for Social Research under the direction of Ihsan Naraqi.

Nāhīd, Manuchehr. **Naqsh-i shirkathā-ye tā'vonī dar pīshraft va tosa'h-ye kishāvarzī.** Tehran: Chāpkhānih-ye Danishgāh, 1967–68, 300 p.
A well-organized and well-written book on the role of rural cooperatives in the agricultural development of Iran, published under the auspices of the Cooperative Research Institute of Iran.

Pārīzī, Bāstānī. **Talāsh-i Āzādī.** Tehran: Muḥammad 'Alī 'Elmī, 1968–69, 626 p.
A biography of Hasan Pirnia, generally known as Mushir al-Dowlih Pirnia, who was repeatedly his country's Prime Minister. In 1920 he started Iran's earliest dialogue with Communist Russia. Hasan Pirnia is also the author of a well-known history of ancient Iran.

Ramazani, Rouhollah Karegar. **The Foreign Policy of Iran: A Developing Nation in World Affairs, 1500–1941.** Charlottesville: University Press of Virginia, 1966, 330 p.
A systematic description and critical analysis by a professor at the University of Virginia.

Ramazani, Rouhollah Karegar. **The Persian Gulf: Iran's Role.** Charlottesville: University Press of Virginia, 1972, 157 p.
Describing the growth of Iran's involvement in the region in the past few years, the author contends that the best insurance for the Gulf's future stability would be an accommodative Iranian policy toward the Arabs and "discriminating" American support to Iran in her active role.

Ṣadrzādih, Zīā'ed-dīn. **Ṣādirāt-i Īrān az dīdgāh-i rushd-i iqtiṣādī.** Tehran: Chāpkhānih-i Shams, 1967–68, 578 p.
A well-informed and non-polemical analysis of the role of Iranian exports in the overall economic growth of the nation.

Sahebjam, Freidoune. **L'Iran des Pahlavis.** Paris: Berger-Levrault, 1966, 405 p.
A history of the Pahlavi dynasty, written under the sponsorship of the Emperor of Iran, Muhammad Reza Shah Pahlavi.

Sanghvi, Ramesh. **The Shah of Iran.** New York: Stein and Day, 1969, 390 p.
An Indian journalist's highly flattering account of the Shah's role in the history of his country.

Shajī'ī, Zahrā. **Nimāyandigān-i Majlis-i Shawrā-ye Millī dar bistuyīk dawrah-ye qānunguzāri.** Tehran: Chāpkhānih-ye Danishgāh, 1965–66, 392 p.
This authoritative examination of the socio-economic background of the Majlis deputies over twenty-one parliamentary sessions is one of the best examples of modern social research in Iran. Published under the auspices of the Institute of Social Research.

Smith, Harvey H. and Others. **Area Handbook for Iran.** Washington: G.P.O., 1971, 653 p.
A useful reference volume with bibliographies, prepared by the Foreign Area Studies at the American University.

Wilber, Donald Newton. **Contemporary Iran.** New York: Praeger, 1963, 224 p.
A brief presentation by a leading American specialist.

Yar-Shater, Ehsan, *ed*. **Iran Faces the Seventies.** New York: Praeger, 1971, 391 p.
A collection of papers originally presented at a conference of the Center for Iranian Studies and the Middle East Institute at Columbia University in November 1968.

Zabih, Sepehr. **The Communist Movement in Iran.** Berkeley: University of California Press, 1966, 279 p.
An Iranian scholar's important study of the oldest communist movement in the Middle East, its history in relation to Iranian political development and the basis for its mass appeal.

Zonis, Marvin. **The Political Elite of Iran.** Princeton: Princeton University Press, 1971, 389 p.

New data, based largely on extensive interviewing and a psycho-sociological approach, on the subject of Iran's unique political system, showing how the Shah has managed to control the potentially powerful elite groups.

CENTRAL ASIA AND THE SUBCONTINENT OF INDIA

GENERAL

See also Comparative Government, p. 18, Problems of New Nations, p. 36; Underdeveloped Economies, p. 78; (The Postwar World) General, p. 178; (Asia and the Pacific Area) General Surveys, p. 607; (China) Foreign Relations, p. 702; other subsections under Central Asia and the Subcontinent of India.

Aiyar, Sadashiv Prabhakar. **The Commonwealth in South Asia.** Bombay: Lalvani Publishing House, 1969, 409 p.

The author, an Indian scholar, states that in this study he has "sought to assess changes in India, Pakistan and Ceylon against the background of the constitutional legacy of British rule."

Barnds, William J. **India, Pakistan, and the Great Powers.** New York: Praeger (for the Council on Foreign Relations), 1972, 388 p.

A Senior Research Fellow at the Council on Foreign Relations traces the evolution of the antagonisms which have plagued South Asia since the end of World War II. The U.S. policy is considered at length.

Brown, W. Norman. **The United States and India, Pakistan, Bangladesh.** Cambridge: Harvard University Press, 1972, 462 p.

The third revised and expanded edition of a classic text (last published in 1962 as "The United States and India and Pakistan").

Hambly, Gavin, *ed.* **Central Asia.** New York: Delacorte Press, 1970, 388 p.

Though only a few chapters in this survey of Central Asian history deal with twentieth century developments, it is a most useful introduction to the area comprising the Kazakh, Kirghiz, Tajik, Turkmen and Uzbek Soviet Socialist Republics, the Mongolian People's Republic, and the three dependencies of China known today as the Inner Mongolian, the Sinkiang-Uighur and the Tibet autonomous regions. The German original was published as "Zentralasien" (Frankfurt/Main: Fischer, 1966, 364 p.).

Lamb, Alastair. **The McMahon Line: A Study in the Relations between India, China and Tibet, 1904 to 1914.** Toronto: University of Toronto Press, 1966, 2 v.

A detailed, careful study of the origins, achievements and failures of the Simla Conference.

Maraini, Fosco. **Where Four Worlds Meet: Hindu Kush 1959.** New York: Harcourt, Brace and World, 1964, 290 p.

Mr. Maraini's description of his expedition to scale Mt. Saraghrar goes far beyond usual travel narration and delves deeply into the secular and religious history of the area. His "four worlds" are Islam, Buddhism, Hinduism and communism. The Italian original appeared as "Paropàmiso: spedizione romana all'Hindu-Kush ed ascensione del Picco Saraghrar" (Bari: Leonardo da Vinci, 1963, 422 p.).

Sen Gupta, Bhabani, *pseud.* **The Fulcrum of Asia: Relations among China, India, Pakistan and the USSR.** New York: Pegasus, 1970, 383 p.

A sophisticated, wide-ranging and thought-provoking study, covering the developments since the 1950s.

Smith, Donald Eugene, *ed.* **South Asian Politics and Religion.** Princeton: Princeton University Press, 1966, 563 p.

These essays by scholars representing the fields of political science, history, anthropology, sociology, law and religion form a comparative study of emerging relationships among India, Pakistan and Ceylon.

Spain, James William. **The Pathan Borderland.** The Hague: Mouton, 1963, 293 p.
   A study of the history and contemporary circumstances of the 11 million Pathans who inhabit the North-West Frontier, living half in Pakistan and half in Afghanistan. The author is an American Foreign Service officer.

Woodman, Dorothy. **Himalayan Frontiers: A Political Review of British, Chinese, Indian and Russian Rivalries.** New York: Praeger, 1970, 423 p.
   A geographer shows how the Himalayas have affected the Asian policies of Britain, China and the U.S.S.R.

AFGHANISTAN

See also (Union of Soviet Socialist Republics) Relations with Other Countries, p. 558; (Middle East) General Surveys and Political Problems, p. 611; (Central Asia and the Subcontinent of India) General, p. 652.

Adamec, Ludwig W. **Afghanistan, 1900-1923: A Diplomatic History.** Berkeley: University of California Press, 1967, 245 p.
   A scholarly monograph describing the skillful handling of Afghanistan's foreign relations by three rulers.

Étienne, Gilbert. **L'Afghanistan; ou, les aléas de la coopération.** Paris: Presses Universitaires, 1972, 294 p.
   A solid survey of economic development in Afghanistan, based on a 1970 study trip by the author.

Fletcher, Arnold. **Afghanistan: Highway of Conquest.** Ithaca: Cornell University Press, 1965, 325 p.
   A solid political history of Afghanistan from its beginnings as a nation in 1747 up to the post-World War II period. Much of the book's insight derives from Professor Fletcher's three years in Kabul with the Afghan Ministry of Education.

Fraser-Tytler, Sir William Kerr. **Afghanistan: A Study of Political Developments in Central and Southern Asia.** New York: Oxford University Press, 3d rev. ed., 1967, 362 p.
   A new edition of a classic volume (originally published in 1950) on the history, diplomacy and strategic importance of this Central Asian kingdom by a one-time British Minister in Kabul. Revised, and with a final chapter which brings the story up to 1964, by M. C. Gillett.

Grassmuck, George and Others, *eds.* **Afghanistan: Some New Approaches.** Ann Arbor: Center for Near Eastern and North African Studies, University of Michigan, 1969, 405 p.
   A collection of papers originally prepared in 1967 for a special seminar at the University of Michigan.

Gregorian, Vartan. **The Emergence of Modern Afghanistan: Politics of Reform and Modernization, 1880-1946.** Stanford: Stanford University Press, 1969, 586 p.
   A distinguished historical work, especially good on the period between the two world wars.

Griffiths, John Cedric. **Afghanistan.** New York: Praeger, 1967, 179 p.
   Brief but balanced treatment of political and social problems, particularly those of disunity versus cohesion and traditionalism versus modernization. The author also weighs both Soviet influence on Afghanistan and the latter's ability to retain its highly prized neutrality and independence.

Hayatullah, Amirzada. **Die wirtschaftlichen Entwicklungsprobleme Afghanistans unter besonderer Berücksichtigung der natürlichen Gegebenheiten und der Bevölkerung.** Nuremberg: Wirtschafts- und Sozialgeographisches Institut, Friedrich-Alexander Universität, 1967, 207 p.
   An economic and demographic survey of Afghanistan.

Klimburg, Max. **Afghanistan: das Land im historischen Spannungsfeld Mittelasiens.** Vienna: Österreichischer Bundesverlag, 1966, 313 p.
   A competent, closely written survey of contemporary Afghanistan growing out of the author's study and travel in 1956-61 at the "crossroads of Asia."

Kraus, Willy, ed. **Afghanistan: Natur, Geschichte und Kultur, Staat, Gesellschaft und Wirtschaft.** Tübingen: Erdmann, 1972, 427 p.
A comprehensive survey of the geography, history, politics, and social and economic conditions of Afghanistan.

Newell, Richard S. **The Politics of Afghanistan.** Ithaca: Cornell University Press, 1972, 236 p.
A handbook with some helpful information on recent political and economic developments.

Rhein, Eberhard and Ghaussy, Abdul Ghanie. **Die wirtschaftliche Entwicklung Afghanistans 1800-1965.** Opladen: Leske, 1966, 208 p.
A study of Afghanistan's economic growth.

Smith, Harvey H. and Others. **Area Handbook for Afghanistan.** Washington: G.P.O., 1969, 435 p.
A useful reference volume with a bibliography, prepared by the Foreign Area Studies at the American University.

Teplinskii, Leonid Borisovich. **50 let sovetskogo-afganskikh otnoshenii 1919-1969.** Moscow: Izd-vo "Nauka," 1971, 237 p.
A survey of fifty years of Soviet-Afghan relations.

Watkins, Mary Bradley. **Afghanistan: Land in Transition.** Princeton: Van Nostrand, 1963, 262 p.
While stating that her book is not a "scholarly treatise," the American author, who knows the country well, nevertheless has produced a highly informative account of external and internal pressures and conflicts in a nation with diverse cultures.

TIBET

See also (Asia and the Pacific Area) General Surveys, p. 607; (Central Asia and the Subcontinent of India) General, p. 652; Indian-Chinese Relations, p. 670; (China) General, p. 683; Sinkiang; National Minority Areas, p. 711.

Barber, Noel. **From the Land of Lost Content: The Dalai Lama's Fight for Tibet.** Boston: Houghton, 1970, 235 p.
A prolific writer of history, biography and travel has here compiled a story of the 1959 Tibetan revolt. Those interviewed include the Dalai Lama and his mother.

Chögyam Trungpa, Trungpa Tulku with Roberts, Esmé Cramer. **Born in Tibet.** New York: Harcourt, Brace and World, 1968, 264 p.
A high-ranking incarnate lama writes nostalgically of the times when feudal tenure, individual peasant proprietorship and nomadism coexisted contentedly in Tibet.

Ginsburgs, George and Mathos, Michael. **Communist China and Tibet: The First Dozen Years.** The Hague: Nijhoff, 1964, 218 p.
An able review of Sino-Tibetan affairs. The authors foresee little hope of severing Tibet from China and have a dim "outlook for a successful containment of Red China at the Indian-Tibetan border."

Lang-Sims, Lois. **The Presence of Tibet.** London: Cresset Press, 1963, 241 p.
A survey of the problems of Tibet by an author who went there following the Chinese invasion.

Mitter, Jyoti Prakash. **Betrayal of Tibet.** Bombay: Allied Publishers, 1964, 192 p.
An indictment of Nehru's Tibetan policies and a description of the Chinese occupation of Tibet in 1950, by an Indian scholar.

Peissel, Michel. **Cavaliers of Kham: The Secret War in Tibet.** London: Heinemann, 1972, 258 p.
The continuing resistance of the Khamba tribesmen to forced integration by China—according to the author, supported by the United States, Soviet Union, India and Taiwan—is colorfully documented in this paean to Tibetan independence. The American edition was published as "The Secret War in Tibet" (Boston: Little, Brown, 1973, 258 p.).

Rahul, Ram. **The Government and Politics of Tibet.** Delhi: Vikas, 1969, 160 p.
A useful introduction.

Shakabpa, Tsepon W. D. **Tibet: A Political History.** New Haven: Yale University Press, 1967, 369 p.
The author, a former government official who has been close to high-ranking lamas, attributes Tibet's fall to lack of understanding of its historical right to independence and of the true nature of the priest-patron relationship. Sources include many original Tibetan documents.

Thubten Jigme Norbu and Turnbull, Colin M. **Tibet.** New York: Simon and Schuster, 1969, 352 p.
Tibet, its history, people, their way of life and thought as interpreted by the elder brother of the Dalai Lama. The co-author, Mr. Turnbull, formerly of the American Museum of Natural History, adeptly records the story.

Tibet 1950-1967. Hong Kong: Union Research Institute, 1968, 848 p.
A massive collection of documents dealing with the establishment of a Chinese-controlled communist regime in Tibet in the period from 1950 to 1967. There is also a detailed chronology.

NEPAL

See also (Asia and the Pacific Area) General Surveys, p. 607; Central Asia and the Subcontinent of India, p. 652; Sikkim; Bhutan, p. 656; (India) Foreign Policy, p. 666.

Chatterji, Bhola. **A Study of Recent Nepalese Politics.** Calcutta: World Press, 1967, 190 p.
In this study by an Indian socialist the emphasis is on the 1950-51 uprising against the Rana regime.

Chauhan, R. S. **The Political Development in Nepal 1950-70: Conflict between Tradition and Modernity.** New York: Barnes & Noble, 1971, 336 p.
The author of this critical survey pleads for the establishment of an alliance between the progressive and traditional forces in Nepalese society.

Donner, Wolf. **Nepal: Raum, Mensch und Wirtschaft.** Wiesbaden: Harrassowitz (for the Institut für Asienkunde, Hamburg), 1972, 506 p.
The physical, industrial and social geography of Nepal is treated here in extraordinary detail; essential for specialists.

Husain, Asad. **British India's Relations with the Kingdom of Nepal 1857-1947: A Diplomatic History of Nepal.** London: Allen and Unwin, 1970, 399 p.
A detailed and carefully documented study. An indispensable reference.

Joshi, Bhuwan Lal and Rose, Leo E. **Democratic Innovations in Nepal.** Berkeley: University of California Press, 1966, 551 p.
An analysis of a political system in transition.

Mihaly, Eugene Bramer. **Foreign Aid and Politics in Nepal: A Case Study.** New York: Oxford University Press (for the Royal Institute of International Affairs), 1965, 202 p.
An analysis of what went on between 1951 and 1962 in a country that has received aid from the United States, the U.S.S.R., China, India, Israel, Switzerland, Western Germany, Japan, Australia, New Zealand, the U.N. and its agencies, and the Ford Foundation.

Morris, John. **A Winter in Nepal.** London: Hart-Davis, 1963, 232 p.
A knowledgeable British journalist presents a study of Nepal and its people.

Pant, Yadav Prasad and Jain, Sharad Chandra. **Agricultural Development in Nepal.** Bombay: Vora, 1969, 248 p.
A critical examination of the major problems confronting Nepal's agriculture, by far the most important segment of the country's national economy.

Rose, Leo E. **Nepal: Strategy for Survival.** Berkeley: University of California Press, 1971, 310 p.

How does a small state—"a root between two stones"—survive? The author presents an object lesson in the politics of buffermanship, and demonstrates that in the Nepali case the tactics of continued existence have remained remarkably constant for two centuries.

Rose, Leo E. and Fisher, Margaret Welpley. **The Politics of Nepal: Persistence and Change in an Asian Monarchy.** Ithaca: Cornell University Press, 1970, 197 p.
The authors note that in the Nepali polity political parties are banned, the bureaucracy is ineffective, the judicial system is at the mercy of the monarchy and the monarchy is "authoritarian." The "process of modernization" is seen as a "tiresome and often discouraging endeavor."

SIKKIM; BHUTAN

Coelho, V. H. **Sikkim and Bhutan.** New Delhi: Indian Council for Cultural Relations, 1970, 138 p.
A compact summary of basic facts on Sikkim and Bhutan, by an Indian diplomat with firsthand experience in the countries he describes.

Karan, Pradyumna Prasad. **Bhutan: A Physical and Cultural Geography.** Lexington: University of Kentucky Press, 1967, 103 p.
The author shows in this well-formulated and excellently illustrated economic and political geography how outside influences are increasingly changing Bhutan's centuries-old personality and individuality.

Karan, Pradyumna Prasad and Jenkins, William M., Jr. **The Himalyan Kingdoms: Bhutan, Sikkim and Nepal.** Princeton: Van Nostrand, 1963, 144 p.
A useful introduction to the geographical and political situation in the three kingdoms.

Olschak, Blanche Christine. **Sikkim: Himalajastaat zwischen Gletschern und Dschungeln.** Zurich: Schweizer Verlagshaus, 1965, 219 p.
A Vienna-born scholar describes life, society and politics in Sikkim.

Rahul, Ram. **Modern Bhutan.** New York: Barnes & Noble, 1972, 173 p.
An introductory survey.

Schappert, Linda G. **Sikkim, 1800-1968: An Annotated Bibliography.** Honolulu: East-West Center Library, 1968, 69 p.
The first detailed bibliography on Sikkim.

INDIA
(SUBCONTINENT AND THE REPUBLIC OF INDIA)

General

See also (Asia and the Pacific Area) General Surveys, p. 607; (Central Asia and the Subcontinent of Asia) General, p. 652; other subsections under India.

Anand, Mulk Raj. **Is There a Contemporary Indian Civilisation?** New York: Asia Publishing House, 1963, 207 p.
The author, a participant in a UNESCO seminar on Indian values, sees the old contrast between a "tolerant" and "compassionate" East and a greedy, materialistic West largely broken down, as India has accepted Western values.

Appadorai, Angadipuram, ed. **India: Studies in Social and Political Development, 1947-1967.** New York: Asia Publishing House, 1968, 342 p.
A collection of essays presented to Pandit Hriday Nath Kunzru, a founder of the Indian Council of World Affairs, on his 80th birthday. The volume includes a useful bibliography on political developments in India from 1947 to 1966.

Bowles, Chester. **The Makings of a Just Society.** Delhi: University of Delhi, 1963, 120 p.
Four lectures, delivered in December 1963, on economic and political development in Asia, Africa and Latin America, with emphasis on India. One of them compares such development in China and in India. The author, a prominent U.S. statesman, was ambassador to India from 1963 to 1969.

ASIA AND THE PACIFIC AREA

Chaudhuri, Nirad C. **The Continent of Circe.** New York: Oxford University Press, 1966, 320 p.
A pessimistic and critical study of India's capability of surviving as an independent nation, by the author of "The Autobiography of an Unknown Indian" (New York: Macmillan, 1951, 506 p.).

Edwardes, Michael. **British India 1772-1947.** New York: Taplinger, 1968, 396 p.
A study of the political ideas of the British and their effects on Indian culture and society.

Lacy, Creighton. **The Conscience of India: Moral Traditions in the Modern World.** New York: Holt, Rinehart and Winston, 1965, 323 p.
An intriguing description of how the basic ideas of the past influence the present.

Lamb, Beatrice Louise (Pitney). **India: A World in Transition.** New York: Praeger, 3rd rev. ed., 1968, 428 p.
A comprehensive survey of contemporary India, produced through scholarly research and numerous trips to India.

Mehta, Ved. **Portrait of India.** New York: Farrar, Straus and Giroux, 1970, 544 p.
An attempt by a gifted journalist and novelist to comprehend and characterize the birthplace from which education and career estranged him.

Nossiter, Bernard D. **Soft State: A Newspaperman's Chronicle of India.** New York: Harper and Row, 1970, 185 p.
For this correspondent of *The Washington Post* lack of social discipline, violence, selfishness and insensitivity are clues to the Indian riddle.

Olivier-Lacamp, Max. **Impasse indienne.** Paris: Flammarion, 1963, 249 p.
A perceptive reporter for the Paris *Le Figaro* offers his observations of India after independence. A general history, designed for the French public, with a chapter on Sino-Indian rivalry.

Santhanam, Kasturirango Iyengar. **Transition in India, and Other Essays.** New York: Asia Publishing House, 1964, 292 p.
Essays on Indian political and economic problems, by an Indian statesman and journalist.

Segal, Ronald. **The Anguish of India.** New York: Stein and Day, 1965, 319 p.
Mr. Segal, founder of the journal *Africa South*, visited India during the Chinese-Indian war. His observations led to most pessimistic conclusions as to India's future.

Singh, Patwant. **India and the Future of Asia.** New York: Knopf, 1966, 264 p.
Believing that the Asian nations will determine their own destiny, and that India and China will determine the future of Asia, Mr. Singh surveys India's history, culture, religious and language problems, criticizing the Indian government on some points, the United States on others, to point to India's pivotal role in Asia.

Varma, Baidya Nath, *ed.* **Contemporary India.** New York: Asia Publishing House, 1965, 362 p.
A collection of articles on India's political, economic and socio-cultural processes, together with an assessment of their sources of strength and weakness.

Zinkin, Taya. **Challenges in India.** New York: Walker, 1967, 248 p.
A discussion of India's leaders, youth's unrest, the status of women, corruption, the 50 million Muslims, and government and private enterprise.

Recent History; Independence and Partition

See also Colonial Problems; Decolonization, p. 36; Second World War, p. 144; The Postwar World, p. 178; (Great Britain) Imperial and Commonwealth Relations; Colonial Policy, p. 367; Biographies, Memoirs and Addresses, p. 369; Foreign Policy, p. 375; Pakistan, p. 675; other subsections under India.

Ahmad, Aziz. **Islamic Modernism in India and Pakistan, 1857-1964.** New York: Oxford University Press (for the Royal Institute of International Affairs), 1967, 294 p.
A solid study, useful as a background for understanding contemporary Muslim attitudes in India and Pakistan.

Aziz, Khursheed Kamal. **Britain and Muslim India.** London: Heinemann, 1963, 278 p.
A carefully developed account of Muslim separatism and the influence of the British on the Muslim-Hindu controversy.

Bhatia, Krishan. **The Ordeal of Nationhood: A Social Study of India Since Independence, 1947-1970.** New York: Atheneum, 1971, 390 p.
A vivid, swift-moving account of India's tortuous struggle to create itself as a modern state, by the Washington correspondent of *The Hindustan Times*.

Bonarjee, N. B. **Under Two Masters.** New York: Oxford University Press, 1970, 317 p.
A general estimate of contemporary India by a civil servant who served many years in high posts, first under the British Raj, then in independent India.

Bose, Sarat Chandra. **I Warned My Countrymen.** Calcutta: Netaji Research Bureau, 1968, 354 p.
Warnings of a major Indian statesman, fiercely opposed to partition, of the threat to India's national aspirations resulting from the Congress leadership's capitulation to the British on the issues of unity and independence. The volume is made up of the author's collected works of the period 1945-50.

Cohen, Stephen P. **The Indian Army: Its Contribution to the Development of a Nation.** Berkeley: University of California Press, 1971, 216 p.
A short discussion of the process by which an instrument of colonial domination becomes a symbol of national unity, suggesting important questions about the civilian-military relationship in new nations.

Das, Durga. **India from Curzon to Nehru and After.** New York: Day, 1970, 487 p.
An urbane survey by a veteran Indian journalist.

Edwardes, Michael. **The Last Years of British India.** Cleveland: World Publishing Co., 1964, 248 p.
An account of the events leading up to India's independence and British, Muslim and Hindu struggles to maintain power.

Elliott, James Gordon. **The Frontier 1839-1947: The Story of the North-West Frontier of India.** London: Cassell, 1968, 306 p.
A substantial historical survey by a British officer with many years of service in the region.

Ghosh, Kalyan Kumar. **The Indian National Army: Second Front of the Indian Independence Movement.** Meerut: Meenakshi Prakashan, 1969, 351 p.
A scholarly history of the Japanese-sponsored Indian National Army during World War II and of its role in establishing independent India. The chief protagonist of this story is Subhas Chandra Bose.

Gopal, Ram. **British Rule in India: An Assessment.** New York: Asia Publishing House, 1963, 364 p.
To counteract works by people with "preconceived prejudices," Mr. Gopal, author of earlier studies on Indian politics, attempts to show what the British did in India and what they deprived her of.

Hodson, H. V. **The Great Divide: Britain—India—Pakistan.** New York: Atheneum, 1971, 563 p.
A first-rate study of the events leading up to the partition of India in 1947. The author, a former constitutional adviser to the British Viceroy in India, particularly emphasizes the achievements of Lord Mountbatten during this critical period.

Majumdar, S. K. **Jinnah and Gandhi: Their Role in India's Quest for Freedom.** Calcutta: Mukhopadhyay, 1966, 310 p.
A sincere attempt to evaluate the personalities and politics of Jinnah and Gandhi and to discover their role in the partition of India. The author, an Indian and a Hindu, argues that Jinnah was primarily responsible for partition, though he absolves him from harboring evil designs for the destruction of India.

Mansergh, Philip Nicholas Seton and Lumby, E. W. R., *eds*. **The Transfer of Power 1942-7.** London: H. M. S. O., 1970—.
The first comprehensive official collection of documents on the last days of British rule in India, modelled upon the Foreign Office series "Documents on British Foreign Policy." Four volumes published through 1973.

Mehrotra, S. R. **India and the Commonwealth, 1885-1929.** New York: Praeger, 1965, 287 p.
An Indian's study of India's role in the shaping of the Commonwealth idea from the establishment of the National Congress Party in 1885 to 1929, when the goal of "complete independence" was set. Particularly valuable are the analyses of the attitudes of the Muslim League and the contribution of the Liberal Federation.

Michel, Aloys Arthur. **The Indus Rivers: A Study of the Effects of Partition.** New Haven: Yale University Press, 1967, 595 p.
Mr. Michel analyzes Indus Basin projects in the context of political and economic developments in West Pakistan and India since partition. Based on field work carried on in 1963 and 1964.

Molesworth, George Noble. **Curfew on Olympus.** New York: Asia Publishing House, 1965, 296 p.
Observations on Indian politics and military affairs by a high-ranking British officer who at his retirement in 1946 had spent well over thirty years in India.

Moon, Sir Edward Penderel. **Gandhi and Modern India.** New York: Norton, 1969, 312 p.
A discussion of Gandhi's life, philosophy, and his decisive influence on the struggle for India's freedom. The author, an Indian scholar, is a Fellow of All Souls College, Oxford.

Panikkar, Kavalam Madhava. **The Foundations of New India.** London: Allen and Unwin, 1963, 259 p.
A valuable judgment on the influences which helped shape independent India; the author has warm praise for the influence of the British.

Philips, Cyril Henry and Wainwright, Mary Doreen, *eds.* **The Partition of India: Policies and Perspectives 1935-1947.** Cambridge: M. I. T. Press, 1970, 607 p.
Papers by historians and leading participants of the partition presented to a seminar of the London School of Oriental and African Studies in 1967. An indispensable collection for the student of the subject.

Rai, Satya (Mehta). **Partition of the Punjab.** New York: Asia Publishing House (for the Indian School of International Studies), 1965, 304 p.
An Indian political scientist covers the 1947–56 period in her scholarly study of the problems arising from the Punjab's becoming overnight a border state. Emphasis is on the effects of the influx of refugees.

Sharma, Jagdish Saran, *ed.* **India's Struggle for Freedom.** Delhi: S. Chand, 1962-65, 3 v.
A compilation of documents and sources relating to India's struggle for political, economic and cultural independence.

Singh, Harbans. **The Heritage of the Sikhs.** New York: Asia Publishing House, 1965, 220 p.
A survey of Sikh history and culture, of which the last chapter deals with the migration and resettlement of the Sikh community after the partition of India.

Singh, Khushwant. **A History of the Sikhs. Volume 2: 1839-1964.** Princeton: Princeton University Press, 1966, 395 p.
The second volume of this general history ends with the great exodus of the Sikhs from Pakistan, their resettlement in independent India and the renewal of the demand for a Sikh state.

Sinha, Sasadhar. **Indian Independence in Perspective.** London: Asia Publishing House, 1964, 311 p.
A thoughtful attempt to place India's independence in perspective, by a former newspaper editor and government official.

South Asian Affairs; Number Two: The Movement for National Freedom in India. New York: Oxford University Press, 1966, 114 p.
A selection of papers read at a St. Antony's seminar in 1964 providing varying interpretations of the movement for national freedom in India. Edited by S. N. Mukherjee.

Tinker, Hugh. **Experiment with Freedom: India and Pakistan, 1947.** New York: Oxford University Press (for the Royal Institute of International Affairs), 1967, 165 p.
A lucid account of the main doctrines of British policy in relation to the objectives of the Indian National Congress and of the Muslim League.

Zinkin, Maurice and Zinkin, Taya. **Britain and India: Requiem for Empire.** Baltimore: Johns Hopkins Press, 1964, 191 p.

    A well-coördinated survey of India's relation to Great Britain. Mr. Zinkin was the representative of Unilevers, Ltd., in India from 1949 to 1960. Mrs. Zinkin is a newspaper correspondent and author.

Biographies, Memoirs and Collected Writings

Abbas, Khwaja Ahmad. **Indira Gandhi: Return of the Red Rose.** Bombay: Popular Prakashan, 1966, 193 p.

    The author attempts to present "the story of Indira Gandhi not in the vacuum of her personal destiny but in the context of the series of revolutionary developments in India and the world." Useful, but not a major contribution.

Andrews, Robert Hardy. **A Lamp for India: The Story of Madame Pandit.** Englewood Cliffs: Prentice-Hall, 1967, 406 p.

    A sympathetic biography of the woman who has been so influential in leading India to independence and sovereignty.

Apsler, Alfred. **Fighter for Independence: Jawaharlal Nehru.** New York: Messner, 1963, 191 p.

    A concise and vivid portrait of the Indian leader by an American admirer.

Ashe, Geoffrey. **Gandhi.** New York: Stein and Day, 1968, 404 p.

    A well-researched, though uncritical, account of Gandhi's personality and influence, by a British writer who concludes his study with the following statement: "He was the only result of Britain's Indian conquests that was quite certainly for her good."

Biswas, S. C., ed. **Gandhi: Theory and Practice.** Simla: Indian Institute of Advanced Study, 1969, 635 p.

    Papers presented at a 1968 seminar discussing Gandhi's views on social change, economics and politics.

Brown, Judith M. **Gandhi's Rise to Power: Indian Politics 1915-1922.** New York: Cambridge University Press, 1972, 384 p.

    A Cambridge trained scholar traces Gandhi's emergence as a leader from his return from South Africa to his first incarceration in an Indian jail.

Char, K. T. Narasimha. **Profile of Jawaharlal Nehru.** Bombay: The Book Centre Private, 1965, 292 p.

    While admiring many aspects of the Indian leader's services to his country, the author criticizes him for having kept too much power in his hands.

Crocker, Walter Russel. **Nehru: A Contemporary's Estimate.** New York: Oxford University Press, 1966, 186 p.

    Personal impressions of Nehru, by a former Australian Ambassador to India, gained from frequent contact over a prolonged period and checked out by documentary sources.

The Emerging World: Jawaharlal Nehru Memorial Volume. New York: Asia Publishing House, 1965, 268 p.

    A volume which reflects the range of interests of the late Indian leader. Among the contributors are: Radhakrishnan, Earl Attlee, Norman Cousins, John Kenneth Galbraith, Mendès-France, Linus Pauling, Daisetz Suzuki, Arnold Toynbee and 18 others.

Erikson, Erik H. **Gandhi's Truth: On the Origins of Militant Nonviolence.** New York: Norton, 1969, 474 p.

    In the words of the author, "This book describes a Westerner's and a psychoanalyst's search for the historical presence of Mahatma Gandhi and for the meaning of what he called Truth."

George, Thayil Jacob Sony. **Krishna Menon: A Biography.** New York: Taplinger, 1965, 272 p.

    A sympathetic biography of India's controversial statesman.

Ghosh, Sudhir. **Gandhi's Emissary.** Boston: Houghton, 1967, 351 p.

    Memoirs by an Indian statesman who as Gandhi's emissary participated in the negotiations with the British at the time when India was divided into two independent states.

Hangen, Welles. **After Nehru, Who?** New York: Harcourt, Brace and World, 1963, 303 p.
Portraits of eight Indian leaders by the late American journalist.

Hutheesing, Krishna (Nehru). **Dear to Behold: An Intimate Portrait of Indira Gandhi.** New York: Macmillan, 1969, 221 p.
This moving biography of India's Prime Minister, as done by her late aunt, serves as well as a tribute to her father, Jawaharlal Nehru, with whose policies she has sometimes disagreed. "Dear to behold" is the English equivalent for Priyadarshini, Indira's middle name.

Hutheesing, Krishna (Nehru) with Hatch, Alden. **We Nehrus.** New York: Holt, Rinehart and Winston, 1967, 343 p.
Jawaharlal Nehru's youngest sister, herself an important Indian revolutionary active in Indian political and civil affairs, describes the lives and personalities of her family.

Mankekar, D. R. **Lal Bahadur: A Political Biography.** Bombay: Popular Prakashan, 1964, 168 p.
A study of the life and career of the late Prime Minister, Mr. Shastri, and of the major influences that shaped Indian politics during his premiership.

Menon, Kumara Padmanabha Sivasankara. **Many Worlds: An Autobiography.** New York: Oxford University Press, 1965, 324 p.
The autobiography of a prominent Indian statesman who was the first Foreign Secretary of India after independence and the Indian Ambassador to Russia from 1952 to 1961.

Nehru, Jawaharlal. **Selected Works of Jawaharlal Nehru.** New Delhi: Orient Longman, 1972–.
Four volumes of this important collection, incorporating much material hitherto unavailable, have been published through 1973.

Norman, Dorothy, *ed.* **Nehru: The First Sixty Years.** New York: Day, 1965, 2 v.
Mrs. Norman, long a student of India and active in the American movement for India's independence, has painstakingly collected the most authoritative versions of Nehru's speeches and writings, issued from 1899 to 1950, which trace the development of his political thought. A valuable compilation, arranged in chronological order.

Patel, Vallabhbhai Jhaverbhai, Sardar. **Sardar Patel's Correspondence, 1945-50.** Ahmedabad: Navajivan Publishing House, 1971–.
A massive collection of correspondence of the late Saradar Patel (1875–1950), a leading Hindu statesman at the time India gained its independence. Nine volumes were published through 1974. Edited by Durga Das.

Payne, Pierre Stephen Robert. **The Life and Death of Mahatma Gandhi.** New York: Dutton, 1969, 703 p.
A very informative biography of the Indian leader by the indefatigable writer of massive biographies of modern statesmen.

Seton, Marie. **Panditji: A Portrait of Jawaharlal Nehru.** New York: Taplinger, 1967, 515 p.
A loosely written portrait of Nehru which includes personal reminiscences of the author, an intimate of the Nehru household.

Tandon, Prakash. **Beyond Punjab, 1937-1960.** Berkeley: University of California Press, 1972, 222 p.
An autobiographical volume by a former chairman of India's State Trading Corporation.

Tendulkar, Dinanath Gopal. **Abdul Ghaffar Khan: Faith is a Battle.** Bombay: Popular Prakashan (for the Gandhi Peace Foundation), 1967, 550 p.
A biography of Gandhi's very close associate who fought for India's freedom and against the oppression and injustice meted out to his Pakhtun brethren in what is now West Pakistan.

Tyson, Geoffrey William. **Nehru: The Years of Power.** New York: Praeger, 1966, 206 p.
The story of Nehru's achievements and failures as a statesman, by a writer who has observed Indian political developments before and after independence.

Varma, Vishwanath Prasad. **The Political Philosophy of Mahatma Gandhi & Sarvodaya.** Agra: Lakshmi Narain Agarwal, rev. ed., 1966, 468 p.
This substantially revised edition of a work first issued in 1959 incorporates new ma-

terial that reveals, says the author, "the growth of the synthesis of spiritual prophesy and political realism in Gandhi's personality."

Werth, Alexander, *ed.* **Der Tiger Indiens: Subhas Chandra Bose.** Munich: Bechtle, 1971, 272 p.
In this study a former member of the German Foreign Office, with the assistance of a few collaborators, surveys, though not in a very scholarly fashion, the endeavors of Subhas Chandra Bose, a leading fighter for India's independence, to enlist German, Soviet and Japanese support for his struggle against the British during World War II.

Governmental, Constitutional and Political Problems

See also Political Factors, p. 12; (Asia and the Pacific Area) General Surveys, p. 607; other subsections under India.

Aiyar, Sadashiv Prabhakar and Srinivasan, R., *eds.* **Studies in Indian Democracy.** New York: Allied Pubs., 1965, 779 p.
A voluminous collection of essays by various authors, both Indian and Western, attempting to assess "the strength and weaknesses of Indian democracy." Most of the contributions were written while Nehru was still alive.

Austin, Granville. **The Indian Constitution: Cornerstone of a Nation.** New York: Oxford University Press, 1966, 390 p.
A political history of the framing of the Indian Constitution.

Baxter, Craig. **The Jana Sangh: A Biography of an Indian Political Party.** Philadelphia: University of Pennsylvania Press, 1969, 352 p.
A well-documented history, by an American Foreign Service officer, of the Indian right-wing political party, the Jana Sangh, from 1951 to 1967.

Bernstorff, Dagmar. **Wahlkampf in Indien.** Düsseldorf: Bertelsmann Universitätsverlag, 1971, 379 p.
The result of the research of an international team of political scientists in the 1967 Andhra Pradesh elections, this well-documented survey tends to confirm the thesis that caste and community organizations in Indian politics can serve as nuclei to structure democratic competition.

Bhambhri, Chandra Prakash. **Bureaucracy and Politics in India.** Delhi: Vikas Publications, 1971, 349 p.
A critical study of the Indian Administrative Service.

Bhargava, G. S. **After Nehru: India's New Image.** Bombay: Allied Publishers, 1966, 447 p.
Reporting on the Indian political scene from April 1964 to September 1965, a period when the Nehru era came to an end and the new Shastri government had to deal with the Chinese challenge and the war over Kashmir.

Bombwall, Kripa Ram. **The Foundations of Indian Federalism.** London: Asia Publishing House, 1967, 348 p.
A thorough and scholarly account of the tension between centralizers and decentralizers in India since early British times.

Brass, Paul R. **Factional Politics in an Indian State: The Congress Party in Uttar Pradesh.** Berkeley: University of California Press, 1965, 262 p.
An analysis of problems of party organizations at the local and district levels, and the means the Indian National Congress has used to cope with them.

Brecher, Michael. **Nehru's Mantle: The Politics of Succession in India.** New York: Praeger, 1966, 269 p.
An account of the events that led to the accession first of Lal Bahadur Shastri and then of Indira Gandhi to the Indian Prime Ministership, by a professor at McGill University. The English original appeared as "Succession in India: A Study in Decision-Making" (London: Oxford University Press, 1966, 269 p.).

Brecher, Michael. **Political Leadership in India: An Analysis of Elite Attitudes.** New York: Praeger (in coöperation with the Centre for Developing-Area Studies, McGill University), 1969, 193 p.

A study of the causes and results of the setback of the Indian National Congress in the Fourth General Elections of 1967 and how they changed India from a one-plus political system to an embryonic multi-party system.

Broomfield, J. H. **Elite Conflict in a Plural Society: Twentieth-Century Bengal.** Berkeley: University of California Press, 1968, 349 p.
This monograph on the unsuccessful struggle of the Bengali high-caste élite to maintain its social and political dominance concentrates on the 1912–1927 period.

Carras, Mary C. **The Dynamics of Indian Political Factions: A Study of District Councils in the State of Maharashtra.** New York: Cambridge University Press, 1972, 297 p.
This painstaking investigation demonstrates that factional alignments, in one Indian state at least, depend primarily on conflicts of economic interest, and that ethnic communalism and power-lust are no more decisive in India than elsewhere.

Chanda, Asok Kumar. **Federalism in India: A Study of Union-State Relations.** New York: Hillary House, 1965, 347 p.
An account of the evolution of the Indian Constitution and a study of the form of federalism adopted therein, by a distinguished Indian civil servant.

Chopra, Pran. **Uncertain India: A Political Profile of Two Decades of Freedom.** Cambridge: M.I.T. Press, 1969, 403 p.
A well-informed Indian writer tells how political institutions shape India's economy, how foreign policy has guided domestic economy and politics and how, in turn, it has been guided by them.

Dash, S. C. **The Constitution of India: A Comparative Study.** Allahabad: Chaitanya Publishing House, rev. ed., 1968, 621 p.
A revised and updated edition of a study, originally published in 1960, of the evolution and functioning of the Indian Constitution.

Doré, Francis. **La République indienne.** Paris: Librairie Générale de Droit, 1970, 499 p.
A systematic survey of the governmental structure of the Republic of India, by a scholar who has served with the French Embassy in New Delhi.

Erdman, Howard L. **The Swatantra Party and Indian Conservatism.** New York: Cambridge University Press, 1967, 356 p.
A study of the background, emergence and growth of the right-wing political party, founded in 1959.

Fartyal, H. S. **Role of the Opposition in the Indian Parliament.** Allahabad: Chaitanya Publishing House, 1971, 260 p.
A pioneering study, covering the period from 1952 to 1970.

Fic, Victor M. **Kerala: Yenan of India: Rise of Communist Power, 1937–1969.** Bombay: Nachiketa Publications, 1970, 555 p.
A lengthy survey of the communist successes in the state of Kerala, based primarily on the strategy of building a united front of the forces of the Left. A continuation of the author's "Peaceful Transition to Communism in India."

Fic, Victor M. **Peaceful Transition to Communism in India: Strategy of the Communist Party.** Bombay: Nachiketa Publications, 1969, 478 p.
A survey of the Kremlin's attempt to set India on the road to communism, with chapters on the origin of the split of the communist movement in India and the establishment of a militant wing calling for the application of revolutionary Maoist techniques.

Franda, Marcus F. **Radical Politics in West Bengal.** Cambridge: M.I.T. Press, 1971, 287 p.
A perceptive analysis of the relations between community, class and political action by a Colgate professor.

Franda, Marcus F. **West Bengal and the Federalizing Process in India.** Princeton: Princeton University Press, 1968, 257 p.
A case study, based on field research, of central and state leaderships, their working relations and the effect on them of political, economic and social conditions.

Ghose, Sankar. **Socialism and Communism in India.** Calcutta: Allied Publishers, 1971, 468 p.

A history of the socialist and communist movements in India, including a very informative description of the aims and policies of both the pro-Soviet and pro-Chinese Indian communist parties.

Ghosh, Pratap Kumar. **The Constitution of India: How It Has Been Framed.** Calcutta: World Press, 1966, 427 p.
The purpose of the author is to show how contemporary political events influenced the deliberations of the Constituent Assembly of India.

Haithcox, John Patrick. **Communism and Nationalism in India: M. N. Roy and Comintern Policy, 1920–1939.** Princeton: Princeton University Press, 1971, 389 p.
A study of the development of communism and nationalism in India from the Second Congress of the Communist International in 1920 to the outbreak of World War II. The protagonist of the story is M. N. Roy, founder of the Indian Communist Party and, subsequently, of the Royist movement.

Hu, Chi-hsi. **Pékin et le mouvement communiste indien.** Paris: Colin, 1972, 152 p.
This thoughtful study finds China's support of Indian revolutionary movements to be directed as much against Moscow as against New Delhi. It argues that the tactics of insurrection perfected in China will not be effective in India, for cultural as well as economic and social reasons.

Husain, Abid. **The Destiny of Indian Muslims.** New York: Asia Publishing House, 1966, 276 p.
An interesting and reasonable analysis of the political, cultural and social problems of the huge Muslim community in India, by an author who deplores the partition of India.

Jain, H. M. **The Union Executive.** Allahabad: Chaitanya Publishing House, 1969, 327 p.
A thorough analysis of the Indian presidency as intended by the framers of the Indian Constitution and as it has worked out since the establishment of Indian independence.

Kaushik, P. D. **The Congress Ideology and Programme, 1920–47: Ideological Foundations of Indian Nationalism during the Gandhian Era.** New York: Allied Publishers, 1964, 405 p.
A lucid and valuable study of the Indian Congress Party written from the nationalist point of view.

Kochanek, Stanley A. **The Congress Party of India: The Dynamics of One-Party Democracy.** Princeton: Princeton University Press, 1968, 516 p.
This work analyzes the relationship between India's Prime Minister and the National Congress President, the evolution of the role of the Congress' Working Committee, sources of the Congress' recruitment and the nature of leadership élite in party and government.

Kumar, Girja and Arora, V. K., eds. **Documents on Indian Affairs, 1960.** New York: Asia Publishing House (for the Indian Council of World Affairs), 1965, 636 p.
A massive collection of documents on Indian politics, economy and foreign relations.

Kumar, R., ed. **Essays on Gandhian Politics: The Rowlatt Satyagraha of 1919.** New York: Oxford University Press, 1971, 347 p.
Essays by a group of Australian, British and Indian scholars exploring the political events in India in 1919 which culminated in the emergence of Gandhi as a dominant figure in Indian politics.

Masani, Minocheher Rustom. **Congress Misrule and the Swatantra Alternative.** Bombay: Manaktalas, 1966, 196 p.
Writings and speeches by a former General Secretary of the Swatantra Party.

Misra, R. N. **The President of the Indian Republic.** Bombay: Vora, 1965, 243 p.
A fine analysis of the prerogatives and obligations of the office of the President. The author thinks that the Constitution of India permits the President to make himself a dictator through legal means.

Morris-Jones, Wyndraeth Humphreys. **The Government and Politics of India.** New York: Hillary House, 1964, 236 p.
A compact study of independent India's political institutions and how they work in practice. Professor Morris-Jones stresses deviations from their British counterparts and their own distinctive character.

Mukherjea, A. R. **Parliamentary Procedure in India.** New York: Oxford University Press, 1967, 497 p.
  A completely revised and updated edition of a standard work, first published in 1958.

Nayar, Baldev Raj. **Minority Politics in the Punjab.** Princeton: Princeton University Press, 1966, 373 p.
  A study of the politics of the Punjab in the period since independence and a discussion of the implications of social diversity in India for national unity and democracy.

Phadnis, Urmila. **Towards the Integration of Indian States, 1919-1947.** New York: Asia Publishing House, 1968, 297 p.
  A study of the events and factors important to the merger of the 600-odd Princely States into the Indian Union.

Philips, Cyril Henry, *ed.* **Politics and Society in India.** New York: Praeger, 1962, 190 p.
  A collection of articles discussing the traditional Indian social and political system and the changes since independence.

Pylee, Moolamattom Varkey. **Constitutional Government in India.** New York: Asia Publishing House, 2d rev. ed., 1965, 824 p.
  A revised edition of a comprehensive survey of the structure and function of the Indian Constitution.

Ram, Mohan. **Indian Communism: Split within a Split.** Delhi: Vikas Publications, 1969, 293 p.
  According to the author, the split within the Indian Communist Party in 1964 was caused not by Maoist influences, but by long-standing divergences among its members.

Ram, Mohan. **Maoism in India.** New York: Barnes and Noble, 1972, 196 p.
  An examination of the Maoist policies toward India and an attempt at the history of the Indian Maoist movement.

Ramachandran, G. and Mahadevan, T. K., *eds.* **Gandhi: His Relevance for Our Times.** Berkeley: World Without War Council, 1970, 393 p.
  A volume of studies.

Ray, Amal. **Inter-Governmental Relations in India: A Study of Indian Federalism.** New York: Asia Publishing House, 1967, 184 p.
  An account of the working relationships between the Union and the states in India, with emphasis on forces and processes rather than the legal structure.

Rudolph, Lloyd I. and Rudolph, Susanne Hoeber. **The Modernity of Tradition: Political Development in India.** Chicago: University of Chicago Press, 1967, 306 p.
  The authors' conviction is that modernity and tradition are not so diametrically opposed as is generally believed but instead infiltrate and transform each other.

Sen, Sirdar D. K. **A Comparative Study of the Indian Constitution.** New York: McKay, 1968, 2 v.
  An authoritative study of the Indian Constitution, by an Oxford-trained Indian scholar and statesman. Volume I is a reprint of the original 1960 edition.

Sen Gupta, Bhabani, *pseud.* **Communism in Indian Politics.** New York: Columbia University Press, 1972, 455 p.
  The author of this study sees communist successes in India as directly related to the impoverishment of the rural poor.

Sharma, Brij Mohan. **The Republic of India: Constitution and Government.** New York: Asia Publishing House, 1966, 655 p.
  A critical and analytical study of the Indian Constitution and government, including chapters on the historical and political background of the Republic of India.

Smith, Donald Eugene. **India as a Secular State.** Princeton: Princeton University Press, 1963, 518 p.
  For the author of this work the fact that India was established as a secular state is "a fundamental aspect of India's democratic experiment."

Turlach, Manfred. **Kerala.** Wiesbaden: Harrassowitz, 1970, 386 p.
  Thorough and conscientious, this account covers the politics since independence of India's most crowded, most Christian, most literate and most communist state.

Venkateswaran, R. J. **Cabinet Government in India.** London: Allen and Unwin, 1967, 200 p.
  After a brief historical introduction, the author deals with the development and working of the Indian cabinet since the attainment of independence in 1947.

Vijayanand Bharathi, S. **Can Indira Accept This Challenge?** Bombay: Vora, 1966, 548 p.
  An Indian doctor and publicist disscusses political and foreign policy issues of India and warns against foreign influences of every kind.

Weiner, Myron. **Party Building in a New Nation: The Indian National Congress.** Chicago: University of Chicago Press, 1967, 509 p.
  A detailed study of the development, organization and successes of the oldest political party in Asia.

Weiner, Myron, *ed.* **State Politics in India.** Princeton: Princeton University Press, 1968, 520 p.
  Political studies of eight of the seventeen Indian states, showing the changing patterns of political participation, problems of integration within the states, the variety of state party systems which have developed and their performances.

Woodcock, George. **Kerala: A Portrait of the Malabar Coast.** London: Faber, 1967, 323 p.
  An introduction to Kerala, a state of particular interest to students of contemporary India because of its sizable communist movement.

Foreign Policy

General

See also General Works, p. 1; International Organization and Government, p. 96; Second World War, p. 144; The Postwar World, p. 178; other subsections under India and the sections for specific countries and regions.

Bains, Joginder Singh. **India's International Disputes: A Legal Study.** New York: Asia Publishing House, 1963, 219 p.
  Competent studies of eight international disputes, including the India-China border conflict.

Bandyopadhyaya, J. **The Making of India's Foreign Policy.** Calcutta: Allied Publishers, 1970, 286 p.
  An analysis of Indian foreign policy and the mechanisms by which it is shaped. The author, an ex-officer of the Department of External Affairs, has strong opinions and does not hesitate to let them appear.

Bose, Arun Coomer. **Indian Revolutionaries Abroad, 1905-1922: In the Background of International Developments.** Patna: Bharati Bhawan, 1971, 268 p.
  A useful survey by an Oxford-trained Indian scholar. Of particular interest is the documentation on German support of Indian revolutionaries during World War I.

Bowles, Chester. **A View from New Delhi.** New Haven: Yale University Press, 1969, 268 p.
  A selection of speeches and articles by the U.S. Ambassador to India, 1963-1969.

Brecher, Michael. **India and World Politics: Krishna Menon's View of the World.** New York: Praeger, 1968, 390 p.
  This volume includes taped interviews with Krishna Menon together with an analysis of his views and their impact on India's foreign policy.

Chakravarty, Birendra Narayan. **India Speaks to America.** New York: Day, 1966, 249 p.
  A defense of India's foreign policies that were devised by Nehru and Krishna Menon, by a former representative of India to the United Nations.

Goroshko, Galina Borisovna. **Bor'ba v Indii po voprosam vneshnei politiki, 1957-1964 gg.** Moscow: Izd-vo "Mezhdunarodnye Otnosheniia," 1966, 143 p.

ASIA AND THE PACIFIC AREA

A Soviet account of the struggle, backed by "foreign and internal reaction," to deflect India from its policy of non-alignment under Nehru.

Gupta, Sisir. **India and Regional Integration in Asia.** New York: Asia Publishing House, 1964, 155 p.
One of India's best scholars in politics and foreign affairs, after analyzing the assumptions and motivations of India's foreign policy, discusses past attempts at coöperation with other Asian states and the problems impeding successful regional integration.

Heimsath, Charles H. and Mansingh, Surjit. **A Diplomatic History of Modern India.** Calcutta: Allied Publishers, 1971, 559 p.
The authors of this broad survey, which is based on published sources, aim "to show the threads of continuity which have run through Indian foreign relations since the First World War." Useful bibliographies and maps.

Kavic, Lorne J. **India's Quest for Security: Defence Policies, 1947-1965.** Berkeley: University of California Press, 1967, 263 p.
A study of the Nehru government's defense policy: how it was conditioned by India's resources and by the thinking of its leaders.

Khera, Sucha Singh. **India's Defence Problem.** Bombay: Orient Longmans, 1968, 330 p.
This survey of the defense problems of India and South Asia provides some information on the Sino-Indian border war of 1962 when the author was Cabinet Secretary of the Indian Government.

Kulkarni, Maya. **Indo-Soviet Political Relations since the Bandung Conference of 1955.** Bombay: Vora, 1968, 216 p.
The author concludes his survey by saying "that as long as it is necessary for the Soviet Union to use India as a counterveiling centre of influence against Chinese ambitions and American presence in Asia, Russia would continue to support India."

Lawrence, Leo. **Nehru Seizes Goa.** New York: Pageant Press, 1963, 226 p.
Born in Goa and educated in India, this Portuguese journalist and diplomat writes an impassioned pro-Goan account of his country's annexation by India. He decries India's military aggressiveness and challenges the legal and moral bases on which action was taken.

Mallik, Deva Narayan. **The Development of Non-Alignment in India's Foreign Policy.** Allahabad: Chaitanya Publishing House, 1967, 342 p.
A discussion of India's concept of non-alignment policy and of its impact on the balance of power among other nations.

Misra, Kashi Prasad. **India's Policy of Recognition of States and Governments.** Bombay: Allied Publishers, 1966, 214 p.
The author states that he has attempted "to study India's application of the general rules of the international law of recognition of states and governments to some concrete and controversial cases."

Murty, K. Satchidananda. **Indian Foreign Policy.** Calcutta: Scientific Book Agency, 1964, 172 p.
An appraisal of Indian foreign policy. The author advocates "vigilant peaceful coexistence" with the United States, the Soviet Union and China and pays particular attention to the problem of Goa and Sino-Indian and Indo-Pakistani relations.

Neelkant, K. **Partners in Peace: A Study in Indo-Soviet Relations.** Delhi: Vikas Publishing House, 1972, 192 p.
A panegyric to Indo-Soviet coöperation. The author notes that Indian policy toward Kashmir, China, Goa and Pakistan has always found Soviet support, and suggests that such support is essential to counteract "Sino-American intervention."

Pillai, K. Raman. **India's Foreign Policy: Basic Issues and Political Attitudes.** Meerut: Meenakshi Prakashan, 1969, 247 p.
An examination of the influence of the opposition parties on the formulation of Indian foreign policy since 1947.

Rajan, Mannaraswamighala Sreeranga. **India in World Affairs, 1954-56.** New York: Asia Publishing House (for the Indian Council of World Affairs), 1964, 675 p.
A third volume in the series (the first two covered the period from 1947 to 1953) giving Indian views of India's role in world affairs.

Rao, P. V. R. **Defence without Drift.** Bombay: Popular Prakashan, 1970, 349 p.
A former Indian Defence Secretary attempts to provide the Indian public with adequate facts to enable it to understand current defense needs and problems.

Ray, Jayunta Kumar. **Security in the Missile Age.** Bombay: Allied Publishers, 1967, 156 p.
The author of this criticism of Indian defense policies argues that India should not rely on foreign assistance in order to repel or deter aggression.

Reddy, T. Ramakrishna. **India's Policy in the United Nations.** Rutherford (N.J.): Fairleigh Dickinson University Press, 1968, 164 p.
In this useful study the focus is on Indian activities in the General Assembly and its main committees.

Rubinoff, Arthur G. **India's Use of Force in Goa.** Bombay: Popular Prakashan, 1971, 134 p.
An American scholar examines the Indian occupation of Portuguese Goa in 1961 in the context of India's contradictory commitments to anti-colonial struggle and the principles of non-aggression.

Sager, Peter. **Moscow's Hand in India: An Analysis of Soviet Propaganda.** Berne: Verlag Schweizerisches Ost-Institut, 1966, 224 p.
A description of Soviet propaganda activities in India, including a listing of the various periodicals and magazines that are widely distributed by the Information Department of the Soviet Embassy in New Delhi.

SarDesai, D. R. **Indian Foreign Policy in Cambodia, Laos, and Vietnam, 1947-1964.** Berkeley: University of California Press, 1968, 336 p.
In this analysis of India's attitude toward former Indochina the author also discusses the role of India as chairman-country in the International Control Commission.

Sherwani, Latif Ahmed. **India, China and Pakistan.** Karachi: Council for Pakistan Studies, 1967, 140 p.
An indictment of India's motivations in foreign policy-making, with emphasis on the roles of Pakistan and China in the formulation of Indian foreign policy.

Stein, Arthur. **India and the Soviet Union: The Nehru Era.** Chicago: University of Chicago Press, 1969, 320 p.
An examination of "the interaction between India and the USSR primarily from the Indian viewpoint, focusing on the rationale underlying India's policy and the factors which led to the close involvement with the Soviet state." There is a valuable bibliography.

Ton-that-Thien. **India and South East Asia, 1947-1960.** Geneva: Droz, 1963, 384 p.
In this study of India's policy toward the Southeast Asian countries, the author concludes that "shorn of its . . . moralising admonitions . . . India's foreign politics, as all politics, was essentially power politics."

Verma, D. N. **India and the League of Nations.** Patna: Bharati Bhawan, 1968, 350 p.
A study of how India influenced international behavior of truly sovereign states through its membership in the League of Nations.

Vinte anos de defesa do Estado Português da Índia (1947-1967). Lisbon: Ministério dos Negócios Estrangeiros, 1967, 4 v.
An official collection of documents dealing with the Portuguese conflict with India over the Goa issue.

Wilcox, Wayne Ayres. **India, Pakistan and the Rise of China.** New York: Walker, 1964, 144 p.
A specialist in South Asian affairs describes his book as "essentially a critique of Indian foreign policy which argues that India since independence has forfeited regional security in the interest of international status."

Indian-Pakistani Relations; Kashmir Dispute

See also (Central Asia and the Subcontinent of India) General, p. 652; Pakistan, p. 675; Bangladesh, p. 679; other subsections under India.

Bazaz, Prem Nath. **Kashmir in Crucible.** New Delhi: Pamposh Publications, 1967, 318 p.
Finding the Kashmiris pawns in the Indo-Pakistani territorial acquisition dispute, the

author pleads for a completely autonomous Kashmir within the framework of the Indian Constitution.

Blinkenberg, Lars. **India-Pakistan: The History of Unsolved Conflicts.** Copenhagen: Munksgaard (for the Dansk Udenrigspolitisk Institut), 1972, 440 p.
A Danish scholar and foreign service officer who knows the Indian subcontinent well surveys in great detail Indo-Pakistani relations "from the political science angle."

Brines, Russell. **The Indo-Pakistani Conflict.** London: Pall Mall Press, 1968, 486 p.
The American author of this extensive study of the 1965 Indo-Pakistani War blames Soviet manipulations for unleashing the conflict.

Choudhury, Golam Wahed. **Pakistan's Relations with India, 1947-1966.** New York: Praeger, 1968, 341 p.
A resumé of Hindu-Muslim problems in pre-partition India and an examination of Pakistan's subsequent search for security.

Das Gupta, Jyoti Bhusan. **Jammu and Kashmir.** The Hague: Nijhoff, 1968, 430 p.
This solid history of Kashmir's accession to India ends with the developments of March 1967. The author is a Dutch-trained Indian scholar.

Gupta, Sisir. **Kashmir: A Study in India-Pakistan Relations.** New York: Asia Publishing House (for the Indian Council of World Affairs), 1967, 511 p.
A detailed tracing of the highly intricate Kashmir dispute by a scholar at the Indian Council of World Affairs. Of the 1965 foray by the Pakistanis (made overconfident, he believes, by large arms shipments from the U.S.) he says, "If anything, Pakistan has only succeeded in demonstrating that the status quo in Kashmir does not depend for its continuance on her peaceful intentions or postures."

Gururaj Rao, H. S. **Legal Aspects of the Kashmir Problem.** New York: Asia Publishing House, 1967, 379 p.
The author charges that those endeavoring to solve the Kashmir dispute have ignored its legal aspects.

Jha, Dinesh Chandra. **Indo-Pakistan Relations (1960-1965).** Patna: Bharati Bhawan, 1972, 418 p.
A survey and analysis of the factors responsible for the deterioration of Indo-Pakistan relations from the signing of the treaty settling the problem of Indus Waters in 1960 to the war over Kashmir in 1965.

Kaul, Brij Mohan. **Confrontation with Pakistan.** New York: Barnes & Noble, 1972, 338 p.
The author, a former Chief of the General Staff of the Indian Army, criticizes in this volume the military High Command in Delhi for preventing victory over Pakistan in 1964 and 1965.

Khan, Rahmatullah. **Kashmir and the United Nations.** Delhi: Vikas Publications, 1969, 199 p.
A critical assessment of the Security Council's handling of the Kashmir problem, especially over the outbreak of hostilities between India and Pakistan in 1965. The author is convinced that Pakistan acted "clearly contrary to international law."

Lamb, Alastair. **The Kashmir Problem.** New York: Praeger, 1967, 163 p.
An historian's view, compactly presented, of the quarrel between the two successors to British rule in the Indian subcontinent, providing essential information on the geography, economy, language and racial makeup of its population.

Noorani, A. G. **The Kashmir Question.** Bombay: Manaktalas, 1964, 125 p.
A Bombay High Court lawyer and well-known political commentator makes clear his belief that the India-Pakistan-Kashmir problem will not be solved until the people of Kashmir have the opportunity to express their own views.

Sharma, Brij Lal E. **The Kashmir Story.** New York: Asia Publishing House, 1967, 271 p.
An attempt to discover, on the basis of a study of official records of the Security Council and reports of its agencies, whether the Kashmir dispute can be solved. The author, closely associated with the question since its inception and a Council adviser from 1948 to 1966, is at times highly critical of the United Nations.

Tinker, Hugh. **India and Pakistan: A Political Analysis.** New York: Praeger, rev. ed., 1968, 248 p.
A considerably revised and enlarged edition of a study published originally in 1962.

The new edition takes account of the end of Nehru's era and of the Indian-Pakistani and Sino-Indian border clashes.

Indian-Chinese Relations

See also (Asia and the Pacific Area) General Surveys, p. 607; (Central Asia and the Subcontinent of India) General, p. 652; (China) Foreign Relations, p. 702; Sinkiang; National Minority Areas, p. 711; other subsections under India.

Bhargava, G. S. **The Battle of NEFA: The Undeclared War.** Bombay: Allied Publishers, 1964, 187 p.
A study of the politics and military operations of the clash between China and India in 1962. The author, a correspondent of the *Hindustan Times*, blames Mr. Krishna Menon for India's unpreparedness and defeats.

Chakravarti, P. C. **The Evolution of India's Northern Borders.** Bombay: Asia Publishing House (for the Indian Council of World Affairs), 1971, 179 p.
In this well-documented study of the frontier in northern India the author pays particular attention to the Sino-Indian border conflicts.

Dalvi, J. P. **Himalayan Blunder.** Bombay: Thacker, 2d ed., 1969, 506 p.
An important and clearly written study of the Sino-Indian war of 1962, by the commander of the Indian brigade that was ordered to attack the superior Chinese forces on the Indian side of the McMahon Line. According to the author, Krishna Menon and General Kaul were the culprits responsible for the Indian debacle.

Fisher, Margaret Welpley and Others. **Himalayan Battleground: Sino-Indian Rivalry in Ladakh.** New York: Praeger, 1963, 205 p.
Evaluation of the claims and counterclaims concerning the Sino-Indian border controversy, by specialists at the Center for South Asia Studies at the University of California's Institute of International Studies.

Gupta, Karunakar. **India in World Politics: A Period of Transition.** Calcutta: Scientific Book Agency, 1969, 324 p.
A useful, though not very carefully prepared study of Indian foreign policy from 1956 to 1960, emphasizing the conflict with China.

Johri, Sitaram. **Chinese Invasion of Ladakh.** Lucknow: Himalaya Publications, 1969, 221 p.
A survey of the limited military operations in Ladakh in 1962 when the Chinese attacked the Indian troops in the territories they claimed and controlled.

Johri, Sitaram. **Chinese Invasion of NEFA.** Lucknow: Himalaya Publications, 1968, 260 p.
A detailed account by an Indian officer of the fighting in the North-East Frontier Agency territories in 1962.

Karnik, V. B., *ed.* **China Invades India.** New York: Allied Publishers, 1963, 316 p.
A discussion by four Indian historians of the background of Sino-Indian relations and the invasion of October-November 1962.

Kaul, Brij Mohan. **The Untold Story.** Bombay: Allied Publishers, 1967, 507 p.
In this bitter study the author, a professional Indian soldier, blames Nehru, Krishna Menon and Morarji Desai for the failure of the Indian Army to withstand the Chinese attack in 1962.

Lamb, Alastair. **The China-India Border: The Origins of the Disputed Boundaries.** New York: Oxford University Press (for the Royal Institute of International Affairs), 1964, 192 p.
A succinct, scholarly treatise on the evolution of the Sino-Indian boundary controversy, based on published and unpublished materials, including available British official records in the India Office Library archives.

Mankekar, D. R. **The Guilty Men of 1962.** Bombay: Tulsi Shah Enterprises, 1968, 184 p.
An attempt to find the scapegoats for the debacle of the Indian Army in the Sino-Indian border war of 1962.

Maxwell, Neville. **India's China War.** New York: Pantheon Books, 1971, 475 p.
  A reconstruction of the diplomatic and military activity surrounding the Chinese punitive expedition of 1962.

Nanporia, N. J. **The Sino-Indian Dispute.** Bombay: Times of India, 1963, 148 p.
  A collection of 33 articles, chronologically arranged by date of original publication in *The Times of India* from September 17, 1962 to June 24, 1963, on the Sino-Indian border controversy. Although completely on India's side in the dispute, Mr. Nanporia is openly frank in criticizing his government's handling of the issue.

Noorani, A. G. **Our Credulity and Negligence.** Bombay: Ramdas G. Bhatkal, 1963, 167 p.
  A documented critique of India's policies toward China from the Tibetan affair in 1950 to the invasion of India in October 1962.

Patterson, George Neilson. **Peking Versus Delhi.** New York: Praeger, 1964, 310 p.
  The author, a missionary turned journalist with long residence in Asia, gives the history of rivalry between China and India in the period from 1947 to 1961.

Rao, Gondker Narayana. **The India-China Border: A Reappraisal.** New York: Asia Publishing House, 1968, 106 p.
  A bitter attack on the pro-China view taken by Alastair Lamb in his "The China-India Border" (1964).

Rowland, John. **A History of Sino-Indian Relations: Hostile Co-existence.** Princeton: Van Nostrand, 1967, 248 p.
  A study of the origin, nature and significance of the tensions between China and India and of their impact on Sino-Soviet rivalry.

Van Eekelen, Willem F. **Indian Foreign Policy and the Border Dispute with China.** The Hague: Nijhoff, 1964, 220 p.
  A Netherlands Foreign Service officer provides a chronological description of the Sino-Indian boundary dispute and then traces the origins and the decline in importance of India's Five Principles of Peaceful Coexistence.

Varma, Shanti Prasad. **Struggle for the Himalayas: A Study in Sino-Indian Relations.** New Delhi: Sterling Publishers, 2d rev. ed., 1971, 316 p.
  An historian and political scientist studies India's foreign policies, especially as affected by the 1962 Chinese invasion, and their influence on the domestic political institutions and processes.

Economic Problems

See also General Economic Conditions and Tendencies, p. 49; Government and Economics; Planning, p. 54; Food and Agriculture, p. 68; Economic Growth and Development, p. 71; Economic Aid and Technical Assistance, p. 81; (The United States) Aid and Assistance, p. 254; (Western Europe) Integration, p. 349; (Union of Soviet Socialist Republics) Foreign Economic Policy, p. 560; (Asia and the Pacific Area) General Surveys, p. 607; other subsections under India.

Banerjee, Arun Kumar. **India's Balance of Payments: Estimates of Current and Capital Accounts from 1921-22 to 1938-39.** New York: Asia Publishing House, 1963, 255 p.
  An extensive study of India's balance of payments during the inter-war years.

Bhatia, B. M. **Famines in India: A Study in Some Aspects of the Economic History of India (1860-1945).** London: Asia Publishing House, 1963, 367 p.
  An inquiry into the history of food shortages in India.

Bhattacharyya, K. N. **India's Fourth Plan: Test in Growthmanship.** New York: Asia Publishing House, 1967, 127 p.
  A critique of India's economic planning, especially of its big industrialization program. In the author's view the strengthening of "the agricultural base is the topmost priority."

Blyn, George. **Agricultural Trends in India, 1891-1947: Output, Availability, and Productivity.** Philadelphia: University of Pennsylvania Press, 1966, 370 p.
  A history of the development of India's agriculture by a professor at Rutgers University.

Braibanti, Ralph J. D. and Spengler, Joseph John, eds. **Administration and Economic Development in India.** Durham: Duke University Press (for the Duke University Commonwealth-Studies Center), 1963, 312 p.

A series of essays treating various aspects of the relationship between administration and economic development—the training of leaders, village and district problems and the tax structure.

Chandrasekhar, Sripati. **American Aid and India's Economic Development.** New York: Praeger, 1965, 243 p.

An Indian social scientist and economist appraises the changes American aid has helped to produce in India's economic and political situation.

Cutt, James. **Taxation and Economic Development in India.** New York: Praeger, 1969, 415 p.

A study of the relationship between India's main tax devices and the growth rate of national income.

Datar, Asha L. **India's Economic Relations with the USSR and Eastern Europe, 1953 to 1969.** New York: Cambridge University Press, 1972, 278 p.

The author concludes his carefully researched book by saying that in purely economic terms Soviet aid and trade were not preferable to those of the West.

Draguhn, Werner. **Entwicklungsbewusstsein und wirtschaftliche Entwicklung in Indien.** Wiesbaden: Harrassowitz (for the Institut für Asienkunde in Hamburg), 1970, 288 p.

After a very substantial and thought-provoking analysis of India's economic development, the author concludes that "only a fundamental social and cultural change can guarantee economic prosperity for India in the future."

Eldridge, Philip John. **The Politics of Foreign Aid in India.** New York: Schocken Books, 1970, 289 p.

An analysis of the basic economic characteristics of aid supplied to India, the objectives of donors of that aid and the political impact of it on the country.

Étienne, Gilbert. **Studies in Indian Agriculture: The Art of the Possible.** Berkeley: University of California Press, 1968, 343 p.

A discussion of the rural economy of India, with emphasis on the factors that influence agricultural production.

Fonseca, A. J. **Wage Determination and Organized Labour in India.** New York: Oxford University Press, 1964, 241 p.

A study of the origins, strengths and weaknesses of the Indian trade union movement and its adjustment to the process of rapid industrialization.

Frankel, Francine R. **India's Green Revolution: Economic Gains and Political Costs.** Princeton: Princeton University Press, 1971, 232 p.

The author of this study thinks that the introduction of high-yield strains of wheat and rice may solve the problem of feeding India, but that the "green revolution" may have also revolutionary and unexpected consequences for Indian society and politics.

Hanson, Albert Henry. **The Process of Planning: A Study of India's Five-Year Plans, 1950-1964.** New York: Oxford University Press (for the Royal Institute of International Affairs), 1966, 560 p.

Professor Hanson, of the University of Leeds, first details the making and implementing of India's three five-year plans and then scrutinizes them from the point of view of the student of politics and public administration.

Johnson, William Arthur. **The Steel Industry of India.** Cambridge: Harvard University Press, 1966, 340 p.

A scholarly study by an economist at the RAND Corporation.

Kapoor, Ashok. **International Business Negotiations: A Study in India.** New York: New York University Press, 1970, 361 p.

A thoroughly researched case study of the negotiation process between an international consortium and the Government of India over the establishment of a large industrial project.

Khan, Mohammed Shabbir. **India's Economic Development and International Economic Relations.** New York: Asia Publishing House, 2d rev. ed., 1966, 229 p.

A revised edition of a balanced discussion of Indian foreign trade, aid and investment problems.

Khera, Sucha Singh. **Government in Business.** New York: Asia Publishing House (for the Indian Institute of Public Administration), 1964, 396 p.
A critical report by a former Indian civil servant of government enterprises since independence.

Kidron, Michael. **Foreign Investments in India.** New York: Oxford University Press, 1965, 368 p.
A fact-laden study which not only surveys the amount and distribution of foreign investment but compares it with the situation just before independence.

Kumar, Dharma. **India and the European Economic Community.** New York: Asia Publishing House (for the Indian Council of World Affairs), 1966, 272 p.
A balanced and sophisticated study showing great knowledge of India's economic problems and their relation to those of the rest of the world.

Kust, Matthew J. **Foreign Enterprise in India: Laws and Policies.** Chapel Hill: University of North Carolina Press, 1964, 498 p.
A comprehensive survey, sponsored by the American Society of International Law, of the laws that govern foreign enterprise in India and of the factors that impede or facilitate foreign participation in the economic development of the country.

Mellor, John W. and Others. **Developing Rural India: Plan and Practice.** Ithaca: Cornell University Press, 1968, 411 p.
Studies on agricultural development in India in the 1950s and the 1960s with a concluding chapter on future prospects.

Pavlov, Vladimir Ivanovich. **India: Economic Freedom Versus Imperialism.** New Delhi: Peoples Publishing House, 1963, 247 p.
A Soviet monograph on the economic development of India.

Pochhammer, Wilhelm von. **Indiens Wirtschaft heute.** Mainz: Krausskopf, 1964, 312 p.
A survey of Indian economic problems, by a former German diplomat with many years of service in India.

Rao, Vijendra Kasturi Ranga Varadaraja and Narain, Dharm. **Foreign Aid and India's Economic Development.** New York: Asia Publishing House, 1963, 111 p.
In this study two Indians have collaborated, at the request of UNESCO, to show the "character, magnitude and organization of foreign aid, the conditions on which it has been received, the impact it has made on the economy, and the problems that it has given rise to."

Rao, Vijendra Kasturi Ranga Varadaraja. **Values and Economic Development: The Indian Challenge.** Delhi: Vikas Publications, 1971, 182 p.
The author–cabinet minister, economic planner and U.N. administrator–examines the role of values in Indian economic development and concludes that economic development is only possible through coercion or conversion away from traditional values.

Röh, Klaus. **Rourkela als Testfall für die Errichtung von Industrieprojekten in Entwicklungsländern.** Hamburg: Verlag Weltarchiv, 1967, 514 p.
A detailed account of the difficulties and successes of the West German aid mission in developing the immense industrial complex in Rourkela in India.

Rosen, George. **Democracy and Economic Change in India.** Berkeley: University of California Press, 1966, 326 p.
An economist with the RAND Corporation analyzes the relationship between political change and economic development in India and comments on the U.S. interest and policies in that country.

Sharma, G. K. **Labour Movement in India.** Jullundur: University Publishers, 1963, 250 p.
A history of "the organized activity of wage-earners" in India from 1785 to 1960.

Singh, Manmohan. **India's Export Trends and the Prospects for Self-Sustained Growth.** New York: Oxford University Press, 1964, 369 p.
The author seeks to explain the stagnation in India's export earnings from 1951 to 1960 and writes about the major policy implications suggested by his analysis.

Singh, Tarlok. **Towards an Integrated Society.** Westport (Conn.): Greenwood, 1970, 554 p.
The author, with long experience in India's national planning, writes in this volume on problems of poverty and economic and social development in India.

Singh, V. B., *ed*. **Economic History of India, 1857–1956.** New York: Allied Publishers, 1965, 795 p.
: A collection of essays on many aspects of the Indian economy. The authors seem to favor the adoption of the socialist pattern of society as the national objective.

Streeten, Paul and Lipton, Michael, *eds*. **The Crisis of Indian Planning: Economic Planning in the 1960s.** New York: Oxford University Press (for the Royal Institute of International Affairs), 1968, 416 p.
: Revised versions of papers on Indian planning and economic conditions originally presented at a conference of British and Indian economists, businessmen and administrators at Sussex University in April 1967. The conference was sponsored by the Royal Institute of International Affairs, the Institute of Development Studies and the University of Sussex.

Venkatasubbiah, H. **The Anatomy of Indian Planning.** Bombay: Vora, 1969, 218 p.
: This volume of essays by the London correspondent of *The Hindu* and sometime Vice-President of the Indian Council on World Affairs contains a great deal of information on the Indian economy and planning since the establishment of independence.

Social Problems

See also Culture; Education; Public Opinion; Communications Processes, p. 42; (Asia and the Pacific Area) General Surveys, p. 607; Burma, p. 753; Fiji; French Polynesia; New Caledonia; Western Samoa; Nauru, p. 775; (Republic of South Africa) Apartheid, p. 838; other subsections under India.

Chand, Gyan. **Population in Perspective: Study of Population Crisis in India in the Context of New Social Horizons.** New Delhi: Orient Longman, 1972, 380 p.
: A sequel to the author's pioneering study "India's Teeming Millions" that was published in 1939.

Das Gupta, Jyotirindra. **Language Conflict and National Development: Group Politics and National Language Policy in India.** Berkeley: University of California Press, 1970, 293 p.
: A useful study of "the complex nature of language politics" in India, written under the auspices of the Institute of International Studies and the Institute of Governmental Studies at the University of California.

Isaacs, Harold Robert. **India's Ex-Untouchables.** New York: Day, 1965, 188 p.
: An examination, based on a visit to India in 1963, of the position of the former "untouchables," a caste legally abolished in that country. The author finds that they still lack social acceptability.

Lambert, Richard David. **Workers, Factories, and Social Change in India.** Princeton: Princeton University Press, 1963, 247 p.
: This study of the workers in five factories in Poona is especially interesting for the light it throws on the interplay between factories and the "traditional society."

Lannoy, Richard. **The Speaking Tree: A Study of Indian Culture and Society.** New York: Oxford University Press, 1971, 466 p.
: An ambitious attempt at a synoptic understanding of Indian culture.

Mandelbaum, David G. **Society in India.** Berkeley: University of California Press, 1970, 2 v.
: The author of this encyclopedic survey denies the Weber-Myrdal thesis that the caste system presents insuperable obstacles to social change in India.

Mason, Philip, *ed*. **India and Ceylon: Unity and Diversity; A Symposium.** New York: Oxford University Press (for the Institute of Race Relations), 1967, 311 p.
: This volume is part of a larger project to compare relations in various parts of the world between ethnic groups inhabiting the same state.

Nayar, Baldev Raj. **National Communication and Language Policy in India.** New York: Praeger (in coöperation with the Centre for Developing-Area Studies, McGill University), 1970, 310 p.
: A solid survey of the very complicated linguistic diversity in India. The author pays particular attention to the controversy concerning the retaining of English as official language.

Srinivas, Mysore Narasimhachar. **Caste in Modern India, and Other Essays.** New York: Asia Publishing House, 1963, 171 p.
Eleven thoughtful essays on the political and sociological impact of the Indian caste tradition on the new India, written between 1952 and 1960 by a leading Indian social anthropologist.

Srinivas, Mysore Narasimhachar. **Social Change in Modern India.** Berkeley: University of California Press, 1966, 194 p.
Essays based on lectures delivered in May 1963 at the University of California, Berkeley.

Taylor, Carl Cleveland and Others. **India's Roots of Democracy.** New York: Praeger, 1966, 694 p.
A comprehensive sociological survey of Indian community development programs since 1947.

PAKISTAN

General Surveys and Political Problems

See also Problems of New Nations, p. 36; (Asia and the Pacific Area) General Surveys, p. 607; (Central Asia and the Subcontinent of India) General, p. 652; (India) General, p. 656; Recent History; Independence and Partition, p. 657.

Ahmad, Kazi Said Uddin. **A Geography of Pakistan.** New York: Oxford University Press, 1965, 216 p.
A handy reference.

Ali, Tariq. **Pakistan: Military Rule or People's Power.** New York: Morrow, 1970, 270 p.
Reviewing contemporary Pakistani history, the author, a Trotskyist leader of the Fourth International, sees mass violent revolution as—happily—inevitable.

Ayub Khan, Mohammad. **Friends Not Masters: A Political Autobiography.** New York: Oxford University Press, 1967, 275 p.
A reëvaluation of the past and an interpretation of significant developments which have influenced the history of Pakistan up to the 1965 presidential elections.

Ayub Khan, Mohammad. **Pakistan Perspective.** Washington: Embassy of Pakistan, 1965, 110 p.
The former President of Pakistan speaks out on the Pakistani-American alliance, Africa and Asia, the Kashmir dispute, India's military build-up, and various aspects of economic development in his country.

Aziz, Khursheed Kamal. **The Making of Pakistan: A Study in Nationalism.** London: Chatto and Windus, 1967, 223 p.
A study of Muslim nationalism in imperial India.

Banerjee, D. N. **East Pakistan: A Case-Study in Muslim Politics.** Delhi: Vikas Publications, 1969, 204 p.
A solid examination of the separatist mood of East Pakistan, by a Cambridge-trained Indian scholar.

Birkhead, Guthrie Sweeney, *ed.* **Administrative Problems in Pakistan.** Syracuse: Syracuse University Press, 1966, 223 p.
A descriptive analysis of development processes by six American and British specialists, all of whom served at the Pakistan Administrative Staff College in Lahore.

Braibanti, Ralph J. D. **Research on the Bureaucracy of Pakistan.** Durham: Duke University Press (for the Program in Comparative Studies on Southern Asia of the Duke University Commonwealth-Studies Center), 1966, 569 p.
An attempt to identify, classify and evaluate source materials for the study of bureaucracy in Pakistan.

Chaudhuri, Muzaffer Ahmed. **Government and Politics in Pakistan.** Dacca: Puthigar, 1968, 416 p.
A detailed and comprehensive survey of contemporary Pakistani politics that was completed before the fall of Ayub Khan. The author is an East Pakistani scholar.

Choudhury, Golam Wahed. **Constitutional Development in Pakistan.** Vancouver: University of British Columbia, Publications Centre, 2d rev. and enl. ed., 1969, 277 p.
A revised edition of a careful study of constitutional developments in Pakistan. An epilogue discusses the abrogation of the 1962 constitution in 1969.

Choudhury, Golam Wahed. **Democracy in Pakistan.** Vancouver: University of British Columbia (for the Social Sciences Research Committee, University of Dacca), 1963, 309 p.
A lucid account of the uncertain development of parliamentary democracy after independence.

Dichter, David with Popkin, Nathan S. **The North-West Frontier of West Pakistan: A Study in Regional Geography.** New York: Oxford University Press, 1967, 231 p.
A systematic study of the province of Pakistan that is inhabited mostly by Pathan tribes.

Feldman, Herbert. **From Crisis to Crisis: Pakistan 1962-1969.** New York: Oxford University Press, 1972, 340 p.
An incisive account of the turbulent and tragic history of Pakistan during its brief experiment with Ayub Khan's new constitution.

Feldman, Herbert. **Revolution in Pakistan: A Study of the Martial Law Administration.** New York: Oxford University Press, 1967, 242 p.
A monograph on the political complications during the period from October 1958 to June 1962.

Gankovskii, Iurii Vladimirovich. **Natsional'nyi vopros i natsional'nye dvizheniia v Pakistane.** Moscow: Nauka, 1967, 267 p.
A Soviet study of the nationality question in Pakistan's politics.

Gankovskii, Iurii Vladimirovich, *ed.* **Pakistan: spravochnik.** Moscow: Nauka, 1966, 478 p.
A Soviet survey of contemporary Pakistan prepared by the Academy of Sciences of the U.S.S.R.

Goodnow, Henry Frank. **The Civil Service of Pakistan: Bureaucracy in a New Nation.** New Haven: Yale University Press, 1964, 328 p.
A case study of the Civil Service of Pakistan and its predecessor, the Indian Civil Service, dealing mainly with conditions prior to 1958, by a member of the team sent by the University of Pennsylvania to establish the Institute of Public and Business Administration at Karachi.

Jahan, Rounaq. **Pakistan: Failure in National Integration.** New York: Columbia University Press, 1972, 248 p.
In this postmortem on Ayub Khan's Pakistan, the author argues that economic growth did not unite the country but divided it.

Loshak, David. **Pakistan Crisis.** New York: McGraw-Hill, 1972, 152 p.
The author argues that all solutions to contemporary Pakistani problems will be unhappy ones.

Muhammad Ali, Chaudhri. **The Emergence of Pakistan.** New York: Columbia University Press, 1967, 418 p.
A Pakistani's account of the events of 1946–48 (immediately preceding and following the partition of British India), the social, economic and political factors shaping them, and the problems facing the new state of Pakistan.

Muqueem Khan, Fazal. **The Story of the Pakistan Army.** Karachi: Oxford University Press, 1963, 250 p.
A history of the Pakistan Army from its beginnings in August 1947 when it was formed from the Muslim troops of the British Indian Army. The author is a former Commandant of the Pakistan Military Academy.

Nyrop, Richard F. and Others. **Area Handbook for Pakistan.** Washington: G.P.O., 1971, 691 p.
A useful reference, with bibliography, prepared by the Foreign Area Studies at the American University.

Peerzada, Syed Sharifuddin, *ed.* **Foundations of Pakistan: All-India Muslim League Documents, 1906-1947.** Karachi: National Publishing House, 1969-70, 2 v.

A valuable collection of documents on the organization that played a decisive role in the creation of a separate Muslim state.

Prakasa, Sri. **Pakistan: Birth and Early Days.** Meerut: Meenakshi Prakashan, 1965, 186 p.
A prominent Indian statesman writes about a period when he was the first Indian High Commissioner in Pakistan (1947-1949).

Ray, Jayanta Kumar. **Democracy and Nationalism on Trial: A Study of East Pakistan.** Simla: Indian Institute of Advanced Study, 1968, 400 p.
A study of the emergence of the new Bengali Muslim élite in East Pakistan.

Sayeed, Khalid Bin. **Pakistan: The Formative Phase, 1857-1948.** New York: Oxford University Press, 2d ed., 1968, 341 p.
A completely revised and updated edition of a solid survey that was originally published in 1961 as "Pakistan: The Formative Phase" (Karachi: Pakistan Publishing House, 1961, 492 p.) and dealt with the period from 1857 to 1960.

Sayeed, Khalid Bin. **The Political System of Pakistan.** Boston: Houghton, 1967, 321 p.
A most useful companion volume to the previous study, with emphasis on the description and analysis of Pakistan's political developments since the establishment of independence.

Schimmel, Annemarie. **Pakistan: ein Schloss mit tausend Toren.** Zurich: Orell Füssli, 1965, 278 p.
A Bonn professor, specialist in oriental and religious studies, made five trips to the eastern and western sectors of Pakistan to collect materials for this book on Pakistani life and thought.

Schuler, Edgar Albert and Schuler, Kathryn R. **Public Opinion and Constitution Making in Pakistan, 1958-1962.** East Lansing: Michigan State University Press, 1967, 286 p.
A chronological account of public reaction to the rewriting of the 1956 constitution.

Siddiqui, Kalim. **Conflict, Crisis and War in Pakistan.** New York: Praeger, 1972, 217 p.
The story of his country's birth and breakup by an outraged Pakistani exile.

Stephens, Ian Melville. **Pakistan.** New York: Praeger, 3rd ed., 1967, 304 p.
A former editor of the Indian *Statesman* (1942-1951) and historian of the Pakistan Army (1957-1960) uses his personal observations and experiences, as well as previously unpublished materials, to write about the creation of Pakistan, the emergence of the new state, the Kashmir dispute and other Indo-Pakistani problems.

Tayyeb, Ali. **Pakistan: A Political Geography.** New York: Oxford University Press, 1966, 250 p.
A valuable study, including an analysis of Pakistan's contemporary foreign relations and an assessment of the country's economic and political performance in the first fifteen years of its existence. The author is a professor of geography at the University of Toronto.

Von Vorys, Karl. **Political Development in Pakistan.** Princeton: Princeton University Press (for the Princeton Center of International Studies), 1965, 341 p.
A detailed description of Ayub Khan's programs of political development.

Waheed-uz-Zaman. **Towards Pakistan.** Lahore: Publishers United, 1964, 248 p.
A survey of major currents of Muslim politics from 1928 (the publication of the Nehru Report) to 1940 (the Lahore Resolution demanding partition of India and the establishment of a separate Muslim state).

Weekes, Richard V. **Pakistan: Birth and Growth of a Muslim Nation.** Princeton: Van Nostrand, 1964, 278 p.
A sketch of the history, politics and social and cultural traditions of the country by a former U.S. information officer in Karachi.

Wheeler, Richard S. **The Politics of Pakistan: A Constitutional Quest.** Ithaca: Cornell University Press, 1970, 346 p.
The author shows how religious conflict, controversies between East and West Pakistan and between central and provincial authorities have resulted in the failure to establish a stable constitutional order.

Wilber, Donald Newton and Others. **Pakistan: Its People, Its Society, Its Culture.** New Haven: Human Relations Area Files Press, 1965, 487 p.

This comprehensive survey is an extensive revision of the 1958 "Area Handbook on Pakistan" which was also prepared by the H.R.A.F.

Wilber, Donald Newton. **Pakistan: Yesterday and Today.** New York: Holt, Rinehart and Winston, 1964, 266 p.
A treatise on a new nation building upon the continuity of ancient history and culture but concurrently patterning its political, social and economic institutions after those of the Western world.

Wilcox, Wayne Ayres. **Pakistan: The Consolidation of a Nation.** New York: Columbia University Press, 1963, 276 p.
A study of the difficult and in part unsuccessful effort to introduce an "effective, uniform, and democratic" government to the new Pakistan nation.

Ziring, Lawrence. **The Ayub Khan Era: Politics in Pakistan, 1958-1969.** Syracuse: Syracuse University Press, 1971, 234 p.
A study of the failure of Ayub Khan to create in Pakistan the sense of nationhood.

Foreign Relations

See also (Great Britain) Imperial and Commonwealth Relations; Colonial Policy, p. 367; Biographies, Memoirs and Addresses, p. 369; Foreign Policy, p. 375; (Central Asia and the Subcontinent of India) General, p. 652; India, p. 656; Bangladesh, p. 679.

Bhutto, Zulfikar Ali. **Foreign Policy of Pakistan.** Karachi: Pakistan Institute of International Affairs, 1964, 125 p.
Speeches (1962-64) by a leading statesman of Pakistan, Prime Minister since 1973, mainly concerned with his country's relations with India, and with Pakistan's adherence to United Nations Charter principles.

Bhutto, Zulfikar Ali. **The Myth of Independence.** New York: Oxford University Press, 1969, 188 p.
The Pakistani leader gives his opinionated views on his achievements as Foreign Minister of Pakistan from 1963 to 1966 and makes proposals for remedying what he considers errors in dealing with the global powers.

Bhutto, Zulfikar Ali. **The Quest for Peace.** Karachi: Pakistan Institute of International Affairs, 1966, 106 p.
A selection of speeches and writings from 1963 to 1965.

Chaudhri, Mohammed Ahsen. **Pakistan and the Great Powers.** Karachi: Council for Pakistan Studies (in coöperation with the Department of International Relations, University of Karachi), 1970, 140 p.
An analysis of Pakistan's relations with the United States, the U.S.S.R. and China.

Sharma, Brij Lal E. **The Pakistan-China Axis.** New York: Asia Publishing House, 1968, 226 p.
An Indian diplomat describes what he thinks were Pakistani-Chinese machinations against unaligned India.

Singh, Sangat. **Pakistan's Foreign Policy.** New York: Asia Publishing House, 1970, 260 p.
The author argues that the foreign policy of Pakistan has been determined by its animosity toward India. He concludes his appraisal by stating that "Pakistan can normalise her relations with India only if she first normalises the political situation within the country."

Economic Problems

See also Economic Growth and Development, p. 71; (Asia and the Pacific Area) General Surveys, p. 607; (Pakistan) General Surveys and Political Problems, p. 675; Republic of Vietnam, p. 746; Burma, p. 753.

Andrus, James Russell and Mohammed, Azizali F. **Trade, Finance and Development in Pakistan.** Stanford: Stanford University Press, 1966, 289 p.
A detailed study based on the authors' "The Economy of Pakistan" (1958).

Brecher, Irving and Abbas, S. A. **Foreign Aid and Industrial Development in Pakistan.** New York: Cambridge University Press, 1972, 271 p.

Well aware of the complexity of the issues and the limits of their study, Professor Brecher of McGill and Mr. Abbas of UNCTAD convincingly demonstrate the substantial contribution aid made to Pakistan's industrial growth in the 1960s.

Étienne, Gilbert. **Progrès agricole et maîtrise de l'eau: le cas du Pakistan.** Paris: Presses Universitaires, 1967, 187 p.
A study of agricultural development in Pakistan, emphasizing the importance of irrigation.

Haq, Mahbubul. **The Strategy of Economic Planning: A Case Study of Pakistan.** New York: Oxford University Press, 1964, 266 p.
A well-organized, analytical study of planning in Pakistan, with evaluation of its first two five-year plans (1955/60–1961/65).

Lewis, Stephen R., Jr. **Economic Policy and Industrial Growth in Pakistan.** Cambridge: M.I.T. Press, 1969, 191 p.
A quantitative and analytical study of how a spectacular industrial growth can occur in an otherwise stagnant economy.

MacEwan, Arthur. **Development Alternatives in Pakistan: A Multisectoral and Regional Analysis of Planning Problems.** Cambridge: Harvard University Press, 1971, 211 p.
The author of this very technical study argues that planning efforts in Pakistan "are of little use until control of the society is wrested from the hands of the present elite."

Mezirow, Jack D. **Dynamics of Community Development.** New York: Scarecrow Press, 1963, 252 p.
A description of the Pakistan government's unsuccessful attempt at rural development from 1952 to 1961, based on the author's observations during two years as adviser to the program.

Norbye, Ole David Koht. **Development Prospects of Pakistan.** New York: Humanities Press, 1968, 336 p.
An evaluation and description of structural alterations in the Pakistani economy.

Papanek, Gustav F. **Pakistan's Development: Social Goals and Private Incentives.** Cambridge: Harvard University Press, 1967, 354 p.
An analysis of Pakistan's economic problems by a member of the Economics Department at Harvard who spent five years in Pakistan as adviser to its Planning Commission.

Raper, Arthur and Others. **Rural Development in Action.** Ithaca: Cornell University Press, 1970, 351 p.
A report on a decade of sustained and impressive efforts by the Academy for Rural Development at Comilla, East Pakistan, to improve the social and economic lot of the Bengalis.

Waterston, Albert with Others. **Planning in Pakistan: Organization and Implementation.** Baltimore: Johns Hopkins Press (for the Economic Development Institute, International Bank for Reconstruction and Development), 1963, 150 p.
This study traces the effective formulation and implementation of development in Pakistan from 1948 to the early 1960s.

BANGLADESH

See also (Central Asia and the Subcontinent of India) General, p. 652; India, p. 656; Pakistan, p. 675.

Ayoob, Mohammed and Subrahmanyam, K. **The Liberation War.** New Delhi: Chand, 1972, 303 p.
An attempt by two Indian scholars to describe the political and military developments which brought about the establishment of the state of Bangladesh.

Chopra, Pran, *ed.* **The Challenge of Bangla Desh: A Special Debate.** New York: Humanities Press, 1971, 159 p.
Members of the Indian opinion-making élite argue against the re-imposition of Pakistani government control over Bangladesh.

Hess, Peter. **Bangladesh: Tragödie einer Staatsgründung.** Frauenfeld (Switzerland): Huber, 1972, 227 p.

A thorough and unbiased survey of the tragic and ironic circumstances surrounding the birth of Bangladesh, by the South Asia correspondent of the *Neue Zürcher Zeitung*.

Kamal, Kazi Ahmed. **Sheik Mujibur Rahman and Birth of Bangladesh**. Dacca: Ahmed, 1972, 204 p.
An admiring biography of the first Prime Minister of Bangladesh who became his country's President on January 25, 1975.

Naik, J. A. **India, Russia, China and Bangla Desh**. New Delhi: Chand, 1972, 163 p.
The author of this study argues that the Bangladesh conflict had "shown not merely a failure of American policy in Asia but also revealed a credibility gap in the U.S. administration's ability for crisis management."

Roy Chowdhury, Subrata. **The Genesis of Bangladesh**. New York: Asia Publishing House, 1972, 345 p.
An analysis of the legal issues involved in the establishment of Bangladesh and a criticism of the policies of the United States and the United Nations toward the new state. The author is a Cambridge-trained Indian scholar.

Singh, Sheelendra Kumar and Others, *eds*. **Bangla Desh: Documents**. New Delhi: Ministry of External Affairs, 1972, 2 v.
Documents, issued under the auspices of the Indian Ministry of External Affairs, dealing with the genesis and progress of the crisis in 1971 that led to the establishment of the state of Bangladesh.

Williams, Laurence Frederic Rushbrook. **The East Pakistan Tragedy**. New York: Drake Publishers, 1972, 142 p.
A pro-Pakistani account of the transmutation of East Pakistan into Bangladesh.

SRI LANKA (CEYLON); MAURITIUS; INDIAN OCEAN

See also (Great Britain) Imperial and Commonwealth Relations; Colonial Policy, p. 367; (Asia and the Pacific Area) General Surveys, p. 607; (Central Asia and the Subcontinent of India) General, p. 652; (India) Social Problems, p. 674; (Southeastern Asia; East Indies) General, p. 733.

Arasaratnam, Sinnappah. **Ceylon**. Englewood Cliffs: Prentice-Hall, 1964, 182 p.
The author states that this survey is "designed as an introduction for general readers, students, and hopefully statesmen."

Bansil, P. C. **Ceylon Agriculture: A Perspective**. Delhi: Dhanpat Rai, 1971, 407 p.
An ambitious and well-documented analysis of the entire problem of agricultural development in Ceylon.

Benedict, Burton. **Mauritius: Problems of a Plural Society**. New York: Praeger (for the Institute of Race Relations, London), 1965, 72 p.
A British anthropologist presents a concise analysis of the religious, linguistic and political problems confronting Mauritius.

Favoreu, Louis. **L'Île Maurice**. Paris: Berger-Levrault, 1970, 119 p.
A study of Mauritius, the former British colony which gained its independence on March 12, 1968.

Gagzow, Burkhard. **Aussenwirtschaftsorientierte Entwicklungspolitik kleiner Länder: das Beispiel Ceylon**. Stuttgart: Gustav Fischer Verlag, 1969, 224 p.
A well-documented study of the interrelationships between foreign trade and economic development in Ceylon.

Jayawardena, Visakha Kumari. **The Rise of the Labor Movement in Ceylon**. Durham: Duke University Press, 1972, 382 p.
A Ceylonese scholar, educated at the London School of Economics, surveys the origins and evolution of the labor movement in Ceylon from 1880 to 1933.

Karunatilake, H. N. S. **Economic Development in Ceylon**. New York: Praeger, 1971, 378 p.
A wide-ranging survey of economic conditions in Ceylon from 1950 to 1970 by a Ceylonese bank official and a former Research Fellow in Economics at Harvard.

ASIA AND THE PACIFIC AREA

Kearney, Robert N. **Trade Unions and Politics in Ceylon.** Berkeley: University of California Press, 1972, 195 p.
The author concludes his study by saying that trade unions in Ceylon "provide one of the few relatively open channels for purposeful participation in the larger social and political realms by persons not born into the small elite and privileged social strata."

Lerski, George Jan. **Origins of Trotskyism in Ceylon: A Documentary History of the Lanka Sama Samaja Party, 1935–1942.** Stanford: Hoover Institution on War, Revolution, and Peace, 1968, 288 p.
A study of how the Trotskyite movement in Ceylon grew from a small group of young London-educated radicals to a formidable political force.

Ludowyk, Evelyn Frederick Charles. **The Modern History of Ceylon.** New York: Praeger, 1966, 308 p.
A survey of the Ceylonese history since 1796, with emphasis on the developments in the twentieth century. The author is a Cambridge-trained Ceylonese scholar.

Ludowyk, Evelyn Frederick Charles. **A Short History of Ceylon.** New York: Praeger, 1967, 336 p.
In the words of the author, this is "the story of the important events and persons crowded into the two thousand years and more of Ceylon's history." The English edition appeared as "The Story of Ceylon" (London: Faber, 2d rev. ed., 1967, 336 p.).

Nyrop, Richard F. and Others. **Area Handbook for Ceylon.** Washington: G.P.O., 1971, 525 p.
A useful reference volume with a bibliography, prepared by the Foreign Area Studies at the American University.

Obeyesekere, Gananath. **Land Tenure in Village Ceylon.** New York: Cambridge University Press, 1967, 319 p.
A University of Ceylon sociologist, on the basis of 1961 field work in Southern Province, analyzes in detail the contemporary system of land tenure and traces the evolution of every land-holding and correlated kinship pattern from the inception of the estate in 1790.

Pakeman, Sidney Arnold. **Ceylon.** New York: Praeger, 1964, 256 p.
A professor, who knows the country well, surveys the period of British rule and the years since World War II.

Sievers, Angelika. **Ceylon: Gesellschaft und Lebensraum in den orientalischen Tropen.** Wiesbaden: F. Steiner, 1964, 398 p.
An impressive geographical description of Ceylon, the first of this scope, with chapters describing at great length the economic, social, cultural and historical problems of the island.

Singer, Marshall R. **The Emerging Elite: A Study of Political Leadership in Ceylon.** Cambridge: M.I.T. Press, 1964, 203 p.
An examination of the patterns of leadership in traditional, colonial and contemporary Ceylon.

Snodgrass, Donald R. **Ceylon: An Export Economy in Transition.** Homewood (Ill.): Irwin, 1966, 416 p.
A former economic adviser to Malaysia's Economic Planning Unit analyzes the structure and growth of Ceylon's export economy from 1840 to the 1960s.

Stoddard, Theodore L. and Others. **Area Handbook for Indian Ocean Territories.** Washington: G.P.O., 1971, 160 p.
A useful reference, prepared for the American University by the Institute for Cross-Cultural Research.

Woodward, Calvin A. **The Growth of a Party System in Ceylon.** Providence: Brown University Press, 1969, 338 p.
The author records the changes in political institutions in Ceylon and analyzes the reasons why they provide for the peaceful and democratic transfer of power in accordance with the preference of its people.

FAR EAST

GENERAL

See also General Works, p. 1; The World Since 1914, p. 129; (The United States) Foreign Policy, p. 229; (Union of Soviet Socialist Republics) Foreign Policy, p. 550; (Asia and the Pacific Area) General Surveys, p. 607; (China) Foreign Relations, p. 702; (Southeastern Asia; East Indies) General, p. 733.

Burnell, Elaine H., *ed.* **Asian Dilemma: United States, Japan and China.** Santa Barbara: Center for the Study of Democratic Institutions, 1969, 238 p.
These papers by Japanese and American politicians discuss the international status of Taiwan, the disposition of military forces in the Pacific, the role of the great powers in Asia and other key issues.

Cowan, Charles Donald, *ed.* **The Economic Development of China and Japan.** New York: Praeger, 1964, 255 p.
Papers originally presented at a study conference in July 1961 at London's School of Oriental and African Studies.

Eliseit, Horst. **Im Schatten des grossen Drachen.** Berlin: Safari-Verlag, 1966, 510 p.
A journalistic description of contemporary Korea, Japan, Taiwan, Hong Kong, Macao and Malaysia.

Fairbank, John King; Reischauer, Edwin Oldfather and Craig, Albert M. **East Asia: The Modern Transformation.** Boston: Houghton, 1965, 955 p.
An historical interpretation of East Asian civilization as it developed in the nineteenth and twentieth centuries, written mostly by Professor Fairbank. Like its predecessor, "East Asia: The Great Tradition," this volume evolved from lecture courses at Harvard dating back to 1937.

Fitzgerald, Charles Patrick. **A Concise History of East Asia.** New York: Praeger, 1966, 306 p.
A succinct survey of 4,000 years of the culture and politics of China, Japan, Korea and Southeast Asia by a leading Asian specialist.

Gushima, Kanesaburō. **Higashi Ajia no kokusai seiji.** Tokyo: Hyōronsha, 1971, 370 p.
A study of the international politics of East Asia.

Ho, Alfred K. **The Far East in World Trade: Developments and Growth Since 1945.** New York: Praeger, 1968, 388 p.
Spotty but useful data; stronger on description than analysis.

Iriye, Akira. **Across the Pacific: An Inner History of American-East Asian Relations.** New York: Harcourt, Brace and World, 1967, 361 p.
Using Chinese, Japanese and Western sources, the author examines the way Chinese, Japanese and Americans have regarded each other since 1780, their misperceptions, their common problems and how all this is related to their historical experiences and to the overall international system.

Iriye, Akira. **After Imperialism: The Search for a New Order in the Far East, 1921–1931.** Cambridge: Harvard University Press, 1965, 375 p.
An attempt at a new interpretation of the history of international relations in the Far East in the 1920s, with emphasis on Japanese and American foreign policies.

Kim, Young Hum. **East Asia's Turbulent Century.** New York: Appleton, 1966, 386 p.
A description of Western-influenced political, social, economic and ideological changes in East Asia from 1840 to 1965; supplemented with 49 major documents on U.S. relations with East Asia.

Kolb, Albert. **Ostasien: China, Japan, Korea; Geographie eines Kulturerdteiles.** Heidelberg: Quelle & Meyer, 1963, 608 p.
A detailed geography of China, Japan and Korea, containing also a wealth of information about historical and cultural developments in these countries.

Naville, Pierre. **La Guerre et la révolution. I: Guerres d'Asie: Vietnam et Corée.** Paris: Études et Documentation Internationales, 1967, 324 p.
A survey of the events of the 1949–56 phase of the Vietnamese and Korean conflicts, chronologically intermingled in one sequence.

CHINA

General

See also (Asia and the Pacific Area) General Surveys, p. 607; (Far East) General, p. 682; other subsections under China.

Adams, Ruth, *ed*. **Contemporary China.** New York: Pantheon Books, 1966, 336 p.
These essays on Communist China's international politics, economy, agriculture, population, science, education and culture by a group of highly respected scholars resulted from the 1966 Chicago China Conference.

Bauer, Wolfgang. **China und die Hoffnung auf Glück.** Munich: Carl Hanser Verlag, 1971, 703 p.
A cultural history of Chinese ideas about the good society and the role of the state. The concluding chapter offers some persuasive insights into the relation of Mao's thought to the long tradition which nourished it.

Bloodworth, Dennis. **The Chinese Looking Glass.** New York: Farrar, Straus and Giroux, 1967, 432 p.
An introduction to Chinese history, culture and contemporary problems by a Far Eastern correspondent for *The Observer* of London.

Bodard, Lucien. **Le Plus grand drame du monde: la Chine de Tseu Hi à Mao.** Paris: Gallimard, 1968, 333 p.
An account of China's rise to power by a well-known China-born journalist.

Buck, Pearl (Sydenstricker). **China as I See It.** New York: Day, 1970, 305 p.
A collection of articles, speeches and other writings by a very well-known writer. Edited by Theodore F. Harris.

Contemporary China. New York: Oxford University Press, 1955–68, 6 v.
A series of historical, geographical, economic and social studies, translations, documents, chronologies and bibliographies on Communist China and Taiwan. Edited by E. Stuart Kirby.

Franke, Wolfgang. **China and the West.** Columbia: University of South Carolina Press, 1967, 165 p.
Professor Franke, resident in China from 1937 to 1950, outlines the historical development of China's relations with the West. The German original appeared as "China und das Abendland" (Göttingen: Vandenhoeck und Ruprecht, 1962, 140 p.).

Geoffroy-Dechaume, François. **China Looks at the World: Reflections for a Dialogue: Eight Letters to T'Ang-Lin.** New York: Pantheon Books, 1967, 237 p.
A Frenchman's imaginative attempt to interpret China's present by examining its past.

Herrmann, Albert. **An Historical Atlas of China.** Chicago: Aldine Publishing Co., new ed., 1966, 88 p.
A new edition of a standard reference.

Hsü, Immanuel C. Y. **The Rise of Modern China.** New York: Oxford University Press, 1970, 830 p.
A masterful work of scholarship tracing political, intellectual, social and economic changes that have affected every phase of Chinese life from 1600 to the present.

Kitagawa, Joseph Mitsuo, *ed*. **Understanding Modern China.** Chicago: Quadrangle Books, 1969, 284 p.
The essays in this volume cover geography, political leadership, economy, ideology, political and foreign policy, Overseas Chinese and American perceptions of China.

Latourette, Kenneth Scott. **China.** Englewood Cliffs: Prentice-Hall, 1964, 152 p.
A succinct, well-coördinated survey by a highly respected China specialist.

Levenson, Joseph Richmond. **Confucian China and its Modern Fate.** Berkeley: University of California Press, 1958–65, 3 v.
A study of modern China in relation to the Confucian past. An important work, based on the study of Chinese, Japanese and Western-language sources.

Lindbeck, John Matthew Henry. **Understanding China: An Assessment of American Scholarly Resources.** New York: Praeger, 1971, 159 p.
Dr. Lindbeck, the Director of Columbia University's East Asian Institute until his

death in 1971, wrote this study at the request of the Ford Foundation. He provides a qualitative and quantitative assessment of the resources for the study of China and indicates subject areas needing further development.

Martin, Helmut. **Chinakunde in der Sowjetunion nach sowjetischen Quellen.** Hamburg: Institut für Asienkunde, 1972, 208 p.
A survey of China studies in the Soviet Union including an annotated bibliography of current Soviet works on China.

Pye, Lucian W. with Pye, Mary W. **China: An Introduction.** Boston: Little, Brown, 1972, 384 p.
A masterly introduction to the history and politics of contemporary China, by a professor at M.I.T.

Pye, Lucian W. **The Spirit of Chinese Politics: A Psychocultural Study of the Authority Crisis in Political Development.** Cambridge: M.I.T. Press, 1968, 255 p.
This work is an "interpretive and largely speculative essay" on the unique national and personality traits that have shaped Chinese political culture from the time of the Manchus to Maoism.

Schurmann, Herbert Franz and Schell, Orville, *eds.* **The China Reader.** New York: Random House, 1967, 3 v.
A comprehensive collection of writings by Chinese and Western scholars illustrating the rise and development of modern China.

Tregear, T. R. **A Geography of China.** Chicago: Aldine Publishing Co., 1966, 342 p.
A thorough survey, arranged in four sections: physical, historical, economic and social, and regional geography. The author also deals with Tibet, Taiwan, Hong Kong and Macao.

Recent History

See also General Works, p. 1; International Organization and Government, p. 96; War and Peace, p. 108; The World Since 1914, p. 129; (The United States) Biographies, Memoirs and Addresses, p. 218; Foreign Policy, p. 229; (Great Britain) Foreign Policy, p. 375; (Union of Soviet Socialist Republics) Relations with China, p. 555; (Asia and the Pacific Area) General Surveys, p. 607; (Far East) General, p. 682; other subsections under China.

Barnett, Arthur Doak. **China on the Eve of Communist Takeover.** New York: Praeger, 1963, 371 p.
In the two years 1947–1949 Mr. Barnett had the opportunity to travel widely through Nationalist-held China and in part of the area under communist control. This work is a selection of 23 field reports he wrote for the Institute of Current World Affairs during that period.

Bates, Miner Searle, *ed.* **China in Change: An Approach to Understanding.** New York: Friendship Press, 1969, 191 p.
Papers selected by a Christian scholar who seeks to correct erroneous stereotyped views of the country.

Belden, Jack. **China Shakes the World.** New York: Monthly Review Press, 1970, 524 p.
An American newspaper correspondent's reporting on the Chinese civil war, introduced by Professor Lattimore.

Berton, Peter Alexander Menquez and Wu, Eugene. **Contemporary China: A Research Guide.** Stanford: Hoover Institution on War, Revolution, and Peace, 1967, 695 p.
A valuable reference volume dealing with Chinese, Japanese, Russian and Western-language sources for the study of post-1949 Communist China and post-1945 Taiwan.

Bianco, Lucien. **Origins of the Chinese Revolution, 1915–1949.** Stanford: Stanford University Press, 1971, 223 p.
A slightly revised translation of a French study of Chinese Revolution, stressing particularly its rural roots. The French original appeared as "Les Origines de la révolution chinoise, 1915–1949" (Paris: Gallimard, 1967, 384 p.).

China Yearbook. Taipei: China Publishing Co.
A useful reference work published annually and containing a wealth of information about both Nationalist and Communist China.

Chou, Tse-tsung. **Research Guide to the May Fourth Movement: Intellectual Revolution in Modern China, 1915-1924.** Cambridge: Harvard University Press, 1963, 297 p.
The author's original study on the May Fourth Movement is supplemented by a bibliography and an annotated list of periodicals.

Clubb, Oliver Edmund. **20th Century China.** New York: Columbia University Press, 2d ed., 1972, 526 p.
A clearly written political history covering the end of the dynastic era, the "abortive experiment in republicanism," the emergence of Communism, and the admission of Communist China to the United Nations in 1971.

Davies, John Paton, Jr. **Dragon by the Tail: American, British, Japanese, and Russian Encounters with China and One Another.** New York: Norton, 1972, 448 p.
In these memoirs history blends with experience in a vivid panoramic picture of 50 years of Chinese war and revolution.

Domes, Jürgen. **Vertagte Revolution: die Politik der Kuomintang in China, 1923-1937.** Berlin: De Gruyter, 1969, 795 p.
A detailed and well-documented study of the policies of the Kuomintang between the death of Sun Yat-sen and the Japanese invasion of 1937. The author concludes that Chiang Kai-shek had laid very strong foundations for the modernization of China which, unfortunately, were destroyed by the Japanese and the subsequent military and political developments.

Fairbank, John King; Banno, Masataka and Yamamoto, Sumiko. **Japanese Studies of Modern China: A Bibliographical Guide to Historical and Social-Science Research on the 19th and 20th Centuries.** Cambridge: Harvard University Press, 1971, 331 p.
A useful reference, originally published in 1953.

Feuerwerker, Albert and Others, *eds*. **Approaches to Modern Chinese History.** Berkeley: University of California Press, 1967, 356 p.
Twelve essays on China's pre-1949 internal political and institutional history, intellectual life, traditional and semi-modern economy, and foreign relations, selected by the editors as a tribute to Professor John King Fairbank of Harvard.

Frillmann, Paul and Peck, Graham. **China: The Remembered Life.** Boston: Houghton, 1968, 291 p.
Mr. Frillmann went to China in 1936 as a Lutheran missionary and stayed on, first as wartime chaplain and soldier, then as peacetime State Department aide until 1953. A lively, informative account as written down by Mr. Peck, himself an old China hand.

Gray, Jack, *ed*. **Modern China's Search for a Political Form.** New York: Oxford University Press (for the Royal Institute of International Affairs), 1969, 379 p.
Essays examining the antecedents of Chinese communism and some of the factors that have shaped China's political climate.

Grieder, Jerome B. **Hu Shih and the Chinese Renaissance: Liberalism in the Chinese Revolution, 1917-1937.** Cambridge: Harvard University Press, 1970, 420 p.
A study of the thought and influence of a leading Chinese liberal. The author, a Harvard-trained scholar, aims particularly "to set forth a record of Hu's views on the great social, political, and intellectual problems that confronted the Chinese in the 1920s and 1930s."

Hahn, Emily. **China Only Yesterday, 1850-1950: A Century of Change.** Garden City: Doubleday, 1963, 423 p.
A broad, general account of China's contacts with the outside world, particularly the Western world.

Hou, Fu-wu. **Chinese Political Traditions.** Washington: Public Affairs Press, 1965, 130 p.
A professor of the University of Massachusetts does not share the view that the communist monolithic system on the mainland is a continuation of traditional Chinese socio-political concepts.

Hsu, Long-hsuen and Chang, Ming-kai, *comps*. **History of the Sino-Japanese War (1937-1947).** Taipei: Chung Wu, 1971, 642 p.
A translation of the Chinese summary of the 100-volume "History of the Sino-Japanese War (1937-1945)," published by the Military History Bureau of the Ministry of National Defense of the Republic of China.

Israel, John. **Student Nationalism in China, 1927-1937.** Stanford: Stanford University Press (for the Hoover Institution on War, Revolution, and Peace), 1966, 253 p.
An examination of the vital role of the university and middle-school élite in Chinese history and politics, and of how student nationalism contributed in a major way to the eventual victory of Mao Tsê-tung.

McAleavy, Henry. **The Modern History of China.** New York: Praeger, 1967, 392 p.
A survey of China since 1840 by a British scholar who lived in China from 1935 to 1950.

Melby, John F. **The Mandate of Heaven: Record of a Civil War, China 1945-49.** Toronto: University of Toronto Press, 1968, 313 p.
A former U.S. Foreign Service officer goes back to his personal letters and diaries to tell of his Chinese assignment during the critical years from Japan's defeat to the founding of the People's Republic of China.

Moseley, George. **China Since 1911.** New York: Harper and Row, 1969, 192 p.
A factual history of China from the revolution of 1911-12 to the present, with little interpretation.

Pye, Lucian W. **Warlord Politics: Conflict and Coalition in the Modernization of Republican China.** New York: Praeger, 1971, 212 p.
A historical case study by a distinguished scholar.

Röper, Erich. **Geteiltes China: eine völkerrechtliche Studie.** Mainz: v. Hase & Koehler, 1967, 320 p.
A study of the claims of Mao Tsê-tung and Chiang Kai-shek to represent the will of the entire Chinese people. The author's sympathies are with the Nationalist regime which, in his opinion, might even regain power on the mainland.

Scharping, Thomas. **Der demokratische Bund und seine Vorläufer, 1939-1949: chinesische Intelligenz zwischen Kuomintang und Kommunistischer Partei.** Hamburg: Institut für Asienkunde, 1972, 155 p.
A solid and well-done study of the China Democratic League.

Shieh, Milton J. T. **The Kuomintang: Selected Historical Documents, 1894-1969.** Jamaica: St. John's University Press, 1970, 434 p.
A useful reference by a leading member of Kuomintang.

Sih, Paul K. T., ed. **The Strenuous Decade: China's Nation-Building Efforts, 1927-1937.** Jamaica: St. John's University, 1970, 385 p.
The contributors to this symposium, sponsored by St. John's University, argue that the National Government of China had established a splendid record during the period from 1927 to 1937.

Tan, Chester C. **Chinese Political Thought in the Twentieth Century.** Garden City: Doubleday, 1971, 390 p.
An examination of the major doctrines of Chinese political thinkers since the Revolution of 1911.

Thomson, James C., Jr. **While China Faced West: American Reformers in Nationalist China, 1928-1937.** Cambridge: Harvard University Press, 1969, 310 p.
A study of the efforts of American Protestant missionaries and foundation representatives to reform Chinese rural society. The author is the son of Presbyterian educational missionaries who were attached to the University of Nanking.

Tien, Hung-mao. **Government and Politics in Kuomintang China, 1927-1937.** Stanford: Stanford University Press, 1972, 226 p.
A study attempting "to determine the effectiveness of the Nationalist party-government in unifying and ruling China" in the period from 1927 to 1937.

Tung, William L. **The Political Institutions of Modern China.** The Hague: Nijhoff, 1964, 408 p.
A former official and professor under the Nationalist regime outlines his country's twentieth-century constitutional development and governmental structure to 1928, and then analyzes Nationalist and communist political ideologies, institutions and programs.

Young, Arthur Nichols. **China's Nation-Building Effort, 1927-1937: The Financial and Economic Record.** Stanford: Hoover Institution Press, 1971, 553 p.

A detailed and favorable account of the economic accomplishments of the Chinese Nationalist government, by an American financial adviser from 1927 to 1947.

Yu, George T. **Party Politics in Republican China: The Kuomintang, 1912-1924.** Berkeley: University of California Press, 1966, 203 p.
A scholarly survey of the development of the Kuomintang from the founding of the Republic in 1912 to 1924, when the Party was reorganized Soviet-style at the First Party Congress.

Chinese Communism: The Communist Regime

General

See also Political Factors, p. 12; (International Law) Miscellaneous, p. 94; The Postwar World, p. 178; Eastern Europe and the Soviet Bloc, p. 358; (The United States) Biographies, Memoirs and Addresses, p. 218; Foreign Policy, p. 229; (Great Britain) Biographies, Memoirs and Addresses, p. 369; Foreign Policy, p. 375; (Union of Soviet Socialist Republics) Relations with China, p. 555; (Asia and the Pacific Area) General Surveys, p. 607; Tibet, p. 654; Indian-Chinese Relations, p. 670; (Far East) General, p. 682; The Korean War, p. 728; The Vietnam War, p. 739; other subsections under China.

Abegg, Lily. **Vom Reich der Mitte zu Mao Tse-tung.** Lucerne: Bucher, 1966, 208 p.
An impressive volume of photographs and commentary describing Mao Tsê-tung's rise to power, by a well-known German journalist.

Barnett, Arthur Doak. **Cadres, Bureaucracy, and Political Power in Communist China.** New York: Columbia University Press, 1967, 563 p.
A foremost China scholar at Columbia University bases this study of the organization and operation of the political system of Communist China mainly on interviews with ex-cadres active within the Communist Party and the government bureaucracy.

Barnett, Arthur Doak. **China after Mao.** Princeton: Princeton University Press, 1967, 287 p.
A discussion of Mao's prescriptions for the future and of the succession to Mao's post. Well over half the book contains key documents translated from the Chinese.

Barnett, Arthur Doak, ed. **Chinese Communist Politics in Action.** Seattle: University of Washington Press, 1969, 620 p.
A volume of essays on China's changing political culture.

Barnett, Arthur Doak. **Communist China: The Early Years, 1949-55.** New York: Praeger, 1964, 336 p.
A leading student of contemporary China bases this book on his reports written on the mainland at the time of the communist takeover of China and later from the vantage point of Hong Kong.

Bartke, Wolfgang. **Das Politbüro des 8. Zentralkomitees der Kommunistischen Partei Chinas.** Wiesbaden: Harrassowitz, 1969, 165 p.
A thorough compendium of biographical information on the members of the Chinese Politburo, 1964-67.

Biehl, Max. **Die chinesische Volkskommune im "Grossen Sprung" und danach.** Hamburg: Verlag Weltarchiv, 1965, 245 p.
A well-documented study of the successes and failures of the commune system in Communist China.

Boorman, Scott A. **The Protracted Game.** New York: Oxford University Press, 1969, 242 p.
An imaginatively argued hypothesis that the Chinese game of *wei-ch'i*, or *go*, provides valuable insights for a deeper understanding of Mao Tsê-tung's revolutionary strategy.

Burlatskii, Fedor Mikhailovich. **Maoizm—ugroza sotsializmu v Kitae.** Moscow: Izd-vo Politicheskoi Literatury, 1968, 192 p.
A Soviet social scientist indicts Maoism as a fundamentally anti-Marxist philosophy, rooted in China's agrarian tradition and constituting a "threat to socialism in China."

Chai, Winberg, ed. **Essential Works of Chinese Communism.** New York: Pica Press, 1970, 464 p.
Introduction to Chinese communism from the first manifesto of 1922 through major works of Mao, Liu and others in 1968. Documents are preceded by explanatory notes.

Chai, Winberg. **The New Politics of Communist China: Modernization Process of a Developing Nation.** Pacific Palisades (Cal.): Goodyear Publishing Company, 1972, 305 p.
An introductory description and analysis of the modernization process of China from the 1950s to the 1970s.

Chassin, Lionel Max. **The Communist Conquest of China: A History of the Civil War, 1945-1949.** Cambridge: Harvard University Press, 1965, 264 p.
A French general, who had access to the most authoritative French sources, including intelligence reports of the Deuxième Bureau, traces the rise of Mao's China. The French original appeared as "La Conquête de la Chine par Mao Tse'-tung (1945-1949)" (Paris: Payot, 1952, 244 p.).

Ch'ên, Hsi-ên, *comp*. **The Chinese Communist Regime: Documents and Commentary.** New York: Praeger, 1967, 344 p.
Texts of laws and directives, with a few official policy statements, selected to show how government and party organizations exercise control in Communist China.

Ch'ên, Jerome. **Mao and the Chinese Revolution.** New York: Oxford University Press, 1965, 419 p.
A scholarly, factual treatise on Mao's role in the Chinese Revolution and its aftermath.

Chen, Yung Ping. **Chinese Political Thought: Mao Tse-tung and Liu Shao-chi.** The Hague: Nijhoff, 1966, 118 p.
The philosophical basis of the Chinese revolution as traced through the thought and theories of its two main ideologists. The Sino-Soviet ideological dispute is also discussed.

Cheng, Peter. **A Chronology of the People's Republic of China from October 1, 1949.** Totowa (N.J.): Littlefield, Adams, 1972, 347 p.
A useful reference covering the events through 1970.

China after the Cultural Revolution. New York: Random House, 1970, 247 p.
A survey, made up of selections from *The Bulletin of the Atomic Scientists*, of how Mao's China fares in the fields of technology, economics, politics and foreign affairs.

China! Inside the People's Republic. New York: Bantam Books, 1972, 432 p.
A comprehensive and informative report of the fifteen-member delegation of the Committee of Concerned Asian Scholars that toured China in the summer of 1971.

Chou, Eric. **A Man Must Choose.** New York: Knopf, 1963, 301 p.
An account by a journalist and intellectual of spying and counterspying in Red China.

Chu, Valentin. **Ta Ta, Tan Tan. "Fight Fight, Talk Talk . . . "** New York: Norton, 1963, 320 p.
A readable and informative analysis of Communist China, including two sprightly chapters on the bizarre quality of Chinese statistics and the vagaries of dragonology (the Chinese counterpart of Kremlinology).

Chūgoku Kyōsantō shiryō shū. Tokyo: Nihon Shuppan Sentā, 1970–.
A collection of documents on the history of the Communist Party of China from 1918 to 1945, prepared by the China Section of the Japanese Institute of International Affairs. The 9th volume appeared in 1974.

Clubb, Oliver Edmund. **Communism in China: As Reported from Hankow in 1932.** New York: Columbia University Press, 1968, 123 p.
The report of an American who, as Vice Consul in Hankow, recognized early the importance of the revolutionary movement in China.

Cohen, Arthur A. **The Communism of Mao Tse-tung.** Chicago: University of Chicago Press, 1964, 210 p.
Mr. Cohen, using Chinese and Russian sources, concludes that Mao's originality lies in the practice of communism, and that he has added little that is new to its basic theories.

Cohen, Jerome Alan, *ed*. **Contemporary Chinese Law: Research Problems and Perspectives.** Cambridge: Harvard University Press, 1970, 380 p.
Thirty specialists in various disciplines survey the developments in Communist Chinese law.

Cohen, Jerome Alan. **The Criminal Process in the People's Republic of China, 1949-1963: An Introduction.** Cambridge: Harvard University Press, 1968, 706 p.

A useful study by a Harvard professor, including excerpts from legal documents, a glossary and a lengthy bibliography.

Collotti Pischel, Enrica. **Storia della rivoluzione cinese.** Rome: Riuniti, 1972, 450 p.
An Italian scholar examines the popular roots of the Chinese Communist Revolution.

Communist China Problem Research Series. Hong Kong: Union Research Institute.
A useful series of monographs on Communist China. Through 1971, 51 volumes have been published. Of special importance is the subseries "Communist China," published annually since 1955 and covering current events. The latest volume, for the year 1970, was published in 1971.

Contemporary China. Toronto: Canadian Institute of International Affairs, 1968, 138 p.
Papers presented at a University of Guelph conference in April 1968.

Croizier, Ralph C., ed. **China's Cultural Legacy and Communism.** New York: Praeger, 1970, 313 p.
A selection of essays and documents showing the development of communist policy toward art, history, philosophy and religion, language and literature.

Crook, Isabel and Crook, David. **The First Years of Yangyi Commune.** New York: Humanities Press, 1966, 288 p.
The authors, long residents of China, insist that communes arose from popular response to needs, not to Peking edicts and that they are a success, and preferable to coöperatives.

Deliusin, Lev Petrovich and Sukharchuk, G. D., eds. **Kitai segodnia.** Moscow: "Nauka," 1969, 336 p.
A comprehensive Soviet study of contemporary China.

Dinić, Jordan and Lazić, Dušan. **Narodna Republika Kina: koncepcije o socijalističkom razvoju i politika u medunarodjnim odnosima.** Belgrade: Institut za medjunarodni radnički pokret, 1970, 370 p.
A Jugoslav survey of Communist China's political development and foreign policy.

Documents of Chinese Communist Party Central Committee, Sept. 1956-Apr. 1969. Volume 1. Hong Kong: Union Research Institute, 1971, 838 p.
A collection of documents of the 8th National Congress and the 8th Central Committee of the Chinese Communist Party. A valuable source for the study of contemporary Chinese affairs.

Domes, Jürgen. **Politik und Herrschaft in Rotchina.** Stuttgart: Kohlhammer, 1965, 183 p.
Basic information on the internal politics, structure of leadership and methods of ruling in Communist China. The author also provides a useful chronology of the Communist Party of China to 1965.

Dutt, Gargi. **Rural Communes of China: Organizational Problems.** New York: Asia Publishing House (for the Indian School of International Studies), 1968, 207 p.
A study, based primarily on Chinese sources, by an Indian scholar who studied at Peking University from 1956 to 1958 and was a Research Associate at the East Asian Research Center, Harvard University, from 1962 to 1963.

Elegant, Robert S. **The Center of the World: Communism and the Mind of China.** New York: Funk & Wagnalls, 2d rev. ed., 1968, 477 p.
Mr. Elegant, who has spent many years in Asia, mostly as correspondent for *Newsweek*, analyzes the psychological and cultural influences on communist leaders and on the nation they have created.

Elegant, Robert S. **Mao's Great Revolution.** New York: World Publishing Co., 1971, 478 p.
This well-narrated attempt to make sense of China's internal politics suffers from the author's assumption that the actors are motivated solely by power considerations and not at all by those that are ideological or patriotic.

Engelborghs-Bertels, M.; Dekkers, R. and Ginsburgh, Victor. **La République Populaire de Chine: cadres institutionels et réalisations.** Brussels: Université Libre de Bruxelles, Institut de Sociologie, 1963, 2 v.
In the first volume, "L'Histoire et le droit," Miss Engelborghs-Bertels discusses contemporary China's continuing revolutions since 1923, foreign affairs and public law,

while Mr. Dekkers deals with civil and penal law. In the second volume, "La Planification et la croissance économique, 1949–1959," Mr. Ginsburgh provides a descriptive view of Chinese economic developments since 1949.

Feuerwerker, Albert, ed. **History in Communist China.** Cambridge: M.I.T. Press, 1968, 382 p.
A review of the work done by communist Chinese historians, sometimes to the dissatisfaction of the political rulers.

Fitzgerald, Charles Patrick. **The Birth of Communist China.** New York: Praeger, rev. and enl. ed., 1966, 288 p.
A completely revised and updated edition of "Revolution in China" (1952) by a leading student of China.

Glaubitz, Joachim, ed. **Opposition gegen Mao: Abendgespräche am Yenshan und andere politische Dokumente.** Olten: Walter-Verlag, 1969, 217 p.
A selection of writings criticizing the policies of Chairman Mao, originally published in the Chinese People's Republic in the early 1960s.

Guillain, Robert. **When China Wakes.** New York: Walker, 1966, 268 p.
A writer, whose knowledge of China dates back to 1937, suggests that, as history is now progressing, Communist China might well dominate the world within the next 30 years. The French original was published as "Dans trente ans, la Chine" (Paris: Éditions du Seuil, 1965, 301 p.).

Guillermaz, Jacques. **Histoire du Parti Communiste Chinois.** Paris: Payot, 1968–72, 2v.
The first volume of this well-documented history of the Chinese Communist Party deals with the bitter struggles of the Party from its origins up to the founding of the People's Republic of China; the second volume, based largely on information brought to light by the Cultural Revolution, traces the history of the Party through March 1, 1972. The English translation of the first volume appeared as "A History of the Chinese Communist Party, 1921–1949" (New York: Random House, 1972, 477 p.).

Harrison, James Pinckney. **The Communists and Chinese Peasant Rebellions: A Study in the Rewriting of Chinese History.** New York: Atheneum, 1969, 363 p.
An analysis of Chinese Communist historiography dealing with Chinese peasant revolts which, in the author's words, are "the only dramatic evidence of class struggle in Chinese history."

Harrison, James Pinckney. **The Long March to Power: A History of the Chinese Communist Party, 1921–1972.** New York: Praeger, 1972, 680 p.
An encyclopedic survey.

Hinton, William. **Fanshen: A Documentary of Revolution in a Chinese Village.** New York: Monthly Review Press, 1967, 637 p.
A former U.S. Office of War Information and UNRRA official, who remained in China until 1953, was an observer to a work team dispatched jointly by the People's Government and the Chinese Communist Party Committee of Lucheng County to investigate progress in land reform. This book is based on extensive notes taken in 1948.

Ho, Ping-ti and Tsou, Tang, eds. **China in Crisis.** Chicago: University of Chicago Press, 1968, 2 v. in 3 pts.
Papers with commentaries resulting from two conferences which assembled 70 world-renowned scholars and non-academic experts who discussed the process of change leading to the establishment of the communist regime in China. Volume I has the title "China's Heritage and the Communist Political System," and volume 2, "China's Policies in Asia and America's Alternatives."

Hou, Fu-wu. **A Short History of Chinese Communism.** Englewood Cliffs: Prentice-Hall, 1967, 245 p.
A leading Sinologist examines the economic, cultural and social policies and accomplishments of the Peking regime since 1949.

Hsiung, James Chieh. **Ideology and Practice: The Evolution of Chinese Communism.** New York: Praeger, 1970, 359 p.
This ambitious survey of Maoist thought contains some interesting ideas about the neo-Confucian and Taoist influences on Chinese Marxism-Leninism.

Hudelot, Claude. **La Longue marche.** Paris: Julliard, 1971, 365 p.
This well-organized collection of primary and secondary source material, with intelli-

gent commentary and narrative, constitutes a useful introduction to a crucial period of modern Chinese Communist history.

Ichiko, Chūzō. **Kindai Chūgoku no seiji to shakai.** Tokyo: Tōkyō Daigaku Shuppankai, 1971, 506 p.
A collection of four essays on the politics and society of modern China, by one of Japan's foremost scholars in the field. There is an appendix providing instructions on how to conduct research on modern China in Japan.

Jacobs, Daniel Norman and Baerwald, Hans H. **Chinese Communism: Selected Documents.** New York: Harper and Row, 1963, 242 p.
A collection of documents, with commentaries, published as background material for the interpretation of Sino-Soviet relations from 1957 to 1962 and their historical origins.

Joffe, Ellis. **Party and Army: Professionalism and Political Control in the Chinese Officer Corps, 1949-1964.** Cambridge: East Asian Research Center, Harvard University, 1965, 198 p.
A detailed analysis, based largely on translated Chinese publications, of the relationship between party leadership and the officer corps in Communist China.

Kao, Chung-yen, *ed.* **Chung-kung Jen-shih Pien-tung (1959-1969).** Hong Kong: Union Research Institute, 1970, 915 p.
A most useful reference volume on the changes of personnel in Communist China (1959-1969).

Karnow, Stanley. **Mao and China: From Revolution to Revolution.** New York: Viking, 1972, 592 p.
A reserved, skeptical and ironic interpretation of Mao Tsê-tung's role in the Chinese Revolution.

Karol, K. S., *pseud.* (Karol Kewes). **China: The Other Communism.** New York: Hill and Wang, 1967, 474 p.
Observations on Chinese Communism, based on a four-months' trip through China in 1965 and interviews with political and intellectual figures. The French edition is entitled "La Chine de Mao: l'autre communisme" (Paris: Laffont, 1966, 483 p.).

Klatt, Werner, *ed.* **The Chinese Model: A Political, Economic and Social Survey.** New York: Oxford University Press (for the Institute of Modern Asian Studies, University of Hong Kong), 1965, 233 p.
A collection of critical essays on Communist China's economic, political, cultural and foreign policy problems.

Kung Fei huo-kuo shih liao hui pien. Taipei: Chung-hua Min-kuo K'ai-kuo Wu-shih Nien Wên-hsien Pien-tsuan Wei-yüan-hui, 1964, 4 v.
An immense compilation of source materials on Chinese Communist seizure of power in China.

Leng, Shao-chuan. **Justice in Communist China: A Survey of the Judicial System of the Chinese People's Republic.** Dobbs Ferry (N.Y.): Oceana Publications, 1967, 196 p.
A pioneering study by a professor of government and foreign affairs at the University of Virginia.

Lewis, John Wilson. **Leadership in Communist China.** Ithaca: Cornell University Press, 1963, 305 p.
A study of the principles and doctrine of party leadership, especially in the period from 1958 to 1962.

Lewis, John Wilson, *ed.* **Major Doctrines of Communist China.** New York: Norton, 1964, 343 p.
Selections from the China mainland press to show the development of the Chinese Communist Party from its formation in 1921.

Lewis, John Wilson, *ed.* **Party Leadership and Revolutionary Power in China.** New York: Cambridge University Press, 1970, 422 p.
Twelve American and British scholars discuss Communist China's political system, the divergent attitudes toward the organization of power, and the changing roles of the Party and its élite.

Lindbeck, John Matthew Henry, *ed.* **China: Management of a Revolutionary Society.** Seattle: University of Washington Press, 1971, 391 p.
A collection of papers given at the 1969 Cuernavaca conference of China scholars.

Liu, Alan P. L. **Communications and National Integration in Communist China.** Berkeley: University of California Press, 1971, 225 p.
An examination of the organization and conduct of Communist Chinese agitation and propaganda.

Liu, William Thomas, *ed.* **Chinese Society under Communism: A Reader.** New York: Wiley, 1967, 496 p.
Selections from writings of Chinese and Western scholars.

Lowe, Donald Ming-dah. **The Function of "China" in Marx, Lenin, and Mao.** Berkeley: University of California Press, 1966, 200 p.
A study of the historical significance of the Marxian, Leninist and Maoist ideas of China.

Macciocchi, Maria Antonietta. **Daily Life in Revolutionary China.** New York: Monthly Review Press, 1972, 506 p.
An admiring report on a visit to China by a Communist member of the Italian Chamber of Deputies. The Italian original appeared as "Dalla Cina: dopo la Rivoluzione Culturale" (Milan: Feltrinelli, 1971, 483 p.).

MacFarquhar, Roderick. **China under Mao: Politics Takes Command.** Cambridge: M.I.T. Press, 1966, 525 p.
A selection of articles from *The China Quarterly*.

MacInnis, Donald E. **Religious Policy and Practice in Communist China: A Documentary History.** New York: Macmillan, 1972, 392 p.
A useful collection of documents and articles translated from original Chinese sources.

Mehnert, Klaus. **Peking and the New Left: At Home and Abroad.** Berkeley: University of California, Center for Chinese Studies, 1969, 156 p.
A brief survey, illustrated with a supplement of documents, of the ideological developments in Red China in 1967 and 1968, and of the relations of Peking with the New Left in the Western World. The German original was published as "Peking und die neue Linke" (Stuttgart: Deutsche Verlags-Anstalt, 1969, 149 p.).

Meisner, Maurice. **Li Ta-chao and the Origins of Chinese Marxism.** Cambridge: Harvard University Press, 1967, 326 p.
A study of the intellectual evolution of China's first Marxist and of the early reception and transformation of Marxist ideas in China. Li, now regarded as a martyr, was executed in 1927.

Myrdal, Jan. **Report from a Chinese Village.** New York: Pantheon Books, 1965, 373 p.
Mr. Myrdal, a Swedish anthropologist, and Mrs. Myrdal lived in the village of Liu Ling, in northern Shensi, for a month in late 1962. The book gives, in the form of biographies of a number of its inhabitants, accounts of changes in life and thought of the villagers. Originally published in Sweden as "Rapport från Kinesisk" (Stockholm: Norstedt, 1963, 371 p.).

Myrdal, Jan and Kessle, Gun. **China: The Revolution Continued.** New York: Pantheon Books, 1971, 201 p.
A sequel to "Report from a Chinese Village," displaying the author's enthusiasm for the Chinese achievements. The original appeared as "Kina: revolutionen går vidare" (Stockholm: Norstedt, 1970, 157 p.).

Nakajima, Mineo. **Gendai Chūgoku ron: ideologi to seiji no nai teki kōsatsu.** Tokyo: Aoki Shoten, 1971, 354 p.
A study of the politics and ideology of contemporary China, written by one of Japan's chief experts on China.

Nomura, Kōichi. **Chūgoku kakumei no shisō.** Tokyo: Iwanami Shoten, 1971, 372 p.
A study of Chinese revolutionary thought, beginning with the May Fourth Movement of 1919.

North, Robert Carver. **Chinese Communism.** New York: McGraw-Hill, 1966, 256 p.
A Stanford professor of political science surveys adaptations of Marxist-Leninist ideas to conditions in China. Useful appendixes include a chronology of China from 1644 to the explosion of the nuclear device in 1964, a biographical register and bibliography.

North, Robert Carver and Eudin, Xenia Joukoff. **M. N. Roy's Mission to China.** Berkeley: University of California Press, 1963, 399 p.

A collection of documentary materials with analysis, relating to Roy's mission to China in 1927 on behalf of the Comintern; a helpful contribution in unraveling the tangled threads of the Communist-Kuomintang rupture in that year.

Ōkubo, Yasushi. **Chūgoku Kyōsantō shi.** Tokyo: Hara Shobō, 1971, 2 v.
A Japanese history of the Communist Party of China.

Pak, Hyobom, *ed*. **Documents of the Chinese Communist Party, 1927-1930.** Hong Kong: Union Research Institute, 1971, 769 p.
Translations of documents published in the internal Party publication "Chung-yang T'ung-hsin," the purpose of which "was to offer clearcut interpretations and explanations of party policies." An important source.

Pang, Thérèse. **Les Communes populaires rurales en Chine.** Fribourg: Éditions Universitaires, 1967, 208 p.
A methodical study of the people's communes in Communist China.

Rue, John Emery. **Mao Tse-tung in Opposition, 1927-1935.** Stanford: Stanford University Press (for the Hoover Institution on War, Revolution, and Peace), 1966, 387 p.
A detailed study based on Chinese and Western sources of Mao's difficult and crucial years from 1927 to the Tsun-yi Conference in 1935, the date when he actually won control of the Party.

Rumiantsev, Aleksei Matveevich. **Istoki i evolutsiia "Idei Mao Tsze-duna" (Ob antimarksistskoi sushchnosti maoizma).** Moscow: Izd-vo "Nauka," 1972, 380 p.
A prominent Soviet social scientist examines critically Chinese Communism and questions whether Mao's China can be considered a socialist country.

Scalapino, Robert Anthony, *ed*. **Elites in the People's Republic of China.** Seattle: University of Washington Press, 1972, 672 p.
A well-documented and wide-ranging collection of essays.

Schram, Stuart R. **The Political Thought of Mao Tse-tung.** New York: Praeger, rev. and enl. ed., 1969, 479 p.
Following a long introduction analyzing the origins of Mao's thought, the direction it is taking and its probable impact on the world, the author gives translations of many of Mao's works which best illustrate his analysis.

Schurmann, Herbert Franz. **Ideology and Organization in Communist China.** Berkeley: University of California Press, enl. ed., 1969, 642 p.
An enlarged edition of a scholarly study, first published in 1966. This important work is based on Chinese and Japanese sources.

Schwartz, Benjamin I. **Communism and China: Ideology in Flux.** Cambridge: Harvard University Press, 1968, 254 p.
A collection of the author's writings showing the evolution of China in terms of its internal development and of its relations with the communist world.

Selden, Mark. **The Yenan Way in Revolutionary China.** Cambridge: Harvard University Press, 1971, 311 p.
A vivid history of the Chinese Communist base areas during the war years. It suggests that the Yenan experience gave the later rulers of China a unique education in, and model for, government.

Sewell, William Gawan. **I Stayed in China.** South Brunswick (N.J.): A. S. Barnes, 1966, 221 p.
Recollections of China from 1947 to 1952, by a Quaker who during that period taught chemistry at a Chinese university.

Sheng, Yueh. **Sun Yat-sen University in Moscow and the Chinese Revolution.** Lawrence: University of Kansas, Center for East Asian Studies, 1971, 270 p.
Reminiscences by one of the Chinese Bolsheviks who lived and studied in the Soviet Union from 1926 through 1932 and was a member of the Central Committee of the Chinese Communist Party.

Shibata, Minoru. **Shū On-rai no jidai.** Tokyo: Chūō Kōronsha, 1971, 268 p.
An analysis of China in the era of Chou En-lai, i.e., since the beginning of the Cultural Revolution.

Sladkovskii, M. I. and Others. **Antimarksistskaia sushchnost' vzgliadov i politiki Mao Tsze-duna.** Moscow: Izd-vo Polit. Lit-ry, 1969, 303 p.
Soviet essays on the anti-Marxist nature of Mao Tsê-tung's views and policies.

Snow, Edgar. **The Long Revolution.** New York: Random House, 1972, 269 p.
  These last notes of the journalist, who for many years has explained China to the world, include interviews with Mao and Chou in 1970.

Snow, Helen Foster (Nym Wales). **The Chinese Communists.** Westport (Conn.): Greenwood, 1972, 398 p.
  In this volume the author has updated her 1937 "Red Dust" interviews with expanded biographical material on the individuals who were to become China's new élite.

Solomon, Richard H. **Mao's Revolution and the Chinese Political Culture.** Berkeley: University of California Press, 1971, 604 p.
  An analysis demonstrating that Mao's principal task in reshaping the Chinese polity has been to change the way people think: to make modern men out of traditional.

Steinhaus, Fritz C. **Rot-Asien 1985: China bereitet die Geschichtskatastrophe vor.** Würzburg: Marienburg-Verlag, 1966, 326 p.
  An attempt to foretell the development of Communist China during the next two decades. In the author's view only around 1985 will Red China become a real threat to the Western World.

Sugino, Akio. **Chūgoku shakaishugi no tenkai.** Tokyo: Mineruba Shobō, 1971, 346 p.
  A study of the development of socialist institutions in China.

Suyin, Han. **China in the Year 2001.** New York: Basic Books, 1967, 268 p.
  A utopian prognosis, by an admirer of Chairman Mao, based partly on conversations with Chinese leaders.

Suyin, Han. **The Morning Deluge: Mao Tsetung and the Chinese Revolution, 1893-1954.** Boston: Little, Brown, 1972, 571 p.
  The first of two volumes of a passionate, enthusiastic and worshipful interpretation of Mao's achievements.

Swarup, Shanti. **A Study of the Chinese Communist Movement.** New York: Oxford University Press, 1966, 289 p.
  A new interpretation of the developments of Chinese Communist policies in the years from 1927 to 1935. The author, an Indian scholar, attributes the communist successes primarily to Mao's ideas that "in China the national and social revolutions were inseparable and must be fought simultaneously."

Terrill, Ross. **800,000,000: The Real China.** Boston: Atlantic (Little, Brown), 1972, 235 p.
  An Australian journalist and Harvard scholar distills his 1971 travel notes into a vivid picture of life in China. His reflections on the shaping of Chinese diplomacy and on the tensions in Chinese intellectual life are particularly instructive.

Thornton, Richard C. **The Comintern and the Chinese Communists, 1928-1931.** Seattle: University of Washington Press, 1969, 246 p.
  A well-documented description of how the Comintern directed the Chinese Communist Party to establish bases (by means of guerrilla warfare and subversion) in areas of the Chinese countryside out of reach of Kuomintang forces.

Townsend, James R. **Political Participation in Communist China.** Berkeley: University of California Press, 1967, 233 p.
  A study of the roles of various classes of people in the task of mobilizing unified popular support behind the communist program.

Trager, Frank N. and Henderson, William, eds. **Communist China, 1949-1969: A Twenty-Year Appraisal.** New York: New York University Press (for the American-Asian Educational Exchange), 1970, 356 p.
  Essays on various aspects of mainland China's society and politics. The editors argue that any preponderant power on the Asian mainland threatens U.S. security.

Ts'ai, Hsiao-ch'ien. **Chiang-hsi Su-ch'ü: Hung Chün Hsi-ts'uan hui-i.** Taipei: Chung Kung Yen-chiu Tsa-chih-shê, 1970, 414 p.
  A former leading Chinese Communist, now residing in Taiwan, describes the Kiangsi Soviet regime and the Long March of the Chinese Red Army in 1934-35.

Ts'ao, Po-i. **Chiang-hsi Su-wei-ai chih chien-li chi ch'i pêng-hui (1931-1934).** Taipei: Kuo-li Chêng-chih Ta-hsüeh Tung-ya Yen-chiu So, 1969, 690 p.
  A well-documented study of the Kiangsi Soviet in China, the first communist regime that was set up in 1931 and was dissolved by the Nationalists in 1934.

ASIA AND THE PACIFIC AREA

Tsien, Tche-Hao. **La République Populaire de Chine: droit constitutionnel et institutions.** Paris: Librairie Générale de Droit, 1970, 646 p.
A study of Red China's constitutional laws and institutions, by an author with Maoist sympathies.

Van Dorn, Harold Archer. **A Decade of Communist Rule.** New York: Pageant Press, 1963, 99 p.
A short, highly critical review of Communist China's revolutionary changes in politics, industry and science, by a retired Kent State University political scientist with extensive experience in China.

Van Slyke, Lyman P., ed. **The Chinese Communist Movement.** Stanford: Stanford University Press, 1968, 274 p.
This report, prepared by the Military Intelligence Division of the U.S. War Department in 1945, was originally published in 1952 as an appendix to the transcript of the Senate hearings on the Institute of Pacific Relations. The critics of the State Department claimed that the conclusions of this report were not taken into consideration by those who decided the United States policy toward China.

Van Slyke, Lyman P. **Enemies and Friends: The United Front in Chinese Communist History.** Stanford: Stanford University Press, 1967, 330 p.
A study of the development of the united front, a principal element of Mao's strategy and one which figures prominently in the Chinese communist movement.

Vogel, Ezra Feivel. **Canton under Communism: Programs and Politics in a Provincial Capital, 1949-1968.** Cambridge: Harvard University Press, 1969, 448 p.
A socio-political history of the building and adapting of a new communist order, based on an official Cantonese communist newspaper and on interviews with former citizens.

Wang, Chien-min. **Chung-kuo kung-ch'an-tang shih kao.** Taipei: The Author, 1965, 3 v.
A massive history of the Chinese Communist Party.

Welch, Holmes. **Buddhism under Mao.** Cambridge: Harvard University Press, 1972, 666 p.
A study of the complex and important consequences of the struggle between God and Caesar in a Chinese setting.

Whitaker, Donald P. and Others. **Area Handbook for People's Republic of China.** Washington: G.P.O., 1972, 729 p.
A useful reference volume with a bibliography, prepared by the Foreign Area Studies at the American University.

Wilson, Dick. **The Long March 1935: The Epic of Chinese Communism's Survival.** New York: Viking, 1972, 331 p.
A study by a veteran journalist and Asian expert.

Wint, Guy. **Communist China's Crusade: Mao's Road to Power and the New Campaign for World Revolution.** New York: Praeger, 1965, 136 p.
Mr. Wint, long a writer on Asia for *The Observer*, analyzes the rise of communism in China and Sino-Soviet relations.

The Cultural Revolution

See also other subsections under China.

Barcata, Louis. **China in the Throes of the Cultural Revolution: An Eye Witness Report.** New York: Hart, 1968, 299 p.
An Austrian correspondent, visitor to China in 1967, reports on the power struggle in Mao's China. The German original was published as "China in der Kulturrevolution: Ein Augenzeugenbericht" (Vienna: Molden, 1967, 318 p.).

Baum, Richard with Bennett, Louise B., eds. **China in Ferment: Perspectives on the Cultural Revolution.** Englewood Cliffs: Prentice-Hall, 1971, 246 p.
A compendium of essays on the Cultural Revolution.

Bennett, Gordon A. and Montaperto, Ronald N. **Red Guard: The Political Biography of Dai Hsiao-ai.** Garden City: Doubleday, 1972, 258 p.
Two American students of sociology and sinology have based this account of the Cultural Revolution on interviews with a leader of the Red Guard who left China for Hong Kong in November 1967.

Blumer, Giovanni. **Die chinesische Kulturrevolution 1965/67.** Frankfurt: Europäische Verlagsanstalt, 1968, 399 p.
   The author of this study thinks that the Chinese Cultural Revolution is a significant advance in the development of communism and that it will strengthen Mao Tsê-tung's position within the world communistic movement. Mr. Blumer was a teacher at the Institute for Foreign Languages in Shanghai at the time of the events he is describing.

Bovin, Aleksandr Evgen'evich and Deliusin, Lev Petrovich. **Politicheskii krizis v Kitae: sobytiia i prichiny.** Moscow: Izd-vo Politicheskoi Literatury, 1968, 182 p.
   A Soviet study of the Cultural Revolution in China, attributing to Mao Tsê-tung and his followers the intent to overthrow the achievements of socialism.

CCP Documents of the Great Proletarian Cultural Revolution, 1966-1967. Hong Kong: Union Research Institute, 1968, 692 p.
   An indispensable collection of documents for the study of Chinese Communism, collected from Chinese Communist publications and published both in Chinese and in English translation.

Chao, Tsung. **Wen Ko yün-tung li-ch'eng shu-lüeh.** Hong Kong: Yu-lien Yen-chiu So, 1971, 413 p.
   The first volume of a detailed and well-documented survey of the Cultural Revolution.

Chiang, Hsüeh-wen. **Chung Kung wen-hua ta ko-ming yü hung-wei-ping.** Taipei: Kuo-chi Kuan-hsi Yen-chiu So, Kuo-li Cheng-chih Ta-hsüeh, 1969, 734 p.
   A detailed account of the Red Guards in China's Cultural Revolution, by a researcher at the Nationalist Chinese Institute of International Relations in Taiwan.

Dutt, Gargi and Dutt, Vidya Prakash. **China's Cultural Revolution.** New York: Asia Publishing House, 1970, 260 p.
   An attempt by two Indian experts on contemporary Chinese history to describe the origins, course and consequences of what they call "one of the most convulsive events in recent history."

Esmein, Jean. **La Révolution culturelle chinoise.** Paris: Éditions du Seuil, 1970, 347 p.
   The author, an attaché at the French Embassy in Peking from 1965 through 1968, gives one of the most convincing and thorough accounts available of the great Chinese Cultural Revolution. The English edition appeared as "The Chinese Cultural Revolution" (Garden City: Anchor Books, 1973, 346 p.).

Fan, Kuang Huan, *ed.* **The Chinese Cultural Revolution: Selected Documents.** New York: Monthly Review Press, 1968, 320 p.
   Official texts from Communist Chinese sources.

Granqvist, Hans. **The Red Guard: A Report on Mao's Revolution.** New York: Praeger, 1967, 159 p.
   A Scandinavian correspondent in Hong Kong reports on the origins and aims of Mao's Cultural Revolution.

Gray, Jack and Cavendish, Patrick. **Chinese Communism in Crisis: Maoism and the Cultural Revolution.** New York: Praeger, 1968, 279 p.
   A study of the Cultural Revolution by two historians.

The Great Cultural Revolution in China. Rutland (Vt.): Tuttle (for the Asia Research Centre, Hong Kong), 1968, 507 p.

The Great Power Struggle in China. Hong Kong: Asia Research Centre, 1969, 503 p.
   Reference materials assembled for studying and assessing the political, ideological, cultural and social consequences of the Cultural Revolution.

Grey, Anthony. **Hostage in Peking.** Garden City: Doubleday, 1971, 365 p.
   The author, who was a Reuters correspondent in Peking, reminisces about his imprisonment from 1967 to 1969 in Mao's China.

Hai, Feng. **Kuang-chou ti-ch'ü wen ko li-ch'eng shu-lüeh.** Hong Kong: Yu-lien Yen-chiu So, 1971, 450 p.
   A detailed account of the Cultural Revolution in Canton from the beginning to late 1968, by a researcher at the Union Research Institute in Hong Kong.

Hoffmann, Rainer. **Entmaoisierung in China: zur Vorgeschichte der Kulturrevolution.** Munich: Weltforum Verlag (for the Arnold-Bergstraesser-Institut), 1972, 239 p.
   An examination of the different tendencies in Chinese politics, administration, industry and culture since 1961 that prepared the ground for Mao's Cultural Revolution.

Hsia, Adrian. **The Chinese Cultural Revolution.** New York: McGraw-Hill, 1972, 254 p.
A study of recent Chinese history by a professor at McGill University emphasizing the crucial contributions of Lin Piao to Mao's success. The German original appeared as "Die chinesische Kulturrevolution" (Neuwied: Luchterhand, 1971, 325 p.).

Hsiung, Yin-Tso. **Red China's Cultural Revolution.** New York: Vantage Press, 1968, 188 p.
The author argues that Mao staged the Cultural Revolution as a nationwide purge against the spreading opposition within his own party.

Hunter, Neale. **Shanghai Journal: An Eyewitness Account of the Cultural Revolution.** New York: Praeger, 1969, 311 p.
A young Australian scholar, who shortly before the Cultural Revolution had arrived in Shanghai as an English instructor at the Foreign Languages Institute, describes his experiences during "one of the most momentous, most complex, and most intriguing developments in modern history."

Important Documents on the Great Proletarian Cultural Revolution in China. Peking: Foreign Languages Press, 1970, 323 p.
An official collection of documents, including the four main Party directives issued during the Cultural Revolution.

Kamibeppu, Chikashi. **Chūgoku Bunka Kakumei no ronri.** Tokyo: Tōyō Keizai Shinpōsha, 1971, 323 p.
A Japanese study of the Cultural Revolution in China.

Kung-fei Wên-hua Ta Ko-ming chung-yao wên-chien hui-pien. Taipei: Kuo-fang Pu Ch'ing-pao Chü, 1968, 338 p.
An important collection of the chief documents of the Cultural Revolution, compiled and published by the Chinese Nationalist Ministry of Defense's Intelligence Bureau.

Lifton, Robert Jay. **Revolutionary Immortality: Mao Tse-Tung and the Chinese Cultural Revolution.** New York: Random House, 1968, 178 p.
A study of Mao's psychology and revolutionary style.

Ling, Ken, *pseud*. **The Revenge of Heaven: Journal of a Young Chinese.** New York: Putnam, 1972, 413 p.
The pseudonymous author, a student leader in the Cultural Revolution who fled China when the military reasserted control, depicts a world of cruel and unpredictable factional conflict.

Pan, Chao-ying and De Jaegher, Raymond J. **Peking's Red Guards: The Great Proletarian Cultural Revolution.** New York: Twin Circle Publishing Co., 1968, 462 p.
A study of the aims, methods and accomplishments of an organization that since early 1966 has specialized in purging all anti-Mao, anti-Party and anti-socialist elements.

Rice, Edward E. **Mao's Way.** Berkeley: University of California Press, 1972, 596 p.
The author, formerly U.S. Deputy Assistant Secretary of State for Far Eastern Affairs and Consul General in Hong Kong, traces the course of Mao's Cultural Revolution from the vantage point of an analyst of political tactics.

Robinson, Thomas W., *ed*. **The Cultural Revolution in China.** Berkeley: University of California Press, 1971, 509 p.
Writing for the RAND Corporation, five scholars discuss the problems of the Cultural Revolution.

Trumbull, Robert, *ed*. **This Is Communist China.** New York: McKay, 1968, 274 p.
A collection of dispatches sent from China to Japan in 1966–67 by correspondents, all of them fluent in Chinese, of one of Japan's largest newspapers, *Yomiuri Shimbun*.

Yao, Wên-yüan. **Yao Wên-yüan wên chi: Kuan-yü Wên-hua Ta Ko-ming (1965–1968).** Hong Kong: Li-shih Tzŭ-liao Ch'u-pan-shê, 1971, 204 p.
A collection of the 1965–68 statements of Yao Wen-yuan, a leading Chinese communist who played a prominent role at the beginning of the Cultural Revolution.

Zhelokhovtsev, Aleksei Nikolaevich. **Chinesische Kulturrevolution aus der Nähe.** Stuttgart: Deutsche Verlags-Anstalt, 1969, 320 p.
An eyewitness account of the Chinese Cultural Revolution by a Soviet sinologue who is very critical of Mao Tsê-tung and his "clique." A Russian version was published as "Kul'turnaia revoliutsiia s blizkogo rasstoianiia" (Moscow: Politizdat, 1973, 262 p.).

Biographies, Memoirs and Collected Writings

Bartke, Wolfgang. **Chinaköpfe: Kurzbiographien der Partei- und Staatsfunktionäre der Volksrepublik China.** Hanover: Verlag für Literatur und Zeitgeschehen, 1966, 454 p.
A Who's Who of Communist China's leadership.

Boorman, Howard Lyon with Howard, Richard C., *eds*. **Biographical Dictionary of Republican China.** New York: Columbia University Press, 1967-71, 4 v.
An important reference work containing biographical articles on Chinese who were prominent during the republican period (1911-1949) in China.

The Case of Peng Teh-huai, 1959-1968. Hong Kong: Union Research Institute, 1968, 494 p.
A documentary history of Marshall Peng's spectacular career as a soldier and how he forfeited Mao's favor by rebelling against an opportunistic agricultural policy that oppressed the broad peasant masses.

Chang, Kuo-t'ao. **The Rise of the Chinese Communist Party, 1921-1927.** Lawrence: University Press of Kansas, 1971, 756 p.
This is the English version of the first volume of the autobiography by one of the founders of the Chinese Communist Party. A most important source, ending with a description of events surrounding the Kuomintang-Communist split in 1927.

Ch'ên, Jerome, *comp*. **Mao.** Englewood Cliffs: Prentice-Hall, 1969, 176 p.
An anthology of statements by Mao Tsê-tung and a series of evaluations of Mao by Chinese and Westerners. Many of the post-1949 statements are taken from Red Guard papers and were not published in official sources.

Ch'ên, Jerome, *ed*. **Mao Papers: Anthology and Bibliography.** New York: Oxford University Press, 1970, 221 p.
A chronologically arranged anthology of selected statements by Mao from 1917 to 1969. It includes many post-1949 writings never published by the Chinese in accessible sources. There is a bibliography of Mao's writings from 1917 to 1967, with 560 entries in Chinese and English.

Ch'ên, Po-ta. **Ch'ên Po-ta wên chi (1949-1967).** Hong Kong: Li-shih Tzǔ-liao Ch'u-pan-shê, 1971, 204 p.
A compilation of the writings of Ch'en Po-ta, a former close and trusted aide of Mao.

Ching Hsüan-t'ung, Emperor of China. **From Emperor to Citizen: The Autobiography of Aisin-Gioro Pu Yi.** Peking: Foreign Languages Press, 1964-65, 2 v.
The autobiography of the last Manchu Emperor, who ascended the throne in 1908, was President of the Japanese puppet state of Manchukuo (Manchuria) from 1934 to 1945, and also a member of the Red Chinese National People's Congress before his death in 1967. The Chinese original was published in 1964 as "Wo ti ch'ien pan shêng" (2 v.). There is also an abridged English edition: "The Last Manchu: the Autobiography of Henry Pu Yi, Last Emperor of China" (New York: Putnam, 1967, 318 p.).

Chou, En-lai. **Quotations from Chou En-lai.** Melbourne: Flesch, 1969, 120 p.
Quotations from speeches of the Premier of the People's Republic of China covering the period from 1946 to 1964. The Chinese edition appeared as "Chou En-lai yü-lu" (Hong Kong: Tzu-lien Ch'u-pan-she, 1968, 128 p.).

Chou En-lai chuan chi. Hong Kong: Tzu-lien Ch'u-pan-she, 1971, 784 p.
Biographical materials on Chou En-lai compiled by the China Problems Research Center of the Union Research Institute, including writings of Chou from the beginning of his political activity through the Cultural Revolution.

Chung, Hua-min and Miller, Arthur C. **Madame Mao: A Profile of Chiang Ch'ing.** Hong Kong: Union Research Institute, 1968, 314 p.
A study of Mao Tsê-tung's wife Chiang Ch'ing, who has played a central role in Chinese politics since the beginning of the Cultural Revolution.

Devillers, Philippe. **Mao.** New York: Schocken, 1969, 317 p.
Selections of Mao's writings as they are being disseminated (not as originally presented) with commentaries. Translated from the French, "Ce que Mao a vraiment dit" (Paris: Stock, 1968, 292 p.).

Ebon, Martin. **Lin Piao: The Life and Writings of China's New Ruler.** New York: Stein and Day, 1970, 378 p.

Lin Piao, chosen by Mao as his successor, was killed, according to a Chinese report, in a plane crash in 1971 while attempting to escape after an unsuccessful attempt to assassinate Mao.

Gillin, Donald G. **Warlord: Yen Hsi-shan in Shansi Province, 1911–1949.** Princeton: Princeton University Press, 1967, 334 p.

A readable and well-documented biography of a warlord who was the ruler of the important province of Shansi in northwestern China from the collapse of the Chinese Empire in 1911 until the establishment of the People's Republic in 1949.

Hsu, Kai-yu. **Chou En-lai: China's Gray Eminence.** Garden City: Doubleday, 1968, 294 p.

A biography of Communist China's Premier who, in pre-Mao days, built the party élite and subsequently the army élite, organized the key party systems and saw to it that they worked.

Huang, Yü-ch'uan. **Mao Tse-tung sheng-p'ing tzu-liao chien-pien, 1893–1969.** Hong Kong: Union Research Institute, 1970, 544 p.

A useful chronology of Mao Tsê-tung's life from 1893 to 1969.

Klein, Donald W. and Clark, Anne B. **Biographic Dictionary of Chinese Communism, 1921–1965.** Cambridge: Harvard University Press, 1971, 2 v.

A thorough and indispensable reference tool.

Klochko, Mikhail Antonovich. **Soviet Scientist in Red China.** New York: Praeger, 1964, 213 p.

An intriguing account by a Soviet scientist (now living in Canada) of his visits to China in 1958 and 1960 to help develop new research and laboratory facilities. He is highly critical of the organization of Chinese science and technology and of conditions of scientific work there.

Lang, Olga. **Pa Chin and His Writings: Chinese Youth between the Two Revolutions.** Cambridge: Harvard University Press, 1967, 402 p.

A carefully researched study of the life and writings of Pa Chin, a Chinese anarchist writer, and how his ideas prepared the young Chinese intellectuals for their role in the revolutions.

Li, T'ien-min. **Chou En-lai.** Taipei: Institute of International Relations, 1970, 426 p.

A biography of Chou En-lai, written by a Chinese Nationalist scholar. The pre-1949 chapters are based on interviews with Chinese public figures who knew Chou personally.

Lin Piao chuan chi. Hong Kong: Tzu-lien Ch'u-pan She, 1970, 354 p.

A volume of biographical materials on Lin Piao, compiled by the China Problems Research Center of the Union Research Institute in Hong Kong.

Liu, Shao-ch'i. **Collected Works of Liu Shao-ch'i.** Hong Kong: Union Research Institute, 1968–69, 3 v.

A collection of letters, speeches, reports and writings of Liu Shao-ch'i, a leading Chinese communist and one-time Chairman of the Republic who was stripped of all his posts in October 1968. Liu Shao-ch'i was a prime target of the Maoist Cultural Revolution.

Liu, Shao-ch'i. **Quotations from President Liu Shao-ch'i.** New York: Walker/Weatherhill, 1968, 223 p.

Writings by Liu Shao-ch'i. The Chinese edition was published as "Liu Chu-hsi yü-lu" (Hong Kong: Tzu-lien Ch'u-pan-she, 1967, 187 p.).

Liu Shao-ch'i wên-t'i tzǔ-liao chuan-chi. Taipei: Chung Kung Yen-chiu Tsa-chih Shê, 1970, 774 p.

A collection of documents and writings on Liu Shao-ch'i.

Loh, Pichon P. Y. **The Early Chiang Kai-Shek: A Study of His Personality and Politics, 1887–1924.** New York: Columbia University Press, 1971, 216 p.

A valuable biographical study.

Mao, Tsê-tung. **Mao Tse-tung Shu.** Tokyo: Hokubosha, 1970–72, 10 v.

A Japanese edition of the complete pre-1949 works of Mao, with texts in Chinese and notes in Japanese. Since no complete set of Mao's works has been published by the Chinese Communists, this collection is a key source for the study of Mao and contemporary China.

Mao, Tsê-tung. **Mō Taku-tō saiko shiji: puroretaria bunka daikakumei ki no hatsugen.** Tokyo: Sanichi Shobō, 1970, 352 p.

A compilation of the many brief quotations and instructions from Mao Tsê-tung which were published in China during the Cultural Revolution. Edited by Atsuyoshi Niijima.

Mao, Tsê-tung. [**Works in English.**]

The official translation of Mao Tsê-tung's selected works was published as "Selected Works of Mao Tse-tung" (Peking: Foreign Languages Press, 1961–65, 4 v.). An earlier edition, published under a similar title in five vols. in London by Lawrence and Wishart and in New York by International Publishers, has now been repudiated by the Chinese. An official version of Mao Tsê-tung's writings on military problems appeared as "Selected Military Writings of Mao Tse-tung" (Peking: Foreign Languages Press, 1963, 408 p.). The index to both official editions was published as "Index to Selected Works of Mao Tse-tung and Selected Military Writings of Mao Tse-tung" (Hong Kong: Union Research Institute, 1968, 180 p.). Other writings by the Chinese communist leader are to be found in the following publications: "Quotations from Chairman Mao Tse-tung (Peking: Foreign Languages Press, 3rd ed., 1972, 311 p.); "Selected Readings from the Works of Mao Tse-tung" (Peking: Foreign Languages Press, 1967, 406 p.) and "Miscellany of Mao Tse-tung Thought (1949–1968)" (Arlington [Va.]: Joint Publications Research Service, 1974, 498 p.).

Payne, Pierre Stephen Robert. **Chiang Kai-shek.** New York: Weybright and Talley, 1969, 338 p.

An undocumented biography of Nationalist China's leader who, according to the author, had been corrupted by power.

Schram, Stuart R. **Mao Tse-tung.** New York: Simon and Schuster, 1967, 351 p.

A leading expert on Mao and Maoism uses, as far as possible, contemporary Chinese texts for this biography, which extends into the 1967 Cultural Revolution.

Sheridan, James Edward. **Chinese Warlord: The Career of Feng Yü-hsiang.** Stanford: Stanford University Press, 1966, 386 p.

A detailed account of the career of one of the most colorful and historically important Chinese warlords who played a leading role in Chinese politics in the 1920s and 1930s.

Takeuchi, Minoru. **Mō Taku-tō nōto.** Tokyo: Shinsensha, 1971, 295 p.

A study of Mao Tsê-tung by a leading Japanese student of Mao and his works.

Wang, Anna. **Ich kämpfte für Mao.** Hamburg: Wegner, 1964, 379 p.

Reminiscences of 20 years in China, by a German woman, the former wife of a Deputy Foreign Minister of Communist China.

Who's Who in Communist China. Hong Kong: Union Research Institute, rev. ed., 1969–70, 2 v.

Biographies of over 3,000 leading personages important to nearly all aspects of Communist China's life and politics. Appendices include rosters of membership in the Central Committee of the Communist Party and government and military organizations.

Tourists' and Correspondents' Reports

Duncan, James S. **A Businessman Looks at Red China.** Princeton: Van Nostrand, 1966, 174 p.

A prominent Canadian industrialist, who does not believe that "we will witness the crumbling of the communist regime" in Red China, reports on his visits to that country in September and October 1964.

Hamm, Harry. **China: Empire of the 700 Million.** Garden City: Doubleday, 1966, 310 p.

A German journalist tells of a 6,000-mile journey through the interior of China, with shrewd observations on political and social situations. German edition, "Das Reich der 700 Millionen: Begegnung mit dem China von Heute" (Düsseldorf: Econ-Verlag, 1965, 358 p.).

Hébert, Jacques and Trudeau, Pierre Elliott. **Two Innocents in Red China.** New York: Oxford University Press, 1969, 152 p.

ASIA AND THE PACIFIC AREA

The diary of a trip made in 1960 by two Québecois, one an author and publisher and the other subsequently the Liberal Party leader and Prime Minister of Canada.

Hevi, Emmanuel John. **An African Student in China.** New York: Praeger, 1963, 220 p.
A disillusioned Ghanaian records his experience with humor as well as acerbity.

Lindqvist, Sven. **China in Crisis.** New York: Crowell, 1965, 125 p.
Mr. Lindqvist records his keen observations on life and politics at Peking University in 1961-62, when he was the Swedish Embassy's Cultural Attaché to the People's Republic. The original appeared as "Kina inifrån: en preliminär rapport" (Stockholm: Bonnier, 1963, 178 p.).

Mackerras, Colin and Hunter, Neale. **China Observed.** New York: Praeger, 1968, 194 p.
Unpretentious reports on Communist China in the years from 1964 to 1967, by two Australians who taught at the Peking Foreign Languages Institute.

Marcuse, Jacques. **The Peking Papers.** New York: Dutton, 1967, 351 p.
A veteran French journalist, with many years of first-hand experience in China, has very little good to say about his sojourn in Mao's empire in the early 1960s.

Mehnert, Klaus. **China Returns.** New York: Dutton, 1972, 322 p.
Observations by a German scholar who toured China in 1971 at the invitation of Cambodia's Prince-in-exile, Sihanouk. The German original appeared as "China nach dem Sturm" (Stuttgart: Deutsche Verlags-Anstalt, 1971, 348 p.).

Portisch, Hugo. **Red China Today.** Chicago: Quadrangle Books, 1966, 383 p.
An eyewitness report of life in Communist China by an Austrian journalist. The Austrian edition appeared as "So sah ich China: Ein Tatsachen- und Erlebnisbericht aus dem Reich Mao Tse-tungs" (Vienna: Kremayr und Sheriau, 1965, 351 p.).

Roper, Myra. **China—The Surprising Country.** Garden City: Doubleday, 1966, 292 p.
Rather favorable impressions of Red China in 1965 by a British-born Australian journalist. This travelogue includes interviews with Mao Tsê-tung, Chou En-lai and other Chinese dignitaries.

Roy, Jules. **Journey Through China.** New York: Harper and Row, 1967, 299 p.
A former French Army officer's account of his journey to Red China in the fall of 1964. He returned convinced that "China's love for peace" was a lie and that Mao Tsê-tung and "his whole silent and mournful court of hirelings dreamed of nothing but revenge." The French original was published as: "Le Voyage en Chine" (Paris: Julliard, 1965, 411 p.).

Stucki, Lorenz. **Behind the Great Wall: An Appraisal of Mao's China.** New York: Praeger, 1965, 154 p.
A Swiss journalist's account of a two months' visit to Red China in 1964 as correspondent for the *Neue Zürcher Zeitung*. The Swiss original appeared as "Land hinter Mauern: China heute" (Zürich: Buchverlag der Neuen Zürcher Zeitung, 1964, 120 p.).

Taylor, Charles. **Reporter in Red China.** New York: Random House, 1966, 208 p.
Impressions of Communist China by a correspondent for the Toronto *Globe and Mail*. During his sojourn in Peking from May 1964 until October 1965 Mr. Taylor was the only North American journalist reporting from China.

Thiess, Frank. **Plädoyer für Peking: ein Augenzeugenbericht.** Stuttgart: Seewald, 1966, 308 p.
A German writer, who does not like what most of the Soviet and American China experts are writing, and who has travelled extensively in Mao's China, writes sympathetically about Chinese civilization and China's role in the world, interspersing his philosophizing with personal impressions.

Topping, Seymour. **Journey between Two Chinas.** New York: Harper and Row, 1972, 459 p.
A senior correspondent of *The New York Times* revisited China in 1971 after a 22-year absence. These discursive memoirs cover the high points of the author's career over that time span and offer some interesting observations on China in an age of rapid change.

Foreign Relations

See also General Works, p. 1; Political Factors, p. 12; International Law, p. 83; International Organization and Government, p. 96; War and Peace, p. 108; The World Since 1914, p. 129; (The United States) Biographies, Memoirs and Addresses, p. 218; Foreign Policy, p. 229; (Union of Soviet Socialist Republics) Relations with China, p. 555; Indian-Chinese Relations, p. 670; Japan, p. 714; The Korean War, p. 728; The Vietnam War, p. 739; other subsections under China and the sections for specific countries and regions.

Ambekar, G. V. and Divekar, V. D., eds. **Documents on China's Relations with South and Southeast Asia (1949-1962).** Bombay: Allied Publishers, 1964, 491 p.
A useful reference.

Amer, Omar Ali. **China and the Afro-Asian Peoples' Solidarity Organization, 1958–1967.** Geneva: Université de Genève, Institut de Hautes Études Internationales, 1972, 258 p.
The author argues that China has failed to turn the A.A.P.S.O. into an instrument of its foreign policy.

Astaf'ev, G. V., ed. **Foreign Policy of the PRC.** Washington: U.S. Joint Publications Research Service, 1971, 180 p.
A translation of a Soviet study on Chinese foreign policy. Although very critical and polemical, it contains information not easily found in non-Soviet sources. The original appeared as "Vneshniaia politika KNR" (Moscow: Mezhdunarodnye Otnosheniia, 1971, 191 p.).

Bartke, Wolfgang. **Die Wirtschaftshilfe der Volksrepublik China.** Hamburg: Institut für Asienkunde, 1972, 251 p.
An examination of the economic aid given by the People's Republic to 26 nations in Africa and Asia, based on data through June 1971.

Bechtoldt, Heinrich. **Die Allianz mit der Armut: Chinas Revolutionsstrategie gegen Russland und Amerika.** Freiburg: Rombach, 1967, 348 p.
A study of Mao's concept of a world communist revolution.

Brahm, Heinz. **Pekings Griff nach der Vormacht: der chinesisch-sowjetische Konflikt von Juli 1963 bis März 1965.** Cologne: Verlag Wissenschaft und Politik, 1966, 255 p.
A chronological survey, supplemented with documents, of the Chinese efforts to achieve leadership within the world communist movement since 1963.

Buchan, Alastair Francis, ed. **China and the Peace of Asia.** New York: Praeger, 1965, 253 p.
Fourteen papers, by Asian, European and American specialists, delivered at the 1964 symposium held at Oxford under the auspices of the Institute for Strategic Studies.

Chin nien lai Kung Fei tui-wai kuan-hsi piao-chieh. Taipei: Chung-kuo Ta-lu Wen-t'i Yen-chiu So, 1972, 538 p.
A handbook on the foreign relations of the People's Republic of China, compiled and published by the China Mainland Research Institute in Taiwan and focusing on the 1969–1971 period.

Chiu, Hung-ta. **The People's Republic of China and the Law of Treaties.** Cambridge: Harvard University Press, 1972, 178 p.
The author, Professor of International Law at the National University in Taipei, argues that China's concept of treaty law does not differ substantially from that of the West, except in her development of the concept of "unequal treaties" out of her own historical experience.

Cho, M. Y. **Die Volksdiplomatie in Ostasien.** Wiesbaden: Harrassowitz (for the Institut für Asienkunde in Hamburg), 1971, 240 p.
A stimulating and well-researched survey of the relations between Mao's China and Japan, with particular attention devoted to problems created by the U.S. involvement in the Far East.

Chung-hua Jen-min Kung-ho-kuo tui-wai kuan-hsi wen-chien chi. Peking: Fa-lü Ch'u-pan She and Shih-chieh Chih-shih Ch'u-pan She, 1957–.
A series of documents on the foreign relations of the People's Republic of China covering the period since 1949. Volume 10, the latest available volume in the West, covers the events of 1963.

Chung-Jih wai-chiao shih-liao ts'ung-pien. Taipei: Chung-hua Min-kuo Wai-chiao Wen-t'i Yen-chiu-hui, 1964–67, 9 v.
A collection of documents on Sino-Japanese relations from 1927 to 1952.

Clark, Gregory John. **In Fear of China.** London: Barrie and Rockliff, 1969, 219 p.
A study of how the West's failure to appraise objectively Chinese politics during the 1959–1965 period has affected China's external behavior.

Communist China and Arms Control: A Contingency Study, 1967–1976. Stanford: Hoover Institution on War, Revolution, and Peace, 1968, 181 p.
A report submitted under contract to the U.S. Arms Control and Disarmament Agency.

Dial, Roger. **Studies on Chinese External Affairs: An Instructional Bibliography of Commonwealth and American Literature.** Halifax: Dalhousie University, Centre for Foreign Policy Studies, 1973, 182 p.
An excellent analytical bibliography of monographic and essay literature.

Domes, Jürgen and Näth, Marie-Luise. **Die Aussenpolitik der Volksrepublik China.** Düsseldorf: Bertelsmann Universitätsverlag, 1972, 221 p.
In a detailed examination the authors predict neither a reanimation of Soviet-Chinese ties nor a return to the politics of militant Afro-Asian solidarity, but a delicate approach to a three-cornered coexistence with the United States and Japan.

Dutt, Vidya Prakash. **China and the World.** New York: Praeger, 1966, 356 p.
An Indian specialist in modern Chinese history discusses domestic politics and foreign policy, factors influencing current international relations in general, and then takes up China's relations with the United States, U.S.S.R., Asia and Africa. A revised version of "China's Foreign Policy, 1958–62" (New York: Asia Publishing House, 1964, 336 p.).

Halpern, Abraham Meyer, *ed*. **Policies Toward China: Views from Six Continents.** New York: McGraw-Hill (for the Council on Foreign Relations), 1965, 528 p.
Sixteen country and area specialists examine the China policies of non-communist countries. Mr. Halpern contributes an introduction and a concluding chapter in which he assesses the implications for U.S. policy.

Hinton, Harold Clendenin. **China's Turbulent Quest: An Analysis of China's Foreign Relations since 1949.** New York: Macmillan, new and enl. ed., 1972, 352 p.
An intelligent appraisal of the many imponderables in China's foreign relations. The analysis includes China's role as a thermonuclear power, the uncertain results of the Cultural Revolution, the Vietnam crisis, the Sino-Soviet border disputes, and Nixon's China policy.

Hinton, Harold Clendenin. **Communist China in World Politics.** Boston: Houghton, 1966, 527 p.
Professor Hinton of George Washington University uses official Chinese sources and, selectively, secondary sources to trace Communist China's foreign policies in all major areas, as well as China's status in international communism.

Hsiung, James Chieh. **Law and Policy in China's Foreign Relations.** New York: Columbia University Press, 1972, 435 p.
Professor Hsiung's study suggests that revolutionary governments are like most of their conservative counterparts: the law will be utilized and obeyed when it is advantageous to do so, ignored or denounced when not.

Iriye, Akira. **Bei-Chū kankei.** Tokyo: Saimaru Shuppankai, 2d ed., 1971, 214 p.
A study of Sino-American relations by one of the leading Japanese students of Far Eastern international relations.

Jih-pên wên-t'i wên-chien hui-pien. Peking: Shih-chieh Chih-shih Ch'u-pan She, 1958–65, 5 v.
A wide-ranging collection of materials on Sino-Japanese relations in the post-World War II period.

Johnston, Douglas M. and Chiu, Hung-ta, *eds*. **Agreements of the People's Republic of China, 1949–1967.** Cambridge: Harvard University Press, 1968, 286 p.
A valuable treaty calendar documenting all official and semi-official exchanges of

international legal commitments involving the People's Republic up to September 30, 1967.

Kapitsa, Mikhail Stepanovich. **KNR: dva desiatiletiia—dve politiki.** Moscow: Izd-vo Politicheskoi Literatury, 1969, 352 p.
A critique of Chinese foreign and domestic policies. The author is a leading Soviet expert in East Asian affairs.

Khalili, Joseph E. **Communist China's Interaction with the Arab Nationalists since the Bandung Conference.** New York: Exposition Press, 1970, 121 p.
A useful introductory survey.

Labin, Suzanne. **Menaces chinoises sur l'Asie.** Paris: Éditions de la Table Ronde, 1966, 329 p.
The author is convinced that the Red Chinese are pursuing an expansionist foreign policy in Asia.

Lall, Arthur Samuel. **How Communist China Negotiates.** New York: Columbia University Press, 1968, 291 p.
One of the six delegates participating in negotiations at the 14-nation Foreign Ministers' Conference on Laos in 1961-62 relates the intricate story of the negotiations and analyzes them in the context of Communist Chinese theory of international relations.

Larkin, Bruce D. **China and Africa, 1949-1970: The Foreign Policy of the People's Republic of China.** Berkeley: University of California Press, 1971, 268 p.
The author concludes his study by stating that "there is virtually no possibility that the African continent will be swept by anti-imperialist and social revolutions led by men who follow Chinese leadership."

Lee, Luke T. **China and International Agreements: A Study of Compliance.** Durham (N.C.): Rule of Law Press, 1969, 231 p.
Professor Lee concludes his well-researched study by saying that the Chinese respect treaty obligations and that Red China should be involved in a network of treaty obligations.

Leng, Shao-chuan and Chiu, Hung-ta, *eds*. **Law in Chinese Foreign Policy: Communist China and Selected Problems of International Law.** Dobbs Ferry (N.Y.): Oceana Publications, 1972, 387 p.
A pioneering collection of essays on the Communist Chinese attitude toward contemporary international law.

Lyons, Daniel, S. J. and Pan, Chao-ying, *eds*. **Voice of Peking: "The Road to Paris..."** New York: Twin Circle Publishing Co., 1967, 332 p.
A collection of official documents, articles and broadcasts from Red China on the foreign policies of Mao Tsê-tung.

McCabe, Robert Karr. **Storm over Asia: China and Southeast Asia—Thrust and Response.** New York: New American Library, 1967, 225 p.
A survey of Chinese penetration and influence in Southeast Asia. The author was *Newsweek*'s bureau chief in Hong Kong from 1962 to 1966.

Matsumoto, Saburō. **Chūgoku gaikō to Tōnan Ajia.** Tokyo: Keiō Tsūshing, 1971, 347 p.
A Japanese study of Chinese diplomacy in Southeast Asia.

Neumann-Hoditz, Reinhold. **Chinas heimliche Fronten: ein Bericht.** Hamburg: Wegner, 1966, 323 p.
A German journalist, who has traveled extensively in the Far East, describes the never-ceasing and many-faceted endeavors of the Chinese communists to increase their influence in the non-communist countries of Asia.

Nieh, Yu-hsi. **Die Entwicklung des chinesisch-japanischen Konfliktes in Nordchina und die deutschen Vermittlungsbemühungen 1937-1938.** Hamburg: Institut für Asienkunde, 1970, 217 p.
A well-documented study of the German mediation attempts in the Sino-Japanese conflict in North China in 1937-38.

Ojha, Ishwer C. **Chinese Foreign Policy in an Age of Transition: The Diplomacy of Cultural Despair.** Boston: Beacon Press, 1969, 234 p.
The author concludes his useful survey by saying that the link between domestic politics and foreign policy in Mao's China is stronger than in other modern states.

ASIA AND THE PACIFIC AREA

Okabe, Tatsumi. **Gendai Chūgoku no taigai seisaku.** Tokyo: Tōkyō Daigaku Shuppankai, 1971, 362 p.
A study of contemporary China's foreign policy.

Richer, Philippe. **La Chine et le Tiers Monde (1949–1969).** Paris: Payot, 1971, 444 p.
An encyclopedic summation of data on Chinese relations with the less developed countries.

Sakamoto, Naomichi. **Chū-So kokkyō funsō no haikei.** Tokyo: Kajima Kenkyūjo Shuppankai, 1970, 409 p.
A Japanese study of the Sino-Soviet border conflicts.

Salisbury, Harrison Evans. **Orbit of China.** New York: Harper and Row, 1967, 204 p.
Mr. Salisbury, of *The New York Times*, traveled the entire periphery of China to gauge its impact on Asia and the world. Key topics are war and peace with America, struggle for Asian leadership, the Sino-Soviet conflict and escalation of war in Southeast Asia.

Simmonds, John Derrington. **China's World: The Foreign Policy of a Developing State.** New York: Columbia University Press, 1971, 260 p.
The Australian author sees Chinese policy as dictated mainly by the need for an external enemy to spur domestic effort.

Tung, William L. **China and the Foreign Powers: The Impact of and Reaction to Unequal Treaties.** Dobbs Ferry (N.Y.): Oceana Publications 1970, 526 p.
A former Chinese diplomat, now professor at Queens College, New York, surveys China's foreign relations from the middle of the nineteenth century to the present. The author argues that "the Chinese attitude toward foreign powers in recent decades has had much to do with the national humiliation endured during the past century."

Van Ness, Peter. **Revolution and Chinese Foreign Policy: Peking's Support for Wars of National Liberation.** Berkeley: University of California Press, 1970, 266 p.
A study of how the Maoists used the lessons gained from the Chinese Communist Party's experience in making revolution in China from 1921 to 1949 to foment the overthrow of governments in Asia, Africa and Latin America.

Watson, Francis. **The Frontiers of China.** New York: Praeger, 1966, 224 p.
The history of Chinese border problems and a description of the major developments of Chinese frontier policy since the communist seizure of power, by a British scholar who emphasizes the problems concerning the Indian-Chinese frontier.

Weng, Byron S. J. **Peking's UN Policy: Continuity and Change.** New York: Praeger, 1972, 337 p.
An attempt to describe the various elements influencing Communist China's attitude toward the United Nations.

Wilbur, Clarence Martin, *ed.* **Documents on Communism, Nationalism, and Soviet Advisors in China, 1918–1927: Papers Seized in the 1927 Peking Raid.** New York: Octagon, 1972, 617 p.
On April 6, 1927, the Peking police raided the offices of the Soviet Military Advisor to China and seized hundreds of secret documents which were published the next year as "Su-lien yin-mou wên-ch'êng hui-pien." The editor has selected 50 of these documents for translation and publication in this volume. An index for the Chinese edition was prepared by David Nelson Rowe: "Index to the Su-lien yin-mou wen-cheng" (Hamden [Conn.]: Shoe String Press, 1965, 400 p.).

Yamamoto, Noboru, *ed.* **Chū-So tairitsu to Ajia shokoku.** Tokyo: Nihon Kokusai Mondai Kenkyūjo, 1969–71, 2 v.
A wide-ranging study of the Sino-Soviet conflict and its effects on Asian countries.

Military Questions

See also War and Peace, p. 108; The World Since 1914, p. 129; (The United States) Biographies, Memoirs and Addresses, p. 218; Foreign Policy, p. 229; (Union of Soviet Socialist Republics) Relations with China, p. 555; Indian-Chinese Relations, p. 670; Japan, p. 714; The Korean War, p. 728; The Vietnam War, p. 739; other subsections under China.

Bueschel, Richard M. **Communist Chinese Air Power.** New York: Praeger, 1968, 238 p.
A historical survey of the growth of China's air strength since 1925 and brief notes on some 100 indigenous and foreign aircraft types which have been in use in Communist China.

Cheng, James Chester and Others, eds. **The Politics of the Chinese Red Army: A Translation of the Bulletin of Activities of the People's Liberation Army.** Stanford: Hoover Institution on War, Revolution, and Peace, 1966, 776 p.
A translation of the secret Communist Chinese military journals for the November 1960–August 1961 period, issued to expedite party instructions to high-ranking cadres in the field.

George, Alexander L. **The Chinese Communist Army in Action: The Korean War and its Aftermath.** New York: Columbia University Press, 1967, 255 p.
A Stanford University professor examines, through interviews with 300 Chinese war prisoners in Korea in 1951, the nature of the political controls and morale of Mao's army.

Gittings, John. **The Role of the Chinese Army.** New York: Oxford University Press (for the Royal Institute of International Affairs), 1967, 331 p.
An examination of the changing character of the People's Liberation Army since 1949, and of the fluctuating position which it occupies in the scale of national priorities.

Griffith, Samuel B., II. **The Chinese People's Liberation Army.** New York: McGraw-Hill (for the Council on Foreign Relations), 1967, 398 p.
A solid study by a retired Marine Corps general and a leading student of China's defense problems.

Griffith, Samuel B., II. **Peking and People's Wars.** New York: Praeger, 1966, 142 p.
Translations with lengthy commentaries of Lin's "Long Live the Victory of the People's War!" and of Lo's "Commemorate the Victory over German Fascism!"—both basic documents, released in 1965, important for understanding China's revolutionary strategy and foreign policy.

Halperin, Morton H. **China and the Bomb.** New York: Praeger (for the Center for International Affairs and the East Asian Research Center, Harvard University), 1965, 166 p.
An analysis of the implications of China's first detonation of an atomic bomb, by a senior fellow at the Brookings Institution.

Huck, Arthur. **The Security of China: Chinese Approaches to Problems of War and Strategy.** New York: Columbia University Press (for the Institute for Strategic Studies, London), 1970, 93 p.
An Australian scholar who visited China in 1965 and 1966 writes about the Communist Chinese views on military and political threats to their country.

Lin, Piao. **Lin Fu Chu-hsi chün-shih lun-wên chi.** Kunming: K'un-ming Chün-ch'ü Ssu-ling Pu, 1970, 582 p.
A collection of Lin Piao's statements on military affairs from 1934 to 1965, published for internal use by the Kunming Military Region.

Liu, Leo Yueh-yun. **China as a Nuclear Power in World Politics.** New York: Taplinger, 1972, 125 p.
The author of this study predicts that the growth of China's thermonuclear intercontinental capacity will accelerate the armament programs of other countries.

Mao, Tsê-tung. **Basic Tactics.** New York: Praeger, 1966, 149 p.
Text of a series of lectures for future guerrilla leaders delivered in 1938. In his foreword Brigadier General Samuel B. Griffith, II, evaluates its significance from a professional soldier's viewpoint; Stuart R. Schram, the translator, traces in his introduction Mao's evolution from politician to guerrilla leader.

Rhoads, Edward J. M. and Others. **The Chinese Red Army, 1927–1963: An Annotated Bibliography.** Cambridge: East Asian Research Center, Harvard University, 1964, 188 p.
A useful reference.

Whitson, William W., ed. **The Military and Political Power in China in the 1970's.** New York: Praeger, 1972, 390 p.
A solid collection of articles by various authors on the role of the military in Communist China. Of particular interest are the discussions of the concepts of Chinese military strategy.

Yin, John. **Sino-Soviet Dialog on the Problem of War.** The Hague: Nijhoff, 1971, 247 p.
A survey of Chinese thinking on questions of war, peace, peaceful coexistence and nuclear armament, including comparisons with Soviet doctrines.

Economic and Social Problems

See also Problems of New Nations, p. 36; Society and Social Psychology, p. 39; Culture; Education; Public Opinion; Communications Processes, p. 42; International Trade, p. 55; Economic Growth and Development, p. 71; (The United States) Foreign Policy, p. 229; (Union of Soviet Socialist Republics) Foreign Economic Policy, p. 560; (Asia and the Pacific Area) General Surveys, p. 607; (Far East) General, p. 682; other subsections under China.

Buchanan, Keith McPherson. **The Transformation of the Chinese Earth.** New York: Praeger, 1970, 336 p.
A confessedly partisan observer celebrates, in a book rich in both data and emotion, the process of transformation of labor into capital, of moral fervor into GNP, which constitutes, as he sees it, the Chinese model for Third World economic development.

Buck, John Lossing and Others. **Food and Agriculture in Communist China.** New York: Praeger (for the Hoover Institution on War, Revolution, and Peace), 1966, 171 p.
Essays on agrarian problems of Communist China, including an evaluation of the country's statistical reporting. The author directed an extensive land utilization survey in China before World War II.

Chang, Tsungtung. **Die chinesische Volkswirtschaft: Grundlagen, Organisation, Planung.** Cologne: Westdeutscher Verlag, 1965, 193 p.
A thorough study of the economy of Communist China, including analyses of its demographic problems and foreign trade and aid.

Chao, Kang. **Agricultural Production in Communist China, 1949-1965.** Madison: University of Wisconsin Press, 1970, 357 p.
The author, a professor of economics at the University of Wisconsin, concludes his study by saying that "the Chinese Communist experience in developing agriculture has been far from successful."

Chao, Kang. **The Rate and Pattern of Industrial Growth in Communist China.** Ann Arbor: University of Michigan Press, 1965, 188 p.
Professor Chao concludes his study by saying that Communist China achieved a higher growth rate than Soviet Russia during its first years of economic planning, and that a Sino-Indian comparison shows even more spectacular success for the Chinese.

Chen, Nai-ruenn. **Chinese Economic Statistics: A Handbook for Mainland China.** Chicago: Aldine Publishing Co., 1967, 539 p.
A compilation of official national and provincial statistics from 1949 to 1959 (when the regime imposed a statistical blackout) culled from a great variety of Communist Chinese sources.

Chen, Nai-ruenn and Galenson, Walter. **The Chinese Economy under Communism.** Chicago: Aldine Publishing Co., 1969, 250 p.
A broad-ranging survey, including a discussion of the prospects for the Chinese economy. A volume in a series commissioned by the Committee on the Economy of China, appointed by the Social Science Research Council.

Cheng, Chu-yüan. **Communist China's Economy, 1949-1962: Structural Changes and Crisis.** South Orange: Seton Hall University Press, 1963, 217 p.
In this study of the structural alterations of the Chinese economy since the communists came to power, the author concludes that they would have done better in following the Japanese rather than the Russian example.

Chesneaux, Jean. **The Chinese Labor Movement, 1919-1927.** Stanford: Stanford University Press, 1968, 574 p.
A massive historical study based on Chinese sources. The French original was published as "Le Mouvement ouvrier chinois de 1919 à 1927," (Paris: Mouton, 1962, 652 p.).

Chou, Shun-hsin. **The Chinese Inflation, 1937-1949.** New York: Columbia University Press, 1963, 319 p.
A Pittsburgh University professor traces the process of the runaway postwar inflation in China, with emphasis on its economic and social effects and as a prime factor causing the downfall of the Nationalist government.

Dawson, Owen L. **Communist China's Agriculture: Its Development and Future Potential.** New York: Praeger, 1970, 326 p.

A survey of basic agricultural resources and trends in Communist China, based primarily on provincial data. The author is a former U.S. Agricultural Attaché in China.

Donnithorne, Audrey Gladys. **China's Economic System.** New York: Praeger, 1967, 592 p.
In this detailed study the focus is on the period from 1957 to 1966.

Dumont, René. **Chine surpeuplée: Tiers-Monde affamé.** Paris: Éditions du Seuil, 1965, 312 p.
A pessimistic view of China's economic future, by a trained agronomist with a remarkable knowledge of China and agriculture in underdeveloped countries all over the world.

Ecklund, George N. **Financing the Chinese Government Budget: Mainland China, 1950–1959.** Chicago: Aldine Publishing Co., 1966, 133 p.
A description and an evaluation of the methods used to raise government revenue for Communist China's rapid industrialization.

Eckstein, Alexander. **Communist China's Economic Growth and Foreign Trade: Implications for U.S. Policy.** New York: McGraw-Hill (for the Council on Foreign Relations), 1966, 366 p.
A long-time student of the Chinese economy looks at economic progress and economic problems on the Chinese mainland from the standpoint of their impact upon Communist China's foreign policy.

Eckstein, Alexander and Others, *eds.* **Economic Trends in Communist China.** Chicago: Aldine Publishing Co., 1968, 757 p.
Studies by twelve experts on population, manpower resources, agriculture, industry, labor and foreign trade in mainland China.

An Economic Profile of Mainland China. New York: Praeger, 1968, 684 p.
A detailed survey of the economic conditions and potentialities of Communist China, prepared by American academic and governmental specialists for the use of the Joint Economic Committee of the U.S. Congress and published originally as a government document in 1967.

Hoffmann, Charles. **Work Incentive Practices and Policies in the People's Republic of China, 1953–1965.** Albany: State University of New York Press, 1968, 148 p.
A description of the complex of material and non-material incentive mechanisms used to motivate China's huge agricultural and industrial labor force.

Hou, Chi-ming. **Foreign Investment and Economic Development in China, 1840–1937.** Cambridge: Harvard University Press, 1965, 306 p.
Professor Hou critically analyzes and challenges the commonly held theory that foreign economic intrusion impeded China's economy and oppressed Chinese-owned enterprises.

Hsiao, Katharine Huang. **Money and Monetary Policy in Communist China.** New York: Columbia University Press, 1971, 308 p.
A professor of economics at Indiana State University concludes her technical study by stating that the official monetary policies of the People's Bank will continue to exercise a moderating and restraining influence on the economic development of China.

Hsiao, Tso-liang. **The Land Revolution in China, 1930–1934.** Seattle: University of Washington Press, 1969, 361 p.
A collection of documents, with annotations, on the agrarian struggle in China.

King, Frank H. H. **A Concise Economic History of Modern China (1840–1961).** New York: Praeger, 1970, 243 p.
A useful survey.

Korbash, E. **Ekonomicheskie "teorii" maoizma.** Moscow: Izd-vo Politicheskoi Literatury, 1971, 184 p.
A Soviet critique of Chinese economic policy since 1955, utilizing Chinese sources to argue that a rational plan to build socialism in China was replaced by an ill-founded course aimed at splitting the socialist camp.

Lewin, Pauline. **The Foreign Trade of Communist China: Its Impact on the Free World.** New York: Praeger, 1964, 128 p.
This brief study appeared under the auspices of the Economist Intelligence Unit.

Li, Choh-ming, *ed.* **Industrial Development in Communist China.** New York: Praeger, 1964, 205 p.
Twelve studies, originally published by *China Quarterly*, on various aspects of China's industrial economy since 1950.

Liu, Ta-chung and Yeh, Kung-chia. **The Economy of the Chinese Mainland: National Income and Economic Development, 1933-1959.** Princeton: Princeton University Press, 1965, 771 p.
The estimates of the authors show an average growth rate well below communist claims.

Mah, Feng-hwa. **The Foreign Trade of Mainland China.** Chicago: Aldine, Atherton, 1971, 270 p.
A detailed survey, supplemented with many statistical tables, covering the period from 1950 to 1967. The author is a professor at the University of Washington.

Meliksetov, A. V. **Biurokraticheskii kapital v Kitae: ekonomicheskaia politika Gomin'dana i razvitie gosudarstvennogo kapitalizma v 1927-1937 gg.** Moscow: Nauka, 1972, 199 p.
A solid study of the economic policy of the Kuomintang and the development of state capitalism in China from 1927 to 1937, by a prominent Soviet China scholar.

Miyashita, Tadao. **The Currency and Financial System of Mainland China.** Seattle: University of Washington Press, 1966, 278 p.
This well-documented study of Communist China's financial policies, sponsored by the Institute of Asian Economic Affairs in Tokyo, is an English version of a work originally published in Japanese in 1965.

Orleans, Leo A. **Every Fifth Child: The Population of China.** Stanford: Stanford University Press, 1972, 191 p.
The author, after estimating China's population at approximately 800 million, suggests that the ratio of Chinese to the world population total is not growing but declining.

Perkins, Dwight Heald and Others. **Agricultural Development in China, 1368-1968.** Chicago: Aldine Publishing Co., 1969, 395 p.
An attempt "to explain how China's farm economy responded to the demands of a rising population" and how "China's agriculture today feeds a quarter of the world's population on 7 per cent of the globe's cultivated land." There is a wealth of statistical information.

Perkins, Dwight Heald. **Market Control and Planning in Communist China.** Cambridge: Harvard University Press, 1966, 291 p.
A technical study, with a historical prologue, by a Harvard professor.

Prybyla, Jan S. **The Political Economy of Communist China.** Scranton: International Textbook Co., 1970, 605 p.
An informative survey of economic development in China during the first two decades of communist power.

Richman, Barry M. **Industrial Society in Communist China.** New York: Random House, 1969, 968 p.
Findings and observations of a Canadian expert made during his 1966 firsthand study of Communist China's management, industry, society and economic development.

Shabad, Theodore. **China's Changing Map: National and Regional Development, 1949-71.** New York: Praeger, rev. ed., 1972, 370 p.
An updated geographical and economic reference tool, first published in 1956. The author is a correspondent for *The New York Times*.

Shiriaev, Stepan Lavrent'evich. **Zheleznodorozhnyi transport Kitaiskoi Narodnoi Respubliki.** Moscow: "Nauka," 1969, 141 p.
A stinging Soviet critique of Chinese railway and transport development economics. Well-documented and including rare statistical material.

Simonis, Udo Ernst. **Die Entwicklungspolitik der Volksrepublik China 1949 bis 1962.** Berlin: Duncker, 1968, 196 p.
A thorough study, with many statistical tables, of the economic development of Communist China from 1949 to 1962. There is a comprehensive bibliography.

Stahnke, Arthur A., *ed*. **China's Trade with the West: A Political and Economic Analysis.** New York: Praeger, 1972, 234 p.
Papers from a symposium of the Association for Asian Studies.

Walker, Kenneth Richard. **Planning in Chinese Agriculture: Socialisation and the Private Sector, 1956–1962.** Chicago: Aldine Publishing Co., 1965, 109 p.
The author of this study argues that home-owned garden plots have come to play a significant part in China's economic life.

Wheelwright, Edward Lawrence and McFarlane, Bruce. **The Chinese Road to Socialism: Economics of the Cultural Revolution.** New York: Monthly Review Press, 1970, 256 p.
The authors of this monograph are fascinated by the Maoist experiment in substituting ideological for material considerations in thinking about development.

Wu, Yuan-li with Ling, H. C. **Economic Development and the Use of Energy Resources in Communist China.** New York: Praeger (for the Hoover Institution on War, Revolution, and Peace), 1963, 275 p.
A solid study by a leading student of China's economy.

Wu, Yuan-li. **The Economy of Communist China.** New York: Praeger, 1965, 225 p.
An outline of China's economic goals and achievements.

Wu, Yuan-li with Others. **The Spatial Economy of Communist China: A Study on Industrial Location and Transportation.** New York: Praeger (for the Hoover Institution on War, Revolution, and Peace), 1967, 367 p.
A study of the problem of how to integrate a vast land area into a viable economy, with emphasis on railways.

Wu, Yuan-li. **The Steel Industry in Communist China.** New York: Praeger (for the Hoover Institution on War, Revolution, and Peace), 1965, 334 p.
A well-documented study of the "overexpanded and unbalanced steel industry" of Communist China. The author concludes his survey by saying that "the overemphasis on steel appears to have been encouraged by the Soviet example."

Yamauchi, Kazuo. **Chūgoku Shakkai shugi keizai kenkyu josetsu.** Tokyo: Hosei Daigaku Shuppankyoku, 1971, 268 p.
A Japanese monograph on the economy of China.

Young, Arthur Nichols. **China and the Helping Hand, 1937–1945.** Cambridge: Harvard University Press, 1963, 502 p.
A senior adviser of the U.S. government, with nearly two decades of service in China, writes on self-help and foreign aid during the crucial war years, relying heavily on his own personal papers and other archival records. He also gives his analysis of the reasons for China's fall to the communists.

Young, Arthur Nichols. **China's Wartime Finance and Inflation, 1937–1945.** Cambridge: Harvard University Press, 1965, 421 p.
A description, analysis and appraisal of the main fiscal and monetary developments in China during the wartime years.

Educational and Cultural Problems

See also other subsections under China.

Chan, Wing-tsit. **Chinese Philosophy, 1949–1963.** Honolulu: East-West Center Press, 1967, 290 p.
An annotated bibliography of books and articles, published in mainland China and Hong Kong.

Chin, Robert and Chin, Ai-li S. **Psychological Research in Communist China, 1949–1966.** Cambridge: M.I.T. Press, 1969, 274 p.
A psychologist-sociologist team surveys the state of psychological research on the Chinese mainland and its effects on the social and political scene.

Fraser, Stewart, *comp*. **Chinese Communist Education: Records of the First Decade.** Nashville: Vanderbilt University Press, 1965, 542 p.
A study of the effects of indoctrination and ideology on Communist Chinese education, with a collection of relevant speeches, articles, official documents and a bibliography.

Goldman, Merle Dorothy. **Literary Dissent in Communist China.** Cambridge: Harvard University Press, 1967, 343 p.
A study of the conflict between the Chinese Communist Party and China's writers in the 1940s and 1950s.

Lutz, Jessie Gregory. **China and the Christian Colleges, 1850-1950.** Ithaca: Cornell University Press, 1971, 575 p.
A detailed study of the work of American Protestant educational missionaries in China. The author concludes that "their contribution to China was of lasting importance; their contribution to Christianizing China or Sinifying Christianity was marginal."

Price, R. F. **Education in Communist China.** New York: Praeger, 1970, 308 p.
An Englishman, who between 1965-67 taught at the Second Foreign Languages Institute in Peking, surveys the educational system of Mao's China.

Tung, Chi-ping and Evans, Humphrey. **The Thought Revolution.** New York: Coward-McCann, 1966, 254 p.
A story of how the Chinese Communists made students abject tools of their system and why Mr. Tung, who defected to the West in 1964, remained immune to their brainwashing.

Wang, Yi Chu. **Chinese Intellectuals and the West, 1872-1949.** Chapel Hill: University of North Carolina Press, 1966, 557 p.
A Peking-born historian details the beginning and development of the Chinese movement to study abroad, what the students accomplished upon their return home and the impact they later made on Chinese society and government.

Yu, Frederick T. C. **Mass Persuasion in Communist China.** New York: Praeger, 1964, 186 p.
The author, professor at Columbia University's School of Journalism, uses communist publications to show how the leaders of mainland China are using the "mass socialization of minds" as an instrument of power and a method of control.

Overseas Chinese

See also Khmer Republic (Cambodia), p. 750; Hong Kong, p. 754; Malaysia, p. 756; Philippines, p. 763; Fiji; French Polynesia; New Caledonia; Western Samoa; Nauru, p. 775; Malagasy Republic, p. 847; other subsections under China.

FitzGerald, Stephen. **China and the Overseas Chinese: A Study of Peking's Changing Policy, 1949-1970.** New York: Cambridge University Press, 1972, 268 p.
In this carefully researched study of a complicated legal, social and political problem, the author finds evidence that a cautious realism balances nationalism and revolutionary imperatives in at least this sphere of Chinese foreign policy.

Purcell, Victor William Williams Saunders. **The Chinese in Southeast Asia.** New York: Oxford University Press (for the Royal Institute of International Affairs), rev. ed., 1965, 623 p.
A new and revised edition of an important history of overseas Chinese, originally published in 1951.

Williams, Lea E. **The Future of the Overseas Chinese in Southeast Asia.** New York: McGraw-Hill (for the Council on Foreign Relations), 1966, 143 p.
In this survey of the Chinese overseas populations, the author finds that instead of a trend to return to China, they are fast assimilating into the countries of their adoption, particularly in Singapore and Malaysia.

Wu, Chun-hsi. **Dollars, Dependents and Dogma.** Stanford: Hoover Institution on War, Revolution, and Peace, 1967, 231 p.
A study of the intricate nature of overseas Chinese remittances to Communist China.

Sinkiang; National Minority Areas

See also (Central Asia and the Subcontinent of India) General, p. 652; Tibet, p. 654; Mongolian People's Republic, p. 713; other subsections under China.

Lattimore, Owen. **Studies in Frontier History.** New York: Oxford University Press, 1963, 565 p.

A selection of Professor Lattimore's papers, written in the years 1928–1958, and dealing chiefly, as the title indicates, with frontiers and frontier peoples in Asia: Sinkiang, Mongolia, Manchuria and China.

Moseley, George, ed. **The Party and the National Question in China.** Cambridge: M.I.T. Press, 1966, 186 p.
This volume includes a translation by the editor of Chang Chih-i's "A Discussion of the National Question in the Chinese Revolution and of Actual Nationalities Policy," written in 1956 by the deputy director of the United Front Work Department of the Chinese Communist Party. The document is an analysis of the Party's theoretical approach to the control of the 40 million Chinese inhabiting national minority areas.

Moseley, George. **A Sino-Soviet Cultural Frontier: The Ili Kazakh Autonomous Chou.** Cambridge: East Asian Research Center, Harvard University, 1966, 163 p.
A study of a sensitive region in Sinkiang on the Soviet border, the one from which 50,000 Kazakh and other Chinese minority people sought refuge in the neighboring Kazakh S.S.R.

Pien-chiang ts'ung-shu. Taipei: Meng Tsang Wei-yüan-hui, 1962– .
A multi-volume series on China's border regions published by the Tibet-Mongolia Commission of the Republic of China.

Tomson, Edgar. **Die Volksrepublik China und das Recht nationaler Minderheiten.** Frankfurt/Main: Metzner, 1963, 201 p.
A valuable collection of documents, translated from Chinese and Russian sources, on laws governing the national minority groups in the People's Republic of China.

Taiwan (Formosa)

See also Economic Growth and Development, p. 71; (Far East) General, p. 682; Philippines, p. 763; other subsections under China.

Chen, Lung-Chu and Lasswell, Harold D. **Formosa, China, and the United Nations.** New York: St. Martin's Press, 1967, 428 p.
The authors of this study recommend General Assembly and Security Council seats for Communist China and subsequent admission to the U.N. of Formosa which, "freed of the fantasies and abuses of Chiang's dictatorial leadership, . . . can become a viable and responsible member of the world community."

Cohen, Jerome Alan and Others. **Taiwan and American Policy: The Dilemma in U.S.-China Relations.** New York: Praeger, 1971, 191 p.
Proceedings of a conference held in March 1971 under the auspices of the League of Women Voters Education Fund and the National Committee on United States-China Relations.

Goddard, William G. **Formosa: A Study in Chinese History.** East Lansing: Michigan State University Press, 1966, 229 p.
A Chinese-speaking, retired Australian government official, who lived most of his life on Formosa, examines that island's past and suggests that it might provide lessons for China's future development.

Ho, Yhi-Min. **Agricultural Development of Taiwan, 1903–1960.** Nashville: Vanderbilt University Press, 1966, 172 p.
An analysis of the sources and patterns of Taiwan's successful agricultural transformation.

Hsieh, Chiao-min. **Taiwan—Ilha Formosa: A Geography in Perspective.** Washington: Butterworths, 1964, 372 p.
Using Chinese, Japanese and Western sources, Mr. Hsieh presents not only the physical environment of this strategic island but also its history as set against the variety of cultural groups that have occupied it.

Jacoby, Neil Herman. **U.S. Aid to Taiwan: A Study of Foreign Aid, Self-Help, and Development.** New York: Praeger, 1967, 364 p.
An analysis of the results of the $1.4 billion U.S. assistance provided Taiwan from 1951–1965, which helped the country to achieve a self-sustaining economic growth.

Kerr, George H. **Formosa Betrayed.** Boston: Houghton, 1965, 514 p.
A critique of U.S. policy toward Formosa and an appeal for better treatment of the indigenous people of the island.

Koo, Anthony Y. C. **The Role of Land Reform in Economic Development: A Case Study of Taiwan.** New York: Praeger, 1968, 197 p.
A study of the land reform in Taiwan, in the author's opinion a highly successful one, that was initiated in 1949 and completed in 1953.

Lin, Ching-ming. **Shirarezaru Taiwan: Taiwan dokuritsu undō no sakebi.** Tokyo: Sanseidō, 1970, 210 p.
A study, by a Chinese advocate of Taiwan's independence, published for a Japanese audience.

Mancall, Mark, ed. **Formosa Today.** New York: Praeger, 1964, 171 p.
Essays on the history, politics and economic and military problems in Taiwan. Most of the contributions originally appeared in *China Quarterly*.

Mendel, Douglas. **The Politics of Formosan Nationalism.** Berkeley: University of California Press, 1970, 315 p.
A study of the political attitudes of native-born Formosans, whose government in Taipei is dominated by the élite of post-1945 Nationalist refugees from China's mainland who account for only 20 percent of the island's population.

Morello, Frank P. **The International Legal Status of Formosa.** The Hague: Nijhoff, 1966, 107 p.
The author concludes his examination of the status of Formosa by saying that "the title to Formosa passed from Japan to the Republic of China at the time of dereliction" after the end of World War II.

Peng, Ming-min. **A Taste of Freedom: Memoirs of a Formosan Independence Leader.** New York: Holt, Rinehart and Winston, 1972, 270 p.
These memoirs provide insights into the relations between the native Formosans and the Nationalist Chinese government on the island.

Sasamoto, Takeji and Kawano, Shigetō, eds. **Taiwan keizai sōgō kenkyū.** Tokyo: Ajia Keizai Kenkyūjo, 1968, 3 v.
A comprehensive study of the economy of Taiwan.

Shen, Tsung-han. **Agricultural Development on Taiwan since World War II.** Ithaca: Comstock Publishing Associates, 1964, 399 p.
A study of the rapid economic growth in post-war Taiwan.

Tai, T'ien-chao. **Taiwan kokusai seiji shi kenkyū.** Tokyo: Hōsei Daigaku Shuppankyoku, 1971, 626 p.
A solid and comprehensive study of the Taiwan problem in international politics from the 16th century to the present, written by a Chinese scholar who teaches at Hosei University in Japan.

Wu, Rong-I. **The Strategy of Economic Development: A Case Study of Taiwan.** Brussels: Vander, 1971, 217 p.
A case study of economic development of Taiwan, based on the theories of J. C. H. Fei and G. Ranis.

Yang, Martin M. C. **Socio-Economic Results of Land Reform in Taiwan.** Honolulu: East-West Center Press, 1970, 555 p.
A study of the role of land reform in improving Nationalist China's agricultural production, rural living conditions and the raising of cultural levels since 1954.

MONGOLIAN PEOPLE'S REPUBLIC

See also (The United States) Foreign Policy, p. 229; Eastern Europe and the Soviet Bloc, p. 358; (Union of Soviet Socialist Republics) Foreign Policy, p. 550; Regional, National and Minority Problems, p. 580; (Central Asia and the Subcontinent of India) General, p. 652; (China) Sinkiang; National Minority Areas, p. 711.

Bawden, Charles R. **The Modern History of Mongolia.** New York: Praeger, 1968, 460 p.
The main object of this study is to show to what extent the Mongol Revolution was a result of native growth and to what extent it reflected the interests of the U.S.S.R.

Bitsch, Jørgen. **Mongolia: Unknown Land.** New York: Dutton, 1963, 159 p.
A sympathetic traveler's report of the Mongolian People's Republic.

Dupuy, Trevor N. and Others. **Area Handbook for Mongolia.** Washington: G.P.O., 500 p.
A useful reference with bibliographies, prepared by the Historical Evaluation and Research Organization for the American University.

Gungaadash, B. **Mongoliia segodniia: priroda, liudi, khoziaistvo.** Moscow: Progress, 1969, 285 p.
A survey of contemporary Mongolia, originally published in Mongolian.

Kapitsa, Mikhail Stepanovich and Ivanenko, Vasilii Ivanovich. **Druzhba, zavoevannaia v bor'be (sovetsko-mongol'skie otnosheniia).** Moscow: Izd-vo "Mezhdunarodnye Otnosheniia," 1965, 218 p.
A record of Soviet relations with Mongolia, "the first country to follow the Soviet Union on the path of socialism."

Murphy, George Gregory S. **Soviet Mongolia: A Study of the Oldest Political Satellite.** Berkeley: University of California Press, 1966, 224 p.
An analysis of the relationship between Outer Mongolia and the Soviet Union between 1921 and 1960.

Petrov, Victor. **Mongolia: A Profile.** New York: Praeger, 1970, 179 p.
An introductory study, containing a useful bibliography.

Rupen, Robert Arthur. **Mongols of the Twentieth Century.** Bloomington: Indiana University Press, 1964, 2 v.
An extensive survey of contemporary Mongolia, with a very useful bibliography.

Sanders, Alan J. K. **The People's Republic of Mongolia: A General Reference Guide.** New York: Oxford University Press, 1968, 232 p.
A useful handbook compiled largely from the Mongolian press.

Shirendyb, Bagaryn. **Istoriia mongol'skoi narodnoi revoliutsii 1921 goda.** Moscow: Nauka, 1971, 400 p.
A history of the political developments in Mongolia in 1921, published under the auspices of the Academy of Science of the U.S.S.R. The study was originally written in Mongolian.

Stolypine, Arcady with Stolypine, Dimitri. **La Mongolie entre Moscou et Pékin.** Paris: Stock, 1971, 238 p.
An historical and political analysis of the international relations of Mongolia, wedged between the three great Asian powers, Russia, China and Japan.

Vidal, Jean-Émile. **La Mongolie.** Paris: Julliard, 1971, 302 p.
An Asian specialist for *L'Humanité* allows his enthusiasm for Mongolia's grandeurs to crowd out any serious consideration of the underlying political and economic realities.

Zhukov, Evgenii Mikhailovich, *ed.* **Istoriia Mongol'skoi Narodnoi Respubliki.** Moscow: Nauka, 2d rev. ed., 1967, 537 p.
A history of the Mongolian People's Republic, published under the auspices of both the Soviet and Mongolian Academies of Science.

JAPAN

General

See also (The United States) Relations with Asia, p. 243; (Asia and the Pacific Area) General Surveys, p. 607; (Far East) General, p. 682; other subsections under Japan.

Beasley, William Gerald. **The Modern History of Japan.** New York: Praeger, 1963, 352 p.
A well-known University of London historian writes about Japan from the early nineteenth century to the present, with particular emphasis on political, social and economic factors.

Hall, John Whitney and Beardsley, Richard King. **Twelve Doors to Japan.** New York: McGraw-Hill, 1965, 649 p.
A useful introduction to Japanese culture and society.

Halloran, Richard. **Japan: Images and Realities.** New York: Knopf, 1969, 281 p.
A study of Japan's history and its political, social and economic order, with the conclusion that the national character of Japan will never become truly Western in essence.

Kennedy, Malcolm Duncan. **A History of Japan.** London: Weidenfeld, 1963, 365 p.
A useful history of Japan, with emphasis on the past century of industrial development.

Kitagawa, Joseph Mitsuo. **Religion in Japanese History.** New York: Columbia University Press, 1966, 475 p.
This scholarly study attempts to describe the role of religion in Japanese society from feudal times to the present.

Lequiller, Jean. **Le Japon.** Paris: Sirey, 1966, 621 p.
A general history.

Moore, Charles Alexander with Morris, Aldyth V., eds. **The Japanese Mind.** Honolulu: East-West Center Press; University of Hawaii Press, 1967, 357 p.
These papers from the Fourth East-West Philosophy Conference held at the University of Hawaii in 1964 attempt to explain the fundamentals of the Japanese mind as expressed in its great philosophies, religions and social customs.

Reischauer, Edwin Oldfather. **Japan: The Story of a Nation.** New York: Knopf, rev. ed., 1970, 345 p.
A thorough revision, with substantial changes, of a classic study, first published in 1946 under the title "Japan: Past and Present." The author was the U.S. Ambassador to Japan from 1961 to 1966.

Reischauer, Edwin Oldfather. **The United States and Japan.** Cambridge: Harvard University Press, 1965, 396 p.
An updated edition of a very thorough work, first published in 1950.

Recent History

General

See also General Works, p. 1; International Organization and Government, p. 96; War and Peace, p. 108; The World Since 1914, p. 129; (Asia and the Pacific Area) General Surveys, p. 607; (Far East) General, p. 682; other subsections under Japan.

Barker, Arthur J. **The March on Delhi.** London: Faber, 1963, 302 p.
An account of the 1944 attempt by the Japanese Imperial Army to invade India.

Bergamini, David. **Japan's Imperial Conspiracy.** New York: Morrow, 1971, 1,239 p.
This giant blend of intuitive speculation and painstaking research offers a radically different picture of twentieth-century Japanese politics that will upset orthodox applecarts right and left.

Gendaishi shiryō. Tokyo: Misuzu Shobō, 1962–72, 43 v. and 3 suppl. v.
A massive collection of source materials dealing with Japan's history from 1921 to the end of World War II in 1945.

Johnson, Chalmers A. **An Instance of Treason: Ozaki Hotsumi and the Sorge Spy Ring.** Stanford: Stanford University Press, 1964, 278 p.
A thorough account of the life and work of the Soviet ranking spy in Japan (concurrently China expert and adviser to high government executives) who was hanged by the Japanese government in 1944. Based primarily on Japanese-language sources, police and court records, and unpublished private materials.

Liang, Chin-tung. **The Sinister Face of the Mukden Incident.** New York: St. John's University Press, 1969, 188 p.
A well-documented study of the Mukden Incident in 1931, planned by a group of young Japanese officers. The author writes "that the spark ignited at Mukden spread until it kindled World War II."

Morley, James William, ed. **The Dilemmas of Growth in Prewar Japan.** Princeton: Princeton University Press, 1971, 527 p.
Essays by Japanese, English and American scholars on the political, economic and foreign policy problems of Japan in the 1930s and 1940s.

Otani, Keijiro. **Gumbatsu.** Tokyo: Tosho Shuppansha, 1971, 270 p.
   A study of the Japanese military establishment and the incident of February 26, 1936, in which young Japanese army men began a three-day abortive *coup d'état*.

Toland, John. **The Rising Sun: The Decline and Fall of the Japanese Empire, 1936-1945.** New York: Random House, 1970, 954 p.
   A solid history of the Japanese Empire's path to self-destruction.

Yoshida, Shigeru. **Japan's Decisive Century, 1867-1967.** New York: Praeger, 1967, 110 p.
   A succinct review of Japan's history since the Meiji Restoration, with emphasis on events following the Manchurian Incident. The late Dr. Yoshida was Foreign Minister in the surrender cabinet and Prime Minister through 1954.

Yoshihashi, Takehiko. **Conspiracy at Mukden: The Rise of the Japanese Military.** New Haven: Yale University Press, 1963, 274 p.
   The author, of American University's School of International Service, has used Tokyo War Crimes Trial materials and other sources, in Japanese and in English, to show how military leadership, with the aid of civilian ideologists and especially of Mori Kaku (the "true molder" of Japan's China policy) engineered the Mukden Incident, sometimes considered the beginning of World War II.

Since 1945

See also The Postwar World, p. 178; (The United States) Biographies, Memoirs and Addresses, p. 218; Foreign Policy, p. 229; (Asia and the Pacific Area) General Surveys, p. 607; (Far East) General, p. 682; other subsections under Japan.

Axelbank, Albert. **Black Star over Japan: Rising Forces of Militarism.** New York: Hill and Wang, 1972, 240 p.
   The author, a former UPI correspondent in Taiwan, argues that Japan will seek the status of a great military power.

Brannen, Noah S. **Sōka Gakkai: Japan's Militant Buddhists.** Richmond: John Knox Press, 1968, 181 p.
   A study of how the 16 million followers of a branch of Nichiren Buddhism threaten to take over Japan and aim to redeem the world, largely through aggressive mass-conversion tactics.

Brzezinski, Zbigniew Kazimierz. **The Fragile Blossom: Crisis and Change in Japan.** New York: Harper and Row, 1972, 153 p.
   A quick and imaginative overview of the Japanese situation in the coming years. Predictions: lower rates of economic growth, social instability, political vacillation, great-power status unattainable.

Emmerson, John K. **Arms, Yen and Power: The Japanese Dilemma.** New York: Dunellen, 1971, 420 p.
   The Deputy Chief of the U.S. Mission in Tokyo, 1962-67, in this attempt to forecast the Japanese future predicts that Japan will remain firmly non-nuclear and that "close coördination and consultation between Tokyo and Washington will continue."

Feis, Herbert. **Contest over Japan.** New York: Norton, 1967, 187 p.
   A leading diplomatic historian assesses the rivalry between the United States and the U.S.S.R. for the right to direct policies of Japan during the occupation, 1945-1952.

Guillain, Robert. **The Japanese Challenge.** Philadelphia: Lippincott, 1970, 352 p.
   A survey of the postwar transformation of Japan and of Japan's role in the world as an economic power. A translation of "Japon troisième grand" (Paris: Éditions du Seuil, 1969, 366 p.).

Johnson, Chalmers A. **Conspiracy at Matsukawa.** Berkeley: University of California Press, 1972, 460 p.
   In the summer of 1949 a passenger train was derailed in Japan after the tracks were sabotaged by persons unknown. Professor Johnson uses this still unsolved mystery as a thread to guide the reader through a labyrinth of speculation about democracy, the law, political culture and social change in postwar Japan.

Kahn, Herman. **The Emerging Japanese Superstate: Challenge and Response.** Englewood Cliffs: Prentice-Hall, 1970, 274 p.
   Speculations about the future of Japan by a well-known futurologist.

Minear, Richard H. **Victors' Justice: The Tokyo War Crimes Trial.** Princeton: Princeton University Press, 1971, 229 p.
Professor Minear argues that the Tokyo trials of 1946–48 were politically motivated, arbitrarily conducted and legally invalid.

Olson, Lawrence Alexander. **Dimensions of Japan.** New York: American Universities Field Staff, 1963, 403 p.
A collection of reports on the political, economic and social aspects of postwar Japan written for the American Universities Field Staff.

Riesman, David and Riesman, Evelyn Thompson. **Conversations in Japan: Modernization, Politics, and Culture.** New York: Basic Books, 1967, 371 p.
Discussions of a Harvard sociologist and his author wife with some of Japan's most gifted intellectuals, revealing the ideas and prejudices that are shaping Japanese thought and attitudes.

Robert, Jacques. **Le Japon.** Paris: Librairie Générale de Droit, 1970, 524 p.
The author of this study on contemporary Japan sees the Japanese re-ascent to world prominence as challenge, example and opportunity for French diplomacy.

Sebald, William Joseph with Brines, Russell. **With MacArthur in Japan: A Personal History of the Occupation.** New York: Norton, 1965, 318 p.
The senior civilian official during the U.S. occupation of Japan, with previous experience there since 1925, reconstructs aspects of the occupation from journals kept from 1945 to 1952. Mr. Brines, the co-author, was Chief of the Bureau of Associated Press in Tokyo during most of that period.

Sheldon, Walter J. **The Honorable Conquerors.** New York: Macmillan, 1965, 336 p.
A description of the U.S. occupation of Japan by a writer with many years of experience in the Far East.

Wendt, Ingeborg Y. **Geht Japan nach links?** Reinbek bei Hamburg: Rowohlt, 1964, 158 p.
An analysis of contemporary Japanese political and cultural trends, and a criticism of the superficiality of the prevalent Western views about modern Japan by a German psychologist.

White Papers of Japan: Annual Abstract of Official Reports and Statistics of the Japanese Government, 1969-70—. Tokyo: Japan Institute of International Affairs, 1971—.
A most useful annual reference volume.

Yamaguchi, Ichirō. **Kindai Chūgoku tainichikan no kenkyū.** Tokyo: Ajia Keizai Kenkyūjo, 1970, 235 p.
A study of contemporary Chinese views of Japan.

Yanaga, Chitoshi. **Big Business in Japanese Politics.** New Haven: Yale University Press, 1968, 371 p.
A study of how Japan's postwar recovery as a major industrial power was accomplished through the coöperation between organized business and government.

Biographies and Memoirs

See also Second World War, p. 144; other subsections under Japan.

Browne, Courtney. **Tōjō: The Last Banzai.** New York: Holt, Rinehart and Winston, 1967, 260 p.
The life of a Japanese militarist who was hanged on December 23, 1948.

Harada, Kumao, Baron. **Fragile Victory: Prince Saionji and the 1930 London Treaty Issue, from the Memoirs of Baron Harada Kumao.** Detroit: Wayne State University Press, 1968, 330 p.
Baron Harado Kumao, the author of these memoirs, was the secretary to Prince Saionji, the last of the Genro, a body of elder statesmen that had to advise and protect the throne. Translated and introduced by Thomas Francis Mayer-Oakes.

Kublin, Hyman. **Asian Revolutionary: The Life of Sen Katayama.** Princeton: Princeton University Press, 1964, 370 p.
The first detailed study of the "father of Asian Communism" who, over a period of 50 years, proceeded from Christian socialism to revolutionary communism to become

a member of the Executive Committee and Praesidium of the Communist International.

Miller, Frank Owen. **Minobe Tatsukichi: Interpreter of Constitutionalism in Japan.** Berkeley: University of California Press, 1965, 392 p.

This study of Minobe's early career shows Japan's lag in adopting democratic ways and institutions (from the 1890s to the 1930s) and discusses his influence on the controversial constitutional strategy of the Japanese government during the occupation.

Miwa, Kimitada. **Matsuoka Yōsuke.** Tokyo: Chūō Kōronsha, 1971, 211 p.

A study of Matsuoka Yōsuke, the Japanese diplomat who represented Japan at the League of Nations during the Manchurian crisis.

Mosley, Leonard Oswald. **Hirohito: Emperor of Japan.** Englewood Cliffs: Prentice-Hall, 1966, 371 p.

A highly readable and well-documented biography of the man whose story necessarily reveals much about the history of the Japanese people over a period of 60 years. The author is a British journalist.

Potter, John Deane. **Yamamoto: The Man Who Menaced America.** New York: Viking, 1965, 332 p.

A commissioned officer in World War II and former newspaper editor in Tokyo writes of the Harvard-educated Admiral Isoroku Yamamoto, Commander-in-Chief of the Combined Japanese Fleet and master-mind of the Pearl Harbor attack. The English edition was published as "Admiral of the Pacific: The Life of Yamamoto" (London: Heinemann, 1965, 332 p.).

Wilson, George Macklin. **Radical Nationalist in Japan: Kita Ikki, 1883-1937.** Cambridge: Harvard University Press, 1969, 230 p.

A careful study of an influential Japanese nationalist that provides a corrective to the pigeonholing of him as a fascist.

Foreign and Defense Policies

See also International Organization and Government, p. 96; War and Peace, p. 108; Inter-War Period, p. 140; Second World War, p. 144; The Postwar World, p. 178; (The United States) Biographies, Memoirs and Addresses, p. 218; Foreign Policy, p. 229; (Great Britain) Foreign Policy, p. 375; (Union of Soviet Socialist Republics) Foreign Policy, p. 550; China, p. 683; other subsections under Japan and the sections for specific countries and regions.

Crowley, James Buckley. **Japan's Quest for Autonomy: National Security and Foreign Policy, 1930-1938.** Princeton: Princeton University Press, 1966, 428 p.

A study of the changing definitions of national security and national objectives within the Japanese government in the 1930s. Emphasis is on attitudes, opinions and policies as articulated by the ministers of state.

Curtis, Gerald L., ed. **Japanese-American Relations in the 1970s.** Washington: Columbia Books, 1970, 204 p.

Seven essays originally prepared as background reading for participants in the Second Japanese-American Assembly, sponsored by the Japan Council for International Understanding and the American Assembly, at Shimoda, Japan, in 1967.

Dunn, Frederick S. **Peace-Making and the Settlement with Japan.** Princeton: Princeton University Press, 1963, 210 p.

This significant work, completed by colleagues after Professor Dunn's death in 1962, deals with the plans for and background to the Japanese Peace Treaty signed in 1951. A concluding chapter considers the effect of this settlement on Pacific security.

Endō, Haruhisa. **Hoppō ryōdo mondai no shinsō: Chishima Rettō to Yalta Kaidan.** Tokyo: Yūshindō, 1968, 274 p.

A noteworthy study of the problems of the Northern Territories (the Kurile Islands), particularly as caused by the decisions of the Yalta Conference.

Hellmann, Donald C. **Japan and East Asia: The New International Order.** New York: Praeger, 1972, 243 p.

A thorough analysis of the choices facing Japanese foreign policy in Asia.

Hellmann, Donald C. **Japanese Foreign Policy and Domestic Politics.** Berkeley: University of California Press, 1969, 202 p.

An important work on the actions and interactions by and among political parties, private pressure groups and governmental institutions which affected the course of negotiations for the Japanese-U.S.S.R. peace agreement.

Hosoya, Chihiro. **Roshia kakumei to Nihon.** Tokyo: Hara Shobō, 1972, 271 p.
A study of the Japanese role in the Allied interventions in Russia beginning in 1918.

Ishikawa, Tadao; Doi, Akira and Wakaizumi, Kei. **Nihon no Kokka Rieki to Chūkyō no Kokka Rieki.** Tokyo: Ajia Chōsakai, 1966, 222 p.
Three prominent Japanese scholars discuss Sino-Japanese relations.

The Japan Annual of International Affairs, 1961—. Tokyo: Japan Institute of International Affairs, 1961—.
A most useful collection of articles, research reports and book reviews dealing with Japanese foreign relations and political and economic conditions. Volume 5, entitled "Japan Institute of International Affairs Annual Review, 1969–70," was published in 1970.

Japan in Current World Affairs. Tokyo: Kajima Institute of International Peace, 1971, 308 p.
A collection of articles by "well-known and authoritative experts of Japan on political or economic international relations."

Kajima, Morinosuke. **A Brief Diplomatic History of Modern Japan.** Rutland (Vt.): Tuttle, 1965, 216 p.
A review of Japan's post-World War II foreign policies, by a Japanese businessman, diplomat and a leading student of his country's foreign relations. Translation of "Nihon gaikō no tembō" (Tokyo: Jiji Tsūshinsha, 1964, 258 p.).

Kajima, Morinosuke. **The Emergence of Japan as a World Power, 1895–1925.** Rutland (Vt.): Tuttle, 1968, 403 p.
A survey of the principles of Japan's diplomacy from the Triple Intervention to the restoration of relations with Soviet Russia. The Japanese original was published as "Nihon gaikō seisaku no shiteki kōsatsu" (Tokyo: Kajima Kenkyūjo, 5th ed., 1958, 490 p.).

Kajima, Morinosuke. **Modern Japan's Foreign Policy.** Rutland (Vt.): Tuttle, 1969, 327 p.
A condensed English version of "Nihon no gaikō seisaku" (Tokyo: Kajima Kenkyūjo, 1966, 501 p.), written on the basis of the author's thirteen-year experience as chairman of the ruling Liberal Democratic Party's Foreign Relations Research Committee and of the Foreign Affairs Committee of the Japanese Diet's House of Councillors.

Kennedy, Malcolm Duncan. **The Estrangement of Great Britain and Japan, 1917–35.** Berkeley: University of California Press, 1969, 363 p.
Captain Kennedy, for many years Reuter's correspondent in Japan and author of a general history of Japan and books dealing with the Japanese army, has written a judicious review, enlivened with personal recollections. The author blames the Chinese for the deterioration of relations between Britain and Japan.

Kesavan, K. V. **Japan's Relations with Southeast Asia, 1952–60: With Particular Reference to the Philippines and Indonesia.** Bombay: Somaiya, 1972, 243 p.
A study of Japanese efforts to win the confidence of two major Southeast Asian countries.

Lensen, George Alexander. **Japanese Diplomatic and Consular Officials in Russia: A Handbook of Japanese Representatives in Russia from 1874–1968.** Tokyo: Sophia University (in coöperation with the Diplomatic Press, Tallahassee), 1968, 230 p.
A useful reference.

Lensen, George Alexander. **Japanese Recognition of the U.S.S.R.: Soviet-Japanese Relations 1921–1930.** Tokyo: Sophia University (in coöperation with the Diplomatic Press, Tallahassee), 1970, 419 p.
The first significant, though ponderous, monograph on the subject, based primarily on published Russian and Japanese sources.

Morley, James William, *ed.* **Forecast for Japan: Security in the 1970's.** Princeton: Princeton University Press, 1972, 249 p.
A collection of papers examining Japan's military options in the 1970s.

Morley, James William. **Japan and Korea: America's Allies in the Pacific.** New York: Walker, 1965, 152 p.

A leading Far Eastern expert interprets the political situations in Japan and Korea and the relationships between the two countries, especially those aspects affecting American policies.

Morris, M. D. **Okinawa: A Tiger by the Tail.** New York: Hawthorn Books, 1969, 238 p.
A study of Okinawa in American-Japanese relations since World War II.

Mushakōji, Kinhide. **Takyokuka jidai no Nihon gaikō.** Tokyo: Tōkyō Daigaku Shuppankai, 1971, 229 p.
A study of contemporary Japanese diplomacy.

Nihon gaikō shi. Tokyo: Kajima Heiwa Kenkyūjo, 1970–71, 33 v., and 5 suppl. v.
A monumental Japanese diplomatic history, covering developments from the middle of the 19th century to the 1970s.

Nitchū kankei kihon shiryō shū, 1949 nen–1969 nen. Tokyo: Kazan, 1970, 447 p.
A collection of documents on Sino-Japanese relations from 1949 to 1969, compiled by the China Section of the Japanese Ministry of Foreign Affairs.

Ogata, Sadako N. **Defiance in Manchuria: The Making of Japanese Foreign Policy, 1931–1932.** Berkeley: University of California Press, 1964, 259 p.
Mrs. Ogata effectively reconstructs the military and civil power struggles within Japan to trace the origins of Japan's "expansionist foreign policy that worked to her own destruction."

Ōhira, Zengo. **Ajia gaikō to Nikkan kankei: taikan rongi o kiru.** Tokyo: Yūshindō, 1965, 272 p.
A study of Japanese Asian policies and Japanese-Korean relations.

Olson, Lawrence Alexander. **Japan in Postwar Asia.** New York: Praeger (for the Council on Foreign Relations), 1970, 292 p.
A scholarly work tracing the shift in the character of Japanese-Asian relations, from one predominantly commercial to one that recognizes the need to promote stability throughout the entire Asian region. The author has made extensive use of Japanese sources.

The Pacific Rivals. New York: Weatherhill/Asahi, 1972, 431 p.
An overview of the Japanese-American relationship, originally published serially in Tokyo's *Asahi Shimbun*.

Packard, George R., III. **Protest in Tokyo: The Security Treaty Crisis of 1960.** Princeton: Princeton University Press, 1966, 423 p.
A former Special Assistant to Ambassador Reischauer examines with painstaking detail the massive Tokyo riots of May and June 1960, held in protest against the revised Security Treaty with the United States. Although communist activity was involved, he finds no single, simple explanation of the disturbances.

Petrov, Dmitrii Vasil'evich. **Vneshniaia politika Iaponii posle Vtoroi mirovoi voiny.** Moscow: "Nauka," 1964, 240 p.
A study of Japanese foreign policy after World War II by a Soviet writer who was *Izvestiia*'s correspondent in Japan for five years.

Rosovsky, Henry, *ed.* **Discord in the Pacific: Challenges to the Japanese-American Alliance.** Washington: Columbia Books (for the American Assembly, Columbia University), 1972, 251 p.
Papers, from the third Japanese-American Assembly (summer 1972), which reflect and analyze the uneasy relationship of the two nations.

Takagi, Yasaka, *ed.* **Nichi-Bei kankei no kenkyū.** Tokyo: Tōkyō Daigaku Shuppankai, 1968–70, 2 v.
Essays by Japanese scholars on various aspects of contemporary Japanese-U.S. relations.

Taoka, Ryōichi. **Kokusaihōjō no jieiken.** Tokyo: Keisō Shobō, 1964, 379 p.
A statement of Japan's right of self-defense according to international law.

Teradaira, Tadasuke. **Rokōkyō jiken.** Tokyo: Yomiuri Shimbunsha, 1970, 454 p.
This study of the Marco Polo Bridge Incident of July 7, 1937, which precipitated the war with China, was prepared by a former special assistant to the Japanese intelligence unit in Peking who was engaged in negotiations with the Chinese at that time. The author bases his work on sources in Japan and China and on extensive interviews.

Ueno, Hideo. **Gendai Nitchū kankei no tenkai.** Tokyo: Futaba Shoten, 1971, 298 p.
  A study of the development of contemporary Sino-Japanese relations.

Watanabe, Akio. **The Okinawa Problem: A Chapter in Japan-U.S. Relations.** Melbourne: Melbourne University Press, 1970, 220 p.
  A useful study by an Australian-trained scholar at the University of Hong Kong.

Weinstein, Martin E. **Japan's Postwar Defense Policy, 1947–1968.** New York: Columbia University Press, 1971, 160 p.
  This concise but thorough study argues that Japanese conservative planners have managed to stick consistently to a military strategy worked out after the end of World War II in Tokyo, not Washington.

Yoshihara, Kōichirō and Others, eds. **Nichi-Bei ampo jōyaku taiseishi.** Tokyo: Sanseidō, 1970–71, 4 v.
  A history of the Japanese-U.S. Security Treaty.

Politics and Government

See also Political Factors, p. 12; other subsections under Japan.

Bakke, Edward Wight. **Revolutionary Democracy: Challenge and Testing in Japan.** Hamden (Conn.): Archon Books, 1968, 343 p.
  A Yale economist studies the significance of the ideas of American democracy for national development in Japan.

Beckmann, George M. and Genji, Okubo. **The Japanese Communist Party, 1922–1945.** Stanford: Stanford University Press, 1969, 453 p.
  This substantial study includes biographical sketches, a chronology and a bibliography.

Cole, Allan Burnett and Others. **Socialist Parties in Postwar Japan.** New Haven: Yale University Press, 1966, 490 p.
  Studies of Japan's non-communist leftist parties from 1945 to 1961.

Curtis, Gerald L. **Election Campaigning Japanese Style.** New York: Columbia University Press, 1971, 275 p.
  Perceptive observations by an author who spent nine months in Japan in 1966.

Duus, Peter. **Party Rivalry and Political Change in Taishō Japan.** Cambridge: Harvard University Press, 1968, 317 p.
  A study of the developments in Japanese Diet politics, from 1912 to 1927, when the established political parties achieved a decisive measure of control over the Cabinet.

Fukui, Haruhiro. **Party in Power: The Japanese Liberal-Democrats and Policy-Making.** Berkeley: University of California Press, 1970, 301 p.
  A pioneering study of policy-making in Japan's most important political party, by a professor at the University of California of Santa Barbara.

Higa, Mikio. **Politics and Parties in Postwar Okinawa.** Vancouver: University of British Columbia, 1963, 128 p.
  A study of U.S. administrative programs and internal politics in Okinawa from 1945 to 1962, with emphasis on the American impact on the party system.

Hori, Kenji. **Gendai Nihon no seiji kōzō.** Tokyo: Mineruba Shobō, 1971, 223 p.
  An analysis of Japanese politics, particularly as conditioned by contemporary international developments.

Ike, Nobutaka. **Japanese Politics: Patron-Client Democracy.** New York: Knopf, 2d ed., 1972, 149 p.
  A completely revised edition of a very solid introduction to Japanese politics, first published in 1957.

Ishida, Takeshi. **Nihon no seiji bunka.** Tokyo: Tōkyō Daigaku Shuppankai, 1970, 228 p.
  The author of this study of the political culture of Japan argues that the main element contributing to Japan's rapid progress and development is the Japanese willingness to conform and to compete.

Kevenhörster, Paul. **Das politische System Japans.** Cologne: Westdeutscher Verlag, 1969, 330 p.
  A comprehensive and critical analysis of contemporary Japanese politics.

Kobayashi, Yoshiaki. **Sengo Kakumei undō ronsō shi.** Tokyo: Sanichi Shobō, 1971, 387 p.

A systematic study of the relations between the Socialist and Communist Parties in postwar Japan, with emphasis on their differing positions on a whole range of domestic and international political issues.

Langer, Paul F. **Communism in Japan: A Case of Political Naturalization.** Stanford: Hoover Institution Press, 1972, 112 p.

A scholar at the RAND Corporation asserts in this study that the Japanese Communist Party must "naturalize" itself as a genuinely independent and native organization if it wishes to prosper.

Maki, John McGilvrey. **Court and Constitution in Japan: Selected Supreme Court Decisions, 1948-60.** Seattle: University of Washington Press, 1964, 445 p.

The decisions selected for translation show the impact which the new Constitution has had on that formerly authoritarian country.

Maruyama, Masao. **Thought and Behaviour in Modern Japanese Politics.** New York: Oxford University Press, rev. ed., 1969, 407 p.

An expanded edition of a volume of essays on Japanese political issues, by an eminent Japanese political scientist. Edited by Ivan Morris.

Monnier, Claude. **Les Américains et Sa Majesté l'Empereur: étude du conflit culturel d'où naquit la constitution japonaise de 1946.** Geneva: Institut Universitaire de Hautes Etudes Internationales, 1967, 222 p.

A comparison of American and Japanese political systems and of their peoples' attitudes toward constitutional revision. Based almost exclusively on English sources.

Nakamura, Kikuo. **Nihon ni okeru seitō to seiji ishiki.** Tokyo: Keiō Gijuku Daigaku Hōgaku Kenkyūkai, 1971, 408 p.

A study of political parties and party consciousness in Japan.

Nihon no fashizumu: keisei ki no kenkyū. Tokyo: Waseda Daigaku Shuppanbu, 1970, 339 p.

A study of the evolution and growth of Japanese fascism in the early twentieth century up to the 1930s.

Scalapino, Robert Anthony. **The Japanese Communist Movement, 1920-1966.** Berkeley: University of California Press, 1967, 412 p.

A detailed history of the Japanese Communist Party: its ideological evolution, relations to other political forces, role in the international communist movement and the reasons why it has failed to attract and to hold a mass following. Emphasis is on the post-1945 period.

Steiner, Kurt. **Local Government in Japan.** Stanford: Stanford University Press, 1965, 564 p.

Following a historical survey from the beginning of the Meiji Era to 1952, Professor Steiner of Stanford describes and analyzes contemporary local government in Japan.

Stockwin, James Arthur Ainscow. **The Japanese Socialist Party and Neutralism.** New York: Cambridge University Press, 1968, 197 p.

A study of the main Japanese opposition party and its foreign policy, based primarily on Japanese-language sources and on interviews with leading members of the Japanese Socialist Party. The author is an Australian scholar.

Thayer, Nathaniel B. **How the Conservatives Rule Japan.** Princeton: Princeton University Press, 1969, 349 p.

A discussion of the Liberal Democratic Party (formed in 1955) and of the role of factions within the party.

Totten, George Oakley, III. **The Social Democratic Movement in Prewar Japan.** New Haven: Yale University Press, 1966, 455 p.

This well-documented study by a professor from the University of Southern California covers the period from 1925 to 1940.

Tsunekawa, Nobuyuki. **Nihon Kyōsantō to Watanabe Masanosuke.** Tokyo: Sanichi Shobō, 1971, 368 p.

A study of the Japanese Communist Party and of Watanabe Masanosuke, a founding member and Comintern activist until his death in 1928.

Von Mehren, Arthur Taylor, ed. **Law in Japan: The Legal Order in a Changing Society.** Cambridge: Harvard University Press, 1963, 706 p.
Papers on Japan's legal system and law processes.

Waga kuni ni okeru kyōsanshugi undōshi gairon. Tokyo: Tōyō Bunkasha (for the Shakai Mondai Shiryō Kenkyūkai), 1971, 327 p.
An introduction to the history of communist movements in Japan.

Ward, Robert Edward. **Japan's Political System.** Englewood Cliffs: Prentice-Hall, 1967, 126 p.
A Stanford University professor uses the theory of comparative politics to evaluate Japan's high level of accomplishments and to point to problems obstructing true parliamentary procedures.

Ward, Robert Edward, ed. **Political Development in Modern Japan.** Princeton: Princeton University Press, 1968, 637 p.
Studies which identify and analyze the principal factors for Japanese political development.

Ward, Robert Edward and Rustow, Dankwart A., eds. **Political Modernization in Japan and Turkey.** Princeton: Princeton University Press, 1964, 502 p.
Essays by leading American scholars on politics, economics, education, mass media and other topics in the effort to account for the success of Japan and Turkey in modernization and for the differences in their rates and patterns. Revisions of papers prepared for a Gould House conference in September 1962.

Economic Problems

See also Problems of New Nations, p. 36; Economic Factors, p. 49; (The United States) Trade, Tariffs and Finance, p. 251; (Asia and the Pacific Area) General Surveys, p. 607; (Far East) General, p. 682; (Africa) Economic and Social Problems, p. 789; other subsections under Japan.

Abegglen, James C., ed. **Business Strategies for Japan.** Tokyo: Sophia University, 1971, 221 p.
This compendium of factual information concerning Japanese business practices and institutions is designed to help foreign firms conduct business operations in Japan. It is the product of the activities of the Boston Consulting Group.

Adams, T. F. M. and Hoshii, Iwao. **A Financial History of the New Japan.** Palo Alto: Kodansha International, 1972, 547 p.
A comprehensive reference manual on Japan's financial development since the conclusion of World War II. There is a wealth of statistical source material.

Adams, T. F. M. and Kobayashi, N. **The World of Japanese Business.** Palo Alto: Kodansha International, 1969, 326 p.
An American, long residing in Japan, and a Japanese, with American experience, offer observations on Japanese business customs.

Allen, George Cyril. **Japan's Economic Expansion.** New York: Oxford University Press (for the Royal Institute of International Affairs), 1965, 296 p.
A treatise on Japan's development in agriculture, industry, finance and trade since World War II; a much enlarged version of the author's "Japan's Economic Recovery" (1958).

Ballon, Robert J. and Lee, Eugene H., eds. **Foreign Investment and Japan.** Tokyo: Sophia University in coöperation with Kodansha International, 1972, 340 p.
This volume contains useful information on Japan and on Japan's own foreign investments.

Bennett, John William and Ishino, Iwao. **Paternalism in the Japanese Economy.** Minneapolis: University of Minnesota Press, 1963, 307 p.
This scholarly work, by two American professors, based on research during the military occupation of Japan, describes relationships among employers and employees in light of the then existing feudal and family systems.

Bieda, Ken. **The Structure and Operation of the Japanese Economy.** New York: Wiley, 1970, 292 p.
A valuable study of the functioning of the modern Japanese economy.

Brochier, Hubert. **Le Miracle économique japonais.** Paris: Calmann-Lévy, 1965, 308 p.
A study of the remarkable achievements of Japanese economy after World War II by a French professor who spent two years in Japan with a French delegation.

Hadley, Eleanor M. **Antitrust in Japan.** Princeton: Princeton University Press, 1970, 528 p.
An account of how and why the United States military government tried to break up Japan's family-owned and operated business giants, the *zaibatsu* companies.

Hollerman, Leon. **Japan's Dependence on the World Economy: The Approach toward Economic Liberalization.** Princeton: Princeton University Press, 1967, 291 p.
A study of the structural difficulties of the Japanese economy during the process of liberalization of its trade and payments, together with an evaluation of the policies with which that liberalization has been associated.

Huh, Kyung-Mo. **Japan's Trade in Asia.** New York: Praeger, 1966, 283 p.
A Korean economist investigates the development of Japan's trade with Asian countries since the mid-1920s and projects the prospects for future trade expansion.

Hunsberger, Warren Seabury. **Japan and the United States in World Trade.** New York: Harper and Row (for the Council on Foreign Relations), 1964, 492 p.
A comprehensive examination of Japan's commercial and financial relations with the United States. The author, an experienced observer of the Asian scene, also provides a careful analysis of Japan's trading and balance-of-payments position with the rest of the world, and offers suggestions on likely trade developments.

Ikeda, Kotaro and Others. **Die industrielle Entwicklung in Japan unter besonderer Berücksichtigung seiner Wirtschafts- und Finanzpolitik.** Berlin: Duncker, 1970, 234 p.
A study of the industrialization of Japan, paying particular attention to the economic doctrines that have influenced its course.

Jéquier, Nicolas. **Le Défi industriel japonais.** Lausanne: Centre de Recherches Européennes, 1970, 189 p.
To the author of this study the Japanese industrial development is both a model and a threat.

Kojima, Kiyoshi. **Japan and a Pacific Free Trade Area.** Berkeley: University of California Press, 1971, 195 p.
This discussion of the problems a Pacific Free Trade Area would raise provides the author also with the opportunity to examine various aspects of Japan's place in the world economy.

Komiya, Ryūtaro, *ed.* **Postwar Economic Growth in Japan.** Berkeley: University of California Press (for the Center for Japanese and Korean Studies), 1966, 260 p.
Translations of papers prepared for the Conference on Japan's Postwar Economic Growth held in January 1963 in Zushi City, Kanagawa Prefecture.

Kurihara, Kenneth K. **The Growth Potential of the Japanese Economy.** Baltimore: Johns Hopkins Press, 1971, 148 p.
Professor Kurihara sees the reasons for Japan's formidable economic growth in the coupling of a "delicate and intricate tradition of state paternalism" with an urgently felt and universally shared need to "catch up."

Lockwood, William W., *ed.* **The State and Economic Enterprise in Japan: Essays in the Political Economy of Growth.** Princeton: Princeton University Press, 1965, 753 p.
Papers resulting from a seminar held under the auspices of the Association for Asian Studies' Conference on Modern Japan in 1963.

Lynch, John. **Toward an Orderly Market: An Intensive Study of Japan's Voluntary Quota in Cotton Textile Exports.** Tokyo: Sophia University (in coöperation with Tuttle, Rutland), 1969, 215 p.
A study by an American Jesuit.

Michalski, Wolfgang and Others. **Perspektiven der wirtschaftlichen Entwicklung in Japan.** Stuttgart: Deutsche Verlags-Anstalt, 1972, 418 p.
A most informative study of Japan's economic prospects by six economists at Hamburg's Institute for the Study of Technological Development.

Nippon: A Chartered Survey of Japan. Tokyo: The Tsuneta Yano Memorial Society.
A very informative survey of Japan's economy, including a wealth of statistics. Published since 1936; the 15th edition was published in 1970.

Ogura, Takekazu, *ed.* **Agricultural Development in Modern Japan.** Tokyo: Fuji Publishing Co., 1963, 688 p.
A compilation of essays concerning the economic, legal and technological aspects of agriculture. Of special importance are the chapters on the land tenure system, small-scale farming, and paddy-field rice culture.

Ohkawa, Kazushi and Others, *eds.* **Agriculture and Economic Growth: Japan's Experience.** Princeton: Princeton University Press, 1970, 433 p.
Papers presented and examined at the International Conference on Agriculture and Economic Development—a Symposium on Japan's Experience, in Tokyo in 1967.

Ozaki, Robert S. **The Control of Imports and Foreign Capital in Japan.** New York: Praeger, 1972, 309 p.
A valuable compendium of Japanese legislation and policy statements and an analysis of how, under certain circumstances, a policy of limited and strategic protectionism can work spectacularly well.

Shinohara, Miyohei. **Growth and Cycles in the Japanese Economy.** Tokyo: Kinokuniya Bookstore (for the Institute of Economic Research, Hitotsubashi University), 1962, 349 p.
A collection of articles on the high rate of growth of the Japanese economy.

Stone, Peter B. **Japan Surges ahead: The Story of an Economic Miracle.** New York: Praeger, 1969, 206 p.
A survey by a British journalist.

Taira, Koji. **Economic Development and the Labor Market in Japan.** New York: Columbia University Press, 1970, 282 p.
The author attempts a wholesale debunking of received ideas about Japanese economic growth. A solid but controversial work.

Yamamura, Kozo. **Economic Policy in Postwar Japan: Growth Versus Economic Democracy.** Berkeley: University of California Press, 1967, 226 p.
A study of the nature and results of the economic democratization that was caused by the U.S. occupation.

Social Problems

See also Labor and Labor Movements, p. 41; Culture; Education; Public Opinion; Communications Processes, p. 42; (Asia and the Pacific Area) General Surveys, p. 607; other subsections under Japan.

Ayusawa, Iwao Frederick. **A History of Labor in Modern Japan.** Honolulu: East-West Center Press, 1966, 406 p.
A detailed history of labor development in Japan from 1868 to 1962, by a leading authority whose specialization in the field goes back to the early days of the I.L.O.

Delassus, Jean-François. **The Japanese: A Critical Evaluation of the Character & Culture of a People.** New York: Hart, 1972, 300 p.
An unfriendly observer depicts Japan as a prototype of a dehumanized society. The French original was published as "Le Japon: monstre ou modèle?" (Paris: Hachette, 1970, 318 p.).

Dimock, Marshall Edward. **The Japanese Technocracy: Management and Government in Japan.** New York: Walker/Weatherhill, 1968, 197 p.
A study based on observations the author made in 1966–67 while he was a Ford Visiting Professor at the International Christian University in Tokyo.

Dore, Ronald Philip, *ed.* **Aspects of Social Change in Modern Japan.** Princeton: Princeton University Press, 1967, 474 p.
A collection of papers delivered at a seminar sponsored by the Conference on Modern Japan in 1963.

Ishida, Takeshi. **Japanese Society.** New York: Random House, 1971, 145 p.
A study by a distinguished Japanese sociologist.

Jansen, Marius Berthus, *ed*. **Changing Japanese Attitudes toward Modernization.** Princeton: Princeton University Press, 1965, 546 p.
Papers by leading world experts, prepared for a 1962 Bermuda seminar sponsored by the Conference on Modern Japan of the Association for Asian Studies.

Passin, Herbert. **Society and Education in Japan.** New York: Teachers College and East Asian Institute, Columbia University, 1965, 347 p.
A Columbia University sociologist, long a resident in Japan and with full command of its language, traces the Japanese educational system from the Tokugawa Period (1603–1867) to the present, illustrating his main points with 43 selected documents.

Plath, David W. **The After Hours: Modern Japan and the Search for Enjoyment.** Berkeley: University of California Press, 1964, 222 p.
A report on a field study project on Honshu Island in 1959–1960 to determine the effect of modernization on the Japanese use of leisure time by a professor at the University of Illinois.

Shively, Donald H., *ed*. **Tradition and Modernization in Japanese Culture.** Princeton: Princeton University Press, 1971, 689 p.
Papers from the fifth seminar of the Conference on Modern Japan, held in Puerto Rico in January 1966.

Vogel, Ezra Feivel. **Japan's New Middle Class.** Berkeley: University of California Press, 1963, 299 p.
The results of field work conducted in Japan from 1958–1960 by trained social scientists to show the emergence of the white-collar worker and the increased importance of his status in the postwar period.

KOREA

General

See also (General Works) General Treatments, p. 7; (Germany) Post-World War II Era, General, p. 487; (Asia and the Pacific Area) General Surveys, p. 607; (Far East) General, p. 682; Republic of Vietnam, p. 746; other subsections under Korea.

Cho, Soon Sung. **Korea in World Politics, 1940–1950: An Evaluation of American Responsibility.** Berkeley: University of California Press, 1967, 338 p.
This study is primarily a discussion of American policy toward Korea from the 1943 Cairo Conference to the end of the Korean War.

Choy, Bong-youn. **Korea: A History.** Rutland (Vt.): Tuttle, 1971, 474 p.
The author concludes his general survey of Korean history with a plea for unification and "for permanent neutrality plus U.N.-supervised nationwide free elections."

Han'guk tongnip undong-sa. Seoul: Kuksa P'yŏnch'an Wiŏnhoe, 1965–68, 4 v.
A history of Korean independence movements.

Hatada, Takashi. **A History of Korea.** Santa Barbara: ABC-Clio, 1969, 182 p.
A study especially concerned with the inter-relationship between Korea's political history and its social and economic development, by a Korean-born Japanese.

Hayashi, Takehiko. **Kita Chōsen to minami Chōsen.** Tokyo: Saimaru Shuppankai, 1971, 256 p.
A Japanese monograph on North and South Korea, with emphasis on the problems concerning the eventual unification.

Hŭngsadan osimnyŏn-sa. Seoul: Taesŏng Munhwasa, 1964, 348 p.
A study of the Hŭngsa Party, founded by An Ch'ang-ho in 1913 for the recovery, development and reformation of the Korean people.

Kazakevich, Igor' Stepanovich and Others, *eds*. **Sovremennaia Koreia: spravochnoe izdanie.** Moscow: "Nauka," 1971, 417 p.
A Soviet handbook on contemporary Korea, published under the auspices of the Institute of Oriental Studies of the U.S.S.R. Academy of Sciences.

Kim, Chong Ik Eugene, *comp*. **Aspects of Social Change in Korea.** Kalamazoo (Mich.): Korea Research and Publications, 1969, 272 p.

A collection of essays, including chapters on the research resources and the state of the social science studies of Korea.

Kim, Pyŏng-sik. **Modern Korea: The Socialist North, Revolutionary Perspectives in the South, and Unification.** New York: International Publishers, 1970, 319 p.
This study, originally published in Japanese by a Korean living in Japan, deals, in the words of the author, "with essential questions concerning present-day Korea on the basis of the ideas and theories, the strategy and tactics, developed by Premier Kim Il Sung."

Kim, Richard E. **Lost Names: Scenes from a Korean Boyhood.** New York: Praeger, 1970, 195 p.
A study of Korea under Japanese occupation, 1910–1945.

Kim, Se-Jin and Cho, Chang-Hyun. **Government and Politics of Korea.** Silver Spring (Md.): Research Institute on Korean Affairs, 1972, 331 p.
A group of expatriate Korean scholars analyze the mechanisms and antagonisms of government in both the northern and southern states, and the outlook for contacts between the two. The collection of essays is perceptive and largely unbiased by ideological preconceptions.

Koh, Hesung Chun with Steffens, Joan, eds. **Korea: An Analytical Guide to Bibliographies.** New Haven: Human Relations Area Files Press, 1971, 334 p.
A most useful annotated bibliography of about 500 bibliographies published from 1896 to 1970 in Korean, English and other languages.

Lee, Chong-sik. **The Politics of Korean Nationalism.** Berkeley: University of California Press (for the Center for Japanese Studies), 1963, 342 p.
A chronicle of Korea's struggle for independence from the fourteenth century to 1945.

McCune, Shannon. **Korea, Land of Broken Calm.** Princeton: Van Nostrand, 1966, 221 p.
An introductory survey of modern Korea by an American geographer who was born in Korea.

Mitchell, Richard H. **The Korean Minority in Japan.** Berkeley: University of California Press, 1967, 186 p.
A study of the Korean minority in Japan and the Korean-Japanese controversies in the post-World War II period.

Mun, Chong-ch'ang. **Kun'guk Ilbon Chosŏn chŏmnyŏng samsibnyungnyŏn-sa.** Seoul: Paengmunsa, 1965–67, 3 v.
This history of the Japanese occupation of Korea from 1910 to 1945 covers both political and economic aspects.

O, So-baek. **Haebang isimnyŏn.** Seoul: Semunsa, 1965, 2 v.
A survey of Korean history in the twenty years after the liberation from Japanese rule in 1945.

Sakurai, Hiroshi. **Chōsen tōitsu eno shidō.** Tokyo: Sanseidō, 1971, 360 p.
A monograph on the problem of Korean unification.

Shabshina, F. I. and Others, eds. **Koreia: sever i iug.** Moscow: "Nauka", 1965, 261 p.
This study of North and South Korea was issued under the auspices of the Institute for the Peoples of Asia of the U.S.S.R. Academy of Sciences.

Shipaev, Viktor Ivanovich. **Kolonial'noe zakabalenie Korei iaponskim imperializmom (1895–1917).** Moscow: "Nauka," 1964, 240 p.
A monograph on the Japanese rule in Korea from 1895 to 1917, issued under the auspices of the Institute for the Peoples of Asia of the U.S.S.R. Academy of Sciences.

Sin, Kuk-chu. **Kŭndae Chosŏn oegyosa.** Seoul: T'amgudang, 1965, 434 p.
A diplomatic history of Korea with an English resumé.

Sŏ, Pyŏng-jo. **Chukwŏnja ŭi chŭngon: Han'guk taeŭi chŏngch'i.** Seoul: Moŭm Ch'ulp'ansa, 1963, 453 p.
A history of the Korean system of representative government since 1936.

Suh, Dae-Sook. **The Korean Communist Movement, 1918–1948.** Princeton: Princeton University Press, 1967, 406 p.
A thorough, scholarly work explaining the reasons for the failure of the old Korean communist revolutionary movement and for the success of North Korea's leader Kim. Based largely on Korean and Japanese sources.

Suh, Dae-Sook, *comp.* **Documents of Korean Communism, 1918–1948.** Princeton: Princeton University Press, 1970, 570 p.
A useful compilation, supplementing the previous study.

The Korean War

See also United Nations, p. 99; War and Peace, p. 108; The Postwar World, p. 178; (The United States) Biographies, Memoirs and Addresses, p. 218; Foreign Policy, p. 229; (China) Foreign Relations, p. 702; Military Questions, p. 705; other subsections under Korea.

Berger, Carl. **The Korea Knot: A Military-Political History.** Philadelphia: University of Pennsylvania Press, rev. ed., 1965, 255 p.
This book analyzes the Korean War as a Soviet experiment in peninsular warfare.

Biderman, Albert D. **March to Calumny: The Story of American POW's in the Korean War.** New York: Macmillan, 1963, 326 p.
A defense of the behavior of American prisoners of war in North Korean captivity.

Blanchard, Carroll Henry, Jr. **Korean War Bibliography and Maps of Korea.** Albany: Korean Conflict Research Foundation, 1964, 181 p.
A useful bibliography of the Korean War.

Carew, Tim, *pseud.* (John Mohun Carew). **Korea: The Commonwealth at War.** London: Cassell, 1967, 307 p.
An account of the military forces of the British Commonwealth in the Korean War.

Collins, J. Lawton. **War in Peacetime: The History and Lessons of Korea.** Boston: Houghton, 1969, 416 p.
An authoritative and well-planned study by an officer who was the U.S. Army Chief of Staff throughout the Korean War.

Fehrenbach, T. R. **This Kind of War.** New York: Macmillan, 1963, 688 p.
An extensive account of the Korean War, a war for which the author feels the American people and its citizen soldiers were not psychologically or politically equipped.

Heinl, Robert Debs, Jr. **Victory at High Tide.** Philadelphia: Lippincott, 1968, 315 p.
In the author's view, the Inchon-Seoul campaign was MacArthur's masterpiece but also led directly to the General's sense of hubris and his ultimate downfall.

Hermes, Walter G. **United States Army in the Korean War: Truce Tent and Fighting Front.** Washington: Department of the Army, Office of the Chief of Military History, 1966, 571 p.
This second volume of a projected five-volume official history covers the last two years in the Korean War and the armistice negotiations.

Kim, Taekhoan. **Die Vereinten Nationen und ihr kollektives Sicherheitssystem.** Munich: Verlag UNI-Druck, 1968, 246 p.
A study by a Korean scholar of the measures taken by the United Nations against the intervention of the Chinese People's Republic in the Korean War.

Meyers, Samuel M. and Biderman, Albert D., *eds.* **Mass Behavior in Battle and Captivity: The Communist Soldier in the Korean War.** Chicago: University of Chicago Press, 1968, 377 p.
A study of Chinese Communist indoctrination and social-control systems and of their influence on prisoner-of-war behavior.

O'Ballance, Edgar. **Korea: 1950–1953.** Hamden (Conn.): Archon Books, 1969, 171 p.
A well-known military historian examines the Korean War and its aftermath.

Paige, Glenn D. **The Korean Decision: June 24–30, 1950.** New York: Free Press, 1968, 394 p.
A University of Hawaii specialist interviewed Truman, Acheson and other major participants to reconstruct this hour-by-hour account of the U.S. decision to support the United Nations "police action" in Korea.

Rees, David. **Korea: The Limited War.** New York: St. Martin's Press, 1964, 511 p.
A detailed history of the Korean situation since the partition in 1945, based on official and semi-official documents, by a British author. Emphasis is on the reasons for the U.S. decision to fight a war of containment.

Ridgway, Matthew Bunker. **The Korean War: How We Met the Challenge.** Garden City: Doubleday, 1967, 291 p.
   This war memoir by the former U.S. Army Chief of Staff includes descriptions of the Truman-MacArthur controversy. The book's central conclusion: "Korea taught us that all warfare from this time forth must be limited."

Schnabel, James F. **United States Army in the Korean War: Policy and Direction, the First Year.** Washington: Department of the Army, Office of the Chief of Military History, 1972, 443 p.
   This third volume in the official military history of U.S. Army participation in the Korean War details the American drive northward and the Chinese Communist riposte.

Sheldon, Walter J. **Hell or High Water: MacArthur's Landing at Inchon.** New York: Macmillan, 1968, 340 p.
   The author attempts to prove that MacArthur not only swayed the President and the Pentagon to go along with the Inchon landing but that the military operation itself overcame the most formidable natural and geographical handicaps.

Thorgrimsson, Thor and Russell, E. C. **Canadian Naval Operations in Korean Waters, 1950-1955.** Ottawa: Naval Historical Section, Canadian Forces Headquarters, Department of National Defence, 1965, 167 p.
   An account of the activities of the eight Canadian destroyers in the Korean conflict.

U.S. Marine Operations in Korea, 1950-1953. Washington: U.S. Marine Corps, Historical Division, 1954-72, 5 v.
   A chronicle of the Marines' participation in the Korean conflict. Since 1962 the following volumes have been published: vol. IV: "The East-Central Front," by Lynn Montross, Hubard D. Kuokka and Norman W. Hicks (1962) and vol. V: "Operations in West Korea," by Pat Meid and James M. Yingling (1972).

Vetter, Hal. **Mutiny on Koje Island.** Rutland (Vt.): Tuttle, 1965, 223 p.
   An analysis of the elements that brought about the 1952 rioting of communist prisoners in Korea, based on interviews conducted during a year and a half's study in Korea.

Wood, Herbert Fairlie. **Strange Battleground: The Operations in Korea and Their Effects on the Defence Policy of Canada.** Ottawa: Queen's Printer, 1966, 317 p.
   The official story of the Canadian Army's part in United Nations' activities in Korea, 1951-53.

Yoo, Tae-ho. **The Korean War and the United Nations: A Legal and Diplomatic Historical Study.** Louvain: Librairie Desbarax, 1965, 215 p.
   A thesis by a graduate of the Institut d'Étude des Pays en Développement on the U.N. intervention in the Korean conflict.

The *Pueblo* Affair

Armbrister, Trevor. **A Matter of Accountability: The Study of the Pueblo Affair.** New York: Coward-McCann, 1970, 408 p.
   The author blames military officials in Washington for the capture of the U.S. intelligence ship *Pueblo* by the North Koreans on January 23, 1968.

Brandt, Ed. **The Last Voyage of USS Pueblo.** New York: Norton, 1969, 248 p.
   A fast-paced narrative, very sympathetic to Commander Bucher and his men, based on the accounts of 15 key members of the crew.

Bucher, Lloyd M. with Rascovich, Mark. **Bucher: My Story.** Garden City: Doubleday, 1970, 447 p.
   Commander Bucher, captain of the U.S. intelligence ship *Pueblo* at the time of its seizure by the North Koreans, describes the capture and the captivity.

Murphy, Edward R., Jr. with Gentry, Curt. **Second in Command.** New York: Holt, Rinehart and Winston, 1971, 452 p.
   The former Executive Officer of the *Pueblo* at the time of its capture charges that the incident "need never have happened" and places responsibility for the ship's seizure squarely on Commander Lloyd M. Bucher.

Naked Act of Aggression by U.S. Imperialism against the Korean People. Pyongyang: Foreign Languages Publishing House, 1968, 4 v.
The official North Korean presentation of the *Pueblo* incident.

Republic of Korea (South Korea)

See also The Postwar World, p. 178; (The United States) Biographies, Memoirs and Addresses, p. 218; Foreign Policy, p. 229; (Asia and the Pacific Area) General Surveys, p. 607; (Far East) General, p. 682; (Japan) Foreign and Defense Policies, p. 718; other subsections under Korea.

Adelman, Irma, *ed*. **Practical Approaches to Development Planning: Korea's Second Five-Year Plan.** Baltimore: Johns Hopkins Press, 1969, 306 p.
American and Korean technicians explain the underlying aspects of South Korea's 1967–1971 development plan and the role it has had in that country's economic and political development.

Chung, Kyung Cho. **Korea: The Third Republic.** New York: Macmillan, 1971, 269 p.
A succinct and well-organized survey of the South Korean political system, plus a passionate plea for reunification.

Cole, David C. and Lyman, Princeton N. **Korean Development: The Interplay of Politics and Economics.** Cambridge: Harvard University Press (for Harvard's Center for International Affairs), 1971, 320 p.
The authors of this study of Korean development confess their inability to predict that more riches will mean more freedom in the years to come.

Henderson, Gregory. **Korea: The Politics of the Vortex.** Cambridge: Harvard University Press, 1968, 479 p.
Mr. Henderson, long with the American Embassy in Korea, studies Korean political culture and development. He urges the decentralization of authority and encouragement of autonomous centers of power at the local level.

Hong, Sŏng-yu. **Han'guk kyŏngje ŭi chabon ch'ukchŏk kwajŏng.** Seoul: Koryŏ Taehakkyo Ch'ulp'anbu, 1965, 406 p.
This study of capital accumulation in the Korean economy includes a discussion of American economic assistance.

Hwang, Pyŏng-jun. **Han'guk ŭi kongŏp kyŏngje: ku yŏksa kujo mit chongch'aek ŭi chungsim ŭro.** Seoul: Koryŏ Taehakkyo, Asea Munje Yon'guso, 1966, 466 p.
A study of the history, structure and policy of the South Korean industrial economy.

Kim, Chong-sin. **Seven Years with Korea's Park Chung-hee.** Seoul: Hollym Corp., 1967, 306 p.
An account of the political activities of South Korea's leader by a South Korean newspaperman. The original was published as "Yŏngsi ŭi hoaetpul" (Seoul, 1966, 325 p.).

Kim, Hyŏng-nyong, *ed*. **Nam Chosŏn haksaeng undong.** Pyongyang: Chosŏn Nodongdang Ch'ulp'ansa, 1964, 222 p.
A study of South Korean student movements, published by the North Korean Workers Party Publishing House.

Kim, Kwan Bong. **The Korea-Japan Treaty Crisis and the Instability of the Korean Political System.** New York: Praeger, 1971, 350 p.
Professor Kim argues in this study that the persistence of an authoritarian culture, endemic factionalism in political parties, and the lack of institutionalized forms for mass political participation has created a basically unstable governmental structure in South Korea.

Kim, Se-Jin. **The Politics of Military Revolution in Korea.** Chapel Hill: University of North Carolina Press, 1971, 239 p.
A detailed and informative study of the internal politics of the South Korean military regime.

Kim, Seung Hee. **Foreign Capital for Economic Development: A Korean Case Study.** New York: Praeger, 1970, 206 p.
A theoretical analysis of the contribution of foreign capital and aid to South Korea's economic development.

Kō, Chun-sōk. **Minami Chōsen seiji shi: Minami Chōsen keizai shi.** Tokyo: Tōkō Shoin, 1970, 470 p., 371 p.

Two studies on South Korean political and economic history, written by a Korean for a Japanese audience.

Koh, Byung Chul, *comp*. **Aspects of Administrative Development in South Korea.** Kalamazoo (Mich.): Korea Research and Publications, 1967, 144 p.
Seven essays on public administration in contemporary South Korea, by South Korean and Korean-American scholars, with a bibliography.

Lee, Hahn-Been. **Korea: Time, Change, and Administration.** Honolulu: East-West Center Press, 1968, 240 p.
Observations on the sweeping changes in Korean politics by a former senior civil servant of the Government of the Republic of Korea from 1951 to 1961.

Mazurov, Viktor Mikhailovich. **Sozdanie antinarodnogo rezhima v Iuzhnoi Koree, 1945–1950 gg.** Moscow: Izd-vo Vostochnoi Lit-ry, 1963, 193 p.
——. **Iuzhnaia Koreia i SShA (1950–1970 gg.).** Moscow: Nauka, 1971, 296 p.
These studies on South Korea were issued under the auspices of the Institute for the Peoples of Asia of the U.S.S.R. Academy of Sciences.

Oh, John Kie-chiang. **Korea: Democracy on Trial.** Ithaca: Cornell University Press, 1968, 240 p.
A survey of governmental systems and processes in the development of Western democracy in South Korea, mostly from 1948 to 1963, with a postscript on the 1967 presidential elections.

Pak, Chŏng-hŭi. **The Country, the Revolution and I.** Seoul: Hollym Corp., 2d ed., 1970, 191 p.
——. **Major Speeches by Korea's Park Chung Hee.** Seoul: Hollym Corp., 1970, 383 p.
——. **Our Nation's Path: Ideology of Social Reconstruction.** Seoul: Hollym Corp., 2d ed., 1970, 240 p.
——. **To Build a Nation.** Washington: Acropolis Books, 1971, 216 p.
In these volumes the leader of South Korea outlines his political ideology and discusses Korea's situation in the modern world.

Reeve, Wilfred Douglas. **The Republic of Korea: A Political and Economic Study.** New York: Oxford University Press (for the Royal Institute of International Affairs), 1963, 197 p.
From materials gathered while adviser to the South Korean Government from 1952 to 1957, the author provides factual information for assessing the results of exposure to Western democracy by an eastern country.

Sinitsyn, Boris Vladimirovich. **Ocherki ekonomiki Iuzhnoi Korei, 1953–1964.** Moscow: Nauka, 1967, 170 p.
A study of the economy of South Korea, sponsored by the Institute for the Peoples of Asia of the U.S.S.R. Academy of Sciences.

Tsutagawa, Masayoshi. **Kankoku no bōeki to sangyō shijō kōzō.** Tokyo: Ajia Keizai Kenkyūjo, 1972, 184 p.
This study of South Korea's trade, industry and market structure covers Korea's economic growth during the 1960s.

Yi, Ch'ang-nyŏl. **Han'guk ŭi kŭmnyung kwa chabon tongwŏn.** Seoul: Koryŏ Taehakkyo, Asea Munje Yŏn'guso, 1966, 414 p.
A monograph on South Korean financial problems.

Yu, T'aek-hŭi. **Han'guk kyŏngje chŏngch'aeknon.** Seoul: Pŏmmunsa, 1965, 447 p.
A study of South Korean economic policies.

Democratic People's Republic of Korea (North Korea)

See also (Union of Soviet Socialist Republics) Foreign Policy, p. 550; (Asia and the Pacific Area) General Surveys, p. 607; (Far East) General, p. 682; Democratic Republic of Vietnam, p. 747; other subsections under Korea.

Burchett, Wilfred Graham. **Again Korea.** New York: International Publishers, 1968, 188 p.
An Australian left-wing journalist, notable for his close contacts with communist sources, recounts his 1967 return visit to North Korea, where he found almost com-

plete reconstruction and recuperation from the 1950 war which, he claims, was started by the South Koreans.

Cho, M. Y. **Die Entwicklung der Beziehungen zwischen Peking und P'Yongyang 1949–1967.** Wiesbaden: Harrassowitz (for the Institut für Asienkunde in Hamburg), 1967, 175 p.
A study, supplemented with documents, of the effect of the Sino-Soviet conflict on the Chinese-North Korean relations in the period from 1949 to 1967.

Griaznov, Genadii Viktorovich. **Sotsialisticheskaia Industrializatsiia v KNDR, 1945–1960 gg.** Moscow: Nauka, 1966, 215 p.
This study of the industrialization of North Korea was published under the auspices of the Institute of the Peoples of Asia of the U.S.S.R. Academy of Sciences.

Hun, Ryu. **Study of North Korea.** Seoul: Research Institute of Internal and External Affairs, 1966, 317 p.
A history, based on materials available from communist sources, by a South Korean scholar.

Kim, Il-sŏng. **Selected Works.** Pyongyang: Foreign Languages Publishing House, 1971–.
A collection of writings by the North Korean leader. The five volumes published through 1972 cover the period from October 1945 to November 1970.

Koh, Byung Chul. **The Foreign Policy of North Korea.** New York: Praeger, 1969, 237 p.
A study of how the Pyongyang regime responds to the stimuli of world politics.

Paek, Pong. **Kim Il Sung: Biography.** Tokyo: Miraisha, 1969–70, 3 v.
An English translation of a biography of the North Korean leader. The Korean original appeared as "Minjok ŭi t'aeyang Kim Il-sŏng changgun" (Pyongyang, 1968, 2 v.).

Pak, Tong-un. **Pukhan t'ongch'i kiguron.** Seoul: Koryŏ Taehakkyo, Asea Munje Yŏn-guso, 1964, 199 p.
A study of the structure of government in North Korea, prepared by the Asia Research Centre of Korea University.

Scalapino, Robert Anthony and Lee, Chong-Sik. **Communism in Korea. Part I: The Movement. Part II: The Society.** Berkeley: University of California Press, 1972, 1,533 p.
A thorough analysis of the history and functioning of the North Korean state. The authors find that traditional Korean society has offered particularly fertile soil for a highly coercive and ideological modernizing bureaucracy.

Scalapino, Robert Anthony, *ed*. **North Korea Today.** New York: Praeger, 1963, 141 p.
A collection of articles, first appearing in a special issue of *The China Quarterly*, on the political, economic, legal, military and educational aspects of North Korea, based largely on Korean and Japanese sources.

Sŏ, Nam-wŏn. **Pukhan ŭi kyŏngje chŏngch'aek kwa saengsan kwalli.** Seoul: Asea Munje Yŏn'guso, 1966, 293 p.
A survey of North Korea's economic policies.

Son, Sŏng-p'il. **Haebang hu uri nara esŏ-ŭi nodong tongmaeng.** Pyongyang: Chosŏn Nodongdang Ch'ulp'ansa, 1965, 215 p.
A study of North Korean labor unions since 1945.

Vaintsvaig, N. K. and Others, *eds*. **Ocherki sotsialisticheskogo stroitel'stva v Koreiskoi Narodno-Demokraticheskoi Respublike.** Moscow: Izd-vo Vostochnoi Lit-ry, 1963, 288 p.
A Soviet monograph on North Korea, issued under the auspices of the Institute for the Peoples of Asia of the U.S.S.R. Academy of Sciences.

Yu, Hon. **Study of North Korea.** Seoul: Research Institute of Internal and External Affairs, 1966, 317 p.
A factual survey of politics, economics, society and foreign policy of North Korea, 1945–1965, by a knowledgeable South Korean researcher.

SOUTHEASTERN ASIA; EAST INDIES
GENERAL

See also Comparative Government, p. 18; Problems of New Nations, p. 36; Second World War, p. 144; The Postwar World, p. 178; (The United States) Foreign Policy, p. 229; (Union of Soviet Socialist Republics) Foreign Policy, p. 550; (Asia and the Pacific Area) General Surveys, p. 607; (India) Foreign Policy, p. 666; (Far East) General, p. 682; (China) Foreign Relations, p. 702; (Japan) Foreign and Defense Policies, p. 718; (Australia) Foreign and Defense Policies, p. 767.

Allen, Sir Richard Hugh Sidley. **A Short Introduction to the History and Politics of Southeast Asia.** New York: Oxford University Press, 1970, 306 p.
A useful work, with detailed bibliographies, by a veteran diplomat who was the British Ambassador to Burma from 1956 to 1962.

Aspects actuels de la situation économique et sociale de l'Asie du Sud-Est. Brussels: Éditions de l'Institut de Sociologie, Université Libre de Bruxelles, 1963, 246 p.
Proceedings of an international colloquium on Southeast Asian economic and social problems that convened in October 1961 in Brussels under the auspices of the Centre d'Études du Sud-Est Asiatique.

Bastin, John and Benda, Harry J. **A History of Modern Southeast Asia.** Englewood Cliffs: Prentice-Hall, 1968, 214 p.
A broad interpretive account of Western colonialism in Southeast Asia from the arrival of the Portuguese to the withdrawal of Western powers and establishment of the independent Southeast Asian governments.

Bechert, Heinz. **Buddhismus, Staat und Gesellschaft in den Ländern des Theravāda-Buddhismus.** Wiesbaden: Harrassowitz, 1966–67, 2 v.
Studies on the influence of organized Buddhism on the political affairs of Ceylon, Burma, Cambodia, Laos, Thailand and Vietnam.

Black, Eugene R. **Alternative in Southeast Asia.** New York: Praeger, 1969, 180 p.
The observations of the former President of the World Bank during his mission to encourage Southeast Asian nations to join in developing their potential resources.

Bloodworth, Dennis. **An Eye for the Dragon: Southeast Asia Observed, 1954–1970.** New York: Farrar, Straus and Giroux, 1970, 414 p.
A journalistic account by a writer who knows the region intimately.

Brackman, Arnold C. **Southeast Asia's Second Front.** New York: Praeger, 1966, 341 p.
The author, who has lived and traveled extensively in Southeast Asia, interviewed leaders of the Malay world to identify the political and strategic problems Moscow, Peking and the West will have to cope with.

Buchanan, Keith McPherson. **The Southeast Asian World.** New York: Taplinger, 1967, 176 p.
An introductory survey, by a professor of geography at the Victoria University of Wellington, New Zealand.

Burling, Robbins. **Hill Farms and Padi Fields: Life in Mainland Southeast Asia.** Englewood Cliffs: Prentice-Hall, 1965, 180 p.
A compact work on the countries east of India and south of China, by a professor of anthropology at the University of Michigan. Emphasis is on village life rather than politics, and on peoples rather than their rulers, although the author does describe the major foreign influences affecting the area.

Cayrac-Blanchard, Françoise and Others. **L'Asie du Sud-Est.** Paris: Sirey, 1970–71, 2 v.
A general survey of contemporary Southeast Asia, published in the series "L'Histoire du XXe siècle" edited by Maurice Baumont.

Chatterji, Bijan Raj. **Southeast Asia in Transition.** Meerut: Meenakshi Prakashan, 1965, 306 p.
In these seminar talks, lectures and papers on various problems in contemporary Southeast Asia stress is laid on the decline of Indian influence and the growth of Chinese influence.

Coedès, George. **The Making of South East Asia.** Berkeley: University of California Press, 1966, 268 p.
An introduction to the history and civilizations of Indochina, Thailand and Burma by a leading French scholar. A translation of "Les Peuples de la péninsule indochinoise," (Paris: Dunod, 1962, 228 p.).

Cowan, Charles Donald, *ed.* **The Economic Development of Southeast Asia.** New York: Praeger, 1964, 192 p.
Papers originally presented at a study conference in July 1961 at London's School of Oriental and African Studies.

Crozier, Brian. **South-East Asia in Turmoil.** Baltimore: Penguin, 3rd rev. ed., 1968, 224 p.
A brief but factual account of the tumultuous events in Southeast Asia since the end of World War II, by a former Asia expert for *The Economist* and the Director of the Institute for the Study of Conflict.

Decornoy, Jacques. **L'Asie du Sud-Est.** Paris: Casterman, 1967, 247 p.
A survey of Southeast Asian history since World War II, by a French journalist.

Dennert, Jürgen. **Verschwiegenes Zeitgeschehen.** Düsseldorf: Econ Verlag, 1970, 399 p.
A West German correspondent presents a competent survey of guerrilla warfare in Southeast Asia.

Dow, Maynard Weston. **Nation Building in Southeast Asia.** Boulder: Pruett Press, 1966, 279 p.
A comparative study of post-World War II resettlement programs in Malaya, the Philippines and South Vietnam that were planned as counterinsurgency measures.

Emery, Robert Firestone. **The Financial Institutions of Southeast Asia: A Country-by-Country Study.** New York: Praeger, 1971, 748 p.
A useful reference, based on data collected in the fall of 1967 and sponsored by the Board of Governors of the U.S. Federal Reserve System.

Fairbairn, Geoffrey. **Revolutionary Warfare and Communist Strategy: The Threat to South-East Asia.** London: Faber, 1968, 286 p.
An attempt at a systematic analysis of the communist insurgency tactics in Southeast Asia. The author, an Australian scholar, defends American policies in Vietnam since 1965.

Fryer, Donald W. **Emerging Southeast Asia: A Study in Growth and Stagnation.** New York: McGraw-Hill, 1970, 486 p.
The author of this study advocates more effective trade, aid and regional coöperation to meet Southeast Asia's pressing problems of food production and overpopulation.

Girling, J. L. S. **People's War: Conditions and Consequences in China and South East Asia.** New York: Praeger, 1969, 244 p.
A study of the factors creating insurgency.

Golay, Frank Hindman and Others. **Underdevelopment and Economic Nationalism in Southeast Asia.** Ithaca: Cornell University Press, 1969, 494 p.
A country-by-country study of the economic and industrial resources and enterprises of the Southeast Asian nations, with emphasis on the role of nationals in the ownership and control of productive assets.

Gordon, Bernard K. **The Dimensions of Conflict in Southeast Asia.** Englewood Cliffs: Prentice-Hall, 1966, 201 p.
Emphasizing that Southeast Asia is a region of separate and quite distinct nations, the author analyzes the various "intra-regional conflicts" and the efforts at collaboration in this region.

Hanna, Willard Anderson. **Eight Nation Makers: Southeast Asia's Charismatic Statesmen.** New York: St. Martin's Press, 1964, 307 p.
Biographic interpretations of the key figures in the making of modern Southeast Asian history and society.

Henle, Hans. **Chinas Schatten über Südost-Asien.** Hamburg: Holsten, 1964, 300 p.
A study of economic and political developments in Southeast Asia after World War II.

Hoang-long-Dien. **L'Inflation en Asie du Sud-Est.** Paris: Génin, 1963, 512 p.
A well-documented analysis of inflation in Southeast Asia, focusing on the years 1948–1958.

Hunter, Guy. **South-East Asia—Race, Culture, and Nation.** New York: Oxford University Press (for the Institute of Race Relations), 1966, 190 p.
An introduction to contemporary Southeast Asia. The author deals particularly with the endeavors of the Southeast Asian nations to establish their national identity and the complications created by race and ethnic diversity.

Insular Southeast Asia, Australia, Indonesia, Malaysia, New Zealand, Philippines, Singapore: Bibliographic Survey. Washington: G.P.O., 1971, 419 p.
A useful reference, compiled by the U.S. Army Library.

Kennedy, Donald Edward. **The Security of Southern Asia.** New York: Praeger, 1965, 308 p.
An assessment of the strategy and consequences of counterinsurgency, mainly in the Philippines, Malaysia and Vietnam. The author also discusses at length Sino-Soviet-American hostilities and their bearing on the security of the region.

Kotovskii, Grigorii Grigor'evich, ed. **Agrarnye otnosheniia v stranakh iugo-vostochnoi Azii.** Moscow: Izd-vo "Nauka," 1968, 236 p.
Essays dealing with problems of land ownership and tenancy in seven Southeast Asian countries and Soviet estimates of the significance of current reform policies for the revolutionary struggle.

Kunstadter, Peter, ed. **Southeast Asian Tribes, Minorities, and Nations.** Princeton: Princeton University Press, 1967, 2 v.
Papers from two 1965 conferences, concentrating largely on Thailand and limited to rural rather than urban minorities.

Leifer, Michael. **Dilemmas of Statehood in Southeast Asia.** Vancouver: University of British Columbia Press, 1972, 161 p.
The author of this study argues that for the new countries of Southeast Asia "state-building" should have precedence over "nation-building."

McCoy, Alfred W. with Others. **The Politics of Heroin in Southeast Asia.** New York: Harper and Row, 1972, 464 p.
A solid study of the intricate history of drug addiction and drug supply in the Southeast Asian "Golden Triangle" and the United States. Its startling thesis: U.S. policies maintain the national security of Asian satellite governments while destroying its own national health.

Mills, Lennox Algernon. **Southeast Asia: Illusion and Reality in Politics and Economics.** Minneapolis: University of Minnesota Press, 1964, 365 p.
A University of Minnesota professor emeritus in political science analyzes the post-independence governments of Southeast Asia and concludes that "all of them are dictatorships or oligarchies controlled by small groups of Western-educated, urban nationalists."

Morgan, Theodore and Spoelstra, Nyle, eds. **Economic Interdependence in Southeast Asia.** Madison: University of Wisconsin Press (for the Center for International Economics and Economic Development), 1969, 424 p.
A study of the prospects for accelerating the rate of national economic growth and promoting trade relationships in Asia through regional coöperation.

Osborne, Milton E. **Region of Revolt: Focus on Southeast Asia.** Baltimore: Penguin, 1972, 201 p.
This concise but wide-ranging analysis puts the chronic Southeast Asian political instability of the last quarter-century in an historical and sociological perspective. The author, an Australian diplomat and history professor, sees little prospect of lasting peace until the transition from economic poverty to sufficiency and from cultural traditionalism to modernity is further advanced.

Saitō, Yoshifumi. **Tōnan Ajia no kōzō.** Tokyo: Asahi Shimbunsha, 1971, 276 p.
A Japanese study of social and political change in South and Southeast Asia.

Schecter, Jerrold. **The New Face of Buddha: Buddhism and Political Power in Southeast Asia.** New York: Coward-McCann, 1967, 300 p.
In this study the former *Time-Life* Tokyo bureau chief identifies Buddhism as the ultimate source of all Asian values, including the political.

Shaplen, Robert. **Time Out of Hand: Revolution and Reaction in Southeast Asia.** New York: Harper and Row, 1969, 465 p.

A revised version of an analysis of each of the Southeast Asian countries and their influence on the Vietnam War; originally published in *The New Yorker*.

Southeast Asia's Economy in the 1970s. New York: Praeger (for the Asian Development Bank), 1971, 684 p.
An exhaustive and well-documented analysis by an expert group headed by Dr. P. Streeten from Oxford University.

Tarling, Nicholas. **A Concise History of Southeast Asia.** New York: Praeger, 1966, 334 p.
A general history of the area including Vietnam, Laos, Cambodia, Thailand, Burma, the Philippines, Malaysia, Indonesia and the Andaman and Nicobar Islands, by a professor at the University of Auckland, New Zealand. The Australian edition appeared as "Southeast Asia: Past and Present" (Melbourne: Cheshire, 1966, 334 p.).

Thompson, Sir Robert Grainger Ker. **Defeating Communist Insurgency: The Lessons of Malaya and Vietnam.** New York: Praeger, 1966, 171 p.
A study of all aspects of counterinsurgency, by a well-known British expert, based on experiences in Malaya (1948–60) and South Vietnam (1961–65).

Trân-minh-Tiêt. **Problèmes de défense du Sud-Est asiatique.** Paris: Nouvelles Éditions Latines, 1967, 156 p.
A critique of communist and American policies toward Vietnam and a proposal for the establishment of a federation of Southeast Asian nations.

Trumbull, Robert. **The Scrutable East: A Correspondent's Report on Southeast Asia.** New York: McKay, 1964, 275 p.
Candid accounts of each of the eight Southeast Asian countries, with appraisals of their leaders, by a veteran *New York Times* foreign correspondent.

Vandenbosch, Amry and Butwell, Richard A. **The Changing Face of Southeast Asia.** Lexington: University of Kentucky Press, 1966, 438 p.
A rewriting of "Southeast Asia among the World Powers," published originally in 1957.

Von der Mehden, Fred R. **Religion and Nationalism in Southeast Asia: Burma, Indonesia, the Philippines.** Madison: University of Wisconsin Press, 1963, 253 p.
A study of the evolving relationships of Buddhism, Mohammedanism and Catholicism with national movements in three newly developed nations.

Wertheim, Willem Frederik. **East-West Parallels: Sociological Approaches to Modern Asia.** Chicago: Quadrangle Books, 1965, 284 p.
A collection of articles on the social structure and dynamics of modern Southeast Asia.

Young, Kenneth Todd, Jr. **The Southeast Asia Crisis.** Dobbs Ferry: Oceana Publications (for the Association of the Bar of the City of New York), 1966, 226 p.
Background papers and proceedings of the Eighth Hammarskjöld Forum held in 1965 and dealing with political, military, economic, social and legal problems of Southeast Asia. Edited by Lyman M. Tondel, Jr.

INDOCHINA

General Surveys and the End of the French Rule

See also Second World War, p. 144; The Postwar World, p. 178; (The United States) Foreign Policy, p. 229; (France) Recent History, p. 396; Biographies, Memoirs and Addresses, p. 400; Foreign Policy, p. 404; Military Policy, p. 407; (Asia and the Pacific Area) General Surveys, p. 607; (Southeastern Asia; East Indies) General, p. 733; Vietnam, p. 738; Laos, p. 749; Khmer Republic (Cambodia), p. 750.

Avon, Anthony Eden, 1st Earl of. **Toward Peace in Indochina.** Boston: Houghton, 1966, 77 p.
A defense of the 1954 Geneva Agreements by the former British Prime Minister who was also Joint Chairman of the 1954 Geneva Conference.

Azeau, Henri. **Ho Chi Minh, dernière chance: la conférence franco-vietnamienne de Fontainebleau, juillet 1946.** Paris: Flammarion, 1968, 310 p.
A thorough study dealing with the meetings of the delegates of the Democratic Republic of Vietnam and France intended to formalize the preliminary convention signed at Hanoi on March 6, 1946.

Bodard, Lucien. **The Quicksand War: Prelude to Vietnam.** Boston: Atlantic (Little, Brown), 1967, 372 p.
This study, concerning the Vietnam crisis from the end of World War II to 1950, is an abridged translation of the first two volumes of "La Guerre d'Indochine" (Paris: Gallimard, 1963-67, 3 v.). The author, a highly regarded foreign correspondent with years of experience in Asia, harshly criticizes U.S. as well as French involvement in the area.

Cameron, Allan W., *ed.* **Viet-Nam Crisis: A Documentary History. Volume I: 1940-1956.** Ithaca: Cornell University Press, 1971, 452 p.
A guide to the documentation on the Vietnam War, covering the period from 1940 to 1956, with succinct and objective introductions to each section.

Chaffard, Georges. **Indochine: dix ans d'indépendance.** Paris: Calmann-Lévy, 1964, 294 p.
A French writer with many years of experience in Indochina surveys the developments in that country during the ten years following the conclusion of the French-Indochinese war.

Devillers, Philippe and Lacouture, Jean. **End of a War: Indochina, 1954.** New York: Praeger, 1969, 412 p.
A study of how battlefield reverses and diplomatic isolation forced the French to the 1954 Geneva Conference negotiations and how France's Asian responsibilities were transferred to the United States. The French original appeared as "La Fin d'une guerre: Indochine 1954" (Paris: Éditions du Seuil, 1960, 384 p.).

Fall, Bernard B. **Hell in a Very Small Place: The Siege of Dien Bien Phu.** Philadelphia: Lippincott, 1967, 515 p.
The late veteran Vietnam specialist attempts an account of what really happened at Dien Bien Phu. Because almost all local documents were destroyed before the siege, he relies largely on French archival material and voluminous correspondence.

Field, Michael. **The Prevailing Wind: Witness in Indo-China.** London: Methuen, 1965, 392 p.
Michael Field, a correspondent for the *Daily Telegraph,* spent the years 1956-1962 observing and analyzing political events in Laos, Cambodia, Thailand and Vietnam.

Kirk, Donald. **Wider War: The Struggle for Cambodia, Thailand, and Laos.** New York: Praeger, 1971, 305 p.
The author of this informative study argues that it is impossible to understand the contemporary struggle for Vietnam without paying attention to the political, military and social developments in other parts of the Indochinese Peninsula.

Langlais, Pierre. **Dien Bien Phu.** Paris: Éditions France-Empire, 1963, 261 p.
A moving and informative account of the defeat of the French Army at Dien Bien Phu, told with restraint by the commander of the French paratroops.

Langlois, Walter G. **André Malraux: The Indochina Adventure.** New York: Praeger, 1966, 259 p.
This account of the sojourn of the prominent French author and statesman in Indochina from 1923 to 1924 contains useful information on French colonial policies and the birth of the Annamite nationalist movement.

Legrand, Julien Joseph. **L'Indochine à l'heure japonaise.** Paris: J. Legrand, 1964, 309 p.
An account of political and military developments in Indochina from 1940 to 1945, a period when the Japanese established their domination in Southeast Asia.

O'Ballance, Edgar. **The Indo-China War 1945-1954: A Study in Guerilla Warfare.** London: Faber, 1964, 285 p.
A leading British student of guerrilla warfare recounts the Vietnam War in its earlier stages, tracing its evolution as expounded in Mao Tsê-tung's famous "Guerrilla Warfare." This study was severely criticized by the British press for its inaccuracies.

Pouget, Jean. **Nous étions à Dien-Bien-Phu.** Paris: Presses de la Cité, 1965, 446 p.
A former aid-de-camp of General Navarre, Commander-in-Chief of the French forces in Indochina from 1953 to 1954, writes with passion on the tragic war that came to a conclusion with the battle of Dien Bien Phu.

Randle, Robert F. **Geneva 1954: The Settlement of the Indochinese War.** Princeton: Princeton University Press, 1969, 639 p.
A very comprehensive and well-documented study of the Geneva Agreements.

Rocolle, Pierre Paul François Marie. **Pourquoi Dien Bien Phu?** Paris: Flammarion, 1968, 604 p.
A graduate of Saint-Cyr, who participated in the French Indochina war, has written a very solid and well-documented account of the battle at Dien Bien Phu and of the French decision to withdraw from Indochina.

Zasloff, Joseph J. and Goodman, Allan E., eds. **Indochina in Conflict: A Political Assessment.** Lexington (Mass.) : Lexington Books, 1972, 227 p.
These papers are products of a Southeast Asia Development Advisory Group (SEADAG) seminar held in May 1971.

VIETNAM
General

See also (Germany) Post-World War II Era, p. 487; (Asia and the Pacific Area) General Surveys, p. 607; (India) Foreign Policy, p. 666; (Southeastern Asia; East Indies) General, p. 733; (Indochina) General Surveys and the End of the French Rule, p. 736; Laos, p. 749; Khmer Republic (Cambodia), p. 750; other subsections under Vietnam.

Buttinger, Joseph. **Vietnam: A Dragon Embattled.** New York: Praeger, 1967, 2 v.
A detailed political history from 1900 up to the fall of Ngo Dinh Diem, based on personal interviews with Vietnamese leaders, primary source materials and a painstaking review of existing literature on the topic.

Buttinger, Joseph. **Vietnam: A Political History.** New York: Praeger, 1968, 565 p.
A combined, abridged and updated edition of "The Smaller Dragon" (1958) and "Vietnam: A Dragon Embattled" (1967).

Chen, King C. **Vietnam and China, 1938-1954.** Princeton: Princeton University Press, 1969, 436 p.
This study deals mainly with Ho Chi Minh's rise to power and with the Vietnamese Communist movement under the impact of the Chinese Communist revolution.

Drachman, Edward R. **United States Policy toward Vietnam, 1940-1945.** Rutherford (N.J.): Fairleigh Dickinson University Press, 1970, 186 p.
This useful study fills a large gap in Vietnam scholarship.

Duncanson, Dennis J. **Government and Revolution in Vietnam.** New York: Oxford University Press (for the Royal Institute of International Affairs), 1968, 442 p.
A standard political history of Vietnam, with emphasis on the post-World War II period.

Fall, Bernard B. **The Two Viet-nams: A Political and Military Analysis.** New York: Praeger, 2d rev. ed., 1967, 507 p.
The late Vietnam specialist analyzes both zones of that divided country, pointing out weaknesses and strengths in each and comparing their governmental and economic institutions.

Hammer, Ellen Joy. **Vietnam Yesterday and Today.** New York: Holt, Rinehart and Winston, 1966, 282 p.
A substantial survey.

Horlemann, Jürgen and Gäng, Peter. **Vietnam: Genesis eines Konflikts.** Frankfurt/Main: Suhrkamp, 3rd ed., 1966, 210 p.
A brief survey of Vietnamese history since the 1930s.

McAlister, John T., Jr. **Viet Nam: The Origins of Revolution.** New York: Knopf (for the Center of International Studies, Princeton University), 1969, 377 p.
In this well-documented attempt to trace the origins of the Vietnam conflict, the author emphasizes the development of Vietnamese revolutionary politics during World War II and the French rule.

McAlister, John T., Jr. and Mus, Paul. **The Vietnamese and Their Revolution.** New York: Harper and Row, 1970, 173 p.
A Princeton professor translates, reorganizes, revises and in some instances rewrites Paul Mus' classic "Viet Nam: sociologie d'une guerre" (Paris: Éditions du Seuil, 1952,

373 p.) in an effort to analyze the cultural and social foundations of Vietnamese politics. Prepared under the auspices of the Center of International Studies, Princeton University.

Marr, David G. **Vietnamese Anticolonialism 1885-1925.** Berkeley: University of California Press (for the Center for South and Southeast Asia Studies), 1971, 322 p.
This study traces the deep roots of Vietnamese nationalism and the Vietnamese relations with their colonial rulers.

Newman, Bernard. **Background to Viet-Nam.** New York: Roy, 1965, 192 p.
A journalistic introduction to the post-World War II history of Vietnam by a writer who knows the country well.

Nguyên-thê-Anh. **Bibliographie critique sur les relations entre le Viêt-Nam et l'Occident.** Paris: G. P. Maisonneuve et Larose, 1967, 310 p.
An annotated bibliography on the relations between Vietnam and the Western World.

Nguyen-van-Hao. **Les Problèmes de la nouvelle agriculture vietnamienne.** Geneva: Droz, 1963, 227 p.
A review of Vietnam's pre-independence agrarian structure and problems followed by a discussion of the aims, methods and results of post-independence "agricultural politics."

Tournaire, Hélène with Bouteaud, Robert. **Livre jaune du Viêt-Nam.** Paris: Perrin, 1966, 349 p.
A journalistic survey of recent Vietnamese history, with emphasis on the role of the Buddhists, by two French writers personally acquainted with the region.

The Vietnam War
General

See also International Organization and Government, p. 96; War and Peace, p. 108; The Postwar World, p. 178; (The United States) Biographies, Memoirs and Addresses, p. 218; Foreign Policy, p. 229; Military and Defense Policy, p. 257; (China) Foreign Relations, p. 702; (Southeastern Asia; East Indies) General, p. 733; (Indochina) General Surveys and the End of the French Rule, p. 736; Laos, p. 749; Khmer Republic (Cambodia), p. 750; (Australia) Foreign and Defense Policies, p. 767; other subsections under Vietnam.

Bain, Chester Arthur. **Vietnam: The Roots of Conflict.** Englewood Cliffs: Prentice-Hall, 1967, 184 p.
An evaluation of the Vietnam conflict within the context of universal communist tactics and Vietnam's historical development.

Fall, Bernard B. **Viet-Nam Witness: 1953-66.** New York: Praeger, 1966, 363 p.
Writings selected to validate the author's conviction that the Vietnam War was not unavoidable and that Paris, Saigon and Washington had repeatedly and mistakenly chosen the easiest ways out in making their policy decisions.

Fallaci, Oriana. **Nothing and So Be It.** Garden City: Doubleday, 1972, 320 p.
This book on the war in Vietnam by an angry and gifted Italian journalist was originally published as "Niente e cosi sia" (Milan: Rizzoli, 2d ed., 1969, 353 p.).

FitzGerald, Frances. **Fire in the Lake: The Vietnamese and the Americans in Vietnam.** Boston: Little, Brown, 1972, 491 p.
For the author of this widely discussed study the weight of South Vietnamese history guarantees not only that East and West will never meet in Vietnam but that the West can only with difficulty understand why.

Glyn, Alan. **Witness to Vietnam.** London: Johnson, 1968, 316 p.
A British writer, who is also a Conservative M.P., urges the West to contain communism in Vietnam and Asia. He is convinced that "without America's help the struggle cannot be won."

Halberstam, David. **The Making of a Quagmire.** New York: Random House, 1965, 323 p.
An account of the Vietnam conflict by a former *New York Times* correspondent who won the 1964 Pulitzer Prize for reporting on the war in Vietnam.

Honey, Patrick James. **Genesis of a Tragedy: The Historical Background to the Vietnam War.** London: Benn, 1968, 86 p.

According to the author, "This short book was written so as to provide a very brief background history of Vietnam to record how the developments there moved, with all the inevitability of a classical Greek tragedy, to the terrible war . . . fought in Vietnam."

Kraslow, David and Loory, Stuart H. **The Secret Search for Peace in Vietnam.** New York: Random House, 1968, 247 p.
An account of missed opportunities to end the war in Vietnam. The main villain of the story is the leadership in Washington.

Lacouture, Jean. **Vietnam: Between Two Truces.** New York: Random House, 1966, 295 p.
A senior correspondent for *Le Monde,* whose solid background on Vietnam dates back to 1945, views the Vietnam conflict as a political one, started locally, and soluble only by the settlement of local issues. French edition, "Le Vietnam entre deux paix" (Paris: Éditions du Seuil, 1965, 269 p.).

Liska, George. **War and Order: Reflections on Vietnam and History.** Baltimore: Johns Hopkins Press (for the Washington Center of Foreign Policy Research), 1968, 115 p.
The author of "Imperial America" (1967) reflects in this study upon the larger historical significance of the Vietnam conflict.

Maneli, Mieczyslaw. **War of the Vanquished.** New York: Harper and Row, 1971, 228 p.
The author of these informative observations on the Vietnam conflict was a member of the Polish delegation to the International Commission for Supervision and Control in Vietnam. Since 1968 Mr. Maneli has lived in the West.

Moore, John Norton. **Law and the Indo-China War.** Princeton: Princeton University Press, 1972, 794 p.
A legal study of the Vietnam conflict, by a professor at the University of Virginia School of Law.

Murti, Bhaskarla Surya Narayana. **Vietnam Divided: The Unfinished Struggle.** New York: Asia Publishing House, 1964, 228 p.
An authoritative record of the workings of the International Commission established in 1954 to implement the provisions of the Geneva Agreement reached at the end of the Indochina war; by the former Public Relations Officer and Deputy Secretary-General of the Commission.

Pan, Chao-ying and Lyons, Daniel, S. J. **Vietnam Crisis.** New York: East Asian Research Institute, 1966, 334 p.
The authors, who have been acquainted with many of the South and North Vietnamese leaders, are convinced that by abdicating in South Vietnam "America will have served notice on the rest of the world that they [sic] cannot count on the United States."

Pike, Douglas. **Viet Cong: The Organization and Techniques of the National Liberation Front of South Vietnam.** Cambridge: M.I.T. Press, 1966, 490 p.
Mr. Pike bases this careful study of the character and nature of the N.L.F. and its relationships with communism and North Vietnam on data personally collected during six years of service as U.S.I.A. official in Vietnam.

Pike, Douglas. **War, Peace, and the Viet Cong.** Cambridge: M.I.T. Press, 1969, 186 p.
The author, who contends that differences between North and South Vietnamese are more emotional than real, updates to 1969 appraisals contained in his earlier "Viet Cong." His information comes from North Vietnamese and National Liberation Front leaders and from documents picked up on the battlefield.

Ray, Sibnarayan, *ed.* **Vietnam: Seen from East and West; An International Symposium.** New York: Praeger, 1966, 192 p.
An examination of the nature and significance of the war in Vietnam, by fifteen Asian, Australian and Western scholars.

Rupen, Robert Arthur and Farrell, Robert Barry, *eds.* **Vietnam and the Sino-Soviet Dispute.** New York: Praeger, 1967, 120 p.
Nine essays resulting from a 1966 international symposium sponsored by the Institute for the Study of the U.S.S.R.

Sansom, Robert L. **The Economics of Insurgency in the Mekong Delta of Vietnam.** Cambridge: M.I.T. Press, 1970, 283 p.

A technical study, based on field work, of the economic reasons for insurgency, by an Oxford-trained American scholar.

Shaplen, Robert. **The Road from War: Vietnam 1965-1970.** New York: Harper and Row, 1970, 368 p.
Reports on the Vietnam War, originally written for *The New Yorker*.

Watt, Sir Alan Stewart. **Vietnam: An Australian Analysis.** Melbourne: Cheshire (for the Australian Institute of International Affairs), 1968, 177 p.
A senior Australian diplomat, with many years of firsthand experience in Southeast Asia, soberly surveys the Vietnam conflict, paying particular attention to the Australian involvement in, and reaction to, the war.

White, Ralph K. **Nobody Wanted War: Misperception in Vietnam and Other Wars.** Garden City: Doubleday, 1968, 347 p.
The author states in the preface of this case study of the Vietnam War that "Its purpose is to explore the psychological forces and rigidities that make any war possible."

Zagoria, Donald S. **Vietnam Triangle: Moscow, Peking, Hanoi.** New York: Pegasus, 1967, 286 p.
In the rivalry among Washington, Moscow and Peking, each, the author argues, has been anxious to keep the others apart. The Vietnam problem is discussed against this background in a sophisticated analytical essay.

U.S. Involvement

See also International Organization and Government, p. 96; War and Peace, p. 108; The Postwar World, p. 178; (The United States) Biographies, Memoirs and Addresses, p. 218; Foreign Policy, p. 229; Military and Defense Policy, p. 257; (China) Foreign Relations, p. 702; (Indochina) General Surveys and the End of the French Rule, p. 736; Laos, p. 749; Khmer Republic (Cambodia), p. 750; (Australia) Foreign and Defense Policies, p. 767; other subsections under Vietnam.

Armbruster, Frank E. and Others. **Can We Win in Vietnam?** New York: Praeger, 1968, 427 p.
A debate among Hudson Institute staff members, specialists in political and military affairs on U.S. involvement in the Vietnam conflict.

Austin, Anthony. **The President's War.** Philadelphia: Lippincott, 1971, 368 p.
A very critical account of how President Johnson obtained congressional authorization for the war in Vietnam.

Bator, Viktor. **Vietnam: A Diplomatic Tragedy.** Dobbs Ferry (N.Y.): Oceana Publications, 1965, 271 p.
The late Hungarian-born international lawyer and diplomat contends in this study that the U.S. involvement in Vietnam stems back to the policies of Eisenhower and Dulles.

Beal, Christopher W. with D'Amato, Anthony, *eds.* **The Realities of Vietnam: A Ripon Society Appraisal.** Washington: Public Affairs Press, 1968, 186 p.
This report, criticizing the policies of the Johnson administration in Vietnam, was prepared by a Republican research and study group.

Brandon, Henry. **Anatomy of Error: The Inside Story of the Asian War on the Potomac, 1954-1969.** Boston: Gambit, 1969, 178 p.
The chief American correspondent of London's *Sunday Times* offers some observations on the personalities and policies that determined the involvement of the United States in Vietnam.

Chomsky, Noam. **At War with Asia.** New York: Pantheon Books, 1970, 313 p.
A passionate indictment of the American role in Vietnam, by a linguist at M.I.T. and a leader of the anti-war movement.

Cooper, Chester L. **The Lost Crusade: America in Vietnam.** New York: Dodd, 1970, 559 p.
One of the best assessments of the Vietnam War by an old Asia hand with many years of service with the U.S. government.

Corson, William R. **The Betrayal.** New York: Norton, 1968, 317 p.
A former Marine officer argues that the United States had failed to supply Vietnam with adequate programs for economic, political and social development.

Draper, Theodore. **Abuse of Power.** New York: Viking, 1967, 244 p.
A polemic against "the supersession of political by military instrumentalities in the conduct of American foreign policy," especially in Vietnam, where the author analyzes seven turning points cutting across four American administrations.

Ellsberg, Daniel. **Papers on the War.** New York: Simon and Schuster, 1972, 309 p.
Memoranda, articles, speeches and testimony prepared between 1965 and 1971, and patched together with footnotes and introductions by the man who made public the Pentagon Papers. The book is an uneven but often compelling source for understanding the author's involvement as participant and then critic in the Vietnam War.

Falk, Richard A., *ed.* **The Vietnam War and International Law.** Princeton: Princeton University Press (in coöperation with the American Society of International Law), 1968-72, 3 v.
A collection of readings and documents by scholars and international lawyers on the legality of the U.S. involvement in the Vietnam War.

Fishel, Wesley R., *ed.* **Vietnam: Anatomy of a Conflict.** Itasca (Ill.): F. E. Peacock Publishers, 1968, 879 p.
An informative survey of how the United States got involved in the Vietnam War.

Galloway, John. **The Gulf of Tonkin Resolution.** Rutherford (N.J.): Fairleigh Dickinson University Press, 1970, 578 p.
This account of the controversial resolution sees it as a symbol of the "stealthful ways" of President Johnson.

Gavin, James M. with Hadley, Arthur T. **Crisis Now.** New York: Random House, 1968, 184 p.
The author, a retired general and a former U. S. Ambassador to France, first proposes to end the Vietnam War through the enclave strategy and then suggests that the money thus saved be spent on the search for solutions to the problem of "the human environment" in the United States.

Goodwin, Richard Naradof. **Triumph or Tragedy: Reflections on Vietnam.** New York: Random House, 1966, 142 p.
A former U.S. government official examines briefly the U.S. involvement in Vietnam.

Goulden, Joseph C. **Truth is the First Casualty: The Gulf of Tonkin Affair—Illusion and Reality.** Chicago: Rand McNally, 1969, 285 p.
A critical survey of the Gulf of Tonkin incidents in 1964.

Gruening, Ernest and Beaser, Wilton Herbert. **Vietnam Folly.** Washington: National Press, 1968, 664 p.
A catalogue of arguments against the American involvement in Vietnam. Ernest Gruening represented Alaska in the U.S. Senate from 1956 to 1969.

Gurtov, Melvin. **The First Vietnam Crisis: Chinese Communist Strategy and United States Involvement, 1953-1954.** New York: Columbia University Press, 1967, 228 p.
A scholarly study, based on many interviews and documentary materials, including the papers of John Foster Dulles. The author was a research associate at the RAND Corporation from 1966 to 1971.

Hammer, Richard. **The Court-Martial of Lt. Calley.** New York: Coward, McCann and Geoghegan, 1971, 398 p.
An account of the widely publicized trial of Lt. Calley for crimes committed in the Vietnam War.

Hersh, Seymour M. **Cover-Up.** New York: Random House, 1972, 305 p.
An exposé of the U.S. Army's concealment of the My Lai atrocities.

Higgins, Marguerite. **Our Vietnam Nightmare.** New York: Harper and Row, 1965, 314 p.
The late Pulitzer Prize winner deplores in this book the U.S. policies in Vietnam which, in her opinion, were determined by conflicting and uninformed advice given to the Kennedy and Johnson administrations.

Hoopes, Townsend. **The Limits of Intervention.** New York: McKay, 1969, 245 p.
This revealing account by a former Under Secretary of the Air Force shows the evolution of the crisis of conscience among a number of men—in particular Paul H. Nitze and Clark M. Clifford—that finally persuaded President Johnson to reverse his Vietnam policy on March 31, 1968.

Hull, Roger H. and Novogrod, John C. **Law and Vietnam.** Dobbs Ferry (N.Y.): Oceana Publications, 1968, 211 p.
A defense of the legality of the American involvement in Vietnam.

The Indochina Story: A Fully Documented Account. New York: Pantheon Books (for the Committee of Concerned Asian Scholars), 1971, 347 p.
A scathing indictment of American policies in Indochina and a plea for an immediate, unilateral and total American withdrawal.

Isard, Walter, ed. **Vietnam: Some Basic Issues and Alternatives.** Cambridge: Schenkman, 1969, 213 p.
An examination of the U.S. involvement in Vietnam by a group of social scientists.

Kahin, George McTurnan and Lewis, John Wilson. **The United States in Vietnam.** New York: Dial Press, rev. ed., 1969, 545 p.
An attempt by two well-known scholars (Professor Kahin is at Cornell and Professor Lewis is at Stanford) to provide the essential facts basic for a better understanding of the Vietnam conflict.

Krause, Patricia A., ed. **Anatomy of an Undeclared War: Congressional Conference on the Pentagon Papers.** New York: International Universities Press, 1972, 271 p.
The proceedings of a 1971 conference on the revelations of the Pentagon Papers. The participants were 17 anti-war Congressmen and 19 other Americans and Vietnamese.

Luce, Don and Sommer, John. **Vietnam—The Unheard Voices.** Ithaca: Cornell University Press, 1969, 336 p.
Two former members of the International Voluntary Services describe their experiences in Vietnam and criticize the U.S. policies there.

McCarthy, Mary Therese. **Vietnam.** New York: Harcourt, Brace and World, 1967, 106 p.
Forceful criticism of the U.S. policies in Vietnam by a well-known writer who was sent to Vietnam in February 1967 by *The New York Review of Books* for firsthand observations.

McGee, Gale W. **The Responsibilities of World Power.** Washington: National Press, 1968, 274 p.
A defense of the U.S. involvement in Vietnam by the Democratic Senator from Wyoming.

Mecklin, John. **Mission in Torment: An Intimate Account of the U.S. Role in Vietnam.** Garden City: Doubleday, 1965, 318 p.
A newsman in Vietnam from 1953 to 1955 and U.S.I.A.'s Public Affairs officer from 1962 to 1964 argues that an important cause of U.S. failure in Vietnam was the breakdown between the American press and government officials.

Menashe, Louis and Radosh, Ronald, eds. **Teach-Ins: U.S.A.** New York: Praeger, 1967, 349 p.
A compilation of reports, opinions and documents concerning the discussion in the United States of the involvement in Vietnam.

Morgenthau, Hans Joachim. **Vietnam and the United States.** Washington: Public Affairs Press, 1965, 112 p.
A collection of writings by an early and most articulate opponent of U.S. policy in Vietnam.

Raskin, Marcus G. and Fall, Bernard B., eds. **The Viet-Nam Reader: Articles and Documents on American Foreign Policy and the Viet-Nam Crisis.** New York: Random House, 1965, 415 p.
A valuable selection from highly diversified sources.

Russell, Bertrand Arthur William Russell, 3rd Earl. **War Crimes in Vietnam.** New York: Monthly Review Press, 1967, 178 p.
A bitter denouncement of U.S. actions in Vietnam by the late British philosopher.

Scott, Peter Dale. **The War Conspiracy: The Secret Road to the Second Indochina War.** Indianapolis: Bobbs-Merrill, 1972, 238 p.
An effort to blame the war in Vietnam on covert machinations by secret intelligence personnel with intimate ties to powerful and sometimes criminal economic interests in the United States.

Shaplen, Robert. **The Lost Revolution.** New York: Harper and Row, 1965, 404 p.
> A severe critique of American military and diplomatic actions in Vietnam. The author, a correspondent for *The New Yorker* with many years of experience in the Far East, believes that the United States lost valuable opportunities to deal realistically with Ho Chi Minh at the outset and to act more effectively at the time of the Diem coup.

Standard, William L. **Aggression: Our Asian Disaster.** New York: Random House, 1971, 228 p.
> An impassioned brief arguing that U.S. conduct of the Vietnam War violated the SEATO treaty, the U.N. Charter, the Hague Convention, the Geneva Convention, the "Nuremberg Principles" and the U.S. Constitution. The author was chairman of the Lawyers Committee on American Policy Towards Vietnam.

Tanham, George Kilpatrick and Others. **War without Guns: American Civilians in Rural Vietnam.** New York: Praeger, 1966, 141 p.
> Mr. Tanham, formerly Director of Provincial Operations for A.I.D., describes American experiences in helping improve social, economic and governmental conditions throughout Vietnam's 43 provinces.

Taylor, Telford. **Nuremberg and Vietnam: An American Tragedy.** Chicago: Quadrangle Books, 1970, 224 p.
> The author of this analysis concludes that "somehow we failed ourselves to learn the lessons we undertook to teach at Nuremberg, and that failure is today's American tragedy."

Thompson, Sir Robert Grainger Ker. **No Exit from Vietnam.** New York: McKay, 1969, 208 p.
> The author, a leading British expert on guerrilla warfare, urges in this study the United States "to keep its pledge and stand by South Vietnam."

Trager, Frank N. **Why Viet Nam?** New York: Praeger, 1966, 238 p.
> A strong defense of the U.S. involvement in Vietnam.

United States-Vietnam Relations, 1945-1967. Washington: G.P.O., 12 v.
> This set of documents, known as the Pentagon Papers, contains the first 43 volumes of the original 47-volume study that was prepared in 1968 for the House Committee on Armed Services by the Department of Defense. A selection of these papers was made public without authorization at first in *The New York Times*. This version, with some additional material, has appeared in book form as "The Pentagon Papers as Published by *The New York Times*" (New York: Quadrangle Books, 1971, 810 p.). Papers from the Department of Defense compilation were also made public by Senator Mike Gravel in the official record of the Senate Subcommittee on Public Buildings and Grounds and were later published, with the addition of material from the published version of *The New York Times* selection, as "The Pentagon Papers: The Senator Gravel Edition; The Defense Department History of United States Decision-making on Vietnam" (Boston: Beacon Press, 1971-72, 5 v.). The last volume of the Gravel edition, edited by Noam Chomsky and Howard Zinn, contains fifteen essays by anti-war journalists and academics on the contents and implication of the Pentagon Papers and also a useful index to the first four volumes.

Van Dyke, Jon M. **North Vietnam's Strategy for Survival.** Palo Alto: Pacific Books, 1972, 336 p.
> A study, originally written for the then Professor Kissinger's Harvard seminar, of the failure of the United States to achieve its objectives in the Vietnam War by bombing North Vietnam between 1965 and 1968.

Warner, Denis Ashton. **The Last Confucian.** Baltimore: Penguin, rev. ed., 1964, 327 p.
> An analytical assessment of American efforts to curb communism in Southeast Asia, with emphasis on Vietnam and Ngo Dinh Diem (the "Last Confucian").

Windchy, Eugene G. **Tonkin Gulf.** Garden City: Doubleday, 1971, 358 p.
> A vividly written critical analysis of the genesis of the Tonkin Gulf resolution, by an author who spent 11 years with the U.S.I.A. in East Asia.

Military Aspects

See also (War) Chemical and Biological Warfare, p. 118; Guerrilla Warfare; Armed Insurrection, p. 118; (The United States) Biographies, Memoirs and Addresses, p. 218; Foreign Policy, p. 229; Military and Defense Policy, p. 257; (China) Foreign Relations, p. 702; Military Questions, p. 705; (Indochina) General Surveys and the End of the French Rule, p. 736; Laos, p. 749; Khmer Republic (Cambodia) p. 750; Malaysia, p. 756; (Australia) Foreign and Defense Policies, p. 767; other subsections under Vietnam.

Broughton, Jack. **Thud Ridge.** Philadelphia: Lippincott, 1969, 254 p.
The story of Thailand-based U.S. fighter pilots who flew against North Vietnam.

Browne, Malcolm W. **The New Face of War.** Indianapolis: Bobbs-Merrill, 1965, 284 p.
A somber book on the war in Vietnam by a journalist who won the Pulitzer Prize for his reporting.

Burchett, Wilfred Graham. **Vietnam: Inside Story of the Guerilla War.** New York: International Publishers, 1965, 253 p.
An Australian pro-communist journalist recounts his experiences with the guerrilla forces in the Vietnam War.

Chaffard, Georges. **Les deux guerres du Vietnam: de Valluy à Westmoreland.** Paris: Éditions de la Table Ronde, 1969, 458 p.
A comparison of the French and American military campaigns in Vietnam, by an author who is convinced that the Vietminh were primarily motivated by nationalistic considerations.

Däniker, Gustav. **Warum sie nicht siegten: der Vietnamkrieg 1965-1969.** Frauenfeld: Huber, 1969, 323 p.
The author of this study reviews the military operations in Vietnam from 1965 to 1969 and tries to discover the reasons for the American failure to achieve a victory.

Doyon, Jacques. **Les Viet Cong.** Paris: Denoël, 1968, 310 p.
A study of the communist Vietcong activities.

Fall, Bernard B. **Last Reflections on a War.** Garden City: Doubleday, 1967, 288 p.
Tape recordings, unpublished works and articles selected by the widow of this highly regarded journalist who was killed, on his sixth visit to Vietnam, on February 21, 1967.

Hosmer, Stephen T. **Viet Cong Repression and Its Implications for the Future.** Lexington (Mass.): Heath Lexington Books, 1970, 176 p.
In this study the author argues that the policy of assassination and abduction is basic to the Vietnamese communists' struggle for power.

Knoebl, Kuno. **Victor Charlie: The Face of War in Viet-Nam.** New York: Praeger, 1967, 304 p.
An Austrian journalist, after five months in Vietnam, reports on the political and military intentions of the Vietcong, many of whose soldiers and leaders he interviewed. A translation of "Victor Charlie: Viet Cong—der unheimliche Feind" (Vienna: Molden, 1966, 454 p.).

Littauer, Raphael and Uphoff, Norman, *eds.* **The Air War in Indochina.** Boston: Beacon Press, rev. ed., 1972, 289 p.
A scholarly appraisal by Cornell University's Air War Study Group of the military techniques that were used by the United States in Indochina to protect its interests and its prestige.

Lucas, Jim Griffing. **Dateline: Viet Nam.** New York: Award House, 1966, 334 p.
Dispatches over a two-year period by a Pulitzer Prize journalist showing how the war was being fought by both the Vietnamese and their American advisers.

McGarvey, Patrick J., *comp.* **Visions of Victory: Selected Vietnamese Communist Military Writings, 1964-1968.** Stanford: Hoover Institution on War, Revolution, and Peace, 1969, 276 p.
A useful collection, compiled by a former research member of the U.S. delegation at the Paris meetings on Vietnam.

Marshall, Samuel Lyman Atwood. **Battles in the Monsoon.** New York: Morrow, 1967, 408 p.

General Marshall, a veteran American war correspondent, visited the II Corps Zone in the Central Highlands in the summer of 1966 to see at first hand how the American forces were coping with the extraordinary conditions of jungle warfare.

Meyerson, Harvey. **Vinh Long.** Boston: Houghton, 1970, 220 p.
A study of the intense warfare in the Mekong Delta.

Oberdorfer, Don. **Tet!** Garden City: Doubleday, 1971, 385 p.
The author of this chronicle of the Tet offensive concludes that the North Vietnamese and Vietcong lost the battle but that the Johnson administration lost the confidence of the American people.

Race, Jeffrey. **War Comes to Long An.** Berkeley: University of California Press, 1972, 299 p.
The author, U.S. Army adviser to a Vietnamese district chief in 1967 and later a graduate student at Harvard, uses interviews and documents to explain the success of insurgent strategies and the failure of Washington and Saigon countermoves. In brief: the revolutionaries understood the situation and the people; the government and its ally were ignorant.

Swearingen, Rodger and Rolph, Hammond. **Communism in Vietnam: A Documentary Study of Theory, Strategy and Operational Practices.** Chicago: American Bar Association, 1967, 195 p.
A survey of unconventional communist doctrines of warfare in Vietnam.

Tregaskis, Richard William. **Vietnam Diary.** New York: Holt, Rinehart and Winston, 1963, 401 p.
An American war correspondent's account of his coverage of all fronts of the war in Vietnam from October 9, 1962 to January 11, 1963.

Vo-nguyen-Giap. **Banner of People's War: The Party's Military Line.** New York: Praeger, 1970, 118 p.
──. **"Big Victory, Great Task."** New York: Praeger, 1968, 120 p.
──. **The Military Art of People's War.** New York: Monthly Review Press, 1970, 332 p.
Major statements on communist strategy in the Vietnam War by the Commander-in-Chief of North Vietnam's Army and Minister of Defense of his country.

Walt, Lewis W. **Strange War, Strange Strategy: A General's Report on Vietnam.** New York: Funk and Wagnalls, 1970, 208 p.
A spirited defense of U.S. military policy in South Vietnam, by a Marine general with command responsibility and long firsthand experience.

Republic of Vietnam (South Vietnam)

See also (Southeastern Asia; East Indies) General, p. 733; (Indochina) General Surveys and the End of the French Rule, p. 736; Laos, p. 749; Khmer Republic (Cambodia), p. 750; other subsections under Vietnam.

Bouscaren, Anthony Trawick. **The Last of the Mandarins: Diem of Vietnam.** Pittsburgh: Duquesne University Press, 1965, 174 p.
An account of the life and political activities of Ngo Dinh Diem, President of South Vietnam who was assassinated in 1963. The author criticizes the U.S. press for prominence given to the accusations against Diem.

Critchfield, Richard. **The Long Charade.** New York: Harcourt, Brace and World, 1968, 400 p.
A *Washington Star* correspondent who covered the war in Vietnam from May 1964 to November 1967 argues that political subversion had placed administrative control of South Vietnam in the hands of a ruthless, self-serving group of generals and politicians whose actions often in fact furthered the interests of Hanoi.

Gheddo, Piero. **The Cross and the Bo-Tree: Catholics and Buddhists in Vietnam.** New York: Sheed and Ward, 1970, 368 p.
A study of the religions in Vietnam and of their influence on contemporary politics. The Italian original was published as "Cattolici e buddisti nel Vietnam" (Florence: Valecchi, 1968, 397 p.).

Hassler, Alfred. **Saigon, U.S.A.** New York: Richard W. Baron, 1970, 291 p.
In this tract, the author takes a dim view of the Saigon regime and its American supporters. There is an introduction by Senator George McGovern.

Hickey, Gerald Cannon. **Village in Vietnam.** New Haven: Yale University Press, 1964, 325 p.
An ethnological study of Khanh Hau in the Mekong basin southwest of Saigon, based on field research in 1958–1959, 1962 and 1964.

Lindholm, Richard Wadsworth. **Economic Development Policy, with Emphasis on Vietnam.** Eugene: University of Oregon Press, 1964, 139 p.
A professor at the University of Oregon, who from 1952 to 1961 was an economic advisor to Southeast Asian governments, discusses first the general problems of development faced by all emerging nations and then the problems of taxation policies, land reform and finance in Pakistan, Korea and especially South Vietnam.

Mole, Robert L. **The Montagnards of South Vietnam.** Rutland (Vt.): Tuttle, 1970, 277 p.
A study of the cross-cultural relations among nine of the 33 Montagnard tribes who, although a minority group, inhabit almost 50 percent of the South Vietnamese land area.

Moore, Frederick T. and Others. **Export Prospects for the Republic of Vietnam.** New York: Praeger, 1971, 389 p.
This volume analyzes the outlook for South Vietnamese exports after the cessation of hostilities. Prepared by the Development and Resources Corporation under a contract with the U.S. Agency for International Development.

Nghiem-Dang. **Viet-Nam: Politics and Public Administration.** Honolulu: East-West Center Press, 1966, 437 p.
A pioneering study by a Vietnamese scholar.

Penniman, Howard R. **Elections in South Vietnam.** Washington: American Enterprise Institute for Public Policy Research; Stanford: Hoover Institution, 1972, 246 p.
A thorough examination of seven national elections in South Vietnam since 1966.

The Postwar Development of the Republic of Vietnam: Policies and Programs. New York: Praeger (in coöperation with Development and Resources Corporation), 1970, 552 p.
This ambitious examination of "the probable problems and opportunities" in South Vietnam of the postwar period was prepared by the Joint Development Group, a body consisting of Vietnamese and American scholars and public figures, and was financed by the U.S. Agency for International Development and the Government of Vietnam.

Scigliano, Robert C. **South Vietnam: Nation under Stress.** Boston: Houghton, 1963, 227 p.
A political history of South Vietnam from 1954 to the assassination of Ngo Dinh Diem, by a professor at Boston College.

Democratic Republic of Vietnam (North Vietnam)

See also (Southeastern Asia; East Indies) General, p. 733; (Indochina) General Surveys and the End of the French Rule, p. 736; Laos, p. 749; Khmer Republic (Cambodia), p. 750; other subsections under Vietnam.

Ashmore, Harry S. and Baggs, William C. **Mission to Hanoi.** New York: Putnam (for the Center for the Study of Democratic Institutions), 1968, 369 p.
A personal account, interspersed with criticisms of the Johnson administration, of two visits to Hanoi in 1967 and 1968 by Mr. Ashmore, a former editor of the "Encyclopedia Britannica," and the late Mr. Baggs, editor of the *Miami News.*

Burchett, Wilfred Graham. **Vietnam North.** New York: International Publishers, 1966, 191 p.
A pro-communist account of travels in North Vietnam in 1966 by an Australian journalist.

Cameron, James. **Here is Your Enemy.** New York: Holt, Rinehart and Winston, 1966, 144 p.

A British journalist, admitted to North Vietnam in December 1965, gives an account of what he saw, heard and learned from lengthy talks with its leaders.

Halberstam, David. **Ho.** New York: Random House, 1971, 118 p.
A short biography of Ho-chi-Minh, the North Vietnamese leader who died in 1969.

Ho-chi-Minh. **On Revolution.** New York: Praeger, 1967, 389 p.
Selected writings dating from 1920 to 1966, edited by Bernard B. Fall.

Hoang-van-Chi. **From Colonialism to Communism: A Case History of North Vietnam.** New York: Praeger, 1964, 252 p.
A description of the communist seizure of control of the patriotic anti-colonial movement in Vietnam and the establishment of a communist regime. Mr. Hoang himself participated in many of the events.

Honey, Patrick James. **Communism in North Vietnam.** Cambridge: M.I.T. Press, 1963, 207 p.
A British scholar examines North Vietnam's internal problems, party leadership and political aspirations in light of its dilemma in choosing sides in the Sino-Soviet dispute.

Huyen, N. Khac. **Vision Accomplished? The Enigma of Ho Chi Minh.** New York: Collier Books, 1971, 377 p.
The author, though characterizing the subject of his very informative biography as "one of the most cunning, ruthless, and dedicated Communists the world has yet known," can not conceal his admiration for the "great patriot whose dedication to Communism never obscured his devotion to his fatherland."

Kux, Ernst and Kun, Joseph Cornelius. **Die Satelliten Pekings: Nordvietnam, Nordkorea.** Stuttgart: Kohlhammer, 1964, 283 p.
A substantial study of the communist republics of North Vietnam and North Korea and their relations with Communist China and the Soviet Union, by two well-informed historians and journalists.

Lacouture, Jean. **Ho Chi Minh: A Political Biography.** New York: Random House, 1968, 313 p.
A biography of the North Vietnamese communist leader by a prominent French writer. The French original appeared as "Hô Chi Minh" (Paris: Éditions du Seuil, 1967, 253 p.).

Lê Châu. **Le Vietnam socialiste: une économie de transition.** Paris: Maspero, 1966, 410 p.
A not very well organized economic history of the Democratic Republic of Vietnam from 1945 to 1965, by a pro-communist Vietnamese author. Uncritical though it is, it provides some useful information.

Lê Duân. **The Vietnamese Revolution.** New York: International Publishers, 1971, 151 p.
A report by the First Secretary of the Vietnam Workers Party on the 40th Anniversary of the establishment of the Indochinese Communist Party.

Lynd, Staughton and Hayden, Thomas. **The Other Side.** New York: New American Library, 1966, 238 p.
A diary of a trip to North Vietnam by two well-known opponents of the American involvement in Indochina.

O'Neill, Robert J. **General Giap: Politician and Strategist.** New York: Praeger, 1969, 219 p.
A biography of the North Vietnamese Army chief and Defense Minister.

Raffaelli, Jean. **Hanoï, capitale de la survie.** Paris: Grasset, 1967, 263 p.
A sympathetic account of a sojourn in North Vietnam in the second half of 1966, with observations on how the Sino-Soviet dispute has affected the war in Vietnam.

Riffaud, Madeleine. **Au Nord Viet-Nam.** Paris: Julliard, 1967, 299 p.
Reporting from North Vietnam by a French journalist who sympathizes with the aims of Ho-chi-Minh.

Riffaud, Madeleine. **Dans les maquis "vietcong".** Paris: Julliard, 1965, 267 p.
Observations by a French journalist who traveled with Wilfred Burchett in North Vietnam from November 1964 to January 1965.

Sainteny, Jean. **Ho Chi Minh and His Vietnam.** Chicago: Cowles Book Co., 1972, 193 p.
A French diplomat who knew Ho for 24 years offers a perceptive account of the personality and politics of a man not easily fathomed. A translation of "Face á Ho Chi Minh" (Paris: Seghers, 1970, 210 p.).

Salisbury, Harrison Evans. **Behind the Lines—Hanoi: December 23, 1966—January 7, 1967.** New York: Harper and Row, 1967, 243 p.
A senior correspondent of *The New York Times* has expanded his dispatches by providing background information and deeper analysis of the situations observed during a brief trip to North Vietnam.

Tru'ó 'ng-Chinh. **Primer for Revolt: The Communist Takeover in Viet-Nam.** New York: Praeger, 1963, 213 p.
A facsimile edition of two major theoretical and political works by a leading communist of North Vietnam.

LAOS

See also (The United States) Foreign Policy, p. 229; (Asia and the Pacific Area) General Surveys, p. 607; (India) Foreign Policy, p. 666; (China) Foreign Relations, p. 702; (Southeastern Asia; East Indies) General, p. 733; (Indochina) General Surveys and the End of the French Rule, p. 736; Vietnam, p. 738; Khmer Republic (Cambodia), p. 750.

Adams, Nina S. and McCoy, Alfred W., *eds.* **Laos: War and Revolution.** New York: Harper and Row, 1971, 482 p.
A collection of articles on Laos and a critical assessment of the U.S. involvement in that country. The volume appeared under the auspices of the Committee of Concerned Asian Scholars.

Caply, Michel. **Guérilla au Laos.** Paris: Presses de la Cité, 1966, 345 p.
Recollections dealing with the French efforts to reëstablish their presence in Indochina in 1945, by an active participant.

Dommen, Arthur J. **Conflict in Laos: The Politics of Neutralization.** New York: Praeger, rev. ed., 1971, 454 p.
A considerably revised and expanded edition of a history of Laos since World War II. The author, with many years of experience as a journalist in the Far East, was a Press Fellow at the Council on Foreign Relations in 1963-64. Mr. Dommen's book is a strong plea for the neutralization of Laos.

Fall, Bernard B. **Anatomy of a Crisis: The Laotian Crisis of 1960-1961.** Garden City: Doubleday, 1969, 283 p.
A study of the origins and probable consequences for Asia, the United States and the world of the controversy between the Pathet Lao and the Royal Laotian government forces. Edited by Roger M. Smith.

Halpern, Joel Martin. **Economy and Society of Laos: A Brief Survey.** New Haven: Yale University, Southeast Asia Studies, 1964, 180 p.

——. **Government, Politics, and Social Structure in Laos: A Study of Tradition and Innovation.** New Haven: Yale University, Southeast Asia Studies, 1964, 184 p.
These companion volumes are based on field data collected in 1957-1959 and subsequent research.

Langer, Paul F. and Zasloff, Joseph J. **North Vietnam and the Pathet Lao: Partners in the Struggle for Laos.** Cambridge: Harvard University Press, 1970, 262 p.
The authors of this study argue that the Pathet Lao is a creation of the North Vietnamese government and a front for its imperialistic designs.

Lee, Chae-jin. **Communist China's Policy toward Laos: A Case Study, 1954-1967.** Lawrence: University of Kansas, Center for East Asian Studies, 1970, 161 p.
The author questions the assumptions that China is expansionist, aggressive and untrustworthy and he concludes his study by stating that China's policy toward Laos has been rational and cautious.

Stevenson, Charles A. **The End of Nowhere: American Policy toward Laos since 1954.** Boston: Beacon Press, 1972, 367 p.
The author argues that U.S. policy toward Laos is not made by the President or

Congress, but by various bureaucratic factions—the State and Defense Departments, CIA, AID—who all have their vested interests.

Toye, Hugh. **Laos: Buffer State or Battleground.** New York: Oxford University Press, 1968, 245 p.
An attempt to discuss the political and military developments of contemporary Laos in their historical context.

Whitaker, David P. and Others. **Area Handbook for Laos.** Washington: G.P.O., 1972, 337 p.
A useful reference, with bibliography, prepared by the Foreign Area Studies at the American University.

KHMER REPUBLIC (CAMBODIA)

See also The Third World; Nonalignment, p. 186; (The United States) Foreign Policy, p. 229; (Asia and the Pacific Area) General Surveys, p. 607; (India) Foreign Policy, p. 666; (China) Foreign Relations, p. 702; (Southeastern Asia; East Indies) General, p. 733; (Indochina) General Surveys and the End of the French Rule, p. 736; Vietnam, p. 738; Laos, p. 749.

Armstrong, John P. **Sihanouk Speaks.** New York: Walker, 1964, 161 p.
Drawing primarily on the words of Cambodia's abdicated King, the former co-director of the Rangoon-Hopkins Center for Southeast Asian Studies provides the reasons for Sihanouk's policies and dealings in international affairs.

Burchett, Wilfred Graham. **The Second Indochina War: Cambodia and Laos.** New York: International Publishers, 1970, 204 p.
A journalist long known for his leftist views asserts that the U.S. incursions into Cambodia and Laos in 1970 represent "a logical extension of policies followed by the United States . . . deliberately planned to 'fill the power vacuum' created by the collapse of French colonialism."

Chhak, Sarin. **Les Frontières du Cambodge. Tome I: Les Frontières du Cambodge avec les anciens pays de la Fédération Indochinoise: Le Laos et le Vietnam (Cochinchine et Annam).** Paris: Dalloz, 1966, 218 p.
A study of Cambodian frontier problems, with a preface by Prince Norodom Sihanouk.

Gour, Claude-Gilles. **Institutions constitutionnelles et politiques du Cambodge.** Paris: Dalloz, 1965, 448 p.
A description of the political institutions in Cambodia as they existed in the early 1960s.

Grant, Jonathan S. and Others, *ed.* **Cambodia: The Widening War in Indochina.** New York: Washington Square Press, 1971, 355 p.
A volume of articles, sponsored by the Committee of Concerned Asian Scholars and dealing with problems caused by "the American thrust into the Cambodian Sanctuaries in the spring of 1970."

Laurent, Maurice. **L'Armée au Cambodge et dans les pays en voie de développement du Sud-Est Asiatique.** Paris: Presses Universitaires, 1968, 315 p.
A French officer, who has served as military advisor to the Cambodian government, surveys the history of the Cambodian army and analyzes its role in the political and economic life of the country. The author argues that in underdeveloped countries the army has to participate actively in social and economic development.

Leifer, Michael. **Cambodia: The Search for Security.** New York: Praeger, 1967, 209 p.
In this study of Cambodia's foreign relations the author focuses on Sihanouk's dilemma in maintaining neutrality while threatened by Thai irredentism and Vietnamese expansionism.

Smith, Roger M. **Cambodia's Foreign Policy.** Ithaca: Cornell University Press (for the Southeast Asia Program, Cornell University), 1965, 273 p.
An examination of the reasons why Cambodia elected a nonalignment policy.

Whitaker, Donald P. and Others. **Area Handbook for Khmer Republic (Cambodia).** Washington: G.P.O., 1973, 389 p.
A useful reference volume with a bibliography, prepared by the Foreign Area Studies at the American University.

Williams, Maslyn. **The Land in between: The Cambodian Dilemma.** New York: Morrow, 1970, 241 p.
This account of a three-month visit to Cambodia by an observant Australian journalist includes a discussion of Prince Sihanouk's politics and foreign policies.

Willmott, William E. **The Chinese in Cambodia.** Vancouver: Publications Centre, University of British Columbia, 1967, 132 p.
A University of British Columbia anthropologist examines the position of the Chinese community in Cambodian society on the basis of research carried out in Cambodia in 1962–63.

THAILAND

See also Political Processes, p. 20; (The United States) Foreign Policy, p. 229; (Asia and the Pacific Area) General Surveys, p. 607; (Southeastern Asia; East Indies) General, p. 733; (Indochina) General Surveys and the End of the French Rule, p. 736.

Darling, Frank C. **Thailand and the United States.** Washington: Public Affairs Press, 1965, 243 p.
A professor at DePauw University analyzes in this study U.S.-Thai relations since their beginnings early in the nineteenth century, with emphasis on the post-World War II period.

Fistié, Pierre. **Sous-développement et utopie au Siam: le programme de réformes présenté en 1933 par Pridi Phanomyong.** The Hague: Mouton, 1969, 254 p.
A discussion of Pridi Panomyong's economic plan of 1933 for revolutionizing Thailand's economic system. The plan, strongly influenced by Marxist ideas, was never implemented.

Fistié, Pierre. **La Thailande.** Paris: Presses Universitaires, 1963, 128 p.
A general work on Thailand in the "Que sais-je" series.

Henderson, John W. and Others. **Area Handbook for Thailand.** Washington: G.P.O., 1971, 413 p.
A useful reference volume with a bibliography, prepared by the Foreign Area Studies at the American University.

Ingram, James C. **Economic Change in Thailand, 1850–1970.** Stanford: Stanford University Press, 1971, 352 p.
An updated and expanded edition of a work originally published in 1955.

Insor, D. **Thailand: A Political, Social, and Economic Analysis.** New York: Praeger, 1963, 188 p.
Basically a political history, with background chapters on the land, its people and influences on their culture.

Jacobs, Norman. **Modernization without Development: Thailand as an Asian Case Study.** New York: Praeger, 1971, 420 p.
An attempt to answer the question why Thailand has not made economic and social progress in spite of various reforms and the considerable aid received.

Jayanama, Direck. **Thailand im Zweiten Weltkrieg.** Tübingen: Horst Erdmann Verlag, 1970, 311 p.
A description of Thailand's politics and foreign relations during World War II. The author of this volume, originally published in a fuller version in Thai, was Thailand's ambassador to Japan and foreign minister during the period described.

Kruger, Rayne. **The Devil's Discus.** London: Cassell, 1964, 260 p.
An investigation of the death of the young King Ananda Mahidol of Thailand in 1946.

Lomax, Louis E. **Thailand: The War That Is, the War That Will Be.** New York: Random House, 1967, 175 p.
The author, who states his stand against U. S. Southeast Asian policies, writes on American military and political involvement in Thailand.

Lovelace, Daniel Dudley. **China and "People's War" in Thailand, 1964–1969.** Berkeley: Center for Chinese Studies, University of California, 1971, 101 p.
A detailed and able study of China's policy toward Thailand from 1964 to 1969.

Muscat, Robert J. **Development Strategy in Thailand: A Study of Economic Growth.** New York: Praeger, 1966, 310 p.

The author states in the introduction that this work evolved from the needs of development planners, foreign aid technicians and administrators for a systematic approach to the problems of Thailand's economic growth.

Nairn, Ronald Charles. **International Aid to Thailand: The New Colonialism?** New Haven: Yale University Press, 1966, 228 p.

An evaluation of U.N. aid programs to Thailand. The author pays particular attention to community development and educational projects and arrives at the conclusion that "the results were less than the aspirations."

Nuechterlein, Donald Edwin. **Thailand and the Struggle for Southeast Asia.** Ithaca: Cornell University Press, 1965, 279 p.

A study of Thailand's foreign relations during and after World War II, its alignment with the West in the Southeast Asia Treaty Organization, and, in particular, the Thai skepticism regarding the long-term American intentions in Southeast Asia.

Poole, Peter A. **The Vietnamese in Thailand: A Historical Perspective.** Ithaca: Cornell University Press, 1970, 180 p.

A study of the legal, political and cultural status of the Vietnamese refugees in Thailand, and of how this group affected Thai relations with North and South Vietnam.

Ray, Jayanta Kumar. **Portraits of Thai Politics.** New Delhi: Orient Longman, 1972, 225 p.

Political memoirs of three Thai civilian leaders, collected and introduced by one of the doyens of Indian political science.

Riggs, Fred Warren. **Thailand: The Modernization of a Bureaucratic Polity.** Honolulu: East-West Center Press, 1966, 470 p.

This work surveys the processes of change in politics and administration from the mid-nineteenth century on in Thailand, a country free from foreign domination and thus able to develop its own form of bureaucracy.

Rozental, Alek A. **Finance and Development in Thailand.** New York: Praeger, 1970, 370 p.

A description and an analysis of the economy of Thailand, based on field research conducted under the auspices of the National Planning Association under contract to the Agency for International Development.

Siffin, William J. **The Thai Bureaucracy.** Honolulu: East-West Center Press, 1966, 291 p.

A study of the institutional characteristics of Thai bureaucracy and their evolution, by a former staff member of the Institute of Public Administration, Thammasat University in Bangkok.

Silcock, Thomas Henry, *comp*. **Thailand: Social and Economic Studies in Development.** Canberra: Australian National University Press (in association with Duke University Press), 1967, 334 p.

A collection of articles on economic, financial, demographic and social problems of modern Thailand. The editor concludes that "the Thais realize, probably more clearly than the people of most less developed countries, that economic progress may demand changes in their social customs and political structure."

Trescott, Paul B. **Thailand's Monetary Experience: The Economics of Stability.** New York: Praeger, 1971, 342 p.

The first scholarly survey of the finances of contemporary Thailand.

Wilson, David A. **The United States and the Future of Thailand.** New York: Praeger, 1970, 181 p.

In the author's estimate, Thailand will be able to sustain its cohesion and to maintain coöperation with the United States after the conclusion of the Vietnam War.

Wit, Daniel. **Thailand: Another Vietnam?** New York: Scribner, 1968, 205 p.

An optimistic survey of Thailand's contemporary politics and foreign relations, by a professor at Northern Illinois University.

BURMA

See also Socialism, p. 24; Economic Growth and Development, p. 71; (Second World War) Southeastern Asia; China; Burma, p. 167; Economic, Technical and Non-Military Aspects, p. 172; (Asia and the Pacific Area) General Surveys, p. 607; (Southeastern Asia; East Indies) General, p. 733.

Ba Maw, U. **Breakthrough in Burma: Memoirs of a Revolution, 1939-1946.** New Haven: Yale University Press, 1968, 460 p.
  The first Prime Minister of Burma records and analyzes his struggle against foreign domination to gain freedom and independence for his country. He had coöperated at first with the Allies but later with the Japanese.

Bixler, Norma. **Burmese Journey.** Yellow Springs (Ohio): Antioch Press, 1967, 238 p.
——. **Burma: A Profile.** New York: Praeger, 1971, 244 p.
  Two volumes on modern Burma by an American journalist who knows the country well.

Butwell, Richard A. **U Nu of Burma.** Stanford: Stanford University Press, 2d ed., 1969, 327 p.
  An evaluation, based largely on interviews and documents not earlier available, of U Nu and his important role in the governing of Burma (1948-1962).

Chakravarti, Nalini Ranjan. **The Indian Minority in Burma: The Rise and Decline of an Immigrant Community.** New York: Oxford University Press (for the Institute of Race Relations, London), 1971, 214 p.
  A study of the political and economic conditions of the sizable Indian community in Burma. The author, an Indian born in Burma, considers the elimination of Indian interests from Burma "a tragedy of the first magnitude."

Cheng, Siok-Hwa. **The Rice Industry of Burma, 1852-1940.** Kuala Lumpur: University of Malaya Press, 1968, 307 p.
  Mrs. Cheng concludes her study by stating that before World War II Burma's rice industry was far more efficient and successful than afterwards.

Donnison, F. S. V. **Burma.** New York: Praeger, 1970, 263 p.
  A former Indian Civil Service officer presents a pessimistic survey of Burma pointing to the ineffective rule of military dictatorship, the prevailing disunion and internal strifes and hardships.

Henderson, John W. and Others. **Area Handbook for Burma.** Washington: G.P.O., 1971, 341 p.
  A useful reference volume with a bibliography, prepared by the Foreign Area Studies at the American University.

Htin Aung, U. **A History of Burma.** New York: Columbia University Press, 1967, 363 p.
  A reinterpretation of the 2,000 year-history of Burma, based mainly on Burmese sources. The author is a former rector of the University of Rangoon.

Htin Aung, U. **The Stricken Peacock: Anglo-Burmese Relations, 1752-1948.** The Hague: Nijhoff, 1965, 135 p.
  Using Burmese historical sources, the author gives the Burmese point of view of relations with Great Britain since the beginnings of Anglo-Burmese diplomatic contacts, revealing numerous contradictions to British versions of the story.

Johnstone, William Crane. **Burma's Foreign Policy: A Study in Neutralism.** Cambridge: Harvard University Press, 1963, 339 p.
  A skillful analysis of Burma's foreign policy since independence, with particular reference to the theme of neutralism.

Maung, Mya. **Burma and Pakistan: A Comparative Study of Development.** New York: Praeger, 1971, 164 p.
  The author, a professor at Boston College, uses the two nations to illustrate his thesis that varying degrees of economic development can be explained at least as much by the cultural factor of "openness" or tolerance of variability as by the more orthodox economic causal factors.

Maung Maung, U. **Burma and General Ne Win.** New York: Asia Publishing House, 1969, 332 p.

A survey of the political events in Burma centering around the endeavors of Ne Win, builder of Burma's modern armed forces who subsequently became Prime Minister and President of the country.

Saimong Mangrai, Sao. **The Shan States and the British Annexation.** Ithaca: Cornell University, Southeast Asia Program, 1965, 319 p.

A former Chief Education Officer of the Shan and Kayah states relates the story of the British occupation of this area from 1885 (the deposition of Thibaw, last king of Burma) and the subsequent annexation of his kingdom to British India.

Sarkisyanz, Emanuel. **Buddhist Backgrounds of the Burmese Revolution.** The Hague: Nijhoff, 1965, 248 p.

A thorough and illuminating study by an Iranian-born student of Asian intellectual history. Introduction by Paul Mus.

Smith, Donald Eugene. **Religion and Politics in Burma.** Princeton: Princeton University Press, 1965, 350 p.

A professor at the University of Pennsylvania describes the interaction of Buddhism and politics from antiquity onward, with emphasis on post-independence; he shows "Burmese attempts to relate Buddhism to the ideologies of nationalism, democracy, and socialism."

Storz, Hans-Ulrich. **Birma: Land, Geschichte, Wirtschaft.** Wiesbaden: Harrassowitz (for the Institut für Asienkunde in Hamburg), 1967, 302 p.

A very thorough survey of the geography, economy and politics of Burma.

Trager, Frank N. **Burma—From Kingdom to Republic: A Historical and Political Analysis.** New York: Praeger, 1966, 455 p.

Professor Trager, Director of Point Four Program, Burma, 1951–1953, and now with New York University, has visited Burma frequently. In this useful book his main themes are the independence of Burma and its relations with major powers (especially China, the U.S.S.R. and the United States).

Trager, Frank N., ed. **Burma: Japanese Military Administration, Selected Documents, 1941–1945.** Philadelphia: University of Pennsylvania Press, 1971, 279 p.

A collection of documents showing that for the Burmese nationalists the Second World War was "simply another opportunity to regain their lost but cherished independence."

HONG KONG

See also (Great Britain) Imperial and Commonwealth Relations; Colonial Policy, p. 367; (Far East) General, p. 682; (China) General, p. 683; Foreign Relations, p. 702; Overseas Chinese, p. 711.

Cooper, John. **Colony in Conflict: The Hong Kong Disturbances, May 1967–January 1968.** Hong Kong: Swindon, 1970, 315 p.

A study of the serious unrest that was caused by the Chinese Communist sympathizers.

Endacott, George Beer. **Government and People in Hong Kong, 1841–1962: A Constitutional History.** Hong Kong: Hong Kong University Press, 1964, 263 p.

A well-documented history of a British community which has existed as a Crown Colony since 1843.

Gleason, Gene. **Hong Kong.** New York: Day, 1963, 318 p.

An American journalist's report on contemporary Hong Kong.

Grantham, Sir Alexander William George Herder. **Via Ports: From Hong Kong to Hong Kong.** New York: Oxford University Press, 1965, 205 p.

British Colonial Service memoirs in outposts of the far-flung empire, from 1922 to the author's retirement as Governor of Hong Kong in 1957.

Hopkins, K., ed. **Hong Kong: The Industrial Colony.** Hong Kong: Oxford University Press, 1971, 422 p.

Critical essays on recent and prospective economic, demographic, social and political developments.

Hughes, Richard. **Hong Kong: Borrowed Place—Borrowed Time.** New York: Praeger, 1968, 171 p.

An introduction to the history and contemporary problems of Hong Kong, by an Australian journalist who is convinced that the future of this territory will be decided by Peking.

Jarvie, Ian C. and Agassi, Joseph, eds. **Hong Kong: A Society in Transition.** New York: Praeger, 1969, 378 p.
An analysis of the economic and socio-cultural effects of an extremely rapid population growth (especially through the influx of refugees) on a colony already experiencing the impact of westernization.

Kobayashi, Susumu, ed. **Honkon no kōgyōka.** Tokyo: Ajia Keizai Kenkyūjo, 1970, 248 p.
A Japanese study of the industrialization of Hong Kong.

Pope-Hennessy, James. **Half-Crown Colony: A Historical Profile of Hong Kong.** Boston: Little, Brown, 1970, 149 p.
The major topics discussed in this study are the influx of refugees from the Chinese mainland, drug traffic, communist-inspired riots and the political situation.

SINGAPORE

See also (Second World War) Southeastern Asia; China; Burma, p. 167; (Great Britain) Imperial and Commonwealth Relations; Colonial Policy, p. 367; (China) Foreign Relations, p. 702; Overseas Chinese, p. 711; (Southeastern Asia; East Indies) General, p. 733; Malaysia, p. 756.

Bellows, Thomas J. **The People's Action Party of Singapore.** New Haven: Yale University Southeast Asia Studies, 1970, 195 p.
A well-written study of a party that achieved total domination of Singapore's political system in 1968.

Chan, Heng Chee. **Singapore: The Politics of Survival, 1965–1967.** Singapore: Oxford University Press, 1971, 65 p.
A study of Singapore's delicate balancing act in the struggle for an autonomous existence and of the development of a community consciousness.

Fletcher, Nancy McHenry. **The Separation of Singapore from Malaysia.** Ithaca: Cornell University Southeast Asia Program, 1969, 98 p.
The first scholarly study of the important event that took place on August 9, 1965.

Hughes, Helen and You, Poh Seng, eds. **Foreign Investment and Industrialization in Singapore.** Canberra: Australian National University Press, 1969, 226 p.
An informative study.

Josey, Alex. **Lee Kuan Yew.** Singapore: Donald Moore, rev. ed., 1971, 630 p.
A biography of the Cambridge-trained statesman who has been Prime Minister of Singapore since 1959; richly interspersed with quotations from his speeches and writings.

Moore, Donald and Moore, Joanna. **The First 150 Years of Singapore.** Singapore: Donald Moore Press (in association with the Singapore International Chamber of Commerce), 1969, 731 p.
A volume published on the occasion of the 150th anniversary of Singapore. The authors, who do not claim to have written a work of scholarship, cover only briefly the developments since World War I.

Ooi, Jin-Bee and Chiang, Hai Ding, eds. **Modern Singapore.** Singapore: University of Singapore, 1969, 285 p.
An informative and well-documented collection of articles on the history, politics, geography, population, and economic and social conditions of contemporary Singapore. There is a very useful bibliography.

Osborne, Milton E. **Singapore and Malaysia.** Ithaca: Cornell University Southeast Asia Program, 1964, 115 p.
"This survey," in the words of the author, "seeks to describe and analyze the events between the assumption of power by the People's Action Party in Singapore in 1959 and that party's decision to contest the Malayan elections in 1964."

Wilson, Dick. **The Future Role of Singapore.** London: Oxford University Press (for the Royal Institute of International Affairs), 1972, 120 p.

A seasoned Southeast Asia correspondent ponders the economic, social and political quantities in the Singapore equation. His solution: Singapore must become a "global city," a neutral mercantile and diplomatic center for all the powers in Asia.

You, Poh Seng and Lim, Chong-Yah, eds. **The Singapore Economy.** Singapore: Eastern Universities Press, 1971, 421 p.

An informative survey.

MALAYSIA

See also (War) Guerrilla Warfare; Armed Insurrection, p. 118; (Second World War) Economic, Technical and Non-Military Aspects, p.172; (The United States) Aid and Assistance, p. 254; (Great Britain) Imperial and Commonwealth Relations; Colonial Policy, p. 367; (Asia and the Pacific Area) General Surveys, p. 607; The Arab World, p. 616; (Far East) General, p. 682; Overseas Chinese, p. 711; (Southeastern Asia; East Indies) General, p. 733; Singapore, p. 755; Philippines, p. 763.

Allen, James de V. **The Malayan Union.** New Haven: Yale University, Southeast Asia Studies, 1967, 181 p.

The author concludes his study of the Malayan Union in the 1940s by characterizing it "as an example of Colonial Office rigidity at its worst."

Allen, Sir Richard Hugh Sidley. **Malaysia: Prospect and Retrospect.** New York: Oxford University Press, 1968, 330 p.

A short general and political survey concentrating on the period after the Japanese invasion, the formation of the Malaysian Federation and confrontation with Indonesia.

Blythe, Wilfred Lawson. **The Impact of Chinese Secret Societies in Malaya: A Historical Study.** New York: Oxford University Press (for the Royal Institute of International Affairs), 1969, 566 p.

A thorough study by a British officer and civil servant with many years of firsthand experience in Southeast Asia. Mr. Blythe was Secretary for Chinese Affairs of the Federation of Malaya from 1946 to 1948.

Boyce, Peter. **Malaysia and Singapore in International Diplomacy: Documents and Commentaries.** University Park: Pennsylvania State University Press, 1968, 268 p.

A useful collection covering primarily the developments from 1963 to 1966.

Clutterbuck, Richard L. **The Long, Long War: Counterinsurgency in Malaya and Vietnam.** New York: Praeger, 1966, 206 p.

A recipient of the Order of the British Empire for service in Malaya from 1956 to 1958 traces the military and political techniques used to defeat communist insurgency in Malaya and documents the guerrilla warfare in Vietnam.

Djojohadikusumo, Sumitro. **Trade and Aid in South-East Asia. Volume I: Malaysia and Singapore.** Melbourne: Cheshire (for the Committee for Economic Development of Australia), 1968, 311 p.

Papers and materials prepared for a seminar in Bangkok on 1966.

Esman, Milton J. **Administration and Development in Malaysia: Institution Building and Reform in a Plural Society.** Ithaca: Cornell University Press, 1972, 341 p.

The author concludes his study of Malaysian administrative developments in the period from 1965 to 1970 by stating that élite-based guided change strategies provide "the most feasible path to human socio-economic development and conflict regulation."

Freeman, Roger A. **Socialism and Private Enterprise in Equatorial Asia: The Case of Malaysia and Indonesia.** Stanford: Hoover Institution on War, Revolution, and Peace, 1968, 130 p.

The author concludes that Malaysia's capitalistic policy accounts largely for her economic growth and stability while Indonesia's socialistic policy has led to her economic deterioration—this despite similarities in climate, natural resources, population and postwar independence for each.

Gould, James Warren. **The United States and Malaysia.** Cambridge: Harvard University Press, 1969, 267 p.

This introduction to contemporary Malaysia is a volume in "The American Foreign Policy Library."

Grossmann, Bernhard, *ed.* **Malaysia.** Frankfurt/Main: Metzner, 1966, 220 p.
A collection of essays on historical, political, social and economic problems of Malaysia.

Gullick, John Michael. **Malaysia.** New York: Praeger, rev. ed., 1969, 304 p.
An account of the making of a modern nation out of different elements and a study of a modern society comprising three major communities, based on firsthand observations of a former Malayan civil service officer.

Gungwu, Wang, *ed.* **Malaysia: A Survey.** New York: Praeger, 1964, 466 p.
Papers by 27 scholarly contributors on the geography, history, society and culture, economy, politics and government of the Malaysian Federation.

Hanna, Willard Anderson. **The Formation of Malaysia: New Factor in World Politics.** New York: American Universities Field Staff, 1964, 247 p.

——. **Sequel to Colonialism: The 1957-1960 Foundations for Malaysia.** New York: American Universities Field Staff, 1965, 288 p.
Two volumes of reports, written *in situ* for the American Universities Field Staff, rearranged to provide information on political developments, key economic activities, international relations and other critical episodes of the Malaysian states, including Singapore.

Henderson, John W. and Others. **Area Handbook for Malaysia.** Washington: G.P.O., 1970, 639 p.
A useful reference, with bibliographies, prepared by the Foreign Area Studies at the American University.

Hyde, Douglas A. **Confrontation in the East.** Chester Springs (Pa.): Dufour, 1965, 127 p.
A study of the conflict between Indonesia and Malaysia by a British writer.

Jackson, James C. **Sarawak: A Geographical Survey of a Developing State.** London: University of London Press, 1968, 218 p.
A monograph on the largest constituent state of the Federation of Malaysia.

Kanapathy, V. **The Malaysian Economy: Problems and Prospects.** Singapore: D. Moore for Asia Pacific Press, 1970, 240 p.
Essays by a Malaysian economist.

Kühne, Dietrich. **Malaysia—ethnische, soziale und wirtschaftliche Strukturen.** Paderborn: Schöningh (for the Geographisches Institut der Ruhr-Universität Bochum), 1970, 286 p.
A substantial survey of the ethnic, social and economic conditions in contemporary Malaysia.

Lim, Chong-Yah. **Economic Development of Modern Malaya.** New York: Oxford University Press, 1968, 388 p.
This useful survey covers the period from 1874 to 1963.

McKie, Ronald Cecil Hamlyn. **The Emergence of Malaysia.** New York: Harcourt, Brace and World, 1963, 310 p.
A journalistic account of Singapore and Kuala Lumpur, of the problems of Malaysia as a member of the British Commonwealth, and of the possibility of a Malaysia-Indonesia-Philippines confederation. The Australian edition is entitled "Malaysia in Focus" (Sydney: Angus, 1963, 236 p.).

Mahathir bin Mohamad. **The Malay Dilemma.** Singapore: D. Moore for Asia Pacific Press, 1970, 188 p.
An informative discussion of the relations among the Chinese, Indians and Malays in Malaysia, and a plea that the Malays should remain "the definitive people of the Malay Peninsula."

Means, Gordon Paul. **Malaysian Politics.** New York: New York University Press, 1970, 447 p.
The author, a Canadian scholar, concludes his detailed examination of Malaysian politics by predicting that "communal tensions and cleavages in Malaysian society will become even more pronounced over the next decade."

Miller, Harry. **A Short History of Malaysia.** New York: Praeger, 1966, 274 p.
This work, by a journalist who lived in Singapore and Malaya from 1933 to 1959,

is actually a history of the Federation of Malaya, including the events that led to the creation of Malaysia. Emphasis is on the period 1940–1965.

Milne, Robert Stephen. **Government and Politics in Malaysia.** Boston: Houghton, 1967, 259 p.
A description and an analysis of the area's parliament, federal-state relations (including Sabah and Sarawak) and local government. Comparisons with other countries are noted.

Newell, William Hare. **Treacherous River: A Study of Rural Chinese in North Malaya.** Kuala Lumpur: University of Malaya Press, 1962, 233 p.
A sociologist's account of an agricultural community in Malaya where 38 percent of the population are Chinese who are economically dominant and who consider themselves as part of the larger Chinese society.

Nihal Singh, S. **Malaysia—A Commentary.** New York: Barnes and Noble, 1971, 268 p.
A firsthand account of developments in Malaysia from 1962 to 1966 by a writer who was the special correspondent of *The Statesman* in Southeast Asia.

O'Ballance, Edgar. **Malaya: The Communist Insurgent War, 1948-60.** Hamden (Conn.): Archon Books, 1966, 188 p.
A leading specialist in guerrilla tactics uses the defeat of the Malayan Races Liberation Army, by Malayan and British government forces, to show how Mao Tsê-tung's formula for protracted warfare is not infallible.

Purcell, Victor William Williams Saunders. **The Chinese in Malaya.** New York: Oxford University Press, 1967, 327 p.
A thorough study by a leading Southeast Asia student who died in 1965.

Purcell, Victor William Williams Saunders. **Malaysia.** New York: Walker, 1965, 224 p.
The emphasis in this work is on the history and on the natural, social, cultural and economic features of Malaysia.

Purcell, Victor William Williams Saunders. **The Memoirs of a Malayan Official.** London: Cassell, 1965, 373 p.
Memoirs by a scholar who served in the Malay Civil Service from 1921 until 1946.

Ratnam, Kanagaratham Jeva. **Communalism and the Political Process in Malaya.** Kuala Lumpur: University of Malaya Press (for the University of Singapore), 1965, 248 p.
A study of the political consequences of communal divisions in the Federation of Malaya, with emphasis on the postwar period up to 1961, which saw the non-Malay population demanding increased political rights.

Ratnam, Kanagaratham Jeva and Milne, Robert Stephen. **The Malayan Parliamentary Election of 1964.** New York: Oxford University Press, 1968, 467 p.
A comprehensive account, with chapters on Malayan politics in the years from 1959 to 1964 and on the role of press and radio in the 1964 campaign.

Roff, William R. **The Origins of Malay Nationalism.** New Haven: Yale University Press, 1967, 297 p.
A study of the effects of British colonial protectorate control on the indigenous Malays, with emphasis on the 1900–1941 period.

Scott, James C. **Political Ideology in Malaysia: Reality and the Beliefs of an Elite.** New Haven: Yale University Press, 1968, 302 p.
This study is based on interviews with 17 Malaysian civil servants.

Silcock, Thomas Henry and Fisk, Ernest Kelvin, *eds.* **The Political Economy of Independent Malaya.** Berkeley: University of California Press, 1963, 306 p.
A case study of the unique aspects of the development of Malaya (Federation of Malaya and Singapore) since independence. The work is the result of a 1962 seminar sponsored by the Research School of Pacific Studies at the Australian National University.

Simandjuntak, B. **Malayan Federalism, 1945-1963.** New York: Oxford University Press, 1970, 347 p.
A study of why the federal system was introduced into Malaya and Malaysia and how it operates, with a survey of major problems posed by a population of differing cultures.

Tilman, Robert Oliver. **Bureaucratic Transition in Malaya.** Durham: Duke University Press, 1964, 175 p.
   The author attempts to demonstrate that the Malayan bureaucracy, a synthesis of the colonial experience and indigenous environment, has provided Malaya with "one of the most stable political systems in Southeast Asia."

Tregonning, Kennedy Gordon. **A History of Modern Malaya.** New York: McKay, 1967, 339 p.
   An introductory history of Malaya since the fifteenth century. The author considers the developments in Malaya since World War II only very briefly.

Tregonning, Kennedy Gordon. **The History of Modern Sabah: North Borneo, 1881–1963.** New York: Oxford University Press, 2d rev. ed., 1965, 275 p.
   An introductory survey.

Tregonning, Kennedy Gordon. **Malaysia and Singapore.** Melbourne: Cheshire (for the Australian Institute of International Affairs), 1966, 113 p.
   A revised and expanded edition of the author's "Malaysia" (1965).

Van der Kroef, Justus Maria. **Communism in Malaysia and Singapore: A Contemporary Survey.** The Hague: Nijhoff, 1967, 268 p.
   A pioneering study of the communist movement in the Singapore-Malaysian area. The emphasis is on the period since the formation of the Federation of Malaysia on September 16, 1963.

Wheelwright, Edward Lawrence. **Industrialization in Malaysia.** New York: Cambridge University Press, 1965, 153 p.
   An analysis of the industrialization policies of the Federation of Malaya and of Singapore, since they gained independence in 1957 and 1959 respectively. An appendix deals with the industrialization problems of the new Malaysia.

Winstedt, Sir Richard Olof. **A History of Malaya.** Singapore: Marican, rev. and enl. ed., 1962, 288 p.
   An enlarged edition of the important introductory history of Malaya which was first published in 1935.

INDONESIA

General

See also Comparative Government, p. 18; (Asia and the Pacific Area) General Surveys, p. 607; (Southeastern Asia; East Indies) General, p. 733; other subsections under Indonesia.

Caldwell, Malcolm. **Indonesia.** New York: Oxford University Press, 1968, 128 p.
   A brief but useful introduction to modern Indonesia.

Henderson, John W. and Others. **Area Handbook for Indonesia.** Washington: G.P.O., 1970, 569 p.
   A useful reference, with bibliographies, prepared by the Foreign Area Studies at the American University.

McVey, Ruth Thomas, *ed.* **Indonesia.** New Haven: Human Relations Area Files Press, 1963, 600 p.
   A survey of Indonesian culture, history, economics, politics and social structure by ten top scholars on the area.

Monteil, Vincent. **Indonésie.** Paris: Horizons de France, 1970, 287 p.
   A travel volume of the best sort.

Palmier, Leslie H. **Indonesia.** New York: Walker, 1966, 240 p.
   A survey of the historical and cultural background of Indonesia, together with an analysis of the more significant contemporary issues.

Williams, Maslyn. **Five Journeys from Jakarta: Inside Sukarno's Indonesia.** New York: Morrow, 1966, 383 p.

An Australian journalist's account of observations made during trips in 1964 from Jakarta to Sulawesi (formerly Celebes), Bali, Sumatra and the hinterlands of Indonesia.

Zainu'ddin, Ailsa. **A Short History of Indonesia.** New York: Praeger, 1970, 299 p.
An introductory survey with emphasis on nationalism and independence, by an Indonesian scholar.

Recent History

See also Second World War, p. 144; (The United States) Foreign Policy, p. 229; The Netherlands, p. 389; (Union of Soviet Socialist Republics) Military Policy, p. 561; (Asia and the Pacific Area) General Surveys, p. 607; (Southeastern Asia; East Indies) General, p. 733; (Japan) Foreign and Defense Policies, p. 718; Malaysia, p. 756; Philippines, p. 763; Papua New Guinea, p. 774; other subsections under Indonesia.

Anderson, Benedict R. O'G. **Java in a Time of Revolution: Occupation and Resistance, 1944-1946.** Ithaca: Cornell University Press, 1972, 494 p.
A detailed analysis of the Indonesian Revolution of 1945 on the island of Java, in which the central role was played by the Indonesian youth, made self-conscious primarily by the efforts of the Japanese occupation authorities.

Brackman, Arnold C. **The Communist Collapse in Indonesia.** New York: Norton, 1969, 264 p.
Emphasizing that the 1965 collapse of the P.K.I. was "not so much a coup as a purge from the top," the author details the downfall of the world's third largest communist party and its effects on the course of world events.

Brackman, Arnold C. **Indonesian Communism.** New York: Praeger, 1963, 336 p.
An informative account of the development of the Indonesian Communist Party.

Dahm, Bernhard. **Sukarno and the Struggle for Indonesian Independence.** Ithaca: Cornell University Press, 1969, 374 p.
A political study of Sukarno, one of the leaders of the Indonesian nationalist struggle, designed to trace his ideological development. Translation, with revisions and updating, of the author's "Sukarnos Kampf um Indonesiens Unabhängigkeit" (Frankfurt/Main: Metzner, 1966, 295 p.).

Feith, Herbert and Castles, Lance, *eds.* **Indonesian Political Thinking, 1945-1965.** Ithaca: Cornell University Press, 1970, 505 p.
A collection of representative writings to show the flow of events affecting post-independence political affairs in Indonesia.

Grant, Bruce. **Indonesia.** New York: Cambridge University Press, 2d ed., 1966, 204 p.
An undocumented political interpretation of Indonesia by an Australian journalist, based largely on articles he wrote during many visits to the country.

Hatta, Mohammad. **Portrait of a Patriot: Selected Writings.** The Hague: Mouton, 1972, 604 p.
A collection of articles and speeches by an elder statesman of Indonesia who played a leading role in establishing the independent state of Indonesia. Hatta served as his country's Vice President from 1945 to 1956 and as Prime Minister from 1949 to 1950.

Hindley, Donald. **The Communist Party of Indonesia, 1951-1963.** Berkeley: University of California Press, 1964, 380 p.
Professor Hindley, of Brandeis University, defines and traces the development of Asia's oldest communist party under the leadership of D. N. Aidit. Based largely on Indonesian sources.

Holt, Claire and Others. **Culture and Politics in Indonesia.** Ithaca: Cornell University Press, 1972, 348 p.
This collection of essays attempts to link traditional values and meanings to contemporary political behavior. Clifford Geertz, a leading student of Indonesian anthropology, has contributed a perceptive afterword.

Hughes, John. **Indonesian Upheaval.** New York: McKay, 1967, 304 p.
A collection of Pulitzer Prize-winning articles, expanded and reworked since their original dispatch to *The Christian Science Monitor*, covering the events that led to the fall of Sukarno in March 1967.

James, Harold and Sheil-Small, Denis. **The Undeclared War: The Story of the Indonesian Confrontation, 1962-1966.** Totowa (N.J.): Rowman and Littlefield, 1971, 201 p.
   An account of how British, Gurkha and Commonwealth troops fought, and defeated, the Indonesian guerrilla forces in Borneo between 1962 and 1966.

Jones, Howard Palfrey. **Indonesia: The Possible Dream.** New York: Harcourt Brace Jovanovich (for the Hoover Institution), 1971, 473 p.
   In this volume the American Ambassador to Indonesia from 1958 to 1965 records his experience with a complex society and its even more complex leader, Sukarno.

Legge, John David. **Indonesia.** Englewood Cliffs: Prentice-Hall, 1964, 184 p.
   A succinct treatise useful for understanding Indonesia's struggle for independence and post-colonial history. Focus is on Sukarno and his "guided democracy," a political system which the author, an Australian professor, thinks is based on Indonesian culture and tradition.

Legge, John David. **Sukarno: A Political Biography.** New York: Praeger, 1972, 431 p.
   A substantial study of the rise and fall of the Indonesian leader.

Lijphart, Arend. **The Trauma of Decolonization: The Dutch and West New Guinea.** New Haven: Yale University Press, 1966, 303 p.
   A study demonstrating that the attempt of the Netherlands to hold on to West New Guinea was motivated solely by an emotional attachment to it as a symbol of national grandeur.

McVey, Ruth Thomas. **The Rise of Indonesian Communism.** Ithaca: Cornell University Press (for the Modern Indonesia Project), 1965, 510 p.
   A solidly documented history of the Indonesian Communist Party (P.K.I.) from its birth in 1914 to 1927, showing its place on Indonesian political movements and its influence on colonial government policy. An important work resulting from research in five countries and in various languages.

Mintz, Jeanne S. **Mohammed, Marx, and Marhaen: The Roots of Indonesian Socialism.** New York: Praeger, 1965, 246 p.
   A study of "guided democracy" in Indonesia. The author sees it as a "weakly structured and poorly functioning attempt at authoritarian rule," successful only because it was in the hands of Sukarno.

Modelski, George Alexander, *ed.* **The New Emerging Forces: Documents on the Ideology of Indonesian Foreign Policy.** Canberra: Australian National University, Department of International Relations, 1963, 131 p.
   Documents illustrating Sukarno's fight for "independence, social justice, and peace."

Muskens, M. P. M. **Indonesië een strijd om nationale identiteit.** Bussum: Paul Brand, 1970, 597 p.
   A comprehensive Dutch study of Indonesia's struggle for a national identity.

Oey, Hong Lee. **Indonesian Government and Press during Guided Democracy.** Zug: Inter Documentation Company, 1971, 401 p.
   A study of the relationship between government and press from July 1959 to September 1965, a period when Sukarno was the dominating influence in Indonesian politics.

Polomka, Peter. **Indonesia since Sukarno.** Ringewood (Vic.): Penguin, 1971, 228 p.
   A most informative study by an author whose knowledge of contemporary Indonesia is exceptional.

Roeder, O. G. **The Smiling General: President Soeharto of Indonesia.** Djakarta: Gunung Agung, 1969, 280 p.
   An admiring biography of the Indonesian leader who has been his country's President since 1968.

Simon, Sheldon W. **The Broken Triangle: Peking, Djakarta, and the PKI.** Baltimore: Johns Hopkins Press (in coöperation with the Institute for Sino-Soviet Studies, George Washington University), 1969, 210 p.
   A study of Chinese efforts to manipulate Indonesian politics through both Sukarno and the Indonesian Communist Party and of the shift from cordiality to enmity between Mao's China and Indonesia.

Sloan, Stephen. **A Study in Political Violence: The Indonesian Experience.** Chicago: Rand McNally, 1971, 107 p.

A case study of the bloody coup that overturned the Indonesian political structure in 1965.

Sukarno with Adams, Cindy (Heller). **Sukarno: An Autobiography.** Indianapolis: Bobbs-Merrill, 1965, 324 p.

A revealing story of Sukarno's private and public life, containing information on Indonesia's relations with the Netherlands and the United States.

Utrecht, Ernst. **Indonesië's nieuwe orde: ontbinding en neokolonisatie.** Amsterdam: Van Gennep, 1970, 208 p.

A Dutch study of contemporary Indonesian politics.

Van der Kroef, Justus Maria. **The Communist Party of Indonesia: Its History, Program and Tactics.** Vancouver: University of British Columbia, 1965, 347 p.

An outline history of the Indonesian Communist Party, its program and organization, its power at home and its role in the international scene—ending before the cataclysm of 1965.

Van der Kroef, Justus Maria. **Indonesia after Sukarno.** Vancouver: University of British Columbia Press, 1971, 253 p.

An Indonesian-born professor at the University of Bridgeport attempts to assess the new directorate of technocrats and military men that came to power after Sukarno's fall.

Vittachi, Tarzie. **The Fall of Sukarno.** New York: Praeger, 1967, 191 p.

A Ceylonese writer who spent 18 months in 1965–66 in Indonesia describes the events leading to Sukarno's downfall.

Weiss, Carl. **Sukarnos tausend Inseln: Indonesien, die gelenkte Demokratie.** Hamburg: Wegner, 1963, 299 p.

Observations on Indonesia by a German journalist who spent a few years in Jakarta as a member of a mission of the Federal Republic of Germany. The author is particularly critical of the Dutch policies toward Indonesia in the years after 1945.

Economic and Social Problems

See also (Union of Soviet Socialist Republics) Foreign Economic Policy, p. 560; (Southeastern Asia; East Indies) General, p. 733; Malaysia, p. 756; other subsections under Indonesia.

Alisjahbana, Sutan Takdir. **Indonesia in the Modern World.** New York: Oxford University Press, 2d enl. ed., 1966, 206 p.

A study of the changes within Indonesian society and culture and their relationship to contemporary events. An expanded edition of a work first published in 1961.

Geertz, Clifford. **Agricultural Involution: The Process of Ecological Change in Indonesia.** Berkeley: University of California Press (for the Association of Asian Studies), 1963, 176 p.

An anthropologist at the Institute for Advanced Study in Princeton analyzes the history of Indonesia with the aim of explaining the country's difficulties in attaining sustained economic growth after 200 years of static conditions under Dutch rule.

Geertz, Clifford. **The Social History of an Indonesian Town.** Cambridge: M.I.T. Press, 1965, 217 p.

A thorough assessment of how the large Dutch-owned sugar enterprises and the smaller peasant agricultural enterprises in Modjokuto integrated into a single, if complex, community. A long epilogue provides a detailed study of the February 1954 election in a town adjoining Modjokuto.

Glassburner, Bruce, *ed*. **The Economy of Indonesia: Selected Readings.** Ithaca: Cornell University Press, 1971, 443 p.

A collection of articles on Indonesia's economic performance and policies since it achieved independence in 1949.

Hicks, George L. and McNicoll, Geoffrey. **The Indonesian Economy, 1950–1965: A Bibliography.** New Haven: Yale University, Southeast Asia Studies, 1967, 248 p.

A useful reference.

Indonesia: Perspective and Proposals for United States Economic Aid. New Haven: Yale University, Southeast Asia Studies, 1963, 250 p.
    A well-organized analysis resulting from the U.S. team visit to Indonesia, arranged by the presidents of both countries, to scrutinize Indonesia's Eight Year Development Plan and to determine in what areas U.S. aid should be concentrated.

Johnson, Rossall J. and Others. **Business Environment in an Emerging Nation: Profiles of Indonesian Economy.** Evanston: Northwestern University Press, 1966, 342 p.
    This book is an outgrowth of the authors' experiences in connection with the establishment of the Executive Development Program at the University of Indonesia.

Liddle, R. William. **Ethnicity, Party, and National Integration: An Indonesian Case Study.** New Haven: Yale University Press, 1970, 238 p.
    The author of this study argues that American-style liberal pluralism is the solution for Indonesia's political problems.

Wander, Hilde. **Die Beziehungen zwischen Bevölkerungs- und Wirtschaftsentwicklung, dargestellt am Beispiel Indonesiens.** Tübingen: Mohr, 1965, 279 p.
    A study of the interrelationship between demographic and economic growth in Indonesia and Southeast Asia.

PHILIPPINES

See also Second World War, p. 144; (The United States) Foreign Policy, p. 229; (Asia and the Pacific Area) General Surveys, p. 607; (Japan) Foreign and Defense Policies, p. 718; (Southeastern Asia; East Indies) General, p. 733; Malaysia, p. 756.

Abueva, Jose V. **Ramon Magsaysay: A Political Biography.** Manila: Solidaridad Publishing House, 1971, 497 p.
    An admiring biography of the Philippine statesman who was the President of his country from 1953 to 1957 when he died in a plane crash.

Averch, Harvey A. and Others. **The Matrix of Policy in the Philippines.** Princeton: Princeton University Press, 1971, 234 p.
    The authors of this well-documented RAND Corporation research study conclude that Philippine political life is basically stable, the economy will continue to grow, the crime problem has been overestimated, and the Huks are not a serious threat.

Chaffee, Frederic H. and Others. **Area Handbook for Philippines.** Washington: G.P.O., 1969, 413 p.
    A useful reference volume with a bibliography, prepared by the Foreign Area Studies at the American University.

Ch'en, Lieh-fu. **Fei-lü-pin ti li-shih yü Chung-Fei kuan-hsi ti kuo-ch'ü yü hsien-tsai.** Taipei: Cheng-chung Shu-chü, 1968, 374 p.
    A history of the Philippines and a study of Sino-Philippine relations, with emphasis on the period since World War I.

Corpuz, Onofre D. **The Philippines.** Englewood Cliffs: Prentice-Hall, 1966, 149 p.
    An introductory study by a Philippine scholar. A volume in the series "The Modern Nations in Historical Perspective."

Farwell, George. **Mask of Asia: The Philippines Today.** New York: Praeger, 1967, 227 p.
    A history of the Philippines, including chapters on the role of the Muslims, prospects of political union with Malaysia and Indonesia and impediments to agricultural and political development.

Friend, Theodore. **Between Two Empires: The Ordeal of the Philippines, 1929–1946.** New Haven: Yale University Press, 1965, 312 p.
    An account of the Philippines' relationship with the United States and Japan during her fight for independence. Based on documentary sources and interviews in all three countries.

Golay, Frank Hindman. **The Philippines: Public Policy and National Economic Development.** Ithaca: Cornell University Press, 1968, 455 p.
    A thorough study by a professor at Cornell University.

Golay, Frank Hindman, *ed*. **The United States and the Philippines.** Englewood Cliffs: Prentice-Hall (for the American Assembly), 1966, 179 p.
Papers, originally designed as background reading for the American Assembly, on various facets of U.S.-Philippine relations.

Grossholtz, Jean. **Politics in the Philippines: A Country Study.** Boston: Little, Brown, 1964, 293 p.
This analysis of the political culture of the Philippines has been based on "the structural functional approach."

Hicks, George L. and McNicoll, Geoffrey. **Trade and Growth in the Philippines: An Open Dual Economy.** Ithaca: Cornell University Press, 1971, 244 p.
A study of post-World War II economic developments in the Philippines.

Huke, Robert E., *ed*. **Shadows on the Land: An Economic Geography of the Philippines.** Manila: Bookmark, 1963, 428 p.
A useful survey, with maps, charts and tables.

Kim, Sung Yong. **United States-Philippine Relations, 1946-1956.** Washington: Public Affairs Press, 1968, 158 p.
The Korean author of this study hopes that an understanding of the forces influencing Philippine-U.S. relations in the decade after World War II will help to "explain the difficulties and rewards awaiting American policy elsewhere in Asia."

Kuhn, Delia and Kuhn, Ferdinand. **The Philippines: Yesterday and Today.** New York: Holt, Rinehart and Winston, 1966, 248 p.
A popular interpretation of the Philippines' period of decolonization in light of its American, Spanish and pre-Spanish past.

Lachica, Eduardo. **The Huks: Philippine Agrarian Society in Revolt.** New York: Praeger, 1971, 331 p.
A description of the Huk revolutionary movement by a Phillipine journalist and a former Nieman Fellow at Harvard University. The author argues that Maoist influences led to the defeat of the movement in 1970.

Landé, Carl Herman. **Leaders, Factions and Parties: The Structure of Philippine Politics.** New Haven: Yale University, Southeast Asia Studies, 1965, 148 p.
This well-researched study of Philippine politics at the national, provincial and local levels is a revised Harvard doctoral dissertation.

Leifer, Michael. **The Philippine Claim to Sabah.** Zug: Inter Documentation, 1968, 75 p.
The emphasis in this informative study is on the political and non-legal aspects of the claim initially associated with the presidency of Macapagal.

Levinson, Georgii Il'ich. **Die Philippinen: gestern und heute.** Berlin: Akademie-Verlag, 1966, 373 p.
A communist history of the Philippine Republic. The German edition is based on the following Russian studies: "Filippiny mezhdu Pervoi i Vtoroi mirovymi voinami" (Moscow: Izd-vo Vostochno Lit-ry, 1958, 287 p.) and "Filippiny vchera i segodnia" (Moscow: Izd-vo Sotsial'no-Ekon. Lit-ry, 1959, 238 p.).

Liang, Dapen. **Philippine Parties and Politics: A Historical Study of National Experience in Democracy.** San Francisco: Gladstone Co., rev. ed., 1971, 486 p.
A completely rewritten and enlarged edition of a study first published as "The Development of Philippine Political Parties" in 1939. The new version covers the political developments up to the elections of November 1969.

Liao, Shubert S. C., *ed*. **Chinese Participation in Philippine Culture and Economy.** Manila: Bookman, 1964, 452 p.
An informative monograph.

Macapagal, Diosdado. **A Stone for the Edifice.** Quezon City: Mac Publishing House, 1968, 560 p.
Reminiscences of the fifth President of the Republic of the Philippines, covering the years of his presidency from 1961 to 1965.

Mahajani, Usha. **Philippine Nationalism: External Challenge and Filipino Response, 1565-1946.** St. Lucia: University of Queensland Press, 1971, 530 p.

In this attempt to provide a topography of the development of the Philippino nationalism, the author pays particular attention to the influence exercised by the Spanish, American and Japanese rulers.

Malay, Armando J. **Occupied Philippines.** Manila: Filipiniana Book Guild, 1967, 304 p.
A defense of Jorge B. Vargas, one of the highest Philippine officials during the Japanese occupation in World War II.

Meyer, Milton Walter. **A Diplomatic History of the Philippine Republic.** Honolulu: University of Hawaii Press, 1965, 321 p.
A study of the origins and development of Philippine diplomacy from the founding of the Republic in 1946.

Nelson, Raymond. **The Philippines.** New York: Walker, 1969, 192 p.
An introduction to Philippine history and politics by a Swedish scientist who has taken part in United Nations technical assistance projects in Southeast Asia.

Power, John H. and Others. **The Philippines: Industrialization and Trade Policies; Taiwan: Industrialization and Trade Policies.** New York: Oxford University Press (for the Development Centre of the Organization for Economic Co-operation and Development), 1971, 324 p.
Studies of economic developments in the Philippines and Taiwan, including useful bibliographies and statistical tables.

Quirino, Carlos. **Quezon: Paladin of Philippine Freedom.** Manila: Filipiniana Book Guild, 1971, 419 p.
An admiring biography of the first President of the Philippine Commonwealth who died in the United States in 1944.

Reynolds, Quentin James and Bocca, Geoffrey. **Macapagal the Incorruptible.** New York: McKay, 1965, 215 p.
A sympathetic biography of the Philippine politician who was his country's President from 1962 to 1965; written from notes left by the late Mr. Reynolds.

Sicat, Gerardo P. **Economic Policy and Philippine Development.** Quezon City: University of the Philippines Press, 1972, 461 p.
A useful survey of contemporary economic conditions in the Philippines.

Spence, Hartzell. **Marcos of the Philippines.** New York: World Publishing Co., 1969, 365 p.
A detailed study of the lawyer, soldier and politician who became President of his nation in 1966. An expanded, updated edition of "For Every Tear a Victory" (1964).

Steinberg, David Joel. **Philippine Collaboration in World War II.** Ann Arbor: University of Michigan Press, 1967, 235 p.
A sympathetic study of the loyalty crisis in a country on the verge of gaining its independence, where choice lay between collaboration with its Japanese conquerors and support for the U.S.

Taruc, Luis. **He Who Rides the Tiger.** New York: Praeger, 1967, 188 p.
The reminiscences of a former Philippine communist guerrilla leader who broke with communism and surrendered to the Philippine government authorities.

Taylor, George Edward. **The Philippines and the United States: Problems of Partnership.** New York: Praeger (for the Council on Foreign Relations), 1964, 325 p.
A study of the problems facing the Republic of the Philippines in the transformation which it has been undergoing since World War II, and of its relations with the United States.

Wernstedt, Frederick L. and Spencer, J. E. **The Philippine Island World: A Physical, Cultural, and Regional Geography.** Berkeley: University of California Press, 1967, 742 p.
A comprehensive, authoritative work on the land and people of the 7,000 islands making up the Philippines. Generous illustrations, maps, charts and tables.

Zaide, Gregorio F. **Philippine Government: Development, Organization and Functions.** Manila: The Modern Book Co., rev. ed., 1965, 301 p.
A useful survey.

AUSTRALIA AND NEW ZEALAND

GENERAL

See also (Southeastern Asia; East Indies) General, p. 733.

Barnes, Victor Dominic Suthers, *ed.* **The Modern Encyclopaedia of Australia and New Zealand.** Sydney: Horwitz-Grahame, 1964, 1,199 p.
A useful reference work covering Australia, New Zealand and Papua New Guinea.

Brown, Bruce, *ed.* **Asia and the Pacific in the 1970s: The Roles of the United States, Australia, and New Zealand.** Canberra: Australian National University Press, 1971, 253 p.
The Australian Institute of International Affairs presents here the position papers and comment from a 1970 conference on ANZUS relations.

Cumberland, Kenneth B. **Southwest Pacific.** New York: Praeger, rev. ed., 1968, 423 p.
A revised edition of a physical and economic geography of Australia, New Zealand and the neighboring Pacific islands.

Grattan, Clinton Hartley. **The Southwest Pacific since 1900: A Modern History; Australia, New Zealand, the Islands, Antarctica.** Ann Arbor: University of Michigan Press, 1963, 759 p.
A volume on the political, economic and cultural developments in the Southwest Pacific. It is a companion volume to an earlier history of the area up to 1900, published in the same series, "The University of Michigan History of the Modern World."

Millar, Thomas Bruce, *ed.* **Australian-New Zealand Defence Co-operation.** Canberra: Australian National University Press, 1968, 125 p.
Australian and New Zealand writers discuss in this volume security problems of their countries that resulted from changes in British and American policies in Asia.

Osborne, Charles, *ed.* **Australia, New Zealand and the South Pacific.** New York: Praeger, 1970, 580 p.
A useful encyclopedic compilation.

Reese, Trevor Richard. **Australia, New Zealand, and the United States: A Survey of International Relations, 1941–1968.** New York: Oxford University Press (for the Royal Institute of International Affairs), 1969, 376 p.
A critical assessment of the benefits of the ANZUS Pact for Australia and New Zealand.

Spender, Sir Percy Claude. **Exercises in Diplomacy.** New York: New York University Press, 1970, 303 p.
A careful, step-by-step account of the creation of the ANZUS Pact and the Colombo Plan, by a former Minister for External Affairs of Australia who was one of the major architects of both.

Starke, Joseph Gabriel. **The ANZUS Treaty Alliance.** New York: Cambridge University Press, 1966, 315 p.
An Australian scholar analyzes the text of the ANZUS Pact linking Australia, New Zealand and the United States and surveys its historical background and purposes.

AUSTRALIA

General

See also (Great Britain) Imperial and Commonwealth Relations; Colonial Policy, p. 367; (Australia and New Zealand) General, p. 766; other subsections under Australia.

Clark, Charles Manning Hope. **A Short History of Australia.** New York: New American Library, 1963, 256 p.
A history of Australia from the early migrations to 1963, enlivened with many sketches of important personalities.

Gunther, John; completed and edited by Forbis, William H. **John Gunther's Inside Australia.** New York: Harper and Row, 1972, 370 p.
The late John Gunther had collected material for this book for several years and he visited Australia and New Zealand before he died in 1970. Mr. Forbis has done an excellent job in completing the volume and in preserving the Gunther style.

Horne, Donald. **The Lucky Country: Australia in the Sixties.** San Francisco: Tri-Ocean Books, 2d rev. ed., 1966, 238 p.
An appraisal of modern Australia by an Australian journalist.

McGregor, Craig. **Profile of Australia.** Chicago: Regnery, 1967, 398 p.
A broad, popularly written but informative survey of contemporary Australian social, economic, cultural and political developments.

Miller, John Donald Bruce. **Australia.** New York: Walker, 1966, 212 p.
A general survey by an Australian professor.

Preston, Richard A., ed. **Contemporary Australia: Studies in History, Politics, and Economics.** Durham: Duke University Press (for Duke University Commonwealth-Studies Center), 1969, 587 p.
Nineteen Australian and American scholars provide a survey of Australia's economic and labor policies and of the problems arising from political ideology, federalism, civil rights and external influences.

Reese, Trevor Richard. **Australia in the Twentieth Century.** New York: Praeger, 1964, 239 p.
A chronicle of the political, constitutional and economic development of Australia from the birth of the federal commonwealth in 1901 to 1962.

Shaw, Alan George Lewers. **A Short History of Australia.** New York: Praeger, rev. ed., 1967, 332 p.
A revised and updated edition of "The Story of Australia" (New York: Roy, 1956, 308 p.).

Spate, Oskar Hermann Khristian. **Australia.** London: Benn, 1968, 328 p.
A lively and informative survey of Australia's history, economy, politics and social conditions.

Venturini, Venturino G., ed. **Australia: A Survey.** Wiesbaden: Otto Harrassowitz (for the Institut für Asienkunde, Hamburg), 1970, 697 p.
A comprehensive and informative volume of articles by Australian scholars on the geography, demography, government, society, economy, the arts and foreign relations of Australia.

Ward, Russel Braddock. **Australia.** Englewood Cliffs: Prentice-Hall, 1965, 152 p.
A general history of Australia by an Australian scholar.

Younger, Ronald M. **Australia and the Australians.** New York: Humanities Press, 1970, 869 p.
A massive survey of Australian history and contemporary political, demographic, economic and social developments.

Foreign and Defense Policies

See also Second World War, p. 144; The Postwar World, p. 178; (The United States) Foreign Policy, p. 229; (Great Britain) Imperial and Commonwealth Relations; Colonial Policy, p. 367; Foreign Policy, p. 375; (Asia and the Pacific Area) General Surveys, p. 607; Nepal, p. 655; The Vietnam War, p. 739; (Australia and New Zealand) General, p. 766; Papua New Guinea, p. 774; other subsections under Australia.

Albinski, Henry Stephen. **Australian Policies and Attitudes toward China.** Princeton: Princeton University Press, 1966, 511 p.
Professor Albinski of Pennsylvania State University interviewed high-ranking officials and consulted official documents of several countries to assess Australia's relations with China in the post-World War II period.

Albinski, Henry Stephen. **Politics and Foreign Policy in Australia: The Impact of Vietnam and Conscription.** Durham: Duke University Press, 1970, 238 p.
A study of the interplay between Australia's external affairs and domestic policies.

Andrews, Eric Montgomery. **Isolationism and Appeasement in Australia.** Columbia: University of South Carolina Press, 1970, 236 p.

A useful and critical study of Australian governmental and public reactions to the Abyssinian crisis, the Spanish Civil War and Munich.

Ball, William Macmahon. **Australia and Japan.** Melbourne: Nelson, 1970, 172 p.

A critical and well-documented appraisal of the relations between the two countries since 1901.

Bellany, Ian. **Australia in the Nuclear Age.** Sydney: Sydney University Press, 1972, 144 p.

A study of Australia's contemporary defense problems. The author argues for nuclear arms for Australia in case India and Japan have them and if the United States withdraws from Asia.

Esthus, Raymond A. **From Enmity to Alliance: U.S.-Australian Relations, 1931–1941.** Seattle: University of Washington Press, 1964, 180 p.

A scholarly work on Australian diplomacy in the crucial decade preceding Pearl Harbor, beginning with disputes over shipping competition and trade and ending with Australia's involvement in World War II.

Firkins, Peter. **The Australians in Nine Wars: Waikato to Long Tan.** New York: McGraw-Hill, 1972, 448 p.

An informative but rather journalistic history of the Australian military achievements during the last hundred years, with emphasis on both world wars.

Gelber, Harry Gregor. **Australia, Britain and the EEC, 1961 to 1963.** New York: Oxford University Press, 1966, 296 p.

A solid study of Australia's reactions to the British attempts to get into the Common Market.

Gelber, Harry Gregor. **The Australian-American Alliance: Costs and Benefits.** Baltimore: Penguin, 1968, 160 p.

The Australian author of this study is convinced that the American-Australian alliance "is the main axis of Australian defence and security policies" and "one of the vital determinants of Australian foreign policy."

Gelber, Harry Gregor, *ed.* **Problems of Australian Defence.** New York: Oxford University Press, 1971, 359 p.

A collection of essays analyzing the factors affecting Australian military security.

Grant, Bruce. **The Crisis of Loyalty: A Study of Australian Foreign Policy.** Sydney: Angus and Robertson (in association with the Australian Institute of International Affairs), 1972, 107 p.

The author of this study urges the Australians to develop new concepts of national interest that would recognize the fact that Australia is no longer a U.S. satellite.

Greenwood, Gordon and Harper, Norman Denholm, *eds.* **Australia in World Affairs.** Melbourne: Cheshire (for the Australian Institute of International Affairs).

A most useful series on the evolution of Australian foreign policies. Two volumes, covering the years from 1956 to 1965, were published in the decade from 1963 to 1972.

Harper, Norman Denholm, *ed.* **Pacific Orbit: Australian-American Relations since 1942.** New York: Humanities Press, 1969, 256 p.

A collection of articles sponsored by the Australian-American Association.

Hudson, W. J. **Australia and the Colonial Question at the United Nations.** Honolulu: East-West Center Press, 1970, 214 p.

A study of the Australian struggle, covering the life span of the United Nations, to remain on good terms with an anti-colonial majority and simultaneously to retain control of Papua and New Guinea.

Millar, Thomas Bruce. **Australia's Defence.** New York: Cambridge University Press, 1965, 198 p.

A monograph on Australia's defense needs, policies, organization and equipment, with particular attention to problems posed by Communist China. Mr. Millar has been the Director of the Australian Institute of International Affairs since 1969.

Millar, Thomas Bruce. **Australia's Foreign Policy.** Sydney: Angus and Robertson, 1968, 361 p.
The author states that his examination of Australia's foreign policy "is an attempt to show what kind of bargains Australia has struck, and what other bargains may be worth considering."

Stockwin, James Arthur Ainscow, *ed*. **Japan and Australia in the Seventies.** Sydney: Angus and Robertson (in association with the Australian Institute of International Affairs), 1972, 223 p.
A collection of papers and discussions of an increasingly important relationship.

Vandenbosch, Amry and Vandenbosch, Mary Belle. **Australia Faces Southeast Asia: The Emergence of a Foreign Policy.** Lexington: University of Kentucky Press, 1968, 175 p.
An account of the effect of British withdrawal from Asia on Australia's foreign policies.

Venturini, Venturino G. **Australien und Asien: einige Aspekte australischer Asienpolitik.** Wiesbaden: Harrassowitz (for the Institut für Asienkunde, Hamburg), 1970, 291 p.
A set of pleas that Australia become an Asian nation rather than an American satellite.

Watt, Sir Alan Stewart. **Australian Diplomat: Memoirs of Sir Alan Watt.** Sydney: Angus and Robertson (in association with the Australian Institute of International Affairs), 1972, 329 p.
Reminiscences by a leading Australian diplomat who has represented his country in the United States, the U.S.S.R., the Federal Republic of Germany and Japan. Sir Alan Watt was also the Director of the Australian Institute of International Affairs from 1963 to 1969.

Watt, Sir Alan Stewart. **The Evolution of Australian Foreign Policy, 1938-1965.** New York: Cambridge University Press, 1967, 387 p.
An authoritative study of how Australia has been meeting the drastic changes in world politics since World War II.

Wilkes, John, *ed*. **Australia's Defence and Foreign Policy.** Sydney: Angus and Robertson, 1964, 172 p.
This volume of proceedings of the 30th Summer School of the Australian Institute of Political Science, held at Canberra in 1964, contains contributions by Sir Garfield Barwick, Roger Hilsman, T. B. Millar, R. I. Downing and B. D. Beddie.

Politics and Government

See also Society and Social Psychology, p. 39; (Australia and New Zealand) General, p. 766; other subsections under Australia.

Atkins, Ruth and Graycar, Adam. **Governing Australia.** New York: Wiley, 1972, 198 p.
A brief introduction to contemporary Australian politics and government.

Davidson, Alastair. **The Communist Party of Australia: A Short History.** Stanford: Hoover Institution Press, 1969, 214 p.
The first scholarly history of the Communist Party of Australia.

Edwards, Cecil. **Bruce of Melbourne: Man of Two Worlds.** London: Heinemann, 1966, 475 p.
A biography of a prominent Australian statesman, Prime Minister of Australia from 1923 to 1929 and High Commissioner of his country in Great Britain from 1933 to 1945.

Ellis, Ulrich Ruegg. **A History of the Australian Country Party.** New York: Cambridge University Press, 1964, 359 p.
A history of an Australian minority party, established in 1916, by a longtime member of it.

Heydon, Peter Richard. **Quiet Decision: A Study of George Foster Pearce.** New York: Cambridge University Press, 1965, 271 p.
A former private secretary to Sir George Pearce uses his own personal recollections, unpublished papers and newspaper and Hansard reports to write of a man of humble

birth who strongly influenced the Australian political scene. Sir George was one of the founders of the Labor Party in Western Australia, a member of the Senate from 1901 to 1937 and Defense Minister during the World War I period.

Jupp, James. **Australian Party Politics.** New York: Cambridge University Press, 1964, 235 p.
A general survey, with emphasis on the relationships between the party machines and the parliamentarians and on the organizational structure and policies of the parties.

La Nauze, John Andrew. **Alfred Deakin: A Biography.** New York: Cambridge University Press, 1965, 2 v.
A biography of Alfred Deakin (1856–1919), who was one of the founding fathers of the Australian Federation and three times Prime Minister of the Commonwealth of Australia.

Menzies, Sir Robert Gordon. **Afternoon Light: Some Memories of Men and Events.** New York: Coward-McCann, 1968, 384 p.
———. **The Measure of the Years.** London: Cassell, 1972, 300 p.
Reminiscences by the Australian statesman who was Prime Minister of his country from 1939 to 1941 and from 1949 to 1966.

Menzies, Sir Robert Gordon. **Central Power in the Australian Commonwealth.** Charlottesville: University Press of Virginia, 1967, 198 p.
An analysis of constitutional development in the Australian Federation and of how the central powers of government have tended to grow beyond original conceptions.

Muirden, Bruce. **The Puzzled Patriots: The Story of the Australia First Movement.** New York: Cambridge University Press, 1969, 200 p.
An Australian journalist reëxamines the background of the Movement and the arrest of its members in 1942 on suspicion of aid to potential Japanese invaders.

O'Collins, Gerald. **Patrick McMahon Glynn: A Founder of Australian Federation.** New York: Cambridge University Press, 1966, 281 p.
A biography of Patrick Glynn (1955–1931), an Irish barrister who arrived in Melbourne at the age of 25 and became a prominent South Australian parliamentarian, delegate at the Federal Convention, and member of three Commonwealth governments.

Palfreeman, A. C. **The Administration of the White Australia Policy.** New York: Cambridge University Press, 1967, 184 p.
An examination of the administrative mechanisms developed by Australia to restrict the immigration of non-whites.

Perkins, Kevin. **Menzies: Last of the Queen's Men.** London: Angus and Robertson; Adelaide: Rigby, 1968, 264 p.
An anecdotal but informative study of a Prime Minister who dominated his country's politics for almost 20 years.

Rawson, Donald Williams. **Australia Votes: The 1958 Federal Election.** Melbourne: Melbourne University Press, 1961, 259 p.
A detailed survey of parties, policies, candidates and the election.

Rivett, Rohan Deakes. **Australian Citizen: Herbert Brookes 1867–1963.** New York: Cambridge University Press, 1966, 217 p.
A biographical study of a prominent Australian who from 1929 to 1930 was also the Australian High Commissioner to the United States.

Economic and Social Problems

See also Population Problems, p. 47; (Australia and New Zealand) General, p. 766; other subsections under Australia.

Appleyard, Reginald Thomas. **British Emigration to Australia.** Toronto: University of Toronto Press, 1965, 255 p.
A study by an Australian scholar of post-World War II British emigration to Australia, including an analysis of interviews with 861 emigrants.

Blainey, Geoffrey. **The Rush That Never Ended: A History of Australian Mining.** New York: Cambridge University Press, 1964, 369 p.
An informative survey.

Boxer, Alan Howard. **Experts in Asia: An Inquiry into Australian Technical Assistance.** Canberra: Australian National University Press, 1969, 180 p.
An investigation of the effectiveness of Australian aid programs, based on data covering the period from 1954 to 1964.

Condliffe, John Bell. **The Development of Australia.** New York: Free Press of Glencoe, 1964, 294 p.
The purpose of this survey was to attract settlers to Australia's underdeveloped areas.

Crawford, Sir John Grenfell with Others. **Australian Trade Policy 1942-1966: A Documentary History.** Canberra: Australian National University Press, 1968, 641 p.
A collection of 14 key government decisions arranged to explain the contrast between the prewar milieu, in which the Ottawa Agreement dominated Australia's external economic relations, and the postwar developments.

Goodwin, Craufurd David Wycliffe. **Economic Enquiry in Australia.** Durham: Duke University Press (for the Duke University Commonwealth-Studies Center), 1966, 659 p.
A history of the importation and adaptation of economic theories and analytical techniques by Australia from the early settlement days to the 1929 depression.

Hughes, Helen. **The Australian Iron and Steel Industry, 1848-1962.** New York: Cambridge University Press, 1964, 213 p.
The first full-length account of the development of Australia's iron and steel industry.

McColl, G. D. **The Australian Balance of Payments: A Study of Post-War Developments.** New York: Cambridge University Press, 1965, 180 p.
An Australian scholar discusses problems in Australia's international economic transactions incurred by increased postwar import demands.

McLeod, Alan Lindsey, ed. **The Pattern of Australian Culture.** Ithaca: Cornell University Press, 1963, 486 p.
A collection of essays.

Rivett, Kenneth, ed. **Immigration: Control or Colour Bar? The Background to "White Australia" and a Proposal for Change.** New York: Cambridge University Press, 1963, 171 p.
A revised edition of a collection of essays, sponsored by the Immigration Reform Group. Changes in official and public attitudes toward non-European immigration are discussed.

Stevens, Frank S., ed. **Racism: The Australian Experience.** New York: Taplinger, 1972-73, 3 v.
Almost 50 authors investigate Australia's racial attitudes in volumes subtitled "Prejudice and Xenophobia," "Black versus White," and "Colonialism."

NEW ZEALAND

See also Political Processes, p. 20; Economic Growth and Development, p. 71; (Second World War) Military Operations, p. 156; (The United States) Foreign Policy, p. 229; (Great Britain) Imperial and Commonwealth Relations; Colonial Policy, p. 367; (Asia and the Pacific Area) General Surveys, p. 607; Nepal, p. 655; (Australia and New Zealand) General, p. 766; Australia, p. 766; Fiji; French Polynesia; New Caledonia; Western Samoa; Nauru, p. 775; The Polar Regions, p. 848.

Burdon, Randal Matthew. **The New Dominion: A Social and Political History of New Zealand, 1918-39.** New York: Hillary House, 1965, 382 p.
The first detailed survey of New Zealand's development between the two world wars, by a New Zealand writer.

Cameron, William James. **New Zealand.** Englewood Cliffs: Prentice-Hall, 1965, 180 p.
Essays on New Zealand, its people, its history, and the forces that have moved the island nation into the twentieth century, by a New Zealand professor of literature.

Farrell, Bryan Henry. **Power in New Zealand.** Wellington: A. H. and A. W. Reed, 1962, 197 p.
A brief survey of New Zealand's power resources and their possible future uses.

Jackson, Keith and Harré, John. **New Zealand.** New York: Walker, 1969, 224 p.
An introductory survey.

Lee, John Alexander. **Simple on a Soap-Box.** London: Collins, 1964, 285 p.
A candid and informative political autobiography of a disillusioned New Zealander of the Left. The author surveys the political scene in New Zealand since the end of World War I.

Lloyd Prichard, Muriel F. **An Economic History of New Zealand to 1939.** Auckland: Collins, 1970, 464 p.
A standard reference.

McLintock, A. H., *ed.* **Encyclopaedia of New Zealand.** Wellington: R. E. Owen, 1966, 3 v.
A most useful reference.

Milne, Robert Stephen. **Political Parties in New Zealand.** New York: Oxford University Press, 1966, 313 p.
A survey of the history, organization and voting behavior of New Zealand's political parties.

New Zealand Foreign Policy: Statements and Documents, 1943-1957. Wellington: A. R. Shearer (for the Ministry of Foreign Affairs), 1972, 495 p.
An indispensable collection of public documents on foreign policy at a time when New Zealand recognized "that the narrow perspectives of the past were no longer adequate to New Zealand's national needs."

Ross, Angus, *ed.* **New Zealand's Record in the Pacific Islands in the Twentieth Century.** Auckland: Longman Paul (for the New Zealand Institute of International Affairs), 1969, 362 p.
A thorough and well-documented discussion of New Zealand's political and administrative responsibilities in the Cook Islands group, Niue, Western Samoa and the Tokelau Islands.

Rowe, James W. and Rowe, Margaret A. **New Zealand.** New York: Praeger, 1968, 192 p.
A survey of New Zealand's history and an account of the country's physical characteristics and its social and economic structures.

Scott, Kenneth John. **The New Zealand Constitution.** New York: Oxford University Press, 1962, 188 p.
A legal study providing useful information on the history and government of New Zealand.

Sinclair, Keith. **A History of New Zealand.** Harmondsworth: Penguin, 1969, 335 p.
A revised edition of a general history first published in 1961.

Sutch, William Ball. **The Quest for Security in New Zealand, 1840 to 1966.** New York: Oxford University Press, 1967, 512 p.
Mr. Sutch, a leading New Zealand economist, tells of the struggle to legislate for and to implement laws for personal, economic and social security from the time that New Zealand was recognized as a separate member of the British Empire. An enlarged revision of the 1942 edition.

Sutch, William Ball. **Takeover New Zealand.** Wellington: A. H. and A. W. Reed, 1972, 142 p.
An examination of foreign ownership in New Zealand.

THE PACIFIC OCEAN

GENERAL

See Second World War, p. 144; (The United States) Foreign Policy, p. 229; (Japan) Foreign and Defense Policies, p. 718; Australia and New Zealand, p. 766; other subsections under the Pacific Ocean.

Brookfield, H. C. **Colonialism, Development and Independence: The Case of the Melanesian Islands in the South Pacific.** New York: Cambridge University Press, 1972, 226 p.

A study of the complicated history of the Melanesian islands—ruled severally or successively by Holland, Germany, Britain, France, Australia, Japan, Indonesia and the United States.

Brookfield, H. C. with Hart, Doreen. **Melanesia: A Geographical Interpretation of an Island World.** London: Methuen, 1971, 464 p.
A pioneering geographical survey of New Guinea, Solomon Islands, New Hebrides, Fiji and New Caledonia.

Henderson, John W. and Others. **Area Handbook for Oceania.** Washington: G.P.O., 1971, 555 p.
A useful reference volume with a bibliography, prepared by the Foreign Area Studies at the American University.

Malakhovskii, Kim Vladimirovich. **Bor'ba imperialisticheskikh derzhav za Tikhookeanskie ostrova.** Moscow: Izd-vo "Nauka," 1966, 368 p.
A Soviet history of great power competition in Oceania since the voyages of exploration.

Pacific Islands Yearbook and Who's Who. Sydney: Melbourne Publishing Co.
A detailed reference, published irregularly since 1932. The 11th edition appeared in 1972. Title varies.

U.S. TERRITORIES

See also Second World War, p. 144; (The United States) Foreign Policy, p. 229; (Japan) Recent History, p. 715; Foreign and Defense Policies, p. 718; Australia and New Zealand, p. 766; (The Pacific Ocean) General, p. 772.

Beardsley, Charles. **Guam: Past and Present.** Rutland (Vt.): Tuttle, 1964, 262 p.
A concise and informative handbook of the largest of the Mariana Islands that is administered as an unincorporated U.S. territory under the jurisdiction of the Department of Interior.

Carano, Paul and Sanchez, Pedro C. **A Complete History of Guam.** Rutland (Vt.): Tuttle, 1964, 452 p.
A detailed political, economic, social and cultural history of Guam since its discovery in 1521.

De Smith, Stanley A. **Microstates and Micronesia.** New York: New York University Press, 1970, 193 p.
In this comprehensive overview of the microstate problem in the contemporary world the author focuses on the U.S. administration of Micronesia.

Kahn, Ely Jacques, Jr. **A Reporter in Micronesia.** New York: Norton, 1966, 313 p.
A staff writer for *The New Yorker* gives a lively account of the successes and failures of the United States in its Trust Territory of the Pacific Islands.

Meller, Norman with Meller, Terza. **The Congress of Micronesia: Development of the Legislative Process in the Trust Territory of the Pacific Islands.** Honolulu: University of Hawaii Press, 1969, 480 p.
An informative study.

Pacific Islands and Trust Territories: A Selected Bibliography. Washington: G.P.O., 1971, 171 p.
A useful reference, including a supplement of maps, prepared by the U.S. Army Library.

Price, Willard DeMille. **America's Paradise Lost.** New York: Day, 1966, 240 p.
A first-hand report on the Trust Territory of the Pacific Islands which, the author contends, has been shamefully neglected through low U.S. appropriations and inadequate, though devoted, staff.

PAPUA NEW GUINEA

See also (Asia and the Pacific Area) General Surveys, p. 607; Indonesia, p. 759; Australia and New Zealand, p. 766; (The Pacific Ocean) General, p. 772.

Bettison, David George and Others, eds. **The Papua-New Guinea Elections 1964.** Canberra: The Australian National University, 1965, 545 p.

A collection of studies on the political history of Papua New Guinea and on how the members of its House of Assembly were chosen in 1964.

Biskup, Peter and Others. **A Short History of New Guinea.** Sydney: Angus and Robertson, 1968, 174 p.

A brief account of the Europeans in New Guinea.

The Economic Development of the Territory of Papua and New Guinea. Baltimore: Johns Hopkins Press, 1965, 468 p.

A report of a mission organized by the International Bank for Reconstruction and Development.

Epstein, A. L. and Others, eds. **The Politics of Dependence: Papua, New Guinea 1968.** Canberra: Australian National University Press, 1971, 398 p.

An Australian research team describes the difficulties of Papua New Guinea on its road toward self-government.

Hastings, Peter. **New Guinea: Problems and Prospects.** Melbourne: Cheshire (for the Australian Institute of International Affairs), 1969, 320 p.

A journalist's survey of New Guinea, its political development and its relations with its neighbors, especially with Australia which underestimated the ease with which Western political and social institutions could be implanted in a Melanesian setting.

Hudson, W. J., ed. **Australia and Papua New Guinea.** Sydney: Sydney University Press, 1971, 198 p.

A collection of essays attempting to provide an overview of Australia's performance as a colonial power.

Kiki, Albert Maori. **Kiki: Ten Thousand Years in a Lifetime: A New Guinea Autobiography.** London: Pall Mall Press, 1968, 190 p.

A native political leader in New Guinea reminisces on his years in government service and on Australian attitudes and policies.

Mair, Lucy Philip. **Australia in New Guinea.** Melbourne: Melbourne University Press, rev. ed., 1970, 254 p.

An updated edition of a classic study first published in 1948.

Ryan, John. **The Hot Land: Focus on New Guinea.** New York: St. Martin's Press, 1970, 390 p.

This general survey by an Australian journalist is best in its description of the formerly Dutch New Guinea, now Indonesian West Irian.

Ryan, Peter, ed. **Encyclopaedia of Papua and New Guinea.** Melbourne: Melbourne University Press in association with the University of Papua and New Guinea, 1972, 3 v.

A most useful reference.

Salisbury, Richard F. **Vunamami: Economic Transformation in a Traditional Society.** Berkeley: University of California Press, 1970, 389 p.

An anthropological-economic study of how a small nonindustrial society in New Guinea, by use of its own resources alone, managed to achieve a sustained economic development over the last 90 years.

Souter, Gavin. **New Guinea: The Last Unknown.** Sydney: Angus and Robertson, 1964, 296 p.

A survey of New Guinea by an Australian journalist.

Van der Veur, Paul W. **Search for New Guinea's Boundaries: From Torres Strait to the Pacific.** Canberra: Australian National University Press, 1966, 176 p.

A thorough study of the boundary problems of New Guinea.

White, Osmar Egmont Dorkin. **Parliament of a Thousand Tribes: A Study of New Guinea.** London: Heinemann, 1966, 256 p.

A useful introduction to New Guinea by a writer who knows the country well, with a discussion of Indonesian and Australian interests in that region.

Willey, Keith. **Assignment New Guinea.** Sydney: Angus and Robertson, 1966, 263 p.
An introduction to New Guinea's history and a survey of the first election held in that country in 1964. The author recommends the establishment of close ties between New Guinea and Australia.

FIJI; FRENCH POLYNESIA; NEW CALEDONIA; WESTERN SAMOA; NAURU

See also (Asia and the Pacific Area) General Surveys, p. 607; New Zealand, p. 771; (The Pacific Ocean) General, p. 772.

Belshaw, Cyril Shirley. **Under the Ivi Tree: Society and Economic Growth in Rural Fiji.** Berkeley: University of California Press, 1964, 336 p.
A Canadian anthropologist did extensive field research for this study of the differentials of economic growth among the Fijians. The Government of Fiji is likened to the ivi tree which, while having large leaves, provides no shelter because the rain quickly drips through.

Coulter, John Wesley. **The Drama of Fiji: A Contemporary History.** Rutland (Vt.): Tuttle, 1967, 230 p.
A geographer and former U.N. Trusteeship official surveys the economic and political problems of the British colony that became independent with Dominion status in the Commonwealth on October 19, 1970.

Davidson, James Wightman. **Samoa mo Samoa: The Emergence of the Independent State of Western Samoa.** New York: Oxford University Press, 1967, 467 p.
A history of Western Samoa, the former German protectorate that was administered by New Zealand from 1920 to 1961 and that became an independent state on January 1, 1962. The volume is also an autobiography of a leading champion of Western Samoan independence.

Fisk, Ernest Kelvin. **The Political Economy of Independent Fiji.** Canberra: Australian National University Press, 1970, 89 p.
In this introduction to Fiji's basic economic and political problems the author discusses the respective roles of the Fijian, Indian, European and Chinese communities in the country's development.

Mayer, Adrian C. **Indians in Fiji.** New York: Oxford University Press (for the Institute of Race Relations), 1963, 142 p.
A study of the tensions and dilemmas brought about by the importation of Indian laborers in Fiji.

Meller, Norman and Anthony, James. **Fiji Goes to the Polls: The Crucial Legislative Council Elections of 1963.** Honolulu: East-West Center Press, 1969, 185 p.
A technical study.

O'Reilly, Patrick and Reitman, Édouard. **Bibliographie de Tahiti et de la Polynésie française.** Paris: Musée de l'Homme, 1967, 1,046 p.
A comprehensive annotated bibliography of Tahiti and French Polynesia.

Pitt, David. **Tradition and Economic Progress in Samoa.** New York: Oxford University Press, 1970, 295 p.
The author concludes this study by saying that Samoan economic development can be achieved mainly through traditional values and institutions.

Snow, Philip A. **A Bibliography of Fiji, Tonga, and Rotuma.** Coral Gables (Fla.): University of Miami Press, 1969, 418 p.
A useful reference containing over 10,000 entries, ranging from the seventeenth century to the mid-1960s.

Thompson, Virginia McLean and Adloff, Richard. **The French Pacific Islands: French Polynesia and New Caledonia.** Berkeley: University of California Press, 1971, 539 p.
The authors of this comprehensive and well-documented study state that their aim has been "to examine the phenomena responsible for the French islands' present transitional situation and to indicate the problems that their inhabitants will inevitably face when and if the islands' status is changed from a quasi-colonial to a sovereign one."

IV. AFRICA
GENERAL
GENERAL SURVEYS

Viviani, Nancy. **Nauru: Phosphate and Political Progress.** Honolulu: University of Hawaii Press, 1970, 215 p.
A pioneering study of Nauru's development toward independence, with emphasis on Australia's economic interests in the island.

See also General Works, p. 1; Political Factors, p. 12; The World Since 1914, p. 129; other subsections under (Africa) General.

Africa 69/70: A Reference Volume on the African Continent. New York: Africana Publishing Corp., 1969, 445 p.
This reference volume includes analytical essays, country profiles, some economic statistics and a variety of maps and charts; also useful information on development projects.

Africa South of the Sahara, 1971—. London: Europa Publications, 1971—.
A most useful reference work on the political, economic, cultural and social conditions of the continent outside North Africa. Through 1973 three volumes have been published.

African Affairs: Number Two. Carbondale: Southern Illinois University Press, 1963, 129 p.
——. **Number Three.** New York: Oxford University Press, 1969, 139 p.
Collections of articles on contemporary Africa, prepared at St. Antony's College, Oxford. Edited by Kenneth Kirkwood.

Anders, Robert. **L'Afrique africaine.** Paris: Les Sept Couleurs, 1963, 230 p.
An author who considers the effect of Portuguese colonization a miracle and U.S. aid exclusively a corrupting force examines the African situation.

Année africaine, 1963—. Paris: Pedone (for the Centre d'Étude d'Afrique Noire de Bordeaux), 1965—.
This annual survey of the political, economic and cultural affairs of Africa contains detailed chronologies. The volume covering the developments in 1972 was published in 1973.

Arkhurst, Frederick S., ed. **Africa in the Seventies and Eighties: Issues in Development.** New York: Praeger (in coöperation with the Adlai Stevenson Institute of International Affairs), 1970, 405 p.
A number of leading students of African affairs were invited in 1969 to project contemporary economic, political and legal problems into the 1980s. This volume includes the resulting papers and comments by other participants.

Barnes, Leonard. **Africa in Eclipse.** New York: St. Martin's Press, 1972, 352 p.
Pessimistic and provocative thoughts on Africa's future by a former British colonial officer who is critical of both the "kleptocratic" regimes of black Africa and the NATO powers.

Bohannan, Paul. **Africa and Africans.** Garden City (N.Y.): Natural History Press, 1964, 259 p.
A survey of African history, geography, culture and contemporary political and economic problems.

Cartey, Wilfred and Kilson, Martin Luther, eds. **The Africa Reader: Colonial Africa.** New York: Random House, 1970, 264 p.
——. **The Africa Reader: Independent Africa.** New York: Random House, 1970, 428 p.
An excellent overview of African society and politics. While the readings on the colonial period include writings both of Europeans and Africans, the volume on independent Africa includes essays written exclusively by Africans.

AFRICA

Davidson, Basil. **The African Genius.** Boston: Atlantic (Little, Brown), 1970, 367 p.
The character of the indigenous cultures of the continent is the central concern of this volume by one of Africa's most prolific and sensitive students.

Davidson, Basil. **Which Way Africa? The Search for a New Society.** Harmondsworth: Penguin, 3rd ed., 1971, 270 p.
A revised survey of contemporary social and political problems of Africa and an attempt to predict future patterns.

Ferkiss, Victor C. **Africa's Search for Identity.** New York: Braziller, 1966, 346 p.
A survey of the cultural, social and political facets of Africa's new role in world affairs.

Fordham, Paul. **The Geography of African Affairs.** Baltimore: Penguin, 1965, 244 p.
This concise volume assembles geographical facts which relate to political and economic problems of those regions south of the Sahara.

Froelich, Jean-Claude. **Les Musulmans d'Afrique noire.** Paris: Éditions de l'Orante, 1962, 406 p.
A study of Islam in African history and contemporary politics.

Ganiage, Jean and Others. **L'Afrique au XXe siècle.** Paris: Sirey, 1966, 908 p.
A comprehensive history of Africa through 1965.

Gann, Lewis Henry and Duignan, Peter. **Burden of Empire: An Appraisal of Western Colonialism in Africa South of the Sahara.** New York: Praeger (for the Hoover Institution on War, Revolution, and Peace), 1967, 435 p.
A provocative, competent evaluation, with emphasis on colonialism's more creative aspects.

Gann, Lewis Henry and Duignan, Peter, *ed.* **Colonialism in Africa 1870–1960.** New York: Cambridge University Press, 1969– .
Four volumes of a projected five-volume series on the history of colonial Africa have been published through 1974, including a bibliographical guide to colonialism in sub-Saharan Africa. Volume 3, "Profiles of Change: African Society and Colonial Rule," was edited by Victor Turner. A Hoover Institution publication.

Grove, Alfred Thomas. **Africa South of the Sahara.** New York: Oxford University Press, 1967, 275 p.
A short general geography illustrated with maps drawn from the "Oxford Regional Economic Atlas of Africa."

Hance, William Adams. **The Geography of Modern Africa.** New York: Columbia University Press, 1964, 653 p.
A most useful reference on the economic geography of the African continent.

Hatch, John Charles. **A History of Postwar Africa.** New York: Praeger, 1965, 432 p.
The former Commonwealth officer of the British Labour Party and the author of "Africa Today—And Tomorrow" has written a critical account, by territories, of shifting colonial policies leading to the present-day "mosaic" of African independent states.

Hennessy, Maurice N. **Africa under My Heart.** New York: Ives Washburn, 1965, 181 p.
An account of personal experiences in Africa by a former British soldier and colonial official.

Hodder, Bramwell William and Harris, D. R., *eds.* **Africa in Transition: Geographical Essays.** New York: Barnes and Noble, 1967, 378 p.
A survey of the changing map of Africa by a group of British geographers.

Howe, Russell Warren. **Black Africa: Africa South of the Sahara from Pre-History to Independence.** New York: Walker, 1966–67, 2 v.
A sweeping, well-written survey of the highlights of sub-Saharan African history from Leakey's terrestrial ape to contemporary Pan-Africanism, intended for readers with a non-scholarly interest in Africa.

Iordanskii, Vladimir Borisovich. **Tupiki I perspektivy tropicheskoi Afriki.** Moscow: Izd-vo "Nauka," 1970, 474 p.
A Soviet analysis of the tropical African tribal, social and national structures.

July, Robert W. **The Origins of Modern African Thought.** New York: Praeger, 1968, 512 p.
A series of intellectual portraits of nineteenth- and twentieth-century African thinkers, comparing their responses to Western ideas and influence.

Junod, Violaine I. with Resnick, Idrian N., eds. **The Handbook of Africa.** New York: New York University Press, 1963, 472 p.

A handbook of information, by country, of 50-odd political units in Africa.

Kitchen, Helen A., ed. **A Handbook of African Affairs.** New York: Praeger (for the African-American Institute), 1964, 311 p.

A concise compendium drawn in great part from *Africa Report*.

Legum, Colin, ed. **Africa: A Handbook to the Continent.** New York: Praeger, rev. and enl. ed., 1966, 558 p.

This comprehensive handbook is divided into two sections: the first consists of a country-by-country survey of basic political and economic information; the second section is organized according to such subject headings as external attitudes toward Africa, art and literature, changing cultural patterns, religion, economics and the role of the United Nations.

Legum, Colin and Others, eds. **Africa Contemporary Record: Annual Survey and Documents, 1968-1969—.** New York: Africana Publishing Corporation, 1969—.

A very useful reference annual on contemporary Africa, consisting of articles on current issues, country surveys and documents. The volume for 1972-73 was published in 1973.

Littell, Blaine. **South of the Moon: On Stanley's Trail through the Dark Continent.** New York: Harper and Row, 1966, 300 p.

An American correspondent gives an impressionistic account of his five-month overland journey through the Congo and East Africa.

Lusignan, Guy de. **French-Speaking Africa since Independence.** New York: Praeger, 1969, 416 p.

This general introduction includes a description of the process of decolonization, a series of short country-by-country essays on post-independence developments and a concluding section on the economies and international relations of francophone Africa.

McCall, Daniel F. **Africa in Time-Perspective.** Boston: Boston University Press, 1964, 175 p.

Lectures given at the University of Ghana to introduce students to the wide range of tools available for historical research.

McEwan, Peter James Michael, ed. **Twentieth-Century Africa.** New York: Oxford University Press, 1968, 517 p.

One of three volumes of readings in African history (the others being concerned with earlier peiods) extracted from books and articles by established scholars.

Meyer, Frank S., ed. **The African Nettle: Dilemmas of an Emerging Continent.** New York: Day, 1965, 253 p.

Among the contributors to this volume there are Gilbert Comte, Elspeth Huxley and K. A. Busia.

Monteil, Vincent. **L'Islam noir.** Paris: Éditions du Seuil, 1964, 367 p.

A fascinating survey of the particular attributes of Islam as interpreted and practiced in black Africa.

Moore, Clark D. and Dunbar, Ann, eds. **Africa Yesterday and Today.** New York: Praeger, 1969, 394 p.

Edited for use in the George School's Afro-Asian Studies Program, this collection of writings by journalists, academics, African leaders and extracts from official publications provides an overview of African society and politics in historical perspective.

Moraes, Francis Robert. **The Importance of Being Black: An Asian Looks at Africa.** New York: Macmillan, 1965, 436 p.

A veteran Indian journalist has written a factual as well as imaginative account of his experiences on the African continent.

Morrison, Donald George and Others. **Black Africa: A Comparative Handbook.** New York: Free Press, 1972, 483 p.

This useful reference contains comparable information for 32 black African nations.

Oliver, Roland Anthony and Atmore, Anthony. **Africa since 1800.** New York: Cambridge University Press, 1967, 304 p.

A well-written history instructively illustrated with interpretive maps analyzing developments in sub-Saharan Africa through the surge of military coups in 1965-66.

Paden, John N. and Soja, Edward W., *eds*. **The African Experience.** Evanston: Northwestern University Press, 1970, 3 v. in 4 pts.
A most useful introduction to African studies, including a volume of essays by eminent Africanists, a syllabus, a comprehensive bibliography and a guide to resources.

Quigg, Philip W., *ed*. **Africa: A Foreign Affairs Reader.** New York: Praeger (for the Council on Foreign Relations), 1964, 346 p.
A collection of 24 articles which have appeared in *Foreign Affairs* over a span of 40 years—from Lord Lugard and W. E. B. Du Bois to Nkrumah, Senghor, Balewa and Sékou Touré—with useful introductions to each article by the editor and a foreword by Hamilton Fish Armstrong.

Sík, Endre. **The History of Black Africa.** Budapest: Akadémiai Kiadó, 1966–74, 4 v.
A massive history of Africa, sponsored by the Hungarian Academy of Sciences and displaying the ideological orientation of that organization. The Hungarian original appeared as "Fekete-Afrika története" (Budapest: Akadémiai Kiadó).

Stokke, Olav, *ed.* **Reporting Africa.** Uppsala: The Scandinavian Institute of African Studies, 1971, 223 p.
Papers delivered at a seminar at Uppsala in October 1970 by Scandinavian, African and British students of the African press.

Trimingham, John Spencer. **The Influence of Islam upon Africa.** New York: Praeger, 1968, 159 p.
A foremost authority on the subject has written a small volume on the process by which Islam spread and the ways in which its norms and practices have gradually come to affect the character of social life in Africa.

Ziégler, Jean. **Le Pouvoir africain.** Paris: Éditions du Seuil, 1971, 227 p.
A discussion of African concepts of time and history as compared with those of industrialized societies, by a professor of sociology at the African Institute in Geneva.

POLITICAL PROBLEMS

See also Political Factors, p. 12; The World Since 1914, p. 129; other subsections under (Africa) General.

Adu, Ammishadai Lawson. **The Civil Service in Commonwealth Africa.** New York: Humanities Press, 1969, 253 p.
——. **The Civil Service in New African States.** New York: Praeger, 1965, 242 p.
Detailed studies of African public administration by the former head of the Ghana Civil Service.

Ainslie, Rosalynde. **The Press in Africa: Communications Past and Present.** New York: Walker, 1967, 264 p.
A study of government-press relations throughout the continent.

Alderfer, Harold Freed. **A Bibliography of African Government, 1950–1960.** Lincoln University (Pa.) : Lincoln University Press, 2d rev. ed., 1967, 163 p.
A useful reference.

Allen, Christopher and Johnson, R. W., *eds.* **African Perspectives.** New York: Cambridge University Press, 1970, 438 p.
A diverse *Festschrift*, presented to Thomas Hodgkin, on contemporary African political parties and politics.

Armah, Kwesi. **Africa's Golden Road.** New York: Humanities Press, 1966, 292 p.
Drawing upon his experience as Ghana's High Commissioner in London, and Minister of Foreign Trade, the author of this "political testament" surveys the struggle for independence, the operation of one-party democracy in Ghana and Guinea, the goal of the Continental Union Government and the role of African states in the world.

Barnes, Leonard. **African Renaissance.** Indianapolis: Bobbs-Merrill, 1970, 304 p.
Combining case studies of individual countries with a continental perspective, a Brit-

ish student of African administration with wide experience in the Colonial Service gives a highly critical assessment of efforts at modernization and development.

Brunschwig, Henri. **L'Avènement de l'Afrique noire du XIXe siècle à nos jours.** Paris: Colin, 1963, 247 p.
A somewhat tendentious survey of European and African contacts from the nineteenth century, with a brief exposition on the growth of nationalist sentiment and ideology.

Busia, Kofi Abrefa. **Africa in Search of Democracy.** New York: Praeger, 1967, 189 p.
The former leader of the parliamentary opposition and one of Ghana's prominent intellectuals analyzes the barriers to the development of democratic forms of government in Africa. He is particularly critical of attempts to combine one-party rule with democracy and of the "Communist prescription of democracy."

Butler, Jeffrey and Castagno, A. A., eds. **Boston University Papers on Africa: Transition in African Politics.** New York: Praeger (for the African Studies Center, Boston University), 1967, 342 p.
A collection of essays, treating in considerable detail such topics as trade unionism, political parties, ideology, and corruption in local government.

Carter, Gwendolen Margaret, ed. **Five African States: Responses to Diversity.** Ithaca: Cornell University Press, 1963, 643 p.
Five political scientists adhere to the same format in analyzing the Congo, Dahomey, the Cameroon Federal Republic, the Rhodesias and Nyasaland and South Africa. The articles on the French-speaking countries are particularly useful.

Carter, Gwendolen Margaret, ed. **National Unity and Regionalism in Eight African States.** Ithaca: Cornell University Press, 1966, 565 p.
The contributors to this volume provide a broad survey of the historical, economic and political forces underlying the tension between national unity and regionalism in Nigeria, Niger, Uganda, Ethiopia, Congo (Brazzaville), Chad, Gabon and the Central African Republic.

Coleman, James Smoot and Rosberg, Carl Gustav, Jr., eds. **Political Parties and National Integration in Tropical Africa.** Berkeley: University of California Press, 1964, 730 p.
Essays by leading authorities, principally political scientists, emphasizing the role of political parties and groups in national integration.

Cowan, Laing Gray. **The Dilemmas of African Independence.** New York: Walker, rev. ed., 1968, 167 p.
This small volume by a professor at Columbia University contains a wealth of political and economic data as well as a general introductory essay on contemporary African developments.

Cowan, Laing Gray and Others, eds. **Education and Nation-Building in Africa.** New York: Praeger, 1965, 403 p.
A valuable collection of papers and documents by African leaders and scholars concerning the relevance of education to political and economic development.

Currie, David P., ed. **Federalism and the New Nations of Africa.** Chicago: University of Chicago Press, 1964, 440 p.
Papers by African scholars on various regions of Africa are complemented by essays on federalism, economic advance, human rights and international legal relations.

Decottignies, Roger and Biéville, Marc de. **Les Nationalités africaines.** Paris: Pedone, 1963, 419 p.
A discussion of the laws of nationality in each of the former possessions of France in Africa.

Emerson, Rupert and Kilson, Martin Luther, eds. **The Political Awakening of Africa.** Englewood Cliffs: Prentice-Hall, 1965, 175 p.
A useful collection of fundamental statements by African leaders and intellectuals who prompted the awakening in the first instance.

Fanon, Frantz. **Toward the African Revolution: Political Essays.** New York: Monthly Review Press, 1967, 197 p.
A collection of essays written between 1952 and 1961, the year of Fanon's death, on such topics as racism, colonialism, the Algerian struggle for independence, and

the struggle of all Africans for liberation from post-colonial as well as pre-colonial élites. Fanon's writings have become a source of intellectual and moral inspiration to the "new left" as well as to a generation of African nationalists. The French original appeared as "Pour la révolution africaine: écrits politiques" (Paris: Maspéro, 1964, 223 p.).

First, Ruth. **Power in Africa.** New York: Pantheon Books, 1971, 513 p.
A thoughtful study of military intervention in Africa, with case-studies of the Sudan, Nigeria and Ghana. Born in South Africa, the author has written extensively on African subjects.

Friedland, William H. and Rosberg, Carl Gustav, Jr., *eds*. **African Socialism.** Stanford: Stanford University Press (for the Hoover Institution on War, Revolution, and Peace), 1964, 313 p.
This interdisciplinary approach to African socialism is enhanced by the inclusion of articles by African leaders setting forth their own interpretations.

Geiss, Imanuel. **Panafrikanismus: zur Geschichte der Dekolonisation.** Frankfurt/Main: Europäische Verlagsanstalt, 1968, 489 p.
A meticulously documented history of Pan-African thinking and politics.

Gifford, Prosser and Louis, William Roger, *eds*. **France and Britain in Africa: Imperial Rivalry and Colonial Rule.** New Haven: Yale University Press, 1971, 989 p.
This collection of historical essays is valuable chiefly for the section devoted to comparative analysis of the British and French colonial administrations.

Gower, Laurence Cecil Bartlett. **Independent Africa: The Challenge to the Legal Profession.** Cambridge: Harvard University Press, 1967, 154 p.
This expansion of the 1966 Oliver Wendell Holmes Lectures at Harvard takes a fresh, pragmatic and open-minded look at the impact of the colonial experience upon English-speaking Africa, and assesses the post-independence innovations and alterations in institutions and practices. The author was formerly a professor of law both at the University of London and at the University of Lagos, Nigeria.

Grundy, Kenneth W. **Guerrilla Struggle in Africa: An Analysis and Preview.** New York: Grossman, 1971, 204 p.
This study, a theoretical treatise on the potential for anti-regime violence in Africa generally, concentrates particularly on the colonial and white-settler regimes and advocates as well as predicts their downfall.

Gueye, Lamine. **Itinéraire africain.** Paris: Présence Africaine, 1966, 243 p.
An elder statesman of Senegal recounts the political, institutional and constitutional evolution of French-speaking Africa from the beginning of this century through 1965.

Gutteridge, William F. **The Military in African Politics.** London: Methuen, 1969, 166 p.
A discussion emphasizing developments in English-speaking tropical Africa. The main stress is on analytical description rather than on the general theory of military intervention.

Hooker, James R. **Black Revolutionary: George Padmore's Path from Communism to Pan-Africanism.** New York: Praeger, 1967, 168 p.
Basing his account on unpublished letters, interviews, newspaper articles and a variety of secondary sources, a Michigan State University historian follows Padmore's wanderings from Trinidad to the United States, Moscow, London and finally Ghana. This itinerary reflects the development of Padmore's thinking, the central concern of this study.

Kaunda, Kenneth D. **A Humanist in Africa: Letters to Colin M. Morris from Kenneth D. Kaunda, President of Zambia.** Nashville: Abingdon Press, 1968, 136 p.
The President of Zambia reveals himself to be a perceptive analyst of the problems of the developing countries as well as an arresting public figure in his own right.

Kesteloot, Lilyan. **Intellectual Origins of the African Revolution.** Washington: Black Orpheus Press, 1972, 128 p.
This brief survey sketches some of the literary roots of Black awareness in the West Indies and Africa.

Lee, John Michael. **African Armies and Civil Order.** New York: Praeger (for the Institute for Strategic Studies), 1969, 198 p.
A general comparative analysis of the reasons for military intervention in African politics, by a British political scientist.

Lefever, Ernest Warren. **Spear and Scepter: Army, Police, and Politics in Tropical Africa.** Washington: Brookings Institution, 1970, 251 p.
A senior fellow in the Brookings Foreign Policy Studies Program compares the roles of the armies and police forces in Ethiopia, Ghana and Congo (Kinshasa).

Lewis, Leonard John. **Education and Political Independence in Africa, and Other Essays.** New York: Nelson, 1963, 128 p.
Essays by a professor at the University of London which emphasize the need for coöperation in educational development.

Lofchie, Michael Frank, ed. **The State of the Nations: Constraints on Development in Independent Africa.** Berkeley: University of California Press, 1971, 305 p.
A collection of papers published under the auspices of the African Studies Center at the University of California (Los Angeles).

Lombard, Jacques. **Autorités traditionnelles et pouvoirs européens en Afrique noire: le déclin d'une aristocratie sous le régime colonial.** Paris: Colin, 1967, 292 p.
An assessment of the changes in the forms of native administration in former British and French colonies in Africa.

Markovitz, Irving Leonard, ed. **African Politics and Society: Basic Issues and Problems of Government and Development.** New York: Free Press, 1970, 485 p.
A political scientist at Queens College has assembled a variety of essays, mostly journal articles, and some extracts from books, to make up an interesting reader for courses in African politics.

Masseron, Jean-Paul. **Le Pouvoir et la justice en Afrique noire francophone et à Madagascar.** Paris: Pedone, 1966, 161 p.
A survey of constitutions, judicial structures and decrees in French Africa, with an introduction by President Senghor of Senegal.

Mazrui, Ali Al'Amin. **The Anglo-African Commonwealth: Political Friction and Cultural Fusion.** New York: Pergamon Press, 1967, 163 p.
Essays on politics, history and culture in English-speaking tropical Africa by the former head of the political science department at Makerere University College in Uganda who is now teaching at the University of Michigan.

Mazrui, Ali Al'Amin. **On Heroes and Uhuru-Worship.** London: Longmans, 1967, 264 p.
Essays on modern African politics. Professor Mazrui is particularly interested in the ideas which motivate the African leaders.

Mazrui, Ali Al'Amin. **Towards a Pax Africana: A Study of Ideology and Ambition.** Chicago: University of Chicago Press, 1967, 287 p.
A historical and analytical exploration of the vocabulary and major concepts of contemporary African thinking about politics.

Milcent, Ernest and Sordet, Monique. **Léopold Sédar Senghor et la naissance de l'Afrique moderne.** Paris: Éditions Seghers, 1969, 271 p.
The development of the Senegalese President's career and political thought is traced by two French journalists. There is a preface by Georges Pompidou.

Molnar, Thomas Steven. **Africa: A Political Travelogue.** New York: Fleet, 1965, 304 p.
A perceptive journalistic account of a nine-month trip on the African continent.

Nkrumah, Kwame. **Africa Must Unite.** New York: Praeger, 1963, 229 p.
The former President of Ghana uses the case of Ghana to exemplify the problems facing a new African state and puts forward suggestions for the future of Pan-Africanism.

Nkrumah, Kwame. **Consciencism.** New York: Monthly Review Press, 1965, 122 p.
An explanation of the causes of social and political unrest in Africa. The book provides insights into the intellect and philosophy of one of Africa's most influential leaders.

Nkrumah, Kwame. **Handbook of Revolutionary Warfare: A Guide to the Armed Phase of the African Revolution.** New York: International Publishers, 1969, 122 p.

The former President of Ghana calls for the formation of an All-African People's Revolutionary Army to liberate the continent from capitalist neo-imperialism, and outlines his blueprint for its organization, tactics and objectives.

Potholm, Christian P. **Four African Political Systems.** Englewood Cliffs: Prentice-Hall, 1970, 308 p.
The author, a professor at Vassar, has written an excellent introductory text for courses on the comparative analysis of African politics. General and theoretical chapters are combined with an examination of politics in South Africa, Tanzania, the Somali Republic and the Ivory Coast.

Quaison-Sackey, Alexander. **Africa Unbound: Reflections of an African Statesman.** New York: Praeger, 1963, 174 p.
A Ghanaian diplomat gives a short political history of the freeing of the African states and of their role in the United Nations.

Rivkin, Arnold. **Nation-Building in Africa.** New Brunswick: Rutgers University Press, 1970, 312 p.
Thoughtful and comprehensive, this general assessment of the problems and prospects of political and economic development by the late American scholar combines case studies of six countries with general theoretical considerations. Edited by John H. Morrow.

Rivkin, Arnold, ed. **Nations by Design: Institution-Building in Africa.** Garden City: Doubleday, 1968, 386 p.
These papers were originally written for a series of meetings of a study group organized at the University of California in 1967.

Rotberg, Robert I. **A Political History of Tropical Africa.** New York: Harcourt, Brace and World, 1965, 440 p.
A solid history of the peoples of tropical Africa from ancient times through the triumph of contemporary nationalism.

Rotberg, Robert I. and Mazrui, Ali Al'Amin. **Protest and Power in Black Africa.** New York: Oxford University Press, 1970, 1,274 p.
A massive collection of essays by outstanding scholars. Political, religious, economic, military, literary and ideological forms of protest from the colonial period to the present are considered. Written under the auspices of The Center for International Affairs, Harvard University.

Said, Abdul A. **The African Phenomenon.** Boston: Allyn and Bacon, 1968, 194 p.
An introduction to the politics of the African continent by a political scientist at the American University.

Senghor, Léopold Sédar. **On African Socialism.** New York: Praeger, 1964, 173 p.
Three essays providing insight into the political philosophy of a distinguished statesman and poet, the President of Senegal.

Sithole, Ndabaningi. **African Nationalism.** New York: Oxford University Press, rev. ed., 1968, 196 p.
The Rhodesian nationalist leader has reorganized, rewritten and brought up to date his thoughtful analysis first published in 1959.

Spiro, Herbert John, ed. **Africa: The Primacy of Politics.** New York: Random House, 1966, 212 p.
A collection of essays on various aspects of contemporary African political development, most of which were originally prepared for the annual meeting of the African Studies Association in October 1963.

Stevenson, Robert F. **Population and Political Systems in Tropical Africa.** New York: Columbia University Press, 1968, 306 p.
The character and complexity of political systems and the average population density are shown to be closely related in a large number of indigenous African political systems studies by an anthropologist at the University of the State of New York at Stony Brook.

Taylor, Sidney, ed. **The New Africans.** New York: Putnam, 1967, 504 p.
A handbook of biographical essays on independent black Africa's political leaders compiled by Reuters' correspondents working in that continent.

Thompson, Vincent Bakpetu. **Africa and Unity: The Evolution of Pan-Africanism.** New York: Humanities Press, 1969, 412 p.
An analysis and assessment of the movement toward African unity which is seen as a distant hope for Africans determined to be independent and to develop their societies. The author is a Nigerian scholar.

Touré, Ahmed Sékou. **L'Afrique et la révolution.** Paris: Présence Africaine, 1967, 398 p.
These writings by the Guinean leader on the history of the Democratic Party of Guinea and on contemporary African problems are intended as guidelines for the revolutionary fight for the political, cultural and economic independence of Africa.

Wallerstein, Immanuel Maurice. **Africa: The Politics of Unity: An Analysis of a Contemporary Social Movement.** New York: Random House, 1967, 274 p.
This volume, in the words of the author, "is an interpretation of the major political developments in Africa between 1957 and 1965 from the perspective of a major social movement on the continent, the movement toward African unity."

Wauthier, Claude. **The Literature and Thought of Modern Africa: A Survey.** New York: Praeger, 1967, 323 p.
This study of contemporary African cultural thought by an African specialist of Agence France-Presse first appeared in French as "L'Afrique des Africains: inventaire de la négritude" (Paris: Éditions du Seuil, 1964, 314 p.).

Welch, Claude Emerson, *comp.* **Soldier and State in Africa: A Comparative Analysis of Military Intervention and Political Change.** Evanston: Northwestern University Press, 1970, 320 p.
A reader combining two general essays and two appendixes on military activity in Africa with case studies of Dahomey and Upper Volta, Congo (Kinshasa), Ghana and Algeria.

Woddis, Jack. **Africa: The Way Ahead.** New York: International Publishers, 1964, 174 p.
Mr. Woddis examines Africa from a Marxist point of view; his information is, however, detailed and his bias lends interest to the interpretation of essentially well-known events.

Zatzépine, Alexandre. **Le Droit de la nationalité des républiques francophones d'Afrique et de Madagascar.** Paris: Librairie Générale de Droit, 1963, 149 p.
A survey of the various laws pertaining to nationality in French-speaking Africa.

INTERNATIONAL RELATIONS

General

See also General Works, p. 1; Political Factors, p. 12; International Law, p. 83; International Organization and Government, p. 96; War and Peace, p. 108; The World Since 1914, p. 129; (The United States) Foreign Policy, p. 229; (Great Britain) Imperial and Commonwealth Relations; Colonial Policy, p. 367; Biographies, Memoirs and Addresses, p. 369; Foreign Policy, p. 375; (France) Recent History, p. 396; Biographies, Memoirs and Addresses, p. 400; Foreign Policy, p. 404; (Italy) Foreign Policy, p. 424; Portugal, p. 439; other subsections under (Africa) General and the sections for specific African countries and regions.

Atwood, William. **The Reds and the Blacks: A Personal Adventure.** New York: Harper and Row, 1967, 341 p.
The author's experiences as U.S. Ambassador to Guinea and then Kenya are related in this readable and sometimes critical account of diplomatic life in two African capitals. Important for students of African politics and American foreign policy.

Aynor, H. S. **Notes from Africa.** New York: Praeger, 1969, 163 p.
An Israeli diplomat, formerly *chargé d'affaires* in what was Leopoldville, and later ambassador to Senegal and Gambia, gives a lively impression of his experiences.

Bandini, Franco. **Gli italiani in Africa: storia delle guerre coloniali (1882-1943).** Milan: Longanesi, 1971, 576 p.
A history of Italian colonial wars in Africa from 1882 to 1943.

Brzezinski, Zbigniew Kazimierz, *ed.* **Africa and the Communist World.** Stanford: Stanford University Press (for the Hoover Institution on War, Revolution, and Peace), 1963, 272 p.

A collection of essays based primarily on communist source materials which presents the various programs of the communist states in Africa. The articles treat the political, social and economic aspects of communist policy toward Africa and the concluding chapter by the editor gives a succinct and provocative summation.

Cervenka, Zdenek. **The Organisation of African Unity and Its Charter.** New York: Praeger, 1969, 253 p.
A full-length study of the O.A.U. from its beginning in May 1963 until late 1968 when it was attempting to mediate the Nigerian Civil War. The author is a Czech-born scholar at the Scandinavian Institute of African Studies at Uppsala.

Cooley, John K. **East Wind Over Africa: Red China's African Offensive.** New York: Walker, 1965, 246 p.
A first-rate treatment by the African correspondent for *The Christian Science Monitor* of Red China's interest and influence in Africa, from the Bandung Conference in 1955 to the failure to hold a second one at Algiers in June 1965.

Corbett, Edward M. **The French Presence in Black Africa.** Washington: Black Orpheus Press, 1972, 209 p.
Modernization will inevitably erode France's influence in her ex-colonies, in the author's view. However, his account indicates in dispassionate detail that French permeation into every phase of institutional life in these ex-colonies is still impressive, as well as profitable for all concerned.

Dumoga, John. **Africa between East and West.** Chester Springs (Pa.): Dufour Editions, 1969, 142 p.
Thoughtful essays on topics such as African socialism, the foreign policies of African states, the role of the press in Africa and problems of economic development, by a Ghanaian journalist.

Emerson, Rupert. **Africa and United States Policy.** Englewood Cliffs: Prentice-Hall, 1967, 117 p.
An up-to-date survey of relations between sub-Saharan Africa and the United States by an eminent student of African politics. The lack of analysis of U.S. policy as a response to Soviet policies in Africa is its major deficiency.

Etinger, Iakov Iakovlevich. **Mezhgosudarstvennye otnosheniia v Afrike.** Moscow: Izd-vo "Nauka," 1972, 319 p.
A Soviet study of contemporary international relations among the African states.

Etinger, Iakov Iakovlevich. **Politicheskie problemy afrikanskogo edinstva.** Moscow: Izd-vo "Nauka," 1967, 176 p.
A Soviet interpretation of international integration and organization in Africa.

Hatch, John Charles. **The History of Britain in Africa: From the Fifteenth Century to the Present.** New York: Praeger, 1969, 320 p.
The Africa correspondent for *The New Statesman* has written an engrossing review of British relations with the African continent beginning with the first contacts and continuing through the Nigerian Civil War.

Hazlewood, Arthur, *ed.* **African Integration and Disintegration.** New York: Oxford University Press (for the Oxford University Institute of Economics and Statistics and the Royal Institute of International Affairs), 1968, 414 p.
While most of the essays in this volume concern aspects of political and economic integration between states, several deal with similar internal problems.

Hevi, Emmanuel John. **The Dragon's Embrace: The Chinese Communists and Africa.** New York: Praeger, 1967, 152 p.
A Ghanaian who spent eighteen months as a student in China tries to make fellow Africans aware of the menace Chinese diplomacy poses to independent Africa.

Hippolyte, Mirlande. **Les États du groupe de Brazzaville aux Nations Unies.** Paris: Colin, 1970, 333 p.
An analysis of the Brazzaville group at the United Nations focusing on three General Assembly issues: the Algerian problem, the Congo problem and the question of Chinese membership in the United Nations.

Hovet, Thomas, Jr. **Africa in the United Nations.** Evanston: Northwestern University Press, 1963, 336 p.

A detailed analysis of the voting records of the African states in the United Nations and of voting records on African issues. Little attempt is made to analyze factors outside the United Nations which influence the voting although some attention is given to Pan-African conferences.

Kirkwood, Kenneth. **Britain and Africa.** Baltimore: Johns Hopkins Press, 1965, 235 p.
A knowledgeable and rather optimistic survey of the historical evolution and contemporary character of British-African relations in different parts of the continent.

Klinghoffer, Arthur Jay. **Soviet Perspectives on African Socialism.** Rutherford (N.J.): Fairleigh Dickinson University Press, 1969, 276 p.
Soviet attitudes and policies toward Africa during the Khrushchev era are the concern of this book by an American political scientist.

McKay, Vernon. **Africa in World Politics.** New York: Harper and Row, 1963, 468 p.
A study of Africa's proliferating relations with the outside world—in the United Nations through various "pan" movements, with the Soviet Union and with the United States. The author, formerly with the State Department, is now a professor at Johns Hopkins University.

McKay, Vernon, ed. **African Diplomacy: Studies in the Determinants of Foreign Policy.** New York: Praeger (for the School of Advanced International Studies, Johns Hopkins University), 1966, 210 p.
This book, by seven social scientists well-known in the African field, contains general essays on the little-understood process of how foreign policy is formed in Africa.

Metrowich, F. R. **Africa and Communism: A Study of Successes, Set-backs, and Stooge States.** Johannesburg: Voortrekkerpers, 1967, 261 p.
The author argues that if the West does not repulse communism from Africa, the Mediterranean will be lost and, consequently, Paris, London and Washington will succumb to the Red rule.

Mortimer, Edward. **France and the Africans 1944–1960: A Political History.** New York: Walker, 1969, 390 p.
The process of decolonization in black Africa is described chronologically by a British journalist.

Nielsen, Waldemar A. **The Great Powers and Africa.** New York: Praeger (for the Council on Foreign Relations), 1969, 431 p.
Europe's partial withdrawal from Africa provides the background for a study of the Chinese and Russian involvement in that continent and a critical history of American policy there. Looking at recent crises, the President of the African-American Institute suggests the lines that American policy should follow in the future.

Padelford, Norman Judson and Emerson, Rupert, eds. **Africa and World Order.** New York: Praeger, 1963, 152 p.
Originally written for a special issue of *International Organization,* these articles treat various aspects of relations among African countries and between African countries and world organizations such as the Commonwealth and the United Nations.

Perham, Dame Margery Freda. **Colonial Sequence 1949 to 1969: A Chronological Commentary upon British Colonial Policy in Africa.** London: Methuen, 1970, 377 p.
A collection of articles and letters by a distinguished British student of African affairs and colonial administration.

Rivkin, Arnold. **The African Presence in World Affairs: National Development and Its Role in Foreign Policy.** New York: Free Press of Glencoe, 1963, 304 p.
The desire for "growth and stability" is seen as the unifying factor in contemporary African states and is treated in both its internal and international setting.

Schatten, Fritz. **Communism in Africa.** New York: Praeger, 1966, 352 p.
An account of the various dimensions of communist foreign policy in Africa. The author, a West German journalist, traces the historical and theoretical background of Sino-Soviet policy differences and stresses the obstacles facing communist activity inherent in the nature of African nationalism.

Scherk, Nikolaus. **Dekolonisation und Souveränität.** Vienna: Braumüller, 1969, 184 p.
In this study an Austrian scholar seeks to discover to what extent the French African states have achieved true independence from Paris. He analyzes the flow of economic

aid and trade, the placement of French troops on African territory, voting patterns in the U.N. General Assembly and a variety of other factors.

Shepherd, George W., Jr. **Nonaligned Black Africa: An International Subsystem.** Lexington (Mass.) : Heath (for the Center on International Race Relations), 1970, 151 p.
A survey of the African role in international politics by a University of Denver political scientist.

Strauch, Hanspeter F. **Panafrika: kontinentale Weltmacht im Werden? Anfänge, Wachstum und Zukunft der afrikanischen Einigungsbestrebungen.** Zurich: Atlantis-Verlag, 1964, 416 p.
This book, by a Swiss lawyer who was born in Africa, is a detailed and objective account of the beginnings and growth of the idea of African unity.

Thiam, Doudou. **The Foreign Policy of African States.** New York: Praeger, 1965, 134 p.
The former Foreign Minister of the Republic of Senegal provides an incisive and lucid assessment of the ideological bases and the political and economic determinants of the foreign policies of African states. The French original appeared as "La Politique étrangère des états africains" (Paris: Presses Universitaires, 1963, 166 p.).

Touval, Saadia. **The Boundary Politics of Independent Africa.** Cambridge: Harvard University Press, 1972, 334 p.
A detailed analysis of independent Africa's relatively pacific border disputes, tracing the evolution of the O.A.U.'s commitment to a status-quo policy for African boundaries.

Williams, G. Mennen. **Africa for the Africans.** Grand Rapids: Eerdmans, 1969, 218 p.
The former U.S. Assistant Secretary of State for African Affairs surveys the continent, highlighting its problems and accomplishments. He calls for a greater U.S. investment in African economies in order to assure the stability and effectiveness of African political systems.

Woronoff, Jon. **Organizing African Unity.** Metuchen (N.J.) : Scarecrow Press, 1970, 703 p.
A comprehensive, detailed historical analysis of the Organization of African Unity from 1963 to 1970.

Youlou, Fulbert. **J'accuse la Chine.** Paris: Éditions de la Table Ronde, 1966, 253 p.
The former president of Congo (Brazzaville) "exposes" the grand conspiracy launched by the Chinese Communists and their African accomplices throughout the continent, and above all in his own country.

Zartman, I. William. **International Relations in the New Africa.** Englewood Cliffs: Prentice-Hall, 1966, 175 p.
An analytical examination of the international relations of African states. The author combines historical perspective with a systematic assessment of the problems of national interest and security, alliance relationships and conflicting ideologies, patterns of regional unity, and the influences on foreign policy emanating from the process of development.

Economic

See also Economic Factors, p. 49; (The United States) Foreign Policy, p. 229; (Israel) Foreign Relations, p. 631; (China) Foreign Relations, p. 702; other subsections under (Africa) General and the sections for specific African countries and regions.

Andreis, Mario. **L'Africa e la Communità Economica Europea.** Turin: Einaudi, 1967, 444 p.
A study of the relationship between African states and the European Economic Community.

Green, Reginald Herbold and Krishna, K. G. V. **Economic Co-operation in Africa: Retrospect and Prospect.** New York: Oxford University Press (for the University College, Nairobi), 1967, 160 p.
Two University of East Africa economists have written a short discussion of the problems of past attempts at African economic integration and an analysis of future prospects.

Green, Reginald Herbold and Seidman, Ann. **Unity or Poverty? The Economics of Pan-Africanism.** Baltimore: Penguin, 1968, 363 p.
Two Americans argue that economic rationality and a stronger bargaining position in the international economy both require the ultimate economic unification of the African continent.

Little, Ian Malcolm David. **Aid to Africa: An Appraisal of U.K. Policy for Aid to Africa South of the Sahara.** New York: Macmillan, 1964, 76 p.
An informative essay.

Mutharika, B. W. T. **Toward Multinational Economic Cooperation in Africa.** New York: Praeger, 1972, 434 p.
This study is strong on data about agricultural and industrial commerce of African countries and the extent of current multinational coöperation among them, and weak on analysis of political and economic factors affecting integration.

Neumark, Solomon Daniel. **Foreign Trade and Economic Development in Africa: A Historical Perspective.** Stanford: Stanford University, Food Research Institute, 1964, 222 p.
An analysis of the impact of foreign trade on the internal development of African countries.

Okigbo, Pius Nwabufo C. **Africa and the Common Market.** Evanston: Northwestern University Press, 1967, 183 p.
The distinguished Nigerian economist and negotiator of the E.E.C.-Nigerian agreement of July 1966 gives a detailed analysis of the opportunities and problems of various forms of economic relationships between African economies and the Common Market. His main emphasis is on the former British territories and their options.

Problems of Foreign Aid. New York: Oxford University Press (for the Institute of Public Administration, University College, Dar es Salaam), 1966, 289 p.
Papers delivered at the Conference on Public Policy at the University of East Africa at Dar es Salaam in November 1964.

Robson, Peter. **Economic Integration in Africa.** Evanston: Northwestern University Press, 1968, 320 p.
An assessment, by a professor of economics at University College, Nairobi, of the various attempts of African states to achieve economic integration.

Saint Marc, Michèle. **Commerce extérieur de développement: le cas de la zone franc.** Paris: Société d'Édition d'Enseignement Supérieur, 1968, 367 p.
A detailed analysis of the external trade and financial problems of the former French possessions.

Stewart, Ian G. and Ord, H. W., *eds.* **African Primary Products and International Trade.** Edinburgh: University Press, 1965, 218 p.
A collection of papers delivered at an international seminar at the University of Edinburgh, September 1964, by economists from Africa, Great Britain and the United States.

Stokke, Baard Richard. **Soviet and Eastern European Trade and Aid in Africa.** New York: Praeger, 1967, 326 p.
In a comprehensive country-by-country study a development economist at the Stanford Research Institute analyzes and describes economic relations during the period 1955 to 1966. The well-organized statistical data make this volume useful both as a reference work and a general analytical study.

Streeten, Paul. **Aid to Africa: A Policy Outline for the 1970's.** New York: Praeger, 1972, 169 p.
This study by an experienced practitioner of development economics combines an incisive critique of current economic indices for measuring the efficacy of aid programs with specific policy proposals.

Vinay, Bernard. **L'Afrique commerce avec l'Afrique.** Paris: Presses Universitaires, 1968, 213 p.
The author argues that Africa needs genuine economic coöperation and joint planning to create complementary economies more than institutional structures such as payments unions.

Zartman, I. William. **The Politics of Trade Negotiations between Africa and the European Economic Community.** Princeton: Princeton University Press, 1971, 243 p.
Weak nations can win considerable concessions in negotiations with stronger nations, argues a professor of political science at New York University. The strategies, techniques and limits of such negotiations are carefully assessed.

ECONOMIC AND SOCIAL PROBLEMS

See also Colonial Problems; Decolonization, p. 36; Problems of New Nations, p. 36; Social, Cultural and Religious Factors, p. 39; Economic Factors, p. 49; (Africa) General Surveys, p. 776; and the sections for specific African countries and regions.

Andreski, Stanislav. **The African Predicament: A Study in the Pathology of Modernisation.** New York: Atherton Press, 1969, 237 p.
Addressing general readers more than his fellow sociologists, Professor Andreski discusses a series of central problems faced by African states. Though the author's pessimism about Africa's future is evident, the lack of an explicit central organizing theme leaves the book's overall argument somewhat out of focus.

Ashby, Sir Eric. **African Universities and Western Tradition.** Cambridge: Harvard University Press, 1964, 113 p.
These thoughtful and perceptive essays challenge many of the premises on which African universities have been founded and set forth patterns of adaptation which merit wide consideration.

Bachelet, Michel. **Systèmes fonciers et réformes agraires en Afrique noire.** Paris: Librairie Générale de Droit, 1968, 679 p.
A massive study of agriculture and agrarian reforms in Black Africa.

Badouin, Robert. **Les Banques de développement en Afrique.** Paris: Pedone, 1964, 271 p.
Detailed documentation on financial institutions and their laws in French-speaking Africa.

Badouin, Robert. **Le Développement économique en Afrique occidentale. I: Structures et caractères communs.** Paris: Le Livre Africain, 1969, 173 p.
A useful analysis of the social, demographic and political factors which influence economic development in Africa.

Bauer, Gebhard. **Die Wirtschaft Afrikas: unter besonderer Berücksichtigung finanzieller Aspekte.** Frankfurt/Main: Knapp, 1963, 441 p.
A guide for the businessman describing the basic economic factors about each African country.

Beling, Willard A., ed. **The Role of Labor in African Nation-Building.** New York: Praeger, 1968, 204 p.
Papers originally presented by a group of academics and government officials at a conference in December 1965 at the University of Southern California.

Biebuyck, Daniel, ed. **African Agrarian Systems.** New York: Oxford University Press (for the International African Institute), 1963, 407 p.
Professor Biebuyck's introductory essay gives continuity and comparability to a series of papers presented at the second International African Seminar held at Lovanium University (Leopoldville) in January 1960.

Bohannan, Paul and Dalton, George, eds. **Markets in Africa.** Evanston: Northwestern University Press, 1962, 762 p.
An analysis of the role of markets in African social and economic life. The papers are based, on the whole, on research done in the 1950s.

Brass, William and Others. **The Demography of Tropical Africa.** Princeton: Princeton University Press, 1968, 539 p.
A group of demographers, all formerly at the Office of Population Research at Princeton University, have collaborated on a comprehensive volume containing a wealth of statistical data. Included are a series of general essays as well as a number of country studies.

Brooks, Hugh C. and El-Ayouty, Yassin, eds. **Refugees South of the Sahara: An African Dilemma.** Westport: Negro Universities Press, 1970, 307 p.
Papers originally presented in connection with St. John's University's 1967 Symposium on Refugees, together with short comments and critiques.

Caldwell, John C. and Okonjo, Chukuka, eds. **The Population of Tropical Africa.** New York: Columbia University Press, 1968, 457 p.
A selection of papers, largely by African scholars, on demographic problems of the continent. The papers were presented at the First African Population Conference at Ibadan in 1966.

Davies, Ioan. **African Trade Unions.** Baltimore: Penguin, 1966, 255 p.
A comprehensive survey providing a scholarly examination of the economic and social forces influencing the trade-union movement, the impact of different colonial policies, the political role of trade unions both before and after independence and the politics of international trade unionism in Africa.

De Gregori, Thomas R. **Technology and the Economic Development of the Tropical African Frontier.** Cleveland: Press of Case Western Reserve University, 1969, 531 p.
An economist argues that the diffusion of ideas, not the investment of foreign capital, generated technological and economic development in Africa.

Dumont, René. **False Start in Africa.** New York: Praeger, 1966, 320 p.
A professional agronomist with a penetrating and critical grasp of the dynamics of social and political change examines the dilemmas of economic and social development in French-speaking Africa. The French original was published as "L'Afrique noire est mal partie" (Paris: Éditions du Seuil, 1962, 286 p.).

Ewing, A. F. **Industry in Africa.** New York: Oxford University Press, 1968, 139 p.
An economist with experience in the U.N. Economic Commission for Africa argues for industrialization projects with linkages which will lead to structural changes in African economies. Primarily addressed to policy-makers and planners.

Farer, Tom J., ed. **Financing African Development.** Cambridge: M.I.T. Press, 1965, 245 p.
A collection of essays dealing with a wide range of economic, administrative, legal and ideological problems concerning African economic development, by members of the M.I.T. Fellows in Africa Program.

Gluckman, Max. **Order and Rebellion in Tribal Africa.** New York: Free Press of Glencoe, 1963, 273 p.
Collected essays by a well-known anthropologist.

Hance, William Adams. **African Economic Development.** New York: Praeger (for the Council on Foreign Relations), rev. ed., 1967, 326 p.
While giving an overall picture of staggering underdevelopment, Professor Hance's revision of his 1958 book isolates certain pockets of measurable progress which encourage one's view of Africa's long-run prospects. This country-by-country survey carries the analysis up to the developments of the mid-1960s.

Hance, William Adams. **Population, Migration, and Urbanization in Africa.** New York: Columbia University Press, 1970, 450 p.
In this excellent volume Professor Hance asserts that there *is* a population problem in Africa, that the land cannot support the needs of the population, despite comparatively low densities in most areas of the continent.

Hausman, Warren H., ed. **Managing Economic Development in Africa.** Cambridge: M.I.T. Press, 1963, 253 p.
A collection of papers presented at an evaluation conference for M.I.T. fellows who had been working with problems of economic development in various parts of Africa. The papers vary widely in quality but raise many of the problems which are encountered by those assisting with economic development.

Herskovits, Melville Jean and Harwitz, Mitchell, eds. **Economic Transition in Africa.** Evanston: Northwestern University Press, 1964, 444 p.
A collection of papers on economic change in Africa delivered at the Conference on Indigenous and Induced Elements in the Economics of Subsaharan Africa held at Northwestern University in 1961 under the auspices of the Social Science Research

Council. Of particular interest is the attempt at an interdisciplinary treatment of economic problems.

Hunter, Guy. **The Best of Both Worlds? A Challenge on Development Policies in Africa.** New York: Oxford University Press (for the Institute of Race Relations), 1967, 132 p.
A concise treatment of the basic problems of modernization in Africa. Among the author's recommendations is a call for a restructuring of African educational systems away from conventional secondary school and university curricula and toward more vocational and technical training oriented to the task of rural economic development.

Jucker-Fleetwood, Erin Elver. **Money and Finance in Africa.** New York: Praeger, 1964, 335 p.
An analysis of monetary policies and a description of the establishment of central banks in Ghana, Morocco, Nigeria, the Rhodesias, Nyasaland, Sudan and Tunisia.

Kamarck, Andrew Martin. **The Economics of African Development.** New York: Praeger, rev. ed., 1971, 352 p.
An excellent, comprehensive survey of sub-Saharan Africa's economic history and contemporary problems by the Director of the Economics Development Institute of the World Bank.

Karefa-Smart, John, *ed.* **Africa: Progress Through Cooperation.** New York: Dodd (for the Council on World Tensions), 1966, 288 p.
Papers on various aspects of social and economic development by distinguished African statesmen, U.N. officials, economists and educators, prepared for a conference sponsored by the Council on World Tensions at Makerere University College in May 1965.

Kuper, Leo and Smith, M. G., *eds.* **Pluralism in Africa.** Berkeley: University of California Press, 1971, 546 p.
Papers dealing "with the nature and social consequences of pluralism, and with problems of social cohesion and change in plural societies," presented by a group of eminent Africanists at a colloquium of the African Studies Center at the University of California in Los Angeles in 1966.

Leduc, Michel. **Les Institutions monétaires africaines: pays francophones.** Paris: Pedone, 1965, 397 p.
A collection of documents dealing with the evolution of monetary institutions in French-speaking Africa.

Lloyd, Peter Cutt, *ed.* **The New Elites of Tropical Africa.** New York: Oxford University Press (for the International African Institute), 1966, 390 p.
Papers presented at the International African Institute's Sixth Seminar on the New Elites of Tropical Africa held at Ibadan in July 1964. The editor provides an informative general introduction.

Lynd, G. E. **The Politics of African Trade Unionism.** New York: Praeger, 1968, 198 p.
An expert on international labor affairs makes a comprehensive survey of trade unions in English-speaking Africa up to 1965.

Lystad, Robert Arthur, *ed.* **The African World: A Survey of Social Research.** New York: Praeger, 1965, 575 p.
Essays by prominent American and British scholars which, by their thoroughness and mastery of the interrelated areas of historical, physical and cultural disciplines, constitute an indispensable handbook. Prepared under the auspices of the African Studies Association.

Mazrui, Ali Al'Amin. **Violence and Thought: Essays on Social Tensions in Africa.** New York: Humanities Press, 1969, 351 p.
These essays reflect the author's capacity for the analysis of political and social behavior in psychological terms. Mazrui, formerly the head of the political science department at Makerere University College in Uganda, is now teaching in the United States.

Meynaud, Jean and Salah Bey, Anisse. **Trade Unionism in Africa: A Study of Its Growth and Orientation.** London: Methuen, 1967, 242 p.
The authors of this useful survey point out to the conflict between European models and African conditions. The French original appeared as "Le Syndicalisme africain: évolution et perspectives" (Paris: Payot, 1963, 260 p.).

Moumouni, Abdou. **Education in Africa.** New York: Praeger, 1968, 319 p.
The author, an African professor, urges a radical restructuring of educational systems in black Africa to rid independent African societies of neo-colonialist influences. Recent reforms in Guinea and Mali are his favored models.

O'Connor, Anthony Michael. **The Geography of Tropical African Development.** New York: Pergamon, 1971, 207 p.
A matter-of-fact survey of the distribution of resources, agricultural and industrial production, trade and income among sub-Saharan nations; it underscores the general conclusion that those who have will get more.

Passin, Herbert and Jones-Quartey, K. A. B., *eds.* **Africa, the Dynamics of Change.** Ibadan: Ibadan University Press (for the Congress for Cultural Freedom), 1963, 262 p.
Excerpts from papers and discussions of the Ibadan Seminar on Representative Government and National Progress sponsored by the Congress for Cultural Freedom in March 1959.

Robinson, Edward Austin Gossage, *ed.* **Economic Development for Africa South of the Sahara.** New York: St. Martin's Press, 1964, 743 p.
A voluminous collection of papers on development problems in Africa, originally presented in 1961 at the Third Regional Conference of the International Economic Association in Addis Ababa.

Robinson, Ronald, *ed.* **African Development Planning.** Cambridge: Cambridge University, Overseas Studies Committee, 1964, 147 p.
Papers on planning in Africa, presented in the fall of 1963 at the Cambridge Conference on Development Planning at Queens' College, Cambridge.

Robson, Peter and Lury, D. A., *eds.* **The Economies of Africa.** Evanston: Northwestern University Press, 1969, 528 p.
Single-economy studies of Algeria, Cameroon, Ghana, Ivory Coast, Liberia, Nigeria and Sudan plus analyses of the East African and Central African economies. In addition to these separate essays by well-known economists, the editors include a general introductory analysis of the African economies.

Samuels, L. H., *ed.* **African Studies in Income and Wealth.** Chicago: Quadrangle Books, 1963, 433 p.
Papers from a Conference of the International Association for Research in Income and Wealth held in Addis Ababa in January 1961 to exchange information on conceptual and practical problems of national income accounting in Africa.

Spiro, Herbert John, *ed.* **Patterns of African Development: Five Comparisons.** Englewood Cliffs: Prentice-Hall, 1967, 144 p.
Essays on general problems of social change and political development in Africa. Claude Welch's comparison of modernization in Japan and Africa is of particular note.

Steward, Julian Haynes, *ed.* **Contemporary Change in Traditional Societies.** Volume I: Introduction and African Tribes. Urbana: University of Illinois Press, 1967, 519 p.
An introductory essay on modernization by the editor is followed by three case studies of individual African societies in transition: the Ukaguru of Tanzania, the Kipsigis of Kenya and the Anaguta of Nigeria.

Tradition et modernisme en Afrique noire. Paris: Éditions du Seuil, 1965, 317 p.
Papers and discussions from a conference dealing with modernization in Africa held in the Ivory Coast in 1962.

Tregear, Peter and Burley, John, *eds.* **African Development and Europe.** New York: Pergamon, 1970, 170 p.
This volume of papers and short accounts of ensuing discussions deals mainly with general development problems in Africa.

Treyer, Claude. **Sahara 1956–1962.** Paris: Société d'Édition "Les Belles Lettres," 1966, 344 p.
An economic survey of the Sahara in the years from 1956 to 1962.

Whetham, Edith H. and Currie, Jean I. **The Economics of African Countries.** New York: Cambridge University Press, 1969, 288 p.
Two economists who have taught in Nigeria have collaborated on an introductory text in economics designed primarily for African students.

Wilde, John C. de and Others. **Experiences with Agricultural Development in Tropical Africa.** Baltimore: Johns Hopkins Press (for the International Bank for Reconstruction and Development), 1967, 2 v.
Case studies of agricultural schemes in Kenya, Mali, Chad, Upper Volta, Ivory Coast and Tanzania. An important, comprehensive work.

NORTH AFRICA

GENERAL

See also Comparative Government, p. 18; Problems of New Nations, p. 36; Second World War, p. 144; The Postwar World, p. 178; (Middle East) General Surveys and Political Problems, p. 611; The Arab World, p. 616; (Africa) General, p. 776.

Amin, Samir. **L'Économie du Maghreb.** Paris: Éditions de Minuit, 1966, 2 v.
Volume I, "La Colonisation et la décolonisation," is a social and economic history of Algeria, Tunisia and Morocco during the period of French control and the beginnings of independence. Volume II, "Les Perspectives d'avenir," deals with the contemporary economic experience of the Maghreb together with a critical analysis and a projection of future development.

Amin, Samir. **Le Maghreb moderne.** Paris: Éditions de Minuit, 1970, 243 p.
Essentially a summary history and handbook of the Maghreb, the small volume is notable for its sharply etched analysis of political forces and their economic and social content.

Annuaire de l'Afrique du Nord, 1962– . Paris: Centre National de la Recherche Scientifique, 1963– .
A most impressive series of annual volumes of articles, documents and bibliographies dealing with Tunisia, Libya, Morocco and Algeria. The tenth volume, covering 1971, was published in 1972.

al-'Aqqād, Ṣalaḥ. **al-Sīyāsah wa-al-mujtama' lī al-Maghrib al-'Arabī.** Cairo: Institute of Arab Studies and Research, League of Arab States, 1971, 214 p.
A general survey of society and politics in Northwest Africa. In addition to the growth of the new governmental systems, the author focuses on two major problems: Arabization and Maghreb unity.

Berque, Jacques. **French North Africa: The Maghrib between Two World Wars.** New York: Praeger, 1967, 422 p.
This penetrating study by a distinguished Arabist combines literary quality with knowledge of the area. The French original appeared as "Le Maghreb entre deux guerres" (Paris: Éditions du Seuil, 1962, 444 p.).

Brace, Richard Munthe. **Morocco, Algeria, Tunisia.** Englewood Cliffs: Prentice-Hall, 1964, 184 p.
A historian's narrative, straightforward and brief, of the Maghreb up to the 1960s.

Brown, Leon Carl, *ed.* **State and Society in Independent North Africa.** Washington: Middle East Institute, 1966, 332 p.
Fourteen essays, some of them brilliant, growing out of a Middle East Institute conference.

Cooley, John K. **Baal, Christ, and Mohammed: Religion and Revolution in North Africa.** New York: Holt, Rinehart and Winston, 1965, 369 p.
A first-rate and highly readable introduction to contemporary North Africa by a well-known American correspondent.

Dresch, Jean and Others. **Industrialisation au Maghreb.** Paris: Maspéro, 1963, 269 p.
Papers presented at a colloquium held in Algiers in January 1963.

Gallagher, Charles F. **The United States and North Africa: Morocco, Algeria and Tunisia.** Cambridge: Harvard University Press, 1963, 275 p.
A solid survey by a long-time associate in North Africa of the American Universities Field Staff.

Gellner, Ernest and Micaud, Charles Antoine, *eds.* **Arabs and Berbers: From Tribe to Nation in North Africa.** Lexington (Mass.): Lexington Books, 1972, 448 p.
A series of contributions on society and politics in the Maghreb, especially significant for new evaluations of the Berbers' role.

Hermassi, Elbaki. **Leadership and National Development in North Africa: A Comparative Study.** Berkeley: University of California Press, 1972, 241 p.
A study of the emergence of Morocco, Algeria and Tunisia as national societies with their own institutions, élites and policies for development. The comparison is instructive, and the discussion of theory and method refreshingly skeptical.

Moore, Clement Henry. **Politics in North Africa: Algeria, Morocco, and Tunisia.** Boston: Little, Brown, 1970, 360 p.
A comparative study of the three Maghreb countries, containing useful information along with much theorizing on political development.

Nehrt, Lee Charles. **The Political Climate for Private Foreign Investment: With Special Reference to North Africa.** New York: Praeger, 1970, 391 p.
This study explores the contrasting behavior of Algeria, Tunisia and Morocco toward foreign investors.

Peyrouton, Bernard Marcel. **Histoire générale du Maghreb: Algérie, Maroc, Tunisie, des origines à nos jours.** Paris: Michel, 1966, 284 p.
A lively historical synthesis from the earliest times up to independence, enriched by the author's quarter-century of experience in North Africa as administrator at the highest level until 1949 and since then as a private businessman and journalist.

Tiano, André. **Le Maghreb entre les mythes: l'économie nord-africaine depuis l'indépendance.** Paris: Presses Universitaires, 1967, 623 p.
A critical study of economic developments in the Maghreb.

Toynbee, Arnold Joseph. **Between Niger and Nile.** New York: Oxford University Press, 1965, 133 p.
Travel impressions of North Africa by the well-known English historian.

Woolman, David S. **Rebels in the Rif: Abd El Krim and the Rif Rebellion.** Stanford: Stanford University Press, 1968, 257 p.
The Berber rebellion in Spanish Morocco in the 1920s was a classic example of guerrilla war, successful until France joined Spain to put it down with overwhelming force. This is the most accurate and detailed account of it to appear.

Zartman, I. William. **Government and Politics in Northern Africa.** New York: Praeger, 1963, 205 p.
A competent comparative survey of contemporary political practices and problems in eight countries of northern Africa, from Morocco to Somalia.

MOROCCO

See also Problems of New Nations, p. 36; Second World War, p. 144; The Postwar World, p. 178; (The United States) Foreign Policy, p. 229; (France) Recent History, p. 396; Biographies, Memoirs and Addresses, p. 400; Foreign Policy, p. 404; (Middle East) General Surveys and Political Problems, p. 611; The Arab World, p. 616; (Africa) General, p. 776; (North Africa) General, p. 793.

Barbour, Nevill. **Morocco.** New York: Walker, 1965, 239 p.
Modern Morocco viewed against its prestigious past by a veteran British commentator on Arab affairs.

Ben Barka, Abdelkader. **El Mehdi ben Barka, mon frère.** Paris: Laffont, 1966, 251 p.
A personal and rather light biography which covers Ben Barka's participation in the nationalist movement and the post-independence politics of Morocco. The story ends before his disappearance.

Ben Barka, El Mehdi. **al-Ikhtīyār al-thawrī fī al-Maghrib.** Beirut: Dār al-Talī'ah, 1966, 206 p.
The author, whose subsequent kidnapping and murder culminated in a big scandal in France, provides a number of reports and documents on the political and social conditions in Morocco and on the political ideology of his party: The National Union of Popular Forces.

Bernard, Stéphane. **The Franco-Moroccan Conflict, 1943-1956.** New Haven: Yale University Press (for the Carnegie Endowment for International Peace), 1968, 680 p.
A careful history and analysis of the Franco-Moroccan "decolonization" dispute by an experienced Belgian administrator and scholar. The original version appeared as "Le Conflit franco-marocain, 1943-1956" (Brussels: Institut de Sociologie de l'Université Libre de Bruxelles, 1963, 3 v.).

Blair, Leon Borden. **Western Window in the Arab World.** Austin: University of Texas Press, 1970, 328 p.
A misleading title for an account by an American military official of U.S.-Moroccan relations during the two decades following the World War II landings. Mohammed V and the U.S. armed forces come out with high marks, in contrast to France and American diplomacy.

Brignon, Jean and Others. **Histoire du Maroc.** Paris: Hatier, 1967, 416 p.
This general history of Morocco, written collectively by a group of French and Moroccan historians, pays particular attention to economic and social factors. There are useful bibliographies.

Cohen, Mark I. and Hahn, Lorna. **Morocco: Old Land, New Nation.** New York: Praeger, 1966, 309 p.
A useful introductory survey.

The Economic Development of Morocco. Baltimore: Johns Hopkins Press, 1966, 356 p.
This informative and well-documented study is a report of a mission organized by the International Bank for Reconstruction and Development at the request of the Government of Morocco.

al-Fāsī, 'Allāl. **al-Naqd al-dhātī.** Beirut, Dār al-Kashshāf, 1966, 447 p.
The leader of the Istiqlāl party in Morocco holds forth on the questions that preoccupy Moroccans in the intellectual, religious, social and economic fields.

Hall, Luella J. **The United States and Morocco, 1776-1956.** Metuchen (N.J.): Scarecrow Press, 1971, 1,114 p.
A book worth noting for its faithful though more or less indiscriminate attention to completeness and detail, reflecting years of research in unpublished and published sources.

Halstead, John P. **Rebirth of a Nation: The Origins and Rise of Moroccan Nationalism, 1912-1944.** Cambridge: Center for Middle Eastern Studies, 1967, 323 p.
A description of the nationalist movement in its early reformist phase, prior to the development of a strong political separatist movement. Especially good on intellectual influences, Eastern and Western, and their adaptation to conditions in Morocco.

Maxwell, Gavin. **Lords of the Atlas: The Rise and Fall of the House of Glaoua, 1893-1956.** New York: Dutton, 1966, 318 p.
A colorful biography of the family which held ruthless sway in parts of Morocco during the French Protectorate.

Muratet, Roger. **On a tué Ben Barka.** Paris: Plon, 1967, 378 p.
An account of the murder of the Moroccan exile politician Ben Barka, an event which had complicated repercussions on Moroccan-French relations. The author thinks that the assassination was primarily a Moroccan undertaking.

Nyrop, Richard F. and Others. **Area Handbook for Morocco.** Washington: G.P.O., 1972, 403 p.
A useful reference volume with a bibliography, prepared by the Foreign Area Studies at the American University.

Renard-Payen, Oliver. **L'Expérience marocaine d'unité de juridiction et de séparation des contentieux.** Paris: Librairie Générale de Droit, 1964, 322 p.
An analysis of the system of administrative justice in Morocco, and its importance as a model for other countries of French-speaking Africa.

Robert, Jacques. **La Monarchie marocaine.** Paris: Librairie Générale de Droit, 1963, 350 p.
A study of government and constitution in modern Morocco.

Scham, Alan. **Lyautey in Morocco: Protectorate Administration, 1912-1925.** Berkeley: University of California Press, 1970, 272 p.

A rather dry and uncritical study of French colonial government in Morocco as exemplified by the achievements of the great hero of French imperial history, Marshal Lyautey, Resident General in Morocco from 1912 to 1925.

Spillmann, Georges. **Du protectorat à l'indépendance: Maroc 1912-1955.** Paris: Plon, 1967, 245 p.
Memoirs of a French official directly involved in Moroccan affairs from the time of Lyautey to the end of the French protectorate. The author places a heavy load of blame on the United States for making impossible a dialogue between France and Morocco and an orderly transfer from protectorate to independence.

Stewart, Charles Frank. **The Economy of Morocco, 1912-1962.** Cambridge: Harvard University Press (distributed for the Center for Middle Eastern Studies), 1964, 234 p.
A solid and well-written economic history.

Tiano, André. **La Politique économique et financière du Maroc indépendant.** Paris: Presses Universitaires, 1963, 284 p.
Studies of economic and financial policies and institutions of Morocco.

Trout, Frank E. **Morocco's Saharan Frontiers.** Geneva: Droz, 1969, 561 p.
A detailed, scholarly study which includes an exhaustive history of the Moroccan-Algerian boundary question up to 1956.

Waterbury, John. **The Commander of the Faithful: The Moroccan Political Elite—A Study in Segmented Politics.** New York: Columbia University Press, 1970, 367 p.
A scholarly treatment of the influence of traditional patterns of behavior on contemporary Moroccan politics, particularly how this has resulted in factionalism and immobilism among the nation's political élite.

Zartman, I. William. **Morocco: Problems of New Power.** New York: Atherton Press (for the American Association for Middle East Studies), 1964, 276 p.
The author makes the decision-making process and the resolution of five major issues an effective vehicle for his exploration of modern Moroccan government and politics.

ALGERIA

See also Socialism, p. 24; (War) General, p. 108; Guerrilla Warfare; Armed Insurrection, p. 118; Second World War, p. 144; The Postwar World, p. 178; (The United States) Foreign Policy, p. 229; (France) Recent History, p. 396; Biographies, Memoirs and Addresses, p. 400; Foreign Policy, p. 404; Military Policy, p. 407; (Middle East) General Surveys and Political Problems, p. 611; The Arab World, p. 616; Arab-Israeli Conflict, p. 633; (Africa) General, p. 776; (North Africa) General, p. 793.

Ait Ahmed, Hocine. **La Guerre et l'après-guerre.** Paris: Éditions de Minuit, 1964, 204 p.
A collection of essays, reports and interviews by one of the leaders of the Algerian Revolution who turned against Ben Bella. His thesis is that within collectivism "bureaucratic authoritarianism" can destroy liberty and that this is what Ben Bella was allowing to happen.

Arcy, François d' and Others. **Essais sur l'économie de l'Algérie nouvelle.** Paris: Presses Universitaires, 1965, 254 p.
Three studies dealing with rural administration, agrarian reform and industrialization in contemporary Algeria.

Bennabī, Malek. **Afāq jazā'iriyah.** Algiers: Maktabat al-Nahḍah, 1964, 231 p.
A leading Algerian intellectual discusses the cultural and ideological directions the Algerian Revolution should take.

Beyssade, Pierre. **La Guerre d'Algérie, 1954-1962.** Paris: Éditions Planète, 1968, 263 p.
Not the definitive history of the Algerian war, but a very informed and dispassionate account, political rather than military, by a high-ranking civil servant in Algeria throughout the period.

Boudiaf, Mohamed. **Où va l'Algérie?** Paris: Éditions Librairie de l'Étoile, 1964, 208 p.
One of the top leaders of the Algerian Revolution, imprisoned by the French in the period 1956-62, tells the story of his imprisonment by the new regime in Algeria in 1963 and explains his militant opposition to it.

Boualam, Saïd. **L'Algérie sans la France.** Paris: Éditions France-Empire, 1964, 382 p.
A narration of the events that took place in Algeria between 1962 and 1964. The

author is an Algerian Muslim who was a prominent leader of the harkis (Muslim soldiers in the French Army).

Brace, Richard Munthe and Brace, Joan. **Algerian Voices.** Princeton: Van Nostrand, 1965, 233 p.
An absorbing account of encounters with Algerians in 1961–62 during the closing stages of the war of independence, by two Americans whose mission was to establish homes for children orphaned by the war.

Buy, François. **La République algérienne démocratique et populaire.** Paris: Librairie Française, 1965, 257 p.
An indignant French documentation of events in Algeria under Ben Bella 1962–65, and of its increasing involvement economically and militarily with the U.S.S.R. and its allies.

Chaliand, Gérard and Minces, Juliette. **L'Algérie indépendante: bilan d'une révolution nationale.** Paris: Maspero, 1972, 175 p.
The authors of this survey of Algeria since 1962 emphasize economic and social aspects and conclude that there has not been a profound economic and social revolution.

Clausen, Ursel, *comp.* **Der algerische Sozialismus.** Opladen: Leske (for the Deutsches Orient-Institut), 1969, 463 p.
A collection of documents, originally published in French from 1962 to 1966 in various Algerian publications, illustrating the views of the governments of Ben Bella and Boumediène on politics, economy and foreign relations. There is an introduction and a useful bibliography.

Courrière, Yves. **La Guerre d'Algérie.** Paris: Fayard, 1968–71, 4 v.
A very detailed account of the last years of French presence in Algeria.

Danan, Yves Maxime. **La Vie politique à Alger de 1940 à 1944.** Paris: Librairie Générale de Droit, 1963, 346 p.
In this volume, the author traces the development of political opinion of Europeans in Algeria from the time of the French capitulation through liberation in 1944.

Gordon, David C. **The Passing of French Algeria.** New York: Oxford University Press, 1966, 265 p.
An able historical analysis of the Algerian struggle for identity.

Guérin, Daniel. **L'Algérie qui se cherche.** Paris: Présence Africaine, 1964, 105 p.
A lucid and sympathetic account of Algeria in 1963 by a pioneer French anti-colonialist.

Henissart, Paul. **Wolves in the City: The Death of French Algeria.** New York: Simon and Schuster, 1970, 508 p.
A journalist's colorful story of the crisis of 1961, the terror campaign of the O.A.S. and the end of French rule in Algeria.

Humbaraci, Arslan. **Algeria: A Revolution That Failed; A Political History since 1954.** New York: Praeger, 1966, 308 p.
A veteran Arabic-speaking journalist whose enthusiasm for the Algerian Revolution gradually gave way to post-independence disillusion has drawn on personal experience and scholarship in this detailed and well-written account.

al-Ibrāhimī, Muḥammad al-Bashīr. **'Uyūn al-baṣā'ir.** Algiers: Société Nationale d'Édition et Diffusion, 1971, 703 p.
A collection of the editorials written for the newspaper *al-Baṣā'ir*, by its editor and president of the Algerian Association of 'Ulama. Mr. al-Ibrāhimī was one of the intellectual and spiritual leaders of the Algerian Revolution.

Jacob, Alain. **D'une Algérie à l'autre.** Paris: Grasset, 1963, 237 p.
A collection of articles by a correspondent for *Le Monde* in Algeria from 1958–1962. While the author has injected some after-thoughts, he has also succeeded in retaining the freshness of his reactions to the harsh events of those years.

Lacheraf, Mostefa. **L'Algérie: nation et société.** Paris: Maspéro, 1965, 346 p.
Essays by an Algerian scholar and nationalist, providing an introduction to the revolutionary history of modern Algeria.

Laffont, Pierre. **L'Expiation.** Paris: Plon, 1968, 349 p.
A prominent French Algerian, editor from 1945 to 1953 of *L'Echo d'Oran*—a news-

paper that was founded by his great-grandfather—reviews the Algerian war, describes the exodus of French and European Algerians in 1962, and criticizes the government and people of France for lack of sympathy for the French in Algeria.

Lapassat, Étienne-Jean. **La Justice en Algérie, 1962-1969.** Paris: Fondation Nationale des Science Politiques, 1968, 184 p.
A balanced analysis of the judicial structure in Algeria through the study of the factors that shaped the independent state of Algeria.

Launay, Michel. **Paysans algériens: la terre, la vigne et les hommes.** Paris: Éditions du Seuil, 1963, 430 p.
The author, who served with the military in Algeria in 1960-61, presents a detailed and documented account of social and economic conditions of the Algerian peasants.

Lebjaoui, Mohamed. **Vérités sur la révolution algérienne.** Paris: Gallimard, 1970, 249 p.
One man's truths about the Algerian war of independence, especially the inside story of the Front de Libération Nationale, its leaders, its victory and its postwar feuds. Lebjaoui was closely associated with Ben Bella.

Massu, Jacques. **La Vraie bataille d'Alger.** Paris: Plon, 1971, 391 p.
France's outspoken "chef des paras" gives his version of the battle of 1957 in Algiers.

Merle, Robert. **Ahmed Ben Bella.** New York: Walker, 1967, 160 p.
A biography of Ben Bella, based on interviews in 1964-65. The French original appeared as "Ahmed Ben Bella" (Paris: Gallimard, 1965, 184 p.).

Nyrop, Richard F. and Others. **Area Handbook for Algeria.** Washington: G.P.O., 1972, 401 p.
A useful reference volume with a bibliography, prepared by the Foreign Area Studies at the American University.

OAS parle. Paris: Julliard, 1964, 355 p.
A collection of documents, arranged chronologically, telling the story of the Organisation de l'Armée Secrète, established by French officers who refused to surrender after the unsuccessful uprising in Algiers in April 1961.

O'Ballance, Edgar. **The Algerian Insurrection, 1954-62.** Hamden (Conn.): Archon Books, 1967, 231 p.
A brief military history concluding that the French won the military struggle, but lost the political and diplomatic one.

Ohneck, Wolfgang. **Die französische Algerienpolitik von 1919-1939.** Opladen: Westdeutscher Verlag, 1967, 195 p.
A well-documented monograph on the colonial regime in Algeria between the two world wars.

Ortiz, Joseph. **Mes Combats: carnets de route, 1954-1962.** Paris: Éditions de la Pensée Moderne, 1964, 311 p.
A leader in the fight to keep Algeria French describes his disenchantment with the French government and his activities on behalf of a French Algeria in the years from 1954 to 1962.

Ottaway, David and Ottaway, Marina. **Algeria: The Politics of a Socialist Revolution.** Berkeley: University of California Press, 1970, 322 p.
An account of Algerian politics since independence, combining scholarship with firsthand journalism. Personalities and ties of clan come through as the real determinants of Algerian socialism.

Pawera, John C. **Algeria's Infrastructure: An Economic Survey of Transportation, Communication, and Energy Resources.** New York: Praeger, 1964, 234 p.
An analysis useful for those interested in the problem of industrialization in less developed countries.

Perroux, François. **Problèmes de l'Algérie indépendante.** Paris: Presses Universitaires, 1963, 207 p.
Essays dealing with education, agrarian reform, economic development and other issues.

Pickles, Dorothy Maud. **Algeria and France: From Colonialism to Cooperation.** New York: Praeger, 1963, 215 p.
A leading British student of France discusses the impact of the Algerian problem on the politics of postwar France. A helpful guide through this very complex question.

AFRICA

Quandt, William B. **Revolution and Political Leadership: Algeria, 1954–1968.**
Cambridge: M.I.T. Press, 1969, 313 p.
A detailed study of the problems of diversity and conflict among Algerian political leaders which the author traces to differences in the "discontinuous process of political socialization."

Sa'd Allāh, Abu al-Qāsim. **al-Ḥarakah al-waṭanīyah al-Jazā'īriyah.** Beirut: Dār al-Adāb, 1969, 556 p.
A historical account of the Algerian nationalist movement between 1900 and 1930.

Susini, Jean-Jacques. **Histoire de l'O.A.S.: avril–septembre 1961.** Paris: Éditions de la Table Ronde, 1964, 396 p.
A history of the O.A.S., by a leading fighter for a French Algeria and an adversary of de Gaulle's policies.

Taleb, Ahmad. **Lettres de prison, 1957–61.** Algiers: Éditions Nationales Algériennes, 1966, 189 p.
Reflections of an Algerian nationalist who later became the Minister of National Education, written while interned during the Algerian War of Independence.

Tricot, Bernard. **Les Sentiers de la paix: Algérie 1958–1962.** Paris: Plon, 1972, 443 p.
Reminiscences by a trusted follower of de Gaulle who helped to execute the General's policies in Algeria from 1958 to 1962.

Trinquier, Roger. **Le Coup d'etat du 13 mai.** Paris: Editions de l'Esprit Nouveau, 1962, 269 p.
An eye-witness account of the Algiers rebellion of May 13, 1958, that prepared the way for de Gaulle's return to power.

Viratelle, Gérard. **L'Algérie algérienne.** Paris: Économie et Humanism, 1970, 309 p.
A comprehensive study of Algerian economic development, by a correspondent of *Le Monde*.

TUNISIA

See also Problems of New Nations, p. 36; Second World War, p. 144; The Postwar World, p. 178; (The United States) Foreign Policy, p. 229; (France) Recent History, p. 396; Biographies, Memoirs and Addresses, p. 400; Foreign Policy, p. 404; (Middle East) General Surveys and Political Problems, p. 611; The Arab World, p. 616; Arab-Israeli Conflict, p. 633; (Africa) General, p. 776; (North Africa) General, p. 793.

'Abd al-Wahab, Hasan Husni. **Waraqāt 'an al-haḍārah al-'Arabīyah bī Ifriqiyah al-Tunisīyah.** Tunis: Maktabat al-Manār, 1964, 2 v.
Studies and essays on various aspects of Tunisian life and culture by the leading Tunisian historian who died recently.

Bégué, Camille. **Le Message de Bourguiba: une politique de l'homme.** Paris: Hachette, 1972, 331 p.
A laudatory presentation of Habib Bourguiba, President of Tunisia, emphasizing his patriotism, his realism and his humanity.

Beling, Willard A. **Modernization and African Labor: A Tunisian Case Study.** New York: Praeger, 1966, 259 p.
An examination of the influence of Tunisian nationalism and trans-national ideological currents (Pan-Arabism, Pan-Maghrebism and Pan-Africanism) on the international relations of the Tunisian labor movement.

Duwaji, Ghazi. **Economic Development in Tunisia: The Impact and Course of Government Planning.** New York: Praeger, 1968, 222 p.
A description of major aspects of Tunisia's economy, with particular emphasis given to the 1962–1971 Ten Year Plan which includes programs for the private as well as the public sectors of the economy.

Ling, Dwight Leroy. **Tunisia: From Protectorate to Republic.** Bloomington: Indiana University Press, 1967, 273 p.
A rather detailed survey of political history from the French occupation in 1881 to the contemporary problems of nationhood, based on considerable research and experience in the area. A useful bibliography is included.

Micaud, Charles Antoine and Others. **Tunisia: The Politics of Modernization.** New York: Praeger, 1964, 205 p.

A study of French colonial impact on Tunisia and an evaluation of the Tunisian modernization.

Moore, Clement Henry. **Tunisia since Independence: The Dynamics of One-Party Government.** Berkeley: University of California Press, 1965, 230 p.
Professor Moore, in a study rich in data and perception, makes a convincing case for the success in Tunisia of a single-party system which differentiates itself from both Western pluralist and totalitarian models.

Ortner-Heun, Irene. **Tunesien als Wirtschaftspartner.** Cologne: Bundesstelle für Aussenhandelsinformation, 1970, 2 v.
A comprehensive survey of Tunisian economic development.

Reese, Howard C. and Others. **Area Handbook for Republic of Tunisia.** Washington: G.P.O., 1970, 415 p.
A useful reference volume with a bibliography, prepared by the Foreign Area Studies at the American University.

Rous, Jean. **Habib Bourguiba, l'homme d'action de l'Afrique.** Paris: Didier, 1969, 188 p.
The first part of an admiring and not very scholarly study of the political career of the President of Tunisia.

Rudebeck, Lars. **Party and People: A Study of Political Change in Tunisia.** New York: Praeger, 1969, 285 p.
The theme of the book is the mobilization of mass support, through the Socialist Destour Party, for the development of Tunisia.

Ruf, Werner Klaus. **Der Burgibismus und die Aussenpolitik des unabhängigen Tunesien.** Bielefeld: Bertelsmann Universitätsverlag, 1969, 279 p.
The first comprehensive study of Tunisian foreign relations.

Sylvester, Anthony. **Tunisia.** Chester Springs (Pa.): Dufour Editions, 1969, 221 p.
A journalist's general account.

Ziadeh, Nicola A. **Origins of Nationalism in Tunisia.** Beirut: Librairie du Liban, 1969, 167 p.
A well-documented study by a professor at the American University of Beirut.

LIBYA

See also Second World War, p. 144; (The United States) Foreign Policy, p. 229; (Middle East) General Surveys and Political Problems, p. 611; The Arab World, p. 616; Arab-Israeli Conflict, p. 633; (Africa) General, p. 776; (North Africa) General, p. 793.

Andersen, Peter. **Die wirtschaftliche Entwicklung Libyens auf der Grundlage seiner Erdölindustrie.** Bamberg: Urlaub, 1969, 184 p.
A study of Libyan oil industry and economic development.

Farley, Rawle. **Planning for Development in Libya: The Exceptional Economy in the Developing World.** New York: Praeger, 1971, 349 p.
One conclusion of this study is that a capital surplus is no panacea for problems of underdevelopment.

Garian, P. + B., *pseud.* **Libyen: Land der Zukunft in Allahs Garten.** Düsseldorf: Econ-Verlag, 1965, 256 p.
An informal and sympathetic account of modern Libya by a well-traveled German couple.

Ḥakim, Sāmī. **Ḥaqiqat Lībiyā.** Cairo: The Anglo-Egyptian Bookshop, 1968, 350 p.
A study of two major problems that faced Libya in the decade of the sixties: the constitutional disputes over the relation of the federal government to the three states of Tripoli, Cyrenaica and Fezzan, and the question of foreign armed forces on Libyan soil.

Khadduri, Majid. **Modern Libya.** Baltimore: Johns Hopkins Press, 1963, 404 p.
A discussion of Libya's political development since liberation, by the Director of Research at the Center for Middle Eastern Studies at Johns Hopkins.

Kubbah, Abdul Amīr Q. **Libya: Its Oil Industry and Economic System.** Baghdad: The Arab Petro-Economic Research Centre, 1964, 274 p.
A technical study.

Mannā', Muḥammad 'Abd al-Rāziq. **Thawrat al-fātiḥ min Sebtimber.** Cairo: al-Hay'ah al-Miṣriyah al-'Āmmah, 1970, 175 p.
A survey of the September 1, 1969 revolution in Libya.

Mikhā'il, Hinri Anis. **al-'Alāqāt al-Inklīzīyah al-Lībīyah ma' taḥlīl lil-mu'āhadah al-Inklīzīyah al-Lībīyah.** Cairo: al-Hay'ah al-Miṣrīyah al-'Āmmah, 1970, 398 p.
A historical survey of the political military and economic relations between Great Britain and Libya, covering the period from 1882 to the departure of the British in 1970.

Norman, John. **Labor and Politics in Libya and Arab Africa.** New York: Bookman Associates, 1965, 219 p.
A well-done study of the Libyan labor movement in a context of desert, poverty, nationalism and new-found oil.

Nyrop, Richard F. and Others. **Area Handbook for Libya.** Washington: G.P.O., 1973, 317 p.
A useful reference volume with a bibliography, prepared by the Foreign Area Studies at the American University.

Pelt, Adrian. **Libyan Independence and the United Nations: A Case of Planned Decolonization.** New Haven: Yale University Press (for the Carnegie Endowment for International Peace), 1970, 1,016 p.
The former U.N. Commissioner in Libya during the transition to unification and independence (1950–52) bases this ponderous work, which comes close to being definitive, on both documents and personal experience.

'Umar, Muḥammad 'Abd al-Khāliq. **al-Qānūn al-dawlī al-Lībī al-khāss.** Cairo: Arab Renaissance Bookshop, 1971, 432 p.
A discussion of Libyan concepts of private international law.

Wright, John. **Libya.** New York: Praeger, 1969, 304 p.
A useful general history and introduction to Libya, with emphasis on the period of Italian rule and the later steps toward independence.

ARAB REPUBLIC OF EGYPT

General Surveys

See also The Postwar World, p. 178; (Middle East) General Surveys and Political Problems, p. 611; The Arab World, p. 616; (Africa) General, p. 776; (North Africa) General, p. 793; other subsections under Arab Republic of Egypt.

Abdel-Malek, Anouar. **Dirāsāt fī al-thaqāfah al-waṭanīyah.** Beirut: Dār al-Tali'ah, 1967, 454 p.
A collection of studies on the Egyptian nationalist movement, culture, youth, university education, national identity and problems of the Egyptian intellectual life.

Ḥamdān, Jamāl. **Shakhṣīyat Miṣr, dirāsah fī 'abqarīyat al-makān.** Cairo: Renaissance Bookshop, 1970, 514 p.
A leading Egyptian geographer discusses the peculiarities of the Egyptian land and people and examines the history and problems of Egypt in the context of its relations to other Arab countries.

Little, Tom. **Modern Egypt.** New York: Praeger, 1967, 300 p.
A rewriting and updating of a competent general survey of modern Egyptian history, politics and foreign relations, first published in 1958.

Mansfield, Peter. **The British in Egypt.** New York: Holt, Rinehart and Winston, 1972, 351 p.
Not a systematic history, but an urbane and perceptive account of Britain's 74 years (1882–1956) on the Nile.

Stevens, Georgiana G. **Egypt: Yesterday and Today.** New York: Holt, Rinehart and Winston, 1963, 234 p.
A well-done introductory handbook by a veteran observer.

Vatikiotis, P. J., *ed.* **Egypt since the Revolution.** New York: Praeger, 1968, 195 p.
Most of the contributions by Western and Egyptian scholars to this symposium cover-

Vatikiotis, P. J. **The Modern History of Egypt.** New York: Praeger, 1969, 512 p.
This survey of Egypt in the nineteenth and twentieth centuries stresses internal politics and the process of cultural change.

Waterfield, Gordon. **Egypt.** New York: Walker, 1967, 230 p.
A brisk popular tour through Egyptian history from the Pharaohs to Arab socialism by a veteran British journalist. The final sixty pages cover the period since 1952, with a generally sympathetic but occasionally skeptical view of Nasser's leadership.

Wilber, Donald Newton and Others, *eds.* **United Arab Republic—Egypt: Its People, Its Society, Its Culture.** New Haven: H.R.A.F. Press, 1969, 461 p.
An expanded and improved version of a 1957 handbook presenting political, economic, geographic, social and cultural data.

Politics and Government

See also Socialism, p. 24; The Problem of Authority; Violence and Revolution, p. 34; (Middle East) General Surveys and Political Problems, p. 611; The Arab World, p. 616; (Africa) General, p. 776; other subsections under Arab Republic of Egypt.

Abdel-Malek, Anouar. **Egypt: Military Society: The Army Regime, the Left, and Social Change under Nasser.** New York: Random House, 1968, 458 p.
An updated translation of a study that originally appeared in French as "Égypte, société militaire" (Paris: Éditions du Seuil, 1962, 379 p.).

'Ashūr, Sa'īd 'Abd al-Fattāḥ. **Thawrat sha'b.** Cairo: Dār al-Nahḍah, 1964, 314 p.
The author, a leading historian of Egypt, traces the development of the nationalist movement in Egypt during the nineteenth and twentieth centuries and focuses on the revolution of July 1952.

'Awad, Luwīs. **al-Jāmi'ah wa al-mujtama' al-jadīd.** Cairo: al-Dār al-Qawmīyah, 1963, 160 p.
The leading literary critic of *al-Ahram* examines the role of the Egyptian universities and concludes that they are not preparing students for the new socialist society.

Badawī, Muḥammad Ṭāha and Muṣṭafā, M. H. **Thawrat yuliyū judhūrahā al-tārīkhīyah wa falsafatuha al-siyāsīyah.** Alexandria: al-Makatab al-Miṣrī, 1966, 515 p.
Two university professors deal with the historical and philosophical roots of the revolution of July 23, 1952.

Berque, Jacques. **L'Égypte: impérialisme et révolution.** Paris: Gallimard, 1967, 749 p.
A study of the waning of British power in Egypt and of Nasser's revolution, by a leading student of the Arab World.

Büren, Rainer. **Die Arabische Sozialistische Union.** Opladen: Leske Verlag (for the Deutsches-Orient Institut), 1970, 304 p.
A history of the Arab Socialist Union and a survey of the constitutional developments in the United Arab Republic.

Dekmejian, R. Hrair. **Egypt under Nasir: A Study in Political Dynamics.** Albany: State University of New York Press, 1971, 368 p.
The reader who is not put off by the charts and jargon of political science can find a great deal in this book to explain the Nasser regime in its various phases.

Estier, Claude. **L'Égypte en révolution.** Paris: Julliard, 1965, 253 p.
A French newspaper editor takes stock of the Nasser regime, its achievements and its failures, and of the fact that Egypt has "finally emerged from its millennial torpor and assumed a vanguard role among the developing nations."

Fahmi, Muṣṭafa Abū Zayd. **al-Niẓām al-Dusturī lil-Jumhūrīyyah al-'Arabīyyah al-muttaḥidah.** Alexandria: Dār al-Ma'ārif, 1966, 615 p.
A study of the constitutional system of Egypt and the changes it underwent since the 1952 revolution.

Harris, Christina Phelps. **Nationalism and Revolution in Egypt.** The Hague: Mouton (for the Hoover Institution on War, Revolution, and Peace), 1964, 276 p.
A careful study of the Muslim Brotherhood in Egypt, the militant fundamentalist

organization dedicated to radical nationalism and reform on an Islamic basis that very nearly wrested control of Egypt from Colonel Nasser and his revolutionary government in 1954.

Hopkins, Harry. **Egypt, the Crucible: The Unfinished Revolution in the Arab World.** Boston: Houghton, 1970, 533 p.
A sweeping and sometimes fleeting treatment of the Arab revolution as it has taken hold since 1952 in Egypt, the country the enthusiastic author sees as the "pivot" and the hope of the Arab world.

Imām, Abd Allāh. **al-Nāṣirīyah: dirāsah bi-al-wathā'iq fī al-fikr al-Nāsirī.** Cairo: Dār al-Sha'b, 1971, 544 p.
A documented study of Nasser's thought explaining its three basic concepts: freedom, socialism and unity.

Lacouture, Jean. **Nasser: A Biography.** New York: Knopf, 1973, 399 p.
This first biography in print following Nasser's death is remarkably balanced and informative, as one would expect of Lacouture, no stranger to his subject. The French original was published as "Nasser" (Paris: Éditions du Seuil, 1971, 354 p.).

Mansfield, Peter. **Nasser's Egypt.** Baltimore: Penguin, 1965, 221 p.
A compressed, balanced and readable discussion by a British journalist with long experience in the Middle East.

Meyer-Ranke, Peter. **Der rote Pharao: Ägypten und die arabische Wirklichkeit.** Hamburg: Wegner, 1964, 334 p.
An able German correspondent's observations, based on four years in Egypt and its Arab neighbors, of Nasser and his regime, and their drive under the banner of "Arab socialism" to build a powerful modern state.

Mitchell, Richard P. **The Society of the Muslim Brothers.** New York: Oxford University Press, 1969, 349 p.
A very solid study of the religious-political movement which challenged—and was outlawed by—both the old regime in Egypt and the new military government after 1952.

Nānū, Jān. **Mawt mushīr.** Beirut: Dār al-I'lām al-'Arabī, 1968, 191 p.
The story of the death of Field Marshal 'Abd al-Ḥakīm 'Amir, who was reported to have committed suidice after a plot against Nasser was discovered.

Quraishi, Zaheer Masood. **Liberal Nationalism in Egypt: Rise and Fall of the Wafd Party.** Allahabad: Kitab Mahal, 1967, 245 p.
A comprehensive, though not definitive, history of the Wafd Party, from its establishment in 1918 to its end in 1953. There are useful appendices of the Wafd Constitution and membership, and of the Egyptian election statistics.

Riad, Hassan. **L'Égypte nassérienne.** Paris: Éditions du Minuit, 1964, 249 p.
An Egyptian Marxist examines modern Egypt and Nasser's "petit-bourgeois" regime with a critical doctrinaire eye.

Rif'at, Kamāl al-Dīn. **Mudhakkirāt Kamāl al-Dīn Rif'at.** Cairo: Dār al-Kātib al-'Arabī, 1968, 390 p.
Memoirs of an Egyptian army officer and participant in the 1952 revolution. Edited by Mustafa Tībah.

al-Sibā'i, Yūsuf. **Ayyām' Abd al-Nāṣir, khwaṭir wa mashā'ir.** Cairo: Maktabat al-Khānji, 1971, 456 p.
Articles on Egyptian political, social and economic issues with special reference to Nasser, by a well-known journalist and Minister of Culture.

Stephens, Robert. **Nasser: A Political Biography.** New York: Simon and Schuster, 1972, 631 p.
This detailed biography of the Egyptian leader is particularly informative on his foreign policies.

Ziadeh, Farhat J. **Lawyers, the Rule of Law and Liberalism in Modern Egypt.** Stanford: Hoover Institution on War, Revolution, and Peace, 1968, 177 p.
A study of the major public role played by Western-minded Egyptian lawyers until their relegation to the status of legal technician after the 1952 revolution.

Foreign Relations

See also International Organization and Government, p. 96; Second World War, p. 144; The Postwar World, p. 178; (The United States) Foreign Policy, p. 229; (Canada) Foreign Relations, p. 282; (Great Britain) Imperial and Commonwealth Relations; Colonial Policy, p. 367; Biographies, Memoirs and Addresses, p. 369; Foreign Policy, p. 375; Political Problems, p. 381; (France) Biographies, Memoirs and Addresses, p. 400; (Middle East) General Surveys and Political Problems, p. 611; The Arab World, p. 616; Arab-Israeli Conflict, p. 633; (Africa) General, p. 776; other subsections under Arab Republic of Egypt.

'Awdah, 'Awdah Buṭrus. **Jamāl 'Abd al-Nāṣir: dawruhu fī al-niḍāl al-'Arabī.** Cairo: al-Matba'ah al-Fannīyah al-Ḥadīthah, 1971, 350 p.
A study of Nasser's role in Arab affairs.

Blaxland, Gregory. **Egypt and Sinai: Eternal Battleground.** New York: Funk & Wagnalls, 1968, 327 p.
Primarily an account of Anglo-Egyptian relations, with accent on military encounters. First published in England as "Objective Egypt" (London: Muller, 1966, 319 p.).

Burj, Muḥammad 'Abd al-Raḥmān. **Qanāt al-Sūways: ahammīyatuhā al-sīyāsīyah wa-al-istrātījīyah.** Cairo: Dār al-Kātib al-'Arabī, 1968, 408 p.
A study of the political and strategic importance of the Suez Canal and its role in Anglo-Egyptian relations from 1914 to 1956.

Copeland, Miles. **The Game of Nations: The Amorality of Power Politics.** New York: Simon and Schuster, 1970, 318 p.
An insider's unorthodox and occasionally hilarious story of the cryptodiplomacy by which American agents and Abdel Nasser allegedly played the "game."

Haykal, Muḥammad Ḥasanayn. **Les Documents du Caire.** Paris: Flammarion, 1972, 314 p.
Disappointing as memoirs or biography because of its episodic structure, Haykal's book nevertheless gives us fascinating glimpses of Nasser's dealings and conversations with world leaders of his day: Dulles, Eden, Khrushchev, Tito and others. Accuracy not guaranteed. The English edition appeared as "The Cairo Documents" (Garden City: Doubleday, 1973, 360 p.).

Haykal, Muḥammad Ḥasanayn. **Naḥnu wa Amrīkā.** Cairo: Dār al-'Aṣr al-Ḥadīth, 1967, 189 p.
A series of articles by the editor of *al-Ahram* on the Egyptian-American relations from 1952 to 1967.

Ismael, Tareq Y. **The U.A.R. in Africa: Egypt's Policy under Nasser.** Evanston: Northwestern University Press, 1971, 258 p.
A review of Egypt's activities in Africa, based largely on the Cairo press. The author describes the grandiose objectives of Nasser's policies and does not gloss over the failures.

Junayd, 'Abd al-Mun'im. **La République Arabe Unie "Egypte" dans l'unité arabe et l'unité africaine.** Cairo: Dār al-Kātib al-'Arabī, 1968, 339 p.
A study of the foreign relations of Egypt with the Arab and African world.

Nutting, Anthony. **Nasser.** New York: Dutton, 1972, 493 p.
The former British Minister of State for Foreign Affairs uses the biographical format to give a well-conceived history of the Middle East crises of Nasser's time. Much is familiar, but from the author's own diplomatic experience and personal acquaintance with Nasser and his cohorts come points of considerable interest.

Economic and Social Conditions

See also Economic Factors, p. 49; (The United States) Aid and Assistance, p. 254; (Union of Soviet Socialist Republics) Foreign Economic Policy, p. 560; The Arab World, p. 616; (Africa) General, p. 776.

'Awad, Luwis. **al-Thawrah wa al-adab.** Cairo: Dār al-Kātib al-'Arabī, 1967, 527 p.
A collection of essays on Egyptian cultural problems published in *al-Ahram* or read at international conferences. One article is dedicated to the affair of the periodical *Ḥiwar*, which was accused of receiving C.I.A. money.

al-Barrāwī, Rāshid. **Economic Development in the United Arab Republic (Egypt).** Cairo: Anglo-Egyptian Bookshop, 1970, 334 p.

An account of Egypt's economic achievements under the impact of the revolution of 1952. This volume by the leading historian of the Egyptian economy surveys the economic policies, techniques and achievements of the Nasserite era.

El-Kammash, Magdi M. **Economic Development and Planning in Egypt.** New York: Praeger, 1968, 408 p.
A comprehensive academic study, with many useful tables, which manages to avoid all political considerations and judgments and to maintain a bland optimism regarding Egypt's economic prospects.

al-Ghazzāli, 'Abd al-Mun'īm. **Tārikh al-harakah al-naqābīyah al-Miṣrīyah 1899-1952.** Cairo: Dār al-Thaqāfah al-Jadidah, 1968, 302 p.
A history of trade unionism in Egypt before the 1952 revolution.

Hansen, Bent and Marzouk, Girgis A. **Development and Economic Policy in the UAR (Egypt).** Amsterdam: North-Holland Publishing Co., 1965, 333 p.
A major study of economic development and economic policies in Egypt since 1945, including an analysis of the mixed government-private system and an appraisal of the first five-year plan.

Issawi, Charles. **Egypt in Revolution: An Economic Analysis.** New York: Oxford University Press (for the Royal Institute of International Affairs), 1963, 343 p.
A very substantial economic study of Egypt, by a leading scholar.

Kardouche, George K. **The U.A.R. in Development: A Study in Expansionary Finance.** New York: Praeger, 1967, 170 p.
Essentially a technical inquiry into Egyptian monetary policy, especially since the revolution of 1952, but with some attempt to relate it to broader economic questions.

Kornrumpf, Hans-Jürgen. **Vereinigte Arabische Republik: Wirtschaftsstrukturwandlung und Entwicklungshilfe.** Opladen: Leske, 1967, 207 p.
An economic handbook with useful statistical material.

Little, Tom. **High Dam at Aswan: The Subjugation of the Nile.** New York: Day, 1965, 242 p.
A veteran observer draws on his quarter-century of experience for the story of this grand enterprise.

Mayfield, James B. **Rural Politics in Nasser's Egypt.** Austin: University of Texas Press, 1971, 288 p.
This description of rural institutions sets out the myriad difficulties that beset Cairo's attempts to bring the tradition-bound fellaheen into the state and party system of the regime.

O'Brien, Patrick Karl. **The Revolution in Egypt's Economic System: From Private Enterprise to Socialism, 1952-1965.** New York: Oxford University Press (for the Royal Institute of International Affairs), 1966, 354 p.
An evaluation of changes in Egypt's economic organization, and the political, legal and institutional framework within which Egyptian economic enterprise has operated since 1952.

Saab, Gabriel S. **The Egyptian Agrarian Reform, 1952-1962.** New York: Oxford University Press (for the Royal Institute of International Affairs), 1967, 236 p.
Dr. Saab's competent and careful analysis of Egyptian agriculture from the revolutionary regime's major reform in 1952 to the second in 1961 draws on his own unique experience in Egypt and a wealth of statistical material. He documents the accomplishments of the reform but is critical of the government's preference for the spectacular.

Shibl, Yusuf. **The Aswan High Dam.** Beirut: The Arab Institute for Research and Publishing, 1971, 128 p.
A general discussion of the history and importance of the dam to Egypt and the Arab World.

Weiss, Dieter. **Wirtschaftliche Entwicklungsplanung in der Vereinigten Arabischen Republik.** Opladen: Westdeutscher Verlag, 1964, 315 p.
A German scholar with two years of experience in one of the U.A.R. planning commissions examines critically the Egyptian economy, U.A.R. development policy, and the ideology of Arab socialism.

SUDAN

See also (Africa) General, p. 776; (East Africa) General, p. 826.

Abdel-Rahim, Muddathir. **Imperialism and Nationalism in the Sudan.** New York: Oxford University Press, 1969, 275 p.
In this study a Sudanese scholar is mainly concerned with institutional and political developments between 1936 and 1956.

Albino, Oliver. **The Sudan: A Southern Viewpoint.** New York: Oxford University Press (for the Institute of Race Relations, London), 1970, 132 p.
A short, competent history of the north-south conflict in the Sudan. The author argues that the division of the country into two sovereign states must ultimately be the outcome of the civil war if peace is to be lasting.

Beshir, Mohamed Omer. **The Southern Sudan: Background to Conflict.** New York: Praeger, 1968, 192 p.
A balanced, scholarly treatment of the ever-present division between North and South. Generous in his criticism of both sides, this northerner concludes that some form of accommodation within a single state must be the ultimate solution.

Hajj Mūsa, Ibrāhīm Muḥammad. **al-Tajribah al-dimūqrāṭīyah wa taṭawūr nuzum al-ḥukm fī al-Sūdān.** Cairo: Cairo University, 1970, 639 p.
A study of the vicissitudes of establishing a democratic system in Sudan since independence. This work is an excellent history of the political and social forces operating in modern Sudan.

Henderson, Kenneth David Druitt. **Sudan Republic.** New York: Praeger, 1965, 256 p.
An account of the training period and preliminary trials of the new Sudan by a veteran of the Sudan political service, author of "Survey of the Anglo-Egyptian Sudan, 1898-1944" (1946) and "The Making of the Modern Sudan" (1953).

Hill, Richard Leslie. **Sudan Transport: A History of Railway, Marine and River Services in the Republic of the Sudan.** New York: Oxford University Press, 1965, 188 p.
An informed, historical account of the establishment, growth and administration of the railway, steamer and port services which have played a major part in the economic development of the Republic of Sudan.

Muḥamadīyah, Aḥmad Saʿīd. **Thawrat Māyū.** Beirut: Dār al-ʿAwdah, 2d ed., 1969, 84 p.
A correspondent of the Lebanese weekly *al-Ṣayyād* explains the reasons and goals of the May 1969 revolution in the Sudan and provides a profile of al-Nemiry and the leftist group that led it.

Nelson, Harold D. and Others. **Area Handbook for Democratic Republic of Sudan.** Washington: G.P.O., 1973, 351 p.
A useful reference volume with a bibliography, prepared by the Foreign Area Studies at the American University.

Oduho, Joseph and Deng, William. **The Problem of the Southern Sudan.** New York: Oxford University Press, 1963, 60 p.
Two Southern Sudanese examine the racial and tribal differences between Northern and Southern Sudan.

Reining, Conrad C. **The Zande Scheme: An Anthropological Case Study of Economic Development in Africa.** Evanston: Northwestern University Press, 1966, 255 p.
An anthropologist provides a first-hand account of the dilemmas of economic and social change encountered by the Zande Scheme in Southern Sudan, a development program initiated in 1945 and designed to promote greater self-sufficiency in manufactured products among remote rural populations.

Said, Beshir Mohammed. **The Sudan: Crossroads of Africa.** Chester Springs (Pa.): Dufour, 1966, 238 p.
A leading Sudanese journalist traces the history of, and apportions blame for, the problem of the South, and calls upon Northern statesmanship and Southern patience to produce a real Sudanese unity.

Stucken, Rudolf, *ed.* **Entwicklungsbedingungen und Entwicklungschancen der Republik Sudan.** Berlin: Duncker, 1963, 265 p.
Articles on the economic situation and potentialities of the Sudan Republic.

Thawrat Shaʻb: sit sanawāt mina al-niḍāl ḍid al-ḥukm al-ʻaskarī al-rujʻī. Khartoum: Dār al-Fikr al-Ishtirākī (for the al-Hizb al-Shuyūʻī al-Sūdānī), 1965, 488 p.
   A collection of documents by the Sudanese Communist Party illustrating its struggle against the government of General Abboud which culminated in a revolution on October 21, 1964.

WEST AFRICA
GENERAL

See also Comparative Government, p. 18; (Union of Soviet Socialist Republics) Relations with Other Countries, p. 558; (Africa) General, p. 776.

Afana, Osendé. **L'Économie de L'Ouest-africain: perspectives de développement.** Paris: Maspéro, 1966, 263 p.
   A survey of West African economy by an African economist of Marxist persuasion.

Amin, Samir. **L'Afrique de l'Ouest bloquée: l'économie politique de la colonisation, 1880–1970.** Paris: Éditions de Minuit, 1971, 322 p.
   Though colonial development is treated in this volume, the emphasis is on the analysis of the economic development of the French-speaking states of West Africa plus Ghana and the Gambia.

Amin, Samir. **Trois expériences africaines de développement: le Mali, la Guinée et le Ghana.** Paris: Presses Universitaires, 1965, 233 p.
   An informative analysis of Malian efforts to restructure the inherited colonial economy and a critical evaluation of economic planning and development in Mali, Guinea and Ghana.

Crowder, Michael. **West Africa under Colonial Rule.** Evanston: Northwestern University Press, 1968, 540 p.
   The author, one of the foremost historians interested in West Africa, has written a book of interest to specialists and generalists alike.

Decker, Henry de. **Nation et développement communautaire en Guinée et au Sénégal.** The Hague: Mouton, 1968, 470 p.
   Based on five months' research in 1963, this study seeks to analyze the plans and achievements of two West African countries in the area of rural, agricultural modernization. The author is a Jesuit and a political scientist.

Fehr, Eugen. **Demokratische Staatsformen in Westafrika.** Vienna: Europa Verlag, 1965, 499 p.
   A survey introducing the reader to the major political institutions of French and British West Africa, by a Swiss scholar.

Foster, Philip and Zolberg, Aristide R., *eds.* **Ghana and the Ivory Coast.** Chicago: University of Chicago Press, 1971, 303 p.
   An excellent collection of original essays on aspects of politics in the two countries.

Grohs, Gerhard. **Stufen afrikanischer Emanzipation: Studien zum Selbstverständnis westafrikanischer Eliten.** Stuttgart: Kohlhammer, 1967, 275 p.
   A discussion of the gradual development of an indigenous modern élite in West Africa as a response to European colonialism.

Hargreaves, John D. **West Africa: The Former French States.** Englewood Cliffs: Prentice-Hall, 1967, 183 p.
   A general history of French-speaking West Africa from the beginnings of recorded history to independence, with particular emphasis on the colonial period.

Jakande, Lateef K., *ed.* **West African Annual, 1962– .** Lagos: John West Publications, 1962– .
   A useful reference. The eighth volume (1972–72) was published in 1973.

Jordan, Robert S. **Government and Power in West Africa.** New York: Africana Publishing Corp., 1970, 336 p.

An excellent general introduction to contemporary politics in English-speaking West Africa by a political scientist at the State University of New York at Binghampton.

Körner, Heiko. **Kolonialpolitik und Wirtschaftsentwicklung: das Beispiel französisch Westafrikas.** Stuttgart: Gustav Fischer Verlag, 1965, 307 p.

A competent, critical assessment of French achievements and failures in economic policy in French West Africa up to 1958, with a useful bibliography of materials in French, English, and German.

Leubuscher, Charlotte. **The West African Shipping Trade, 1909-1959.** Dobbs Ferry (N.Y.): Oceana, 1963, 109 p.

A close examination of shipping patterns and practices to and from Nigeria and Ghana over a fifty-year period.

Lewis, Sir William Arthur. **Politics in West Africa.** New York: Oxford University Press, 1965, 90 p.

In these three lectures Professor Lewis offers a provocative and critical analysis of basic issues in African politics—the problem of national integration, the centralizing tendencies of single-party regimes, and the prospects for democratic institutions in Africa.

Lewis, William Hubert, ed. **French-Speaking Africa: The Search for Identity.** New York: Walker, 1965, 256 p.

These papers were given at a colloquium on French-speaking Africa held in Washington in the late summer of 1964.

Lloyd, Peter Cutt. **Africa in Social Change.** Baltimore: Penguin, 1967, 362 p.

A competent analysis of the major aspects of social change, modernization and class differentiation in the new states of West Africa, by a prominent British social anthropologist.

Morgan, William Basil and Pugh, J. C. **West Africa.** London: Methuen, 1969, 788 p.

A comprehensive, general geography by two British scholars.

Morgenthau, Ruth Schachter. **Political Parties in French-Speaking West Africa.** New York: Oxford University Press, 1964, 445 p.

A survey of the establishment and disintegration of Afrique Occidentale Française and a detailed analysis of the political changes in the new states that superseded the federation, particularly in Senegal, Ivory Coast, Guinea and Mali.

November, András. **L'Évolution du mouvement syndical en Afrique occidentale.** Paris: Mouton, 1965, 282 p.

A study of the trade union movement in West Africa.

Peterec, Richard J. **Dakar and West African Economic Development.** New York: Columbia University Press, 1967, 206 p.

A geographer at Bucknell University analyzes the special administrative position of Dakar in the French colonial structure and foresees that the independence of neighboring countries will gradually modify its preëminent position.

Post, Kenneth William John. **The New States of West Africa.** Baltimore: Penguin, 1964, 206 p.

A well-written analysis of factors which affect and will affect internal political changes in West Africa for years to come.

Price, Joseph Henry. **Political Institutions of West Africa.** New York: Humanities Press, 1968, 266 p.

A treatment of the legal and constitutional development of the English-speaking West African states from the colonial period through independence.

Seck, Assane and Mondjannagni, Alfred. **L'Afrique occidentale.** Paris: Presses Universitaires, 1967, 290 p.

A general introductory economic geography by two West African scholars.

Serreau, Jean. **Le Développement à la base au Dahomey et au Sénégal.** Paris: Librairie Générale de Droit, 1966, 358 p.

A detailed study of the problems and policies in rural development of two West African states, devoting considerable attention to their respective economic plans since 1959-60.

Stahn, Eberhard. **Kommunistische Modelle für Afrika? Ghana und Guinea.** Hanover: Verlag für Literatur und Zeitgeschehen, 1967, 192 p.

The author argues that while the party organizations and terminologies of the P.D.G. (Parti Démocratique de Guinée) and C.P.P. (Convention People's Party, Ghana) owe much to communist theory, they should be seen essentially as pragmatic adaptations to the tasks of national unification and rapid industrialization, prerequisites to democratization.

Sy, Seydou Madani. **Recherches sur l'exercice du pouvoir politique en Afrique noire (Côte-d'Ivoire, Guinée, Mali).** Paris: Pedone, 1965, 230 p.
The author, a Senegalese scholar, traces the inapplicability of Western models of constitutional democracy to the economic conditions and social structures which have decisively influenced the organization and exercise of political power in Guinea, Mali and the Ivory Coast.

Thompson, Virginia McLean. **West Africa's Council of the Entente.** Ithaca: Cornell University Press, 1972, 313 p.
A much-needed survey of the five-country regional grouping dominated by the Ivory Coast. The author is a political scientist at the University of California at Berkeley.

Wade, Abdoulaye. **Économie de l'Ouest africain (zone franc).** Paris: Présence Africaine, 1964, 371 p.
A detailed analysis of the economy of West Africa. Particular attention is paid to the conditions of production, agriculture, industrialization, problems of capital and foreign investment, and the role of international trade in West Africa's development.

Wallerstein, Immanuel Maurice. **The Road to Independence: Ghana and the Ivory Coast.** The Hague: Mouton, 1964, 200 p.
The sections on the formation and role of voluntary associations distinguish this book from other studies of Ghana and the Ivory Coast.

Welch, Claude Emerson. **Dream of Unity: Pan-Africanism and Political Unification in West Africa.** Ithaca: Cornell University Press, 1966, 396 p.
A careful analysis of several attempts at unification. Of particular interest are the sections on Ewe nationalism, the amalgamation of British Togo with Ghana, the Senegambia proposals and the development of the Federal Republic of Cameroon.

Wilson, John. **Education and Changing West African Culture.** New York: Teachers College, Bureau of Publications, 1963, 125 p.
A British scholar presents a survey of education in English-speaking Africa and documents the need for an African, not a transplanted European, system of education.

Wraith, Ronald Edward. **Local Government in West Africa.** New York: Praeger, 1964, 184 p.
A study of local government in English-speaking West Africa.

Zolberg, Aristide R. **Creating Political Order: The Party-States of West Africa.** Chicago: Rand McNally, 1966, 168 p.
In an important contribution to the literature of comparative politics, Professor Zolberg surveys the development of parties and government since independence in Mali, Guinea, Ivory Coast, Senegal and Ghana, calling attention to the basic similarity in their patterns of evolution.

GUINEA; PORTUGUESE GUINEA; MALI; MAURITANIA

See also Socialism, p. 24; (Union of Soviet Socialist Republics) Relations with Other Countries, p. 558; (Africa) General, p. 776; (West Africa) General, p. 807.

Cabral, Amilcar. **Revolution in Guinea.** New York: Monthly Review Press, 1970, 174 p.
Speeches, interviews and statements of the leader of the P.A.I.G.C., the liberation movement in Portuguese Guinea which began an armed insurrection in 1963.

Curran, Brian Dean and Schrock, Joann. **Area Handbook for Mauritania.** Washington: G.P.O., 1972, 185 p.
A useful reference volume with a bibliography, prepared by the Foreign Area Studies at the American University.

Davidson, Basil. **The Liberation of Guiné: Aspects of an African Revolution.** Baltimore: Penguin, 1969, 166 p.

This work is concerned largely with the activities, strategies and ideology of the P.A.I.G.C. (African Independence Party of Guiné and the Cape Verde Islands) in the Portuguese enclave on the west coast of Africa.

Foltz, William Jay. **From French West Africa to the Mali Federation.** New Haven: Yale University Press, 1965, 235 p.

A well-written and stimulating study of the formation and failure of the Mali Federation. Illuminates the continuing efforts in Africa toward unity.

Gerteiny, Alfred G. **Mauritania.** New York: Praeger, 1967, 243 p.

A general introduction to the history, geography and social development of one of Africa's least-known countries, which has a population of under a million and a huge land area, most of it desert.

Hopkins, Nicholas S. **Popular Government in an African Town: Kita, Mali.** Chicago: University of Chicago Press, 1972, 246 p.

This very detailed delineation of both the traditional and contemporary political structure of a Malian town illustrates some of the conflicts that may arise when a new and poor nation tries to combine the goals of participatory government and economic development.

Mauritania: Guidelines for a Four-Year Development Program. Washington: International Bank for Reconstruction and Development, 1968, 146 p.

A revised version of a report prepared by a World Bank mission, headed by R. M. Westebbe, which visited Mauritania in 1967 at the request of its government.

Morrow, John H. **First American Ambassador to Guinea.** New Brunswick: Rutgers University Press, 1968, 291 p.

The experiences of an academic who was President Eisenhower's ambassador to Guinea from 1959 to 1961.

Pujos, Jérôme. **Croissance économique et impulsion extérieure: étude sur l'économie mauritanienne.** Paris: Presses Universitaires, 1964, 314 p.

An analysis and prescription for Mauritanian development. The author was an adviser to the president of that country.

Snyder, Frank Gregory. **One-Party Government in Mali: Transition toward Control.** New Haven: Yale University Press, 1965, 178 p.

A detailed analysis of the growth of the Union Soudanaise and the problems confronting it in power.

Touré, Ahmed Sékou. **La révolution guinéenne et le progrès social.** Conakry: Imprimerie Nationale Patrice Lumumba, 1963, 812 p.

The political history of the Parti Démocratique de Guinée, and thereby of Guinea, as chronicled by the President of the Republic. The book contains full reports on the conferences at Kissidougou in 1960 and at Conakry in 1961. A detailed diagram compares the structure and functions of the party with those of the administration.

Voss, Joachim. **Der progressistische Entwicklungstaat: seine rechts- und verwaltungstechnische Problematik; das Beispiel der Republik Guinea.** Hanover: Verlag für Literatur und Zeitgeschehen, 1971, 448 p.

A massive and well-documented study of the legal and administrative problems of the Republic of Guinea.

IVORY COAST; TOGO; DAHOMEY; UPPER VOLTA

See also (Union of Soviet Socialist Republics) Relations with Other Countries, p. 558; (Africa) General, p. 776; (West Africa) General, p. 807.

Amin, Samir. **Le Développement du capitalisme en Côte d'Ivoire.** Paris: Éditions de Minuit, 1967, 330 p.

A survey of the rapid development of the Ivory Coast economy since 1950.

Balima, Salfo Albert. **Genèse de la Haute-Volta.** Ouagadougou: Presses Africaines, 1970, 253 p.

A general history of the Republic of Upper Volta which gained its independence on August 5, 1960.

Bassolet, François Djoby. **Évolution de la Haute Volta de 1898 au 3 janvier 1966.** Ouagadougou: Imprimerie Nationale, 1968, 131 p.
A brief history of twentieth-century Upper Volta.

Cornevin, Robert. **Histoire du Togo.** Paris: Berger-Levrault, 3rd rev. and enl. ed., 1969, 555 p.
A considerably revised and expanded edition of a general history of Togo, with emphasis on contemporary developments.

La Côte-d'Ivoire: chances et risques. Brussels: La Conférence Olivaint de Belgique, 1967, 2 v.
Papers and proceedings of a conference dealing with contemporary problems of the Ivory Coast.

Glélé, Maurice-A. **Naissance d'un état noir.** Paris: Librairie Générale de Droit, 1969, 537 p.
Attributing the instability of politics in Dahomey to certain features of colonial experience as well as to a lack of effective leadership, Glélé argues for the development of a two-party system with a strong presidency. He studies developments through the coup of December 1965.

Hammond, Peter B. **Yatenga: Technology in the Culture of a West African Kingdom.** New York: Free Press, 1966, 231 p.
A well-written analysis of one of the four major peoples who make up the Mossi of Upper Volta, by an American anthropologist.

Wülker, Gabrielle (Weymann). **Togo: Tradition und Entwicklung.** Stuttgart: Klett, 1966, 159 p.
A survey of economic and social conditions in contemporary Togo.

Zeller, Claus. **Elfenbeinküste: ein Entwicklungsland auf dem Wege zur Nation.** Freiburg: Rombach, 1969, 520 p.
A general political history of the Ivory Coast with emphasis on the period from 1939 to 1963.

Zolberg, Aristide R. **One-Party Government in the Ivory Coast.** Princeton: Princeton University Press, rev. ed., 1969, 400 p.
The need for unity in a political entity affected by ethnic cleavages is analyzed with special reference to the role of the single party and the directions of political change.

SENEGAL

See also Government and Economics; Planning, p. 54; (The Postwar World) General, p. 178; (Union of Soviet Socialist Republics) Relations with Other Countries, p. 558; (Africa) General p. 776; (West Africa) General, p. 807.

Behrman, Lucy C. **Muslim Brotherhoods and Politics in Senegal.** Cambridge: Harvard University Press, 1970, 224 p.
Professor Behrman of the University of Pennsylvania has written a first-rate study of the sources of power of traditional religious leaders and the complicated relationships of dependence and competition between these leaders and the party politicians.

Crowder, Michael. **Senegal: A Study in French Assimilation Policy.** New York: Oxford University Press (for the Institute of Race Relations, London), 1962, 104 p.
A brief study of Senegal, with emphasis on France's policy of assimilation of the natives.

Diarassouba, Valy-Charles. **L'Évolution des structures agricoles du Sénégal.** Paris: Éditions Cujas, 1968, 298 p.
The interaction between agricultural techniques on the one hand and the character of social and economic organization on the other is the concern of this work. It begins with pre-colonial times and carries through to the post-independence period.

Fougeyrollas, Pierre. **Où va le Sénégal?** Dakar: IFAN; Paris: Éditions Anthropos, 1970, 274 p.

Using public opinion polls and interviews, this French sociologist argues that Senegal made considerable progress in economic and social development in its first decade of independence and that the dichotomy between revolutionary and neocolonial regimes in the Third World is a false one.

Markovitz, Irving Leonard. **Léopold Sédar Senghor and the Politics of Negritude.** New York: Atheneum, 1969, 300 p.
A study of the development of Senghor's philosophical ideas and a description of their relevance to the political affairs of Senegal.

Milcent, Ernest. **Au Carrefour des options africaines: le Sénégal.** Paris: Éditions du Centurion, 1965, 223 p.
An introductory survey of Senegal.

O'Brian, Rita Cruise. **White Society in Black Africa: The French of Senegal.** Evanston: Northwestern University Press, 1972, 320 p.
A history of the relationship between colonialists and natives in Senegal, culminating in an inquiry into contemporary French attitudes toward the Senegalese. In a curious twist, the author attempts to demonstrate the debilitating effects of the continued African dependency by showing us the Senegalese through the eyes of the French, who continue to dominate them economically if not politically.

Pfeffermann, Guy. **Industrial Labor in the Republic of Senegal.** New York: Praeger, 1968, 325 p.
An attempt to apply contemporary economic standards to the performance of the Senegalese economy. The author finds that the family system, the colonial past and agreements with France render government labor policies ineffective. The work supports a neocolonialist view of the Senegalese political system.

Skurnik, W. A. E. **The Foreign Policy of Senegal.** Evanston: Northwestern University Press, 1972, 308 p.
A somewhat abstruse analysis of the foreign policy of Senegal, with emphasis on Senghor's central role.

Traoré, Bakary; Lô, Mamadou and Alibert, Jean-Louis. **Forces politiques en Afrique noire.** Paris: Presses Universitaires, 1966, 312 p.
This volume contains a study of the evolution of the political parties of Senegal since 1946, by Bakary Traoré; a survey of the Union Progressiste Sénégalaise, by Mamadou Lô; and a study of the political opposition in Black Africa, by Jean-Louis Alibert.

Zuccarelli, François. **Un Parti politique africain: l'Union Progressiste Sénégalaise.** Paris: Librairie Générale de Droit, 1970, 401 p.
A detailed study of Senegal's only active political party, the Senegalese Progressive Union, which was established in 1949 by Léopold Sédar Senghor.

SIERRA LEONE; GAMBIA

See also Economic Growth and Development, p. 71; (The United States) Aid and Assistance, p. 254; (Africa) General, p. 776; (West Africa) General, p. 807.

Fyfe, Christopher. **A History of Sierra Leone.** London: Oxford University Press, 1962, 773 p.
———. **A Short History of Sierra Leone.** London: Longmans, 1962, 193 p.
———. **Sierra Leone Inheritance.** London: Oxford University Press, 1964, 352 p.
Comprehensive surveys of the history of Sierra Leone from the arrival of the Portuguese until the establishment of independence in 1961. The last volume is a collection of documents and writings supplementing the general accounts.

Gailey, Harry A. **A History of the Gambia.** New York: Praeger, 1965, 244 p.
A political history of the small West African country that became independent on February 18, 1965.

Kilson, Martin Luther. **Political Change in a West African State: A Study of the Modernization Process in Sierra Leone.** Cambridge: Harvard University Press, 1966, 301 p.
This study of the political process in Sierra Leone through 1964 lays great emphasis on the significance of groups and their interrelations. It contains illuminating com-

parisons with other African political systems. Prepared under the auspices of the Center for International Affairs, Harvard University.

Mühlenberg, Friedrich and Breitengross, Jens Peter. **Fallstudie Sierra Leone: Entwicklungsprobleme in interdisziplinärer Sicht.** Stuttgart: Ernst Klett Verlag, 1972, 2 v.
A comprehensive and very well-documented survey of the economic development of Sierra Leone.

Rice, Berkeley. **Enter Gambia: The Birth of an Improbable Nation.** Boston: Houghton, 1967, 389 p.
A spirited, impressionistic report on the problems of Gambia by a former *Newsweek* correspondent.

Saylor, Ralph Gerald. **The Economic System of Sierra Leone.** Durham: Duke University Press (for Duke University Commonwealth-Studies Center), 1968, 231 p.
A scholarly study with particular emphasis on the impact of government policies on the course of economic development. The author is a project specialist at the Ford Foundation.

LIBERIA

See also Economic Growth and Development, p. 71; (Africa) General, p. 776; (West Africa) General, p. 807.

Clifford, Mary Louise. **The Land and People of Liberia.** New York: Lippincott, 1971, 160 p.
An introductory survey.

Clower, Robert W. and Others. **Growth without Development: An Economic Survey of Liberia.** Evanston: Northwestern University Press, 1966, 385 p.
A comprehensive study of the Liberian economy prepared under the auspices of Northwestern University. The authors argue that the growth in production since 1950 has had little or no impact upon the structure of the society or economy.

Fraenkel, Merran. **Tribe and Class in Monrovia.** New York: Oxford University Press (for the International African Institute), 1964, 244 p.
A significant anthropological study of the capital of Liberia in which a caste-like society of ex-slave expatriates and indigenous natives has persisted for over a century. The author's field work demonstrates the postwar turn toward social mobility.

Liebenow, J. Gus. **Liberia: The Evolution of Privilege.** Ithaca: Cornell University Press, 1969, 247 p.
A first-rate analysis of Liberia's political system and its historical development. The author is a professor at Indiana University.

Lynch, Hollis Ralph. **Edward Wilmot Blyden: Pan-Negro Patriot, 1832-1912.** New York: Oxford University Press, 1967, 272 p.
A sympathetic biography of a nineteenth-century West Indian immigrant to Liberia who became one of the foremost proponents of the Negro "return" to Africa, and later Liberia's first ambassador in London.

McLaughlin, Russell U. **Foreign Investment and Development in Liberia.** New York: Praeger, 1966, 217 p.
In this informative study of the structure of the Liberian economy, the author explores the relationship between foreign public and private investment and domestic economic growth.

Marinelli, Lawrence A. **The New Liberia.** New York: Praeger (for the Africa Service Institute of New York), 1964, 244 p.
A general survey of the internal and external affairs of Liberia, with a supplement of documents.

Roberts, Thomas D. and Others. **Area Handbook for Liberia.** Washington: G.P.O., 1972, 387 p.
A useful reference volume with a bibliography, prepared by the Foreign Area Studies at the American University.

Unger, Marvin H. **Pawpaw, Foofoo, and Juju: Recollections of a Peace Corps Volunteer.** New York: Citadel Press, 1968, 210 p.

An account of the author's experiences as a teacher in a teacher training institute in Liberia from 1964 to 1966.

Wilson, Charles Morrow. **Liberia: Black Africa in Microcosm.** New York: Harper and Row, 1971, 249 p.

Written by a journalist who worked for nearly five years for Firestone and occasionally for the Liberian Government, this work is devoid of concern with the implications of political and economic domination of the country by the Americo-Liberian minority.

GHANA

See also Comparative Government, p. 18; Economic Growth and Development, p. 71; (The Postwar World) General, p. 178; The Third World; Nonalignment, p. 186; (Union of Soviet Socialist Republics) Relations with Other Countries, p. 558; (Africa) General, p. 776; (West Africa) General, p. 807; Zaïre, p. 822.

Afrifa, Akwasi Amankwa. **The Ghana Coup: 24th February 1966.** New York: Humanities Press, 1966, 144 p.

A shrill denunciation of Nkrumah, the former President of Ghana, by one of the three principal figures who engineered the coup against him. The author's devotion to British concepts and culture make him sound strangely unlike the usual concept of an African nationalist of the 1960s.

Alexander, Henry Templer. **African Tightrope: My Two Years as Nkrumah's Chief of Staff.** New York: Praeger, 1966, 152 p.

In addition to his illuminating account of the political strains underlying the Africanization and modernization of Ghana's armed forces, General Alexander critically discusses his experiences in the Congo.

Ansprenger, Franz and Others. **Die politische Entwicklung Ghanas von Nkrumah bis Busia.** Munich: Weltforum Verlag, 1972, 246 p.

A brief, straightforward account of the three Ghanaian regimes which preceded the military government that came to power in January 1972.

Anyane, Seth La. **Ghana Agriculture.** New York: Oxford University Press, 1963, 228 p.

A Ghanian economist traces the development of agriculture products and institutions in Ghana from the eleventh century to the present.

Apter, David Ernest. **Ghana in Transition.** New York: Atheneum, rev. ed., 1963, 432 p.

A revised edition of the author's "Gold Coast in Transition" (1955).

Austin, Dennis. **Politics in Ghana, 1946–1960.** New York: Oxford University Press (for the Royal Institute of International Affairs), 1964, 459 p.

This excellent political history combines factual richness with felicity of style.

Balogun, Kolawole. **Mission to Ghana: Memoir of a Diplomat.** New York: Vantage Press, 1964, 73 p.

A delightful account of his tenure in Ghana, by the former Nigerian High Commissioner.

Bing, Geoffrey. **Reap the Whirlwind: An Account of Kwame Nkrumah's Ghana from 1950 to 1966.** London: MacGibbon and Kee, 1968, 519 p.

A partisan survey by one of Nkrumah's most faithful advisors.

Birmingham, Walter Barr and Others, *eds.* **A Study of Contemporary Ghana.** Evanston: Northwestern University Press (for the Ghana Academy of Sciences), 1966–67, 2 v.

A major study of the economy and social structure of Ghana.

Bretton, Henry L. **The Rise and Fall of Kwame Nkrumah: A Study of Personal Rule in Africa.** New York: Praeger, 1966, 232 p.

Professor Bretton has written a highly critical account of Nkrumah's rule with particular emphasis on the later years. While the book contains much general material of interest, it lacks the balance and detail which will be required of the definitive study of Ghana's first ten years of independence.

Dowse, Robert E. **Modernization in Ghana and the U.S.S.R.** New York: Humanities Press, 1969, 107 p.
A British political scientist argues that Ghana and the U.S.S.R. dealt with the fundamental problem of economic development in remarkably similar manners despite differences in political ideology. A suggestive, if somewhat forced, comparative study.

Fitch, Robert Beck and Oppenheimer, Mary. **Ghana: End of an Illusion.** New York: Monthly Review Press, 1966, 130 p.
This assessment, written from a neo-Marxist viewpoint, argues that Nkrumah's downfall was the result of his failure to liquidate the essential features of a foreign-dominated capitalist economy.

Garlick, Peter C. **African Traders and Economic Development in Ghana.** New York: Oxford University Press, 1971, 172 p.
An attempt "to illuminate some problems of economic development in Ghana by studying the behavior and social background of the biggest African traders dealing in manufactured goods."

Kaplan, Irving and Others. **Area Handbook for Ghana.** Washington: G.P.O., 1971, 449 p.
A useful reference volume with a bibliography, prepared by the Foreign Area Studies at the American University.

Moxon, James. **Volta: Man's Greatest Lake.** New York: Praeger, 1969, 256 p.
A retired British civil servant has written a political and economic history of the Volta River project, designed for the general reader.

Nkrumah, Kwame. **Dark Days in Ghana.** New York: International Publishers, 1968, 163 p.
Dealing with the coup of February 1966 and subsequent developments in Ghana, this book by the deposed President of Ghana is passionate and full of controversy. His indictment of the military government is unqualified.

Nsarkoh, J. K. **Local Government in Ghana.** New York: Oxford University Press, 1964, 309 p.
A valuable study of the Ghanaian local government system, including chapters on general background and recent developments.

Oertly, Walter Viktor. **Wirtschaftliche Zentralprobleme Ghanas seit der Unabhängigkeit.** Berne: Lang, 1971, 305 p.
A study of Ghana's economy and foreign trade.

Omari, T. Peter. **Kwame Nkrumah: The Anatomy of an African Dictatorship.** London: C. Hurst, 1970, 229 p.
An attempt to assess the role of the controversial Ghanian leader in the contemporary history of Africa and his own country.

Pinkney, Robert. **Ghana under Military Rule, 1966-1969.** London: Methuen, 1972, 182 p.
According to the author of this study, Ghana's soldiers behaved like statesmen after deposing Nkrumah, working effectively with civilians to promote austerity and a return to elected government. Pinkney's study was written before the 1972 coup; therefore the symmetry of his success story is not marred by the evidence of its transitory quality.

Thompson, Willard Scott. **Ghana's Foreign Policy, 1957-1966: Diplomacy, Ideology, and the New State.** Princeton: Princeton University Press, 1969, 462 p.
Foreign-policy objectives and strategies to reach those objectives have to be developed in relationship to the resources available to a country. Nkrumah is criticized for his failure to grasp this basic fact. A first-rate analysis by a professor at the Fletcher School of Law and Diplomacy.

NIGERIA

Politics and Government

See also (Great Britain) Imperial and Commonwealth Relations; Colonial Policy, p. 367; (Union of Soviet Socialist Republics) Relations with Other Countries, p. 558; (Africa) General, p. 776; (West Africa) General, p. 807; other subsections under Nigeria.

Adedeji, Adebayo. **Nigerian Administration and Its Political Setting.** London: Hutchinson, 1968, 162 p.
A collection of papers on Nigerian politics given at the Institute of Administration, University of Ife, in 1966.

Arikpo, Okoi. **The Development of Modern Nigeria.** Baltimore: Penguin, 1967, 176 p.
A searing critique of political life in Nigeria through the early months of 1966, by a Nigerian author whose legal training and use of almost exclusively British sources lead him to an overemphasis on constitutional developments.

Awa, Eme O. **Federal Government in Nigeria.** Berkeley: University of California Press, 1964, 349 p.
A Nigerian political scientist describes the structure of the federal government and of the regional governments in Nigeria. A useful reference book.

Awolowo, Obafemi. **The People's Republic.** New York: Oxford University Press, 1969, 356 p.
A well-known Nigerian politician analyzes the effects of the colonial period upon his country, develops some general principles by which its constitutional crisis should be resolved and gives his own personal blueprint for a new constitution.

Awolowo, Obafemi. **Thoughts on Nigerian Constitution.** New York: Oxford University Press, 1967, 196 p.
The author proposes a fragmented federation of eleven states organized along linguistic lines. Written before his release from prison, this proposal for a new constitution was put forward in the period between the two 1966 coups and the Biafra secession.

Azikiwe, Nnamdi. **My Odyssey: An Autobiography.** New York: Praeger, 1971, 452 p.
The former President of Nigeria reminisces on his formative years, the extended sojourn in the United States in the 1920s and 1930s, and on his political, journalistic and publishing activities.

Blitz, L. Franklin, *ed.* **The Politics and Administration of Nigerian Government.** New York: Praeger, 1965, 281 p.
An introduction to the structure and operation of Nigerian political and administrative institutions.

Brown, Charles V. **Government and Banking in Western Nigeria.** New York: Oxford University Press (for the Nigerian Institute of Social and Economic Research), 1964, 141 p.
A brief analysis of the political and economic history of Western Nigeria.

Campbell, Michael J. **Law and Practice of Local Government in Northern Nigeria.** Lagos: African Universities Press, 1963, 236 p.
A detailed description of local government and local authorities in Northern Nigeria.

Dudley, Billy J. **Parties and Politics in Northern Nigeria.** London: Frank Cass, 1968, 352 p.
A scholarly analysis, based on research carried out in 1963-64, of the ineffectiveness of political parties and parliamentary rule in Northern Nigeria before the outbreak of the civil war.

Enahoro, Anthony Eronsele Oseghale. **Fugitive Offender: The Story of a Political Prisoner.** London: Cassell, 1965, 436 p.
Chief Enahoro, a Nigerian political leader, writes about his political activities in Western Nigeria and his flight to Great Britain, from where he was sent back to Nigeria to stand trial on treason charges.

Hatch, John Charles. **Nigeria: The Seeds of Disaster.** Chicago: Regnery, 1970, 313 p.
A general history of Nigeria by a British author.

Jakande, Lateef K. **The Trial of Obafemi Awolowo.** London: Secker and Warburg, 1966, 354 p.
The bulk of this work on the trial in 1962 and 1963 of a leading Nigerian politician consists of verbatim extracts from the proceedings of the trial. The author himself was one of the accused.

Jones-Quartey, K. A. B. **A Life of Azikiwe.** Baltimore: Penguin, 1966, 272 p.
The career of one of Nigeria's outstanding nationalists and first President is traced against the background of the turbulent transition from empire to commonwealth in this informative though drily written biography by a professor at the University of Ghana.

Kaden, Wolfgang. **Das nigerianische Experiment.** Hanover: Verlag für Literatur und Zeitgeschehen, 1968, 188 p.
A competent survey of Nigerian political development since independence, with particular emphasis on factors leading to the coups of 1966 and the ensuing civil war.

Kirk-Greene, A. H. M. **Crisis and Conflict in Nigeria: A Documentary Sourcebook, 1966–1970.** New York: Oxford University Press, 1971, 2 v.
The book-length introduction to these two volumes of documents provides a lucid and closely substantiated account of the important events leading up to and spanning the civil war; the collection of primary source material is a significant tool for students of Nigeria.

Luckham, Robin. **The Nigerian Military: A Sociological Analysis of Authority and Revolt, 1960–67.** New York: Cambridge University Press, 1971, 376 p.
Comprehensive and detailed, this study focuses on the training, organization and functions of the military in order to explain its fateful political interventions in 1966.

Mackintosh, John Pitcairn. **Nigerian Government and Politics: Prelude to the Revolution.** Evanston: Northwestern University Press, 1966, 651 p.
Professor Mackintosh's treatment of the complicated ethnic-political struggles in Nigeria gives an excellent picture of politics before the January 1966 coup.

Melson, Robert and Wolpe, Howard, *eds.* **Nigeria: Modernization and the Politics of Communalism.** East Lansing: Michigan State University Press, 1971, 680 p.
Distinguished Africanists comment on the impact of what Geertz calls "primordial" attachments to modernization and political development. A contribution to the literature on Nigeria as well as to the discipline of political science.

Miners, N. J. **The Nigerian Army, 1956–1966.** London: Methuen, 1971, 290 p.
A description of the transfer of colonial armed forces to the new Nigerian government, the "Nigerianization" of these forces and their use in the Congo, Tanganyika and elsewhere. However, the major focus of this work by a political scientist who spent nine years at King's College, Lagos, is on the army's increasing involvement in politics, culminating in the coups of 1966.

Murray, D. J., *ed.* **Studies in Nigerian Administration.** London: Hutchinson Educational (for the Institute of Administration, University of Ife), 1970, 324 p.
Six short studies by Nigerian and foreign scholars on various administrative processes in Nigeria in the 1950s and 1960s.

Nelson, Harold D. and Others. **Area Handbook for Nigeria.** Washington: G.P.O., 1972, 485 p.
A useful reference volume with a bibliography, prepared by the Foreign Area Studies at the American University.

Nicolson, I. F. **The Administration of Nigeria, 1900–1960: Men, Methods and Myths.** Oxford: Clarendon Press, 1969, 326 p.
A thorough study of the development of the public services and of public administration in Nigeria.

Niven, Sir Cecil Rex. **Nigeria.** New York: Praeger, 1967, 268 p.
A standard, non-academic introduction to Nigerian development from the beginning of the colonial period, by a Briton whose long service in Nigeria included several posts in the Northern Region government up until 1962.

Odumosu, Oluwole Idowu. **The Nigerian Constitution: History and Development.** London: Sweet and Maxwell, 1963, 407 p.
A capable presentation by a Nigerian legal scholar who expresses his concern that constitutional rights have been violated by the federal government.

Park, Andrew Edward Wilson. **The Sources of Nigerian Law.** Lagos: African Universities Press, 1963, 161 p.
This study examines the conflicting influence of the English law and the Nigerian customary law in the development of the Nigerian legal system.

Phillips, Claude S., Jr. **The Development of Nigerian Foreign Policy.** Evanston: Northwestern University Press, 1964, 154 p.
An analysis of the formation and implementation of foreign policy in Nigeria from the period preceding the federal election of 1959 to mid-1963.

Post, Kenneth William John. **The Nigerian Federal Election 1959.** New York: Oxford University Press (for the Nigerian Institute of Social and Economic Research), 1963, 518 p.
An election study which entails examination of political, administrative and judicial structures in Nigeria.

Schwarz, Frederick August Otto, Jr. **Nigeria: The Tribes, the Nation, or the Race—The Politics of Independence.** Cambridge: M.I.T. Press, 1965, 316 p.
This study of Nigerian political history is focused on the implications of regional and ethnic diversity for the creation of a new nation and the operation of democratic institutions.

Schwarz, Walter. **Nigeria.** New York: Praeger, 1968, 328 p.
This study of post-independence Nigeria stresses the factors leading up to the 1966 coups and to the civil war beginning in July 1967.

Sklar, Richard L. **Nigerian Political Parties: Power in an Emergent African Nation.** Princeton: Princeton University Press, 1963, 578 p.
A detailed analysis, employing case-study techniques, of party structures and functions in a new state.

Smith, Sir Bryan Sharwood. **Recollections of British Administration in the Cameroons and Northern Nigeria, 1921-1957: "But Always as Friends."** Durham: Duke University Press, 1969, 460 p.
The memoirs of the former Governor of Northern Nigeria.

Smock, Audrey C. **Ibo Politics: The Role of Ethnic Unions in Eastern Nigeria.** Cambridge: Harvard University Press, 1971, 274 p.
A "micropolitical study" by an American political scientist.

Whitaker, C. Sylvester, Jr. **The Politics of Tradition: Continuity and Change in Northern Nigeria, 1946-1966.** Princeton: Princeton University Press (for the Center of International Studies), 1970, 563 p.
Addressing himself to his fellow political scientists, a Princeton professor argues that "modernity" and "tradition" have a far more complicated relationship to one another than is commonly recognized: the former does not inexorably replace or supplant the latter; rather, they achieve, at least in Northern Nigeria, what he calls a "stable symbiosis."

White, Stanhope. **Dan Bana: The Memoirs of a Nigerian Official.** New York: James H. Heineman, 1967, 268 p.
This personal account of a colonial district officer posted in Northern Nigeria from 1936 to 1954 captures much of the spirit of British colonial policy before the surge to independence.

The Civil War

See also (War) General, p. 108; (Africa) International Relations, p. 784; other subsections under Nigeria.

Akpan, Ntieyong U. **The Struggle for Secession, 1966-1970.** London: Frank Cass, 1972, 225 p.
The former leader of the civil service in what was once Biafra, and an opponent of Biafra's secession, describes the tragic civil war in Nigeria in the 1960s.

Červenka, Zdenek. **The Nigerian War, 1967–1970.** Frankfurt/Main: Bernard und Graefe Verlag für Wehrwesen, 1971, 459 p.
   A useful collection of documents and a comprehensive bibliography, with an extensive introduction.

Debré, François. **Biafra, an II.** Paris: Julliard, 1968, 222 p.
   A sympathetic glimpse through the eyes of a French journalist into war-torn Biafra during mid-1968. Includes an interview with Colonel Ojukwu.

De St. Jorre, John. **The Brothers' War: Biafra and Nigeria.** Boston: Houghton Mifflin, 1972, 437 p.
   A comprehensive account of the Nigerian Civil War. The author manages to combine clear-cut analyses of the main issues with a mass of authenticated detail about the major figures, motives and events.

Forsyth, Frederick. **The Biafra Story.** Baltimore: Penguin, 1969, 236 p.
   Generally sympathetic to the Biafran cause, this work describes the origins and analyzes the issues in the Nigerian Civil War. The author, a British journalist with wide African experience, covers developments through early 1969.

Niven, Sir Cecil Rex. **The War of Nigerian Unity, 1967–1970.** Totowa (N.J.): Rowman and Littlefield, 1971, 175 p.
   A brief and quite general analysis of the administrative and political sources of the civil war.

Nwankwo, Arthur Agwuncha and Ifejika, Samuel Udochukwu. **Biafra: The Making of a Nation.** New York: Praeger, 1970, 361 p.
   Two supporters of Colonel Ojukwu's movement present the case for Biafra's secession and independence. Written before the Federal victory over Biafra.

Ojukwu, Chukuemeka Odumegwu. **Biafra: Selected Speeches and Random Thoughts of C. Odumegwu Ojukwu, with Diaries of Events.** New York: Harper and Row, 1969, 613 p.
   A collection of speeches by the Ibo leader of the Biafran independence movement.

Okpaku, Joseph, *ed.* **Nigeria: Dilemma of Nationhood; An African Analysis of the Biafran Conflict.** New York: The Third Press, 1972, 426 p.
   An uneven collection of essays on Nigerian institutions and the civil war, by eight African authors.

Renard, Alain. **Biafra, naissance d'une nation?** Paris: Aubier-Montaigne, 1969, 255 p.
   A general treatment of Nigeria's post-independence difficulties which culminated in the attempted secession of Biafra in July 1967. The author describes events through January 1969.

Uwechue, Raph. **Reflections on the Nigerian Civil War: Facing the Future.** New York: Africana Publishing Corp., 1971, 206 p.
   The author, an Ibo, describes the origins of the civil war, his own reasons for supporting the secession, and then his gradual alienation from Ojukwu's leadership. A thoughtful, fair-minded book.

Economic and Social Conditions

See also Economic Growth and Development, p. 71; (Africa) General, p. 776; other subsections under Nigeria.

Aboyade, Ojetunji. **Foundations of an African Economy: A Study of Investment and Growth in Nigeria.** New York: Praeger, 1966, 366 p.
   In this informed study of the development of the Nigerian economy since World War I, an economist at the University of Ibadan discusses major theoretical and methodological problems involved in the measurement of development. His critical appraisal concludes with several proposals for a reorientation of economic planning in Nigeria.

Brown, Charles V. **The Nigerian Banking System.** Evanston: Northwestern University Press, 1966, 214 p.
   A survey of the accomplishments and deficiencies of Nigerian banking from 1950 to 1963.

Damachi, Ukandi Godwin. **Nigerian Modernization: The Colonial Legacy.** New York: Third Press, 1972, 145 p.
A Nigerian social scientist looks at what the West has wrought in his country, accepting as inevitable the growth of social stratification, the decline of family and tribal ties, and the increasing urbanization.

Dill, Kurt. **Industrialisierung Nigerias.** Basel: Institut für Angewandte Wirtschaftsforschung der Universität Basel, 1965, 252 p.
A study of Nigeria's industrialization. Issued under the auspices of the Basel Centre for Economic and Financial Research.

Eicher, Carl K. and Liedholm, Carl, *eds.* **Growth and Development of the Nigerian Economy.** East Lansing: Michigan State University Press, 1970, 456 p.
A collection of studies on Nigerian economy.

Ikejiani, Okechukwu, *ed.* **Education in Nigeria.** New York: Praeger, 1965, 234 p.
Three Nigerian educators and an American collaborator offer specific suggestions and remedies.

Kilby, Peter. **Industrialization in an Open Economy: Nigeria 1945-1966.** New York: Cambridge University Press, 1969, 399 p.
A solid study by a professor at Wesleyan University.

Mummery, David R. **The Protection of International Private Investment: Nigeria and the World Community.** New York: Praeger, 1968, 198 p.
A survey of bilateral and multilateral efforts to protect foreign investments in Nigeria.

Okigbo, Pius Nwabufo C. **Nigerian Public Finance.** Evanston: Northwestern University Press, 1965, 245 p.
A Nigerian economist, charged with the negotiations leading to Nigeria's association with the E.E.C., examines fiscal relationships in his country.

Onyemelukwe, Clement Chukwukadibia. **Problems of Industrial Planning and Management in Nigeria.** New York: Columbia University Press, 1966, 330 p.
A survey of the central problems and deficiencies in Nigeria's 1962-68 Development Plan.

Pearson, Scott R. **Petroleum and the Nigerian Economy.** Stanford: Stanford University Press, 1970, 235 p.
A Stanford University economist calculates that the net direct and indirect benefits of foreign investment in the petroleum industry amount to about seven percent of prewar national income and might increase considerably in the coming years.

Proehl, Paul O. **Foreign Enterprise in Nigeria: Laws and Policies.** Chapel Hill: University of North Carolina Press, 1965, 250 p.
This study was sponsored by the American Society of International Law.

Seibel, Hans Dieter. **Industriearbeit und Kulturwandel in Nigeria.** Opladen: Westdeutscher Verlag, 1968, 503 p.
A study of the relationships between social change and industrialization in Southern Nigeria. A major piece of systematic, empirical research.

Smock, David R. and Smock, Audrey C. **Cultural and Political Aspects of Rural Transformation: A Case Study of Eastern Nigeria.** New York: Praeger, 1972, 387 p.
A study emphasizing the effectiveness of demonstrated economic advantage in stimulating Ibo and Ibibio farmers in Nigeria to adopt new social, political and economic habits.

Sokolski, Alan. **The Establishment of Manufacturing in Nigeria.** New York: Praeger, 1965, 373 p.
A factual and statistical study of industrial growth.

Weiler, Hans N., *ed.* **Erziehung und Politik in Nigeria—Education and Politics in Nigeria.** Freiburg im Breisgau: Rombach, 1964, 294 p.
A collection of papers on education, social change and politics in Nigeria, by English, American and German scholars.

CHAD; NIGER

See also (Africa) General, p. 776; (West Africa) General, p. 807; (Central Africa) General, p. 821.

Diguimbaya, Georges and Langue, Robert. **L'Essor du Tchad.** Paris: Presses Universitaires, 1969, 400 p.
A comprehensive study of economic and social development of Chad through 1966. There is a very useful bibliography.

Donaint, Pierre and Lancrenon, François. **Le Niger.** Paris: Presses Universitaires, 1972, 126 p.
An introduction to contemporary Niger.

Hugot, Pierre. **Le Tchad.** Paris: Nouvelles Éditions Latines, 1965, 155 p.
An introduction to the Republic of Chad.

Le Cornec, Jacques. **Histoire politique du Tchad de 1900 à 1962.** Paris: Librairie Générale de Droit, 1963, 374 p.
Focusing on the role of the chiefs and the place of chieftaincies, the author describes the legal and administrative changes that have taken place in Chad in the twentieth century. The book's documentation will be valuable for future comparative analysis.

Nelson, Harold D. and Others. **Area Handbook for Chad.** Washington: G.P.O., 1972, 261 p.
A useful reference volume with a bibliography, prepared by the Foreign Area Studies at the American University.

Séré de Rivières, Edmond. **Histoire du Niger.** Paris: Berger-Levrault, 1965, 311 p.
Surveying the physical and cultural inheritance of Niger since prehistoric times, the author describes in detail the history of the peoples of Niger from the early medieval kingdoms through the period of twentieth-century colonial rule.

CENTRAL AFRICA

GENERAL

See also Ethnic Problems; The Jews, p. 46; United Nations, p. 99; (Africa) General, p. 776.

Anguilé, André G. and David, Jacques E. **L'Afrique sans frontières.** Monaco: Éditions Paul Bory, 1965, 311 p.
An account of economic regionalism in Central Africa devoting considerable attention to the formation in 1964 of an economic union between Chad, Gabon, the Central African Republic, Congo-Brazzaville and the Cameroons.

Dreux-Brézé, Joachim de. **Le Problème du regroupement en Afrique équatoriale.** Paris: Librairie Générale de Droit, 1968, 211 p.
A study of the development of the Union Douanière et Économique de l'Afrique Centrale, with emphasis on its structural aspects.

Gussman, Boris. **Out in the Mid-Day Sun.** New York: Oxford University Press, 1963, 179 p.
An appraisal of the role and attitudes of the European settler in Central Africa.

Ranger, Terence Osborn, *ed.* **Aspects of Central African History.** Evanston: Northwestern University Press, 1968, 291 p.
A series of essays by members of the History Department at the University College at Dar es Salaam on the indigenous political systems of Portuguese, Belgian and British Central Africa, especially during the colonial period.

Sautter, Gilles. **De l'Atlantique au fleuve Congo: une géographie du sous-peuplement.** Paris: Mouton, 1966, 582 p.
This massive study, sponsored by the École Pratique des Hautes Études at the Sorbonne, contains a wealth of information on the physical, economic and social geography of the Republic of Congo and the Republic of Gabon.

ZAÏRE (CONGO-KINSHASA)

See also United Nations, p. 99; (The United States) Foreign Policy, p. 229; Belgium, p. 391; (Africa) General, p. 776; (Central Africa) General, p. 821.

Anstey, Roger. **King Leopold's Legacy: The Congo under Belgian Rule, 1908-1960.** New York: Oxford University Press (for the Institute of Race Relations, London), 1966, 293 p.
A scholarly examination of the origins and nature of Belgian rule in the Congo and of its social, economic and political impact.

Bouvier, Paule. **L'Accession du Congo Belge à l'indépendance: essai d'analyse sociologique.** Brussels: Éditions de l'Institut de Sociologie, Université Libre de Bruxelles, 1965, 392 p.
An account of the Congo's swift move from a politically underdeveloped colony to an independent state; much attention is paid to the years immediately preceding independence.

Colvin, Ian Goodhope. **The Rise and Fall of Moïse Tshombe: A Biography.** London: Leslie Frewin, 1968, 263 p.
A sympathetic biography of the late leader of secessionist Katanga.

Congo. Brussels: Centre de Recherche et d'Information Socio-Politiques.
Annual collections of official documents and surveys relating to political developments in the Congo (Kinshasa), covering the years since 1959. The 1964 and 1965 volumes were published in the United States in 1966-67 by Princeton University Press.

Cornevin, Robert. **Histoire du Congo (Léopoldville).** Paris: Berger-Levrault, 1963, 336 p.
A detailed history of the Congo by a well-known Africanist.

Ganshof van der Meersch, W. J. **Fin de la souveraineté belge au Congo.** Brussels: Institut Royal des Relations Internationales, 1963, 684 p.
The Belgian Minister of General Affairs in Africa from May 15 to July 20, 1960, gives a detailed account of the events of those days in Congo, as well as his reflections on them. Invaluable documentation for this critical period.

Gendebien, Paul-Henry. **L'Intervention des Nations Unies au Congo, 1960-1964.** Paris: Mouton, 1967, 292 p.
In assessing the work of the United Nations in the Congo, this Dutch legal scholar and economist concludes that despite its many difficulties, the U.N. intervention did maintain the territorial integrity of the Congo and probably prevented an even more protracted period of violence and chaos.

Gérard-Libois, Jules. **Katanga Secession.** Madison: University of Wisconsin Press, 1966, 377 p.
A detailed study of the secession of Katanga. The author considers the situation in Katanga prior to independence, the period of secession, and the province's potential role in the Republic of Congo. The French original appeared as: "Sécession au Katanga" (Brussels: Centre de Recherche et d'Information Socio-Politiques, 1963, 363 p.).

Germani, Hans. **Weisse Söldner im schwarzen Land: ein Erlebnisbericht.** Frankfurt/Main: Ullstein, 1966, 175 p.
A sympathetic account, by a German correspondent, of the activities of Michael Hoare's white mercenaries during their suppression of the Mulele rebellion against the Leopoldville government in 1964-65.

Heinz, G. and Donnay, H. **Lumumba Patrice: les cinquante derniers jours de sa vie.** Brussels: Centre de Recherche et d'Information Socio-Politiques, 1966, 196 p.
A memoir of the last days of Lumumba, first Premier of the Republic of Congo in 1960.

Hoskyns, Catherine. **The Congo since Independence.** New York: Oxford University Press (for the Royal Institute of International Affairs), 1965, 518 p.
A detailed and carefully researched record of the events from January 1960 to the end of 1961.

Kanza, Thomas. **Conflict in the Congo: The Rise and Fall of Lumumba.** Baltimore: Penguin, 1972, 345 p.

A narrative of Patrice Lumumba's brief, turbulent career as Prime Minister of the newly independent Republic of the Congo related by his Minister for U.N. Affairs.

Kashamura, Anicet. **De Lumumba aux colonels.** Paris: Buchet/Chastel, 1966, 270 p.
A former Minister of Information and close associate of Lumumba gives an impassioned history of the frustrations of African nationalists in the Congo and elsewhere.

Kestergat, Jean. **Congo, Congo.** Paris: Éditions de la Table Ronde, 1965, 196 p.
An eye-witness account of the Congo crisis by a correspondent of the Belgian newspaper, *La Libre Belgique*.

Kitchen, Helen A., ed. **Footnotes to the Congo Story: An "Africa Report" Anthology.** New York: Walker, 1967, 175 p.
A collection of short essays on the Congo written since 1960.

Lacroix, Jean Louis. **Industrialisation au Congo: la transformation des structures économiques.** Paris: Mouton, 1967, 358 p.
An economist who was at the Institut de Recherches Économiques et Sociales of the University of Lovanium at Kinshasa attempts to examine Congolese development in the light of contemporary theories of economic growth. The incapacity of the indigenous political structure to make the key decisions in the foreign-dominated economy is seen as a major barrier to rational economic planning.

La Fontaine, Jean Sybil. **City Politics: A Study of Léopoldville, 1962-63.** New York: Cambridge University Press, 1970, 246 p.
An anthropologist at the London School of Economics has written an interesting study of politics and social relations in a major African city shortly after independence.

LeClercq, Claude. **L'ONU et l'affaire du Congo.** Paris: Payot, 1964, 367 p.
A chronological rather than analytical examination of the U.N. actions in the Congo.

Lefever, Ernest Warren. **Crisis in the Congo: A United Nations Force in Action.** Washington: Brookings Institution, 1965, 215 p.
A detailed review and analysis of the U.N. peace-keeping effort in the Congo.

Lefever, Ernest Warren. **Uncertain Mandate: Politics of the U.N. Congo Operation.** Baltimore: Johns Hopkins Press, 1967, 254 p.
A well-researched assessment of the United Nations' activities in the Congo from 1960 to 1964.

Lemarchand, René. **Political Awakening in the Belgian Congo.** Berkeley: University of California Press, 1964, 357 p.
A lucid and detailed study of the history of the Congo in the pre-colonial and colonial periods.

Lopez Alvarez, Luis. **Lumumba ou l'Afrique frustrée.** Paris: Cujas, 1964, 233 p.
An admiring biography of the Congolese political leader Patrice Lumumba, assassinated in Katanga on January 17, 1961. There is a useful chronology covering the events in Congo from 1958 to 1961.

Lumumba, Patrice. **Lumumba Speaks: The Speeches and Writings of Patrice Lumumba, 1958-1961.** Boston: Little, Brown, 1972, 433 p.
This collection of speeches and lectures has been edited by Jean Van Lierde. In his introduction, Jean-Paul Sartre portrays Lumumba in existentialist terms as a doomed symbol of his country's future. The French original appeared as "La Pensée politique de Patrice Lumumba" (Paris: Présence Africaine, 1964, 401 p.).

Martelli, George Ansley. **Experiment in World Government.** London: C. Johnson Publications, 1966, 244 p.
A very critical account of the operations of the United Nations forces in Congo from 1960 to 1964.

Nkrumah, Kwame. **Challenge of the Congo.** New York: International Publishers, 1967, 304 p.
This work by the former President of Ghana contains many documents exchanged between him and various important figures involved in the political affairs of the Congo. The volume includes a secret agreement between Lumumba and Nkrumah to unite their two countries with a capital at Leopoldville.

Okumu, Washington A. Jalango. **Lumumba's Congo: Roots of Conflict.** New York: Obolensky, 1963, 250 p.

In this analysis of the Congo crisis a Kenyan political economist emphasizes that independence can be won only through struggle.

Saïd, Shafik-G. **De Léopoldville à Kinshasa: la situation économique et financière au Congo ex-belge au jour de l'indépendance.** Brussels: Centre National d'Étude des Problèmes Sociaux de l'Industrialisation en Afrique Noire, 1969, 262 p.
An assessment of the economic and political difficulties Congo faced at independence.

Scott, Ian. **Tumbled House: The Congo at Independence.** New York: Oxford University Press, 1969, 142 p.
An account of the turbulent period from January 1960 to July 1961, by the senior British diplomat in what was then Leopoldville, who later became the first British ambassador to the independent Congo.

Tshombe, Moise. **My Fifteen Months in Government.** Plano (Tex.): University of Plano, 1967, 117 p.
The former Prime Minister makes a highly personal defense of his attempt to restore order and central control in the Congo in 1964-65.

Valahu, Mugur. **The Katanga Circus: A Detailed Account of Three UN Wars.** New York: Speller, 1964, 364 p.
An impassioned advocate of Katanga's separatism castigates the role of the United Nations. The French original appeared as "Ci-gît le Katanga" (Paris: Nouvelles Éditions Latines, 1964, 418 p.).

Verbeek, Roger. **Le Congo en question.** Paris: Présence Africaine, 1965, 223 p.
Mr. Verbeek offers some penetrating reflections on his first-hand experiences in the Congo. Bitterly condemning the cultural debasement inherent in colonial rule, he argues, with Fanon, that true emancipation and decolonization must entail the rejection of Europe.

Verhaegen, Benoît. **Rébellions au Congo.** Brussels: Centre de Recherche et d'Information Socio-Politiques, 1966-69, 2 v.
A massive survey, with a supplement of documents, of the contemporary history of Congo, particularly of the violent events in 1963 and 1964 which were, in the author's opinion, often influenced by the followers of the revolutionary doctrines of Marxism, Leninism and Chinese communism.

Weiss, Herbert F. **Political Protest in the Congo: The Parti Solidaire Africain during the Independence Struggle.** Princeton: Princeton University Press, 1967, 326 p.
Professor Weiss suggests that rural radicalism in the Congo was only temporarily harnessed by the political parties in the struggle against the European élite, but that after independence rural radicals (politicized peasants) have come to resist African élite domination in the same way.

Young, Crawford. **Politics in the Congo: Decolonization and Independence.** Princeton: Princeton University Press, 1965, 659 p.
A perceptive and penetrating analysis of political evolution in the Congo.

CONGO-BRAZZAVILLE

See also (Africa) General, p. 776; (Central Africa) General, p. 821.

Amin, Samir and Coquery-Vidrovitch, Catherine. **Histoire économique du Congo 1880-1968.** Paris: Éditions Anthropos, 1969, 204 p.
The process of economic development in the Congo (Brazzaville) is examined with particular emphasis on the period between 1960 and 1968 and the development of a customs union among the countries of former French Equatorial Africa.

McDonald, Gordon C. and Others. **Area Handbook for People's Republic of Congo (Congo Brazzaville).** Washington: G.P.O., 1971, 255 p.
A useful reference volume with a bibliography, prepared by the Foreign Area Studies at the American University.

Vennetier, Pierre. **Géographie du Congo-Brazzaville.** Paris: Gauthier-Villars, 1966, 170 p.
An informative geographical survey.

Wagret, Jean-Michel. **Histoire et sociologie politiques de la République du Congo (Brazzaville).** Paris: Librairie Générale de Droit, 1963, 250 p.
A study of the historical background and political forces in Congo (Brazzaville).

CAMEROON

See also (Africa) General, p. 776; (Nigeria) Politics and Government, p. 816; (Central Africa) General, p. 821.

Gardinier, David E. **Cameroon: United Nations Challenge to French Policy.** New York: Oxford University Press (for the Institute of Race Relations), 1963, 142 p.
A descriptive study of the development of Cameroon under French trusteeship and of the effect of U.N. presence and activity.

Hugon, Philippe. **Analyse du sous-développement en Afrique noire: l'exemple de l'économie du Cameroun.** Paris: Presses Universitaires, 1968, 327 p.
A well-organized and comprehensive survey of the economy of Cameroon, by a French scholar with first-hand knowledge of the country.

Johnson, Willard R. **The Cameroon Federation: Political Integration in a Fragmentary Society.** Princeton: Princeton University Press, 1970, 426 p.
A political scientist at M.I.T. argues that there are important distinctions between the processes of integration required for building a state and the processes of integration required for developing a nation.

Le Vine, Victor Theodore. **The Cameroon Federal Republic.** Ithaca: Cornell University Press, 1971, 205 p.
A compact introductory survey by a political scientist at Washington University. The basic argument is that President Ahidjo's able leadership accounts for a decade of internal political stability and steady economic progress.

Le Vine, Victor Theodore. **The Cameroons: From Mandate to Independence.** Berkeley: University of California Press, 1964, 329 p.
A detailed analysis of political developments in the Cameroons, with particular attention to the structure and role of political parties.

Mveng, Englebert. **Histoire du Cameroun.** Paris: Présence Africaine, 1963, 533 p.
A history of Cameroon, stressing the pre-colonial period but describing also the colonial administrations, the establishment of independence and the reunification of the country.

Rubin, Neville. **Cameroun: An African Federation.** New York: Praeger, 1971, 259 p.
A study of Cameroon from its colonization by Germany and its division into separate French and British mandates through the reunification of the two disparate cultural areas under the present independent regime.

GABON; CENTRAL AFRICAN REPUBLIC

See also (Africa) General, p. 776; (Central Africa) General, p. 821.

Darlington, Charles Francis and Darlington, Alice Benning. **African Betrayal.** New York: McKay, 1968, 359 p.
An account of the political developments which confronted the first U.S. Ambassador to Gabon, and a personal memoir about life in Libreville by his wife.

Kalck, Pierre. **Central African Republic: A Failure in Decolonization.** New York: Praeger, 1971, 206 p.
The author, a French scholar with first-hand experience in the new African state that was established in 1960, concludes his informative survey by stating that "the inhabitants do not really distinguish between colonial regime and the government that came with independence."

Weinstein, Brian. **Gabon: Nation-Building on the Ogooué.** Cambridge: M.I.T. Press, 1967, 287 p.
A somewhat abstract study of Gabonese political development.

EAST AFRICA

GENERAL

See also International Finance, p. 59; (First World War) The Conduct of the War, p. 136; (Second World War) North and East Africa; Near and Middle East, p. 165; (Africa) General, p. 776.

Archer, Sir Geoffrey Francis. **Personal and Historical Memoirs of an East African Administrator.** Edinburgh: Oliver and Boyd, 1963, 260 p.
Reminiscences by a British governor of three different territories, British Somaliland, Uganda and the Anglo-Egyptian Sudan, from 1914 to 1926.

Cox, Richard Hubert Francis. **Pan-Africanism in Practice: An East African Study; PAFMECSA 1958-1964.** New York: Oxford University Press (for the Institute of Race Relations), 1964, 95 p.
A somewhat uncritical examination of attempts made by the Pan-African Freedom Movement of Eastern, Central and Southern Africa toward political unity.

Diamond, Stanley and Burke, Fred G., *eds.* **The Transformation of East Africa: Studies in Political Anthropology.** New York: Basic Books, 1967, 623 p.
Issued by the Program of Eastern African Studies at Syracuse University, this comprehensive volume contains sixteen essays by distinguished Africanists.

Doob, Leonard W., *ed.* **Resolving Conflict in Africa: The Fermeda Workshop.** New Haven: Yale University Press, 1970, 209 p.
In 1969 a session was held in Fermeda, Italy, with participants from Somalia, Kenya and Ethiopia, with the aim of finding ways of resolving border problems among the three countries. This volume includes assessments of these sessions by participants.

Franck, Thomas M. **East African Unity through Law.** New Haven: Yale University Press, 1964, 184 p.
A description and analysis of the institutions which have laid the foundations for unity in East Africa, prepared under the auspices of the American Society of International Law.

Ghai, Dharam P., *ed.* **Portrait of a Minority: Asians in East Africa.** New York: Oxford University Press, 1966, 154 p.
This volume of essays by six Asian intellectuals, residents or students of East Africa, provides information on the Asians' dilemma in Kenya, Uganda and Tanzania.

Gulliver, Philip Hugh, *ed.* **Tradition and Transition in East Africa.** Berkeley: University of California Press, 1969, 378 p.
Papers from an inter-disciplinary seminar on the role of tribalism in contemporary East African society presented during 1966–67 at the School of Oriental and African Studies at the University of London.

Harlow, Vincent and Chilver, E. M., *eds.* **History of East Africa. Volume II.** New York: Oxford University Press, 1965, 766 p.
This volume, the second in a three-part work on East African history, is an authoritative, scholarly study of the period from about 1890 through the Second World War.

Horrut, Claude. **Les Décolonisations est-africaines.** Paris: Pedone, 1971, 231 p.
A history of the withdrawal of British authority from Kenya, Uganda, Tanganyika and Zanzibar, with particular attention to problems of tribe, region, race and separatism. There is an extensive bibliography.

Hughes, Anthony John. **East Africa: The Search for Unity—Kenya, Tanganyika, Uganda, and Zanzibar.** Baltimore: Penguin, 1964, 277 p.
An analysis of East Africa's political development and of the tendencies toward federation through 1961, with a concluding chapter on events of 1962.

Hunter, Guy. **Education for a Developing Region: A Study in East Africa.** London: Allen and Unwin (for Political and Economic Planning and the Institute of Race Relations), 1963, 119 p.
A study of manpower needs in East Africa and a survey of the sources for manpower training and development.

Huxley, Elspeth Josceline (Grant). **With Forks and Hope: An African Notebook.** New York: Morrow, 1964, 398 p.

An examination of the East African peoples and places by a well-known English writer.

Leys, Colin Temple and Robson, Peter, *eds.* **Federation in East Africa: Opportunities and Problems.** New York: Oxford University Press, 1966, 244 p.
A collection of papers originally prepared for a conference on public policy in East Africa at the University College, Nairobi, in 1963.

Mangat, J. S. **A History of the Asians in East Africa, c. 1886 to 1945.** New York: Oxford University Press, 1969, 216 p.
A most useful historical survey of the Indian communities in the former British possessions in East Africa.

Mazrui, Ali Al'Amin. **Cultural Engineering and Nation-Building in East Africa.** Evanston: Northwestern University Press, 1972, 301 p.
A straightforward and detailed study by an eminent East African political scientist who sees fewer pitfalls in Kenya's version of "African capitalism" than in Tanzania's self-reliant (and -denying) communalism or Uganda's mixture of the two.

Meister, Albert. **Le Développement économique de l'Afrique orientale (Kenya, Ouganda, Tanzanie).** Paris: Presses Universitaires, 1966, 156 p.
After surveying the general problems of development and the national economic plans of Kenya, Uganda and Tanzania, the author concludes that the prospects for development in East Africa are dim.

Meister, Albert. **East Africa: The Past in Chains, the Future in Pawn.** New York: Walker, 1968, 282 p.
This book by a perceptive French sociologist presents a sobering discussion of Kenya, Uganda and Tanzania, and their plans and prospects for economic and social development. The French original appeared as "L'Afrique peut-elle partir? Changement social et développement en Afrique orientale" (Paris: Éditions du Seuil, 1966, 449 p.).

Nye, Joseph Samuel, Jr. **Pan-Africanism and East African Integration.** Cambridge: Harvard University Press, 1965, 307 p.
Mr. Nye's informative account of the social, economic and political bases of East African integration and his analysis of the reasons for the failure of attempts at federation in 1963 underscore the complex and significant role of ideological factors.

O'Connor, Anthony Michael. **An Economic Geography of East Africa.** New York: Praeger, 1966, 292 p.
A detailed survey of the physical, demographic, economic and political features which determine the character and distribution of economic activities in East Africa.

Pearson, D. S. **Industrial Development in East Africa.** New York: Oxford University Press, 1970, 213 p.
A description of some of the basic features of the process of economic development in East Africa.

Vente, Rolf E. **Planning Processes: The East African Case.** New York: Humanities Press, 1970, 233 p.
A study of the decision-processes involved in the formulation and implementation of economic planning in East Africa. Published under the auspices of the Munich Institute for Economic Development.

ETHIOPIA

See also Inter-War Period, p. 140; (Second World War) North and East Africa; Near and Middle East, p. 165; (The United States) Foreign Policy, p. 229; (Italy) Foreign Policy, p. 424; (Australia) Foreign and Defense Policies, p. 767; (Africa) General, p. 776; (East Africa) General, p. 826.

Baer, George W. **The Coming of the Italian-Ethiopian War.** Cambridge: Harvard University Press, 1967, 404 p.
An authoritative diplomatic and political history, well-documented and with a comprehensive bibliography.

Barker, Arthur J. **The Civilizing Mission: A History of the Italo-Ethiopian War of 1935–1936.** New York: Dial Press, 1968, 383 p.
A monograph by a British soldier-historian.

Boca, Angelo del. **The Ethiopian War, 1935–1941.** Chicago: University of Chicago Press, 1969, 289 p.
This history includes descriptions of the major battles and an evocative account of the Emperor's appearance before the League of Nations. Translated from "La guerra d'Abissinia" (Milan: Feltrinelli, 1965, 284 p.).

Clapham, Christopher. **Haile-Selassie's Government.** New York: Praeger, 1969, 218 p.
The author, a British scholar, argues that post-liberation Ethiopia has a dual structure of government in which traditional modes of politics are carried on behind a front of modern institutions.

Davy, André. **Éthiopie d'hier et d'aujourd'hui.** Paris: Le Livre Africain, 1970, 254 p.
A general political history from the pre-Axum period to the present.

Ginzberg, Eli and Smith, Herbert A. **Manpower Strategy for Developing Countries: Lessons from Ethiopia.** New York: Columbia University Press, 1967, 188 p.
An investigation by an American and an Israeli economist, sponsored by the U.S. Agency for International Development.

Greenfield, Richard. **Ethiopia: A New Political History.** New York: Praeger, 1965, 515 p.
A history of the ancient empire with emphasis on postwar developments, including the attempted *coup d'état* of 1960.

Harris, Brice, Jr. **The United States and the Italo-Ethiopian Crisis.** Stanford: Stanford University Press, 1964, 187 p.
A monograph on the role of the United States in the Ethiopian crisis of 1935–36.

Hess, Robert L. **Ethiopia: The Modernization of Autocracy.** Ithaca: Cornell University Press, 1970, 272 p.
A general overview of both history and contemporary politics.

Kaplan, Irving and Others. **Area Handbook for Ethiopia.** Washington: G.P.O., 1971, 525 p.
A useful reference volume with a bibliography, prepared by the Foreign Area Studies at the American University.

Levine, Donald Nathan. **Wax and Gold: Tradition and Innovation in Ethiopian Culture.** Chicago: University of Chicago Press, 1965, 315 p.
An examination, using various sociological techniques, of the dominant Ethiopian ethnic group, the Amhara.

Marcus, Harold G. **The Modern History of Ethiopia and the Horn of Africa: A Select and Annotated Bibliography.** Stanford: Hoover Institution Press, 1972, 641 p.
A most useful reference volume.

Mosley, Leonard Oswald. **Haile Selassie: The Conquering Lion.** Englewood Cliffs: Prentice-Hall, 1965, 288 p.
An informed and well-balanced biography of the Emperor.

Pankhurst, Richard Keir Pethick. **Economic History of Ethiopia, 1800–1935.** Addis Ababa: Haile Selassie I University Press, 1968, 772 p.
A massive survey by a leading student of Ethiopia.

Perham, Dame Margery Freda. **The Government of Ethiopia.** Evanston: Northwestern University Press, 1969, 531 p.
A re-issue of the now classic 1948 study with an additional chapter on developments since 1947, a chapter on central government by Christopher Clapham, and a new chronology of Ethiopian history.

Redden, Kenneth R. **The Legal System of Ethiopia.** Charlottesville: Michie Co., 1968, 290 p.
An American law professor surveys the legal, judicial and administrative structure of Ethiopia. This volume was sponsored by the University of Virginia School of Law.

Rochat, Giorgio. **Militari e politici nella preparazione della Campagna d'Etiopia: studio e documenti, 1932–1936.** Milan: Franco Angeli, 1971, 514 p.

This collection of letters and memoranda by De Bono, Badoglio and Graziani, three leading Italian participants in the Ethiopian conflict, reveals the lack of coherence in the planning and direction of the invasion of Ethiopia. The author guides the reader through the documents by providing interpretive commentary.

SOMALI REPUBLIC; THE FRENCH TERRITORY OF THE AFARS AND THE ISSAS

See also Comparative Government, p. 18; (Africa) General, p. 776; (East Africa) General, p. 826.

Contini, Paolo. **The Somali Republic: An Experiment in Legal Integration.** London: Frank Cass, 1969, 92 p.
A study of the legislative unification of the former British and Italian administered territories that formed the new Somali Republic.

Drysdale, John Gordon Stewart. **The Somali Dispute.** New York: Praeger, 1964, 183 p.
A discussion of the problems of the Somali peoples, by a former adviser to the Prime Minister of Somalia.

Hess, Robert L. **Italian Colonialism in Somalia.** Chicago: University of Chicago Press, 1966, 234 p.
A careful, factual account of Italian activities in "Africa Orientale Italiana" from 1885 to Somali independence in 1960.

Kaplan, Irving and Others. **Area Handbook for Somalia.** Washington: G.P.O., 1970, 455 p.
A useful reference volume with a bibliography, prepared by the Foreign Area Studies at the American University.

Laurence, Margaret. **New Wind in a Dry Land.** New York: Knopf, 1964, 295 p.
A Canadian novelist reports on the two years she and her engineer husband lived and worked in Somaliland. The English edition was published as "The Prophet's Camel Bell" (London: Macmillan, 1963, 239 p.).

Lewis, Ioan Myrddin. **The Modern History of Somaliland: From Nation to State.** New York: Praeger, 1965, 234 p.
This history of the Somalis chronicles their growth as a nation: from the nineteenth century partition to national consciousness and independence, from cultural to political identity.

Thompson, Virginia McLean and Adloff, Richard. **Djibouti and the Horn of Africa.** Stanford: Stanford University Press, 1968, 246 p.
An excellent analysis of the history, politics and economy of what used to be French Somaliland, now officially called the Territoire Français des Afars et des Issas. The authors suggest that Ethiopia's economic stake in the port of Djibouti and Somalia's irredentist claims to the area make continued French control of the territory a temporary convenience to both countries.

Touval, Saadia. **Somali Nationalism: International Politics and the Drive for Unity in the Horn of Africa.** Cambridge: Harvard University Press, 1963, 214 p.
A political history of the various constituent parts of contemporary Somalia and French Somaliland which gives full emphasis to the Pan-Somali fervor; overly optimistic in its hope for a peaceful resolution of border disputes.

KENYA

See also Food and Agriculture, p. 68; Economic Growth and Development, p. 71; (War) Guerilla Warfare; Armed Insurrection, p. 118; (Africa) General, p. 776; (East Africa) General, p. 826.

Barnett, Donald L. and Njama, Karari. **Mau Mau from within: Autobiography and Analysis of Kenya's Peasant Revolt.** New York: Monthly Review Press, 1966, 512 p.
An account of the Mau Mau movement by an American anthropologist and a former Mau Mau rebel.

Blundell, Sir Michael. **So Rough a Wind: Kenya Memoirs.** London: Weidenfeld, 1964, 340 p.
Important memoirs, containing a wealth of information on Kenya's move for independence, by a man who played a prominent role in the politics of the country after the Second World War.

Carey Jones, Norman Stewart. **The Anatomy of Uhuru: Dynamics and Problems of African Independence in an Age of Conflict.** New York: Praeger, 1967, 231 p.
An extended interpretive essay on the problems of Kenya's independent government by the Director in Development Administration at the University of Leeds.

Cox, Richard Hubert Francis. **Kenyatta's Country.** New York: Praeger, 1966, 203 p.
A foreign correspondent of *The Sunday Times* of London provides a vivid and competent account of the political transformation of Kenya since independence.

The Economic Development of Kenya. Baltimore: Johns Hopkins Press (for the International Bank for Reconstruction and Development), 1963, 380 p.
The report of the mission sent by the World Bank to help the government of Kenya plan its program of economic development.

Gatheru, R. Mugo. **Child of Two Worlds: A Kikuyu's Story.** New York: Praeger, 1964, 216 p.
An autobiography by a Western-educated Kenyan.

Gertzel, Cherry. **The Politics of Independent Kenya 1963-8.** Evanston: Northwestern University Press, 1970, 180 p.
A study by a political scientist at the University of Zambia.

Huxley, Elspeth Josceline (Grant). **White Man's Country: Lord Delamere and the Making of Kenya.** New York: Praeger, new ed., 1968, 2 v.
This new edition of an excellent biography of Lord Delamere, covering the period from 1870 to 1931, constitutes a history of the development of Kenya as a settlement for white men. The first edition appeared in 1935.

Kaplan, Irving and Others. **Area Handbook for Kenya.** Washington: G.P.O., 1967, 707 p.
A useful reference volume with a bibliography, prepared by the Foreign Area Studies at the American University.

Kariuki, Josiah Mwangi. **Mau Mau Detainee.** New York: Oxford University Press, 1963, 188 p.
A record of the experiences of a young Kikuyu detained from 1953 to 1960 as an activist in the Mau Mau movement in Kenya.

Kenyatta, Jomo. **Harambee! The Prime Minister of Kenya's Speeches 1963-1964, from the Attainment of Internal Self-Government to the Threshold of the Kenya Republic.** New York: Oxford University Press, 1964, 114 p.
Speeches illuminating the political philosophy of one of Africa's leading elder statesmen.

Kenyatta, Jomo. **Suffering without Bitterness: The Founding of the Kenya Nation.** Nairobi: East African Publishing House, 1968, 348 p.
The father of modern Kenya describes in this volume his struggle for the independence of his country. He devotes particular attention to his arrest, imprisonment and release by the British. There is an appendix of speeches.

MacPhee, Archibald Marshall. **Kenya.** New York: Praeger, 1968, 238 p.
A concise descriptive analysis of Kenya's embattled path from British colony to independent state, by a British journalist formerly associated with the East African Standard Group.

Mboya, Tom. **The Challenge of Nationhood.** New York: Praeger, 1970, 278 p.
This volume by the late Kenyan political leader contains mainly speeches made during the period 1961-67.

Mboya, Tom. **Freedom and After.** Boston: Little, Brown, 1963, 288 p.
An autobiography which expresses the attitudes, plans and vision of Africa by one of Kenya's best-known leaders.

Murray-Brown, Jeremy. **Kenyatta.** London: Allen & Unwin, 1972, 381 p.
A major biography of the Kenyan leader by a British author.

Odinga, Ajuma Oginga. **Not Yet Uhuru: The Autobiography of Oginga Odinga.** New York: Hill and Wang, 1967, 323 p.
    In this volume the former Vice President of Kenya and an opponent of the Kenyatta government devotes most of his attention to the struggle for independence and comments on the events leading up to his resignation from the Kenya African National Union in April 1966.

Ominde, Simeon H. **Land and Population Movements in Kenya.** Evanston: Northwestern University Press, 1968, 204 p.
    The author, a professor of geography at the University College in Nairobi, aims "to demonstrate the importance of accurate demographic statistics" for any kind of economic planning in Kenya.

Roberts, John S. **A Land Full of People: Life in Kenya Today.** New York: Praeger, 1968, 240 p.
    A British journalist with considerable African experience presents an informal introduction to life in contemporary Kenya.

Rosberg, Carl Gustav, Jr. and Nottingham, John C. **The Myth of "Mau Mau": Nationalism in Kenya.** New York: Praeger (for the Hoover Institution on War, Revolution, and Peace), 1966, 427 p.
    This study shows that the dominance of Kikuyu in the Mau Mau movement often led Europeans in Nairobi and London to mistake the rebellion as an atavistic resurgence of tribalism. The authors argue that Mau Mau was an important stage in the development of nationalist demands and capabilities.

UGANDA

See also Food and Agriculture, p. 68; (Africa) General, p. 776; (East Africa) General, p. 826.

Burke, Fred G. **Local Government and Politics in Uganda.** Syracuse: Syracuse University Press, 1964, 274 p.
    A theoretical analysis of local government and politics in selected Ugandan communities.

Fallers, Lloyd Ashton, *ed.* **The King's Men: Leadership and Status in Buganda on the Eve of Independence.** New York: Oxford University Press (for the East African Institute of Social Research), 1964, 414 p.
    Studies by prominent scholars of the various facets of social change among the Baganda, the most populous group in Uganda.

Fischer, Wolfgang E. **Die Entwicklungsbedingungen Ugandas.** Munich: Weltforum Verlag, 1969, 274 p.
    A study of the economy of Uganda by a German East Africa specialist.

Gukiina, Peter M. **Uganda: A Case Study in African Political Development.** Notre Dame: University of Notre Dame Press, 1972, 190 p.
    A brief history of how the ethnic divisions of Uganda have influenced the country's political development.

Herrick, Allison Butler and Others. **Area Handbook for Uganda.** Washington: G.P.O., 1969, 456 p.
    A useful reference volume with a bibliography, prepared by the Foreign Area Studies at the American University.

Low, Donald Anthony. **Buganda in Modern History.** Berkeley: University of California Press, 1971, 265 p.
    A historian at the University of Sussex traces the rise and fall of Buganda as a model of social and political organization within Uganda.

Low, Donald Anthony. **The Mind of Buganda: Documents of the Modern History of an African Kingdom.** Berkeley: University of California Press, 1971, 234 p.
    A collection of documents on the Kingdom of Buganda covering the period from 1844 to 1966.

Morris, H. S. **The Indians in Uganda.** Chicago: University of Chicago Press, 1968, 230 p.
A thorough analysis of the economic, religious and social life of Indians in Uganda, by an anthropologist at the London School of Economics.

Morris, Henry Francis and Read, James S. **Uganda, the Development of Its Laws and Constitution.** London: Stevens, 1966, 448 p.
A well-documented and comprehensive study of the legal system of Uganda, providing useful information on the country's development from a British protectorate to independence.

Mutesa II, Kabaka of Buganda. **Desecration of My Kingdom.** London: Constable, 1967, 194 p.
Though the bulk of this book concerns the history and political maneuverings in Uganda before independence, there is a short account of the Kabaka's dramatic flight to England and his indictment of the Obote government.

O'Connor, Anthony Michael. **Railways and Development in Uganda: A Study in Economic Geography.** New York: Oxford University Press (for the East African Institute of Social Research), 1966, 176 p.
A very detailed study of a principal form of transport in Uganda.

RWANDA; BURUNDI

See also (Africa) General, p. 776; (East Africa) General, p. 826.

Lacroix, B. **Le Rwanda.** Montreal: Éditions du Lévrier, 1966, 96 p.
A brief account of social life and customs in Rwanda.

Lemarchand, René. **Rwanda and Burundi.** New York: Praeger, 1970, 562 p.
A historical study of the two little-known states, with emphasis on the character of revolution and social change.

Leurquin, Philippe. **Agricultural Change in Ruanda-Urundi, 1945-60.** Stanford: Stanford University Press, 1963, 93 p.
A survey of economic development.

Louis, William Roger. **Ruanda—Urundi, 1884-1919.** New York: Oxford University Press, 1964, 290 p.
A detailed administrative and diplomatic history of Ruanda-Urundi to the end of World War I.

McDonald, Gordon C. and Others. **Area Handbook for Burundi.** Washington: G.P.O., 1969, 203 p.
A useful reference volume with a bibliography, prepared by the Foreign Area Studies at the American University.

Nyrop, Richard F. and Others. **Area Handbook for Rwanda.** Washington: G.P.O., 1969, 212 p.
A useful reference volume with a bibliography, prepared by the Foreign Area Studies at the American University.

Paternostre de La Mairieu, Baudouin. **Le Rwanda: son effort de développement.** Brussels: De Boeck, 1972, 413 p.
A study of the economic and political development of the state of Rwanda.

UNITED REPUBLIC OF TANZANIA (TANGANYIKA; ZANZIBAR)

See also Food and Agriculture, p. 68; (Africa) General, p. 776; (East Africa) General, p. 826.

Abrahams, R. G. **The Political Organization of Unyamwezi.** New York: Cambridge University Press, 1967, 208 p.
An analytical description of the political life of the inhabitants of the area around Tabora, in pre-independence Tanganyika, by a Cambridge University anthropologist.

Austen, Ralph A. **Northwest Tanzania under German and British Rule: Colonial Policy and Tribal Politics, 1889-1939.** New Haven: Yale University Press, 1968, 307 p.
An "attempt to investigate the relationship of German and British forms of colonial adaptation to the traditional politics of the Haya and the Sukuma" in Tanzania.

Bienen, Henry. **Tanzania: Party Transformation and Economic Development.** Princeton: Princeton University Press (for the Center of International Studies), 1967, 446 p.
A solid political study of Tanzania's single-party system.

Cliffe, Lionel, *ed.* **One Party Democracy: The 1965 Tanzania General Elections.** Nairobi: East African Publishing House, 1967, 470 p.
Studies on Tanzanian politics and a favorable assessment of President Nyerere's one-party rule.

Cole, J. S. R. and Denison, W. N. **Tanganyika: The Development of Its Laws and Constitution.** London: Stevens, 1964, 339 p.
A comprehensive description of the constitutional structure and legal system of Tanganyika as of April 1, 1963.

Hawkins, H. C. G. **Wholesale and Retail Trade in Tanganyika.** New York: Praeger, 1965, 168 p.
A detailed analysis of the distribution system in Tanganyika, prepared by *The Economist* Intelligence Unit.

Herrick, Allison Butler and Others. **Area Handbook for Tanzania.** Washington: G.P.O., 1968, 522 p.
A useful reference volume with a bibliography, prepared by the Foreign Area Studies at the American University.

Hopkins, Raymond F. **Political Roles in a New State: Tanzania's First Decade.** New Haven: Yale University Press, 1971, 293 p.
Based on extensive interviews with political leaders, this volume by a Swarthmore College political scientist attempts to measure the degree of institutionalization of the roles of legislator, administrator and president.

Ingle, Clyde Reid. **From Village to State in Tanzania: The Politics of Rural Development.** Ithaca: Cornell University Press, 1972, 279 p.
The point of this study (reiterated in somewhat excessive detail) is that ties between the central government and the village in Tanzania, necessary to rural development, are still only tenuous.

Kainzbauer, Werner. **Der Handel in Tanzania.** New York: Springer-Verlag (for the IFO-Institut für Wirtschaftsforschung), 1968, 239 p.
After a survey of economic, social and geographic conditions, the author analyzes commercial organization in Tanzania.

Kimambo, I. N. and Temu, A. J., *eds.* **A History of Tanzania.** Evanston: Northwestern University Press (for the Historical Association of Tanzania), 1969, 276 p.
Papers presented at a conference at the University College in Dar es Salaam in 1967.

Leslie, John Arthur Kingsley. **A Survey of Dar es Salaam.** New York: Oxford University Press (for the East African Institute of Social Research), 1963, 305 p.
Interviews and discussions from 1957, supplemented by a random sample survey conducted in 1956, form the foundation for this detailed analysis of African life in the rapidly-growing capital of Tanzania.

Liebenow, J. Gus. **Colonial Rule and Political Development in Tanzania: The Case of the Makonde.** Evanston: Northwestern University Press, 1971, 360 p.
An examination of the factors that have contributed to the political, economic and social backwardness of the Makonde people, Tanzania's third largest tribal group, by a professor at Indiana University.

Listowel, Judith (Márffy-Mantuano) Hare, Countess of. **The Making of Tanganyika.** New York: London House and Maxwell, 1966, 451 p.
A well-written political history of Tanganyika, beginning with the growth of the Arab slave trade and German colonization and extending through the achievement of independence.

Lofchie, Michael Frank. **Zanzibar: Background to Revolution.** Princeton: Princeton University Press, 1965, 316 p.

A well-informed examination of the historical, sociological and political origins of the January 1964 revolution in Zanzibar.

MacDonald, Alexander. **Tanzania: Young Nation in a Hurry.** New York: Hawthorn Books, 1966, 253 p.

A sympathetic journalist presents an informative survey of the major features of contemporary politics and society in Tanzania.

Maguire, G. Andrew. **Toward 'Uhuru' in Tanzania: The Politics of Participation.** New York: Cambridge University Press, 1970, 403 p.

By focusing on one area—Sukumaland—the author analyzes the political development of Tanzania as a whole. Mr. Maguire is an American political scientist who was with the U.S. Mission to the United Nations from 1966 to 1969.

Morris-Hale, Walter. **British Administration in Tanganyika from 1920 to 1945.** Geneva: Imprimo, 1969, 352 p.

The main concern of this study is the British educational policy and its effects upon the character of indigenous leadership.

Nellis, John R. **A Theory of Ideology: The Tanzanian Example.** New York: Oxford University Press, 1972, 217 p.

The author asserts that Nyerere's government is buying time by appealing to the masses over the heads of the self-seeking élites and concludes that this policy will eventually backfire by creating more politically aware citizens aspiring to élite prerogatives.

Nyerere, Julius Kambarage. **Freedom and Unity. Uhuru Na Umoja.** New York: Oxford University Press, 1967, 366 p.

——. **Ujamaa—Essays on Socialism.** New York: Oxford University Press, 1969, 186 p.

——. **Freedom and Socialism. Uhuru Na Ujamaa.** New York: Oxford University Press, 1970, 422 p.

Speeches and writings that set forth the ideology of Tanzania's President and his ruling party.

Okello, John. **Revolution in Zanzibar.** Nairobi: East African Publishing House, 1967, 222 p.

The leader of the January 1964 revolution gives his version of the events surrounding the uprising. Clyde Sanger of the Manchester *Guardian* provides an excellent introduction.

Rutman, Gilbert L. **The Economy of Tanganyika.** New York: Praeger, 1968, 190 p.

The author, a professor at the Southern Illinois University, believes that Tanzania's economic plans are unrealistically ambitious.

Smith, William Edgett. **We Must Run while They Walk: A Portrait of Africa's Julius Nyerere.** New York: Random House, 1972, 296 p.

This political biography was written by a *Time* correspondent who has reported on East African affairs for many years.

Stephens, Hugh W. **The Political Transformation of Tanganyika, 1920-67.** New York: Praeger, 1968, 225 p.

Macro-political and economic change are the focal points of this study by a political scientist who attempts to render operational Karl Deutsch's concept of "social mobilization."

Taylor, James Clagett. **The Political Development of Tanganyika.** Stanford: Stanford University Press, 1963, 254 p.

This is a brief political history of Tanganyika from the German entry into East Africa in the 1880s to the attainment of independence in 1961. The author was an educational missionary in Southern Rhodesia.

Tordoff, William. **Government and Politics in Tanzania.** Nairobi: East African Publishing House, 1967, 257 p.

A collection of essays covering developments in Tanzania from 1960 to 1966.

Urfer, Sylvain. **Ujamaa, espoir du socialisme africain en Tanzanie.** Paris: Aubier-Montaigne, 1971, 239 p.

Analyzing the ideology of President Nyerere, the author argues that it constitutes the most comprehensive and distinctively African approach to the problems of building a polity on the continent.

Yaffey, M. J. H. **Balance of Payments Problems of a Developing Country: Tanzania.** Munich: Weltforum Verlag, 1970, 290 p.
This study was sponsored by the Economic Research Bureau of the University College, Dar es Salaam, and the IFO-Institut für Wirtschaftsforschung, Munich.

Yu, George T. **China and Tanzania: A Study in Cooperative Interaction.** Berkeley: University of California, Center for Chinese Studies, 1970, 100 p.
A well-researched study.

SOUTHERN AFRICA

GENERAL

See also Ethnic Problems; The Jews, p. 46; (Africa) General, p. 776.

Davis, John Aubrey and Baker, James K., eds. **Southern Africa in Transition.** New York: Praeger (for the American Society of African Culture), 1966, 427 p.
A collection of papers, first presented in 1963 at the Fourth International Conference of the American Society of African Culture. Topics include: the nature of nationalist movements, violent and non-violent tactics, the role of expatriate economic interests, the significance of Pan-Africanism, U.S. policy toward southern Africa, and the problems of racial adjustment after independence.

Gibson, Richard. **African Liberation Movements.** New York: Oxford University Press (for the Institute of Race Relations), 1972, 350 p.
This study of the internal politics of the southern African liberation organizations recounts in great detail their separate histories of internecine strife, seeming to stem more from tribalism and personal ambition than from ideology.

Marquard, Leo. **A Federation of Southern Africa.** New York: Oxford University Press, 1971, 142 p.
A proposal for a federation of 11 districts including what is now the Republic of South Africa, Namibia (South West Africa), and the states of Botswana, Lesotho and Swaziland.

Nielsen, Waldemar A. **African Battleline: American Policy Choices in Southern Africa.** New York: Harper and Row (for the Council on Foreign Relations), 1965, 156 p.
An analysis of situations of present and future crisis in the white-controlled areas of southern Africa, paying special attention to the international implications of racial conflict. The author of this book, President of the African-American Institute, gives his specific conclusions on American interests and policies.

Tindall, P. E. N. **A History of Central Africa.** New York: Praeger, 1968, 348 p.
Limited to Rhodesia, Zambia and Malawi, this work by a historian at the University of Rhodesia is largely a description of the major institutional developments of the colonial period, with little analysis of their significance.

Tötemeyer, Gerhard. **Südafrika, Südwestafrika; South Africa, South West Africa: Eine Bibliographie 1945–1963.** Freiburg i. Br.: Arnold-Bergstraesser-Institut für Kulturwissenschaftliche Forschung, 1964, 284 p.
A useful bibliography on South and South West Africa.

Wills, Alfred John. **An Introduction to the History of Central Africa.** New York: Oxford University Press, 2d ed., 1967, 412 p.
The emphasis in this useful survey is on European activities in Rhodesia and Nyasaland, particularly before World War II.

REPUBLIC OF SOUTH AFRICA

General

See also Society and Social Psychology, p. 39; (Great Britain) Imperial and Commonwealth Relations; Colonial Policy, p. 367; Foreign Policy, p. 375; (Africa) General, p. 776; (Southern Africa) General, 835; Lesotho; Botswana; Swaziland, p. 841; South West Africa, p. 841.

Adam, Heribert, ed. **South Africa: Sociological Perspectives.** New York: Oxford University Press, 1971, 340 p.
Fifteen general essays by internationally known students of South African society dealing with such topics as racism, social change and modernization, nationalism and education.

Barber, James P. **South Africa's Foreign Policy, 1945-1970.** New York: Oxford University Press, 1973, 325 p.
This well-documented study by an English scholar emphasizes the relationship between internal and external developments.

Drury, Allen. **"A Very Strange Society." A Journey to the Heart of South Africa.** New York: Trident Press, 1967, 465 p.
Interviews with the European "establishment" in South Africa and with a limited number of Pretoria-approved Africans.

Hance, William Adams, ed. **Southern Africa and the United States.** New York: Columbia University Press, 1968, 171 p.
These essays assess the advisability of U.S. disengagement from South Africa and survey U.S. policies in southern Africa.

Hancock, Sir William Keith. **Smuts: The Fields of Force, 1919-1950.** New York: Cambridge University Press, 1968, 589 p.
The second and final volume of a major biography of Jan Smuts written by the eminent Commonwealth historian.

Hepple, Alexander. **South Africa: A Political and Economic History.** New York: Praeger, 1966, 282 p.
To the authors of this account of the historical background of South African society, the real issues in South African politics are determined not by racial but by economic factors.

Hepple, Alexander. **Verwoerd.** Baltimore: Penguin, 1967, 253 p.
A former South African M.P. recounts the major events of the late Prime Minister's life.

Horwitz, Ralph. **The Political Economy of South Africa.** New York: Praeger, 1967, 522 p.
The author of this well-documented analysis interprets the economic development of South Africa from the Boer Trek to the present as the product of South African responses to two influences—the forces of international and domestic markets, and the determination of Afrikanerdom to maintain a racially stratified society, whatever the cost.

Houghton, D. Hobart. **The South African Economy.** New York: Oxford University Press, 1964, 261 p.
Making use of Walt Rostow's concepts of economic growth, a professor at Rhodes University has written a valuable study of South African economy.

Hyam, Ronald. **The Failure of South African Expansion, 1908-1948.** New York: Africana Publishing Company, 1972, 219 p.
The author states that this study "is an attempt to explain the failure of South Africa to complete and extend its provisional area, to turn widespread expectations and expansive ambitions into the reality of a 'Greater South Africa.'"

Karis, Thomas and Carter, Gwendolen Margaret, eds. **From Protest to Challenge: A Documentary History of African Politics in South Africa, 1882-1964.** Stanford: Hoover Institution Press, 1972– .
Two volumes of this most useful reference have been published through 1973: vol. I, "Protest and Hope, 1882-1934" (378 p.), was prepared by Sheridan Johns, III; vol. II, "Hope and Challenge, 1935-1952" (536 p.), by Thomas Karis.

Krüger, D. W. **The Making of a Nation: A History of the Union of South Africa, 1910-1961.** New York: Humanities Press, 1970, 348 p.
A well-written general history of white South Africa.

Kuper, Leo. **An African Bourgeoisie: Race, Class, and Politics in South Africa.** New Haven: Yale University Press, 1965, 452 p.
An exhaustive study of an important section of the African population by a well-known scholar.

Louw, Eric Hendrik. **The Case for South Africa.** New York: MacFadden Books, 1963, 189 p.
A collection of public statements on his country's policies by a former Foreign Minister. Compiled and edited by H. H. Biermann.

Marquard, Leo. **A Short History of South Africa.** New York: Praeger, rev. ed., 1968, 272 p.
A revised edition of a general history, originally published in 1955, with additional material in the final chapter covering developments up to 1967.

Mathews, Anthony S. **Law, Order and Liberty in South Africa.** Berkeley: University of California Press, 1972, 318 p.
The author, a professor at the University of Durban, South Africa, demonstrates in this painstaking analysis of the South African internal-security legislation that freedom is indivisible. He shows how the process which has shorn non-whites of their individual and civil liberties has also deprived white citizens of these same liberties.

Munger, Edwin Stanton. **Notes on the Formation of South African Foreign Policy.** Pasadena: Castle Press, 1965, 102 p.
Useful insights into the principles and procedures which underlie the formation of South African foreign policy.

Newman, Bernard. **South African Journey.** London: Jenkins, 1965, 222 p.
A vivid but rambling travelogue touching on many aspects of contemporary South African society.

Paton, Alan. **South African Tragedy: The Life and Times of Jan Hofmeyr.** New York: Scribner, 1965, 424 p.
The dilemmas of contemporary South African history are masterfully interwoven into this penetrating portrait of the liberal South African leader, Jan Hofmeyr (1894-1948).

Potholm, Christian P. and Dale, Richard, *eds.* **Southern Africa in Perspective.** New York: Free Press, 1972, 418 p.
A collection of essays offering a comprehensive picture of South Africa's relations with the Portuguese territories, Rhodesia, Malawi, Zambia, the O.A.U. and the liberation movements.

Robertson, Janet. **Liberalism in South Africa, 1948-1963.** New York: Oxford University Press, 1971, 252 p.
The author depicts in dispassionate detail the struggle of white and black liberals for traditional civil rights as well as against racial separation.

Segal, Ronald, *ed.* **Sanctions against South Africa.** Baltimore: Penguin, 1964, 272 p.
A collection of papers, given at the International Conference on Economic Sanctions against South Africa, held in London in April 1964.

Smuts, Jan Christiaan. **Selections from the Smuts Papers.** New York: Cambridge University Press, 1966-73, 7 v.
A massive collection of the South African leader's papers and letters, covering the years from 1886 to 1950. Edited by Sir William Keith Hancock and Jean Van Der Poel. Volume 7 includes biographical notes and an index.

Spence, John Edward. **Republic under Pressure: A Study of South African Foreign Policy.** New York: Oxford University Press (for the Royal Institute of International Affairs), 1965, 132 p.
The author examines the domestic context, economic factors and external influences as they affect South African foreign policy.

State of South Africa: Economic, Financial and Statistical Year-Book for the Republic of South Africa. Johannesburg: De Gama Publishers.
A useful reference, published annually since 1957.

Suermann, Josef. **Die weltwirtschaftliche Bedeutung der Südafrikanischen Republik.** Göttingen: Vandenhoeck, 1964, 111 p.
A study of the economy and foreign trade of the Republic of South Africa.

Thompson, Leonard Monteath. **Politics in the Republic of South Africa.** Boston: Little, Brown, 1966, 230 p.
An examination of the unique features of the South African political system and of the internal and external reactions that it has evoked.

Van den Berghe, Pierre Louis. **South Africa, A Study in Conflict.** Middletown (Conn.): Wesleyan University Press, 1965, 371 p.
A study of the problems of South Africa which are analyzed in a sociological framework.

Vandenbosch, Amry. **South Africa and the World: The Foreign Policy of Apartheid.** Lexington: University Press of Kentucky, 1970, 303 p.
A comprehensive survey of South African foreign policy since its beginnings in 1910, by a professor emeritus at the University of Kentucky.

Van Jaarsveld, Floris Albertus. **The Afrikaner's Interpretation of South African History.** Cape Town: Simondium Publishers, 1964, 199 p.
A discussion by a professor at the University of South Africa in Pretoria.

Villiers, H. H. W. de. **Danger en Afrique du Sud.** Paris: Les Sept Couleurs, 1966, 181 p.
An analysis of the communist menace in Africa, and a description of events of the Rivonia Trial of 1963, by a retired Cape Province judge.

Wilson, Monica and Thompson, Leonard Monteath, *eds.* **The Oxford History of South Africa. II: South Africa 1870-1966.** New York: Oxford University Press, 1971, 584 p.
A series of essays by eminent scholars on basic topics such as urbanization, political history, economic development, agriculture and foreign relations.

Apartheid

See also (Africa) General, p. 776; (Southern Africa) General, p. 835; (Republic of South Africa) General, p. 836; Lesotho; Botswana; Swaziland, p. 841; South West Africa, p. 841.

Adam, Heribert. **Modernizing Racial Domination: South Africa's Political Dynamics.** Berkeley: University of California Press, 1971, 203 p.
The author of this study disputes the widespread claim that racial discrimination and continued growth and industrialization are increasingly incompatible.

Ballinger, Margaret. **From Union to Apartheid: A Trek to Isolation.** New York: Praeger, 1970, 499 p.
A distinguished South African politician, who from 1938 until 1960 represented in Parliament the African population of her country, traces the origin and demise of this form of representation.

Benson, Mary. **South Africa: The Struggle for a Birthright.** New York: Funk & Wagnalls, 1969, 314 p.
A partially rewritten and updated version of the author's 1963 work "The African Patriots." She discusses the African struggle for emancipation in South Africa emphasizing the activities of the African National Congress.

Brookes, Edgar Harry, *ed.* **Apartheid: A Documentary Study of Modern South Africa.** New York: Barnes and Noble, 1968, 228 p.
A collection of speeches, extracts from statutes, letters, party declarations and other sources compiled by a historian, formerly a Senator in the South African Parliament. Notable by their absence are documents concerning black politics.

Brown, Douglas. **Against the World: Attitudes of White South Africa.** Garden City: Doubleday, 1968, 253 p.
An analysis of the predicament of being a white South African, written by an editor of London's *Sunday Telegraph*.

Bunting, Brian Percy. **The Rise of the South African Reich.** Baltimore: Penguin, rev. ed., 1969, 552 p.

A survey emphasizing fascist tendencies in the government of the Republic of South Africa, by a South African journalist.

Carter, Gwendolen Margaret and Others. **South Africa's Transkei: The Politics of Domestic Colonialism.** Evanston: Northwestern University Press, 1967, 200 p.
An analysis of South African "domestic colonialism" in the Transkei. While the authors welcome the new opportunities for legitimate African participation in politics, they nevertheless doubt South Africa's often-stated determination to make this first Bantustan a viable entity.

Cope, John Patrick. **South Africa.** New York: Praeger, 1965, 236 p.
Mr. Cope, a South African journalist and parliamentarian, traces the historical, economic and sociological roots of the racial crisis. He concludes that the sheer preponderance and economic indispensability of the African population assure the inevitable destruction of the apartheid order.

Desmond, Cosmas. **The Discarded People: An Account of African Resettlement in South Africa.** Baltimore: Penguin, 1971, 264 p.
A first-hand report of the appalling conditions of life in many of the South African "homelands," and their effect upon the South African blacks resettled there.

Feit, Edward. **African Opposition in South Africa: The Failure of Passive Resistance.** Stanford: Hoover Institution on War, Revolution, and Peace, 1967, 223 p.
A University of Massachusetts political scientist argues that African opposition to the removal program in the Western areas and to the Bantu Education Act failed because of poor leadership, deficient physical resources, faulty strategy and an inability to induce increasingly prosperous Africans to risk reprisals.

Frye, William R. **In Whitest Africa: The Dynamics of Apartheid.** Englewood Cliffs: Prentice-Hall, 1968, 222 p.
An American journalist calls for foreign pressure and intervention to destroy apartheid.

Gandhi, Arun. **A Patch of White.** Bombay: Thacker, 1969, 191 p.
An Indian who lived for 25 years in South Africa writes a description of apartheid and its human costs.

Giniewski, Paul. **The Two Faces of Apartheid.** Chicago: Regnery, 1965, 373 p.
The author pleads ardently for the independence of the South African Reserves, the Bantustans, Dr. Verwoerd's answer to criticism of his apartheid policy. The South African edition was entitled "Bantustans: A Trek Towards the Future" (Cape Town: Human and Rousseau, 1961, 257 p.).

Hill, Christopher Richard. **Bantustans: The Fragmentation of South Africa.** New York: Oxford University Press (for the Institute of Race Relations), 1964, 112 p.
An account and an evaluation of the policies underlying the formation of Bantustans. Particular attention is given to the territory of Transkei.

Hoagland, Jim. **South Africa: Civilizations in Conflict.** Boston: Houghton Mifflin, 1972, 428 p.
The Africa correspondent for *The Washington Post* surveys South Africa and advocates a unified attempt on the part of the United States and the Soviet Union to gain concessions from the white minority.

Horrell, Muriel and Others, *comps.* **A Survey of Race Relations in South Africa.** Johannesburg: South African Institute of Race Relations.
A detailed and informative reference, published annually since 1952. The volume for 1972 was published in 1973.

Hutt, William Harold. **The Economics of the Colour Bar.** London: Deutsch (for the Institute of Economic Affairs), 1964, 189 p.
Professor Hutt's thesis is that the color bar, which limits a competitive market situation, works to the economic disadvantage of South Africa.

Joseph, Helen. **Tomorrow's Sun: A Smuggled Journal from South Africa.** New York: Day, 1967, 319 p.
An account of the misery inflicted on rural African leaders exiled to remote places on charges of trying to retribalize and oppress their own people.

Kahn, Ely Jacques, Jr. **The Separated People.** New York: Norton, 1968, 276 p.
A well-written analysis of life and politics in contemporary South Africa by a staff writer of *The New Yorker*.

Laurence, John. **The Seeds of Disaster.** New York: Taplinger, 1968, 333 p.
A survey of contemporary South African society and the attempts of the government to hide the facts of social and political life both at home and abroad.

Lewin, Julius. **Politics and Law in South Africa.** New York: Monthly Review Press, 1963, 115 p.
The collected essays of a South African lawyer and lecturer on race relations who comes to the conclusion that "a government determined at all costs to enforce apartheid in the teeth of all legal or practical difficulties will abandon the rule of law itself."

Mandela, Nelson Rolihlahla. **No Easy Walk to Freedom.** New York: Basic Books, 1965, 189 p.
Articles, speeches and trial addresses by the South African nationalist leader who was sentenced to life imprisonment during the Rivonia trial in May 1964.

Marquard, Leo. **The Peoples and Policies of South Africa.** New York: Oxford University Press, 4th ed., 1969, 266 p.
Since its original appearance in 1952 this work has become a standard source on South Africa. Many portions of the text have now been rewritten and updated. This edition presents a balanced analysis of South African society, a society organized in a form sometimes called "domestic colonialism."

Mokgatle, Naboth. **The Autobiography of an Unknown South African.** Berkeley: University of California Press, 1971, 349 p.
Living in self-imposed exile in London since 1954, the author describes his upbringing in a Sesutho-speaking tribe of the Transvaal, his move to Pretoria and his gradual immersion in politics and the trade union movement.

Munger, Edwin Stanton. **Afrikaner and African Nationalism: South African Parallels and Parameters.** New York: Oxford University Press (for the Institute of Race Relations), 1967, 142 p.
An analysis of competing nationalisms by a professor at the California Institute of Technology. He sees Afrikaner nationalism approaching its "maturity," while African nationalism is still largely an élite movement.

Ngubane, Jordan K. **An African Explains Apartheid.** New York: Praeger, 1963, 243 p.
An African's view of the African's place under the encroachment of apartheid.

Paton, Alan. **The Long View.** New York: Praeger, 1968, 295 p.
A collection of essays on South African themes by a well-known writer and the former President of the South African Liberal Party.

Segal, Ronald. **Into Exile.** New York: McGraw-Hill, 1963, 319 p.
The personal story by an author who was editor of the now defunct *Africa South* and worked unceasingly on behalf of the black African.

Taubenfeld, Rita F. and Taubenfeld, Howard J. **Race, Peace, Law, and Southern Africa.** Dobbs Ferry (N.Y.): Oceana Publications (for the Association of the Bar of the City of New York), 1968, 211 p.
A collection of papers on political and legal questions in South Africa by American and African experts. Edited by John Carey.

Vatcher, William Henry. **White Laager.** New York: Praeger, 1965, 309 p.
A description of some of the factors which have contributed to and strengthened the development of Afrikaner nationalism.

Walshe, Peter. **The Rise of African Nationalism in South Africa: The African National Congress, 1912-1952.** Berkeley: University of California Press, 1971, 480 p.
A general history of the major nationalist party by a professor at the University of Notre Dame.

LESOTHO; BOTSWANA; SWAZILAND

See also (Africa) General, p. 776; Republic of South Africa, p. 836.

Barker, Dudley. **Swaziland.** London: H.M.S.O., 1965, 145 p.
A popular introduction to Swaziland under British rule.

Fair, Thomas J. D. and Others. **Development in Swaziland.** Johannesburg: Witwatersrand University Press, 1969, 155 p.
An economic survey.

Hailey, Malcolm Hailey, 1st Baron. **The Republic of South Africa and the High Commission Territories.** New York: Oxford University Press, 1963, 136 p.
A historical survey of relations among the High Commission Territories, the Republic and the British Government.

Halpern, Jack. **South Africa's Hostages: Basutoland, Bechuanaland and Swaziland.** Baltimore: Penguin, 1965, 495 p.
A survey of the historical background and political problems of Britain's three former High Commission Territories.

Holleman, Johan Frederick, *ed.* **Experiment in Swaziland.** New York: Oxford University Press, 1964, 352 p.
A detailed report on the Swaziland socio-economic survey of 1960.

Khaketla, B. M. **Lesotho 1970: An African Coup under the Microscope.** Berkeley: University of California Press, 1972, 350 p.
An anecdotal narrative about a post-election day *putsch* by the incumbent—but allegedly defeated—Prime Minister. The author's "inside" vantage point as Secretary-General of an opposition political party makes this a useful primary source.

Matsebula, J. S. M. **A History of Swaziland.** Cape Town: Longman Southern Africa, 1972, 131 p.
A useful introduction.

Munger, Edwin Stanton. **Bechuanaland: Pan-African Outpost or Bantu Homeland?** New York: Oxford University Press (for the Institute of Race Relations), 1965, 114 p.
A well-written history.

Potholm, Christian P. **Swaziland: The Dynamics of Political Modernization.** Berkeley: University of California Press, 1972, 183 p.
The story of King Sobhuza II, the traditional ruler of the Swazi people, who was elected head of state when his country became independent.

Spence, John Edward. **Lesotho: The Politics of Dependence.** New York: Oxford University Press (for the Institute of Race Relations), 1968, 86 p.
An analysis of the young state's internal and external difficulties.

Stevens, Richard P. **Lesotho, Botswana, and Swaziland: The Former High Commission Territories in Southern Africa.** New York: Praeger, 1967, 294 p.
A history and analysis of contemporary developments by a political scientist who finds the economic and political dominance of the Republic of South Africa to be the single most important factor shaping political life in the three territories.

SOUTH WEST AFRICA

See also International Court of Justice, p. 93; (Africa) General, p. 776; (Southern Africa) General, p. 835; Republic of South Africa, p. 836.

Bruwer, J. P. van S. **South West Africa: The Disputed Land.** Johannesburg: Nasionale Boekhandel Beperk, 1966, 147 p.
This brief survey includes a useful bibliography.

Carroll, Faye. **South West Africa and the United Nations.** Lexington: University of Kentucky Press, 1967, 123 p.

A short introductory survey by a political scientist who sees the elimination of apartheid and South African domination as inevitable.

Dugard, John, ed. **The South West Africa/Namibia Dispute: Documents and Scholarly Writings on the Controversy between South Africa and the United Nations.** Berkeley: University of California Press, 1973, 585 p.

An indispensable reference, edited by a professor at the University of the Witwatersrand.

First, Ruth. **South West Africa.** Baltimore: Penguin, 1963, 269 p.

A journalistic treatment of South West Africa which details the history of the territory to the end of 1962.

Hidayatullah, M. **The South-West Africa Case.** New York: Asia Publishing House, 1968, 144 p.

This volume by an Indian Supreme Court Judge contains a useful analytical description and some of the historical documents surrounding the case.

Horrell, Muriel. **South-West Africa.** Johannesburg: South African Institute of Race Relations, 1967, 94 p.

A brief survey.

Jenny, Hans. **Südwestafrika: Land zwischen den Extremen.** Stuttgart: Kohlhammer, 2d rev. ed., 1967, 301 p.

A Swiss journalist and specialist in African affairs pleads for a chance for South Africa to pursue its policy of "separate development" in South West Africa, a policy he sees as a middle way between the extremes of white colonial dictatorship on the one hand, and black and/or communist dictatorship on the other.

Molnar, Thomas Steven. **South West Africa: The Last Pioneer Country.** New York: Fleet, 1966, 160 p.

A professor at Brooklyn College and frequent traveler in Africa gives an unqualified, conventional defense of the South African government's policies in South West Africa.

Segal, Ronald and First, Ruth, eds. **South West Africa: Travesty of Trust.** London: André Deutsch, 1967, 351 p.

Papers and proceedings of the International Conference on South West Africa, held at Oxford in March 1966. At this conference the demand was voiced that the United Nations' General Assembly should formally strip South Africa of its mandate over South West Africa.

Wellington, John Harold. **South West Africa and Its Human Issues.** New York: Oxford University Press, 1967, 461 p.

An authoritative, scholarly analysis of South West African history, geography and politics from the pre-European period to the present, by a South African geographer whose balanced study leads him to conclude: "We White South Africans have to face the facts, and the facts are against us."

FEDERATION OF RHODESIA AND NYASALAND

See also (Great Britain) Imperial and Commonwealth Relations; Colonial Policy, p. 367; (Africa) General, p. 776; (Southern Africa) General, p. 835; Rhodesia, p. 843; Zambia, p. 845; Malawi (Nyasaland), p. 846.

Alport, Cuthbert James McCall Alport, Baron. **The Sudden Assignment.** London: Hodder, 1965, 255 p.

Lord Alport, who served as British High Commissioner in Salisbury from January 1961, gives his personal account of the final dismemberment of the Federation of Rhodesia and Nyasaland.

Franklin, Henry. **Unholy Wedlock: The Failure of the Central African Federation.** London: Allen and Unwin, 1963, 239 p.

An inside look at a brief historical episode - the ill-fated British imposed Federation of Rhodesia and Nyasaland (1953-1963)—as told by a member of the British Colonial Service who was consistently opposed to the creation of the Federation and the policy of white supremacy.

Keatley, Patrick. **The Politics of Partnership.** Baltimore: Penguin, 1963, 527 p.
A political history of the countries that constituted the Federation of Rhodesia and Nyasaland.

Sowelem, R. A. **Towards Financial Independence in a Developing Economy.** New York: Humanities Press, 1968, 329 p.
An analysis of the establishment, impact and experience of the central banking system in the Federation of Rhodesia and Nyasaland. The period covered is 1952-1963.

Welensky, Sir Roland. **Welensky's 4000 Days: The Life and Death of the Federation of Rhodesia and Nyasaland.** London: Collins, 1964, 383 p.
The former Prime Minister of the extinct Federation gives his personal account of its formation and dissolution.

RHODESIA

See also (Great Britain) Imperial and Commonwealth Relations; Colonial Policy, p. 367; (Africa) General, p. 776; (Southern Africa) General, p. 835; (Republic of South Africa) General, p. 836; Federation of Rhodesia and Nyasaland, p. 842; Zambia, p. 845.

Barber, James P. **Rhodesia: The Road to Rebellion.** New York: Oxford University Press (for the Institute of Race Relations), 1967, 338 p.
An analysis of European politics in Rhodesia and of Anglo-Rhodesian relations from the beginnings of federal dissolution in 1960 until the unilateral declaration of independence in November 1965.

Bull, Theodore, ed. **Rhodesia: Crisis of Color.** Chicago: Quadrangle Books, 1968, 184 p.
A survey of Rhodesia's history and politics by contributors to the former *Central African Examiner*. British diplomats in Salisbury and their superiors in London are taken to task for deficiencies in their information, planning and tactics.

Clements, Frank. **Rhodesia: A Study of the Deterioration of a White Society.** New York: Praeger, 1969, 286 p.
A well-informed, critical history of white Rhodesia by the former mayor of Salisbury.

Gann, Lewis Henry. **A History of Southern Rhodesia.** London: Chatto and Windus, 1965, 354 p.
Complementing the author's "History of Northern Rhodesia," published in 1964, this important and well-documented volume traces "the history of Southern Rhodesia from prehistoric times to 1934 when Dr. Godfrey Huggins (now Lord Malvern) became Prime Minister."

Lardner-Burke, Desmond. **Rhodesia: The Story of the Crisis.** London: Oldbourne Press, 1966, 101 p.
A former Minister of Justice of the Smith government describes the negotiations between the Rhodesian and British governments before the unilateral declaration of independence in 1965.

Marshall, Charles Burton. **Crisis Over Rhodesia: A Skeptical View.** Baltimore: Johns Hopkins Press (for the Washington Center of Foreign Policy Research), 1967, 75 p.
This is an unequivocal indictment of British and U.N. policies toward Ian Smith's Rhodesia by a Johns Hopkins University professor of international relations.

Mtshali, B. Vulindlela. **Rhodesia: Background to Conflict.** New York: Hawthorn Books, 1967, 255 p.
A critical account of Ian Smith and his regime in Rhodesia, by a South African Zulu educated in the Netherlands and the United States.

Murray, D. J. **The Governmental System in Southern Rhodesia.** New York: Oxford University Press, 1970, 393 p.
Adopting a group-politics perspective, the author analyzes politics in Southern Rhodesia in terms of six occupational sectors and changes in their interrelationships.

Orcival, François d' with Laroche, Fabrice. **Rhodésie, pays des lions fidèles.** Paris: Éditions de la Table Ronde, 1966, 261 p.
A survey of the contemporary history of Southern Rhodesia. The author sympathizes with the settlers' case against the British government. Introduction by the Rhodesian Premier, Ian Smith.

Palley, Claire. **The Constitutional History and Law of Southern Rhodesia, 1888-1965.** New York: Oxford University Press, 1966, 872 p.
A thorough scholarly analysis of the constitutional and legal development of Southern Rhodesia in which the author seeks to illuminate the legal techniques of British imperial control and demonstrate the actual extent of internal self-government enjoyed by Southern Rhodesia for over 40 years.

Ranger, Terence Osborn. **The African Voice in Southern Rhodesia, 1898-1930.** Evanston: Northwestern University Press, 1971, 252 p.
A well-known Rhodesian historian surveys the politics among the indigenous inhabitants in the period between the consolidation of colonial power and the emergence of the nationalist movement.

Ransford, Oliver. **The Rulers of Rhodesia: From Earliest Times to the Referendum.** London: John Murray, 1968, 345 p.
A study of the political history of Rhodesia, ending with a discussion of the 1922 referendum when the electorate decided for self-government with British ties and against incorporation into the Union of South Africa.

Rea, Frederick Beatty, *ed.* **Southern Rhodesia—The Price of Freedom.** Bulawayo: Stuart Manning, 1964, 141 p.
Nine Rhodesians advocate non-violent forms of change for the future, emphasizing the need for a rapid transition to majority rule.

Reed, Douglas. **The Battle for Rhodesia.** New York: Devin-Adair, 1967, 150 p.
A South African contends that the whites of southern Africa are struggling alone against a communist-led, international conspiracy against peace, dignity and freedom centered at the United Nations. The English edition is entitled "Insanity Fair '67" (London: Gibbs, 1967, 224 p.).

Shamuyarira, Nathan M. **Crisis in Rhodesia.** New York: Transatlantic Arts, 1966, 240 p.
A member of the Zimbabwe African National Union discusses sympathetically the nationalist movement in Rhodesia up to early 1965.

Sithole, Ndabaningi. **Obed Mutezo: The Mudzimu Christian Nationalist.** New York: Oxford University Press, 1971, 210 p.
A portrait of a Rhodesian nationalist.

Todd, Judith. **Rhodesia.** London: MacGibbon, 1966, 170 p.
An account of Rhodesia's political problems up to the declaration of independence in November 1965, by the daughter of former Prime Minister Garfield Todd.

Tredgold, Sir Robert Clarkson. **The Rhodesia That Was My Life.** London: Allen and Unwin, 1968, 271 p.
An autobiography of a former Federal Chief Justice of Rhodesia. The author is quite critical of Rhodesian politics.

Young, Kenneth. **Rhodesia and Independence.** London: Dent, new ed., 1969, 684 p.
A history of the events surrounding Rhodesia's declaration of independence in November 1965, by an adviser to the Beaverbrook newspapers and an unqualified defender of white Rhodesia.

Yudelman, Montague. **Africans on the Land.** Cambridge: Harvard University Press, 1964, 288 p.
A well-documented study, with special reference to Southern Rhodesia, of the vital problem of increasing African agricultural productivity.

ZAMBIA

See also (Great Britain) Imperial and Commonwealth Relations; Colonial Policy, p. 367; (Africa) General, p. 776; (Southern Africa) General, p. 835; (Republic of South Africa) General, p. 836; Federation of Rhodesia and Nyasaland, p. 842; Rhodesia, p. 843; Malawi (Nyasaland), p. 846.

Baldwin, Robert Edward. **Economic Development and Export Growth: A Study of Northern Rhodesia, 1920–1960.** Berkeley: University of California Press, 1966, 254 p.
Professor Baldwin's comprehensive study shows that the groundwork for general development in Zambia has yet to be built, especially in the agricultural sector and in marketing, but that the country's long-term potential is outstanding.

Bostock, Mark and Harvey, Charles, *eds.* **Economic Independence and Zambian Copper: A Case Study of Foreign Investment.** New York: Praeger, 1972, 274 p.
Papers examining the Zambian nationalization of the copper industry.

Caplan, Gerald L. **The Elites of Barotseland 1878–1969: A Political History of Zambia's Western Province.** Berkeley: University of California Press, 1971, 270 p.
Though this work by a Canadian historian is largely devoted to the colonial period, it also deals with Barotseland's absorption into the Zambian provincial structure.

Dotson, Floyd and Dotson, Lillian O. **The Indian Minority of Zambia, Rhodesia, and Malawi.** New Haven: Yale University Press, 1968, 444 p.
The authors of this study conclude that since independence the Indians have become politically less influential and more insecure than either Europeans or Africans.

Faber, Michael L. O. and Potter, J. G. **Towards Economic Independence.** New York: Cambridge University Press, 1971, 134 p.
Two former members of the Zambian government provide an anatomy of the corporate structure of the mining industry up to 1963 and an insider's view of negotiations with the British South Africa Company at the establishment of independence in 1964.

Gann, Lewis Henry. **A History of Northern Rhodesia.** New York: Humanities Press, 1964, 478 p.
An authoritative history of European policies in southern Africa and Northern Rhodesia, from the sixteenth century through 1953.

Hall, Richard Seymour. **The High Price of Principles: Kaunda and the White South.** London: Hodder, 1969, 256 p.
The author of this study argues that the Zambian leader Kaunda was betrayed by British policy toward Rhodesia, and that the result has been to drive Zambia into closer economic relations with South Africa.

Hall, Richard Seymour. **Zambia.** New York: Praeger, 1965, 357 p.
This useful, comprehensive study examines the cultural and geographic setting of Zambian history, the establishment and impact of colonial rule, the rise of African nationalism, the abortive efforts at federation, the consolidation of independence, and the decisive influence of the Copperbelt on Zambia's economic and political development.

Kaplan, Irving and Others. **Area Handbook for Zambia.** Washington: G.P.O., 1969, 482 p.
A useful reference volume with a bibliography, prepared by the Foreign Area Studies at the American University.

Kaunda, Kenneth D. **Zambia, Independence and Beyond: The Speeches of Kenneth Kaunda.** London: Nelson, 1966, 265 p.
A collection of President Kaunda's speeches made in the period from 1962 to 1966. Edited by Colin Legum.

Kay, George. **A Social Geography of Zambia: A Survey of Population Patterns in a Developing Country.** London: University of London Press, 1967, 160 p.
An introductory survey, with useful information on the history, politics and economy of the country. Many charts.

Mulford, David C. **The Northern Rhodesia General Election, 1962.** New York: Oxford University Press, 1964, 205 p.
A detailed study.

Mulford, David C. **Zambia: The Politics of Independence, 1957-1964.** New York: Oxford University Press, 1968, 362 p.
    In this study the development of political parties is described in relation to major constitutional changes.

MALAWI (NYASALAND)

See also (Great Britain) Imperial and Commonwealth Relations; Colonial Policy, p. 367; (Africa) General, p. 776; (Southern Africa) General, p. 835; (Republic of South Africa) General, p. 836; Federation of Rhodesia and Nyasaland, p. 842; Zambia, p. 845.

Jones, Griffith Bevan. **Britain and Nyasaland.** London: Allen and Unwin, 1964, 314 p.
    An impassioned and documented critique of British policy in Nyasaland, now Malawi, by a former administrative officer.

Mwase, George Simeon. **Strike a Blow and Die: A Narrative of Race Relations in Colonial Africa.** Cambridge: Harvard University Press, 1967, 135 p.
    This heretofore unknown account of the Chilembwe revolt in Nyasaland in 1915 by an African nationalist was discovered in the Malawi national archives by the Harvard historian Robert I. Rotberg, who prepared it for publication under the auspices of the Center for International Affairs.

Pike, John George and Rimmington, G. T. **Malawi: A Geographical Study.** New York: Oxford University Press, 1965, 229 p.
    A textbook in two parts: a section of detailed physical geography is followed by chapters on history, population, agriculture and subjects of economic and social significance.

Pike, John George. **Malawi: A Political and Economic History.** New York: Praeger, 1968, 248 p.
    A basic introductory account by a former member of the British Colonial Service who was posted in what was then Nyasaland.

Rotberg, Robert I. **The Rise of Nationalism in Central Africa: The Making of Malawi and Zambia, 1873-1964.** Cambridge: Harvard University Press, 1965, 362 p.
    A very well-written and well-documented study.

ANGOLA; MOZAMBIQUE

See also Portugal, p. 439; (Africa) General, p. 776; (Republic of South Africa) General, p. 836.

Abshire, David M. and Samuels, Michael A., eds. **Portuguese Africa: A Handbook.** New York: Praeger (in coöperation with the Center for Strategic and International Studies, Georgetown University), 1969, 480 p.
    In this collection of original essays contemporary political and economic issues as well as historical topics are dealt with.

Barnett, Donald L. and Harvey, Roy. **The Revolution in Angola.** Indianapolis: Bobbs-Merrill, 1972, 312 p.
    These recorded autobiographies of four Angolan guerrillas, which constitute the major part of this book, offer vivid insights into the sources of the conflict in that Portuguese colony.

Boavida, Américo. **Angola: Five Centuries of Portuguese Exploitation.** Richmond (B.C.): L.S.M. Information Center, 1972, 124 p.
    A significant Angolan nationalist critique of Portuguese rule in Angola by a medical doctor trained in Portugal. The Portuguese original appeared as "Angola: cinco séculos de exploração portuguesa" (Rio de Janeiro: Civilizacão Brasileira, 1967, 138 p.).

Chilcote, Ronald H. **Portuguese Africa.** Englewood Cliffs: Prentice-Hall, 1967, 149 p.
    A compact survey of Portugal's colonial theory and practice in her overseas provinces in Africa.

Costa, Pereira da. **Um mês de terrorismo (Angola–marco-abril de 1961).** Lisbon: Polis, 1969, 145 p.
   A journalist's account of the 1961 crisis in Angola, including revelations not found in the standard account by Hélio Felgas.

Davezies, Robert. **Les Angolais.** Paris: Éditions de Minuit, 1965, 259 p.
   Abbé Robert Davezies, a partisan of the anti-colonialist struggle in Angola, seeks to present the people of Angola by means of personal portraits of individual peasants, students, teachers and political leaders.

Davidson, Basil. **In the Eye of the Storm: Angola's People.** Garden City: Doubleday, 1972, 367 p.
   A prolific historian looks at Angola's past and present struggles through the eyes of the African insurgents.

Ehnmark, Anders and Wästberg, Per. **Angola and Mozambique: The Case against Portugal.** New York: Roy, 1964, 176 p.
   Two Swedish authors treat separately and journalistically the conditions of African life in both territories.

Felgas, Hélio. **Guerra em Angola.** Lisbon: Classica Editora, rev. ed., 1963–64, 227 p.
   A former Governor of Portuguese Congo describes the major events in northern Angola in 1961. Best general account in the language.

Herrick, Allison Butler and Others. **Area Handbook for Angola.** Washington: G.P.O., 1967, 439 p.
   A useful reference volume with a bibliography, prepared by the Foreign Area Studies at the American University.

Herrick, Allison Butler and Others. **Area Handbook for Mozambique.** Washington: G.P.O., 1969, 351 p.
   A useful reference volume with a bibliography, prepared by the Foreign Area Studies at the American University.

Marcum, John. **The Angolan Revolution. Volume 1: The Anatomy of an Explosion (1950–1962).** Cambridge: M.I.T. Press, 1969, 380 p.
   A scholarly and detailed analysis of the growth of Angolan nationalism and the development of the nationalist movement. The author is a professor at the Merrill College of the University of California.

Mondlane, Eduardo. **The Struggle for Mozambique.** Baltimore: Penguin, 1969, 221 p.
   A first-hand account of the nationalist movement, its origins and its problems. Until his assassination in early 1969, the author was the President of the Mozambique Liberation Front and a leading spokesman for Africans generally.

Neto, João Pereira. **Angola: meio século de integração.** Lisbon: Instituto Superior de Ciências Sociais e Política Ultramarina, 1964, 332 p.
   A well-documented study on colonial administration of Angola from 1912 to 1960, by a Portuguese sociologist at the Technical University of Lisbon.

Valahu, Mugur. **Angola, clef de l'Afrique.** Paris: Nouvelles Éditions Latines, 1966, 315 p.
   A pro-Portuguese survey of the contemporary history of Angola, by a Rumanian-born writer.

Wheeler, Douglas L. and Pélissier, René. **Angola.** New York: Praeger, 1971, 296 p.
   This study is divided into two main sections—the first is a historical survey to the year 1961; the second, a more detailed account of the consequences of the insurrection which began in that year.

MALAGASY REPUBLIC (MADAGASCAR)

See also (France) Foreign Policy, p. 404; (Africa) General, p. 776.

Heseltine, Nigel. **Madagascar.** New York: Praeger, 1971, 334 p.
   One of the few English language books on Madagascar, this study is particularly strong in its synthesis of social and economic developments in the period before 1960. The author served as economic adviser to the President of the country.

Massiot, Michel. **L'Administration publique à Madagascar.** Paris: Librairie Générale de Droit et de Jurisprudence, 1971, 472 p.
A study of the development of the territorial administration in Madagascar from 1896 to the proclamation of independence.

Nelson, Harold D. and Others. **Area Handbook for Malagasy Republic.** Washington: G.P.O., 1973, 327 p.
A useful reference volume with a bibliography, prepared by the Foreign Area Studies at the American University.

Slawecki, Leon M. S. **French Policy Towards the Chinese in Madagascar.** Hamden (Conn.): Shoe String Press, 1971, 265 p.
An analysis of the role played by overseas Chinese in the internal politics of colonial Madagascar and in domestic and foreign policy of the Malagasy Republic.

Spacensky, Alain. **Madagascar: 50 ans de vie politique.** Paris: Nouvelles Éditions Latines, 1970, 526 p.
A study of the politics of twentieth-century Madagascar by an author who was born on the island.

Stratton, Arthur. **The Great Red Island.** New York: Scribner, 1964, 368 p.
A personal and informative account of Madagascar.

Thompson, Virginia McLean and Adloff, Richard. **The Malagasy Republic: Madagascar Today.** Stanford: Stanford University Press, 1965, 504 p.
This detailed and comprehensive study of Malagasy history includes sections dealing with political developments, religion, education, economic policy, transportation, finances, industry, trade and labor.

V. POLAR REGIONS

See also (Great Britain) Biographies, Memoirs and Addresses, p. 369; (Australia and New Zealand) General, p. 766.

Antarctic Bibliography, 1965—. Washington: Library of Congress, 1965—.
A very thorough annotated bibliography, sponsored by the Office of Antarctic Programs of the National Science Foundation. Five volumes, and a supplementing volume covering the years from 1951 to 1961, have been published through 1972.

Arctic Bibliography. Washington: Department of Defense, 1953–67; Montreal: McGill University Press, 1967—.
A most comprehensive annotated bibliography prepared by the Arctic Institute of North America. Beginning with volume 13, the bibliography—co-sponsored by U.S. and Canadian government agencies—has been published in Canada. Fifteen volumes have appeared through 1971.

Baird, Patrick D. **The Polar World.** New York: Wiley, 1964, 328 p.
An advanced geographic study of the Arctic and Antarctic regions.

Barkov, N. I. and Tarasova, Zh. A. **Desiat' let sovetskikh issledovanii v Antarktike.** Leningrad: Ordena Lenina Arkticheskii i Antarkticheskii Nauchno-Issledovatel'skii Institut, 1968, 167 p.
A bibliographical survey of Soviet activities in Antarctica from 1956 to 1965.

Battaglini, Giovanni. **La condizione dell'Antartide nel diritto internazionale.** Padua: CEDAM, 1971, 477 p.
A study of the Antarctic Treaty of 1959 and of Antarctica as a problem in international law.

Bertrand, Kenneth John. **Americans in Antarctica, 1775-1948.** New York: American Geographical Society, 1971, 554 p.
A most thorough survey by a professor at the Catholic University of America in Washington, sponsored by the National Science Foundation.

Hatherton, Trevor, *ed*. **Antarctica**. New York: Praeger, 1965, 511 p.
  This substantial collaborative study covering the activities of the various nations in Antarctica, the Southern Ocean and the South Polar atmosphere is a New Zealand Antarctic Society survey.

Macdonald, Ronald St. John, *ed*. **The Arctic Frontier**. Toronto: University of Toronto Press (in association with the Canadian Institute of International Affairs and the Arctic Institute of North America), 1966, 311 p.
  Essays on the geography, administration, defense problems and the scientific exploration of the Arctic territories belonging to Canada, United States, Soviet Union, Denmark, Iceland and Norway. Canadian aspects of the Arctic problems are emphasized.

Nudel'man, Aizik Vol'fovich. **Soviet Antarctic Expeditions, 1961–1963**. Jerusalem: Israel Program for Scientific Translations, 1968, 220 p.
  An account, sponsored by the Academy of Sciences of the U.S.S.R., of Soviet activities in Antarctica from 1961 to 1963. The Russian original was published as "Sovetskie ekspeditsii v Antarktiku, 1961–1963 gg." (Moscow: Nauka, 1965, 271 p.).

Petrow, Richard. **Across the Top of Russia**. New York: McKay, 1967, 374 p.
  A description of the attempt of the U.S. Coast Guard icebreaker *Northwind* to traverse the Northeast Passage on the northern coast of Siberia from the Atlantic to the Pacific and of the Soviet objections that prevented the completion of the mission.

Polar Research: A Survey. Washington: National Research Council, 1970, 204 p.
  A summary of the current knowledge of the polar regions, prepared by the Committee on Polar Research. A valuable reference.

Priestley, Sir Raymond and Others, *eds*. **Antarctic Research: A Review of British Scientific Achievement in Antarctica**. London: Butterworths, 1964, 360 p.
  A useful reference.

San Martín, C. **Argentinos en la Antártida**. Buenos Aires: Editorial Librería Mitre, 1969, 191 p.
  A survey of the developments in the Argentinian sector of Antarctica.

Treshnikov, Aleksei Fedorovich. **Istoriia otkrytiia i issledovaniia Antarktidy**. Moscow: Gos. Izd-vo Geogr. Lit-ry, 1963, 430 p.
  A Soviet monograph on the exploration of Antarctica.

Victor, Paul-Émile. **Man and the Conquest of the Poles**. New York: Simon and Schuster, 1963, 320 p.
  In this study the French explorer pays attention also to the political and economic factors that have determined the exploration of the polar regions. The French original appeared as "L'Homme à la conquête des pôles" (Paris: Plon, 1962, 376 p.).

INDEX TO AUTHORS

Aaken, W. van, 161
Åmlid, J., 444
Abadie-Aicardi, R. F., 322
Abaeva, D. M., 585
Abbas, K. A., 660
Abbas, S. A., 678
Abd al-Hakim, M. S., 616
'Abd al-Mun'im, M. F., 633, 638
'Abd al-Wahab, H. H., 799
Abdel-Malek, A., 616, 801, 802
Abdel-Rahim, M., 806
Abdulrahman, A. J., 617
Abegg, L., 687
Abegglen, J. C., 723
Abel, E., 180, 245
Abelein, M., 463
Abellá Blasco, M., 317
Abellan, V., 78
Abels, J., 264
Abert, J. G., 389
Abidi, A. H. H., 643
Aboltin, V. Ia., 122
Aboyade, O., 819
Abraham, H. J., 267
Abrahams, R. G., 832
Abrahams, W. M., 436
Abramowitz, M., 246
Abramowski, G., 468
Abrikosov, D. I., 533
Abshire, D. M., 257, 846
Absolon, R., 475
Abu-Izzedin, H. S., 628
Abu Jaber, K. S., 617
Abu-Lughod, I., 633, 638
Abū Yasīr, S. M., 633
Abueva, J. V., 763
Accoce, P., 169
Acedo Mendoza, C., 341
Acheson, D. G., 223, 227
Achminow, G. F., 545, 547
Achminow, H. F. See Achminow, G. F.
Achterberg, E., 254
Aćimović, L., 186
Ackermann, J., 480
Ackley, C. W., 257
Acosta Hermoso, E., 70
Aczél, T., 514
Adam, E. P., 231
Adam, H., 836, 838
Ádám, M., 515
Adamec, L. W., 653
Adamović, M., 594
Adams, A. E., 358, 362, 582
Adams, B. D., 258
Adams, C. H., 762
Adams, H. E., 201
Adams, H. H., 146, 156
Adams, J. S., 362
Adams, Michael, 611, 617
Adams, Mildred, 200
Adams, N. S., 749
Adams, R., 683
Adams, R. N., 297
Adams, T. F. M., 723

Adams, T. W., 418
Adams, W., 42
Adamson, D., 645
Adamson, H. C., 169
Adedeji, A., 816
Adelman, I., 71, 730
Adelman, M. A., 70
Adenauer, K., 496
Adizes, I., 594
Adleman, R. H., 159, 163
Adler, J. H., 59, 72
Adler, M. J., 12
Adler, S., 229
Adler-Karlsson, G., 185
Adloff, R., 775, 829, 848
Adolph, W., 475
Adu, A. L., 779
Ady, P. H., 387
Afana, O., 807
Afrifa, A. A., 814
Agaev, S. L., 649
Ağaoğlu, S., 622
Agar, A. W. S., 136
Agassi, J., 755
Agor, W. H., 203
Ágoston, I., 365
Agudelo Villa, H., 197, 333
Aguilar, L. E., 302
Aguilar Monteverde, A., 193, 208
Agulla, J. C., 314
Agwani, M. S., 617, 628
Agzamkhodzhaev, A., 585
Aharoni, Y., 251
Ahearn, D. S., 274
Ahlberg, R., 578
Ahluwalia, K., 105
Ahmad, A., 657
Ahmad, K. S. U., 675
Ahtokari, R., 449
Aigner, D., 140
Ailleret, C., 407
Ainslie, R., 779
Airapetian, M. E., 550
Ait Ahmed, H., 796
Aitchison, J. H., 285
Aitken, T., Jr., 311
Aiyar, S. P., 652, 662
Aizsilnieks, A., 458
Ajnenkiel, A., 525
Ake, C. E., 13
Akehurst, M., 83
Akimova, V. V. V., 555
Akpan, N. U., 818
Akzin, B., 13, 641
'Alam al-Dīn, W., 626
Alba C., M. M., 299
Alba, V., 197, 200, 203, 208, 289
Albaharna, H. M., 646
Albert, M., 413
Albertini, R. von, 36
Albino, O., 806
Albinski, H. S., 767
Albonetti, A., 349
Albrecht-Carrié, R., 349

851

Alcock, A., 105
Aldcroft, D. H., 385
Alderfer, H. F., 36, 779
Alderman, R. H., 297
Aldouby, Z., 633
Alemann, R. T., 208
Alencastre, A., 324
Alende, O. E., 314
Alessandri Palma, A., 329
Alexander, H. T., 814
Alexander, L. M., 90, 345
Alexander, R. J., 200, 203, 208, 313, 341
Alexander, S. S., 613
Alexander, Y., 105
Alexander-Frutschi, M. C., 72
Alexandersson, G., 55
Alexandre, P., 408
Alexandrowicz, C. H., 90
Alford, R. R., 39
Ali, T., 675
Āli-i Aḥmad, Jalāl, 649
Aliber, R. Z., 59, 60
Alibert, J.-L., 812
Alisjahbana, S. T., 762
Alisky, M., 340
Alker, H. R., Jr., 99
Allard, S., 509
Allardt, E., 13
Allemann, F. R., 503
Allen, C., 779
Allen, G. C., 723
Allen, J. de V., 756
Allen, Sir R. H. S., 733, 756
Allen, R. V., 31, 257
Allilueva, S., 533
Allison, G. T., 180
Allon, Y., 639
Allworth, E., 580, 585
Alman, K., 168
Almaraz Paz, S., 322
Almond, G. A., 23
Alnasrawi, A. A.-K., 644
Alonso Avila, A., 302
Alperovitz, G., 148
Alpert, P., 72
Alport, C. J. McC. A., Baron, 842
Alsop, S. J. O., 268
Althoff, P., 125
Alting von Geusau, F. A. M., 55, 60, 188, 349
Alton, T. P., 513, 529
Alvarez Díaz, J. R., 302
Alves, E. R., 329
Amal'rik, A., 533, 568
Ambekar, G. V., 702
Ambler, J. S., 408
Ambrose, S. E., 156, 159, 268
Amer, O. A., 702
Ames, E., 569
Amin, M., 615
Amin, S., 793, 807, 810, 824
Aminov, A. M., 585
Aminova, R. Kh., 585
Amirkhanyan, S. M., 585
'Ammash, S. M., 617
Amme, C. H., Jr., 188
Amoia, A., 2

Amoros, Robert, 291
Amort, Č., 516
Amselek, P., 415
Amuzegar, J., 649
Anabtawi, M. F., 617
Anand, M. R., 656
Ananiadès, L. C., 353
Anchieri, E., 424
Andenæs, J., 444
Anderle, A., 554
Anders, L., 172
Anders, R., 776
Andersen, P., 800
Anderson, B. R. O'G., 760
Anderson, C. W., 208, 293, 438
Anderson, J. B., 269
Anderson, J. N. D., 37
Anderson, M., 42
Anderson, P., 269
Anderson, R. W., 311
Anderson, S. V., 441
Anderson, T., 531
Andersons, E., 458
Andic, F. M., 336
Andic, S., 336
Andics, H., 507, 508, 566
Andolenko, S., 561
Andrade S., F., 333
Andrassy, J., 90
Andreassen, T., 444
Andreen, P. G., 447
Andreev, E. P., 576
Andreis, M., 787
Andrén, N. B. E., 441, 447
Andreski, S., 200, 789
Andrews, E. M., 768
Andrews, R. H., 660
Andrieu, R., 408
Andronov, S. A., 578
Andrus, J. R., 678
Angell, A., 329
Angermann, E., 129
Anglin, D. G., 148
Angress, W. T., 468
Anguilé, A. G., 821
Ansel, W., 168
Anson, R. S., 218
Ansprenger, F., 129, 814
Anstey, R., 822
Anthony, J., 775
Antoine, C., 325
Antonio, J., 318
Antonovsky, A., 642
Anweiler, O., 578
Anyane, S. L., 814
Apel, H., 489
Apih, E., 431
Apostol, G. P., 588
Appadorai, A., 656
Appleton, S., 229
Appleyard, R. T., 770
Apsler, A., 660
Apter, D. E., 21, 31, 37, 814
Apunen, O., 452
al-'Aqqād, Ṣ., 793
Aquarone, A., 426

AUTHOR INDEX

Araldi, V., 422
Aranda, S., 303
Arango, E. R., 391
Aranibar, E., 320
Arapey, *pseud.*, 340
Arasaratnam, S., 680
Arasteh, A. R., 649
Arasteh, J., 649
Arazi, A., 640
Arbatov, G. A., 181, 241, 550
Archer, Sir G. F., 826
Arcy, F. d', 796
Ardagh, J., 396
Arendt, H., 34, 269, 484
Arévalo, J. J., 193
Arfa, H., 645, 649
Argenti, P. P., 172
Arian, A., 640, 642
Arias, J., 212
Arias Sánchez, O., 297
Arikpo, O., 816
Arismendi, R., 340
Arkes, H., 255
Arkhurst, F. S., 776
Armacost, M. H., 258
Armah, K., 779
Armajani, Y., 649
Armand, L., 347
Armangué Rius, G., 437
Armbrister, T., 226, 729
Armbruster, F. E., 741
Armitage, S., 385
Armstrong, H. F., 129, 140
Armstrong, J. A., 176, 564
Armstrong, J. P., 750
Armstrong, M., 288
Armstrong, T., 581
Arnhym, A. A., 184
Arnold, G., 367
Arnold, H. J. P., 81
Arnoni, M. S., 633
Arntz, H., 495
Aroma, N. d', 422
Aron, Raymond, 4, 18, 39, 115, 408, 629
Aron, Robert, 396, 400
Aronowitz, D. S., 123
Aronson, J., 278
Aronson, S., 480
Arora, S. K., 20
Arora, V. K., 664
Arpi, G., 447
Arredondo, A., 303
Arsić, D., 544
al-Arsūzī, Z., 617
Art, R. J., 108, 258
Arumäe, H., 456
Aruri, N. H., 643
Ash, B., 159
Ashabranner, B., 255
Ashby, Sir E., 42, 789
Ashby, J. C., 292
Ashe, G., 660
Asher, R. E., 255
Ashford, D. E., 37
Ashkenasi, A., 498
Ashmore, H. S., 747

'Ashūr, Saʿīd 'Abd al-Fattāḥ, 802
Aspaturian, V. V., 550
Aspelmeier, K. F. D., 452
Asprey, R. B., 137, 227
Assaf, M., 633
Assah, A., 646
Assarson, V., 447
Astaf'ev, G. V., 702
Astier, E. d'. *See* Astier de la Vigerie, E. d'.
Astier de la Vigerie, E. d', 396, 544
Astiz, C. A., 193, 338
Atanasov, S., 596
Atatürk, K., 622
Athay, R. E., 569
Atherton, A. L., 97
Atkin, R., 290, 769
Atkins, G. P., 307
Atmore, A., 778
Attia, G. el D., 106
Atwood, W., 784
Aubrey, H. G., 55, 60
Audénas, J., 461
Aufricht, H., 60
Augier, M. *See* Saint-Loup, S. de, *pseud.*
Augstein, R., 496
Aulén, G., 99
Ausch, K., 509
Austen, R. A., 833
Austin, A., 741
Austin, D., 375, 814
Austin, G., 662
Auty, P., 591, 594
Avakumović, I., 594
Avantaggiato Puppo, F., 148
Avcıoğlu, D., 622
Averch, H. A., 763
Avery, P., 649
Avineri, S., 633
Avnery, U., 633
Avon, A. E., 1st Earl of, 369, 736
Avramov, P., 596
Avrich, P. H., 541
Avril, P., 409
Avtorkhanov, A., 546
Awa, E. O., 816
'Awad, L., 802, 804
'Awdah, 'Awdah Buṭrus, 804
Awolowo, O., 816
Axelbank, A., 716
Aya, R., 187, 269
Aydemir, Ş. S., 622, 623
Ayearst, M., 388
Ayer, F., Jr., 218
Aynor, H. S., 784
Ayoob, M., 679
Ayub Khan, M., 675
Ayusawa, I. F., 725
al-Ayyūbī, H., 639
Azaña, M., 434
Azaola, J. M. de, 439
Āzarī, S. 'Alī, 649
Azcárate y Flórez, P. de, 633
Azeau, H., 159, 736
Azikiwe, N., 816
Aziz, K. K., 658, 675
al-'Azm, S. J., 617

Azrael, J. R., 564
Azzam, A. R., 617

Ba Maw, U., 753
Baade, F., 49
Baban, C., 623
Baby, J., 556
Bachelet, M., 789
Bachmann, H., 78
Back, P.-E., 447
Backer, J. H., 488
Backmann, R., 413
Bacon, E. E., 585
Badalyan, Kh. H., 585
Badawī, M. Ṭ., 802
Badeau, J. S., 81, 242
Bader, W. B., 116, 509
Badgley, J., 607
Badi, J., 640
Badia, G., 468, 489
Bădina, O., 589
Badouin, R., 68, 789
Baer, G., 617
Baer, G. W., 827
Baer, W., 327
Baerresen, D. W., 208
Baerwald, H. H., 691
Baggs, W. C., 747
Bagramian, I. K., 161
Bagú, S., 318
Bahār, M., 650
al-Bahi, M., 617
Bahne, S., 346
Bahr, E., 530
Bahrampour, F., 623
Baik, B. *See* Paek, P.
Bailey, D. L., 284
Bailey, N. A., 200
Bailey, R., 50
Bailey, S. D., 89, 99
Bailey, T. A., 249
Bain, C. A., 739
Bain, J. S., 50, 102
Bains, J. S., 666
Baird, P. D., 848
Bairoch, P., 72
Baishev, S. B., 585
Baker, J. C., 60
Baker, J. K., 835
Baker, J. V. T., 157
Baker, L., 144, 214, 264, 274
Baker, W. G., 99
Bakhīt, Abd, al-Ḥamīd, 617
Bakke, E. W., 721
Baklanoff, E. N., 323
Bakojannis, P., 602
Balabanoff, A., 533
Balabkins, N., 489, 641
Balagurov, Ia. A., 584
Balandier, G., 39
Balassa, B. A., 55, 56, 78
Balawyder, A., 282
Balcerak, W., 527
Baldwin, D. A., 255
Baldwin, G. B., 650
Baldwin, H. W., 156, 258

Baldwin, R. E., 53, 56, 845
Baldwin, W. L., 258
Balekjian, W. H., 353
Balfour, M. L. G., 466, 495
Balima, S. A., 810
Balinky, A., 569
Ball, A., 145
Ball, G. W., 229
Ball, M. M., 197, 367
Ball, W. M., 768
Ballaloud, J., 106
Ballinger, J., 633
Ballinger, M., 838
Ballon, R. J., 723
Balogh, T., 50
Balogun, K., 814
Bambirra, V., 203
Bandera, V. N., 79
Bandini, F., 422, 784
Bandulet, B., 498
Bandyopadhyaya, J., 666
Banerjee, A. K., 671
Banerjee, D. N., 675
Bangs, R. B., 72
Banks, A. S., 13
Bankwitz, P. C. F., 407
Banno, M., 685
Bansil, P. C., 680
Banton, M. P., 46
Bar-Yaacov, N., 633
Bar-Zohar, M., 181, 630, 631,634
Barale, J., 409
Barangé, 339
Baranson, J., 79
Barber, J. P., 836, 843
Barber, N., 167, 654
Barber, W. F., 193
Barbour, N., 794
Barcata, L., 634, 695
Barclay, C. N., 156
Barclay, G. St. J., 193, 375
Barghoorn, F. C., 550, 564
Baring, A., 490, 498
Barjonet, A., 409
Bark, D. L., 493
Barker, A. J., 137, 165, 637, 715, 828
Barker, C. A., 123
Barker, C. M., 264
Barker, D., 841
Barker, E., 375
Barkov, N. I., 848
Barkovskii, A. N., 365
Barkun, M., 85
Barm, W., 490
Barman, T., 369
Barna, T., 53
Barnaby, C. F., 116
Barnds, W. J., 652
Barnes, J., 372
Barnes, L., 776, 779
Barnes, V. D. S., 766
Barnes, W. S., 193
Barnet, R. J., 123, 181, 229, 258
Barnett, A. D., 243, 607, 684, 687
Barnett, C., 137, 367
Barnett, D. L., 829, 846
Barnett, V. M., Jr., 249

AUTHOR INDEX

Baron, S. W., 581
Barraclough, G., 129
al-Barrāwī, R., 615, 617, 804
Barringer, R. E., 112
Barrios, G., 342
Barros, J., 96, 99, 140, 425, 452, 606
Barros, M., 332
Barry, E. E., 385
Barsalou, J., 396
Bartke, W., 687, 698, 702
Bartlett, C., 239
Bartlett, R. J., 229
Bartolotta, F., 426
Barton, R., 319
Bartošek, K., 516
Bartoszewski, W., 176
Bartz, F., 68
Barucci, P., 430
al-Barūdī, 'Alī, 618
Barwich, E., 532
Barwich, H., 532
Barzanti, S., 353
Barzel, R., 495
Barzīn, M., 650
Barzini, L. G., 419
Basalykas, A. B., 463
Basch, A., 72
Basgil, A. F., 623
Bashir, al-Shāfi'ī Muhammad, 618
Basov, G. F., 584
Bass, L. W., 81
Bassani, M., 426
Bassolet, F. D., 811
Bastin, J., 733
Bastjānis, V., 458
Bastos, J. J. A., 325
Batailler, F., 416
Bates, M. S., 684
Bateson, C., 165
Batista y Zaldivar, F., 302
Batlle Berres, L., 340
Bator, V., 741
Batowski, H., 525
Battaglia, R., 176
Battaglini, G., 848
Batty, P., 463
Baudhuin, F., 391
Baudino, C., 163
Baudissin, W., Graf von, 502
Bauer, E., 147
Bauer, G., 789
Bauer, P. T., 72
Bauer, R. A., 274
Bauer, W., 683
Baum, R., 695
Baumer, W. H., 259
Baumgart, W., 131
Baumont, M., 140, 485, 733
Baus, H. M., 269
Bawden, C. R., 713
Bawly, D., 639
Baxter, C., 662
Baxter, R. R., 90
Bayar, C., 623
Bayh, B. E., 264
Bayne, E. A., 18, 650
Bazant, J., 293

Bazaz, P. N., 668
Bazna, E., 170
Beal, C. W., 741
Beal, J. R., 243, 285
Beardsley, C., 773
Beardsley, R. K., 714
Beaser, W. H., 742
Beasley, W. G., 714
Beaton, L., 7
Beaufre, A., 112, 118, 159, 178, 189, 400, 638
Beaulac, W. L., 208, 249
Beaver, D. R., 137
Beaverbrook, W. M. A., 1st Baron, 369
Bechert, H., 733
Bechtel, G., 397
Bechtoldt, H., 702
Beck, C., 13
Beck, R. H., 349
Becker, A. S., 569
Becker, B. M., 99
Becker, S., 585
Becker, T. L., 20
Beckerman, W., 385
Beckford, G. L., 79
Beckman, R., 449
Beckmann, G. M., 721
Bédard, C., 282
Bedregal, G., 322
Beer, F. A., 189
Be'eri, E., 618
Beglov, S. I., 42
Bégué, C., 799
Béguin, J.-P., 65
Behrendt, R. F. W., 79
Behrens, E., 532
Behrman, J. N., 65
Behrman, L. C., 811
Behrmann, L.-R., 510
Beichman, A., 249
Beilenson, L. W., 8, 118
Beitzell, R., 148
Bejarano, R. C., 337
Bekker, C., *pseud*., 167
Belaúnde, V. A., 193
Belaúnde Terry, F., 338
Belden, J., 684
Beling, W. A., 789, 799
Bell, C., 8, 181, 189, 353
Bell, D., 276
Bell, H. H., 208
Bell, J., 214
Bell, J. B., 118, 388
Bell, J. P., 297
Bell, W., 300, 310
Bellah, R. N., 607
Bellany, I., 768
Bello, J. M., 323
Bellows, T. J., 755
Bellush, B., 218
Beloff, M., 13, 240, 360, 375
Belshaw, C. S., 775
Ben Barakah, el-Mehdi. *See* Ben Barka, El Mehdi.
Ben Barka, A., 794
Ben Barka, El Mehdi, 794
Ben-Elissar, E., 482
Ben-Gurion, D., 630, 631, 634
Benanti, F., 600

Benda, H. J., 172, 733
Bender, P., 358, 498
Benedick, R. E., 650
Benedict, B., 680
Benediktsson, B., 454
Beneš, E., 516
Beneš, V. L., 523
Bennabī, M., 796
Bennecke, H., 478
Bennett, E. M., 241
Bennett, G. A., 695
Bennett, G. M., 137
Bennett, J., 176
Bennett, J. C., 8
Bennett, J. W., 723
Bennett, L., Jr., 276
Bennett, L. B., 695
Bennett, M., 255
Bennett, M. T., 276
Bennett, R. L., 293
Bennigsen, A., 585
Benoit, E., 123
Benoit-Guyod, G., 397
Benson, L. G., 22
Benson, M., 838
Benton, W., 578
Bentwich, H., 631
Bentwich, N. de M., 631
Benum, E., 444
Benvenuto, L. C., 340
Benz, E., 607
Berding, A. H. T., 249
Berelson, B., 47
Berenbrok, H. D. See Bekker, C., pseud.
Bereshkow, V. See Berezhkov, V. M.
Berezhkov, V. M., 148, 533
Berg, M. von, 186
Berg, P., 473
Bergamini, D., 715
Berger, C., 728
Berger, E., 634
Berger, J., 533
Berger, M., 618
Berger, P. L., 39
Berger, S., 409
Bergeron, G., 181, 285
Berggrav, E. J., 444
Bergson, A., 569
Bergstraesser, A., 13
Bergström, V., 447
Berio, A., 420
Berkeley, H., 379
Berkes, N., 623
Berkhin, I. B., 538
Berl, E., 397
Berle, A. A., Jr., 13, 274
Berler, A., 642
Berlin, Sir I., 369
Berman, H. J., 564
Bermúdez, A. J., 293
Bernard, J.-P., 204
Bernard, M., 285
Bernard, P. J., 569
Bernard, S., 795
Bernhardt, F., 173
Bernikow, L., 566
Bernstein, B. J., 269

Bernstorff, D., 662
Berov, L., 596
Berque, J., 36, 618, 793, 802
Berrill, K., 72
Berstein, S., 426
Berti, G., 427
Berton, P. A. M., 684
Bertrand, K. J., 848
Bērziņš, A., 181, 459
Bērziņš, V., 459
Beshir, M. O., 806
Besson, W., 498
Bestuzhev-Lada, I. V., 550
Betancourt, R., 200, 342
Bethel, P. D., 193
Bethell, N., 524
Béthouart, M. É., 148, 510
Bettison, D. G., 774
Beugel, E. H. van der, 349
Beyen, J. W., 389
Beyme, K. von, 503
Beyssade, P., 618, 796
Bezymenskii, L. A., 480
Bhagwati, J. N., 50, 56, 79, 81
Bhambhri, C. P., 662
Bhargava, G. S., 662, 670
Bharier, J., 650
Bhatia, B. M., 671
Bhatia, K., 658
Bhattacharyya, K. N., 671
Bhutto, Z. A., 678
Bialek, R. W., 335
Bialer, S., 154
Bianco, L., 684
Biase, C. de, 131
Bidault, G., 401
Biddle, W. F., 123
Biderman, A. D., 4, 728
Biebuyck, D., 789
Bieda, K., 724
Biehl, M., 687
Bielecki, T., 524
Bienen, H., 37, 833
Biermann, H. H., 837
Biéville, M. de, 780
Biewer, G., 466
Bihl, W., 131
Bilandžić, D., 594
Bilger, F., 506
Bilinsky, Y., 582
Bill, J. A., 650
Billig, J., 484
Billington, J. H., 578
Bilsborrow, R., 78
Binder, G., 487
Binder, L., 13, 611, 628
Bing, G., 814
Bingham, J. R., 99
Binkley, W. E., 264
Binswanger, H. C., 351
Birch, A. H., 379
Bird, R. M., 333
Birdsell, D., 175
Biriuzov, S. S., 154, 597
Birkenfeld, W., 465, 475
Birkenhead, F. W. F. S., 2nd Earl of, 369
Birkhead, G. S., 675

AUTHOR INDEX

Birmingham, W. B., 72, 814
Birnbaum, E., 640
Birnbaum, I., 498
Birnbaum, K. E., 181
Birse, A. H., 148
Bishop, D. G., 102, 241
Biskup, P., 774
Biskup, R., 560
Biswas, S. C., 660
al-Biṭār, N., 618
Bitsch, J., 714
Bittman, L., 519
Bixler, N., 753
Bjerke, J., 444
Bjøl, E., 404
Björkman, L., 447
Björnsson, Ó., 454
Black, C. E., 8, 26, 84, 129
Black, C. V. de B., 310
Black, E. R., 733
Black, J. E., 8
Black, L. D., 255
Blackmer, D. L. M., 427
Blackstock, P. W., 120, 121
Blainey, G., 770
Blair, L. B., 795
Blake, B. B., 353
Blake, H. M., 353
Blake, R., 381
Blakeley, T. J., 547
Blanchard, C. H., Jr., 728
Blancké, W. W., 249
Blanckenhagen, H. von, 455
Blanco Moheno, R., 291
Blasier, S. C., 208
Blauhorn, K., 506
Blaxland, G., 804
Bleek, W., 492
Blet, P., 148
Bleton, P., 415
Bletz, D. F., 258
Blinkenberg, L., 669
Blinnikka, A., 452
Blit, L., 524
Blittersdorf, W., Freiherr von, 94
Blitz, L. F., 816
Bliven, B., 129
Bloch, R., 96, 409
Bloch-Morhange, J., 409
Bloema, K. P., 390
Bloes, R., 349
Blomstedt, Y., 450
Bloodworth, D., 683, 733
Bloomfield, L. P., 106, 178, 248, 561
Blouet, B., 418
Bluhm, G., 530
Blum, A. A., 209
Blum, J. M., 213, 219
Blum, L., 401
Blum, R., 243
Blum, Y. Z., 94
Blumenfeld, Y., 358
Blumenson, M., 159, 165, 227
Blumer, G., 696
Blundell, Sir M., 830
Blutstein, H. I., 297, 298, 300, 302
Blyn, G., 671

Blythe, W. L., 756
Board, J. B., Jr., 447
Boarman, P. M., 506
Boavida, A., 846
Boban, L., 591
Bobbio, N., 420
Bobe, M., 459
Boberach, H., 475
Bobrow, D. B., 258
Boca, A. del, 32, 828
Bocca, G., 176, 765
Bocheński, I. M., 26, 548
Bocheński, J. M. *See* Bocheński, I. M.
Bochud, F., 60
Bodard, L., 683, 737
Bodenheimer, S. J., 353
Böhme, H., 149
Böhmler, R., 163
Böhning, W. R., 347
Boelcke, W. A., 170
Bölling, K., 503
Børde, K., 444
Boettcher, E., 545
Böttcher, W., 178
Boffa, G., 541
Bohannan, P., 776, 789
Boheman, E., 447
Bohlen, C. E., 241
Bohmann, A., 530
Bokarev, V.A., 112
Bolin, L. A., 434
Bolintineanu, A., 100
Bolling, R., 265
Bollmus, R., 478
Bombelles, J. T., 594
Bombwall, K. R., 662
Bonachea, R. E., 303, 304
Bonanni, M., 424
Bonante, L., 8
Bonarjee, N. B., 658
Bonham-Carter, V., 369
Bonham-Carter, Lady V. A., 369
Bonifaz, M., 320
Bonilla, F., 330, 343
Bonin, B., 288
Bonjour, E., 393
Bonnaud, J., 415
Bonnefous, É., 397, 405
Bonnet, G. É., 401
Bonnin, G., 478
Bonsal, P. W., 303
Booms, H., 468
Boorman, H. L., 698
Boorman, S. A., 687
Boorstein, E., 303
Bor, M. Z., 570
Borch, H. von, 178
Borg, D., 243
Borg, O., 450
Borgese, E. M., 90
Borgstrom, G. A., 48
Boris, G., 401
Borisov, E. F., 570
Borisov, I. V., 178
Borisov, O. B., 556
Borkowski, J., 524
Borodin, B. A., 556

Boros, F., 515
Borowsky, P., 132
Borre, O., 442
Borries, K., 466
Borroni, O., 317
Bortoli, G., 409
Bosc, R., 123
Bosch, J., 300, 308
Bosch, W. J., 173
Bose, A. C., 666
Bose, N. S., 243
Bose, S. C., 658
Bose, T. C., 241
Boserup, A., 116
Boserup, E., 72, 81
Boskey, B., 116
Bosman, H. W. J., 60
Bostock, M., 845
Bosworth, A. R., 267
Bot, B. R., 92
Bott, H., 503
Botting, D., 532
Bottome, E. M., 181
Boualam, S., 796
Boudiaf, M., 796
Boulding, K. E., 50, 123, 129
Bourdeaux, M., 578
Bourne, C. B., 84
Bourne, R., 204
Bourricaud, F., 338
Bourrinet, J., 353
Bouscaren, A. T., 48, 746
Bouteaud, R., 739
Bouthoul, G., 48
Bouvier, P., 822
Boveri, M., 478
Bovin, A. E., 696
Bovis, H. E., 634
Bowett, D. W., 84, 106
Bowie, R. R., 229
Bowles, C., 223, 656, 666
Boxer, A. H., 771
Boyce, D. G., 388
Boyce, P., 756
Boyd, A., 100
Boyd, F., 381
Boyd, J. M., 107
Boyer de Latour, P., 397
Boyle, J. H., 149
Bozeman, A. B., 84
Božić, I., 591
Brace, J., 797
Brace, R. M., 793, 797
Bracher, K. D., 13, 464, 475, 495
Brackman, A. C., 733, 760
Braden, S., 224
Bradley, G. E., 251
Bradley, J., 541
Bräker, H., 81
Braeman, J., 230
Bräutigam, O., 480
Braham, R. L., 511, 539, 588
Brahm, H., 541, 702
Brahmananda, P. R., 60
Braibanti, R. J. D., 607, 672, 675
Braisted, P. J., 278
Braisted, W. R., 258

Bramsted, E. K., 478
Brand, C. F., 381
Brandes, D., 516
Brandes, H., 60
Brandon, D. W., 230
Brandon, H., 385, 741
Brandt, E., 729
Brandt, W., 181, 214, 485, 499
Brannen, N. S., 716
Brannon, R. H., 340
Brass, P. R., 662
Brass, W., 789
Bratland, P., 444
Braun, W. von. See Von Braun, W.
Braunias, K., 87
Braunthal, G., 503, 506
Braunthal, J., 24
Braverman, H., 545
Bravo, A., 176
Brecher, I., 678
Brecher, M., 607, 632, 662, 666
Bredow, W. von, 181
Bregman, A., 527
Breitengross, J. P., 813
Brelis, D., 167
Bremmer, R. H., 230
Brentano, H. von, 499
Breslauer, G. W., 27
Bretton, H. L., 814
Breyer, S., 561
Brezhnev, L. I., 545
Briano, J. P., 200
Bridel, R., 94
Bridges, E. E. B., Baron, 379
Briefs, H. W., 189
Briggs, E. O., 224, 249
Briggs, H. W., 84
Brignon, J., 795
Brines, R., 669, 717
Bringolf, W., 393
Brinkhorst, L. J., 104
Brinkley, G. A., 541
Brinton, C. C., 396
Brisby, L., 130
Brisk, W. J., 312
Brissenden, P. F., 609
Brito Figueroa, F., 342
Brittan, S., 60, 385
Britten, M., 257
Brochier, H., 724
Brod, T., 517
Brodie, B., 116
Brodrick, A. H., 369
Brody, D., 230
Broek, J. O. M., 45
Broekmeijer, M. W. J. M., 189
Broekmeyer, M. J., 594
Brogan, Sir D. W., 18, 213
Bromage, M. C., 388
Bromberger, M., 349, 401
Bromberger, S., 349
Brome, V., 434
Bromke, A., 181, 358, 524, 556
Broner, J., 318
Bronger, D., 574
Brook, D., 634
Brook-Shepherd, G., 508. See also Shepherd, G.

AUTHOR INDEX

Brooke, M. Z., 65
Brookes, E. H., 838
Brookfield, H. C., 772, 773
Brooks, H., 280
Brooks, H. C., 790
Brooks, L., 147
Broomfield, J. H., 663
Broszat, M., 129, 592
Brothers, D. S., 293
Brougher, W. E., 173
Broughton, J., 745
Brower, D. R., 409
Brown, A. A., 56
Brown, B., 421
Brown, B. E., 399
Brown, Bruce, 766
Brown, C., 8
Brown, C. V., 816, 819
Brown, C. W., Jr., 35
Brown, D., 838
Brown, E. C., 576
Brown, E. D., 90
Brown, E. H. P., 50
Brown, F. J., 118
Brown, J. A. C., 121
Brown, J. F., 358, 597
Brown, J. M., 660
Brown, L. C., 793
Brown, L. R., 8, 68
Brown, N., 112, 116, 131
Brown, R. T., 209
Brown, S., 230
Brown, S. D., 610
Brown, W. N., 652
Browne, C., 717
Browne, M., 582
Browne, M. H., 50
Browne, M. W., 745
Browning, D., 300
Brownlie, I., 89, 92
Brownlow, D. G., 165
Brucan, S., 8
Bruce-Briggs, B., 179
Brügel, J. W., 522
Brüning, H., 468, 469
Brugmans, H., 349
Brumberg, A., 545
Brundage, P. F., 274
Brundtland, A. O., 11, 444
Brunner, E. E., 346
Brunschwig, H., 780
Bruwer, J. P. van S., 841
Bryant, E. H., 1
Bryant, J., 79
Bryce, M. D., 72
Brynes, A., 255
Brzezinski, Z. K., 18, 230, 240, 358, 564, 716, 784
Buber-Neumann, M., 26
Buchan, A. F., 108, 116, 189, 346, 702
Buchanan, A. R., 147
Buchanan, K. McP., 707, 733
Bucher, L. M., 729
Buchheim, H., 33, 476, 486
Buchhofer, E., 530
Buck, J. L., 707
Buck, P. S., 683
Buckley, K. A. H., 282

Buckley, T. H., 230
Buckley, W. F., Jr., 269
Budkevich, S. L., 170
Budrys, J., 461
Budurowycz, B. B., 527
Buehrig, E. H., 634
Bülent, N. E., 623
Büren, R., 802
Buergenthal, T., 90
Buerstedde, S., 349
Bueschel, R. M., 705
Buhite, R. D., 243
Bukšs, M., 459
Bulavas, J., 461
Bull, G., 432
Bull, T., 843
Bullitt, O. H., 227
Bullitt, W. C., 220
Bullock, A. L. C., 369
Bulmer-Thomas, I., 379
Bundy, McG., 265
Bunker, G. E., 149
Bunn, R. F., 503
Bunting, B. P., 838
Bunyan, J., 567
Burchett, W. G., 731, 745, 747, 750
Burden, H. T., 478
Burdett, W., 634
Burdick, C. B., 149
Burdon, R. M., 771
Burenstam Linder, S., 56
Burg, D., 546
Burger, N., 426
Burgess, P. M., 444
Burgess, W. R., 178
Burggraaff, W. J., 342
Burj, Muḥammad 'Abd al-Raḥmān, 804
Burke, F. G., 826, 831
Burke, L. H., 249
Burke, W. T., 90
Burks, D. D., 207
Burks, R. V., 344
Burlatskii, F. M., 578, 687
Burley, J., 792
Burling, R., 733
Burman, B. L., 397
Burnell, E. H., 682
Burnett, B. G., 204, 330
Burnham, F., 336
Burnham, J., 24
Burns, Sir A. C., 367
Burns, A. L., 107
Burns, E. B., 323, 325
Burns, J. MacG., 219, 227, 265, 269
Burns, R. M., 286
Burokevičius, M., 461
Buron, R., 397
Burr, R. N., 194
Burrowes, R. A., 336
Burrows, Sir B., 189
Burt, A., 309
Burton, J. W., 4, 186
Bury, J. P. T., 375
Busch, B. C., 375
Busey, J. L., 204
Bush, V., 224
Busia, K. A., 780

Busk, Sir D. L., 87
Bustos Fierro, R., 314
al-Būṭī, M. S. R., 618
Butler, D. E., 381
Butler, J., 780
Butler, Sir J. R. M., 156, 157
Butler, R., 375
Butler, W. E., 91, 564
Butler of Saffron Walden, R. A. B., Baron, 369
Butshek, F., 510
Butt, R., 23, 379
Butterfield, H., 4
Butterwick, M., 353
Buttinger, J., 738
Butwell, R. A., 37, 736, 753
Buy, F., 797
Buzzetti, J. L., 340
Byford-Jones, W., 639
Bykov, O. N., 240
Byrnes, R. F., 241

Cable, J., 114
Cabral, A., 809
Caccia Dominioni di Sillavengo, P., Conte, 165
Cademártori, J., 330
Cadogan, Sir A. G. M., 149
Caetano, M., 439
Café Filho, J., 325
Cahén, F. M., 473
Cahill, H. A., 251
Caillet-Bois, R. R., 314
Caillot, J., 365
Cairns, J. C., 396
Calamandrei, P., 420
Caldas Villar, J., 313
Calder, A., 173
Calder, N., 108
Caldwell, J. C., 790
Caldwell, L. K., 45
Caldwell, M., 759
Calic, É., 480
Callado, A., 325
Callcott, W. H., 194
Calleo, D. P., 240, 346, 366
Calmann, J., 346
Calvert, P., 200, 290
Calvocoressi, P., 147, 178
Cameron, A. W., 737
Cameron, J., 747
Cameron, R., 60
Cameron, W. J., 771
Cammett, J. M., 420
Campbell, Alan, 353
Campbell, Alex, 244
Campbell, Arthur, 119
Campbell, J. C., 241, 594
Campbell, J. F., 249
Campbell, J. K., 602
Campbell, M. J., 816
Campbell, R. W., 570, 575
Campbell of Eskan, Baron, 353
Campiglia, N., 340
Campillo Pérez, J. G., 308
Campos, R. de O., 209, 327
Camps, M., 354
Camu, P., 288

Candilis, W. O., 602
Canelas O., A., 197, 322
Cang, J., 582
Canham, E. D., 230
Cannon, L., 219
Cannon, M. W., 271
Canton, D., 314
Cantril, A. H., 39, 230, 270
Capelle, R., 391
Caplan, G. L., 845
Caply, M., 749
Capps, F. H., 278
Caradon, H. M. F., Baron, 369
Caraley, D., 258
Carano, P., 773
Cárdenas, G., 317
Cardif, M. *See* Lincoln, J., *pseud*.
Cardinale, I., 432
Cardona, M. E., 201
Cardonnel, J., 22
Cardoso, F. H., 327
Cardozo, E., 337
Carell, P., *pseud*., 161
Carew, J. M. *See* Carew, T., *pseud*.
Carew, T., *pseud*., 728
Carey, A. G., 602
Carey, J., 100, 840
Carey, J. C., 338
Carey, J. P. C., 602
Carey, R. G., 255
Carey Jones, N. S., 830
Caridi, R. J., 244
Carley, M. M., 310
Carlton, R. G., 202
Carmichael, J., 618, 631
Carmichael, S., 277
Carmona, F., 293
Carmoy, G. de, 405
Carneiro, G., 325
Carneiro, L., 325
Carnoy, M., 209
Carocci, G., 424
Carone, E., 325
Carr, D. W., 286
Carr, E. H., 539, 544, 570
Carr, R., 433, 434
Carras, M. C., 663
Carreau, D., 60
Carrère d'Encausse, H., 586, 610
Carri, R., 315
Carrigan, D. O., 286
Carrillo, E. A., 420
Carrillo Batalla, T. E., 342
Carroll, B. A., 476
Carroll, E. M., 550
Carroll, F., 842
Carsten, F. L., 33, 141, 469
Carter, G. M., 780, 836, 839
Carter, J. R., 560
Carter, W. H., 375
Cartey, W., 776
Cartier, R., 147
Cartou, L., 349
Carver, M., 165
Cary, W. L., 265
Casadio, G. P., 354
Casella, A., 141

AUTHOR INDEX

Cassell, F., 60
Cassels, A., 424
Castagno, A. A., 780
Castañeda, J., 100
Castiglione, L., 432
Castillero R., E. J., 299
Castillo, C. M., 295
Castles, L., 760
Castor, S., 309
Castro, F., 303
Catalano, F., 347, 427, 429
Cate, J. L., 158
Cater, D., 269
Catlin, G. E. G., 189
Cattan, H., 615, 634
Catti de Gasperi, M. R., 420
Catudal, H. M., Jr., 493
Caulfield, M. F., 388
Caute, D., 409
Cavallari, A., 432
Cavendish, P., 696
Caves, R. E., 288, 385
Cayrac-Blanchard, F., 733
Ceauşescu, N., 588
Cecil, L., 466
Cecil, R., 481
Čejka, E., 517
Cem, İ., 623
Ceresole, N., 315, 317, 338
Černý, B., 522
Cerny, K. H., 189
Červenka, Z., 785, 819
Cervi, M., 163, 602
Červinková, M., 518
Cerych, L., 81
Ceuppens, H. D., 337
Ceva, B., 163
Chadwick, G. W. St. J., 286
Chadwin, M. L., 149
Chaffard, G., 737, 745
Chaffee, F. H., 763
Chai, W., 687, 688
Chakravarti, N. R., 753
Chakravarti, P. C., 670
Chakravarty, B. N., 666
Chaliand, G., 639, 797
Challe, M., 401
Chalmers, D. A., 503
Chambe, R., 401
Chamberlaine, N. W., 48
Chamberlin, W. H., 495
Chambers, W., 227
Chambre, H., 570
Chamorro Cardenal, P. J., 298
Chamoun, C., 628
Champenois, L., 648
Chan, H. C., 755
Chan, Wing-tsit, 710
Chand, G., 674
Chanda, A. K., 663
Chandos, O. L., 1st Viscount, 370
Chandrasekhar, S., 608, 672
Chaney, O. P., Jr., 533
Chang, Hsin-Hai, 244
Chang, Kuo-t'ao, 698
Chang, Ming-kai, 685
Chang, Tsungtung, 707

Chang-Rodríguez, E., 308
Chantebout, B., 407
Chao, Kang, 707
Chao, T., 696
Chapal, P., 94
Chapaprieta Torregrosa, J., 434
Chapelle, J., 575
Chapman, B. K., 270
Chapman, G., 397
Chapman, J. G., 576
Chapman, J. W., 35
Char, K. T. N., 660
Charles, S. F., 265
Charlot, J., 409
Charlot, M., 379
Charnay, J.-P., 36, 409
Chary, F. B., 597
Chase, A., 45
Chassin, L. M., 688
Chatterji, B., 655
Chatterji, B. R., 733
Chaudet, P., 393
Chaudhri, M. A., 678
Chaudhuri, M. A., 675
Chaudhuri, N. C., 657
Chauhan, R. S., 655
Chaunu, P., 200
Chautemps, C., 149
Chauvel, J., 401
Chauvel, J.-F., 602
Chayes, A., 84, 258
Cheever, D. S., 82
Ch'ên, Hsi-ên, 688
Ch'ên, J., 688, 698
Chen, K. C., 738
Ch'en, Lieh-fu, 763
Chen, Lung-Chu, 712
Chen, Nai-ruenn, 707
Ch'ên, Po-ta, 698
Chen, T. H. E. See Ch'ên, Hsi-ên.
Chen, Yung Ping, 688
Chenery, H. B., 72
Chêng, Chu-yüan, 556, 707
Cheng, Hang-sheng, 61
Cheng, J. C., 706
Cheng, P., 688
Cheng, Siok-Hwa, 753
Chennault, A., 154
Cherepanov, A. I., 556
Cherepanov, N. M., 164
Cherepnin, L. V., 584
Chériff Vanly, I., 645
Chernenko, K. U., 562
Chernikov, G. P., 405
Chernikova, D. A., 405
Chersheev, D., 586
Chesneaux, J., 707
Chester, L., 215, 381
Cheverny, J., 27
Chew, A. F., 454
Chhak, S., 750
Chiang, Hai Ding, 755
Chiang, Hsüeh-wen, 696
Ch'ien, Ts'un-hsün, 278
Chilcote, R. H., 438, 846
Childs, D., 490, 503
Childs, J. R., 224

Chilver, E. M., 826
Chin, Ai-li S., 710
Chin, R., 710
Chin, Shen-pao, 556
Ch'ing, Ju-chi, 244
Ching Hsüan-t'ung, Emperor of China, 698
Chittick, W. O., 249
Chiu, Hung-ta, 92, 702, 703, 704
Chkhikvadze, V. M., 548, 564
Cho, Chang-Hyun, 727
Cho, M. Y., 702, 732
Cho, S. S., 726
Chögyam Trungpa, T. T., 654
Chomsky, N., 230, 741, 744
Chonchol, J., 209
Chopard, T., 393
Chopra, P., 663, 679
Chornovil, V., 582
Chou, Chih-ming, 244
Chou, E., 688
Chou, En-lai, 698
Chou, Keng-sheng, 84
Chou, Shun-hsin, 707
Chou, Tse-tung, 685
Choudhry, L. P., 16
Choudhury, G. W., 669, 676
Choukas, M., 121
Choy, Bong-youn, 726
Christiakov, O. I., 544
Christian, G., 224
Christian, W. A., Jr., 397
Christidis, C., 606
Christman, H. M., 596
Chu, V., 688
Chubar'ian, A. O., 550
Chubb, B., 388
Chuikov, V. I., 154
Chulanov, G. C., 585
Chung, Hua-min, 698
Chung, K. C., 730
Churchill, R. S., 370, 639
Churchill, W. S., 639
Churchward, L. G., 564
Ciałowicz, J., 528
Ciani, A., 427
Ciechanowski, J. M., 525
Cielēns, F., 459
Cienciala, A. M., 145
Cierva y de Hoces, R. de la, 434, 435
Cioranesco, G., 588
Ciria, A., 194, 315, 317
Čirković, S., 591
Citrine, W. McL., 1st Baron, 370
Clabaugh, S. F., 251
Clague, C. K., 310
Clapham, C., 828
Clapp, C. L., 265
Clark, A., 161
Clark, A. B., 699
Clark, C., 50, 68
Clark, C. M. H., 766
Clark, D., 454
Clark, D. M. J., 638
Clark, G., 204, 281
Clark, G. J., 703
Clark, J. S., 265
Clark, K. C., 249

Clark, M. See Clark, C. M. H.
Clark, P. G., 255
Clark, R. W., 129, 370
Clark, W. H., 354
Clarke, R., 108, 118
Clarke, S. V. O., 274
Clarkson, S., 283
Clausen, U., 797
Clawson, M., 70, 613
Clayton, Sir G. F., 618
Clemens, D. S., 149
Clemens, W. C., Jr., 556
Clements, F., 843
Cleveland, H., 189, 230
Cleveland, H. Van B., 240
Cleveland, W. L., 618
Clews, J. C., 121
Cliffe, L., 833
Clifford, J.M., 82
Clifford, M. L., 813
Clifford, N. R., 375
Clifford-Vaughan, M., 389
Cline, C. A., 381
Cline, H. F., 200
Clissold, S., 433, 558, 591
Clogg, R., 602
Closon, F.-L., 415
Clough, S. B., 419, 429
Clower, R. W., 813
Clubb, O. E., 556, 685, 688
Clutterbuck, R. L., 756
Clytus, J., 303
Coakley, R. W., 159
Coats, W. J., 112
Cobb, R. C., 396
Cobban, A., 396
Čobeljić, N., 53
Cocatre-Zilgien, A., 405
Cochran, B., 219, 258
Cochrane, J. D., 295
Cochrane, W. W., 68
Cockburn, P. A., 387
Codding, G. A., 96
Coedès, G., 734
Coelho, V. H., 656
Coffey, J. I., 258
Coffey, P., 354
Coffey, T. M., 166
Coffin, F. M., 255
Coffin, T., 219
Coffman, E. M., 137
Cohen, A., 634
Cohen, A. A., 688
Cohen, B. C., 278
Cohen, B. J., 251, 385
Cohen, J. A., 84, 688, 712
Cohen, J. B., 252
Cohen, M. I., 795
Cohen, S. B., 45
Cohen, S. D., 61
Cohen, S. F., 567
Cohen, S. P., 658
Cohen, S. S., 415
Cohen, W. I., 132, 244
Cohn, E. J., 626
Cohn, H. D., 558
Cohn-Bendit, D., 31

AUTHOR INDEX

Cohn-Bendit, G., 31
Colapietra, R., 431
Colby, C. C., 67
Colby, R., 27
Cole, A. B., 721
Cole, D. C., 730
Cole, H., 401
Cole, H. M., 161
Cole, J. A., 370
Cole, J. P., 209, 531
Cole, J. S. R., 833
Cole, W. E., 293
Colebrook, M. J., 350
Coleman, J. S., 42, 780
Coles, H. L., 175
Collier, B., 156, 167, 375
Collier, D. S., 358
Collier, R., 420
Colligan, F. J., 279
Collins, J. L., 728
Collins, L., 397
Collotti Pischel, E., 689
Colombo, E., 429
Colotti, E., 422, 487
Colton, J., 401
Colvin, I. G., 141, 375, 822
Comfort, R. A., 469
Comín Colomer, E., 433
Comitas, L., 300
Compton, J. V., 141
Conan, A. R., 385
Conant, J. B., 224
Condliffe, J. B., 771
Confer, V., 397
Confino, B., 597
Conil Paz, A., 314
Conn, S., 158, 159
Connell, C., 164
Connell, J., *pseud.*, 370
Connell-Smith, G., 197
Connery, D. S., 442
Connolly, W. E., 22
Connor, W. D., 576
Conolly, V., 581
Conquest, R., 24, 545, 548, 565, 566, 567, 576, 581
Constant, S. C., 354
Constantinescu-Iași, P., 589
Consuegra, J., 333
Conte, A., 149
Contini, P., 829
Conway, J. S., 476
Coogan, T. P., 388
Cook, D., 350
Cook, F. J., 267
Cook, J. W., 317
Cooke, A., 227
Cookridge, E. H., *pseud.*, 170, 496
Cookson, J., 118
Cooley, J. K., 785, 793
Coombes, D. L., 354
Coombs, P. H., 278
Cooper, C. A., 613
Cooper, C. L., 741
Cooper, J., 754
Cooper, J. M., Jr., 230
Cooper, R. N., 189
Cope, J. P., 839

Copeland, M., 804
Coplin, W. D., 84
Coppock, J. O., 68
Coquery-Vidrovitch, C., 824
Corbet, H., 56, 354, 368, 385
Corbett, E. M., 286, 785
Corbino, E., 429, 431
Corden, W. M., 56
Cordier, A. W., 100, 123
Corkran, H., Jr., 301
Cornelius, W. A., Jr., 204
Cornevin, R., 811, 822
Cornwell, E. E., Jr., 217, 278
Corominas, E. V., 290
Corpuz, O. D., 763
Corson, W. R., 741
Cosgrove, C. A., 100
CosíoVillegas, D., 194, 290
Costa, J. M. da, 440
Costa, P. da, 847
Coste, R., 108
Cot, J.-P., 8
Cotta, M., 397
Cottam, R. W., 87, 650
Cottrell, A. J., 189
Coudenhove-Kalergi, R. N., Graf von, 350
Couloumbis, T. A., 606
Coulter, J. W., 775
Courrière, Y., 797
Courthéoux, J.-P., 415
Cousins, N., 227
Coutsoumaris, G., 602
Couve de Murville, M., 405
Cowan, C. D., 682, 734
Cowan, L. G., 780
Cowie, H., 382
Cowling, M., 382
Cox, A., 265
Cox, A. M., 107
Cox, D. W., 280
Cox, R. H. F., 826, 830
Cox, R. W., 96
Coyle, D. C., 100
Coyne, J. R., Jr., 227
Crabb, C. Van M., Jr., 187
Cragg, K., 44
Craig, A. M., 682
Craig, G. A., 108
Craig, G. M., 283
Craig, W., 166
Crane, R. D., 182
Crankshaw, E., 533, 556
Cranston, M., 31
Cras, H. *See* Mordal, J., *pseud.*
Crassweller, R. D., 301, 308
Craven, W. F., 158
Crawford, E. T., 4
Crawford, Sir J. G., 771
Crawford, O., 350
Crawford, W. R., 292
Crawley, A., 401
Creighton, D., 282
Cremeans, C. D., 618
Crépeau, P. A., 286
Creswell, J., 168
Crick, B. R., 366, 380
Crick, W. F., 61

Crispo, J. H. G., 283
Critchfield, F., 746
Crochat, M., 61
Crocker, W. R., 660
Cromwell, W. C., 190
Cronin, T. E., 265
Crook, D., 689
Crook, I., 689
Croome, D. R., 385
Cross, C., 367, 370
Cross, J. E., 119
Crosser, P. K., 123
Crossman, R. H. S., 24, 380
Crouzet, M., 346
Crow, J. A., 433
Crowder, M., 807, 811
Crowley, E. L., 533, 539, 550, 574
Crowley, J. B., 718
Crozier, B., 13, 27, 37, 437, 734
Crozier, M., 417
Crozier, R. C., 689
Cruz Costa, J., 323
Cuadra Pasos, C., 298
Cuccorese, H. J., 318
Čulinović, F., 592
Cumberland, C. C., 289
Cumberland, K. B., 766
Cummings, M. C., Jr., 215, 265
Cúneo, D., 194, 314, 318
Cunill Grau, P., 201
Curran, B. D., 809
Currie, A. W., 288
Currie, D. P., 780
Currie, J. I., 792
Currie, L. B., 72, 73
Curry, R. L., Jr., 13
Curti, M. E., 255
Curtis, G. L., 718, 721
Curtis, M., 611
Curtis, R., 116
Curtis, T. B., 252
Curtiss, J. S., 531
Curzon, G., 56
Cutajar, M. Z., 56
Cutler, R., 224
Cutt, J., 672
Czempiel, E. O., 8, 230
Czernin, F. See Czernin von und zu Chudenitz, F., Graf.
Czernin von und zu Chudenitz, F., Graf, 132
Czerwinski, E. J., 358

Daalder, H., 380
Däniker, G., 112, 745
Dafnis, G., 604
Dagan, A., 632
Dahl, H. F., 444
Dahl, R. A., 20, 265
Dahm, B., 760
Dahm, H., 113, 548
Dahms, H. G., 147
Dahrendorf, R., 464
Dain, B. M., 8
Daix, P., 520
Dakin, D., 375
Daland, R. T., 328

Dalberg, T., 496
Dale, R., 837
Dalla Tana, L., 422
Dallek, R., 219
Dallin, A., 27, 132, 545, 562
Dallin, D. J., 539
Dalton, G., 789
Dalvi, J. P., 670
Dam, K. W., 56
Damachi, U. G., 820
D'Amato, A., 94, 741
Damm, U., 499
Damm, W., 67
D'Amoja, F., 424
Danan, Y. M., 797
Danglis, G. P., 604
Danielian, N. R., 252
Daniels, J., 215, 227
Daniels, R. V., 541
Daniloff, N., 563
Dann, U, 644
Dansette, A., 410
Danstrup, J., 443, 444
D'Antonio, W. V., 201
Dantsig, B. M., 405
Dapčević-Oreščanin, S., 556
Dargeant, R., 393
Darin-Drabkin, H., 642
Darling, F. C., 751
Darlington, A. B., 825
Darlington, C. F., 825
Darmstadter, J., 70
Das, D., 658, 661
Dasbach, A. M., 490
Das Gupta, J., 674
Das Gupta, J. B., 669
Dash, S. C., 663
Datar, A. L., 672
Dau, M., 442
Davenport, M. G., 517
Davet, M.-C., 626
Davezies, R., 847
David, J. E., 821
David, W. L., 336
Davids, J., 231, 239
Davidson, A., 769
Davidson, B., 777, 810, 847
Davidson, E., 484
Davidson, I., 354
Davidson, J. W., 775
Davies, I., 790
Davies, J. P., Jr., 685
Davies, R. W., 570
Davis, B., 166
Davis, F., 244
Davis, H. E., 201
Davis, J. A., 835
Davis, J. H., 634
Davis, K., 48
Davis, K. S., 156, 219
Davis, N. P., 219
Davis, V., 259
Davison, W. P., 121
Davy, A., 828
Davydov, I. P., 230
Dawidowicz, L. S., 269
Dawson, F. G., 94

AUTHOR INDEX

Dawson, O. L., 707
Day, A. T., 277
Day, L. H., 277
Dayan, D., 640
Dayan, M., 638
Dayez, É.-C., 391
Deakin, F. W., 170
Deakin, N., 382, 387
Dean, A. H., 123
De Biase, C., 422, 424
Debray, R., 204, 330
Debré, F., 819
Debré, M., 410
Decker, H. de, 807
Decornoy, J., 734
Decottignies, R., 780
Dederke, K., 469
Dedijer, V., 132, 591, 594
Deener, D. R., 283
De Felice, R., 420
Deffarge, C., 647
De Gaury, G., 647
De George, R. T., 27, 548, 579
Degras, J. T., 27, 570
De Grazia, A., 267
De Gregori, T. R., 790
De Guingand, Sir F. W., 154
De Guinsbourg, V., 100
Dehousse, J.-M., 350
Deitchman, S. J., 259
De Jaegher, R. J., 697
De Kadt, E. J., 301, 378
Dekkers, R., 689
Dekmejian, R. H., 802
De la Mahotière, S., 350
Delarue, J., 478
Delassus, J.-F., 725
Delaume, G. R., 61
Delcoigne, G., 116
Delgado, H., 440
Delgado, O., 209
Deliusin, L. P., 689, 696
Dell, S. S., 79, 197
Delperrie de Bayac, J., 435
De Mauny, E., 532
Demeter, K., 464
Deng, W., 806
Denis, H., 176
Denison, E. F., 73
Denison, W. N., 833
Dennert, J., 734
Dennis, P., 378
Denno, T. F., 548
DeNovo, J. A., 242
Denton, G., 347
DePorte, A. W., 405
Derogy, J., 642
Desai, A. R., 79
Desai, R. H., 387
De St. Jorre, J., 819
De Smith, S. A., 773
Desmond, C., 839
Despres, L. A., 336
Destler, I. McA., 250
De Toledano, R., 219
Deuerlein, E., 149, 466
Deutsch, H. C., 485

Deutsch, K. W., 4, 17, 37, 190, 350
Deutscher, I., 27, 178, 534, 539
Deutschkron, I., 632
Devillers, P., 698, 737
Devlin, B., 370
Dew, E., 338
Dewart, L., 304
Dewdney, J. C., 623
DeWeerd, H. A., 137
Dexter, B., 1, 141
Dey, R., 450
Dhahab, S., 615
Diab, M. A., 618
Dial, R., 703
Diamond, S., 826
Diarassouba, V.-C., 811
Díaz Alejandro, C. F., 318
Díaz Araujo, E., 315
Díaz Ordaz, G., 291
Dibb, P., 581
Di Capua, G., 424
Dichter, D., 676
Dickey, J. S., 283
Dickie, J., 370
Dickson, P., 278
Didden, H., 644
Diebold, J., 40
Diebold, W., Jr., 252
Diederich, B., 309
Dietze, G., 265
Díez Alegría, M., 437
Diggins, J. P., 33
Diguimbaya, G., 821
Dill, K., 820
Dillon, W., 81
Dimitrov, I., 597
Dimock, M. E., 725
Dines, A., 325
Dinić, J., 689
Dinur, B.-Z., 640
Dīrī, A., 639
Dirscherl, D., 545
Ditmas, E. M. R., 3
Divekar, V. D., 702
Divine, R. A., 149, 248
Dix, R. H., 333
Dixon, P., 370
Dizard, W. P., 42
Djilas, M., 22
Djojohadikusumo, S., 756
Djordjevic, J., 592
Dmitriev, B. D., 231
Dobell, P. C., 283
Dobie, E., 418
Dobney, F. J., 227
Dod, K. C., 175
Dodd, C. H., 623, 634
Dodge, N. T., 576
Dodic, L., 600
Doehring, K., 488
Dönhoff, M., Gräfin, 178, 179, 490, 495, 499
Dönitz, K., 481
Doernberg, S., 490
Doi, A., 719
Doig, J. W., 266
Dolci, D., 178, 431
Doležal, J., 517

AUTHOR INDEX

Dollmann, E., 481
Domarus, M., 481
Dombrowski, J., 297
Domdey, K. H., 186
Domenach, J.-M., 417
Domergue, M., 81
Domes, J., 503, 685, 689, 703
Domhoff, G. W., 277
Dommen, A. J., 749
Donahoe, B. F., 215
Donaint, P., 821
Donaldson, P., 385
Donelan, M. D., 11, 231
Donlagić, A., 592
Donnay, H., 822
Donnelly, D., 182
Donner, W., 655
Donneur, A., 25
Donnison, F. S. V., 157, 753
Donnithorne, A. G., 708
Donovan, F. R., 100
Donovan, J., 204
Donovan, J. A., 259
Donovan, J. B., 566
Donovan, J. C., 269
Doob, L. W., 17, 826
Dopfer, K., 186
Doré, F., 663
Dore, R. P., 725
Dormann, M., 502
Dorn, F., 167
Dornberg, J., 490, 532
Dorpalen, A., 469
Dósa, R., 511
Dos Passos, J. R., 323
Dotson, F., 845
Dotson, L. O., 845
Dougherty, J. E., 123, 189
Douglas, P.H., 224, 252
Douglas, S., Baron Douglas of Kirtleside, 370
Douglas, W. O., 96, 178, 201, 269
Douglas-Hamilton, J., 149
Douglas-Home, C., 634
Douma, J., 93
Dow, J. C. R., 385
Dow, M. W., 734
Dowse, R. E., 815
Doxey, M. P., 96
Doyon, J., 745
Drachkovitch, M. M., 25, 27, 29, 31, 539
Drachman, E. R., 738
Dragoicheva, T., 597
Draguhn, W., 672
Drancourt, M., 347, 417
Draper, T., 304, 308, 632, 742
Dreher, K., 503
Dresch, J., 793
Dress, H., 522
Dreux-Brézé, J. de, 821
Driberg, T. E. N., 22
Driver, C. P., 124
Drīzulis, A., 459
Dröge, H., 102
Drogichinskii, N. E., 570
Dror, Y., 641
Drouin, P., 354
Droz, J. H. *See* Humbert-Droz, J.

Druks, H., 241
Drury, A., 836
Drysdale, J. G. S., 829
Dubnic, V. R. de, 325
Dubois, J., 204
Du Bois, W. E. B., 224
Dubos, R., 46
Dubyna, K. K., 582
Duchacek, I. D., 4
Duché, J., 130
Duclos, J., 401
Ducouloux, C., 415
Ducret, J., 612
Ducros, B., 55
Dudley, B. J., 816
Duff, C., 388
Duff, E. A., 333
Dugard, J., 842
Duhamel, A., 410
Duignan, P., 777
Duisberg, C.-J., 127
Dulac, A., 407
Dulles, A. W., 121, 122, 170
Dulles, E. L., 182, 219, 250, 487, 493
Dulles, F. R., 244
Dulles, J. W. F., 326
Dumoga, J., 785
Dumont, R., 68, 304, 574, 708, 790
Dunbar, A., 778
Duncan, F., 281
Duncan, J. S., 700
Duncan, W. R., 559
Duncanson, D. J., 738
Duncker, J. Z., 113
Dunn, F. S., 718
Dunn, J., 34
Dunning, J. H., 66
Duocastella, R., 438
Dupuy, R. E., 147, 259
Dupuy, T. N., 108, 714
Duquesne, J., 397
Durán, J. L., 340
Ďurica, M. S., 523
Duroselle, J.-B., 11, 37, 231, 426
Du Roy, A., 391
Duscha, J., 259
Dutoit, B., 85, 350
Dutt, G., 689, 696
Dutt, V. P., 696, 703
Dutton, F. G., 270
Duus, P., 721
Duvalier, F., 309
Duverger, M., 13
Duwaji, G., 799
Dyck, H. L., 473
Dzhamgerchinov, B. D., 586
Dzhaoshvili, V. S., 586
Dziewanowski, M. K., 528
Dziuba, I., 582
Dzyuba, I. *See* Dziuba, I.

Eagleton, W., Jr., 646
Eayrs, J. G., 283, 367
Eban, A. S., 629
Ebb, K., 353
Ebel, A., 482

AUTHOR INDEX

Ebel, R. E., 362
Ebert, F., 492
Ebert, T., 119
Ebon, M., 698
Eby, C. de G., 435
Eccles, H. E., 113
Echaiz, R. L., 330
Echavarría Olózoga, F., 333
Ecklund, G. N., 708
Eckstein, A., 708
Eckstein, H. H., 34, 444
Eckstein, S., 293
Edel, M., 209
Eden, A. *See* Avon, A. E., 1st Earl of.
Eder, G. J., 322
Edinger, L. J., 18, 497
Edwardes, M., 657, 658
Edwards, C., 769
Edwards, D. V., 124
Edwards, E. O., 274
Edwards, J. E., 231
Edwards, M. L., 132
Edwards, S. F., 328
Eells, R., 66
Efimov, A. N., 570
Efrat, E., 630
Eggleston, W., 285
Egorov, V. N., 182
Ehlers, D., 485
Ehlert, N., 497
Ehni, R., 393
Ehnmark, A., 847
Ehrenberg, H., 506
Ehrenburg, I. G., 534
Ehrlich, A., 48
Ehrlich, P., 48
Ehrlich, S., 20
Ehrlich, T., 84
Eichelberger, C. M., 100
Eicher, C. K., 820
Eide, A., 93
Einaudi, L., 420
Einstein, L., 224
Einzig, P., 61, 382
Eisenberg, D., 33
Eisenhower, D. D., 154, 224
Eisenhower, J. S. D., 159
Eisenhower, M. S., 194
Eisenstadt, S. N., 642
Eismann, B., 270
Ekmečič, M., 591
El-Ayouty, Y., 100, 790
Eldem, V., 626
Elder, R. E., 278
Eldredge, H. W., 270
Eldridge, H. T., 274
Eldridge, P. J., 672
Elegant, R. S., 689
Elgey, G., 397
Elias, T. O., 85
Eliav, A. L., 582
Eliseit, H., 682
El-Kammash, M. M., 805
Eller, E. McN., 562
Elliott, J. G., 658
Elliott, W. Y., 255
Elliott-Bateman, M., 122, 608

Ellis, C. H., 541
Ellis, H. B., 354
Ellis, H. S., 328, 603
Ellis, L. E., 231
Ellis, L. F., 157
Ellis, U. R., 769
Ellman, M., 570
Ello, P., 520
Ellsberg, D., 742
Ellul, J., 23, 121
Ellwein, T., 503
El Mallakh, R., 647
Elmer, Å., 447
Elon, A., 487, 643
Elstob, P., 159
Elston, D. R., 629
Elvander, N., 448
Ély, P., 401
Emanuel, M., 629
Embree, G. D., 554
Émelianidès, A., 418
Emerson, R., 237, 780, 785, 786
Emerson, T. I., 42
Emery, R. F., 734
Emme, E. M., 114
Emmerson, D K., 32
Emmerson, J. K., 716
Enahoro, A. E. O., 816
Encina, F. A., 332
End, H., 499
Endacott, G. B., 754
Endō, H., 718
Enepekidis, P., 605
Engel, S., 85
Engelborghs-Bertels, M., 689
Engelman, R. C., 159
Englebardt, S. L., 259
Enke, S., 73
Enzensberger, H. M., 13
Epstein, A. L., 774
Epstein, L. D., 19, 382
Epstein, W., 124
Erdei, F., 513
Erdman, H. L., 663
Erdmann, K. D., 468, 469
Erdmenger, K., 499
Eremenko, A. I., 161
Eren, N., 623
Erényi, T., 513
Erger, J., 469
Erhard, L., 506
Erickson, E. E., 335
Erickson, J., 108
Erickson, R. J., 85
Eriksen, K. E., 445
Erikson, E. H., 660
Erkin, F. C., 625
Erlander, T., 448
Erler, F., 504
Erlikh, A. N., 142
Ernst, F., 466
Ernst, H., 354
Ernst, H. W., 222
Eschenburg, T., 469, 478
Escobari Cusicanqui, J., 320
Esman, M. J., 82, 756
Esmein, J., 696

AUTHOR INDEX

Espinosa Moraga, O., 320
Essame, H., 160
Esthus, R. A., 768
Estier, C., 802
Estruch, J., 438
Eterovich, F. H., 592
Étienne, G., 653, 672, 679
Etinger, I. I., 785
Etzioni, A., 40, 96, 182, 280
Etzioni, M. M., 97
Eubank, K., 88, 141
Eubanks, G. J., 363
Eudes, D., 605
Eudin, X. J., 551, 692
Euler, H., 92
Evalenko, R., 391
Evans, F. T., 115
Evans, Sir G. C., 370
Evans, H., 711
Evans, J. W., 252
Evans, L., 242
Evans, R., 215, 219
Evers, T. T., 315
Ewing, A. F., 790
Eyzaguirre, J., 332
Ezcurdia, M., 291

Faaland, J., 56
Fabela, I., 291
Fabela, J. E., 291
Faber, H., 215
Faber, M. L. O., 845
Fabian, L. L., 107
Fabre-Luce, A., 398, 410
Fabry, P. W., 161, 554
Facchi, P., 427
Fagen, R. R., 204, 304
Fagerberg, E. P., 405
Fahmi, M. A. Z., 802
Faillant de Villemarest, P., 398
Fainsod, M., 565
Fair, T. J. D., 841
Fairbairn, G., 734
Fairbank, J. K., 244, 682, 685
Fairchild, B., 159
Fairhall, D., 562
Fakhrā'ī, I., 650
Falconi, C., 150, 432
Faldella, E., 137
Falin, V. M., 146
Falk, R. A., 45, 84, 85, 89, 94, 123, 742
Falkowski, M., 73
Fall, B. B., 737, 738, 739, 743, 745, 748, 749
Fallaci, O., 739
Fallers, L. A., 831
Falls, C. B., 137
Fals Borda, O., 333
Fan, K. H., 696
Fanon, F., 780
Farago, L., 145, 219
Farahmand, S., 650
Farajallah, S. B., 101
Faraone, R., 340
Farer, T. J., 790
Farley, R., 209, 800
Farnie, D. A., 612

Farnsworth, B., 241
Farrell, B. H., 771
Farrell, R. B., 14, 283, 358, 740
Farrugia, L., 312
Fartyal, H. S., 663
Farwell, G., 763
al-Fāsī, 'Allāl, 795
Fatemi, N. S., 252
Faure, E., 14, 396
Faust, J.-J., 323, 326
Fauvet, J., 410
Favoreu, L., 680
Fawcett, J. E. S., 93
Fawdah, 'Izz al-Dīn, 634
Fayerweather, J., 66
Fayt, C. S., 315, 317
Feddersen, D., 490
Fediukin, S. A., 541
Fedoseev, P. N., 548
Fedyshyn, O. S., 132
Fehr, E., 807
Fehrenbach, T. R., 150, 728
Feibleman, J. K., 14
Feierabend, L. K., 517
Feifer, G., 565
Fein, L. J., 629
Feinberg, N., 635
Feis, H., 150, 182, 215, 255, 632, 716
Feit, E., 839
Feith, H., 760
Feiwel, G. R., 519, 529, 570
Fejtö, F., 358, 410, 556
Feld, B. T., 109
Feld, W. J., 354, 355, 499
Feldman, G. D., 137
Feldman, H., 676
Felgas, H., 847
Felice, R. de. *See* De Felice, R.
Felix, C., *pseud.*, 259
Felker, J. L., 570
Fellman Velarde, J., 319
Fellner, W., 61
Fenet, A., 426
Fenno, R. F., Jr., 265
Fenyo, M. D., 515
Ferguson, J. H., 204
Fergusson, J. *See* Fergusson of Kilkerran, Sir J.
Fergusson of Kilkerran, Sir J., 383
Ferkiss, V. C., 777
Ferlet, T., 448
Fermi, L., 277
Fernandes, F., 328
Fernández, C. J., 320
Fernández Cabrelli, A., 340
Fernández-Carvajal, R., 437
Fernández-Shaw, F. G., 197, 296, 299
Ferniot, J., 410
Ferns, H. S., 313
Féron, B., 545
Ferrara, M., 424
Ferrari, G., 314
Ferreira, P., 328
Ferrell, R. H., 231
Ferrer, A., 318
Ferris, P., 61
Ferro, M., 541
Fest, J. C., 481

AUTHOR INDEX

Fetscher, I., 33
Feuer, L. S., 32
Feuerwerker, A., 685, 690
Feulner, E. J., Jr., 251
Fic, V. M., 663
Fiechter, G.-A., 326
Field, G. L., 19
Field, M., 737
Field, M. G., 576
Fields, A. B., 410
Fienup, D. F., 318
Fifer, J. V., 319
Fifield, R. H., 244
Fijalkowski, J., 493
Filene, P. G., 241
Filippi, J., 415
Finer, H., 638
Fink, T. M. T., 442
Finkelstein, L. S., 248
Finker, K., 485
Finlay, D. J., 14
Finletter, T. K., 231
Finley, D. D., 553
Fiori, G., 420
Fireside, H., 173
Firkins, P., 768
Firpo, L., 421
Firpo, M. E., 317
First, R., 781, 842
Firth, R. W., 79
Fiš, T., 517
Fischer, A., 150
Fischer, E., 27
Fischer, F., 355
Fischer, Fritz, 132
Fischer, George, 576
Fischer, Georges, 124, 367
Fischer, H. D., 42
Fischer, L., 534, 551
Fischer, W. E., 831
Fischer-Galati, S. A., 359, 589
Fishel, W. R., 742
Fisher, B. S., 68
Fisher, G. H., 88
Fisher, J. C., 594
Fisher, M. W., 656, 670
Fisher, R., 635
Fisher, R. D., 8, 88
Fisher, S. N., 203, 231, 405, 612
Fisk, E. K., 758, 775
Fistié, P., 751
Fitch, R. B., 815
Fitte, E. J., 314
Fitzgerald, C. P., 682, 690
FitzGerald, F., 739
FitzGerald, G., 388
FitzGerald, S., 711
FitzGibbon, C., 489
Fitzpatrick, S., 579
FitzSimons, L., 231
Fitzsimmons, M. A., 612
Flanagan, R. J., 348
Flanner, J., 402
Flash, E. S., Jr., 265
Flechtheim, O. K., 4, 27, 548
Fleiner, T., 97
Fleischman, H., 220

Fleisher, F., 448
Fleming, D. F., 244
Fleming, J. M., 53
Fleming, P. *See* Fleming, R. P.
Fleming, R. P., 534
Flender, H., 176
Fleron, F. J., Jr., 27
Flerov, V. S., 542
Fletcher, A., 653
Fletcher, N. McH., 755
Fletcher, W. C., 579
Fliess, P. J., 9
Flinn, W. L., 333
Florit, C. A., 315
Flory, M., 619
Flory, T., 56
Floyd, D., 556, 589
Flynn, G. Q., 277
Förtsch, E., 490
Foley, C., 418
Foltz, W. J., 37, 810
Fonseca, A. J., 672
Fontaine, A., 182, 410
Foor, R., 363
Foot, Sir H. *See* Caradon, H. M. F., Baron.
Foot, M. R. D., 170
Foot, P., 371
Foote, W., 100, 123
Forbis, W. H., 767
Ford, A. G., 72
Ford, C., 170
Fordham, P., 777
Form, W. H., 209
Fornari, H., 421
Forndran, E., 124
Forrester, J. W., 73
Forster, D. F., 287
Forster, T. M., 490
Forsyth, F., 819
Forsythe, D. P., 635
Forte, F., 430
Forward, N., 5
Fosdick, R. B., 228
Fossaert, R., 410
Foster, P., 807
Fostervoll, K., 445
Fouchet, C., 402
Fougeyrollas, P., 410, 811
Fourastié, J., 415
Fowler, W. B., 132
Fox, A. B., 240
Fox, M. H., 264
Fox, U., 362
Fox, W. T. R., 240, 278
Foxley, A., 330
Fraenkel, E., 19
Fraenkel, H., 482, 486
Fraenkel, M., 813
Fraga Iribarne, M., 437
Francis-Williams, E. F. W., Baron, 382
Franck, T. M., 57, 97, 826
Franco, F. J., 308
Franco, P., 194
Franco, P. A., 308
Franco, V., 304
François-Poncet, J., 507
Franda, M. F., 663

Frank, A. G., 204, 209
Frank, C. R., Jr., 79
Frank, E., 19
Frank, H. J., 615
Frank, J. D., 109
Frank, L. A., 109
Frank, T. M., 9
Franke, W., 683
Frankel, C., 224, 232
Frankel, F. R., 672
Frankel, J., 9
Frankel, P. H., 421
Frankenberg und Proschlitz, E. von, 154
Frankland, M., 534
Franklin, H., 842
Franklin, J. H., 46
Franks, A., 56
Franz, G., 9
Fraser, B., 282
Fraser, D., 48
Fraser, R., 435
Fraser, S., 42, 710
Fraser-Tytler, Sir W. K., 653
Frederica, Queen of the Hellenes, 604
Frederik, H., 497
Frederiksen, B. W., 442
Fredette, R. H., 137
Free, L. A., 270
Freed, F., 168 -
Freedman, M., 228
Freedman, R. O., 560
Freeland, R. M., 215
Freeman, J., 381
Freeman, O. L., 69
Freeman, R. A., 756
Freeth, Z., 649
Frei, B. 629
Freidel, F., 261
Freisberg, E., 355
Freitas, J.-I. de, 328
Freithaler, W. O., 293
Frenzke, D., 359
Freud, S., 220
Freudenheim, Y., 640
Freund, L., 190, 464
Frey, F. W., 623
Frey, R. L., 641
Freymond, J., 28, 346
Freyre, G., 326
Frías, I., 338
Fricke, K. W., 490
Fried, M., 109
Fried, R. C., 427
Friedeberg, A. S., 105
Friedensburg, F., 70, 493
Friedländer, S., 432, 483, 485, 632
Friedland, W. H., 781
Friedlander, S. L., 311
Friedman, E., 245
Friedman, M., 53, 274
Friedmann, G., 46
Friedmann, W. G., 66, 82, 85, 91
Friedrich, C. J., 14, 19, 34, 350
Friend, T., 763
Frigerio, R., 318
Frillmann, P., 685
Fritsch, B., 79

Fritzsche, B., 507
Froelich, J.-C., 777
Froese, L., 495
Fromm, E., 25
Fromm, G., 61
Frondizi, A., 315, 318
Frowein, J. A., 95
Frutkin, A. W., 115
Fry, M. G., 141
Frydenlund, K., 445
Frye, A., 483
Frye, W. R., 839
Fryer, D. W., 734
Fuchs, L. H., 255, 277
Führ, C., 137
Fuentes Irurozqui, M., 197
Fürstenberg, H., 469
Fujiwara, I., 170
Fukui, H., 721
Fulbright, J. W., 182, 228, 232, 251, 259
Fumoto, M., 581
Funke, M., 141
Furgurson, E. B., 220
Furler, H., 350
Furlonge, Sir G., 631
Furniss, E. S., Jr., 190, 407
Furre, B., 445
Furtado, C., 73, 209
Furtak, R. K., 304
Fusiler, R., 442
Futrell, M., 133
Fyfe, C., 812
Fyzee, A. A. A., 44

Gaal, M., 489
Gabriel, P. P., 79
Gabrieli, F., 619
Gabrielsen, B. V., 445
Gaddis, J. L., 242
Gäng, P., 738
Gaetani d'Aragona, G., 430
Gafurov, B. G., 187, 586
Gagzow, B., 680
Gaigalaitė, A., 461
Gailey, H. A., 812
Gál, G., 91
Galante, P., 493
Galarza Arízaga, R., 335
Galbraith, J. K., 53, 225
Galbraith, W. O., 333
Galeano, E., 297
Galenson, W., 707
Galkin, A. A., 33, 554
Gall, F., 297
Gallagher, C. F., 793
Gallagher, H. G., 232
Gallagher, T., 168
Galli, G., 427
Gallman, W. J., 644
Gallo, M., 422, 437
Gallois, P. M., 116
Galloway, J., 742
Galloway, J. F., 280
Galula, D., 113
Gamarnikow, M., 362
Gambini, H., 304
Gambino, A., 150

Gamboa, M. J., 88
Gamson, W. A., 182
Gandhi, A., 839
Ganiage, J., 777
Ganier-Raymond, P., 170
Gankovskii, I. V., 676
Gann, L. H., 119, 777, 843, 845
Gannon, F. R., 141
Ganshof van der Meersch, W. J., 350, 822
Garaudy, R., 25, 28, 520
Garbo, G., 445
García, A., 210
García Angulo, E., 311
García Durán, J., 435
García-Echevarría, S., 438
García Lupo, R., 314, 318
García Martínez, C., 318
García Montes, J., 302
García Passalacqua, J. M., 311
García Robles, A., 124, 194
García Venero, M., 437, 439
García Zamor, J. C., 318
Garder, M., 171, 562
Gardiner, L., 600
Gardinier, D. E., 825
Gardner, B., 137, 138, 150, 371
Gardner, J. W., 213
Gardner, L. C., 182, 242, 252
Gardner, M. A., 197
Gardner, R. B. *See* Gardner, B.
Gardner, R. N., 61, 97, 124, 248
Garelli, F., 62
Garfield, B. W., 165
Garian, P.+B., *pseud.*, 800
Garland, A. N., 165
Garlick, P. C., 815
Garliński, J., 171
Garner, W. R., 320
Garretson, R. C., 252
Garrié Faget, R., 197
Garst, J., 69
Garthoff, R. L., 557, 562
Gascar, P., 173
Gasperi, M. R. Catti de. *See* Catti de Gasperi, M. R.
Gasteyger C., 562
Gatheru, R. M., 830
Gatti, A., 138
Gaucher, R., 568
Gaulle, C. A. J. M. de, 402, 407
Gavin, J. M., 742
Gavshon, A. L., 101
Gay, P., 469
Gaya Delrue, M., 435
Gazsi, J., 511
Gazzera, M., 317
Gečys, C. G. *See* Gečys, K.
Gečys, K., 565
Geertz, C., 37, 762
Gehl, J., 508
Gehlen, M. P., 546, 551
Gehlen, R., 497
Gehrke, U., 644
Geiger, T., 179
Geismann, G., 390
Geiss, I., 133, 781
Gelber, H. G., 768

Gelber, L. M., 376
Gelberg, L., 526
Geldard, F. A., 42
Gelfand, L. E., 224, 232
Gellhorn, W., 20
Gellner, E., 22, 794
Gemzell, C.-A., 168
Gendebien, P.-H., 822
Genelin, R. S., 559
Genêt. *See* Flanner, J.
Genji, O., 721
Genovés, S., 124
Gentry, C., 262, 729
Geoffroy-Dechaume, F., 683
George, A.L., 232, 706
George, M., 376
George, T. J. S., 660
George-Brown, G. A. G.-B., Baron, 371
Georgeoff, P. J., 597
Georgescu, T., 589
Georghiades, A., 418
Georgiev, V., 597
Gérard-Libois, J., 391, 822
Gerassi, J., 32, 204
Gerberding, W. P., 250
Gerhardsen, E., 445
Gerhardt, J. M., 259
Gerken, E., 495
Gerken, R., 504
Gerlach, A., 89
Germani, G., 319
Germani, H., 822
Gerson, L. L., 231, 270
Gerstenmaier, C., 568
Gerstenmaier, E., 504
Gerteiny, A. G., 810
Gertzel, C., 830
Gerutis, A., 461
Gervasi, F., 629
Getlein, F., 109
Getzler, I., 534
Geyelin, P. L., 232
Geyer, D., 359, 551, 552
Geyer, G. A., 210
Ghai, D. P., 826
Ghālī, S., 619
Ghālib, Ṣubayḥ 'Ali, 644
al-Ghamrāwī, A. S., 646
Ghassemlou, A. R., 646
Ghaussy, A. G., 79, 654
al-Ghazzāli, 'Abd al-Mun'īm, 805
Ghébali, V.-Y., 405
Gheddo, P., 746
Ghose, S., 663
Ghosh, K. K., 658
Ghosh, P. K., 664
Ghosh, S., 660
Giap, Vo Nguyen. *See* Vo-nguyen-Giap.
Gibbs, Sir P. H., 138
Gibson, C. R., 335
Gibson, R., 835
Gidney, J. B., 586
Giffen, J. H., 560
Giffin, S. F., 5
Gifford, P., 781
Gil, F. G., 330
Gil-Robles y Quiñones, J. M., 435

Gilbert, B. B., 366
Gilbert, M., 1, 141, 344, 370
Gilbert, S. P., 562
Gilder, G. F., 270
Giles, J. H., 160
Gill, G. H., 156
Gillett, M. C., 653
Gillin, D. G., 699
Gilmore, K. O., 306
Gilmour, I. H. J. L., 382
Gilpin, R. G., 280, 415
Gimbel, J., 489
Giménez Landínez, V. M., 342
Giniewski, P., 839
Ginsburg, R. B., 353
Ginsburgh, R. N., 259
Ginsburgh, V., 689
Ginsburgs, G., 184, 654
Ginzberg, E., 73, 828
Ginzburg, E. S., 534
Giosan, N., 589
Giovana, M., 32
Giovanna di Bulgaria, 597
Giovannitti, L., 168
Girardet, R., 407
Giraudy, J.-L., 357
Girdner, A., 173
Girling, J. L. S., 734
Gisevius, H. B., 481
Gitelman, Z. Y., 582
Gittings, J., 557, 706
Glad, B., 232
Glade, W. P., Jr., 210, 293
Gladwyn, H. M. G. J., 1st Baron, 350, 351, 371
Glasebock, W., 145
Glaser, H., 504
Glaser, K., 145, 358
Glassburner, B., 762
Glaubitz, J., 690
Glaus, B., 393
Glazer, M., 330
Gleason, G., 754
Gleitze, B., 490
Glélé, M.-A., 811
Glick, E. B., 21
Gligorijević, B., 592
Glinkin, A. N., 194
Glubb, Sir J. B., 629
Gluckman, M., 790
Glyn, A., 739
Gniffke, E. W., 490
Goddard, W. G., 712
Godechot, T., 427
Godinho, V. de M., 440
Göhring, M., 476
Görlich, J. W., 491
Görlitz, W., 154, 481
Goerner, E. A., 23
Goguel, F. *See* Goguel-Nyegaard, F.
Goguel-Nyegaard, F., 398, 410
Goichon, A. M., 643
Golan, G., 520
Golay, F. H., 734, 763, 764
Goldberg, A. J., 228
Goldberg, G., 133
Goldenberg, B., 205, 210, 304
Goldhagen, E., 581

Goldhamer, H., 194
Goldman, E. F., 215
Goldman, M. D., 711
Goldman, M. I., 561, 570, 571
Goldmann, K., 5
Goldmann, N., 631
Goldschmidt, B., 116
Goldsen, J. M., 115
Goldsmith, R. W., 62
Goldstein, L. J., 269
Goldsworthy, D, 367
Goldwater, B., 270
Goldwert, M., 315
Goldwin, R. A., 232
Golembiewski, R. T., 14
Golinkov, D. L., 542
Gollin, A. M., 371
Gollin, J., 432
Gologlu, M., 623
Gómez Robledo, A., 290
González, L. J., 320
Gonzalez, R. F., 328
González Casanova, P., 291
González Navarro, M., 291
Good, R. C., 179
Goodfriend, A., 232
Goodhart, P. C., 150
Goodman, A. E., 738
Goodman, P., 213
Goodman, W., 267
Goodnow, H. F., 676
Goodrich, L. M., 101
Goodsell, C. T., 311
Goodspeed, D. J., 138
Goodwin, C. D. W., 771
Goodwin, R. N., 742
Gopal, R., 658
Gorbanevskaya, N., 568
Gorbatov, A. V., 534
Gorden, M., 346
Godenker, L., 101
Gordon, B. K., 245, 734
Gordon, D. C., 17, 797
Gordon, H. J., Jr., 479
Gordon, J. K., 283
Gordon, K., 270
Gordon, L., 197
Gordon, M. R., 376
Gordon, R. L., 348
Gordon, W. C., 210
Gordon, W. L., 283
Gornenski, N., 597
Goroshko, G. B., 666
Gosovic, B., 105
Gostyńska, W., 528
Gotlieb, A., 124, 286
Gotovitch, J., 391
Gott, R., 141, 205
Gottwald, R., 474
Gould, J., 1
Gould, J. M., 280
Gould, J. W., 756
Gould, W. L., 85
Goulden, J. C., 742
Goulding, P. G., 259
Goulet, D., 73
Gounelle, C., 398

Gour, C.-G., 750
Gowda, K. G. V., 62, 367
Gower, L. C. B., 781
Gowing, M. M., 366
Gozard, G., 210
Grabendorf, W., 308
Grabert, H., 487
Grabill, J. L., 612
Graham, B. D., 411
Graham, L. R., 579
Graham, L. S., 326
Graham, R., 323
Graham, R. A., 148
Graml, H., 129, 485
Granqvist, H., 696
Grant, A. T. K., 386
Grant, B., 760, 768
Grant, C. P. *See* Harris, C. P.
Grant, J. S., 750
Grant, M., 608
Grantham, Sir A. W. G. H., 754
Granzow, B., 483
Grassmuck, G., 653
Grattan, C. H., 766
Graubard, S. R., 346
Gravel, M., 744
Gray, C. S., 82, 285
Gray, E., 288
Gray, J., 685, 696
Gray, T., 384, 388
Graycar, A., 769
Grayson, G. W., Jr., 330
Graziano, L., 425
Greaves, C. D., 388
Grebing, H., 504
Grechko, A. A., 154, 161
Green, A. W., 355
Green, D., 194
Green, H. P., 268
Green, P., 116
Green, R. H., 787, 788
Green, T., 62
Greenberg, S. D., 265
Greene, F., 245
Greene, N., 411
Greenfield, K. R., 156, 158
Greenfield, R., 828
Greenstein, F. I., 14
Greenwood, G., 768
Greep, R. O., 48
Gregg, A. R., 297
Gregg, R. W., 198, 232
Gregor, A. J., 33
Gregorian, V., 653
Gregory, J. S., 531
Gregory, R., 220
Greig, I., 182
Grenholm, G., 448
Grenville, J. A. S., 233
Gretton, Sir P., 114
Grewe, W. G., 9
Grey, A., 696
Grey, I., 539
Griaznov, G. V., 732
Grieder, J. B., 685
Grieswelle, D., 479
Grieve, M. J., 11

Grieves, F. L., 95
Griffin, K., 210
Griffith, R., 267
Griffith, S. B., II, 166, 706
Griffith, W. E., 237, 344, 557, 600
Griffiths, F., 566
Griffiths, J. C., 454, 653
Griffiths, Sir P. J., 367
Griffiths, R., 402
Grigoriadis, Ph. N., 605
Grigoropoulos, T., 605
Grimm, C., 455
Grimond, J., 382
Grindrod, M., 419
Gripenberg, G. A., 452
Grivas, G., 119, 418
Grňa, J., 517
Grobba, F., 467
Grodzins, M. M., 280
Gröndal, B., 455
Grohs, G., 807
Gromyko, Anatolii A., 178, 215
Gromyko, Andrei A., 88, 146, 553
Grondona, M. C., 313
Groscurth, H., 485
Gross, B., 28
Gross, B. M., 277
Gross, F., 9
Gross, F. B., 248
Gross, J., 495
Gross, L., 330
Grosser, A., 14, 405, 410, 487, 495
Grossholtz, J., 764
Grossman, G., 362
Grossmann, B., 757
Grossmann, K. R., 469, 507
Grossner, C., 179
Grottian, W., 565
Groueff, S., 116
Grove, A. T., 777
Grubb, P. D., 66
Grubbe, P., *pseud.*, 187
Grubcheva-Ogniana, M., 597
Gruber, C., 393
Gruber, H., 28
Gruchmann, L., 129
Gruening, E., 742
Grünwald, L., 521
Grundy, K. W., 781
Gruner, E., 393
Grunewald, J., 135, 194, 210
Grunwald, C. de, 554
Grzybowski, K., 85, 365
Guardo, R. C., 317
Günter, H., 66
Günther, M., 93
Guérin, D., 411, 797
Guernier, M., 73
Guerra y Sánchez, R., 302
Guerry, É. M., 432
Guetzkow, H., 5
Guevara, E. (Guevara, Che), 304, 321
Gueye, L., 781
Gueyt, R., 520
Guggenheim, Paul, 85
Gugushvili, P. V., 586
Guhin, M. A., 220

Guillain, R., 690, 716
Guillén, A. See Arapey, pseud.
Guillén Martínez, F., 333
Guillén Romo, A., 293
Guillermaz, J., 690
Guinn, P. S., 138
Guitton, H., 55
Guizado, J. R., 299
Gukiina, P. M., 831
Guldescu, S., 593
Guliev, D. B. ogly, 586
Gullick, J. M., 757
Gullion, E. A., 45
Gulliver, P. H., 826
Gumpel, W., 361
Gungaadash, B., 714
Gungwu, W., 757
Gunther, J., 201, 767
Gunzenhäuser, M., 122
Gupta, D. C., 245
Gupta, K., 670
Gupta, K. R., 57
Gupta, S., 667, 669
Gureev, S. A., 91
Gurevich, S. M., 579
Gurr, T. R., 34
Gurtov, M., 245, 742
Gururaj Rao, H. S., 669
Guseinov, I. A., 586
Gushima, K., 682
Guske, C., 469
Gussman, B., 821
Gusti, D., 589
Gutiérrez, M. R., 321
Gutmann, G., 507
Gutscher, J. M., 504
Guttenberg, K. T., Freiherr zu, 487, 495
Gutteridge, W. F., 37, 781
Guttsman, W. L., 380
Guyol, N. B., 70
Guzmán Campos, G., 333
Gvishiani, L. A., 559
Gwertzman, B. M., 220
Gwyer, J. M. A., 157

Haan, R. L., 73
Haas, E. B., 93, 97, 237, 248
Haas, L., 393, 542
Haas, M., 97
Haas, W., 499
Habegger, N., 333
Haberer, J., 42
Hachem, N., 628
Hacker, A., 213
Hacker, J., 150, 365
Hackett, A.-M., 415
Hackett, J., 415
Hadawi, S., 635, 641
Haddad, G. M., 612
Hadenius, S., 448
Hadley, A. T., 742
Hadley, E. M., 724
Haefs, H., 520
Hägglöf, G., 448
Hänsch, K., 398
Hæstrup, J., 442
Hättich, M., 504

Haffner, S., 470
Haftendorn, H., 502
Hagemann, M., 179
Hagen, E. E., 73
Hagras, K. M., 105
Hague, D. C., 20, 57
Hahlweg,W., 119
Hahn, E., 685
Hahn, G., 571
Hahn, L., 795
Hahn, L. A., 62
Hahn, W. G., 574
Hai, F., 696
Haight, J. McV., Jr., 173
Hailey, M. H., 1st Baron, 841
Haithcox, J. P., 664
Hajj Mūsa, I. M., 806
Hakalehto, I., 450
Ḥakim, S., 800
Hako, H., 600
Halasi-Kun, T. T., 624
Halasz de Beky, I. L., 515
Halbecq, M., 411
Halberstam, D., 215, 739, 748
Halder, F., 154
Halderman, J. W., 101, 635
Hale, O. J., 479
Halevi, N., 641
Halévy, É., 25
Hall, G., 9
Hall, H. D., 367
Hall, J. W., 714
Hall, L. J., 795
Hall, P. G., 382
Hall, R. S., 845
Hall, W., 450
Halle, L. J., 182
Haller, A. von, 79
Halliday, F., 178
Halloran, R., 715
Hallowell, J. H., 73
Hallstein, W., 355
Halm, G. N., 62
Halperin, E., 330
Halperin, M., 304
Halperin, M. H., 124, 259, 260, 557, 706
Halperin Donghi, T., 316
Halpern, A. M., 703
Halpern, J., 841
Halpern, J. M., 749
Halpern, M., 612
Halstead, J. P., 795
Halsti, W. H., 452, 454
Hambly, G., 652
Hambro, C. J., 445
Hambro, E., 101
Ḥamdān, J., 615, 801
Hamel, H., 491
Hamilton, A., 33
Hamilton, B. L. St. J., 310
Hamilton, C. V., 277
Hamilton, E. K., 276
Hamilton, F. E. I., 594
Hamilton, W. B., 368
Hamm, H., 600, 700
Hammarskjöld, D., 101
Hammer, E. J., 738

AUTHOR INDEX

Hammer, R., 742
Hammerschmidt, H., 495
Hammerstein-Equord, K., Freiherr von, 481
Hammond, P. B., 811
Hammond, P. Y., 613
Hammond, T. T., 551
Hamon, L., 9
Hamšík, D., 521
Hamzeh, F. S., 97
Han, H. H., 101
Hanak, H., 551
Hance, W. A., 777, 790, 836
Hancock, M. D., 233, 237
Hancock, Sir W. K., 173, 836, 837
Hanfstaengl, E., 481
Hangen, W., 491, 661
Hanham, H. J., 384
Hankey, M. P. A. H., 1st Baron, 133
Hanna, W. A., 734, 757
Hannak, J., 508
Hanrieder, W. F., 499
Hansen, B., 805
Hansen, H., 336
Hansen, H. W., 455
Hansen, N. M., 415
Hansen, R., 150
Hansen, R. D., 293
Hanson, A. H., 672
Hanson, P., 571
Hanson, S. G., 198
Hansson, Ó., 455
Hantsch, H., 133
Hapgood, D., 69, 255, 256
Haq, M., 679
Harada, K., Baron, 717
Haraldsson, E., 646
Harbeck, K.-H., 468
Harbeck, W., 185
Harbison, F. H., 73, 74
Harbottle, M., 107
Harbron, J. D., 362
Harcourt, F. d', 608
Harcourt, R. d', 495
Hardin, C. M., 69
Hardy, M., 88
Hargreaves, J. D., 807
Harkabi, Y., 109, 116, 635
Harkness, D. W., 389
Harlow, V., 826
Harmon, R. B., 2, 88
Harper, G. T., 435
Harper, N. D., 768
Harr, J. E., 250
Harré, J., 771
Harriman, W. A., 242
Harrington, M., 25, 270
Harris, B., 386
Harris, B., Jr., 828
Harris, C. D., 531
Harris, C. P., 802
Harris, David R., 777
Harris, Dixie R., 175
Harris, E. E., 97
Harris, G. S., 624, 625
Harris, R., 270, 321
Harris, S. E., 275
Harris, T. F., 683

Harrison, A. J., 50
Harrison, H. V., 5
Harrison, J. P., 690
Harrison, M., 414
Harrod, Sir H. R. F., 57, 62, 386
Harrod, J., 310
Hart, D., 773
Hart, J., 270
Hartcup, G., 173
Hartendorp, A. V. H., 173
Hartl, H., 554
Hartley, A., 366, 411
Hartmann, F. H., 233
Hartmann, K., 524
Hartog, F., 390
Hartz, L., 40
Harvey, C., 845
Harvey, J., 371
Harvey, M. L., 252, 551
Harvey, O., 371
Harvey, R., 846
Harwitz, M., 790
al-Hasan, H., 628
Haseeb, K., 645
Haselmayr, F., 133
Hashavia, A., 639
al-Hāshimi, T., 645
Haskins, C. P., 40
Hasluck, P., 156
Hassler, A., 747
Hasson, J. A., 116
Hastings, M., 384
Hastings, P., 774
Haswell, M. R., 68
Hatada, T., 726
Hatch, A., 661
Hatch, J. C., 777, 785, 816
Hatherton, T., 849
Hatta, M., 760
Hattori, T., 166
Hauberg, C. A., 205
Hauck, C. W., 488
Haungs, P., 506
Haupt, G., 534, 544
Haupt, W., 160, 161
Hauser, O., 141
Hauser, P. M., 48
Hausman, W. H., 790
Hausner, G., 484
Havemann, R., 491
Havens, A. E., 333
Havighurst, C. C., 121
Havighurst, R. J., 328
Haviland, H. F., Jr., 192
Havrincourt, H. d', 395
Ḥawātimah, N., 647
Hawkins, F., 282
Hawkins, H. C. G., 833
Hawkins, R. G., 64, 252
Hawley, D., 647
Hay, P., 57, 97
Hayami, Y., 69
Hayashi, F., *pseud.*
Hayashi, T., 726
Hayatullah, A., 653
Hayden, T., 748
Hayes, P. M., 445

Hayes, S. P., 256
Hayit, B., 586
Haykal, M. H., 638, 804
Hayter, T., 82, 406
Hayter, Sir W. G., 534, 551
Hayward, M., 566, 579
Hazard, J. N., 28
Hazlehurst, C., 133
Hazlewood, A., 785
Head, I. L., 85, 94
Headlam-Morley, Sir J. W., 133
Hearder, H., 419
Heath, D. B., 322
Heath, E. R. G., 346
Heathcote, N., 107
Heaton, L. E., 342
Heberle, R., 479
Hébert, J., 700
Hector, C., 201
Heeney, A., 286
Heer, D. M., 48
Heer, F., 22
Heer, N. W., 579
Hehn, J. von, 455
Heiber, H., 129, 481
Heikal, M. H. *See* Haykal, M. H.
Heikkilä, T., 450
Heilbroner, R. L., 50, 74, 275
Heilbrunn, O., 117, 119
Heilperin, M. A., 62
Heimsath, C. H., 667
Heinl, R. D., Jr., 728
Heinrichs, W. H., Jr., 220
Heinz, G., 476, 822
Hekhuis, D. J., 9
Helfritz, H., 296
Heller, David, 233
Heller, Deane, 233
Heller, W. W., 275
Hellmann, D. C., 718
Hellmann, M., 461
Hellmann, R., 66, 253
Hempel, G., 464
Hendel, S., 539
Henderson, G., 730
Henderson, J. W., 278, 751, 753, 757, 759, 773
Henderson, K. D. D., 806
Henderson, W., 245, 694
Henig, S., 346
Henissart, P., 797
Henkin, L., 85, 250
Henkys, R., 484, 499
Henle, H., 612, 734
Hennessy, M. N., 777
Henriques, A., 326
Henry, Z., 301
Henry-Haye, G., 150
Hentsch, G., 150
Hepple, A., 836
Heradstveit, P. Ø., 445
Heren, L., 215, 266
Hergel, H. H., 438
Hermann, C. F., 5
Hermassi, E., 794
Hermens, F. A., 470
Hermes, W. G., 728
Hermet, G., 433

Herngård, K.-E., 448
Hero, A. O., Jr., 233
Herrera Lane, F., 194, 198, 201
Herrick, A. B., 831, 833, 847
Herrick, R. W., 562
Herrington, J., 156
Herrmann, A., 683
Hersch, S. M., 260, 742
Hershlag, Z. Y., 612, 626
Herskovits, M. J., 790
Herter, C. A., 190
Hertzman, L., 470
Herz, M. F., 182
Herzfeld, H., 129
Herzog, A., 109, 215
Heseltine, N., 847
Hess, G. R., 245
Hess, J. L., 398
Hess, P., 679
Hess, R. L., 828, 829
Hess, S., 220, 221
Hesse, E., 177
Hesse, H., 57
Hesse, K., 54
Heuss, T., 470, 497
Heussler, R., 380
Heuston, R. F. V., 371
Hevesy, P. de, 97
Hevi, E. J., 701, 785
Hewins, R., 445
Hewlett, R. G., 281
Heydon, P. R., 769
Hezlet, Sir A. R., 114, 115
Hickel, W. J., 270
Hickey, G. C., 747
Hicks, G. L., 762, 764
Hicks, Sir J. R., 53
Hicks, N. W., 729
Hicks, U. K. W., 74
Hidalgo, C. F., 298
Hidas, A., 513
Hidayatullah, M., 842
Higa, M., 721
Higgins, B., 74
Higgins, M., 250, 742
Higgins, R., 85, 95, 102, 107
Higgins, T., 138, 150, 164
Higham, R. D. S., 109, 371, 378
Hilan, R., 627
Hilberg, R., 484
Hildebrand, G. H., 430
Hildebrand, K., 483
Hildebrandt, W., 608
Hill, C. R., 839
Hill, F. E., 67, 276
Hill, N. L., 250
Hill, R. L., 806
Hillel, M., 629
Hillgruber, A., 147, 150, 156, 158
Hilliker, G., 338
Hillmann, G., 28
Hills, G., 433, 437
Hilsman, R., 179, 233, 250
Hilton, R., 198
Hindley, D., 760
Hindrichs, A., 491
Hindus, M. G., 545

AUTHOR INDEX

Hinkel, G., 256
Hinshaw, R. W., 62, 253
Hinsley, F. H., 9, 17
Hinton, H. C., 703
Hinton, W., 690
Hippolyte, M., 785
Hirsch, F., 62
Hirsch, S., 57
Hirsch-Weber, W., 195
Hirschman, A. O., 74, 210
Hirst, D., 615
Hirzowicz, Ł., 483
Hiscocks, C. R., 495, 526
Hiscocks, R. *See* Hiscocks, C. R.
Hitch, C. J., 260
Hitler, A., 481
Hitti, P. K., 628
Hla Myint, U, 80
Hnilicka, K., 161
Ho, A. K., 682
Ho, Ping-ti, 690
Ho, Yhi-Min, 712
Hoagland, J., 839
Hoang-long-Dien, 734
Hoang-van-Chi, 748
Hobbs, J. P., 228
Ho-chi-Minh, 748
Hodder, B. W., 74, 777
Hodgkin, T., 779
Hodgson, G., 215
Hodgson, J. H., 450
Hodson, H. V., 658
Höglinger, F., 133
Höglund, B., 125
Hoehling, A. A., 145
Höhmann, H.-H., 362, 364
Höhn, R., 464
Höhne, H., 171, 479, 497
Höjer, K. J., 448
Hoensch, J. K., 515, 523, 552
Hoepke, K.-P., 470
Höpker, W., 417, 562
Hoetzsch, O., 559
Hofer, W., 179, 470, 488
Hoffman, A. S., 43
Hoffman, G. W., 359, 362
Hoffman, J. D., 382
Hoffmann, C., 708
Hoffmann, J., 499
Hoffmann, P., 485
Hoffmann, R., 696
Hoffmann, S., 5, 113, 240, 396
Hoffmann, W. G., 464
Hoffschmidt, E. J., 168
Hogan, E., 116
Hogan, G., 286
Hogan, J. D., 253
Hogan, W. N., 351
Hohenberg, J., 43, 245, 608
Holbik, K., 488, 500
Holborn, H., 479
Holbraad, C., 179
Holcombe, A. N., 125
Holden, D., 603, 647
Hollander, A. N. J. den, 390
Hollander, G. D., 548
Holleman, J. F., 841

Hollerman, L., 724
Holley, I. B., Jr., 175
Hollós, E., 511
Hollyday, F. B. M., 550
Holst, J. J., 260, 445
Holsti, K. J., 5
Holsti, O. R., 5
Holt, C., 760
Holt, D., 589
Holt, P. M., 334
Holt, S., 355
Holzer, J., 525
Holzweissig, G., 466
Homan, P. T., 613
Homze, E. L., 476
Hondius, F. W., 594
Honey, J. C., 54
Honey, P. J., 739, 748
Hong, Sŏng-yu, 730
Hooker, J. R., 781
Hoopes, R., 256
Hoopes, T., 742
Hoor, E., 508
Hoover, C. B., 225
Hoover, H. C., 256
Hopcraft, A., 69
Hope, A. G., 245
Hope, M., 32
Hopkins, H., 387, 803
Hopkins, K., 754
Hopkins, N. S., 810
Hopkins, R. F., 833
Hopper, J. H., 328
Hopwood, D., 647
Horák, S., 528
Horecky, P. L., 359, 531
Horelick, A. L., 562
Hori, K., 721
Horie, S., 62
Horlemann, J., 738
Horn, C. C. von, 107
Horn, H. R., 291
Horn, S., 266
Horn, W., 479
Horne, A., 160, 330
Horne, D., 767
Hornstein, E. von, 491
Hornykiewicz, T., 582
Horowitz, D., 50, 199, 233, 641
Horowitz, D. L., 430
Horowitz, G., 286
Horowitz, I. J., 10, 326
Horowitz, I. L., 205, 210, 281
Horrell, M., 839, 842
Horrut, C., 826
Horsburgh, H. J. N., 109
Horta, A. P. d', 291
Horthy, M., 511
Horvat, B., 595
Horwitz, R., 836
Hory, L., 592
Hoselitz, B. F., 40, 51, 53
Hoshii, I., 723
Hoskyns, C., 822
Hosmer, S. T., 745
Hosoya, C., 719
Hottinger, A., 612, 619

Hou, Chi-ming, 708
Hou, Fu-wu, 685, 690
Houben, P. H. J. M., 355
Houdbine, A.-M., 355
Hough, J. F., 547
Houghton, D. H., 836
Houn, F. W. *See* Hou, Fu-Wu.
Hourani, A. H., 614
Houssiaux, J., 190
Houtart, F., 44, 205
Hovannisian, R. G., 586
Hovet, T., Jr., 785
Hovey, H. A., 260
Hovey, J. A., Jr., 97
Howard, A., 382
Howard, F., 213
Howard, H. D., 115
Howard, H. N., 242
Howard, M. E., 109, 113, 157, 164, 379
Howard, N., 14
Howard, R. C., 607, 698
Howarth, D. A., 647
Howe, J. T., 260
Howe, Q., 179
Howe, R. W., 777
Howlowitsch, J., 363
Hoxha, E., 601
Hoyle, M. B., 157
Hoyt, E. P., 138, 168, 517
Hsia, A., 697
Hsiao, K. H., 708
Hsiao, Tso-liang, 708
Hsieh, Chiao-min, 712
Hsiung, J. C., 690, 703
Hsiung, Yin-Tso, 697
Hsu, F. L. K., 40
Hsu, Kai-yu, 699
Hsu, Long-hsuen, 685
Hsü, I. C. Y., 683
Htin Aung, M. *See* Htin Aung, U
Htin Aung, U, 753
Hu, Chi-hsi, 664
Huang, Yü-ch'uan, 699
Hubatsch, W., 158, 470
Huber, H., 476
Hubert-de Perrot, F., 393
Huck, A., 706
Hudelot, C., 690
Hudson, G. F., 179, 539, 608
Hudson, J. A., 218
Hudson, M., 253
Hudson, M. C., 628
Hudson, W. J., 768, 774
Hümmelchen, G., 147, 169
Huet, P., 386
Huggett, F. E., 391
Hughes, A. J., 826
Hughes, E. J., 225
Hughes, H., 755, 771
Hughes, H. S., 417, 419
Hughes, J., 760
Hughes, J. M., 408
Hughes, R., 754
Hughes, S., 419
Hugo, G., 5, 376
Hugon, P., 825
Hugot, P., 821

Huh, Kyung-Mo, 724
Ḥujayr, M., 619
Huke, R. E., 764
Hulkko, J., 450
Hull, R. H., 743
Hulse, J. W., 28
Humbaraci, A., 797
Humbert-Droz, J., 25, 28, 411
Humphrey, H. H., 268
Humphreys, R. A., 205
Hun, R., 732
Hundley, N., Jr., 290
Hunsberger, W. S., 724
Hunt, C. L., 74
Hunt, R. N., 470
Hunter, G., 74, 735, 791, 826
Hunter, H., 571
Hunter, N., 697, 701
Hunter, R. A., 244
Hunter, R. E., 190, 256
Huntington, S. P., 18, 33, 37
Huntley, J. R., 178
Hurewitz, J. C., 612
Hurtado, A., 439
Hurtado, O., 335
Husain, Abid, 664
Husain, Asad, 655
Husák, G., 523
al-Ḥusarī, A. K. S., 619, 627
al-Husary, K., 619
Husayn, A., 619
Hussein, King of Jordan, 644
Hutchings, R., 571
Hutchison, B., 286
Huter, F., 426
Hutheesing, K. N., 661
Hutt, W. H., 53, 839
Hutten, K., 44
Huxley, E. J. G., 387, 826, 830
Huyen, N. K., 748
Huyn, H., Graf, 500
Hwang, Pyong-jun, 730
Hyam, R., 836
Hyde, D. A., 119, 551, 757
Hyde, H. M., 371, 534
Hyland, W., 545
Hymoff, E., 107
Hyvämäki, L., 450

Iachino, A., 168
Iakovlev, A. N., 233
Ianni, O., 326, 328
Iarmukhamedov, M. S., 586
Iatrides, J. O., 359
Ibarra, D., 293
Ibarruri, D., 435
al-Ibrāhimī, Muḥammad al-Bashīr, 797
Ichiko, C., 691
Idyll, C. P., 69
Ierodiakonou, L., 418
Ifejika, S. U., 819
Iglesias Selgas, C., 437
Ignotus, P., 513
Ike, N., 145, 721
Ikeda, K., 724
Ikejiani, O., 820

AUTHOR INDEX

Iklé, F. C., 5, 109
Iklé, M., 393
Il'ichev, L. F., 515, 597
Il'ina, N. G., 334
Ilsemann, S. von, 470
Imām, A. A., 803
Imam, Z., 36
'Imārah, M., 619
Imaz, J. L. de, 319
Imbert, A., 351
Imhoff, C. H., Freiherr von, 612, 643
Ind, A., 122
Infield, G. B., 260
Ingebrigtsen, A., 445
Ingle, C. R., 833
Inglis, B., 380
Ingo, W., 355
Ingram, D., 47, 571
Ingram, J. C., 751
Ingrams, W. H., 647
Inkeles, A., 577
Inman, S. G., 198
İnönü, İ., 624
Inoiatov, K. S., 586
Insor, D., 751
Ioffe, A. E., 551, 552
Ionescu, G., 22, 359, 589, 590
Iordanskii, V. B., 777
Ipsen, K., 190
Iriye, A., 682, 703
Irizarry, C., 438
Irving, B., 336
Irving, D. J. C., 168, 171, 173
Irwin, C., 189
Isaacs, H. R., 674
Isard, W., 743
İsen, C. K., 624
Ishida, T., 721, 725
Ishikawa, T., 719
Ishino, I., 723
Ismael, T. Y., 804
Ismā'il, 'Adil, 619
Israel, F. L., 220
Israel, J., 245, 686
Israelian, V. L., 151, 178
Issawi, C., 616, 805
Isusov, M., 597
Italiaander, R., 601, 608
Iturralde Chinel, L. de, 320
Iurkov, S. G., 557
Iusopov, I. A., 650
Ivanenko, V. I., 714
Iwan J. H., 125
Iyer, R., 10

Jabłoński, H., 525
Jackson, D. B., 205
Jackson, G., 433, 435
Jackson, G. D., 359
Jackson, H. M., 190, 250
Jackson, J. C., 757
Jackson, K., 771
Jackson, Lady. *See* Ward, B.
Jackson, W. A. D., 69
Jackson, W. G. F., 164, 371
Jacob, A., 797

Jacob, H., 464
Jacob, P. E., 97
Jacobs, D. N., 32, 691
Jacobs, N., 650, 751
Jacobs, P., 635
Jacobs, W. D., 562
Jacobsen, C. G., 552
Jacobsen, H.-A., 147, 157, 158, 467, 483, 508
Jacobson, H. K., 125, 561
Jacobson, J., 141
Jacobsson, P., 62
Jacoby, C. F., 74
Jacoby, E. H., 74
Jacoby, N. H., 712
Jacomini di San Savino, F., 425
Jados, S. S., 242
Jäckel, E., 398
Jaeger, F., 57
Jägerskiöld, S., 450
Jaenicke, W. A., 142
Jagan, C., 336
Jaguaribe, H., 328
Jahan, R., 676
Jain, H. M., 664
Jain, S. C., 655
Jakande, L. K., 807, 817
Jakobson, M., 452
Jalanti, H., 452
Jalée, P., 182
al-Jamal, S., 619
al-Jamālī, M. F., 645
James, A., 107
James, D., 290, 304, 321
James, D. C., 173, 220
James, H., 761
James, R. R., 138, 371, 382
Jamet, C., 398
Jamgotch, N., Jr., 359
Jancar, B. W., 521
Janeway, E., 275
Janis, I. L., 233
Janos, A. C., 513
Janowitz, M., 37
Jansen, G. H., 187, 632
Jansen, M. B., 726
Jansen, M. E., 632
Jansen, T., 502
Janson, D., 270
Janssen, G., 174
Janssen, K.-H., 133
Janus, E. *See* Stawar, A., *pseud.*
Jarausch, K. H., 142
Jargy, S., 635
Jarvie, I. C., 755
al-Jāsim, Muḥamad 'Ali Rida, 647
Jasny, N., 570, 571, 574
Jaspers, K., 496
Javits, J. K., 270
Jawdat, 'Ali, 645
Jaworskyj, M., 548
Jayanama, D., 751
Jayawardena, V. K., 680
Jeanneney, J.É., 398
Jeantet, G., 398
Jedlicki, W., 526
Jędrzejewicz, W., 529
Jeffries, Sir C. J., 43

Jegouzo, Y., 355
Jenkins, R., 371, 372
Jenkins, W. M., Jr., 656
Jenks, C. W., 86, 95
Jennings, R. Y., 84, 95
Jenny, H., 842
Jensen, F. B., 355
Jéquier, N., 724
Jervis, R., 5
Jessup, J. K., 228
Jessup, P. C., 86
Jha, D. C., 669
Jiménez Lazcana, M., 198
Jochmann, W., 479
Jørgensen, H., 443
Joffe, E., 691
John, O., 497
John, W., 466
Johnpoll, B. K., 220, 525
Johns, C. J., Jr., 263
Johns, S., III, 836
Johnson, A. R., 595
Johnson, C. A., 28, 34, 715, 716
Johnson, C. A. T., 225
Johnson, C. E., 201
Johnson, E. A. J., 74, 88, 225
Johnson, H. B., 220, 304
Johnson, H. G., 50, 57, 82, 288, 385
Johnson, J. J., 205, 210
Johnson, K. F., 204
Johnson, L. B., 225
Johnson, P., 579
Johnson, R., 411
Johnson, R. A., 250
Johnson, R. J., 763
Johnson, R. W., 779
Johnson, W., 223, 279
Johnson, W. A., 672
Johnson, W. R., 825
Johnston, B. F., 77
Johnston, Sir C. H., 647
Johnston, D. M., 703
Johnston, G. A., 105
Johnston, V. B., 435
Johnstone, A. W., 66
Johnstone, W. C., 753
Johri, S., 670
Joliat, J., 330
Joll, J., 31, 32
Jonas, M., 233
Jones, G., 74
Jones, G. B., 846
Jones, H. P., 761
Jones, J. H., Jr., 271
Jones, J. M., 105
Jones, R. H., 174
Jones, T., 372
Jones, W. G., 443
Jones-Quartey, K. A. B., 792, 817
Jong, L. de, 390
Jonkman, J. A., 390
Jónsson, A. K., 455
Joravsky, D., 544, 579
Jordan, A. A., Jr., 260
Jordan, D. C., 207
Jordan, R. S., 190, 807
Jordan, Z. A., 527

Jorrín, M., 205
José, F., 201
Jose, J. R., 198
Joseph, H., 839
Josey, A., 755
Joshi, B. L., 655
Joshua, W., 562
Joslin, D., 210
Journalist M., *pseud.*, 521
Jowitt, K., 590
Joxe, A., 330
Joyce, J. A., 10
Jucker-Fleetwood, E. E., 791
Juhász, G., 515, 516
Jukić, I., 592
Julien, C., 23, 234, 284
Julliard, J., 398
July, R. W., 777
Jum'ah, S., 644
Junayd, 'Abd al-Mun'im, 804
Junckerstorff, H. A. K., 355
Jung, H., 160
Junker, E. U., 504
Junnila, T., 450
Junod, V. I., 778
Jupp, J., 770
Jurema, A., 326
Just, W., 260
Justo, L. *See* Quebracho, *pseud.*
Jutikkala, E. K. I., 450
Juviler, P. H., 565

Kaarsted, T., 443
Kabel, R., 491
Kadare, I., 601
Kaden, A., 504
Kaden, W., 817
Käkönen, U. A., 452, 454
Kagan, B., 640
Kahin, G. McT., 743
Kahl, J. A., 211
Kahn, D., 122
Kahn, E. J., Jr., 773, 840
Kahn, H., 109, 179, 716
Kahn, H. W., 502
Kahng, Tae Jin, 101
Kainzbauer, W., 833
Kaiser, K., 355, 376, 500
Kajima, M., 719
Kalb, M., 245, 532
Kalbe, E., 470
Kalck, P., 825
Kalela, J., 452
Kallas, H., 450
Kalmanoff, G., 82
Kaltakhchian, S. T., 548
Kaltefleiter, W., 19, 469
Kamal, K. A., 680
Kamarck, A. M., 791
Kamibeppu, C., 697
Kamman, W., 299
Kanapathy, V., 757
Kane, W. E., 195
Kaneko, T., 166
Kanellopoulos, P., 605
Kanet, R. E., 29

AUTHOR INDEX

Kann, R. A., 133
Kannapin, H.-E., 174
Kanovsky, E., 635, 642
Kantor, MacK., 225
Kantorowicz, H., 133
Kanza, T., 822
Kao, Chung-yen, 691
Kapitsa, M. S., 704, 714
Kaplan, I., 815, 828, 829, 830, 845
Kaplan, J. J., 256
Kaplán, M., 198, 201
Kaplan, M. A., 6, 271
Kapoor, A., 66, 672
Kapur, H., 559
Karalis, K., 605
Karan, P. P., 656
Karaosmanoğlu, A. L., 107
Karcz, J. F., 363
Kardouche, G. K., 805
Karefa-Smart, J., 791
Karis, T., 836
Kariuki, J. M., 830
Karl, B. D., 266
Karnik, V. B., 670
Karnow, S., 691
Karol, K. S., *pseud.*, 305, 691
Karpat, K. H., 613
Karryev, A., 587
Karst, H., 502
Kartunova, A. I., 557
Karunatilake, H. N. S., 680
Karup Pedersen, O., 443
Kase, F. J., 359
Kaser, M. C., 363, 365
Kash, D. E., 115
Kashamura, A., 823
Kasperson, R. E., 45
Kaspi, A., 398
Kassalow, E. M., 41
Kassof, A. H., 577
Katcher, L., 220
Katkov, G., 542, 566
Katona, G., 50
Katris, J. A., 603
Katz, A., 571
Katz, D., 446
Katz, M., 14, 94
Katz, R., 177
Katz, S., 631
Kaufman, R. R., 331
Kaufmann, J., 88
Kaufmann, W. W., 260
Kaul, B. M., 669, 670
Kaunda, K. D., 781, 845
Kaushik, P. D., 664
Kautsky, J. H., 21, 29
Kavic, L. J., 667
Kawano, S., 713
Kay, D. A., 45, 101, 102
Kay, G., 845
Kay, H., 440
Kay, R. L., 157
Kazakevich, I. S., 726
Kazamias, A. M., 624
Kearney, J. R., 220
Kearny, R. N., 681
Keatley, P., 843

Kedourie, E., 613
Kédros, A., 177
Kedward, H. R., 33
Kee, R., 389
Keefe, E. K., 601
Keeffe, G. M., 252
Keeley, J. C., 221
Keenleyside, H. L., 82
Keep, J. L. H., 130
Keese, D., 361
Keeton, G. W., 3
Kegley, C. W., Jr., 232
Kehrberger, H. P., 91
Keitel, W., 481
Keith, H. H., 328
Kele, M. H., 479
Kelen, E. *See* Kelen, I.
Kelen, I., 102
Kelf-Cohen, R., 386
Kellas, J. G., 384
Kellenberger, E., 57
Keller, J. W., 493
Kellermann, V., 474
Kelly, G. A., 35, 408
Kelly, J. B., 647
Kelly, W. B., Jr., 253
Kelman, H. C., 6
Kempner, B. M., 485
Kendall, W., 24
Kende, P., 513
Kendrick, A., 221
Kenen, P. B., 57
Kenez, P., 542
Kennan, G. F., 145, 182, 225, 271
Kennedy, D. E., 735
Kennedy, E. M., 213
Kennedy, J., 608
Kennedy, M. D., 715, 719
Kennedy, P. P., 296
Kennedy, R. F., 183, 228
Kent, G. O., 467
Kenyatta, J., 830
Keohane, R. O., 97
Kepplinger, H. M., 32
Kerblay, B. H., 574
Kerbusch, E.-J., 340
Kerekes, L., 508, 515, 516
Kerensky, A. F., 535
Kermani, T. T., 613
Kernig, C. D., 2
Kerr, G. H., 713
Kerr, M. H., 619
Kerstiens, T., 19
Kertesz, S. D., 43, 179
Kesavan, K. V., 719
Keshales, H., 598
Kessel, J. H., 271
Kessle, G., 601, 692
Kessler, H., 470
Kessler, M.-C., 411
Kesteloot, L., 781
Kestergat, J., 823
Ketchian, S., 575
Keuning, H. J., 390
Kevenhörster, P., 721
Kewes, K. *See* Karol, K. S., *pseud.*
Khadduri, M., 619, 645, 800

Khadduri, M. D., 635
Khadzhinikolov, V., 598
Khaitsman, V. M., 125
Khaketla, B. M., 841
Khalikov, A. Kh., 584
Khalili, J. E., 704
Khan, M. S., 672
Khan, R., 669
al-Kharbutly, 'Ali Husnī, 620
Khatskevich, A. F., 535
Khaṭṭāb, M. S., 640
Kheifets, A. N., 559
Khera, P. N., 158
Khera, S. S., 667, 673
Kholodkovskii, V. M., 450
Khouri, F. J., 635
Khristov, K., 598
Khrushchev, N. S., 535, 571
al-Khūlī, L., 636
Khvostov, V. M., 553
Kidron, M., 609, 673
Kieft, D. O., 391
Kielmansegg, P., Graf von, 138
Kiep, W. L., 500
Kiernan, B. P., 234
Kiewisz, L., 459
Kiikbaev, N., 587
Kiki, A. M., 774
Kilbourn, W., 288
Kilby, P., 820
Kilmuir, D. P. M. F., 1st Earl of, 372
Kilson, M. L., 776, 780, 812
Kilty, D. R., 338
Kim, C. I. E., 726
Kim, Chong-sin, 730
Kim, Hyŏng-nyong, 730
Kim, Il-sŏng, 732
Kim, K. B., 730
Kim, M. P., 577, 581
Kim, Pyŏng-sik, 727
Kim, R. E., 727
Kim, S. H., 730
Kim, S. Y., 764
Kim, Se-Jin, 727, 730
Kim, T., 728
Kim, Y. H., 682
Kimambo, I. N., 833
Kimball, L. K., 645
Kimball, W. F., 174
Kimber, R., 380
Kimche, D., 639
Kimche, J., 160, 613, 632
Kimmich, C. M., 474
Kimminich, O., 109
Kindermann, G. K., 129
Kindleberger, C. P., 51, 63, 66, 74, 253, 348
King, A., 381
King, E. J., 29
King, E. L., 260
King, F. H. H., 708
King, G., 647
King, G. J., 459
King, J. A., Jr., 75
King, R., 32
King, R. R., 592
Kinghorn, A., 165
Kingsbury, R. C., 202, 531

Kingston-McCloughry, E. J., 113
Kinnane, D., 646
Kinross, J. P. D. B., 3rd Baron, 624
Kintner, W. R., 260, 562
Kirakosyan, J. S., 587
Kirby, E. S., 608, 683
Kirby, S. W., 157, 167
Kirdar, Ü., 105
Kirk, D., 737
Kirk, R., 271
Kirk-Greene, A. H. M., 817
Kirkendall, R. S., 216
Kirkman, W. P., 368
Kirkpatrick, Sir I. A., 421
Kirkpatrick, J. J., 29, 317
Kirpatrick, L. B., Jr., 171, 260
Kirkwood, K., 776, 786
Kirova, K. E., 425
Kirsch, B., 183
Kirschen, É. S., 51, 355
Kis, A., 516
Kissel, H., 162
Kissinger, H. A., 190, 234
Kitagawa, J. M., 683, 715
Kitchel, D., 94
Kitchen, H. A., 778, 823
Kitsikes, D., 606
Kitson, F., 119
Kitzinger, U. W., 346
Kivimäki, T. M., 450
Klafkowski, A., 151
Klass, P. J., 115
Klatt, W., 691
Klatzmann, J., 642
Kleber, B. E., 175
Kleiman, R., 240
Klein, D. W., 699
Klein, F., 138
Klein, H. S., 321
Klein, J., 125
Klein, R. A., 10
Klein, S., 557
Kleinwaechter, F. F. G., 508
Kleps K., 348
Klette, I. J., 299
Klieman, A. S., 613, 620
Klietmann, K.-G., 157
Klimburg, M., 653
Klimeš, M., 517
Klineberg, O., 6
Klinghoffer, A. J., 786
Klink, E., 162
Klinov-Malul, R., 641
Klīve, Ā., 459
Klocho, M. A., 699
Klonis, N. I., pseud., 119
Klose, W., 479
Knapp, V., 519
Knapp, W., 130
Kneese, A. V., 45
Knoebl, K., 745
Knoll, E., 260, 279
Knorr, K. E., 6, 110
Knowles, Y. K., 301
Knütter, H.-H., 470
Knusel, J. L., 500
Knutson, J. N., 14

Kō, Chun-sōk, 730
Kobayashi, N., 723
Kobayashi, S., 755
Kobayashi, Y., 722
Kobliakova, I. K., 510
Koch, H., 443, 444
Koch, H. W., 134
Koch, T., 216, 496
Kochan, L., 467, 582
Kochanek, S. A., 664
Kock, K., 57
Kocman, A., 517
Koebner, R., 10
Köhler, H., 363
Koeltz, L., 138
König, H., 427, 552
König, K., 530
Koenig, L. W., 266
Koenig, M. P. J. F., 165
Koenig, P. *See* Koenig, M. P. J. F.
Köprülü, M. F., 624
Körner, H., 808
Kofos, E., 603
Kogan, N., 425, 427
Koginos, M. T., 142
Kogon, E., 488
Koh, B. C., 105, 731, 732
Koh, H. C., 727
Koh, S. J., 608
Kohl, W. L., 406
Kohler, F. D., 531
Kohn, H., 17
Kohnstamm, M., 356
Kojima, K., 724
Kolarov, V., 598
Kolarz, W., 29
Kolasky, J., 583
Kolb, A., 682
Kolb, W. L., 1
Kolesnikov, M. S., 566
Kolesnikova, M. V., 566
Kolko, G., 151, 234
Kolko, J., 234
Kolkowicz, R., 125, 547
Kolodziej, E. A., 260
Koloskov, B. T., 556
Komarnicki, T., 525
Komiya, R., 724
Konanau, H. M., 584
Kondrat'ev, N. D., 535
Konev, I. S., 154
Konstantinov, F. V., 6
Konstantinov, O. A., 577
Konvitz, M. R., 268
Kónya, I., 512
Kónya, S., 512
Koo, A. Y. C., 713
Kool, F., 549
Kopański, S., 155
Kopanskii, I. M., 590
Kopp, F., 491
Kopp, O., 485, 495
Korablev, I. I., 562
Korbash, E., 708
Korbel, J., 183, 528
Korbonski, A., 530
Korboński, S., 524

Korhonen, K., 453
Koritzinsky, T., 445
Korn, Y., 629
Kornrumpf, H.-J., 805
Korol, A. G., 579
Korolivskii, S. M., 583
Koropeckyj, I. S., 583
Korozis, A., 606
Kosev, D., 598
Kositsyn, A. P., 565
Kosmas, G., 605
Kostov, T., 598
Kotovskii, G. G., 735
Kottman, R. N., 240
Koury, E. M., 620
Kousoulas, D. G., 603
Kovar, R., 356
Kovrig, B., 513
Kowalczyk, S., 524
Kowalski, W. T., 528
Kozeński, J., 528
Koziebrodski, L. B., 95
Kozlov, V. I., 577
Kraft, J., 271
Krakau, K., 305
Král, V., 142, 523
Kramarz, J., 485
Kramish, A., 117
Kraslow, D., 740
Krastiņš, J., 459, 460
Krasuski, J., 528
Kraus, W., 654
Krause, L. B., 253
Krause, P. A., 743
Krausnick, H., 476, 485
Kravchenko, G. S., 174
Kravis, I. B., 57
Krebs, A., 486
Krecker, L., 625
Kreinin, M. E., 275, 632
Kreisky, B., 179
Kreissler, F., 508
Krejčí, J., 519
Krekeler, H. L., 88
Křen, J., 517
Kretschmar, R. S., Jr., 363
Kretzschmar, W. W., 256
Kriegel, A., 411, 566
Krieger, L., 15
Krieviņš, E., 460
Kripens, A., 460
Krippendorff, E., 234
Krishna, K. G. V., 787
Kristol, I., 276
Krivine, D., 80
Krock, A., 216, 225
Krockow, C., Graf von, 183
Kroek, P. C., 115
Kroeger, E., 460
Kroll, H., 497
Kronfol, Z. A., 66
Krosby, H. P., 453
Krüger, D. W., 837
Krülle, S., 488
Krug von Nidda, R., 134
Kruger, R., 751
Krummacher, F. A., 555

AUTHOR INDEX

Krupenikov, I. A., 584
Kruse-Rodenacker, A., 198
Kruszewski, Z. A., 530
Kubbah, A. A. Q., 800
Kubek, A., 246
Kubijovyč, V., 583
Kublin, H., 717
Kuby, E., 494, 497
Kuby, H., 351
Kučas, A., 461
Kuehl, W. F., 234
Kühne, D., 757
Kühnl, R., 480, 504
Küng, A., 457
Kuenne, R. E., 114, 261
Kürkçüoğlu, Ö. E., 625
Kuhn, A., 483
Kuhn, D., 764
Kuhn, F., 764
Kuhn, G., 644
Kuhn, H., 519
Kukiel, M., 524
Kuklick, B., 489
Kukov, K., 598
Kukułka, J., 528
Kulichenko, M. I., 565
Kuliev, N. M., 587
Kulkarni, M., 667
Kulski, W. W., 10, 406
Kulundžić, Z., 592
Kumar, G., 664, 673
Kumar, R., 664
Kumykin, P. N., 561
Kun, B., 513
Kun, J. C., 748
Kunstadter, P., 735
Kunz, F. A., 286
Kunz, J. L., 86
Kuokka, H. D., 729
Kuper, L., 791, 837
Kurihara, K. K., 724
Kurman, M. V., 577
Kurowski, F., 164
Kurz, H. R., 171, 394
Kurzman, D., 29, 308, 639
Kusin, V. V., 519, 521
Kust, M. J., 673
Kutakov, L. N., 142, 151
Kutner, L., 93
Kutzner, G., 198
Kuusinen, A., 451
Kux, E., 748
Kuz'min, M. S., 580
Kuźmiński, T., 528
Kuznets, I. L., 151
Kuznets, P. W., 59
Kuznets, S. S., 75, 569
Kvaček, R., 518
Kwavnick, D., 286
Kwiet, K., 174
Kyre, J., 261
Kyre, M., 261
Kyriakides, S., 418
Kyrou, A. A., 606

Laaman, E., 457
Labedz, L., 29, 557, 569, 579

Labin, S., 187, 704
Labini, S., 431
Labuda, G., 530
La Cascia, J. S., 294
Lacerda, C., 326
La Chapelle, P. de, 93
Lacharrière, G. de. *See* Ladreit de Lacharrière, G.
Lacheraf, M., 797
Lachica, E., 764
Lackó, M., 512
Lacoste Lareymondie, M. de, 408
Lacouture, J., 187, 402, 737, 748, 803
Lacroix, B., 832
Lacroix, J. L., 823
Lacy, C., 657
Lador-Lederer, J. J., 98
Ladreit de Lacharrière, G., 57
Laeuen, H., 527
LaFave, W. R., 57, 565
LaFeber, W., 183
Laffargue, A. C. V., 138
Laffin, J., 46
Laffont, P., 797
La Fontaine, J. S., 823
Lafore, L. D., 142
La Gorce, P. M. de, 402, 406, 408
Lagos Carmona, G., 332
Lagutkin, V. M., 571
Laidler, H. W., 25
Laird, B. A., 574
Laird, M. R., 24, 271
Laird, R. D., 539, 574
Lall, A. S., 88, 636, 704
Laloy, J., 180, 549
La Malfa, U., 430
Lamb, A., 608, 652, 669, 670
Lamb, B. L. P., 657
Lamberg, R. F., 205
Lambert, J., 201, 352
Lambert, M. E., 375
Lambert, R. D., 51, 674
Lambrinidis, J. S., 356
Lambton, A. K. S., 650
Lamfulussy, A., 386
Lamont, L., 117
Lampe, D., 177
La Nauze, J. A., 770
Lancrenon, F., 821
Landau, D., 221
Landau, J. M., 641
Landau, Z., 530
Landauer, C., 488
Landé, C. H., 764
Landecker, M., 250
Landelius, T., 41
Landen, R. G., 647
Landis, A. H., 435
Landívar Flores, H., 321
Landqvist, Å., 447
Landsberg, H. H., 275
Landsberger, H. A., 205
Landy, E. A., 105
Lane, D., 577
Lane, M., 216
Lane, R. E., 15
Lane, T. A., 234
Lang, G., 320
Lang, J. T., 356

AUTHOR INDEX

Lang, O., 699
Lang-Sims, L., 654
Langbein, H., 484
Lange, H., 555
Lange, K., 481
Lange, O. R., 51
Lange, P. H., 22
Lange-Prollius, H., 186
Langer, P. F., 722, 749
Langer, W. L., 2
Langlade, P. de, 402
Langlais, P., 737
Langley, L. D., 303
Langlois, W. G., 737
Langrod, G. See Langrod, J. S.
Langrod, J. S., 98, 389
Langue, R., 821
Lannoy, R., 674
Lansdale, E. G., 246
La Palombara, J. G., 21, 427, 430
Lapassat, É.-J., 798
Lapenna, I., 565
Lapie, P. O., 402
Lapierre, D., 397
LaPorte, R., Jr., 195
Lapp, R. E., 261
Laqueur, W. Z., 47, 180, 346, 542, 555, 559, 636
Lardner-Burke, D., 843
Lare, J., 228
Laretei, H., 457
Lareymondie, M. de L. See Lacoste Lareymondie, M. de.
Larin, P. A., 457
Larios, J. See Lerma, J. L. F. de V., Duque de.
Larkin, B. D., 704
Larmour, P. J., 411
Laroche, F., 844
Laron, R., 636
Laroui, A., 620
Larriqueta, D. E., 318
Larson, A., 91, 121, 216
Larson, D. L., 183
Larson, T. B., 545, 563
Larssen, O., 445
Larus, I. J. See Larus, J.
Larus, J., 107, 117
Lary, H. B., 58, 253
Lasby, C. G., 183
Lasch, O., 155
Lash, J. P., 221
Lasky, V., 221
Lasmanis, A., 460
Lasswell, H. D., 15, 20, 35, 92, 712
Lataste Hoffer, A., 305
Latey, M., 35
Latham, D. C., 110
Latham, E., 268
Latour, A., 629
Latourette, K. S., 683
Lattimore, O., 711
Lattre, A. de, 416
Lau-Lavie, N., 631
Laue, T. H. von. See Von Laue, T. H.
Lauer, P., 644
Laufer, L., 632
Launay, J. de, 130, 398
Launay, M., 798
Laundy, P., 380, 381

Laurence, J., 840
Laurence, M., 829
Laurens, F. D., 425
Laurent, J., 398
Laurent, M., 750
Lauterbach, A. T., 211
Lavenère-Wanderley, N. F., 326
Laves, W. H. C., 280
Lavrishchev, A. A., 187
Lawrence, L., 667
Lawrence, R., 57
Lawrence, R. J., 384
Lawrence, S. A., 67, 253
Layton, C., 351
Lazareff, S., 89
Lazarev, A. M., 584
Lazić, D., 689
Lazitch, B., 27, 29
Lazo, M., 305
Leacacos, J. P., 250
Leach, R. H., 282
Leachman, R. B., 125
Leal, F. P. da C., 440
Leasor, J., 167
Lebbin, H.-A., 457
Lebedev, V. V., 552
Lebedinskii, I. V., 577
Lebjaoui, M., 798
Lebovics, H., 471
Lebra, J. C., 151
Lebret, L. J., 80
Lê Châu, 748
Leckie, R., 110, 166, 261
LeClerq, C., 823
Lecoeur, A., 402
Le Corbeiller, J., 627
Le Cornec, J., 821
Leczyk, M., 525
Ledeen, M. A., 33
Lederer, I. J., 361, 592
Ledesma Ramos, R., 437
Lednicky, R., 567
Lê Duân, 748
Leduc, M., 791
Lee, Chae-jin, 749
Lee, Chong-Sik, 727, 732
Lee, E. H., 723
Lee, Hahn-Been, 731
Lee, J., 43, 372
Lee, J. A., 772
Lee, J. M., 368, 782
Lee, L. T., 88, 91, 704
Lee, M. J., 102
Lee, R. E., 151
Lee, U., 175
Lees, J. D., 380
Lefever, E. W., 782, 823
Lefèvre, J., 96
Leff, N. H., 328
Lefranc, G., 411
LeFranc, P., 489
Legault, A., 107, 113
Legere, L. J., 249
Legg, K. R., 603
Legge, J. D., 761
Legrand, A., 442
Legrand, J. J., 737
Legrand-Lane, R., 356

Le Gris, C., 284
Legum, C., 82, 778, 845
Legvold, R., 559
Lehman, J. F., Jr., 123
Lehndorff, H., Graf von, 488
Leichter, O., 508
Leiden, C., 35
Leifer, M., 735, 750, 764
Leighton, R. M., 159
Leiss, A. C., 178
Leite, A. D., 328
Leites, N., 35, 412
Lejiņš, J., 460
Lejiņš, P., 460
Lekachman, R., 54
Lemarchand, R., 823, 832
LeMay, C. E., 225, 261
Lenczowski, G., 613
Lendvai, P., 47, 359
Lenecka, H. P., 393
Leng, Shao-chuan, 691, 704
Lengyel, E., 29
Lenin, V. I., 542, 559
Lensen, G. A., 151, 533, 559, 719
Lent, J. A., 608
Lenti, L., 430
Lenz, F., 51
Leon, D. E., 389
Léon, P., 211
Leonard, R. L., 380
Leone, G., 421
Leonhard, W., 535
Leonhardt, R. W., 490, 496
Leoni, F., 427
Leonidov, S. M., 418
Leontief, W. W., 54
Lequiller, J., 715
Lerche, C. O., 183, 234, 240
Le Riverend, J., 303
Lerma, J. L. F. de V., Duque de, 436
Lermercier-Quelquejay, C., 585
Lerner, D., 35, 80, 346
Lerner, W., 535
Lerski, G. J., 681
Leruez, J., 386
Leser, N., 25
Leslie, J. A. K., 833
Lesser, J., 467
L'Etang, H., 35
Leubuscher, C., 808
Leuchtenburg, W. E., 216
Leurquin, P., 832
Levenson, J. R., 683
Lévesque, J., 557
Levi, A., 539
Levi, W., 609
Levin, B., 387
Levin, M. B., 216, 268
Levin, N., 47
Levin, N. G., Jr., 234
Levine, D. N., 828
Levine, I. D., 532
Levine, R. A., 261
Levine, R. M., 326
Le Vine, V. T., 825
Levinson, G. I., 764
Levinson, J., 198

Levit, I. E., 590
Levitt, K., 288
Levkovskii, A. I., 609
Levy, F. D., Jr., 342
Levy, L., 115
Levy, L. W., 214
Levy, M. J., Jr., 10
Lewandowski, J., 528
Lewin, J., 840
Lewin, L., 448
Lewin, M., 535, 539
Lewin, P., 708
Lewin, R., 155
Lewin, Z., 176
Lewinówna, Z. See Lewin, Z.
Lewis, B., 613, 624
Lewis, F., 360
Lewis, G. K., 311, 312
Lewis, I. M., 829
Lewis, J. W., 691, 743
Lewis, L. J., 782
Lewis, N., 277
Lewis, P. H., 337
Lewis, S. R., Jr., 679
Lewis, Sir W. A., 75, 808
Lewis, W. C., Jr., 229
Lewis, W. H., 808
Lewy, G., 476
Lewytzkyj, B., 547, 563, 567, 583
Leyburn, J. G., 309
Leyen, F., Prinz von der, 157
Leys, C. T., 827
Li, Choh-ming, 709
Li, T'ien-min, 699
Liang, Chin-tung, 167, 715
Liang, D., 764
Liao, S. S. C., 764
Libal, M., 145
Liberman, E. G., 571
Librach, J., 552
Lichtheim, G., 36, 344, 347, 412
Licklider, R. E., 261
Liddell Hart, Sir B. H., 157, 372
Liddle, R. W., 763
Lie, T., 445
Liebenow, J. G., 813, 833
Lieber, H. J., 549
Lieber, R. J., 6, 376
Lieberman, J. I., 125
Liebich, F. K., 58
Liebman, A., 206, 311
Liedholm, C., 820
Liehm, A. J., 521
Lierde, J. Van, 823
Liess, O. R., 360, 513
Lieuwen, E., 195, 206, 291, 307
Lifschitz, Y., 642
Lifton, R. J., 117, 697
Lijphart, A., 390, 761
Lilienthal, A. M., 636
Lilienthal, D. E., 117, 225
Lillich, R. B., 66
Lim, Chong-Yah, 756, 757
Lin, Ching-ming, 713
Lin, Piao, 706
Lincoln, G. A., 11
Lincoln, J., *pseud.*, 289

AUTHOR INDEX

Lindbeck, A., 448
Lindbeck, J. M. H., 683, 691
Lindberg, L. N., 351, 356
Lindbergh, C. A., 225
Lindblom, C. E., 23
Lindboe, A., 446
Linde, G., 462
Linden, C. A., 545
Lindholm, R. W., 747
Lindqvist, S., 701
Lindsay, J. V., 228
Lineberry, W. P., 239
Ling, D. L., 799
Ling, H. C., 710
Ling, K., *pseud.*, 697
Liniger-Goumaz, M., 394
Link, A. S., 221
Link, M., 294
Link, W., 474
Linke, H. G., 474
Linkomies, E., 451
Lipfert, H., 63
Lipgens, W., 351
Lipiansky, E., 416
Lippincott, B. E., 23
Lippmann, H., 491
Lippmann, W., 228, 234
Lipschits, I., 406
Lipset, S. M., 15, 19, 32, 35, 206, 213, 271
Lipsey, R. E., 253
Lipski, J., 528
Lipson, L., 21
Liptai, E., 513
Lipton, M., 674
Lisagor, P., 250
Liska, G., 234, 351, 740
Lisón Tolosana, C., 439
Liss, S. B., 290, 299
Listowel, J. M.-M. H., Countess of, 833
Littauer, R., 745
Littell, B., 778
Littell, R., 521
Little, I. M. D., 82, 788
Little, T., 647, 801, 805
Litvinoff, B., 47, 631
Litvinskov, B. A., 586
Liu, A. P. L., 692
Liu, Kwang-Ching, 246
Liu, Leo Yueh-yun, 706
Liu, Shao-ch'i, 699
Liu, Ta-chung, 709
Liu, W. T., 692
Liubimov, N. N., 51, 142
Liulevičius, V., 462
Livermore, H. V., 440
Livermore, S. W., 216
Livingston, W. S., 368
Livingstone, J. M., 386
Lleras Restrepo, C., 334
Llosa M., J. A., 321
Lloyd, P. C., 791, 808
Lloyd, P. J., 58
Lloyd, T., 283
Lloyd Prichard, M. F., 772
Lô, M., 812
Lochman, J. M., 44
Lockhart, Sir R. H. B., 535

Lockwood, C. A., 169
Lockwood, D., 166
Lockwood, L., 305
Lockwood, W. W., 724
Lodge, G. C., 195
Loeber, D. A., 456
Löbl, E., 25, 519, 521
Løchen, E., 446
Løkkegaard, F., 443
Loewenberg, G., 464
Loewenheim, F. L., 235
Loewenstein, H., Prince, 497
Löwenthal, R., 29, 546, 609
Löwy, A. G., 535
Lofchie, M. F., 782, 834
Loftis, A., 173
Logan, R. W., 310
Logsdon, J. M., 281
Loh, P. P. Y., 699
Lomax, Sir J. G., 171
Lomax, L. E., 751
Lombard, J., 782
Lombardi, G, 164
Lombardo Toledano, V., 291
London, A. G., 519
London, K., 187, 360, 539
Long, B., 226
Long, G. M., 156, 221
Longford, F. A. P., 7th Earl of, 389
Longrigg, S. H., 613
Loock, H.-D., 446
Loory, S. H., 740
Lopez Alvarez, L., 823
López Contreras, E., 342
López-Fresquet, R., 305
López Michelson, A., 334
López Rosado, D. G., 294
López Tamés, R., 311
Lopukhov, B. R., 427
Lora, G., 321, 322
Lord, W., 166
Lorenzo, C. M., 436
Loshak, D., 676
Lototskii, S. S., 563
Lottich, K. V., 361
Louis, J. A., 341
Louis, W. R., 134, 376, 781, 832
Louw, E. H. 837
Love, K., 638
Lovelace, D. D., 751
Low, D. A., 831
Lowe, A., 54
Lowe, D. M., 692
Lowe, G. E., 261
Lowe, P., 134
Lowenfeld, A. F., 84
Lowenstein, L., 235
Lowenthal, A. F., 308
Lowenthal, R. *See* Löwenthal, R.
Lowi, T. J., 271
Lozoya, J. A., 291
Luard, D. E. T., 89, 93, 95, 98, 125, 183
Luard, E. *See* Luard, D. E. T.
Lubachko, I. S., 584
Lubell, H., 616
Lubell, S., 271
Lucas, J. G., 745

Lucas, J. R., 15
Luce, D., 743
Luce, H. R., 228
Luchsinger, F., 504
Luckett, R., 542
Luckham, R., 817
Ludowyk, E. F. C., 681
Ludz, P. C., 491
Lüthy, H., 344
Lufti, A., 71
Lukács, G., 29
Lukacs, J. A., 129, 344
Lukas, R. C., 168
Łukasiewicz, J., 529
Lukaszewski, J., 360
Lumby, E. W. R., 658
Lumumba, P., 823
Luna, F., 317
Lundberg, E., 75, 448
Lundborg, E. P. A. M., 457
Lundestad, G., 445
Lundgreen, P., 142
Luns, J. M. A. H., 390
Lunt, R. D., 221
Lupi, L. C., 440
Lurie, L., 216
Lury, D. A., 792
Lusignan, G. de, 778
Lussu, E., 422
Luther, H., 471
Luttwak, E., 110, 119
Lutz, J. G., 711
Lutz, V. C., 416
Lutzhöft, H.-J., 480
Luvaas, J., 379
Lux Wurm, P. C., 317
Luykx, T., 10, 391
Luža, R., 523
Luzardo, R., 342
Lvová, M., 518
Lyautey, P., 628, 644
Lyman, P. N., 730
Lynch, H. R., 813
Lynch, J., 724
Lynd, G. E., 791
Lynd, S., 748
Lyng, J., 446
Lynn, K. S., 214
Lyon, M., 391
Lyon, P. V., 283, 284
Lyons, D., S. J., 704, 740
Lyons, E., 221, 539
Lyons, G. M., 213, 279
Lystad, R. A., 791

Maamägi, V., 457
Maas, H. H., 104
Maasing, R., 457
Maass, W. B., 390, 508
Macadam, Sir I., 1
McAleavy, H., 686
McAlister, J. T., Jr., 738
MacArthur, D., 226, 228
McArthur, J. H., 416
Macaulay, N., 299, 305
McAuley, M., 576

MacBean, A. I., 75
McBride, J. H., 261
McCabe, R. K., 704
McCall, D. F., 778
MacCallum Scott, J. H., 24
McCamant, J. F., 296
McCamy, J. L., 251
Macapagal, D., 764
McCarthy, A., 226
McCarthy, E. J., 216, 235
McCarthy, M. F., 193
McCarthy, M. T., 743
McCarthy, R. D. 118
Macciocchi, M. A., 692
McClellan, J., 271
McClelland, D. H., 296
McClintock, R., 110
MacCloskey, M., 261
McCloy, J. J., 190
McColl, G. D., 771
McConville, M., 413
McCord, W., 38
McCormack, A., 48
McCormick, D., 110, 372
MacCormick, N., 384
McCoy, A. W., 735, 749
McCoy, D. R., 221
McCreary, E. A., 66
McCuen, J. J., 119
McCune, S., 727
McDaniels, J. F., 63
McDermott, G. L., 376, 494
MacDonald, A., 834
MacDonald, C. B., 157, 161
McDonald, G. C., 824, 832
Macdonald, R. St. J., 849
MacDonald, R. W., 620
McDougal, M. S., 91, 92
MacEoin, G., 195
Macesich, G., 595
MacEwan, A., 679
McEwan, P. J. M., 778
McFadden, J. N., 260
McFadyean, Sir A., 372
McFarlane, B., 710
Macfarlane, L. J., 382
MacFarquhar, R., 246, 692
McGaffin, W., 279
McGarvey, P. J., 745
McGee, G. W., 743
McGeehan, R., 502
McGovern, G. S., 69, 747
McGovern, J., 482
McGregor, C., 767
MacGregor-Hastie, R., 421
McGuire, E., 256
McGuire, M. C., 113
Machlup, F., 61, 63
Machotka, O., 518
MacInnis, D. E., 692
McInnis, M., 266
McIntyre, I. C., 629
McIntyre, W. D., 368
MacIver, R. M., 10
Mack Smith, D., 422
McKay, V., 786
McKechnie, J. T., 13

AUTHOR INDEX

McKee, A., 160
McKenzie, K. E., 30
Mackerras, C., 701
McKie, R. C. H., 757
Mackintosh, J. P., 380, 817
Mackintosh, M., 563
McLachlan, D., 171
McLane, C. B., 559
McLaughlin, R. U., 813
MacLeish, R., 639
MacLennan, M., 348
McLeod, A. L., 771
McLin, J. B., 285
McLintock, A. H., 772
McMahon, C. W., 386
McMillan, C., Jr., 328
MacMillan, H., 372
McMillan, J., 386
McNamara, R. S., 261
McNaught, K., 282
McNeal, R. H., 360, 535, 544
McNeil, E. B., 110
MacNeil, N., 266
McNeill, W. H., 130
McNicoll, G., 762, 764
Macovescu, G., 591
MacPhee, A. M., 830
Macpherson, C. B., 286
McPherson, H., 271
MacRae, D., Jr., 412
McRae, K. D., 394
Macridis, R. C., 399, 402
Macro, E., 648
McSherry, J. E., 145
McVey, R. T., 759, 761
McWhinney, E., 183
Madajczyk, C., 526
Madan, B., 75
Madariaga, S. de, 180
Maddison, A., 75
Maddox, R. J., 235
Mader, J., 171
Madison, B. Q., 577
Mägi, A., 457
Mäkelä, J. L., 454
März, E., 510
Maestre Alfonso, J., 297
Maggs, P. B., 564
Maginnis, J. J., 174
Magnelia, P. F., 43
Magnúss, G. M., 455
Maguire, G. A., 834
Mah, Feng-hwa, 709
Mahadevan, T. K., 665
Mahajani, U., 764
Mahas, D., 164
Mahathir bin Mohamad, 757
Maheu, R., 105
Mahncke, D., 502
Mahr, H., 627
Maichel, K., 531
Maier, F. G., 418
Maier, J. B., 206
Maier, R., 497
Mair, L. P., 38, 774
Maiskii, I. M., 535
Maizels, A., 58

Majdalany, F., 157, 165
Majonica, E., 500
Major, J., 268
Majumdar, S. K., 658
Makarov, A. D., 549
Makarova, G. P., 581
Makharadze, N. B., 587
Maki, J. McG., 722
Malafeev, A. N., 549
Malakhovskii, K. V., 773
Malay, A. J., 765
Maldonado-Denis, M., 311, 312
Male, D. J., 577
Malefakis, E. E., 438
Malik, C., 10
Malinovskii, R. I., 162
Malinschi, V., 589
Maliṭa, M., 100, 590
Mallaby, Sir H. G. C., 151
Mallan, L., 125
Mallik, D. N., 667
Mallin, J., 119, 305
Mallinson, V., 392
Mallory, J. R., 287
Mallory, W. H., 2
Malloy, J. M., 319, 321
Malmgren, H. B., 79, 253
Malpica Silva Santisteban, C., 338
Malraux, A., 402
Mamalakis, M., 331
Mammarella, G., 427
Mampel, S., 494
Manacorda, G., 428
Mancall, M., 713
Manchester, W. R., 216
Mancisidor, J. M., 436
Mandel, E., 58
Mandela, N. R., 840
Mandelbaum, D. G., 674
Mandel'shtam, N., 536
Mandelstam, N. See Mandel'shtam, N.
Mander, J., 206, 211, 376
Manderson-Jones, R. B., 376
Maneli, M., 740
Mangabeira, F., 329
Mangat, J. S., 827
Manger, W., 195, 199
Mangone, G. J., 105
Manin, P., 412
Mankekar, D. R., 611, 670
Mann, B., 456
Mann, C., 648
Mann, D. E., 266
Mann, G., 464
Mann, R., 490
Mannā', Muḥammad 'Abd al-Rāziq, 801
Manners, G., 71
Manning, B., 300
Mannoni, E., 403
Mansergh, P. N. S., 368, 389, 658
Mansfield, P., 801, 803
Mansingh, S., 667
Mansoor, M., 620
Manṣūr, 'Ali 'Ali, 86
Mantoux, P. J., 134
Mantran, R., 619
Manvell, R., 482, 486

Manzanarès, H., 356
Mao, Tsê-tung, 699, 700, 706
Mar, N. I., 440
Maraini, F., 652
al-Marayati, A. A., 613
Marceau, M., 603
Marcelle, J., 521
Marchal, J., 55
Marchenko, A. T., 568
Marcic, R., 510
Marcum, J., 847
Marcus, H. G., 828
Marcuse, J., 701
Marder, A. J., 138
Marek, F., 35
Marer, P., 363
Marett, Sir R. H. K., 338, 376
Margach, J. D., 374
Margiotta Broglio, F., 432
Margolis, J., 55
Margulies, S. R., 540
Mariaca Bilboa, E., 322
Marianetti, B., 315
Mariano, E., 420
Marie, J.-J., 534, 536
Marienfeld, W., 151
Marighela, C., 119
Marín Madrid, A., 332
Mariñas Otero, L., 298
Marinelli, L. A., 813
Mario, V., *pseud.*, 327
Maritano, N., 199
Mark, D. E., 125
Mark, M., 10
Markert, W., 467, 552, 571
Markezinis, S. V., 603
Markham, J. W., 43, 75, 214, 253
Markiewicz, S., 527
Markovitz, I. L., 782, 812
Márkus, L., 512
Marlowe, J., *pseud.*, 651
Marof, T., *pseud.*, 321
Marosán, G., 513
Marotta, S., 319
Marquard, L., 835, 837, 840
Marques, A. H. de O., 440
Márquez, P., 342
Marr, D. G., 739
Marrero, L., 342
Marshall, C. B., 10, 843
Marshall, S. L. A., 745
Martellaro, J. A., 431
Martelli, G. A., 823
Martin, A., 492
Martin, B., 151
Martin, H., 684
Martin, J. B., 308
Martin, J. J., 235
Martin, L. W., 114
Martin, M.-M., 392
Martin, P. J. J., 284
Martin, T. L., Jr., 110
Martin Saunders, C., 339
Martinet, G., 25
Martinez, 399
Martinez, A. R., 342
Martínez Codó, E., 120

Martini, A., 148
Martinkevich, F. S., 584
Martins, L., 329
Marton, E., 514
Martyn, H., 66
Martz, J. D., 205, 342
Maruyama, M., 722
Marwick, A., 387
Marx, J. L., 166
Marx, W., 554
Marzouk, G. A., 805
Masani, M. R., 664
Maschke, A., 199
Maser, W., 480, 482
Mashezerskov, V. I., 584
Masnata, A., 572
Masnata, F., 394
Mason, E. S., 82
Mason, J. B., 2
Mason, P., 40, 674
Masseron, J.-P., 782
Massey, V., 287
Massigli, R. L. D., 625
Massiot, M., 848
Massip, R., 406
Masson, P., 82
Massu, J., 798
Mast, C. E., 165
Masterman, J. C., 171
Masters, R. D., 235
Mastny, V., 518
Masur, G., 206
Matei, H. C., 590
Matern, H., 492
Mates, L., 187
Mathews, A. S., 837
Mathisen, T., 10
Mathos, M., 654
Matloff, M., 158
Matras, J., 643
Matsebula, J. S. M., 841
Matsumoto, S., 704
Matt, A., 157
Matte, N. M., 91
Matthews, H. L., 226, 305
Matthews, K., 605
Matthews, M., 577
Matusow, A. J., 275
Mau, H., 476
Maude, A., 383, 609
Mauersberg, H., 464
Maugham, B., 156
Maung, M., 753
Maung Maung, U, 753
Maurach, R., 86, 565
Maurer, G., 201
Mauriac, C., 403
Mauriac, F., 403
Mauriès, R., 646
Mavestiti, P., 351
Maxa, J. *See* Journalist M., *pseud.*
Maxelon, M.-O., 474
Maxwell, G., 795
Maxwell, K. L., 100
Maxwell, N., 671
May, A. J., 508
May, E. R., 214, 246

AUTHOR INDEX

May, H. K., 199
May, J. M., 363
Mayer, A. C., 775
Mayer, A. J., 134
Mayer, D., 177
Mayer, G. H., 271
Mayer, P., 30
Mayer-Oakes, T. F., 717
Mayfield, J. B., 805
Mayne, R., 347
Mayo, L., 175
Mayobre, J. A., 199, 343
Mayrzedt, H., 183, 351
Maza Zavala, D. F., 343
Mazanova, M. B., 575
Mazlakh, S., 583
Mazlish, B., 221
Mazo, E., 221
Mazrui, Ali Al'Amin, 782, 783, 791, 827
Mazurov, V. M., 731
Mboya, T., 830
Mead, W. R., 451
Meadows, D. H., 76
Meagher, R. F., 82
Means, G. P., 757
Mecklin, J., 743
Medding, P. Y., 641
Medlicott, W. N., 366, 375
Medvedev, R. A., 544, 546
Medvedev, Z. A., 546, 580
Meerhaeghe, M. A. G. van, 98
Meersch, W. J., Ganshof van der. *See* Ganshof van der Meersch, W. J.
Mehdi, M. T., 636
Mehnert, K., 467, 557, 692, 701
Mehrotra, S. R., 659
Mehta, V., 657
Meid, P., 729
Meier, G. M., 58, 80
Meier, H. K., 394
Meier, J., 363
Meier, R. L., 76
Meier, V. E., 360, 532
Meier, W., 90
Meier-Welcker, H., 162, 471
Meijer, J. M., 542
Meisel, J. H., 35
Meisner, M., 692
Meissner, B., 86, 95, 365, 500, 552, 565, 577
Meister, A., 294, 595, 827
Melas, M. K., 606
Melby, J. F., 686
Melchior de Molènes, C., 356
Meléndez, H. T., 294
Melgunov, S. P., 542
Meliksetov, A. V., 709
Melito, A., 428
Mellander, G. A., 299
Meller, N., 773, 775
Meller, T., 773
Mellnik, S. M., 155
Mellor, J. W., 673
Mellor, R. E. H., 531
Melman, S., 261, 275
Mel'nikov, D. E., 554
Mel'nikov, I. M., 235
Melo, C. R., 315

Melograni, P., 423, 428
Melson, R., 817
Melville, M., 297
Melville, T., 297
Menard, O. D., 399
Menashe, L., 743
Mendel, A. P., 536
Mendel, D., 713
Mendès-France, P., 412
Mendl, W., 408
Meneses, E., 305
Mengin, R., 403
Menjívar, R., 211
Menon, K. P. S., 536, 661
Mensbrugghe, Y. van der, 91
Men'shikov, S. M., 275
Menz, G., 572
Menzhinskii, V. I., 365
Menzies, Sir R. G., 770
Meo, L. D., 171
Meo, L. M. T., 628
Meraviglia, P., 87
Méray, T., 515, 557
Mercader, A., 341
Merchant, L. T., 284
Mercier Vega, L., 206
Meretskov, K. A., 536
Merhav, P., 643
Merillat, H. C. L., 86
Merino, H. Z., 331
Merk, F., 261
Merkelis, A., 462
Merkl, P. H., 496, 504
Merle, M., 36
Merle, R., 798
Merleau-Ponty, M., 30
Merlin, S., 613, 636
Merritt, R. L., 19, 43
Mesa-Lago, C., 305
Meskauskas, K., 462
Meskill, J. M. M., 152
Métall, R. A., 85
Metrowich, F. R., 786
Metzger, S. D., 95, 254
Meyer, A., 394
Meyer, A. G., 565
Meyer, F. S., 24, 778
Meyer, G., 555
Meyer, L., 290
Meyer, M. C., 291
Meyer, M. W., 765
Meyer, R. H., 63
Meyer-Ranke, P., 803
Meyers, J. S., 226
Meyers, S. M., 728
Meyerson, H., 746
Meynaud, J., 22, 356, 392, 603, 791
Meyriat, J., 37
Mezirow, J. D., 679
Micaud, C. A., 794, 799
Micewski, A., 525, 526
Michaels, A. L., 292
Michalski, W., 724
Michel, A. A., 659
Michel, H., 147, 177, 399
Michelmore, P., 221
Michener, J. A., 433

Michie, A. A., 121
Mickelson, S., 279
Mickiewicz, E. P., 580
Middlemas, K., 142, 372
Middleton, D., 191, 246, 377
Miège, J.-L., 425
Mieres, F., 343
Mieroszewski, J., 527
Miguel, A. de, 438, 439
Mihajlov, M., 532
Mihaly, E. B., 655
Mihanovich, C. S., 355
Mijares, A., 343
Mikdashi, Z., 71, 616
Mikesell, R. F., 63, 66, 256
Mikhā'il, H. A., 801
Mikoian, A. I., 536
Miksche, F. O., 183, 184
Mikus, J. A., 523
Milcent, E., 782, 812
Milenkovitch, D. D., 595
Miles, M. E., 152
Miliband, R., 15, 25
Miliukov, P. N., 536
Millar, J. R., 574
Millar, T. B., 766, 768, 769
Millen, B. H., 41
Miller, A. C., 698
Miller, F. O., 718
Miller, H., 757
Miller, J., 493
Miller, J. C., 92
Miller, J. D. B., 187, 368, 609, 767
Miller, K. E., 377, 443
Miller, L. B., 102
Miller, M., 363
Miller, N., 187, 269
Miller, R. F., 575
Miller, W. J., 222
Millers, V., 460
Millikan, M. F., 55, 69, 97
Millis, W., 125, 126
Millon, R. P., 291, 292
Mills, C. A., 46
Mills, C. W., 15
Mills, L. A., 735
Milne, R. S., 758, 772
Milward, A. S., 174, 446
Milza, P., 426
Minces, J., 797
Minear, R. H., 717
Minerbi, S., 425
Miners, N. J., 817
Minghi, J. V., 45
Minkel, C. W., 297
Minogue, K. R., 24
Minor, D., 279
Minott, R. G., 160
Mints, I. I., 542, 584
Mintz, J. S., 761
Mintz, S. W., 302
Mironov, N. V., 552
Mirskii, G. I., 187
Miscaud, C. A., 412
Misra, K. P., 611, 667
Misra, R. N., 664
Mitchell, A., 471

Mitchell, Sir H. P., 1st Bart., 301
Mitchell, R. H., 727
Mitchell, R. P., 803
Mitchell, W. B., 336
Mitin, M. B., 22
Mitrany, D., 126
Mitrović, A., 592
Mittelstädt, A., 416
Mitter, J. P., 654
Mitterand, F., 403, 412
Mitzscherling, P., 492
Miwa, K., 718
Miyamoto, K., 174
Miyashita, T., 709
Mizov, N., 598
Mlynář, Z., 519
Mňačko, L., 521
Mnogolet, N. I., 275
Moch, J. S., 126, 403, 408, 502
Moczulski, L., 526
Modelski, G. A., 15, 761
Modigliani, A., 182
Modrzhinskaia, E. D., 188
Mörner, M., 211
Mohammed, A. F., 678
Mohler, A., 399, 504
Mohr, H. J., 334
Moisuc, V., 590
Mokgatle, N., 840
Molas, I., 439
Molchanov, N. N., 403
Mole, R. L., 747
Molenda, J., 525
Molesworth, G. N., 659
Moley, R., 216
Moley, R., Jr., 271
Molin, B., 448
Mollet, G., 399
Molnár, M., 515
Molnar, T. S., 782, 842
Mommsen, H., 477
Mommsen, W., 468
Monahan, J., 306
Moncrieff, A., 638
Mondjannagni, A., 808
Mondlane, E., 847
Moneta, J., 412
Monnerville, G., 403
Monnier, C., 722
Monroe, E., 377
Monsen, R. J., Jr., 271
Montalais, J. de, 412
Montaperto, R. N., 695
Monteil, V., 620, 759, 778
Montfort, H. A. de, 526
Montgomery, J. D., 76, 82, 237
Montgomery of Alamein, B. L. M., 1st Viscount, 110
Montias, J. M., 590
Monticone, A., 134
Montigny, J., 142
Montross, L., 729
Montvalon, R. de, 417
Moomaw, I. W., 256
Moon, Sir E. P., 659
Moore, B., Jr., 40
Moore, C. A., 715

Moore, C. D., 778
Moore, C. H., 33, 794, 800
Moore, D., 755
Moore, F. T., 747
Moore, J., 755
Moore, J. E., 114
Moore, J. N., 740
Moore, O. E., 310
Moore, W. E., 40
Moorsteen, R. H., 246, 572
Morača, P., 592
Moraes, F. R., 778
Moran, C. McM. W., Baron, 372
Moran, W. E., Jr., 48
Morandi, R., 430
Mordal, J., *pseud.*, 160
Mordecai, Sir J., 301
Moreira, A., 440
Moreira, J. R., 328
Morel, E., 324
Morello, F. P., 713
Moreno, D., 292
Morenoff, J., 91
Morgan, K. O., 384
Morgan, R., 6, 351, 376
Morgan, T., 735
Morgan, W. B., 808
Morgenthau, H. J., 182, 214, 235, 743
Morgenthau, R. S., 808
Morison, D. L., 560
Morison, S. E., 169, 214, 261
Morland, 399
Morley, J. W., 715, 719
Morozov, G. I., 98, 102, 106
Morozow, M., 546
Morris, A. V., 715
Morris, B. S., 235
Morris, C., 117
Morris, C. T., 71
Morris, H. F., 832
Morris, H. S., 832
Morris, I., 722
Morris, J., 655
Morris, M. D., 720
Morris-Hale, W., 834
Morris-Jones, W. H., 664
Morrison, D. G., 778
Morrison, DeL. S., 195
Morrison, J. L., 222
Morrow, J. H., 783, 810
Morrow, W. L., 266
Morse, A. D., 47
Morse, D. A., 106
Morse, R. McG., 81
Morsey, R., 469, 471
Mortimer, E., 786
Morton, H. W., 565, 580
Morton, L., 279
Morton, W. L., 282
Moscati, R., 424
Moscow, W., 216
Moseley, G., 686, 712
Mosely, Sir O. E., 6th Bart., 372
Mosely, P. E., 540
Mosler, H., 488
Mosley, L., 145, 168
Mosley, L. O., 139, 718, 828

Moss, N., 117
Moss, R., 120
Mosse, G. L., 480
Mossé, R., 26, 63
Mosse, W. E., 471
Mossuz, J., 412
Moulton, J. L., 110, 160
Moumouni, A., 792
Mountjoy, A. B., 80
Moura, F. P. da, 440
Mourin, M., 406, 433
Mousa, S., 620
Moussa, F., 88
Mowat, C. L., 130
Mowat, R. C., 130
Mowrer, E. A., 216
Moxon, J., 815
Moya Palencia, M., 292
Mtshali, B. V., 843
Mudd, S., 49
Mühlen, P. von zur, 174
Mühlenberg, F., 813
Müller, A., 476
Müller, C., 486
Müller, H., 477
Müller, K., 83
Müller, K.-J., 477
Müller-Hillebrand, B., 157
Münch, F., 102
Mughraby, M. A., 616
Muḥamadīyah, A. S., 806
Muhammad Ali, C., 676
Muḥyī al-Dīn, K., 620
Muirden, B., 770
Mukerjee, T., 50
Mukherjea, A. R., 665
Mukhlis, J., 645
Mulford, D. C., 845, 846
Mullenbach, P., 117
Muller, H. J., 22, 222
al-Mumayyiz, A., 645
Mummery, D. R., 820
Mun, Chong-ch'ang, 727
Munch, P., 443
Mundell, R. A., 54, 63
Munger, E. S., 837, 840, 841
Munier, B., 63
Munk, F., 191
Munro, D. G., 195
Munson, F. P., 313
Muqueem Khan, F., 676
Muratet, R., 795
Murillo Valladares, G., 299
Murphy, E. R., Jr., 729
Murphy, G. G. S., 714
Murphy, P. L., 266
Murphy, R. D., 226
Murqus, I., 620
Murray, D. J., 817, 844
Murray, J. L., 1
Murray, J., 139
Murray-Brown, J., 830
Murrow, E. R., 228
Murti, B. S. N., 740
Murty, B. S., 121
Murty, K. S., 667
Mury, G., 601

Mus, P., 738
Muscat, R. J., 752
Musgrave, R. A., 63
Musgrove, P., 210
Mushakōji, K., 720
Muskens, M. P. M., 761
Musrey, A. G., 620
Mussolini, B., 421
Muṣṭafā, M. H., 802
Musteikis, K., 462
Mutchler, D. E., 206
Mutesa II, Kabaka of Buganda, 832
Mutharika, B. W. T., 788
Mutton, A. F. A., 344
Mužić, I., 592
Mveng, E., 825
Mwase, G. S., 846
Mydans, C., 110
Mydans, S., 110
Myer, D. S., 174
Myers, C. A., 73, 74
Myers, H. A., 488, 500
Myint, Hla. See Hla Myint, U
Myrdal, G., 51, 54, 609
Myrdal, J., 601, 692

Nader, C., 614
Näth, M.-L., 703
Nagle, J. D., 505
Nagy, M. H., 512
Nagy-Talavera, N. M., 512
Nahayewsky, I., 583
Nāhīd, M., 651
Naik, J. A., 560, 680
Naimy, M., 184
Nair, K., 69
Nairn, R. C., 752
Nakajima, M., 692
Nakamura, H., 609
Nakamura, K., 722
Nalin, I., 184
Nanporia, N. J., 671
Nantet, J., 403
Nānū, J., 803
Narain, D., 673
Narkiewicz, O. A., 543
Narr, W.-D., 505
Narsarski, P., 142
Nascimento, C. A., 336
Nascimento e Silva, G. E. do, 89
Nash, G. D., 275
Nasser, D., 327
Nassmacher, K.-H., 510
Natan, Z., 598
Nathan, H., 466
Naumann, B., 484
Navarro, G. A. See Marof, T., pseud.
Navarro Gerassi, M., 315
Navasky, V. S., 266
Naville, P., 682
Nawfal, al-S. M. A., 621, 648
Nayar, B. R., 665, 674
Nayir, Y. N., 624
Naylor, J. F., 377
Neamṭu, O., 589
Neatby, H. B., 287

Nedelmann, C., 505
Needler, M. C., 206
Neelkant, K., 667
Neelsen, K., 507
Nehemkis, P., 202
Nehring, W. K., 467
Nehrt, L. C., 95, 794
Nehru, J., 661
Nekrasov, V. P., 536
Nelkin, D., 262
Nellessen, B., 436
Nellis, J. R., 834
Nelson, H. D., 806, 817, 821, 848
Nelson, H. I., 143
Nelson, J., 155
Nelson, J. M., 256
Nelson, L., 306
Nelson, R., 765
Nelson, R. R., 334
Nelson, W. H., 266
Nême, C., 351
Nême, J., 351
Nenni, P., 428
Nerhood, H. W., 532
Nerlich, U., 110
Nesterenko, O. O., 583
Neto, J. P., 847
Nettl, J. P., 15, 30, 540
Nettleford, R. M., 310
Netzband, K.-B., 471
Netzer, H.-J., 496
Neubauer, H., 471
Neuberg, A., 120
Neuberger, E., 56
Neufeld, E. P., 67
Neufeld, M. F., 38
Neuhaus, R., 272
Neumann, W. L., 152, 246
Neumann-Hoditz, R., 704
Neumark, S. D., 788
Neunreither, K., 356
Neustadt, R. E., 191
Nevakivi, J., 453, 614
Neven-du Mont, J., 496
Nevins, A., 222, 276
Newcomb, R. F., 166
Newell, R. S., 654
Newell, W. H., 758
Newfield, J., 222
Newhouse, J., 191, 356, 406
Newman, A. H., 216
Newman, B., 739, 837
Newman, P. C., 287
Newman, P. K., 337
Newman, W. J., 143, 272
Newth, J. A., 587
Nghiem-Dang, 747
Ngubane, J. K., 840
Nguyên-thê-Anh, 739
Nguyen-van-Hao, 739
Ni, Chêng-yü, 95
Nicholas H. G., 377
Nicholls, A., 180
Nichols, P., 433
Nichols, R. F., 272
Nicholson, I., 289
Nicholson, M., 380

AUTHOR INDEX

Nickels, S., 450
Niclauss, K., 555
Nicolaevsky, B. I., 540
Nicolson, Sir H. G., 372
Nicolson, I. F., 817
Nicolson, N., 372
Niebuhr, R., 23
Niedergang, M., 308
Nieh, Yu-hsi, 704
Niekisch, E., 471
Nielsen, W. A., 279, 786, 835
Niemeier, J. G., 299
Niemeyer, G., 26, 30, 40
Nihal Singh, S., 758
Niijima, A., 700
Nikhamin, V. P., 552
Nikolaev, A., 184
Nikolaev, P. A., 555
Niri, A., 590
Nisbet, C. T., 211
Nish, I. H., 377
Nish'at, Ş., 648
Nissen, H., 443
Nitschke, A., 130
Nittner, E., 523
Niv, D., 641
Niven, Sir C. R., 817, 819
Nixon, E. B., 235
Nizer, L., 216
Njama, K., 829
Nkrumah, K., 36, 782, 815, 823
Nobécourt, J., 160, 412, 433
Nobécourt, R. G., 139
Noble, G. B., 231
Nogly, H., 170
Nógrádi, S., 514
Nogueira, A. F. See Nogueira, F.
Nogueira, F., 440
Noguères, H., 143, 399
Nolde, O. F., 44
Nollau, G., 560
Nolte, E., 33, 34, 129
Nolte, R. H., 614
Nomura, K., 692
Noonan, L. G., 412
Noorani, A. G., 669, 671
Norbye, O. D. K., 679
Nordahl, K., 446
Norden, A., 492
Nordlinger, E. A., 383
Norgren, C., 449
Norgren, M., 449
Norman, A., 139
Norman, D., 661
Norman, J., 801
Norström, G., 55
North, R. C., 692
Northedge, F. S., 11, 377
Nossiter, B. D., 276, 657
Notkin, A. I., 572
Nottingham, J., 118
Nottingham J. C., 831
Noudel, E., 457
Nourissier, F., 396
Nousiainen, J., 451
Novak, B. C., 426
Novak, R. D., 215, 219

Nove, A., 572, 587
November, A., 808
Novick, P., 399
Novikov, K. V., 552
Novogrod, J. C., 743
Nowlan, K. B., 389
Nsarkoh, J. K., 815
Nudel'man, A. V., 849
Nuechterlein, D. E., 752
Nuñez, C., 341
Nunn, C., 69
Nunn, F. M., 331
Nunn, G. R., 609
Nunnerly, D., 240
Nurmukhamedov, S. B., 587
Nutting, A., 621, 638, 804
Nwankwo, A. A., 819
Nye, J. S., Jr., 97, 126, 827
Nyerere, J. K., 834
Nyers, R., 514
Nyman, O., 449
Nyrop, R. F., 627, 676, 681, 795, 798, 801, 832

O, So-baek, 727
Oakley, S., 449
Obaid, A. H., 199
O'Ballance, E., 563, 606, 639, 648, 728, 737, 758, 798
Oberdorfer, D., 746
Oberländer, E., 540, 549
Obeyesekere, G., 681
O'Brian, R. C., 812
O'Brien, C. C., 389
O'Brien, P. K., 805
O'Brien, W. V., 95, 110, 117
O'Collins, G., 770
O'Connell, D. P., 86
O'Connor, A. M., 792, 827, 832
O'Connor, J. R., 306
O'Connor, R., 246
O'Connor, R. G., 152
O'Connor, W. E., 68
Oda, S., 91
Oddone, J. A., 341
Odell, P. R., 71
Odinga, A. O., 831
O'Donnell, K. P., 226
Oduho, J., 806
Odumosu, O. I., 818
Oertly, W. V., 815
Ørvik, N., 446, 453
Oey, H. L., 761
Ofer, G., 642
Offner, A. A., 143
Ogata, S. N., 720
Oglesby, C., 38
O'Grady, J. P., 134
Ogura, T., 725
Oh, John Kie-chiang, 731
Ōhira, Z., 720
Ohkawa, K., 725
Ohlin, B. G., 58, 449
Ohlin, G., 49
Ohneck, W., 798
Ojha, I. C., 704
Ojukwu, C. O., 819

Okabe, T., 705
Okello, J., 834
Okigbo, P. N. C., 788, 820
Okinshevich, L., 202
Okonjo, C., 790
Okpaku, J., 819
Ōkubo, Y., 693
Okumu, W. A. J., 823
Okumura, F., 152, 609
Olarra Jiménez, R., 319
Oldenburg, F., 493
Oldman, O. S., 294
O'Leary, M. K., 257
Oliver, K. D., 598
Oliver, R. A., 778
Olivier-Lacamp, M., 657
Ollenhauer, E., 497
O'Loughlin, C., 312
Olschak, B. C., 656
Olson, K. E., 344
Olson, L. A., 717, 720
Olson, M., Jr., 55
Omari, T. P., 815
Omarovskii, A. G., 572
Ominde, S. H., 831
O'Neill, R. J., 477, 748
O'Neill, T. N., 384
O'Neill, T. P., 389
O'Neill, W. L., 217
Onís, J. de, 198
Onslow, C., 609
Onufriev, I. G., 211
Onyemelukwe, C. C., 820
Ooi, Jin-Bee, 755
Opat, J., 360
Ophuls, M., 399
Oppenheimer, M., 815
Orantes, I. C., 296
Orcival, F. d', 523, 844
Ord, H. W., 788
Ordzhonikidze, Z. B., 536
O'Reilly, P., 775
Oren, N., 598
Organski, A. F. K., 15
Orleans, L. A., 709
Orlov, A., 122
Orlow, D., 152, 480
Orni, E., 630
Orona, J. V., 315
Orsolini, M. H., 316
Ortiz, J., 798
Ortner-Heun, I., 800
Osakwe, C., 552
Osborn, R. J., 578
Osborne, C., 766
Osborne, J., 217
Osborne, M. E., 735, 755
Oser, J., 76
Osgood, R. E., 15, 235
Osipov, G. V., 576
Ospina Vásquez, L., 334
Ossenbeck, F. J., 115
Osswald, K.-D., 406
Osterroth, F., 467
Ostrý, A., *pseud.*, 521
Ostry, S., 289
Oswald, J. G., 202, 560

Otáhalová, L., 518
Otani, K., 716
Ottaway, D., 798
Ottaway, M., 798
Ottone, P., 572
Oudenhove, G. van, 356
Overstreet, B. W., 272
Overstreet, H. A., 272
Owen, D., 110
Owen, W., 68
Owens, R. J., 339
Oxaal, I., 312
Oya, S., 166
Ozaki, R. S., 725
Oznobishin, D. V., 553

Paasikivi, J. K., 453
Paasivirta, J., 453
Pabón y Suárez de Urbina, J., 433
Pachter, H. M., 184
Pack, H., 642
Packard, G. R., III, 720
Paddock, P., 69, 80
Paddock, W., 69, 80
Padelford, N. J., 11, 786
Paden, J. N., 779
Padgett, L. V., 292
Padilla Aragón, E., 294
Pächter, H., 553
Paek, P., 732
Paetel, K. O., 471
Page, B., 122, 215
Page, D. M., 284
Page, M., 546
Paget, J., 120, 648
Paige, G. D., 728
Paikert, G. C., 360
Paillat, C., 399
Pajewski, J., 529
Pak, Chŏng-hŭi, 731
Pak, H., 693
Pak, Tong-un, 732
Pakaslahti, A., 454
Pakeman, S. A., 681
Paklons, L. L., 352
Palermo, I., 423
Palfreeman, A. C., 770
Palit, D. K., 111
Palley, C., 844
Palmer, M., 352
Palmer, N. D., 246
Palmer, R. W., 311
Palmer, S. E., Jr., 592
Palmier, L. H., 759
Pan, Chao-ying, 697, 704, 740
Pan, S. *See* Pan, Chao-ying.
Pan, S. C. Y. *See* Pan, Chao-ying.
Pando Monje, M., 321
Pang, T., 693
Paniker, S., 437
Panikkar, K. M., 659
Pankhurst, R. K. P., 828
Panksejev, A., 458
Pano, N. C., 601
Pansa, G., 423
Pant, Y. P., 655

AUTHOR INDEX

Pantaleone, M., 431
Panter-Downes, M., 155
Paolucci, H., 272
Papakonstantinou, T., 164
Papandreou, A. G., 603
Papanek, G. F., 75, 76, 679
Papanicolaou, E. E., 51
Papen, F. von, 471
Papi, U., 69
Paredes, L., 298
Paredes Moreira, J. L., 298
Parenti, M., 236
Parera, R. G., 316
Paret, P., 408
Pariseau, E. J., 201
Pǎrīzī, B., 651
Park, A. E. W., 818
Park, C. H. See Pak, Chŏng-hŭi.
Parker, F. D., 296
Parker, G., 356
Parker, R. A. C., 344
Parkin, F., 40, 383
Parkinson, C. N., 383
Parkinson, G. H. R., 30
Parkinson, R., 146
Parmet, H. S., 236
Parra Aranguren, G., 343
Parra Sandoval, R., 334
Parry, A., 549
Parsons, T., 15
Pašic, N., 595
Passin, H., 246, 726, 792
Pastorelli, P., 425
Patel, V. J. S., 661
Paternostre de la Mairieu, B., 832
Paterson, T. G., 242
Paton, A., 837, 840
Patrick, C. W., 279
Pattee, R., 309
Patterson, G., 58
Patterson, G. N., 671
Patterson, J. T., 222
Paucker, A., 471
Paulsen, H., 446
Paulson, B. H., 428
Paulu, B., 43
Paustovskii, K. G., 536
Pavett, D., 118
Pavlov, D. V., 162
Pavlov, V. I., 673
Pavlowitch, S. K., 593
Pawera, J. C., 798
Pawle, G., 155
Paxton, J., 3, 357
Paxton, R. O., 399
Payne, J. L., 236, 334, 339
Payne, P. S. R., 536, 661, 700
Payne, R. See Payne, P. S. R.
Payne, S. G., 434, 436
Payton-Smith, D. J., 173
Pazos y Roque, F., 211
Peabody, J. B., 228
Peach, C., 387
Pearlman, M., 484, 630
Pearson, D. S., 827
Pearson, L. B., 11, 83, 126, 287
Pearson, S. R., 820

Pearton, M., 590
Peaslee, A. J., 19
Peccei, A., 51
Peck, G., 685
Pedreira, F., 327
Pedroncini, G., 139
Peers, W. R., 167
Peerzada, S. S., 676
Peikert, H., 416
Peirce, N. R., 214, 266
Peissel, M., 654
Pejovich, S., 595
Pelikán, J., 521
Pélissier, R., 847
Pelling, H. M., 386
Pelt, A., 801
Peltier, M. A., 454
Peña, M., 316
Peña, M. T. de la, 294
Peñaloza, L., 321
Pendle, G., 337
Peng, Ming-min, 713
Penkov, P., 599
Penkovskii, O. V., 567
Penna, J. O. de M., 324
Penniman, H. R., 747
Pennock, J. R., 35, 38
Penrose, E. F., 11, 71
Pentzopoulous, D., 603
Pereira, L. C. B., 323
Pereira, P. T., 441
Perera, P., 63
Peres, S., 640
Peretz, D., 614
Perez Alfonzo, J. P., 343
Pérez Concha, J., 335
Pérez López, E., 294
Perham, Dame M. F., 368, 786, 828
Perillo, J. M., 353
Perkins, D., 226, 236, 301
Perkins, D. H., 124, 709
Perkins, J. O. N., 51
Perkins, K., 770
Perko, T., 454
Perlmutter, A., 640
Perloff, H. S., 199, 266
Pernack, H.-J., 601
Perón, J. D., 317
Perrault, G., 172
Perrone Capano, R., 177
Perroux, F., 798
Perroy, H., 80
Perry, H. D., 143
Pertot, V., 593
Peschaut, T., 513
Pesonen, P., 451
Pesti, M., 458
Peterec, R. J., 808
Peters, I. A., 143
Petersen, W., 49
Peterson, A. F., 476
Peterson, E. N., 477
Peterson, H.-C., 339
Peterson, H. F., 314
Pethybridge, R. W., 540
Petit, A. G., 306
Petrakov, N. I., 572

Petran, T., 627
Petranović, B., 595
Petras, J., 195, 207, 331
Petrie, Sir C., 434
Petrov, D. V., 720
Petrov, F. P., 184
Petrov, P. S., 272
Petrov, V., 714
Petrov, Vladimir, 146, 174
Petrova, D. V., 599
Petrow, R., 849
Petuchowski, J. J., 630
Peyrouton, B. M., 794
Pfaff, W., 32, 131, 238
Pfahlberg, B., 102
Pfahlmann, H., 174
Pfaltzgraff, R. L., Jr., 191, 377
Pfeffer, R. M., 236
Pfeffermann, G., 812
Pflimlin, P., 356, 396
Phadnis, U., 665
Pham-Thi-Tu, 98
Phelps-Fetherston, I., 553
Philby, H. St. J. B., 616
Philip, A., 412
Philips, C. H., 659, 665
Phillips, C. B. H., 217
Phillips, C. S., Jr., 818
Phillips, H. S., 76
Phillips, K. P., 272
Phillips, R. H., 306
Phillips, W., 648
Phillips, W. A. P., 477
Pichlík, K., 518
Pickersgill, J. W., 287
Pickles, D. M., 23, 406, 413, 798
Pickles, W., 377
Pidhainy, O. S., 583
Piedra, A. M., 211
Piekalkiewicz, J. A., 358, 521
Pierce, R., 413
Pierre, A. J., 379
Pierre-Charles, G., 310
Pietromarchi, L., 540
Pietsch, W., 543
Piip, A., 458
Pike, D., 740
Pike, F. B., 201, 207, 332, 339, 434
Pike, J. G., 846
Pillai, K. R., 667
Pin, E., 205
Pincus, J., 337
Pincus, J. A., 83
Pinder, J., 346
Pineau, C., 536
Pinkney, R., 815
Pinney, E. L., 505
Pintér, I., 511, 512
Pinto, A., 331
Pinto, L. de A. C., 334
Pinto, R., 352
Pinto-Duschinsky, M., 381
Piper, D. C., 284
Pipes, R., 543
Pippin, L. LaR., 300
Pirages, D. C., 527
Pirie, N. W., 69

Pirker, T., 30, 34, 505
Pisar, S., 186
Piterskii, N. A., 169
Piti, B., 599
Pitt, D., 775
Pittoni, B., 422
Pizzuto de Rivero, M. R., 317
Planchais, J., 412
Planck, C. R., 184, 191
Plank, J. N., 303
Plano, J. C., 98
Plaschka, R. G., 139
Plath, D. W., 726
Platig, E. R., 6
Platt, D. C. St. M., 377
Playfair, I. S. O., 157
Plaza, G., 202
Plehwe, F.-K. von, 152
Plender, R., 91
Plischke, E., 98, 494
Ploncard d'Assac, J., 441
Ploss, S. I., 575
Plotnick, A. R., 254
Poats, R. M., 257
Poblete Tronsoso, M., 211
Pochhammer, W. von, 673
Poel, J. Van Der, 837
Poggi, G., 430
Pogue, F. C., 222
Pois, R. A., 464
Pokshishevskii, V. V., 578
Polach, J. G., 357
Poleman, T. T., 294
Polenberg, R., 174
Polikeit, G., 492
Polk, J., 254
Polk, W. R., 38, 243
Polomka, P., 761
Polonsky, A., 526
Polsby, N. W., 272
Polvinen, T., 453
Pomaret, C., 399
Pomeroy, W. J., 120
Pomian, J., 525
Pommer, H. J., 365
Pommerening, H., 557
Pomper, G., 266
Ponomarev, B. N., 547, 549, 553
Pool, I. de S., 43
Poole, P. A., 752
Pope-Hennessy, J., 755
Popişteanu, C., 590
Popkin, N. S., 676
Popov, V. I., 184, 553, 555
Popović, N. D., 595
Popperwell, R. G., 446
Poppinga, A., 498
Poppino, R E., 207, 324
Poretsky, E. K., 567
Porter, B. E., 11, 377
Portes Gil, E., 292
Portisch, H., 701
Poska, J. G., 456
Posner, C., 413
Posner, M. V., 430
Pospelov, P. N., 157, 537
Possony, S. T., 130, 262, 537

AUTHOR INDEX

Post, K. W. J., 808, 818
Postan, M. M., 173, 348
Posvar, W. W., 262
Potash, R. A., 316
Potholm, C. P., 783, 837, 841
Potichyj, P. J., 583
Potre, R., 417
Potter, C. E., 268
Potter, J. D., 718
Potter, J. G., 845
Pouget, J., 737
Poulantzas, N. M., 90
Poullier, J.-P., 73
Poulsen, H., 443
Pound, R., 372
Pounds, N. J. G., 345, 360, 507, 523, 614
Pournelle, J. E., 262
Powell, J. E., 373
Powell, R. P., 572
Powelson, J. P., 76, 211
Power, J. H., 765
Power, T. S., 184
Powers, D. F., 226
Powers, F. G., 262
Powers, P. W., 262
Pozdniakov, V. S., 561
Prado Júnior, C., 324
Prakasa, S., 677
Prandi, A., 427
Prasad, B., 158
Pratt, J. W., 231, 236
Prcela, J., 593
Prebisch, R., 212
Prečan, V., 523
Preece, R. J. C., 506
Preeg, E. H., 58
Preradovich, N. von, 509
Prescott, J. R. V., 2
Presley, J. R., 354
Presser, J., 390
Preston, R. A., 283, 284, 285, 767
Preston, W., Jr., 268
Pribičević, B., 595
Price, J. H., 808
Price, R. F., 711
Price, W. DeM., 773
Priestland, G., 214
Priestley, Sir R., 849
Prieto, R., 316
Primakov, E. M., 180
Pritt, D. N., 380
Prittie, T. C. F., 497, 630, 631
Pritzel, K., 492
Proché, P., 510
Prochnow, H. V., 51, 63
Proctor, J. H., 44
Proehl, P. O., 820
Prokof'ev, B. P., 102
Propp, P. D., 492
Pross, H., 467
Prosser, M. H., 102
Proxmire, W., 276
Pruitt, D. G., 111
Prybyla, J. S., 77, 709
Pryde, P. R., 572
Pryor, F. L., 51, 363
Psaros, D., 603

Psomiades, H. J., 606
Puaux, G., 510
Pünder, H., 471
Pünder, T., 489
Puga Vega, M., 331
Pugh, J. C., 808
Puhle, H.-J., 322
Puiggrós, R., 316
Pujos, J., 810
Puławski, M., 529
Pulzer, P. G. J., 380
Puntila, L. A., 451
Purcell, H. D., 418
Purcell, V. W. W. S., 711, 758
Pusey, M. J., 236, 267
Pushkarev, S. G., 542
Pusta, K. R., 456, 458
Pustay, J. S., 120
Puttkamer, E. von, 102
Pye, L. W., 16, 21, 684, 686
Pye, M. W., 684
Pylee, M. V., 665
Pyromaglou, K., 605

Quaison-Sackey, A., 783
Quandt, W. B., 799
Quaroni, P., 421, 558
Quazza, G., 177
Qubain, F. I., 621
Quebracho, *pseud*., 321
Querejazu Calvo, R., 320
Quester, G. H., 115, 184
Quet, P., 169
Queuille, P., 188, 195
Quigg, P. W., 236, 779
Quigley, J. B., Jr., 564
Quijada, R., 343
Quinn, H. F., 287
Quintero, C. A., 316
Quirarte, M., 294
Quirino, C., 765
Quraishi, Z. M., 803

Raab, E., 271
Ra'anan, U., 563
Rabinovich, I., 627
Rabinowitch, A., 543
Rabinowitch, E., 280
Race, R., 746
Rachocki, J., 529
Rachkov, B. V., 71
Račić, O., 106
Radcliffe, S., 488
Radice, G., 26
Radkau, J., 241
Radkey, O. H., 543
Radó, S., 172
Radosh, R., 236, 743
Rădulescu, I., 590
Radványi, J., 515
Radzhabov, Z. S., 587
Raffaelli, J., 748
Ragionieri, E., 419
Rahl, J. A., 353
Rahm, W., 394

Rahman, F., 621
Rahul, R., 655, 656
Rai, S. M., 659
Raina, P. K., 525, 527
Raiola, G., 169
Raïssac, G., 400
Rajan, M. S., 16, 667
Rákosi, S., 513
Rakowska-Harmstone, T., 358, 587
Rallis, K., 603
Ram, M., 665
Rama Rao, T. S. See Rao, T. S. R.
Ramachandran, G., 665
Ramazani, R. K., 357, 614, 651
Ramers, R. K., 112
Ramírez, G., 341
Ramírez Necochea, H., 195, 331, 332
Ramírez Novoa, E., 339
Ramos, A. G., 327
Ramos, J. A., 202, 313, 316
Ramos, J. R., 212
Ramos de Santiago, C., 312
Ramsett, D. E., 296
Ramsey, P., 111
Ramundo, B. A., 86
Randall, F. B., 544
Randle, R. F., 738
Rangel, D. A., 343
Ranger, T. O., 821, 844
Rangnekar, D. K., 357
Ranis, G., 51, 76
Ránki, G., 516
Rankin, K. L., 246
Ranney, A., 380
Ransford, O., 844
Ransom, H. H., 262, 272
Rao, G. N., 671
Rao, P. V. R., 668
Rao, R. P., 441
Rao, T. S. R., 2
Rao, V. K. R. V., 76, 673
Raper, A., 679
Rapoport, A., 113, 242, 246
Raposo, B.-H., 329
Rapp, A., 501
Rasch, H., 500
Rascovich, M., 729
Rashidov, S. R., 581
Raskin, M. G., 181, 743
Rasmussen, E., 443
Raštikis, S., 462
Rataj, M., 525
Rathenau, W., 472
Ratnam, K. J., 758
Raton, P., 395
Rauch, G. von, 456
Rauchensteiner, M., 160
Raupach, H., 361, 363
Raux, J., 357
Ravenal, E. C., 247
Rawski, T., 162
Rawson, D. W., 770
Rawson, R. R., 609
Ray, A., 665
Ray, J. K., 668, 677, 752
Ray, S., 740
Raymond, J., 262

Raynolds, D. R., 300
Rea, F. B., 844
Read, H., 32
Read, J. S., 832
Real, J., 125
Reck-Malleczewen, F. P., 486
Record, W., 272
Reddaway, P., 537, 569
Redden, K. R., 828
Reddy, T. R., 668
Reed, B., 373
Reed, D., 844
Reed, E., 23
Reed, L. D., 348
Reedy, G. E., 267
Rees, D., 728
Rees, G. L., 348
Reese, H. C., 644, 800
Reese, T. R., 766, 767
Reeve, W. D., 731
Reford, R. W., 284
Rehm, G. W., 126
Rei, A., 456
Reich, C. A., 277
Reid, R. W., 111
Reifenberg, J., 272
Reimann, G., 363
Reimann, V., 509
Reinhardt, K., 162
Reining, C. C., 806
Reischauer, E. O., 243, 247, 682, 715
Reisman, M., 636
Reitman, É., 775
Remington, R. A., 365, 521
Remmers, H. L., 65
Rémond, R., 413, 417
Rémy, pseud., 400
Renard, A., 819
Renard-Payen, O., 795
Renault-Roulier, G. See Rémy, pseud.
Renesse, E. A. von, 19
Reno, P., 337
Renouvin, P., 11, 130, 134
Renoux, Y., 92
Répaci, A., 423
ReQua, E. G., 80
Resnick, I. N., 778
Ressing, G., 152
Reston, J. B., 217, 279
Retinger, J. H., 525
Rettenbach, B., 416
Reuber, G. L., 288
Reuss, H. S., 236
Reuther, H., 500, 558
Revel, J.-F., 272, 396
Revell, J., 386
Reventlow, R., 434
Reynaud, P., 406
Reynolds, C. W., 294, 331
Reynolds, L. G., 52
Reynolds, Q. J., 765
Rhein, E., 654
Rhoads, E. J. M., 706
Rhode, G., 524, 552
Rhode, H., 175
Rhyne, C. S., 86
Riad, H., 803

AUTHOR INDEX

Ribbentrop, A. von, 146
Ribeiro, D., 202
Ribi, R. C., 365
Ricci, A., 428
Rice, B., 813
Rice, E. E., 697
Richards, D. J., 549
Richards, P. G., 377, 380
Richardson, J. L., 191
Richer, P., 705
Richert, E., 492
Richert, F., 505
Richman, B. M., 575, 709
Richter, J. H., 59
Rickards, C., 301
Rico, G., 437
Riḍā, 'Adil, 648
Riddle, D. H., 267
Ridgway, M. B., 729
Ridley, F. F., 413
Riegle, D., 226
Rieker, J., 303
Riekhoff, H. von. See Von Riekhoff, H.
Rielly, J. E., 256
Riencourt, A. de, 236
Riera Hernández, M., 303
Ries, J. C., 262
Riesman, D., 40, 717
Riesman, E. T., 717
Riezler, K., 134
Rifā'ī, Muḥammad 'Ali, 621
Rif'at, Kamāl al-Dīn, 803
Riffaud, M., 748
Rigby, T. H., 547
Riggs, F. W., 38, 76, 752
Riggs, R. E., 98, 248
Rijkens, P., 390
Riklin, A., 494
Rimmington, G. T., 846
Ringer, F. K., 465
Rings, W., 394
Rintala, M., 451
Rio Cisneros, A. del, 438
Rioux, L., 413
Ristić, D. N., 593
Ritchie-Calder, P. R. R.-C., Baron, 43
Ritsch, F. F., 413
Ritschel, K. H., 426
Ritter, G. A., 21, 465, 563
Rivera, J. H. de, 236
Rivers, W. L., 279
Rivett, K., 771
Rivett, R. D., 770
Rivkin, A., 783, 786
Rivkin, M. D., 626
Rivlin, B., 614
Rizk, C., 628
Rizzo Romano, A., 314
Roa, R., 306
Robbins, K., 143
Robbins, L. C. R., Baron, 16, 52
Robert, J., 717, 795
Roberts, A., 111, 522
Roberts, B. C., 41
Roberts, C. M., 126
Roberts, E. C., 654
Roberts, G. K., 505

Roberts, H. L., 3, 361
Roberts, H. S., 609
Roberts, J. S., 831
Roberts, P. C., 572
Roberts, T. D., 309, 813
Robertson, A. H., 93, 352
Robertson, D., 354
Robertson, E. M., 477
Robertson, J., 837
Robertson, J. H. See Connell, J., *pseud.*
Robertson, T., 638
Robichon, J., 160
Robien, L., Comte de, 537
Robinson, A. N. R., 312
Robinson, D., 120
Robinson, D. A., 339
Robinson, E. A. G., 76, 80, 609, 792
Robinson, G. T., 531
Robinson, J., 47, 86
Robinson, R., 76, 792
Robinson, R. A. H., 436
Robinson, R. D., 80, 620
Robinson, S. W., Jr., 254
Robinson, T. W., 697
Robock, S. H., 329
Robson, P., 788, 792, 827
Rochat, G., 430, 828
Roche, J. P., 214, 268
Rochefort, R., 403
Rock, V. P., 184
Rock, W. R., 373
Rocolle, P. P. F. M., 738
Rodberg, L. S., 262
Rodinson, M., 621, 636
Rodman, S., 298, 309
Rodney, W., 287
Rodrigues, J. A., 329
Rodrigues, J. H., 324, 325
Rodrigues, L. M., 329
Rodríguez, M., 296
Rodríguez de Martínez Paiva, C. E., 317
Roeder, O. G., 761
Röder, W., 486
Röh, K., 673
Röhrs, H.-D., 482
Roel Pineda, V., 339
Rönnefarth, H. K. G., 92
Röper, E., 686
Röpke, W., 24, 52, 54
Roesler, K., 139
Rössler, H., 134, 139, 143
Roethlisberger, E., 394
Roett, R., 324
Roff, W. R., 758
Rogers, E. M., 77
Rogers, J., 331
Rogers, W. D., 199
Rogers, W. T., 373
Rogger, H., 345
Rogin, M. P., 272
Rogow, A. A., 222
Roh, F., 477
Rohe, K., 472
Roherty, J. M., 262
Rohr, J., 394
Rohwer, J., 157, 169
Rojo, R., 306

Rokach, A., 642
Rokkan, S., 13, 19
Rokossovskii, K. K., 155
Rolfe, E. N., 353
Rolfe, S. E., 64, 67
Roll, Sir E., 52
Rolón Anaya, M., 321
Rolph, H., 746
Romano, A., 599
Romano, S., 420
Romanovskii, S. K., 580
Romanus, C. F., 175
Romasco, A. U., 276
Romé, H., 183
Romensky, S., 572
Romeo, R., 430
Romero, L. A., 316
Romualdi, S., 195
Ronart, N., 621
Ronart, S., 621
Ronblöm, H. K., 122
Ronchey, A., 532
Rondière, P., 324
Ronning, C. N., 193, 195
Roon, G. van, 486
Roos, H., 524
Roosa, R. V., 53, 64
Roosevelt, A. E., 229
Rooy, S. van, 646
Roper, M., 701
Ropp, F. von der, 134
Rosberg, C. G., Jr., 780, 781, 831
Roscoe, T., 262
Rose, A. M., 277
Rose, E. J. B., 387
Rose, L. E., 655, 656
Rose, R., 384
Rose, S., 118, 610
Rosecrance, R. N., 6, 113, 117, 379
Rosen, E. A., 216
Rosen, G., 673
Rosenau, J. N., 6, 11, 111, 236, 251
Rosenbaum, H. J., 324
Rosenbaum, K., 474
Rosengarten, F., 423
Rosenko, I. A., 555
Rosenko, M. N., 572
Rosenne, S., 94
Rosenstein-Rodan, P. N., 76
Rosenthal, E. I. J., 44
Rosenthal, M., 298
Rosier, B., 68
Rosinski, H., 16
Roskamp, K. W., 507
Roskill, S. W., 143, 373
Rosmer, A., 537
Rosner, G., 107
Rosovsky, H., 720
Ross, A., 102, 772
Ross, D. R. B., 175
Ross, I., 217
Ross, J. B., 294
Ross, T., 361
Ross, T. B., 122
Ross, W. B., 269
Ross, W. F., 175
Rossi, M., 188

Rossiter, C. L., 228
Rostow, E. V., 236, 237
Rostow, W. W., 77, 180, 237
Rotberg, R. I., 310, 783, 846
Rotblat, J., 126, 184
Rothberg, A., 569
Rothschild, J., 526
Rothschild, J. H., 118
Rothstein, R. L., 7, 11
Rothwell, V. H., 135
Rotondaro, R., 319
Roucek, J. S., 361
Rougemont, D. de, 130, 345, 394
Rouhani, F., 71
Rouleau, E., 639
Rous, J., 800
Rousseas, S. W., 603
Rousseau, A., 44
Roussinov, S., 599
Rout, L. B., Jr., 320
Rovere, R. H., 237
Rovine, A. W., 98
Rowat, D. C., 21
Rowe, D. N., 705
Rowe, J. W., 772
Rowe, J. W. F., 69
Rowe, M. A., 772
Rowland, J., 671
Rowles, J. P., 300
Roy, J., 400, 701
Roy Chowdhury, S., 680
Rozanov, G. L., 146
Rozental, A. A., 752
Rozmaryn, S., 527
Rubenstein, R. E., 273
Rubin, J. A., 257
Rubin, N., 825
Rubin, R. I., 279, 582
Rubin, S. J., 77, 96
Rubinoff, A. G., 668
Rubinstein, A. Z., 184, 553, 595
Rubinstein, G., 116
Ruches, P. J., 602
Rudebeck, L., 800
Rudel, C., 202, 441
Rudman, H. C., 580
Rudnev, V. S., 230
Rudolph, L. I., 665
Rudolph, S. H., 665
Rue, J. E., 693
Rueff, J., 53, 64
Rühle, J., 30
Ruf, W. K., 800
Ruffmann, K. H., 129, 549
Ruge, F., 113, 191
Ruin, O., 449
Ruiz, R. E., 306
Ruiz García, E., 212
Ruiz Novoa, A., 334
Rumi, G., 425
Rumiantsev, A. M., 549, 693
Rupen, R. A., 714, 740
Rush, M., 562, 566
Rusinow, D. I., 426
Rusis, A., 456
Rusk, D., 229
Russell, B. A. W. R., 3rd Earl, 743

Russell, E. C., 729
Russell, R. B., 248
Russett, B. M., 7, 11, 16, 54, 99, 152, 262, 378
Rustow, D. A., 38, 233, 237, 723
Rutkis, J., 460
Rutman, G. L., 834
Ruttan, V. W., 69
Ryan, C., 160
Ryan, J., 774
Ryan, J. M., 299
Ryan, P., 774
Ryan, S., 403
Ryan, S. D., 312
Ryan, W. L., 117
Ryder, A. J., 472
Rynne, X., *pseud.*, 433
Rywkin, M., 587

Saab, É., 627, 642
Saab, G. S., 805
Ṣaab, H., 621
Sabaliūnas, L., 462
Sable, M. H., 202
Saborit, A., 436
Sachar, H. M., 614, 630
Sachs, I., 77, 80, 81
Saʿd Allāh, Abu al-Qāsim, 799
Sáder Pérez, R., 343
Ṣadrzādih, Z., 651
Safarian, A. E., 288
Safran, N., 632, 637
Sager, P., 668
Ságvári, A., 514
Sahebjam, F., 651
Saiadov, S. A. O., 581
Said, A. A., 7, 783
Said, B. M., 806
Saïd, S.-G., 824
Saimong Magrai, S., 754
St. George, G., 581
Saint-Geours, J., 55
St. John, R., 631
Saint-Loup, S. de, *pseud.*, 162
Saint Marc, M., 64, 788
Saint-Paulien, J., *pseud.*, 400
Saint Phalle, T. de, 252
Saint Robert, P. de, 406
Sainteny, J., 749
Saitō, T., 146
Saitō, Y., 735
Sakai, R. K., 610
Sakamoto, N., 705
Sakharov, A. D., 185
Sakurai, H., 727
Saladino, S., 419
Salah Bey, A., 791
Salan, R., 404
Salant, W. S., 254
Salcedo, J., 439
Saldern, A. von, 472
Salem, D., 404
Sales, M. E., 634
Salewski, M., 169, 474
Salgado, G., 335
Saliba, S. N., 637
Salibi, K. S., 628
Salih, H. I., 418
Salin, E., 54
Salinger, P. E. G., 217
Salis, J. R. von, 147
Salisbury, H. E., 162, 214, 540, 558, 705, 749
Salisbury, R. F., 774
Salomon, M., 417, 521
Salvadori, M., 420, 421
Salvemini, G., 421
Samedov, T. G., 587
Samedov, V. I., 587
Sametz, A. W., 77
Sampedro, J. L., 52
Sampson, A., 347, 373, 380
Samuel, A., 207
Samuelli, A., 591
Samuels, L. H., 792
Samuels, M. A., 846
Samuelson, P. A., 59
San Martín, C., 849
Sanakoev, S. P., 152
Sánchez, J. M., 436
Sanchez, P. C., 773
Sánchez Jáuregui, F. J., 319
Sánchez Salazar, G. A., 320
Sánchez Tarniella, A., 312
Sanders, A. J. K., 714
Sanders, R., 630
Sanders, S., 247
Sandoval Rodríguez, I., 321
Sanger, R. H., 35, 644
Sanghvi, R., 651
Sanguinetti, T., 114
Sanjian, A. K., 627
Sansom, R. L., 740
Santarelli, E., 423, 428
Santhanam, K. I., 657
Santos, T. dos, 212
Santovenia, E. S., 303
Sanz de Santamaría, C., 196, 334
Sapin, B. M., 251
Saraceno, P., 430
Saragat, G., 421
Saran, V., 558
SarDesai, D. R., 668
Sarkis, N., 616
Sarkisyanz, E., 754
Šarmaitis, R., 462
Sarmet, M., 357
Sarti, R., 428
Sartorelli, F., 352
Sasamoto, T., 713
Sathyamurthy, T. V., 106
Satō, K., 166
Sattler, A., 352
Saunders, J., 324
Sautter, G., 821
Sauvage, L., 306
Sauvy, A., 416
Savarius, V., *pseud.*, 514
Savasis, J., 462
Saville, J., 25
Saville, L. B., 431
Savinkin, N. I., 562
Sawer, G., 16
Sawyer, C. A., 186
Sayeed, K. B., 677

Sayegh, F. A., 621
Sayegh, K. S., 616
Sayers, R. S., 441
Sayf al-Dawlah, 'Ismat, 621
Saylor, R. G., 813
Scalapino, R. A., 610, 693, 722, 732
Scammon, R. M., 272, 277
Scargill, D. I., 416
Schachter, G., 431
Schaedel, R. P., 310
Schäfer, E. P., 146
Schäfer, F., 505
Schäfer, G., 505
Schaefer, H. W., 366
Schärf, A., 510
Schaffter, D., 281
Scham, A., 795
Schapiro, L. B., 537, 547, 566
Schappert, L. G., 656
Schapsmeier, E. L., 222
Schapsmeier, F. H., 222
Scharlau, W. B., 136
Scharndorff, W., 567
Scharping, T., 686
Schatten, F., 558, 786
Schaull, R., 38
Schechtman, J. B., 49, 621
Schecter, J., 735
Scheer, R., 307
Scheffer, P., 532
Scheingold, S. A., 352, 356
Scheinman, L., 86, 408
Schell, O., 684
Schellenger, H. K., Jr., 505
Schelling, T. C., 111
Schenk, F., 492
Scherer, A., 135
Scherer, F. M., 262
Scherk, N., 786
Schermerhorn, W., 390
Schettini, M., 139
Scheurig, B., 172, 486
Schick, A., 276
Schick, J. M., 494
Schickele, R., 77
Schickling, W., 553
Schieder, T., 345, 470
Schierbaum, H., 466
Schiller, H. I., 279
Schiller, K., 494, 507
Schiller, U., 532
Schimmel, A., 677
Schirach, B. von, 482
Schlabrendorff, F. von, 486
Schlarp, K.-H., 135
Schleicher, C. P., 102
Schleifer, A., 637
Schlesinger, A. M., Jr., 182, 217, 237, 267, 273
Schlesinger, J. A., 273
Schlesinger, T. O., 510
Schlüter, H. W., 102
Schmädke, J., 472
Schmeltz, G. W., 180
Schmid, K., 352
Schmid-Ammann, P., 394
Schmidt, D. A., 646, 648
Schmidt, G., 505

Schmidt, H. D., 10
Schmidt, Hans, 310
Schmidt, Helmut, 500
Schmidt, P. K. *See* Carell, P., *pseud.*
Schmidt, R. J., 143
Schmitt, K. M., 35, 207, 292
Schmitter, P. C., 329
Schmitthenner, W., 486
Schmitz, W., 64
Schmokel, W. W., 467
Schnabel, J. F., 729
Schnabel, R., 172
Schneider, B., 148
Schneider, F. M. T., 191
Schneider, H., 357
Schneider, R. M., 202, 327
Schneider, W., 30
Schneider, W., Jr., 260
Schnitzer, M., 449
Schoenbaum, D., 477, 505
Schoenbrun, D., 404
Schöneburg, K.-H., 492
Schoenfeld, M. P., 158
Schöpflin, G., 361
Schokking, J. J., 390
Scholl-Latour, P., 413
Schorn, H., 477
Schou, A., 11, 93
Schram, S. R., 610, 693, 700, 706
Schramm, P. E., 158, 481
Schramm, W., Ritter von, 486
Schramm, W. L., 44, 80
Schreiber, A. P., 199
Schrock, J., 809
Schröder, A., 505
Schröder, D., 188
Schroeder, F. von, 130
Schröder, G., 500
Schröder, H.-J., 483
Schröder, J., 164
Schubert, G., 483
Schubert, K. von, 503
Schubert, P. V., 502
Schütz, W. J., 89
Schütz, W. W., 501
Schuh, G. E., 329
Schuler, E. A., 677
Schuler, K. R., 677
Schulmeister, O., 510
Schulte, H. F., 434
Schultz, T. W., 70
Schultze, C. L., 276
Schulz, E., 501
Schulz, G., 129, 492
Schulze, H., 468, 472
Schuman, R., 352
Schumann, K., 394
Schurmann, H. F., 684, 693
Schurr, S. H., 613
Schurz, W. L., 202
Schuschnigg, K. von, 509
Schuster, D., 467
Schuster, D. V., 18
Schuster, R., 489
Schwabe, K., 474
Schwartz, A. J., 274
Schwartz, B. I., 693

AUTHOR INDEX

Schwartz, H., 521, 558, 573
Schwartz, M. A., 282
Schwartz, M. D., 91
Schwartzenberg, R.-G., 413
Schwarz, F. A. O., Jr., 818
Schwarz, H.-P., 488
Schwarz, J., 472
Schwarz, M., 465
Schwarz, U., 262
Schwarz, W., 818
Schwarzenberger, G., 3, 67, 86
Schwarzkopf, D., 90, 501
Schweisfurth, T., 92
Schweitzer, A., 477
Schweitzer, C.-C., 247
Schwoebel, J., 494
Scigliano, R. C., 747
Scitovsky, T., 64, 77
Scobie, J. R., 313
Scoppola, P., 428
Scott, A. M., 12, 120
Scott, B. R., 416
Scott, C. P., 373
Scott, H. D., 273
Scott, H. F., 562
Scott, I., 924
Scott, J. C., 21, 758
Scott, K. J., 772
Scott, M. F., 386
Scott, P. D., 743
Screen, J. E. O., 451
Seabury, P., 185, 237
Seale, B., 273
Seale, P., 413, 627
Seaman, L. C. B., 366
Seaton, A., 162
Sebald, W. J., 717
Secchia, P., 143, 428
Seck, A., 808
Sedlmeyer, K., 531
Sedwick, F., 436
Seelbach, J., 501
Seers, D., 306
Segal, A., 301
Segal, R., 47, 214, 657, 837, 840, 842
Segesvary, V., 560
Segre, V. D., 643
Segundo, J. L., 341
Segundo Silioni, R., 325
Seibel, H. D., 820
Seidman, A., 788
Seidman, H., 267
Seifert, J., 505
Sekistov, V. A., 158
Selden, M., 245, 693
Selek, S., 624
Seligman, L. G., 217
Sell, M., 395
Sellars, R. W., 16
Selltiz, C., 279
Selser, G., 316
Selucky, R., 363
Selzer, M., 643
Semidei, M., 306
Sen, B., 89
Sen, C. *See* Sen Gupta, B., *pseud.*
Sen, S., 103

Sen, S. D. K., 665
Sen Gupta, B., *pseud.*, 652, 665
Senger und Etterlin, F. von, 482
Senghor, L. S., 783
Senn, A. E., 395, 462
Seoane Corrales, E., 294, 339
Šepić, D., 593
Seppälä, H., 454
Sepúlveda Niño, S., 334
Sérant, P., 347, 417
Séré de Rivières, E., 821
Serfaty, S., 407
Serfőző, L., 512
Sergeev, A. N., 538
Sergeev, P. I., 111
Sergeichuk, S., 247
Serrão, J., 441
Serreau, J., 808
Serres, J., 89
Servan-Schreiber, J.-J., 348, 413
Service, J. S., 247
Seth, R., 162, 567
Sethe, P., 501
Seton, M., 661
Seton-Watson, C., 428
Seton-Watson, H., 22, 531
Settembrini, D., 428
Sevigny, P., 287
Sewell, J. P., 106
Sewell, W. G., 693
Seymour, C., 135
Sezer, D., 625
Shabad, T., 575, 709
Shabshina, F. I., 727
Shafer, B. C., 18
Shafer, R. J., 294
Shaffer, E. H., 254
Shaffer, H. G., 77, 361
Shajī'ī, Z., 651
Shakabpa, T. W. D., 655
Shakhrai, V., 583
Shamsul Huq, M., 610
Shamuyarira, N. M., 844
Shand, R.T., 610
Shanks M., 386
Shannon, W. V., 222
Shapiro, S., 196, 202
Shaplen, R., 735, 741, 744
Sharabi, H. B., 622, 637
Sharf, A., 484
Sharma, B. L. E., 669, 678
Sharma, B. M., 16, 665
Sharma, D. N., 103
Sharma, G. K., 673
Sharma, J. S., 659
Sharova, K., 599
Sharp, D. A., 339
Sharp, W. R., 103
Sharpe, M. E., 573
Shashin, V. D., 575
Shaw, A. G. L., 767
Shaw, R. d'A., 79
Shawcross, W., 522
al-Shaybānī, M. ibn al-H., 87
Shchetinin, V. D., 188
Sheahan, J., 416
Shearer, D., 262

Shears, D. J. A., 489
Sheehy, E. P., 3
Sheil-Small, D., 761
Sheldon, C. S., II, 564
Sheldon, W. J., 717, 729
Shelton, R. M., 303
Shen, Tsung-han, 713
Sheng, Y., 693
Shepherd, G., 135. *See also* Brook-Shepherd, G.
Shepherd, G. W., Jr., 237, 787
Shepperd, G. A., 164
Sheridan, J. E., 700
Sherlock, P. M., 301
Sherman, H. J., 54, 573
Sherrard, P., 602
Sherrill, R., 222
Sherwani, L. A., 668
Sherwin, M., 273
Shewmaker, K. E., 247
Shibata, M., 693
Shiber, S. G. *See* Shibr, S. J.
Shibl, Y., 805
Shibr, S. J., 648
Shieh, M. J. T., 686
Shinnar, F. E., 632
Shinohara, M., 725
Shipaev, V. I., 727
Shirendyb, B., 714
Shirer, W. L., 400
Shiriaev, S. L., 709
Shishkin, V. A., 561
Shively, D. H., 726
Shkunaev, V. G., 106
Shonfield, A., 51, 52
Shore, W. I., 126
Short, J. F., Jr., 277
Shoup, C. S., 64
Shoup, P., 595
Shryock, R. W., 545
Shtemenko, S. M., 155
Shterev, P., 599
al-Shu'aybī, Muḥammad 'Ali, 648
Shub, A., 361, 532
Shukman, H., 543
Shulman, M. D., 553
Shuster, G. N., 106
Shvedkov, I. A., 251
al-Sibā'i, Y., 803
Sicard, M.-I. *See* Saint-Paulien, J., *pseud.*
Sicat, G. P., 765
Siddiqui, K., 677
Sidey, H., 217
Sidjanski, D., 352, 356
Siegert, H., 599
Siegler, H., Freiherr von, 103, 126, 352, 466, 501, 510
Sierra, E., 331
Sievers, A., 681
Siffin, W. J., 76, 752
Sigmund, P. E., 23, 38, 207
Sih, P. K. T., 686
Siilivask, K., 458
Sik, E., 514, 779
Šik, O., 26, 519, 522
Silberstein, G. E., 135
Silcock, T. H., 752, 758
Šilde, Ā., 461

Silk, L., 276
Sills, D. L., 2
Silone, I., 16
Silva, H., 327
Silva, R. E., 336
Silva Herzog, J., 289, 295
Silva Michelena, J. A., 343
Silverlight, J., 543
Silvert, K. H., 16, 18, 331
Silvestri, S., 345, 417
Simai, M., 52, 59
Simandjuntak, B., 758
Simão, A., 327
Simeon, R., 287
Simirenko, A., 578, 580
Simmonds, G. W., 537
Simmonds, J. D., 705
Simmons, H. G., 414
Simms, P., 337
Simon, S. W., 761
Simonen, S., 451
Simonis, U. E., 709
Simons, A. P., 101, 102, 249
Simonsen, M. H., 329
Simpson, S., 251
Šimutis, L., 462
Sin, Kuk-chu, 727
Sinai, I. R., 38
Sinclair, K., 772
Singer, D., 414
Singer, G., 527
Singer, H. W., 77
Singer, J. D., 7, 111
Singer, L., 543
Singer, M., 295
Singer, M. R., 7, 681
Singer, S. F., 49
Singh, H., 659
Singh, K., 659
Singh, L. P., 610
Singh, M., 673
Singh, N., 20
Singh, P., 610, 657
Singh, S., 678
Singh, S. K., 680
Singh, T., 673
Singh, V. B., 674
Singham, A. W., 313
Singleton, F. B., 361
Sinha, K. K., 610
Sinha, N. C., 158
Sinha, S., 659
Sinitsyn, B. V., 731
Siotis, J., 98
Sīpols, V., 460
Sipos, P., 512
Sithole, N., 783, 844
Sitton, S., 643
Sjøqvist, V., 443
Skaba, A. D., 583
Skendi, S., 602
Skidelsky, R. J. A., 383
Skidmore, T. E., 327
Skilling, H. G., 361, 566
Skipitis, R., 462
Sklar, R. L., 818
Skodvin, M., 446

AUTHOR INDEX

Skolnikoff, E. B., 12, 45, 281
Skorov, G. E., 77
Skriver, A., 604
Skurnik, W. A. E., 812
Sladkovskii, M. I., 558, 561, 693
Slater, J., 199, 309
Slawecki, L. M. S., 848
Šliogeris, V., 463
Sloan, S., 762
Slottman, W. B., 513
Slusser, R. M., 551
Small, M., 111
Smets, P. F., 188
Smiley, D. V., 287
Smirnov, V., 537
Smith, A. D., 18
Smith, A. K., 281
Smith, A. L., Jr., 483
Smith, B. F., 482
Smith, B. L. R., 20, 280
Smith, Sir B. S., 818
Smith, D., 373
Smith, D. E., 652, 665, 754
Smith, D. O., 261, 263
Smith, D. S., 247
Smith, E. E., 537, 567
Smith, E. E. T., 306
Smith, Gaddis, 135, 152, 231
Smith, Gene, 222
Smith, H., 537
Smith, H. A., 828
Smith, H. H., 645, 651, 654
Smith, J. E., 492, 494
Smith, L., 373
Smith, M. C., 229
Smith, M. E., III, 263
Smith, M. G., 791
Smith, P. H., 319
Smith, P. McC., 263
Smith, R. H., 263
Smith, R. M., 434, 749, 750
Smith, R. R., 167
Smith, T. L., 212, 324, 334
Smith, W. E., 834
Smith, W. W., 169
Smock, A. C., 818, 820
Smock, D. R., 820
Smolar, B., 582
Smouts, M.-C., 103
Smoydzin, W., 505
Smuts, J. C., 837
Smyth, H. McG., 165
Snell, J. L., 152
Snodgrass, D. R., 681
Snow, C. P., 41
Snow, E., 694
Snow, H. F. N. W., 694
Snow, P., 644
Snow, P. A., 775
Snowman, D., 214
Snyder, F. G., 810
Snyder, L. L., 18
Snyder, R. C., 111
Snyder, W. P., 379
Sŏ, Nam-wŏn, 732
Sŏ, Pyŏng-jo, 727
Soares, M., 441

Sobolev, A. I., 30
Sodre, N. W., 327, 329
Södersten, B., 449
Sømme, A. C. Z., 442
Sørensen, M., 87, 443
Soja, E. W., 779
Sokolovskii, V. D., 563
Sokolski, A., 820
Solari, A. E., 206, 341
Solís M., L., 293, 295
Solo, R. A., 77
Solomon, R. H., 694
Solov'ev, A. A., 547
Sommer, J., 743
Sommer, T., 490
Sommer, W., 237
Son, Sŏng-p'il, 732
Sonninno, S., 421
Sontag, R. J., 144
Sontheimer, K., 492, 630
Sopher, D. E., 45
Sordet, M., 782
Sorell, W., 395
Sorensen, T. C., 217, 222, 267, 280
Sorlin, P., 540
Sosa-Rodriguez, R., 212
Sosnovskyi, M., 583
Soulié, G. J.-L., 648
Soustelle, J., 400, 630
Souter, G., 774
Southworth, H. M., 77
Southworth, H. R., 436
Sowelem, R. A., 843
Spaak, P.-H. C., 392
Spacensky, A., 848
Spaeth, C. B., 300
Spaey, P., 339
Spain, J. W., 653
Spalatin, C., 592
Spanier, J. W., 16
Sparring, Å., 442
Sparrow, G., 373
Spartaro, G., 429
Spate, O. H. K., 767
Spears, Sir E. L., 1st Bart., 373
Specovius, G., 533
Speer, A., 482
Speier, H., 111
Spekke, A., 461
Spence, H., 765
Spence, J. E., 837, 841
Spencer, D. L., 83
Spencer, F., 131
Spencer, J. E., 765
Spencer, R. F., 610
Spender, Sir P. C., 766
Spengler, E., 144
Spengler, J. J., 672
Spenz, J., 474
Spicer, K., 284
Spiegel, S. L., 7, 12
Spillmann, G., 796
Spindler, J. von, 77
Spinelli, A., 352
Spiro, E. *See* Cookridge, E. H., *pseud.*
Spiro, H. J., 16, 783, 792
Spoelstra, N., 735

AUTHOR INDEX

Spriano, P., 429
Springer, A., 494
Sprudzs, A., 456
Spulber, N., 364, 573
Srinivas, M. N., 675
Srinivasan, R., 662
Staar, R. F., 31, 361
Stacey, C. P., 285
Stacey, F. A., 381
Stachko, P. I., 461
Stackelberg, K.-G., Freiherr von, 506
Stadler, K. R., 509
Stahl, K. H., 504
Stahl, W., 496
Stahn, E., 808
Stahnke, A. A., 710
Štajner, K., 568
Stakman, E. C., 70
Staley, E., 81
Stalin, I. V., 544
Stallings, L., 139
Stambuk, G., 263
Standard, W. L., 744
Standke, K.-H., 186
Stanger, R. J., 494
Stanisławska, S., 529
Stanley, E. J., 576
Stanley, T. W., 185, 191
Stansky, P. D. L., 436
Starke, J. G., 766
Starobin, J. R., 273
Starodubrovskii, B. G., 570
Starr, E., 233
Statham, J., 80
Stawar, A., *pseud.*, 30
Stawecki, P., 526
Stebbins, R. P., 2, 231, 239
Steel, R., 237, 238, 241
Steele, A. T., 247
Steenberg, S., 172
Stefanov, G., 599
Stefánsson, B., 455
Stefánsson, S. J., 455
Steffens, J., 727
Stegenga, J. A., 419
Steglich, W., 135
Stehle, H., 501, 527
Stehlin, P., 191
Stehouwer, J., 442
Šteimanis, J., 461
Stein, A., 668
Stein, B. H., 212
Stein, E., 125
Stein, G. H., 158
Stein, H., 263
Stein, L., 631
Stein, S. J., 212
Steinberg, A., 222
Steinberg, D. J., 765
Steinberg, S. H., 3
Steiner, J., 395
Steiner, J.-F., 484
Steiner, K., 511, 722
Steiner, Z. S., 378
Steinert, M. G., 175, 477
Steinhaus F. C., 694
Steinicke, D., 185

Stennis, J. C., 251
Stepan, A., 327
Stephens, H. W., 834
Stephens, I. M., 677
Stephens, R., 803
Stephens, R. H., 339, 419
Stephenson, H., 67
Sterling, C., 520
Stern, B., 643
Stern, C., *pseud.*, 492
Stern, F. R., 15, 465
Stern, P. M., 268
Stern, R. M., 430
Sternberg Montaldi, A., 191
Sternberger, A., 506
Sternsher, B., 223
Stevens, F. S., 771
Stevens, G. G., 81, 243, 801
Stevens, R. P., 841
Stevenson, A. E., 103, 223
Stevenson, C. A., 749
Stevenson, F., 373
Stevenson, R. F., 783
Steward, J. H., 792
Stewart, C. F., 796
Stewart, D. E. J., 201
Stewart, I. G., 788
Stewart, I. McD. G., 164
Stewart, J. D., 417
Stewart, M., 383
Stewart, W., 288
Stikker, D. U., 391
Stillman, E. O., 131, 238
Stock, E., 637
Stocking, G. W., 616
Stockton, B., 604
Stockwin, J. A. A., 722, 769
Stoddard, T. L., 681
Stoessinger, J. G., 17, 103, 185
Stoetzer, O. C., 199
Stohler, J., 357
Stoicoiu, V., 591
Stoiko, M., 564
Stojadinović, M. M., 593
Stojanović, R., 53
Stojanović, S., 26
Stojkov, T., 593
Stojković, M. M., 364
Stokes, D. E., 381
Stokke, B. R., 788
Stokke, O., 779
Stoleru, L., 416
Stolper, G., 465
Stolypine, A., 714
Stolypine, D., 714
Stone, I. F., 217
Stone, J. J., 126
Stone, P. B., 725
Stone, R. A., 248
Storbeck, D., 493
Storing, H. J., 273
Storry, G. R., 170
Storz, H.-U., 754
Stošić, B. D., 98
Stoyanovitch, C., 26
Strachey, E. J. St. L., 126
Strackbein, O. R., 254

AUTHOR INDEX

Strandmann, H. P. von, 472
Strange, S., 387
Strasser, W., 510, 511
Strassmann, W. P., 295
Stratton, A., 848
Stratulat, N. P., 584
Strauch, H. F., 787
Strauch, R., 192
Strauss, E., 575
Strauss, F. J., 345, 501
Strausz-Hupé, R., 192, 226
Streeten, P., 77, 368, 674, 788
Streit, G., 605
Strel'nikov, V. S., 164
Strik-Strikfeldt, W., 172
Ströhm, C. G., 361
Strokov, A. A., 111
Stromberg, R. N., 238
Strong, J. W., 546
Strong, Sir K., 122, 172
Strover, A. J., 560, 579
Stroyen, W. B., 580
Stucken, R., 465, 806
Stucki, L., 701
Studnitz, H.-G. von, 501
Stürmer, M., 472
Stumpf, R., 472
Sturmthal, A. F., 41
Sturzo, L., 421
Stuvel, G., 50
Stycos, J. M., 212
Suárez, A., 306
Subrahmanyam, K., 679
Suchlicki, J., 307
Sud, U., 103
Suda, Z., 520
Sūduvis, N. E., *pseud.*, 463
Suermann, J., 838
Sugar, P. F., 34, 361
Sugino, A., 694
Suh, Dae-Sook, 727, 728
Sukarno, 762
Sukharchuk, G. D., 689
Sukhodeev, V. V., 550
Sukijasović, M., 595
Suleiman, M. W., 628
Sullivan, M., 288
Sulzberger, C. L., 226, 238
Summerlin, S., 117
Sun-tzŭ, 113
Sundquist, J. L., 273
Suny, R. G., 543
Suprunenko, N. I., 584
Surányi-Unger, T., 364
Surilov, A. V., 584
Susini, J.-J., 799
Susmel, D., 421, 429
Susmel, E., 421
Sutch, W. B., 772
Sutherland, E., 307
Sutton, A. C., 573
al-Suwaydī, T., 645
Suyin, Han, 694
Šveics, V., 113
Svensson, B., 443
Sviták, I., 522
Swanson, R. F., 284

Swarup, S., 694
Swe, T., 607
Swearingen, R., 180, 746
Sweet-Escott, B., 172
Swerdlow, I., 38
Swianiewicz, S., 568
Swing, R., 226
Swinson, A., 167
Swinton, P. C.-L., 1st Earl of, 374
Swoboda, A. K., 63
Swomley, J. M., Jr., 238, 263
Sworakowski, W. S., 30
Sy, S. M., 809
Syed, A. H., 12
Sykes, C., 487, 630
Sylvester, A., 800
Symonds, R., 36
Symonenko, R. H., 584
Syrkin, M., 631
Syrop, K., 524
Szabolcs, O., 512
Szász, B. S. *See* Savarius, V., *pseud.*
Szawlowski, R., 98
Szczepański, J., 527
Széchényi, G., Graf, 514
Szembek, J., 525
Szent-Miklósy, I., 192
Szikszoy, J. A., 515
Szinai, M., 511, 512
Szklarska-Lohmannowa, A., 529
Szokolóczy-Syllaba, J., 416
Szűcs, L., 511, 512
Szulc, T., 207, 301 309, 438, 520
Szyliowicz, J. S., 614, 624

Taaffe, R. N., 531
Ṭaher, A. H., 648
Tai, T'ien-chao, 713
Taira, K., 725
Takagi, Y., 720
Takeuchi, M., 700
Talbott, J. E., 417
Taleb, A., 799
Talmon, J. L., 630
Tamagna, F. M., 212
al-Ṭamāwī, S. M., 622
Tamboer, K., 646
Tamburrano, G., 428
Tamedly, E., 26
Tan, C. C., 686
Tanaka, M., 153
Tandon, P., 661
Tanham, G. K., 744
Tansky, L., 83
Tanter, R., 7
Tantum, W. H., IV, 168
Tanzer, M., 71, 276
Taoka, R., 720
Tarasov, K. S., 196
Tarasova, Zh. A., 848
al-Ṭarīqī, 'Abd Allah, 637
Tarling, N., 736
Tarrow, S., 431
Taruc, L., 765
Tarulis, A. N., 456
Tarvydas, S. S., 463
Tasca, C., 558

Tassoulis, G., 604
Tatu, M., 522, 546
Taubenfeld, H. J., 115, 840
Taubenfeld, R. F., 840
Tauber, K. P., 506
Tavares de Sá, H., 103
Taÿ, H., 414
Taylor, A., 108
Taylor, A. H., 238
Taylor, A. J. P., 139, 345, 366, 373, 374
Taylor, C., 701
Taylor, C. C., 675
Taylor, E. L., 227
Taylor, G. E., 765
Taylor, G. R., 46
Taylor, J. C., 834
Taylor, M. D., 227, 238
Taylor, S., 783
Taylor, T., 160, 744
Tayyeb, A., 677
Tedder, A. W. T., Baron, 155
Tedeschi, M., 429
Teich, G., 366
Teitelboim Volsky, S., 332
Tella, G. di, 319
Tella, T. S. di, 313, 316, 319
Temu, A. J., 833
Ten Eyck, J. C., 112
Tendulkar, D. G., 661
Ténékidès, G., 419
TePaske, J. J., 203
Teplinskii, L. B., 654
Teradaira, T., 720
Terchek, R. J., 238
Terpstra, V., 254
Terraine, J., 139
Terrill, R., 694
Tervasmäki, V., 454
Terzić, V., 163
Teske, H., 159, 474
Tetlow, E., 103, 307
Tevetoğlu, F., 624
Textor, R. B., 13, 257
Tezer, Ş., 622
Thalheim, K. C., 364, 493
Thant, U, 126
Thayer, C. W., 120
Thayer, G., 263, 273, 383
Thayer, N. B., 722
Thayer, R. C., Jr., 263
Theberge, J. D., 78, 302
Theobald, R., 54
Theodoulou, C., 606
Theoharis, A. G., 153, 268
Thiam, D., 787
Thiesenhusen, W. C., 331
Thiess, F., 701
Thimme, A., 472
Thirlway, H. W. A., 87
Thoenes, P., 17
Thomas, A. J., Jr., 118, 199, 309
Thomas, A. Van W., 118, 199, 309
Thomas, D. A., 169
Thomas, D. S., 274
Thomas, G. R., 465
Thomas, H., 303, 638

Thomas, J. I., 602
Thomas, N. M., 26
Thomas, S., 494
Thompson, C. A., 280
Thompson, G. R., 175
Thompson, J. C., Jr., 246
Thompson, J. M., 135
Thompson, K. W., 8, 17, 257
Thompson, L. M., 838
Thompson, L. V., 144, 155
Thompson, N., 378
Thompson, Sir R. G. K., 120, 736, 744
Thompson, R. W., 158, 289, 374
Thompson, V. B., 784
Thompson, V. McL., 775, 809, 829, 848
Thompson, W. S., 815
Thomsen, A., 568
Thomsen, E., 175
Thomsen, N., 443
Thomson, D. C., 284, 288
Thomson, J. C., Jr., 686
Thórarinsson, T., 455
Thorbecke, W. J. R., 17
Thordarson, B., 284
Thorgrimsson, T., 729
Thorn, R. S., 319
Thornburg, M. W., 614
Thorne, C., 144, 146
Thornton, A. P., 381
Thornton, R. C., 694
Thornton, T. P., 26, 188
Thorp, W. L., 257
Thubten Jigme Norbu, 655
Thunig-Nittner, G., 518
Thygesen, N., 443
Thyraud de Vosjoli, P. L., 404
Tiano, A., 794, 796
Tibah, M., 803
Tibawi, A. L., 627
Tibi, B., 622
Tickner, F. J., 106
Tien, Hung-mao, 686
Tietze, W., 46
Tigrid, P., 522
Tilford, R. B., 506
Tilkovszky, L., 512
Tillett, L., 581
Tillmann, H., 153
Tilman, R. O., 759
Timasheff, N. S., 112
Tinbergen, J., 55
Tindall, P. E. N., 835
Tinker, H., 23, 610, 611, 659, 669
Tinker, J. M., 120
Tint, H., 407
Tito, J. B., 596
Titulescu, N., 591
Tjaden, K. H., 473
Tobias, F., 473
Tobiassen, L. Kr., 103
Todd, J., 844
Tökés, R. L., 514
Törnudd, K., 553
Tötemeyer, G., 835
Togan, A. Z. V., 587
Togliatti, P., 422

Toivonen, A. L., 451
Toker, M., 624
Toland, J., 716
Tolkachev, A. S., 573
Toma, P. A., 257, 361
Tomashpol'skii, L. M., 71
Tomasson, R. E., 449
Tomaszewski, J., 530
Tomingas, W., 458
Tomioka, S., 167
Tompkins, C. D., 223
Tompkins, E. B., 21
Tompkins, J. S., 112
Tompkins, P., 423
Tompkins, S. R., 543
Tomson, E., 712
Ton-that-Thien, 668
Tondel, L. M., Jr., 736
Topping, S., 701
Tordoff, W., 834
Tornquist, D., 596
Torre, A., 424
Torres Ramírez, B., 307
Torres Restrepo, C., 335
Torres-Rivas, E., 296
Torrey, G. H., 627
Toscano, M., 3, 131, 153, 424, 425, 426
Tóth, I., 514
Totten, G. O., III, 722
Toulat, J., 203
Touraine, A., 41, 414
Touré, A. S., 784, 810
Tournaire, H., 739
Tournoux, J.-R., 404
Touval, S., 787, 829
Townley, R., 103
Townsend, J. R., 694
Toye, H., 750
Toynbee, A. J., 41, 131, 203, 374, 794
Tracy, M., 348
Trager, F. N., 694, 744, 754
Traina, R. P., 438
Trân-minh-Tiêt, 736
Traoré, B., 812
Trapeznikov, S. P., 549, 584
Trask, D. F., 135, 196
Trask, R. R., 626
Travis, W. P., 59
Treadgold, D. W., 31, 540
Tredgold, Sir R. C., 844
Tregaskis, R. W., 746
Tregear, P., 792
Tregear, T. R., 684
Tregonning, K. G., 759
Tremblay, R., 289
Tremelloni, R., 430
Treml, V. G., 573
Trescott, P. B., 752
Treshnikov, A. F., 849
Trevaskis, Sir G. K., 648
Trevelyan, H. T., Baron, 374, 614
Treviranus, G. R., 473
Trevor-Roper, H. R., 158
Trewhitt, H. L., 263
Treyer, C., 792
Triantis, S. G., 604

Trías, V., 196, 341
Tricot, B., 799
Triffin, R., 61, 64, 65
Trimingham, J. S., 779
Trinquier, R., 120, 799
Triska, J. F., 31, 362, 553
Trivers, H., 238
Troeller, G., 647
Trommer, A., 443
Trout, F. E., 796
Trudeau, P. E., 288, 700
Truman, D. B., 267
Trumbull, R., 697, 736
Trumpener, U., 135
Trunk, I., 175
Trunski, S., 599
Tru'ó 'ng-Chinh, 749
Trythall, J. W. D., 437
Ts'ai, Hsiao-ch'ien, 694
Tsakalotos, T., 606
Ts'ao, Po-i, 694
Tsapkin, N. V., 573
Tschebotarioff, G. P., 537
Tschopp, P., 395
Tsereteli, I. G., 537
Tshombe, M., 824
Tsien, Tche-Hao, 695
Tsien, Tsuen-Hsuin. *See* Ch'ien, Ts'un-hsün.
Tsirmokos, I., 605
Tsou, Tang, 247, 690
Tsoucalas, C., 604
Tsunekawa, N., 722
Tsur, J., 632
Tsutagawa, M., 731
Tsybulevskii, B. L., 152
Tuchman, B. W., 247
Tucker, F. H., 41
Tucker, R. C., 31, 544, 567
Tucker, R. W., 15, 238
Tütsch, H. E., 615, 622
Tugendhat, C., 67
Tugwell, R. G., 217, 239
Tuker, Sir F. I. S., 165
Tulchin, J. S., 196
Tuleja, T. V., 263
Tullis, F. LaM., 339
Tully, A., 257
Tuma, E. H., 70
Tumiati, P., 71
Tunçay, M., 625
Tung, Chi-ping, 711
Tung, W. L., 87, 104, 686, 705
Tunkin, G. I., 87
Tuñón de Lara, M., 439
Tuompo, W. E., 454
Tupper, S. R., 284
Turan, O., 625
Turati, F., 422
Turlach, M., 666
Turnbull, C. M., 655
Turner, F. C., 207, 292
Turner, H. A., Jr., 473
Turner, V., 777
Turney, A. W., 163
Tweedy, O., 615
Twining, N. F., 263

Twitchett, K. J., 100, 104
Tyler, W. G., 324
Tyrmand, L., 214
Tys-Krokhmaliuk, Y., 177
Tyson, G. W., 661

Ülken, H. Z., 625
Ueno, H., 721
Uexküll, G. von, 453
Uhlin, Å., 449
Uhrich, R., 396
Ulam, A. B., 242, 543, 546, 553
Ulč, O., 520
Ul'ianovskii, R. A., 31, 560
Ullman, R. H., 7, 378
Ulloa Ortiz, B., 290
Ulman, L., 348
Ulrich, J. W., 125
'Umar, Muḥammad 'Abd al-Khāliq, 801
Umbreit, H., 175
Unāms, Ž., 461
Undén, Ö., 449
Unger, M. H., 814
Unger, T., 339
Uphoff, N., 745
Upton, A. F., 451
Urban, G. R., 362, 557
Uren, P. E., 181, 186
Urfer, S., 834
Uri, P., 59, 352
Urquhart, B., 104
Urquhart, M. C., 282
Urquidi, A. *See* Urquidi Morales, A.
Urquidi, V. L., 212
Urquidi Morales, A., 322
Urrutia, M., 335
Urrutia Lleó, M., 307
'Urwadkī, Y., 622
Urzúa Valenzuela, G., 331
Uschakow, A., 359, 365, 366
Ushakov, G., 263
Usher, D., 52
Utechin, S. V., 532
Utrecht, E., 762
Uustalu, E., 458
Uwechue R., 819

Vacca, R., 317
Väyrynen, R., 453
Vagts, A., 89
Vaidyanath, R., 588
Vaintsvaig, N. K., 732
Vaitkevičius, B., 463
Vaitkus, M., 463
Vajda, I., 59
Valadés, J. C., 292
Valahu, M., 824, 847
Valdés, N. P., 303, 304, 307
Valen, H., 446
Valentei, D. I., 49
Valentinov, N., *pseud.*, 537
Váli, F. A., 489, 626
Valiani, L., 423
Valori, F., 163
Vance, V., 644

Vandegrift, A. A., 227
Van den Berghe, P. L., 838
Vandenbosch, A., 736, 769, 838
Vandenbosch, M. B., 769
Van den Bulcke, D., 392
Van der Kroef, J. M., 759, 762
Van der Post, L., 533
Van der Veur, P. W., 774
Van Doorn, J., 112
Van Dorn, H. A., 695
Van Dusen, H. P., 104
Van Dyke, J. M., 744
Van Dyke, V., 93, 281
Van Eekelen, W. F., 671
Vanek, J., 59, 78
Vanezis, P. N., 419
Van Jaarsveld, F. A., 838
Van Langenhove, F., 104, 392
Van Ness, P., 705
Van Panhuys, H. F., 104
Van Slyke, L. P., 695
Van Wauwe, L., 392
Vardys, V. S., 463
Varga, E. S., 52
Varma, B. N., 657
Varma, S. P., 611, 671
Varma, V. P., 661
Vasak, K., 93
Vásárhelyi, M., 364
Vasari, E., 509, 512
Vasconcelos, J., 292
Vass, H., 514
Vasser, M. M., 542
Vastine, J. R., Jr., 252
Vatcher, W. H., 840
Vatikiotis, P. J., 615, 644, 801, 802
Vaudiaux, J., 414
Vazeilles, J., 317
Vegesack, S. von, 175
Vehaegen, B., 824
Vehviläinen, O., 555
Vekemans, R., 213
Velarde Fuertes, J., 439
Velden, D. van, 175
Véliz, C., 203, 207
Vellas, P., 348
Vel'tov, N., 560
Veneroni, H. L., 199
Venezis, I., 605
Venkataramani, M. S., 239
Venkatasubbiah, H., 674
Venkateswaran, R. J., 666
Vennetier, P., 824
Venohr, W., 177
Vente, R. E., 827
Venturini, V. G., 767, 769
Vera, J. de, 341
Verba, S., 16, 23
Verbeek, R., 824
Verein, A. V., 257
Verg, E., 637
Vergès, J.-R., 355
Verkade, W., 20
Verma, D. N., 668
Vernekohl, W., 469
Verney, D. V., 18
Vernier, B., 615, 645

Vernon, R., 67, 196, 254, 295
Verre, É., 575
Verrier, A., 168, 379
Verzijl, J. H. W., 94
Vetiška, R., 519
Vetter, H., 729
Veyrassat, P., 395
Viansson-Ponté, P., 414
Viard, R., 400
Viatkin, M. P., 588
Victor, P.-É., 849
Vidal, J.-É., 714
Vierheller, V., 529
Vietsch, E. von, 136
Vigezzi, B., 140
Vigor, P. H., 549
Vijayanand Bharathi, S., 666
Vilar, S., 437
Villagrán Kramer, F., 296
Villanueva, V., 339
Villard, H. S., 251
Villarroel Claure, R., 322
Villaveces, J., 335
Villemarest, P. F. de. *See* Faillant de Villemarest, P.
Villiers, H. H. W. de, 838
Vinay, B., 788
Vinarov, I., 599
Vinaver, V., 593
Vinterhalter, V., 596
Vîntu, I., 591
Viorst, M., 153
Virally, M., 98
Viratelle, G., 799
Vishniak, M. V., 537
Visine, F., 345
Visscher, C. de, 87, 94, 392
Vital, D., 12, 378
Vitale, L., 332
Viteles, H., 643
Vito, F., 431
Vittachi, T., 762
Vittone, L., 320
Vivarelli, R., 423
Viviani, N., 776
Vladimirov, L., 578
Vladimirtsev, I. N., 543
Vlahov, D., 593
Vodopivec, A., 511
Vogel, B., 506
Vogel, E. F., 695, 726
Vogel, G., 498
Vogel, H., 546
Vogel, R., 632
Vogel, R. M. W., 395
Vogelsang, T., 129, 473
Vogt, H., 468
Vogt, M., 144, 468
Voïcu, I., 92
Volin, L., 575
Volkmann, H.-E., 49, 362, 456
Volkmann, K. *See* Grubbe, P., *pseud.*
Volkov, F. D., 555
Volkov, N. V., 407
Volle, H., 127
Vol'skii, N. V. *See* Valentinov, N., *pseud.*
Von Braun, W., 115

Von der Mehden, F. R., 39, 736
Von der Porten, E. P., 169
Vo-nguyen-Giap, 746
Von Klemperer, K., 509
Von Laue, T. H., 540
Von Mehren, A. T., 723
Von Riekhoff, H., 192, 474
Von Vorys, K., 677
Voorhis, J., 217
Vorontsov, V. B., 247, 248
Voroshilov, K. E., 538
Voss, E. H., 264
Voss, J., 810
Votaw, D., 431
Voyenne, B., 345
Vranchev, P., 600
Vrtačič, L., 596
Vucinich, W. S., 596
Vukadinović, R., 239, 362
Vukmanović-Tempo, S., 596
Vygodskii, S. I., 554

Wadbrook, W. P., 507
Wade, A., 809
Wade, L. L., 13
Wade, R. A., 544
Wadsworth, J. J., 104
Wädekin, K.-E., 575
Waelder, R., 17
Waelès, R., 641
Wästberg, P., 847
Wagar, W. W., 23
Wagener, C., 163
Wagener, H.-J., 573
Wagenheim, K., 312
Wagenlehner, G., 637
Wagley, C., 203, 324
Wagner, F. S., 515
Wagner, H., 637
Wagner, R. H., 196
Wagner, U., 451
Wagner, W., 129
Wagner de Reyna, A., 339
Wagret, J.-M., 825
Wagt, G. de, 336
Waheed-uz-Zaman, 677
Wahlbäck, K., 449
Wainhouse, D. W., 104, 127
Wainwright, M. D., 659
Wakaizumi, K., 719
Walder, D., 606
Waldman, E., 494, 503
Waldock, Sir H., 84
Walendy, U., 146, 153
Waley, D. P., 419
Walker, K. R., 710
Walker, R., 157
Walker, R. L., 231
Wallerstein, I. M., 784, 809
Walpole, N. C., 649
Walsdorff, M., 475
Walsh, A. E., 357
Walshe, P., 840
Walt, L. W., 264, 746
Walter, E. V., 35
Walter, I., 252, 357

Walters, R. S., 83
Walton, G., 159, 163
Walton, R. J., 223, 239
Waltz, K. N., 12, 20, 108
Wandel, E., 475
Wander, H., 763
Wandycz, P. S., 529
Wang, A., 700
Wang, Chien-min, 695
Wang, Yi Chu, 711
Wannow, M., 566
Warburg, J. P., 239, 637
Ward, B., 12, 46, 78
Ward, B. E., 611
Ward, R. B., 767
Ward, R. E., 723
Ward, R. J., 65
Ware, R. M., 65
Warlimont, W., 155
Warma, A., 458
Warmbrunn, W., 391
Warnecke, S. J., 347
Warner, D. A., 744
Warner, G., 400
Warner, O., 155, 451
Warnock, J. W., 285
Warren, F. A., III, 218
Warren, S., 218, 239
Warriner, D., 70
Warth, R. D., 538, 554
Wasowski, S., 186
Wasserman, M. J., 65, 357
Watanabe, A., 721
Waterbury, J., 796
Waterfield, G., 802
Waterman, H., 414
Waters, M., 89, 104
Waterston, A., 679
Watkins, K. W., 383
Watkins, M. B., 654
Watkins, R. J., 336
Watson, F., 705
Watt, Sir A. S., 741, 769
Watt, D. C., 131, 378
Watt, R. M., 140
Wattenberg, B. J., 273, 277
Watters, W. E., 436
Wauthier, C., 784
Weatherhead, R. W., 206
Weaver, J. D., 223
Weaver, J. H., 83
Webb, J. W., 45
Weber, E., 364
Weber, E. J., 345
Weber, F. G., 136
Weber, H., 140, 468, 493
Weber, W., 511
Wechsberg, J., 484
Weekes, R. V., 677
Weeks, A. L., 554
Weidenfeld, W., 475
Weidner, E. W., 83, 611
Weigley, R. F., 264
Weiker, W. F., 625
Weil, G. L., 93, 347, 357
Weil, T. E., 300, 324, 335, 336, 337, 340, 341, 344
Weiler, H. N., 820

Weiler, L. D., 102, 249
Weiller, J., 53
Weinberg, A. K., 175
Weinberg, G. L., 483
Weiner, M., 21, 666
Weingartner, T., 555
Weingrod, A., 643
Weinstein, B., 825
Weinstein, M. E., 721
Weintal, E., 239
Weintraub, S., 254, 436
Weisband, E., 9, 57
Weisgal, M. W., 631
Weiss, C., 762
Weiss, D., 805
Weiss, H. F., 824
Weit, E., 529
Weitz, R., 70, 642
Weizmann, C., 631
Welch, C. E., 784, 809
Welch, H., 695
Welensky, Sir R., 843
Welles, B., 434
Wellington, J. H., 842
Wellisz, S. H., 364
Wells, H., 312
Wells, L. T., Jr., 65
Wells, S. J., 387
Wendt, B. J., 144
Wendt, F., 444
Wendt, H., 203
Wendt, I. Y., 717
Weng, B. S. J., 705
Wenk, E., Jr., 46
Wenner, M. W., 649
Wentz, W. B., 117
Wepf, R., 649
Wernstedt, F. L., 765
Werth, A., 147, 404, 540, 544
Werth, Alexander, 662
Wertheim, W. F., 736
Wesson, R. G., 185, 554, 578
West, Dame R., 35
West, R., 382
Westebbe, R. M., 810
Westen, K., 547
Westergård Andersen, H., 444
Westerlind, E., 449
Westin, A. F., 17, 44
Westwood, J. N., 540, 574
Wetter, G. A., 549
Wettig, G., 488, 554
Whan, V. E., Jr., 228
Wheare, K. C., 20
Wheaton, E. B., 478
Wheeler, D. L., 847
Wheeler, G. E., 264, 588
Wheeler, H., 24
Wheeler, R. S., 677
Wheeler-Bennett, Sir J. W., 131, 180, 374
Wheelwright, E. L., 710, 759
Whetham, E. H., 792
Whetten, L. L., 501
Whitaker, A. P., 207, 313
Whitaker, C. S., Jr., 818
Whitaker, D. P., 695, 750
White, D. S., 153

AUTHOR INDEX

White, G. M., 96
White, I. L., 92
White, J., 65, 502
White, O. E. D., 774
White, R. K., 741
White, S., 818
White, T. H., 218
White, W. S., 267, 273
Whitehouse, A. G. J., 114
Whiteman, M. M., 87
Whiteside, T., 449
Whiting, K. R., 532
Whitman, A. R., 223
Whitman, M. Von N., 67
Whitney, T. P., 546
Whitson, W. W., 706
Whitt, D. M., 185
Whitton, J. B., 121, 185
Whitwell, J., 374
Whitworth, W., 239
Wiarda, H. J., 309
Wicker, T., 273
Widdicombe, S. H., Jr., 311
Widmaier, H. P., 471
Wiehe, H. J., 560
Wiener, A. J., 179
Wieslander, H., 448
Wiesner, J. B., 258, 281
Wight, M., 4
Wightman, D., 611
Wighton, C., 498
Wigmans, J. H., 568
Wigny, P. L., 392
Wilber, C. K., 81
Wilber, D. N., 651, 671, 678, 802
Wilbur, C. M., 705
Wilcox, F. O., 192, 251
Wilcox, W. A., 237, 611, 668, 678
Wilczynski, J., 186, 364
Wildavsky, A. B., 237, 272
Wilde, J. C. de, 793
Wildenmann, R., 506
Wilding, N., 381
Wilensky, H. L., 122
Wiles, P. J. de la F., 54
Wilgus, A. C., 289, 302, 344
Wilhelm, D., Jr., 23
Wilke, J. W., 323
Wilkes, J., 769
Wilkie, J. W., 292, 295
Wilkins, M., 67, 254
Wilkinson, D., 86
Willars, C., 519
Willemsen, A., 357
Willener, A., 41
Willey, K., 775
William, J., 161
Williams, D., 389
Williams, E. E., 302, 313
Williams, E. J., 207
Williams, G., 373
Williams, G. M., 787
Williams, L. E., 711
Williams, L. F. R., 680
Williams, M., 374, 751, 759
Williams, P. M., 400, 414
Williams, R. N., 278

Williams, T. D., 389
Williams, W. A., 218
Williams, W. L., 108
Williamson, S. R., Jr., 136
Willis, F. R., 353, 425
Willmott, W. E., 751
Willner, D., 643
Willoquet, G., 329
Willrich, M., 71, 116, 180, 185
Wills, A. J., 835
Wills, G., 223
Willtse, C. M., 175
Wilmington, M. W., 176
Wilson, A., 114
Wilson, C. E., 89
Wilson, C. M., 814
Wilson, D., 611, 695, 755
Wilson, D. A., 752
Wilson, E., 282
Wilson, E. M., 637
Wilson, F. H., 280
Wilson, F. L., 414
Wilson, G. M., 718
Wilson, G. W., 78, 289
Wilson, H., 374
Wilson, H. E., 280
Wilson, H. R., Jr., 144
Wilson, J., 809
Wilson, J. H., 254
Wilson, L. C., 307
Wilson, M., 838
Wilson, R. R., 368
Wilson, T., 373, 383
Wilson, T. A., 153
Wilson, T. W., Jr., 46, 264
Winchell, C. M., 3
Windchy, E. G., 744
Windelen, H., 502
Windsor, P., 189, 495, 522
Winger, H. W., 278
Winstedt, Sir R. O., 759
Winstone, H. V. F., 649
Wint, G., 147, 611, 695
Winter, E., 433
Winton, J., *pseud.*, 169
Wionczek, M. S., 59, 200, 295
Wirth, J. D., 329
Wise, D., 122
Wiseman, H. V., 381
Wiskemann, E., 345
Wiśniewski, E., 526
Wit, D., 752
Witcover, J., 218, 223
Withers, W., 213, 274
Witos, W., 525
Witte, B. C., 496
Wittlin, T., 538
Wittner, L. S., 239
Wlatnig, F., 511
Woddis, J., 32, 784
Wohl, R., 415
Woitzik, K.-H., 493
Wojciechowski, M., 529
Wojcik, A., 153
Wolf, C., Jr., 35, 239
Wolf, D., 404
Wolf, E. R., 112

Wolfe, B. D., 26, 31, 538, 540
Wolfe, J. N., 384
Wolfe, T. W., 555, 563
Wolfers, A., 185, 264
Wolfgang, M. E., 277
Wolfskill, G., 218
Wolpe, H., 817
Wolpin, M. D., 332
Womack, J., Jr., 292
Wonnacott, G. P., 289
Wonnacott, P. *See* Wonnacott, G. P.
Wonnacott, R. J., 289
Wood, B., 196
Wood, H. F., 729
Wood, J., 373
Wood, J. R., 89
Woodcock, G., 666
Woodhouse, C. M., 99, 604
Woodman, D., 653
Woods, H. D., 289
Woods, W. H., 524
Woodward, C. A., 681
Woodward, D., 563
Woodward, Sir E. L., 140, 153
Woolf, S. J., 34, 423, 430
Woolman, D. S., 794
Wootton, G. *See* Wootton, J. G. G.
Wootton, J. G. G., 383
Wormser, G., 404
Wormser-Migot, O., 485
Woroniak, A., 83
Woronoff, J., 787
Worsley, P., 188
Worswick, G. D. N., 387
Woytinsky, E. S., 276, 538
Wraith R. E., 809
Wrangel, G. von, 364
Wrangel, O. von, 501
Wriggins, W. H., 21
Wright, C., 280
Wright, G., 147
Wright, H. K., 295
Wright, J., 801
Wright, Sir M., 127
Wright, R., 370
Wright, T. P., 196
Wriston, H. M., 274
Wrzesiński, W., 530
Wu, Chun-hsi, 711
Wu, E., 684
Wu, Rong-I, 713
Wu, Yuan-li, 710
Wülker, G. W., 811
Wuescht, J., 593
Wüst, R.-H., 395
Wulf, J., 478
Wulf, P., 468
Wuorimaa, A., 453
Wuorinen, J. H., 442, 452
Wurfel, S. W., 335
Wylie, J. C., 114
Wyller, T. C., 446
Wyman, D. S., 49
Wynia, G. W., 296
Wythe, G., 196

Xydis, D. P., 19
Xydis, S. G., 419, 607

Yaffey, M. J. H., 835
Yahil, L., 444
Yalem, R. J., 99
Yalman, A. E., 625
Yamaguchi, I., 717
Yamamoto, N., 705
Yamamoto, S., 685
Yamamura, K., 725
Yamauchi, K., 710
Yamey, B. S., 79
Yanaga, C., 717
Yang, M. M. C., 713
Yannopoulos, G., 602
Yao, Wên-yüan, 697
Yar-Shater, E., 651
Yarmolinsky, A., 264
Yarwood, A. T., 49
Yates, J., 92
Ydígoras Fuentes, M., 298
Yeganeh, M., 616
Yeh, Kung-chia, 709
Yglesias, J., 307
Yi, Ch'ang-nyŏl, 731
Yin, J., 706
Yingling, J. M., 729
Yogev, G., 631
Yoo, Tae-ho, 729
York, H., 117
Yoshida, S., 716
Yoshihara, K., 721
Yoshihashi, T., 716
Yost, C. W., 12, 239
You, P. S., 755, 756
Youlou, F., 787
Young, A. N., 686, 710
Young, C., 824
Young, E., 127
Young, G. B., 233
Young, K., 374, 604, 844
Young, K. T., 248, 736
Young, O. R., 7, 12
Young, P., 159, 639
Younger, C., 389
Younger, K. G., 378
Younger, R. M., 767
Yu, F. T. C., 711
Yu, G. T., 687, 835
Yu, H., 732
Yu, T'aek-hŭi, 731
Yudelman, M., 213, 844
Yu, Tê-chi. *See* Yu, F. T. C.

Zabiełło, S., 526
Zabih, S., 651
Zablocki, C. J., 558
Zacher, M. W., 104
Zagladin, V. V., 31
Zagoria, D. S., 558, 741
Zagoria, J. D., 540

AUTHOR INDEX

Zahlan, A. B., 614
Zahn, G. C., 487
Zaide, G. F., 765
Zaidi, M. A., 289
Zainu'ddin, A., 760
Zakharov, M. V., 163, 167, 563
Zaldívar Guzmán, R., 298
Zaleski, E., 574
Zamboni, G., 425
Zangrandi, R., 423
Zarański, J., 525
Žarko, D., 596
Zarnitskii, S. V., 538
Żarnowski, J., 526
Zartman, I. W., 522, 787, 789, 794, 796
Zaslavskaia, T. I., 578
Zasloff, J. J., 738, 749
Zatko, J. J., 580
Zatzépine, A., 784
Zauberman, A., 364
Zawadzki, K. K. F., 65
Zawodny, J. K., 4
Zdziechowski, G., 530
Zea, L., 208
Zebot, C. A., 78
Zechlin, E., 136
Zeitlin, M., 207, 307
Zeledón, M. T., 296
Zelinsky, W., 46
Zeller, A., 357
Zeller, C., 811
Zeller, E., 487
Zeman, Z. A. B., 136, 480, 522
Zenz, G., 561
Zhelokhovtsev, A. N., 697
Zhilin, P. A., 163
Zhukov, E. M., 26, 131, 714
Zhukov, G. K., 163, 538
Zhukov, I. A., 538
Zhurkin, V. V., 180
Ziadé, P., 629

Ziadeh, F. J., 803
Ziadeh, N. A., 800
Zidon, A., 641
Ziebura, G., 21, 404, 502
Ziégler, J., 779
Ziemer, G., 473
Ziemke, E. F., 163
Zimmerman, W., 554
Zimmermann, L., 407
Zinkin, M., 660
Zinkin, T., 657, 660
Zinn, H., 744
Zinner, P. E., 520
Zipfel, F., 487
Ziring, L., 678
Zischka, A., 507
Žiugžda, J., 463
Zivier, E. R., 96
Živković, D., 593
Živojnović, D. R., 136
Zlatopol'skii, D. L., 544
Zöller, J. O., 506
Zolberg, A. R., 807, 809, 811
Zolling, H., 497
Zolōtas, X. E., 78
Zondag, C. H., 323
Zonis, M., 652
Zook, D. H., 336
Zorgbibe, C., 442
Zorina, I. N., 332
Zorrilla, L. G., 290
Zotos, S., 604, 606
Zsigmond, L., 475
Zsoldos, L., 514
Zsolnay, V. von, 362
Zuccarelli, F., 812
Zuckerman, S. Z., Baron, 44
Zürn, P., 415
Zuwiyya-Yamak, L., 627
Zverev, A. G., 574
Zymelman, M., 319

INDEX TO TITLE ENTRIES

Included here are *only* titles which are not listed under an author's name

Acta Baltica, 455
Actes et documents du Saint Siège relatifs à la Seconde guerre mondiale, 148
L'Adaptation de L'O.N.U. au monde d'aujord'hui, 99
Africa 69/70, 776
Africa South of the Sahara, 1971-, 776
African Affairs, 776
Akten der Reichskanzlei: Weimarer Republik, 468
Akten zur deutschen auswärtigen Politik, 1918-1945, 465
L'altra Europa 1922–45: momenti e problemi, 140
A'māl mu'tamar al-iqtiṣādiyīn al-'Arab al-thānī, 617
The Amerasia Papers: A Clue to the Catastrophe of China, 243
American Foreign Policy: Current Documents, 1956–67, 229
Amerika no taigai seisaku, 229
Année Africaine, 1963-, 776
L'Année politique, économique, sociale et diplomatique en France, 395
Annuaire de l'Afrique du Nord, 1962-, 793
Annuaire de l'U.R.S.S.: droit, économie, sociologie, politique, culture, 1965-, 538
Annuaire français de droit international, 84
The Annual Register of World Events, 1
Annual Review of United Nations Affairs, 99
Antarctic Bibliography, 1965-, 848
Arab Political Documents, 622
Aramco Handbook, 615
Arctic Bibliography, 848
Area Handbook for Peripheral States of Arabian Peninsula, 646
The Arms Trade with the Third World, 108
Asian Development after Vietnam, 607
Aspectos financieros de las economías latinoamericanas, 208
Aspects actuels de la situation économique et sociale de l'Asie du Sud-Est, 733
Das atlantische Dilemma: Aggresivität und Krise der NATO, 1949–1969, 189
Aussenpolitische Perspektiven des Westdeutschen Staates, 498
Australia in the War of 1939–1945, 156
Die auswärtige Politik der Bundesrepublik Deutschland, 498

Basic Principles of Romania's Foreign Policy, 588
Bibliography of Asian Studies, 1969-, 607
The Black Man in Search of Power, 46
Les Bolchéviks et la révolution d'octobre, 541
Bol'shaia Sovetskaia Entsiklopediia, 531
The British Yearbook of International Law, 84

CCP Documents of the Great Proletarian Cultural Revolution, 1966–1967, 696
Canada in World Affairs, 283
Canadian Annual Review, 281

The Canadian Yearbook of International Law, 84
Carl Melchior: ein Buch des Gedenkens und der Freundschaft, 469
The Case of Peng Teh-huai, 1959–1968, 698
The Changing Values on Campus, 277
Chile: A Critical Survey, 330
Chin nien lai Kung Fei tui-wai kuan-hsi piao-chieh, 702
China after the Cultural Revolution, 688
China! Inside the People's Republic, 688
China, Vietnam, and the United States, 244
China Yearbook, 684
Chou En-lai chuan chi, 698
Chūgoku Kyōsantō shiryō shū, 688
Chung-hua Jen-min Kung-ho-kuo tui-wai kuan-hsi wen-chien chi, 702
Chung-Jih wai-chiao shih-liao ts'ung-pien, 703
Communist China and Arms Control, 703
Communist China Problem Research Series, 689
Conferinṭa naṭională a Partidului Comunist Român, 588
Congo, 822
Les Conséquences d'ordre interne de la participation de la Belgique aux organisations internationales, 391
The Conservative Papers, 24
Contemporary China, 683
Contemporary China [Canadian Institute of International Affairs], 689
La Côte-de'Ivoire: chances et risques, 811
La cuestión del Río Lauca, 332
Current Biography, 1

Dai Tōa sensō senshi sōsho, 166
Dansk sikkerhedspolitik 1948–1966, 442
Deutsch-sowjetische Beziehungen von den Verhandlungen in Brest-Litowsk bis zum Abschluss des Rapallovertrages, 473
Der deutsche Faschismus in Lateinamerika: 1933–1943, 201
Deutsche Geschichte seit dem Ersten Weltkrieg, 466
Die deutsche Justiz und der Nationalsozialismus, 476
Development Problems in Latin America, 209
Doz anos de política externa (1936–1947), 440
Dezvoltarea economică a României, 1944–1964, 589
Diagnóstico de la economía venezolana, 342
Diplomáciai iratok Magyarország külpolitikájához, 1936–1945, 515
Documente din Istoria Partidului Comunist şi a Mişcării Muncitoreşti Revoluţionare din România, 589
I documenti diplomatici italiani, 424
Documentos históricos de la Revolución Mexicana, 291
Documents diplomatiques français, 1932–1939, 405

TITLE INDEX 919

Documents of Chinese Communist Party Central Committee, Sept. 1956-Apr. 1969, 689
Documents on American Foreign Relations, 231
Documents on British Foreign Policy, 1919-1939, 375
Documents on Canadian External Relations, 283
Documents on Disarmament, 123
Documents on International Affairs, 1
Documents on Polish-Soviet Relations, 1939-1945, 528
Documents on Swedish Foreign Policy, 447
Dokumenta kryesore të Partisë së Punës të Shqipërisë, 600
Dokumentation zur Deutschlandfrage, 466
Dokumente zur Aussenpolitik der Regierung der Deutschen Demokratischen Republik, 490
Dokumente zur Deutschlandpolitik, 466
Dokumentumok a magyar forradalmi munkásmozgalom történetéből, 513
Dokumenty i materiały do historii stosunków polsko-radzieckich, 528
Dokumenty Vneshnei Politiki SSSR, 550
Droga przez półwiecze, 524

Economic Development Issues: Greece, Israel, Taiwan, and Thailand, 73
The Economic Development of Kenya, 830
The Economic Development of Kuwait, 647
The Economic Development of Morocco, 795
The Economic Development of Spain, 438
The Economic Development of the Territory of Papua and New Guinea, 774
The Economic Effects of Disarmament, 124
An Economic Profile of Mainland China, 708
Eesti nõukogude entsüklopeedia, 456
Eight European Central Banks, 347
Ekonomia politike e socializmit, 600
L'Élection présidentielle des 5 et 19 décembre 1965, 410
O Ellinikos Stratos kata ton B'Pagkosmion Polemon, 164
The Emerging World: Jawaharlal Nehru Memorial Volume, 660
Las empresas estatales en el Perú, 338
En hommage á Paul Guggenheim: recueil d'études de droit international, 85
Die Erhebung der österreichischen Nationalsozialisten im Juli 1934, 508
Estonian Official Guide, 457
The Europa Year Book, 1
The European Free Trade Association and the Crisis of European Integration, 354
European Resistance Movements, 1939-45, 176
Everyman's United Nations, 101

Facts on File, 1
The Far East and Australasia, 1969-, 1
Far Eastern Affairs, 608
Les Fondements philosophiques des systèmes économiques, 53
Foreign Affairs Bibliography, 3
The Foreign Affairs 50-Year Bibliography, 1
Foreign Relations of the United States, 231
La Fusion des communautés européennes, 350

Gendaishi shiryō, 715
Gosudarstvennyi piatiletnii plan razvitiia narodnogo khoziaistva SSSR na 1971-1975 gody, 571
Il governo dei C.L.N., 422
The Great Cultural Revolution in China, 696
The Great Power Struggle in China, 696

Handbook of Latin American Studies, 201
Han'guk tongnip undong-sa, 726
Harakat al-muqāwamah al-Filasṭīnīyah fī waqi'ihā al-rāhin, 639
Historia argentina contempóranea, 1862-1930, 313
History of the Party of Labor of Albania, 601
History of the Second World War: United Kingdom Civil Series, 173
History of the Second World War: United Kingdom Military Series, 156
Hŭngsadan osimnyŏn-sa, 726

The Impact of the Russian Revolution, 1917-1967, 548
Important Documents on the Great Proletarian Cultural Revolution in China, 697
Index to the Correspondence of the Foreign Office, 1920-, 376
The Indian Year Book of International Affairs, 2
The Indochina Story, 743
Indonesia: Perspective and Proposals for United States Economic Aid, 763
Informe sociológico sobre la situación social de España, 438
Informe sociológico sobre la situación social de España 1970, 438
Insular Southeast Asia, Australia, Indonesia, Malaysia, New Zealand, Philippines, Singapore: Bibliographic Survey, 735
International Documents on Palestine, 1967-, 635
International Encyclopedia of the Social Sciences, 2
International Meeting of Communist and Workers' Parties, Moscow, 1969, 28
The International Migration of High-Level Manpower, 48
The International Who's Who, 2
Die internationale Politik: Jahrbücher des Forschungsinstituts der deutschen Gesellschaft für Auswärtige Politik, 2
Israel Economic Development, 642
Israel Government Yearbook, 640
Israel Yearbook, 641
Istoriia Velikoi otechestvennoi voiny Sovetskogo Soiuza, 1941-1945, 157
L'Italia in Africa, 425
Izvestiia na instituta po istoriia na Bulgarskata Komunisticheska Partiia, 597

Jahrbuch für internationales Recht, 86
Jane's Fighting Ships, 114
The Japan Annual of International Affairs, 1961-, 719

Japan in Current World Affairs, 719
Jewish Resistance during the Holocaust, 177
Jih-pên wên-t'i wên-chien hui-pien, 703

K novym rubezham (razvitie narodnogo khoziaistva SSSR v deviatoi piatiletke), 571
Keesing's Contemporary Archives, 2
Kongresi i pestë i Partisë së Punës të Shqipërisë, 601
Kultura, nauka, iskusstvo SSSR, 579
Kung Fei huo-kuo shih liao hui pien, 691
Kung-fei Wên-hua Ta Ko-ming chung-yao wên-chien hui-pien, 697

Lateinamerika und Europa: Probleme und Möglichkeiten der Zusammenarbeit, 211
Latvijas PSR mazā enciklopēdija, 460
Letopis' sovetskoi vneshnei politiki 1917–1967, 552
Lietuvių enciklopedija, 462
Lin Piao chuan chi, 699
Liu Shao-ch'i wên-t'i tzŭ-liao chuan-chi, 699

M. V. Frunze: vospominamiia druzei i soratnikov, 535
Man in the Living Environment, 46
La Marina Italiana nella Seconda Guerra Mondiale, 169
Masa'il-i ijtimā'ī-ye shahr-i Tihrān, 651
Materialy XXIII s'ezda KPSS, 547
Materialy XXIV s'ezda KPSS, 547
Mauritania: Guidelines for a Four-Year Development Program, 810
The Maxwell School Series on the Administration of Foreign Policy through the United Nations, 102
Mažoji lietuviškoji tarybinė enciklopedija, 462
México: realidad política de sus partidos, 291
Mezhdunarodnye otnosheniia posle Vtoroi Mirovoi Voiny, 552
Mezhdunarodnyi ezhegodnik: politika i ekonomika, 1958–, 2
The Middle East and North Africa, 620
The Middle East: Economic and Political Problems and Prospects, 613
Middle East Record, 613
Middle Eastern Affairs, 614
Mikhail Vasil'evich Frunze: vospominaniia rodnykh, blizkikh, soratnikov, 535
The Military Balance, 1960–, 110

Naked Act of Aggression by U.S. Imperialism against the Korean People, 730
Národní fronta a komunisté: Československo, Jugoslávie, Polsko, 1938–1945, 360
National Studies on International Organization, 102
Nederlandse buitenlandse politiek: aspecten en achtergronden, 390
New Directions for World Trade, 58
New Zealand Foreign Policy, 772
Niḍāl al-Ba'th fī sabīl al wiḥdah, al-ḥurrīyah, al-istirākīyah, 621

Nihon gaikō shi, 720
Nihon no fashizumu, 722
Nippon: A Chartered Survey of Japan, 725
Nitchū kankei kihon shiryō shū, 1949 nen - 1969 nen, 720
Norges økonomi etter drigen, 446
Northern Ireland: A Report on the Conflict, 384

OAS parle, 798
L'occupazione in Europa, 177
Odboj a revoluce, 1938–1945, 518
Official History of New Zealand in the Second World War, 1939–45, 157
Official History of the Indian Armed Forces in the Second World War, 1939–45, 158
The Official Warren Commission Report on the Assassination of President John F. Kennedy, 216
Olaylarla Türk dış Politikası 1919–1965, 625
L'Opinion publique belge, 392
Organizații de masă legale și ilegale create, conduse sau influențate de P.C.R., 1921–1944, 590
Otechestvenata voina na Bulgariia, 1944–1945, 162
Oxford Regional Economic Atlas: Western Europe, 348

Pacific Islands and Trust Territories, 773
Pacific Islands Yearbook and Who's Who, 773
The Pacific Rivals, 720
Palestine: International Documents on Human Rights, 1948–1972, 636
The Palestine Question, 636
Panamá y los Estados Unidos de América ante el problema del Canal, 299
Parliaments, 19
The Pentagon Papers. *See* United States-Vietnam Relations, 1945–1967.
Pien-chiang ts'ung-shu, 712
Pobeda sovetskoi vlasti v Srednei Azii i Kazakhstane, 587
Polar Research, 849
The Polemic on the General Line of the International Communist Movement, 557
Political Handbook and Atlas of the World, 1963–, 2
Politicheskie partii zarubezhnykh stran: spravochnik, 15
The Politics of Change in Venezuela, 343
The Postwar Development of the Republic of Vietnam, 747
Los presidentes de México ante la nación, 292
Problemas de pagos en América Latina, 212
Problems of Foreign Aid, 788
Problems of Modern Strategy, 113
El proceso económico del Uruguay, 341
The Professional School and World Affairs, 279
Psychiatry and Public Affairs, 40
Public Papers of the Presidents of the United States, 228

Rapid Population Growth: Consequences and Policy Implications, 49

TITLE INDEX

Le Régime et les institutions de la Roumanie, 590
Les Relations militaires franco-belges de mars 1936 au 10 mai 1940, 392
Report of the Royal Commission on Bilingualism and Biculturalism, 282
Republika Popullore e Shqipërisë në jubileun e 30 vjetorit të themelimit të PPSH, 601
La resistenza e gli alleati in Toscana, 177
Revisão constitucional 1971, 441
La "Revolución Argentina": análisis y prospectiva, 316
The Role of Science in the Development of Natural Resources with Particular Reference to Pakistan, Iran and Turkey, 610
România în războiul antihitlerist, 23 august 1944–9 mai 1945, 591
Rudé právo, 1939–1945, 518
Russian Oppression in Ukraine, 583

Scandinavian Political Studies, 1966–, 442
Schweizerisches Jahrbuch für internationales Recht, 86
SIPRI Yearbook of World Armaments and Disarmament, 1968/69—, 111
Social Sciences in the USSR, 580
Sociología española de los años setenta, 439
South Asian Affairs; Number Two: The Movement for National Freedom in India, 659
Southeast Asia's Economy in the 1970s, 736
Sovetskii ezhegodnik mezhdunarodnogo prava, 87
Sovetsko-Bolgarskie otnosheniia, 1944–1948, 599
Soviet Intelligence and Security Services, 1964–70, 567
Soviet Peace Efforts on the Eve of World War II, 146
SSSR v Velikoi otechestvennoi voine 1941–1945gg., 147
State of South Africa, 837
Statement on the Stand of the Romanian Workers' Party Concerning the Problems of the World Communist and Working-Class Movement, 591
The Statesman's Year Book, 3
Strategic Survey, 1966–, 111
Studies on Asia 1960–1967, 610
Survey of International Affairs, 1920/23–, 3
Symposium on Latin America, 203

Taiheiyō Sensō Shi, 610
The Technology Gap: U.S. and Europe, 52
Thawrat Sha'b: sit sanawāt mina al-niḍal ḍid al-ḥukm al-'askarī al-rujʻī, 807
Tibet 1950–1967, 655
Tradition et modernisme en Afrique noire, 792
Treaties and Alliances of the World, 92
The Turkish Yearbook of International Relations, 1960–, 626

The Ulster Debate, 384
The United Nations and Human Rights, 93
U.S. Marine Operations in Korea, 1950–1953, 729
United States Army in World War II, 158
United States Army in World War II: The European Theater of Operations, 161
United States Army in World War II: The Mediterranean Theater of Operations, 165
United States Army in World War II: Special Studies, 175
United States Army in World War II: The Technical Services, 175
United States Army in World War II: The War Department, 158
United States Army in World War II: The War in the Pacific, 167
United States Army in World War II: The Western Hemisphere, 159
The United States in World Affairs, 239
United States-Vietnam Relations, 1945–1967, 744
The University Looks Abroad, 280
Ustanoviavane i ukrepvane na narodnodemokratichnata vlast, septembri 1944–mai 1945, 599

Veröffentlichungen der Kommission für Zeitgeschichte bei der Katholischen Akademie in Bayern, 467
Vinte anos de defesa do Estado Português da Índia (1947–1967), 668
The Violations of Human Rights in Soviet Occupied Lithuania, 463
Vneshniaia politika Sovetskogo Soiuza i mezhdunarodnye otnosheniia, 553
Vneshniaia torgovlia SSR: statisticheskii sbornik, 1918–1966, 561
Vunshna politika na Narodna Republika Bulgaria, 600

Waga kuni ni okeru kyōsanshugi undōshi gairon, 723
al-Wathā'iq al-'Arabīyah, 1963–, 622
Die Wehrmacht im Kampf, 159
Westermann Lexikon der Geographie, 46
Westeuropäische Verteidigungskooperation, 192
White Papers of Japan, 717
Who's Who, 3
Who's Who in America, 3
Who's Who in Communist China, 700
Who's Who in the Arab World, 1971–1972, 622
Who's Who in the World, 3
World Communist Movement: Selective Chronology 1818–1957, 31
World Index of Social Science Institutions, 3
The World of Learning, 3

The Year Book of World Affairs, 3
Yearbook [International Court of Justice], 94
Yearbook on International Communist Affairs, 1966–, 31
Yearbook of International Organizations, 4
Yearbook of the United Nations, 104

Za chistotu marksizma-leninizma, 550
Zbornik dokumenata i podataka o narodnooslobodilačkom ratu jugoslovenskih naroda, 593

JX
1305
.K73

Kreslins, Janis A.
    Foreign affairs
bibliography